FOOTBALL LEAGUE PLAYERS' RECORDS 1888 to 1939

Michael Joyce

A SoccerData publication from Tony Brown

Published in Great Britain by Tony Brown,
4 Adrian Close, Toton, Nottingham NG9 6FL.
Telephone 0115 973 6086. E-mail soccer@innotts.co.uk
www.soccerdata.com

First published in hardback 2002, ISBN 1899468633
Second, paperback edition, with revisions, published 2004
This third edition, with revisions, published 2012

Dedicated to Derek Hyde, with many thanks for his contribution to this book.

Front cover photographs are, left to right, top, Steve Bloomer and Alf Common; bottom, Willie Foulke and Ernest Needham. On the back cover is action from the game between Notts County and Aston Villa on April 16, 1910, the last time Notts played a home fixture at the Trent Bridge cricket ground.

Tony Brown is a specialist publisher of books and computer databases on association football. Publications include 'Definitive' club histories, season-by-season line-ups from 1888/89 to the 1960s, players' records and complete results from the Football League, F.A. Cup and League Cup. Please write to the address above for a catalogue or visit the web site.

Printed by 4Edge, Hockley, Essex

ISBN 978-1-905891-61-0

INTRODUCTION

This book lists the career records of all players who appeared in at least one match in the Football League between its formation in 1888 and the outbreak of the Second World War in 1939.

Even today a player can slip into obscurity soon after his career has finished. The youngest players in these pages were performing two or three generations ago when rewards for their services were far less generous. Many died young, often in tragic circumstances. There is not room to tell any of their stories here, but the intention is that, alongside the big name players, Stanley Matthews, Dixie Dean and Billy Meredith, there is a brief mention for the likes of Albert Smith, whose League career began and ended for Loughborough in a 12-0 defeat one March afternoon in 1900. In the introduction to the first edition of this book I noted that we knew little about him, and we still don't, but he and all the others on these pages played their part in establishing the traditions of the sport which dominates the thoughts and emotions of so many of us.

If we stand back we can see that, for all the changes in football in the past century and more, it is still fundamentally the same game. Albert Smith would instantly recognise the skills of today's players. Eventually they too will depart from the field, though perhaps not all of them into obscurity. The chances are that football will still be around in 100 years, and it will be different in ways we cannot imagine. But if some twenty-second century statistician tries putting together a book, or whatever has succeeded books, listing all players up to that point, Carlos Tevez will probably be next to the pre-war amateur goalkeeper Ken Tewkesbury.

Now to this book. It has been eight years since the last edition. Surely, some will say, the book covers a fixed period in the past. Can anything have changed in that time? Well, yes, plenty. There has been an enormous amount of additional research during the interval, covering clubs and players at all levels of League football. The availability of genealogical data has improved; the 1911 census is now in the public domain, and we can see far more entries for those with occupation "professional footballer". As a result it has been possible to track many more places of birth and dates of birth and death.

Since last time the details of some players' careers have merged into one, and a few others have split in two. Similarly-named brothers have been the bane of the football statistician's life since day one. All of these changes have added more than thirty densely worded pages to this book since it last appeared.

And is it complete now? Of course not. It will always be a work in progress, and what is published here will yield more valuable information from our readers, and so our knowledge base will continue to grow.

Last time I referred to the vexed issue of the abandoned 1939-1940 season and whether or not to include appearances and goals in players' records. I decided to do so for completeness, but this was not universally approved. This time I have opted to included them but on a separate line in the player's career details, and in brackets. I have included the records of Wigan Borough for the 12 matches in the 1931-1932 season before their expulsion from the League. All their players, with the exception of Harry Hurst, made League appearances elsewhere. Records for their opponents for these matches are not included in player totals, though a list of the affected players appears on page 323. Appearances for Leeds City, expelled in 1919-1920, and Port Vale, who took over their League record for the rest of that season, are of course included.

This book is a by-product of a player database which I have been developing and maintaining in one form or another for something like thirty years. It has been used to assist the publication of numerous reference books. It now forms a constituent part of the English National Football Archive at www.enfa.co.uk. The archive includes full line-up and scorer data for nearly 200,000 matches in League and cups. The continual updating of this data, which so far has only been visible when a new edition of this book appears, will be more readily visible on the website. So is this book out of date? Well, yes, but it was ever thus; almost every book of record goes out of date immediately it is published. What follows is based on our best information in late 2012.

Michael Joyce
October 2012

DETAILS OF THE PLAYER PAGES

Name: The full name where known. The surname given is the one by which the player was known for most of his career, though occasionally he may have had a different surname at his birth or at some other time. Alternative surnames appear in brackets. The first name by which the player was usually known also appears in brackets where it was different from his full first name. The fact that a player called William has nothing in brackets merely means that I have never seen him called Bill or Billy in any document. Widely used nicknames also appear in brackets. Some titles and honours are included – even if acquired after the playing career – these pages contain 17 doctors, 4 knights, 4 ordained ministers, 2 VCs and 2 MPs.

Position: For the period in question it is simplest to use the 'old' positional names such as right half, centre forward and outside left. Over a player's career I have recorded the position in which he appeared most in each season. The position shown first is the one in which he played most, then the second most, then the third. Only positions in which he appeared in more than 5% of his career are shown.

Born: The place and date of birth are shown as accurately as possible. When a date is quoted simply as a year, it is possible that this could be a year earlier or later. Inaccuracies in birth and death data previously published in various sources are continually coming to light. Correcting them is an ongoing process.

Died: The year of death is shown where known.

Caps: The number of full caps is shown for countries within the British Isles. For internationals with other countries, and there were a few even then, the number of caps is usually not known. Representative matches are also recorded: for the Football League (FLge), Football Alliance (FAlliance), Scottish League (SLge), Welsh League (WLge), Southern League (SoLge), League of Ireland (LoI) and Irish League (IrLge). Wartime internationals are listed, including appearances for the Northern Ireland Regional League (NIRL).

Appearances: The year shown is the one in which the season started; e.g. 1888 means the 1888-1889 season. The start and end seasons are the first and last in which the player appeared for the club either in the League or the FA Cup. No season is shown against clubs that were not in the Football League at the time. Appearance and goals totals refer only to League matches, and are based on the line-ups for individual matches.

The club name shown is the one by which the club was known at the start of the player's spell with them, unless there was significant name change in which case both old and new names appear; i.e. Ardwick/Manchester City, Newton Heath/Manchester United, Small Heath/Birmingham. No distinction is made for minor name changes during the player's spell, e.g. Woolwich Arsenal/Arsenal, Stoke/Stoke City. Burton United, formed by the merging of Burton Swifts and Burton Wanderers has been shown separately from its two constituents.

Test matches were used to settle promotion and relegation issues from 1893 to 1898. Players' appearances in these games are listed on page 324.

There is one more anomaly that should be mentioned. The 1898-1899 match between Sheffield Wednesday and Aston Villa on 26 November was abandoned after 79 minutes because of poor light with Wednesday leading 3-1. The Football League decreed that the remaining 11 minutes be played on a separate occasion. It eventually took place on 13 March 1899. Wednesday scored again to win 4-1. However both teams had changed during the interval. Billy Garraty of Aston Villa, and Samuel Bosworth, Bob Ferrier, Ambrose Langley, Jack Pryce and Fred Richards (who scored the final goal) of Wednesday all played only in the final 11 minutes. In effect they became the first substitutes used in a League match. These appearances have not been included in the totals shown in this book, but the players are listed here for completeness.

From To Apps Goal

Aaron, Arthur Frederick IR
b Liverpool q4 1885
Southport Central
1907 Stockport County 2 1
St Helens Recreation
Accrington Stanley
Ashton Town

Abbott, H CH/LH
1894 1896 Nottingham Forest 5

Abbott, Henry (Harry) IL
b Crawshawbooth 31/12/1879 d 1970
Padiham
1901 Blackburn Rovers 0
Queen's Park Rangers
1904 Bolton Wanderers 1
Swindon Town
Darwen

Abbott, Henry (Harry) GK
b Preston q3 1897 d 1968
Lancaster Town
1922 Portsmouth 0
1922 1926 Nelson 154
1927 1928 Luton Town 55
1929 Exeter City (trial) 0
Lancaster Town
1931 Rochdale 32
Wigan Athletic

Abbott, James Arthur IR
b Patricroft q4 1892 d 1952
Barton Albion
Eccles Borough
1913 Manchester City 3 2

Abbott, Shirley Wray CH/LB/RH
b Alfreton 19/2/1889 d 1947
Alfreton Town
1910 Sheffield Wednesday 0
1911 Derby County 1
1920 1922 Portsmouth 96 3
1923 Queen's Park Rangers 12
1924 1927 Chesterfield 117 5

Abbott, Walter LH/IL
b Small Heath 7/12/1877 d 1941
Caps: FLge 4/England 1
Rosewood Victoria
1895 1898 Small Heath 76 57
1899 1907 Everton 257 32
1908 1909 Burnley 57 15
1910 Birmingham 1

Abbott, Walter A IL
b Birmingham q1 1899
1919 Grimsby Town 5
Chesterfield Municipal
Worcester City
Redditch
Oakengates Town
Tamworth Castle
Stewart Street Old Boys (Birmingham)

Abbott, William Lee OL
Riddings
1893 Derby County 4 1
Poolsbrook United
Riddings
Chesterfield Town
Riddings
Clowne Rovers
Walgrave
Market Harborough

Abdallah, Tewfik IR
b Cairo, Egypt 23/6/1897
International Sporting Club
1920 1921 Derby County 15 1
Cowdenbeath
Bridgend Town
1923 Hartlepools United 11 1
Providence Clamdiggers
Fall River Marksmen
Hartford Americans
New York Nationals
Fall River Marksmen
Montreal Carsteel

Abel, Christopher Robert (Robert) RB/LB
b Chorlton 28/4/1912 d 1986
1934 Leeds United 1
1936 Bradford City 14
Stalybridge Celtic
Hurst

From To Apps Goal

Abel, Samuel Charles (Sam) CF/OR
b Neston 30/12/1908 d 1959
Neston Brickworks
1929 Bury 0
1930 Accrington Stanley 26 18
1930 1932 Chesterfield 70 39
1933 Fulham 9 1
1934 1938 Queen's Park Rangers 36 6
Tunbridge Wells Rangers

Abraham, Evan OL
b Swansea 1899
1922 1925 Merthyr Town 57 1
1926 Walsall 13

Abrahams, James OR
b New Mills q1 1868 d 1947
1891 Notts County 4 1
Stockton
Middlesbrough

Abram, Robert Lawrence (Lol) LH/IL/OL
b Banks 14/5/1889 d 1966
Southport Central
Colne Town
1907 1910 Stockport County 67 9
Heart of Midlothian
1914 1919 Chelsea 44 7
1920 Cardiff City 1
1921 1922 Southport 46 7

Abrams, Jack RH
1888 Burnley 13 1
Burnley Union Star

Abrines, James Watson (Jimmy) IR
b Renfrew 31/12/1900 d 1976
Muirpark Amateurs
Glengarnock Vale
Parkhead
Albion Rovers
Dundee (trial)
Sittingbourne (trial)
1923 Barrow 7
King's Park
Duntocher Hibs

Ackerley, George IL
b West Derby 21/5/1887 d 1958
1908 Liverpool 0
1909 Leeds City 2

Ackroyd, Haughton GK
b Todmorden 24/6/1894 d 1979
1921 Wigan Borough 5
Lytham

Ackroyd, John OR/IL
b Heanor 1868 d 1927
Notts County
Heanor Town
1892 1893 Grimsby Town 38 17
1894 Rotherham Town 16 3
Heanor Town

Ackroyd, John William (Jack) LB/RB
b Rotherham q2 1895
Norland
Halifax Town
1919 Rotherham County 1
Scunthorpe & Lindsey United
1922 Exeter City 30
1923 Grimsby Town 6

Acquroff, John (Jack) CF/IL
b Chelsea 9/9/1911 d 1987
Willesden Polytechnic
1931 Tottenham Hotspur 0
Northfleet
Folkestone
1934 1936 Hull City 70 25
1936 1938 Bury 56 15
1938 Norwich City 17 6
1939 (Norwich City) (3) (1)
Metro (Tasmania)

Adams, Amos RB/LB
b West Bromwich 6/1880 d 1941
George Salter's Works
Springfields
1898 1907 West Bromwich Albion 209 3

Adams, Arthur Edward (Edward) OR
b Bromborough 12/11/1908 d 1981
Bromborough Pool
1929 1932 Tranmere Rovers 6 1
Bromborough Pool

From To Apps Goal

Adams, Edward Fairclough (Ted) GK
b Anfield 30/11/1906 d 1991
Oakmere
Earle
1927 Liverpool 0
Burscough Rangers
Manchester Central
Connah's Quay & Shotton
1931 Barrow 0
1931 1934 Wrexham 87
1935 Southport 13
1935 1938 Burnley 111
1939 (Burnley) (2)

Adams, George RH/LH
b Ayrshire
Kilmarnock
Cowlairs
Kilmarnock
1895 1896 Newcastle United 13 1
Hebburn Argyle
Darlington St Augustine's

Adams, James RB
b Edinburgh 1864 d 1943
Caps: SLge 2/Scotland 3
Norton Park
Heart of Midlothian
1894 1895 Everton 40 1
Heart of Midlothian
St Bernard's

Adams, James (Jimmy) GK
b Norton Canes 3/1/1908 d 1983
Cannock Chase Colliery
Cannock Town
1929 1938 West Bromwich Albion 100
1939 (West Bromwich Albion) (3)

Adams, James Henry OR
b Chesterfield 7/7/1896 d 1973
Staveley Wesleyans
Lowgates United (Eckington)
Staveley Town
1921 Chesterfield 6
Staveley Town
Matlock Town

Adams, Percy IR
b Stoke-on-Trent 12/7/1914 d 1984
1936 Port Vale 1

Adams, Robert James (Bob) GK
b Coleford 28/2/1917 d 1970
Coleford
Chepstow
1932 1933 Cardiff City 11
1934 Bristol Rovers 2
1935 Millwall 6
1936 Bristol City 0

Adams, Walter OR
1893 Middlesbrough Ironopolis 23 6

Adams, William (Bill) RB/RH
b Tynemouth 3/11/1902 d 1963
Sunderland Colliery
Guildford United
1927 1935 Southampton 196 4
1936 West Ham United 3 1
1936 Southend United 13

Adams, William (Billy) LB
b Blackheath, Worcestershire 20/3/1897 d 1945
Blackheath United
Rowley Victoria
1920 1926 West Bromwich Albion 92
1927 1928 Barrow 23
1929 Newport County 0
Cradley Heath
Kidderminster Harriers

Adams, William Edward (Billy) LB/CH
b Smethwick q1 1903 d 1953
1924 West Bromwich Albion 0
1925 1927 Walsall 45 1

Adamson, Harry OL
Bishop Auckland
1909 Gainsborough Trinity 12

Adamson, Harry CF
b Grimsby 15/9/1912 d 1989
Upton Colliery
1933 1936 Bradford City 29 19
1937 Aldershot 4 1

Adamson, Hugh Muir LH/RH
b Halbeath 21/4/1885
Dunfermline Athletic
Lochgelly United
1907 1909 Everton 25
1909 1910 Bolton Wanderers 15
South Liverpool

From To Apps Goal

Adamson, Robert McClellan (Bert) IL
b Balbeggie 21/5/1914 d 1995
Perth Craigie
Dundee Violet
Heart of Midlothian
Dundee
1938 Wrexham 35 13
1939 1945 Carlisle United (2)
Dundee United
East Fife

Adamson, Thomas Kay (Tom) LB/RB
b Mossend 12/2/1901
Blantyre Celtic
1920 1928 Bury 271
1929 1933 Brentford 141
1934 Stockport County 0
Ards

Adcock, Hugh OR
b Coalville 10/4/1903 d 1975
Caps: FLge 1/England 5
Ravenstone United
Coalville Town
Loughborough Corinthians
1923 1934 Leicester City 434 51
1935 Bristol Rovers 13 1
Folkestone
Ibstock Penistone Rovers

Adcock, Josiah CF
b Loughborough q2 1878 d 1944
1899 Loughborough 2

Adcock, W IR
1899 Loughborough 9

Adcock, William (Willie) IL
b Cudworth
Ecclesfield
1900 Barnsley 2
1901 Grimsby Town 0

Addenbrooke, John Edwin IR/CF
b Sheffield 1/1900 d 1961
Beighton
1924 1925 Chesterfield 21 5
Wath Athletic
Tinsley Working Mens Club
Fulwood

Addinall, Percy LH
b Hull q2 1888 d 1932
West End (Lincoln)
1919 Lincoln City 15
Grantham

Addy, George William LH
b Carlton, West Yorkshire 27/4/1891 d 1971
Carlton Victoria
1919 Barnsley 1
1920 1921 Norwich City 31 6

Adey, George W RH
b Handsworth 1869
Bournbrook
1898 1901 Small Heath 71 1
Kettering

Adey, Thomas William (Tom) LH/CH
b Hetton-le-Hole 22/2/1901 d 1986
Hetton Celtic
1919 Sunderland (trial) 0
1921 Bristol City (trial) 0
Bedlington United
1923 Hull City 16
1925 Swindon Town 25
1926 Northampton Town 10
1927 Durham City 32 6
Wombwell
Mansfield Town
Newark Town
Crook Town

Adey, Wilfred (Wilf) LB/RB
b Featherstone 6/7/1909 d 1975
Thurcroft Church
Thurcroft Main
1930 Huddersfield Town 0
Thurcroft Main
Norton Woodseats
1931 1932 Sheffield United 2
1934 1936 Barnsley 66
1936 1937 Carlisle United 74 5
Aberdeen

Adlam, Leslie William (Les) RH
b Guildford 24/6/1897 d 1968
Farnham United Breweries
Guildford United
1922 1931 Oldham Athletic 279 9
1931 1932 Queen's Park Rangers 56
1933 Cardiff City 4
Guildford Post Office

From To Apps Goal

Adlington, James H OR
b Shifnal 5/1872
Ironbridge
1895 Small Heath 6 4
Berwick Rangers (Worcester)
Stourport Swifts

Affleck, David Roy (Dave) CH
b Coylton 26/7/1912 d 1984
Crosshouse Castle Rovers
1933 Notts County 0
1934 Bristol City 3
1935 1936 Clapton Orient 66
1937 1938 Southampton 61
1939 (Southampton) (3)
Yeovil Town

Affleck, George LB/RB
b Auchendinny 1/7/1888
Penicuik
1909 1919 Leeds City 182 1
1919 1924 Grimsby Town 197

Agar, Alfred (Alf) OR
b Esh Winning 28/8/1904 d 1989
Shildon
Esh Winning
West Stanley
Dundee
1927 Barrow 31 7
1928 1929 Carlisle United 49 11
1930 1931 Accrington Stanley 73 27
1932 1935 Oldham Athletic 96 28
1936 York City 24 4
Scarborough

Agnew, William (Billy) IL/CF
b Pollokshaws 9/1/1898
Pollok
Ayr United
Falkirk
Bo'ness (loan)
1921 1922 Port Vale 42 6
Arthurlie
1925 1926 Luton Town 35 8
Providence Clamdiggers

Agnew, William Barbour LB/RB
b New Cumnock 16/12/1880 d 1936
Caps: SLge 2/Scotland 3
Afton Lads
Kilmarnock
1902 1903 Newcastle United 43
1904 1905 Middlesbrough 66 2
Kilmarnock
1908 1909 Sunderland 28
Falkirk
Third Lanark
East Stirlingshire

Aiken, Albert Victor (Bert) RH
Glentoran
1938 Brentford 3
Dundalk

Aimer, George Anderson LB
b Dundee 27/10/1897 d 1935
Glenisla
Dundee Celtic
Dundee Hibernian
Dundee
1923 1924 Fulham 16
Third Lanark
Providence Clamdiggers
Fall River Marksmen
New York Giants

Ainsley, George Edward CF/IR
b South Shields 15/4/1915 d 1985
South Shields St Andrew's
1932 1933 Sunderland 4
1936 Bolton Wanderers 7
1936 1947 Leeds United 89 30
1939 (Leeds United) (2)
1947 1948 Bradford Park Avenue 44 29

Ainsworth, Alphonso (Alf) IR/IL
b Manchester 31/7/1913 d 1975
Ashton Athletic
1933 Manchester United 2
Great Harwood
1935 1938 New Brighton 150 39
1939 (New Brighton) (3) (1)
1939 Oldham Athletic 0
1946 1947 New Brighton 31 9
Congleton Town
Ashton United

Ainsworth, Charles OL
b Ashbourne q1 1885 d 1955
Queen's Park Rangers
1908 Derby County 8
1909 Grimsby Town 3

From To Apps Goal

Ainsworth, Edgar Ward GK
b Hull q4 1910 d 1952
Caps: England Amat
Old Boulevardiers
Bridlington Town
1932 Hull City 1
1933 York City 0
1935 Hull City 1

Ainsworth, Fred IL
b Loughborough 29/6/1894 d 1981
Loughborough
1919 Derby County 1
Ashington

Airey, Frank GK
b Gainsborough q4 1887 d 1948
Trinity Institute
1905 Gainsborough Trinity 2

Aistrup, Sidney Roy (Sid) IR
b Sheffield 7/5/1909 d 1996
1928 Halifax Town 2

Aitken, Andrew (Andy 'Daddler') CH/IL/RH
b Ayr 27/4/1877 d 1955
Caps: Scotland 14
Annbank
Ayr Thistle
Ayr Parkhouse
1895 1906 Newcastle United 312 32
Kilmarnock (loan)
1906 1908 Middlesbrough 76 1
1908 1910 Leicester Fosse 64 2
Dundee
Kilmarnock
Gateshead Town

Aitken, Andrew Liddell GK
b Newcastle 25/8/1909 d 1984
Wallsend
1930 Liverpool 1
Mickley
Newburn Athletic
1935 Hartlepools United 1

Aitken, Fergus McKenna (Fergie) OR/OL
b Glasgow 5/6/1896 d 1989
Petershill
Glasgow Benburb
Third Lanark
1919 1920 Bury 75 5
1921 Blackburn Rovers 8 1
1922 Cardiff City 2
1922 Birmingham 0
1923 1925 Southport 78 3
1926 Bradford Park Avenue 11

Aitken, James CF
b Scotland 1907 d 1931
Markinch
Milton Violet
Kettering Town
1929 York City 4 1
Dartford

Aitken, John OL
b Dumfries 1870
5th King's Rifle Volunteers
1895 Newton Heath 2 1

Aitken, John Gordon (Jock) OL
b Govan 19/9/1897 d 1967
St Anthony's (Glasgow)
St Roch's
Clyde
1921 1923 Bury 80 8
1924 Southport 42 1
1925 Crewe Alexandra 28 3
1926 Norwich City 42 8
1927 Northampton Town 10 5
Kilmarnock
St Mirren
Morton

Aitken, Samuel RH/CH
b Ayr 1878 d 1930
Ayr Parkhouse
Ayr
1903 1909 Middlesbrough 227 6
Raith Rovers

From To Apps Goal

Aitken, William John OR/IR
b Peterhead 2/2/1894 d 1973
Kirkintilloch Harp
Kirkintilloch Rob Roy
Kilsyth Rangers
Queen's Park
Rangers
1919 Port Vale (loan) 30 4
1920 1923 Newcastle United 104 10
1924 1925 Preston North End 56 11
Chorley
1926 Norwich City 14
Bideford Town
Juventus
AS Cannes
Stade de Reims
Antibes

Aitkenhead, Walter Campbell Allison IL/LH/CF
(Wattie)
b Maryhill 21/5/1877 d 1966
Caps: Scotland 1
Maryhill Harp
Partick Thistle
1906 1914 Blackburn Rovers 210 75

Akers, George OL
b Preston 26/8/1912 d 1976
Preston St Luke's
1932 Preston North End 1
Clitheroe (loan)
Clitheroe

Akers, Walter (Wally) OR
b West Auckland 29/9/1917 d 1975
1934 Wolverhampton Wanderers 0
1935 Newport County 0
1935 Bournemouth & Boscombe Ath 15 4
1937 Chelsea 0
1939 1945 Mansfield Town (3) (3)
Gillingham
Corby Town

Albinson, George RH/LH
b Manchester 14/2/1897 d 1975
1920 Manchester United 0
1921 Manchester City 3
1922 Accrington Stanley 0
1923 1924 Crewe Alexandra 24 1

Alcock, Edward OL
b Hanley 7/9/1913 d 1981
Congleton Town
1935 Tranmere Rovers 5 1
Congleton Town

Alcock, George Leonard CF/IL
b Chorlton 15/8/1902 d 1976
Wombwell
1924 1926 Bradford City 15 9
1927 Crewe Alexandra 3
1928 Torquay United 0
1929 Doncaster Rovers 3

Alcock, Harry OL/CF
b Walsall q4 1905 d 1953
1925 1926 Walsall 45 13

Alcock, John Thomas IL/OL
b Wolverhampton q4 1869 d 1940
1892 1893 Walsall Town Swifts 10 4

Alden, Norman Ernest (Norrie) IR
b Caerphilly 3/11/1909 d 1980
Llanbradach Colliery
Mount Carmel Juniors
Merthyr Town
1933 Liverpool 0
1935 Oldham Athletic 1
1936 Southport 7 2
Hereford United

Alderman, Albert Edward IR/OR
b Alvaston 30/10/1907 d 1990
Alvaston House
1928 1933 Derby County 21 5
1934 Burnley 19 2

Alderson, John Henry OL
b Bowburn 5/3/1910 d 1986
Bowburn
Bishop Auckland
1930 Stoke City 0
Bowburn
1932 Darlington 2 1

From To Apps Goal

Alderson, John Thomas (Jack) GK
b Crook 28/11/1891 d 1972
Caps: WLge 1/England 1
Crook Juniors
Crook Town
Shildon Athletic
1912 Middlesbrough 0
Shildon Athletic
1912 Newcastle United 1
1920 1923 Crystal Palace 150
Pontypridd
1925 1928 Sheffield United 122
1929 Exeter City 36
1930 Torquay United 0
Worcester City
Crook Town

Alderson, Thomas (Tom) IL
b Leasingthorne 8/12/1908
West Auckland
1927 Bradford City (trial) 0
Cockfield
1929 Huddersfield Town 0
1930 Leeds United 4 2
1932 Luton Town 14 5
1933 1935 Darlington 116 39
1936 1937 Chester 44 4
1937 1938 Darlington 35 7

Aldridge, Albert James LB
b Walsall 13/4/1864 d 1891
Caps: England 2
Walsall Swifts
West Bromwich Albion
Walsall Town Swifts
1889 Aston Villa 15

Alexander, David CF
b Falkirk
Caps: Scotland 1
East Stirlingshire
1891 Darwen 21 9
1892 Accrington 6 1
Rossendale United
East Stirlingshire

Alexander, David B RH
b Glasgow
Clydebank
1938 Chelsea 1

Alexander, G GK
1895 Bolton Wanderers 2

Alexander, John William (Jack) OR
b Percy Main 25/8/1899 d 1976
Percy Main Amateurs
Preston Colliery
1924 Ashington 5
Percy Main
1926 Hull City 0
1928 Ashington 31 1
Workington
1929 Bury 0
Workington
Throckley Welfare
Wills Sports (Mitcham)

Alexander, Stanley (Stan) IR/OR/CF
b Percy Main 17/9/1905 d 1961
Percy Main Amateurs
1926 1931 Hull City 98 41
1931 1933 Bradford City 61 23
1933 1935 Millwall 88 11
1936 Tottenham Hotspur 9 1
1938 Accrington Stanley 22 2

Alford, Francis James (Frank) OL
b Swindon 14/5/1901 d 1982
Swindon Town
Darwen
Barrow
1921 Everton 2
1923 1924 Barrow 64 3
1925 Lincoln City 20 3
Scunthorpe & Lindsey United
Northfleet
Dartford
Sheppey United
Sittingbourne

Allan, Adam McIlroy CH/RH/LH
b Newarthill 12/9/1904
Regent Star
Rutherglen Glencairn
Falkirk
1927 1929 Sunderland 63
1930 1932 Reading 106 3
Queen of the South

Allan, Charles Edward LB
b Darlington q1 1908 d 1947
1931 Darlington 3
1932 1933 Northampton Town 15
1934 1936 Darlington 66 1

From To Apps Goal

Allan, George Horsburgh CF
b Linlithgow Bridge 23/4/1875 d 1899
Caps: Scotland 1
Vale of Avon
Linlithgow Athletic
Broxburn Shamrock
Bo'ness
Leith Athletic
1895 1896 Liverpool 49 42
Celtic
1898 Liverpool 30 8

Allan, James (Jimmy) RB/LB
b Airdrie 29/8/1899
Glasgow Ashfield
Airdrieonians
1925 1927 Leeds United 70
Third Lanark
1929 Coventry City 0

Allan, John IL/OR/IR
b Glasgow 1872
Glasgow Thistle
1893 1894 Derby County 36 8
1894 1897 Notts County 79 27
Heanor Town

Allan, John (Jack) RH
b Carlisle 11/5/1890
Benwell St James
Bentwick Mission
Newcastle North End
Bedlington United
Carlisle United
1909 1911 Everton 19
1912 Leeds City 14
Rochdale
1919 Coventry City 5
Walsall

Allan, John LB
b Cardenden 1891
Bowhill Thistle
Hibernian
East Fife
1913 1921 Bury 132 1
1922 Reading 42
J & P Coats (Rhode Island)

Allan, John IR
b Glasgow
1925 Leicester City 0
1926 1927 Manchester City 8 1
Scottish Interim League

Allan, John Thomas (Jack) IR/CF
b South Shields 2/1883
Bishop Auckland
1904 1906 Manchester United 35 21
Bishop Auckland

Allan, Richard OR
b Preston
Motherwell
1894 Preston North End 2 1
Chorley
Dundee
1897 Newcastle United 24 4
Bristol St George

Allan, Richard LB
1903 Stockport County 22

Allan, Robert GK
Cronberry Eglington
1907 Sunderland 11
Heart of Midlothian

Allan, Stanley James E (Jack) CF/IL
b Wallsend 28/12/1886 d 1919
Wallsend
1907 Sunderland 0
1908 1910 Newcastle United 15 5
1911 West Bromwich Albion 19 4
1912 1913 Nottingham Forest 22 3
Worcester City

Allan, Thomas E GK
b Glasgow
Caps: SLge 1
Wellwood Star
Rutherglen Glencairn
Heart of Midlothian
1908 1910 Sunderland 24
Heart of Midlothian
Motherwell

From To Apps Goal

Allan, Walter (Watty) IR/IL
b Paisley 1864
Fairfield
Chorley
Stalybridge Rovers
Northfleet
Kettering
Berry's
1898 Manchester City 0
Thames Ironworks
1898 1899 Loughborough 18 7
Watford
1901 Blackpool 6

Allan, William (Bill) GK
b Montrose 1870 d 1948
Montrose Belmont
Aberdeen Orion
Victoria United (Aberdeen)
1892 1895 Sheffield Wednesday 102
Victoria United (Aberdeen)
Millwall Athletic
Montrose
Camelon
East Stirlingshire
Montrose

Allan, William (Billy) LB
b Kilbarchan
Kilbarchan Athletic
Morton
Johnstone
Morton
Bethlehem Steel
1931 Hartlepools United 1
St Mirren
Dunfermline Athletic

Allcock, Clarence William (Bill) RH/LH/RB
b Codnor 18/7/1907 d 1971
Codnor
Ilkeston Rangers
Ilkeston United
Heanor Town
Grantham
1930 1933 Bradford Park Avenue 64
1935 1938 Barrow 127 5
1939 (Barrow) (3)

Allcock, HG LH
1895 Crewe Alexandra 15

Alldis, Gilbert John (Gillie) RH/OL
b Birkenhead 26/1/1920 d 1998
1938 1948 Tranmere Rovers 75 4
1939 (Tranmere Rovers) (3)
1950 New Brighton 12
Prescot Cables
Bangor City

Allen, Albert IR/IL
b Aston 4/1867 d 1899
Caps: England 1
St Philip's (Aston)
1888 1890 Aston Villa 44 27

Allen, Albert John (Jack) RB/LB
b Moston 16/10/1891 d 1971
Higher Blackley
Barrowfields
Hurst
1914 Glossop 23
1919 1923 Manchester City 52
1924 Southport 36
1925 Crewe Alexandra 30
1926 Southport 35
Lancaster Town

Allen, Albert Robert (Bob) OL/LB
b Bromley-by-Bow 11/10/1916 d 1992
Caps: England Sch
1932 Tottenham Hotspur 0
Leytonstone
1933 Clapton Orient 1
1934 1936 Fulham 11
1937 Doncaster Rovers 31 6
1938 Brentford 0
Dartford
1946 Northampton Town 5
1950 Colchester United 29 1
Bedford Town

Allen, Arthur Reginald (Reg) GK
b Marylebone 3/5/1919 d 1976
Caps: FLge 2
Corona
1938 1949 Queen's Park Rangers 183
1939 (Queen's Park Rangers) (3)
1950 1952 Manchester United 75
Altrincham

From To Apps Goal

Allen, Edward (Ned) LB
b Montrose 31/8/1875
Dundee Wanderers
Millwall Athletic
1900 Newcastle United 4
Dundee
Watford
Dundee

Allen, Edward IL
b London
1920 Southend United 4

Allen, Frank IR/RH
b Altofts 5/5/1901 d 1989
Altofts West Riding Colliery
Castleford Town
1925 1927 Barnsley 68 2
Bangor City
Port Vale 0
1928 Clapton Orient 0
1929 Southport 31 6
1930 Nelson 14
1930 1932 Barrow 67 11
1933 1934 New Brighton 53 18
Le Havre
Ollerton Colliery

Allen, Harry CH
b Walsall 19/1/1866 d 1895
Caps: England 5
Walsall Swifts
1888 1893 Wolverhampton Wanderers 123 9

Allen, Henry (Harry) OL
b Spondon 1879 d 1939
Alvaston
1898 1899 Derby County 15 3
1899 Leicester Fosse 13 2
1900 Derby County 0
Alvaston & Boulton
(Rhodesia)

Allen, Henry Albert OR/OL
b Hackney 28/6/1898 d 1976
Gnome Athletic
1920 1921 Southend United 23
1923 Gillingham 6
1924 1925 Charlton Athletic 38 1
Grays Thurrock

Allen, Herbert IL
b Shifnal q2 1899
Wellington St George's
1923 Notts County 1
Stourbridge
Burton Town
1928 Charlton Athletic 0
Wellington Town
Wellington St George's
Oswestry Town
Darlaston
Wellington Town

Allen, James (Jimmy) RH
b Amble 18/8/1913 d 1979
Stakeford United
1934 Huddersfield Town 1
1935 1936 Queen's Park Rangers 44 1
1937 Clapton Orient 5

Allen, James Phillips (Jimmy) CH
b Poole 16/10/1909 d 1995
Caps: FLge 2/England 2
Poole Central
Poole
1930 1933 Portsmouth 132 1
1934 1938 Aston Villa 147 2
1939 (Aston Villa) (3)

Allen, James Thomas (Jack) RB/RH/LB
b Sneinton q1 1900
Walker Celtic
1921 1923 Crystal Palace 16
1924 Hartlepools United 29 3
Jarrow

Allen, John CF
b Bishop Auckland
Bishop Auckland
1897 Newcastle United 1

Allen, John (Jack) RB
Colne
1907 Chesterfield Town 11 1
Doncaster Rovers

From To Apps Goal

Allen, John William Alcroft (Jack) CF/OL/IL
b Newburn 31/1/1903 d 1957
Prudhoe Castle
1923 Leeds United 2
1924 1926 Brentford 54 24
1926 1930 Sheffield Wednesday 104 76
1931 1934 Newcastle United 81 34
1934 Bristol Rovers 6 2
1935 Gateshead 23 12
Ashington

Allen, Joseph (Joe) IR/IL
b Bilsthorpe 30/12/1909 d 1978
Bilsthorpe Colliery
Mansfield Town
Bilsthorpe Colliery
1932 Tottenham Hotspur 0
Northfleet (loan)
1932 Tottenham Hotspur 1 1
1933 1934 Queen's Park Rangers 51 6
1935 Mansfield Town 8 5
Racing Club de Roubaix
Nancy

Allen, Mervyn John LB/IR/RH
b Bargoed 16/10/1909 d 1976
Gilfach
1931 1933 Hull City 15 1
1934 Carlisle United 16
1934 Barrow 0

Allen, Percy William RH
b West Ham 2/7/1895 d 1969
1919 1922 West Ham United 80 5
1923 1924 Lincoln City 59 4
1925 1926 Northampton Town 44 3
Weymouth
Peterborough & Fletton United
Stamford Town

Allen, Philip John LB
b Brentford 5/11/1902 d 1992
Grenadier Guards
1922 1923 Brentford 3
Peterborough & Fletton United
Wellingborough Town
Stamford Town

Allen, Ralph Slack Littlewood CF
b Newburn 30/6/1906 d 1981
Walbottle
Elswick
Wombwell
1927 Hartlepools United (trial) 0
1927 Sheffield Wednesday (trial) 0
Dipton United
1928 1930 Fulham 16 8
1930 1933 Brentford 13 4
1934 1935 Charlton Athletic 52 47
1936 Reading 10 7
1936 1937 Northampton Town 52 41
1938 Torquay United 28 15
Annfield Plain

Allen, Robert H IR
b Dundee
Dundee
1919 West Ham United 1 1

Allen, Thomas (Tommy) GK
b Moxley 1/5/1897 d 1968
Bilston United
1919 Sunderland 19
1920 1927 Southampton 291
1928 1931 Coventry City 154
1932 Accrington Stanley 35
1933 Northampton Town 19
Kidderminster Harriers
Cradley Heath

Allen, Thomas (Tom) RH
1928 Darlington 3

Allen, Thomas S IL
Bath City
1912 Bristol City 1 1
Bath City

Allen, W IL
1893 Rotherham Town 1

Allen, William (Bill) LH/IR
b Newburn 22/10/1917 d 1981
1938 Chesterfield 2
1939 1949 York City 130 23
1939 (York City) (3) (2)
1950 1951 Scunthorpe United 64 1
Goole Town

From To Apps Goal

Allen, William B (Barney) OR
b Birmingham 1882 d 1946
Icknield Street Old Boys
1905 Aston Villa 3 1
Westbourne Celtic
1906 Chesterfield Town 20 1
Kidderminster Harriers
Stafford Rangers

Allin, Tom CF
b Boston q2 1862
Boston
1888 Notts County 6 2

Allinson, Charles (Charlie) CF
b Accrington 24/11/1901 d 1975
St Mary's RC (Oswaldtwistle)
1922 Accrington Stanley 1
Darwen

Allison, Arthur OR
Wisbech Town
1896 Lincoln City (trial) 1

Allison, John IL
b Glasgow
Parkhead Juniors
Kilmarnock
St Johnstone
Stenhousemuir
East Stirlingshire
Airdrieonians
Queen of the South (loan)
Cowdenbeath
Morton
1929 Barrow 11
Armadale
Shelbourne

Allison, John William IL
b Brigg q4 1884
1907 Gainsborough Trinity 3
Pinxton
Sutton Junction
Mansfield Town
Kiveton Park

Allison, Thomas (Tommy) LH
b Edinburgh 1875 d 1961
Strathclyde
1898 1900 New Brighton Tower 66 1
Reading
West Ham United

Allison, William Martin Laws (Bill) LB
b Shildon 13/1/1908 d 1981
Shildon
1929 Arsenal 0
1931 Clapton Orient 14
1932 1933 Darlington 52
Eden Colliery
1935 1937 Hartlepools United 107
Spennymoor United

Allman, Arthur RB
b Milton, Staffordshire 24/12/1890 d 1956
Smallthorne
Shrewsbury Town
1912 Wolverhampton Wanderers 0
Swansea Town
1914 Manchester United 12
1920 Millwall Athletic 6
1921 Port Vale (trial) 0
Aberaman Athletic
1922 1923 Crewe Alexandra 22
Aberaman Athletic

Allman, Leslie GK
b Burton-on-Trent 26/5/1902 d 1979
Moulton Alexandra
Northwich Victoria
Llandudno Town
Ellesmere Port Town
Lancaster Town
1926 1927 Norwich City 15
1928 Merthyr Town 5
Kettering Town
Shrewsbury Town

Allman, Messina Wilson (Dick) CF
b Burslem q2 1883 d 1943
Burslem Higherhave
1903 1904 Burslem Port Vale 35 11
Reading
Portsmouth
Plymouth Argyle
1908 Liverpool 1
Wrexham
Grantham
Ton Pentre
1911 Leicester Fosse 7 3
Croydon Common
Crystal Palace
Maidstone United

From To Apps Goal

Allmark, John Joseph OR/CF
b Liverpool 26/5/1912 d 1981
Colwyn Bay United
Witton Albion
1937 Manchester City 1
Altrincham (loan)
1938 New Brighton 5 2

Allon, Thomas George (George) RH
b Blyth 27/8/1899 d 1983
Usworth Colliery
1921 1924 Coventry City 74 2
Nuneaton Town
Peterborough & Fletton United
1926 1931 Northampton Town 185 7
Wigan Athletic

Allport, Austin RB
b Darlington 18/10/1905 d 1986
1927 Darlington 0
1928 Stockport County 3
1929 Wolverhampton Wanderers 0
1930 Crewe Alexandra 0
Spennymoor United
Rhyl Athletic
Northwich Victoria

Allport, George Harry (Harry) RH/LH
b North Ormesby q4 1873 d 1943
1893 Middlesbrough Ironopolis 21 1
1899 Middlesbrough 31

Allsebrook, Richard (Dick) LH
b Newstead 25/9/1892 d 1961
Newstead Amateurs
1912 1919 Notts County 97 2
Ebbw Vale
Hucknall Byron

Allsop, Edwin Thomas RH
b Chesterfield 6/12/1887 d 1974
Eckington Red Rose
1909 1911 Gainsborough Trinity 3

Allsop, William Henry (Bill) RB
b Ripley 29/1/1912 d 1997
Ripley Town
1930 Bolton Wanderers 0
1931 1932 Port Vale 6
1934 1946 Halifax Town 239
1939 (Halifax Town) (3)

Allsopp, Dennis Watkin (Dan) GK
b Derby 13/2/1871 d 1921
Derby Junction
1892 1899 Nottingham Forest 206

Allsopp, Elijah OR/RH/IR
b Wymeswold q3 1877 d 1958
Bury
1893 1896 Notts County 59 20

Allsopp, Thomas Charlesworth (Tommy) OL
b Leicester 18/12/1880 d 1919
1900 1901 Leicester Fosse 34 3
Luton Town
1904 Leicester Fosse 30 4
Brighton & Hove Albion
Norwich City

Allum, Leonard Hector (Len) RH
b Reading 16/7/1907 d 1980
1929 Fulham 0
1930 Reading (trial) 0
Maidenhead United
1932 1938 Chelsea 93 2
1939 Clapton Orient (1)

Allwright, Charles Russell S OR
b Brentford q3 1888 d 1966
Brentford
1919 Bristol City 11
1920 Swindon Town 0

Almond, Alfred LB
b Alderley Edge 28/4/1907 d 1981
Sandbach Ramblers
1928 Leeds United 0
1929 1930 Carlisle United 22
1930 Barnsley 0

Almond, James LH
b Clayton-le-Moors 9/1874 d 1923
Nelson
1896 Burnley 1
Swindon Town

Almond, John (Jack) CF/IL
b Darlington 6/11/1876 d 1912
Darlington
Bishop Auckland
1896 1900 Sheffield United 109 23
Gainford
Millwall Athletic
1904 Bradford City 0
Doncaster Rovers
Doncaster GNR Loco

From To Apps Goal

Almond, John (Jack) OL
b Prescot 21/11/1915 d 1993
Prescot Cables
1934 1935 Stoke City 3 1
1936 Tranmere Rovers 22 5
Shrewsbury Town

Almond, William (Willie) CH/RH
b Blackburn 5/4/1868
Witton (Blackburn)
1888 1892 Blackburn Rovers 58 3
1892 Accrington 9 1
1893 Northwich Victoria 5
Middlesbrough
Nelson
Millwall Athletic
Tottenham Hotspur
Millwall Athletic
Tottenham Hotspur
Clapton
Wandsworth

Alsford, Walter John (Wally) LH/RH
b Edmonton 6/11/1911 d 1968
Caps: England 1
1929 Tottenham Hotspur 0
Cheshunt (loan)
Northfleet (loan)
1930 1936 Tottenham Hotspur 81
1936 1937 Nottingham Forest 30
Grantham

Alsop, Gilbert Arthur CF/IR
b Frampton Cotterell 10/9/1908 d 1992
Bath City
1929 1930 Coventry City 16 4
1931 1935 Walsall 160 126
1935 West Bromwich Albion 1
1938 Ipswich Town 9 2
1938 1946 Walsall 35 25
1939 (Walsall) (3) (1)

Alsop, Leonard (Len) OL
b Richmond, North Yorkshire 28/10/1905 d 1993
1930 Darlington 1

Alstead, Anthony LB
b Preston 15/7/1893 d 1973
Bamber Bridge Corinthians
1914 1919 Preston North End 14
Lancaster Town

Alston, William (Bill) RH
b Scotland 19/4/1884 d 1971
Maxwelltown Volunteers
1907 Lincoln City 18 2
Rochdale

Alton, Charles LB/RB
b Brampton, Derbyshire 24/12/1891 d 1969
Spital Olympic
Chesterfield Town
Castleford Town
Doncaster Rovers
Stalybridge Celtic
1919 1920 Rotherham County 55 1
1921 1924 Brentford 126 5
Northfleet

Alton, Thomas William RB
b Chesterfield q4 1917 d 1964
New Tupton Ivanhoe
1937 Derby County 3

Ambler, Alfred RH/LH
b Manchester q3 1879 d 1940
Hawktown Juniors
Hyde
1899 Newton Heath 9 1
Colne
1906 1907 Stockport County 24
Exeter City
Colne

Ambler, Charles James (Charlie) GK
b Alverstoke 1868 d 1952
Bostall Rovers
Royal Arsenal
Clapton
Dartford
Luton Town
Tottenham Hotspur
1895 Woolwich Arsenal 1
Tottenham Hotspur
Gravesend United
New Brompton
West Ham United
Millwall Athletic

Ambridge, Frederick William GK
b Wellingborough 16/6/1892 d 1966
Royal Navy
1921 Northampton Town 13
Wellingborough Town

From To Apps Goal

Ambrose, D OL
1896 Burton Swifts 1

Amery, Charles Siddall (Charlie) LB/CH/IL
b Heswall 16/9/1910 d 1979
Heswall
West Kirby
1931 Tranmere Rovers 0
1932 1935 New Brighton 117 9
1935 1937 Tranmere Rovers 47
1937 Stockport County 1
Waterford
Heswall

Ames, Leslie Ethelbert George (Les) OL/OR
b Elham 3/12/1905 d 1990
Folkestone
1926 1930 Clapton Orient 14
1931 Gillingham 5 1

Amos, Alfred Herbert (Alf) LH/RH/CH
b Forest Hill 9/2/1893 d 1964
Kingstonian
1920 1921 Brentford 74 4
1922 1929 Millwall Athletic 217 13
Hitchin Town

Amos, Stanley Thomas CF/RH
b Cradley Heath 1907
Cradley Heath St Luke's
1926 1927 Gillingham 31 12
Cradley Heath St Luke's

Amos, Walter Robert (Wally) OL
b Grimsby 3/9/1899 d 1967
Caps: FLge 1
Worksop Town
1923 1934 Bury 455 122
1935 Accrington Stanley 0

Ancell, Robert Francis Dudgeon (Bobby) LB
b Dumfries 16/6/1911 d 1987
Caps: Scotland War 1/Scotland 2
Mid Annandale
St Mirren
Queen of the South (loan)
1936 1938 Newcastle United 97 1
1939 (Newcastle United) (3)
Dundee
Aberdeen
Dundee
Berwick Rangers

Anderson, Alfred James (Alf) OL
b Old Cumnock 1915
Yoker Athletic
Hibernian
1936 1938 Bolton Wanderers 52 4
Aberdeen
Third Lanark

Anderson, Andrew Lyle OL
b Glasgow 27/2/1885 d 1969
Glasgow Ashfield
St Mirren
1908 1911 Newcastle United 61 5
Third Lanark
1914 Leicester Fosse 25 1
Abercorn

Anderson, David Robert McLean LH/CF/IR
b Lasswade 1/11/1891
Heart of Midlothian
Bonnyrigg Rose
1910 1911 Preston North End 9 3
Queen's Park Rangers
Swansea Town
Rosewell
1921 Halifax Town 10 2

Anderson, Douglas Nicol LB
b Stonehaven 25/3/1914 d 1989
Stonehaven
Aberdeen
Dundee United
Hibernian
1938 Brentford 1
Derry City

Anderson, Edward OL
b Beith 27/1/1879 d 1954
Beith
St Mirren
Beith
St Mirren
1903 Woolwich Arsenal 2
Fulham

Anderson, Edward Totty CF
b Newcastle q1 1884
Willington
1905 Sheffield United 1
Queen's Park Rangers

From To Apps Goal

Anderson, Edward Walton (Ted) RH/RB/LH
b Dudley, Northumberland 17/7/1911 d 1979
Dudley (Northumberland)
Framwellgate Moor
Durham Victoria
Jarrow
Worksop Town
1930 Wolverhampton Wanderers 3
1931 1932 Torquay United 61 2
1933 1934 West Ham United 26
1935 1936 Chester 23
1937 1947 Tranmere Rovers 73

Anderson, Ferguson GK
b Newcastle q2 1887
North Shields Athletic
1911 Bristol City 7
Jarrow Caledonians

Anderson, Frank (Ernie) LH
b Scotland 1896
Distillery
Clydebank
Cardiff City
1920 Stockport County 24 3
1921 Cardiff City 1
1922 Aberdare Athletic 14 1

Anderson, George Albert GK
b Haydon Bridge 1887 d 1954
Haydon Bridge
Mickley Colliery Welfare
1911 1912 Sunderland 10
Aberdeen
Dundee
Aberdeen

Anderson, George E (Geordie) CH/IR/IL
b Edinburgh 1870
Caps: SLge 1
Leith Athletic
1892 1896 Blackburn Rovers 131 11
New Brighton Tower
1897 Blackburn Rovers (loan) 2
1898 Blackburn Rovers 26 7
1898 New Brighton Tower 8
1899 Blackburn Rovers 19 1
1900 1903 Blackpool 91 29

Anderson, George Edward OL
b Sunderland 1881
Sunderland Albion
Sunderland Royal Rovers
1905 1908 Birmingham 74 10
Brentford

Anderson, George Russell IR/IL/CF
b Saltcoats 29/10/1904 d 1974
Dalry Thistle
Airdrieonians
1926 Brentford 8 2
1927 1928 Chelsea 9
1929 Norwich City 28 12
1930 Carlisle United 2 1
1930 Gillingham (trial) 0
Cowdenbeath
Yeovil & Petters United
1933 1934 Bury 25 10
1934 Huddersfield Town 14 4
1935 1936 Mansfield Town 36 16
Newark Town
Ayr United
Saltcoats Victoria

Anderson, George Walter CF
b Cheetham q1 1893
Broughton St James
Broughton Wellington
Salford United
1909 1910 Bury 3
1911 1914 Manchester United 80 37

Anderson, James (Jock) IR
d 1991
Arthurlie
Mossley
Morton
Mossley
Hurst
Winsford United
Ashton National
1938 Rotherham United 8
Stalybridge Celtic

Anderson, James (Jimmy) LB
b Felling 25/7/1913 d 1993
Blyth Spartans
1933 Darlington 0
Wigan Athletic
Blyth Spartans
Queen of the South
1939 Brentford (3)
1946 Carlisle United 11

From To Apps Goal

Anderson, James Ballantine (Jimmy) RH
Musselburgh Bruntonians
1922 Hartlepools United 13

Anderson, John CH
b Rothesay 1879
Morton
Rothesay Royal Victoria
1901 Chesterfield Town 2

Anderson, John RH
Vale of Clyde
Port Glasgow Athletic
1904 Notts County 9
Port Glasgow Athletic
Hamilton Academical

Anderson, John OR
b Hedleyhope q4 1900
Crook Town
Workington
Shildon (trial)
West Stanley
1924 Ashington 1
West Stanley

Anderson, John IR
b South Molton
South Molton
1925 Exeter City 1
South Molton

Anderson, John Curr (Jock) IR/CF
b Dundee 8/5/1915 d 1987
Stobswell
1933 1945 Portsmouth 81 33
1939 (Portsmouth) (3) (1)
1946 Aldershot 4 1
Newport (Isle of Wight)

Anderson, John William (Jack) LH/CH
b Crook 1875
Crook Town
1896 1902 Woolwich Arsenal 144 10
Portsmouth
Crook Town

Anderson, Joseph (Joe) CF
b Bishopton 1895
Thornliebank
Vale of Leven
Airdrieonians
Dumbarton Harp
Clydebank
1919 1923 Burnley 121 64
Clydebank
Pollok
Vale of Leven
Pollok

Anderson, Nicholas CF
b Wolverhampton 1865
1888 Wolverhampton Wanderers 2

Anderson, Reginald S IR
b Greenwich q4 1912 d 1942
Caps: England Amat
Dulwich Hamlet
1938 Cardiff City 2 1

Anderson, Robert Nicol Smith (Bobby) RB
b Ardrossan 26/2/1897 d 1974
Caps: WLge 1
Ardrossan Winton Rovers
1923 1925 Luton Town 74
1926 1929 Newport County 137
1930 1931 Lincoln City 27

Anderson, Samuel IL
b Glasgow
Shettleston
Hamilton Academical
South Shields
Hamilton Academical
1914 Bradford City 14 3
Bathgate
Airdrieonians
Hamilton Academical
Third Lanark
St Bernard's
Nithsdale Wanderers

Anderson, Samuel MJ (Sam) OL
Stockton
1933 Luton Town 10 5
West Stanley

Anderson, T IL
1903 Blackpool 2

From To Apps Goal

Anderson, Thomas Coldwell IR/CF
b Shettleston 12/1/1895
Shettleston
Hamilton Academical
Johnstone
Bathgate
Albion Rovers
1920 1921 Bradford City 2
Third Lanark
Bathgate

Anderson, Thomas D GK
b Gateshead
1938 Grimsby Town 1

Anderson, Thomas W OR
1932 Rotherham United 1

Anderson, Walter (Wattie) CF/IL
b Thornaby q4 1879 d 1904
Darlington
Thornaby Utopians
1899 1901 Sheffield United 4
1901 1902 Woolwich Arsenal 28 10
Plymouth Argyle

Anderson, William (Bill) LB
b High Westwood 12/1/1913 d 1986
Medomsley Juniors
1931 Nottingham Forest 0
Chopwell Institute
1933 1934 Sheffield United 23
1935 Barnsley 14
Hartlepools United 0

Anderton, William OR/OL
b Blackpool q4 1879 d 1942
1901 1906 Blackpool 104 10
Rossendale United
Blackpool Athletic

Andrews, Arthur LH
b Sunderland 12/1/1901 d 1971
Lambton Star
1921 1922 Durham City 13 2
1922 1930 Sunderland 228 2
Blyth Spartans (loan)
Ashington
Spennymoor United

Andrews, Charles RB/LH
Lincoln Liberal Club
1905 1907 Lincoln City 5
Rotherham Town

Andrews, Frederick Edgar (Fred) CF
b King's Norton q3 1896
Burton All Saints
1923 Bristol City 1
Burton All Saints

Andrews, Harold IL/LH/CF
b Lincoln 13/8/1903 d 1988
St Botolph's Old Boys (Lincoln)
1924 1927 Lincoln City 75 41
1927 1931 Notts County 134 55
1932 1934 Barnsley 110 42
1935 Luton Town 1
1936 1937 Accrington Stanley 65 2
Players (Nottingham)

Andrews, Harold Edgar Ramsden CF/IF
b Earby 8/6/1897 d 1984
St Cuthbert's
1921 Nelson 8 1
1922 Bury 0
1922 Luton Town 0
Rushden Town
Chorley
Torquay United
1927 Exeter City 2
1928 Merthyr Town 7 1
Bath City
Tunbridge Wells Rangers

Andrews, Harry OR/OL
b Oldham
1926 Oldham Athletic 0
Bacup Borough
1928 Wolverhampton Wanderers 0
1929 1930 Chesterfield 8 1

Andrews, John Henry (Jack) LH/LB
b Darlington 26/5/1898 d 1974
Darlington Rise Carr
Darlington Railway Athletic
1922 1923 Darlington 4
1924 Durham City 0
1924 Grimsby Town 0
Shildon
1925 1928 Southend United 74 1
1929 Darlington 0

From To Apps Goal

Andrews, Leonard Thomas Alford (Len) IL/OL
b Reading 9/12/1888 d 1969
Reading University
Reading
Southampton
1920 Reading 33 5
1921 1923 Southampton 59 3
1924 Watford 38 6

Andrews, William IR/IL
Dumbarton
1894 Bolton Wanderers 12 3
1895 1896 Loughborough 46 11

Andrews, William (Willie) RH/IR
b Kansas City, USA 1886
Caps: IrLge 6/Ireland 3
Stranmillis
Distillery
Glentoran
1908 Oldham Athletic 9 3
1908 1909 Stockport County 13
Glentoran
1912 1914 Grimsby Town 105 2
Distillery
Belfast United
Darlington
Leadgate Park
Belfast Bohemians

Angus, Hugh OL
West Manchester
1892 Ardwick 2

Angus, James (Jimmy) CF
Morpeth Harriers
1908 1909 Stockport County 9
West Stanley

Angus, John (Jack) OL
Newcastle West End
1888 Everton 5
Gainsborough Trinity
Newcastle West End

Angus, John (Jack) CH/LH
b Amble 12/3/1909 d 1965
Amble Welfare
1928 Wolverhampton Wanderers 0
Wath Athletic
Scunthorpe & Lindsey United
1930 1947 Exeter City 246 1
1939 (Exeter City) (3)
Sidmouth

Angus, John Alexander (Jack) GK
b King Edward 1868 d 1891
King's Park
Sunderland Albion
1890 Everton 11

Angus, John William CF
b Blythswood 1/12/1868
Third Lanark
1892 Ardwick 7 3
Southampton St Mary's
Fulham

Annables, Walter (Wally) RB/LB
b Swinton 31/10/1911 d 1979
Mexborough Athletic
1932 1934 Grimsby Town 6
1936 1938 Hull City 62 1
1939 Carlisle United (2)

Annan, Walter Archibald (Archie) RB/LB
b Bathgate 1880
West Calder
St Bernard's
1902 Sunderland 1
1903 1904 Sheffield United 27
1905 1909 Bristol City 143
Burslem Port Vale

Annis, William (Billy) LH/RH
b Darlaston 1877
1898 1904 Wolverhampton Wanderers 137 1

Ansell, George Thomas Leonard IL/IR/CF
b Worthing 28/11/1909 d 1988
Worthing
Oxford University
1931 1932 Brighton & Hove Albion 6 1
Corinthians
1935 Norwich City 4
Kimbolton Town
Eynesbury Rovers

From To Apps Goal

Anstey, Brendel GK
b Bristol 11/1887 d 1933
Hanham Athletic
Bristol Rovers
1910 1914 Aston Villa 42
1919 Leicester City 7
Mid-Rhondda
Wednesbury Old Athletic

Anstiss, Henry Augustus (Harry) IL/IR/OR
b Chiswick 22/8/1899 d 1964
Hammersmith Athletic
1920 1921 Brentford 42 19
1922 Millwall Athletic 19 3
1923 Watford 18 5
1924 1925 Rochdale 72 39
1926 Sheffield Wednesday 12 5
1926 1930 Port Vale 109 36
1931 1932 Swansea Town 28 6
1933 Crewe Alexandra 30 7
1934 Gillingham 33 6
Tunbridge Wells Rangers
Cray Wanderers

Anthoney, Charles RB/LB
b Mansfield 15/4/1902 d 1982
Mansfield Town
1929 1931 Northampton Town 81
1932 Mansfield Town 39 2

Anthony, A CH
1899 Bolton Wanderers 3

Anthony, Walter OL
b Basford 21/11/1879 d 1950
Osmaston
Heanor Town
1903 1904 Nottingham Forest 7
Brighton & Hove Albion
1907 1913 Blackburn Rovers 149 11
Stalybridge Celtic

Antonio (Rowlands), George Antonio IR/RH/IL
b Whitchurch 20/11/1914 d 1997
Oswestry Town
1935 1946 Stoke City 84 13
1946 1947 Derby County 18 2
1948 1949 Doncaster Rovers 34 7
1949 1950 Mansfield Town 67 2
Oswestry Town
Wellington Town
Stafford Rangers
Oswestry Town
Berriew

Appleby, Arthur Benjamin (Ben) CF
b Burton-on-Trent q3 1877 d 1961
Shobnall Albion
Trinity Strollers
1898 Derby County 0
Chatham
1900 Burton Swifts 33 5
1901 West Bromwich Albion 1
Bristol Rovers
Leighton

Appleby, John (Jack) IR/OL/IL
b New Seaham 4/7/1906 d 1987
Beds & Herts Regiment
Aldershot
Aldershot Command
1932 1934 Southport 81 20
South Shields
Seaham Colliery

Appleby, Thomas Alexander (Tommy) OR
b Wolverhampton 5/10/1916 d 1977
Beechwood Corries
Windsor Juniors
1935 1936 Newport County 14 3
Glenavon
Yeovil & Petters United
Folkestone
1939 Southport 0
1939 Tranmere Rovers 0
Merthyr Tydfil

Appleton, Frederick (Fred) RB/LB
b Hyde 22/6/1904 d 1932
Marple
1925 1927 Manchester City 2

Appleton, Leonard (Len) OR/IR
b Bamfurlong 16/11/1892 d 1970
Scowcroft's Colliery
Atherton
1914 1919 Blackpool 33 3
1920 Exeter City 37 2
1921 Southport 25

Appleyard, Fred LH/IL
b Rochdale 13/6/1909 d 1995
Norden St James
1928 1931 Rochdale 6
Norden Congregationalists

From To Apps Goal

Appleyard, George Charles CF
b Rawmarsh 31/5/1900 d 1967
Rotherham Forge
Rotherham Town
Rawmarsh Athletic
1923 Barnsley 4 2
1924 Exeter City 8 1
Torquay United
1926 Wrexham 5 2

Appleyard, William (Bill) CF
b Cleethorpes 16/11/1878 d 1958
Cleethorpes Town
Cleethorpes Rovers
Grimsby Tradesmen
1901 1902 Grimsby Town 44 19
1902 1907 Newcastle United 128 71
1908 Oldham Athletic 4
1908 Grimsby Town 13 2
Mansfield Mechanics

Apsey, Thomas Leonard (Len) CF
b Ynyshir 11/2/1910 d 1967
Trethomas Bluebirds
1930 Newport County 2
1930 Burnley 0
1931 Arsenal 0
Porth

Arblaster, William (Bill) IL
b Brownhills q4 1900 d 1958
Darlaston
Bilston United
1923 1925 Merthyr Town 92 29
1926 1927 Gillingham 54 24
Darlaston
Leamington Town
Darlaston

Arch, William Henry (Harry) RB
b Tipton 29/11/1894 d 1978
Great Bridge Celtic
Pensnett
1919 West Bromwich Albion 0
1921 Newport County 28
Willenhall
1923 1925 Grimsby Town 91
1926 Hartlepools United 23
Bilston United

Archer, Archie Allen Edgar LH/RH/CH
b Swindon 7/3/1899 d 1982
Caps: England Sch
Swindon Rovers
1920 1930 Swindon Town 189 4

Archer, Arthur RB/LB
b Ashby-de-la-Zouch q4 1877 d 1940
Burton St Edmund's
Tutbury Hampton
Swadlincote Town
1894 1896 Burton Wanderers 42 1
1897 1901 Small Heath 154 4
New Brompton
Wingfield House
Queen's Park Rangers
Tottenham Hotspur (loan)
Norwich City
Brighton & Hove Albion
Millwall Athletic

Archer, Frederick John IL/CF
b Aston-upon-Trent 28/2/1900 d 1973
1919 Rotherham County 2 1
1920 Aston Villa 0
1922 1923 Walsall 29 10
1924 Sheffield United 0

Archer, George Thompson CH/RH
b Corbridge 19/8/1899 d 1993
Hexham Town
1922 1925 Ashington 12

Archer, John William (Bill) LH
b Wednesbury 24/7/1908 d 1985
1929 1930 Walsall 26
1932 1935 Everton 15 2
1936 1938 Coventry City 76
1938 Plymouth Argyle 19
1939 (Plymouth Argyle) (2)

Archer, William J (Bill) LH
Freetown
1901 1902 Bury 2

Archibald, David Kerr RB/LB
b Glasgow 20/9/1902
Parkhead
Morton
New York Nationals
Clyde (trial)
1929 1932 York City 85
Shelbourne

From To Apps Goal

Archibald, James Mitchell (Jimmy) LH/CH/RH
b Falkirk 18/9/1892 d 1975
Cambuslang Rangers
Bellshill Athletic
Motherwell
1919 1921 Tottenham Hotspur 24 1
1922 Aberdare Athletic 30 2
1923 1925 Clapton Orient 49 1
1926 Southend United 0
Margate
Tunbridge Wells Rangers
Ashford Town (Kent)

Archibald, John (Jock) GK
b Strathaven 23/8/1895
Albion Rovers
Reading
1919 Chelsea 0
St Bernard's
1921 Newcastle United 1
1923 1926 Grimsby Town 111
1926 1927 Darlington 41
Albion Rovers
Airdrieonians
East Stirlingshire

Archibald, Robert Fleming (Bobby) OL
b Strathaven 6/11/1894 d 1966
Rutherglen Glencairn
Albion Rovers
Hibernian (loan)
Third Lanark
Aberdeen
Rangers (loan)
Ayr United (loan)
Albion Rovers
Dumbarton
Aberdeen
Raith Rovers
Third Lanark
1925 1931 Stoke City 262 37
1932 Barnsley 6 1

Ardley, George Henry RH
b Langley Park q4 1897 d 1927
Langley Park
1919 Sunderland 1
Shildon Athletic

Ardron, Walter (Wally) CF
b Swinton-on-Dearne 19/9/1918 d 1978
Denaby United
1938 Rotherham United (trial) 1
Denaby United
1945 1948 Rotherham United 122 98
1949 1954 Nottingham Forest 182 123

Argue, James (Jimmy) IR
b Glasgow 26/11/1911 d 1978
St Roch's
1931 Birmingham 0
1933 1946 Chelsea 118 30
1939 (Chelsea) (1)
Shrewsbury Town

Arkesden, Arthur Thomas GK
b Warwick q1 1873 d 1944
1896 Burton Wanderers 15

Arkesden, Thomas (Tom) IL/IR
b Warwick q3 1878 d 1921
1895 1896 Burton Wanderers 25 5
1898 1900 Derby County 50 14
1901 1902 Burton United 53 26
1902 1905 Manchester United 70 28
1907 Gainsborough Trinity 6
Burton United

Armand, John Edward (Jack) IR/IL/CF
b Sabathu, India 11/8/1898 d 1974
Caps: WLge 1
West Stanley
1922 1928 Leeds United 74 23
1929 1930 Swansea Town 54 10
Ashton National
1932 Southport 0
1932 Newport County 3 1
Scarborough
Denaby United

Armes, Samuel (Sammy) OR
b New Seaham 30/3/1908 d 1958
Howden
Dawdon Colliery
1929 1931 Carlisle United 76 19
1932 1933 Chester 31 13
1933 Blackpool 4
Wigan Athletic
1935 1938 Leeds United 79 8
1938 Middlesbrough 3

From To Apps Goal

Armeson, Lawrence Raymond LH/CH
b Rotherham 28/2/1917 d 1964
Rotherham YMCA
1934 Sheffield United 0
1935 Rotherham United 4
1938 Coventry City 7

Armfield, William Christopher Wassell OR
(Billy)
b Handsworth 7/7/1903 d 1985
Ellisons
1923 1927 Aston Villa 12 2
1929 1931 Exeter City 72 14
1932 Gillingham 30 7
Droitwich
Brierley Hill Alliance

Armitage, George Henry CH
b Stoke Newington 17/1/1898 d 1936
Caps: England Amat/England 1
St Saviour's (Chelsea)
Wimbledon
1923 1929 Charlton Athletic 165 4
Leyton

Armitage, Harold Arthur RB
b Sheffield 16/8/1901 d 1973
Hathersage
1920 1921 Sheffield Wednesday 3
1922 1925 Bristol Rovers 122
1926 Lincoln City 9
Scarborough

Armitage, John Henry (Jack) CH
b Chapeltown 21/8/1896 d 1940
Thorncliffe Works
Mexborough Town
1924 1925 Burnley 44 1
1926 1928 Oldham Athletic 90 3
1929 Southend United 9 2
1930 Northampton Town 4
Wombwell

Armitage, John W GK
1931 Halifax Town 8

Armitage, Leonard (Len) RH/CF/IR
b Sheffield 20/10/1899 d 1972
Wadsley Bridge
1919 Sheffield Wednesday 3
1920 1922 Leeds United 48 11
1923 Wigan Borough 28 21
1923 1931 Stoke 194 19
Rhyl Athletic
1932 1933 Port Vale 11 2

Armitt, Caesar Charles Edward (Charles) OL
b Bollington q2 1866 d 1942
Macclesfield
Liverpool Police Athletic
Bootle
Gorton Villa
1892 Blackburn Rovers 0
Chester
Gorton Villa
1892 Ardwick 1

Armitt, Thomas (Tom) CH
b Pendleton 1/4/1904 d 1972
Pendleton
1925 Accrington Stanley 1

Armory, Wilfred (Wilf) IL
b Hunwick 23/1/1911 d 1996
New Brancepeth
1929 Norwich City 0
Spennymoor United
Ayr United
1932 Aldershot 3
Spennymoor United
Nuneaton Town
Folkestone

Armour, Andrew D OR
b Irvine 24/7/1883 d 1955
Caps: SLge 1
Irvine Meadow
Queen's Park
Kilmarnock
Queen's Park
Kilmarnock
1911 1913 Huddersfield Town 93 7
Kilmarnock
Clydebank (loan)

Armson, Herbert IL
b Leek q4 1875
Ogden's (Liverpool)
1899 Barnsley 13 2

Armstrong, ? LH
1893 Northwich Victoria 1

Armstrong, ? GK
1899 Glossop 2

From To Apps Goal

Armstrong, Arthur Singleton OR
b Southwell q1 1887 d 1962
Ripley Athletic
Bakewell
1906 1907 Derby County 4 1
Ripley Athletic
Heanor Town
Brighton & Hove Albion
Pontypridd
Loughborough Corinthians
Heanor Town

Armstrong, Harold Arthur (Harry) OR
b 1885
Southwick (Co Durham)
1907 1908 Sheffield Wednesday 6
West Ham United
Darlington

Armstrong, James Donald (Jimmy) RB
b Chester-le-Street 12/6/1899
Chester-le-Street
1921 1924 Barnsley 59
1925 1926 Bournemouth & Boscombe Ath 15
1927 1933 Accrington Stanley 260 7
Stalybridge Celtic

Armstrong, James Harris (Jimmy) CH
b Lemington 8/3/1904 d 1971
Easington Colliery
1926 Clapton Orient 2
1928 1932 Queen's Park Rangers 122 5
1933 1938 Watford 187 2
1939 (Watford) (3)

Armstrong, James William (Jimmy) IR/IL/CF
b Swalwell 6/9/1901 d 1977
Spen Black & White
1922 1925 Chelsea 29 9
1927 1929 Tottenham Hotspur 28 5
1930 Luton Town 10 1
1930 Bristol Rovers 9 2

Armstrong, John (Jack) LH/RH
b Tollerton 4/2/1884 d 1963
Keyworth United
1905 1922 Nottingham Forest 431 9
Sutton Town

Armstrong, John LH
b Felling
1927 Darlington 1

Armstrong, John Busby CF
b Gateshead q3 1890 d 1950
Shildon Athletic
1912 Grimsby Town 4 1

Armstrong, Joseph (Joe) OL
b Boldon Colliery 20/10/1910
Jarrow
1930 1931 Bury 2

Armstrong, Joseph Williams (Joe) IL
b Blaydon 10/10/1892 d 1966
Hedgefield
Scotswood
1920 Portsmouth 13 2
1921 Sheffield Wednesday 7
1921 Norwich City 18 7
Clapton (trial)
Scotswood
1923 Bournemouth & Boscombe Ath 29 2
Portsmouth Tramways

Armstrong, Matthew RH/LH
b High Spen 1914
1936 1938 Darlington 38 2
1939 Aston Villa 0

Armstrong, Richard Johnstone (Dick) LH/IR/RH
b Newburn 31/8/1909 d 1969
Willington
Easington Colliery
1929 1934 Nottingham Forest 17
1935 1938 Bristol City 112 18
1939 (Bristol City) (3) (1)

Armstrong, Thomas GK
b Preston 1898
1919 Liverpool 1
1920 Preston North End 0

Armstrong, Thomas Hart (Tommy) IR/CF
b Cathcart 11/5/1906 d 1967
Potch Juniors
Airdrieonians
Cowdenbeath (loan)
1933 1934 Swindon Town 64 30
1935 1936 Crewe Alexandra 68 10
Hyde United

From To Apps Goal

Armstrong, Walter Bedford (Wally) CF
b Bolton q2 1906 d 1950
1925 Bolton Wanderers 0
Atherton
1927 Watford 1
Atherton
BTH (London)

Armstrong, William (Bill) CH
b Throckley 3/7/1913 d 1995
Throckley Welfare
1931 1932 Rochdale 14
1933 Aston Villa 0
1934 1935 Swindon Town 59
1936 1937 Gillingham 61
Shorts Sports
Betteshanger

Arnold, Harold Stanley (Stanley) OL
b St Helens 4/6/1904 d 1976
Davies Athletic
1928 Accrington Stanley 1
Oxford City

Arnold, John (Johnny) OL
b Cowley 30/11/1907 d 1984
Caps: England 1
Morris Motor Works (Cowley)
Oxford City
1928 1932 Southampton 116 46
1932 1938 Fulham 202 57
1939 (Fulham) (2)

Arnold, Thomas OR
b Coventry 1878
Foleshill Great Heath
Coventry City
1905 Woolwich Arsenal 2
Coventry City

Arnold, Walter OR/LH/IR
b Brimington1876 d 1955
New Whittington Exchange
1899 1900 Chesterfield Town 41 4
New Whittington Exchange
Denaby United
1903 Chesterfield Town 19 3
Denaby United
1906 1907 Chesterfield Town 48 1
Mexborough Town
New Whittington Exchange

Arnold, William John IL
b Bromley 1/3/1900 d 1977
Bromley
1922 Gillingham 2 1

Arnott, H IL
1895 Burton Swifts 17 4

Arnott, James GK
Fair City Athletic
1897 1899 Burnley 12

Arnott, Walter (Wattie) RB
b Pollokshields 12/5/1861 d 1931
Caps: Scotland 14
Matilda (Pollokshields)
Pollokshields Athletic
Ashfield
Queen's Park
Pollokshields Athletic
Kilmarnock Athletic
Queen's Park
Newcastle West End
Queen's Park
Corinthians
Ballina
Queen's Park
Linfield Athletic
Third Lanark
Queen's Park
St Bernard's
Celtic
1894 Notts County 1
Corinthians

Arridge, Smart LB
b Southwick, County Durham 21/6/1872 d 1947
Caps: Wales 8
Bangor City
1892 Bootle 21
1893 1896 Everton 51
1898 1900 New Brighton Tower 83 2
1901 1902 Stockport County 63
Bangor City

Arrowsmith, Arthur IR
b Wolverhampton 1880 d 1954
Compton
Coventry City
1906 1907 Stoke 41 8
1908 Wolverhampton Wanderers 1
Willenhall Swifts

From To Apps Goal

Arrowsmith, John Thomas (Tony) LB
b North Staveley 6/7/1887 d 1950
Anston United
Anston Colliery
Worksop Town
1911 1914 Grimsby Town 137

Arthern, Thomas (Tommy) IL
b Hanley 1868
Hanley Town
1891 Stoke 1
Congleton Hornets

Arthur, John (Jackie) OR
b Edenfield 14/12/1917 d 1986
1935 Blackburn Rovers 0
1936 Everton 0
1938 Stockport County 2
1946 Chester 24 3
1946 1953 Rochdale 170 25

Arthur, John William Herbert (Herbie) GK
b Blackburn 14/2/1863 d 1930
Caps: England 7
King's Own
1888 1889 Blackburn Rovers 19
Southport Central
1891 1892 Blackburn Rovers 21

Arthur, Joseph Ord (Joe) OL
b South Shields 11/7/1891 d 1975
South Shields Parkside
1910 1911 Sunderland 2
South Shields
Southport Central

Arthurs, Charles Henry LH/RH
b Kilnhurst 1881
Rotherham County
1907 Gainsborough Trinity 27 1
New Brompton
1909 Preston North End 8 1
New Brompton
Rotherham County
Worksop Town
Merthyr Town
Mardy
Pontypridd
Ebbw Vale

Arthurs, George OL/IL
b Rotherham 1890
Worksop Town
1909 1910 Barnsley 19 2
Rotherham County

Asbury, A IL
1896 Burton Wanderers 2

Ascroft, John Herbert OL
b Bebington 2/2/1907 d 1990
Connah's Quay & Shotton
Flint Town
1926 Oldham Athletic 0
Flint Town
1927 Arsenal 0
Bangor City
1929 Wrexham 10 6
Workington
Runcorn

Ash, John William (Jack) CH/RB/CF
b Hebburn 31/12/1911 d 2003
Hebburn St Cuthbert's
1935 Norwich City (trial) 0
1935 Carlisle United (trial) 0
1935 1937 Accrington Stanley 29
1938 Southport 4
1939 1945 (Accrington Stanley) (3)

Ashall, George Henry OL
b Killamarsh 29/9/1911 d 1998
Caps: FLge 1
Brodsworth Main Colliery
1932 Huddersfield Town 0
Upton Colliery
Frickley Colliery
1935 1937 Wolverhampton Wanderers 84 14
1938 1947 Coventry City 62 10
1939 (Coventry City) (3)

Ashall, Thomas IL
1934 Mansfield Town 2
Nuneaton Town

Ashbridge, Kenneth (Ken) GK
b Burnley 12/11/1916 d 2002
Burnley Lads Club
1935 Burnley 1
1938 Halifax Town 1

From To Apps Goal

Ashby, Henry Radford (Harry) RB/LB
b Derby q4 1875 d 1926
Derby Athletic
1896 1898 Burton Swifts 88 6
Brighton United
1901 1903 Burton United 92
Plymouth Argyle
1905 1906 Leicester Fosse 66

Ashcroft, Gordon GK
b Lea 7/9/1902 d 1982
Coppull Central
1925 Burnley 1
Burscough
Lancaster Town

Ashcroft, J OL
1896 Darwen 16 4

Ashcroft, James (Jimmy) GK
b Liverpool 12/9/1878 d 1943
Caps: FLge 2/England 3
Wilbyn's United
Anfield Recreation Club
Garston Copperworks
1897 Everton 0
Gravesend United
1900 1907 Woolwich Arsenal 273
1908 1912 Blackburn Rovers 114
Tranmere Rovers

Ashford, Herbert Edwin LH
b Fulham 18/2/1896 d 1978
Southall
Brentford
1920 1921 Queen's Park Rangers 10
1922 Notts County 0
Ayr United (trial)
Dartford
Guildford City
Tunbridge Wells Rangers

Ashford, James William LB/RB
b Bamburgh 24/5/1897 d 1970
Brodsworth Main Colliery
Ebbw Vale
1920 1924 Chelsea 8
1925 Doncaster Rovers 25
1926 Bristol Rovers 12
Scunthorpe & Lindsey United

Ashley, Harry IR
b Smethwick 7/1/1913 d 1985
Smethwick Highfield
1935 West Bromwich Albion 0
1937 Derby County 0
1939 Darlington (3) (1)

Ashley, John Albert (Jack) RB/CH
b Clowne 13/10/1912 d 1992
Clowne Miners Welfare
1931 Notts County (trial) 0
Bolsover Colliery
Shirebrook
1933 1935 Mansfield Town 69
1935 1938 Sheffield Wednesday 106 3
1939 (Sheffield Wednesday) (3)

Ashman, Donald (Don) LB/LH/RB
b Staindrop 9/10/1902 d 1984
Cockfield
1924 1931 Middlesbrough 160 2
1932 1934 Queen's Park Rangers 78
1935 Darlington 14

Ashmole, William George OL
b Winshill q2 1892 d 1968
Burton United
1913 1914 Stockport County 37 9
Watford

Ashmore, George Samuel Austin GK
b Plymouth 5/5/1898 d 1973
Caps: England 1
Nineveh Wesley
1920 1930 West Bromwich Albion 246
1931 1932 Chesterfield 71

Ashmore, John Wilfred OR
b Chesterfield q1 1886
New Tupton Ivanhoe
1905 1906 Chesterfield Town 9
New Tupton Ivanhoe

Ashmore, Richard A (Dick) CH/IR
b Rotherham 28/11/1892
Bristol Rovers
1920 Barnsley 12
1920 1921 Nottingham Forest 11 1
1923 Doncaster Rovers 4
Scunthorpe & Lindsey United
Denaby United

From To Apps Goal

Ashmore, Walter William GK
b West Smethwick 1867 d 1940
West Bromwich Standard
1888 Aston Villa 1
Aston Unity

Ashmore, William LB
b Tibshelf 1884
Tibshelf Church
1907 Chesterfield Town 2
Rotherham County

Ashton, Edward (Teddy) OL/OR
b Kilnhurst 19/1/1906 d 1978
Kilnhurst WMC
Mexborough Town
1927 1936 Barnsley 289 70
1936 1937 Sheffield United 35 4
1938 Carlisle United 29 8
1939 Barnsley 0
Grantham

Ashton, Edwin OL/IL
b Hindley 9/2/1893 d 1970
Haslingden
1911 1912 Grimsby Town 8
Portsmouth
Haslingden
Nelson

Ashton, Frank Cuckson OR/RB/LH
b Gainsborough q3 1879 d 1952
1900 1904 Gainsborough Trinity 10

Ashton, Herbert OR/OL
b Blackburn q3 1885 d 1927
Caps: SoLge 1
Padiham
Accrington Stanley
1905 1906 Preston North End 4
Accrington Stanley
West Ham United

Ashton, (Sir) Hubert (MP) LB/RB
b Calcutta, India 13/2/1898 d 1979
1919 West Bromwich Albion 0
Corinthians
1924 Bristol Rovers 1
1926 Clapton Orient 5

Ashton, Percy GK
b Bolton-on-Dearne 28/3/1909 d 1985
West Melton Excelsior
1930 1938 Nottingham Forest 176
1939 (Nottingham Forest) (3)
Grantham Road

Ashurst, Elias RB
b Willington 28/12/1901 d 1927
Stanley United
Shildon Athletic
1921 1925 Birmingham 66 1

Ashurst, William (Bill) RB
b Willington 4/5/1894 d 1947
Caps: FLge 1/England 5
Willington
Durham City
1919 Leeds City 0
1919 Lincoln City 24
1920 1926 Notts County 200
1926 West Bromwich Albion 22 1
Newark Town
Bestwood Colliery

Ashurst, William Edward IL
b Wigan q1 1896 d 1956
Ince Labour Club
1921 Wigan Borough 5
Burscough Rangers

Ashworth, James Ernest OL
b Warrington 28/1/1902 d 1977
1924 Everton 0
1925 Nottingham Forest 3
1926 Blackpool 0

Ashworth, James Joseph (Jimmy) CF
b Ireland 1/3/1918 d 1990
1938 Blackpool 4
Morecambe
Netherfield

Ashworth, John OR
Lowerhouse
1889 Burnley 3 2

Ashworth, Leonard CF
1898 Darwen 5 1
1900 Stockport County 15 4

From To Apps Goal

Ashworth, Samuel Bolton (Sam) CH/RH/LH
b Fenton 3/1881 d 1925
Caps: FLge 1
Stoke Alliance
Fenton Town
Stafford Wednesday
Stafford Rangers
Stoke Nomads
1901 1902 Stoke 34
Oxford City
Reading
1903 Manchester City 18
Reading
1904 Everton 11
1905 Burslem Port Vale 4
North Staffs Nomads
Northern Nomads
Sheffield
Richmond Association

Askew, Hubert Frank RH
b Rugby 23/7/1908 d 1988
Warwick Town
1926 1927 Coventry City 8
Morton
Hinckley United
1930 Birmingham 0
Warwick Town
Coventry Strollers
Atherstone Town
Leamington Town

Askew, James GK
b North Shields
Percy Main Amateurs
1933 1936 Gateshead 28

Askew, Leslie William (Billy) LH
b Marylebone q4 1886 d 1955
Xylonite
Tottenham Gothic Works
Chadwell Heath
Finchley
Southend United
Norwich City
1911 Aston Villa 2
West Ham United

Askew, William RH/CH
b Coundon 23/8/1911 d 1992
West Auckland
1934 1936 Chesterfield 5 1
1937 1938 Walsall 26 2
1939 Lincoln City (3)

Asnip, John IR
b Sheffield 17/7/1881 d 1943
1901 Lincoln City 1

Asnip, Thomas OL
b Sheffield 18/2/1883 d 1918
St Catherine's
1904 Lincoln City 1
Adelaide (Lincoln)

Aspden, Thomas Eccles (Tommy) OR
b Liverpool q1 1881 d 1959
1900 Preston North End 0
Kettering
1903 Burnley 29 4
Brighton & Hove Albion
Oldham Athletic

Aspden, Thomas G RB/CH/LH
b Darwen 1868
1891 1893 Darwen 15 1

Aspin, James Cressy (Jim) IR/OR
b Blackburn 13/9/1914 d 1963
1934 Accrington Stanley 1
1934 Wolverhampton Wanderers 0
1935 Accrington Stanley 2
Jiffy

Aspinall, John (Jack) LH/CH/LB
b Ashton-under-Lyne 27/4/1916 d 1996
Ferguson Pailin
Mossley
Stalybridge Celtic
1936 1938 Oldham Athletic 11
Ashton National
1946 1949 Bolton Wanderers 14

Aspinall, Wilfred (Wilf) IL
b Hartford, Cnnecticut, USA 22/8/1910 d 1960
Mill Street Rovers (Frizington)
Whitehaven Athletic
Workington
1931 Sheffield Wednesday 0
Workington
1934 Stockport County 1 1
1935 Southport 6

From To Apps Goal

Asquith, Beaumont IL/LH/CF
b Painthorpe 16/9/1910 d 1977
Painthorpe Albion
1934 1938 Barnsley 105 40
1939 Manchester United (1)
1945 1947 Barnsley 40 5
1948 1949 Bradford City 31 4
Scarborough

Astill, Leonard Victor IL/OL
b Wolverhampton 30/12/1916 d 1990
Heath Town
1934 Wolverhampton Wanderers 2
1935 Blackburn Rovers 3 1
Ipswich Town
Colchester United

Astill, Thomas (Tommy) IL
b Brightside 9/12/1889 d 1970
Sheffield Douglas
1909 Leeds City 1
Doncaster Rovers
Mexborough Town

Astin, James LB
b Hapton 16/8/1900 d 1979
1921 Burnley 13
1922 Bury 0

Astley, David John (Dai) IR/IL/CF
b Dowlais 11/10/1909 d 1989
Caps: Wales Sch/Wales War 4/Wales 13
Dowlais Welfare
1927 Merthyr Town 5 3
1927 1930 Charlton Athletic 96 27
1931 1936 Aston Villa 165 92
1936 1938 Derby County 93 45
1938 Blackpool 18 6
1939 (Blackpool) (3)
Metz

Astley, Henry (Harry) CF/IL/IR
b Bolton q2 1882 d 1968
1900 1901 Bolton Wanderers 6
Millwall Athletic
1904 Middlesbrough 14 4
Crystal Palace
Heywood United
1907 Bury 1
Heywood United

Astley, John (Jack) RB
b Warrington 3/12/1909 d 1984
Caps: LoI 1
St Elfin's Parish Church
Chadwick Recreation
Warrington Bedouins
Elmwood Avenue Methodists
1931 Southport 2
Shelbourne
1933 1935 Brentford 49
1935 1938 Coventry City 140
1939 (Coventry City) (3)

Astley, Joseph Emmanuel LB
b Cradley Heath q2 1899 d 1969
Cradley Heath
1925 1926 Manchester United 2
1928 Notts County 4
Nantwich
Hyde United

Aston, Alfred CF
1904 1906 Burton United 49 12
Tutbury Town
Wellington Town
Tutbury Town

Aston, Charles Lane (Charlie) LB/RB
b Bilston q4 1875 d 1931
Bilston United
1896 1897 Walsall 52 1
1897 1900 Aston Villa 23
Queen's Park Rangers
1902 Burton United 30 2
Gresley Rovers
1904 Burton United 30
Watford
Leyton
Redditch
Cradley Heath St Luke's

Aston, J Harold CF
b Redditch 1881 d 1938
Silver Star
Redditch Town
Quinton Victoria
Coventry City
Ironbridge
Durham Light Infantry
1903 1904 West Bromwich Albion 25 9
Willenhall Swifts
Clifton Victoria

From To Apps Goal

Aston, James (Jack) IR/CH
b Walsall 1/7/1877 d 1934
Walsall White Star
Fullbrook Saints
Willenhall Pickwick
Bloxwich Strollers
Wednesfield
1896 1898 Walsall 88 38
1899 Woolwich Arsenal 11 3
1899 1901 Small Heath 55 24
1902 Doncaster Rovers 30 3
Walsall
Bilston United
Walsall
Blakenhall St Luke's
Walsall Wood

Aston, James CH
1903 Stockport County 1

Aston, Thomas OL
b Ironbridge 1876
Ironbridge
1900 Burslem Port Vale 4 1

Aston, Walter Vivien (Viv) LB/RB/CH
b Coseley 16/10/1918 d 1999
1935 Wolverhampton Wanderers 0
1936 Bournemouth & Boscombe Ath 0
1938 1947 Bury 23
1948 1951 Oldham Athletic 30 1
1951 Chester 0

Atack, Sidney (Sid) RH/CH
b Methley 10/5/1918 d 1983
1937 1938 Halifax Town 4 1

Atherley, Robert CF
b Leicester q4 1878 d 1963
Anstey Town
Leicester Imperial
1901 Leicester Fosse 1
Leicester Imperial
Humberstone Victoria
St Andrew's (Leicester)

Athersmith, William Charles (Charlie) OR
b Bloxwich 10/5/1872 d 1910
Caps: FLge 9/England 12
Bloxwich Wanderers
Bloxwich Strollers
Unity Gas
1890 1900 Aston Villa 269 75
1901 1904 Small Heath 100 12

Atherton, James LH
b Lancashire 1872
South Shore
Blackpool
1895 Leicester Fosse 2
Kettering
New Brompton

Atherton, James OR
b Adlington 1877
Pemberton Wanderers
Wigan Nondescripts
South Shore
Wigan County
1899 Preston North End 13
Southport Central
Brynn Central
Ashton Recreational

Atherton, John James (Jack) IL/IR
b Preston q3 1917
1936 Preston North End 4 1
1938 Brighton & Hove Albion 9 2

Atherton, Robert William IR
b Bethesda 29/7/1876 d 1917
Caps: Wales 9
Dalry Primrose
Heart of Midlothian
Hibernian
1903 1904 Middlesbrough 60 13
1905 Chelsea 0

Atherton, Thomas Henry (Tommy) OR
b West Derby q1 1879 d 1955
Caps: SLge 1
Dunfermline Juniors
Dundee
Hibernian
Tottenham Hotspur
St Bernard's
Raith Rovers
Partick Thistle
Dundee
1902 Grimsby Town 2
Brentford
Motherwell

Atherton, W LH
1898 Blackpool 8

From To Apps Goal
Atherton, William Jackson (Billy) IR/CF/IL
b Bradford 4/5/1905 d 1976
1928 1930 Bradford Park Avenue 36 20
1931 1933 Doncaster Rovers 54 21
1934 Halifax Town 15 2
1935 Preston North End 0

Atkin, Arthur William RB/LH/RH
b Skegness 14/5/1893 d 1952
Skegness
1912 1923 Lincoln City 96 2
Boston Town

Atkin, Fred RB
b Caistor q1 1887 d 1964
1910 Tottenham Hotspur 0
Kingston-on-Thames
1913 Grimsby Town 0
Scunthorpe & Lindsey United
1914 Grimsby Town 12

Atkin, John Thomas (Jack) RB/LB
b Newhall q1 1883 d 1961
Newhall Swifts
1907 1921 Derby County 308 3

Atkin, Thomas Lowes (Tommy) OR
b Darlington 19/8/1906 d 1986
Albert Hill
1925 Darlington 0
Chilton Colliery Recreation Athletic
1927 Bolton Wanderers 0
1928 1931 Doncaster Rovers 99 6
1932 1933 Gateshead 54 16
1934 1935 Darlington 26 3
Wigan Athletic
Peterborough United

Atkinson, Frank LB/RB
b North Shields
Rosehill Villa
1925 1927 South Shields 3
1929 Accrington Stanley 0
Dundee
Scunthorpe & Lindsey United

Atkinson, George OR
1904 Burnley 14

Atkinson, George Arthur (Arthur) IR/OR
b Goole 30/9/1909 d 1983
Goole LMS
Goole Town
1932 Lincoln City 9 5
1933 Hull City 5
1934 1936 Mansfield Town 120 32
1937 Southport 37 7
Thorne Colliery

Atkinson, James IR/CH
b Manchester 1886
Newton Heath Athletic
Sale Holmfield
1905 1906 Bolton Wanderers 3 1
Brighton & Hove Albion
Exeter City
Barrow

Atkinson, John Edward (Jack) CH
b New Washington 20/12/1913 d 1977
Caps: England Sch
Washington Colliery
1932 1947 Bolton Wanderers 240 4
1948 1949 New Brighton 52

Atkinson, Joshua Whitehead (Josh) LH/RH
b Blackpool 28/3/1902 d 1983
South Shore
1923 Blackpool 0
1924 1927 Leeds United 52
1928 1929 Barnsley 61 2
1931 Chester 7
Fleetwood
Macclesfield

Atkinson, Robert Armstrong OL
b Ashington 4/9/1906
Preston Colliery
1928 Rotherham United 14 3

Atkinson, Thomas (Tom) RH
b Ulverston q1 1903 d 1966
Aberaman Athletic
1921 Accrington Stanley 0
1921 1922 Barrow 58
Aberaman Athletic
1925 Barrow 27 1

Atkinson, Thomas GK
1933 Gateshead 2

Atter, John Tom (Tom) GK
b Dinnington 9/5/1901 d 1958
Dinnington Main Colliery Welfare
1922 1925 Grimsby Town 48
1926 1929 Rotherham United 108

From To Apps Goal
Atterbury, Septimus (Sep) LB
b Allestree 18/10/1880 d 1964
Caps: SoLge 2
Kettering
1898 Loughborough 2
1899 1900 Barnsley 34 1
Wellingborough
1902 Leicester Fosse 21
Swindon Town
1920 Plymouth Argyle 30

Attley, Leonard James (Len) IL
b Cardiff 21/4/1914 d 1979
1934 1935 Cardiff City 12 2
Yeovil & Petters United

Attwell, Frederick Reginald (Reg) RH/LH
b Shifnal 23/3/1920 d 1986
Caps: FLge 1
Denaby United
1937 1946 West Ham United 5
1946 1954 Burnley 244 9
1954 Bradford City 24
Darwen

Attwood, Arthur Albert CF
b Walsall 1/12/1901 d 1974
Walsall LMS
1928 Walsall 14 13
1928 1929 Everton 3
1930 1931 Bristol Rovers 51 27
1931 1934 Brighton & Hove Albion 87 55
Northfleet
Hove

Auld, John Robertson CH
b Lugar 7/1/1862 d 1932
Caps: Scotland 3
Kilmarnock
Lugar Boswell
Third Lanark
Queen's Park
Third Lanark
1890 1894 Sunderland 99 6
1896 Newcastle United 14 3

Austin, ? OR
1902 Burton United 3

Austin, Percy Charles LH
b Watford 1/7/1903 d 1961
Farnham United Breweries
1927 Tottenham Hotspur 1

Austin, Sydney William (Billy) OR
b Arnold 29/4/1900 d 1979
Caps: SoLge 1/England 1
Arnold United
1919 Sheffield United (trial) 0
Arnold St Mary's
1920 1923 Norwich City 152 35
1924 1930 Manchester City 160 43
Worcester City
1931 1932 Chesterfield 45 6
Kidderminster Harriers
Racing Club de Roubaix

Avey, Frederick George (Fred) CF/IR
b Poplar 31/8/1909 d 1999
Leytonstone
Leyton
1927 1930 Fulham 62 28
1932 Torquay United 3
Tunbridge Wells Rangers

Axcell, Charles Edward (Charlie) OL/IL
b Leigh-on-Sea 14/3/1880 d 1949
Leigh Ramblers
Fulham
Grays United
1905 1906 Burton United 31 10
1906 Stoke 3
1906 Burton United 1
Southend United

Ayre, Herbert Wilkinson (Bert) LB
b Grimsby q4 1882 d 1966
Old Humberstonians
Grimsby St John's
1904 Grimsby Town 3
Cleethorpes Town
Grimsby Rangers
Grimsby Rovers
Cleethorpes Town
Old Humberstonians

Ayres, George Alexander IL/CH/CF
b Islington 5/9/1901 d 1983
RAF
1922 1923 Charlton Athletic 33 5
1923 1925 Sheffield Wednesday 27 11
1926 1927 Blackpool 39 4

From To Apps Goal
Aytoun, George LH
b Dalkeith 1880
Clydebank
1905 Burslem Port Vale 4

Bach, Philip (Phil) RB
b Ludlow 9/1872 d 1937
Caps: England 1
Middlesbrough
Reading
1897 1898 Sunderland 44
1899 Middlesbrough 0
1903 Bristol City 3

Bache, Harold Godfrey CF
b Churchill 20/8/1889 d 1916
Caps: FLge 1
Cambridge University
Corinthians
West Bromwich Springfield
Eastbourne
1913 1914 West Bromwich Albion 12 4

Bache, Joseph William (Joe) IL/OL
b Stourbridge 8/2/1880 d 1960
Caps: FLge 7/England 7
Bewdley Victoria
Stourbridge
1900 1914 Aston Villa 431 167
Mid-Rhondda
1920 Grimsby Town 5 1

Bacon, Arthur CF/IL
b Birdholme 1905 d 1942
New Tupton Ivanhoe
1923 Chesterfield 0
1925 1927 Derby County 8 3
1928 Manchester City 5 1
1929 1931 Reading 69 44
1932 Chesterfield 30 6
1933 1935 Coventry City 16 17
Burton Town

Bacon, Arthur Parnell CF
b Basford q4 1884 d 1937
Sutton Junction
1906 Lincoln City 4
Sutton Town

Bacon, Clarence George (Clarrie) OR/RB
b Grimsby 9/11/1889 d 1954
Haycroft Rovers
Grimsby Rangers
1908 1911 Grimsby Town 11
Cleethorpes Town
Doncaster Rovers
Goole Town
North Shields Athletic

Bacon, Ernest Frederick RH/LB/IL
b Leicester 19/2/1896 d 1972
Caps: England Sch
St Andrew's (Leicester)
1919 Leicester City 4
1920 Watford 12
1921 1922 Charlton Athletic 5
Nuneaton Town
Kettering
Barwell United
Erith & Belvedere
Callendar Athletic

Bacuzzi, Giuseppe Luigi Davide (Joe) RB/LB
b Holborn 25/9/1916 d 1995
Caps: FLge 1/England War 13
Tufnell Park
1936 1955 Fulham 283 2
1939 (Fulham) (3)

Baddeley, Amos OL/IL
b Fegg Hayes q2 1885 d 1946
Fegg Hayes
1906 1907 Stoke 19 6
1908 Blackpool 32 3
Stoke
Walsall
Abertillery
Ebbw Vale

Baddeley, George RH
b Fegg Hayes q4 1878 d 1952
Pitshill
Biddulph
1901 1907 Stoke 208 14
1908 1913 West Bromwich Albion 145 2

Baddeley, Samuel (Sam) CH
b Norton-in-the-Moors q4 1884 d 1958
Ball Green
Endon
Norton
1906 Burslem Port Vale 30
1907 Stoke 1
Kidsgrove Wellington

From To Apps Goal
Baddeley, Thomas (Tom) GK
b Bycars 2/11/1874 d 1946
Caps: FLge 4/England 5
Burslem Swifts
1893 1895 Burslem Port Vale 62
1897 1906 Wolverhampton Wanderers 296
1908 Bradford Park Avenue 9
Stoke
Whitfield Colliery

Badenoch, George Huntly OR
b Castle Douglas 9/4/1882 d 1915
Douglas Wanderers
Heart of Midlothian
1901 1902 Glossop 48 4
Watford
Tottenham Hotspur
Northampton Town
Indian Head (Canada)

Badger, Herbert Osborne (Bert) RH
b Islington 4/10/1882 d 1965
Clacton Town
Colchester Town
Ilford
Tottenham Hotspur
1904 Woolwich Arsenal 0
Watford
Brentford
1909 Nottingham Forest 2
Brentford

Bagge, Henry John (Harry) LH/RH
b Tottenham 15/9/1896 d 1967
1914 Tottenham Hotspur 0
1919 1925 Fulham 179 1
Northfleet
1927 Sheffield Wednesday (loan) 0
1928 Clapton Orient (trial) 0
Athletic Bilbao
Hinckley Amateurs

Baggett, Walter John (Bill) IR/IL
b Potterspury 29/5/1902 d 1978
Victoria Ironworks
1922 Wolverhampton Wanderers 0
1923 1926 Bolton Wanderers 24 10
1927 1929 Reading 46 12
Colwyn Bay
1930 1931 Reading 31 8
Tunbridge Wells Rangers

Bagley, Thomas Henry (Tommy) OR
b Tranmere 19/10/1909 d 1995
Bangor City
1933 1936 Bury 53 7
1936 1937 Bradford City 31 4
1938 Stockport County 40 13
1939 (Stockport County) (1)

Bagley, William (Billy) IL/IR
b Wolverhampton 8/7/1909 d 1976
Caps: WLge 1
Newport Excelsior
1929 1932 Newport County 71 12
1933 1938 Portsmouth 129 12

Bagnall, Samuel (Sam) OR
b Neepsend q4 1892 d 1916
Clowne Rising Star
Mansfield Town
Chesterfield Town
1913 Sheffield United 7 1
South Liverpool
Welbeck Colliery

Bagshaw, James Edward (Jim) GK
b Grimsby q1 1874 d 1941
Britannia
Grimsby Thursdays
1893 Grimsby Town 0
Grimsby All Saints
1896 1897 Gainsborough Trinity 58
1898 Grimsby Town 34
Scarborough
1899 1908 Gainsborough Trinity 289

Bagshaw, John James (Jimmy) RH/LH/CH
b Derby 25/12/1885 d 1966
Caps: England 1
Graham Street Primitives
Fletchers Athletic
1906 1919 Derby County 226 6
1919 1920 Notts County 24
1921 Watford 14
Ilkeston United
Grantham

Baguley, Christopher RH
1910 Stockport County 1

From To Apps Goal

Baguley, William Ewart IL
b Hucknall q1 1887 d 1938
Hucknall
1907 Bolton Wanderers 0
Moore's Athletic (Shirebrook)
1908 Gainsborough Trinity 8
Stanton Hill Victoria
Mansfield Mechanics
Shirebrook

Bailey, A CF
1892 Crewe Alexandra 7 3

Bailey, Arthur IL
b Ancoats 11/1/1911 d 2006
Chapel-en-le-Frith
Manchester North End
1933 1935 Oldham Athletic 53 11
Stalybridge Celtic
1939 Oldham Athletic (1)
Shrewsbury Town

Bailey, Daniel (Dan) IR
b East Ham 26/6/1893 d 1967
Custom House
1919 1920 West Ham United 35 9
1921 Charlton Athletic 33 8
1922 Clapton Orient 18 4

Bailey, Frank OL
Darnall Rovers
1901 Doncaster Rovers 22 6
Worksop Town

Bailey, Frank RH
b Burnley 2/8/1907 d 1969
Knowlwood
1924 Burnley 0
1925 1926 Nelson 4
Great Harwood
Lancaster Town
Rossendale United
Morecambe

Bailey, Frederick Henry LB
b Loughborough q2 1878
1896 1899 Loughborough 52 1

Bailey, George Samuel James (Jerry) OL
b Swindon 18/1/1905 d 1964
Swindon Butchers
1926 Swindon Town 7 1

Bailey, H CF
1894 Darwen 3 1

Bailey, Harold RB/LB
b Congleton 13/1/1915 d 1994
1934 Leeds United 0
1935 1937 Swindon Town 5
Cheltenham Town

Bailey, Hedley LH/RH
b Sutton-in-Ashfield 25/6/1895
Sutton Junction
1919 1927 Rotherham County 333 12

Bailey, Henry (Harry) GK
b Macclesfield 1897
Millwall Athletic
1920 1922 Luton Town 82
1923 1926 Exeter City 143
1927 1928 Brentford 44
1930 1931 Thames 29

Bailey, Herbert Albert LB
b Amble 7/11/1894 d 1955
Amble
1922 Ashington 2

Bailey, Horace Peter GK
b Derby 3/7/1881 d 1960
Caps: England Amat/England 5
1899 Derby County 0
Crich
Ripley Athletic
Leicester Imperial
1907 1909 Leicester Fosse 68
Northern Nomads
1909 Derby County 3
1910 Blackburn Rovers 0
Stoke
1910 1912 Birmingham 50

Bailey, James William (Billy) OL
b Basford q4 1884
South Normanton St Michael's
Clown Parish Church
Ilkeston Town
1907 Chesterfield Town 15 1
Mansfield Wesleyans
Mansfield Mechanics
South Normanton
Ripley Town
Shirebrook
Mansfield Mechanics

From To Apps Goal

Bailey, John (Jack) IR/IL
b Grays 1901
Sittingbourne
1926 1930 Southend United 78 22
1931 Thames 11 1

Bailey, John Henry (Jack) GK
b 1901
Bostall Heath
Tilbury
1925 Charlton Athletic 4
Sittingbourne
Dartford

Bailey, John Herbert (Herbert) CF
b Melton Mowbray q3 1869
Melton Town
Birmingham St George's
1891 Wolverhampton Wanderers 1
Melton Town
Leicester Fosse
Melton Town

Bailey, Leslie Albert (Les) CH/RH
b Worksop 2/10/1916 d 1980
Manton Colliery
Gainsborough Trinity
1936 Bradford Park Avenue 22 1
1937 1938 Derby County 26
Llandudno Town

Bailey, LF CF
1888 Notts County 1 1

Bailey, Rowland Miles OL
b Bradford 10/8/1903 d 1972
1921 Rotherham County 0
Harrogate AFC
1923 1924 Doncaster Rovers 17 1
1924 Barnsley 0
1925 Wrexham 11 2
Llandudno

Bailey, Sidney (Sid) LB
b London
1921 Queen's Park Rangers 1

Bailey, T CF
1892 1893 Northwich Victoria 17 7

Bailey, Thomas CF
Overseal Swifts
Burton United
1907 Lincoln City (trial) 1
Walsall
Gresley Rovers

Bailey, Thomas W RH
b Ebbw Vale
1927 Merthyr Town 0
1928 Rochdale 1
Buckley

Bailey, Walter IR
b Birmingham 1876
1895 Grimsby Town 2

Bailey, Walter George (Joe) IR/IL
b Thame 9/2/1890 d 1974
Caps: England Amat
Thame United
1910 Nottingham Forest 4 1
Oxford City
1920 Reading 41 17
Boscombe
Sittingbourne

Bailey, Wilfred William IL
b Leiston q2 1898
Ipswich Town
Kilmarnock
1922 Chesterfield 3
1923 Stockport County (trial) 0

Bailey, William Henry (Harry) LB
b Melton Mowbray 2/10/1870 d 1930
Melton Rovers
Melton Town
Birmingham St George's
Melton Rovers
1894 1899 Leicester Fosse 47

Bailiff, William Ellis GK
b Ruabon 19/3/1882 d 1972
Caps: SoLge 1/Wales 4
Ruabon
Druids
Northampton Town
Treharris
1910 Bristol City 7
Treharris
Llanelly
Bargoed

From To Apps Goal

Baillie, David Arthur GK
b Ilford 6/6/1905 d 1967
Coryton
1925 1928 West Ham United 16
Chester

Baillie, James (Jim) RH
b Hamilton 18/2/1900 d 1966
Motherwell Boys Brigade
Wishaw Thistle
1926 1927 Cardiff City 5
New York Giants
Derry City
1930 Fulham 2
Dundee United (trial)
Falkirk (trial)
1931 Preston North End (trial) 0
Lille

Bain, David RH/CF/CH
b Rutherglen 5/8/1900
Rutherglen Glencairn
1922 1923 Manchester United 22 9
1924 1927 Everton 38 3
1928 1929 Bristol City 50 2
1930 1931 Halifax Town 60 5
1932 1933 Rochdale 52 5

Bain, James CF
b Dundee 1878
Dundee
1899 Newton Heath 2 1

Bain, James (Jimmy) CH
b Rutherglen 6/2/1899 d 1969
Rutherglen Glencairn
Strathclyde
1924 1927 Manchester United 4
Manchester Central
1928 1933 Brentford 191 2

Bain, Kenneth (Ken) LB
b Scotland 26/5/??
Mid-Rhondda
1921 1923 Queen's Park Rangers 91

Bainbridge, John Robert (Jack) OR
b Seaham q2 1880 d 1960
Silksworth
Sunderland Royal Rovers
1903 Glossop 34 4
Reading
Portsmouth
Southampton
Hartlepools United
Horden Athletic

Bainbridge, John Taylor OR
b North Shields 17/8/1900 d 1945
1922 Ashington 1
Gateshead Town
Birtley

Bainbridge, Joseph (Joe) RH/LB/CF
b South Shields 11/3/1888 d 1954
South Shields Parkside
1908 Newcastle United (trial) 0
Blyth Spartans
1910 1920 Blackpool 111 11
1921 1924 Southport 65

Bainbridge, Robert (Bob) GK
b Jarrow 5/1/1897 d 1967
Jarrow
1921 1922 Lincoln City 35
Sittingbourne
Gateshead Town
Leadgate

Bainbridge, Simpson OR/OL
b Silksworth 3/4/1895 d 1988
Caps: England Sch
Seaton Delaval
1912 1919 Leeds City 64 15
1919 Preston North End 14 1
1920 South Shields 13 3
Aberdeen
Wheatley Hill Alliance
Shildon
Hylton Colliery

Baines, Charles Edwin (Charlie) LH
b Ardsley 9/2/1896 d 1954
Ardsley Athletic
1920 1930 Barnsley 322 5

Baines, Frederick (Fred) LB
b Leeds q4 1898
1919 Rotherham County 7
Rochdale
1921 Accrington Stanley 2

From To Apps Goal

Baines, Reginald (Reg) CF
b York 3/6/1906 d 1974
York City
Selby Town
Scarborough
Selby Town
1931 1932 York City 71 57
1933 Sheffield United 10 5
1934 1936 Doncaster Rovers 80 43
1937 York City 39 23
1938 Barnsley 1
1939 Halifax Town (2) (1)

Baines, Stanley Norman (Stan) OL/LH
b Syston 28/7/1920 d 1990
Syston Methodists
Syston St Peter's
Coalville Town
1938 Leicester City 7 1
1946 Northampton Town 1
Syston Imperial
Hinckley Athletic

Baird, Henry HC (Harry) LH/RH/IR
b Belfast 17/8/1913 d 1973
Caps: IrLge 2/NIRL 2/Ireland 1
Bangor
Dunmurry
Linfield
1936 1937 Manchester United 49 15
1938 Huddersfield Town 19 4
Linfield
1946 1951 Ipswich Town 216 6

Baird, John RB/LB/LH
b Alexandria 20/2/1870 d 1905
Vale Athletic
Vale of Leven
1888 Aston Villa 0
Kidderminster Olympic
Kidderminster Harriers
1891 1894 Aston Villa 60
1895 Leicester Fosse 13
Clyde
Vale of Leven

Baird, Richard OR
b Nelson 20/2/1892 d 1977
Nelson
Bacup Borough
Rossendale United
1921 Nelson 2
Chorley
Rossendale United
Great Harwood
Colne Carltons
Colne Town

Baird, Ronald Arthur RB
b Grays 14/10/1908 d 1989
Royal Naval Depot (Chatham)
1929 Gillingham 1
Redhill

Baird, Thomas Skinner (Tam) RB
b Lugar 7/6/1911
Cumnock Townhead
Lugar Boswell
St Mirren
1937 1938 Rochdale 79

Baird, Walter Young LB
b Cambuslang 8/1/1913 d 1958
Caps: Scotland Sch
Lesmahagow
Partick Thistle
Larkhall Thistle
1934 Sheffield Wednesday 1
Hamilton Academical
Morton
1938 Doncaster Rovers 0

Baird, William (Billy) CF
b Glasgow 1876
Morton
1896 Stoke 3

Baker, Aaron RH
b Basford Green 23/12/1904 d 1963
Ilkeston Town
1927 Leeds United 2
1928 Sheffield Wednesday 0

Baker, Albert OL
b 1912
Redhill
1929 Luton Town 1

Baker, Alfred (Alf) RH/RB
b Ilkeston 27/4/1898 d 1955
Caps: FLge 2/England 1
Eastwood Rangers
1919 1930 Arsenal 310 23

From To Apps Goal

Baker, Arthur OR
b Dalton 3/6/1911 d 1992
Ulverston GS
1929 1937 Barrow 67 6

Baker, Arthur Lewis (Billy) OR
b Plumstead 8/1/1894 d 1972
Royal Navy
1920 Brentford 4
1921 Manchester City (trial) 0
Hampstead Town

Baker, Benjamin Howard (Howard) GK
b Aigburth 12/2/1892 d 1987
Caps: FLge 1/England Amat/England 2
Marlborough Old Boys (Liverpool)
Liverpool Balmoral
1913 Blackburn Rovers 0
1914 Preston North End 0
Northern Nomads
Corinthians
1919 Liverpool 0
1920 Everton 2
1921 1925 Chelsea 92 1
Corinthians
1926 Everton 11
1928 Oldham Athletic 1

Baker, Cecil (Cis) IL/IR
b Darnall
Beighton
Eckington Athletic
1920 Blackpool 2
Creswell Colliery
1925 Chesterfield 2
Shirebrook
Beighton Miners Welfare

Baker, Charles (Charlie) IR/CF/IL
b Stafford 10/2/1870 d 1940
Stafford Rangers
1888 1889 Stoke 13 2
1891 1892 Wolverhampton Wanderers 37 6
1892 Stoke 4
Southampton St Mary's
Stafford Rangers

Baker, Frank OL/IL
b Stoke-on-Trent 22/10/1918 d 1989
1935 Port Vale 0
1936 1949 Stoke City 162 32
1939 (Stoke City) (3)
Stafford Rangers
Leek Town

Baker, Frederick (Fred) RH
b Caergwrle 7/5/1905 d 1980
Oak Alyn Rovers
Mold Town
Rhyl
1930 Wrexham 0
1930 New Brighton 4
Cross Street

Baker, George LB/RB
b Chesterfield q2 1883
New Tupton Ivanhoe
1905 1906 Chesterfield Town 63 2
Clay Cross
1908 Chesterfield Town 17
1909 1912 Preston North End 24
Shirebrook

Baker, Henry GK
b Sheffield 23/1/??
St John's Institute
1921 Halifax Town 20
1922 Brighton & Hove Albion 0

Baker, Horace Anthony OR
b Fenton 1/9/1910 d 1974
Longton Hall Town
1932 1933 Port Vale 10 1
1934 1935 Tranmere Rovers 23 10
Shrewsbury Town
1937 Southport 20 3
Shrewsbury Town

Baker, J LH
1893 Ardwick 3 1

Baker, J OL
1900 Walsall 6 1

Baker, James Edward (Jimmy) RH/CH
b Trethomas 5/5/1904 d 1979
Caps: WLge 1
Lovells Athletic
1926 1928 Wolverhampton Wanderers 16
1929 1931 Coventry City 108 8
Lovells Athletic
1932 1934 Coventry City 74 3
1935 1936 Bristol City 10
Colchester United

From To Apps Goal

Baker, James Edward (Jim) LB/RB/CF
b Wolverhampton 3/8/1911 d 1974
Darlaston
Chillington Athletic
Shrewsbury Town
Sedgley Rovers
Cradley Heath
1930 Wolverhampton Wandrs (trial) 0
1931 1932 Charlton Athletic 25
1934 1935 Port Vale 18 8
1936 1937 Barrow 52 3

Baker, James Seymour (Jimmy) LH/IR
b Aston Clinton 24/11/1897 d 1975
Aylesbury
Wycombe Wanderers
1924 1925 Watford 9 2
Wolverton Town

Baker, James William (Jim) LH/RH/CH
b Basford Green 15/11/1891 d 1966
Eastwood Rangers
Ilkeston Town
1910 Derby County 0
Portsmouth
Hartlepools United
1914 1919 Huddersfield Town 56 3
1920 1925 Leeds United 200 2
1926 Nelson 28 6
Colne Valley

Baker, John RB
1890 Derby County 8

Baker, John (Johnny) LH
Stockton
1899 Gainsborough Trinity 7

Baker, Langford IR
b Lowestoft 29/3/1879 d 1964
Lowestoft North End
Lowestoft Harriers
Lowestoft Town
Norwich City
1903 1905 Grimsby Town 59 16
Norwich City
East Halton Rovers

Baker, Lawrence Henry (Lawrie) CH/RH/LH
b Sheffield 18/11/1897 d 1979
Darnall Old Boys
Beighton
1919 1922 Blackpool 20
1923 1924 Leeds United 11
1924 1928 Barnsley 78 1
1929 Rochdale 34
1930 Nelson 7

Baker, Norman OL
b Buckley 21/6/1909 d 1980
Oak Alyn Rovers
Normal College (Bangor)
Mold Town
1929 Wrexham 1
1929 New Brighton 0
Connah's Quay & Shotton

Baker, Thomas William (Billy) GK
b Seaham Harbour 17/8/1905 d 1975
Usworth Colliery
Crook Town
Shotton Colliery
Chilton Colliery Recreation Athletic
1929 1931 Southport 59
1932 1933 Brentford 64
1934 Northampton Town 13
1935 Rochdale 38
Horden Colliery Welfare

Baker, William Edward (Billy) OL
b Woolwich 11/5/1892 d 1980
Plumstead
Northfleet
Queen's Park Rangers
Dartford
1913 Woolwich Arsenal (trial) 0
1914 1920 Derby County 44 7
1921 1926 Plymouth Argyle 85 11
Bude

Baker, William George (Billy) RH/LH
b Penrhiwceiber 3/10/1920 d 2005
Caps: Wales Sch/WLge 4/Wales 1
Troedyrhiw
1938 1954 Cardiff City 292 5
1955 Ipswich Town 20
Ton Pentre

Bakewell, George OR
b Derby 13/5/1864
Derby Midland
1888 1890 Derby County 49 9
1891 Notts County 5 1

From To Apps Goal

Balcombe, Leslie OR
b Romney Marsh q1 1914 d 1938
Tunbridge Wells Rangers
1934 1935 Gillingham 14 1
Ashford Town (Kent)

Balderston, W CH
1895 Crewe Alexandra 1

Baldock, John William N LH
b Shadwell q3 1893
1920 Queen's Park Rangers 1

Baldry, George William OR
b Cleethorpes 26/5/1911 d 1987
Humber United
1935 Grimsby Town 20 7
1936 Hull City 5 2
Scunthorpe & Lindsey United
Chelmsford City
Shrewsbury Town

Baldwin, Edmund CF
b Preston q4 1902 d 1968
Eanam Celtic (Blackburn)
1921 Tranmere Rovers 1

Baldwin, Harold (Harry) GK
b Saltley 17/7/1920 d 2010
Sutton Town
1937 West Bromwich Albion 5
1939 1951 Brighton & Hove Albion 164
1939 (Brighton & Hove Albion) (1)
Kettering Town
1953 1954 Walsall 37
Wellington Town

Baldwin, Harry OR
b Bolton
Bolton League
1920 1921 Southend United 14 2
1922 Bolton Wanderers 0
Altrincham
Northwich Victoria

Baldwin, Joseph IR
b Blackburn 1/4/1902 d 1983
1929 Nelson 1

Baldwin, W IR/CF
Sale Holmfield
1906 1907 Manchester City 2
Reading

Baldwin, William (Bill) CF/IL
b Leigh 31/1/1907 d 1982
Abram Wanderers
Leigh
Scunthorpe & Lindsey United
1930 Chesterfield 4 3
1931 Barrow 6 1
1932 Oldham Athletic 1
1933 Southport 23 13
1934 1935 Gillingham 60 23
1936 Crewe Alexandra 1

Balkwill, Alexander Forbes CF
b Inverness 1878 d 1947
Alvaston
1900 Derby County 0
Ripley Town
1901 Derby County 11 1

Ball, Alfred (Alf) OL
b Clowne 1890 d 1952
Clowne Rising Star
Creswell Athletic
1913 1919 Lincoln City 97 13
Mansfield Town
Ilkeston United

Ball, Aloysius (Alf) RH/LH
b Preston q1 1874 d 1940
1893 Preston North End 5
Kettering
1897 1899 Leicester Fosse 75 3
Nelson

Ball, Charles RB
b Yeovil q1 1871
1898 Loughborough 16

Ball, Christopher George (Chris) IR/OR
b Leek 31/10/1906 d 1987
Leek St Luke's
1927 1928 Coventry City 10
Colwyn Bay
1930 Bristol Rovers 15
1931 Bristol City 3
1931 1934 Walsall 112 20
Colwyn Bay United
Cradley Heath
Brierley Hill Alliance

From To Apps Goal

Ball, Harold (Harry) IR
b Liverpool 9/2/1908 d 1990
Wavertree
Runcorn
Colwyn Bay United
1932 New Brighton 1

Ball, Herbert James IR
b Bristol q2 1889 d 1923
Cardiff City
1911 Bristol City 2 1

Ball, John (Jack) IL/IR/CF
b Hazel Grove 29/9/1899 d 1989
Caps: England 1
Silverwood Colliery
1919 1920 Sheffield United 6
1921 Bristol Rovers 23 4
Wath Athletic
1923 1928 Bury 203 93
1929 West Ham United 15 9
1930 Coventry City 23 4
Stourbridge
Hinckley Athletic
Atherstone Town
Coventry Gas

Ball, John Thomas (Jack) CF
b Banks 13/9/1907 d 1976
Banks Juniors
Croston (trial)
1925 1926 Southport 25 7
Darwen
Chorley
1929 Manchester United 23 11
1930 1933 Sheffield Wednesday 132 90
1933 1934 Manchester United 24 6
1934 Huddersfield Town 5 1
1934 1935 Luton Town 50 39
Excelsior Roubaix
1936 Luton Town 15 8
Vauxhall Motors
St Albans City
Biggleswade Town

Ball, Joseph (Joe) OL
b Clowne 1882
Clowne White Star
1903 Chesterfield Town 7 2
1903 1904 Bury 4
1905 Chesterfield Town 29 5
Worksop Town
Denaby United
Clowne Town
Mansfield Mechanics
Clowne Rising Star

Ball, Samuel CF/IR
b Newsham 21/8/1907 d 1984
Seghill Colliery Welfare
Blyth Spartans
New Delaval Villa
West Stanley
1925 Chelsea (trial) 0
Seghill Colliery Welfare
1926 1928 Ashington 44 22
New Delaval Villa
Blyth Spartans

Ball, Thomas Edgar (Tommy) CH/LH
b Usworth 11/2/1899 d 1923
Felling Colliery
1919 Newcastle United 0
1919 1923 Aston Villa 74

Ball, William (Billy 'Kosher') RB
b Dudley 9/4/1886 d 1942
Dudley Welfare
Stourbridge
Leamington Town
Wellington Town
1911 1920 Birmingham 152
Cannock Town
Wellington Town

Ball, William Henry RH
b West Derby q2 1876 d 1929
Florence Institute
Liverpool South End
Rock Ferry
1897 Blackburn Rovers 17
1898 Everton 0
1899 1900 Notts County 65 2
1901 Blackburn Rovers 3
1902 Manchester United 4
Tranmere Rovers

Ballantyne, James IL
1921 Stalybridge Celtic 1

From To Apps Goal

Ballantyne, John OR
b Riccarton 30/6/1892
Kenmuirhill Athletic
Kilmarnock
Vale of Leven
1912 1913 Birmingham 20 2
Vale of Leven
Rangers
Vale of Leven
Dumfries

Ballantyne, John (Johnny) IL/IR
b Glasgow 27/10/1899
Caps: SLge 1
Glasgow Ashfield
Partick Thistle
Boston Wonder Workers
Partick Thistle
Falkirk (loan)
1935 1936 Queen's Park Rangers 25 3

Ballantyne, John T LB
b Norton
Stockton
1921 Bradford City 0
1922 Halifax Town 2

Ballantyne, William RH
b Broxburn
Broxburn
Reading
1899 1900 Chesterfield Town 35 3

Ballard, Frank RB
b Long Eaton q4 1876 d 1902
Long Eaton Rangers
1898 Leicester Fosse 2
Ilkeston Town

Ballham, Joseph Louis OR
b Stoke-on-Trent q1 1866 d 1948
Stoke Locomotive
Stoke
Burslem Port Vale
1891 Stoke 18 5

Ballsom, William George (George) RB/CH
b Trealaw 30/10/1912 d 1983
Tunbridge Wells Rangers
1935 1937 Gillingham 45
1938 Cardiff City 34
1939 (Cardiff City) (3)

Balmer, John (Jack) IL/IR/CF
b Liverpool 6/2/1916 d 1984
Caps: England War 1
Collegiate Old Boys
1934 Everton 0
1935 1951 Liverpool 289 98
1939 (Liverpool) (3) (1)

Balmer, Robert (Bob) RB/LB
b West Derby q1 1882
Caps: FLge 1
1902 1911 Everton 165

Balmer, William Atherton RB/LB
b West Derby q3 1875 d 1961
Caps: FLge 1/England 1
Aintree Church
South Shore
1897 1907 Everton 293 1
Croydon Common
Chester

Balmforth, George William RH
b Denaby 1/9/1906 d 1995
Wombwell
1929 Sheffield Wednesday 0
1930 1931 Reading 9
Sete (France)
Oswestry Town

Bamber, John (Jack) LH/CH/RH
b St Helens 11/4/1895 d 1971
Caps: FLge 2/England 1
St Helens Recreation
Alexandra Victoria
Heywood
St Helens Town
1919 1923 Liverpool 72 2
1923 1926 Leicester City 113 7
1927 1929 Tranmere Rovers 86 1
Prescot Cables

Bamber, John Belfield (Jack) CH/RH
b Preston 8/6/1912 d 2000
1931 Preston North End 0
Fleetwood
1933 1938 Stoke City 24 1

From To Apps Goal

Bambrick, Joseph Gardiner Absolom (Jo CF
b Belfast 3/11/1905 d 1983
Caps: IrLge 12/Ireland Amat/Ireland 11
Ulster Rangers
Glentoran
Linfield
1934 1937 Chelsea 59 33
1938 Walsall 35 15

Bamford, Harold Walley LH
b Hull q4 1886 d 1915
1907 Sunderland 0
Southampton
1912 1913 Glossop 14

Bamford, John AE OL
b Weedon 1880 d 1941
Wellingborough
1904 West Bromwich Albion 3
Wellingborough

Bamford, Thomas (Tom) RB/LB
b Horwich q4 1886
Darwen
1909 1914 Burnley 137
Rochdale

Bamford, Thomas (Tommy) CF
b Port Talbot 2/9/1905 d 1967
Caps: Wales 5
Cardiff Docks
Cardiff Wednesday
Bridgend Town
1928 1934 Wrexham 204 175
1934 1937 Manchester United 98 53
1938 Swansea Town 36 14
1939 (Swansea Town) (3) (4)

Bamford, Walter Phillip OR
b Port Talbot
Cardiff Wednesday
1930 Wrexham 1
1932 Carlisle United 0

Bamforth, Geoffrey Charles RH
b Swindon, Staffordshire 21/10/1896 d 1985
Saltley College
1921 Wigan Borough 1

Bamlett, Thomas (Tommy) RB
b Kimblesworth q4 1880 d 1913
Kimblesworth
1901 Newcastle United 2
West Ham United
West Stanley

Bamsey, Hiley Royal CH
b Woodbury 8/10/1916 d 1943
Woodbury
1934 1937 Exeter City 42
1938 Barrow 0

Bancroft, Arthur CH
b Darlington 10/7/1903 d 1984
Tow Law Town
1926 1927 Bradford City 30 1
Aldershot

Bancroft, John Gill IR/CF
b Shardlow q4 1898 d 1958
Heanor Town
1923 Walsall 10
Rugby Town
1926 Walsall 8 1

Banes, Claude Stanley GK
b Beeston Green 1/7/1904 d 1977
Biggleswade Town
1928 1930 Luton Town 57
Biggleswade Town

Banfield, Albert John IR
b Bristol 5/5/1912 d 1970
St Philip's Marsh
1933 1934 Bristol City 38 8
1935 York City 30 10
1936 Clapton Orient 0

Banfield, Laurence LB
b Paulton 11/11/1889 d 1979
Paulton Rovers
1911 1924 Bristol City 259 6
Ilfracombe Town

Banks, Frederick William OR/OL
b Aston 9/12/1888 d 1957
Park Road
Myrtle Villa
1909 Birmingham 1
Stourbridge
Wellington Town
1911 1913 Nottingham Forest 56 5
Stalybridge Celtic
1919 Nottingham Forest 15
Worksop Town

From To Apps Goal

Banks, George Ernest CF/IR
b Wednesbury 28/3/1919 d 1991
Brownhills Athletic
1938 West Bromwich Albion 1 2
1939 (West Bromwich Albion) (3) (1)
1947 1948 Mansfield Town 63 21
Hereford United

Banks, Herbert Ernest (Bert) IL/CF
b Coventry q2 1874 d 1947
Caps: England 1
72nd Seaforth Highlanders
1896 Everton 2
St Mirren (loan)
Third Lanark
Millwall Athletic
1901 Aston Villa 5
1901 1902 Bristol City 42 18
Watford
Coventry City
Stafford Rangers
Verity's Athletic

Banks, J IR/LH
1897 1898 Blackpool 9

Banks, James Andrew (Jimmy) IR/OR/IL
b Wigan 28/4/1893 d 1942
Starcliffe Celtic
St Gregory's
All Saints
Spennymoor United
Willington
1913 1922 Tottenham Hotspur 68 6
1923 1926 Norwich City 124 22
1927 Luton Town 13 2
London Public Omnibus Company

Banks, John (Jack) LH/OL/RH
b West Bromwich 14/6/1875 d 1947
Oldbury Broadwell
1893 1900 West Bromwich Albion 119 5
1901 1902 Newton Heath/Manchester Utd 40
Plymouth Argyle
Leyton
Exeter City

Banks, Reginald (Reg) OL/OR
Caps: England Amat
Birmingham University
1934 West Bromwich Albion 0
1935 1936 Queen's Park Rangers 12 3
Tunbridge Wells Rangers

Banks, Richard IR
b Preston q4 1878
Lostock Hall
Kettering
Skerton
1899 Preston North End 4
Chorley
Kettering
Oswaldtwistle Rovers
Ashton Town
Chorley
St Helens Town
Clitheroe Central

Banks, William (Willie) LH
b Riccarton 2/11/1880 d 1966
Glenbuck Athletic
Rugby XI
Kilmarnock
1905 1906 Manchester City 25 1
Atherton Combe
Hurlford
Portsmouth
Alberta
1911 Manchester City 0
Kilmarnock
Nithsdale Wanderers

Banks, William (Billy) IR
b Cramlington q1 1893
Hartford Burden
Bedlington
Ashington
Tranmere Rovers
1913 1914 Liverpool 26 6
Tranmere Rovers
1919 1920 Fulham 40 12
Bedlington United

Bann, Fred CH
b Rotherham q3 1879 d 1954
1901 Doncaster Rovers 1
Thornhill United

Bann, William Edward (Bill) RB/LB
b Broxburn 15/8/1902 d 1973
Broxburn United
1925 1928 Tottenham Hotspur 12
1930 1931 Brentford 7
1932 Bristol Rovers 1
1933 1934 Aldershot 7

From To Apps Goal

Banner, Arthur RB/LB/CH
b Sheffield 28/6/1918 d 1980
Lopham Street
1936 Doncaster Rovers 0
1938 1947 West Ham United 27
1947 1952 Leyton Orient 164 1
Sittingbourne

Banner, Henry Samuel (Harry) OR
b Marshside 14/8/1905 d 1963
Crossens
1926 1927 Southport 9
Burscough Rangers
Fleetwood Hesketh

Banner, T CF
1899 Burton Swifts 4

Banner, William Arthur LB
b Warrington 20/5/1907 d 1974
Manchester North End
1934 Halifax Town 9

Banner, William Henry (Billy) CH/RH/RB
b Barnsley q4 1878 d 1936
Poolsbrook United
Dronfield Town
New Whittington Exchange
1901 1902 Chesterfield Town 52 4
Queen's Park Rangers
1904 1907 Chesterfield Town 129 8
Hardwick Colliery
Denaby United
Hardwick Colliery

Bannister, Charles (Charlie) CH/RH
b Burton-on-Trent 1875 d 1947
Newtown
1896 Manchester City 18 2
Oldham County
1897 1900 Lincoln City 106 1
Swindon Town
Reading
Swindon Town
Perth YMCA (Australia)

Bannister, Ernest LH
b Buxton q4 1883
Buxton
1907 Manchester City 1
1910 Preston North End 0
Port Vale
Darlington
Heart of Midlothian
Ayr United

Bannister, James (Jimmy) IR
b Leyland 20/9/1880 d 1953
Leyland Temperance
Leyland
Chorley
1902 1905 Manchester City 45 21
1906 1909 Manchester United 57 7
1909 1911 Preston North End 65 12
Lancaster Town
Leyland
Darlington
Heywood
Lancaster Town

Bannister, Thomas IL
1908 Gainsborough Trinity 1
1908 Nottingham Forest 0

Bannister, William (Billy) CH
b Burnley q4 1878 d 1942
Caps: FLge 2/England 2
Earby
1899 1901 Burnley 50 3
1901 1902 Bolton Wanderers 28 3
1902 1903 Woolwich Arsenal 18
1904 1909 Leicester Fosse 149 15
1910 1911 Burnley 5 1
Crewe Alexandra
Leicester Imperial

Barber, Arthur William OR
b Weston-super-Mare 25/1/1919 d 1995
1938 Everton 2

Barber, Bernard RB
b Worsborough q3 1905 d 1966
Wombwell
1927 Halifax Town 1

Barber, George Frederick RB/LB
b West Ham 1/8/1908 d 1974
1929 Luton Town 0
1930 1938 Chelsea 262
1939 (Chelsea) (3)

From	To	Club	Apps	Goal
Barber, John (Jack)			CH/IL/LH	
b Salford 8/1/1901			d 1961	
		Clayton		
1922	1923	Manchester United	3	1
1924	1925	Southport	43	18
1926		Halifax Town	12	1
1927	1930	Rochdale	142	4
1931		Stockport County	16	
1932		Hull City (trial)	0	
1932		Stockport County	0	
		Bacup Borough		
Barber, John Foster			LH	
b Felling 5/9/1893			d 1969	
		Washington United		
		Seaton Delaval		
1914		Burnley	0	
1921		Ashington	23	3
		Workington		
Barber, Joseph			OL	
b Barnsley q2 1909				
		Barnsley Milton Street		
1930		Doncaster Rovers	6	1
		Wombwell		
Barber, Lewis Frederick			GK	
b Darfield 11/4/1906			d 1983	
		Broomhill WMC		
1925	1926	Halifax Town	35	
1927	1930	Manchester City	92	
Barber, Stanley (Stan)			LH	
b Wallsend 28/5/1908			d 1984	
		Wallsend		
1927		Newcastle United	1	
1928	1929	Bristol City	23	1
1930	1933	Exeter City	118	10
1934		Brighton & Hove Albion	0	
Barber, Thomas (Tommy)			LH/RH/IL	
b West Stanley 22/7/1886			d 1925	
Caps: FLge 1				
		Shankhouse		
		West Stanley		
		Hamsterley		
1908	1912	Bolton Wanderers	102	14
1912	1914	Aston Villa	57	9
		Belfast Celtic (loan)		
		Celtic (loan)		
		Partick Thistle (loan)		
		Linfield (loan)		
		Distillery (loan)		
		Stalybridge Celtic		
		Crystal Palace		
1920		Merthyr Town	2	
		Ton Pentre		
		Pontypridd		
1921		Walsall	5	2
		Darlaston		
		Hinckley United		
		Barwell		
Barber, William Arthur Joseph			RH	
b Lincoln 20/12/1908			d 1954	
		Army		
1933		Luton Town	0	
1933	1934	Lincoln City	13	
1935		Crewe Alexandra	0	
		Peterborough United		
		Truro City		
Barbour, Alexander (Alec)			CF/OR	
b Dumbarton 7/6/1862			d 1930	
Caps: Scotland 1				
		Renton		
1888	1891	Bolton Wanderers	34	17
		Glossop North End		
1892		Nottingham Forest	1	
Barbour, John R			IR	
b Glasgow 1891			d 1916	
		Glasgow Perthshire		
		Queen's Park		
		Dundee		
1914		Preston North End	12	2
Barbour, Thomas Parkhill (Tommy)			LB/RH/RB	
b Largs 13/11/1887			d 1967	
		Kilbirnie Ladeside		
1908	1920	Derby County	273	3
1921		Darlington	29	
1922		Derby County	0	
		Burton All Saints		

From	To	Club	Apps	Goal
Barbour, William (Billy)			CF/RB/LB	
b Kilmarnock 21/9/1865			d 1900	
		Queen of the South Wanderers		
1888	1890	Accrington	53	33
		Sunderland Albion (loan)		
		Stockton		
		Annbank		
1894	1897	Bury	101	11
		Gravesend		
Barclay, John Birrell			OL	
b Thornton 22/1/1904			d 1978	
		Wellesley Juniors		
		Dundee		
		Forfar Athletic (loan)		
1926		Reading	4	
1927	1928	Accrington Stanley	76	11
		Yeovil & Petters United		
		Guildford City		
		Armadale		
		Albion Rovers		
		Boston United		
Barclay, Robert (Bobby)			IR	
b Scotswood 27/10/1906			d 1969	
Caps: England 3				
		Scotswood United Church		
		Bell's Close Amateurs		
		Allendale		
		Scotswood		
1928	1930	Derby County	61	23
1931	1936	Sheffield United	231	67
1936	1938	Huddersfield Town	74	19
1939		(Huddersfield Town)	(2)	
		Hurst		
Barcroft, Thomas Arthur (Tom)			GK	
b Rossendale q3 1871			d 1946	
1901		Blackpool	1	
Bardsley, Edwin			OL	
b Hadfield q4 1883			d 1958	
1903		Glossop	10	1
1905	1906	Stockport County	43	3
Bardsley, John C			LB	
b Southport 1886				
		Northern Nomads		
1909		Everton	1	
1911		Manchester City	0	
Bargh, George Wolfenden			IR/IL	
b Bilsborrow 27/5/1910			d 1995	
		Fulwood Amateurs		
		Garstang		
1928	1934	Preston North End	142	42
1935		Sheffield Wednesday	5	
1936	1938	Bury	90	13
1939		Chesterfield	(2)	
1946		Bury	1	
Barkas, Edward (Ned)			LB/RB	
b Wardley Colliery 21/1/1901			d 1962	
		Bedlington		
1919		South Shields	0	
		Hebburn Colliery		
1920		Norwich City	1	
		Bedlington United		
1921	1928	Huddersfield Town	119	4
1928	1936	Birmingham	256	9
1937	1938	Chelsea	27	
		Solihull Town		
Barkas, Henry Brown (Harry)			CF	
b Wardley Colliery 21/1/1906			d 1974	
		Wardley Juniors		
		Spennymoor United		
1929		South Shields	21	15
1930		Gateshead	19	7
1930	1931	Liverpool	5	
		Jarrow		
Barkas, Samuel (Sam)			LB/LH	
b Wardley Colliery 29/12/1909			d 1989	
Caps: FLge 3/England 5				
		Middle Dock		
1927	1933	Bradford City	202	8
1933	1946	Manchester City	175	1
		Workington		
Barkas, Thomas (Tommy)			IL/IR	
b Gateshead 27/3/1912			d 1991	
		Washington Colliery		
1932	1934	Bradford City	16	2
1934	1945	Halifax Town	169	36
1939		(Halifax Town)	(2)	
1946	1947	Rochdale	44	17
1947	1948	Stockport County	44	18
1948		Carlisle United	14	5

From	To	Club	Apps	Goal
Barke, John Lloyd (Lloyd)			CH/RH	
b Nuncargate 16/12/1912			d 1976	
		Annesley Colliery		
1930		Chesterfield	0	
		East Kirkby Welfare		
		Bleakhall United		
		Scunthorpe & Lindsey United		
1934	1936	Sheffield United	6	
1937	1946	Mansfield Town	114	
1939		(Mansfield Town)	(3)	
		Denaby United		
		Sutton Town		
		Heanor Town		
		Ilkeston Town		
		Belper Town		
Barker, Donald (Don)			IL/IR	
b Long Eaton 17/6/1911			d 1979	
1932		Notts County	0	
		Johnson & Barnes		
1933	1936	Bradford Park Avenue	55	15
1936	1938	Millwall	62	18
1939		(Millwall)	(1)	
1946		Brighton & Hove Albion	14	4
Barker, Frederick Charles			IR/IL	
b Shardlow q4 1883			d 1904	
1903	1904	Derby County	4	2
Barker, Frederick Malcolm			RB	
b Thirsk q2 1882				
		South Bank		
1906		Middlesbrough	1	
Barker, George			RB/LB	
b Blakenhall 2/1875				
1896	1897	Everton	10	
		Bristol City		
		Bedminster		
1900		Wolverhampton Wanderers	13	
Barker, J			OR	
1897		Darwen	6	
Barker, Jeffrey (Jeff)			RB/LB	
b Scunthorpe 16/10/1915			d 1985	
		Goole Town		
		Scunthorpe & Lindsey United		
1937		Aston Villa	3	
1945	1947	Huddersfield Town	67	
1950	1951	Scunthorpe United	73	1
Barker, John			OR	
1901		Stockport County	2	
Barker, John William (Jack)			CH	
b Denaby 27/2/1907			d 1982	
Caps: FLge 3/England 11				
		Denaby Rovers		
		Denaby United		
1928	1938	Derby County	326	2
1939		(Derby County)	(3)	
Barker, R			CF	
1902		Burton United	3	1
Barker, William (Billy)			OL/OR	
b Shincliffe 20/12/1904			d 1993	
		Bowburn Juniors		
		Hamsteels Colliery		
1921		Walsall (trial)	0	
		Willington United		
		Kelloe St Helen's		
1923		Burnley (trial)	0	
1923	1925	Durham City	21	2
		Ferryhill Athletic		
		St Johnstone (trial)		
1926		Grimsby Town (trial)	0	
		Cockfield		
		Spennymoor United		
		Bishop Auckland		
		Crook Town		
		Bishop Auckland		
Barker, William Clement (Billy)			RH/LH	
b Linthorpe q4 1883			d 1937	
		South Bank		
1905	1912	Middlesbrough	104	2
Barklam, Horace			OL	
b Newport 18/2/1912			d 1984	
		Somerton Park		
1933		Newport County	3	1
		Newport Rangers		
Barks, Wilfred			IL/IR	
b Chesterfield 27/3/1905			d 1968	
		Dinnington Athletic		
1932		Chesterfield	7	
1934		Mansfield Town	4	
		Mexborough		
1935		Rotherham United	0	
		Denaby United		
		Dinnington Colliery		
1937		Rochdale	3	

From	To	Club	Apps	Goal
Barley, Henry Frank (Harry)			OR	
b Grimsby q1 1905			d 1958	
		Humber United		
1929	1930	Grimsby Town	5	1
1931		Hull City	13	2
1932	1933	New Brighton	21	4
1933		Notts County	11	1
		Scunthorpe & Lindsey United		
1935		Bristol Rovers	17	5
1936		Barrow	40	8
		Kidderminster Harriers		
		Frickley Colliery		
		Bath City		
Barley, John Charles (Charlie)			LH/IL	
b Staveley 30/10/1904			d 1962	
		Staveley Town		
1926	1928	Arsenal	8	1
1929	1936	Reading	194	16
		Maidenhead United		
Barley, Peter			LH	
b Staveley q3 1877			d 1933	
		Hartington Colliery		
		Sheepbridge Works		
		Hartington Colliery		
1899		Chesterfield Town	3	
		Staveley Town		
		Poolsbrook United		
		Grassmoor Red Rose		
		Thornhill United		
		Seymour Colliery		
		Lowgates United		
Barlow, A			OL	
1900		Glossop	12	5
Barlow, C Arthur			RB	
		Northern Nomads		
1919	1921	Manchester United	29	
		New Cross (Blackley)		
Barlow, Cyril			RB	
		Newton Heath Parish Church WM		
1922		Manchester United	0	
1924		Stockport County	1	
Barlow, George Arthur			LB/RB	
b Langwith Junction 1914				
		Langwith Miners Welfare		
1934	1935	Mansfield Town	11	
Barlow, George Herbert			OL	
b Wigan q4 1885			d 1921	
Caps: England Amat				
		Wigan Grammar School OB		
1906	1907	Preston North End	10	2
1908	1910	Everton	34	5
1912	1914	Preston North End	79	5
Barlow, Herbert (Bert)			IR/IL	
b Kilnhurst 22/7/1916			d 2004	
		Silverwood Colliery		
1935	1937	Barnsley	58	12
1938		Wolverhampton Wanderers	3	1
1938	1949	Portsmouth	104	34
1939		(Portsmouth)	(3)	(1)
1949	1951	Leicester City	42	9
1952	1953	Colchester United	60	16
		Crittall Athletic		
		Long Melford		
Barlow, JM			CF/OR	
1890	1891	Accrington	5	
Barlow, John			OL/IR	
b Prescot q4 1875				
		Prescot		
1897	1898	Everton	4	
		Reading		
		Tottenham Hotspur		
		Reading		
1903		Leicester Fosse	22	2
		St Helens Recreation		
		Oldham Athletic		
Barlow, Patrick Joseph (Paddy)			OR	
b Athlone 1915				
Caps: LoI 1				
		Athlone Town		
		Newry Town		
1938		Huddersfield Town	7	1
		Sligo Rovers		
		Dundalk		
		Limerick		
		Chelmsford City		
		Wisbech Town		
Barlow, Ralph			CH	
1895		Burslem Port Vale	29	1
Barlow, T			RH	
1893		Northwich Victoria	1	
Barlow, T			OR	
1903		Burton United	2	

From	To	Club	Apps	Goal
Barlow, Thomas Henry (Tom)			IL	
b Bolton q1 1875				
		Halliwell Rovers		
1898	1901	Bolton Wanderers	81	24
		Southampton		
1903		Bolton Wanderers	5	1
		Millwall Athletic		
		Atherton Church House		
		Oldham Athletic		
Barlow, W			OR	
1899		Loughborough	1	
Barnard, Cecil			CF	
		Aylesbury United		
1921		Watford	2	1
Barnard, Frank Edwin			OR/RH	
b Gainsborough q2 1885				
1901	1902	Gainsborough Trinity	8	
Barnard, Frederick William (Fred)			OL	
b Gainsborough q2 1882			d 1925	
1902		Gainsborough Trinity	1	
Barnard, Sidney			IR	
b Aigburth 10/7/1914			d 1999	
		Aigburth Parish Church		
1934		Blackburn Rovers	0	
1935		Stockport County	0	
		Bangor		
1937		Wrexham	2	1
Barnard, Walter Eric (Wally)			RB	
b Tottenham 9/10/1898			d 1982	
1922		Tottenham Hotspur	0	
1923		Gillingham	3	
1926		Brentford	0	
Barnes, Charles			OR/OL	
b Chesham q1 1879			d 1960	
		Chesham Town		
		Reading		
1902	1903	Bristol City	23	5
		Watford		
Barnes, Edward			GK	
b Royston, Hertfordshire 21/7/1898			d 1975	
		St Albans City		
		Watford		
1920		Southend United	1	
1921		Charlton Athletic	21	
1922		Queen's Park Rangers	0	
Barnes, G			OL	
1903		Glossop	5	
Barnes, George			OL/OR	
b Liverpool 1878				
		All Saints (Liverpool)		
1897	1898	Darwen	31	6
1898		Bolton Wanderers	9	1
		Portsmouth		
1900		New Brighton Tower	7	1
Barnes, George Henry			OL/IR	
b Chesham 22/5/1899			d 1961	
		Chesham United		
1921	1923	Watford	5	1
Barnes, Harold			IR	
b Aldridge				
1921		Aston Villa	0	
1922		Southend United	4	
Barnes, Horace			IL	
b Wadsley Bridge 3/1/1891			d 1961	
Caps: FLge 2				
		Wadsley Bridge		
1908	1913	Derby County	153	74
1914	1924	Manchester City	217	120
1924	1925	Preston North End	39	16
1925	1926	Oldham Athletic	41	16
		Ashton National		
Barnes, Howard Ellington			IR	
b Clapham 1/11/1909			d 1992	
Caps: England Amat				
		Wimbledon		
1934		Crystal Palace	1	
		Wimbledon		
		Boulogne		
		Wimbledon		
Barnes, J			CH	
1895		Burton Wanderers	2	1
Barnes, James			OL	
b Earsdon 21/7/1900				
		Harkford		
1921		Derby County	4	
1923		Rochdale	0	

From	To	Club	Apps	Goal
Barnes, John Benjamin (Jack)			OL/OR	
b Atherstone 28/4/1908			d 2008	
		Atherstone Town		
1927		Coventry City	8	
1929	1930	Walsall	68	18
1931	1932	Watford	75	12
1933		Exeter City	18	1
1934		York City	15	1
		Atherstone Town		
		Wilstaff Sports (Birmingham)		
Barnes, Joseph			CH	
1921		Rochdale	3	
		New Church		
Barnes, Kossuth Seed			GK	
b Preston 5/1892			d 1965	
		Durham City		
1921		Bristol Rovers	17	
		Houghton		
1922		Accrington Stanley (trial)	2	
Barnes, Victor Herbert Burrow			OL	
b New Eltham 12/9/1905			d 1971	
		Kingstonian		
1926	1927	Crystal Palace	4	1
Barnes, Walter T			RH	
1899		Luton Town	6	
Barnes, William Edwin (Billy)			OL/IL/IR	
b Stratford 28/7/1877			d 1962	
Caps: SoLge 1				
		Thames Ironworks		
		South West Ham		
		Leyton		
1899	1901	Sheffield United	23	7
		West Ham United		
		Luton Town		
		Queen's Park Rangers		
		Southend United		
Barnett, Albert			IL/LH/LB	
b Altrincham q1 1892			d 1941	
		Altrincham		
		Macclesfield		
1913		Glossop	20	2
1920	1921	Cardiff City	17	1
1924		Aberdare Athletic	22	1
		Fordsons		
1926		Wigan Borough	3	
		Altrincham		
Barnett, Charles			GK	
b Derby q2 1890				
		Newark		
1912	1914	Leicester Fosse	20	
		Mansfield Town		
		Alfreton Town		
Barnett, Frederick William (Fred)			OR	
b Dartford 13/4/1898			d 1982	
		Hawley		
1919		Bolton Wanderers (trial)	0	
1920		Tottenham Hotspur	0	
		Northfleet		
1922	1928	Tottenham Hotspur	16	1
1929	1933	Southend United	174	35
1934		Watford	0	
		Dartford		
Barnett, Harry			IR	
		Talk o' th' Hill Club		
1920		Bury	2	
Barnett, Laurence Hector (Laurie)			LB/RB/LH	
b Bramley, Rotherham 8/5/1900			d 1982	
1920	1921	Bradford Park Avenue	33	
		Gainsborough Trinity		
1924	1925	Barnsley	28	
1926	1928	Blackpool	47	
1930	1934	Manchester City	84	
Barnett, Samuel (Sammy)			IR/IL/OR	
b Nantwich q2 1871				
		Nantwich		
1892	1895	Crewe Alexandra	62	7
Barnett, Thomas Andrew (Tommy)			IR	
b Salford 11/11/1908			d 1986	
		Longsight		
1927		Manchester United	0	
1928	1938	Watford	395	144
1939		(Watford)	(3)	
Barnett, William Thomas (Thomas)			IR/CF	
b Sherwood 29/12/1876				
		Beeston Rangers		
1900	1901	Nottingham Forest	2	

From	To	Club	Apps	Goal
Barnfather, Percy			OR	
b Newcastle 17/12/1879			d 1951	
		Wallsend Park Villa		
1903		Barnsley	27	3
		New Brompton		
		West Stanley		
		Croydon Common		
		Norwich City		
		Croydon Common		
		West Stanley		
		Croydon Common		
		Merthyr Town		
Barnie-Adshead, (Dr) William Ewart			CH	
b Dudley 10/4/1901			d 1951	
Caps: England Amat				
		Birmingham University		
		Corinthians		
1922		Aston Villa	2	1
		Corinthians		
Barnsdale, John Davison			RH/CH	
b Nottingham 24/5/1878			d 1960	
1903	1904	Nottingham Forest	25	
Barnshaw, Robert James (Bob)			CH	
b Hebburn 14/3/1889			d 1974	
		Jarrow Croft		
		Hebburn Argyle		
1911		Sheffield Wednesday	0	
		Hebburn Argyle		
1913		Sheffield United	3	
1920		Watford	12	1
1921		Aberdare Athletic	24	2
Baron, Frederick John (Fred)			CF/IL/IR	
b Prudhoe 29/12/1901			d 1993	
		Prudhoe Castle		
1922		Leicester City	0	
		Mid-Rhondda United		
1924	1926	Liverpool	20	7
1926	1931	Southend United	62	42
Baron, Harold			LH	
b Hindley 23/10/1894			d 1963	
		Hindley Central		
		Stalybridge Celtic		
		Wigan United		
		Burscough Rangers		
1921		Wigan Borough	7	
Barr, Albert McDonald			CF/IL	
b Ballymena				
Caps: IrLge 1				
		Glentoran		
1937	1938	Manchester City	4	2
		Ballymena United		
Barr, John			OR	
b Lanark 1885				
		Motherwell		
		Partick Thistle		
		Lanemark		
1906		Grimsby Town	2	1
Barr, John			OR	
b Chatham 1902				
		Folkestone		
1922		Clapton Orient	8	
		Chatham Town		
Barr, Joseph Hilrick (Joe)			RH	
b Glasgow 1868			d 1894	
		Elderslie		
		Burslem Port Vale		
1891		Accrington	12	
		Northwich Victoria		
1893		Rotherham Town	28	
Barr, JW			RH	
		Grantham Rovers		
1893		Newcastle United	1	
		Ashington		
Barr, Robert (Bob)			IR/CF	
b Paisley 1865				
		Hurlford		
1888		Stoke	3	
		Abercorn		
1894	1895	Preston North End	29	9
1895		Bury	15	6
		Reading		
		Abercorn		
Barr, William			IR	
		London Caledonians		
1925		Queen's Park Rangers	2	
Barraclough, Arthur			OL	
b Moorthorpe 7/11/1916			d 2005	
		Peterborough United		
1937		Chelsea	0	
1938		Swindon Town	21	6
1939		Clapton Orient	0	

From	To	Club	Apps	Goal
Barraclough, William (Billy)			OL	
b Hull 3/1/1909			d 1969	
		Bridlington Town		
1927		Hull City	9	
1928	1934	Wolverhampton Wanderers	172	18
1934	1936	Chelsea	74	8
		Colchester United		
1938		Doncaster Rovers	8	
		Peterborough United		
Barrass, Cuthbert (Chris)			IL	
b South Shields 11/2/1898			d 1978	
		Pandon Temperance		
		Jarrow		
1921		Grimsby Town	4	
		Jarrow		
Barrass, Matthew Williamson (Matt)			IL/IR/RH	
b Seaham Harbour 14/2/1899			d 1953	
		Seaham Harbour		
1919	1924	Blackpool	162	53
1924	1925	Sheffield Wednesday	48	14
1926	1932	Manchester City	162	14
		Ashton National		
Barrass, Richard Kendrick			CF	
b Gateshead 23/8/1914			d 1972	
1938		Gateshead	4	1
Barratt, Alfred George (Alf)			CH/LH	
b Weldon 13/4/1920			d 2002	
		Weldon		
		Kettering Town		
1938		Northampton Town	1	
		Stewart & Lloyds		
1947	1948	Leicester City	4	
1950		Grimsby Town	23	
1951	1955	Southport	198	
Barratt, Harold (Harry)			RB/RH/IR	
b Headington 25/12/1918			d 1989	
		Herberts Athletic		
1935		Coventry City	0	
		Cheltenham Town (loan)		
1937	1951	Coventry City	170	12
Barratt, John			RH	
b Stafford 1916				
		Stafford Rangers		
1938		Rochdale	1	
Barratt, Josiah (Jos)			OR	
b Bulkington 21/2/1895			d 1968	
		Nuneaton Town		
1920	1921	Southampton	52	5
1921	1922	Birmingham	30	1
		Pontypridd		
1924	1925	Lincoln City	74	8
1926		Bristol Rovers	21	4
		Nuneaton Town		
Barratt, Percy Marriott			LB/RB	
b Annesley 6/10/1898			d 1974	
		Annesley St Albans		
1919	1929	Nottingham Forest	217	17
		Grantham		
Barratt, Peter			IL	
b Edinburgh				
		Edinburgh Emmet		
		East Fife		
1927		Newport County	17	4
		Dundee		
		East Fife		
		Arbroath (trial)		
Barrell, George			IL/LH/CF	
b Lincoln 7/7/1888			d 1960	
		Rustons Engineers		
1909	1914	Lincoln City	141	26
		Rustons Engineers		
		Boston Town		
Barrett, Albert Frank (Bert)			LH/LB	
b Stratford 11/11/1903			d 1989	
Caps: England Amat/England 1				
		Fairbairn House		
		Leytonstone		
1923		West Ham United	0	
		Leytonstone		
1924		Southampton	1	
1925	1936	Fulham	389	16
Barrett, Alfred Edward			OL	
b Narborough, Leicestershire q2 1896				
1914		Leicester Fosse	1	
Barrett, Arthur Kingston			LH	
b Stratford 4/12/1901			d 1990	
		Leytonstone		
		Ilford		
1929		Millwall	1	
		Margate		

From To Apps Goal

Barrett, Claude LB/RB
b Rawdon 5/12/1907 d 1976
Rawdon Old Boys
1932 1935 Bradford Park Avenue 47
1936 Port Vale 19
1937 1938 York City 41

Barrett, Francis (Frank) GK
b Dundee 2/8/1872 d 1907
Caps: Scotland 2
Dundee Harp
Dundee
1896 1899 Newton Heath 118
1900 New Brighton Tower 34
Arbroath
1901 Manchester City 5
Dundee Wanderers
Aberdeen

Barrett, Frederick K (Fred) LB/RB
b Woodford 12/4/1896
Caps: IrLge 1
Belfast Celtic
1920 1926 Chelsea 64 6
Dundalk
Ards

Barrett, James William (Jim) CH
b West Ham 19/1/1907 d 1970
Caps: England 1
Fairbairn House
1924 1938 West Ham United 442 49

Barrett, William Henry (Billy) RB
b Stockingford q3 1893
Stockingford Congregationals
Bromsgrove Rovers
Nuneaton Town
1919 1924 Leicester City 143 1
1925 Derby County 0
Hinckley United
Hereford United

Barrick, Harry Rowley CF
b Skegness q3 1883 d 1955
Scunthorpe United
1906 Lincoln City 5 2
Scunthorpe & Lindsey United

Barrie, Alexander W (Alex) CH
b Parkhead 1881 d 1917
Glasgow Parkhead
St Bernard's
1902 1906 Sunderland 66 1
Rangers
Kilmarnock
Abercorn

Barrie, George CH/LB
b Coaltown of Balgonie 17/7/1904
East Fife
Kettering Town
1929 1933 Crystal Palace 77
1933 1936 Gillingham 87 1

Barrie, James William LB
b Old Kilpatrick 20/10/1902
Duntocher Hibs
Kirkintilloch Rob Roy
Duntocher Hibs
Dumbarton
Queen's Park
Clydebank
Queen's Park
Boston Wonder Workers
Bethlehem Steel
New Bedford Whalers
Boston Wonder Workers
New Bedford Whalers
Fall River Marksmen
Providence Gold Bugs
Celtic
1930 1932 Halifax Town 91
Worcester City
Cowdenbeath

Barrie, Walter Bartholomew RB
b Kirkcaldy 9/8/1909
Hibernian
1931 West Ham United 0
1932 1937 Queen's Park Rangers 157 1
1938 Carlisle United 10

Barrington, James (Jimmy) LB
b Lower Ince 15/11/1901 d 1968
Wigan United
1920 1921 Bradford City 2
Hamilton Academical
Atherton
Runcorn (trial)
1925 1926 Wigan Borough 71 1
Winsford United
1929 1936 Nottingham Forest 210 1
Ollerton Colliery

From To Apps Goal

Barron, Charles William RB
b Prudhoe q3 1889
Durham City
1914 Leicester Fosse 16
Scotswood

Barron, Fred RH/RB
b Stockton 7/6/1879
Stockton St Mary's
1898 1910 Burnley 400 13
Portsmouth

Barron, George Ward OR
b Darlington q4 1883 d 1961
Wallsend Park Villa
1902 Sheffield Wednesday 1

Barron, James (Jim) GK
b Burnhope 19/7/1913 d 1969
Durham City
Blyth Spartans
1935 1938 Blackburn Rovers 76
1939 (Blackburn Rovers) (3)
1946 Darlington 23

Barron, William (Bill) LB/OL
b Houghton-le-Spring 26/10/1917 d 2006
Hetton Juniors
Bishop Auckland
Annfield Plain
1936 Hartlepools United 0
1936 Wolverhampton Wanderers 0
Annfield Plain
1937 Charlton Athletic 3 2
1938 1950 Northampton Town 166 4
1939 (Northampton Town) (3)
Kettering Town

Barrott, William (Willie) OL
b Oldham 6/10/1908 d 1971
Royton
1933 Rochdale 1

Barrow, William Henry (Billy) OR/OL
b Cardiff 28/1/1911 d 2000
Caps: Wales Sch
1929 Clapton Orient 0
Margate
1933 1934 Southend United 34 3
1935 Bournemouth & Boscombe Ath 26 4
1936 Wrexham 13 2
Barry

Barrowman, William (Bill) GK
b Wigan 28/8/1905 d 2000
Station Road Athletic
1927 Wigan Borough 5

Barry, Leonard James (Len) OL
b Sneinton 27/10/1901 d 1970
Caps: England Amat/England 5
RAF Cranwell
1920 1927 Notts County 146 10
1927 1932 Leicester City 203 25
1933 Nottingham Forest 17 1

Barsby, Ernest LH
b Stanton, Derbyshire q1 1886 d 1962
Overseal
1906 Burton United 1
Midway Albion
1908 Birmingham 0
Watford

Barson, Frank CH/RH
b Grimesthorpe 10/4/1891 d 1968
Caps: England 1
Albion (Sheffield)
Cammell Laird (Sheffield)
1911 1919 Barnsley 91
1919 1921 Aston Villa 92 10
1922 1927 Manchester United 140 4
1928 Watford 10 1
1929 Hartlepools United 9 2
1930 Wigan Borough 19
Rhyl Athletic

Bartholomew, Frederick Charles (Fred) OR
b Reading 3/1/1885 d 1979
Reading Biscuits
1920 Reading 8

Bartholomew, Roland OL
b Great Harwood 15/1/1915 d 2001
Urmston Old Boys
1934 Leeds United 0
1935 1937 Bradford City 100 14
1938 Grimsby Town 12 4

Bartlett, AE LH
1893 Rotherham Town 4

From To Apps Goal

Bartlett, Albert Burdon OR/IR
b Newcastle 10/4/1884 d 1969
Morpeth Harriers
1906 1908 Bradford City 52 18
Brentford
Reading
1912 Bradford City 0
Heckmondwike
Halifax Town
Castleford Town

Bartlett, Frederick Leslie (Fred) CH
b Reading 5/3/1913 d 1968
Club Francais
1934 1936 Queen's Park Rangers 48
1937 1947 Clapton Orient 96
Gloucester City

Bartlett, John W LB
b South Wales
1933 Cardiff City 1

Bartlett, Thomas IL
b Tyneside
St Thomas
Science & Art
Arthur's Hill
1893 Newcastle United 3 3
Willington Athletic
1894 Walsall Town Swifts 0
Willington Athletic
1896 Newcastle United 0
Hebburn Argyle

Bartlett, William John (Billy) LH
b Newcastle 13/4/1878 d 1939
Caps: IrLge 1
Brandling
Gateshead NER
1903 1909 Sheffield Wednesday 176 2
1910 1911 Huddersfield Town 65 2
Linfield

Bartley, James William E (Jim) RB
b Bilston q2 1902 d 1939
Bilston United
1926 1929 Gillingham 25
Canterbury Waverley

Bartley, John (Jack) LH
b Houghton-le-Spring 15/1/1909 d 1929
Hetton Juniors
Chester-le-Street
1926 1929 Sunderland 19 1

Bartley, John Patrick (Jack) IR
b New Washington 26/12/1907 d 1999
Spennymoor United
1929 Wolverhampton Wanderers 2
1930 Walsall 5
Usworth Colliery
1932 Stockport County 0
Altrincham

Bartley, Philip James CF
b Bentley 23/12/1914 d 1978
1933 Norwich City 0
1934 Rochdale 14 3
1935 Mansfield Town 2

Bartley, Thomas OR
b Flint 1874 d 1951
Caps: Wales 1
Flint
Port Sunlight
1898 Glossop North End 7 2
Llandudno
Earlestown
Ashton Wanderers
Earlestown

Barton, Edward Victor (Teddy) RH
b Liverpool q1 1904 d 1941
1924 Everton 0
1925 1934 Tranmere Rovers 237 5

Barton, Fred RH
b Southport 9/8/1899 d 1958
Maple Crescent
Haskayne
1920 Bury 0
1921 Southport 2

Barton, George McIntosh RB
b Newtongrange 15/10/1899 d 1970
Newbattle
Midlothian United
Newtongrange Star
Raith Rovers
1928 1930 Bristol Rovers 66 5
Bedminster Down Sports

From To Apps Goal

Barton, Harold OR
b Leigh 3/8/1910 d 1969
Whitegate Juniors (Blackpool)
Prescot Cables
1929 1933 Liverpool 101 25
1934 1938 Sheffield United 184 42
Denaby United

Barton, Harry OL
b Northwich 1874 d 1954
Castle True Blues
Fairfield
1897 Grimsby Town 3 1
Witton Albion
Middlewich Athletic Rangers
Northwich Victoria
Watford
Witton Albion

Barton, John (Jack) RH
b Blackburn 5/10/1866 d 1910
Caps: England 1
Witton (Blackburn)
Blackburn West End
1888 1891 Blackburn Rovers 40 2

Barton (Fishwick), John (Jack) OR
b Preston 9/6/1869 d 1953
Lytham
1893 Preston North End 2

Barton, John William (Jack) RB
b Southport q3 1895 d 1965
Southport Park Villa
1912 Burnley 0
Rochdale
1919 Blackburn Rovers 1
1920 Merthyr Town 0
Pontypridd
1921 Rochdale 19
Colwyn Bay
Chester
Manchester North End
Ashton National
Lytham St Annes

Barton, Percival Harry (Percy) LH/RB/LB
b Edmonton 19/8/1895 d 1961
Caps: England 7
Tottenham Thursday
Edmonton Amateurs
Sultan
1913 1928 Birmingham 331 13
Stourbridge

Barton, Thomas IR
1923 Rotherham County 1

Barton, Walter RB
b Westhoughton
1921 Stalybridge Celtic 13

Barton, William (Kenny) CH/LH
Adelaide (Lincoln)
1898 Lincoln City 1
Grantham
1900 Lincoln City 1
Adelaide (Lincoln)

Barton, William RB
b Perkinsville q1 1902
Felling Colliery
1925 1926 Durham City 13

Bartram, James Leslie (Jimmy) CF
b South Shields 8/3/1911 d 1987
Boldon Colliery Welfare
1932 Portsmouth 0
North Shields
Falkirk
1935 Northampton Town 12 3
Queen of the South
North Shields
South Shields

Bartram, Samuel (Sam) GK
b Simonside 22/1/1914 d 1981
Caps: England War 3
Boldon Villa
North Shields
Boldon Villa
Jarrow
Boldon Villa
1931 Reading (trial) 0
Easington Colliery
Boldon Villa
1934 1955 Charlton Athletic 579
1939 (Charlton Athletic) (3)

Bartrop, Charles Henry Wilfred (Wilf) OR
b Worksop 22/11/1887 d 1918
Worksop Town
1909 1913 Barnsley 160 15
1914 Liverpool 3

From To Apps Goal

Basford, George IR
1919 Wolverhampton Wanderers 1

Basnett, Alfred (Alf) RH/CH
b St Helens 10/4/1893 d 1966
Star Rovers
Skelmersdale
St Helens Town
Eccles Borough
1919 1926 Burnley 147 5
1926 1928 Lincoln City 89 6
Ballymena
Hereford United
Nelson

Bassett, Edward John (Ted) OR
b Deptford 1/1/1889 d 1970
Deptford Invicta
1907 Woolwich Arsenal 0
Dartford
Croydon Common (trial)
Metrogas
Charlton Athletic
1911 Tottenham Hotspur 0
Millwall Athletic
Newark Stanley Works
Dartford
1913 1914 Notts County 44 5
1920 Watford 33 3
1921 Luton Town 21 3
Dartford
Fordsons
Finchley

Bassett, Idris Charles Henry RB
b Brithdir 31/3/1915 d 1978
Sutton Town
1937 1938 West Bromwich Albion 8

Bassett, Spencer Thomas RH
b Blackheath q3 1885 d 1917
Maidstone United
1909 Woolwich Arsenal 1
Exeter City
Swansea Town
Southend United

Bassett, William Edward George (Billy) CH
b Brithdir 8/6/1912 d 1977
Aberaman Athletic
1933 Wolverhampton Wanderers 0
1934 1938 Cardiff City 154 2
1945 1948 Crystal Palace 70
Portmadoc

Bassett, William Isaiah (Billy) OR
b West Bromwich 1/1869 d 1937
Caps: FLge 3/England 16
West Bromwich Strollers
Old Church
1888 1898 West Bromwich Albion 261 61

Bassindale, Isaac Bradley (Ike) RH/IL
b Harrington 26/1/1896 d 1985
Loftus Albion
Hartlepools United (trial)
1920 1925 Oldham Athletic 50
Mossley
Ashton National

Bastin, Clifford Sydney (Cliff) OL/IL/IR
b Exeter 14/3/1912 d 1991
Caps: England Sch/FLge 4/England 21
1927 1928 Exeter City 17 6
1929 1946 Arsenal 350 150
1939 (Arsenal) (3) (1)

Bastow, Rowland CF/IR
b Altofts 9/4/1913 d 1995
Goole Town
1934 1938 Rotherham United 113 57
1939 (Rotherham United) (3) (2)

Batchelor, James William OL
b Hoo q1 1890 d 1951
Chatham Town
1922 Gillingham 3
1923 Brentford 0

Bate, Arthur OR
b Little Hulton 14/10/1908 d 1993
Walkden Primitive Methodists
1927 Bury (trial) 0
Little Hulton United
Chorley
Winsford United (trial)
1930 Nelson 24 6
Chorley
Bacup Borough
Fleetwood
Bacup Borough

From To Apps Goal

Bate, Thomas OL
1905 1906 Blackpool 18 1
Brynn Central
Garston Gasworks
Wallasey Village
African Royal

Bate, Thomas Edward (Tommy) IL/IR
b Willenhall 14/12/1911 d 1984
Bentons Works
1934 1938 Walsall 78 24
Worcester City

Bate, Walter (Wally) CF
b West Bromwich 1895
Darlaston
Dumbarton
1919 Wolverhampton Wanderers 11 5
West Smethwick

Bateman, Arthur LB/RB
b Grimsby 15/3/1908 d 1988
Cleethorpes Town
1929 1932 Grimsby Town 18
1933 Southend United 19
1933 1938 Brentford 145 3

Bateman, Benjamin John (Ben) OR
b Chelsea 20/11/1892 d 1961
Caps: England Amat
Sutton Court
1920 1923 Crystal Palace 99 6
Dartford

Bateman, George Henry LB
b Wolstanton q1 1865 d 1953
Burslem Port Vale
1888 Stoke 0
Burslem Port Vale
1891 Stoke 5
1892 Northwich Victoria 0

Bates, Charles (Charlie) CF/IL
b West Bromwich q3 1885
Darlington
1910 1911 Burnley 15 5

Bates, Edric Thornton (Ted) IR/IL/LH
b Thetford 3/5/1918 d 2003
Thetford Town
1936 Norwich City 0
1937 1952 Southampton 202 65
1939 (Southampton) (1)

Bates, Francis George (Frank) GK
b Eckington q4 1890 d 1947
Eckington Rovers
Beighton Recreation
1920 Barnsley 7
Scunthorpe & Lindsey United

Bates, Henry Joseph (Harry) OR
b Sutton Coldfield q2 1891
Ravensmoor
Coventry City
1911 1912 Birmingham 3
1913 Leicester Fosse 0
Walsall

Bates, Philip William (Phil) CH
b Penge 16/11/1897 d 1974
Beckenham Wanderers
1920 Crystal Palace 40 2
Scunthorpe & Lindsey United

Bates, Sydney IR/IL
b Wardley Colliery 17/5/1912 d 1984
Eighton Banks
1934 Lincoln City 6
1935 Millwall 2 1
1936 Stockport County 0

Bates, William Edric (Billy) RB/CF
b Kirkheaton 5/3/1884 d 1957
1906 Bolton Wanderers 2
1907 1908 Leeds City 15

Bateson, Edward OR
b Melling 2/7/1902 d 1972
1923 Blackburn Rovers 2

Bateup, Edwin GK
b Horley q2 1881 d 1939
Croydon Glenrose
Faversham
1905 1907 Woolwich Arsenal 6
New Brompton
1910 Woolwich Arsenal 28
Port Vale

Batey, John Clarke LH/LB/RB
b Carlisle q3 1911
1934 Carlisle United 11
1936 Preston North End 9
1937 Carlisle United 2

From To Apps Goal

Batey, Robert (Bob) CH/LH
b Greenhead 18/10/1912 d 1988
Greenhead South Tyne Rangers
1932 1933 Carlisle United 23
1934 1938 Preston North End 90
1939 (Preston North End) (3)
1946 Leeds United 8
1947 Southport 29
Annfield Plain
Leyland Motors
Chorley

Batey, Thomas OL
b Ushaw Moor 18/10/1894 d 1971
Willington Athletic
Esh Winning
1914 Bristol City 7 1
Norwich City
Hartford Colliery

Batho, George RH
b Willaston q4 1875 d 1957
Nantwich
1895 Crewe Alexandra 15

Batt, Edgar IL
b Bradford 20/2/1909 d 1969
1926 Bradford Park Avenue 5 3
1927 Doncaster Rovers 0

Batten, Herbert George (Bert) IL/OL/IR
b Bedminster 14/5/1898 d 1956
Paulton Rovers
1920 Bristol City 7
1921 1925 Plymouth Argyle 88 26
1925 1926 Everton 15 1
1926 Bradford City 24 5
1927 Reading 12 2
1927 1928 Clapton Orient 31 6
Northfleet

Batten, John (Jock) IR/CF
b Galston 28/5/??
1920 1922 Bradford Park Avenue 33 5
1923 Exeter City 9 1
Kidderminster Harriers
Castleford Town
Poole

Battiste, Walter (Wally) OR/RH
b Worksop 11/6/1892 d 1965
Worksop Town
Shirebrook
1914 Notts County (trial) 0
1919 Grimsby Town 31
1920 1923 Gillingham 149 8
1924 1927 Millwall Athletic 43 5
1930 Gillingham 3
Sittingbourne
Aylesford Paper Mills

Battles, Bernard (Barney) RH
b Springburn 13/1/1875 d 1905
Caps: SLge 2/Scotland 3
Linlithgow Juniors
Bathgate Rovers
Broxburn Shamrock
Bathgate
Heart of Midlothian
Celtic
1895 Liverpool 2
Celtic
Dundee
1897 Liverpool 1
Celtic
Kilmarnock

Battles, Charles LH
Stockport County
1905 Burton United 24
Hyde
Lancaster

Batty, William (Billy) IL/IR
b Killamarsh 13/7/1886
Caps: SoLge 4
Thorncliffe
Mortomley
High Green Swifts
1907 1909 Sheffield United 38 7
1909 1910 Bristol City 5
Lincoln City
1920 1921 Swindon Town 41 18
1922 Barnsley 1

From To Apps Goal

Batty, William (Billy) RB/LB
b South Bank 4/6/1905 d 1974
St Peter's (South Bank)
Bishop Auckland
Ferryhill Athletic
Willington
1926 1928 Barnsley 39 5
1930 Swindon Town 18 1
1931 Southport 3
1933 Clapton Orient 0
Nelson
Firestone Tyres

Baty, Henry (Harry) GK
b South Hetton 24/5/1914 d 1977
South Hetton
1933 Sunderland (trial) 0
1933 Southport 1
1934 Hull City (trial) 0
South Hetton
Marton Colliery
Brandon Social
1939 Hartlepools United 0

Bauchop, James Rae (Jimmy) IL/CF
b Sauchie 22/5/1886 d 1948
Sauchie
Alloa Athletic
Celtic
Norwich City
Crystal Palace
1909 1912 Derby County 126 68
1913 Tottenham Hotspur 10 6
1913 1921 Bradford Park Avenue 157 68
Celtic (loan)
Doncaster Rovers
1923 Lincoln City 28 11

Bauchop, William Fotheringham (Willie) OL
b Alloa 18/1/1882 d 1948
Abercorn
East Stirlingshire
Alloa Athletic
Plymouth Argyle
Heart of Midlothian
Carlisle United
1909 1910 Stockport County 41 6
1911 Leicester Fosse 18 1
Norwich City
1913 Fulham 0
1913 Grimsby Town 0
Alloa Athletic

Baugh, Richard (Dick) RB
b Wolverhampton 14/2/1864 d 1919
Caps: England 2
Rose Villa
Wolverhampton Rangers
Stafford Road
1888 1895 Wolverhampton Wanderers 185 1
1896 Walsall 6

Baugh, Richard Horace (Dicky) RB/LB
b Wolverhampton 6/3/1898 d 1972
Stafford Road
1919 1923 Wolverhampton Wanderers 108 4
1923 Cardiff City 0
1924 1927 West Bromwich Albion 61
1929 1931 Exeter City 53 5
Kidderminster Harriers

Bauld, Robert (Bobby) LH
b Cowdenbeath 14/3/1902
Glencraig Celtic
1921 Tottenham Hotspur (trial) 0
Raith Rovers
Dundee United
1927 1934 Bradford City 217 34
1935 Chesterfield 2

Baum, Samuel (Sam) OR
b Sunderland 4/5/1914 d 2002
South Shields
1936 Bolton Wanderers 0
Darwen (loan)
1937 Port Vale 3

Baverstock, Herbert (Bert) RB/LB
b Dudley 1/1883 d 1951
Netherton St James
Brierley Hill Alliance
1905 1921 Bolton Wanderers 366 4
1921 1922 Blackpool 18 1

Baverstock, John James GK
b Willenhall 1889
Grantham
1913 Bolton Wanderers 2

From To Apps Goal

Bavin, Arthur RH
b Nottingham 5/2/1887 d 1961
Lincoln Liberal Club
1907 Lincoln City 5
Worksop Town
Grantham Avenue
Mansfield Mechanics
Grantham
1914 Lincoln City 0
1919 Barnsley 0
Llanelly
Grantham

Baxendale, Frank OL/OR
b Leyland 28/12/1913 d 1990
1932 Preston North End 0
Dick, Kerr's XI
Leyland Motors
1935 1936 Blackburn Rovers 12 3
Falkirk
1939 Carlisle United 0

Baxendale, James IR
1900 Blackpool 10
Atherton
Barrow

Baxter, Arthur George IL
b Dundee 28/12/1911 d 1944
Dundee North End
1933 Portsmouth 0
Falkirk
Dundee
1938 Barnsley 6 2

Baxter, Frank IR
b Newton, Midlothian 1898
Bo'ness
1923 Barrow 13 2

Baxter, James (Jimmy) LH/RH
b Glasgow 1904
Parkhead
1925 1928 Leicester City 6 1
1929 Reading 0
1930 Torquay United 0
Boston United

Baxter, Leslie (Les) RH
b Clay Cross q2 1905 d 1943
Williamthorpe Colliery
West Auckland Town
1932 Chesterfield 0
Scarborough
1935 New Brighton 11
Shirley Town
Dartford

Baxter, Robert Denholm (Bob) CH/IL
b Gilmerton 23/1/1911 d 1991
Caps: SLge 1/Scotland War 4/Scotland 3
Tranent Juniors
Musselburgh Bruntonians
1932 1938 Middlesbrough 247 19
1939 (Middlesbrough) (3)
Heart of Midlothian
Leith Athletic

Baxter, Thomas James Charles (Tom) RH
b Wandsworth 22/10/1893 d 1955
1919 Chelsea 1
1920 Gillingham 21

Baxter, Thomas Thornton RB
b Blackburn 18/4/1907 d 1981
Blackburn Works XI
1928 1931 Blackburn Rovers 36
Blackburn Borough Police Force

Baxter, Thomas William OL
b Warsop 1/2/1903 d 1987
Welbeck Colliery
Newark Town
Worksop Town
Mexborough
Mansfield Town
1927 1928 Wolverhampton Wanderers 50 14
1929 1930 Port Vale 54 11
1931 Mansfield Town 14 1
Margate
1933 Carlisle United 5
Distillery

Baxter, William Amelius (Bill) CH/LH
b Nottingham 6/9/1917 d 1992
Wilson's FC
Vernon Athletic
Berridge Road Institute
1937 1946 Nottingham Forest 15
1946 1953 Notts County 140
Grantham

From To Apps Goal

Bayes, Archibald William Clayton (Archie) GK
b Bedford 25/4/1896 d 1980
RAF
Ilford
1927 1929 Torquay United 55

Bayley, John Thomas (Tom) RB
b Walsall 8/1868
Walsall Swifts
Walsall Town Swifts
1892 Small Heath 18
1893 Walsall Town Swifts 23
1896 1898 Gainsborough Trinity 89 1
South Shields
Watford
Leamington Town

Bayley, Samuel IL
b Rugby 11/1878
St Saviour's
Rugby
Leamington
1899 Small Heath 1 1
Leamington

Bayley, SE CH
1898 1899 Burslem Port Vale 5 1

Bayliss, Albert Edward James Mathias (Jem) RH/IR/CF
b Tipton 8/1863 d 1933
Caps: England 1
Great Bridge Unity
Tipton Providence
Wednesbury Old Athletic
1888 1891 West Bromwich Albion 56 12
1892 Walsall Town Swifts 0

Bayliss, Hervey Hugo Robert (Robert) OL
b Burton-on-Trent 17/4/1895 d 1943
Overseal Swifts
Burton All Saints
Gresley Rovers
1920 Derby County 1
Gresley Rovers

Bayliss, Leonard Richard (Dick) LH/RH
b Alfreton 28/4/1899 d 1947
Alfreton Rose Villa
1920 Luton Town 1
Mansfield Town
1925 1926 Southend United 8

Bayman, Albert CH
b Preston 1869 d 1951
1893 1894 Crewe Alexandra 15

Baynham, Albert OR
b Smethwick 1874
Halesowen
1903 1905 Wolverhampton Wanderers 71 2

Baynham, David Morton LB/RB
b Aberdare 12/6/1902 d 1974
1926 Aberdare Athletic 16
1927 Bournemouth & Boscombe Ath 7
Yeovil & Petters United
Scunthorpe & Lindsey United

Baynton, John (Jack) GK
b Rushock Wood 20/3/1859 d 1939
1888 Wolverhampton Wanderers 18
Kidderminster Olympic

Beach, Cyril Howard IL/IR/RH
b Nuneaton 28/3/1909
Hounslow Town
1928 1931 Charlton Athletic 29 4
1932 Sunderland 3
Hayesco
Peterborough United

Beacham, Albert John (Jack) RH/CH
b Birmingham 15/8/1902 d 1982
Wolseley Motors
Weymouth
1925 1928 Brentford 62 2
1929 1931 Gillingham 109
Worcester City
Evesham Town

Beachill, Arthur LB/RB
b Monk Bretton 21/5/1905 d 1943
1924 Rotherham County 0
Frickley Colliery
1926 1933 Stoke City 128
1934 Millwall 12

From To Apps Goal

Beadles, George Harold (Harry) IL/CF/IR
b Llanllwchaiam 28/9/1897 d 1958
Caps: Wales 2
Newtown
Cardiff City (trial)
1920 Liverpool 0
Grayson's
1921 1923 Liverpool 17 6
1924 1925 Cardiff City 31 14
1925 Sheffield Wednesday 0
1926 1928 Southport 92 61
Workington
Dundalk

Beadling, William OR
b Sunderland q4 1885 d 1944
Ashington
1908 Grimsby Town 25 5
Northampton Town
1909 Grimsby Town 10
Ashington
Wallsend Park Villa
Blyth Spartans

Beadsworth, Arthur OL/IR/IL
b Leicester 9/1876 d 1917
Leicester Fosse
Leicester YMCA
Hinckley Town
1900 Leicester Fosse 4
Coventry City
1902 Preston North End 0
1902 Manchester United 9 1
Swindon Town
1905 Blackburn Rovers 0
New Brompton
1906 Burton United 18
Hinckley United
Nuneaton Town
Hinckley United

Beak, Clifford George (Cliff) IL
b Bristol 22/12/1902 d 1991
Hanham Athletic
1929 Bristol City 1

Beale, Percy Ernest OL
b Poplar q1 1886
Peterborough GN Loco
Leyton
1908 Clapton Orient 5 1
New Brompton

Beale, Robert Hughes (Bobby) GK
b Maidstone 8/1/1884 d 1950
Caps: FLge 1
Maidstone United
Brighton & Hove Albion
Norwich City
1912 1914 Manchester United 105
Gillingham
Maidstone United

Bean, Alfred Samuel (Alf 'Billy') LB/RH
b Lincoln 25/8/1915 d 1993
Lincoln Corinthians
1934 1948 Lincoln City 171 10
1939 (Lincoln City) (3)

Beard, Arthur H OR
1904 Burnley 1

Beard, Ernest (Ernie) OR
b Barrow 2/9/1907 d 1994
Barrow Pulp Works
1926 Barrow 1

Beardsell, Arthur OR
b Padiham 5/4/1891 d 1976
Lytham
Fleetwood
Lytham
1921 Southport 3
Fleetwood

Beardshaw, Ernest Colin (Colin) CH/RB
b Crawcrook 26/11/1912 d 1977
Shadforth St Cuthbert's
South Hetton Juniors
South Hetton Colliery Welfare
1935 Gateshead 12
1937 Stockport County 18
1938 1945 Bradford City 42
1939 (Bradford City) (1)
Distillery
Peterborough United
Distillery
Cork United
1948 1950 Southport 61

From To Apps Goal

Beardsley, Godfrey Leonard (Goff) GK
b Barrow-on-Soar q2 1879 d 1912
1897 Loughborough 20
Loughborough Corinthians (loan)
1898 1900 Leicester Fosse 69
Reigate Priory
Old Rossallians
Corinthians

Beare, George OR/OL
b Southampton 2/10/1885 d 1970
Shirley Warren
Southampton
1908 1910 Blackpool 76 18
1910 1913 Everton 104 18
1920 Cardiff City 23 3
1921 Bristol City 14 2
1922 Cardiff City 0
Oswestry Town

Beasley, Albert Edward (Pat) OL/LH/IL
b Stourbridge 27/7/1913 d 1986
Caps: England 1
Cookley St Peter's
Stourbridge
1931 1936 Arsenal 79 19
1936 1938 Huddersfield Town 108 24
1939 (Huddersfield Town) (3)
1945 1949 Fulham 152 13
1950 1951 Bristol City 66 5

Beasley, John (Jack) CF
b Wednesbury 1916
1934 Birmingham 0
1935 Torquay United 4 2
Worcester City
Halesowen Town

Beaton, Simon RH
b Inverness 1888
Inverness Thistle
1907 Aston Villa 0
1908 Newcastle United 0
1909 Middlesbrough (loan) 2
1910 1913 Huddersfield Town 111

Beats, Edwin (Eddie) CF
b Bristol q2 1906 d 1965
Caps: England Sch
1926 Aston Villa 0
1927 Queen's Park Rangers 1 1

Beats, William Edwin (Billy) CF
b Wolstanton 13/11/1871 d 1939
Caps: FLge 5/England 2
Porthill Victoria
Port Vale Rovers
1892 1894 Burslem Port Vale 77 25
1895 1902 Wolverhampton Wanderers 199 67
Bristol Rovers
1906 Burslem Port Vale 33 13
Reading

Beattie, Andrew (Andy) LB/RB/RH
b Kintore 11/8/1913 d 1983
Caps: Scotland War 5/Scotland 7
Inverurie Loco
1934 1946 Preston North End 125 4

Beattie, David RH/CH
b Renton 23/8/1903
Renton Victoria
Dumbarton Harp (loan)
East Fife
1926 1928 New Brighton 8
Clydebank
1927 1928 New Brighton 21
Dumbarton

Beattie, James LB
b Wishaw 24/8/1910
Shieldmuir Celtic
1931 Rochdale 14
Glentoran

Beattie, James Falconer (Jimmy) CF
b Brechin 15/5/1916 d 1965
Forfar Academy
Forfar West End
St Johnstone
1936 1938 Portsmouth 57 27
1939 Millwall (3) (1)

Beattie, John Murdoch (Jack) IR/CF
b Newhills 28/5/1912 d 1992
St Machars
Hall, Russell & Co
Aberdeen
1933 1934 Wolverhampton Wanderers 44 13
1934 1936 Blackburn Rovers 76 17
1936 1937 Birmingham 36 10
1937 Huddersfield Town 3
1937 1938 Grimsby Town 56 13
1939 (Grimsby Town) (3)
1939 Walsall 0

From To Apps Goal

Beattie, Robert (Bobbie) IL/IR
b Stevenston 24/1/1916 d 2002
Caps: Scotland 1
Ardeer Mission
Kilwinning Rangers
Kilmarnock
1937 1953 Preston North End 264 57
1939 (Preston North End) (3)
Wigan Athletic

Beattie, Stephen OR
b Birkenhead 22/6/1898 d 1980
Runcorn
1920 Stockport County 20 1
New Brighton

Beaumont, Leonard (Len) OL/OR
b Huddersfield 4/1/1915 d 2002
1932 1935 Huddersfield Town 12 1
1936 Portsmouth 6 3
1938 Nottingham Forest 34 3
Peterborough United

Beaumont, Percy CH
b Mexborough 3/9/1897 d 1967
Mexborough Rovers
1919 1920 Sheffield United 34 3
1921 1925 Barnsley 138 7
1926 Southend United 30
Mexborough Athletic

Beaumont, Sydney (Syd) OL/RH
b Wrestlingworth q4 1883 d 1939
Colchester Town
1904 Lincoln City 5
Biggleswade & District
Watford
1911 Preston North End 1
Merthyr Town
Troedyrhiw
Barry

Beaver, John OL/RH
b Chorley q2 1876
1900 1902 Preston North End 21 2
Wellingborough
Chorley
Lancaster
Chorley
Clitheroe Central

Beby, John Victor (Jack) GK
b Gillingham 23/8/1907 d 1976
Cuxton
1924 Charlton Athletic 0
Grenadier Guards
1929 Gillingham 20
1929 1931 Leicester City 29
Ashford Town (Kent)
1932 Bristol Rovers 24
1933 Crystal Palace 0
1933 1935 Darlington 74
1935 Exeter City 10
Ashington
Vickers Aviation
Shorts Sports

Beck, Henry Alfred (Harry) CH/RH/LH
b Walsall Wood 21/2/1901 d 1979
Rushall
1921 Walsall 3 1
Darlaston
Cannock Town
Burton Town
1921 1927 Walsall 41
Stafford Rangers
1928 Barrow 29
1929 1931 York City 119 12
1932 1933 Wrexham 30 2
Ards (trial)
Glentoran
Dudley Town

Beck, Norman RH
b Burnopfield 070/7/1906 d 1979
Tanfield Lea Institute
1930 Bradford City 3
1931 Barnsley (trial) 0
West Stanley

Beck, William LH
b Silvertown 1905
South West Ham
1934 Luton Town 2
1935 Carlisle United 2

Beckett, Charles IR
Atherton Church House
1905 Bolton Wanderers 1

Beckett, Ernest IR
b Knutton q3 1869 d 1952
Newcastle Swifts
1895 Burslem Port Vale 23 8
Newcastle Swifts
1898 Burslem Port Vale 21 9

From To Apps Goal

Beckett, William (Billy) OL/IL
b Kirkdale 4/7/1915 d 1999
Litherland
1934 1935 New Brighton 25 4
1936 Tranmere Rovers 0
South Liverpool
1937 Blackpool 0
1938 Bradford City 5 1
1945 1946 Watford 7 1
1947 Northampton Town 0

Beckram, John George IR
b Sunderland q3 1881 d 1933
Sunderland Selbome
1901 Sheffield United 0
1903 1904 Bradford City 25 6

Becton, Francis (Frank) IL/CF
b Preston 28/10/1873 d 1909
Caps: FLge 2/England 2
Preston Juniors
Fishwick Ramblers
1891 1894 Preston North End 87 37
1894 1897 Liverpool 70 37
1898 Sheffield United 11 3
Bedminster
1900 Preston North End 26 9
Swindon Town
Nelson
Swindon Town
Ashton Town
New Brighton Tower

Becton, John IL
b Preston 1872
1893 Middlesbrough Ironopolis 3

Becton, Martin OR
b Preston 25/3/1883 d 1965
Christ Church (Preston)
Lytham
1906 1907 Preston North End 23 3
Nelson
Chorley
Watford

Becton, Thomas (Tommy) IL/OL
b Preston q1 1878 d 1957
1897 Preston North End 4
1898 New Brighton Tower 24 7
1899 Sunderland 15 5
Kettering
Bristol Rovers
Kettering
Accrington Stanley
Oswaldtwistle Rovers
Colne
Rossendale United
Leyland

Beddow, Harry OL
b Rogerstone q1 1901 d 1972
Bassaleg
1922 Newport County 1

Beddow, John Harry (Clem) OR/IR
b Burton-on-Trent q4 1885 d 1949
Trent Rovers
1904 Burton United 21 2
1904 1906 Manchester United 33 12
1907 1909 Burnley 16 7

Bedford, Fred OR/CF
b Blackburn 25/6/1902 d 1972
1923 Blackburn Rovers 0
1924 Accrington Stanley 25 5
1925 Barnsley 9 2
Lancaster Town
1927 Tranmere Rovers 3 2
Morecambe
1928 Bradford City 9 8
Morecambe

Bedford, George CH/IL
b Chesterfield 12/4/1916 d 1984
Williamthorpe Colliery
Temple Normanton
1934 Chesterfield 0
1935 1936 Leicester City 4
Stamford Town
Hinckley Athletic

Bedford, Henry (Harry) CF/IR/IL
b Calow 15/10/1899 d 1976
Caps: FLge 2/England 2
Grassmoor Ivanhoe
1919 1920 Nottingham Forest 18 8
1920 1925 Blackpool 171 112
1925 1930 Derby County 203 142
1930 1931 Newcastle United 30 17
1931 Sunderland 7 2
1932 Bradford Park Avenue 33 15
1933 Chesterfield 25 12
Heanor Town

From To Apps Goal

Bedford, Lewis (Lew) OL/OR
b Tyburn, Warwickshire q3 1899 d 1966
1920 1921 West Bromwich Albion 3
1922 1924 Walsall 97 5
1925 Sheffield Wednesday 11 2
1926 Walsall 23 6
1926 1927 Nelson 32 7
1927 Walsall 16 1
1928 1929 Luton Town 49 15
1929 Walsall 6 1
Bloxwich Strollers
Walsall Wood

Bedford, Samuel (Sam) OR
b Scarborough q3 1881 d 1952
Scarborough
1904 Doncaster Rovers 1
Rawmarsh

Bedford, Sidney George (Syd) CH/RH/LH
b Northampton q1 1897 d 1958
1920 1923 Northampton Town 70 1
1924 Brighton & Hove Albion 14
1925 Luton Town 1
Rushden Town

Bedingfield, Francis Robert (Frank) CF
b Monkwearmouth q1 1878 d 1904
Yarmouth Town
Rushden
1898 Aston Villa 1 1
Queen's Park Rangers
Portsmouth

Beeby, Augustus Richard GK
b Ashbourne 24/1/1889 d 1974
Osmaston
1909 1910 Liverpool 16
1911 Manchester City 11

Beech, ? OR
1904 Burton United 1

Beech, Albert LH/IR
b Fenton 24/9/1912 d 1985
Stoke St Peter's
Leek Alexandra
1931 Port Vale 1
Altrincham
1934 1936 Huddersfield Town 22 4
1937 Notts County 13
Northwich Victoria

Beech, George LB
b Sheffield q2 1892 d 1964
Attercliffe Sports Club
1911 Sheffield Wednesday 0
Brighton & Hove Albion
Bridgend
Ebbw Vale
1924 Brighton & Hove Albion 2

Beech, George Charles (Jack) IR/IL
b Sheffield 5/1872 d 1945
Attercliffe
1896 1903 Sheffield Wednesday 20 6
1904 1905 Barnsley 61 9

Beech, Harry RH
1911 Stockport County 6

Beech, Herbert Harold LH/IL
b Hasland q2 1886 d 1932
Hasland Wild Rose
1905 1906 Chesterfield Town 6

Beech, James (Jim) CH
b Smallthorne 1871
Smallthorne St Saviour
Smallthorne Albion
1894 1901 Burslem Port Vale 119 7

Beecham, Ernest Cromwell (Ernie) GK
b Hertford 23/7/1906 d 1985
Ward End Works
Hertford Town
1925 1931 Fulham 174
1932 1934 Queen's Park Rangers 86
1935 Brighton & Hove Albion 0
1935 Swindon Town 8

Beedall, Frederick (Fred) IR/IL/RH
b North Wingfield 15/8/1911 d 1976
Ling's Row Primitives
1932 Chesterfield 7
1934 1937 Torquay United 122 21

Beedie, William Alexander Clark OL
b Montrose 22/4/1894
Clyde
Blantyre Celtic
1920 1925 Portsmouth 202 29
1926 Oldham Athletic 0

From To Apps Goal

Beedles, Norman LB/RB
b Ardwick 13/6/1907 d 1972
Altrincham
1930 1933 Stockport County 42
1934 Barnsley 1
1935 New Brighton 19 1

Beel, George William CF/IR/IL
b Bracebridge Heath 26/2/1900 d 1980
1919 Manchester United (trial) 0
1919 Lincoln City 23 6
1920 1921 Merthyr Town 54 22
1922 Chesterfield 35 23
1922 1931 Burnley 316 179
1931 Lincoln City 9 6
1932 Rochdale 20 8
Tunbridge Wells Rangers

Beer, Walter John IL
b Bideford 10/5/1900 d 1981
Chepstow
1922 Newport County 1
Lovells Athletic

Beer, William John (Billy) RH/IR
b Saltburn 4/1/1879 d 1942
Staveley Town
Poolsbrook United
1896 Sheffield United 0
Chesterfield Town
1898 1901 Sheffield United 73 18
1901 1909 Small Heath/Birmingham 236 34

Beeson, George William RB
b Clay Cross 31/8/1906 d 1999
Caps: FLge 2
Clay Cross
North Wingfield
1927 1928 Chesterfield 43
1929 1933 Sheffield Wednesday 74
1934 1936 Aston Villa 70
1938 Walsall 34 1
1939 (Walsall) (1)

Beever, Alfred (Alf) LH/RH/CH
b Birley Carr 7/9/1899 d 1982
Caps: WLge 1
Grenoside
1922 Sheffield United 0
Mid-Rhondda United
1925 Wrexham 35 1
1926 Aberdare Athletic 31 3
1927 Wrexham 3
1928 Merthyr Town 7
Scunthorpe & Lindsey United

Beever, Lewis LH
b Grenoside 9/11/1901 d 1977
1924 Rotherham County 12

Behan, William GK
b Dublin 3/8/1911 d 1991
Shelbourne
1933 Manchester United 1
Shelbourne
Shamrock Rovers

Beilby, Norman William RH
b Hartlepool 21/9/1900 d 1988
Wood Skinners
1921 Ashington 2
Low Fell
1923 Sheffield Wednesday 0
Wardley Colliery
Ravenswood Welfare
Newcastle Blue Star

Belfield, Frederick (Fred) OL
b Burslem q2 1876 d 1921
1894 1898 Burslem Port Vale 12 3

Bell, A IR
1895 Bury 1

Bell, Albert RB/LB
b Sunderland 8/2/1898 d 1973
South Pontop Villa
Anfield Plain
West Stanley
1920 Aston Villa 0
1923 Leeds United 1
1925 1926 Accrington Stanley 70
1927 Durham City 18
Anfield Plain
Consett

Bell, Albert Edward RB
b Sheffield 30/1/1905 d 1988
Hallam
1926 Cardiff City (trial) 0
1930 Chesterfield 9
St Timothy's Church (Sheffield)

From To Apps Goal

Bell, Alexander (Alex) LH
b Cape Town, South Africa 1882 d 1934
Caps: Scotland 1
Ayr Parkhouse
1902 1912 Manchester United 278 10
1913 1914 Blackburn Rovers 11

Bell, Andrew CF
1904 Glossop 2

Bell, Andrew (Andy) RB
b Buckhaven 11/5/1910 d 1992
Bangor City
1933 1938 Bury 111
Motherwell

Bell, Arthur IL
b Burnley 11/1882 d 1923
Caps: England Amat
Burnley Belvedere
1902 1908 Burnley 101 29

Bell, Charles Oliver (Charlie) CF
b Dumfries 18/5/1894 d 1939
Dumfries Wanderers
Douglas Wanderers
Carlisle City
1913 Woolwich Arsenal 1 2
Chesterfield Town
Barrow
1921 Queen's Park Rangers 0

Bell, Clifford (Cliff) OL
b Bowness 30/9/1908 d 1998
Bowness Rovers
1928 Barrow 7 1
1929 Queen's Park Rangers 0

Bell, David (Dave 'Daniel') RB/RH/CH
b Gorebridge 24/12/1909 d 1986
Arniston Rangers
Musselburgh Bruntonians
Wallyford Bluebell
1931 1933 Newcastle United 21 1
1934 1938 Derby County 52
1938 1949 Ipswich Town 171 3
1939 (Ipswich Town) (3)

Bell, Donald Simpson, VC RB/LB
b Harrogate 3/12/1890 d 1916
Harrogate Christ Church
Starbeck
Westminster Methodist Training Coll
Crystal Palace
Starbeck
1910 Newcastle United 0
Bishop Auckland
Mirfield United
1912 1913 Bradford Park Avenue 5

Bell, Edward (Ted) RB/LB
b Burnopfield 23/12/1883
West Stanley
Bishop Auckland
Seaham White Star
1905 1907 Sunderland 19
Spennymoor United

Bell, Edward Dorman (Dorman) LH/RH
b Hartlepool 22/3/1908 d 1958
Belle Vue Congregationalists
1929 Hartlepools United 4
1930 Sheffield Wednesday 0
Tunbridge Wells Rangers
1932 Rotherham United 3
Colwyn Bay United
1933 Carlisle United 23

Bell, Edwin LB
b Bristol 1895
Welton Rovers
1922 Exeter City 1
Bath City

Bell, Ernest IL
1891 Notts County 5

Bell, Ernest (Ernie) IR/IL/OR
b Hull 22/7/1918 d 1968
Blundell Street Old Boys
1936 1937 Hull City 22 4
1938 Mansfield Town 28 1
1945 Aldershot 0
1946 Hull City 5 1
Scarborough
Hessle Old Boys

Bell, F William (Nobby) LH
1899 Middlesbrough 1

Bell, Fred RH/CH
b Bolton
1900 1901 Bolton Wanderers 5
Brynn Central
1906 Bury 2
Pendlebury

From To Apps Goal

Bell, Fred IL
b Blackburn 29/9/1901 d 1978
Church of the Saviour
Clayton Church Institute
1922 Blackburn Rovers 0
1923 Southport 11
Lancaster Town
Great Harwood
Clitheroe
Stalybridge Celtic
Leyland Motors

Bell, George IL
1906 Glossop 1

Bell, Gordon OL
b Sunderland 9/1/1906 d 1979
Caps: England Sch
Newcastle United Swifts
Chilton Colliery Recreation Athletic
1922 Darlington 0
1925 Durham City 0
Carlisle United
1928 Leeds United 0
1929 Wrexham 24 7
1930 Swansea Town 19 6
1931 Carlisle United 1
Consett

Bell, Harold IL
b Thurlstone 11/7/1898 d 1992
Craven Sports
1919 Barnsley 15 6
1920 Bristol Rovers 2
Castleford Town

Bell, Henry Parkin GK
b Stanhope 30/4/1901 d 1976
Caps: England Amat
Cambridge University
Corinthians
1926 Durham City 3

Bell, J RB
1893 Middlesbrough Ironopolis 18

Bell, Jack IL
b Ryhope 1884
Ryhope Villa
1905 1906 Barnsley 23 6

Bell, James (Jim 'Daisy') IR
b Eston 25/10/1883 d 1962
Grangetown
1904 Middlesbrough 10 3
Eston United
Barrow
Exeter City
Portsmouth
Barrow

Bell, James IL
1920 Nottingham Forest 1

Bell, John (Jack) OL/IL/IR
b Dumbarton 6/10/1869
Caps: SLge 2/Scotland 10
Dumbarton Union
Dumbarton
1892 1897 Everton 130 52
Tottenham Hotspur
Celtic
1900 New Brighton Tower 22 9
1901 1902 Everton 47 10
1903 1907 Preston North End 109 25

Bell, John (Jock) OR/IR/CF
b Forfarshire 3/1873 d 1934
Dundee Wanderers
Renton
1894 Wolverhampton Wanderers 6 2
1895 1896 Grimsby Town 48 11
Swindon Town

Bell, John (Jack) CH/RH
b Dundee 1876
Bacup
1897 1898 Grimsby Town 28 3
1899 1900 Chesterfield Town 51 2
Millwall Athletic
1903 Leicester Fosse 21

Bell, (Dr) John Barr OR
b Barrow 5/4/1901 d 1973
Queen's Park
1920 1922 Chelsea 43 9
Hamilton Academical
Cowdenbeath

From To Apps Goal

Bell, John Carr (Jack) GK
b Seaham Harbour q1 1904
Ryhope Colliery
Seaham Colliery
1926 1930 Sunderland 41
1930 Walsall 2
1931 Accrington Stanley 28
1931 1935 Bradford Park Avenue 66

Bell, John Greenhorn IL
b Hamilton 14/7/1909 d 1983
Beith
Ayr United
Beith
Queen of the South
1933 1934 Preston North End 20 5
Queen of the South
Beith
Albion Rovers

Bell, John James (Jack) IL/IR/CF
b Basford 2/3/1891
Sherwood Foresters
St Bartholomew's
Christ Church
1909 Nottingham Forest (trial) 0
Sutton Town
Royal Engineers
Reading
Plymouth Argyle
1913 1914 Nottingham Forest 54 6
1919 South Shields 4 1
Merthyr Town
1920 Grimsby Town 3
Loughborough Corinthians
1921 1922 Rotherham County 15 2
Weymouth
1923 Hartlepools United 12 4

Bell, John James (Johnnie) CF
b Dundee 1891
Glasgow Ashfield
West Ham United
Army
Heart of Midlothian
Third Lanark
Dundee
Albion Rovers
Hamilton Academical
1923 Newport County 21 9
1924 1925 Watford 20 6
Arbroath

Bell, Joseph (Joe) RH
b Shettleston
Dumbarton
1924 1925 Clapton Orient 2
1926 Aberdare Athletic 20

Bell, Joseph LH
1932 Walsall 6
1933 Halifax Town 0

Bell, Joseph Nicholson (Jackie) OR/OL
b Pegswood 30/8/1912 d 1994
Northern Traction
United Omnibus Co
Pegswood United
1932 Barrow 1
1934 Middlesbrough 2
1935 West Ham United 0
1936 Walsall 6
Ashington

Bell, Mark Dickson CH
b Edinburgh 8/2/1881 d 1961
Roseberry Juniors
St Bernard's
Heart of Midlothian
St Bernard's
Heart of Midlothian
Southampton
Heart of Midlothian
Fulham
1907 1909 Clapton Orient 88 4
Leyton
New Brompton

Bell, Matthew (Matt) LB/RB
b West Hartlepool 8/7/1897 d 1962
East Yorkshire Regiment
1919 1930 Hull City 393 1
1931 1933 Nottingham Forest 85 1

Bell, Peter Norton OR/IR
b Ferryhill 3/3/1897
Willington Athletic
Durham City
Willington Athletic
1919 1921 Oldham Athletic 18 2
1922 Darlington 16 4
Raith Rovers
1926 1927 Manchester City 42 7
Falkirk
Burton Town
1930 Darlington 11 1

From To Apps Goal

Bell, Richard (Dick) IL/OL
b Greenock
Dawdon Juniors
Port Glasgow Athletic
1936 Sunderland 1
1938 West Ham United 1 1

Bell, Robert Charles (Bunny) CF
b Birkenhead 10/4/1911 d 1988
Carlton Athletic
1930 1935 Tranmere Rovers 114 102
1935 1938 Everton 14 9

Bell, Robert William (Billy) IL
b Walker
1927 Millwall 0
1928 Walsall 1

Bell, Samuel (Sam) IR/IL/OR
b Burnhope 6/2/1909 d 1982
Burnhope Institute
1930 1933 Norwich City 76 26
1933 1934 Luton Town 30 20
1934 1936 Tottenham Hotspur 15 6
1937 1938 Southend United 68 16
1939 (Southend United) (3) (1)
1945 Millwall 0
Tonbridge

Bell, Stanley Lawrence T (Laurie) CF/OR
b Langbank 5/1875 d 1933
Langbank
Dumbarton
Third Lanark
1895 1896 Sheffield Wednesday 47 10
1897 1898 Everton 41 17
1899 1902 Bolton Wanderers 99 44
Brentford
1904 West Bromwich Albion 16 6
Hibernian

Bell, Sydney G OR
Herrington Colliery
1932 Rochdale 2

Bell, T CF
1900 Glossop 4

Bell, Thomas (Tommy) IR/CF/RH
b Seaham Harbour 9/11/1906 d 1983
Dawdon Colliery
1924 Bristol City 0
Torquay United (loan)
1926 Merthyr Town 10 1
1927 1929 Halifax Town 89 26
1930 1931 Chesterfield 55 22
1931 1932 Southport 47 6
1933 1934 Luton Town 34 15
1934 1937 Northampton Town 73 31
Wellingborough Town
Spalding United

Bell, Thomas Dawson IL
b West Stanley q1 1885 d 1951
West Stanley
1909 1911 Grimsby Town 32 9
Scunthorpe & Lindsey United
Cleethorpes Town

Bell, Thomas Gilbert (Tommy) LB/RB
b Usworth 11/4/1899 d 1975
Birtley
1922 Leeds United 1
1925 1927 Southend United 91 2
1928 1929 Portsmouth 26
1930 Carlisle United 12
Burton Town
Usworth Colliery

Bell, Walter Charles (Wally) IL
b Norwich 26/2/1896 d 1982
Norwich Priory
1920 Norwich City 3 2
Norwich Priory
City Wanderers

Bell, William CH
1898 Burton Swifts 4
1899 West Bromwich Albion 0

Bell, William Cumming (Billy) LH
b Prestwich 9/12/1906 d 1990
1926 Manchester City 0
1927 1930 Coventry City 120 5
1931 Portsmouth 1
1932 1934 Chester 46 2

From To Apps Goal

Bell, William John OL
b Backworth q3 1906
Chopwell Institute
Blyth Spartans
1923 Aston Villa (trial) 0
1924 Lincoln City 20 3
Mansfield Town
1925 1929 Leicester City 41 5
1930 Torquay United 28 6

Bell, William Todd RB/LH
b North Seaton 17/3/1905
Blyth Spartans
1926 Sheffield United 5
1930 1931 Grimsby Town 11
1932 Hull City 4

Bellamy, Benjamin Walter (Ben) OL
b Wollaston 22/4/1891 d 1985
Wollaston
1920 Northampton Town 3
Kettering

Bellamy, Herbert (Bert) LH/RH
b Kettering 6/4/1896 d 1978
Kettering White Cross
Kettering
1921 1922 Watford 36 2
1923 1925 Swansea Town 90 2
1926 Brentford 33
Wellingborough
United Counties Bus Company
Kidderminster Harriers

Bellamy, James Francis (Jim) RH/OR
b Bethnal Green 11/9/1881 d 1969
Barking
Grays United
Reading
1904 1906 Woolwich Arsenal 29 4
Portsmouth
Norwich City
Dundee
Motherwell
1912 1913 Burnley 21 3
1914 Fulham 17 1
Southend United
Ebbw Vale
Barking Town

Bellamy, Samuel Charles RB
b Small Heath 2/11/1913 d 2005
St Andrew's OSL
1937 Birmingham 1
Tamworth

Bellamy, Walter Richard OL
b Tottenham 6/11/1904 d 1978
Caps: England Amat
Ilford
Tufnell Park
Dulwich Hamlet
1926 1934 Tottenham Hotspur 70 9
1935 Brighton & Hove Albion 3

Bellamy, William Ernest (Bill) LB
b Creswell q3 1912 d 1963
Creswell
1934 Bristol City 0
1935 Grimsby Town 0
1937 1938 Wrexham 68

Bellas, John Edward (Jack) RB
b Bishop Auckland 16/9/1895 d 1977
Shildon Athletic
1920 1922 Sheffield Wednesday 45
Mansfield Town
1924 1925 Coventry City 33
Heanor Town
Sutton Junction
Peasley College
New Houghton Church

Bellhouse, Ernest Walter CH
b Sale 15/7/1871 d 1920
Repton School
1888 Derby County 2

Bellingham, F James CH
b Stirlingshire 1878
Falkirk Excelsior
Falkirk Hawthorn
Woodbine Rovers
Falkirk
Queen's Park Rangers
1901 Grimsby Town 4
Brentford
Willesden Town
Tunbridge Wells Rangers
Brentford

From To Apps Goal

Bellis, Alfred (Alf) OL
b Ellesmere Port 8/10/1920
Shell Juniors
Burnell's Ironworks
1937 1947 Port Vale 82 18
1939 (Port Vale) (2)
1947 1950 Bury 95 18
1951 1952 Swansea Town 41 11
1953 Chesterfield 13 3
Rhyl Athletic
Colwyn Bay
Penmaenmawr

Bellis, George Alfred CH/LB
b Khadki, India 8/6/1904 d 1969
Waterloo
Formby LMS
Seaforth Fellowship
1924 1926 Southport 41 4
1927 1928 Wrexham 82 5
1929 1932 Wolverhampton Wanderers 42
1932 1934 Burnley 86
1935 1936 Bournemouth & Boscombe Ath 56
Wellington Town

Bellis, Thomas Gilbert (Gib) LH
b Mold 21/4/1919 d 2000
Buckley Town
1938 1948 Wrexham 95 1
1939 (Wrexham) (1)
Colwyn Bay
Holywell Town
Caernarvon Town
Mold Alexandra

Belton, John (Jackie) RH/CF
b Loughborough 1/5/1895 d 1952
Quorn Emmanuel
Loughborough Corinthians
1914 1927 Nottingham Forest 322 17
Loughborough Corinthians

Belton, Thomas (Tom) IL
b Loughborough q4 1878 d 1944
Woodhouse United
Loughborough Emmanuel
Whitwick White Cross
1902 1903 Leicester Fosse 49 12
Coventry City
Loughborough Corinthians
Hinckley United
Mansfield Wesleyans
Sutton Town
Mansfield Town
Loughborough Corinthians

Bembridge, Charles William RB/LB
b Basford q4 1908 d 1967
Mexborough
1930 Barnsley 0
1931 1933 Rotherham United 6

Bemment, Frederick Charles (Fred) LH/CH
b Lowestoft 12/10/1884 d 1957
Lowestoft IOGT
Kirkley
Norwich City
1907 Notts County 9
1907 1908 Chesterfield Town 29 1
Hardwick Colliery

Benbow, John Albert IR
b Newtown 6/4/1879
Oswestry United
1897 Nottingham Forest 2

Benbow, Leonard (Len) CF
b Oswestry 3/5/1876 d 1946
Oswestry United
Shrewsbury Town
1897 1899 Nottingham Forest 54 20
1900 Stoke 21 2
Northampton Town

Beney, Albert CF/IR/IL
b Hastings q1 1883 d 1915
Hastings & St Leonards
1908 1909 Woolwich Arsenal 16 6
Carlisle United
1910 1911 Bury 4
Tunbridge Wells Rangers

Benfield, Thomas Charles (Tommy) OR/IR/IL
b Leicester q1 1889 d 1918
Leicester Old Boys
Leicestershire Regiment
Leicester Nomads
1910 1913 Leicester Fosse 106 23
1914 Derby County 38 15

Bennett, A IR
1893 Ardwick 12 6

From To Apps Goal

Bennett, Alfred GK
b Clowne 13/11/1898
Clowne Rising Star
1920 1925 Nottingham Forest 83
1927 1928 Port Vale 35

Bennett, Charles R OL/IR/IL
b 1882
Fleetwood Amateurs
1903 Blackpool 31 9
Accrington Stanley
1905 Blackpool 12 4
1905 Bradford City 14 1

Bennett, Edward Thomas RB/LB
b Barton Regis 10/8/1904 d 1957
1922 Bristol City 0
1922 1924 Swansea Town 11
1925 Wrexham 37
1926 1928 Manchester City 19
1929 1930 Norwich City 11

Bennett, Frederick (Fred) RB/LB
b Bristol 2/10/1906 d 1990
Fry's
HJ Packers Ltd
1925 1929 Bristol Rovers 128 2
1931 1935 Chester 158 1
Nantwich

Bennett, G OL
1906 Burton United 2

Bennett, George James OR
b Mexborough q2 1881
Mexborough Thursday
1901 Barnsley 9 3

Bennett, Henry Edward (Harry 'Tip') RH
b Mexborough q4 1871 d 1905
Mexborough Town
1899 1904 Barnsley 115 4

Bennett, Jesse RB
b Dronfield q4 1903
Dronfield Woodhouse
1929 Sheffield United 9
1932 Coventry City 25
1933 1935 Northampton Town 56
Folkestone

Bennett, John Benjamin (Jack) RB
b Basford 2/1911 d 1972
1930 Birmingham 0
1931 Blackburn Rovers 0
1932 1937 Walsall 182
Wellington Town
Long Eaton

Bennett, John H IL
Brechin Nomads
1921 Reading 9

Bennett, John William (Jack) RB/LH
b Liverpool 29/11/1879
Wavertree
Wellingborough
1900 Lincoln City 4
Northampton Town
Luton Town
1904 Leicester Fosse 27 1
1904 Blackburn Rovers 1

Bennett, Joseph LB
Porthill
1899 Burslem Port Vale 1

Bennett, Reuben Mitchell GK
b Aberdeen 21/12/1913 d 1989
Aberdeen East End
1935 Hull City 3
Queen of the South
Dundee
Ayr United
Dundee

Bennett, S OR/OL
Walmersley
1898 1899 Bury 2 1

Bennett, Thomas (Tom) OR
Heeley Friends
1902 Sheffield United 2
Doncaster Rovers

Bennett, Thomas Samuel (Tommy) CF/IR
b Walton q3 1891 d 1923
1919 Liverpool 1
Halifax Town
1921 Rochdale 3

From To Apps Goal

Bennett, Walter OR
b Mexborough q2 1874 d 1908
Caps: England 2
Mexborough Town
1895 1904 Sheffield United 195 61
1904 1906 Bristol City 48 22
Denaby United

Bennett, Walter RH/IR
b Sheffield 17/4/1901 d 1988
1921 Birmingham 0
1922 1923 Chelsea 5
1924 Southend United 6
1925 Doncaster Rovers 0
1926 Portsmouth 0
Gainsborough Trinity
1928 1929 Bristol City 20
Ballymena

Bennett, Wilfred (Wilf) RB
b Barrow 12/4/1900 d 1984
Barrow YMCA
1925 Barrow 17
Barrow Novocastrians

Bennett, William IR
b Leyland 1896
Leyland Motors
1920 Sheffield United 0
Leyland Motors
Chorley
1922 Nelson 1
Leyland Motors
Lytham
Leyland Motors

Bennett, William (Bill) IL
b Manchester 27/7/1910 d 1971
Winsford United
1931 Leeds United 10 4
1933 Southport 13
Rossendale United

Bennett, William Ambrose OR/IR
b Altrincham 4/1872
Summerfield
1892 1895 Crewe Alexandra 33 5
1896 1901 Small Heath 70 12
Stafford Rangers

Bennie, John CF
b Polmont 30/11/1896
Slamannan
Falkirk
Bo'ness
1921 Nelson 12 6
Bo'ness

Bennie, Peter OR
b Polmont 1872
Airdrieonians
1893 Sheffield United 1
Royal Albert
Wishaw Thistle
Slamannan
St Mirren
Dunipace

Bennie, Peter OR
b Larkhall 10/6/1898
Larkhall Thistle
Bellshill Athletic
Royal Albert
Albion Rovers
1923 Burnley 36 7
1924 1926 Bradford City 73 3

Bennie, Robert Brown (Bob) RB
b Polmont 1873 d 1945
Airdrieonians
Heart of Midlothian
St Mirren
1901 1903 Newcastle United 33
Morpeth Harriers

Bennion, Samuel (Sam) LB
b Burslem 1871 d 1941
1893 Burslem Port Vale 1

Bennion, Samuel Raymond (Ray) RH
b Summerhill 1/9/1896 d 1968
Caps: Wales 10
Crichton's Athletic
1921 1931 Manchester United 286 2
1932 1933 Burnley 31

Bennison, Thomas John (Jack) RH
b Barrow Hill q3 1874
Poolsbrook
Chesterfield Town
1899 Sheffield United 0
1900 Chesterfield Town 2
Poolsbrook Rangers
Royston Colliery

From To — Apps Goal

Benskin, Frank Sidney (Sam) IL
b Leicester q1 1879 d 1938
Leicester Old Boys
Belgrave Thursday United
1902 Leicester Fosse 1 1
Leicester British United
South Wigston Albion
Leicester Old Boys
Leicester British United

Benskin, William Ewart (Ewart 'Benny') LH/CH
b Leicester 8/4/1880 d 1956
Hugglescote Robin Hoods
Wigston Excelsior
Thursday Wanderers
Leicester Old Boys
1901 1903 Leicester Fosse 11
Leicester British United
South Wigston Albion
Northampton Town
Leicester Pilgrims
Leicester Imperial
St Johnstone

Benson, Charles Graydon OL
b Sunderland 19/4/1890 d 1970
Sunderland College
1912 Clapton Orient 1
Bishop Auckland
Durham City

Benson, George Herdman OL
b Burnley 25/6/1893 d 1974
Accrington Stanley
1920 Blackburn Rovers 0
1921 1922 Stalybridge Celtic 66 2
1923 Queen's Park Rangers 17
1923 Port Vale 1
Chorley

Benson, Harry Lewis LB/RB
b Hartshill 22/1/1883 d 1953
Shelton Albion
Porthill
1901 1906 Stoke 87
Northampton Town
Port Vale

Benson, James Robertson CF/IL
b Newmains 25/9/1914 d 1989
Markinch Victoria Rovers
St Johnstone
Brechin City (loan)
St Johnstone
1934 1935 Blackburn Rovers 2 1
East Fife
Falkirk
Dunfermline Athletic
Dundee United
Durham City
1938 Hartlepools United 0

Benson, John GK
Storey Brothers
Lancaster Town
1931 Accrington Stanley 1

Benson, Robert William (Bob) RB/LB
b Whitehaven 9/2/1883 d 1916
Caps: FLge 1/England 1
Dunston Villa
Shankhouse
Swalwell
1902 Newcastle United 1
Southampton
1905 1913 Sheffield United 273 20
1913 1914 Woolwich Arsenal 52 7

Bentham, Stanley Joseph (Stan) RH/IR
b Leigh 17/3/1915 d 2002
Lowton St Mary's
1932 Bolton Wanderers (trial) 0
Wigan Athletic
1935 1948 Everton 110 17
1939 (Everton) (3)

Bentley, Alec RB
b Saltaire 2/1/1907 d 1975
Guiseley
1929 1930 Bradford Park Avenue 12

Bentley, Alfred (Alf) CF/IR/IL
b Alfreton 9/1886 d 1940
Alfreton Town
1906 1910 Derby County 151 99
1911 1912 Bolton Wanderers 51 15
1913 1921 West Bromwich Albion 97 46
Burton Town
Alfreton Town

Bentley, Arthur IR
b Longton 1871
Sandbach Ramblers
1898 Stoke 5
Sandbach Ramblers

Bentley, E CH
1901 Stockport County 4

Bentley, Edgar RH
b Wolstanton q3 1892
Kidsgrove Wellington
1919 Port Vale 2

Bentley, Edwin LB/RB
b Lincoln q2 1876 d 1955
St Mary's (Lincoln)
1901 1907 Lincoln City 10

Bentley, Frank William LH/RH/CH
b Butt Lane 9/10/1886 d 1958
Butt Lane
1907 Stoke 1
1909 1911 Tottenham Hotspur 36
Brentford

Bentley, Handel OL/IL
b Eddgworth q4 1871 d 1945
1891 1894 Bolton Wanderers 44 17

Bentley, Harold (Harry) LH/RB/RH
b Heeley 9/3/1885 d 1949
Heeley Friends
1913 1919 Sheffield Wednesday 50 3
1920 1921 Brighton & Hove Albion 64
1922 1923 Swindon Town 11
Maltby Main Colliery

Bentley, Joseph LH
b Knutsford
Knutsford
Chester
Macclesfield
1911 Manchester City 1
Macclesfield
Hartlepools United

Bentley, Roland CF
b Rotherham q2 1904 d 1967
1925 1926 Rotherham United 4 2

Bentley, Thomas (Tom) IL
b Radcliffe
Eccles United
1922 Crewe Alexandra 27 12

Bentley, Walter B LH/RH
b Accrington q3 1907
Barnoldswick Town
Manchester Central
1932 1933 Accrington Stanley 22 1
Nelson

Benton, John (Jack) LH
b Wolverhampton 1865 d 1932
St Philip's
Stafford Royal
Willenhall White Star
1888 Wolverhampton Wanderers 1
Blakenhall
Wightwick

Benton, John Dutton (Jack) GK
b Newcastle-under -Lyme q4 1875 d 1926
Newcastle Swifts
North Staffordshire Regiment
Glentoran
Transvaal Police
1903 1905 Stoke 4
Glentoran
Stoke

Benton, William Henry (Billy) LH
b Walsall 5/12/1895 d 1967
Walsall
1920 1930 Blackpool 352 23
Fleetwood
1932 1933 Rochdale 48 8
Rossendale United

Benwell, Louis Andrew (Lou) GK
b Birmingham q2 1870 d 1936
Berwick Rangers (Worcester)
1893 Aston Villa 1
1894 Walsall Town Swifts 15
Berwick Rangers (Worcester)

Benyon, Joseph (Joe) OL
Atherton
Chorley
1925 Norwich City (trial) 0
Runcorn
Chorley (trial)
1926 Accrington Stanley 4 1

Benzie, Robert LH
b Greenock 19/9/1900 d 1977
Greenock HS
1923 1924 Doncaster Rovers 57
1924 1926 Manchester City 13
Flint Town

Beren, Hugh Gray RH
b Leith 9/10/1892 d 1961
Musselburgh
1909 Leeds City 3

Beresford, Frank Edgar IR/IL
b Chesterfield 8/10/1910 d 1974
Owston Park Rangers
1931 1933 Doncaster Rovers 56 10
1933 1934 Preston North End 36 4
1935 Luton Town 12 1
1936 Crystal Palace 3
1937 1938 Carlisle United 68 10
1939 Bradford City (1)

Beresford, James OR
Staveley
Church
Accrington
1888 Blackburn Rovers 12 4
Hyde

Beresford, Joseph (Joe) IR
b Chesterfield 26/2/1906 d 1978
Caps: FLge 2/England 1
Askern Road WMC
Bentley Colliery
Mexborough
Mansfield Town
1927 1935 Aston Villa 224 66
1935 1937 Preston North End 76 10
1937 Swansea Town 13 1
Stourbridge

Bernard, Eugene Henri Georges GK
b Southampton 3/6/1914 d 1973
Tauntons School
1936 Southampton 2
Winchester City

Berridge, Thomas Reginald (Reginald) RH
b Northampton 18/4/1904 d 1977
Northern Nomads
1929 Northampton Town 1
Wellingborough Town

Berrington, William Alfred (Alf) LB
b Ruabon q2 1887 d 1957
Army
Aberdare Town
1913 Leicester Fosse 2

Berry, Alfred (Alf) IL
Freetown
1905 Bury 3 2
Rossendale United
Haslingden

Berry, Arthur RH/LH
b Leicester q1 1877 d 1940
Leicester Imperial
1900 1903 Leicester Fosse 24

Berry, Arthur OR
b Liverpool 3/1/1888 d 1953
Caps: England Amat/England 1
Wrexham
1907 1908 Liverpool 3
Oxford University
1909 Fulham 12
1909 1910 Everton 27 7
Wrexham
Oxford City
1912 Liverpool 1
Northern Nomads
Wrexham

Berry, Clarence Herbert GK
b Macclesfield q4 1885 d 1954
1908 1911 Everton 3

Berry, Edmund OL
1919 Blackpool 5 1
Leyland
Leyland Motors

Berry, George Albert CF
b Bristol 1/9/1909 d 1985
Rose Green
1930 Bristol City 0
1934 Bristol Rovers 1
1935 Bristol City (loan) 0
Yeovil & Petters United

Berry, George Leslie (Les) GK
b Dorking 28/4/1906 d 1985
Market Harborough
1929 Sheffield Wednesday 0
1930 Bristol Rovers 34
1932 Swindon Town 22
Nuneaton Town

Berry, James IR
1922 Stalybridge Celtic 1
Mansfield Town

Berry, John (Jack) LB/RB
1892 1893 Burton Swifts 50
1895 1896 Loughborough 46 1

Berry, John RH
b Upholland 13/3/1904 d 1987
Wigan YMCA
1929 Wigan Borough 1
Burscough Rangers
Upholland

Berry, John L IL
b Bury 20/3/1878
Moulding Wesleyans
1897 1902 Bury 37 8

Berry, William Alexander (Bill) OR/CF
b Monkwearmouth 1884
Oakhill
Sunderland Royal Rovers
1902 Sunderland 0
Tottenham Hotspur
1906 1908 Manchester United 13 1
1908 1909 Stockport County 14 3
Sunderland Royal Rovers

Berry, William George (Bill) OL
b Hackney 18/8/1904 d 1972
Royal Naval Depot (Chatham)
1923 Charlton Athletic 11 2
1923 1925 Gillingham 79 9
1926 1932 Brentford 133 40
1932 Crystal Palace 17 4
1933 Bournemouth & Boscombe Ath 13 2
Fives (France)

Bertram, Ernest LH
b 20/1/1885
South Shields
1903 Sunderland 1
South Shields
Darlington

Bertram, George IL/OR
b Brandon, County Durham 15/1/1896 d 1963
Durham City
1919 Middlesbrough 0
1919 1920 Fulham 15 2
1921 Brentford 10 2
Sittingbourne
1924 Rotherham County 1
Leadgate Park
Whitchurch
Oswestry Town
1926 Wrexham 0
Whitchurch
Fitzgerald's Athletic (Surrey)

Bertram, William (Billy) IR/IL
b Brandon, County Durham 31/12/1897 d 1962
Browney Colliery
Durham City
1919 Newcastle United 3
1921 Norwich City 25 2
Leadgate Park (trial)
1922 1924 Durham City 100 28
1925 1930 Rochdale 198 72
1931 Accrington Stanley 0

Berwick, John William (William) IR
b Northampton q3 1887 d 1948
1910 1912 Glossop 25 7
1919 Everton 1

Best, Charles IR/OR
b Boosbeck q4 1888 d 1965
Eston United
1910 Middlesbrough 5 1
Eston United
1911 1912 Hull City 35 4

Best, Edward LB
b Mickley Square 27/9/1899 d 1975
Mickley
1927 Ashington 17
Mickley
Chopwell Institute
Mickley (trial)

Best, George Arthur GK
b Worksop 20/3/1904 d 1970
Worksop Town
1925 1926 Blackpool 27
Worksop Town

Best, Harry Orlando CF
b Poolstock q1 1892 d 1940
Appley Bridge
1910 Preston North End 4
Fleetwood
Altrincham
Wigan United

From To Apps Goal

Best, Jeremiah (Jerry) GK
b High Spen 22/8/1897 d 1955
Mickley Colliery Welfare
1920 1925 Coventry City 224
1926 Halifax Town 9
1927 1928 Rotherham United 25
Worksop Town
Newark Town
Worksop Town

Best, Jeremiah (Jerry) OL/CF/OR
b Mickley 23/1/1901 d 1975
Mickley Colliery Welfare
1919 Newcastle United 2
1920 Leeds United 11 1
Providence Clamdiggers
New Bedford Whalers
Fall River Marksmen
Pawtucket Rangers
New Bedford Whalers
1931 1932 Clapton Orient 51 17
1933 1936 Darlington 109 67
1936 Hull City 31 11
Hexham

Best, Robert (Bobby) OR
b Mickley 12/9/1891 d 1947
Mickley Colliery Welfare
1911 1921 Sunderland 93 23
1922 Wolverhampton Wanderers 22
1923 Durham City 33 2
1924 1926 Hartlepools United 72 8
Bedlington United (loan)
Robert Thompson's Works
West Stanley

Bestall, John Gilbert (Jackie) IR
b Beighton 24/6/1900 d 1985
Caps: FLge 3/England 1
Beighton Miners Welfare
1924 1926 Rotherham County 61 16
1926 1937 Grimsby Town 427 76

Beston, James CF
b Houghton-le-Spring q1 1880
Herrington Swifts
Houghton Rovers
Hebburn Argyle
1907 Lincoln City 3
Darlington
Houghton Rovers
Blyth Spartans
Wallsend Park Villa

Bestwick, Thomas Henry (Harry) GK
b Long Eaton q3 1864 d 1946
Long Eaton Rangers
1888 Derby County 1
Long Eaton Rangers

Beswick, David (Dave) GK
b Stoke-on-Trent 18/6/1910 d 1991
Mount Pleasant
1929 1932 Stoke City 9
1933 Walsall 0

Beswick, John Ewart (Ewart) CH
b Macclesfield 5/4/1897 d 1978
Longton
Congleton Town
1921 1923 Stoke 25
Congleton Town
1925 1926 Stoke City 33 1
Congleton Town

Beswick, Joseph CF
1906 Stockport County 10

Beswick, Samuel McAdam (Sammy) IR/IL/OR
b Macclesfield 8/3/1903 d 1966
Caps: England Amat
Northern Nomads
1920 Bury 0
1921 Stockport County 0
1922 1928 Tranmere Rovers 44 12
Northern Nomads
1926 1928 Tranmere Rovers 23 19
Rhyl
1929 1932 Bournemouth & Boscombe Ath 54 11
Poole Town

Bethell, Roy IL/OR
b Watford 9/8/1906 d 1976
St Albans City
1927 1928 Charlton Athletic 3
1929 1934 Gillingham 165 32

From To Apps Goal

Bethune, John (Jack) LB/RB
b Milngavie 19/10/1888 d 1955
Milngavie Allander
Vale of Clyde
Glasgow Ashfield
Heart of Midlothian
Hamilton Academical
Bonnyrigg Rose Athletic
Darlington
1912 1919 Barnsley 103 1
1919 Fulham (trial) 0
1920 Bristol Rovers 30
1921 Brentford 10
Sittingbourne
Sittingbourne Paper Mills

Betmead, Harry CH
b Grimsby 11/4/1912 d 1984
Caps: England 1
Cleethorpes Town
Haycroft Rovers
1931 1946 Grimsby Town 296 10
1939 (Grimsby Town) (3)

Bett, Frederick (Fred) IR/IL
b Scunthorpe 5/12/1920
Scunthorpe & Lindsey United
1937 1938 Sunderland 3
1946 1948 Coventry City 27 11
1948 Lincoln City 14 2
Spalding United
Holbeach United
Bourne Town

Betteley, Richard H (Dick) LB/RB
b Bradley, Staffordshire 14/7/1880 d 1942
Bradley Athletic
Priestfield Albion
Bilston St Leonard's
Bilston United
1901 1905 Wolverhampton Wanderers 115 1
1906 1911 West Bromwich Albion 85
Bilston United

Betteley, William (Billy) OL
b Nantwich q1 1877 d 1917
Nantwich Church House
Nantwich
Congleton
Nantwich
1899 Glossop 0
1900 1901 Stockport County 44 6
Nantwich
Crewe Alexandra
Nantwich
Stafford Rangers
Stafford Albion
Whitchurch
Nantwich
Stafford Rangers
Stafford St Mary's Institute

Betteridge, Frank OL
b Worksop 12/1/1911 d 1972
Manton Colliery
Denaby United
Worksop Town
1930 1935 Halifax Town 109 33
1936 Barrow 29 4
Goole Town

Betteridge, Walter RB
b Romsey 24/12/1896 d 1979
Boscombe
1920 Exeter City 2
Maidstone United
Peterborough & Fletton United
1928 Crystal Palace 1
Loughborough Corinthians

Bettison, Frederick Harold (Harry) RB
b Hucknall Torkard 20/12/1890 d 1982
Mapperley
Netherfield Rangers
1910 Notts County 1
Grantham

Betton, Alexander (Alec) CH/LB
b New Tupton 28/11/1903 d 1965
New Tupton Ivanhoe
1927 1928 Chesterfield 31
Scarborough
1930 1933 Newcastle United 61 1
1934 Stockport County 2
Scarborough

Bettridge, Walter RB/LB
b Oakthorpe 10/1886 d 1931
Oakthorpe Albion
Measham United
Worksop Town
Burton United
1909 1920 Chelsea 224
1922 Gillingham 19

From To Apps Goal

Betts, Arthur Charles (Charlie) LB
b Scunthorpe 2/1/1886 d 1967
North Lindsey
1905 1906 Gainsborough Trinity 64 1
Watford
1910 Gainsborough Trinity 29 1
1911 Newcastle United 0
1911 1913 Derby County 71
1914 1919 Hull City 51
Scunthorpe & Lindsey United
Normanby Park Steelworks

Betts, Arthur R OR
b Huthwaite 17/5/1916
Huthwaite CWS
1936 1938 Nottingham Forest 65 10

Betts, Herbert RH
b Woodford, Northamptonshire q3 1879
Belgrave St Michael's
Leicester Imperial
1901 Leicester Fosse 2
Leicester Imperial

Betts, William (Billy) CH
b Sheffield 26/3/1864 d 1941
Caps: England 1
Parkwood Rovers
Clarence
Pyebank Rovers
The Wednesday
Lockwood Brothers
1892 1894 Sheffield Wednesday 49 3

Bevan, Frederick Walter (Fred) CF/IL
b Poplar 27/2/1879 d 1935
Millwall St John's
Millwall Athletic
1901 1902 Manchester City 8 1
Reading
Queen's Park Rangers
1906 Bury 31 16
1907 Fulham 5 1
1907 1909 Derby County 51 17
1909 1912 Clapton Orient 118 35
Chatham

Bevan, Harry Frederick IL
b Birkenhead 23/2/1906 d 1970
Runcorn
1927 Tranmere Rovers 3 2
Prescot Cables
Northwich Victoria

Beveridge, David RH/OR
b Scotland 1872
Albion Rovers
1896 1898 Burnley 20
1899 Grimsby Town 5 2
Albion Rovers

Beveridge, Robert CF
b Polmadie 24/6/1877 d 1901
Maryhill Harp
Third Lanark
1899 1900 Nottingham Forest 28 5
1900 Everton 4

Beverley, Joseph (Joe) RB
b Blackburn 12/11/1856 d 1897
Caps: England 3
James Street
Blackburn Olympic
Blackburn Rovers
Blackburn Olympic
1888 Blackburn Rovers 8

Bevin, Frederick Walter (Fred) IL
b Walsall 1880 d 1940
Walsall Dynamos
Darlaston
1903 1905 Wolverhampton Wanderers 35 8
Stourbridge
Bilston
Bloxwich Strollers

Bevis, William Ernest (Billy) OR
b Warsash 29/9/1918 d 1994
1936 Portsmouth 0
Gosport Athletic
1937 1946 Southampton 82 16
1939 (Southampton) (2)
Winchester City

Bew, Daniel Crombie (Danny) CH
b Sunderland 22/3/1896 d 1951
Lambton Star
1921 Sunderland 0
1922 Hull City 11
1923 1929 Swindon Town 209 6

From To Apps Goal

Bewick, James CH
b Southwick, County Durham 31/12/1906 d 1979
Herrington Swifts
1932 Newcastle United 0
1935 Port Vale 3
1936 Walsall 3
Yeovil & Petters United
South Shields

Beynon, Benjamin (Ben) CF
b Swansea 14/3/1894 d 1969
1920 1921 Swansea Town 25 11
Mid-Rhondda United

Beynon, David Robert RB/LB
b New Tredegar q3 1914 d 1942
1936 Watford 0
1937 1938 Chester 13

Beynon, John Alfred OL/OR
b Pontypridd q2 1909 d 1937
Great Western Colliery
1927 West Bromwich Albion 0
1928 Halifax Town 20 4
Scunthorpe & Lindsey United
1930 1931 Rotherham United 50 10
1932 Doncaster Rovers 23 13
Aberdeen

Bibby, C CF
1898 Darwen 5 3

Bibby, Joseph (Joe) RB/LB
b Rishton q1 1897 d 1968
Blackburn Trinity
1920 Blackburn Rovers 8
1921 Wigan Borough 9
Dundee Hibernian
Bridgend Town

Bicknell, Charles (Charlie) RB/LB
b Pye Bridge 6/11/1905 d 1994
New Tupton Ivanhoe
1928 1929 Chesterfield 79
1930 1935 Bradford City 240 2
1935 1946 West Ham United 137 1
1939 (West Ham United) (3)
Bedford Town

Biddlestone, Thomas Frederick (Fred) GK
b Pensnett 26/11/1904 d 1982
Bilston Boys Club
Hickman Park Rangers
Moxley Wesleyans
Wednesbury Town
Sunbeam Motors
Bloxwich Strollers
1929 Walsall 21
1929 1938 Aston Villa 151
1939 Mansfield Town (3)

Bidewell, Sidney Harry (Sid) IR
b Wymondham 6/6/1918 d 2003
St Albans City
Wealdstone
1937 Chelsea 4 2
Gravesend & Northfleet
Chelmsford City

Bidmead, William Harold LB/RB
b West Bromwich 12/1882 d 1961
Elwells
1900 Walsall 0
Stourbridge
Brierley Hill Alliance
1903 1905 Small Heath/Birmingham 3
Leyton
1908 Grimsby Town 1
Brierley Hill Alliance

Bigden, James Henry RH/LH
b Poplar q2 1880 d 1918
Old St Luke's
Thames Ironworks
Gravesend United
West Ham United
1904 1907 Woolwich Arsenal 75 1
1908 Bury 3
Southend United

Bigg, Robert James (Bob) OL
b Egypt 11/3/1911 d 1991
Redhill
1934 1938 Crystal Palace 109 41
1939 Aldershot (2) (1)

Biggar, Alex OL
b Lanark
Lanemark
1912 Bradford City 1
1913 Tottenham Hotspur 0

From To Apps Goal

Biggar, Frederick William (Billy) GK
b Blaydon q4 1877 d 1935
Birtley
1899 1901 Sheffield United 14
West Ham United
Fulham
Watford
Rochdale
Leyland Motors

Biggin, Horace IR
b Shirebrook q2 1897 d 1984
Whitwell St Lawrence
Whitwell Colliery
1919 West Ham United 2
Ilkeston United
Shirebrook
Retford Town
Mansfield Town
Whitwell Colliery

Biggins, Francis Joseph (Fred) OR/RH
b Brownhills q3 1884
South Kirkby
1908 1910 Barnsley 29 2

Biggs, Arthur Gilbert IR/CF
b Wootton 26/5/1915 d 1996
1936 1937 Arsenal 3
Heart of Midlothian
Aberdeen
Bedford Town
Colchester United
Vauxhall Motors

Bilcliff, Bernard GK
b Chapeltown 6/6/1904 d 1955
Chapeltown Primitives
1925 1928 Chesterfield 60
Scarborough
1930 1931 Halifax Town 66
Shelbourne

Billam, George Thomas (Bobbie) RB
b Jarrow q1 1884 d 1962
Jarrow
1908 Bury 5
Hartlepools United
Ashington Alliance

Billingham, John (Jack) CF/OR/RH
b Daventry 3/12/1914 d 1981
Stead & Simpson
1935 Northampton Town 3
1937 Bristol City 7
1938 1948 Burnley 93 36
1949 1950 Carlisle United 65 17
1950 1954 Southport 150 37

Billington, Hugh John Richard CF/IL/IR
b Ampthill 24/2/1916 d 1988
Luton Cocoa Works
Chapel Street Methodists
Waterlows
1938 1947 Luton Town 86 63
1939 (Luton Town) (3) (5)
1947 1950 Chelsea 82 28
Worcester City

Billington, S OR
1901 Blackpool 1

Bimson, James (Jimmy) LH
b Lathom 9/2/1899 d 1966
Stormy Albion (Skelmersdale)
Westhead Juniors
Ormskirk DS & S
1922 1926 Southport 109 5
Chester
Ashton National
1930 Wigan Borough 41 1
Skelmersdale United
1931 Rochdale 12 1

Bingham, Harold W OL
b 1903
1923 Cardiff City 0
Pembroke Dock
Chester
1927 Wrexham 3
Caernarvon Athletic
Burton Town

Bingham, Samuel (Sam) OR
b Northern Ireland
Belfast
1920 Bradford Park Avenue 7

Binks, Edward G OL
1928 Merthyr Town 1
1929 Rochdale 0

Binks, George Frederick (Fred) LH/CH
b West Bromwich 3/1899
1921 Birmingham 0
1922 1926 Walsall 107 1

Binks, Louis RB/LB
b Sheffield 23/10/1898 d 1969
Tinsley Amateurs
1919 1920 Coventry City 15
1922 Grimsby Town 3
Rotherham Town

Binks, Sidney (Sid) CF/CH
b Bishop Auckland 25/7/1899 d 1978
Caps: England Amat
Spennymoor United
Bishop Auckland
1922 1924 Sheffield Wednesday 76 29
1924 1925 Huddersfield Town 4 1
1925 1926 Blackpool 55 9
1927 Portsmouth 0
1928 Southend United 14
1928 1929 Fulham 27
1930 1931 Chesterfield 44 12
1932 Sheffield Wednesday 0
Ashington

Binney, Charles (Chas) IR/OR/IL
b Sheffield 24/2/1901 d 1952
Leadmill St Mary's
1919 1922 Sheffield Wednesday 40 6
Worksop Town
Wombwell Town
Frickley Colliery

Binney, John IL
Worksop Town
1902 Leicester Fosse 2
Worksop Town
Denaby United
Worksop Town

Binnie, Alexander (Alex) GK
b Kilsyth 1905
Kilsyth Rangers
Partick Thistle
1926 Port Vale (trial) 4
Hamilton Academical

Binns, Clifford Herman (Cliff) GK
b Cowling 9/3/1907 d 1977
Knott United
Portsmouth Rovers
1927 Burnley (trial) 0
1927 Preston North End (trial) 0
1927 1929 Halifax Town 34
1929 1932 Blackburn Rovers 94
Workington
1933 1935 Blackburn Rovers 89
1936 1938 Barnsley 95
1939 (Barnsley) (3)
1945 Carlisle United 0
Gainsborough Trinity

Binns, Ernest Dalton CF
b Wombwell 27/3/1901 d 1975
Wombwell
1922 Barnsley 0
Wombwell
Shirebrook
1928 Doncaster Rovers 1 1
Shirebrook
Newark Town
Wombwell

Bint, Albert John OR
b Guisborough 8/11/1912 d 1983
Whitby United
1934 Doncaster Rovers 7 2
Thorne Colliery

Birch, Arnold GK
b Grenoside 12/7/1891 d 1964
Grenoside Bible Class
Tankersley Colliery
Be Quick (Groningen)
1919 1922 Sheffield Wednesday 27
1923 1926 Chesterfield 141 5
Denaby United
Grenoside Sports

Birch, Arthur H RB
Wombwell
1901 1904 Doncaster Rovers 34
Rawmarsh

Birch, Edwin (Ted) LH/IL/OL
b Newhall 7/10/1869
1893 1894 Burton Swifts 41 10
1897 1898 Luton Town 29 10

Birch, Frank OR
b Hednesford
Wellington Town
1922 West Bromwich Albion 0
1923 1924 Walsall 35 1

Birch, James (Jimmy) IR/OR
b Blackwell 1888 d 1940
Stourbridge
1911 Aston Villa 3 2
1920 1925 Queen's Park Rangers 183 60
1926 Brentford 0

Birch, Joseph (Joe) RB/LB
b Hednesford 6/7/1904 d 1980
Cannock Chase
Hednesford Town
1928 Birmingham 1
1929 1931 Bournemouth & Boscombe Ath 26
1931 1937 Fulham 185
Colchester United

Birch, Wallace IR/OR
b Grenoside 6/3/1910 d 1987
Grenoside Sports
1929 Luton Town 15 3
1930 Sheffield Wednesday 0
1931 Accrington Stanley 2 1
1932 Blackpool 0
Kidderminster Harriers

Birch, William (Birch) OL
b Rainford 1887 d 1968
1907 Blackpool 13 3
1908 Nottingham Forest 14 2
Reading
St Helens Town
Eccles Borough
1912 1913 Grimsby Town 34 1
Gainsborough Trinity
Steam Trawler Co
Charlton's (Grimsby)

Birchall, John (Jack) LH/CH
b Prescot 1876
St Helens Recreation
1899 Liverpool 0
1900 1902 Blackpool 81 3
1902 1906 Blackburn Rovers 39 3
Leyton

Birchall, Joseph OL
1901 1902 Burnley 12 1
1903 Preston North End 0

Birchall, Richard (Dick) OL
b Prescot 14/10/1887
Newton-le-Willows
St Helens Town
1909 Bradford City 1
Carlisle United
Hyde
Norwich City
Rochdale
1912 Lincoln City 7 1
Worksop Town
Rotherham Town
Mexborough
1919 Bradford City 0

Birchenough, Frank GK
b Crewe 1898
Nantwich
1919 West Ham United 1
1920 Burnley 2
Whitchurch
Nantwich

Birchenough, Herbert GK
b Haslington 21/9/1874 d 1942
Caps: FLge 1
Haslington Villa
1892 Crewe Alexandra 0
Nantwich
Sandbach St Mary's
Audley
Crewe Alexandra
Nantwich
1898 1899 Burslem Port Vale 51
1899 1902 Glossop 81
1902 Manchester United 25
Crewe Alexandra

Bird, Anthony (Tony) CF/IR
b Dublin 1910
Richmond United
Dundalk
Bray Unknowns
1930 1933 Plymouth Argyle 26 7
1934 Newport County 29 15
1935 Tranmere Rovers 0
Boston United
Brideville

Bird, Charles Denton (Charlie) GK
b Hoylake 1/10/1914 d 1984
Hoylake
1934 Newport County 0
1934 1935 New Brighton 31
Northwich Victoria

Bird, Donald William Carlton OL
(Don 'Dickie')
b Rhayader 5/1/1908 d 1987
Llandrindod Wells
1929 1930 Cardiff City 13 4
1931 Bury 0
1932 1933 Torquay United 73 15
1934 1935 Derby County 5 2
1935 1936 Sheffield United 13 3
1936 Southend United 10 1

Bird, Horace OR
b Smethwick
1919 Wolverhampton Wanderers 3

Bird, Isaac (Ike) IL
b Kimberley 14/7/1895 d 1984
Ilkeston United
1919 Lincoln City 8 2
Ilkeston United

Bird, Jesse Herbert OR
b Hoylake q1 1904 d 1968
Hoylake
1923 1924 Wrexham 8
Mold Town
Buckley Town
Mold Town
Connah's Quay & Shotton

Bird, Kenneth Benjamin (Ken) GK
b Norwich 25/9/1918 d 1987
Caps: England Sch
Willenhall Rovers
1937 Wolverhampton Wanderers 0
1938 1952 Bournemouth & Boscombe Ath 249
Dorchester Town

Bird, Sidney (Sid) LB
b Lemington q4 1906
Scotswood
1928 1931 Fulham 43
1932 1934 Walsall 90 2
Spennymoor United
Brandon

Bird, Sidney Albert (Sid) GK
b Luton q1 1904
Luton Amateurs
1922 Luton Town 1
Kettering

Bird, Sidney J OR
b Bristol 1910
Ashton Gate Old Boys
Bath City
1928 Huddersfield Town 0
Bath City
1930 Thames 2
Shrewsbury Town

Bird, Walter Smith IR/CF
b Hugglescote q3 1891 d 1965
Ellistown St Christopher's
Hugglescote United
Coalville Swifts
1912 1914 Notts County 10 2
1919 Grimsby Town 7 2
1920 Bristol Rovers 20 5
Dundee
Heart of Midlothian
Kilmarnock
Loughborough Corinthians

Bird, William (Billy) RH/CF
b Broughton Astley
Hinckley United
1926 1927 Coventry City 37 11
Hinckley United
Atherstone Town
Nuneaton Town

Birds, Joseph (Joe) GK
b Youlgreave 29/10/1887 d 1966
Hazel Grove
Macclesfield
1910 1912 Stockport County 15
1913 Manchester City 0
1919 1920 Stockport County 22
Macclesfield
1922 1923 Nelson 40

Birdsall, George LB
b Saxton 30/9/1891 d 1936
Brompton
Brighton & Hove Albion
Brompton
Harpenden Town
1921 Derby County 8

Birkbeck, John William IR
b Wellingborough q3 1885 d 1961
Irthlingborough Town
1906 Gainsborough Trinity 21 4
Rushden Fosse
Irthlingborough Town

From To Apps Goal

Birket, Richard (Bob) RB/CF/IR
b Weeton, Lancashire q1 1879 d 1962
Fleetwood Rangers
1896 1906 Blackpool 219 44

Birkett, Ralph James Evans OR
b Newton Abbot 9/1/1913 d 2002
Caps: FLge 2/England War 1/England 1
Dartmouth United
1929 1932 Torquay United 95 19
1933 1934 Arsenal 19 7
1934 1937 Middlesbrough 93 35
1938 Newcastle United 23 3
1939 (Newcastle United) (1)

Birkett, William Cunningham (Bill) LB
b Carlisle 29/10/1910 d 1973
Crescent Rangers
1930 1931 Carlisle United 13
1932 1933 Southport 34
1934 1938 Rotherham United 173
1939 (Rotherham United) (3)

Birkhead, Alfred GK
b Deepcar 10/1/1904 d 1978
Stocksbridge Church
1930 Sheffield United 0
1931 1933 Rotherham United 64

Birks, Clifford (Cliff) RH/OR
b Hanley 13/12/1910 d 1998
Stoke St Peter's
1932 1935 Port Vale 58 7
1936 Torquay United 1 1
1937 Halifax Town 2

Birks, Leonard (Len) LB/RB
b Stoke-on-Trent 6/10/1896 d 1975
Butt Lane Star
1920 1924 Port Vale 101
1924 1930 Sheffield United 195
1930 1932 Plymouth Argyle 49
1933 Bristol City 30
Yeovil & Petters United

Birnie, Alexander Kelmar (Alex) OR
b Aberdeen 11/1/1884
Commercial Athletic
Chatham Dockyard
West Ham United
Sittingbourne
1905 Everton 3
Norwich City
Sittingbourne
Southend United
1908 1911 Bury 80 2
Tunbridge Wells Rangers

Birnie, Edward Lawson (Ted) LH/CH/OL
b Sunderland 25/8/1878 d 1935
Sunderland Seaburn
1898 1903 Newcastle United 19
Crystal Palace
1906 1909 Chelsea 101 3
1910 Tottenham Hotspur 4 1
Mulheim
Rochdale
Leyton

Birnie, John (Jack) LH
Fraserburgh
1923 Hartlepools United 5
Fraserburgh

Birrell, William (Billy) IR/OR
b Cellardyke 13/3/1897 d 1968
Inverkeithing United
Raith Rovers
1920 1927 Middlesbrough 225 59
Raith Rovers

Birtles, Daniel (Danny) OR
b Barton-on-Irwell 24/2/1904 d 1986
1922 Bury 0
Lancaster Town
1924 Tranmere Rovers 10
Lancaster Town

Birtles, Fred IL/OL/CF
b Stockport 6/4/1903 d 1985
1922 1924 Crewe Alexandra 28 9
1925 Hartlepools United 15 6
1926 1927 Crewe Alexandra 52 13
Chester
Altrincham
Stalybridge Celtic
Mossley

From To Apps Goal

Birtles (Birtel), Thomas James Denton (Tommy) OR
b Higham, West Yorkshire 26/10/1886 d 1971
Higham
1903 1905 Barnsley 35 7
Swindon Town
Portsmouth
1910 Barnsley 3 1
Rotherham County
Northampton Town
Doncaster Rovers

Birtley, Robert (Bob) IR/OR/LH
b Easington 15/7/1908 d 1961
1933 Everton 0
1934 Coventry City 30 6
1935 1938 Crystal Palace 65 15
1939 Gateshead (3) (2)

Birtwhistle, Thomas (Tom) RB
b Halifax 10/8/1892 d 1970
Hebden Bridge
1921 Halifax Town 2

Bisby, Clarence Charles (Charlie) LB
b Mexborough 10/9/1904 d 1977
Denaby United
1926 1931 Notts County 206 1
1932 1935 Coventry City 100
1935 Mansfield Town 9
Peterborough United

Bisby, Fred OL/OR
b Ecclesfield q3 1880 d 1948
Kilnhurst Town
Rawmarsh
Kilnhurst Town
1905 1907 Grimsby Town 12 1
Cleethorpes Town
Worksop Town
Grimsby Rangers
Denaby United

Bisby, John Charles LH/IL
b Rawmarsh q1 1877 d 1945
Kilnhurst Town
Highthorne
1905 Sheffield United 1
1906 1907 Grimsby Town 7 1
Denaby United

Bishop, Albert John LH/CH
b Stourbridge 8/4/1886 d 1938
Halesowen
1906 1919 Wolverhampton Wanderers 357 6
Wrexham

Bishop, Alfred (Alf) IR/IL
b Aston 17/7/1902 d 1944
Royal Air Force
St Albans City
1926 Southampton 7
Wellington Town
Cradley Heath St Luke's
1928 Barrow 11 2
Cradley Heath St Luke's
Wellington Town
Leamington Town
Stafford Rangers
Bromsgrove Rovers
BSA (Birmingham)
Billesley Estates

Bishop, George Arthur CH/LH/LB
b Tredegar q2 1901
1925 Rochdale 0
1926 1928 Merthyr Town 109 3
1929 1931 Gillingham 94
1932 Southampton 0
Ebbw Vale

Bishop, Matthew (Matt) OL
b Melton Mowbray 1876
Melton Town
1895 1896 Leicester Fosse 10 2
Warmley
1898 1899 Leicester Fosse 3
Coalville Town
Melton Town
South Wigston Albion
Melton Mowbray
Melton Working Mens Club

Bishop, Robert OR
Winchburgh
1921 Portsmouth 11 1
Aberaman Athletic

Bishop, Sidney Macdonald (Sid) LH/RH/IR
b Stepney 10/2/1900 d 1949
Caps: FLge 1/England 4
Ilford
Crystal Palace
1920 1926 West Ham United 159 10
1926 1927 Leicester City 49 7
1928 1932 Chelsea 103 5

From To Apps Goal

Bispham, Thomas Minnican (Tom) GK
b Barrow 21/8/1907 d 1981
Dalton Casuals
1926 Barrow 3

Bissett, George IR
b Cowdenbeath 25/1/1897
Glencraig Thistle
Third Lanark
St Mirren (loan)
1919 1921 Manchester United 40 10
1921 1922 Wolverhampton Wanderers 41 10
Pontypridd
1924 1925 Southend United 59 14
Lochgelly United
Dunfermline Athletic

Bissett, James Thompson (Jimmy) RB
b Lochee 19/6/1898
Dundee
1920 Everton 0
Ebbw Vale
1922 Southend United 33
1923 Rochdale 42 3
1924 1925 Middlesbrough 33
1926 1927 Lincoln City 32 6
Dundee
Raith Rovers

Bissett, John GK
Dalbeattie
1898 Lincoln City 18

Biswell, George William IR/LH/CF
b Watford 1/9/1904 d 1981
1923 Watford 0
St Albans City
1925 1927 Charlton Athletic 63 19
1927 1929 Chelsea 24 10
Chester
1931 1933 Charlton Athletic 28 3

Bithell, Samuel Herbert (Bert) IL/OL
b Hindley 19/11/1900 d 1969
St Philip's Old Boys
Crossens
Burscough Rangers
1921 1922 Southport 5
1923 Burnley (trial) 0
High Park

Black, Adam Hudson RB/LB
b Denny 18/2/1898 d 1981
Bathgate
1919 1934 Leicester City 528 4

Black, Alec LH
b Edinburgh 1867
Edina
Rangers
St Bernard's
1898 Barnsley 4

Black, Alfred George (Alf) OL
b Milton Regis 15/3/1902 d 1972
Sittingbourne
1924 1930 Millwall Athletic 110 19
1931 Luton Town 1
Folkestone

Black, Arthur Richard (Dick) CF/OL
b Airdrie 18/2/1907
Gartsherrie Juniors
Stenhousemuir
Blantyre Victoria
Morton
1931 1933 Manchester United 8 3
St Mirren
Morton
Queen of the South

Black, Daniel GK
b Whitehaven 16/4/1911 d 1978
Kells
1933 1934 Carlisle United 21
1934 Rotherham United 0
1935 1938 Mansfield Town 46
Peterborough United

Black, David CF
1894 Blackburn Rovers 0
1895 Burslem Port Vale 7 1

Black, David George OL/IR
b Irvine 22/3/1868 d 1940
Caps: Scotland 1
Hurlford
Grimsby Town
Middlesbrough
1893 1896 Wolverhampton Wanderers 74 15
1896 Burnley 12 5
Tottenham Hotspur
1898 Woolwich Arsenal 0
Clyde

From To Apps Goal

Black, Edward CH
Aberdeen
1931 Rochdale 8
1932 Gateshead 0

Black, James RH
b Scotland
Arbroath Ardenlea
1924 Newport County 3
Forfar Athletic

Black, James (Jim) IL/IR
b Motherwell 4/5/1906
Carluke Rovers
St Johnstone
Cowdenbeath
1931 1932 Charlton Athletic 31 3
Burton Town
1934 Aldershot 32 3
Cheltenham Town
Cowdenbeath

Black, John Ross RH/CF/OR
b Denny 26/5/1900 d 1993
Denny Hibernian
1921 Sunderland 2
1922 1923 Nelson 29 5
1923 Accrington Stanley 14 5
1924 1925 Chesterfield 21
1926 1929 Luton Town 91 4
1930 1931 Bristol Rovers 49 2

Black, Robert Watson (Bobby) LH/RH
b Washington 17/7/1915 d 1979
1936 1937 West Ham United 2
1938 1945 Clapton Orient 23
1939 (Clapton Orient) (3)

Black, Samuel (Sammy) OL
b Motherwell 18/11/1905 d 1977
Kirkintilloch Rob Roy
1924 1937 Plymouth Argyle 470 176
1938 Queen's Park Rangers 5

Black, Thomas (Tommy) LH
b Holytown 1/12/1908
Strathclyde
1932 Arsenal 0
1932 1938 Plymouth Argyle 162
1939 Southend United (3)

Black, William RH
b Flemington 16/5/1878
Enfield Star
Dalziel Rovers
Queen's Park
Celtic
1905 1906 Everton 20
Broxburn (loan)
Kilmarnock (loan)
Dumbarton
Kilmarnock
Hamilton Academical
Ayr Parkhouse
Ayr United
Annbank
Thornhill

Black, William (Bill) CF
b Airdrie 15/1/1916
Wishaw Juniors
Airdrieonians
Blantyre Victoria
Wishaw Juniors
Hibernian
1937 Watford 16 3
Dunfermline Athletic

Black, William F (Willie) IL
b Linlithgow 1905
Linlithgow Rose
Heart of Midlothian
Hamilton Academical
1928 Swansea Town 11 1
Forfar Athletic
Bo'ness
Morton
East Stirlingshire
Dundee United
Raith Rovers

Black, William (Bill) CF
b Airdrie 15/1/1916
Wishaw Juniors
Airdrieonians
Blantyre Victoria
Wishaw Juniors
Hibernian
1937 Watford 16 3
Dunfermline Athletic

From To | Apps Goal

Blackadder, Frederick (Fred) CH
b Carlisle 13/1/1916 d 1992
Penrith
1937 1946 Carlisle United 3
Blackhall Colliery Welfare
1947 Hartlepools United 0

Blackadder, William (Bill) LH
b Padiham 9/1/1899 d 1977
1922 Burnley 0
1924 Accrington Stanley 17
Chorley
Clitheroe
Lancaster Town

Blackburn, Arthur RB/LB
b Blackburn q2 1876
Mellor
1894 Blackburn Rovers 0
Wellingborough
1899 Blackburn Rovers 2
Southampton
1901 Blackburn Rovers 2

Blackburn, Frederick (Fred) OL/IL
b Mellor 9/1879
Caps: FLge 1/England 3
Mellor
1897 1904 Blackburn Rovers 192 25
West Ham United

Blackburn, George OR
b Worksop q2 1888
Denaby United
1908 Glossop 5 3
Denaby United
1909 Bradford Park Avenue 11 6
1910 1911 Huddersfield Town 37 6

Blackburn, George Frederick LH
b Willesden Green 8/3/1899 d 1957
Caps: WLge 1/England 1
Hampstead Town
1920 1925 Aston Villa 133 1
1926 1930 Cardiff City 115 1
1931 Mansfield Town 14
Cheltenham Town

Blackburn, Robert OR
b Edinburgh 1885
Raith Rovers
Hamilton Academical
Leith Athletic
1906 1907 Newcastle United 5
Aberdeen
1909 Grimsby Town 6

Blackburn, Robert Ernest (Ernie) RB/LB
b Crawshawbooth 23/4/1892 d 1964
Loveclough
Manchester Youth Club
1919 1921 Aston Villa 32
1922 1923 Bradford City 40

Blackburn, Stanley IL
b York 4/10/1909 d 1987
Rowntree's
Selby Town
1931 York City 1
Scarborough
Selby Town
Goole Town

Blackburn, William RB
b Bury
Black Lane Rovers
1930 Rochdale 3

Blackburne, Charles (Charlie) OR
b Knottingley 24/1/1910 d 1980
1929 Leeds United 0
1930 Doncaster Rovers 4
Aldershot

Blackett, Joseph (Joe) LB/RB/IL
b Newcastle 20/6/1875
1894 Newcastle United 0
Gateshead
Willington Athletic
1896 Loughborough 21 8
1897 1899 Wolverhampton Wanderers 96 11
1900 Derby County 17 1
1900 Sunderland 0
1901 1904 Middlesbrough 78 4
Luton Town
1906 1908 Leicester Fosse 78
Rochdale
Barrow

Blackham, Ernest GK
b Stoke-on-Trent 4/7/1898 d 1966
1921 Port Vale 1

Blackham, Robert Bert T OL
b Wolverhampton 2/11/1912 d 1989
1935 Walsall 10 4

From To | Apps Goal

Blackham, Samuel (Sam) LB/RB
b Edmonton 19/8/1890 d 1956
1909 Tottenham Hotspur 0
Barrow
1911 1921 Bradford Park Avenue 221
1922 Halifax Town 6
1923 Bradford Park Avenue 0

Blackie, A IL
1897 Burton Swifts 11 1

Blackie, Sydney (Syd) CF
b Gateshead q1 1900 d 1966
Hebden Bridge
1924 Stoke 2
1926 Southend United 0

Blackman, Frederick Ernest (Fred) RB/LB
b Kennington 8/2/1884 d 1942
Caps: SoLge 2
1907 Woolwich Arsenal 0
Hastings & St Leonards United
Brighton & Hove Albion
1911 1913 Huddersfield Town 92
1913 1914 Leeds City 44
1920 1921 Queen's Park Rangers 42

Blackman, John James (Jack) CF
b Bermondsey 25/11/1911 d 1987
Weston United
1931 1935 Queen's Park Rangers 108 62
1935 1945 Crystal Palace 99 52
Guildford City

Blackmore, Harold Alfred CF/IL
b Silverton 13/5/1904 d 1989
Silverton
1924 1926 Exeter City 71 45
1926 1931 Bolton Wanderers 153 111
1932 Middlesbrough 19 9
1933 1934 Bradford Park Avenue 60 32
1934 Bury 6 4
1935 Exeter City 0

Blackmore, Peter CF
b Gorton q3 1879 d 1937
Ross Place OB
1899 Newton Heath 1

Blackshaw, Herbert Kitchener (Bert) IL/OL
b Altrincham 8/6/1916 d 1999
Altrincham
1936 Sheffield United (trial) 0
1937 1938 Oldham Athletic 59 14
1939 (Oldham Athletic) (3) (1)
Wisbech Town

Blackshaw, John CF
b Blackburn q1 1881 d 1962
Park Road
1900 Blackburn Rovers 2
Darwen
Trawden Forest

Blackshaw, William (Bill) OR/IR
b Ashton-under-Lyne 6/9/1920 d 1994
Audenshaw United
Ashton National
1938 Manchester City 3
Audenshaw United
1946 1948 Oldham Athletic 67 22
1949 1950 Crystal Palace 32 5
1951 Rochdale 0
Stalybridge Celtic

Blackstock, Thomas (Tommy) LB
b Kirkcaldy 1881 d 1907
Dunniker Rangers
Blue Bell
Raith Athletic
Leith Athletic
Cowdenbeath
1903 1906 Manchester United 34

Blackwell, Clifford Harry (Harry) GK
b Sheffield q1 1902
Heeley Friends
Scunthorpe & Lindsey United
Aberdeen
1930 1931 Clapton Orient 15
1932 Preston North End 0
Forfar Athletic

Blackwell, Ernest GK
b Sheffield 19/7/1894 d 1964
Atlas & Norfolk
Scunthorpe & Lindsey United
1919 1924 Sheffield United 47

From To | Apps Goal

Blackwell, John (Jack) IL/IR
b Eccleshall 28/10/1909
Chapel-en-le-Frith
1931 1932 Huddersfield Town 3
1932 1933 Charlton Athletic 34 7
1933 1934 Port Vale 24 5
Boston United
Ipswich Town

Blackwell, William Arthur OR
1932 Rotherham United 1

Blackwood, John CF
b Maine, USA 1877
Petershill
Celtic
Partick Thistle (loan)
1900 Woolwich Arsenal 17 6
Reading
Queen's Park Rangers
West Ham United
Royal Albert

Blades, William James OR
b Lincoln q4 1872 d 1926
1894 Lincoln City 3 1

Bladon, Ernest Albert CH
b Burton-on-Trent q1 1875 d 1923
1895 Burton Wanderers 19

Bladon, John James C IL
b Burton-on-Trent q3 1876 d 1942
Burton Wanderers
1900 Burton Swifts 22

Blagden, Jonathan IR
b Sheffield 12/4/1900 d 1964
Creswell Colliery
1921 West Bromwich Albion 16 2
Worksop Town

Blair, Charles Henry CH
b Chesterfield q4 1881 d 1961
Brampton Juniors
1903 Chesterfield Town 1
North Wingfield Red Rose

Blair, Daniel (Danny) RB/LB
b Parkhead 2/2/1905 d 1985
Caps: SLge 3/Scotland 8
Rasharkin
Cullybackey
Davenport Albion (Toronto)
Toronto Scottish
Willys Overland Motor Works
Providence Clamdiggers
Parkhead Juniors
Clyde
1931 1935 Aston Villa 129
1936 1938 Blackpool 121

Blair, Hugh OR
b Belfast 21/5/1909
Caps: IrLge 1/WLge 1/Ireland 4
Ivy Swift
Ballyclare Comrades
Queen's Island
Portadown
1931 Manchester City 0
1932 1934 Swansea Town 57 11
1935 Millwall 6 1

Blair, James (Jimmy) LH/IL
b Dumfries 1885 d 1913
Dumfries Volunteer
5th Kings Own Highlanders
Kilmarnock
1905 1906 Woolwich Arsenal 13 3
1906 1909 Manchester City 76
1910 1911 Bradford City 39 4
1912 Stockport County 23 1

Blair, James (Jimmy) LB
b Glenboig 11/5/1888 d 1964
Caps: SLge 3/Scotland 8
Bonnybridge Thistle
Glasgow Ashfield
Clyde
1914 Sheffield Wednesday 18
Clydebank (loan)
Alloa Athletic (loan)
Rangers (loan)
Rangers
1919 1920 Sheffield Wednesday 39
1920 1925 Cardiff City 177
1926 1927 Bournemouth & Boscombe Ath 61

From To | Apps Goal

Blair, James Alfred (Jimmy) IR/IL
b Whiteinch 6/1/1918 d 1983
Caps: Wales Sch/Scotland 1
1934 Cardiff City 0
1937 1946 Blackpool 53 8
1947 1949 Bournemouth & Boscombe Ath 80 8
1949 1952 Leyton Orient 104 26
Ramsgate Athletic
Canterbury City
Sheppey United

Blair, John CH
b Glasgow
Glasgow Benburb
1895 Grimsby Town 1
Stalybridge Rovers
1897 Sheffield United 1
Gravesend United
New Brompton

Blair, John (Jock) LB
b Kilwinning
Kilwinning Rangers
1919 1920 Coventry City 10
Caerphilly
Kilwinning Rangers

Blair, John Elliott CF
b Liverpool 21/10/1898 d 1974
Caps: England Amat
Liverpool University
Northern Nomads
1919 1921 Everton 5 3
Congleton Town
1922 1924 Oldham Athletic 26 16
Mold Town
Northern Nomads
1926 Arsenal 0
Ilford
Northern Nomads
Derbyshire Amateurs

Blair, John Guthrie IR/CF
b Neilston 23/8/1905 d 1972
Caps: LoI 1
Thornliebank
Neilston Park Villa
Neilston Victoria
Pollok
Third Lanark
1926 1927 Tottenham Hotspur 29 15
1927 1928 Sheffield United 26 7
Fordsons
Cork FC

Blair, Thomas GK
b Glasgow 24/2/1892 d 1961
Vale of Clyde
Kilmarnock
1921 Manchester City 38
Edmonton CNR (Canada)
Cumberland United (Canada)
Boston Wonder Workers
Fall River Marksmen
Hartford Americans
New Bedford Whalers
Fall River Marksmen
Pawtucket Rangers
Ayr United
Linfield
Sheppey United
Sittingbourne
Dundee United

Blake, Albert George LH
b Fulham q1 1900 d 1968
1928 Fulham 0
1929 1932 Watford 28
1933 1935 Queen's Park Rangers 81 9
Tunbridge Wells Rangers

Blake, Andrew LH/CH
b West Lothian 1904
Rosslyn Juniors
Cowdenbeath
Broxburn United
1927 1928 Crewe Alexandra 14
Chester
Nantwich
Stafford Rangers
Wardle & Barbridge

Blake, D IR
1897 Darwen 5 2

From To Apps Goal

Blake, Ernest OL
b Hednesford q2 1895 d 1965
Grimsby Rovers
1920 Grimsby Town 7
Grimsby Rovers
Haycroft Rovers
Grimsby Rovers

Blake, Gardner Wallis RH
b Linlithgow 1911
St Andrews United
Airdrieonians
Cowdenbeath
Airdrieonians
1933 Carlisle United 33 1
1934 1938 Crewe Alexandra 176 5

Blake, Herbert Charles Edwin (Bert) CH
b Bristol 16/3/1908 d 1986
Brislington Old Boys
1930 Bristol City 0
Yeovil & Petters United
1931 1932 Bristol Rovers 31 2
Bath City
Trowbridge Town

Blake, Herbert Edwin GK
b Bristol 26/8/1894 d 1958
Fishponds
1914 Bristol City 1
1919 Preston North End (trial) 0
Mid-Rhondda
1921 1923 Tottenham Hotspur 51
Kettering Town

Blake, John GK
b Stoneclough 1899
Farnworth Town
1924 Accrington Stanley 5
Herrington Swifts
Durham City
Ballymena

Blake, Ronald RH
b Eston 16/11/1901 d 1977
Lazenby
1924 Middlesbrough 0
1925 Wigan Borough 13
Eston United

Blake, Sydney (Syd) GK/OL
b Whitley Bay 1883 d 1929
Willington Athletic
Whitley Athletic
1905 Newcastle United 1
Queen's Park Rangers
Whitley Athletic
North Shields
1909 1912 Newcastle United 13
Coventry City

Blake, William Henry RB
b Worcester q2 1901 d 1963
Kidderminster Harriers
1924 1925 Crystal Palace 34
Kidderminster Harriers

Blakemore, Cecil IL
b Stourbridge 8/12/1897 d 1963
Redditch Town
Fairfield Villa
Stourbridge
Redditch Town
1922 1926 Crystal Palace 133 54
1927 1928 Bristol City 42 20
1929 1930 Brentford 77 28
1931 1932 Norwich City 70 29
1933 Swindon Town 26 8
Brierley Hill Alliance

Blakemore, Leonard (Len) GK
b Wheatley Hill q4 1904 d 1960
Washington Colliery
1926 Fulham 0
1927 1930 Newport County 72
Hereford United
Worcester City

Blakemore, Ralph Golding LB
b Cardiff 24/12/1908 d 1992
1930 Cardiff City 1
1931 Bradford City 0

Blakeney, James (Jim) CF
b Crawcrook 26/9/1919 d 1999
Spen Juniors
1937 Accrington Stanley 20 11
1938 Arsenal 0
Annfield Plain
Crawcrook Albion
Mickley Colliery Welfare

From To Apps Goal

Blakey, Charles Henry Smithson GK
b Lincoln q1 1896 d 1962
Lincoln YMCA
Newland Athletic
1919 Lincoln City 30
Doncaster Rovers
Boston Town

Blanchard, John William (William) RB/GK/LB
b Grimsby q2 1889 d 1963
Caps: England Amat
1907 1909 Grimsby Town 4
Grimsby Rangers
1911 1912 Grimsby Town 3
1913 Fulham 0
1913 1914 Grimsby Town 4

Blanckley, Herbert Sidney RH
b Penshaw 9/5/1899 d 1973
Houghton Rovers
Annfield Plain
Fatfield Albion
1922 Durham City 4
Scarborough

Bland, George Patrick (Pat) GK
b Tutbury 24/2/1915 d 1970
Horncastle Town
1936 Lincoln City 1
1938 Bradford Park Avenue 0
1945 Watford 0
Ransome & Marles

Bland, William Henry (Harry) RB/CH/RH
b Leeds 12/1/1898
Royal Navy
1927 1933 Plymouth Argyle 122 2
1934 Cardiff City 8

Blaney, George LH
b Workington 1905
1938 Carlisle United 2

Blanthorne, Robert (Bob) CF/IR
b Rock Ferry 8/1/1884 d 1965
Rock Ferry
Birkenhead
1906 Liverpool 2
1907 Grimsby Town 28 14
1908 Newcastle United 1
Hartlepools United

Bleakley, Thomas (Tommy) LH/CH
b Little Hulton 16/5/1893 d 1951
Clegg's Lane
Walkden Central
1914 Bolton Wanderers 0
1919 1929 Hull City 368 5
Goole Town
Bridlington Town
Wombwell

Bleasdale, G IR/CF
1897 1898 Darwen 32 2

Blencowe, Arthur George CF
b Brackley 5/11/1916 d 2005
Brackley Town
1937 Northampton Town 2
Banbury Spencer

Blenkinsop, Ernest (Ernie) LB
b Cudworth 20/4/1902 d 1969
Caps: FLge 8/England 26
Brierley Colliery
Cudworth United Methodists
1921 1922 Hull City 11
1922 1933 Sheffield Wednesday 393 5
1933 1937 Liverpool 71
1937 Cardiff City 10
Buxton
Hurst

Blessington, James (Jimmy) IR
b Linlithgow 28/2/1874 d 1939
Caps: SLge 6/Scotland 4
Harp Athletic
Hibernian
Leith Hibernian
Leith Athletic
St Bernard's (loan)
Celtic
1897 1898 Preston North End 15 1
1899 Derby County 2
Bristol City
Luton Town
1903 1908 Leicester Fosse 100 19

Blew, Frank William Elford LB/CF
b Wrexham q1 1902 d 1968
Caps: Wales Amat
1921 Wrexham 5 1
Llandudno
1923 Wrexham 7
Llandudno
1925 1926 Wrexham 16

From To Apps Goal

Blew, Horace Elford RB
b Wrexham q1 1878 d 1957
Caps: Wales Amat/Wales 22
Wrexham Old Boys
Rhostyllen
Wrexham
1905 Manchester United 1
Wrexham
1906 Manchester City 1
Wrexham

Blezzard, Rupert Joseph OL
b Manchester q4 1912
Kells
1935 Bournemouth & Boscombe Ath 1
Nuneaton Town

Blight, Albert Benjamin (Abe) CF
b Blackhill 5/1/1912 d 1961
Blackhill
1933 1934 Barnsley 45 36
Annfield Plain
Ashington

Blinkhorn, Frederick (Fred) LB
b Bolton 2/8/1901 d 1983
Horwich RMI
1925 1926 Burnley 15

Bliss, Arnold Percy Donald CH/RB
b Wolstanton 8/11/1909 d 1975
Dartford
1931 1932 Port Vale 9
Stalybridge Celtic
1933 Rochdale 5
Stafford Rangers

Bliss, Herbert (Bert) IL
b Willenhall 29/3/1890 d 1968
Caps: England 1
New Invention
Bilston United
Willenhall Swifts
Willenhall Pickwick
1911 1922 Tottenham Hotspur 194 92
1922 1924 Clapton Orient 70 20
1925 Bournemouth & Boscombe Ath 6

Bliss, Wallace CF
b Shrewsbury q4 1871 d 1951
1892 Burslem Port Vale 13 3

Blood, John Foster (Jack) LB
b Nottingham 2/10/1914 d 1992
Johnson & Barnes
1938 Notts County 8
1939 1947 Exeter City 39 1
1939 (Exeter City) (3)
Peterborough United

Blood, Robert (Bobby) CF/IR
b Harpur Hill 18/3/1894 d 1988
Buxton
Buxton Lime Firms
Leek Alexandra
1919 1920 Port Vale 53 44
1920 1924 West Bromwich Albion 53 26
1924 1926 Stockport County 42 15
Winsford United
Mossley
Buxton
Ashton National

Bloomer, Philip LB
b Cradley q4 1875 d 1896
1895 Derby County 1

Bloomer, Stephen (Steve) IR
b Cradley 20/1/1874 d 1938
Caps: FLge 15/England 23
Derby Swifts
Tutbury Hawthorn
1892 1905 Derby County 376 240
1905 1909 Middlesbrough 125 59
1910 1913 Derby County 98 53

Blore, Vincent (Vince) GK
b Uttoxeter 25/2/1907 d 1997
Uttoxeter Amateurs
Burton Town
1932 Aston Villa 0
1933 1934 Derby County 15
1935 West Ham United 9
1936 1937 Crystal Palace 33
1938 Exeter City 4

Blott, Cyril Leslie Coldham CF
b Southend-on-Sea 10/8/1917 d 1994
Romford
1937 1938 Charlton Athletic 16 4

From To Apps Goal

Blott, Samuel Prince (Prince) LH/OL/IL
b Holloway 1/1/1886 d 1969
Southend Athletic
Southend United
Bradford Park Avenue
Southend United
1909 1912 Manchester United 19 2
Plymouth Argyle
1920 1921 Newport County 16 1
Dartford

Blow, Edward Percy (Percy 'Corky') LH
b North Hykeham 16/11/1877 d 1938
Blue Star (Lincoln)
1900 1905 Lincoln City 162 1
Horncastle United
Bracebridge

Blower, Samuel (Sam) CF
b South Kirkby 1887
Wath Athletic
1907 Gainsborough Trinity 4 2
Mexborough Town

Bloxham, Albert OR
b Solihull 29/11/1905 d 1996
Overton-on-Dee
Oswestry Town
Torquay United
1927 Birmingham 3 1
Rhyl Athletic
1928 Chesterfield 7 1
Raith Rovers
Yeovil & Petters United
1931 1932 Millwall 70 11

Bluer, Alfred William (Alf) CH/LH
b Rotherham q1 1890 d 1947
Rotherham County
1913 1914 Stockport County 32
Gillingham

Bluff, Edgar Underwood IR
b Sheffield 19/3/1882 d 1952
High Hazels (Sheffield)
Yorkshire Light Infantry
Reading
1st Army Corps
Southampton
1905 1907 Sheffield United 65 18
1907 Birmingham 9 1
St Helens Town

Blunt, Edwin (Eddie) LH/RH
b Tunstall 21/5/1918 d 1993
Lichfield Town
1936 Port Vale 0
1937 1948 Northampton Town 87 2
1939 (Northampton Town) (1)
1949 Accrington Stanley 9 1
Northwich Victoria
Congleton Town
Macclesfield

Blunt, John Arthur RH
b Wolverhampton
Caps: England Sch
1924 Wolverhampton Wanderers 0
1925 Stockport County 10

Blunt, Sidney LH
b Bilston 13/4/1902 d 1965
1920 Wolverhampton Wanderers 0
Worcester City
Bilston United
Lichfield City
1924 1925 Port Vale 61 1
Shrewsbury Town
Hednesford Town

Blunt, William (Billy) CF
b Stafford q2 1889 d 1935
Stafford Rangers
1908 1911 Wolverhampton Wanderers 58 38
Bristol Rovers
Stafford Rangers
Hednesford Town
Stafford Rangers

Bly, William (Billy) GK
b Newcastle 15/5/1920 d 1982
Walker Celtic
1938 1959 Hull City 403
Weymouth

Blyth, George GK
b Motherwell 18/10/1906 d 1984
Perth Roselea
Perth YMCA
Newburgh West End
Hibernian
St Johnstone
1935 1937 Notts County 99
Grantham

From	To		Apps	Goal
		Blyth, James Banes (Jim)	CH	
		b Gorebridge 9/8/1911	d 1979	
		Newtongrange		
		Arniston Rangers		
1936		Tottenham Hotspur	11	
1937	1938	Hull City	72	
		Heart of Midlothian		
		Falkirk (loan)		
		St Johnstone		
		Blyth, Robert Fleming (Bob)	RH/OL/LH	
		b Muirkirk 16/10/1869	d 1941	
		Glenbuck Athletic		
		Middlesbrough Ironopolis		
		Cowlairs		
		Rangers		
1894	1896	Preston North End	73	7
		Dundee		
1897	1898	Preston North End	41	1
		Portsmouth		
		Blyth, Robert Roberts Taylor	OR	
		b Muirkirk 2/6/1900		
1921		Portsmouth	8	2
1922		Southampton	8	
		Boston Wonder Workers		
		Blyth, Thomas Hope	CF	
		b Seaham Harbour 16/10/1876	d 1949	
		Durham University		
1896		Newcastle United	1	1
		Blyth, William John (Billy)	RH	
		b Glenbuck 1883		
		Glenbuck Athletic		
		Portsmouth		
1905		Preston North End	1	
		Carlisle United		
		Blyth, William Naismith (Billy)	IL/LH/IR	
		b Dalkeith 17/6/1895	d 1968	
		Wemyss Athletic		
1913		Manchester City	0	
1914	1928	Arsenal	314	45
		Third Lanark (loan)		
1929	1930	Birmingham	21	4
1931		Arsenal	0	
		Blythe, James R (Jim)	CF	
1911		Nottingham Forest	1	
		Blythe, John (Joe)	LH	
		b Tweedmouth 1877		
		Delaval Villa		
		Blyth		
		Jarrow		
1898	1901	Everton	34	1
		West Ham United		
		Millwall Athletic		
		Watford		
		Blyth Spartans		
		Blythe, Thomas Henry (Tom)	IL/CF	
		b Shoreham q4 1872	d 1944	
		Grimsby All Saints		
1897		Grimsby Town	3	1
		Cleethorpes Swifts		
1898		Grimsby Town	1	
		Grimsby All Saints		
		Boag, John M	CF	
		b Glasgow 6/4/1874	d 1954	
		Cowlairs		
		Glasgow Ashfield		
		East Stirlingshire		
1896	1903	Derby County	117	27
		Brentford		
		Boardman, Albert Charles	GK/LB	
		b Stoke-on-Trent q1 1872	d 1943	
1894		Burslem Port Vale	0	
1895	1896	Stoke	4	
		Dresden United		
		Boardman, Benjamin (Ben)	IR/OR	
		b Ashton-under-Lyne 28/4/1899	d 1968	
		Macclesfield		
1924	1930	Stockport County	185	31
1931		Manchester City	0	
		Boardman, Harry C	RB	
		b Newcastle		
		Caps: England Amat		
		Grangetown Athletic		
1909		Middlesbrough	4	
		Bishop Auckland		
		Middlesbrough		
		Boardman, William (Billy)	OL/IR	
		b Urmston 14/10/1895	d 1968	
		Eccles Borough		
1920		Leeds United	4	
1923	1926	Doncaster Rovers	122	20
1927		Crewe Alexandra	13	2
		Chester		

From	To		Apps	Goal
		Boast, Ernest	GK	
		b Sheffield q2 1880	d 1961	
		Chelmsford Town		
1903		Lincoln City	21	
		Bocking, William (Bill)	RB	
		b Stockport 11/6/1902	d 1985	
		Hyde United		
1924	1930	Stockport County	262	6
1930	1933	Everton	15	
1934	1937	Stockport County	104	
		Boddington, Harold	OL	
		b Darlington		
1903		Middlesbrough	1	
		Darlington		
		Boden, John William	CH	
		b Northwich q1 1882	d 1946	
		Northwich Victoria		
1902	1904	Glossop	91	4
1905		Clapton Orient	27	5
1905	1906	Aston Villa	17	2
		Reading		
		Croydon Common		
		Plymouth Argyle		
		New Brompton		
		Northwich Victoria		
		Boden, Rowland	LB	
		b Northwich q1 1883	d 1952	
		Earlestown		
1909		Burnley	5	
		Witton Albion		
		Halifax Town		
		Bodle, Harold	IL/LH/RH	
		b Adwick-le-Street 4/10/1920	d 2005	
		Ridgehill Athletic		
1938		Rotherham United	9	
1938	1948	Birmingham	94	32
1948	1951	Bury	119	40
1952		Stockport County	29	6
1953	1956	Accrington Stanley	94	13
		Boe, James	GK	
		b Gateshead 5/1/1891	d 1973	
		Gateshead Rodsley		
1914		Sunderland	1	
		Southport Central		
		Boggie, Alexander (Alex)	CF	
		b Abbotshall 31/1/1870	d 1923	
		Burton Swifts		
		Ardwick		
		West Manchester		
1893	1895	Burton Swifts	68	29
		Swindon Town		
		Kirkcaldy		
		Bohills, George Henry	RH	
		b New Delaval q4 1890	d 1964	
		Bedlington		
1912		Barnsley	1	
		Boileau, Henry Arthur (Harry)	LH	
		b Bedworth 31/7/1910	d 1981	
		Bedworth Town		
1931	1938	Coventry City	157	
1939		(Coventry City)	(3)	
		Bokas, Frank	RH/LH	
		b Bellshill 13/5/1914	d 1996	
		Kirkintilloch Rob Roy		
1935		Blackpool	6	
1936	1938	Barnsley	89	4
1939		(Barnsley)	(1)	
1945		Carlisle United	0	
		Gainsborough Trinity		
		Grantham		
		Bolam, David Robert	IL/IR	
		b Newcastle 24/1/1898	d 1983	
		Chester-le-Street		
1924		Lincoln City	3	1
1925		Exeter City	1	
		Chester-le-Street		
		Bolam, Robert Coltman (Bob)	OR	
		b Tynemouth q2 1896	d 1964	
		Lewin's Temperance (Birtley)		
		Birtley		
1919	1921	Sheffield United	33	2
1922		Darlington	12	2
1923		South Shields	32	1
1924		Queen's Park Rangers	2	
		Lewin's Temperance (Birtley)		
		Birtley		
		Bolan, Leonard Arthur (Len)	OR/IR	
		b Lowestoft 16/3/1909	d 1973	
		Lowestoft Town		
1930		Norwich City	0	
1931		West Ham United	0	
1933	1934	Tottenham Hotspur	10	3
1935	1938	Southend United	104	20

From	To		Apps	Goal
		Boland, Charles	IL	
		b Kilmarnock 5/10/1895	d 1969	
		Lilymont		
		Kilmarnock		
		Queen of the South		
1921		Fulham	2	1
		Queen of the South		
		Galston		
		Arthurlie		
		Galston		
		Beith		
		Boland, George (Dicky)	OL	
		b Marley Hill 6/10/1902	d 1977	
		White-le-Head Rangers		
1925	1927	Hartlepools United	64	9
1928		Reading	1	
1929		Fulham	6	
1931	1933	Gateshead	92	16
1934		Crewe Alexandra	20	2
		Walker Celtic		
		Boland, Nicholas (Nick)	IL	
		b Bradford, Lancashire 28/4/1910	d 2007	
		Northwich Victoria		
1933		Wolverhampton Wanderers	0	
1934	1935	Southport	29	2
		Altrincham		
		Brockhouses		
		Bolland, William Thomas (Tommy)	OL	
		b Darlington 12/1884	d 1967	
		Washington United		
1907	1908	Sheffield Wednesday	13	1
1920		Swindon Town	6	
		Bath City		
		Bollington, John Edward (Jack)	RH	
		b Belper q2 1892	d 1924	
1920		Southend United	1	
1920		Brighton & Hove Albion	14	
		Bolsover, Henry	GK	
		b Sheffield 1875	d 1939	
		Sheffield		
1893		Sheffield United	0	
		Sheffield		
1899		Sheffield Wednesday	2	
		Sheffield		
		Bolt, J	OR	
1897		Darwen	4	
		Bolton, Arthur Frederick	CF	
		b Hexham 21/11/1912	d 2001	
		Ashington		
1938		Sunderland	8	1
		Bolton, Fred	OL	
		Great Harwood		
1921		Accrington Stanley	1	
		Bolton, Hugh	IR/IL	
		b Port Glasgow 1881		
		Clydeville		
		Port Glasgow Athletic		
1905		Newcastle United	1	
1905	1908	Everton	75	27
1908	1909	Bradford Park Avenue	30	7
		Morton		
		Glentoran		
		Johnstone		
		Bolton, James McFarlane (Jimmy)	LH	
		b Clydebank 22/3/1906		
		Bridgeton Waverley		
		St Johnstone		
1930	1931	Clapton Orient	37	1
1932		York City	7	
		Coleraine		
		Bolton, Ronald	IR	
1898		Bolton Wanderers	2	
		Bolton, William	OL	
1914		Burnley	1	
		Bonar, James (Jim)	IR	
		b Scotland 1866		
		Thornliebank		
1888		Accrington	17	
		Bonass, Albert Edward	OL	
		b Great Ouseburn q2 1911	d 1945	
		Dringhouses		
		York Wednesday		
1932		Darlington	6	1
1933		York City	6	
1934	1935	Hartlepools United	77	31
1936	1938	Chesterfield	98	26
1939		Queen's Park Rangers	(3)	

From	To		Apps	Goal
		Bond, Anthony	OR	
		b Preston q3 1888	d 1944	
		Oswaldtwistle Rovers		
1907		Preston North End	0	
		Ashton Town		
1909		Bradford City	1	
		Lancaster Town		
		Dick, Kerr's XI		
		Bond, Anthony (Tony)	OR	
		b Preston 27/12/1913	d 1993	
1930		Preston North End	0	
		Dick, Kerr's XI		
1932		Blackburn Rovers	0	
		Dick, Kerr's XI		
		Chorley		
1936		Wolverhampton Wanderers	0	
1937		Torquay United	15	
		Chorley		
		Preston North End		
1945		Southport	0	
1946		Accrington Stanley	29	4
		Fleetwood		
		Bacup Borough		
		Bamber Bridge		
		Bond, Benjamin (Benny)	OR	
		b Wolverhampton 10/1904		
		Upper Gornal		
1926	1930	Birmingham	82	13
		Bond, George Albert	CF/OR	
		b Ilford 11/2/1910	d 1982	
		Redhill		
1931	1933	Millwall	60	23
		Northfleet		
1935		Gillingham	9	2
		(Malta)		
		Bond, John	OR	
		b Preston 5/1894		
1913		Preston North End	1	1
		Motherwell		
		Lancaster Town		
		Dick, Kerr's XI		
		Lancaster Town		
		Morecambe		
		Bond, Richard (Dickie)	OR	
		b Preston 14/12/1883	d 1955	
		Caps: FLge 1/England 8		
		Royal Field Artillery		
1902	1908	Preston North End	148	34
1909	1921	Bradford City	301	60
1922		Blackburn Rovers	24	2
		Lancaster Town		
		Garstang		
		Bond, Samuel (Sam)	LH	
		b Stockport		
		Eccles United		
1927		Stockport County	1	
		Bond, Thomas (Tommy)	OR/IR	
		b Barrow		
		Barrow Butchers		
1922	1923	Barrow	4	
		Bone, John (Johnnie)	IL	
		b Ayr		
1901		Everton	2	
		Bonham, John William	IR	
		b Wallsend 11/1/1895	d 1973	
		Wallsend Park Villa		
1921		Lincoln City	1	
		Bonsall, Cyril	OL	
		b East Kirkby q3 1903		
		New Hucknall Colliery		
1922	1923	Luton Town	8	2
		Sutton Town		
		Bonthron, Robert Pollock	RB	
		b Burntisland 1880		
		Raith Athletic		
		Raith Rovers		
		Dundee		
1903	1906	Manchester United	119	3
1907		Sunderland	22	1
		Northampton Town		
1910		Birmingham	11	1
		Airdrieonians (loan)		
		Leith Athletic		
		Boocock, Irvine	LB	
		b Cleckheaton 27/2/1890	d 1941	
		Caps: FLge 3		
		Sunfield Rovers		
1909	1921	Bradford City	169	1
1922		Darlington	13	
		Booker, ?	RB	
1893		Northwich Victoria	1	

From	To		Apps	Goal
		Booker, ?	IR	
1901		Burton United	1	1
		Booker, John W	LH	
		Civil Service		
		Poole		
		Nunhead		
1924		Millwall Athletic	1	
		Nunhead		
		Erith & Belvedere		
		Booker, Kenneth (Ken)	CH/LH	
		b Sheffield 3/3/1918	d 1997	
		Dronfield Town		
1938	1951	Chesterfield	183	4
1939		(Chesterfield)	(2)	
1952		Shrewsbury Town	9	
		Winsford United		
		Bookman (Buckhalter), Louis James Arthur Oscar	OL	
		b Zagaren, Lithuania 6/11/1890	d 1943	
		Caps: Ireland Amat/Ireland 4		
		Dublin Adelaide		
		Frankfort (Dublin)		
		Belfast Celtic		
1911	1913	Bradford City	32	2
1914		West Bromwich Albion	16	1
1920	1921	Luton Town	72	4
1923		Port Vale	10	
		Shelbourne		
		Boon, Reginald (Reggie)	CF	
		b Wolverhampton 1880		
		Stafford Rangers		
1905		Wolverhampton Wanderers	3	1
		Tettenhall		
		Featherstone Rangers		
		Boot, Edmund (Eddie)	LH	
		b Laughton Common 13/10/1915	d 1999	
		Aughton		
		Denaby United		
1935	1936	Sheffield United	41	
1936	1951	Huddersfield Town	305	5
1939		(Huddersfield Town)	(3)	
		Boot, Leonard George William	GK	
		b West Bromwich 4/11/1899	d 1937	
		York City		
1923	1924	Huddersfield Town	10	
1925		Fulham	9	
1926		Bradford City	7	
1927		Nottingham Forest	2	
		Caernarvon Athletic		
		Worcester City		
		Boote, George	GK	
		b Stoke-on-Trent q2 1878	d 1930	
		St Peter's Bards		
1901		Stoke	1	
		Lonsdale Rovers		
		Halmerend Rovers		
		Silverdale Town		
1905		Burslem Port Vale	3	
		Knutton Rovers		
		Booth, C	RH	
1914		Glossop	3	
		Booth, Charles	OL/IR	
		b Gainsborough 1869	d 1898	
		Gainsborough Trinity		
		Hurst		
1889	1891	Wolverhampton Wanderers	61	9
1893		Woolwich Arsenal	16	2
		Loughborough		
		Booth, Curtis (Tommy)	IL	
		b Gateshead 12/10/1891	d 1949	
		Wallsend Elm Villa		
1914	1919	Newcastle United	34	6
1920	1922	Norwich City	62	11
1923		Accrington Stanley	1	
		Booth, Frank	OL/IL	
		b Hyde q1 1882	d 1919	
		Caps: England 1		
1900		Glossop	0	
1901		Stockport County	6	1
1902	1905	Manchester City	94	18
1906	1908	Bury	58	4
		Clyde		
1911		Manchester City	4	
		Booth, George R	CF	
		b Edgworth 1882		
		Turton		
1902		Bury	5	1
		Booth, Jeremiah (Jerry)	RB	
		Burnley Belvedere		
1903		Burnley	1	

From	To		Apps	Goal
		Booth, Joseph (Joe)	IL/CH	
		b Edgworth		
		Rochdale		
1898	1899	Bury	7	1
		Booth, Llewellyn	IR/IL	
		b Merthyr Tydfil 28/2/1912	d 1984	
		Merthyr Town		
1934		Swansea Town	1	
		Bangor City		
1936	1938	Bristol City	63	22
1939		(Bristol City)	(2)	
		Booth, Robert (Bobby)	LH/RH	
		b West Hartlepool 22/5/1892	d 1974	
		Spennymoor United		
1912	1919	Blackpool	95	5
1920	1921	Birmingham	8	1
1922		Southend United	28	1
1923	1924	Swansea Town	36	4
1924		Merthyr Town	13	1
1925		New Brighton	12	1
		Fleetwood		
		Skelmersdale United		
		Pleasley Cross Athletic		
		Booth, Samuel (Sam)	RB/LB	
		b Northwich 30/1/1910	d 1956	
		Northwich Victoria		
		Witton Albion		
		Lostock		
1930		Middlesbrough (trial)	0	
		Margate		
1935	1937	Crystal Palace	24	
1938		Southport	2	
		Yeovil & Petters United		
		Booth, Thomas Edward (Tom)	CH/RH	
		b Ardwick 25/4/1874	d 1939	
		Caps: FLge 4/England 2		
		Hooley Hill		
		Ashton North End		
1896	1899	Blackburn Rovers	111	10
1900	1907	Everton	175	9
1908		Preston North End	0	
		Carlisle United		
		Booth, William	OL	
		b Stockport 10/1880		
		Edge Lane		
1900		Newton Heath	2	
		Booth, William (Billy)	CH	
		b Sheffield 9/5/1886	d 1963	
		Caps: SoLge 7		
		Thorpe Hesley Parish Church		
1907		Sheffield United	1	
		Brighton & Hove Albion		
		Castleford Town		
		Worthing		
		Booth, William Samuel (Sam)	CH	
		b Hove 7/7/1920	d 1990	
		Hove Penguins		
1938		Brighton & Hove Albion	0	
1938		Port Vale	9	
1939		Cardiff City	(3)	
1947	1948	Brighton & Hove Albion	28	6
		Hastings United		
		Boothman, James	LB	
		b Blackburn q2 1890		
		Blackburn Trinity		
1919		Blackburn Rovers	2	
		Lancaster Town		
		Fleetwood		
		Lancaster Town		
		Darwen		
		Booton, Harold	RB	
		b Annesley 2/3/1906	d 1976	
		Annesley Colliery		
		Shirebrook		
1929	1935	Birmingham	150	2
1935		Luton Town	7	
		Atherstone Town		
		Boots, George Horace	GK	
		b Newport 5/5/1911	d 1971	
		Somerton Park Juniors		
1930	1933	Newport County	3	
		Lovells Athletic		
		Boreham, Frederick (Fred)	GK	
		b Rye 8/7/1885	d 1951	
		Tunbridge Wells Rangers		
		Leyton		
1908	1909	Tottenham Hotspur	20	
		Leyton		

From	To		Apps	Goal
		Boreham, Reginald Walter (Reg)	IL	
		b High Wycombe 27/5/1896	d 1976	
		Caps: England Amat		
		Wycombe Wanderers		
1920		Notts County	3	
		Wycombe Wanderers		
1921	1923	Arsenal	51	18
		Wycombe Wanderers		
		Borland, John Thompson Mathieson	OL	
		b Rutherglen 9/11/1903	d 1979	
		Rutherglen Glencairn		
		Raith Rovers		
		Kilmarnock		
		Cowdenbeath (loan)		
		Hamilton Academical		
1927		Charlton Athletic	5	1
1928		Merthyr Town	41	2
1929		Southend United	21	3
1929		Barrow (trial)	0	
		Alloa Athletic		
		Rutherglen Glencairn		
		Stenhousemuir		
		Borland, William Barr (Billy)	CH	
		b Darvel 21/8/1888	d 1915	
		Darvel Juniors		
1910		Fulham	3	
		Galston		
		Dumfries		
		Borrows, John Edward	RB	
		b Manchester 19/1/1917	d 1989	
1938		Chelsea	0	
1939		Mansfield Town	(2)	
		Borthwick, John James Blacklaw	CH	
		b Leith 15/2/1886	d 1942	
		Royal Oak		
		Edinburgh Clifton		
		Wemyss Violet		
		Lochgelly United		
		Hibernian		
1907	1910	Everton	25	
		Millwall Athletic		
		East Fife		
		Cowdenbeath		
		Hibernian		
		Borthwick, Walter	RB/IR	
		b Newington 9/1/1899		
		Broxburn Shamrock		
		East Fife		
		Cowdenbeath		
		Hibernian		
		Partick Thistle		
1921		Bristol City	1	
		Cowdenbeath		
1922		Hartlepools United	2	
		Nithsdale Wanderers		
		Bosbury, Charles Edwin (Charlie)	OR	
		b Newhaven 5/11/1897	d 1929	
		Pemberton Billings		
1921		Southampton	0	
1922		Birmingham	15	
1925		Preston North End	2	
1926	1928	Lincoln City	85	30
		Bosomworth, Alexander Charles (Alex)	RH/IR	
		b Guisborough 22/9/1904	d 1987	
		Eston Juniors		
		Redcar		
1923		Middlesbrough	0	
1924	1925	Darlington	8	
1926		Barrow	35	6
1927		Bradford Park Avenue	0	
		West Stanley (trial)		
		Grantham Town		
		Woolwich Borough Council Ath		
		Bosse, Percy Llewellyn	RH	
		b Cardiff 18/10/1914	d 1994	
1935		Cardiff City	0	
1936		Arsenal	0	
1937	1938	Northampton Town	34	3
		Bossons, William Horace	GK	
		b Talke q2 1901	d 1970	
1924		Stockport County	0	
		Macclesfield		
1927		Nelson	4	
		Whitchurch		
		Winsford United		
		Oswestry Town		
		Bostock, Archibald Millership E (Archie)	CF	
		b Brecon 7/1869	d 1926	
		Caps: Wales 1		
		Singers		
		Smethwick		
		Birmingham St George's		
		Shrewsbury Town		
1892	1893	West Bromwich Albion	26	11
1895		Burton Wanderers	1	1

From	To		Apps	Goal
		Bostock, Joseph	LB	
1905		Stockport County	1	
		Boston, Henry James (Harry)	OR	
		b Nantwich 20/10/1899	d 1973	
		Shavington Town		
		Nantwich		
1923	1928	Bolton Wanderers	37	2
1929	1930	West Bromwich Albion	27	6
1931		Swansea Town	19	
		Nantwich		
		Boswell, William (Bill)	IR/CF/CH	
		b Cradley Heath 5/8/1902	d 1977	
		Tansey Green Rovers		
		Coombs Wood Colliery		
1924		Walsall	8	1
1926	1927	Wolverhampton Wanderers	9	5
1927		Gillingham	17	4
		Worcester City		
		Burton Town		
1931		Oldham Athletic	2	1
		Burton Town		
		Kidderminster Harriers		
		Shirley Town		
		Solihull Town		
		Bosworth, Samuel	OR	
		b Annesley q2 1877	d 1945	
		Castle Donington		
		Long Eaton Rangers		
1898		Loughborough	8	1
1898		Derby County	2	1
1898		Sheffield Wednesday	6	
		Ilkeston United		
		Castle Donington		
		Whitwick White Cross		
		South Wigston Albion		
		Bott, Vincent Eric (Eric)	IR	
		b Grantham 3/5/1916	d 1975	
		Grantham		
1935	1936	Doncaster Rovers	8	1
		Peterborough United		
		Grantham		
		Bott, Wilfred (Wilf)	OL/OR	
		b Featherstone 25/4/1907	d 1992	
		Edlington Colliery Welfare		
1926	1930	Doncaster Rovers	111	32
1930	1934	Huddersfield Town	110	25
1934	1935	Newcastle United	37	11
1936	1938	Queen's Park Rangers	75	34
		Lancaster Town		
		Colchester United		
		Guildford City		
		Botto, Lewis Anthony	GK	
		b Jarrow 12/7/1898	d 1953	
		Jarrow Rangers		
		Hebburn Colliery		
1923	1924	Durham City	49	
		Shildon		
1926		Durham City	32	
1927		Wolverhampton Wanderers	16	
1928		Norwich City	2	
1929		Nelson	1	
		Jarrow		
		Bottomley, William (Bill)	RH/CH	
		b Mossley q3 1886		
		Greenfield Athletic		
		Edgehill (Delph)		
		Mossley Britannia		
		Oldham Athletic (trial)		
		Failsworth		
1907		Oldham Athletic	13	
1908	1914	Manchester City	98	2
		Bottrill, Allan	OL	
		b Eston q1 1905	d 1929	
		Whitby Town		
1921		Middlesbrough	0	
1924		Nelson	1	
		York City		
		South Bank East End		
		Bottrill, Walter Gibson (Billy)	IR/OR/CF	
		b Eston 8/1/1903	d 1986	
		South Bank		
1922	1923	Middlesbrough	17	
1924	1927	Nelson	121	35
1928		Rotherham United	30	11
1929		York City	39	18
1930	1932	Wolverhampton Wanderers	101	42
1933	1934	Huddersfield Town	12	1
1934		Chesterfield	16	5

From	To		Apps	Goal
Boucher, Thomas Charles (Tom)			CF/IL	
b West Bromwich 1873				
		Stourbridge		
1896	1898	Notts County	79	32
		Bedminster		
		Bristol Rovers		
1901	1902	Bristol City	51	14
		New Brompton		
		Maidstone United		
Boughey, Joseph			RH/OL	
b Audley q3 1873				
1893	1895	Burslem Port Vale	12	
		Audley		
Bould, George			IR	
b Tettenhall 1885			d 1951	
		Goldthorn Alexandra		
		St Saviour's		
		Penkridge		
1907		Wolverhampton Wanderers	6	1
		Darlaston		
		Bilston Town		
Boullemier, Leon Autonin			GK	
b Stoke-on-Trent q3 1874			d 1954	
1892		Stoke	0	
1893		Burslem Port Vale	0	
		Stockport County		
1895	1896	Lincoln City	49	
		Reading		
		Brighton United		
		Northampton Town		
Boullemier, Lucien Emile			RH/CH	
b Stoke-on-Trent q1 1877			d 1949	
		Stoke Alliance		
		Chesterton White Star		
		Stone Town		
1896		Stoke	7	
1898	1902	Burslem Port Vale	136	6
		Philadlphia Hibernians		
		Northampton Town		
1905		Burslem Port Vale	1	
		Northern Nomads		
		North Staffs Nomads		
Boulter, Leslie Mervyn (Les)			IL	
b Ebbw Vale 31/8/1913			d 1975	
Caps: Wales Sch/Wales 1				
		Cwm Athletic		
1932	1938	Charlton Athletic	167	27
1938		Brentford	16	1
1939		(Brentford)	(3)	(1)
		Yeovil Town		
Boulton, Alfred			RB	
b Kirkham q3 1879			d 1916	
1900	1901	Blackpool	54	1
Boulton, Frank Preece			GK	
b Chipping Sodbury 12/8/1917			d 1987	
1934		Bristol City	0	
		Bath City		
1936	1937	Arsenal	36	
1938	1945	Derby County	39	
1939		(Derby County)	(3)	
1946	1949	Swindon Town	97	
1950		Crystal Palace	0	
		Bedford Town		
Boulton, John William Charles			LB	
b Southwick, County Durham q4 1899			d 1959	
		Southwick (Co Durham)		
1923		Hartlepools United	4	
		Southwick (Co Durham)		
Boulton, Redvers Wilfred			CF/OR	
b Rotherham 8/3/1900			d 1976	
		Greasborough WMC		
1923	1925	Rotherham County	11	
Boundy, Ronald H			IL	
b Wallasey q1 1911			d 1934	
		Wallasey		
1933		Exeter City	2	
1934		Southport	0	
Bourne, Alfred			GK	
b Kidsgrove 1898				
1919	1921	Port Vale	55	
Bourne, AWB			OR	
		Liverpool Road		
1902		Burslem Port Vale	3	
Bourne, Hubert E			IL/RH	
b Bromsgrove 1/1/1895			d 1965	
		Manchester United		
1919	1920	Aston Villa	7	2

From	To		Apps	Goal
Bourne, John Thomas (Jack)			GK	
b Wolstanton 29/1/1901			d 1992	
		Kidsgrove Wellington		
1924		Bolton Wanderers	3	
		Eccles United		
1926	1927	Swindon Town	41	
		Sandbach Ramblers		
		Manchester North End		
Bourne, Richard (Dickie)			OL/IL	
b Manchester q3 1878			d 1957	
		Roundel (Sheffield)		
1900	1901	Sheffield United	8	1
1902		Barnsley	19	
1902	1904	Preston North End	62	6
1905	1906	Clapton Orient	56	2
1906	1907	West Bromwich Albion	9	1
		Walsall		
Bourton, Clarence Frederick Thomas (Clarrie)			CF/IR	
b Paulton 30/9/1908			d 1981	
		Paulton United		
1927		Bristol City	4	1
1928	1930	Blackburn Rovers	63	37
1931	1937	Coventry City	228	173
1937		Plymouth Argyle	8	3
1937	1938	Bristol City	54	13
1939		(Bristol City)	(3)	(1)
Boutwood, John Robert			OR	
b Luton q1 1879			d 1958	
1898		Luton Town	1	
Bovill, John McKeown			IR/CF	
b Rutherglen 21/2/1886			d 1935	
		Strathclyde Juniors		
		Rangers		
1907		Blackburn Rovers	0	
1908		Chesterfield Town	18	3
1911	1913	Liverpool	27	7
		Linfield		
Bow, James (Jimmy)			IL	
b Lochore 14/12/1910			d 1973	
		Lochore Welfare		
		Hearts o' Beath		
		Hamilton Academical		
		St Cuthbert Wanderers (loan)		
		Leith Athletic		
		St Bernard's		
1934		Clapton Orient	0	
1936		Gateshead	1	
		Lochore		
Bow, William			IR	
b Edinburgh 1884			d 1929	
		Broxburn		
		St Bernard's		
1902	1903	Blackburn Rovers	20	2
		Darwen		
		Nelson		
		Oswaldtwistle		
		Great Harwood		
Bow, William John			GK	
b Penrhiwceiber 14/11/1900			d 1985	
1923	1924	Merthyr Town	9	
1925		Bournemouth & Boscombe Ath	1	
1926		Coventry City	0	
		Merthyr Town		
Bowater, George Albert			OL	
b Shirebrook 26/10/1911			d 1966	
		Shirebrook		
1931	1932	Mansfield Town	60	28
1933		Bradford Park Avenue	6	1
1934		York City	30	11
		Burton Town		
		Frickley Colliery		
		Peterborough United		
Bowden, Edwin Raymond (Ray)			IR/CF/IL	
b Looe 13/9/1909			d 1998	
Caps: FLge 2/England 6				
		Looe		
1926	1932	Plymouth Argyle	145	83
1932	1937	Arsenal	123	42
1937	1938	Newcastle United	48	6
1939		(Newcastle United)	(3)	(3)
Bowden, Frederick (Frank)			OL	
b King's Heath 11/1904				
		Darwen (Shirebrook)		
1925		Birmingham	1	
		Kidderminster Harriers		
		Stourbridge		
1928		West Ham United	0	
1929	1931	Coventry City	38	8
		Evesham Town		
		Kidderminster Harriers		
1933		Chesterfield	0	
1934		Coventry City	0	
1935		West Ham United	0	

From	To		Apps	Goal
Bowden, James William			CH	
b Wolverhampton 8/1880			d 1951	
		Yardley Methodists		
		Erdington		
		Handsworth Rovers		
1904		West Bromwich Albion	8	
		Southampton		
1907		Grimsby Town	19	
		Stourbridge		
Bowden, Joseph (Joe)			CF	
		Thornsett United		
1906		Bury	1	
		Rossendale United		
		Hyde		
		Rochdale		
		Thornsett United		
Bowden, Joseph			CH/IL	
1912	1913	Glossop	6	
Bowden, Oswald (Ossie)			IR/IL	
b Byker 7/9/1912			d 1977	
		Newcastle United Swifts		
1932	1933	Derby County	10	1
1935	1936	Nottingham Forest	14	3
1937		Brighton & Hove Albion	1	
1938		Southampton	2	
Bowdler, John Charles Henry (Charlie)			OL	
b Shrewsbury 12/1868			d 1927	
Caps: Wales 4				
		Shrewsbury Town		
1890	1891	Wolverhampton Wanderers	24	3
1892		Blackburn Rovers	22	5
		Shrewsbury Town		
Bowen, David			OL	
1925		Walsall	2	
Bowen, Edward (Ted)			CF	
b Goldthorpe q3 1901				
		Wath Athletic		
1926		Arsenal	1	
1927	1931	Northampton Town	162	114
1932	1933	Bristol City	55	33
Bowen, George			OR/CF/OL	
b Walsall 7/1875				
		Bridgetown Amateurs		
1899	1900	Wolverhampton Wanderers	48	13
1901		Liverpool	2	
1902		Wolverhampton Wanderers	3	1
1904		Burslem Port Vale	6	1
		Bloxwich Strollers		
Bowen, Lionel Francis William			LB	
b Sholing 31/12/1915			d 1996	
		Sholing St M		
1935		Crystal Palace	0	
1936		Southampton	2	
		Metropolitan Police		
		Winchester City		
Bowen, Samuel Edward (Teddy)			LB/RB	
b Hednesford 17/11/1903			d 1981	
		Hednesford Rovers		
		Hednesford Primitives		
		Hednesford Congregationals		
		Rugeley		
		Hednesford Town		
1923	1933	Aston Villa	191	
1934	1937	Norwich City	129	2
Bowen, Thomas George (Tommy)			IR/IL	
b West Bromwich 16/1/1900				
		Bush Rangers		
1920		Birmingham	0	
1921	1923	Walsall	74	16
1923	1927	Wolverhampton Wanderers	86	24
1928	1929	Coventry City	11	3
		Kidderminster Harriers		
Bowen, Walter Edward (Tod)			CH	
b Hednesford 1891			d 1944	
		Nuneaton Town		
1914		West Bromwich Albion	1	
		Hednesford Town		
		Stamford Town		
Bowen, William L			CF	
b 16/3/1909				
1929		Tranmere Rovers	3	
Bower, Alfred George (Baishe)			LB/RB	
b Bromley 10/11/1895			d 1970	
Caps: England Amat/England 5				
		Old Carthusians		
		Corinthians		
1923		Chelsea	3	
		Corinthians		
1925		Chelsea	6	
		Corinthians		
		Casuals		

From	To		Apps	Goal
Bower, Ronald William Charles (Ronnie)			RB	
b Wrexham 17/11/1911			d 1998	
1932	1934	New Brighton	24	
		South Liverpool		
1936		Bolton Wanderers	3	
1937		Millwall	0	
		Folkestone Town (trial)		
		Colchester United		
		Sudbury Town		
Bower, William Alfred (Billy)			GK	
b Dalston 18/9/1887			d 1954	
		Peel Institute		
1905	1914	Clapton Orient	171	
		Gillingham		
Bowering, Ernest George (Ernie)			LH	
b Wandsworth 30/3/1891			d 1961	
		Tottenham Thursday		
1911		Tottenham Hotspur	7	
1912		Fulham	1	
		Merthyr Town		
Bowers, Alfred George Walter (Alf)			CH/RH	
b Bethnal Green 2/4/1895				
		Bromley Celtic		
1924		Charlton Athletic	5	
1925		Bristol Rovers	3	
1926		Queen's Park Rangers	1	
Bowers, John William Anslow (Jack)			CF	
b Low Santon 22/2/1908			d 1970	
Caps: FLge 2/England 3				
		Appleby Works		
		Scunthorpe & Lindsey United		
1928	1936	Derby County	203	167
1936	1938	Leicester City	79	52
1939		(Leicester City)	(3)	
Bowes, John Thomas			IL	
b Middlesbrough q4 1876				
		Darlington		
1896		Sheffield United	4	2
		Darlington		
Bowes, William (Billy)			IL/IR	
b Armadale 1870				
		Armadale Wanderers		
		Bathgate Rovers		
		Broxburn		
1890	1900	Burnley	269	80
		Bank Hall Colliery		
		Trawden Forest		
Bowie, Alexander (Alex)			CF	
b Newcastle 21/9/1903			d 1978	
		Rosehill Villa		
		Wallsend		
1923	1924	Barnsley	5	
		Aberdeen		
		Kettering Town		
		Guildford City		
1928		Nelson (trial)	0	
		Gainsborough Trinity		
		Market Harborough Town		
		Loughborough Corinthians		
		Goole Town		
		Stamford Town		
		Waterford Celtic (trial)		
		Walker Celtic		
		Usworth Colliery		
		Biggleswade Town		
		Evesham Town		
Bowie, W			RH	
1892		Accrington	9	1
Bowl, Henry Thomas (Harry)			CF/IL	
b Faringdon 14/4/1914			d 1991	
		Stanford-in-the-Vale		
1933	1935	Swindon Town	44	8
1936		Blackpool	2	1
1937	1938	Exeter City	76	42
1939		(Exeter City)	(3)	(1)
		Lancaster Town		
Bowler, Albert (Bertie)			IL/CF	
b Nottingham q4 1887				
Caps: SoLge 5				
		Sherwood Foresters		
1920	1922	Plymouth Argyle	54	15
Bowler, George Frederick			LB	
b Grantham				
1893		Lincoln City	6	
Bowler, George Henry			RH	
b Newhall 23/1/1890			d 1948	
		Gresley Rovers		
1912		Derby County	1	
1913		Tottenham Hotspur	3	
		Luton Town		

From To Apps Goal

Bowles, John Charles (Jack) GK
b Cheltenham 4/8/1914 d 1987
Cheltenham Town
1936 Newport County 4
1937 Accrington Stanley 12
1938 1952 Stockport County 275
1939 (Stockport County) (2)
Winsford United

Bowman, Adam IL/CF
b Forfar 4/8/1880 d 1937
St Johnstone
East Stirlingshire
1901 1902 Everton 9 3
1902 1906 Blackburn Rovers 99 43
Brentford
1908 Leeds City 15 6
Brentford
Portsmouth
Leith Athletic
Forfar Athletic
Accrington Stanley

Bowman, J OR
b Scotland
Dundee East End
1893 Newcastle United 1

Bowman, John William (Jack) RH
b Middlesbrough 23/4/1879 d 1943
Shelton Juniors
Hanley St Jude's
Burslem Park
1898 Burslem Port Vale 0
1899 1900 Stoke 4
Queen's Park Rangers
Norwich City
Shepherds Bush

Bowman, Joseph (Joe) LB/RB
b Evenwood 7/11/1902 d 1941
Evenwood Town
1924 1931 Doncaster Rovers 189 1
1931 1932 Chesterfield 29
Broad Oaks Works

Bowman, Thomas (Tommy) RH/LB/RB
b Tarbolton 26/10/1873 d 1958
Annbank
1896 1897 Blackpool 38 2
1897 1900 Aston Villa 100 2
Southampton
Portsmouth
Eastleigh Athletic

Bowman, Walter Wells CH/RH/IL
b Waterloo, Ontario, Canada 11/8/1870 d 1948
Caps: Canada
Berlin Rangers (Canada)
Toronto Scottish
1891 Accrington 5 3
1892 1898 Ardwick/Manchester City 47 3

Bown, Archibald James William (Archie) LH/IL
b Swindon 7/1882 d 1958
Caps: SoLge 1
Swindon Casuals
Swindon Town
Whitehead Torpedo Works
Swindon Town
1919 1921 Bristol City 35 5
Weymouth

Bown, Herbert Arthur GK
b East Ham 3/5/1893 d 1959
Squirrels Heath
Roneo Works
Romford Town
West Ham United (trial)
1913 1921 Leicester Fosse 143
1922 1923 Halifax Town 80 1
1924 Hull City 4

Bowring, John Westray CF
b Tideswell q4 1874 d 1964
Blackwell Colliery
1895 Sheffield Wednesday 0
Stanton Hill Town
Blackwell Colliery
1901 Chesterfield Town 3 1
Blackwell Colliery

Bowron, Stephen (Steve) RB
b Ferryhill 5/5/1903 d 1963
Ferryhill Athletic
1929 1933 Hartlepools United 194
1934 Aldershot 6
Gainsborough Trinity

From To Apps Goal

Bowser, Sidney (Sid) CH/IL/IR
b Handsworth 6/4/1891 d 1961
Caps: IrLge 1/England 1
Astbury Richmond
Willenhall
1907 Birmingham (trial) 0
1908 1912 West Bromwich Albion 123 44
Distillery
1913 1923 West Bromwich Albion 218 20
1924 Walsall 27

Bowser, William IL
b Handsworth 5/11/1886 d 1975
1905 Everton (trial) 0
Dudley Town
1907 West Bromwich Albion 1
Walsall
1911 Birmingham 0
Shrewsbury Town

Bowsher, Stanley James (Stan) CH/LH
b Newport 3/10/1899 d 1968
Caps: WLge 2/Wales 1
Lovells Athletic
1925 1928 Newport County 118 3
1928 1932 Burnley 82 2
1932 Rochdale 10
1933 Newport County 5

Bowyer, Samuel (Sam) IL/OL
b Northwich 12/10/1887 d 1961
Earlestown
1907 1911 Liverpool 45 14
1911 1912 Bristol City 49 14
Bedminster
South Liverpool

Bowyer, Thomas William (Tommy) OR/IR
b Stoke-on-Trent
1919 Stoke 0
1919 Clapton Orient 21 6
1920 Gillingham 0
1921 Walsall 34 5
Shrewsbury Town

Box, Arthur GK
b Hanley 9/1884
Hanley Villa
Northwood Mission
1903 Stoke 0
1904 1906 Burslem Port Vale 50 1
1907 Stoke 33
1908 1909 Birmingham 28
Leek Victoria
Croydon Common
Crewe Alexandra

Boxley, David CF
b Cradley Heath 17/6/1890 d 1941
Cradley Heath St Luke's
1919 Stoke 8 4
Dudley Town

Boxley, Fred GK
b Cradley Heath q3 1886 d 1955
Cradley Heath
1909 1911 Wolverhampton Wanderers 67
Shrewsbury Town

Boxley, George Harry (Harry) RH/CF
b Cradley Heath 4/10/1891 d 1966
Stourbridge
Shrewsbury Town
Wellington Town
1919 Derby County 7
1920 1922 Bristol Rovers 48 8
1923 Bournemouth & Boscombe Ath 0
Darlaston
Oswestry Town
Stourbridge

Boyce, Thomas Dodd (Tommy) GK
b Edinburgh 2/8/1905 d 1991
Ardrossan Winton Rovers
St Mirren
1927 Southend United 7
Clydebank
Partick Thistle
1930 Bristol Rovers 8
Leith Athletic
East Fife
Bo'ness
Partick Thistle
King's Park

Boyd, David IL
b Greenock 1871
Abercorn
Rangers
1896 1897 Preston North End 37 14
Third Lanark
Abercorn
Linfield

From To Apps Goal

Boyd, Henry CF
b Pollokshaws 1868
Sunderland Albion
1892 Burnley 4 1
1892 West Bromwich Albion 7 1
1894 1896 Woolwich Arsenal 40 32
1896 1898 Newton Heath 51 30
Falkirk

Boyd, Hugh LH
b Glasgow
East Stirlingshire
Portadown
1936 Luton Town (trial) 0
1936 Clapton Orient 2
East Stirlingshire

Boyd, J CF
1897 Burton Swifts 2

Boyd, James Murray (Jimmy) OR
b Glasgow 29/4/1907 d 1991
Caps: Scotland 1
Petershill
St Bernard's
1926 1934 Newcastle United 198 58
1935 1936 Derby County 9 1
1936 Bury 9 2
Dundee
1938 Grimsby Town 37 9
1939 (Grimsby Town) (1)

Boyd, John LH
Hurlford Thistle
1902 1908 Bolton Wanderers 189 7
Plymouth Argyle
Accrington Stanley

Boyd, Malcolm S OR
Harpole
1926 Northampton Town 2
Rushden

Boyd, William Gillespie (Willie) CF/IL
b Cambuslang 27/11/1905 d 1967
Caps: SLge 3/Scotland 2
Regent Star (Rutherglen)
Rutherglen Glencairn
Royal Albert
Larkhall Thistle
Clyde
1933 1934 Sheffield United 42 30
1934 Manchester United 6 4
Tunbridge Wells Rangers
1935 Carlisle United (trial) 0
Workington
1935 Luton Town 13 11
1936 Southampton 19 7
Weymouth
Workington
Nuneaton Borough

Boyes, Kenneth Cecil (Ken) OL
b Southampton 17/11/1895 d 1963
Shirley Warren
1921 Southampton 4
1922 Bristol Rovers 2
Poole
Weymouth
Southampton Civil Service
Pirelli General
Romsey Town
Pirelli General

Boyes, Walter Edward (Wally) OL/LH/IR
b Killamarsh 5/1/1913 d 1960
Caps: FLge 2/England 3
Woodhouse Mills United
1931 1937 West Bromwich Albion 151 35
1937 1948 Everton 66 11
1939 (Everton) (3)
1949 Notts County 3 1
1950 Scunthorpe United 13 2
Retford Town

Boylan, EJ LB
1895 Rotherham Town 7

Boylan, Patrick A CH
b Greenock 26/1/1876
Greenock Volunteers
1896 Woolwich Arsenal 11
Morton

Boyle, Fred LH
b 1888
Cambridge House
Darlington
1909 Gainsborough Trinity 14
Bristol Rovers

From To Apps Goal

Boyle, James CH/GK
b Springburn 11/7/1866
Towerhill
Celtic
Clyde
1893 1896 Woolwich Arsenal 61 7
Dartford

Boyle, Michael John (Mike) RB/LB
b Bearpark 11/10/1908 d 2005
Bearpark Welfare
1931 1932 Bolton Wanderers 13
1933 1934 Reading 15
1936 Exeter City 23
1937 1938 Darlington 74 3
1939 York City (3)

Boyle, Owen RH
b South Bank 1895 d 1959
Grangetown St Mary's
1919 Bradford Park Avenue 1

Boyle, Peter LB
b Carlingford 26/4/1876 d 1939
Caps: Ireland 5
Coatdyke Gaelic
Albion Rovers
1896 1898 Sunderland 29
1898 1903 Sheffield United 150 1
Motherwell
1905 Clapton Orient 11
Wigan Town
Chorley
Eccles Borough
Brodsworth Colliery
York City
Brodsworth Colliery

Boyle, Richard H (Dickie) RH/CH
b Dumbarton 1870
Caps: SLge 1
Dumbarton Episcopalians
Dumbarton Union
Methlan Park (Dumbarton)
Dumbarton
1892 1901 Everton 229 7
Dundee

Boyle, Thomas IR/RH
b Sheffield 2/1901
Bullcroft Main Colliery
1921 1928 Sheffield United 127 38
1928 1929 Manchester United 16 6
1930 1934 Northampton Town 142 33
Scarborough

Boyle, Thomas William (Tommy) CH/RH
b Hoyland 29/1/1886 d 1940
Caps: FLge 4/England 1
Hoyland Star
Elsecar Athletic
1906 1911 Barnsley 160 17
1911 1921 Burnley 210 36
1923 Wrexham 7

Boylen, John OR
b Hamilton 13/3/1900 d 1961
Newmains Juniors
Wishaw
1921 1922 Lincoln City 59 4
1923 Wigan Borough 1
1923 Grimsby Town 4
Armadale
Kettering Town (trial)

Boylen, Robert Hunter OR/OL
b Newcastle 5/1/1907 d 1992
St Peter's Albion
1928 1929 Luton Town 11 1
1930 Gillingham 3
1931 Gateshead 0

Boyman, William Richard CF/IL
b Richmond, Surrey 10/8/1891 d 1970
Cradley Heath
1919 1921 Aston Villa 22 11
1921 1922 Nottingham Forest 12 3
Stourbridge
Kidderminster Harriers
Worcester City

Boyne, Reginald (Reg) CF/IR/IL
b Leeds 10/1891 d 1939
(New Zealand)
1913 1914 Aston Villa 8
Loughborough Brush Works
1920 Brentford 21 10

Boyton, John IR/OL
b Glasgow 1891
Kilsyth Emmet
1912 1913 Hull City 13 1
Linfield
Clyde
Arthurlie

From To Apps Goal

Brace, Thomas Frederick IL
b Bristol 8/3/1908 d 1983
1929 Bristol City 1

Bracegirdle, Ernest OL
b Knutsford q1 1886 d 1954
Knutsford
Northwich Victoria
1906 1909 Blackburn Rovers 59 6
Crewe Alexandra
Northwich Victoria
Altrincham
Winsford United

Bracelin, J IL
1894 Bolton Wanderers 1

Bracey, Frederick Cecil (Fred) OL/OR
b Derby 20/7/1887 d 1960
1903 Small Heath 0
Holbrook Swifts
1905 1907 Leicester Fosse 10
1908 Bradford Park Avenue 7
Rochdale

Bradbrook, Charles LB/RH/CH
b Overstrand 19/1/1902 d 1982
Yarmouth Town
1920 1925 Norwich City 96 1
Yarmouth Town

Bradburn, George LH/CH
b Wolverhampton q2 1894
Caps: SoLge 1
Walsall
1920 1921 Southampton 6
1922 Walsall 12

Bradburn, Richard OR/OL
b Hapton q1 1903
1922 1923 Accrington Stanley 14 1
Great Harwood

Bradbury, E LH
1896 Burton Wanderers 2

Bradbury, George RB/LB
b Matlock 26/4/1897 d 1974
Hackney Foresters (Darley Dale)
Hartshay Colliery
1920 1921 Clapton Orient 32 2
1922 Chesterfield 2
Scunthorpe & Lindsey United

Bradbury, John Joe Longstaff OR
b Normanby q1 1875 d 1942
1895 Lincoln City 2
Stockport County
Ashton North End
1897 Blackburn Rovers 2
Ashton North End
1899 Derby County 7 1
1900 Barnsley 16 2
1901 Bristol City 30 4
New Brompton
Millwall Athletic
Carlisle United
Penrith
Monckton Athletic

Bradbury, Leonard (Len) IL
b Northwich q3 1914 d 2007
Caps: England Amat
Manchester University
Northwich Victoria
Corinthians
Birmingham University
Moor Green
Corinthians
1938 Manchester United 2 1

Bradbury, Noah OL
b Stockingford 8/1/1910 d 1971
1931 Rotherham United 1
1932 Walsall 0

Bradbury, Thomas (Tom) LH
1939 Crewe Alexandra (1)

Bradbury, Thomas (Tom) IL
Gresley Rovers
1938 Derby County 0
1939 Wrexham (3)

From To Apps Goal

Bradbury, William Henry (Bill) RH/RB/LH
b Sudbury, Derbyshire 1884
Tutbury
Maybank
Newcastle Swifts
1903 1906 Burslem Port Vale 12
Fegg Hayes
Stoke
Aberdare Town
1911 1912 Oldham Athletic 7 2
Scunthorpe & Lindsey United
1919 1920 Oldham Athletic 67 3
1922 Rochdale 12
Burton Town
Bass & Co

Bradford, Alexander (Alex) RB
b Broomhill q1 1892 d 1963
Broomhill
East Chevington
1921 1922 Ashington 38 1
Amble
East Chevington Black Watch
North Broomhill Welfare
Eshott
Hauxley United

Bradford, Bernard LB
b Walker 13/2/1906 d 1975
Walker Park
1929 Hull City 1
1930 Walsall 11
Cork FC
Nuneaton Town
Jarrow
Throckley Colliery Welfare
Horden Colliery Welfare
Walker Celtic

Bradford, James (Jimmy) RB
b Walker 26/3/1914 d 1990
Birtley
1934 Huddersfield Town 0
1935 1936 Hartlepools United 9
Frickley Colliery

Bradford, James Arthur (Arthur) CH/RB
b Walsall 3/7/1902 d 1944
Talbot Stead Tube Works
1923 1935 Southampton 306 6
Cowes

Bradford, John (Jack) LH/RH
b Pilsley 9/4/1895 d 1969
Hucknall Byron
1920 1923 Grimsby Town 108
1923 1927 Wolverhampton Wanderers 77
1927 1930 Bournemouth & Boscombe Ath 113 1
Letchworth Town

Bradford, John William (Bill) LH/RH/CH
b Peggs Green 6/11/1903 d 1984
Peggs Green Victoria
1923 Birmingham 0
1924 Brighton & Hove Albion 3
1925 Preston North End 1
1926 1937 Walsall 318 21

Bradford, Joseph (Joe) CF/IL
b Peggs Green 22/1/1901 d 1980
Caps: FLge 5/England 12
Coalville
1919 Aston Villa (trial) 0
1919 Derby County (trial) 0
1920 1934 Birmingham 414 249
1935 Bristol City 5 1

Bradford, Leo OR
b Patricroft q3 1895 d 1947
Prestwich
Hurst
1925 Manchester City 5 1
Ashton National

Bradley, Albert CF
b Bradford 10/5/1896 d 1969
College AFC (Undercliffe)
1922 1925 Bradford Park Avenue 39 22
Selby Town
1926 Southport 11 7

Bradley, CH IR
b Smethwick 1/1882
Invention Street Boys
1904 West Bromwich Albion 3
Dudley Town

Bradley, Claude RH
b Walsall 1868
Burchills
1891 Wolverhampton Wanderers 6
Dudley Town

Bradley, Clifford RB
1906 Stockport County 1

From To Apps Goal

Bradley, Cromwell Marland (Cecil) OR
b Hemsworth 18/11/1904 d 1968
Truro City
Falmouth Town
1927 1928 Norwich City 4 1
1929 Sheffield Wednesday 0
Margate
Truro City
Wadebridge
Falmouth Town
Helston

Bradley, Edward OL
b Doncaster
Hyde Park Rangers (Doncaster)
1904 Doncaster Rovers 4
Doncaster St James

Bradley, Eli CF/CH
b Dudley q4 1883 d 1964
Caps: SoLge 3
Bilston United
Dudley Town
1905 1907 West Bromwich Albion 25 6
Luton Town
Coventry City
Heart of Midlothian
Dudley Town

Bradley, George Joseph LH/RH/RB
b Maltby 7/11/1917 d 1998
Maltby Hall Old Boys
1937 1938 Rotherham United 28
1938 Newcastle United 1
1946 1949 Millwall 74 2
Guildford City

Bradley, Herbert OL
b Padiham q2 1887
Colne
1906 1909 Bury 18
1910 Notts County 3
Padiham
1911 Preston North End 2
Great Harwood
Nelson

Bradley, James (Jimmy) RH
b Clayton 23/4/1897 d 1972
1921 Manchester City 0
1923 Chesterfield 8
1924 Wigan Borough 3 1
1925 Crewe Alexandra 9
Colwyn Bay
Ashton National

Bradley, James Edwin (Jimmy) LH
b Goldenhill 5/1881 d 1954
Caps: FLge 1
Goldenhill Wanderers
1898 1904 Stoke 199 4
1905 1910 Liverpool 169 5
Reading
Stoke
Goldenhill Wanderers

Bradley, James Leslie (Jimmy) IR
b Lesmahagow 1892
Luton Town
Dundee Hibernian
1920 Luton Town 5 1
1920 Clapton Orient 5 1

Bradley, John (Jack) IL
b Hemsworth 27/11/1916 d 2002
South Kirkby Colliery
1935 Huddersfield Town 0
1936 1937 Swindon Town 25 6
1938 Chelsea 0
1945 1947 Southampton 49 22
Grantham (loan)
1947 1950 Bolton Wanderers 92 19
1950 1951 Norwich City 6
Yarmouth Town

Bradley, Martin IR
b Wolstanton q4 1886 d 1958
South Kirkby
1907 1908 Grimsby Town 28 6
Mexborough Town
1910 Sheffield Wednesday 2
Bristol Rovers

Bradley, Patrick John OL
b Coatbridge 1901
1924 1926 Wolverhampton Wanderers 5
1926 1927 Gillingham 33 3
Walsall Wood
Brownhills Albion

Bradley, Percy GK
b Hull q3 1887 d 1967
Day Street Old Boys
1911 1912 Grimsby Town 6
Goole Town
Gainsborough Trinity

From To Apps Goal

Bradley, Robert (Bob) RB
b Washington 16/9/1906 d 1934
Bishop Auckland
1927 Newcastle United 1
1929 Fulham 6
Tunbridge Wells Rangers
1932 1933 Carlisle United 70

Bradley, William (Bill) GK
b Wardley 1/3/1893
Dunston Wednesday
Fatfield Albion
Jarrow Caledonians
Portsmouth
Jarrow
1919 1925 Newcastle United 133
1927 1928 Ashington 36
North Shields

Bradley, William (Willie) IR
b Glasgow 1/3/1893
Pollok Juniors
Cowdenbeath
1922 1923 Barrow 48 6
Queen of the South

Bradshaw, Albert Ernest GK
b Staveley q2 1872
Eckington Works
1895 1898 Sheffield United 5
1899 New Brighton Tower 27

Bradshaw, Ernest LH/OL
b Padiham q4 1887
Accrington Stanley
1906 Blackburn Rovers 0
Nelson
1911 1913 Burnley 8

Bradshaw, Francis (Frank) IL/RB/IR
b Sheffield 31/5/1884
Caps: SoLge 1/FLge 4/England 1
Oxford Street Sunday School
1905 1909 Sheffield Wednesday 87 37
Northampton Town
1911 1913 Everton 66 19
1914 1922 Arsenal 132 14

Bradshaw, George LB/RB
b Trimdon Grange 12/3/1904 d 1951
Chilton Colliery Recreation Athletic
1924 1926 Blackpool 43
1927 1933 Bury 140 1
1935 Tranmere Rovers 5

Bradshaw, George Frederick GK
b Southport 10/3/1913 d 1989
High Park Villa
1932 1934 New Brighton 83
1934 Everton 2
1935 Arsenal 0
1936 1937 Doncaster Rovers 53
1938 1949 Bury 118
1950 Oldham Athletic 1

Bradshaw, Harold OL
1925 Northampton Town 2

Bradshaw, Harold Bruce (Harry) OL
b Leicester 8/8/1896 d 1967
1919 1920 West Ham United 14

Bradshaw, Henry (Harry) GK
b Liverpool 22/1/1895 d 1979
South Liverpool
1921 1922 Tranmere Rovers 59
Ellesmere Port Cement Works

Bradshaw, John Henry (Jack) OR
b Burnley 28/6/1892 d 1970
Southend United
Watford
Luton Town
Aberdare Athletic
1921 Queen's Park Rangers 5
1922 Burnley 0
1922 Southend United 1
1923 Swansea Town 0

Bradshaw, Joseph (Joe) IR
b Burnley q3 1880
Woolwich Polytechnic
1901 Woolwich Arsenal 0
West Norwood
Southampton
1907 1908 Fulham 3
1909 Chelsea 6 3
Queen's Park Rangers
Southend United

Bradshaw, Richard LH/RH
b Padiham
Accrington Stanley
Padiham
1908 1911 Blackpool 30

From To Apps Goal

Bradshaw, Thomas IL
b Woodhouse Eaves q4 1875
1897 Loughborough 1

Bradshaw, Thomas (Tom 'Tiny') CH
b Bishopton 7/2/1904 d 1986
Caps: Scotland 1
Woodside Juniors
Hamilton Academical
1922 1929 Bury 208 8
1929 1937 Liverpool 277 3
Third Lanark
South Liverpool

Bradshaw, Thomas Dickinson (Tom) OR/IR/OL
b Hambleton 15/3/1876 d 1953
Lostock Hall
1896 Preston North End 0
1896 Blackpool 18 5
1897 Sunderland 14 2
1897 1898 Nottingham Forest 18
1898 1899 Leicester Fosse 28 7
1900 New Brighton Tower 11 3
Swindon Town
Reading
1902 Preston North End 0
Wellingborough
Southport Central
Earlestown
Accrington Stanley
1905 Leicester Fosse 15 2
Rossendale United
1907 Glossop 0
Penrith
Peterborough City
Darwen

Bradshaw, Thomas Henry (Harry) OL/CF
b Liverpool 24/8/1873 d 1899
Caps: FLge 2/England 1
Liverpool Nomads
1892 1893 Northwich Victoria 22 8
1893 1897 Liverpool 118 46
Tottenham Hotspur
Thames Ironworks

Bradshaw, William (Will) OR
b Burnley q2 1882
Burnley Belvedere
1902 1903 Woolwich Arsenal 4 2
Fulham
1905 1906 Burton United 67 14
1907 Burnley 11 1
Burnell's Ironworks
Chester
Ton Pentre

Bradshaw, William (Billy) LH
b Padiham 4/1884
Caps: FLge 4/England 4
Padiham
Accrington Stanley
1903 1919 Blackburn Rovers 386 36
Rochdale

Brady, Alexander (Alec) IL/IR/OR
b Cathcart 2/4/1865 d 1913
Dundee Harp
Renton Thistle
Partick Thistle
Sunderland
1888 Burnley 20 7
Sunderland
1889 1890 Everton 34 17
Broxburn Shamrock (loan)
Celtic
1892 1898 Sheffield Wednesday 158 34
Clydebank
Renton

Brady, Arthur OR
1892 1893 Burnley 24 10

Brady, Frank CF
b Glasgow
Shelbourne
1934 Aldershot 4 2

Brady, W IR
Renton
1888 Burnley 9 2
Newcastle West End

Brae, James CH
1896 Burnley 6

Brae, William (Billy) IL
b Kelvin 4/11/1902 d 1968
Petershill
Ayr United
Lille (trial)
Clyde (trial)
1935 Swindon Town 6
Cheltenham Town
Evesham Town

From To Apps Goal

Braidford, Lowingham (Lowe) CF/IR
b Wallsend 17/11/1894 d 1926
Wallsend Town
Clydebank
Dundee Hibernian
1922 Hartlepools United 29 9
Philadelphia Field Club
1923 Northampton Town 5 1
Preston Colliery

Braidwood, Ernest (Ernie) CH/RH/LH
b Heywood 14/4/1895 d 1968
Heywood York St Congregationals
Chesterfield Municipal
1920 1921 Oldham Athletic 10 1
1922 1925 Nelson 128 10
1925 1928 Rochdale 87 1
Great Harwood
New Mills

Brailsford, J CF/IL
1896 1897 Loughborough 25 5

Brailsford, James Robert CH/RH
b Lincoln q2 1877 d 1946
Casuals FC
Newark Town
1895 1896 Lincoln City 20
1897 Notts County 1
1906 Lincoln City 0

Brain, James (Jimmy) CF/IR
b Bristol 11/9/1900 d 1971
1921 Cardiff City (trial) 0
Ton Pentre
1924 1930 Arsenal 204 125
1931 1934 Tottenham Hotspur 45 10
King's Lynn

Brain, Joseph (Joe) CF/IL
b Ebbw Vale 28/1/1910 d 1981
Ebbw Vale
1930 Sunderland 0
1931 Norwich City 13 5
1932 Barrow 29 17
1933 Preston North End 7 2
1934 1936 Swansea Town 49 26
1937 1938 Bristol City 32 9

Braithwaite, Edward (Ted) LH/IR/IL
b Salford 12/12/1900 d 1990
New Cross
1921 1923 Bradford City 17 2
1924 1928 Reading 133 22
1929 1932 Swindon Town 142 6
Margate

Braithwaite, John CF
b Barrow 12/11/1902
Barrow St George's
1920 Southampton (trial) 0
1922 Barrow 2

Brallisford, Albert CF/OR
b Belle Vue, Hartlepool 9/10/1911 d 1991
West Hartlepool Perseverance
Trimdon Grange
1932 Southport 1 1
1933 1935 Blackpool 17 8
1936 1937 Darlington 39 26
1937 Gillingham 14 3
Glentoran
Blackhall Colliery Welfare

Bramham, Arnold CF
b West Melton 16/1/1912 d 1989
West Melton
Silverwood Colliery
1934 1935 Notts County 18 10
1936 1938 Rotherham United 89 52
1939 (Rotherham United) (3) (2)
Peterborough United
Sutton Town

Bramham, Samuel Snelson OR
b Burton-on-Trent q1 1875 d 1965
1895 Burton Wanderers 2

Bramley, Charles (Charlie) RH
b Nottingham 1870 d 1916
Nottingham Jardines
Notts St John's
Notts Rangers
1891 1897 Notts County 126 8

Bramley, Cyril OR
1924 Rotherham County 20

Bramley, Ernest RB/CF
b Mansfield 29/8/1920 d 1993
Bolsover Colliery
1938 1947 Mansfield Town 45 1
1939 (Mansfield Town) (1)

From To Apps Goal

Bramley, John (Jack) RB/CH
b East Kirkby 1898
Mansfield Town
Welbeck Colliery
1922 1923 Bradford City 6
1924 1925 Rotherham County 23
Sutton Town

Brammer, George W LB
b Lincoln 1873
Lincoln Ramblers
1892 Lincoln City 2

Brand, Robert (Bob) OL/IL
b Wishaw 1865
Queen of the South Wanderers
Rangers
Heart of Midlothian
Queen of the South Wanderers
1888 Accrington 16 11
Sunderland Albion (loan)
Sunderland Albion
1889 Accrington 2
Rotherham Town
Carlisle
1890 Derby County 3
Sunderland Albion

Brand, Robert A CF
b Dumfries 1887
Argyll & Sutherland Highlanders
Motherwell
1911 Bristol City 8
King's Park

Brandon, Harry RH
b Kilbirnie 26/3/1870 d 1936
Caps: FAlliance 1
Heywood Wanderers
St Mirren
Clyde
1892 1897 Sheffield Wednesday 147 15
Chesterfield Town

Brandon, James CF
b Kilbirnie 2/1870 d 1934
Port Glasgow Athletic
St Mirren
Port Glasgow Athletic
1890 Preston North End 8 3
The Wednesday
Chesterfield Town
1892 Bootle 8 5

Brandon, Thomas (Tom) RB/LB
b Kilbirnie 26/2/1869 d 1921
Caps: FLge 1/Scotland 1
Clipsons
Johnstone
Port Glasgow Athletic
Renfrew Athletic
St Mirren
1889 1890 Blackburn Rovers 39 1
1892 Sheffield Wednesday 30 2
Nelson
1893 1899 Blackburn Rovers 177 1
St Mirren

Brandon, Thomas (Tom) RB/IR/LB
b Blackburn 28/5/1893 d 1956
1909 Blackburn Rovers 0
Rossendale United
Darwen
South Liverpool
West Ham United
Bristol Rovers
1920 1921 Hull City 56 3
1922 1924 Bradford Park Avenue 85
1925 Wigan Borough 8
Bootle Borough

Branfield, Jack GK
b Gillingham 25/10/1891 d 1957
1920 1921 Gillingham 57
Sheppey United

Brankson, ? RH
1895 Rotherham Town 1

Brannan, Edward (Teddie) RB
Stockton
1899 Gainsborough Trinity 15

From To Apps Goal

Brannan, Frank RH
b Walker
Chester-le-Street
Shildon
1925 Ashington 4
Walker Celtic
Spen Black & White

Brannan, Michael H (Mike) GK
b Brampton Bierlow q1 1911
Dearne Valley Old Boys
Rotherham Road
Wombwell
Denaby United
1933 Arsenal 0
1933 Hull City 0
1934 1935 Barnsley 5
1937 Notts County 3
Grantham
Peterborough United

Brannick, James IR
b Manchester 1889 d 1917
1912 Everton 3 2
St Mirren

Brannigan, Daniel McKay LH
b Dunasken 22/12/1902 d 1990
Glenburn Rovers
1927 Halifax Town 15
Peterborough & Fletton United
1931 1933 Gateshead 56 2

Branston, James Hart (Jimmy) GK
b Sutton-in-Ashfield 22/2/1894 d 1970
1913 Grimsby Town 0
Sutton Junction
1919 1921 Rotherham County 111
1921 1926 Preston North End 129

Brant, Henry (Harry) IL
b Motherwell 11/6/1905 d 1979
New Stevenston
Cambuslang Rangers
Newarthill Thistle
Albion Rovers
1929 Bury 22 6
Dundee United

Brash, Archibald Taylor (Archie) OR
b Uphall 18/1/1873 d 1942
St Mirren
1894 1897 Sheffield Wednesday 93 14
Crewe Alexandra
1899 Sheffield Wednesday 26 6
1900 Leicester Fosse 14 5
Aberdeen

Bratby, John Lewis IR/IL
b Belper 15/5/1895 d 1982
Belper Cow Hill
Luton Town (trial)
Matlock Town
1920 1922 Clapton Orient 27 1

Bratley, George William CH/RB/LB
b Wickersley 17/1/1909 d 1978
Wickersley
Rotherham St Peter's
Rotherham YMCA
1929 1932 Rotherham United 85 9
1932 Sheffield Wednesday 3
1933 Rotherham United 14 3
Gainsborough Trinity
Bath City
1936 1937 Barrow 82 9
1938 Swindon Town 0
Tunbridge Wells Rangers

Bratley, Philip Wright (Phil) CH/RH/LB
b Rawmarsh 26/12/1880 d 1959
Rawmarsh
1902 Doncaster Rovers 3
Rotherham Town
Rotherham County
1910 1913 Barnsley 107 7
1914 Liverpool 13
1919 1920 Rotherham County 10
Worksop Town

Bratt, Halford James GK
b Walsall 16/9/1900 d 1970
Oakengates Town
1923 Walsall 2
Rugby Town
Leamington Town
Bloxwich Strollers

Bratt, William (Bill) CF/RH
b West Hartlepool 11/6/1896
Christ Church (Hartlepool)
West Hartlepool Expansion
1921 1922 Hartlepools United 15 2
Wingate Albion
Wheatley Hill

From To Apps Goal

Brawn, Charles Edwin OR
b Wolverhampton q1 1882 d 1958
1905 Wolverhampton Wanderers 0
1906 1907 Gainsborough Trinity 42 7
Portsmouth
Wellington Town
Cheddleton Asylum

Brawn, William Frederick (Billy) OR
b Wellingborough 1/8/1878 d 1932
Caps: England 2
Wellingborough
Northampton Town
1899 1901 Sheffield United 14 4
1901 1905 Aston Villa 95 19
1905 1907 Middlesbrough 56 5
1907 1910 Chelsea 93 10
Brentford

Bray, EH OL/OR
1894 1895 Crewe Alexandra 18

Bray, Eric OL
b Barugh Green 22/7/1915 d 1994
Barugh Green
1935 1938 Barnsley 37 12

Bray, George LH
b Oswaldtwistle 11/11/1918 d 2002
Great Harwood
1938 1951 Burnley 241 8
1939 (Burnley) (2)

Bray, HE OL
1893 Northwich Victoria 7

Bray, John (Jackie) LH
b Oswaldtwistle 22/4/1909 d 1982
Caps: FLge 5/England 6
Oswaldtwistle
Clayton Olympia
Manchester Central
1929 1938 Manchester City 257 10
1939 (Manchester City) (3)

Brayshaw, Edward (Teddy) CF
b Kirkstall q2 1863 d 1908
Caps: England 1
Walkley All Saints
The Wednesday
1892 Grimsby Town 2

Brayshaw, Walter (Wally) IR/IL
b Mexborough q3 1898 d 1935
Mexborough Rovers
Denaby United
1919 Sheffield United 4
1920 Exeter City 5
Denaby United
Mexborough
Wath Athletic
Denaby United
1924 1925 Blackburn Rovers 9 1
1926 Southend United 13 5
Denaby United
Wombwell

Brayson, Joseph Hayes (Joe) OL
b Newcastle 12/12/1901 d 1970
Newburn
Wallsend
1919 South Shields 2
Newburn
1921 Ashington 2
Scotswood
1926 Hull City 3
Annfield Plain
West Stanley

Breakwell, Arthur James OL/IL
b Wolverhampton q4 1881 d 1930
Sedgley
1905 1906 Wolverhampton Wanderers 24 3
Brierley Hill Alliance
Bilston

Breakwell, Thomas (Tom) LH
b Stourport 3/7/1915 d 2003
1933 Blackpool 0
Lytham
1935 Bolton Wanderers 0
1936 Bradford Park Avenue 18
1937 Wrexham 3
Fleetwood

Brealey, Harry OL
b Nottingham q2 1874 d 1929
1894 1895 Notts County 8 3
Hucknall St John's

Brealey, WB OR
1898 Gainsborough Trinity 1

From To Apps Goal

Brearley, John IR/RH
b West Derby q4 1875 d 1944
Liverpool South End
1897 Notts County 1
Kettering
Chatham
Millwall Athletic
1900 Notts County 8
1900 1901 Middlesbrough 32 22
1902 Everton 22 7
Tottenham Hotspur
Crystal Palace
Millwall Athletic
Chatham

Brebner, Ronald Gilchrist (Ron) GK
b Darlington 23/9/1881 d 1914
Caps: England Amat
Edinburgh University
Elgin City
1905 Sunderland 2
Rangers
Darlington
1906 Chelsea 1
London Caledonians
Darlington
Elgin City
Pilgrims
Stockton
Northern Nomads
Queen's Park
Darlington
1911 Huddersfield Town 23
1912 Chelsea 17
1913 Leicester Fosse 18

Breckin, Charles Edward RH
b Rotherham 1/5/1902 d 1971
1921 Rotherham County 1

Breedon, John (Jack) GK
b South Hiendley 29/12/1907 d 1977
South Hiendley
1928 1930 Barnsley 8
1930 1933 Sheffield Wednesday 45
1935 1938 Manchester United 35
1939 (Manchester United) (3)
1945 Burnley 0

Breen, Thomas (Tom) GK
b Drogheda 27/4/1912 d 1988
Caps: IrLge 3/NIRL 5/LoI 3/Ireland War 3/ Ireland 9/Eire 5
Drogheda United
Newry Town
Belfast Celtic
1936 1938 Manchester United 65
Belfast Celtic
Linfield
Shamrock Rovers
Glentoran

Breeze, Ernest Clarence LB
b Burslem 8/5/1910 d 1984
1933 1935 Port Vale 39
Shrewsbury Town

Brelsford, Benjamin H (Ben) LB
b Attercliffe q4 1896 d 1968
1922 Sheffield Wednesday 0
1924 1925 Barrow 63 2
1926 1927 Oldham Athletic 9
1928 1929 Watford 25 1
Bray Unknowns
Shelbourne
Manchester North End
Rossendale United
Larne
Newton Heath Loco
New Mills

Brelsford, Charles (Chas) RB/LB
b Attercliffe q4 1890 d 1959
Kilnhurst Town
Buxton
1912 1913 Sheffield Wednesday 6
1919 South Shields 0
Castleford Town
Mansfield Town

Brelsford, Thomas William (Tom) LH/RH/CH
b Attercliffe 21/4/1894 d 1946
Wombwell
Castleford Town
Bird-in-Hand
1919 1923 Sheffield Wednesday 117 6
1924 Barrow 31 1
1925 Rotherham United 36 2
Wombwell Town
Station Hotel (Sheffield)

From To Apps Goal

Brelsford, William Henry (Bill) RH/CH
b Darnall q1 1885 d 1954
Attercliffe United
Tinsley Park
Lodge Inn
Rawmarsh Albion
Doncaster Rovers
1909 1921 Sheffield United 277 1
Taunton

Bremner, Gordon Hutton IR/OR
b Glasgow 12/11/1917
Caps: Scotland War 2
Cartha Athletic
1937 1938 Arsenal 15 4
1939 (Arsenal) (1)
Motherwell

Brenen, Albert (Bert) RH/CH/LH
b South Shields 5/10/1915 d 1995
South Shields
St John's College (York)
1938 1950 York City 204 13
Scarborough

Brennan, James Francis IR
b Templemore 10/9/1884
Prior Park College (Bath)
Valkyrie (Liverpool)
Africa Royal (Liverpool)
1907 Bury 1
Brighton & Hove Albion

Brennan, John (Jack) LH/RH/CH
b Manchester 13/12/1892 d 1942
Ancoats Lads Club
Hollinwood United
1910 Manchester City (trial) 0
Denton
1912 1913 Glossop 21
1913 Bradford City 11
1914 1921 Manchester City 56
1922 Rochdale 0

Brennan, Thomas CF
b Goldenhill
1919 Stockport County 1
Stafford Rangers

Brennan, Thomas James IL/IR
b Calderbank 7/2/1911
Caps: Scotland Sch
Longriggend Rob Roy
1928 Brentford 0
1929 1930 Gillingham 16 2
1930 Crystal Palace 2
Leith Athletic
Tunbridge Wells Rangers
1933 1934 Blackburn Rovers 13 1
1935 Stockport County 10 2

Brentnall, Arthur Allen RB
b Basford q2 1877 d 1948
1899 Nottingham Forest 2

Brentnall, Charles Frederick GK
b Burton-on-Trent 3/1871 d 1934
1894 1896 Burton Wanderers 16

Breslin, Thomas G (Tom) OR/IL
b Kirkcaldy 1906
Glasgow Shawfield
1925 1926 Coventry City 22 2

Brett, Frank Bernard LB/CH
b King's Norton 10/3/1899 d 1988
Redditch Town
1921 Manchester United 10
1922 Aston Villa 0
1923 1929 Northampton Town 254 4
1930 1934 Brighton & Hove Albion 131
Tunbridge Wells Rangers
1936 Brighton & Hove Albion 0
Hove

Brett, Ralph S CF
b Chester 6/1878 d 1940
Southport Central
Royal Army Medical Corps
1898 West Bromwich Albion 12 3
Wellingborough
Brentford
Stoke Newington

Brett, Samuel Stephen (Sammy) IR/CF
b St Asaph 25/12/1879 d 1939
St Asaph YMCA
Southport Central
1898 1899 West Bromwich Albion 8 2
Wellingborough
Brentford

Brettie, Arthur CH
Walsall Unity
1893 1894 Walsall Town Swifts 31 2
1895 1896 Burton Wanderers 39 2

From To Apps Goal

Brewis, John Thomas (Tom) IR/RH/IL
b Tynemouth 21/4/1907 d 1975
Preston Colliery
West Stanley
Newark Town
1930 1931 York City 26 11
1931 1936 Southampton 118 18
Newport (Isle of Wight)

Brewis, Robert CF/IR
b Newcastle 1885
Scotswood
Queen's Park Rangers
1907 Lincoln City 22 11
1908 Burnley 2
Merthyr Town
Hartlepools United
Luton Town

Brewster, George (Dod) CH
b Culsalmond 7/10/1893 d 1963
Caps: Scotland 1
Mugiemoss
Aberdeen
Ayr United (loan)
Falkirk (loan)
1919 1922 Everton 64 4
1922 Wolverhampton Wanderers 11
Lovells Athletic
Wallasey United
Brooklyn Wanderers
Inverness

Brickenden, Norman Ralph GK
b Isle of Sheppey 20/7/1914 d 1972
Sheppey United
1937 Gillingham 3
Sittingbourne

Bricker, Frank CF
b Bradford-on-Avon q4 1897 d 1967
1921 1922 Crewe Alexandra 30 14
Macclesfield
Bath City

Briddon, Samuel (Sam) RH
b Alfreton 26/7/1915 d 1975
1934 Port Vale 0
Stanton Hill
1938 Brentford 6
1939 1946 Swansea Town 18
1939 (Swansea Town) (3)

Bridge, Cyril LB/RB
b Keynsham 28/8/1909 d 1988
St Philip's Marsh
1932 1938 Bristol City 155

Bridge, John (Jock) OR
1910 Stockport County 5 1

Bridge, R OR
1893 Darwen 1

Bridgeman, William Walter (Billy) OL/IR
b Bromley-by-Bow 24/12/1882 d 1947
Adam & Eve
West Ham United
1906 1914 Chelsea 147 20
Southend United

Bridges, Alexander OL
1932 Blackpool 7

Bridges, Harold IL
b Burton-on-Trent 30/6/1915 d 1989
Burton Town
1937 Manchester City 0
1939 1947 Tranmere Rovers 33 9
1939 (Tranmere Rovers) (3) (2)
Ashton National

Bridgett, George Arthur (Arthur) OL/IR
b Fordbrook 11/10/1882 d 1954
Caps: FLge 2/England 11
Burslem Park
Trentham
1902 Stoke 7
1902 1911 Sunderland 320 108
South Shields
1923 Port Vale 14 7
Sandbach Ramblers

Bridgett, Harry OL
b Longton q3 1889
Stoke
1909 1912 Leeds City 13 2
West Stanley

From	To	Player / Club	Apps	Goal
		Briercliffe, Thomas (Tommy)	OR	
		b Blackburn q2 1874	d 1948	
		St Luke's Wheelton		
		Clitheroe		
1897	1899	Blackburn Rovers	56	10
		Stalybridge Rovers		
1901	1904	Woolwich Arsenal	122	33
		Plymouth Argyle		
		Brentford		
		Darwen		
		Brierley, ?	OR	
1894		Crewe Alexandra	1	
		Brierley, Harold (Harry)	LH/OL	
		b Rochdale 2/8/1914	d 1988	
		Duckworths		
1935	1936	Rochdale	20	2
		Mossley		
		Brierley, Herbert James	OR	
1898		Burnley	2	
		Brierley, John	IL	
		b Rochdale q2 1908		
1928		Rochdale	14	7
		Witton Albion		
		Briggs, Arthur Henry	OR/IL	
		b Bow 1899		
		Woolwich		
1921	1924	Charlton Athletic	9	1
		Guildford United		
		Briggs, Arthur Lionel	GK	
		b Newcastle 27/5/1900	d 1987	
		Jesmond Villa		
		Walker Celtic		
1922	1923	Hull City	5	
1923		Manchester City	0	
1924	1931	Tranmere Rovers	233	
		Ashton National		
1932	1934	Swindon Town	69	
1935		Newport County	40	
		Colwyn Bay		
		Briggs, Charles Edward (Charlie)	GK	
		b Newtown 4/4/1911		
		Haywards Sports		
		Guildford City		
1935		Fulham	0	
1935		Tottenham Hotspur	0	
		Guildford City		
1936		Crystal Palace	0	
		Guildford City		
1937		Bradford Park Avenue	0	
1937	1938	Halifax Town	53	
1939		(Halifax Town)	(3)	
		Clyde		
1946	1947	Rochdale	12	
1947		Chesterfield	0	
		Briggs, Frank	LH	
		b Salford 1/2/1917	d 1984	
		Altrincham		
1937		Port Vale	8	
1938		Aston Villa	0	
1939		Wrexham	(3)	
		Oswestry Town		
		Briggs, Fred	IL/OR/CF	
		b Wombwell 1/5/1908	d 1998	
		Mexborough Town		
		Wombwell		
1932	1934	Rotherham United	74	17
1935	1937	Reading	27	6
1938		Southampton	36	14
1939		(Southampton)	(3)	(1)
		Briggs, George Richard	OR/CF/IL	
		b Wombwell 23/5/1903	d 1972	
		Denaby United		
1923	1932	Birmingham	298	98
1933	1935	Plymouth Argyle	58	11
		Briggs, Harold (Harry)	RH/OR/OL	
		b Middlesbrough q3 1904		
1925	1926	Darlington	6	
1927		Luton Town	2	
		Newark Town		
1928		Hartlepools United	18	3
1930		Barrow	35	7
		Crook Town		
		Briggs, HF	GK	
1893	1895	Darwen	51	
1895	1896	Everton	11	
		Briggs, Jack Christopher	IL	
		b Blackburn 15/7/1911	d 2009	
		Scarborough		
1934		Tottenham Hotspur	0	
		Northfleet		
		Peterborough United		
		Northampton Town	0	
		Wisbech Town		
1938		Rochdale	1	
		Grantham		
		Briggs, James (Jim)	IR	
		b West Moor, Newcastle 1893		
		Craghead United		
1912		Hull City	2	
		West Stanley		
		Leadgate Park		
		Briggs, John W	OR	
1919		Stockport County	5	1
		Briggs, Roy	OL	
		b Mansfield 1/11/1920	d 1995	
		Mansfield Shoe Company		
1936		Mansfield Town	2	
		Briggs, Stanley	CH	
		b Stamford Hill 7/2/1871	d 1935	
		Folkestone		
		Hermitage		
		Tottenham		
		Tottenham Hotspur		
1893		Woolwich Arsenal	2	
		Tottenham Hotspur		
		Corinthians		
		Friars		
		Tottenham Hotspur		
		London Caledonians		
		Richmond		
		Tottenham Hotspur		
		Upton Park		
		Clapton		
		Millwall Athletic		
		Shepherds Bush		
		Brigham, Harold (Harry)	RB	
		b Selby 19/11/1914	d 1978	
		Frickley Colliery		
1936	1946	Stoke City	104	
1939		(Stoke City)	(3)	
1946	1947	Nottingham Forest	35	2
1948	1949	York City	56	5
		Gainsborough Trinity		
		Selby Town		
		Bright, Samuel (Sam)	LB/RB/CH	
		b Clowne q4 1875		
		Clowne Rovers		
1900	1901	Sheffield United	3	
1903		Bradford City	6	
		Worksop Town		
		Moore's Athletic (Shirebrook)		
		Bright, Stanley	LB	
		b Hemyock		
		Cullompton		
1931		Exeter City	1	
1932		Bournemouth & Boscombe Ath	0	
		Brimblecombe, William Henry	OR/IR	
		b Burnley 5/6/1876	d 1917	
		Bacup		
1897	1899	Bury	57	12
		Brindle, Rowland	RH/CH	
		b Bolton 9/1896	d 1963	
		Horwich RMI		
1919	1920	Bury	2	
		Darwen		
		Lancaster Town		
		Brindley, Horace	OL	
		b Knutton 1/1/1885	d 1971	
		Knutton Villa		
1904		Stoke	4	
		Crewe Alexandra		
		Norwich City		
1907		Blackpool	17	2
		Crewe Alexandra		
		Queen's Park Rangers		
		Luton Town		
1912	1913	Lincoln City	50	4
		Chester		
		Brinton, Ernest James (Ernie)	LH	
		b Bristol 26/5/1908	d 1981	
		Avonmouth Town		
1929	1936	Bristol City	249	7
1937	1945	Newport County	75	3
1939		(Newport County)	(3)	
1946		Aldershot	12	
		Street		
		Brinton, John Victor (Jack)	OL	
		b Avonmouth 11/7/1916	d 1997	
		Shell-Mex & BP		
		Avonmouth Town		
1935	1936	Bristol City	12	1
1937		Newport County	6	
1937		Derby County	8	2
1946	1947	Stockport County	58	9
1948		Leyton Orient	4	1
		Street		
		Chippenham Town		
		Briscoe, James (Jimmy 'Tim')	RB	
		b Skelmersdale 25/1/1914	d 1944	
		Skelmersdale Shoe Company		
		Skelmersdale United		
1937		Southport	2	
		Skelmersdale United		
		Briscoe, James Edward Rotherham	CF/OR	
		b Clock Face 23/4/1917	d 1981	
		St Helens Town		
1936		Preston North End	5	
		Heart of Midlothian		
1946	1948	Northampton Town	53	17
		Nuneaton Borough (loan)		
		Wolverton Town		
		Briscoe, James Norman Robinson (Jim)	RB	
		b Miles Platting 15/11/1901	d 1966	
		Royal Marines (Chatham)		
1925		Manchester United	0	
		Ashton National		
1925		Southport	5	
		Congleton Town		
1926		Manchester United	0	
1927		Accrington Stanley	0	
		Briscoe, William (Billy)	LH/OL/IL	
		b Longton 6/11/1896	d 1994	
1919	1922	Port Vale	118	9
		Congleton Town		
1923	1929	Port Vale	179	34
		Congleton Town		
		Briscoe, William Henry	IL	
1888		Everton	3	
		Brittain, John Walter	LB	
		b Aston q1 1880		
		Hednesford Swifts		
		Wednesbury Old Athletic		
1902	1905	West Bromwich Albion	9	
		Willenhall Swifts		
		Brittain, William	LB	
		Grantham Rovers		
1894		Lincoln City	17	
		Grantham Rovers		
		Brittan, Charles Healy (Charlie)	OR/CF	
		b Farnham 19/4/1898	d 1983	
		Caps: WLge 2		
		Marshes Hall		
1921	1923	Newport County	22	3
		Bridgend Town		
		Barry		
1927		Newport County	19	6
		Bath City		
1929		Newport County	0	
		Brittan, Harold Pemberton (Harry)	CF/IL	
		b Derby q1 1894	d 1964	
		Ilkeston United		
1913	1919	Chelsea	24	7
		Bethlehem Steel		
		Philadelphia Field Club		
		Fall River Marksmen		
		New Bedford Whalers		
		Fall River Marksmen		
		Brittan, Richard Charles (Charlie)	RB/LB	
		b Newport, Isle of Wight 7/8/1887	d 1949	
		Caps: SoLge 6/WLge 2		
		Portsmouth		
		Northampton Town		
1911	1912	Tottenham Hotspur	40	
1920	1922	Cardiff City	75	
		Brittleton, John Thomas (Tom)	RH/LB/RB	
		b Winsford 23/4/1882	d 1955	
		Caps: FLge 2/England 5		
		Winsford Juniors		
		Winsford Celtic		
		Winsford United		
1902	1903	Stockport County	45	10
1904	1919	Sheffield Wednesday	343	30
1920	1924	Stoke	114	5
		Winsford United		
		Brittleton, John Thomas	RB/LB	
		b Winsford 5/5/1906	d 1982	
		Winsford Celtic		
		Chester		
1927	1929	Aston Villa	10	
		Winsford United		
		Britton, Clifford Samuel (Cliff)	RH	
		b Hanham 29/8/1909	d 1975	
		Caps: FLge 4/England War 12/England 9		
		Hanham Athletic		
		Hanham VM		
		Bristol St George		
1928	1929	Bristol Rovers	50	1
1930	1938	Everton	221	2
1945		Burnley	0	
		Britton, Francis George (Frank)	LH/CF	
		b Bristol 4/6/1911	d 1999	
		Bristol St George		
1929		Bristol Rovers	1	
1930	1933	Blackburn Rovers	45	8
1934		Oldham Athletic	1	
1934		Accrington Stanley	11	9
1935		Reading (trial)	0	
1935		Aldershot	1	
		Worcester City		
		Hereford United		
		Cradley Heath		
		Stourbridge		
		Evesham Town		
		Britton, John (Jack)	GK	
		b Lennoxtown 18/3/1900	d 1953	
		Duntocher Hibs		
		Albion Rovers		
		Dundee		
1925	1927	Tottenham Hotspur	40	
		Derry Celtic		
		Kirkintilloch Rob Roy		
		Broad, James (Jimmy)	CF/IR	
		b Stalybridge 10/11/1891	d 1963	
		St Mark's (West Gorton)		
		Stalybridge Celtic		
1909		Manchester City	0	
1910		Manchester United	0	
		Royal Corunna		
1912		Manchester City	0	
1913	1914	Oldham Athletic	15	5
		Morton		
		Bacup Borough		
1920		Millwall Athletic	9	6
		Las Palmas		
1921	1923	Stoke	108	62
		Barcelona		
		Sittingbourne		
1924	1925	Everton	18	8
1925		New Brighton	11	3
1926		Watford	1	1
		Peterborough & Fletton United		
		Caernarvon Athletic		
		Taunton Town		
1929		New Brighton	0	
		Geneva		
		Fleetwood		
		Morecambe		
		Broad, Thomas Higginson (Tommy)	OR	
		b Stalybridge 31/7/1887	d 1966	
		Caps: FLge 1		
		Redgate Albion		
		Denton Wanderers		
1903		Manchester City (trial)	0	
		Openshaw Lads Club		
1906		West Bromwich Albion	11	
1907	1908	Chesterfield Town	48	5
1909	1911	Oldham Athletic	96	9
1912	1914	Bristol City	106	8
1919	1920	Manchester City	42	
1921	1923	Stoke	83	4
1924		Southampton	9	
		Weymouth		
		Rhyl Athletic		
		Broadbent, Frederick (Fred)	CF	
		b Hollinwood 9/11/1900	d 1959	
		Ferranti (Hollinwood)		
1921	1922	Oldham Athletic	12	4
1923		Southport	19	3
		Broadbent, John	GK	
		b Great Gonerby 1864	d 1949	
		Grantham		
		Grantham Rovers		
1894		Lincoln City	2	
		Broadbent, William Henry (Billy)	RH/RB	
		b Oldham 20/11/1901	d 1979	
		Wellington Albion		
1920	1923	Oldham Athletic	12	1
1924		Brentford	17	
1925	1931	Clapton Orient	198	8
1932		Preston North End	2	
		Manchester North End		
		Broadfoot, John George	LH	
		b Newcastle q1 1893	d 1963	
1925		Barrow	1	
		Broadgate, Leonard Archer	OR	
		b Brigg q4 1879	d 1952	
1901		Gainsborough Trinity	5	

From	To		Apps	Goal
		Broadhead, Arnold	IR	
		b Darnall 19/2/1900	d 1973	
1920	1921	Brighton & Hove Albion	8	2
1923		Swindon Town	1	2
		Broadhead, James Edward (Jimmy)	LH	
		b Rotherham 25/8/1894	d 1955	
		Kimberworth Old Boys		
		Rotherham County		
		Norwich City		
1920		South Shields	0	
		Scunthorpe & Lindsey United		
1922	1925	Nelson	66	1
		Barnoldswick Town		
1927		Nelson	1	
		Horwich RMI		
		Morecambe		
		Broadhead, W	LH/CH	
1893	1895	Rotherham Town	53	4
		Broadhead, William	IR	
1924		Rotherham County	3	
		Broadhurst, Albert	OR	
		b 1897		
1919		Port Vale	4	
		Broadhurst, Charles (Charlie)	CF/IR	
		b Moston 31/1/1906	d 1971	
		Newton Heath LMS		
		Hurst		
		Ashton National		
1926	1928	Manchester City	33	25
1929	1930	Blackpool	18	6
		Manchester North End		
		Ashton National		
		Hyde United		
		Droylsden		
		Newton Heath Loco		
		Broadhurst, Fred	RB/LB	
		b Aspull 30/11/1888	d 1953	
		Hindley Central		
1910	1921	Preston North End	107	3
		Hindley Central (loan)		
1922		Stalybridge Celtic	36	
1923		Stockport County	4	
1924		Barrow	38	
1925	1926	Nelson	61	
		Chorley		
		Broadhurst, John William (Jack)	CF	
		b Birkenhead 11/3/1918	d 1979	
		Brookville		
1937		Tranmere Rovers	0	
1938		Southend United	1	
1938		New Brighton	1	
		Brobbins, Sydney (Syd)	LH	
		b Salford 29/12/1911	d 1979	
		Altrincham		
1934		Halifax Town	1	
		Brock, Frederick	LB	
		b Huddersfield		
1920		Huddersfield Town	1	
		Brock, George Wallace	LH	
		b Glasgow 27/7/1915	d 1971	
		Kirkintilloch Rob Roy		
		Partick Thistle (trial)		
		Airdrieonians (trial)		
1935	1936	New Brighton	66	4
1937		Wolverhampton Wanderers	0	
		Brock, James	OR	
		b Scotland		
		East Stirlingshire		
1896	1898	Woolwich Arsenal	57	20
		Cowes		
		Clyde		
		Abercorn		
		Brock, John George Graham	GK	
		b Bromsgrove 15/12/1915	d 1976	
		Bristol University		
		Forest Green Rovers		
1936		Swindon Town	5	
		Brock, John Robert Eadie	OR	
		b Cargill 4/10/1897		
		Edinburgh City		
1920		Leeds United	6	
		Brock, John S	IR/OR	
		b Glasgow 12/1/1878		
		Vale of Clyde		
1898	1899	Luton Town	52	14
		Clyde		
		Brockhurst, William James (Bill)	CH	
		b Brownhills 25/11/1913	d 1995	
		Cannock Chase Colliery		
1936		West Bromwich Albion	5	
		Hednesford Town		

From	To		Apps	Goal
		Brocklebank, Robert Edward (Bob)	IR/CF/IL	
		b Finchley 23/5/1908	d 1981	
		Finchley		
1929	1935	Aston Villa	19	2
1935	1938	Burnley	121	33
1939		(Burnley)	(2)	
		Brocklesby, Herbert Ernest (Bert)	RB	
		b Grimsby q3 1879	d 1959	
		White Star Rangers		
		St James United		
1897		Grimsby Town	3	
		Grimsby All Saints		
		Brocksopp, Arthur	OL/OR	
		b Walsall q3 1872		
		Ironbridge		
1894		Wolverhampton Wanderers	3	
1896		Walsall	2	
		Willenhall		
		Brodie, D	RB	
1900		Glossop	3	
		Brodie, David (Davy)	LH/RH	
		b Paisley 9/11/1863	d 1938	
		Abercorn		
1889	1896	Stoke	170	2
		Burslem Port Vale		
		Brodie, Duncan	RH	
		b Lugar 23/4/1878	d 1915	
		Cronberry Eglington		
		Lugar Boswell		
		Partick Thistle		
		Cumnock		
1904		Barnsley	1	
		Thornhill		
		Brodie, George Woolven	OL/IR	
		b Castle Douglas 17/12/1898	d 1982	
		Castle Douglas		
		Fleetwood Town		
1921		Wigan Borough	11	2
		Castle Douglas		
1922		Notts County	1	
		Castle Douglas	0	
		Queen of the South		
		Brodie, John Brant	CF/LH	
		b Wightwick 30/8/1862	d 1925	
		Caps: England 3		
		Saltley College		
1888	1890	Wolverhampton Wanderers	42	22
		Brodie, John Charles	IR	
		b Kilmarnock 1868	d 1901	
		Hurlford		
		Kilmarnock		
1890		Burnley	2	
		Kilmarnock		
		Third Lanark		
		Kilmarnock		
1893		Nottingham Forest	9	5
		Kilmarnock		
		Kilmarnock Athletic		
		Brogan, James	IR/OR	
		b Beith 1865		
		Beith		
		Hibernian		
		Heart of Midlothian		
1888	1891	Bolton Wanderers	74	26
		Broley, John Fair	GK	
		b Liverpool 15/11/1872	d 1944	
		Tranmere Rovers		
1900		Barnsley	3	
		Brolly, Thomas Henry (Tom)	RH/CH/LH	
		b Belfast 1/6/1912	d 1986	
		Caps: NIRL 4/Ireland 4		
		Crusaders		
		Glenavon		
1933		Sheffield Wednesday	2	
1935	1938	Millwall	136	6
1939		(Millwall)	(3)	(1)
		Linfield		
1945	1949	Millwall	93	2
		Bromage, Enos	GK	
		b Mickleover 1865	d 1947	
		Derby Junction		
1888	1889	Derby County	17	
		Derby Junction		
		Bromage, Enos	OL	
		b Mickleover 22/10/1898	d 1978	
		Stapleford Town		
1922		Sheffield United	0	
1923	1926	Derby County	4	2
1927		Gillingham	21	6
1927		West Bromwich Albion	10	2
1929		Nottingham Forest	1	
		Chester		
		Wellington Town		

From	To		Apps	Goal
		Bromage, George	OL	
		b Derby q1 1899		
1919		Derby County	0	
		Doncaster Rovers		
1922	1923	Sheffield United	5	1
		Buxton		
		Shirebrook		
		Bromage, George Edward	GK	
		b Doncaster 10/8/1902	d 1990	
		Bentley Colliery		
1924		Barnsley	0	
1925		Doncaster Rovers	3	
		Frickley Colliery		
		Scunthorpe & Lindsey United		
		Bromage, Henry (Harry)	GK	
		b Derby 17/5/1879		
		Derby Constitutional		
1899	1901	Derby County	5	
1903	1904	Burton United	67	
1905	1910	Leeds City	143	
		Doncaster Rovers		
		Bentley Colliery		
		Bromage, William (Billy)	OL/IL	
		b Derby 31/3/1881		
1900		Derby County	0	
		Derby Hills Ivanhoe		
1902		Gainsborough Trinity	20	3
		Whitwick White Cross		
1905	1908	Sheffield United	30	5
		Doncaster Rovers		
		Bromilow, Thomas George (Tom)	LH	
		b Liverpool 7/10/1894	d 1959	
		Caps: FLge 6/England 5		
		West Dingle		
		United West Dingle Presbyterians		
1919	1929	Liverpool	341	11
		Bromilow, William	GK	
		b Liverpool q4 1889	d 1965	
		Lingdale		
1912		Everton	1	
1920		Oldham Athletic	0	
1921		Wigan Borough	33	
		Skelmersdale United		
		Chorley		
		Brook, Eric Fred	OL	
		b Mexborough 27/11/1907	d 1965	
		Caps: FLge 7/England War 1/England 18		
		Wath Athletic		
1925	1927	Barnsley	78	18
1927	1938	Manchester City	450	158
1939		(Manchester City)	(3)	(1)
		Brook, Lewis	RB/CF/RH	
		b Northowram 27/7/1918	d 1996	
		Northowram		
1935		Halifax Town	0	
1937	1946	Huddersfield Town	18	6
1947	1956	Oldham Athletic	189	14
		Brook, Reginald (Reg)	RB/LB	
		b Nottingham 20/7/1912	d 1989	
		Loughborough Corinthians		
1934		Coventry City	9	
1936		Southend United	3	
1937	1938	Bristol City	71	1
1939		(Bristol City)	(3)	
		Brooke, Percy	LB/RB	
		b Kidsgrove 5/1893	d 1971	
		Caps: WLge 1		
		Kidsgrove Wellington		
1919	1920	Stoke	11	
1921	1925	Aberdare Athletic	123	
1926		Swindon Town	3	
1927		Accrington Stanley	2	
		Brookes, Arthur Goodreid	LH	
		b Wednesbury 24/3/1914	d 2001	
1936		West Bromwich Albion	0	
1937	1938	Halifax Town	47	
		Brookes, Arthur Walter	CH/LH	
		b Small Heath 1888		
		Bordesley Rangers		
		Small Heath Taveners		
		Cradley Heath St Luke's		
1911	1914	Wolverhampton Wanderers	13	
		Newport County		
		Brookes, Gilbert Henry	GK	
		b Kidderminster 2/4/1895	d 1952	
		Kidderminster Harriers		
		Shrewsbury Town		
1922		Stoke	12	
1923		Swansea Town	37	
1924		Luton Town	42	
1925		Merthyr Town	38	
		Kidderminster Harriers		

From	To		Apps	Goal
		Brookes, Isaac (Ike)	GK	
		b Bilston 1861		
1891		Stoke	2	
1893		Northwich Victoria	6	
		Brookes, J	LB	
1894	1895	Crewe Alexandra	10	
		Brookes, Sydney (Syd)	IL/LH	
		b Ashby-de-la-Zouch 19/7/1907	d 1975	
		Scunthorpe & Lindsey United		
1927	1931	Blackpool	24	4
1932		Swindon Town	30	6
		Scarborough		
		Brookes, Thomas	LH	
1900		Stockport County	2	
		Brookes, William Norman (Norman)	OR	
		Highley		
		Kidderminster Harriers		
1930	1931	Walsall	16	2
		Brookfield, Arthur	OR	
		b Longton q4 1873		
		Longton Atlas		
1894	1895	Stoke	8	2
1895		Crewe Alexandra	0	
		Brooks, Albert	RB	
		b Parkgate 1888		
		Rotherham County		
		Rotherham Town		
		Rotherham County		
1913	1914	Wolverhampton Wanderers	15	
		Brooks, Arthur Frederick	CF	
		b Henstead 4/10/1891	d 1976	
		Yarmouth Town		
		Gorleston		
		Norwich City		
1909		Grimsby Town	4	2
		Doncaster Rovers		
		Brooks, Charles Edward (Charlie)	RB	
		b Kent		
1930		Arsenal	0	
		Nunhead		
		Folkestone		
1937		Clapton Orient	4	
1938		Crystal Palace	0	
		Brooks, Edward A (Ned)	CF/IL	
		Caps: IrLge 1/LoI 1/Ireland 1		
		Shelbourne		
		Bohemians		
1920	1921	Stockport County	12	1
		Bohemians		
		Athlone Town		
		Brideville		
		Brooks, Ernest William	OR	
		b Brierley Hill 4/3/1894	d 1962	
1919		Blackburn Rovers	3	
1921		Wolverhampton Wanderers	0	
		Brierley Hill Alliance		
		Brooks, George	RH/LH/CH	
		b Tottington 1/1893		
		Ramsbottom		
1919	1925	Bury	69	3
		Brooks, George Harold	LH/CH/CF	
		b Radcliffe q2 1887	d 1918	
		Longfield		
1910	1911	Manchester City	3	1
1911	1912	Bury	2	
		South Shields		
1914		Derby County	33	
		Brooks, Harry	CF/IR	
		b Tibshelf 2/6/1915	d 1994	
		Heanor Town		
1936	1938	Doncaster Rovers	5	
1945	1947	Aldershot	23	14
		Brooks, John (Jack)	RB	
		b Stockton 13/3/1904	d 1973	
		Stillington St John's		
1924		Fulham	9	
		Shildon		
1926	1928	Darlington	54	
1928		Nelson	6	
1929	1931	York City	82	
		Bacup Borough		
		ICI (Durham)		
		Brooks, Joseph (Joe)	LB	
		b Stalybridge q3 1878		
		Stalybridge Rovers		
1900		Glossop	4	
		Watford		
1907	1911	Sheffield United	126	
		Stalybridge Celtic		

From To Apps Goal

Brooks, Joseph (Joe) OL
b Stairfoot 11/1886 d 1955
Ardsley Nelson
1904 1906 Barnsley 48 7
1907 West Bromwich Albion 21 1
1908 Barnsley 4
Rotherham County

Brooks, Joseph Ernest (Ernie) OR
b Heanor 20/11/1892 d 1975
Langley Heanor
1919 Grimsby Town 3
Shirebrook
1921 Leicester City 4
Shirebrook
Kettering
Shirebrook

Brooks, Joseph T OR
Melbourne Town
1894 Derby County 3
Heanor Town
Melbourne Town

Brooks, JS RH
1901 Blackpool 3 1

Brooks, L CH
1914 Blackpool 2

Brooks, Leonard Walter (Len) GK
b Manningtree 13/12/1913 d 1994
Fleet Amateurs
1935 1936 Fulham 2
1937 1938 Bournemouth & Boscombe Ath 39
Colchester United

Brooks, Samuel Ernest (Sammy) OL/OR
b Brierley Hill 28/3/1890 d 1960
Caps: FLge 1
Brierley Hill Corinthians
Brierley Hill Alliance
Bilston United
Cradley Heath
1910 1921 Wolverhampton Wanderers 224 50
1922 1923 Tottenham Hotspur 10 1
1924 Southend United 12 2
Kidderminster Harriers
Cradley Heath
Stourbridge

Brooks, William Henry CF
b Stalybridge q3 1873
Stalybridge Rovers
1895 Newton Heath (trial) 0
1898 Newton Heath 3 3
Stalybridge Rovers

Brooksbank, Clifford CF
b Halifax q1 1889 d 1955
1908 Blackburn Rovers 0
Oswaldwistle Rovers
Exeter City
1914 Bristol City 10 7

Broom, William IL
b Grimsby 26/2/1895 d 1971
Brigg Town
Box Company (Grimsby)
1919 Grimsby Town 3 2
Charlton's (Grimsby)
Brigg Town

Broome, Albert Henry (Harry) IR
b Unsworth 30/5/1900 d 1989
Manchester University
Northern Nomads
1921 Oldham Athletic 0
1922 Manchester United 1
1924 Oldham Athletic 4
Welshpool
Sandbach Ramblers
1926 1927 Stockport County 4
Mossley
Chester
Altrincham
Northwich Victoria

Broome, Frank Henry OR/OL/CF
b Berkhamsted 11/6/1915 d 1994
Caps: England War 1/England 7
Boxmoor United
Berkhamsted Town
1934 1946 Aston Villa 133 78
1939 (Aston Villa) (3)
1946 1949 Derby County 112 45
1949 1952 Notts County 105 35
1953 Brentford 6 1
1953 1954 Crewe Alexandra 36 17
Shelbourne

Broome, Samuel (Sam) IL
Kidderminster Harriers
1907 Bury 1
Plymouth Argyle

From To Apps Goal

Broome, Thomas Alfred (Tommy) LH/RH/CF
b Pendleton q1 1892 d 1956
Salford United
Rochdale
1913 1919 Preston North End 65 2
Caernarvon
1920 Grimsby Town 7
Nelson
1920 Bolton Wanderers (trial) 0
1921 Chesterfield 14 2
Sandbach Ramblers
CWS Balloon Street
Stourbridge

Broome, William Henry (Harry) IR/IL/OR
b Chorlton 16/4/1904
Altrincham
1926 Bury 0
Colwyn Bay
Bangor City
Caernarvon Athletic
1929 Crewe Alexandra 30 5
1930 Accrington Stanley 33 9
1931 1932 Mansfield Town 48 9

Broomfield, Ernest CF
1903 Stockport County 5 1

Broomfield, Herbert C GK
b Audlem 11/12/1878
Northwich Wednesday
Northwich Victoria
1902 1906 Bolton Wanderers 28
1907 Manchester United 9
1908 Manchester City 4

Brophy, Henry Frederick (Harry) LH
b Leicester 22/10/1916 d 1996
1934 Arsenal 0
Canterbury Waverley (loan)
Margate (loan)
1937 Brighton & Hove Albion 0
1938 Southampton 37 5
1939 (Southampton) (1)
Follands
Nuneaton Town
Corinthian Club (Queensland)

Brophy, Thomas (Tom) LB/LH/RH
b St Helens 8/1/1897 d 1979
St Helens Town
1920 Burnley 3
St Helens Town
1923 1926 Aberdare Athletic 133 5
1927 1929 Southend United 42

Broskom, George Richard OR
b Rotherham 4/12/1896 d 1984
1919 Coventry City 0
1920 Reading 15 1
1921 Halifax Town 1
Castleford Town
Rotherham Town
Wombwell
Scunthorpe & Lindsey United
Frickley Colliery
Shirebrook

Broster, John RH
b Burtonwood q1 1889 d 1959
Chorley
Queen's Park Rangers
1921 Rochdale 1
1921 Wigan Borough 31 3
1922 Rochdale 8
Earlestown LMS

Brough, Albert RB
b Barrow 20/7/1895 d 1980
Barrow RFC
1921 1922 Barrow 15
1923 Oldham Athletic 0
Mossley

Brough, Henry Burton (Harry) RH/LH
b Guisborough 27/12/1896 d 1975
Kilnhurst
1913 Huddersfield Town 6 2
York City
1919 1922 Huddersfield Town 54
1922 Manchester United 0
1922 1925 Stoke 84 1

Brough, Joseph (Joe) IR/RH
b Burslem 9/11/1886 d 1968
Burslem Park
Smallthorne
1906 Burslem Port Vale 11 1
1907 Stoke 1
1908 Tottenham Hotspur 1
Burslem Port Vale
1910 Liverpool 10 3
1911 1912 Bristol City 22 11
1919 1921 Port Vale 61 5

From To Apps Goal

Broughton, Matthew (Matt) OR
b Grantham 8/10/1880 d 1957
Grantham
1901 1902 Nottingham Forest 27 5
Grantham
1904 Notts County 2 1
Watford
Grantham

Broughton, Thomas William (Tom) RH
b Port Clarence 7/6/1888
Grangetown
1912 Leeds City 4

Browell, Anthony (Andy) CH
b Walbottle 17/9/1888 d 1964
Newburn Juniors
1908 1911 Hull City 101 5
1912 Everton 1
West Stanley
Lintz Institute

Browell, George RH
b Walbottle q4 1884 d 1951
West Stanley
1905 1910 Hull City 194 3
1911 Grimsby Town 23
West Stanley

Browell, Thomas (Tommy) CF/IR/IL
b Walbottle 19/10/1892 d 1955
Caps: FLge 1
Newburn Grange
1910 1911 Hull City 48 32
1911 1913 Everton 50 26
1913 1925 Manchester City 222 122
Motherwell (loan)
1926 1929 Blackpool 66 27
Lytham
Morecambe

Brown, ? RH
1901 Glossop 1

Brown, Alan Winston CH/LH
b Corbridge 26/8/1914 d 1996
Caps: FLge 1
Corbridge United
Spen Black & White
1934 1938 Huddersfield Town 57
1946 1948 Burnley 88
1948 Notts County 13

Brown, Albert Alfred OR/IR
b Aston 1862 d 1930
Mitchell St George's
1888 1893 Aston Villa 86 37

Brown, Albert CF
b Tamworth q2 1879 d 1955
Atherstone Star
Tamworth
1900 Aston Villa 2 2
Southampton
Queen's Park Rangers
1904 1905 Preston North End 22 7
1905 Blackpool 3

Brown, Albert Charles CF
b Bedford q2 1895
Kettering
1922 Luton Town 1
Kettering

Brown, Albert Richard (Dick) OL/OR
b Pegswood 14/2/1911
Alnwick United
1928 1929 Rochdale 40 10
1930 Sheffield Wednesday 0
Blyth Spartans
1932 1933 Queen's Park Rangers 60 20
1934 1935 Northampton Town 79 23
1935 1936 Nottingham Forest 20 2

Brown, Albert Roy (Roy) OL/OR
b Nottingham 14/8/1917 d 2005
Sneinton
1936 1938 Nottingham Forest 51 7
1939 1946 Wrexham 24 3
1939 (Wrexham) (3) (1)
1947 Mansfield Town 17 2
Stafford Rangers
Goole Town

From To Apps Goal

Brown, Alexander (Sandy) CF
b Beith 7/4/1879
Caps: Scotland 1
Glenbuck Athletic
Kilsyth Wanderers
St Bernard's
1896 1898 Preston North End 63 25
Portsmouth
Tottenham Hotspur
Portsmouth
1903 1904 Middlesbrough 44 15
Luton Town
Kettering
Nithsdale Wanderers
Ayr United

Brown, Alexander Roy (Alex) OL/OR/IR
b Seghill 21/11/1914
West Cramlington Welfare
Blyth Spartans
Ashington
Normanby Magnesite
1932 Hartlepools United 0
Seghill Colliery Welfare
1934 Chesterfield 8 1
1935 Darlington 5
Shrewsbury Town
1939 Gateshead (1)
1946 Mansfield Town 5

Brown, Alfred (Alf) RH/LH
b Chapeltown 19/10/1898 d 1979
Carbrook Reform
Sheffield United
Rotherham Town
1921 1922 Blackpool 9
1923 1925 Barnsley 12
1926 Swindon Town 14 1
1927 Nelson (trial) 2
1927 Barnsley (trial)
Hurst
Manchester Central
Stalybridge Celtic

Brown, Alfred (Alf) CF
Ashton National
1921 Crewe Alexandra 11 4

Brown, Alfred (Alf) RH
b Chadderton 22/2/1907 d 1994
Chamber Colliery
1928 1932 Oldham Athletic 44
1933 1935 Northampton Town 55 1
1935 1936 Mansfield Town 46

Brown, Ambrose Robert IL
b Burton-on-Trent 15/2/1911 d 1989
Newhall Swifts
1934 Chesterfield 27 10
1935 Portsmouth 1
1936 Wrexham 27 5
Bath City
Tunbridge Wells Rangers

Brown, Andrew Robert IL
b Coatbridge 20/2/1915 d 1973
Cumbernauld Thistle
1936 1937 Cardiff City 2
1938 1946 Torquay United 34 5
Colchester United
Kidderminster Harriers
Bury Town

Brown, Arthur IL
b Preston 1896 d 1974
Lancaster Town
1922 Portsmouth 5 1
Guildford United
Lancaster Town
Morecambe
Lancaster Town
Morecambe Victoria
Morecambe

Brown, Arthur Ivor GK
b Aberdare 10/10/1903 d 1971
Caps: Wales 1
1925 1926 Aberdare Athletic 42
1928 Reading 14
1929 Port Vale 1
1929 1932 Crewe Alexandra 117
Merthyr Town

Brown, Arthur Samuel CF/IL
b Gainsborough 6/4/1885 d 1944
Caps: England 2
1901 Gainsborough Trinity 3 2
1902 1907 Sheffield United 178 104
1908 1909 Sunderland 50 21
1910 1911 Fulham 41 9
1912 Middlesbrough 4

Brown, Bertie R OR
1937 Bournemouth & Boscombe Ath 3
1938 Barrow 0

From To | Apps Goal

Brown, C IR/OL
1896 1897 Gainsborough Trinity 2 1

Brown, Charles RB
Mossend Swifts
Leith Athletic
1898 Blackburn Rovers 1
Mossend Swifts
Leith Athletic

Brown, Charles (Charlie) OR
b Stakeford 14/1/1898 d 1979
Stakeford United
1920 1923 Southampton 80 8
1924 1925 Queen's Park Rangers 67 3
Poole

Brown, Charles George RH
b Earlsfield 7/12/1909
Hayes
1932 1933 Crystal Palace 29
1934 Watford 0
Dartford
1936 Clapton Orient 1

Brown, Charles Marshall (Charlie) LH/LB
b Tinsley 1915
1937 Bolton Wanderers 0
1938 1945 Hartlepools United 5
1939 (Hartlepools United) (2)

Brown, Charles V LB
b Hodthorpe
1924 1925 Millwall Athletic 10

Brown, Craig LB/RH
b Muirkirk 22/1/1893
Caps: SLge 1
Lesmahagow
Carluke Milton Rovers
Leith Athletic
St Bernard's
Armadale
1914 1919 Bradford City 9 1
Bathgate (loan)
Motherwell (loan)
Hibernian (loan)
Motherwell
Cowdenbeath
Morton
Peebles Rovers
Mid Annandale

Brown, David IR
1895 Loughborough 3

Brown, David C CF
1896 Burnley 4 1

Brown, David Carre (Davie) CF/IR
b Dundee 26/11/1887
Dundee St Joseph's
Dundee
Morton
Peebles Rovers
Dundee
Rangers (loan)
1919 1920 Stoke 50 17
1921 Notts County 14 7
Kilmarnock
1923 1925 Darlington 97 74
1926 Crewe Alexandra 37 21
1927 Barrow 23 7

Brown, David Crichton CF
b Broughty Ferry 26/7/1889
Forthill Athletic
1909 Tottenham Hotspur 1
Reading (trial)
1909 Birmingham (trial) 0
Merthyr Town (trial)
Morton
Northampton Town

Brown, Edward OL
b Ormskirk 22/1/1899 d 1972
Ormskirk DS & S
1921 Wigan Borough 1

Brown, Edward G RH
b Dudley
1919 West Bromwich Albion 0
1920 1921 Merthyr Town 38 2

Brown, Edward H CF/OR
1903 1904 Lincoln City 37 9

Brown, Frank CH/LH
b Rotherham q4 1890
1913 Barnsley 0
Rotherham County
1920 Blackpool 1
1921 Exeter City 6
Pontypridd
Torquay United

From To | Apps Goal

Brown, Frederick (Fred) IR/CF/IL
b Gainsborough 28/6/1895 d 1960
Gainsborough Trinity
1919 1922 Sheffield United 38 8
1923 Brighton & Hove Albion 19 3
1924 1926 Gillingham 95 26
Gainsborough Trinity

Brown, Frederick Walter (Fred) IR/CF
b Birmingham 1911
Hinckley Juniors
1931 Sunderland 0
1931 Rochdale 21 6
1932 1933 Halifax Town 54 13
1934 1935 Accrington Stanley 76 25
1936 Torquay United 10 3
Newark Town
Grantham

Brown, George IL
b Barnsley
Hoyle Mill
1906 Barnsley 1
Hoyle Mill
1913 Barnsley 0

Brown, George CF/IR
b Mickley 22/6/1903 d 1948
Caps: FLge 3/England 9
Mickley Colliery Welfare
1921 1928 Huddersfield Town 213 142
1929 1934 Aston Villa 116 79
1934 1935 Burnley 35 24
1935 1936 Leeds United 37 19
1936 1937 Darlington 44 12

Brown, George A RH/LH
b Whitton Park 1913
Cockfield
1933 1935 Hartlepools United 51
1936 Halifax Town 10
Spennymoor United

Brown, George Gerald OL
b Lowestoft 1/1884
Kirkley
Dulwich Hamlet
1903 Woolwich Arsenal 0
1904 Stoke 8
Norwich City
Millwall Athletic
1907 Gainsborough Trinity 16
1908 Sheffield United 2

Brown, George H RH
Nottingham Forest
1888 Notts County 19 1
Nottingham Forest

Brown, George H GK
b Southampton
Ebbw Vale
1922 Birmingham 0
Mid-Rhondda United
1925 Aberdare Athletic 13

Brown, GL LB
1896 1897 Gainsborough Trinity 13

Brown, Harold OR
1931 Oldham Athletic 1 1
British Dyes
1934 Oldham Athletic 0
Stalybridge Celtic
Mossley

Brown, Harold Archer (Harry) CF
b Shildon q4 1897 d 1958
Shildon Athletic
1921 Sunderland 6 1
Leadgate Park
Chilton Colliery Recreation Athletic
Shildon
1924 Queen's Park Rangers 13 3

Brown, Harry GK
1901 Burnley 7

Brown, Harry Russell LH
b Stoke-on-Trent q3 1888
Tredegar
Crewe Alexandra
1910 Manchester City 2
Tredegar
Crewe Alexandra

From To | Apps Goal

Brown, Henry (Harry) IL
b Northampton 11/1883 d 1934
St Sepulchre's (Northampton)
Northampton Town
1903 1904 West Bromwich Albion 35 5
Southampton
1906 1907 Newcastle United 24 8
Bradford Park Avenue
1907 1909 Fulham 53 21
Southampton
Woolston

Brown, Henry IL
b Bebside q2 1886
Bedlington United
Heart of Midlothian
1910 Stockport County 2

Brown, Henry (Ernie) IR/OR
b Aberaman 17/3/1902 d 1984
Caps: WLge 1
Aberaman Athletic
1921 Merthyr Town 0
Caerphilly
1922 1923 Aberdare Athletic 44 9
1924 Liverpool 0
1925 Southport 24 7
1926 Aberdare Athletic 31 8
1928 Merthyr Town 36 5
1929 Charlton Athletic 2
1930 Newport County 35 3
1931 Thames 17 1

Brown, Henry Stanford (Harry) CH/OR
b Workington 23/5/1918 d 1963
Workington
1938 Wolverhampton Wanderers 2
1946 Hull City 22

Brown, Henry Summers (Harry) IR/OR/IL
b Kirkcaldy 18/9/1907 d 1963
Wemyss Athletic
Hibernian
1932 1933 Darlington 57 17
1933 1936 Chesterfield 111 25
1936 1938 Plymouth Argyle 45 12
1938 Reading 26 4

Brown, Herbert Archibald LB
b Witton Park
Shildon
1928 1931 Darlington 139 7
Spennymoor United

Brown, Herbert Edward (Bert) OR
b Nottingham
Crewe Alexandra
Welbeck Colliery
1922 Bradford City 6 1
1923 Middlesbrough 0
York City

Brown, HS CH
1893 1894 Rotherham Town 17

Brown, Hugh Allan RH
b Glasgow 11/3/1896 d 1952
Anderson Thornbank
St Anthony's (Glasgow)
Celtic
Clackmannan (loan)
Dunfermline Athletic
Partick Thistle
1921 Merthyr Town 19 1
Caerphilly Town
Dunkeld & Birnam

Brown, Ivor Ronald John CF
b Shardlow 1/4/1888 d 1966
Ripley Town
1909 1910 Tottenham Hotspur 12
Ilkeston United
Coventry City
Reading
Swansea Town
Porth Athletic

Brown, J LH
1898 Darwen 7

Brown, J OL
1903 Stockport County 5

Brown, James (Jimmy) IL
b Blackburn 31/7/1862 d 1922
Caps: England 5
1888 Blackburn Rovers 4

Brown, James LB
Dundee Our Boys
1892 Newton Heath 7
Dundee Our Boys
Dundee

From To | Apps Goal

Brown, James LB
b Scotland
1892 1893 Sheffield Wednesday 10

Brown, James (Jimmy) CH/RH
b Alexandria 17/6/1869 d 1924
Renton Union
Renton Thistle
Renton
1893 Aston Villa 0
1894 1898 Leicester Fosse 116 5
1899 Loughborough 13 2

Brown, James LH/OL
b Luton 1880
1899 Luton Town 13 1
1900 Middlesbrough 2

Brown, James (Jimmy) RB
Lambton Star
1923 Hartlepools United 1

Brown, James IR
Workington
1926 1927 Crewe Alexandra 35 11

Brown, James (Jimmy) RH/LH
b Motherwell 1907
Belhavenock
Maryhill
Wishaw Juniors
East Fife
1927 1934 Burnley 228 5
1935 1938 Manchester United 102 1
1938 Bradford Park Avenue 13
1939 (Bradford Park Avenue) (1)

Brown, James Benjamin GK
b Barnard Castle q4 1902
Barnard Castle United
1921 1922 Darlington 5

Brown, James Frederick (Freddie) IR/CF
b Brierley Hill 1886 d 1939
Kidderminster Harriers
1906 1907 Stoke 23 8
1908 1909 West Bromwich Albion 8 1
Kidderminster Harriers
Willenhall Swifts

Brown, James J (Jimmy) OR/IL
b Kilmarnock 31/12/1908 d 1994
Caps: USA
Plainfield
Bayonne Rovers (New Jersey)
Newark Skeeters
New York Nationals
New York Giants
New York Soccer Club
Brooklyn Wanderers
Newark Americans
1932 1933 Manchester United 40 17
1935 Brentford 1
1936 Tottenham Hotspur 4
Guildford City
Clydebank
Greenport United (Connecticut)

Brown, James Richard RH
b Birmingham 1868 d 1934
Bordesley Green Victoria
Small Heath
1890 1892 Aston Villa 52 3
Stourbridge

Brown, James William CH/RH
b Wigan 18/1/1903 d 1982
Adlington
Atherton
1924 1925 Wigan Borough 7
Runcorn
Hurst
Clitheroe
Chorley
Middlewich
Hurst
1930 Wigan Borough 0

Brown, John (Jock) CF/IR
b Motherwell 1876
Motherwell Star
Dalziel Rovers
1897 1898 Sunderland 33 9
Portsmouth
1900 Middlesbrough 22 5
Luton Town
Kettering

Brown, John RH
1904 1905 Glossop 52 8

From To Apps Goal

Brown, John IR
b Rutherglen 1890
Rutherglen Castle Bank
Rutherglen Glencairn
Parkhead
1911 1913 Bury 41 10

Brown, John CF
1922 Rochdale 2

Brown, John (Jack) IR/IL
b Belfast 1/9/1900
Caps: IrLge 1/Ireland 3
Glenavon
1923 1924 Tranmere Rovers 47 11
Mid-Rhondda United
1926 Merthyr Town 26 5
1927 Crystal Palace 8 2
Aberdare & Aberaman

Brown, John OR
b Glasgow
Broxburn
Armadale
Shawfield
East Stirlingshire
St Johnstone
Brechin City
Morton
1926 Burnley (trial) 0
1926 Nelson (trial) 2
Manchester Central

Brown, John (Jack) GK
Marley Hill
1927 Hartlepools United 5
West Stanley

Brown, John RB
b Dumfries 1898
Kello Rovers
1928 Carlisle United 1

Brown, John (Jackie) OR/OL
b Belfast 8/11/1914
Caps: IrLge 2/Ireland 10/Eire 1
Belfast Celtic
1934 1936 Wolverhampton Wanderers 27 6
1936 1937 Coventry City 69 26
1938 Birmingham 34 6
1939 (Birmingham) (3) (1)
Barry Town
1948 1950 Ipswich Town 98 25

Brown, John Alexander OL
b Dysart 5/1887 d 1943
Caps: SLge 1
Clackmannan Juniors
Hearts o' Beath
Alloa Athletic
Falkirk
Celtic
1912 1914 Chelsea 16 4
Falkirk (loan)
Raith Rovers
Dunfermline Athletic
Falkirk (loan)
Clackmannan
Falkirk
Clackmannan
Lochgelly United

Brown, John Alfred OL
b Nottingham 20/3/1866
1888 Notts County 1

Brown, John B RH/CH
b Edinburgh
Heart of Midlothian
Bathgate
1920 1921 Portsmouth 39
Leith Athletic
St Bernard's

Brown, John Emery (Jack) OL
b Burslem q3 1890
Orrell
1908 1909 Manchester City 6
Stoke
Port Vale

Brown, John Henry (Jack) GK
b Worksop 18/3/1899 d 1962
Caps: FLge 2/England 6
Worksop Town
1922 1936 Sheffield Wednesday 465
1937 Hartlepools United 1

Brown, John Robert (Bobby) RB/OR
b South Bank 11/1887
South Bank
1906 1907 Middlesbrough 25
1908 Bristol City 3
Warrenby Athletic

From To Apps Goal

Brown, John Thomas (Jack) LB/RB
b Eastwood 15/6/1901 d 1977
Kirkby Colliery
1925 1930 Leicester City 114
1931 1933 Wrexham 85
Nuneaton Town
Heanor Town

Brown, John Thomas OR
b Sheffield
Shrewsbury Town
1927 Gillingham (loan) 2

Brown, Jonathan LH
b Clayton-le-Moors d 1916
Great Harwood
1914 Burnley 1

Brown, Joseph (Joe) OR
b Jarrow q2 1912 d 1962
Jarrow St Bede's
1929 Sunderland 0
Jarrow Imperial
1929 Middlesbrough 0
Jarrow
1931 Darlington 0
Jarrow
1932 Gateshead 0
Jarrow
1935 New Brighton 16 3
Ballymena United
Reyrolles

Brown, Joseph (Joe) OL
b Troon 10/4/1913
Troon Athletic
Shawfield
Aberdeen
1937 Watford 6 2
Frickley Colliery

Brown, Lennox S CF
b South Africa 24/11/1910
1935 Millwall 1

Brown, Maurice CH
b Barrow q1 1917
1937 Barrow 27

Brown, McAndrew RH
1923 Lincoln City 17

Brown, Noel OR
1907 Newcastle United 1

Brown, Norman CH
b Ulverston 17/5/1907 d 1992
Ulverston Town
1927 Barrow 3
Dick, Kerr's XI
Rossendale United

Brown, Norman IL/IR
b New Brancepeth
Willington
1929 1931 Stockport County 46 9
Ashton National

Brown, Norman Liddle OR/CF
b Willington Quay q1 1885
Willington Athletic
1904 1906 Sunderland 26 1
Brentford
Luton Town
Southend United
Millwall Athletic
Newcastle City
North Shields
1913 Blackpool 13 2

Brown, Oliver Maurice (Buster) CF
b Burton-on-Trent 10/10/1908 d 1951
Trent Villa
Robirth Athletic
Burton Town
1930 Nottingham Forest 9 6
1931 1932 Norwich City 51 33
1932 West Ham United 0
1933 1936 Brighton & Hove Albion 58 38

Brown, R OL
1930 Walsall 1

Brown, Richard Harold (Dick) LH
b Sheffield 1870 d 1940
1893 Sheffield Wednesday 2

Brown, Richard Robert RH
1927 South Shields 1

From To Apps Goal

Brown, Robert OR/IR
b Dublin 11/1869
1894 1896 Burton Wanderers 84 19
Southampton
Bristol Rovers
Queen's Park Rangers
Swindon Town

Brown, Robert Alan John (Sailor) IR/OL/IL
b Great Yarmouth 7/11/1915 d 2008
Caps: England War 6
Gorleston
1937 1945 Charlton Athletic 47 21
1939 (Charlton Athletic) (3)
1946 1947 Nottingham Forest 45 17
1947 1948 Aston Villa 30 9
Gorleston

Brown, Robert George (Bob) OR/CF
b Hathersage 1902
Hathersage
1920 Bradford City 0
1921 Accrington Stanley 5 1
Hathersage
1923 Rotherham County 1

Brown, Robert Neil (Bob) CH/IR/RH
b Cambuslang 8/1870 d 1943
Blantyre Thistle
Cambuslang
1892 1893 Sheffield Wednesday 45 8
Third Lanark
1895 1901 Bolton Wanderers 125 12
1896 Burnley (loan) 4

Brown, Robert Samuel (Bob) LB
b Southampton 16/10/1895 d 1980
Thorneycrofts
1919 1923 Tottenham Hotspur 37
Aldershot

Brown, Samuel (Sam) LB
b Glasgow 1901
Rutherglen Glencairn
Third Lanark
King's Park (loan)
East Stirlingshire (loan)
1929 1930 Bournemouth & Boscombe Ath 59
1931 Brighton & Hove Albion 4
1932 Chester 0
1932 Swindon Town 2
Stranraer (trial)

Brown, Samuel IR/CF
b Lincoln 1/5/1908 d 1961
Lincoln Corinthians
1933 1934 Tranmere Rovers 13 2
Prescot Cables

Brown, Sidney GK
b Brierley Hill
1923 1925 Port Vale 16
1927 Gillingham 8
Congleton Town
Dudley Town

Brown, T OL
1892 Northwich Victoria 1

Brown, Thomas IR
b Sunderland
Sunderland Royal Rovers
1907 Sunderland 1
St Mirren
Hamilton Academical

Brown, Thomas (Tommy) CF
b Beith 1880
Glenbuck Cherrypickers
1899 1901 Leicester Fosse 49 21
1901 Chesterfield Town 10 10
Third Lanark
1902 Leicester Fosse 23 14
Portsmouth
Dundee

Brown, Thomas OR
b Middlesbrough q3 1898
1920 1922 Middlesbrough 5
1923 Accrington Stanley 16 1

Brown, Thomas Bertie LB
b Troedyrhiw 7/1912 d 1974
Folkestone
1934 Crystal Palace 5

Brown, Thomas E GK
1929 South Shields 2

From To Apps Goal

Brown, Thomas Francis (Tommy) RB
b Sunderland q3 1906
Percy Main
Crook Town
1925 Newcastle United 0
1926 Fulham 11
1927 Charlton Athletic 0
York City

Brown, Thomas Henry (Tommy) OL
b Darlington 1896
Darlington Close Works
Portsmouth
Spennymoor United
Norwich City
1920 Brighton & Hove Albion 14
1921 Cardiff City 2
1922 Bristol City 8
1923 South Shields 20 1
1924 Luton Town 15
Poole

Brown, Thomas Walter (Tommy) LH/RH
b Sheffield 27/3/1897
1919 1921 Bradford Park Avenue 19
Rotherham Town

Brown, Victor Charles (Vic) RB
b Bedford 26/7/1903 d 1971
Bedford Town
1930 Leeds United 1
1933 1936 Coventry City 100
1939 Chester (3)

Brown, Wilfred (Wilf) CF/OR
b Rotherham 6/6/1912 d 1986
Tinsley Park
Boston Town
1934 New Brighton 11 2
Rawmarsh Welfare
1936 Rotherham United 16 7

Brown, William OL
b Liverpool 1865
Stanley
1888 Everton 6 1

Brown, William GK
b Nottingham
Notts Rangers
1892 1893 Nottingham Forest 22
1894 Notts County (loan) 1

Brown, William CH
1895 Loughborough 3

Brown, William CF
b Darwen 1873
Clyde
Thornliebank
1895 Preston North End 1
Tottenham Hotspur
1896 Lincoln City 1

Brown, William CF
Stalybridge Rovers
Chester
1896 Newton Heath 7 2
Stockport County
Hurst Ramblers

Brown, William RB/LB
b Hurlford 1876
Hurlford Thistle
Beith
1899 1903 Bolton Wanderers 106
1904 1905 Aston Villa 12
Plymouth Argyle
Crystal Palace

Brown, William CH
Gateshead NER
1904 Bury 1

Brown, William RH
b Cambuslang 10/5/1897
Flemington Hearts
Cambuslang Rangers
Partick Thistle
1914 1927 Everton 170
1928 Nottingham Forest 4
Liverpool Cables

Brown, William (Billy) IR/IL
b Fencehouses 22/8/1900 d 1985
Caps: England 1
Hetton
1920 1923 West Ham United 60 15
1923 1927 Chelsea 54 20
1929 Fulham 2
1930 Stockport County 4
1931 Hartlepools United 13 3
Annfield Plain
Blackhall Colliery Welfare

From To Apps Goal

Brown, William (Bill) RH
b Burnbank 17/11/1902 d 1985
Bellshill Athletic
1925 1927 Coventry City 55
1928 Wolverhampton Wanderers 33
1929 1930 Norwich City 50 2
Boulton & Paul

Brown, William CF
b Liverpool
1925 Wrexham 1
Rhyl

Brown, William (Bill) RB
b Bishop Auckland 27/2/1907 d 1976
Bishop Auckland
Crook Town
1927 Huddersfield Town 0
1928 1935 Watford 220
1936 1938 Exeter City 86
1939 Darlington (3)
Dickinson's (Apsley)

Brown, William LH
1929 Nottingham Forest 1

Brown, William Henry RB
b Barrow q2 1906 d 1960
St Matthew's RFC
1924 Barrow 1

Brown, William Hutchinson (Billy) RH/RB
b Choppington 11/3/1909 d 1996
West Stanley
1931 1945 Middlesbrough 256 2
1946 1947 Hartlepools United 80
Stockton

Brown, William Ian (Billy 'Buster') RH/RB/OR
b Silvertown 6/9/1910 d 1993
Fairbairn House
Silvertown
1930 1934 Luton Town 49 4
1934 1935 Huddersfield Town 20 2
1936 1946 Brentford 92 2
1939 (Brentford) (2)
1946 1947 Leyton Orient 26
Chingford Town

Brown, William John (Willie) LB/RB
b Dundee 25/12/1900
Dundee
Llanelly
1923 1927 Rochdale 178
1928 Torquay United 16
Dundalk

Brown, William P RH
1900 Stockport County 23 2

Brown, William Roland (Roland) OR
b Luton 1875 d 1940
Luton Town
St Albans Town
Woodville
1899 Luton Town 26 3
Watford
Luton Town

Brown, William Walker (Billy) LB/RB
b Coatbridge 24/6/1912 d 2008
Strathclyde
1933 Chelsea 0
Dunfermline Athletic
1935 1937 Stockport County 8
1938 Bradford City 4
1939 (Bradford City) (2)

Brown, William Young (Billy) IL/IR
b Dysart 23/2/1889 d 1963
Kettering
Queen's Park Rangers
1911 1912 Chelsea 9 2
1913 1914 Bristol City 62 23
1920 1921 Swansea Town 65 16
1922 Portsmouth 0
1922 Northampton Town 2
Sittingbourne

Browne, Robert James (Bobby) LH
b Derry 2/2/1912 d 1994
Caps: IrLge 1/Ireland 6
Maleven
Clooney Rovers
Derry City
1935 1946 Leeds United 107
1939 (Leeds United) (3)
1947 York City 5
Thorne Colliery

Browning, Alfred Sidney CF
b Derby q4 1877
Belper Town
1900 Chesterfield Town 3 1

From To Apps Goal

Browning, Donovan Albert (Don) RB
b Ashley 9/5/1916 d 1997
New Milton
1936 1937 Southampton 26

Browning, John OL
b Dumbarton 29/1/1888
Caps: SLge 2/Scotland 1
Mossfield Amateurs
Glasgow Perthshire
Bonhill Hibernian
Dumbarton Harp
Vale of Leven
Celtic
Dumbarton Harp (loan)
Vale of Leven (loan)
1919 Chelsea 5 1
Vale of Leven
Dumbarton
Vale of Leven

Browning, John LH
b Alexandria 27/1/1915 d 1971
Bridgeton Waverley
Dunoon Athletic
1934 1938 Liverpool 19
Albion Rovers (trial)
Cowdenbeath

Browning, William Clarence GK
b Whitburn, County Durham 6/1893 d 1950
1919 South Shields 1

Brownley, John LH
Bristol St George
Southampton
1899 Chesterfield Town 1

Brown-Sim, (Dr) James (Jim) CF
b Nottingham q3 1884 d 1957
Queen's Park
1908 Sheffield United 1
Sheffield

Bruce, Daniel (Dan) IL/OL/CF
b Bonhill 20/10/1870 d 1931
Caps: Scotland 1
Vale of Leven
Rangers
1892 1895 Notts County 89 47
1895 Small Heath 9 2
St Mirren
Perth
Vale of Leven
St Mirren

Bruce, David OR
b Perth 23/2/1911 d 1976
Perth Thistle
East Fife
Dundee East Craigie
1935 Leicester City 1
1936 Bristol Rovers 12 2
St Mirren
Airdrieonians

Bruce, Henry (Harry) CH/RH/LB
b Coundon 5/1905
1922 Durham City 0
Bishop Auckland
1924 1927 Birmingham 8
1928 Gillingham 30
1929 Torquay United 28
Colwyn Bay
Bankhead Albion
1930 Rochdale 2
1930 Darlington 0
Bankhead Albion
1931 Reading 7
Colwyn Bay United
Macclesfield

Bruce, James IR
Albion Rovers
1896 Gainsborough Trinity 2

Bruce, John (Jackie) GK
b Trimdon 16/7/1908 d 1998
Trimdon Rising Star
Station Town United Methodists
1928 Huddersfield Town 0
Station Town United Methodists
1930 Hartlepools United 0
Tunbridge Wells Rangers
1932 Clapton Orient 19
Whitecrofts (Isle of Wight)
Leavesden Mental Hospital

From To Apps Goal

Bruce, Robert Fotheringham GK
b Bridge of Allan 11/3/1895
Cowie Wanderers
Kirkintilloch Rob Roy
Raith Rovers
Partick Thistle
Alloa Athletic
Kirkintilloch Rob Roy
1921 Nelson 7
Plean
Stenhousemuir
Broxburn United

Bruce, Robert Frederick (Bobby) IL/IR
b Paisley 29/1/1906
Caps: Scotland 1
St Anthony's (Glasgow)
Aberdeen
1927 1934 Middlesbrough 237 65
1935 Sheffield Wednesday 5
Ipswich Town
Mossley

Bruce, Ronald (Ron) IL
b Walker 4/3/1918 d 1997
North Shields
1938 Bradford Park Avenue 1
Consett

Bruce, Walter IR/OR/IL
b Sunderland 15/5/1912 d 1984
Southwick St Columba's
Silksworth Colliery
Workington
1933 1937 Bradford City 76 17
1938 Swansea Town 13 1
1939 West Ham United 0

Bruce, Walter A IR
Caps: Ireland Amat
Bangor
Belfast Celtic
1939 Halifax Town (3) (1)

Brueton, Edward M GK
b Penn 1871
Stafford Rangers
1894 Small Heath 1
Willenhall Swifts

Brumley, Edward CH
b Grimsby 2/1878 d 1942
Humber Rovers
Grimsby All Saints
1900 1902 Grimsby Town 5 2
Hull Comets
West Marsh
Reading

Brunskill, Norman RH
b Dipton 14/6/1912 d 1988
South Moor Juniors
Lintz Colliery
1930 Huddersfield Town 0
1932 1936 Oldham Athletic 143 10
1936 1938 Birmingham 63 2
1938 Barnsley 28 2
1939 (Barnsley) (3)
Workington

Brunt, John Arthur (Jack) IL
b Dartford 6/12/1904 d 1981
Mizpah Mission
Wombwell
1928 Southport 2
Manchester Central
Fulwood Sports
Norton Woodseats

Brunton, Matthew (Matt) IR/CF
b Burnley 20/4/1878 d 1962
Vale XI (Burnley)
South Lancs Regiment
1899 Preston North End 8 2
Accrington Stanley
1901 Burnley 30 8
Accrington Stanley
1904 Leicester Fosse 5
Nelson
Accrington Stanley
1907 Oldham Athletic 1
Southport Central
Great Harwood
Haslingden
Darwen
Accrington Stanley
Rossendale United

From To Apps Goal

Bruton, John (Jack) OR
b Westhoughton 21/11/1903 d 1986
Caps: FLge 2/England 3
Hindley Green
1922 Wigan Borough 0
1923 Bolton Wanderers 0
Horwich RMI
1924 1929 Burnley 167 42
1929 1938 Blackburn Rovers 324 108
1939 Preston North End 0

Bruton, Leslie Hector Ronald (Les) CF/IR/IL
b Foleshill 1/4/1903 d 1989
Bell Green Wesleyans
Foleshill
1921 Coventry City 0
1921 West Bromwich Albion (trial) 0
Peterborough & Fletton United
1923 1925 Southampton 7
Peterborough & Fletton United
Raith Rovers
1929 1931 Blackburn Rovers 38 23
1931 1932 Liverpool 7 1
Leamington Town
1935 Coventry City (trial) 0

Bryan, James OL
b Manchester
Stalybridge Celtic
1929 Bolton Wanderers 1 1
1929 Crewe Alexandra 24 7

Bryan, John Joseph (Jack) RH
b Langwith 22/8/1897 d 1978
Langwith Red Rose
Mansfield Swifts
Shirebrook
1919 1921 Lincoln City 75 1
Mansfield Town
Worksop Town
Mexborough

Bryan, JT CF
1895 Darwen 4 5

Bryan, John Thomas OR
1899 Wolverhampton Wanderers 9 2
Blakenhall

Bryan, Raymond OR
b Bishop Auckland 26/7/1916 d 1984
Bishop Auckland
1936 Middlesbrough 1
1939 Hartlepools United (trial) 0

Bryan, Thomas OL
b Plumstead 1873
Woolwich Ordnance Factory
1893 Woolwich Arsenal 9 1
Royal Ordnance
New Brompton

Bryan, William (Billy) GK
b Doncaster 6/9/1912 d 1944
1934 Sunderland 0
1935 Walsall 9
1935 West Ham United 0
1936 Southend United 7
1937 1938 Swindon Town 22
1939 Wrexham (3)

Bryant, Clifford Samuel A (Cliff) RH/CH/LH
b Kingswood 6/8/1913 d 1997
Caps: England Sch
Wesley Rangers
1930 Bristol Rovers 1
1932 1935 Blackburn Rovers 4
1936 Wrexham 8
Cheltenham Town
Glastonbury

Bryant, James Marshall IL
b Saltcoats
1928 Merthyr Town 23 6
1929 Southend United 2
Taunton Town

Bryant, William (Willie) OR/IR/IL
b Rotherham q3 1874
Caps: FLge 1
Wath Athletic
Chesterfield Town
1894 1895 Rotherham Town 54 22
1896 1899 Newton Heath 108 26
1900 1901 Blackburn Rovers 25 8

Bryant, William (Bill) OR
b Shildon 26/11/1913 d 1975
Cockfield
1932 1933 Wolverhampton Wanderers 5
1933 1934 Wrexham 40 11
1934 1938 Manchester United 148 42
1939 (Manchester United) (3) (2)
1945 Bradford City 0
Altrincham
Stalybridge Celtic

From To Apps Goal

Bryant, William Ingram (Billy) CH/RH
b Ghent, Belgium 1/3/1899 d 1986
Caps: England Amat/England 1
Clapton
1925 1930 Millwall 132 30
Clapton

Bryce, Frederick (Ted) GK
1927 Wolverhampton Wanderers 2

Bryce, John McPheators LB
b Cambuslang 4/10/1898
Cambuslang Rangers
Hibernian
1927 Wigan Borough 3
Northwich Victoria

Bryce, Robert Stuart (Bob) OL
b Grangemouth 17/11/1904 d 1970
Grange Rovers
Falkirk
East Stirlingshire
Stenhousemuir
Grange Rovers
1928 1929 Bournemouth & Boscombe Ath 63 24
1930 1931 Luton Town 34 8
King's Park
Bo'ness

Bryden, Thomas OL
b Tynemouth q2 1891
1912 Stockport County 1
Gateshead Town
Jarrow

Bryson, George Maxwell IL
b Liverpool 11/11/1900 d 1953
Seaforth Fellowship
South Liverpool
1923 New Brighton 2
Port Sunlight
Northwich Victoria

Buchan, Charles Murray (Charlie) IR
b Plumstead 22/9/1891 d 1960
Caps: FLge 10/England 6
Woolwich Polytechnic
Plumstead St Nicholas
Plumstead
1908 Woolwich Arsenal 0
Northfleet
Leyton
1910 1924 Sunderland 379 209
1925 1927 Arsenal 102 49

Buchan, James RH/LH
b Perth 1881
St Johnstone
Hibernian
1904 Woolwich Arsenal 8
1904 1910 Manchester City 155 8
Motherwell
Kilmarnock
Forfar Athletic
St Johnstone

Buchan, Thomas Murray (Tom) LH/RH/IR
b Plumstead 9/1889 d 1952
Woodhall Thistle
1910 Sunderland 0
Leyton
Sunderland Rovers
1913 Blackpool 24 2
1914 1922 Bolton Wanderers 116 14
1923 Tranmere Rovers 36
Runcorn
Atherton

Buchan, William Ralston Murray (Willie) IR/IL
b Grangemouth 17/10/1914 d 2003
Caps: SLge 2/Scotland War 1
Cowie Thistle Juveniles
Grange Rovers
Celtic
1937 1947 Blackpool 91 35
1939 (Blackpool) (3)
1947 1948 Hull City 40 12
1949 1951 Gateshead 89 16
Coleraine
East Stirlingshire

Buchanan, Alexander D CF
1930 Thames 2 2
Hampstead Town

Buchanan, David M (Dave) RH
b Bellshill 1873
Third Lanark
Bellshill Athletic
Brentford
1904 Middlesbrough 0
Plymouth Argyle
1906 1907 Clapton Orient 65 2
Leyton

From To Apps Goal

Buchanan, George OL
b Paisley 1888 d 1934
Levern Victoria
St Mirren
Heart of Midlothian
1910 1912 Bradford Park Avenue 52 9
Morton
St Mirren

Buchanan, James (Jim) IR/OR
b Kirkliston 10/10/1898
Bellstane Birds
Winchburgh Violet
Broxburn United
Aberdeen (trial)
Hibernian
1924 1927 Bournemouth & Boscombe Ath 65 10
Raith Rovers (loan)
East Stirlingshire
1928 1929 Nelson 66 15
Ashton National (trial)
Clitheroe
1930 Accrington Stanley 0
Bray Unknowns
Shamrock Rovers
Leith Athletic
Bangor

Buchanan, Peter Symington OR
b Glasgow 13/10/1915 d 1977
Caps: Scotland 1
St Mungo (Glasgow)
1933 Chelsea 0
Wishaw Juniors
1936 1938 Chelsea 39 6
1946 Fulham 20 1
1947 1948 Brentford 74 13
Headington United

Buchanan, Robert RB
b Bellshill
Bellshill Athletic
Leyton
1911 Chelsea 3
Southend United
Gillingham

Buchanan, Robert John (Bob) IR/CF/IL
b Johnstone 1868 d 1907
Johnstone
Abercorn
Sunderland Albion
1892 1893 Burnley 40 12
1894 1895 Woolwich Arsenal 42 16
Southampton St Mary's
Sheppey United

Buchanan, William OR
Clydebank
1929 Darlington 3
1930 Bury 0

Buck, Edward (Teddy) LH
b Dipton 29/10/1904 d 1993
West Stanley
1928 Leeds United 8
1929 1938 Grimsby Town 354 4
1939 (Grimsby Town) (3)

Buck, Frederick Richard (Fred) IL/IR/CH
b Newcastle-under-Lyme 12/7/1880 d 1952
Caps: FLge 2
Newcastle-under-Lyme
Stafford Wesleyans
Stafford Rangers
1900 1902 West Bromwich Albion 22 6
1903 Liverpool 13 1
Plymouth Argyle
1905 1913 West Bromwich Albion 265 84
Swansea Town

Buck, Harry Shaw OR
b Liverpool q2 1884
Tranmere Rovers
1908 Everton 1
Tranmere Rovers
Hoylake

Buck, Henry Samuel (Harry) CF
b Poplar q2 1888 d 1962
Caps: England Amat
Dulwich Hamlet
1920 Millwall Athletic 4
1922 Charlton Athletic 0

Buckby, Leonard Curtis CH
b Kettering 27/8/1904 d 1978
1926 Northampton Town 4
Wellingborough Town

From To Apps Goal

Buckenham, William Elijah CF
b Woolwich 3/2/1888 d 1954
Plumstead Park Villa
Plumstead Melrose
Farnham
86th Batallion Royal Artillery
1909 Woolwich Arsenal 21 5
Southampton
12th Royal Field Artillery

Buckingham, Victor Frederick (Vic) LB/LH/RH
b Greenwich 23/10/1915 d 1995
Caps: England War 2
1931 Tottenham Hotspur 0
Northfleet
1935 1948 Tottenham Hotspur 204 1
1939 (Tottenham Hotspur) (3)

Buckland, William Albert (Bill) LH
b Shipston-on-Stour q1 1900
Cinderford Town
1924 Bristol City 1

Buckle, George Frederick GK
b Lewisham 3/7/1907 d 1992
Army
1931 Gillingham 29
1932 Aldershot 0

Buckle, Henry Redmond (Harry) OL
b Belfast 6/3/1882
Caps: SoLge 1/IrLge 4/Ireland 3
Cliftonville Casuals
Cliftonville Olympic
Cliftonville
1902 1905 Sunderland 44 13
Portsmouth
Bristol Rovers
Coventry City
Belfast Celtic
Glenavon
Belfast United
Fordsons

Buckler, Thomas C CF
b Cardiff
1928 Newport County 1 1

Buckley, Ambrose (Amby) LB
b Brinsley 31/1/1909 d 1968
Sherwood Foresters
1934 1938 Fulham 6
1939 Doncaster Rovers 0
Dartford
1946 Stockport County 11

Buckley, Arthur OL
b Greenfield 3/7/1913 d 1992
Greenfield
1934 1936 Oldham Athletic 47 10
1936 1938 Leeds United 81 20
1939 (Leeds United) (2)
1945 Oldham Athletic 0
Mossley
Ashton United

Buckley, Christopher Sebastian (Chris) CH
b Urmston 9/9/1886 d 1974
Caps: FLge 2
Victoria Park
Manchester Ship Canal
1903 Manchester City 0
Xavieran Brothers College
1904 West Bromwich Albion (trial) 0
Brighton & Hove Albion
1906 1912 Aston Villa 136 3
1914 1920 Arsenal 56 3

Buckley, Edward Colston (Ted) CF
b Trethomas 13/9/1912 d 1971
Trethomas
1933 Sunderland (trial) 0
1934 Wolverhampton Wanderers 0
1935 Bristol Rovers 8 2
Bath City
1936 Bournemouth & B Ath (trial) 0
1937 1938 Tranmere Rovers 35 12
Birkenhead Fire Service

Buckley, Franklin Charles (Frank) CH
b Urmston 9/11/1882 d 1964
Caps: England 1
1904 Aston Villa 0
Brighton & Hove Albion
1906 Manchester United 3
1907 1908 Manchester City 11
1909 1910 Birmingham 55 4
1911 1913 Derby County 92 3
1914 Bradford City 4
Norwich City

From To Apps Goal

Buckley, John William (Jack) RB
b Prudhoe Castle 24/11/1903 d 1985
Prudhoe Castle
1924 1931 Doncaster Rovers 257
1932 1934 Lincoln City 92
Grantham

Buckley, Seth CF
b Moulton, North Yorkshire q4 1874 d 1923
Haverton Hill
1899 Middlesbrough 1

Buckley, Walter LH
b Ecclesall 30/4/1906 d 1985
Caps: England Sch
Birley Carr
1923 Arsenal 0
1926 Bournemouth & Boscombe Ath 0
Mansfield Town
1928 Bradford Park Avenue 5
1930 1932 Lincoln City 81 1
1933 1935 Rochdale 108 2
Runcorn

Bucknall, Wilfred (Wilf) RB/LB
b Lichfield
1933 Wolverhampton Wanderers 0
Wellington Town
1935 1936 Bournemouth & Boscombe Ath 5

Budd, Herbert Reece IL/CF
b Bristol 26/2/1904 d 1979
Hanham Athletic
1926 Exeter City 0
1927 1928 Torquay United 9 2
Kettering Town
Bath City

Budden, Wilfrid Lionel (Wilf) OL/IR
b Southampton 12/2/1902 d 1971
Bournemouth FC
1923 1924 Bournemouth & Boscombe Ath 10 1

Buddery, Harry IL/CF
b Sheffield 6/10/1889 d 1962
Denaby United
Doncaster Rovers
1920 1921 Portsmouth 21 3
1921 Southend United 25
Rotherham Town

Buist, Alfred George (George) GK
b 1884
Willington Quay
1904 1907 Lincoln City 83
North Shields Athletic

Buist, George RB
b Glasgow 1873
Morton
1896 Woolwich Arsenal 6
East Stirlingshire

Buist, Robert W (Bobby) CH
b Govan 5/10/1869 d 1944
Fairfield Rangers (Glasgow)
Cowlairs
Clyde
1893 Woolwich Arsenal 17 1
Leith Athletic
Royal Ordnance
Gravesend United

Bulcock, Joseph (Joe) RB
b Burnley q2 1880 d 1917
Caps: SoLge 1
Brynn Central
1906 Bury 5
Macclesfield
Exeter City
Crystal Palace
Swansea Town

Bulger, Charles Guest (Charlie) OL
b Manchester 19/1/1915 d 1976
1931 Manchester United 0
Congleton Town
1934 Birmingham 0
1935 Lincoln City 22 10
1936 1945 Walsall 78 11
1939 (Walsall) (3) (2)

Bull, Benjamin Henry (Ben) OL/OR
b Shardlow q1 1872
1895 Loughborough 7 1
1895 Liverpool 1 1

Bull, TA OR
1895 Burton Swifts 2 1

From To Apps Goal

Bull, Walter CH/OL/RH
b Nottingham 19/12/1874 d 1952
Caps: FLge 1
Nuncargate
Newstead Byron
St Andrew's (Nottingham)
1894 1903 Notts County 282 53
1908 Tottenham Hotspur 12
Heanor United

Bullen, Edward (Teddy) LH
b Warrington 1884 d 1917
Altrincham
1906 1914 Bury 188 7

Buller, Joseph (Joe) RH/LH
b Chilton Colliery 25/10/1909 d 1986
Chilton Colliery Recreation Athletic
Spennymoor United
1929 1931 Hartlepools United 86 2
1931 1934 Stoke City 6
1936 Aldershot 22

Bulling, Evelyn (Ed) RB
b Retford q4 1888 d 1963
Nottingham Olympic
1910 Tottenham Hotspur 2

Bulling, Harold Montague (Harry) RB
b Horncastle 19/9/1890 d 1933
Bridgford Juniors
Heanor Town
Watford
1919 1924 Nottingham Forest 186 2
Shirebrook

Bulling, James (Jim) RH
b West Bridgford 12/2/1909 d 1992
1926 Nottingham Forest 0
Shirebrook
1930 1931 Leicester City 12
1932 1935 Wrexham 121 3
Shrewsbury Town

Bullivant, Edward Rufus IR/IL/CF
b Lincoln 21/4/1888 d 1960
Rustons Engineers
South End Athletic (Lincoln)
1908 1911 Gainsborough Trinity 35 5

Bullivant, Thomas GK
b Sheffield q2 1876 d 1965
Montrose Works (Sheffield)
1901 Gainsborough Trinity 11
1904 Sheffield United 0
Bacup
Southport Central

Bulloch, Hugh Cairns CH
b Larkhall 2/6/1908
Royal Albert
Morton
Portadown
1935 Newcastle United 5
1936 1937 New Brighton 48 2
Portadown
1938 New Brighton 34 1
1939 (New Brighton) (3) (1)
Portadown
Aircraft United
Portadown

Bullock, Arthur OL
b Hull 7/10/1909 d 1997
Caps: England Sch
1932 1934 Hull City 18 3
1934 York City 6
Bridlington Town

Bullock, Eli CF
b Newcastle-under-Lyme 4/9/1895 d 1984
Crewe Alexandra
Macclesfield
1921 Exeter City 27 4

Bullock, Frederick Edwin (Fred) LB
b Hounslow 7/1886 d 1922
Caps: England Amat/England 1
Hounslow Town
Custom House
Ilford
1910 1920 Huddersfield Town 202 1

Bullock, George Frederick OR
b Wolverhampton q1 1916 d 1943
1934 Birmingham 0
Stafford Rangers
1936 1938 Barnsley 68 12
1939 (Barnsley) (3)

From To Apps Goal

Bullock, James CF/IR
b Gorton 25/3/1902 d 1977
Caps: WLge 1
Gorton
1922 Manchester City 0
1923 Crewe Alexandra 4 1
1924 1927 Southampton 32 13
1929 1930 Chesterfield 45 32
1930 Manchester United 10 3
Dundalk
Llanelly
Hyde United

Bullock, JH RH
1892 Nottingham Forest 1

Bullock, Norman CF/CH/IR
b Monton Green 8/9/1900 d 1970
Caps: FLge 1/England 3
Broughton St John's
Sedgley Park Amateurs
Prestwich Amateurs
1920 1934 Bury 505 123

Bullock, Samuel OL
1934 Stockport County 2

Bullough, Dennis Reginald (Denny) CF/OR/IR
b Allerton Bywater 29/11/1895 d 1975
Castleford Town
1914 Glossop 2
1919 1920 Stockport County 17 2
Doncaster Rovers
1921 Tranmere Rovers 9 5
1921 Southport 12
Hoylake
Cadby Hall

Bullough, Peter Adam RH
b Lostock q2 1865 d 1933
1888 1892 Bolton Wanderers 38 4

Bumford, Bertie LH
b Ton Pentre 27/4/1907 d 1981
1929 Bristol City 0
1930 1931 Bradford City 10
Bangor City

Bumphrey, James (Jim) RH/LH/IR
b Morpeth q2 1884 d 1946
Bedlington United
Ashington Alliance
1908 1914 Birmingham 137 7
Durham City

Bunce, William RB
Rochdale Athletic
1900 1901 Stockport County 14
1902 Manchester United 2

Bunce, William Newman (Newman) GK
b Pill 17/4/1911 d 1981
Pill
1932 Bristol City 0
1933 Leicester City 0
1934 Bristol Rovers 2
Bath City
1936 Bristol City 0
Crewkerne United

Bunch, Arthur William IR
b Bloemfontein, South Africa 30/9/1909 d 1978
Wellington Works
Aldershot
Blyth Spartans
1934 Aldershot 16 3
Blyth Spartans

Bunch, Walter RB/LB
b Weston-super-Mare 1872
Compton Colts
1895 1896 Wolverhampton Wanderers 7
Eastville Rovers
1899 1900 Walsall 61
1901 Small Heath 2

Bungay, Frank CF
b Ecclesfield 31/3/1909 d 1990
Ecclesfield Red Rose
Mexborough Athletic
1931 1932 Huddersfield Town 18 5
1932 1933 Southend United 2
Boston United
Grantham

Bungay, Reginald Harold (Reg) LB/CF
b Reading 5/2/1911 d 1986
Oxford City
1932 Tottenham Hotspur 0
1933 1934 Plymouth Argyle 3
1935 Bristol City 8 3
1936 1938 Mansfield Town 87 5
1939 Clapton Orient (3)

Bunting, HW IR/GK
1899 1900 Burton Swifts 28 2

From To Apps Goal

Bunting, John Baden (Jack) GK
b Bingham q3 1900 d 1951
Grantham
1921 Nottingham Forest 0
Sneinton
Grantham
1922 Leicester City 0
Boston Town
1924 Brighton & Hove Albion 8
Mansfield Town

Bunyan, Charles (Charlie) GK
b Campton q1 1869 d 1922
Old Horns (Chesterfield)
Spital Olympic
Chesterfield
Hyde
1889 1891 Derby County 9
Chesterfield Town
1893 Sheffield United 0
1894 Derby County 0
Ilkeston Town
Heanor Town
1896 1897 Walsall 44
New Brompton
1899 Newcastle United 0
Ripley Athletic
(Canada)
Grassmoor Red Rose
Brimington Athletic

Burbage, Robert William CF
b Peterborough q3 1875 d 1952
Hertford
1899 Luton Town 3 1
Bedford Queens Engineers

Burbanks, William Edwin (Eddie) OL
b Campsall 1/4/1913 d 1983
Doncaster YMCA
Thorne Town
Denaby United
1934 1947 Sunderland 132 25
1939 (Sunderland) (3) (1)
1948 1952 Hull City 143 21
1953 Leeds United 13 1

Burden, Frederick (Fred 'Ike') CH/RH
b Birmingham q1 1883
Walsall
1908 1910 Stockport County 58 1
Heart of Midlothian
St Mirren

Burder, John R LB
1900 1901 Blackpool 35

Burdett, George Walter Robert GK
b Tottenham q3 1883
Royal Fusiliers
1910 1911 Woolwich Arsenal 28
Royal Artillery

Burdett, Thomas John (Tom) CF/IR
b Hetton-le-Hole 29/10/1915 d 2001
Station Town Welfare
Blyth Spartans
Wheatley Hill Juniors
1933 1934 Hull City 3
1935 Fulham 0
1936 1938 Lincoln City 27 12
1939 Bury 0

Burditt, Frederick Charles Kendall (Ken) OR/IR/CF
b Ibstock 12/11/1906 d 1977
Ibstock Penistone Rovers
Bloxwich Strollers
Gresley Rovers
1930 1935 Norwich City 162 58
1936 1937 Millwall 54 22
1937 1938 Notts County 20
Colchester United
Ibstock Penistone Rovers

Burditt, George Leslie CF
b Ibstock 27/2/1910 d 1981
Ibstock Penistone Rovers
1933 Norwich City 0
1934 1935 Nottingham Forest 18 10
1936 Millwall 1
1937 1938 Wrexham 67 35
1939 Doncaster Rovers 0

Burgess, Caleb LB
b Presteigne 1/12/1908 d 1978
1931 Sunderland 0
1932 Aldershot 1
1934 Gateshead 16
Hereford United
Yeovil & Petters United

Burgess, Charles (Charlie) RB/LB
b Church Lawton 25/12/1883 d 1956
Butt Lane Swifts
1901 1907 Stoke 179
1908 1910 Manchester City 32

From To Apps Goal

Burgess, Charles Millar RB
b Montrose 20/11/1873 d 1960
Montrose
Dundee
1895 Sunderland 0
Dundee
Millwall Athletic
1900 Newcastle United 30
Portsmouth
Montrose

Burgess, Daniel (Dick) IL/IR
b Goldenhill 23/10/1896 d 1983
1919 Port Vale 0
1919 1921 Arsenal 13 1
1922 West Ham United 2
1923 1924 Aberdare Athletic 77 24
1925 1926 Queen's Park Rangers 46 9
Sittingbourne
Dartford
Sheppey United

Burgess, George LB
b Talke
Macclesfield
1925 1927 Stockport County 18
Caernarvon Athletic

Burgess, Harry IL/IR/CF
b Alderley Edge 20/8/1904 d 1957
Caps: England 4
Alderley Edge
Nantwich Ramblers
1925 1928 Stockport County 115 71
Sandbach Ramblers (loan)
1929 1934 Sheffield Wednesday 215 70
1934 1938 Chelsea 142 33
1939 (Chelsea) (1)

Burgess, Herbert LB/RB
b Openshaw 25/2/1883 d 1954
Caps: FLge 7/England 4
Openshaw United
Edge Lane
Moss Side
1899 1902 Glossop 81
1903 1905 Manchester City 85 2
1906 1909 Manchester United 49
Kristiania (Norway)
MTK-VM Budapest

Burgess, John William (Billy) LH/RH/IL
b Southport 11/1/1908 d 1989
Caps: WLge 1
1927 Southport 0
Burscough Rangers
Chester
1931 Tottenham Hotspur 0
Colwyn Bay United
Kidderminster Harriers
1933 1935 Newport County 103 15
1936 Barrow 41 3
Rhyl

Burgess, Reginald (Reg) OL
b Swindon 8/2/1910 d 1978
Purton
1931 Swindon Town 7 1

Burgess, Thomas OR
b Leicester q2 1874
Belgrave St Michael's
Leicester Imperial
1901 Leicester Fosse 3 1
Leicester Imperial
Hinckley United
Nuneaton Town
Hinckley United
Leicester Imperial

Burgess, William Arthur Ronald (Ron) LH/RH
b Cwm 9/4/1917 d 2005
Caps: FLge 1/Wales War 10/Wales 32
Cwm Villa
1935 Cardiff City 0
1936 Tottenham Hotspur 0
Northfleet (loan)
1938 1953 Tottenham Hotspur 297 15
1939 (Tottenham Hotspur) (3) (1)
1954 1955 Swansea Town 46 1

Burgess, William Walter OR
b Wellingborough 22/9/1919 d 2003
Rushden Town
1938 Luton Town 5

Burgin, Meynell CF/IR/IL
b Sheffield 29/11/1911 d 1994
Rossington Main
1933 Wolverhampton Wanderers 0
1934 Tranmere Rovers 31 21
1935 Bournemouth & Boscombe Ath 5 1
1936 1937 Nottingham Forest 22 11
1938 West Bromwich Albion 14 9

From To Apps Goal

Burgon, Frederick Archibald (Archie) OL
b Nottingham 28/3/1912 d 1994
Colwick
Burton Joyce
1930 Notts County (trial) 0
Newark Town
Grantham
1932 1933 Notts County 26 7
Grantham
1934 Tottenham Hotspur 4
1935 1938 Wrexham 140 36
1939 Carlisle United (2)

Burgoyne, Emmanuel IR
b Gibraltar 1870
Lancashire Fusiliers
Distillery
1895 Crewe Alexandra 25 3
Lancashire Fusiliers

Burke, James (Jimmy) LH/IL/IR
b Scotland 1870
Cowlairs
Third Lanark
Newark Town
1892 Notts County 15 4
Grantham Rovers
1894 1896 Lincoln City 52 7
Grantham Rovers
Ilkeston Town

Burke, John OL
b London
1929 Southend United 1
1930 West Ham United 0

Burke, John Joseph (Johnny) GK
b Dublin 28/5/1911 d 1987
Shelbourne
1931 1935 Chester 91
1936 1946 Millwall 24
1950 Gillingham 5

Burke, Joseph William (Joe) LH/IL
b Jarrow 23/3/1913 d 1988
Jarrow St Bede's
1932 Sunderland 0
1933 1934 Gateshead 13
1935 New Brighton 2
Jarrow
Blyth Spartans
Wigan Athletic
1936 Exeter City (trial) 0
Belfast Celtic
Cork City
North Shields
Scarborough
1938 Torquay United (trial) 0

Burke, Michael (Micky) IR/OR
b Blythswood 28/6/1904 d 1984
Dumbarton Harp
Old Kilpatrick
Glasgow Ashfield
Clyde
Dunfermline Athletic
Aberdeen
Dundalk
1934 1935 Lincoln City 27 2
1936 Southport 20 2
1937 Rochdale 8
Morton
Burton Town

Burke, Patrick (Pat) RH/LH
b Hebburn q3 1892
Hebburn Argyle
1912 1920 Blackpool 19
1921 Darlington 2

Burke, Peter Joseph CH
b Fazakerley 1/2/1912 d 1979
Bootle Joint Ordnance Corps
Fazakerley ROF
1929 Liverpool 0
Prescot Cables
1933 1935 Oldham Athletic 93 6
1935 1938 Norwich City 114
1939 Luton Town 0
1946 Southport 1
Prescot Cables

Burke, Richard (Dick) LB/RB
b Ashton-under-Lyne 28/10/1920 d 2004
Droylsden
1938 1945 Blackpool 1
1946 Newcastle United 15
1947 1948 Carlisle United 77 8
Ashton United

Burkinshaw, Abraham (Abe) IR
b Kilnhurst q1 1884 d 1954
Mexborough Town
1908 Barnsley 9 5
Mexborough Town
Rotherham Town

From To Apps Goal

Burkinshaw, John Dean Lewis (Jack) RH/IR/LH
b Kilnhurst 12/5/1890 d 1947
Kilnhurst Town
1907 1908 Grimsby Town 5 3
Rotherham Town
Swindon Town
1913 1919 Sheffield Wednesday 56 8
Rotherham Town
1920 Bradford Park Avenue 23 2
1921 Accrington Stanley 31 1
Denaby United
Wath Athletic
Chicago

Burkinshaw, Laurence (Laurie) OR
b Kilnhurst 2/12/1893 d 1969
Kilnhurst Town
Mexborough Town
1911 1913 Sheffield Wednesday 23 6
Rotherham Town
Stalybridge Celtic
1919 1921 Birmingham 71 11
1922 Halifax Town 26 2
Mexborough Town

Burkinshaw, Ralph RH/IL/IR
b Kilnhurst 26/3/1898 d 1951
1914 Barnsley 0
1919 South Shields 2
Wath Athletic
1920 Northampton Town 0
Gainsborough Trinity
1920 1924 Bury 104 20
1925 1929 Bradford City 166 30
1930 1931 Wrexham 64 1
Scarborough
Mexborough
Denaby United

Burkinshaw, William (Willie) IL
b Camelon 7/7/1911
Falkirk
1933 Rotherham United 11

Burleigh, J CH
Glossop North End
1898 Barnsley 25
Scarborough

Burleigh, James OL
b Wolverhampton 1869
1891 Wolverhampton Wanderers 2

Burley, Benjamin (Ben) OL/IL
b Sheffield 2/11/1912 d 2003
Woodhouse Mills United
1931 Sheffield United 0
1933 Southampton 2
1934 Grimsby Town 22 5
1935 1937 Norwich City 35 4
1938 Darlington 35 7
Chelmsford City

Burley, George Marcus CF/IL
b West Ham 23/12/1900 d 1978
Ellesmere Port Town
Chester
1926 1927 Burnley 4
Chester
Stalybridge Celtic
Colwyn Bay

Burley, William Roberts Elliott IL/IR
b Devonport 3/1/1899 d 1976
Torquay Town
Torquay United
1922 Swansea Town 0
Peterborough & Fletton United
1924 Grimsby Town 5
Peterborough & Fletton United
1925 1926 Millwall 15 3
1927 Norwich City 0

Burluraux, Frederick (Fred) RB
b North Skelton 22/12/1911 d 1977
St Peter's (North Skelton)
Lingdale
South Bank
1931 Middlesbrough (trial) 0
Whitby Town
1932 Hartlepools United 1
Scarborough
Thurnscoe Victoria

Burn, Frederick (Fred) OL
b Annfield Plain
Annfield Plain
1921 Hartlepools United 9 1
Whickham Athletic

From To Apps Goal

Burn, John Edward (Jack) OR
b South Hetton 15/11/1904 d 1991
1927 Birmingham 0
Worcester City
1929 Torquay United 7
Hereford United
Jarrow

Burn, Joshua Robinson (Josh) RB
b Whickham q1 1883 d 1930
1903 Newcastle United 0
1904 Doncaster Rovers 19

Burnand, Walter Thomas W IR
b Northampton 29/9/1894 d 1974
1920 1921 Northampton Town 25 5
Rushden

Burnell, Albert Edward IL
b Bristol 12/5/1901 d 1987
1923 Charlton Athletic 0
Barton Hill Sports
1925 Bristol Rovers 9 3
Dockland Settlement

Burnett, James J (Jimmy) CF/IL
b Aberdeen
Victoria United (Aberdeen)
Aberdeen
Portsmouth
Dundee
1905 1906 Grimsby Town 51 13
Brighton & Hove Albion
1908 1909 Leeds City 20 2

Burnett, Norman GK
b Dundee d 1982
1930 Sunderland 0
1931 Gillingham 7

Burnett, Thomas (Tom) RB
b Leyburn 9/2/1913 d 1986
1935 1937 Darlington 16

Burnham, Harry IL
b Sunderland
1920 Portsmouth 0
1925 1926 Aberdare Athletic 38 6

Burnham, John Robert (Jack) LH/RH/CH
b Southwick, County Durham 11/1/1896 d 1973
Sunderland Comrades
1920 Brighton & Hove Albion 1
1921 1922 Queen's Park Rangers 31
1923 Durham City 20
Scunthorpe & Lindsey United
1926 Durham City 3
West Stanley
Jarrow

Burnicle (Burnikell), William Frederick (Billy) LH/RH
b Southwick, County Durham 9/12/1910 d 1980
Newcastle Juniors
1929 1932 Lincoln City 25
1933 1936 Bradford City 53 2
1937 1938 Aldershot 63 2
1939 (Aldershot) (2)

Burnip, John Douglas CH
b Tanfield q4 1903 d 1946
Hobson Wanderers
1922 Preston North End 0
1923 Rotherham County 3

Burnison, Joseph (Joe) LH
b Belfast 12/12/1880
Caps: IrLge 3/Ireland 1
Glenavon
Distillery
1900 1901 Bolton Wanderers 18
Distillery
Derry Celtic
Glenavon

Burnison, Samuel (Sam) RB
b Belfast 1891
Caps: IrLge 5/Ireland 8
Distillery
1910 Bradford Park Avenue 15
Distillery
Glenavon

Burniston, Gordon Edmondson IR
b Knaresborough q3 1885 d 1934
Darlington
1910 Huddersfield Town 3 1
Merthyr Town

Burns, George CF
1928 Merthyr Town 2 1

From To Apps Goal

Burns, Hugh CH
b Dumbarton
St Anthony's (Glasgow)
Dumbarton Harp
Rutherglen Glencairn
Dumbarton
Renton
1921 Rochdale 15
1922 Oldham Athletic (trial) 0

Burns, J LH
1892 Bootle 1

Burns, James OL
b Dromore
Caps: IrLge 4/Ireland 1
Glenavon
1924 Reading 4

Burns, James Arthur (Jimmy) OL/IR
b Liverpool 20/6/1865 d 1957
Hurst
London Caledonians
1890 West Bromwich Albion 15 5
1891 Notts County 1
South Weald

Burns, John IR
b Walsall 1871 d 1933
Fairfield Villa
1893 West Bromwich Albion 1
Stafford Rangers
Bilston United

Burns, John Charles (Jack) IR/LH/IL
b Fulham 27/11/1906 d 1986
Caps: England Amat
Crypto
1927 1930 Queen's Park Rangers 117 29
1931 1935 Brentford 145 14
Leyton

Burns, Michael Thomas (Mick) GK
b Leeholme 7/6/1908 d 1982
Chilton Colliery Recreation Athletic
1927 1935 Newcastle United 104
1936 1937 Preston North End 12
1938 1951 Ipswich Town 157
1939 (Ipswich Town) (3)

Burns, Peter IR
1893 Lincoln City 2

Burns, Robert CH
Abercorn
1897 Lincoln City 1

Burns, Robert (Bobby) CF
b Edinburgh 8/1882
Royal Field Artillery
Salisbury City
Heart of Midlothian
1909 1910 Fulham 18 7
Broxburn Athletic

Burns, Roy OR
b Wolverhampton q4 1916
1935 Wolverhampton Wanderers 0
1935 Port Vale 2
Bournemouth Tramways
1936 Bournemouth & Boscombe Ath 18 3
Bournemouth Tramways

Burns, Thomas LB
b Fulham q4 1890 d 1921
Clapham
Shaftesbury Athletic
Tooting Graveney
1910 1912 Fulham 35

Burns, William CH
b Newtownards 1904
Caps: IrLge 1
Nortonville
Ards
Glentoran
1925 Wolverhampton Wanderers 1
Philadelphia Celtic
J & P Coats (Rhode Island)
Shelbourne
1928 Wolverhampton Wanderers 3
Ards
Workington
Glentoran
Ards
Belfast St Peter's

Burns, William CF
b Durham 1907
Crook Town
1930 Stoke City 3 2
1931 Stockport County 6
1932 Rotherham United 0

From To Apps Goal

Burrell, George OL
b Newcastle 1892
Shildon Athletic
South Shields
Leyton
1912 1913 Woolwich Arsenal 23 3
South Shields

Burridge, Ben James Herbert (Bert) RH/LH
b Beamish 11/3/1898 d 1977
Oxhill Villa
Houghton Rovers
Annfield Plain
1921 1925 Darlington 92 7
1926 1929 Sheffield Wednesday 26
1930 Oldham Athletic 6
Macclesfield
Hyde United
Hurst
Ashton National

Burrill, Frederick (Frank) IR/IL
b Manor Park 20/4/1894 d 1962
West Ham United
Southend United
1920 1922 Wolverhampton Wanderers 61 16
1923 Charlton Athletic 13 4
1924 Walsall 39 14

Burrows, Arthur RB
b Stockport q3 1896
1920 Stockport County 4
Mossley

Burrows, Arthur LH/OR/IL
b Stockport 4/12/1919 d 2005
1938 1946 Stockport County 5 1
Ashton United
1948 Accrington Stanley 9
Mossley
Winsford United
Buxton

Burrows, George Baker CF/IL
b Hetton-le-Hole 2/3/1900 d 1979
Hetton Celtic
1919 1920 Oldham Athletic 7 1
1921 West Ham United 0

Burrows, Horace LH
b Sutton-in-Ashfield 11/3/1910 d 1969
Caps: England 3
Sutton Junction
1930 Coventry City 0
1931 Mansfield Town 0
1932 1938 Sheffield Wednesday 233 8
1939 (Sheffield Wednesday) (3)
Ollerton Colliery

Burrows, JL OR/OL
Crewe Alexandra
1892 Northwich Victoria 1
1893 Crewe Alexandra 9 3

Burrows, Leslie George (Les) CF
b Exeter 29/12/1905 d 1976
Taunton Town
1929 Bristol City 1
1930 Torquay United 2

Burrows, Lycurgus LB/RB
b Ashton-under-Lyne 26/6/1875 d 1952
Woolwich Polytechnic
1893 1894 Woolwich Arsenal 9
Tottenham Hotspur
1895 Woolwich Arsenal 1
Tottenham Hotspur
1897 Sheffield United (trial) 0

Burrows, Wilfred (Wilf) GK
b Castleford 16/021902 d 1985
Castleford Town
Selby Town
1926 1930 Tranmere Rovers 49
1931 1932 Wrexham 28
1933 York City 3
Bangor City
1934 Bury 0
Colwyn Bay United
Shrewsbury Town

Burrows, William GK
1893 Notts County 1
Notts Olympic

Burt, John CF
b Guildford q4 1888 d 1960
1909 1910 Blackpool 7 2

Burtenshaw, James CF
1913 Stockport County 1

From To Apps Goal

Burton, Andrew Douglas (Andy) IL
b Lochgelly 1884
Thomson Rovers
Lochgelly Rangers
Lochgelly United
Motherwell
1905 1910 Bristol City 192 45
1911 Everton 12 4
Reading
East Fife

Burton, Edward Charles OR
b Birmingham 1881
Walsall
1904 West Bromwich Albion 1
Walsall
1906 Burton United 0

Burton, Edwin IL/OL
b Dunston-on-Tyne q1 1893 d 1916
Shildon Athletic
1913 1914 Bristol City 18 4

Burton, F IR/IL/OR
1898 1900 Burton Swifts 82 22
1901 1905 Burton United 35 1

Burton, Frank James RB/LB
b Luapango, Mexico 1891
Queen's Park Rangers
1919 1920 West Ham United 64 2
1921 1924 Charlton Athletic 97
Grays Thurrock

Burton, George CF
b South Bank 1889
Grangetown
1909 Middlesbrough 2
Cardiff City
Hartlepools United

Burton, George Frank (Frank) RH/LH
b Aston 6/1868 d 1935
Birmingham St Luke's
Walsall Town Swifts
1892 1897 Aston Villa 52 2

Burton, Henry Arthur (Harry) LB/RB
b West Bromwich 1881 d 1923
Attercliffe
1903 1908 Sheffield Wednesday 171
1908 1909 West Bromwich Albion 32
Scunthorpe & Lindsey United

Burton, Horace Arthur LH/RH
b Melton Mowbray 28/7/1887 d 1969
Melton Mowbray
Holwell Works
1910 1914 Leicester Fosse 78 1
Loughborough Corinthians
Mountsorrel Town
Melton Working Mens Club

Burton, J OR
1895 Darwen 4 3

Burton, John Henry (Jack) LH/RH
b Handsworth 9/1863 d 1914
Handsworth Victoria
Aston Park Unity
1888 1890 Aston Villa 28 1

Burton, John Henry (Jack) IR
b Derby 13/8/1875 d 1949
Caps: SoLge 1
Derby St Andrew's
1897 1898 Derby County 10 3
Chatham
Tottenham Hotspur
1906 Preston North End 0
Lancaster

Burton, John Henry (Jack) IL/OR
b Normanby 31/7/1885
Grangetown
1905 1907 Blackburn Rovers 3
West Ham United
1909 Birmingham 4 3
Nelson
Cardiff City
Southend United

Burton, John William (Billy) RB
b Shirebrook 1/4/1908 d 1975
Mansfield Woodhouse Albion
Woodhouse Comrades
Sutton Junction
1931 1935 Nottingham Forest 36
1936 Brighton & Hove Albion 6
Bilsthorpe Colliery

From To Apps Goal

Burton, Matthew (Matt) OR/OL/IL
b Grassmoor 8/2/1897 d 1940
Grassmoor Athletic
1919 Everton 0
1919 1920 Stoke 8 1
1921 1922 Wrexham 54 10
1923 1924 New Brighton 16 6
Oswestry Town
Rhos Athletic
Llandudno
Rhos Athletic
Connah's Quay & Shotton
Staveley Town
Grassmoor Athletic

Burton, Noah IL/LH/OL
b Old Basford 18/12/1896 d 1956
Bulwell St Albans
Ilkeston United
1919 1920 Derby County 56 16
1921 1931 Nottingham Forest 296 57

Burton, Oliver (Ollie) LB
b Derby 27/5/1879 d 1929
1908 1909 Tottenham Hotspur 37

Burton, Ridley LH
b Amble 21/12/1893 d 1974
Gateshead Rodsley
Seaton Delaval
1912 Middlesbrough (trial) 0
Windy Nook
Newcastle City
Close Works (Gateshead)
1919 Grimsby Town 13
West Stanley
1920 Birmingham (trial)
1922 Ashington 29 1
Chester-le-Street
Preston Colliery

Burton, Stanley (Stan) OR
b Wombwell 3/12/1912 d 1977
Thurnscoe Victoria
1932 1938 Doncaster Rovers 196 50
1938 Wolverhampton Wanderers 28 3
1938 West Ham United 1
1939 (West Ham United) (3)
Frickley Colliery
Peterborough United
Wombwell Athletic
Shipcroft United
Ship Inn Rovers

Bury, William Henry RB/LB
b Darwen 1865
Padiham
1888 1890 Burnley 43
Brierfield

Busby, (Sir) Matthew William (Matt) RH
b Orbiston 26/5/1909 d 1994
Caps: SLge 1/Scotland War 7/Scotland 1
Alpine Villa
Denny Hibernian
1929 1935 Manchester City 202 11
1935 1938 Liverpool 115 3
1939 (Liverpool) (3)

Busby, Walter OL
b Spratton q1 1881 d 1945
Wellingborough Britons
Wellingborough
Queen's Park Rangers
1903 Woolwich Arsenal 5 2
Leyton

Bush, George Edward OL
b Canning Town q4 1883
Leyton
1907 Grimsby Town 12 2

Bush, Robert James LH
b West Ham 1879
Britannia
West Ham United
1906 Chelsea 4 1

Bush, William Thomas (Tom) CH
b Hodnet 22/2/1914 d 1969
Shrewsbury Amateurs
1933 1946 Liverpool 61 1
1939 (Liverpool) (3)

Bushby, Thomas William (Billy) CF/IR
b Shildon 21/8/1914 d 1997
1932 Wolverhampton Wanderers 0
Shildon
1934 1938 Southend United 40 12
1945 Portsmouth 0
1946 Southampton 2
Cowes

From To Apps Goal

Bushell, William (Willie) OR
b Wednesbury q3 1905
Darlaston
1926 West Bromwich Albion 0
Willenhall
1929 Leicester City 3 1
1931 Walsall 30 4

Bussey, Walter IR
b Eckington 6/12/1904 d 1982
Aughton Common Celtic
Dinnington Main Athletic
Anston Athletic
Denaby United
1925 1932 Stoke City 185 46
1933 Blackpool 25 8
1934 1936 Swansea Town 72 18
1936 1938 Exeter City 75 16

Bussingham, Charles LB
b Pontefract 31/3/1902 d 1962
Bentley Colliery
1928 Doncaster Rovers 1
Dartford

Butcher, Fred LB
b Hemingfield 14/8/1913 d 1996
Wombwell
1934 Aston Villa 2
1937 Blackpool 4
1938 Swindon Town 36

Butcher, George Thomas IL/IR
b St Albans 25/10/1890 d 1970
Caps: SoLge 1
St Albans City
1919 1920 West Ham United 34 8
1920 1924 Luton Town 121 24

Butcher, Joseph (Joe) CF
d 1958
Wolverhampton West End
1892 1894 Wolverhampton Wanderers 65 26
1895 West Bromwich Albion 0

Butcher, Reginald (Reg) RB/LH/RH
b Prescot 13/2/1916 d 2000
Shrewsbury Town
1937 Liverpool 0
1938 1949 Chester 155 1
1939 (Chester) (3)

Butcher, Ronald Walter (Ron) GK
b Shirley 23/2/1916 d 1997
Shirley Town
Shrewsbury Town
1935 Aston Villa 0
1936 1937 Reading 18

Butler, Arthur CF
b Norton, County Durham q3 1892
Stockton
Stillington Athletic
1921 Hartlepools United 2
Stockton

Butler, Charles Joseph W (Charlie) LB/RB
b Watford q4 1897
Caps: England Sch
1922 Manchester United 0
1923 1926 Gillingham 76
Grays Thurrock (loan)
1926 1927 Brentford 67
Montreal Carsteel

Butler, Charles Reginald (Charlie) LH/IR
b Barry 20/3/1908 d 1983
Caps: Wales Sch
Barry
1927 Charlton Athletic 0
Chatham (loan)
Sittingbourne (loan)
1929 Charlton Athletic 1
1930 Cardiff City (trial) 0
1930 Thames 3 1
Bath City
1931 Blackburn Rovers 0
Bath City (loan)
1933 1934 New Brighton 69
1935 Oldham Athletic 13
1936 Tranmere Rovers 1
Tunbridge Wells Rangers
Cork FC
South Liverpool

Butler, Edward Leslie (Leslie) CH
b Pinxton 25/2/1908 d 1985
1930 Derby County 0
1931 Southend United 0
1932 1933 Mansfield Town 46 5
Ollerton Colliery

From	To		Apps	Goal
Butler, Ernest (Ernie)			OL/OR	
b Stillington 17/6/1896			d 1969	
		Scunthorpe & Lindsey United		
		Ebbw Vale		
1922	1923	Queen's Park Rangers	34	
1924	1925	Hartlepools United	58	4
1926	1927	Durham City	65	10
Butler, Herbert			IL	
b Atherton 11/7/1903			d 1967	
		Atherton Collieries		
1923	1925	Blackpool	45	13
1927		Southport	0	
		Chorley		
1928	1931	Crystal Palace	109	31
1932		Chester	2	1
1933		Crewe Alexandra	2	
		Horwich RMI		
Butler, Herbert (Dick)			CH	
b Eastwood 18/11/1911			d 1984	
		Bestwood Colliery		
1936	1938	Birmingham	10	
1938		Crewe Alexandra	6	
Butler, Jack			CH	
		Rossendale United		
1933		Rochdale	5	
		Darwen		
Butler, John (Jack)			LB/CF	
b Sheffield 1885				
		Kiveton Park		
1904	1906	Grimsby Town	44	2
		Plymouth Argyle		
Butler, John Dennis (Jack)			CH	
b Colombo, Sri Lanka 14/8/1894			d 1961	
Caps: England 1				
		Fulham Thursdays		
1913		Fulham	0	
		Dartford		
1919	1929	Arsenal	267	7
1930	1931	Torquay United	50	2
		Daring		
Butler, John Thomas (Jock)			CF	
b Kirkmabreck 8/8/1888				
		Creetown Volunteers		
		Rangers		
		Morton		
		Rangers		
		Creetown Volunteers		
		Motherwell		
1911	1912	Bristol City	43	12
		Newport County		
		Third Lanark		
Butler, Joseph Henry (Joe)			GK	
b Dawley Bank q1 1879			d 1939	
1900	1903	Stockport County	100	
1905		Clapton Orient	20	
1905	1907	Stockport County	74	
1907	1911	Glossop	161	
1912	1913	Sunderland	65	
1914		Lincoln City	37	
		Macclesfield		
Butler, Malcolm Partridge			LB/RB/CF	
b Belfast 6/8/1913			d 1987	
Caps: Ireland 1				
		Elmgrove		
		Belfast Celtic		
		Bangor		
1935	1938	Blackpool	23	
1939		(Blackpool)	(3)	
1947		Accrington Stanley	32	
Butler, Reuben			CF/IR	
b Stillington 10/10/1890			d 1958	
		Stillington St John's		
		Stockton		
		Spennymoor United		
1912		Middlesbrough	0	
		Hartlepools United (loan)		
1919		Middlesbrough	27	11
1920	1922	Oldham Athletic	77	34
1923		Bury	20	13
1924	1925	Bradford City	40	16
1925		Crewe Alexandra	11	2
1926		Rochdale	5	
1927		Accrington Stanley	28	9
		Great Harwood		
		Northwich Victoria		
		Bacup Borough		
		Rossendale United		
Butler, Richard (Dick)			LH	
b Shepshed q1 1885			d 1956	
		Shepshed Albion		
1906	1909	Nottingham Forest	3	
1910	1911	Leicester Fosse	26	
		Loughborough Corinthians		

From	To		Apps	Goal
Butler, Stanley (Stan)			OL	
b Stillington 7/1/1919			d 1979	
		Flixborough Town		
		Scunthorpe & Lindsey United		
1938	1946	West Bromwich Albion	4	
1947		Southport	4	1
		Appleby Frodingham		
		Ashby Institute		
		Appleby Frodingham		
Butler, Thomas (Tommy)			IL	
b Darlaston			d 1923	
		Willenhall		
1921		Walsall	28	12
		Darlaston		
1922	1923	Port Vale	32	11
Butler, Thomas (Tommy)			OR/IR/IL	
b Atherton 28/4/1918			d 2009	
		Astley & Tyldesley Collieries		
1936		Bolton Wanderers	0	
		Macclesfield		
1937	1938	Oldham Athletic	45	9
1938		Middlesbrough	2	
1946		Oldham Athletic	30	3
1947	1952	Accrington Stanley	218	26
		Wigan Athletic		
Butler, Walter John			IL	
b Skirlaugh 19/10/1902			d 1976	
		Leeds Steelworks		
1920		Leeds United	1	
		Doncaster Rovers		
1922		Darlington	0	
Butler, William			LB/RB	
b 1883				
		Doncaster St James		
1904		Doncaster Rovers	7	
1906		Preston North End	3	
		Denaby United		
		Conisbrough St Peter's		
		Doncaster St James		
Butler, William (Billy)			OR	
b Atherton 27/3/1900			d 1966	
Caps: England 1				
		Howe Bridge		
		Atherton Collieries		
1921	1932	Bolton Wanderers	407	65
1933	1934	Reading	57	13
Butler, William			OR	
b Stockton 12/1/1901				
1922		Darlington	13	1
1922		Middlesbrough	2	
Butt, Harold Herbert (Harry)			IL/OL	
b Bristol 3/3/1910			d 1988	
		Bath City		
1933	1934	Charlton Athletic	28	8
1936	1937	Aldershot	40	7
		Cheltenham Town		
1939		Bristol Rovers	0	
Butt, Leonard (Len)			IR	
b Wilmslow 26/8/1910			d 1994	
		Wilmslow Albion		
		Ashton National		
1929	1930	Stockport County	8	1
		Macclesfield		
1935	1936	Huddersfield Town	67	11
1936	1946	Blackburn Rovers	110	44
1939		(Blackburn Rovers)	(3)	
1946	1947	York City	25	2
1947		Mansfield Town	15	4
		Mossley		
Butt, Leonard George (Len)			RH/LH	
b Freemantle 20/12/1893			d 1993	
		Malmesbury United		
		Shirley St James		
		Southampton		
		Thorneycrofts		
1920	1921	Southampton	17	
1923	1927	Bournemouth & Boscombe Ath	136	2
		Cowes		
Butterwick, H			IR	
1893		Middlesbrough Ironopolis	3	
Butterworth, Albert			OR/IR	
b Ashton-under-Lyne 20/3/1912			d 1991	
		Droylsden		
		Hurst		
1930		Manchester United (trial)	0	
1932	1933	Blackpool	22	5
1934	1935	Preston North End	14	4
1936	1945	Bristol Rovers	95	13
1939		(Bristol Rovers)	(3)	
		Stalybridge Celtic		
		Ashton United		

From	To		Apps	Goal
Butterworth, Charles Edward			OR	
b Derby q2 1871				
		Derby Midland		
1891		Derby County	1	
		Loughborough		
		Long Eaton Rangers		
		Heanor Town		
Butterworth, Herbert			RH/IR	
b Unsworth 1/1/1885				
		Unsworth Parish Church		
1904		Preston North End	0	
		Barrow		
1908	1909	Oldham Athletic	12	
		Queen's Park Rangers		
		Millwall Athletic		
Butterworth, Herbert			LH	
b Higham, Lancashire q3 1902				
		Higham		
1920		Wolverhampton Wanderers	0	
1924	1925	Nelson	9	
		Colne Town		
		Great Harwood		
		Wellington Town		
		Colne Town		
		CPR Calgary		
		Trent Motors (Derby)		
Butterworth, Thomas (Tommy)			LH	
1904		Bury	0	
1905	1908	Stockport County	118	
Buttery, Arthur			IL	
b Hednesford 20/12/1908			d 1990	
		Hednesford Town		
1931		Wolverhampton Wanderers	10	6
1932	1936	Bury	104	38
1936	1937	Bradford City	35	13
1938		Walsall	15	4
1939		Bristol Rovers	(3)	
		Stafford Rangers		
Buttrell, Charles Edward			IR	
b Sheffield 5/9/1894			d 1970	
1921		Chesterfield	9	3
		Mexborough		
		Mansfield Town		
Buxton, Arthur			LB/CH	
b Barlborough 15/5/1908			d 1979	
		Barlborough Welfare		
		Worksop Town		
1930	1931	Wrexham	15	
		Ripley Town (trial)		
1931		Lincoln City	0	
1932		Wrexham	0	
1932		Luton Town (trial)	0	
		Bangor City		
		Wellington Town		
1937	1938	New Brighton	54	
1939		(New Brighton)	(1)	
Buxton, Stephen (Steve)			LB	
b South Bank 3/2/1888			d 1953	
		South Bank		
		Brentford		
1911	1912	Oldham Athletic	27	
		Darlington		
1921		Ashington	24	1
		Workington		
		South Bank Gasworks		
Bycroft, Sydney (Syd)			CH	
b Lincoln 19/2/1912			d 2004	
1931		Notts County	0	
		Grantham		
1932		Bradford City	0	
1932		Hull City	0	
		Grantham		
		Newark Town		
1935	1951	Doncaster Rovers	333	2
1939		(Doncaster Rovers)	(3)	
Bye, James Henry			RH	
b Aston 11/2/1920			d 1995	
		Shirley Juniors		
1938		Birmingham	1	
1939		(Birmingham)	(3)	
Bye, Leslie			LH	
b Bedwellty 30/6/1913			d 1970	
1937	1938	Swansea Town	3	
		Dartford		
		Lovells Athletic		
Byers, John Edwin (Jack)			OL	
b Selby q3 1897			d 1931	
		Knaresborough		
		Selby Town		
1921	1922	Huddersfield Town	12	4
1922	1923	Blackburn Rovers	27	2
1923	1927	West Bromwich Albion	104	11
		Worcester City		
1929		Torquay United	0	
		Kidderminster Harriers		

From	To		Apps	Goal
Byrne, Andrew			OL	
b Dublin 1891				
		Shelbourne		
1913		Hull City	3	
		Shelbourne		
Byrne, David			CF	
b Dublin 28/4/1905				
Caps: Eire 3				
		St Brendan's		
		Shamrock Rovers		
1927		Bradford City	3	1
		Shelbourne		
		Shamrock Rovers		
1932		Sheffield United	0	
		Shamrock Rovers		
1933		Manchester United	4	3
		Coleraine		
		Larne		
		Shamrock Rovers		
		Hammond Lane		
		Brideville		
		Shelbourne		
1939		Sheffield United (trial)	0	
Byrne, J			OL	
		South Bank		
1905		Gainsborough Trinity	2	
Byrne, Michael Patrick (Mick)			GK	
b Bristol q2 1880			d 1931	
		Grenadier Guards		
		Bristol Rovers		
		Southampton		
1905	1906	Chelsea	4	
1907		Glossop	11	
Byrom, Thomas (Tom)			IR	
b Blackburn q1 1889			d 1958	
		Blackburn St Philip's		
		Blackburn Victoria Cross		
1914	1919	Blackburn Rovers	13	3
		Rochdale		
1920		Oldham Athletic	5	
		Chorley		
Byrom, Thomas George (Tom)			LH	
b Upton 17/3/1920			d 1997	
		Heswall		
1939	1946	Tranmere Rovers	3	
1939		(Tranmere Rovers)	(3)	
Bytheway, George			OL/OR	
b Chesterfield 27/3/1908			d 1979	
		Staveley Town		
1927	1930	West Bromwich Albion	16	2
1933		Coventry City	7	2
1933	1935	Mansfield Town	87	23
		Guildford City		
Bytheway, William			OR	
1921		Walsall	1	
Cable, Thomas Henry (Tommy)			CH	
b Barking 27/11/1900			d 1986	
Caps: England Amat				
		Barking		
		Leyton		
1925	1926	Queen's Park Rangers	18	2
		Middlesex Wanderers		
		Leyton		
1928	1931	Tottenham Hotspur	41	
1932		Southampton	0	
		Kettering Town		
Caddick, George Frederick R			CH/LH/RH	
b Liverpool 2/3/1900			d 1984	
1924		Everton	0	
1925		Stockport County	11	1
1925	1931	Barnsley	169	
		Llanelly		
Caddick, William (Bill)			CH	
b Wellington 14/3/1903				
		Wellington Town		
1920	1926	Wolverhampton Wanderers	147	4
		Wellington Town		
Cadwell, Albert Frank			LH	
b Edmonton 1/11/1900			d 1944	
Caps: FLge 1				
		Nunhead		
1923	1932	West Ham United	272	1
Cadwell, James (Jimmy 'Midge')			OR	
b High Park 12/1/1894			d 1969	
		Churchtown Congegationals		
		High Park		
		Norwood Crescent		
		Skelmersdale Mission		
1922		Southport	5	
		Fleetwood Hesketh		

From To Apps Goal

Caesar, William Cecil (Bill) CH
b Battersea 25/11/1899 d 1988
Caps: England Amat
Dulwich Hamlet
1924 Darlington 0
1925 Fulham 1
Harwich & Parkeston
London Caledonians
1926 Chelsea 0
1927 Walsall 8
Dulwich Hamlet
1929 Brentford 1
Hayes
Wimbledon
Egham
Leyton
Civil Service

Cahill, Richardson Gibbins (Richard) OR
b Sunderland q1 1885 d 1949
Houghton Rovers
1911 Blackpool 20
Houghton Rovers

Caie, Alexander S (Alex) RH/CF
b Nigg 25/6/1877 d 1914
Victoria United (Aberdeen)
1896 Woolwich Arsenal 8 4
Bristol City
Millwall Athletic
1901 1902 Newcastle United 31 1
Brentford
Motherwell
Westmount (Canada)
Sons of Scotland (Canada)
Rosedale (Canada)

Caiels, Alfred Leonard OL
b Walthamstow 21/1/1909 d 1991
Epsom Town
Leytonstone
1931 Tottenham Hotspur 0
Linfield
Olympique Marseille
1933 Notts County 0
1934 Stockport County 2 1

Caig, Hugh IR
b Dalry 1894
Kilwinning
1914 Middlesbrough 1

Cail, Samuel George (Sammy) CF/IL
b Middlesbrough q3 1887 d 1950
Army
1906 1912 Middlesbrough 136 52
Stalybridge Celtic
Aberdeen
Scotswood

Cain, Robert (Bob) LB/RH
b Slamannan 13/2/1866
Airdrieonians
1889 Everton 10
Bootle
1892 1897 Sheffield United 164 3
Tottenham Hotspur
Albion Rovers
1899 Small Heath 0

Cain, Thomas (Tom) GK
b Sunderland 12/10/1874 d 1897
Hebburn Argyle
1893 Stoke 11
1894 Everton 11
Southampton
1896 Grimsby Town 2
Hebburn Argyle
West Stanley

Cain, Thomas LH
b Ealing q1 1895
Richmond YMCA
Queen's Park Rangers
Guildford United
Dartford
Sheppey United
1924 1925 Brentford 11

Caine, James (Jimmy) CH
b Brierfield 24/6/1908 d 1971
1928 Burnley 0
1929 1930 Nelson 5
1931 Bury 0
Barnoldswick Town
William Fell & Co (Nelson)

Cainey, William Percival (Percy) OL
b Bristol 12/12/1908 d 1960
Wesley Rovers
1932 1935 Bristol City 76 12
1936 Bradford Park Avenue 11 1
Bath City

Cairns, J IR
1894 Burton Swifts 7

From To Apps Goal

Cairns, James RH/LB
1893 Ardwick 1
1894 Newton Heath 1

Cairns, James IR
Stevenston Thistle
Glossop North End
1897 Lincoln City 0
1898 Newton Heath 1
Berry's Association

Cairns, John CF/IR
b Glasgow 1902 d 1965
St Bernard's
Broxburn United
Dunfermline Athletic
Kettering Town
1926 Charlton Athletic 7 2
1927 Brentford 1 1
1928 Leicester City 0
1929 Portsmouth 0
Kettering Town
Margate
1933 Rochdale 5
Toronto Scottish
Ramsgate

Cairns, Thomas IR
1904 Glossop 22 2
Distillery
Oldham Athletic

Cairns, Thomas (Tommy) IL/IR
b Merryton 30/10/1890 d 1967
Caps: SLge 6/Scotland 8
Burnbank Athletic
Larkhall Thistle
1911 Bristol City 11 1
Peebles Rovers
St Johnstone
Rangers
Hamilton Academical (loan)
1927 1931 Bradford City 135 32

Cairns, Thomas IL
b Newcastle q1 1896 d 1917
Chopwell Villa
Newcastle City
1914 Newcastle United 1

Cairns, William Hart (Billy) CF/IL
b Newcastle 7/10/1914 d 1988
Holborn Rangers
Stargate Rovers
1934 1938 Newcastle United 87 51
1939 (Newcastle United) (2) (1)
1945 Gateshead 0
1946 1953 Grimsby Town 221 121

Calder, John (Jack) CF
b Glengarnock 19/10/1913
Glengarnock YMCA
Dalry Thistle
1931 Leicester City 1
Falkirk
St Johnstone
Dunfermline Athletic
Alloa Athletic (trial)
Morton
1936 1937 Bolton Wanderers 27 11
1938 Barnsley 9 5
Morton

Calder, John H LH/LB
b Lochgelly 13/10/1911
Montrose
Leith Athletic
1937 Torquay United 5 1
1938 Hartlepools United 4

Calder, Leslie Adair CF
b Southampton q4 1888
Army
1910 Woolwich Arsenal 1

Calder, Robert (Bob) RB/LB
b Glasgow 2/1/1907 d 1973
Bell Telephone (Toronto)
Toronto Scottish
Montreal Carsteel
Rangers
1933 Cardiff City 37
1934 Bradford City 0
1934 Cardiff City (trial) 0
1934 Southend United (trial) 0
1935 Newport County 14
1936 1937 Barrow 7
1937 Clapton Orient (trial) 0
Milford United

Calderbank, J RH
Horwich
1900 Bolton Wanderers 3

From To Apps Goal

Calderhead, David CH
b Hurlford 19/6/1864 d 1938
Caps: FLge 1/Scotland 1
Wishaw Swifts
Wishaw Thistle
Queen of the South Wanderers
1889 1899 Notts County 278 12
1900 Lincoln City 2

Calderhead, David CH/LH
b Dumfries 25/10/1889 d 1965
Dumfries Primrose
Maxwelltown Volunteers
1906 Lincoln City 0
1910 1913 Chelsea 34 1
Motherwell
1919 Clapton Orient 1

Calderwood, James Cuthbertson LB/RH/RB
b Busby 19/12/1898 d 1968
Manchester Calico Printers
1922 1925 Manchester City 35
1927 1929 Grimsby Town 74

Caldow, G CF
1889 Burnley 6

Caldwell, Arthur John OL
b Salford 24/2/1913 d 1989
1932 Manchester United 0
Winsford United
1934 1938 Port Vale 92 21

Caldwell, James (Jimmy) OL
b London
Willesden
1907 Clapton Orient 12
Hastings & St Leonards
Queen's Park Rangers
Reading

Caldwell, James Henry GK
b Carronshore 1886
Carron Thistle
Dunipace
East Stirlingshire
1908 Tottenham Hotspur 0
Reading
1912 Everton 31
1913 Woolwich Arsenal 3
Reading

Caldwell, John (Jock) LB
b Shawwood 28/11/1874
Newmilns
Hibernian
1894 1895 Woolwich Arsenal 59 1
Third Lanark
1896 1897 Woolwich Arsenal 34 1
Brighton United
Galston
Brighton & Hove Albion

Caldwell, Robert RH/LH
b South Kirkby 22/6/1909 d 1974
South Kirkby Colliery
1935 Doncaster Rovers 3
1936 1938 Bristol City 39 3
1939 Bristol Rovers 0

Caldwell, Thomas (Tommy) OL
b West Ham q3 1885
Ilford Alliance
West Ham St Paul's
1907 Clapton Orient 7
Southend United
West Ham United
New Brompton
Reading

Caldwell, Thomas Somerville (Tommy) LB
b Glasgow 30/1/1909
Caps: WLge 2
Newmains Juniors
1928 1936 Swansea Town 55

Cale, Frederick (Fred) IL
b Hucknall Torkard q4 1875 d 1950
Hucknall St John's
1895 Notts County 1
Red Hill United

Callachan, Henry (Harry) LB
b Madras, India 9/4/1903 d 1990
Kirkintilloch Rob Roy
Parkhead
Celtic
Alloa Athletic (loan)
Beith (loan)
1927 Leicester City 3
Tunbridge Wells Rangers
Burton Town
Wigan Athletic
Market Harborough Town

From To Apps Goal

Calladine, Charles Frederick (Charlie) OR
b Wessington q2 1888
Notts Olympic
1907 Notts County 3

Calladine, Charles Frederick (Charlie) LH/IL/RH
b Wessington 24/1/1911 d 1983
Ivanhoe
Scunthorpe & Lindsey United
1930 1935 Birmingham 114 5
1935 1937 Blackburn Rovers 48 6
Guildford City

Calladine, John OR
1920 West Ham United 1

Callaghan, Ernest (Ernie 'Mush') RB/CH
b Birmingham 21/1/1910 d 1972
Walmer Athletic
Hinckley Athletic
Atherstone Town
1932 1946 Aston Villa 125
1939 (Aston Villa) (3)

Callaghan, George RH
b Southampton
1923 1924 Merthyr Town 15

Callaghan, J OL
1893 Middlesbrough Ironopolis 3 1

Callaghan, James IR
South Bank
1899 Middlesbrough 2

Callaghan, John RH/IL
b Scotland
Hunslet
1895 1896 Sheffield Wednesday 4 2

Callaghan, Patrick J OL
b Longbridge, Ireland 1904
Aberaman Athletic
1926 Aberdare Athletic 40 4
1927 Bristol City 12 1
Aberdare & Aberaman

Callaghan, Thomas OR
b Birmingham 1886 d 1917
Halesowen
1904 1906 Glossop 73 8
1907 Manchester City 2
Partick Thistle
St Mirren
Partick Thistle

Callaghan, Thomas T (Tom) OL
b Govan 1901
St Anthony's (Glasgow)
Third Lanark
Nithsdale Wanderers (loan)
Dunfermline Athletic
1927 Middlesbrough 0
Third Lanark
Glentoran
Cork FC
1932 Darlington 2
Third Lanark (trial)
Raith Rovers (trial)
Coleraine

Callagher, John CH
b Glasgow 3/4/1898 d 1980
St Roch's
1921 1923 Bury 60 1
1924 Southampton 1
1925 Wigan Borough 8 2
1926 Norwich City 0
Horwich RMI
Mossley

Callan, William IL
b Glasgow 10/6/1900
Shawland Thistle
Pollok
1921 Derby County 1

Callanan, William D CH
b Featherstone, Staffordshire 6/1885
Oxley St Mark's
Willenhall Pickwick
1907 Wolverhampton Wanderers 3
Bilston Town

Calland, Ralph LB
b Lanchester 5/7/1916
Annfield Plain
1937 Charlton Athletic 0
1939 1953 Torquay United 207 14
1939 (Torquay United) (1)

From To Apps Goal

Callender, John OR
b West Wylam 3/9/1912 d 1980
Walker Celtic
1933 Brighton & Hove Albion 0
Walker Celtic
1934 Chesterfield 5 1
Ashington
1936 1937 Lincoln City 75 26
1938 Port Vale 3 1
1939 Gateshead (3) (2)

Callender, Reginald Henry (Reg) OL
b Stockton q4 1892 d 1915
Caps: England Amat
St John's College (Cambridge)
Stockton
1912 Glossop 1
1913 Derby County 5

Callender, Thomas Sanderson (Tom) CH/LH/LB
b Bywell 20/9/1920 d 2002
Caps: England Sch
Crawcrook Albion
1938 Lincoln City 23
1939 (Lincoln City) (3)
1946 1956 Gateshead 439 58

Callender, William (Billy) GK
b Prudhoe 5/1/1903 d 1932
Prudhoe Castle
1923 1931 Crystal Palace 203

Calvert, Frederick John IR
b Ipswich 7/8/1891 d 1976
Army
1910 1911 Woolwich Arsenal 2 1

Calvert, James (Jim) RH
b Blackburn 15/5/1917 d 1988
1936 Blackburn Rovers 0
1938 Accrington Stanley 8

Calvert, Joseph William Herbert (Joe) GK
b Beighton 3/2/1907 d 1999
Owston Park Rangers
Bullcroft Main Colliery
Frickley Colliery
1931 Bristol Rovers 42
1932 1947 Leicester City 72
1947 Watford 5
Brush Sports

Calvey, John (Jack) IR/CF
b South Bank 23/8/1875 d 1937
Caps: FLge 1/England 1
South Bank Juniors
Millwall Athletic
1899 1903 Nottingham Forest 131 48
Millwall Athletic

Calvey, Mitchell CF
b Blackburn
Lancashire Fusiliers
Distillery
1893 Blackburn Rovers 6 3
1894 Manchester City 7 5
Bacup
Baltimore

Cameron, David Francis LH/CH
b Partick 12/9/1902 d 1978
Cameron Highlanders
Akeld
Queen's Park
1920 1924 Chelsea 73 2
Heart of Midlothian
Helensburgh (loan)
1926 Portsmouth 0
Heart of Midlothian
Dunfermline Athletic
1928 1929 Nottingham Forest 21 1
Colwyn Bay

Cameron, Duncan IL
b Menstrie 1898
Stenhousemuir
1920 Reading 26 1
1921 Rotherham County 5 1

Cameron, Edward S (Eddie) OL
b Glasgow 1895
Clydebank
1921 Birmingham 6 1
1922 1923 Walsall 63 4
1923 1924 Nelson 46 10
Stafford Rangers
1928 Exeter City 24 9
Stafford Rangers
1929 Nelson (trial) 0
Cradley Heath
Hednesford Town
Stafford Rangers

Cameron, Hugh IL
1920 Burnley 0
1921 Rochdale 11 2

From To Apps Goal

Cameron, James (Jock) LB
b Glasgow 1868 d 1934
Caps: SAll 1
Cardonald Juniors
Glasgow Perthshire
Liverpool
Linthouse
Rangers
1894 Liverpool 4
Pollokshields

Cameron, James LH
b Inverness
Cameron Highlanders
Third Lanark
Inverness Clachnacuddin
Mitcham Athletic
Heart of Midlothian
1923 Queen's Park Rangers 24
Indiana Flooring
New York Nationals
New York Giants

Cameron, John IL
b Glasgow 1868
Renton
1891 Stoke 9 4
Hibernian

Cameron, John CF/IL
b Ayr 13/4/1872 d 1935
Caps: Scotland 1
Ayr Parkhouse
Queen's Park
1895 1897 Everton 42 12
Tottenham Hotspur

Cameron, John (Jack) CF
Dornoch
1911 Huddersfield Town 2 1

Cameron, John Bell (Jock) LB/RB
b Kirkwood 1880 d 1945
Caps: SLge 3/Scotland 2
Kirkwood Thistle
St Mirren
1903 1907 Blackburn Rovers 64
1907 1912 Chelsea 179
Port Vale

Cameron, John R CF
b Currie 1875 d 1944
1896 West Bromwich Albion 13 2
1897 Blackburn Rovers 0

Cameron, Kenneth (Ken) IR/OL/IL
b Hamilton 1905
Parkhead
1926 1928 Preston North End 24 5
1929 1933 Middlesbrough 99 30
1933 1934 Bolton Wanderers 24 3
1935 Hull City 30 12
1936 Queen's Park Rangers 8 1
1937 Rotherham United 0

Cameron, Kenneth A (Ken) CH
b Inverness 1913
Inverness Clachnacuddin
1934 Aldershot 1

Cameron, R CF
b Glasgow
1892 Lincoln City 15 3

Cameron, William Smith (Kilty) CF/IR/OL
b Mossend 15/5/1886 d 1958
Burnbank Athletic
Albion Rovers
Renton
1904 1905 Glossop 51 23
1906 1907 Bolton Wanderers 26 5
1907 1912 Blackburn Rovers 70 18
1912 1913 Bury 38 16
1913 1914 Hull City 47 10
Clydebank
Hamilton Academical
Vale of Leven
1919 Bury 2

Cameron, William T (Bill) IR
b Glasgow 11/4/1914
1933 Middlesbrough 0
1934 Bournemouth & Boscombe Ath 1
Stenhousemuir

From To Apps Goal

Camidge, Walter IR
b York 2/1/1912 d 1987
Dringhouses
1932 York City 2
Scarborough
Peterborough United

Cammack, Francis John OR
b Prescot 24/4/1900 d 1984
Hallam
1920 Sheffield United 6
Houghton Main Colliery
Worksop Town
Scunthorpe & Lindsey United
Mansfield Town
Mexborough Athletic

Campbell, Alex RB
b Glasgow
Parkhead
Albion Rovers
1926 1927 Clapton Orient 23
Connah's Quay & Shotton

Campbell, Alexander IR
b Perth
Holyhead Swifts
1899 Barnsley 6 1
Dearne

Campbell, Alexander (Alex) LB/RB
b Inverness 7/3/1883
Inverness Clachnacuddin
1906 1908 Middlesbrough 34
Inverness Clachnacuddin
1911 Leeds City 1

Campbell, Alexander (Alex) LB
b Ayr
Glenburn Rovers
1925 Halifax Town 10

Campbell, Alexander Ferguson (Sandy) IL/IR
b Dalmuir 24/1/1897 d 1975
Old Kilpatrick
Glasgow Ashfield
Queen's Park
1920 1921 Oldham Athletic 37 6
1922 Swansea Town 7 2
1923 Oldham Athletic 4 2
Mossley

Campbell, Alistair Kenyon (Alec) CH
b South Stoneham 29/5/1890 d 1943
Caps: England Amat
Southampton
1909 1912 Glossop 10
West Ham United
Boscombe
1920 1925 Southampton 157 13
Poole

Campbell, Allan Fletcher GK
b Hebburn 2/2/1914 d 1984
Jarrow Imperial
Jarrow
Washington Colliery
1934 Bolton Wanderers 0
1935 Southport 8
1936 Middlesbrough 0
Walker Celtic
Jarrow
Blyth Spartans
South Shields

Campbell, Andrew IL/IR
b Dunfermline
Dunfermline Athletic
1924 1926 Doncaster Rovers 44 7
1927 Brighton & Hove Albion 0
1927 Lincoln City 5 4

Campbell, Archibald (Archie) RH/CH
b Crook 8/1904
Leadgate Park
Craghead United
Spennymoor United
1923 1924 Aston Villa 4
1925 1926 Lincoln City 54 4
Craghead United
Washington Colliery
Dundee
Washington Colliery
Birmingham City Transport

Campbell, Archibald MacEachern (Archie] RB/LB
b Johnstone 21/11/1897 d 1987
Kilbarchan Athletic
Paisley Vulcan
1921 Derby County 0
1924 1927 Norwich City 87
Gothic
CEYMS (Norwich)

From To Apps Goal

Campbell, Austen Fenwick LH
b Hamsterley 5/5/1901 d 1981
Caps: FLge 5/England 8
Spen Black & White
Leadgate Park
1920 Coventry City 1
Leadgate Park
1922 1929 Blackburn Rovers 161 7
1929 1934 Huddersfield Town 194 5
1935 Hull City 11
Darwen

Campbell, Charles J CF/LH
b Blackburn 1903
Pembroke Dock
1925 Queen's Park Rangers 4 1
1926 Reading 1

Campbell, Charles William George (Charlie) LH
b Chatham 27/3/1917 d 2002
Gillingham Nomads
1937 Gillingham 7

Campbell, Francis Stephen (Frank) RH/CH
b Camlachie 3/3/1907
Irvine Meadow
1931 1934 Southampton 86 5
Newport (Isle of Wight)

Campbell, George LH
b Largs 28/3/1871 d 1898
Renton
1890 1892 Aston Villa 51 2
Dundee
Renton

Campbell, Henry (Harry) IR/IL
b Renton 1867 d 1915
Caps: Scotland 1
Renton
1889 1893 Blackburn Rovers 98 22

Campbell, Hugh OL
b Glasgow 1916
Shawfield Juniors
Morton
Rangers
Ballymena United
1935 Clapton Orient 8 1
Distillery
1936 Cardiff City 1
Distillery
Stranraer
Ballymena United
1937 Halifax Town 25 1

Campbell, J IR
Darwen
1889 Burnley 14 3

Campbell, James RH
Strathclyde Juniors
1907 1908 Chesterfield Town 8
Bethlehem Steel
Todd Shipyards (USA)
Harrison FC (USA)
Newark Skeeters

Campbell, James GK
Custom House
1910 Huddersfield Town (trial) 1
Custom House

Campbell, James (Jimmy) LH
b Newhaven, Midlothian 12/11/1886 d 1925
Caps: Scotland 1
Leith Athletic
1910 1919 Sheffield Wednesday 144 3
1920 Huddersfield Town 1
St Bernard's

Campbell, James GK
b Dalry
Partick Thistle
1928 Exeter City 17

Campbell, John OL
b Govan 1877
Caps: SLge 1/Scotland 4
Renton Union
Linthouse
Partick Thistle
1896 1897 Blackburn Rovers 55 10
Rangers
West Ham United
Hibernian
New Brompton
Partick Thistle
Dumbarton Harp

From To Apps Goal

Campbell, John CF
b South Shields 12/5/1901 d 1983
Berwick Rangers
Wood Skinners
Jarrow
1923 1927 West Ham United 28 11
Hibernian
1929 Clapton Orient 25 9

Campbell, John (Johnny) CF/OR
b Ardrossan 7/3/1910 d 1999
Dalry Thistle
1932 1933 Leicester City 21 12
1933 1938 Lincoln City 184 104
Scunthorpe & Lindsey United
Lincoln Co-op

Campbell, John Henry (Johnny) RH/LH
b Birkenhead 14/10/1894
Ocean Athletic
1921 1929 Tranmere Rovers 189 10

Campbell, John James (Johnny) CF
b Glasgow 9/1871 d 1947
Caps: SLge 4/Scotland 12
Possil Hawthorn
Glasgow Benburb
Possil Hawthorn
Celtic
1895 1896 Aston Villa 55 39
Celtic
Third Lanark

Campbell, John Middleton (Johnny) CF
b Renton 19/2/1870 d 1906
Renton Union
Renton
1890 1896 Sunderland 186 136
1897 1898 Newcastle United 23 9

Campbell, Joseph (Joe) OR
b Blackburn 13/4/1894 d 1976
Heywood United
1920 Oldham Athletic 0
1921 Wigan Borough 7
1921 Blackburn Rovers 0
1922 1926 Rochdale 34 4
Stalybridge Celtic
Morecambe
Great Harwood

Campbell, Joseph (Joe) RH/LH
b Walker 31/10/1903 d 1981
Walker Park
Walker Celtic
1925 1926 Hull City 11
1927 Bradford City 1
Yeovil & Petters United
1929 Southend United 7
Dartford

Campbell, Kenneth (Kenny) GK
b Cambuslang 6/9/1892 d 1977
Caps: SLge 1/Scotland 8
Clyde Vale
Rutherglen Glencairn
Cambuslang Rangers
1911 1919 Liverpool 125
Partick Thistle (loan)
Partick Thistle
New Brighton
1922 1925 Stoke 35
1925 1928 Leicester City 79
1929 South Shields 0
1929 1930 New Brighton 55

Campbell, Lewis OL/OR/IL
b Edinburgh 4/1864 d 1938
Dumbarton
Helensburgh
Glasgow United
Hibernian
1889 1892 Aston Villa 40 20
Dumbarton
1893 Burslem Port Vale 27 13
1894 Burton Swifts 23 9

Campbell, Peter LH
b Greenock 1866
Glasgow Perthshire
1894 1898 Burton Swifts 40 1
Morton
1898 Burton Swifts 33 1
Morton

Campbell, Robert (Bob) RB
b Lugar 1882 d 1931
Caps: SLge 1
Lugar Boswell
Craigston Strollers
Partick Thistle
Rangers
Millwall Athletic
1906 1914 Bradford City 223 1

From To Apps Goal

Campbell, T OR
1894 Newcastle United 2

Campbell, T Fred RB
b Burnley
Queen's Park
1905 Burnley 9
Queen's Park

Campbell, WC LH/CH
Bootle
1890 1891 Everton 17 1
1892 Bootle 0

Campbell, William Cecil IR/CF/IL
b Inverness 25/10/1865
Royal Arsenal
1890 Preston North End 4 4
Middlesbrough
1892 Darwen 22 8
1893 Blackburn Rovers 1
1893 Newton Heath 5 1
1893 Notts County 0
Newark
1896 Everton 3 1
Clyde

Campbell, William R (Willie) RH
b Dunfermline
Townhill
Cowdenbeath
Clackmannan
Beith
Canadian Pacific Railroad
Alloa Athletic
1927 1928 Huddersfield Town 3
Raith Rovers

Campling, A Harold (Harry) RB
b Grimesthorpe
Grimethorpe Colliery
1922 1924 Coventry City 10

Camsell, George Henry CF
b Framwellgate Moor 27/11/1902 d 1966
Caps: FLge 1/England 9
Durham Chapel
Framwellgate Moor
Tow Law Town
Esh Winning
1923 Durham City 0
Esh Winning
1924 1925 Durham City 21 20
1925 1938 Middlesbrough 418 325
1939 (Middlesbrough) (1)

Canavon, Alfred (Alf) GK
b Coventry 26/8/1903 d 1991
Stafford Rangers
1925 1927 Wolverhampton Wanderers 13
Shrewsbury Town

Candy, George William OL
b Stockbridge q3 1885
Salisbury Town
1908 Clapton Orient 3

Cann, Harry GK
b Tintagel 31/3/1905 d 1980
Tintagel
1927 1938 Plymouth Argyle 225
1939 Fulham 0

Cann, Sidney Thomas (Syd) RB/CH
b Torquay 30/10/1911 d 1996
Caps: England Sch
Babbacombe
1928 1929 Torquay United 44 3
1929 1933 Manchester City 42
1935 1938 Charlton Athletic 15

Cannell, John Barker CF
b Laxey 1892 d 1961
Laxey
1911 Bury 3
Altrincham

Cannon, Alec LH
1888 Wolverhampton Wanderers 7
Kidderminster Olympic

Cannon, Charles (Charlie) RH
b Coatbridge 7/2/1903 d 1955
Shillighmuir Celtic
Baillieston Juniors
Bellshill Athletic
1926 Manchester City 0
1928 Southport 9
St Bernard's

From To Apps Goal

Cannon, George Frederick IR
b Hammersmith q1 1891
Richmond St Elizabeth
Mortlake Church Wanderers
Mortlake Institute
Mortlake Wednesday
Tooting
1914 Fulham 6 5
Brentford
Wimbledon
Margate

Cannon, Thomas (Tom) RH
b Tonge q2 1891
Turton
1911 Bury 13

Cant, Andrew Fairweather CF
b Kirkton of Auchterhouse 6/10/1899
Dunfermline Discharged Soldiers
Raith Rovers
Alloa Athletic
East Fife
1922 1923 Bradford City 14 3
East Fife
Dunfermline Athletic
Dundee United
1924 Barnsley (trial) 0
King's Park

Cant, John Leslie (Les) GK
b Medomsley 20/2/1908 d 1943
Shotton Colliery Welfare
Crook Town
1932 York City 0
Chester-le-Street
1933 Bury 4
1934 Stockport County 1
1934 Southport 11
Northwich Victoria
Consett
South Shields
Whitley & Monkseaton

Cantrell, James (Jimmy) CF/IR/IL
b Sheepbridge 7/5/1882 d 1960
Bulwell Red Rose
Bulwell White Star
Hucknall Constitutionals
1904 1907 Aston Villa 48 22
1907 1912 Notts County 131 64
1912 1922 Tottenham Hotspur 159 74
Sutton Town

Cape, John Phillips (Jackie) OR
b Carlisle 16/11/1911 d 1994
Penrith
1929 Carlisle United 15 2
1929 1933 Newcastle United 51 18
1933 1936 Manchester United 59 18
1937 1938 Queen's Park Rangers 61 12
1939 1945 Carlisle United 0
Scarborough
1946 Carlisle United 3

Capener, RH IR
1898 Burslem Port Vale 1

Capes, Adrian CF/IL/IR
b Burton-on-Trent 18/4/1873 d 1955
1894 1895 Burton Wanderers 54 32
1896 1897 Nottingham Forest 30 7
1897 1898 Burton Swifts 14 7
1900 1905 Burslem Port Vale 164 60
1905 1906 Stoke 17 2
Burslem Port Vale

Capes, Arthur John (Sailor) IL/IR/OR
b Burton-on-Trent 23/2/1875 d 1945
Caps: FLge 1/England 1
1894 1895 Burton Wanderers 57 23
1896 1901 Nottingham Forest 169 33
1902 1903 Stoke 61 18
1904 Bristol City 29 7
Swindon Town

Capewell, Leonard King (Len) CF/IL
b Bordesley Green 8/6/1895 d 1978
Saltley Baptists
Wolseley Athletic Works
Wellington Town
1921 1928 Aston Villa 144 88
1929 Walsall 7
Wellington Town

Capewell, William (Billy) RB/RH/LB
b Stoke-on-Trent 2/1878
1895 Stoke 1
Reading
1899 1902 Stoke 57

Cappendale, Thomas William (Tommy) IL
b Whittington 1882 d 1950
New Whittington Exchange
1903 Chesterfield Town 4 1
New Whittington Exchange

From To Apps Goal

Capper, Alfred (Freddy) OR
b Knutsford 2/1891 d 1955
Northwich Church Lads
Northwich Victoria
1911 Manchester United 1
Witton Albion
1914 1920 Sheffield Wednesday 59 4
1921 1923 Brentford 96 5

Capper, Thomas (Tommy) GK
b Newton-le-Willows 14/7/1891 d 1971
Atherton
South Liverpool
Dundee
1920 1921 Southend United 78
1922 Wigan Borough 5
Wallasey United

Capstick, William GK
b South Kirkby 25/3/1903 d 1965
South Kirkby
Frickley Colliery
1931 Barnsley 6
Mexborough Athletic

Cardwell, George LB
b Blackpool 1877 d 1939
1897 Blackpool 5

Cardwell, Louis CH
b Blackpool 20/8/1912 d 1986
Whitegate Juniors
1930 1937 Blackpool 131 6
1938 1946 Manchester City 39
1939 (Manchester City) (3)
Netherfield (loan)
Ashton United
Netherfield
1947 1948 Crewe Alexandra 25

Carey, Andrew P CF
b New Cumnock
1922 Merthyr Town 1

Carey, John Joseph (Johnny) RB/RH/IL
b Dublin 23/2/1919 d 1995
Caps: Ireland War 2/Ireland 7/Eire 29
St James's Gate
1937 1952 Manchester United 304 16
1939 (Manchester United) (2) (1)
Shamrock Rovers (loan)

Carey, William Anderson (Billy) RH
b Govan 14/8/1898
Harland & Wolff
Kirkintilloch Rob Roy
Glasgow Benburb
Peebles Rovers
1926 Clapton Orient 3

Carey, William James GK
b Manchester 21/9/1913 d 1998
Sedgley Park
Hereford United
1937 1938 Aston Villa 3
1939 (Aston Villa) (1)
1945 Bury 0

Cargill, James (Jimmy) IL/OR
b Arbroath 21/11/1914
Arbroath Roselea
Arbroath Woodside
1934 1935 Nottingham Forest 10 1
1936 1938 Brighton & Hove Albion 66 19
1939 Barrow (1) (1)

Carless, Ernest Francis (Ernie) IR
b Barry 9/9/1912 d 1987
Caps: Wales Sch
1931 Wolverhampton Wanderers 0
Barry
1932 Cardiff City 1
Altrincham
Barry
1946 Plymouth Argyle 4

Carlin, John Charles (Jack) OR/IL
b Southport q4 1876 d 1935
Tranmere Rovers
1899 Glossop 8 1
1900 1901 Barnsley 48 9
1902 1906 Liverpool 31 8
1907 1908 Preston North End 32 5

Carlisle, Richard Wright (Dick) CH
b Preston 9/9/1889 d 1975
South Liverpool
1909 Preston North End 0
Padiham
South Liverpool
1919 1920 Oldham Athletic 5
1921 Wigan Borough 32 3
Morecambe

From	To		Apps	Goal
Carlton, John			IL/RH/IR	
b Ashington 29/1/1902			d 1983	
		Pegswood		
1925	1928	Ashington	67	11
		Frickley Colliery		
		Ashington		
		Bedlington United		
Carlton, William			RB/RH	
b Washington 15/7/1908			d 1973	
		Washington Colliery Welfare		
1927	1928	Newcastle United	5	1
1929		Merthyr Town	15	
		West Stanley		
		Ashington		
		Annfield Plain		
Carman, James			OR/IR	
b Manchester q2 1875				
1895		Darwen	3	1
		Oldham County		
1897		Newton Heath	4	2
Carmedy, Thomas Owen (Tom)			OR/CF	
b Gainford 23/6/1904			d 1985	
		Gainford		
1927		Darlington	1	
		Cockfield		
		Bishop Auckland		
1928	1930	Nelson	66	20
1931		Barrow	7	
		Boston Town		
		Northwood United		
Carmichael, Harvey W			GK	
b Tillicoultry 20/8/1881				
		Tillicoultry Rovers		
		Clackmannan Juniors		
		East Stirlingshire		
1906	1907	Grimsby Town	36	
		Millwall Athletic		
		Hartlepools United		
Carmichael, James (Jimmy)			CF/CH	
b Bridgeton 14/12/1894			d 1967	
		Strathclyde		
		Mid-Rhondda		
1920	1926	Grimsby Town	227	137
		Worksop Town		
Carmichael, Robert (Bob)			IL/IR	
b Paisley 1885				
		Baillieston Thistle		
		Shettleston		
1906		Sunderland	1	
		Heart of Midlothian		
		St Mirren		
1909		Oldham Athletic	6	1
		Third Lanark		
		Clyde		
		Shelbourne		
		Dumbarton		
Carnaby, Thomas Easton			CH	
b Newsham 25/12/1913			d 1971	
		New Delaval United		
		Blyth Spartans		
1938		Southampton	14	
Carnegie, James			CF	
		Linfield		
1904		Doncaster Rovers	14	3
Carnelly, Albert			IR/IL	
b Nottingham 29/12/1870			d 1920	
		Westminster Amateurs (Nottingham)		
		Notts Mapperley		
1892		Notts County	0	
		Loughborough		
1894	1895	Nottingham Forest	52	24
1896		Leicester Fosse	28	10
		Bristol City		
		Ilkeston Town		
		Bristol City		
		Thames Ironworks		
		Millwall Athletic		
		Ilkeston Town		
Carney, Eugene (Gene)			OL	
b Bootle q3 1895			d 1952	
1914		Everton	0	
		South Liverpool		
		Pontypridd		
1921		Rochdale	10	6
		New Brighton		
1923		Reading	23	
		Mold Town		
1924		New Brighton	33	1
		Caernarvon Athletic		
1925		New Brighton	13	2
		Caernarvon Athletic		
		St James CYMS		
		Sandbach Ramblers		

From	To		Apps	Goal
Carney, James Michael (Jimmy)			LH/RH	
b Bolton 4/12/1891			d 1980	
1908		Bolton Wanderers	0	
1909		Blackpool	0	
1910	1914	Glossop	138	6
1919		Bolton Wanderers	0	
1921	1922	Stalybridge Celtic	72	14
1923	1926	Newport County	118	13
Carnie, J			IR	
		Stalybridge		
1898		Bury	4	
Carr, Andrew Hughes			CH/LB	
b Burradon 13/3/1908			d 1983	
		Percy Main		
1930	1932	Middlesbrough	5	
1934		Mansfield Town	12	
1935		Crewe Alexandra	36	2
1936		Rochdale	32	
Carr, Anthony Grey (Tony)			GK	
b Old Hartley 18/5/1901			d 1968	
		Seaton Delaval Villa		
1920		Sunderland (trial)	0	
1922	1923	Newport County	80	
1924		Sheffield Wednesday	0	
		Seaton Delaval Villa		
1926	1927	Preston North End	59	
		Craghead United		
1929		South Shields	40	
		Blyth Spartans		
1934		New Brighton	12	
Carr, Edward Miller (Eddie)			IL/CF	
b Wheatley Hill 3/10/1917			d 1998	
		Wheatley Hill Colliery		
1934		Arsenal	0	
		Margate		
1937	1938	Arsenal	12	7
1945	1946	Huddersfield Town	2	
1946	1949	Newport County	98	48
1949	1952	Bradford City	94	49
1953		Darlington	7	
Carr, George			CH/IL/IR	
b South Bank 19/1/1899				
		South Bank East End		
1919	1923	Middlesbrough	67	23
1923	1931	Leicester City	179	24
1932		Stockport County	18	
		Nuneaton Town		
Carr, Henry (Harry)			CF	
b South Bank q1 1887			d 1942	
Caps: England Amat				
		South Bank		
1910		Sunderland	1	
		South Bank		
1910		Middlesbrough	3	3
		South Bank		
		Hartlepools United		
		South Bank		
		Hartlepools United		
		South Bank		
Carr, James Edward Charles (Jimmy)			OL	
b Maryhill 19/12/1893			d 1980	
		Watford Orient		
		Watford		
		West Ham United		
1920	1922	Reading	116	8
1923	1925	Southampton	86	10
1926		Swansea Town	7	1
		Southall		
1927		Queen's Park Rangers	0	
Carr, James Proctor (Jimmy)			CF	
b Ferryhill 27/12/1912			d 1976	
		Spennymoor United		
		Ferryhill Athletic		
1933		Arsenal	0	
		Spennymoor United		
1935		Leeds United	2	
1937		York City	2	2
		Spennymoor United		
Carr, John (Jack)			LH/LB	
b Seaton Burn q2 1876			d 1948	
Caps: FLge 1/England 2				
		Seaton Burn		
1899	1911	Newcastle United	252	5
Carr, John (Jackie)			IR/OR/IL	
b South Bank 26/11/1891			d 1942	
Caps: FLge 3/England 2				
		South Bank East End		
		South Bank		
1909		Sunderland (trial)	0	
1910	1929	Middlesbrough	421	75
1930		Blackpool	14	2
1931		Hartlepools United	10	1

From	To		Apps	Goal
Carr, John James			LB/RB	
b Gateshead 1909				
		Felling Colliery		
		Crawcrook Albion		
1928		Chelsea	1	
		Crawcrook Albion		
1932		Chester	0	
1933	1935	Gateshead	55	2
Carr, John Robert			LH/RH	
b Newcastle				
		Science & Art		
1895	1897	Newcastle United	4	
		Kilmarnock		
Carr, Joseph (Joe)			LB	
b Sheffield q1 1919			d 1940	
1937	1938	Sheffield United	26	
1939		(Sheffield United)	(3)	
Carr, Lance Lanyon			OL	
b Johannesburg, South Africa 18/2/1910			d 1983	
		Johannesburg Calies		
		Boksburg		
1933	1935	Liverpool	31	8
1936		Newport County	25	5
		South Liverpool		
1938	1945	Newport County	39	9
1946		Bristol Rovers	42	8
		Merthyr Tydfil		
Carr, Laurence Ashdown			IL	
b Ashton-under-Lyne q2 1887				
1905		Glossop	7	1
		Vale of Leven		
Carr, Leonard William (Len)			LB	
b Sheffield 19/9/1901			d 1981	
		St Bart's		
		Norton Woodseats		
1924		Rotherham County	0	
1925		Sheffield Wednesday	0	
		Mansfield Town		
1926		Barnsley	0	
1927	1934	New Brighton	302	2
		South Liverpool		
Carr, Robert			LH	
b Spennymoor q4 1900				
		Spennymoor United		
1920		Derby County	0	
1921		Durham City	7	1
		Shiney Row Swifts		
		Nettleston Church Institute		
Carr, RS			OR	
1902		Glossop	4	
Carr, SR			OR	
1898		Bolton Wanderers	2	
Carr, Thomas (Tommy)			RB/CF/IR	
b Burnhope 1903				
		Burnhope Institute		
		Annfield Plain		
1924	1928	Hartlepools United	131	13
		West Stanley		
Carr, William (Willie)			CH	
b South Bank 1889			d 1943	
		South Bank		
1910	1923	Middlesbrough	116	3
Carr, William			LH	
		Scotswood		
1930		Doncaster Rovers	3	
Carr, William Edward (Billy)			LH/RH	
b Framwellgate Moor 7/3/1905			d 1989	
		Horden Colliery Welfare		
		Horden Athletic		
1926	1934	Huddersfield Town	93	1
1934	1938	Southend United	95	1
Carr, William Patterson (Billy)			RB/LB	
b Cambois 6/11/1901			d 1990	
		Seaton Delaval		
1925	1932	Derby County	102	
1935	1936	Queen's Park Rangers	28	
1937		Barrow	0	
Carr, Zachariah			LB	
b Preston q1 1869				
		Preston Hornets		
1890		Burnley	1	
Carrick, Christopher (Chris)			OL	
b Stockton 8/10/1882			d 1927	
1900	1903	Middlesbrough	26	6
		West Ham United		
		Tottenham Hotspur		
		Reading		
		Bradford Park Avenue		
		Glentoran		

From	To		Apps	Goal
Carrick, J			RB	
1893		Middlesbrough Ironopolis	1	
Carrick, James H (Jim)			CH/LB/RH	
b Boothstown 17/2/1901				
		Blackburn Wanderers (Leigh)		
		Astley Wanderers		
		Plank Lane		
1919		Manchester City	0	
		Airdrieonians (trial)		
1920		Exeter City	41	3
1921	1922	Oldham Athletic	6	
1923		Stockport County	1	
1924		Barrow	27	2
1926		Bradford Park Avenue	18	
1927		Accrington Stanley	27	1
1928		Torquay United	29	2
1929		Accrington Stanley	6	
		Burton Town		
		Stalybridge Celtic		
Carrier, William			RB	
b Ashington 1887				
1904		Manchester United	0	
		Merthyr Juniors		
		Troedyrhiw Stars		
1909		Birmingham	7	
		Kidderminster Harriers		
		Pontypridd		
		Worcester City		
Carrigan, John			GK	
b Glasgow 1902				
		Vale of Clyde		
1926		Barnsley	6	
Carrigan, Patrick (Pat)			CH	
b Cleland 5/7/1898			d 1957	
		Douglas Water Thistle		
1923	1929	Leicester City	75	3
1929	1932	Sheffield United	52	
1933		Southend United	0	
		Hinckley United		
Carrington, George Albert			GK	
b Bow 20/6/1888			d 1954	
		Ford Sports		
1919		Clapton Orient	1	
1920		Millwall Athletic (trial)	0	
Carris, Bertima			OL	
b Nuneaton q3 1878			d 1946	
1898		Loughborough	5	
Carroll, Ernest James (Ernie)			CH/CF	
b Barrow 20/4/1899			d 1974	
1923	1924	Barrow	18	
		Barrow YMCA		
		Barrow Shop Assistants		
		Penrith		
Carroll, Francis (Frank)			IR/RH	
b Bessbrook 11/6/??				
		Bessbrook Strollers		
		Cliftonville		
		Belfast Celtic		
1920	1923	Manchester City	18	
		Newry Town		
		Dundee United		
		Newry Town		
Carroll, James			CH	
b Dumbarton				
		Renton		
1901		Barnsley	13	1
Carroll, James Tony (Tony)			OR	
b Maryhill 31/10/1906			d 1983	
		Strathclyde		
		Newry Town		
		Belfast Celtic		
		Shelbourne		
		Belfast Celtic		
		Clyde		
1934	1937	Leicester City	94	25
1938		Luton Town	13	
1939		(Luton Town)	(3)	
Carroll, John Patrick			CF	
b North Bierley q2 1896				
		Fryston Colliery		
		Castleford Town		
		Selby Town		
1924		Oldham Athletic	7	2
		Selby Town		
Carroll, John Patrick			OL	
b Wolviston 9/1/1902			d 1986	
1925		Durham City	1	
Carroll, Joseph (Joe)			LH	
		Keighley		
		Harrogate AFC		
1919		Bradford City	1	
		Harrogate AFC		

From To Apps Goal

Carruthers, Alexander Neilson (Alec) OR
b Loganlea 12/5/1914 d 1977
Heart of Midlothian
Falkirk
1936 1937 Bolton Wanderers 26 4
Falkirk
1946 Rochdale 13 4
Rossendale United

Carruthers, John Clement CF/IR
b Howden-on-Tyne q2 1900 d 1959
Preston Colliery
1920 South Shields 2 1
1921 1922 Bradford City 4
1923 Blackpool 2
1923 1924 Crewe Alexandra 20 4
Preston Colliery

Carruthers, John Walter (Jack) CF/RB
b Fulham 29/11/1901 d 1947
Southdown Athletic
Eastbourne
Brighton Tramways
1928 1932 Brighton & Hove Albion 23 9
Brighton Tramways

Carson, A LB
b 1886
1907 Lincoln City 1

Carson, Adam IL/CF
Caps: SAll 1
Cowlairs
Glasgow Thistle
1892 Newton Heath 14 3
1892 1893 Ardwick 9 3
1894 Liverpool 0
Fairfield

Carson, James (Jim) OR
b Clydebank 1912
Yoker Athletic
1933 Bradford Park Avenue 12
1934 1935 Crystal Palace 52 17
1936 Burnley 6
Alloa Athletic

Carswell, Frederick (Fred) OL
b Elham q2 1898 d 1959
Southport 0
Ulverston Town
1926 Barrow 2
Folkestone
Barrow Shipbuilders
Ulverston Town
Morecambe
Kirkby United

Carswell, Robert CF
b Port Glasgow 27/2/1892 d 1962
Morton
1923 Hartlepools United 2

Carte, Robert RB
b Denaby 11/10/1913 d 1986
Denaby United
Gainsborough Trinity
1937 Bristol Rovers 0
1937 1938 Luton Town 6
1938 Bristol Rovers 2

Carter, Albert James OL
b Milton q2 1898
Zion
1920 Gillingham 2

Carter, Alfred Burton IR/RH
b Basford q4 1877 d 1951
Newstead Byron
1896 1898 Notts County 20 5
Kettering
Newstead Byron

Carter, Anthony John H RB/LB
b Sunderland 14/12/1881 d 1970
1902 Sunderland 0
1903 1905 Bradford City 30
Carlisle United

Carter, Ernest T LH
b Herrington
Ashington
1921 1923 Wolverhampton Wanderers 17

Carter, George OR
b Princes Park 24/3/1914 d 1964
Littlewoods
Everton Colts
Prescot Cables
1934 1936 Southport 86 19
1937 Chester 0
Littlewoods

From To Apps Goal

Carter, George William RH/OR/CH
b West Ham 19/10/1900 d 1981
Green & Siley Weir
1919 1926 West Ham United 136 1
1927 Fulham 0
Grays Thurrock

Carter, Henry GK
b Bristol 1889
Aberdare Town
Workington
Millom Town
Barrow
West Ham United
Ton Pentre
1921 1922 Barrow 60

Carter, Herbert John (Bert) RH/CH
b Liverpool q3 1906
1931 1932 New Brighton 5
Winsford United

Carter, Horatio Stratton (Raich) IR/IL
b Sunderland 21/12/1913 d 1994
Caps: England Sch/FLge 4/LoI 2/England War 17/ England 13
Whitburn St Mary's
Sunderland Forge
Esh Winning
1932 1938 Sunderland 245 118
1939 (Sunderland) (3) (3)
1945 1947 Derby County 63 34
1947 1951 Hull City 136 57
Cork Athletic

Carter, James GK
b Preston
1894 Preston North End 0
Sheppey United
Millwall Athletic
1897 1898 Blackburn Rovers 43
New Brompton

Carter, John Henry (Jock) CF
b Aylesbury 11/11/1910 d 1992
Hazels
Aylesbury United
1932 1934 Watford 15 7
1935 Reading 2
Ipswich Town
Yeovil & Petters United

Carter, Joseph Henry (Joe) IR
b Aston 27/7/1899 d 1977
Caps: FLge 1/England 3
Westbourne Celtic
1922 1935 West Bromwich Albion 414 145
1935 Sheffield Wednesday 0
1936 Tranmere Rovers 6 1
1936 Walsall 20 4
Vono Sports

Carter, Robert (Bob) OR
b Hendon, County Durham q1 1881 d 1927
Sunderland Royal Rovers
Selbourne
1904 1906 Burslem Port Vale 83 23
1907 Stockport County 27 8
1907 1908 Fulham 10 7
Southampton

Carter, Robert (Bob) RH/CH
b Bolton 1911
Army
1930 1932 Chelsea 18 1
1933 Plymouth Argyle 3
1934 Watford 0

Carter, Roger GK
b Leicestershire
Hugglescote Robin Hoods
Bristol St George
Whitwick Town
1899 Leicester Fosse 1
Whitwick Town
Whitwick White Cross

Carter, Sydney Youles (Syd) CF
b Chesterfield 28/7/1916 d 1978
Bolsover Colliery
1935 Sheffield United 0
1936 Wolverhampton Wanderers 0
Macclesfield
1938 1946 Mansfield Town 39 10

Carter, Wilfred (Wilf) LH/RH
b Annesley 19/6/1896 d 1975
Bolsover Colliery
1920 1925 Watford 126 4

Carthy, John CF
1903 Blackpool 14 1

From To Apps Goal

Carthy, T OL
b Liverpool
Liverpool White Star
1898 Barnsley 1

Cartledge, Samuel Henry (Sam) GK
b Basford q2 1882 d 1938
Hainton Swifts
West Marsh Social
Grimsby St John's
1904 1906 Grimsby Town 52
Queen's Park Rangers
Worksop Town
Hainton Swifts
Grimsby St John's
Grimsby Rangers

Cartlidge, Arthur GK
b Stoke-on-Trent 12/6/1880 d 1940
Penkell Victoria
Market Drayton
1899 1900 Stoke 10
Bristol Rovers
1908 1910 Aston Villa 52
Stoke
South Shields

Cartlidge, Francis Arthur CF
b Burslem q1 1899 d 1946
Ravenside Mission
1920 1921 Port Vale 18 1
Congleton Town

Cartman, Herbert Redvers (Bert) OL/OR
b Bolton 28/2/1900 d 1955
Waterloo Temperance
1919 1921 Bolton Wanderers 22
1922 Manchester United 3
1923 1929 Tranmere Rovers 217 32
Chorley
Burscough Rangers
Westhoughton Collieries

Cartmell, J (Scottie) IR
Fleetwood Rangers
1898 Blackpool 12 1

Cartmell, John Range (Jack) OL
b Blackpool 28/8/1890 d 1979
1911 Huddersfield Town 0
1912 Blackpool 0
Mardy
Abertillery Town
Heart of Midlothian
1920 Brentford 29
Boscombe
1923 Gillingham 4
1924 Brentford 0

Cartwright, Archibald IR
b Wolverhampton 1885
Bankside Wanderers
Willenhall Pickwick
1907 Wolverhampton Wanderers 2
Walsall
Bilston Town
Worcester City
Willenhall Swifts
Wednesbury Old Athletic

Cartwright, Herbert IR
b Pleasley 1916
Brunts Old Boys
1934 Rotherham United 0
Brunts Old Boys
1936 Mansfield Town 5 1
Brunts Old Boys
Woodhouse Mills United

Cartwright, Herbert Philip (Phil) OR/OL
b Scarborough 8/2/1908 d 1974
Scarborough
1925 Middlesbrough 6
1927 1928 Bradford Park Avenue 20 3
1929 Hull City 20
1930 1932 Lincoln City 86 21
1933 Bournemouth & Boscombe Ath 0
Scarborough
1934 Carlisle United (trial) 3
1935 Rotherham United 0

Cartwright, James Ernest (Joe) OL
b Lower Walton 11/12/1888 d 1955
Northwich Victoria
1913 1920 Manchester City 38 3
1921 1922 Crystal Palace 19 4
Llanelly

Cartwright, Sidney RH/LH
b Kiveton Park 16/7/1910 d 1988
High Moor
Kiveton Park
1935 1938 Arsenal 16 2
Atlas Steel Works

From To Apps Goal

Cartwright, Walter LH/LB
b Nantwich q1 1871 d 1930
Nantwich
Heywood Central
Nantwich
1893 1894 Crewe Alexandra 50 1
1895 1903 Newton Heath/Manchester Utd 228 9

Cartwright, William (Bill) LB/RB
b Burton-on-Trent 24/6/1884 d 1971
Trent Rovers
1906 1907 Gainsborough Trinity 60 5
1908 1912 Chelsea 44
1913 Tottenham Hotspur 13
Swansea Town
Gillingham

Carty, J IL
1891 Darwen 8 1

Carvell, Arthur LB
b Birkenhead 26/5/1911 d 1991
Planters (Birkenhead)
1932 Tranmere Rovers 11

Carver, George LB
1896 Woolwich Arsenal 1

Carver, Jesse CH
b Aigburth 7/7/1911 d 2003
1930 1935 Blackburn Rovers 143 2
1936 1938 Newcastle United 70
1939 Bury 0

Carver, T CF
1900 Walsall 2

Cashmore, Arthur CF/IR
b Birmingham 30/10/1893 d 1969
Sparkhill Avondale
Bromsgrove Rovers
Stourbridge
1913 Manchester United 3
1914 Oldham Athletic 16 8
Darlaston
1920 1921 Cardiff City 30 10
1921 Notts County 14 6
Darlaston
Nuneaton Town
Shrewsbury Town
Hereford United

Caskie, James (Jimmy) OL
b Possilpark 30/1/1914 d 1977
Caps: SLge 3/Scotland War 9
Glasgow Ashfield
St Johnstone
1938 Everton 5 1
Rangers
Forfar Athletic
Berwick Rangers

Cassell, Leo Eugene CF
b Sittingbourne 10/4/1895 d 1976
1921 Gillingham 5 1

Cassels, A CF
1892 Northwich Victoria 4 2

Cassidy, Daniel RH/OR/IR
b Felling 15/6/1907 d 1995
Hebburn
1926 Southampton 0
1927 1936 Darlington 165 15

Cassidy, Francis Arthur Michael CF
b Woodton 5/5/1917 d 1983
Gorleston
Lowestoft Town
1937 Norwich City 1
Lowestoft Town

Cassidy, Hugh RB
Army
1896 Woolwich Arsenal 1

Cassidy, James (Jimmy) CF/IR/OL
b Dalry 2/12/1869
Kilmarnock Athletic
Kilmarnock
Glasgow Hibernian
1889 1897 Bolton Wanderers 194 84
Carfin Shamrock (loan)
Celtic (loan)

Cassidy, James Alexander (Jim) IR/IL
b Lurgan 22/7/1912
Newry Town
1935 1936 Manchester City 3
1937 1938 Tranmere Rovers 51 9
Newry Town
Dundalk
Limerick

From To Apps Goal

Cassidy, Joseph IL/OL/CF
b Dalziel 30/7/1872
Motherwell Athletic
Blythe
1892 Newton Heath 4
Celtic
1894 1899 Newton Heath 148 91
1899 1900 Manchester City 31 14
1901 1905 Middlesbrough 126 33
Workington

Cassidy, Joseph (Joe) IL/CF
b Calder 10/8/1896 d 1949
Caps: SLge 3/IrLge 3/Scotland 4
Vale of Clyde
Celtic
Vale of Atholl (loan)
Kilmarnock (loan)
Abercorn (loan)
Ayr United (loan)
Clydebank (loan)
Clydebank (loan)
1924 Bolton Wanderers 22 7
1925 Cardiff City 24 6
Dundee
Clyde
Ballymena United
Dundalk
Morton
Dundalk
Morton

Cassidy, Joseph (Joe) IL
b Glasgow
Glasgow Ashfield
1935 1936 Hull City 8 1

Cassidy, Patrick (Pat) CH/IR
b Willington Quay q3 1886 d 1945
North Shields Athletic
1907 Sheffield United 1
South Shields
1910 1911 Bradford City 4
Cardiff City
Willington St Aidan's

Cassidy, Patrick Joseph (Joe) GK
b Dublin 1891
Bohemians
Shelbourne
1912 Grimsby Town (trial) 1

Cassidy, William (Bill) LH/RH
b Gateshead 30/6/1917
Close Works
1935 1952 Gateshead 133 6
1939 (Gateshead) (3)

Casson, Walter CF
b Blyth q1 1895 d 1965
Blyth Spartans
1921 South Shields 9 2
1921 1923 Grimsby Town 19 5
Pontypridd
1925 Exeter City 8 3
1926 South Shields (trial) 0

Castle, Frederick Charles CF
b King's Norton 29/1/1899 d 1974
Smethwick Highfield
1925 1926 Birmingham 3
Shrewsbury Town

Castle, Frederick Richard (Fred) CF
b Pen-y-graig 10/4/1902 d 1982
Pontypridd
Mid-Rhondda United
1926 1927 Cardiff City 3
1928 Chesterfield 24 9
1929 Gillingham 16 4
Mid-Rhondda United
Derry City
1930 Doncaster Rovers 8 3
Nelson
Broad Oaks Works

Castle, John RH
b Hall Green 2/1871 d 1929
Yardley Wood Vics
Birmingham St George's
1891 West Bromwich Albion 4
Brierley Hill Alliance

Castle, Sidney Ernest Rowland (Sid) OR
b Basingstoke 12/3/1892 d 1978
Basingstoke Town
Thorneycrofts
Guildford United
1919 1920 Tottenham Hotspur 5
1921 1922 Charlton Athletic 66 10
1923 1924 Chelsea 32 2
Guildford United

Caterall, VA OL
1900 Blackpool 1

From To Apps Goal

Catesby, William Henry IL
b Aigburth q4 1874 d 1933
1894 Crewe Alexandra 1

Catlin, Arthur Edward (Ted) LB
b Middlesbrough 11/1/1911 d 1990
Caps: FLge 1/England 5
South Bank
1930 1938 Sheffield Wednesday 206
1939 (Sheffield Wednesday) (3)
Scunthorpe & Lindsey United

Catlin, Norman John OR
b Liverpool 8/1/1918 d 1941
Caps: England Sch
Bitterne Boys Club
1934 Arsenal 0
1935 1936 Southampton 6
Ryde Sports

Catlin, Walter Henry CF
b St Albans q1 1876 d 1947
1897 Luton Town 1 1
Watford

Catlow, Thomas RH/CH
Southend United
Barry
1920 Swansea Town 1
Mid-Rhondda United
1921 Rochdale 1

Catterall, John OL/IL
b Leyland q4 1884
Leyland Amateurs
Chorley
1904 Preston North End 4
Fulham
Leyland
Chorley
Nelson
1907 Notts County 0
1909 Preston North End 2 1
Haslingden
Leyland
Leyland Motors

Catterall, R RH
1895 Darwen 1

Catterick, Henry (Harry) CH
b Darlington q3 1897 d 1972
Chilton Colliery Recreation Athletic
1926 Stockport County 13 1

Catton, Edward IR
b Langley Park 25/5/1906 d 1981
Trimdon Grange Colliery
Eden Colliery
1933 Hartlepools United 8 3
Blackhall Colliery Welfare

Caulfield, William (Billy) IR/OR
b St Helens 20/3/1892 d 1972
Ormskirk
Southport Central
1914 Blackburn Rovers 0
1921 1922 Crewe Alexandra 59 23
1923 Nelson 18 5
1924 Crewe Alexandra 29
Chester

Caunce, Lewis GK
b Earlestown 20/4/1911 d 1978
Earlestown White Star
1931 Huddersfield Town 0
1932 Rochdale 18
Wigan Athletic
1935 1938 Oldham Athletic 134
1939 (Oldham Athletic) (3)

Causer, Arthur Haden GK
b Wolverhampton q4 1884 d 1927
Wellington Town
1912 1914 Glossop 109
1919 1921 Preston North End 46
Shrewsbury Town

Cavanagh, John Andrew (Jack) IL
b Newcastle q2 1891 d 1962
Ashington
Jarrow Caledonians
1911 Clapton Orient 0
Ashington
1914 Lincoln City 2

Cave, George Harold RB
b Great Bridge q1 1874 d 1904
Horseley Heath
Great Bridge Unity
1895 1900 West Bromwich Albion 77

Cave, William GK
b Northampton 18/6/1907 d 1978
1927 1936 Northampton Town 93

From To Apps Goal

Cawdry, Walter RB
b Bradford 12/6/1884 d 1970
1908 Bradford Park Avenue 1

Cawley, Edward RH/CH
b Hanley 1904
1927 1930 Stockport County 8
Ashton National
1932 Carlisle United 25 1
Distillery

Cawley, Thomas Edward (Tom) IR/OR
b Sheffield 21/11/1891 d 1980
Sheffield
1912 Sheffield Wednesday 0
1914 Leeds City 0
1919 1921 Rotherham County 36 6
Worksop Town
Scunthorpe & Lindsey United

Cawthorne, Harold Henry (Harry) RH/LB
b Darnall q2 1900 d 1966
Dronfield Woodhouse
1921 1926 Huddersfield Town 74 2
1926 1928 Sheffield United 27
Connah's Quay & Shotton
Mansfield Town
Manchester Central
Middlewich
Kettering Town
Denaby United
Woodhouse Alliance

Cawthorne, Rupert CH/LB/LH
b Clitheroe q2 1879 d 1965
1898 Darwen 10
Clitheroe Central
1906 Burnley 20
Clitheroe Central
1908 1909 Burnley 4
Bacup

Cawthra, Jack GK
b Halifax 15/8/1904 d 1974
Leyland Motors
1924 1925 Rochdale 5

Ceney, John OR
b Sheffield 2/2/1906 d 1984
1922 1923 Walsall 7 1

Chadbourne, Joe Henry CF
b Halifax q1 1885 d 1958
Halifax Boys Brigade
Halifax Whitehall
Elland Ramsdenians
1905 Bradford City 0
1905 Barnsley 1
1906 Bradford City 0
Heckmondwike
1909 Burnley 9 4
Mirfield United
Halifax Town

Chadburn, John Lucas OR/LB
b Mansfield 12/2/1873 d 1923
Leicester Fosse
Mansfield Unitarians
Mansfield Greenhalgh's
1893 Lincoln City 25 8
1894 1896 Notts County 50 15
1897 1898 Wolverhampton Wanderers 11 1
1899 1902 West Bromwich Albion 43 3
1903 Liverpool 2
Plymouth Argyle
Mansfield Mechanics (loan)
Swindon Town
Mansfield Mechanics
Woodhouse Rangers

Chadderton, Albert LB
b Oldham 22/11/1894 d 1963
Woodhouses (Failsworth)
1919 Oldham Athletic 1

Chadwick, Andrew Charlton CF
b Ashbourne q1 1877 d 1950
Ashbourne
1906 Chesterfield Town 1

Chadwick, Arthur LB
b Liverpool q1 1866 d 1937
1888 1892 Everton 5

Chadwick, Arthur RH
b Church q3 1875 d 1936
Caps: England 2
Church
Accrington
1895 1896 Burton Swifts 55 7
Southampton
Portsmouth
Northampton Town
Accrington Stanley
Exeter City

From To Apps Goal

Chadwick, Clifton (Cliff) OL/OR
b Bolton 26/1/1914
Turton
Fleetwood
1933 Oldham Athletic 18 6
1933 1945 Middlesbrough 93 27
1939 (Middlesbrough) (3)
1946 Hull City 23 7
1947 Darlington 37 5
Stockton

Chadwick, Edgar IL/OR
b Blackburn 3/1891 d 1963
Nelson
Accrington Stanley
Seedhill
Great Harwood
Bacup Borough
1923 1925 Nelson 36 19
Lancaster Town
Clitheroe
Barnoldswick Town
Morecambe
Bacup Borough
Nelson
Nelson Town

Chadwick, Edgar Wallace IL
b Blackburn 14/6/1869 d 1942
Caps: FLge 3/England 7
Little Dots
Blackburn Olympic
Blackburn Rovers
1888 1898 Everton 270 97
1899 Burnley 31 10
Southampton
1902 1903 Liverpool 43 7
1904 Blackpool 34 8
1905 Glossop 35 5
Darwen

Chadwick, Frederick William (Fred) CF/IR/IL
b Manchester 8/9/1913 d 1987
British Dyes
1935 Wolverhampton Wanderers 0
1936 1937 Newport County 40 19
1938 1946 Ipswich Town 40 18
1939 (Ipswich Town) (3) (2)
1946 West Ham United 0
1946 Nottingham Forest (trial) 0
1947 Bristol Rovers 6 1
Street

Chadwick, Harry IL
b Rochdale
Bagslate Methodists
1933 Rochdale 1

Chadwick, John (Jack) IR/IL
b Burnley 25/8/1905 d 1974
Hapton Valley Miners
1925 Burnley 0
1926 1929 Accrington Stanley 46 12
Stalybridge Celtic
Chorley
Clitheroe
Nelson
Frickley Colliery
Lancaster Town

Chadwick, Miles OL
b Blackburn q2 1880 d 1940
Blackburn St Philip's
Darwen
1905 1907 Blackburn Rovers 51 7
Darwen

Chadwick, Thomas CH/LH/RH
b Blackburn 2/3/1882 d 1960
Blackburn St Philip's
1901 1907 Everton 21
1908 Preston North End 9
Everton 0
Great Harwood

Chadwick, Walter Russell RB
b Haslingden q4 1903 d 1966
St Saviour's
Burnley 0
Barnoldswick Town
1924 Burnley 0
1925 Nelson 2
Darwen

Chadwick, Wilfred (Wilf) IL
b Bury 7/10/1900 d 1975
1919 Bury 0
Nelson
Accrington Stanley
Rossendale United
1921 1925 Everton 102 50
1925 1926 Leeds United 16 3
1926 1928 Wolverhampton Wanderers 97 44
1929 Stoke City 7 2
1930 Halifax Town 5

From To | Apps Goal

Chadwick, William Floyd GK
b Hanley q3 1881 d 1936
Hanley Swifts
1901 1903 Burslem Port Vale 9

Chalcraft, Harry IR
b Gosport 29/10/1905 d 1972
Emsworth
1926 Reading 0
1927 Barrow 2 1
Emsworth

Chalk, Norman William CH
b Bitterne 28/10/1916 d 2005
Woolston Wednesday
1937 1938 Southampton 5
Southampton Police

Chalkley, Alfred George (Alf) RB/LB
b Plaistow 16/8/1904 d 1971
1931 1936 West Ham United 188 1

Challinor, John (Jack) LB
b Middlewich 5/8/1916 d 1981
Witton Albion
1937 1938 Stoke City 43
Linfield

Challinor, Samuel (Sam) LH/CH
b Middlewich 2/4/1890 d 1963
Middlewich
Witton Albion
1913 Everton 0
1920 Brentford 31 2
1921 Halifax Town 23 2
1922 Accrington Stanley 23 1
1923 New Brighton 40 2
Mold Town
Llandudno

Chalmers, Andrew IL/IR
b Girvan 15/2/1897
Girvan
Dumbarton
1921 1925 Bradford City 118 19
Kettering Town

Chalmers, Bruce RH/LH/CH
b Whifflet 1868
Albion Rovers
1890 Derby County 20 1
Albion Rovers
1892 1893 Sheffield Wednesday 24 1
Albion Rovers

Chalmers, David C CF
b Buckhaven 22/7/1891 d 1920
Leven Celtic
Buckhaven
Kilmarnock
Arthurlie (loan)
Third Lanark
Raith Rovers
East Fife
York City
1913 1914 Grimsby Town 5
East Fife
Gillingham

Chalmers, James (Jimmy) OL/IL
b Old Luce 3/12/1877
Beith
Morton
1897 1898 Sunderland 26 6
1898 Preston North End 10 2
1899 Notts County 25 2
Beith
Partick Thistle
Watford
Tottenham Hotspur
Swindon Town
Norwich City
Bristol Rovers
Clyde
Beith

Chalmers, John (Jackie) CF
b Beith 16/10/1886
Rutherglen Glencairn
Rangers
Beith
1905 1907 Stoke 40 19
Bristol Rovers
Clyde
1910 1911 Woolwich Arsenal 48 21
Morton
West Stanley
Clyde
Shelbourne

Chalmers, Thomas Kennedy (Tommy) CH/LH
b Beith 1883 d 1918
Beith
1905 1908 Notts County 18 1
Ilkeston United
Shirebrook

From To | Apps Goal

Chalmers, William (Willie) IR
b Bellshill 25/7/1904
Bellshill
Queen's Park
Rangers
1927 1930 Newcastle United 41 13
1931 Grimsby Town 6 1
1932 1935 Bury 98 23
1936 1937 Notts County 65 17
1938 Aldershot 36 9
1939 (Aldershot) (3)

Chalmers, William Green (Billy) OL
b Aberdeen 3/4/1901
Old Aberdeen
1924 Liverpool 2
1925 Tranmere Rovers 23 4

Chalmers, William Ritchie IL
b Kirkcaldy 11/2/1912 d 1943
Newburgh West End
Kirkcaldy Waverley
Raith Rovers
1932 1937 Bournemouth & Boscombe Ath 153 17
1938 Barrow 36 2
1939 (Barrow) (3) (1)

Chalmers, William Stewart IR
b Glasgow 5/3/1907
Caps: Scotland Sch/Scotland Amat/Scotland 1
Mount Florida
Queen's Park
Heart of Midlothian
Cowdenbeath
1932 1933 Manchester United 34 1
Dunfermline Athletic

Chamberlain, Arthur Stanley RH
b Barton in Fabis 10/12/1907 d 1977
1927 Notts County 0
1928 Torquay United 11
Worksop Town

Chamberlain, Hubert George (Bert) LB
b Langley 10/11/1899 d 1975
Langley St Michael's
Cradley Heath
1922 1923 West Bromwich Albion 4
1927 1928 Brighton & Hove Albion 9
Dartford
Shoreham

Chambers, Benjamin OL
Sheffield Falcon
1919 Rotherham County 1
Scunthorpe & Lindsey United
New Stubbin Colliery

Chambers, Bernard CH
b Bramcote q2 1903 d 1936
Langwith Athletic
New Stubbin Colliery
Warsop Colliery
1924 Nottingham Forest 0
Shirebrook
1926 Rotherham United 34
Boston Town
1931 1932 Mansfield Town 10
Ilkeston Town

Chambers, Frank RB/LB
b Bramcote 1/4/1900 d 1970
1919 Derby County 0
1921 1924 Bolton Wanderers 12

Chambers, Henry (Harry) IL/CF/IR
b Willington Quay 17/11/1896 d 1949
Caps: England Sch/FLge 5/England 8
Willington United Methodists
North Shields Athletic
1919 1927 Liverpool 310 135
1927 1928 West Bromwich Albion 40 4
Oakengates Town
Hereford United

Chambers, James CH
b Alcester 1/4/1918 d 1987
1936 Bolton Wanderers 0
1937 1938 Swindon Town 4
Worcester City

Chambers, Leonard OL
b Northampton
Rushden
1920 1921 Northampton Town 28
Rushden

Chambers, Peter LH
b Workington 9/2/1877 d 1952
Black Diamonds
1897 1898 Blackburn Rovers 33
Bedminster
1901 1905 Bristol City 131 10
Swindon Town

From To | Apps Goal

Chambers, Reuben GK
b New Basford 2/8/1908 d 1973
Beeston Ericssons
1926 Lincoln City 7

Chambers, Robert (Bob) CH/IR
b Newcastle 11/12/1899 d 1972
Brighton West End
1921 Lincoln City 23 12
1922 Burnley 4
1923 1925 Rotherham County 100 6
Carlisle United
1927 Exeter City 1
1928 New Brighton 1
Colwyn Bay
Hurst
Morecambe
Burnley Corporation Highways

Chambers, Robert James (Jimmy) OR/OL
b Mullaghglass 26/7/1908 d 1977
Caps: Ireland 12
Newry Town
1925 1929 Bury 28 7
1931 Nottingham Forest 9 1

Chambers, Thomas IR
Caps: Scotland 1
St Bernard's
Heart of Midlothian
1892 Burnley 16 4
Heart of Midlothian
1896 Burnley 10 5
St Bernard's

Chambers, William Alfred RH/IR/IL
b Rotherham 16/9/1900
Mexborough
1919 1922 Rotherham County 96 8
Denaby United
1924 Rotherham County 9 1

Chambers, William Thomas (Bill) IR/CF/IL
b Wednesbury 10/8/1906 d 1978
1925 West Bromwich Albion 0
Wednesbury
Worcester City
Shrewsbury Town
Darlaston
1929 Burnley 2
Lovells Athletic
Lancaster Town
Shrewsbury Town
Darlaston
1932 1933 Halifax Town 70 50
1934 Bolton Wanderers 2 1
1935 Oldham Athletic 10 2
1936 1937 Chester 48 18
Bath City

Champion, ? GK
Nantwich
1895 Crewe Alexandra 1

Champion, Ernest Frank RB
b Lewisham 23/5/1894 d 1974
Catford Southend
1923 Charlton Athletic 2
Catford Southend
Tunbridge Wells Rangers

Champion, Percy Arthur Gordon OL
b Lewes 3/1887 d 1957
1st East Lancs Regiment
Woking
1st East Lancs Regiment
1912 1913 Fulham 2

Chance, George Harold OR
b Stourbridge 25/12/1896 d 1952
Brierley Hill Alliance
1920 1923 Bristol Rovers 80 11
1924 Gillingham 40 4
1925 1929 Millwall 175 22
Brierley Hill Alliance

Chandler, Albert (Bert) RB
b Carlisle 15/1/1897 d 1963
Dalston Beach Reds
Carlisle United
1919 1924 Derby County 169
1925 1926 Newcastle United 33
1926 1928 Sheffield United 70
Mansfield Town
Northfleet
Manchester Central
Holme Head (Carlisle)
Queen of the South

From To | Apps Goal

Chandler, Arthur Clarence Hillier CF/IL
b Paddington 27/11/1895 d 1984
Caps: FLge 1
Handley-Page
Hampstead Town
1920 1922 Queen's Park Rangers 78 16
1923 1934 Leicester City 393 259
1935 Notts County 10 6
1936 Leicester City 0

Chandler, Frederick Ernest John (Fred) IL/OL/LB
b Hythe, Hampshire 2/8/1912 d 2005
1930 Portsmouth 0
Newport (Isle of Wight)
1932 1935 Reading 41 14
1935 Blackpool 15 2
1936 Swindon Town 21 7
1937 1946 Crewe Alexandra 80 21
1939 (Crewe Alexandra) (2) (2)

Chandler, Robert Walter GK
b Calcutta, India 9/1894 d 1964
Aston Town
Upper Thomas Street Boys
1911 Glossop 0
1913 Aston Villa 1
Walsall

Chandler, Sidney Ellis (Sid) RH/IR
b Paddington 30/5/1901 d 1961
Southall
1925 Aston Villa 0
1926 1928 Preston North End 65 12
1928 1930 Reading 84 1
Canterbury Waverley

Channell, Frederick Charles (Fred) RB
b Edmonton 5/5/1910 d 1976
Harwich & Parkeston
Haywards Heath
1930 Tottenham Hotspur 0
1931 Clapton Orient (trial) 0
Peterborough & Fletton United
Northfleet
1933 1935 Tottenham Hotspur 95 1

Channon, Hubert Victor (Vic) OL
b Brighton 1/12/1899 d 1983
Vernon Athletic
1921 Brighton & Hove Albion 2
Vernon Athletic
Shoreham
Tunbridge Wells Rangers
Horsham

Chantry, Harry OR
b Caistor 21/11/1885 d 1971
White Cross United
Albert Swifts
Hagerup & Doughty
Grimsby Rovers
1906 Grimsby Town 4
Grimsby Rovers
Grimsby Rangers
Scunthorpe & Lindsey United
Rotherham Town
Grimsby Victoria
Immingham

Chape, George Henry RH
b Longhoughton q2 1901 d 1968
1923 South Shields 1
1924 Hartlepools United 4
Robert Thompson's
Houghton Colliery

Chapelhow, Harry OR
b Thrimby q1 1886 d 1957
Penrith
Lancaster
Chorley
1909 Manchester City 7
Darlington
1911 Middlesbrough 0

Chaplin, Alexander Balfour (Alec) LB
b Dundee 6/2/1892 d 1986
Dundee Hibernian
1919 1925 Fulham 259 1
Northfleet

Chaplin, Alfred (Fred) RH
b Foleshill q4 1882
St Paul's Bible Class
Foleshill Great Heath
Coventry City
1903 Small Heath 4
1904 Woolwich Arsenal 0
Coventry City

From To Apps Goal

Chaplin, George Duncan LB/RB
b Dundee 26/9/1888 d 1963
Caps: Scotland 1
Dundee Arnot
Dundee
1908 1914 Bradford City 88
1919 1922 Coventry City 106

Chaplin, John Fowler LB
b Dundee 10/10/1882 d 1952
Caps: SLge 1
Dundee Wanderers
Dundee
Tottenham Hotspur
Dundee
1910 Manchester City 15
1913 Leeds City 0

Chapman, Albert T (Bert) IR/CH/CF
Chatham
1907 1911 Bristol City 7 1
Maidstone United
Bath City

Chapman, Edwin (Eddie) CF/OR
b Blackburn 2/5/1919 d 1976
Darwen
1936 Blackburn Rovers 0
1938 Accrington Stanley 4 1
1939 1945 Oldham Athletic (3)
1946 Stockport County 9 3

Chapman, Frerderick William CH/RH/RB
b Nottingham 10/5/1883 d 1951
Caps: England Amat
1904 1906 Nottingham Forest 3
Nottingham Magdale
Oxford City
South Nottingham

Chapman, George R CF/CH
b Broxburn 23/10/1886
Edinburgh Myrtle
Heart of Midlothian
Raith Rovers
1908 1909 Blackburn Rovers 67 5
Rangers
1911 1914 Blackburn Rovers 71 29
Accrington Stanley

Chapman, H LB
1895 1896 Burton Swifts 28

Chapman, Henry (Harry) IR/OR
b Kiveton Park 23/2/1880 d 1916
Kiveton
Worksop Town
1900 1910 Sheffield Wednesday 270 94
1910 1911 Hull City 32 7

Chapman, Herbert IR/OR
b Kiveton Park 19/1/1878 d 1934
Kiveton Park
Ashton North End
Stalybridge Rovers
Rochdale
1898 Grimsby Town 10 4
Swindon Town
Sheppey United
Worksop Town
Northampton Town
1902 Sheffield United 21 2
1903 Notts County 7 1
Northampton Town
Tottenham Hotspur
Northampton Town

Chapman, John (Jack) CF
b Islington 1895
Caps: England Amat
Southall
Brentford
Southall
1919 Clapton Orient 9 2
Excelsior (Middlesex)

Chapman, John RH
b Lumley 1917
Ouston Wanderers
1935 Hartlepools United 0
1937 Bury 0
1938 Hartlepools United 9
Consett
Ashington

Chapman, Joseph Ralph (Joe) IR
b Whittington Moor q2 1908
Bolsover Town
1931 Luton Town 1
Scunthorpe & Lindsey United

Chapman, Josiah CH
b 12/10/??
1922 Rochdale 5
Rossendale United

From To Apps Goal

Chapman, Ralph OR
b Salford 26/1/1906 d 1999
1929 1930 Nelson 10

Chapman, Richard IR
1912 Blackpool 2
Hurst
Stalybridge Celtic

Chapman, Thomas CH/LH
b Newtown q1 1871 d 1929
Caps: FLge 1/Wales 7
Newtown Excelsior
Newtown
1895 Manchester City 26 3
1896 1897 Grimsby Town 50
Chatham
Maidstone United

Chapman, Walter John CH
b Rothwell q4 1899 d 1959
Rothwell Town
1924 Northampton Town 8
Rothwell Town

Chapman, William (Billy) OR
b Murton 21/9/1902 d 1967
Murton Democratic Club
1923 1924 Sheffield Wednesday 4
1926 1927 Manchester United 26
1928 1933 Watford 210 10
Murton Colliery Welfare

Chappell, Archibald (Archie) IR
b Hucknall 14/4/1910 d 1977
Hucknall Church
1927 Sunderland 0
1928 Norwich City 10 2
1929 Charlton Athletic 0
Mansfield Town
Guildford City

Chappell, Sydney RH
b Bridgend 13/11/1915 d 1987
1938 York City 1

Chappell, Thomas GK
Buxton
1894 Leicester Fosse 0
West Manchester
1897 1898 Manchester City 8

Chappell, Thomas Alfred LB
b Sheffield q4 1901
1922 Rotherham County 2

Chapple, Frederick John (Fred) IL/CF/LH
b Bristol q1 1884 d 1965
Treharris Boys Club
1906 1907 Aston Villa 10 3
1908 1909 Birmingham 50 15
Crewe Alexandra
Brentford
1913 1914 Bristol City 20 10
Blyth Spartans

Charles, Alfred Pious (Alf) IL
b Trinidad 11/7/1909 d 1977
1933 Burnley 0
Nelson
Darwen
Stalybridge Celtic
1936 Southampton 1
Stalybridge Celtic

Charles, Frederick IR
b High Garrett 10/5/1889 d 1976
Doncaster Rovers
Mexborough
1910 1911 Sheffield United 7
Castleford Town
Halifax Town

Charles, John William OR
b Crook 10/3/??
Crook Town
1912 1923 Blackpool 227 30

Charleston, Thomas (Tom) RB
1923 Wrexham 0
1924 Bournemouth & Boscombe Ath 7
Poole

Charlesworth, Arthur Laurence CF
b Hull q1 1898 d 1966
1919 1920 Hull City 15 7
Worksop Town
Doncaster Rovers
York City

Charlesworth, George RB
b Bolsover q3 1893 d 1964
Sutton Junction
1919 Notts County 30 4
Sutton Town

From To Apps Goal

Charlesworth, George James OR/OL/CF
b Bristol 29/11/1901 d 1965
St Philip's Adult School
Barton Hill Sports
1924 1925 Bristol Rovers 21 2
1926 Queen's Park Rangers 23 3
Kettering Town
1928 1931 Crystal Palace 21 8
Kettering Town

Charlesworth, Stanley (Stan) CH
b Conisbrough 8/3/1920 d 2003
Conisbrough Welfare
Wath Wanderers
1938 1946 Grimsby Town 2
1946 Barnsley 7
Gainsborough Trinity
Wellingborough Town

Charlton, Arthur IR
Brentford
1898 Nottingham Forest 3

Charlton, Edward (Ted) RB
b Southwick, County Durham 15/1/1888 d 1978
1905 Sunderland 0
Southwick (Co Durham)
1907 1919 Fulham 229 7
Robert Thompson's Munitions Works
Carlisle United

Charlton, George OR
1933 Darlington 6 1
Shildon

Charlton, John Browell LB
b Leadgate 23/3/1908 d 1969
Caps: IrLge 1
Wallsend
1928 Bradford City 0
1931 Liverpool 3
Derry City

Charlton, Joseph CF
b Choppington q2 1907
Frickley Colliery
1929 Carlisle United 1

Charlton, Stanley (Stan) LB
b Little Hulton 16/11/1900 d 1971
Little Hulton United
1920 Oldham Athletic 6
1922 Rochdale 38
1923 1927 Exeter City 163 10
1928 1931 Crystal Palace 122 7
1932 Newport County 32
Margate
Streatham Town
Greenbroom Athletic
Venner Sports (Surrey)

Charlton, Thomas (Tommy) OR/IR/IL
b Hexham q1 1889
Darlington
1909 1912 Stockport County 93 26
1912 1913 Burnley 7 3
1913 Blackpool 22 3

Charlton, Thomas (Tom) LH
b West Sleekburn q1 1907
West Sleekburn Welfare
Bebside Gordon
Blyth Spartans
Bebside Gordon
Bedlington United (trial)
Stakeford United
Bebside Gordon
Ashington (trial)
Heart of Midlothian (trial)
1927 Grimsby Town (trial) 0
1928 Ashington 17
Seaton Delaval
Bedlington United
Blyth Spartans
Hexham

Charlton, Thomas OR
b Jarrow
1929 South Shields 16 5
1930 1932 Gateshead 91 28
Jarrow

Charlton, William (Bill) CF
b South Stoneham 4/1/1912 d 1998
Caps: England Amat
Oxford University
1931 Southampton 2 1
Corinthians
1934 Hull City 3 1
Wimbledon
1936 1937 Queen's Park Rangers 20 10
Barnet
1939 Fulham 0

From To Apps Goal

Charlton, William George (Billy) OR/IR/CF
b Sunderland 10/10/1900 d 1981
Caps: England Sch
Southwick St Columba's
Robert Thompson's
1919 1921 South Shields 50 12
1922 West Ham United 8
1922 1924 Newport County 90 20
1924 Cardiff City 0
1925 1929 Tranmere Rovers 130 72
Workington

Charnley, Samuel (Sam) CH
b Craigneuk 18/8/1903 d 1980
Burnbank Athletic
1925 1927 Wolverhampton Wanderers 52 1
York City
Dartford
Kettering Town

Charnley, William (Will) OR
b Kirkham 4/1895
Great Eccleston
1919 Stoke 2
Abercorn
Musselburgh

Charsley, Charles Christopher (Chris) GK
b Leicester 7/11/1864 d 1945
Caps: England 1
Stafford Town
Stafford Rangers
Aston Villa
Small Heath
1891 West Bromwich Albion 1
1892 1893 Small Heath 18

Chatburn, Frederick William OL
b Grimsby q1 1878
Weelsby Alexandra
White Star
Grimsby All Saints
1898 Grimsby Town 1 1
Grimsby All Saints
Grimsby Rovers

Chatburn, Herbert Mills LH
b Grimsby q1 1877 d 1963
Weelsby Alexandra
Grimsby All Saints
1897 Grimsby Town 1
Harrogate
Grimsby All Saints
North Lindsey United
Grimsby Rovers

Chatt, Robert (Bob) RH/IR/CH
b Barnard Castle q4 1869 d 1935
Caps: FLge 1
Cleator Moor
Middlesbrough Ironopolis
1892 1897 Aston Villa 86 19
Stockton
South Shields
Willington Athletic

Chatterton, Walter CF
b Ferryhill q3 1911
Ferryhill St Luke's
Chilton St Aidan's
Chilton Colliery Recreation Athletic
Trimdon Colliery
1934 West Bromwich Albion (trial) 0
1935 Hartlepools United 2 1
Blackhall Colliery Welfare

Chatterton, William IR
b Thornsett 27/12/1861 d 1913
1888 Derby County 5 1

Cheater, John Henry RB
b Blaby q3 1881 d 1950
South Wigston Albion
1903 Leicester Fosse 6
South Wigston Albion
South Wigston Primitive Methodists

Checkland, Francis Joseph (Frank) RH
b Seaforth 31/7/1895 d 1960
1921 Liverpool 5
1923 1924 Tranmere Rovers 17

Chedgzoy, Samuel (Sam) OR
b Ellesmere Port 27/1/1889 d 1967
Caps: FLge 5/England 8
Burnell's Ironworks
1910 1925 Everton 279 33
New Bedford Whalers
Montreal Carsteel

From	To	Club	Apps	Goal
Chedgzoy, Sydney			OR	
b Liverpool 17/2/1912			d 1983	
1932		Everton	0	
1933		Burnley	5	1
1934		Millwall	3	
		Runcorn		
1935		Halifax Town (trial)	0	
		Runcorn		
1937		Sheffield Wednesday	4	
		Runcorn		
1938		Swansea Town	17	2
Cheesmur, Frederick Harold (Fred)			IR/IL/CF	
b Wandsworth 16/1/1908			d 1987	
		Dartford		
1927		Arsenal	0	
1928		Charlton Athletic	0	
1929	1930	Gillingham	55	19
1930	1933	Sheffield United	17	2
1934	1935	Southend United	31	8
		Folkestone		
Cheetham, John (Jackie)			CF/IR	
b Wishaw 25/3/1904			d 1987	
		Linotype		
		Broxburn United		
1925		Brighton & Hove Albion	8	
1926		West Ham United (trial)	0	
		Eccles Borough		
		Hurst		
1928	1929	Swansea Town	25	11
		Connah's Quay & Shotton		
		Ashton National		
		Hyde United		
1933	1934	Accrington Stanley	39	15
		Stalybridge Celtic		
		Witton Albion		
		Linotype		
Cheetham, Samuel			RB/CF/LB	
b St Helens 3/12/1896			d 1967	
		Thatto Heath		
1920	1921	Hull City	28	1
1921	1926	Bradford City	57	9
		Colwyn Bay		
		Macclesfield		
		Yeovil & Petters United		
Cheetham, Thomas Miles (Tommy)			CF	
b Byker 11/10/1910			d 1993	
		Byker		
		Royal Artillery		
1935	1938	Queen's Park Rangers	115	81
1938		Brentford	17	8
1939		(Brentford)	(2)	
1945	1947	Lincoln City	47	29
Chell, Joseph Arthur			CF	
b Stoke-on-Trent 20/6/1911			d 1992	
1930		Port Vale	2	1
		Witton Albion		
		Stafford Rangers		
Cherrett, Percy Albert Mark			CF/IR	
b Christchurch 12/9/1899			d 1984	
		Boscombe		
1920	1922	Portsmouth	67	36
1923	1924	Plymouth Argyle	61	36
1925	1926	Crystal Palace	75	58
1927		Bristol City	25	15
1928		Bournemouth & Boscombe Ath	36	19
		Cowes		
Cherry, James			OR	
b Stockport q1 1903			d 1966	
		Wigan Borough		
		Skelmersdale United		
		Chorley		
		Burscough Rangers		
		Morecambe		
		Colwyn Bay		
1931		Wigan Borough	4	
		Prescot Cables		
		Rushden Town		
1933		Northampton Town	10	2
		Wigan Athletic		
1935		Cardiff City	0	
1935		Southport (trial)	0	
1935		Walsall	1	
Cherry, Thomas			RH	
b Torphichen 1873				
		East Benhar Heatherbell		
		Motherwell		
		Hamilton Academical		
1898		Grimsby Town	7	
		East Benhar Heatherbell		
Chesser, James Monteith (Jimmy)			LH	
b Stockton 27/12/1899			d 1970	
		Stockton		
1922	1923	Hartlepools United	41	

From	To	Club	Apps	Goal
Chesser, William Etheridge (Billy)			IL	
b Stockton 11/8/1893			d 1949	
		Stockton		
1912	1913	Bradford City	7	2
1913	1919	Lincoln City	76	18
1920		Merthyr Town	28	7
1921		Wigan Borough	13	1
1923		Lincoln City	0	
		Lincoln Claytons		
Chester, Albert Edward N			IL	
b Hexham q2 1886				
		Wingate Albion		
1910		Preston North End	2	1
		Croydon Common		
		Queen's Park Rangers		
		Brentford		
Chester, John Utrick Carlisle (Carlisle)			RH	
b Linton, Northumberland 14/11/1904			d 1979	
1924		Luton Town	0	
1925	1926	Ashington	15	
		Ulverson Town		
Chester, Reginald Arthur (Reg)			OL/OR	
b Long Eaton 21/11/1904			d 1977	
		Long Eaton Rangers		
1920		Notts County (trial)	0	
		Mansfield Town (trial)		
		Peterborough & Fletton United		
		Stamford Town		
1925	1934	Aston Villa	93	34
1935		Manchester United	13	1
1935	1936	Huddersfield Town	25	7
1937		Darlington	31	10
		Arnold Town		
		Woodborough United		
Chester, Thomas Holland (Tommy)			RB/LB	
b Glasgow 7/11/1907			d 1979	
		Baillieston Juniors		
1926	1936	Bury	249	
1936	1938	Burnley	51	1
1939		Notts County	(1)	
Chesters, Arthur			GK	
b Salford 14/2/1910			d 1963	
		Irlam o' the Heights		
		Bangor City		
		Sedgley Park		
1929	1931	Manchester United	9	
1933	1936	Exeter City	95	
1937	1938	Crystal Palace	78	
1939		(Crystal Palace)	(2)	
1945		Rochdale	0	
Chesters, Ralph Frederick (Eddie)			OR	
b Nantwich q1 1907			d 1966	
		Whitchurch		
		Northwich Victoria		
1929		Crewe Alexandra	1	
		Macclesfield		
		Altrincham		
		Nantwich		
Chesworth, Frank			IL	
b Nantwich q4 1873			d 1907	
		Nantwich		
		Stockport County		
1900		Glossop	28	6
1901		Stockport County	28	6
		Nantwich		
		Witton Albion		
		Stretford		
Cheyne, Alexander George (Alec)			IR	
b Glasgow 28/4/1907			d 1983	
Caps: SLge 1/Scotland 5				
		Shettleston Juniors		
		Aberdeen		
1930	1931	Chelsea	53	10
		Nimes		
1934	1935	Chelsea	9	2
		Colchester Town		
		Colchester United		
Chilcott, Kenneth (Ken)			OR/IR	
b Rhondda 17/3/1920			d 2001	
		Eastville United		
1937	1948	Bristol City	46	6
		Bridgwater Town		
Childs, Harold (Harry)			LB/RB	
b Acomb 7/11/1908			d 1977	
		Ferryhill Athletic		
1927		Darlington	0	
		St Columba's (Sunderland)		
		West Stanley		
1928		Notts County	1	
1929		Halifax Town	16	

From	To	Club	Apps	Goal
Childs, John Arthur (Arthur)			CH/RH	
b Acomb 25/4/1899			d 1964	
		Shildon Athletic		
1923	1927	Darlington	26	2
1928	1930	Hull City	74	8
1931	1933	Exeter City	62	4
1934		Accrington Stanley	0	
1934	1935	Darlington	16	4
		Durham City		
Childs, Walter			RB	
b Hapton 8/11/1900			d 1985	
		Hapton		
1922	1924	Accrington Stanley	22	
		Clitheroe		
Chilton, Allenby			CH	
b South Hylton 16/9/1918			d 1996	
Caps: England 2				
		Hylton Colliery		
		Seaham Colliery		
		South Shields		
1938		Liverpool	0	
1939	1954	Manchester United	352	3
1939		(Manchester United)	(1)	
1954	1956	Grimsby Town	63	
Chilton, Charles			CF	
b Mansfield 5/3/1899			d 1970	
		Mansfield Colliery		
		Shirebrook		
1926	1927	Rotherham United	25	12
		Pleasley Colliery		
		Sutton Junction		
		Pleasley Colliery		
		Bolsover Town		
Chippendale, Harry			OR/OL	
b Blackburn 2/10/1870			d 1952	
Caps: England 1				
1889		Accrington	0	
		Nelson		
1891	1896	Blackburn Rovers	134	50
Chippendale, Peter			CH	
b Church q4 1862			d 1941	
		Church		
1888	1889	Accrington	6	1
Chipperfield, Francis (Frank)			LH/LB/CH	
b Shiremoor 2/12/1895			d 1979	
		Bates United		
		South Shields (trial)		
		Blyth Spartans		
1919		Leeds City	0	
1919		Lincoln City	23	
1920		Middlesbrough	1	
		Blyth Spartans (loan)		
		Carlisle United		
1923	1928	Ashington	164	9
		Frickley Colliery		
Chipperfield, John James (Jimmy)			OL	
b Bethnal Green 4/3/1894			d 1966	
		Commercial Cars		
		Luton Clarence		
		Luton Town		
1919		Tottenham Hotspur	15	6
1921		Notts County	18	2
		Northfleet		
1923		Charlton Athletic	3	
		Chatham Town		
Chirnside, James Edward			OR	
b Bolton q2 1872			d 1945	
1891		Bolton Wanderers	1	
Chisem, Frank			RB	
b Darlington 4/10/1907			d 1978	
		Chilton Colliery Recreation Athletic		
1927		Birmingham	0	
		Spennymoor United		
1928		Nottingham Forest (trial)	0	
		Tunbridge Wells Rangers		
1932		Clapton Orient	1	
		Shildon		
Chisholm, Norman W			RB	
b Arbroath 1888				
1908		Woolwich Arsenal	3	
Chitty, Wilfred Sidney (Wilf)			OL/OR/RB	
b Walton-on-Thames 10/7/1912			d 1997	
		Wycombe Wanderers		
		Woking		
1931	1937	Chelsea	45	16
1938		Plymouth Argyle	3	1
1939	1947	Reading	23	7
1939		(Reading)	(3)	(1)

From	To	Club	Apps	Goal
Chivers, Francis Cornelius (Frank)			CF/LH/IL	
b Drybrook q4 1909			d 1942	
		Goldthorpe United		
1930	1935	Barnsley	79	16
1935	1937	Huddersfield Town	50	16
1937	1938	Blackburn Rovers	48	2
1939		(Blackburn Rovers)	(3)	
Chivers, William			LH/RH	
1912	1913	Stockport County	21	1
		Eccles Borough		
Chivers, William			RH/IL	
b Merthyr Tydfil 23/6/1903			d 1976	
1925		Merthyr Town	0	
1926		Newport County	0	
1927		Swindon Town	1	
1927		Bournemouth & Boscombe Ath	1	
Chiverton, Edward James (Ted)			CH/RH	
b Birkenhead 24/12/1912			d 1979	
1931		New Brighton	0	
1932	1934	Tranmere Rovers	6	
1935		Sheffield Wednesday	0	
		Peterborough United		
1937	1938	Millwall	65	
1939		(Millwall)	(3)	
Chorlton, Charles (Charlie)			RB/CH	
b Heaton Mersey q1 1886			d 1956	
1906		Manchester United	0	
		Denton		
1909	1910	Bury	5	1
1921	1923	Crewe Alexandra	65	
		Nantwich		
Chorlton, Francis			OL	
b Rawmarsh 27/2/1908			d 1984	
		Calderbrook St James		
1930		Rochdale	3	
Chorlton, Frank Hurst			LH	
b Bolton q2 1878			d 1959	
		Southport Central		
1906		Bury	1	
Chorlton, Henry Herman			OR/OL/IL	
b Bolton q1 1874			d 1933	
1897	1900	Bolton Wanderers	9	2
Chorlton, James Gilbert (Gilbert)			RH/OR	
b Bolton q1 1883			d 1939	
		St Helens Town		
1905	1907	Bury	15	1
		Rossendale United		
		Tyldesley Albion		
		Banks St Stephen's		
Chorlton, Thomas (Tom)			RB/LB/LH	
b Heaton Mersey q4 1880			d 1952	
		All Saints (Stockport)		
		Northern		
1900	1902	Stockport County	27	
		Accrington Stanley		
1904	1910	Liverpool	118	8
1913		Manchester United	4	
		Stalybridge Celtic		
Christie, Alexander Gray (Alex)			RH/LH	
b Glasgow 27/6/1896			d 1981	
		Paisley Central YMCA		
		Larkhall Thistle		
		Hamilton Academical		
1920		Reading	31	1
1921		Walsall	30	1
1922		Southampton	5	
1923		Norwich City	5	
1924	1927	Rochdale	137	5
1928		Exeter City	4	
		Aldershot		
		H & G Simons Athletic		
Christie, David (Davy)			RH/LH	
b Forfar 1867				
		Forfar Athletic		
1889	1894	Stoke	101	2
		Dresden United		
Christie, David			IL	
		Hurlford		
1908		Manchester United	2	
		St Helens Recreation		
Christie, David Fiddes			CF	
b Arbroath 1/4/1899			d 1973	
		Arbroath St Thomas		
		Forfar Athletic		
		Arbroath		
		Albion Rovers		
		Celtic		
		Arbroath Athletic		
		Third Lanark		
		East Stirlingshire		
1925		Port Vale (trial)	0	
1926		Barrow	21	5

From	To		Apps	Goal
		Christie, Gilbert David	CF	
		b Dundee 18/11/1891	d 1973	
		Fairfield		
1913		Huddersfield Town	2	
		Halifax Town		
		Christie, John	RB/LH	
		b 1884		
		Sale Holmfield		
1902		Manchester United	1	
1904	1906	Manchester City	10	
		Bradford Park Avenue		
		Croydon Common		
		Brentford		
		Christie, Norman T	CH	
		b Jarrow 24/11/1913	d 1938	
		Bishop Auckland		
1930		Newcastle United (trial)	0	
1931	1934	Huddersfield Town	47	
1934	1936	Blackburn Rovers	43	
		Christon, Leonard (Len)	CF	
		b Skelton 14/6/1906	d 1988	
		Brotton		
1925		Durham City	0	
		Carlin How		
1928		Hartlepools United	2	
		Church, Henry Boyce (Harry)	GK	
		b Castleford 24/11/1904	d 1984	
		Castleford Town		
1930	1934	Bolton Wanderers	41	
1935		Oldham Athletic	23	
1937	1938	Exeter City	66	
		Church, John	OL/OR/CF	
		b Lowestoft 17/9/1919	d 2004	
		Lowestoft Town		
1937	1949	Norwich City	110	16
1939		(Norwich City)	(3)	(1)
1950	1953	Colchester United	118	21
		Crittall Athletic		
		Beccles		
		Eastern Counties Coachworks		
		Churchman, Ernest Arthur	IR	
		b Northampton q1 1891	d 1925	
		Rushden Town		
		Market Harborough Town		
1920		Northampton Town	2	1
		Wellingborough Town		
		Churchman, Herbert	LH	
		b Burton-on-Trent q1 1887	d 1963	
1905		Burton United	1	
		Civil, Harry	LH	
		b Northampton 1/4/1902	d 1971	
1922		Northampton Town	2	
		Clacher, John	RH/LH	
		b Kirkcaldy 28/2/1909	d 1980	
		St Andrews Athletic		
		Alloa Athletic		
		Altrincham		
1934	1936	Burnley	30	1
1937		Darlington	36	2
		Clack, Charles Edward (Ted)	OR	
		b Highworth 4/6/1896	d 1984	
		Pontypridd		
1921	1922	Sunderland	9	
1923		Bristol City	2	
		Nuneaton Town		
		Hinckley Town		
		Holywell Amateurs		
		Clack, Frank Edward	GK	
		b Witney 30/3/1912	d 1995	
		Witney Town		
1933	1938	Birmingham	60	
1939		Brentford	0	
1946	1948	Bristol City	67	
		Guildford City		
		Clamp, Arthur	CH	
		b Sneinton 1/5/1884	d 1918	
		Sneinton		
1906	1914	Notts County	275	3

From	To		Apps	Goal
		Clare, Joseph (Joe)	OL/LB	
		b Westhoughton 4/2/1910	d 1987	
		Westhoughton Town		
1930		Manchester City	0	
1931		Wigan Borough	0	
		Westhoughton Town		
1933	1934	Accrington Stanley	25	1
1935		Arsenal	0	
		Margate		
1936		Norwich City	22	5
1937	1938	Lincoln City	68	23
1939		(Lincoln City)	(3)	(2)
		Ruston-Bucyrus		
		Clare, Thomas (Tommy)	RB	
		b Congleton q1 1865	d 1929	
		Caps: FAlliance 1/FLge 1/England 4		
		Talke Rangers		
		Goldenhill Wanderers		
		Burslem Port Vale		
1888	1896	Stoke	198	4
		Burslem Port Vale		
1897		Manchester City	1	
1898	1900	Burslem Port Vale	18	
		Clare, William Edwin (Edwin)	RB	
		b Basford q4 1883	d 1944	
		Kirkby Rovers		
		Bentinck Colliery		
		Mansfield Woodhouse		
1903	1904	Notts County	6	
		Brighton & Hove Albion		
		Mansfield Wesleyans		
		Clark, Andrew (Andy)	LB	
		b Leith 16/3/1880		
		Hamilton Academical		
		Buckhaven United		
		Heart of Midlothian		
1901	1902	Stoke	52	
		Plymouth Argyle		
1906		Leeds City	24	
		East Fife		
		Brentford		
		Southend United		
		Clark, Archie	CH/RH	
		b Shoreham, Kent 4/4/1902	d 1967	
		Aylesford Paper Mills		
		Grays Thurrock		
1926		Brentford	1	
1927		Arsenal	1	
1928	1930	Luton Town	87	11
1931	1934	Everton	41	1
1935	1938	Tranmere Rovers	104	1
		Gillingham		
		Clark, Benjamin	OL	
		b Wednesbury 1/1900	d 1970	
		Seaforth Highlanders		
		Wednesbury Old Athletic		
1920		West Bromwich Albion	1	
		Wednesbury Old Athletic		
		Blakenhall		
		Wednesbury Old Athletic		
		Clark, Charles	RH/CH	
		b 1881		
1901	1902	Everton	6	1
		Plymouth Argyle		
		Crystal Palace		
		Clark, Charles (Charlie)	OR/IR	
		b Fleet q2 1917	d 1943	
1935	1937	Queen's Park Rangers	6	
1938		Luton Town	14	6
		Clark, David Cleland	GK	
		b Sligo 1880		
		Northampton Town		
1902	1903	Glossop	67	
		Bristol Rovers		
		West Ham United		
1909		Bradford Park Avenue	7	
		Southend United		
		Bristol Rovers		
		Clark, Ernest	RB	
1899		Middlesbrough	1	
		Clark, Frederick Donald (Don)	CF/RH	
		b Bristol 25/10/1917		
		North Bristol Old Boys		
1938	1950	Bristol City	117	67
		Clark, Gordon Vincent	RB	
		b Gainsborough 15/6/1913	d 1997	
		Goldthorpe United		
1934		Southend United	0	
		Denaby United		
1936	1945	Manchester City	55	
		Hyde United		
		Waterford		
		Clark, H	OR	
1892		Walsall Town Swifts	3	

From	To		Apps	Goal
		Clark, Harold	GK	
		b 2/1/1905	d 1975	
		Ulverston Town		
1925	1926	Barrow	40	
1927		Tranmere Rovers	0	
		Ulverston Town		
1930		Barrow	5	
		Bo'ness		
		Clark, Hector	OR	
		b Morpeth 8/12/1904	d 1983	
1928		Ashington	2	
		Clark, Herbert	LB	
		b 1896		
		Abertillery		
		Halifax Town		
1921		Rochdale	1	
		Clark, James	OR	
		b Tyneside		
		Newburn		
		Throckley Welfare		
		Margate		
1935		Arsenal	0	
		Hibernian		
1936		Barnsley	11	
		Distillery		
		Waterford		
		Derry City		
		Clark, James Ferguson (Jimmy)	OL	
		b Kilwinning 5/5/1911		
		Kilwinning Eglinton		
		Partick Thistle		
		Benburb Star		
1934		Southend United	23	6
		Denny Hibernian		
		Derry City		
		Clark, James M	CH/LH	
		Bostall Rovers		
1897	1898	Woolwich Arsenal	4	
		Clark, James McNicholl Cameron (Jimmy)	CH	
		b Glasgow 1913		
		Clydebank Juniors		
1934	1936	Sunderland	49	
1937	1938	Plymouth Argyle	37	
1939		(Plymouth Argyle)	(1)	
		Clark, James Robinson (Jimmy)	IL/CF	
		b Bensham 20/10/1895	d 1947	
		Annfield Plain		
		Jarrow		
1922	1923	Newcastle United	11	2
1924		Leeds United	3	
1925		Swindon Town	18	7
		Morton		
1926		Ashington	5	
		Shelbourne		
		Clark, John (Jack)	CF/IL	
		b Durham		
		Bathgate		
1911	1912	Bradford City	6	1
		Cardiff City		
		Clark, John	OL/OR	
		b Bo'ness 4/3/1900		
		Black Watch		
		Bo'ness		
1922	1924	Arsenal	6	
1926		Luton Town	29	2
		Bo'ness		
		Third Lanark		
		Bo'ness		
		Clark, John Forsythe	CH	
		b Dumbarton		
1932		Wolverhampton Wanderers	0	
1933		Gillingham	5	
		Clark, John L	IR	
		b Bradley		
		Bradley United		
1925		Walsall	26	5
		Clark, John Robinson (Bob)	IR/OL	
		b Newburn 6/2/1903	d 1977	
		Spencer's Welfare		
		Hawthorn Leslie		
		Newburn Grange		
		Newburn		
		Prudhoe Castle		
1922	1927	Newcastle United	77	16
1927	1930	Liverpool	40	11
1931		Nottingham Forest	5	2
		North Shields		

From	To		Apps	Goal
		Clark, Joseph	IR	
		b Dundee 14/4/1874		
1895		Loughborough	15	3
		Dundee		
		Brighton United		
		Dundee		
1899		Newton Heath	8	
1899		Middlesbrough (trial)	1	
		Lochee United		
		Dunfermline Athletic		
		East Fife		
		Clark, Joseph Walter (Joe)	OL	
		b Willington Quay 15/2/1890	d 1960	
		Hebburn Argyle		
1920	1921	Cardiff City	14	
		Aberaman Athletic		
1922		Southampton	20	
1923		Rochdale	16	1
		Clark, Ronald Newton	GK	
		b Gateshead q4 1909	d 1966	
		Whitehall Juniors		
1932	1933	Gateshead	30	
1934		Manchester United	0	
		Clark, Samuel James Hugh	LB	
		b Whitletts 15/11/1912	d 1987	
		Petershill		
1935		Blackburn Rovers	1	
1937	1938	Halifax Town	20	2
		Clark, Thomas George	LH/RH	
		b Trehafod 31/10/1913	d 1994	
		Bargoed		
		Aberaman Athletic		
1935	1936	Bolton Wanderers	21	
1938		Nottingham Forest	27	
1939		(Nottingham Forest)	(3)	
		Clark, Wallace (Wally)	OL	
		b Jarrow 14/7/1896	d 1975	
		Durham City		
1919	1920	Middlesbrough	8	
1921	1922	Leeds United	13	
1922	1923	Birmingham	32	
1924		Coventry City	8	
		Boston Town		
1926		Barrow	16	2
1927		Torquay United	3	
		Weymouth		
		Whitchurch		
		Connah's Quay & Shotton		
		Clark, William (Willie)	OR	
		b Whifflet 1881	d 1937	
		Port Glasgow Athletic		
		Bristol Rovers		
1908	1909	Sunderland	41	4
1910		Bristol City	24	1
1911		Leicester Fosse	6	1
		Clark, William	OL	
		Notts County		
1919		Hull City	1	
		Clark, William	OL	
		b Beith 16/9/1900		
		Beith		
1924		Clapton Orient	4	
		Beith		
		Arthurlie (loan)		
		Clyde (loan)		
		Carlisle United (trial)		
		Kilmarnock		
		Beith		
		Clarke, Albert	CH/IR	
		b Chesterfield q1 1887	d 1948	
		Brampton United		
		Hasland Wild Rose		
1905	1908	Chesterfield Town	4	
		Doncaster Rovers		
		Clarke, Albert W	IL/OR/CF	
		b Sheffield 25/12/1916	d 1944	
		Mexborough Town		
		Frickley Colliery		
1934	1935	Torquay United	12	9
1935	1937	Birmingham	31	9
1938		Blackburn Rovers	38	21
1939		(Blackburn Rovers)	(3)	
		Clarke, Alfred William (Alfie)	IL	
		b Newport q3 1914	d 1953	
		Caps: Wales Sch/Wales Amat		
1932		Newport County	0	
		Lovells Athletic		
1934	1936	Newport County	29	7
		Lovells Athletic		

From To Apps Goal

Clarke, Benjamin (Ben) RB/LB
b Dungannon 6/8/1911 d 1981
Caps: Ireland Amat
Portadown
1934 1936 Sheffield United 10
1937 1938 Exeter City 40 1
1939 Carlisle United (2)

Clarke, Bernard M RB
b Leicester 1897 d 1941
St Peter's
1920 Leicester City 3
1921 Halifax Town 0
Barwell United

Clarke, Bruce Mitchell RH
b Johannesburg, South Africa 4/10/1910
Hillside Junior Club
Montrose
Third Lanark
Corale A (Paris)
1934 1938 Fulham 112 1
Worcester City

Clarke, Charles (Charlie) GK
b Bentham q1 1904 d 1933
Bentham Wanderers
Morecambe
1928 1929 Barrow 40
Ingleton
Morecambe

Clarke, George OR
1908 1909 Burnley 3
Hyde

Clarke, George RH
b Willaston 3/12/1894 d 1960
Nantwich
1919 1923 Stoke 156 4
1926 Crewe Alexandra 2

Clarke, George LH
b Nottingham 1902
Redditch Town
1924 Bristol City 0
1925 1926 Merthyr Town 66 2
1927 Coventry City 5
1928 Torquay United 0
Leamington Town

Clarke, George Baden OL
b Pleasley 24/7/1900 d 1977
Nottingham Royal
Welbeck Colliery
Mansfield Town
1924 Aston Villa 1
1925 1932 Crystal Palace 274 99
1933 Queen's Park Rangers 15 6

Clarke, Harold CF/OR
b Walsall 1875
1898 Everton 12 2
Portsmouth
1901 Burton United 31 8

Clarke, Horace RH/LH
b Sheffield 2/2/1892 d 1972
Ripley Town
Shirebrook
1914 Sheffield Wednesday 0
Scunthorpe & Lindsey United
1919 Coventry City 17
1920 Merthyr Town 29 1
1921 Chesterfield 35 4
1922 Exeter City 16
Mansfield Town
Pleasley Central School Old Boys
British Celanese (Spondon)

Clarke, Isaac (Ike) CF/IR/IL
b Tipton 9/1/1915 d 2002
Coseley Juniors
Toll End Wesley
1937 1947 West Bromwich Albion 108 39
1947 1952 Portsmouth 116 49
Yeovil Town

Clarke, James Henry OR
b Barnsley 6/10/1913 d 1978
Mexborough Athletic
1933 1935 Bradford City 9
Goole Town
1937 1938 Rotherham United 54 13
1939 (Rotherham United) (3)
Chesterfield

Clarke, John CF
Rangers
Fairfield
1896 Bury 6
1896 Blackpool 13 6
1897 Luton Town 1

From To Apps Goal

Clarke, John CF
b Annfield Plain
1912 Middlesbrough 0
Brentford
Durham City
1919 1920 Grimsby Town 39 12
Leadgate Park
1922 Coventry City 0

Clarke, John CH
b Rosewell 1905
Rosewell Rosedale
St Mirren
Hibernian
Dunfermline Athletic
Third Lanark
1933 Carlisle United 28 1
Cowdenbeath

Clarke, John Theodore Knight OR
b Lancaster 19/1/1917 d 1989
New Mills
Lancaster Town
1936 Oldham Athletic 1 1

Clarke, Leonard (Len) CF/IR
b Manchester
1932 Accrington Stanley 0
1934 1935 Rochdale 29 17

Clarke, Patrick (Pat) LB
b Dundalk 1914
Dundalk
1934 Leicester City 1
1938 Bristol City 0
1939 Hull City 0
Sligo Rovers
Leicester Frith

Clarke, Percy R IL
1923 Luton Town 1
Peterborough & Fletton United

Clarke, Philip Joseph C (Paddy) LH
b Dublin 3/3/1910 d 1988
Pembroke Celtic
Queen's Park (Dublin)
Brideville
1932 Southport 5
ESB (Dublin)

Clarke, Reginald Leonard (Reg 'Nobby') RH/LH
b Heavitree 4/9/1907 d 1981
Friernhay
Southern Railway
1927 1936 Exeter City 315 18
1937 1938 Aldershot 62 3
1939 (Aldershot) (1)

Clarke, Sidney (Sid) OR
b Swansea
Shrewsbury Town
1936 Halifax Town 2

Clarke, T RH
1893 Northwich Victoria 8

Clarke, Tom LH
b Bury q2 1881
1906 1911 Blackpool 137

Clarke, W CH
1895 Darwen 8 1

Clarke, Walter E CH
b Rushden 1874
Rushden Town
1898 Luton Town 4

Clarke, Walter Henry Leonard (Wally) OL
b Southwark 13/3/1908 d 1981
Blackheath
Wimbledon
Blackheath
1933 Crystal Palace 16
Folkestone

Clarke, William IL
1898 1899 Lincoln City 35 7

Clarke, William IL
b Newcastle
Jarrow Caledonians
1911 Blackpool 8 1

Clarke, William Arthur CF
b Manchester q4 1908
1926 Oldham Athletic 0
Hurst
1927 Oldham Athletic 0
Hyde United
1928 Bradford City 1
Morecambe
Hurst

From To Apps Goal

Clarke, William George CH/RH/LH
Wednesbury
Shrewsbury Town
Dudley Town
1930 West Bromwich Albion 0
1933 1935 Notts County 37 1
Dudley Town
Oakengates Town
Brierley Hill Alliance

Clarke, William Gibb (Willie) OR
b Mauchline 1880 d 1940
Third Lanark
East Stirlingshire
Bristol Rovers
1901 1904 Aston Villa 42 6
1905 1908 Bradford City 92 15
1909 1910 Lincoln City 35 1
Croydon Common

Clarke, William Harry OL
b Leicester 2/7/1916 d 1986
Melbourne Hall
Leicester Nomads
1936 Leicester City 0
1937 Exeter City 12 1
1938 Southampton 2
Cheltenham Town
Hinckley United
Anstey Methodists

Clarke, William Henry LB
b Kettering q1 1880
Kettering
Kettering St Mary's
Kettering
1902 Sheffield United 2
Northampton Town
Southampton

Clarke, William Vincent (Billy) RH/IR
b Newport 17/1/1911 d 1970
Pontymister
1930 Newport County 7
1931 Charlton Athletic 0
1932 1933 Newport County 41 1
1934 Portsmouth 1
1935 Brighton & Hove Albion 1
1936 Aldershot 21 4
1937 Crewe Alexandra 6
Hereford Town
1938 Accrington Stanley 3 1
Rhyl
Ebbw Vale
1945 Newport County 0

Clarkin, John OR
b Neilston 1872
Neilston
1892 Bootle 10 9
Glasgow Thistle
1893 1895 Newton Heath 67 23
1896 1897 Blackpool 56 11

Clarkin, John IL
b Ireland
Shelbourne
1911 Leeds City 1
Belfast Celtic

Clarkson, Clifford Stanbury (Cliff) OR
b Barrow 12/1/1917 d 1986
1937 1945 Barrow 1
Netherfield
Lancaster City

Clarkson, Richard CF/IR
b Lytham 30/10/1904 d 1978
Lytham
1926 1927 Accrington Stanley 38 17
Darwen
Lytham

Clarkson, Thomas RH/LH
b Stourbridge 4/1865 d 1915
Stourbridge Invicta
Halesowen Town
1889 1892 Aston Villa 17
Oldbury Town

Clarkson, William (Billy) OL
b Wombwell 22/9/1891 d 1954
Padiham
Nelson
1919 Burnley 2
1920 1921 Rotherham County 63 2
1922 Luton Town 32 3
Pontypridd
1923 Southport 19 1
Scunthorpe & Lindsey United

Claugh, CW OL
1904 Glossop 1

Claussen, DC OR
1898 Darwen 2

From To Apps Goal

Clawley, George GK
b Scholar Green 10/4/1875 d 1920
1893 Crewe Alexandra 3
1894 1895 Stoke 49
Southampton
1898 Stoke 34
Tottenham Hotspur
Southampton

Clay, George IR
1909 Preston North End 0
Hindley Central
South Liverpool
1913 Glossop 7

Clay, Henry (Harry) GK
b Kimberley 29/1/1881 d 1964
Kimberley St John's
1901 1912 Bristol City 310

Clay, Thomas (Tommy) RB
b Leicester 19/11/1892 d 1949
Caps: FLge 1/England 4
Belvoir Street Sunday School
Leicester Belvoir
1911 1913 Leicester Fosse 63
1913 1928 Tottenham Hotspur 318 23
Northfleet

Clay, William Edward LB
b Belfast 31/10/1880
Caps: IrLge 1
Belfast Celtic
1903 Sheffield United 7
Belfast Celtic
1905 Leeds City 0
Derry Celtic

Clayson, William James (Billy) IR
b Wellingborough 12/7/1897 d 1973
Northampton Compton
Wellingborough Town
1922 1924 Brentford 81 15
1925 Crewe Alexandra 33 12
1926 Barnsley 10 2
1927 Chesterfield 22 11
Scarborough
1930 1931 Torquay United 75 28
Scarborough
1933 York City 7
Scarborough
Scarborough Junior Imperial

Clayton, Harry RH
b Nelson 22/10/1904 d 1974
Hebden Bridge
Chorley
1925 Nelson 4
Morecambe
Manchester Central
Central (Belle Vue)
Bacup Borough
James Clark Ltd (Nelson)
Lustrafil Ltd (Nelson)

Clayton, Horace Leonard IR/IL
b Hackney 4/7/1898 d 1985
1920 1921 Queen's Park Rangers 6 1

Clayton, James Gordon CF/IL
b Sunderland 14/5/1913 d 1998
Shotton Colliery
1933 1937 Wolverhampton Wanderers 47 34
1937 1938 Aston Villa 11 1
1938 Burnley 16 10
1939 (Burnley) (2)
Barry Town

Clayton, John RH/IR
b Sheffield 23/4/1904 d 1973
Anston Athletic
Mansfield Town
Frickley Colliery
1927 1929 Rotherham United 98 11

Clayton, John RH/LH
b Mansfield 23/4/1907
Loughborough Corinthians
1929 Chesterfield 5
1930 1931 Wrexham 51 1
1932 Carlisle United 24
1933 Mansfield Town 15 1
Grantham
Gainsborough Trinity

Clayton, Rex CF/IR
b Retford 4/1/1916 d 1993
Retford Town
1937 Manchester City 3 2
1938 Bristol City 13 3
1939 Lincoln City (3) (1)

From To Apps Goal

Clayton, Roland IR/IL
b Ulverston 24/7/1904 d 1976
1922 1925 Barrow 11 7
Vickers Sports
1929 Barrow 9
Vickers Sports

Clayton, Stanley (Stan) IR
b Castleford 21/11/1912 d 2002
Castleford Town
Bradford Park Avenue 0
Leeds United 0
Upton Colliery
1937 1938 Notts County 31 3

Cleaver, Frederick Louis (Fred) CF
b Ashbourne 22/4/1885 d 1968
Ashbourne Town
1905 1906 Derby County 11 3
1907 Preston North End (trial) 0
Watford
Redditch
Atherstone Town
Washford Mills

Cleaver, Harry Patrick CF
b Walworth q4 1879 d 1953
Desborough
1902 Manchester United 1
Darlington

Clegg, Harry GK
b Burnley 1898
Burnley Tramways
1921 Nelson 5
Burnley Tramways

Clegg, John GK
b Sheffield q1 1890 d 1916
1908 1910 Bristol City 13
1910 1911 Barnsley 33
1912 Sheffield Wednesday 0
1913 Clapton Orient 8
1914 Bradford Park Avenue 0

Clegg, Joseph (Joe) CH
b Burnley q2 1869 d 1902
1891 Accrington 1
1894 1898 Bury 104 6

Cleghorn, Thomas (Tom) LH
b Leith 13/2/1870
Leith Athletic
1894 1895 Blackburn Rovers 45 3
1895 1898 Liverpool 56
Portsmouth
Plymouth Argyle

Cleland, James H IR
b Kilsyth 1889
1912 Preston North End 0
1914 Hull City 1

Clement, Archibald Ernest (Archie) RB
b Grays 27/11/1901 d 1984
Grays Athletic
Whitstable
Dartford Town
Chatham Town
1928 Millwall 2
1930 Watford 14
1931 1932 New Brighton 78
Yeovil & Petters United
1934 Southport 19
Sittingbourne
Canterbury Waverley
Sittingbourne
Chatham Town

Clements, Harry OR
b Worcester 22/7/1883 d 1939
Worcester City
1903 West Bromwich Albion 10
Worcester City
Shrewsbury Town
St Mirren
Third Lanark

Clements, John LB
b East Markham q4 1867
St Saviour's (Nottingham)
1888 1889 Notts County 14
1892 1893 Newton Heath 36
1894 Rotherham Town 27 3
1895 Newcastle United 0

From To Apps Goal

Clennell, Joseph (Joe) IL
b New Silksworth 19/2/1889 d 1965
Caps: FLge 3
Silksworth United
Seaham Harbour
1910 Blackpool 32 18
1910 1913 Blackburn Rovers 26 12
1913 1921 Everton 68 30
1921 1924 Cardiff City 118 36
1924 1925 Stoke 33 9
1926 Bristol Rovers 19 5
1927 Rochdale 13 2
Ebbw Vale
Barry
Bangor
Great Harwood

Clenshaw, Leslie James (Les) OL
b Poplar 29/9/1905 d 1985
Westcliff
1924 Southend United 0
Chelmsford Town (loan)
1926 1933 Southend United 132 28
1934 Barrow 33 8
1935 Mansfield Town 27 6
Chelmsford City
Gaslight (Rayleigh)

Clent, Herbert Edward RH
b Brixton 1/4/1918 d 1997
1935 Fulham 0
1937 Barrow 2
Dartford

Cleugh, William (Billy) LH
b Gateshead 27/4/1914 d 1981
1934 Hartlepools United 1
Horden Colliery Welfare
Jarrow
Annfield Plain

Clews, Alfred Herbert (Alf) CF
b Coventry 27/7/1900 d 1971
Stoke Dairymen
1922 Coventry City 3

Cliff, J OR
1895 Burton Swifts 2

Cliffe, John William OR
b Lincoln 4/2/1912 d 1982
1932 Lincoln City 0
1933 Bradford City 0
1934 Barnsley 3
1935 1938 Carlisle United 108 16

Clifford, George RB
b New Sawley 10/2/1896
Sutton Junction
1924 1930 Portsmouth 175
1931 Mansfield Town 39
Ilkeston United

Clifford, Hugh (Hughie) CH/RH
b Carfin 8/4/1873
Caps: FAlliance 1
Carfin Shamrock
1891 Stoke 13 1
Celtic
1893 Stoke 1
Carfin Shamrock
Motherwell
1894 Liverpool
1895 Manchester City 4 1
Carfin Rovers

Clifford, John Charles GK
1937 Crystal Palace 0
1938 Northampton Town 11
1939 (Northampton Town) (3)

Clifford, John Charles Thomas (Jack) RH/LH/CH
b Newport 24/9/1906 d 1961
1927 1930 Newport County 41
1931 1932 Crystal Palace 12
1933 Newport County 2
Lovells Athletic

Clifford, Patrick (Pat) OR
b Pontlottyn q1 1903 d 1948
1924 Merthyr Town 11
1924 1929 Bournemouth & Boscombe Ath 189 16
Chester
Stalybridge Celtic
Prescot Cables
Bacup Borough

Clifford, Robert (Bob) CH/RH/RB
b Rankinston 12/11/1883
Rankinston
Trabboch
1903 1908 Bolton Wanderers 152 5
1908 1910 Everton 37
South Liverpool
1911 Fulham 8

From To Apps Goal

Clifford, George Thomas (Thomas) IR
b Sawley q3 1877 d 1960
1899 Loughborough 20 2

Clifford, Thomas CH
b Kilbirnie 1875
Annbank
1897 Newton Heath 0
Ayr
1898 1899 Glossop North End 39 1
Luton Town
Celtic
Beith
Motherwell
1905 Nottingham Forest 0

Clifton, G RH
Long Eaton Rangers
1888 Derby County 1
Long Eaton Rangers

Clifton, Henry (Harry) IR/IL/CF
b Marley Hill 28/5/1914 d 1998
Caps: England War 1
Lintz Colliery
1932 West Bromwich Albion 0
Annfield Plain
Scotswood
1933 1937 Chesterfield 121 67
1938 1945 Newcastle United 29 15
1946 1948 Grimsby Town 69 23
Goole Town
Sutton Town

Clifton, William OR
b Leyland q3 1891 d 1953
Leyland
1914 1919 Preston North End 4
1921 Rochdale 13

Clinch, Thomas (Tom) RB
b Guisborough q2 1875 d 1956
Chorley
Nelson
Halliwell Rovers
1899 Sheffield United 9
Reading
1904 Notts County 6

Clint, Thomas GK
b Gateshead q4 1892 d 1965
Felling Colliery
1921 Lincoln City 1

Clipson, Roy RB/LB
b Lincoln 18/4/1909 d 1970
Newark Town
1930 1933 Bury 7
1934 Bristol City 17
Dartford
Altrincham
1936 Rochdale 31

Clitheroe, William Wilson (Bill) CH
b Otley q1 1905 d 1954
1927 Leeds United 0
1928 1929 Torquay United 6

Clotworthy, Hugh RH
b Kilwinning 8/3/1914 d 1984
Kilwinning Rangers
1938 Lincoln City 2

Clough, Albert Eric LB
b Blackburn q1 1901 d 1957
Great Harwood
1919 Blackburn Rovers 1
1921 Blackpool 1
Great Harwood

Clough, H OR
Nelson
1903 Burton United 4

Clough, James K (Jimmy) OL
b Hazlerigg 30/8/1918 d 1998
Seaton Burn
Blyth Spartans
Seaton Burn
1938 1946 Southport 45 10
1947 1948 Crystal Palace 67 12
1949 Southend United 34 7
1950 Barrow 18 3
Blyth Spartans

Clough, John H (Jack), MM GK
b Murton 13/5/1902
Fatfield Albion
1922 1925 Middlesbrough 124
1926 1931 Bradford Park Avenue 208
1932 Mansfield Town 30
1933 Brentford 20
1934 1936 Rotherham United 91

From To Apps Goal

Clunas, William McLean (Billy) RH
b Johnstone 29/4/1899 d 1967
Caps: Scotland 2
Kilbarchan Athletic
Johnstone
Luton Town (trial)
St Mirren
1923 1930 Sunderland 256 42
Morton
Inverness Thistle

Clutterbuck, Henry James GK
b Wheatenhurst 6/1873 d 1948
Hereford Thistle
1897 1898 Small Heath 59
Queen's Park Rangers
1901 Grimsby Town 1
1902 Chesterfield Town 29
New Brompton
Fulham

Clutton, James RB
b Goldenhill q2 1869 d 1943
1892 1893 Burslem Port Vale 29

Coates, Charles OL/IL
b Esh Winning 18/4/1912 d 1991
Hamsteels
1931 1933 Darlington 46 9

Coates, Frederick (Fred) LH
b Sheffield q4 1879 d 1956
1901 1903 Glossop 64 3

Coates, Herbert James Leopold (Rigger) IL
b West Ham q4 1901 d 1965
Caps: England Amat
Royal Navy
1928 1933 Southampton 99 22
Leyton

Coates, Walter Albert OR
b Burnhope 4/4/1895
Burnhope
Craghead United
Sacriston United
1919 Fulham 2
Leadgate Park
1921 1924 Leeds United 47 3
1925 Newport County 26 7
Linfield
1928 Hartlepools United 2
Chester-le-Street
Newport (Isle of Wight)
Burnhope Institute
Consett

Cobain, Sydney Percival OL
b Newtownards 6/8/1896 d 1971
1921 Halifax Town 1

Cobley, William Arthur LB
b Countesthorpe 31/12/1909 d 1989
Countesthorpe United
Solus
Nuneaton Town
1936 1938 Aston Villa 44
Solus (Leicester)
1946 Notts County 0

Cobourne, Ernest (Ernie) IL
b Toxteth Park 30/11/1911 d 2003
Northwich Victoria
1936 1938 Crewe Alexandra 20 7

Cochrane, Alexander Fraser (Sandy) IL/IR/OR
b Glasgow 8/8/1903
Caps: WLge 1
Shawfield Juniors
Alloa Athletic
1922 1925 Middlesbrough 67 8
1926 1928 Darlington 100 24
1928 1930 Bradford City 69 27
1931 Chesterfield 27 1
Llanelly
1933 1934 Northampton Town 42 7
1935 Swindon Town 13 1
Partick Thistle
East Stirlingshire
Dumbarton
Rothwell Town
Brigstock

Cochrane, Andrew F GK
b Belfast 1905
Ayr Fort
Ayr United
1927 Barrow 15

From To Apps Goal

Cochrane, David Andrew (Davy) OR
b Portadown 14/8/1920 d 2000
Caps: NIRL 8/LoI 4/Ireland 12
Portadown
1937 1938 Leeds United 28 3
1939 (Leeds United) (3)
Portadown
Shamrock Rovers
Linfield
Shamrock Rovers
1946 1950 Leeds United 144 25

Cochrane, David Stobbie CF
b Dunblane 30/1/1910
Dunblane Rovers
Denny Hibernian
1927 Nelson 2 2
Bo'ness
Armadale

Cochrane, Michael (Mick) RB
b Belfast d 1912
Caps: IrLge 4/Ireland 8
Milltown
Distillery
Glentoran
Belfast Celtic
Distillery
1900 Leicester Fosse 27
1900 Middlesbrough 6
Distillery
Belfast Celtic

Cochrane, Thomas (Tom) OL
b Newcastle 7/10/1908 d 1976
St Peter's Albion
1928 1936 Leeds United 244 23
1936 1938 Middlesbrough 80 16
1939 Bradford Park Avenue (3)

Cock, Donald James CF/IL
b Phillack 8/7/1896 d 1974
Camborne Boys Brigade
Gwynne's Foundry
1919 1922 Fulham 87 43
1922 1924 Notts County 85 32
1924 1925 Arsenal 3
1925 1926 Clapton Orient 64 28
1927 Wolverhampton Wanderers 3 1
1927 Newport County 0

Cock, Herbert CF
b Burnham 7/10/1900 d 1977
1920 Brentford 1

Cock, John Gilbert (Jack) CF
b Phillack 14/11/1893 d 1966
Caps: FLge 2/England 2
West Kensington United
Forest Gate
Old Kingstonians
Brentford
1914 1919 Huddersfield Town 18 9
1919 1922 Chelsea 99 47
1922 1924 Everton 69 29
1924 1927 Plymouth Argyle 90 72
1927 1930 Millwall 115 77
Folkestone
Walton & Hersham

Cockburn, George William OL
b Gateshead 18/10/1903 d 1983
1925 West Ham United 0
1926 Northampton Town 1
Jarrow

Cockburn, William Old (Bill) CH/RH
b Craghead 8/1899 d 1958
Rosehill Villa
1921 1923 Stockport County 73
1924 1926 Liverpool 63
1928 1929 Queen's Park Rangers 57
1930 Swindon Town 38 1

Cockerill, Henry Leslie (Harry) LH
b Ryhope 14/1/1894 d 1960
1919 Arsenal 0
1920 Luton Town 8
Mid-Rhondda United
1921 1922 Bristol City 16
1923 1924 Reading 55 2
1925 Merthyr Town 3 1

Cockle, Ernest Samuel (Ernie) CF/IL
b East Ham 12/9/1896 d 1966
Green & Siley Weir
1920 Clapton Orient 20 4
Margate
Maidstone United
1923 Arsenal 0
1924 Luton Town 7 1
1924 1927 Northampton Town 97 46
1928 1929 Wigan Borough 75 16
Sittingbourne (trial)
Guildford City
1931 Wigan Borough 6

From To Apps Goal

Cockroft, Joseph (Joe) LH
b Barnsley 20/6/1911 d 1994
Yorkshire Paper Mills
Ardsley Athletic
Wombwell
1930 1931 Rotherham United 3 1
Gainsborough Trinity
1932 1938 West Ham United 251 3
1939 (West Ham United) (3)
1945 1948 Sheffield Wednesday 87 2
1948 Sheffield United 12
Wisbech Town
Goole Town

Cockshutt, James William CF
b Darwen q2 1872 d 1938
1891 Blackburn Rovers 1
Brierfield
1892 Burnley 0
Nelson
Reading
1898 1899 Grimsby Town 61 21
Nelson

Codd, Henry (Harry) CH/RH/RB
b Aberdare 18/1/1903 d 1975
1924 Aberdare Athletic 9
Ebbw Vale
1927 1928 Charlton Athletic 19
1929 Wigan Borough 26
Connah's Quay & Shotton

Codd, Thomas Henry (Tommy) OL
b Grimsby q3 1890 d 1961
Goole Town
1914 Leicester Fosse 13
Harrogate AFC

Codling, Allan OL
b Guisborough 24/2/1911 d 1991
Whitby Town
1932 Bolton Wanderers 0
1932 Hartlepools United 0
Scarborough
Folkestone
1936 1937 Clapton Orient 32 3
1938 Darlington 7
1939 Hartlepools United 0

Codling, Rowland (Ralph) LH
b Norton-on-Tees 22/2/1880 d 1956
Stockton
Swindon Town
1903 Stockport County 28
1905 Clapton Orient 28 1
1905 1908 Aston Villa 77
Northampton Town
Croydon Common
1910 Manchester City 5

Coe, Fred CH
b Canklow
Atlas Hotel
1911 Gainsborough Trinity 26
1919 1920 Rotherham County 24 3

Coen, Joseph Leo (Joe) GK
b Glasgow 4/12/1911 d 1941
Mosspark Amateurs
Parkview United
Clydeholm Juniors
Celtic
Clydebank (loan)
Nithsdale Wanderers (loan)
Stenhousemuir (loan)
Guildford City
1932 1933 Bournemouth & Boscombe Ath 36
1934 1938 Luton Town 142
1939 (Luton Town) (3)

Coen, Lawrence (Laurie) LB/OL/OR
b Lowestoft 4/12/1914 d 1972
Caps: England Sch
Milford Haven
1936 West Bromwich Albion 7 4
1938 1947 Coventry City 20 3
1939 (Coventry City) (3)
South Liverpool
Dudley Town

Coggins, William Herbert (Billy) GK
b Bristol 16/9/1901 d 1958
Victoria Albion
Bristol St George
1925 1929 Bristol City 171
1929 1933 Everton 51
1935 Queen's Park Rangers (trial) 6
Bath City

From To Apps Goal

Coglin (Cocklin), Stephen (Steve) IL
b Wolverhampton 14/10/1899 d 1965
Moxley White Star
Darlaston
Lichfield City
Wednesbury Old Athletic
Willenhall
1924 1926 Sunderland 20 9
1926 1930 Grimsby Town 118 39
1931 Notts County 13 3
Worcester City
Hereford United
Cannock Town
Bromsgrove Rovers
Archdales (Worcestershire)

Coid, David CF
b Kilbarchan 13/9/1891 d 1966
Pollok
Petershill
Kilbarchan Athletic
Clyde
East Stirlingshire
Cowdenbeath
Armadale (trial)
1920 Portsmouth 7 3

Colclough, Ephraim CF
b Stoke-on-Trent q4 1875 d 1914
1898 1899 Stoke 3
Watford
Brighton & Hove Albion

Colclough, William (Billy) IR
b Woodvale 9/2/1917 d 1982
Kent Road Juniors
Southport United
1936 Oldham Athletic 0
Rhyl Athletic
1937 Southport 1
1938 Blackburn Rovers 0
Queen of the South
Spennymoor United
North Shields
Prescot Cables
Skelmersdale United
Burscough
Brockhouse

Coldicott, Thomas William IR
b Solihull 5/10/1911 d 1993
1933 Walsall 1 1
Fives (France)

Cole, E John LB
1899 Gainsborough Trinity 18

Cole, George Douglas (Doug) RB/LH
b Heswall 2/7/1916 d 1959
1936 Sheffield Wednesday 0
1937 Sheffield United 1
1945 1947 Chester 20
Stalybridge Celtic

Cole, John Samuel IR
b West Bromwich 1885 d 1933
Bloxwich Strollers
1902 1903 West Bromwich Albion 9 3
Wellingborough
Northampton Town

Cole, Norman Philip CF
b Woolston 7/11/1913 d 1976
Itchen Sports
Thorneycrofts
Newport (Isle of Wight)
1933 1934 Southampton 34 13
1935 Norwich City 1

Cole, Samuel CF
b Smethwick 9/1874
1896 Stoke 0
Smethwick Centaur
1899 Small Heath 1
Harborne

Cole, William Walter OR/RB
b Sheffield 1874
1898 1900 Sheffield Wednesday 8 1
1901 Doncaster Rovers 0
Worksop Town

Colebourne, Joseph (Joe) RB
b Tyldesley 15/3/1893 d 1979
Atherton
1920 Exeter City 30
1921 1922 Swindon Town 57
1923 1924 Exeter City 45 3
Taunton United

Coleman, Albert Edward OR
b South Kirkby
Frickley Colliery
1928 Rotherham United 2
Mexborough
Gainsborough Trinity

From To Apps Goal

Coleman, Ernest (Tim) CF/IL/IR
b Blidworth 4/1/1908 d 1984
Hucknall Colliery
1925 Nottingham Forest (trial) 0
1926 1928 Halifax Town 48 15
1928 1931 Grimsby Town 87 57
1931 1933 Arsenal 45 26
1934 1936 Middlesbrough 85 21
1936 1938 Norwich City 63 25
Linby Colliery

Coleman, John George (Tim) IR/IL
b Kettering 26/10/1881 d 1940
Caps: FLge 3/England 1
Kettering St Mary's
Kettering
Northampton Town
1902 1907 Woolwich Arsenal 172 79
1907 1909 Everton 69 30
1910 Sunderland 32 21
1911 1913 Fulham 94 45
1914 Nottingham Forest 38 14
Tunbridge Wells Rangers
Maidstone United

Coleman, Macdonald Arthur (Arthur) OL
b Chesterfield 8/3/1907 d 1990
Frickley Colliery
1928 Rotherham United 0
Gainsborough Trinity
1932 Bradford Park Avenue 2
Gainsborough Trinity

Coles, Arthur CH
b Crediton 27/1/1914 d 1997
Copplestone
1937 Exeter City 2
Coleraine
1946 1948 Exeter City 14
Barnstaple Town

Coles, Donald Stratton RB
b Plymouth 29/7/1879 d 1941
Ardingly College
Burgess Hill
Brighton Athletic
Brighton & Hove Rangers
Brighton & Hove Albion
1902 Leicester Fosse 1
Brighton & Hove Albion
St Leonards United

Coles, Frederick Gordon (Gordon) RH/CH
b Nottingham q4 1875 d 1947
Nottingham Post Office
1895 Notts County 1
1899 Nottingham Forest 1
1900 1903 Woolwich Arsenal 78 2
1904 1907 Grimsby Town 44
1908 Clapton Orient (trial) 0

Coles, Walter Theodore (Theo) LH
b Bedford Park 17/8/1895 d 1969
Cambridge University
1920 Watford 1
Corinthians

Coley, William Ernest (Bill) LH
b Wolverhampton 17/9/1916 d 1974
1936 Wolverhampton Wanderers 2
1937 Bournemouth & Boscombe Ath 13
1938 1946 Torquay United 61 1
1939 (Torquay United) (3)
1947 1950 Northampton Town 104 7
1951 Exeter City 8
St Austell

Colledge, Ernest (Ernie) OL
b Chesterfield 12/5/1902 d 1974
Bolsover Colliery
1924 Watford 1
Leavesden Mental Hospital

Collett, Ernest (Ernie) LH
b Sheffield 17/11/1914 d 1980
Oughtibridge WMC
1937 1946 Arsenal 20

Colley, Robert OR/IR
b Sedgley q2 1879 d 1954
1899 1900 Wolverhampton Wanderers 8 2
Newton

Colley, William Booth RH
b Sheffield 12/6/1905 d 1976
Sheffield Victoria
1928 Rotherham United 4

From To Apps Goal

Collier, Austin RH/LH
b Dewsbury 24/7/1914 d 1991
Upton Colliery
Frickley Colliery
1938 Mansfield Town 21
1946 York City 10
Queen of the South
1946 1947 Rochdale 6
1947 Halifax Town 1
Goole Town
Scarborough

Collier, Christopher James (Chris) OR
b Blackrod 16/1/1906 d 1993
Blackrod White Star
Horwich Lee Congregational
Adlington United
Hindley Green
Winsford United
1926 Southport 2
Middlewich

Collier, David John (Dai) IR
b Llwynypia 12/4/1894 d 1973
Caps: Wales 1
St Cynon's
Mid-Rhondda
1920 1921 Grimsby Town 44 13
Llanelly
Mid-Rhondda United
Barry

Collier, James CF
1906 Blackpool 3

Collier, James LH
b Seaton Delaval 3/4/1897 d 1980
Blyth Spartans
1919 Burnley (trial) 0
1920 Crystal Palace 1
1922 Ashington 17

Collier, John C (Jock) RH
b Dysart 1/2/1897 d 1940
Victoria Hawthorn
Denbeath Star
Inverkeithing United
1920 1925 Hull City 168
1926 1927 Queen's Park Rangers 36 1
York City

Collier, Samuel GK
b Ince-in-Makerfield 17/9/1906 d 1975
Ince Parish Church
Ince St Mary's
1925 1929 Wigan Borough 12
Bacup Borough
Rossendale United
Prescot Cables
Leyland Motors
Ince St Mary's

Collier, Thomas (Tom) GK
b Barnsley
1936 1937 Halifax Town 5

Collier, William (Bill) LH
b Portmoak 11/12/1889 d 1954
Caps: Scotland 1
Black Watch
Forfar Yeomanry
Inverkeithing Juniors
Raith Rovers
1924 Sheffield Wednesday 14
Kettering Town
Dartford

Collin, George LB
b Oxhill 13/9/1905 d 1989
1922 West Ham United 0
West Stanley
1923 Arsenal 0
West Stanley
1925 1926 Bournemouth & Boscombe Ath 48
West Stanley
1927 1935 Derby County 309
1936 Sunderland 31
1938 Port Vale 1
Burton Town

Colling, Fred IR
b Crook 23/11/1897 d 1973
Darlington Railway Athletic
1921 Darlington 2 1
1922 Durham City 14 4
Shildon
Chopwell Institute

Collinge, Arthur IL
b Rochdale 20/7/1897 d 1971
Rochdale Tradesmen
1921 Rochdale 10 1
Rochdale Tradesmen

From To Apps Goal

Collinge, Ernest RH/LH
b Blackley 5/2/1895 d 1960
1921 1925 Port Vale 143 9

Collinge, Thomas Edward CF
b Blackley q3 1897 d 1960
1921 Port Vale 1

Collins, Albert John CH
b Sheerness 16/1/1899 d 1969
1923 1928 Millwall Athletic 24 3
1929 1933 Gillingham 170 4
Tunbridge Wells Rangers
Canterbury Waverley

Collins, Arthur (Pat) RH/CH/LH
b Chesterfield 29/5/1882 d 1953
Leicester Old Boys
1901 1904 Leicester Fosse 82 5
1907 1913 Fulham 197 8
Norwich City

Collins, Arthur Henry GK
b Smethwick q4 1902
Clay Cross
1924 Derby County 0
1926 Brentford 4
Scarborough
Mansfield Town

Collins, David OR
b Dumbarton 1912
Dumbarton Fern
Dumbarton
1932 Bradford Park Avenue 7 2
Dumbarton
Morton

Collins, Edward (Ted) LB/RB
b Wolverhampton q3 1882
Bilston United
Verity Athletic
Brownhills Albion
1907 1914 Wolverhampton Wanderers 284
Newport County
Hednesford Town

Collins, Henry Edward (Harry) GK
b Winlaton q2 1876 d 1937
Birtley
Hebburn Argyle
1900 Burnley 30
Queen's Park Rangers
1905 Everton 3

Collins, James IL/IR/OR
b Scotland 1872 d 1900
Newcastle East End
Newcastle West End
Newcastle East End
Newcastle United
1893 1894 Nottingham Forest 40 15
1895 1896 Newcastle United 34 9
Sheppey United
Chatham

Collins, James (Jimmy) RH/CH
b Dundee
Caps: WLge 2
Lochee Harp
1920 1929 Swansea Town 275 9

Collins, James (Jack) OL
b London
1931 Liverpool 0
1932 Cardiff City 7
Merthyr Town
1933 Millwall 0
Bangor

Collins, James Frederick Arthur (Jimmy) RH/LH
b Brentford 14/7/1903 d 1977
Chelmsford
Clapton
Leyton
1923 1935 West Ham United 311 3
Colchester United

Collins, James Henry (Jimmy) CF/IR
b Bermondsey 30/1/1911 d 1983
Tooting Town
1931 1932 Queen's Park Rangers 22 4
Tunbridge Wells Rangers
1933 Rochdale 30 6
1934 Stockport County 6 1
1935 Walsall 22 14
1935 1936 Liverpool 7
1937 1938 Cardiff City 76 41
1939 (Cardiff City) (3) (4)
Aberaman

Collins, John LB
b Scotland 1870
Cambuslang
1891 1892 Everton 15

From To Apps Goal

Collins, John CH
b Carlisle q4 1907
1929 1930 Carlisle United 9

Collins, Legh Richman LH
b Liverpool q2 1901
Grassendale St Mary's
1921 1922 Wigan Borough 5
1923 Nelson 13
1924 New Brighton 11
1925 Crewe Alexandra 0
Stalybridge Celtic

Collins, Nicholas OL
b Hamilton
Blantyre Celtic
1926 Charlton Athletic 1
Alloa Athletic

Collins, Nicholas LH/IL
b Chopwell 7/9/1911 d 1990
Canterbury Waverley
1934 1938 Crystal Palace 143 7
1939 (Crystal Palace) (1)
Yeovil Town

Collins, Robert CF
b St Helens 4/6/1910 d 1999
Whiston Parish Church
1928 Bolton Wanderers (trial)
1928 Manchester United (trial)
Chorley
Prescot Cables
1929 1930 Wigan Borough 19 7

Collins, Thomas (Tom) RB/LB
b Leven 16/4/1882 d 1929
Caps: SLge 2/Scotland 1
Leven Thistle
Heart of Midlothian
Bathgate (loan)
East Fife
Heart of Midlothian
1910 1914 Tottenham Hotspur 113 1

Collins, Walter Edmund IL
b Newbold q2 1885
Sutton Town
1907 Barnsley 1

Collins, W Arthur (Pat) RH/CH/LH
b Leicester 1883
Leicester Old Boys
1901 1904 Leicester Fosse 82 5
1907 1913 Fulham 197 8
Norwich City

Collins, William Charles Elvet (Elvet) OR
b Bedwellty 16/10/1902 d 1977
Caps: WLge 3/Wales 1
Rhymney Town
1923 1926 Cardiff City 12
1927 1928 Clapton Orient 39 1
Lovells Athletic
Rhymney Town
Llanelly
1932 Newport County 6 1
Llanelly
Oakdale Welfare

Collinson, CF OL/CH
1894 Everton 0
1895 Bury 1 1
1898 Darwen 9

Collinson, James IR/RB/LB
b Prestwich q1 1876
1895 1900 Newton Heath 63 15

Colman, Edgar GK
b Oldham 1/6/1905 d 1979
Mossley
1925 Oldham Athletic 2
Mossley
Eccles United
Bacup Borough
Congleton Town

Colquhoun, David Wilson (Davie) RH
b Motherwell 9/1/1906 d 1983
Blantyre Victoria
St Mirren
1931 1934 Tottenham Hotspur 81 2
1934 1935 Luton Town 16
1936 Rochdale 0

From To Apps Goal

Colquhoun, Duncan Morton OL
b Glenfruin 24/7/1915 d 2005
Dunoon Athletic
Partick Thistle
1932 Fulham (trial) 0
1933 Millwall 0
Raith Rovers
Dumbarton
1934 Sheffield Wednesday (trial) 0
1934 Hartlepools United (trial) 0
King's Park
Queen of the South
Hibernian
Wigan Athletic
1937 Bristol City 3
1938 Southport 36 9
1939 Bradford City (1)
Wigan Athletic
Hurst
Runcorn
Crompton Recreation

Colville, George RH
b Tarbolton 1876
Annbank
1896 Blackpool 5
Hibernian
Annbank
1898 1901 Glossop North End 105 2
Fulham
Annbank
Port Glasgow Athletic

Colville, James OL
b Coylton 1868
Annbank
1892 Newton Heath 9 1
Fairfield
1894 Notts County (trial) 0
Annbank

Colvin, Robert (Bobby) OR/CF
b Kirkconnel 5/12/1876 d 1940
Coatbridge
1897 Liverpool 3
1898 Glossop North End 15 2
1899 1900 New Brighton Tower 34 5
Luton Town
Queen's Park Rangers
Swindon Town
Maxwelltown Volunteers
African Royal

Combes, John William CH
b Holborn q2 1908
1930 Thames 2

Comery, Harold OL
b Basford q4 1883
1903 Nottingham Forest 1

Common, Alfred (Alf) IR/CF/IL
b Millfield, County Durham 25/5/1880 d 1946
Caps: FLge 1/England 3
South Hylton
Jarrow
1900 1901 Sunderland 18 6
1901 1903 Sheffield United 67 23
1904 Sunderland 20 6
1904 1909 Middlesbrough 168 58
1910 1912 Woolwich Arsenal 77 23
1912 1913 Preston North End 35 9

Common, Edward Winchester (Ted) RB/LB
b Seaton Delaval 25/1/1907 d 1958
New Delaval Villa
Blyth Spartans
1928 1929 Everton 14
1933 Preston North End 1
1935 1938 Chester 142

Common, John (Jack) RH
b Sunderland q1 1902
Robert Thomson's
Chester-le-Street
1922 South Shields 0
1923 Hartlepools United 32 4
St Bernard's
Chester-le-Street
Aldershot
Derry City
Waterford
1934 Darlington (trial)

Compstey, James William IL/IR
b Darwen q4 1874 d 1900
1894 1897 Darwen 25 1

Compton, Denis Charles Scott OL
b Hendon 23/5/1918 d 1997
Caps: England War 12
Golders Green
Nunhead
1936 1949 Arsenal 54 15

From To Apps Goal

Compton, Leslie Harry (Les) CH/RB/LB
b Woodford 12/9/1912 d 1984
Caps: FLge 1/England War 5/England 2
Bell Lane Old Boys (Hendon)
Hampstead Town
1931 1951 Arsenal 253 5

Compton, William Alfred (Bill) OL
b Bedminster 5/4/1896 d 1976
Bristol Motor Works
1919 1923 Bristol City 14
1924 1927 Exeter City 151 39
1928 Bristol Rovers 21 3
Bath City

Comrie, George Smart LH
b Denny 31/3/1885
Dunipace Juniors
Third Lanark
Millwall Athletic
Dundee
1912 Huddersfield Town 15
Forfar Athletic

Comrie, James (Jock) CH
b Denny 31/3/1881 d 1916
Caps: SoLge 2
Third Lanark
Reading
1907 1908 Glossop 38 1
1908 1909 Bradford City 43 3
1910 Lincoln City 12 1
Grantham
Stenhousemuir
Reading

Comrie, Malcolm IL/IR
b Denny 26/8/1906
Dunipace Juniors
Denny Hibernian
1931 Brentford 0
1932 1933 Manchester City 17 1
1934 Burnley 8
1935 Crystal Palace 2
1936 1937 York City 79 20
1938 Bradford City 0

Conaty, Thomas Philip LH/CH
b North Shields q3 1906 d 1964
Preston Colliery
1923 Ashington 0
Preston Colliery
Raith Rovers (trial)
1927 South Shields 3
1928 Crystal Palace 3
1929 Barrow 14
North Shields

Condon, Bernard Clive CF
b Swansea 14/10/1902 d 1987
Barry
Taunton
Barry
1926 Swansea Town 0
1926 Merthyr Town 0
Bridgend United
1927 Clapton Orient 0
1927 Wrexham 2
Mold Town
Bath City
Barry
1928 Manchester City (trial) 0
Llanelly
Barry

Condrey, James Frederick (Fred) CF
b Wrexham q1 1883 d 1952
Willaston White Star
Nantwich
Wellington Town
1911 Nottingham Forest 7 2

Coneys, James John (Jimmy) IR
b Rochdale 12/6/1908 d 1974
1928 Bolton Wanderers 0
1933 Rochdale 1
1933 Southport (trial) 2
1933 Rochdale 1
Hurst
Witton Albion
Bacup Borough

Congdon, James (Jim) IL/OL
b Plymouth
Millbrook Rangers
1921 Exeter City 6
1922 Accrington Stanley 5
Torquay United

Conley, John Joseph (Jack) CF
b Whitstable 27/9/1920 d 1991
1938 Charlton Athletic 0
1939 1950 Torquay United 156 72
1939 (Torquay United) (3) (2)
Whitstable Town

From To Apps Goal

Conlin, James (Jimmy) OL
b Durham 6/7/1881 d 1917
Caps: FLge 2/England 1
Captain Colt's Rovers
Cambuslang
Hibernian
Falkirk
Albion Rovers
1904 1905 Bradford City 61 5
1906 1910 Manchester City 161 28
1911 Birmingham 21 2
Airdrieonians
Broxburn United

Conlin, John Francis RB
b Barrow 17/3/1901 d 1967
Barrow St Mary's
1925 Barrow 28
Barrow St Mary's

Conn, Luke (Leslie) CF
b Houghton-le-Spring q2 1909 d 1940
Easington Colliery
1934 Gillingham (trial)
1934 Millwall (trial) 0
1934 1935 Barrow 15 4
Lancaster Town

Connaboy, Michael (Mick) LH/IR
b Edinburgh 29/11/1901 d 1948
Loanhead Mayflower
Dunfermline Athletic
Alloa Athletic
Raith Rovers
Cowdenbeath
New York Nationals
Yeovil & Petters United
1931 Wolverhampton Wanderers 0
1932 Exeter City 4 1
1933 Darlington 10
Arbroath

Connaboy, Thomas IR
b Straiton 10/11/1911 d 1974
Arniston Rangers
Arbroath
Leith Athletic
1937 Darlington 1
Bangor City
1938 Southampton 0

Connachan, James CF/IR/RH
b Glasgow 29/8/1874
Duntocher Hibs
Glasgow Perthshire
Duntocher Hibs
Celtic
Airdrieonians
1898 Newton Heath 4
1898 1899 Glossop North End 28 8
1900 Leicester Fosse 29 7
1901 Nottingham Forest (trial) 0
Morton
Renton
Britannia (Canada)
Dumbarton Harp

Connell, Archibald (Archie) IR
b Darvel 22/4/1900
Darvel
Motherwell
Queen of the South
1927 Notts County 4 1

Connell, David RH
Morton
1922 Hartlepools United 15
Morton

Connell, Herbert CF
1907 Stockport County 1

Connell, John IR
b Scotland
Caps: SLge 1
St Mirren
Galston
1896 Newcastle United 24 3

Connell, William C (Billy) GK
b Liverpool
West Kirby
Port Sunlight
Flint Town
1924 Wrexham 3
Flint Town
Mold Town
1926 Wrexham 7
1927 Crewe Alexandra 2
1929 New Brighton 0

From To Apps Goal

Connelly, Edward John (Eddie) IL/IR
b Dumbarton 9/12/1916 d 1990
Rosslyn
1935 1937 Newcastle United 25 8
1937 1938 Luton Town 50 16
1939 1945 West Bromwich Albion (3) (1)
1946 1947 Luton Town 38 8
1948 1949 Leyton Orient 32 5
1949 Brighton & Hove Albion 6 1

Connelly, Fred H IL
1906 1907 Bristol City 13 6
Brentford

Connelly, John IL
b Cleckheaton
1910 Bradford City 1

Connelly, Robert CH/CF
b Glasgow
Shettleston Juniors
1921 1931 Port Vale 323 18
Congleton Town

Conner, John (Jack) CF/IR/OR
b Rutherglen 27/12/1891
Centre Half Holiday
Perth Violet
Perth Co-operative
1912 1913 Sunderland 5 2
Distillery
1920 1922 Crystal Palace 61 37
1922 1924 Newport County 85 26
1924 Bristol City 16 3
1925 Millwall 2
Chatham Town
Yeovil & Petters United
1927 Southend United 0
Yeovil & Petters United

Conner, John Cuthbertson Tippet (Jack) LH/CH
b Kirkmuirhill 26/4/1898 d 1967
Blantyre Celtic
Celtic
Alloa Athletic
Dykehead (loan)
1925 Plymouth Argyle 0
1926 Newport County 14
1927 Torquay United 24
Guildford City

Conner, William (Bill) RB
b St Ninians, Stirlingshire 3/12/1902 d 1999
St Johnstone
1930 Tranmere Rovers 2

Connolly, J CF
1893 Walsall Town Swifts 4

Connor, EA IR
1893 Preston North End 1
1894 Liverpool 0
Warrington

Connor, J RH
1893 Nottingham Forest 5

Connor, J Edward OL/OR/IL
b Weaste 1884 d 1955
Eccles Borough
1907 Lincoln City 4
Eccles Borough
Walkden Central
1909 1910 Manchester United 15 2
1911 Sheffield United 14
1912 1914 Bury 89 4
Fulham
Exeter City
Rochdale
Nelson
1921 Chesterfield 9 2
Saltney Athletic

Connor, James LH
b Birmingham 1/4/1867 d 1929
Warwickshire County
1889 1890 Aston Villa 4
Burslem Port Vale

Connor, James (Jimmy) OL
b Renfrew 1/6/1909 d 1980
Caps: Scotland 4
Paisley Celtic
Glasgow Perthshire
St Mirren
1930 1938 Sunderland 254 48

Connor, James GK
b Cleland 1917
Glenavon
Coltness United
1938 Lincoln City 7

From To Apps Goal

Connor, John OR
b Durham 1893
Houghton Rovers
1914 Huddersfield Town 3

Connor, John LB
b Ashton-under-Lyne 1/2/1914 d 2000
Mossley Methodists
Mossley
1934 1938 Bolton Wanderers 29
Hurst
Mossley
1947 1948 Tranmere Rovers 46 3

Connor, John (Jack) CF/IL
b Garngad 7/9/1911 d 1994
St Roch's
Alloa Athletic (loan)
Celtic
Airdrieonians (loan)
Airdrieonians
Albion Rovers (loan)
1936 1937 Plymouth Argyle 42 19
1938 Swansea Town 12 1
Queen of the South
Alloa Athletic
St Johnstone
British Railways Works XI

Connor, John Henry (Jack) RB
b Staincross q4 1875 d 1939
Newstead Rovers
Newstead Byron
Newark
1895 Notts County 17
Newark

Connor, Joseph CH/LH/IL
b Stirling 1885
Bathgate
1905 1914 Blackpool 287 30

Connor, Maurice Joseph John (Joe) IR
b Lochee 14/7/1877 d 1934
Caps: Ireland 3
Dundee Fereday
Gordon Highlanders
1897 1898 West Bromwich Albion 10
1899 1900 Walsall 48 14
1901 Bristol City 25 8
1902 Woolwich Arsenal 14 2
Brentford
New Brompton
Fulham
Colne
1905 Blackpool 0
Treharris
Wednesbury Old Athletic

Connor, Robert OL
b Newcastle 1913
1934 Queen's Park Rangers 5
Yeovil & Petters United

Conroy, Richard Maurice (Maurice) RB/RH
b Bradford 26/4/1919 d 2006
1937 Fulham 0
1939 1948 Accrington Stanley 87 1
1939 (Accrington Stanley) (3) (2)
1949 Rotherham United 0
1950 Scunthorpe United 1

Conroy, Thomas RB
b Walker q3 1913
Walker Celtic
1933 Darlington 0
1934 1938 Gateshead 183
1939 (Gateshead) (3)

Constantine, Clarence LB
b Bury q1 1909 d 1967
Black Lane Rovers
1931 Rochdale 2
Rossendale United

Conway, Arthur Joseph RH/CH
b Stirchley 1/4/1885 d 1954
1907 Aston Villa 0
1908 1909 Wolverhampton Wanderers 30
Worcester City

Conway, Herman GK
b Gainsborough 11/10/1908 d 1983
Gainsborough Trinity
1930 1933 Burnley 81
1934 1938 West Ham United 122
Tunbridge Wells Rangers
1945 Southend United 0

Conway, Thomas RB/RH
b Belfast
Willowfield
1928 Burnley 3
1932 Northampton Town 3

From	To		Apps	Goal
		Conwell, Laurence Doyle (Laurie)	IR	
		b Airdrie 26/9/1909	d 1972	
		Caps: IrLge 1		
		Arthurlie		
		Aberdeen		
		Portadown		
1935	1936	West Ham United	8	1
1937		Coventry City	2	
		Hinckley United		
		Cooch, Henry (Harry)	GK	
		b Wellingborough q1 1879	d 1944	
		Wellingborough		
		Finedon		
		Rushden		
		Kettering		
1901	1907	Aston Villa	25	
		Walsall		
		Coode, Jack	RH	
		b Oldham 8/3/1910	d 1972	
1934		Manchester United	0	
1935		Halifax Town	19	
		Cook, Albert	RB/CH/LH	
		b Stoke-on-Trent 1880	d 1949	
		North Staffs Nomads		
1901	1905	Burslem Port Vale	26	4
1906		Stoke	1	
1907		Stockport County	4	
		Northern Nomads		
		Burslem Port Vale		
		Stoke		
		Burslem Port Vale		
		Cook, Arthur Frederick	RB/LB	
		b Stafford q2 1889	d 1930	
		Old Wesleyans		
		Stafford Rangers		
		Wrexham		
1911	1921	West Bromwich Albion	38	
1921		Luton Town	0	
1922		Swansea Town	17	
		Whitchurch		
		Cook, Charles (Charlie)	OL/IL	
		b Glasgow 3/6/1898		
		Bellshill Athletic		
1920	1921	Bradford City	7	
1922		Bury	1	
		Morton		
		Queen of the South (loan)		
1923		Wigan Borough	3	
1923		Coventry City	3	
		Philadelphia Field Club		
1924		Bradford Park Avenue	2	
		Shawsheen Indians		
		Fall River Marksmen		
		New York Giants		
		Ayr United (trial)		
		Cook, Colin	CF	
		b North Shields 8/1/1909	d 1976	
		Percy Main		
1927	1928	South Shields	9	3
		North Shields		
1931		Bradford City	1	
		Crook Town		
1932	1933	Chesterfield	50	38
1934	1935	Luton Town	8	5
1936	1937	Northampton Town	12	3
		Horden Colliery Welfare		
		Cook, Eric James	RB	
		b 1914		
		Letchworth		
1933		Tottenham Hotspur	0	
1934		Newport County	4	1
		Cook, Frederick C (Fred)	OL	
		b Aberdare 20/1/1902	d 1966	
		Caps: Wales 8		
		Albions		
1922		Aberdare Athletic	8	1
1923	1925	Newport County	119	9
1925	1932	Portsmouth	247	41
1933		Southampton (trial)	0	
		Waterford		
		Cook, Frederick Charles (Fred)	OR	
		b Liverpool		
		South Liverpool		
1921	1922	Tranmere Rovers	19	
		Cook, Frederick William (Fred)	GK	
		b Hardingstone q1 1880	d 1934	
		Northampton Town		
1903	1904	West Bromwich Albion	28	
		Portsmouth		
		Cook, George	LB/RB/LH	
		b Shankhouse 20/11/1904		
		Bedlington United		
1924		Gillingham	7	
1924	1925	Preston North End	23	
1927		Torquay United	29	
1928		Carlisle United	23	
		Sittingbourne		
		Blyth Spartans		
1930		Everton	0	
1931		Tranmere Rovers	1	
1932		Carlisle United	5	
		Cook, George William (Billy)	IR/IL/CF	
		b Evenwood 27/2/1895	d 1980	
		Bishop Auckland		
1922		Rotherham County	42	8
1923	1926	Huddersfield Town	87	35
1926	1928	Aston Villa	57	35
1929	1930	Tottenham Hotspur	63	22
1931		Brentford	14	3
		Colwyn Bay United		
		Cook, Harry E	IL	
		b Liverpool 1882		
1905		Everton	7	3
		Cook, Henry (Harry)	LH/RH	
		b Middlesbrough q4 1893	d 1917	
1912	1914	Middlesbrough	23	
		Cook, Herbert (Bert)	IL	
		b Sheffield		
		Thorpe Hesley		
1910		Sheffield United	3	1
		Doncaster Rovers		
		Chesterfield Town		
		Mexborough Town		
		Halifax Town		
		Sheffield Old Boys		
		Cook, James	OR	
		b Kilbirnie 1885		
		Kilbirnie		
		Vale of Garnock		
		Celtic		
		Morton		
		Glasgow Benburb		
		Airdrieonians		
1906	1907	Grimsby Town	8	
		Plymouth Argyle		
		Cook, James Alexander (Alec)	IL/IR	
		b Trimdon Grange q4 1900		
		Trimdon Grange		
1922	1924	Hartlepools United	28	3
		Trimdon Grange		
		Spennymoor United		
		Cook, James Reginald (Jim)	LH	
		b Herrington q2 1904		
		Chester-le-Street		
1922		Grimsby Town	5	
		West Stanley		
		Cook, John (Jack)	IR/OL	
		b Sunderland 27/7/1887	d 1952	
		South Bank		
		Seaham Harbour		
1911	1914	Middlesbrough	52	3
1919	1923	Notts County	98	13
1924		Northampton Town	20	2
		Sneinton Thursday		
		Cook, Lawrence Whalley (Lol)	CF/OR/RB	
		b Preston 28/3/1885	d 1933	
		Nelson		
1904		Blackpool	7	
1905	1906	Preston North End	4	
		Lancaster		
		Southport Central		
1908		Gainsborough Trinity	9	3
		Rossendale United		
		Bacup		
		Chester		
1912		Stockport County	10	4
		Chester		
		Cook, R	CH/RB	
1893	1894	Walsall Town Swifts	32	1
		Cook, Reginald (Reg)	LB	
		b Scunthorpe		
		Scunthorpe & Lindsey United		
1933		Huddersfield Town	0	
1934		Rochdale	5	
		Cook, Robert	CF/LH	
		b Ardrossan		
		Ardrossan Winton Rovers		
		Kilmarnock		
		Galston		
1921		Chesterfield	6	
1922		Merthyr Town	5	
		Cook, Robert	LH	
		b Stockton		
1922		Darlington	1	
		Cook, Ronald (Ron)	IR	
		b South Normanton 23/9/1917	d 1998	
		Ripley Town		
1936		Mansfield Town	2	1
		Cook, Stanley	RB	
		Tunbridge Wells Rangers		
1936		Rochdale	1	
		Cook, Stanley	RH	
1939		Rotherham United	(2)	
		Scunthorpe & Lindsey United		
		Cook, Thomas Edwin Reed (Tommy)	CF/IL	
		b Cuckfield 5/2/1901	d 1950	
		Caps: England 1		
		Cuckfield		
1922	1928	Brighton & Hove Albion	190	114
		Northfleet		
1931	1932	Bristol Rovers	42	21
		Cook, W	OR	
1911		Bristol City	3	
		Bath City		
		Cook, Walter Charles	GK	
		b Welton 1/7/1894	d 1973	
		Castleford Town		
1921	1922	Plymouth Argyle	7	
1924	1925	Brighton & Hove Albion	52	
1926		Darlington (trial)	0	
1928		Stockport County	9	
		Harrogate AFC		
		Cook, William (Billy)	LB/RB	
		b Preston 16/1/1882	d 1947	
		Caps: FLge 1		
		St Stephen's (Preston)		
1901		Preston North End	0	
		Ashton Town		
		Rossendale United		
1907	1919	Oldham Athletic	157	16
		Rossendale United		
		Cook, William (Bill)	RB	
		b Usworth 2/3/1890	d 1974	
		Hebburn Argyle		
1912	1926	Sheffield United	264	
		Worksop Town		
		Cook, William (Billy)	RB/LB	
		b Coleraine 20/11/1909	d 1993	
		Caps: FLge 1/Ireland 15		
		Port Glasgow Athletic		
		Celtic		
1932	1938	Everton	225	5
1939		(Everton)	(3)	
1945		Wrexham	0	
		Ellesmere Port Town		
		Rhyl		
		Cook, William	IL/IR	
		b Darlington		
		Willington		
1930		Stoke City	0	
		Meadowfield		
1932		Darlington	15	2
		Spennymoor United		
		Crook Town		
1935		Gateshead	4	
		Horden Colliery Welfare		
		Cook, William Lawrence (Willie)	OL	
		b Dundee 11/3/1906	d 1981	
		Caps: SLge 2/Scotland 3		
		Dundee North End		
		Forfar Athletic		
		Dundee		
1928	1935	Bolton Wanderers	233	35
1936		Blackpool	19	1
1937		Reading	33	2
		Dundee		
		Cooke, Albert	LH/CH	
		b Royston, Yorkshire 11/4/1908	d 1988	
		Royston		
1928		Rochdale	1	
		Scunthorpe & Lindsey United		
1930	1931	Hull City	35	
1932	1935	Halifax Town	135	4
		Cooke, Edward	IR	
		b Govan 6/4/1896		
		St Anthony's (Glasgow)		
		Third Lanark		
		Abercorn (loan)		
		Armadale		
		Renton		
1920		Millwall Athletic	1	
		Dartford		
		Cooke, Edward	CF	
		Bolton Albion		
1930		Rotherham United	2	
		Cooke, Edwin	RB	
		b Kirkby-in-Ashfield 26/2/1903	d 1978	
		Kirkby Colliery		
		Mansfield Town		
1923		Barnsley	0	
1924		Brentford	6	
		Grantham		
		Mansfield Town		
		Cooke, Frederick Robert (Fred)	CF/IL	
		b Kirkby-in-Ashfield 5/7/1896	d 1976	
		East Kirkby		
1919	1920	Sunderland	12	5
1921	1922	Swindon Town	33	14
1923		Accrington Stanley	25	5
		Bangor City		
		Cooke, George Harry	OL	
		b Clowne 20/11/1899	d 1977	
		Clowne Colliery		
		Creswell White Star		
		Bolsover Town		
		Bolsover Colliery		
1921		Chesterfield	0	
		Shirebrook		
1923		Norwich City	4	
1924		Portsmouth	2	
1925		Southend United	2	
1926	1927	Wigan Borough	61	10
		Mansfield Town		
1929		Bradford Park Avenue	0	
		Connah's Quay & Shotton		
		Grantham		
		Cooke, J	LB	
1897		Darwen	1	
		Cooke, John Alfred	OL	
		Mansfield Wesleyans		
1898	1899	Derby County	11	2
		Cooke, Reuben James (James)	OR	
		b Ilkeston 1897		
		Ilkeston United		
		Mansfield Mechanics		
1919		Notts County	12	
		Ilkeston United		
		Cooke, Thomas	OR	
		Notts Rangers		
1888		Notts County	1	
		Cooke, Thomas S	CH	
1925		Aberdare Athletic	2	
		Cooke, Thomas Vincent	LB/CH	
		b Melton Mowbray 10/9/1913	d 1974	
		Sheepbridge		
1933		New Brighton	0	
1934	1935	Mansfield Town	13	
1936	1937	Bournemouth & Boscombe Ath	19	
1938		Luton Town	0	
		Sutton Town		
		Cooke, Wilfred Hudson (Wilf)	IL/RH/LH	
		b Crewe 10/10/1915	d 1985	
1934		Leeds United	0	
1936	1937	Bradford City	21	2
1938		Leeds United	0	
1939		Fulham	0	
1946		Crewe Alexandra	9	2
		Cooke, William	IR/CF	
1896	1897	Gainsborough Trinity	6	1
		Cooke, WJ	IR	
1898		Burton Swifts	1	
		Cookson, Alfred Ernest	LH	
		b Nottingham q2 1873	d 1910	
1896		Notts County	3	
		Newark		
1904		Nottingham Forest	0	
		Cookson, GH	OR	
1898		Gainsborough Trinity	2	

From	To	Club	Apps	Goal
Cookson, James (Jimmy)			CF	
b Manchester 6/12/1904			d 1970	
		South Salford Lads Club		
		Clayton		
		Manchester North End		
1923		Manchester City	0	
1924		Southport (trial)	0	
1925	1926	Chesterfield	74	85
1927	1931	West Bromwich Albion	122	103
1933	1935	Plymouth Argyle	46	37
1936	1937	Swindon Town	50	31
		Swindon Wednesday Corinthians		
Cookson, James Henry (Harry)			CF	
b Blackpool q1 1869			d 1922	
		South Shore		
		Burslem Port Vale		
		South Shore		
1892		Accrington	27	14
		South Shore		
Cookson, Samuel (Sam)			RB	
b Manchester 22/11/1896			d 1955	
		Stalybridge Celtic		
		Macclesfield		
1919	1927	Manchester City	285	
1928	1932	Bradford Park Avenue	136	
1933	1934	Barnsley	30	
Cookson, Samuel Percy			LH	
b Shrewsbury 17/1/1891			d 1974	
		Bargoed Town		
1914		Manchester United	12	
Cookson, Walter Stanley			IR/CF	
b South Shore q4 1879			d 1948	
		Nelson		
1901		Bristol City	16	5
1902		Blackpool	32	8
		Wellingborough		
		Brentford		
		Portsmouth		
1907		Blackpool	2	1
		Huddersfield Town		
Coomber (Comber), George Stephen			CH/RH	
b West Hoathly 19/1/1890			d 1960	
		Tottenham Thursday		
1912		Tottenham Hotspur	0	
		Tufnell Park		
1920	1924	Brighton & Hove Albion	168	1
Coombs, Ernest Howard			CF/OL	
b Writhlington 21/12/1912			d 2008	
		Writhlington		
		Coleford Athletic		
1931		Bristol Rovers	1	
1932		Bristol City	0	
		Bath City		
1933		Blackburn Rovers	6	
		Bath City		
		Cheltenham Town		
Coombs, Joseph (Joe)			RH	
b Ashington 2/3/1902			d 1971	
		Ashington Welfare		
1927	1928	Ashington	26	
		Wallaw United		
		Pegswood United		
Cooper, Alfred (Alf)			OL	
b Manchester				
		Middleton		
1919		Sheffield Wednesday	3	
		Rotherham Town		
Cooper (Routledge), Anthony			IR	
b Derby 7/4/1893			d 1974	
		Hetherington Colliery		
1919		Sheffield Wednesday	1	
1920		Barnsley	0	
Cooper, Arthur			GK	
b Sheffield 1895				
		Beighton		
1914		Birmingham	0	
1919	1921	Barnsley	99	
1922		Oldham Athletic	9	
Cooper, Arthur			CF	
b Manchester				
		Ashton National		
1927		Crewe Alexandra	9	3
		Mossley		
		Buxton		
Cooper, C			RH	
1906		Burton United	1	
Cooper, Charles Robert			RB	
b Belper 10/1894				
1921		Derby County	0	
1922		Portsmouth	4	
1923		Queen's Park Rangers	0	

From	To	Club	Apps	Goal
Cooper, Duncan			LB	
b Middlewich 1880				
		Witton Albion		
1901		Burslem Port Vale	5	
Cooper, E			CF	
1899		Gainsborough Trinity	4	1
Cooper, Edward			OR	
b Walsall q4 1891				
		Stafford Rangers		
1912		Glossop	24	5
1912	1919	Newcastle United	45	2
1920		Notts County	4	
		Stafford Rangers		
Cooper, Frank B			IL	
1900		Bury	1	
Cooper, Fred			OR	
b Bolton 1900				
		Bolton St Mary's		
1921		Accrington Stanley	1	
Cooper, Harry G			OL	
1929		Stockport County	1	
Cooper, Horace George Humphrey			GK	
b Maidenhead 16/4/1899			d 1962	
		Reading Phoenix		
		Reading Liberal Club		
1920		Reading	1	
Cooper, J			CF/IL	
1899	1900	Burton Swifts	25	7
Cooper, John			CF/IR	
b Wednesbury				
		Darlaston		
1921	1922	Southampton	5	
1923		Notts County	0	
Cooper, John (Jack)			CF	
b Smethwick				
1929		Birmingham	0	
1930		Walsall	14	15
1931		Torquay United	14	7
Cooper (Holloway), John Denman (Jack)			GK	
b Nottingham 25/2/1887			d 1952	
		Sutton Town		
1908	1914	Barnsley	172	
1920	1921	Newport County	81	
Cooper, John Henry (Jack)			CH/LH	
b Smethwick 22/10/1904			d 1980	
1929		Walsall	3	
1930	1931	Bristol Rovers	22	
Cooper, John William			OR	
b Bebside q3 1906				
		Bebside Gordon		
		Blyth Spartans		
1924		Ashington	2	
		Bebside Gordon		
		Blyth Spartans		
		New Delaval Villa		
		Bebside Gordon		
Cooper, Joseph			IR/CF/OR	
b Wolverhampton 1865				
		Milton		
1888	1890	Wolverhampton Wanderers	24	6
1893		Woolwich Arsenal	6	
Cooper, Joseph (Joe)			IR/IL	
b Newbold q3 1899			d 1959	
		Sheepbridge Works		
1919		West Bromwich Albion (trial)	0	
		Saltley College		
1920		Sheffield Wednesday (trial)	1	
1921	1922	Chesterfield	53	14
1922	1923	Notts County	31	4
1924	1931	Grimsby Town	154	47
1932		Lincoln City	24	5
Cooper, Joseph (Joe)			LB/RB	
b Reddish 16/2/1918			d 1992	
1935		Oldham Athletic	0	
		Hurst		
1938		Blackpool	0	
1939	1946	Crewe Alexandra	3	
1939		(Crewe Alexandra)	(1)	
		Ashton United		
		Hyde United		
		Mossley		
Cooper, Kenneth Herbert Lionel (Ken)			OR	
b Ilford 20/2/1911			d 1971	
		Corinthians		
1932		Clapton Orient	4	
1933		Tottenham Hotspur	0	
		Corinthians		
		Stockton		

From	To	Club	Apps	Goal
Cooper, Lewis			OL/IL	
b Belper q4 1864			d 1937	
		Darley Dale		
		Derby County		
		Grimsby Town		
1888	1891	Derby County	50	23
Cooper, Reginald (Reg)			RH	
b Highworth 3/2/1899			d 1970	
		Swindon Victoria		
1922	1927	Swindon Town	92	
		Bath City		
Cooper, Robert			IR/OL	
b Southend-on-Sea				
1893		Middlesbrough Ironopolis	2	2
1894		Grimsby Town	2	
Cooper, Sedley			OL/IL	
b Garforth 17/8/1911			d 1981	
		Carlton Athletic		
1928	1930	Halifax Town	79	19
1933	1935	Sheffield Wednesday	18	4
1936		Huddersfield Town	5	1
1936	1938	Notts County	56	14
1939		(Notts County)	(2)	
Cooper, Sidney Mathew			IR	
b Carlisle 23/1/1902			d 1972	
		Carlisle Holmehead		
1928		Carlisle United	11	2
Cooper, Thomas (Tommy)			RB	
b Fenton 9/4/1904			d 1940	
Caps: FLge 5/England 15				
		Longton		
		Trentham		
1924	1925	Port Vale	32	
1925	1934	Derby County	248	1
1934	1938	Liverpool	150	
Cooper, Thomas A (Tommy)			CH	
		Burton Town		
1931		Walsall	3	
		Leamington Town		
Cooper, W			CF	
1906		Burton United	1	
		SS Mary & Modwens		
Cooper, William (Willie)			LH	
b Mexborough 1886				
		Denaby United		
1906		Barnsley	2	
		Portsmouth		
		Dundee		
		Castleford Town		
		Rochdale		
		Lincoln City		
Cooper, William George Edward			IL/OR/CF	
b York 2/11/1917			d 1978	
1938		Halifax Town	2	
1946	1947	Bradford City	7	4
1948		Rochdale	0	
Cooper, William Thomas			OL	
b Denaby				
		Bangor City		
1928		Rotherham United	4	
Cooperthwaite, John			LB/IL	
b Gosforth 21/8/1901			d 1982	
		Coxlodge		
		Durham City (trial)		
		Carlisle United		
		Gosforth		
1921		Ashington	0	
		Coxlodge British Legion		
1922	1927	Durham City	41	3
1928	1929	Carlisle United	5	2
		Spennymoor United		
Coopland, Walter Ernest (Ernest)			RH/OL	
b Sheffield 1/3/1900				
		Birley Carr		
1919		Arsenal	1	
1922		Exeter City	9	
1923		Aberdare Athletic	0	
Coote, Stanley Arthur (Stan)			CH/RB	
b Harpenden 7/5/1909			d 1973	
		Arden Wednesday		
1932		Luton Town	1	
1935	1936	Reading	6	
Cope, Alfred George (Alf)			LB	
b Coppenhall q3 1867			d 1932	
1892	1895	Crewe Alexandra	87	
Cope, Ernest			LB	
b Coppenhall q4 1875			d 1918	
1894	1895	Crewe Alexandra	5	

From	To	Club	Apps	Goal
Cope, George			CH	
b Crewe 26/1/1915			d 1988	
		Crewe Alexandra	0	
		Nantwich		
1936	1945	Crewe Alexandra	14	
Cope, Harold			GK	
b Rawmarsh 9/2/1902			d 1980	
		Parkgate Works		
		Rawmarsh Athletic		
		Mexborough Town		
1921		Birmingham (trial)	0	
1922	1924	Barnsley	32	
		Mexborough Town		
1926	1929	Blackburn Rovers	25	
1930	1931	Swindon Town	68	
		Stalybridge Celtic		
		Harrow Sheet Metal Works		
Cope, Horace Walter			LB	
b Treeton 24/5/1899			d 1961	
		Treeton Reading Rooms		
		Treeton United		
1920	1926	Notts County	125	6
1926	1932	Arsenal	65	
1933		Bristol Rovers	0	
Cope, John James (Jack)			LH/OL	
b Ellesmere Port 1/8/1908			d 1995	
		Llanelly		
1933	1937	Bury	67	2
1938		Ipswich Town	4	
Cope, John Thomas (Tom)			GK	
b Bilston q1 1880				
		Clowne White Star		
1905	1908	Chesterfield Town	127	
		Portsmouth		
1910		Sunderland	0	
		Frickley Colliery		
		Clowne Rising Star		
Cope, John William			RH/CH	
b Milton 23/11/1899			d 1979	
		Leek Alexandra		
1925	1928	Bolton Wanderers	79	
1929	1933	Port Vale	121	
Cope, T			GK	
1894		Crewe Alexandra	5	
Cope, William Arthur (Billy)			LB/RB	
b Stoke-on-Trent 25/11/1884			d 1937	
		Mount Pleasant		
1904	1906	Burslem Port Vale	73	1
1907		Stoke	25	
1908	1913	Oldham Athletic	62	1
1919	1921	West Ham United	106	
1922		Wrexham	13	
Copeland, Charles William (Charlie)			RB	
b Grangetown 12/3/1892				
		South Bank		
1912	1914	Leeds City	44	
1919		Coventry City	32	
1920		Merthyr Town	8	
Copeland, David Campbell			CF/IL/IR	
b Ayr 2/4/1875			d 1931	
		Ayr Parkhouse		
1893	1897	Walsall Town Swifts	76	19
		Bedminster		
		Tottenham Hotspur		
1905	1906	Chelsea	26	9
1907		Glossop	2	
		Ayr Parkhouse		
Copeland, H			GK	
1897	1898	Gainsborough Trinity	6	
Copeland, James Leslie (Leslie)			CF	
b Chorlton-cum-Hardy 1/10/1909			d 1991	
		Polygon Electric		
1930		Manchester United	0	
		Mossley		
		Park Royal		
1932		West Ham United	0	
1933	1934	Chelsea	2	1
		Linfield		
1937		Halifax Town	22	6
Copeman, Robert (Bobby)			RB	
b Washington q1 1912			d 1953	
		Washington Colliery		
1937		Hartlepools United	1	
		Washington Chemical Works		
Copestake, Levi			OL/OR	
b Kiveton Park q4 1886			d 1968	
		Worksop Town		
1905	1906	Blackpool	21	1
1907		Bristol City	2	1
		Exeter City		
1910	1912	Bristol City	41	5

From To Apps Goal

Copitch, Israel (Jack) GK
b High Cheetham q2 1903 d 1962
Ancoats Lads Club
1925 Southport 2
Manchester North End
Hyde United
Grove House (Manchester)

Copitch, Woolf (Bill) IR
b High Cheetham q1 1901 d 1974
Macclesfield
Stalybridge Celtic
1920 Blackburn Rovers 0
1921 Tranmere Rovers 0
Darwen
Bath City
Hurst
1924 Stockport County 0
1925 New Brighton 3 1
Bootle
Colwyn Bay United
Connah's Quay & Shotton
Northwich Victoria
Boston Town (trial)

Copley, Sydney Herbert OL
b Hucknall Torkard 1/11/1905 d 1986
Grantham
1926 Rotherham United 2

Copping, Wilfred (Wilf) LH
b Middlecliffe 17/8/1909 d 1980
Caps: FLge 2/England War 1/England 20
Dearne Valley Old Boys
Middlecliffe & Darfield Rovers
1929 Barnsley (trial) 0
1930 1933 Leeds United 159 4
1934 1938 Arsenal 166
1938 Leeds United 12
1939 (Leeds United) (3)

Coquet, Ernest (Ernie) RB/LB
b Dunston-on-Tyne 6/1/1883 d 1946
Seaham White Star
Gateshead Town
1905 Sunderland 0
Reading
1908 1910 Tottenham Hotspur 76
Port Vale
1912 1914 Fulham 47
Leadgate Park

Corbett, David John RH
b Camelon 1/2/1910 d 1995
Old Plean Amateurs
Linlithgow Rose
Heart of Midlothian
Camelon Juniors
Ayr United
Dundee United
1936 West Ham United 4
1938 Southport 1

Corbett, Francis James (Frank) RB/LB
b Willenhall 27/8/1903 d 1970
Hednesford Primitives
Hednesford Town
1926 1929 West Bromwich Albion 12
1931 Coventry City 6
Burton Town
Hednesford Town

Corbett, Frederick Herbert (Fred) CF/IR
b Stepney 8/1880 d 1924
Old St Luke's
Thames Ironworks
Bristol Rovers
1903 1904 Bristol City 49 14
Bristol Rovers
Brentford
Bristol Rovers
New Brompton
Merthyr Town

Corbett, Frederick William (Fred) LB/RB
b Birmingham 8/10/1909 d 1974
1927 Birmingham 0
Worcester City
1929 Torquay United 21 1
1932 1935 Manchester City 15
1936 1938 Lincoln City 103

Corbett, Joseph LH
b Brierley Hill 19/6/1902 d 1973
Cradley Heath Victoria
1919 Aston Villa (trial) 0
Brierley Hill Alliance
1923 1926 Aston Villa 7
Stourbridge

Corbett, Norman George (Norrie) RH/RB
b Falkirk 23/6/1919 d 1990
Musselburgh
Heart of Midlothian
1936 1949 West Ham United 166 3

From To Apps Goal

Corbett, Percy Baxter IL
b Penn 2/1885 d 1948
Caps: England Amat
Old Wulfrunians
1906 1907 Wolverhampton Wanderers 6 3
Old Wulfrunians

Corbett, Richard Turner RB
b Lawley Bank q2 1883 d 1942
Willenhall Swifts
1909 West Bromwich Albion 3
Walsall
Bilston United

Corbett, Victor John Stanley (Vic) LB/RB
b Birmingham 27/1/1908 d 1984
Bromsgrove Rovers
Worcester City
Hereford United
1933 Manchester City 5
1935 Southend United 1
Brierley Hill Alliance

Corbett, Walter Samuel (Watty) RB/RH/LB
b Wellington 26/11/1880 d 1960
Caps: England Amat/England 3
Thornhill
Astbury Richmond
Headingley
Soho Villa
Queen's Park Rangers
1904 1906 Aston Villa 13
1907 Birmingham 11
Queen's Park Rangers
1908 Birmingham 15
Wellington Town
1909 1910 Birmingham 20
Wolverhampton Old Church

Corcoran, Patrick (Patsy) OR
b Glasgow 16/6/1893
Mossend Hibernian
Clyde
Shelbourne (loan)
Royal Albert (loan)
Hamilton Academical (loan)
Renton (loan)
Albion Rovers (loan)
Celtic (loan)
Royal Albert (loan)
Hamilton Academical
Bathgate
1920 1925 Plymouth Argyle 188 27
Torquay United
1926 Luton Town 0
Bathgate
East Stirlingshire

Corcoran, Thomas (Tommy) LB/RB
b Earlestown 9/1/1907 d 1969
1926 Bolton Wanderers 0
Horwich RMI
Atherton
1929 Bradford City 3
1930 Rochdale 24
Guildford City
1932 1934 Accrington Stanley 64 1
Prescot Cables

Corfield, Samuel George (Sam) CH/RH
b Tipton q1 1883 d 1951
Toll End Wesley
1903 West Bromwich Albion 8
1905 1906 Wolverhampton Wanderers 44 3
Wrexham
Tipton Victoria

Corfield, William RH
1893 Burslem Port Vale 3 1

Corkhill, William Grant (Bill) RH/LB/CH
b Belfast 23/4/1910 d 1978
Northern Nomads
Marine
1930 Liverpool
1931 1937 Notts County 166 9
1938 Cardiff City 23
1939 (Cardiff City) (3)
1945 1951 Notts County 98

Corkindale, William Joseph (Billy) OL/OR
b Langley Green 19/5/1901 d 1972
Wellington Town
1923 1925 Swansea Town 18 2
1926 1928 Clapton Orient 96 17
1929 1930 Millwall 40 4
1932 Luton Town 1
Shrewsbury Town

From To Apps Goal

Cornan, Francis (Frank) IL/LH
b Sunderland 5/5/1880 d 1971
Sunderland Black Watch
Willington
1902 1904 Barnsley 87 18
1905 1907 Birmingham 54 1
1908 Aston Villa 16
Spennymoor United
1909 Barnsley 0
Nelson
Exeter City
1912 Barnsley 6

Cornock, Matthew CF
b Chapelhall 23/6/1890 d 1961
Douglas Park (Hamilton)
Airdrieonians
Darlington
1911 Barnsley 12 5
Castleford Town

Cornthwaite, Christopher GK
b Bury 13/7/1917 d 1991
1935 1936 Rochdale 6

Cornthwaite, Thomas (Tommy) GK
b Sedbergh 1/5/1891 d 1956
1919 1922 Bury 90

Cornwell, Ralph Leslie LB
b Nottingham 7/9/1901 d 1988
Sneinton Institute
1923 1925 Notts County 42
1926 Norwich City 2
Mansfield Town
Sneinton Church Institute

Corrin, Thomas OL
b Liverpool q3 1878 d 1936
1900 Everton 3
Portsmouth
1903 Everton 8 1
Reading
Plymouth Argyle
Millwall Athletic
Reading

Cosgrove, Frederick (Fred) RB
b Hartlepool 14/11/1896
Felling
Durham City
1920 1930 Plymouth Argyle 103

Cosgrove, Michael Docherty (Mick) RH/CH
b Dundee 20/5/1901 d 1972
Dundee North End
Dundee Hibernian
1921 Tottenham Hotspur 0
Celtic
Brooklyn Wanderers
1924 Barnsley (trial) 0
Aberdeen
1928 1929 Bristol Rovers 58 6

Cosgrove, William Henry IR
b London 1898
Custom House
1923 Gillingham 15 3

Coshall, John William Macdonald LB
b Erith 21/1/1901 d 1975
Erith
1928 West Ham United 2
AS Cannes

Costelli, John RB
Altrincham
Rochdale
1913 Glossop 7

Costello, J OL
1893 Middlesbrough Ironopolis 1

Costigan, Thomas Stephen IL
b Tynemouth q1 1881 d 1962
Wallsend Park Villa
Seaham Harbour
1910 Lincoln City 2 1
Wallsend Park Villa

Costley, James L OL
b Liverpool q1 1862 d 1931
Blackburn Olympic
1888 Everton 6 3

Cothliff, Harold Thomas RH/IL
b Liverpool 24/3/1916 d 1976
Prescot Cables
1936 Manchester City 0
1937 Nottingham Forest 0
1938 1947 Torquay United 65 1
1939 (Torquay United) (3)
Ilfracombe Town

Cotterill, Thomas CF
b Chilvers Coton 1874
1895 Loughborough 6 3

From To Apps Goal

Cottingham, Thomas McLanaghan (Tom) IR
b Camlachie 1/10/1901
Parkhead Juniors
Hamilton Academical
1922 Luton Town 1
Airdrieonians
Dundee United
Carlisle United
Weymouth
Bo'ness
Queen of the South
Alloa Athletic

Cottle, Joseph Richard (Joe) LB
b Bedminster q3 1886 d 1958
Caps: England 1
Eclipse
Dolphins (Bristol)
1905 1910 Bristol City 204
Bristol Rovers

Cotton, ? OL
1898 Blackpool 1

Cotton, Francis Charles T (Charlie) GK
b East Stonehouse q1 1881 d 1910
Sheppey United
Reading
West Ham United
1903 Liverpool 12
West Ham United
Southend United

Cotton, Henry (Harry) GK
b Crewe 5/4/1882 d 1921
Nantwich
1901 1904 Burslem Port Vale 124
Crewe Alexandra
Stoke
Eccleshall AS

Cotton, R OL/OR
1895 1896 Burton Swifts 3 1

Cotton, William Charles (Billy) IR/CF
b Liverpool 10/4/1894 d 1971
South Liverpool
Garston
1921 1923 Wrexham 88 34
Kettering Town
1925 Port Vale 0
Connah's Quay & Shotton
Buckley United
1925 Halifax Town 5 3
1926 Crewe Alexandra 14 5
Connah's Quay & Shotton
Yeovil & Petters United
Buckley United
Prescot Cables
Brenka

Cottrell, Alfred Thomas LH
b Bristol 18/2/1913 d 1997
Dockland Settlement
1933 1934 Bristol City 4
1937 Northampton Town 1
Worcester City

Cottrell, Ernest Herbert IR
b Grantham 31/1/1877 d 1929
1895 Nottingham Forest 0
Newark
Hucknall St John's
Sheppey United
Stockport County
1898 1900 Woolwich Arsenal 24 12
Watford
Fulham
1903 Stockport County 1
Workington
Coventry City
Nuneaton Town

Couchlin, David LH
b Inchinnan 1879
Renfrew Victoria
1901 Barnsley 11
Thornliebank

Coulbeck, Thomas (Toy) IR/IL
b Caistor q3 1885 d 1955
Cleethorpes Town
1907 1909 Grimsby Town 13 4
1910 1911 Gainsborough Trinity 56 9
Cleethorpes Town
Gainsborough Trinity
Cleethorpes Town
Haycroft Rovers

Coule, John CF
b Stockport
1920 Sheffield United 0
1921 Crewe Alexandra 1

From To Apps Goal

Coull, Charles (Charlie 'Chic') CH
b Dundee 27/11/1912 d 1991
Stobswell Juniors
Arden Lea
Celtic
1934 Clapton Orient 4
1935 Southport 2
1935 Clapton Orient 0
Portadown
Stobswell
Dundee Corporation Transport

Coulson, Ernest OR
b Leicester q4 1878 d 1964
Leicester Excelsior
1898 Leicester Fosse 0
Hugglescote Robin Hoods
Ratby Swifts
1900 1901 Burton Wanderers/Burton United 0
Allsopp's Brewery
1902 Chesterfield Town 0
1903 Leicester Fosse 1
Leicester Imperial

Coulson, William Henry (Henry) IR
b Hugglescote q2 1876 d 1939
Leicester Excelsior
1897 Leicester Fosse 1 1
Hugglescote Robin Hoods
Ratby Swifts
1900 1901 Burton Wanderers/Burton United 0
Allsopp's Brewery
1902 Chesterfield Town 0
1903 Leicester Fosse 0
Leicester Imperial
Syston Robin Hoods

Coulston, Walter OR
b Wombwell 31/1/1912 d 1990
Hemsworth West End
South Kirkby Colliery
1933 Manchester City 0
1936 Crystal Palace 12 1
1937 Exeter City 32 2
1938 Barnsley 0
1938 Notts County 1
1939 (Notts County) (2)

Coulter, H IL/IR
1895 1896 Darwen 6

Coulter, John (Jackie) OL
b Whiteabbey 1912 d 1981
Caps: IrLge 2/Ireland 11
Carrickfergus
Brantwood
Dunmurry
Cliftonville
Distillery
Belfast Celtic
1933 1937 Everton 50 16
1937 Grimsby Town 25 11
1938 Chester 4
1939 Swansea Town (3)
Chelmsford City

Coulthard, ? CF
1893 Middlesbrough Ironopolis 8 4

Coulthard, Ernest Talbot OR
b South Hylton q4 1884 d 1968
Sunderland West End
1908 1909 Barnsley 31 2
Sunderland Rovers

Coulthard, Frank OL
b Cockerton q4 1910
Bushbury
Featherstone (Staffs)
1930 Wolverhampton Wanderers 0
Stanhope
Evenwood Town
1934 Hartlepools United 4
Worcester City
Hereford United

Coulthard, Thomas de Aar (Tom) RB/LB/RH
b Darlington 12/2/1900 d 1971
Darlington Railway Institute
1921 Newcastle United 0
1924 1925 Norwich City 40 1
Ebbw Vale
1928 1930 Carlisle United 97 1
Wallsend
West Stanley

Coulthard, William (Billy) RB
b Cockerton 27/9/1906 d 1978
Ferryhill Athletic
Ebbw Vale
1932 Tottenham Hotspur 0
Spennymoor United
1934 1936 Darlington 119
South Shields

From To Apps Goal

Coulton, Charles Crighton LB
b Birmingham q2 1868 d 1948
Mitchell St George's
1888 Aston Villa 0
Birmingham St George's
1892 Lincoln City 12

Coulton, Francis (Frank) LB
b Birmingham q3 1866 d 1929
Walsall Swifts
1888 1893 Aston Villa 38

Coundon, Cuthbert OR
b Sunderland 3/4/1905 d 1978
Jarrow
1925 1927 Southampton 26 3
1928 Wolverhampton Wanderers 13 1
1929 Southend United 0
Guildford City
Tunbridge Wells Rangers

Counsell, Henry James (Harry) RB
b Preston 10/4/1909 d 1990
Chorley
1930 Nelson 3
Great Harwood
Clitheroe
Lancaster Town

Coupar, James (Jimmy) IR/CF/LH
b Dundee 3/1869 d 1953
Dundee Our Boys
1892 Newton Heath 21 5
St Johnstone
1894 Rotherham Town 19 9
1897 Luton Town 26 9
Swindon Town
Linfield
Swindon Town
1901 Newton Heath 11 4

Coupar, Peter CF
b Dundee 1867
Dundee
1889 Stoke 11 3
Dundee
1892 Newton Heath 0

Coupar, Thomas CF/OL
b Dundee 1862
1888 1889 Bolton Wanderers 5 1

Coupe, Daniel RB
b Worksop q2 1885 d 1954
Worksop Town
1909 Manchester City 1

Coupe, John Clement (Jack) CH
b Walton-le-Dale 11/6/1913 d 1988
1933 Preston North End 0
Fleetwood
1938 Accrington Stanley 1

Coupe, Thomas GK
b Rishton
Great Harwood
1899 Blackburn Rovers 1
Accrington Stanley
1901 Blackburn Rovers 0
Chorley
Great Harwood
Accrington Stanley
Padiham

Coupe, W OR
1898 New Brighton Tower 7

Couper, George OR
b Scotland 1880
Heart of Midlothian
1906 1907 Everton 4 1

Coupland, Clifford (Baggy) RH
b Grimsby 29/5/1900 d 1969
Haycroft Rovers
Grimsby Rovers
1921 1922 Grimsby Town 43 2
Mansfield Town
1925 1926 Manchester City 24 2
1927 Grimsby Town 13
Caernarvon Athletic
Sittingbourne
1930 Crystal Palace 0

Court, Harold John (Jack) IR
b Tir Phil 13/6/1919 d 1975
Llanbradach
1938 Cardiff City 1
Dundee
1950 Swindon Town 16 2
Weymouth

From To Apps Goal

Court, Richard Charles (Dick) CF
b India 23/10/1916
Ryde Sports
1937 1938 Aldershot 10 1
1939 Brighton & Hove Albion 0

Courtney, Frederick Hubert OL
b Barnstaple 15/6/1910 d 1988
South Molton
1930 1931 Exeter City 3
South Molton

Courts, Frank CH
b Rotherham 19/2/1909 d 1976
Dinnington Athletic
1935 Blackburn Rovers 0
1936 1945 Rotherham United 34
1939 (Rotherham United) (3)

Cousins, Harold (Harry) RH/LH
b Pilsley 25/9/1907 d 1981
North Wingfield
1926 1931 Chesterfield 86
1932 1946 Swindon Town 272 1
1939 (Swindon Town) (1)

Cousins, Harry Douglas IR
b Coundon Grange 6/12/1896 d 1978
Tanfield Lea Institute
West Stanley
Annfield Plain
1921 Durham City 37 17
1922 Stockport County 14 3
1923 1924 Southport 44 13
Bangor City
1925 Ashington 8 3
1926 Nelson 0
Stalybridge Celtic

Cousins, William Alfred OR
b Norwich 1/12/1902 d 1983
Boulton & Paul
City Wanderers
Gorleston
1926 1928 Norwich City 26
Boulton & Paul
Gorleston

Coutanche, Wilfred John LB
b Sherborne q2 1895 d 1960
Callow Land
Watford Orient
St Albans City
1921 1922 Watford 6
Tufnell Park
Ilford

Coutts, Thomas (Tom) LH/RH
b Gateshead 10/5/1902 d 1968
Saltwell Villa
1923 1925 Ashington 46
Dunston Atlas Villa
1927 Leeds United 1
1928 Southampton 0
Newport (Isle of Wight)

Coutts, William Farquharson (Billy) IL
b Edinburgh 26/6/1909 d 1991
Edinburgh Ashton
Dunbar United
Heart of Midlothian
Leith Athletic (loan)
1934 1938 Leicester City 48 4
1939 (Leicester City) (2)

Coverdale, Robert LH/IR/RH
b West Hartlepool 16/1/1892 d 1959
Rutherglen Glencairn
1914 1920 Sunderland 21
1921 1923 Hull City 63 5
1924 Grimsby Town 30 1
Bridlington Town

Covey, Albert Sidney (Bert) IL
b Swindon q1 1895 d 1969
Eastcott Hill
1920 Swindon Town 1
Trowbridge Town
Bath City

Cowan, David IL
b West Carron 30/11/1910
Alva Albion Rovers
1930 Rochdale 24 2
Stenhousemuir
Falkirk
Arbroath
Dumbarton

Cowan, J LH
1896 Darwen 12 1

From To Apps Goal

Cowan, James (Jimmy) CH
b Jamestown 17/10/1868 d 1918
Caps: Scotland 3
Vale of Leven
1889 1901 Aston Villa 316 22
Queen's Park Rangers

Cowan, James RB
1899 Middlesbrough 17

Cowan, John OL/OR
b Dumbarton 12/1870 d 1937
Vale of Leven
1892 1893 Preston North End 55 8
Rangers
1895 1898 Aston Villa 66 25
Dundee Harp

Cowan, Peter CH
Aberaman
1924 Merthyr Town 13

Cowan, Robert Bruce (Bob) CF/IR
b Wheatley Hill 14/1/1907 d 1996
Thornley Albion
Wheatley Hill Alliance
Crook Town
1925 Durham City 1
1926 Huddersfield Town 0
1928 1929 Watford 6 1
Rhyl Athletic
Blackhall Colliery Welfare
Leavesden Mental Hospital
1932 Aldershot 0
1933 Bristol Rovers 0

Cowan, Samuel (Sam) CH
b Chesterfield 10/5/1901 d 1964
Caps: FLge 1/England 3
Aldwark Juniors
1920 Huddersfield Town 0
Bullcroft Main Colliery
Denaby United
1923 1924 Doncaster Rovers 48 13
1924 1934 Manchester City 369 19
1935 1936 Bradford City 57 1
1937 Doncaster Rovers 0
Mossley

Cowan, Walter Gowans IR
b Dalziel 1874
Motherwell
1895 1896 Sunderland 17 7
Motherwell

Cowan, William CF
b Gateshead 28/11/1900 d 1979
High Fell
1925 1926 Hull City 11 8
1927 Blackpool 1
1928 Chesterfield 7 6
1929 York City 0
National Radiator (Hull)

Cowan, William Duncan (Billy) IR/IL
b Edinburgh 9/8/1896 d 1965
Caps: Scotland 1
Dalkeith Thistle
Tranent Juniors
Dundee
1923 1925 Newcastle United 87 23
1926 Manchester City 22 11
St Mirren
Peebles Rovers
Harrogate Town
Northfleet (trial)
North Shields
1930 Hartlepools United 3 2
1930 Darlington 7 1
Bath City
Wolviston St Peter's

Coward, William Charles (Billy) OR
b Windsor 28/12/1905 d 1995
Windsor & Eton
Wycombe Wanderers
1927 1931 Queen's Park Rangers 126 24
1932 Walsall 35 8
Yeovil & Petters United
Bath City

Cowell, ? RH
1920 South Shields 1

Cowell, Arthur LB
b Lower Darwen 20/5/1886 d 1959
Caps: FLge 1/England 1
Blackburn St Peter's
Nelson
1905 1919 Blackburn Rovers 280

Cowell, Herbert IR
1920 West Ham United 1

From To Apps Goal

Cowell, John (Jack) CF
b Blyth 9/6/1887
Caps: IrLge 3
Springwell
Rowland's Gill
Spen Black & White
Castleford Town
Selby Mizpah
Rotherham Town
1908 1910 Bristol City 37 20
1910 Sunderland 14 5
Distillery
Belfast Celtic
Durham City

Cowell, William (Billy) GK
b Acomb, Northumberland 7/12/1902 d 1999
Caps: England Sch
Newburn
Mickley
Newburn
1922 1923 Huddersfield Town 9
1924 1925 Hartlepools United 78
1926 Derby County 1
1926 1927 Grimsby Town 39
1928 Millwall 0
1929 Carlisle United 1

Cowen, James (Jimmy) LH
b North Wingfield
Bentley United
Sheffield Wednesday 0
Doncaster Rovers
1921 Chesterfield 1
Doncaster Rovers
Gainsborough Trinity

Cowen, James Ernest (Jimmy) IL/CF
b Distington 22/1/1902 d 1950
Hensingham
Whitehaven Athletic
1925 Nelson 3 4
Barnoldswick Town
1927 1928 Northampton Town 1
1929 1932 Southport 129 55
1933 Aldershot 3 1
Peterborough United
Westwood Works
Peterborough PO Engineers

Cowen, Robert William IR
b Chester-le-Street 21/9/1886 d 1949
Spen Black & White
1914 Leeds City 2
Spen Black & White

Cowie, Andrew OL
b Lochee 21/10/1878
Dundee Harp
Thames Ironworks
Gravesend United
1898 Manchester City 11 3
Queen's Park Rangers
1900 Woolwich Arsenal 0

Cowie, Charles (Charlie) CH
b Carron 23/4/1907 d 1971
Carron Welfare
St Ninian's Thistle
Heart of Midlothian
1930 Barrow 33
Dunfermline Athletic
1933 1935 Barrow 80
1938 Ipswich Town 6

Cowie, James George (Jimmy) CF
b Keith 8/6/1904 d 1966
Keith Strathlisa
Raith Rovers
Arbroath (loan)
1929 1930 York City 18 9
Keith

Cowie, Stanley IR
b Sunderland 1891
King's Liverpool Regiment
Herrington Swifts
1911 Blackpool 3
Seaham Harbour
Exeter City
Barry

Cowley, Arthur OR
Brentford
Nunhead
1911 Huddersfield Town 5 2
Aberdare Town

Cowley, John Bennett (Jack) LH
b Winshill 3/2/1877 d 1926
Hinckley Town
1899 1901 Lincoln City 68 3
Swindon Town

From To Apps Goal

Cowley, John S GK
b Mexborough 1886
Mexborough Town
1907 Barnsley 1

Cownley, Francis Frederick RB
b Swallownest 13/11/1892 d 1962
Scunthorpe & Lindsey United
1919 1921 Arsenal 15

Cowper, Peter Poole OR
b Tyldesley 1/9/1902 d 1962
Burns Celtic
Parkside Rangers
Atherton Collieries
1921 Bolton Wanderers (trial) 0
1923 Wigan Borough (trial) 0
Rossendale United
1924 West Ham United 2
1927 Grimsby Town 4
Lancaster Town
1928 1929 New Brighton 71 19
1930 1931 Southampton 5
1931 Southport 2 1
1932 Carlisle United 12 1
Wigan Athletic
Altrincham
Prescot Cables

Cox, Albert Edward Harrison LB
b Treeton 24/6/1917 d 2003
Woodhouse Mills United
1935 1951 Sheffield United 267 5
1952 1953 Halifax Town 54 1

Cox, Arthur OR
b Nottingham
Mexborough Town
1922 Southend United 1

Cox, Eric CH
Nunhead
1932 Bristol City 1

Cox, Frederick James Arthur (Freddie) OR
b Reading 1/11/1920 d 1973
St George's Lads Club
1936 Tottenham Hotspur 0
Northfleet
1938 1948 Tottenham Hotspur 99 15
1949 1952 Arsenal 79 9
1953 West Bromwich Albion 4 1

Cox, George CF
b Warnham 23/8/1911 d 1985
Horsham
1933 1935 Arsenal 7 1
1936 Fulham 5 3
1937 Luton Town 0

Cox, Gershom RB/LB
b Birmingham 3/1863 d 1940
Excelsior
Walsall Town (trial)
1888 1892 Aston Villa 86
Willenhall Pickwick
Walsall Brunswick
Bloxwich Strollers

Cox, John (Jackie) LH
b Darvel 9/5/1910 d 1990
Darvel Juniors
Hamilton Academical
1938 Preston North End 5 1
Ayr United
Stranraer

Cox, John Davies (Jack) RH
b Spondon 1870 d 1957
Caps: England 1
Spondon
Long Eaton Rangers
1890 1899 Derby County 212 7

Cox, John Thomas (Jack) OL/OR
b Liverpool 21/12/1877 d 1955
Caps: FLge 3/England 3
South Shore Standard
South Shore
1897 Blackpool 17 12
1897 1908 Liverpool 327 72
1909 1911 Blackpool 66 6

Cox, S IL/OL
1893 1894 Walsall Town Swifts 4 1

Cox, Thomas Charles (Tommy) LH
b Woodford Bridge q3 1908
1928 West Ham United 0
1929 Fulham 5 1
West Ham Mental Hospital
North Ockendon

From To Apps Goal

Cox, Walter GK
b Scotland 1863
Hibernian
1888 1889 Burnley 27
1889 Everton 4
Nottingham Forest

Cox, Walter GK
b Southampton 1876
Southampton
Bristol St George
Bedminster
Millwall Athletic
1900 Manchester City 1
1901 Bury 0

Cox, William (Billy) CF
b Falkirk 22/10/1897
Govan YMCA
Renfrew Juniors
Whiteinch Glenbuck
Clydebank
Cardiff City
1920 Newport County 6 2
Vale of Leven
Workington
1922 Nottingham Forest 1
Workington

Cox, William Charles (Bill) OL/CF/IR
b Watford 19/3/1899 d 1987
Caps: England Sch
Leavesden Mental Hospital
Watford
1921 1925 Charlton Athletic 98 18
Sittingbourne

Cox, William Charles (Charlie) LB/LH/CH
b West Ham 31/7/1905 d 1978
Glico Works
Ilford
1927 1931 West Ham United 89
1932 Southend United 2

Cox, William James (Bill) CF
b Liverpool q2 1880 d 1915
Rossendale United
1903 Bury 4
Plymouth Argyle
1905 Leicester Fosse 3
Accrington Stanley
Oldham Athletic
1905 Preston North End 0
Dundee
Heart of Midlothian
Bradford Park Avenue

Coxford, John (Jack) CH/LH
b Seaton Hirst 25/7/1901 d 1978
North Seaton Colliery
Stakeford United
1924 1926 Sunderland 10
1927 1929 Birmingham 16
1930 1933 Bournemouth & Boscombe Ath 134 3
Poole Town
Northfleet

Coxon, Leybourne Wilson OL
b Lanchester 1/10/1914 d 2001
Burnhope Institute
1933 Barnsley 1

Coxon, Thomas (Tommy) OL
b Hanley 10/6/1883 d 1942
1902 1903 Burslem Port Vale 5 4
1903 1904 Stoke 25 5
Hanley Town
1905 Middlesbrough 11 1
1906 Burslem Port Vale 37 9
1907 Stoke 9 1
1908 1909 Grimsby Town 61 6
Cleethorpes Town
Leyton
Grimsby Rovers

Coyle, Terrance CH
b Broxburn 16/7/1897
Broxburn Athletic
Broxburn United
Heart of Midlothian
St Johnstone
Broxburn United
Heart of Midlothian
St Johnstone
East Fife
1925 1926 Crystal Palace 29 2
Stafford Rangers
Bromsgrove Rovers
Cookley

Coyle, WB IR
Glasgow Hibernian
1889 Burnley 2

From To Apps Goal

Coyne, J IR
Vale of Leven
1888 Everton 2 1

Crabtree, Frederick William OR
b West Bromwich 1865
Christ Church
1888 West Bromwich Albion 1 1
Old St Stephen's (Shepherds Bush)

Crabtree, James Joseph (Jimmy) GK
b Clitheroe 2/1895 d 1965
Caps: England Amat
Stronghurst Colliery
Clitheroe Amateurs
1913 1919 Blackburn Rovers 12
1921 1922 Rochdale 58 2
1923 1924 Accrington Stanley 7

Crabtree, James William (Jimmy) LH/LB/RB
b Burnley 23/12/1871 d 1908
Caps: FLge 9/England 14
Burnley Royal Swifts
1889 Burnley 3 1
Rossendale
Heywood Central
1892 1894 Burnley 69 9
1895 1901 Aston Villa 178 6
Plymouth Argyle

Crabtree, John (Jack) LH
1912 1913 Wolverhampton Wanderers 10
Worcester City

Crack, Frederick William (Fred) OL
b Lincoln 12/1/1919 d 2002
Lincoln CSOB
1935 1938 Grimsby Town 28 7
1939 (Grimsby Town) (1)
Lincoln CSOB

Cracknell, Richard (Dick) CH/RH
b Newcastle q4 1893
1914 Newcastle United 0
Crystal Palace
Maidstone United
1923 1925 Crystal Palace 47
Dartford

Craddock, Claude William (Joe) IR/CF/OR
b Grimsby 2/8/1902 d 1976
Chatham Central
1924 1925 Gillingham 16 3
Sittingbourne (loan)
Grays Thurrock (loan)
1926 1927 Brentford 23 11
Dundee
Sheppey United
1930 Rochdale 34 10
1931 Darlington 10 2
Tunbridge Wells Rangers

Cragg, Richard Hartley IR/CF
b Burnley 21/1/1891 d 1978
1919 Burnley 15 5
1920 Stockport County 21 3
1921 Accrington Stanley 6

Craggs, John (Jack) OR
b Trimdon Grange 1880
Trimdon Grange
1901 Sunderland 6 2
Reading
1903 1904 Sunderland 36 11
1904 1906 Nottingham Forest 52 7
Sutton Town
Houghton Rovers
West Stanley

Craig, Allan CH/LH
b Paisley 7/2/1904
Caps: SLge 2/Scotland 3
Paisley Carlisle
Saltcoats Victoria
Motherwell
1932 1938 Chelsea 196
Dartford

Craig, Arnott CH
b Motherwell
Wishaw
Motherwell
1929 1930 Swansea Town 3
Glentoran
Bangor
Waterford Celtic
Coleraine
Newry Town

From To | Apps Goal

Craig, Benjamin (Benny) RB/LB
b Leadgate 6/12/1915 d 1982
Medomsley Juniors
Leadgate
Ouston Juniors
Eden Colliery
1933 1938 Huddersfield Town 98
1938 1949 Newcastle United 66
1939 (Newcastle United) (3)

Craig, Charles Thomson (Charlie) RB/LB
b Dundee 11/7/1876 d 1933
Dundee Our Boys
Dundee
Dundee Wanderers
Dundee
Silvertown
Thames Ironworks
1902 1906 Nottingham Forest 136 2
1908 Bradford Park Avenue 6
Norwich City
Southend United
Merthyr Town

Craig, Edward Freeman (Teddy) CH/IR/IL
b Stewarton 9/2/1903 d 1982
Stewarton Thistle
1924 1929 Fulham 151 29
1930 1931 Bristol City 47 4
1932 1938 Halifax Town 287 5
1939 (Halifax Town) (3)

Craig, Francis G (Frank) IL
b Swansea
Llanelly
1924 Merthyr Town 0
1925 Fulham 0
1926 Bournemouth & Boscombe Ath 7 1

Craig, Frederick Glover (Fred) GK
b Larkhall 16/1/1891
Larkhall Thistle
Plymouth Argyle
Hamilton Academical
Ayr United
Motherwell
1920 1929 Plymouth Argyle 361 5
1930 Barrow 14

Craig, H CF
1895 Burton Swifts 6

Craig, John IR
b Lintz Colliery
Dipton United
1925 1926 Hartlepools United 30 6
1927 Crewe Alexandra 6 1
Chester

Craig, Thomas RB
b Scotland
1904 Middlesbrough 2
Falkirk
1906 Sunderland 0
1906 1907 Stockport County 36
Exeter City

Craig, Thomas (Tom) CF
b Tullibody
Rowlands Gill
Welbeck Athletic
1925 Ashington 1

Craigie, Charles M RH
b Dundee 1888
1909 1910 Glossop 32 3
1911 Notts County 0
1912 Fulham 0

Craik, Herbert Clark LH
b Greenock 1880
Morton
1903 Liverpool 1
Newton Swifts
Heart of Midlothian
Paisley Academicals

Crane, ? CH
b Liverpool
1900 Chesterfield Town 1

Crane, John Pringle LH
b Newcastle 23/12/1903 d 1990
Jesmond Villa
Durham University
Durham County Amateurs
Wallsend
Bede College
1925 Ashington 1
Annfield Plain
Jarrow Town

From To | Apps Goal

Crank, Joseph RB
b Leigh q3 1876 d 1946
Manchester Fairfield
1896 Notts County 1
Glossop North End
Manchester Fairfield
Oldham County
Berry's

Crapper, Christopher LB
b Rotherham 5/07/1884 d 1933
South Kirkby
1905 Sheffield Wednesday 1
1907 Grimsby Town 3
South Kirkby

Crapper, Joseph (Joe) OL/OR
b Wortley 3/3/1899 d 1989
Swallownest
1921 Notts County 2
1922 Huddersfield Town 0
Doncaster Rovers
1923 Swansea Town 3

Crate, Charles RH
b Newcastle q4 1894 d 1946
1922 Rotherham County 1

Crate, Thomas IR/CF
b Kilmarnock 1872
Newcastle East End
1893 1894 Newcastle United 39 14
Hebburn Argyle
Blyth Town
Seaton Burn
Morpeth
Ashington

Craven, Charles (Charlie) IL/IR
b Boston 2/12/1909 d 1972
Boston Trinity
Boston Town
1930 1937 Grimsby Town 256 95
1938 Manchester United 11 2
1938 Birmingham 17 2
Tamworth
Sutton Town

Craven, George GK
b York q4 1917
Fishergate Old Boys
1935 York City 3

Craven, John Rodger LH/OL
b Low Valley, Wombwell q1 1875 d 1952
1898 1899 Barnsley 20 1
Monk Bretton

Craven, Joseph Gerard (Joe) CH
b Preston 28/12/1903 d 1972
Frenchwood Villa
Preston YMCA
St Augustine's (Preston)
Croston
1923 1924 Stockport County 5
1925 1930 Preston North End 65 1
1931 1933 Swansea Town 49
1934 Port Vale 11
1935 Newport County 28
1936 1937 Accrington Stanley 57
Leyland Motors

Craven, Joseph McNae LB
b Paisley 15/2/1910
Mosspark Amateurs
Parkhead
Partick Thistle
1934 1935 Northampton Town 2
St Mirren

Craven, R IL
1891 Darwen 5 1

Craven, Richard OL
Oswaldtwistle Rovers
Rochdale
1908 Bolton Wanderers 2
Chorley

Crawford, Edmund Charles (Ted) CF/IL
b Filey 31/10/1906 d 1977
Scarborough Town
Scarborough Penguins
Filey Town
1931 Halifax Town 29 20
1932 Liverpool 7 4
1933 1938 Clapton Orient 200 67

Crawford, Gavin RH/OR
b Galston 24/1/1869 d 1955
Ash Lea
Fairfield Rangers (Glasgow)
Sheffield United
1893 1897 Woolwich Arsenal 122 13
Millwall Athletic
Queen's Park Rangers

From To | Apps Goal

Crawford, George William CH
b Sunderland 10/12/1905 d 1975
1926 Sunderland 0
1927 1928 Gillingham 40 1
1929 Bournemouth & Boscombe Ath 4
1930 Northampton Town 2

Crawford, Harold Sidney (Sidney) GK
b Dundee 7/10/1887 d 1979
1907 Newcastle United 0
Hebburn Argyle
1911 1912 Woolwich Arsenal 26
1920 1921 Reading 73
1922 1924 Millwall Athletic 77
Workington

Crawford, Herbert RH
Nantwich
Heywood Central
Nantwich
1893 1895 Crewe Alexandra 57
Nantwich

Crawford, James OR
b Leith 1877
Rangers
Abercorn
Reading
1898 1899 Sunderland 55 4
1900 1901 Derby County 42 1
1901 1902 Middlesbrough 24 1
1903 Sunderland 0

Crawford, James CF/IR
b Stirling
King's Park
1902 1903 Burnley 45 4
Colne

Crawford, John CH/LH
b Renton 23/2/1880 d 1934
Renton
1900 1902 Lincoln City 85 1
1902 1904 Nottingham Forest 13
Dumbarton

Crawford, John A OR
b Mossend
Newarthill Thistle
1928 Bury 1

Crawford, John Chalmers (Jock) GK
b Stirling 11/10/1902 d 1973
Fallin Violet
Stenhousemuir
Alloa Athletic
1924 1931 Blackburn Rovers 155
East Stirlingshire

Crawford, John Forsyth (Jackie) OR/OL
b Jarrow 26/9/1896 d 1975
Caps: England 1
Palmer's (Jarrow)
Jarrow Town
1919 1922 Hull City 126 9
1923 1932 Chelsea 288 25
1934 1936 Queen's Park Rangers 53 15

Crawford, Robert (Bob) CF
Clyde
1895 Bury 2
Clyde

Crawford, Robert (Bobby) LH
b Glespin 4/2/1901 d 1965
Glenbuck Cherrypickers
Raith Rovers
1921 1932 Preston North End 392 17
1932 1933 Blackpool 56 5
1934 1935 Blackburn Rovers 5
1936 1937 Southport 47 1
Lancaster City

Crawford, Robert Stuart (Bob) LB/RB
b Blythswood 4/7/1886
Barrhead Boys Club
Arthurlie
1908 1914 Liverpool 108 1

Crawford, Ronald RB
b South Africa
Lochee Central
St Johnstone
1930 Thames 3
1931 Rotherham United 3
St Johnstone
Arbroath

Crawford, William Alfred (Bill) IR
b Darlington q2 1872
Stockton
1893 Grimsby Town 7 6

From To | Apps Goal

Crawley, Felix Patrick (Frank) LB
b Paisley 22/5/1894 d 1945
Croy Celtic
Kirkintilloch Rob Roy
1921 1922 Blackburn Rovers 24 1
1923 Lincoln City 1
1924 Accrington Stanley 11
Toronto Dunlops
Toronto Bell Telephone
New Bedford Whalers
Brooklyn Wanderers

Crawley, Thomas Andrew (Tommy) CF/LH/CH
b Hamilton 10/11/1911 d 1976
Blantyre Victoria
St Mirren (trial)
Third Lanark (trial)
Hamilton Academical
Motherwell
1935 Preston North End 2
1935 1946 Coventry City 45 16
1939 (Coventry City) (3) (2)

Crawshaw, Aaron William (Billy) RH/LH
b Darwen 11/8/1895 d 1963
Royal Artillery (Topsham)
1920 Exeter City 28
1921 1922 Accrington Stanley 59
1923 1924 Exeter City 11
Taunton United

Crawshaw, Cyril OR/IR
b Barton-on-Irwell 2/3/1916 d 2003
Newton Heath Loco
Rossendale United
1936 Rochdale 2
Fleetwood
Rossendale United
Queen of the South
1945 Exeter City 0
1945 Stockport County 0
1946 Hull City 2 2
Stalybridge Celtic

Crawshaw, Harold William CF
b Prestwich 18/2/1912 d 1975
Newton Heath Loco
Ashington
1936 Portsmouth 1
1937 Mansfield Town 41 25
1938 Nottingham Forest 22 9

Crawshaw, Percy RH
b Sheffield 7/8/1879 d 1944
Worksop Town
1899 1904 Sheffield Wednesday 9

Crawshaw, Raymond (Ray) CH
b Padiham 12/8/1908 d 1975
Great Harwood
1929 Southport 0
Great Harwood
1931 Burnley 0
Great Harwood
1933 Accrington Stanley 19
1934 Birmingham 4
Bromsgrove Rovers

Crawshaw, Richard Leigh (Dick) IL/IR
b Manchester 21/9/1898 d 1965
Woodhouses
1919 1921 Manchester City 25 6
1922 Halifax Town 7
1922 1923 Nelson 32 10
Stalybridge Celtic
Mossley

Crawshaw, Thomas Henry (Tommy) CH
b Sheffield 27/12/1872 d 1960
Caps: FLge 8/England 10
Park Grange
Attercliffe
Heywood Central
1894 1907 Sheffield Wednesday 418 25
1908 Chesterfield Town 25
Castleford Town

Crayston, William John (Jack) RH/CH
b Grange-over-Sands 9/10/1910 d 1992
Caps: FLge 1/England War 1/England 8
Ulverston Town
1928 1929 Barrow 77 1
1930 1933 Bradford Park Avenue 96 15
1934 1938 Arsenal 168 16
1939 (Arsenal) (3)

Craythorne, Reuben (Ben) LH/IL
b Aston 21/1/1882 d 1953
Caps: FLge 1
Small Heath Athletic
Kidderminster Harriers
Coventry City
Walsall
1904 1913 Notts County 282 12
Darlington

From To Apps Goal

Creasor, Walter Cuthbert OL
b Middlesbrough 31/10/1902 d 1975
1923 Middlesbrough 0
1924 Darlington 6 1

Creegan, Walter Warden OR
b Manchester 4/6/1902 d 1967
1921 Arsenal 5

Creek, Frederick Norman Smith (Norman) CF
b Darlington 12/1/1898 d 1980
Caps: England Amat/England 1
Cambridge University
Corinthians
1921 Darlington 1 1
Corinthians
1923 Darlington 1
Corinthians

Creighton, Alexander (Alec) LB
b Greenock 7/7/1885
Distillery
1910 1911 Leeds City 66
Glenavon

Creighton, Thomas LB
b Springburn 29/7/1908
Strathclyde
Bo'ness
Armadale
1928 South Shields 1
1929 Merthyr Town 26

Crelley, John (Jack) LB
b Kirkdale q4 1881 d 1946
1899 1900 Everton 2
Millwall Athletic
1902 1907 Everton 114
Exeter City
St Helens Recreation

Cresser, Ernest (Eddie) LH
b Aston q2 1883 d 1926
Walsall
1905 1906 Stockport County 12
Leyton
Worcester City
Peterborough City
Barrow

Cresswell, Frank IL
b South Shields 5/9/1908 d 1979
Caps: England Sch
Tyne Dock
1925 South Shields 0
1926 1928 Sunderland 13 1
1929 West Bromwich Albion 30 6
1931 1933 Chester 97 26
1933 Notts County 16 4
1934 1937 Chester 76 31

Cresswell, Warneford (Warney) RB/LB
b South Shields 5/11/1897 d 1973
Caps: England Sch/FLge 5/England 7
North Shields Athletic
Heart of Midlothian
Hibernian
1919 1921 South Shields 99
1921 1926 Sunderland 182
1926 1935 Everton 290 1

Cretney, Jonathan T RH/IL
b Harrington 1879
1904 Newcastle United 0
1905 1910 Burnley 167 7
1911 Gainsborough Trinity 5
Croydon Common
Padiham

Crewdson, Robert (Bob) RB
b Lancaster q1 1881 d 1956
Fleetwood Mechanics
1904 1912 Blackpool 210

Crewe, William (Billy) RH/IR
b Little Lever 26/11/1901 d 1981
Great Lever
1922 Bolton Wanderers 4
1923 Wolverhampton Wanderers 7
1924 Tranmere Rovers 19
Pontypridd
1925 1928 Merthyr Town 131 10
1929 Southend United 1
1929 Merthyr Town 1
1930 Wigan Borough 24 4
Rhyl Athletic
Colwyn Bay United
Yeovil & Petters United
Burton Town
Mossley
Rhyl

From To Apps Goal

Crews, Alexander Norman (Alex) CH
b East Stonehouse 6/11/1888 d 1987
Green Waves
Plymouth Argyle
1911 Chelsea 0
1912 Leicester Fosse 1
1913 Stockport County 0

Cribb, Stanley Roy (Stan) OL
b Gosport 11/5/1905 d 1989
Gosport Athletic
1924 1929 Southampton 70 22
1930 West Ham United 0
1931 Queen's Park Rangers 28 12
1932 Cardiff City 27 11
Gosport Borough

Crichton, Alexander (Alec) LH
b Bellshill 12/6/1899
Blantyre Victoria
1924 Bradford Park Avenue 0
1925 Bristol Rovers 7

Crichton, William OL
b Paisley
1922 Rotherham County 8

Crielly, Robert RH
b Scotland
Newcastle East End
1893 1894 Newcastle United 54 1
Hebburn Argyle

Crilly, Thomas (Tommy) LB/RB
b Stockton 20/7/1895 d 1960
Stockton
1921 Hartlepools United 37
1922 1927 Derby County 197
1928 1932 Crystal Palace 116 1
1933 1934 Northampton Town 46 1
Scunthorpe & Lindsey United

Cringan, James A (Jimmy) RH/LH
b Douglas Water 12/1918
Armadale Thistle
1937 Bradford Park Avenue 6
1938 Wolverhampton Wanderers 0
1939 Cardiff City (3)

Cringan, James Anderson (Jimmy) CH/RH/LH
b Douglas Water 16/12/1904 d 1972
Douglas Water Thistle
1921 Sunderland (trial) 0
Dunfermline Athletic (trial)
Falkirk (trial)
1922 Bury 0
1923 1933 Birmingham 260 12
Boston United

Cringan, Robert OR
b Muirkirk
Ayr United
Hamilton Academical
Parkhead Athletic
1921 Portsmouth 1

Cringan, William (Billy) LH/RH
b Muirkirk 15/5/1890 d 1958
Caps: SLge 4/Scotland 5
Douglas Water Thistle
1910 1914 Sunderland 77 3
Wishaw Thistle (loan)
Ayr United
Celtic
Third Lanark
Motherwell
Inverness Thistle
Bathgate

Crinson, William James (Billy) GK
b Sunderland 6/1883 d 1951
Southwick (Co Durham)
1906 1907 Sheffield Wednesday 4
Huddersfield Town
Brighton & Hove Albion
Sunderland Rovers

Crisp, George Henry OL
b Pontypool 30/6/1911 d 1982
Melbourne Stars
Llanelly
1933 1934 Coventry City 8
1935 Bristol Rovers 22 6
1936 Newport County 10 1
Colchester United
1939 Nottingham Forest 0
Merthyr Tydfil

From To Apps Goal

Crisp, John (Jack) OR/OL/IR
b Hamstead 27/11/1896 d 1939
Caps: England Sch/FLge 1
Walsall
1913 Aston Villa (trial) 0
1913 Leicester Fosse 0
Ordnance
1914 1922 West Bromwich Albion 115 22
1922 1926 Blackburn Rovers 98 18
1926 1927 Coventry City 22 3
1928 Birmingham 0
Stourbridge
Bromsgrove Rovers
Cheltenham Town

Critchley, Edward (Ted) OR
b Ashton-under-Lyne 31/12/1904 d 1996
Cheadle
Witton Albion
1922 1926 Stockport County 118 10
1926 1933 Everton 217 37
1934 Preston North End 11 1
1934 Port Vale 18 1
South Liverpool

Critchley, James OR
b Bolton-on-Dearne 4/4/1909 d 1996
Goldthorpe United
Denaby United
1931 1932 Doncaster Rovers 15 1
Thurnscoe Victoria

Critchlow, Richard Harold (Dick) RB/LB
b Birkenhead q2 1897
Runcorn
1923 1924 New Brighton 10
Chester
Congleton Town
Northwich Victoria

Croal, James Anderson (Jimmy) IL
b Glasgow 27/7/1885 d 1939
Caps: SLge 3/Scotland 3
Falkirk Juniors
Rangers
Ayr Parkhouse (loan)
Alloa Athletic (loan)
Dunfermline Athletic (loan)
Falkirk
1914 1921 Chelsea 113 22
Falkirk (loan)
Dunfermline Athletic (loan)
1921 1923 Fulham 36 6

Crockford, Harold Arthur CF/IL/IR
b Derby 25/9/1893 d 1983
Chatham
1919 1920 Fulham 26 9
1922 Exeter City 30 17
1923 Port Vale 6 2
1923 1924 Chesterfield 52 28
1924 Gillingham 7 1
1925 Accrington Stanley 11 5
1925 Walsall 24 17
1926 Darlington 18 8
1927 Norwich City 2
Bedford Town
Tunbridge Wells Rangers

Croft, Henry (Harry) IL/OL
b Bolton 1898
Astley Bridge
1920 1921 Preston North End 2
1922 Portsmouth 5
Atherton
Horwich RMI
Chorley
Darwen

Croft, Thomas William GK
b Gainsborough
1898 Gainsborough Trinity 5

Crombie, Alexander (Alex) OL
b Berwick-on-Tweed q2 1876
Morpeth Harriers
Reading
1905 Burslem Port Vale 17 1

Crompton, Arthur OL/OR
b Birmingham 9/1/1903 d 1987
Devon County
Army
1928 1929 Tottenham Hotspur 15 3
1930 1931 Southend United 56 20
1931 1932 Brentford 43 14
1933 1934 Crystal Palace 26 6
1935 Tranmere Rovers 12 2
Northwich Victoria

From To Apps Goal

Crompton, George Ellis (Ellis) CH/IR/RH
b Ramsbottom 17/7/1886 d 1953
Padiham
1906 1910 Blackburn Rovers 35 20
1910 1911 Tottenham Hotspur 8
Exeter City
1920 Bristol Rovers 41 10
1921 1925 Exeter City 145 6
1921 Bristol Rovers (loan) 0
Barnstaple Town
Llanelly
Barry

Crompton, Leonard (Len) GK
b Tottington 26/3/1902 d 1966
Rossendale United
1924 1927 Blackpool 88
Lancaster Town
1929 Rochdale 11
1930 Barnsley 17
1931 Norwich City 0

Crompton, Norman CH/IR
b Farnworth 7/4/1904 d 1991
Worsley Road (Bolton)
Walkden Alliance
Little Hulton United
Denbigh United
1926 1927 Oldham Athletic 9
1927 Queen's Park Rangers 1
Dartford
Horwich RMI
Darwen
Lancaster Town
Rossendale United
Wigan Athletic

Crompton, Robert (Bob) RB/LB
b Blackburn 26/9/1879 d 1941
Caps: FLge 17/England 41
Rose & Thistle
Blackburn Trinity
1896 1919 Blackburn Rovers 530 14

Crompton, Thomas CF
1898 Everton 3 1

Crompton, Wilfred (Wilf) OR/OL
b Blackburn 1/4/1908 d 1971
1929 1930 Blackburn Rovers 20 5
1932 1933 Burnley 31 9
1934 Gillingham 14 6
1934 1936 Luton Town 48 15

Crompton, Wynne LB/RB
b Cefn-y-Bedd 11/2/1907 d 1988
Caps: Wales 3
Oak Alyn Rovers
1927 1931 Wrexham 64
Tunbridge Wells Rangers
1933 1934 Clapton Orient 79
1934 Crystal Palace 0
1935 Exeter City 7
Oswestry Town
Cross Street (Wrexham)

Crone, Robert (Bob) LB/RB/RH
b Belfast 1876 d 1942
Caps: Ireland 4
Distillery
Middlesbrough
1892 1894 West Bromwich Albion 40
1895 Burton Swifts 30 2
1896 1897 Notts County 32
Bedminster

Cronin, William Joseph IR
b Scotland 10/10/1912 d 1986
1931 Gillingham 2

Crook, AJ IR
1896 1897 Darwen 23 9

Crook, Frederick James CF
b Clapton q3 1901 d 1960
Enfield
1922 Millwall Athletic 5
1925 Clapton Orient 0

Crook, James Albert IR
Stalybridge Rovers
1899 Blackburn Rovers 9 2
Stalybridge Rovers

Crook, Mark Stanley OR/IL
b Morley 29/6/1903 d 1977
Wombwell
1925 1928 Blackpool 55 12
1929 Swindon Town 1
1929 1934 Wolverhampton Wanderers 78 14
1935 Luton Town 5 1

From To Apps Goal

Crook, Walter LB/RB
b Whittle-le-Woods 28/4/1912 d 1988
Caps: England War 1
Blackburn Nomads
1931 1946 Blackburn Rovers 218 2
1939 (Blackburn Rovers) (3)
1947 Bolton Wanderers 28

Crooks, Samuel Dickinson (Sammy) OR
b Bearpark 16/1/1908 d 1981
Caps: FLge 5/England 26
Bearpark Colliery
Brandon Juniors
Tow Law Town
Bishop Auckland (trial)
1926 Durham City 16 4
1927 1946 Derby County 408 101
Retford Town
Gresley Rovers

Crooks, William James (Billy) IR
b Belfast 12/12/1899 d 1956
Caps: IrLge 3/Ireland 1
University FC
Glentoran
1922 Manchester United 0
1923 1924 New Brighton 33 7
Belfast Celtic
Larne
Glentoran
Bangor

Croot, Frederick Richard (Fred) OL
b Little Harrowden 30/11/1885 d 1958
Wellingborough
1905 1906 Sheffield United 8
1907 1914 Leeds City 218 37
Stevenston United
Rangers (loan)
Clydebank

Croot, James Edward (Jimmy) RH
b Smalley Green 24/6/1906 d 1993
Denaby United
1926 1927 Bradford Park Avenue 7

Cropper, Arthur IR/IL/CF
b Brimington 2/1/1906 d 1949
Matlock Town
1924 Luton Town (trial) 0
Staveley Town
Alfreton Town
1927 1929 Norwich City 23 3
Guildford City
1930 1931 Clapton Orient 27 10
1932 Gillingham 16 2
Yarmouth Town

Cropper, Reginald (Reg) IR/IL
b Brimington 21/1/1902 d 1942
Staveley Town
1924 Watford (trial) 0
1925 Notts County 0
1926 1927 Norwich City 49 16
Guildford City
1929 Tranmere Rovers 18 4
Guildford City
1931 Crystal Palace 3 1
1932 Mansfield Town 6 1
Hollingwood Rangers

Crosbie, John Anderson (Johnny) IR
b Gorbals 3/6/1896 d 1982
Caps: Scotland 2
Glenbuck Cherrypickers
Muirkirk Athletic
Saltcoats Victoria
Ayr United
1920 1931 Birmingham 409 71
1932 Chesterfield 3
Stourbridge

Cross, Alfred (Alf) CH
Northwich Victoria
1897 Darwen 4

Cross, Arthur George (Archie) RB/LB
b Dartford q3 1881 d 1956
Dartford
1900 1909 Woolwich Arsenal 132
Dartford

Cross, Benjamin (Benny) IL/IR
b Birkenhead 23/8/1898 d 1984
Caps: England Sch/FLge 2
Runcorn
1920 1927 Burnley 237 57

Cross, C Edward (Ted) LH
Northwich Victoria
Rotherham Town
Sheffield United
Northwich Victoria
Rotherham Town
Chesterfield Town
1894 Rotherham Town 2

From To Apps Goal

Cross, Charles Alan (Charlie) LB/RB
b Nuneaton 15/5/1897 d 1981
Siddeley-Deasy
1919 1921 Coventry City 12
1922 1927 Crystal Palace 221
1928 Wolverhampton Wanderers 3
1929 Merthyr Town 16

Cross, George J OL
b London
RAMC
1936 Aldershot 6 2

Cross, J RB
1893 Nottingham Forest 1

Cross, Robert Samuel OR
b York 10/8/1901 d 1988
1st West Royal Regiment
York City
1924 Durham City 4
Harrogate AFC
Newport Recreation
South Cave
Newport Recreation
York Wednesday

Cross, William IL
b Dumfries 1904
Queen of the South
1933 Carlisle United 2
Queen of the South

Crossan, Bernard (Bernie) IL
b Glasgow 1870 d 1917
Glasgow Benburb
Celtic
1890 Preston North End 7 3
Third Lanark
St Bernard's
Celtic

Crossan, Daniel (Danny) LB
b Motherwell 1888 d 1918
Abercorn
1908 1909 Bradford Park Avenue 23
Rochdale

Crossley, Charles Arthur (Charlie) IL/IR
b Short Heath 17/12/1891 d 1965
Willenhall Swifts
Siemens Institute
Willenhall Swifts
Hednesford Town
Walsall
1913 1919 Sunderland 43 17
1920 1921 Everton 50 18
1922 West Ham United 15 1
1923 1924 Swindon Town 38 11
Ebbw Vale

Crossley, Frederick OL
b Gomersal q3 1891
Elswick St Andrew's
Birtley
Newburn
1912 Fulham 1
Newcastle City

Crossley, Thomas H OR
1890 Burnley 1

Crossthwaite, Harold (Harry) OR
b Stockport 9/8/1890 d 1939
Heywood United
1912 1919 Stockport County 75 7
1919 1920 Stoke 30
1921 1922 Stockport County 52 4
Stalybridge Celtic

Crossthwaite, Herbert GK
b Preston 4/4/1887 d 1944
Preston Post Office
1905 Preston North End 0
1906 Blackpool 1
1907 Fulham 2
Exeter City
1911 1913 Birmingham 49

Crowe, Alfred CF
b Woolwich 1885
North Woolwich Invicta
1904 1905 Woolwich Arsenal 6 4

Crowe, Edward Wilfred (Ted) GK
b Stourport 27/11/1911 d 1982
Stourport Swifts
1933 1935 West Bromwich Albion 15
1936 Swansea Town 1
1937 1938 Aldershot 19
Wilden

From To Apps Goal

Crowe, Frank LH/RH/IL
b Birmingham q3 1893
Caps: WLge 1
Apollo Works
1914 Birmingham 0
1919 Coventry City 2
1920 1921 Merthyr Town 72 7
1922 Chesterfield 20 1
1923 Rochdale 18 5
1924 Merthyr Town 0
Penrhiwceiber

Crowl, Sydney Robert (Syd) OL
b Islington 18/3/1888 d 1971
Enfield
1913 Tottenham Hotspur 1

Crown, Lawrence (Laurie) RB/LB
b Fulwell 25/2/1898 d 1984
Furness Athletic
Sunderland All Saints
Redcar
1922 1925 South Shields 87 3
1925 Newcastle United 2
1927 Bury 17
1928 1930 Coventry City 112

Crownshaw, George IL
b Sheffield 17/4/1908 d 1992
Wombwell
1929 1931 Huddersfield Town 26 8
1932 Luton Town 0

Crowther, George Edward GK
b Pudsey 7/9/1901 d 1979
Pudsey Celtic
Pudsey Athletic
Armley
Leeds Malvern
Leeds Harehills
Liversedge
1924 Leeds United 0
1925 Bradford Park Avenue 8
York City
1928 1929 Stockport County 47
1930 1932 Gateshead 62
Linfield

Crowther, George Lisle CF/IL
b Bishop Middleham q2 1892 d 1957
Shildon
1911 Manchester United 0
1912 Huddersfield Town 2
Rotherham Town
Halifax Town
Hurst
1919 Bradford Park Avenue 9
1920 West Ham United 3
1921 1922 Hartlepools United 25 10
1922 Tranmere Rovers 10 2

Crowther, John IR/CF
b Walsden
1930 Halifax Town 1
1931 Rochdale 1 1
Bacup Borough

Crowther, Reuben IR
b Blackburn q1 1875 d 1931
1894 Bury 2
Tonge

Croxon, William James F OR/IR
b West Ham q1 1871 d 1949
Royal Arsenal
Millwall Athletic
Ilford
1892 1893 Sheffield United 3
1894 Rotherham Town 9 1

Croxton, Harry Clement RH
b Stoke-on-Trent 2/1880 d 1965
Burslem Park
1901 1905 Burslem Port Vale 116 7
1905 1906 Stoke 22 1
Burslem Port Vale

Crozier, James GK
Clyde
Partick Thistle
1894 Woolwich Arsenal 1
Partick Thistle

Crozier, James Paterson Lyle OL
b Glasgow 29/10/1906
Glasgow Ashfield
1927 Hull City 3
Celtic
Forfar Athletic (loan)
Ayr United (loan)
Derry City
Linfield
Glasgow Ashfield
Brechin City
Morton (trial)

From To Apps Goal

Crozier, Joseph (Joe) RH/LH
b Middlesbrough 4/12/1889 d 1960
1910 1913 Middlesbrough 27
1914 1921 Bradford Park Avenue 115 4
1922 Grimsby Town 14

Crozier, Joseph (Joe) GK
b Coatbridge 2/12/1914 d 1985
Caps: Scotland War 3
Strathclyde
East Fife
1937 1948 Brentford 200
1939 (Brentford) (3)
Chelmsford City
Kidderminster Harriers
Ashford Town (Kent)

Crozier, RW CH
1893 Darwen 4

Crozier, W CH
Northwich Victoria
Sunderland Albion
1892 Northwich Victoria 19

Cruickshank, Alexander (Alec) OR
b Haddington 12/8/1900 d 1972
Port Glasgow Athletic
1924 Derby County 0
1925 Merthyr Town 42 7
1926 Sheffield Wednesday 2
Guildford City
1929 Merthyr Town 33 4
1930 Swindon Town 26 5
St Johnstone

Cruise, James Arthur GK
b Bradford q1 1895 d 1968
Halifax Town
Yorkshire Amateurs
1921 Halifax Town 1
Yorkshire Amateurs

Crumley, James Brymer GK
b Dundee 17/7/1898 d 1981
Dundee Hibernian
1920 1922 Swansea Town 28
1923 Bristol City 2
1924 1925 Darlington 66
1926 1928 Bournemouth & Boscombe Ath 51

Crumley, Robert J (Bob) GK
b Lochee 1878
Lochee United
1904 1905 Newcastle United 4
Dundee
Darlington
Arbroath

Crump, Arthur RB
b Smethwick q2 1887 d 1960
Birmingham Casuals
Smethwick Old Church
1906 Manchester City 0
Reading
1909 West Bromwich Albion 1
Dudley Town
Shrewsbury Town
Wellington Town

Crump, Frederick (Fred) CF/IR
b Stourbridge 1880
Stourbridge
1899 Derby County 6 1
1900 1901 Glossop 65 27
Northampton Town
Stourbridge
Stalybridge Rovers
1905 1907 Stockport County 89 29
Brighton & Hove Albion
Walsall
Darlaston

Crump, Herbert RH
1912 Glossop 6

Crump, James Arthur RB
b Elsecar q2 1883 d 1959
Elsecar Main
1906 Barnsley 1
Rotherham Town
Elsecar Athletic
Mexborough Town

Crump, Leslie Victor OL
b Wolverhampton 10/10/1902 d 1983
Sunbeam Motors (Wolverhampton)
Kilmarnock
1927 Bournemouth & Boscombe Ath 4

From To Apps Goal

Crump, William Harold (Harry) LH
b Smethwick 10/2/1874 d 1943
Smethwick Centaur
West Smethwick
Wednesfield
1894 Wolverhampton Wanderers 1
Hereford Thistle
Bloxwich
Tottenham Hotspur
1898 Luton Town 25
Tottenham Hotspur
Thames Ironworks
Doncaster Rovers
Brentford
Watford

Crussell, James Freshwater (Jimmy) IL
b Watford 19/2/1904 d 1983
Caps: England Amat
Old Fullerians
Leavesden Road Baptists
Sun Engraving
1924 Watford 1
Tufnell Park
Clapton

Crutchley, Arthur Victor (Vic) RB
b Birkenhead q3 1910 d 1961
Carlton Athletic
1930 Tranmere Rovers 1

Cubberley, Stanley Morris (Stan) LH/IR/IL
b Edmonton 18/7/1882 d 1933
Enfield
Cheshunt
Asplin Rovers
Crystal Palace
1906 1912 Leeds City 181 6
Swansea Town
1914 Manchester United 0

Cuff, William Peter (Billy) RH
b Bristol 3/3/1901 d 1969
Victoria Albion
1923 Bristol Rovers 2

Cuffe, John Alexander LB/RB
b Sydney, Australia 26/6/1880 d 1931
1905 1914 Glossop 282 3

Cuggy, Francis (Frank) RH
b Walker 16/6/1889 d 1965
Caps: FLge 3/England 2
Willington Athletic
1909 1920 Sunderland 164 4
Wallsend

Cull, John Ernest (Ernie) OR
b Aston 18/11/1900 d 1964
Bloxwich Strollers
Nuneaton Town
Shrewsbury Town
1925 1930 Stoke City 75 9
1931 Coventry City 17 3
Shrewsbury Town
1933 Crewe Alexandra 30 13
1934 Accrington Stanley 38 6
1935 Gateshead 19 5
1935 Aldershot 3

Cullen, Joseph (Joe) GK
b Glasgow 1870 d 1905
Caps: SLge 1
Stanley Swifts
Glasgow Benburb
Celtic
Tottenham Hotspur
1899 Lincoln City 12

Cullen, William McKenzie OL
b Gorbals 18/12/1896
Petershill
Glasgow Perthshire
Third Lanark
King's Park
1923 Reading 1
King's Park
Bathgate

Culley, James GK
b Condorrat 20/7/1915 d 1981
Camelon Juniors
Hibernian
1938 Lincoln City 5
Alloa Athletic

From To Apps Goal

Culley, William Neill (Bill) CF/IR
b Kilwinning 26/8/1892 d 1955
Caps: SLge 1
Kilwinning Eglinton
Kilwinning Rangers
Ardrossan Winton Rovers
Kilmarnock
Third Lanark (loan)
Renton (loan)
Clyde
Weymouth
1925 1927 Bristol Rovers 57 42
1928 Swindon Town 3 1
Weymouth
Kilmarnock
Galston (loan)
Kilwinning Eglinton

Cullis, Stanley (Stan) CH
b Ellesmere Port 25/10/1915 d 2001
Caps: FLge 3/England War 20/England 12
1932 Bolton Wanderers 0
Ellesmere Port Wednesday
1934 1946 Wolverhampton Wanderers 152
1939 (Wolverhampton Wanderers) (3)

Cullum, Charles IR
b West Cornforth 21/7/1897 d 1972
Cornforth United
Durham City
Norwich City
1919 Derby County 0
West Stanley
1921 Tranmere Rovers 0
1922 Walsall 22 9
1923 Barrow 3 1
Spondon

Culshaw, Alexander (Alex) RH
b Blackpool q2 1891
Chorley
1913 Bury 1
Chorley

Cumberland, Thomas William GK
b Derby q4 1882
Southwell St Mary's
1902 Lincoln City 5
Southwell St Mary's
Grantham Avenue
Southwell St Mary's
Brentford
Sutton Junction
Sutton Town

Cumberlidge, Arthur Leonard LB/IR
b Wolstanton 5/4/1914 d 1983
1935 Stoke City 0
1936 1938 Port Vale 66
1939 (Port Vale) (2)
Northwich Victoria

Cumming, David Douglas OR
b Glasgow 1900
Dundee
1922 Grimsby Town 6

Cumming, David Scott (Dave) GK
b Aberdeen 6/5/1910 d 1993
Caps: Scotland War 1/Scotland 1
Woodside Thistle
Hall, Russell & Co
Aberdeen
Arbroath
1936 1946 Middlesbrough 135
1939 (Middlesbrough) (3)

Cumming, James Ferguson OR
b Alexandria 9/7/1891
Clydebank Juniors
Glasgow Benburb
Maryhill
1913 1914 Manchester City 35 3
Aberdeen
Dumbarton
1919 1920 West Ham United 15

Cumming, John LH
b Muirkirk
Cowdenbeath
1920 Portsmouth 8 1
King's Park

From To Apps Goal

Cumming, Lawrence Stanley Slater (Lawrie) IR/IL
b Derry 10/4/1905
Caps: Ireland 3
St George's Church
Dunoon United
Alloa Athletic
1927 1929 Huddersfield Town 19 6
1929 Oldham Athletic 25 11
1930 Southampton 20 4
Alloa Athletic
Queen of the South
St Mirren
Hamilton Academical

Cummings, Daniel IL
Accrington Stanley
Parkhead
1921 Wigan Borough 0
1922 Accrington Stanley 1
Fall River Marksmen
Boston Wonder Workers

Cummings, George Wilfred LB
b Thornbridge 5/6/1913 d 1987
Caps: SLge 2/Scotland War 1/Scotland 9
Thornbridge Waverley
Thornbridge Welfare
Grange Rovers
Partick Thistle
1935 1948 Aston Villa 210
1939 (Aston Villa) (3) (1)

Cummins, Joseph Henry IR
b Plympton 8/4/1910
Jersey Wanderers
1933 Southampton 1
Sportive Union Tourcoing
Newport (Isle of Wight)

Cumner, Reginald Horace (Horace) OL/IL/IR
b Cwmaman 31/3/1918 d 1999
Caps: Wales War 10/Wales 3
Aberaman Athletic
1935 Arsenal 0
Margate (loan)
1937 Hull City (loan) 12 4
1938 1945 Arsenal 12 2
1946 1947 Notts County 66 11
1948 1950 Watford 62 7
1950 1952 Scunthorpe United 102 21
1953 Bradford City 0
Poole Town
Bridport

Cunliffe, Arthur OL
b Blackrod 5/2/1909 d 1986
Caps: England 2
Adlington
Chorley
1929 1932 Blackburn Rovers 129 47
1932 1935 Aston Villa 69 11
1935 1936 Middlesbrough 27 5
1937 Burnley 9
1938 Hull City 42 20
1939 (Hull City) (2)
1945 1946 Rochdale 23 5

Cunliffe, Daniel (Dan) OR/IR/CF
b Bolton 11/6/1875 d 1937
Caps: England 1
Little Lever
Middleton Borough
Oldham County
1897 Liverpool 14 6
1898 New Brighton Tower 30 15
Portsmouth
1900 New Brighton Tower 28 9
Portsmouth
New Brompton
Millwall Athletic
Heywood
Rochdale

Cunliffe, James Nathaniel (Jimmy 'Nat') IR
b Blackrod 5/7/1912 d 1986
Caps: England 1
Adlington
1932 1938 Everton 174 73
1946 Rochdale 2

Cunliffe, Thomas (Tommy) OL
b Simms Lane End 1886
Audenshaw
Hooley Hill
Earlestown
1905 Blackburn Rovers 1
St Helens Recreation
Chorley
1919 Oldham Athletic 2
Mossley

From To Apps Goal

Cunningham, Andrew Nisbet (Andy) IR
b Galston 30/1/1890 d 1973
Caps: SLge 10/Scotland 12
Galston Riverside Rangers
Newmilns
Kilmarnock
Rangers
1928 1929 Newcastle United 12 2

Cunningham, Charles (Charlie) IL
b Manchester q1 1890 d 1942
Whitfield United
1912 Manchester City 0
1921 Tranmere Rovers 32 6
Ashton National

Cunningham, G RB
1894 1896 Burton Wanderers 75 1
1897 Burton Swifts 8

Cunningham, George IL
Cambuslang
1935 1936 Walsall 10 2

Cunningham, George P OR
b Dublin 1891
Caps: IrLge 2
Shelbourne
1910 Leeds City 3
Crewe Alexandra

Cunningham, Joel (Joey) GK
b Logie 1905
Logie United
Aberdeen
1925 Newport County 2
1926 1931 Queen's Park Rangers 168
1932 1933 Walsall 49
1934 York City 42
Dartford
Folkestone
Dartford

Cunningham, John IL/IR
b Glasgow 1873 d 1910
Glasgow Benburb
Celtic (trial)
1889 Burnley (trial) 0
Glasgow Hibernian
Celtic
Partick Thistle
Heart of Midlothian
Rangers
Glasgow Thistle
1893 1896 Preston North End 51 8
1897 Sheffield United 24 7
1898 Aston Villa 0
1898 Newton Heath 15 3
Wigan County
Barrow

Cunningham, Joseph Bernard (Bernard) RH
b Cwmbran 20/4/1905 d 1988
1932 Newport County 3

Cunningham, Peter CF
b Glasgow 13/7/1906 d 1934
Glasgow Ashfield
Clyde
Partick Thistle
Cork FC
Rangers
1932 Barnsley 14 17
1933 Port Vale 2
1933 Crewe Alexandra 15 13

Cunningham, Thomas GK
b Sunderland 9/9/1884
Sunderland Juniors
1908 Leeds City 1

Cunningham, William (Willie) LH
b Radcliffe 27/10/1893 d 1934
Blyth Spartans
1920 1921 Liverpool 3
1923 Barrow 39 1
Mid-Rhondda United

Cupit, William W (Billy) OR
b Huthwaite 1912
Sutton Junction
1931 Luton Town 8 1
1932 Mansfield Town 2
Sutton Town

Curle, William (Willie) CF
b Glasgow 1886
Rutherglen Glencairn
1908 Woolwich Arsenal 3
Cowdenbeath
Abercorn
Albion Rovers
Bathgate
Renton

From To Apps Goal

Curley, Michael RH
b Northwich 15/5/1912 d 1973
Northwich Victoria
1934 Manchester City 0
1935 1936 Port Vale 27 1
Colwyn Bay United
Macclesfield
Northwich Victoria
Mossley

Curnow, Jack GK
b Lingdale 31/1/1910 d 1990
Pease & Partners
South Bank East End
Whitby United
1935 Wolverhampton Wanderers 6
1936 Blackpool 0
1937 1938 Tranmere Rovers 52
1939 Hull City (2)
1945 Tranmere Rovers 0

Curr, Robert RB/LB
b Liverpool 13/2/1906 d 1985
Orrell
1926 Everton 0
Lancaster Town
1928 1931 New Brighton 33

Curr, Wallace (Wally) RH/CF
b Liverpool 4/4/1908 d 1981
1926 Everton 0
1929 1930 New Brighton 8

Curran, Andrew Eltringham (Andy) CH/RH
b Ryton-on-Tyne 5/7/1898 d 1967
Mickley
1920 Sunderland 0
1921 1926 Blackpool 97 3
1926 1930 Accrington Stanley 136 5
Lytham

Curran, Frank IL/IR/CF
b Ryton-on-Tyne 31/5/1917 d 1998
Spen Black & White Juniors
Washington Colliery
1935 1936 Southport 16 3
1936 1937 Accrington Stanley 34 14
1938 Bristol Rovers 27 21
1939 1945 Bristol City (3) (1)
1946 Bristol Rovers 10 3
Shrewsbury Town
1947 Tranmere Rovers 17 7
Shrewsbury Town
Hyde United
Ashton United
Hyde United
Darwen

Curran, James (Jimmy) OR
b Ryton-on-Tyne 2/8/1902 d 1979
Crawcrook Albion
Spen Black & White
1921 1931 Barnsley 244 71
1932 Southend United 2 1

Curran, John RB
b Bellshill 3/1864 d 1933
Glasgow Benburb
Celtic
1894 1895 Liverpool 20
Hibernian
Motherwell
Celtic

Curran, John Joseph (Jack) LB/RB
b Belfast 1898
Caps: IrLge 4/WLge 2/Ireland 5
Queen's Park (Lurgan)
Glenavon
Pontypridd
Glenavon
1925 1930 Brighton & Hove Albion 180
Linfield

Curran, Patrick Joseph (Pat) IR/IL
b Sunderland 13/11/1917 d 2003
Sunderland St Patrick's
1937 Sunderland 1
1938 Ipswich Town 7 1
1939 1945 Watford (1)
1947 Bradford City 5 1

Currie, Ford LH
b Innerleithen
1924 Arsenal 0
1925 Charlton Athletic 7 1

Currie, James Blair (Blair) IR
b Galston 14/2/1896
Prestwick
Glenleven Rovers
1919 Notts County 8 1

From To Apps Goal

Currie, Peter OL
b Armadale
St Bernard's
Armadale
1913 1914 Bradford City 17 2
Armadale
Falkirk
Broxburn United
Dumbarton

Currie, Robert (Bob) IL/IR/CF
b Kilwinning 1884
Arthurlie
1902 Middlesbrough 3 1
Abercorn
Kilwinning Rangers
Morton
1906 1911 Bury 116 33
Heart of Midlothian
Darlington

Currie, Samuel Percy (Sam) LB
b Kilwinning 22/11/1887 d 1962
Kilwinning Rangers
St Mirren (trial)
1909 1921 Leicester Fosse 236 4
1922 1923 Wigan Borough 33 2

Currie, Walter Robertson (Wattie) LH/RH
b Auchterderran 5/10/1895 d 1965
Denbeath Star
Cowdenbeath
East Fife
Raith Rovers
1919 1921 Leicester City 32 1
1922 Bristol Rovers 42
Clackmannan
Lochgelly United

Currier, James (Jim) CF
b Wednesbury 24/1/1913 d 1991
Cheltenham Town
1935 1938 Bolton Wanderers 26 14
Ashton National
Ashton United

Curry, Joseph CH/LH
b Newcastle q1 1887
Scotswood
1908 1910 Manchester United 13
Southampton
West Stanley

Curry, Luke LH
b Dudley, Northumberland 8/8/1905 d 1970
Jarrow
1927 1931 Bury 14

Curry, Robert (Bob) IR
b Gateshead 2/11/1918 d 2001
1936 Gateshead 0
1937 Sheffield Wednesday 1
Gainsborough Trinity
1950 Colchester United 32 13
Clacton Town
Halstead Town

Curry, Robert Vickers RH
b Chopwell q3 1912
Ouston Park
1933 1938 Rotherham United 189 2
1939 Carlisle United 0

Curry, Thomas (Tom) RH/LH
b South Shields 1/9/1894 d 1958
Caps: FLge 1
South Shields St Michael's
South Shields Parkside
1919 1928 Newcastle United 221 5
1928 1929 Stockport County 19 1

Curry, Thomas IL
b Newcastle
Clarence Wesleyans
1919 Barnsley 1
Scotswood
Jarrow
Pandon Temperance
1923 Aberdare Athletic 4

Cursham, Henry Alfred (Harry) RB
b Wilford 27/11/1859 d 1941
Caps: England 8
Notts County
Corinthians
Grantham
Thursday Wanderers
1888 1890 Notts County 9 2

Curtis, Albert Victor LH
b Bradford q1 1899 d 1967
Robeys
1922 Lincoln City 1
Gainsborough Trinity

From To Apps Goal

Curtis, Charles (Charlie) RH
b Sunderland 22/11/1910 d 1985
1933 Stoke City 0
1934 1935 Tranmere Rovers 21
Boston Town

Curtis, Ernest Robert (Ernie) OL/IL/IR
b Cardiff 10/6/1907 d 1992
Caps: Wales Sch/Wales Amat/Wales 3
Severn Road Old Boys
Cardiff Corinthians
1926 1927 Cardiff City 46 8
1927 1933 Birmingham 165 44
1933 Cardiff City 16 6
1934 1936 Coventry City 21 2
1937 Hartlepools United 16 1

Curtis, Frank CF/IR
b Llanelli 1890
South Liverpool
West Ham United
Llanelly
1914 1919 Wolverhampton Wanderers 40 25
1920 Reading 1
Bilston United
Kidderminster Harriers

Curtis, George Edward IR/RH/IL
b West Thurrock 3/12/1919 d 2004
Anglo (Purfleet)
1937 Arsenal 0
Margate (loan)
1938 1946 Arsenal 13
1947 1951 Southampton 174 11
Valenciennes
Chelmsford City

Curtis, John Joseph (Jack) OR
b South Bank 13/12/1888 d 1955
Eston United
South Bank St Peter's
1906 Sunderland 1
South Bank
Shildon Athletic
1908 Gainsborough Trinity 30 2
1908 1912 Tottenham Hotspur 82 5
1913 Fulham 2
Brentford
1914 Stockport County 15 1
1919 Middlesbrough 5
Shildon Athletic

Curtis, Leslie H CF
b Yorkshire
1936 Barnsley 0
Army
1938 Northampton Town 2 1
Northwich Victoria

Curtis, Thomas (Tom) RB
b South Bank 1901
South Bank
1920 Bradford Park Avenue 9

Curwen, William (Billy) OL/LB
b High Spen q3 1905 d 1950
Willington
1928 Luton Town 1
1929 Queen's Park Rangers (trial) 0
1930 Thames 2

Curwood, Albert CF
b Bridgwater 21/12/1910 d 1971
Llanelly
1933 Blackpool 0
1934 Bournemouth & Boscombe Ath 7
1935 Swansea Town 0

Cust, John OR
b Bonhill 1875
Vale of Leven
1897 Bury 9 1
Clyde

Cuthbert, Westgarth (Wes) LB
b Morpeth 3/11/1913 d 1985
South Elmsall
1933 1934 Rotherham United 2
1935 Hull City 0
1936 Carlisle United 0
1937 Accrington Stanley 6
Frickley Colliery
Grantham

Cutler, A OL
1895 Loughborough 1

Cutler, Eric Richmond IR
b Codsall q1 1900
Caps: England Sch
1919 1920 Wolverhampton Wanderers 18 4

From To Apps Goal

Cutting, Stanley William (Stan) RH
b St Faiths 21/9/1914 d 2004
1936 Norwich City 0
1938 Southampton 3
1946 1947 Exeter City 38 2

Cutts, Arthur CF
1895 Rotherham Town 15 3
Chesterfield Town

Cutts, Edward Robert IR
b Sheffield 1869 d 1920
1892 Sheffield Wednesday 0
1893 1894 Rotherham Town 24 8

Cutts, George Henry GK
b Nottingham 11/3/1900 d 1975
Arnold Town
Mansfield Town
1920 1922 Watford 5
Sutton Town
Grantham
Hucknall Byron
Hucknall British Legion
Loughborough Corinthians
Raleigh Athletic

Dabbs, Benjamin Edwin (Ben) LB/RB
b Oakengates 17/4/1909 d 2001
Oakengates Town
1933 1937 Liverpool 54
1938 Watford 3
1939 (Watford) (2)

Dackers, William LB/RB
b Dunkeld 20/10/1874 d 1945
St Johnstone
Victoria United
1898 1899 New Brighton Tower 12
Aberdeen
Watford

Dackins, Haydn Vernon IL/OL
b Pontypridd 18/7/1912 d 1943
1934 Swansea Town 2
1935 Port Vale 9 1
Northwich Victoria
Macclesfield Town
Hurst

Dadley, Benjamin James LH
b Great Baddow 1/6/1898 d 1962
Croydon Juniors
1921 Charlton Athletic 8
Chatham

Daft, Harry Butler OL/IL
b Radcliffe-on-Trent 5/4/1866 d 1945
Caps: FLge 2/England 5
Notts County
Nottingham Forest
Newark
Corinthians
1888 Notts County 19 8
Corinthians
1889 1892 Notts County 82 39
1892 Nottingham Forest 4 1
1893 1894 Notts County 36 11
Newark

Daft, Thomas IR
Sawley q4 1868 d 1939
Derby Midland
1890 Derby County 3

Daglish, John LH/LB/CH
b South Moor
White-le-Head Rangers
1930 1932 Darlington 14 1
Annfield Plain
1934 Gateshead 14

Dagnall, Walter IL
b Prescot q2 1883
Prescot
St Helens Recreation
1906 Hull City 8 2
St Helens Recreation
Prescot Athletic
Skelmersdale United
Prescot Athletic
Rossendale United

Dailey, William S (Bill) RH
b Coatbridge
Shieldmuir Celtic
1924 Bradford Park Avenue 8 1
1926 Coventry City 5 1

Dailly, Hugh (Jock) OL
b Dundee 1879
Dundee North End
1898 Woolwich Arsenal 8 4
Dundee Wanderers
1898 Wolverhampton Wanderers 0
1899 Walsall 28 5

From To Apps Goal

Daily, John IL
Hibernian
Motherwell
1897 Lincoln City 1

Dainty, Herbert Charles CH/RH
b Geddington 6/2/1879 d 1957
Caps: SLge 1
Kettering
1899 Leicester Fosse 30 3
1900 New Brighton Tower 33 3
1901 Leicester Fosse 23
Northampton Town
1903 Notts County 20
Southampton
Dundee
1911 1913 Bradford Park Avenue 63 1
Ayr United
Dundee Hibernian

Dale, George RB/LB
b Kidsgrove q4 1883
Kidsgrove Wellington
1909 1912 Blackpool 40

Dale, George Henry IR
b Nottingham 2/5/1883 d 1957
Newark Athletic
Stanley Works (Newark)
Newark Town
1914 Notts County 18 5
1919 1921 Chelsea 49 1
Weymouth
Vickers (Crayford)

Dale, Guy Bailey GK
b Newcastle-under-Lyme q1 1895 d 1920
1920 Clapton Orient 1

Dale, Harry James GK
b Woolwich 23/4/1899 d 1985
1920 Reading 1

Dale, James (Jimmy) RH
b Motherwell 7/1869
1893 Sunderland 0
1894 Stoke 4
Southampton St Mary's

Dale, Richard Armstrong (Dickie) LH/RH/CH
b Low Fell 21/5/1896 d 1975
Stanley United
North Walbottle
West Hartlepool
1922 1928 Birmingham 146
1928 1929 West Bromwich Albion 19
1931 Tranmere Rovers 7
Crook Town

Dale, William (Billy) RB/LB
b Manchester 17/2/1905 d 1987
Sandbach Ramblers
1928 1931 Manchester United 64
1931 1937 Manchester City 237
1938 Ipswich Town 40
1939 (Ipswich Town) (3)

Dalkin, Arthur Ernest LH/RH
b Ashington 6/3/1906 d 1990
Ashington Colliery Welfare
Bedlington United
1926 Ashington 9
Preston Colliery
1928 Ashington 26
Frickley Colliery
South Kirkby Colliery

Dalkin, Joseph William (Joe) OR
b Ashington q1 1901
Bedlington United
1925 1926 Ashington 32 6
Preston Colliery
1928 Ashington 14
Walker Celtic
Bedlington United
Pegswood United
Wallaw United
Bedlington United

Dallison, Arthur Redvers RB
b Sutton-in-Ashfield 6/4/1900 d 1985
Sutton Junction
1921 Rotherham County 2
Mansfield Town
Sutton Town
Newark Town
Mansfield Town
Sutton Town

From To Apps Goal

Dalrymple, Robert Rodie (Bob) IR
b Paisley 2/1/1880 d 1970
Westmarch
Abercorn
Heart of Midlothian
Kilbarchan (loan)
Plymouth Argyle
Rangers
Portsmouth
1907 1910 Fulham 98 39
1910 1919 Clapton Orient 139 38
Ton Pentre

Dalton, Bryan Lovall OL
b Arundel 9/1/1917 d 2004
Littlehampton
1935 Portsmouth 1
1936 Reading 7 2
1937 Gillingham 6

Dalton, Edward LB
b Manchester
Pendlebury
1907 Manchester United 1
Pendlebury
Brighton & Hove Albion
St Helens Recreation
Chorley
Pontypridd
Vernon Athletic

Dalton, James J RB
b Ontario, Canada
Canadian Touring Team
Pawtucket
1893 Sunderland 3
Nelson

Dalton, Joseph LH/RH
b Bradford 2/8/1915 d 1984
1935 1937 Bradford City 17 3
Shrewsbury Town

Dalton, Reginald (Reg) RH/CH
b Foleshill 19/7/1896 d 1979
Edgewick
1919 1922 Coventry City 54 4
1924 Halifax Town (trial) 0
Foleshill Great Heath
Nuneaton Town
Foleshill Great Heath

Dalton, Thomas Victor (Tom) CF
b Cardiff q1 1897
Pontypridd
Cardiff City
Bargoed
Dalton Casuals
1922 Barrow 1 1

Daly, Joseph (Joe) OR
b Lancaster 28/12/1897 d 1941
Cliftonville
1920 1926 Notts County 139 12
1927 Northampton Town 33 4
1928 1929 Luton Town 70 4
1930 Gillingham 0
Notts Corinthians

Dance, Thomas OR
b Prestwich 1/1/1898 d 1973
1921 Stalybridge Celtic 11 1

Dand, Reginald (Reggie) RH/LH
b Ilford 30/6/1896 d 1981
Caps: England Amat
Ashford Railway Works
Ilford
1921 1922 Reading 54
1924 Queen's Park Rangers 1
Margate
Tunbridge Wells Rangers

Dando, Maurice CF
b Bristol 7/1905 d 1949
Kingswood
Bath City
Bracknell's
1928 1932 Bristol Rovers 18 5
1933 1934 York City 82 46
1935 Chesterfield 27 29
1937 Crewe Alexandra 16 2

Daniel, AG CF
1896 Burton Wanderers 1 1

Daniel, Cyril Henry CF/IL/IR
b Swindon 10/1899 d 1964
Swindon Victoria
1922 1928 Swindon Town 70 31
Chippenham Town
Bath City

From To Apps Goal

Daniel, David LH/CF
b Porth q1 1899
Porth
1925 Preston North End 1
Mid-Rhondda United
1927 Torquay United 15 2

Daniels, Arthur WC OL
b Mossley 9/5/??
Salford Lads Club
Mossley
1922 1925 Manchester City 31 1
1926 1929 Watford 136 16
1930 Queen's Park Rangers 14 3

Daniels, George OL
b Chorlton q1 1899
Bury
1919 Preston North End 12 1
1920 Bury 0
1921 1922 Rochdale 35 1

Daniels, George RH/CH
b Winsford q4 1912
1931 Leeds United 0
Altrincham
1933 Stoke City 2
1935 1936 Torquay United 49 3
1937 1938 Crystal Palace 7
1939 Hartlepools United (1)
Carlisle United

Daniels, John IR/OR
b Kent 1915
Bexleyheath
1935 1938 Millwall 25 6

Daniels, John Francis (Jack) GK
b Prestwich 6/10/1913 d 1970
1932 Stockport County 0
Manchester North End
Ashton National
1934 Leeds United 1
Ashton National (loan)
1935 1937 Stockport County 9
1938 Accrington Stanley 10
1939 Tranmere Rovers (3)
Leeds United
1945 Bradford City 0
1946 Lincoln City 17

Daniels, Norman LH
South Manchester
1922 Stalybridge Celtic 1

Danks, Richard OR
b Bilston 3/1865 d 1929
Wolverhampton Wanderers
1893 Wolverhampton Wanderers 1

Dann, Reginald Walter (Reg) LH
b Maidstone 6/6/1916 d 1948
1933 Blackpool 0
Aylesford Paper Mills
1935 Gillingham 8
1936 Tottenham Hotspur 0
1939 Bradford Park Avenue (1)

Danskin, Charles (Charlie) OL
b Lemington q1 1893 d 1968
Lemington Mission
Scotswood
Ashington
1913 Sunderland 0
Scotswood
1919 1920 Stockport County 56 6
1921 1922 Aberdare Athletic 73 5
1923 Luton Town 11
Dragon (Pontypridd)

Danskin, Robert (Bob) CH
b Scotswood 28/5/1908 d 1985
Throckley
Wallsend
1930 1931 Leeds United 5 1
1932 1947 Bradford Park Avenue 260 4
1939 (Bradford Park Avenue) (3)

Danson, Herbert (Herbie) OL/IL
b Preston 21/6/1883 d 1963
1902 Preston North End 0
Southport Central
1905 1911 Preston North End 156 23
Lancaster Town

Darby, Albert OL
b Wombwell 1896
1919 Rotherham County 1

From To Apps Goal

Darby, Ernest William GK
b Leicester 20/3/1886 d 1974
Leicester Nomads
Clarendon Park Congregational
Leicester Old Boys
Leicester British United
Clarendon Park Congregational
Leicester Nomads
1909 Leicester Fosse 4
Loughborough Corinthians
Market Harborough Town
Belvoir Street Sunday School
Stafford's FC

Darcey, Harry Carlill H IL
b Lincoln q2 1874 d 1930
Nondescripts
1894 1896 Lincoln City 3
Adelaide (Lincoln)

Dargan, James IR
b Manchester 28/8/1906 d 1985
Northwich Victoria
1927 Nelson 2
Northwich Victoria
Clitheroe
Barnoldswick Town
Morecambe
McMahon's (Manchester)

Dargue, James Henderson IL
b Blantyre 1882 d 1937
Burnbank Athletic
Hamilton Academical
1905 Glossop 7
Airdrieonians
Heart of Midlothian
Bristol Rovers
Royal Albert
Hamilton Academical

Dargue, Thomas Johnson (Tom) IL
b Morpeth 11/8/1893 d 1951
Stakeford United
1921 Ashington 15 7
Stakeford United
Guide Post United

Dark, Alfred James (Alf) CH/RH
b Keynsham 21/8/1893 d 1964
Seaton Delaval
Wallsend
1919 Newcastle United 0
1922 Leeds United 3
1923 Port Vale 25 1
1924 1927 Halifax Town 129 1
1928 Barrow 15
Sittingbourne
North Shields

Darke, Thomas William (Tom) IL
Eastville Athletic
Bristol Rovers
1904 Bristol City 3 2

Darling, Benjamin Stones (Ben) GK
b South Shields 23/3/1916 d 1974
South Shields St Andrew's
South Shields
1938 Hull City 2

Darling, Henry Leonard (Len) RH/LH
b Gillingham 9/8/1911 d 1958
Colchester Town
Tufnell Park
Chatham Town
1932 Gillingham 14
1933 1947 Brighton & Hove Albion 199 5
1939 (Brighton & Hove Albion) (3)

Darlington, Edward OL
1905 Blackpool 4

Darnell, Jabez LH
b Potton 28/3/1884 d 1950
Northampton Town
1908 1914 Tottenham Hotspur 150 3

Darnell, Leonard (Len) LH/RH
b Irchester 14/9/1905 d 1968
Rushden Town
1925 1929 West Bromwich Albion 57
1930 1932 Reading 85 4
1934 Carlisle United 7

Darroch, John (Jack) RB/LB
b Alexandria 1872 d 1949
Dumbarton
Renton
Vale of Leven
1892 1893 Sheffield Wednesday 16
Dundee
1896 1901 Bury 143 1
1901 Blackburn Rovers 17
Dundee
Dundee Hibernian

From To Apps Goal

Dart, Elijah RH
b Chesterfield 12/3/1880 d 1954
Skinningrove
1909 Grimsby Town 3

Dartnell, Bertie IL/OL
b Wellingborough q1 1877 d 1943
Wellingborough
1899 1900 Manchester City 4
1901 Barnsley 18 6
Wellingborough

Darvill, Alfred Ronald CF
b Berkhamsted 27/10/1897 d 1960
Watford Corinthians
Ilford
1924 Watford 1

Darvill, Gerald Moffatt LB
b High Wycombe 20/3/1916 d 1973
Wycombe Wanderers
1934 Reading 0
1935 Mansfield Town 13
1936 Wolverhampton Wanderers 0

Darvill, Harvey Arthur IL/OL
b Watford 7/4/1896 d 1924
Ilford
1921 1924 Fulham 69 10

Date, Marmaduke (Marmy) IR
b Englishcombe q2 1884 d 1957
Frome Town
1910 Bristol City 1
Frome Town

Daughtrey, George Arthur IL
b Masbrough q4 1874 d 1939
1897 Gainsborough Trinity 1

Daughtrey, John Thomas CH
b Masbrough q4 1876 d 1938
1895 Rotherham Town 13

Davenport, James Kenyon (Kenny) OR/IR
b Bolton 23/3/1862 d 1908
Caps: England 2
1888 1892 Bolton Wanderers 56 25
Southport Central

Davey, Hugh Henry CF/IL
b Belfast 14/6/1897
Caps: IrLge 1/Ireland 5
Glentoran
1922 Blackburn Rovers 0
1923 1924 Bournemouth & Boscombe Ath 43 22
1924 1927 Reading 61 46
1927 Portsmouth 7 2
Belfast Celtic

Davidson, Alexander GK
b Strathclyde
1904 Woolwich Arsenal 1

Davidson, Alexander IR
Brynn Central
1907 Gainsborough Trinity 5 1
Macclesfield

Davidson, Alexander Godwin (Alex) GK
b Newcastle 22/9/1899
Close Works (Gateshead)
1921 1923 Ashington 42
Workington
Annfield Plain

Davidson, Alexander Laude (Alex) CF
b Beith 27/9/1878 d 1929
Beith
Third Lanark
New Brompton
1899 Glossop 13 1
1899 1900 Manchester City 7 1
Reading
West Ham United
Luton Town
Fulham
New Brompton
Kilmarnock
Aberdeen
Stockport County
Atherton Church House
1906 Bolton Wanderers 0
Wigan Town
Nelson
Macclesfield
Denton

From To Apps Goal

Davidson, Andrew IR/LH
Duntocher Hibs
Clyde
Leyton
1905 1906 Burnley 47 10
Croydon Common
Partick Thistle
Belfast Celtic
Distillery
Croydon Common

Davidson, (Dr) Andrew LH
b 1892
Rutherglen Glencairn
Celtic
Vale of Atholl (loan)
Wishaw Thistle (loan)
St Mirren
1919 South Shields 1
Glasgow University

Davidson, Andrew Crawford (Andy) LH/CH
b Auchinleck 24/2/1878
Ayr
1900 1905 Middlesbrough 181 8
1906 1907 Bury 64 1
1908 Grimsby Town 31
Southampton
1909 Grimsby Town 28
Grimsby Rovers
Mexborough Town
Grimsby Rovers

Davidson, Charles Alfred (Alf) OL
b Kirkdale 10/10/1904 d 1978
Kirkdale
Congleton Town
1928 1929 New Brighton 34 6
1931 Southport 6 1
Blundellsands
Macclesfield

Davidson, David Leighton (Dave) CH/LH
b Aberdeen 4/6/1905 d 1969
Garthdee
Aberdeen Argyle
Forfar Athletic
1928 1929 Liverpool 58 2
1929 1936 Newcastle United 128
1937 Hartlepools United 6
1937 Gateshead 14 2

Davidson, George Hedley CF
b Lanchester q3 1894 d 1948
Tow Law Town
1922 Durham City 1

Davidson, James (Jack) OR/IR
b Throckley 14/3/1901
1930 1931 Carlisle United 9 3

Davidson, James Wilkie (Jimmy) IL/IR
b Edinburgh 25/10/1873
Leith Athletic
Celtic
1895 1896 Burnley 20 2
1896 Lincoln City (loan) 9 1
Tottenham Hotspur
Brighton United
1899 1901 Burnley 45 5

Davidson, John Campbell IR
b Glenbuck 31/1/1894
Glenbuck Athletic
Solway Star
1922 Coventry City 4
Kilmarnock
Nithsdale Wanderers
Thornhill

Davidson, Nicholas Tiesdell (Nichol) IL
b Tynemouth q2 1901 d 1956
Backworth United
Blyth Spartans
1921 Middlesbrough 0
1922 Ashington 13 1
Carlisle United
Mold Town
Caernarvon Athletic
Washington Colliery Welfare
Wallsend

Davidson, Robert LB/RB
b Whitburn, West Lothian 1876 d 1935
West Benhar Juveniles
Albion Rovers
Dykehead
Celtic
Belfast Celtic (loan)
Heart of Midlothian (loan)
Airdrieonians (loan)
1902 1903 Manchester City 32
Airdrieonians
Bathgate
Balimba Rangers (Queensland)

From To Apps Goal

Davidson, Robert Trimming (Bobby) IR/IL
b Lochgelly 23/4/1913 d 1988
Caps: SLge 1
Prinlaws United
Hamilton Academical (trial)
Bowhill Rovers
St Bernard's
St Johnstone
1934 1937 Arsenal 57 13
1937 1947 Coventry City 47 9
1939 (Coventry City) (1)
Hinckley Athletic
Redditch Town
Rugby Town

Davidson, Stewart RH
b Aberdeen 1/6/1886 d 1960
Caps: Scotland 1
Aberdeen Shamrock
Aberdeen
1913 1922 Middlesbrough 208 4
Aberdeen
Forres Mechanics

Davidson, Thomas (Tommy) LB/RB
b West Calder 1873 d 1949
Dykehead
1894 1899 Bury 116
Millwall Athletic
1901 1902 Newcastle United 38
Brentford

Davidson, William (Willie) OL
b Glasgow
Queen's Park
Falkirk
Airdrieonians
1910 Middlesbrough 16
1911 1912 Everton 38 3
St Mirren

Davidson, William R LH
Annbank
1893 1894 Newton Heath 40 2

Davie, George Alexander CF
b Cardross 19/4/1864
Renton
1888 Everton 2
Sunderland
Renton
Woolwich Arsenal

Davie, John (Jock) CF
b Dunfermline 19/2/1913 d 1994
St Bernard's
St Johnstone
Dunfermline Wednesday
Hibernian
1934 Arsenal 0
Margate
1936 1945 Brighton & Hove Albion 89 39
1939 (Brighton & Hove Albion) (2) (2)
Stockton
1946 Barnsley 6
Kidderminster Harriers
Shrewsbury Town

Davies, Albert IL
Maltby Main Colliery Welfare
1927 1928 Rotherham United 8 1

Davies, Albert Brynley (Bryn) IL/IR
b Cardiff 17/12/1913 d 1990
Army
1935 1937 Cardiff City 9
1938 Ipswich Town 32 7

Davies, Albert Stanley (Bert) OL
b Swindon 1/3/1894 d 1976
Caps: SoLge 1
West End Juniors
Swindon Town
1914 Middlesbrough 1
1920 1926 Swindon Town 217 19
1927 Luton Town 4
Garrards Athletic

Davies, Alfred CH
b 1889 d 1954
Alderley
Hurst
1919 Bolton Wanderers 8 1
1921 Bury 3
Hurst
Macclesfield

Davies, Arthur OR
b Bod Howell 1886 d 1949
Caps: Wales 2
Wrexham St Giles
Wrexham
Druids
1904 West Bromwich Albion 12 1
1904 Middlesbrough 10
Wrexham Nomads

From To Apps Goal

Davies, Arthur Leonard GK
b New Brighton 3/1/1905 d 1940
Caps: FLge 1
Harrowby
1923 New Brighton 0
Flint Town
1926 1929 Everton 90
1930 1934 Exeter City 165
1935 1936 Plymouth Argyle 21
1937 Southport 7
1938 Plymouth Argyle 14

Davies, Arthur Thomas OL
b Nelson q2 1893
Caps: England Amat
Corinthians
1921 Northampton Town 10 1
1922 Nelson 0
Corinthians

Davies, Benjamin (Ben) GK
b Wolverhampton
Wellington St George's
1925 1929 Crewe Alexandra 162
1929 1932 Port Vale 102

Davies, Benjamin IR
Merthyr Thursdays
1927 Merthyr Town 7 1

Davies, Benjamin Edward (Ben) GK
b Middlesbrough 9/6/1888 d 1958
Middlesbrough United
Shildon Athletic
1910 1914 Middlesbrough 31
1920 1922 Cardiff City 73
1923 Leicester City 3
1924 Bradford Park Avenue 0

Davies, Cecil Joseph LH/RH
b Bedwellty 26/3/1918 d 1994
Caps: Wales Sch
Fleur-de-Lis Welfare
Lovells Athletic
1935 Charlton Athletic 0
1938 1946 Barrow 75 3
1939 (Barrow) (3)
1947 1948 Millwall 31
Dartford

Davies, Cyril CH
b West Bromwich 13/5/1917 d 1998
Kidderminster Harriers
1937 1938 West Bromwich Albion 7
Stourbridge

Davies, David (Dai) GK
b Llanelli 1880 d 1944
Caps: Wales 3
1902 1909 Bolton Wanderers 123

Davies, David Daniel (Dai) IL/IR
b Aberdare 5/12/1914 d 1984
Aberaman Athletic
1935 1946 Hull City 141 30
1939 (Hull City) (2) (1)
Scarborough (loan)
Scunthorpe & Lindsey United
Barton Town

Davies, David Walter (Walter) CF/IL
b Treharris 1/10/1888
Caps: Wales 2
Merthyr Town
Treharris
1912 Oldham Athletic 10 3
1912 Stockport County 11 2
1913 1914 Sheffield United 27 9
Millwall Athletic
Merthyr Town
Treharris Albion

Davies, Edward (Charlie) OR
b Pen-y-ffordd 11/5/1910 d 1982
Castleford Town
1929 1935 Halifax Town 195 29
1936 1937 Chesterfield 2
1938 Walsall 12 1
1939 Darlington 0

Davies, Edwin Lloyd (Lloyd) LB/OL/CH
b Cefn Mawr 23/2/1877 d 1957
Caps: SoLge 1/Wales 16
Rhosymedre St John's
Druids
1903 Stoke 7 3
Wellington Town
Swindon Town
1905 1907 Stoke 27
Northampton Town

From To Apps Goal

Davies, Ernest (Ernie) RH
b Heswall q1 1916 d 1942
Heswall
1936 1938 Tranmere Rovers 44 1
1939 (Tranmere Rovers) (3) (1)
1939 York City 0

Davies, Frank GK
b Birkenhead
Birkenhead
1902 Derby County 1
1904 1905 Glossop 61
1906 1909 Manchester City 6

Davies, Frank Palmer LH/CH
b Swansea 1/8/1903 d 1970
Bath City
1923 1925 Bristol City 54
1926 1927 Charlton Athletic 25 1
1928 Portsmouth 0
Nantwich
1930 1933 Northampton Town 144 7
Burton Town

Davies, Fred H IL
Ardwick
1892 1893 Sheffield United 16 6
Baltimore (USA)

Davies, G IR
1896 Walsall 2 2

Davies, G OL
1903 Blackpool 1

Davies, George OL
b Wellington St Georges 2/1900
Ironbridge
1919 1921 Birmingham 29 7
Wellington Town
1922 1923 Southend United 63 11
Wellington Town

Davies, George CF
b Earlestown 4/4/1916 d 1980
Earlestown Bohemians
1937 1945 Bury 54 35
1946 Stockport County 0
Northwich Victoria
Earlestown

Davies, George Albert LH
b Prescot 19/1/1897 d 1956
Prescot
1920 1921 Hull City 11
1922 Merthyr Town 18
1923 1924 Grimsby Town 12 1
Whiston
Llandudno
Caernarvon Athletic
Ashton National
Northwich Victoria

Davies, Glyn Ivor OL
b Swansea 24/11/1909 d 1985
Caps: Wales Amat
1929 1930 Swansea Town 3
Casuals
Bristol University
1932 Brentford 0
1934 Norwich City 3

Davies, Glyn Owen OL
b Holyhead 31/10/1910 d 1971
Connah's Quay & Shotton
Prescot Cables
1931 New Brighton 3
Marine
Rhyl Corinthians

Davies, Gordon Owen RH
b Woolwich 26/4/1903 d 1991
Old Pastonian
1925 Norwich City 1
Metropolitan Police
Waterlow's

Davies, Harry CF
b Chorley
Chorley
1922 Port Vale 12 1
Chorley
Bacup Borough
Chorley

Davies, Harry Augustus IL/IR
b Gainsborough 29/1/1904 d 1975
Bamfords Athletic (Uttoxeter)
1922 1928 Stoke 225 68
1929 1931 Huddersfield Town 55 17
1931 1936 Stoke City 164 24
1937 1938 Port Vale 44 4

From To Apps Goal

Davies, Haydn LH
b Troedyrhiw
Troedyrhiw
1929 Southend United 7
1930 Lincoln City 0

Davies, Henry James (Harry) LB/RB
b Tibberton q1 1876
Bamford's Athletic
1897 1900 Wolverhampton Wanderers 66
Shrewsbury Town
1902 1903 Gainsborough Trinity 46 3
1904 Doncaster Rovers 26 1
1905 1906 Hull City 34
1907 Leicester Fosse 0
Oldfields (Uttoxeter)

Davies, (Rev) Hywel C OL/OR
b Llanddulas 20/11/1902 d 1976
Caps: Wales Amat/Wales 1
Oxford University
Abergele
Llanddulas
Oxford University
1924 1926 Wrexham 11
1926 Chesterfield 0
1927 Wrexham 2
Brynffordd

Davies, Jack GK
b Chorley 1902
Caps: WLge 1
Horwich RMI
1925 1926 Bury 5
1928 Swansea Town 5
Horwich RMI
Wigan Athletic
Horwich RMI

Davies, James OL
b Fife 1895
1920 Millwall Athletic 23 2

Davies, James CH/LH/RH
b Northwick 20/11/1901
Gnome Saltney
1925 Huddersfield Town 0
1926 Charlton Athletic 17
1927 1929 South Shields 106
1930 1931 Gateshead 51
1932 Chesterfield 0
Eden Colliery

Davies, John GK
Hurst
Burslem Port Vale
1892 Newton Heath 7

Davies, John CH
b Rhosllanerchrugog
Rhos Athletic
1922 Wrexham 1
Rhos Athletic

Davies, John Howard CH/RH
b Machynlleth q3 1916
Merthyr Town
1934 1935 Newport County 36

Davies, John Oscar (Jack) IR/OL/OR
b Liverpool 7/1881
1900 1902 Liverpool 9
1903 Blackpool 0

Davies, John William (Jack) LH
b Holt 14/11/1916
Caps: Wales Sch
Troedyrhiw
Ruthin Town
1935 1936 Chester 18 1
1946 Everton 1
1946 1947 Plymouth Argyle 33
1948 Bristol City 30 1

Davies, Jonathan OL
b Rhosllanerchrugog 21/0/1904 d 1978
Caps: Wales Amat
Rhos Athletic
1924 Wrexham 1
Rhos Athletic
Denbigh United
Bangor City
Blaenau Ffestiniog
Llanerch Celts
Oswestry Town
Colwyn Bay United
Wellington Town
Macclesfield Town
Bangor City
Runcorn
Whitchurch

From To Apps Goal

Davies, Joseph (Joe) IR/OR/IL
b Chirk 1870 d 1943
Caps: Wales 11
Chirk
1888 Everton 8 2
Chirk
1892 1893 Ardwick 16 8
1894 1895 Sheffield United 12 4
1895 Manchester City 11 4
Millwall Athletic
Reading
1900 Manchester City 8 1
1901 Stockport County 29 7
Chirk

Davies, Joseph RH/LH
b Cefn Mawr 7/1864 d 1943
Caps: Wales 7
Druids
Newton Heath
1890 1892 Wolverhampton Wanderers 34
Druids

Davies, Joseph (Joe) OR
b Burslem 10/11/1917
1937 Wolverhampton Wanderers 0
1938 Bradford Park Avenue 5

Davies, JW LH
1892 Bootle 7
1893 Walsall Town Swifts 6

Davies, Leonard Stephen (Len) IR/CF/IL
b Splott 28/4/1899 d 1945
Caps: Walses Sch/WLge 2/Wales 23
Victoria Athletic
1920 1930 Cardiff City 305 128
1931 Thames 28 12
Bangor City
Hurst

Davies, Llewellyn Charles (Llew) LB
b Wrexham 1881 d 1961
Caps: Wales Amat/Wales 13
Wrexham
Druids
Wrexham
1904 West Bromwich Albion 3
Wrexham
Northern Nomads
Wrexham
1910 Everton 0
St Helens Town
Wrexham

Davies, Llewellyn John LH
b Northampton 17/5/1894 d 1965
Northampton Town
Cambridge University
1921 Northampton Town 1
Corinthians

Davies, Matthew IL
1926 Aberdare Athletic 7 2

Davies, Oliver T IL
b St Albans
St Albans City
1933 Northampton Town 1

Davies, Raymond RH
b Leicester
1919 Stockport County 1

Davies, Reginald (Reg) RH
b Stanton Hill 29/9/1897 d 1977
Sutton Town
1922 1927 Portsmouth 201 3
1928 1930 Brentford 116
1932 Mansfield Town 18

Davies, Richard H IR/IL
b Hanley 1876
Wrexham
1894 Manchester City 0
Hanley Town
1895 Leicester Fosse 7 4
South Shields
Glossop North End
1898 Wolverhampton Wanderers 11 2
Reading

Davies, Robert RH
b Chirk q2 1886
Caps: Wales Amat
Cammell Laird
Stafford Rangers
Watford
1911 Manchester City 6
Pontypridd

Davies, Robert G IR/OR
b Oswestry
Stoke St Peter's
1932 1933 Port Vale 7
1934 1935 Torquay United 5 1

From To Apps Goal

Davies, Robert Griffith CH
b Blaenau Ffestiniog 19/10/1913 d 1978
Caps: Wales War 6
Blaenau Ffestiniog
1936 1946 Nottingham Forest 55
1939 (Nottingham Forest) (2)

Davies, Robert H (Bob) LB/RB
b Bolton 1876
Tonge Lower End
Haugh Albion
Bolton Lads Club
Halliwell Rovers
1895 1898 Bolton Wanderers 29
Bedminster
1901 1902 Bristol City 36 2
1903 Bolton Wanderers 0

Davies, Robert Idwal (Idwal) CF/IL
b Ewloe Green 17/8/1899 d 1980
Caps: Wales Amat/Wales 1
Conway
Buckley United
1919 West Bromwich Albion 0
Southport
Marine
1921 Southport 9 4
Marine
1923 Liverpool 0
Marine
1924 1925 Bolton Wanderers 3
Rhyl Athletic
Welsh Dragons

Davies, Royston (Roy) OL/OR
b Penydarren 19/10/1903 d 1944
Cyfartha Stars
Aberaman Athletic
1924 Merthyr Town 0
1925 Manchester United 0
1925 Southport 5
Cyfartha Stars
Barry
1927 Bristol Rovers 2
Ebbw Vale
1929 Wolverhampton Wanderers 9
1929 1931 Reading 67 7
Guildford City
Aberaman Athletic
Bangor City
Cyfartha Athletic
Troedyrhiw Welfare
Barry

Davies, Samuel (Sam) LB/RH
b Nantwich q4 1870 d 1913
Nantwich
Crewe Alexandra
Chester
Nantwich
Rossendale
New Brompton
1894 1895 Bury 42 5
1897 Luton Town 25 1
Gravesend United
Nantwich

Davies, Samuel Herbert LB
b Wrexham 5/11/1894 d 1972
Queen's Park
Morton
1924 Manchester United 0
1927 Crewe Alexandra 3
Altrincham
Sandbach Ramblers

Davies, Septimus OL
1912 Blackpool 3

Davies, Seymour RH
1914 Stockport County 16

Davies, Stanley Charles (Stan) CF/IL/IR
b Chirk 24/3/1898 d 1972
Caps: Wales 18
Chirk
Manchester United (trial)
Rochdale
1919 1920 Preston North End 24 11
1920 1921 Everton 20 9
1921 1926 West Bromwich Albion 147 77
1927 Birmingham 14 2
1928 Cardiff City 14 2
1929 Rotherham United 1
1930 Barnsley 1
Manchester Central
Dudley Town

Davies, Thomas LB
Nantwich
1899 1902 Burslem Port Vale 58
Nantwich

From To Apps Goal

Davies, Thomas (Tommy) LH/CH/RH
b Troedyrhiw
1924 Luton Town 0
1925 Bournemouth & Boscombe Ath 5
Columbia
1929 Chelsea 0
1933 1936 Watford 58 3
1937 Exeter City 14
1938 Walsall 1

Davies, Thomas E (Tom) RB
b Briton Ferry q3 1912
Briton Ferry Athletic
Garthmoor (Neath)
1933 Swansea Town 3
1935 Torquay United 5
Bangor City

Davies, Thomas John LB
b 26/5/1908 d 1998
1933 Torquay United 1

Davies, Thomas Osborne (Tom) OR
b Highworth 27/3/1882 d 1967
Swindon Town
1903 1905 Nottingham Forest 40 1
Reading
Salisbury City
Southampton

Davies, Thomas S (Tom) OL
Cross Street (Wrexham)
1938 Wrexham 1
Shotton Athletic

Davies, Vincent (Vince) OL
b Aberaman 2/7/1906 d 1980
1926 Aberdare Athletic 0
1927 Merthyr Town 0
Llanelly
1930 Newport County 22 6
1931 Accrington Stanley 0
Llanelly

Davies, Walter (Wally) IL/IR
b Manchester
Crossley's
Hurst
1914 Bolton Wanderers 0
1914 Manchester United 0
1921 1923 Crewe Alexandra 34 8
Nantwich
Whitchurch
Sandbach Ramblers

Davies, Walter OR
1938 Torquay United 2

Davies, Wilfred Gordon (Gordon) RB/LB
b Swansea 31/7/1915 d 1992
1934 1946 Swansea Town 54
1939 (Swansea Town) (3)
Barry Town
Llanelly
Haverfordwest Athletic
Pembroke Borough

Davies, Wilfred James (Jim) OL
b South Wales
Troedyrhiw
1938 Cardiff City 1

Davies, William (Bill 'Tinker') CF
b Wrexham 13/4/1882 d 1966
Caps: Wales 11
Wrexham St Giles
Wrexham Victoria
Wrexham
1905 1911 Blackburn Rovers 132 66

Davies, William (Billy) IR
b Longton 1884
Newcastle Rangers
1907 Stoke 10 2

Davies, William (Willie) OR
b Troedyrhiwfuwch 16/2/1900 d 1953
Caps: WLge 1/Wales 17
Rhymney
Swansea Amateurs
1921 1923 Swansea Town 43 4
1924 1927 Cardiff City 87 17
1927 1929 Notts County 71 9
1929 1932 Tottenham Hotspur 109 19
Bargoed
1933 1935 Swansea Town 85 18
Llanelly

Davies, William (Taffy) OR/OL/IR
b Troedyrhiw 22/6/1910 d 1995
Caps: Wales War 1
Troedyrhiw
New Tredegar
1930 1949 Watford 283 69
1939 (Watford) (3) (1)

From To Apps Goal

Davies, William Charles (Billy) OL/OR
b Forden 1883
Caps: Wales 4
Rhayader
Llandrindod
Knighton
Shrewsbury Town
1905 1906 Stoke 16 1
Crystal Palace
1908 1909 West Bromwich Albion 53 4
Crystal Palace

Davies, William H RH
b Blakeley 1877
1898 Bolton Wanderers 21
Bedminster
Bristol Rovers

Davies, William T (Bill) OL
b Barry
1923 Bristol City 0
Barry
1925 1926 Merthyr Town 38 3
1927 Walsall 0
Barry

Davin, Martin IR
b Dumbarton 9/5/1905 d 1957
Vale of Clyde
Dumbarton
1927 1929 Bury 38 8
1930 Bolton Wanderers 3
1930 Hull City 8 1
Yeovil & Petters United
Airdrieonians
1933 Clapton Orient 15 2
Guildford City
Ashford Town (Kent)
Briggs Motor Bodies

Davis, Arthur George IL/IR
b Birmingham q1 1898 d 1955
Birmingham St George's
Evesham Town
1919 1921 Aston Villa 5 1
1922 1923 Queen's Park Rangers 62 21
1923 1927 Notts County 140 51
1928 Crystal Palace 5 2
Kidderminster Harriers

Davis, Charles F (Charlie) CH
b Bristol 1905
Bath City
1927 1928 Torquay United 28
1929 1930 York City 61 1
1931 Mansfield Town 5 1
Glastonbury
Bath City

Davis, Charles Harrison CH
b Tynemouth 22/9/1902 d 1987
1923 Liverpool 0
1924 Gillingham 5
West Stanley

Davis, Edward IR
b Larne
Larne
1938 Southend United 5 4

Davis, Edwin (Ted) GK
b Bedminster 1/1892 d 1954
1911 Bristol City 0
Brentford (trial)
1912 Clapton Orient 4
Portsmouth
1913 1921 Huddersfield Town 50
1922 1923 Blackburn Rovers 24
1925 Bristol City 3
Bath City

Davis, Eric CF
b Sheffield
Bangor City
1936 Bournemouth & Boscombe Ath 2
Bath City

Davis, Felix Charles LB
b Wolverhampton q1 1871 d 1950
Brampton Works
Chesterfield Town
Brampton Works
Ilkeston
1895 Nottingham Forest 0
1895 1896 Grimsby Town 29 1
Warmley

Davis, Frederick A (Freddie) OL
b Hackney 1913
Walthamstow Avenue
1935 Clapton Orient 2
Walthamstow Avenue

From To Apps Goal

Davis, Frederick William LH/RH
b Smethwick 1871
Soho Villa
Birmingham St George's
1893 1898 Woolwich Arsenal 137 8
1899 Nottingham Forest 0

Davis, George GK
b Birmingham 1868
St Philip's
1889 Aston Villa 1
Witton White Star

Davis, George CH/RH/LH
b Sheffield 10/2/1907 d 1990
Norton Woodseats
1928 1929 Sheffield United 6
1931 1933 Rotherham United 55

Davis, George Archibald CF
b Handsworth 1870
Victoria
Aston Manor
1892 Aston Villa 1 1
Smethwick Centaur
Wesleyans

Davis, George Henry OL
b Alfreton 5/6/1881 d 1969
Caps: England 2
Alfreton Town
1900 1907 Derby County 134 27
Alfreton Town
Mansfield Mechanics
Calgary Hillhurst

Davis, Harry OR/CF
b Wombwell 11/1879 d 1945
Caps: FLge 1/England 3
Ardsley
1898 1899 Barnsley 49 21
1899 1906 Sheffield Wednesday 214 58

Davis, Henry (Harry) IR/IL/OR
b Smethwick 11/1873 d 1938
Caps: FAlliance 1
Summer Hall
Birmingham St George's
1892 1898 Sheffield Wednesday 159 35

Davis, Henry LB
Cambuslang Hibernian
1898 1899 Walsall 60
Coventry City

Davis, Herbert (Bert) OR
b Bradford 11/8/1906 d 1981
Guiseley
1927 1931 Bradford Park Avenue 172 40
1932 1936 Sunderland 150 38
1936 Leicester City 8
1937 1938 Crystal Palace 26 4
1939 Bradford Park Avenue 0

Davis, Herbert Alfred (Bert) IL/IR/OR
b Arnold 30/3/1897
Arnold St Mary's
1919 1920 Nottingham Forest 20 7
Boston Town
1923 1924 Reading 33 8
Mansfield Town

Davis, James CH
1905 Burton United 33
Coventry City

Davis, James Edgar (Jimmy) GK
b Burneside q3 1905
Burneside
Kendal Town
Bowness Rovers
1928 1931 Barrow 70

Davis, John Alfred Robert (Jack) CF/IL
b Plymouth 29/12/1898 d 1979
1920 Plymouth Argyle 0
Torquay United
1922 1924 Exeter City 68 18
1925 Newport County 34 20
1927 Plymouth Argyle 2

Davis, John William (Jack 'Pimmy') OR/OL
b Ironville 10/4/1882 d 1963
1902 Grimsby Town 0
Somercotes
1904 1909 Derby County 138 9
Ilkeston United
Eastwood Rangers
Sutton Junction
Ilkeston United

Davis, John William IR
Beredbury United
1920 Port Vale 1
Macclesfield

From To Apps Goal

Davis, P OL
1893 Middlesbrough Ironopolis 1

Davis, Samuel George (Sam) RB
b Plymouth 1895
Oreston
Gillingham
Plymouth Argyle
1920 Newport County 13
Torquay United

Davis, Samuel Storey (Sam) RB/LB
b Marsden 25/5/1900 d 1978
Whitburn Colliery
1923 Stoke 2
1925 Tranmere Rovers 5
1926 Accrington Stanley 2
1927 Darlington (trial) 0
Spennymoor United

Davis, Thomas OL
1923 Wigan Borough 7 1
Blythe Bridge

Davis, Thomas John CH
b Bucknall 1901
1923 Port Vale 14
Stafford Rangers

Davis, Thomas Lawrence (Tommy) CF/IR
b Dublin 3/2/1911 d 1987
Caps: Ireland 1/Eire 4
Beaumont
Frankfort
Shelbourne
Midland Athletic
Cork FC
1931 Exeter City (trial) 0
Boston Town
1932 Torquay United 4 1
1933 1934 New Brighton 77 50
FC de Metz
1935 1937 Oldham Athletic 72 51
1937 Tranmere Rovers 10 6
Cork City
Dundalk
Workington
Dundalk
Drumcondra
Shelbourne
Distillery

Davis, W GK
1911 Bristol City 1

Davis, WR OR
1892 1893 Walsall Town Swifts 17 5

Davison, Albert IR
b 1888
Target Club (Chesterfield)
1908 Chesterfield Town 2
Ilkeston United

Davison, John Edward (Teddy) GK
b Gateshead 2/9/1887 d 1971
Caps: England 1
Gateshead St Chad's
Gateshead Town
1908 1924 Sheffield Wednesday 397
Mansfield Town

Davison, John W (Joe) LB/RB
b Byers Green 6/7/1897
Blyth Spartans
1919 1922 Middlesbrough 7
1923 1925 Portsmouth 30
1927 1931 Watford 135 2

Davison, Joseph Hood IR
b Ashington 5/12/1905 d 1991
Ashington Colliery Welfare
1924 Ashington 0
Ashington Colliery Welfare
1928 Ashington 1

Davison, Thomas (Tom) IR
b Edmondsley q1 1901
Sacriston
Bishop Auckland
1922 1923 Durham City 18 4
Sacriston
Bishop Auckland

Davison, Thomas Reay (Tommy) CH
b West Stanley 3/10/1901 d 1971
Tanfield Lea Juniors
Stanley United
1921 1922 Durham City 62 3
1923 1924 Wolverhampton Wanderers 9 1
1925 1930 Derby County 83 5
1930 1931 Sheffield Wednesday 17
1932 1934 Coventry City 100 5
Rhyl Athletic
Bath City

From To Apps Goal

Davy, Harry RB
b Padiham 1872
Padiham
Heywood Central
Blackpool
1895 1896 Leicester Fosse 50
Bristol City

Daw, Edwin Charles (Teddy) GK
b Doncaster 23/1/1875 d 1944
Doncaster Congregationals
Hexthorpe Wanderers
1895 Sheffield United (trial) 0
1896 Grimsby Town 2
Barnsley St Peter's
Rushden
1899 Luton Town 34
1900 1901 Leicester Fosse 55
New Brompton
1904 Doncaster Rovers 2
1905 Bradford City 16
Oldham Athletic
Belmont Works
Merthyr Town
1909 Leicester Fosse 1

Dawe, Edgar Robert (Eddie) RH/LH
b Swindon 3/4/1899 d 1983
Swindon Corinthians
Swindon Victoria
1921 1923 Swindon Town 33 2
Weymouth

Dawes, Albert George (Bert) IL/IR/CF
b Frimley Green 23/4/1907 d 1973
Frimley Green
Guildford City
Aldershot
1929 1933 Northampton Town 164 82
1933 1936 Crystal Palace 105 75
1936 1937 Luton Town 44 18
1937 1938 Crystal Palace 44 16
1939 Aldershot (3)

Dawes, Frederick William (Fred) LB
b Frimley Green 2/5/1911 d 1989
Frimley Green
Aldershot
1929 1935 Northampton Town 162 1
1935 1949 Crystal Palace 222 2
1939 (Crystal Palace) (3)
Beckenham

Dawes, John (Jack) OL
b Smethwick 1881
Smethwick Centaur
1904 West Bromwich Albion 1
Smethwick Centaur
Redditch Albion

Daws, James (Jimmy) RH
b Mansfield Woodhouse 27/5/1898 d 1985
1919 Notts County 0
Mansfield Woodhouse
Mansfield Town
1920 1923 Birmingham 46 1
1924 Bristol Rovers 29
Mansfield Woodhouse
Poole

Dawson, ? RH
1899 Luton Town 2

Dawson, Adam IR/CF/IL
b Craster 23/12/1912 d 2004
Seahouses
Blyth Spartans
Pegswood United
1934 1935 Chesterfield 17 3
1936 Torquay United 9 2
1937 Halifax Town 6
1937 Rochdale 12 6
1938 Southport 0

Dawson, Arthur OL
b Rishton q1 1882
Blackburn Crosshill
1903 1906 Blackburn Rovers 18 4
Nelson
1908 Burnley 1
Accrington Stanley

Dawson, Arthur OL
b Cliviger 22/4/1907 d 1985
Portsmouth Rovers
1928 Burnley 0
Lancaster Town
1930 Nelson 10

Dawson, Charles OR/OL/IL
Southport Central
1906 1909 Preston North End 67 23
Ashton Town

From To Apps Goal

Dawson, Edward GK
b Chester-le-Street 16/1/1913 d 1970
Annfield Plain
Blyth Spartans
1934 Manchester City 0
1936 1938 Bristol City 66
1939 (Bristol City) (3)
1946 1948 Gateshead 83

Dawson, F OL
1893 Rotherham Town 5 1

Dawson, Frank LB
b Bolton 17/10/1909 d 1991
Darwen
1932 Manchester United 0
1933 1935 Tranmere Rovers 77

Dawson, Frederick Henry Herbert (Frankie LH
b Birmingham 12/1858 d 1938
Aston Unity
1888 Aston Villa 3

Dawson, G OR
1914 Glossop 2

Dawson, George LH/OL
b Bedlington d 1927
Dudley Rovers
Seghill United
Bedlington United
1912 1920 Preston North End 123 3
Bedlington United

Dawson, Harold (Harry) OL
b Bolton q1 1886
Rossendale United
1908 Everton 4
1908 1910 Blackpool 26 4
Croydon Common
West Ham United
Croydon Common
Gillingham

Dawson, James Maxwell (Jimmy) IR
b Edinburgh 13/8/1890
Edinburgh Emmet
1913 Liverpool 13 3
St Bernard's
Albion Rovers
Alloa Athletic
St Mirren
Bo'ness

Dawson, Jeremiah (Jerry) GK
b Holme-in-Cliviger 18/3/1888 d 1970
Caps: FLge 4/England 2
Portsmouth Rovers
Holme-in-Cliviger
1906 1928 Burnley 522

Dawson, Jonathan IL
b Todmorden q1 1884
1906 Burnley 1

Dawson, Joseph Reginald (Reg) OL
b Sheffield 4/10/1914 d 1973
Dinnington Athletic
1938 1946 Rotherham United 32 2
Denaby United

Dawson, Kenneth (Kenny) IL
b Forres
Forres Thistle
Nairn County
1933 Sheffield United 0
Forres Mechanics
Falkirk
1938 Blackpool 12 1
Falkirk

Dawson, Percival Hall (Percy) CF
b Cullercoats 4/12/1889 d 1974
Whitley Athletic
North Shields Athletic
Heart of Midlothian
1913 1922 Blackburn Rovers 140 71
Dumbarton (loan)
Preston Colliery
1923 Barrow 4

Dawson, Sidney RB
b Mexborough q4 1893
Denaby United
1912 Sheffield Wednesday 0
Kilnhurst Town
Northampton Town
1919 1920 Grimsby Town 48
Denaby United

From To Apps Goal

Dawson, Thomas (Tommy) LB/CH
b Springwell 15/12/1901 d 1977
Washington Colliery
Chopwell Institute
1924 1929 Stoke 23
1932 Clapton Orient 19
1933 1935 Gateshead 20

Dawson, Thomas (Tommy) IR/IL/OR
b Middlesbrough 6/2/1915 d 1972
Whitby United
1936 1937 Darlington 23 3
Spennymoor United
1938 1946 Charlton Athletic 23 2
1939 (Charlton Athletic) (2) (1)
1947 Brentford 36 10
1948 1949 Swindon Town 65 15
Chippenham Town

Dawson, William Henry (Billy) IL
b Farnworth q4 1880
1900 Everton 0
Southport Central
1905 Gainsborough Trinity 2

Dawson, William John (Digger) LB
b Newbiggin 1905
Newbiggin West End
1930 Carlisle United 18
1931 1932 Crewe Alexandra 54
1933 York City 28 1
Workington

Day, Albert Ernest (Dapper) OR
b Cardiff 4/5/1918 d 1992
Caps: Wales Sch
1937 Cardiff City 0
1938 Torquay United (loan) 20 2
1939 Torquay United (3)

Day, Alfred (Alf) RH/LH
b Ebbw Vale 2/10/1907 d 1997
Caps: Wales 1
Ebbw Vale
Cheshunt
Northfleet
1933 1935 Tottenham Hotspur 13
1936 Millwall 5
1937 Southampton 22
1938 Tranmere Rovers 32
1939 Swindon Town (1)

Day, Horace CF
1923 Walsall 1

Day, John William GK
b Sutton-on-Trent 16/9/1882 d 1949
Newark
1906 Nottingham Forest 0
1907 1909 Gainsborough Trinity 62

Daykin, Harry Reginald OL
b Somercotes 25/7/1909 d 1985
Alfreton Town
1927 Southend United 1
1928 Fulham 0
Mansfield Town

Daykin, Thomas (Tom) RB/LB/LH
b Shildon 8/1882 d 1960
Eldon Albion
Bishop Auckland
1902 Newcastle United (trial) 0
Hobson Wanderers
1904 1908 Sunderland 46
1908 1911 Birmingham 88 1
Spennymoor United
South Shields

Deacey, Charles (Charlie) CH
b Wednesbury 6/10/1889 d 1952
Wednesbury Town
Wednesbury Old Athletic
1910 1913 West Bromwich Albion 18
1914 1920 Hull City 75 4
1920 1922 Grimsby Town 90 4
Pontypridd
1924 Merthyr Town 0

Deacon, Henry (Harry) IR/IL
b Darnall 25/4/1900 d 1946
Caps: WLge 2
Hallam
1919 Sheffield Wednesday 0
1921 Birmingham 2
1922 1930 Swansea Town 319 86
1931 1933 Crewe Alexandra 118 47
1934 Southport 9 2
1934 Accrington Stanley 25 11
1935 Rotherham United 6

From To Apps Goal

Deacon, James (Jimmy) IL/RH
b Glasgow 23/1/1906 d 1968
Albert Hill United
1927 Darlington 2
1929 1934 Wolverhampton Wanderers 149 51
1934 1938 Southend United 100 3
1939 Hartlepools United (3)

Deacon, Leslie Claude (Les) CH/LH
b Plymouth 22/12/1895 d 1982
Devon County
1921 1928 Plymouth Argyle 5 1
Devon County

Deacon, Richard (Dickie) IL
b Glasgow 26/6/1911 d 1986
Darlington Juniors
Cockfield
1928 Fulham (trial) 0
1930 Wolverhampton Wanderers 3 1
1932 West Ham United 3
1933 Chelsea 0
Glentoran
1935 Northampton Town 3
1936 1938 Lincoln City 110 22
1939 (Lincoln City) (3)

Deakin, Enoch IL
b Wolverhampton
1910 Wolverhampton Wanderers 5 1

Deakin, George Aubrey OL
b Holywell 21/2/1915 d 2000
Caps: Wales Amat
Caergwrle
1937 Chester 1

Deakin, JG OL
1893 Middlesbrough Ironopolis 6 1

Deakin, John (Jack) CH
b Stoke-on-Trent 1873
Dresden United
1898 Stoke 2
Hanley Swifts

Deakin, John (Jack) CF
b Altofts 27/9/1912
Altofts WR Colliery
1936 1938 Bradford City 62 45
1939 (Bradford City) (1)

Dean (Deanes), Alfred (Alf) OR/CF
b Hednesford 24/5/1877 d 1959
Tantany Rovers
West Bromwich Standard
Walsall
1896 1897 West Bromwich Albion 7 3
1898 1900 Walsall 65 29
1900 Nottingham Forest 7
1901 Grimsby Town 17 1
1902 1904 Bristol City 84 35
Swindon Town
Millwall Athletic
Dundee
Millwall Athletic
Wellington Town

Dean, Arthur IL
b Stoke-on-Trent q3 1904
1930 Crewe Alexandra 1

Dean, Cyril George IR
b Bournemouth 27/7/1915 d 1997
Caps: England Sch
1935 Aston Villa 0
1936 1937 Reading 16 3
Rouen
1939 Southampton 0
Gloucester City
Cheltenham Town
Trowbridge Town
Dursley Town

Dean, Harold CF
b Hulme
1931 Manchester United 2
Mossley

Dean, John Thomas (Jerry) OR/IR
b Hadley 13/2/1881
Trench Victoria
1901 1902 Wolverhampton Wanderers 4
Ironbridge
Wellington Town
1904 1911 Notts County 254 49

Dean, Luke IL/OR
b Hanley 21/6/1913 d 1975
Downings Tileries
1934 1936 Port Vale 32 9
Northwich Victoria

Dean, Meshach IR
b Burslem q4 1872 d 1916
1892 1895 Burslem Port Vale 75 21

From To Apps Goal

Dean, William Ralph (Bill 'Dixie') CF
b Birkenhead 22/1/1907 d 1980
Caps: FLge 6/England 16
Pensby Institute
1923 1924 Tranmere Rovers 30 27
1924 1937 Everton 399 349
1937 1938 Notts County 9 3
Sligo Rovers
Hurst

Dearden, Robert LH/CH
Leyland
1902 1905 Manchester City 21

Dearn, Stephen LH/IL
b Halesowen 3/1901 d 1947
Halesowen Town
1922 Aston Villa 0
1923 1925 Portsmouth 21 4
1926 1928 Brentford 82 9

Dearnaley, Irvine LB
b Ashton-under-Lyne q2 1883 d 1965
1908 Glossop 1

Dearnaley, Robert Harold LB
b Glossop q4 1886 d 1951
1909 1914 Glossop 54

Dearson, Donald John (Don) IR/LH/RH
b Ynysybwl 13/5/1914 d 1990
Caps: Wales Amat/Wales War 15/Wales 3
Llantwit Major Juniors
Barry
1934 1946 Birmingham 131 17
1939 (Birmingham) (3) (1)
1946 1949 Coventry City 84 10
1949 1950 Walsall 51 12
Nuneaton Borough
Bilston

Death, William George (Billy) OL
b Rotherham 13/11/1899 d 1984
Broome Athletic
Rotherham Town
1920 1922 Notts County 21 4
Mansfield Town
1924 1927 Sunderland 53 12
1928 1929 Exeter City 25 6
1930 Gillingham 27 6
1931 Mansfield Town 14 2
Grantham
Heanor Town
Sutton Town
Heanor Town
City Transport (Nottingham)

Dee, Amos LH/OR/IL
b Merthyr Tydfil 19/12/1904 d 2000
1924 Merthyr Town 2
1925 Manchester United 0
1926 Wolverhampton Wanderers 0
1927 Gillingham 4
1928 Bradford City 1

Deeley, James OL
b Evesham 1871
Worcester Rovers
1895 Small Heath 1
Hereford Thistle

Deeming, Henry (Harry) OR
b Bedworth 24/7/1901 d 1984
Exhall Colliery
1924 Coventry City 1
Nuneaton Town
Foleshill Great Heath

Deighton, Alexander (Alex) OL
b Gateshead q2 1876 d 1908
Liverpool South End
Rock Ferry
1897 Notts County 10 1
Rock Ferry
Haydock

Deighton, James (Jack) GK
1934 Everton 0
1935 Cardiff City 18

Delea, William (Bill) CF
b Cork 12/9/1910 d 1985
Glenview
Cork Bohemians
1932 Southport 7 3
Cork Bohemians
Dundalk
Ford Sports

Dell, Frederick (Fred) IR
b Dartford 10/12/1915 d 1970
Dartford
1936 1937 West Ham United 4
1938 Doncaster Rovers 27 12
1939 (Doncaster Rovers) (2)

From To Apps Goal

Dellow, Reginald Charles IL/CF
b Farnham, Essex 28/9/1902 d 1981
Caps: England Amat
Barking Town
1925 1926 Millwall 4 1
Ilford

Dellow, Ronald William (Ron) OR
b Crosby 13/7/1914
1931 Liverpool 0
Bootle St Mary's
Bootle Celtic
1933 Blackburn Rovers 0
1934 Mansfield Town 24 10
1934 Manchester City 10 4
1935 1938 Tranmere Rovers 105 29
1939 1946 Carlisle United 16 5
1939 (Carlisle United) (2) (1)
Ards

Dellow, Stanley Philip (Stan) RB/LB
b Aylesbury q4 1898 d 1923
Willesden
1920 Bradford City 0
1921 1922 Southend United 21

Delves, William (Billy) LH
b Wolstanton q4 1870 d 1908
1892 Burslem Port Vale 2

Demellweek, John William (Jack) OR
b Turnchapel 10/1/1907 d 1994
Royal Navy
1926 Plymouth Argyle 1
Royal Navy
1931 1934 Plymouth Argyle 31 2
1935 Southend United 6

Demmery, William GK
b Kingswood q2 1877 d 1955
Warmley
Bristol East
1905 1907 Bristol City 38
Bristol Rovers

Dempsey, Alfred CF
b Lancaster 1864
1888 Preston North End 0
1888 Stoke (loan) 1

Dempsey, Edwin IR
Accrington Stanley
1906 Bolton Wanderers 7 1
Accrington Stanley

Dempsey, James OR/OL/IL
b Pentrebach q3 1897 d 1984
1920 1921 Millwall Athletic 16
1922 1923 Merthyr Town 37 1

Dempsey, Mark LB
b 14/10/1887
1914 Bradford Park Avenue 1

Dempsey, William Watson (Bill) LB
b St Germans 10/9/1896 d 1967
Cawsand
Portland United
RAF Felixstowe
Ipswich Town
1925 Norwich City 8
London Prison OS
1927 Brentford 0
1928 Queen's Park Rangers 0
Tunbridge Wells Rangers
Grays Thurrock
Canterbury Waverley
Weymouth

Dempster, James Barclay GK
b Newarthill 30/1/1896
Newarthill Thistle
1919 1921 Sunderland 40
Airdrieonians
St Johnstone
Dundee United
Bo'ness
Bathgate
Bo'ness

Denby, Stanley LH/RH
b Goole 19/6/1912 d 1995
Goole Territorials
Goole Town
1932 1936 Hull City 124 3
Guildford City

Denholm, George Anderson LB/LH/CH
b Hill o' Beath 8/1915
Park View Rangers (Cowdenbeath)
Hearts o' Beath
Raith Rovers
1936 1938 York City 8

From To Apps Goal

Denmark, James (Jimmy) CH
b Glasgow 30/5/1913 d 1978
Tollcross Clydesdale
Parkhead Juniors
Third Lanark
1937 1938 Newcastle United 51
1939 (Newcastle United) (3)
Queen of the South
Ashington

Dennington, Charles (Charlie) GK
b Beccles 7/10/1899 d 1943
Beccles Town
1922 1928 Norwich City 195
1929 Bradford City 18
Kirkley
Beccles Town
Kirkley
Gorleston

Dennington, Leslie Arthur (Les) LH/CH
b West Bromwich 4/1/1903 d 1988
Wolseley Motors
1924 Aston Villa 1
1926 1928 Reading 11
1928 1930 Exeter City 65

Dennis, George Thomas OL/LB
b Moira 12/9/1897 d 1969
Coalville Swifts
Newhall Swifts
1920 1923 Nottingham Forest 30 3
1924 1928 Luton Town 139 42
1929 Norwich City 1
1930 Bristol Rovers 26 4
Burton Town

Dennis, Harold T OR
b Newark 1903
Newark Town
Grantham
1925 Huddersfield Town 1
1926 Southend United 11 2
Grantham

Dennis, William (Billy) LB/RB
b Mossley 21/9/1895 d 1952
Ashton PSA
Denton (trial)
1919 Blackburn Rovers 5
1921 1922 Stalybridge Celtic 72
1923 Manchester United 3
1923 1927 Chesterfield 165 6
1928 1929 Wigan Borough 67
Macclesfield
Hurst
Mossley

Dennison, Harry IL/CF
b Bradford 4/11/1894 d 1947
Blackburn Trinity
1910 1919 Blackburn Rovers 3
Accrington Stanley
1921 Rochdale 33 17
1922 Wigan Borough 30 13
Stalybridge Celtic
1924 Stockport County 11 3
Stalybridge Celtic
Hurst
Macclesfield
Barnoldswick Town
Lytham
Stalybridge Celtic

Dennison, James CF
Sale Holmfield
1903 Manchester City 1 2

Dennison, John S (Jack) RH
b Castle Douglas
Amble
1922 Coventry City 4

Dennison, Robert (Bob) IR/IL/CF
b Arnold 6/10/1900 d 1973
Arnold St Mary's
1920 1923 Norwich City 117 34
1924 Brighton & Hove Albion 25 10
1925 Manchester City 8 4
1926 1928 Clapton Orient 70 28
1929 Chesterfield 28 7
Yarmouth Town

Dennison, Robert Smith (Bob) CH/CF/LB
b Amble 6/3/1912 d 1996
Radcliffe Welfare United
1932 1933 Newcastle United 11 2
1934 Nottingham Forest 15 5
1935 1938 Fulham 31
1939 (Fulham) (1)
1945 1947 Northampton Town 55

From To Apps Goal

Denoon, John (Jock) GK
b Inverness 10/4/1890
Tockgorm
Nelson (Inverness)
Inverness Thistle
1909 Chelsea 0
Motherwell
Norwich City
1920 1926 Swansea Town 173
Mid-Rhondda United
New Tredegar

Densley, Arthur Herbert (Bert) GK
b Bristol 11/5/1903 d 1972
YMCA
1927 1929 Bristol Rovers 23
Bath City

Dent, Frederick (Fred) IL/CF/IR
b Sheffield 24/1/1896 d 1983
Caps: WLge 1
St Cuthbert's
1920 Sheffield Wednesday 4 1
1921 1922 Halifax Town 38 12
1923 Chesterfield 0
Mid-Rhondda United
1925 Bristol City 12 1
1926 1927 Exeter City 48 29
1928 Merthyr Town 13 1
1928 Norwich City 24 12
1929 Swindon Town 21 6
1930 Luton Town 13 5
Sheffield Employment Exchange
Barnsley Ministry of Labour

Dent, George Henry IL
b Hull 9/3/1899 d 1983
Clee Rangers
Humber Graving Dock
1923 1924 Grimsby Town 24 12
Cleethorpes Town
Mexborough Athletic
Haycroft Rovers

Dent, John George (Johnny) CF
b Spennymoor 31/1/1903 d 1979
Spennymoor Rangers
Tudhoe United
Thornley Albion
1923 1924 Durham City 18 8
Tow Law Town
1925 Durham City 28 18
1926 1929 Huddersfield Town 48 22
1929 1936 Nottingham Forest 196 119
Kidderminster Harriers

Denton, Arthur CF
b Chorlton 9/1907 d 1979
1928 Crewe Alexandra 1
Chorley
Hurst
Mossley
Hurst
Droylsden

Denton, Frederick George (Fred) IL
b Barnet 7/5/1899 d 1969
1920 Clapton Orient 3
Chatham Town

Denwood, Wilfred (Wilf) OL
b Bury 26/3/1900 d 1959
Bacup Borough
1924 New Brighton 5
1925 Nelson (trial) 3
Witton Albion
Heywood Street United Methodists
Horwich RMI
Heywood St James

Denyer, Albert Edward Curly (Bertie) OR/CF
b Plaistow 9/4/1893 d 1969
Caps: England Sch
Ilford
Leyton
West Ham United
Swindon Town
Heart of Midlothian
1920 1929 Swindon Town 324 49
Evesham Town
West End Sports

Depledge, Joseph (Joe) CH
b Sheffield 15/4/1897 d 1974
Rotherham Town
1923 Stoke 5
Mansfield Town

Depledge, Robert Percy GK
b Litherland q3 1882 d 1930
1906 Everton 1

From To Apps Goal

Derbyshire, James Edward LB
b Tottington q2 1882 d 1945
Hawks Lane St Mary's
Turton
1902 Blackburn Rovers 11
Nelson
Darwen
Turton

Derbyshire, Joseph RB
b Turton q3 1880
Darwen
1902 1908 Preston North End 126 8
Rossendale United
Darwen
Great Harwood

Derrick, Albert Edward CF/OR
b Newport 8/9/1908 d 1975
1935 1945 Newport County 125 43
1946 Swindon Town 1
Ebbw Vale
Girlings

Derrick, John Henry IR/CF/IL
b Nottingham 8/12/1891 d 1938
Christ Church
1909 1919 Nottingham Forest 139 35
Aberaman

Devan, Charles F (Charlie) OR/OL
b Girvan 22/4/1901 d 1980
Glasgow Ashfield
St Anthony's (Glasgow)
Clydebank
Morton
1924 South Shields 12
1925 1926 Grimsby Town 50 13
1927 Fulham 7 2

Devan, William Gemmill (Bill) IL/OL
b Whitletts 23/2/1909 d 1966
Caps: IrLge 2
Whitletts
Ayr United
1929 Nelson (trial) 0
Ards (trial)
Mansfield Town (trial)
Sanquhar
Coleraine
Linfield
Coleraine Caledonians
1933 1937 Watford 90 33
Ayr United (trial)
Scammells

Deverall, Harold Reginald (Jackie) LH/OL/RH
b Petersfield 5/5/1916 d 1999
Caps: England Sch
Maidenhead United
1938 1947 Reading 74 9
1948 1952 Leyton Orient 115 2
Sittingbourne

Devey, Edwin James (Ted) LH/IR/RH
b Small Heath 8/1862 d 1946
Excelsior
1892 1895 Small Heath 75 2
1895 1896 Burton Wanderers 56 11

Devey, Harry Percival CH/LH/RH
b Birmingham 3/1860 d 1924
Aston Clarendon
Montrose (Birmingham)
Excelsior
1888 1892 Aston Villa 73 1

Devey, John Henry George (Jack) IR/CF/IL
b Birmingham 26/12/1866 d 1940
Caps: FAlliance 1/FLge 4/England 2
Wellington Road
Excelsior
Aston Unity
Aston Manor
1889 West Bromwich Albion 0
Birmingham St George's
1891 1901 Aston Villa 268 168

Devey, William (Will) CF/IR/OL
b Perry Barr 12/4/1865 d 1948
Clarendon Montrose
Wellington Town
Aston Unity
Mitchell St George's
Small Heath Alliance
1891 1892 Wolverhampton Wanderers 41 17
1892 1893 Aston Villa 10 2
1894 Walsall Town Swifts 21 7
1896 Burton Wanderers 22 7
1896 1897 Notts County 14 3
1897 Walsall 11 6
Burton Wanderers
1898 Walsall 0
1898 Small Heath 2 1

From To Apps Goal

Devine, Archibald F (Archie) IL
b Lochore 2/4/1887 d 1964
Caps: SLge 1/Scotland 1
Minto Rovers
Lochgelly Rangers
Lochgelly United
Heart of Midlothian (trial)
Raith Rovers
Heart of Midlothian
Falkirk
1910 1912 Bradford City 48 9
1912 1913 Woolwich Arsenal 24 5
Shelbourne
1914 Bradford City 0
Lochgelly United
Dunfermline Athletic
Lochgelly United

Devine, Daniel RH
b Dumbarton 1870
Dumbarton
Renton
1893 Woolwich Arsenal 2
Partick Thistle

Devine, John (Jock) LB
b Twechar 10/6/1899 d 1949
Kilsyth Rangers
1921 1922 Plymouth Argyle 14 2
1923 Exeter City 0
East Stirlingshire
Kettering Town
1926 Charlton Athletic 19
Dundee
1927 Southport 34 1
1928 Crewe Alexandra 0
Kilsyth Rangers
Croy Celtic

Devine, John Stephen IR
b Aberdeen
St Roch's
Aberdeen
1938 Queen's Park Rangers 7 3

Devine, Joseph Cassidy (Joe) IL/LH/IR
b Motherwell 8/9/1905 d 1980
Motherwell Watsonians
Cleland Juniors
Bathgate
1925 1929 Burnley 114 27
1929 1930 Newcastle United 22 11
1930 1932 Sunderland 68 7
1933 1934 Queen's Park Rangers 57 9
1934 1936 Birmingham 55 2
1937 Chesterfield 23

Devlin, Hugh LB
b Glasgow 1875
Cambuslang
1896 Blackburn Rovers 1

Devlin, James (Jimmy) CF
Blackstoun R
Celtic
Abercorn
Paisley Celtic
Celtic
Royal Albert
Chorley
Dundee
1897 Sunderland 0
1897 Woolwich Arsenal 1 1
Airdrieonians
Third Lanark
Albion Rovers
Army
Albion Rovers

Devlin, Thomas (Tom) IR/IL/OR
b Bellshill 6/10/1903 d 1979
Vale of Clyde
Shawfield Juniors
Kilsyth Rangers
Third Lanark
King's Park
1924 Birmingham 2 1
1925 1926 Preston North End 8 1
1927 Liverpool 0
1928 Swindon Town 1
Brooklyn Wanderers
Aberdeen
1932 Walsall 4
Fall River Marksmen
Zurich
Fleetwood
1934 Oldham Athletic 2
Racing Club de Roubaix
Fleetwood

From To Apps Goal

Devlin, William (Billy) CF/IR
b Hebburn q1 1891 d 1965
Wallsend
1911 Stockport County 20 2
Cardiff City
1920 1921 Newport County 57 21
1922 Exeter City 12 5

Devlin, William OL
b Belfast
Belfast Celtic
1920 1921 Coventry City 9

Devlin, William Alexander (Bill) CF
b Bellshill 30/7/1899 d 1972
Vale of Clyde
Clyde
King's Park (loan)
Cowdenbeath
1925 1926 Huddersfield Town 32 14
1926 1927 Liverpool 19 15
Heart of Midlothian
Macclesfield
Cowdenbeath
Mansfield Town
Cowdenbeath
Burton Town
Shelbourne
Olympique Marseille
Bangor City
Boston Town
Ashton National
Olympique Marseille
Zurich

Devonshire, William James OR
b Catford 1/1890 d 1946
Lewisham Park
Catford South End
1914 Derby County 7 1

Dewar, George (Geordie) RH/CH
b Dumbarton 20/7/1867 d 1915
Caps: FLge 1/Scotland 2
Dumbarton Athletic
Dumbarton
1889 1896 Blackburn Rovers 174 7
New Brighton Tower
Southampton

Dewar, John LB
b Glasgow 12/1866
Well Park
Third Lanark
Glasgow Thistle
Third Lanark
Sunderland Albion
1892 Everton 1

Dewar, Neil Hamilton CF
b Lochgilphead 11/11/1908 d 1982
Caps: SLge 2/Scotland 3
Lochgilphead United
Third Lanark
1932 1933 Manchester United 36 14
1933 1936 Sheffield Wednesday 84 43
Third Lanark

Dewey, Joseph IR/IL
b Burton-on-Trent q4 1873 d 1926
1892 1895 Burton Swifts 65 21
1896 Nottingham Forest 1
1896 Burton Swifts 17 5

Dewhurst, Frederick (Fred) IL/CF
b Fulwood 16/12/1863 d 1895
Caps: England 9
Preston Juniors
Preston North End
Corinthians
Preston North End
Corinthians
1888 Preston North End 16 12
Corinthians
1889 1890 Preston North End 8 1

Dewhurst, Gerard Powys CF
b London 14/2/1872 d 1956
Caps: England 1
Cambridge University
Liverpool Ramblers
1893 Liverpool 1
Corinthians

Dewhurst, John (Jack) CH/CF/RH
b Padiham q3 1877
Padiham
1898 Darwen 8 3
1899 1904 Blackburn Rovers 169 43
Brentford
1905 1911 Bury 186 6
Accrington Stanley
Morecambe

Dewhurst, WA GK
1898 Blackpool 1

From To Apps Goal

Dewick, Leonard F (Len) GK
b Watford 24/2/1900 d 1981
1923 1924 Watford 7
Chesham United
Tufnell Park
Chesham United
Barnet

Dewis, George Renger CF/IL
b Burbage 22/1/1913 d 1994
Stoke Golding
Nuneaton Town
1933 1949 Leicester City 116 45
1939 (Leicester City) (1) (1)

Dewsnap, George Henry OR
b Bolton 13/12/1905 d 1974
Rossendale United
Bacup Borough
Rhyl
Runcorn
1932 Accrington Stanley 18 3
Rossendale United

Dexter, Arthur (Alf) GK
b Nottingham 11/1/1905 d 1997
Highbury Vale
Vernon Athletic
Stapleford Brookhill
1923 1936 Nottingham Forest 256

Dexter, George RB
b Hucknall Torkard 5/8/1896 d 1972
Bestwood Colliery
Coventry City
1914 Preston North End 1
Hucknall Byron
Norwich City

Diamond, John James (Jack) CF
b Middlesbrough 30/10/1910 d 1961
Bethesda (Hull)
East Riding Amateurs
Beverley White Star
1931 Hull City 1
Newark Town
Shelbourne
1933 1934 Southport 48 28
1934 Barnsley 4 1
1935 Cardiff City 18 9
1936 Bury 0
1936 1938 Oldham Athletic 50 22
1938 Hartlepools United 9 1
Hyde United

Diaper, Bertie William F (Bert) LH/RH
b Woolston 11/2/1909 d 1995
Cowes
1928 Arsenal 0
1932 Luton Town 3
1933 Fulham 3
1935 Charlton Athletic 0
1936 1938 Aldershot 64
Guildford City

Dick, Alexander (Alec) RB
b Kilmarnock 1865 d 1925
Kilmarnock Athletic
Liverpool Stanley
1888 Everton 9

Dick, Andrew RH
b Larkhall 26/3/1900 d 1970
Larkhall Thistle
Armadale
Airdrieonians
Aberdeen
1925 Bristol Rovers 19
Motherwell
Ayr United
Aberdeen

Dick, Douglas Charles IR
b Greenock 12/1868 d 1950
Morton
Rangers
1893 Liverpool 11 2
Third Lanark
Morton

Dick, John RH/CH
b Eaglesham 1876
Airdrieonians
1898 1909 Woolwich Arsenal 262 12

Dick, William Russell RH
b Harthill 12/6/1901
Armadale
Airdrieonians
Hibernian
1931 Bradford Park Avenue 11
Raith Rovers

From To Apps Goal

Dicken, Harold CH
b Wednesbury 18/7/1891 d 1972
Bilston United
1909 West Bromwich Albion 1
Bilston United

Dickenson, James (Jimmy) LH/LB
b Pittington 1908
Murton Colliery Welfare
Easington Colliery
1930 Hartlepools United 23 1
1931 Blackpool 0
1932 1933 Oldham Athletic 6
1934 Torquay United 18 1
Scarborough
Horden Colliery Welfare
Walker Celtic

Dickenson, Joseph (Joe) OL
b Chatham
1892 1893 Bolton Wanderers 42 11
New Brompton
Chatham
Grays United
New Brompton

Dickie, George OR
b Montrose 1906
Forres Mechanics
1925 Stoke City 1
St Johnstone
Forres Mechanics

Dickie, James (Jimmy) OL
b Montrose 22/9/1903 d 1960
Buckie Thistle
1924 Preston North End (trial) 0
1925 Preston North End 3 1
Forres Mechanics
1927 1928 New Brighton 56 15
1928 1929 Bristol City 48 4
Chester
Macclesfield
1932 Chester 1
1932 New Brighton 27 4
Forres Mechanics

Dickie, John Wilkie CF
b Dundee 25/1/1900 d 1976
Glasgow Perthshire
1923 1925 Barrow 30 15
Taunton United
1926 Barrow 0
Caernarvon Athletic

Dickie, Murdoch McFarlane OR
b Dumbarton 28/12/1919 d 2004
1937 Crewe Alexandra 0
1939 Port Vale (2)
Guildford City
1946 Chelsea 1
1946 1947 Bournemouth & Boscombe Ath 17 1
Tonbridge
Chingford Town
Merthyr Tydfil

Dickie, Percy RH/IR
b Aberdeen 11/12/1907
Mugiemoss
Aberdeen
St Johnstone
1937 1938 Blackburn Rovers 19 1
Aberdeen
Peterhead

Dickie, William Campbell (Bill) RH
b Maryhill 22/11/1903 d 1977
Poole
Weymouth
Portland
Poole
1927 Everton 0
1928 1929 Southport 31 1
Connah's Quay & Shotton
1929 Wrexham 19
Connah's Quay & Shotton
Llanelly
Connah's Quay & Shotton
Poole Town
Worgret Wanderers
Poole Municipal Sports

Dickie, William Cunningham (Bill) RH/CH
b Kilmarnock 2/5/1893 d 1960
Riccarton
Kilbirnie Ladeside
Kilmarnock
1919 1920 Chelsea 35
1920 1921 Stoke 14
Sittingbourne
Sheppey United

From To Apps Goal

Dickinson, Alfred IL
b Saltney Ferry 10/2/1914 d 1998
1934 Everton 1
1936 Port Vale 5
1937 1938 Northampton Town 19 5

Dickinson, Arthur William RB
b Darlington 7/10/1907 d 1976
Ferryhill Athletic
1930 Brighton & Hove Albion 0
Folkestone
1932 Darlington 3

Dickinson, H James OL
b Padiham
1901 Burnley 2
Padiham

Dickinson, Harry CF
b London
1920 Southend United 3

Dickinson, James (Jimmy) RH/LH
b Crawshawbooth 11/11/1899 d 1971
Royal Navy
1920 1924 Plymouth Argyle 111
1925 Wigan Borough 0
Rossendale United
1926 Norwich City 16
Peterborough & Fletton United
Guildford City

Dickinson, Joseph Henry (Joe) IR
b Choppington q4 1900 d 1951
Choppington
Hartlepools United (trial)
1919 South Shields (trial) 0
1920 Sunderland 0
1921 Ashington 3 1
Bedlington United
Amble

Dickinson, Percival Edward OR
b Langley Moor 19/1/1902 d 1985
Willington Athletic
1924 Middlesbrough 6 1
Annfield Plain
Durham City

Dickinson, Samuel IR
1936 Gateshead 1

Dickinson, Sydney (Syd) LH/OL
b Nottingham 17/8/1906 d 1984
Dale Rovers
1923 Nottingham Forest 0
Mansfield Town
1926 1933 Bradford Park Avenue 156 19
1933 Port Vale 12 2
1934 Lincoln City 14 3
Grantham

Dickinson, Thomas Septimus OR
b Ormskirk q1 1890
Kippax Parish Church
1908 Bolton Wanderers 0
Southport YMCA
1910 Preston North End 1
1911 Stockport County 0

Dickinson, Walter (Wally) RB/LB
b Sheffield 22/12/1895 d 1968
Craven Sports
1919 1921 Bradford Park Avenue 113
1922 Sheffield Wednesday 7
1923 1929 Swindon Town 230 20

Dickinson, William (Billy) IL/IR/OR
b Wigan 18/2/1904 d 1968
New Springs
Tophock
1925 1927 Wigan Borough 104 61
1928 1933 Nottingham Forest 136 68
1934 1935 Rotherham United 70 43
1936 1937 Southend United 59 26
1938 Hull City 18 5

Dicks, JT CF
1894 1895 Crewe Alexandra 5

Dickson, Charles OL/OR
b Dundee
Dundee
1893 Preston North End 3 1
1894 Newcastle United 21 12
1895 Loughborough 17 1

Dickson, Henry (Harry) IL
b Blyth
Newburn
1936 Aldershot 4 2

From To Apps Goal

Dickson, Hubert (Hughie) RH/RB
b Gainsborough 14/7/1895 d 1965
Gainsborough Trinity
Worksop Town
1921 1933 Darlington 402 37
Newburn

Dickson, Ian William CF/IR
b Maxwelltown 9/1902 d 1956
Queen of the South
1920 1923 Aston Villa 76 30
1923 1924 Middlesbrough 37 12
Wesbrough

Dickson, J LH
1898 Blackpool 1

Dickson, William Alexander (Billy) IR/LB/IL
b Crail 27/8/1866 d 1910
Dundee Strathmore
Sunderland
1889 1891 Aston Villa 58 33
1892 1896 Stoke 119 40

Didymus, Edward John IR
b Portsmouth 13/4/1885 d 1918
Portsmouth
Northampton Town
Huddersfield Town
1909 Blackpool 2
Burslem Port Vale

Digweed, Harry LH
b Portsmouth q2 1878 d 1965
Portsmouth
1902 Burton United 34
Plymouth Argyle
Portsmouth

Dilks, Frank Thomas OL
b Lamport q2 1881 d 1937
Daventry Town
Northampton Town
Reading
1903 Leicester Fosse 8
Wellingborough
Northampton Town

Dilley, Ernest Edward (Ernie) CF
b Dorking q3 1896 d 1968
1920 Reading 2

Dillimore, James William N IL/CF
b Canning Town 19/12/1894 d 1980
Barking Town
1922 1925 Millwall Athletic 98 41
Weymouth

Dillon, Francis Richard OR
b Bury q2 1913
Manchester North End
1938 Sheffield Wednesday 7

Dilly, Thomas (Tommy) OL/IL/CF
b Arbroath 11/1882 d 1960
Forfar County
Arbroath
Heart of Midlothian
1902 1905 Everton 9 2
1905 1907 West Bromwich Albion 30 9
1907 Derby County 10 2
1908 Bradford Park Avenue 1
Walsall
Shrewsbury Town
Worcester City
Kidderminster Harriers

Dimbleby, Stanley (Stan) LH
b Killingholme 27/11/1916 d 1992
South Killingholme
1935 1936 Hull City 20
1937 Port Vale 1

Dimmick, Edmund (Ted) LB/RB
b Blaina q4 1896
Blaina
Abertillery
Houghton Rovers
Lambton Star
1922 1925 Newport County 84
Abertillery
1926 Chesterfield 3

Dimmock, Ernest OL
1899 Luton Town 12 2

From To Apps Goal

Dimmock, James Henry (Jimmy) OL
b Edmonton 5/12/1900 d 1972
Caps: England 3
Park Avenue
Gothic Works
Edmonton Ramblers
1919 1930 Tottenham Hotspur 400 100
1931 Thames 37 12
1932 Clapton Orient 18 3
Ashford Town (Kent)
Tunbridge Wells Rangers

Dimmock, W RH
1903 Burton United 4

Dinan, J LH
1894 Crewe Alexandra 5

Dines, Joseph Oscar (Joe) LH
b King's Lynn 12/4/1886 d 1918
Caps: England Amat
King's Lynn
Queen's Park Rangers
1909 Woolwich Arsenal 0
1910 Bradford City 0
King's Lynn
Ilford
1912 Liverpool 1
Millwall Athletic
Walthamstow Avenue

Dingwall, George Lennox CF
b Gateshead q3 1895 d 1962
1919 Stockport County 6 3

Dinnie, Charles RH
b Arbroath 1887
Dundee
1911 1912 Huddersfield Town 17

Dinsdale, Norman CH
b Hunslet 20/6/1898 d 1970
Anston Athletic
1920 1927 Notts County 267 11
1927 1929 Coventry City 90 10
1930 Bristol Rovers 31 3
Kidderminster Harriers

Dinsdale, William Arthur (Billy) CF
b Guisborough 12/7/1903 d 1984
Rise Carr
1921 Darlington 2
Darlington Railway Athletic
York City (trial)
Crook Town
1924 1925 Aston Villa 8
1926 1928 Lincoln City 92 69
1928 1929 Bradford Park Avenue 17 4
1930 Lincoln City 34 20
1931 Darlington 4 1

Ditchburn, John Hurst (Jock) RH/CH
b Leeds 13/3/1897 d 1992
Blantyre Thistle
Cambuslang
Blantyre Victoria
1923 1925 Sunderland 6
1926 1928 Exeter City 51
Exeter Loco
1929 1931 Exeter City 34

Ditchfield, J Charles RB
1892 Accrington 29
Rossendale
1895 1896 Manchester City 12 1

Ditchfield, James Henry CH/IL
b Bolton q1 1865 d 1933
Rossendale
1892 1895 Burslem Port Vale 12

Diver, Edwin James GK
b Cambridge 20/3/1861 d 1924
Surrey AFC
1891 Aston Villa 3

Divers, John OL/IR
b Glasgow 19/9/1873 d 1910
Caps: SLge 1/Scotland 1
Vale of Clyde
Glasgow Benburb
Hibernian
Celtic
1897 1898 Everton 30 11
Celtic
Hibernian

Dix, Joseph (Joe) OL
b Geddington q4 1884
Kettering
Portsmouth
1910 1914 Clapton Orient 148 11

From To Apps Goal

Dix, Ronald William (Ronnie) IL/IR
b Bristol 5/9/1912 d 1998
Caps: England Sch/FLge 1/England 1
Bedminster
1927 1931 Bristol Rovers 100 33
1932 Blackburn Rovers 38 14
1932 1936 Aston Villa 97 30
1936 1938 Derby County 94 35
1939 1947 Tottenham Hotspur 36 5
1939 (Tottenham Hotspur) (3) (1)
1947 1948 Reading 44 13

Dixon, Alan M CF
b Nantwich q4 1912
1933 Crewe Alexandra 1
Oswestry Town

Dixon, Andrew Gillfilling GK
b Ashington 23/5/1905 d 1987
Ashington Welfare
1928 Ashington 1
Ashington Welfare

Dixon, Arthur LB/LH/RB
b Barrowford 5/10/1879 d 1946
Trawden Forest
Nelson
1901 1906 Burnley 175 7
Tottenham Hotspur
1908 1912 Bradford Park Avenue 115 2
Nelson

Dixon, Arthur RH
b Chadderton q3 1892 d 1965
Washbrook Primitives
Woodhouse
Tonge
1913 1914 Oldham Athletic 30
St Mirren (loan)
St Mirren (loan)
Rangers
St Mirren (loan)
Cowdenbeath

Dixon, Arthur Albert RH
b Matlock 7/1867 d 1933
Derby Midland
1888 Aston Villa 3 1
1889 Stoke 0

Dixon, Charles (Charlie) RB/LB
b Sacriston 22/7/1891
Darlington
1919 1920 Middlesbrough 12
1922 1925 Hartlepools United 66

Dixon, Charles Hubert (Charlie) CH
b Ansley 16/6/1903 d 1983
Rugeley Villa
Cannock Town
1926 Sunderland 0
1928 Bournemouth & Boscombe Ath 25
Connah's Quay & Shotton
1929 Southport 19
1930 Nelson 16 1
Hednesford Town

Dixon, Cyril RB/LB
b Rawmarsh 1/2/1901 d 1978
Rawmarsh Athletic
1924 1931 Barnsley 251 7
1932 Reading 4
Scarborough

Dixon, David P RB
b North Shields 11/1898
1920 South Shields 0
1921 1924 Birmingham 4
1925 Southend United 4
Rhyl Athletic

Dixon, Edward (Ted) RB/CF
b Easington q3 1884
Tynevale
1904 Sunderland 0
1905 1906 Lincoln City 35 3
1906 Hull City 3

Dixon, Edward Stanley (Stan) CH/IR/RH
b Choppington 26/5/1894 d 1979
Barrington Albion
1913 1922 Newcastle United 49 7
1922 1925 Blackburn Rovers 29 1
1926 1929 Hull City 99 3
East Riding Amateurs
Choppington Rovers

From To Apps Goal

Dixon, Ernest (Ernie) CF
b Pudsey 10/7/1901 d 1941
Calverley
1921 Bradford City 1
1922 1923 Halifax Town 58 33
1923 Burnley 3
1924 1929 Halifax Town 179 94
1929 Huddersfield Town 5 1
1929 Nelson 28 10
1930 1932 Tranmere Rovers 83 53
Gresley Rovers
Mossley

Dixon, Frederick (Fred) LB
b Lincoln 31/5/1917 d 1979
Lincoln Corinthians
1936 Lincoln City 1
Newark Town

Dixon, Harry OL
b Kettering q4 1870 d 1949
Kettering
1893 Notts County 3
Kettering

Dixon, J CH
1902 Stockport County 1

Dixon, John (Jack) RH/CF/OR
b Lincoln q1 1882 d 1942
St Mary's (Lincoln)
1901 Lincoln City 17 4
1902 1906 Gainsborough Trinity 127 23
Newark Town

Dixon, Joseph GK
b 1902
Penrhiwceiber
1925 Lincoln City 1
Boston Town

Dixon, Matthew (Matt) CH
b Byker 1906
Walker Park
1928 Everton 0
1929 Preston North End 0
1929 Barrow 7
1930 New Brighton 2
Connah's Quay & Shotton
Nantwich
Lancaster Town
Wigan Athletic
Bacup Borough

Dixon, R LH
1895 Crewe Alexandra 12

Dixon, Robert Hall (Bobby) OL/OR
b Pelton 8/2/1908 d 1993
Birtley
1928 1932 Hartlepools United 114 27
Rhyl Athletic
Annfield Plain

Dixon, Robert Hewitson (Bob) GK
b Whitehaven 30/8/1901 d 1967
West Stanley
1922 1928 Stoke 189
1928 1932 West Ham United 65

Dixon, T OL
1893 Middlesbrough Ironopolis 1

Dixon, Thomas (Tommy) OR/IL/IR
b Cramlington q4 1882 1941
Bedlington United
1907 1910 Middlesbrough 27 8
Watford
Bristol Rovers
Blyth Spartans

Dixon, Thomas Henry (Tommy) RH
b Seaham Harbour 17/9/1899
Murton Colliery Welfare
1919 Sunderland (trial) 0
1919 1926 Clapton Orient 234 15
1927 1933 Southend United 249 7

Dixon, Wilfred Hall (Wilf) LH
b Silksworth q4 1919
Ouston United
1938 Aldershot 12

Dixon, William Armour (Will) OL
b Newcastle 2/1887 d 1964
Willington Athletic
Crawcrook Villa
Newcastle City
1909 Fulham 1
1920 Plymouth Argyle 17 2
1921 Barrow 4

From To Apps Goal

Dixon, William Harrison (Billy) LH
b Grimsby q2 1905 d 1956
Caps: England Sch
1923 Middlesbrough 0
Craghead United
1923 1925 Grimsby Town 9
1926 1927 Barrow 46 1
Poole
Boston Town
Bridlington Town
LNER (Grimsby)
Anlaby United

Dobbin, Stewart Alexanda GK
b Dungannon 12/2/1906 d 1992
1930 Thames 29

Dobbs, Arthur CF
b 1913
Yoker Athletic
St Roch's
1933 Derby County 3 1
Larne
Third Lanark
Stranraer
Workington

Dobell, Donald (Danny) LH/CF
b Church Fenton 23/5/1906 d 1976
Easington Colliery
Chilton Colliery Recreation Athletic
1926 1929 Hartlepools United 62 5
Spennymoor United
Blackhall Colliery Welfare

Dobie, Robert Tulloch OR
b Edinburgh 1875
Leith Athletic
St Bernard's
1896 1897 Bury 10
Reading
Leith Athletic

Dobinson, Harold (Harry) CF
b Darlington 2/3/1898 d 1990
Sunderland West End
1921 Durham City 15 5
1921 Burnley 2
1922 Chesterfield (trial) 0
1923 Queen's Park Rangers 2
Thornley Albion
Heaton-on-Tyne Sports Club

Dobson, Charles Frederick (Charley) CH
b Basford 9/9/1862
Caps: England 1
Corinthians
1888 Notts County 1

Dobson, George RB
Bolton Wanderers
1888 Everton 18

Dobson, George Frederick OL/OR
b Handsworth, Yorkshire 7/11/1910 d 2001
Northedge Amateurs
1930 Huddersfield Town 0
1931 1932 Southport 38 12
1933 Sheffield United (trial) 0
1933 Bradford City 0
1934 Sheffield Wednesday (trial) 0
1934 Southport 3 2
1934 Rochdale 15 5
1935 Rotherham United 26 5
Worksop Town
Ipswich Town

Dobson, George Walter OL
b Rotherham 7/10/1897
Kimberworth Old Boys
1919 Barnsley 25
1920 Norwich City 27 1
1921 1922 Rotherham County 19 1
Worksop Town
South Yorkshire Chemical Works

Dobson, Harry IR/IL
b Newcastle 1894
Caps: WLge 1
North Shields Athletic
Coventry City
1920 1921 Newport County 66 8
1921 1924 Southend United 101 20
Rugby Town

Dobson, Henry Arthur (Arthur) LH/RH
b Chesterton 4/1893 d 1918
Chesterton Foresters
Audley
1912 1914 Aston Villa 6

Dobson, Samuel (Sammy) IL/IR
b Preston q2 1870 d 1927
Crewe Alexandra
1890 Preston North End 8 5
1892 Sheffield United 6 1

From To Apps Goal

Dobson, William LB
b Coxhoe q1 1892
Spennymoor United
Southampton (trial)
1921 Durham City 4
Coxhoe United
Wingate Albion Comrades

Docherty, Archibald (Archie) IR
b Hebburn q1 1881
Hebburn Argyle
1904 Barnsley 3 1
Denaby United

Docherty, Edward IR/OL
b Glasgow 1871
Jordanhill
Partick Thistle
1892 Notts County 6 1
Duntocher Harp
1895 Lincoln City 5 2

Docherty, Francis J (Frank) OR
b Glasgow 28/5/1898
St Bernard's
1921 South Shields 2
Dykehead

Docherty, J CH
1894 Bolton Wanderers 2

Docherty, James LH
b Pollokshaws
Pollokshields
1893 1894 Derby County 35
1897 Luton Town 30
Cowes

Docherty, John CF/IR
Motherwell
1894 1895 Sheffield United 17 9
1895 Bury 4 1

Dockery, George GK
b Glasgow 1866 d 1931
Third Lanark
1893 Derby County 5

Docking, Stanley Holbrook (Stan) IL
b Chopwell 13/12/1914 d 1940
Birtley
1934 1937 Newcastle United 21 3
1938 Tranmere Rovers 31 7

Dockray, John OL
b Carlisle q1 1892 d 1939
Caps: SoLge 2
Carlisle United
1912 1913 Bury 5
Solway Star
1920 1923 Exeter City 141 12
Bideford Town

Dodd, Ernest Lloyd (Ernie) RB
b Wirral 1/5/1914 d 2003
Port Sunlight Gym
1933 1936 Tranmere Rovers 14
South Liverpool

Dodd, George Francis IL/OL
b Whitchurch 7/2/1885 d 1960
Wallasey United
Rock Ferry
1905 Stockport County 27 5
Workington
1907 1910 Notts County 91 20
Tunbridge Wells Rangers
1911 1912 Chelsea 29 8
Millwall Athletic
Brighton & Hove Albion
Darlington
West Ham United
Luton Town
Treherbert
1921 Charlton Athletic 1

Dodd, Robert RH
b Blackburn q1 1887 d 1958
Clitheroe
1910 Burnley 5

Dodd, Robert J CF
b Chester-le-Street 1900
1935 Carlisle United 1

Dodd, Ronald Ivor (Ronnie) CF
b Chester-le-Street 25/4/1911 d 1955
Usworth Colliery
West Stanley
1933 1936 Doncaster Rovers 68 38
1937 Walsall 18 9
Shrewsbury Town
1939 New Brighton (3) (3)

From To Apps Goal

Dodd, Samuel (Sammy) CH
b Birkenhead
Birkenhead
1904 Sheffield Wednesday 0
1905 1907 Stockport County 73 3
Coventry City

Dodds, Christopher (Chris) RH
b Gateshead 24/3/1904 d 1990
Greenfield Locomotive Athletic
1925 Middlesbrough 0
1926 1928 Accrington Stanley 41 3
1930 Sheffield Wednesday 1
Colwyn Bay United
1932 1935 Accrington Stanley 116 6
Great Harwood
Charter Street

Dodds, Ephraim (Jock) CF
b Grangemouth 7/9/1915 d 2007
Caps: Scotland War 8
Medomsley Juniors
1932 Huddersfield Town 0
1933 Lincoln City 0
1934 1938 Sheffield United 178 114
1938 1945 Blackpool 12 10
1939 (Blackpool) (3) (3)
Shamrock Rovers
1946 1948 Everton 55 36
1948 1949 Lincoln City 60 39

Dodds, James Angus (Jim) OR
b Belfast 7/9/1914
Model
Linfield
1935 Fulham 1
1936 Gillingham 25 6
Glentoran
Worcester City
Kidderminster Harriers

Dodds, John Thomas (Jack) OR/OL/IR
b Hexham q3 1885 d 1940
Northern Star (Hexham)
1905 1906 Newcastle United 5
1908 Oldham Athletic 8
Heart of Midlothian
Darlington
Merthyr Town
Stalybridge Celtic

Dodds, Leslie Smith (Les) OL
b Newcastle 20/9/1912 d 1967
Newcastle Swifts
1931 1933 Grimsby Town 14 1
1933 1934 Hull City 20 4
1935 Torquay United 34 4
Wellington Town
1937 1938 Clapton Orient 53 4
1939 Hartlepools United (3)
Peterborough United

Dodds, William (Billy) IR
b Sunderland 1/1885
Caps: IrLge 2
Sunderland Royal Rovers
Southwick (Co Durham)
1906 Burslem Port Vale 38 11
1907 Oldham Athletic 13 3
Linfield

Dodgin, William (Bill) LH/RH
b Gateshead 17/4/1909 d 1999
Gateshead High Fell
Wallsend
Kirkley & Waveney
Lowestoft Town
1930 1932 Huddersfield Town 10
1932 1933 Lincoln City 46 1
1934 1935 Charlton Athletic 29
1936 Bristol Rovers 30 1
1937 1938 Clapton Orient 62 1
1939 1945 Southampton (2)

Dodson, Albert RH
b Bingham q2 1891 d 1966
1911 Nottingham Forest 1

Dodsworth, John George RH
b Darlington 6/3/1907 d 1998
1927 Darlington 1
1928 Nelson 2
Shildon
Crook Town

Dodsworth, Victor Edward (Vic) CH/LH/RH
b Mexborough 2/10/1911 d 1986
Gainsborough Trinity
1932 Grimsby Town 4 1
1933 Manchester United 0
1935 1936 Doncaster Rovers 16
Grimsby Borough Police

From To Apps Goal

Doggart, Alexander Graham (Graham) IL
b Bishop Auckland 2/6/1897 d 1963
Caps: England Amat/England 1
Corinthians
Cambridge University
1921 Darlington 2 4
Corinthians
Bishop Auckland

Doherty, John LH/IL
b Belfast 12/4/1908
Caps: Ireland Amat/Ireland 1
Park End
Belfast Celtic
Park End
Woodburn
Portadown
Ards
Cliftonville
1932 1933 Charlton Athletic 8

Doherty, Peter Dermont IL/OR
b Magherafelt 5/6/1913 d 1990
Caps: FLge 1/Ireland War 2/Ireland 16
Station United (Coleraine)
Coleraine
Glentoran
1933 1935 Blackpool 83 28
1935 1938 Manchester City 119 74
1939 (Manchester City) (3) (2)
1945 1946 Derby County 15 7
1946 1948 Huddersfield Town 83 33
1949 1952 Doncaster Rovers 103 56

Doig, John Edward (Ned) GK
b Letham 29/10/1866 d 1919
Caps: Scotland 5
St Helens (Arbroath)
Arbroath
1889 Blackburn Rovers 1
Arbroath
1890 1903 Sunderland 417
1904 1907 Liverpool 51
St Helens Recreation

Doig, Thomas RH
1900 Middlesbrough 3

Dolby, Hugh Ryde H OR
b Agra, India 1888 d 1964
Clapham
Nunhead
1909 1910 Chelsea 2
Brentford

Dollery, Horace Edgar (Tom) CF
b Reading 14/10/1914 d 1987
St Marks Wednesday (Reading)
1935 Reading 1

Dollin, James William IR/CH/CF
b Hull q3 1890
Fleetwood
1909 Burnley 8
Fleetwood
1911 1912 Blackpool 18 1

Dolman, Humphrey William (Bill) GK
b Bloxwich 30/8/1906 d 1964
Blakenhall Congregationals
Bloxwich
Willenhall Pickwick
1928 1932 Chesterfield 103
1934 1935 Bristol City 61
1935 1938 Luton Town 62

Dolphin, Alfred (Alf) OR
b Redditch q2 1890 d 1940
Nuneaton Town
1919 Oldham Athletic 16
1920 Notts County 24 3
1921 Darlington 33 3
1922 Stockport County 11
1923 Walsall 13 1
Weymouth

Dominy, Arthur Albert (Art) IR/IL
b South Stoneham 11/2/1893 d 1974
Caps: SoLge 1
Weston Grove
Peartree Athletic
Bitterne Guild
Woolston
1920 1925 Southampton 222 68
1926 1927 Everton 29 12
1927 1928 Gillingham 55 17
1929 Clapton Orient 5 1
Newport (Isle of Wight)

Domleo, William George (Bill) LB
b Sutton Bonington q4 1883 d 1918
Sandiacre Olympic
Nottingham Jardines Athletic
Mansfield Mechanics
1908 Gainsborough Trinity 33
1909 1910 Bury 14

From To Apps Goal

Don, Robert Perrett RH
b Glasgow 22/3/1914 d 1982
Glasgow Ashfield
Glasgow Perthshire
1935 1936 Hull City 21
Galston SA
Stranraer
1938 Hartlepools United 4
South Shields

Donagher, Michael (Mick) RH/CH
b Kilmarnock 1880
Cronberry
1904 1905 Barnsley 66 1
Lochgelly United
Raith Rovers
Lochgelly United

Donaghey, Bernard IR
b Derry 23/12/1882 d 1916
Caps: IrLge 2
Derry Celtic
Ulster
Derry Celtic
Belfast Celtic
Glentoran
Hibernian
Derry Celtic
1905 Manchester United 3
Derry Celtic
1907 Burnley 5 2
Derry Celtic

Donaghy, Charles IR/OL
b Meerut, India 1883 d 1949
Rangers
1905 1906 Chelsea 2 1
Royal Albert
Rochdale
(USA)

Donaghy, Edward LH
b Grangetown 8/1/1900 d 1956
Grangetown
1922 Middlesbrough 0
1923 1925 Bradford City 13
1926 Derby County 6
1927 Gillingham 4
AS Cannes

Donaghy, John OL
b Grangetown q1 1896
Caps: England Amat
South Bank
1920 Middlesbrough 0
1921 Bradford Park Avenue 8

Donaghy, Peter CF/LH
b Grangetown 13/1/1898 d 1939
Grangetown St Mary's
1919 1922 Middlesbrough 30 2
1923 1924 Bradford City 22 5
Carlisle United

Donal, Henry LH
b Liverpool q2 1895 d 1956
Northern Nomads
1921 Crewe Alexandra 1

Donald, Alexander (Alec) LB
b Kirkintilloch 29/5/1900 d 1949
Kirkintilloch Harp
Partick Thistle
Indiana Flooring
Heart of Midlothian
New York Nationals
1930 1931 Chelsea 24
1932 1935 Bristol Rovers 136
Dunfermline Athletic

Donald, David Morgan (Davie) OL/OR
b Coatbridge 21/7/1885 d 1932
Albion Rovers
1908 1909 Bradford Park Avenue 27 2
1909 1911 Derby County 45 2
Chesterfield Town
Watford
1920 Queen's Park Rangers 22
Ilkeston United
Coalville Swifts
Hamilton Academical

Donald, Robert Stephenson (Bob) OL
b Selby q1 1899 d 1951
Caps: England Amat
Durham University
1920 South Shields 10
1921 Hartlepools United 8
Wallsend
Bishop Auckland

Donaldson, ? IR
1894 Newcastle United 2

From To Apps Goal

Donaldson, Alexander Pollock (Alex) OR
b Barrhead 4/12/1890 d 1972
Caps: Scotland 6
Belgrave Primitive Methodists
Belgrave
Balmoral United
Ripley Athletic
1910 Sheffield United (trial) 0
1912 1921 Bolton Wanderers 139 5
1921 1922 Sunderland 43 1
1923 Manchester City 7
1924 Crystal Palace (trial) 0
Chorley
Ashton National
Chorley

Donaldson, David Edwin (Dave) OR
b Selby 28/2/1911 d 1974
Selby Town
1931 Grimsby Town 1
1932 York City 18 1
Yeovil & Petters United
Boston United

Donaldson, John IL
b Glasgow 1909 d 1939
Kilsyth Rangers
1931 Bristol City 4

Donaldson, John McFarlane (Jack) LH
b Glasgow 4/1884
King's Park Thistle
1905 Everton 2
1907 Preston North End 1
Amble
1908 Bradford Park Avenue 6
King's Park
Bedlington United
Amble

Donaldson, Joseph (Joe) GK
b Scotland
Holytown Thistle
1898 Notts County 3

Donaldson, Robert CF/IR
Dundee Our Boys
Airdrieonians
1891 Blackburn Rovers 0
1892 1897 Newton Heath 129 56
1897 Luton Town 17 10
1898 Glossop North End 32 18
Ashford

Donaldson, Thomas Arthur (Tom) IL/OR
b Selby 24/12/1905 d 1976
Selby Town
1930 1931 Halifax Town 10 3
Bridlington Town

Donbavand, Albert Edward B CF
b Stockport 18/8/1898 d 1976
Mardy
1920 Stockport County 1

Doncaster, Richard Arthur (Dick) OL/IL
b Barry Dock 13/5/1908 d 1973
Caps: Wales Sch
Barry
1927 Bolton Wanderers 0
1928 1931 Exeter City 126 31
1932 Crystal Palace 15 4
1933 Reading 2
1934 1935 Gillingham 68 16
Yeovil & Petters United

Doncaster, Stuart CF
b Gainsborough 9/1890 d 1955
Buxton
Stourbridge
1912 Aston Villa 2 1
1913 Glossop 15 7
Matlock

Doncaster, Thomas William (Tommy) LB
b Retford 18/1/1889 d 1974
Dinnington Colliery
1911 Barnsley 4
Cardiff City

Done, Cyril Charles CF/IL
b Liverpool 21/10/1920 d 1993
Bootle Boys Brigade
1939 1951 Liverpool 93 32
1939 (Liverpool) (1) (1)
1952 1954 Tranmere Rovers 87 61
1954 1956 Port Vale 52 34
Winsford United

From	To	Club	Apps	Goal
Done, Robert (Bob)			LB/RB	
b Runcorn 27/4/1904			d 1982	
		Runcorn		
1926	1934	Liverpool	147	13
1935	1936	Reading	13	1
1937		Chester	37	
1938		Accrington Stanley	6	
		Bangor City		
Donkin, George William Cope			OR	
b Carlton, West Yorkshire 1/12/1892			d 1927	
		Wharncliffe Woodmoor		
		Royston Midland		
		Monckton Athletic		
1913	1924	Barnsley	231	20
Donkin, William (Billy)			RB	
b Annfield Plain 22/6/1900			d 1974	
		Twizell United		
		Annfield Plain		
		West Stanley		
		Craghead United		
		Preston Colliery		
		West Stanley		
		Chester-le-Street		
		Annfield Plain		
		Spennymoor United		
1928		Nelson	8	
		Spennymoor United		
		Annfield Plain		
		Shildon		
		Blackhall Colliery Welfare		
Donnachie, Charles			LH	
b Invergowrie 1869			d 1923	
		Dundee		
1889		West Bromwich Albion	2	
		Cambuslang Rangers		
Donnachie, Joseph (Joe)			OL/OR	
b Kilwinning 1883			d 1967	
Caps: Scotland 3				
		Rutherglen Glencairn		
		Morton		
		Albion Rovers		
		Morton		
1905		Newcastle United	2	
1905	1908	Everton	40	
1908	1914	Oldham Athletic	216	19
1919		Everton	16	
1920		Blackpool	19	1
		Chester		
Donnelly, Anthony (Tony)			LB/RB	
b Middleton q2 1886			d 1947	
		Heywood United		
1908	1912	Manchester United	34	
		Heywood United		
		Glentoran		
		Heywood United		
		Chester		
		Southampton		
		Middleton Borough		
Donnelly, James (Jimmy)			OR/IR	
b South Bank q3 1879				
		South Bank		
		Darlington St Augustine's		
1902	1906	Sheffield United	89	26
1907	1909	Leicester Fosse	74	25
		Darlington		
Donnelly, James (Jim)			RB/LB	
b Mayo 18/12/1899				
		Royal Artillery		
1920		Blackburn Rovers	8	
1922	1923	Accrington Stanley	54	
1924		Southend United	42	
1925	1927	Brentford	79	1
1930	1931	Thames	36	3
		Grajanski		
		Gunes		
Donnelly, John			OR	
1920		Stockport County	1	
Donnelly, Robert			CH/LB	
b Craigneuk 1908				
		Wishaw Juniors		
		Partick Thistle		
1935	1936	Manchester City	37	1
		Morton		
		Stranraer		
Donnelly, Samuel (Sam)			IR	
b Annbank 1874				
		Annbank		
1893	1894	Notts County	32	7
1896		Blackpool	14	5
		Annbank		
Donnelly, William Walter (Willie)			GK	
b Magherafelt 1872			d 1948	
		St Mungo Juniors		
		Vale of Clyde		
		Hibernian		
		Clyde		
1896		Liverpool	6	
		Clyde		
		Celtic		
		Belfast Celtic		
Donoghue, Frank			CH	
b Openshaw 1916				
1936		Portsmouth	0	
1937		Gillingham	1	
		Yeovil & Petters United		
Donoghue, John			LH	
b New York, USA 22/1/1903			d 1971	
		St Francis Juniors		
		Shawfield Juniors		
		Celtic		
		Third Lanark (loan)		
		Cowdenbeath (loan)		
		Belfast Celtic (loan)		
1930	1931	Wrexham	67	2
		Celtic		
		Excelsior Roubaix		
Donoghue, Patrick			OR	
		Celtic		
1921		Millwall Athletic	0	
1922		Port Vale	3	
Donoven, Alfred Ernest (Dickie)			IL/LH	
b Bulwell 20/6/1900			d 1978	
		Bulwell		
1920		Nottingham Forest	3	
		Mansfield Town		
1925	1934	Southend United	318	55
Donowa, George William			OL	
b Southampton 31/12/1900			d 1973	
		Harland & Wolff		
1923		Bournemouth & Boscombe Ath	1	
		Salisbury City		
Doolan, Alexander (Sandy)			LB/RB	
b Tarbolton 7/8/1889			d 1937	
		Annbank		
		Kilmarnock		
		Beith (loan)		
1912	1919	Bradford City	22	
1920	1922	Preston North End	77	
		Mold Athletic		
Dooley, Thomas Edward			RH	
b Accrington 15/12/1914			d 1975	
		Bacup Borough		
1934		Blackpool	0	
		Bacup Borough		
1938		Accrington Stanley	28	2
1939		(Accrington Stanley)	(3)	
		Rochdale		
Doran, John Francis (Jack)			CF/CH	
b Belfast 3/1/1896			d 1940	
Caps: Ireland 3				
		Gillingham		
		Pontypridd		
		Newcastle Empire		
		Coventry City		
		Norwich City		
1920	1921	Brighton & Hove Albion	71	44
1922		Manchester City	3	1
1923		Crewe Alexandra	18	1
		Mid-Rhondda United		
		Shelbourne		
		Boston Town		
Doran, Sam			OR	
b Bradford 22/12/1912			d 1995	
		Sunfield Rovers		
1934	1937	Bradford Park Avenue	54	4
1938		Reading	27	8
1939	1945	Halifax Town	(2)	(1)
Dorey, Charles William (Charlie)			CH	
b Brentford q1 1900			d 1967	
1922	1924	Southend United	30	
		Guildford United		
Dorrans, Owen			IL/IR	
b Stevenston 12/12/1897			d 1972	
		Saltcoats Victoria		
		Cowdenbeath		
		Raith Rovers		
		Morton		
		Connah's Quay & Shotton		
1930		Wigan Borough	17	4
		Falkirk		
		Stevenston United		
1931		New Brighton (trial)	3	
		East Stirlingshire		
		Stalybridge Celtic		
		Shelbourne		
Dorrell, Arthur Reginald			OL	
b Small Heath 30/3/1896			d 1942	
Caps: FLge 2/England 4				
		Carey Hall		
1919	1929	Aston Villa	355	60
1931		Port Vale	34	4
Dorrell, William (Billy)			OL/OR	
b Coventry q4 1872			d 1953	
Caps: FLge 1				
		Singers		
		Leicester Fosse		
1894	1895	Aston Villa	11	5
1895	1898	Leicester Fosse	59	22
		Belper		
1905		Burslem Port Vale	0	
Dorrell, William Ernest (Billy)			OR	
b Leicester 9/5/1893			d 1973	
		Carey Hall		
		Belgrave Primitive Methodists		
1919		Leicester City	1	
		Hinckley United		
		Coalville Swifts		
		Loughborough Corinthians		
		Coalville Swifts		
Dorrington, John (Jack)			GK	
b Smethwick 5/1881			d 1944	
		West Smethwick		
1899		West Bromwich Albion	0	
		Kidderminster Harriers		
1902	1912	Small Heath/Birmingham	106	
Dorrington, Joseph Ralph (Joe)			GK	
b Lichfield q1 1878				
1899		Blackburn Rovers	0	
1900	1904	Blackpool	78	
		Colne		
		Oswaldtwistle		
Dorsett, George			OL/OR/IR	
b Brownhills 8/1881			d 1943	
Caps: FLge 1				
		Shireoaks Athletic		
1899		Small Heath (trial)	0	
		Brownhills Albion		
1901	1904	West Bromwich Albion	95	22
1904	1911	Manchester City	193	62
Dorsett, Joseph Arthur Harold (Joe)			OL/OR/CF	
b Brownhills 11/4/1888			d 1951	
		Brownhills Albion		
1908	1909	West Bromwich Albion	18	3
1910	1919	Manchester City	132	17
		Colne		
1920		Southend United	34	3
1921	1922	Millwall Athletic	55	
Dorsett, Richard (Dickie)			LB/LH/IL	
b Brownhills 3/12/1919			d 1999	
		Walsall Juniors		
1937	1946	Wolverhampton Wanderers	46	32
1939		(Wolverhampton Wanderers)	(3)	(2)
1946	1952	Aston Villa	257	32
Dougal, David Wishart			OR	
b Dundee 22/3/1882			d 1937	
		Dundee Harp		
		Dundee		
1904		Preston North End (trial)	0	
1904		Grimsby Town (trial)	0	
1905	1906	Clapton Orient	50	3
		Reading		
		Brighton & Hove Albion		
1908	1909	Leeds City	25	1
		Montrose		
Dougal, James (Jimmy)			OR/IL/CF	
b Denny 3/10/1913			d 1999	
Caps: Scotland War 1/Scotland 1				
		Kilsyth Rangers		
		Falkirk		
1933	1946	Preston North End	170	51
1946	1948	Carlisle United	71	13
1948		Halifax Town	21	2
		Chorley		
Dougal, Peter G			IL	
b Denny 21/3/1909			d 1974	
		Dunipace Thistle		
1927		Burnley	6	2
		Clyde		
1929	1931	Southampton	29	5
		Sete		
1933		Chesterfield (trial)	0	
1933	1935	Arsenal	21	4
1937		Everton	11	2
1938		Bury	16	2
1939		(Bury)	(3)	
Dougal, William (Billy)			LH	
b Denny 25/10/1895			d 1966	
Caps: SLge 1				
		Denny Hibernian		
		Falkirk		
1925	1927	Burnley	60	1
		Clyde		
Dougall, David Reid			IL/CF	
b Eyemouth 29/6/1908			d 1968	
		Chirnside		
1932	1934	Carlisle United	28	5
		Ashington		
Dougall, George			OL	
b Eyemouth 1876				
		Hibernian		
1897	1900	Manchester City	75	13
1901		Glossop	10	
Dougall, James H (Jimmy)			OR	
b Wishaw 1900				
		Cleland Juniors		
		Motherwell		
1919	1925	Coventry City	227	13
1926		Reading	11	
Dougall, Robert			RH	
b Falkirk 1910				
		Forth Rangers		
		Bo'ness (loan)		
		Hamilton Academical		
1933	1935	Blackpool	74	2
1937	1938	Reading	74	7
1939		(Reading)	(3)	
Dougan, Patrick			OL	
		East Fife		
1909		Burnley	1	
		East Fife		
		Heart of Midlothian		
Dougan, Thomas (Tommy)			OR	
b Holytown 22/11/1915				
		Alloa Athletic		
		Tunbridge Wells Rangers		
1936	1938	Plymouth Argyle	42	6
1938		Manchester United	4	
		Heart of Midlothian		
		Kilmarnock		
		Dunfermline Athletic		
		Waterford		
		Chingford Town		
		Stirling Albion		
Dougherty, James (Jim)			LH/RH	
b New Brighton 19/11/1878				
		Chorley		
1900		New Brighton Tower	12	
1901	1907	Small Heath/Birmingham	130	3
		Coventry City		
		Stirchley United		
		Worcester City		
Dougherty, Joseph (Joe)			LH/CF	
b Cockerton 11/11/1894			d 1959	
		Darlington Forge Albion		
1913		Leeds City	1	
1919		Oldham Athletic	15	5
		Shildon Athletic		
1921		Hartlepools United	32	
1923		Lincoln City (trial)	2	
Douglas, Angus			OR	
b Lochmaben 1/1/1889			d 1918	
Caps: Scotland 1				
		Castlemilk		
		Lochmaben Rangers		
		Dumfries		
1908	1912	Chelsea	96	11
1913	1914	Newcastle United	49	2
Douglas, Edward Alfred C (Eddie)			OL	
b Hebburn 26/3/1899				
		Crook Town		
1922		Crystal Palace	2	1
		Crook Town		
		Washington Colliery		
1925	1928	Brentford	102	21
1929	1930	Reading	6	
		Guildford City		
Douglas, George Harold			OR	
b Stepney 18/8/1893			d 1979	
Caps: England Amat				
		St Saviour's (Forest Gate)		
		Custom House		
		Ilford		
1912	1920	Leicester Fosse	127	10
1920	1921	Burnley	5	
1922	1925	Oldham Athletic	134	8
1926	1927	Bristol Rovers	45	5
		Tunbridge Wells Rangers		
		Dover United		

From To Apps Goal

Douglas, Harry OR
b Hartlepool
South Bank
1902 Middlesbrough 4
Darlington
Bishop Auckland

Douglas, James (Jimmy) RH/RB
b Renfrew 3/9/1859 d 1919
Caps: Scotland 1
Paisley Institution
Renfrew
Barrow Rangers
1888 1891 Blackburn Rovers 34

Douglas, John Stuart LH/CH
b West Hartlepool 1/12/1917 d 2001
Belle Vue Congregationalists
Stockton
Trimdon Grange
Ferryhill Athletic
Houghton Colliery Welfare
1938 Hartlepools United 5
1945 1946 Middlesbrough 2
1948 1949 Hartlepools United 27 1
1950 Halifax Town 0

Douglas, Robert (Bob) IL
b Mickley 26/3/1908
Gainsborough Trinity
1932 Aldershot 4 1
Kreuzelngen

Douglas, Thomas Alexander (Tom) IL/IR
b Whitletts 11/9/1910 d 1943
Kilwinning
Motherwell
1931 1933 Blackpool 60 17
1933 1935 Burnley 63 13
Witton Albion
1938 Rochdale 8

Douglas, William GK
b Dundee
Dundee Our Boys
1892 1893 Ardwick 36
1893 1895 Newton Heath 55
1895 Derby County 0
1896 1897 Blackpool 60
Warmley
Dundee

Douglas, William (Billy) CF
b Porth 1892
Cardiff City
1913 Oldham Athletic 2 1
Wrexham

Douglas, William J IL
1933 Blackburn Rovers 0
1934 Rochdale 1

Dover, Harold OR/CF
1935 1936 Walsall 5

Dovey, Donald OR/IR
b Lincoln 13/4/1900 d 1979
Horncastle Town
1925 1926 Lincoln City 14 3
Newark Town

Dow, Hugh Connor RB
b Herrington 2/4/1906 d 1987
1925 Sunderland 0
1931 Grimsby Town 2
1932 1933 Darlington 40 1
Houghton Rovers
Easington Colliery Welfare

Dow, James Frazer LH
b Sunderland 27/3/1889 d 1972
Southwick (Co Durham)
1912 1914 Huddersfield Town 47
Carlisle United

Dow, John M RB/CF
b Dundee 1874
Dundee Our Boys
Dundee
1893 1895 Newton Heath 47 6
Fairfield
Glossop North End
1898 1899 Luton Town 56 3
1900 1901 Middlesbrough 34
West Ham United
Luton Town

Dow, William (Billy) CF
b Edinburgh 15/11/1884
Leith Athletic
1905 Bury 15 6
Tottenham Hotspur

From To Apps Goal

Dowall, William (Bill) OL/LB
b Thornliebank
Kilbirnie Ladeside
Motherwell
St Mirren (loan)
1935 Bury 10 2
1936 Lincoln City 5
Red Star (Paris)
Ballymena United
1938 Notts County 6

Dowdall, Charles (Charlie) IR
b Dublin 7/4/1898
Caps: LoI 2/Eire 3
Wasps (Dublin)
St James's Gate
Fordsons
1928 Barnsley 3
1929 Swindon Town 8 2
Cork FC
St James's Gate

Dowdall, Walter OL
b Stockport 1884
1902 Stockport County 16 2

Dowden, William Walter (Bill) CF
b Wandsworth 29/8/1902 d 1976
Spalding Athletic
Wimbledon
1927 Southend United (trial) 0
1929 Crystal Palace 0
1930 Fulham 1 1
Wimbledon

Dowds, Peter LH/CH
b Johnstone 12/12/1867 d 1895
Caps: Scotland 1
Broxburn Shamrock
Celtic
1892 Aston Villa 19 3
1893 Stoke 17
Celtic

Dowell, Leonard IL
b Edinburgh 13/6/1902
Portobello Thistle
Partick Thistle
Sittingbourne
1927 1930 Gillingham 55 7
Ashford Town (Kent)

Dowen, John Stewart (Jack) LB/RB
b Wolverhampton 31/10/1914 d 1994
Caps: England Sch
Courtaulds
1934 1935 Wolverhampton Wanderers 8
1935 West Ham United 1
1936 1937 Wolverhampton Wanderers 4
1938 Hull City 39

Dowling, Michael IR/CF/OR
b Jarrow 30/3/1890 d 1969
Jarrow Croft
St Mirren
1910 Sheffield Wednesday 7
Portsmouth
Jarrow
1914 1919 Lincoln City 28 4
Ebbw Vale

Dowling, Thomas P (Tommy) RH
b Ireland 1893 d 1945
Plumstead Hibernians
Woolwich
1921 1923 Charlton Athletic 21 1
Indiana Flooring
Newark Skeeters
Calpe American

Down, William (Billy) GK
b Ryhope 22/1/1898 d 1977
Ashington
1920 1924 Leeds United 96
1925 1926 Doncaster Rovers 50
1927 1929 Burnley 80
1930 Torquay United 0
1930 Wigan Borough (trial) 2
Ashington

Downes, Percy OL
b Langold 19/9/1905 d 1989
Dinnington Main Colliery Welfare
Gainsborough Trinity
1925 1930 Blackpool 149 32
1931 Hull City 11 3
1932 1933 Stockport County 82 27
1934 1935 Burnley 61 6
1936 1937 Oldham Athletic 51 4
Gainsborough Trinity

From To Apps Goal

Downey, Alfred Francis (Alf) LH
b Dublin 20/8/1898 d 1985
Bohemians
1920 Bradford City 1
1922 Halifax Town 1
1923 Blackpool 0

Downie, Alexander Leek Brown (Alex) RH/LH
b Glasgow 8/10/1876 d 1953
Glasgow Perthshire
Third Lanark
Bristol City
Swindon Town
1902 1909 Manchester United 172 12
1909 1910 Oldham Athletic 48
Crewe Alexandra

Downie, Edwin LH/RB
b Montrose 1876
Montrose
Heart of Midlothian
Tottenham Hotspur
1899 Chesterfield Town 21
1900 Stockport County 7

Downie, James OR
1895 Blackburn Rovers 0
1895 Burslem Port Vale 12 2

Downie, Robert OL
Caps: Scotland 1
Third Lanark
Albion Rovers
1897 Lincoln City 6 1

Downie, William LH
1936 Gateshead 11

Downing, John GK
b Royston, West Yorkshire q3 1894
Monckton Athletic
1919 Barnsley 7
Hednesford Town

Downing, John Westnes (Jack) IL
b Darlington q2 1913 d 1962
Evenwood Town
1932 Darlington 2 3
Spennymoor United
Stockton
Shildon

Downing, Samuel (Sam) LH
b Willesden Green 19/1/1883 d 1974
Willesden Green
Willesden Town
Park Royal
West Hampstead
Queen's Park Rangers
1908 1913 Chelsea 134 9
Croydon Common

Downs, John Thomas (Dickie) RB/LB
b Middridge 13/8/1886 d 1949
Caps: FLge 2/England 1
Crook Town
Shildon Athletic
1908 1919 Barnsley 274 10
1919 1923 Everton 92
1924 Brighton & Hove Albion 16

Downwood, William LB
b Burslem 1872
1892 Burslem Port Vale 3

Dowsey, John (Jack) RH/IR
b Willington 1/5/1905 d 1942
Hunswick Villa
1925 Newcastle United 3
1926 West Ham United 1
Carlisle United
1927 1928 Sunderland 11 1
1928 1931 Notts County 98 4
1931 1933 Northampton Town 86 5
Nuneaton Town

Dowson, Ernest LH
b Doncaster q4 1877 d 1960
Wheatley Rangers
1901 Doncaster Rovers 2
Denaby United

Dowson, Francis LH/IL
b North Ormesby q3 1897
1920 Middlesbrough 7 2
1922 Hartlepools United 18
Spennymoor United

From To Apps Goal

Doyle, Daniel (Dan) LB
b Paisley 16/9/1864 d 1918
Caps: SLge 10/Scotland 8
Rawyards Juniors
Darngavil
Slamannan Barnsmuir
Broxburn Shamrock
Hibernian
Broxburn Shamrock
East Stirlingshire
Sunderland
Hibernian
Heart of Midlothian (loan)
Newcastle East End
Grimsby Town
1889 Bolton Wanderers 0
1889 1890 Everton 42
Celtic
Dykehead
Celtic

Doyle, Dermot Patrick OL
b Dublin
Shelbourne
Pontypridd
1921 1922 Hull City 6

Doyle, Francis (Frank) IL
b Glasgow 20/11/1901 d 1965
Glasgow Benburb
Rutherglen Glencairn
Vale of Clyde
Airdrieonians
1923 1924 Fulham 30 9
Celtic
Ayr United

Doyle, Thomas GK
b Uddingston 15/1/1916
New Stevenston Athletic
Blantyre Celtic
Celtic
Arbroath (loan)
1938 Rochdale 29
1939 Stockport County 0

Doyle, Thomas Christopher (Tommy) CF
b Ringsend 24/12/1910 d 1991
Home Farm
Alton (Donnybrook)
Shamrock Rovers
1933 Southport 6 3
Wigan Athletic
Reds United
Fearon's Athletic
Distillery (Dublin)

Doyle, William (Bill) CF
b Wishaw 19/11/1913
Forth Wanderers
1937 Bradford Park Avenue 1

Drabble, Frank GK
b Southport 8/7/1888 d 1964
Bloxwich Wesleyans
Southport YMCA
1909 Tottenham Hotspur 1
1910 Nottingham Forest 8
1912 Burnley 2
1913 1914 Bradford Park Avenue 32
Southport Central
1919 1920 Bolton Wanderers 29
1921 Southport 5
1923 Queen's Park Rangers 2

Drain, Thomas (Tom) CF/IR/CH
b Pollokshaws 26/6/1879 d 1952
Drongan Juniors
Celtic
Ayr
Maybole
1903 1904 Bradford City 32 12
1905 Leeds City 9 3
Kilmarnock
Aberdeen
Vale of Leven
Carlisle United
Exeter City
1909 Woolwich Arsenal 2
1909 Blackpool 4
Nithsdale Wanderers
Galston

Drake, Alonzo IL/CF
b Rotherham 16/4/1884 d 1919
Parkgate
1901 1902 Doncaster Rovers 36 7
1903 1907 Sheffield United 95 20
1907 Birmingham 11 2
Queen's Park Rangers
Huddersfield Town

From To | Apps Goal

Drake, Edward Joseph (Ted) CF
b Southampton 16/8/1912 d 1995
Caps: England 5
Winchester City
1931 1933 Southampton 71 47
1933 1938 Arsenal 168 124
1939 (Arsenal) (1) (4)

Dransfield, Edward (Ted) RB/LB
b High Green 28/11/1906 d 1986
High Green Swifts
1927 1929 Rotherham United 31
1930 Birmingham 0
1931 1932 Swindon Town 64 3
1933 Southampton 0
1934 1936 Mansfield Town 78 1
Bath City

Dransfield, George Ronald OR
b Ecclesfield 12/10/1914 d 1941
High Green Athletic
1935 Lincoln City 3 1
Macclesfield

Dransfield, Walter IL/IR/CF
b Sheffield 1/2/1901 d 1969
Attercliffe United
1925 Doncaster Rovers 2 2
Worksop Town
1927 Bristol City 2
1929 Merthyr Town 23 4

Draper, Cyril CH
b Tibshelf q2 1896 d 1963
1920 Derby County 0
1921 Chesterfield 2
Mansfield Town
Shirebrook
Sutton Town
Ilkeston United
Upper Pleasley United
Pleasley Colliery

Draper, Frederick (Bob) CF
b Luton 1876 d 1901
1898 1899 Luton Town 9 3

Draper, Harry IL
b Chesterfield 1887
Stag's Head (Rotherham)
Rotherham County
1910 Birmingham 3
Merthyr Town
Denaby United

Draper, James Walter IR
b Kimberley q1 1878
Kimberley
1895 1896 Sheffield United 12 3
Ilkeston Town
Kimberley
Ilkeston Town
Kimberley

Draper, John Percy CF
b Lanchester 18/6/1901 d 1978
Usworth Colliery
1922 Middlesbrough (trial) 0
1922 Ashington 5 1

Draper, W LB
1894 Burton Wanderers 30

Draper, William LB
1920 Reading 3
1921 Southampton 0

Draycott, Levi William (Billy) RH
b Newhall 15/2/1869
Burslem Port Vale
1891 1893 Stoke 2
1894 1895 Burton Wanderers 50 3
1896 1898 Newton Heath 81 6
Bedminster
Bristol Rovers
Wellingborough
Luton Town

Drew, William A OR
b Willesden 1905
Caps: England Sch
Barnet
1926 Queen's Park Rangers 1
Tufnell Park
Hampstead Town

Dreyer, Frederick (Fred) RH
b Woodburn 19/3/1908 d 1975
Army
1928 Portsmouth 0
1929 Fulham 0
1930 Southampton 0
1931 Gateshead 0
1932 Newport County 1

From To | Apps Goal

Dreyer, Gordon RH/CH
b Whitburn, County Durham 1/6/1914 d 2003
Whitburn St Mary's
Washington Colliery
1934 Hartlepools United 15
1935 Hull City 5
1936 Hartlepools United 26
1937 1938 Luton Town 23
1939 (Luton Town) (3)
Bedford Town
Gravesend & Northfleet United
Rushden Town

Dreyer, Henry (Harry) LH/RH
b Sunderland 9/3/1892 d 1953
1919 1920 South Shields 58 2
1921 1922 Crystal Palace 55 2
1923 Southend United 22
Boston Town
Seaham Harbour

Drinkwater, Charles John (Charlie) OL
b Willesden 25/6/1914 d 1998
Hendon FC
Golders Green
Middlesex Wanderers
1933 Brentford 0
Walthamstow Avenue
1935 Aston Villa 2 1
1938 Charlton Athletic 3
1945 1946 Watford 1
Pinner
Ruislip Manor

Drinkwater, GA IL
1892 1893 Northwich Victoria 30 4

Drinnan, James McKay (Jimmy) IL
b Harthill 28/5/1906 d 1936
Larkhall Thistle
1923 Bristol City 2
Aberaman Athletic
1924 Merthyr Town 15 2
1925 1926 Newport County 42 11
1927 1928 Brentford 43 11
1929 Luton Town 31 12
1930 Burnley 6 2
Worcester City

Driscoll, John Henry (Jack) IL
b Grays 27/7/1909 d 1997
Rodington
Oakengates Town
Oswestry Town
Shrewsbury Town
1936 West Bromwich Albion 0
1937 Sheffield Wednesday 5 2
Wellington Town

Driver, Allenby IL/IR/CF
b Blackwell, Derbyshire 29/9/1918 d 1997
Mansfield Shoes
1937 1945 Sheffield Wednesday 6 3
1939 (Sheffield Wednesday) (1)
1946 1947 Luton Town 41 13
1947 1949 Norwich City 49 19
1949 1951 Ipswich Town 86 25
1952 Walsall 26 2
Corby Town
Frickley Colliery

Driver, Fred IL/IR
1900 1902 Burnley 16 2
Trawden
1904 Burnley 1

Driver, Robert GK
b Summit 14/7/1914 d 2001
Thorneham
1935 Rochdale 2

Drummond, George (Geordie) OL/CF/OR
b Edinburgh 8/1/1865 d 1914
St Bernard's
1888 1898 Preston North End 139 36
South Shore

Drummond, James (Jimmy) IL
b Bellshill 24/4/1881
Bellshill Athletic
Celtic
1901 1903 Manchester City 28 5
Partick Thistle

Drummond, John (Jack) OR/OL
b Edinburgh 1870
Partick Thistle
1890 Preston North End 11 4
1892 1893 Sheffield United 40 9
1894 Liverpool 14
Barnsley St Peter's

From To | Apps Goal

Drummond, Robert Cray (Bob) IR/IL/CF
b Dalmeny 1898
Caps: WLge 1
Kingseat Juniors
Bathgate
1924 Burnley 3
Pembroke Dock
1926 Bristol City 2 1
1927 Bournemouth & Boscombe Ath 7 1
Bathgate

Drury, George Benjamin IL/OR/IR
b Hucknall 22/1/1914 d 1972
Hucknall Congregationalists
Hucknall Villa
Loughborough Corinthians
Heanor Town
1936 1937 Sheffield Wednesday 44 9
1937 1946 Arsenal 38 3
1939 (Arsenal) (2) (1)
1946 1947 West Bromwich Albion 29 8
1948 1949 Watford 35 3
Linby Colliery
Darlaston
South Normanton

Dryburgh, William (Willie) OR
b Cowdenbeath 22/5/1876 d 1951
Dunfermline Juniors
Cowdenbeath
1897 1898 Sheffield Wednesday 36 8
Millwall Athletic
1901 Sheffield Wednesday 11 2
Cowdenbeath
Tottenham Hotspur
Cowdenbeath
Lochgelly United

Dryden, John (Jack) OL
b Broomhill 21/8/1908 d 1975
Pegswood United
Ashington
Aberdeen (trial)
1932 1933 Newcastle United 5 1
1934 Exeter City 20 5
1935 Sheffield United 19 5
1936 1937 Bristol City 63 13
1938 Burnley 4 2
1939 (Burnley) (2)
Peterborough United

Dryden, William (Billy) CF
b Amble
Broomhill
Blyth Spartans
Ashington
East Chevington Institute United
Choppington
1912 Clapton Orient 13 6
Watford
Portsmouth

Drysdale, J OR
1895 Burton Swifts 19 3

Ducat, Andrew (Andy) RH/CF/RB
b Brixton 16/2/1886 d 1942
Caps: England 6
Westcliff Athletic
Southend Athletic
1904 1911 Woolwich Arsenal 175 19
1912 1920 Aston Villa 74 4
1921 1923 Fulham 64
Casuals

Duckers, Samuel Edward (Sam) IL
b Stafford 28/11/1903 d 1972
Stafford Rangers
1925 Bristol Rovers 1
Stafford Rangers

Duckett, Donald Thwaites (Don) LH/RH
b Bradford 20/4/1894 d 1970
Wibsey
Thornton
Queensbury
1919 1924 Bradford City 155 6
1924 1927 Halifax Town 119
1927 1928 Bradford Park Avenue 36

Duckhouse, Edward (Ted) CH
b Walsall 9/4/1918 d 1978
Shelfield
Streetly Works
Walsall Wood
Cannock Chase Colliery
1937 West Bromwich Albion 0
1938 1949 Birmingham 119 4
1939 (Birmingham) (3) (1)
1950 1951 Northampton Town 68
Rushden Town

Duckworth, Allan CF
b Darwen q4 1914
Darwen Juniors
1934 Accrington Stanley 1 1

From To | Apps Goal

Duckworth, Frederick (Fred) LB
b Blackburn q3 1892
Blackburn YMCA
1919 1920 Blackburn Rovers 60

Duckworth, Harry IL
1902 Burnley 9 2

Duckworth, Harry LH
b Manchester
1921 Stalybridge Celtic 4

Duckworth, Joseph Cullen (Joe) GK
b Blackburn 29/4/1898
Accrington Stanley
1919 Blackburn Rovers 5
1921 1923 Aberdare Athletic 84
1924 1929 Reading 202
1930 1931 Brighton & Hove Albion 37
1932 York City 7

Duckworth, Richard (Dick) RH
b Manchester q4 1878
Caps: FLge 5
Newton Heath
1903 1913 Manchester United 225 11

Duckworth, Richard (Dick) LH/RH/LB
b Harpurhey 6/6/1906 d 1983
Castleton Juniors
1925 Rochdale 0
1926 Manchester United 0
1927 Oldham Athletic 0
1929 1931 Chesterfield 89 4
1932 Southport 25 1
1932 1933 Chester 30
1934 1935 Rotherham United 46
1936 1938 York City 88
Newark Town

Duckworth, Robert William IR
b Burnley q3 1870 d 1924
Royal Swifts
1888 1889 Burnley 5 1
Rossendale
1894 Lincoln City 24 5
Rossendale

Duckworth, Thomas Crook OR
b Blackburn 1881
1902 Blackpool 9 3
West Ham United
1903 1904 Blackburn Rovers 1
1905 Blackpool 19 2
Nelson

Duckworth, Thomas Cullen (Tommy) RB
b Tonge 2/10/1908 d 2001
Tonge United
Darwen
1930 Blackpool 0
1931 1932 Bolton Wanderers 28
1933 1936 Swindon Town 124
1937 Southport 9
Darwen
Horwich RMI

Dudgeon, Andrew CH
b Newcastle 23/12/1913 d 1993
1935 Sheffield Wednesday 0
Throckley Welfare
1937 1938 Gateshead 79 2
1939 (Gateshead) (3)
North Shields

Dudley, George OL
b Gartcosh 26/2/1916 d 1979
Twechar United
Albion Rovers
King's Park
Vono Sports
1938 West Bromwich Albion 6 2
Banbury Spencer
Cradley Town
Netherton
Cradley Heath
Accles & Pollock

Dudley, John Oswald Charles CH/LH
b Forest Gate 1910 d 1975
Great Eastern Railway (Romford)
1930 1931 Fulham 14
Leytonstone

Dudley, Robert (Bob) LH
1888 Wolverhampton Wanderers 1

From	To		Apps	Goal
Dudley, Reginald Arthur (Reg)			RB/LB	
b Hemel Hempstead 3/2/1915			d 1994	
Caps: England Amat				
		Boxmoor St John's		
		Apsley		
1935	1946	Millwall	42	
1946	1949	Queen's Park Rangers	58	
1950		Watford	1	
		Dover		
		Margate		
Dudley, Samuel Morton (Sam)			LH/IL/OL	
b Dudley Port 26/11/1907			d 1985	
1927		Preston North End	0	
1928		Bournemouth & Boscombe Ath	2	
		Coleraine		
1930	1931	Clapton Orient	12	1
1932		Chelsea	1	
1934		Exeter City	8	1
Dudley, Walter William			RB/LB	
b Rotherham q2 1882				
1902	1913	Nottingham Forest	278	
Dudley, William E			CH	
1923		Charlton Athletic	2	
		Erith & Belvedere		
1925		Bradford City	0	
Duerden, James			RB/OL	
		Livesey		
1888		Blackburn Rovers	2	
1890		Burnley	3	
		Rossendale		
Duff, Hugh			OL	
		Millwall Athletic		
1896	1897	Woolwich Arsenal	1	1
		Millwall Athletic		
1899		Woolwich Arsenal	0	
Duff, James (Jimmy)			OR	
b Bowhill 20/2/1908				
		Renton Thistle		
		Celtic		
1931		New Brighton (trial)	4	1
1931		Southport (trial)	0	
1931		Bristol Rovers (trial)	0	
		East Stirlingshire		
Duff, Joseph Hunter (Joe)			IR/LH	
b Ashington 1/5/1913			d 1985	
1934		Newcastle United	0	
1935	1945	Rochdale	132	26
1939		(Rochdale)	(3)	
		Cheltenham Town		
Duff, Stanley Douglas (Stan)			OL	
b Liverpool q1 1919			d 1941	
		Earle		
1935		Liverpool	0	
1935		Leicester City	0	
1937		Tranmere Rovers	7	2
		Waterford		
1938		Chester	2	
1938		New Brighton	3	
Duff, Thomas Edwin (Tommy)			OL	
b West Cornforth q4 1905			d 1951	
1927		Huddersfield Town	0	
1928		Bournemouth & Boscombe Ath	3	
1930		Darlington	2	
		Crook Town		
Duffield, Albert (Bert)			RB	
b Owston Ferry 3/3/1894			d 1981	
		Gainsborough Trinity		
		Castleford Town		
1920	1925	Leeds United	203	
1925	1927	Bradford Park Avenue	51	
Duffus, John Murison (Jack)			RH/LH/CF	
b Aberdeen 10/5/1901			d 1975	
		Aberdeen Richmond		
		Dundee		
		Dumbarton		
		Bo'ness (loan)		
		Scunthorpe & Lindsey United		
		Llanelly		
		Caerau		
1922		Clapton Orient	6	
1923		Tottenham Hotspur	0	
1924	1926	Norwich City	77	4
1927		Stockport County	6	3
		Hyde United		
		Hurst		
		Congleton Town		
Duffus, Robert Maurice Duncan (Bob)			LH/RB	
b Aberdeen 28/2/1891			d 1949	
		Aberdeen East End		
		Aberdeen Richmond		
		Aberdeen		
		Dundee		
		Dumbarton		
		Scunthorpe & Lindsey United		
1921		Millwall Athletic	5	
1922		Clapton Orient	5	
1923		Accrington Stanley	29	
		Bangor City		
Duffy, Bernard (Barney)			LH	
b Burnbank 9/2/1898			d 1978	
		Blantyre Caledonians		
		Burnbank		
		Bellshill Athletic		
1923	1925	Chelsea	3	
1926	1928	Clapton Orient	70	1
		Ards		
		Shelbourne		
		Dundalk		
Duffy, Christopher Francis (Chris)			OL	
b Jarrow 24/1/1884			d 1971	
		Jarrow		
		St Mary's College (Hammersmith)		
		Brentford		
		Jarrow		
1905		Middlesbrough	4	
1906	1907	Newcastle United	16	1
1908	1912	Bury	123	13
		North Shields Athletic		
1914		Bury	22	2
		Bradford City		
1919		Leicester City	4	1
		Chester-le-Street		
Duffy, James (Jimmy)			CH	
b Lochgelly 23/3/1908			d 1940	
		Cowdenbeath		
		Shelbourne		
		Dundalk		
1931		Wrexham	0	
		Cork Bohemians		
1932		Southport	3	
		Drumcondra		
		Waterford		
		Brideville		
		Rossville		
Duffy, John			CH	
b Cleator Moor 1886				
		Workington		
1909		Bradford City	1	
		Exeter City		
		Swansea Town		
Duffy, Richard			IL	
b Dumbarton 24/9/1914				
		Yoker Athletic		
1933		Millwall	5	
		Alloa Athletic		
		Falkirk		
Duffy, William K			RH	
b Workington				
1930	1931	Thames	2	
Duggan, Henry Anthony (Harry)			OR/IR/CF	
b Dublin 8/6/1903			d 1968	
Caps: Ireland 8/Eire 5				
		Richmond United		
1926	1936	Leeds United	187	45
1936	1938	Newport County	88	13
1939		(Newport County)	(3)	
Duggins, Alfred Edward (Alf)			OL/IL	
b Aston 2/11/1897			d 1969	
		Tamworth Castle		
1920		Southampton (trial)	0	
		Walsall		
		Kingsbury Colliery		
		Redditch Town		
		Aberdeen		
		Heart of Midlothian		
1923		Preston North End	2	
1924		Walsall	12	
1925		New Brighton	13	3
		Redditch Town		
		Gresley Rovers		
		Stafford Rangers		
		Harlaston United		
Dugnolle, John Henry (Jack)			LH/CH	
b Peshawar, India 24/3/1914			d 1977	
		Hove		
		Southwick (Sussex)		
1935	1937	Brighton & Hove Albion	7	
		Tunbridge Wells Rangers		
1938		Plymouth Argyle	4	
1939		(Plymouth Argyle)	(1)	
1946	1947	Brighton & Hove Albion	59	
		Horsham		
Duguid, William Charles			LH/RH/CH	
b Wishaw				
		Heart of Midlothian		
		Albion Rovers		
		Hibernian		
		Wishaw Thistle		
1910	1912	Middlesbrough	23	
Duhig, Robert			RH	
b Athlone 8/2/1914			d 2005	
1932		Gillingham	0	
		Maidstone United		
		Sheppey United		
1935		Grimsby Town	0	
		Sheppey United		
1936		Brentford (trial)	0	
1938		Barrow	2	
		Margate		
Duke, James			CH/RH	
b Mauchline				
1919	1920	Grimsby Town	6	
		Scunthorpe & Lindsey United		
1922		Bristol City	0	
1922		Exeter City	1	
Dukes, Harry Parkinson			GK	
b Portsmouth 31/3/1912			d 1988	
		Sleaford		
		Martlesham		
		Melton		
		Orwell Works		
		Ipswich Town		
1934	1938	Norwich City	105	
1939		(Norwich City)	(3)	
		Bedford Town		
1946		Norwich City	13	
		Guildford City		
		Newmarket Town		
Dulson, Joseph (Joe)			IL/CF	
b Basford 31/1/1913			d 1990	
		Newstead Colliery		
1930		Accrington Stanley (trial)	0	
1931		Nottingham Forest	1	2
1933		Accrington Stanley	11	1
1934		Bournemouth & B Ath (trial)	0	
Dumbrell, George			LB/RB/CF	
b Catford 23/9/1906			d 1990	
		Botwell Mission		
		Nunhead		
		Catford South End		
		Cray Wanderers		
		Dartford		
1928	1929	Brentford	12	
1930	1933	Leicester City	37	
1933		Bournemouth & Boscombe Ath	13	2
1935	1936	Brentford	5	
Dumper, James			OR	
b Sunderland q4 1898			d 1923	
		Seaham Harbour		
1919		Blackpool	1	
1922		Hartlepools United (trial)	0	
Duncan, Adam Scott Mathieson (Scott)			OR	
b Dumbarton 2/11/1888			d 1976	
		Dumbarton Oakvale		
		Dumbarton Corinthians		
		Clydebank Juniors		
		Shettleston Juniors		
		Dumbarton		
1907	1912	Newcastle United	73	10
		Rangers		
		Celtic (loan)		
		Partick Thistle (loan)		
		Dumbarton		
		Cowdenbeath		
		Dumbarton		
Duncan, Alexander L			OL	
b Glasgow 1891				
		Cambuslang		
		Portsmouth		
1912		Grimsby Town	2	
Duncan, Andrew (Andy)			IR/IL	
b Renton 25/1/1911			d 1983	
		Renton Thistle		
		Dumbarton		
		Renton Thistle		
1930	1934	Hull City	105	31
1934	1938	Tottenham Hotspur	93	22
		Chelmsford City		
Duncan, Charles Stanley			CF	
b Kinross 1889				
Caps: SLge 1				
		Kelty Rovers		
		Dunfermline Athletic		
1912	1914	Birmingham	22	6
		East Fife		
		Rangers		
		Third Lanark		
		St Mirren		
		Clyde		
		Dundee		
		Arbroath		
Duncan, David			OL/CF	
b Glasgow 4/1892				
		St Anthony's (Glasgow)		
		Bellshill Athletic		
		Albion Rovers		
1911		Fulham	9	
1912		Woolwich Arsenal	3	1
		Albion Rovers		
		Bathgate		
		Heart of Midlothian		
		Dundee Hibernian		
		Peebles Rovers		
Duncan, Douglas (Dally)			OL/IL	
b Aberdeen 14/10/1909			d 1990	
Caps: Scotland 14				
		Aberdeen Richmond		
1928	1931	Hull City	111	47
1931	1946	Derby County	261	63
1939		(Derby County)	(3)	(1)
1946	1947	Luton Town	32	4
Duncan, Ernest (Ernie)			GK	
b Bootle 3/12/1915			d 1979	
		Orrell		
1935		Southport	6	
		Miranda		
Duncan, John (Johnny)			IR/RH	
b Lochgelly 14/2/1896			d 1966	
Caps: Scotland 1				
		Denbeath Star		
		Kirkcaldy United		
		Lochgelly United		
		Raith Rovers		
1922	1929	Leicester City	279	88
		Solus		
Duncan, John Grant			OR	
b Aberdeen 3/2/1898			d 1963	
		Aberdeen		
1920		Norwich City	4	
Duncan, Peter			IL	
b Scotland				
		Broxburn Rangers		
1922		Brentford	13	2
		Armadale		
Duncan, Thomas Grossett (Tom)			IR/OR	
b Lochgelly 1/9/1897			d 1940	
		Lochgelly United		
		Raith Rovers		
1922	1923	Leicester City	41	6
1924	1925	Halifax Town	32	5
1926		Bristol Rovers	13	2
		Kettering Town		
Duncan, William McKiddie			IL	
b Dundee 20/7/1913				
		Dundee Stobswell		
1933		Blackburn Rovers	2	
1934		Carlisle United	13	
1935	1937	Gillingham	51	10
Duncan, William Wilson (Bill)			CH	
b Aberdeen 14/7/1895				
		Aberdeen		
1920		Norwich City	2	
		Montrose		
1924		Barrow	0	
		Peterhead		
Dunderdale, William Leonard (Len)			CF	
b Willingham-by-Stow 6/2/1915			d 1989	
1933		Sheffield Wednesday	0	
		Goole Town		
1935	1937	Walsall	32	19
1938		Watford	30	19
1938		Leeds United	3	
1939		(Leeds United)	(1)	
1946	1947	Watford	44	15
		Margate		
		Sittingbourne		

From To Apps Goal

Dunkerley, John OL
b Manchester 20/8/1912 d 1986
Newton Heath Loco
Ashton National
1933 Manchester United 0
1934 Stockport County 9 3
1934 Exeter City (trial) 0
1935 Barrow 19 5
Macclesfield
British Dyes

Dunkley, Albert Edward OL
b Earls Barton q3 1877 d 1949
Earls Barton Wesleyans
Rushden
Northampton Town
1900 Leicester Fosse 10
Northampton Town
New Brompton
Queen's Park Rangers
1903 Blackburn Rovers 4 1
Bristol Rovers
1906 Blackpool 17 3
Northampton Town
St Michael's Thursday

Dunkley, Maurice Edward Frank OR
b Kettering 19/2/1914 d 1989
Kettering Town
1936 1937 Northampton Town 26 5
1937 1946 Manchester City 51 5
1939 (Manchester City) (3) (1)
Kettering Town
1949 Northampton Town 4
Corby Town

Dunlop, Thomas RH
b Annbank 7/5/1872
Port Glasgow (trial)
Annbank
1895 1898 Small Heath 59 2
Dundee Harp

Dunlop, Walter OL
b Saddleworth q1 1862
1892 Sheffield Wednesday 1
1893 Darwen 6 1

Dunlop, William (Billy) RH/LH/CH
b Annbank
Annbank
1892 1898 Sunderland 137 6
Rangers
Partick Thistle
Annbank

Dunlop, William Theodore P (Billy) LB
b Hurlford 14/7/1871 d 1945
Caps: Scotland 1
Sandyford
Hurlford
Annbank
Kilmarnock
Abercorn
1894 1908 Liverpool 321 2

Dunmore, Alfred (Alf) OR
b South Shields 1/1/1911 d 1991
Newcastle Swifts
1930 Newcastle United 0
1931 Derby County 0
1932 Southampton 1
1933 Mansfield Town 0
Blyth Spartans
Horden Colliery Welfare

Dunn, Archibald RH/LH/LB
b Bridgeton 14/12/1876 d 1943
Avenue Thistle
Queen's 2nd Gordon Highlanders
1898 1900 West Bromwich Albion 71 2
Bristol Rovers
Millwall Athletic
1902 1903 Grimsby Town 45 1
Wellingborough

Dunn, Bertie OR
b Montrose 15/8/1893
Blantyre Victoria
Alloa Athletic
1924 1925 Clapton Orient 4
Carlisle United

Dunn, Bertram Scott (Bert) LH
b Carshalton 29/9/1893 d 1976
Carshalton Athletic
1921 Charlton Athletic 8

Dunn, Edwin IR
Cannock Town
1914 Wolverhampton Wanderers 14 3

Dunn, Ernest RH
b 1909
Trowbridge Town
1932 1933 Bristol City 27 1

From To Apps Goal

Dunn, George IL
1890 Derby County 1
Ilkeston Town

Dunn, George Appleby LB
b North Shields 13/5/1902 d 1952
1926 1928 South Shields 40
North Shields
Crook Town

Dunn, Hugh RB/LB
b Johnstone 20/12/1874 d 1947
Johnstone
1893 1900 Preston North End 164
Bristol Rovers
1906 Burslem Port Vale 27

Dunn, James (Jimmy) IR/IL
b Glasgow 25/11/1900 d 1963
Caps: SLge 1/Scotland 6
St Anthony's (Glasgow)
Hibernian
1928 1934 Everton 140 42
1935 Exeter City 22 4
Runcorn

Dunn, John IR
b Cambuslang 7/12/1902 d 1968
Cambuslang Rangers
1925 Wigan Borough 13 6
1926 Coventry City 29 4
1927 Crewe Alexandra (trial) 0
King's Park

Dunn, John Henry RB
b Eccles 11/1888
Eccles Borough
1913 Leeds City 0
Luton Town
1920 Sheffield Wednesday 8

Dunn, Robert CH
b West Bromwich q3 1887
Cannock Town
1912 Wolverhampton Wanderers 1
1921 Crewe Alexandra 5

Dunn, Ronald Victor GK
b Southall 24/11/1908 d 1994
2nd Dorset Regiment
Wealdstone
1931 1936 Crystal Palace 167
Colchester United

Dunn, Stephen GK
b Darlaston 31/1/1893
Army
1919 1922 Arsenal 43

Dunn, Thomas (Tommy) LB/RB
b Falkirk 2/6/1873 d 1938
1891 1896 Wolverhampton Wanderers 88
1896 1897 Burnley 7
Chatham
Thames Ironworks

Dunn, William (Billy) OL/IL
b Scotland 1865
East Stirlingshire
1889 1892 Stoke 39 7
Hednesford Town
1893 Walsall Town Swifts 2

Dunn, William OL
b Middlesbrough 1877
South Bank
1897 Newton Heath 10
Reading

Dunn, William Marshall (Billy) CF
b Lambhill 9/10/1910 d 1980
Newton Villa
Glasgow Ashfield
Celtic
1935 1936 Brentford 3 1
1937 Southampton 14 3
Bo'ness (loan)
Raith Rovers

Dunne, James (Jimmy) CF
b Ringsend 3/9/1905 d 1949
Caps: LoI 6/Ireland 7/Eire 15
Park View
Riverside Athletic
Shamrock Rovers
1925 New Brighton 8 6
1926 1933 Sheffield United 173 143
1933 1935 Arsenal 28 10
1936 Southampton 36 14
Shamrock Rovers

From To Apps Goal

Dunne, John Joseph (Jack) LB
b Donnybrook 8/1890 d 1974
Caps: IrLge 1
Shelbourne
1914 Lincoln City 23
Mid-Rhondda
Boston Town
Horncastle Town

Dunne, Leo RB/LB
b Dublin 1908
Caps: Eire 2
Drumcondra
1933 1934 Manchester City 3
1935 Hull City 8
Shelbourne
(Malta)
Drumcondra

Dunning, William (Willie) GK
b Arthurlie 2/1/1865 d 1902
Johnstone
Celtic
Glasgow Hibernian
Bootle
1892 1894 Aston Villa 64

Duns, Leonard (Len) OR
b Newcastle 28/9/1916 d 1989
West End Albion
Newcastle West End
1935 1951 Sunderland 215 46
1939 (Sunderland) (3)
Ashington

Dunsbee, Charles Richard LH
b Willington, Warwickshire 1873
Kidderminster Harriers
1899 Woolwich Arsenal 8

Dunsire, Andrew IL
b Buckhaven 11/10/1902 d 1980
Abbotshill Juniors
Kinhorn Athletic
Raith Rovers
Abbotshill Juniors
Dunniker
Third Lanark
Anstruther Rangers
Raith Rovers
Broxburn United
Kettering Town
1928 1929 Crystal Palace 5 1
Dartford
Raith Rovers
Forfar Athletic

Dunsmore, Thomas Hamilton (Tom) LB
b Motherwell 23/5/1914
Motherwell Miners Welfare
Bellshill Athletic
Royal Albert
Hibernian
1938 1945 Luton Town 40
Albion Rovers

Durber, Peter LB/LH
b Wood Lane, Staffordshire q2 1873 d 1963
Audley Town
1896 1897 Stoke 27
Southampton
1900 Stoke 33
1901 Glossop 33
Northampton Town

Durkan, James (Jack) RB
b Bannockburn 14/7/1915 d 1990
King's Park
1933 Cardiff City 6
1934 Bristol Rovers 2

Durnin, John RH
b Campbeltown 10/11/1894
Campbeltown Academical
Plymouth Argyle
Partick Thistle
Vale of Leven
Dumbarton
1920 1921 Swansea Town 24
Llandrindod Wells
1924 Northampton Town (trial) 0

Durnion, Andrew Joseph (Andy) CF/IL
b Hamilton 18/2/1907 d 1985
1928 Brentford 2 1
1929 Gillingham 19 9
1930 Thames 2

Durrant, Arthur Francis (Jimmy) OR/IR
b Luton q1 1880 d 1927
Luton Stanley
1897 1899 Luton Town 32 8
1904 1908 Leicester Fosse 140 23
Leyton
Luton Town

From To Apps Goal

Durston, Frederick John (Jack) GK
b Clophill 11/7/1893 d 1965
1920 Brentford 24
Northfleet

Duthie, John Flett LH/RH/IL
b Fraserburgh 7/1/1903 d 1969
Roselee
Fraserburgh Town
1922 Hartlepools United 0
Clydebank
1923 Hartlepools United 3
1924 1926 Norwich City 27 4
Fraserburgh Town
1927 Queen's Park Rangers 11
York City
1929 Crystal Palace 13 3
1930 York City 22
1931 Crewe Alexandra 19 1
Aberdeen
Workington
1933 Cardiff City 13
Caerau
Peterborough United

Dutton, Henry Robert (Harry) LH
b Edmonton 16/1/1898 d 1972
Tufnell Park
1922 1926 West Bromwich Albion 57 2
1926 1928 Bury 37 1
1929 1931 Brighton & Hove Albion 93 4
Shoreham

Dutton, Thomas (Tommy) IL/OL
b Southport 11/11/1906 d 1982
Chorley
1933 Leicester City 0
1934 Queen's Park Rangers 23 6
1935 1937 Doncaster Rovers 48 9
1938 Mansfield Town 39 12
1939 Rochdale (1)

Dutton, Thomas Theodore IL
b West Bromwich 4/1860 d 1922
Wednesbury Old Athletic
1891 Aston Villa 1
1892 Walsall Town Swifts 0

Duxbury, Robert RB
b Darwen q1 1890
1910 Huddersfield Town 6

Duxbury, Thomas (Tom) RH
b Accrington 1898
Accrington Stanley
1920 1923 Preston North End 51 1
1924 Leeds United 3
Fleetwood

Dwane, Edwin John (Eddie) IL/LH
b Valletta, Malta 17/7/1896 d 1973
Royal Engineers (Chatham)
1921 1923 Lincoln City 46 2
Boston Town
Newark Town
1926 Lincoln City 0
Worksop Town

Dwight, Arthur George LH
b Berkhamsted q1 1897 d 1952
1897 Burton Swifts 1

Dwight, Fred LB
b Chesham q3 1879 d 1958
Chesham Town
Fulham
1904 Woolwich Arsenal 1
Nelson
Stalybridge Rovers

Dyal, Edwin OR
b Ecclesfield 1881 d 1953
Worksop Town
Heeley Friends
1905 Chesterfield Town 24 2
Heeley Friends
Denaby United
Rotherham Town
Denaby United
Doncaster Rovers

Dycke, S CF/IL
1895 1896 Burton Wanderers 8

Dye, Lewis IL
b Pilsley 24/11/1904 d 1975
Clay Cross
Waterloo United
1924 Chesterfield 3
Staveley Town
Mansfield Town
Loughborough Corinthians
Matlock Town
Sutton Town

From To Apps Goal

Dyer, F RH
1888 Bolton Wanderers 1

Dyer, Frank LH/LB
b Bishopbriggs 1870 d 1940
Warwickshire County
1890 1891 West Bromwich Albion 41 2
Woolwich Arsenal
1893 1897 Ardwick/Manchester City 36 3

Dyer, Herbert Reginald IR
b Filey 27/1/1917
1937 Bradford Park Avenue 0
1938 Torquay United 10 1

Dyer, James Arthur (Jimmy) CH/CF
b Blacker Hill 24/8/1880
Wombwell Town
1901 Barnsley 2
Doncaster Rovers
Ashton Town
1905 Manchester United 1
West Ham United
1909 Bradford Park Avenue 0
Wombwell Town
Mexborough
Castleford Town
Harrogate AFC

Dyer, Joseph Alexander (Alec) OL/LB
b Crewe 13/4/1913 d 1984
1933 1936 Crewe Alexandra 51 10
1936 1946 Plymouth Argyle 53 3

Dyer, Reginald Ernest (Reg) RB/LB
b Bristol 18/4/1900 d 1990
Ashton City
1921 1924 Bristol City 49
1925 1928 Fulham 98
Yeovil & Petters United
(France)
(Czechoslavakia)
Tunbridge Wells Rangers
Ashford Town (Kent)

Dyke, Archibald Samuel (Archie) OR
b Newcastle-under-Lyme 9/1886 d 1955
Chesterton
Newcastle Congregational
Newcastle PSA
Stoke
Port Vale
Stoke
1913 1914 Aston Villa 9
Port Vale
Stafford Rangers
1920 Coventry City 3
1921 Blackpool 1
Congleton Town

Dyke, J OR
1902 Glossop 1 1

Dyson, J LH
1897 1898 Darwen 21 1

Dyson, James Middleton (Jimmy) OR/IR
b Middleton 4/3/1907 d 2000
Park Villa
British Dyestuffs
Northwich Victoria
1927 1931 Oldham Athletic 122 40
1931 1937 Grimsby Town 139 38
1937 1938 Nottingham Forest 15
1939 Accrington Stanley 0

Dyson, Samuel IR
1936 Rotherham United 8 3
1937 West Ham United 0

Eades, John LB
b Goldthorpe
Rotherham Town
1906 Sheffield United 2
Rotherham Town
Goole Town
Goldthorpe Institute

Eadie, William Phillip (Bill) CH
b Greenock 1882
Greenock Overton
Morton
1906 1913 Manchester City 185 6
1914 Derby County 31

Eadon, John Pollock GK
b Glasgow 3/9/1889 d 1961
Maryhill
1914 Tottenham Hotspur 5
Ayr United

Eardley, Bertram Cooper OR/RH
b Newcastle-under-Lyme q4 1879 d 1929
1899 1906 Burslem Port Vale 148 24

From To Apps Goal

Eardley, William George (Billy) OR/CF
b Stoke-on-Trent 1871
1894 1895 Burslem Port Vale 17 7
1896 Stoke 10 1
Burslem Port Vale

Earl, Albert Thomas (Sam) IR/IL/OR
b Gateshead 10/2/1915 d 2000
Dunston CWS
1933 1935 Bury 35 7
Rhyl Athletic
1937 1938 York City 58 9
1939 Hartlepools United (3)
1946 1947 Stockport County 42 12
1947 Rochdale 4 1
1947 New Brighton 9 1
Northwich Victoria

Earl, Alfred Thomas (Alf) RB/LB
b Earlsfield 19/3/1903 d 1951
Summerstown
1925 1932 West Ham United 191
Streatham Town

Earl, Arthur (Mick) OL/IL
b Loughborough q4 1878 d 1949
Coalville Albion
1899 Loughborough 5
Coalville Town
1900 1901 Chesterfield Town 44 3
Walsall
West Ham United
1903 Chesterfield Town 16 3
Grassmoor Red Rose
1906 Chesterfield Town 0
Moore's Athletic (Shirebrook)
Shirebrook Athletic

Earl, Sidney Ernest (Sid) LH
b Norwich 25/4/1902 d 1992
Lamberts
1923 1925 Norwich City 29 1
City Wanderers
CEYMS (Norwich)

Earle, Edwin OL
b Newbiggin 17/6/1905
Newbiggin United
Blyth Spartans
1925 1926 Nelson 54 15
1926 Burnley 3 1
Boston Town
1933 Crystal Palace 10 3
Gresley Rovers
Boston United
Wisbech Town

Earle, Harry Thomas GK
b East Grinstead 23/11/1868 d 1951
Poplar Trinity
Millwall Athletic
Royal Arsenal
Clapton
1904 Notts County 23

Earle, Stanley George James (Stan) IR
b Stratford 6/9/1897 d 1971
Caps: England Sch/England Amat/England 2
Clapton
1921 1923 Arsenal 4 3
1924 1931 West Ham United 258 56
1932 Clapton Orient 15 1

Earnshaw, John CF
b Tottington
Bacup
1895 Bury 1 2
1895 Blackburn Rovers 0
1896 1897 Darwen 24 6

Earnshaw, John RB/LB
1903 1905 Glossop 10

Earp, Martin John (Jack) RB
b Nottingham 6/9/1872
Caps: FLge 1
Nottingham Forest
1891 Everton 9
1892 Nottingham Forest 13
1893 1899 Sheffield Wednesday 155 7
1900 Stockport County 15 1

From To Apps Goal

Easson, James Ferrier (Jimmy) IL
b Brechin 3/1/1906 d 1983
Caps: Scotland 3
Grange (Arbroath)
Carnoustie Panmure
East Craigie
1928 1938 Portsmouth 292 102
1938 Fulham 3

Eastham, George Richard IR/IL/OR
b Blackpool 13/9/1914 d 2000
Caps: England 1
Cambridge Juniors (Blackpool)
South Shore Wednesday
1932 1936 Bolton Wanderers 114 16
1937 1938 Brentford 49 1
1938 1946 Blackpool 45 9
1947 Swansea Town 15
1948 Rochdale 2
1948 1949 Lincoln City 27 1
Hyde United
Winsford United
Ards

Eastham, Henry (Harry) IL/IR/OR
b Blackpool 30/6/1917 d 1998
1934 Blackpool 0
1936 1946 Liverpool 63 3
1948 1952 Tranmere Rovers 154 12
1953 Accrington Stanley 42 3
Netherfield
Rolls Royce

Eastham, John Bilborough (Jack) LB/RB
b Blackburn q1 1883 d 1932
St Peter's School
1901 1903 Blackburn Rovers 48
1905 Glossop 26
Southampton

Eastman, George Frederick CH
b Leyton 7/4/1903 d 1991
1924 1925 West Ham United 2
Chatham Town
1928 1929 Clapton Orient 13
Sochaux
Fives (France)
Boulogne

Easton, Andrew RB
b Armadale 14/3/1877
Leith Athletic
Airdrieonians
Leith Athletic
Heart of Midlothian
Millwall Athletic
Rangers
1905 Bradford City 14

Easton, William (Bill) IR/IL
b Newcastle 10/3/1904 d 1960
Caps: WLge 1
Blyth Catholic Young Mens Soc
Blyth Spartans
1923 Rotherham County 6 1
Montreal Maroons
Blyth Spartans
1927 1928 Everton 15 3
1929 1930 Swansea Town 56 18
1931 1932 Port Vale 25 6
1933 Aldershot 5
Workington
Walker Celtic
North Shields
Walker Celtic

Eastwood, Cecil Milner LH/CH
b Castleford 7/5/1894 d 1968
Castleford Town
1920 1923 Plymouth Argyle 108 3
1925 Preston North End 20 2
1926 1927 Stoke City 46
1927 Stockport County 0

Eastwood, Edmund (Eddie) RB/OR
b Barrowfield 7/1/1902 d 1981
Barrowford
1921 1922 Nelson 3
Morecambe
Clitheroe
Rossendale United
Heywood St James
Darwen

Eastwood, Eric CH/LB/RH
b Heywood 24/3/1916 d 1991
Chorley Road Congregationals
Little Lever
Westhoughton
Heywood St James'
1938 1946 Manchester City 16
1946 1948 Port Vale 28 1

From To Apps Goal

Eastwood, James (Jimmy) RH/IR
b Heywood 12/4/1915 d 1995
1936 Crewe Alexandra 4
1937 Rochdale 28
Tunbridge Wells Rangers

Eastwood, Raymond (Ray) RB
b Moston 1/1/1915 d 1999
Newton Heath Loco
Bacup Borough
Hurst
1936 Oldham Athletic (trial) 0
Altrincham
1938 Aldershot 9
1939 (Aldershot) (3)
1946 Accrington Stanley 3
Nelson
Mossley

Eatock, Thomas (Tom) OL/IL
b Wigan q2 1895 d 1944
1921 1922 Wigan Borough 10 1
1924 1925 Bolton Wanderers 11 1

Eaton, Clifford (Cliff) IL
b Oldham 15/10/1910 d 1979
Lees Road Lads
Hurst
1933 Portsmouth 0
1934 1935 Rochdale 31 3
1936 Oldham Athletic 2
Macclesfield
Chelmsford City

Eaton, Frank IR/CF
b Stockport 12/11/1902 d 1979
Cressbrook
1923 Oldham Athletic 0
New Mills
1925 1929 Barnsley 150 59
1930 1932 Reading 101 33
1933 Queen's Park Rangers 15 2

Eaton, Samuel Llewellyn L (Sam) IR/OR
b Derby q4 1878
Derby St James
1894 Derby County 0
Derby St Luke's
Hinckley Town
1897 1899 Leicester Fosse 31 9
Hinckley Town
1901 Stockport County 10 1
1901 1902 Leicester Fosse 21 4
Luton Town
Watford
Earlestown
Accrington Stanley
Maidstone United

Eaton, Walter RB
b Sheffield q3 1881 d 1917
1904 Sheffield Wednesday 1
Rotherham County
Rotherham Town

Eaves, R OR
1898 Blackpool 5

Eaves, Thomas Albert (Bert) LB/RB
b Mawdesley 1/1/1914 d 2001
Leyland Motors
1936 1938 Oldham Athletic 28
1945 Reading 0
Leyland Motors
Stalybridge Celtic
Hyde United

Eaves, William Henry (Bill) IL
b Blackpool q4 1893 d 1957
1919 Manchester United 0
Darwen
1921 Barrow 25 5
Lytham

Ebdon, Richard George (Dick 'Digger') CF/IL
b Ottery St Mary 3/5/1913 d 1987
Ottery St Mary
1935 1947 Exeter City 138 50
1939 (Exeter City) (1) (2)
1948 Torquay United 5 1

Eccles, Arthur P OR
1908 Bradford Park Avenue 1

From	To		Apps	Goal
Eccles, George Samuel			RB/LB	
b Newcastle-under-Lyme q3 1872			d 1945	
Caps: FLge 1				
		Wolstanton Brotherhood		
		Stoke St Peter's		
		Titbury Town		
		Middleport		
1893	1895	Burslem Port Vale	50	
1896	1897	Wolverhampton Wanderers	36	1
1898	1901	Everton	56	
1901		Preston North End	0	
		West Ham United		
1904		Bolton Wanderers	6	
Eccles, John (Jack)			LB	
b Stoke-on-Trent 31/3/1869			d 1932	
Caps: FLge 1				
		London Road (Stoke)		
1889	1900	Stoke	160	1
Eccles, Joseph (Joe)			OR	
b Stoke-on-Trent 2/1906			d 1970	
1922		Walsall	0	
		Wolseley Motors		
1924		Aston Villa	10	
1926		West Ham United	0	
1928		Northampton Town	15	1
1929		Coventry City	0	
Eccles, Robert			OL	
			d 1916	
1898		Darwen	6	1
Eccles, Thomas Edward			IL/CF	
b Hull q1 1900			d 1968	
		Hargreaves (Hull)		
1921	1922	Hull City	9	2
		Bridlington Town		
Eccleston, Thomas			RH/LH	
b Preston q4 1875				
1895		Preston North End	2	
		Reading		
1899	1900	Preston North End	24	2
Eccleston, William			RH/IR/OR	
b Preston q4 1873			d 1937	
		North Meols		
1894		Grimsby Town	29	13
1895	1899	Preston North End	72	6
		Kettering		
		Oldham Athletic		
		Barrow		
		Lancaster		
		Clitheroe		
Ecclestone, Arthur			IL	
b Stafford 1902				
		Stone Lotus		
1925	1926	Port Vale	2	
Eckersley, Frank			GK	
b Manchester 12/11/1912			d 1992	
		Pelaw CWS		
1930		Derby County	0	
		Linfield		
		Wigan Athletic		
1937		Manchester City	0	
1938		Oldham Athletic	1	
Eckford, John			OL	
b Buckhaven 13/2/1878				
		Raith Rovers		
1899		Luton Town	34	4
1900		Middlesbrough	3	
		Raith Rovers		
Eddleston, Joseph (Joe)			CF/IR/IL	
b Oswaldtwistle 29/12/1896			d 1959	
		St Mary's RC (Oswaldtwistle)		
1919		Blackburn Rovers	7	3
1921	1925	Nelson	183	97
1926	1931	Swindon Town	202	66
1932		Accrington Stanley	40	12
		Fleetwood		
Edelston, Joseph (Joe)			RH/LH	
b Appley Bridge 27/4/1891			d 1970	
		Appley Bridge		
		St Helens Recreation		
1912	1919	Hull City	109	
1920		Manchester City	6	
1920	1924	Fulham	67	
Edelston, Maurice			IR/IL	
b Hull 27/4/1918			d 1976	
Caps: England Amat/England War 5				
1935	1937	Fulham	3	
		Wimbledon		
1937	1938	Brentford	21	6
		Corinthians		
1939	1951	Reading	202	70
1939		(Reading)	(3)	(2)
1952	1953	Northampton Town	40	17

From	To		Apps	Goal
Eden, Edwin			LH	
b Blockley 21/4/1893			d 1939	
1921		Walsall	9	
Eden, J			LB	
1911		Manchester City	1	
Eden, William (Billy)			OR/OL	
b Stockton 1/7/1905			d 1993	
		Loftus Albion		
1928	1929	Darlington	40	15
1929	1931	Sunderland	60	19
1932	1934	Darlington	79	16
1934	1938	Tranmere Rovers	139	30
1939		New Brighton	0	
Edgar, Daniel (Danny)			RB/LH	
b Jarrow 3/4/1910			d 1991	
		Jarrow St Bede's		
1930		Walsall	9	
1931	1934	Sunderland	43	
1935	1937	Nottingham Forest	100	1
Edgar, David James (Dave)			OL	
b Edinburgh 5/2/1902			d 1976	
		Raith Rovers		
1920		Burnley	0	
		East Fife		
		Heart of Midlothian		
		Airdrieonians (loan)		
		East Fife (loan)		
		(USA)		
1932		Aldershot	4	
1933	1935	Darlington	88	20
		Cannock Town		
		Hexham		
		Workington		
Edgar, James Henry			OR	
b Birtley q4 1882				
		Birtley		
1905		Sunderland	2	
		Birtley		
		Hebburn Argyle		
		Birtley		
Edgar, John			IR	
b Scotland				
		Parkhead		
1901		Woolwich Arsenal	10	1
		Airdrieonians		
		Aberdeen		
		Hibernian		
		Aberdeen		
Edge, Alfred (Alf)			IL/OL	
b Stoke-on-Trent 1866			d 1941	
Caps: FAlliance 1				
		Goldenhill Wanderers		
1888	1889	Stoke	30	4
		Newton Heath		
		Nottingham Jardines Athletic		
1892		Stoke	1	1
1893		Northwich Victoria	3	
1893		Ardwick	1	
		Macclesfield		
Edge, Arthur Stanley			GK	
b Freshfields 24/9/1892			d 1932	
		Cambridge University		
1914		Blackburn Rovers	9	
Edge, Robert (Bob)			OL/CF/IR	
1893	1896	Wolverhampton Wanderers	24	8
1897		Loughborough	0	
Edge, Thomas (Tommy)			OR	
b Leigh 28/4/1898			d 1966	
		Brook Valley		
1919		Manchester City	0	
		Treherbert		
1920		Oldham Athletic	3	
1921		Exeter City	3	
1922		Blackpool	5	
1923		New Brighton	26	2
		Rossendale United (trial)		
		Winsford United		
		Stockport Wednesday		
		Stockport Thursday		
Edgley, Frank			IL/CF	
b Crewe q3 1880			d 1910	
		Crewe Alexandra		
1903	1904	Sheffield United	5	
		Fulham		
		Reading		
		Hartlepools United		

From	To		Apps	Goal
Edgley, Harold Horace			OL/OR	
b Crewe 1/1892			d 1966	
		Whitchurch		
		Crewe Alexandra		
1911	1919	Aston Villa	75	15
		Stourbridge (loan)		
1921	1922	Queen's Park Rangers	69	6
1923		Stockport County	29	4
		Worcester City		
Edmed, Richard Alfred (Dick)			OR	
b Gillingham 14/2/1904			d 1983	
		Chatham Central		
		Rochester Sports		
1923	1925	Gillingham	24	7
1926	1930	Liverpool	160	44
1931	1932	Bolton Wanderers	4	1
Edmonds, Alfred John (Alf 'Eddie')			RH/CH/IR	
b Brighton 16/10/1902			d 1942	
		Vernon Athletic		
		Allen West		
1925	1928	Brighton & Hove Albion	14	
1929	1931	Clapton Orient	89	18
1932	1933	Bury	13	
1934		Mansfield Town	33	4
		Manchester North End		
Edmonds, Frederick Henry A (Fred)			GK	
b Swindon 9/5/1915			d 2003	
		Swindon Rangers		
1935	1936	Swindon Town	8	
1937		Reading	0	
		Cheltenham Town		
Edmonds, George William Neville (Eddie)			CF/IL	
b Holborn 4/4/1893			d 1989	
		St Stephen's (Watford)		
		Andre & Sleigh		
		Watford Wednesday		
		St Albans City		
		Watford		
1920	1923	Wolverhampton Wanderers	115	38
1923	1925	Fulham	66	23
1926		Watford	22	12
		Northfleet		
Edmonds, Hugh			GK	
b Chryston 1884				
Caps: IrLge 1				
		Smithson		
		Hamilton Academical		
		Distillery		
		Linfield		
1909	1910	Bolton Wanderers	10	
1910	1911	Manchester United	43	
		Glenavon		
		Distillery		
		Jarrow		
		Distillery		
		Whitehall		
Edmondson, John			CF	
b Carleton				
Caps: WLge 1				
		Leyland		
1914	1919	Leeds City	11	6
1919		Sheffield Wednesday	14	2
1920	1922	Swansea Town	60	33
1923		Exeter City	6	1
Edmondson, John Henry			GK	
b Accrington 1882				
		Accrington Stanley		
1902	1905	Manchester City	38	
1906	1914	Bolton Wanderers	239	
Edmondson, T			LB	
1898		Darwen	13	
Edmondson, William			OL	
		Briercliffe Rovers		
1902		Burnley	2	
Edmunds, Alec			OL	
b Birmingham				
		Royal Navy		
1927		Plymouth Argyle	5	
1928		Torquay United	6	
Edmunds, Charles Trevor (Trevor)			IR/CF	
b Merthyr Tydfil 7/12/1903			d 1975	
1926		Aberdare Athletic	0	
		Aberaman Athletic		
1928		Bradford City	19	11
1929		Chesterfield	8	1
		Yeovil & Petters United		
1931		Charlton Athletic	6	4
		Red Star (France)		
		Worcester City		
		Redditch Town		

From	To		Apps	Goal
Edmunds, William (Bill)			CF	
		Spennymoor United		
		Shildon Athletic		
1921		Darlington	8	6
		Trimdon Grange		
Edrich, William John (Bill)			OL	
b Lingwood 26/3/1916			d 1986	
1932		Norwich City	0	
1934		Tottenham Hotspur	0	
		Northfleet		
1935	1936	Tottenham Hotspur	20	4
		Chelmsford City		
Edwards, Albert			RH	
			d 1918	
1912		Aston Villa	0	
1912		Bristol City	4	
		Newport County		
Edwards, Alfred			CH	
b Coventry 4/1890			d 1949	
		Stourbridge		
1911		Aston Villa	6	
		Dudley Town		
		Netherton		
		Cradley Heath St Luke's		
Edwards, Charles Robert (Charlie)			GK	
b Brandon Colliery 11/1/1891			d 1959	
		Edmondsley		
1919		Burnley	0	
		Tranmere Rovers		
1921	1922	Durham City	9	
		Spennymoor United		
Edwards, David Samuel (Dai)			OL	
b Bargoed 11/9/1916			d 1990	
		Deri		
1937		Newport County	2	
		Gloucester City		
1945		Ipswich Town	0	
1946		Swindon Town	3	1
		Bath City		
Edwards, Edmund Clifford (Eddie)			IR/IL/OL	
b Durham q3 1909			d 1991	
		Thurcroft Main		
		Worksop Town		
1933		Rotherham United	1	
1934		Bury	0	
1935		Clapton Orient	1	
1936		Hull City	10	1
		Mossley		
1938		Carlisle United	2	
Edwards, Ernest Arthur (Ernie)			LH/CH	
b Stourbridge 17/2/1892				
		Old Hill Unity		
1912		West Bromwich Albion	0	
		Kidderminster Olympic		
		Redditch Town		
1913	1914	Birmingham	17	
		Tipton Excelsior		
		Merthyr Town		
1920	1922	Newport County	112	
1923	1925	Southend United	92	4
		Dudley Town		
1927		Merthyr Town	0	
Edwards, Ernest J (Ernie)			IR	
b Dudley Port 1893				
		Old Hill Unity		
1913		West Bromwich Albion	7	3
		Walsall		
Edwards, Evan Jenkin			OL	
b Bedlinog 14/12/1896			d 1958	
Caps: Wales Amat				
1920	1922	Merthyr Town	87	10
1923	1924	Wolverhampton Wanderers	63	12
		Mid-Rhondda United		
1925		Swansea Town	11	1
1926		Northampton Town	11	2
1927		Halifax Town	0	
		Ebbw Vale		
1928		Darlington	25	3
1929		Clapton Orient	4	
Edwards, George			OL	
b Treherbert 2/12/1920			d 2008	
Caps: Wales Amat/WLge 3/Wales War 3/Wales 12				
1938		Swansea Town	2	
1945	1948	Birmingham City	84	9
1948	1954	Cardiff City	195	36
Edwards, George Robert			OR/IL/IR	
b Great Yarmouth 1/4/1918			d 1993	
		Yarmouth Caledonians		
1935	1937	Norwich City	9	1
1938	1950	Aston Villa	138	34
1939		(Aston Villa)	(3)	(1)
		Bilston United		
		Yarmouth Town		

From To Apps Goal

Edwards, Gerald Gething GK
b Hong Kong 18/12/1911 d 1992
Cambridge University
1930 Luton Town 2

Edwards, Henry Roby (Harry) IR
b Birmingham q4 1872 d 1940
Singers
1892 Small Heath 5 1
Ryton Rovers
Leicester Fosse
1894 Derby County 0
Wolverton LNWR
Watford
Bedford Queens Engineers

Edwards, Herbert P CF
1925 Walsall 3

Edwards, James (Jimmy) LH/IL
b Tipton 11/12/1905 d 1982
Caps: FLge 1
Tipton Park
Newport Foundry
Stourbridge
Great Bridge Celtic
Stourbridge
1927 1936 West Bromwich Albion 182 9
1937 Norwich City 2
Bilston United
Kingswinford
Dudley Town

Edwards, JH IL
b 1876
Aberystwyth
1894 Bury 2 1
1895 West Bromwich Albion 0

Edwards, John RH
b Staffordshire 1875
1893 1894 Burslem Port Vale 12 3
Stockport County
1895 Burslem Port Vale 3 1
Grays United
Queen's Park Rangers
Plymouth Argyle

Edwards, John Bentley (Jack) OL
b Preston 1867 d 1960
1888 Preston North End 4 3

Edwards, John S RH
Buckley
1937 Chester 1

Edwards, John W IR
Carr Vale
Bolsover
1908 Derby County 2 1

Edwards, Joseph Arthur (Joe) GK
b Hillstown 5/3/1907 d 1997
Bolsover Town
Staveley Town
1930 Chesterfield 0
1931 Derby County 0
Bolsover Colliery
1933 Mansfield Town 20
Ollerton Colliery

Edwards, Joseph H OR
1925 Queen's Park Rangers 3

Edwards, Joseph Noel (Noel) LB
b Johnstown 26/11/1898 d 1952
Rhos Athletic
1921 1925 Wrexham 80 3
Llandudno
Oswestry Town
Holywell Town
1929 Carlisle United (trial) 0

Edwards, Leonard (Len) LH
b East Ham q1 1920
Caps: England Sch
1938 Fulham 0
1939 Reading (1)

Edwards, Leslie (Les) RH
b Nuneaton 29/10/1910 d 1996
Bradbury's (Hinckley)
1931 Leicester City 3
Folkestone
1933 1935 Crystal Palace 23 2
1936 1937 Newport County 41 1
Hinckley United

Edwards, Martin LB
b East Boldon q2 1882 d 1944
Darnell
Gateshead NER
1903 1904 Barnsley 65 3
Crystal Palace
Doncaster Rovers

From To Apps Goal

Edwards, Moses William IR
b Alverstoke q4 1893 d 1958
Gosport Athletic
1921 Portsmouth 1
Gosport Athletic

Edwards, Oliver OL/OR
b Rhymney
Caps: Wales Amat
Rhymney
1920 1921 Merthyr Town 5

Edwards, Reginald T CF/IL
b Coseley 1912
Brierley Hill Alliance
1931 1932 Burnley 18 5
1933 Walsall 1

Edwards, Samuel (Sam) OR
b Dudley Port 5/1898
Old Hill Unity
1919 West Bromwich Albion 0
Kidderminster Harriers
1924 Bristol Rovers 32 5
Stourbridge

Edwards, Samuel H (Sam) RH
b Wolverhampton 1885 d 1938
Brades Park
1904 West Bromwich Albion 1
Stafford Rangers

Edwards, Sydney Charles OR
b Northampton 16/8/1912 d 1995
Wellingborough Town
1934 1935 Northampton Town 4 1
Rushden Town
Kettering Town

Edwards, Tudor S IL/CF
b Aberdare
1926 Aberdare Athletic 15 2
1927 Exeter City 3

Edwards, W CF
Crewe Alexandra
1904 Burslem Port Vale 1

Edwards, Wilfred James (Wilf) OL
b Fenton 22/8/1905 d 1976
1923 Stoke 0
1924 Crewe Alexandra 10 1
Stafford Rangers
1928 Crewe Alexandra 2 1
Burton Town
Loughborough Corinthians
1931 Lincoln City 1

Edwards, William OL
Colwyn Bay United
1936 Tranmere Rovers 1
1937 Everton 0

Edwards, William Francis (Billy) OR
b Aston q3 1896 d 1952
Shrewsbury Town
Brentford
Watford
Llanelly
1919 Fulham 0
1920 1922 Newport County 79 12
1922 1925 West Ham United 37 3
Hereford United

Edwards, William H OL
b Coventry 2/1874
Singers
1896 Small Heath 5 1
Rugby

Edwards, William John Thomas (Tom) OR/RH
b Merthyr Tydfil 22/8/1905 d 1976
Aberaman Athletic
1924 Merthyr Town 10
1926 1927 Walsall 34 5
1928 Millwall 4

Edwards, Willis RH
b Newton, Derbyshire 28/4/1903 d 1988
Caps: FLge 11/England 16
Newton Rangers
1922 1924 Chesterfield 70 1
1924 1938 Leeds United 417 6

Egan, George Douglas (Doug) IL
b Tibshelf 6/6/1919 d 1995
1937 Derby County 0
1938 Aldershot 10

Egan, Henry (Harry) IL/CF
b Tibshelf 23/2/1912 d 1979
Sutton Town
1933 1935 Brighton & Hove Albion 19 8
1936 Southend United 6
1937 1938 Aldershot 59 19
1938 Cardiff City 17 9

From To Apps Goal

Egan, Thomas William (William) CF/OL/IR
b Chirk q2 1872 d 1946
Caps: Wales 1
Chirk
Fairfield
1893 Ardwick 7
1893 1894 Burnley 10 3
Ashton North End
1895 Sheffield United 15 4
1896 Lincoln City 16
Birdwell
Altofts
Darwen
Royston United
1901 Stockport County 0
Chirk

Egan, William Henry (Bill) LB
b Birkenhead 27/12/1908 d 1972
1932 New Brighton 1

Egerton, William (Billy) CF
b Bollington q3 1891 d 1934
Bollington
1911 Bolton Wanderers 2
Chesterfield Town
1913 1919 Lincoln City 76 25
Mid-Rhondda

Eggett, John Henry (Jack) GK
b Wisbech 19/4/1874 d 1943
Wisbech Town
1901 1902 Doncaster Rovers 67
1903 Woolwich Arsenal 0
West Ham United
Tottenham Hotspur
Croydon Common

Eggleston, Arthur IL/IR/RH
b Chopwell 4/1/1910 d 1990
Spen Black & White
1930 1934 Bury 100 31
1935 1936 Plymouth Argyle 45 16
1937 1938 Sheffield United 24 2

Eggleton, James Arthur Edward (Jimmy) CH
b Heston 29/8/1897 d 1963
Army
1921 1923 Charlton Athletic 26
1923 1925 Watford 48 2
1925 Lincoln City 0
1926 1928 Queen's Park Rangers 42

Eggo, Robert Mollison (Bert) RB/RH/CH
b Brechin 22/11/1895 d 1977
Caps: SoLge 1
Brechin North End
Heart of Midlothian
Dunfermline Athletic
1919 1920 Sheffield Wednesday 23
1921 1928 Reading 289 2

Eglington, Robert IL
b Stockton q4 1874 d 1950
Thornaby
1899 Middlesbrough 5 2

Ekins, Frederick George OL/IL
b New Brompton 27/9/1871 d 1960
New Brompton Rovers
Chatham
1891 1892 Derby County 18 3
1893 1894 Burton Swifts 52 17
1897 1898 Luton Town 33 5

Eley, William OR
b Matlock Bath q3 1883
Matlock Town
1906 Bradford City 1

Elkes, Albert John (Jack) IL/CH
b Snedshill 31/12/1894 d 1972
Caps: FLge 3
Wellington St George's
Stalybridge Celtic
Shifnal Town
1919 1921 Birmingham 34 15
1921 1922 Southampton 33 7
1923 1928 Tottenham Hotspur 190 50
1929 1932 Middlesbrough 105 4
1933 Watford 9 1
Stafford Rangers
Oakengates Town

Elkin, Bertie Henry West RB
b Neasden 14/1/1886 d 1962
Fulham
Luton Town
1908 1909 Stockport County 47
1909 1910 Tottenham Hotspur 26

Elkins, Arthur CF
b Grimsby q3 1880 d 1920
1903 1904 Grimsby Town 18 7

From To Apps Goal

Elleman, Allan Richard OR
b Birmingham 3/11/1862 d 1939
Caps: Ireland 2
Stoke St Peter's
Glentoran
Cliftonville
1889 West Bromwich Albion 0
1891 Notts County 6 2
Grimsby Town
Mansfield Town

Elleray, James Alfred OR
b Burneside 12/2/1909 d 1976
Staveley
1929 Accrington Stanley (trial) 0
1929 Barrow 9 1
Lancaster Town
1931 Barrow 0
1931 Carlisle United 0

Ellerington, William (Bill) CH/LH
b Sunderland q3 1892 d 1948
Caps: WLge 1
Fatfield Albion
Darlington South Bank
Darlington
1919 1923 Middlesbrough 127 1
1924 Nelson 26 2
Pontypridd
Mid-Rhondda United
Ebbw Vale
Basingstoke Town

Elliott, Alex OL
b Liverpool 1898
Northwich Victoria
Wigan Borough
1921 Southend United 8
1923 Crewe Alexandra 10 2

Elliott, Arthur IL
b Nottingham 1870
Notts Rangers
Gainsborough Trinity
1891 Accrington 24 7
1893 Woolwich Arsenal 24 10
Tottenham Hotspur

Elliott, Charles CF
b Sheffield
Rotherham Town
1921 Rotherham County 5 1
York City

Elliott, Charles Standish (Charlie) LB/RB
b Bolsover 24/4/1912 d 2004
Bolsover Colliery
1929 Sheffield Wednesday 0
1930 Chesterfield 0
1931 1947 Coventry City 95 2

Elliott, Edward (Ted) GK
b Carlisle 24/5/1919 d 1984
1937 1938 Carlisle United 11
1946 1947 Wolverhampton Wanderers 7
1948 1950 Chester 59
1950 1951 Halifax Town 33

Elliott, George Washington CF/IR/IL
b Sunderland 7/1/1889 d 1948
Caps: FLge 3/England 3
Redcar Crusaders
South Bank
Grangetown
1909 1924 Middlesbrough 345 203
Celtic (loan)

Elliott, Hugh Bell RB
b Annfield Plain q2 1899 d 1966
South Pontop Villa
West Stanley (trial)
1921 Arsenal 0
Margate (loan)
1922 1923 Durham City 47
Shildon
South Pontop Villa
Usworth Colliery
White-le-Head Rangers

Elliott, Jack OL/LH/OR
1890 1895 Everton 14 1

Elliott, James Alexander E LB
b Middlesbrough 20/10/1869 d 1899
Middlesbrough Ironopolis
1893 1895 Aston Villa 19

Elliott, James Edward (Jimmy) RH/CF
b Peterborough 1891
South Weald
Peterborough City
1911 1919 Tottenham Hotspur 13 4
1920 1921 Brentford 65 2

From To Apps Goal

Elliott, John William GK
b Scotswood 21/5/1899
Scotswood
1920 1921 Preston North End 12
1923 Watford 0
Scotswood
Jarrow
1925 1926 Ashington 56
Scotswood
Jarrow
Walker Park
Scotswood
Newcastle Tramways

Elliott, Joseph (Joe) LH/RH
b Paisley 1876
Haywood Wanderers
1898 1901 Preston North End 80 4
Plymouth Argyle
New Brompton

Elliott, Robert (Bob) OL/IL
b Carlisle q2 1912 d 1955
London & North Western Railway
1933 1934 Carlisle United 10 1
1934 Preston North End 0
1935 New Brighton 38 1
Bath City
1937 Aldershot 12 1
1938 Carlisle United 0

Elliott, Sidney (Sid) CF/IL/IR
b Sunderland 14/1/1908 d 1986
FG Minter Sports
Arcade Mission
Margate
1926 Durham City 28 10
1927 Fulham 42 26
1928 1929 Chelsea 30 9
1930 1931 Bristol City 50 24
1931 1933 Notts County 51 16
1934 Bradford City 15 7
1935 Rochdale 11 1
FG Minter Sports

Elliott, Thomas William (Tom) IR/CF
b Annfield Plain 6/4/1890
Annfield Plain
West Stanley
1910 Gainsborough Trinity 9
West Stanley
1912 1919 Huddersfield Town 72 18
1919 Grimsby Town 0
1920 Nottingham Forest 28 7
1921 1922 Brentford 49 8
1923 Durham City 27 13
1924 Crewe Alexandra 16 4
Annfield Plain
Crawcrook Albion
Newcastle Tramways

Elliott, William Bethwaite (Billy) OR
b Harrington 6/8/1919 d 1966
Caps: England War 2
1936 Carlisle United 0
Dudley Town
1937 Wolverhampton Wanderers 0
1938 Bournemouth & Boscombe Ath 10 1
1938 1950 West Bromwich Albion 170 39
Bilston

Ellis, Brinley (Bryn) LB/OL
b Pontypridd 12/3/1917 d 1992
1936 1937 Newport County 2
Gloucester City

Ellis, David OR
b Glasgow 2/3/1900
Cameron Highlanders
Glasgow Ashfield
Airdrieonians
Maidstone United
1923 Manchester United 11
St Johnstone
1927 Bradford City 0
1928 Brighton & Hove Albion (trial)
Arthurlie

Ellis, Ernest Edgar RB
b Sprowston 30/11/1885 d 1916
Norwich City
Doncaster Rovers
1909 Barnsley 4
Hartlepools United
Heart of Midlothian

Ellis, Frederick Charles (Fred) LH/LB
b Sheerness 7/11/1900 d 1970
Sheppey United
1925 1930 Gillingham 108 1
1931 Watford 32 1
1932 Clapton Orient 27
Ashford Town (Kent)

From To Apps Goal

Ellis, John (Jack) GK
b Tyldesley 25/1/1908 d 1994
Tyldesley United
Atherton
Winsford United
1930 West Bromwich Albion 0
1932 1933 Wolverhampton Wanderers 26
1934 1937 Bristol Rovers 86
1938 Hull City 32
1939 Clapton Orient (3)
Winsford United
Stalybridge Celtic
Mossley

Ellis, John A OL
1921 Stalybridge Celtic 17 2

Ellis, Jonathan (Jack) RB
b Flint 20/11/1890 d 1941
Flint Church Guild
Flint Town
Connah's Quay
Flint Alliance
Connah's Quay & Shotton Alliance
Tranmere Rovers
1921 Wrexham 19
Rhos Athletic

Ellis, Percy RB/RH
b Hanley
1919 Port Vale 12
1921 Walsall 1
Stafford Rangers

Ellis, Robert (Bob) IR
b Parkhead 1885
Vale of Leven
Workington
1908 Blackburn Rovers 1 1
Workington

Ellis, Thomas (Tom) GK
b Coxhoe
Deaf Hill
1928 Middlesbrough 0
South Bank
Coxhoe
1931 Wolverhampton Wanderers 0
1932 1938 Barnsley 169

Ellis, William Thomas (Billy) OL
b Wolverhampton 5/11/1895 d 1939
Caps: FLge 1
Highfield Villa
Willenhall Swifts
Bilston Juniors
Willenhall
1919 1927 Sunderland 190 32
1927 1928 Birmingham 32 8
1929 Lincoln City 31 11
1930 York City 3 1

Ellison, Irvin LB
b Stocksbridge 27/8/1914 d 2006
1934 Chesterfield 3

Ellison, James RB
b Manchester 4/2/1906 d 1986
St Helens Town
1924 Tranmere Rovers 0
1925 Rotherham United 0
Rhyl Athletic
1927 Southampton 1
1928 Rochdale 16
Connah's Quay & Shotton

Ellison, R CH
1899 New Brighton Tower 2

Ellson, Merton Frederick (Matt) IR
b Thrapston 10/7/1890 d 1958
Frickley Colliery
1920 1921 Leeds United 37 8
Frickley Colliery
1922 1923 Halifax Town 23 6

Ellwood, Reginald John IL
b Worcester 1/1/1919
1935 Fulham 0
Tunbridge Wells Rangers
Worcester City
1938 Northampton Town 19 2
1939 (Northampton Town) (3)
Guildford City

Elmore, E IL
Lincoln Liberal Club
1903 Lincoln City 1
Lincoln Liberal Club

From To Apps Goal

Elmore, George IL/CF/OR
b Northwich q3 1880 d 1916
Witton Albion
Broadheath
1902 West Bromwich Albion 3 1
Bristol Rovers
Witton Albion
Altrincham
1907 1908 Glossop 34 14
1909 Blackpool 34 6
Partick Thistle
St Mirren
Witton Albion
St Bernard's

Elsdon, William Rowell OL
b Hexham 19/4/1900 d 1984
1928 Ashington 1

Elson, William (Billy) LH
1892 1893 Burslem Port Vale 42 2
West Manchester

Elston, Arthur Edward OL
b Liverpool 7/1882 d 1950
Crownhills
1905 Aston Villa 1
Portsmouth
St Helens Recreation

Elston, H OR
1898 Blackpool 4

Elvey, John Richard RB
b Sharpenhoe 1890
Luton Clarence
Luton Town
1920 1921 Bolton Wanderers 11
1922 Arsenal 1

Elvidge, Christopher (Chris) IL
b Stourbridge q2 1892
Hereford Town
1921 Wrexham 12 2
Shrewsbury Town

Elwell, Thomas Dennis Oakly (Dennis) CH
b Wolverhampton 20/9/1901 d 1974
Orb United
Somerton Park
1925 1926 Newport County 4
Lovells Athletic

Elwood, James H (Jimmy) CH
b Belfast 12/6/1901 d 1937
Caps: Ireland 2
Glentoran
1923 1926 Manchester City 31
1927 Chesterfield 38 4
1928 1932 Bradford Park Avenue 106 1
Derry City

Emberton, Frederick Percival (Teddy) RH
b Thryston 23/6/1884 d 1957
Stafford Wesleyans
Stafford Rangers
1904 1914 Notts County 365 2

Embleton, Edward (Eddie) IL
b South Moor q2 1916 d 1962
Ouston Juniors
1934 Norwich City 0
1935 Bradford City 3 1
1937 Hartlepools United 22 6
1938 Gateshead 17 9
1939 Doncaster Rovers 0

Embleton, George OR
b Sacriston 3/4/1918 d 1983
1938 Carlisle United 10 1

Embleton, Sidney William (Sid) OR
b Poplar 16/3/1905 d 1987
Walthamstow Avenue
1930 Queen's Park Rangers 2

Embrey, Sydney (Syd) OR
b Bury 16/2/1903 d 1981
Horwich RMI
1923 Halifax Town 3
Horwich RMI

Emerson, Arthur CF
b Bury 21/7/1913 d 1997
Red Lumb
1935 Rochdale 1

Emerson, William RH
b Enniskillen 16/12/1891 d 1961
Caps: IrLge 4/Ireland 11
Glentoran
1921 1923 Burnley 44
Glentoran

From To Apps Goal

Emery, Donald Kenneth James (Don) LB/OL
b Cardiff 11/6/1920 d 1993
Caps: Wales Sch
Ely Rangers
1936 Cardiff City 0
1937 1947 Swindon Town 69 3
Aberdeen
East Fife
Fraserburgh

Emery, Frederick David (Fred) LH
b Lincoln 19/5/1900 d 1959
1921 Lincoln City 0
Wibsey
1923 Bradford City 5
1924 1935 Doncaster Rovers 417 30

Emery, Herbert John C (Bert) GK
b Bristol 18/2/1910 d 1995
Ely United
Cardiff Corinthians
1928 Clapton Orient 0
1929 1930 Rotherham United 36
1931 1932 Clapton Orient 62
1933 1934 Newport County 77

Emery, Samuel (Sam) IR
1892 1893 Burton Swifts 25 11

Emmanuel, David Leonard (Len) LB/LH/RB
b Treboeth 3/9/1917 d 2010
Caps: Wales Sch
1937 1946 Swansea Town 49 1
1939 (Swansea Town) (3)
1946 1947 Newport County 33 7
1948 Bristol Rovers 0
Kidderminster Harriers
Llanelly
Carmarthen Town

Emmanuel, Thomas (Tom) LB
b Treboreth 1/8/1915 d 1997
ICI Works
1935 1938 Swansea Town 45 1
1938 1945 Southampton 33
1939 (Southampton) (3)
Milford United
Llanelly

Emmerson, George Arthur Heads OR
b Bishop Auckland 15/5/1906 d 1966
Palmer's (Jarrow)
Jarrow
1928 1929 Middlesbrough 7 3
1930 1932 Cardiff City 120 16
1933 1934 Queen's Park Rangers 52 13
1935 1936 Rochdale 66 12
Tunbridge Wells Rangers
1937 Gillingham 10

Emmerson, J CF
1906 Burton United 6 1
Midway Albion
Measham United

Emmett, Charles P LB
b Newcastle
St Anthony's (Newcastle)
1926 Bradford City 1
Dipton United

Emmett, Herbert RH
b Rotherham 24/4/??
Rotherham Town
1920 1926 Rotherham County 170

Emmitt, Herbert William RH
b Nottingham 6/8/1857 d 1901
1888 Notts County 4
Nottingham Forest

Emptage, Albert Taylor LH/IR
b Grimsby 26/12/1917 d 1997
Caps: FLge 1
Scunthorpe & Lindsey United
1937 1950 Manchester City 136 1
1950 1952 Stockport County 36 1

England, Ernest (Ernie) LB
b Shirebrook 3/2/1901 d 1982
Shirebrook
1919 1929 Sunderland 336
1930 West Ham United 5
1931 1934 Mansfield Town 130 3
Frickley Colliery

From To Apps Goal

England, John Thomas IR
b Newstead q1 1879
Newstead Byron
Kirkby Town
Hucknall Town
Sutton Town
Stanton Town
1901 Chesterfield Town 17 9
Blackwell Colliery
Creswell United
Ilkeston United
New Hucknall Colliery

English, John Cogal (Jack) LB/RB
b Hebburn 13/12/1886 d 1953
Caps: FLge 1
Hebburn Argyle
Wallsend Park Villa
1910 1911 Preston North End 6
Watford
1913 1914 Sheffield United 55
Darlington

English, Samuel (Sam) CF
b Coleraine 18/8/1908 d 1967
Caps: Ireland 2
Port Glasgow Juniors
Old Kilpatrick
Yoker Athletic
Rangers
1933 1934 Liverpool 47 24
Queen of the South
1936 1937 Hartlepools United 69 27
Duntocher Hibs

Enright, Joseph (Joe) IL/OR
b Athlone 1891
Caps: IrLge 2/Ireland 1
Shelbourne
1910 1912 Leeds City 77 23
Newport County
Coventry City

Entwistle, Harry CH
b Bolton
Heaton
1924 Manchester United (trial)
Horwich RMI
Little Lever
1930 Wigan Borough 2

Entwistle, Jonathan T (Jonty) OL/OR
b Darwen 1868
Darwen Rovers
Haslingden
Darwen
1889 Accrington 19 9
1891 1893 Darwen 40 15
Accrington
Nelson
Padiham

Entwistle, RH GK
1891 Darwen 2

Entwistle, William LH
b Leeds
West Riding Amateurs
1922 1924 Accrington Stanley 29 2

Ephgrave, George Arthur GK
b Reading 29/4/1918
Guernsey Rangers
Northfleet
1936 Aston Villa 0
1938 Swindon Town 1
1946 1947 Southampton 36
1948 1950 Norwich City 5
1951 Watford 4
Deal Town
March Town

Erentz, Fred Charles LB/LH
b Broughty Ferry 3/1870 d 1938
Dundee Our Boys
1892 1901 Newton Heath 280 9

Erentz, Henry B (Harry) RB
b Dundee 17/9/1874 d 1947
Dundee
Oldham County
1897 Newton Heath 6
Tottenham Hotspur
Swindon Town

Errington, Albert (Darkie) LB
b Low Walker q3 1901
Scotswood
1926 1930 Hartlepools United 81
Spennymoor United

From To Apps Goal

Erskine, George Rowlands CH
b Aberdeen 22/10/1914
Hall, Russell & Co
Aberdeen
1937 Carlisle United 1
Forfar Athletic

Eslor, John (Jack) LB
b Scotland
Heart of Midlothian
1936 Cardiff City 3
Workington

Espie, John (Jock) CH/CF
b Hamilton 1868
Rangers
Motherwell
Queen's Park
Burnbank Swifts
1891 1895 Burnley 93 11
1895 Manchester City 1
Dundee

Essex, John Reginald IR
b Crewe 14/2/1917 d 1988
Nantwich
1937 Crewe Alexandra 13 6
1938 Stockport County 41 13
1939 (Stockport County) (2)

Essom, Walter LB
b Leicester 11/1895 d 1966
Carey Hall
Leicester Imperial
British United
1919 Leicester City 2
Ashby Town

Etches, Henry (Harry) IR
b Nottingham 1875
Adelaide (Lincoln)
Boston Town
Adelaide (Lincoln)
1902 Lincoln City 2
Adelaide (Lincoln)

Etherington, Robert Dilworth OR
b Croston 19/6/1899 d 1981
Leyland
1921 1922 Manchester City 12
1924 Rotherham County 14 1
Hurst
Manchester North End
1927 Crewe Alexandra (trial) 0
Chester
Mossley

Ette, Clifford Albert (Cliff) IR
b Northampton 17/6/1910 d 1995
Northampton Nomads
1933 West Ham United 1 1
St Albans City
Park Royal
Southall

Evans, Albert CF/IR
b Camberwell 17/1/1901 d 1969
Woking
1927 1928 Tottenham Hotspur 5
Grantham

Evans, Albert H LH/IR
b South Wales
1931 1932 Cardiff City 22
Dundalk

Evans, Albert James LB
b Barnard Castle 3/1874 d 1966
Caps: FLge 1
Barnard Castle
1896 1905 Aston Villa 179
1907 1908 West Bromwich Albion 37

Evans, Aneurin CF
Porth
1922 Merthyr Town 4 1

Evans, Arthur LH/CH
Rossendale United
1909 1911 Blackpool 37

Evans, Arthur OR
b Barking 1906
Caps: England Amat
Barking Town
1930 West Ham United 1
Barking Town

From To Apps Goal

Evans, Arthur Richard GK
b Wrexham 1905
Miners' Institute (Wrexham)
Denbigh United
1927 Wrexham 2
Denbigh United
Bangor City
Llanelly
Whitchurch

Evans, Arthur Victor (Vic) RB
b Mold 1918
Caps: Wales Sch
1934 1937 Wrexham 84

Evans, Arthur W GK
b Stoke-on-Trent 1868
1893 Stoke 9
Barlaston Saints

Evans, B OR
1896 1897 Burton Swifts 32 3

Evans, Charles IR
b Luton
1929 Queen's Park Rangers 1

Evans, Charles H IR
1927 Crewe Alexandra 14 5

Evans, Charles John H RH
b Cardiff 31/1/1897
Cardiff Camerons
1922 Cardiff City 0
1924 Northampton Town 18 2
1925 Grimsby Town 5
Barry

Evans, David (Dai Gethin) LH
b Abercanaid 28/1/1902 d 1951
Caps: Wales 4
Troedyrhiw Stars
1921 Merthyr Town 0
1922 Nelson 0
1923 Bolton Wanderers 0
1924 1927 Reading 122 11
1928 Huddersfield Town 18
1929 Bury 19
Merthyr Town
Burton Town

Evans, David B IR
1926 Aberdare Athletic 7 4

Evans, David Richard RB/LB
b Merthyr Vale
1925 1926 Aberdare Athletic 18
1927 Merthyr Town 6

Evans, Denzil Ralph (Ralph) IL/CF/OL
b Hungerford 9/10/1915 d 1996
1935 Bury 0
Yeovil & Petters United
1936 Halifax Town 21 1
1937 1947 Watford 88 30
1939 (Watford) (2) (1)

Evans, Evan Thomas RH
b Llanidloes 23/7/1903 d 1982
Llanidloes
1925 Brentford 7
Chatham Town
Gaslight (Brentford)

Evans, George CF
b Sutton-in-Ashfield 1865 d 1930
Derby Midland
St Luke's
Derby County
1889 West Bromwich Albion 13 8
Brierley Hill Alliance
Oldbury Town
Oldbury St John's

Evans, Herbert Price (Herbie) RH
b Llandaff 30/8/1894 d 1982
Caps: WLge 1/Wales Amat/Wales 6
Cardiff Corinthians
1920 1925 Cardiff City 93 1
1926 1927 Tranmere Rovers 44

Evans, Jabez OL
b Holywell 29/4/1895 d 1966
Buckley United
1922 1924 Tranmere Rovers 46 5
Mold Town

From To Apps Goal

Evans, James Henry (Jimmy) LB
b Rhyl 29/11/1894 d 1975
Caps: Wales 4
Rhyl Athletic
Ton Pentre
1920 1922 Southend United 96 14
1922 1924 Burnley 20
1925 Swansea Town 7
Rhyl
Kinmel Bay United

Evans, James Llewellyn (Jim) RH
b Merthyr Tydfil 18/2/1911 d 1993
Presteigne
Merthyr Town
Hereford United
Margate
1936 Arsenal 0
1937 1938 Fulham 71 5
1939 (Fulham) (3)
Margate

Evans, John (Jack) OL
b West Bromwich 12/7/1900
West Bromwich Standard
Ewells (Wednesbury)
1921 Walsall 1
Shrewsbury Town
1923 Sheffield United 2
1924 Stoke 12
Nantwich
Shrewsbury Town
Stalybridge Connaughts

Evans, John IL
1929 Merthyr Town 2 1

Evans, John Edward (Ted) IR/IL
b Fenton 4/1868
Newcastle Swifts
1891 1894 Stoke 55 18
1895 Bury 2
Burslem Port Vale

Evans, John Henry (Jack) CH
b Grangetown 19/1/1903 d 1989
1920 Cardiff City 0
Barry
Cadoxton
1922 Newport County 4
Leghorn
Gibraltar
Boca Juniors
British Cellophane

Evans, John Hugh (Jack) OL
b Bala 31/1/1889 d 1971
Caps: SoLge 2/Wales 8
Bala Wanderers
Welshpool
Wrexham
Cwmparc
Treorchy
Rhondda
1920 1925 Cardiff City 184 6
1926 1927 Bristol Rovers 63 8

Evans, Jonathan IL
b Denbighshire 1898
Brymbo Green
1921 Wrexham 3 1
Brymbo Green
Rhos Athletic

Evans, Joseph LH
b Cwmbach
Aberaman
1926 Merthyr Town 2

Evans, Joseph Thomas CH
b Darlaston 6/2/1906 d 1971
Caps: England Sch
Darlaston
1925 1929 West Bromwich Albion 88 8

Evans, L Thomas (Tommy) GK
1913 1914 Stockport County 72

Evans, Lewis M OL
b Aberdare
Aberaman Albions
Aberdare Amateurs
1923 Aberdare Athletic 2

Evans, Lorenzo OL
b Prestwich q2 1878 d 1945
1898 Blackburn Rovers 2
1899 Glossop 19 3
1900 1902 Blackpool 54 6

Evans, Nolan Edwin (Peggy) LB
b Ashton-in-Makerfield q4 1885 d 1948
Brynn Central
St Helens Recreation
Exeter City
1912 1914 Clapton Orient 111 1

From To Apps Goal

Evans, Orlando RH
b Penkridge q1 1875 d 1954
Hednesford Town
Hednesford Swifts
1902 Aston Villa 2
1903 1904 Burton United 62 1
Leyton
Hednesford Town

Evans, R William (Bill) IL
b Thornaby 1875
Whitby Town
1898 Bury 5 2
1898 Gainsborough Trinity 0
1899 Middlesbrough 2

Evans, Richard (Dick) OR/IL
b Smallthorne 1875 d 1942
Newcastle White Star
1894 1898 Burslem Port Vale 59 21
Reading
Southampton
1904 Burslem Port Vale 1

Evans, Robert RB
b Islington
1912 Woolwich Arsenal 1
1913 Clapton Orient 0

Evans, Robert Ernest (Bobby) OL
b Chester 21/11/1885 d 1965
Caps: Wales 10/England 4
Bretton
Saltney Works
Wrexham
1906 1907 Aston Villa 16 4
1908 1914 Sheffield United 204 39
Tranmere Rovers
Sandycroft
Crichton's Athletic
Saltney Ferry
Brookhurst

Evans, Robert Owen (Bob) GK
b Wrexham 8/1881 d 1962
Caps: Wales 10
Olympic Juniors
Stansty Villa
Wrexham
1903 1907 Blackburn Rovers 104
Croydon Common
Coventry City
1913 Birmingham 3
Nuneaton Town

Evans, Robert Spencer (Spencer) LH
b St Asaph 24/9/1911 d 1981
Rhyl Athletic
1931 Chester 1
Altrincham
1936 1937 Port Vale 68
Northwich Victoria

Evans, Roland (Rollo) LH
b Cardiff
1930 Bradford City 0
1931 Bristol Rovers 0
1932 Cardiff City 1

Evans, Samuel (Sam) OR
b Glasgow 8/2/1904
Clydebank
St Mirren
Clydebank
1927 1928 Reading 13
Ballymena
1929 1930 York City 66 12
Scarborough
1932 Darlington 2

Evans, Sidney John Vivian Leonard (Len) GK
b Llandaff 20/5/1903 d 1977
Caps: WLge 1/Wales Amat/Wales 4
Cardiff Corinthians
1926 Aberdare Athletic 24
1927 Merthyr Town 5
Cardiff Corinthians
Lovells Athletic
Barry
1930 1932 Cardiff City 8
1933 Birmingham 2
Svenborg

Evans, Sidney Thomas (Sid) OR
b Darlaston q3 1897
Darlaston
1920 1922 Cardiff City 9 1
1923 Manchester United 6 2
Pontypridd

From To Apps Goal

Evans, Thomas (Tom) RH
b Ton Pentre 28/11/1907 d 1993
Ton Pentre
Leytonstone
1927 Tottenham Hotspur 0
Northfleet
1929 1936 Tottenham Hotspur 95 4
1937 West Bromwich Albion 0

Evans, Thomas E RH
b Skelmersdale 1907
Skelmersdale Albion
Atherton
Clitheroe
1929 Oldham Athletic 0
Clitheroe
Chorley
Burscough Rangers
Vickerstown Athletic
1932 Barrow 1
Morecambe

Evans, Thomas Edward (Tom) RH
b Dudley q4 1892
Bradley United
Cradley Heath St Luke's
1919 Birmingham 6
1921 Brighton & Hove Albion 5
Cradley Heath

Evans, Thomas J (Tommy) RH/LH
b Durham
1922 Rotherham County 4
1923 Southend United 27

Evans, Thomas J LH
Aberaman Athletic
1924 Aberdare Athletic 10

Evans, Thomas John RB
b Wolverhampton 1872
Fairfield
1896 West Bromwich Albion 21
Wellington Town
Tottenham Hotspur

Evans, Thomas John (Tom) LB
b Maerdy 7/4/1903
Caps: WLge 1/Wales 4
Maerdy
1924 1927 Clapton Orient 53 1
1927 1928 Newcastle United 13 1
1930 1931 Clapton Orient 26
Merthyr Town

Evans, Trevor John OL
b South Wales
Caerau Athletic
1937 Cardiff City 1
1938 Brighton & Hove Albion 0

Evans, Walter Gwynne RB/LB
b Builth Wells q3 1867 d 1897
Caps: Wales 3
Builth
Bootle
1890 1892 Aston Villa 61
Builth

Evans, William CF
b Llansaintffraid
London Welsh
Queen's Park Rangers
1900 Lincoln City 3

Evans, William OL
d 1963
Clay Cross Zingari
1904 Chesterfield Town 17 2
Clay Cross Zingari
Clay Cross Works
1907 Derby County 1
Clay Cross Works

Evans, William (Willie) OL
b Waunllwyd 7/11/1912 d 1976
Caps: Wales 6
Tottenham Juniors
Barnet
Hayward Sports
1930 Cardiff City 0
1931 1936 Tottenham Hotspur 177 78
1937 Fulham 0

Evans, William (Bill) CF/IL/OL
b Cannock 1914
Cannock Chase Colliery
Hednesford Town
1934 1938 Walsall 114 54
1939 Tranmere Rovers (3)

From To Apps Goal

Evans, William B (Billy) RB/LB
b Llanidloes 1895
Caps: SoLge 1
1919 Everton 2
Llanelly (loan)
1920 Swansea Town 1
1921 1923 Southend United 65
1924 Queen's Park Rangers 17

Evans, William Percy IL
b Shrewsbury q3 1885
Shrewsbury Town
1907 Bolton Wanderers 1

Evenson, Isaac (Ike) IL/CH/LH
b Manchester q4 1877 d 1936
Tonge
1898 Glossop North End (trial) 2
Tonge
1900 1902 Stockport County 34 9
1903 1904 Leicester Fosse 42 14
Luton Town
1905 1906 Clapton Orient 63 8
1907 West Bromwich Albion 8 1
Plymouth Argyle
Stalybridge Celtic

Everest, John (Jack) LB/CF/CH
b Kilcullen 20/7/1908 d 1979
Dunnington
Heslington
York City
1928 1929 Stockport County 7 7
1930 1931 Rochdale 38 8
1931 1933 Blackpool 42 1
1934 1935 Cardiff City 73 5
1936 1937 Southend United 49 2
1937 1938 Barnsley 37
1939 (Barnsley) (3)

Ewart, John (Jock) GK
b Oakbank 14/2/1891 d 1943
Caps: SLge 2/Scotland 1
Douglas Park
Bellshill Rovers
Bellshill Athletic
Larkhall Thistle
Airdrieonians
1912 1922 Bradford City 255
Airdrieonians
1927 Bradford City 28
1928 1929 Preston North End 35

Ewing, David Alexander (Dave) LB
b Elsecar q2 1881
Firth Park Wesleyans
Worksop Town
Meadowhall
Tinsley
Ranmoor Wesleyans
Workington
Brunswick Mission
1907 Chesterfield Town 32 1
Brentford
Huddersfield Town
Castleford Town
Machen
Queen's Park Rangers
Newport County

Ewing, George RH
Airdrieonians
1895 Bury 1

Ewington, Charles (Charlie) RB/LB
b Watford 1/1/1914 d 1978
St Albans City
1933 1936 Watford 12

Eyre, Claude Roland (Ronnie) CF
b Skegby 26/11/1901 d 1969
Hucknall Colliery
1923 Sheffield Wednesday 1
1924 1932 Bournemouth & Boscombe Ath 304 202
Christchurch
Bournemouth Electric

Eyre, Edmund OL
b Worksop 12/1884 d 1943
Worksop West End
Worksop Town
Rotherham Town
1906 1908 Birmingham 48 12
1908 1910 Aston Villa 44 8
1911 1913 Middlesbrough 63 13
1913 1914 Birmingham 29 2

Eyre, Frank Michael B IL
b Northampton 29/9/1903 d 1988
Wolverton
1930 Northampton Town 1
Rushden Town

From To Apps Goal

Eyre, Isaac John CF
b Heeley q1 1875 d 1947
Sheffield
1903 Sheffield Wednesday 1

Eyre, Thomas LB
Glasgow Ashfield
1895 1897 Lincoln City 65 1
Hamilton Academical

Eyres, C CH
1893 Northwich Victoria 9

Eyres, John (Jack) IL/IR
b Northwich 20/3/1899 d 1975
Nantwich
Witton Albion
1922 1928 Stoke 64 23
1929 1930 Walsall 81 34
1931 Brighton & Hove Albion 11 3
1932 1933 Bristol Rovers 64 12
1934 York City 37 13
Gainsborough Trinity

Eyres, Samuel CF
b Droylsden q2 1887
Failsworth
1906 Manchester City 1 1
Colne
Hyde
Crewe Alexandra

Fabian, Aubrey Howard (Howard) IR/OR
b Barnet 20/3/1909 d 1984
Caps: England Amat
Casuals
Cambridge University
Corinthians
1931 1932 Derby County 12 1
Sutton United
1934 Fulham 3
Corinthians
Sutton United

Facer, Albert CH
b Northampton 15/7/1901 d 2002
Wellingborough Town
1923 Northampton Town 2
Higham Town

Fagan, Stephen LB/RB
b Attercliffe 28/10/1886 d 1966
Rawmarsh Athletic
1908 Sheffield United 0
Plymouth Argyle
1910 1911 Bristol City 34
1912 1914 Stockport County 109

Fagan, William (Willie) IL/CF/OR
b Inveresk 20/2/1917 d 1992
Caps: Scotland War 1
Balgonia Scotia
Wellesley Juniors
Celtic
1936 1937 Preston North End 35 6
1937 1951 Liverpool 158 47
1939 (Liverpool) (3)
Distillery
Weymouth

Fairbairn, James CF/IR
b Stockton q3 1872
Stockton
1893 Middlesbrough Ironopolis 1
1894 Grimsby Town 2 2
Stockton

Fairbrother, (Dr) Ronald Wilson CH
b Poulton-le-Fylde 28/4/1902 d 1969
Caps: England Amat
Manchester University
Northern Nomads
1922 Manchester City 0
1922 Manchester United 0
1923 Blackburn Rovers 1
Northern Nomads

Fairburn, Arthur Millward OL
b Sheffield q2 1870 d 1902
Sheffield United
1893 Rotherham Town 12 3

Fairburn, James IL
Darlington
1899 Burnley 1

Fairchild, Clifford Charles RB
b Romford 23/10/1917 d 1974
Barking
Northfleet
Colchester United
1938 Arsenal 0
1939 Southend United (2)
Yarmouth Town
Lowestoft Town

From To Apps Goal

Fairclough, Albert CF
b St Helens 4/10/1891 d 1958
Windle Villa
St Helens Town
St Helens Recreation
Eccles Borough
1913 1919 Manchester City 5 1
1920 Southend United 24 15
1920 1923 Bristol City 91 44
1924 1926 Derby County 37 26
1926 Gillingham 11 3

Fairclough, Peter LH/CF
b St Helens 19/10/1886 d 1973
Cammell Laird
St Helens Town
Eccles Borough
1914 1919 Manchester City 5
1921 Tranmere Rovers 8

Fairclough, William Oliver (Bill) GK
b 1869 d 1911
1st Scots Guards
1895 1896 Woolwich Arsenal 26
New Brompton

Fairfoul, Thomas (Tom) RH
b West Calder 16/1/1881 d 1952
Caps: SLge 1
Lanark Athletic
Patna
Kilmarnock
Third Lanark
1913 1914 Liverpool 62

Fairgray, Norman Murray (Norrie) OL
b Dumfries 28/10/1880 d 1968
Dumfries Primrose
Maxwelltown Volunteers
Kilmarnock
Maxwelltown Volunteers
1905 1907 Lincoln City 60 6
1907 1913 Chelsea 79 5
Motherwell
Queen of the South

Fairgrieve, Robert Walter (Walter) CF
b Edinburgh 30/8/1874 d 1923
Dalry Primrose
Glasgow Perthshire
1897 Liverpool 0
1897 Everton (trial) 0
Southampton
1899 Luton Town 15 5
Hibernian
Partick Thistle
Heart of Midlothian
Dunfermline Athletic

Fairhurst, David Liddle LB/RB
b Blyth 20/7/1906 d 1972
Caps: England 1
New Delaval Villa
Blyth Spartans
1927 1928 Walsall 56
1928 1938 Newcastle United 266 2

Fairhurst, Horace LB
b Bolton 2/6/1893 d 1921
Bolton Juniors
Darwen
1919 1920 Blackpool 47

Fairhurst, Richard (Dick) LB/CH
b St Helens 5/9/1911
Skelmersdale United
1931 1932 Burnley 23 3
1934 Hartlepools United 11
1935 1936 Tranmere Rovers 30

Fairhurst, William Gerard (Bill) GK
b St Helens 23/9/1907 d 1984
St Helens Town
1927 Liverpool 0
Runcorn (trial)
1930 Wigan Borough 22
Rhyl Athletic
1934 1938 Bury 88
1939 (Bury) (3)
1945 Bristol City 0
Rhyl

Fairhurst, William Shaw (Bill) LB/RB
b Blyth 1/10/1902 d 1979
Bebside Gordon
Blyth Spartans
1925 Middlesbrough 0
1928 Southport 18
1929 1930 Nelson 76
1932 Northampton Town 13
1933 1934 Hartlepools United 58
1935 Tranmere Rovers 0

Fairley, Peter Lindsey IL
b Morpeth q1 1882 d 1964
1907 Lincoln City 4

From To Apps Goal

Fairley, William LH
b Scotland
Dunmow Thistle
St Mirren
1892 Grimsby Town 17

Fairman, Robert Samuel (Bob) LH/LB/RB
b Southampton q3 1883 d 1968
Southampton
1907 1908 Birmingham 22 2
West Ham United
1912 1913 Birmingham 16

Falconer, Fleming LH/RH
b Hutchesontown 24/5/1899 d 1991
Glasgow Ashfield
1923 Nottingham Forest 2
Bo'ness
J & P Coats (Rhode Island)
New Bedford Whalers
1927 1928 Bristol Rovers 20

Fall, Joseph William GK
b Miles Platting q1 1872 d 1945
Leigh Street
Middlesbrough Ironopolis
1893 Newton Heath 23
Altrincham
1895 Small Heath 2
Altrincham
Stockton

Fall, William LH
b Tyne Dock q3 1900 d 1965
Tyne Dock
1924 Sunderland 4
West Stanley

Fallon, William Joseph (Bill) OL
b Larne 14/1/1912 d 1989
Caps: LoI 6/Eire 9
Brideville
Dolphin
1933 1937 Notts County 120 20
1937 1938 Sheffield Wednesday 44 12
1939 (Sheffield Wednesday) (1)
Shamrock Rovers
Shelbourne
Dundalk
1946 Notts County 15 3
1947 Exeter City 8 2
Peterborough United

Fallows, J GK
1892 Northwich Victoria 1

Fallows, John CF
1895 Burslem Port Vale 8 1

Fantham, John Thomas LH
b Sheffield q4 1908 d 1958
Manchester Central
1930 Stockport County 3
1931 1933 Rotherham United 100 2
1934 Chester 15
1935 Exeter City 6 1
Rhyl Athletic

Fare, Harold Vautin (Harry) RB
b Wallasey 1/5/1896 d 1963
Harrowby
1920 Everton 0
1922 1924 Wigan Borough 112 12
1926 Bury 2
Flint Town
Stalybridge Celtic
Liverpool Warehousing Company
Congleton Town

Farman, Alfred Henry (Alf) OR/IR
b King's Norton q2 1869 d 1926
Birmingham Excelsior
Aston Villa
1888 Bolton Wanderers 0
1892 1894 Newton Heath 51 18

Farman, H GK
1901 Burton United 1

Farmer, Albert CH
b Stoke-on-Trent 7/1864
Everton
1888 1889 Stoke 3
Newton Heath

Farmer, Alexander (Alec) CH/IL/LH
b Lochgelly 9/10/1908 d 1986
Kettering Town
1930 1931 Nottingham Forest 16
1931 Leicester City 0
Yeovil & Petters United
1933 1938 Queen's Park Rangers 79 10
1939 (Queen's Park Rangers) (1)

From To Apps Goal

Farmer, Andrew Richmond IL
b Paisley 11/7/1915
Paisley Mossvale YMCA
Glasgow Benburb
Rangers (trial)
1934 Sunderland (trial) 0
Motherwell
1936 Aldershot 17 1
Portadown
King's Park
Dunfermline Athletic

Farmer, George LH
b Oswestry q1 1863
Caps: Wales 5
Oswestry
1888 1889 Everton 31 1
Liverpool Caledonians

Farmer, George Alfred IR
b Derby 25/1/1874 d 1951
Derby Swifts
Derby Bedford Rangers
Belper Town
1896 Woolwich Arsenal 1

Farmery, Lionel John Victor (Jack) GK
b Bentley 25/4/1901 d 1971
1924 Hull City 0
1925 Bradford City 0
1926 1928 Doncaster Rovers 33
1929 1930 York City 67
Bentley Colliery

Farnall, Thomas (Tot) LH/RH
b Birmingham q2 1874 d 1927
Eastville Rovers
1895 1896 Small Heath 26 1
Bristol Eastville Rovers
1899 Small Heath 19 1
Worcester City
Watford
Bristol Rovers
Watford
1903 Bradford City 25 1
Walsall
Barrow
Gloucester

Farne, Frederick Charles (Fred) IR
b Chickerell 1881
Weymouth Town
Eastleigh Town
Aberaman
1900 Notts County 0
1901 Chesterfield Town 2
Weymouth

Farquhar, James William (Billy) RH/CF/LH
b Elgin 1879 d 1916
Elgin City
1898 1906 Sunderland 189 17

Farquharson, Hugh Hamilton GK
b Paisley 27/9/1910 d 1940
Renfrew Juniors
1934 1935 Hull City 7
Dunfermline Athletic

Farquharson, Thomas G (Tom) GK
b Dublin 4/12/1900 d 1974
Caps: WLge 1/Ireland 7/Eire 4
Abertillery
1921 1934 Cardiff City 445

Farr, Andrew Martin IR
b Larkhall 7/8/1911
Larkhall Thistle
Clyde
Yoker Athletic
Margate
1938 Arsenal 2 1
Airdrieonians
Heart of Midlothian

Farr, Frank Edgar CH/IR
b Bristol 23/10/1913 d 1981
Bristol CED
1931 1933 Bristol City 9
Bath City
1935 Northampton Town 2
1936 Southampton 0
Street

Farr, Harry GK
1898 Luton Town 1
Southend

Farr, Thomas Francis (Chick) GK
b Bathgate 19/2/1914 d 1980
Broxburn Athletic
1934 1949 Bradford Park Avenue 294
1939 (Bradford Park Avenue) (3)

From To Apps Goal

Farrage, Thomas Oysten OL
b Chopwell 11/1917 d 1944
Walker Celtic
1938 Birmingham 7 2
1939 (Birmingham) (3) (1)

Farrant, Samuel George IR
b Bristol 1885
Bristol St George
Grays United
1904 Bristol City 0
1905 Stockport County 2
Workington
Luton Town
Coventry City
Aberdare Town
Bath City

Farrar, Peter RH
b St Helens 6/5/1897 d 1972
Prescot
1920 Everton 0
1921 Rochdale 12

Farrell, Francis (Frank) CH
b Salford 24/6/1907 d 1992
Pendlebury
Mossley
1930 Aston Villa 0
1930 Sunderland 0
Mossley
1932 Accrington Stanley 2
Altrincham
Northwich Victoria

Farrell, Francis IL
b Wishaw 1916
Caps: Scotland Amat
Hibernian
1938 Clapton Orient 2

Farrell, John (Jack) CF
b Tunstall 1873 d 1947
Caps: FLge 1
Dresden United
1894 Stoke 16 6
Southampton St Mary's
1898 Stoke 22 4
Southampton
1900 New Brighton Tower 31 6
Northampton Town
West Ham United

Farrell, Patrick (Paddy) CH
b Belfast 3/4/1872 d 1950
Caps: IrLge 1/Ireland 2
Ligoniel
Belfast Celtic
Distillery
Celtic
1897 Woolwich Arsenal 19 2
Brighton United
Belfast Celtic
Distillery
Brighton & Hove Albion

Farrell, Robert (Bobby) OR/IR/IL
b Dundee 1/1/1906 d 1971
Dundee North End
Dundee
1928 Portsmouth (trial) 0
1928 1938 Brighton & Hove Albion 382 66

Farrell, Thomas IL
b Earlestown
1904 Woolwich Arsenal 0
1906 Manchester City 3
Airdrieonians
Eccles Borough

Farrell, Vincent (Vince) IL/LH/OL
b Preston 11/9/1908 d 1987
Dick, Kerr's XI
1930 1932 Preston North End 16 5
1934 1936 Clapton Orient 79 21
1937 Exeter City 6 4
Leyland Motors

Farren, Fred William LB
b Kettering q7 1885 d 1959
Kettering
1906 1911 Bradford City 87
Halifax Town
Kettering

Farrington, Frederick (Fred) RH
b Newcastle-under-Lyme q4 1867 d 1924
1892 1893 Burslem Port Vale 22 4

From To Apps Goal

Farrington, George Samuel CF
b Burslem 7/1884 d 1946
Stoke Priory
1901 Glossop 1
Hanley Swifts
1902 West Bromwich Albion 1 1
Castleford Town
Southampton
1904 Bristol City 0
Smallthorne
1906 Preston North End 2
Smallthorne
Leek United

Farrington, Robert IR
b Radcliffe 19/2/1902 d 1980
Little Lever
1921 Accrington Stanley 1
1922 Bolton Wanderers 0

Farrow, Albert Ernest LH
b Gainsborough q4 1886 d 1916
Gainsborough WMC & Institute
1906 1907 Gainsborough Trinity 35 1
Watford
Worksop Town

Farrow, George Henry RH/IR/LH
b Whitburn, County Durham 4/10/1913 d 1980
Whitburn
1931 Stockport County 6
1932 Wolverhampton Wanderers 11
1933 1935 Bournemouth & Boscombe Ath 107 12
1936 1947 Blackpool 143 15
1939 (Blackpool) (3)
1947 Sheffield United 1
Bacup Borough
Whitburn St Mary's
Whitburn

Faulconbridge, George Henry IL
b Nottingham 29/6/1902 d 1983
Ilkeston United
1927 1928 Southend United 19 2
Grantham

Faulds, W OR
1891 Accrington 10 2

Faulkner, Robert OR
b Glasgow 1895
Caps: Canada
St Anthony's (Glasgow)
Maryhill
1919 Blackburn Rovers 9
1920 1921 Queen's Park Rangers 50 1
1922 South Shields 18
Toronto Clarkes
Philadelphia Field Club
Providence Clamdiggers
Toronto Ulster

Fawcett, Desmond Hallimond (Des) GK
b Carlin How q1 1905 d 1968
Normanby Magnesite
Loftus Albion
1922 Middlesbrough 0
Loftus Albion
1926 1927 Darlington 30
1928 Nelson 23
1929 1931 Preston North End 44
1932 1933 York City 74
1934 1935 Mansfield Town 72
1936 1938 Rochdale 93
Wellington Town

Fawcett, George CH
b Great Houghton q1 1902
1927 Doncaster Rovers 1

Fawcett, Robert Elliott OR
b Usworth 31/7/1903 d 1972
Usworth Colliery
1929 1930 Hull City 6

Fawcett, T GK
1897 Blackburn Rovers 0
1898 Barnsley 1

Fawcett, William Fraser OR
b Bradford 27/5/1898 d 1971
1919 Blackburn Rovers 5 1

Fay, James Albert (Jimmy) CH/IR/RH
b Southport 29/3/1884 d 1957
Caps: FLge 3
Southport Crescent
Southport Blue Star
Southport Working Lads
Chorley
Oswaldtwistle Rovers
1907 1911 Oldham Athletic 154 37
1911 1920 Bolton Wanderers 128 5
1921 1922 Southport 25 1
Hesketh Park

From To Apps Goal

Fayers, Fred 'Tiny' CH/RH
b King's Lynn 29/1/1890 d 1954
Caps: England Amat
St Albans City
Watford
1910 1914 Huddersfield Town 154 15
1919 Stockport County 42 2
1920 1922 Manchester City 73 5
1923 Halifax Town 8

Fazackerley, Stanley Nicholas (Stan) IR/IL
b Preston 3/10/1891 d 1946
Lane Ends United
1909 Preston North End 0
Charlestown (Boston, USA)
Accrington Stanley
1911 1912 Hull City 29 19
1912 1920 Sheffield United 105 44
1920 1922 Everton 51 21
1922 1924 Wolverhampton Wanderers 70 28
Kidderminster Harriers
1925 Derby County 3 2

Fearn, ? OR
1900 Burton Swifts 1

Fearns, William (Billy) RH
b Glasgow 1871
Corinthians
1896 Stoke 4
Corinthians

Featherby, Stanley (Stan) IL
b Chesterfield 29/12/1914 d 1989
1936 Carlisle United 2

Featherby, Walter Leonard (Len) IL/OR/IR
b King's Lynn 28/7/1905 d 1972
Whitefriars
South Lynn Wednesday
Lynn Town
Rangers (trial)
1924 1925 Norwich City 26 3
Northfleet
1927 Millwall 0
Peterborough & Fletton United
1928 Merthyr Town 8 2
1928 1929 Wolverhampton Wanderers 21 6
1930 Reading 25 3
1931 Queen's Park Rangers 0
1931 Mansfield Town 22 5
1932 Crewe Alexandra 16 1
Merthyr Town
1933 1934 Plymouth Argyle 8 1
1935 Notts County 3
1936 Carlisle United (trial) 0
Scarborough
King's Lynn

Featherstone, Frederick (Fred) OR/CF
b Stockton q1 1882
Darlington
1903 Middlesbrough 1
1904 Bolton Wanderers 2 1
Leyton

Featherstone, George IR
b Middlesbrough q1 1885
Darlington St Hilda's
Darlington
Stockton
1907 1908 Sheffield United 29 11
Brighton & Hove Albion
Hartlepools United

Featherstone, Henry Wilson (Harry) LB
b Wallsend 20/6/1885 d 1956
Wallsend Park Villa
St Mirren
Cardiff City
Ashington
Belfast United
1921 1922 Ashington 66 3
1923 Halifax Town 20 2
Victoria Garesfield
Stanley United

Fecitt, Herbert Lincoln (Harry) IL/OL/CF
b Blackburn q1 1865 d 1946
King's Own
Blackburn Rovers
Accrington
1888 1890 Blackburn Rovers 21 13
1892 Northwich Victoria 13 7

Feebery, Albert LH
b Hucknall 9/4/1891 d 1964
Hucknall
1910 Nottingham Forest 0
Coventry City
1920 1923 Crystal Palace 91 7
Folkestone

From To Apps Goal

Feebery, Alfred (Alf) LB
b Hucknall 10/9/1909 d 1989
Hucknall Congregationalists
1929 1938 Notts County 221 1
Newark Town (loan)
1939 Bristol Rovers (3)

Feebery, John Henry (Jack) LB/RH
b Hucknall 10/5/1888 d 1960
Hucknall
Bulwell White Star
1909 1919 Bolton Wanderers 180 16
1920 Exeter City 42 2
1921 1923 Brighton & Hove Albion 62 3
Mid-Rhondda United

Feenan, John Joseph RB
b Newry 1/7/1914 d 1994
Caps: Eire 2
Newry Town
Belfast Celtic
1936 1938 Sunderland 28

Feeney, Wilfred Thomas (Tom) CF/IR/IL
b Grangetown 26/8/1910 d 1973
Normanby Magnesite
Whitby United
1931 Newcastle United 4 1
1932 Notts County 17 2
1933 Lincoln City 10
1933 Stockport County 2
1934 1936 Halifax Town 52 11
1937 Chester 5
1937 1938 Darlington 40 22

Felix, Evan Jones OR
b Aberdare q4 1901 d 1964
1925 Walsall 25 3
1926 Aberdare Athletic 0

Fell, Gerald (Gerry) CH/RH
b Barnsley 3/12/1898 d 1977
Elsecar
1919 1921 Barnsley 61 3
1921 1927 Bradford Park Avenue 184 6
1928 Chesterfield 42 4
Gainsborough Trinity
Mexborough Athletic
Newark Town

Fell, John Wilson (Jackie) OL
b Quebec, County Durham 14/5/1902 d 1979
Tow Law Town
1922 1923 Durham City 8
Spennymoor United
Crook Town
1925 1926 Leeds United 13 1
1927 Southend United 30 3
1928 Hartlepools United 21
Connah's Quay & Shotton
1930 Southport 6
Connah's Quay & Shotton
West Stanley
Hamsteels
Blackwell Colliery Welfare

Fellowes, William James (Billy) LH/CH
b Bradford 15/3/1910 d 1987
Tavistock Town
1929 1932 Plymouth Argyle 5
1933 1934 Clapton Orient 78 1
1935 1937 Luton Town 110 3
1938 1946 Exeter City 56 1
1939 (Exeter City) (3)
Tavistock Town

Fellows, Arthur (Archie) OR
b Wednesfield 1880
Willenhall Pickwick
1901 1902 Wolverhampton Wanderers 54 8
Darlaston
Halesowen
Netherton

Fellows, J Ernest IL/CF/OL
b West Bromwich 1870 d 1933
Cooper's Hill Methodists
1892 1896 West Bromwich Albion 9
King's Heath
1898 West Bromwich Albion 2
Studley Rovers

Fellows, Percy James OL
b Dudley q2 1894 d 1958
Dudley
1913 Derby County 2 1
Walsall

Felstead, Thomas (Tom) GK
b Sutton-in-Ashfield 1889
1909 Bradford City 0
1910 Huddersfield Town 2
Mirfield United

From To Apps Goal

Felton, Edward Taylor (Teddy) IL/IR/OR
b Gateshead 12/11/1907 d 1970
Wardley Colliery Welfare
1931 1932 Carlisle United 20 3
1932 Darlington 0
Wigan Athletic
1936 Huddersfield Town 0
1937 Gateshead 4 1

Felton, Robert Francis Foster RB
b Gateshead 12/8/1918 d 1982
1937 Everton 0
1938 1945 Port Vale 10
1946 Crystal Palace 1
South Liverpool
Northwich Victoria

Felton, William (Billy) RB/LB
b Heworth 1/8/1900 d 1977
Caps: England 1
Wardley Colliery Welfare
Jarrow
1921 1922 Grimsby Town 43
1922 1928 Sheffield Wednesday 158
1928 1931 Manchester City 73
1931 1933 Tottenham Hotspur 73 1
Altrincham

Fenner, Thomas (Tom) IR/CF/OR
b Uxbridge 12/5/1904
Warrington Juniors
1924 1927 Wigan Borough 92 36
1927 1933 Notts County 158 69
1933 1934 Bradford City 7 3

Fenner, William Edward (Bill) RB
b New Ferry 1/7/1889 d 1950
Wrexham
1910 1912 Bury 57
Wrexham

Fenoughty, Thomas (Tom) IL/IR
b Rotherham 7/7/1905 d 2001
1925 Rotherham United 0
1929 1933 York City 147 56
1933 Sheffield United 0
1934 1935 Rotherham United 65 22
Gainsborough Trinity

Fenton, Benjamin Robert Vincent (Benny) RH/IL/LH
b West Ham 28/10/1918 d 2000
Colchester Town
1937 1938 West Ham United 21 9
1938 1946 Millwall 20 7
1946 1954 Charlton Athletic 264 22
1954 1957 Colchester United 104 15

Fenton, Edward Benjamin Ambrose (Ted) RH/CF
b Forest Gate 7/11/1914 d 1992
Caps: England Sch/England War 1
Ilford
Colchester Town
1932 1945 West Ham United 163 18
1939 (West Ham United) (3) (1)
Colchester United

Fenton, Frederick (Freddie) OL
b Gainsborough 2/1879 d 1958
1898 1899 Gainsborough Trinity 36 5
West Ham United
1901 Gainsborough Trinity 25 2
1901 1902 Preston North End 20
1903 West Bromwich Albion 6 1
1904 1906 Bristol City 36 1
Swindon Town
Croydon Common

Fenton, Isaac OR
b Birtley 30/081910 d 1997
Birtley
1934 Burnley 0
1936 Brentford 0
1937 Hartlepools United 1
Consett

Fenton, Michael (Micky) CF/IR
b Stockton 30/10/1913 d 2003
Caps: England War 1/England 1
Portrack Shamrocks
South Bank East End
1932 1949 Middlesbrough 240 147
1939 (Middlesbrough) (3) (3)

Fenwick, Alfred Leslie (Alf) LB
b West Ham 23/5/1915 d 1985
1938 Sheffield Wednesday 0
1939 Reading (1)

From To Apps Goal
Fenwick, Alfred Randolph (Alf) LH/CH/CF
b Hamsterley 26/3/1891 d 1975
Craghead United
1911 1913 Hull City 17 7
1919 West Ham United 2
1919 1920 Coventry City 50 1
Craghead United
Blyth Spartans
1924 Ashington 12
Blyth Spartans
1925 Halifax Town 0
Bedlington United

Fenwick, George OL
b Bishop Auckland q2 1892
Shildon Athletic
1912 Leeds City 5 3

Fenwick, Harrison CH
b Tynemouth q3 1893 d 1951
Shildon
1924 Queen's Park Rangers 19

Fenwick, Robert William (Bob) CH
b Walker 29/9/1894 d 1973
Ashington
1921 1922 Lincoln City 49 2
1922 1924 Notts County 6
1924 1925 Lincoln City 27
Shirebrook
Newark Town
Horncastle Town
Shildon

Fereday, David Thomas OR
b Walsall Wood 6/7/1908 d 1995
Walsall Wood
1927 Walsall 10
1928 1929 Derby County 16 2
1931 West Ham United 0
Yeovil & Petters United

Fergus, Alexander (Alex) RB
b Kilsyth 17/2/1898
Kirkintilloch Rob Roy
Bathgate
1924 1926 Burnley 38
1926 1927 Coventry City 30

Ferguson, Alex (Sandy) RH/LH
b Glasgow 1867 d 1894
Rangers
1889 1890 Notts County 22
Newark

Ferguson, Alexander (Alex) OR
b Monifieth
Heart of Midlothian
1939 Rochdale (1)

Ferguson, Alexander Stirling Brown (Alex GK
b Lochore 5/8/1903 d 1974
Caps: WLge 2
Vale of Clyde
1924 Wigan Borough 1
1925 1926 Gillingham 67
1926 1935 Swansea Town 280
1936 1937 Bury 63
1938 1945 Newport County 41
1939 (Newport County) (3)
1946 Bristol City 32
1947 Swindon Town 7
Milford United

Ferguson, Archibald LB
Heart of Midlothian
1888 1890 Derby County 49
1891 Preston North End 0
1894 Manchester City 2
Baltimore

Ferguson, Archibald (Archie) OR
Rhyl Athletic
1931 Chester 1 1
Rhyl Athletic

Ferguson, Charles (Charlie) OR/IL
b Dunfermline 22/11/1910 d 1995
Yoker
Glasgow Benburb
1933 1935 Middlesbrough 19 7
1936 Notts County 22 8
1937 1938 Luton Town 29 10
Aberdeen
North Shields

Ferguson, Christopher (Chris) IR/LH
b Kirkconnel
1927 Chelsea 1
1930 Queen's Park Rangers 15 1
1931 Wrexham 18 4
Guildford City
Post Office Engineers (Beddington)

From To Apps Goal
Ferguson, Daniel (Danny) RH/IR
b Flint 25/1/1903 d 1971
Rhyl Athletic
1927 Manchester United 4
1928 Reading 2
1929 1931 Accrington Stanley 113 12
1931 1932 Chester 29 3
1933 1934 Halifax Town 69 1
1935 Stockport County 15
Macclesfield
Hurst
Macclesfield

Ferguson, Edward (Ted) RB/OR
b Seaton Burn 2/8/1895 **d 1978**
Seaton Burn
Ashington
1920 1922 Chelsea 11
1924 1927 Ashington 119 4
1928 1929 Nelson 67
Annfield Plain
Seaton Burn Welfare

Ferguson, G IL/CH/OL
1893 1895 Bolton Wanderers 16 3

Ferguson, George Clifford (Cliff) IR
b Langley Moor 1/6/1909 d 1988
Durham City
1930 Hartlepools United 1
Crook Town
1931 Tottenham Hotspur 0
Northfleet
Crook Town
Blackhall Colliery Welfare
Horden Colliery Welfare
Blackhall Colliery Welfare

Ferguson, Hugh (Hughie) CF
b Motherwell 2/3/1898 d 1930
Caps: SLge 3
Motherwell Hearts
Parkhead
Helensea
Vale of Leven
Motherwell
Third Lanark (loan)
Mid Annandale (loan)
St Mirren (loan)
1925 1928 Cardiff City 117 77
Dundee

Ferguson, James OL
b Scotland
Cambuslang Hibernian
1906 Woolwich Arsenal 1
Partick Thistle

Ferguson, James RH/CH
b Glasgow 1885
Strathclyde
Airdrieonians
1907 1910 Blackburn Rovers 32 1
St Johnstone

Ferguson, James Stirling (Jim) GK
b Longriggend 30/8/1896 d 1952
Airdriehill Shamrock
Partick Thistle
St Roch's
1926 1927 Brentford 65
1927 1931 Notts County 158
Ayr United

Ferguson, John (Jock) LB
b Dundee 1887 d 1973
Arbroath
St Johnstone
Dundee
1912 Leeds City 17
Gateshead
Clydebank
Bethlehem Steel
Philadelphia Field Club
J & P Coats (Rhode Island)
Bethlehem Steel

Ferguson, John James OR
b Rowlands Gill 1904
1926 Grimsby Town 3
Workington
Spen Black & White
1928 Wolverhampton Wanderers 20 4
1929 Watford 4
Burton Town
1931 Manchester United 8 1
Derry City
1934 Gateshead 21 5

Ferguson, Matthew RH
b Bellshill 1873 d 1902
Bellshill Hawthorn
Mossend Brigade
1896 1901 Sunderland 167 5

From To Apps Goal
Ferguson, Pearson OL
b Coalburn 28/8/1909 d 1985
Kello Rovers
Ayr United
Cork FC
Ayr United
Queen of the South
1933 1934 Carlisle United 67 19
Montrose
Morton
East Stirlingshire

Ferguson, Robert CF
1906 Bradford City 9 3

Ferguson, Robert (Bob) LH/CH
b Cleland 6/1886 d 1962
Cleland Rangers
Third Lanark
1912 1914 Liverpool 92 2
Wishaw Thistle

Ferguson, Robert IL
b Seaton Burn q2 1908
Seaton Burn
1926 West Bromwich Albion 0
Blyth Spartans
Annfield Plain
1929 Nelson 1
Annfield Plain
Jarrow
Seaton Burn Welfare

Ferguson, Robert (Bob) GK
b Grangetown 25/7/1917 d 2006
1933 Sunderland 0
Hurworth Juniors
1936 1937 Middlesbrough 10
1939 1946 York City 26
1939 (York City) (3)
Peterborough United
Goole Town

Ferguson, Robert Gibson CH/RH/RB
b Blythswood 5/1/1902
Battlefield
Queen's Park
Cambuslang Rangers
1921 1924 Sunderland 32 1
1924 1930 Middlesbrough 139 2
1932 Crystal Palace (trial) 0
1932 Barrow (trial) 0
Northwich Victoria

Ferguson, Robert Lemon OL
b Stewarton 15/11/1895 d 1983
Stewarton Thistle
1925 Fulham 17 3
1926 Coventry City 40 4
1927 Fulham 4 2

Ferguson, William (Willie) OL
Caps: SLge 1
Jordanhill Juniors
Maryhill Juniors
Celtic
1896 1899 Burnley 33 7
1899 Manchester City 0

Ferguson, William Copeland (Willie) LH/OL/IL
b Muirkirk 13/2/1901 d 1960
Kellsbank Juveniles
Kello Rovers
Queen of the South
1923 1932 Chelsea 263 11
Queen of the South

Fergusson, William Alexander (Billy) CF
b Willenhall 2/3/1900 d 1986
Sunbeam Motors
1922 1923 Oldham Athletic 5 1
1924 Reading 24 8
1925 Rochdale 21 19
1926 Rotherham United 19 2
Worcester City

Fern, Thomas Edward (Tommy) GK
b Measham 1/4/1886 d 1966
Mafeking Rovers
Worksop Albion
Worksop Town
1909 1913 Lincoln City 127
1913 1923 Everton 219
1924 1926 Port Vale 86
Colwyn Bay

Ferne, George Edward OL
b Burton-on-Trent q1 1874 d 1955
Hinckley Town
1898 Lincoln City 24 3
Millwall Athletic
Watford
Fulham
Coventry City

From To Apps Goal
Fernyhough, Ernest (Ernie) GK
b Barnsley 5/7/1918 d 1999
Great Houghton
1938 Halifax Town 1

Ferrans, Robert LB
b New Cumnock 20/6/1894 d 1970
1920 1925 Merthyr Town 191 2
1926 Sheffield Wednesday 0

Ferrari, Frederick Joseph (Fred) CF/CH/LB
b Stratford 22/5/1901 d 1976
Barking Town
Leyton
1925 Northampton Town 18
1926 Sheffield Wednesday 0
Flint Town
1927 Norwich City 4
1928 Barrow 26 14
1929 Nelson 7 3
1929 Chesterfield (trial)
Bedouins
Burton Town
Mansfield Town
1930 Queen's Park Rangers 0
Hillsborough Old Boys
Darwin's Sports

Ferrier, David RB
Dundee
1894 Notts County 2

Ferrier, Robert (Bob) RH/IR
b Dumbarton 7/1874 d 1947
L'Homme Qui Rit (Dumbarton)
Dumbarton
1894 1904 Sheffield Wednesday 307 16

Ferrier, Ronald Johnson (Ron) CF/IL
b Cleethorpes 26/4/1914 d 1991
Grimsby Wanderers
1933 Grimsby Town 0
1935 1937 Manchester United 18 4
1937 1946 Oldham Athletic 45 25
1939 (Oldham Athletic) (3)
1947 Lincoln City 0
Lysaght's Sports

Ferris, James (Jimmy) IL/IR
b Belfast 28/11/1894 d 1932
Caps: IrLge 5/Ireland 6
Belfast Celtic
Distillery
Belfast Celtic
1920 1921 Chelsea 33 8
1921 1923 Preston North End 53 11
Pontypridd
Belfast Celtic

Ferris, Walter Joseph (Wally) GK
b Bloxwich q1 1887 d 1943
Willenhall Swifts
1907 Wolverhampton Wanderers 2
Wednesfield
Darlaston
Greets Green Primitives
Cradley Town

Fidler, Albert GK
b Newcastle q4 1906
Spen Black & White
Gosforth & Coxlodge British Legion
1929 Newcastle United 5
Newburn

Fidler, Joseph Edward (Joe) LB
b Sheffield q1 1885 d 1948
Caps: SoLge 1
South Steer New Connexion
1903 1904 Sheffield United 2
Fulham
Queen's Park Rangers
1912 1913 Woolwich Arsenal 25
Port Vale
Bird-in-Hand
Industry Sports (Sheffield)
Turton Platts

Field, Charles William Frederick (Oakey) OL/IL
b Hanwell q1 1879 d 1949
Hanwell
Royal Ordnance Factory
Brentford
1898 1901 Sheffield United 54 19
1901 1905 Small Heath/Birmingham 86 14
Brentford

Field, Frederick Stanley (Fred) CF
b Mansfield 12/6/1914 d 2004
Welbeck Colliery
1933 Bradford Park Avenue 1 1
1935 Mansfield Town 2
Sutton Town

From To Apps Goal

Field, Richard (Dick 'Rusty') CH/RH/LH
b Sunderland 2/8/1891 d 1963
Kings Hall Wesleyan Club
Lambton Star
Willington
1914 Sunderland 0
Barry
Dumbarton
1922 Aberdare Athletic 24
1923 Norwich City 28
1924 Grimsby Town 32
1925 1926 Accrington Stanley 52 1
Boston Town
West Stanley

Field, William Henry GK
b Oxford 21/9/1902 d 1972
Oxford City
1923 1925 Queen's Park Rangers 29

Fielden, Alwyn CF
b Oldham 12/5/1920 d 2012
Denshaw
Hurst
Manchester CWS
Droylsden
1938 Oldham Athletic 1 1
Witton Albion
Droylsden

Fielden, Leonard William (Len) GK
b Stockton 22/12/1903 d 1966
South Bank
Stockton
1931 1933 Darlington 39

Fielding, Arthur Ross (Ross) OR/OL
b Trentham 1881 d 1947
Stoke Priory
1901 Stoke 2
1902 Nottingham Forest 10
1903 1907 Stoke 99 11
1908 West Bromwich Albion 9
Burton United

Fielding, Horace OL/IR/OR
b Heywood 14/10/1906 d 1969
Mossley
1926 1929 Stockport County 92 16
1930 1932 Grimsby Town 69 13
1933 1936 Reading 132 36
1936 1937 Crystal Palace 22 1
1938 Mansfield Town 0
Peterborough United

Fielding, Howitt OR
b Selston 22/8/1914 d 1982
Ilkeston Town
1936 Reading 0
1937 Mansfield Town 4
Peterborough United

Fielding, P CF
1902 Glossop 1

Fielding, William J (Bill) GK
b Broadhurst 17/6/1915 d 2006
Hurst
1936 1938 Cardiff City 50
1939 (Cardiff City) (3)
1945 Bolton Wanderers 0
1946 Manchester United 6
Ashton United

Fields, Alfred George (Alf) CH
b Canning Town 15/11/1918 d 2011
West Ham Youth Club
Margate
1938 1950 Arsenal 19

Fieldsend, George Henry LB
b Ecclesall Bierley 19/1/1908 d 1988
Chorley
1933 Burnley 0
1934 1935 Accrington Stanley 57
1936 Rotherham United 1
Scarborough

Fife, ? GK
1889 Derby County 2

Fillingham, Thomas (Tom) CH/LH
b Bulwell 6/9/1904 d 1960
Bromley United
1929 1937 Birmingham 183 8
1938 Ipswich Town 29 1

Filliston, Joseph William (Joe) CF/OR
b Shoreditch 12/5/1894 d 1981
Mildmay Athletic
Redhill
1920 Clapton Orient 0
1921 1923 Charlton Athletic 30 8
1924 Luton Town (trial) 0

From To Apps Goal

Finan, Robert Joseph (Bobby) CF/IL/OL
b Old Kilpatrick 1/3/1912 d 1983
Caps: Scotland War 1
Yoker Athletic
1933 1938 Blackpool 171 83
1939 (Blackpool) (3) (2)
1947 1948 Crewe Alexandra 62 14
Wigan Athletic

Finch, Abel Robert (Bob) RB
b Hednesford 31/8/1908 d 2000
Hednesford Primitives
Hednesford Town
1925 1937 West Bromwich Albion 216
1938 Swansea Town 0
Hednesford Town
Tamworth

Finch, John (Jack) OR/OL/IL
b West Ham 3/2/1909 d 1993
Walthamstow Avenue
Lowestoft Town
Walthamstow Avenue
1929 Aston Villa (trial) 0
1930 1938 Fulham 280 50
1939 (Fulham) (1)
Colchester United

Findlay, Alex OR
Arbroath
1896 Preston North End 2 1

Findlay, Alexander (Alex) RH/IR/IL
b Wishaw 26/12/1902 d 1985
Musselburgh Rose
Musselburgh Bruntonians
1929 1931 Bristol Rovers 37 9
1932 1934 Wrexham 22 4
Cheltenham Town
Gloucester City

Findlay, Andrew LH
b Newburn 6/11/1896 d 1969
Newburn
1919 Tottenham Hotspur 0
1922 1923 Wigan Borough 30 1
1924 Darlington (trial) 0
Dundee
1926 Portsmouth 0

Findlay, John (Jock) RH
b Scotland
Knibshill United
1905 Newcastle United 2
Vale of Leven

Findlay, Norman GK
b Walker
Newcastle City
Blyth Spartans
Heart of Midlothian
Walker Celtic
1921 1925 Coventry City 9

Findlay, Thomas RB/LB
b Port Glasgow 26/2/1900
Port Glasgow Athletic
1922 1923 Derby County 4
1925 Merthyr Town 24
Morton
Brechin City

Findlay, William (Billy) RH
b Musselburgh 17/2/1900 d 1949
Preston Grange Athletic
Musselburgh Bruntonians
Third Lanark
1924 Liverpool 0
1925 1931 Leicester City 100
1932 1935 Watford 128 6

Findlay, William RH
b Wishaw 1901
Peebles Rovers
1926 Clapton Orient 2

Finlay, Andrew IR
b Hutchesontown 10/2/1901
Shawfield Juniors
1921 Port Vale 1
St Roch's
Airdrieonians
1923 Manchester City
1923 Crewe Alexandra 12 3
Third Lanark
Dundee United
Hibernian
Portadown
Cork FC
Shawfield Juniors
Coleraine

Finlay, James (Jim) OR
b Scotland
Bute Athletic
1937 Cardiff City 1

From To Apps Goal

Finlay, John (Jack) LH
b Riccarton 19/10/1882 d 1933
Kilmarnock Shawbank
Celtic (trial)
Rangers
Airdrieonians
1909 1923 Newcastle United 153 8

Finlayson, Evan LB
b Applecross 1876
Rangers
1899 Grimsby Town 5

Finlayson, John OR
b Glasgow
Middlesbrough
1892 Bootle 9
Luton Town

Finlayson, John RH/RB
b Cowdenbeath 14/6/1912
Thornliebank
Motherwell
East Stirlingshire
Cowdenbeath
1933 1934 Clapton Orient 11
Ashford Town (Kent)
1935 1938 Luton Town 154 9
1939 (Luton Town) (3)

Finlayson, William (Bill) IL/CF
b Thornliebank 29/3/1899
Glasgow Ashfield
Thornliebank
1921 1923 Chelsea 5 1
1924 Clapton Orient 21 2
1925 Brentford 21 5
Springfield Babes
Providence Clamdiggers
Montreal CNR
Providence Clamdiggers
Montreal CNR
Bethlehem Steel
Montreal CNR
Montreal Carsteel

Finn, Arthur Charles LH
b Folkestone 24/3/1911 d 1996
Folkestone
1933 Crystal Palace 9
Cannes

Finn, John (Jack) LB
b Accrington 18/4/1907 d 1984
St Anne's (Accrington)
1930 Accrington Stanley 5
Barnoldswick Town

Finnerhan, Patrick (Pat) IR
b Northwich 3/1872 d 1951
Caps: FLge 1
Winnington
1892 1893 Northwich Victoria 48 13
1894 1896 Manchester City 85 27
1897 Liverpool 5 1
Bristol City
Northwich Victoria

Finney, Alexander (Alex) LB
b St Helens 13/3/1902 d 1982
Caps: FLge 1
Sutton Juniors
Peasley Cross
South Liverpool
New Brighton
1922 1936 Bolton Wanderers 483 2
Darwen

Finney, James IL/CH
b Wigan 28/12/1906 d 1988
1926 1928 Wigan Borough 7
Rossendale United (trial)
Congleton Town
Hurst
Stalybridge Celtic
Mossley

Finney, John (Jack) RH/CH
b Prescot 1880 d 1904
Accrington Stanley
1899 1900 Bury 3
Accrington Stanley

Finney, John T OL
1925 Crewe Alexandra 1

Finney, William Arthur (Arthur) CH/LH/RH
b Nottingham 17/7/1900 d 1976
Wath Athletic
1923 1929 Bury 70 1
1930 1931 Oldham Athletic 30
Hereford United
Goldthorpe United

From To Apps Goal

Finnigan, Fred IR
b Sheffield 10/2/1903 d 1987
1923 Rotherham County 6

Finnigan, Joseph RH
b Lanchester 20/3/1909 d 1976
Blackhill
1933 Hartlepools United 3
Blackhill
Annfield Plain

Finnigan, Richard Prytherch (Dick) GK
b Wrexham 16/5/1904 d 1979
Caps: Wales 1
Oswestry Town
Holyhead Town
Connah's Quay & Shotton
1922 1923 Wrexham 3
Holyhead Town
Connah's Quay & Shotton
1926 Manchester City 8
1927 1928 Accrington Stanley 42
Connah's Quay & Shotton
1929 1931 Wrexham 98
Colwyn Bay United
1932 1933 Chester 13
1933 1934 Stockport County 26
Winsford United
1935 Swindon Town 0
Bala Town

Firman, John R OL
b Evenwood 1915
Evenwood Town
1935 Hartlepools United 2
South Shields

Firth, John (Jack) RH/IL/IR
b Doncaster 8/8/1907 d 1987
Woodlands Primitives
Brodsworth Main Colliery
1926 Doncaster Rovers 0
1927 1932 Birmingham 93 7
1933 1935 Swansea Town 102 16
1936 Bury 7 4
Brodsworth Main Colliery

Firth, Joseph (Joe) IR
b Glasshoughton 27/3/1909 d 1983
Glasshoughton
1928 1934 Leeds United 72 25
1935 1936 Southend United 33 12
1938 York City 6 1
1938 Rochdale 18 6

Firth, Robert Edwin OR
b Hanley 20/2/1887 d 1966
Birmingham Corporation Transport
Golders Green
1909 1910 Birmingham 25 2
Wellington Town
1911 1920 Nottingham Forest 141 14
1921 Port Vale 39 5
1922 Southend United 37 1

Fish, Ivor OR/IR
b Cardiff q3 1913 d 1954
GWR Institute
1934 1935 Bristol City 7 1
Barry

Fish, Kenneth Henry Albert (Ken) CF
b Cape Town, South Africa 20/2/1914 d 2005
Caps: South Africa
Railway Association (South Africa)
1936 Aston Villa 0
1937 Port Vale 5 1
Young Boys Berne
1939 Port Vale 0

Fish, Robert LH/RH/CF
b Darwen q3 1871 d 1944
1891 1898 Darwen 69 2

Fish, Thomas LH
b Birtley q2 1877
Birtley
1900 1901 Sheffield Wednesday 7
Thornhole

Fisher, ? RB
1895 Rotherham Town 2

Fisher, Albert IR/IL
b Glasgow 6/1879 d 1937
1902 Aston Villa 1
1903 1904 Bristol City 50 21
Brighton & Hove Albion
1906 Manchester City 5 2
Bradford Park Avenue
Coventry City
Merthyr Town

From To Apps Goal

Fisher, Albert James (James) OL/CF
b Denny 23/12/1876 d 1921
Vale of Forth
King's Park
East Stirlingshire
St Bernard's
1897 Aston Villa 18 5
Celtic
1898 Preston North End (loan) 0
East Stirlingshire (loan)
1900 1901 Newton Heath 42 3
King's Park
Vale of Leithen
Fulham
Woodville United
Grays United

Fisher, Alfred RB/RH/LB
Nottingham Olympic
1909 1914 Nottingham Forest 100 1

Fisher, Charles RH
b Handsworth
1919 Aston Villa 0
Kidderminster Harriers
1921 Brentford 6
Margate

Fisher, Frederick (Fred) IL/IR
b Hucknall 29/1/1910 d 1955
Hucknall YMCA
Staveley Town
Newark Town
1929 Notts County 3 1
1930 Torquay United 7 1
1931 1932 Mansfield Town 10 6
1933 1934 Swindon Town 46 16
1935 Gillingham 17 6
1936 Clapton Orient 2
Dudley Town
Bestwood Colliery
Newport (Isle of Wight)

Fisher, Frederick Thomas (Fred) LB
b Wednesbury 12/1/1920 d 1993
Fallings Heath
1938 1950 Grimsby Town 166
1951 Rochdale 1
Boston United
Spalding United
Wisbech Town
Barton Town
Alford United

Fisher, Frederick William (Fred) OR/CF/IR
b Barnsley 11/4/1910 d 1944
Caps: England War 1
Monckton Athletic
1933 1937 Barnsley 66 16
1937 1938 Chesterfield 16 1
1938 Millwall 12 6
1939 (Millwall) (3)

Fisher, George GK
1909 Woolwich Arsenal (trial) 2
1910 Manchester United 0

Fisher, J IR
1903 Glossop 3

Fisher, John (Jackie) OR
b Hodthorpe 4/8/1897 d 1954
Brodsworth Main Colliery
Highfields United
1921 Chesterfield 19 5
1921 1922 Burnley 32 3
1922 1926 Chesterfield 154 26
Mansfield Town
Staveley Town
1928 1929 Lincoln City 19 3
Denaby United
Hurst

Fisher, Lawrence G OR
1923 Merthyr Town 2

Fisher, Lewis IL
b Barnsley 18/10/1904 d 1975
Worsborough Dale WMC
1923 Barnsley 1
Wombwell Town
Ardsley Athletic

Fisher, Peter IL/IR
b Glasgow
St Anthony's (Glasgow)
Clyde
Stenhousemuir
1936 Watford 3 1
1936 1938 Burnley 23 2
Dunfermline Athletic

From To Apps Goal

Fisher, William IR/IL
b 1873
Dalry
Kilmarnock
1896 Derby County 11 5
1897 Aston Villa 0
1897 Burton Swifts 23 4
Bristol Rovers
1900 Derby County 0
Stevenston Thistle

Fisher, William RH
b Preston q4 1904 d 1953
Skerton Athletic
Preston Butchers
Leyland
Lancaster Town
1925 Preston North End 0
Darwen (trial)
1927 Wigan Borough 4
Horwich RMI
Dick, Kerr's XI
Municipal Offices (Preston)
Ashton Institute Sports

Fishlock, Laurence Barnard (Laurie) OL
b Battersea 2/1/1907 d 1986
Caps: England Amat
Dulwich Hamlet
1928 Fulham 0
1929 1931 Crystal Palace 18 2
1932 Aldershot 38 14
1933 Millwall 34 7
1934 1935 Southampton 69 14
1936 Fulham 0
1937 Gillingham 20 2

Fishwick, Albert Edward (Bert) IR/CH
b Chorley q1 1899 d 1961
Hamilton Central
Leyland
Chorley
1923 1924 Plymouth Argyle 7 1
Chorley
1925 1927 Blackpool 58 36
1927 1930 Port Vale 39 15
1930 1933 Tranmere Rovers 83 9
Chorley

Fiske, William A GK
b Beccles 7/8/1885 d 1918
Bungay
Norwich City
1907 1913 Blackpool 212
1914 Nottingham Forest 4

Fitchett, John (Jack) RH/LB
b Chorlton q4 1874
Caps: FLge 3
Talbot
1897 1901 Bolton Wanderers 76 4
Southampton
1902 Manchester United 5 1
Plymouth Argyle
1904 Manchester United 11
1905 Manchester City 0
Fulham
Sale Holmfield
Exeter City

Fitchford, William Henry IL
b Wolstanton q2 1896 d 1966
Porthill St Andrew's
1919 1922 Port Vale 70 8
1923 Stoke 0
Glossop
Congleton Town
Northern Nomads

Fitchie, Thomas Tindal (Tom) IL/IR
b Edinburgh 11/12/1881 d 1947
Caps: Scotland 7
West Norwood
1901 Woolwich Arsenal 3 3
Tottenham Hotspur
1902 Woolwich Arsenal 1
London Caledonians
1904 Woolwich Arsenal 9 6
Queen's Park
Fulham
London Caledonians
1905 Woolwich Arsenal 22 9
West Norwood
Queen's Park
Norwich City
Queen's Park
Brighton & Hove Albion
1908 Woolwich Arsenal 21 9
1909 1911 Glossop 41 9
1912 Fulham 8 2
London Caledonians
Pilgrims

From To Apps Goal

Fitton, Fred CF/IR/IL
b Bury 12/1/1905 d 1970
Adlington
1925 Bolton Wanderers (trial) 0
Darwen (trial)
1927 Stoke City (trial) 0
1928 1929 Burnley 15 2
1930 1931 Oldham Athletic 9 4
1931 Southend United 3 1
1932 1933 Accrington Stanley 45 24
1933 Rochdale 13 6
Nelson
Runcorn

Fitton, Frederick (Fred) CF
High Crompton St Mary's
1930 Rochdale 1
Northwich Victoria

Fitton, George Arthur (Arthur) OL
b Melton Mowbray 30/5/1902 d 1984
Kinver Swifts
Cookley St Peter's
Kidderminster Harriers
1922 1930 West Bromwich Albion 96 11
1931 1932 Manchester United 12 2
1932 1934 Preston North End 62 18
1935 1937 Coventry City 54 21
Kidderminster Harriers

Fitzgerald, Alfred (Alf) IL/RH/LH
b Conisbrough 25/1/1911 d 1981
Denaby United
1934 1935 Reading 6 1
1936 1938 Queen's Park Rangers 94 43
1939 (Queen's Park Rangers) (3)
1945 1947 Aldershot 59 1
Chingford Town
Tonbridge

Fitzpatrick, Harold James (Harry) IL
b Ayr 2/1880
Vale of Garnock Strollers
Luton Town
1907 Liverpool 4 2
1908 Chesterfield Town 17 1

Fitzsimmons, David RH/CH
b Annbank 1875
Annbank
1895 Newton Heath 27
Fairfield
Chorley
Wigan County
1899 Newton Heath 2

Fitzsimmons, James A (Jim) CF
b Salford 23/11/1888
Hurst
Chorley
Buxton
Northwich Victoria
1912 Bury 1
Northwich Victoria
Mardy
Northwich Victoria

Fitzsimmons, Matthew Joseph (Matt) CH
b Toxteth Park 10/12/1913
Mather United
1938 Liverpool 1
1939 Ipswich Town 0

Fitzsimmons, Stephen LB
b 1901
West Calder
1921 Halifax Town 1

Fitzsimmons, Thomas IL
b Annbank 21/10/1870
Annbank
Celtic (trial)
1892 1893 Newton Heath 27 6
Annbank
St Mirren
Annbank
Fairfield
Glossop North End
Fairfield
Oldham County
Chorley
Wigan County
Annbank

Flack, Hugh David RB
b Belfast 26/4/1903
Caps: Ireland 1
Crusaders
1928 Burnley 3
1929 Swansea Town 0
Distillery
1932 1933 Halifax Town 74

From To Apps Goal

Flack, William Leonard Wallace (Len) RB/LH/LB
b Cambridge 1/6/1916
Caps: England Sch
Cambridge Town
1934 1946 Norwich City 49
Bury Town

Flaherty, Jack IL
b Mexborough
1934 Wolverhampton Wanderers 0
1935 Bournemouth & Boscombe Ath 1

Flanagan, John (Jack) CF
b Lostock Hall 3/2/1902 d 1989
Lostock Hall
Leyland Motors
Leyland
1924 Manchester United 0
1926 1928 Tranmere Rovers 64 42
Chorley
1930 Barrow 5
1930 Wigan Borough 1
Lancaster Town
Burscough Rangers
Lancaster Town
Stalybridge Celtic
Rhyl Atletic
Northwich Victoria
Leyland Motors

Flanagan, John Thomas (Pat) IR/IL
b Aston q2 1887 d 1917
Verity's
Stourbridge
Norwich City
1909 1910 Fulham 11 1
1910 1914 Woolwich Arsenal 114 28

Flanagan, William IL/IR
b Birmingham 1876
Smethwick Carriage Works
Oldbury Town
1895 Aston Villa 0
1896 Burton Wanderers 9 1
1897 Leicester Fosse 4
Glentoran
Morton
Port Glasgow Athletic
Distillery

Flanagan, William Joseph Augustus (Bud OL
b Plymouth 8/4/1908 d 1993
Bath City
1933 1934 Swindon Town 41 2
Trowbridge Town

Flanaghan, Henry Nixon (Harry) OL
b Nottingham q1 1896 d 1938
Bedlay Juniors
Third Lanark
Aberdeen
Maidstone United
1923 Grimsby Town 3
Scunthorpe & Lindsey United (trial)
Adams Athletic
York City (trial)
Denaby United

Flanders, Frederick (Fred) LB
b Derby 1/1/1894 d 1967
Caps: England Sch
Shelton United
1910 Derby County 13
Ilkeston Town
Newport County
Mansfield Town
1921 Newport County 16
1922 Hartlepools United 3
Nuneaton Town

Flannigan, David LH
b Glasgow 1906
Third Lanark
1928 Newcastle United 3
East Stirlingshire

Flannigan, Patrick (Pat) CH
b Cowdenbeath 19/5/1909
Rosyth Dockyard
Kelty Rangers
Cowdenbeath
Lochgelly United (loan)
1928 Liverpool 0
1929 Bradford City 1
1930 Liverpool 0
New York Giants
Glenavon
Rosyth Recreation

From	To		Apps	Goal
Flannigan, Thomas (Tommy)			IR/IL	
b Edinburgh 27/5/1908			d 1981	
		Edinburgh Emmet		
		Dundee		
1928		Stoke City	4	
1929		Hull City	2	
		Loughborough Corinthians		
1931		Darlington (trial)	0	
1931		Rochdale	2	
		Stafford Rangers		
		Buxton		
		St Etienne		
		Shrewsbury Town		
Flatley, Albert Austin			IL	
b Bradford 5/9/1919			d 1987	
1937		Wolverhampton Wanderers	0	
1938		York City	4	
1939		Port Vale	(2)	
1945		Bradford Park Avenue	0	
1946		Bury	0	
		Alessandria		
1951		Workington	8	
Flavell, Arthur E			GK	
b West Bromwich 1875				
		West Bromwich Baptists		
1896		West Bromwich Albion	2	
		Bournbrook		
Flavell, Frederick (Fred)			CF/IL	
b Northwich 5/9/1904			d 1981	
		Northwich Victoria		
		Witton Albion		
1930		Oldham Athletic	4	
1932	1935	Torquay United	42	22
		Witton Albion		
Fleet, Albert Edward			LH	
b Great Yarmouth q3 1880			d 1953	
		Grimsby Corinthians		
		Grimsby Rangers		
1906		Grimsby Town	4	
		Rotherham County		
		Grimsby Rangers		
Fleetwood, Edric Denton (Eddie)			IR/CF	
b Barnsley q2 1910			d 1969	
		Mexborough Athletic		
1930		Blackburn Rovers	0	
		Mexborough Athletic		
1932	1934	Barnsley	14	8
		Denaby United		
		Scunthorpe & Lindsey United		
Fleetwood, Thomas (Tom)			CH/RH	
b Toxteth Park 6/12/1888			d 1945	
Caps: FLge 5				
		St George the Martyr (Bolton)		
		Atherton		
		Hindley Central		
		Rochdale		
1910	1922	Everton	264	9
1923		Oldham Athletic	5	
		Chester		
Fleming, George			LH/RH/LB	
b Broxburn 20/5/1869				
		East Stirlingshire		
1894	1900	Wolverhampton Wanderers	171	7
1901	1905	Liverpool	79	5
Fleming, George S			OR	
1888		Everton	4	2
Fleming, Harold John			IR/CF	
b Downton 30/4/1887			d 1955	
Caps: SoLge 6/England 11				
		Swindon Amateurs		
1920	1923	Swindon Town	69	34
Fleming, James			CF	
b Leith 9/1864			d 1934	
		Vale of Leven		
		Southampton St Mary's		
1892		Aston Villa	4	2
1892		Lincoln City	11	5
		Larkhall Saints		
Fleming, John			RH/IR/CF	
b Slamannan 1890			d 1916	
		Musselburgh Union		
		Armadale Thistle		
		Bonnyrigg Rose Athletic		
		St Bernard's		
1912		Newcastle United	4	
1913	1914	Tottenham Hotspur	19	3
		Rangers		
Fleming, Thomas N (Tom)			RB	
b Glasgow 15/11/1901			d 1965	
		Shettleston		
		Dundee		
1921	1925	Fulham	111	
1925	1926	Wigan Borough	22	
		Dundee United		

From	To		Apps	Goal
Fleming, William Thomas (Billy)			IL	
b Renton 11/12/1871			d 1934	
		Darlington		
1893		Sheffield United	21	7
		Abercorn		
1895		Bury	2	1
		Tottenham Hotspur		
Fletcher, Alan Frederick			IL/IR	
b Pendleton 28/10/1917			d 1984	
1937		Blackpool	0	
1937		Port Vale (trial)	0	
1938		Bournemouth & Boscombe Ath	12	
1939		Bristol Rovers	(3)	
1947		Crewe Alexandra	1	
		Mossley		
Fletcher, Albert Thomas			RH	
b Wolverhampton 4/6/1867			d 1938	
Caps: England 2				
		Willenhall Pickwick		
1888	1892	Wolverhampton Wanderers	59	1
Fletcher, Albert William (Bert)			RH/CF	
b Wolverhampton q2 1898				
1921		Brentford	0	
1922	1923	West Ham United	8	1
1927		Brentford	33	1
1928		Norwich City (trial)	0	
Fletcher, Alfred Henry (Alf)			CH/RH	
b Ripley 6/9/1892			d 1984	
		Ilkeston		
1913		Glossop	2	
1914		Arsenal	3	
		Chesterfield Municipal		
		Heanor Town		
1921		Chesterfield	4	
		Shirebrook		
		Kettering		
		Glossop		
Fletcher, Brough			IR/RH	
b Mealsgate 9/3/1893			d 1972	
		Chilton Colliery Recreation Athletic		
		Shildon Athletic		
1914	1925	Barnsley	249	51
		Partick Thistle (loan)		
		Partick Thistle (loan)		
1925		Sheffield Wednesday	2	
1926	1929	Barnsley	62	21
Fletcher, Charles Alfred (Charlie)			OL/LH	
b Homerton 28/10/1905			d 1980	
1927		Clapton Orient	0	
1928		Crystal Palace	7	
1929		Merthyr Town	23	1
1930	1932	Clapton Orient	120	32
1933	1935	Brentford	104	25
1935	1937	Burnley	62	21
1937	1938	Plymouth Argyle	23	6
1938	1945	Ipswich Town	29	9
1939		(Ipswich Town)	(3)	
1945		Clapton Orient	0	
Fletcher, David John (Jack)			LB	
b Stonebroom 1878				
		Stonebroom & Morton		
1899	1900	Chesterfield Town	46	
		Alfreton Town		
Fletcher, EA			GK	
1898		Blackpool	32	
Fletcher, Eli			LB	
b Tunstall 15/12/1887			d 1954	
Caps: FLge 2				
		Earlestown		
		Crewe Alexandra		
		Northwich Victoria		
		Goldenhill Wanderers		
		Hanley Swifts		
		Crewe Alexandra		
1911	1925	Manchester City	301	2
		Clydebank (loan)		
1926		Watford	23	
		Sandbach Ramblers		
		Ards		
Fletcher, Ernest			LB	
1903		Stockport County	4	
Fletcher, Frank			OL	
b Caversham 1874			d 1936	
		Shiplake United		
		Reading		
1895		West Bromwich Albion	1	
1896		Grimsby Town	0	
Fletcher, Frederick (Fred)			OL/CF	
b Ripley q1 1877				
1894		Derby County	3	
1894	1895	Notts County	9	3
		Worcester Rovers		

From	To		Apps	Goal
Fletcher, Harry W			CH	
b Willenhall				
		Ellesmere Port		
		Southport Central		
		Chester		
		Willenhall		
1920		Birmingham	0	
1922		Newport County	1	1
		Barry		
Fletcher, Henry Handley (Harry)			IL/OR	
b Birmingham 13/6/1873			d 1923	
Caps: FLge 1				
		Albion Swifts		
1892	1897	Grimsby Town	154	73
1897	1899	Notts County	60	17
1900	1902	Grimsby Town	79	12
		Fulham		
		Brentford		
1905	1909	Grimsby Town	40	7
		RTM		
		Grimsby Rangers		
Fletcher, Horace Robert (Robert)			IL	
b Rotherham q3 1876			d 1931	
		Mexborough		
1897		Lincoln City	28	6
		Rotherham Town		
Fletcher, J			IR	
1897		Darwen	5	
Fletcher, Jack			OL/OR	
b Padiham 6/8/1905				
		Colne Town		
1927	1928	Nelson	11	1
		Clitheroe		
1930		Accrington Stanley	1	
1931		Burnley	0	
		Fleetwood		
Fletcher, James			LB	
1905		Chelsea	1	
Fletcher, John (Jack)			IR	
b Tyne Dock 1910				
		Hedworth St Nicholas		
		West Boldon Church Institute		
		Boldon Colliery Welfare		
1929		Portsmouth (trial)	0	
		Chopwell Institute		
		Aldershot		
		Guildford City		
1933	1934	Bournemouth & Boscombe Ath	26	3
1935		Queen's Park Rangers	20	
1936	1937	Clapton Orient	55	11
1938		Southampton	0	
1938		Barrow	18	5
		Peterborough United		
Fletcher, Leonard (Len)			CF	
b Overton, Cheshire				
		Mersey Power		
		Frodsham		
		Helsby Athleitc		
		Warrington		
1932	1934	Manchester City	5	1
1935	1936	Watford	36	22
		Runcorn		
Fletcher, S Ernest			CH	
1914		Nottingham Forest	1	
Fletcher (Younger), Samuel (Adam)			GK	
1920		Rotherham County	0	
1921		Bury	1	
Fletcher, Thomas (Tommy)			IL/CF	
b Heanor 15/6/1881			d 1954	
		Hill's Ivanhoe		
		Derby Nomads		
1901	1903	Leicester Fosse	5	2
		Derby Nomads		
1904	1906	Derby County	33	8
		Derby Thornhill		
Fletcher, Thomas Wilberforce			IL	
b Wednesfield 1878				
		Willenhall		
1900		Small Heath	2	
		Cradley Heath St Luke's		
		Bellswood Rangers		
Flewin, Reginald (Reg)			CH	
b Portsmouth 28/11/1920			d 2008	
Caps: England War 1				
		Ryde Sports		
1938	1953	Portsmouth	150	

From	To		Apps	Goal
Flewitt, Albert William			IR/IL/CF	
b Beeston 2/1872			d 1943	
Caps: FLge 1				
		Mansfield Greenhalgh's		
1893	1894	Lincoln City	56	28
1895		Everton	3	1
1895	1898	West Bromwich Albion	65	18
		Bedminster		
Flinn, George			OL	
1919		South Shields	1	1
Flint, William			OR	
b Elswick q2 1883				
		Scotswood		
		Hebburn Argyle		
1909		Middlesbrough	1	
		Watford		
		Gateshead		
		Ashington		
Flint, William Arthur (Billy)			RH/IR/CF	
b Underwood 21/3/1890			d 1955	
		Underwood & Bagthorpe		
		Eastwood Rangers		
1908	1925	Notts County	376	40
Flitcroft, W			RB	
1888	1889	Bolton Wanderers	8	
Flood, Charles William (Charlie)			IL/IR	
b Newport, Isle of Wight 18/7/1896			d 1978	
		Plymouth Argyle		
1920	1921	Hull City	54	25
1922		Bolton Wanderers	8	2
1922	1925	Nottingham Forest	97	21
		York City		
1926	1927	Swindon Town	8	3
Flood, John Joseph (John Joe)			OR	
b Dublin				
Caps: LoI 8/Eire 5				
		Windsor Rangers		
		St Patrick's (Ringsend)		
		Shamrock Rovers		
		Shelbourne		
		Shamrock Rovers		
1924		Leeds United	0	
		Shamrock Rovers		
1926	1927	Crystal Palace	34	5
		Shamrock Rovers		
		Reds United		
Flood, Leslie Thomas Brooking (Les)			GK	
b Bristol 13/10/1904			d 1967	
		Wallasey Trams		
1927	1933	New Brighton	38	
		Thorndale		
Flower, Thomas (Tom)			GK	
b Liverpool q4 1915			d 1962	
		Cadby Hall		
1934		Liverpool	0	
1938	1945	Notts County	36	
1939		(Notts County)	(2)	
Flowers, Alfred H (Alf)			OL	
b Southend-on-Sea				
1921		Southend United	5	
Flowers, George Alfred			RH/LH	
b Darlaston 7/5/1907			d 1991	
		Edlington		
1929	1935	Doncaster Rovers	149	7
1936		Bradford Park Avenue	10	1
1937	1938	Tranmere Rovers	40	1
1939		Rochdale	0	
Flowers, Ivan Joseph			IL	
b Mutford 21/2/1919			d 1944	
		Eastern Coach Works		
1937		Wolverhampton Wanderers	0	
1938		Mansfield Town	7	2
1939		(Mansfield Town)	(1)	(1)
Flowitt, Charles			IL	
b Doncaster q2 1884				
1904		Doncaster Rovers	3	
		Goole Town		
		Huddersfield Town		
		Doncaster Saracens		
		Goole Town		
Floyd, Peter			GK	
b Burnley 8/7/1899			d 1979	
		Huncoat Baptists		
1921	1922	Accrington Stanley	34	
		Clitheroe		
		Lancaster Town		
1928		Oldham Athletic	3	
		Lancaster Town		

From To Apps Goal

Floyd, William Bertram (Bill) LB
b Scunthorpe q3 1885 d 1932
1904 Gainsborough Trinity 24
New Brompton
Bristol Rovers
1909 1911 Gainsborough Trinity 72 3

Flynn, Andrew (Andy) LB
b Sheffield
Mexborough Town
1922 1925 Exeter City 34 1
York City
Boston Town

Flynn, John Arthur (Jack) OL
b 1875
1898 1900 Walsall 38 6
1901 Bristol City 31 1
Reading
West Ham United

Fogg, William Henry (Billy) RH/LH/IR
b Birkenhead 9/3/1903 d 1991
Wirral Railways
1924 1925 Tranmere Rovers 22 6
Bangor City
1928 1932 Huddersfield Town 62 3
1933 1935 Clapton Orient 81 2
1936 1937 New Brighton 70 1

Foley, George OR
Ashford
1899 Newton Heath 7 1

Foley, James (Jimmy) GK
b Cork 19/3/1914 d 1952
Caps: Eire 7
Cork Celtic
Cork FC
Belfast Celtic
Cork FC
Celtic
1936 1937 Plymouth Argyle 39
Cork City
Cork United
St Joseph's
Cork United

Foley, Michael (Mick) LH/CF
b Dublin 1890
Caps: LoI 5/Eire 1
Shelbourne
1910 1919 Leeds City 127 6
Shelbourne

Folks, William Thomas OR
b Tottenham 1/1886 d 1944
Clapton
1903 West Bromwich Albion 1
Clapton

Foot, George GK
b Chorley 15/8/1887 d 1975
Heaton Park
1911 1912 Bury 8
Eccles Borough
1919 Preston North End 5

Foote, Ernest CH
b Ebbw Vale q1 1916 d 1944
Ebbw Vale
1937 Newport County 1
Gloucester City

Forbes, Alexander S (Alex) RH/CH
b Bo'ness
Musselburgh Bruntonians
1928 Luton Town 1
1929 1931 Bournemouth & Boscombe Ath 47 1
1932 1934 Gillingham 69 1

Forbes, Frederick James (Fred) IR/CF/OR
b Leith 5/8/1894
Leith Benburb
Heart of Midlothian
1922 1924 Everton 14 4
1924 1928 Plymouth Argyle 159 52
1929 1930 Bristol Rovers 63 10
Leith Athletic
Workington
1932 Northampton Town 35 3
Airdrieonians

Forbes, George Parrott CH
b Dukinfield 21/7/1914 d 1964
Cresent Road Congregational
Mossley
Hyde United
1936 1945 Blackburn Rovers 2 1
Hurst
1946 1950 Barrow 177 3

From To Apps Goal

Forbes, James (Jimmy) CH
b Walker 14/3/1896 d 1939
Walker Celtic
Carlisle United
1921 1922 Lincoln City 16
Leadgate Park
Scunthorpe & Lindsey United
1923 Blackpool 20
1924 Southport 15 2
1924 1925 Bolton Wanderers 3
1926 1927 Bristol Rovers 59 5
Workington
North Shields

Forbes, John LB/RB
b Bonhill 13/1/1862 d 1928
Caps: Scotland 5
Star of Leven
Vale of Leven
1888 1893 Blackburn Rovers 106 1

Forbes, John (Johnny) OL
b Scotland 1892
Dundee Violet
1911 Bristol City 27 5

Forbes, William (Billy) RB/LH
b Denny
Denny Hibernian
1920 1923 Plymouth Argyle 134
Fall River Marksmen

Ford, Alfred (Alf) OR/OL
b Newcastle 2/8/1901 d 1976
People's Hall
Spen Black & White
1921 Manchester City 4
Seaton Delaval
1923 Norwich City 1
Peterborough & Fletton United
Stamford Town
Peterborough Westwood Works

Ford, Arthur OR
Ancoats
1920 Southend United 7

Ford, Arthur IL
b Wolstanton q3 1911
1936 Port Vale 3
1937 Wolverhampton Wanderers 0
1938 Northampton Town 0

Ford, C OL
1897 Burton Swifts 1

Ford, Charles RH
b Arbroath 4/3/1878
Arbroath
1898 Luton Town 24
Reading

Ford, David GK
b Belper 1878 d 1914
1898 Derby County 6
1899 Chesterfield Town 7

Ford, Ernest Frederick OL
b Chingford 1/1896 d 1960
Woodford Town
Ilford
1922 West Bromwich Albion 1

Ford, Ewart OL
b Walsall 8/12/1901 d 1982
Hinckley United
1924 1925 Queen's Park Rangers 55 4
1927 Merthyr Town 35 4

Ford, Frederick George Luther (Fred) RH/LH/CH
b Dartford 10/2/1916 d 1981
Erith & Belvedere
1935 Arsenal 0
1936 1937 Charlton Athletic 22
1945 1946 Millwall 9
1947 Carlisle United 28

Ford, George E LB
b Woolwich 1891
Gravesend United
Dartford
1912 1914 Woolwich Arsenal 9

Ford, Henry Thomas (Harry) OR/IR
b Fulham q1 1893
Tunbridge Wells Rangers
1912 1923 Chelsea 221 41

Ford, John OR
b Wishaw 1893 d 1917
Bellshill Athletic
1913 1914 Preston North End 43 4

Ford, John IR
1920 Liverpool 0
1921 Tranmere Rovers 15 4

From To Apps Goal

Ford, Joseph RB
Atherton
1921 Blackpool 1

Ford, Joseph Bertram (Joe) OL
b Northwich 7/5/1886
Witton Albion
Crewe Alexandra
1908 1909 Manchester United 5
1910 1913 Nottingham Forest 102 12

Ford, Joseph Charles (Joe) CF
b Canongate 20/9/1910 d 1951
Rosewell Rosedale
1931 Newcastle United 1
Partick Thistle
Leith Athletic
Penicuik Athletic
Gala Fairydean
Benford

Ford, Louis LB/RB
b Cardiff 18/5/1914 d 1980
1936 1938 Cardiff City 35

Ford, T OR
1899 New Brighton Tower 3 1

Ford, William Gracey (Bill) IL/CF
b Dundee 7/5/1876 d 1948
Dundee Our Boys
Dundee
1896 West Bromwich Albion 12 1
Hereford Thistle
New Brompton
1898 Luton Town 23 7
Gravesend United

Forde, Stephen (Steve) LB/RB
b South Kirkby 29/8/1914 d 1992
South Elmsall
1932 Sheffield Wednesday 0
1932 1936 Rotherham United 116 1
1937 1951 West Ham United 170 1

Fordham, Norman Mills CF
b Willesborough 5/12/1890 d 1929
Ashford Railway Works
1913 1914 Derby County 13 5

Foreman, Alexander George (George) CF
b Walthamstow 1/3/1914 d 1969
Caps: England Amat
Leyton
Walthamstow Avenue
1938 1945 West Ham United 6 1
1946 Tottenham Hotspur 36 14

Foreman, John James OR
b Tanfield q4 1913 d 1964
Tanfield Lea
West Stanley
Crook Town
1933 Sunderland 2
1934 1936 West Ham United 49 7
1936 Bury 4 1
1937 Swansea Town 14 2
Workington
1939 Hartlepools United (3)

Foreman, Reginald George (Reg) RH
b Louth 3/9/1917 d 1978
1938 Lincoln City 2
Gainsborough Trinity
Louth Town
Louth United

Forester, Reginald (Reg) LH
b Penkhull 12/5/1892 d 1959
Kidsgrove Wellington
1919 Manchester City 0
1920 Stoke 7
Macclesfield
Congleton Town

Forgan, Thomas Albert CF
b Middlesbrough q2 1886 d 1964
South Bank
1908 Gainsborough Trinity 2
Crystal Palace

Forman, F GK
1906 Burton United 2

From To Apps Goal

Forman, Frank RH/CH/LH
b Aston-upon-Trent 23/5/1875 d 1961
Caps: FLge 2/England 9
Aston-upon-Trent
Beeston Town
1894 Derby County 8
1894 1905 Nottingham Forest 219 23

Forman, Frederick Ralph (Fred) OR/OL
b Aston-upon-Trent 8/11/1873 d 1910
Caps: England 3
Beeston Town
1892 Derby County 4 3
1894 1902 Nottingham Forest 155 34

Forman, Thomas (Tom) OL
b Basford 26/10/1879
1900 1902 Nottingham Forest 5
1903 Manchester City 0
Sutton Town
1907 1910 Barnsley 126 16
1910 1911 Tottenham Hotspur 8 1
Sutton Junction

Forrest, Alexander (Alex) LH
b Hamilton 2/4/1908
Cadzow St Anne's
Bo'ness
1927 1932 Burnley 108 4
1933 1934 Chesterfield 42 1

Forrest, Alfred OL
1920 Stockport County 1

Forrest, Ernest (Ernie) LH/RH
b Sunderland 19/2/1919 d 1987
Usworth Colliery
1938 1947 Bolton Wanderers 69 1
1948 Grimsby Town 33 1
1949 Millwall 37 4
Darwen

Forrest, George A RH/CH
b Wallyford
Caps: Canada
Heart of Midlothian
Alloa Athletic
Toronto Ulster
Bethlehem Steel
York City
St Bernard's
Heart of Midlothian
Raith Rovers
Peterhead
1933 1934 Plymouth Argyle 3
1935 Mansfield Town 0

Forrest, James (Jack) CF/OR
b Glasgow 1878
Wishaw United
Motherwell
1902 Stoke 6 3
1903 1905 Bradford City 53 18
Hamilton Academical
Ayr

Forrest, James (Jim) CH/RH
b Lesmahagow 1/1/1897
Caps: SLge 1
Nethanvale Thistle
Maryhill
Clyde
1923 1925 Preston North End 51
Bethlehem Steel
Cowdenbeath
Providence Clamdiggers
Providence Gold Bugs

Forrest, James Henry (Jimmy) LH/RH/LB
b Blackburn 24/6/1864 d 1925
Caps: England 11
Witton (Blackburn)
King's Own
1888 1894 Blackburn Rovers 148 2
1895 Darwen 10 1
Imperial United

Forrest, James Henry (Jack) RH
b Shildon q4 1892
Shildon Athletic
1913 1920 Clapton Orient 126 10
1922 Northampton Town 2
Spennymoor United

Forrest, James Henry LB/RH/RB
b Blackburn 28/10/1895
Tramways
1921 1925 Blackburn Rovers 16

Forrest, John Reid OR/IR
b Tranent 3/5/1908
Rosewell Rosedale
1930 1932 Nottingham Forest 14 2
Distillery

From To Apps Goal

Forrest, Samuel (Sam) CH/RH
b Paisley 29/12/1890 d 1967
Westmarch
Petershill
1912 1913 Fulham 7
Reading
1914 Fulham 1
Raith Rovers
Clydebank

Forrest, William (Billy) LH
b Tranent 28/2/1908 d 1965
Haddington
Musselburgh Bruntonians
Tranent
St Bernard's
1929 1938 Middlesbrough 307 7
1939 (Middlesbrough) (2)

Forrester, Thomas (Tom) CF/IR
b Stoke-on-Trent 6/1864
Trentham
1888 Stoke 0
Stoke St Peter's
1892 1893 Ardwick 10 2

Forrester, William OL
b Stoke-on-Trent 1869
Hanley Town
1891 Stoke 1
Hanley Town

Forshaw, Allen RB
South Liverpool
1921 Tranmere Rovers 1
South Liverpool

Forshaw, Arthur OR
b q3 1913
1932 Tranmere Rovers 1

Forshaw, Edward CH
1901 Preston North End 2

Forshaw, Hugh CF
b Southport q3 1906 d 1965
1924 Wigan Borough 1 1
1926 Accrington Stanley 0
Burscough Rangers
Crompton Road (Southport)
Kent Road (Southport)
Crossens
St Paul's (Southport)

Forshaw, Richard (Dick) IR/CF/IL
b Preston 20/8/1895
Gateshead St Vincent's
Middlesbrough
1919 1926 Liverpool 266 117
1926 1928 Everton 41 8
1929 Wolverhampton Wanderers 6 4
Hednesford Town
Rhyl Athletic
Waterford

Forster, Arthur RB
b Stoke-on-Trent 1869
Hanley Town
1893 1894 Stoke 7
Oswestry Town

Forster, Henry (Harry) LB/RB/LH
b Annfield Plain 1883
West Stanley
Annfield Plain Celtic
1906 1911 Sunderland 101
West Ham United

Forster, Leslie James OR
b Byker 22/7/1915 d 1986
Walker Celtic
1938 Blackpool 2
1946 York City 10 2
1946 1947 Gateshead 14 3
Blackhall Colliery Welfare

Forster, Matthew (Matt) RB/LB
b Newburn 24/8/1900 d 1976
Newburn
1920 1929 Tottenham Hotspur 236
1930 1932 Reading 70
1933 Charlton Athletic 1
Bexleyheath & Welling

Forster, Robert Hudson OL
b Throckley 3/11/1909 d 1990
Throckley
Frickley Colliery
1931 Rochdale 2

Forster, Thomas LH/RH
b Northwich q2 1894
Northwich Victoria
1919 1921 Manchester United 35
Northwich Victoria

From To Apps Goal

Forster, William Birkett (Billy) RB/LB
b Walker 28/5/1909 d 1975
Howdon British Legion
1935 1936 Newcastle United 3
1938 Southend United 6
1939 Bristol Rovers (3)

Forster, William E (Bill) LH/RH
b 1882
North Wingfield
Grassmoor Red Rose
1903 1905 Sheffield United 4
Crystal Palace
1908 Grimsby Town 5

Forsyth, James (Jim) LH/IL
b Armadale 18/10/1904 d 1982
Armadale
Bathgate
1925 Portsmouth 3
1928 Gillingham 34
1929 1938 Millwall 321 47

Forsyth, Norman LH
b Walsall 11/1869
Darlaston
1892 1894 Walsall Town Swifts 78 9
Willenhall

Fort, John (Jack) RB
b Leigh 13/4/1888 d 1965
Caps: SoLge 1/England 1
St Andrew's Mission
Atherton
Exeter City
1920 1929 Millwall Athletic 250

Fort, Paul Smith LB
b Wigan 19/8/1901 d 1966
Plank Lane
1922 Wigan Borough 1
Hindley Green Athletic
1926 Millwall (trial) 0

Fortune, James J (Jimmy) OL
b Dublin 1890
Shelbourne
Distillery
1911 Leeds City 1
Shelbourne
Barrow
Queen's Park Rangers
Bristol Rovers
Shelbourne

Forward, Frederick John (Fred) OR/OL
b Croydon 8/9/1899 d 1977
Brighton Railway
1921 1923 Crystal Palace 6
1924 1926 Newport County 101 10
1926 1931 Portsmouth 183 27
1932 Hull City 39 6
Bath City (trial)
Margate
Ramsgate
Ford Sports

Foss, Sidney Lacy Richard (Dick) IL/LH
b Barking 28/11/1912 d 1995
1931 Thames 0
1932 Tottenham Hotspur 0
Enfield
Southall
1936 1947 Chelsea 41 3

Foster, Allen IL
b Rawmarsh q4 1887 d 1916
Parkgate Athletic
Rotherham Town
1909 1910 Bristol City 13 1
Reading

Foster, Albert William (Bertie) OR
b Sleaford 1885 d 1959
Grantham Avenue
1906 1910 Lincoln City 67 1
Grantham
1914 Lincoln City 0

Foster, Arthur Webster IL
b Deritend 12/11/1894 d 1954
Corinthians
1913 Birmingham 2 1
Acocks Green

Foster, Bernard Osborne CF
b Watford 10/12/1907 d 1993
1928 Arsenal 0
1929 Halifax Town 23 4

Foster, Bertram Ernest (Bert) CH
b Wrexham q4 1898 d 1922
1921 Wrexham 2

From To Apps Goal

Foster, Clifford Lake (Cliff) OL
b Rotherham q2 1904 d 1959
Scunthorpe & Lindsey United
1924 Rotherham County 5
1925 Bournemouth & Boscombe Ath 4
Shirebrook
Morecambe
1927 Manchester City 3
1928 Oldham Athletic 1
1928 Halifax Town 8 3

Foster, Cyril James IR/IL/RH
b Aylesbury q2 1903 d 1968
Aylesbury
Wycombe Wanderers
1925 1927 Watford 70 24
1928 1929 Queen's Park Rangers 5

Foster, HA OL
1896 1897 Manchester City 7 1
1898 Darwen 8

Foster, Harry OR
Sudden Villa
1921 Rochdale 2

Foster, Harry CH
b Newark 1903
Grantham
1930 1932 Doncaster Rovers 29
Grantham

Foster, Isaac CH
b 1881
1900 Newton Heath 0
1901 Bury 1

Foster, Isaiah OR
b Greets Green 3/9/1905 d 1966
1924 West Bromwich Albion (trial) 0
1924 Birmingham (trial) 0
Wesley Chapel
Greets Green Primitives
1927 Southport 2
Flint Town

Foster, J LH
1903 Bolton Wanderers 2

Foster, Jabez OR
b Darlaston q4 1878 d 1945
Berwick Rangers (Worcester)
1898 West Bromwich Albion 1

Foster, Jabez OL
b Darlaston 15/9/1902 d 1971
Brownhills Town
1923 West Bromwich Albion 0
Kettering Town
1925 Bristol Rovers 3 1
1926 Gillingham 21 4
Wellington Town

Foster, James RH
b Preston 1874
Reading
Northampton Town
1900 Leicester Fosse 20
Kettering

Foster, James CH
b Sherburn Hill q1 1903
Wheatley Hill
1923 Arsenal 0
1925 Barrow 7
West Stanley (trial)

Foster, James (Jimmy) GK
b Wigan
Washington Colliery
1929 Preston North End 1
Manchester Central
1932 1933 Crewe Alexandra 63
1935 Barnsley 6
Wigan Athletic

Foster, John Henry (Jack) IR
1900 Stockport County 12 5

Foster, John Henry (Jack) RH/CH/LH
b Wombwell 24/1/1889 d 1972
Worksop Town
1919 Notts County 32 1
1921 1923 Luton Town 47 3
1924 1926 Hartlepools United 54 2

From To Apps Goal

Foster, John Samuel (Jack) IL/CF
b Rawmarsh 19/11/1877 d 1946
Rotherham Church Institute
Thornhill United
1901 Blackpool 28 6
Rotherham Town
Watford
1907 Sunderland 8 3
West Ham United
Southampton
Huddersfield Town
Castleford Town
Morley

Foster, John Thomas (Jackie) OR
b Southwick, County Durham 21/3/1902
Murton Colliery Welfare
1920 Sunderland 5
1921 1922 Ashington 68 5
1923 1924 Halifax Town 73 2
1925 Grimsby Town 10 1
1926 1928 Bristol City 47 4
1929 1932 Brentford 141 21
1933 1935 Barrow 87 21
Colwyn Bay United
Ashford (trial)

Foster, Joseph (Joe) LH
b Church
1921 Accrington Stanley 6
Great Harwood

Foster, Leyland Dean LH
b Cannock 4/10/1898 d 1986
1921 Walsall 4

Foster, Robert (Bobby) IR
b Kelloe 8/1900
Kello St Helen's
Morton
Petershill
1920 Sunderland 0
1922 Blackburn Rovers 0
Shildon
1924 Durham City 11 2

Foster, Robert (Bob) GK
b Dean, Lancashire q2 1911
Farnworth Standard
1931 Accrington Stanley 11
1932 Southampton 1
1933 Wrexham 29
1934 Bury 0
1936 Oldham Athletic 10
Mossley

Foster, Samuel Bernard (Bernard) CF
b Southwell 12/11/1897 d 1965
Southwell Federation
1919 Lincoln City 1
Mansfield Town
1920 Coventry City 10 4
Mansfield Town
Newark Town

Foster, Thomas CH/RH
b Hull 20/11/1913 d 1986
Ranks
1934 1936 Hull City 25 1
Guildford City

Foster, Thomas Curtis (Tom) CF/IR
b Easington 30/6/1908 d 1982
Page Bank Rovers
Crook Town
Stanley United
1933 Reading 1
1934 1935 Clapton Orient 19 11
1936 Swansea Town 14 3
1937 1938 Crewe Alexandra 62 27

Foster, William CF
b Birkenhead q2 1918
St James Old Boys
1936 Tranmere Rovers 1

Foster, William H OL
b Hucknall 1913
Newstead Colliery
1932 1933 Mansfield Town 10 2
Newstead Colliery

Foster, William Joseph (Joe) IL/IR
b Crewe
Coppenhall
1900 1902 Stockport County 31 10

Fotheringham, Alexander (Alex) LB
Inverness Caledonian
1898 Sunderland (trial) 1
Inverness Caledonian
1900 Nottingham Forest 0

From To Apps Goal

Foulds, Frederick (Fred) GK
b Woodhouse Eaves q4 1870 d 1939
Woodhouse Rovers
Quorn
Barrow Rising Star
1896 1899 Loughborough 7

Foulds, Jack LH
b Glasgow 1874
Partick Thistle
1899 Barnsley 5 1

Foulke, William Henry (Willie) GK
b Dawley 12/4/1874 d 1916
Caps: FLge 2/England 1
Blackwell Colliery
1894 1904 Sheffield United 299
1905 Chelsea 34
1905 1906 Bradford City 22

Foulkes, Charles Edward CH
b Bilston 7/2/1905 d 1986
Fryston Colliery
1923 Bradford City 0
1924 Bournemouth & Boscombe Ath 0
1927 1929 Lincoln City 64 1
Boston Town
Hurst

Foulkes, Hugh Edward LB
b Llandudno 13/4/1909 d 1981
Caps: Wales 1
Llandudno Town
1931 1936 West Bromwich Albion 15
Guildford City
1938 Darlington 35 1
1939 (Darlington) (3)

Foulkes, Jabez OR
b Fryston 28/8/1913 d 2004
Fryston Colliery
1929 Huddersfield Town 0
1932 1935 Stockport County 143 31
1936 1937 Bradford Park Avenue 47 3
1938 Halifax Town 27 2
1939 Crewe Alexandra 0

Foulkes, James (Jim) GK
b Prescot 14/8/1900 d 1970
Prescot
1925 1926 New Brighton 6
Nutgrove Athletic

Foulkes, Richard RH
b Pelsall 9/2/1903 d 1983
Frickley Colliery
1923 1924 Bradford City 35
1925 Bournemouth & Boscombe Ath 0

Foulkes, William David OL/IR
b Flint q1 1909 d 1964
Caps: Wales Amat
Flint Town
Chester
Connah's Quay & Shotton
Witton Albion
1931 Southport 0
1932 Arsenal 0
Flint Town
1936 1937 New Brighton 18 3
Witton Albion
Northwich Victoria (trial)

Foulstone, Edward (Teddy) RH
b Sheffield 1869
1896 1899 Gainsborough Trinity 50 1

Fountain, Edwin Joseph IL/OL
b Aston q4 1871
Calthorpe
1894 1895 Small Heath 3
Birmingham St George's

Fountain, Richard Ernest IL
b Leeds q3 1882
Scarborough
1905 Notts County 1
Accrington Stanley

Foweather, Vincent James (Vince) IR
b Oldham q4 1896 d 1966
Albert Mount
Crewe Alexandra
1920 Oldham Athletic 5 1
1922 Rochdale 4 1
Macclesfield
Stalybridge Celtic
Macclesfield

From To Apps Goal

Fowler, Alan IR/CF
b Rothwell 20/11/1911 d 1944
Whitehall Printeries
1927 Leeds United 0
Whitehall Printeries (loan)
Brodsworth Main Colliery (loan)
1932 1933 Leeds United 15 8
1934 1938 Swindon Town 172 65
1939 (Swindon Town) (1) (2)

Fowler, Arthur Joseph OR
b Strood 13/12/1913 d 2001
1935 1937 Gillingham 28 2
Dartford

Fowler, Henry Norman (Norman) LB/RB
b Stockton 3/9/1919 d 1990
Caps: England Sch
South Bank
1937 1938 Middlesbrough 7
1946 1949 Hull City 52
1949 1951 Gateshead 64
Scarborough
Stockton

Fowler, John (Jack) CF/IL/CH
b Cardiff 3/12/1898 d 1975
Caps: Wales 6
Mardy
1921 1923 Plymouth Argyle 37 25
1923 1929 Swansea Town 167 102
1930 1931 Clapton Orient 75 15

Fowler, John Collier (Jack) LB/RB
b Salford 17/11/1902 d 1979
Droylsden
1926 1927 Bradford City 13
1928 1933 Torquay United 180 10

Fownes, William Joseph (Billy) RB/LB
b Coseley q4 1882 d 1935
Wednesbury St Paul's
Wood Green Rovers
1907 1911 Wolverhampton Wanderers 12
Willenhall
Darlaston
Wednesbury Old Athletic

Fox, Frederick Samuel (Fred) GK
b Highworth 22/11/1898 d 1968
Caps: England 1
Swindon Town
Abertillery
1921 Preston North End 3
1922 1924 Gillingham 106
1925 1926 Millwall 28
1927 Halifax Town 13
1928 1930 Brentford 74
Truro City

Fox, Oscar IR/IL
b Sheffield q3 1892 d 1946
Castleford Town
1910 1921 Bradford City 164 57

Fox, Walter Cyril GK
b Derby 3/4/1901 d 1972
Matlock Town
Alfreton Town
1925 Derby County 1
Grantham
Shirebrook

Fox, William CF
b Scotland
Carfin
1894 Sheffield Wednesday 4
Carfin
Albion Rovers

Fox, William Stanley (Stan) RH/RB
b Sheffield 4/7/1906 d 1979
Sheffield
1926 Reading 0
1927 Sheffield United 0
1930 Bury 0
1931 1937 York City 136 4

Fox, William Victor (Victor) LB/RB/LH
b Middlesbrough 8/1/1898 d 1949
South Bank Juniors
1919 1923 Middlesbrough 107 1
1924 1927 Wolverhampton Wanderers 44
1930 Newport County 37
1931 Exeter City 0
Manchester Central
Nantwich

Foxall, Abraham (Abe) OL
b Sheffield q4 1874 d 1950
Tinsley
1897 1898 Gainsborough Trinity 55 13
1899 Liverpool 1
Queen's Park Rangers
1901 Woolwich Arsenal 31 3
1903 1905 Gainsborough Trinity 71 8

From To Apps Goal

Foxall, Arthur Thomas IL/LH
b Halesowen 27/5/1897 d 1980
Pontypridd
1921 1922 Merthyr Town 23 5
1923 Watford 3 1
1924 Portsmouth 1
Kidderminster Harriers

Foxall, Francis (Frank) IL/OL
b Sheffield q2 1883 d 1968
Roundel
Wombwell Town
1902 Doncaster Rovers 12 2
1903 1906 Gainsborough Trinity 126 41
1906 1909 Sheffield Wednesday 45 9
1910 Birmingham 21 3
Shrewsbury Town
Willenhall Swifts

Foxall, Frederick Howard (Fred) OL
b Halesowen 2/4/1898 d 1926
1914 Aston Villa 0
Blackheath Town
1920 1921 Southampton 67 8
1921 1922 Birmingham 28 4
1923 Watford 32 2

Foxall, Harry CH
b Birmingham 9/11/1901 d 1976
Cradley Heath
Pontypridd
1922 1923 Merthyr Town 64 2
1923 1927 Portsmouth 155 10
Cradley Heath
Stourbridge

Foxall, John William IL
b Sheffield q2 1889 d 1961
1910 1911 Gainsborough Trinity 24 4
1919 Rotherham County 6

Foxall, Joseph Stanley (Stan) OR
b Crowle 8/10/1914 d 1991
Gainsborough Trinity
1934 1938 West Ham United 106 38
Colchester United
Chelmsford City

Foy, John IR
1925 Crewe Alexandra 7 1

Foy, Thomas Gerard (Tommy) OL
b Croydon q2 1911
Caps: Eire 2
Bohemians
St James's Gate
1931 Bradford City 0
Scarborough
1933 1934 Bristol City 10 2
1935 Barrow 32 2
Shamrock Rovers
Limerick
Shamrock Rovers

Foyers, Robert (Bob) LB
b Hamilton 22/6/1868 d 1942
Caps: SAll 1/Scotland 2
Burnbank Swifts
St Bernard's
Heart of Midlothian
St Bernard's
1895 1896 Newcastle United 34
St Bernard's
Clyde
Hamilton Academical

Foyne, John OL
b Chorlton 23/11/1914 d 1984
1933 Wrexham 1
Colwyn Bay United
Winsford United

Frail, Martin Joseph (Joe) GK
b Burslem 1869 d 1939
1892 1893 Burslem Port Vale 29
Gorton Villa
Glossop North End
1897 Derby County 10
Chatham
1900 1901 Middlesbrough 62
Luton Town
Brentford
Stalybridge Rovers
1904 Middlesbrough 1
1905 Stockport County 7
1905 1906 Glossop 16

Frame, Thomas (Tommy) CH
b Burnbank 5/9/1902 d 1988
Burnbank Athletic
Cowdenbeath
Lochgelly United (loan)
1932 1933 Manchester United 51 4
1936 Southport 38
Rhyl Athletic
Bridgnorth Town

From To Apps Goal

Frame, William G GK
b Larkhall 1898
Larkhall Thistle
Clyde
St Bernard's (loan)
Motherwell
St Mirren (trial)
Dunfermline Athletic
1931 Gateshead 6
Bray Unknowns
Linfield
Motherwell

Frame, William Lammie (Billy) RB
b Carluke 7/5/1912 d 1992
Overton Athletic
Shawfield Juniors
1934 1949 Leicester City 220
Rugby Town

Frampton, Harry John RB
b Freemantle 3/8/1896 d 1979
Thorneycrofts
1920 Portsmouth 3
Chatham

France, Herbert CF/IL
b Stalybridge q1 1884 d 1926
Stalybridge Albion
Stalybridge Rovers
Hooley Hill
Earlestown
1905 1906 Blackburn Rovers 4
St Helens Recreation
Earlestown
Bacup
Hurst
Stalybridge Celtic

France, John (Jack) RH
b Stalybridge 30/11/1913 d 1995
Stalybridge Celtic
Hurst
Stalybridge Celtic
1937 Swindon Town 1
Bath City
1946 1947 Halifax Town 51 1
Stalybridge Celtic
Macclesfield Town

Francis (Albon), Albert Francis IR
b St Albans 15/7/1902 d 1961
Spalding United
1923 Sheffield United 0
1924 Watford 1

Francis, Alfred William IL
b Scunthorpe q1 1881 d 1930
Hickleton Main Colliery
1907 Barnsley 1
Scarborough

Francis, Clifford Thomas (Cliff) IR
b Merthyr Tydfil 28/12/1915 d 1961
Aberaman Athletic
1937 Leeds United 1
1938 1945 Swindon Town 41 16
1939 (Swindon Town) (3)

Francis, Ernest (Ernie) CF
b King's Norton 1/4/1886
1904 Aston Villa 0
1905 1906 Blackpool 38 11
Worcester City
Walsall
Worcester City
1913 Wolverhampton Wanderers 10 3
Bournville
Worcester City

Francis, George James CH
b Poplar 18/6/1896 d 1923
1919 Clapton Orient 1
Folkestone

Francis, Percy Ollivant IR/OR/RH
b Derby q1 1875 d 1947
1893 1895 Derby County 16 6

Franklin, John Leonard (Jack) IR
b Aston q4 1896 d 1967
1921 Walsall 6 4

Franks, Albert Edward OL
b Aston q2 1888 d 1957
Cradley Heath
1912 Oldham Athletic 1

Franks, Anthony Turnbull (Tony) RB/LB
b Middlesbrough q3 1885 d 1934
West Hartlepool
Greatham
Christ Church
Spennymoor United
1921 1922 Hartlepools United 45

From To Apps Goal

Franks, Charles Robert CF
b Gateshead 15/10/1892 d 1978
Close Works
1922 Lincoln City 1

Fraser, Adam LH
b Paisley 1871
Glasgow Nomads
Northern
1895 Small Heath 19
Heart of Midlothian

Fraser, Alexander (Alec) IL/CH
b Inverness 1883
Inverness Thistle
1903 Newcastle United 0
1907 Fulham 10 5
1908 Bradford Park Avenue 17 5
Darlington
1911 1912 Middlesbrough 5
Newcastle City

Fraser, Charles Roderick LH
b Plaistow q2 1907 d 1944
Caps: England Sch
Fairbairn House
1926 1934 Luton Town 246 4

Fraser, David IR
St Bernard's
Leith Athletic
1896 Lincoln City 1

Fraser, George RH
b Elgin 1874 d 1951
Elgin City
1899 Sunderland 0
1901 1910 Lincoln City 265 4
Nettleham

Fraser, John (Jack) OL
b Dumbarton 10/11/1876 d 1952
Caps: SLge 1/Scotland 1
Dumbarton
Motherwell
1897 1898 Notts County 41 5
1899 1900 Newcastle United 49 9
St Mirren
Southampton
Dundee

Fraser, Nathan James IR/CF
b Glasgow 16/4/1913 d 1997
Glasgow Ashfield
1935 Blackburn Rovers 0
1937 Wrexham 18 2
Dumbarton
1938 Tranmere Rovers 1

Fraser, William (Billy) OR
b Glasgow 6/1868
Renton
1891 Stoke 3
Renton

Fraser, William Clark OR
b Perth 9/12/1906
Kirkcaldy
Dunipace
Raith Rovers (trial)
East Stirlingshire (trial)
1926 1927 Northampton Town 17 4
St Johnstone
East Stirlingshire

Fraser, William Cuthbert (Billy) IR/CF
b Cowpen 3/7/1905 d 1977
Blyth Juniors
New Delaval Temperance
Cowpen Celtic
Royal Tank Corps
Aldershot
1929 1931 Southampton 56 11
1932 Fulham 0
1933 Northampton Town 3 1
1934 Hartlepools United (trial) 0
Salisbury City

Frater, David Thomas IL
b Tonteg 8/2/1911 d 1986
Pontypool
1931 Cardiff City 0
Pontypridd
1933 Swindon Town 1
1934 Cardiff City 0
1935 Bristol Rovers 1 1

Freebairn, Archibald (Archie) LH/RH
b Whiteinch 1870 d 1917
Wheatburn
Partick Thistle
1894 1906 Bolton Wanderers 286 9

From To Apps Goal

Freebairn, William Alexander (Willie) OR
b Partick 9/1/1875 d 1900
Partick Thistle
Abercorn
1896 1897 Leicester Fosse 44 14
East Stirlingshire
Partick Thistle

Freeborough, James (Jimmy) RB/CH/RH
b Stockport 13/2/1879 d 1961
1902 1903 Stockport County 26
Tottenham Hotspur
1905 1907 Leeds City 24
1908 Bradford Park Avenue 10
Rochdale
Macclesfield
Denton

Freeman, Albert IR/LH/IL
b Preston 21/10/1899
Leyland
1922 1928 Burnley 78 19
1929 Swansea Town 23
Chorley

Freeman, Bertram Clewley (Bert) CF
b Handsworth 10/10/1885 d 1955
Caps: FLge 4/England 5
Gower Street Old Boys
Aston Manor
1904 Aston Villa 0
1905 1907 Woolwich Arsenal 44 21
1907 1910 Everton 86 61
1910 1920 Burnley 166 103
1921 Wigan Borough 25 13
Kettering
Kidderminster Harriers
Dudley Bean

Freeman, Charles Redfern (Charlie) IL/IR
b Overseal 22/8/1887 d 1956
Overseal Swifts
1906 Burton United 31 3
Overseal Swifts
1907 Fulham 0
1908 1919 Chelsea 95 21
1921 1922 Gillingham 82 21
Maidstone United

Freeman, Edwin (Neddy) OL
b Northampton 5/6/1886 d 1945
Caps: SoLge 3
1904 Stoke 0
Regent Templars
1920 Northampton Town 25 2

Freeman, Henry George (Harry) RB
b Worcester 4/11/1918 d 1997
Woodstock Town
1938 1951 Fulham 179 6
1952 Walsall 20 1
Dover
Ashford United
1954 Fulham 0
Windsor & Eton

Freeman, James Alfred (Alf) RH
b Ilkeston 13/7/1904 d 1986
Sutton Town
1925 Blackpool 0
1927 Lincoln City 2
Mansfield Town
Frickley Colliery

Freeman, Joseph OR
Shrewsbury Town
1902 Glossop 2
Chester
Hamilton Academical
Walsall

Freeman, Raymond Harry CF/IL
b Droitwich 24/7/1918 d 1985
Bromsgrove Rovers
1936 1938 Manchester City 4 1
1939 Exeter City (1)

Freeman, Reginald Fidelas Vincent (Reg) LB/RB
b New Brighton 20/12/1893 d 1955
Wallasey Rovers
Harrowby
Yorkshire Amateurs
Northern Nomads
1920 Liverpool 0
1920 1922 Oldham Athletic 101
1923 1929 Middlesbrough 179
1930 1933 Rotherham United 95 3

Freeman, Thomas (Tom) LB
b Brandon, County Durham 26/1/1907
Durham City
1930 1932 Middlesbrough 74
1933 Chester 17
Blyth Spartans

From To Apps Goal

Freeman, Walter CF/IR
b Handsworth 21/1/1884 d 1971
Aston Manor
Lowestoft Town
1904 Aston Villa 0
1907 1908 Fulham 21 10
1909 1910 Birmingham 37 11
Walsall
Wellington Town
Walsall

Freer, Wilfred Laurence (Wilf) RH
b Birmingham 10/9/1909 d 1973
1929 Birmingham 0
1930 1931 Torquay United 9 1

French, Alfred (Alf) CF
b St Helens 8/9/1908 d 1980
1929 Everton 0
1930 Crewe Alexandra 30 17

French, James John Buchanan (Jim) IR/CF
b Tannochside 31/12/1907
Airdrieonians
1930 Gillingham 18 1
Tunbridge Wells Rangers
1933 Clapton Orient 4 1

French, John Proctor (Jackie) RB
b Stockton q3 1903 d 1952
1924 Middlesbrough 1
1925 1931 Southend United 174 2
1932 Brentford 5
Tunbridge Wells Rangers

French, P RB
Seacombe Swifts
1899 New Brighton Tower 2

French, P Archibald IR
Airdrieonians
1897 Sheffield United 1
Albion Rovers

Frettingham, John Henry Abel (Jimmy) OL
b Nottingham q3 1871 d 1904
Beeston St John's
Stapleford
Basford
Newark
1892 Nottingham Forest (trial) 0
Leicester Fosse (trial)
Long Eaton Rangers
1894 1895 Lincoln City 56 20
New Brompton

Frew, James (Jimmy) CH
b Ballochmyle 16/3/1900
Lugar Boswell
Lanemark
Hurlford
Nithsdale Wanderers
Kilmarnock
Nithsdale Wanderers (loan)
Nithsdale Wanderers (loan)
1922 1925 Chelsea 42
1927 1928 Southend United 56
1929 Carlisle United 24 2

Frew, James Harty (Jimmy) LB/RB
b Kinghorn 21/5/1892 d 1967
Kilsyth Emmet
Alloa Athletic
Newcastle City
Heart of Midlothian
1920 1923 Leeds United 96
1924 1926 Bradford City 48
Harrogate AFC

Frew, Joseph IL
b Stevenston 1873
Stevenston Thistle
1895 Sheffield United 4 1
Glossop North End
Stevenston Thistle
Wishaw Thistle
Stevenston Thistle

Frewin, George William IR/IL
b Fulham 6/2/1907 d 1984
Caps: IrLge 2
1929 Fulham 0
Belfast Celtic
1932 1935 Wrexham 88 30
Venner Sports (London)

From To Apps Goal

Friar, John (Jack) OR
b Newmains 22/7/1911 d 1979
Carluke Rovers
1930 Bradford City 0
Hibernian
1932 Portsmouth 1 1
1933 Bournemouth & Boscombe Ath 34 11
1934 Port Vale 18 10
1934 1935 Preston North End 26 8
1935 1938 Norwich City 82 18
1939 Ipswich Town 0

Friel, Daniel (Dannie) CH/RH
b Bonhill 1860 d 1911
Vale of Leven
Accrington
1888 1889 Burnley 27 1
Nelson
Vale of Leven

Friend, Harold LH
b Cardiff 5/5/1909 d 1987
Cardiff Corinthians
1933 Cardiff City 3

Frith, Charles (Charlie) RH
b Grimsby q3 1868 d 1942
Humber Rovers
1893 Grimsby Town 9 1
Fleetwood Rangers

Frith, Robert William CH/LH
b Hassop q3 1892 d 1939
Caps: WLge 1
1908 Bradford Park Avenue
1909 Sheffield United 0
1910 Derby County 1
Luton Town
1919 South Shields 19 1
1919 1920 Rotherham County 21
Mansfield Town
Mid-Rhondda United
1924 Rochdale 0

Frith, Thomas (Tom) LB
b Grimsby q4 1870 d 1915
Humber Rovers
1892 1898 Grimsby Town 125

Frith, William (Billy) RH/LH/IL
b Sheffield 9/6/1912 d 1996
Worksop Town
Mansfield Town
1931 Chesterfield 9 3
1932 1938 Coventry City 162 4
1939 (Coventry City) (3)
1946 Port Vale 0
1946 Coventry City 7

Froehlich, William RB
b Manchester 20/1/1890 d 1970
1911 1912 Stockport County 6

Froggatt, Frank CH/LH
b Sheffield 21/3/1898 d 1944
Rose Athletic
Attercliffe
Denaby United
Worksop Town
1921 1927 Sheffield Wednesday 90 1
1927 1930 Notts County 115 1
1931 1933 Chesterfield 28
Scarborough
Manchester North End

Frosdick, Albert Walter OL
b Trowse 3/10/1893 d 1973
Trowse
Carrow Works
1920 1921 Norwich City 5

Frost, Arthur Douglas CF
b Walton 1/12/1915 d 1998
Army
1938 New Brighton 23 18
1938 Newcastle United 5 1
1939 New Brighton 0
South Liverpool

Frost, Benjamin (Ben) RH
b Hessle q4 1883
Hessle
1905 Hull City 1

Frost, H RH
1904 1905 Burton United 16

Frost, Harry Victor RH/IR
b King's Lynn q1 1893 d 1962
Wath Athletic
1919 1920 Barnsley 4
Boscombe

From To Apps Goal

Frost, James (Jack) RH
b Oakenshaw, County Durham q4 1908
Bishop Auckland
Durham City
1929 Arsenal 0
1930 Crystal Palace 4 2

Frost, James Lewis (Jimmy) OR
b Wolverton q1 1880 d 1928
Wolverton
Northampton Town
1906 1907 Chelsea 22 4
West Ham United
Croydon Common
Leyton

Frost, Samuel (Sammy) RH
b Poplar q1 1879 d 1926
Caps: FLge 2/SoLge 1
Millwall St John's
Millwall Athletic
1901 1905 Manchester City 103 4
Millwall Athletic

Frost, Walter OL/IL
b Middlesbrough
Middlesbrough
South Bank
1894 Grimsby Town 14 5
Middlesbrough
1897 Grimsby Town 2
Middlesbrough

Frost, William George (George) LB
b Gillingham 17/9/1888 d 1986
Gillingham
1920 Plymouth Argyle 1
Chatham Town

Frost, Winston Harvey GK
b Congleton 22/4/1911 d 1979
Bromborough Pool
1936 Tranmere Rovers 1

Fryar, Albert Frederick George (Buck) CF/IL
b Shoeburyness 25/7/1911 d 1993
Shoebury Town
1931 1938 Southend United 39 19

Fryatt, Arthur William LB
b Matlock q3 1905 d 1968
Brentwood & Warley
1930 1932 West Ham United 3

Fryer, Edward Reginald LH
b South Yardley 8/1904 d 1987
Harborne Lynwood
1927 1928 West Bromwich Albion 21
Shrewsbury Town

Fryer, Henry Charles (Harry) GK
b Luton 26/9/1897 d 1975
Luton Clarence
1921 1922 Exeter City 58
Torquay United
1924 Halifax Town 31

Fryer, John Leavy (Jack) IR/IL
b Widnes 23/9/1911
Runcorn
1930 Everton 0
1933 1936 Wrexham 82 26
1937 Hull City 40 23
1938 Nottingham Forest 22 8

Fryer, John Spencer (Jack) GK
b Cromford q2 1877 d 1933
Abbey Rovers
Cromford
Clay Cross Town
1897 1902 Derby County 173
1908 1909 Fulham 19

Fryer, Joseph CF
b Lancaster 12/1/1896
Fleetwood
1922 Stalybridge Celtic 9 4

Fryer, William (Bill) CH/IR
b Burradon 22/7/1895 d 1960
Byker West End
1919 1920 Barnsley 9
Tebo Yacht Basin
Todd Shipyards (USA)
Paterson Silk Sox (New Jersey)
New York Giants
Fall River Marksmen
Brooklyn Wanderers
Newark Americans
Clan Gordon

Fuge, Thomas William (Tom) IR
b Barton Regis q1 1888 d 1944
Llanelly
1913 Bristol City 6 3

From To Apps Goal

Fullam, Robert (Bob) IL
b Ringsend 17/9/1897 d 1974
Caps: LoI 6/Eire 2
St Brendan's
North End
Olympic
Shelbourne
Shamrock Rovers
1923 Leeds United 7 2
Shamrock Rovers
Philadelphia Celtic
Holley Carburetors (Detroit)
Shamrock Rovers

Fullarton, William Millwright CH
b Glasgow 1882
Vale of Leven
Queen's Park
1903 1905 Sunderland 31 1
1905 Nottingham Forest 20
Plymouth Argyle
New Brompton

Fuller, Edward William (Eddie) CF/CH/LH
b Staines q3 1900 d 1966
London Caledonians
1921 1925 Brighton & Hove Albion 72 20
1927 1928 Watford 55
1929 Brighton & Hove Albion 2
Worthing
1931 Brighton & Hove Albion 0

Fuller, Richard James (Dick) CF/IR
b Burwell 2/3/1913 d 1983
1937 Stockport County 3 1
1938 Port Vale 1
1939 Darlington (3)

Fulljames, William CH
b Cleethorpes q1 1889 d 1959
Grimsby Rovers
St James' United
Grimsby Rovers
1911 Grimsby Town 1
Cleethorpes Victoria (loan)
Goole Town
Scunthorpe & Lindsey United
Coventry City
Nuneaton Town
Caerphilly

Fullwood, James LB
b Ilkeston 17/2/1911 d 1981
Thorne Colliery
1934 1937 Tottenham Hotspur 34 1
1938 Reading 42
1939 (Reading) (2)

Fulton, David CF
b Gorbals 16/10/1895
St Mark's
Pollok Athletic
Kilmarnock
Dumbarton Harp (loan)
St Mirren
Clydebank
Bo'ness
Dunfermline Athletic
1921 Tranmere Rovers 8 3

Fulton, John Wilson (Jack) RB
b Kilmaurs 10/3/1876 d 1947
Dean Park (Scotland)
Swindon Town
Trowbridge Town
1898 New Brighton Tower 14
Swindon Town
Swindon Thistle

Fulton, John J CH/RH
b Knockentiber 22/12/1903 d 1963
Kilbirnie Ladeside
1927 1929 Luton Town 81
1930 Norwich City 1
Vauxhall Motors

Fulton, William IL/CF
b Alva 1877
Alva Albion Rovers
1897 Preston North End (trial) 0
1898 1899 Sunderland 26 3
Bristol City
1901 Derby County 13 1
Alloa Athletic

Fulwood, Benjamin (Bennie) OL
b Long Eaton q4 1876 d 1948
Long Eaton Rangers
1898 Leicester Fosse 11 3
Ilkeston Town
Stapleford Town
Castle Donington Town
Long Eaton St Helen's

From To Apps Goal

Fulwood, Walter LB
b Whittington Moor q4 1877 d 1963
Newbold White Star
1903 Chesterfield Town 4
Newbold White Star
North Wingfield Red Rose
Hardwick Colliery

Furness, William Isaac (Billy) IL/IR
b New Washington 8/6/1909 d 1980
Caps: England 1
Washington Colliery
Usworth Colliery
1929 1936 Leeds United 243 62
1937 1946 Norwich City 93 21
1939 (Norwich City) (3) (2)

Furniss, Samuel (Sam) RH/CH
b Sheffield 9/3/1895 d 1977
1920 Sheffield United 3
1921 1923 Bristol Rovers 91 2
1924 1926 Swindon Town 36 1
Boston Town
Scarborough

Furniss, WH RB
1892 1894 Burton Swifts 47

Furr, George Melville OR
b Barnet q4 1885 d 1967
Hitchin St John's
Hitchin Town
Biggleswade
Watford
1909 Manchester City 3
Watford
Croydon Common
Watford

Furr, Harold Frederick (Harry) GK
b Barnet 23/1/1887 d 1971
Hitchin St John's
Hitchin Town
Hitchin Union Jack
Hitchin Blue Cross Brigade
Hitchin Town
Croydon Common
Brentford
Croydon Common
1912 Leicester Fosse 8
Letchworth Town

Furr, Victor Reginald (Vic) OR
b Hitchin 26/4/1897 d 1976
Hitchin Town
1924 Watford 1
Hitchin Town

Furr, William Stanley (Willie) OR
b Barnet 22/7/1891 d 1975
Hitchin Town
Brentford
1912 Leicester Fosse 1
Luton Town
Letchworth Town

Fursdon, Roy Harry OR
b Saskatchewan, Canada 7/9/1918 d 2003
Tiverton Town
1938 Torquay United 15 2

Fursland, Sydney Albert (Syd) LH/OL
b Llwynypia 31/7/1914 d 1990
1934 Cardiff City 2
Bangor City
1935 1938 Stoke City 4 1

Fyfe, James RB
b Scotland
Alloa Athletic
1898 Woolwich Arsenal 7

Fyfe, James IL
1906 Glossop 11 4

Gabbitas, Henry CF
b Arkwright Town 1903 d 1992
Mansfield LMS
Army (India)
1935 Mansfield Town 1
Worksop Town

From To Apps Goal

Gadsby, Ernest (Ernie) IR/IL/CF
b New Whittington q3 1884 d 1963
New Whittington Exchange
1904 1907 Chesterfield Town 15 2
Denaby United
Mexborough Town
1909 1910 Barnsley 44 13
1910 Bristol City 10 1
Castleford Town
Reading
Worksop Town
1914 Glossop 32 5
New Whittington Exchange
Clay Cross Town
Clay Cross Zingari
Bentley Colliery

Gadsby, Kenneth Joseph (Ken) LB
b Chesterfield 3/7/1916 d 2003
Middlecliffe Rovers
Scarborough
1936 1947 Leeds United 78
1939 (Leeds United) (3)
King's Lynn

Gadsby, Walter IR
b Bromsgrove 1872
Redditch Town
1896 1897 Small Heath 4 3
Watford

Gadsby, Walter LB/RB
b Whittington q2 1882 d 1961
New Whittington Exchange
1904 1906 Chesterfield Town 16
Old Whittington Mutuals
New Whittington Exchange

Gadsden, Ernest (Ernie) LB
b Bulwell 22/12/1895 d 1966
Bulwell St Albans
1920 Norwich City 19
Shildon Athletic
1922 Portsmouth 0
1923 1924 Blackpool 7
1925 1927 Halifax Town 82

Gaffney, Peter CH/CF
b Kirknewton 9/11/1897
Loanhead Mayflower
Bo'ness
Hamilton Academical
Alloa Athletic
Dunfermline Athletic
1923 Doncaster Rovers 2
Denaby United
1924 Barrow 17
1924 1925 New Brighton 18 3
1926 Coventry City 2
1927 Ashington 1
1927 Torquay United 0
Aldershot

Gager, Horace Edwin CH
b West Ham 25/1/1917 d 1984
Caps: NIRL 2
Vauxhall Motors
1939 Luton Town (3)
Glentoran
1945 1947 Luton Town 59 2
1947 1954 Nottingham Forest 258 11

Gair, Donald G RH
b Valletta, Malta 1880 d 1964
Portsmouth
1903 Burton United 6

Galbraith, ? CF
Dundee
1888 Notts County 1

Galbraith, David OR/OL
b Coatbridge 1889
Bellshill Athletic
1909 1910 Preston North End 4
Albion Rovers
Airdrieonians

Galbraith, Hugh OR/CF/IR
b Govan 22/12/1868 d 1930
1888 Accrington 1
Bootle
Middlesbrough Ironopolis
1891 Burnley 5 2
1898 Luton Town 3
1899 Glossop 0

Galbraith, John McDonald (Jack) CH/LH
b Renton 4/4/1898
Vale of Leven
Shawfield
1921 1930 Clapton Orient 277 9
1930 1934 Cardiff City 143 2
Milford United

From To Apps Goal

Galbraith, Thomas D (Tommy) OR/IR
b Bonhill 15/1/1875
Renton
Vale of Leven
1897 Sunderland 2
1898 1899 Leicester Fosse 62 17
Vale of Leven

Gale, Arthur Reuben OR/IR/CF
b Salford 16/11/1904 d 1976
South Salford Lads Club
Sedgley Park
1925 1929 Bury 39 5
Chester
1931 1936 West Bromwich Albion 23 8
1936 1938 Chester 35 16
Macclesfield

Gale, Ernest Walter Henry (Ernie) CH
b Feltham 14/8/1911 d 1972
Southall
1930 1931 Luton Town 11

Gale, George Warrington GK
b Merthyr Tydfil 15/3/1915 d 1996
1934 Cardiff City 0
1935 Bradford Park Avenue (trial) 0
Bangor City
Northwich Victoria
1938 New Brighton 18
1939 Reading (2)
Northwich Victoria

Gale, Thomas (Tom) RB/LB
b Falkirk
Rotherham Main Institute
1906 1907 Bristol City 3
1908 Grimsby Town 0
Rotherham Main Institute
Rotherham Town

Gale, Thomas (Tommy) GK
b Castleford 12/10/1895 d 1976
Castleford Town
Harrogate AFC
1922 1930 Barnsley 296
1931 1932 Stockport County 57
Denaby United

Gall, Leonard (Leon) OR
b Alloa 1878
Caps: IrLge 2
1896 Gainsborough Trinity 13 2
Doncaster Rovers
South Shields
Doncaster Rovers
Wellingborough
Luton Town
Belfast Celtic
1904 Glossop 19 2
Belfast Celtic
Distillery
Doncaster Rovers

Gall, Thomas William George (Tommy) OL
b Dennistoun 5/5/1906
Bridgeton Waverley
Clyde
King's Park
Falkirk
Aberdeen
1934 West Ham United 1
St Mirren

Gallacher, Francis (Frank) IR/IL
b Paisley 1913
Hamilton Academical
1935 1937 Barnsley 40 9
1937 1938 Bristol City 22 5
1939 (Bristol City) (1) (1)

Gallacher, Hugh Kilpatrick (Hughie) CF
b Bellshill 2/2/1903 d 1957
Caps: SLge 2/Scotland 20
Tannochside Athletic
Hattonrigg Thistle
Bellshill Athletic
Queen of the South (trial)
Airdrieonians
1925 1929 Newcastle United 160 133
1930 1934 Chelsea 132 72
1934 1935 Derby County 51 38
1936 1937 Notts County 45 32
1937 Grimsby Town 12 3
1938 Gateshead 31 18
1939 (Gateshead) (3)

From To Apps Goal

Gallacher, Hugh Morgan OL/IL
b Girvan 11/5/1870 d 1941
Maybole
Celtic
1890 1892 Preston North End 55 12
Lanemark
1892 1893 Sheffield United 38 9
1894 1895 Leicester Fosse 47 11
Rossendale United
Nelson
New Brompton

Gallacher, Patrick (Patsy) IL/IR
b Bridge of Weir 21/8/1909 d 1992
Caps: Scotland 1
Linwood St Conval's
Bridge of Weir
1929 1938 Sunderland 273 100
1938 Stoke City 3
1939 (Stoke City) (3) (1)
Weymouth

Gallacher, Patrick (Pat) IL/RH
b Glasgow 9/1/1913 d 1983
St Agnes Welfare
Dunoon Athletic
1933 Millwall 0
Third Lanark
1936 1937 Blackburn Rovers 11
1938 1947 Bournemouth & Boscombe Ath 35 3
1939 (Bournemouth & Boscombe Ath) (3) (2)
Weymouth
Dundalk

Gallacher, Samuel (Sam) CH/RH/IR
b Annbank 23/12/1904
Larkfield Juveniles
Cadzow St Anne's
1924 1926 Bradford City 40 2
1927 Crystal Palace 0
1928 Lincoln City 13
1929 York City (trial) 3

Gallacher, William (Willie) OR/IR
Vale of Leven
1892 Bootle 22 9
1897 Luton Town 30 7
1898 1899 Glossop North End 54 18

Gallacher, William IL
b Dalmuir
Renton
1919 Burnley 4

Gallagher, Hugh Samuel RH
b Clydebank 1901
St Anthony's (Glasgow)
Clyde
1926 1927 Crystal Palace 35
Clydebank
Leith Athletic

Gallagher, James (Jim) LB
b Dipton 17/2/1897 d 1982
Dipton United
1920 Middlesbrough 1
1921 Millwall Athletic 1
Wallsend Town
1923 1925 Durham City 73 3
Workington

Gallagher, James (Jimmy) CH/CF
b Bury 2/9/1911 d 1972
Grenadier Guards
1935 Bury 0
Lancaster Town
1937 1938 Notts County 23 2
1945 Exeter City 0
1948 Exeter City 1

Gallagher, John CF
b Newcastle
Benwell
1926 Durham City 4 3

Gallagher, Patrick LH
Smallthorne United
1900 Burslem Port Vale 1

Gallagher, Patrick (Patsy) IR
b Limavady 16/1/1908 d 1979
Glenavon
Dundalk
Belfast Celtic
Newry Town
Cork Bohemians
1933 Southport 19 2

Gallagher, Thomas H (Tom) CH
b Oldbury
Oldbury Town
1919 Coventry City 1

From To Apps Goal

Gallantree, William Leslie (Les) OR
b East Boldon 25/12/1913 d 2006
Harton Colliery Welfare
1932 1934 Newcastle United 9 2
1936 Aldershot 3
1937 Gateshead 13 2

Galley, Thomas (Tom) RH/IR/CH
b Hednesford 4/8/1915 d 1999
Caps: FLge 1/England 2
Cannock Town
1933 Notts County 0
1934 1947 Wolverhampton Wanderers 183 41
1939 (Wolverhampton Wanderers) (3)
1947 1948 Grimsby Town 32 2
Kidderminster Harriers
Clacton Town

Galley, W LH
Nantwich
Shrewsbury Town
1903 Glossop 11
Chester

Gallimore, Frank RB
b Northwich 19/10/1908 d 1977
Northwich Victoria
Witton Albion
1931 1938 Preston North End 241
1939 (Preston North End) (3)

Gallimore, George IL/OL/CF
b Hanley 8/1886 d 1949
Ashwood Vale
East Vale
1903 1907 Stoke 77 15
1908 1909 Sheffield United 16 2
1910 Birmingham 18 1
Leek Town
East Vale

Gallimore, H IL
1893 Northwich Victoria 6

Gallimore, Leonard (Len) LB/LH
b Northwich 14/9/1912 d 1978
Dick, Kerr's XI
Bainton Victoria
1933 1936 Preston North End 9
1936 Liverpool 0
1937 1946 Watford 64

Gallimore, Stanley Hugh IR/IL
b Bucklow Hill 14/4/1910 d 1994
1930 1933 Manchester United 72 19
Altrincham
Northwich Victoria
Altrincham

Gallocher, Patrick (Pat) OR/IL/CF
b Glasgow 1866 d 1916
Padiham
1888 Burnley 20 6
1888 1890 Accrington 40 6
Vale of Leven

Gallogley, Thomas (Tommy) IR/IL
b Larkhall 9/4/1890 d 1976
Bedlay Juniors
Plymouth Argyle
Royal Albert
Motherwell
Albion Rovers
Airdrieonians
Vale of Leven
1920 1922 Plymouth Argyle 62 9
1923 Exeter City 21 1
Queen of the South
Albion Rovers

Gallon, James LH
b Burslem q1 1894 d 1948
Hanley
1919 Chelsea 2
Yeovil & Petters United

Gallon, John William (Jack) IR/OR
b Burradon 12/2/1914 d 1993
Burradon Welfare
Blyth Spartans
Bedlington United
Carlisle United 0
1936 1937 Bradford City 20 5
1937 1938 Bradford Park Avenue 31 4
1939 Swansea Town (3)
1946 Gateshead 20 2
North Shields

From To Apps Goal

Galloway, David Wilson (Dave) IL/IR
b Kirkcaldy 6/5/1905 d 1979
Wellesley Juniors
Raith Rovers
Aberdeen
1932 1933 Preston North End 31 1
1934 Port Vale 12
1935 1937 Carlisle United 109 11
1938 Clapton Orient 2
Tunbridge Wells Rangers

Galloway, Herbert LH
b Bramley q3 1908 d 1975
1926 Halifax Town 1
Wombwell
1928 Leicester City 0

Galloway, Septimus Randolph (Randolph) CF
b Sunderland 22/12/1896 d 1964
Sunderland Tramways
1922 1924 Derby County 66 25
1924 1926 Nottingham Forest 39 8
1927 Luton Town 2 1
1927 Coventry City 4 1
1928 Tottenham Hotspur 3 2
Grantham

Galloway, Thomas (Tommy) RH/CH/IL
b Kilmarnock 1887
Kilmarnock Athletic
Kilmarnock
Hurlford (loan)
Arthurlie (loan)
Ayr
1907 1910 Stockport County 77
1911 1912 Preston North End 24
Portsmouth
Galston

Galloway, William Walton IR
b Newcastle 13/11/1894 d 1969
Newcastle Bohemians
Northumberland County Amateurs
1921 Ashington 11 6

Gallyer, Richard LH
b Prescot q1 1908 d 1943
1927 Liverpool 0
1928 Rotherham United 12 1
Colwyn Bay

Galt, James Hill (Jimmy) CH
b Saltcoats 11/8/1885 d 1935
Caps: SLge 2/Scotland 1
Stevenston
Ardrossan Winton Rovers
Ardeer Thistle
Rangers
1914 Everton 32 2
Partick Thistle
Third Lanark

Galvin, Patrick, MM CH
b Stockport q4 1882 d 1918
1906 1907 Glossop 20 4
Rochdale
Eccles Borough

Gamble, Frank IR
b Sheffield q3 1870 d 1939
Heeley
Sheffield United
Worksop Town
1895 Sheffield United 3
Oldham County
Worksop Town
Ilkeston Town
Wombwell Town
Mexborough

Gamble, Frederick Charles (Fred) CF
b Charing Cross 29/5/1905 d 1965
Southall
1928 1930 Brentford 13 5
1930 West Ham United 2 2
1931 Brentford 0
1932 Aldershot 24 15
1932 1933 Reading 10 3

Gamble, GF IR
1898 Blackpool 5 3

Gambles, John C IR
1923 Crewe Alexandra 3

From	To		Apps	Goal
		Gane, George	LB/LH	
		b Kingswood 2/1886	d 1967	
		Kingswood Rovers		
		Lodge Hill		
		Watchet		
		Bridgend		
		Bristol Rovers (trial)		
		Workington		
1910	1913	Bradford City	35	
		Airdrieonians		
1914	1919	Bristol City	2	
		Douglas		
1920		Bristol Rovers	1	
1921		Bradford City	0	
		Gara, Andrew (Andy)	IR/CF/IL	
		b Roscommon 15/8/1878		
		Caps: Ireland 3		
		Wigan County		
1898	1901	Preston North End	66	27
1902		Nottingham Forest	6	1
1902		Bristol City	18	6
		Ashton Town		
		Garbutt, Henry Penty (Harry)	CF/IR	
		b Pontefract 12/11/1907	d 1986	
		Castleford Town		
1927		Tottenham Hotspur	0	
1930		Clapton Orient	9	1
1931		Accrington Stanley	12	7
		Garbutt, J	RH	
1893		Middlesbrough Ironopolis	3	
		Garbutt, William Thomas (Billy)	OR	
		b Stockport 9/1/1883	d 1964	
		Caps: FLge 1		
		Royal Artillery		
		Reading		
1905	1907	Woolwich Arsenal	52	8
1908	1911	Blackburn Rovers	82	10
		Gard, Alfred	OR	
		b Reading 1876		
		Trowbridge Town		
1900		Small Heath	3	
		Maidenhead		
		Garden, Henry Whitworth	CH	
		b Curragh Camp 1869	d 1949	
		Derby Midland		
1892		Derby County	1	
		Long Eaton Rangers		
		Gardiner, A Charles (Charlie)	IR/IL/OR	
		b Perth 1915	d 1943	
		Roselea		
1935	1937	Nottingham Forest	38	8
1938		Mansfield Town	27	4
		Montrose		
		Gardiner, Archibald (Archie)	CF/IR	
		b Penicuik 17/3/1913		
		Burnbank Athletic		
		Penicuik Athletic		
1930		Clapton Orient (trial)	0	
		Heart of Midlothian		
1933	1934	Leicester City	18	11
1934	1935	Wrexham	45	12
		Hamilton Academical		
		Olympique Lille (trial)		
		Brideville		
		Morton (trial)		
		Inverness Thistle		
		Gardiner, Henry (Harry)	CH	
		b Kilmarnock 1868	d 1922	
		Caps: FLge 1		
		Renton		
1890	1893	Bolton Wanderers	80	5
		Rangers		
		St Bernard's		
		Gardiner, John Graham (Jack)	LH	
		b Hamilton 14/11/1904	d 1977	
		Blantyre Victoria		
		Motherwell		
1926	1927	Coventry City	51	
1928		Wolverhampton Wanderers	3	
1928		Norwich City	1	
1928		Walsall	0	
		Kettering Town		
		Workington		
1932		Barrow	2	
		Lancaster Town		
		Gardiner, Joseph (Joe)	LH	
		b Durham q1 1916		
		Caps: FLge 1		
		Bearpark		
1934	1938	Wolverhampton Wanderers	121	2
1939		(Wolverhampton Wanderers)	(3)	

From	To		Apps	Goal
		Gardiner, Leslie Lickley (Les)	OL	
		b Dundee 10/8/1918		
		Broughty Ferry Ex-Service Club		
		Hibernian		
1937		Torquay United	14	5
1938		Clapton Orient	0	
		Gardiner, Robert	IR	
		b Motherwell 1895		
		Blantyre Victoria		
		Motherwell		
1921	1923	Reading	96	20
		King's Park		
		East Stirlingshire		
		Gardiner, Robert (Bobby)	OL/IL	
		b Dundee 2/9/1912	d 1993	
		East Craigie		
		Broughty Ex-Service Club		
		Dundee United		
		Dartford		
1937	1938	Bristol Rovers	67	10
1939		(Bristol Rovers)	(3)	
		Dundee United		
1945		Bristol Rovers	0	
		Union Sportive Valenciennes		
		Arbroath		
		Gardner, Albert Edward (Edward)	RH	
		b King's Heath 4/1887	d 1923	
		BSA Sports		
1908	1919	Birmingham	113	4
		King's Heath		
		Gardner, Alexander (Alec)	RH/IR/OR	
		b Leith 1877	d 1952	
		Leith Ivanhoe		
		Leith Athletic		
1899	1908	Newcastle United	279	22
		Blyth Spartans		
		Gardner, Alexander (Alec)	IR	
		b Glasgow 12/2/1876		
1898		Small Heath	16	9
		Swindon Town		
		Gardner, Andrew (Andy)	OL	
		b Oban 17/4/1877		
		Kilbarchan Victoria		
		Kilbarchan		
		Clyde		
1901		Grimsby Town	31	4
1902		Newcastle United	9	3
1903		Bolton Wanderers	8	1
		Brighton & Hove Albion		
		Queen's Park Rangers		
		Carlisle United		
		Johnstone		
		Carlisle United		
		Gardner, Andrew (Andy)	CH	
		b Airdrie 1886	d 1934	
		Petershill		
1909	1919	Lincoln City	151	9
		Gardner, Charles Richard (Dick)	IR	
		b Birmingham 22/12/1912	d 1997	
		Evesham Town		
1933		Notts County	0	
		Stourbridge		
1935	1936	Manchester United	16	1
1937		Sheffield United	11	1
		Stourbridge		
		Gardner, David Richmond (Dave)	LB/RB	
		b Glasgow 31/3/1873	d 1931	
		Caps: Scotland 1		
		Third Lanark		
1899	1901	Newcastle United	76	2
1902	1903	Grimsby Town	51	
		West Ham United		
		Croydon Common		
		Gardner, James (Jimmy)	CF/OR	
		b London 29/7/??		
		Caps: WLge 1		
		Walton United		
		Ipswich Town		
1921		Norwich City (trial)	0	
		Yeovil & Petters United		
1925		Bristol Rovers	32	4
1926	1928	Clapton Orient	31	17
		Lovells Athletic		
1932		Newport County	13	12
		Lovells Athletic		
		Felixstowe Town		
		Parkland's Welfare		
		Billingham		
		Basle		

From	To		Apps	Goal
		Gardner, James Robert (Jimmy 'Rufus')	CH	
		b West Hartlepool 5/3/1905	d 1977	
		Shotton		
1926		Hartlepools United	0	
1928		Middlesbrough	0	
1929		Charlton Athletic	0	
		Aldershot		
		Belfast Celtic		
1932		Newport County	3	
		Lancaster Town		
		Gardner, Thomas (Tommy)	RH/OR	
		b Huyton 28/5/1910	d 1970	
		Caps: England 2		
		Orrell		
1929		Liverpool	5	
1931		Grimsby Town	13	
1932	1933	Hull City	66	2
1933	1937	Aston Villa	74	1
1938		Burnley	39	3
1939		(Burnley)	(2)	
1945	1946	Wrexham	33	4
		Wellington Town		
		Oswestry Town		
		Saltney		
		Gardner, William (Bill)	IR/CF	
		b Langley Moor 7/6/1893	d 1973	
		Caps: England Amat		
		Redworth		
		St Helen's United		
		Brandon Institute		
		St Helen's WM Club		
		Durham City		
		Crook Town		
		Bishop Auckland		
1920		Derby County	5	1
1921		Stockport County	0	
		Spennymoor United		
1922		Queen's Park Rangers	2	
1923	1925	Ashington	84	38
1925	1926	Grimsby Town	20	4
1927		Darlington	19	16
1928		Torquay United	23	8
1929	1930	York City	51	26
1931		Crewe Alexandra	12	2
1932		Rochdale	1	
		Garfield, Benjamin Walter (Ben)	OL	
		b Higham Ferrers 8/1872	d 1942	
		Caps: England 1		
		Finedon		
		Kettering		
1894	1895	Burton Wanderers	59	27
1896	1901	West Bromwich Albion	109	34
		Brighton & Hove Albion		
		Tunbridge Wells Rangers		
		Garfield, James Herbert	OR	
		b Wellingborough q2 1874	d 1949	
		Gravesend United		
1899		Aston Villa	1	1
		Northampton Town		
		Kettering		
		Garland, Graham Edwin	IL/IR/OL	
		b Barton Regis 7/1/1898	d 1972	
		Bath City		
		Kingswood		
1927	1929	Bristol City	7	2
		Garland, J	CF	
1893		Middlesbrough Ironopolis	1	
		Garland-Wells, Herbert Montandon (Mont	GK	
		b Brockley 14/11/1907	d 1993	
		Caps: England Amat		
		Oxford University		
1929		Clapton Orient	11	
1930		Fulham	0	
		Corinthians		
		Garlick, James Stanley (Dick)	LH/GK	
		b Kidderminster q2 1880	d 1915	
		Kidderminster Harriers		
1898	1899	Burton Swifts	22	
1901		Burton United	27	
		Kidderminster Harriers		
		Garner, Charles	OR	
1892		Burslem Port Vale	1	
		Garner, Herbert Arthur (Bert)	LB	
		b Horwich 27/3/1899	d 1977	
		Denaby United		
1921		Lincoln City	6	
		Wombwell		
		Rotherham Town		
		Mansfield Town		
1926		Leicester City	0	
1930		Stockport County	2	
1931		Mansfield Town	0	
		Hereford United		
		Midland Red Sports		

From	To		Apps	Goal
		Garner, James Albert (Jimmy)	LB/RB	
		b Swinton 18/7/1895	d 1975	
		Army		
1924	1925	Liverpool	5	
1926		Southport	26	
1927		New Brighton	0	
		Garner, William	CH/LH	
		b Manchester		
		Heaton Park		
1912	1914	Manchester City	5	
		Southport		
		Garnett, John	RH	
		Nantwich		
1893		Northwich Victoria	1	
		Garnett, Tom	OL	
		b Burnley q2 1900	d 1950	
1921		Nelson	1	
		Garnham, Alfred	LH/LB/RH	
		b Birtley 22/6/1914	d 1998	
		Fatfield Albion		
		Herrington Colliery		
		Birtley		
1935	1938	Newcastle United	45	1
		Queen of the South		
		West Stanley		
		Garnish, Thomas Frederick (Tom)	OR	
		b Wandsworth 3/5/1900	d 1991	
		Wandsworth Town		
1923	1924	Brentford	44	5
1925		Fulham (trial)	1	
		Sheppey United		
		Garratly, George	LB/RB	
		b Walsall 10/1888	d 1929	
		Walsall Constitutional		
		Bloxwich Strollers		
		Chapel End United		
		Walsall		
1909	1919	Wolverhampton Wanderers	217	6
		Hednesford Town		
		Garratt, A	RH	
1899		Luton Town	1	
		Garratt, Frederick CH (Fred)	CF	
		b Wolverton		
		Wolverton Town		
1922		Reading	2	
		Garratt, Frederick Howard (Fred)	CH/LB	
		b Stanton Hill q4 1888	d 1967	
		Stanton Hill Victoria		
1909	1911	Notts County	8	
1912	1920	Stockport County	137	8
		Garratt, George T	OR	
		b Byker 4/1884	d 1960	
		Cradley Heath St Luke's		
		Brierley Hill Alliance		
		Crewe Alexandra		
1905		Aston Villa	13	
		Plymouth Argyle		
1907		West Bromwich Albion	29	3
		Crystal Palace		
		Millwall Athletic		
		Kidderminster Harriers		
		Garratt, John	RH/LH/CH	
		b Old Hill 23/3/1890		
		Halesowen Town		
		Cradley Heath		
1920		Everton	0	
1921	1922	Chesterfield	25	
		Dragon (Pontypridd)		
		Torquay United		
1925	1926	Exeter City	10	
		Aldershot		
		Sheppey United		
		Worcester City		
		Garraty, William (Billy)	IR/CF/IL	
		b Saltley 6/10/1878	d 1931	
		Caps: England 1		
		Highfield Villa		
		Lozells		
		Aston Shakespeare		
1897	1907	Aston Villa	224	96
1908		Leicester Fosse	6	
1908	1909	West Bromwich Albion	53	20
1910		Lincoln City	16	2

From To Apps Goal

Garrett, Archibald Campbell Elson (Archie CF/IL
b Lesmahagow 17/6/1919 d 1994
Burnbank Athletic
Lesmahagow Juniors
Larkhall Saints
Airdrieonians
1937 Preston North End 2 2
Heart of Midlothian
1946 1947 Northampton Town 51 35
1947 1948 Birmingham City 19 5
1948 1950 Northampton Town 43 15
Wisbech Town
Holbeach United

Garrett, Sydney (Syd) CH/RH
b Hull q1 1899 d 1929
1920 1922 Hull City 8
Goole Town

Garry, Edward (Ted) RH/IR/OL
b Renton 7/3/1885 d 1955
Dumbarton Harp
Galston
Celtic
Ayr (loan)
Stenhousemuir (loan)
1907 1912 Derby County 120 18
1913 1914 Bradford Park Avenue 44
Dumbarton

Garside, James Arthur (Jimmy) OL/CF
b Manchester q1 1885
Caps: SoLge 1
1902 Preston North End 0
Accrington Stanley
1904 1905 Liverpool 5
Accrington Stanley
Exeter City
Horwich RMI

Garside, William IR
Third Lanark
1897 Bury 5

Garstang, Frank Bramley OL
b Blackburn 2/11/1904 d 1977
Clitheroe
1925 Nelson 0
Clitheroe
1929 Southport 12 2
Clitheroe
Lancaster Town

Garstang, Harry RB
b Blackburn
1890 Blackburn Rovers 3

Garstang, John CF/IR
b Blackburn
Blackburn Etrurians
1897 1898 Blackburn Rovers 4
Chorley
Witton
Blackburn Crosshill

Gartland, Peter LB
b Seaham 14/5/1893 d 1973
Seaham Harbour
1914 Manchester City 1

Garton, James OL/IR
b 1887
Kettering
1905 1906 Bradford City 11 1
Huddersfield Town

Garton, John RB
b Castle Donington 1879
1898 Woolwich Arsenal 5

Gartside, Robert (Bob) CF
b Nelson 21/1/1906 d 1970
Barnoldswick Town
Trawden
1929 Nelson 1
Clitheroe
Bacup Borough
Clitheroe
Nelson
Hodge House (Nelson)
St Mary's Mission (Nelson)
G Smith's Sports Club (Colne)

Garvey, Batty Walter OL/IL
b Aston 12/1864 d 1932
Aston Hall Swifts
Aston Shakespeare
1888 1889 Aston Villa 7 4

From To Apps Goal

Garvey, James (Jim) LH/IL/RH
b Motherwell 4/6/1919 d 2009
Corby Town
1937 Queen's Park Rangers 0
Stewart & Lloyds
1939 Northampton Town (1) (1)
1946 1948 Leicester City 15
Corby Town
Hinckley Athletic

Garvey, James Patrick GK
b Hulme q1 1878
Wigan County
1900 Newton Heath 6
Middleton
Stalybridge Rovers
Southport Central
1904 1905 Bradford City 22

Garvey, William G (Bill) LH
b London 1888
Metrogas
1913 Fulham 2
Livesey United

Gascoigne, James William (Jim) CH
b Chester-le-Street 26/7/1902 d 1980
Chester-le-Street
Ferryhill Athletic
1923 Durham City 2
1924 South Shields 3
Spennymoor United
Craghead United
Chester-le-Street
Brown's Building Works

Gascoigne, Thomas Clinton (Tom) CH/RH
b Scotswood 4/11/1899 d 1991
Scotswood
1921 1923 Leeds United 20
1924 1925 Doncaster Rovers 55 3
1925 1926 Bradford City 21 1
1927 Tranmere Rovers 0
Hurst

Gash, Robert RH/CH
Grantham
Grantham Rovers
1894 Lincoln City 14 1
Grantham Rovers
1896 Gainsborough Trinity 13 3
Grantham Avenue
Hornsby's Engineers (Lincoln)

Gaskell, Arthur RH
b Bollington q2 1886
1905 1909 Bolton Wanderers 105 2
Macclesfield

Gaskell, JR FB
1911 Blackpool 1

Gaskell, Richard (Dick) RB
b Ashton-under-Lyne
Ashton National
1921 Exeter City 14
Torquay United

Gaskell, Richard Halliwell IR/CF
b Wigan 11/10/1905 d 1983
Upholland
1926 Wigan Borough 3 1
1927 Nelson 3
Westhoughton Collieries
1928 Bolton Wanderers 0
Darwen
Chorley
Parbold
Chorley (trial)

Gastall, John William Holden CF/OR
b Oswaldtwistle 25/5/1913 d 1997
1930 Blackburn Rovers 0
Burscough Rangers
St Luke's College
Darwen
1934 Oldham Athletic (trial) 0
Bacup Borough
1935 Aston Villa (trial) 0
1936 1937 Burnley 21 7
1938 Accrington Stanley 8 2
1938 Rochdale 4 1

Gate, Henry William (William) OL
1899 Newton Heath 0
Darwen
1901 Blackburn Rovers 4 1
Southport Central
Chorley

Gates, Basil Hibble RB
b Portchester 10/5/1896 d 1974
Caps: England Amat
London Caledonians
1924 Southend United 1
London Caledonians

From To Apps Goal

Gates, George James RH/IL/CF
b Hammersmith q3 1883
Brentford
1906 1908 Clapton Orient 53 7
1909 Grimsby Town 17 2
Merthyr Town

Gatland, William James (Bill) OR
b Marylebone 6/7/1898 d 1989
Caps: England Amat
Ilford
1920 West Ham United 1
Ilford
Dulwich Hamlet
Barnet

Gaudie, James Ramsey OR
b Glasgow
1936 Plymouth Argyle 0
1937 Torquay United 14
1938 Bradford Park Avenue 0

Gaudie, Ralph CF/IR/OR
b Guisborough q1 1876 d 1951
South Bank
1897 Sheffield United 6 2
1898 Aston Villa 5 1
1899 1900 Woolwich Arsenal 47 23
1903 Manchester United 7
Darlaston
Stourbridge

Gaughan, William Bernard (Billy) OL
b Stoke D'Abernon 20/1/1892 d 1956
Cardiff City
1914 Manchester City 10
1920 1923 Newport County 95 8

Gaughran, Bernard Michael (Benny) CF
b Dublin 29/9/1915 d 1977
Bohemians
Celtic
1937 Southampton 7 4
1937 Sunderland 2
1938 Notts County 2 1
Dundalk
St James's Gate
Distillery
Brideville

Gault, William Ernest (Ernie) IR/CF/IL
b Wallsend 20/9/1889 d 1980
Jarrow Caledonians
1912 Everton 8 1
1913 1914 Stockport County 64 20
1919 Everton 21 12
1920 Cardiff City 2
1920 1921 Stockport County 41 12
New Brighton

Gavigan, Peter OR
b Gorbals 11/12/1896 d 1977
Vale of Clyde
1920 1924 Fulham 72 1
1925 1926 Clapton Orient 62 4
Bilston United
St Johnstone
Dundee
Montrose
Dundee United

Gavin, Patrick (Peter) LB
b Belfast 31/10/??
Caps: Ireland Amat
Cliftonville
1920 1921 Blackpool 48

Gay, James McLean (Jimmy) LB
b Stanley, Perthshire 17/3/1897 d 1967
Perth Celtic
Clydebank
St Bernard's
Lochgelly United
Dunfermline Athletic
East Fife
St Bernard's
Rhyl Athletic
1926 1927 Coventry City 30
1928 1929 Clapton Orient 40
1930 Watford 4
Raith Rovers

Gear, Francis John RH
b Tottenham q3 1897 d 1960
Ashford Railway Works
1924 Millwall Athletic 0
1925 Gillingham 3
Ashford Railway Works

From To Apps Goal

Geary, Fred CF/IR/OR
b Hyson Green 23/1/1868 d 1955
Caps: FLge 2/England 2
Balmoral (Nottingham)
Notts Rangers
Grimsby Town
Notts Rangers
1888 Notts County 0
Notts Rangers
1889 1894 Everton 91 78
1895 1898 Liverpool 39 14

Geary, George OL
b Hyson Green 1/3/1876 d 1970
Notts Rangers
1893 1894 Nottingham Forest 7 3
Long Eaton Rangers
1899 1901 Chesterfield Town 59 12

Gebbie, Allan Alexander IR
b Muirkirk 11/11/1901
Muirkirk Ex-Servicemen
Kilmarnock (trial)
Muirkirk Athletic
St Mirren
1936 Aldershot 12

Gechern (Geehrin), Patrick RB
b Musselburgh 1889
Bonnyrigg Thistle
Celtic
Alloa Athletic (loan)
1911 Bristol City 4 1
Alloa Athletic
Armadale

Geddes, Alfred John (Alf 'Jasper') OL
b West Bromwich 4/1871 d 1927
Causeway Green Villa
1891 1893 West Bromwich Albion 70 22
Clapham Rovers
Millwall Athletic
1894 West Bromwich Albion 3 3
Millwall Athletic
Bedminster
Bristol City
Bristol Rovers

Geddes, Archibald Campbell (Archie) RH
b Bridgeton 22/1/1904 d 1966
Glenboig Cameronians
1928 Barrow 8

Geddes, James (Jimmy) RH
b Stane Shotts 1902 d 1937
East Benhar
Shotts United
Dykehead
Beith
St Mirren
Albion Rovers
1926 1927 Bristol City 5 1
Morton
Brechin City
Forfar Athletic

Geddes, John LB
b Lochgelly 11/4/1908 d 1937
Lochgelly Celtic
Celtic
1929 Gillingham 11 1
Rhyl Athletic
Tunbridge Wells Rangers
1933 Bolton Wanderers (trial) 0
1933 Rotherham United (trial) 0
East Stirlingshire
Newry Town

Geddes, Robert (Bob) CF
b Salford 1899
Macclesfield
Hurst
1921 Stalybridge Celtic 6 2
Chorley

Gedney, Charles (Charlie) CH
b Wombwell q4 1885 d 1967
Hoyland Town
1906 Barnsley 1
Castleford Town
Fryston Colliery
Castleford Town
Harrogate AFC

Gee, Arthur CF/IL/IR
b Earlestown 6/1892 d 1959
Earlestown
1911 1920 Oldham Athletic 112 43
1921 Stalybridge Celtic 28 12
1922 Rochdale 8 2
Ashton National
1923 Crewe Alexandra 1
Nuneaton Town
Ferranti
Mossley
Witton Albion

From To Apps Goal

Gee, Charles William (Charlie) CH
b Reddish 6/4/1909 d 1981
Caps: FLge 1/England 3
Reddish Green Wesleyans
1929 Stockport County 25 1
1930 1938 Everton 196 2

Gee, Ellis OL
b Grassmoor 15/6/1877 d 1948
Grassmoor Red Rose
Sheepbridge Works
Chesterfield Town
1897 1899 Everton 31
1900 1906 Notts County 214 21
Reading
Ilkeston United

Gee, Frederick (Freddie) IR/RH
b Handsworth 6/1872
Edgbaston
1888 1889 Stoke 17 4
Pershore Swifts
King's Heath

Gee, Harold (Harry) LH
b Haydock 25/12/1895 d 1990
Haydock St James
Newton Common Recs
1922 Burnley 5
1923 1926 New Brighton 87 7
1927 Exeter City 29 2
Runcorn

Gee, James (Jimmy) IR
b Wigan 30/9/1898
Kirk Bobbin Works
1922 Blackburn Rovers 0
1922 Accrington Stanley 0
1922 Blackburn Rovers 0
1924 1926 Accrington Stanley 86 35
Clitheroe
Rossendale

Gee, James H (Jimmy) IR
Willenhall Pickwick
1893 1894 Walsall Town Swifts 10 6
Willenhall Pickwick

Geldard, Albert OR
b Bradford 11/4/1914 d 1989
Caps: England Sch/FLge 1/England 4
Manningham Mills
1929 1932 Bradford Park Avenue 34 6
1932 1937 Everton 167 31
1938 1946 Bolton Wanderers 29 1
1939 (Bolton Wanderers) (3)
Darwen

Geldart, Thomas Septimus (Tom) LH/IL
b Barrow 15/2/1905 d 1985
Barrow Novocastrians
1928 1929 Barrow 2
Egremont
Kendal Town
Crow Nest Sports

Gellatly, Charles Thelluson (Charlie) LB
b Brodsworth 18/4/1910 d 1973
Norwood Rangers
Shirebrook
1928 Halifax Town 0
Shirebrook
1930 Leicester City 0
1931 1933 Gillingham 56
Darenth Training Colliery

Gemmell, Duncan OR
b Glasgow 1870
Elderslie Ranger Swifts
The Wednesday
1893 Woolwich Arsenal 5

Gemmell, James (Jimmy) IL/IR/CF
b Glasgow 17/11/1880
Duntocher Hibs
Clyde
1900 1906 Sunderland 176 43
1907 Stoke 11 2
1907 1909 Leeds City 67 14
1910 1911 Sunderland 36 3
Third Lanark
West Stanley

Gemmell, James (Jimmy) LB/CH
b Sunderland 17/11/1911 d 1992
Ouston Juniors
Annfield Plain
West Stanley
1930 1938 Bury 255
1939 (Bury) (3)
1945 1946 Southport 25

Genever, ED OL
1898 Walsall 4 1

From To Apps Goal

Gentle, Philip GK
b Luton q1 1881
Luton Amateurs
1898 Luton Town 5

George, Frank Noel (Noel) GK
b Lichfield 26/12/1897 d 1929
Hednesford Town
1920 1927 Wolverhampton Wanderers 222

George, Herbert Stewart OL/OR
b Wellingborough 23/2/1905 d 1986
Wellingborough Town
Irchester
1924 1927 Northampton Town 22 2
Rushden
Bedford Town

George, John Spencer CH/RH
b Irchester 4/2/1884 d 1931
Kettering
Tottenham Hotspur
1905 1906 Leeds City 8
Croydon Common
Hastings & St Leonards

George, William (Billy) GK
b Atcham 29/6/1874 d 1933
Caps: FLge 1/England 3
Woolwich Ramblers
Royal Artillery (Trowbridge)
Trowbridge Town
1897 1910 Aston Villa 356
1911 Birmingham 1

George, William Samuel (Billy) RH
b Aston q3 1895 d 1962
Austin Motor Works
Merthyr Town
1920 Sunderland 2
Shildon Athletic
Burton All Saints
Birmingham Corporation Trams

German, Arthur Clive Johnson (Clive) IR/CF
b Ashby-de-la-Zouch 28/6/1905 d 1968
Oxford University
Corinthians
1927 1930 Nottingham Forest 25 10
Corinthians

Gerrard, Edward D RH
b Hindley 1/12/1903
Hindley Colliery
1925 Preston North End 10

Gerrard, Edwin David (Ted) RH/CH
b Farnham 10/10/1908 d 1984
Royal Tank Corps
1932 1936 Aldershot 97
Guildford City

Gerrish, William Webber Walter (Billy) IR/IL
b Bristol 12/1884 d 1916
Freemantle
Bristol Rovers
1909 1911 Aston Villa 55 17
1912 Preston North End 3
Chesterfield Town

Gerry, James CF
Larkhall Thistle
1910 Lincoln City 2
Scunthorpe & Lindsey United
Leicester Imperial

Getgood (Goodman), George RH/CH/LH
b Coylton 15/11/1892 d 1970
Ayr Seaside
Ayr United
Reading
Ayr United
1920 Reading 36 1
Willenhall Swifts
1921 Birmingham 10
1921 1922 Southampton 35 1
1922 1924 Wolverhampton Wanderers 55 1
Kidderminster Harriers
1926 Aberdare Athletic 5
Shrewsbury Town
Gala Fairydean
Bathgate
Bo'ness
Nuneaton Town
Midland Red Sports

Gettins, Edward (Eddie) IR/LB/OR
b Darlaston 1881 d 1925
1898 1902 Gainsborough Trinity 110 29
1903 1904 Middlesbrough 44 5
Reading
1907 1908 Glossop 41
1909 1910 Stockport County 62
Haslingden

From To Apps Goal

Gettins, Joseph Holmes (Joe) CF
b Middlesbrough 19/11/1874 d 1954
Millwall Athletic
Middlesbrough
Millwall Athletic
Corinthians
Millwall Athletic
1899 Middlesbrough 3
Millwall Athletic
1900 Middlesbrough 3 1
Millwall Athletic
1902 Middlesbrough 4
Millwall Athletic

Getty, John OR
b Bonhill 23/4/1918
Glasgow Ashfield
1936 1938 Nottingham Forest 18 2
Dumbarton

Ghee, Thomas (Tommy) RH/CH/LH
b Kilmarnock 1873 d 1939
Kilmarnock
1893 1894 Darwen 19
Kilmarnock
St Mirren
1897 1901 Newcastle United 130 2

Gibb, James M IR
b East Calder 1918
Newtongrange
1937 Manchester United 0
1938 Lincoln City 3
Hibernian

Gibbins, William Vivian Talbot (Viv) CF/IL
b Forest Gate 7/1/1901 d 1979
Caps: England Amat/England 2
Clapton
1923 1931 West Ham United 129 58
Clapton
1931 Brentford 8 4
1932 Bristol Rovers 37 15
1933 Southampton 2
Leyton
Catford Wanderers

Gibbon, Aaron LH
b Penrhiwceiber 17/7/1891 d 1969
1921 1922 Aberdare Athletic 6

Gibbon, Henry (Harry) OR
b Hetton-le-Hole 19/4/1906 d 1972
Bishop Auckland
1926 Sunderland 0
1927 Notts County 3
Seaham Harbour

Gibbon, John OR
Cowlairs
1895 Bury 1

Gibbon, Samuel (Sonny) RB/LB/CF
b Merthyr Tydfil 9/1/1910 d 1935
Caps: Wales Amat/WLge 1
1925 Merthyr Town 0
1926 Aberdare Athletic 0
1928 Merthyr Town 25 12
1928 1933 Fulham 114 1

Gibbon, Thomas (Tommy) GK
b West Hartlepool 24/3/1891 d 1975
Hartlepool St Joseph's
Houghton Rovers
1913 Glossop 5
Merthyr Town
Dundee
1922 1923 Luton Town 69
1924 Queen's Park Rangers 0
Mid-Rhondda United
Torquay United

Gibbons, Albert Henry (Jackie) CF/IL
b Fulham 10/4/1914
Caps: England Amat/England War 1
Hayes
Uxbridge Town
Kingstonian
1937 Tottenham Hotspur 27 13
1938 Brentford 11 1
1939 Tottenham Hotspur 0
1945 1946 Bradford Park Avenue 42 21
1947 1948 Brentford 56 16

Gibbons, Albert S IL
b London
Dartford
1921 Southend United 5 1

From To Apps Goal

Gibbons, Sydney (Syd) CH
b Darlaston 24/3/1907 d 1953
Cradley Heath
1924 Wolverhampton Wanderers 0
1925 Walsall 4
Cradley Heath
1927 1929 Manchester City 10
1930 1937 Fulham 299 13
Worcester City

Gibbs, Arthur LB
b Tipton 1898
Brierley Hill Alliance
1924 Bristol Rovers 19
Weymouth

Gibbs, George Henry William OL/OR
b Chester-le-Street 11/12/1907 d 1990
Caps: England Sch
1927 Leicester City 0
1928 Barnsley 1
Scarborough
1929 1930 Barnsley 36 5
Worcester City
1932 Carlisle United 28 2
Folkestone
Denaby United

Gibson, Adam Paton OL
b Kilmarnock 3/6/1890
Cronberry Eglington
Glasgow Rangers
Portsmouth
St Mirren
York City
Chesterfield Municipal
Rotherham Town
1921 Chesterfield 1
Scunthorpe & Lindsey United
Mansfield Town
Sutton Town

Gibson, Albert IR
b Kilmarnock 1898
1923 Rotherham County 7

Gibson, Andrew (Andy) IL
b Glasgow 1/7/1890
Kelvinhaugh
Strathclyde
Southampton
Celtic (trial)
1912 Leeds City 5

Gibson, David LB
b Kilmarnock 29/9/1895 d 1964
Shawfield Juniors
Kilmarnock
1925 Preston North End 13
Springfield Babes
Fall River Marksmen
Providence Clamdiggers
Providence Gold Bugs
Fall River FC
Queen of the South
Galston

Gibson, Frederick Thomas Bertrand (Fred OL
b Pilgrim's Rest, South Africa 8/12/1888 d 1952
Iona Star
Bedworth Town
Sunderland Royal Rovers
1909 Sunderland 2
Raith Rovers
Dunfermline Athletic
Raith Rovers
Heart of Midlothian
1919 1921 Coventry City 54 5
Nuneaton Town
Atherstone Town
Collycroft United

Gibson, Frederick William (Fred) GK
b Somercotes 18/6/1902
Laughton Common
Frickley Colliery
Denaby United
Dinnington Colliery
1927 1932 Hull City 101
1932 1936 Middlesbrough 112
1937 Bradford City 10
Boston United
Denaby United

Gibson, George Bennett IL/IR
b Hamilton 29/9/1903
Dundee
St Johnstone (loan)
Hamilton Academical
1926 1932 Bolton Wanderers 236 76
1932 1938 Chelsea 130 23

From To Apps Goal

Gibson, George Eardley CF/IL
b Biddulph 29/8/1912 d 1990
Kidderminster Harriers
Frickley Colliery
1932 Sunderland 2 1
1934 Leicester City 2
US Valenciennes
Distillery
Racing Club de Roubaix
Shelbourne
Workington
1938 Bradford City 3

Gibson, Harold Thomas (Harry) LH
b Hoxton
Hoxton Hall
1913 1914 Clapton Orient 30

Gibson, James CF
b Airdrie
Baillieston Thistle
1925 1926 Charlton Athletic 5 3
Thames
Dartford
Shepherds Bush

Gibson, James Davidson (Jimmy) RH
b Larkhall 12/6/1901 d 1978
Caps: SLge 2/Scotland 8
Larkhall Thistle
Kirkintilloch Rob Roy
Glasgow Ashfield
Partick Thistle
1926 1935 Aston Villa 215 10

Gibson, John Rutherford (Jock) RB/LB
b Philadelphia, USA 23/3/1898 d 1974
Netherburn
Blantyre Celtic
1920 1921 Sunderland 4
1922 1928 Hull City 210
1928 1932 Sheffield United 74
1933 Luton Town 3
Vauxhall Motors

Gibson, Kenneth J OR
b Hackney q2 1883
Saracens
1905 Clapton Orient 5 1
Saracens

Gibson, Richard Samuel OR/IR
b Holborn 2/1889
Sultan
1911 1920 Birmingham 110 16
1921 Manchester United 11

Gibson, Robert James (Bob) OR
b Brownieside q2 1887
Scotswood
North Shields Athletic
1908 Bury 14 1
Crystal Palace
1910 Middlesbrough 28 3
1911 Newcastle United 2
1912 Lincoln City 1
Chesterfield Town
Third Lanark
Durham City
1919 Newcastle United 0

Gibson, Sidney George (Sid) OR
b Walgrave 20/5/1899 d 1938
Kettering
1921 1928 Nottingham Forest 252 53
1928 1931 Sheffield United 106 24

Gibson, Thomas (Tommy) LB/CF/RB
b Maxwelltown 23/10/1888
Maxwelltown Volunteers
Morton
1907 1919 Nottingham Forest 186 32
1919 1922 Notts County 63 5
1923 Southend United 5

Gibson, Thomas D CF
b Glasgow 1901
Bridgeton Waverley
1926 Manchester City 2 2
1927 South Shields 4

Gibson, (Dr) Thomas Maitland (Tom) IL
b Dennistoun 11/5/1902 d 1974
Parkhead
1927 1928 Leicester City 4 1
Ashby White Rose
Burton Town
Ashby Town

From To Apps Goal

Gibson, William (Will) LB/LH
b Cambuslang 1869 d 1911
Caps: SLge 1
Flemington Thistle
Cambuslang
1890 1893 Sunderland 75 5
Rangers
1895 Sunderland 16 1
1896 1897 Notts County 41
Bristol City
1898 1902 Lincoln City 130 1

Gibson, William Kennedy RB
b Ireland 1876
Caps: IrLge 5/Ireland 14
Cliftonville
1901 Sunderland 1
Bishop Auckland
Cliftonville
Sunderland Royal Rovers

Gibson, William M (Billy) RB
b Manchester
Glossop
1927 Leeds United 0
1928 1929 Blackpool 14
1930 Southend United 10
Macclesfield

Gibson, William Muir (Willie) LH
b Larkhall 21/7/1898
Larkhall Thistle
Cadzow St Anne's
St Anthony's (Glasgow)
Ayr United
1923 1928 Newcastle United 124 2
Inverness Clachnacuddin

Gilbert, Albert G (Bert) GK
Civil Service
1924 Brentford 10
Park Royal

Gilberthorpe, Alfred Edward (Ted) IR/IL/CF
b Bolsover 1/1886 d 1960
1905 1907 Chesterfield Town 49 8
1908 Hull City 18 4
Bolsover Colliery

Gilbey, Thomas Edmund (Tom) CF
b Bishop Auckland 20/1/1898 d 1962
Darlington
1920 Gillingham 11 6
Spennymoor United
Thornley Albion

Gilboy, Bertram Tollett IL
b Islington 15/8/1894 d 1974
1911 Tottenham Hotspur 0
1912 Huddersfield Town 3
1913 Preston North End 0
Swansea Town

Gilchrist, Albert Edward IR
b Sheffield
1926 Sheffield United 0
1927 Bradford City 0
1928 Arsenal 0
1929 Halifax Town 15 4
Denaby United

Gilchrist, Donald LH
b Campbeltown
1922 Portsmouth 0
1923 Exeter City 29 1
Workington

Gilchrist, Duncan OL
b Campbeltown 1903 d 1924
Heart of Midlothian
1922 1923 Portsmouth 3

Gilchrist, George RB/LB/RH
b Crewe
Sandbach Ramblers
1933 Wolverhampton Wanderers 0
1934 1938 Crewe Alexandra 159
1939 (Crewe Alexandra) (1)

Gilchrist, John Wotherspoon RH
b Glasgow 30/3/1899 d 1950
Caps: SLge 2/Scotland 1
St Anthony's (Glasgow)
Celtic
1922 1923 Preston North End 19
Carlisle United
Third Lanark
Dunfermline Athletic
Bathgate
Brooklyn Wanderers
Chicago Bricklayers
J & P Coats (Rhode Island)

From To Apps Goal

Gilchrist, Leonard IL/IR
b Burton-on-Trent q4 1881
1902 1903 Burton United 34 12
1904 Derby County 11

Gildea, Henry (Harry) IR
b Uphall 1890 d 1917
Lochgelly St Patrick's
Hibernian
1909 Grimsby Town 3
1910 Bristol City 1
Lochgelly United
East Fife
Lochgelly United
Dumbarton
York City
Lochgelly United

Gildea, Peter OR
b Uphall 1883 d 1940
Lochgelly Rangers
Lochgelly United
Cowdenbeath
Airdrieonians
1906 1907 Bury 44 4
Lochgelly United

Gildea, William Franklyn (Willie) CH
b Uphall 11/1884
Lochgelly St Patrick's
Falkirk
1910 Bradford City 7
1911 Birmingham 18 1
Belfast Celtic

Giles, Sidney GK
b Cricklade 21/1/1909 d 1938
Cricklade
1931 1932 Swindon Town 20
Purton

Gilfillan, D OL
1896 Darwen 1

Gilfillan, Hector McDonald OL
b Winlaton 26/2/1903 d 1970
Workington
1927 Darlington 7

Gilfillan, John GK
b Townhill 29/9/1897 d 1976
Woodend Juveniles
Musselburgh Bruntonians
Inverkeithing United
Heart of Midlothian
East Stirlingshire (loan)
East Fife (loan)
1928 1936 Portsmouth 331
1937 Queen's Park Rangers 21
1937 Clapton Orient (loan) 0
Portsmouth Electricity

Gilgun, Patrick (Pat) CF/IR
b West Shotts 30/12/1901 d 1981
Newmains
Law Scotia
Celtic
Vale of Leven (loan)
East Stirlingshire (loan)
1925 Brighton & Hove Albion 3 3
1926 Norwich City 12 4
Sittingbourne
Lloyds Paper Mills

Gilhespy, Thomas William Cyril (Cyril) OR
b Fencehouses 18/2/1898 d 1985
Chester-le-Street
Fencehouses
1920 Sunderland 15 1
1921 1924 Liverpool 19 3
1925 1928 Bristol City 117 25
1929 Blackburn Rovers 5 1
1930 Reading 21 3
1931 Mansfield Town 19 4
1932 Crewe Alexandra 3

Gilhooley, Michael (Mike) CH
b Glencraig 26/11/1896
Caps: Scotland 1
Glencraig Celtic
Celtic (trial)
Abercorn
Vale of Leven
Clydebank
1920 1921 Hull City 65 1
1921 1923 Sunderland 19
1925 1926 Bradford City 52
1927 Queen's Park Rangers 9
Troon Athletic

From To Apps Goal

Gilhooly, Patrick (Paddy) IR
b Draffan 6/7/1876 d 1907
Caps: SLge 1
Vale of Avon Juveniles
Larkhall Thistle
Cambuslang Hibernian
Celtic
1900 Sheffield United 15 3
Tottenham Hotspur
Brighton & Hove Albion

Gill, Ernest Harry LB
b Mountsorrel 24/8/1877 d 1950
Poole White Star
Bridgwater
Southampton
Freemantle
1901 Leicester Fosse 1
Melton Amateurs
Excelsior Thursday

Gill, Francis GK
b Witton q1 1897 d 1959
1921 Blackburn Rovers 0
1922 Tranmere Rovers 17

Gill, George Arthur GK
b Heaton 1894
Newcastle City
Kelloe St Helen's
1921 1923 Hartlepools United 65
South Durham Steel & Ironworks

Gill, James (Jimmy) IR/OL
b Sheffield 9/11/1894 d 1964
1913 1919 Sheffield Wednesday 38 9
1920 1925 Cardiff City 184 82
1925 Blackpool 16 4
1925 1927 Derby County 65 35
1928 Crystal Palace 10 3
Scarborough

Gill, James OL
b Bloxwich
1919 Bury 0
Exeter City
1921 Wolverhampton Wanderers 7

Gill, James Edward (Jimmy) RB
b Halesowen 1884
Halesowen Town
1903 1904 Barnsley 29
Swindon Town
1908 Bury 1

Gill, James Joshua Allison (Jimmy) GK
b Crook 21/7/1903 d 1985
Crook Town
Bearpark Welfare
1926 1929 Bolton Wanderers 40
1930 1932 Bradford City 86
1933 Clapton Orient 19
1934 1935 Accrington Stanley 62
Great Harwood

Gillam, Samuel Gladstone GK
b Swindon q1 1867 d 1938
Caps: Wales 5
Wrexham Lever
Wrexham Olympic
Wrexham
1888 Bolton Wanderers 2
Shrewsbury Town
Chirk
London Welsh
Wrexham
Clapton
Brighton Athletic
West Hampstead

Gillan, Felix Joseph CH
b Colchester q4 1903 d 1986
St Anthony's (Glasgow)
Ayr United
Queen of the South
1928 Nelson 11
Raith Rovers
Galston

Gillan, James Stanley LH
b Derby 12/1870 d 1944
1892 Burton Swifts 0
1893 Aston Villa 3
Brierley Hill Alliance
Cradley Heath

Gillatt, Ernest (Ernie) IR/OR
b Wensley 15/1/1897 d 1971
Hartshay Colliery
Matlock Town
1920 1922 Clapton Orient 61 6
1923 Burnley 1
Mansfield Town
1924 1925 Barnsley 13 1

From To Apps Goal

Gillespie, Alexander T (Sandy) CH
b Denny
Denny Athletic
Alloa Athletic
Cowdenbeath
Ayr United
Ton Pentre
1922 Aberdare Athletic 32
Ton Pentre
Ayr United
Ashton National

Gillespie, Ian Colin IR/IL
b Plymouth 6/5/1913 d 1988
Harwich & Parkeston
1936 1945 Crystal Palace 21 4
1946 Ipswich Town 6 1
Colchester United
Leiston

Gillespie, James OR
b Dunbartonshire 1870 d 1932
Caps: SLge 1/Scotland 1
Renton
Morton
1890 Sunderland 2 2
Sunderland Albion
1892 1896 Sunderland 127 48
Third Lanark
Ayr

Gillespie, John LB/RB
b Larbert 1873
Morton
1892 Sunderland 5
Sunderland Albion
1894 Bury 5

Gillespie, Matthew (Matt) IL/OL/IR
b Strathclyde 24/12/1869
Glasgow Thistle
1892 Blackburn Rovers 6 1
Accrington
Strathclyde
Leith Athletic
1895 1896 Lincoln City 36 10
1896 1899 Newton Heath 74 17

Gillespie, Robert (Bob) IL/IR
b Manchester 20/10/1904 d 1971
Newton Heath Loco
1924 Oldham Athletic 27 5
1926 Luton Town 0
1927 1929 Port Vale 38 14
1930 Wrexham 0
Northwich Victoria
1931 Barrow 9
Boston United
Nelson
Brierley Hill Alliance
Ashton National

Gillespie, Thomas Bennett (Tom) OR/IL
b Girvan 28/2/1901
Hurlford
Queen of the South
Hamilton Academical
Queen of the South
1925 Preston North End 19 2
Bethlehem Steel
Newark Americans
1931 Preston North End 4 1
Queen of the South (trial)

Gillespie, William Ballantrae (Billy) IL/CF/IR
b Kerrykeel 6/8/1891 d 1981
Caps: Ireland 25
Derry Institute
1910 1911 Leeds City 24 10
1911 1931 Sheffield United 448 128
Derry City

Gillespie, William Blyth (Wally) LB
b Fife 29/10/1903
Leven R
Buckhaven Victoria
East Fife
1927 1928 Newcastle United 9
1929 Bristol Rovers 2
St Mirren
East Fife
Distillery
Bangor
East Fife

Gillespie, William Jardine (Billy) CF
b Strathclyde 2/10/1873 d 1942
Strathclyde
1895 1896 Lincoln City 37 16
1896 1904 Manchester City 218 126
General Electric (Lynn, USA)

From To Apps Goal

Gillespy, Toby IL
b Tyneside
Arthur's Hill (Newcastle)
1893 Newcastle United 4
Hebburn Argyle

Gillett, Nicholas OR/CF
b Lytham q3 1874 d 1920
1896 1901 Blackpool 5

Gillibrand, Charles Sydney OR
b Preston q1 1881 d 1958
Longridge
1907 Preston North End 3 2
1908 Blackpool 0
Barrow

Gillibrand, Ernest Percival OL
b Prestwich 27/8/1901 d 1976
Compstall
Northwich Victoria
Glossop
1922 Aston Villa 0
1923 Nelson 2
Rossendale United
Manchester North End
Stalybridge Celtic
Buxton
Denton United
Hyde United
Denton United
Buxton
Ashton National
Stalybridge Celtic
Droylsden
Droylsden United
Denton

Gillick, Torrance (Torry) OR/OL
b Airdrie 19/5/1915 d 1971
Caps: SLge 3/Scotland War 3/Scotland 5
Petershill
Rangers
1935 1938 Everton 121 40
1939 (Everton) (3)
Rangers
Partick Thistle

Gillies, Alexander (Alec) OL/IL/CF
b Cowdenbeath 14/6/1875 d 1932
Lochgelly United
1895 Bolton Wanderers 6
1895 Manchester City 3
Lochgelly United
Heart of Midlothian
1896 Sheffield Wednesday 2
1897 Leicester Fosse 4
Lochgelly United
Dumbarton
Lochgelly United
Dumbarton
Lochgelly United

Gilligan, Alexander (Sandy) IR/OL
b Dundee 1873
Dundee East End
Dundee
1893 Bolton Wanderers 1
Dundee
1896 1899 Bolton Wanderers 98 17

Gilligan, Samuel Anderson (Sammy) CF/IR/IL
b Dundee 18/1/1882 d 1965
Dalry
Belmont Athletic
Dundee Violet
Dundee
Celtic
1904 1909 Bristol City 188 78
1910 1912 Liverpool 41 16
Gillingham
Dundee Hibernian
Forfar Athletic
Mahoning Valley
Republican Iron & Steel

Gilligan, William (Billy) LH
1898 Bolton Wanderers 3

Gillott, Edward CH
b Sheffield 14/12/1902 d 1984
Sheffield Forge
1924 1927 Lincoln City 14
Shirebrook
Scarborough

From To Apps Goal

Gillow, Wilfred Bernard (Wilf) RH/IL
b Preston 8/7/1892 d 1944
Lancaster Town
1910 Preston North End 0
Fleetwood
1912 1913 Blackpool 26 3
1914 1919 Preston North End 7 1
Partick Thistle (loan)
1919 1921 Grimsby Town 80 2
Lancaster Town
1923 1924 Grimsby Town 23 3

Gilmer, William GK
b Ireland 1875
Royal Ordnance
1895 Woolwich Arsenal 3

Gilmore, Henry Patrick (Patrick 'Mike') RH/LH
b West Hartlepool 17/11/1913 d 1966
West Hartlepool St Joseph's
Shotton Colliery Welfare
1934 Hull City 0
1935 Mansfield Town 20
1936 Bournemouth & Boscombe Ath 13
Runcorn
1938 Queen's Park Rangers 6
1939 Hull City (1)
1946 Queen's Park Rangers 0

Gilson, Thomas Aubrey (Alf) RB
b Lichfield 6/1879 d 1912
Whittington Royal
1899 Burton Swifts 0
1900 Aston Villa 2
Brentford
1903 1904 Bristol City 47 1
1905 Clapton Orient 2
Brentford

Gimblett, Arthur John OR
b Merthyr Tydfil q1 1889 d 1957
Merthyr Town
1913 Grimsby Town 4

Gimblett, Gwilym Stanford RH
b Merthyr Tydfil q2 1891
Swansea Town
Morriston
1911 1919 Bolton Wanderers 32

Gipps, Thomas Savill (Tommy) RH/CH
b Walthamstow q1 1888 d 1956
Walthamstow Avenue
Tottenham Hotspur
Barrow
1912 1914 Manchester United 23

Girvan, Hector McDonald LB
b Glasgow 10/12/1899 d 1969
Parkhead Juniors
Bo'ness
1926 1928 Reading 33
1929 1932 Swindon Town 148
Margate

Gittins, Alfred CF/IR
b Manchester q1 1885 d 1960
Adlington
1903 Bolton Wanderers 0
1904 Blackpool 1
Atherton Church House
Luton Town
Queen's Park Rangers
1908 Aston Villa 1
Croydon Common
Brighton & Hove Albion
1910 Fulham 0
Portsmouth
Partick Thistle
Dumbarton

Gittins, James (Jimmy) IR
b West Bromwich 8/10/1900 d 1975
1920 1932 Newport County 254 64
Shrewsbury Town
Brierley Hill Alliance

Gittins, John Henry (Jack) RB/LB/CH
b Stanton Hill 11/11/1893 d 1956
Bentley Colliery
1914 1926 Barnsley 261 7
1926 Chesterfield 10
Wombwell Town

Gittos, John E CF
b Chesterfield 1901
Staveley Town
Scunthorpe & Lindsey United
1923 Coventry City 5 1
Frickley Colliery

Givens, James CF/IL
b Glasgow 1/1870 d 1940
Dalry
1893 1894 Liverpool 10 3
Abercorn

From To Apps Goal

Gladding, Charles OL
b Louth q4 1874
1894 Lincoln City 2
1896 Gainsborough Trinity 4
Blue Star

Gladwin, Charles Edward (Charlie) LB/RB
b Worksop 9/12/1887 d 1952
Dinnington Main Colliery Welfare
1908 1912 Blackpool 87
1912 1914 Sunderland 54
Watford

Gladwin, George William E (Willie) RH/IL/IR
b Worksop 28/3/1907
Worksop Town
1930 1936 Doncaster Rovers 226 22
1936 1938 Manchester United 27 1

Glasper, William H LH/OR
b Middlesbrough q4 1910
South Bank
1931 Sheffield Wednesday 0
Mexborough Town
1933 1934 Tranmere Rovers 18 1
1935 1936 Darlington 8

Glassey, Robert John (Bob) IL/IR
b Chester-le-Street 13/8/1914 d 1984
Horden Colliery Welfare
1935 1936 Liverpool 9 4
Horden Colliery Welfare
1937 Stoke City 0
1939 Mansfield Town (3) (1)
Horden Colliery Welfare
Stockton
West Stanley

Gledhill, Samuel (Sammy) LH/LB/RH
b Castleford 7/7/1913 d 1995
West Riding Amateurs
Castleford Town
Altofts
1936 1948 York City 123 6
1939 (York City) (3)

Glen, Alexander (Alex) IL
b Kilsyth 11/12/1878
Fitzhugh Rovers
Glasgow Parkhead
Clyde
1902 Grimsby Town 13 1
1903 Notts County 20 3
Tottenham Hotspur
Southampton
Portsmouth
Brentford

Glen, Robert (Bob) LH
b Renton 16/1/1875 d 1949
Caps: SLge 2/Scotland 1
Renton
1893 Sheffield Wednesday 1
Renton
Rangers
Hibernian

Glendenning, Robert (Bob) RH
b New Washington 6/6/1888 d 1940
Washington United
1908 1912 Barnsley 141 1
1912 1914 Bolton Wanderers 73
Accrington Stanley

Glenn, Ernest LB/RB
b Redditch 12/4/1902 d 1965
Willenhall
1923 1930 Bristol City 276

Glennie, James RB
b Aberdeen 1905
Park Vale (Aberdeen)
1924 Accrington Stanley (trial) 0
1924 Oldham Athletic 1
Scunthorpe & Lindsey United

Glennon, Joseph Edward (Teddy) IR/CF/IL
b Whitwick 17/10/1889 d 1926
Kilnhurst Town
1907 1908 Grimsby Town 10
Denaby United
1910 1914 Sheffield Wednesday 121 41
1919 1920 Rotherham County 65 17
Rotherham Town

Glew, Joseph OR
b Chapeltown 28/10/1903 d 1998
Elsecar
1923 Sheffield United 0
Frickley Colliery
1925 Rotherham United 4

From To Apps Goal

Glidden, Gilbert Swinburne IL/RB/IR
b Sunderland 15/12/1915 d 1988
Caps: England Sch
1932 Sunderland 0
1935 Port Vale 5 1
1936 1949 Reading 111 24
1950 Leyton Orient 1

Glidden, Sidney (Syd) IL/IR
b Coxlodge 30/1/1908
Sunderland West End
1926 West Bromwich Albion 0
1928 Halifax Town 3
Worcester City
1929 Doncaster Rovers (trial) 1
1929 York City (trial) 2
Peterborough & Fletton United
1930 Newport County 5 2
Loughborough Corinthians
Larne
Wigan Athletic
Blyth Spartans
Colwyn Bay United
Hereford United

Glidden, Thomas William (Tommy) OR
b Coxlodge 11/7/1902 d 1974
Caps: England Sch
1919 Sunderland 0
1919 Bristol City (trial) 0
Colliery Old Boys
Boldon Villa
Sunderland West End
1922 1935 West Bromwich Albion 445 135

Glover, Arthur LH/CH/RB
b Barnsley 27/3/1918 d 1998
Regent Street Congregationals
1937 1952 Barnsley 186 5

Glover, Charles Edward (Ted) RB/LB
b Bootle 7/4/1902 d 1993
South Liverpool
Stanley
1923 New Brighton 32
1924 Everton 0
1925 1926 Southport 54
1927 Wigan Borough 10
New York Giants
1928 Accrington Stanley (trial) 0
1928 Leeds United (trial) 0
Harrogate
New York Soccer Club
New York Giants
New York Americans
Brookhatton
Phalzer Sports Club

Glover, Ernest William Matthew (Pat) CF
b Swansea 9/9/1910 d 1971
Caps: Wales Sch/Wales War 1/Wales 7
Forward Movement
1928 Swansea Town 0
1929 1938 Grimsby Town 226 180
1939 Plymouth Argyle (3) (1)

Glover, John William RB/LB
b West Bromwich 28/10/1876 d 1955
Caps: FLge 4
West Bromwich Unity
Great Bridge Celtic
Halesowen
Rudge-Whitworth
Newton Albion
1896 West Bromwich Albion 0
1897 1898 Blackburn Rovers 25
New Brompton
1900 1902 Liverpool 59
1903 1907 Small Heath/Birmingham 116 2
Brierley Hill Alliance

Glover, John William (Billy) IR/CF/IL
b Blowick 29/10/1896 d 1962
St Paul's
Maple Crescent
Blowick Working Lads
Lancaster Town
1921 1922 Southport 54 33
1922 1925 Wigan Borough 94 33
1926 Southport 0
Mold Town
Burscough Rangers

Goates, J OR
1906 Gainsborough Trinity 1

Goddard, Arthur OR
b Heaton Norris 14/6/1878 d 1956
Caps: FLge 4
Heaton Norris Albion
Stockport County
1899 1901 Glossop 77 20
1901 1913 Liverpool 388 75
Cardiff City

From To Apps Goal

Goddard, Charles Percy IL/CF/IR
b Rauceby 6/4/1909 d 1991
Mansfield Town (trial)
Shirebrook
Clipstone Colliery Welfare
1928 Sheffield Wednesday 0
Worksop Town
Mansfield Town
Northfleet
1932 1935 Crystal Palace 24 8
1935 Fulham 0
Tunbridge Wells Rangers

Goddard, George CF
b Gomshall 20/12/1903 d 1987
Redhill
1926 1933 Queen's Park Rangers 243 174
1933 Brentford 0
1933 1934 Wolverhampton Wanderers 17 12
1934 1935 Sunderland 14 5
1935 1937 Southend United 34 18

Goddard, Howard Vincent GK
b Warsop Vale 24/1/1905 d 1966
Warsop Rovers
Shirebrook
1927 Aston Villa 1
Mansfield Town
Frickley Colliery
Worksop Town

Goddard, Raymond (Ray) CH/RH
b Ecclesfield 17/10/1920 d 1974
Red Rovers
1938 Wolverhampton Wanderers 4
1946 1947 Chelsea 14 1
1948 1949 Plymouth Argyle 43 1
1949 1953 Exeter City 130 2
Bideford Town

Goddard, Robert James GK
b Bristol 22/11/1898 d 1968
Charles Hill
1921 1923 Bristol City 21
1924 Reading 0

Godderidge, Albert Edward GK
b Tamworth 29/5/1902 d 1976
Tamworth Twogates
1923 1926 Leicester City 50
1927 Barnsley 16
Newark Town
Hinckley United
Nuneaton Town
Tamworth

Godding, George Alfred GK
b Caergwrle 3/5/1896 d 1960
Caps: Wales 2
Caergwrle
Crichton's Athletic
1921 1925 Wrexham 160
Llandudno Town
Oak Alyn Rovers

Godfrey, Clifford (Cliff) LH/CH/RH
b Baildon 17/2/1909 d 1986
Guiseley
1928 1934 Bradford Park Avenue 55 1
1935 1937 Cardiff City 104 1
1938 Walsall 27 1
1939 (Walsall) (3)

Godfrey, Edward John (Ted) OR
b West Ham 17/9/1903 d 1977
UBG
Erith & Belvedere
1925 1926 Charlton Athletic 31 7
Dundee
Peterborough & Fletton United
Folkestone
Bexleyheath & Welling

Godfrey, Joseph (Joby) CF/IR
b Waleswood 9/1894
Beighton Recreation
1914 Nottingham Forest 0
1919 Birmingham 3 1
1919 Coventry City 6
1919 Manchester City 9 1
1920 Merthyr Town 7 2
Rotherham Town
Denaby United
Mexborough
Denaby United

From To Apps Goal

Godfrey, Thomas (Tommy) RH/CH
b Stenhousemuir 15/1/1904 d 1983
Dunipace Juniors
Stenhousemuir (trial)
Falkirk Amateurs
East Stirlingshire
Falkirk
Bo'ness
Clackmannan
Forfar Athletic
Stenhousemuir
1927 1929 Stoke City 9
1930 Walsall 38 2
1931 1932 Swindon Town 49
Folkestone
Worcester City

Godfrey, William Paterson Binnie (Will) LH
b Stenhousemuir 29/4/1910 d 1978
Alva Albion Rovers
Aberdeen
1933 1935 Plymouth Argyle 15
1935 1936 Luton Town 6
Vauxhall Motors

Godley, William (Bill) IL/CF/OL
b Durham 1879
South Bank
1902 1903 Middlesbrough 2
1904 Stoke 2
Plymouth Argyle
Reading
New Brompton
Darlington

Godsmark, Gilbert IR
b Derby q1 1877 d 1901
Ashford
1899 Newton Heath 9 4

Goffey, Herbert Henry (Bert) IL/IR
b Sundridge 9/5/1911 d 1991
Sevenoaks
Higham Ferrers Town
1930 Northampton Town (trial) 0
1931 Bristol Rovers (trial) 0
Northampton Nomads
1935 1936 Norwich City 32 9
1937 1938 Brighton & Hove Albion 52 9

Goffin, Richard Robert (Dick) IR/CF
b Clapton 1886
Eton Mission
Peel Institute
1907 1910 Clapton Orient 65 12
New Brompton
Uxbridge

Gofton, George CF
b Hartlepool 28/2/1912 d 1990
1931 Newcastle United 0
1932 Queen's Park Rangers 7 8
Dunkirk United
Grantham

Golby, Joseph Allen CH
b Burton-on-Trent q1 1897 d 1937
Burton All Saints
1922 Derby County 1
1926 Halifax Town 0

Gold, William (Billy) GK
b Birkenshaw
Baillieston Juniors
1931 1935 Bournemouth & Boscombe Ath 77
1936 Wolverhampton Wanderers 10
1937 Chelsea 0
1937 1938 Doncaster Rovers 36
1939 (Doncaster Rovers) (3)

Goldberg (Gaunt), Leslie (Les) RB
b Leeds 3/1/1918
Caps: England Sch
1937 1946 Leeds United 31
1939 (Leeds United) (2)
1946 1949 Reading 71
Newbury Town

Goldie, Alexander (Alex) IL
b Hurlford 1901 d 1958
Caps: WLge 1
Worcester City
Stourbridge
Nuneaton Town
1923 Reading 4 1
Llanelly

Goldie, Archibald (Archie) RB
b Hurlford 5/1/1874 d 1953
Clyde
1895 1899 Liverpool 126 1
1900 New Brighton Tower 34
1901 1903 Small Heath 77
Crewe Alexandra

From To Apps Goal

Goldie, Edward IR
b Motherwell 15/5/1873
Newton Thistle
Cambuslang Hibernian
Motherwell
1897 Grimsby Town 26 5
Reading
Bristol City

Goldie, Hugh RH
b Dalry 10/2/1874 d 1935
Caps: SLge 1
Hurlford Thistle
St Mirren
1895 1896 Everton 18 1
Celtic
Dundee
Barry
Millwall Athletic
Dundee
New Brompton

Goldie, John IR
b Hurlford 1899
Ayr Juniors
1921 Preston North End (trial) 0
1921 Accrington Stanley 1
Akron Goodyear

Goldie, John Wyllie (Jock) CH/RH/LH
b Hurlford 10/11/1889
Hurlford Thistle
1908 1910 Fulham 31
1911 Glossop 33
1912 1919 Bury 142 5
Kilmarnock (loan)
Kilmarnock (loan)
Kilmarnock (loan)
Dundee (loan)
Kilmarnock (loan)
Kilmarnock
Clyde (loan)

Goldie, William Glover (Billy) LH
b Hurlford 22/1/1878 d 1952
Hurlford Thistle
Clyde
1897 1902 Liverpool 158 6
1907 Fulham 36
1908 1910 Leicester Fosse 82 2
Leicester Imperial

Golding, Charles (Charlie 'Chick') IR
b Birkdale 28/8/1913 d 1994
Birkdale South End
St Paul's
1935 Southport 4 1
Marine
Banks Rangers
High Park
St Paul's

Golding, Percy Albert LB
b Bristol q4 1883 d 1961
1909 1910 Blackpool 14

Goldsborough, John (Jack) GK
b Sheffield q3 1892 d 1952
Industry (Sheffield)
1913 1919 Lincoln City 36
Boston Town
Llanelly

Goldsmith, George RB
b Loftus 11/3/1905 d 1974
Bishop Auckland
Loftus Albion
1928 1933 Hull City 172
1934 Tottenham Hotspur 1
1934 1935 Bolton Wanderers 19

Goldthorpe, Ernest Holdroyd (Ernie) CF/IR
b Middleton, West Yorkshire 8/6/1898 d 1929
1919 Bradford City 15 3
1920 Leeds United 6 2
1921 Bradford City 0
1922 1924 Manchester United 27 15
1925 Rotherham United 2 1

Golightly, Lambert RB
b Gateshead 9/3/1895 d 1987
Caps: England Amat
1922 1923 Darlington 7

Golightly, Martin IL
b Lintz q4 1891 d 1953
Fatfield Albion
Gateshead
Exeter City
Bideford Town
Durham City
1919 Grimsby Town 9
Charlton's (Grimsby)

From To Apps Goal

Golledge, Leslie Howard (Les) RH/CF/IR
b Chipping Sodbury 3/8/1911 d 1989
Kingswood
1931 1934 Bristol City 25 3
1934 1936 Bristol Rovers 9 1
1937 Lincoln City 0

Gollings, Platts Shadrach (Platt) LH/RH
b Winson Green q1 1878 d 1935
Hereford Thistle
1899 1900 West Bromwich Albion 5
Brierley Hill Alliance
Hereford Town

Gomersall, B LB
1898 Darwen 1

Gomm, Archibald Frank (Archie) CH/IR
b Beaconsfield 1/5/1897 d 1978
Chesham
Wycombe Wanderers
Reading
1920 1930 Millwall Athletic 187 14
1931 1932 Carlisle United 67
Lancaster Town

Gooch, Percival George (Percy) CF/OR
b Lowestoft 1/9/1882 d 1956
Lowestoft Fearnoughts
Kirkley Juniors
Lowestoft Harriers
Lowestoft IOGT
Lowestoft Town
Norwich City
1906 1907 Birmingham 4 1
1907 Notts County 3 1
Norwich City

Good, Hugh Jardine CH/RH
b Motherwell 2/7/1901 d 1958
Wishaw YMCA
Kilmarnock
Wishaw YMCA
1924 1925 Middlesbrough 10
1926 Exeter City 4
1927 Bristol City 0
1927 Torquay United 16
Raith Rovers
Bo'ness (loan)
Lovells Athletic
Glentoran
Larne
Montrose

Good (Sullivan), Michael HS (Micky) CH/IR
b Cork 1873 d 1959
Airdrie Hill
Airdrieonians
1896 1898 Small Heath 15 1
Watford
1901 Preston North End 24 2
1902 Bristol City 32 5
Reading
Brighton & Hove Albion
Southern United

Goodacre, Reginald (Reg) RB
b Billingborough 24/7/1908 d 1998
Billingborough
Boston Town
1930 1932 West Ham United 20
1933 Mansfield Town 18 1
Peterborough United
Gainsborough Trinity

Goodall, Archibald Lee (Archie) CH/CF
b Belfast 19/6/1864 d 1929
Caps: Ireland 10
Liverpool Stanley
St Jude's
1888 Preston North End 2 1
1888 Aston Villa 14 7
1889 1902 Derby County 380 48
Plymouth Argyle
1903 1904 Glossop 26 13
1905 Wolverhampton Wanderers 7

Goodall, Edward Ilderton (Ed) GK
b South Shields 13/10/1913 d 1978
Middle Dock
Jarrow
1936 Chesterfield 0
North Shields
1937 Hull City 26
1938 Bolton Wanderers 12

Goodall, Frederick Roy (Roy) RB
b Dronfield 31/12/1902 d 1982
Caps: FLge 9/England 25
Dronfield Woodhouse
1922 1936 Huddersfield Town 403 19

From To Apps Goal

Goodall, John CF/OR/IL
b Westminster 19/6/1863 d 1942
Caps: FLge 4/England 14
Kilmarnock Athletic
Great Lever
1888 Preston North End 21 20
1889 1898 Derby County 211 76
1899 New Brighton Tower 6 2
1900 1902 Glossop 35 8
Watford
Racing Club de Roubaix
Mardy

Goodall, Richard OR
b Ashton-under-Lyne
Ashton National
1936 Halifax Town 5 1

Goodburn, Harold OR
b Preston q1 1887 d 1907
1906 Preston North End 2

Goodchild, Andrew James (Jim) GK
b Southampton 4/4/1892 d 1950
St Paul's Athletic
Southampton
1911 1926 Manchester City 204
Guildford City
Stoneham Nomads

Goodchild, George OR/IR
b Ryhope q1 1875
Ryhope Colliery
1894 Sunderland 1
1896 Derby County 2
1896 1897 Nottingham Forest 4
1897 Burton Swifts 9 1
Jarrow
Whitburn
South Shields Athletic
Ashington

Goodcliffe, William G CF
b London
Dulwich Hamlet
1932 1935 Crystal Palace 2 1
Dulwich Hamlet

Goode, Bertram John (Bert) IR
b Chester 11/8/1886 d 1955
Old St Mary's
Hoole
Saltney
Chester
1908 1909 Liverpool 7 1
Wrexham
1911 Aston Villa 7 3
1912 Hull City 28 10
1921 Wrexham 32 5
Rhos Athletic
Chester
1923 1925 Wrexham 21 5

Goodfellow, Derwick Ormond GK
b Shilbottle 26/6/1914 d 2001
Amble
1934 1935 Gateshead 29
1936 1946 Sheffield Wednesday 69
1947 Middlesbrough 36
1948 Exeter City 0

Goodfellow, Sydney (Syd) RH/LH/IL
b Wolstanton 6/7/1915 d 1998
Silverdale
Hanley
1936 Port Vale 16 1
Glentoran
1938 Rochdale 41 2
1945 1947 Chesterfield 80
1948 1949 Doncaster Rovers 66 2
1950 1951 Oldham Athletic 72 2
1952 Accrington Stanley 28 3
Wellington Town
Stafford Rangers
Oswestry Town

Goodier, Edward (Ted) LH/CH
b Farnworth 15/10/1902 d 1967
Worsley Primitive Methodists
Brookhouse United
1922 Huddersfield Town 0
Lancaster Town
1925 1931 Oldham Athletic 113 2
1931 1934 Queen's Park Rangers 139 2
1935 Watford 1
1936 Crewe Alexandra 41
1937 1938 Rochdale 67 1

Goodin, Walter RB
b Hull q2 1883
Grangetown
Beverley Barracks
1905 Hull City 1

From To Apps Goal

Goodison, Percy IL
b Burnley
Livingstone
1911 Burnley 1
Accrington Stanley

Goodman, Albert Abraham (Bert) LH/LB/CF
b Dalston 3/9/1890 d 1959
London Fields
Tufnell Park
Tottenham Thursday
Maidstone United
Croydon Common
1919 Tottenham Hotspur 16 1
Margate
1921 1924 Charlton Athletic 126 15
1925 Gillingham 6
1925 1926 Clapton Orient 12
Guildford City

Goodman, William Robert OL
b Islington q2 1894
Margate
Tufnell Park
Northfleet
1923 Queen's Park Rangers 1

Goodson, Leonard George (Len) IL/OL
b Doncaster q2 1880 d 1922
Marshgate Institute
1901 1902 Doncaster Rovers 38 6
1902 1904 Middlesbrough 35 6
Doncaster Rovers

Goodwill, Thomas OL
b Bates Cottages 1894 d 1916
Seaton Delaval
1913 1914 Newcastle United 52 4

Goodwin, A CH/RH
1899 1900 Burton Swifts 49 1
1901 Burton United 1

Goodwin, Ernest William OR
b Gateshead 20/7/1894
Spennymoor United
1914 1919 Leeds City 20 3
1919 1920 Manchester City 20 3
1921 Rochdale 0

Goodwin, Fred OL
1906 Burnley 1

Goodwin, Harry B OR
b Glasgow 4/12/1903
Bo'ness
1925 1926 Portsmouth 38 10
1927 1929 Reading 89 15
Dolphin
Colwyn Bay United
Worcester City
Glentoran

Goodwin, James W OR
1905 1906 Stockport County 16 1

Goodwin, John GK
b Hallside 10/12/1903
St Anthony's (Glasgow)
Dumbarton
Dumbarton Harp
1924 Wigan Borough 41
1925 Barnsley 2
1926 Wigan Borough (trial) 3
Horwich RMI
Ashton National
Poole's Central
Chorley

Goodwin, Ralph RB
b Hanley 1887
1906 Glossop 14
Stalybridge Rovers
Tunstall Park
1907 1914 Stockport County 179
1919 Preston North End 7
1920 Stockport County 1

Goodwin, William (Bill) LB/RB
b Mold 16/1/1892 d 1972
Caps: Wales Amat
Mold Town
Bangor College
Holywell
Wrexham
1914 1920 Oldham Athletic 40
1921 1924 Crewe Alexandra 149 2
1925 Oldham Athletic 2
Congleton Town
Mossley

From To Apps Goal

Goodwin, William (Billy) CF/IR
b Staveley q1 1892 d 1951
Staveley Primitives
1913 Blackburn Rovers 0
Exeter City
1920 1921 Manchester United 7 1
1922 1926 Southend United 84 32
Dartford

Gooing, William Henry (Bill) CF
b Penistone q2 1874 d 1969
Wath
1895 Sheffield Wednesday 3 1
Wath
1899 1901 Chesterfield Town 71 26
1901 1904 Woolwich Arsenal 94 45
Northampton Town

Goonan, Michael OL
b Gosforth 9/6/1901 d 1991
West Sleekburn
1922 Ashington 1
Bedlington United
Seaton Delaval
Stakeford United
Cramlington Rovers
Stakeford United
Blyth Spartans
Bedlington United
Blyth Spartans
Bedlington United

Gooney, William Henry (Harry) RH/LH
b Sheffield 8/10/1910 d 1978
Caps: England Sch
Norton Woodseats
1930 1934 Sheffield United 132 2
1935 Plymouth Argyle 14
1935 Luton Town 4

Goord, George William CF
b Brighton q1 1897 d 1961
Vernon Athletic
Civil Service Club
1925 Brighton & Hove Albion 1 1

Gordon, Andrew (Andy) RH
1901 Newcastle United 0
1902 1904 Doncaster Rovers 43

Gordon, Arthur OR
1926 Doncaster Rovers 1

Gordon, Daniel (Dan) RB
b West Calder 7/1/1881 d 1958
Broxburn
Heart of Midlothian
Broxburn
1903 Everton 0
Southampton
Falkirk
St Mirren
1908 Middlesbrough 1
1908 1909 Bradford Park Avenue 50
1909 1910 Hull City 11
Southampton

Gordon, David Smith (Davy) LH
b Leith 29/12/1882
Leith Athletic
1905 1913 Hull City 275 17
St Bernard's
Leith Athletic
Hibernian
Kilmarnock
Hibernian

Gordon, George CF
b 1880
Wallsend Park Villa
1901 Barnsley 14 6
1902 Gainsborough Trinity 3 2

Gordon, James (Jimmy) LH/RH
b Fauldhouse 23/10/1915 d 1996
Wishaw Juniors
1934 1938 Newcastle United 132 2
1939 (Newcastle United) (1)
1945 1953 Middlesbrough 231 3

Gordon, James Thornton (Jimmy) CH
b Barking q1 1886 d 1959
Barking Victoria
Barking
West Ham United
1909 1914 Grimsby Town 126 7

Gordon, John IR/RH
b Kirkcudbright 11/4/1899
Bellshill Juniors
Queen's Park
1922 Port Vale 21 3
Morton
1926 1927 Luton Town 14
Dunfermline Athletic

From To Apps Goal

Gordon, John B (Jack) OR
b Port Glasgow 1863
1888 1894 Preston North End 113 27
1895 Loughborough 3 1
Wigan County

Gordon, John George (Jack) RH
b South Shields 25/9/1911
Boldon Colliery Welfare
1931 Leeds United 0
1932 1933 Rochdale 66 1
Queen of the South
South Shields
Jarrow
Blyth Spartans

Gordon, Leslie William (Les) LH
b Barking 13/7/1903
Grimsby Rovers
1923 Sheffield United 0
1925 Crystal Palace 0
Shirebrook
1927 Nottingham Forest 2
Shirebrook
1928 Brighton & Hove Albion 18
Cleethorpes UDC Buses

Gordon, Patrick OR/IR
b Renton 1864
Renton
1890 1892 Everton 18 3
1893 1894 Liverpool 26 7
1894 Blackburn Rovers 12 2
Liverpool South End

Gordon, Robert (Bob) CF
b Leith 7/1870 d 1938
Edinburgh Thistle
Leith Rangers
Leith Athletic
Heart of Midlothian
Middlesbrough Ironopolis
Heart of Midlothian
1894 Aston Villa 4 2
1894 Leicester Fosse 21 12
1895 Woolwich Arsenal 20 6
Reading
Forfar Athletic
St Bernard's

Gordon, Robert Henry RH
b 1917 d 1940
Shankhouse
1937 1938 Huddersfield Town 7

Gore, Frederick Leslie (Les) OR
b Coventry 21/1/1914 d 1991
Morris Motor Works
1935 Fulham 0
1936 Stockport County 7 1
1937 Carlisle United 3
1937 1938 Bradford City 33 8
1939 1945 Clapton Orient (3) (1)
Yeovil Town
Gillingham
Gravesend & Northfleet

Gore, Reginald (Reg) OL
b Hepthorne Lane 1/8/1913 d 1997
Hepthorne Lane Primitives
1932 Chesterfield 0
1933 Birmingham 0
1934 Southport 16 2
South Liverpool
Rhyl
Frickley Colliery
1938 West Ham United 5 1
St Mirren
Cowdenbeath

Gore, Sidney Percy (Sid) OL
b Faversham 23/9/1900 d 1987
Faversham Rangers
1920 Gillingham 8
Sittingbourne
1923 1926 Millwall Athletic 113 12
Chatham Town
1929 Gillingham 32
Ashford Town (Kent)

Gore, Thomas (Tommy) CH/RB
b Hindley 25/5/1901 d 1955
Hindley Green
Horwich RMI
1925 Bolton Wanderers 0
1926 1928 Barrow 113 1
Connah's Quay & Shotton
Hindley Parish Church
Ramsgate Press Wanderers
Margate
Horwich RMI

From To Apps Goal

Gorman, Archibald Macdonald (Archie) RH/LH
b Lochore 10/4/1909 d 1992
Edinburgh City
1931 1945 Plymouth Argyle 237 2
1939 (Plymouth Argyle) (3)

Gorman, James (Jimmy) CH
b Middlesbrough q2 1882
St Mary's (Middlesbrough)
Newport Celtic
South Bank
Darlington St Augustine's
Darlington
1905 1907 Liverpool 19
1908 Leicester Fosse 3
Hartlepools United
Stockton

Gorman, James Joseph (Jimmy) RB
b Liverpool 3/3/1910 d 1991
Burscough Rangers
Skelmersdale United
1930 1936 Blackburn Rovers 213
1936 1938 Sunderland 82
1939 (Sunderland) (3)
1945 Hartlepools United 0

Gorman, John IL
b Dudley 1882
1905 1906 Wolverhampton Wanderers 9 4
Halesowen Town
Stoke
Croydon Common
Dudley Town

Gorman, William (Bill) LH
b Brentwood 1896
Monks Hall
1921 1922 Bury 28 1

Gorman, William Charles (Bill) RB/LB
b Sligo 13/7/1911 d 1978
Caps: Ireland 4/Eire 13
Shettleston Juniors
1936 1938 Bury 52
1938 1949 Brentford 125
1939 (Brentford) (3)
Deal Town

Gormlie, William Joseph (Bill) GK
b Blackpool 4/1911 d 1976
Fleetwood Windsor Villa
1931 1933 Blackburn Rovers 44
1935 1938 Northampton Town 138
1939 Lincoln City (3)

Gorringe, Frederick Charles (Fred) OL/IL
b Salford q4 1903 d 1965
Manchester Ship Canal
1927 Manchester City 1 2
1928 Lincoln City 6 3
1929 Crewe Alexandra 17 8
1930 Bolton Wanderers 1
1931 Reading 1

Goslin, Henry (Harry) RH
b Willington 9/11/1909 d 1943
Caps: England War 4
Boots Athletic
1930 1938 Bolton Wanderers 303 23
1939 (Bolton Wanderers) (3)

Gosling, G CH
1898 Blackpool 1

Gosling, Tom RH
b Ardsley q3 1876 d 1943
Wombwell Town
1899 Barnsley 14 1

Gosling, W OL
1899 Gainsborough Trinity 1 1

Gosling, William Walter LB/RB
b Hexham 1879
Jarrow
1900 1901 Sheffield Wednesday 5

Gosnell, Albert Arthur (Bert) OL
b Colchester 10/2/1880 d 1972
Caps: England 1
The Albion (Colchester)
Colchester Town
New Brompton
Chatham
1904 1909 Newcastle United 106 15
1910 Tottenham Hotspur 5
Darlington
Port Vale

From To Apps Goal

Goss, Frederick Charles (Fred) OR
b Shardlow 25/5/1914 d 1983
Ilkeston St Clare's
Ilkeston Town
1936 Aston Villa 2
1938 Wrexham 9 1
1939 Aston Villa 0

Goss, William IL
b Nottingham q1 1879
Nottingham St Peter's
Heanor Town
1899 Notts County 16 1
Portsmouth
Newark Town

Gott, Edward GK
Rawdon
1905 Bradford City 8

Goucher, George Henry LB/RB
b Shirebrook 18/5/1902 d 1987
Hawthorn Exchange
Norwood Rangers
Shirebrook
1926 Notts County 1
1928 Nottingham Forest 1
1929 Torquay United 6
Shirebrook
Sutton Town
Ilkeston United

Goudie, Peter Augustus GK
b Derby q2 1879
Derby YMCA
Derby Nomads
1898 Leicester Fosse 1
Derby Nomads
Derby Hills Ivanhoe

Gough, Arthur Victor (Tony) CF/OL
b Cirencester 20/1/1900 d 1975
Swindon Victoria
1923 Bristol Rovers 0
1925 1926 Brighton & Hove Albion 9 4
1928 Walsall 16 4
1929 Merthyr Town 11 4

Gough, Cecil William McKinley RH/LH
b South Cerney 14/9/1901 d 1963
South Cerney
Cirencester Town
Cirencester Victoria
Tetbury Town
Cirencester Town
1924 Bristol Rovers 0
1925 Clapton Orient 6
1926 Queen's Park Rangers 19
1927 Torquay United 28
1928 Clapton Orient 1
Canterbury Waverley
Park Royal
Ealing Celtic

Gough, Claude Francis OL/IR
b Rhayader 17/10/1900 d 1990
Llandrindod Wells
1920 Swansea Town 2 1
1921 Coventry City 15 1
1922 Swansea Town 10 3

Gough, Harold GK
b Chesterfield 31/12/1890 d 1970
Caps: England 1
Spital Olympic
Castleford Town
1910 Bradford Park Avenue 3
Castleford Town
1913 1923 Sheffield United 242
Hibernian (loan)
Hibernian (loan)
Castleford Town
Harrogate AFC
1926 Oldham Athletic 4
1927 Bolton Wanderers 4
1928 1929 Torquay United 56

Gould, Charles (Charlie) OR
b Bristol q4 1889
Bath City
1911 1912 Bristol City 27
Bath City

Gould, Harry L GK
b London
Metropolitan Police
1920 Queen's Park Rangers 2

Gould, James A IL
1904 Doncaster Rovers 2

From To Apps Goal

Gould, William (Willie) OL/IL/OR
b Burton-on-Trent q3 1884
1903 1904 Burton United 38 8
1905 Leicester Fosse 6 1
Bristol Rovers
1907 1908 Glossop 33 6
1908 Bradford City 18 2
1909 1910 Manchester City 8 2
Tranmere Rovers

Goulden, John Thomas OR
b Sunderland 26/12/1903 d 1981
North Hull Liberals
Needler's
1924 Hull City 2
Raith Rovers
Yeovil & Petters United
1928 Middlesbrough 0

Goulden, Leonard Arthur (Len) IL/RH
b Hackney 9/7/1912 d 1995
Caps: England Sch/FLge 2/England War 6/ England 14
Dagenham
1931 West Ham United 0
Chelmsford
Leyton
1932 1938 West Ham United 239 54
1939 (West Ham United) (3)
1945 1949 Chelsea 99 17

Gourlay, James Walter IL/RH
b Annbank 1888
Caps: SLge 2
Annbank Juniors
Cambuslang Rangers
Port Glasgow
Morton
1909 1912 Everton 54 8
Morton
Third Lanark

Gourlay, John OR/CH
b Annbank 1876
Annbank
1896 Loughborough 4 1
Motherwell
1898 Newton Heath 1

Gow, Donald Robertson LB
b Blair Atholl 8/2/1868 d 1945
Caps: FLge 1/Scotland 1
Cessnock Bank
Rangers
1891 Sunderland 16
Rangers
1893 1896 Sunderland 82 1
New Brighton Tower
Millwall Athletic
Girvan

Gow, John OR/IR
1903 Liverpool 0
1904 1907 Blackpool 62 4

Gow, John GK
Vale of Leven
Renton
1890 Blackburn Rovers 15
1892 Northwich Victoria 17
West Manchester

Gowdy, William Alexander (Bill) RH/LH
b Belfast 24/12/1903 d 1958
Caps: IrLge 4/Ireland 6
Duncairn Old Boys
Cliftonville Olympic
Highfield
Duncairn Old Boys
Cliftonville Olympic
Dundalk
Ards
Brantwood
Ards
1929 1931 Hull City 65 1
1931 Sheffield Wednesday 1
1932 Gateshead 4
Linfield
Hibernian
Goole Town
Altrincham
1938 Aldershot 3

Gower, Frank GK
b Tunbridge Wells
Tunbridge Wells Rangers
1938 Darlington 7

From To Apps Goal

Gower, Herbert Henry LB
b Acton q2 1899 d 1959
Ealing Celtic
1923 Brentford 2
Southall
Dulwich Hamlet
Botwell Mission
Dulwich Hamlet
Hayes
Uxbridge Town

Gowland, Norman GK
b Butterknowle q1 1902
Chilton Colliery Recreation Athletic
1925 1928 Middlesbrough 5
1930 Stockport County 14
1931 Rotherham United 5

Gracie, Thomas (Tommy) IL/CF
b Glasgow 12/6/1889 d 1915
Caps: SLge 1
Wellwood Star
Strathclyde
Airdrieonians
Hamilton Academical
Arthurlie
Morton
1910 1911 Everton 13 1
1911 1913 Liverpool 32 5
Heart of Midlothian

Gradwell, T IR
1898 Darwen 2

Graham, A OL
b Belfast
1922 Accrington Stanley 1 1

Graham, Alexander Cameron (Alex) IR
b Coatbridge 26/8/1912
Burnbank Amateurs
Vale of Clyde
1934 West Ham United 0
Albion Rovers
Cowdenbeath
Stenhousemuir
Morton
1937 Rochdale 11 4
1937 Bradford Park Avenue 7
1938 Halifax Town 14 3

Graham, Charles John (Jack) RH/LH
b Newcastle 1911
1930 Newcastle United 0
1931 Gillingham 2
Shelbourne
1934 Hartlepools United 5
1935 Stockport County 0
Walker Celtic

Graham, Ernest IR
b New Delaval q3 1906 d 1968
New Delaval Villa
Dundee (trial)
1927 Ashington 14 6
Blyth Spartans
Ashington
New Delaval Villa

Graham, Frederick Todd IR
b Tynemouth 24/3/1912 d 1973
1935 Wolverhampton Wanderers 0
1936 Sheffield United 2 1

Graham, George OL
b North Shields 1900
Preston Colliery
1925 Newcastle United 0
1927 South Shields 0
1928 Carlisle United 7 1

Graham, George Kretchen IL
b Glasgow
Vale of Clyde
Shettleston
Morton
1928 Bournemouth & Boscombe Ath 17 2
Caernarvon Athletic
Boston Town
Waterford
Morton
East Stirlingshire
Ards
Jarrow

Graham, Harry OL
b Belfast 1902
Pill United
1921 1922 Newport County 6 1
Lovells Athletic

From To Apps Goal

Graham, Harry Nicol IL/IR
b Edinburgh 16/12/1887 d 1940
Caps: SLge 1
Granton Oakvale
St Bernard's
1909 1910 Bradford City 11
1911 Birmingham 12 4
Raith Rovers
Heart of Midlothian
1920 1923 Leicester City 110 14
St Bernard's
1925 1926 Reading 12

Graham, Jack IL/CF
b Smethwick 8/1868 d 1932
Smethwick Centaur
Oldbury Broadwell
1889 1891 Aston Villa 18 5
Brierley Hill Alliance
Dudley

Graham, James LH/CH/RH
Stockton
1893 1896 Grimsby Town 84 2
New Brompton

Graham, James Arthur (Jimmy) CF
b Rothwell, Northamptonshire 13/1/1911 d 1987
Desborough Town
1932 1934 Nottingham Forest 32 13
1935 York City 7
1935 Hartlepools United 18 3
1935 1936 Southend United 4 2
1937 Clapton Orient 9 1
Yeovil & Petters United

Graham, John (Johnny) LH
b Ayr 23/2/1857 d 1927
Caps: Scotland 1
Annbank
1888 1889 Preston North End 39

Graham, John CF
b Northumberland 1873
Blyth
1893 Newton Heath 4

Graham, John (Jack) RB
b Derby 12/4/1873 d 1925
Magpie (Clapham)
Cray Wanderers
Millwall Athletic
1897 Woolwich Arsenal 0
Millwall Athletic
1899 Woolwich Arsenal 1
Brentford
Fulham

Graham, John Alexander (Alex) CH/LH/RH
b Hurlford 11/7/1890 d 1943
Caps: Scotland 1
Hurlford
Hamilton Academical
Larkhall United
1912 1924 Woolwich Arsenal 51 2
Vale of Leven
Hamilton Academical
1919 1923 Arsenal 115 15
1924 1925 Brentford 47 10
Folkestone

Graham, John R OL/OR
b Newcastle
Black Diamonds
1901 Newcastle United 6
1903 1904 Bradford City 54 8

Graham, Joseph Gilpin LH
b Hebburn q2 1889 d 1968
Wallsend
1911 1920 Stockport County 86 3
1921 Exeter City 12
New Brighton
Ashton National

Graham, Joseph William LB
b Newcastle q4 1885 d 1969
Bedlington United
Heart of Midlothian
1911 1912 Stockport County 42
Hartlepools United
Durham City

Graham, Leonard (Len) LH
b Leyton 20/8/1901 d 1962
Caps: FLge 1/England 2
Capworth
Leytonstone
1923 1933 Millwall Athletic 313 8

From To Apps Goal

Graham, Robert (Bobby) IR
b Glasgow 1882
Cartha
Queen's Park Strollers
Third Lanark
Fulham
Third Lanark
1906 1907 Everton 2
1907 Bolton Wanderers 0
Third Lanark
Partick Thistle
St Johnstone

Graham, Robert Currie (Bob) RB/LB
b Muirkirk 25/8/1900 d 1965
Kilwinning Rangers
1921 1928 Luton Town 164 5
1929 1930 Norwich City 50
1931 Thames 30
Bedford Town
Luton Davis Athletic

Graham, Robert Henry (Bob) LH/LB
b Middlesbrough 12/10/1900 d 1965
1923 Middlesbrough 0
1924 1925 Darlington 5
1926 1929 Wrexham 126 2
1930 1931 Halifax Town 39
Workington

Graham, Samuel (Sam) CH
Morton
1895 Bury 9

Graham, Samuel (Sam) OR
b Galston 7/4/1878
Galston
Shankhouse
1902 1904 Newcastle United 5
Norwich City
Kilmarnock
Galston
Ayr
Ayr Parkhouse (loan)
Ayr United
Galston

Graham, Samuel J (Sam) LH
Walker Celtic
1936 Hartlepools United 12
Walker Celtic
1938 Bristol Rovers (trial) 0
North Shields

Graham, Thomas (Tommy) CH/LH
b Hamsterley 12/3/1905 d 1983
Caps: FLge 2/England 2
Hamsterley Swifts
Consett Celtic
1927 1938 Nottingham Forest 372 7
1939 (Nottingham Forest) (1)

Graham, Thomas Henry CF
b South Shields q3 1887
1909 Barnsley 1
Castleford Town
Allerton Bywater Colliery
Brentford
Castleford Town

Graham, William (Willie) CH
b Ayr
New Cumnock
1888 Preston North End 5
New Cumnock
Newcastle East End
1893 1896 Newcastle United 88 10

Graham, William OL
1891 1892 Burnley 24 3
1892 1893 Lincoln City 21 2

Graham, William (Bill) IR/OL
b Preston 14/10/1893 d 1984
Dick, Kerr's XI
Lancaster Town
1921 1923 Northampton Town 45 10
1924 Wrexham 6 2
Lancaster Town
Great Harwood
Burscough Rangers
Lytham

Graham, William (Billy) IL/IR
b Hetton-le-Hole 3/10/1914 d 1996
Hetton Juniors
Blyth Spartans
1933 1934 Burnley 5 2
1935 1938 Bury 81 29
1938 1945 Norwich City 17 4
1939 (Norwich City) (3)
Barry Town
Aberaman
Holywell Town

From To Apps Goal

Grainger, Arthur OL
Wath Athletic
1926 Lincoln City 1
Wath Athletic

Grainger, Dennis OR/OL
b Royston, West Yorkshire 5/3/1920 d 1986
South Kirkby
1939 Southport (1)
1945 1947 Leeds United 37 5
1947 1950 Wrexham 98 12
1951 Oldham Athletic 3
Bangor City
Flint Town

Grainger, John RB
b Norton Canes q3 1891 d 1963
Crystal Palace
1921 Tranmere Rovers 1

Grainger, John (Jack) LB
b Royston, West Yorkshire 17/7/1912 d 1976
Frickley Colliery
Royston Athletic
1932 Barnsley 1
1933 1946 Southport 222
Prescot Cables
Hyde United
Clitheroe
Bangor City

Grant, Alick Frank GK
b Peasedown St John 11/8/1916 d 2008
1935 Doncaster Rovers 0
1936 Sheffield United 0
1937 Bury 0
1938 Aldershot 5
1946 Leicester City 2
1946 1947 Derby County 12
1948 Newport County 20
1949 Leeds United 0
1949 York City 3
Matlock Town
Worksop Town
Corby Town

Grant, Duncan C CF
1914 Preston North End 9 3

Grant, Ebenezer OL
b Wolstanton q4 1881
Tunstall Park
1905 Burslem Port Vale 5 1
Stafford Rangers
Burslem Liverpool Road
Tunstall Park

Grant, George OR
b Bonnyrigg
Bonnyrigg Rose Athletic
Stoneyburn
Tranent
Falkirk
Workington
Tranent
Leith Athletic
Albion Rovers
St Bernard's
1938 Clapton Orient 19 4
Ballymena United

Grant, George Melton RH
b Plumstead q2 1891
Woolwich Wesley Guild
Northumberland Oddfellows
Dartford Invicta
1911 1914 Woolwich Arsenal 54 4
Millwall Athletic
1920 1921 Queen's Park Rangers 69 1
Northfleet

Grant, John Wyllie CF
b Strood q1 1891
Cliftonville
(Sweden)
Southport Central
1911 Woolwich Arsenal 4 3
Genoa

Grant, Leonard (Len) LB/RB
b Reading 1892 d 1967
Caps: England Sch
Reading United
1921 1924 Reading 77 1

Grant, Reginald CF
1931 Rochdale 1

Grant, Walter IL/IR
b Cleethorpes q1 1884 d 1961
1903 Grimsby Town 1
Grimsby Rangers
1905 Grimsby Town 8 2
1906 Chesterfield Town 4 2
Grimsby Rangers
Cleethorpes Town

From To Apps Goal

Grant, Walter A IR/CF
b Aberdeen 1890 d 1940
Balnagask
Banks o' Dee
Aberdeen
Raith Rovers
1926 1927 Crystal Palace 21 5
Bedford Town
Walthamstow Grange
Bexleyheath & Welling
Swanley

Grant, William Middleton RB/RH/CH
b Bo'ness 14/11/1904
Vale of Grange
Bo'ness
East Stirlingshire
1927 1934 Blackpool 220
Motherwell

Granville, Arthur David RB/RH
b Llwynypia 8/5/1911 d 1987
Porth United
1934 1938 Cardiff City 98 6

Grapes, Leslie Onslow GK
b Bromley q3 1887
Shepherds Bush
1912 Clapton Orient 2
Shepherds Bush

Grass, George IL
b Morecambe 23/10/1905 d 1988
Bolton-le-Sands
Morecambe
1927 Blackburn Rovers 0
Lancaster Town
1930 1931 Bury 27 6
Lancaster Town

Grassam, William (Billy) OR/CF/IR
b Larbert 20/11/1878
Redcliffe Thistle
Maryhill
1899 Burslem Port Vale 31 5
West Ham United
Celtic
1903 1904 Manchester United 29 13
Leyton
West Ham United
Brentford

Graver, Frederick (Fred) IR/CF
b Craghead 8/9/1897 d 1950
Burnhope Institute
Darlington
Shildon Athletic
1922 Grimsby Town 6 1
West Stanley
1924 Leeds United 3
1925 Southend United 10 1
Wallsend

Gray, Albert (Bert) GK
b Tredegar 23/9/1900 d 1969
Caps: WLge 1/Wales 24
Rhyd Welfare
Rhyd Athletic
Ebbw Vale
1923 1926 Oldham Athletic 97
1926 1928 Manchester City 68
Manchester Central
1930 Coventry City 0
1931 1935 Tranmere Rovers 192
1936 1937 Chester 73
Waterford
Congleton Town

Gray, Alexander Duncan IL
b Glasgow 4/5/1901
Glasgow Perthshire
Johnstone
Vale of Leven
Kilmarnock
1926 Bristol City 8 3
Queen of the South
Morton
Queen of the South

Gray, Alfred (Alf) CH/LH/RH
b Westhoughton 30/8/1910 d 1974
Daisy Hill
1931 Oldham Athletic 0
1932 Torquay United 22 1
1933 Liverpool 0
1934 1935 Lincoln City 32
Newark Town

Gray, Andrew Dunsmore OR
b Newcastle 6/1/1894
Jesmond Villa
1920 Newcastle United 2
Leadgate Park
1921 1922 South Shields 35 5

From To Apps Goal

Gray, Archibald (Archie) RB/LB
b Govan 24/8/1878
Caps: SLge 1/Scotland 1
Govan Columbia
Glasgow Ashfield
Hibernian
1904 1911 Woolwich Arsenal 184
1911 1914 Fulham 24

Gray, Arthur Ernest (Ernie) OL/IL
b Cleethorpes 10/3/1894 d 1973
Cleethorpes Town
1919 Grimsby Town 1
Cleethorpes Town
1924 1926 Grimsby Town 5 1

Gray, D CH
1893 Middlesbrough Ironopolis 2

Gray, Ernest LH
b 1875
Mexborough
1898 Lincoln City 6
New Brompton

Gray, Ernest F (Ernie) OR
1922 Darlington 1

Gray, Frederick John Swithin OL
b Rugeley 15/7/1869 d 1933
Walsall Town Swifts
1889 Aston Villa 2
Birmingham St George's
Warwick County
1889 Preston North End 1 1
Warwick County
Walsall Town Swifts
Edgbaston Crusaders (rugby)
1892 Walsall Town Swifts 7 1
Walsall YMCA

Gray, George RH/LH
b Bolton
1919 1920 Manchester City 3
Chorley
Fleetwood

Gray, George Robert LH/RH/CF
b South Hylton 4/1/1894 d 1972
New Riddick Colliery
Seaham Harbour
Gillingham
Hartlepools United
1920 1921 Swansea Town 39 2
1921 Bury 0
1923 Northampton Town 11
1924 Durham City (trial) 2
Clydebank (trial)
Yoker Athletic
Rushden Town

Gray, George Willie RB
b Ecclesfield 27/2/1896 d 1962
Eastwood Bible Class
1919 Grimsby Town 0
1920 1921 Norwich City 50
1921 1922 Sheffield Wednesday 32

Gray, James A LH
b Bristol 1878 d 1937
Royal Albert
Bristol Rovers
1904 Aston Villa 7
Rangers
Tottenham Hotspur
Leyton

Gray, Matthew (Matt) IL/CH/LH
b Westhoughton 18/4/1907 d 1985
Hindley Green
1927 Tranmere Rovers 1
Atherton
1928 1938 Oldham Athletic 289 59

Gray, Peter (Paddy) CH
b Partick 13/9/1878
Yoker Athletic
Partick Thistle
1897 Liverpool 0
1898 1902 Grimsby Town 121 5
Fulham
Leyton
1906 Burton United 22
Parkgate & Rawmarsh United
Leyton

Gray, Richard GK
b Derby q1 1877
1895 1898 Burton Swifts 93 3
Bristol Rovers
1901 1902 Burton United 50

From To Apps Goal

Gray, Robert OL/IL
b Scotland 1878
Lenzie
Meadowside
Partick Thistle
1899 1900 Everton 20 1
Southampton
Partick Thistle

Gray, Robert Alexander (Alec) IL/IR
b Cowpen 7/10/1903 d 1954
Bishop Auckland
1925 Huddersfield Town 0
1927 1928 Tranmere Rovers 3 1
Northwich Victoria
Mansfield Town
1930 1931 Rotherham United 69 13
1932 Chester 6 1
1932 Southport 7 2
1932 1933 Carlisle United 37 7
1934 Gateshead 11 2
1935 York City 4 1
Bridlington

Gray, Robert SM (Bob) OL
b Stirling 27/2/1872 d 1926
King's Park
1894 Aston Villa 0
1895 1897 Grimsby Town 69 25
Bedminster
1899 Middlesbrough 3
Luton Town

Gray, Thomas (Tom) IL/OR
b Grimsby 1876 d 1944
1898 Gainsborough Trinity 8 1
New Brompton
Queen's Park Rangers
1901 1902 Bury 25 5

Gray, Thomas (Dolly) GK
b Portsmouth 1891
Portsmouth
1919 1920 Clapton Orient 12
Guildford United

Gray, Thomas (Tom) RB
b 1901
1923 Huddersfield Town 0
1924 Hartlepools United 11

Gray, William James (Jimmy) RB
b Glasgow 16/9/1900 d 1978
Glasgow Boys Club
Transvaal
1928 Liverpool 1
1929 1935 Exeter City 213

Grayer, Frank RB
b Brighton 13/2/1890 d 1961
Fazeley
St Mary's Athletic (Southampton)
Southampton
1913 Liverpool 1

Grayson, William (Bill) RH
b Peasley Cross
1925 Lincoln City 0
1926 Crewe Alexandra 1

Greathead, William (Billy) LH
b Grangetown, Sunderland q2 1893 d 1964
Seaham Harbour
Grangetown
Durham City
Dawdon
1921 1922 Durham City 4

Greatorex, George Arthur IR
b Huthwaite 4/12/1899 d 1964
Sutton Junction
1921 Leicester City 11 2
Mansfield Town
Sutton Town
Frickley Colliery
Scarborough
Shirebrook

Greatorex, Lawrence (Laurie) CF
b Unstone q1 1901 d 1960
Sutton Junction
1922 Lincoln City 0
Dronfield
1924 Notts County 4
1925 Southend United 0
Mansfield Town

Greatorex, William Alphonso Henry (Billy) RB
b Preston 3/1/1895 d 1971
Preston Winckley
1919 1920 Preston North End 24
1921 1922 Southport 58
1923 Chesterfield 13
Morecambe

From To Apps Goal

Greatrex, George Kenneth William (Ken) GK
b Liverpool 16/5/1904 d 1981
Orrell
Marine
Burscough Rangers
1928 1929 Wrexham 17
1930 1932 New Brighton 25
1933 Crewe Alexandra (trial) 0
Workington
Runcorn
Stoneycroft St Paul's
Manchester North End

Greatwich, Frank Ernest OR
b Wednesbury q1 1876 d 1936
Wednesbury Old Athletic
Wednesbury Excelsior
1897 Wolverhampton Wanderers 2
1898 Walsall 4 2
Wednesbury Old Athletic

Greaves, Arthur LH
b Doncaster 1908
Drumcondra
1933 Crewe Alexandra 27
1934 Barnsley 3
1935 Watford 0
Boston United
Bath City
Hertford Town

Greaves, Edward RH/LH
b Cardiff q2 1898 d 1964
Porth
1922 Swansea Town 1
1923 Swindon Town 1
Bridgend Town

Greaves, George GK
b Darfield
1935 1936 Rotherham United 35
1937 1938 Aldershot 53
1939 (Aldershot) (3)

Greaves, George Henry RB/LB
b Nottingham 20/6/1897 d 1972
Lincoln Rovers
Chesterfield Municipal
1921 1923 Lincoln City 72
Scunthorpe & Lindsey United
Boston Town
Lincoln Claytons

Greaves, Joseph (Joe) GK
b Ecclesfield q3 1871
1892 Sheffield Wednesday 0
1898 1902 Barnsley 105

Greaves, Thomas (Tommy) RB
b Springwell Colliery 26/3/1892
Hylton Colliery
1911 1919 Bury 66
1921 1927 Darlington 227 1

Greechan, James IL
b Glasgow 1883
Petershill
Hibernian
Bo'ness
Brentford
1907 Clapton Orient 30 8
1907 1908 Glossop 19 3
1909 Stockport County 16 4
Albion Rovers
Carlisle United
Bathgate

Green, A RH/OL
1892 1893 Crewe Alexandra 14

Green, A CF
1895 Wolverhampton Wanderers 2

Green, Adrian (Haydn) IR
b Greasley 18/3/1887 d 1957
Stanton Hill Victoria
1907 Nottingham Forest 0
1908 Chesterfield Town 21 5
Ilkeston United
1910 Manchester United 0
Worksop Town
1912 Aston Villa 0
Newport County
Reading

Green, Albert IR/IL
b Rickmansworth 7/10/1892
Rickmansworth
Watford Orient
Watford
Crystal Palace
Sheppey United
1921 Charlton Athletic 17 3
1922 Millwall Athletic 0
1923 Reading 10 1

From To Apps Goal

Green, Albert IL
b Hanley 1907
Denaby Rovers
Denaby United
1927 Sheffield Wednesday 0
Denaby United
Gainsborough Trinity
1934 West Ham United 0
1935 Lincoln City 23 6
Newark Town
Gainsborough Trinity

Green, Albert Willis (Willie) OL
b Sheffield 12/3/1912 d 2000
Dore
1936 1937 Sheffield Wednesday 6 1
1938 Barnsley 0
Gainsborough Trinity

Green, Alfred V (Alf) LH
b Rotherham
Rotherham Town
1920 1921 Exeter City 43

Green, Arthur LB
b Grantham 1885
1911 Birmingham 1
1912 Lincoln City 0
Mansfield Town

Green, Arthur William CF
b Aberystwyth 12/5/1881 d 1966
Caps: Wales 8
Aberystwyth
Swindon Town
1900 Aston Villa 0
Ebbw Vale
Walsall
1902 1906 Notts County 134 56
1906 1908 Nottingham Forest 38 19
1909 Stockport County 7 1
Brierley Hill Alliance

Green, Benjamin Haigh (Benny) IR
b Barnsley 23/2/1882 d 1917
Penistone Juniors
1901 1903 Barnsley 45 18
1903 1908 Small Heath/Birmingham 185 44
1909 1910 Burnley 71 29
1911 1913 Preston North End 73 23
1913 1914 Blackpool 31 4

Green, Ellis OL
b Whittle-le-Woods q2 1882 d 1942
Chorley
1900 1901 Preston North End 27 8
Chorley
Colne
Pendlebury

Green, Francis (Frank) IR/IL
b Ashington 5/1902 d 1982
Choppington
1925 Ashington 0
Frickley Colliery
1927 1929 Wolverhampton Wanderers 37 17
1929 Crewe Alexandra 30 7
Peterborough & Fletton United
1930 Crewe Alexandra 11 2
1931 Barnsley 4
Racing Club de Paris
Northwich Victoria
Rhyl Athletic
Nantwich

Green, Frederick Zeanes (Freddie) RB/LB
b Sheffield 9/9/1916 d 1998
Mosborough Trinity
1935 1937 Torquay United 86
1938 1947 Brighton & Hove Albion 26

Green, George Frederick LH/RH
b Northowram 21/12/1914 d 1995
1936 Bradford Park Avenue 2
1945 1947 Huddersfield Town 9 1
1947 1948 Reading 44 6

Green, George Henry LH
b Leamington Spa 2/5/1901 d 1980
Caps: FLge 3/England 8
Leamington St John's
Leamington Imperial
Leamington Town
Nuneaton Town
1923 1933 Sheffield United 393 10
Leamington Town

Green, George Henry RH
b Barry Dock 12/11/1912 d 1994
Caps: Wales War 2/Wales 4
Barry
1934 Charlton Athletic 0
Espanyol Barcelona
1936 1938 Charlton Athletic 57 3
1939 (Charlton Athletic) (3)

From To Apps Goal

Green, Harold (Harry) LB/RB
b West Bromwich 1860 d 1900
George Salter's Works
1888 1890 West Bromwich Albion 33
Old Hill Wanderers

Green, Harold (Harry) RH/CH/LH
b Sedgley 3/8/1904 d 1975
Coseley Amateurs
Redditch
1925 Sheffield United 1
1927 Nottingham Forest 4
1928 Halifax Town 1
Hereford United
Kidderminster Harriers

Green, Harold (Harry) OR
b Sheffield 8/10/1909
1928 Oldham Athletic 1
Mexborough Town
1930 1933 Leeds United 19 4
1934 Bristol City 12 1
1935 York City 42 8
Frickley Colliery

Green, Harry CH
b Billinge 18/11/1908 d 1978
Burscough Rangers
Northwich Victoria
1928 Wigan Borough 3
Orrell YMCA
Billinge Juniors

Green, Horace RB/RH/LB
b Barnsley 23/4/1918 d 2000
Worsborough Bridge Old Boys
1937 1948 Halifax Town 155 5
1939 (Halifax Town) (3)
1948 1954 Lincoln City 212 14

Green, J LB
1894 Darwen 1

Green, James OR
b Wheelton
1898 1899 Preston North End 6
Chorley

Green, James OL/CF
b Whittle-le-Woods q3 1879
1919 1920 Preston North End 7
1921 Exeter City 6
Bideford Town

Green, James Huntley IL
b Shilbottle 12/6/1915 d 1984
1934 Gateshead 0
1935 Accrington Stanley 15 2
1936 Walsall 5
Queen of the South

Green, John IR/CF
b Blackburn d 1927
1919 Blackburn Rovers 0
Fleetwood
1921 1922 Nottingham Forest 11 2
1923 Luton Town 26 5
1924 Southend United (trial) 0
Lancaster Town

Green, John LB
b Atherton 1919
1936 Plymouth Argyle 0
1937 Manchester City 0
Altrincham (loan)
1938 Accrington Stanley 13

Green, John A IR
b St Helens 9/1894 d 1966
1919 Wolverhampton Wanderers 6 1

Green, John H CH
b Newcastle 19/3/??
1929 Newcastle United 0
1930 Gateshead 2
Usworth Colliery
1933 1935 Doncaster Rovers 47
1936 Darlington 7
Denaby United

Green, Joseph (Joe) LB
1914 Leeds City 1

Green, Joseph James GK
Derby q1 1871
Derby Bedford Rangers
1894 Derby County 7
Belper Town

Green, Robert Edward (Bob) IL
b Tewkesbury q1 1912 d 1949
1929 1930 Bournemouth & Boscombe Ath 6
1931 Derby County 1
1933 Manchester United 9 4
1934 1935 Stockport County 48 19
Cheltenham Town

From To Apps Goal

Green, Ronald Clarence George (Ronnie) OL/IL/IR
b Frampton Cotterell 12/3/1912 d 1979
Coalpit Heath
Bath City
1932 Bristol Rovers 22 2
1933 Arsenal 0
1934 1935 Notts County 36 5
1936 Charlton Athletic 3 2
1937 Swansea Town 8 4
Coalpit Heath

Green, Thomas IR/CF
b King's Heath 1873
Coles Farm Unity
Birmingham St George's
1894 1895 West Bromwich Albion 8 2
1896 Small Heath 0
Oldbury Town

Green, Thomas (Tommy) OR/CF
b Liverpool 1879
Tranmere Rovers
1899 1900 New Brighton Tower 7 3
1901 1902 Liverpool 7 1
Swindon Town
Stockport County
1904 1905 Middlesbrough 37 9
Queen's Park Rangers
1907 1908 Stockport County 61 12
Exeter City
St Helens Town
Tranmere Rovers

Green, Thomas (Tommy) CF
b Liverpool 25/11/1893 d 1975
Southport Vulcan
1919 West Ham United 3
Southport
South Liverpool
1921 Accrington Stanley 30 23
1922 Stockport County 31 16
1923 Clapton Orient 24 10
Heart of Midlothian
Third Lanark
Flint Town
Wavertree Albion
Milners Safe Works

Green, Thomas (Tommy 'Toby') OL
b Preston 26/2/1900 d 1973
Leyland
Hamilton Central
Dick, Kerr's XI
1920 Preston North End 1
1922 Southport 9
Dick, Kerr's XI
Colne

Green, Thomas (Tommy) IR
b Droitwich 5/1913
Droitwich Spa
Droitwich Comrades
1933 1936 West Bromwich Albion 13 3
1936 1938 West Ham United 40 6
1938 Coventry City 9 2
1939 (Coventry City) (1) (2)
Worcester City
Bromyard

Green, Thomas Foster (Tommy) OR/IR
b Easington 24/8/1907 d 1972
Easington Rovers
Easington Colliery
1932 1935 Newport County 56 17
Easington Colliery

Green, Thomas W (Tommy) IR
b Worcester 8/1863 d 1921
Dreadnought
Mitchell St George's
Small Heath Alliance
Wolverhampton Wanderers
Church Villa
Mitchell St George's
Aston Unity
Great Lever
Mitchell St George's
West Bromwich Albion
1888 Aston Villa 22 14
Kidderminster Harriers
Birmingham St George's
Worcester Rovers

Green, W IL
1903 1904 Glossop 16 3

Green, William OR
Gateshead NER
1903 Bury 1
Colne

From To Apps Goal

Green, William LB
b Billinge
Skelmersdale United
Burscough Rangers
1929 Wigan Borough 12
Connah's Quay & Shotton
Billinge Juniors

Green, William John (Billy) GK
b Gravesend q1 1881
Gravesend United
Brentford
1903 1908 Burnley 147
1908 1909 Bradford Park Avenue 31

Greenaway, David OR
b Coatdyke 24/12/1889
Shettleston
1908 1919 Woolwich Arsenal 161 13

Greene, Christopher (Christy) RH/IR/LH
b Dublin 1/12/1911 d 1975
Brideville
Shelbourne
1933 1934 Southport 49 1
1934 1935 Wolverhampton Wanderers 7 2
1936 Swansea Town 4
1937 Bury 0
Workington

Greener, Robert (Bob) LH/IR
b Birtley 17/7/1899 d 1970
Birtley Colliery
1921 1931 Crystal Palace 292 5
1932 York City 24

Greenfield, George William IL
b Hackney 4/8/1908 d 1981
Lea Bridge Gasworks
1931 1934 Tottenham Hotspur 31 11

Greenhalgh, ? FB
1900 Blackpool 1

Greenhalgh, Harry Woodgate RB/LB
b Bolton 27/6/1900 d 1982
Chorley Old Road Congregational
Atherton
1924 1928 Bolton Wanderers 70

Greenhalgh, John Stanley IR/OR/IL
b Bolton 16/7/1898 d 1987
St Augustine's
Leyland
1922 1924 Burnley 7
1925 Barrow 0
1925 Accrington Stanley 13 3

Greenhalgh, Norman LB/RB
b Bolton 10/8/1914 d 1995
Caps: FLge 1/England War 1
1933 Bolton Wanderers 0
1935 1937 New Brighton 77 8
1937 1948 Everton 106 1
1939 (Everton) (3)
Bangor City

Greenhalgh, Samuel (Sam) CH/RH
b Eagley 7/1882 d 1955
Caps: FLge 4
Eagley
Turton
1902 1905 Bolton Wanderers 96 6
1905 1907 Aston Villa 46 2
1907 1913 Bolton Wanderers 163 13
Chorley

Greenhalgh, Samuel CH/LH
b Basford q2 1883
Sutton Town
1904 1905 Gainsborough Trinity 11
Denaby United
Eastwood Rangers

Greensill, Edwin IR
b Rotherham q3 1877 d 1950
Swallownest Rovers
Swallownest Bible Class
Ulley Church
Royston United
1901 Sheffield United 4 1
1902 1903 Gainsborough Trinity 34 6
Thornhill United
Aughton

Greenwell, Ernest Edward (Ernie) IL
b Wardley Colliery 4/1/1901 d 1965
Easington Colliery Welfare
1920 1925 South Shields 60 15
1927 Durham City 36 5
Easington Colliery Welfare

From To Apps Goal

Greenwell, John Wilfred (Jack) CH
b Crook 18/2/1901
Stanhope
Crook Town
Ferryhill Athletic
Annfield Plain
1928 1930 Norwich City 47 2
1931 Swindon Town 15 2
Bath City
Durham City
Western House

Greenwood, JC OL
1893 Darwen 1

Greenwood, Jonathan W RB
b Todmorden
1905 Burnley 11
Nelson

Greenwood, Thomas OR
1899 Burnley 1

Greenwood, Wilson OL
b Halifax q3 1871 d 1943
Blue Star (Burnley)
Brierfield
Accrington
1894 Sheffield United 1
Rossendale
Nelson
Rochdale
Warmley
1898 1899 Grimsby Town 57 13
1900 Newton Heath 3

Greer, Thomas Gershom CF
b Bathgate 1889
Coatbridge Rob Roy
1910 1911 Birmingham 2
Reading

Greer, William Henry (Billy) CH/RH
b Preston 28/2/1872 d 1937
1891 1896 Preston North End 107 7
1898 Darwen 6

Gregg, Robert Edmund (Bob) IL/IR
b Ferryhill 4/2/1904 d 1991
Ferryhill Athletic
Cornford Juniors
Spennymoor United
Chilton Colliery Recreation Athletic
1926 1927 Darlington 40 21
1928 1930 Sheffield Wednesday 37 7
1930 1933 Birmingham 66 11
1933 1937 Chelsea 48 5
Boston United
Sligo Rovers

Gregg, Willis RB/LB
b Woodhouse 21/7/1908 d 1989
Mexborough Town
1932 Chesterfield 1
1934 1935 Torquay United 48
1936 Accrington Stanley 33
1937 1938 Manchester City 9
1938 Chester 29 2
1939 (Chester) (3)
Beighton Miners Welfare
Buxton

Gregory, Albert LH/OL
b New Moston 1913
Manchester North End
1934 Bury 6
Manchester North End
1938 Rochdale 9

Gregory, Charles Frederick (Fred) RB/LB/CF
b Doncaster 24/10/1911 d 1985
Brodsworth Main Colliery
1929 Doncaster Rovers 13 3
1931 1933 Manchester City 21 2
1933 1937 Reading 129 6
1937 1945 Crystal Palace 43 9
1946 Hartlepools United 21
1946 Rotherham United 1

Gregory, Clarence OL
b Aston Manor 27/10/1900 d 1975
Caps: England Sch
Wellington Town
1920 Sunderland 1
1922 Queen's Park Rangers 24 1
Yeovil & Petters United
Wellington Town
Hereford United
Leamington Town
Rugby Town

From To Apps Goal

Gregory, Edward (Ted) LB
b Radcliffe 1902
Rossendale United (trial)
1923 Oldham Athletic 0
1925 1926 Accrington Stanley 10
Hurst
Manchester Central
Witton Albion
Mossley
Stalybridge Celtic

Gregory, Frederick J RB
b London
Caps: England Amat
Wimbledon
1927 Millwall 3
Wimbledon
Leyton

Gregory, Frederick James (Fred) LB
b Pinner 21/10/1886 d 1937
Pinner
1920 1925 Watford 168 1

Gregory, George LB
b Hyde q4 1873
1893 Grimsby Town 1

Gregory, Howard OL/IL/IR
b Aston Manor 6/4/1893 d 1954
Aston Manor
Birchfield Trinity
1911 1924 West Bromwich Albion 162 39

Gregory, J OL
1897 1898 Bolton Wanderers 6

Gregory, John (Jack) OL/IL/LH
b Birmingham
Willenhall Swifts
1920 1922 Queen's Park Rangers 112 21
Yeovil & Petters United

Gregory, John Thomas (Jack) OR
b Dudley q4 1886
Victoria Road Swifts
Darlaston
1908 Wolverhampton Wanderers 1
Dudley Town
St Philip's

Gregory, Julius LB/RB
b Romiley q3 1881 d 1916
Unsworth
1903 1904 Bury 14
1905 Manchester City 3
Brighton & Hove Albion
Luton Town

Gregory, Robert James (Bob) LB
b Croydon 26/8/1902 d 1973
Croydon Juniors
1924 Crystal Palace 0
1925 1927 Fulham 37
1928 Norwich City 0
Commerce House (Croydon)

Gregory, Valentine Francis (Val) RH/RB
b Hendon 14/2/1888 d 1940
Caps: SoLge 3
Reading
Watford
1920 1922 Wolverhampton Wanderers 96 2

Gregson, Alfred (Alf) IL
b Bury q2 1889 d 1968
Unitarians (Rochdale)
Rochdale
1913 1914 Grimsby Town 49 12
1919 1920 Bury 15 1
Rossendale United

Gregson, William RB
Herrington Colliery
1932 Rochdale 1
Horden Colliery Welfare

Gregson, William Cameron Smart (Bill) IL
b Stockton 8/3/1890 d 1977
Stockton
1914 Blackpool 3
1920 Sunderland 0
1921 Hartlepools United 1
Chilton Colliery Recreation Athletic
Kelloe
Trimdon Grange Colliery
(USA)

Greig, Andrew CF
b Inverness 1887
Inverness Clachnacuddin
1909 Lincoln City 2
Inverness Clachnacuddin

From To Apps Goal

Greig, Andrew John Smith GK
b Aberdeen 19/10/1893
Mugiemoss
Aberdeen
Raith Rovers (loan)
1921 1923 Darlington 95
Shildon
Montrose

Grendon, Frank Joseph W RH
b Farnham 5/9/1891 d 1984
Queen's Park Rangers
1920 1921 Northampton Town 38
Rushden Town

Grenyer, Alan LH
b North Shields 31/8/1892 d 1953
Caps: FLge 1
North Shields Athletic
1910 1922 Everton 142 9
1924 1928 South Shields 41 5

Gresham, James OL
b Branston q1 1869
Lincoln City
Doncaster Rovers
1892 Lincoln City 22 5
Rossendale
1894 Lincoln City 5 1
Gainsborough Trinity
Thames Ironworks

Gresham, William Henry GK
b Potterhanworth q2 1864
Gainsborough Trinity
1892 1893 Lincoln City 35

Gretton, Thomas (Tommy) GK
b Cannock q2 1907 d 1964
Wolverhampton United
1929 Queen's Park Rangers 4
1930 Walsall 3

Grewer, James (Jimmy) CH
b Dundee 2/1865 d 1950
Sunderland Albion
1893 Middlesbrough Ironopolis 26 2
1894 1897 Stoke 75 1
Gravesend United

Grey, Thomas (Tom) CH
b Whitley Bay q1 1885
Caps: England Amat
Whitley Bay Athletic
1907 Sunderland 1
Bedlington United
1907 Newcastle United 0
Blyth Spartans
1913 Newcastle United 1
Newcastle Bohemians

Gribben, William Howat (Bill) CH
b Glasgow 28/10/1906 d 1969
Beeston Parish Church
1928 Leeds United 3
Harrogate AFC

Grice, Frank LH/CH
b Derby 13/11/1908 d 1988
Caps: IrLge 1
Linby Colliery
Linfield
1931 1935 Notts County 102 4
1935 1938 Tottenham Hotspur 47 1
Glentoran
Dundalk
Glentoran

Grice, Neve Joseph OR
b Acton q2 1881 d 1950
Ealing
1905 Woolwich Arsenal 1

Grice, Reuben OL
b Ruddington q1 1886 d 1967
Grove Celtic
1910 1911 Notts County 4
Rotherham County
1914 Burnley 2

From To Apps Goal

Grice, Robert (Bob) CH/LB
b Sutton, Lancashire 12/4/1907 d 2004
Peasley Cross Athletic
St Helens Town
Runcorn
Conway
Sutton Commercial
Colwyn Bay
Flint Town
1929 Liverpool 0
Skelmersdale United
Ashton National
Peasley Cross Athletic
1932 New Brighton (trial) 3
Peasley Cross Athletic
1932 1934 Oldham Athletic 26
1935 Southport 39 2
Stalybridge Celtic
Clitheroe
Ashton National

Grice (Le Grice), Thomas William (Tommy RH/CH
b Sutton-in-Ashfield 17/3/1908 d 1996
Worksop Town
Mansfield Town
Worksop Town
1932 Birmingham 0
1933 Torquay United 4
1934 Walsall 5
Dunkirk Olympique
Teversal Colliery

Grierson, George LH
b Lesmahagow
1926 1929 Preston North End 5
1930 Rochdale 31
Ashton National

Grierson, Robert Tuck (Bob) IR
b Newcastle q1 1887 d 1944
Scotswood
1907 Newcastle United 0
1908 Bradford Park Avenue 4 1
Seaham Harbour
Rochdale
Hartlepools United
Swansea Town
Rochdale

Grierson, W LH
1892 Bootle 18 3

Grieve, James CF
b Walkergate 1906
Wallsend
1931 1932 Darlington 29 13
St Johnstone

Grieve, Robert B (Bob) IR/CF
b Greenock 28/3/1884
Greenock Volunteers
Morton
1906 1908 Manchester City 44 18
Accrington Stanley
1910 Leicester Fosse 4 2
Accrington Stanley
Southport Central
Accrington Stanley
Crewe Alexandra
Witton Albion

Grieve, Stanley Edawrd CH
b Sunderland 8/4/1902 d 1978
Bishop Auckland
1923 Durham City 1
Esh Winning
Crook Town
Southwick (Co Durham)
Sunderland Co-operative
Roker St Andrew's

Grieve, Thomas (Tom) OR
b Leith 7/7/1875 d 1948
Northfleet
New Brompton
Gravesend United
1900 Woolwich Arsenal 6
Brentford
Watford
Brighton & Hove Albion
Northfleet

Grieves, James RB/CH
b North Seaton 13/1/1905 d 1984
Seaton Delaval
Stakeford United
1924 Ashington 0
Seaton Delaval
Sheppey United
1926 1928 Ashington 47 1
Cramlington Village
Durham Divisional Police
East Cramlington Black Watch
Dudley United

From	To	Club	Apps	Goal
Griffin, Albert			CF	
1902		Stockport County	2	
Griffin, Arthur			OL/CF/OR	
b Walsall 3/6/1871			d 1945	
		Brierley Hill Alliance		
		Walsall Town Swifts		
1892	1895	Wolverhampton Wanderers	69	12
1896	1899	Walsall	82	30
Griffin, Henry (Harry)			IR	
b Swindon q4 1878			d 1957	
1902		Aston Villa	1	
Griffin, J			IL	
1892		Burton Swifts	3	
Griffin, James Henry (Jimmy)			LB	
b Newport q4 1898			d 1974	
		Oak Villa		
1920	1922	Newport County	77	
1923		Stockport County	2	
		Ebbw Vale		
Griffin, Michael (Mick)			OL	
b Middlesbrough q4 1886				
		Darlington St Augustine's		
1907	1908	Liverpool	4	
		Crystal Palace		
		Hartlepools United		
1912	1914	Barnsley	69	7
Griffin, Ronald Henry George			OR	
b Camberwell Green 18/10/1919			d 1987	
		Larkhall Thistle		
		St Mirren		
1938		Lincoln City	1	
1938		Brentford	0	
1939		Watford	0	
Griffith, Robert (Bob)			OR	
b Dublin 28/9/1907			d 1976	
Caps: Eire 1				
		Hillview		
		Great Southern Railway		
1931		Tottenham Hotspur	0	
		Drumcondra		
		Shelbourne		
1932	1934	Southport	57	10
1934		Walsall	8	1
Griffiths, Arthur			RB/LB/LH	
b Aston 16/3/1879				
		Park Mills		
		Lozells		
		Bristol Eastville Rovers		
1903	1911	Notts County	163	1
Griffiths, Arthur			IR/OR/OL	
b Stoke-on-Trent 1885				
		Hartshill		
1905	1907	Stoke	13	1
1908		Oldham Athletic	25	4
		Stoke		
		Wrexham		
Griffiths, Arthur Alexander			OL/IL	
b Tonypandy 23/4/1908			d 1995	
		Barry		
1931		Torquay United	5	1
1933		Newport County	1	
		Barry		
		Cheltenham Town		
		Barry		
		Newry Town		
		Glentoran		
1938		Rochdale	14	5
1938		Stoke City	4	
Griffiths, Charles			IL	
b Shropshire 1882				
		Oswestry Olympics		
		Chirk		
		Oswestry United		
		St Helens Town		
1903		Barnsley	0	
		Luton Town		
		Coventry City		
		Barrow		
1907		Preston North End	0	
1907		Lincoln City	1	
		Wellington Town		
		Wrexham		
Griffiths, David			OR	
b Coatbridge 1889				
		Renfrew Victoria		
		Petershill		
		Blantyre Victoria		
		Third Lanark		
1908		Bolton Wanderers	4	
		Plymouth Argyle		

From	To	Club	Apps	Goal
Griffiths, Edward Oliver			OR	
b Tipton 5/3/1916			d 2003	
		Stourbridge		
1937		Luton Town	6	1
Griffiths, Elwyn			RB	
1924		Merthyr Town	3	
Griffiths, Frederick John (Fred)			GK	
b Presteigne 13/9/1873			d 1917	
Caps: Wales 1				
		South Shore		
		Clitheroe		
		South Shore		
		Blackpool		
		Stalybridge Rovers		
		Millwall Athletic		
		Tottenham Hotspur		
1901		Preston North End	10	
		West Ham United		
		New Brompton		
1906		Middlesbrough	0	
		Moore's Athletic (Shirebrook)		
Griffiths, George E			LB	
		Hoole Alexandra		
1938		Chester	6	
Griffiths, Harold (Harry)			RB/LB	
b Middlesbrough 2/1/1886				
1905	1907	Liverpool	6	
1908		Chesterfield Town	22	1
		Partick Thistle		
Griffiths, Harry Stanley			CH	
b Liverpool 17/11/1912			d 1981	
1932		Everton	0	
1935	1946	Port Vale	103	3
1939		(Port Vale)	(2)	
Griffiths, Henry			IL	
b Aston 29/11/1876				
1898	1899	Burton Swifts	68	23
		Bristol Rovers		
		Reading		
1903		Nottingham Forest	8	1
		Bristol Rovers		
		Millwall Athletic		
		Kidderminster Harriers		
Griffiths, Hillary (Hill)			RH	
b Wednesfield 8/1871			d 1940	
Caps: FLge 1				
		Wednesfield Rovers		
1889	1900	Wolverhampton Wanderers	181	1
Griffiths, Isaac (Ike)			GK	
1890		Wolverhampton Wanderers	1	
Griffiths, James Stephen (Steve)			IR	
b Stairfoot 23/2/1914			d 1998	
		Ardsley Athletic		
		Barnsley Main Colliery Welfare		
		Thurnscoe Victoria		
1934		Chesterfield	0	
1937	1938	Halifax Town	76	14
1939		Portsmouth	0	
1946		Aldershot	42	9
1947	1950	Barnsley	65	29
1951	1952	York City	74	12
		Denaby United		
Griffiths, Jeremiah Albert			RH/LH	
b Birmingham 9/1872			d 1940	
		Birmingham St George's		
1895	1896	Aston Villa	2	
		Bilston United		
		Bloxwich Strollers		
Griffiths, John			RB/LB	
b Fenton 15/9/1909				
		Shirebrook		
1929	1931	Wolverhampton Wanderers	5	
1932	1933	Bolton Wanderers	24	
1933	1938	Manchester United	165	1
1939		(Manchester United)	(3)	
		Hyde United		
Griffiths, John Charles Ruskin (Jack)			CF	
b Hednesford 1888			d 1966	
		Bushbury White Star		
		Goldthorn Park		
		Willenhall		
		Green Heath Albion		
		Hednesford Town		
1913	1914	Wolverhampton Wanderers	13	2
		Hednesford Town		
		Wellington Town		
		Hednesford Town		

From	To	Club	Apps	Goal
Griffiths, John Edward			RH	
b Aston q2 1876			d 1953	
		Soho Villa		
		Halesowen		
1895		Aston Villa	0	
1898	1901	Grimsby Town	85	5
		Wellingborough		
		Northampton Town		
Griffiths, John Evan			OL	
b Gwersyllt 30/6/1916			d 1997	
		Druids		
1935		Chester	0	
1936	1938	Tranmere Rovers	16	1
Griffiths, Joseph A			RH	
1920		Gillingham	5	
		Sheppey United		
Griffiths, Joseph Leonard (Joe)			OL	
b Wolverhampton q3 1890				
		Dudley Town		
		Bristol Rovers		
1920		Bury	12	
1920	1923	Stockport County	50	3
1924		Tranmere Rovers	8	
Griffiths, Joseph Russell (Joe)			CF	
b New Tredegar				
1930		Wolverhampton Wanderers	1	
1931	1932	Stockport County	48	33
Griffiths, Lewis Henry (Lew)			CF	
b Tonypandy 7/9/1903			d 1985	
		Mid-Rhondda United		
1925		Bristol Rovers	1	
		Mid-Rhondda United		
1927		Torquay United	12	8
1928	1929	Crystal Palace	36	20
1930		Fulham	2	
1931		Cardiff City	0	
1932		Gateshead	0	
Griffiths, Philip Henry			OR	
b Tylorstown 25/10/1905			d 1978	
Caps: Wales 1				
		Tylorstown		
		Wattstown		
1925		Stoke City (trial)	0	
1926	1930	Port Vale	85	30
1931	1932	Everton	8	3
1933		West Bromwich Albion	0	
1934		Cardiff City	12	1
		Folkestone		
Griffiths, Richard W			LH	
b London				
		Barking Town		
1920	1921	Millwall Athletic	16	
Griffiths, Robert (Bob)			LH	
b Brynteg 27/3/1889			d 1983	
		Stansty Juniors		
		Brymbo Victoria		
		Summerhill Victoria		
1911		Bolton Wanderers	0	
		Chester		
		Garston		
		Wrexham		
		Shrewsbury Town		
1921		Wrexham	1	
		Holyhead Town		
		Holyhead Railway Institute		
Griffiths, Robert (Bob)			CH	
b Chapeltown 9/11/??				
		Pollok Juniors		
1932	1938	Chelsea	42	
Griffiths, Stanley (Stan)			IL/OL	
b Pentre 8/2/1911			d 2003	
1931		Cardiff City	0	
1932		Chester	0	
1933		Gillingham	4	
1934		Cardiff City	2	2
		Bangor City		
		Dundalk		
		Grantham		
Griffiths, Thomas (Tom)			LH	
b Wavertree 1888				
1909		Blackburn Rovers	0	
		Exeter City		
1912	1913	Clapton Orient	12	
		Llanelly		
Griffiths, Thomas (Tommy)			CF	
b Willington Quay q3 1901				
		Willington St Aidan's		
1922		Lincoln City	22	7
		Jarrow		
1922		Darlington (trial)	0	
1922		Hartlepools United (trial)	0	
1923		Ashington	1	
		Jarrow		

From	To	Club	Apps	Goal
Griffiths, Thomas Percival (Tom)			CH/RB/RH	
b Moss 21/2/1906			d 1981	
Caps: Wales 21				
		Ffrith Valley		
		Wrexham Boys Club		
1922	1926	Wrexham	35	2
1926	1930	Everton	76	9
1931	1932	Bolton Wanderers	48	6
1932	1935	Middlesbrough	88	1
1935	1936	Aston Villa	65	1
1938		Wrexham	10	
Griffiths, William (Billy)			CH	
b Manchester q4 1876				
		Berry's Association		
1898	1904	Newton Heath/Manchester Utd	157	27
		Atherton Church House		
Griffiths, William			CF	
b Wombwell				
		Mitchell's Main		
1906		Barnsley	7	4
Griffiths, William (Walter)			IL	
b Nottingham 1886				
		Ilkeston		
1907	1908	Barnsley	16	3
Griffiths, William Malwyn (Mal)			OR	
b Merthyr Tydfil 8/3/1919			d 1969	
Caps: Wales 11				
		Merthyr Thursday		
1936		Arsenal	0	
		Margate		
1937		Arsenal	9	5
1938	1955	Leicester City	373	66
1939		(Leicester City)	(1)	(1)
		Burton Albion		
Griffiths, William Thomas (Billy)			CF	
b Pontefract 9/6/1912			d 1987	
		Upton Colliery		
		Goole Town		
1933		Sunderland	0	
1935	1936	New Brighton	24	7
Griggs, Philip Ronald			IR	
b Southampton 12/6/1918			d 1980	
		Spring Albion		
1938		Southampton	1	
Grime, John			GK	
1902		Bolton Wanderers	3	
Grimes, William John (Billy)			OR/OL	
b Hitchin 27/3/1886			d 1936	
		Hitchin St John's		
		Hitchin Town		
		Watford		
1907	1908	Glossop	45	10
1908	1909	Bradford City	17	1
1909	1914	Derby County	161	11
		Luton Town		
Grimsdell, Arthur			LH	
b Watford 23/3/1894			d 1963	
Caps: England Sch/FLge 1/England 6				
		Watford St Stephen's		
		Watford		
		St Albans City		
		Watford		
1911	1928	Tottenham Hotspur	324	26
1929		Clapton Orient	11	
Grimsdell, Ernest Frederick (Ernie)			LB	
b Watford q3 1892			d 1947	
Caps: England Amat				
		Watford St Stephen's		
		Watford		
		Watford Orient		
		St Albans City		
		Reading		
		Watford		
1920		Queen's Park Rangers	20	
		Guildford United		
1922		Queen's Park Rangers	2	
		Chatham		
		Dartford		
Grimshaw, William (Billy)			OR	
b Burnley 30/4/1890			d 1968	
Caps: FLge 1				
		Livingstone United		
		Barnoldswick United		
1910		Burnley	0	
		Colne		
1912	1914	Bradford City	7	1
1920	1923	Cardiff City	108	17
1923	1926	Sunderland	70	6
		JS Driver's (Bradford)		

From To Apps Goal

Grimwood, John Barton (Jack) LH/CH/RH
b South Shields 25/10/1898 d 1977
South Shields
1919 1926 Manchester United 196 8
Aldershot Town
1927 Blackpool 7
Altrincham
Taylor Brothers (Trafford)

Gripton, Ernest William (Billy) CH
b Tipton 2/7/1920 d 1981
Brownhills Albion
Toll End Wesley
1938 1947 West Bromwich Albion 15
1939 (West Bromwich Albion) (3)
1948 Luton Town 3
1950 1951 Bournemouth & Boscombe Ath 79
Worcester City

Grocock, JE OR
1894 Burton Wanderers 1

Grocott, Frederick RB
b Paisley 1900
Walker Celtic
1922 1924 Lincoln City 60

Grogan, John (Johnny) CH/RH
b Paisley 30/10/1915 d 1976
St Mirren Boys Guild
Paisley Carlisle
Shawfield Juniors
1935 1946 Leicester City 46
1947 1951 Mansfield Town 201
Bentley Engineering

Groome, Joseph Phoenix George (Joe) CF
b Apsley 1/9/1901 d 1956
Apsley Town
1926 Northampton Town 13 6
1927 1928 Watford 17 14
1929 Queen's Park Rangers 0

Grosvenor, Arthur Thomas (Tom) IR
b Netherton 22/11/1908 d 1980
Caps: FLge 1/England 3
Tippity Green Victoria
Vono Works
Stourbridge
1927 West Bromwich Albion (trial) 0
1927 Wolverhampton Wandrs (trial) 0
1931 1935 Birmingham 108 17
1935 1936 Sheffield Wednesday 22 1
1937 1938 Bolton Wanderers 53 7
Dudley Town

Grosvenor, Percy LH
b Dudley 17/3/1911 d 1999
Dudley Works
Evesham Town
1933 1938 Leicester City 168 1
1939 (Leicester City) (1)

Grosvenor, Sydney Morris RB
b Dudley 18/8/1881 d 1971
Willenhall Swifts
1904 Wolverhampton Wanderers 2
Crewe Alexandra
Worcester City
Stafford Royal
Walsall

Groves, Albert CH/RH
b Newport 1/1886 d 1960
Aberdare Town
1909 1919 Wolverhampton Wanderers 200 18
1921 1923 Walsall 79 15

Groves, Arthur IR/IL
b Killamarsh 27/9/1907 d 1979
Langwith Colliery
1927 1928 Halifax Town 30 5
1928 1932 Blackburn Rovers 65 26
1933 1935 Derby County 64 17
1935 1938 Portsmouth 80 13
1939 Stockport County (2)
Atherstone Town
Heanor Athletic

Groves, Edwin (Teddy) RB/CF/RH
b Walsall q4 1900 d 1968
Talbot Stead Tube Works
1921 1929 Walsall 244 25
Shrewsbury Town
Wellington Town

From To Apps Goal

Groves, Frederick (Fred) IR
b Lincoln 6/5/1892 d 1980
South Bar
1909 Lincoln City 7 1
Worksop Town
1911 Sheffield United 0
1912 Huddersfield Town 4
Worksop Town
Pontypridd
1921 Tranmere Rovers 12 7
1921 1922 Stoke 41 13
1924 1925 Crystal Palace 14 2
Rhyl Athletic
Sutton Town

Groves, Frederick William (Freddie) OR/IR
b Shadwell 13/1/1891 d 1965
Barnet Alston
1911 Glossop 9
1912 1920 Woolwich Arsenal 50 6
1921 1923 Brighton & Hove Albion 53 2
1924 Charlton Athletic 7
Dartford

Groves (Lucas), George RH/LH
b Wolverhampton 8/10/1894 d 1963
Caps: WLge 1
Lysaght's Amateurs
Newport County
Llanelly
Abertillery
Llanelly
1920 1923 Newport County 100 4
Taunton United
Watchet
Newport Excelsior

Groves, George Jasper IR
b Nottingham 19/10/1868 d 1941
Heeley
Sheffield
Sheffield United
Gainsborough Trinity
Woolwich Arsenal
Vampires
1895 Sheffield United 1

Groves, James Albert (Albert) RB/LB
b South Bank 7/1883 d 1939
South Bank
1903 Lincoln City 29 2
1903 1906 Sheffield United 62
1907 1909 Middlesbrough 27 2
Wingate Albion

Groves, William (Willie) LH/CF
b Leith 9/11/1869 d 1908
Caps: FLge 1/Scotland 3
Stella Maris CYMS
Hibernian
Edinburgh Thistle (loan)
Leith Harp (loan)
Celtic
1889 Everton 0
Celtic
1890 1892 West Bromwich Albion 58 7
1893 Aston Villa 22 3
Hibernian
Celtic
Rushden Town

Grozier, Thomas (Tommy) OR
b Rutherglen 25/8/1902 d 1960
Rutherglen Glencairn
1927 1935 Plymouth Argyle 211 57
St Austell

Grundy, Harry OL
Chirk
Neston
1905 Everton 2
Reading
1907 1909 Lincoln City 6

Grundy, Harry RB/LB
b Little Hulton 18/9/1893 d 1979
Rothwells Athletic
Wharton Lads
Little Lever Colliery
1914 1928 Oldham Athletic 279

Grundy, J IR
1897 Blackpool 1

Grundy, John (Jack) OL
b Egerton q2 1873
Wigan County
1894 Newton Heath 0
Halliwell
1899 1900 Newton Heath 11 3
1900 Bolton Wanderers 0

From To Apps Goal

Grundy, John Arnold (Arnold) LH
b Bishop Auckland 19/9/1919 d 1989
Dunston CWS
1936 1937 Newcastle United 2
Chingford Town

Grundy, William LH/RH
b Kirkby-in-Ashfield 1913
Annesley Colliery Welfare
1934 Coventry City 1
1935 Mansfield Town 5
Annesley Colliery Welfare

Grundy, William Alfred CF
b Bolton q2 1884
1906 1908 Blackpool 57 28
1908 Bolton Wanderers 2
Northern Nomads
Port Vale
1910 Huddersfield Town 1
1911 Blackpool 0
Northern Nomads

Gueran, Sidney F IR
b Grays 2/10/1916 d 1944
1934 Arsenal 0
Margate
1936 1937 Southampton 3
1938 Exeter City 0

Guest, A OL
1894 Bolton Wanderers 1

Guest, W RB
1893 Northwich Victoria 27 4

Guest, William Francis (Billy) OL
b Brierley Hill 8/2/1914 d 1994
Bromley Juniors (Kingswinford)
1933 1936 Birmingham 76 15
1936 1946 Blackburn Rovers 88 30
1947 Walsall 5
Peterborough United
Kidderminster Harriers
Lovells Athletic
Hinckley United
Bilston United

Guest, William Richard (Joe) OL
b Denaby 2/2/1914 d 1973
Silverwood Colliery
1932 New Brighton (trial) 0
1934 Chesterfield (trial) 0
Denaby United
1936 West Ham United 3 1

Gullen, George IR
b Newcastle
1902 Newcastle United 0
1903 Barnsley 16 3

Gumm, Alfred James (Jimmy) OR
b Barnstaple 15/11/1907 d 1985
St James (Exeter)
1930 1933 Exeter City 5
Sidmouth

Gummery, Walter Harry OL
b Worcester 1/5/1900 d 1974
Worcester City
1924 Wolverhampton Wanderers 10 1
1925 Accrington Stanley 31 3
Worcester City

Gundry, Reginald Leonard (Reg) RB
b Eastleigh 4/10/1917
Dorchester Town
1935 Portsmouth 1
Dorchester Town

Gunn, John IL/IR
1895 Bolton Wanderers 6 5
1896 Manchester City 21 4
Clyde

Gunn, Kenneth (Ken) IL/RB/RH
b Dunfermline 9/4/1909 d 1991
Newmains
1927 1932 Swansea Town 95 35
1933 1936 Port Vale 134 10
1937 1938 Northampton Town 74 1

Gunn, William (Billy) OR/RB
b Nottingham 4/12/1858 d 1921
Caps: England 2
Nottingham Forest
1888 1892 Notts County 3 1

Gunnell, Richard Charles OL
b Harpenden 10/4/1899 d 1977
Hertford Town
1926 Northampton Town 11
Bedford Town

From To Apps Goal

Gunson, Fred LH
b Middle Rasen q3 1874 d 1963
St Catherine's (Lincoln)
Lincoln City
Casuals (Lincoln)
1896 Lincoln City 1
Adelaide (Lincoln)

Gunson, Joseph Gordon (Gordon) OL
b Chester 1/7/1904 d 1991
Brickfields
1923 Nelson 0
1926 1928 Wrexham 116 32
1929 Sunderland 19 11
1929 1932 Liverpool 81 24
1934 Swindon Town 31 8
1935 Wrexham 15 5
Bangor City

Gunton, Samuel Arthur RB
b Norwich q3 1883 d 1959
Norwich St James
Norwich City
Doncaster Rovers
1911 Gainsborough Trinity 30
1912 Burnley 1

Gurkin, John CH/LH
b Murton 9/9/1895 d 1976
Dean Bank
South Hetton Royal Rovers
1921 West Ham United 1
1922 Norwich City 10
Stalybridge Celtic
Spennymoor United
1924 1927 Durham City 160 3
Stalybridge Celtic
1929 Exeter City 2
Hyde United
Jarrow
Murton

Gurney, Robert (Bobby) CF/IL
b Silksworth 13/10/1907 d 1994
Caps: England 1
Hetton Juniors
Seaham Harbour
Bishop Auckland
1925 1938 Sunderland 348 205

Gurry, John William RH/IR
b Barking 17/7/1907 d 1983
1930 West Ham United 0
Barking Town
1932 1934 Leicester City 23
1935 Southampton 9
1936 Chester 6 3

Guthrie, George Robert GK
b Gateshead 1/12/1899 d 1981
Scotswood
Felling
West Stanley
1924 Ashington 2
Chilton Colliery Recreation Athletic
1925 South Shields 0

Guthrie, James Eric (Jimmy) RH/LH
b Luncarty 13/6/1913 d 1981
Luncarty
Scone Thistle
Dundee
1937 1945 Portsmouth 76 2
1946 Crystal Palace 5
Guildford City

Guttridge, Frank Herbert RB
b Nottingham 12/4/1866 d 1918
Heanor Town
1888 Notts County 17
Nottingham Forest
1894 Notts County 1
Nelson

Guttridge, George CH
b Prescot 6/1/1897 d 1974
Clock Face
1920 Everton 0
Prescot Cables
1924 New Brighton 3
Prescot Cables
Bootle
Sacred Heart CYMS

Guttridge, H IL
1905 Burton United 17 2

Guy, George CF/IR
b Bolton 1/11/1896 d 1975
1920 Bolton Wanderers 2 1
1922 Rochdale 15 7
Aberaman Athletic
Chorley

From To | Apps | Goal

Guy, Richard William (Dickie) OR
b Madeley, Shropshire 4/8/1877 d 1938
1902 Manchester City 0
1903 Bradford City 6 1
Hastings & St Leonards
1908 Leeds City 18 3
Portsmouth
Hastings & St Leonards

Guy, Stanley Walton OR
b Liverpool 2/9/1914 d 1996
Liverpool 0
1936 Bristol City 1

Guyan, George Wood CF
b Aberdeen 5/4/1901
Banks o' Dee
Dundee
1922 1925 South Shields 42 11
1926 1927 Hull City 19 9
Connah's Quay & Shotton
1929 Exeter City 28 14
1930 Swindon Town 2
1931 Rochdale 4 1
Bath City
Drumcondra
Distillery

Gwilliam, ? IL
Shrewsbury
Wellington Town
1901 Wolverhampton Wanderers 2 1
Wellington Town

Gwynne, Ernest CF
b Dowlais q2 1882 d 1965
1903 Leicester Fosse 1

Gwyther, Bertie Perseus IR/CF
b Merthyr Tydfil 22/8/1906 d 1981
Cardiff Corinthians
Roath Villa
1925 Newport County 1
1926 Merthyr Town 2
1933 Cardiff City 0

Hackett, A IL
Leicester Imperial
1901 Leicester Fosse 2
Leicester Imperial
Hinckley United

Hackett, Christopher Edward (Chris) OR/IL
b Mansfield 9/2/1903 d 1983
Langwith Colliery
Mansfield Town
Welbeck Colliery
Newark Town
Grantham
1924 Leicester City 0
Caernarvon Athletic
Grantham
1928 Bury 0
Scunthorpe & Lindsey United
1930 Bristol Rovers 1
Loughborough Corinthians
1932 Accrington Stanley 7
Leicester Tramways

Hackett, Ernest GK
b Royston 1908
Monckton Athletic
Frickley Colliery
1930 Wolverhampton Wanderers 0
1931 Coventry City 4
1932 Newport County 4
Frickley Colliery

Hackett, Oliver LB/LH
b Lichfield q1 1870
1892 1895 Burton Swifts 55

Hackford, George Frederick OL
b Wath-on-Dearne q4 1908
1930 1932 Rotherham United 4
1933 Barnsley 0

Hacking, John (Jack) GK
b Blackburn 23/12/1897 d 1955
Caps: FLge 2/England 3
Grimshaw Park Co-operative
1921 1924 Blackpool 32
Fleetwood
1926 1933 Oldham Athletic 223
1933 1934 Manchester United 32
1935 Accrington Stanley 17

From To | Apps | Goal

Haddleton, Arthur CF/OR/IR
b Chester-le-Street 6/4/1910 d 1971
West Hartlepool Belle Vue Congs
Horden Athletic
Easington Colliery Welfare
Horden Colliery Welfare
1930 1931 Southampton 17 10
1932 Fulham 4 4
1933 Swindon Town 7
1934 Walsall 15 4
Pirelli General

Haddon, Harry CF
b Pelsall 1871
Pelsall Villa
Lichfield
1895 1896 Small Heath 8 2
Walsall Wood

Haddon, Percy RH
b Walsall 18/5/1895 d 1972
1919 Rotherham County 1

Haddow, Andrew Sorbie CF
b Glasgow 8/4/1903
Strathclyde
Morton
1927 Burnley 1
New York Nationals
Clyde
Dundee United (loan)
Dundee United
Clyde
Ballymena
Etoile Rouge (Switzerland)

Haddow, David (Davie) GK
b Dalserf 12/6/1869
Caps: SLge 1/Scotland 1
Albion Rovers
1890 Derby County 16
Albion Rovers
Rangers
Motherwell
1895 1897 Burnley 38
1898 New Brighton Tower 34
Tottenham Hotspur

Haddow, James CH/RH/LH
b Kilmarnock 1872 d 1943
1891 1895 Darwen 43 4

Haden, Samson (Sam) OL/IL
b Royston, West Yorkshire 17/1/1902 d 1974
Castleford Town
1923 1926 Arsenal 88 10
1927 1935 Notts County 289 36
Peterborough United

Hadfield, George CH
b Grassmoor 7/3/1908 d 1988
1930 Crewe Alexandra 1

Hadley, Arthur OR
b Reading 5/5/1876 d 1963
Reading Abbey
Reading
1898 1901 Notts County 76 22
1902 1904 Leicester Fosse 64 4
1906 Notts County 0

Hadley, Benjamin (Ben) CH/RH/LH
b West Bromwich 1871 d 1937
Hereford Thistle
1892 1895 West Bromwich Albion 7 1
Hereford Town

Hadley, E GK
Birmingham St George's
1892 Burton Swifts 22
Stourbridge

Hadley, George A LH/RH
b West Bromwich 5/6/1893 d 1963
Willenhall Swifts
Southampton
1919 Aston Villa 4
1920 1922 Coventry City 72 3

Hadley, Harold (Harry) LH/RH
b Barrow 26/10/1877 d 1950
Caps: England 1
Colley Gate United
Halesowen
1897 1904 West Bromwich Albion 167 2
1905 Aston Villa 11
1905 1906 Nottingham Forest 12 1
Southampton
Croydon Common
Halesowen
Merthyr Town

Hadlington, James Edward IR
b Cannock 27/3/1904 d 1982
1926 Walsall 1

From To | Apps | Goal

Hafekost, Charles Henry (Charlie) RH
b Sunderland 22/3/1890 d 1967
Sunderland Royal Rovers
New Brompton
1914 Liverpool 1
Darlington Forge Albion
Hamilton Academical
Hartlepools United

Hagan, Alfred (Alfie) IR/IL
b Usworth 10/11/1893 d 1980
Washington Colliery
1919 1922 Newcastle United 21 5
1923 1925 Cardiff City 9 2
1926 Tranmere Rovers 12

Hagan, James (Jimmy) IL/IR/OR
b Washington 21/1/1918 d 1998
Caps: England Sch/FLge 3/England War 16/ England 1
Washington Colliery
Usworth Colliery
1933 Liverpool 0
1935 1938 Derby County 30 7
1938 1957 Sheffield United 361 117
1939 (Sheffield United) (3) (1)

Haggan, John LH
b Boldon 16/12/1896 d 1982
Pelaw
1919 Sunderland 2
1922 Brentford 18 1
Preston Colliery
Hamilton United (Canada)
Usworth Colliery
Washington Co-op Wednesday

Haggart, William RB/LB
b Edinburgh 8/1874 d 1934
Dalry Primrose
Edinburgh Royal
1898 1899 Aston Villa 2
Partick Thistle
Edinburgh Thistle

Hagley, Ernest John RB
b Burton-on-Trent q1 1874 d 1957
1896 Burton Wanderers 1

Hague, Eric Montague OR/OL/CF
b Sheffield 21/7/1901 d 1972
1924 Birmingham 0
1925 Blackpool 0
1926 Swindon Town 0
Gainsborough Trinity
1928 Nottingham Forest 4
1928 West Ham United 0
1928 1929 Walsall 8 1
1930 Crewe Alexandra 2

Hague, Joseph Keith (Keith) CH
b Duffield 13/11/1913 d 1980
1935 Derby County 0
1936 1938 Southend United 39 1
1939 (Southend United) (3)

Haig, James (Jimmy) RH
b Rothesay 1876
Rothesay Royal Victoria
St Mirren
1898 Derby County 3
Kilbarchan
1900 1907 Chesterfield Town 228 2

Haig, Paul OL
b Nottingham q4 1888
Mapperley
Eastwood Rangers
Mansfield Mechanics
1910 Leicester Fosse 12 2
Mansfield Mechanics
Stanton Hill Victoria
Eastwood Rangers
1913 Notts County 1
Long Eaton St Helen's
Mansfield Town
Loughborough Corinthians
Grantham

Haigh, Charles CH
b Leicester 14/8/1903 d 1973
Caps: England Sch
Fairweather Green
Calverley
Yorkshire Amateurs
1923 1924 Accrington Stanley 12
1925 Bradford City (trial) 0
Selby Town
Lancaster Town

Haigh, George CH
b Reddish q3 1915
1938 Stockport County 2
1939 Burnley 0

From To | Apps | Goal

Haigh, Kenneth Jack RB/RH/LB
b Sheffield 17/9/1913 d 1997
Wincobank
1932 Sheffield Wednesday 0
1933 Bradford City 0
1934 1935 Stockport County 10
1936 1938 Rotherham United 96

Haigh, Maurice OR
b Sheffield q3 1877 d 1955
Sheffield
1897 Sheffield United 0
St Mark's College (Chelsea)
1899 Gainsborough Trinity 26 4
1900 Chesterfield Town 6 2
Rotherham Town

Haigh, William RB
b Dodworth q3 1880
1903 Barnsley 1

Haigh-Brown, Alan Roderick OR
b Godalming 6/9/1877 d 1918
Old Cathusians
Cambridge University
Corinthians
Tottenham Hotspur
Worthing
Brighton & Hove Albion
Shoreham
Brighton & Hove Albion
1905 Clapton Orient 4 1

Hails, George IL
b South Shields q3 1889 d 1964
Gateshead Town
South Shields Adelaide
1909 Gainsborough Trinity 7
South Shields

Haines, Wilfred Henry (Wilf) OR
b Stone 6/1882
Newcastle Swifts
1904 Stoke 3 1
Hanley Swifts
Stafford Rangers
1908 Birmingham 3
Leek United
West Ham United
Stafford Rangers

Haines, Wyndham William Pretoria (Willie CF
b Warminster Common 14/7/1900 d 1974
Warminster Town
Frome Town
1922 1927 Portsmouth 164 119
1928 1931 Southampton 70 47
Weymouth
Frome Town

Hainsworth, Leonard (Len) RB/CH/LB
b Rotherham 25/1/1918 d 1990
1938 1947 Rotherham United 33 7
1948 1950 Doncaster Rovers 67
1951 1952 Workington 75 1
Corby Town
Grantham

Hair, Alexander (Sandy) CF/IL
b Glasgow 9/3/1902
Strathclyde
Partick Thistle
Queen of the South (loan)
Third Lanark (loan)
Alloa Athletic (loan)
1928 1929 Preston North End 45 22
Shelbourne
Bray Unknowns
Colwyn Bay United
Worcester City
Burton Town
Shirley Town

Hair, William OR
b Edinburgh 1904
Newtongrange Star
Broxburn United
Bo'ness
Rangers
1928 Grimsby Town 6 2
Peebles Rovers
Rhyl Athletic
Flint Town
Leith Athletic

Hakin, John Thomas (Tommy) IL
b Mexborough 17/10/1882 d 1950
Mexborough United
Mexborough Town
1906 1907 Grimsby Town 58 16
Plymouth Argyle
Portsmouth
Rotherham County

From To Apps Goal

Haldane, James (Jim) GK
b Edinburgh 17/9/??
Peebles Rovers
Penicuik
1921 Halifax Town 8

Hale, Alfred (Alf 'Pally') LH/LB
b Kiveton Park 24/1/1906 d 1972
Kiveton Park Colliery
1925 1929 Lincoln City 156 4
1930 1931 Luton Town 22
Llanelly
1934 1935 Halifax Town 27
Dinnington Athletic

Hale, Walter LB
b Ormskirk 8/6/1903 d 1997
Coppull Central
1923 Preston North End (trial)
1924 Wigan Borough 1
Chorley

Hales, Archibald OL
b Leicester q2 1880 d 1952
1902 Leicester Fosse 1
Leicester Old Boys

Hales, Frank F IR
1920 Wolverhampton Wanderers 2 1

Hales, Herbert (Bert) OL
b Kettering 21/11/1908 d 1982
Desborough Hotspur
Desborough Town
1928 Nottingham Forest 3
1929 Northampton Town (trial) 0
Peterborough & Fletton United
1930 Stoke City 1
1931 1932 Preston North End 57 10
1933 1934 Chesterfield 42 10
1934 Stockport County 16
1935 Rochdale 38 4
Burton Town
Kidderminster Harriers

Hales, Leonard (Len) IL/IR
b Crewe 1872
Crewe Alexandra
1898 Stoke (loan) 1
Crewe Alexandra
1901 Stoke 15 2

Hales, William CH
b London
Walthamstow Grange
1910 Clapton Orient 1
Walthamstow Grange

Hales, William OL
1934 Gateshead 14 4

Hales, William Alfred OR/OL
b Poplar 24/7/1910 d 1986
Leytonstone
1930 Thames 3
1931 1932 Clapton Orient 13 3

Hales, William Harry RH
b Bristol
1903 Bristol City 1
Bristol Rovers
New Brompton

Haley, William Thomas (Bill) IR
b Bexleyheath 16/2/1904 d 1960
Bostall Athletic
Bostall Heath
1924 Charlton Athletic 18 6
1924 1926 Derby County 9 1
Dartford
1928 1930 Fulham 93 50
1931 Queen's Park Rangers 17 5
Dartford
Sheppey United

Halford, David OL
b Croxley Green 19/10/1915 d 2007
Caps: England Sch
Rowntree's
Scarborough
1935 Derby County 6 3
1936 1937 Bolton Wanderers 6 1
1938 Oldham Athletic 26 11
1939 (Oldham Athletic) (2)

From To Apps Goal

Halkyard, Cecil LH
b Rochdale 17/4/1902 d 1989
Bacup Borough
Rochdale All Saints
1923 Accrington Stanley 0
1924 1927 Rochdale 15
Connah's Quay & Shotton
1930 Reading 8
Rhyl Athletic
Colwyn Bay United
1932 Charlton Athletic 1
1934 Barrow 1
Hyde United
Mossley
Macclesfield

Hall, AJ OR
1893 1895 Crewe Alexandra 6

Hall, Albert Edward (Bert) OL
b Wordsley 2/1882 d 1957
Caps: FLge 2/England 1
Stourbridge
1903 1913 Aston Villa 195 52
Millwall Athletic

Hall, Albert Edwards Benjamin IL/IR/OR
b Cadoxton 3/9/1918 d 1998
Caps: Wales Sch
Tottenham Juniors
1935 1946 Tottenham Hotspur 40 10
1947 Plymouth Argyle 9
Chelmsford City

Hall, Alexander Frank (Alec) RH
b Grimsby 17/9/1909 d 1992
Cleethorpes Town
1929 1947 Grimsby Town 358 4
1939 (Grimsby Town) (1)
Alford United

Hall, Alexander Noble (Alex) CF
b Peterhead 26/4/1906
Toronto Scots
Galt (Canada)
St Bernard's
1907 Newcastle United 6 2
Dundee
Portsmouth
Motherwell
Dunfermline Athletic

Hall, Alexander Richmond (Sandy) LH
b Kirkcaldy 1865 d 1938
Raith Rovers
1892 Sheffield Wednesday 17 1
Raith Rovers
Heart of Midlothian
Dundee
Tottenham Hotspur
Aberdour

Hall, Alexander Webster (Alex) LB/RB
b East Calder 6/11/1908 d 1991
East Calder Swifts
Oakbank Amateurs
Wallyford Bluebell
Dunfermline Athletic
1928 1938 Sunderland 206 1
1939 (Sunderland) (3)
Hibernian

Hall, Alfred W OL
1905 Burslem Port Vale 1

Hall, Almeric George (Almer) IR/IL
b Hove 12/11/1912 d 1994
Southwick (Sussex)
1930 Brighton & Hove Albion 0
1934 1935 Tottenham Hotspur 16 3
1937 1938 Southend United 37 10
1939 Bradford City (1)
1945 1948 West Ham United 50 11
Margate

Hall, Benjamin (Ben) CH
b Ecclesfield 6/3/1879 d 1963
1900 1902 Grimsby Town 39 4
1903 1910 Derby County 245 11
1911 Leicester Fosse 14
Hyde
Heywood United
South Shields

Hall, Berthold Allan Couldwell (Allan) CF
b Deepcar 29/3/1908 d 1983
Park Labour
1926 1927 Doncaster Rovers 30 22
1927 1929 Middlesbrough 7 2
1930 Bradford City 11 4
1931 1932 Lincoln City 72 63
1933 Tottenham Hotspur 2
1933 1934 Blackpool 16 9
Gainsborough Trinity

From To Apps Goal

Hall, Bertie RH
b Newburn 18/12/1902 d 1990
Gateshead Victoria
1924 Newcastle United (trial) 0
Lemington Glass Works
1926 1928 Hartlepools United 88 3
Peterborough & Fletton United
1931 Norwich City 2
1932 Bristol City 2

Hall, Claude Francis GK
b Gainsborough q1 1883 d 1955
1903 1905 Gainsborough Trinity 6

Hall, Coombe IL
b North Leith 1871 d 1932
St Bernard's
1890 1894 Blackburn Rovers 79 26
St Bernard's
Wanderers (South Africa)
Port Elizabeth

Hall, Edward OR
Beeston Humber
1897 Lincoln City 18 3
1897 Loughborough 8 1
Wellingborough

Hall, Ellis CH
b Ecclesfield 22/6/1889 d 1947
Ecclesfield Bible Class
1905 1906 Hull City 8
Millwall Athletic
Hastings & St Leonards
Stoke
1910 1911 Huddersfield Town 39 2
South Shields
Hamilton Academical
1922 Millwall Athletic (trial) 0
1922 1924 Halifax Town 115 2
1925 Rochdale 0
Consett

Hall, Ernest (Ernie) CH
b Crawcrook 6/8/1916
West Wylam
1935 Newcastle United 2
1937 Brighton & Hove Albion 3
1938 Stoke City 0

Hall, Ernest William (Ernie) LB
b Bedworth 23/2/1904 d 1979
Bedworth Town
1931 1932 Queen's Park Rangers 62
1934 1937 Chester 118

Hall, Frederick (Fred) GK
b Drayton 20/10/1914 d 2003
Hellesdon Hospital
1935 1946 Norwich City 90

Hall, Frederick Wilkinson (Fred) CH
b Chester-le-Street 18/11/1917 d 1989
Ouston Juniors
1936 1938 Blackburn Rovers 29
1946 1954 Sunderland 215 1
1955 Barrow 16 1
Ransome & Marles

Hall, Fretwell LH/RH
b Wortley q3 1892 d 1937
South Shields
Goole Town
Norwich City
1920 Brighton & Hove Albion 12
1921 1922 Halifax Town 52 2
Torquay United
Peterborough & Fletton United

Hall, George IR
b Northern Ireland
Caps: IrLge 5/Ireland 1
Distillery
Glentoran
Distillery
1897 Blackburn Rovers 1 1

Hall, George IR/OR
b Herrington
Herrington Swifts
1922 1923 Hull City 12 4
1925 Durham City 0
Hesleden Rising Star

Hall, George LH
1939 Accrington Stanley (1)

Hall, George W RH/IR
b Shildon
Bishop Auckland
1929 Huddersfield Town 0
1930 1932 Darlington 21 4
Spennymoor United

Hall, George William LH/RH
1897 1905 Gainsborough Trinity 241 2

From To Apps Goal

Hall, George William (Willie) IL/IR
b Newark 12/3/1912 d 1967
Caps: FLge 3/England War 3/England 10
Ransome & Marles
1930 1932 Notts County 34 7
1932 1938 Tottenham Hotspur 202 27
1939 (Tottenham Hotspur) (3)

Hall, George William E LH
b Worksop 5/9/1912 d 1989
Worksop Town
1932 1934 Sheffield United 22
1935 Coventry City 0
1936 Newport County 28
1937 1938 Bristol City 13
Scarborough

Hall, Harry OR/IR
b Ecclesfield q1 1887
1906 Hull City 1
Rotherham Town
1910 Huddersfield Town 20
1911 Grimsby Town 0

Hall, Harry IR/CF
b Newark q4 1893
1910 Gainsborough Trinity 0
Newark
Long Eaton St Helen's
1913 Sheffield United 5
Long Eaton
Worksop Town
Ilkeston United
1920 1921 Sheffield Wednesday 31 1
Gainsborough Trinity
Newark Town
Long Eaton St Helen's
Grantham
Ransome & Marles

Hall, Harry OR
b 1900
Pinxton
1921 Lincoln City 16
1923 Darlington 13 1

Hall, James RH
1923 Halifax Town 2

Hall, James GK
b Durham
West Stanley
1937 1938 Portsmouth 9

Hall, James Henry (Jim) RH/LH
b 1914
Bath City
1936 1938 Blackpool 26 1
Fleetwood

Hall, Jeffrey CF
1933 Halifax Town 2 1

Hall, John RH/IL
b Heywood
Heywood St James'
1923 1929 Rochdale 74 2
Great Harwood

Hall, John (Jack) OR/IR
b Bolton 1905
1923 Lincoln City 1
1924 Accrington Stanley 5 1
1925 Manchester United 3

Hall, John OL
b Hetton-le-Hole
Hetton United
1930 1932 Burnley 38 4

Hall, John CH
b Southend-on-Sea
1932 Southend United 2
Sochaux
CA Paris
Le Havre

Hall, John (Jack) GK
b Prestwich 23/10/1912 d 2000
Failsworth
Newton Heath Loco
1933 1935 Manchester United 67
1936 1938 Tottenham Hotspur 53
Stalybridge Celtic
Runcorn
Stalybridge Celtic

Hall, John (Jack) LB
b Accrington 1916
Clarendon Villa
1937 1938 Accrington Stanley 43 3
1939 Hull City 0

From To Apps Goal

Hall, John Edward (Jack) OR
b Tyne Dock 1885
Harton Star
Kingston Villa
1905 1907 Barnsley 74 14
Jarrow
1908 Hull City 0
Brighton & Hove Albion
Rochdale
South Shields
1910 1911 Preston North End 18 3
Doncaster Rovers
Pontypridd
South Shields

Hall, John Edward (Jack) RH
b Bermondsey q1 1898
Hampstead Town
Metrogas
1919 Fulham 1
Maidstone United
1921 Luton Town 0
Millwall United

Hall, John G OL
b Sheffield
Kirkby Bentinck Rangers
1927 Chesterfield 2

Hall, John Halpin OR
b Houghton-le-Spring q1 1895
South Shields
1921 1923 Durham City 41 4

Hall, John Henry (Jack) CF/IL/IR
b Hucknall 3/7/1883 d 1949
Newstead Byron
Newark
1903 Nottingham Forest (trial) 0
1904 1905 Stoke 53 18
Brighton & Hove Albion
1908 1909 Middlesbrough 59 30
1910 Leicester Fosse 15 5
1910 1914 Birmingham 97 47
Hucknall Town

Hall, Joseph (Jack) RB/LB
b Boldon Colliery q3 1892
1909 Preston North End 0
Jarrow Croft
1910 Hull City 0
1911 1912 Barnsley 5
1914 Manchester City 1
Darlington
1920 1921 Bristol Rovers 28
1922 Newport County 0
Bristol Aeroplane Company

Hall, Joseph (Joe) CH
b Bentley 25/10/1909 d 1976
Winterwell Athletic
1933 Huddersfield Town 0
1934 1936 Doncaster Rovers 66
Boston United

Hall, Joseph H (Joe) GK
b East Holywell
Backworth Percy
1921 1923 Southend United 57

Hall, Lancelot (Lance) LB/CH
b Darlington 23/1/1915 d 1985
Cockfield
1937 Luton Town 0
1938 1948 Barrow 108 1
1939 (Barrow) (3)

Hall, Matthew IL
b Renfrew 1884
St Mirren
1906 Sunderland 8
Clyde
Alloa Athletic
Third Lanark

Hall, Proctor IR/IL/CF
b Blackburn q1 1883 d 1957
Oswaldtwistle Rovers
1903 Manchester United 8 2
Brighton & Hove Albion
1906 Aston Villa 0
1906 Bradford City 28 7
Luton Town
1907 1908 Chesterfield Town 44 13
Hyde
Nelson
Rossendale United
Chorley
Fleetwood
1911 Preston North End 0
Newport County
Mardy

From To Apps Goal

Hall, Robert CH
b Preston
Leyland
1923 Burnley 0
1925 1927 Accrington Stanley 7

Hall, Stanley Arthur (Stan) GK
b Southgate 18/2/1917 d 1999
Finchley
1938 1946 Clapton Orient 26
Yeovil Town

Hall, Thomas (Tommy) LH/CH/RH
b Macclesfield q1 1877
Macclesfield
Stockport County
1900 1901 Glossop 53 2
1902 1906 Stockport County 76 6

Hall, Thomas (Tom) IL/CF
b Newburn 4/9/1891
Newburn Manor
Newburn Grange
Newburn Alliance
1909 1912 Sunderland 30 8
1913 1919 Newcastle United 54 15
1920 1925 Gillingham 190 47

Hall, Thomas (Tom) CF
b Darnall
Darnall Working Mens' Club
1927 Rotherham United 16 6
Shirebrook
Scunthorpe & Lindsey United

Hall, Thomas Henry IL
b Birtley q2 1904
Stobswood St John's
1922 Ashington 2

Hall, Thomas L (Tom) RB
b Crawcrook
Crawcrook Albion
1931 Coventry City 2

Hall, Thomas Williamson Sidney (Tommy) LH
b Darlington 15/6/1908 d 1973
1929 1930 Darlington 23 1

Hall, William IL
1920 Fulham 9 3

Hall, William Coulson (Billy) OL
b Consett 1906
Tow Law Town
Consett
1929 1930 Blackpool 23 3
1931 Southend United 1
Crook Town
Consett

Hall, William Henry RB
1894 Notts County 2

Hall, William John GK
1904 Bolton Wanderers 0
Bristol Rovers
1906 Manchester City 11
Crystal Palace

Hallam, Charles (Cliff) IL/OL
b Longton 17/1/1902 d 1970
Sandford Hill Primitives
1922 Port Vale 1
Sandbach Ramblers
1924 1926 Stoke 31 2
1927 Crystal Palace 2 2
Sandbach Ramblers
Stafford Rangers
Bilston United

Hallam, Harry RB
b Sleaford 22/8/1892 d 1976
Grantham
Peterborough GN Loco
1913 Lincoln City 2

Hallam, Jack RH
b Hadfield 23/5/1910 d 1995
Hadfield Star
1930 1931 Wigan Borough 12 1
1931 Oldham Athletic 1
1932 Stockport County (trial) 0
1932 Fulham (trial) 0
Hyde United
Hadfield Star
Hollingworth

Hallam, John (Jack) OR
b Oswestry 6/1869 d 1949
Caps: Wales 1
Oswestry
1892 1895 Small Heath 82 33
Swindon Town
Trowbridge Town
Swindon Town

From To Apps Goal

Hallard, William (Billy) LH
b St Helens 28/8/1913 d 1980
Runcorn
1935 Bury 1
1937 1945 Bradford Park Avenue 69 5
1939 (Bradford Park Avenue) (1)
1946 Rochdale 17 2
1946 Accrington Stanley 3

Halley, George RH/LB
b Cronberry 29/10/1887 d 1941
Caps: SLge 1
Glenbuck Cherrypickers
Kilmarnock
1911 1912 Bradford Park Avenue 62 8
1912 1921 Burnley 137 4
1922 Southend United 21 2
Bacup Borough

Halley, William RB
1897 Bolton Wanderers 1
Bedminster
1899 1900 Bolton Wanderers 39
Millwall Athletic

Halliday, David (Dave) CF
b Dumfries 11/12/1901 d 1970
Caps: SLge 1
Tayleurians
Queen of the South
St Mirren
Albion Rovers (loan)
Dundee
1925 1929 Sunderland 166 156
1929 Arsenal 15 8
1930 1933 Manchester City 76 47
Folkestone
1933 1934 Clapton Orient 53 33
Yeovil & Petters United

Halliday, John Frederick (Fred) LB/RB
b Chester 19/4/1880 d 1953
Chester
Crewe Alexandra
1900 Everton 0
1901 1902 Bolton Wanderers 27
1903 1905 Bradford City 72

Halliday, John Hastings (Jack) IL/CF
b Dumfries 20/2/1908
Queen of the South
Boston Town
1930 1931 Lincoln City 9 7
1931 Doncaster Rovers 12 4
Boston Town
1933 Stockport County 0
Hurst

Halliday, Thomas (Tom) RB/RH/CH
b Browney Colliery 11/9/1909 d 1975
Caps: England Sch
Esh Winning
Meadowfield
1927 Sunderland 0
Tursdale Sports Club
1928 1932 Darlington 118 2
1933 1938 Norwich City 191
1938 Exeter City 14

Halliday, William (Billy) IL
b Dumfries 14/11/1906
Noblehill
Queen of the South
1927 Newcastle United 1
Third Lanark
Connah's Quay & Shotton
Boston Town
1930 1931 Exeter City 11 1
Gainsborough Trinity
Queen of the South
Hyde United
St Cuthbert Wanderers

Halligan, William (Billy) IL/CF/IR
b Athlone 18/2/1886 d 1950
Caps: IrLge 1/Ireland 2
Old St Mary's (Dublin)
Cliftonville
Belfast Celtic
Distillery
1909 Leeds City 24 11
1909 1910 Derby County 22 8
1911 1912 Wolverhampton Wanderers 67 34
1913 1914 Hull City 65 28
1919 Preston North End 16 2
1919 1920 Oldham Athletic 28 9
1921 Nelson 17 6
Boston Town
Wisbech Town

Halliwell, Jonathan Clifford (Cliff) RH/LH
b Sheffield 20/5/1898 d 1984
Darnall Old Boys
1921 1925 Sheffield United 25
1926 1931 Bournemouth & Boscombe Ath 216 2

From To Apps Goal

Halliwell, Joseph Adam (Joe) CF/RH/IL
b Preston 17/1/1892 d 1964
Lostock Hall Loco
1912 1913 Preston North End 26 10
1913 1926 Barnsley 312 83
1927 1928 Nelson 74 9
Barnoldswick Town
St Paul's (Preston)

Hallows, Herbert CH
Southport Central
1900 Manchester City 1
Southport Central

Hallows, John Henry (Jack) CF/IR/IL
b Chester 16/2/1907 d 1963
Liverpool Bluecoats
Willenhall Swifts
1928 West Bromwich Albion 0
Grays Thurrock
1930 1935 Bradford City 164 74
1935 1936 Barnsley 13 4

Hallworth, Arthur LH
b Stoke-on-Trent 1884
Twyford Youth Club
1906 Birmingham 1
Leek Alexandra
Barlaston Manor

Hallworth, Ralph Sutherland OR
b Manchester 28/7/1888 d 1971
Macclesfield
Great Harwood
Hurst
1919 Stockport County 2
Barrow

Halsall, Laurence OL/IL
b Ormskirk q1 1872 d 1919
Southport Central
1897 Blackpool 5 1
1897 1899 Preston North End 54 6
Southport Central

Halsall, Walter Gerard LH/CH/RH
b Liverpool 29/3/1912 d 1996
Bootle Celtic
1929 Liverpool 0
Marine
Burscough Rangers
1931 Bolton Wanderers 0
1933 1937 Blackburn Rovers 63 4
1938 Birmingham 21
1939 Chesterfield 0

Halsall, William (Billy) GK
b Birkdale 2/5/1897 d 1968
Lyndhurst
Birkdale Working Lads
1921 1930 Southport 334

Halse, Harold James IR/LH
b Leytonstone 1/1/1886 d 1949
Caps: FLge 5/England 1
Newportians (Leyton)
Wanstead
Barking
1905 Clapton Orient 2 1
Southend United
1907 1911 Manchester United 109 41
1912 Aston Villa 31 21
1913 1920 Chelsea 96 23
1921 1922 Charlton Athletic 21 5

Halshaw, John Thomas (Jack) IR
b Preston 30/6/1896 d 1975
Croston
1923 Accrington Stanley 1
Dick, Kerr's XI

Halstead, Fred Douglas CH
b Crawshawbooth q4 1896 d 1978
Welbeck Colliery
1920 Blackpool 1
1921 Southend United 24 3
1922 Hartlepools United 8
1922 1924 Tranmere Rovers 81 2
Folkestone
Mossley

Halton, Reginald Lloyd (Reg) LH
b Leek 11/7/1916 d 1988
Cheddleton Mental Hospital
Stafford Rangers
Buxton
1936 Manchester United 4 1
1937 Notts County 6
1937 1948 Bury 114 19
1939 (Bury) (3) (1)
1948 1950 Chesterfield 61 10
1950 1951 Leicester City 64 3
Scarborough
Goole Town
Symingtons
Brush Sports

From	To		Apps	Goal
Hamblett, George			CH	
b Barton-on-Irwell q3 1879				
		Gorton St Francis		
1906		Manchester City	1	
		St Helens Recreation		
Hamer, Arnold			LB	
b Huddersfield 8/12/1916			d 1993	
1938		York City	8	
Hamill, Alexander (Alex)			CF/RH	
b Dumbarton 1912				
		Hamilton Welfare		
		Renton Thistle		
		Cowdenbeath		
1935	1936	Blackburn Rovers	21	4
1936	1937	Barnsley	24	4
1938		Carlisle United	25	1
Hamill, Kevin Joseph			GK	
b Liverpool 6/3/1914			d 1975	
		Seaforth Social Club		
1934		Liverpool	0	
1935		Blackburn Rovers	1	
		Seaforth Social Club		
Hamill, Michael (Mickey)			LH/CH/IR	
b Belfast 19/1/1889			d 1943	
Caps: IrLge 3/Ireland 7				
		St Paul's Swifts		
		Belfast Rangers		
		Red Hand		
		Belfast Celtic		
		Celtic (loan)		
1911	1913	Manchester United	57	2
		Belfast Celtic		
		Distillery		
		Celtic (loan)		
		Celtic		
		Belfast Celtic		
1920	1923	Manchester City	118	1
		Fall River Marksmen		
		Boston Wonder Workers		
		New York Giants		
		Belfast Celtic		
Hamilton, Alexander McCline			GK	
b Bulwell 26/12/1890			d 1971	
		Bestwood		
1911	1912	Nottingham Forest	7	
Hamilton, Andrew			OL	
b Glasgow 1874			d 1929	
		Cambuslang		
		Falkirk		
1896		Sunderland	7	2
		New Brighton Tower		
		Warmley		
		Ryde		
		Watford		
Hamilton, David Stewart			IR/OR	
b Carlisle 8/2/1919				
		Shawfield Juniors		
1939		Newcastle United	(2)	(1)
1946		Southend United	4	
Hamilton, E			LB	
1895		Bolton Wanderers	1	
Hamilton, Edward McDonald			OR	
b Paisley 31/3/1886				
		Petershill		
1909		Leeds City	3	
Hamilton, George William			LB	
b Shankhouse 1899				
Caps: England Sch				
		Stakeford Albion		
		Watford (trial)		
		Stakeford United		
		Blyth Spartans		
1921	1927	Ashington	162	
		Shankhouse (loan)		
		Frickley Colliery		
		South Kirkby Colliery		
		Shankhouse		
Hamilton, Harold			CF	
1924		Rotherham County	9	3
Hamilton, Henry Gilhespy			CF/IL	
b South Shields q3 1887			d 1938	
		Craghead United		
1909		Sheffield Wednesday	7	
1910		Huddersfield Town	16	10
		Haslingden		
		Southampton		
		Belfast Celtic		
		South Shields		

From	To		Apps	Goal
Hamilton, Herbert Harold (Duke)			RB	
b Wallasey 27/3/1906			d 1951	
		New Brighton Baptists		
		Harrowby		
		Poulton Rovers		
1923		New Brighton	1	
1926		Everton	1	
1927	1930	Preston North End	24	
1931	1936	Chesterfield	192	6
1937	1938	Tranmere Rovers	47	1
1938		Accrington Stanley	10	
		Bangor City		
		Marine		
Hamilton, James (Snowy)			LB	
b Burslem 1884				
		Burslem Town		
1903	1906	Burslem Port Vale	96	
1907	1910	Oldham Athletic	105	5
Hamilton, James (Jimmy)			RH/CH	
b Hetton-le-Hole 1904				
		Coldstream Guards		
1923	1930	Crystal Palace	180	4
1931	1932	Hartlepools United	48	2
		City of Durham		
1934		Gateshead	4	
Hamilton, James (Jimmy)			LB	
b Bargeddie 16/6/1901			d 1975	
Caps: SLge 1/Scotland 1				
		Vale of Clyde		
		St Mirren		
		Rangers		
1928	1929	Blackpool	28	
1929	1930	Barrow	43	2
		Armadale		
		Galston		
Hamilton, James Stevenson (Jimmy)			LB/RB	
b New Cumnock 16/8/1906				
		Girvan Juniors		
		Hamilton Academical		
		Ayr United		
1931	1932	Rochdale	77	
1933	1937	Wrexham	163	1
1938		Carlisle United	23	
1939		Chester	0	
Hamilton, John			CF	
1894		Derby County	12	2
Hamilton, John (Jock)			CH/LH	
b Ayr 31/7/1869			d 1931	
		Ayr		
1894		Wolverhampton Wanderers	4	
1895	1896	Loughborough	59	2
		Bristol City		
1900		Leicester Fosse	28	
		Watford		
		Wellingborough		
		Fulham		
Hamilton, John Eley (Jack)			OR/IR	
b Nottingham 23/1/1902			d 1980	
		Heanor Athletic		
		Welbeck Colliery		
1921		Watford	2	
		Sutton Town		
1924	1925	Blackpool	3	
1926		Queen's Park Rangers	10	
		Sutton Town		
		Loughborough Corinthians		
Hamilton, John H (Jock)			CH	
b Bonnyton, Fife 1879				
		Leith Athletic		
		Brentford		
1908		Leeds City	21	
		Brentford		
		Swansea Town		
		Barry		
Hamilton, John Haggarty			OR	
b Glasgow 1880				
1897	1898	Burton Swifts	42	8
1900		Gainsborough Trinity	34	1
		Millwall Athletic		
		Queen's Park Rangers		
		West Ham United		
Hamilton, John Peden			LH	
b Armadale 25/4/1909			d 1983	
		Penicuik Juniors		
1929	1930	Bristol Rovers	63	2
		Thornbury Town		

From	To		Apps	Goal
Hamilton, Robert Templeton			LB	
b Newry 11/11/1903			d 1964	
Caps: IrLge 1/Ireland 5				
		Darnolly Rovers		
		Portadown		
		Newry Town		
		Rangers		
1933	1934	Bradford City	23	
		Third Lanark		
		Morton		
		Bangor		
Hamilton, Samuel			IR	
b Belfast 1/1902			d 1925	
		Mount Pottinger		
		Dundela		
		Bangor		
		Ebbw Vale		
1924		Hull City	27	7
Hamilton, Sydney			OL	
b Penrith q2 1913			d 1961	
		Penrith		
		Morecambe		
1937	1945	Carlisle United	38	10
Hamilton, Thomas (Tom)			RH	
b Ayrshire				
Caps: Scotland 1				
		Kilmarnock		
		Hurlford		
1892		Nottingham Forest	7	
Hamilton, Thomas (Tommy)			RB/LB	
b New Cumnock 10/2/1893			d 1959	
Caps: SLge 1				
		New Cumnock Afton Lily		
		Cronberry Eglington		
		Kilmarnock		
1920	1928	Preston North End	267	
		Dick, Kerr's XI (loan)		
		Manchester Central		
		Great Harwood		
		Leyland Motors		
Hamilton, Thomas (Tommy)			OR	
b Stevenston				
		Ardrossan Winton Rovers		
		Kilmarnock		
		Clydebank		
		Stevenston United		
		Falkirk		
		Llanelly		
1923		Hull City (trial)	2	
Hamilton, Thomas S			GK	
		Stockton		
1898	1899	Woolwich Arsenal	7	
		Gravesend United		
Hamilton, William (Billy)			OR	
b Musselburgh 24/10/1904			d 1984	
		Tollcross YMCA		
		Vale of Clyde		
		Shettleston		
		Bellshill Athletic		
1925	1926	Bradford City	13	3
1927		Southport	31	8
1928		Barrow	41	11
1929		Accrington Stanley	41	14
1930		Notts County	2	
		Alloa Athletic		
Hamilton, William			OL	
b Belfast 1906				
		Dundela		
1926	1927	Lincoln City	15	3
1928		Notts County	0	
		Gainsborough Trinity		
Hammerton, John Daniel			CF	
b Sheffield 22/3/1900			d 1968	
		Oughtibridge		
1920	1922	Barnsley	30	9
1923	1925	Rotherham County	67	35
1926		Barnsley	0	
1926		Crewe Alexandra (trial)	0	
1927		Oldham Athletic	0	
		York City		
		Mansfield Town		
Hammond, George			IR/CF	
b Sunderland 1880				
		Barrow		
1902		Lincoln City	1	
		Clapton Orient		
1905		Gainsborough Trinity	1	
1905		Clapton Orient	4	
		Croydon Common		
Hammond, Herbert Edward (Jim)			IR/IL	
b Hove 7/11/1907			d 1985	
Caps: England Amat				
		Robin's Athletic		
		Lewes		
1928	1937	Fulham	316	142

From	To		Apps	Goal
Hammond, Jack			GK	
b Birtley				
		RAF Cranwell		
1934		Lincoln City	1	
Hammond, Jonathan Arnold			GK	
b Congleton q2 1890				
		Butt Lane Star		
1919	1920	Port Vale	6	
Hammond, Joseph Henry (Joe)			OR	
b Stepney 2/6/1909			d 1993	
		London Paper Mills		
		Leytonstone		
1933	1935	Queen's Park Rangers	18	6
Hammond, Leonard (Len)			GK	
b Rugby 12/9/1901			d 1983	
		Rugby Town		
1924	1932	Northampton Town	301	
1933		Notts County	26	
		Rugby Town		
		Nuneaton Town		
Hammond, Norman			LH	
b Mexborough 10/2/1910			d 1975	
		Denaby United		
1930		Sunderland	0	
1931		Swindon Town	2	
		Denaby United		
Hammond, Walter Harry (Harry)			CF/IL/CH	
b Chorlton q3 1868			d 1921	
Caps: FLge 1				
		Edge Hill		
1889		Everton	1	
1892	1896	Sheffield United	108	53
1898	1899	New Brighton Tower	58	29
1900		Leicester Fosse	4	1
Hammond, Walter Reginald (Wally)			IR/CF	
b Buckland 19/6/1903			d 1965	
		Union Jacks		
		Cowes		
1920		Southampton (trial)	0	
1921	1923	Bristol Rovers	19	2
		Ryde Sports		
		Yorkshire Amateurs		
Hampshire, John George			CH	
b Goldthorpe 5/10/1913			d 1997	
		Mexborough		
1934		Manchester City	0	
1935	1937	Bristol City	21	
		Bath City		
Hampson, Harold			IR/IL	
b Little Hulton 8/6/1918			d 1942	
		Walkden Methodists		
1935		Everton	0	
		Walkden Methodists		
1936	1937	Southport	31	13
1938		Sheffield United	39	13
1939		(Sheffield United)	(2)	(1)
Hampson, James (Jimmy)			CF/IR	
b Little Hulton 23/3/1906			d 1938	
Caps: FLge 4/England 3				
		Little Hulton St John's		
		Ogden Primitive Methodists		
		Walkden Park Primitive Methodists		
1925	1927	Nelson	64	42
1927	1937	Blackpool	361	248
Hampson, John			CH/LH	
b Oswestry 28/12/1887			d 1960	
		Oswestry Town		
		Northampton Town		
1913	1919	Leeds City	71	8
1919	1920	Aston Villa	14	
1921	1923	Port Vale	99	9
		Hanley Sports Club		
Hampson, Thomas (Tommy)			GK	
b Bury 2/5/1898				
Caps: WLge 1				
		South Shields		
		Walker Celtic		
1920	1924	West Ham United	70	
1925		Blackburn Rovers	0	
		Annfield Plain		
1925		Burnley	6	
		West Stanley		
1926		Darlington	3	
		West Stanley		
1926	1928	Cardiff City	8	
1929		Notts County	1	
		Notts Co-op Dairy		
Hampson, Thomas (Tom)			RH	
b Salford 10/8/1916			d 1947	
		Droylsden		
1938		Leeds United	2	
1939		Oldham Athletic	0	

From To Apps Goal

Hampson, Walker LH/CH
b Radcliffe 24/7/1889 d 1959
Black Lane St Andrew's
Colne
1914 Burnley 4
Scotswood
1919 1920 South Shields 50 2
1921 Charlton Athletic 15
1922 Hartlepools United 22 4
1923 Chesterfield 12
1924 Rochdale (trial) 0
1924 Grimsby Town (trial) 0

Hampson, William (Billy) RB/LB
b Radcliffe 26/8/1884 d 1966
Woolfold Wesleyans
Ramsbottom
Rochdale Town
1907 Bury 2
Norwich City
1913 1926 Newcastle United 163 1
1927 South Shields 25

Hampton, Colin McKenzie GK
b Brechin 1/9/1888
Caps: SLge 1
Brechin Rovers
Brechin City
Motherwell
1913 1923 Chelsea 79
Brechin City
1925 Crystal Palace 3

Hampton, George RB
b Wellington, Shropshire q2 1890 d 1951
1909 1913 Glossop 110 1
1914 Aston Villa 3
Shrewsbury Town

Hampton, Henry Vernon (Harry) RH/LH
b Dublin 1/5/1890
Caps: Ireland 9
Dundee
1909 1913 Bradford City 47
Distillery

Hampton, John William GK
b Wolverhampton q2 1901 d 1939
Wellington Town
Oakengates Town
1922 1926 Wolverhampton Wanderers 49
1927 1929 Derby County 12
1930 Preston North End 37
Dundalk

Hampton, Joseph Henry (Harry) CF/IR/IL
b Wellington, Shropshire 21/4/1885 d 1963
Caps: FLge 3/England 4
Shifnal Juniors
Wellington Town
1904 1919 Aston Villa 339 215
1919 1921 Birmingham 57 31
1922 Newport County 14 2
Wellington Town

Hancock, Edmund (Ted) OR/IR/CF
b Denaby Main 29/3/1907
Denaby United
Gainsborough Trinity
1931 Liverpool 9 2
1932 1936 Burnley 112 23
1936 1937 Luton Town 26 3
Northwich Victoria
1938 Lincoln City 30 4
Frickley Colliery

Hancock, Frank Leslie CH
b Garforth 13/7/1906 d 1971
Castleford & Allerton United
1928 Bradford Park Avenue 0
Peterborough & Fletton United
1930 1934 Millwall 162 5
Wigan Athletic
1936 Millwall 3
Goole Town

Hancock, Frederick LH
1905 Stockport County 9

Hancock, Henry Bentley (Harry) IL/CF
b Levenshulme q4 1874 d 1924
Melrose (Cheshire)
Port Sunlight
Stockport County
1905 Blackpool 29 6
1907 Oldham Athletic 27 7
1907 Manchester City 0
1908 West Bromwich Albion 2
Brierley Hill Alliance
Tranmere Rovers

From To Apps Goal

Hancock, James (Jim) GK
b Methley 1875
Denaby United
Mexborough
1899 1900 Chesterfield Town 59
Denaby United
1901 Chesterfield Town 1
Denaby United

Hancock, JB IR
1894 Nottingham Forest 1

Hancock, Joseph RB
1902 1903 Glossop 26

Hancocks, John (Johnny) OR
b Oakengates 30/4/1919 d 1994
Caps: FLge 2/England 3
Oakengates Fellowship
Oakengates Town
1938 1945 Walsall 30 9
1939 (Walsall) (3)
1946 1955 Wolverhampton Wanderers 343 158
Wellington Town
Cambridge United
Oswestry Town
GKN Sankey

Hand, John (Jacky) CH
b Middlesbrough q4 1885
Grangetown Athletic
Darlington St Augustine's
1906 Blackburn Rovers 2
Shildon Athletic
Hartlepools United
Seaham Harbour
Wallsend Park Villa

Hand, William R (Bill) OL/IL/IR
b Codnor 5/7/1898
Sutton Town
1920 1925 Crystal Palace 100 15

Handford, Thomas LB
1895 Burton Wanderers 26
1898 Bury 1

Handley, Charles Harold James (Charlie) IL/OR/OL
b Edmonton 12/3/1899 d 1957
Edmonton Juniors
1921 1928 Tottenham Hotspur 120 26
1929 Swansea Town 19 4
Sittingbourne
Sheppey United
1931 Thames 29 3
Sittingbourne
1932 Norwich City 0
Berne

Handley, George OR/IR
b Burton-on-the-Wolds q4 1868
Loughborough
1895 Notts County 1
Coalville Town
1897 1898 Derby County 15 2
Northampton Town
Newark Town

Handley, George Albert OL
b Totley q1 1886 d 1952
Hallam
1904 Sheffield United 0
1904 1906 Chesterfield Town 25 4
1906 1910 Bradford City 86 29
Southampton
Goole Town
1913 Bradford City 1
Barrow
1919 1920 Bradford City 16 1
Bruhl

Handley, George H IR
b Wednesbury q3 1912 d 1943
Hednesford Town
1933 West Bromwich Albion 0
1934 Crystal Palace 5
Brierley Hill Alliance
Darlaston

Handley, Hamlet CH/OR
b Burslem q2 1873 d 1918
1895 Burslem Port Vale 5 1
1896 Burton Wanderers 18 5

Handley, John C CH
1926 Aberdare Athletic 1

Handley, Thomas Henry (Tom) CH/LH
b Aston q2 1886
King's Norton Monks
1907 1908 Birmingham 13
1909 1910 Bradford Park Avenue 26

From To Apps Goal

Hands, Thomas (Tommy) OL
b Small Heath 4/1/1870
Small Heath Unity
1892 1895 Small Heath 104 32
King's Heath

Hanford, Harold (Harry) CH
b Blaengwynfi 9/10/1907 d 1995
Caps: Wales Sch/WLge 1/Wales 7
Ton Pentre
Blaengwynfi Juniors
1927 1935 Swansea Town 201
1935 1938 Sheffield Wednesday 85 1
1939 (Sheffield Wednesday) (3)
1946 Exeter City 36
Haverfordwest Athletic

Hanger, Harold (Harry) LH
b Kettering 1886 d 1918
Caps: SoLge 1
Kettering
Northampton Town
Kettering
1905 1908 Bradford City 73 3
Crystal Palace

Hanger, Percy Kemshed CH
b Kettering q3 1889 d 1939
Kettering St Mary's
Kettering
1909 1912 Leicester Fosse 54
Kettering
Stamford Town

Hankey, Albert Edward (Ted 'Gunner') GK
b Stoke-on-Trent 24/5/1914 d 1998
1935 Charlton Athletic 0
Army
1937 1949 Southend United 125
Tonbridge

Hankey, Harry Barker CH/LH
b St Albans 28/3/1899 d 1952
1922 1923 Millwall Athletic 6

Hanks, Albert IL
b Rotherham 26/4/1908 d 1979
Brodsworth Main Colliery
1931 1932 Halifax Town 14 2

Hanks, Ernest CF
b York Town q2 1888 d 1965
Army Service Corps
1912 Woolwich Arsenal 4 1
Southend United

Hanlin, Patrick (Pat) LH
b West Calder 1885
Burnbank Athletic
1904 Everton 0
1905 1910 Bristol City 163 3

Hanlon, Edward (Eddie) CH
b Darlington q3 1886 d 1925
Darlington
1906 Middlesbrough 1
Darlington
1911 Barnsley 12 1
Darlington

Hanlon, John James (Johnny) CF/IR
b Manchester 12/10/1917 d 2002
St Wilfrid's (Hulme)
1938 1948 Manchester United 63 20
1939 (Manchester United) (1)
1948 1949 Bury 31 1
Northwich Victoria
Rhyl

Hann, Charles William (Billy) OL
b Bedwellty 11/4/1904 d 1998
1925 1926 Wolverhampton Wanderers 14 2

Hann, James IL
b Birtley q1 1897
Birtley
1920 Coventry City 1
Leadgate Park
Birtley
Warrington

Hann, Leslie IL/LH
b Gateshead 3/6/1911 d 1988
Windy Nook
Ashington
1934 West Ham United (trial) 0
Blyth Spartans
Felling Red Star
1936 1938 Accrington Stanley 29 1
1939 Clapton Orient (2)

From To Apps Goal

Hann, Ralph LH/RH/CH
b Whitburn, County Durham 4/7/1911 d 1990
Marsden Colliery Welfare
Whitburn St Mary's
1929 Sunderland 0
1930 Newcastle United 0
Newcastle Swifts
1932 1938 Derby County 115
1939 (Derby County) (2)
1946 Crystal Palace 1

Hanna, A John (Jack) GK
b Belfast
Caps: IrLge 1/Ireland 2
Linfield
1911 1913 Nottingham Forest 97
Scunthorpe & Lindsey United
Workington

Hannaford, Charles William (Charlie) OL/CF/OR
b Finsbury Park 8/1/1896 d 1970
Caps: England Sch
Page Green Old Boys
1914 Tottenham Hotspur 0
Tufnell Park
Maidstone United
1920 1922 Millwall Athletic 37 12
1923 Charlton Athletic 20 2
1923 1925 Clapton Orient 63 10
1925 1926 Manchester United 11
1928 Clapton Orient 4

Hannah, Andrew Boyd RB
b Renton 17/9/1864 d 1940
Caps: SLge 1/Scotland 1
Renton
1888 West Bromwich Albion 0
Renton
1889 1890 Everton 42
Renton
1893 1894 Liverpool 40 1
Rob Roy

Hannah, David (Davy) IL/OL/IR
b Raffrey 28/4/1867 d 1936
Renton
1890 1894 Sunderland 78 17
1894 1896 Liverpool 31 12
Dundee
1897 1898 Woolwich Arsenal 46 17
Renton

Hannah, Gardiner RH
b Baillieston 4/2/1871
Baillieston Thistle
Airdrieonians
1895 Blackburn Rovers 3
1896 1897 Lincoln City 56

Hannah, George Lamb RH
b Sunderland 25/9/1914 d 1977
Caps: England Sch
Washington Colliery
1937 Derby County 0
1938 Port Vale 42
1939 (Port Vale) (2)

Hannah, George William OL
b Leith 11/10/1895 d 1968
Loanhead Mayflower
Hamilton Academical
Cowdenbeath
Broxburn United
Dundee United
1925 New Brighton 6
Loanhead Mayflower

Hannah, James (Jimmy) OL/IL/OR
b Glasgow 1868 d 1917
Caps: FAlliance 1/Scotland 1
Third Lanark
Sunderland Albion
1891 1896 Sunderland 152 68
Third Lanark
Queen's Park Rangers
Dykehead
Sunderland Royal Rovers

Hannah, James Henry (Joe) RB/RH
b Sheringham 30/11/1898 d 1975
Sheringham Teachers
Royal Engineers
Sheringham
1920 1934 Norwich City 398 18

Hannah, John LB
Celtic
1905 Everton 1

Hannay, John OR
b Newcastle
1920 Derby County 1

From To Apps Goal

Hanney, Terence Percival (Ted) CH
b Bradfield 19/1/1889 d 1964
Caps: SoLge 1/England Amat
Wokingham Town
Reading
1913 1919 Manchester City 68 1
1919 1920 Coventry City 32
1921 Reading 41 2
Northfleet

Hanney, William Patrick Edward (Mick) CF
b Wigston 7/5/1904 d 1990
1927 Derby County 0
1928 Gillingham 11 4
1929 Birmingham 0
Market Harborough Town
Nuneaton Town

Hannible, Charles IR
b Stockport q1 1906 d 1960
1930 Crewe Alexandra 3 1
Hurst

Hannigan, Richard OR
Morton
1898 Notts County 15 2
1899 Woolwich Arsenal 1
1899 Burnley 8 3
Ilkeston Town
Newton Rovers
Somercotes United

Hanning, James IR
Dalziel Rovers
1897 Sunderland 1
Hamilton Academical
Carfin Emmet

Hanson, Adolph Jonathan (Alf) OL
b Bootle 27/2/1912 d 1993
Caps: Lol 3/England War 1
Bootle Joint Ordnance Corps
1930 Everton (trial) 0
1932 1937 Liverpool 166 50
1938 Chelsea 37 8
1939 (Chelsea) (3)
South Liverpool
Shelbourne
Ellesmere Port Town

Hanson, Frederick (Fred) OL/LB
b Sheffield 23/5/1915 d 1967
Indus Sports
1933 Sheffield United 0
1934 Bradford City 0
Mexborough Town
1934 Wolverhampton Wanderers 0
1935 Crystal Palace 1
1936 1946 Rotherham United 106 29
1939 (Rotherham United) (3)

Hanson, James (Jimmy) IR/RH/GK
b Little Hulton q2 1877
Little Hulton
1898 1903 Bolton Wanderers 64 9
1904 Doncaster Rovers 14 2
Oldham Athletic

Hanson, James (Jim) IR/CF
b Manchester 6/11/1904
Manchester YMCA
Bradford Parish
1922 Stalybridge Celtic 0
Manchester North End
1924 1929 Manchester United 138 47

Hanson, Stanley (Stan) GK
b Bootle 27/12/1915 d 1987
1933 Liverpool 0
1934 Southport 0
Litherland
1936 1955 Bolton Wanderers 384
1939 (Bolton Wanderers) (3)
Rhyl Athletic

Hanson, Thomas (Tot) OR
b Bearpark 1/3/1902 d 1983
Bearpark
1922 1923 Durham City 3
Shildon
Malton
Annfield Plain
1927 Durham City 0

Hanson, William (Bill) LB
b Rushall 1887
Rushall Red Cross
1907 Aston Villa 0
Coventry City
1910 Bradford Park Avenue 1

Hanwell, James (Jimmy) IR
b Rotherham 9/6/1901 d 1982
Guildford United
1923 Rotherham County 19 6
1924 Doncaster Rovers 7 2

From To Apps Goal

Hapgood, Edris Albert (Eddie) LB
b Bristol 27/9/1908 d 1973
Caps: FLge 4/England War 15/England 30
1926 Bristol Rovers (trial) 0
Kettering Town
1927 1938 Arsenal 393 2
1939 (Arsenal) (3)
Shrewsbury Town

Happs, Roland RB
b Birdwell 2/8/1909 d 2004
Platts Common
Denaby United
1931 1933 Barnsley 12
Mexborough Athletic

Harbidge, Charles William (Charlie) LH
b Tipton 15/7/1891 d 1980
Caps: England Amat
Civil Service Strollers
Corinthians
1920 Reading 19
1921 Charlton Athletic 6

Harbot, James Willie (Jimmy) LB/RB
b Bolton 16/8/1907 d 1992
Royal Naval Depot (Chatham)
1930 Gillingham 2 1
1932 Charlton Athletic 1 1
1933 Barrow 23
1936 Stoke City 1
1937 Torquay United 15
Chorley

Harbottle, Albert Norman GK
b Newcastle 30/3/1915 d 1997
1935 1936 Gateshead 35

Harbour, William RH
b Liverpool q4 1869 d 1928
1888 Everton 0
1888 Derby County 1

Hardaker, James OL
b Bradford 1901
Calverley
1922 Halifax Town 3

Hardcastle, Douglas Scott IL
b Worksop q1 1886 d 1915
Worksop Town
1905 Derby County 5 1
Worksop Town

Hardie, Alexander Shaw (Alex) LH
b Kilsyth 8/7/1898
Kilsyth Rangers
Third Lanark
1925 Charlton Athletic 28 3
1925 1932 Plymouth Argyle 232 4
1933 Exeter City 18 1
Truro City

Hardie, George GK
b Stanley, Derbyshire 1873
West Hallam
Denaby Wanderers
Conisbrough
Mexborough
1896 Grimsby Town 6
Mexborough
1898 Lincoln City 12

Harding, Albert GK
Nantwich
1921 Crewe Alexandra 1

Harding, Augustus William (Gus) RB/LB
b Ash, Kent q2 1885 d 1916
Tottenham Hotspur
1907 1909 Chelsea 4
Exeter City

Harding, William LB
1900 Stockport County 2

Hardinge, Harold Thomas William (Wally) IL/IR
b Greenwich 25/2/1886 d 1965
Caps: England 1
Eltham
Tonbridge
Maidstone United
1905 Newcastle United 9 1
1907 1912 Sheffield United 147 45
1913 1919 Woolwich Arsenal 54 14

From To Apps Goal

Hardman, Harold Payne OL/OR
b Kirkmanshulme 4/4/1882 d 1965
Caps: FLge 1/England Amat/England 4
Worsley Wanderers
Chorlton-cum-Hardy
South Shore Choristers
Northern Nomads
1900 1902 Blackpool 73 10
1903 1907 Everton 130 25
1908 Manchester United 4
1908 1909 Bradford City 20 2
Stoke

Hardman, John Andrew (Jack) LH/CH
b Miles Platting q2 1889 d 1917
Longfield
1911 Oldham Athletic 2
Pontypridd
1913 1914 Derby County 14
Bristol Rovers

Hardstaff, Joseph (Joe) IR
b Kirkby-in-Ashfield 9/11/1882 d 1947
1904 1905 Nottingham Forest 12 1
Mansfield Mechanics

Hardware, James (Jimmy) RH
b Wolverhampton 9/1886 d 1957
Tettenhall Institute
Hurst Lane Social
1908 1909 Wolverhampton Wanderers 9
Bilston United
Willenhall Pickwick
Wightwick Star

Hardwick, George Francis Moutry LB/IL
b Saltburn 2/2/1920 d 2004
Caps: FLge 3/England War 17/England 13
South Bank East End
1937 1950 Middlesbrough 143 5
1950 1955 Oldham Athletic 190 14

Hardy, Alfred (Alf) CF/OR
b Seaton Delaval 13/5/1897 d 1970
Cramlington Rovers
Ashington
1920 Watford 0
1921 Durham City 1
Pontypridd
Porth Athletic
1922 Barrow 16 8
Mold Town
Scotswood
Vono Sports
Truro City

Hardy, Allen LB
b Ilkeston q1 1873 d 1950
Ilkeston Town
Wigan County
1899 1901 Blackburn Rovers 42

Hardy, Arthur IL
Derby Midland
1891 1892 Derby County 3 1
Heanor Town

Hardy, Cecil IL
b Kimblesworth 1/1/1898 d 1975
Blackhall Colliery Welfare
1921 1927 Hartlepools United 124 45
Blackhall Colliery Welfare
Horden Colliery Welfare
Blackhall Colliery Welfare

Hardy, Edgar OL
b Sutton-in-Ashfield 14/8/1903 d 1988
1925 1926 Rotherham United 11 4
Mansfield Town

Hardy, George G CH/LH
b Newbold Verdon 4/1912
Nuneaton Town
1936 1937 Aston Villa 6 1
1938 Blackburn Rovers 7

Hardy, Harry GK
b Stockport 14/1/1895 d 1969
Caps: FLge 2/England 1
Alderley Edge
1920 1925 Stockport County 207
1925 1927 Everton 40
1929 1930 Bury 27

Hardy, Jacob Henry OR
b Bishop Auckland q3 1898
Shildon Athletic
1922 Blackburn Rovers 1

From To Apps Goal

Hardy, John Henry (Jack) LH/RH
b Chesterfield 15/6/1910 d 1978
Unstone
1934 1936 Chesterfield 48 1
1937 1938 Hull City 65
1939 1946 Lincoln City 18
1939 (Lincoln City) (1)
Skellingthorpe

Hardy, John James CH
b Sunderland 10/2/1899 d 1932
Wearmouth Colliery
Sunderland Celtic
1921 1923 South Shields 102 5
1924 Derby County 3
1925 1926 Grimsby Town 46 4
1926 Oldham Athletic 2
1927 South Shields 11
Boldon Colliery
Scarborough
West Stanley
1931 Clapton Orient 0
Silksworth Colliery

Hardy, Lawrence Richard (Dick) IR/CH
b South Bank 28/2/1913 d 1995
South Bank East End
1931 1936 Hartlepools United 150 26
1937 Bradford City 12 2
Shrewsbury Town

Hardy, Robert (Bob) OR/OL/IR
b South Bank 16/6/1885
Caps: England Amat
South Bank Celtic
South Bank
1908 1910 Bristol City 74 13
Wingate Albion
Olympique (France)

Hardy, Robert RH
b Hemsworth
1932 1933 Rotherham United 12

Hardy, Robert M (Bob) IR
b Hemsworth 1914
Dinnington Colliery
1937 Rochdale 7

Hardy, Sam GK
b Newbold 26/8/1882 d 1966
Caps: FLge 10/England 21
Newbold White Star
1902 1904 Chesterfield Town 71
1905 1911 Liverpool 219
1912 1920 Aston Villa 159
1921 1924 Nottingham Forest 102

Hardy, Stanley (Stan) IL
b Newcastle 1890
Rutherford College
1913 Newcastle United 3 1

Hardy, Sydney (Sid) OL
b Kimblesworth q1 1902
Blackhall Colliery Welfare
Hartlepools United
Horden Colliery Welfare
1924 1927 Hartlepools United 62 19
Spennymoor United
Blackhall Colliery Welfare

Hardy, Walter RB/LB/RH
1896 1899 Loughborough 99 1

Hardy, William (Billy) LH
b Bedlington 18/4/1892 d 1981
Caps: WLge 2/FLge 1
Bedlington United
Heart of Midlothian
1910 Stockport County 1
1920 1931 Cardiff City 354 6
1932 Bradford Park Avenue 0

Hardy, William RH
b Stockport
1925 Crewe Alexandra 1

Hardy, William Henry IR
b Denaby 25/10/1915 d 1990
1935 1936 Rotherham United 46 11
1936 Nottingham Forest 1
Gainsborough Trinity
Grantham

Hare, Charles Boyd (Charlie) IR/CF/OR
b Birmingham 6/1870 d 1934
Warwick County
Birmingham United
1891 1894 Aston Villa 25 13
1894 1895 Woolwich Arsenal 19 7
1896 1897 Small Heath 43 14
Watford
Fulham
Plymouth Argyle
Green Waves

From To Apps Goal

Haresnape, Robert OR
b Blackburn 1866
Darwen
Witton (Blackburn)
1888 Blackburn Rovers 9 2
1889 1891 Burnley 26 7
Irwell Springs

Harford, George Balloch GK
b Abbey Wood 1910
Bexleyheath
1927 1928 Millwall 57
1929 1933 Luton Town 99
1935 Carlisle United 26
Rhyl Athletic

Harget, Andrew CF/LB
b Wolverhampton q2 1879
Army
1903 1904 Bristol City 16 3
Bath City

Harget, George Henry LB
b Wolverhampton q2 1883
Bristol St George
Bristol Rovers
1904 Bristol City 3

Hargraves, J Fred CF/RH
b Yorkshire 1884
1903 1904 Burton United 56 14
1905 1907 Leeds City 63 12
Stoke

Hargreaves, A CF
1892 Blackburn Rovers 2

Hargreaves, A IR
1894 Burnley 2

Hargreaves, Alfred OR
1905 Burnley 1

Hargreaves, Ellis IL/OR
1896 Burnley 1
Tottenham Hotspur
1898 Darwen 14 1

Hargreaves, Frank IL/IR/OL
b Ashton-under-Lyne 17/11/1902 d 1987
New Moss Colliery
Ashton National
Hurst
Stalybridge Celtic
Droylsden United
Manchester North End
1923 Oldham Athletic 33 3
1924 Everton 9 2
1925 1929 Oldham Athletic 70 14
1930 Rochdale 9 3
1931 Bournemouth & Boscombe Ath 0
1931 Watford 0
1932 Oldham Athletic 5

Hargreaves, Harold (Harry) IL
b Higham, Lancashire 15/3/1896
Higham
Great Harwood
1921 Nelson 13 2
1921 1922 Wolverhampton Wanderers 53 8
Pontypridd
1923 1925 Tottenham Hotspur 34 7
1925 1927 Burnley 26 6
1928 Rotherham United 0
Rossendale United
Barnoldswick Town
Nelson Town

Hargreaves, Harold CH
b Sheffield 1906
Worksop Town
1926 Blackpool 2
Stalybridge Celtic
1928 Lincoln City 0
Wath Athletic
1928 Rotherham United 0
1929 Merthyr Town 25 1
Mansfield Town
Worksop Town

Hargreaves, J OL
1893 Ardwick 8

Hargreaves, John (Jackie) OL
b Rotherham 1/5/1915 d 1978
Sheffield Juniors
1935 1938 Leeds United 45 10
1939 (Leeds United) (1)
1945 1946 Bristol City 26 9
1946 1947 Reading 15 1
Yeovil Town

Hargreaves, Joseph Jackson CF
1895 Rotherham Town 2 1

From To Apps Goal

Hargreaves, Joseph Langard (Joe) RH
b Enfield, Lancashire 4/3/1890 d 1924
Clayton YMCA
Great Harwood
Accrington Stanley
1911 1923 Bradford City 188 6

Hargreaves, Joshua (Josh) CF/IR/OR
b Blackburn 1870
1891 Blackburn Rovers 0
1892 Northwich Victoria 14 1
1893 1896 Blackburn Rovers 52 18
1898 1900 New Brighton Tower 90 26
1897 Blackburn Rovers (loan) 2 1
Accrington Stanley

Hargreaves, Leonard (Len) OL
b Kimberworth 7/3/1906 d 1980
Blackburn Wesleyans (Doncaster)
1925 1926 Doncaster Rovers 36 12
1927 1928 Sunderland 35 11
1928 Sheffield Wednesday 2 1
Workington
1932 Doncaster Rovers 8 2
1933 Luton Town 0
Peterborough United

Hargreaves, Robert IR/IL
Clitheroe
1897 1898 Preston North End 11
South Shore
Oswaldtwistle Rovers

Hargreaves, Thomas (Tom) CH/CF
b Blackburn 29/10/1917 d 1997
Crosshill
1937 Blackburn Rovers 4 2
1946 Rochdale 7
Nelson

Hargreaves, Walter Oscar (Oscar) CH
b Rawmarsh q2 1893
Frickley Colliery
1920 1921 Rotherham County 42
Scunthorpe & Lindsey United

Hargreaves, WG IR
1904 Burton United 30

Hargreaves, William Vesey LH
b Wombwell 1888
Darfield United
1908 1909 Grimsby Town 18 1
Mexborough Town

Harker, Edward (Ted) IR
b Plumtree q4 1862
1888 Notts County 2

Harker, George F OL
1926 Walsall 1

Harker, J IR
Thornaby
1898 Sunderland 1
Thornaby

Harker, James H (Jim) OL
1931 1932 Darlington 9 3
Bishop Auckland

Harker, Stanley Jefferson (Stan) OL
b Bradford 1/10/1909 d 1973
Wyke
1931 1932 Halifax Town 5

Harker, Willie IR/LH
b Brierfield 21/12/1910 d 1973
1929 Burnley 0
1930 Nelson 18 5
1931 1932 Burnley 24 6
1933 Torquay United 9
1934 1935 Accrington Stanley 62 23
1936 Portsmouth 0
1936 1938 Stockport County 35 3
1939 Rochdale 0

Harkin, James (Jim) RH/IL
b Brinsworth 8/8/1913 d 1988
Rossington Main
Denaby United
1934 Doncaster Rovers 1
1935 Rotherham United (trial) 0
Shrewsbury Town
1938 1946 Mansfield Town 23 5
1939 (Mansfield Town) (3)
Gainsborough Trinity
Peterborough United

From To Apps Goal

Harkins, James IL
b Paisley 1905
Dalbeattie Star
Petershill
Third Lanark
Solway Star
1927 Luton Town 4 3
1927 Port Vale 0
Bo'ness
Solway Star

Harkins, John Anderson RH/LH
b Milton, Glasgow 10/4/1881 d 1916
Black Watch Regiment
1906 1907 Middlesbrough 39
Broxburn Athletic
Bathgate
1910 1911 Leeds City 63
Darlington
Coventry City

Harkins, John F IL/IR
b Bathgate 21/2/1909
St Mary's Guild
Dalkeith Thistle
Albion Rovers
1930 1934 Millwall 26 1
Albion Rovers

Harkus, George Cecil CH/RH/LH
b Newcastle 25/9/1898 d 1950
Nun's Moor
Edinburgh Emmet
Scotswood
1921 1922 Aston Villa 4
1923 1929 Southampton 218 3
Fives (France)
New Milton
1931 Southampton 2
1932 Southport 0

Harland, Alfred Ireland (Alfie) GK
b Cookstown 26/11/1897
Caps: IrLge 2/Ireland 2
Linfield
1922 1925 Everton 64
Runcorn

Harland, Thomas Henry (Tommy) RB/LB
b Wingate 8/4/1904 d 1985
Wingate United Methodist Church
Station Town United Methodists
1928 Huddersfield Town (trial) 0
1928 1930 Hartlepools United 16
Shotton Colliery Welfare
1931 1933 Hartlepools United 23
Gas & Water
Wingate United

Harley, Alexander John (Alex) CF/IL
b Edinburgh 17/9/1898 d 1984
Bonnyrigg Rose Athletic
Bathgate
Heart of Midlothian
Caernarvon Athletic
1927 New Brighton 27 14
1928 Millwall 7 4
Rhyl Athletic
Connah's Quay & Shotton
1930 Norwich City (trial) 1

Harley, Charles C (Charlie) OR
b Birmingham 1873
Aston Victoria
1890 Aston Villa 1
Burton Wanderers
Lozells
1893 1894 Walsall Town Swifts 10 3
Soho Villa
Worcester Rovers

Harley, James (Jim) LB/RB
b Methil 2/2/1917 d 1989
Caps: Scotland War 2
Hearts o' Beath
1935 1947 Liverpool 114
1939 (Liverpool) (3)

Harling, Edwin GK
1904 Doncaster Rovers 1

Harmsworth, Frederick (Fred) RH
b Croxton Kerrial 1877
1902 Newcastle United (trial) 0
1903 Grimsby Town 5

Harper, Bernard CH/RH/LH
b Gawber 23/11/1911 d 1994
Caps: England War 1
Gawber Sunday School
Barugh Green
West Ward
1932 1938 Barnsley 215 2
1939 (Barnsley) (3)
Scunthorpe & Lindsey United

From To Apps Goal

Harper, Charles Henry IL/IR
Lower Gornal
1921 1923 Walsall 41 9

Harper, Edward Cashfield (Ted) CF
b Sheerness 22/8/1901 d 1959
Caps: England 1
Whitstable Town
Sheppey United
1923 1927 Blackburn Rovers 144 106
1927 1928 Sheffield Wednesday 18 13
1928 1931 Tottenham Hotspur 63 62
1931 1933 Preston North End 75 67
1933 1934 Blackburn Rovers 27 15

Harper, Ernest RB
1893 Northwich Victoria 2

Harper, Ernest LB
b Hugglescote q3 1883
Coalville United
Coalville Town
Coalville Wednesday
Hugglescote United
Coalville Town
1904 Leicester Fosse 1
1904 Derby County 0
Hugglescote United

Harper, George Spencer IR/IL
b Birmingham 5/1877 d 1949
Saltley Gas Company
1894 Burton Wanderers 0
1895 Aston Villa 0
Hereford Thistle
1897 1900 Wolverhampton Wanderers 61 19
1901 1902 Grimsby Town 21 3
1902 Sunderland 10 1

Harper, James RB/LB
Newtown
1895 1897 Manchester City 33
Chatham

Harper, John OR
b Ayrshire 1883
Beith
Maybole
Vale of Glengarnock Strollers
1903 Bradford City 2

Harper, Kenneth (Ken) RB
b Worsborough 15/4/1917 d 1994
1937 1938 Walsall 22 2
1939 (Walsall) (2)
1946 1948 Bradford City 50

Harper, Rowland Richard G OR
b Lichfield 4/1881 d 1949
Walsall Wood
1905 1906 Birmingham 22 1
1906 Burton United 0
1907 Aston Villa 2
1907 1908 Notts County 10 1
Mansfield Invicta

Harper, Theophilus (Fay) RB/LB
b Brierley Hill q3 1866
Mansfield Greenhalgh
Mansfield Town
Notts Rangers
1892 1894 Notts County 46
Mansfield Town

Harper, Thomas OR
b Marsden q4 1903
1926 South Shields 0
1927 1928 Newport County 24 5
Whitburn
1929 Accrington Stanley 0
Marsden
Whitburn Villa

Harper, William (Billy) RB
b Blackburn 17/8/1897 d 1982
Feniscowles
1924 Nelson 6
Darwen
Chorley

Harper, William (Bill) GK
b Tarbrax 19/1/1897 d 1989
Caps: SLge 3/Scotland 11
Winchburgh Thistle
Winchburgh Violet
Broxburn St Andrew's
Edinburgh Emmet
Hibernian
1925 1926 Arsenal 42
Fall River Marksmen
Boston Wonder Workers
Boston Bears
Boston (USA)
New Bedford Whalers
1930 1931 Arsenal 21
1931 1938 Plymouth Argyle 78

From	To	Club	Apps	Goal
Harper, William E (Billy)			OL	
b Nechells 1876			d 1944	
		Smethwick Wesleyan Rovers		
1901	1902	West Bromwich Albion	8	
1903		Leicester Fosse	4	
		Stourbridge		
Harper, William George (Bill)			GK	
b Bothwell 15/11/1900				
		Wishaw		
1921	1922	Sunderland	28	
1923		Manchester City	4	
1924	1925	Crystal Palace	57	
1926		Luton Town	31	
		Weymouth		
		Callender Athletic		
Harries, Edward R			CH	
1924		Stockport County	1	
Harrington, James Christopher (Chris)			OL/IL	
b Edge Hill 25/12/1896			d 1978	
		South Liverpool		
1920		Liverpool	4	
		South Liverpool		
1921	1922	Wigan Borough	21	4
1922		Southport	17	1
1923		Crewe Alexandra	10	2
		Mold Town		
		Prescot Cables		
		New York Giants		
		Aysgarth		
Harrington, John W (Jack)			OR	
b Hednesford				
		Hednesford Town		
1923	1927	Wolverhampton Wanderers	107	10
1928		Northampton Town	8	
		Brierley Hill Alliance		
Harris, Albert			OR/OL	
b Horden 16/9/1912			d 1995	
		Hetton United		
		Herrington Swifts		
1930		Hull City	5	
		Blackhall Colliery Welfare		
1935		Newcastle United	12	4
1936		Barnsley	15	1
1936	1938	Darlington	60	7
		Scunthorpe & Lindsey United		
Harris, Ambrose			LH/RH	
b Harle Syke 29/10/1902			d 1952	
		Briercliffe		
1924	1927	Nelson	58	1
		Barnoldswick Town		
		Brierfield Central		
Harris, Arthur			OR	
b Atherton 15/9/1903			d 1970	
		Hindley Green Colliery		
		Atherton		
		Atherton Collieries		
1926		Norwich City	1	
		Poole		
		Bacup Borough		
Harris, Arthur			RH	
b Coventry 28/7/1914			d 1973	
		Nuneaton Town		
1936	1946	Southend United	114	1
1939		(Southend United)	(3)	
		Nuneaton Town		
Harris, Bernard (Bernie)			LB/RB	
b Sheffield 1901				
		Upperthorpe Comrades		
		Gainsborough Trinity		
1922		Rotherham County	30	
1924	1926	Sheffield United	44	
1928		Luton Town	19	
1929	1931	Queen's Park Rangers	60	
		Llanelly		
1933		Swindon Town	25	
		Margate		
		Ramsgate		
Harris, Cecil Norman			GK	
b Madeley, Shropshire q4 1905				
		Hibernian		
1929	1930	Darlington	21	
Harris, Cecil Vernon			RB/LB	
b Grantham 1/9/1896			d 1976	
		Grantham		
		Llandrindod Wells		
1922	1925	Aston Villa	26	
1926	1927	Grimsby Town	47	1
		Gainsborough Trinity		
Harris, Charles (Charlie)			CH	
b Wanstead 1/12/1885				
1905		Chelsea	1	
Harris, Charles Herbert			OL	
b Lewisham q2 1899			d 1965	
		Nunhead		
1925	1927	Millwall	12	
Harris, Francis (Frank)			RH/IR	
b Catshill 5/4/1908				
		Cradley Heath		
		Bromsgrove Rovers		
1928	1932	Cardiff City	130	10
1933	1935	Charlton Athletic	82	8
		Brierley Hill Alliance		
		Bromsgrove Rovers		
Harris, Francis Edgar (Frank)			RH/CH	
b Urmston 1/12/1899				
		Urmston Congregational		
		Urmston Old Boys		
1919	1921	Manchester United	46	2
		Bethlehem Steel		
Harris, Frederick (Fred)			IL/RH/IR	
b Sparkbrook 2/7/1912			d 1998	
Caps: FLge 1				
		Sparkbrook		
		Birmingham City Transport		
		Osborne Athletic		
1934	1949	Birmingham	280	61
1939		(Birmingham)	(3)	
Harris, Frederick McKenzie (Fred)			OR/CF	
b Rothwell 1884				
		Rothwell Congregationals		
1900		Burton Swifts	0	
		Desborough Town		
		Kettering		
		Northampton Town		
		Kettering		
1913	1914	Nottingham Forest	48	12
		Swansea Town		
		Kettering		
1921		Southend United	20	2
		Kettering		
		Rushden Town		
		Rothwell Town		
Harris, George			GK	
b Headless Cross, Redditch q3 1875			d 1910	
		Headless Cross		
		Redditch Excelsior		
1895		Aston Villa	1	
1897	1899	Wolverhampton Wanderers	7	
1900		Grimsby Town	13	
		Portsmouth		
		Redditch Town		
		Tunbridge Wells Rangers		
		Kidderminster Harriers		
Harris, George			IL/OL	
b Rocester 1877				
		Uttoxeter Town		
1900	1902	Stoke	23	5
		Reading		
		Southampton		
		Tutbury Town		
Harris, George			CF	
		Wingate St Mary's		
		Hesleden Rising Star		
1935		Hartlepools United	1	1
		Horden Colliery Welfare		
		Trimdon Colliery Welfare		
		Hartlepool Paper Mills		
Harris, George Abner			LH	
b Halesowen 1/1/1878			d 1923	
		Haden Hill Rose		
		Halesowen		
		Coombs Wood		
		Halesowen		
1901	1907	Aston Villa	20	1
1908	1909	West Bromwich Albion	19	
		Wellington Town		
		Coventry City		
Harris, George Buller			RH	
b Grays q1 1900				
Caps: England Sch				
		Barking Town		
1921		Southend United	3	
Harris, George Thomas			LH/LB	
b High Wycombe 14/6/1904			d 1986	
		Wycombe Wanderers		
1922	1923	Notts County	2	
1924	1925	Queen's Park Rangers	38	
1926	1927	Fulham	8	1
		Margate		
		Watford Wednesday		
Harris, J			OL	
1898		Loughborough	1	
Harris, James Somerville			GK	
b Gorbals 17/5/1906				
		Shawfield		
		Hamilton Academical		
		Dunfermline Athletic		
1929		Manchester City	0	
1930		Rotherham United	10	
		Waterford		
		Cork Bohemians		
		Glentoran		
		Bangor		
Harris, James William (Jimmy)			OL	
b Tunbridge Wells q2 1907				
		Folkestone		
1930	1931	West Ham United	7	1
1932		Southampton	2	
Harris, John (Jack)			RH/IL	
b Hesleden 1901				
		Hesleden Celtic		
1921	1922	Hartlepools United	4	
Harris, John			OL/CF	
b Redcar 19/3/1896			d 1933	
1920		Middlesbrough	0	
1924		Wolverhampton Wanderers	6	2
1925		Watford	29	5
1927		Darlington	1	1
1927		Hartlepools United	1	
1928		Barrow	12	1
		Spennymoor United		
Harris, John			CH/RB/RH	
b Glasgow 30/6/1917			d 1988	
Caps: Scotland War 1				
1933		Swindon Town	0	
1934	1938	Swansea Town	29	4
1938		Tottenham Hotspur	0	
1939		Wolverhampton Wanderers	0	
1945	1955	Chelsea	326	14
1956		Chester	27	1
Harris, Joseph (Joe)			RH/LH	
b Glasgow 19/3/1896			d 1933	
Caps: Scotland 2				
		Strathclyde Juniors		
		Partick Thistle		
1922	1924	Middlesbrough	56	
1925	1930	Newcastle United	149	2
1931	1932	York City	62	
Harris, Joseph (Joe)			LH	
1938		Doncaster Rovers	0	
1939		Brighton & Hove Albion	(3)	
Harris, Joshua (Jack)			OL/OR	
b Glasgow 5/11/1891			d 1966	
		Vale of Clyde		
		Glasgow Ashfield		
1910	1911	Burnley	57	5
1912	1921	Bristol City	205	26
		Partick Thistle (loan)		
		Clydebank (loan)		
1922	1925	Leeds United	126	15
1925	1926	Fulham	42	2
Harris, Neil L			CF/IR	
b Tollcross 30/10/1894			d 1941	
Caps: Scotland 1				
		Vale of Clyde		
		Partick Thistle		
		Kilmarnock (loan)		
		Rangers (loan)		
		St Mirren (loan)		
1920	1925	Newcastle United	174	87
1925	1926	Notts County	49	23
		Shelbourne		
1927	1928	Oldham Athletic	39	16
		Third Lanark		
		Burton Town		
		Distillery		
Harris, Robert			OR	
		Dunfermline Athletic		
1923		Doncaster Rovers	11	
		Bullcroft Colliery		
Harris, SG			OR	
1906		Gainsborough Trinity	2	
Harris, Thomas (Tommy)			OR/IR/IL	
b Ince-in-Makerfield 18/9/1905			d 1985	
		Skelmersdale United		
1926		Manchester United	4	1
1928		Wigan Borough	24	8
1929		Rotherham United	6	1
1929	1930	Crewe Alexandra	41	6
		Chorley		
		Gresley Rovers		
		Prescot Cables		
Harris, Thomas Frank Fearnley (Tom)			CF	
b Plymouth 26/6/1913			d 1987	
		Devon Corinthians		
		Plymouth Kitto		
1934	1937	Bristol Rovers	28	16
1937		Southampton	0	
1938		Barrow	41	24
1939		(Barrow)	(3)	(1)
Harris, Valentine (Val)			RH	
b Dublin 1885				
Caps: IrLge 4/LoI 2/Ireland 20				
		Shelbourne		
1907	1913	Everton	190	1
		Shelbourne		
Harris, Wallace Norman			OR/IR	
b Hockley 22/2/1900			d 1933	
		Ada Road Social		
		Burton All Saints		
1923	1927	Birmingham	89	12
1929		Walsall	6	1
Harris, Walter Henry			CF	
b Plymouth q1 1904				
		Plymouth Ivanhoe		
		Torquay Town		
1924	1927	Aston Villa	20	4
1929		Bristol City	26	15
		Loughborough Corinthians		
		Bath City		
Harris, Walter T (Wally)			CF	
b Wolverhampton 1887				
		Queen's Park Athletic		
		Willenhall		
		Redditch		
1908		Wolverhampton Wanderers	5	1
		Dudley Town		
		Blakenhall		
Harris, William			LB	
b Glasgow 25/9/1890				
		Glasgow Benburb		
		Rutherglen		
1909		Tottenham Hotspur	7	
Harris, William (Bill)			GK	
b Dudley 1/12/1918			d 1996	
		Oakham Juniors		
		Whiteheath		
1937		West Bromwich Albion	2	
1946		Oldham Athletic	32	
1947	1949	Accrington Stanley	99	
		Dudley Town		
		Bilston		
Harris, William Henry G			LB	
b Axbridge 6/4/1920			d 2001	
		Hallam Athletic		
1939		Ipswich Town	(1)	
Harris, William J			IR	
b Plymouth				
1929		Millwall	1	
1930		Gateshead	0	
Harris, William James (Bill)			IR	
b Cramlington 25/4/1900			d 1969	
		Whitley Bay Athletic		
1923		Coventry City	0	
1924		South Shields	2	
		Walker Celtic		
		Colwyn Bay		
1926		Ashington	21	11
1926		Huddersfield Town	0	
1927		Wrexham	9	2
1928		Ashington	19	2
Harris, William Thomas (Tommy)			RB/OL	
b Aberbargoed 30/6/1913			d 1997	
		New Tredegar		
1935	1948	Watford	94	6
		De Havilland Leavesden		
		Biggleswade Town		
Harrison, Albert			CH	
b Leigh 15/2/1904				
		West Leigh		
1922	1923	Wigan Borough	6	
		Atherton Collieries		
		Chorley		
1927	1929	Nottingham Forest	77	5
1929	1930	Leicester City	32	1
		Dundalk		
		Drumcondra		
		Wigan Athletic		
		Lugano		
Harrison, Albert			RH	
b Birches Head 19/8/1909			d 1989	
1932		Port Vale	3	
		Leek Alexandra		

From To Apps Goal

Harrison, Albert W OR
Ruddington
1905 Notts County 3

Harrison, Alvern (Jerry) LH
b Gainsborough q2 1878
1899 1901 Gainsborough Trinity 28
Worksop Town

Harrison, Arthur OR
b Birmingham 9/1878
Linton
1902 Small Heath 4 3
Brownhills Athletic

Harrison, Arthur LH
1903 Gainsborough Trinity 1

Harrison, Charles Edwin (Charlie) GK
b Newton Heath q3 1861
Newton Heath
1888 1889 Bolton Wanderers 24
Newton Heath

Harrison, Eugene IR/LH
b Bolton-on-Dearne q3 1893
1919 1920 Rotherham County 7 4

Harrison, F LH
1898 Blackpool 1

Harrison, Fred Parker LH
b Bradford 21/6/1911 d 1986
1934 1935 Bradford Park Avenue 8
1936 Halifax Town 3

Harrison, Frederick (Fred) CF
b Winchester 2/7/1880 d 1969
Fitzhugh Rovers
Bitterne Guild
Southampton
1907 1910 Fulham 120 47
West Ham United
1913 Bristol City 15 5

Harrison, George OL
b Church Gresley 18/7/1892 d 1939
Caps: England 2
Gresley Rovers
1910 1912 Leicester Fosse 59 9
1913 1923 Everton 177 17
1923 1930 Preston North End 274 72
1931 Blackpool 16 2

Harrison, George (Ginger) RH/LH/CF
b South Moor q4 1900
Tanfield Lea Institute
Houghton Rovers
1920 Sunderland 0
Annfield Plain
1922 1923 Durham City 10 1
1924 Darlington 1
West Stanley
1928 Carlisle United 28
Lancaster Town
Lancaster Corporation Omnibus Co

Harrison, Harry LB/RB/RH
b Millfield, County Durham 26/6/1917 d 2000
Millfield
Durham City
Houghton Colliery Welfare
1936 Hartlepools United 0
1937 Chesterfield 0
1939 1950 Southport 135 1
1939 (Southport) (3)

Harrison, Henry (Harry) GK
b Redcar 21/11/1893 d 1975
Redcar
Grangetown Athletic
1911 Newcastle United 0
1919 1923 Middlesbrough 31
1924 Darlington 0
1925 Durham City 36
1926 1927 Hartlepools United 68
1928 Darlington 22

Harrison, Horace Frank (Frank) OR
b Bournemouth
Bournemouth Tramways
1923 Bournemouth & Boscombe Ath 4
Bournemouth Tramways

Harrison, Jack OR
Sneyd Colliery
1936 Port Vale 2

Harrison, James IL
b Bolton 1914
Army
Hibernian
1937 Cardiff City 1
1937 Rochdale (trial) 0
Chorley

From To Apps Goal

Harrison, John CH
b Rotherham
1919 Rotherham County 12
Rotherham Town
Boston Town
Wath Athletic
Shirebrook

Harrison, John RB
b New Brancepeth q1 1901
White-le-Head Rangers
Leadgate Park
West Stanley
1927 Durham City 4
Stanley United
1928 Barnsley 0
Kettering Town

Harrison, John Richardson (Jack) OL/IL
b Rhyl q2 1908 d 1966
Llandudno Junction
Rhyl Athletic
1929 Manchester City 2 1
1930 Sheffield United 5 1
1932 1933 Brighton & Hove Albion 5 3
Distillery
Northwich Victoria

Harrison, John T IR/CF
b Parkgate
1925 1926 Rotherham United 10 3

Harrison, Joseph J (Joe) LB
b Betley
Altrincham
1930 Crewe Alexandra 6
Stafford Rangers

Harrison, Percy GK
b Huthwaite q1 1902
1921 1922 Grimsby Town 8
Denaby United

Harrison, Rennie RB
b Burnley q2 1897 d 1951
1919 Huddersfield Town 1

Harrison, Richard RH
b 1881
Accrington Stanley
1904 Bury 1
Bacup
Haslingden
Nelson
Carlisle United

Harrison, Thomas OL
b Birmingham 4/1867 d 1942
Coombs Wood
1888 Aston Villa 1
Halesowen
Handsworth Richmond

Harrison, Thomas CF
1896 Darwen 8 5

Harrison, Thomas CF
1899 Loughborough 8 1

Harrison, Thomas LH
1902 Glossop 1

Harrison, Thomas IL/IR
1914 1919 Stockport County 7

Harrison, Thomas William GK
South Normanton Town
Stanton Hill Town
South Normanton Town
Ripley Athletic
1901 Derby County 1
Pinxton

Harrison, Walter RH/IR
b Langley Moor
Coxhoe United
Ferryhill Athletic
Wingate Albion
Kelloe St Helen's
1926 Durham City (trial) 0
Shildon
Bishop Auckland
1929 1930 Hartlepools United 10 2
1931 Darlington 0

Harrison, William OR
1898 Blackpool 2

Harrison, William (Billy) GK
b Lancaster 26/9/1901 d 1984
Scotforth
Marsh Wesleyans
Lancaster Town
1924 1932 Bury 127
Lancaster Town

From To Apps Goal

Harrison, William Ewart (Billy) OR
b Wybunbury 27/12/1886 d 1948
Caps: FLge 2
Hough United
Crewe South End
Willaston White Star
Crewe Alexandra
1907 1920 Wolverhampton Wanderers 317 43
1920 1921 Manchester United 44 5
1922 Port Vale 22 2
1923 Wrexham 29

Harrisson, Alfred Everson GK
b Holbeach q1 1872 d 1947
1893 Nottingham Forest 0
1894 Notts County 1

Harrold, James George William (Jimmy) CH
b Poplar 26/3/1892 d 1950
Caps: England Amat
Custom House
1911 Huddersfield Town (trial) 0
West Ham United
1912 1922 Leicester Fosse 206 7
1923 Millwall Athletic 2 1
1925 Clapton Orient 0

Harrold, Sidney (Sid) OR/OL
b Stourbridge 5/9/1895
Willenhall
Stourbridge
Wednesbury
1919 Leicester City 18 2
1920 1921 Nottingham Forest 50 8
1922 Accrington Stanley 6 1

Harron, Joseph (Joe) OL
b Langley Park 14/3/1900 d 1961
Langley Park
1920 Hull City 2
1921 Northampton Town 18 1
York City
1922 1924 Sheffield Wednesday 61 5
York City
Kettering Town
Scarborough
1928 1929 Barnsley 28 4
Dartford

Harrop, James (Jimmy) CH/LH
b Heeley 5/2/1884 d 1954
Caps: FLge 4
Ranmoor Wesleyans
1903 Sheffield Wednesday 0
Denaby United
Rotherham Town
1907 1911 Liverpool 133 4
1912 1920 Aston Villa 153 4
1920 1921 Sheffield United 14
Burton All Saints

Harrop, John OR
1922 Stalybridge Celtic 2

Harrow, Jack Harry LB/RB/RH
b Beddington 8/10/1888 d 1958
Caps: FLge 1/England 2
Mill Green Rovers
Croydon Common
1911 1925 Chelsea 304 5

Harry, Albert Ernest (Bert) OR
b Kingston 8/3/1897 d 1966
Kingstonian
1921 1933 Crystal Palace 410 53
Dartford
Mulhouse
Nancy
Shrewsbury Town

Harston, Edwin (Ted) CF/IL
b Monk Bretton 27/2/1907 d 1971
Barnsley Co-op
Cudworth Village
1928 Sheffield Wednesday 0
1930 Barnsley 12 4
1931 1933 Reading 18 11
1934 1935 Bristol City 28 17
1935 1936 Mansfield Town 70 81
1937 Liverpool 5 3
Ramsgate
Ramsgate Press Wanderers

Hart, Adam OR
Port Glasgow Juniors
1922 Bristol City 2

Hart, Ernest (Ernie) IL
b Huddersfield
Folkestone
1922 Queen's Park Rangers 5 2
Guildford United

From To Apps Goal

Hart, Ernest Arthur (Ernie) CH
b Overseal 3/1/1902 d 1954
Caps: FLge 3/England 8
Overseal Juniors
Woodland Wesleyans
1920 1935 Leeds United 447 14
1936 Mansfield Town 28
Tunbridge Wells Rangers

Hart, George RH/LH
b Gosforth q3 1899
Bedlington Colliery Welfare
1923 1924 Queen's Park Rangers 6 1
1924 1927 Durham City 78 1
Workington
Tunbridge Wells Rangers

Hart, Harry RH
St Andrew's (Lincoln)
1894 Lincoln City 1

Hart, Horace Alfred IR
b Nottingham 16/8/1894
Stalybridge Celtic
1919 Nottingham Forest 6 1

Hart, Hunter LH/CH
b Glasgow 11/3/1897 d 1954
Parkhead White Rose
Parkhead
Airdrieonians
1921 1929 Everton 289 5

Hart, James (Jimmy) CF/IR
b Glasgow 2/1/1903
Vale of Clyde
1926 Hull City 2
Flint Town
1927 1928 Bradford Park Avenue 12 10
1928 Crewe Alexandra 19 13
Connah's Quay & Shotton
1930 Charlton Athletic 5 1
Chester (loan)
East Stirlingshire
Hibernian
Portadown
Dundee United
Cowdenbeath

Hart, James Patrick (Jimmy) IL
b Dalziel 1915
Clydesdale Corinthians
St Roch's
Wishaw Juniors
1935 Preston North End 0
1937 Torquay United 5 1
Hibernian

Hart, John IL
b Bo'ness 1/1/1903
Shettleston
Troon Athletic
Bo'ness
1928 Nelson (trial) 0
1928 Barrow 9 3

Hart, John Leslie (Leslie) CF
b Bolsover 21/11/1904 d 1974
New Hucknall Colliery
Bolsover Colliery
Worksop Town
1924 Chesterfield 4 1
Mansfield Town
1925 1926 Derby County 4 3
Newark Town
Ebbw Vale

Hart, John Leslie (Les) CH/RH/RB
b Ashton-in-Makerfield 28/2/1917 d 1996
Ashton National
Earlestown White Star
1938 1953 Bury 280 2
1939 (Bury) (3)

Hart, John Thomas GK
St Andrew's (Lincoln)
1894 Lincoln City 1

Hart, Joseph RB
b Bulwell
1920 West Ham United 1
1921 Millwall Athletic 0

From To Apps Goal

Hartford, Alfred Elliott OR
b Boldon Colliery q1 1902 d 1963
Craghead United
Hebburn Colliery
1923 Durham City 4
Hebburn Colliery
1924 South Shields 0
Craghead United
1924 South Shields 0
Ferryhill Athletic
Crook Town
North Shields
Crook Town
Murton Colliery Welfare

Hartill, William John (Billy) CF
b Wolverhampton 18/7/1905 d 1980
Royal Horse Artillery
1928 1934 Wolverhampton Wanderers 221 162
1935 Everton 5 1
1935 Liverpool 5
1935 1937 Bristol Rovers 36 19
Street

Hartland, Frederick GK
1920 Wolverhampton Wanderers 1

Hartles, Wilfred (Wilf) OL
b Warrington q4 1890
Runcorn
1920 Bradford Park Avenue 2 1
1921 Accrington Stanley 14

Hartley, Abraham (Abe) CF/IR/OL
b Dumbarton 8/2/1872 d 1909
Artizan Thistle
Dumbarton
1892 1897 Everton 50 24
1897 Liverpool 7 1
Southampton
1899 Woolwich Arsenal 5 1
1899 Burnley 13 5

Hartley, Arthur RB
b Hollingworth 4/8/1907 d 1990
Glossop
1930 1931 Wigan Borough 7
1932 Fulham (trial) 0
1932 Crystal Palace (trial) 0
Rhyl Athletic
Nelson
Hadfield Star
Hollingworth
Leyland Motors

Hartley, Dilworth OR/RH
b Clitheroe q3 1870
1891 1892 Blackburn Rovers 6
1894 Darwen 20 9

Hartley, Frank IL/IR
b Shipton-under-Wychwood 7/2/1896 d 1965
Caps: England Amat/England 1
Oxford City
1922 Tottenham Hotspur 1
Corinthians
1927 1929 Tottenham Hotspur 6 1

Hartley, Geoffrey Alfin IL/RH
b Wakefield 11/5/1915 d 1991
1936 1937 Rotherham United 5

Hartley, James Milburn (Jimmy) IL/IR
b Dumbarton 29/10/1876
Dumbarton
1895 1896 Sunderland 11 1
1896 Burnley 1
1896 Lincoln City (loan) 9 5
Tottenham Hotspur
1899 1902 Lincoln City 129 47
Rangers
Port Glasgow Athletic
Brentford
New Brompton
Port Glasgow Athletic

Hartley, Percy Wilding LH/RH
b Bolton q1 1885
Atherton Church House
1905 1906 Preston North End 3
Atherton
Rochdale
Chorley
Exeter City
Rochdale

Hartley, Roy RH
b Brierfield 6/1/1897 d 1984
1921 Nelson 1

From To Apps Goal

Hartley, Sydney (Syd) RB
b Gomersal 22/1/1914 d 1987
Heckmondwike
1932 Huddersfield Town 0
1933 Grimsby Town 0
Tunbridge Wells Rangers
1935 Burnley 0
1935 Clapton Orient 0
1936 1937 Gillingham 77 2
1938 Bristol Rovers 4 1
Tunbridge Wells Rangers

Hartley, Thomas W IL
b Newcastle
Norwich City
1919 Stockport County 7

Hartley, Thomas William (Tom) IL/IR
b Gateshead 7/5/1917 d 1984
Birtley Boys Club
1935 1936 Gateshead 5 1
1938 Bury 0
1939 Chesterfield 0
North Shields
Stockton
1947 Leicester City 0
1947 Watford 6 1

Hartness, George IR
Monkwearmouth
1896 Sunderland 2

Hartshorne, Arthur LB
b Moxley 1881
Moxley White Star
1900 Wolverhampton Wanderers 0
1902 Burslem Port Vale 28 3
1902 1904 Stoke 53
1905 Aston Villa 0
Southampton
Northampton Town

Hartshorne, Jack RB
b Willenhall 25/3/1907 d 1971
Short Heath
1932 Stoke City 0
Macclesfield
1936 1938 Lincoln City 91
1939 (Lincoln City) (2)
Grantham
Boston United

Hartwell, Ambrose Francis George Broderic CH/RB
b Exeter q3 1879
Caps: SoLge 2
Budleigh Town
Erdington
1901 1907 Small Heath/Birmingham 50 1
1908 Bradford Park Avenue 21 2
Queen's Park Rangers
Kidderminster Harriers
Shrewsbury Town

Hartwell, William OL
b 1885
Kettering
1903 1904 Manchester United 3
Northampton Town
Peterborough City

Harvey, Albert J IR/OL
b Southend-on-Sea
Southchurch
1923 1926 Southend United 3

Harvey, Arthur LB
Shildon Athletic
1906 Blackburn Rovers 1
Hartlepools United
Shildon Athletic

Harvey, Benjamin LH
b Ashton-under-Lyne 6/11/1874
Hulme Swifts
Greenhill
Hulme
Stockport Association
Stockport County
West Manchester
Nelson
1900 Stockport County 12

Harvey, Charles OR
b Small Heath 1879
St Philip's YMCA
1904 1906 Small Heath/Birmingham 2
Leek
Shrewsbury Town
Redditch

From To Apps Goal

Harvey, Edmund OR
b Kiveton Park 8/9/1900
Kiveton Park
1924 1926 Birmingham 13
York City
1927 1928 Bradford City 45 15

Harvey, Edward Lee OL
b Sheffield 5/7/1892 d 1965
Hallam
Heeley
1919 1920 Sheffield Wednesday 12
1921 Bristol Rovers 5
Retford Town

Harvey, Ernest Alfred RB
b Chesterfield q4 1883
New Brompton
1908 Glossop 5
Hyde

Harvey, George MH OR
b South Shields q1 1919
1937 1938 Gateshead 6

Harvey, Howard CF/IR/IL
b Birmingham 1877
1897 Aston Villa 11 3
1898 1899 Burslem Port Vale 49 19
1899 1900 Manchester City 7 1
Watford
Glentoran

Harvey, James D GK
b York 7/8/1911
1930 Sheffield Wednesday 0
Wombwell Town
Frickley Colliery
1931 Rotherham United 0
Frickley Colliery
1932 Bristol Rovers 1
Frickley Colliery
1934 Gillingham 15
Frickley Colliery

Harvey, John Arthur H CH
Partick Thistle
1894 Derby County 5
Ilkeston Town
Abercorn

Harvey, John Howard (Jack) IL/IR
b Maidenlaw 6/4/1915
Annfield Plain
1934 Aston Villa (trial) 0
1934 Stoke City (trial) 0
1934 Port Vale (trial) 0
1935 Manchester City 0
1936 Bradford Park Avenue 3
1937 Bristol City 2
1938 Newport County 2

Harvey, Joseph CF
b Kilnhurst
1929 Doncaster Rovers 7 1
Wombwell

Harvey, Joseph (Joe) RH
b Edlington 11/6/1918 d 1989
Caps: FLge 3
Edlington Rangers
1936 Bradford Park Avenue 0
1936 Wolverhampton Wanderers 0
1937 Bournemouth & Boscombe Ath 1
1938 Bradford City 0
1945 1952 Newcastle United 224 12

Harvey, William Arthur (Bill) IL/CF/IR
b Chopwell 2/5/1908 d 1978
Chopwell Institute
Annfield Plain
Eden Colliery
1929 1931 Barnsley 42 12
Eden Colliery
1935 Chesterfield 14 4
Boston United
1938 Darlington 14 7
Stockton

Harvey, William Henry (Bill) OR
b Netley 22/12/1896 d 1972
Caps: England Amat
Yorkshire Amateurs
West Riding Regiment
1919 Sheffield Wednesday 19 1
1921 1924 Birmingham 78 2
1925 Southend United 0

Harvie, John IR/OR
b Scotland
Renton
1890 Sunderland 15 1
Clyde
1892 1896 Sunderland 80 11
1897 1898 Newcastle United 26 6

From To Apps Goal

Harwood, Alfred James (Alf) CF
b Bishop Auckland 16/4/1879
Bishop Auckland
Crook Town
Bishop Auckland
Fulham
1906 Leeds City 1 1
West Ham United
Spennymoor United
Bishop Auckland
Hartlepools United
Bishop Auckland YMCA

Harwood, Irvine IL/CF/IR
b Bradford 5/12/1905 d 1973
Manningham Mills
1929 1931 Bradford Park Avenue 49 27
1931 1932 Bradford City 5
1933 Wolverhampton Wanderers 6
1934 1935 Bristol Rovers 51 14
1936 Walsall 28 6
Burton Town

Harwood, John A (Jack) CH
b Somerstown 1/2/1891 d 1956
Tooting Town
Southend United
1912 Chelsea 4
1920 1921 Portsmouth 41 2
1922 1923 Swansea Town 45 3
1924 1926 Aberdare Athletic 103 8
1927 Barrow 3
Royal Naval Volunteer Reserve

Harwood, Richard CH
1894 Darwen 3

Haseldon, Peter CH
1898 Darwen 1

Hasell, Albert Arthur GK
b Bristol 5/1885 d 1955
1906 Bolton Wanderers 0
1907 Middlesbrough 1
1909 1910 Nottingham Forest 33
Plymouth Argyle
Swindon Town

Haslam, Frank LH
b Mansfield q2 1872
Mansfield Town
1894 Burslem Port Vale 8
1894 Notts County 0

Haslam, Frederick Gill (Fred) GK
b Blackpool 6//1/1899 d 1971
Lytham
1925 Stockport County 31
Chorley

Haslam, George (Tiny) CH
b Turton 4/1898
Darwen
1921 1927 Manchester United 25
1927 Portsmouth 4
Ashton National
Whitchurch
Lancaster Town
Chorley
Burscough Rangers
Northwich Victoria

Haslam, Harry B RH/OL
Gresley Rovers
Belper Town
1900 1901 Derby County 8
Belper Town

Haslam, Robert CH
1900 Bolton Wanderers 1

Hassall, Harry OL
b Crewe 1899
1921 1924 Crewe Alexandra 103 10
Hednesford Town

Hassall, Joshua (Joe) GK
b Wednesfield 11/1871 d 1895
St George's
Stafford Rangers
Heath Moor
1892 1894 Wolverhampton Wanderers 48

Hasson, William Craig (Bill) OL
b Glasgow 12/6/1905 d 1976
Shettleston Juniors
Clyde
1928 1933 Oldham Athletic 134 22
1934 Millwall 13 2
1935 Chesterfield 2

From To Apps Goal

Hastie, Archibald IL
b Shotts 1913
Douglas Water Thistle
Partick Thistle
1936 1937 Huddersfield Town 13 1
Motherwell
1938 1945 Bradford City 31 9
1939 (Bradford City) (3) (1)

Hastie, George IL
b Kelvin 13/1/1892
Govan Glentoran
Glasgow Ashfield
Kilmarnock
Bristol Rovers
Bath City
Kilmarnock
St Johnstone
Abercorn
1914 Leicester Fosse 17 1
Belfast United
Arthurlie
Abercorn
Belfast Celtic
Abercorn
Johnstone

Hastie, Henry (Harry) LB
b Padiham
1919 Burnley 7
Fleetwood
Morecambe

Hastie, Ian Scott OR
b London 1887
Edmonton Royal
1911 Birmingham 1
Wycombe Wanderers

Hastie, John OR
d 1933
Eastwood Juniors
St Mirren
Reading
Plymouth Argyle
1920 Middlesbrough 1
Dundee

Hastings, Alexander Cockburn (Alex) LH/RH
b Falkirk 17/3/1912 d 1988
Caps: Scotland 2
Carron Welfare
Rosewell Rosedale
Stenhousemuir
1930 1945 Sunderland 262 2
1939 (Sunderland) (3) (2)

Hastings, John (Jack) LH
b Whitburn, County Durham q4 1903 d 1963
Whitburn
Esh Winning
Spennymoor United
1928 1929 Rotherham United 43 1
1930 Barrow 2
Crook Town
Jarrow
Blyth Spartans

Hastings, John George RB
b Thornaby q2 1887
Darlington St Augustine's
1908 Sunderland 1

Hastings, William (Bill) OL
b West Hartlepool 22/8/1888
Greenbank
West Hartlepool
West Hartlepool Expansion
Brighton & Hove Albion
1911 1913 Birmingham 40 7
Watford
Hartlepool Old Boys

Hatch, Thomas Henry (Tom) OR/RB
b Barrow 14/11/1903 d 1972
Barrow Thursdays
1924 Blackburn Rovers 0
1925 1928 Barrow 103 5
Sheppey United
Frickley Colliery

Hateley, Andrew IL
1898 Blackpool 1 1

Hateley, Charles Bernard (Charlie) OL
b Aston q2 1890
1913 Bolton Wanderers 1

From To Apps Goal

Hatfield, Sidney Ernest (Ernie) RB
b Basford 16/1/1902
Frickley Colliery
Wombwell
1928 Sheffield Wednesday 1
Sheppey United
1930 Wolverhampton Wanderers 3
1931 1932 Southend United 51 3
Dartford
Upton Colliery

Hatfield, Thomas (Tom) GK
b Woolwich q3 1874
1894 1895 Woolwich Arsenal 2
Tottenham Hotspur
Royal Engineers

Hathway, Edward Albert (Ted) IL/LH/RH
b Bristol q1 1910
1930 Bristol City 0
1931 Bristol Rovers 0
1932 Bolton Wanderers 0
1933 1938 York City 218 38
1939 (York City) (3)

Hatton, Albert LH
b Nottingham q4 1879 d 1963
Sutton Junction
1907 1909 Grimsby Town 74 2
Crystal Palace
Aberdare Town
Rotherham Town

Hatton, Cyril IL/IR
b Grantham 14/9/1918 d 1987
Notts Corinthians
Grantham Co-operative
1936 1938 Notts County 62 15
1939 (Notts County) (2) (2)
1946 1952 Queen's Park Rangers 163 64
1953 Chesterfield 36 10
Grantham

Hatton, George OL/IL
1892 1893 Northwich Victoria 8

Hatton, John W IR
b Goldthorpe
1929 Doncaster Rovers 1

Hatton, Sidney Edward Oscar (Sid) LH/RH/CF
b West Bromwich 22/1/1892 d 1961
West Bromwich Baptists
1919 1921 West Bromwich Albion 6
Shrewsbury Town

Hauser, Stanley (Stan) GK
b Handsworth, Yorkshire 20/2/1893 d 1945
Caps: England Amat
Handsworth GSOB
Handsworth Oakhill
Stockton
1913 1921 Birmingham 31
Stourbridge
Netherton
Cradley Heath St Luke's

Havelock, John CF
b Hartlepool 11/5/1904 d 1981
Folkestone
1929 Crystal Palace 0
Northcliffe
Folkestone
1933 1934 Bristol Rovers 20 11
Aylesford Paper Mills

Havelock, Peter Henry W (Harry) IR/CF
b Hartlepool 20/1/1901 d 1973
Army
1923 Hull City 6 2
1925 Lincoln City 27 17
1925 1926 Portsmouth 11 8
1927 1930 Crystal Palace 67 39
1931 Hull City 3
Folkestone
Margate
Crown Athletic

Hawarden, Andrew LH/IL
b Bolton 30/6/1895 d 1978
1921 Southend United 10 1
1922 1923 Tranmere Rovers 21

From To Apps Goal

Hawes, Arthur Robert IL
b Swanton Morley 2/10/1895 d 1963
CEYMS (Norwich)
Boulton & Paul
Norwich City
1920 1921 South Shields 52 18
1921 1926 Sunderland 139 39
1927 1928 Bradford Park Avenue 52 17
1929 Accrington Stanley 39 9
1930 Nelson 26 3
Hyde United
Wombwell
1931 Rochdale 13
Goole Town
Frost's Athletic

Hawke, William CH
1893 Rotherham Town 1

Hawkes, Frederick (Fred) IR
b Luton 17/4/1881
Luton Stanley
1899 Luton Town 2 1

Hawkes, Thomas RB/LB
b Luton q3 1878
1898 1899 Luton Town 2

Hawkings, Thomas William (Tom) OL
b Edmonton q2 1899
Walthamstow Grange
Leyton
1924 Arsenal 0
1925 Charlton Athletic 10 1
Leyton
Chelmsford Town
Leytonstone
Enfield

Hawkins, Alfred Thorn IL
b Malden 10/1904
Southall
1925 1926 Crystal Palace 20 8

Hawkins, Arthur CF
Bloxwich Strollers
1906 Wolverhampton Wanderers 20 9
Kidderminster Harriers
Halesowen

Hawkins, Ernest RB
Middleton
1895 Bury 7
1896 Burton Wanderers 6

Hawkins, George Harry (Harry) IL/IR/CF
b Middlesbrough 24/11/1915 d 1992
South Bank Princess Street
South Bank East End
1935 Middlesbrough 1
1937 Watford 5
1938 1946 Southport 79 30
1939 (Southport) (3) (1)
1947 Gateshead 27 12
1947 1948 Hartlepools United 30 4
Blyth Spartans
Murton Colliery

Hawkins, Harold H RB
1903 Aston Villa 0
1904 Doncaster Rovers 1
Denaby United

Hawkins, Horace LB
b Mexborough
Denaby United
1925 Exeter City 4

Hawkins, John Thomas (Tom) GK
b West Bromwich 4/1869
Great Bridge Unity
Elwells
1892 1897 Walsall Town Swifts 67
Walsall Wood
Bloxwich
Willenhall Olympic

Hawkins, Joseph CH
b Sheffield 1911
Swallownest
Woodhouse Mill
1934 1938 Rotherham United 153 2
1938 York City 21 1
1939 (York City) (3)

Hawkins, Joseph Frederick Vincent IR
b East Ham 5/10/1904 d 1972
Barking Town
1927 1929 Millwall 16 8
1930 Thames 2

From To Apps Goal

Hawksworth, Ernest IL
b Rochdale 6/12/1894 d 1961
Sudden Villa
Rochdale
1919 1923 Blackburn Rovers 96 34
Macclesfield
1926 New Brighton 17 2

Hawley, Frederick (Fred) CH
b Darlington 28/10/1890 d 1954
Derby Midland
Ripley Town & Athletic
1912 1914 Sheffield United 57 1
1919 Coventry City 14
1919 Birmingham 3
1920 1922 Swindon Town 90 4
1922 1924 Bristol City 75 1
1925 Brighton & Hove Albion 37 4
1926 1927 Queen's Park Rangers 29 1
Loughborough Corinthians

Hawley, Sydney IR
b Langwith 1912
Langwith Welfare
Bolsover Colliery
Shirebrook
1933 Sheffield Wednesday 0
1934 Mansfield Town 4 1
Sutton Town
Stewart & Lloyds

Hawley, William (Bill) RB
b Sheffield
1919 Huddersfield Town 0
1920 Blackpool 0
1921 Halifax Town 7
Rotherham Town

Haworth, George RH/CH
b Accrington 17/10/1864 d 1943
Caps: England 5
Christ Church
Accrington
Preston North End (loan)
Blackburn Rovers (loan)
1888 1891 Accrington 74 3

Haworth, Harry LH
b Ramsbottom
Ramsbottom
1926 1929 Accrington Stanley 4
Horwich RMI

Haworth, James (Jimmy) OL
b Accrington
1928 1930 Accrington Stanley 20 4
Stalybridge Celtic
Nelson
Bacup Borough

Haworth, John (Jack) CF
b Nelson 1883
Colne
1903 1904 Stoke 6 2
Netherfield
Darwen Institute

Haworth, John GK
b Huncoat
1925 Accrington Stanley 1

Haworth, John Houghton (Jack) RB/LH
b Bolton q4 1887
Turton
Brighton & Hove Albion
1911 1914 Middlesbrough 61
Chorley
Darwen

Haworth, P GK
1889 Accrington 1

Haworth, Ralph LB/RB
b Crawshawbooth q2 1907
Ramsbottom
1929 1930 Accrington Stanley 3

Haworth, Richard OR
Manchester North End
1938 Rochdale 9 1

Haworth, Robert (Bob) CH/RH
b Blackburn 1879
Christ Church
1897 Darwen 0
1898 1903 Blackburn Rovers 122 5
Fulham
Brentford
Chorley
Clitheroe Central

From To Apps Goal

Haworth, Robert (Bob) RB
b Atherton 26/6/1897 d 1962
Howe Bridge
Atherton Collieries
1921 1930 Bolton Wanderers 322
1932 Accrington Stanley 3

Haworth, Roland LH
b Ramsbottom 1914
Manchester North End
1937 Rochdale 2

Haworth, Ronald IL
b Lower Darwen 10/3/1901 d 1973
1921 1923 Blackburn Rovers 25 7
1924 1925 Hull City 36 10
1926 Manchester United 2
Darwen

Haworth, TE LB
1896 1897 Darwen 39

Hawthorn, William (Willie) GK
b Glasgow 3/2/1908
Grangemouth Welfare
Maryhill Hibernian
Kilsyth Rangers
Alloa Athletic
1932 1933 Bradford Park Avenue 32
Airdrieonians
1936 1938 New Brighton 108
1939 (New Brighton) (3)

Hawtin, Leonard Charles LB/RB
b Northampton 2/7/1892 d 1937
1920 1922 Northampton Town 10

Hawtin, Thomas Arthur (Tom) OR
b Barrow 23/9/1903 d 1979
Thorneycrofts
Barrow Novocastrians
1926 Barrow 4
Dalton Casuals
Lancaster Town

Hay, James (Jimmy) RB/LB
b Lanark 1876 d 1940
Renfrew Victoria
1901 1907 Barnsley 146
1908 Chesterfield Town 37
Stoke

Hay, James (Jimmy) LH
b Beith 12/12/1880 d 1940
Caps: SLge 6/Scotland 11
Woodside Annbank
Celtic (trial)
Annbank
Ayr
Celtic
Annbank (loan)
1911 1914 Newcastle United 132 8
Ayr United
Heart of Midlothian
Clydebank
Ayr United

Hay, John RB
b Renfrew 2/10/??
Wemyss Athletic
St Bernard's
Bathgate
1921 Bradford City 3
St Bernard's
Arbroath

Hay, John OL
b Glasgow 1912
Lanark United
St Bernard's
1937 Aldershot 7 1
Distillery

Hay, Thomas (Tom) GK
b Staveley 1857
Staveley
Bolton Wanderers
Great Lever
Halliwell
Burslem
Newton Heath
1890 1892 Accrington 70
1893 Burton Swifts 1

Haycock, Frederick Joseph (Freddie) IR
b Liverpool 19/4/1912 d 1989
Waterford
Prescot Cables
1936 1938 Aston Villa 99 28
1939 (Aston Villa) (1)
1945 1946 Wrexham 6 1
Hednesford Town
Stourbridge
Sutton Coldfield Town

From To Apps Goal

Haycock, George Frederick (Fred) IR/OR
b Smethwick q4 1885 d 1953
Smethwick Victoria
Coombs Wood
1904 1905 West Bromwich Albion 15 8
Crewe Alexandra
Luton Town
Portsmouth
1910 Lincoln City 25 5
Port Vale
Dudley Town
Shrewsbury Town

Haycox, John Harold (Jack) CF
b Hampstead 6/3/1907 d 1992
Cheltenham Town
1933 1934 Newport County 13 4
1936 1937 Bristol City 43 25
1937 1938 Torquay United 24 12
1938 1945 Northampton Town 17 6
Peterborough United

Haydock, J RB
1888 1889 Bolton Wanderers 2
Ardwick

Haydock, James (Jimmy) OR/IR/IL
b Blackburn q4 1872 d 1900
Borough Road College
1890 1896 Blackburn Rovers 66 21

Haydon, James Gilbert (Jimmy) LB
b Bristol 4/5/1901 d 1969
Newton Old Boys
1921 1930 Bristol Rovers 291 5
Kingswood

Hayes, Charles William (Charlie) RB
b Buckley 7/12/1893 d 1978
Caps: Wales Amat
Buckley Town
1921 1923 Tranmere Rovers 24
Mold Town

Hayes, Frederick Albert (Fred) IL/RH/CF
b Liverpool 1895
Liverpool Badgers
1920 1921 Port Vale 3
1922 1923 Tranmere Rovers 11 1

Hayes, George Edward CF
b Hartley Wintney 10/10/1910 d 1993
Ferndale Athletic
1932 Swindon Town 5 1
Cricklade Road Primitives

Hayes, James Vincent (Vince) LB/RB/IL
b Miles Platting q2 1879
Caps: FLge 1
Newton Heath Athletic
1900 1904 Newton Heath/Manchester Utd 62 2
Brentford
1908 1910 Manchester United 53
1910 1911 Bradford Park Avenue 29
Rochdale

Hayes, John P OL
Liverpool Badgers
1923 Tranmere Rovers 3

Hayes, Joseph William GK
b Oldbury 1894
Hednesford Town
1913 Wolverhampton Wanderers 2
Cradley Heath
Lye Town

Hayes, Lawrence LH
b Hemsworth 6/3/1916 d 1990
South Kirkby Colliery
1935 Halifax Town 1

Hayes, Thomas George (George) CF
b Port Talbot 25/9/1909 d 1984
Port Talbot
Bridgend Town
1927 Barnsley 0
1927 Nelson 9 5

Hayes, Thomas William (Billy) GK
b Eccleston 28/5/1895 d 1979
Eccleston
1912 Preston North End 0
Chorley (loan)
1914 Preston North End 10
1920 1923 Brighton & Hove Albion 167
1924 1925 Southend United 51
1926 Accrington Stanley 41
1927 Stockport County 16
Winsford United
Burscough Rangers
Stalybridge Celtic
Bacup Borough

From To Apps Goal

Hayes, William (Bill) LH/CH/IL
b Runcorn 8/6/1919 d 2002
Halton Juniors
1938 1950 Oldham Athletic 126 3
1939 (Oldham Athletic) (3)
Mossley

Hayes, William Edward (Bill) RB/LB
b Cork 7/11/1915
Caps: LoI 2/Ireland 4/Eire 2
St Vincent's (Sheffield)
1934 1949 Huddersfield Town 69 5
1939 (Huddersfield Town) (3)
Cork United
1946 1949 Huddersfield Town 112
1949 1950 Burnley 12

Hayhurst, Albert (Bert) CH/RB
b Birdwell 17/9/1905 d 1991
Frickley Colliery
1931 Barnsley 0
1932 Luton Town 1
1933 1938 Reading 219 10

Haynes, ? LB
(possibly John Hynd)
1894 Newcastle United 1

Haynes, Alfred Edward RH/CH/RB
b Oxford 4/4/1907 d 1953
Oxford City
1929 1933 Arsenal 29
1933 1935 Crystal Palace 47 1

Haynes, George Harold OL/IL
b West Bromwich 1865 d 1937
West Bromwich Sandwell
1888 1891 West Bromwich Albion 12 1
Coles Farm Unity

Haynes, Harry CH/OR
b Walsall 21/4/1873 d 1902
Walsall Unity
1892 Walsall Town Swifts 3
1893 1894 Wolverhampton Wanderers 24 2
1895 Small Heath 9
Southampton

Haynes, Robert IL
b Desborough
Desborough
1920 Southend United 1

Hays, Christopher John (Jack) OL
b Ashington 12/12/1918 d 1983
Ashington
Ipswich Town
1938 Bradford Park Avenue 17
1939 1950 Burnley 146 12
1939 (Burnley) (2)
1951 1952 Bury 27 2
Bury Town

Hayward, Douglas Wilfred (Doug) OL
b Bournemouth q2 1902
1924 Bournemouth & Boscombe Ath 1

Hayward, Jack RB
b Warsop Vale 21/5/1904 d 1974
Warsop Main Byrons
Shirebrook
Welbeck Colliery
1924 Bradford City 0
1925 1932 Bournemouth & Boscombe Ath 247 26
1933 Crystal Palace 19 1

Hayward, Lionel Eric (Eric) CH/RB
b Newcastle-under-Lyme 2/8/1917 d 1976
Hanley
Wardles
1934 1936 Port Vale 35
1937 1951 Blackpool 269
1939 (Blackpool) (3)

Hayward, Thomas LH
1900 Walsall 1

Hayward, William Arthur (Willie) LH
b Blaina 16/11/1907 d 1976
Abertillery
Blaina West Side
1925 Newport County 4
1926 Clapton Orient 1
1927 Tottenham Hotspur 0
1931 Clapton Orient 9

From To Apps Goal

Haywood, Adam IR/IL
b Horninglow 23/3/1874 d 1932
Burton Ivanhoe
1894 Burton Wanderers 9
Swadlincote
1895 1898 Woolwich Arsenal 84 31
1899 Glossop 0
Queen's Park Rangers
New Brompton
1901 1904 Wolverhampton Wanderers 107 28
1905 1907 West Bromwich Albion 62 25
1907 Blackpool 15 1
Crystal Palace

Haywood, Amos LB
b Burton-on-Trent q4 1868
Burton Wanderers
1899 1900 Burton Swifts 65

Haywood, Frederick CF
Mexborough Town
1906 Derby County 1

Haywood, George CF
b Coleorton 11/12/1906 d 1992
Coleorton Bible Class
Whitwick Imperial
Gresley Rovers
1928 Southend United (trial) 0
1928 Chesterfield (trial) 0
1929 1933 Birmingham 38 15
1934 Chesterfield 16 7
Cradley Heath
1935 Southport 6 1
Cradley Heath

Haywood, Johnson William (Billy) OR/IR/LH
b Eckington q2 1899
Eckington Works
1921 1923 Chelsea 23 2
1924 Halifax Town 1
Yeovil & Petters United
1926 Portsmouth 0
1926 Barrow 9 1
Weymouth
Scunthorpe & Lindsey United
Wombwell
Denaby United

Haywood, Joseph Francis RH/LH
Hindley Central
1913 1914 Manchester United 26

Haywood, Norman Scott Carmichael (Norrie) CF
b Portobello 7/9/1910 d 1979
Peebles Rovers
1933 Watford 1
Peebles Rovers
Queen of the South
Leith Athletic
Raith Rovers
Leith Athletic
Peebles Rovers

Haywood, Samuel LH
1925 Walsall 3

Haywood, Thomas (Tom) CH/RH
b Walsall 1880 d 1952
Walsall Co-op
Stourbridge
1904 Aston Villa 0
1904 1906 West Bromwich Albion 15
Crewe Alexandra
Darlaston

Hazard, AJ LH
1899 Loughborough 9 1

Head, Bertram James (Bert) CH/RB
b Midsomer Norton 8/6/1916 d 2002
Midsomer Norton
Welton Rovers
1936 1950 Torquay United 222 6
1939 (Torquay United) (3)
1951 1952 Bury 22

Heald, James Frederick (Freddie) OR
b Sheffield q2 1907 d 1930
1925 Rotherham United 1
Shirebrook
Mexborough Athletic

Heald, JT IL
1896 Burton Swifts 11 4

Heale, James Arthur (Jimmy) IL/IR/CF
b Bristol 19/9/1914 d 1997
South Bristol Central
1931 1933 Bristol City 26 8
1933 1938 Manchester City 84 39
1939 (Manchester City) (2)
1945 Doncaster Rovers 0

From	To	Club	Apps	Goal
Healey, Richard (Dick)			IR/CF	
b Darlington 20/9/1890			d 1974	
Caps: England Amat				
		Bishop Auckland		
1909		Sunderland	2	1
		Stockton		
		Bishop Auckland		
1911		Sunderland	1	
		Bishop Auckland		
		Darlington		
1913	1914	Middlesbrough	4	2
1921	1922	Darlington	21	5
Healless, Henry (Harry)			RH/CH/LH	
b Blackburn 10/2/1893			d 1972	
Caps: FLge 1/England 2				
		Blackburn Athletic		
		Victoria Cross		
		Blackburn Trinity		
1919	1932	Blackburn Rovers	360	12
Healy, James (Jimmy)			OR	
b Craigneuk 14/9/1901			d 1969	
		Shieldmuir Celtic		
		Celtic		
		Montrose (loan)		
		Stenhousemuir (loan)		
		Motherwell (loan)		
		Montrose (loan)		
1925	1929	Plymouth Argyle	28	4
1930		Bristol City	0	
Heames, William Henry (Billy)			OL	
b Burslem q2 1871				
		Middleport Athletic		
1893	1896	Stoke	16	2
1898	1903	Burslem Port Vale	191	18
Heaney, Frank			RB	
b Ireland				
		St James's Gate		
1911		Leeds City	2	
Heap, Clifford			LB/RB	
b Burnley 14/2/1906			d 1984	
1928		Burnley	5	
1930		Thames	13	
		Clitheroe		
		Manchester Central		
1931		Millwall	0	
1931		Accrington Stanley	4	
1931		Southend United (trial)	0	
		Stalybridge Celtic		
		Tunbridge Wells Rangers		
Heap, Dennis			IL	
b Padiham 2/3/1902			d 1980	
1923	1924	Accrington Stanley	10	4
Heap, Frederick (Fred)			RB/OR/CF	
b Ashton-in-Ribble 12/10/1897			d 1981	
		Rochdale		
1919	1929	Bury	268	5
Heap, Lawrence			OR	
1898		Darwen	6	
Heap, Robert			IR	
1891		Darwen	5	
Heap, Robert (Bob)			RH/LH/CH	
b Haslingden 1891				
		Failsworth		
		Rochdale		
1910	1921	Bury	110	4
Heap, William Victor (Victor)			LH/RH	
b Bury q1 1878				
1900	1901	Bury	3	
Heard, Leslie Henry (Les)			IR	
b Hendon 25/5/1893			d 1970	
		Southall		
1923		Fulham	19	3
Hearty, Hugh			LB	
b Lesmahagow 22/3/1913			d 1992	
		Royal Albert		
		Heart of Midlothian		
		Clyde		
1935		Cardiff City	18	
1936	1938	Clapton Orient	98	2
		Rochester City Police		
Heaselgrave, Samuel Ernest (Sammy)			IR/IL	
b Smethwick 1/10/1916			d 1975	
		Bearward Swifts		
		Warley Lions		
		Smethwick Highfield		
		Brierley Hill Alliance		
1936	1938	West Bromwich Albion	49	16
1945	1947	Northampton Town	42	4
		Boston United		
		Northwich Victoria		

From	To	Club	Apps	Goal
Heath, A			RB	
1895		Crewe Alexandra	3	
Heath, Ernest C (Ernie)			GK	
b Rotherham				
		Denaby United		
		Gainsborough Trinity		
1914	1920	Bradford City	3	
1921		Bury	23	
		Bullcroft Main Colliery		
Heath, Joseph Frederick (Billy)			CF	
b Bristol 1869				
		Walsall Town Swifts		
		Wednesbury Old Athletic		
1891		Wolverhampton Wanderers	8	4
1893	1894	Woolwich Arsenal	10	5
		Gravesend United		
1896		Woolwich Arsenal	0	
Heath, Thomas W			GK	
1936		Crewe Alexandra	1	
Heath, Westby			CH/CF	
b Horton-in-Ribblesdale 22/2/1891			d 1961	
		Luton Town		
1919	1922	Stockport County	84	14
		Chester		
Heath, William			LB/RB	
		Lindum		
1893	1895	Lincoln City	10	
Heathcock, Joseph Bert (Bert)			CF	
b Cradley Heath 5/12/1903				
		Cradley Heath		
		Leamington Town		
1926		Leicester City	1	2
1928	1929	Nottingham Forest	20	15
		Cradley Heath		
		Hereford United		
		Nuneaton Town		
Heathcote, James (Jimmy)			IL/IR/CF	
b Bolton 17/1/1894				
1914		Bolton Wanderers	0	
1919	1921	Blackpool	95	33
1922		Notts County	12	1
		Pontypridd		
1924		Lincoln City	33	13
		Mansfield Town		
1926	1927	Coventry City	63	36
1928		Accrington Stanley	0	
Heathcote, Joseph			IR/IL	
b Elton q3 1879				
		Berry's Association		
1899	1901	Newton Heath	7	
Heaton, C			OL	
1889		Preston North End	2	1
Heaton, Frederick (Fred)			OR	
b Westhoughton				
		Westhoughton Colliery		
1929	1931	Preston North End	13	1
		Chorley		
		Lancaster Town		
Heaton, John Hagues			OL	
b Preston 11/4/1916			d 1979	
		Northern Nomads		
1938		Oldham Athletic	2	1
Heaton, Sidney			CF/OR	
b Lancashire				
1903		Bolton Wanderers	4	1
		Millwall Athletic		
1906		Bury	3	
		Chorley		
Heaton, Thomas (Tommy)			LH/CH/RH	
b Blackburn 2/6/1897				
1919	1922	Blackburn Rovers	57	1
1923	1926	Oldham Athletic	59	3
		Manchester North End		
		Toronto District		
Hebden, George Horace Robert			GK	
b West Ham 2/6/1900			d 1973	
Caps: England Sch				
		Clapton		
		Barking Town		
1920	1924	Leicester City	101	
1925	1926	Queen's Park Rangers	59	
1927	1928	Gillingham	70	
1929		Queen's Park Rangers	1	

From	To	Club	Apps	Goal
Hebden, Jack			RB/LB	
b Castleford 12/11/1901			d 1956	
		Castleford Town		
1920		Bradford City	3	
1920	1927	West Ham United	110	
1927	1928	Fulham	23	
		Thames		
		Hereford United		
1932		Clapton Orient	4	
1932		Halifax Town	1	
1932		Chesterfield	0	
		Sheppey United		
		Dorman Long (Westminster)		
Hedley, Foster			OL	
b Monkseaton 6/1/1908			d 1983	
		St Andrew's (Newcastle)		
1925		South Shields	0	
		Corinthians (Newcastle)		
		Jarrow		
1928		Hull City	2	
1929		Nelson	26	5
1929		Manchester City	2	2
1931	1933	Chester	88	29
1933	1934	Tottenham Hotspur	4	1
1937	1938	Millwall	11	6
1938		Swindon Town	1	
1939		(Swindon Town)	(3)	
Hedley, George			OL	
b Newcastle				
1907		Newcastle United	1	
		Knaresborough		
1910		Newcastle United	0	
Hedley, George			CH	
1909		Bradford City	2	
Hedley, George Albert			CF/IR/IL	
b South Bank 20/7/1876			d 1942	
Caps: FLge 1/England 1				
		South Bank		
1897	1902	Sheffield United	120	34
		Southampton		
1906	1912	Wolverhampton Wanderers	193	65
Hedley, George Thomas (Tot)			RB	
b Lanchester q3 1882			d 1937	
		West Stanley		
1905		Middlesbrough	3	
		Chester-le-Street		
		Heart of Midlothian (trial)		
1905	1907	Hull City	78	2
1907	1908	Leicester Fosse	35	1
		Luton Town		
		Hartlepools United		
		Crook Town		
		Jarrow Caledonians		
		Brandesburton		
Hedley, Ralph Bickerton			RB/LB	
b Cambois q3 1897			d 1966	
		Pandon Temperance		
		Newburn		
1923		Hull City	9	
1924	1925	Crystal Palace	4	
1926		Durham City	4	
		Tyne Tees		
Hedley, Richard (Dick)			OR	
b Newcastle q3 1873			d 1908	
		Marlborough (Newcastle)		
		Arthur's Hill		
		Newcastle Albion		
1894		Newcastle United	3	1
		Jarrow		
1895		Newcastle United	0	
		Hebburn Argyle		
Hedley, Thomas			CF	
b Jarrow 1890				
1910		Woolwich Arsenal	0	
		Plymouth Argyle		
		Jarrow Caledonians		
1911		Birmingham	0	
1911		Hull City	2	
Heelbeck, Leslie Walter (Les)			LH	
b Scarborough 5/7/1909			d 1998	
		Scarborough		
		Newark Town		
		Grantham		
1931		Carlisle United	12	1
1932	1933	Wolverhampton Wanderers	8	
1934	1936	Rotherham United	102	6
		Scarborough		
Heeley, Charles Jones			LB	
b Ecclesall q4 1880				
1902		Sheffield United	1	

From	To	Club	Apps	Goal
Heeps, Andrew			CH	
b Muiravonside 15/12/1899				
		Banknock Juniors		
		Dunfermline Athletic		
		Airdrieonians		
1928		Brentford	2	
		Camelon		
		Bo'ness		
		Dumbarton		
Heeps, James (Jimmy)			IL	
b Glen Village 30/11/1894			d 1989	
		Banknock Juniors		
1920		Plymouth Argyle	16	1
		Airdrieonians		
		Hamilton Academical		
		New York Giants		
		Bathgate		
Hegarty, Richard (Dick)			RB	
b Stockton q2 1885			d 1917	
		Belle Vue Athletic		
		West Hartlepool Perseverance		
		West Hartlepool		
1905		Stockport County	1	
		Sunderland Royal Rovers		
		Hartlepools United		
		North Shields Athletic		
		West Hartlepool St Joseph's		
Hegarty, Thomas (Tom)			LB	
b Stockton q1 1883			d 1954	
		West Hartlepool Perseverance		
		West Hartlepool		
1905		Stockport County	2	2
		Sunderland Royal Rovers		
		West Hartlepool		
		Hartlepools United		
		Heart of Midlothian		
Hegazi, Hassan (Hussein)			CF	
b Cairo, Egypt 14/9/1891			d 1958	
Caps: Egypt Amat				
		National Sporting Club (Cairo)		
		University College (London)		
		Dulwich Hamlet		
1911		Fulham	1	1
		Dulwich Hamlet		
		Millwall Athletic		
		University College (London)		
		St Catherine's College		
		Cambridge University		
		Sekka (Egypt)		
		Al-Ahly		
		Zamalek (Cairo)		
		Al-Ahly		
		Zamalek (Cairo)		
Heigh, Robert (Bob)			IL/CF/OR	
b Bathgate 11/7/1904			d 1981	
		Bathgate		
		Tranent Juniors		
1926	1927	Coventry City	8	
		Arbroath		
		Armadale		
1929		Grimsby Town	0	
1930		Carlisle United	6	
		Armadale		
Heightley, Nicholas Temperley			CH	
b Hamsteels 20/1/1893			d 1970	
		Quebec United		
		Esh Winning		
		Ashington		
		South Shields (trial)	0	
		Norwich City (trial)	0	
		Watford	0	
1921		Durham City	1	
		Houghton		
Heinemann, Charles Adolph			IR	
b Stafford 29/2/1904			d 1974	
Caps: LoI 2				
		EEC Siemens Works		
		Riverscote		
		Stafford Rangers		
1925		Bristol Rovers	3	
1926		Port Vale	0	
		Stafford Rangers		
		Fordsons		
1927		Port Vale	0	
		Oakengates Town		
		Wallingford Town		
Heinemann, George Henry			LH/RH	
b Stafford 17/12/1905			d 1970	
		Stafford Rangers		
1928	1930	Manchester City	21	
1931	1933	Coventry City	52	1
1934		Crystal Palace	26	
1935	1937	Clapton Orient	86	1
		Wellington Town		

From To Apps Goal

Hellewell, Albert CF
b Huddersfield 1880
Greenock Overton
1902 Barnsley 27 5

Hellewell, Alexander (Alec) CF/OR/IR
b Sheffield q1 1880 d 1934
Mexborough Town
1899 1909 Barnsley 237 53

Hellier, William James (Bill) CH
b Tonypandy q1 1910
Stalybridge Celtic
1937 1945 Torquay United 52

Helliwell, Charles RB/LB
b Barnsley
1931 1932 Halifax Town 30 1

Helliwell, Ernest LH
b Sheffield 25/11/1905 d 1958
Wycliffe Bible Class
1924 Bradford City 0
1925 Sheffield Wednesday 0
1926 1930 Stockport County 83 3
1931 1932 Chesterfield 51 1
1933 Brighton & Hove Albion 0

Helliwell, Sidney (Sid) CH
b Sheffield 30/1/1904 d 1939
Wycliffe
1923 Sheffield Wednesday 0
1926 Reading 5 2
1927 1928 Tottenham Hotspur 8
1929 1931 Walsall 98 8
Hednesford Town
1933 Halifax Town 1
Goole Town

Helliwell, Tim OL
b Sowerby Bridge 19/1/1897 d 1985
Mytholmroyd
Halifax Town
West Riding Amateurs
1922 1923 Accrington Stanley 18 1
Darwen

Hellyer, Charles Edward (Percy) OL
b Greenwich 18/6/1909 d 1976
Caps: England Sch
Tunbridge Wells Rangers
1930 Rochdale 1
1931 Bradford City 0

Helme, James Albert (Jack) IL
b Altrincham 1887
Altrincham
1920 Stoke 4 1
Altrincham

Helsby, Thomas (Tom) RH/IR/LH
b Runcorn 4/4/1904 d 1961
Rhyl Athletic
1925 1926 Wigan Borough 29
Ellesmere Port Town
1926 Nelson (trial) 0
Northwich Victoria
Runcorn
1928 1930 Cardiff City 46 2
1931 1932 Bradford City 34
1933 Swindon Town 34
1934 Hull City 22
1935 Newport County 10
Caerau
Parr & Harland

Hemingway, Cyril Francis IL/OL
b Rotherham
1925 1927 Rotherham United 67 22
1928 Torquay United 38 11
1929 Exeter City 39 19
1930 Wolverhampton Wanderers 4
1931 Torquay United 23 4
Dartmouth United

Hemmingfield, William Edmund (Bill) RH/CF/OL
b Wortley 1875 d 1953
Mexborough Town
1898 Sheffield Wednesday 22 8
1899 1902 Grimsby Town 94 9
1903 1906 Sheffield Wednesday 21 4

Hempsall, Ernest RH
b Lincoln q4 1901 d 1941
Lincoln Claytons
1925 Lincoln City 1
1926 Luton Town 0
Lincoln Claytons

Hempshall, W Harry LB/LH
1901 1904 Gainsborough Trinity 61

From To Apps Goal

Hemsley, Charles James CF/LB
b Brighton 17/8/1888 d 1986
Ewbank
Accrington Stanley
1919 1920 Oldham Athletic 7 1

Henderson, Adam OL
b Darlington 16/7/1873
Airdrie Fruitfield
Airdrieonians
1893 1896 Preston North End 77 28
Celtic
Bristol St George
Gravesend
1899 1900 Preston North End 41 13

Henderson, Alastair Ian RH
b Shettleston 1910
Yoker Athletic
1931 Liverpool 5
1933 1934 Clapton Orient 18

Henderson, Charles John (Charlie) IR/CF
b Durham 4/1870
Darlington
South Bank
1892 Grimsby Town 12
Leith Athletic
1894 Bolton Wanderers 28 14
1895 Wolverhampton Wanderers 30 9
1896 Sheffield United 14 4
New Brighton Tower
South Bank
Dundee Harp
Edinburgh Thistle

Henderson, Crosby Gray LB
b South Hylton 12/5/1885 d 1970
Hylton Rangers
Hylton Star
1906 Newcastle United 0
1908 1909 Grimsby Town 65
1910 Birmingham 6
Brighton & Hove Albion
Luton Town

Henderson, David (Davy) RH/CF
b Stirling 1868 d 1933
King's Park
1893 Liverpool 20 10
Callendar Rob Roy

Henderson, David LB
b Bellshill
Shettleston Juniors
1938 Bury 1
Ayr United

Henderson, Douglas (Doug) RB/RH/LB
b Southampton 6/3/1913 d 2002
South Avenue
1935 1938 Southampton 22
1939 Bristol City 0

Henderson, Frank LH/RH
1923 Stockport County 3
1924 Brentford 8

Henderson, George LH/RH/CH
b High Blantyre 15/12/1873
Coatbridge St Patrick's
Burnbank Swifts
Motherwell
Airdrieonians
1897 Preston North End 2
Swindon Town
Millwall Athletic
1901 1905 Nottingham Forest 103 6
Hamilton Academical
Girvan

Henderson, George Brown CH
b Kelty 9/1/1902
Kelty Athletic
St Bernard's
1925 1928 Sunderland 45 1
1928 1936 Barnsley 258 11
Glenavon (trial)
Cowdenbeath

Henderson, George Donald (Geordie) CF
b Forfar 15/4/1897 d 1953
Caps: SLge 1
Forfar Celtic
Forfar Athletic
Dundee
Rangers
1926 Darlington 14 6
New York Nationals
Dundee United
Rhyl

From To Apps Goal

Henderson, George Turnbull RH
b Ladhope 2/5/1880 d 1930
Caps: Scotland 1
Queen's Park
Dundee
Rangers
1905 Middlesbrough 10
1905 1908 Chelsea 60 1
1909 Glossop 6

Henderson, Hugh CF
Third Lanark
1894 Liverpool 2
Partick Thistle

Henderson, James IR
b Thornhill, Dumfriesshire 1867
5th Kirkcudbright Rifle Volunteers
Rangers
1893 1894 Woolwich Arsenal 38 19

Henderson, James IR/IL
b Newcastle
Scotswood
Cardiff City
1919 Newcastle United 6 1
Scotswood
1921 Ashington 1
Scotswood
Spennymoor United

Henderson, James R RH
b Scotland 1870 d 1940
Annbank
1893 Liverpool 1
Broxburn Athletic
Edinburgh Thistle

Henderson, James Thomas (Jimmy) LH/RH
b Morpeth 10/6/1877
Morpeth Harriers
Morpeth Town
Reading
1904 Bradford City 14
1905 1907 Leeds City 75
1908 Preston North End 7
1909 Clapton Orient 26 4
Rochdale
South Liverpool
Rochdale
Rochdale Pioneers

Henderson, James Thomas CF/IL
b Sunderland
Derby County 0
1913 1914 Glossop 23 7
Bristol Rovers
1920 Derby County 0

Henderson, John GK
b Scotland d 1932
Clyde
1895 Newcastle United 30
Clyde
Burnbank Swifts

Henderson, John CF
Abercorn
1901 Manchester City 5 1

Henderson, John (Jock) CH
b Kelty 1895
Kelty Rangers
Cowdenbeath Hibs
Bathgate
St Bernard's
1914 1919 Manchester City 5
1920 Southend United 23
Mid-Rhondda United
1922 1923 Gillingham 76 9
Dunfermline Athletic

Henderson, John Neil (Jock) IR/OL
b Dumfries 1871 d 1930
5th Kirkcudbright Rifle Volunteers
Dumfries
Celtic
Victoria United (Aberdeen)
1898 1900 Lincoln City 76 9
1900 Leicester Fosse 13
1900 Small Heath 4
Maxwelltown Volunteers
Carlisle United
Maxwelltown Volunteers
King's Own Scottish Borderers
Annan United
Nithsdale Wanderers

Henderson, Joseph (Joe) IL
b 1872
Leith Athletic
1894 1897 Bury 87 27

From To Apps Goal

Henderson, Joseph Robert RB/LB
b Washington 1902
1929 Charlton Athletic 0
Washington Colliery
1931 1934 Carlisle United 55 1

Henderson, Lauchlan LH
b Kilbarchan
Paisley Juniors
1921 Hartlepools United 2

Henderson, Robert LB
Bee Hole
1904 Burnley 10
Clitheroe

Henderson, Robert Duff (Bob) OL/IR
b Clackmanan
Wee County Juvenile Rovers
1929 1930 Burnley 3
Dunfermline Athletic (loan)
Bangor (loan)
1931 New Brighton 11
Cork FC
Dumbarton

Henderson, Samuel Joplin (Sam) RH
b Willington Quay 3/11/1901 d 1980
Willington Quay
1925 1927 South Shields 14 1
1928 Chelsea 0
1929 Fulham 18
Tunbridge Wells Rangers
North Shields

Henderson, Thomas (Tommy) RB/LH
b Black Callerton q3 1902
North Walbottle
1919 Newcastle United 0
1920 Southampton 0
Leadgate Park
Workington
1923 1924 Ashington 40 3
Annfield Plain
Wallsend

Henderson, Thomas (Tommy) LH
b Lemington
Lemington Glass Works
1925 Hartlepools United 1

Henderson, William CF
1893 Middlesbrough Ironopolis 1

Henderson, William RB
b Broxburn 1878
Broxburn Athletic
1896 Everton 0
Reading
Southampton
1902 1903 Everton 15
Reading
1906 1907 Clapton Orient 47
New Brompton

Henderson, William RH
b Morpeth
Morpeth Town
1910 1911 Clapton Orient 16

Henderson, William (Billy) RB/LB
b Whitburn, County Durham 5/1/1900 d 1934
Whitburn
Brighton & Hove Albion
1921 Aberdare Athletic 19 2
1921 1927 West Ham United 162

Henderson, William (Bill) CF
b Edinburgh 1898 d 1964
St Bernard's
Airdrieonians
1921 1924 Manchester United 34 17
1924 Preston North End 9 1
1925 Clapton Orient 29 7
Heart of Midlothian
Morton
1928 Torquay United 15 10
1929 Exeter City 5

Henderson, William (Bill) IR
b Accrington
Stanhill
1931 Accrington Stanley 1

Henderson, William IL
1935 Carlisle United 3

Henderson, William James (Bill) OR
b Carlisle 11/1/1899 d 1934
Carlisle United
1921 1922 Arsenal 7
1922 1923 Luton Town 2
1923 1927 Southampton 152 10
1928 Coventry City 15 1
1929 Carlisle United 9 2

From To Apps Goal

Henderson, William James (Jim) CF
b Kilbirnie
Penicuik Athletic
St Bernard's
Penicuik Athletic
1932 1933 Cardiff City 43 25

Henderson, William M LH
b Houghton-le-Spring
Houghton Rovers
1913 1919 Preston North End 11 1

Henderson, William Pirrie (Bill) LH/CF
b Dundee 1883
Norwood (Dundee)
Dundee
Heart of Midlothian
New Brompton
1909 Bradford City 4
1911 Grimsby Town 4
Scunthorpe & Lindsey United
Dundee Hibernian

Hendren, Elias Henry (Patsy) OL/OR
b Turnham Green 5/2/1889 d 1962
Caps: SoLge 1
Sandersons
Queen's Park Rangers
Brentford
1908 Manchester City 2
Coventry City
1920 1926 Brentford 138 15

Hendrie, Richard (Dick) LB
b Airdrie 22/11/1895 d 1964
Royal Navy
Petershill
Heart of Midlothian
Queen's Park
Airdrieonians
Maidstone United
1923 1925 Gillingham 71
Margate
Grays Thurrock
1927 Brentford 0

Hendry, Connell Nicholson (Nick) GK
b York q1 1887 d 1949
North Eastern Railway (York)
1907 Middlesbrough 0
Darlington
1911 1919 Hull City 140
Doncaster Rovers
York City

Hendry, James OL
Alloa Athletic
1892 Newton Heath 2 1

Hendry, John (Jack) LB
b Scotland 1867
Uddingston
Rangers
1890 1895 Notts County 163 1
Heanor Town
Sheppey United
Rushden Town
Northampton Town

Hendry, Robert CF
b Dumbarton 1876
Dumbarton
Rangers
1897 Everton 0
1897 Notts County 7
Morton
Dumbarton
Renton

Hendry, William Harold (Billy) CH/CF
b Dundee 6/1864 d 1901
Dunblane Thistle
Dundee Wanderers
1888 West Bromwich Albion 16 4
Kidderminster Harriers
1888 1889 Stoke 16 1
1889 1890 Preston North End 15
1892 1894 Sheffield United 69 4
Dundee
1896 Bury 8 1
West Herts
Brighton United
Shrewsbury Town

Henery, John OL
b Sunderland
Houghton Rovers
1920 Brentford 20 1
1921 Darlington 1

Henry, Charles E (Charlie) RH
1930 Leicester City 0
1931 Walsall 18

From To Apps Goal

Henry, Gerald Robert (Gerry) IR/IL/RH
b Hemsworth 5/10/1920 d 1979
Outwood Stormcocks
1938 1947 Leeds United 44 4
1947 1949 Bradford Park Avenue 79 31
1949 1951 Sheffield Wednesday 40 7
1951 1952 Halifax Town 24 3

Henry, Thomas (Tom) RH/LH
b South Bank
South Bank
1913 1914 Bristol City 3

Henry, William Armstrong (Billy) RB
b Glasgow 6/9/1884
Blantyre Victoria
Rangers
Falkirk
1909 1911 Leicester Fosse 89
1911 1919 Manchester City 143 1
St Bernard's

Henrys, Arthur LH/CH
b Radford q2 1866 d 1922
Notts Rovers
Notts St John's
Nottingham Jardines
Nottingham Forest
Gainsborough Trinity
1892 Newton Heath 5
1894 1895 Leicester Fosse 37 1
1896 Notts County 7

Henshall, Albert V IR
1905 Wolverhampton Wanderers 2

Henshall, Horace Vincent OL
b Hednesford 14/6/1889 d 1951
Caps: FLge 1
Bridgetown Amateurs
Crewe Alexandra
1910 1911 Aston Villa 45 8
1912 1921 Notts County 164 27
1922 Sheffield Wednesday 14 1
1923 Chesterfield 33 3

Henshall, James Cecil (Jim) OR/OL
b Packmoor q1 1907
1930 1932 Port Vale 37 6
1932 Crewe Alexandra 19 3
1933 Stockport County 0
Ashton National
Mossley

Henshall, John IR
Hanley Swifts
1900 Burslem Port Vale 5

Henshaw, Ernest (Ernie) CH
b Ellesmere Port 28/11/1910 d 1995
Burton Town
1931 Tranmere Rovers 1

Henson, Adam IL
b Carlisle 25/8/1911 d 1987
1934 Carlisle United 7

Henson, George Horace CF
b Stony Stratford 25/12/1911 d 1988
Stony Stratford
Wolverton
1932 1934 Northampton Town 43 23
1935 Wolverhampton Wanderers 6 1
1936 Swansea Town 23 5
1937 1938 Bradford Park Avenue 60 33
1938 Sheffield United 10 5
1939 (Sheffield United) (3) (1)
Bedford Town
Stony Stratford

Henzell, William Henry IR
b Newcastle 9/6/1897 d 1985
Blyth Spartans
Walker Celtic
1920 Hull City 2 1
South Shields Employment Exchange

Heppell, George GK
b West Hartlepool 2/9/1916 d 1993
1936 Wolverhampton Wanderers 0
1937 1951 Port Vale 193
Witton Albion

Heppinstall, Frank OL
b Huddersfield 1874
1893 Rotherham Town 1

Heppinstall, Frank OL/IL
b Worsborough Dale 31/1/1883 d 1969
Denaby United
1904 Barnsley 8 1
Denaby United
Swindon Town
1909 1910 Woolwich Arsenal 23
Stalybridge Celtic
Hamilton Academical

From To Apps Goal

Hepple, Robert OR/IL
b Mickley 18/1/1898 d 1970
Mickley
1920 Bradford City 3
1921 Reading 19
Mickley
1923 Ashington 10 1
West Wylam Colliery
South Tyne Rangers
1927 Ashington 2
Mickley
Prudhoe Castle Welfare

Hepworth, Arthur LH
b Dodworth 28/2/1908 d 1988
1926 Barnsley 0
1927 1928 Nelson 16
Wombwell
E & A Smith's Sports (Cleckheaton)
Battyeford Wanderers

Hepworth, Ronald (Ronnie) LB/RB
b Barnsley 25/1/1919 d 2006
1936 Chesterfield 0
1939 1950 Bradford Park Avenue 101
1939 (Bradford Park Avenue) (3)

Hepworth, Walter IR
b Dodworth 1878
Worsborough Common St Luke's
1898 1899 Barnsley 26 9

Herbert, Frederick (Fred) IL/OL
b Longford, Warwickshire q4 1897
Foxford United
Bedworth Town
Exhall Colliery
1922 1928 Coventry City 187 82
Brierley Hill Alliance

Herbert, Frederick Walter (Fred) CF
b Cliffe 6/1/1920 d 1996
Kent Alloys
1937 Gillingham 17 7

Herbert, Joseph Henry OR
b Kimberworth 21/1/1895 d 1959
Rotherham County
Kimberworth Old Boys
Norwich City
1920 Swansea Town 0
1921 Rochdale 16 4
Guildford United

Herbert, Selwyn Lucmore CF
b Crickhowell q2 1908
Crickhowell
1929 Merthyr Town 1

Herbert, William Edward (Billy) IR/IL
b Canning Town q4 1888
Walthamstow Grange
Barnet Alston
1909 Woolwich Arsenal 0
1910 1911 Glossop 17 3
Gravesend United
1919 Stoke 11 3
1919 1921 Bolton Wanderers 34 7
1921 Wigan Borough 24 6

Herd, Alexander (Alex) IR/IL
b Bowhill 8/11/1911 d 1982
Caps: Scotland War 1
Hearts o' Beath
Hamilton Academical
1932 1947 Manchester City 257 107
1939 (Manchester City) (3)
1947 1951 Stockport County 111 35

Herdman, Henry CH
1938 Rotherham United 11

Herod, Edwin Redvers Baden (Baden) LB/RB
b Ilford 16/5/1900 d 1973
Barking Town
Ilford
Great Eastern Railway Works
1921 1927 Charlton Athletic 213 2
1928 Brentford 28
1928 1930 Tottenham Hotspur 57
1931 1932 Chester 79 1
1933 1934 Swindon Town 81
1935 1936 Clapton Orient 53

Heron, Alexander Agnew (Alec) GK
b Pershore q3 1889 d 1964
1923 1925 Bournemouth & Boscombe Ath 26

Herring, Clifford LH
b Chesterfield 13/10/1911 d 1997
1932 Mansfield Town 2
Ollerton Colliery

From To Apps Goal

Hesford, Robert Taylor (Bob) GK
b Bolton 13/4/1916 d 1982
1931 Blackpool 0
South Shore
1934 1949 Huddersfield Town 203
1939 (Huddersfield Town) (3)
Stalybridge Celtic

Hesham, Frank James OR
b Manchester 1879 d 1915
1896 Manchester City 2
Gorton St Francis
1900 Manchester City 1
Crewe Alexandra
Accrington Stanley
1904 Stoke 17 1
Leyton
1907 1908 Oldham Athletic 34 9
1909 Preston North End 0
Hyde
Croydon Common
Crewe Alexandra
Newton Heath Alliance

Heslop, Archibald Sorbie (Archie) OR
b Annfield Plain q1 1903
South Pontop Villa
Annfield Plain
1927 1929 Burnley 24 4
West Stanley
1930 1931 Luton Town 27 7
Spennymoor United

Heslop, John J OR
1932 Gateshead 2

Heslop, Robert IL/IR/RH
b Annfield Plain 5/2/1907
Annfield Plain
1928 1933 Nottingham Forest 92 23
Annfield Plain
1935 1938 Gateshead 95 13

Heslop, Thomas W (Tom) IR/LH
1912 1913 Blackpool 29 4
1913 1914 Bolton Wanderers 7
Accrington Stanley
1921 Tranmere Rovers 8

Hesmondhalgh, Thomas (Tom) CF
b Bolton q4 1896 d 1957
Horwich RMI
Rochdale
1920 Exeter City 1
Horwich RMI

Hetherington, John Arthur (Arthur) OL/IL/IR
b Rotherham 7/8/1906 d 1977
Dalton & Eastwood
Shirebrook
Mexborough Athletic
Denaby United
Dalton & Eastwood
1928 1934 Wolverhampton Wanderers 95 24
1934 1935 Preston North End 15 3
1936 1937 Swindon Town 65 13
1937 1938 Watford 8 1

Hetherington, Joseph (Jos) CF/IR
b Sunderland 11/4/1892 d 1971
Sunderland Royal Rovers
Southwick (Co Durham)
1920 1923 South Shields 64 15
1924 Preston North End 5
1925 Lincoln City 3 1
1926 Durham City 0
1927 Norwich City 1
Guildford City
Walker Celtic
Sunderland Employment Exchange

Hetherington, Sidney IR/IL
b Monkwearmouth
1920 Exeter City 8 1
Southwick (Co Durham)
1921 Halifax Town 27 11

Hetherington, Thomas Burns (Tom) GK
b Walker 22/1/1911 d 1968
Walker Celtic
1933 1937 Burnley 67
Jarrow
1938 Barnsley 0
1946 Gateshead 1

Hetherington, William CF
1935 Darlington 1

Heward, Harold Aubrey (Aubrey) LH
b Hetton-le-Hole 31/8/1910 d 1985
Herrington Swifts
1932 Newcastle United 5
1934 Bradford Park Avenue 0
1935 Hartlepools United 28
Yeovil & Petters United

From To Apps Goal

Hewett, Joseph Thomas (Joe) GK
b Coventry 1902
Coventry Motor Sundries
1927 1930 Watford 104
1931 Coventry City 5

Hewish, Henry IL
b Houghton-le-Spring q1 1886
New York United (Northumberland)
Bedlington United
1909 Gainsborough Trinity 10
West Allotment
New Hartley Rovers

Hewison, Robert (Bob) RH/LB/IL
b Backworth 25/3/1889 d 1964
East Holywell Villa
Whitley Athletic
1910 1914 Newcastle United 64
1914 Leeds City 0
1919 Newcastle United 3
1920 1924 Northampton Town 99 8

Hewitson, Isaac W IL
1893 Middlesbrough Ironopolis 2

Hewitson, Robert (Bob) GK
b Blyth 26/2/1884 d 1957
Morpeth Harriers
1903 1904 Barnsley 62
Crystal Palace
1907 Oldham Athletic 27
1908 Tottenham Hotspur 30
Croydon Common
Doncaster Rovers

Hewitson, Robert OL
b Newburn 1888 d 1957
Newburn
1912 Hull City 1
Newburn

Hewitson, William John (Bill) CF
b Prestwich q3 1915
1934 Oldham Athletic 0
Shrewsbury Town
1936 York City 2 1
Burton Town

Hewitt, Arthur Harper LB
b Beeston 10/1/1900
Ilkeston Town
1924 Nottingham Forest 4
1925 Watford 0

Hewitt, Charles William (Charlie) IR/OR
b Greatham 10/4/1884 d 1966
Christ Church
West Hartlepool
1904 1905 Middlesbrough 33 12
Tottenham Hotspur
1907 Liverpool 16 6
1907 1909 West Bromwich Albion 60 26
Spennymoor United
Crystal Palace
1921 Hartlepools United 6

Hewitt, Edgar Donald (Don) RH/LH/CH
b Coventry
1929 Coventry City 0
1930 1933 Torquay United 42
Nuneaton Town

Hewitt, George IL
b Burslem 1878
Burslem Port Vale
1898 Luton Town 12 6

Hewitt, John IR
1903 Glossop 1

Hewitt, John Joseph (Joss) CF/IR/RH
b Evenwood 15/6/1911 d 1984
Raby United
Evenwood Town
Cockfield
1929 Everton 0
1930 1933 Hartlepools United 110 53
1934 1935 Norwich City 13 2
1935 1938 Northampton Town 83 14
1939 Southport (3) (1)

Hewitt, Joseph (Joe) CF/IL/IR
b Chester 3/5/1881 d 1971
1901 1903 Sunderland 36 9
1903 1909 Liverpool 153 67
1910 Bolton Wanderers 11 3
Reading
South Liverpool

From To Apps Goal

Hewitt, Thomas John RB
b Connah's Quay 26/4/1889 d 1980
Caps: Wales 8
Sandycroft
Connah's Quay
Saltney
Wrexham
1911 Chelsea 8
South Liverpool
Swansea Town

Hews, Harold Burston GK
b Honiton q1 1888 d 1922
Sleaford Town
1909 Lincoln City 2

Hey, Charles (Charlie) OR/LB
b Salford q1 1899 d 1942
Gorton
Hurst
1926 1929 Oldham Athletic 11 1
Hurst
1931 Stockport County 0
Rossendale United

Heydon, Cecil RH/OR
b Birkenhead 24/5/1919 d 2007
Victory Social
1938 New Brighton 1
1939 Derby County 0
1945 1947 Doncaster Rovers 6
1948 Rochdale 1

Heyes, Edward GK
b Aspull 16/3/1899
Aspull
1922 1923 Wigan Borough 34

Heyes, Henry (Harry) GK
b Aspull q1 1894 d 1962
Chorley
Coppull
Horwich RMI
1921 Nelson 26
Chorley
Horwich RMI

Heyes, James (Jack) IR
b Northwich 1902
Northwich Victoria
1925 Sunderland 3
1926 West Ham United 0
Connah's Quay & Shotton
Bangor City
Ashton National
Mossley

Heyes, L IL
Darwen
1889 Burnley 11 2
Hyde

Heyes, Lawrence (Lol) IR
1892 Northwich Victoria 5
Chester

Heys, Richard IR/CF
b Clitheroe q4 1904
Blackburn Olympic
1923 1924 Accrington Stanley 15 3
Clitheroe
Chorley

Heys, Stephen LB
b Haslingden q3 1879
Colne
1907 Burnley 1
Haslingden
Accrington Stanley
Rossendale United

Heywood, Albert Edwards (Napper) GK
b Hartlepool 12/5/1913 d 1989
West Hartlepool Expansion
Trimdon Grange
1933 Manchester City (trial) 0
1934 Luton Town (trial) 0
Spennymoor United
1936 Wolverhampton Wandrs (trial) 0
1938 Sunderland 4
1946 Hartlepools United 39
Horden Colliery Welfare

Heywood, Archibald OL
b Oldham 1878 d 1972
Oldham Athletic
Accrington
1894 Blackburn Rovers 0
1895 West Bromwich Albion 3
Chorley
Colne

From To Apps Goal

Heywood, Frederick (Fred) IR/IL
b Edgworth q1 1879
Turton
1900 Newcastle United 13 3
1902 Blackpool 33 4
Reading
1904 Blackpool 2
Oldham Athletic
Darwen
Turton
Chorley
Hyde
Nelson

Heywood, George RB
b Clayton 12/1/1907 d 1985
Caps: England Sch
South Salford Lads Club
1928 Manchester City 0
South Salford Lads Club
Altrincham
1935 1936 Port Vale 23
1936 Southport 14
Hyde United
Northwich Victoria
Stalybridge Celtic
Altrincham

Heywood, Herbert (Bert) OR
b Little Hulton q3 1913
Turton
1930 Oldham Athletic 0
Northwich Victoria
1932 1933 Manchester United 4 2
1934 Tranmere Rovers 9 1
Altrincham
Wigan Athletic
Astley & Tyldesley Collieries

Heywood, James (Jimmy) RB/LB
b Stockport q1 1881
1903 1906 Stockport County 65
1906 1908 Blackburn Rovers 15
1909 1911 Glossop 39
Nelson

Heywood, Roger CH/RH
b Chorley 4/5/1909 d 1985
Chorley St James
Chorley
1929 1938 Leicester City 228 2
1939 (Leicester City) (1)
Corby Town

Hibberd, Cyril Marples GK
b Sheffield 8/5/1895 d 1980
Valley Road Juniors
1921 1922 Chesterfield 58
1923 Rochdale 2

Hibberd, William OL
1898 Sheffield United 1
Sheffield
Wycliffe

Hibbert, Henry Crookes (Harry) LH/CH
b Dore q2 1887 d 1947
Hathersage
1907 Sheffield Wednesday 2
1908 Stockport County 1
1909 Lincoln City 4 1
Rotherham County
1913 Sheffield United 0
Rotherham County
Halifax Town

Hibbert, Jack T OR
b Darwen
1888 Burnley 1

Hibbert, James William RH/IL
b Windy Nook q1 1889
Windy Nook
Pelaw
1910 1911 West Bromwich Albion 3
Hartlepools United

Hibbert, William (Billy) CF/IR
b Golborne 21/9/1884 d 1949
Caps: FLge 3/England 1
Golborne Juniors
Newton-le-Willows
Brynn Central
1906 1911 Bury 178 99
1911 1919 Newcastle United 139 46
1920 1921 Bradford City 53 26
1922 Oldham Athletic 16 4
Fall River Marksmen
J & P Coats (Rhode Island)
Burscough Rangers

From To Apps Goal

Hibbs, Henry Edward (Harry) GK
b Wilnecote 27/5/1906 d 1984
Caps: FLge 3/England 25
Tamworth Castle
1925 1938 Birmingham 358
1939 (Birmingham) (3)

Hick, John B (Jack) LB/RB/LH
b Birmingham 1912
1933 Birmingham 0
1934 1938 Bristol City 83
1939 Ipswich Town (2)

Hick, William Morris (Billy) CF
b Beamish 13/2/1903 d 1972
Consett Celtic
1921 Hartlepools United 1
1922 South Shields 0
1923 1924 Middlesbrough 16 7
1924 1927 Southend United 106 69
1928 Bristol City 10 1
1928 Exeter City 16 8
Grays Athletic
Scunthorpe & Lindsey United
1929 Notts County 0
1930 1931 Rotherham United 47 36

Hickie, William (Bill) LB/RB
b Larkhall 9/12/1902 d 1957
Waterloo Rovers
Larkhall Thistle
1924 1925 Aberdare Athletic 14
Aberaman Athletic
Ebbw Vale
Peebles Rovers
Aberdeen
1930 Newport County 21 2
1931 Fulham 9
1932 Aldershot 3
Guildford City
Basingstoke Town

Hickinbotham, W RB/LB
1898 1899 Walsall 7

Hickinbottom, Ernest Thomas RH/CH/LH
b Derby q4 1865 d 1939
Darley Abbey
Derby Midland
1888 1893 Derby County 50

Hickling, William (Billy) LB
Somercotes United
Ashby
1903 Derby County 9
Tottenham Hotspur
1906 Middlesbrough 5
Mansfield Mechanics
Ilkeston United

Hickman, George OR
b Lanchester 17/1/1909 d 1978
Caps: England Sch
Lintz Colliery
1927 West Bromwich Albion 0
1928 1929 Halifax Town 50 8
Scarborough
Horden Colliery Welfare
Blyth Spartans
Shrewsbury Town
Blyth Spartans

Hickman, John Edward Arthur W (Arthur) IR
b Golds Hill 25/3/1915 d 1985
1932 West Bromwich Albion 0
1936 1938 Newport County 71 21
1939 (Newport County) (3) (2)

Hickman, Joseph (Joe) GK
b Tanfield 5/9/1905 d 1980
Horden Athletic
Lintz Colliery
1926 1927 Hartlepools United 7
1927 Aston Villa 2
1928 Hartlepools United 20
Scarborough
1930 Clapton Orient 0
Horden Colliery Welfare
Durham City
Spennymoor United
Connah's Quay & Shotton
Horden Colliery Welfare
Ashington
Blackhall Colliery Welfare

Hickman, William CH
b Wolverhampton
Burton Town
1927 Coventry City 9 2
Oakengates Town

From	To	Club	Apps	Goal
Hicks, George Wolstenholme			OL	
b Salford 30/4/1902			d 1954	
		Droylsden		
		Manchester Central		
1923	1928	Manchester City	123	40
1928	1931	Birmingham	76	18
1931		Manchester United	0	
1932		Bristol Rovers	0	
1933		Swindon Town	4	
1933		Rotherham United	28	6
		Manchester North End		
Hicks, Leslie Walter			RB	
b Swindon 9/12/1907			d 1991	
		Stratton St Philip's		
1926		Swindon Town	1	
		Swindon Corinthians		
		Bath City		
		Street		
Hicks, Thomas George			LB	
b Trehafod 1903				
		Pontypridd		
1924	1926	Preston North End	9	
1927		Nottingham Forest	8	
1928		Northampton Town	5	
		Chester		
Hickton, Arthur Joseph			CH	
b Birmingham 6/1867			d 1940	
		Birmingham Waterworks		
1889		Aston Villa	1	
		Rugby Wanderers		
		Coventry Standard		
		Nuneaton Welfare		
Hickton, Edward Henry			GK	
b Nantwich q4 1868				
1892	1895	Crewe Alexandra	72	
Hiftle, Jacob Ernest			IL	
b Newcastle q1 1889			d 1966	
1911		Stockport County	4	1
Hiftle, William Adam (Bill)			OL	
b Byker 16/1/1917			d 2008	
1935		Charlton Athletic	0	
		Walker Celtic		
1937	1938	Doncaster Rovers	10	3
Higginbotham, Ernest			LH/IL/LB	
b Sheffield				
1925	1927	Rotherham United	25	9
		Mexborough Athletic		
1929		Bradford City	0	
		Loughborough Corinthians		
Higginbotham, Henry (Harry)			IR/OR	
b Ashfield, NSW, Australia 27/7/1894			d 1950	
		Kilsyth Rangers		
		Petershill		
		Third Lanark		
		St Mirren		
1919		South Shields	7	
1920	1922	Luton Town	80	26
1922	1923	Clapton Orient	19	1
1923		Nelson	4	
1924		Reading	24	3
		Mid-Rhondda United		
		Pontypridd		
Higgins, Alexander (Sandy)			IL/IR	
b Kilmarnock 4/11/1885			d 1939	
Caps: Scotland 4				
		Belle Vue Juniors		
		Kilmarnock		
1905	1914	Newcastle United	126	36
		Kilmarnock		
1920		Nottingham Forest	33	7
		Jarrow		
1921		Norwich City	7	2
		Wallsend		
		Workington		
		Preston Colliery		
Higgins, Alexander F (Sandy)			CF/IR	
b Kilmarnock 7/11/1863			d 1920	
Caps: Scotland 1				
		Kilmarnock		
1888	1889	Derby County	42	25
1892	1893	Nottingham Forest	47	18
		Kilmarnock		

From	To	Club	Apps	Goal
Higgins, Andrew Kincade (Andy)			IR/IL	
b Gartsherrie 26/4/1909			d 1966	
		Gartsherrie Athletic		
		Stoneyburn Juniors		
		Dunblane Rovers		
		Cowdenbeath		
		Gartsherrie Athletic (loan)		
1930		West Bromwich Albion	0	
1931		Millwall	5	
1932		Exeter City	22	9
1933	1934	Newport County	40	13
1934		Notts County	10	2
		Lille		
		Racing Club d'Arras		
1938		Newport County	2	
Higgins, Dennis			OR	
b Wolstanton q4 1915			d 1942	
		Leek Alexandra		
		Tamworth		
1935	1938	Fulham	30	12
1939		(Fulham)	(2)	
Higgins, Francis (Frank)			LH/CH/RH	
b Birkenhead 3/10/1901			d 1982	
		Wirral Railways		
		Flint Town		
1926	1929	New Brighton	13	
Higgins, James			CF	
b Cradley Heath 1874				
		Stourbridge		
1897		Small Heath	6	3
		Netherton		
		Halesowen Town		
Higgins, John Bernard (Bernard)			IL	
b Harborne 31/12/1885			d 1970	
1906		Aston Villa	0	
1907		Birmingham	1	
		Brierley Hill Alliance		
Higgins, John Thomas (Tom)			CH/CF	
b Halesowen 1874			d 1916	
Caps: FLge 2				
		Albion Swifts		
		Stourbridge		
1894	1897	West Bromwich Albion	78	4
Higgins, Martin			LH/CH/IL	
b Consett q3 1879				
		Bishop Auckland		
1904	1907	Grimsby Town	95	8
		Bristol Rovers		
		New Brompton		
1911		Grimsby Town	1	
		Scunthorpe & Lindsey United		
Higgins, Michael (Mike)			LH	
1888		Everton	1	
Higgins, Thomas (Tommy)			CF	
		Darlington St Augustine's		
1903		Lincoln City	6	
		Spennymoor United		
		Hartlepools United		
Higgins, Thomas			LH	
b Glasgow				
		Baillieston Juniors		
		Heart of Midlothian		
1934		Northampton Town	3	
		Scarborough		
Higgins, William (Sandy)			CH/RH/IR	
b Smethwick q2 1869				
Caps: FLge 1				
		Woodfield		
		Albion Swifts		
		Birmingham St George's		
1892	1896	Grimsby Town	126	27
		Bristol City		
1898	1899	Newcastle United	35	3
1900		Middlesbrough	24	1
1901		Newton Heath	10	
Higgins, William			LH	
b Rutherglen 21/6/1916			d 1989	
		Blantyre Celtic		
		Rutherglen Glencairn		
1934		Hull City	5	
Higginson, Jack			IL/OL	
b Dudley 1876				
		Dudley Town		
1900	1901	Small Heath	14	4
		Stourbridge		
Higginson, Levi			GK	
b Wolstanton q4 1867				
1892		Burslem Port Vale	1	
		Goldenhill		

From	To	Club	Apps	Goal
Higginson, Samuel (Sam)			IR/CH/CF	
b Goldenhill 1880			d 1930	
		Goldenhill Wanderers		
1899	1903	Stoke	110	21
		Reading		
1906	1908	Bradford City	56	6
Higginson, William			GK	
1901		Blackpool	3	
Higgs, Frank Jary			GK	
b Willington Quay q4 1907			d 1956	
		Howden Stead Memorial		
		East Howden		
		Bedlington United		
		Seaton Delaval		
1929		Chelsea	2	
		Linfield		
1931		Barnsley	35	
1932		Manchester City	1	
1933		Aldershot	0	
1934		Walsall	2	
1935	1936	Carlisle United	49	
1937		Southend United	2	
1938		Barrow	8	
Higgs, Harold			GK	
1919		Wolverhampton Wanderers	3	
Higgs, Sydney A (Syd)			IL/IR	
1923	1924	Crewe Alexandra	19	6
1924		Walsall	13	2
High, Stanley (Stan)			RH/LH	
b Hetton-le-Hole 18/2/1908			d 1982	
		Easington Colliery		
1928		Leicester City	0	
1929	1930	Torquay United	44	1
1931		Accrington Stanley	28	1
1932		Gillingham	11	
		Dartford		
Higham, Frank			RH/CH	
b Daventry 9/1905				
		Daventry		
1924		Walsall	2	
1926	1927	Wolverhampton Wanderers	37	2
1928	1929	Coventry City	35	2
1930		Lincoln City	0	
		Worcester City		
		Nuneaton Town		
		Evesham Town		
		Hereford United		
Higham, Norman			IL/IR	
b Chorley 14/2/1912			d 1994	
		Chorley		
1931		Bolton Wanderers	0	
		Chorley		
1933	1934	Everton	14	6
1935	1938	Middlesbrough	49	10
1939		Southampton	(2)	(2)
Higham, Walter			OL	
1892		Accrington	2	2
Hignett, Samuel (Sam)			RH	
b Liverpool 9/1885				
1907		Liverpool	1	
Higson, James (Jamie)			IR	
b Newton Heath				
		Manchester Wednesday		
1901		Newton Heath	5	1
Higson, Richard			GK	
b Wigan 9/8/1901			d 1978	
		Ince Parish Church		
		Skelmersdale United		
1922		Wigan Borough	2	
		Chorley		
		Hindley Green Athletic		
Hilditch, Clarence George (Clarrie)			RH/CH/LH	
b Hartford 2/6/1894			d 1977	
		Hartford		
		Witton Albion		
		Altrincham		
1919	1931	Manchester United	301	7
Hiles, Arthur			GK	
1896		Bolton Wanderers	1	
Hiles, Ernest Cuthbert			CH	
b Little Birch 11/9/1913			d 1976	
		Hereford Town		
1934	1938	Fulham	49	
1939		(Fulham)	(2)	

From	To	Club	Apps	Goal
Hiles, William Robert George (Billy)			OL/OR	
b Cardiff 28/11/1901			d 1978	
Caps: WLge 3				
		Lovells Athletic		
1924	1926	Newport County	28	4
1927		Swansea Town	7	2
1928		Merthyr Town	0	
		Lovells Athletic		
		Evesham Town		
		Lovells Athletic		
Hill, Albert Edward			CH/CF	
b Conisbrough q2 1906				
		Mexborough		
		Denaby United		
1928		Huddersfield Town	0	
1929		Wolverhampton Wanderers	2	
1930		Wrexham	4	
		Peterborough & Fletton United		
		Tunbridge Wells Rangers		
		Bolton Albion		
		Conisbrough Welfare		
		Edlington Welfare		
Hill, Albert Victor William Percy (Percy)			RB/LB	
b Wilton 2/1885			d 1940	
		Southampton		
1905	1906	Everton	14	
1906	1907	Manchester City	38	
		Airdrieonians		
		Swindon Town		
		Weymouth		
Hill, Amos Montague			OL	
b Wath-on-Dearne 21/6/1910			d 1973	
		Hawson Street		
1935	1936	Lincoln City	14	5
1936		Mansfield Town	1	
Hill, Charles John (Charlie 'Midge')			IL/LH	
b Cardiff 6/9/1918			d 1998	
1938	1946	Cardiff City	19	3
1947	1949	Torquay United	63	15
1948	1949	Queen's Park Rangers	21	1
1950		Swindon Town	4	
		Barry Town		
Hill, David Fairbairn			CH	
b Prestwick 2/6/1904			d 1989	
		Barr & Stroud		
		Anniesland Young Methodists		
		Yoker Athletic		
		Alloa Athletic		
		Hamilton Academical		
1934	1936	Plymouth Argyle	14	
1937	1938	Southport	73	1
Hill, F			IR	
1893		Rotherham Town	1	
Hill, Francis William (Frank)			LB	
b Grimsby q4 1910				
		Scunthorpe & Lindsey United		
1929		Portsmouth	0	
1931		Bristol Rovers	16	
1932		Crewe Alexandra	0	
		Scunthorpe & Lindsey United		
Hill, Frank Robert			LH/OL/RH	
b Forfar 21/5/1906			d 1993	
Caps: SLge 1/Scotland 3				
		Forfar West End		
		Forfar Athletic		
		Aberdeen		
1932	1935	Arsenal	76	4
1936	1937	Blackpool	45	8
1937	1938	Southampton	51	3
1939		Preston North End	0	
1945	1947	Crewe Alexandra	20	
Hill, Frank W Percival (Percy)			IR	
b Luton 25/3/1895			d 1970	
		Luton Clarence		
1920		Luton Town	6	4
1921		Exeter City	14	2
		Torquay United		
		Chatham		
Hill, Fred A (Freddie)			IR/OL	
b Cardiff q3 1913				
1932	1935	Cardiff City	67	15
Hill, George			OL	
b Dronfield				
		Simplex Motor Works (Sheffield)		
		Rotherham Town		
1920		Leeds United	7	

From To Apps Goal

Hill, Harold IL/IR
b Blackwell, Derbyshire 24/9/1899 d 1969
Birdholme Rovers
New Hucknall Colliery
1919 1924 Notts County 151 50
1924 1928 Sheffield Wednesday 91 37
Scarborough
1932 Chesterfield 11 2
1933 Mansfield Town 22 5
Sutton Town
Bolsover Colliery

Hill, Haydn Henry Clifford GK
b Creswell 4/7/1913 d 1992
Caps: England Amat
Sheffield University
1934 1935 Sheffield Wednesday 4
Yorkshire Amateurs
Corinthians
Weymouth
Dulwich Hamlet

Hill, James (Jimmy) OL/IR/IL
b Paisley 1872
St Mirren
1889 1896 Burnley 151 36
1896 1897 Stoke 31 11
1898 1899 New Brighton Tower 53 7
Wellingborough

Hill, James OL/OR
b Hanley
1919 1920 Port Vale 18 1
Shrewsbury Town

Hill, James Thomas (Jim) GK
1909 Wolverhampton Wanderers 1

Hill, John (Jacky) OR
b Kirkcaldy 18/3/1871
Leith Rangers
Leith Athletic
Middlesbrough Ironopolis
1894 Leicester Fosse 20 2
Glossop North End
West Herts

Hill, John Henry (Jack) CH
b Hetton-le-Hole 2/3/1897 d 1972
Caps: SoLge 1/FLge 3/England 11
Durham City
1920 1922 Plymouth Argyle 101 10
1923 1928 Burnley 184 13
1928 1930 Newcastle United 74 2
1931 Bradford City 8 1
1931 1933 Hull City 94 2

Hill, John Thomas (Jack) CF
b Monkwearmouth q1 1908
Esh Winning
Jarrow
1928 Newport County 1
1929 1930 Darlington 22 14
West Stanley
Spennymoor United

Hill, John William (Jack) RH/IR
b Rochdale 2/6/1895
Brights
1921 1922 Rochdale 43 11
Bacup Borough

Hill, Joseph (Joe) IR/CF
b Sheffield 1906
1927 Leeds United 0
1928 1929 Torquay United 49 14
Mansfield Town
Newark Town
1931 Barnsley 8 3
1932 Queen's Park Rangers 15 1
1933 1937 Stockport County 133 63
1938 Walsall 8 2

Hill, Leonard George (Len) GK
b Islington 15/2/1899 d 1979
Cranley Rovers
Southend United
1920 1924 Queen's Park Rangers 162
1925 Southampton 10
1926 Rochdale 34
1927 1928 Lincoln City 69
Grays Thurrock

Hill, Matthew Aaron RH
b Haltwhistle q2 1915
1935 Carlisle United 0
1936 Mansfield Town 1

Hill, Reginald (Reg) RH/CH/LH
b Gibraltar 6/5/1907 d 1961
1930 1931 Carlisle United 5
Lancaster Town
1932 Tranmere Rovers 1
1932 1936 Hartlepools United 139 6
1936 Darlington 12

From To Apps Goal

Hill, Richard Henry (Dick) LB/RB
b Mapperley 26/11/1893 d 1971
Caps: England 1
Grenadier Guards
1920 1929 Millwall Athletic 313
1930 Torquay United 28 1
Newark Town

Hill, Robert CF/IL
b Forfar 3/7/1867 d 1938
Linfield
1892 1895 Sheffield United 58 21
1895 1896 Manchester City 21 9
Watford St Mary's
Millwall Athletic
Brighton United
Dundee
Forfar Athletic

Hill, Roland LH
Greenbank
1931 Rochdale 2
Rochdale St Mary's
Mossley
Hurst
Stalybridge Celtic
Droylsden
Ashton United

Hill, Thomas (Tom) CF
b Market Drayton q1 1871
Market Drayton
1897 Stoke 5 2
Leicester Nomads

Hill, Thomas (Tommy) LH/RH
b Bradford 1901
Bolton United
1921 1923 Bradford City 12
1924 Walsall 15
York City

Hill, Thomas IL
Castleton
1932 Rochdale 7

Hill, WA (Jim) GK
1910 Wolverhampton Wanderers 2

Hill, Walter RB/LH/RH
Grimethorpe
1892 1895 Sheffield United 15

Hill, William T LB
1927 Walsall 1

Hillam, Charles Emmanuel (Charlie) GK
b Burnley 6/10/1908 d 1958
Clitheroe
1930 Nelson 3
Clitheroe
1932 Burnley 19
1933 Manchester United 8
1934 1937 Clapton Orient 125
1938 Southend United 13
1939 (Southend United) (3)
Ekco Sports
Chingford Town

Hilley, Cornelius (Con) LH/OL
b Glasgow 29/9/1902 d 1959
St Anthony's (Glasgow)
Raith Rovers
Third Lanark
1926 1927 Crystal Palace 43 4
Thames
Derry City
1931 Rochdale 3
Coleraine
Ruskin (Croydon)

Hillhouse, John T RH
b Hurlford 14/1/1898
Hurlford
1921 Middlesbrough 0
Nithsdale Wanderers
Workington
1925 1926 Rochdale 52
1926 Notts County 4
1927 Bury 0
Arthurlie

Hillier, Ernest John Guy (Joe) GK
b Bridgend 10/4/1907 d 1979
Bridgend Town
1926 Swansea Town (trial) 0
1927 1929 Cardiff City 9
1929 1934 Middlesbrough 63
1936 Newport County 22

Hillier, Stanley (Stan) IL/LH
b London 1904
Erith & Belvedere
1924 1925 Bradford City 11 2
1926 1927 Gillingham 26 4
Cannes

From To Apps Goal

Hilligan, Samuel Henry GK
b Maryhill 13/10/1902
Glasgow Perthshire
St Mirren
Bo'ness
1926 Reading 1
Arthurlie
St Bernard's

Hillman, Alfred George (George) CH
b Newport q3 1892
Abertillery
1920 Newport County 16
Chepstow Standard Institute

Hillman, John (Jack) GK
b Tavistock 30/10/1870 d 1955
Caps: FLge 1/England 1
1891 1894 Burnley 100
1894 1895 Everton 35
Dundee
1897 1901 Burnley 75
1901 1905 Manchester City 116
Millwall Athletic

Hills, Jack L OL
b London
1905 Clapton Orient 2

Hills, Joseph John (Joe) GK
b Plumstead 14/10/1897 d 1969
Great Eastern Railway Works XI
Bexleyheath
Northfleet
1924 1925 Cardiff City 14
1926 Swansea Town 8
1927 Fulham 0

Hills, Walter John LH/IR
b Ferozopore, India 18/7/1898 d 1985
Meadow Thursday
1924 1926 Notts County 3
Grantham
Radford Thursday
Notts Corinthians

Hills, William Ralph (Ralph) OR
b Ely 16/12/1904 d 1970
St Peter's Albion
Bishop Auckland
1924 Middlesbrough 0
1926 Huddersfield Town 0
1927 1928 Watford 30 3
1929 1931 Southport 108 26
1932 Barrow 28 7
1933 1934 Crewe Alexandra 17 4

Hilsdon, George Richard CF
b Bromley-by-Bow 10/8/1885 d 1941
Caps: FLge 2/England 8
South West Ham
Castle Swifts
Clapton Orient
Luton Town
West Ham United
1906 1911 Chelsea 150 98
West Ham United
Heart of Midlothian (loan)
Chatham

Hilton, Frank OL
b Worsborough Dale q2 1882
Caps: FLge 1
Doncaster St James
1905 1909 Bristol City 116 21

Hilton, Frederick (Fred) CH/LH/RH
b Sheffield 8/7/1903
Lopham Street
1922 1924 Grimsby Town 71
1924 1928 Notts County 109 3
Scunthorpe & Lindsey United
Gainsborough Trinity
Lincoln Wednesday

Hilton, Harold IR/IL
b Birkenhead 13/11/1889 d 1971
Tranmere Rovers
1909 1919 Bolton Wanderers 62 23
1921 1923 Tranmere Rovers 52 4

Hilton, Percival (Percy) LH
b Eagley 24/10/1897 d 1991
1919 Everton 0
1920 Exeter City 1
Torquay United

Hilton, William Ashton (Billy) RB
b Oldham 14/4/1911 d 1989
Coldhurst Sunday School
Bedford Lads
New Mills
1934 1938 Oldham Athletic 129 4
1939 (Oldham Athletic) (3)

From To Apps Goal

Hinchcliffe, Thomas (Tom) IR/IL
b Denaby 6/12/1913 d 1978
Denaby United
1936 1937 Grimsby Town 27 5
1937 1938 Huddersfield Town 13 4
1938 Derby County 6 1
1946 Nottingham Forest 1
Gainsborough Trinity
Denaby United

Hinchley, Albert Aubrey GK
b Warwick 8/1869 d 1922
Warwickshire County
1891 Aston Villa 11
Cape Hill

Hinchliffe, Alfred G (Alf) LH
b Wadsley Bridge 26/8/1896
Craven Sports
1919 Sheffield Wednesday 1

Hinchliffe, Arthur G RH/CH
b Bolton 26/8/1897
1921 1922 Rochdale 26

Hind, Arthur LH
b Sheffield q2 1879 d 1929
Owlerton Swifts
1898 Barnsley 1

Hind, F RB
Derby Junction
1889 Derby County 1
Derby Junction

Hind, William (Billy) RH/RB
b Percy Main q2 1885 d 1963
Willington Athletic
1907 Fulham 3
1908 1919 Clapton Orient 198 7
Ton Pentre

Hind, William (Billy) OR
b Percy Main q2 1885
1924 South Shields 0
1925 Southend United 6 2

Hindle, Fred IR
1927 Crewe Alexandra 1

Hindle, Harry CH/LH
b Wilpshire 1883
St James' Road (Blackburn)
Oswaldtwistle Rovers
1901 1902 Blackburn Rovers 2
Nelson
West Ham United
Hurst

Hindley, Frank Charles CF
b Worksop 2/11/1915 d 2003
Netherton United
1938 Nottingham Forest 6 3
1939 1946 Brighton & Hove Albion 10 4
1939 (Brighton & Hove Albion) (2) (1)
Peterborough United (loan)

Hindley, Robert Andrew (Bob) GK
b Leigh 17/3/1907 d 1997
Mossley
Atherton
1927 Southampton 0
Mossley
1930 Swansea Town 3
1931 Barrow 37
Ramsgate Press Wanderers
Folkestone

Hindmarsh, James Lyons (Jimmy) LH
b Whitburn, County Durham q2 1885 d 1959
Whitburn Colliery
1905 Sunderland 1
Fulham
Watford
Plymouth Argyle
1910 1912 Stockport County 69 2
1913 1914 Manchester City 28 1
Newport County

Hindmarsh, John Smith RH/LH
b Ashington 29/1/1914 d 1990
Ashington Welfare
Ashington
1934 Sheffield Wednesday 0
1935 1936 Burnley 39 1
1937 1938 Notts County 57
Ashington

Hindmarsh, Joseph M RB
1920 South Shields 0
1921 1922 Aberdare Athletic 32

Hindson, Edward OR
b Easington q4 1882
Southwick (Co Durham)
1903 Lincoln City 11

From	To	Club	Apps	Goal
Hindson, James Bell			RB/LB	
b Sunderland 15/7/1908			d 1950	
		Hylton Colliery		
1928		Sunderland	0	
		Spennymoor United		
1930		Middlesbrough	0	
1931	1937	Fulham	104	
Hine, Ernest William (Ernie)			IR/IL	
b Smithy Cross 9/4/1901			d 1974	
Caps: FLge 5/England 6				
		New Mills		
		Staincross Station		
1921	1925	Barnsley	161	82
1925	1931	Leicester City	247	148
1932		Huddersfield Town	23	4
1932	1934	Manchester United	51	12
1934	1937	Barnsley	127	42
Hine, John Robert Adams			RH	
b Burradon q3 1895				
1921		Ashington	1	
Hingerty, James (Jim)			CF	
b Walsall q3 1875				
Caps: IrLge 1				
		North Staffordshire Regiment		
1896	1897	Stoke	20	6
		Rushden		
Hinks, Charles William (Charlie)			IL/OL	
b Manchester q2 1880				
		Darwen		
1901		Stockport County	1	
1902		Manchester City	0	
1903		Stoke	1	
		Altrincham		
		Southport Central		
		Hyde		
		Haslingden		
		Sale Holmfield		
		Haslingden		
		Eccles Borough		
Hinsley, George			RH/IR/CH	
b Sheffield 19/7/1914			d 1989	
		Denaby United (trial)		
1934		Fulham (trial)	0	
1934		Sheffield Wednesday (trial)	0	
1935	1938	Barnsley	9	
1938	1948	Bradford City	114	17
1939		(Bradford City)	(2)	(1)
1949		Halifax Town	32	
		Nelson		
Hinson, Ronald Henry			IR/OR	
b Chelveston 9/10/1915				
		Rushden		
1933		Northampton Town	1	
		Irchester		
1935		Northampton Town	7	4
		Rushden		
Hinton, Ivor Francis			LB/RB	
b Barry q1 1897			d 1936	
		Barry		
1926	1928	Newport County	84	
		Barry		
Hinton, John (Jack)			IL	
b Southampton q1 1891				
		Sholing Athletic		
		Southampton		
		Thorneycrofts		
		Barnstaple Town		
1920		Exeter City	4	1
		Thorneycrofts		
Hinton, Robert George (Tim)			IR	
b High Wycombe q4 1899				
		Wycombe Wanderers		
1926		Millwall	5	3
Hinton, William Frederick Weston (Bill)			GK	
b Swindon 25/12/1895			d 1976	
		Swindon Town		
1920	1923	Bolton Wanderers	34	
1924	1925	Tottenham Hotspur	57	
1928		Swindon Town	0	
Hinton, William George (Bill)			IR/OR	
b Sholing 22/6/1913			d 1954	
		Sholing		
		Salisbury City		
		Frost's Athletic		
1934		Norwich City	3	
1936		Aldershot	9	2
		Bitterne Nomads		

From	To	Club	Apps	Goal
Hipkin, Augustus Bernard			GK	
b Branchester 8/8/1900			d 1957	
		Bostall Heath		
1922		Charlton Athletic	0	
1923		Brentford	0	
1924		Clapton Orient	0	
		Leyton		
1926		Charlton Athletic	1	
		Margate		
		Chatham		
Hird, Alexander (Alex)			RH/LH/CH	
b Montrose 2/9/1900			d 1988	
		Montrose		
		Dundee		
1922	1926	South Shields	69	2
1927	1930	Charlton Athletic	130	1
Hird, Henry (Harry)			IR	
b Bolton 30/7/1896			d 1974	
		Horwich RMI		
1919	1921	Bury	63	19
1922		Blackpool	4	
		Horwich RMI		
1924	1925	New Brighton	13	3
		Horwich RMI		
		Rossendale United		
		Burscough Rangers		
		Horwich RMI		
Hird, Thomas (Tommy)			OR	
b Crook 31/12/1912			d 1989	
		Roddymoor Juniors		
		Stanley United		
1930		Bolton Wanderers (trial)	0	
		West Stanley		
		Spennymoor United		
1933	1934	Hartlepools United	84	22
1935		Portsmouth	1	1
		Selsey		
		St Johnstone		
Hirons, John William			OL/LH	
b Sheffield q3 1878			d 1938	
		Erdington		
		Pleck Ramblers		
		Walsall		
1902	1903	Small Heath	5	
		Walsall		
Hirst, George			OR	
b Barnsley				
1901		Barnsley	1	
Hirst, Henry (Harry)			RH/LB	
b Horbury 24/10/1899				
1921	1922	Rotherham County	3	1
1924		Preston North End	2	
1925		Queen's Park Rangers	26	
1926		Charlton Athletic	4	
		Thames		
Hisbent, Joseph Samuel (Joe)			RB	
b Plymouth 5/1882			d 1949	
		Green Waves		
1905		Aston Villa	2	
		Portsmouth		
		Brentford		
		Darlington		
1911	1914	Middlesbrough	44	
Hislop, Percy David			IL	
b Glasgow 9/1870			d 1929	
		Glasgow Royal		
1891		Aston Villa	8	3
		Forfar Athletic		
		Perth		
Hitch, Alfred (Alf)			RH	
b Walsall 3/1877			d 1962	
		Walsall Unity		
1897		Walsall	2	
		Wellington Town		
		Thames Ironworks		
		Grays United		
		Queen's Park Rangers		
1901		Nottingham Forest	13	2
		Queen's Park Rangers		
		Watford		
Hitchcock, Ernest			IR	
1907		Aston Villa	0	
1908		Manchester City	1	
Hitchins, Arthur Williams			CH	
b Devonport 1/12/1913			d 1975	
		Walthamstow Avenue		
		Lea Bridge Gasworks		
1934		Tottenham Hotspur	0	
		Northfleet		
1937	1938	Tottenham Hotspur	35	1
1939		(Tottenham Hotspur)	(2)	

From	To	Club	Apps	Goal
Hoad, Sidney James (Sid)			OR	
b Eltham 27/12/1890			d 1973	
Caps: England Amat				
		St Annes		
1909	1910	Blackpool	26	3
1911	1914	Manchester City	64	1
1921		Rochdale	17	2
1921	1926	Nelson	152	13
		Hurst		
Hoadley, Dermot			OL	
b Leeds 7/12/1910			d 1994	
		Birtley		
1933		Rochdale	2	
Hoar, Sidney Walter (Sid)			OR/OL	
b Leagrave 28/11/1895			d 1969	
		Luton Clarence		
1920	1924	Luton Town	160	26
1924	1928	Arsenal	100	16
		Bedford Town		
1929		Clapton Orient	26	3
Hoare, Gordon Rahere			IL/CF/IR	
b Blackheath 18/4/1884			d 1973	
Caps: England Amat				
		Westcombe Park		
		West Norwood		
		Woolwich Polytechnic		
		Bromley		
1907	1909	Woolwich Arsenal	13	5
1909	1910	Glossop	11	2
		Bromley		
1910	1911	Woolwich Arsenal	17	7
1911	1913	Glossop	40	14
		West Norwood		
		Bromley		
		Queen's Park		
1914		Arsenal	0	
		Northfleet		
		West Norwood		
1919		Fulham	2	
Hoare, Joseph Henry (Joe)			LB	
b Southampton 11/1881			d 1947	
		Southampton Oxford		
		Southampton		
1903		Liverpool	7	
		Southampton		
		Bitterne Guild		
		Salisbury City		
		Bitterne Guild		
		Woolston		
Hoare, William			OL	
1899		New Brighton Tower	5	3
Hobbins, Sydney George (Syd)			GK	
b Plumstead 6/5/1916			d 1984	
		Bromley		
1937	1946	Charlton Athletic	2	
1948		Millwall	15	
1949		Leyton Orient	11	
Hobbis, Harold Henry Frederick			OL	
b Dartford 9/3/1913			d 1991	
Caps: England 2				
		Bromley		
1931	1947	Charlton Athletic	248	76
1939		(Charlton Athletic)	(3)	
		Tonbridge		
Hobbs, Ernest Charles			CH/CF	
b Wellingborough 30/4/1910			d 1984	
		Wellingborough Town		
1934	1935	Northampton Town	9	
1936		Exeter City	11	
		Tunbridge Wells Rangers		
1938		Rochdale	6	
Hobbs, Ralph Victor			IL	
b Toddington q4 1898				
		Toddington		
1923		Northampton Town	1	
Hobbs, William T			IL	
b Lurgan 1904				
		Lurgan		
1926		Lincoln City	1	
		Belfast Celtic		
Hobby, Frank Edward			IR	
b St Pancras q2 1902				
1921		Millwall Athletic	1	
Hobson, Alfred (Alf)			GK	
b Leamside 9/9/1913			d 2004	
		Ferryhill Athletic		
		Shildon		
1936	1937	Liverpool	26	
1938		Chester	17	
1939		(Chester)	(3)	
1945		Liverpool	0	
		South Liverpool		

From	To	Club	Apps	Goal
Hobson, Alfred Frank (Fred)			CF/IR	
b Tipton 1878				
		Wednesbury Town		
1902	1903	West Bromwich Albion	13	4
		Brentford		
		Crewe Alexandra		
1906		Gainsborough Trinity	0	
		Darlington		
Hobson, Ernest			CF	
1932		Bolton Wanderers	0	
1932		Accrington Stanley	1	1
Hobson, Herbert Bertie (Bert)			RB	
b Tow Law q1 1890			d 1963	
		Tow Law Town		
		Stanley United		
		Crook Town		
1912	1921	Sunderland	160	
1922		Rochdale	0	
		West Stanley		
		Jarrow		
1924	1925	Darlington	5	
		Jarrow		
		Spennymoor United		
Hobson, James			OR	
b Ecclesfield 1886				
		Ecclesfield Church		
		Rotherham County		
		Ecclesfield Town		
		Worksop Town		
1907	1908	Sheffield United	15	2
1909		Leicester Fosse	0	
		New Brompton		
		Grimsby Town		
1911		Bolton Wanderers	0	
Hobson, John William			CH	
b High Green, Sheffield q3 1888			d 1948	
1921		Wigan Borough	3	
Hobson, Joseph			RB	
1893		Middlesbrough Ironopolis	3	
Hobson, Mark			GK	
b Gornal q3 1867				
1895		Rotherham Town	2	
Hobson, Robert George E (George)			RH	
b Leeds				
		Bishop Auckland		
1925		Huddersfield Town	2	
1927		Bradford City	24	2
		Dulwich Hamlet		
Hobson, Walter			RB/RH	
		Owlerton		
		Sheffield United		
		Owlerton		
1893	1894	Rotherham Town	20	1
Hodder, William (Bill)			OR	
b Stroud 10/1865			d 1897	
		Notts Rangers		
1888		Notts County	20	3
		Nottingham Forest		
		Kidderminster Olympic		
		The Wednesday		
		Lincoln City		
		Mansfield Town		
Hoddinott, Francis Thomas (Frank)			CF/IR/IL	
b Brecon 26/11/1894			d 1980	
Caps: Wales 2				
		Brecon Sports Club		
		Aberdare Athletic		
1920		Watford	39	22
1921	1922	Chelsea	31	4
1923	1925	Crystal Palace	79	20
		Rhyl		
1927		New Brighton	23	6
		Newark Town		
		Grantham		
		Ilkeston United		
Hodge, James (Jimmy)			LB/RB/CH	
b Stenhousemuir 5/7/1891			d 1970	
		Stenhousemuir		
1910	1919	Manchester United	79	2
1920		Millwall Athletic	17	1
1921	1922	Norwich City	51	1
1923		Southend United	18	
		Buxton		
		Buxton Medical Institution		
Hodge, John			RB/CH	
b Stenhousemuir				
		Stenhousemuir		
1913	1914	Manchester United	30	

From To Apps Goal

Hodge, John (Jack) OR
b Plymouth
1933 Plymouth Argyle 0
1934 1935 Bristol City 62 8
1935 1936 Luton Town 20 1
Colchester United
Hereford United
1945 Plymouth Argyle 0

Hodge, William RB
1892 Accrington 9

Hodge, William GK
b Kilwinning
1912 1913 Everton 10

Hodge, William (Billy) RB/LB/RH
b Twechar 31/8/1904
Baillieston
Rangers
1927 1933 Brentford 119 1

Hodges, Frank Charles OR/IR/CF
b Nechells Green 20/1/1891 d 1985
Alum Rock All Souls
Birmingham City Gas
1913 1914 Birmingham 27 4
St Mirren (loan)
1919 1920 Manchester United 20 4
1921 Wigan Borough 33 5
1922 1923 Crewe Alexandra 22 1
Stalybridge Celtic
Manchester North End
Sandbach Ramblers
Middlewich
Winsford United

Hodges, Harry James CF
b Edmonton q4 1897 d 1966
Sterling Athletic
1923 West Ham United 2 1
1924 Lincoln City 7

Hodgetts, Alfred IL
1925 Rotherham United 2

Hodgetts, Dennis (Denny) IL/OL
b Birmingham 28/11/1863 d 1945
Caps: FLge 1/England 6
Mitchell St George's
Great Lever
Mitchell St George's
1888 1895 Aston Villa 181 62
1896 Small Heath 22 9

Hodgetts, Joseph Harold OL
b Forest Town 2/6/1916 d 2008
Forest Town St Albans
Mansfield Colliery
1937 Brighton & Hove Albion 0
1938 Mansfield Town 1
Ollerton Colliery
Bilsthorpe
Huthwaite CWS

Hodgkin, William CH
b Castle Donington 1874
Castle Donington
1897 1899 Loughborough 89 3

Hodgkins, Thomas Reginald (Reg) CH
b Nuneaton q2 1903 d 1927
Hinckley United
1925 1926 Stoke City 5

Hodgkinson, Albert Victor (Bert) CF/OL
b Pembroke Dock 4/8/1884 d 1939
Caps: Wales 1
Old Normanton
1901 Derby County 0
Hinckley Town
1903 Grimsby Town 16 4
Plymouth Argyle
1905 Leicester Fosse 33 5
1906 Bury 17 3
Southampton
Croydon Common
Southend United
Ilkeston United

Hodgkinson, Charles Frith OR
1898 Burslem Port Vale 6

Hodgkinson, Herbert (Bert) LB
b Penistone 26/12/1903 d 1974
Penistone Juniors
1923 1929 Barnsley 200
1930 1931 Tottenham Hotspur 56
Colwyn Bay United
1933 1934 Crewe Alexandra 46 2

From To Apps Goal

Hodgkinson, John Chapman IL/OR
b Stockport q4 1883 d 1915
1905 1908 Stockport County 19 3
Haslingden
Nelson
Rochdale
1911 Grimsby Town 12 3

Hodgkinson, Joseph (Joe) IR
b Bolton 7/1882
Rossendale United
1905 Bury 7
Crystal Palace

Hodgkinson, Joseph (Joe) LB
b Wigan 15/3/1905 d 1975
New Springs Conservative Club
1924 Wigan Borough 0
New Springs Conservative Club
1926 Wigan Borough 1

Hodgkinson, Robert (Bob) CF
b Burton-on-Trent 1902
Loughborough
Burton All Saints
1924 Wrexham 6 2
Oswestry Town
1926 Wrexham 9 2
Whitchurch (trial)
Llandudno (trial)
Middlewich

Hodgkinson, Vincent Arthur IR
b Wollaton 1/11/1906 d 1990
Magdalene Amateurs
1925 Nottingham Forest 9 1
1926 Blackpool 0
Grantham
Loughborough Corinthians
1933 Lincoln City 1
Lysaght's Sports

Hodgkinson, William H CF
Hinckley Town
1901 Derby County 0
Hinckley Town
1903 Derby County 16 9
Plymouth Argyle

Hodgkiss, Jack GK
b Bolton
1914 Bolton Wanderers 0
1919 Stockport County 22
Wrexham

Hodgkiss, Robert (Bob) RB
b Little Hulton 22/3/1918 d 2003
Walkden Methodists
1938 Southport 10
1939 (Southport) (3)
1946 Everton 0
1947 1948 Southport 20

Hodgkiss, Samuel N (Sam) IR
b Little Hulton q1 1895
Walkden Amateurs
1919 Bury 1
Walkden Amateurs
Hurst

Hodgkiss, Thomas (Tom) RB
b Sheffield q3 1903
Wincobank CFC
1927 Sheffield Wednesday 2
1930 1931 Reading 48 1

Hodgkiss, William LH
b Bolton 1878
1900 Bolton Wanderers 1

Hodgson, Edward (Teddy) IL
b Chorley q4 1885 d 1919
Caps: FLge 1
Chorley
1911 1914 Burnley 120 53

Hodgson, Frederick (Fred) LB
b Lytham 19/10/1903
1920 Blackburn Rovers 0
Lytham
1923 1924 Rotherham County 43 2

Hodgson, George OL
1923 Halifax Town 3 1

Hodgson, George F GK
Brotton
Saltburn Swifts
1900 Middlesbrough 4

From To Apps Goal

Hodgson, Gordon IR/CF
b Johannesburg, South Africa 16/4/1904 d 1951
Caps: South Africa Amat/FLge 1/England 3
Benoni
Rustenberg
Pretoria
Transvaal
1925 1935 Liverpool 359 233
1935 1936 Aston Villa 28 11
1936 1938 Leeds United 81 51
1939 (Leeds United) (1)

Hodgson, Harold LB/RB
b Bradford 24/10/1903
1922 1925 Bradford Park Avenue 32

Hodgson, James GK
1903 Blackpool 2

Hodgson, John Venner (Jack) LB/CH
b Seaham Harbour 30/9/1913 d 1970
Dawdon Colliery Welfare
Seaham Colliery
1931 Hartlepools United (trial) 0
1932 1947 Grimsby Town 212 2
1939 (Grimsby Town) (3)
1947 1951 Doncaster Rovers 95 2

Hodgson, John William R LB
b Sunderland q1 1900
Holden Welfare
1925 Sunderland 0
1926 Brentford 4
1927 Hartlepools United 0
Canadian National Railways

Hodgson, Joseph (Joe) LH
b South Moor
Twizell United
Easington Colliery
1933 1938 Darlington 160 2
1939 (Darlington) (3)

Hodgson, Joseph C OL
b 1894
Rawmarsh Town
1913 Grimsby Town 1

Hodgson, Thomas RH/CH
1899 1900 Preston North End 4

Hodgson, Thomas (Tommy) LB/RB
b Hetton-le-Hole 19/1/1903 d 1989
Hetton Colliery
1921 1929 West Ham United 87
1930 1932 Luton Town 67
Luton Postal

Hodgson, Thomas CF
Alnwick Town
1924 Ashington 2 2

Hodgson, William (Bill) CF
b West Hartlepool
West Hartlepool Perseverance
1928 Hartlepools United 4 1
West Hartlepool Perseverance
St Oswald's (Hartlepool)

Hodgson, William H IL
1908 1909 Preston North End 3

Hodkin, Ernest (Ernie) RH
b Alfreton q3 1889
Clay Cross Works
Mansfield Mechanics
1910 Sunderland 2
Stoke
Billingham
Shirebrook
Mansfield Mechanics

Hodkinson, Joseph (Joe) OL
b Lancaster q2 1889 d 1954
Caps: FLge 2/England 3
Lancaster Town
1909 1912 Glossop 84 6
1912 1922 Blackburn Rovers 228 19
Lancaster Town

Hodnett, Joseph Edward (Joe) CH/RH
b Bilston 18/7/1896 d 1943
Willenhall
1919 1922 Wolverhampton Wanderers 75 5
Pontypridd
1924 Chesterfield 12 1
1925 Merthyr Town 22
1926 Brentford 9
1927 Gillingham 16 1
Stafford Rangers
Stourbridge
Halesowen
Dudley Town
Brierley Hill Alliance

From To Apps Goal

Hodson, AS OL
1893 Walsall Town Swifts 3

Hodson, F OR
1897 Walsall 1

Hodson, James (Jimmy) RB
b Horwich 5/9/1880 d 1938
St Helens Recreation
1903 Bury 2
1907 1914 Oldham Athletic 252 1
Belfast Celtic
1920 Brentford 33
Guildford United

Hodson, James LB
b Wigan
Garswood Hall
1919 1921 Bolton Wanderers 22

Hodson, Robert J CF
1905 Glossop 3

Hodson, TJ IL
1892 Walsall Town Swifts 2

Hoffman (Holt), Ernest Henry (Ernie) GK
b South Shields 16/7/1892 d 1959
Caps: England Amat
Hebburn Wesleyans
Hebburn Old Boys
Hebburn Argyle
1919 1920 South Shields 23
1922 Derby County 1
1923 Ashington 35
1924 Durham City 0
1924 Darlington 0
Wood Skinners
1929 York City 0

Hofton, Leslie Brown RB
b Sheffield q2 1888 d 1971
Caps: FLge 2
Kiveton Park
Worksop Town
Denaby United
1907 1909 Glossop 53 6
1910 1920 Manchester United 17
Denaby Main

Hogan, Cornelius CF/CH
b Malta 1878 d 1909
1897 Aston Villa 0
Millwall Athletic
1899 1900 New Brighton Tower 18 1
Watford
1901 1902 Burnley 43 17
Fulham
Swindon Town
St Helens Recreation
Nelson
Rossendale United

Hogan, James (Jimmy) IR/IL
b Nelson 16/10/1882 d 1974
Burnley Belvedere
Nelson
Rochdale Town
1903 1904 Burnley 50 12
Nelson
1907 Fulham 4
Swindon Town
1908 1912 Bolton Wanderers 54 18

Hogan, James (Jimmy) IL
b Dublin 2/7/1911
Bray Unknowns
1933 Bradford Park Avenue 4 1
Bray Unknowns
Fearons

Hogan, William OL
b Aldershot q1 1871
Church Town (Southport)
Fleetwood Rangers
1895 Leicester Fosse 0
1896 Grimsby Town 1
Nelson

Hogg, Anthony (Tony) GK
b Walker 9/1/1890 d 1957
Walker Church Lads
1909 1914 Leeds City 96
Houghton Rovers
Palmer's (Jarrow)
1920 Newcastle United 0

Hogg, Charles IL
b Leicester q1 1895 d 1964
Knighton Sunday School
St Andrew's (Leicester)
1914 Leicester Fosse 7 2
Whitwick Imperial
J Pick & Sons

From	To	Club	Apps	Goal
Hogg, Charles George (George)			RB	
b Kiveton Park 1900				
		Anston		
1925		Lincoln City	5	
1926		Southend United	2	
		Peterborough & Fletton United		
		Mansfield Town		
Hogg, Frederick (Freddie)			IL	
b Bishop Auckland 24/4/1918			d 2001	
		West Auckland		
1937		Luton Town	4	
1945	1947	Mansfield Town	45	8
1947	1949	Halifax Town	49	2
		Wigan Athletic		
Hogg, James Anthony			OR	
b Sunderland q2 1891				
		South Shields		
1920		Portsmouth	16	2
		Guildford United		
Hogg, James William			CF	
b Sunderland 9/8/1900			d 1974	
		Whitburn		
1923	1924	Sunderland	9	8
1925		Sheffield United	0	
Hogg, John			RB	
b West Calder 25/8/1879				
		West Calder Swifts		
		Heart of Midlothian		
1902	1905	Middlesbrough	90	
		Luton Town		
Hogg, John (Jack)			RH	
b Sunderland 22/5/1881			d 1944	
1900		Sunderland	0	
		Morpeth Harriers		
1903		Sheffield United	3	
		Southampton		
		West Stanley		
		Hartlepools United		
Hogg, Robert			IR/CF	
b Whitburn, County Durham q2 1877			d 1963	
Caps: FLge 1				
		Whitburn		
		Selbourne Rovers		
1899	1902	Sunderland	67	18
1902		Grimsby Town	3	1
1904		Blackpool	26	5
		Luton Town		
Hogg, Thomas (Tommy)			OR/IR	
b Brampton 21/3/1908			d 1965	
		Durham City		
1929	1930	Bradford Park Avenue	3	
1931		Rochdale	10	1
Hogg, William (Billy)			OR/IR/CF	
b Newcastle 29/5/1879			d 1937	
Caps: FLge 3/England 3				
		Rosehill		
		Willington Athletic		
1899	1908	Sunderland	281	82
		Rangers		
		Dundee		
		Raith Rovers		
		Montrose		
		Dundee		
		Dundee Hibernian		
		Brooklyn Wanderers		
		Providence Clamdiggers		
		Philadelphia Field Club		
		Newark Skeeters		
		New York Giants		
		Brooklyn Wanderers		
Hogg, William (Billy)			OL	
		Bishop Auckland		
1935		Gateshead	1	
		Willington		
1936		Bradford City	0	
Hoggan, Matthew (Matt)			CH	
b Grangemouth 14/7/1905			d 1981	
		Grange Rovers		
		Raith Rovers		
		East Stirlingshire		
1935		New Brighton	38	
Holbeach, Frederick David G (Fred)			OR	
b Mansfield 17/3/1910			d 1935	
		Welbeck Colliery		
		Grantham		
1933		Luton Town	2	
		Yeovil & Petters United		

From	To	Club	Apps	Goal
Holbem, Walter			LB/CH	
b Sheffield q4 1884			d 1930	
		Heeley Friends		
1906	1910	Sheffield Wednesday	86	
1911	1912	Everton	18	
		St Mirren		
1913	1914	Preston North End	37	
		Southport Central		
Holborn, Henry F (Harry)			LB	
b Bishop Auckland q2 1915				
		Stanley United		
1934		Southend United	1	
Holcroft, Sidney (Sid)			IL	
b Aston 8/1901			d 1934	
		Britannia		
		Small Heath United		
		Hednesford Town		
		Stourbridge		
1924	1926	Bristol Rovers	33	9
		Willenhall		
		Birmingham Corporation Trams		
Holdcroft, George Henry (Harry)			GK	
b Burslem 23/1/1909			d 1983	
Caps: FLge 1/England 2				
		Biddulph		
		Norton Druids		
		Whitfield Colliery		
1926	1927	Port Vale	10	
1928	1930	Darlington	83	
1931		Everton	0	
1932	1938	Preston North End	263	
1939		(Preston North End)	(3)	
1945		Barnsley	0	
		Morecambe		
		Chorley		
		Leyland Motors		
Holdcroft, Hugh Edwin (Teddy)			IL/CH/CF	
b Stoke-on-Trent q2 1883			d 1952	
1902		Burslem Port Vale	16	1
1902	1905	Stoke	43	11
Holdcroft, James Henry			RH	
b Burslem				
1894	1895	Burslem Port Vale	36	
Holden, Arthur			OL	
b Billingshurst 23/9/1882				
		Portsmouth		
		Southend United		
		Plymouth Argyle		
1908	1909	Chelsea	20	1
		Plymouth Argyle		
		Aberdeen		
Holden, J			IL/IR	
1888	1890	Accrington	7	4
Holden, J			IL	
1898		Darwen	4	1
Holden, Ralph			CH/LH	
b Blundellsands 1890				
		St Helens Recreation		
1912	1913	Liverpool	2	
		Tranmere Rovers		
Holden, Richard H (Dick)			LB/RB	
b Middleton 12/6/1885			d 1971	
		Parkfield Central		
		Tonge		
1904	1912	Manchester United	106	
Holden, Thomas (Tom)			GK	
b Leyland				
		Leyland		
		Lancaster Town		
		Fleetwood		
1925	1926	Accrington Stanley	34	
		Hurst		
Holden, Thomas H			OR	
1906		Burnley	1	
Holden, William			GK	
b Darwen 1860				
		Darwen		
1888		Blackburn Rovers (loan)	1	
Holding, William			OR	
		Castle Donington		
1908	1909	Leicester Fosse	3	
Holdstock, Herbert Frederick			CH/LH	
b St Albans 29/10/1879			d 1965	
		Luton Star		
1899		Luton Town	13	1
1904		Nottingham Forest	1	

From	To	Club	Apps	Goal
Holdsworth, Edward			RH	
b Halifax q1 1888			d 1967	
		Southport Central		
1907	1919	Preston North End	222	3
1920		Swansea Town	7	
Holdsworth, Harold			CF	
b Sedgefield 28/9/1906			d 1978	
		West Stanley		
1928		Notts County	0	
1929		Carlisle United	1	
Hole, William James (Billy)			OR	
b Swansea 1/11/1897			d 1983	
Caps: WLge 2/Wales 9				
		Hillside (Swansea)		
1920	1930	Swansea Town	341	36
		Llanelly		
Holford, Thomas (Tom)			CH/LH/CF	
b Hanley 28/1/1878			d 1964	
Caps: England 1				
		Cobridge		
1898	1907	Stoke	248	30
1907	1913	Manchester City	172	34
		Stoke		
1919	1923	Port Vale	56	1
Holland, George Alfred			LH	
b Wolverhampton 11/12/1917			d 1997	
1936		Bradford Park Avenue	0	
1937		Gillingham	10	
		Shrewsbury Town		
Holland, John (Jack)			IL/IR	
b Preston q2 1897			d 1944	
Caps: WLge 1				
1920	1921	Preston North End	6	
1923	1924	Swansea Town	21	2
1925		Wrexham	9	2
1925		Crewe Alexandra	23	3
1926		Newport County	10	2
1927	1928	Clapton Orient	19	4
1929		Carlisle United	33	13
1930		Barrow	7	
Holland, John Henry (Jack)			GK	
b Bulwell q3 1861			d 1898	
1888		Notts County	9	
		Nottingham Forest		
Holland, Peter Byrom			IR/OR/IL	
b Hindley 5/10/1898			d 1963	
Caps: England Sch				
		New Herrington Swifts		
		Houghton Rovers		
		Hull City		
1919	1927	Blackburn Rovers	116	24
1928	1930	Watford	21	3
1930		West Ham United	0	
		Tunbridge Wells Rangers		
Holland, Thomas (Tom)			GK	
b Sheffield 16/7/1902			d 1987	
		Rotherham Town		
1925		Doncaster Rovers	2	
		Weymouth		
1927	1929	Exeter City	59	
1930	1931	Watford	62	
1932	1935	Gillingham	119	
		Aylesford Paper Mills		
		Weymouth		
Holland, Walter (Wally)			IL	
b Tonge 1879				
		Tonge		
1899		Bury	1	
Holleworth, Walter Harry			GK	
b Nottingham q1 1881			d 1946	
		Grassmoor Red Rose		
1900		Chesterfield Town	2	
		Grassmoor Red Rose		
		Hasland Wild Rose		
1904		Chesterfield Town	0	
		Old Whittington Mutuals		
		Grassmoor Red Rose		
		Clay Cross Works		
Holley, George			IL/IR	
b Seaham Harbour 25/11/1885			d 1942	
Caps: FLge 5/England 10				
		Seaham Athletic		
		Seaham Villa		
		Seaham White Star		
1904	1914	Sunderland	280	151
		Brighton & Hove Albion		
Holley, Thomas (Tom)			CH/RH	
b Sunderland 15/11/1913			d 1992	
1931		Sunderland	0	
1933	1935	Barnsley	72	4
1936	1948	Leeds United	162	1
1939		(Leeds United)	(2)	

From	To	Club	Apps	Goal
Holliday, John William (Jack)			CF/IL	
b Cockfield, County Durham 19/12/1908			d 1987	
		Cockfield		
1930	1931	Middlesbrough	6	4
1932	1938	Brentford	213	116
1939		(Brentford)	(1)	(1)
Hollingsworth, Hubert			RB	
b Chapeltown 28/12/1911			d 1983	
1936		Newcastle United	0	
1937		Brighton & Hove Albion	0	
1938		Barrow	39	
1939		(Barrow)	(3)	
Hollingworth, James (Jim)			IL	
b Manchester 1914				
		Manchester North End		
1934		Halifax Town	6	
Hollingworth, John D			OL	
1905		Blackpool	10	
Hollingworth, Reginald (Reg)			CH/RB	
b Rainworth 17/10/1909			d 1969	
		Nuffield Colliery		
		Mansfield Town		
		Sutton Junction		
1928	1935	Wolverhampton Wanderers	167	7
Hollis, Ellis			RH	
b Darwen				
		Darwen		
		Nelson		
1912		Oldham Athletic	2	
Hollis, George			GK	
b Kenilworth 1869				
		Warwickshire County		
1892	1893	Small Heath	31	
		Bournbrook		
Hollis, Joshua Norris			OR	
b Bradford q2 1875			d 1944	
1896		Nottingham Forest	1	1
Holmes, Edward (Eddie)			LB	
b Manchester 15/11/1900			d 1975	
		Altrincham		
1927		Crystal Palace	17	
1928		Reading	0	
1929		Barrow	11	1
		Winsford United		
		Altrincham North Western		
Holmes, Ernest			CH	
		Bolton L & Y		
1920		Bury	3	
Holmes, Ezra			IL/IR	
b West Bromwich 1882				
		Wombwell		
1906	1907	Gainsborough Trinity	40	12
1907		Birmingham	2	
		Stamford Town		
Holmes, George Albert (Albert)			OL	
b Mansfield q3 1885				
		Hucknall Constitutional		
1905		Nottingham Forest	5	
		Mansfield Wesleyans		
1907	1908	Chesterfield Town	51	9
		Nelson		
		Mansfield Mechanics		
		Coventry City		
		Heart of Midlothian		
		Coventry City		
		Portsmouth		
Holmes, George William			RB	
b Goldenhill q3 1892				
		Goldenhill Wanderers		
		Leek Alexandra		
1920		Merthyr Town	18	
1921		Sheffield Wednesday	20	
1922		Wrexham	34	
Holmes, Henry James (Harry)			LH	
b Reading q4 1901			d 1975	
1920		Reading	4	1
Holmes, James (Jim)			CH/LH	
b Skelmersdale 27/12/1908			d 1971	
		Sutton Commercial		
		Sutton Parish		
1927		Liverpool	0	
1928		Wigan Borough	0	
		Prescot Cables		
1930		Chesterfield	26	1
1931	1935	Sheffield United	135	
1936		West Ham United	2	
1937	1938	Reading	70	5
1939		(Reading)	(3)	

From To Apps Goal

Holmes, John RH/LH/CH
b Preston 1874
1891 1893 Preston North End 20
1895 1897 Liverpool 42
1898 Burton Swifts 27
1899 1900 New Brighton Tower 58 3

Holmes, John Thomas (Tom) OR
b Chesterfield q2 1880
Sheffield Brunswick
Roundel
1901 Sheffield United 3
Fulham
Southern United
Fulham
Tunbridge Wells Rangers

Holmes, John V OL
1930 Thames 5 1

Holmes, Maxey Martin OL/CF/RH
b Pinchbeck 24/12/1908 d 1999
Spalding United
1931 1934 Grimsby Town 37 17
1935 1936 Hull City 29 10
1937 Mansfield Town 17 4
1938 Lincoln City 20 1
1939 (Lincoln City) (1)

Holmes, Norman IL
b Grange-over-Sands q3 1905
Willington
Broughton Athletic
1928 Barrow 1

Holmes, Norman Arnold RB
b Darley Hillside q3 1890
1909 Leeds City 0
1910 1911 Clapton Orient 4
1913 Huddersfield Town 3
York City

Holmes, Robert (Bob) RB/LB
b Preston 23/6/1867 d 1955
Caps: FLge 3/England 7
Preston Olympic
1888 1902 Preston North End 300 1

Holmes, Samuel IL
Crich
1889 1890 Derby County 21 8

Holmes, Samuel (Sammy) RH/OR/IR
b Walsall 1870
1892 1900 Walsall Town Swifts 214 28
Dudley

Holmes, Thomas (Tommy) LH
b Spennymoor 20/4/1902 d 1997
Caps: LoI 1
Coundon United
Willington
1926 Bury 4
Spennymoor United
1928 Grimsby Town 0
1929 1931 Southport 104 2
Shelbourne
1933 Southport 34 4
Spennymoor United

Holmes, Walter RB/LB
b Willington 9/5/1892 d 1978
Bede College
Willington
1914 1926 Middlesbrough 167 1
1928 Darlington 22

Holmes, William Harold (Harry) OR
b Ambergate 18/8/1908 d 1976
Milford Ivanhoe
Heanor Town
1931 1932 Coventry City 22 12
Heanor Town
1933 Notts County 2
Heanor Town
1934 Birmingham 1
Heanor Town

Holmes, William Marsden (Billy) LH/LB/RB
b Darley Hillside 1875 d 1922
Caps: FLge 1
Darley Dale
Chesterfield Town
1896 1904 Manchester City 156 4
1905 1907 Clapton Orient 46

Holroyd, Eric OL
b Rochdale 24/7/1905 d 1987
1927 Rochdale 1

From To Apps Goal

Holt, Arnold (Andy) OR
b Scunthorpe q4 1891
Kidderminster Harriers
Denaby United
1911 Sheffield United 0
Southport Central
Newport County
Cardiff City
Merthyr Town
Linfield
Belfast Celtic
Clyde
Distillery
Linfield
Chesterfield Municipal
1920 Gillingham 6
Mansfield Town
Sutton Town
Wath Athletic

Holt, Arthur George IL
b Southampton 8/4/1911 d 1994
Bitterne Park Congregationals
Totton
1932 1938 Southampton 206 46
1939 (Southampton) (1) (2)

Holt, David Edward IR
b Brixworth 13/9/1912 d 2005
1936 Northampton Town 1

Holt, J Edward OR
b Newton Heath 1880
Newton Heath Athletic
1899 Newton Heath (trial) 1 1

Holt, James William (Jim) GK
b Elton, Lancashire q2 1888
Summerseat
1910 Bury 21
Nelson
Haslingden

Holt, John (Johnny) CH
b Church 10/4/1865
Caps: FLge 2/England 10
Blackpool St John's
Bootle
1888 1897 Everton 225 3
Reading

Holt, John RB/LB
Hurst
1921 1922 Stalybridge Celtic 7

Holt, Sidney IR
Willenhall Pickwick
1907 Wolverhampton Wanderers 8

Holt, Stanley (Stan) CH
1927 Manchester City 0
Altrincham
Ashton National
Macclesfield
1931 Cardiff City 2
Berne

Holt, Thomas (Tommy) RH/LH
b West Bromwich 2/1901
Bush Rangers
1923 1926 Walsall 82
Dudley Town
Brierley Hill Alliance
Cradley St Peter's

Holyhead, Joseph CH/LH
b West Bromwich 7/1879
Wednesbury Old Athletic
1902 Wolverhampton Wanderers 6
1903 1904 Burslem Port Vale 60 2
Swindon Town
1905 1906 Burslem Port Vale 63 4
Wednesbury Old Athletic
Kidderminster Harriers

Holyoake, James Ernest LB
b Derby q4 1879
1901 Derby County 1
Ripley Town
Ripley Athletic

Homer, Sydney (Syd) OR
b Bloxwich 14/1/1903 d 1983
Bloxwich White Star
1925 1926 Wolverhampton Wanderers 29 2
1927 1929 Bristol Rovers 38 5
1929 1933 Bristol City 179 18
Worcester City

Homer, Thomas Percy (Tom) CF
b Winson Green q2 1886 d 1945
Soho Caledonians
Erdington
Stourbridge
Kidderminster Harriers
1909 1911 Manchester United 25 14

From To Apps Goal

Honeyman, John William OR
b Middlesbrough 29/12/1893 d 1972
Cargo Fleet & Cochrane Works
1919 Middlesbrough 1
Dundee
Maidstone United
1923 Grimsby Town 21 1
Chatham
Margate
New Bedford Whalers
J & P Coats (Rhode Island)
Maidstone United
Folkestone
Kreemy Works

Hood, Clarence OR
b Mansfield 28/4/1912 d 1977
Bilsthorpe Colliery
1934 Nottingham Forest 3

Hood, Richard Parker CH/RB
b Seaham q2 1881
Seaham Rovers
1904 1907 Lincoln City 130 1

Hood, William (Billy) IR
b Ashton-under-Lyne q1 1873
1892 1893 Newton Heath 33 6
Stalybridge Rovers

Hood, William John (Billy) RB
b Belfast 3/11/1914
Caps: Ireland Amat
Cliftonville
1937 Liverpool 3
Derry City

Hook, Albert Edward LH
b Sittingbourne
Maidstone United
1924 Gillingham 20
Sittingbourne

Hooker, Evan LH/CH
b Chadderton q2 1901 d 1962
1921 1922 Stalybridge Celtic 7
1924 1928 Stockport County 36
1929 Rochdale 25
Ashton National

Hookings, Frank Henry RH
b Dover 10/12/1906 d 1976
Army
1932 Millwall 4

Hooley, A OR
Stapleford
1891 Notts County 3 1
Stapleford

Hooley, Samuel OR
New Mills
1931 Stockport County 18 1

Hooper, Alexander (Alex) LB/RB
b Darlington 5/1/1900 d 1978
Shildon
1925 Charlton Athletic 7
St Johnstone
1928 Nelson 9
Bangor City
Barnoldswick Town
Bangor City
1931 Accrington Stanley 0
Barnoldswick Town

Hooper, Arthur Henry IL/CF
b Brierley Hill q1 1889
Kidderminster Harriers
1909 1913 Manchester United 7 1
Crystal Palace

Hooper, Charles (Carl) IR/IL
b Darlington 23/3/1903 d 1972
Darlington
Cockfield
Darlington Railway Athletic
Crook Town
1924 1925 Lincoln City 34 6
Shildon
1926 Notts County 0
York City
1927 Chesterfield 3
Willington
1928 Norwich City 3
Darlington Wire Works
1929 Sheffield Wednesday 0
Worksop Town
West Stanley

From To Apps Goal

Hooper, Daniel (Danny) CH
b Newton Aycliffe 15/9/1893 d 1973
Darlington Rise Carr
1919 Oldham Athletic 5
Shildon Athletic
Darlington Rise Carr
Darlington Wednesday
1927 Lincoln City (trial) 0

Hooper, Frederick William (Bill) IR/IL
b Darlington 14/11/1894 d 1982
Darlington Rise Carr
1919 Oldham Athletic 5 1
1921 1925 Darlington 141 60
1926 Rochdale 20 1
Consett

Hooper, Harold (Harry) LB/RB
b Aston 18/8/1900 d 1963
Brierley Hill Alliance
1921 1923 Southampton 19
1924 1925 Leicester City 33
1926 Queen's Park Rangers 16

Hooper, Harry Reed RB/LB
b Burnley 16/12/1910 d 1970
Nelson Tradesmen
1928 1929 Nelson 21
1930 1945 Sheffield United 269 10
1947 1949 Hartlepools United 66 4

Hooper, Mark OR/IL
b Darlington 14/7/1901 d 1974
Cockfield
1923 1926 Darlington 116 43
1926 1937 Sheffield Wednesday 384 125
1939 1945 Rotherham United (3) (1)

Hooper, Percy William George GK
b Lambeth 17/12/1914 d 1997
Cheddington Athletic (Edmonton)
Tufnell Park
Leyton
Islington Corinthians
Northfleet
1934 1938 Tottenham Hotspur 97
1939 (Tottenham Hotspur) (3)
1946 1947 Swansea Town 12
Chingford Town
King's Lynn

Hooper, William George (Bill) OR
b Lewisham 20/2/1884 d 1952
Catford Southend
Service Corps
1905 1906 Grimsby Town 33 5
1906 1911 Nottingham Forest 147 22
1912 Notts County 16 1
Barrow
Gillingham
Southport Central
Lancaster Town

Hoose, William RH
b Burton-on-Trent
1892 Burton Swifts 1 1

Hooton, Alfred Alexander (Alf) RH
b Hythe, Hampshire 19/11/1910 d 1970
Howards Athletic
1935 Bournemouth & Boscombe Ath 4
Poole Town

Hope, Henry (Harry) IR/IL
b Newcastle 1914
Crawcrook Albion
1933 Rochdale 2
Chopwell Institute
1934 Bristol Rovers 1
1934 Bristol City 0
Bath City
Weymouth

Hope, James Prentice RH
b East Wemyss 22/7/1905 d 1971
East Fife
1928 1929 South Shields 38 2
1930 Gateshead 0
1931 Chelsea 1

Hope, James Richard (Jimmy) OR
b Weston 22/7/1907 d 1967
Northwich Victoria
Witton Albion
Winsford United
1931 Oldham Athletic 4
Runcorn
Winsford United
Stalybridge Celtic
Clayton Aniline

From	To		Apps	Goal
Hope, James William			IR	
b Kelloe				
		Kelloe		
		Southmoors Violet		
		Birtley		
		West Stanley		
		Horden Colliery		
		Horden Athletic		
1908		Sunderland	1	
Hope, John (Jack)			IR	
b Bishop Auckland 10/6/1905			d 1982	
		Bishop Auckland		
		Crook Town		
1926	1929	Derby County	9	2
1929	1930	Bury	34	4
		Spennymoor United		
		Washington Colliery		
		Falkirk		
Hope, Philip (Phil)			RB	
b Kimblesworth 24/4/1897			d 1969	
		Croxdale Colliery		
1919		Sunderland (trial)	0	
		Durham City		
1920	1923	Norwich City	98	1
1924	1925	Blackburn Rovers	6	
1926		Southend United	9	
1927		Clapton Orient	18	
		Washington Colliery		
1929		Rochdale	13	1
Hopewell, Thomas Henry (Harry)			LH/RH	
b Basford 12/8/1896			d 1968	
		Bagnall Rovers		
		Basford United		
1914		Nottingham Forest	0	
		Bulwell		
1920	1921	Norwich City	27	
		Ilkeston United		
		Newark Town		
		Grantham		
		Loughborough Corinthians		
Hopewell, W			CH	
		Long Eaton Rangers		
		Grimsby Town		
1888		Derby County	5	
		Grimsby Town		
		Doncaster Rovers		
Hopkin, Frederick (Fred)			OL	
b Dewsbury 23/9/1895			d 1970	
		Darlington		
1919	1920	Manchester United	70	8
1921	1930	Liverpool	335	9
1931		Darlington	26	2
Hopkins, Arthur G			RB	
b Ebbw Vale				
		Ebbw Vale		
1924	1927	Rochdale	36	
Hopkins, George Henry			GK	
b Sheffield 11/5/1901			d 1974	
		Normanton Springs		
		Wombwell		
1924		Rotherham County	16	
		Normanton Springs		
		Newark Town		
1926	1927	Notts County	28	
		Scarborough		
1929		Oldham Athletic	0	
		Hurst		
1931		Stockport County	0	
Hopkins, Henry			CF/RB	
b Pontypridd				
		Bridgend		
		Barry		
1926	1927	Crystal Palace	40	14
Hopkins, Idris Morgan (Dai)			OR	
b Merthyr Tydfil 11/10/1910			d 1994	
Caps: Wales War 9/Wales 12				
		New Road Amateurs		
		Gellifaelog Amateurs		
1927		Merthyr Town	0	
1929		Sheffield Wednesday	0	
		Dartford Town		
		Ramsgate Press Wanderers		
1932		Crystal Palace	4	
1932	1946	Brentford	290	77
1939		(Brentford)	(3)	
1947		Bristol City	24	
Hopkins, Jack			OR/OL	
1902		Liverpool	0	
1904	1906	Wolverhampton Wanderers	43	14
		New Brompton		
Hopkins, James			IR	
b Manchester 1873				
		Berry's Association		
1898		Newton Heath	1	
Hopkins, James (Jimmy)			IL	
b Ballymoney 23/2/1900			d 1943	
Caps: Ireland 1				
		Willowfield United		
		Belfast United		
1920	1922	Arsenal	21	7
1922	1928	Brighton & Hove Albion	220	72
		Aldershot		
Hopkins, Thomas Edward (Tom)			LH/RH	
b Broad Lanes 1911				
		Bilston Borough		
1933	1936	Gillingham	87	1
		London Paper Mills		
Hopkins, William			LH/RB	
b Derby 1871				
		Derby Junction		
1890		Derby County	8	
1892	1893	Ardwick	23	
Hopkins, William (Bill 'Pop')			CH	
b Esh Winning 11/11/1888			d 1938	
		Esh Winning Rangers		
		Crook Town		
		Esh Winning Rangers		
		Stanley United		
1913	1914	Sunderland	10	
1919		Leeds City	7	
1919	1920	South Shields	61	2
1921	1922	Hartlepools United	53	1
1923	1924	Durham City	52	3
Hopkins, William J (Bill)			OR	
b Queensferry				
		Chester		
1930	1931	Halifax Town	20	3
Hopkinson, Charles (Charlie)			GK	
b Tibshelf				
		Tibshelf Colliery Church		
1907		Chesterfield Town	11	
		Rotherham County		
Hopkinson, Frederick (Fred)			LH/RH/IR	
b Royton 26/4/1908			d 1986	
		Haswell Plough Rangers		
		Thornley Albion		
		Shotton Colliery Welfare		
		Seaham Harbour		
1927		Sheffield Wednesday (trial)	0	
		Wombwell		
1928	1933	Darlington	157	10
1934	1935	Barrow	63	2
		Horden Colliery Welfare		
		South Shields		
		Stockton		
Hopkinson, Samuel (Sammy)			CH	
		Kent Road Mission		
		Denaby United		
1919		Rotherham County	1	
Hopkinson, Samuel (Sam)			OL/LH	
b High Moor 9/2/1903			d 1958	
Caps: England Sch				
		Valley Road Boys Club (Sheffield)		
		Shirebrook		
1924	1926	Chesterfield	76	18
		Shirebrook		
		Ashton National		
1930	1933	Manchester United	51	10
1935		Tranmere Rovers	10	
Hopley, Harold			RB	
b Barrow 25/5/1913			d 1975	
		Submarine Engine Athletic		
		Vickers Sports		
1931		Barrow	0	
		Lancaster Town		
1934		Barrow	8	
		Lancaster Town		
Hopper, Matthew			OR	
b Ashington 17/1/1893			d 1978	
		Annfield Plain		
		Esh Winning		
		Percy Main Colliery		
		Ashington		
		Lincoln City		
1920	1922	Millwall Athletic	48	1
		Catford Southend		
		Sittingbourne		
1926		Coventry City	15	1
1927		Ashington	19	1
		Annfield Plain		
		Northfleet United		
		Consett		
		West Moor Welfare		
Horler, George Henry			LB/RB	
b Coleford 10/2/1895			d 1967	
		Coleford		
		Frome Town		
1920	1921	Reading	56	
1922	1927	West Ham United	47	
1927		Fulham	8	
		Aldershot		
Horn, George			IL	
b West Ham 1886				
		Army & Navy (Anchor FC)		
		Tunbridge Wells Rangers		
		West Ham United		
1909		Chelsea	2	
		Peterborough & Fletton United		
Hornby, Cecil Frederick			LH/IR/RH	
b West Bromwich 25/4/1907			d 1964	
		Oakengates Town		
1930	1935	Leeds United	88	5
1935	1936	Sunderland	12	2
		Oakengates Town		
		Brierley Hill Alliance		
		Cradley Heath		
Hornby, George			GK	
1893		Northwich Victoria	18	
Hornby, Ronald (Ron)			OL/IL	
b Rochdale 13/4/1914			d 1962	
		Rochdale St Clement's		
1931		Rochdale	2	
1933		Oldham Athletic	0	
		Stalybridge Celtic		
1934	1947	Burnley	123	16
1939		(Burnley)	(2)	(1)
Hornby, William			CF	
b Fleetwood q4 1899				
		Fleetwood		
1921		Wigan Borough	1	1
		Fleetwood		
Horne, Alfred (Alf)			OR/IL/IR	
b Birmingham 16/3/1904			d 1976	
		Alvechurch		
1923		West Bromwich Albion	0	
		Stafford Rangers		
		Bromsgrove Rovers		
1925	1926	Hull City	25	2
1927		Southend United	30	10
1927	1928	Manchester City	11	2
1929	1931	Preston North End	40	5
1932	1936	Lincoln City	166	36
1936	1937	Mansfield Town	44	9
Horne, John Kay (Johnny)			GK	
b Huncoat q1 1862			d 1926	
		Accrington		
		Windsor		
		Grimsby Town		
		Bury		
		Accrington		
		Burslem Port Vale		
		Accrington		
		Burslem Port Vale		
1888		Accrington	22	
1889		Blackburn Rovers	2	
1890		Notts County	0	
1890		Accrington	1	
		Burton Swifts		
1892		Accrington	3	
1893		Darwen	1	
Horne, William E			GK/IR	
b Huncoat				
1890		Accrington	1	
1891		Blackburn Rovers	7	
		Nelson		
Horner, James			GK	
b Kirkby 1880				
1903		Grimsby Town	1	
		Grimsby Rovers		
		Grimsby Rangers		
1905	1906	Grimsby Town	13	
		Grimsby Thursday		
		Rotherham County		
		Grimsby Rovers		
		Rotherham County		
		Grimsby Rovers		
Hornsby, Stanley			LB	
1936		Gateshead	8	
Horobin, Daniel (Dan)			OR	
1896	1897	Walsall	23	3
Horrocks, Harry			IR/OR	
b Manchester 10/5/1897			d 1973	
		Norman Athletic		
		Cleckheaton		
1920		Manchester City	0	
1921		Bolton Wanderers	0	
1922	1923	Oldham Athletic	23	2
1924		Crewe Alexandra	1	
Horrocks, John			OL	
b Lees 9/1887				
1908		Stockport County	32	5
1909	1910	Nottingham Forest	22	
1911		Bury	1	
Horrocks, Stanley (Stan)			LH/RH	
b Wigan 7/5/1910			d 1993	
		Queen's Hall		
1929	1930	Wigan Borough	16	
1931		West Bromwich Albion	0	
1934	1935	Swindon Town	24	1
		Calne & Harris United		
Horrocks, Victor (Vic)			LH/OL	
b Goldenhill q4 1883			d 1922	
		Goldenhill Wanderers		
1901		Stoke	0	
		Talke United		
		Sandyford United		
		Goldenhill United		
1904	1906	Burslem Port Vale	33	2
		Goldenhill United		
		Whitchurch		
		Stoke		
		Port Vale		
		Congleton Town		
Horsfall, Walter			GK	
1930		Stockport County	8	
1931		Liverpool	0	
Horsley, James Edward			CH/RH	
b Newark 20/3/1890				
		Grantham Avenue		
		Newark		
1909	1910	Leeds City	29	
		Grantham		
Horsman, Frederick (Fred 'Ginger')			RB/LB	
b Leeds 12/12/1889			d 1959	
		Mansfield Town		
		Sutton Junction		
		Grantham		
		Mansfield Town		
1920	1923	Watford	100	
1924		Doncaster Rovers	38	
		Peterborough & Fletton United		
1925		Luton Town	0	
		Ashford		
		Chatham		
Horsman, William (Bill)			OR	
b Doncaster 18/12/1906			d 1982	
		Selby Town		
1928	1934	Birmingham	79	3
1935	1938	Chester	151	34
1939		(Chester)	(3)	
		Chester Nomads		
Horton, Ezra			RH	
b West Bromwich 10/8/1861			d 1939	
		George Salter's Works		
		West Bromwich		
1888	1890	West Bromwich Albion	46	
Horton, George			CF	
b Aston q2 1887				
		Dudley		
1910		Fulham	1	
		Dudley		
Horton, James Colin (Jimmy)			RB	
b Rotherham q4 1909				
		Newark Town		
1934		Bradford City	3	
		Boston United		
1938	1945	Aldershot	3	
		Ebbw Vale		
Horton, James William George (Sonny)			OR/CF/IR	
b Farnham 6/1/1907			d 1972	
		Aldershot Traction		
		Woking		
		Aldershot		
1929	1933	Millwall	49	8
1934		Southampton	4	1
1935		Aldershot	0	
Horton, John Henry (Jack)			RB/LB	
b West Bromwich 15/2/1866			d 1946	
		Oak Villa		
		Burslem Port Vale		
		Wednesbury Old Athletic		
		West Bromwich Albion		
		Burslem Port Vale (loan)		
1888	1897	West Bromwich Albion	130	

From To Apps Goal

Horton, John William (Jackie) OL
b Castleford 14/7/1905
1924 Bury 0
Castleford Town
1926 1932 Charlton Athletic 252 54
1932 1936 Chelsea 59 15
1937 1938 Crystal Palace 38 7

Horton, John Wooldridge CF
b Thurnscoe 11/8/1902 d 1984
Wombwell
1921 Southampton 1

Horton, Ralph IR
b South Wales
Lovells Athletic
1932 Cardiff City 1

Hosey, Edward (Ted) CH/RH
b Whittington Moor q3 1876
New Whittington Exchange
1898 Sheffield United 0
1899 1901 Chesterfield Town 41
Denaby United
New Whittington Exchange
Old Whittington Mutuals
Bolsover Town

Hosie, Alexander (Alec) RB
b Kirk Merrington q2 1895 d 1928
Mrrington Lane
Spennymoor United
1921 Durham City 26
Shildon Athletic
Spennymoor United (trial)

Hosie, James CH/LH
b Glasgow 1876
Glasgow Perthshire
Reading
1900 Blackburn Rovers 3
1900 1902 Manchester City 39 3
1902 Stockport County 25 3
1903 1904 Bristol City 53 10

Hosker, John IL
b Preston 15/2/1894
Lancaster Town
1919 1920 Preston North End 12 2
1921 1923 Accrington Stanley 104 29
Morecambe

Hoskins, Albert Henry IR/OL
b Southampton q1 1886 d 1955
Freemantle
Southampton
1908 1909 Wolverhampton Wanderers 14 2
Dudley
Shrewsbury Town

Host, William Wilkinson (Billy) RB/LB
b Parton 13/1/1906 d 1990
Parton
1928 1935 Barrow 235 1
Lancaster Town
Netherfield

Hoten, Ralph Vincent IL/LH
b Pinxton 27/12/1896 d 1978
Caps: SoLge 1
Lady Bay
Pinxton Colliery
1919 1920 Notts County 4 1
1921 1922 Portsmouth 39 9
1922 1924 Luton Town 59 13
1924 1929 Northampton Town 197 75
1930 Queen's Park Rangers 9 4

Hough, Edward (Ted) RB/LB/CH
b Walsall 4/12/1899 d 1978
Talbot Stead Tube Works
1921 1930 Southampton 175
1931 Portsmouth 1
1932 Bristol Rovers 1
Portsmouth Electricity

Hough, William Arthur (Billy) RB/LH/RH
b Greenfield 10/6/1908 d 1988
Connah's Quay & Shotton
Holywell Arcadians
1930 New Brighton 4 1
1931 1936 Preston North End 69
1937 1938 Blackburn Rovers 49
1939 (Blackburn Rovers) (3)

Hougham, Henry Victor (Harry) OL
b Southwark q4 1879
South Wigston Albion
1903 Leicester Fosse 2
South Wigston Albion
South Wigston Imperial

Houghton, Fred LB/LH
b Stockport d 1918
1911 1914 Stockport County 29

From To Apps Goal

Houghton, Harold IL/IR
b Liverpool 26/8/1906 d 1986
Caps: England Sch
Anfield Social Club
1927 Everton 1
1928 1933 Exeter City 207 79
1933 1935 Norwich City 52 10
1935 1936 Bristol Rovers 63 23
South Liverpool

Houghton, John (Jack) LB/RB/CH
b Wallsend q4 1888 d 1950
Wallsend Park Villa
Wallsend Elm Villa
Wallsend Park Villa
1910 1912 Hull City 28 3
1913 1920 Fulham 63
Newburn

Houghton, John (Jack) LB/CH
b Prescot 14/9/1891 d 1991
Prescot
St Helens Town
Norwich City
Rangers
1919 Fulham 2
1921 Wigan Borough 29
Mistletoe Lodge (Chicago)
Canadian Club (Chicago)

Houghton, Joseph Cyril (Cyril) GK
b Walsall q1 1896
1921 1922 Walsall 15

Houghton, Roy OR
b Billingborough 31/3/1921
1937 1938 Notts County 8
Grantham
Boston United
Peterborough United

Houghton, William Eric (Eric) OL/OR
b Billingborough 29/6/1910 d 1996
Caps: FLge 4/England 7
Billingborough
Bourne Town
Boston Town
1929 1946 Aston Villa 361 160
1946 1948 Notts County 55 10

Houldey, Charles Arthur (Charlie) LB/RB
b Birmingham 29/8/1901 d 1972
Barble
Harborne Lynwood
1925 1928 Coventry City 59 2
1928 1930 Walsall 100
1931 Coventry City 0
Lea Hall Rangers
Oswestry Town
Evesham Town
Halesowen Town
Shirley Town

Houldsworth, Frederick Charlton (Freddie GK
b Henley-on-Thames 29/5/1911 d 1994
Army
1934 Swindon Town 30
1934 Stoke City 2
Ipswich Town
1938 1945 Reading 8
1939 (Reading) (1)

Houlker, Albert Edward (Kelly) LH/CH
b Blackburn 27/4/1872 d 1962
Caps: FLge 1/England 5
Blackburn Hornets
Park Road (Blackburn)
1896 1901 Blackburn Rovers 121 2
Portsmouth
Southampton
1906 1908 Blackburn Rovers 31
Colne

Hoult, Alfred Aubrey (Aubrey) IR/OR
b Whitwick 17/7/1915 d 1998
Oaks Parish Church
1934 1935 Notts County 8
1937 Northampton Town 9
1938 Millwall 0

Hounsfield, Reginald E OR
b Sheffield 14/8/1882
Sheffield
1902 Sheffield Wednesday 2
1904 1905 Derby County 23 4

Housam, Arthur RH
b Sunderland 10/10/1917 d 1975
Hylton Colliery
1937 1947 Sunderland 55 2
1939 (Sunderland) (3)
Horden Colliery Welfare

From To Apps Goal

Housley, Herbert IR/IL
b Greasley 3/12/1894 d 1980
Warsop Rovers
Mansfield Town
Loughborough Corinthians
1923 Halifax Town 36 9
Loughborough Corinthians
1926 1927 Halifax Town 35 12
Loughborough Corinthians

Houston, John (Johnny) OR/CF
b Ahoghill 17/9/1889
Caps: IrLge 2/Ireland 6
Linfield
1912 1914 Everton 26 2
Linfield
Ulster Rangers
Partick Thistle
Belfast Bohemians

Houston, William McR (Billy) IR/RH
b Stirling
St Ninian's Thistle
1921 Crewe Alexandra 9 2
Macclesfield
1923 Wrexham 3 1
Nantwich
Llandudno
Rhyl
1925 Crewe Alexandra 3 1
Runcorn
Stafford Rangers

Howard, ? OL
1895 Crewe Alexandra 1

Howard, ? RH
Measham
1901 Burton United 3 1

Howard, David Cecil CF
b Doncaster q1 1883
Doncaster Thursday
1904 Doncaster Rovers 1
Doncaster Thursday

Howard, Frank CH
b Hardingstone 12/3/1878
Northampton Town
1899 Derby County 1
Ripley Town
Wellingborough
Northampton Town

Howard, Frederick (Fred) RH
b Blacker Hill q1 1877 d 1910
Hoyland Silkstone
1895 Sheffield United 0
1897 Lincoln City 1
1898 1899 Barnsley 49 1

Howard, Frederick (Fred) CF
b Walkden q3 1891
Walkden Wednesday
1912 1919 Manchester City 79 40
Mid-Rhondda
Pontypridd
1921 Gillingham 0
Dundee Hibernian (trial)
Ayr United (trial)
Clyde
1923 Port Vale 12 2
1923 New Brighton 10 4
1924 Wrexham 1
Sittingbourne (trial)
Welshpool
Holyhead Town

Howard, Frederick Julian (Fred) IR/CF
b Long Eaton q1 1895
Stapleford Brookhill
Long Eaton
1919 Derby County 5
1920 1921 Gillingham 18 3
Long Eaton

Howard, Gordon IR
b Worsborough 11/9/1886
Hoyland Town
1905 Leeds City 1

Howard, Harry LH
b Blacker Hill q1 1875
1893 Rotherham Town (trial) 0
1894 Sheffield Wednesday (trial) 0
1895 1900 Sheffield United 48 2
1902 1905 Small Heath/Birmingham 48 1
Wisbech Town

Howard, John H OR
Burton All Saints
1911 Blackpool 1

From To Apps Goal

Howard, Stephen RH/LH
b Sunderland 1897
1919 1920 Blackpool 9
1921 Southend United 15 1

Howard, William (Bill) CH
b High Park 18/1/1899 d 1965
St Simon's & St Jude's
Park Villa
1922 Southport 2
Leyland
Boys Brigade Old Boys
High Park Villa

Howarth, Archibald (Archie) OL
b Bury q1 1911 d 1966
1930 Nelson 8 2
Great Harwood

Howarth, Harold LH/RH/CH
b Little Hulton 25/11/1908 d 1973
Little Hulton
Little Lever
1929 1933 Bolton Wanderers 59
1934 1938 Chester 175 7
1939 (Chester) (3)
1945 Southport 0

Howarth, Harold (Harry) OR
b Shaw 1912
1930 Stockport County 0
1931 Rochdale 20 4
Mossley
New Mills
1934 Burnley 0
1934 Oldham Athletic 0
Hurst
Mossley
1938 Rochdale 4

Howarth, Horace R IL/IR
b Liverpool
1914 1919 Everton 8 2

Howarth, Jack Mitchell GK
b Bolton 14/1/1900 d 1979
1919 Bolton Wanderers 1

Howarth, James Thomas (Tommy) CF/IR
b Bury 15/4/1890 d 1969
1912 Bury 0
1913 1920 Bristol City 52 17
1920 1922 Leeds United 45 19
1922 Bristol Rovers 21 4
Lovells Athletic

Howarth, John Thomas RB
b Darwen 1899
Darwen
1921 Manchester United 4

Howarth, Nelson LH
b Irlams o' th' Height q4 1904
Urmston Old Boys
1922 1925 Bolton Wanderers 35 2
1926 1928 West Bromwich Albion 61 1
Runcorn
Loughborough Corinthians

Howarth, P IL
1900 Burnley 5

Howarth, Robert Henry (Bob) RB/LB
b Preston 20/6/1865 d 1938
Caps: FLge 2/England 5
1888 1891 Preston North End 47
1891 1893 Everton 59
1894 1898 Preston North End 3

Howarth, Thomas Grimshaw RH/RB
1901 1902 Burnley 9

Howarth, William LB
b Bury
1908 Burnley 9
Southport Central
Haslingden

Howat, David LH
b Preston 1/10/1870 d 1941
Fishwick Ramblers
Preston North End
1893 1895 Woolwich Arsenal 56 2
Third Lanark

Howcroft, H RH
1898 Bolton Wanderers 3

Howe, Donald (Don) RH/IL/LH
b Outwood 26/11/1917 d 1978
Whitehall Printeries
1936 1951 Bolton Wanderers 266 35
1939 (Bolton Wanderers) (3) (2)

From To Apps Goal

Howe, Frederick (Fred) LH/RH
b Rotherham 1895
Kimberworth Old Boys
1919 Coventry City 5
1920 1921 Brentford 3
Peterborough & Fletton United
Wellingborough Town
Peterborough & Fletton United

Howe, Frederick (Fred) CF
b Bredbury 24/9/1912 d 1984
Wilmslow
Hyde United
1931 1932 Stockport County 2
Hyde United
1934 1937 Liverpool 89 36
1938 Manchester City 6 5
1938 Grimsby Town 29 15
1939 (Grimsby Town) (3) (2)
1946 Oldham Athletic 30 20
Hyde United
Ashton United

Howe, Harold George OL/OR
b Hemel Hempstead 9/4/1906 d 1976
1928 Watford 0
1929 1932 Queen's Park Rangers 69 13
1933 Crystal Palace 2
1934 Rochdale 24 3
Dartford
Tunbridge Wells Rangers

Howe, Herbert OR
b Sheffield q4 1906
Ecclesfield United
1928 Chesterfield 17 1
Denaby United
Wombwell
Handsworth United
Lopham Street Methodists

Howe, Herbert Alexander (Bert) LB
b Rugby 1/4/1916 d 1972
Braunston
Rugby Town
Market Harborough Town
Leicester Nomads
1938 1946 Leicester City 28
1947 1948 Notts County 52
Rugby Town
Hinckley Athletic

Howe, John Robert (Jack) LB
b West Hartlepool 7/10/1915 d 1987
Caps: England 3
West Hartlepool Expansion
Wingate United
1934 1935 Hartlepools United 24
1935 1949 Derby County 223 2
1939 (Derby County) (3)
1949 1950 Huddersfield Town 29 1
King's Lynn
Long Sutton United
Wisbech Town

Howe, Leslie Francis (Les) RH/CH/OR
b Bengeo 5/3/1912 d 1999
Caps: England Sch
Enfield
Northfleet
1930 1938 Tottenham Hotspur 165 26

Howe, Peter Mortimer IL
b South Shields q3 1884 d 1958
Harton Old Boys
Kingston Villa
Reading
1905 1906 Hull City 32 15

Howe, Thomas (Tom) LB
b Wolverhampton 26/5/1892
Sunbeam Motors
1921 1925 Stoke 56 2
Featherstone

Howell, Albert Louis IR
b Ladywood 26/7/1898 d 1958
Hednesford Town
1920 Coventry City 4 1
Jarrow

Howell, Henry (Harry) IR/CF
b Hockley, Warwickshire 29/11/1890 d 1932
Burslem Swifts
1913 1919 Wolverhampton Wanderers 38 6
1920 Southampton 0
Northfleet
1922 Accrington Stanley (trial) 3
Mansfield Town

Howell, Henry Robert OL
b Norwich 28/6/1895 d 1935
Norwich City Supporters Club
1925 Norwich City 4

From To Apps Goal

Howell, Raby (Rabbi) RH
b Wincobank 12/10/1867 d 1937
Caps: England 2
Ecclesfield
Rotherham Swifts
1892 1897 Sheffield United 155 6
1897 1900 Liverpool 59
1901 1903 Preston North End 60 1

Howell, William Thomas Richard LB
Wellington Town
1900 Wolverhampton Wanderers 1
Willenhall Pickwick

Howells, Archie Baden GK
b Aberdare q1 1901
1924 Aberdare Athletic 19

Howes, Arthur GK
b Leicester q4 1876
Leicester Waverley
1896 1897 Leicester Fosse 12
Reading
1897 Lincoln City (trial) 0
1898 Leicester Fosse 3
Brighton United
Dumbarton
Dundee
Brighton & Hove Albion
Queen's Park Rangers

Howes, Denis RH
b Bristol 23/3/1898 d 1970
1920 1921 Bristol Rovers 22
Bath City

Howes, George Albert RH
b Jarrow 5/1/1906 d 1993
Jarrow
1928 Barnsley 0
1930 Nelson 35
Tunbridge Wells Rangers
1932 Burnley 0

Howgate, Archibald Wallace (Archie) IL
b Lanchester 6/9/1898 d 1965
Fatfield Albion
Ferryhill Athletic
Craghead United
1922 Aston Villa (trial) 0
1924 Durham City 14 1

Howie, Charles OR
b Larbert 25/4/1906
Stenhousemuir
1928 1930 Nottingham Forest 23 2
Stenhousemuir

Howie, David CH/IL/LH
b Galston 15/7/1886 d 1930
Galston Athletic
Kilmarnock
1911 1924 Bradford Park Avenue 306 21

Howie, James (Jimmy) IR
b Galston 19/3/1878 d 1962
Caps: SLge 1/Scotland 3
Galston Athletic
Kilmarnock
Galston Athletic (loan)
Kettering
Bristol Rovers
1903 1910 Newcastle United 198 68
1910 1913 Huddersfield Town 84 18

Howieson, James (Jimmy) IL
b Rutherglen 7/6/1900 d 1974
Caps: LoI 1/Scotland 1
Rutherglen Glencairn
Airdrieonians
St Johnstone
Dundee United
St Mirren
1926 1927 Hull City 39 7
New Bedford Whalers
1929 Hull City 28 5
Shelbourne
Clyde
Alloa Athletic
Glenavon
Belfast Celtic

Howlett, Charles Edward (Charlie) CF/RH
b Shildon 26/9/1906 d 1990
Evenwood United
Middleton-in-Teesdale United
1927 Durham City 8 4
1928 Rochdale 2
1929 Halifax Town 2 1
Annfield Plain
Shildon

From To Apps Goal

Howlett, Charles Herbert (Charlie) GK
b Glanford Brigg q3 1864 d 1906
Gainsborough Trinity
1892 1893 Sheffield United 38
Gainsborough Trinity

Howlett, Harry CF/OL
b Evenwood q4 1910
Evenwood Town
1928 Rochdale 1
Evenwood Town
Cockfield
1931 Portsmouth (trial) 0
1932 Nottingham Forest 1
Crook Town
West Stanley

Howling, Edward (Teddy) GK
b Stockton q4 1885 d 1955
Caps: England Amat
South Bank St Peter's
South Bank
1910 Middlesbrough 1
South Bank
1913 1914 Bristol City 55
1919 1920 Bradford Park Avenue 2
Pontypridd

Howshall, A Samuel (Sam) OR/OL
b Cobridge 9/1883
Newcastle Swifts
1903 Burslem Port Vale 2
Salisbury City
1907 Clapton Orient 2
Salisbury City
Stoke
Merthyr Town

Howshall, John Henry (Jack) LH/CH/RH
b Normacot 12/7/1912 d 1962
Dresden Juniors
Longton Juniors
Dresden United
1933 Stoke City 1
1934 Chesterfield 25
1935 1936 Southport 51
1937 Bristol Rovers 21
1938 Accrington Stanley 8
1938 Carlisle United 32
1939 (Carlisle United) (2)
Northwich Victoria
Wigan Athletic

Howson, Charles (Charlie) RB
b Wombwell 18/7/1896 d 1976
Rotherham Town
Wombwell
1922 Nelson (trial) 1
1922 Port Vale (trial)
Mansfield Town

Howson, Edward Bamber RH
b Blackpool q2 1876 d 1947
1898 Blackpool 8

Howson, George Sharples RB/LB
b Little Lever 24/8/1904 d 1975
Little Hulton United
1925 Bristol City 3
1927 New Brighton 11
Bath City
1929 Exeter City 13
Bath City
Warminster Town

Howson, Horace LH/RH
b Hunslet 2/2/1899 d 1972
Caerau
1921 1923 Halifax Town 35
Castleford Town
Harrogate AFC
Selby Town

Howson, Richard LH/OR
b Blackpool q4 1877 d 1929
Fleetwood Rangers
1898 1900 Blackpool 18

Howson, William (Billy) CF/IR/IL
b Garforth 22/10/1893 d 1959
Castleford Town
1920 1922 Bradford City 58 16
1923 Oldham Athletic 21 5
1924 1925 Halifax Town 48 18

Hoyland, Ernest (Ernie) OL/OR
b Thurnscoe 17/1/1914 d 1986
Firbeck
Thurnscoe Victoria
1935 Lincoln City (trial) 0
1936 1937 Halifax Town 30 8
1937 Blackpool 0
1938 West Bromwich Albion 1
1939 Lincoln City (2)
Grantham

From To Apps Goal

Hoyland, Frederick (Fred) OR
b Moorthorpe 10/12/1897 d 1971
Frickley Colliery
1920 1921 Swansea Town 9
1922 Bury 0
Glossop
1923 Birmingham 6
1924 1925 Brighton & Hove Albion 5

Hoyland, George A OR/CF
Sheffield
1903 1904 Sheffield Wednesday 3 1

Hoyland, Walter IL/IR
b Sheffield 14/8/1901 d 1985
1921 1926 Sheffield United 24 4
1926 1927 Fulham 22 4
Boston Town
Loughborough Corinthians
Peterborough & Fletton United
1932 Mansfield Town 25 9
Spalding United
Seymour Cobley (Spalding)

Hoyle, George CF
b Rochdale q2 1896
Sudden Villa
1921 Rochdale 3 1

Hoyle, Thomas RH
1898 Blackpool 19 1

Hoyle, Victor Frederick W (Vic) OL
b Exeter 20/6/1912 d 1969
1935 Exeter City 6 1
Dawlish Town
1936 Torquay United 6

Hoyne, James IR
b Chorlton q1 1883 d 1940
Sale Holmfield
1901 Blackburn Rovers 2
Stalybridge Rovers
Heywood United

Hubbard, Archibald (Archie 'Ranji') IL/RH/IR
b Leicester 7/2/1883 d 1967
South Wigston Albion
Humberstone Victoria
Leicester Imperial
St Andrew's (Leicester)
1904 1906 Leicester Fosse 58 21
1907 Fulham 5 1
Watford
Norwich City
1911 Grimsby Town 25 13
1912 Lincoln City 12 3
Leicester Imperial

Hubbard, Arthur A LB
b Erdington 1911
Wright & Eagle Range Co
1934 Birmingham 5
1935 1936 Luton Town 4
Dunstable Town

Hubbard, Clifford (Cliff) OR/IR
b Worksop q2 1911 d 1962
Shireoaks
Netherton United
Manton Colliery
Scunthorpe & Lindsey United
1933 1938 Hull City 183 56
1938 West Ham United 1 1
1939 (West Ham United) (3) (2)
Ransome & Marles
Goole Town
Worksop Town
Grantham

Hubbard, Shirley IL/CF/IR
b Leicester 18/2/1885 d 1963
St Andrew's (Leicester)
17th Regimental District
Leicester Imperial
1906 1912 Leicester Fosse 137 36
Darlington
South Shields
1919 Leicester City 3 1
Ashby Town

Hubbert, Hugh LH/LB
b Bradford 12/10/1899 d 1966
1922 1926 Bradford Park Avenue 135 4
1927 1928 Halifax Town 59 4

From To Apps Goal

Hubbick, Henry Edward (Harry) LB
b Jarrow 12/11/1910 d 1992
Jarrow
Blyth Spartans
Spennymoor United
1935 1936 Burnley 58 1
1936 1946 Bolton Wanderers 128
1939 (Bolton Wanderers) (3) (1)
1947 1948 Port Vale 50 1
1948 1950 Rochdale 90
Lancaster City
Caernarvon Town
Llandudno
Rhyl Athletic

Hubery, Robert (Bob) RB
b Kelloe 1895
Kelloe St Helen's
1921 Hartlepools United 1
Thornley Albion
Wingate Albion

Huddart, William Leitch (Billy) LB
b Workington 16/9/1898 d 1959
Cleator Moor Celtic
Workington
1923 Barrow 35 1
Gateshead Town
Workington

Hudson, Charles Herbert LB
b Birmingham q2 1872 d 1955
1895 Grimsby Town 5

Hudson, Edward Kearsley LB/RB
b Bolton q1 1887
Walkden Central
Ashton National
1913 1914 Manchester United 11
Tranmere Rovers
1919 Stockport County 11
Aberdare Athletic

Hudson, George OR
1908 Preston North End 0
1909 Gainsborough Trinity 6

Hudson, John B GK
b Barnsley
1930 Halifax Town 1

Hudson, Robert Sanford (Bob) IR
b Liverpool q2 1902 d 1965
Marine
Earle
Wallasey United
Earle
Mold Town
1928 1929 Wrexham 36 12
Runcorn
1931 Crewe Alexandra 0

Hudspeth, Francis Carr (Frank) LB
b Percy Main 20/4/1890 d 1963
Caps: England 1
Scotswood
Newburn
Clara Vale
North Shields Athletic
1910 1928 Newcastle United 430 34
1928 1929 Stockport County 14 2
Crook Town

Hufton, Arthur Edward (Ted) GK
b Southwell 25/11/1892 d 1967
Caps: England 6
Atlas & Norfolk
1912 1914 Sheffield United 15
1919 1931 West Ham United 371
1932 Watford 2

Hufton, Clarence RH
b Sutton-in-Ashfield 25/3/1912 d 2002
Shirebrook
Bolsover Colliery
Sutton Junction
Langwith Wagon Works
1934 1935 Mansfield Town 4
Sutton Town

Hugall, James Cockburn (Jimmy) GK
b Whitburn, County Durham 26/4/1889 d 1927
Sunderland Co-operative Wednesday
Sunderland Royal Rovers
Whitburn
1910 1921 Clapton Orient 140
Hamilton Academical
1923 Durham City 35
Seaham Colliery
Sunderland Co-operative Wednesday

From To Apps Goal

Huggins, Albert IL/CF
b Grange Villa 5/2/1913 d 1975
Birtley Welfare
1934 1935 Hartlepools United 11 2
Spennymoor United
Ouston United

Huggins, John Warwick (Jack) OL
b Shap q3 1886 d 1915
Bede College
Leadgate
1906 1907 Sunderland 14 2
Reading
1909 Sunderland 0

Hugh, Arthur Ronald (Ron) RB
b Rogerstone 5/8/1909 d 2000
Caps: WLge 1/Wales 1
Newport YMCA
Lovells Athletic
1929 1933 Newport County 61
Lovells Athletic
1935 Newport County 0

Hughes, ? OR
1898 Darwen 2 1

Hughes, Abel FB
b Rhosllanerchrugog q4 1869 d 1946
Caps: Wales 2
Rhosllanerchrugog
1893 Liverpool 1
Rhosllanerchrugog
Rhosllanerchrugog Rangers

Hughes, Alan OR
b South Shields 1909
North Shields Athletic
1929 Blackpool 0
Wigan Athletic
1933 1934 Chesterfield 37 8
1934 Derby County 2 1
1935 Everton (trial) 0
Fleetwood
South Liverpool
Wigan Athletic
South Liverpool
Fleetwood

Hughes, Alexander LB
b Hetton-le-Hole
Hetton Juniors
Heart of Midlothian
1931 Burnley 3
1933 Accrington Stanley 0

Hughes, Archibald (Archie) CH
b Arthurlie 1871
Barrhead
Arthurlie
Middlesbrough Ironopolis
1893 Bolton Wanderers 15 2
1894 Leicester Fosse 18 2
Glossop North End
Chatham

Hughes, Archibald Morris (Archie) IR
b Neilston 1886
Arthurlie
1908 Bury 6 3
1909 Manchester City 0
Exeter City
Bristol Rovers

Hughes, Arthur Robert CF
b Abermorddu
Oak Alyn Rovers
1923 Wrexham 3 1
Oak Alyn Rovers
1924 1925 Wrexham 15 4
Llandudno
Oak Alyn Rovers

Hughes, Bernard OL
b Dudley q3 1880
Humberstone Victoria
1905 Leicester Fosse 1
Leicester Nomads

Hughes, Clarence Leslie IL/RH
b Cardiff q1 1896
1914 Bristol City 2
Bristol Rovers
1919 Bristol City 3

Hughes, David LH
1903 Blackpool 1

Hughes, Duncan IL
1898 Gainsborough Trinity 9 2

From To Apps Goal

Hughes, Edward (Teddy) LH
b Ruabon 1876
Caps: Wales 14
Formby
1898 Everton 8
Tottenham Hotspur
Clyde

Hughes, Edwin (Teddy) RH
b Wrexham 1886 d 1949
Caps: Wales 16
Wrexham St Giles
Wrexham Victoria
Wrexham
1905 1910 Nottingham Forest 163 5
Wrexham
1912 1919 Manchester City 77 2
1921 1922 Aberdare Athletic 32 1
Colwyn Bay
Llandudno Town

Hughes, George GK
Runcorn
1931 Preston North End 11

Hughes, Harold (Harry) LH
b Nantwich 1881
Crewe Alexandra
1905 Wolverhampton Wanderers 9
Leamington Town
Stafford Rangers
Hanley Swifts

Hughes, Harry IR
1921 Merthyr Town 7
1923 Aberdare Athletic 9 2
1924 Brentford 14 1

Hughes, Henry IL
b Merthyr Tydfil
1924 Merthyr Town 0
1925 Chesterfield 0
Torquay United
1927 Walsall 16 5
Taunton Town
Staveley Town

Hughes, Herbert CH
1902 Stockport County 2

Hughes, James (Jimmy) LH/RH
b Bootle 12/1885 d 1948
Caps: SoLge 1
1904 1908 Liverpool 14
Crystal Palace
Chatham

Hughes, James (Jimmy) IR/IL/CF
b Coxhoe 29/8/1909 d 1966
Northumberland Fusiliers
1934 York City 15 5
1935 Hartlepools United 8 3
1935 1938 York City 91 25
1939 Hartlepools United 0

Hughes, James Henry CH
b Cuddington 1911
Northwich ICI
1933 Birmingham 0
1934 Bristol City 10

Hughes, John OL
1893 Ardwick 2

Hughes, John (Jack 'Geezer') LH
b Flint 4/1877 d 1950
Caps: Wales 3
1898 New Brighton Tower 1
Seacombe
Aberdare Town
1903 Liverpool 31 2
Plymouth Argyle

Hughes, John (Jack) LH/RH
b Tanfield
Tanfield Lea Institute
1933 Newcastle United 5
1935 1936 Aldershot 50
1937 Hartlepools United 36 1
Consett

Hughes, John Henry (Jack) OR/IR
b Oswestry 25/9/1912 d 1991
Llangollen
1929 1932 Wrexham 79 15
1933 Bolton Wanderers 9 3
1933 1935 Chester 82 21
1936 1938 Chesterfield 102 17
1939 Bradford Park Avenue (3)
Oswestry Town
Towyn

From To Apps Goal

Hughes, John Iorwerth (Jack) GK
b Rhosllanerchrugog 29/1/1913 d 1993
Caps: Wales Amat/Wales 1
Plas Bennion
Llanerch Celts
Aberystwyth Town
Afongoch
Druids
Llanerch Celts
Rhos
Dick, Kerr's XI (loan)
1932 1936 Blackburn Rovers 47
1937 1938 Mansfield Town 76
Nelson
Bacup Borough
Rossendale United
Darwen
Third Lanark

Hughes, Joseph (Joe) GK
b London 1892
Tufnell Park
South Weald
West Ham United
1919 Chelsea 0
1919 1920 Bolton Wanderers 40
1921 Charlton Athletic 19
1922 Clapton Orient 0

Hughes, Joseph (Joe) GK
b Tylorstown 1898
Porth Athletic
1921 Bristol City 3
1921 1922 Grimsby Town 31

Hughes, Joseph CF
b Manchester 4/6/1902
Gorton
New Cross (Manchester)
1922 Bolton Wanderers 0
1923 Chelsea 0
Guildford United
1924 Arsenal 1

Hughes, Joseph (Joe) CF
b Rhyl 18/3/1901 d 1983
Jollyboys
Rhyl
1922 Birmingham (trial) 0
1925 1926 Bury 8 6
1927 Southport 9 1
Rhyl Athletic
Bangor City
Rhyl Athletic

Hughes, Leonard Chester (Len) LH
b Edmonton q2 1899
Leyton
1924 1925 Burnley 28 1
1926 Accrington Stanley 33
Folkestone

Hughes, Martin GK
b Fauldhouse
1899 Middlesbrough 24

Hughes, Richard Gwynedd (Dick) RB/LB
b Sunderland 2/8/1902 d 1984
Caps: England Sch
1919 Sunderland 0
1920 1931 Bristol City 268
1932 1933 Exeter City 26

Hughes, Robert (Bobby) OL/OR
b Pelaw 5/8/1892 d 1955
Caps: SoLge 1
Pelaw
Northampton Town
1919 1921 Hull City 66 9
1922 Sheffield United 2
1923 Brentford 16 7
1924 1927 Rochdale 127 48
1928 1929 Wigan Borough 66 15
Ashton National

Hughes, Robert Arthur (Bobby) OL/RH
b Wrexham 26/9/1901 d 1973
Caps: Wales Amat
Flint Town
Chester
1927 Blackpool 2
1929 Clapton Orient 6 1
Altrincham
Mossley

Hughes, Stephen Hamer (Steve) CH
b Aigburth 11/11/1919 d 1981
Old Collegians
1936 Liverpool 0
1937 Oldham Athletic 0
Stalybridge Celtic
1938 New Brighton 17
1939 (New Brighton) (3)
Shrewsbury Town
Worksop Town

From To Apps Goal

Hughes, Thomas (Tom) IL
b Wallsend 1892 d 1915
Wallsend Park Villa
1912 Newcastle United 2

Hughes, Thomas John OL
b Rhyl q3 1896 d 1966
Halifax Town
Rhyl
Aberdare Athletic
1921 Tranmere Rovers 3

Hughes, William CH
b Caernarvon 1865 d 1919
Caps: Wales 3
Oakfield Rovers
1892 Bootle 22 1

Hughes, William CF
1893 Middlesbrough Ironopolis 1

Hughes, William Henry (Billy) CF
b West Bromwich 1888
Stourbridge
1908 1912 Bolton Wanderers 100 51
1913 Wolverhampton Wanderers 21 10

Hughes, William John (Jack) RH
b Rhyl 1889 d 1955
Rhyl Athletic
1907 Newcastle United 1
1910 Huddersfield Town 0
Oswestry United
Norwich City
Halifax Town
1913 Bradford City 1
Barrow
Halifax Town

Hughes, William Marshall (Billy) LB
b Llanelli 6/3/1918 d 1981
Caps: Wales War 14/Wales 10
Archer Corinthians
Watchers Celtic
Llanelly
1934 Swansea Town (trial) 0
1935 1946 Birmingham 105
1939 (Birmingham) (3)
1947 Luton Town 31
1947 1950 Chelsea 93
Hereford United
Flint Town United

Hulbert, Robert (Bob) OL
b Westhoughton 1/4/1914 d 1985
Westhoughton Colliery
1936 1938 Bury 39 15
1939 (Bury) (3)
1945 Southport 0

Hull, Arthur Alexander (Tishy) GK
b Birkenhead q2 1878 d 1952
1902 1905 Blackpool 116

Hull, Archibald James (Archie) RH/CH/LH
b East Ham 8/8/1902 d 1978
Ilford
1926 1928 West Ham United 2
1930 Clapton Orient 1
Ilford

Hull, Frank LB
b Dunstable 1896
Luton Amateurs
1920 Luton Town 3
Torquay United

Hull, John Smellie (Jack) RH
b Motherwell 22/4/1913
Wishaw White Rose
1935 Sheffield Wednesday 1

Hullett, William Alexander (Bill) CF
b Liverpool 19/11/1915 d 1982
1935 Everton 0
1936 New Brighton (loan) 13 8
1937 1938 Plymouth Argyle 29 20
1939 Manchester United 0
Merthyr Tydfil
1947 1948 Cardiff City 27 15
1948 Nottingham Forest 13 2
Merthyr Tydfil
Worcester City (trial)
Treharris

Hulley, Thomas (Tom) GK
b Whitefield
1922 Bury 3

Hulligan, John CF
White Star Wanderers (Liverpool)
1900 Stockport County 1 1

From To Apps Goal

Hullock, James RH
b Maryport q3 1886 d 1965
Crystal Palace
Third Lanark
1914 Stockport County 20
Croydon Common

Hullock, Lawrence CF
b Penrith q2 1907 d 1961
Bowness Rovers
1925 Barrow 7 1
Bowness Rovers
Morecambe

Hulm, George William OR
b Southport 8/11/1903 d 1964
Mornington Road
1929 Southport 1
Clitheroe
Formby
Cheshire Lines Railway
Formby

Hulme, ? OR
1898 Darwen 1

Hulme, Aaron RB/LB
b Manchester q2 1883 d 1933
Newton Heath Athletic
Colne
Oldham Athletic
1907 1908 Manchester United 4
Nelson
Hyde
St Helens Recreation
Newton Heath Athletic

Hulme, George RB
1898 Burslem Port Vale 8

Hulme, Joseph Arthur (Arthur) IR
b Leek 18/12/1877 d 1916
1897 Lincoln City 29 12
Gravesend United
Wellingborough
Bristol Rovers
Brighton & Hove Albion

Hulme, Joseph Harold Anthony (Joe) OR
b Stafford 26/8/1904 d 1991
Caps: FLge 5/England 9
Stafford YMCA
York City
1923 1925 Blackburn Rovers 73 6
1925 1937 Arsenal 333 107
1937 Huddersfield Town 8

Hulme, William RH
b Bolton
1914 Bury 0
1919 Bolton Wanderers 3
New Brighton
Chorley

Hulmes, Samuel (Bob) LH
Heywood
1899 Lincoln City 2
New Brompton

Hulmes, Samuel (Sam) LB
b Bolton
1905 Bury 15
Nelson

Hulse, Benjamin Daniel (Ben) IR/IL/CF
b Liverpool q3 1875 d 1950
Liverpool South End
Rock Ferry
1897 1899 Blackburn Rovers 85 22
1900 New Brighton Tower 31 14
Millwall Athletic
Brighton & Hove Albion

Hulse, Joseph (Joe) GK
Christian Church
1920 Bury 1

Humble, Geoffrey CF
b Chester-le-Street q4 1912
1935 Gateshead 3 1

Humpage, Joseph GK
1896 Burton Wanderers 7

Humpage, William Leonard Frederick GK
b Birmingham 1870
Wednesbury Old Athletic
1893 1895 West Bromwich Albion 4
Hereford Thistle

Humphrey, Douglas Vincent (Duggie) OL
b Ecclesall Bierlow 27/9/1897 d 1965
1921 Bradford Park Avenue 7 1
1922 1923 Stockport County 29 2
1923 Nelson 8
Selby Town

From To Apps Goal

Humphrey, Eric Thomas H IL/IR
b Mansfield 14/12/1907 d 1995
Brodsworth Main Colliery
1927 Leeds United 0
1928 Torquay United 6 2
Frickley Colliery
Upton Colliery
1937 Rotherham United 6 2

Humphreys, Joseph (Joe) CH
b Newhall
1921 Aston Villa 0
1922 Southend United 17
Burton Town

Humphreys, Percy IR/CF/CH
b Cambridge 3/12/1880 d 1959
Caps: FLge 1/England 1
Cambridge St Mary's
Queen's Park Rangers
1901 1906 Notts County 189 66
1907 Leicester Fosse 26 19
1907 1909 Chelsea 45 13
1909 1911 Tottenham Hotspur 45 24
1911 Leicester Fosse 14 2
Hartlepools United
Norwich City

Humphreys, Reginald Harry RB
b Oswestry q2 1888
Oswestry Town
1910 Manchester City 3

Humphreys, William IR
b St Helens
1931 Bradford City 1

Humphreys, William T (Billy) RH/CH
b Bolton q2 1884
Chorley
1905 1914 Bury 240 1
Barrow

Humphries, Brinley CH
b Swansea 26/12/1901 d 1972
Stepney (Swansea)
1925 1926 Swansea Town 11 1
1927 1929 Swindon Town 55 2
Mynydd Newydd Colliery

Humphries, Howard J IL/LB/OL
b Aston 2/1894 d 1960
Handsworth Amateurs
1914 1921 Aston Villa 20 2
1921 Southend United 0
1921 1922 Rotherham County 10 1

Humpish, Albert Edward (Bert) RH/IR/IL
b Heaton 3/4/1902 d 1986
1921 Halifax Town 8 1
Walker Celtic
1924 Bury 2
1925 1929 Wigan Borough 161 15
1929 Arsenal 3
1930 1931 Bristol City 36 1
1932 1933 Stockport County 58 11
1934 Rochdale 31 2
Ashton National
Wigan Athletic

Hunt, A LB
1895 Nottingham Forest 1

Hunt, Archibald (Archie) CF
Bulwell United
Whitwick White Cross
1904 1905 Derby County 15 1
Walsall
Mansfield Wesleyans
Walsall

Hunt, Ashley Kenneth GK
b Kirkby-in-Ashfield 24/11/1921
Hawleys Athletic
1938 Nottingham Forest 2

Hunt, Douglas Arthur (Doug) CF/IR
b Shipton Bellinger 19/5/1914 d 1989
Winchester City
1931 Southampton 0
Northfleet
1934 1936 Tottenham Hotspur 17 6
1936 1937 Barnsley 36 18
1937 1938 Sheffield Wednesday 42 30
1939 (Sheffield Wednesday) (3) (1)
1946 1947 Leyton Orient 61 16
Gloucester City

Hunt, E LB
1891 Darwen 1

From To Apps Goal

Hunt, Fergus IR/OR/CF
b Masbrough q1 1875
Mexborough
1893 Middlesbrough Ironopolis 11 5
1895 1896 Darwen 57 27
1897 1899 Woolwich Arsenal 69 29
West Ham United
1902 Woolwich Arsenal 3 1
Fulham
1905 1906 Burton United 60 13
Shildon Athletic

Hunt, George Samuel CF/IR
b Barnsley 22/2/1910 d 1996
Caps: England 3
1927 Barnsley (trial) 0
1927 Sheffield United (trial) 0
1928 Port Vale (trial) 0
Regent Street Congregationals
1929 Chesterfield 14 9
1930 1936 Tottenham Hotspur 185 125
1937 Arsenal 18 3
1937 1946 Bolton Wanderers 45 24
1939 (Bolton Wanderers) (3) (1)
1946 1947 Sheffield Wednesday 32 8
1948 Bolton Wanderers 0

Hunt, Harold (Harry) CF
1905 Clapton Orient 1

Hunt, Herbert CF
1902 Glossop 16 7

Hunt, Herbert OL
b West Bromwich 7/1916
1935 West Bromwich Albion 0
1936 Walsall 6
Darlaston

Hunt, John RH/LH
Alvaston & Boulton
Derby Hills Ivanhoe
1901 Derby County 3
Ripley Athletic
1903 Glossop 3
1905 Derby County 2

Hunt, Joseph Frederick IR
b Ireland
1934 Nottingham Forest 1

Hunt, (Rev) Kenneth Reginald Gunnery RH/CH
b Oxford 24/2/1884 d 1949
Caps: FLge 1/England Amat/England 2
Oxford University
Corinthians
1906 1908 Wolverhampton Wanderers 34 1
Leyton
1909 Wolverhampton Wanderers 7
Leyton
1910 Wolverhampton Wanderers 4
Leyton
1911 Wolverhampton Wanderers 2
Leyton
1912 Wolverhampton Wanderers 2
Crystal Palace
Oxford City
Crystal Palace
1919 Wolverhampton Wanderers 1
Crystal Palace
Corinthians

Hunt, Michael H GK
b Croydon
North Croydon
1925 1927 Crystal Palace 3
North Croydon

Hunt, Patrick CH
b Glasgow
Shawfield Juniors
Hamilton Academical
1928 Burnley 8
Belfast Celtic
Alloa Athletic

Hunt, Richard CH
b Jarrow 1912 d 1963
Blyth Spartans
1934 1935 Torquay United 31
1936 Brighton & Hove Albion 0

Hunt, Robert OR
Farnworth PM
1933 Tranmere Rovers 8 2

Hunt, Samuel (Sam) CF
b Smithies 1866
Mexborough
Doncaster Rovers
Lincoln City
Barnsley St Peter's
Mexborough
Barnsley St Peter's
1895 Darwen 9 4
1899 Barnsley 1

Hunt, Samuel Walter (Wally) CF/IL
b Doe Lea 9/1/1909 d 1963

From	To	Club	Apps	Goal
		Welbeck Colliery Welfare		
1933		Lincoln City	3	
1934		Mansfield Town	29	14
1935		Torquay United	27	8
1936	1937	Rochdale	58	31
1937		Stockport County	11	2
1938		Accrington Stanley	5	1
1938		Carlisle United	31	33
1939		(Carlisle United)	(2)	(1)

Hunt, Thomas (Tommy) CF
b West Bromwich 23/6/1908 d 1975

From	To	Club	Apps	Goal
		Wednesbury Town		
		Stourbridge		
1926		Birmingham	0	
		Wednesbury Town		
1928		Wolverhampton Wanderers	0	
1929	1932	Norwich City	50	33
		Drumcondra		
1934		Watford	0	

Hunt, Thomas Richardson (Tom) OR
b Shiney Row q2 1901

From	To	Club	Apps	Goal
		Seaham Harbour		
1923		Hartlepools United	2	
		Carlisle United		
		Shildon		

Hunter, Albert CF
b Hartlepool

From	To	Club	Apps	Goal
		West Hartlepool St Oswald		
		Shildon		
1925		Hartlepools United	1	
		Horden Colliery Welfare		
		Hartlepool Gas & Water		

Hunter, Albert Edward RB
b Sheffield 7/8/1902 d 1982

From	To	Club	Apps	Goal
		Norton Woodseats Amateurs		
1924		Sheffield United	0	
1925		Brighton & Hove Albion	0	
		Scarborough		
		Denaby United		
1930		Bradford Park Avenue	0	
1931		Walsall	35	
1932	1933	Doncaster Rovers	58	
1934		Accrington Stanley	38	1
1935		Barrow	35	1
		Frickley Colliery		
		Goole Town		

Hunter, Alexander Campbell (Alex) GK
b Renfrew 27/9/1895 d 1984

From	To	Club	Apps	Goal
		Renfrew Juniors		
		Queen's Park		
1920	1921	Tottenham Hotspur	23	
1922	1923	Wigan Borough	39	
		Armadale		
		New Bedford Whalers		

Hunter, Andrew (Andy) OR
b Belfast 11/10/1883
Caps: IrLge 7/Ireland 8

From	To	Club	Apps	Goal
		Distillery		
		Belfast Celtic		
1908	1909	Sheffield Wednesday	14	3
		Distillery (loan)		
		Glentoran		
		Distillery		

Hunter, Archibald (Archie) CF
b Ayr 23/9/1859 d 1894

From	To	Club	Apps	Goal
		Third Lanark		
		Ayr Thistle		
1888	1889	Aston Villa	32	8

Hunter, Cyril CH/RH
b Pelaw 1898 d 1962

From	To	Club	Apps	Goal
		Leadgate Park		
1921	1923	Brentford	78	2
1924	1927	South Shields	105	3
		Fall River Marksmen		
1929		Lincoln City	14	1

Hunter, George RH
b Hylton Colliery 1902

From	To	Club	Apps	Goal
		Walker Parish Church		
		Hylton Colliery		
1921	1922	Sunderland	10	
1923		Exeter City	18	
		Workington		
1924		Southend United	0	
1925		Doncaster Rovers	0	
		Scunthorpe & Lindsey United		

Hunter, George Charles LH/CH/RH
b Peshawar, India 16/8/1886 d 1934
Caps: FLge 2

From	To	Club	Apps	Goal
		Maidstone United		
		Croydon Common		
1908	1911	Aston Villa	91	1
1911	1912	Oldham Athletic	40	1
1912	1913	Chelsea	30	2
1913	1914	Manchester United	22	2
		Portsmouth		

Hunter, Herbert GK
b Trimdon Colliery 1884

From	To	Club	Apps	Goal
		Deaf Hill United		
		Darlington		
1905		Middlesbrough	3	
		Crystal Palace		
		Wingate Albion		
		Deaf Hill United		

Hunter, James Alton LB
b Balfron 5/7/1898
Caps: SLge 2

From	To	Club	Apps	Goal
1919		Newcastle United	0	
		Motherwell		
		Falkirk		
1923	1924	Newcastle United	10	
		Heart of Midlothian (trial)		
		New Bedford Whalers		

Hunter, James Boyd (Jimmy) OR
b Dunfermline 1913

From	To	Club	Apps	Goal
		Wheeldons United		
		Stanton Ironworks		
		Ilkeston United		
1932		Fulham (trial)	0	
		Ripley Town		
1934	1935	Mansfield Town	26	5
1935	1938	Plymouth Argyle	95	15
1939		Preston North End	(3)	

Hunter, John (Jock) RH
b Paisley 1875

From	To	Club	Apps	Goal
		Troon		
		St Mirren		
1897	1898	Preston North End	16	
		Portsmouth		
		Distillery		

Hunter, John CH
b Preston 1881 d 1928

From	To	Club	Apps	Goal
1902	1907	Preston North End	186	5

Hunter, John IL
b Stenhousemuir 11/4/1905

From	To	Club	Apps	Goal
		Burnhead Hearts		
		Falkirk		
1928	1930	Reading	86	7
		Brideville		
		Guildford City		

Hunter, John Bryson (Sailor) IL/CF
b Johnstone 6/4/1878 d 1966
Caps: Scotland 1

From	To	Club	Apps	Goal
		Westmarch		
		Abercorn		
1899	1901	Liverpool	37	10
		Heart of Midlothian		
1904		Woolwich Arsenal	22	4
		Portsmouth		
		Dundee		
		Clyde		
		Motherwell		

Hunter, Norman IR
b Sheepwash 25/5/1905

From	To	Club	Apps	Goal
		Wreckenden Blue Star		
		Blyth Spartans		
1922		Ashington	9	1
		Washington Colliery		
1928		Sheffield United	0	
		Washington Colliery		
		Ashington		
		Blyth Spartans		
		Chopwell Institute		

Hunter, Robert RB/LB/RH

From	To	Club	Apps	Goal
1900	1901	Manchester City	7	
1902		Stockport County	3	

Hunter, Robert OR
b Silpho q1 1883 d 1962

From	To	Club	Apps	Goal
		Filey		
1904		Grimsby Town	8	1

Hunter, Robert CH

From	To	Club	Apps	Goal
		Ashton National		
1926		Stockport County	7	

Hunter, Thomas (Tommy) OR
b 1863 d 1918

From	To	Club	Apps	Goal
		Walsall Town		
1888		Wolverhampton Wanderers	20	4
		Kidderminster Olympic		
		Kidderminster		
		Walsall Town Swifts		
		Kidderminster Harriers		

Hunter, Thomas OL

From	To	Club	Apps	Goal
1893		Middlesbrough Ironopolis	27	6

Hunter, Thomas CF
b Birkenhead

From	To	Club	Apps	Goal
1919	1920	Blackpool	13	4

Hunter, Thomas John (Jack) CH/OR

From	To	Club	Apps	Goal
1899	1901	Liverpool	5	

Hunter, William (Bill) CF
b Sunderland 1888
Caps: SLge 1

From	To	Club	Apps	Goal
		Sunderland West End		
1908		Liverpool	1	
1909		Sunderland	0	
1909	1910	Lincoln City	32	8
		Wingate Albion		
		South Shields		
1912		Barnsley	2	1
1912		Manchester United	3	2
1913		Clapton Orient	9	1
		Exeter City		

Hunter, William (Bill) CH/LB
b Falkirk 16/8/1900

From	To	Club	Apps	Goal
		Bowhill		
1921	1926	Birmingham	41	
1926	1927	Grimsby Town	6	
1927		Coventry City	31	1
1928		Walsall	10	
1929		Torquay United	6	

Hunter, William B (Billy) OL
b Alva 1885

From	To	Club	Apps	Goal
		Millwall Athletic		
1908	1911	Bolton Wanderers	53	15

Huntley, Edward (Ed) RH
b Dawdon 20/9/1913 d 2000

From	To	Club	Apps	Goal
		Dawdon Colliery Welfare		
		Deneside Recreation		
		Easington Colliery Welfare		
1933		West Bromwich Albion		
1935	1936	Rochdale	30	
		Newry Town		

Hurdman, Arthur Stanley OR
b Sunderland q3 1882 d 1953

From	To	Club	Apps	Goal
		Sunderland Black Watch		
1906	1907	Sunderland	8	3
		Darlington		
		Wingate Albion		
		Sunderland Rovers		

Hurel, Eli CF/IR
b Val de Mar, Jersey 10/4/1915

From	To	Club	Apps	Goal
		St Helier		
1936		Everton	5	1
1938		Northampton Town	12	2

Hurley, Albert Victor OL
b Tiverton q2 1901

From	To	Club	Apps	Goal
		Oxford University		
		Oxford City		
		Dulwich Hamlet		
1921		Reading	2	
		Yorkshire Amateurs		
		Corinthians		

Hurst, Aaron RB
b Bolton 1/12/1912 d 1979

From	To	Club	Apps	Goal
1934		Blackpool	0	
1935		Clapton Orient	1	
1936		Bury	0	
		South Liverpool		

Hurst, Daniel James OL
b Cockermouth q4 1876
Caps: FLge 1

From	To	Club	Apps	Goal
		Black Diamonds		
1897	1899	Blackburn Rovers	53	17
		Workington		
1901		Manchester City	15	
1902		Manchester United	16	4

Hurst, George IL/IR
b Lanchester

From	To	Club	Apps	Goal
		Consett		
		Leadgate Park		
1930	1932	Darlington	63	21
		Eden Colliery		

Hurst, George John (Jack) CH/LH
b Lever Bridge 27/10/1914 d 2002

From	To	Club	Apps	Goal
		Lever Bridge Juniors		
1934	1946	Bolton Wanderers	60	2
1939		(Bolton Wanderers)	(3)	
1946	1950	Oldham Athletic	98	2
		Chelmsford City		

Hurst, George M IR

From	To	Club	Apps	Goal
1930		Walsall	11	2
		Altrincham		
		Manchester North End		
		Stalybridge Celtic		
		Mossley		

Hurst, Henry (Harry) LH
b Wigan 28/4/1910 d 1988

From	To	Club	Apps	Goal
		Hindley St Peter's		
1931		Wigan Borough	2	
		Wigan Athletic		
		Chorley		
		Rossendale United		

Hurst, Stanley Charles (Stan) OL/OR/CF
b Newton St Cyres 21/6/1911 d 1993

From	To	Club	Apps	Goal
		Jackson's United (Crediton)		
		Newton Poppleford		
		Tipton St John's		
1932	1935	Exeter City	107	25
1936		Watford	29	12
1937	1938	Brighton & Hove Albion	33	11
1939		Aldershot	(1)	(1)
		Crediton United		

Hurst, William (Bill) CF/IR
b Newcastle

From	To	Club	Apps	Goal
		Walker Celtic		
1922		Derby County	3	
1923	1924	Queen's Park Rangers	10	4

Husband, William OL
b Kilmarnock

From	To	Club	Apps	Goal
		Kilmarnock Celtic		
		St Mirren		
1912	1913	Burnley	39	7
		Hamilton Academical		
		Vale of Leven		

Husler, Horace Henry GK
b Ecclesall q1 1890 d 1959

From	To	Club	Apps	Goal
1911		Sheffield Wednesday	0	
1912		Huddersfield Town	1	
		Doncaster Rovers		

Hutcheson, David High LH
b Dundee 1894

From	To	Club	Apps	Goal
		Dundee North End		
		Dundee Stobswell		
		Dundee		
1921	1927	South Shields	188	4

Hutcheson, John Hughes McGeavy (Jock) LH
b Larbert 31/3/1909 d 1979
Caps: SLge 1

From	To	Club	Apps	Goal
		Preston Athletic		
		Falkirk		
1933	1935	Chelsea	22	1
1938		Ipswich Town	0	
		Crittall Athletic		

Hutchins, Arthur Victor LB/RB
b Bishop's Waltham 15/9/1890 d 1950

From	To	Club	Apps	Goal
		Croydon Common		
1919	1922	Arsenal	104	1
1923		Charlton Athletic	21	1

Hutchinson, Albert IL/LB/LH
b Sheffield 30/9/1910 d 1974

From	To	Club	Apps	Goal
		Atlas & Norfolk		
1929		Luton Town	5	1
1930	1938	Torquay United	317	80
1939		(Torquay United)	(3)	(1)

Hutchinson, Alexander (Alex) OL
b Musselburgh 1908

From	To	Club	Apps	Goal
		Bo'ness		
1929		Burnley	5	2
1930		Blackpool	6	2
		Bo'ness		
1933		Cardiff City	23	4
		Bo'ness		

Hutchinson, Frank CF

From	To	Club	Apps	Goal
1894		Burton Swifts	2	

Hutchinson, GW GK

From	To	Club	Apps	Goal
1894		Manchester City	7	

Hutchinson, J RB

From	To	Club	Apps	Goal
1892		Bootle	20	

From To Apps Goal

Hutchinson, Robert (Bobby) OL/IR
b Blyth 22/12/1894 d 1971
Gosforth
Palmer's (Jarrow)
St Mirren
1919 Newcastle United 0
1921 Ashington 22 4
1922 1923 Nelson 60 1
1923 Stockport County 4 1
1924 Chesterfield 13 1
1925 Barrow 37 4
New Bedford Whalers
Springfield Babes
Fall River Marksmen
Newark Skeeters
Hartford Americans
1927 Darlington 3
West Stanley
Gosforth & Coxlodge British Legion

Hutchinson, Thomas (Tom) CF
b Glasgow 1872 d 1933
Govan
Stockton
Govan Whitefield
Darlington
1893 Newcastle United 0
Nelson
1894 1895 West Bromwich Albion 45 19
Celtic
Abercorn
Stockport County
Ellesmere Port

Hutchinson, William (Billy) OR
b Stoke-on-Trent 7/1870
Fenton RS
1888 Stoke 1
Long Eaton Rangers

Hutchinson, William IL
Alston
1904 Burnley 1

Hutchinson, William L (Billy) OL
b Chester-le-Street
Chester-le-Street
1929 Birmingham 0
1930 Bournemouth & Boscombe Ath 2
1931 Leeds United 0
1932 Darlington 3 1
1932 Halifax Town 2

Hutchison, David Campbell (Davie) IR/OL
b Shotts 29/10/1908
Dykehead
Albion Rovers
Motherwell
1928 1931 Carlisle United 149 63
1932 1934 Luton Town 55 21
Airdrieonians
1936 Bournemouth & Boscombe Ath 2 1
Stenhousemuir

Hutchison, Duncan CF/OR/IR
b Kelty 3/3/1903 d 1973
Leathens Heatherbell
Rosewell Rosedale
Dunfermline Athletic
Dundee United
1929 1931 Newcastle United 40 16
1931 1933 Derby County 29 4
1934 Hull City 38 8
Dundee United

Hutson, Sidney John IR
b Willesden q1 1906 d 1949
1930 Millwall 1

Hutton, Harry OL
b Bolton q2 1915
Hebble Motor Services
1938 Halifax Town 7

Hutton, James OL
1897 Burton Swifts 11 1

Hutton, John (Jock) RB
b Dalziel 29/10/1898
Caps: SLge 4/Scotland 10
Motherwell
Heart of Midlothian
Larkhall Thistle
Bellshill Athletic
Hall, Russell & Co
Aberdeen
1926 1931 Blackburn Rovers 127 4

Hutton, Robert CF/IR
b Sheffield
St Andrew's (Sheffield)
1898 1901 Sheffield Wednesday 5 1
Worksop Town
1903 Chesterfield Town 8 1
Worksop Town

From To Apps Goal

Huxford, Augustus Thomas (Gus) OL
b Brixham 29/7/1889 d 1961
Grimsby St John's
1909 1911 Grimsby Town 12 1
Goole Town
Castleford Town
1914 1919 Grimsby Town 6 1
Charlton's (Grimsby)
Worksop Town
Charlton's (Grimsby)
Brigg Town
Louth Town

Huxford, Harold CF
b Grimsby 2/2/1916 d 2001
Grimsby YMCA
1936 Grimsby Town 0
1938 Hull City 10 1
Boston United
Peterborough United

Huxley, Frank Ronald LB
b Chester 18/4/1911 d 1995
Northern Nomads
1935 Rochdale 1
Horden Colliery Welfare

Huyton, James CF
1919 Stockport County 2 1

Hyam, James William (Jim) CF
b Shoreditch 1891 d 1951
Bristol Rovers
Aberdare Athletic
1921 Tranmere Rovers 1
Clevedon

Hyde, Jack IL
b Leek q2 1899
Leek Town
1924 Port Vale 2

Hyde, Leonard Joseph (Leon) OR/OL
b Birmingham 6/5/1876 d 1932
Harborne
Kidderminster Harriers
1897 Grimsby Town 4
Bristol St George
Wellingborough
Tottenham Hotspur
Wellingborough
Brighton & Hove Albion
1904 Doncaster Rovers 32 1

Hyde, Lincoln OL/CF
b Stockport q3 1892
1913 1914 Stockport County 13 1

Hyde, Wilfred CF
1900 Glossop 1

Hydes, Arthur CF/IR
b Barnsley 24/11/1910 d 1990
Ardsley United
1928 Barnsley 0
1929 Southport (trial) 0
Ardsley Athletic
1930 1936 Leeds United 127 74
Scunthorpe & Lindsey United
1938 1945 Newport County 27 13
1939 (Newport County) (3) (3)
1946 Exeter City 4
Scunthorpe & Lindsey United

Hyett, James CF
Stapleford Town
1904 Leicester Fosse 1
Stapleford Town
Ripley Town
Stapleford Town
Long Eaton St Helen's

Hynd, John (Jock) GK
Cowdenbeath
1894 Newcastle United 9

Hynds, Thomas (Tommy) CH
b Hurlford 1880
Caps: SLge 1
Hurlford Thistle
Celtic
1898 Bolton Wanderers (loan) 8
Clyde (loan)
1900 Bolton Wanderers (loan)
1901 1905 Manchester City 158 9
1906 Woolwich Arsenal 13
1907 Leeds City 37
Heart of Midlothian
Dumbarton
Ladysmith (Canada)
Musselburgh

From To Apps Goal

Hyslop, Thomas (Tommy) IL
b Mauchline 22/9/1874 d 1936
Caps: Scotland 2
Elderslie
Army
Millwall Athletic
1893 1894 Sunderland 19 10
1894 1895 Stoke 31 24
Rangers
1898 Stoke 12
Rangers
Partick Thistle
Dundee Wanderers
Johnstone
Abercorn
Philadelphia Thistle
Tacony (Philadelphia)

Ibbotson, Ernest Edward CF
b Hathersage q2 1885 d 1949
Hathersage
1908 Sheffield United 1

Iceton, Jacob (Jake) GK
b West Auckland 22/10/1903 d 1981
Cockfield
1925 Hull City 0
Shildon
1930 1933 Fulham 90
1935 Aldershot 10
1937 1938 Clapton Orient 40
Worcester City

Iddon, Richard CF/IR
b Tarleton 21/6/1901 d 1975
Tarleton
Leyland
1921 Preston North End 0
Tarleton
Chorley
1925 1926 Manchester United 2
Chorley
Morecambe
1928 New Brighton 11 2
Morecambe
Lancaster Town
Horwich RMI
Altrincham

Igoe, John LH
b Bonhill 1907
Lochgelly Celtic
Airdrieonians
1929 Charlton Athletic 0
1930 Thames 20
Cork (trial)
Cork Bohemians
Larne
Lochgelly Amateurs
St Bernard's
Brechin City

Iles, Albert Kitchener (Bert) CF
b Tunbridge Wells 9/10/1914 d 1979
Tunbridge Wells Rangers
1937 1938 Bristol Rovers 46 19
1939 (Bristol Rovers) (1)
Street

Illingworth, John William RB
b Castleford 3/9/1904 d 1964
Castleford Town
Northfleet
1929 1934 Tottenham Hotspur 10
1935 Swansea Town 1
Barry

Imrie, David CF
b Scotland
Chicago
1931 1932 Clapton Orient 12 7

Imrie, James J GK
b Markinch
Dunbeath Star
Kettering Town
1928 1930 Crystal Palace 35
1931 1932 Luton Town 63
1933 1938 Doncaster Rovers 126

Imrie, William Noble (Bill) RH/LH/CH
b Methil 4/3/1908 d 1944
Caps: Scotland 2
Kirkcaldy Juniors
East Fife Juniors
Dunniker Juniors
St Johnstone
1929 1933 Blackburn Rovers 165 23
1933 1937 Newcastle United 125 24
1938 Swansea Town 27 1
1939 Swindon Town (2)

From To Apps Goal

Ince, John GK
b Morpeth q4 1908
Walker Celtic
St Peter's Albion
1932 Exeter City 0
1933 Darlington 29
1934 Gateshead 22

Ing, Alfred Archibald (Jack) RH/OR
b Long Crendon 16/9/1887 d 1975
Swindon Victoria
1920 1923 Swindon Town 9

Ing, Joseph Henry Charles (Joe) RH
b Clapton 16/10/1890 d 1977
Clapton Warwick
1919 Clapton Orient 17
Northfleet

Ingham, Thomas Lawrence (Tom) OL
b Prestwich 22/7/1917 d 1996
Manchester North End
1935 Bolton Wanderers 0
1935 1936 New Brighton 2
Altrincham

Ingham, Thomas William CF
b Hulme 12/5/1896 d 1960
1921 Manchester City 2 1
1923 Chesterfield 8 1

Ingham, William E (Billy) CF
b 1882
Caps: SoLge 2
Aberdare Town
West Ham United
Aberdare Town
1905 Bristol City 1
1906 Gainsborough Trinity 28 7
Plymouth Argyle
Accrington Stanley
Norwich City

Ingledew, George Edward IL
b Sheffield 3/1/1903 d 1979
Wombwell
1925 1926 Bradford City 4
Wath Athletic

Inglis, Douglas G OL
Rosewell
1925 Charlton Athletic 2

Inglis, James Allen OR
b Kirkland 1872
Airdrieonians
1896 1898 Small Heath 56 24
1899 Luton Town 4
Sanquhar

Inglis, John (Jock) IR
1888 1889 Preston North End 3 2

Inglis, John OL
b Scotland
Dalmuir Thistle
1893 Newcastle United 3

Inglis, William John (Bill) RH/CH/LH
b Hebburn 4/9/1899 d 1968
1920 Derby County 0
Hebburn Colliery
1922 1924 Brentford 80 1
1925 1929 Reading 120 1
1930 Exeter City 15
1931 Stockport County 35 1
1932 Watford 12
Dartford
Cray Wanderers

Inglis, William White (Bill) RB
b Kirkcaldy 2/3/1897 d 1968
Inverkeithing United
Kirkcaldy United
Raith Rovers
1924 Sheffield Wednesday 29
1925 1928 Manchester United 14 1
1930 1931 Northampton Town 62

Ingram, John IL
b Bamfurlong 29/9/1909 d 1970
Ashton St Thomas
1929 Wigan Borough 11 1
Loughborough Corinthians
Chorley
Burscough Rangers

Innerd, Wilfred Lawson (Wilf) CH/RH
b Newcastle q4 1878 d 1967
Wallsend Park Villa
1900 1904 Newcastle United 3
Crystal Palace
Shildon Athletic

From To Apps Goal

Innes, Robert A (Bob) RH
b Lanark 23/7/1878 d 1959
Royal Ordnance Factory
Gravesend United
New Brompton
1901 1902 Notts County 48
1903 1904 Nottingham Forest 26
Brighton & Hove Albion
Swindon Town
Swindon Victoria

Inns, Thomas Frederick William (Tommy) LB
b Plaistow 30/1/1911 d 1987
Clapton
1933 West Ham United 4
1936 1938 Millwall 88

Inskip, John LH
b Glengarnock
South Shields
1912 Lincoln City 1

Inskip, Joseph Barton (Joe) CH/RH/LH
b South Shields 31/12/1912 d 2001
St Andrew's Church
1932 Sunderland 0
1933 1938 Gateshead 158 12
1939 (Gateshead) (3)

Ions, William Thomas IL
b Newcastle q1 1903 d 1975
Bedlington United
White-le-Head Rangers
West Stanley
Newcastle United Swifts
Annfield Plain
Preston Colliery
1928 Ashington 21 2
St Peter's Albion
Crook Town

Ireland, Robert Johnstone (Bob) RH
b Darvel 22/7/1900 d 1962
Darvel
Rangers
Peebles Rovers (loan)
1930 Liverpool 1
St Johnstone
Brechin City (loan)
Workington
Airdrieonians

Ireland, Walter CF
b Clitheroe q2 1904
Rossendale United
1927 Crewe Alexandra 3
1928 Accrington Stanley 0
Lancaster Town

Iremonger, Albert GK
b Wilford, Nottinghamshire 15/6/1884 d 1958
Caps: FLge 2
1903 Nottingham Forest (trial) 0
Nottingham Jardines Athletic
1904 1925 Notts County 564
1926 Lincoln City 35

Iremonger, Harold (Harry) GK
b Wilford, Nottinghamshire q1 1894 d 1957
1913 1914 Nottingham Forest 11

Iremonger, James (Jim) LB/RB/GK
b Norton, West Yorkshire 5/3/1876 d 1956
Caps: FLge 4/England 2
Wilford
Nottingham Jardines Athletic
1895 1909 Nottingham Forest 276 2

Iremonger, James GK
b Wilford, Nottinghamshire 5/6/1901 d 1980
Clifton Colliery
1924 Hull City 1

Ironmonger, Sidney OR
b Lincoln 19/1/1896 d 1977
1919 Lincoln City 3 1
Grantham
Newark Town

Irvine, Albert Walter RB
b Newcastle 7/5/1898 d 1975
Walker Celtic
Mid-Rhondda
1920 Grimsby Town 3
Boston Town

Irvine, George Wilson (Peter) RB
b Barrow q1 1889 d 1952
Barrow St Luke's
Barrow
West Ham United
Barrow
1921 Chesterfield 20
Shirebrook

From To Apps Goal

Irvine, Joseph CF
1891 Accrington 16 7

Irvine, Joseph (Joe) OL
Distillery
Port Glasgow Athletic
Johnstone
Abercorn
Thornliebank
1904 1905 Glossop 48 6
Hamilton Academical
Morton
Johnstone

Irvine, Robert William (Bobby) IR/IL/CF
b Lisburn 29/4/1900 d 1979
Caps: IrLge 2/Ireland 15
Dunmurry
1921 1927 Everton 199 54
1927 1929 Portsmouth 35 10
Chester
Connah's Quay & Shotton
Derry City
1933 Watford 22 2
Waterford
Brideville

Irvine, Thomas Bennett (Tommy) IL
b Dreghorn 6/7/1898 d 1964
Springside
Dreghorn
1922 Luton Town 8
Bedford Town
Dreghorn
Ayr United

Irving, John IR
b 1867 d 1942
Queen of the South Wanderers
1892 1894 Lincoln City 44 9
Newark Town
1896 Lincoln City 7 1

Irving, Joseph LH
b Hobson 1898
Langley Park
1921 Preston North End 15
1922 Arsenal 0
1925 Aberdare Athletic 8

Irving, Samuel Johnstone (Sam) RH/IR
b Belfast 28/8/1894 d 1969
Caps: Ireland 18
Shildon Athletic
1910 Newcastle United (trial) 0
Galashiels United
Esh Winning
1913 1914 Bristol City 18 4
Blyth Spartans
Shildon Athletic
Dundee
1926 1927 Cardiff City 47 3
1927 1931 Chelsea 89 5
1932 Bristol Rovers 21 1
Brechin City

Irwin, George William GK
b Smethwick 7/1/1891
1920 West Bromwich Albion 0
1921 1922 Crystal Palace 17
1923 Reading 36
Brierley Hill Alliance
Worcester City
Brierley Hill Alliance

Isaac, Arthur Hector M IR
b Swansea q2 1902
Ealing Association
1924 Brentford 2 1
Corinthians
Casuals
Ealing Celtic

Isaac, James (Jimmy) IR/IL/OR
b Cramlington 23/10/1916 d 1993
Cramlington
1936 1938 Huddersfield Town 33 8
1939 (Huddersfield Town) (3)
1945 1946 Bradford City 24 3
1947 1948 Hartlepools United 56 9

Isaac, William James (Bill) IL
b Tynemouth q3 1918 d 1941
1938 Newcastle United 0
1939 Brighton & Hove Albion (3)

Isherwood, Harold (Harry) LB
b Darwen 1901
Fleetwood
1925 Sunderland 0
1926 Birmingham 1
1928 Bournemouth & Boscombe Ath 18
Worcester City

From To Apps Goal

Islip, Ernest (Ernie) IL/CF
b Parkwood Springs 31/10/1892 d 1941
Sheffield Douglas
1913 1923 Huddersfield Town 152 44
1923 1926 Birmingham 83 23
1927 Bradford City 6 1
Kidderminster Harriers
Ashton National
1928 Wrexham 14 1

Ison, Ernest (Ernie) OL
b Hartshill 12/6/1903 d 1983
Nuneaton Town
1925 1930 Brighton & Hove Albion 16
1931 Southport 10 1
1932 Watford 3 1
Ramsgate

Iverson, Robert Thomas James (Bob) LH/IR/RH
b Folkestone 17/10/1910 d 1953
Folkestone
1932 Tottenham Hotspur 0
Northfleet
Ramsgate Press Wanderers
1933 1934 Lincoln City 41 13
1934 1936 Wolverhampton Wanderers 35 7
1936 1947 Aston Villa 135 9
1939 (Aston Villa) (3)

Ives, Albert Edward (Bert) LB
b Newcastle 18/12/1908 d 1980
Spen Black & White
1932 1933 Sunderland 12
1935 1937 Barnsley 9
Blyth Spartans

Ives, Arthur LB
b Lincoln 23/10/1910 d 1984
1932 Sunderland 0
Gainsborough Trinity
1934 Rochdale 7
Worcester City
Evesham Town

Ives, Charles Benjamin (Ben) OL
b Tottenham q1 1888 d 1962
Page Green Old Boys
Romford
Tufnell Park
1910 Tottenham Hotspur 0
Barrow
Exeter City
Queen's Park Rangers
1919 Clapton Orient 17 4
Ton Pentre

Ivey, Lawrence Albert CH
b Abingdon 5/10/1900 d 1969
Sutton United
1927 Crystal Palace 1
Sutton United
Metropolitan Police

Ivill, Edward (Teddy) RB/LB
b Little Hulton 7/12/1898 d 1979
New Lester Colliery
Brookhouses
Williams Temperance
Boothstown
1922 Bolton Wanderers 0
Atherton
1924 1932 Oldham Athletic 276 2
1932 Wolverhampton Wanderers 4
1932 1934 Charlton Athletic 35
1935 1936 Accrington Stanley 16
Clitheroe

Ivison, Noel Wilson IR
b Keswick 25/12/1903 d 1991
Keswick
Workington
1925 Barrow 12 1
Lancaster Town
Whitehaven
Millom

Ivory, George William Albert IR
b Sittingbourne 21/4/1910 d 1992
Sheppey United
1932 Millwall 3 2
1933 York City 31 9
1934 Tottenham Hotspur 0
Sittingbourne

Izon, Charles John CF/OL
b Aston q3 1872
Old Hill Wanderers
Halesowen
1893 1896 Small Heath 25 8
1897 Walsall 7

From To Apps Goal

Izon, Denis George LH/CH
b Colwich 1/4/1907 d 1967
Rugeley
Colwich
1929 1931 Port Vale 17
Hyde United
Stafford Rangers

Izzard, William (Bill) OR
b Hitchin q3 1911
Royal Tank Corps
1932 1934 Aldershot 52 7
Courages (Alton)

Jack, Archibald OL
b Grangemouth 15/8/1889
Forth Rangers
Falkirk
1919 South Shields 7 1

Jack, David Bone Nightingale IR/CF
b Bolton 3/4/1898 d 1958
Caps: FLge 5/England 9
Plymouth Presbyterians
1920 Plymouth Argyle 14 3
1920 1928 Bolton Wanderers 295 144
1928 1933 Arsenal 181 113
1936 Southend United 0

Jack, Robert (Bob) OL
b Alloa 2/4/1876 d 1943
Alloa Athletic
1895 1900 Bolton Wanderers 110 29
1901 Preston North End 22 6
1902 Glossop 30 6
Plymouth Argyle
Southend United
Plymouth Argyle

Jack, Robert Rollo (Rollo) IR/OR/CF
b Bolton 4/4/1902 d 1994
Argyle Juniors
1922 1923 Plymouth Argyle 15 4
1923 1928 Bolton Wanderers 29 9
1929 1931 Clapton Orient 79 22
Yeovil & Petters United
1934 Swindon Town 20 2

Jack, Samuel CF
b Scotland 1884
Arthurlie
Third Lanark
1907 Grimsby Town 1

Jack, Walter Robert IL
b Grangemouth 1875
Leith Athletic
Bristol Rovers
1904 West Bromwich Albion 25 13
Clyde

Jacketts, George Arthur LH
b Hull q2 1887 d 1957
Hull Tivoli
1919 Hull City 2
Ebbw Vale
Bridlington Town
Holderness Athletic

Jacklin, Alfred LH
b Lincoln q4 1883 d 1951
Lincoln Liberal Club
1903 Lincoln City 3

Jacklin, Harold GK
b Chesterfield 6/2/1897 d 1966
1919 Blackpool 1
1920 1921 Leeds United 3
1923 1925 Doncaster Rovers 63

Jacklin, Thomas Henry (Harry) IR/IL
b Lincoln q1 1882 d 1949
Adelaide (Lincoln)
1902 1904 Gainsborough Trinity 49 15
Newark

Jackson, A LB
1892 Lincoln City 2
Lindum

Jackson, Albert CF
1921 Stalybridge Celtic 1

Jackson, Albert R RB
Ward End
1921 Walsall 18

From To Apps Goal

Jackson, Alexander Skinner (Alex) OR
b Renton 12/5/1905 d 1946
Caps: Scotland 17
Renton Victoria
Shawfield Juniors
Dumbarton
Bethlehem Steel
Aberdeen
1925 1930 Huddersfield Town 179 70
1930 1931 Chelsea 65 26
Ashton National
Margate
Nice
Le Touquet Olympique
Nimes

Jackson, Alfred Clement (Clem) RB
b Kimberley q3 1886 d 1960
Kimberley St John's
Eastwood Rangers
1909 1919 Lincoln City 184

Jackson, Alfred Gordon (Alf) OL
b Bradford 30/1/1920 d 2000
1938 Halifax Town 3

Jackson, Archibald (Archie) CH
b Plumstead 25/1/1901 d 1985
Rutherglen Glencairn
1922 1923 Sunderland 6
1924 Southend United 0
Third Lanark
Chester
1928 1929 Tranmere Rovers 37
1930 Accrington Stanley 0
1930 Walsall 0
1930 Southport 0
Northwich Victoria
Manchester North End
Rossendale United

Jackson, Bertram Harold LB
b Manchester q4 1882 d 1940
Luton Town
1907 1910 Manchester City 91
Stalybridge Celtic

Jackson, Ernest RB/LB
b Sheffield 1903
Stag Athletic
Boston Town
1925 1926 Grimsby Town 20
Mansfield Town
Wombwell
Hathersage

Jackson, Ernest RH
b Sheffield 11/6/1914 d 1996
1930 Sheffield Wednesday 0
1930 Grimsby Town (trial) 0
Atlas & Norfolk
1932 1948 Sheffield United 229 8
1939 (Sheffield United) (3)
Boston United

Jackson, George RB
b Liverpool 14/1/1911 d 2002
Walton Parish Church
1933 Everton 0
Marine (loan)
1934 1947 Everton 75
Caernarvon Town

Jackson, George Alexander LB/RB
b Liverpool 17/6/1893 d 1985
Pontypridd
1921 1922 Merthyr Town 49
1923 1929 Tranmere Rovers 104
South Liverpool

Jackson, Harold LB/OR
b Halifax 20/7/1917 d 1996
Sowerby Bridge
1936 1946 Halifax Town 83 3
1939 (Halifax Town) (3)
1947 Stockport County 2

Jackson, Harry CF
b Nottingham 23/4/1864
Sneinton Wanderers
1888 Notts County 5 3
Nottingham Forest

Jackson, Henry IL
1935 Millwall 8 1

Jackson, Horace LB
b Wrexham 21/11/1905 d 1977
New Broughton
Chester
Middlewich
Rhyl Athletic
1930 Wrexham 1
Gwersyllt

From To Apps Goal

Jackson, Horace OL
1931 Rotherham United 1

Jackson, J Thomas CF
b Padiham
Padiham
1897 1898 Blackburn Rovers 26 10

Jackson, James LH/LB
1897 1898 Darwen 9

Jackson, James (Jimmy) LB
b Cambuslang 15/9/1875
Hamilton Academical
Adamstown Rosebuds (Australia)
Newton Thistle
Cambuslang
Rangers
1897 1898 Newcastle United 58
1899 1904 Woolwich Arsenal 183
Leyton
West Ham United
Rangers

Jackson, (Rev) James (Jimmy) RB/CH/LB
b Newcastle 4/12/1899
Caps: SLge 1/FLge 1
Queen's Park Strollers
Queen's Park
Motherwell
Aberdeen
1925 1932 Liverpool 212 2

Jackson, James Herbert CF
b Bollington 27/12/1897 d 1964
Bollington Cross
Macclesfield
1921 Derby County 13 4
Bollington Cross
1923 1927 Norwich City 111 54

Jackson, James Robert (Bob) CF
b Farnworth 14/4/1896 d 1968
Caton Engineering
Lancaster Town
Darwen
White Lund
Lancaster YMCA
Lancaster Town
1923 Bury 0
1924 Tranmere Rovers 6 1
Northwich Victoria
1926 Nelson 0

Jackson, Jeremiah (Jerry) OR
b Burnley 1876 d 1927
1900 Burnley 0
1923 Sheffield Wednesday 1

Jackson, John GK
1892 Bootle 1

Jackson, John (Johnny) GK
b Glasgow 29/11/1906 d 1965
Caps: SLge 4/Scotland 8
Kirkintilloch Rob Roy
Partick Thistle
1933 1938 Chelsea 49
Guildford City

Jackson, John Bertram IR
b Dalry 21/6/1890
Caps: SLge 1
Ardeer Thistle
Clyde
Celtic (loan)
Celtic (loan)
1913 1914 Leeds City 54 10
Ayr United (loan)
Clyde (loan)
Rangers (loan)
Celtic
Clydebank (loan)
Motherwell
Dundee
Stevenston United (loan)

Jackson, Richard RB
b Spennymoor 4/7/1900
Crook Town
1922 1931 Rotherham County 344 1
1932 1933 Gillingham 63
Canterbury Waverley

Jackson, Richard William (Dicky) LH
b Middlesbrough q1 1877
Ripley Athletic
Middlesbrough
1898 1904 Sunderland 162 10
Portsmouth
Darlington

From To Apps Goal

Jackson, Robert Gristwood (Bob) CH/LH/RB
b Cornsay 12/5/1915 d 1991
Stanley United
1935 1947 Southend United 93
Folkestone Town

Jackson, Samuel (Sam) OL
b Belfast q3 1900
Caps: Ireland Amateur/ IrLge 2
Distillery
Cliftonville
1920 1921 Swansea Town 6 1
1922 Barnsley 1
Barn
Portadown
Ards
Broadway United

Jackson, T Andrew CH
b Paisley 1891 d 1918
Ardrossan Rovers
1910 1914 Middlesbrough 123 3

Jackson, Thomas (Tom) IL
b Sunderland q2 1896
Sunderland West End
1919 Burnley 1
Dundee
1921 West Ham United 3 1
Jarrow

Jackson, Thomas (Tommy) GK
b Benwell Village 6/3/1897 d 1973
Rutherford College Old Boys
Durham University
1920 1929 Aston Villa 172
Kidderminster Harriers

Jackson, Thomas F (Tom) IL
1920 Reading 2 2

Jackson, Thomas John CF
1899 Glossop 3

Jackson, Walter E CF/OR
b Renton 19/1/1897
Yoker Athletic
Kilmarnock
Bethlehem Steel
Aberdeen
1925 1926 Preston North End 45 13
Bethlehem Steel
Philadelphia Centennials (loan)

Jackson, Walter S OR
b Birmingham 1870
Harborne
1893 Small Heath 4 1
Berwick Rangers (Worcester)

Jackson, Wilbert (Peter) CH/RH/LH
b Luddenden Foot 4/8/1904 d 1986
Luddenden Foot
Hebden Bridge
1924 1933 Stoke 72 1
Congleton Town
1934 Southend United 3

Jackson, William (Billy) OL/OR
b Farnworth 5/7/1902 d 1974
Leyland
Altrincham
Darwen
1924 Sunderland 0
1925 1926 Leeds United 38 2
1927 West Ham United 2
1927 1930 Chelsea 26 6
1931 Leicester City 4
Ashford Town (Kent)
1932 1933 Bristol Rovers 37 14
1934 Cardiff City 12
1934 Watford 4 1
Chorley
Netherfield

Jackson, William RB/LB
b Earlestown
Witton Albion
1936 Tranmere Rovers 7
1937 1938 Stockport County 11

Jackson, William H (Bill) CF
b Oldbury 1894 d 1917
Oldbury Town
Langley St Michael's
1912 West Bromwich Albion 3

From To Apps Goal

Jackson, William James IL
b Flint 27/1/1876 d 1954
Caps: Wales 1
Flint
Rhyl
Flint
St Helens Recreation
1899 1900 Newton Heath 61 11
Barrow
1903 1904 Burnley 22 6
Flint
Wrexham

Jackson, William Kennedy (Billy) CF
b Renton 24/12/1900 d 1986
Vale of Leven
Duntocher Hibs
1921 Everton 0
1922 1923 Wrexham 52 10
Vale of Leven
Aberdeen
Vale of Leven

Jacobson, Hugh (Hughie) LB
b Hepscott 20/2/1903 d 1974
Newbiggin Athletic
Blyth Spartans
1925 1934 Grimsby Town 360 1
1935 1936 Doncaster Rovers 43

Jacques, Robert (Robin) CF
b Newcastle q1 1897 d 1923
RAF
West Norwood
1922 Clapton Orient 4 2
1923 Fulham 0

Jacques, Thomas Edgar (Edgar) CH/LH
b Skipton 13/11/1890 d 1968
Victoria Cross
Blackburn Trinity
Mill Hill Woodfold
Accrington Stanley
Darwen
Blackburn Trinity
1912 Blackburn Rovers 2
1921 Nelson 17 1
Great Harwood
Barnoldswick Park Villa
Earby

Jacques, William (Bill) GK
b Erith 8/12/1888 d 1925
Gravesend United
Coventry City
1914 1922 Tottenham Hotspur 123

Jakeman, George John William RH/RB/LH
b Small Heath 19/5/1903 d 1973
Wolseley Motor Works
Metropolitan Carriage Works
1924 1928 Aston Villa 8
1929 1932 Notts County 70
Kidderminster Harriers
Cradley Heath

James, Albert Edward OL
b Redcar
Clulows
1933 Hartlepools United 0
1936 Darlington 3
1937 Chesterfield 0
1938 Torquay United 31 2
1939 Crystal Palace 0

James, Alexander Wilson (Alex) IL
b Mossend 14/9/1901 d 1953
Caps: Scotland 8
Brandon Amateurs
Orbiston Celtic
Bellshill Athletic
Glasgow Ashfield
Motherwell (trial)
Raith Rovers
1925 1928 Preston North End 147 53
1929 1936 Arsenal 231 26

James, Alfred OR
1923 Cardiff City 0
1924 Merthyr Town (trial) 3

James, Andrew Foster (Andy) IL
b Lemington 31/12/1902 d 1986
Blucher
Crawcrook Albion
1926 Middlesbrough 0
1927 Southport 17 3
Peterborough & Fletton United
Scunthorpe & Lindsey United

James, David (Dai) OR/IL/IR
b Aberdare 16/11/1890
1921 1926 Aberdare Athletic 171 16
1926 1928 Brighton & Hove Albion 30 8

From To Apps Goal

James, David (Dai) CF
b Swansea 29/9/1917 d 1981
Midland Athletic (Morriston)
1935 Leeds United 0
1936 Bradford City 5
Mossley
1939 Chelsea (3) (1)
1947 Swansea Town 12 7
Haverfordwest Athletic

James, E IL
1893 Northwich Victoria 1

James, Ernest John (Jack) LH
b Wednesbury 25/3/1883 d 1956
Wednesbury Brunswick
Darlaston
1905 Wolverhampton Wanderers 17
Wednesbury Old Athletic

James, Evan GK
b London
1929 Merthyr Town 4
Clapton
1929 Southend United 1

James, Francis Edward (Frank) CF
b Brownhills 1888
1907 West Bromwich Albion
Whitchurch
Halesowen
1909 Manchester City 2
Exeter City

James, George CF
Aberaman
1933 Swansea Town 4 1
Aberaman

James, George Charles CF
b Oldbury 14/2/1899 d 1976
Bilston United
1921 1928 West Bromwich Albion 106 52
1929 Reading 19 7
1929 1932 Watford 82 68

James, Griffith GK
b Cwmaman
1923 Aberdare Athletic 16

James, Joseph (Joe) CH
b Battersea 13/1/1910 d 1993
Battersea Church
1931 1938 Brentford 240 2
1939 (Brentford) (3)

James, Lancelot (Lance) RB/LB
b Nottingham 11/1/1890 d 1983
1910 1913 Notts County 6

James, Norman Leslie CH
b Bootle 25/3/1908 d 1985
Bootle St James
Braby's Athletic
1930 1932 Liverpool 8
1933 1935 Bradford City 4
1936 1938 Queen's Park Rangers 68 1

James, Ralph GK
b Crewe q2 1875 d 1948
1900 Preston North End 3

James, Robert Kenneth IR
b Merthyr Tydfil 16/1/1901 d 1984
1923 Merthyr Town 1

James, Robert William LB
b Bow q1 1896
Royal Ordnance
1920 Millwall Athletic 0
1921 Barrow 8
Woolwich
Bexleyheath Town

James, Roland William (Roly) LH/RH/CF
b Smethwick 4/5/1897 d 1979
Smethwick Highfield
1920 1921 West Bromwich Albion 9 4
1922 1923 Brentford 35 1
1924 1927 Stockport County 33 3
Manchester Central
Stalybridge Celtic

James, Sidney CF/LH
b Sheffield d 1916
Bird-in-Hand
1913 1914 Huddersfield Town 12 2

James, Walter John W CF
b Stratford 8/10/1904 d 1971
1927 1928 Crystal Palace 4 1
1929 Merthyr Town 1

From To Apps Goal

James, Wilfred Bernard (Wilf) IL/RH/CF
b Cross Keys 19/2/1907 d 1996
Caps: Wales 2
Abercarn Welfare
Ynysddu Crusaders
1925 1926 Newport County 19 8
Thorne Colliery
Owston Park Rangers
1928 1929 Notts County 16 5
1930 1931 West Ham United 40 7
1931 1932 Charlton Athletic 28 3
Workington
1935 1936 Carlisle United 39 4

James, William Ebsworth (Billy) OL/CF/IL
b Stockton q1 1892 d 1960
Eston United
1910 1912 Middlesbrough 24 8
1920 Portsmouth 22 3
1920 1921 West Ham United 54 7

Jameson, Joseph Burn (Joe) RH/RB
b Newcastle q2 1882 d 1948
Wallsend Park Villa
1906 1908 Sheffield Wednesday 7
Castleford Town
Newcastle City
Hartlepools United

Jameson, Percy CF
b Sunderland 21/7/1917 d 1981
1937 Sunderland 0
1938 Darlington 1

Jamieson, Harold John IL/IR/OR
b Wallsend 9/12/1908
Wallsend United
1928 Bradford City 2
Crawcrook Albion
1929 Crystal Palace 4
1930 1931 Gillingham 17 1
Kilwinning Rangers

Jamieson, James (Jimmy) LH
b Lockerbie 3/11/1867
1892 Everton 14
1893 1898 Sheffield Wednesday 125 3

Jamieson, John Pretsel (Jock) IL
b Newtongrange 9/12/1898 d 1974
Lochgelly United
1921 1922 Halifax Town 17 4
St Bernard's

Jamieson, R CF
1889 Everton 1
Bootle

Jaques, George H OL
b Rushden 1875
Rushden
1893 Woolwich Arsenal 2 2

Jardine, David GK
b Scotland 1868
Mid Annandale
Bootle
1890 1893 Everton 37
Nelson

Jardine, Robert J (Bob) OL/IL
b Partick 1864 d 1941
Halliwell
1888 Notts County 18 9
Heanor Town
1889 Derby County 1 1
Nottingham Forest
Heanor Town
Sheffield United
Mellors United

Jarps, Joseph Henry (Joe) GK
b Hartlepool 14/5/1907 d 1955
Hartlepool St James'
West Hartlepool Perseverance
1931 Hartlepools United 2
Blackhall Colliery Welfare

Jarrett, George CF/IL
1900 Stockport County 1
Hooley Hill
1901 Manchester City 1

Jarrett, Richard Herbert OR
b Corwen q4 1870
Caps: Wales 2
Ruthin
Rhyl
Ardwick
1890 Bolton Wanderers 5
Ruthin

From To Apps Goal

Jarvie, Gavin LH
b Newton, Lanarkshire 1879
Cambuslang Rangers
Airdrieonians
Bristol Rovers
1907 1911 Sunderland 93 2
Hamilton Academical

Jarvie, John GK
b Old Monkland 19/10/1900 d 1985
Tannochside United
Bellshill Athletic
Third Lanark
1925 Leicester City 5
1926 1927 Portsmouth 4
1927 Southend United 13
1929 Watford 0
1929 Norwich City 42
Chester
Shrewsbury Town
Solus

Jarvis, Ambrose GK
b Kenilworth 20/4/1895 d 1980
Edgewick
1919 Coventry City 3
Nuneaton Town

Jarvis, George Henry CF/RH
b Glasgow 3/12/1889 d 1969
Glasgow Benburb
Cambuslang Rangers
Celtic
Motherwell (loan)
Vale of Leven (loan)
Ayr United (loan)
Ayr United (loan)
Clyde (loan)
St Mirren (loan)
Falkirk (loan)
Clydebank (loan)
Stevenston United (loan)
1919 1920 Stoke 32 10
Clydebank
Dunfermline Athletic
Ayr United
Ayr Fort

Jarvis, Harold RH
b Manchester q3 1895
Caps: England Sch
1919 1920 Manchester City 2

Jarvis, Leonard Richard (Len) LH/CH
b Grays q2 1884
West Ham United
1909 1911 Bury 55

Jarvis, Sidney (Sid) RB/LB
b Sheffield q4 1905 d 1994
Ecclesall Church
Nether Edge Amateurs
1925 Hull City 0
1926 Darlington 0
Kettering Town
Raith Rovers
1927 1934 Middlesbrough 86 1
Dunkerque
1936 Darlington 0

Jarvis, Thomas Richard (Richard) GK
b 1881 d 1924
Whitwick White Cross
1903 1904 Sheffield Wednesday 6
St Leonards United
Luton Town

Jasper, Frederick Sampson OR
b Camelford 11/11/1910 d 1979
Budleigh Salterton
1933 Exeter City 1
Budleigh Salterton

Jay, James (Jimmy) LH
b Kingswood q3 1879 d 1927
Bristol East
1901 1902 Bristol City 21 4
Brentford

Jeacock, Thomas LH/OR
b Hinckley q4 1866
Mellors Ltd
Nottingham Forest
1892 Burton Swifts 2
1894 Nottingham Forest 1

Jeavons, William LH
b Wolverhampton
Hurst Hill
1907 1908 Wolverhampton Wanderers 8
Dudley Town
Halesowen

From To Apps Goal

Jeavons, William Henry (Billy) OR
b Woodhouse Mill 9/2/1912 d 1992
Woodhouse Working Mens Club
Woodhouse Brunswick
1930 Huddersfield Town (trial) 0
1931 Chesterfield 4
1932 Burnley 1
1933 Accrington Stanley 17 7
1933 Oldham Athletic 3 1
1934 Southport 16 1
1935 Wrexham 2
Shrewsbury Town
Burton Town
Worcester City

Jebb, Alfred James (Alf) LH/RH
b Hyson Green q2 1886 d 1931
Ilkeston United
1909 1911 Barnsley 9
Watford

Jee, Joseph William (Joe) OL
b Chorlton-cum-Hardy q1 1883 d 1959
1907 Bolton Wanderers 6 1
Brighton & Hove Albion
1910 1914 Huddersfield Town 171 30
Nelson

Jefferies, Charles Edward (Charlie) IR/OL
b Swindon 27/12/1906 d 1986
Swindon Corinthians
1926 1927 Swindon Town 5 3
1928 Charlton Athletic 0
Bath City

Jefferies, Sydney William (Syd) GK
b Hackney q4 1897
Green & Siley Weir
1921 Southend United 2

Jefferis, Frank IR/IL
b Fordingbridge 3/7/1884 d 1938
Caps: England 2
Fordingbridge Turks
Southampton
1910 1919 Everton 125 22
1919 1922 Preston North End 79 12
1923 1924 Southport 52 6
1925 Preston North End 0
1926 Southport 2 1

Jefferson, Arthur LB/RB
b Goldthorpe 14/12/1916 d 1997
Goldthorpe Working Mens Club
Peterborough United
1936 1949 Queen's Park Rangers 211 1
1939 (Queen's Park Rangers) (3)
1949 1954 Aldershot 170

Jefferson, Robert William (Bob) OR/IR
b Sunderland 6/1882 d 1966
Caps: SoLge 11
Sunderland Royal Rovers
1904 1905 Bradford City 30 6
1906 1907 Leeds City 17 5
1920 1921 Swindon Town 54 7
Bath City

Jeffery, Alfred Howard (Alf) OL
b Sheffield 3/1895 d 1921
Trinity Wesleyans
1919 Sheffield United 4 2

Jeffery, Harold (Harry) RB
b Newcastle 3/1867 d 1930
Newcastle West End
Drysdale (Newcastle)
1890 Sunderland 0
Third Lanark
Newcastle West End
Newcastle East End
1893 1894 Newcastle United 45 4
South Shields

Jeffery, William Walls LB/RB
b Dalderby q1 1866 d 1932
West Manchester
Horncastle
Lincoln City
Boston Town
Grimsby Town
Gainsborough Trinity
Lincoln City
1891 Burnley 7
1893 Woolwich Arsenal 22
Southampton St Mary's

Jeffes, Albert Stanley (Bert) RH
b Liverpool 20/10/1897 d 1974
Orrell
1921 Liverpool 0
1922 Everton 0
1923 Barnsley 5
1924 Tranmere Rovers 15
Bangor City

From To Apps Goal

Jeffrey, George IL
b Motherwell 15/8/1916 d 1979
Wishaw Juniors
1937 Tottenham Hotspur 1 1
Motherwell

Jeffrey, William Alexander H (Alec) CH
b Madeley, Shropshire q3 1875 d 1934
Bacup
Madeley Institute
Wrockwardine Wood
Wellington Town
Ashford United
Watford
1901 1902 Stockport County 43
Dudley
Heckmondwike

Jeffries, Alfred (Alf) OR
b Bishop Auckland 27/9/1915 d 2004
Leasingthorne Colliery Welfare
Willington
1934 Norwich City 0
1935 1936 Bradford City 55 11
1936 1938 Derby County 15 1
1939 Sheffield United (3)
Basingstoke Town

Jeffs, Thomas Edmond LB/RB
b Peterborough 3/8/1900 d 1971
Rugby Town
1921 1927 Northampton Town 143

Jenkins, Edward Jonathan (Eddie) LH/RB/LB
b Cardiff 16/7/1909 d 2005
Caps: Wales Sch
Cardiff East
1930 1933 Cardiff City 77
1934 Bristol City 10
1935 Newport County 34

Jenkins, Edwin Samuel (Eddie) LH/CH
b Cardiff 6/7/1895 d 1976
Caps: WLge 4/Wales Amat/Wales 1
Cardiff Corinthians
1921 1923 Cardiff City 12
Lovells Athletic
1925 Cardiff City 0
1926 Bristol City 0
Lovells Athletic

Jenkins, Eric Trevor CF
b Wallasey 31/7/1904 d 1972
1925 New Brighton 0
1931 New Brighton 1

Jenkins, Evan Thomas OR
b Ynyshir 26/6/1906 d 1990
Denaby United
1928 1929 Lincoln City 30 12
1930 1932 Burnley 66 16
1933 Lincoln City 14 1
1933 Barnsley 0
1934 York City 28 10
Crittall Athletic

Jenkins, John (Jack) LB/RB
b Gwersyllt 20/3/1892 d 1946
Caps: SoLge 1/Wales 8
Mold Town
Mardy
Wrexham
Gwersyllt
Pontypridd
Mardy
Pontypridd
1922 1928 Brighton & Hove Albion 216 4
Brighton Hotels

Jenkins, John Edward (Eddie) OR
b Aberfan
1924 Merthyr Town 2

Jenkins, Reginald (Reg) OR
Chester
1926 Lincoln City 5
Chester

Jenkins, Richard George Christopher OR
b Chelsea 27/11/1903 d 1978
Caps: England Amat
London Polytechnic
London University
1924 Chelsea 4
Corinthians
Oxford University
Casuals

Jenkins, S Harold OR
b Newport
Risca
1924 Newport County 3 1
Ebbw Vale

From To Apps Goal

Jenkins, Thomas W OR
b Merthyr Tydfil
Cyfarthfa Stars
1926 Merthyr Town 20 1
1927 Exeter City 4
1928 Southend United 0

Jenkins, Walter LB
b Chesterfield q3 1905
Staveley Town
1928 Coventry City 6
Staveley Town

Jenkinson, Frederick (Fred) LB/RB
b Chapeltown 7/4/1910 d 1990
Chapeltown
Intake WMC
1928 Sheffield United (trial) 0
1929 Huddersfield Town 0
Intake WMC
1931 1938 Stockport County 269 1
1939 Bury 0

Jenkinson, Matthew (Matt 'Sailor') OR/IR
b Filey 31/10/1906 d 1979
Filey Town
Scarborough
1930 1931 York City 18 6
Scarborough
1932 1933 York City 54 14
Filey Town
Scarborough
Filey Town

Jenkinson, Thomas Henry OL
b Bradford 15/5/1895 d 1974
Wapping
1914 Bradford City 1
Halifax Town

Jenkinson, Thomas Iddo OR
b Sheffield q2 1877 d 1949
Sheffield Heeley
1896 Gainsborough Trinity 0
1897 Sheffield United 2
1898 1900 Grimsby Town 66 24

Jenkinson, William (Bill) CF/LB
b Chesterfield 1877
Antwerp
1898 1900 Burnley 33 11
West Ham United
1903 Burnley 17 1
Colne

Jenkinson, William CH/CF
b Wombwell 1883
Wombwell Town
1901 1910 Gainsborough Trinity 280 14

Jenkinson, William (Bill) RB/LB
b Golborne 2/3/1892 d 1967
Golborne United
1912 Manchester City (trial) 0
South Liverpool
St Helens Recreation
Nelson
1919 Liverpool 13
1921 Wigan Borough 11
Wallasey United

Jenkyns, Caesar Augustus Llewellyn CH
b Builth Wells 24/8/1866 d 1941
Caps: Wales 8
Builth
Small Heath St Andrew's
Walsall Swifts
Unity Gas
1892 1894 Small Heath 75 11
1895 Woolwich Arsenal 27 6
1896 1897 Newton Heath 35 5
1897 1900 Walsall 80 2
Coventry City
Unity Gas
Saltley Wednesday

Jennings, Alfred W (Alf) OR
b Finsbury Park 30/5/1904 d 1994
Barnet
Granville (Sydney)
1922 Tottenham Hotspur 0
Poole
1926 Oldham Athletic 2
Poole

From To Apps Goal

Jennings, Dennis Bernard OR/LB/IR
b Habberley 20/7/1910 d 1996
Franche (Kidderminster)
St Barnabas
Foley Park
Stourport Swifts
Romsley Village
1927 West Bromwich Albion 0
Kidderminster Harriers
1930 1932 Huddersfield Town 33 5
1932 1935 Grimsby Town 99 29
1935 1949 Birmingham 192 12
Kidderminster Harriers
Lockheed Leamington

Jennings, Henry William (Bill) CF/IR
b Norwich 7/1/1920 d 1969
1938 1946 Northampton Town 11 2
1939 (Northampton Town) (3)
1947 1950 Ipswich Town 102 41
1951 Rochdale 3 1
1951 Crystal Palace 0

Jennings, John (Jack) RB/RH/LB
b Platt Bridge 27/8/1902 d 1997
Caps: WLge 1
Platt Bridge Wesleyans
1923 1924 Wigan Borough 47 1
1925 1929 Cardiff City 94
1929 1936 Middlesbrough 195 10
1936 Preston North End 19 1
1937 Bradford City 28

Jennings, Percy RB/LB
b Consett 27/3/1907 d 1996
Consett
1929 Blackpool 3
1930 1931 Clapton Orient 19
Annfield Plain
Consett

Jennings, Samuel (Sam) CF/IR/IL
b Cinderhill 18/12/1898 d 1944
Coldstream Guards
Basford United
Norwich City
1919 1920 Middlesbrough 10 2
1921 1923 Reading 110 45
1924 West Ham United 9 3
1924 1927 Brighton & Hove Albion 110 61
1928 Nottingham Forest 27 15
1929 1931 Port Vale 63 42
1931 Stockport County 14 2
1931 Burnley 6 2
Olympique Marseille
Club Francais
Scarborough
(Switzerland)

Jennings, Thomas Hamilton Oliver (Tomn CF
b Strathaven 8/3/1902 d 1973
Strathaven Academy
Earnock Rovers
Glasgow Ashfield
Cadzow St Anne's
1919 Tottenham Hotspur (trial) 0
Raith Rovers
1924 1930 Leeds United 167 112
1931 1932 Chester 48 33
Bangor City

Jennings, Walter GK
b Grimsby 20/10/1897 d 1970
Welholme Old Boys
1919 Grimsby Town 2
1920 1921 Swansea Town 3
1922 Southend United 15
Boston Town
1925 Blackpool 4

Jennings, Walter Henry (Wally) RH/RB/CH
b Bristol 1/4/1909 d 1993
Caps: WLge 1
1926 Bristol Rovers 0
1927 Blackburn Rovers (trial) 0
South Bristol COB
1929 1933 Bristol City 122 1
Cheltenham Town
1934 1935 Cardiff City 30
Bristol St George

Jennings, William (Billy) LH/LB/RB
b Barry 25/2/1893 d 1968
Caps: Wales Sch/Wales 11
Barry
Bethel Baptists
Barry
1912 1929 Bolton Wanderers 267 2

From To Apps Goal

Jennings, William (Bill) CH
b Cinderhill 25/2/1891 d 1953
Rigby Athletic
Arnold St Mary's
1913 1914 Notts County 42
Norwich City
1920 1921 Merthyr Town 66 3
1922 1925 Luton Town 114 2
1926 Northampton Town 3
Peterborough & Fletton United
Hearts of Winnipeg

Jephcott, Alan Claude (Claude) OR
b Smethwick 31/10/1890 d 1950
Caps: FLge 2
Olive Mount
Brierley Hill Alliance
Stourbridge
Brierley Hill Alliance
1911 1922 West Bromwich Albion 174 15

Jepson, Albert Edward (Bert) OR
b Glasshoughton 9/5/1902 d 1981
Frickley Colliery
1927 Huddersfield Town 0
1928 1931 Southampton 92 18
1932 Fulham 0
1933 1934 Brighton & Hove Albion 45 8
Belgravia Dairy
Hove

Jepson, Arthur GK
b Selston 12/7/1915 d 1997
Newark Town
1934 Mansfield Town 2
Grantham
1938 1945 Port Vale 39
1939 (Port Vale) (2)
1946 1947 Stoke City 28
1948 1949 Lincoln City 58
Northwich Victoria
Gloucester City
Hinckley United

Jepson, John James CF
b Heaton Norris 19/8/1899 d 1987
New Mills
Atherton
New Mills
Stalybridge Celtic
1924 Notts County 0
1925 1926 Accrington Stanley 56 41
Carlisle United
1928 1929 Accrington Stanley 61 41
1930 Wigan Borough 35 28
1931 Mansfield Town 1
Macclesfield
Altrincham
Nelson
Rossendale United
1934 New Brighton (trial) 0
Hurst
Rhyl Athletic

Jessop, Frederick Samuel (Freddie) LB/LH/CH
b Barrow Hill 7/2/1907 d 1979
Staveley Works
1930 1937 Derby County 84 7
1937 1938 Sheffield United 25 1
Atherstone Town

Jewell, John OR
b Brierfield q4 1909
Colne Town
1930 Burnley 0
1930 Nelson 3
Bacup Borough

Jewell, William OL
b 1884
Royal Engineers
1907 Grimsby Town 19 2

Jewett, Alfred William (Alf) CH
b Bitterne 15/11/1899 d 1980
Bitterne United
1921 Southampton 0
Thorneycrofts
1922 Arsenal 0
1923 Lincoln City 37 3
1926 Wigan Borough (trial) 1
1926 Bournemouth & Boscombe Ath 0

Jewett, George LH
b Bitterne 2/5/1906 d 1997
Cowes
1927 1928 Watford 29
1929 Southampton 0
1931 Crystal Palace 1
Basingstoke Town
Cowes

From To | Apps Goal

Jewhurst, Frederick Harold (Fred) RH
b Hoxton 30/9/1897 d 1949
Northfleet
1921 1923 Charlton Athletic 9
1923 1926 Southend United 118
1927 Clapton Orient 1
Dartford

Jex, William IR
b Norwich 23/3/1885 d 1934
Thorpe Village
CEYMS (Norwich)
Norwich City
Doncaster Rovers
Rotherham Town
Doncaster Rovers
1911 Gainsborough Trinity 6
Croydon Common
Doncaster Rovers

Jeyes, James LH
b London
1914 Clapton Orient 1

Jinks, James Thomas (Jimmy) CF
b Camberwell 19/8/1916 d 1981
Downham Common
1938 1947 Millwall 45 16
1948 1949 Fulham 11 3
1949 1950 Luton Town 9 2
1951 Aldershot 5
Ashford Town (Kent)

Jobe, Thomas Samuel OL
b Newcastle q1 1904 d 1962
1929 Chesterfield 2
1930 Wigan Borough 0
Ashton St Thomas
Haydock Athletic
Strubshaw Cross (Ashton)
Crompton Recreation

Jobey, George RH/CH
b Heddon 13/7/1885 d 1962
Morpeth Harriers
1906 1912 Newcastle United 47 2
1913 Woolwich Arsenal 28 3
1914 Bradford Park Avenue 14 3
Hamilton Academical
Hartlepools United
1919 Leicester City 30
1920 1921 Northampton Town 78 2

Jobling, Joseph (Joe) RH/LH
b Annfield Plain 29/7/1906 d 1969
Sunderland Co-operatives
South Pontop Villa
Langley Park
Annfield Plain
Gorleston
1929 1931 Norwich City 71 1
1931 1938 Charlton Athletic 211 5

Jobling, Leonard (Len) OR
b Sunderland 26/3/1884 d 1967
Roker Wednesday
Sunderland Co-operative
Spennymoor United
Carlisle United
Sheffield United 0
Norwich City
1912 Manchester City 2
Hartlepools United

Jobson, John Thomas (Jack) CH/RH
b Hebburn 8/8/1900 d 1983
Washington Colliery
1922 Plymouth Argyle 1
1924 1926 Hartlepools United 102 2
1927 1931 Stockport County 171 7
1932 Queen's Park Rangers 4
1933 Gateshead 8

Jobson, John William OL
b Burradon 29/7/1908 d 1974
Hatfield Main Colliery
Bedlington United
Walker Celtic
Burradon Colliery Welfare
Blyth Spartans
1930 Hull City 2
Frickley Colliery
Hatfield Main Colliery
Seaton Burn Welfare
Burradon Colliery Welfare

John, Emlyn James LH/CH/LB
b Tonypandy q3 1907
Mid-Rhondda United
1928 1931 Cardiff City 15
1932 1933 Newport County 55 2
Barry
Drumcondra

From To | Apps Goal

John, Reginald (Reg) RH
b Aberdare 22/7/1899
Aberdare Athletic
1920 1925 Queen's Park Rangers 131 1
1926 Charlton Athletic 8
Folkestone

John, Robert Frederick (Bob) LH/LB
b Barry Dock 3/2/1900 d 1982
Caps: Wales 15
Caerphilly
Barry
1922 1936 Arsenal 421 12

John, William Ronald (Roy) GK/LB
b Briton Ferry 29/1/1911 d 1973
Caps: Wales War 1
Briton Ferry Athletic
1927 Swansea Town 0
1928 Manchester United (trial) 0
1928 1931 Walsall 88
1931 1933 Stoke City 71
1934 Preston North End 0
1934 1935 Sheffield United 29
1936 Manchester United 15
1936 Newport County 10
1937 1938 Swansea Town 40
Briton Ferry Athletic

Johnman, John LB
b Cambusnethan
Carluke Milton Rovers
Motherwell
1932 Stockport County 1
1933 Halifax Town 36
Dunfermline Athletic

Johnson, Albert LB/RB
b Sheffield 1885
Attercliffe
1906 1907 Barnsley 11

Johnson, Alexander (Alex) RB
b Gateshead 5/12/1917 d 1944
Birtley
1938 Norwich City 5

Johnson, Arthur OL
b Atherstone 1/1904
Atherstone Town
1924 Huddersfield Town 0
1925 Barnsley 23 4
1927 Birmingham 9
1928 1930 Bristol City 60 7
1931 Coventry City 5 1

Johnson, Arthur John RH
b Grays q1 1885
Grays United
Southend United
1907 Sheffield United 2
Southend United
New Brompton

Johnson, Charles LB
b North Shields 29/4/1884
Hylton Rovers
Wallsend Park Villa
Willington Athletic
1905 1909 Sheffield United 71
South Shields
Jarrow Caledonians
1919 South Shields 4

Johnson, Clifford (Cliff) OR/IR
b Hessle 24/2/1914 d 1989
Hessle
1934 York City 4 2
1934 Wolverhampton Wanderers 0
1935 Port Vale 5
1936 Torquay United 8 1

Johnson, Cyrus William CF
b Hoylake 6/5/1906 d 1980
Nantwich
Manitoba
Nantwich
1935 New Brighton 10 6
United Western (Winnipeg)

Johnson, David RH
Barrow
1906 Burnley 4

Johnson, Edward William OL
Rochdale
1898 Sheffield United 3

Johnson, Ernest Leslie (Ernie) LH
b Sheffield 27/1/1917 d 2003
1935 Sheffield United 0
1937 Nottingham Forest 0
1937 1938 New Brighton 8
Scunthorpe & Lindsey United
1945 Rotherham United 0
Worksop Town

From To | Apps Goal

Johnson, Frank GK
1914 Stockport County 2
Hurst

Johnson, Frederick RH/IR
1899 1902 Gainsborough Trinity 81 4

Johnson, Frederick J (Freddie) OR
b Stoke-on-Trent 1877
Caps: FLge 1
Stoke St Peter's
1895 1902 Stoke 175 19

Johnson, Garnet Joseph Wolsley OL
b Pudsey 8/10/1882
Upper Armley Christ Church
1906 Leeds City 1

Johnson, George CF/IL/IR
b West Bromwich 11/1871 d 1934
West Bromwich Baptists
Wrockwardine Wood
1895 West Bromwich Albion 0
1896 1897 Walsall 55 23
1897 1904 Aston Villa 99 38
Plymouth Argyle
Crystal Palace

Johnson, George RB
b Newcastle 6/1/1907 d 1989
Walker Celtic
1925 Wigan Borough 3
Walker Celtic
1926 Darlington 2
1927 Chelsea 0
Northfleet
LGOC Sports Association

Johnson, George Alfred RH/CF/IL
b Ashington 20/7/1904 d 1985
Ashington Welfare
Bedlington United
1924 1928 Ashington 167 67
1930 Sheffield Wednesday 1 1
1932 1936 Reading 161 8
1937 1938 Watford 23 8

Johnson, George Edward CH
b Sheffield 15/7/1913 d 1989
1935 1936 Torquay United 3
Waterford
1938 Watford 1

Johnson, George Henry LB
b Stepney q1 1888
Southend United
1908 1911 Clapton Orient 82 4
1911 1912 Chelsea 4
Portsmouth
Boscombe

Johnson, George Henry OR
b Darnall q4 1903
Darnall Old Boys
1922 Swansea Town 1
1923 1925 Southend United 62 13
1926 Newport County 39 9
1927 Coventry City 14 2
1928 Torquay United 0

Johnson, George W OR
Eckington Sunday School
1906 Sheffield United 0
1907 Chesterfield Town 3
Rotherham County

Johnson, Harold CH/LH
b Manchester
1930 1932 Stockport County 12

Johnson, Harry CF
b Ecclesfield 4/1/1899 d 1981
Caps: FLge 1
Ecclesfield
1919 1930 Sheffield United 313 201
1931 1935 Mansfield Town 163 104

Johnson, Harry CF/IR
b Radcliffe 4/12/1910 d 1981
Heywood St James'
Great Harwood
Winsford United
Stalybridge Celtic
1931 1933 Oldham Athletic 37 13
1934 1935 Southend United 26 15
1936 Exeter City 11 1
Scunthorpe & Lindsey United

Johnson, Henry (Harry) RB/LB
b Walker 8/8/1913 d 1976
Walker Park
1935 Newcastle United 5
1937 Port Vale 19
1938 Hartlepools United 24

From To | Apps Goal

Johnson, Henry Edward (Harry) IL/CF
b Birmingham 1897
1919 Coventry City 2
Darlaston
1921 1923 Southampton 38 8
1923 1925 Queen's Park Rangers 50 15
Cradley Heath

Johnson, J CH
1892 1893 Crewe Alexandra 5

Johnson, James Tennant OR
b Newcastle 3/5/1892
Bedlington
1913 Leeds City 1
North Leeds Athletic

Johnson, John Charles (Jack) RH/CH/LH
b South Kirkby 3/10/1905 d 1991
South Kirkby Colliery
Denaby United
1927 Sheffield Wednesday 0
1928 1929 Bournemouth & Boscombe Ath 12 4
1930 1932 Rotherham United 90 3
1933 Barnsley 9
1934 1937 Carlisle United 139 2
1938 Accrington Stanley 39
1939 (Accrington Stanley) (3)

Johnson, John George CF
b Ryhope 12/1906
Ryhope
1924 Sunderland 0
1925 Tranmere Rovers 2
Blyth Spartans

Johnson, John Henry (Jack) IL
b Bristol 28/5/1897 d 1974
Fry's
1921 1926 Swindon Town 151 63
1927 1928 Queen's Park Rangers 18 7

Johnson, John James (Jack) GK
b Gateshead 1911
Davison Villa
1933 1934 Hartlepools United 52
1935 Chesterfield 0
Blyth Spartans
West Stanley

Johnson, John William (Jack) OR
b Newcastle 12/2/1919 d 1975
Leicester Nomads
1936 1938 Huddersfield Town 18 2
1939 1947 Grimsby Town 44 2
1939 (Grimsby Town) (2)
Shrewsbury Town

Johnson, Joseph (Joe) OL/IL
b Rossendale 1882
Rossendale United
1905 Grimsby Town 19 3
Carlisle United
Millwall Athletic
Luton Town
1912 Clapton Orient 3
Brentford

Johnson, Joseph (Josh) GK
b Tibshelf 1883
Caps: SoLge 3
Ripley Athletic
1905 Aston Villa 0
Plymouth Argyle
Crystal Palace
1919 1920 Nottingham Forest 53
Sutton Town

Johnson, Joseph (Joe) RB/LB
b Stamford
Stamford Town
Mansfield Mechanics
1919 Notts County 10
1920 1923 Watford 94 1
1924 Luton Town 11

Johnson, Joseph LB
b Felling
Felling Colliery
1919 1920 Sunderland 5
Ebbw Vale

Johnson, Joseph IR
b Liverpool 1903
Northwich Victoria
1925 Stockport County 7
Scunthorpe & Lindsey United
1927 Bradford City 1 1

From To Apps Goal

Johnson, Joseph Alfred (Joe) OL
b Grimsby 4/4/1911 d 1983
Caps: England 5
Scunthorpe & Lindsey United
1931 Bristol City 7
1931 1937 Stoke City 184 54
1937 1938 West Bromwich Albion 52 22
1939 (West Bromwich Albion) (3)
Northwich Victoria
Hereford United

Johnson, Joseph James (Joe) IL/IR
b Wednesbury 23/6/1900 d 1976
Bradley United
Talbot Stead Tube Works
Cannock Town
1922 1924 Crystal Palace 29 6
1925 Barnsley 17 2
1926 1927 West Ham United 15 7
1928 Southend United 0
1929 Walsall 0
1930 Wigan Borough 30 9
1931 Halifax Town 27 6
1932 Accrington Stanley 26 7
Cannock Town
Cradley Heath

Johnson, Martin John James IL
b Windy Nook 21/3/1906
Felling Colliery
1924 Sunderland (trial) 0
1925 Durham City 11 2
1925 1926 Bradford Park Avenue 37 6
1927 Sheffield United 6
Durham City
1928 Wolverhampton Wanderers 8 2
Spennymoor United
Murton Colliery Welfare
North Shields
Wardley Colliery Welfare
Pelaw
Blyth Spartans

Johnson, Matthew Harrison (Matt) OL/CF
b South Shields 26/7/1910 d 1988
White Lea Juniors
Harton Colliery
1932 Sheffield Wednesday 0
1933 Hartlepools United 6
Northwich Victoria
1934 Brentford 0
1935 1936 Rochdale 19 5
Darwen
1937 1938 Crewe Alexandra 83 25
1939 (Crewe Alexandra) (2)

Johnson, Nathan Victor (Nat) CF
b Gateshead q3 1887 d 1963
Windy Nook
1912 Grimsby Town 1
Castleford Town
Charlton's (Grimsby)
Cleethorpes Town
Haycroft Rovers

Johnson, Patrick LB
b Wingate
Crook Town
1910 Barnsley 1

Johnson, Percy Raymond LB/RB
b Northampton 13/12/1899 d 1983
1921 1922 Northampton Town 11
Wellingborough Town
Higham Ferrers

Johnson, Reginald (Reg) CH/LH
b Cradley Heath 15/4/1904 d 1984
Stourport Swifts
Cradley Heath
1926 1927 Fulham 4 1
1929 Swindon Town 11
Cradley Heath
Wednesbury St Paul's

Johnson, Richard Kemp (Dick) CF/IR/IL
b Gateshead q2 1895 d 1933
Victoria Adelaide
Bensham
Hebburn Argyle (trial)
Marley Hill United
Bensham
Felling Colliery
1919 1924 Liverpool 77 28
1924 1928 Stoke 78 21
1929 1930 New Brighton 74 23
Connah's Quay & Shotton
Brenka

From To Apps Goal

Johnson, Robert Emmerson Oliver (Bob) CH
b Fencehouses 25/10/1911 d 1982
Lambton Coke Works
1931 Blackburn Rovers (trial) 0
1932 Blackpool (trial) 0
Bishop Auckland
1934 1948 Burnley 78
Nelson
1950 Rochdale 0

Johnson, Robert James (Bob) CF/OR
b Chester-le-Street 27/3/1905 d 1987
Ushaw Moor
Moor Ends Thorne
Firbeck Colliery
Spennymoor United
1930 Southport 6
Derry City
Thorne Colliery
1932 Darlington 33 15
1933 Barnsley 0
Spennymoor United
Eden Colliery
Walker Celtic
Shell-Mex (trial)

Johnson, Samuel (Sam) LB/LH
b Kidsgrove 19/10/1901 d 1975
Goldenhill Wanderers
1924 1925 Stoke 38
1926 1928 Swindon Town 35 1
1929 1932 York City 124
1933 Southport 1
1933 Crystal Palace 0
Scarborough

Johnson, Samuel C IR
Tonge
1900 Newton Heath 1
1901 Barnsley 0
Heywood

Johnson, Samuel Clay (Sam) LH/RH
b Manchester q3 1881
Newton Heath Albion
Colne
1905 1906 Blackpool 33 1
Colne
Exeter City
Coventry City
1911 Leeds City 7 1

Johnson, Sydney (Syd) CF
Barnoldswick Town
1930 Accrington Stanley 7 3
Barnoldswick Town

Johnson, Thomas RB
b 1867
1889 Wolverhampton Wanderers 1

Johnson, Thomas (Tom) CH/LH
b Ecclesfield 4/5/1911 d 1983
Ecclesfield United
1929 1938 Sheffield United 183
1939 (Sheffield United) (3)
1946 1948 Lincoln City 75

Johnson, Thomas Clark Fisher (Tommy) IL/CF
b Dalton-in-Furness 19/8/1901 d 1973
Caps: FLge 3/England 5
Dalton Athletic
Dalton Casuals
1919 1929 Manchester City 328 158
1929 1933 Everton 146 56
1933 1935 Liverpool 37 8
Darwen

Johnson, Thomas O (Tom) GK
b 1917
Houghton-le-Spring
1937 Hartlepools United 12
1938 Southport 0

Johnson, W IL
1894 Crewe Alexandra 1

Johnson, William OR
b Beverley
Beverley Barracks
1919 Hull City 5
Bridlington Town

Johnson, William RH
b Aberdeen
Aberdeen
1919 West Ham United 2

Johnson, William (Bill) LH/RH
b Seaton Delaval 1900
Seaton Delaval
1923 1925 Hull City 46
Blyth Spartans

From To Apps Goal

Johnson, William (Bill) GK
b Sheffield
Wombwell
1923 1930 Leeds United 72
1931 1932 Chester 54
Bangor City
1933 1934 Crewe Alexandra 16
Oswestry Town

Johnson, William Frederick GK
b Bradley, Staffordshire 29/8/1902
Leek Alexandra
Buxton
1926 1927 Aston Villa 4
1928 Charlton Athletic 10
Yeovil & Petters United

Johnson, William H CF
1933 Rotherham United 1

Johnson, William Harrison (Harry) RH
b Ecclesfield 4/1/1876 d 1940
Caps: FLge 1/England 6
Ecclesfield Church
1897 1908 Sheffield United 242 6

Johnson, William Joseph (Bill) LH/RH
b Leigh-on-Sea 9/11/1909 d 1982
Leigh Amatuers
1928 1931 Southend United 45
1932 West Ham United 5

Johnson, William T OL
1939 Darlington (3) (1)

Johnson, William Thomas (Tommy) OL
Wrockwardine Wood
1896 Walsall 17 4
Gravesend United
Chatham
1901 Lincoln City 6

Johnston, Charles (Charlie) OL
b Glasgow 26/11/1912
Blantyre Victoria
Motherwell
1935 1936 Doncaster Rovers 36 3
1937 Mansfield Town 36 4
Dunfermline Athletic
Rangers
Queen of the South

Johnston, Ezekiel (Zeke) GK
b Belfast 1871
Caps: IrLge 3
Glentoran
1893 1894 Burnley 9
Glentoran
Belfast Celtic
1896 1897 Stoke 38
Belfast Celtic

Johnston, Henry IR
b Manchester
1919 Port Vale 0
1920 Grimsby Town 1

Johnston, Henry (Harry) RH/LH/CH
b Manchester 26/9/1919 d 1973
Caps: FLge 4/England 10
Droylsden
Droylsden Athletic
1937 1954 Blackpool 386 11
1939 (Blackpool) (3)

Johnston, Henry Wallace (Harry) LH/LB
b Glasgow 1871 d 1936
Airdrieonians
Clyde
1894 1896 Sunderland 60 3
1896 Aston Villa 0
1897 Grimsby Town 8
Gravesend United
Third Lanark

Johnston, Herbert (Bert) OR
b Dundee 3/4/1912
Dundee Violet
Aberdeen
1935 Fulham 4 1
London Paper Mills

Johnston, J OL
1897 Walsall 2 1

Johnston, James (Jack) OL
b Edinburgh 1869
St Bernard's
1891 1892 Wolverhampton Wanderers 16 5
East Stirlingshire

Johnston, James RB
b Rothesay 1886 d 1953
Rothesay Royal Victoria
Maryhill
1910 1913 Blackburn Rovers 14

From To Apps Goal

Johnston, James Watson RH
b Forfar 1888
1911 1913 Preston North End 10

Johnston, John RB
Dalziel Rovers
Cambuslang Rangers
1908 Sunderland 1
Motherwell

Johnston, John B RB
b Muirkirk
1921 Sunderland 0
1922 Bolton Wanderers 1

Johnston, John Murray CF
b Durham q2 1905
Seaton Delaval
1923 Derby County 1
1924 Rotherham County 15 1

Johnston, John Shand RH
b Lennoxtown 1878 d 1955
Stalybridge Rovers
1901 1906 Bury 180 2
Southampton
Stalybridge Celtic

Johnston, John Thompson RB
b Sunderland 1882
Caps: FLge 1
Sunderland Royal Rovers
1907 Middlesbrough 0
1908 1914 Clapton Orient 218 1

Johnston, Leslie IL
b Liverpool 1890
1913 Everton 8 1

Johnston, Robert (Bert) CH
b Falkirk 2/6/1909 d 1968
Caps: Scotland 1
Alva Albion Rovers
1930 1938 Sunderland 146
1939 (Sunderland) (1)

Johnston, Septimus (Sep) LH
b Percy Main q1 1890 d 1944
1920 South Shields 0
1921 Barrow 2

Johnston, William Gifford (Billy) IL/IR/LH
b Edinburgh 16/1/1901 d 1964
Caps: Scotland Sch
Dalkeith Thistle
Selby Town
1920 1923 Huddersfield Town 46 6
1924 1927 Stockport County 72 27
1927 1928 Manchester United 43 13
Macclesfield
1931 Manchester United 28 11
1932 1934 Oldham Athletic 67 8
Frickley Colliery

Johnstone, Gordon Stewart LH/CF
b Felling q2 1900 d 1961
Houghton Rovers
1922 1924 Brentford 45 7
Felling Colliery

Johnstone, Harold OL
b Manchester
1920 Port Vale 8 1

Johnstone, James (Jimmy) RH
b Troon 25/3/1896 d 1924
Motherwell
St Johnstone
1921 Barrow 4

Johnstone, John Arthur CF/OL
b Manchester
1920 Manchester City 0
1920 1921 Port Vale 6

Johnstone, John Charles (Jock) RH
b Dundee 4/1896 d 1952
Dundee Hibernian
Dundee
1921 1926 Aston Villa 105 1
1928 Reading 6

Johnstone, Robert (Bob) OL
b Renton
Renton
1896 Sunderland 12 1
Third Lanark
Dunfermline Athletic

Johnstone, Robert (Bob) LB/RB/OR
b Coldstream 18/9/1908
Coldstream
Heart of Midlothian
1935 1938 Bradford Park Avenue 120 1
1939 (Bradford Park Avenue) (1)

From To Apps Goal

Johnstone, TC OR
1927 Bournemouth & Boscombe Ath 1

Johnstone, Walter Campbell CF/IL
b Glasgow 29/1/1908
Shawfield
Falkirk (trial)
1927 1928 Coventry City 29 12
1928 Walsall 3
Morton

Johnstone, William IL
1889 Preston North End 2

Johnstone, William (Bill) CF/IL
b Markinch 18/5/1901 d 1975
Rosyth Juniors
King's Park
Clyde
1926 1928 Reading 78 33
1929 1930 Arsenal 9 4
1930 1932 Oldham Athletic 68 28
Clyde
Northwich Victoria

Johnstone, William K (Bill) IL
Irvine Meadow
1932 Plymouth Argyle 1
1933 Coventry City 0

Johnstone, William R CF
b Kirriemuir 1867
Dundee Harp
1889 West Bromwich Albion 3
Alloa Athletic
Arbroath

Joliffe, Cyril Alfred GK
b Portsmouth 15/1/1907 d 1990
South Hants Nomads
1932 Portsmouth 2
South Hants Nomads

Jolley, Alfred OR
1904 Blackpool 5

Jolley, Edwin CH/RB/LH
b Birmingham 6/1871
Lozells
1893 1895 Small Heath 23 2
Berwick Rangers (Worcester)

Jolliffe, Charles James GK
b Liverpool q1 1861 d 1943
1888 1889 Everton 5

Jolly, Henry (Harry) CH/LH
b Ushaw Moor 5/4/1908 d 1976
Ushaw Moor
1927 Leeds United 0
1932 Chester 9
1932 Southport 9
1933 1934 Bury 3
1935 Rotherham United 5
Rhyl Athletic
Scarborough

Jonas, William (Willie) CF/IL
b Blyth q3 1890 d 1916
Havana Rovers
Jarrow Croft
Washington United
1912 1914 Clapton Orient 70 21

Jones, A IR
b Llandudno
Small Heath
1893 Ardwick 2 1

Jones, A Fred (Freddie) IL
b Newstead 25/12/1888
Annesley
Sutton Junction
1907 1910 Notts County 66 24
Coventry City
1912 Notts County 20 3
Coventry City
Southampton
1919 Coventry City 1
Wrexham
Pembroke Dock
Ebbw Vale

Jones, Aaron CF/IL
b Walsall q3 1881 d 1950
Newstead Byron
Royston United
1903 1904 Barnsley 32 16
1905 1906 Birmingham 5
1906 1907 Notts County 22 6

From To Apps Goal

Jones, Abraham CH
b Tipton 1875 d 1942
Cameron Highlanders
1897 1900 West Bromwich Albion 104 6
1901 1905 Middlesbrough 140 9
Luton Town

Jones, Abraham (Abe) CF/IR
b West Bromwich 4/1899
West Bromwich Sandwell
1919 Birmingham 3 2
1921 Reading 24 5
1922 Brighton & Hove Albion 6 1
1923 Merthyr Town 19 6

Jones, Albert Thomas RB/LB
b Talgarth 6/2/1883 d 1963
Caps: Wales Amat/Wales 2
Builth Town
Talgarth
Harborne Lynwood
1901 Aston Villa (trial) 0
Swindon Town
1903 1904 Nottingham Forest 12
1905 1906 Notts County 30
Norwich City
Wellington Town
Swansea Town

Jones, Alfred (Alf) OL
b Hanley 1902
1920 Port Vale 0
1921 Crewe Alexandra 5
Congleton Town
1924 Stoke 5 1
Congleton Town

Jones, Alfred (Alf) RB
b Chester 10/1/1900 d 1959
Chester
Brickfields
Saltney Athletic
1923 1935 Wrexham 503 5
Winsford United

Jones, Arthur LB
b Birmingham
Heywood
1927 Nelson 1

Jones, Arthur OR
b Gwersyllt 22/8/1912 d 2002
Cross Street Church
Holyhead
1931 1932 Wrexham 7
Hyde United
1935 1938 Oldham Athletic 98 30

Jones, Arthur Ernest CH
b St Pancras q1 1878 d 1939
Shrewsbury Town
Market Drayton
Tottenham Hotspur
1901 Doncaster Rovers 21 1

Jones, Ben CH
b Alsagers Bank 1880
Alsagers Bank Church
1904 Burslem Port Vale 1
Alsagers Bank United
Halmerend Gymnastics
Alsagers Bank Church

Jones, Benjamin (Ben) CF
b Rotherham
Rotherham Town
1906 Aston Villa 0
Doncaster Rovers
1908 Barnsley 16 5
Denaby United
Doncaster Rovers
Worksop Town
Mansfield Town

Jones, Bertram OR
b Merthyr Tydfil
Ewyllrhysdyn
1934 Southend United 1

Jones, Brynmor (Bryn) IL
b Penyard 14/2/1912 d 1985
Caps: Wales War 8/Wales 17
Merthyr Amateurs
Plymouth United
1931 Southend United (trial) 0
1931 Swansea Town (trial) 0
Glenavon
Aberaman Athletic
1933 1937 Wolverhampton Wanderers 163 52
1938 1948 Arsenal 71 7
1939 (Arsenal) (3)
1949 Norwich City 23 1

From To Apps Goal

Jones, Charles (Charlie) OL/RH/IL
b Troedyrhiw 12/12/1899 d 1966
Caps: Wales 8
Troedyrhiw
1920 Cardiff City 1
1921 1922 Stockport County 48 9
1922 1924 Oldham Athletic 56 5
1925 1927 Nottingham Forest 100 22
1928 1933 Arsenal 176 8

Jones, Charles (Charlie) CH
b Penmaen 20/11/1911
Ebbw Vale
Northfleet
1934 1935 Tottenham Hotspur 18
1937 1945 Southend United 22 2

Jones, Charles Edward (Charlie) GK
b Manchester 1889
Northwich Victoria
1913 1919 Preston North End 34
Northwich Victoria
Witton Albion

Jones, Charles H (Charlie) IL/OL
b Swansea 1911
Northend
1932 1933 Queen's Park Rangers 16 1

Jones, Charles Reginald OL
b Wrexham q4 1907
Chirk
1925 Wigan Borough 1
1926 Wolverhampton Wanderers 0
Altrincham

Jones, Charles T OL
b Birmingham 7/1888
Verity Works
1908 Birmingham 1
Bristol Rovers

Jones, Charles Wilson (Wilson) CF
b Pentre Broughton 29/4/1914 d 1985
Caps: Wales 2
Brymbo Green
1930 Blackburn Rovers (trial) 0
1931 Bolton Wanderers (trial) 0
1932 1934 Wrexham 7 3
1934 1946 Birmingham 134 63
1947 Nottingham Forest 7 5
Kidderminster Harriers
Redditch United

Jones, Christopher IR/IL
b Merthyr Tydfil
Gellifaelog Amateurs
1928 1929 Rochdale 2

Jones, Clifford (Cliff) LB/RB
b Rotherham 1891
1911 Gainsborough Trinity 12
1912 1921 Burnley 82
1922 Accrington Stanley 0

Jones, David (Di) LB
b Trefonen 1867 d 1902
Caps: Wales 14
Oswestry
Chirk
Newton Heath
1888 1897 Bolton Wanderers 228 4
1898 1901 Manchester City 114 1

Jones, David RH
b Hodthorpe 9/4/1914 d 1998
Worksop Town
1934 1949 Bury 257 12

Jones, David GK
b Blaenau Ffestiniog 8/9/1914
Blaenau Ffestiniog
1935 Everton 0
Colwyn Bay United
1938 Stoke City 1
1939 1947 Carlisle United 66
1939 (Carlisle United) (2)
1948 Rochdale 0
Northwich Victoria

Jones, David Gwilym (Dai) OL/CH
b Ynysddu 10/6/1914 d 1988
Ynysddu
1930 Newport County 0
1931 Tottenham Hotspur 0
Northfleet
1934 Cardiff City 9
1934 Fulham (trial) 0
1935 Newport County 15 1
Wigan Athletic
1937 Manchester United 1
1938 Swindon Town 15
Cheltenham Town

From To Apps Goal

Jones, David Oswald Edwards (Ossie) IR/OL
b Ruabon 15/7/1909 d 2002
Afongoch Chums
1929 Wrexham 1
Aberystwyth
Llanerch Celts
Gywffia
Connah's Quay & Shotton
1931 Nottingham Forest 0
1932 Wrexham 2
Oswestry Town
Macclesfield
1936 1937 Tranmere Rovers 54 12
1938 Watford 2
1938 Southport 7 2
1939 Crewe Alexandra 0
Monsanto

Jones, David Owen (Dai) LB/RB
b Cardiff 28/10/1910 d 1971
Caps: Wales 7
Ely United
Ebbw Vale
1929 Millwall (trial) 0
1929 Charlton Athletic (trial) 0
1930 Millwall (trial) 0
1931 1932 Clapton Orient 55
1933 1946 Leicester City 226 4
1939 (Leicester City) (3)
1947 1948 Mansfield Town 74
Hinckley Athletic

Jones, David Thomas (Dai) GK
b Troedyrhiw
1921 Merthyr Town 8
1922 Chesterfield 6
1923 Lincoln City 3
Penrhiwceiber
Barry
1925 Stockport County 0

Jones, Dennis RH
b Bolsover 14/5/1894 d 1961
Shirebrook
1921 1923 Leicester City 64 2
1924 Southampton 7
Mansfield Town
Shirebrook
Sutton Town
Wombwell

Jones, E John LH
1937 Gillingham 5

Jones, Edward L IR/OR
b Merthyr Tydfil
1926 Aberdare Athletic 0
1927 1928 Merthyr Town 22 3

Jones, Edwin OL
b Tyldesley
1923 Brighton & Hove Albion 0
1924 Crystal Palace 4

Jones, Edwin Morris (Eddie) OR
b Abercynon 20/4/1914 d 1984
Caps: Wales Sch
Abercynon
1933 Bolton Wanderers 1 1
1936 1946 Swindon Town 124 17
1939 (Swindon Town) (2)
Chippenham Town

Jones, Ellis IR/IL
b Spennymoor 5/4/1900 d 1972
Stanley United
Willington
Crook Town
Spennymoor United
1925 Hull City 8 1
Annfield Plain
1927 1928 Oldham Athletic 7 3
Workington
Spennymoor United
Crook Town
Blackwell Colliery Welfare

Jones, Emlyn (Mickey) IR
b Merthyr Tydfil 29/11/1906 d 1973
Dowlais
1927 Merthyr Town 21 3
1927 Bournemouth & Boscombe Ath 6 2
1927 Everton 0
1929 1935 Southend United 220 30
Northwich Victoria
Shirley Town
Nuneaton Borough
1938 Barrow 3

From To Apps Goal

Jones, Eric Norman OL/OR
b Stirchley 5/2/1915 d 1985
Kidderminster Harriers
1936 Wolverhampton Wanderers 3
1937 Portsmouth 1
1938 Stoke City 0
1939 West Bromwich Albion (3) (4)
1945 Brentford 0
1946 1947 Crewe Alexandra 37 9
Kidderminster Harriers

Jones, Evan IR/CF
b Trehafod 20/10/1888 d 1972
Caps: Wales 7
Trehafod
Aberdare Town
1909 1910 Chelsea 21 4
1910 1911 Oldham Athletic 50 25
1912 1914 Bolton Wanderers 90 24
Swansea Town
Pontypridd
Porth
Llanbradach

Jones, Frank IR
1900 Blackpool 1

Jones, Frank OL/IL
b Chester
Brickfields Athletic
1924 1926 Wrexham 35 9
Wellington Town
Chester
Caernarvon Athletic
Connah's Quay & Shotton
Flint Town
Runcorn
LMS Sheds (Chester)

Jones, Frederick (Fred) CF/RH
b Pontypool 26/8/1909 d 1994
Pontnewydd
Aberaman Athletic
Pontypridd
1932 Swansea Town 6
1934 Notts County 1
1934 1935 Millwall 9 1
Folkestone
1938 Ipswich Town 21 8

Jones, Frederick C GK
b Disley
1929 Manchester City 0
1930 Exeter City 5
Yeovil & Petters United

Jones, Frederick John (Fred) IL/OL
b Greenwich 11/2/1898 d 1990
Royal Naval Depot (Chatham)
1923 Arsenal 2
1924 Aberdare Athletic 12 2
1925 Charlton Athletic 10 2
1926 Blackpool 0

Jones, Frederick R (Fred) IF
b Halesowen q2 1913
Old Hill White Star
Halesowen Town
1933 Leeds United 0
1934 Birmingham 1
Cheltenham Town

Jones, Frederick S CF/IL
b Oswestry
Barry
1925 1933 Stockport County 24 11

Jones, Frederick William (Fred) LB/GK
b Llandudno 1869 d 1910
Caps: Wales 1
Llandudno Swifts
Burslem Port Vale
Newton Heath
West Manchester
1892 Small Heath 8
1893 Lincoln City 7
Reading
Llandudno Swifts

Jones, George Benjamin (Benny) IL/CF/RH
b Newtown 29/1/1907 d 1982
Newtown
1927 Bolton Wanderers 0
Hamilton Academical
1930 Swindon Town 4 1
1931 Rochdale 19 3
1931 Oldham Athletic 2
Wigan Athletic
Nelson
1934 Southend United 3
Horwich RMI
Crusaders
Portadown
Bangor
Crusaders

From To Apps Goal

Jones, George Henry OL
b Sheffield 27/11/1918 d 1995
Woodburn Alliance
1936 1950 Sheffield United 141 36
1950 1951 Barnsley 22 6

Jones, George Wilfred OR
b Crook 28/6/1895 d 1970
Crook Town
Gwersyllt
1919 1922 Everton 36 2
1922 1924 Wigan Borough 89 7
1925 Middlesbrough 24 1
1926 1928 Southport 56 7
Yeovil & Petters United
Great Harwood

Jones, George William CH
b Carlton, Nottinghamshire 30/11/1896
1920 Nottingham Forest 8
Mansfield Town
Grantham

Jones, Glyn OL/IL
b South Wales 1916
1934 1935 Cardiff City 12

Jones, Gordon IR/RH
b Birkenhead 1/2/1889
Bebington St Andrew's
Melrose (Cheshire)
Birkenhead
1909 1911 Bolton Wanderers 22 6
1912 Tottenham Hotspur 7
Hurst
Chester
South Liverpool
Chester
Crichton's Athletic
1921 Wrexham 1 1
Connah's Quay & Shotton
Flint Town

Jones, Gwyn Thomas LB
b Troedyrhiw q1 1912 d 1968
Merthyr Town
1933 Huddersfield Town 1
1934 1936 Rochdale 88
1936 1937 Stockport County 30
1938 Tranmere Rovers 16
1939 Walsall 0

Jones, Harold (Harry) GK
b West Bromwich 1881
Leamington
1900 Walsall 0
Brierley Hill Alliance
1902 West Bromwich Albion 0
Brierley Hill Alliance
1906 West Bromwich Albion 2
Shrewsbury Town

Jones, Harold (Harry) OL
b Codsall 1889
1910 Wolverhampton Wanderers 4
Darlaston
Walsall Comrades

Jones, Harry LB/RB
b Blackwell, Derbyshire 24/3/1891
Caps: FLge 1/England 1
Blackwell Wesley Guild
Mansfield Wesleyans
Blackwell Colliery
1912 1923 Nottingham Forest 224 7
Sutton Town

Jones, Harry Joseph CF/IR/IL
b Haydock 10/1911 d 1957
Haydock Athletic
1932 Preston North End 1 1
1934 1938 West Bromwich Albion 117 52
1939 (West Bromwich Albion) (3) (2)

Jones, Henry Norman LB
b Bangor q3 1909 d 1964
Bangor City
1933 Chester 8

Jones, Herbert LB/LH
b Blackpool 3/9/1896 d 1973
Caps: FLge 3/England 6
South Shore Strollers
South Shore
Fleetwood
1922 1925 Blackpool 94
1925 1932 Blackburn Rovers 247
1934 Brighton & Hove Albion 37
Fleetwood

Jones, Herbert OR
b Wolverton
Wolverton
1926 Northampton Town 5
Wolverton
1935 Northampton Town 0

From To Apps Goal

Jones, Herbert (Bert) GK
b Mostyn 5/10/1910 d 1990
Rhyl Athletic
1935 1936 Wrexham 18
Rhyl Athletic

Jones, Herbert (Herbie) GK
b St Helens 1915
Wargrave
Warrington
1936 Bradford Park Avenue 10
1937 Sheffield United 0
Worcester City
Runcorn

Jones, Horace RH/CF
b Stafford
Ton Pentre
1922 1924 Brentford 31
Hednesford Town

Jones, Ivor IR
b Merthyr Tydfil 31/7/1899 d 1974
Caps: Wales Sch/WLge 1/Wales 10
Merthyr Town
Caerphilly
1920 1921 Swansea Town 65 14
1921 1925 West Bromwich Albion 63 9
1926 Swansea Town 0
Aberystwyth
Aldershot
Thames
Eastside
Aberavon Harlequins

Jones, J OL
1899 Bolton Wanderers 2

Jones, Jackery RB
b Wellington, Shropshire 16/3/1877 d 1945
Caps: FLge 1
Wrockwardine Wood
Lanesfield
1901 1912 Wolverhampton Wanderers 314 16

Jones, James (Jimmy) LB/RB
1899 1901 Middlesbrough 7
Millwall Athletic

Jones, James (Jimmy) LB
b South Bank 9/7/1888
Gateshead Co-op
Gateshead
1912 1919 Blackpool 113
1919 1921 Bolton Wanderers 70
1923 1926 New Brighton 141 1

Jones, James (Jimmy) CF
b Treorchy 1901 d 1977
Caps: WLge 2/Wales 1
Ton Pentre
1923 Cardiff City 12 2
1924 1925 Wrexham 40 23
1926 Aberdare Athletic 32 18
1927 Torquay United 20 6
Worcester City (trial)

Jones, James (Jimmy) OL
Colwyn Bay United
1937 Bolton Wanderers 6 1
South Liverpool
1939 Torquay United (2)

Jones, James Walter Edmund (Walter) CF
b Wellington 4/1890 d 1951
Wellington Ravenhurst
Shrewsbury Town
Wellington Town
1910 Aston Villa 2 1
Bristol Rovers

Jones, James Willie (Jimmy) OL
b Warsop q4 1896
Welbeck Colliery
1919 1920 Notts County 11
Mansfield Town (trial)
Alfreton Town
1922 1923 Brighton & Hove Albion 17 3
Mansfield Town
Crystal Palace (trial)
Worksop Town
Welbeck Colliery
Shirebrook

Jones, John IL
Fleetwood Rangers
1898 Blackpool 4

Jones, John LH/OL
1903 1905 Blackpool 17

From To Apps Goal

Jones, John Edward (Jack) LB
b Bromborough 3/7/1913 d 1995
Bebington
Bromborough Pool
Ellesmere Port Town
1933 1937 Everton 98
1945 1946 Sunderland 24

Jones, John Hubert GK
b Holyhead 1900
Caps: Wales Amat
Holyhead
1924 Liverpool 4
Llandudno

Jones, John Joseph Alfred RB
b Wolverhampton 1887 d 1940
1911 Wolverhampton Wanderers 0
Wellington Town
1913 1914 Bristol City 19
1919 1920 Wolverhampton Wanderers 36 1
Bilston Town

Jones, John Leonard (Jack) OL/CH/LH
b Rhuddlan 1869 d 1931
Caps: Wales 21
Rhuddlan
Bootle
Stockton
1893 Grimsby Town 28 6
1894 1896 Sheffield United 31 5
Tottenham Hotspur
Worcester City

Jones, John Lewis (Jack) RH/CH/IR
b Penrhiwceiber q4 1909
Caps: WLge 1
Pentwyn Albion
Penrhiwceiber
1931 1933 Swansea Town 34 5
1934 1937 Torquay United 157 8
1938 Bournemouth & Boscombe Ath 12 1
1939 Chester 0

Jones, John Lewis Mansfield OR/RH/CF
b Abergele 11/2/1900
Abergele
Atherton
1922 1925 Bolton Wanderers 12 3
1926 Chesterfield 4

Jones, John Love (Love) OL/CF
b Rhyl q4 1884 d 1913
Caps: Wales 2
Rhyl
1905 1906 Stoke 13 3
Crewe Alexandra
1908 1909 Middlesbrough 14
Portsmouth

Jones, John Owen CF/IR
b Bangor 1869 d 1955
Caps: Wales 2
Bangor City
1892 1895 Crewe Alexandra 46 17
Chorley
1898 Newton Heath 3
Bangor City
Earlestown
Stalybridge Rovers

Jones, John R (Jack) IL/IR
b Hawarden
Whitchurch
1922 1923 Wrexham 55 13
1924 1925 Crewe Alexandra 8 1
Sandbach Ramblers

Jones, John Thomas IR
b West Bromwich 10/1874 d 1904
Sandwell Albion
Dudley
Halesowen
1894 1896 Small Heath 35 15
Bristol Eastville Rovers
Tottenham Hotspur

Jones, John Thomas GK
b Holywell 25/11/1916 d 1978
Caps: Wales Sch
Flint Town
1936 Port Vale 3
1938 1947 Northampton Town 71
1948 Oldham Athletic 22

From To Apps Goal
Jones, John William (Jack) LB
b Rotherham 8/2/1891 d 1948
Caps: FLge 1
Allerton Bywater Colliery
Industry FC
Bird-in-Hand
Maltby Main Colliery Welfare
1914 Sunderland 0
1920 1926 Birmingham 228 1
1927 Nelson 12
1927 1929 Crewe Alexandra 90 7
Scarborough

Jones, Joseph Thomas (Joey) CH/RH
b Rhosymedre 1887 d 1941
Caps: Wales 15
Cefn Albion
Wrexham
Treharris
1919 Stoke 15 3
1920 1921 Crystal Palace 61 6
1922 1923 Coventry City 50 1
1924 Crewe Alexandra 15 1
Wellington St George's

Jones, Joseph William OR/OL
b Wellington, Shropshire 1880
Lanesfield
1900 1901 Wolverhampton Wanderers 15 1

Jones, Leonard OL/IL
Eastwood
1901 1902 Burslem Port Vale 4 1

Jones, Leonard (Len) CH/LH
b Birkenhead 1910
Holywell
Flint
Rhyl Athletic
1932 Huddersfield Town 0
1933 1938 Stockport County 202 1
1939 (Stockport County) (1)

Jones, Leonard (Len) OR/RH
b Barnsley 9/6/1913 d 1998
Wombwell
1932 Huddersfield Town 0
1934 1937 Barnsley 57
Chelmsford City
1939 1948 Plymouth Argyle 39 2
1939 (Plymouth Argyle) (1)
1949 Southend United 29
1950 1952 Colchester United 71 3
1953 Ipswich Town 0
Clacton Town
Great Bentley

Jones, Leslie IL
Wombwell
1932 Rotherham United 7 1

Jones, Leslie Jenkin (Les) IL/IR
b Aberdare 1/7/1911 d 1981
Caps: Wales Sch/Wales War 5/Wales 11
Aberdare & Aberaman
1929 1933 Cardiff City 142 31
1933 1937 Coventry City 139 69
1937 1945 Arsenal 46 3
1939 (Arsenal) (3)
1946 Swansea Town 2
Barry Town
1948 Brighton & Hove Albion 3

Jones, Norman Edward RH
b Liverpool
Walker Celtic
1922 Derby County 3
1923 1926 Gillingham 98 2

Jones, Ormond Henry GK
b Towyn 24/8/1910 d 1972
Caps: Wales Sch
Wednesbury Town
1928 Stoke City 0
Towyn Town
Bilston
Wednesbury Town
1932 Blackpool 0
Yeovil & Petters United
1933 Port Vale 14
1934 Norwich City 9
1935 Watford 8
1936 Mansfield Town 14
1937 Norwich City 0
Queen of the South
Yarmouth Town

Jones, Percival (Percy) CF
b Acrefair
Acrefair United
1922 Wrexham 1
Acrefair United
Colwyn Bay
Druids United
Buckley

From To Apps Goal
Jones, Percy Oswald LB
b Aston q1 1897 d 1960
Ellisons Works
Birmingham University Old Boys
1921 1923 Aston Villa 15

Jones, Price IR
b Brymbo 21/5/1903 d 1983
Brymbo Juniors
Brymbo Green
Llandudno
Buckley Town
1926 Wrexham 1
Rhos Athletic
Buckley United
Mold Alexandra
Holywell United
Brymbo Green

Jones, Reginald LH/OL
b Burslem 1/9/1902 d 1967
Middleport
Ravensdale
1923 1936 Port Vale 326 19

Jones, Reginald Warneford (Reg) CF
b Swindon 26/5/1915 d 2001
Wroughton
1935 Swindon Town 1 1
Cheltenham Town

Jones, Richard (Dick) LH
b Wales 1875
Caps: Wales 1
Hanley Swifts
South Shore
1897 1900 Leicester Fosse 104 1
1901 Burton United 4
Royston United
Leeds City

Jones, Richard (Dickie) OL/IL
b Liverpool 1874
Liverpool White Star
1898 Barnsley 30 10
Liverpool White Star
1899 Glossop 7
1899 1900 Barnsley 34 9
1900 Glossop (loan) 2

Jones, Richard (Dicky) LH
b Ashton-in-Makerfield 6/6/1901 d 1962
Skelmersdale United
1920 1921 Oldham Athletic 25
1922 Rochdale 32
1923 Stockport County 6
1924 Exeter City 10
1925 Bristol Rovers 8
Colwyn Bay
Bath City
1926 Wigan Borough 0
Northwich Victoria
Ashton St Thomas (Wigan)

Jones, Richard TW (Dick) IL
b Montgomeryshire 1879 d 1943
Caps: Wales 2
Millwall St John's
Millwall Athletic
1901 Manchester City 8 2
Millwall Athletic

Jones, Robert (Bobby) CH
b Glasgow
Saltcoats Victoria
Celtic
Dumbarton (loan)
1925 Coventry City 7
Stourbridge
Worcester City
Workington
Olympique Marseille
Nithsdale Wanderers
Brechin City

Jones, Robert (Bob) GK
b Everton 9/1/1902 d 1989
Ferndale
1924 Everton 3
1926 1929 Southport 16
1929 1936 Bolton Wanderers 219
1937 1938 Cardiff City 58
1939 Southport 0

Jones, Robert LB
b Liverpool 1911
1931 Huddersfield Town 0
1932 Tranmere Rovers 2

Jones, Robert Reuben OR
b Gateshead q2 1902
High Fell
1921 Huddersfield Town 2 1

From To Apps Goal
Jones, Robert Samuel RB/CH
b Wrexham q3 1868 d 1939
Caps: Wales 1
Wrexham Grosvenor
1888 1892 Everton 7 1
1894 Manchester City 18
South Shore

Jones, Robert Trevor (Bob) IR
b Bethesda d 1930
Holyhead Town
1927 Wrexham 1 1
Holyhead Town
Bethesda Athletic

Jones, Ronald (Ronnie) OR
b Mold 6/1914
Mold Alexandra
1935 1937 Wrexham 78 21
1937 1938 Liverpool 5 1
1945 Wrexham 0
Peterborough United

Jones, Ronald (Ron) OL
b Crewe 9/4/1918 d 1987
Heslington Victoria
1936 1946 Crewe Alexandra 18 7

Jones, Samuel GK
b Wrexham 1870 d 1931
Caps: Wales 6
Wrexham
1893 1895 Burton Swifts 85
Shrewsbury Town
New Brompton
Druids

Jones, Samuel (Sammy) LH
b Lurgan 11/6/1911 d 1993
Caps: Ireland War 1/Ireland 2
Distillery
1933 1946 Blackpool 166 6

Jones, Samuel E (Sam) OL
b Newport
Caps: Wales Amat
1932 Newport County 2
Lovells Athletic
1934 Bristol Rovers 0
Epsom Town
Lovells Athletic

Jones, Sidney (Sid) OR
b Langley Park 10/8/1915 d 1984
Gretna
1934 Carlisle United 3 1
1935 Gateshead 3
1935 Manchester United 0
1935 Burnley 0
1936 Oldham Athletic 1

Jones, Stephen CF
1903 Glossop 6

Jones, Steven CF
Aberdare Town
1901 Bristol City 5 2

Jones, Thomas CF/IL
1893 1895 Crewe Alexandra 26 8

Jones, Thomas (Tom) LB
b Newport, Shropshire 1877
Shrewsbury Town
Belfast Celtic
1901 West Bromwich Albion 0
Bristol Rovers
1905 Hull City 26 2
Wigan County
Heywood
Wrockwardine Wood

Jones, Thomas CF/OR/IL
b Prescot 1885
1905 1909 Everton 15 5
1910 1911 Birmingham 31 12
Southport Central

Jones, Thomas (Tom) IR
b Rhosymedre 1896
1919 Oldham Athletic 10 2
Accrington Stanley

Jones, Thomas GK
b Stanton Hill 1889 d 1923
Mansfield Wesleyans
Huthwaite Colliery
1921 Grimsby Town 3
New Hucknall Colliery

From To Apps Goal
Jones, Thomas (Tom) RB/LB
b Penycae 6/12/1899 d 1978
Caps: Wales 4
Rhosymedre
Acrefair
Druids
1922 Everton (trial) 0
Oswestry Town
1924 1936 Manchester United 189
Scunthorpe & Lindsey United

Jones, Thomas (Tommy) IL
b Anfield 3/1/1915 d 1995
Stoneycroft
Westminster Amateurs (Nottingham)
Bedford Amateurs
1933 Southport 0
West Kirby
Bedford Amateurs
1934 Blackburn Rovers 0
1934 Southport 4
Prescot Cables
South Liverpool
1939 Chesterfield 0
Prescot Cables
South Liverpool

Jones, Thomas (Tom) CH
b Little Hulton 1916
Little Hulton
1937 1938 Accrington Stanley 10 1
1938 Oldham Athletic 1

Jones, Thomas Cledwyn (Tommy) OR
b Trehafod
Guildford City
1938 Bradford Park Avenue 1

Jones, Thomas Daniel IL
b Aberaman 1884 d 1958
Caps: Wales Amat/Wales 1
Aberaman Athletic
Aberdare Town
1903 1904 Nottingham Forest 3
Aberdare Town
Grantham

Jones, Thomas Edward (Tommy) LH/RH/IR
b Cardiff
1914 Wolverhampton Wanderers 0
1919 1920 Bristol City 16
1921 Southend United 3
1922 Wolverhampton Wanderers 0

Jones, Thomas Edwin (Eddie) LB
b Tyldesley 1886 d 1953
1907 Bolton Wanderers 0
Tyldesley
Penrith
Chorley
Exeter City
1910 1922 Bristol City 101 4
Weymouth

Jones, Thomas George (Tommy 'TG') CH
b Connah's Quay 12/10/1917 d 2004
Caps: Wales Sch/Wales War 10/Wales 17
Primrose Hill Athletic
Llanerch Celts
1935 Wrexham 6
1936 1949 Everton 165 4
1939 (Everton) (3)
Pwllheli & District

Jones, Thomas James (Jimmy) IL/OL
b Newcastle 1876
Newcastle Swifts
Congleton Hornets
1899 1900 Stoke 26 9
Crewe Alexandra

Jones, Thomas John (Tommy) OR/IL/OL
b Tonypandy 6/12/1909
Caps: Wales 2
Mid-Rhondda United
1926 1928 Tranmere Rovers 90 28
1929 1933 Sheffield Wednesday 29 6
1934 Manchester United 20 4
1935 1945 Watford 118 23
1939 (Watford) (3)
Guildford City

Jones, Thomas Robert LH
b Blackpool
Llandudno
1902 Blackburn Rovers 11

Jones, Thomas Trevellyan OL
b Shrewsbury 1879
1902 Wolverhampton Wanderers 0
Shrewsbury Town
1904 Small Heath 2
Shifnal Town

From To Apps Goal

Jones, Thomas W (Tommy) LH/CH
b Birmingham 6/1905
Caps: England Sch
Birmingham St George's
Oakengates Town
1924 1925 Aston Villa 5
1926 Burnley 0

Jones, Thomas William (Tommy) IL/IR
b Oakengates 23/3/1907 d 1980
Oakengates Town
1929 West Bromwich Albion 0
1930 1933 Burnley 94 24
1933 1937 Blackpool 153 38
1938 1946 Grimsby Town 48 8
1939 (Grimsby Town) (3)
1947 Accrington Stanley 0

Jones, Trevor RB RB
b Cefn Coed 1913
Barry
1934 1935 Walsall 2
1935 Newport County 11
1936 Walsall 4
Barry

Jones, Verdun Aubrey IR
b Edmonton 22/6/1916 d 1987
1936 Aston Villa 0
1937 Derby County 2
1948 Southend United 0

Jones, Vincent Wellfield (Vince) RH/LH/OL
b Carmarthen q3 1900 d 1950
1922 Cardiff City (trial) 1
1923 Merthyr Town 22 1
Ebbw Vale
1927 1930 Millwall 42 1
1931 Luton Town 3
1932 Norwich City 0
1933 Newport County 33 1
1934 Cardiff City 0

Jones, W OL
1892 Burslem Port Vale 1

Jones, Walter LB
Buckley
1931 Chester 2

Jones, Walter H IR
1908 Stockport County 3 1

Jones, William (Billy) RH/IL
b Brighton 6/3/1876 d 1959
Caps: England 1
Long Eaton Rangers
Willington Athletic
1895 1896 Loughborough 35 18
1901 1905 Bristol City 148 9
Tottenham Hotspur
Swindon Town

Jones, William CF
1898 Burton Swifts 1

Jones, William (Lot) IL/CF/IR
b Chirk 4/1882 d 1941
Caps: Wales 20
Chirk
Druids
1903 1914 Manchester City 281 69
Southend United
1921 Aberdare Athletic 18
1921 Wrexham 7 2
Oswestry Town
Chirk

Jones, William RB
1905 Burslem Port Vale 4

Jones, William LB
b Farndon
1929 Crewe Alexandra 1

Jones, William David (Dai) RH
b Hafod 4/4/1905 d 1946
1920 Swansea Town 0
Hafod United Methodists
1926 Preston North End 0
1927 Barnsley 12
Denaby United
1929 Southport 40 1
Lovells Athletic
1931 York City 12
1932 Clapton Orient (trial) 0
1933 Charlton Athletic (trial) 0
Llanelly

Jones, William George LH/OR/RH
b Chatham
Chatham Town
1929 1931 Gillingham 46 2
Sittingbourne

From To Apps Goal

Jones, William Henry (Billy) CF/IR/OL
b Tipton 24/3/1881 d 1948
Caps: FLge 1/SoLge 1
Smethwick Town
Halesowen
1901 1908 Small Heath/Birmingham 183 77
Brighton & Hove Albion
1911 1913 Birmingham 53 22
Brighton & Hove Albion

Jones, William Lewis G (Bill) LH
b Ynysddu 26/11/1910 d 1993
Ynysddu Crusaders
1930 Newport County 4
1930 Notts County 0
1932 Newport County 2
Barry

Jones, William W (Bill) IL
b Little Hulton 1910
1928 Aston Villa 0
Scarborough
Manchester Central
Bacup Borough
1931 Accrington Stanley 22 3
Altrincham (trial)
Rossendale United
Wigan Athletic

Jordan, Alfred Ralph (Alf) RH
b Lisburn 1900
Willowfield
1923 Stoke 2
1924 1925 Hull City 9
1926 Bristol Rovers 0
Worcester City
Dundalk
Barton Town

Jordan, David CF/RH/RB
b Belfast 1908
Caps: Eire 2
Glentoran
Ards
1932 1935 Hull City 24 15
1936 Wolverhampton Wanderers 3
1937 1938 Crystal Palace 7

Jordan, George CH
b Methil 2/10/1905
Rosslyn
Connah's Quay & Shotton
1929 Bury 1
Yeovil & Petters United
1932 Bradford City 0
1933 Newport County 32
1934 Rochdale 17
Prescot Cables
Shirley Town

Jordan, Hugh McNaughton IR
b Musselburgh 24/7/1908
Falkirk
1930 Norwich City 18 3
Margate
Stade de Reims
Dunkerque
Stade de Reims

Jordan, (Rev) William Charles (Willie) CF/IR
b Langley 9/12/1885 d 1949
Caps: England Amat
Langley St Michael's
1903 Liverpool 0
1906 West Bromwich Albion 10 8
Oxford University
1907 1908 West Bromwich Albion 21 5
1911 Everton 2
1912 Wolverhampton Wanderers 3 2
St George's (Isle of Man)

Joslin, Philip James (Phil) GK
b Kingsteignton 1/9/1916 d 1981
1935 Plymouth Argyle 0
1935 1947 Torquay United 135
1939 (Torquay United) (3)
1948 1950 Cardiff City 108

Jowett, Charles Herbert B (Charlie) GK
b Liverpool q2 1876 d 1941
1896 Liverpool 1

Joy, Bernard CH/LB
b Fulham 29/10/1911 d 1984
Caps: England Amat/England War 1/England 1
London University
Corinthians
Casuals
1930 Southend United 0
1933 Fulham 1
1935 1946 Arsenal 86
1939 (Arsenal) (3)
Corinthian Casuals

From To Apps Goal

Joy, Fred OR
b Bradford 7/1/1905 d 1999
Malton Colliery
Langley Park
1927 Durham City 17 4
Annfield Plain
Malton Colliery
Burnhope Institute

Joy, William Joseph (Billy) GK
b Preston 1864 d 1947
1895 Preston North End 9
1896 Blackburn Rovers 3
1897 1898 Darwen 2

Joyce, Edward Patrick OR
b Bradford 31/5/1908 d 1992
Yorkshire Amateurs
1929 Bradford City 1

Joyce, John William (Tiny) GK
b Burton-on-Trent 26/6/1877 d 1956
Burton Pioneers
Woodville
Overseal Town
Southampton
Millwall Athletic
1901 Burton United 0
Millwall Athletic
1902 Blackburn Rovers 14
Millwall Athletic
1909 1914 Tottenham Hotspur 73 1
Millwall Athletic
Gillingham (loan)
1920 Tottenham Hotspur 0

Joyce, Martin LB
b Jarrow 24/1/1894 d 1960
Jarrow St Bede's
1921 1926 Darlington 166
1927 Durham City 15

Joyce, Patrick (Pat) RB
b Jarrow q1 1902
Jarrow St Bede's
1926 Doncaster Rovers 4
1927 Hartlepools United (trial) 0

Joyce, Thomas GK
b Burton-on-Trent q4 1878 d 1950
1898 1900 Burton Swifts 55

Joyce, Thomas (Tom) IR
b Wardley 30/8/1907 d 1995
Wardley Welfare
West Stanley
Washington Colliery
1930 Grimsby Town 0
Tunbridge Wells Rangers
1932 Barrow 1
Tunbridge Wells Rangers
Washington Colliery
Hexham

Joyce, William (Bill) CF
b Burslem q2 1873
Morton
1894 1896 Bolton Wanderers 30 16
Tottenham Hotspur
Thames Ironworks
Portsmouth
1901 1902 Burton United 52 16
Morton
Motherwell

Joyce, William LH
b Hebden Bridge
1935 Halifax Town 1 1
1936 Southport 0

Joyner, Francis McNab (Frank) OL
b St Andrews 20/8/1918 d 1997
Strathkinnes Amateurs
St Andrews United
Dundee (trial)
Hamilton Academical (trial)
Raith Rovers
1938 Sheffield United 2
Kidderminster Harriers
Dundee
Raith Rovers
Hamilton Academical
Kettering Town
Falkirk
Forfar Athletic
Stirling Albion

Joynes, Richard Albert (Dickie) OR/IR
b Grantham 16/8/1877 d 1949
Newark Avenue
Newark
1901 1902 Notts County 46 3
Newark
Brighton & Hove Albion
1908 1909 Leeds City 22 1

From To Apps Goal

Joynson, George Edward IL/IR
b Wallasey q3 1889 d 1914
Wallasey Rovers
1912 1913 Oldham Athletic 5

Joynt, Fred IL
b Salford 12/4/1894 d 1980
1921 Stalybridge Celtic 2 1

Juggins, Eleader (Ted) RB/CH
b Birmingham q3 1882 d 1966
Willenhall Swifts
Darlaston
1904 1906 Wolverhampton Wanderers 22
Coventry City

Jukes, Bernard IL
b Sheffield 10/6/1899 d 1977
Nether Edge
1922 Chesterfield 0
1923 1924 Barnsley 16 1
Gainsborough Trinity
Scarborough

Julian, Eric CF
b Sheffield q2 1903 d 1966
1925 Rotherham United 1

Julian, Samuel (Sam) LB
b Eastwood 31/10/1901 d 1972
Eastwood Town
Newthorpe Rangers
1926 Notts County 0
Ilkeston United
Heanor Town
1929 1930 Halifax Town 32
1931 Wigan Borough 11

Julian, Walter RB/LH
b Hucknall 24/12/1914 d 1972
West Bridgford
1934 1937 Notts County 14
1938 Crewe Alexandra 3
Scunthorpe & Lindsey United

Juniper, Edward James (Ted) CF
b Mile End 1/5/1896 d 1977
1920 Clapton Orient 9 1

Kaine, William Edward John Charles (Bill) GK
b East Ham 27/6/1900 d 1968
Sterling Athletic
1924 West Ham United 7
1925 Tottenham Hotspur 11
1926 Luton Town 0
1927 Bradford City 0

Kane, Alexander (Alex) GK
b Aberdeen 17/10/1897
King's Own Scottish Borderers
Broxburn United
Heart of Midlothian
1922 Reading 42
1923 1925 Portsmouth 96
1925 1926 West Ham United 2
Congasgo (Toronto)
Bredins Bread (Toronto)

Kane, Edward T CH
Gordon Highlanders
1896 Woolwich Arsenal 1

Kane, Robert (Bob) CH
b Cambuslang 11/5/1911 d 1985
Rutherglen Rosebank
Celtic
St Roch's
1935 1946 Leeds United 57
1939 (Leeds United) (1)

Kane, Stanley (Stan) GK
b Workington 17/4/1912 d 1976
1933 Birmingham 0
1934 1935 Liverpool 6
1935 Southend United (trial) 2

Kasher, Joseph William Robinson (Joe) CH
b Crook 14/1/1894 d 1992
Hunwick Juniors
Willington
Crook Town
1919 1922 Sunderland 86
1922 1923 Stoke 52 1
Carlisle United
1925 1926 Accrington Stanley 47 2

Kavanagh, ? RB
1888 Burnley 1
Nelson

From To Apps Goal

Kavanagh, Peter Joseph OL
b Dublin 11/9/1909 d 1993
Caps: LoI 2/Ireland 1/Eire 2
Melrose Celtic of Fairview
Drumcondra
Bohemians
Celtic
1932 Northampton Town 1
Guildford City
Hibernian
Stranraer
Waterford
Witton Albion
Babcock & Wilcox

Kavanagh, Terrence (Terry) RH/LH
b Dublin 1912
Drumcondra
Wigan Athletic
1933 Everton 0
1936 Notts County 2
1937 Exeter City 6

Kavanagh, William J CF
b Ireland 27/10/1917 d 1991
Fearon Athletic
Tunbridge Wells Rangers
1937 Fulham 0
Tunbridge Wells Rangers
1938 Bristol Rovers 6

Kay, Albert Edward LH/LB
b Sheffield 22/11/1895
Willenhall
1922 1931 Wolverhampton Wanderers 278 2

Kay, Alexander (Alec) LB
Dalry Primrose
St Bernard's
Partick Thistle
1901 Sheffield United 6

Kay, Fred (Freddie) RB
b Hindley q2 1901
Ramsbottom British Legion
1921 1922 Accrington Stanley 30

Kay, George CH
b Manchester 21/9/1891 d 1954
Caps: IrLge 2
Eccles Borough
1910 Bolton Wanderers 3
Distillery
1919 1925 West Ham United 237 15
1927 Stockport County 2
1928 Luton Town 0

Kay, Harold RH
b Chapeltown 24/4/1897 d 1966
Thorncliffe United
1920 1922 Barnsley 14
1923 Southend United 11 1
1924 Barrow 39 3
1925 1927 Crewe Alexandra 119 24
Mansfield Town
Wombwell Town
Barnsley Ministry of Labour

Kay, Harry RB
b Unsworth 3/1883 d 1954
1906 Bolton Wanderers 0
1907 Leeds City 31
1920 1921 Swindon Town 31

Kay, Harry IL
b Elsecar
Elsecar
1907 1909 Barnsley 14 5
Rotherham Town
Rotherham County
Bristol Rovers

Kay, John Sharp (Jacky) IL
b Dalmellington 1908 d 1963
Motherwell Juniors
Dundee United
1933 Blackpool (trial) 0
1933 Crystal Palace (trial) 0
1933 Chester 2
Dundee United
Brechin City
Alloa Athletic

Kay, Robert GK
1888 Burnley 5

Kay, Thomas (Tom) IL/CF/IR
b Ramsbottom 24/4/1883
1902 Blackburn Rovers 0
Nelson
1904 1913 Bury 221 75

From To Apps Goal

Kay, Thomas (Tom) GK
b Mossley Common
Walkden
1913 Bolton Wanderers 0
1919 1921 Stoke 74

Kay, Thomas (Tommy) OL
b Ramsbottom 1904
Ramsbottom British Legion
1923 1924 Accrington Stanley 33 5
1925 Southport (trial) 0
1926 Manchester City (trial) 0
Hurst

Kaye, Albert CF
b Staveley 1875 d 1935
Staveley
Eckington
1897 1898 Sheffield Wednesday 41 12
Chatham
West Ham United
Distillery
1903 Stockport County 16 2

Kaye, Archibald GK
b Glasgow 1869
Glasgow Thistle
1889 1890 Burnley 27

Kaye, George CH
b Huddersfield
1938 Bradford Park Avenue 3
1939 Liverpool 0

Kean, Archibald (Archie) IR/IL
b Barrhead 30/9/1894
Parkhead
Croy Celtic
1921 Clapton Orient 11
1922 1923 Lincoln City 76 11
1924 Blackburn Rovers 0
Grantham

Kean, Frederick William (Fred) RH/CH
b Sheffield 10/12/1898 d 1973
Caps: FLge 4/England 9
Hallam
1920 1928 Sheffield Wednesday 230 8
1928 1930 Bolton Wanderers 80 1
1931 1934 Luton Town 117 5
Sutton Town

Keane, John OR
b Clydebank 1910
Clydebank Corinthians
Yoker Athletic
Kilmarnock
Falkirk (trial)
1936 Exeter City 13 1
1937 1938 Gateshead 5
1939 Hartlepools United 0
Yoker Athletic

Kearney, Joseph Leo (Joe) IR
b Belfast 28/9/1899 d 1981
Glentoran
Ards
1923 Barrow 2

Kearney, Robert (Bob) CH
b Ashton-in-Makerfield 6/3/1903 d 1931
Burnbank Athletic
Kirkintilloch Rob Roy
Dundee
1929 1930 Portsmouth 60

Kearney, Sydney Francis (Syd) LH/IL/RH
b Liverpool 28/3/1917 d 1982
Crowndale
1936 Leicester City 0
1937 1938 Tranmere Rovers 9 2
1938 1946 Accrington Stanley 30 7
1939 (Accrington Stanley) (3)
1946 1949 Bristol City 65 5
Street

Kearney, Terence Patrick (Terry) GK
b Blackpool 8/7/1913 d 1993
St Theresa's
Birkdale South End
1931 Barrow 0
Our Lady of Lourdes
St Theresa's
1933 Southport 2
Our Lady of Lourdes

Kearney, William RB
b Sunderland
Sunderland Celtic
1920 Brentford 6

From To Apps Goal

Kearns, Alfred (Alfie) IR
b Belfast 7/2/1877
Caps: IrLge 3/Ireland 6
Belfast Celtic
Distillery
1904 Blackpool 15 3
St Helens Recreation
Distillery

Kearns, John (Jack) RB
b Talke Pits 4/1/1914 d 1945
Downing Tileries
1936 Millwall 0
1937 Wolverhampton Wanderers 0
1938 Tranmere Rovers 21 1

Kearns, John H RB/LB
b Nuneaton 4/1880 d 1949
Brownhills Albion
Coventry City
1905 1908 Birmingham 61 1
1908 1911 Aston Villa 39
1912 1914 Bristol City 93 1

Kearslake, Joseph George (Joe) OR/CF
b Southampton 9/2/1901 d 1972
1919 Everton 1 1
Wigan Borough
1921 1922 Stockport County 15 2
Chester
Ashton National
Hurst
Ward Street Old Boys
Denton United

Keary, Albert IL
b Liverpool 1889
Violet (West Derby)
Bootle
Africa Royal (Liverpool)
Liverpool Dominion
Accrington Stanley
1911 Manchester City 8 1
Port Vale

Keary, J OR
1898 Darwen 2 1

Keating, Albert Edward IL/IR/OL
b Swillington Common 28/6/1902 d 1984
Prudhoe Castle
1923 1924 Newcastle United 12 3
1925 1927 Bristol City 79 47
1928 1929 Blackburn Rovers 17 5
1930 1932 Cardiff City 45 22
1932 Bristol City 21 6
North Shields
Throckley Welfare

Keating, Reginald (Reg) CF/IR/OR
b Halton 14/5/1904 d 1961
Caps: WLge 1
Annfield Plain
Scotswood United
1926 Newcastle United 0
1927 Lincoln City 2
Gainsborough Trinity
Scarborough
1930 Stockport County 5
1931 Birmingham 5 1
1932 Norwich City 2
North Shields
Bath City
1933 1935 Cardiff City 70 35
1936 Doncaster Rovers 3
1936 Bournemouth & Boscombe Ath 11 5
1937 Carlisle United 5 1
Blyth Spartans

Keay, Richard Henry LB
b Capenhurst q3 1873
Nantwich
1892 Crewe Alexandra 1
Nantwich

Keay, Walter (Wattie) OL
b Whiteinch 8/1871 d 1943
Partick Thistle
Darlington
1893 1894 Derby County 24 7
Southampton

Kedens, James Anderson OL
b Auchinleck 19/4/1901 d 1975
Glenburn Rovers
Sherburn Rovers
Ardeer Thistle
1926 Bristol Rovers 1

From To Apps Goal

Keeble, Albert George CF
b Romford 18/4/1904 d 1984
Ilford
Leytonstone
Great Eastern (Romford)
Barking Town
Leyton
1929 Fulham (trial) 1
Barking Town
Finchley

Keech, William (Bill) CF/RH
b Irthlingborough 22/2/1872 d 1948
Wellingborough
Finedon
Kettering Hawks
Irthlingborough Wanderers
Kettering
Barnsley St Peter's
1895 Liverpool 6
Barnsley St Peter's
1897 Blackpool 16
1897 1898 Leicester Fosse 15 4
1898 Loughborough 13 6
Queen's Park Rangers
Brentford
Kensal Rise United

Keedwell, John Henry (Jack) CF
b Ellesmere Port 12/2/1901 d 1958
1922 Liverpool 0
1924 Oldham Athletic 16 4
Llandudno (loan)
Chester
Colwyn Bay
Runcorn
Mold Town
Llandudno Planters
New Ferry
Bebington

Keeffe, Edward George CH
b Exminster 3/8/1913 d 1990
Exminster
1934 Exeter City 2

Keegan, James Edward (Jimmy) OL
b Barrow 23/10/1896 d 1973
1923 Barrow 7
1924 Gillingham 4
Peterborough & Fletton United
Kettering Town
Poole
Barrow YMCA
Morecambe
Barrow Shipbuilders
Ulverston Town
Barrow Green Athletic
Prescot Cables

Keeley, Arthur CF/OR
b Ellesmere Port 26/9/1916 d 1944
Ellesmere Port Town
1936 Wolverhampton Wanderers 2
1937 Bournemouth & Boscombe Ath 2
1938 Chester 36 18
1939 Portsmouth 0

Keeley, Ernest (Ernie) RH/IR
b Ellesmere Port 1/10/1908 d 1974
Ellesmere Port Town
1931 Chester 19
1931 1932 Leicester City 4

Keeley, S CF
1895 Crewe Alexandra 1

Keeley, Samuel CF
b Scotland 1874
1897 Everton 1
Dundee

Keeling, Alfred John (Alf) OR
b Bradford 14/12/1920 d 1942
1937 Bradford Park Avenue 1
1938 Portsmouth 0

Keeling, Harold (Harry) IL
b Huthwaite 10/2/1906 d 1988
Huthwaite CWS
Sutton Town
Grantham
Mansfield Town
1926 Luton Town 0
1927 Wolverhampton Wanderers 0
1928 Notts County 0
1929 1930 Torquay United 26 10
1931 Swindon Town 24 7
1932 Norwich City 5 1
1933 Mansfield Town 8
Bath City
Sutton Town
Hereford United
Tamworth
Brierley Hill Alliance
Hereford United

From To Apps Goal

Keeling, Percy OR
b Basford q1 1903 d 1939
New Hucknall Colliery
Alfreton Town
1924 Notts County 6
Ilkeston Town

Keen, Errington Ridley Liddell(Eric 'Ike') LH
b Walker 4/9/1910 d 1984
Caps: FLge 1/England 4
Nun's Moor
1930 Newcastle United 1
1930 1937 Derby County 219 4
Chelmsford City
Hereford United
1945 Leeds United 0
Bacup Borough
1946 Hull City 0
IFK Norrkoping

Keen, Herbert Jackson OL
b Ulverston q4 1900 d 1955
Vickerstown
1922 Barrow 2
Dalton Casuals

Keen, James Frederick OR
b Walker 25/11/1895 d 1980
Walker Celtic
Carlisle United
1920 1921 Bristol City 9 1
1922 Newcastle United 2
1923 Queen's Park Rangers 31
1924 Hull City 17
1925 Darlington (trial) 0
1925 Wigan Borough 12
Walker Celtic

Keen, Stanley OR
b Walker 1905
1932 Everton 0
1933 Carlisle United 1 1
1933 Tranmere Rovers 0

Keen, Walter James (Wally) CH/RB/LB
b Loudwater q2 1904 d 1968
Wycombe Wanderers
1926 1928 Millwall 6
1931 Fulham 0
1932 1934 Clapton Orient 53 2
London Transport (Tramways)

Keen, William Joseph (Billy) CF
b Hazlemere 19/6/1901 d 1971
1920 1923 Millwall Athletic 64 24
1924 Luton Town 3

Keenan, Arnold IL
b Belfast
Glentoran
1925 Crystal Palace 4
Philadelphia Celtic
Fall River Marksmen
New York Nationals
Providence Clamdiggers

Keenan, Harold CH/RH
b Warrington 20/12/1893 d 1956
Atherton
1912 1922 Blackpool 100 3

Keenan, John (Jack) LH
b Clitheroe 1864 d 1906
Clitheroe
1888 1892 Burnley 68

Keenan, William G RB
b Torbray 1916
West Calder
1938 Rochdale 9
1939 (Rochdale) (3)
1945 Newport County 0

Keenlyside, George OL/OR
b Jarrow 4/8/1889 d 1967
Jarrow Royal Oak
Jarrow Park Villa
Jarrow Croft
1908 Sunderland 0
Jarrow
Partick Thistle
Jarrow Croft
1919 1922 South Shields 98 11
1923 Hartlepools United 24 1
Jarrow

Keenor, Frederick Charles (Fred) CH/RH
b Cardiff 31/7/1894 d 1972
Caps: Wales Sch/WLge 2/Wales 32
Roath Wednesday
1920 1930 Cardiff City 371 13
1931 1933 Crewe Alexandra 116 5
Oswestry Town
Tunbridge Wells Rangers

Keeping, Alexander Edwin Michael (Mike) LB
b Milford-on-Sea 22/8/1902 d 1984
Caps: FLge 1
Milford-on-Sea
1924 1932 Southampton 265 10
1932 1938 Fulham 205 7
1939 (Fulham) (2)

Keers, John Mandell (Manny) OL
b Tow Law 2/1900 d 1963
Chopwell Colliery
Langley Park
Tow Law Town
1925 Hull City 8 1
Annfield Plain
1926 Nelson 8 3
Boston Town
Hyde United

Keetley, Albert E OR
b Derby q4 1885 d 1946
1906 Burton United 2

Keetley, Charles Frederick (Charlie) CF/IR
b Derby 10/3/1906 d 1979
Alvaston & Boulton
1927 1934 Leeds United 160 108
1934 Bradford City 22 4
1935 Reading 9 3

Keetley, Frank IR/OR
b Derby 23/3/1901 d 1968
Victoria Ironworks
1921 1925 Derby County 76 8
1926 1929 Doncaster Rovers 110 28
1929 1930 Bradford City 28 8
1931 1932 Lincoln City 42 28
1932 Hull City 0
Margate
Worcester City

Keetley, Harold CF/IL
b Derby 9/4/1903 d 1982
Victoria Ironworks
Matlock Town
1924 1926 Doncaster Rovers 47 25
Mansfield Town

Keetley, Joseph Frederick (Joe) IL/OR
b Derby 28/6/1897 d 1958
Victoria Ironworks
1921 Bolton Wanderers 1
1923 Accrington Stanley 13 8
1923 Liverpool 9 3
1925 Wolverhampton Wanderers 10 5
1925 Wrexham 7 3
1925 Doncaster Rovers 2
Horwich RMI
Lancaster Town
Ribble Motors

Keetley, Thomas (Tom) CF/OR
b Derby 16/11/1898 d 1958
Victoria Ironworks
1919 Derby County 0
1919 1922 Bradford Park Avenue 21 5
1923 1928 Doncaster Rovers 231 180
1929 1932 Notts County 103 94
1933 Lincoln City 10 5
Gresley Rovers
Heanor Town

Keeton, Albert (Bob) RB/LB
b Chesterfield 15/1/1918 d 1996
Gainsborough Trinity
Mosborough Trinity
1937 1947 Torquay United 77
Yeovil Town

Keeton, William Walter (Walter) IR
b Shirebrook 30/4/1905 d 1980
Loughborough Corinthians
Grantham
1930 1931 Sunderland 12 1
1932 Nottingham Forest 5
Grantham

Keggans, Henry (Harry) IR
b Cambuslang 1888
Sanquhar
Nithsdale Wanderers
1911 Bradford City 1
1912 Lincoln City 0
Cardiff City
Nithsdale Wanderers

Keightley, Arthur OR
b Cromford 7/12/1908 d 1976
Brimington Juniors
1928 Chesterfield 20 1
Shirebrook
Heanor Town
Sutton Junction

Keir, Charles RB
1904 1905 Glossop 14

Keir, Matthew OR
b Old Kilpatrick 23/2/1871
Dalmuir Thistle
1893 Newcastle United 1

Keizer, Gerrit Pieter (Gerry) GK
b Amsterdam, Holland 18/8/1910 d 1980
Caps: Holland 2
1929 Millwall 0
Margate
1930 Arsenal 12
1931 Charlton Athletic 17
1932 Queen's Park Rangers 0
Ajax

Kelham, Harold James LH
b Derby 22/9/1888 d 1969
1908 Derby County 1

Kell, George RB/LB
b Gateshead 13/7/1896 d 1985
Allhusen Works (Gateshead)
1920 Sheffield Wednesday 5
1922 1924 Brentford 76
1925 1927 Hartlepools United 71 1
Gainsborough Trinity

Kellard, Thomas (Tom) OR/IR/IL
b Oldham 30/11/1904 d 1986
Limehurst
Chamber Colliery
Hurst
Ashton National
Glossop
Hurst
1927 Oldham Athletic 2
1927 1928 Queen's Park Rangers 5 1
Burton Town
Hurst
Mossley
Stalybridge Celtic
Ashton National
Ashton United

Kellett, Alfred CH
b Preston 22/5/1903 d 1970
Dick, Kerr's XI
1926 Rochdale 1
Rossendale United

Kellett, Charles Arthur CF
b Grassmoor 26/12/1908 d 1990
1929 Halifax Town 2

Kellett, Thomas William (Tom) RB
b Crewe 24/1/1890 d 1969
1921 Crewe Alexandra 5
Nantwich

Kellock, William (Billy) IL/OL
b Stockport 18/4/1889 d 1966
1920 Plymouth Argyle 6 1
Torquay Town
1921 Aberdare Athletic 15 4
1922 Barrow 29 12
Torquay United
Poole
Green Waves
St Austell
Mayflower Press

Kelly, Bernard RB
b Wishaw 1889
Glasgow Ashfield
1910 Middlesbrough 4

Kelly, Charles IR
b Sandbach 14/6/1894 d 1969
Sandbach Ramblers
1923 1925 Stoke 27 5
1927 Tranmere Rovers 1

Kelly, Christopher (Chris) RH/CH
b Tunstall 10/9/1887 d 1950
Goldenhill Wanderers
Stoke
Denaby United
1910 1911 Leeds City 4
Denaby United

Kelly, Daniel (Dan) IR/OR/OL
b Blantyre 25/6/1904 d 1941
Blantyre Victoria
Hamilton Academical
1926 1927 Derby County 5
1928 1929 Torquay United 53 13
1930 1931 York City 48 12
1932 1933 Doncaster Rovers 13 4
Dundalk
1935 Clapton Orient 0

Kelly, Dominic (Dom) CH
b Sandbach 23/6/1917 d 1982
Sandbach Ramblers
1937 Leeds United 4
1938 Newcastle United 1

Kelly, Francis (Frank) OL
b Liverpool 1883
White Star Wanderers
Chester
1903 Barnsley 10 3
1904 Chesterfield Town 9 1
Watford
Leyton
Watford
1909 1910 Stockport County 46 11
Nelson
1911 Everton 0

Kelly, Gerard (Gerry) OR/CF
b Castletown 18/11/1909 d 1986
Castletown
Hylton Colliery
1927 Sunderland 0
1928 1929 Nelson 47 15
1929 1931 Huddersfield Town 37 15
1931 1932 Charlton Athletic 20 6
1932 1935 Chester 73 27
1936 Port Vale 20 2
1937 1938 Southampton 19 2
1939 (Southampton) (1)

Kelly, Hugh OL
Cadzow Oak
Motherwell Celtic
Cambuslang Rangers
Motherwell
1914 Preston North End 4 1
Clyde
Armadale

Kelly, James IL
b Glasgow 1870
Shettleston
1892 Lincoln City 8 1
Liverpool

Kelly, James CF
Overton Rangers
Airdrieonians (trial)
Wishaw United
1926 Blackpool 1 1
Airdrieonians

Kelly, James Edward (Jimmy 'Ned') RB/LB
b Seaham Harbour 29/12/1907 d 1984
Langley Park
Seaham Harbour
Blyth Spartans
Dawdon Colliery
Murton Colliery Welfare
1928 1930 Southport 7
Chorley (trial)
1931 1932 Barrow 55
1932 1937 Grimsby Town 160 3
1938 Bradford Park Avenue 2
1938 York City 24
1939 (York City) (3)
Trondheim
1946 Barrow 1

Kelly, James Steen IL
b Ballymacarrett q2 1902
Mountpottinger
Dundela
Castlereagh
Willowfield
Bangor
Barn
St Johnstone
Fall River Marksmen
Bangor
1929 Barrow 2
Glentoran
Portadown
Ards
Fall River Marksmen
Trocadero

Kelly, Jeremiah (Jerry) RH/CH
b Hamilton 1900
Uddingston St John's
Blantyre Victoria
Ayr United
1926 1929 Everton 81 1
Celtic
1930 Carlisle United 32
Rennes University Club
Dolphin
Stranraer
Glentoran
Dunfermline Athletic (trial)

From	To		Apps	Goal
Kelly, John			GK	
b Wishaw 4/5/1902				
		Wishaw YMCA		
		Vale of Fleet		
1922		Preston North End	0	
		Motherwell		
		Peebles Rovers		
1925		Brighton & Hove Albion	2	
1926		Gillingham	16	
1927		Crystal Palace	22	
		Thames		
1928		Tottenham Hotspur (trial)	0	
		Nithsdale Wanderers		
		Celtic		
		Nithsdale Wanderers (loan)		
1930	1932	Carlisle United	77	
		Coleraine		
		Motherwell		
		Beith		
Kelly, John			OL	
b Clydebank				
		St Roch's		
1927	1928	Darlington	18	1
Kelly, John			IL	
b 1909				
		Durham City		
1930		York City	6	4
		Yorkshire Amateurs		
Kelly, John (Jack)			CF/IR	
b Hetton-le-Hole 2/3/1913			d 2000	
		Hetton Juniors		
1930	1932	Burnley	30	12
1933	1934	Newcastle United	5	1
1934	1937	Leeds United	59	17
1937	1938	Birmingham	12	1
1939		Bury	(3)	(1)
Kelly, John (Mick)			CF/IR	
b Sandbach 1913				
1932		Accrington Stanley	0	
1934	1935	Leeds United	4	
1935		Barnsley	3	
1935		Bradford City	5	
		Bedford Town		
Kelly, John Norman (Norman)			IL	
b Liverpool 1909				
		Seaforth Ribble Motors		
1931		Blackburn Rovers	0	
1933		Southport (trial)	0	
1933		Accrington Stanley	14	8
Kelly, Lawrence (Lawrie)			LB/RB	
b Bellshill 19/11/1911			d 1979	
		St Anthony's (Glasgow)		
1934	1935	Southend United	20	
1936		Bristol City	1	
1937	1938	Aldershot	40	
1939		(Aldershot)	(3)	
Kelly, Martin			IL	
		Lincoln Liberal Club		
1905	1906	Lincoln City	24	3
1907		Oldham Athletic	0	
		Lincoln Liberal Club		
Kelly, Michael J			OL/IL	
b Blackburn 1877				
		Clitheroe		
		Ashton North End		
1897	1898	Bury	25	7
		Reading		
1900		Blackburn Rovers	3	
Kelly, Nicholas			OL	
1925	1926	Walsall	2	
Kelly, Patrick J (Paddy)			OR	
b Kilcoo 7/9/1896				
Caps: Lol 1/Ireland 1				
		Belfast Celtic		
1920	1922	Manchester City	25	1
1923		West Ham United	0	
		Fordsons		
Kelly, Peter			IR	
		Kirkintilloch Rob Roy		
1920		Millwall Athletic	11	1
		Dundee Hibernian		
Kelly, Peter			IR/IL	
b Tyldesley 20/3/1901			d 1950	
		Tyldesley Celtic		
		Chorley		
1924	1925	New Brighton	54	18
1925	1927	Notts County	69	19
1929		New Brighton	8	2
		Chorley		
		Hindsford		

From	To		Apps	Goal
Kelly, Peter W			LB	
		North Shields Athletic		
1908		Sunderland	1	
		Merthyr Town		
Kelly, Robert (Bob)			IR/OR	
b Ashton-in-Makerfield 16/11/1893			d 1969	
Caps: FLge 7/England 14				
		Ashton White Star		
		Ashton Central		
		Earlestown Rovers		
		St Helens Town		
1913	1925	Burnley	277	88
1925	1926	Sunderland	50	11
1926	1931	Huddersfield Town	186	39
1932	1934	Preston North End	78	17
1934	1935	Carlisle United	12	1
Kelly, Thomas			LH	
		Seaham White Star		
1905		Sunderland	1	
		Murton Red Star		
		Seaham Albion		
		Seaham Harbour		
Kelly, Thomas			RH/CH	
b Tunstall q2 1884			d 1916	
		Denaby Main		
1906		Glossop	23	1
		Denaby United		
1908	1909	Grimsby Town	26	3
		New Brompton		
		Silverwood Town		
Kelly, Thomas			CF	
b Manchester 13/1/1902			d 1979	
		Corpus Christi		
		Ancoats Lads Club		
		Bradford Road Gasworks		
		Hadfield		
		Stalybridge Celtic		
1923	1924	Barnsley	15	5
		Rhyl Athletic		
1930		Wigan Borough	1	
Kelly, Thomas (Tim)			IR	
b Belfast 14/9/1907			d 1975	
Caps: Ireland Amat				
		RAF		
1930		Fulham	1	
		Vauxhall Motors (Luton)		
Kelly, Thomas William (Tom)			CH/RH/RB	
b Darlington 22/11/1919			d 1970	
		Deneside Juniors		
1937	1950	Darlington	157	2
1951		York City	0	
Kelly, William (Willie)			RH	
b Kirkintilloch 27/3/1880				
		Cadzow Oak		
		Hamilton Academical		
		West Ham United		
1903		Notts County	2	
		Brighton & Hove Albion		
		Bathgate		
		Maxwelltown Volunteers		
Kelly, William			GK	
1919		South Shields	1	
Kelly, William Bainbridge			IR	
b Newcastle q4 1890			d 1920	
		Benwell Adelaide		
		Newcastle Balmoral		
		Blaydon		
		North Shields Athletic		
		Watford		
1911		Newcastle United	6	
1911	1912	Manchester City	10	
		Blyth Spartans		
		Rochdale		
Kelsall, Josiah			CF	
b Maryport 20/5/1892			d 1974	
		Maryport		
1913		Sunderland	1	
		Houghton Rovers		
		Spennymoor United		
Kelsey, Arthur George			IL	
b Dudley q4 1871			d 1955	
		Reading		
		29th Worcestershire Regiment		
1895		West Bromwich Albion	11	
		Brierley Hill Alliance		
1897		Wolverhampton Wanderers	0	
Kelsey, William John (Billy)			GK	
b Durham q4 1887			d 1952	
		Boldon Juniors		
		Boldon Star		
1906		Newcastle United	2	
		Boldon Colliery		

From	To		Apps	Goal
Kelso, James (Jimmy)			LB/RB/LH	
b Cardross 8/12/1910			d 1987	
		Helensburgh		
		Dumbarton		
1933		Bradford Park Avenue	11	
1934		Port Vale	15	
1935	1937	Newport County	119	1
1938		Cardiff City	41	
1945		Swindon Town	0	
		Ebbw Vale		
Kelso, Robert Robinson (Bob)			RB/RH	
b Cardross 2/10/1865			d 1942	
Caps: SLge 1/Scotland 8				
		Renton		
		Newcastle West End		
1888		Everton	1	
1889	1890	Preston North End	38	
1891	1895	Everton	88	5
		Dundee		
		Bedminster		
Kelso, Thomas (Tommy)			RB	
b Renton 5/6/1882			d 1974	
Caps: Scotland 1				
		Rangers (trial)		
		Third Lanark		
1906	1911	Manchester City	138	3
		Dundee		
		Rangers		
		Dumbarton		
		Abercorn		
Kelson, Harry James			LH	
b Bath q4 1889			d 1966	
1914		Bristol City	0	
1920		Newport County	11	1
		Mardy		
Kemp, Frederick (Fred)			OL	
b Tottenham 1887				
		Ethelburga's		
		Barking St Andrew's		
		Newportonians		
		Barking Victoria		
1905		Woolwich Arsenal	2	
		West Ham United		
		Dundee		
		Falkirk		
Kemp, Gilbert			IL/CF	
b Wallasey q1 1888			d 1951	
		Wallasey Rovers		
1912	1914	Oldham Athletic	64	23
1919		Bradford City	1	
1919		Coventry City	3	2
1919		Grimsby Town	9	1
		Doncaster Rovers		
Kemp, Haydn			LH/RH	
b Mosborough 17/1/1897			d 1982	
		New Bolsover Wesleyans		
		Staveley West End		
		Anston United		
		Bolsover Colliery		
		Bolsover Town		
		Chesterfield Municipal		
1920	1930	Notts County	286	6
1931		Thames	28	2
		Grantham		
		Heanor Town		
Kemp, Richard James (Dirk)			GK	
b Cape Town, South Africa 15/10/1913				
		Sea Point Boys Club		
		Arcadia		
		Transvaal		
1936	1938	Liverpool	27	
1939		(Liverpool)	(3)	
Kemplay, James			CF	
b Middlesbrough 17/1/1876				
		Middlesbrough St John's		
		Middlesbrough		
1898		Luton Town	29	11
Kempton, Arthur Richard			GK	
b West Thurrock 29/1/1892				
		Hastings & St Leonards		
		Tufnell Park		
1914		Arsenal	0	
1921		Reading	9	
		Folkestone		
		Tunbridge Wells Rangers		
Kendall, John William (Jack)			GK	
b Broughton, Lincolnshire 9/10/1905			d 1961	
		Broughton Rangers		
1922	1923	Lincoln City	71	
1923	1925	Everton	21	
1927		Preston North End	2	
1928	1929	Lincoln City	46	
1929	1933	Sheffield United	80	
		Peterborough United		

From	To		Apps	Goal
Kendrick, Kenny			CF/OR	
b Bartley Green 28/4/1913			d 1988	
		Halesowen Town		
1936	1938	Birmingham	10	3
Kennedy, Andrew Lynd (Andy)			LB/CH	
b Belfast 1/9/1895			d 1963	
Caps: Ireland 2				
		Belfast Celtic		
		Glentoran		
1920	1921	Crystal Palace	4	
1922	1927	Arsenal	122	
1928		Everton	1	
1930		Tranmere Rovers	36	
Kennedy, Fred			IL/IR	
b Black Lane 23/10/1902			d 1963	
		Rossendale United		
1923	1924	Manchester United	17	4
1924	1926	Everton	35	11
1927	1928	Middlesbrough	23	5
1929		Reading	23	8
1930		Oldham Athletic	5	
		Rossendale United		
		Northwich Victoria		
		Racing Club de Paris		
1933		Blackburn Rovers	29	8
		Racing Club de Paris		
1937		Stockport County	6	1
Kennedy, George			LH/CH	
b Dumfries 1885			d 1917	
		Maxwelltown Volunteers		
1906	1907	Lincoln City	42	
1908		Chelsea	10	
		Brentford		
Kennedy, James			IR	
1913		Preston North End	3	1
Kennedy, James			OR	
b Burradon 20/2/1897			d 1988	
		Bedlington United		
1921	1924	Portsmouth	22	
1925		Reading	6	
Kennedy, James John (Jimmy)			CH/LH/RH	
b Dundee 8/5/1883			d 1947	
		Celtic		
		Brighton & Hove Albion		
1906	1908	Leeds City	58	1
1909		Stockport County	18	1
1909	1911	Tottenham Hotspur	13	1
		Swindon Town		
		Norwich City		
		Watford		
		Gillingham		
Kennedy, John (Jack)			IR	
b Edinburgh 1873				
Caps: SLge 1/Scotland 1				
		Hibernian		
1897	1899	Stoke	58	8
1900	1902	Glossop	39	7
Kennedy, John (Jack)			IL/IR	
b Blyth				
		Blyth Spartans		
1929		Sheffield United	0	
1930	1931	Tranmere Rovers	65	45
1932	1933	Exeter City	16	3
1933		Torquay United	19	1
1934		Watford	0	
		Blyth Spartans		
Kennedy, Robert			IL/CF	
b Glasgow				
		Kirkintilloch Rob Roy		
		Petershill		
		Shettleston		
		Falkirk		
		Raith Rovers (loan)		
1928	1929	South Shields	70	25
1930	1933	Gateshead	134	53
		Third Lanark		
Kennedy, Samuel (Sam)			CF/RH	
b Platts Common 1896			d 1963	
		Wombwell		
1920		Huddersfield Town	0	
1921		Burnley	0	
		Denaby United		
		Wombwell		
1923		Nelson	6	
1924	1925	Fulham	6	1
1926		Barnsley	9	5
		Mexborough Athletic		
		Shirebrook		
		Scunthorpe & Lindsey United		
		Brigg Town		
		Broughton Rovers		

From To Apps Goal

Kennedy, Stephen Patrick (Steve) RH/LH
b Edge Hill 26/12/1914 d 1982
Prescot Cables
1933 1934 Southport 2
St Vincent's CYMS

Kennedy, William (Billy) IL
b Scotland
Renton
Clyde
1904 Bradford City 0
Brighton & Hove Albion
1906 Stockport County 18 2
Stenhousemuir

Kennedy, William (Bill) CH/OR
b Saltcoats 2/2/1912 d 1989
Royal Albert
1931 Portsmouth 1
1933 Carlisle United 8
Portadown
1935 Crewe Alexandra 6
1936 1937 Southampton 43
Colchester United
Hamilton Academical

Kennedy, William John IR
b Scotland
Ayr Parkhouse
1895 1896 Newton Heath 30 11
Stockport County
Morton

Kennie, George OL
b Bradford 17/5/1904 d 1994
1921 1923 Bradford Park Avenue 10
Mansfield Town
1925 Halifax Town 28 2

Kenny, David Brown CH/CF
b Maybole 22/5/1891
Maybole
Girvan
Falkirk
Barrow
1913 1919 Grimsby Town 58
1920 Bristol Rovers 11
Nainamo City (Canada)

Kent, Ernest RB
1924 Rotherham County 1

Kent, Henry (Harry) CH
b Foleshill 22/10/1879 d 1948
Heanor Town
Ilkeston Town
Newark
Brighton & Hove Albion
1908 Middlesbrough 6
Watford

Kent, Jack LB
1891 Everton 1
Loughborough

Kent, Percy W OL
b 1897
1919 Blackpool 5
1920 Grimsby Town 1

Kent, Thomas OR
Carrington
1898 Nottingham Forest 2

Kent, William Edward LB/RB
b Middlesbrough q1 1875
Middlesbrough Grange
Jarrow
1899 Sheffield United 2
1900 Glossop 14

Kenworthy, Ernest G OR/IR
b Sutton Junction 1888
Matlock
Manningham Recreational
1906 1908 Bradford City 2 1
Sutton Junction
Huddersfield Town

Kenyon, Arthur GK
b Birmingham q1 1868 d 1895
Birmingham St George's
1892 1893 Darwen 46
Worcester Rovers

Kenyon, Frank OR
b Chorlton 22/2/1912 d 1978
Usworth Colliery
1931 Bolton Wanderers 0
Usworth Colliery
Wardley Colliery Welfare
1933 Charlton Athletic 1
1934 New Brighton 13 3
Ashington
Blyth Spartans
Newbiggin Welfare

From To Apps Goal

Kenyon, GB LH/RH
1897 1898 Darwen 11

Kenyon, James (Jimmy) CF/IR
b Glossop q1 1888
1908 1909 Stockport County 18 3
1910 Bradford Park Avenue 1
Rochdale
Millwall Athletic
1913 Glossop 1
Hurst
1914 Stockport County 3 2

Kenyon, Joseph OR
Failsworth
1906 Burnley 29

Keogh, George A LB
b Leicester
St Andrew's (Leicester)
Leicester Imperial
1905 Leicester Fosse 1
Leicester Imperial
Hinckley United
Leicester Imperial
Aylestone Park Adult School

Kerns, Frederick IR
b Paddington 1883
1907 Aston Villa 0
1908 Birmingham 1
Bristol Rovers

Kerr, Albert Wigham OR
b Lanchester 11/8/1917 d 1979
Lanchester CRC
Gateshead Colts
Medomsley Juniors
1936 1946 Aston Villa 29 4

Kerr, Andrew (Andy) CF
b Ardrossan 1900
Ardrossan Winton Rovers
Partick Thistle
Ardrossan Winton Rovers
1923 1924 Luton Town 68 25
1925 Reading 3 1
1925 Queen's Park Rangers 2

Kerr, Daniel (Danny) IL
b Hamilton 1915
Carluke Rovers
1934 Manchester United 0
1935 Accrington Stanley 2
1937 Birmingham (trial) 0

Kerr, David (Jock) CF
b Wishaw 1913
Wishaw Thistle
Stonehouse Violet
Clyde
Glentoran
Bangor
Drumcondra
Bangor
1937 Lincoln City 5
Newark Town

Kerr, Edward Joseph (Ned) OL
b Belfast
Wilton Amateurs
Logan Celtic
Barn
Belfast Celtic
1919 Preston North End 2
Wallsend

Kerr, George IR
Annbank
Kilmarnock
1893 Notts County 23 6
Annbank

Kerr, Hugh CF
b 1882
Westerlea
Ayr
1903 Manchester United 2

Kerr, Jasper Howat LB/RB
b Burnbank 1898
Burnbank Athletic
Larkhall Thistle
Bathgate
1924 1926 Everton 18 1
1926 1931 Preston North End 121
1933 New Brighton 10
Lancaster Town

Kerr, John RH/LH
b Sanquhar 4/11/1894
Queen's Park
1919 1920 Blackburn Rovers 16
1921 1923 Brentford 85 1
Solway Star

From To Apps Goal

Kerr, Neil OR/CF
b Bowling 13/4/1871 d 1901
Cowlairs
Rangers
1894 Liverpool 12 3
1895 Nottingham Forest 1
Falkirk
Rangers

Kerr, Robert Charles (Bobby) CF
b Larkhall 1904
Netherton Recreation
Wishaw YMCA
Third Lanark
Larkhall Thistle
Wishaw YMCA
Heart of Midlothian
Oadby Town
1925 1926 Wolverhampton Wanderers 18 7
1927 1928 Clapton Orient 31 8
Worcester City
Kettering Town
Grantham

Kerr, Thomas McDonald (Tommy) RB
b New Cumnock 5/1/1909
Kello Rovers
Partick Thistle (trial)
1933 Notts County (trial)
Queen of the South
1935 1938 Carlisle United 136
Kello Rovers

Kerry, Arthur Henry Gould OL
b Headington 21/7/1879 d 1967
Caps: England Amat
Tottenham Hotspur
Oxford City
1909 Tottenham Hotspur 1
Oxford University

Kerry, Edward (Ned) IL
b Creswell 16/6/1905 d 1976
Creswell United Methodists
Creswell Colliery
Long Eaton
Creswell United Methodists
Shirebrook
Long Eaton
Matlock Town
1927 Liverpool 0
Mansfield Town
1928 Notts County (trial) 0
1929 1931 Barnsley 48 6
Llanelly
1933 Barnsley 0
1933 Mansfield Town 0
Creswell Boys Brigade

Kerry, J OL
1900 Burton Swifts 23 5

Kershaw, John RB/CF
b Standish 7/4/1899 d 1977
Standish St Wilfred's
St Marie's
Wigan United
1921 1923 Wigan Borough 40 1
Chorley
1924 Wigan Borough 1
Runcorn
Hurst
Winsford United (trial)
Congleton Town

Kessler, Lawrence P (Laurie) OL
b Woolwich 1889
RAF
1921 Hartlepools United 13
Shildon Athletic

Kettle, E IL
1893 Northwich Victoria 4

Kettle, William Walderham (Billy) OL/IL
b South Shields 10/9/1898 d 1980
Leeds City
1919 South Shields
1919 Newcastle United 0
Ebbw Vale
1921 Southend United 31 1
1922 Grimsby Town 16 3
1923 Southport 18 1
1923 1925 Wigan Borough 39 13

Key, George Brown RH/LH
b Dennistoun 11/2/1882 d 1958
Caps: Scotland 1
Baillieston Rangers
Parkhead Juniors
Heart of Midlothian
1905 1908 Chelsea 54 2
Baillieston Rangers

From To Apps Goal

Keys, John (Jack) CF
b 1866 d 1890
1888 Everton 1
Everton Athletic

Kidd, Ernest OR
b Dunston-on-Tyne 25/5/1895 d 1974
Scotswood
1919 Newcastle United 0
Dunston Atlas Villa
1920 Bolton Wanderers 0
1921 1922 Wigan Borough 26
1923 Ashington 28
Workington

Kidd, George Imlay LH/CF
b Dundee 20/5/1909 d 1988
Dundee North End
1931 Charlton Athletic 6 1
1931 1934 Gillingham 119 2
1934 1935 Luton Town 9

Kidd, James (Jimmy) GK
b Darlington 1884
Spennymoor United
1910 1914 Blackpool 65
1914 Bolton Wanderers 9
1919 1921 Derby County 20
Fleetwood

Kidd, John W (Jack) IR/IL
b Glasgow 1884 d 1927
Maryhill
Third Lanark
Swindon Town
Third Lanark
St Johnstone
1910 1911 Birmingham 40 8
Brierley Hill Alliance

Kidd, William Edward (Billy) LB
b Pegswood 31/1/1907 d 1978
Pegswood Juniors
Pegswood United
Bedlington United
Pegswood United
1931 1947 Chesterfield 316 2
1939 (Chesterfield) (2)

Kiddier, James Frederick CF
b Nottingham q3 1874 d 1935
1895 Notts County 15 4
Bulwell United
Sutton Town

Kidger, Edmund Alt IR
b Derby 16/7/1892 d 1976
1913 Sheffield United 0
Worksop Town
1920 Norwich City 4
Peterborough & Fletton United

Kifford, John (Jackie) RB/LB
b Paisley 20/10/1875 d 1921
Abercorn
1898 1899 Derby County 6
Bristol Rovers
1901 1904 West Bromwich Albion 96 8
Millwall Athletic
Carlisle United
Coventry City

Kilborn, Cecil IL/IR
b Desborough 18/3/1902 d 1983
Desborough Town
1921 1923 Bradford City 40 5

Kilbourne, Amos IR/IL
b Long Eaton q1 1881 d 1940
Sawley Rangers
1905 1906 Bury 26 8
1907 1909 Grimsby Town 66 16

Kilcar, Stephen P (Steve) IL/IR
b Bo'ness 22/12/1907
Linlithgow Rose
East Stirlingshire
1929 1931 Bradford Park Avenue 27 9
1932 Coventry City 4
1933 1934 Mansfield Town 31 14
1934 Chester 3 4
1935 1936 Burnley 24 7
1936 Bournemouth & Boscombe Ath 6
1937 Watford 0

Killean, Edward (Ted) LH/LB/IL
b Blackburn 1874
3rd Coldstream Guards
1894 1897 Blackburn Rovers 88 6
1898 1899 Glossop North End 54 4
Southampton
New Brompton
1903 Blackpool 3

From To Apps Goal

Killourhy, Michael Joseph (Mick) IR/IL
b New Springs 19/2/1911 d 2002
Coldstream Guards
Kirklees Stars
Darwen
1929 1931 Wigan Borough 17 5
1931 1935 Sheffield United 27 6
1936 1938 Doncaster Rovers 63 28
Denaby United
Goole Town

Kilner, A CF
1899 Barnsley 2 1
Penistone

Kilsby, Reginald Harry Robert (Reg) OL/OR/LH
b Wollaston 23/8/1910 d 1992
Wellingborough Town
1934 Northampton Town 1
Scunthorpe & Lindsey United
1936 Rotherham United 1
1937 Aldershot 31 5
Tunbridge Wells Rangers
1938 Rochdale 23 6
1939 (Rochdale) (3)

Kilshaw, Edmund Ainsworth (Eddie) OR
b Prescot 25/12/1919 d 2006
Prescot Cables
1937 1948 Bury 147 17
1948 Sheffield Wednesday 17 1

Kimberley, John B CF
b Birkenhead q2 1899
Port Sunlight
1922 Tranmere Rovers 2

Kimberley, Walter LB/RH
b Birmingham q4 1884 d 1917
Tower Unity
Selly Oak St Mary's
Coldstream Guards
Aston Manor
1907 1908 Aston Villa 7
Coventry City
Walsall

King, Alexander IL
b Dykehead 27/7/1871 d 1957
Dykehead
Airdrieonians
Albion Rovers
Wishaw Thistle
1894 Darwen 21 10
Dykehead
Rangers (trial)
Heart of Midlothian
Celtic
Dykehead
St Bernard's
Dykehead
Airdrieonians
Dykehead

King, Alfred (Alf) OL
b Wallyford 6/6/1906
Wallyford Bluebell
1927 1929 Bristol Rovers 45 10
1930 Tranmere Rovers 0
St Bernard's

King, Alfred Page GK
b Swardeston 26/11/1895 d 1975
CEYMS Thursday
1921 Norwich City 3

King, Arthur CF
1900 Gainsborough Trinity 30 7
Queen's Park Rangers

King, Arthur GK
b Kentore 6/8/1887
Aberdeen East End
Aberdeen
1913 Tottenham Hotspur 19
Belfast Celtic
Dunfermline Athletic
Dumbarton
Forres Mechanics
Inverness Caledonian

King, Charles Thomas (Charlie) CH
b Johannesburg, South Africa 18/5/1897 d 1973
Metrogas
1922 Millwall Athletic 0
1923 Southport 35 1
Blaenau Ffestiniog
Northwich Victoria

King, Cyril William RH
b Plymouth q3 1915
Plymouth United
1934 1938 Southampton 93 2
1939 Darlington 0
Plymouth Argyle

From To Apps Goal

King, Edgar Frederick (Eddie) LB
b Hackney 25/2/1914 d 1993
Tottenham Juniors
Tufnell Park
Northfleet
1934 Tottenham Hotspur 1

King, Edward (Eddie) RH
b Blyth 1890
Leyton
1912 Woolwich Arsenal 11
1914 Clapton Orient 17

King, Edwin (Teddy) LH/CH/RH
b Leicester 7/7/1884 d 1952
Aylestone Swifts
St Andrew's (Leicester)
Leicester Imperial
1906 1921 Leicester Fosse 227 26

King, EH OL
1902 1905 Burton United 121 17
Stafford Rangers
Burton Town
Oldfields (Uttoxeter)
Chesterton White Star
Wetmoor County
Gresley Rovers

King, Ernest Stanley RB/RH
b Southampton 6/12/1902 d 1993
Hamilton House
1924 Bournemouth & Boscombe Ath 0
1925 1926 Southampton 2
Guildford City

King, Ernest William (Ernie) RB/LB
b Brockley 25/11/1907 d 2001
Wyke Sports
Weymouth
1930 West Bromwich Albion 0
1931 1937 Brighton & Hove Albion 186

King, Francis Oliver (Frank) GK
b Alnwick 13/3/1917 d 2003
Blyth Spartans
1934 1936 Everton 13
1937 Derby County 3

King, Frederick Alfred Bobby (Bobby) OR/IL/IR
b Northampton 19/9/1919 d 2003
1937 1938 Northampton Town 42 6
1939 (Northampton Town) (3)
1945 1946 Wolverhampton Wanderers 6 3
1947 1949 Northampton Town 56 17
Rushden Town

King, George RH
b Dunblane
Sunderland Albion
1892 1893 Burnley 33 2
Millwall Athletic

King, George Colin IL
b Combs 8/12/1900 d 1991
Old Chorltonians
1922 Oldham Athletic 4 1
Old Chorltonians
Dick, Kerr's XI

King, George Edwin LB
b Coalville q1 1890
Mansfield Woodhouse
Langwith Colliery
Coalville Town
1910 Leicester Fosse 1
Mansfield Mechanics
Mansfield Town

King, H LB
1905 Bolton Wanderers 1

King, Henry Edward (Harry) CF/IR
b Northampton 4/1/1886 d 1968
Evesham Star
Worcester City
1907 1909 Birmingham 29 6
Crewe Alexandra
Northampton Town
1914 Arsenal 37 26
1919 Leicester City 8 1
1920 Brentford 33 16
Stourbridge

King, Henry Walter IR
b Houghton-le-Spring 25/1/1905 d 1992
West Stanley
Jarrow
1929 Wolverhampton Wanderers 0
1930 Walsall 11 4
Scarborough

From To Apps Goal

King, Herbert John (Bert) IR/IL
b Bristol 21/12/1910 d 1998
Bath City
Bristol St George
1933 York City 1
Dartford
Cork FC
Waterford
1937 Tranmere Rovers 11 4
1938 Barrow 38 14
1939 (Barrow) (2)

King, Horace Herbert IL
b Norwich 10/7/1883 d 1940
Norwich St James
Catton
Norwich City
1907 Blackpool 10 1

King, John CF
b Shotts 19/1/1874
Cleland Thistle
Dykehead
Wishaw Thistle
Airdrieonians
Dykehead
1894 Darwen 5 1
Dykehead
Celtic
East Stirlingshire
Dykehead
Albion Rovers
Scots Guards

King, John IR
b Dykehead
Caps: SLge 1
Renfrew
Shotts United
Partick Thistle
1913 1914 Newcastle United 33 6
Third Lanark
Motherwell
Partick Thistle (loan)
1919 1920 Newcastle United 21 2
Dykehead (loan)
Dykehead
Clydebank

King, John (Jack) IL
b Birmingham 1901
Hockley St George
Hinckley United
1921 1923 Leicester City 7 4
1924 Halifax Town 12 5
Nuneaton Town
Kidderminster Harriers
Hinckley United

King, John (Jack) OR
b Pendlebury 8/12/1902 d 1988
Newton United
Mossley
1926 1930 Oldham Athletic 80 12
Rossendale United
Ashton National
Mossley
Ashton National
1933 Huddersfield Town 0
Stalybridge Celtic
Ashton National
Pendlebury
Bacup Borough
South Liverpool

King, Louis Henry IR/OR
b Nottingham q2 1873 d 1952
Mansfield Greenhalgh's
Notts County Rovers
1892 1893 Notts County 3

King, Robert (Rab) OL/CF
Wishaw Thistle
Airdrieonians
1897 1899 Leicester Fosse 81 28
1900 Glossop 16 2
1901 Leicester Fosse 34 7
Hamilton Academical
Dykehead

King, Seth CH/LB
b Penistone 14/2/1897 d 1958
Penistone
1919 Huddersfield Town 0
Penistone Church
1922 1928 Sheffield United 107
1929 1931 Oldham Athletic 91
Denaby United

King, T RH
1896 Burton Wanderers 15 1
1898 Barnsley 3

King, TF CF
1898 Blackpool 1

From To Apps Goal

King, Thomas Parkinson (Tom) RB
b Woolsthorpe-by-Belvoir 29/6/1909 d 1993
Woolsthorpe-by-Belvoir
1930 Notts County 0
Sneinton
1934 Notts County 2
1935 1936 Bournemouth & Boscombe Ath 66
1936 1938 Luton Town 55
1939 (Luton Town) (3)

King, William (Willie) CF
b Hull q2 1890
1910 Hull City 0
1911 Leicester Fosse 7 4
Goole Town
Mexborough Town
Goole Town

King, William George (George) OR
1905 Derby County 1

Kingaby, Herbert Charles (Bert) OR
b Hackney q1 1880 d 1934
West Hampstead
1905 Clapton Orient 26 4
1905 Aston Villa 4
Fulham
Leyton
Peterborough City
Croydon Common

Kingdon, William Issacher Garfield (Billy) LH/RH/CH
b Worcester 25/6/1905 d 1977
Kepex (Worcester)
Kidderminster Harriers
1926 1935 Aston Villa 224 5
1936 1937 Southampton 48 1
Yeovil & Petters United

Kingham, Henry Ronald RB
b Harpenden 19/11/1904 d 1948
St Albans City
1926 1935 Luton Town 250
Yeovil & Petters United
Worcester City

Kinghorn, Henry McGill (Harry) GK
b Midlothian 1886 d 1955
Arniston Rangers
Alloa Athletic
Leith Athletic
1908 1910 Sheffield Wednesday 25
1928 Bournemouth & Boscombe Ath 1

Kinghorn, William John Darroch (Bill) OL
b Strathblane 27/2/1912
Caps: Scotland Amat
Kirkintilloch Rob Roy
Pollok
Queen's Park
1938 Liverpool 19 4

Kingsley, Alfred John (Alf 'Scotty') OR
b Barbados 25/10/1891 d 1967
Vanbrugh Park
Blackheath St John's
1921 Charlton Athletic 20 2
1921 1922 Fulham 29 2
1923 1924 Millwall Athletic 44 2
Sittingbourne
Sheppey United
Hendon

Kingsley, Matthew (Matt) GK
b Turton 1876 d 1960
Caps: FLge 3/England 1
Edgworth
Turton
1895 1897 Darwen 72
1898 1903 Newcastle United 180
West Ham United
Queen's Park Rangers
Rochdale
Barrow

Kingwell, Leonard Edward L (Len) CH
b Rosyth 31/5/1918 d 1998
1935 Plymouth Argyle 0
1937 1938 Torquay United 3
Bath City

Kinloch, Joseph CF
Our Boys (Dundee)
1892 Newton Heath 1

Kinsella, J IL
1896 Darwen 15 4
1896 Newcastle United 2

From To Apps Goal
Kinsey, George LH
b Burton-on-Trent 27/11/1866 d 1936
Caps: England 4
Barton FC
Burton Crusaders
Burton Swifts
Mitchell St George's
1891 1893 Wolverhampton Wanderers 72 3
1894 Aston Villa 3
1895 1896 Derby County 36
1896 Notts County 4
Bristol Eastville Rovers
1900 Burton Swifts 8 1
Gresley Rovers
Burton Early Closing

Kirby, Conyers OR
b Bordesley Green q2 1884 d 1946
Army Medical Corps
Fulham
1906 Birmingham 1
1907 Blackpool 2
Worcester City
Kidderminster Harriers
Willenhall Pickwick
1913 Fulham 0

Kirby, Frederick (Fred) CF
b Bishop Auckland q3 1891
Caps: England Amat
Bishop Auckland
1911 Sunderland 1
Bishop Auckland
Durham City
1913 Middlesbrough 2
Bishop Auckland
Halifax Town
1914 Bradford Park Avenue 10 3
Bishop Auckland
Halifax Town

Kirby, Herbert Hely OR
b Barry 23/3/1903
Barry
1924 Bristol City 5
1925 Charlton Athletic 7
St Johnstone
Sittingbourne
1928 Cardiff City 0
Derry City
Dartford
Folkestone

Kirby, John (Jack) GK
b Overseal 30/9/1910 d 1960
Newhall United
1929 1937 Derby County 173
Folkestone

Kirby, Norman Rufus OL/IL
b Cockfield 24/6/1908 d 1977
Caps: IrLge 2
Shildon
Cockfield
1926 Doncaster Rovers (trial) 0
1927 Stockport County (trial) 1
1927 Manchester United (trial)
Crook Town
1928 Bury 5 1
Crook Town
1930 1931 Swindon Town 66 10
Distillery
Dundee

Kirby, Reginald John Stanley (Reg 'Badge OL
b Wealdstone 13/8/1893 d 1960
Wealdstone
Hampstead Town
1922 Watford 1
Hampstead Town

Kirby, William (Bill 'Sunny Jim') IL
b Preston q3 1882 d 1917
Oswaldtwistle Rovers
Swindon Town
West Ham United
Swindon Town
Portsmouth
1911 1912 Preston North End 55 22
Exeter City
Merthyr Town

Kirby, William (Bill) GK
b Trimdon Grange 2/7/1898 d 1974
Caps: England Sch
Haswell United
Easington Colliery Welfare
Trimdon Grange Colliery
1925 1927 Durham City 28
Trimdon Grange Colliery
Shotton Colliery
Hetton United
1930 Middlesbrough (trial) 0
Trimdon Colliery United

From To Apps Goal
Kirchen, Alfred John (Alf) OR
b Shouldham 26/4/1913 d 1999
Caps: England War 3/England 3
Shouldham
1933 1934 Norwich City 14 7
1934 1938 Arsenal 92 38
1939 (Arsenal) (3) (1)

Kirk, Clifford John GK
b Cardiff 7/8/1910 d 1982
1934 Liverpool 0
1935 Exeter City 3
1936 Barnsley 0
Barry

Kirk, Frank V OL
b Greenock 1873 d 1950
1893 Woolwich Arsenal 1
Royal Ordnance

Kirk, Gerald CH
b Ingleton 14/7/1883 d 1915
Pocklington Grammar School
1905 1906 Bradford City 40 2
1906 Leeds City 8 1
1907 Bradford City 3

Kirk, Henry (Harry 'Jazzo') IR/IL
b Sheffield 22/4/1899
Dinnington Main Athletic
Worksop Town
Sherwood Rangers
1919 1920 Bristol City 17 7
1921 Plymouth Argyle 1
1921 Exeter City 14 9
1922 Plymouth Argyle 0
1922 1925 Exeter City 126 36
1926 Charlton Athletic 8 2
Bath City
1928 New Brighton 27 9
1929 South Shields 12 3
Bath City

Kirk, James John RB/LH
b Southwell q1 1879 d 1953
Southwell St Mary's
1902 Notts County 1
Newark Town
1909 1910 Lincoln City 5
Worksop Town

Kirk, Robert Hastings OL
b Clydebank 22/2/1899
Clydebank Juniors
Albion Rovers
1924 1926 Bristol City 54 5
1927 1928 Exeter City 10
1928 Blackpool 0

Kirk, William Henry OR
b Grantham 11/10/1912 d 1991
Caythorpe
Grantham
1933 Mansfield Town 7 1
Gainsborough Trinity
1935 West Ham United 0
Yeovil & Petters United
Worcester City

Kirkaldie, John (Jack) OR
b Coventry 2/8/1917 d 1985
Leamington St John's
1936 Southend United 1
1936 1938 West Ham United 11 1
1938 1947 Doncaster Rovers 53 17
1939 (Doncaster Rovers) (3)
Bedworth Town
Rugby Town

Kirkaldy, James William LH
b Newcastle 8/11/1885
Northern Temperance
1905 1906 Newcastle United 11 1
Kilmarnock (trial)
Huddersfield Town

Kirkbride, John Patterson (Jacky) OL
b Hetton-le-Hole 14/7/1897 d 1989
Horden St Mary's
Horden Athletic
1919 1920 South Shields 25 1
Horden Athletic
1922 Hartlepools United 0
Armadale
Stenhousemuir
St Bernard's

Kirkham, James OL
1895 Burslem Port Vale 1

From To Apps Goal
Kirkham, John (Jack) CF/OL
b Ellesmere Port 16/6/1918 d 1982
Ellesmere Port Town
1937 1938 Wolverhampton Wanderers 13 5
1938 1946 Bournemouth & Boscombe Ath 48 27
1939 (Bournemouth & Boscombe Ath) (3) (4)
Wellington Town

Kirkham, John Batty (Jack) OL/IL/IR
b Blackburn q1 1868 d 1930
Oswaldtwistle Rovers
1888 1892 Accrington 104 33
Blackpool
Accrington
Oswaldtwistle Rovers

Kirkham, Thompson Noble OR
b Gateshead 10/12/1901 d 1986
1923 Darlington 19 1

Kirkham, Wilfred Thomas (Wilf) CF/IL
b Cobridge 26/11/1901 d 1974
Caps: FLge 1
Cobridge Church
Congleton Town
Shelton United
Sheffield TTC
1923 1928 Port Vale 211 134
1929 1931 Stoke City 51 30
1931 1932 Port Vale 49 19
Kidderminster Harriers

Kirkland, Alexander (Alex) IR
b Dublin 26/8/1897
Caps: LoI 5/Eire 1
Shelbourne
Pontypridd
1921 1922 Bradford Park Avenue 27 6
Shamrock Rovers

Kirkland, Edward LB/RB
b Burton-on-Trent q1 1877
1897 1900 Burton Swifts 84
1901 1906 Burton United 174 1
Burton All Saints
Burton United
Byrkley
Burton United
Byrkley
Burton Town

Kirkland, J RH
1892 Bootle 1

Kirkland, Joseph (Joe) CH
b County Longford 1873
Duntocher
1894 Bury 5
Duntocher

Kirkland, William CH
b Carluke 21/6/1914
Carluke Rovers
Stonehouse Violet
1936 Birmingham (trial) 0
Partick Thistle (trial)
Third Lanark
1938 Lincoln City 3
Partick Thistle

Kirkman, Gerald (Gerry) LH/RH
b Bolton 20/4/1912 d 1972
Bolton YMCA
1935 Bolton Wanderers 1
1936 Reading 1
1938 New Brighton 2

Kirkman, Samuel (Sam) OR
b Bury q3 1889 d 1960
Ramsbottom
Carlisle United
1909 1919 Sheffield Wednesday 188 37
Mid-Rhondda
1920 Bury 1
Wombwell

Kirkpatrick, Ernest (Ernie) IL/RH
b Farnworth 27/2/1899 d 1971
All Saints (Newton Heath)
Wyre Port
Newton Heath Parish Church
Fleetwood
1925 1926 Oldham Athletic 15 4
Fleetwood
Chorley
1929 Bournemouth & Boscombe Ath 2
Chorley
Windsor Villa (Fleetwood)

From To Apps Goal
Kirkpatrick, James Maxwell (Jim) LB
b Annan 7/12/1901
Annan
Queen of the South
Solway Star
Workington
1925 1926 Leeds United 10
1927 Watford 9
Solway Star

Kirkpatrick, James Nodwell (Jimmy) OR
b Dumfries
Dumfries
1920 1923 Plymouth Argyle 40
Torquay United

Kirkpatrick, John IL
b Annan 1900
Workington
1924 Accrington Stanley 4

Kirkup, Richard RH
b Ashington 7/4/1908 d 1978
Ashington Welfare
1927 Ashington 5
1928 Carlisle United 0
Bedlington United
Annfield Plain
Newbiggin West End

Kirkwood, Daniel (Dan) IR
b Dalserf 24/12/1900 d 1977
Ashgill YMCA
Airdrieonians
Rangers
St Johnstone (loan)
1926 1927 Sheffield Wednesday 18 1
1928 1932 Brighton & Hove Albion 168 74
1933 Luton Town 2 1
1933 Swindon Town 7

Kirkwood, David RH/IR
1889 1891 Everton 35 1
Broxburn

Kirkwood, Joseph Josiah RB
b Pinxton q2 1885
Caps: SoLge 2
Pinxton
Sutton Town
Chesterfield Town
1910 Fulham 1
Millwall Athletic
Hartshay Colliery

Kirkwood, Samuel James (Sam) RB/CH
b Belfast 31/7/1910 d 1980
Caps: IrLge 1
Cook Island
Portadown
1933 Arsenal 0
1934 1938 Plymouth Argyle 109 1
1939 (Plymouth Argyle) (3)
Linfield

Kirkwood, Walter George (Wally) IL
b Belfast 13/8/1919
1938 Torquay United 3

Kirrage, Frank Bernard IR
b Bromley 3/3/1893 d 1933
Mapperley
Bulwell
1919 Nottingham Forest 1
Ilkeston United

Kirsop, William Smeaton OL
b Gateshead 15/7/1890 d 1973
Rome Hill Villa
Wallsend Park Villa
New Hartley Rovers
Kilmarnock
Gateshead Athletic
1914 Barnsley 3

Kirsopp, William Henry James (Billy) IR
b Liverpool 21/4/1892 d 1978
Wallasey Borough
1914 1920 Everton 58 28
1921 Bury 20 1
1922 Grimsby Town 6 2
1923 New Brighton 14 1
1924 Crystal Palace (trial) 0
Oswestry Town
Llandudno (trial)

From To Apps Goal

Kirtley, Edward (Ted) CH
b Houghton-le-Spring 25/8/1911 d 1992
Lambton Star
Brickley Colliery
Lumley & Sixth Pit Welfare
1931 Southport 1
1932 Hartlepools United 0
Lumley & Sixth Pit Welfare
Horden Colliery Welfare
Throckley Welfare
Hetton United
Blyth Spartans
Spennymoor United
Horden Colliery Welfare

Kirtley, William (Bill) GK
Workman's Hall (Monkwearmouth)
1890 Sunderland 2
Sunderland Albion

Kirton, John (Jock) LH
b Aberdeen 4/3/1916 d 1996
Caps: Scotland War 1
St Marchers
Banks o' Dee
1936 1952 Stoke City 219 2
1953 Bradford City 8
Hinckley Athletic
Downings Tileries

Kirton, John William (Jack) OL
b Chorlton 18/7/1871 d 1939
Glossop North End
Oldham County
1896 Lincoln City 27 5
1897 Small Heath 18 2
Swindon Town
1899 Sunderland 0
Swindon Town
Millwall Athletic

Kirton, William John (Billy) IR
b Newcastle 2/12/1896 d 1970
Caps: England 1
Pandon Temperance
1919 Leeds City 1
1919 1926 Aston Villa 229 53
1928 1929 Coventry City 16
Kidderminster Harriers
Leamington Town

Kirwan, John Henry (Jack) OL
b Wicklow 25/4/1872 d 1959
Caps: Ireland 17
Kirkdale
Southport Central
1898 Everton 24 5
Tottenham Hotspur
1905 1907 Chelsea 73 17
Clyde
Leyton

Kissock, Joseph Gartshore (Joe) LB/RB
b Coatbridge 5/6/1893 d 1959
Caps: New Zealand
Vale of Clyde
1919 1920 Bury 6
1921 Bristol Rovers 17
Peebles Rovers
(USA)
(New Zealand)

Kitchen, George William GK
b Fairfield, Derbyshire q2 1876
Caps: SoLge 3
Buxton
Stockport County
1898 1903 Everton 87
West Ham United
Southampton
Boscombe

Kitchen, Harry IR
b Bolsover q4 1914
Bolsover Colliery
1933 Luton Town 1 1

Kitchen, Joseph Ernest (Joe) CF/OR/IL
b Brigg 20/6/1890 d 1974
Ancholme United
Brigg Britannia
Brigg Town
1906 1907 Gainsborough Trinity 33 13
1907 1919 Sheffield United 235 105
1920 Rotherham County 18 1
1920 Sheffield United 13 3
1921 1922 Hull City 30 5
Scunthorpe & Lindsey United
Gainsborough Trinity
Shirebrook
Gainsborough Trinity
Barton Town

From To Apps Goal

Kitchen, Norman (Norrie) OL/OR
b Sunderland 26/7/1911 d 1998
Millfield
Eden Colliery Welfare
Ferryhill Athletic
1934 Sheffield Wednesday (trial) 0
1935 Hull City 4 1
Ferryhill Athletic (loan)
1936 1937 Southport 58 15
1938 Bristol Rovers 2
Workington

Kitching, Harold (Harry) IL/IR/CF
b Grimsby 2/8/1905 d 1970
Municipal College
Leeds University
1923 1925 Grimsby Town 16 1
Boston Town
Worksop Town
1928 1930 Lincoln City 58 28
1931 Tranmere Rovers 5
1932 1935 New Brighton 37 7

Kite, Percy Albert GK
b Warrington q3 1892 d 1960
Thelwall
Eccles Borough
Lancashire Tool (Lymm)
1919 Sheffield Wednesday 1
Lancashire Tool (Lymm)

Kitson, George RB
b Newport 16/5/1911 d 1993
1934 Newport County 6
1935 1936 Barrow 48
Kidderminster Harriers
Bangor City
Tunbridge Wells Rangers

Kivlichan, (Dr) William Fulton (Willie) OR/IR
b Galashiels 11/3/1886 d 1937
Caps: SLge 3
Dumfries St Joseph's
Maxwelltown Juniors
Dumfries
Rangers
Celtic
1911 1914 Bradford Park Avenue 88 5
Queen of the South

Knapman, Alfred (Alf) OR
b Plymouth 1902
1927 Torquay United 1
Dartmouth United

Knapman, Alfred Leonard (Len) OR
b Newton Abbot 18/3/1910 d 1983
1938 Torquay United 1 1

Kneale, Charles Henry LB
b Queensferry 2/1/1912 d 1999
1933 Liverpool 0
1934 1938 Crewe Alexandra 154 1
1939 (Crewe Alexandra) (2) (1)

Kneeshaw, Herbert Justin (Jack) GK
b Beckhill 13/1/1883 d 1955
Caps: WLge 1
Heaton
1903 Bradford City 0
St Cuthbert's
Guiseley Celtic
1907 Bradford City 1
Colne Town
1920 1923 Cardiff City 34

Knibbs, ? OL
1898 1899 Burton Swifts 29 5

Knight, Arthur Egerton LB
b Godalming 7/9/1887 d 1956
Caps: England Amat/England 1
Godalming
Corinthians
1920 1921 Portsmouth 34
Corinthians

Knight, Bertram Harold OL
b North Woolwich 23/12/1893 d 1978
Caps: England Sch
1912 Woolwich Arsenal 0
Llanelly
1922 Charlton Athletic 3
Dartford

Knight, Frederick Charles (Fred) CF
b Hillingdon 11/2/1895 d 1973
Botwell Mission
1921 Queen's Park Rangers 2 1
Uxbridge Town
Staines Town
Hayes

From To Apps Goal

Knight, George Rollinson IL/OR
b Bolton 12/5/1921
Holdens Temperance
1938 1946 Burnley 9 2

Knight, J LH
1893 Northwich Victoria 1

Knight, John George CH
b Edmonton 18/8/1902 d 1990
Caps: England Amat
Casuals
Corinthians
1928 Tottenham Hotspur 1

Knight, John Herbert OL
b Blackley q2 1889 d 1958
Heaton Park
Crewe Alexandra
1913 1914 Glossop 65 5
1919 1920 Preston North End 3
1921 Wigan Borough 15

Knight, Thomas (Tommy) OL/OR
b Wolverhampton 1865
1888 1889 Wolverhampton Wanderers 21 7
Willenhall
Bilston
Darlaston

Knighton, Thomas (Tom) CF/IL
1914 Glossop 2
Manchester United
1919 Lincoln City 2

Knipton, F OL
1904 Burton United 4

Knott, Herbert (Bert) IR/CF
b Goole 5/12/1914 d 1986
Goole Town
1932 Arsenal 0
1936 Brentford 0
Brierley Hill Alliance
1937 Walsall 9 2
Stourbridge (loan)
Brierley Hill Alliance
1945 Bradford Park Avenue 0
1946 Hull City 6 1
Hinckley Athletic

Knott, Percy GK
b Hartshill 1899
Hartshill White Star
1920 1921 Stoke 27
1922 Queen's Park Rangers 0
1925 Stoke City 1

Knowles, Albert GK
Clitheroe
Whalley & District
1897 1899 Blackburn Rovers 31

Knowles, Frank CH/LH/RH
b Hyde q2 1891 d 1951
Hyde St Thomas
Hyde
Skelmersdale United
Stalybridge Celtic
1911 1914 Manchester United 46 1
Hartlepools United
1919 Manchester City 2
Stalybridge Celtic
1921 Ashington 34 3
1922 Stockport County 15 1
1923 Newport County 16
1923 1924 Queen's Park Rangers 35
Ashton National
Macclesfield

Knowles, Frederick Edmund CF
b Derby 21/6/1901 d 1991
Derby YMCA
1921 Derby County 3 1

Knowles, Harold E IR
b Rotherham q1 1914
Goole Town
1937 Rotherham United 7 1
1938 Rochdale 0

Knowles, Herbert OL
1920 Stockport County 2

Knowles, James Henry IL
1902 Bolton Wanderers 3 3
Turton

Knowles, John Walter OR/IL
b Wednesbury 1879
1897 West Bromwich Albion 2
Dudley Town
1900 West Bromwich Albion 1
Dudley Town

From To Apps Goal

Knowles, Joseph (Joe) LB
b Monkwearmouth 1872
Monkwearmouth
1896 Sunderland 1
Tottenham Hotspur
South Shields
Queen's Park Rangers

Knowles, W IR
1893 Middlesbrough Ironopolis 2 1

Knox, James Phillips (Jimmy) IR
b Ibrox 8/8/1910
Bellahouston Academy
Queen's Park Strollers
1928 Portsmouth 0
1930 Charlton Athletic 1
St Mirren
1939 Notts County (1)

Knox, Thomas (Tommy) GK
b Ushaw Moor 11/11/1905 d 1954
Ushaw Moor Labour Party
Bearpark
1926 Darlington 0
Chilton Colliery Recreation Athletic
1928 Bolton Wanderers 0
West Stanley
1930 Norwich City (trial) 0
1930 Bradford City (trial) 0
1930 Leeds United (trial) 0
Durham City (trial)
Crook Town
1931 1932 Darlington 48
1933 Hartlepools United 25
1933 1935 Notts County 72
1936 Crystal Palace 3
1936 Norwich City 0
1937 1938 Carlisle United 63

Knox, William RB
b Douglas Water
Bathgate
1927 1929 Burnley 23
1930 Luton Town 0
1932 Bristol City 19 1
1933 Stockport County 0

Knox, William (Bill) OR
b Old Cumnock 2/5/1904 d 1985
Kilbarchan Athletic
Kilbirnie Ladeside
Dundee
St Mirren
Third Lanark
1927 Reading 4
1929 Norwich City 3
1930 Carlisle United 0
Stenhousemuir

Knox, William P RH
b Glasgow 8/10/1904
Shettleston
1925 1926 Bradford City 11

Koerner, Charles Frederick (Frederick) LB/RB
b Eccleshill q1 1878 d 1933
Army
1898 1899 Lincoln City 3 1

Kurz, Frederick John (Fred) CF
b Grimsby 3/9/1918 d 1978
Grimsby YMCA
1938 Grimsby Town 3
1945 1950 Crystal Palace 148 48
Boston United
Wisbech Town
Gainsborough Trinity

Kyle, Archibald (Archie) IL
Caps: SLge 2
Parkhead
Rangers
1907 1908 Blackburn Rovers 36 8
1909 Bradford 0
Bo'ness
Linfield
Clyde
St Mirren
Hamilton Academical

From To Apps Goal

Kyle, Peter CF/IR
b Cadder 21/12/1878 d 1957
Linton Villa
Glasgow Parkhead
Clyde
Thames Ironworks (trial)
Heart of Midlothian (trial)
Larkhall Thistle
1899 Liverpool 4
1900 Leicester Fosse 31 3
West Ham United
Kettering
Wellingborough
Aberdeen
Cowdenbeath
Heart of Midlothian
Port Glasgow Athletic
Royal Albert
Partick Thistle
Tottenham Hotspur
1906 1907 Woolwich Arsenal 52 21
1907 1908 Aston Villa 5
1908 Sheffield United 10 4
Royal Albert
Watford
Royal Albert

Lacey, Arthur Darrell (Darrell) RH
b Chesterfield 1895 d 1952
1921 Chesterfield 18 3
Shirebrook
Matlock Town

Lacey, Reginald William James (Dick) CF
b Chesham 18/9/1901 d 1970
Chesham United
1923 Watford 3 1
Chesham United

Lacey, William (Billy) OR/OL/RH
b Wexford 24/9/1889 d 1969
Caps: LoI 3/Ireland 23
Lansdowne
Shelbourne
1908 1911 Everton 37 11
1911 1923 Liverpool 229 18
1924 New Brighton 7
Shelbourne
Hereford United
Shelbourne
Cork Bohemians

Lafferty, Hugh LH
b Rutherglen 16/11/1901 d 1971
Bellshill Athletic
1923 1924 Fulham 4
1925 Arsenal 0
St Johnstone
New York Nationals
New York Giants
Aberdeen (trial)
King's Park

Lager, Ellis Walter CF/IR
b Mansfield 14/1/1918 d 1995
Mansfield Rovers
Sutton Junction
1935 1938 Coventry City 50 25
1939 (Coventry City) (3) (2)

Laidlaw, James A (Jimmy) OL/IR
b Scotland 1873
1895 Burnley 0
Leith Athletic (loan)
1900 Newcastle United 10 3
1901 Woolwich Arsenal 3 2

Laidlaw, John W IR
b Muirkirk 12/1891 d 1954
Muirkirk Athletic
South Shields
1913 Aston Villa 2
Kilmarnock
Chesterfield Town

Laidler, John Ralph (Jackie) OL
b Windermere 5/1/1919
Windermere
1936 1938 Barrow 40 6
Netherfield
1946 Carlisle United 27 3
Morecambe

Laidman, Frederick (Fred) IL/IR
b Durham 20/6/1913 d 1987
1936 Everton 0
1938 Bristol City 10 1
Stockton
1949 Darlington 2

From To Apps Goal

Laing, David Buick Peter OL
b Dundee 14/11/1913 d 1981
East Craigie
Dundee United
East Craigie
Portadown
Forfar Athletic
1936 Liverpool 0
1937 Watford 15 5
Yeovil & Petters United
Barry

Laird, Alexander (Sandy) IL/IR
b Denny 21/10/1901
Longcroft Thistle
Rangers
1922 1923 Preston North End 28 4
Falkirk
Armadale

Laird, J William CF/IL
b Larkhall
Kirkmuirhill
Blantyre Celtic
1931 Sunderland 2
1932 Gateshead 2 1
Excelsior Roubaix

Lake, Christopher Edwin (Ned) OL
b Thurlstone q2 1880
Thurlstone
1899 1900 Barnsley 29 8
Thurlstone
1903 Barnsley 8 2
Rotherham Town

Lake, George A LH
b Manchester d 1918
1912 Manchester City 0
1913 Chelsea 1

Lake, William Henry (Billy) IL
b Birmingham 1908
Yardley White Star
1927 1928 Walsall 25 8
1928 1938 Coventry City 225 113

Lakey, Thomas Frederick OL
b Stockton q2 1874 d 1932
Stockton
1899 1900 Grimsby Town 30 12

Lakin, George William (William) RH
b Bulwell 11/6/1890 d 1971
Woodhouse
1919 Barnsley 5
1920 Exeter City 6
Doncaster Rovers

Lakin, John Henry IL
b Loughborough q2 1876
1897 Loughborough 3

Laking, George Edward RB/LB
b Harthill, Yorkshire 17/3/1913 d 1997
Kiveton Park
Dinnington
1935 1936 Wolverhampton Wanderers 27
1936 1946 Middlesbrough 94 1
1939 (Middlesbrough) (3)
Shrewsbury Town

Lamb, Albert Edward GK
b Auchtermuchty 26/10/1908
Caps: IrLge 2
East Craigie
Dundee Violet
Dundee United
Dundee
Portadown
1936 Chesterfield 8

Lamb, James Frank LB
b Fulham q4 1893
1923 1924 Bournemouth & Boscombe Ath 63

Lamb, John A (Jack) IR
b Birmingham 1893
Long Eaton
Birmingham Tramways
Worcester City
Brierley Hill Alliance
Worcester City
1913 1914 Notts County 8 3
Worcester City

Lamb, John William LH/CH
b Worksop q4 1893
Bolsover Colliery
1913 1919 Sheffield Wednesday 5
1920 Luton Town 24
Matlock Town

From To Apps Goal

Lamb, Joseph (Joe) RH
b Chilton 28/11/1898 d 1982
Caps: England Amat
Chilton Colliery Recreation Athletic
1922 Northampton Town (trial) 0
Bishop Auckland
Willington Athletic
1924 Liverpool (trial) 0
1925 Durham City 34
1926 Stockport County 5
1927 1929 Norwich City 80 3
Walker Celtic
Jarrow
Crook Town
Lumley 6th Pit
North Shields
West Stanley
Lumley Colliery Welfare
Hoffman Athletic

Lamb, Sam (Sammy) OL
b Alfreton 11/1885 d 1960
Caps: SoLge 2
Alfreton Town
1905 1906 Derby County 30 1
Alfreton Town
Sutton Town
Plymouth Argyle
Swindon Town
Millwall Athletic
1919 Rotherham County 35 2
Caerphilly

Lamb, Thomas John IR
1898 Newcastle United 0
1899 Middlesbrough 23 6
Willington Athletic

Lamb, Walter Charles LB/RB
b Tarleton 8/8/1897 d 1973
1919 Liverpool 0
Fleetwood
1921 Sheffield Wednesday 2
1923 1924 Swansea Town 3
1925 Southend United 1
Rhyl
Abergele

Lambert, John (Jack) CF/IR/IL
b Greasbrough 22/5/1902 d 1940
Army
Greasborough
Methley Perseverance
1921 Sheffield Wednesday (trial) 0
1922 Rotherham County 1 1
1923 Leeds United 1
1924 1925 Doncaster Rovers 44 13
1926 1933 Arsenal 143 98
1933 1934 Fulham 34 4
Margate

Lamberton, George IR
b Rossendale 24/12/1880 d 1954
Berry's Association
Tonge
1901 1903 Bury 22 7
Luton Town
1905 Clapton Orient 26 3
Norwich City
1907 Bury 0
Haslingden
Colne
Hyde
Chorley

Lamberton, James RB/LB
b Haslingden 9/2/1877 d 1929
Middleton
Berry's Association
1899 Bury 7
Crewe Alexandra
1902 Bristol City 3
Wellingborough
Stalybridge Rovers
1905 Clapton Orient 33
Norwich City
1907 West Bromwich Albion (trial) 0
Haslingden

Lambie, Alexander (Alec) CH
b Troon 15/4/1897 d 1963
Caps: SLge 1
Dreghorn Juniors
Glenburn Rovers
Kilmarnock
Troon Athletic
Ayr United (trial)
Partick Thistle
1931 Chester 1
1931 1933 Swindon Town 83 1
1934 Newport County (trial)
Lovells Athletic
Distillery (trial)

From To Apps Goal

Lambie, Claude CF
b Glasgow 1868 d 1921
Glasgow Thistle
1889 1890 Burnley 25 21
Clyde
Cowlairs
Highland Light Infantry
1892 Burnley 4
Auchterarder Thistle

Lambie, William Allan IL
b Govan 10/1/1873
Caps: Scotland 9
Queen's Park
Ardwick
Queen's Park
Ardwick
Queen's Park
1892 Ardwick 3 1
Queen's Park
Hamilton Academical
1901 Burnley 1

Lambourne, Albert LH/IL
b Altrincham
Linotype Works
1929 1932 Stockport County 61 10

Lamming, Walter George OL/OR
b Lincoln 2/9/1896 d 1962
Boston Town
Rustons Staff
1919 Lincoln City 2
1920 Merthyr Town 0
1921 Lincoln City 4
Robeys

Lammus, William Christmas James RB
b East Ham 14/8/1898 d 1982
Barking Town
1922 West Bromwich Albion 0
1923 Nelson 8
Nuneaton Town
Tunbridge Wells Rangers
New Beckton Baptists

Lampard, Alfred James (Alf) GK
b Felixstowe 16/8/1908 d 1969
Nailsworth
1929 Bournemouth & Boscombe Ath 2
1930 1931 Barnsley 2

Lamph, Thomas (Tommy) RH/LH
b Gateshead 16/11/1892 d 1926
Pelaw United
Spennymoor United
1913 1919 Leeds City 11 1
1919 Manchester City 11
1919 1920 Derby County 16
1920 Leeds United 6

Lancaster, Wilfred OL
b Backbarrow 27/9/1904 d 1987
Dick, Kerr's XI
1924 Burnley 4
Dick, Kerr's XI

Lanceley, Ernest (Ernie) RB/LB
b Rotherham 10/4/1910 d 1992
Mexborough Athletic
1931 Charlton Athletic 0
Dartford
1933 1938 Blackburn Rovers 52

Lanceley, Francis James (Frank) GK
b Bristol 13/9/1909 d 1963
Bristol St George
Bath City
1932 Bristol City 5

Lancelotte, Eric Charles IR/IL
b Jhansi, India 26/2/1917 d 2007
Romford
1937 1947 Charlton Athletic 40 6
1947 1949 Brighton & Hove Albion 60 14
Chippenham Town
Hastings United
Ashford Town (Kent)
Folkestone Town

Landells, John (Jack) IR/CF/IL
b Gateshead 11/11/1904 d 1960
Thames Board Mills
Grays Athletic
Grays Thurrock
1925 1932 Millwall 176 69
1933 West Ham United 21 3
1934 Bristol City 21 2
1935 Carlisle United 33 6
1936 Walsall 19 1
1937 Clapton Orient 2
Chelmsford City

Lander, John F (Johnny) IR
1892 Burslem Port Vale 3 2

From To Apps Goal

Lander, Thomas James (Tommy) LH
b Burslem q1 1875 d 1956
Talke Alexandra
1898 1901 Burslem Port Vale 61 2

Lane, Edward RB
b 1908
1932 West Bromwich Albion 0
1933 Notts County 0
1934 Cardiff City 30

Lane, Harry William RH/RB/LH
b Stoney Stanton 23/10/1894
Stoney Stanton Swifts
Hinckley United
1913 Nottingham Forest 0
1914 Notts County 0
Sutton Town
1919 1920 West Ham United 19
1921 Charlton Athletic 3
1922 Queen's Park Rangers 5

Lane, Henry (Harry) IL/OL/IR
b Hednesford 21/3/1909 d 1977
Hednesford Town
Bloxwich Strollers
1930 Birmingham 2
1933 1937 Southend United 155 50
1937 1938 Plymouth Argyle 47 8
1939 (Plymouth Argyle) (3) (1)
1946 1948 Southend United 65 14
Chelmsford City

Lane, James Charles (Joe) CF/IL/OL
b Hereford 11/7/1892 d 1959
Watford
Ferencvaros Torna
Watford
1913 Sunderland 2
1913 1919 Blackpool 94 65
1919 1921 Birmingham 67 26
1922 1923 Millwall Athletic 28 6
Barcelona
Bournville
Watford Printing Works

Lane, John William (Jack) IR/IL
b Birmingham 29/5/1898 d 1984
Cradley Heath
1920 1922 Burnley 5
1923 1924 Chesterfield 65 19
1924 1930 Brentford 215 72
1930 1931 Crystal Palace 34 10
1932 Aldershot 36 8

Lane, Moses Alexander Edmund CF/IL
b Willenhall 17/2/1895 d 1949
Willenhall Pickwick
Willenhall Town
Walsall
Willenhall Town
1922 1923 Birmingham 15 4
1924 Derby County 0
Wellington Town
Worcester City
1927 1928 Walsall 57 51
Brierley Hill Alliance
Netherton
Dudley Town

Lane, William Henry Charles (Billy) CF
b Tottenham 23/10/1904 d 1985
London City Mission
Gnome Athletic
Park Avondale
1922 Tottenham Hotspur 0
Summerstown
Barnet
Northfleet
1924 1926 Tottenham Hotspur 26 7
1926 1927 Leicester City 5 2
1927 Walsall (trial) 0
1928 Reading 6 2
1929 1931 Brentford 112 83
1932 1935 Watford 124 68
1935 1936 Bristol City 30 11
1937 Clapton Orient 12 1
Gravesend United

Lang, Alexander (Sandy) LB/CH
b Bridge of Weir 1864 d 1901
Padiham
1888 1894 Burnley 123 2
Nelson

Lang, Clifford RH
b Cardiff 1/9/1908 d 1978
Ely United
1930 Swansea Town 1
1931 Clapton Orient 0
Clifton
Cheltenham Town

Lang, James OL
1935 Halifax Town 1

From To Apps Goal

Lang, John (Johnny) OR
b Kilbirnie 16/8/1882 d 1934
Govan
Co-operative United (Glasgow)
1902 Barnsley 14 2
1902 1908 Sheffield United 103 13
1909 Leicester Fosse 17 2
Denaby United

Lang, John (Johnny) IL/OL
b Dumbarton 9/6/1908
Maryhill
Dumbarton
Forthbank
King's Park
Aberdeen
1937 1938 Barnsley 43 10
1939 (Barnsley) (3)
Dumbarton

Lang, Thomas (Tommy) OL
b Larkhall 3/4/1905 d 1988
Larkhall Thistle
1927 1934 Newcastle United 215 53
1934 1935 Huddersfield Town 24 5
1935 1936 Manchester United 12 1
1937 Swansea Town 33 1
Queen of the South
1946 Ipswich Town 5 1

Langenove, Eugene E IR
b Paris, France 1898
Caps: France
Olympique de Paris
Le Havre
1922 Walsall 2

Langford, Albert Edward (Sammy) RB/LB
b Tipton 16/10/1899 d 1965
Caps: WLge 1
1920 1923 Merthyr Town 106 1
1923 1926 Swansea Town 78
Worcester City
1928 1931 Charlton Athletic 135 1
1932 Walsall 24 1
Dudley Town

Langford, Joseph (Joe) GK
b Mexborough 1911
Darwen
Tyldesley Alexandra
Conisbrough Welfare
Shirebrook
Denaby United
Scarborough
1933 1934 Torquay United 19
Yeovil & Petters United

Langford, Leonard (Len) GK
b Alfreton 30/5/1899 d 1973
Attercliffe Victory
Rossington Main
1924 1929 Nottingham Forest 136
1930 1933 Manchester City 112
1934 1935 Manchester United 15

Langford, Thomas Sidney (Tom) RH/LH/IL
b Wolverhampton 4/10/1892 d 1965
Bargoed Town
1914 Wolverhampton Wanderers 7 3
Stalybridge Celtic
1920 1921 Swindon Town 41
1922 Halifax Town 27

Langford, Walter IL/LH
b Wolverhampton 24/3/1905 d 1976
Sunbeam Motors
Wellington Town
1928 1932 Leicester City 13 5
1933 1934 Queen's Park Rangers 11
Wellington Town
Kidderminster Harriers

Langham, Francis (Frank) CH
b Nottingham 12/3/1889
South Nottingham
1911 Nottingham Forest 2
Northampton Town
Rushden Town

Langham, William (Billy) OR/IR
b Lenton q2 1876
Notts County Rovers
Stapleford
Hucknall Portland
South Shore
1896 1897 Notts County 47 15
Bristol City
1900 Leicester Fosse 14 2
1901 1902 Doncaster Rovers 62 16
1903 1905 Gainsborough Trinity 91 27
Doncaster Rovers
1906 1909 Lincoln City 58 21

Langland, Albert Edward IL
1889 Derby County 2

From To Apps Goal

Langley, Ambrose LB
b Horncastle 10/3/1870 d 1937
Caps: FLge 1
Horncastle
Boston
Grimsby Town
Middlesbrough Ironopolis
1893 1903 Sheffield Wednesday 293 14
1905 Hull City 14

Langley, Ronald OL
b Basford 8/3/1912
Quarry Road Old Boys
1932 Nottingham Forest 5 1

Langley, William Ernest (Bill) CF
b Wolverhampton
Tunbridge Wells Rangers
1937 Wolverhampton Wanderers 7 3
1938 Bournemouth & Boscombe Ath 22 12
Yeovil & Petters United
Poole Town

Langton, James Robinson (Jimmy) RH
b Burscough 20/3/1910 d 1976
Knowsley Cons
1930 Everton (trial) 0
1931 Liverpool (trial) 0
Litherland Amateurs
1934 Southport 12
South Liverpool

Langton, Joseph RH/LH
b Crook
1920 1921 Chelsea 3

Langton, Robert (Bobby) OL
b Burscough 8/9/1918 d 1996
Caps: England B/FLge 9/NIRL 1/England 11
Burscough Victoria
1938 1947 Blackburn Rovers 107 24
1939 (Blackburn Rovers) (3) (1)
Glentoran (loan)
1948 1949 Preston North End 55 14
1949 1952 Bolton Wanderers 118 16
1953 1955 Blackburn Rovers 105 33
Ards
Wisbech Town
Kidderminster Harriers
Wisbech Town
Colwyn Bay

Langton, Walter LB
b Leabrooks q1 1867 d 1952
1901 1902 Doncaster Rovers 45

Lansdale, Arthur OL
b Willenhall q2 1905 d 1966
1927 Walsall 8 1

Lansdale, Joseph (Joe) GK
b Little Lever 4/3/1894 d 1977
Caps: SoLge 1
Little Lever Congregational
Norwich City
1920 1929 Millwall Athletic 237
1930 Accrington Stanley 26
Folkestone

Lanyon, William James (Billy) OR/RB
b Abercwmboi q2 1906 d 1962
Caps: Wales Sch
1926 Aberdare Athletic 7
Aberaman Athletic
1928 Portsmouth 0
1929 1930 Walsall 21 3
Peterborough & Fletton United
1932 Wrexham 2

Lapham, Edgar Harold (Harold) CF
b Liverpool 3/9/1909
Peter Lunt Athletic Club
Marine
Netherton
1932 Everton (trial) 0
1935 Blackburn Rovers 2
1935 Accrington Stanley 7 2
1936 1938 Wrexham 69 40
1939 Barrow 0
Ribble Motors (Bootle)

From To Apps Goal

Lappin, Hubert Henry OL
b Manchester q1 1879 d 1925
Springfield
Oldham Athletic
1900 1902 Newton Heath/Manchester Utd 27 4
1903 Grimsby Town 20 4
Rossendale United
1906 Clapton Orient 38 1
Rhyl
Chester
1909 Birmingham 11 2
Chirk
Oswestry United
Wrexham
Hurst
Macclesfield
Hurst
Mossley

Large, Herbert (Herbie) IR
b Brymbo 18/7/1901 d 1968
Brymbo Green
Druids
Brymbo Green
Llandudno
1924 Wrexham 1
Llandudno
Connah's Quay & Shotton
Denbigh United
Rhos Athletic
Mold Alexandra
Blaenau Ffestiniog
Bangor City

Latham, Albert RH
b Hucknall q4 1904
Newark Town
1927 Wolverhampton Wanderers 0
1928 1929 Accrington Stanley 52 3
1930 Rochdale 8 1
Hurst
1931 York City 0
Barnoldswick Town
Fleetwood
Clitheroe
Morecambe
Lancaster City

Latham, Arthur RB/LB
b 1863 d 1929
St Luke's
Derby Midland
1888 1901 Derby County 48 1

Latham, Frederick (Fred) GK
b Crewe 7/1876
1894 1895 Crewe Alexandra 18
1896 Stoke 5
Tottenham Hotspur (trial)
Crewe Alexandra

Latham, Frederick H (Frank) CF
b Bristol
Bristol Rovers
1908 Bristol City 1

Latham, George RH/LH/CH
b Newtown 1/1/1881 d 1939
Caps: Wales 10
Newtown
1904 1907 Liverpool 18
Caledonian (South Africa)
Southport Central
Stoke
1921 Cardiff City 1

Latham, George IL
b Blackburn q1 1915
1936 Blackburn Rovers 0
1937 Liverpool 0
1938 Accrington Stanley 2
Bangor City

Latham, Nicholas IR
b Tarleton q2 1899 d 1958
Croston
1921 Preston North End 1

Latheron, Edwin Gladstone (Eddie) IR/IL
b Brotton q2 1887 d 1917
Caps: FLge 5/England 2
Grangetown
1906 1914 Blackburn Rovers 257 94

Latheron, Robert OL
b Brotton q3 1879 d 1957
1908 Blackpool 1

From To Apps Goal

Latheron, Wilfred (Ed) CF
b Ferryhill q3 1890 d 1945
Dean Bank Villa
1921 Durham City 0
Ferryhill Athletic
1923 Durham City 1
Ferryhill Athletic
Tow Law Town
Ferryhill Athletic

Latimer, John OR
b Hill o' Beath 3/2/1905 d 1979
Hearts o' Beath
1928 1929 Portsmouth 8 1
Derry City
East Stirlingshire
St Mirren
Dundee
Queen of the South
1938 Rochdale (trial) 1
Leith Athletic

Latimer, John George GK
b Newcastle 10/11/1904 d 1977
Prudhoe Street Mission
Benwell Colliery
1928 Ashington 22
Benwell Colliery
Washington Colliery
Benwell Colliery

Latta, Alexander (Alex) OR
b Dumbarton 9/1867 d 1928
Caps: Scotland 2
Dumbarton
1889 1895 Everton 136 69
1896 Liverpool 0

Lauder, Alexander IR
b Glasgow 1899
Glasgow Ashfield
Partick Thistle
1921 Port Vale 21 3

Lauderdale, John Herbert (Jock) IR/IL
b Dumfries 27/11/1908 d 1965
Parkhead
Third Lanark
Stenhousemuir
Queen of the South
1929 1930 Blackpool 19 6
1931 1936 Coventry City 171 59
1936 1938 Northampton Town 47 10
Nuneaton Borough

Lavender, Horace (Harry) OR/OL
b Dudley q2 1904
Dudley Town
1926 1927 Coventry City 9 1

Laverick, Charles RB/LB
b 1881
1900 Newcastle United 0
Wallsend Park Villa
1902 Doncaster Rovers 8
1904 1906 Lincoln City 66
West Stanley
Newburn

Laverick, J LB/RB
b Tyneside
1893 1894 Newcastle United 4
Hebburn Argyle

Laverick, William (Bill) OL
b Pelton Fell 11/9/1897 d 1975
Annfield Plain
Darlington
Chester-le-Street
1923 1924 Ashington 79 12
Annfield Plain
West Stanley
1926 1927 Ashington 13 1
1928 Halifax Town 2
Murton Colliery Welfare

Lavery, James IL/CF
1905 1906 Blackpool 23 2

Lavery, John OL
b Gateshead q4 1872
Gateshead NER
1897 Sunderland 1
Gateshead NER
1898 Burton Swifts 30 8
Hebburn Argyle

Lavery, John (Jack) IL/IR
b Newcastle 1/3/1882 d 1937
Jarrow
1903 Barnsley 4 2
Denaby United
1905 1907 Leeds City 56 20
Swindon Town
South Shields

From To Apps Goal

Lavery, Patrick OL
b Hebburn q2 1884 d 1915
Gateshead
1905 Hull City 2
West Stanley
South Shields Athletic
Bedlington United
Coxlodge Villa
Pelaw
Marley Hill United

Lavery, William RB
b Thornton, Lancashire 1887
Caps: IrLge 5
Fylde
1906 1908 Preston North End 22
1907 Leicester Fosse (trial) 0
West Ham United
Belfast Celtic
1913 Middlesbrough 0
Raith Rovers
Heart of Midlothian
Belfast Celtic (loan)
St Mirren
Johnstone (trial)
1921 1922 Port Vale 5
Alkali Works

Law, Abraham GK
b Wealdstone 1874
Millwall Athletic
1896 West Bromwich Albion 1
Stafford Rangers

Law, Alexander (Alec) CF
b Bathgate 28/4/1910
Bathgate
Fauldhouse United
Bo'ness (loan)
1933 1934 Sheffield Wednesday 9 4
1935 1938 Brighton & Hove Albion 66 36
1939 Chester (2) (1)

Law, Dudley George (George) CF
b Wellingborough 12/5/1912 d 1970
Beau Ideal FC
Irchester
Wellingborough Town
1935 Northampton Town 0
Rushden Town
1937 1938 Norwich City 6 2
Colchester United
Lowestoft Town
Folkestone Town

Law, George RH/RB
b Arbroath 13/12/1885
Caps: Scotland 3
Arbroath
Rangers
1912 1914 Leeds City 105 1
Rangers
Partick Thistle
Arbroath

Law, George Bramley RB
b Ramsbottom 10/10/1905 d 1975
Ramsbottom United
1928 Oldham Athletic (trial) 0
1930 1931 Accrington Stanley 4

Law, James OR
1899 Blackburn Rovers 3 1

Law, JH CF
1892 Bootle 4 1

Law, John OL
b Dumfries 1887
Maxwelltown Volunteers
1906 Sunderland 1
Rangers
1907 Lincoln City 19
King's Own Scottish Borderers
1908 Gainsborough Trinity 9 1
King's Own Scottish Borderers
Leith
Carlisle United
Rangers
King's Own Scottish Borderers
Kilmarnock
Falkirk
Abercorn
Queen of the South

Law, John H OL
b Scotland
Rangers
1893 Everton 0
1893 Newcastle United 8 2

From To Apps Goal

Law, Thomas (Tommy) LB
b Glasgow 1/4/1908 d 1976
Caps: Scotland 2
Claremont
Bridgeton Waverley
1926 1937 Chelsea 293 15

Law, William Daniel (Billy) OL/OR
b Pleck 3/1882 d 1952
Rushall Olympic
Walsall
1904 Doncaster Rovers 26 2
1905 West Bromwich Albion 10
Watford
Queen's Park Rangers
1909 1913 Glossop 95 4

Law, William George McKenzie (Billy) CF
b Leith 26/4/1914
Penicuik Athletic
1937 Bradford Park Avenue 2 1
1938 Stockport County 1
1939 Watford (2) (1)

Lawie, Charles Robert IL
b Glenlivet 25/2/1911
Inverurie Rovers
Forfar Athletic
1934 Crewe Alexandra 41 5
1935 York City 10 1

Lawless, Patrick Joseph Henry (Henry) CH
b Sheffield q2 1906 d 1968
Calthorpe
1929 Notts County 2
Loughborough Corinthians
Boston Town
Distillery
Coleraine
Distillery

Lawley, George Harry OR/OL
b Wolverhampton 10/4/1903 d 1987
Bloxwich All Saints
Talbot Stead Works
Darlaston
Bloxwich Strollers
1925 Walsall 26 3
Burton Town
1927 Merthyr Town 18 2
Dundee
1929 1930 Sunderland 10 1
1931 Swindon Town 28 3
Worcester City
Shrewsbury Town
Brierley Hill Alliance
Dudley Town
Hednesford Town
Cannock Town
Nuneaton Town

Lawley, William IL
b Mexborough
Denaby United
1902 Barnsley 1
Denaby United

Lawrance, Raymond Stanley (Ray) CH/RH
b Gainsborough 18/9/1911 d 1987
Gainsborough Trinity
1933 1935 Hull City 34 1
1936 1938 Newport County 38
Haarlem

Lawrence, E RH/LB
1892 1897 Burton Swifts 68

Lawrence, Edward (Eddie) LH/RH
b Cefn Mawr 24/8/1907 d 1989
Caps: Wales 2
Druids
1925 1927 Wrexham 21
1928 1930 Clapton Orient 100 2
1931 1935 Notts County 138 2
1936 Bournemouth & Boscombe Ath 39 1
1937 Clapton Orient 21
Players Athletic
1939 Notts County 0
Grantham

Lawrence, Everard Thomas OL
b Kettering q4 1878
Wellingborough
Northampton Town
Kettering
Northampton Town
1902 Woolwich Arsenal 20 3
Fulham
1904 Glossop 11 4
Elsecar Athletic
Market Harborough Town
Kettering
Kettering Working Men's Club

From To Apps Goal

Lawrence, George Harold GK
b Basford 10/3/1889 d 1959
Ilkeston Primitives
Ilkeston United
1910 1923 Derby County 137
1924 Bristol City 14
1925 Lincoln City 5
Ilkeston Town

Lawrence, James (Jimmy) GK
b Glasgow 16/2/1885 d 1934
Caps: Scotland 1
Partick Athletic
Glasgow Perthshire
Hibernian (loan)
1904 1921 Newcastle United 432

Lawrence, James (Jimmy) LB
b Earlestown 6/1892 d 1937
Earlestown Boys Club
1919 Aston Villa 13
1920 1924 Coventry City 128 2

Lawrence, Joseph (Joe) OR
b Willenhall 1871
Wolverhampton Rangers
1892 Wolverhampton Wanderers 2
Darlaston

Lawrence, Matthew (Matt) LH/RH
b Cefn-y-Bedd 3/4/1909 d 1999
Cross Street Church
1930 1937 Wrexham 132 4
1937 1938 Hull City 25 1

Lawrence, Sidney Wilfred (Sid) RB
b Penrhiwceiber 16/3/1909 d 1949
Caps: WLge 1/Wales 8
Penrhiwceiber Rangers
1930 1938 Swansea Town 312 11
1939 Swindon Town (1)
Haverfordwest Athletic

Lawrence, Thomas (Tommy) OR/OL
b Hoylake 23/11/1909 d 1992
Runcorn
Hoylake
1932 Everton 0
Runcorn
1934 1936 New Brighton 55 7
South Liverpool
Wigan Athletic (trial)
Hoylake
Witton Albion

Lawrence, Valentine (Val) RH/CH
b Arbroath 5/5/1889 d 1961
Dundee Violet
1909 Newcastle United (trial) 0
Forfar Athletic
1911 1912 Manchester City 20
Arbroath
1913 Oldham Athletic 1
1914 Leeds City 6
Morton
Dumbarton
Darlington
Shildon Athletic
Hartlepools United
1921 Southend United 18
Abertillery
Tunbridge Wells Rangers

Lawrence, Walter GK
Heaton Stannington
1937 1938 Gateshead 10
Stockton

Lawrence, Walter Henry IL
b Richmond, Surrey q2 1884 d 1952
Summerstown
Crystal Palace
1909 Woolwich Arsenal 25 5
Crystal Palace
Merthyr Town

Lawrie, Hugh LB
1905 Bolton Wanderers 3
Queen's Park Rangers

Lawrie, John OR
b Knightsbridge, Glasgow
Clydebank Juniors
Partick Thistle
Workington
1908 Blackburn Rovers 2
Workington
Bristol Rovers

From To Apps Goal

Laws, Joseph Minto (Joe) OL
b Cornsay Colliery 6/7/1897 d 1952
Spennymoor United
1921 1922 Grimsby Town 53 5
Worksop Town
York City
1926 Nottingham Forest 7 1
1927 1928 Southport 81 11
Macclesfield
Ashton National
Macclesfield
Chorley

Laws, Thomas (Tommy) RH
b Summerstown 28/1/1890 d 1980
De Nevers Rubber Mills
Summerstown
1913 Fulham 6
Morton
Clydebank

Lawson, Denis OR
b Campsie 11/12/1897 d 1968
Caps: Scotland 1
Kilsyth Emmet
Kilsyth Rangers
St Mirren
1923 1925 Cardiff City 64 2
Springfield Babes
Providence Clamdiggers
1927 Wigan Borough 28 2
Clyde
Brechin City

Lawson, George William CF
b Durham 29/11/1898 d 1980
Langley Park
Cornsay Park Albion
Esh Winning
1924 Durham City 2
Esh Winning
Chilton Colliery Recreation Athletic

Lawson, Hector Stewart Ramsay LH/CH/OR
b Shettleston 21/5/1896 d 1971
Shettleston
Cambuslang Rangers
Rangers
Third Lanark (loan)
Hamilton Academical (trial)
Clyde (loan)
Vale of Leven (loan)
Third Lanark (loan)
Clyde (loan)
1923 1924 Liverpool 12
Airdrieonians
Aberdeen
1928 Brighton & Hove Albion 7
1929 1930 Newport County 55 1
Shamrock Rovers

Lawson, Herbert (Bert) OR/RH
b Luton 12/4/1905
Frickers Athletic
Luton Clarence
1925 Arsenal 13 2
1926 1931 Brentford 61 11
1933 Luton Town 1
Bedford Town

Lawson, Herbert Thomas IR/IL/CF
b Sunderland 31/1/1913 d 1975
1934 Reading 2 1
1934 Bournemouth & Boscombe Ath 3
1935 1936 Barrow 24 9
Frickley Colliery

Lawson, James (Jim) RB
b Glasgow 1897
Port Glasgow Juniors
St Mirren
Kilsyth Rangers
1920 Bolton Wanderers 0
Hartlepools United
1920 1921 Southend United 19

Lawson, Reginald Openshaw IR
b Halliwell 11/1880
Halliwell St Paul's
Cheshire College
1900 Newton Heath 3
1901 Bolton Wanderers 0
Southport Central

Lawson, Richard R IR/OR
1893 1894 Bolton Wanderers 2 2
South Shore

From To Apps Goal

Lawson, Thomas (Tommy) LH
b Boldon Colliery 1907 d 1936
1925 Newcastle United 0
Scotswood
Boldon Colliery Welfare
1927 1929 Fulham 30 2
1931 West Ham United 0
1932 1933 Aldershot 68
1934 Newport County 11

Lawton, George OR
b Stoke-on-Trent 8/1862
Stoke St Peter's
Stoke
Burslem Port Vale
1888 Stoke 13 1
Altrincham
Belvedere

Lawton, George GK
b Tunstall 1880
Burslem Port Vale
Porthill
1901 Stoke 1
Tunstall
Porthill

Lawton, Jack OR
Manchester North End
1935 Burnley 3
Altrincham

Lawton, James Allsop CH
b Ripley 27/9/1893 d 1975
Caps: England Sch
Openwoodgate
Ripley Athletic
Portsmouth
Brampton Ironworks
Chesterfield Town
Ilkeston United
1919 Nottingham Forest 3

Lawton, John Wesley (Jack) IL
b Wallasey 6/11/1909 d 1974
Wallasey Grocers
1935 Bradford Park Avenue (trial) 0
1935 New Brighton 18 4

Lawton, Robert LB
b Barnsley
Monk Bretton
1899 Barnsley 2

Lawton, Thomas (Tommy) CF
b Bolton 6/10/1919 d 1996
Caps: FLge 3/England War 23/England 23
Rossendale United
1935 1936 Burnley 25 16
1936 1938 Everton 87 65
1939 (Everton) (3) (4)
1945 1947 Chelsea 42 30
1947 1951 Notts County 151 90
1951 1953 Brentford 50 17
1953 1955 Arsenal 35 13
Kettering Town

Lax, George RH/LB
b Barnsley q1 1905
Frickley Colliery
1929 1931 Wolverhampton Wanderers 61 1
1931 1932 Barnsley 48 1
1933 Bournemouth & Boscombe Ath 7 1
Worcester City
Evesham Town
Bohemians (Worcester)

Lax, Walter OL
b Gainsborough 22/3/1912 d 1967
Albion Works
1929 1930 Lincoln City 45 18
1931 1932 Blackpool 25
1933 Coventry City 0
1933 York City 28 5
Scunthorpe & Lindsey United
Lysaght's Sports

Laxton, Edward George OR
b Brazil 1896 d 1961
Netherfield Rangers
1914 Nottingham Forest 0
1920 Norwich City 16
Shildon Athletic
Bohemians
Grantham
Heanor Town

Laycock, Alfred (Alf) GK
b Low Moor 29/9/1895 d 1964
Hill Top Sunday School
Calverley
Wibsey United
1921 1924 Bradford Park Avenue 7
1925 Southport 9

From To Apps Goal

Laycock, Frederick Walter (Fred) IR/IL
b Sheffield 31/3/1897 d 1989
St Mary's (Sheffield)
Shirebrook
Rotherham Town
1922 Sheffield Wednesday 0
1924 Barrow 31 10
1924 1925 Nelson 23 12
Mansfield Town
1927 New Brighton 28 14
Peterborough & Fletton United
1929 Darlington 35 14
1930 York City 27 12
1931 Swindon Town 16 2
Derry City
Witton Albion
Nuneaton Town
Cannock Town
Northwich Victoria (trial)
Shrewsbury Town (trial)
Hereford United

Layton, Arthur Edmund D LB/RB
b Gornal 2/1885 d 1959
Royston United
1905 Sheffield United 0
South Kirkby
Rotherham Town
1908 1910 Aston Villa 16
1911 Middlesbrough 7
Whitby Town
1920 Cardiff City 2
1920 1922 Stockport County 59

Layton, Arthur Richard CF/IR
b West Ham q1 1890 d 1962
North Sydney
Spitalfields Athletic
1914 1919 Clapton Orient 26 4
Northfleet
1922 Millwall Athletic 9 1

Layton, George LH
b Stourbridge 1865
Stourbridge Royal
Cradley Heath St Luke's
1898 1900 Small Heath 17 3
Dudley Town
Soho Villa

Layton, George William (Billy) IR/OR
b Newtown 1881
Shrewsbury Town
1904 1905 Wolverhampton Wanderers 29 4
Coventry City
Wolverhampton Swifts
Willenhall Pickwick

Layton, William (Willie) RB/LB
b Gornal 1875 d 1944
Caps: FLge 1
Blackwell Colliery
Chesterfield Town
1897 1909 Sheffield Wednesday 331 4
Whitwell St Lawrence

Layton, William Herbert (Bill) LH/IL
b Shirley 13/1/1915 d 1984
Shirley Town
1937 1946 Reading 51 17
1946 1948 Bradford Park Avenue 47 5
1950 Colchester United 7
Harwich & Parkeston

Lea, Alfred Ernest CF
b Edgbaston q1 1894
1920 West Bromwich Albion 0
1921 Merthyr Town 7 1

Lea, Harry IL
1892 Accrington 28 10
West Manchester

Lea, Isaac George RH/RB/CH
b Donnington Wood 17/2/1911 d 1972
Oswestry Town
Oakengates Town
1932 1936 Birmingham 27 1
1937 1938 Millwall 37
1939 (Millwall) (1)

Lea, Thomas (Tom) OR
1892 Accrington 29 6
West Manchester

Lea, Thomas (Tancy) OL/OR/CF
b Shrewsbury 2/9/1890 d 1979
Whitchurch
Chester
Oswestry Town
1913 1921 Wolverhampton Wanderers 47 3
1922 1923 Bristol Rovers 49 2
Shrewsbury Town

From To Apps Goal

Leach, James McIntyre (Jimmy) LH
b Spennymoor q1 1891
Newcastle St Wilfred's
Spennymoor United
Spen Black & White
1912 1921 Aston Villa 67 3
1922 Queen's Park Rangers 1

Leach, John Ralph RB/LB/CH
b Darwen 15/5/1866 d 1931
1891 1897 Darwen 176 7
Whitehall (Darwen)

Leach, Samuel LB
1897 Derby County 1
Heanor Town

Leach, Samuel LH
b Carrville
Belmont
1926 Durham City 1

Leach, Thomas (Tommy 'Tony') CH/RH
b Wincobank 23/9/1903 d 1968
Caps: FLge 1/England 2
Blackburn Wesleyans (Doncaster)
Retford Town
Wath Athletic
1925 Liverpool (trial) 0
1926 1933 Sheffield Wednesday 238 11
1934 1935 Newcastle United 51 2
1936 Stockport County 16 4
1936 1937 Carlisle United 52
1938 Lincoln City 25 2

Leadbetter, John (Jack) OL
Fleetwood Rangers
Chorley
1897 1900 Blackpool 63 10
Fleetwood Amateurs

Leadbetter, John Herbert (Jack) RH
b Prescot 28/12/1898 d 1985
Whiston Parish
1923 New Brighton 1
Connah's Quay & Shotton
Prescot Cables
Brenka

Leafe, Alfred Richard (Dicky) OR/IR/IL
b Boston q4 1891 d 1964
Boston Town
1909 Grimsby Town 1
Boston Town
1911 1912 Sheffield United 28 15
1919 1921 West Ham United 31 7

Leahy, Edward John GK
b West Ham q3 1891 d 1962
Caps: WLge 1
Walthamstow Grange
1913 Leicester Fosse 0
Southend United
1921 1926 Aberdare Athletic 37
Mansfield House
Silvertown Rubber Works

Leake, Alexander (Alex) CH/LH
b Small Heath 11/7/1871 d 1938
Caps: FLge 1/England 5
King's Heath Albion
Saltley Gas Company
Singers Hoskins & Sewell
Old Hill Wanderers
1895 1901 Small Heath 199 21
1902 1907 Aston Villa 127 7
1907 1909 Burnley 81 2
Wednesbury Old Athletic

Lealman, Frederick William (Fred) OR
b Hackforth q1 1912
Hartlepool Gas & Water
1936 York City 0
Blackhall Colliery Welfare
1938 Hartlepools United 7 2
Blackhall Colliery Welfare

Leaning, Joseph GK
b Grimsby q2 1874 d 1949
St Andrew's (Grimsby)
Grimsby United
West Marsh Wanderers
Grimsby All Saints
1897 Grimsby Town 2
Grimsby Rovers
1900 Grimsby Town 3
Grimsby Rovers
West Marsh Social
Grimsby Rovers

Leary, Reginald Samuel C (Rex) CH
b Everton q4 1897 d 1964
1921 Everton 0
1922 1923 Tranmere Rovers 5

From To Apps Goal

Leather, George Robert (Bob) OR
b Northwich q1 1867 d 1935
1892 Northwich Victoria 0
1893 Rotherham Town 1 1

Leather, John (Jack) GK
b 1875
Macclesfield Swifts
Macclesfield
1896 Woolwich Arsenal 8
Queen's Park Rangers

Leather, John George GK
b Bethnal Green 9/5/1901 d 1967
1926 Clapton Orient 1

Leatherbarrow, Charles (Charlie) IR/CF
b Liverpool 1869
1893 Rotherham Town 12 3
1893 1894 Walsall Town Swifts 24 12
1894 Small Heath 5 3
Millwall Athletic
Chatham

Leaver, James (Jimmy) RB/CH
b Blackburn 26/12/1897 d 1959
1919 Blackburn Rovers 0
1920 1925 Blackpool 103 4
1926 1927 Watford 35 3
Mossley
Stalybridge Celtic

Leavey, Herbert James (Bert) OL/IL/OR
b Guildford 5/11/1886 d 1954
Woodland Villa
Plymouth Argyle
1908 Derby County 0
Plymouth Argyle
1910 Liverpool 5
1911 Barnsley 28 2
1913 Bradford Park Avenue 19 1
Llanelly
1920 Portsmouth 13
Boscombe

Leck, Reginald (Reg) IL
b Aigburth 29/1/1890 d 1966
Aigburth Vale
Zalkyrie
Tranmere Rovers
1921 Wrexham 13 3

Leckie, Charles T LH/RH
b Alva 1876
Dundee
1898 1904 Derby County 126 1

Leckie, John Thompson (Jock) GK
b Alva 3/3/1906
Caps: Lol 1
Alva Albion Rovers
St Johnstone
Alloa Athletic
Raith Rovers
Bray Unknowns
1931 1932 Port Vale 24
1933 Stockport County 5
1934 1935 Cardiff City 46
1936 Walsall 26
1937 Carlisle United 8

Ledbrooke, L IL
1893 Walsall Town Swifts 6 2

Leddy, Henry Christopher (Harry) CH
b Dublin 1888
Caps: IrLge 1
Belfast Celtic
Distillery
Glenavon
Shelbourne
Clyde
Shelbourne
Belfast United
Distillery
Glenavon
Tranmere Rovers
1921 Everton 0
1921 1922 Chesterfield 45 7
1923 Grimsby Town 13
Shamrock Rovers
Frankfort (Dublin)

Ledger, R GK
1893 Rotherham Town 1

Ledger, Robert CH
Mickley (Ripon)
1913 Huddersfield Town 1
Chopwell Villa

Ledingham, William Denis CH
b Newtongrange 1891 d 1960
Tranent Juniors
1913 Barnsley 1

From To Apps Goal

Ledwidge, John (Johnny) IR
Richmond Rovers
Shelbourne
Bray Unknowns
1932 Bournemouth & Boscombe Ath 17 7
Dolphin (Dublin)

Lee (Evans), Abel RH
b North Staveley 1884 d 1929
Wombwell Rising Star
Darfield United
1906 1909 Grimsby Town 86
New Brompton

Lee, Albert George IL
b Leicester q3 1883
Oxford Victoria (Leicester)
1904 Leicester Fosse 1
Thursday Excelsior
Leicester Imperial
Leicester Nomads
Thursday Excelsior

Lee, Arthur G GK
b Plymouth
Woodland Villa
1926 1927 Plymouth Argyle 4

Lee, Bernard James (Barney) IR/OR
b Alloa 5/3/1873
Leith Athletic
1894 1895 Bury 23 11
1896 Newcastle United 0
Nelson
Bo'ness
King's Park
Brighton & Hove Albion
Broxburn

Lee, Bert CF
Hesleden Celtic
1921 Hartlepools United 3 1

Lee, Edward OL
1902 Burnley 26 3

Lee, Edwin CF
b Lymm
Hurst Ramblers
1898 1899 Newton Heath 11 5
Hyde St George

Lee, Frank (Frankie) OR
b Heeley
1907 Gainsborough Trinity 13 1
1919 Rotherham County 7 1

Lee, Frederick (Freddie) OL
b Yardley
Yardley White Star
1930 1931 Coventry City 7
1932 1934 Walsall 85 24
1935 Blackpool 0
1936 Mansfield Town 0

Lee, Garnet Morley RB
b Calverton 7/6/1887 d 1976
1910 Notts County 4

Lee, George OR
b Stockton q3 1876 d 1906
Stockton
Rotherham Town
1899 Sheffield Wednesday 5 1
Amberley (Sheffield)

Lee, George Thomas OL
b York 4/6/1919 d 1991
Acomb
1935 Tottenham Hotspur (trial) 0
Scarborough
1936 1946 York City 37 11
1939 (York City) (3)
1947 1948 Nottingham Forest 76 20
1949 1957 West Bromwich Albion 271 59
Lockheed Leamington
Vauxhall Motors

Lee, Harold Godfrey OR/IR/CF
b Erith q1 1884
Erith Albion
Erith Town
Cray Wanderers
Sittingbourne
1907 1909 Woolwich Arsenal 41 15
1909 1911 Bury 50 4
Dartford

From To Apps Goal

Lee, Henry (Harry) CF/OR
b Preston q2 1887
Moor Parts (Preston)
Leyland
St Helens Recreation
1907 1908 Fulham 7 2
Reading
1912 1914 Fulham 58 30
Gillingham
Chorley

Lee, James Alfred (Alf) RB/LB
b Rotherham q1 1892
Rotherham County
1913 1914 Grimsby Town 15
1919 1921 West Ham United 26
1922 Newport County 4

Lee, James Thomas (Jimmy) GK
b Brierley Hill 4/1892 d 1955
Cradley Heath St Luke's
Wulfrunians
1919 1920 Aston Villa 18
1921 Stoke 22
Macclesfield

Lee, John (Jack 'Dump') LB
b Tranmere 1876 d 1938
Tranmere Rovers
1902 Everton 2
Tranmere Rovers

Lee, John (Jack) OL/IL
b Sheffield 1890 d 1955
Bird-in-Hand
1913 1919 Hull City 75 19
1919 1922 Chelsea 7 1
1924 Watford 8
1925 Rotherham United 17 2

Lee, John Charles OL
b Morpeth q3 1889
Morpeth Town
1909 1912 Clapton Orient 20 1
Exeter City
1913 Newcastle United 0

Lee, John S IR
b Walsall Wood 1869
Walsall Unity
1893 Small Heath 7 3
Darlaston
Bilston United
Darlaston

Lee, John W CF
b Newcastle 1906
Preston Colliery
1927 Newcastle United 0
1928 Chesterfield 4 1
Bedlington United
Wallsend

Lee, John William (Jack) OL
b Tynemouth 26/6/1903 d 1990
Blackhall Wesleyans
Horden Athletic
1924 Hartlepools United 2
1925 Luton Town (trial) 0
Horden Athletic
1926 Arsenal 7
1928 1932 Chesterfield 172 49
1933 1934 Aldershot 61 19
Ollerton Colliery
Broad Oaks Works

Lee, Joseph (Joe) GK
Earlestown
Stockport County
1897 1898 Bolton Wanderers 6
Haydock

Lee, Patrick Francis (Pat) LH/IL
b Uddingston 20/1/1903 d 1981
Uddingston Rep
Vale of Clyde
1925 1926 Hull City 25 6
1927 1929 Accrington Stanley 112 4
1930 Southport (trial) 2
Ballymena
Dolphin
Albion Rovers
Ballymena
Dundee
Hamilton Academical
St Mirren
Invernss Caledonian (trial)
Babcock & Wilcox

From To Apps Goal

Lee, Thomas LH
b Alnwick q1 1876
Alnwick Town
1897 Sunderland 2
Bristol Rovers
Hebburn Argyle
South Shields
Bristol Rovers
Hebburn Argyle
Millwall Athletic
Ashington

Lee, William (Billy) CF
b West Bromwich 8/1878 d 1934
West Bromwich Baptists
West Bromwich Standard
Bournville Athletic
1901 1903 West Bromwich Albion 71 25
Bournemouth Wanderers
Portsmouth
New Brompton
1907 Chesterfield Town 26 6
Darlaston

Lee, William Richard (Billy) RH
b Darwen 24/10/1919 d 1996
Feniscowles
Pleasington
1938 Blackburn Rovers 1
1946 1952 Barrow 158 1

Lee, Willis IL
b Sheffield 1904
1924 Sheffield Wednesday 0
1925 Rotherham United 2

Leech, William (Billy) RH/LH
b Newcastle-under-Lyme 15/7/1875 d 1934
Newcastle White Star
Newcastle Swifts
Tottenham Hotspur
1899 Burslem Port Vale 26 1
1900 1901 Stoke 46 2
Plymouth Argyle
Reading
1906 1910 Leicester Fosse 84 3

Leedham, Frederick Arthur (Fred) IL
b Lye 21/2/1909 d 1996
Kidderminster Harriers
1928 West Bromwich Albion 4
Kidderminster Harriers
1931 1932 Bradford Park Avenue 49 6
1933 1934 Accrington Stanley 51 9
1934 1936 Oldham Athletic 48 11
Cheltenham Town
Revo Electric

Leedham, Harry LH
b Stourbridge q3 1898
1921 1923 Walsall 65 2
Brierley Hill Alliance
Worcester City
Kidderminster Harriers

Leedham, Thomas William CF
b Sunderland q4 1905 d 1966
Southwick (Co Durham)
1926 Sunderland (trial) 0
1927 Durham City 13 9
Jarrow
1928 Preston North End (trial) 0
Durham City
Jarrow
Murton
Easington Colliery Welfare
Maple Amateurs (Sunderland)

Leeds, William Henry
b Blaby q3 1896 d 1961
Southend Corinthians
1920 Southend United (trial) 1

Leeming, Albert OL
b Preston 11/12/1902 d 1943
1924 Wigan Borough 1
Lytham
Darwen

Leeming, Joseph (Joe) CH/IL/LB
b Preston 22/9/1876 d 1962
Caps: FLge 1
Turton
1897 1907 Bury 258 18
Brighton & Hove Albion
Chorley

Leeming, William Brian (Bill) LB
b Blean 23/3/1909 d 1997
1929 Wrexham 1
Oswestry Town
Camberley & York Town

From To Apps Goal

Lees, Andrew Anderson RH
b Motherwell 30/4/1896
Renfrew Juniors
Motherwell
Kilmarnock (loan)
Aberdeen
1922 Swindon Town 1
St Bernard's
Alloa Athletic
Lochgelly United
Queen of the South
Dykehead
Broxburn United

Lees, Harry Hamilton IL
b Wandsworth q3 1900 d 1966
Ebbw Vale
1922 1927 Wolverhampton Wanderers 120 40
1927 1928 Darlington 54 21
Shrewsbury Town
Stourbridge
Leamington Town

Lees, John IR
Sawley Rangers
1888 1889 Derby County 10 2

Lees, John William (Jack) RB/RH
b Northwich 26/7/1892 d 1984
Northwich Victoria
1919 1920 Preston North End 31
1922 1929 Halifax Town 248 1

Lees, Joseph William Drury (Joe) IL/IR
b Coalville q1 1892 d 1933
Coalville PSA
Whitwick Imperial
1914 Barnsley 10 2
1919 1920 Rotherham County 53 19
1921 Lincoln City 33 9
Guildford United
1923 Halifax Town 5 1
Scunthorpe & Lindsey United
1925 Newport County (trial) 0
Wombwell Town
Shirebrook

Lees, William (Don) CH/CF/IR
b Cronberry 1873
Cronberry Eglington
Celtic
1893 Lincoln City 28 17
Celtic
1894 Lincoln City 24 7
Barnsley St Peter's
1896 Darwen 20 8
1898 1903 Barnsley 187 42
Watford
1904 Barnsley 1
Denaby United
South Kirkby
Monk Bretton
South Kirkby

Lees, William Harry OL
1906 Stockport County 13 1

Leese, Harry IL
b Pitts Hill q1 1887
Smallthorne
Goldenhill Villa
1908 Bradford City 1
Stoke
Port Vale
Crewe Alexandra
Goldenhill Wanderers

Legg, Henry George W RB
b Swindon 6/8/1910 d 1985
1929 Swindon Town 0
1930 Crystal Palace 1
Dartford
Bath City

Legge, Albert Edward CF/OR/IR
b Hednesford 19/6/1901 d 1998
Lewisham Athletic
1923 1927 Wolverhampton Wanderers 53 5
1928 Gillingham 31 5
1929 Charlton Athletic 10 2
1930 Queen's Park Rangers 9
Wellington Town
Hednesford Town
Cradley Heath

Legge, Arthur CF
b London
Custom House
1914 Leicester Fosse 2
Millwall Athletic
Charlton Athletic

From To Apps Goal

Legge, Edward Daniel (Eddie) LB/RB
b Bridge of Dee 3/12/1907 d 1947
Balmoral Thistle
Aberdeen Park Vale
Arbroath
Aberdeen
1932 1934 Carlisle United 104 1
1935 1937 York City 82 2
Burton Town
Aberdeen Park Vale

Legge, Samuel G OL/IL
b Willenhall 1883 d 1973
Willenhall Swifts
1906 West Bromwich Albion 7 3
Worcester City
1908 West Bromwich Albion 2 1
Coventry City

Leggett, Sidney IR
b Clapton q1 1897
1913 Fulham 0
1920 Clapton Orient 1
Tunbridge Wells Rangers

Leigh, Alfred Sidney (Syd) CF
b Shardlow 8/1893 d 1958
Osmaston
1919 Derby County 2
1920 1921 Bristol Rovers 67 37

Leigh, Charles Henry (Charlie) RH
b New Springs 4/2/1903 d 1972
Standish St Wilfred's
1922 1923 Wigan Borough 2
Lancaster Town
New Springs IM

Leigh, Harold (Harry) OR
b Oughtrington q2 1877
1908 Aston Villa 0
1908 Barnsley 1
Stoke
Winsford United

Leigh, J OR
1903 Bolton Wanderers 2

Leigh, Thomas (Tommy) CF
b Derby q1 1875
1895 Derby County 0
1896 1898 Burton Swifts 73 26
1898 1899 New Brighton Tower 12 4
1899 1900 Newton Heath 43 16
New Brompton
Brentford

Leigh, Thomas (Ginger) RB/LB
b Hollins q2 1887 d 1914
Heywood Springfield
Haslingden
Ashton Town
Oldham Athletic
1908 1909 Fulham 6
Queen's Park Rangers
Croydon Common
Rochdale
South Liverpool

Leigh, Walter IR/CF/IL
b Birmingham q4 1876 d 1958
Cadishead Amateurs
1898 Aston Villa 1
Altrincham
1900 1901 Grimsby Town 48 12
1902 Bristol City 30 5
New Brompton
1905 Clapton Orient 23 8
Hastings & St Leonards
1907 Clapton Orient 17 3
Kettering

Leightley, Joseph (Joe) CF
b Cramlington 7/11/1913 d 1985
Ashington
1930 Bury 4 1

Leighton, John (Jock) LH
b Scotland
Newton Thistle
Hibernian
1896 Leicester Fosse 14

Leighton, William Alexander (Bill) IR/LH
b Walker 8/12/1914 d 1981
Walker Park
1932 1937 Newcastle United 39 8
1938 Southend United 16
Ekco Sports
1945 Southend United 0
Colchester United
Chingford Town

From To Apps Goal

Leiper, Joseph (Joe) LB
b Govan 15/3/1873
Minerva
Partick Thistle
1892 1899 Derby County 157
1900 1901 Grimsby Town 46
1902 Chesterfield Town 25
Partick Thistle
Motherwell
Hull City
Aberdare Town
Belper Town

Leitch, William (Billy) LH/IR
b Glasgow
Greenock Overton
Port Glasgow Athletic
Partick Thistle
Distillery (loan)
1920 1922 Coventry City 27 2
1923 1925 Bournemouth & Boscombe Ath 81 1
Helensburgh

Le Maitre, Albert E (Bert) OL
b Guernsey
Army
1933 Aldershot 2 1

Le May, Frederick John Sidney (Fred) OR
b Bow 2/2/1907 d 1988
Bulphan
Laindon Hills
Tilbury
1926 Southend United 0
Grays Thurrock
Grays Athletic
Woking
1930 Thames 34 4
1931 Watford 4
1932 Clapton Orient 10
Margate
Chelmsford

Le May, Leslie George (Les) OL
b Bow 17/9/1912 d 1992
1930 Thames 1
1931 Watford 0
1932 Clapton Orient 0

Lemoine, Harold Meredith GK
b Royston 4/10/1877
Caps: England Amat
Shepherds Bush
Clapton
Southend United
1912 1913 Nottingham Forest 9
Woking

Lemons, Charles George (Charlie) CF
b Sheffield 3/12/1887 d 1952
Beighton Recreation
Scunthorpe & Lindsey United
1921 Lincoln City 22 4
York City
Gainsborough Trinity

Lenney, Ralph Curry OL
b South Shields 11/1/1895 d 1971
Hebburn Colliery
1922 West Bromwich Albion 0
1923 Wrexham 15 1
Carlisle United

Lennon, George Ferguson RB
b Kilwinning 24/5/1889 d 1984
Kilwinning Rangers
Third Lanark
Abercorn
Third Lanark
St Mirren
Ayr United (loan)
1920 1922 Luton Town 107
1922 1923 Stoke 3
Weymouth
1925 Bristol Rovers 4
Airdrieonians
Llandudno (trial)
Colwyn Bay United

Lennox, Malcolm OR
b Glasgow 6/4/1874
Glasgow Perthshire
1895 1897 Newcastle United 46 16
New Brompton

Lennox, William OR
b Holytown 24/5/1901
Shildon
1928 Nottingham Forest 9 1
Washington Colliery

From To Apps Goal

Lennox, Wilson (Billy) CF/IR/RH
b Lanark 27/5/1901 d 1976
Glasgow Ashfield
Mid Annandale
1927 1930 Charlton Athletic 71 41
1931 Thames 23 10
1932 Newport County 22 1
1933 Accrington Stanley 31 9
Enschede

Lenton, A IR/IL
1895 1896 Burton Swifts 8 2

Leonard, Anthony Michael (Micky) IR
b Ireland
Caps: Ireland Amat
Reading
1906 Clapton Orient 37 7
Plymouth Argyle
Reading

Leonard (Bamford), Arthur Ralph IR/OL
b Leicester 1874 d 1950
17th Leicestershire Regiment
1897 Leicester Fosse 0
Rushden Town
Sheppey United
Glentoran
1901 1903 Small Heath 68 25
1903 1904 Stoke 14 3
St Bernard's

Leonard, Henry Doxford (Harry) CF
b Sunderland q3 1886 d 1951
Sunderland West End
Southwick (Co Durham)
1907 Newcastle United 0
Sunderland West End (loan)
1908 1909 Grimsby Town 53 23
1910 1911 Middlesbrough 13 3
1911 1919 Derby County 144 72
1920 Manchester United 10 5
Heanor Town

Leonard, James (Jimmy 'Hookey') IL
b Paisley 1906 d 1959
Saltcoats Victoria
Cowdenbeath
Indiana Flooring
Cowdenbeath
New York Nationals
Cowdenbeath
1930 Sunderland 26 17
Rhyl Athletic
Colwyn Bay United
1931 Sunderland 9 2
Morton
Shelbourne
Shamrock Rovers
Dolphin
Fearons Athletic
Brideville
Shelbourne

Leonard, John (Jack) OR
b Gloucester 1876
St Mirren
1897 Derby County 1 1
1897 Notts County 1 1
Bedminster
Bristol Eastville Rovers
1899 Small Heath 7 1
Cheltenham Town

Leonard, John (Jack) CF
b Paisley 30/9/1911
Renfrew Juniors
Lanark United
Partick Thistle (trial)
Hibernian
1936 Southport (trial) 0
1936 New Brighton 8 2

Leonard, Patrick OL
b Scotland 1877
St Mirren
1897 Manchester City 15 4
New Brompton
Thames Ironworks
1899 Manchester City 1 1
St Bernard's

Leslie, Alexander J (Alex) RH/CH
b Methil 1902
1923 Manchester City 1
1925 Tranmere Rovers 14
Crossley Brothers

From To Apps Goal

Leslie, Alfred James (Alec) LH
b Arbroath 11/7/1896 d 1974
Greenock Wayfarers
Port Glasgow Juniors
St Mirren
Houghton-le-Spring
St Mirren
Morton
Torquay United
1926 1931 Birmingham 132

Leslie, George William John CH
b Eton 9/7/1907 d 1986
Slough Town
1930 Charlton Athletic 0
(France)
1932 1935 Walsall 88 2
Guildford City

Leslie, James (Jim) IR
b Barrhead 1875 d 1920
Neilston
Clyde
1894 Bolton Wanderers 0
Clyde
1897 1900 Sunderland 92 24
1901 Middlesbrough 7 3
Clyde
Arthurlie

Leslie, John Francis (Jack) IL
b Canning Town 17/8/1901 d 1988
Barking Town
1921 1934 Plymouth Argyle 383 131

Leslie, Thomas Scott (Tom) RB/LH/RH
b Tollcross 26/2/1885 d 1948
Vale of Clyde
1908 1910 Tottenham Hotspur 10
Leyton
New Brompton
Clyde
Bathgate
Gillingham
Caerphilly

Lessons, George Frederick (Fred) CF
b Stockport 30/8/1883 d 1918
Nottingham Jardines Athletic
1904 1906 Nottingham Forest 31 8
Northampton Town

Lester, Edmund CF
Fleetwood Rangers
1898 Burnley 1

Lester, Frank RB/LB
b Wednesbury 1870
Fallings Heath
1894 Wolverhampton Wanderers 1
Walsall Unity
1895 1900 Small Heath 68
Walsall

Lester, Frederick Charles (Fred) LB
b Rochester 20/2/1911 d 1974
Chatham Town
1930 1937 Gillingham 201
1937 1938 Sheffield Wednesday 17

Lester, Hugh LB/RH/OL
b Lehigh, Pennsylvania, USA 1891
St Helens Recreation
1911 1912 Liverpool 2
1914 Oldham Athletic 1
Reading
Hurst

Letham, Crawford RH
b Montrose 9/5/1894 d 1930
Newtongrange Star
Dalkeith Thistle
Dundee
Cowdenbeath (loan)
Hamilton Academical
1927 Barrow 31 1
Sittingbourne (trial)
Montrose

Levene, David Jack LH/CH
b Bethnal Green 25/2/1908 d 1970
Hugonians
Northfleet
1932 1934 Tottenham Hotspur 8
1935 1936 Crystal Palace 22
Olympique Lillois
1938 Clapton Orient 0

Lever, A CH
1893 Bolton Wanderers 1

From To Apps Goal

Lever, John Edward (Eddie) LH
b Burnopfield 5/4/1911 d 1994
White-le-Head Rangers
1933 Portsmouth 0
1934 Aldershot 5
Alton Town

Levick, Frank IR
b Eckington q3 1882 d 1908
Tinsley
1905 Sheffield Wednesday 0
Rotherham Town
1907 Sheffield United 18 6

Levick, Oliver LH/CH
b Rotherham q3 1899 d 1965
Woodhouse
1920 1923 Sheffield Wednesday 21
1926 Stockport County 5
York City
Boston Town
Hurst

Levitt, Ernest (Ernie) CH
b Silksworth 2/4/1893 d 1979
New Silksworth
1920 Brentford 7
West Stanley
Thornley Albion
Wingate Albion

Lewins, George Albert RB/LB
b Walker 16/7/1906 d 1991
Newcastle United Swifts
1925 Newcastle United 0
1927 Reading 0
1928 Rochdale 34
1928 Manchester City 0
1930 Wigan Borough 26
1930 1931 Tranmere Rovers 30
Rhyl
Walker Celtic
Jarrow
Walker Celtic
West Stanley
South Shields
Ouston United

Lewis, Albert E OL/IL
b Wolverhampton 1884 d 1923
Caps: SoLge 1
Stafford Rangers
1904 1905 West Bromwich Albion 29 6
Coventry City
Northampton Town
1913 West Bromwich Albion 18 3
South Shields

Lewis, Arthur Cyril (Cyril) OL/OR
b Tonypandy 10/4/1909 d 1999
Trealaw Rangers
Treorchy Juniors
Merthyr Town
1932 Tranmere Rovers 8
1933 1938 Grimsby Town 75 31
1939 Plymouth Argyle (1)

Lewis, Arthur Norman (Norman) GK
b Wolverhampton 13/6/1908 d 1968
Sunbeam Motors
1928 Wolverhampton Wanderers 29
1929 1935 Stoke City 159
1936 Bradford Park Avenue 2
1936 1938 Tranmere Rovers 58

Lewis, Benjamin (Ben) GK
b Cafor 1898
Aberaman
1926 1927 Merthyr Town 21
1928 Portsmouth 2
1929 Merthyr Town 20 3
Folkestone
Dundalk
Bray Unknowns (loan)
Glentoran
Nargs

Lewis, Charles Henry (Charlie) IR/OL/OR
b Plumstead 15/8/1886 d 1967
East Wickham
Eltham
Maidstone United
1907 1919 Woolwich Arsenal 206 30
Margate

Lewis, Daniel (Dan) GK
b Mardy 11/2/1902 d 1965
Caps: Wales 3
Mardy
1923 Clapton Orient 0
1924 1929 Arsenal 142
1931 Gillingham 6

Lewis, Daniel W IR
1937 Stockport County 1

From To Apps Goal

Lewis, David Bryn (Bryn) OL
b Tonypandy 16/5/1913
1937 Torquay United 0
1938 Rochdale 1
Newry Town
1945 Torquay United 0

Lewis, David James (Jim) LB/RB
b Troedyrhiwfuwch 21/6/1909 d 1980
New Tredegar
1930 1938 Watford 111
1939 (Watford) (1)

Lewis, David Jenkin (Dai) OL/OR
b Merthyr Tydfil 2/2/1912 d 1997
Caps: WLge 1/Wales 2
Gellifaelog Amateurs
1930 1935 Swansea Town 112 5
1936 Bury 8
1937 Crystal Palace 0
1938 Bristol Rovers 0
Bath City

Lewis, Dudley Reginald James LH/RH
b Kensington 19/11/1909 d 1987
1931 Queen's Park Rangers 0
1932 1933 Bristol Rovers 27 4
1934 Exeter City 16 2
Bath City
1935 Newport County 10
Milford United

Lewis, Ernest G IL
b South Wales
1933 Cardiff City 14 1

Lewis, George LB/RB
b Chasetown q1 1875
1894 1896 Walsall Town Swifts 32 1
Wellingborough
1897 1901 Notts County 129 1
1902 Bristol City 30 1
Stourbridge
1903 Leicester Fosse 10
Stourbridge

Lewis, Harold Howell (Harry) IL/IR
b Merthyr Tydfil 25/10/1910 d 2006
Caps: Wales Sch
Dowlais United
1928 1930 Rochdale 62 16
1931 Arsenal 0
1932 Southend United 18 6
1933 1934 Notts County 32 7
1935 West Ham United 4 4
1936 1938 Swansea Town 45 13
Queen of the South

Lewis, Henry (Harry) IL/CF
b Birkenhead 19/12/1896 d 1976
The Comets (Liverpool)
1919 1921 Liverpool 59 10
1923 1924 Hull City 36 5
Mold Town

Lewis, Idris OR
b Tonypandy 26/8/1915 d 1996
Gelli Colliery
1935 1937 Swansea Town 66 4
1938 Sheffield Wednesday 18 7
1939 (Sheffield Wednesday) (2)
1939 Swansea Town 0
1946 Bristol Rovers 13 2
1946 1947 Newport County 27 4
1947 Sheffield Wednesday (trial) 0
Haverfordwest Athletic
Pembroke Borough

Lewis, Ivor Samuel OL
b Merthyr Tydfil 1/1/1920 d 1991
Langford St Thomas
1938 Coventry City 1

Lewis, James IR
1933 1934 Rotherham United 3 1

Lewis, James John (Jack 'Ginger') LH/LB
b Newport q1 1902
Caps: Wales 1
Somerton Park Juniors
1922 1923 Newport County 26
1924 Cardiff City 1
1925 1933 Tranmere Rovers 266 9

Lewis, James William (Jim) IR
b Hackney 2/12/1905 d 1976
Caps: England Amat/England War 1
Walthamstow Avenue
1930 1931 Queen's Park Rangers 12 5
Walthamstow Avenue

From To Apps Goal

Lewis, John (Jack) CH
b Gwersyllt
Gwersyllt
1933 1937 Wrexham 96 2
1937 Luton Town 2
1939 (Crewe Alexandra) (2)
Barmouth & Duffryn United

Lewis, John (Jack) RH/LH
b Walsall 26/8/1919 d 2002
Brownhills Albion
1937 West Bromwich Albion 0
1938 1949 Crystal Palace 124 5
1949 1950 Bournemouth & Boscombe Ath 45 1
1951 1952 Reading 74 17
Kettering Town
Worcester City

Lewis, John E (Jack) LH
b Porthcawl 1912
Trethomas
Merthyr Town
1934 Stoke City 2

Lewis, John Richard (Jack) IR
b Aberystwyth 8/1881 d 1954
Caps: Wales 1
Kidderminster Harriers
Bristol Rovers
Portsmouth
1901 1903 Burton United 74 24
Bristol Rovers
Brighton & Hove Albion
Southampton
Croydon Common
Burton United

Lewis, Joseph RB
b Buckley q1 1902
Buckley Town
1923 1924 Tranmere Rovers 11
Mold Town

Lewis, Reginald (Reg) CF/IL/IR
b Bilston 7/3/1920 d 1997
Caps: England B
Nunhead
Dulwich Hamlet
1936 Arsenal 0
Margate (loan)
1937 1951 Arsenal 154 103
1939 (Arsenal) (2) (1)

Lewis, Sidney GK
1929 Walsall 2

Lewis, Thomas George (George) CF/LB
b Troedyrhiwfuwch 20/10/1913 d 1981
Troedyrhiwfuwch
New Tredegar
1936 1945 Watford 25 11
1939 (Watford) (1) (1)
1946 1947 Southampton 43 12
1948 Brighton & Hove Albion 24 8
Dartford

Lewis, Thomas Henry (Tommy) RH
b Greenfield 1903
St Mary's (Greenfield)
Connah's Quay & Shotton
1922 Manchester United (trial) 0
Chester
1923 Crewe Alexandra 0
Holywell Arcadians
Rhyl Athletic
1927 1930 New Brighton 99 4
Connah's Quay & Shotton (trial)
Holywell Arcadians
1931 New Brighton 11
Holywell Arcadians
Mostyn YMCA

Lewis, Thomas Hewitt (Tommy) OL/IL
b Ellesmere Port 11/10/1909 d 1962
1928 Everton 1
1930 1932 Wrexham 105 40
1933 1938 Bradford Park Avenue 193 66
1938 Blackpool 10 3

Lewis, Thomas J LH/RH
b Merthyr Tydfil
1922 1928 Merthyr Town 41

Lewis, Wilfred Leslie (Wilf) CF/IL/IR
b Swansea 1/7/1903 d 1979
Caps: WLge 3/Wales 6
Baldwins Welfare
Swansea Amateurs
1925 1928 Swansea Town 65 43
1928 1930 Huddersfield Town 15 7
1931 Derby County 8 3
Yeovil & Petters United
Bath City
1934 1935 Cardiff City 35 6
Haverfordwest Athletic

From To Apps Goal

Lewis, William CF
b Bangor 1864 d 1935
Caps: Wales 27
Bangor Rovers
Bangor City
1888 Everton 3 1
Bangor City
Crewe Alexandra
Chester
1896 Manchester City 12 4
Chester

Lewis, William John (Bill) IR/OR
b Bordesley Green q1 1871
Windsor Street Gasworks
1894 1895 Small Heath 2 1
Nechells
Stourbridge
1902 Leicester Fosse 30 3
Stourbridge

Lewis, Wilson Arnold CF
b Evesham 1873
Hereford Thistle
1897 Small Heath 20 7
Bromyard

Lewry, William George CF
b Alverstoke 1/1896 d 1956
Gosport Athletic
1920 Portsmouth 4 1
Boscombe

Leyfield, Charles (Charlie) OL/OR
b Chester 30/10/1911 d 1982
Chester Brickfields
1934 1936 Everton 38 13
1937 1938 Sheffield United 36 13
1938 Doncaster Rovers 28 11
1939 (Doncaster Rovers) (3) (2)

Leyland, ? OR/OL
1893 1894 Crewe Alexandra 10 1

Leyland, John CH
b Northwich 1889
Witton Albion
1920 1921 Manchester City 3
Manchester North End

Leyland, Peter CH
b Golborne q3 1911
1932 Bolton Wanderers 0
Chorley
1934 Sheffield Wednesday 0
1935 1938 Swansea Town 25
Runcorn

Liddell, Edward (Ned) CH/LH/RH
b Sunderland 27/5/1878 d 1968
East End Blackwatch
Whitburn
Seaham White Star
1904 Sunderland 0
Southampton
1906 Gainsborough Trinity 9
1907 1912 Clapton Orient 193 3
Southend United
1914 Arsenal 2
Southend United

Liddell, George M RH/RB/LH
b Murton 14/1/1895
Yorkshire Amateurs
South Shields
1920 1931 Birmingham 323 6

Liddell, James Brown (Jimmy) IL
b Partick 10/1/1898 d 1963
1920 Liverpool 0
1921 1922 Bristol Rovers 31 4
1923 Preston North End 0
Albion Rovers

Liddell, Robert RH/CH/LH
b Blaydon 5/1877
Caps: SoLge 4
Heaton Rothbury
Westwood
1905 1909 Newcastle United 14 2
Millwall Athletic

Liddle, Daniel Hamilton Sneddon (Danny) OL/IL
b Bo'ness 19/2/1912 d 1982
Caps: Scotland 3
Bo'ness
Wallyford Bluebell
East Fife
1932 1945 Leicester City 255 64
1939 (Leicester City) (3)
1946 Mansfield Town 1
Stamford Town
Hinckley Athletic
South Wigston WMC

From To Apps Goal

Liddle, George OL
1936 Bradford City 0
1937 Accrington Stanley 4
Frickley Colliery

Liddle, Isaac IR
b Sunderland
South Hetton
1927 Hartlepools United 12 2

Liddle, James Frederick (Fred) OL
b Dunston-on-Tyne 18/9/1904
Crawcrook Albion
1927 Queen's Park Rangers 0
1928 Huddersfield Town 0
1929 Rotherham United 13
Crawcrook Albion
1931 Newcastle United 0
1932 1933 Gillingham 81 18
1934 1936 Coventry City 62 12
1937 1938 Exeter City 43 9

Liddle, James Sigsworth (Jimmy) OR
b Felling 31/5/1912 d 1994
West Stanley
1931 Middlesbrough 0
1932 1935 Reading 66 35
1936 Crystal Palace 13 1

Liddle, Robert (Bobby) OR/IR
b Gateshead 11/4/1908 d 1972
Washington Colliery
1928 1938 Stoke City 297 61

Lievesley, Ernest Frederick (Fred) IL/IR
b Netherthorpe 24/7/1899 d 1974
Staveley
1919 1921 Manchester City 2
1922 Southend United 4 1
1923 Exeter City 0
1925 1929 Rotherham United 108 28

Lievesley, Harold CH
b Chesterfield 28/2/1913
Rossington Main
1934 Doncaster Rovers 1

Lievesley, Joseph (Joe) GK
b Staveley 25/7/1883 d 1941
Caps: FLge 1
Poolsbrook United
1904 1912 Sheffield United 278
1913 1914 Woolwich Arsenal 73
Rossington Colliery

Lievesley, Leslie (Les) RH/LH/CF
b Staveley 7/1911 d 1949
Rossington Main
1929 1931 Doncaster Rovers 66 21
1931 Manchester United 2
1932 Chesterfield 0
1933 1936 Torquay United 131 4
1936 1938 Crystal Palace 75 3
1939 (Crystal Palace) (3)

Lievesley, Walter CH
b Haydock
Haydock Colliery
1919 Everton 5
1920 Reading 0

Lievesley, Wilfred (Wilf) IL/IR/OR
b Staveley 6/10/1902 d 1979
Staveley Old Boys
1920 Derby County 1
1922 Manchester United 2
1923 1927 Exeter City 97 38
1928 Wigan Borough 26 13
1929 Cardiff City 3
Macclesfield
Matlock Town

Liggins, Alfred George (Alf) OR
b Aston 23/4/1911 d 2003
Little Sutton
1929 Everton 0
1931 Liverpool 0
1931 1933 New Brighton 76 13
South Liverpool

Liggins, John Granville (Jack) CF
b Altrincham 26/3/1906 d 1976
Rotherham YMCA
1930 Rotherham United 0
Mossley
Hyde United
1934 1935 Leicester City 8 5
1935 Burnley 4 1
Mossley
Shrewsbury Town
Worksop Town
Bridlington Town

From To Apps Goal

Light, William Henry (Billy) GK
b Woolston 21/6/1913 d 1993
Thorneycrofts
Harland & Wolff
1933 1935 Southampton 45
1935 1937 West Bromwich Albion 28
Colchester United
Clacton Town

Lightbody, John William CF
b Newcastle 10/3/1905 d 1979
Lambton Star
Bank Head Albion
1925 Sunderland 0
Fatfield Albion
1926 Liverpool 0
1927 New Brighton 1 1
1928 Fulham (trial) 0
Grays Thurrock

Lightbody, Thomas (Tom) CH
b Shotts 2/7/1891 d 1918
Law Volunteers
1911 1912 Leicester Fosse 3
Peebles Rovers

Lightfoot, Edward John LH/CH
b Liverpool 13/11/1889 d 1918
Harrowby
Southport Central
1911 1914 Tottenham Hotspur 61 2

Lill, Alfred Edward CF
b Newton-on-Trent q4 1886 d 1968
Sturton
1905 Gainsborough Trinity 2
Moore's Athletic (Shirebrook)

Lilley, Edward Henry (Harry) RB/LB
b Staveley q3 1868 d 1900
Caps: England 1
Staveley
1892 1893 Sheffield United 19
Gainsborough Trinity

Lilley, Ernest RB
b Rotherham q1 1900
1924 Rotherham County 1

Lilley, James William (Will) GK
b Staveley q4 1865 d 1933
Staveley
1892 1893 Sheffield United 13
1894 Rotherham Town 9

Lilley, Robert (Bob) RB
b Bolton 3/4/1893 d 1964
Bridge Street Wesleyans
Bolton West End
Bolton North End
Little Lever Lads
Rochdale
Horwich RMI
1921 1924 Nelson 66

Lilley, Thomas (Tom) RB/LB
b New Herrington q1 1900 d 1964
Methley Perseverance
1922 Huddersfield Town 3
1923 Nelson 14
1924 1925 Hartlepools United 60
1927 Sunderland 1
St Mirren
1930 Fulham 7
Annfield Plain
New Herrington Welfare
Shiney Row Swifts
Sunderland District Omnibus Co

Lillie, John LB
b Newcastle
1923 Liverpool 0
1924 Queen's Park Rangers 3
1925 Clapton Orient 5
Blyth Spartans
1926 New Brighton 0

Lillycrop, George Beanland CF
b Gosport 7/12/1886 d 1962
South Shields Adelaide
North Shields Athletic
1907 1912 Barnsley 195 92
1913 1914 Bolton Wanderers 52 31
1919 1920 South Shields 44 16

Limond, Thomas Andrew (Andrew) CH
b Newton-in-Makerfield q2 1877
Wigan County
1900 Stockport County 30
Earlestown
Altrincham

From To Apps Goal

Linacre, James Henry (Harry) GK
b Aston-upon-Trent 26/3/1881 d 1957
Caps: FLge 1/England 2
Aston-upon-Trent
Draycott Mills
1898 Derby County 2
1899 1908 Nottingham Forest 305

Linaker, Frederick (Fred) IL
b Southport 7/2/1901 d 1971
St Simon's & St Jude's
Dick, Kerr's Juniors
St Michael's
Milton Athletic
Park Villa
1922 Southport 1
Tarleton

Lincoln, Andrew (Andy) IL
b Seaham Harbour 17/5/1902 d 1977
Speedwell
Glen Rose
Lincoln City
1921 Halifax Town 1
Boldon Villa
Peterborough & Fletton United
1924 1927 Millwall Athletic 27 9
1928 Northampton Town 2
1929 1930 Stockport County 81 39
1931 Lincoln City 3 2
1932 Gateshead 1
Workington

Lindley, A LH
1896 Gainsborough Trinity 1

Lindley, Frank Louis OR
b Sheffield q4 1885 d 1947
Midland Athletic (Sheffield)
Dundee
Motherwell
1912 Sheffield United 1
Newport County
Luton Town

Lindley, Richard (Dick) IR/IL
b Bolton q1 1885 d 1941
Little Hulton United
Oswaldtwistle Rovers
1908 1919 Burnley 137 42
1920 Bradford City 15 4
1921 Coventry City 15 1

Lindley, Tinsley (Dr) CF
b Nottingham 27/10/1865 d 1940
Caps: England 13
Nottingham Forest
Cambridge University
Corinthians
Casuals
Crusaders
1889 Notts County 2
Nottingham Forest
Swifts
Nottingham Forest
1891 Preston North End 1

Lindley, Urban RB
b Sheffield 7/12/1912 d 1994
1936 Preston North End 0
1937 1938 Bradford Park Avenue 60

Lindley, William (Manny) OR
Marshgate Wanderers
1901 Doncaster Rovers 1
Denaby United

Lindon, Albert Eric GK
b King's Norton 24/1/1891 d 1976
Birmingham Fruiterers
Delta Metal Works
1910 Birmingham 7
1911 Aston Villa 1
1912 Barnsley 0
1919 Coventry City 29
1920 1927 Merthyr Town 253 1
1927 1929 Charlton Athletic 34

Lindsay, Albert Fowler GK
b West Hartlepool 26/9/1881 d 1961
Park Villa
St James'
West Hartlepool
1902 1903 Sunderland 3
Luton Town
1905 Glossop 2
Sunderland Royal Rovers

Lindsay, Alexander Findlay (Alex) CF/LH/RH
b Dundee 8/11/1896 d 1971
Dundee Violet
Raith Rovers
1919 1929 Tottenham Hotspur 212 42
1930 Thames 25 1
Dundee
Elgin City (trial)

From To Apps Goal

Lindsay, Archibald (Archie) LB
b Rosneath 1882
Rutherglen Glencairn
Parkhead
Renton
Reading
1907 1910 Fulham 78 1
Dundee
St Johnstone
Third Lanark
Lochgelly United
St Johnstone
St Johnstone YMCA

Lindsay, Denis GK
b Benoni, South Africa 1916
Transvaal
1937 Huddersfield Town 1
(South Africa)

Lindsay, Duncan Morton CF
b Cambuslang 21/3/1903 d 1972
Cambuslang Rangers
East Fife
Cowdenbeath
1930 Newcastle United 19 12
1931 1933 Bury 45 17
Ashton National (loan)
1933 Northampton Town (trial) 1
Hurst
1934 Hartlepools United 37 21
1935 Barrow 8 3
1935 York City 25 8
Ashton National
Hurst

Lindsay, James (Jimmy) RB
b Stockton 28/8/1880 d 1925
Stockton St John's
Jarrow
1899 Newcastle United 2
1900 Burnley 30
1900 1909 Bury 247 27

Lindsay, James J IL/IR/OL
b Johnstone 16/10/1890 d 1959
Caps: IrLge 1
Strathclyde
Clyde
Glentoran
1914 Burnley 13 4
St Mirren
Linfield
1919 1922 Burnley 61 14
Llanelly
Larne
1925 Accrington Stanley 5

Lindsay, John GK
Caps: Scotland 3
Renton
1889 Accrington 21
Renton
St Bernard's

Lindsay, John LH/OR/IR
b Cardenden 1900
Bowhill Juniors
Inverkeithing
Clyde (trial)
Partick Thistle
Rhyl Athletic
1928 1929 Liverpool 14 2
1929 1930 Swansea Town 16 2
Rhyl Athletic
Bangor City
Lochgelly Amateurs

Lindsay, Neil CF
b 1875
Thornliebank
1894 Burnley 2
Clitheroe

Lindsay, Thomas (Tommy) OL/IL
b Laighpark 11/3/1903 d 1979
Babcock & Wilcox
Renfrew Juniors
Pollok
Ardeer Thistle
Kilmarnock
Alloa Athletic
1927 Reading 11 3
1928 Wigan Borough 22 5
1929 Rochdale 7
1930 Watford 7
1931 New Brighton (trial) 7
1931 Southport (trial) 2
1931 Chester (trial) 0
Prescot Cables
1933 Wrexham 0
Leyland Motors

From To Apps Goal

Lindsay, William (Billy) RB/LB
b Stockton 10/12/1872 d 1933
Stockton St John's
Stockton
1893 Everton 9
1894 1897 Grimsby Town 106 1
1897 1899 Newcastle United 59 1
Luton Town
Watford
Luton Town
Hitchin Town

Linfoot, Frederick (Fred) OR
b Whitley Bay 12/3/1901 d 1979
Smith's Dock
1919 Leeds City 0
1919 Lincoln City 29 3
1920 1923 Chelsea 34 1
1923 1925 Fulham 41 4
Blyth Spartans
Shiremoor Albion
Columbia (London)
Dorman Long (Westminster)
Ashington

Ling, Arthur Samuel (Archie) GK
b Cambridge 14/3/1881 d 1943
Albert Institute (Cambridge)
1902 1904 Leicester Fosse 59
Swindon Town
Brentford

Linkson, Oscar Horace Stanley RB
b Barnet q2 1888 d 1916
Barnet Alston
The Pirates
1908 1912 Manchester United 55
Shelbourne

Linley, Edward OL/IL
b Retford 26/9/1894
Worksop Town
1920 1925 Birmingham 113 11
1926 Nottingham Forest 29 5
Sutton Town
Mansfield Town
Shirebrook

Linley, Harry LH/CH/RH
b Sheffield
Silverwood Colliery
1913 1920 Huddersfield Town 48 1
1921 Halifax Town 22 1

Linnell, William Henry RH
b Crewe q1 1871
1892 Crewe Alexandra 1

Linton, J OL
b Scotland
Dundee
1892 Grimsby Town 1

Linton, Thomas CF
b Whitby q4 1878 d 1955
Stockton Vulcan
1899 Middlesbrough 4

Lintott, Evelyn Henry CH/LH/RH
b Godalming 2/11/1883 d 1916
Caps: FLge 1/England Amat/England 7
St Luke's College
Woking
Surrey County
Plymouth Argyle
Queen's Park Rangers
1908 1911 Bradford City 53 2
1912 1913 Leeds City 43 1

Linward, William Henry (Bill) OL
b Hull 8/02/1877 d 1940
Grimsby All Saints
Doncaster Rovers
West Ham United
1902 1904 Woolwich Arsenal 47 10
Norwich City
Kilmarnock
Maidstone United
Dartford

Lipsham, Herbert Broughall (Bert) OL
b Chester 29/4/1878 d 1932
Caps: FLge 2/SoLge 2/England 1
St Oswald's (Chester)
Chester
Rock Ferry
Crewe Alexandra
1899 1907 Sheffield United 235 29
1907 1909 Fulham 56 5
Millwall Athletic

From To Apps Goal

Lipsham, John Reginald (Jack) OL
b Chester q4 1881 d 1959
Chester St John's
Chester
1906 Liverpool 3
Chester
Wrexham
Chester

Lishman, William Joseph RH
b Newcastle 28/4/1899
Hebburn Argyle
Close Works
1921 Lincoln City 4
Gateshead Town
Leadgate Park

Lisle, Joseph Temple OL
b Dinnington 14/7/1910
Pegswood United
1935 Bury 6
1936 Carlisle United 3

Lister, Charles Albert OL
b Halifax 4/9/1917 d 1997
1937 Rotherham United 1

Lister, James S (Jimmy) CF/IR
b Glasgow 1895
Glasgow Perthshire
Kilmarnock
Rangers
Renton (loan)
Armadale (loan)
Morton
1919 Bury 14 6
1921 Hartlepools United 8 2
Llanelly
1923 Bournemouth & Boscombe Ath 28 7
1924 Aberdare Athletic 16 7
Ebbw Vale

Lister, Robert S (Bobby) OL
b Glasgow 1901
Kirkintilloch Rob Roy
Heart of Midlothian
Queen of the South
Hamilton Academical
Queen of the South
Dunfermline Athletic
1927 Stoke City 1
1929 West Ham United 0
1930 Exeter City 8 1
Rhyl Athletic
Shrewsbury Town

Litherland, Edgar Harold (Harry) CF
b Carlisle 28/10/1911 d 1971
Caps: Lol 1
Cockfield
1933 Everton 0
1934 Newport County 1
Witton Albion
Mossley
Sligo Rovers
Glentoran
Sligo Rovers
Drumcondra

Little, George OR
b Newcastle 1/12/1915 d 2002
Throckley Welfare
1936 1947 Doncaster Rovers 49 11
1947 York City 15 2
Scunthorpe & Lindsey United
Frickley Colliery
Worksop Town

Little, James (Jimmy) IL/RH/CF
b Blowick 2/12/1901 d 1976
Blowick Working Lads
1922 1926 Southport 14
Burscough Rangers

Little, John (Jack) RB
b Seaton Delaval 1888 d 1965
Clara Vale
Scotswood
1908 1910 Barnsley 47
Crystal Palace
Croydon Common
1920 1925 Crystal Palace 200
Sittingbourne

From To Apps Goal

Little, John (Jack) RB/LB
b Dunston-on-Tyne 18/9/1904 d 1988
Leeholme Juniors
Sheldon Athletic
Crook Town
1927 Newcastle United 3
1928 1932 Southport 160
1933 1934 Chester 36
Le Havre
1935 1937 Northampton Town 57 1
1938 Exeter City 25
1939 (Exeter City) (1)
1939 Southport 0
Fleetwood Hesketh
High Park

Little, John Adams (Jackie) OL/IR/IL
b Gateshead 17/5/1912
Needham Market
1938 1949 Ipswich Town 146 20
1939 (Ipswich Town) (3) (1)
Stowmarket

Little, John James (Jack) GK
b Carlisle q3 1903
Solway Star
1928 1929 Carlisle United 6

Little, Joseph (Joe) CF
b Dumfries
1912 Bradford Park Avenue 6

Little, Joseph (Joe) OL/LH
b Leeds 25/1/1902 d 1965
Castleford Town
1920 1923 Plymouth Argyle 7
1925 1926 Darlington 62 13
1927 Bradford Park Avenue 2 1
1929 Rotherham United 24 1

Little, Richard (Dick) RB
b Ryton-on-Tyne 30/5/1895
Clara Vale Juniors
Jarrow Croft
1912 1914 Newcastle United 3
Hamilton Academical
Cowdenbeath
Motherwell
Morton
Dunfermline Athletic
Glentoran
Newry Town

Little, Robert Alcock (Rob) GK
b Sunderland 31/12/1902 d 1981
Sunderland West End
Lambton Star
1924 Hartlepools United (trial) 0
1926 Hartlepools United 4

Little, Thomas (Tommy) CF/OL/IL
b Dumfries 4/1872
Nithsdale Wanderers
1892 1893 Derby County 16 1
1894 Manchester City 7 3
Baltimore
1895 Manchester City 9 2
Ashton North End
Wellingborough
1897 Luton Town 22 9
Swindon Town
1899 Barnsley 14 2
Dumfries

Little, Thomas Stewart Colquhoun (Tomm IR/IL/CF
b Ilford 27/2/1890 d 1927
Ilford
Southend United
1908 1920 Bradford Park Avenue 231 106
1920 1921 Stoke 21 1

Little, Walter James (Wally) LH/LB
b Southall 10/11/1897 d 1976
1920 1928 Brighton & Hove Albion 285 32
1929 Clapton Orient 24

Little, William (Billy) CH/LH
b Blowick 19/6/1893 d 1977
Norwood Crescent
Blowick Working Lads
1921 1925 Southport 158 8
Lancaster Town
Burscough Rangers
Skelmersdale United
Hesketh Park

Littledyke, Robert CF/IL
b Chester-le-Street 5/7/1913 d 1990
City of Durham
1935 Lincoln City 9
1936 Mansfield Town 9 1
Grantham

From	To	Club	Apps	Goal
Littlefair, James (Jim)			OL	
b Cambo q1 1876			d 1958	
		Burradon		
1900		Newcastle United	2	
Littleford, Arthur George			RB	
b Wellington, Shropshire q4 1868			d 1934	
		South Yardley		
1893		Small Heath	3	
		Berwick Rangers (Worcester)		
Littlehales, Henry (Harry)			IL/LH/CF	
b Burslem 26/8/1901			d 1989	
		Goldenhill Wanderers		
		Rudyard		
1921		Port Vale	0	
1922		Reading	6	1
1923	1931	Tranmere Rovers	162	50
1932		Wrexham	5	
Littler, Oswald (Ossie)			IR/CF/OR	
b Billinge 15/2/1907			d 1970	
		Billinge		
		Skelmersdale United		
1927		Notts County	0	
		Northwich Victoria		
1928		Rochdale	4	1
1929		Southampton	12	3
		Guildford City		
1930		Southport	15	3
1931	1932	Barrow	15	3
		Winsford United		
Littlewood, Alfred John (Alf)			CH	
b Esh Winning 28/1/1902			d 1975	
		Stanley United		
		Willington		
		Esh Winning		
		Waterhouses		
		Tow Law Town		
1928	1929	South Shields	8	1
1930		Gateshead	3	
		Tunbridge Wells Rangers		
1932		Southport	6	
		Guildford City		
		Tunbridge Wells Rangers		
		Aylesford Paper Mills		
		Shorts Sports		
Littlewood, George Charles (Charles)			RB	
b Tipton q4 1899			d 1965	
		Brierley Hill Alliance		
1927		West Bromwich Albion (trial)	0	
		Worcester City		
1929	1930	Bristol Rovers	2	
		Badminton & Acton Turville		
Littlewood, Stewart Christopher			CF	
b Treeton 7/1/1905			d 1977	
		Hardwick Colliery		
1923		Chesterfield	0	
		Matlock Town		
1924		Sheffield Wednesday	0	
1925		Luton Town	6	2
		Alfreton Town (trial)		
1926	1928	Port Vale	18	18
1928	1930	Oldham Athletic	78	45
1930	1932	Port Vale	35	17
1933		Bournemouth & Boscombe Ath	18	11
		Altrincham		
		Mossley		
		Northwich Victoria		
Littlewood, Wilfred Albert			LB/RB	
b Aston 23/4/1892			d 1969	
		Verity Works		
		Worcester City		
		Wellington Town		
1911	1914	Aston Villa	49	
		Wellington Town		
		GKN Sankey		
Littlewort, Henry Charles (Harry)			RH/CH	
b Elmsett 7/7/1882			d 1934	
Caps: England Amat				
		West Norwood		
		Crystal Palace		
		West Norwood		
1908		Fulham	4	
		Shepherds Bush		
		West Norwood		
1909	1913	Glossop	73	3
1919		Arsenal	0	
Livesey, B			CH	
1898		Darwen	12	

From	To	Club	Apps	Goal
Livingstone, Alan McKenzie			IL/RH/CH	
b Alexandria 2/12/1899			d 1970	
		Vale United		
1920		Everton (trial)	0	
		Dumbarton Harp		
1922		Hull City	1	
		Scunthorpe & Lindsey United		
1924		Hartlepools United (trial)	3	1
1925		Crewe Alexandra (trial)	0	
1925		New Brighton	6	
1926		Clapton Orient	1	
1927		Merthyr Town	27	3
1928		Swansea Town	0	
		Ayr United		
1930		Chelsea	0	
		Armadale		
		East Fife		
1931		Walsall (trial)	1	
		Oswestry Town (trial)		
		Colwyn Bay United (trial)		
1931		Chester (trial)	0	
		Colwyn Bay United		
		Dumbarton (trial)		
		Ayr United (trial)		
1933	1934	Mansfield Town	43	1
1934		Stockport County	0	
Livingstone, Andrew Bowie			IL	
b Dennistoun 6/2/1893				
		Strathclyde		
		Rangers		
		Stevenston United (loan)		
		Dumbarton Harp (loan)		
		Vale of Leven		
		Bathgate		
1920		Port Vale	1	
		Vale of Leven		
Livingstone, Angus			LB	
b Wallsend q4 1912			d 1968	
		Walker Celtic		
1935	1938	Gateshead	94	1
1939		(Gateshead)	(3)	
Livingstone, Archibald (Archie)			IL/RH/IR	
b Pencaitland 15/11/1915			d 1961	
		Musselburgh Lewisvale		
		Ormiston Primrose		
		Dundee		
1935	1937	Newcastle United	33	5
1938		Bury	24	8
1939		(Bury)	(3)	
		Peterborough United		
1946		Everton	4	2
1947		Southport	23	2
		Glenavon		
		Dundee		
		Worksop Town		
Livingstone, Archibald Lang (Archie)			LH/CH	
b Kilpatrick 30/8/1872				
		Greenock		
		Glasgow Whitefield		
		Third Lanark		
1892	1899	Burnley	169	3
		Nelson		
1901	1903	Burton United	71	2
		Brighton & Hove Albion		
		Norwich City		
		Peterborough City		
Livingstone, Dugald (Duggie)			LB/RB	
b Alexandria 25/2/1898			d 1981	
		Parkhead		
		Glasgow Ashfield		
		Celtic		
		Dumbarton Harp (loan)		
		Dumbarton Harp (loan)		
		Dumbarton Harp (loan)		
		Clydebank (loan)		
		Dumbarton Harp (loan)		
1921	1925	Everton	95	
1925	1926	Plymouth Argyle	22	
		Aberdeen		
1930	1932	Tranmere Rovers	88	
Livingstone, George Turner (Geordie)			IR/IL/RH	
b Dumbarton 5/5/1876			d 1950	
Caps: SLge 1/Scotland 2				
		Sinclair Swifts		
		Artizan Thistle		
		Parkhead		
		Dumbarton		
		Heart of Midlothian		
1900		Sunderland	30	12
		Celtic		
1902		Liverpool	31	4
1903	1905	Manchester City	81	19
		Rangers		
1908	1913	Manchester United	43	4
Livingstone, James			OL	
b Wallsend 12/1/1898			d 1984	
		Walker Celtic		
1922		Lincoln City	2	

From	To	Club	Apps	Goal
Llewellyn, Richard George (George)			RH	
b Abercwmboi 16/10/1910			d 1968	
		Caerphilly		
1936		Hull City	4	
		Scarborough		
Lloyd, ?			RH	
1898		Burton Swifts	2	
Lloyd, Arthur			CH	
		Ripley Athletic		
1903		Derby County	1	
		Gresley Rovers		
Lloyd, Arthur Amos			LH	
b Smethwick 1881			d 1945	
		Smethwick St Mary's		
		Oldbury Broadwell		
		Halesowen Town		
1905	1907	Wolverhampton Wanderers	79	3
		Brighton & Hove Albion		
		Barrow		
Lloyd, Charles Frederick (Charlie)			RB	
b North Shields 27/9/1906			d 1979	
		Percy Main Colliery		
1926		Hull City	7	
1928		Southend United	1	
		Loughborough Corinthians		
1931	1932	Mansfield Town	5	
		Ripley Town		
Lloyd, Clifford (Cliff)			OR	
b Brymbo 27/12/1913			d 1973	
		Lodge (Brymbo)		
		Oswestry Town		
		Brymbo Steelworks		
1935		Liverpool (trial)	0	
1937	1945	Wrexham	12	2
		Bangor City		
Lloyd, Clifford John			LH	
b Swansea 30/9/1902			d 1975	
1927	1929	Swansea Town	39	
1930		Nottingham Forest	4	
1931		Crystal Palace	0	
		Waterford		
1932		Barrow	0	
		Ammanford Corries		
Lloyd, Edward Hugh			LB	
b Oldham 25/7/1905			d 1976	
		Oldham Juniors		
1930	1932	Stockport County	67	
1933		Hull City	1	
1935		Carlisle United	42	
		Scunthorpe & Lindsey United		
		Droylsden		
		Hurst		
Lloyd, Ernest (Ernie)			OL	
b Chester 12/2/1894			d 1979	
		Chester		
1914		Stockport County	10	
		Winsford United		
1921		Wrexham	31	2
		Ellesmere Port Cement Works		
		Rhyl Athletic		
		Chester		
		Rhos Athletic		
		Flint Town		
Lloyd, Evan			CF/IL	
b Middlesbrough q3 1892			d 1948	
		Grangetown		
1919		Middlesbrough	2	
1920		Bradford Park Avenue	0	
1921		Tranmere Rovers	11	2
Lloyd, Frank			OR	
b King's Norton 18/9/1876			d 1945	
		Finsbury Park		
		Wednesbury Old Athletic		
1899		Woolwich Arsenal	18	3
1900	1901	Aston Villa	5	1
		Dundee		
		Dudley Town		
		Rangers		
Lloyd, George Henry			RH	
b Derby q2 1877				
1901	1902	Derby County	10	1
		New Brompton		
Lloyd, Herbert			RH/IR	
b Cannock Chase 1888			d 1960	
		Cannock Town		
		Walsall		
		Rotherham County		
		Crystal Palace		
1913		Wolverhampton Wanderers	8	1
		Hednesford Town		
		Walsall Wood		
1919		Rotherham County	17	
		Scunthorpe & Lindsey United		

From	To	Club	Apps	Goal
Lloyd, James Clifford (Jack)			LH/IR	
b Bristol				
		Yeovil & Petters United		
1929		Southend United	4	
1930	1931	Crystal Palace	14	
		Bath City		
		Salisbury City		
Lloyd, John			RB/CH	
1924	1926	Aberdare Athletic	4	
Lloyd, John Amos (Amos)			OL	
b Pelsall 5/1889			d 1943	
		Nuneaton Town		
		Halesowen		
		Hednesford Town		
1910	1913	West Bromwich Albion	45	8
		Swansea Town		
		Porth Athletic		
		Eastside (Swansea)		
Lloyd, John Edgar (Eddie)			LH/RH	
b Middlesbrough 6/9/1902				
		Stockton		
1922		Middlesbrough	0	
1923	1928	Bradford City	157	4
		Derry City		
Lloyd, John Henry (Jackie)			OR/OL	
b Lodge 20/6/1916			d 1999	
Caps: Wales Amat				
		Lodge (Brymbo)		
		Brymbo Steelworks		
		Llanerch Celts		
1937		Chester	1	
1938		Wrexham	1	
		Bangor City		
		Oswestry Town		
		Connah's Quay Nomads		
		Brymbo Steelworks		
Lloyd, Joseph Millington (Joe)			LH/RH	
b Shotton 30/9/1910			d 1996	
		Connah's Quay & Shotton		
1931		Everton	0	
1933	1938	Swansea Town	211	1
1946		Wrexham	20	
Lloyd, Norman			LB/LH	
b Salford q4 1912				
		Manchester Central		
1933		Manchester City	3	
1935		New Brighton	5	
		Hyde United		
		Denton		
		Hurst		
Lloyd, Rhys			IR/OR	
b Wrexham				
		Rhosymedre		
1920	1921	Rotherham County	7	2
Lloyd, Thomas (Tommy)			LB	
b Wednesbury 17/11/1903			d 1984	
		Willenhall		
1925	1926	Sunderland	4	
1927	1936	Bradford Park Avenue	328	17
		Burton Town		
Lloyd, Thomas W			RB	
b Sheffield				
1923		Walsall	5	
Lloyd, William (Billy)			RH/OR/IR	
b South Hylton 1885				
		Jarrow		
1906	1912	Sheffield Wednesday	79	6
		Rotherham County		
1914		Sheffield Wednesday	0	
Loasby, Harry			CF	
b Kettering 13/10/1911			d 1990	
		Wellingborough Town		
1927	1929	Northampton Town	27	25
1930		Gillingham	35	19
1931		Luton Town	15	14
		Kettering Town		
Lochhead, Alexander (Alex)			LH/RH	
b Johnstone 12/5/1866				
Caps: Scotland 1				
		Arthurlie		
		Third Lanark		
		Morton		
1890	1891	Everton	6	
		Third Lanark		
		Clyde		
Lochhead, Arthur William			IL/IR	
b Busby 8/12/1897			d 1966	
		Heart of Midlothian		
		Clyde (loan)		
1921	1925	Manchester United	147	50
1925	1934	Leicester City	303	106

From To Apps Goal

Lochhead, Dougald (Doug) LH
b Partick 16/12/1904 d 1968
St Peter's Boys Guild
Eaglesham
Maryhill
St Anthony's (Glasgow)
St Johnstone
1928 Walsall 42
1929 1935 Norwich City 210 5

Lochhead, Matthew (Matty) CH
b Anderston 19/8/1884 d 1964
Beith Hibernians
Beith
St Mirren
Swindon Town
1908 Leicester Fosse 0
1909 Manchester City 0
Beith
Swindon Town
Bath City
1921 1922 Reading 6
Bath City

Lock, Herbert GK
b Southampton 21/1/1886 d 1957
St Mary's Guild
Southampton
Rangers
Kilmarnock (loan)
Ayr United (loan)
Kilmarnock (loan)
St Mirren (loan)
Partick Thistle (loan)
1921 Queen's Park Rangers 6
1922 Southampton 11
1923 Bournemouth & Boscombe Ath 13

Locker, William (Billy) IL
b Long Eaton 16/2/1866 d 1952
Long Eaton Rangers
1889 Stoke 1
Long Eaton Rangers
1889 Derby County 0
1890 1891 Notts County 21 12
Loughborough

Lockett, Aaron IR
b Newcastle-under-Lyme q4 1892 d 1965
Kidsgrove Wellington
Stoke
1919 Port Vale 9 3
Audley

Lockett, Arthur OL/RB
b Alsagers Bank 11/3/1877 d 1957
Caps: FLge 1/England 1
Alsgars Bank Friendly
Audley
Cross Heath
Audley
Crewe Alexandra
1900 1902 Stoke 65 7
1902 1904 Aston Villa 41 5
1905 1907 Preston North End 64 5
Watford
Mardy

Lockett, Henry (Harry) LH/IR
b Market Drayton 27/12/1887
Wilmslow
Crewe Alexandra
Whitchurch
1909 Bolton Wanderers 16 4
1910 Nottingham Forest 23 5
Exeter City
Chesterfield Town
1921 1922 Stalybridge Celtic 70 1

Lockett, William Curfield CF/IL
b Tipton 23/4/1893 d 1974
Caps: England Sch
1913 Wolverhampton Wanderers 6 2
1920 1925 Northampton Town 185 68
Kidderminster Harriers

Lockhart, Alec OL
1913 Bolton Wanderers 2

Lockhart, George LB
b Beith 1874
1897 1899 Bolton Wanderers 26
1900 1902 Burnley 93

Lockie, Alexander James (Alex) CH
b South Shields 11/4/1915 d 1974
South Shields St Andrew's
Reyrolles
1936 1945 Sunderland 40 1
1939 (Sunderland) (2)
1946 Notts County 23

From To Apps Goal

Lockie, James RB
b Newcastle 4/1/1874 d 1955
St Thomas' (Newcastle)
Caxton (Newcastle)
Trafalgar (Newcastle)
Willington Athletic
1897 1898 Newcastle United 1
1898 Grimsby Town 6
New Brompton
Gravesend United
New Brompton
Hebburn Argyle

Lockie, Thomas (Tom) CH
b Duns 13/1/1906 d 1977
Duns
Rangers
Leith Athletic
1932 Barnsley 14 1
1933 York City 29 1
1934 Accrington Stanley 36
1935 Mansfield Town 14 1

Lockton, John Henry (Johnnie) IL
b Peckham 22/5/1892 d 1972
London University
Ilford
1913 1914 Nottingham Forest 20 2
Casuals
Nunhead

Lockyer, Thomas William GK
b East Stour q2 1873 d 1937
Hucknall St John's
1899 Nottingham Forest 1

Lodge (Barrass), James William (Jimmy) LB/RB
b Felling 11/1/1895 d 1971
Coxlodge
Scotswood
Newburn
1919 1923 Hull City 81
1924 Halifax Town 42
Nuneaton Town
York City

Lodge, Lewis Vaughan (Vaughan) RB
b Darlington 21/12/1872 d 1916
Caps: England 5
Casuals
Corinthians
Cambridge University
1895 Small Heath 1
Corinthians
Newbury Town
Durham Town

Lofthouse, James (Jimmy) OL
b St Helens 24/3/1894 d 1954
St Helens Recreation
Stalybridge Celtic
Reading
1920 1922 Sheffield Wednesday 95 13
1922 1923 Rotherham County 26 7
1923 1925 Bristol Rovers 105 16
1926 1927 Queen's Park Rangers 80 27
Aldershot
GPO (Reading)

Lofthouse, Joseph Morris (Joe) OR/OL
b Blackburn 14/4/1865 d 1919
Caps: England 7
King's Own
Blackburn Rovers
1888 Accrington 21 2
1889 1891 Blackburn Rovers 51 18
1892 Darwen 8 1
1893 1894 Walsall Town Swifts 33 4

Loftus, Joseph Leo (Leo) IL
b Ferryhill 24/1/1906 d 1992
Chilton Lane United
Cornforth United
Bishop Auckland
Willington
1925 Stockport County 0
Willington
1926 1928 South Shields 30 6
1929 1931 Nottingham Forest 54 14
1932 1934 Bristol City 93 29
1935 Gillingham 2
Burton Town
1936 Barrow 27 9

From To Apps Goal

Logan, Alexander (Alec) IL/CF
b Barrhead 2/1880 d 1938
Caps: SLge 2
Barrhead Fereneze
Hibernian
Airdrieonians
Arthurlie
Falkirk
1906 1908 Aston Villa 24 11
Falkirk
1910 1911 Bristol City 37 9
Kilmarnock
Partick Thistle

Logan, Henry Morrison (Harry) IR
b Glasgow 5/1888
Cathcart Windsor
Myrtle XI (Glasgow)
Glasgow Benburb
Shettleston
1909 Sunderland 1
1910 Woolwich Arsenal 11

Logan, James (Jimmy) CF
b Troon 24/6/1870 d 1896
Caps: Scotland 1
Ayr
1891 Sunderland 2
Ayr
1892 1893 Aston Villa 14 8
1893 1894 Notts County 41 31
Ayr
Dundee
1895 Newcastle United 7 5
1895 Loughborough 11 5

Logan, James (Jimmy) IL
b Parkhead 1900
St Anthony's (Glasgow)
1919 1920 Bury 7 2
1921 Southend United 3

Logan, James (Jimmy) RH
b Lochgelly 10/8/??
Glencraig Celtic
Cowdenbeath
1920 1928 Plymouth Argyle 228 14
Yeovil & Petters United

Logan, James Henry (Jimmy) LH/RH/CH
b Dunbar 17/10/1885
St Bernard's
1905 Bradford City 5 1
1906 1908 Chesterfield Town 94 9
1909 1911 Bradford Park Avenue 59 3
Raith Rovers

Logan, James Lochhead CH/LH/LB
b Barrhead 8/8/1885 d 1948
Caps: SLge 1
Barrhead Fereneze
Queen's Park
1905 1911 Aston Villa 145 4
Rangers
Partick Thistle
St Mirren
Arthurlie

Logan, John Theodore OL
b Edinburgh 1871
Partick Thistle
1896 Small Heath 1
Musselburgh

Logan, John William RH/LH
b Horden 16/8/1912 d 1980
Horden Colliery Welfare
1934 Charlton Athletic 0
1935 1936 Darlington 65 5
1936 1946 Barnsley 99 5
1939 (Barnsley) (3)
1946 Sheffield Wednesday 4

Logan, Neil CH/CF
b Burnbank 16/12/1875 d 1949
Blantyre
Rutherglen Glencairn
1897 Sheffield United 5 4
Swindon Town
1902 Blackburn Rovers 22 2
Swindon Town

Logan, Peter (Paddy) IR/CF
b Glasgow 1877
Motherwell
1898 Notts County 16 6
1899 Woolwich Arsenal 23 6
Reading
1901 Woolwich Arsenal 5 1
Brentford

Logan, Peter OL/IR/OR
b Edinburgh 3/4/1889 d 1944
Alva Albion Rovers
St Bernard's
1908 1924 Bradford City 271 37

From To Apps Goal

Logan, Thomas (Tom) CH
b Barrhead 17/8/1888 d 1960
Caps: Scotland 1
Arthurlie
Falkirk
1913 1920 Chelsea 107 7
Partick Thistle (loan)
Dunfermline Athletic (loan)
Falkirk (loan)
Arthurlie

Logan, W IR
1896 Gainsborough Trinity 10 2

Logie, James IL
b Inverness 1904
Inverness Clachnacuddin
1924 Swansea Town 2 1
Dunfermline Athletic

Lomas, Harold (Harry) LH
b Leek q2 1903
Congleton Town
Leek Town
1924 Port Vale 1

Lomas, William (Billy) CF/IL/LH
b Pendleton 4/7/1885 d 1976
Heywood United
1909 1910 Burnley 36 21
1910 1911 Bury 15 1
1912 Manchester City 0
York City
1913 Clapton Orient 5
Tranmere Rovers
1919 1922 Bury 52 8

Lomax, H RB/RH
1895 1896 Darwen 29
1898 Glossop North End 12

Lomax, James (Jimmy) IL/IR
b Bury q2 1888
1908 1911 Stockport County 72 17

Lomax, John Neale IL
b Birkenhead 1/4/1901 d 1970
1921 Everton 0
1922 Tranmere Rovers 5 2
Winsford United

London, George Walter RB
b Romford 21/8/1901 d 1991
Barking Town
1923 Fulham 7
1925 Clapton Orient (trial) 0

Long, Henry Robert OL/LH
b Southampton 15/10/1914 d 1989
Ryde Sports
1936 1937 Southampton 5
Newport (Isle of Wight)

Long, James (Jimmy) IR/OR/CF
b Glasgow 1880
Clyde
1901 1903 Grimsby Town 57 13
Reading
1906 1907 Derby County 61 18

Long, John P OR
Bohemians
1921 Bolton Wanderers 1

Long, William Kenneth LB
b Wednesbury q2 1912
1931 Walsall 3
1932 Wolverhampton Wanderers 0
Folkestone
1934 Brighton & Hove Albion 0

Long, William Richard (Billy) OR
b Tividale 4/1899 d 1960
Hednesford Town
1920 West Bromwich Albion 2
Hednesford Town
Brierley Hill Alliance

Longair, William (Plum) CH
b Dundee 19/7/1870 d 1926
Caps: Scotland 1
Rockwell (Dundee)
Dundee East End
Dundee
1894 Newton Heath 1
Dundee
1896 Sunderland 2
1896 Burnley 12
Dundee
Brighton United
Dundee

Longbottom, Harry RH
Trinity Methodists
1933 Rochdale 2

From	To	Club	Apps	Goal
Longden, Eric			IR/RH/IL	
b Goldthorpe 18/5/1904			d 1983	
		Goldthorpe United		
1926	1928	Doncaster Rovers	32	9
1928	1930	Leeds United	28	7
1930		Hull City	14	7
1930	1932	Blackpool	61	7
1932	1934	Hull City	74	5
		Scarborough		
Longden, William (Billy)			RH/OR	
1893	1895	Rotherham Town	78	2
1901		Doncaster Rovers	31	2
Longdon, Samuel (Sam)			OL	
b Derby 22/11/1895			d 1971	
1920		Norwich City	3	
Longmore, Samuel James (Jimmy)			RB	
b Hartlepool q4 1899			d 1968	
		Central Machine Engine Works		
1922		Hartlepools United	12	
1923		Derby County	0	
Longmuir, Archibald MacDonald (Archie)			OR/IR	
b Ardrossan 17/4/1897				
		Hall, Russell & Co		
		Aberdeen		
		Ardrossan Winton Rovers		
		Celtic		
1921	1922	Blackburn Rovers	24	2
1923		Oldham Athletic	22	4
1924	1929	Wrexham	223	34
		Cowdenbeath (loan)		
Longstaff, Albert Edward (Bert)			OR	
b Shoreham 9/10/1885			d 1970	
		Shoreham		
1920	1921	Brighton & Hove Albion	41	4
		Shoreham		
Longstaff, Geoffrey			OR	
b Middlesbrough q1 1876			d 1953	
1899		Middlesbrough	19	3
1901		Stockport County	5	2
1902		Burton United	12	
Longstaff, James William			OL	
b Dumfries 12/9/1914			d 1983	
1932		Carlisle United	1	
Longthorn, Albert Edward			IR	
b Leeds 29/8/1910			d 1985	
		Carlton Athletic		
1931		Halifax Town	2	
Longworth, Bruce			RH	
b Lanchester q2 1898			d 1955	
		Hopley's All Blacks		
1919	1923	Bolton Wanderers	77	
1924	1925	Sheffield United	13	1
1926		Bury	0	
		Darwen		
		Clitheroe		
Longworth, Ephraim			RB/LB	
b Halliwell 2/10/1887			d 1968	
Caps: FLge 6/England 5				
		Chorley Road Congregationals		
		Bolton St Luke's		
		Halliwell Rovers		
		Hyde		
1907		Bolton Wanderers	0	
		Leyton		
1910	1927	Liverpool	342	
Lonie, Arthur			RH	
b Wingate 22/9/1898			d 1973	
		Trimdon Grange		
1923		Hartlepools United	10	
		Spennymoor United		
Lonie, Thomas (Tom)			CF	
b Dundee 26/11/1874			d 1941	
		Dundee Harp		
		Johnstone Wanderers		
1893		Notts County	0	
1894		Darwen	8	2
		Dundee Wanderers		
		Dundee		
1895		Stoke	9	4
1896		Leicester Fosse	7	3
Lonsdale, David			CH/LH	
b Carlisle 25/5/1905			d 1991	
1930	1938	Carlisle United	30	2
Lonsdale, George			CF	
1895		Preston North End	2	1

From	To	Club	Apps	Goal
Lonsdale, Thomas Stewart (Tommy)			GK	
b Bishop Auckland 21/9/1882			d 1973	
		West Auckland		
		Bishop Auckland		
1908	1913	Grimsby Town	87	
		West Ham United		
		Southend United		
1921	1922	Stalybridge Celtic	75	
1923		Port Vale	31	
Lord, Jabez John P (Jack)			LH/CH	
b Derby q4 1869			d 1934	
		Derby St Luke's		
		Derby Junction		
1894	1896	Leicester Fosse	29	2
Lorimer, Hugh Harper			OR	
b Paisley 11/11/1896			d 1939	
		St Mirren Juniors		
1919	1921	Tottenham Hotspur	5	
		Dundee		
		Dalbeattie Star		
		Carlisle United		
		Boston Wonder Workers		
		J & P Coats (Rhode Island)		
		Mahoning Valley		
Louch, Lionel Arthur			CF	
b Brentford 4/7/1888			d 1967	
Caps: England Amat				
		Shepherds Bush		
		Portsmouth		
1908	1909	Clapton Orient	36	10
		Portsmouth		
		Shepherds Bush		
		Southend United		
Loughlin, James William (Jimmy)			CF	
b Darlington 9/10/1904			d 1954	
		Darlington Railway Athletic		
1924	1926	Newcastle United	12	5
1927		West Ham United	10	4
1928	1930	Coventry City	61	32
		Dolphin (loan)		
		Bray Unknowns (loan)		
		Worcester City (loan)		
		Northwich Victoria (loan)		
1933		Darlington	11	5
Loughran, James (Jimmy)			LH	
b Seaham Colliery 10/9/1897			d 1970	
		Easington Colliery Welfare		
1922	1923	Hull City	4	
1924		Barrow	24	1
		York City		
		Newark Town		
1930		York City	1	
		Goole Town		
		Fulford United		
Loughran, Joseph Lane (Joe)			RB/LH/RH	
b Consett 12/8/1915			d 1994	
		Medomsley Juniors		
		Dudley College		
1935	1936	Birmingham	31	2
1937	1938	Luton Town	25	
1945	1949	Burnley	65	
1949	1952	Southend United	147	1
		Newhaven		
Loughran, Thomas (Tommy)			IR/IL/CH	
b South Bank 2/11/1893			d 1972	
		South Bank		
1919	1921	Bradford Park Avenue	22	3
1922		Sunderland (trial)	0	
1923		Doncaster Rovers	10	1
Loughran, Thomas Henry (Tom)			CH	
b Sunderland q1 1904			d 1957	
		Usworth Colliery		
1922		Ashington	7	
		Workington		
		Usworth Colliery		
		Sunderland West End		
		Carlisle United		
		Spennymoor United		
		Usworth Colliery		
		St Joseph's CYMS (Sunderland)		
Lounds, Herbert Ernest			OR	
b Masbrough 30/5/1889			d 1964	
		Silverwood Colliery		
1911		Gainsborough Trinity	23	
1919		Leeds City	8	
1919	1922	Rotherham County	89	6
1923	1924	Halifax Town	5	

From	To	Club	Apps	Goal
Lovatt, Harold Albert (Harry)			CF	
b Audley 18/8/1905			d 1984	
		Wood Lane United		
		Red Street St Chad's		
		Audley		
1923		Port Vale	0	
1924		Preston North End	0	
1925		Crewe Alexandra	27	14
1925	1926	Bradford City	13	3
1926		Wrexham	11	5
		Scarborough		
1928	1930	Leicester City	10	9
1930	1931	Notts County	9	3
1931		Northampton Town	14	7
		Macclesfield		
		Stafford Rangers		
		Winsford United		
Love, Andrew Robb			OR	
b Renfrew 26/3/1905			d 1962	
Caps: SLge 1/Scotland 3				
		Kirkintilloch Rob Roy		
		Aberdeen		
1935		Aldershot	12	2
		Montrose		
Love, Robert William (Bob)			CF	
b Llay Main 14/3/1914			d 1990	
1934		Manchester City	0	
		Frickley Colliery		
		Winsford United		
1938		Hartlepools United	13	2
1939		(Hartlepools United)	(1)	
		Blackhall Colliery Welfare		
Love, Thomas			CF	
		Dumbarton		
1925		Luton Town	2	
		Alloa Athletic		
Lovelady, Edward Richard (Eddie)			OR	
b Liverpool 24/6/1898			d 1983	
		Bangor City		
1924		Wrexham	10	
		Bangor City		
		Marine		
		Bangor City		
		Winsford United		
Loverseed, William Henry			CF	
b Basford q1 1876			d 1914	
		Newark		
1902	1904	Burslem Port Vale	36	6
Lovery, James Bernard (Jimmy)			OL/OR	
b Stockport 26/7/1915			d 2004	
1935		Wolverhampton Wanderers	0	
1936		Stockport County	0	
1937	1938	Bournemouth & Boscombe Ath	30	9
1939		Bradford City	(3)	
Lovett, Albert William			OL	
b Rotherham 13/2/1911			d 1975	
		Dinnington Athletic		
1934		Chesterfield	17	2
1935		Rotherham United	4	
		Dinnington Athletic		
		Worksop Town		
Lovett, Jonathan			GK	
1905		Burnley	1	
Lovett, William (Billy)			IR	
b Bolton				
		Hindley Central		
		Rochdale		
		Exeter City		
1920		Blackpool	2	
		Horwich RMI		
Low, Archibald B			LH	
b Forfar 1885				
		Glasgow Ashfield		
1906		Woolwich Arsenal	3	
		Partick Thistle		
		Johnstone		
Low, David			RH/LH	
b New Herrington 20/4/1900			d 1971	
		New Herrington Swifts		
1924	1926	Blackburn Rovers	13	
1927	1931	Swindon Town	148	1
		Crook Town		
Low, Henry Forbes (Harry)			LH/CF/CH	
b Old Machar 1882			d 1920	
		Orion		
		Aberdeen		
1907	1914	Sunderland	203	36

From	To	Club	Apps	Goal
Low, James (Jimmy)			OR	
b Kilbirnie 9/3/1894				
Caps: SLge 2				
		Bishopmill United		
		Elgin City		
		Edinburgh University		
		Heart of Midlothian		
		Elgin City		
		Rangers		
1921	1927	Newcastle United	108	8
		Buckie Thistle		
Low, John			OL	
b Newtongrange				
		Denbeath Star		
		Heart of Midlothian		
		Dunfermline Athletic		
		Ayr United		
		Mid-Rhondda United		
		Ayr United		
1923		Manchester United	0	
		Dunfermline Athletic		
1925		Halifax Town	5	1
Low, John Hamilton			RH	
b Dundee 29/10/1874				
		Dundee		
		Brighton United		
1900		Bolton Wanderers	1	
Low, Norman Harvey			CH	
b Aberdeen 23/3/1914			d 1994	
		Rosehill Villa		
1932		Newcastle United	0	
1934	1936	Liverpool	13	
1936	1946	Newport County	112	
1939		(Newport County)	(3)	
1946	1949	Norwich City	150	
Low, Thomas Pollock			OR	
b Cambuslang 3/10/1874				
Caps: SLge 1/Scotland 1				
		Parkhead		
		Celtic (trial)		
		Rangers		
		Dundee		
1900		Woolwich Arsenal	24	1
		Abercorn		
		Rangers		
		Dunfermline Athletic		
		Morton		
Low, Wilfred Lawson (Wilf)			CH	
b Aberdeen 8/12/1884			d 1933	
Caps: Scotland 5				
		Abergeldie		
		Montrose (trial)		
		Aberdeen		
1909	1923	Newcastle United	324	9
Low, William Ross (Willie)			LH	
b Aberdeen 21/9/1889			d 1970	
		Aberdeen Shamrock		
		Aberdeen		
		South Shields		
		Aberdeen		
1919		Grimsby Town	0	
		Gainsborough Trinity		
1920	1921	Barnsley	42	
		Wombwell		
		Truro City		
		Mabe		
Lowdell, Arthur Edward			RH/IR/OR	
b Edmonton 7/11/1897			d 1979	
		Ton Pentre		
1921	1926	Sheffield Wednesday	108	6
1927	1929	Tottenham Hotspur	87	
Lowder, Arthur			LH	
b Wolverhampton 11/2/1863			d 1926	
Caps: England 1				
1888	1891	Wolverhampton Wanderers	46	1
Lowe, Charles Bernard (Bernard)			IL/OL	
b Cradley Heath q2 1888			d 1941	
		Harborne Lynwood		
		Halesowen		
1908	1910	Birmingham	16	3
		Darlaston		
		Netherton		
Lowe, David (Davey)			OR	
b Dudley 1899				
		Tividale White Star		
		Cradley Heath		
1921	1922	Sheffield United	2	
		Cradley Heath		
		Old Hill Wanderers		
Lowe, Edward (Ted)			GK	
b Newport q4 1901				
		Newport County		
		Marshes Hall		
		Caerphilly		
1921	1922	Newport County	5	

From To Apps Goal

Lowe, George CF
b Mastin Moor 25/5/1915 d 2008
Mastin Moor Juniors
1938 Chesterfield 5

Lowe, Henry (Harry) LB
b Skelmersdale 19/2/1907 d 1975
Skelmersdale Mission
1927 1929 Southport 72
1930 1931 Everton 5
1932 1938 Preston North End 182
1939 Swindon Town (3)
Skelmersdale United

Lowe, Henry Charles (Harry) LH/CH/RH
b Whitwell 20/3/1886 d 1958
Whitwell St Lawrence
1907 1910 Gainsborough Trinity 106 3
1911 1919 Liverpool 122 2
1919 Nottingham Forest 9
Mansfield Town
Newark Town
Grantham

Lowe, Henry Pratt (Harry) IR/IL/RH
b Kingskettle 24/2/1907 d 1988
St Andrews United
1929 1934 Watford 120 39
1935 1938 Queen's Park Rangers 159 40
1939 (Queen's Park Rangers) (3)
Guildford City

Lowe, HG IL
1894 Sheffield Wednesday 2

Lowe, Horace (Harry) CH/LH
b Northwich 10/8/1886 d 1966
Northwich Victoria
Brighton & Hove Albion
1914 1926 Tottenham Hotspur 65
1927 Fulham 3
Beckenham

Lowe, John GK
b Denton 1866 d 1911
Denton
1890 Blackburn Rovers 2
1894 1895 Bury 26

Lowe, John (Jack) OR
b Ripley 1900
Ripley Colliery
Hartshay Colliery
Chesterfield Municipal
1921 1922 Bolton Wanderers 5
1923 1927 Port Vale 163 17
1928 Oldham Athletic 7 2
1929 Rotherham United 1
Ripley Town

Lowe, Joseph A GK
b West Bromwich 1876 d 1931
Coombs Wood
1900 1902 West Bromwich Albion 4
Willenhall Pickwick

Lowe, Luke OL
b Wigan 14/8/1888 d 1971
Eccles Borough
1911 Burnley 1
Accrington Stanley

Lowe, Richard Ernest CF
b Cannock 13/7/1915 d 1986
1936 Leeds United 0
1937 Sheffield United 1
1939 Hull City (2) (2)

Lowe, Robert H IL/OL
Congleton
1903 1904 Burnley 3

Lowe, T LH/LB/RB
1894 1896 Burton Wanderers 81 6
1897 1899 Burton Swifts 34

Lowe, Wallace RB
b Blackpool q2 1884
1904 1907 Blackpool 11
Blackpool Athletic
Colne

Lowe, William (Kiddy) CF
b Long Eaton q1 1870
Long Eaton Midland
Long Eaton Rangers
Notts Rangers
Loughborough
Leicester Fosse
Long Eaton Rangers
1895 Loughborough 3
Long Eaton Rangers

From To Apps Goal

Lowe, William Chantry RH
b Boston q1 1877 d 1957
Grimsby United
Grimsby All Saints
1898 Grimsby Town 2
Grimsby All Saints

Lowe, William Henry OL
b Clay Cross 1882
Clay Cross Zingari
1903 Chesterfield Town 1
Clay Cross Zingari

Lowery, Bernard LH/RH
b Kirkdale q3 1907 d 1957
1930 Liverpool 0
1932 Rochdale 1
1932 Chester (trial) 0
Yeovil & Petters United
1934 Southport 0
1934 Accrington Stanley 7
South Liverpool
1936 Notts County 0

Lowery, Edward (Ted) IR/IL
b Tynemouth 24/10/1907 d 2000
Walker Park
Usworth Colliery
East Fife
1932 1933 Leicester City 14 1
Yeovil & Petters United (loan)
1934 1935 Torquay United 36 11
1936 Darlington 11 3
Frickley Colliery
Burton Town

Lowery, Harry RH/CH
b Moor Row 26/2/1918 d 2004
Cleator Moor Celtic
1937 West Bromwich Albion 17
1945 1948 Northampton Town 76 2
Bromsgrove Rovers

Lowery, W GK
b Tyneside
Trafalgar (Newcastle)
Gateshead NER
Blyth FC
1893 1894 Newcastle United 28

Lowes, Arnold Richardson RH/LH/IR
b Sunderland 27/2/1919 d 1994
Washington Chemicals
1938 1947 Sheffield Wednesday 42 8
1947 1950 Doncaster Rovers 72 3

Lowes, John (Jacky) IL
b Coxlodge q2 1897
Coxlodge United Methodists
Gosforth & Coxlodge British Legion
1921 1922 Durham City 5 4
Chester-le-Street
1922 Durham City 6 1
Craghead United
Gosforth & Coxlodge British Legion
1927 Durham City 0
Trimdon Colliery United
Gosforth & Coxlodge British Legion
Coxlodge Welfare
Gosforth & Coxlodge British Legion

Lowes, Robert Graham CF
b Gateshead 18/2/1902 d 1985
Lintz Colliery
1928 Darlington 13 3
Jarrow

Lowes, Thomas (Tommy) IL
b Walker 9/4/1892 d 1973
Walker Church Lads
Wallsend Park Villa
1911 1913 Newcastle United 16 3
1919 Coventry City 10 2
Nuneaton Town
Caerphilly
1922 1925 Newport County 110 34
Yeovil & Petters United

Lowndes, William (Billy) CF
b Wallasey 6/2/1909 d 1977
Egremont United
1932 1933 New Brighton 13 10

Lowrie, George CF/IL/IR
b Tonypandy 19/12/1919 d 1989
Caps: Wales War 9/Wales 4
Tonypandy
1936 1937 Swansea Town 19 3
1937 Preston North End 5
1939 1947 Coventry City 56 44
1939 (Coventry City) (1) (1)
1947 1949 Newcastle United 12 5
1949 1951 Bristol City 48 21
1951 1952 Coventry City 27 12
Lovells Athletic

From To Apps Goal

Lowry, Sydney Harold (Syd) OL/IL
b Hay-on-Wye 29/8/1912 d 1982
South Wales Borderers
Hereford Town
Merthyr Town
1932 1934 Swansea Town 60 21
1935 Swindon Town 30 14
1936 Newport County 14 2
Burton Town
Wellington Town

Lowson, Edmund 'Venner' RH/LH
b Evenwood 21/3/1895 d 1955
Cockfield Swifts
Crook Town
Spennymoor United
1921 Nottingham Forest (trial)
1921 1922 Blackpool 5
1923 Doncaster Rovers 18
1924 1925 Bournemouth & Boscombe Ath 4
Poole
1927 Durham City 42
1928 1929 Halifax Town 59

Lowson, Frank IL
b Forfar 13/12/1895 d 1969
Forfar Celtic
Dundee
1921 1922 Bradford Park Avenue 12 2
1923 Exeter City 4
1924 Barrow 25 2
Poole

Lowton, Wilfred George (Wilf) RB/LB
b Exeter 3/10/1899 d 1963
Heavitree United
1925 1928 Exeter City 75 9
1929 1934 Wolverhampton Wanderers 198 25
1935 Exeter City 18

Loynes, John (Jock) RH
Dundee Wanderers
1897 Walsall 8 1

Lucas, Arthur GK
b Gwersyllt 28/2/1904 d 1949
Conway
Runcorn
1927 1928 Wrexham 4
Caernarvon Athletic
Burton Town
Runcorn

Lucas, Francis James (Frank) CF
b Barrow 17/3/1907 d 1982
Barrow YMCA
Barrow Shipbuilders
1928 Blackburn Rovers (trial) 0
1929 Barrow 17 6
Lancaster Town
Glentoran
Ballymena
Glentoran

Lucas, Thomas (Tommy) RB/LB
b St Helens 20/9/1895 d 1953
Caps: FLge 4/England 3
Sherdley Villa
Sutton Commercial
Heywood United
Peasley Cross
Eccles Borough
Manchester United (trial)
1919 1932 Liverpool 341 3
1933 Clapton Orient 21

Lucas, William Henry (Billy) RH/IR/IL
b Newport 15/1/1918 d 1998
Caps: Wales Sch/WLge 3/Wales War 8/Wales 7
Brookside Athletic
Treharris
1936 Wolverhampton Wanderers 0
1937 1947 Swindon Town 141 32
1939 (Swindon Town) (3)
1947 1953 Swansea Town 205 35
1953 1957 Newport County 94 6

Luckett, William (Bill) LH/OL
b St Helens 6/9/1903 d 1985
Skelmersdale
1927 1936 Southampton 211 10
Cowes

Ludford, George Albert RH/CF/LH
b Barnet 22/3/1915 d 2001
Tottenham Juniors
Enfield
Northfleet
1936 1949 Tottenham Hotspur 75 7
1939 (Tottenham Hotspur) (2)

Ludkin, Daniel (Dan) CH
b Ryton-on-Tyne 1/5/1894 d 1945
Close Works
1922 1923 Lincoln City 14 1

From To Apps Goal

Luke, Charles (Charlie) OR/IL/OL
b Esh Winning 16/3/1909 d 1983
Esh Winning Juniors
Ushaw Moor
Tow Law Town
1927 Portsmouth (trial) 0
1928 Darlington 2
Esh Winning
Bishop Auckland
1931 1935 Huddersfield Town 130 40
1935 1937 Sheffield Wednesday 42 8
1937 Blackburn Rovers 10 2
1938 Chesterfield 13 4
Whitstable

Luke, William (Billy) OR
b Acklington 17/12/1890 d 1992
Trimdon Grange
Bedlington United
1912 Preston North End 8 2
Hartlepools United

Lumberg, Arthur Albert (Bert) LB/RB
b Connah's Quay 20/5/1901 d 1986
Caps: Wales 4
Flint Town
Connah's Quay & Shotton
1924 Liverpool (trial) 0
Mold Town
1924 1929 Wrexham 170
1930 1932 Wolverhampton Wanderers 20
1933 Brighton & Hove Albion 21
1934 Stockport County 2
1934 Clapton Orient 0
Lytham
1935 New Brighton 2
Winsford United
Newry Town
Rhyl
Newry Town
Mold Alexandra

Lumby, Walter Charles William RH/IR/CF
b Milton Regis 16/1/1915 d 2001
Caps: NIRL 1
Lloyds Paper Mills
Murston Town
Sittingbourne
1937 Grimsby Town 3
1937 1938 Stockport County 15 1
1939 (Stockport County) (1)
Distillery
Park United
Weelsby Social

Lumley, J RH
1893 Middlesbrough Ironopolis 1

Lumley, Sydney (Syd) CF
b Esh Winning 13/10/1906 d 1973
Esh Winning
Sunderland District Omnibus Co
1931 Newcastle United (trial) 0
1931 Hartlepools United 25 18
1932 Newport County 14 2
1933 Barrow 1
Sunderland District Omnibus Co

Lumley, William Read CF/IR
b Swalwell 27/12/1898 d 1975
Swalwell
1920 1921 Norwich City 24 6
Leadgate Park

Lumsden, James Boyd IR
b West Calder
West Calder Juniors
1928 Preston North End 0
1929 Bournemouth & Boscombe Ath 2

Lumsden, Joseph (Joe) OL/IL
b Derby 1875
1896 Burton Wanderers 29 5
1897 Liverpool 6 2
1898 1899 Glossop North End 53 19

Lumsden, Robert RH
b West Calder 10/7/1902 d 1974
West Calder Swifts
1927 Luton Town 1

Lumsdon, Francis (Frank) OR
b Sunderland q4 1913 d 1965
Castletown
1933 Huddersfield Town 1
1935 1936 Queen's Park Rangers 38 8
1937 Burnley 1

Lundie, James (Jimmy) RB
b Edinburgh 20/4/1857 d 1942
Caps: Scotland 1
Hibernian
1892 1894 Grimsby Town 49

From To Apps Goal

Lunn, Enoch IR
b Barnsley q1 1886 d 1961
Clowne White Star
1905 Chesterfield Town 24 3
New Brompton

Lunn, Frederick Levi (Fred) CF
b Marsden 8/11/1895 d 1972
Marsden
1920 Huddersfield Town 6 2
1921 Sheffield Wednesday 11 4
1922 Bristol Rovers 31 10
1923 Southend United 7 2
Nuneaton Town

Lunn, Laurence GK
b Huddersfield q3 1896 d 1946
Royton Amateurs
Rochdale (trial)
1921 Oldham Athletic 0
Ashton National
Royton Amateurs
1923 Crewe Alexandra 12
1924 Nelson 0
1925 Barrow 12
Llandudno
1925 Accrington Stanley 5
1926 Crewe Alexandra 4
Ashton National
Mossley

Lunn, Thomas Henry (Tommy) GK
b Bishop Auckland 9/7/1883 d 1960
Caps: FLge 1
Brownhills Albion
1904 1909 Wolverhampton Wanderers 129
1909 1912 Tottenham Hotspur 86
1913 Stockport County 2

Lupton, John CH/LH
b Liverpool q3 1878
1899 1900 Glossop 42

Lutterloch, Bertie Richard IR/LB
b Poplar 12/8/1910 d 1996
Tufnell Park
Lille
1934 Wolverhampton Wanderers 2
1934 1935 Aldershot 55 15
1936 1938 Luton Town 10
1939 (Luton Town) (3)
Vauxhall Motors

Lyall, John (Jack) GK
b Dundee 16/4/1881 d 1944
Caps: Scotland 1
Jarrow
1901 1908 Sheffield Wednesday 263
1909 1910 Manchester City 40
Dundee
Ayr United
Palmer's (Jarrow)

Lyall, Thomas IR
b Eckington 14/9/1899 d 1978
Nottingham Forest
Eckington Red Rose
1920 Nottingham Forest 1
Eckington Works
1922 Chesterfield 0

Lyden, J IR
1894 Bolton Wanderers 3 1
1896 Wolverhampton Wanderers 8 3
Darlaston

Lydon, George LH/RH
b Newton Heath 24/6/1902 d 1953
Nelson United
Mossley
1930 1931 Manchester United 3
1932 Southport 4
Burton Town
Hurst
Great Harwood

Lydon, Thomas CH
St Bernard's
Celtic
1901 Barnsley 1

Lyle, Archibald IR
b 10/2/1886
Maryhill
1909 Tottenham Hotspur 1

Lyle, David IL
1890 Notts County 2

Lyle, Robert Chalmers CH
b Glasgow 1889
Maryhill
Glasgow Perthshire
Partick Thistle
1910 Derby County 7

From To Apps Goal

Lyman, Colin Charles OL/IR
b Northampton 9/3/1914 d 1986
Rushden Town
1932 West Bromwich Albion (trial) 0
1933 Southend United 1
1934 1937 Northampton Town 86 29
1937 1945 Tottenham Hotspur 46 10
1939 (Tottenham Hotspur) (1)
1946 Port Vale 11 1
1946 Nottingham Forest 23 9
1947 Notts County 21 5
Nuneaton Borough
Long Eaton Town
British Timken

Lynas, John (Johnny) OR
b Bothwell 18/1/1907 d 1988
Linlithgow Port
Shettleston
Rutherglen Glencairn
Bo'ness
1928 Sunderland 10 1
Third Lanark

Lynas, Ralph John Langtrey IL
b Belfast 29/2/1904
Caps: IrLge 1/Ireland Amat
Cliftonville
1925 1926 Nottingham Forest 20 2
Ards

Lynch, Joseph William LH
b Tweedmouth
1936 Sheffield Wednesday 0
1937 Rotherham United 18

Lynch, Thomas John (Tom 'Paddy') GK
b Tredegar 31/8/1907 d 1976
Rhymney
1929 1930 Rochdale 58
Colwyn Bay United
1932 Barnsley 19
1933 Barrow 4
Yeovil & Petters United
1935 Brentford 0
1936 Watford 2
Guildford City
Bangor City

Lynch, Walter CH
b Castleford 1896
York City
Castleford Town
1920 Bradford City 4
Pontypridd
York City

Lyner, David (Davy) OL/OR
b Belfast 9/1/1893 d 1973
Caps: IrLge 7/Ireland 6
Owen O'Cork
Glentoran
Dundela
Distillery
Glentoran
1922 Manchester United 3
Kilmarnock
Queen's Island
Dundela
Clydebank
Dundela
Clydebank
Mid-Rhondda United
1926 New Brighton 21 1
Glentoran
Queen's Island
Dundela

Lynes, James (Jimmy) OR/CF
b Coleshill q2 1869
Liskeard
Avenue FC
Plymouth St James the Less
Plymouth United
Home Park
Argyle FC
Warmley
Weymouth
1895 Leicester Fosse 7 3
1896 Lincoln City 19 4
Halifax
Warrington
Bacup

Lynex, James IR
b Walsall q4 1878 d 1941
1900 Walsall 17 2

Lyon, Frank RB
b Crewe 23/9/1879 d 1917
1900 Stockport County 0
Crewe Alexandra
Watford
Queen's Park Rangers
1907 Chelsea 6
Crewe Alexandra

From To Apps Goal

Lyon, Herbert Henry Saxon Bertie Cordey (Bertie) IL/IR
b Masbrough 18/5/1875 d 1927
Overseal Town
Gresley Rovers
1898 1899 Leicester Fosse 15 4
Nelson
Watford
Reading
West Ham United
Brighton & Hove Albion
Swindon Town
Carlisle United
Swindon Town
1908 Blackpool 8 2
Walsall
Tredegar

Lyon, John (Jack) IL/CF/IR
b Prescot 3/11/1893 d 1975
Prescot
1913 1919 Hull City 37 6
1920 Leeds United 33 3
Prescot Cables
1923 New Brighton 28 5
Mold Town
Prescot Cables

Lyon, RE CH
1895 Crewe Alexandra 3

Lyon, Samuel (Sam) CF
b Prescot 20/11/1890 d 1916
Prescot
1912 1913 Hull City 6 1
1914 Barnsley 8 3

Lyon, Thomas King (Tom) IR/IL
b Clydebank 17/3/1915 d 1998
Clydebank Juniors
Motherwell (trial)
Yoker Athletic
Albion Rovers
Airdrieonians (loan)
1936 1937 Blackpool 6
1938 1947 Chesterfield 41 22
1939 (Chesterfield) (2) (1)
1948 New Brighton 36 7
Prescot Cables
Oswestry Town

Lyon, William John (Billy) LH
b Inverness 1880
Dundee
1898 1900 Walsall 44 1
Bristol Rovers
1903 Manchester City 6
1903 1910 Preston North End 210 8

Lyons, Albert Thomas (Bert) RB/LB
b Hednesford 5/3/1902 d 1981
1924 Port Vale 0
1925 Walsall 0
1926 1929 Clapton Orient 76
1930 1931 Tottenham Hotspur 54 3
Colwyn Bay United

Lyons, Alfred Thomas (Tommy) RB
b Littleworth 5/7/1885 d 1938
Hednesford Town
Hednesford Victoria
Bridgetown Amateurs
1907 1914 Aston Villa 217
1919 1920 Port Vale 63
1922 Walsall 1

Lyons, George IR
Black Lane Temperance
1903 1905 Manchester United 4
Oldham Athletic
Rossendale United
Salford United

Lyons, James (Jimmy) IR
b Hednesford 27/9/1897 d 1970
Hednesford Town
1919 1922 Derby County 80 31
1925 Wrexham 34 13
Hednesford Town
Stourbridge
Cannock Town

Lythgoe, Alfred Peter (Alf) CF
b Nantwich 16/3/1907 d 1967
Caps: FLge 1
1927 Crewe Alexandra 0
Whitchurch
Sandbach Ramblers
Congleton Town
Ashton National
1932 1934 Stockport County 69 80
1932 Wolverhampton Wandrs (trial) 0
1934 1937 Huddersfield Town 73 42
1937 1938 Stockport County 50 24
Ashton National

From To Apps Goal

Lythgoe, John (Jack) IL/CF/OL
b Dixon Fold 3/4/1892 d 1969
Newbury FC
Walkden Central
1913 1914 Bury 38 17
1919 1920 Nottingham Forest 61 13
1920 Manchester City 0
1921 Newport County 35 4
1922 Norwich City 14 3
Ebbw Vale
Eccles United
Chorley
1924 Crewe Alexandra 0
Margate
Horwich RMI
Kearsley Celtic

Mabbott, John OR/IR
b Nottingham q3 1872 d 1955
Mellors Ltd
Nottingham Forest
Newark
Grantham
Kettering
Leicester Fosse
1892 Notts County 0
Leicester Fosse
1892 1893 Notts County 2
Newark
Mansfield
Long Eaton Rangers
Whitwick White Cross

McAdam, Thomas E (Tom) OR
b Shadwell q2 1917 d 1955
Tufnell Park
1937 Southend United 2 1
Gillingham

McAdam, W CH
1891 Darwen 4

McAinsh, James OR
b Clackmannan 13/10/1913 d 1978
1933 Hull City 7
1934 1935 Gateshead 45 6

McAleer, Joseph (Joe) OL/CF/OR
b Blythswood 8/3/1910
Glenboig St Joseph's
Bridgeton Waverley
Arbroath
1931 1932 Rochdale 35 8
Glenavon
1933 Northampton Town 8 6
1934 Lincoln City 6 5
1935 Clapton Orient 18 4
1936 Gillingham 9 3
Brideville
1937 Wrexham 7 1

McAlinden, James (Jimmy) IR/IL
b Belfast 31/12/1917 d 1993
Caps: IrLge 5/NIRL 8/LoI 1/Ireland 4/Eire 2
Glentoran
Belfast Celtic
1938 Portsmouth 20 4
1939 (Portsmouth) (3)
Belfast Celtic
Shamrock Rovers (loan)
1946 1947 Portsmouth 33 5
1947 1948 Stoke City 33 2
1948 1953 Southend United 217 12
Glenavon

McAllister, Alexander (Sandy) CH
b Kilmarnock 1878 d 1918
Dean Park (Kilmarnock)
Carrington Vale
Kilmarnock
1896 1903 Sunderland 210 4
1904 Derby County 24
Oldham Athletic
Spennymoor United

McAllister, Thomas (Tom) RH
b Govan 1882
Castleford Town
1905 Blackburn Rovers 2
Brentford
1908 1909 Leeds City 53
Castleford Town
Halifax Town
(Scotland)
Halifax Town

From To Apps Goal

McAllister, William (Billy) RH/IL/IR
b Glasgow
Milngavie Allander
Maryhill
Hamilton Academical
Renton
St Mirren
Johnstone (loan)
Ebbw Vale
1921 1924 Brighton & Hove Albion 89 6
1924 1925 Middlesbrough 33
1926 Queen's Park Rangers 26 1
Raith Rovers
Heart of Midlothian
Dolphin
Glentoran

McAloon, Gerald Padua (Gerry) IR
b Gorbals 13/9/1916 d 1987
St Francis Juniors
1937 1938 Brentford 21 8
1938 Wolverhampton Wanderers 2 1
1945 1946 Brentford 7 4
Celtic
Belfast Celtic

McAlpine, C LB
Burslem Port Vale
Darlington
1892 Burslem Port Vale 10

McAlpine, James Walker (Jim) LH/RH
b Ravenscraig 5/2/1887 d 1946
Craigneuk Heatherbell
Dalziel Rovers
Vale of Clyde
Strathclyde Juniors
Southampton
Kilmarnock
Wishaw Thistle
1920 Millwall Athletic 17
1921 1922 Gillingham 47

McAninly, Joseph (Joe) IR
b Tow Law 15/1/1913 d 1989
Tow Law Town
West Stanley
1934 Huddersfield Town 0
1935 Clapton Orient 0
Eden Colliery Welfare
1936 Chesterfield 2
1937 1938 Darlington 72 7

McArdle, J LB
1895 Rotherham Town 7

McArdle, Peter OL
b Lanchester 8/4/1911 d 1979
Trimdon Grange
Durham City
1933 1934 Stoke City 7 1
1935 Exeter City 9 1
1936 Carlisle United 27 12
1936 1937 Barnsley 16 3
1937 Stockport County 4
1938 Gateshead 20 5
1939 Crewe Alexandra 0

McArthur, Edward Stanley Smith (Ted) OL/IL
b Cowdenbeath 30/4/1908
Edinburgh Emmet
Crossgates Primrose
Raith Rovers
Alloa Athletic
Crossgates Primrose
Raith Rovers
1933 Middlesbrough 0
1934 1935 Exeter City 23 7
Dawlish
1936 Torquay United 14
Bath City
Raith Rovers

McArthur, Walter (Wally) LH
b Denaby 21/3/1912 d 1980
Denaby United
Goldthorpe United
1932 1949 Bristol Rovers 261 14
1939 (Bristol Rovers) (3)

McArthur, William (Willie) CF/IR
b Neilston 17/8/1870
Renton Union
Sunderland Albion
Middlesbrough Ironopolis
1893 Bolton Wanderers 19 6
1894 1895 Leicester Fosse 55 27
Dundee
Brighton United
Worthing

From To Apps Goal

McAteer, Thomas CH/CF
b Glasgow 8/8/1878
Kilsyth Wanderers
Smithston Hibernian
1898 1901 Bolton Wanderers 59 10
West Ham United
Brighton & Hove Albion
Dundee
Carlisle United
Clyde (loan)
Clyde
Carlisle United
Clyde
Celtic
Wishaw Thistle
Albion Rovers
Abercorn
Broxburn United
Cameron Highlanders

Macaulay, Archibald Renwick (Archie) RH/IR/CF
b Falkirk 30/7/1915 d 1993
Caps: Scotland War 5/Scotland 7
Comely Park
Lauriston Villa
Camelon Juniors
Rangers
1937 1946 West Ham United 83 29
1939 (West Ham United) (3)
1946 Brentford 26 2
1947 1949 Arsenal 103 1
1950 1952 Fulham 49 4
Guildford City

McAulay, Robert (Bob) LB/RB
b Wishaw 28/8/1904 d 1994
Caps: SLge 1/Scotland 2
Bellshill Athletic
Montreal Carsteel
Montreal Grenadier Guards
Providence Clamdiggers
Fall River Marksmen
Clyde (trial)
Rangers
1932 1935 Chelsea 66 1
1936 Cardiff City 4
Sligo Rovers
Workington
Raith Rovers

Macaulay, William (Willie) IR
b Glasgow 1/11/1879 d 1935
Cambuslang Hibernian
Celtic
1898 Sheffield Wednesday 0
Dundee
1899 Walsall 24 7
1900 Aston Villa 6
Portsmouth
1902 Middlesbrough 21 2
Aberdeen
Falkirk
Hibernian
Alloa Athletic

McAuley, James RB
b Scotland
Morton
1897 Woolwich Arsenal 23 1

McAuley, James Lowry (Jim) IL
b Portarlington 24/11/1889 d 1945
Caps: IrLge 5/Ireland Amat/Ireland 6
Cloughfern
Cliftonville Olympic
Cliftonville
Rangers
1910 1913 Huddersfield Town 95 32
1913 1914 Preston North End 59 23
Belfast Celtic (loan)
1919 Leicester City 19 2
1920 Grimsby Town 16 4
Lancaster Town
Morecambe

McAvoy, Francis (Frank) LH/OL
b Ayr 16/11/1875
Ayr
1895 1897 Woolwich Arsenal 44 8
Brighton United
Gravesend United
Brighton & Hove Albion
Watford
St Mirren
Ayr

McAvoy, John LB/RB
b Scotland 1878
Celtic
Airdrieonians
1898 Woolwich Arsenal 25
1899 1900 Grimsby Town 26

McAvoy, M LH
1891 1895 Darwen 94 7

From To Apps Goal

McBain, Neil CH/IL
b Campbeltown 15/11/1895 d 1974
Caps: Scotland 3
Campbeltown Academicals
Hamilton Academical (trial)
Ayr United
Kilmarnock
Third Lanark (trial)
1921 1922 Manchester United 42 2
1922 1925 Everton 97 1
St Johnstone
1927 1928 Liverpool 12
1928 1931 Watford 85 5
1946 New Brighton 1

McBain, Thomas (Tom) IL/OR
b Whifflet 1902
Whifflet Emerald
1931 Newcastle United 1
1932 1933 Carlisle United 39 12
Glenavon

McBeath, Andrew OR
b South Shields q4 1884 d 1965
1904 Barnsley 1

Macbeth, Robert IL/OL
St Bernard's
1888 Accrington 1
Grimsby Town
1890 Accrington 3
Grimsby Town
Burton Swifts
1892 Northwich Victoria 13 3
1893 Rotherham Town 2

McBride, James (Jim) LH
b Renton 30/12/1873 d 1899
Caps: SLge 1
Renton Wanderers
Renton
1893 1894 Liverpool 30 3
1894 1896 Manchester City 70 1
Ashton North End

McBride, Peter GK
b Ayr 15/9/1877
Caps: Scotland 6
Westerlea
Ayr
1897 1911 Preston North End 442

McBride, Robert CF
Ayr
1896 Loughborough 3 1

McCabe, Arthur OL
b Sheffield q3 1871
Heeley
Rotherham Town
Sheffield United
1895 Rotherham Town 18 4
1895 Manchester City 1
Ilkeston Town
Rochdale

McCabe, James (Jim) IL
b Paisley 25/4/1909 d 1955
Kilbirnie Ladeside
Hamilton Academical
1929 Barrow 11
East Stirlingshire
St Mirren
Babcock & Wilcox

McCabe, Thomas Bernard (Barney) CF/IR
b Middleton St George 15/1/1903 d 1963
Teesdale United
Middleton Athletic
1928 Darlington 1
Ferryhill Athletic
1929 Newcastle United (trial) 0
Spennymoor United
1930 1931 York City 21 10
Wigan Athletic
1933 Wrexham 5
Burton Town
Worcester City
Stourbridge
Heevans

McCafferty, James (Joe) OL/OR
b Stevenston 1900
Wishaw Juniors
Larkhall Thistle
Duntocher Hibs
Shieldmuir Celtic
Motherwell
1925 1926 Halifax Town 20 5
1927 Brentford 1
Shieldmuir Celtic
1929 Gillingham 14
Vale of Leithen

From To Apps Goal

McCafferty, Michael CH
Celtic
1898 Sheffield Wednesday 1

McCafferty, William (Bill) OL/IR
b Rutherglen 9/12/1882
Rutherglen Glencairn
Celtic
1902 Bolton Wanderers 8
Stenhousemuir
Dunfermline Athletic
Bathgate
Reading
1906 Birmingham 4
Bathgate
Portsmouth
Brentford
Bathgate

McCaig, Alexander Reid (Alex) IL/IR
b Larbert 18/10/1895
Larbert Central
Law Volunteers
Newarthill Thistle
Falkirk
Alloa Athletic
Stenhousemuir
1921 Coventry City 10 2
1922 Reading 16 2
Cowdenbeath
Stenhousemuir
St Bernard's
Stenhousemuir

McCaig, David RH/LH
b Carluke 26/11/1906 d 1982
Law Scotia
Raith Rovers
1928 1929 Bristol Rovers 15
East Fife

McCairns, Thomas (Tommy) CF
b Dinsdale 22/12/1873 d 1932
Caps: FLge 1
Middlesbrough Ironopolis
Whitby
1893 1897 Grimsby Town 137 86
Bristol Rovers
1899 Notts County 4
1899 1900 Lincoln City 35 14
1901 Barnsley 23 9
Wellingborough
Queen's Park Rangers
Brighton & Hove Albion
Southern United
Kettering

McCall, Andrew Johnstone IL/IR
b Cumnock 12/10/1908
Cumnock Juveniles
Cumnock Townend Thistle
Ayr United
St Johnstone
1938 Huddersfield Town 5
1939 Nottingham Forest (3) (1)
Huntly

McCall, John OR
b Muirkirk 1877
Muirkirk Athletic
Strathclyde
Kilmarnock Deanpark
Hibernian
Bristol Rovers
1903 Notts County 3

McCall, John (Johnny) IL
b Glasgow 29/9/1918 d 1992
Workington
1937 1947 Bradford Park Avenue 41 5
Shrewsbury Town

McCall, Joseph (Joe) CH
b Kirkham 6/7/1886 d 1965
Caps: FLge 2/England 5
Kirkham
1906 1924 Preston North End 370 15

McCall, Robert Henry (Bob) LB/RH/CF
b Worksop 29/12/1915 d 1992
Worksop Town
1935 1951 Nottingham Forest 162 1
1939 (Nottingham Forest) (3)
Worksop Town

McCall, William (Bill) OL/IL
b Wallacetown 5/5/1898
Queen of the South
1920 1921 Blackburn Rovers 11
1922 Wolverhampton Wanderers 15 1
1922 Southampton 8 2
Queen of the South
Carlisle United

From To Apps Goal

McCallum, Charles OL
Workington
1910 Burnley 4
Renton

McCallum, Cornelius Joseph (Neil) IR/OR
b Bonhill 3/7/1868 d 1921
Caps: SLge 1/Scotland 1
Renton Athletic
Renton
Rangers (loan)
Celtic
1889 Blackburn Rovers 2
Nottingham Forest
Celtic
1892 1893 Nottingham Forest 36 10
Loughborough
Newark Town
1895 Notts County 13 3
Heanor Town
Middleton
Folkestone
Gravesend United
Celtic

McCallum, Donald RB
b Glasgow 6/1880 d 1959
Strathclyde
Queen's Park
1902 Liverpool 2
Morton
1904 Sunderland 3
1904 1905 Middlesbrough 25
Port Glasgow Athletic
Kilmarnock
Renton
Lochgelly United
East Fife
Mid-Rhondda
East Fife

McCallum, Donald LH/RH
b Dunfermline
Caps: WLge 1
Mid-Rhondda
1920 1922 Swansea Town 60 2
Clackmannan

McCambridge, James (Jimmy) CF/IL/IR
b Larne 24/9/1905 d 1980
Caps: IrLge 2/Ireland 4
Larne
Ballymena
1930 Everton 1
1930 1932 Cardiff City 95 51
Ballymena
1933 1935 Bristol Rovers 58 23
1935 Exeter City 23 14
1936 Sheffield Wednesday 2
1936 Hartlepools United 16 4
Cheltenham Town

McCamon, Patrick Logan IL
b Kilmarnock 23/5/1912 d 1974
Irvine Victoria
Largs Thistle
St Mirren
1937 Barrow 7 1
Dundee United

McCandless, John (Jack) OL/OR/IL
b Coleraine 29/2/1892 d 1940
Caps: Ireland 5
Coleraine Alexandra
Belfast Celtic
Linfield
1911 1922 Bradford Park Avenue 190 21
Hibernian (loan)
Linfield (loan)
1923 Accrington Stanley 2
Barn
Mid-Rhondda United
Lovells Athletic
Coleraine

McCandless, Thomas Black (Tom) LB
b Belfast
Barn
1928 Bradford Park Avenue 6
1929 Charlton Athletic 0

McCann, Daniel (Dan) IR
b Hurlford 18/3/1888
Hurlford Thistle
Galston
Nithsdale Wanderers
Hurlford Athletic
Dundee
Celtic
Ayr United (loan)
Dundee Hibernian
1911 Nottingham Forest 1
Hurlford Athletic
Galston
Dundee

From To Apps Goal

McCann, Henry IL
b Falkirk 1888
Carron Thistle
Glasgow Ashfield
Hibernian
1907 Lincoln City 17 6
Birtley
1912 Barnsley 1
Exeter City
Bristol Rovers

McCann, John IR
b Uphall 6/9/1867
Broxburn Shamrock
Bathgate Rovers
Newcastle West End
Broxburn Shamrock
Celtic
Hibernian
1893 Preston North End 6 1
Broxburn Shamrock

McCann, William (Billy) GK
b Renfrew 1871 d 1924
Renfrew Juniors
Abercorn
1894 Liverpool 15
Paisley Celtic

McCappin, Samuel Alfred (Sam) GK
b Kilburn q3 1875 d 1945
Barking Excelsior
St Luke's (Canning Town)
Barking Woodville
Ilford
Vampires
1899 Notts County 7

McCarthy, Bernard Roy IR
Margate
1935 Barnsley 0
Bangor City
1937 Chester 1
1938 Wolverhampton Wanderers 0

McCarthy, Kenneth (Ken) IL
1938 Reading 3

McCarthy, Leonard Daniel (Len) IR/IL
b Caerau
Caerau Harlequins
1929 Crystal Palace 0
1930 1931 Thames 58 17
1932 1936 Portsmouth 24 5
1937 1938 Queen's Park Rangers 22 9

McCarthy, Michael GK
b Cork 22/12/?? d 1973
Caps: LoI 1/Eire 1
Blackrock Rovers
Fordsons
Cork Bohemians
Shamrock Rovers
1934 Sheffield United 9
Brideville
Shamrock Rovers

McCarthy, Patrick CF
b 1888
Chester
Skelmersdale
1911 Manchester United 1
Skelmersdale
Tranmere Rovers
Chester

McCarthy, Patrick (Paddy) OL
b Liverpool 2/2/1914 d 1999
St Sylvester's Boys Club
St Sylvester's CYMS
Sidley Hill
1934 Liverpool 0
1934 Burnley 0
1935 1936 Southport 37 8
1937 Chester 2

McCarthy, Thomas (Tom) CH
b Dundee
Dundee Logie
Lochee United
Dundee
Montose (loan)
1935 Brighton & Hove Albion 1
Dundee United
Fraserburgh

MacCartney, Charles William (Charlie) CF
b Stamford 4/2/1910 d 1982
Stamford Town
1932 1934 Notts County 50 19
1935 1936 Wrexham 48 26
1937 Carlisle United 4
1937 York City 1
1937 Darlington 2
Peterborough United
Grantham

From To Apps Goal

McCartney, David (Dave) CH
b Ayrshire 1880
Cronberry
Dalbeattie
Lugar Boswell
1900 1902 Glossop 73 5
Watford
1906 Chelsea 1
Northampton Town

McCartney, James (Jimmy) IL/OR/OL
b Washington 30/3/1909 d 1976
Washington Colliery
1928 Newcastle United 0
1929 1930 Swindon Town 37 5
Bath City
Wardley Colliery Welfare
1933 1937 Millwall 161 33
1938 Northampton Town 22 7
South Shields

McCartney, John RH
b Newmilns 1870
Newmilns
St Mirren
1893 1897 Liverpool 123 4
1898 1899 New Brighton Tower 18

McCartney, W James IR
b Cronberry 1881
Cronberry
1904 Barnsley 1

McCartney, Walter John RB
b Glasgow 1866 d 1933
Cartvale
Glasgow Thistle
Rangers
Cowlairs
1894 Newton Heath 19 1
1897 Luton Town 27
1898 1900 Barnsley 63 3

McCartney, William (Bill) IL
b Newmilns
Caps: SLge 2/Scotland 1
Rutherglen Glencairn
Ayr
Hibernian
1903 Manchester United 13 1
West Ham United
Broxburn
Lochgelly United
Clyde
Broxburn
Clyde

McCartney, William James (Willie) LH/CH
b Cronberry 14/11/1879 d 1969
Lugar Boswell
1901 1903 Barnsley 7

McCaughey, Cecil RH
b Bootle q4 1909
Liverpool St James'
Burscough Rangers
1933 Liverpool 0
1934 Blackburn Rovers 0
1935 1936 Coventry City 31
1937 1938 Cardiff City 66 5
1939 Southport 0

McClarence, Joseph P (Joe) IL/CF/IR
b Newcastle q3 1885
Wallsend Park Villa
1904 1907 Newcastle United 30 13
1907 1908 Bolton Wanderers 15 6
1908 1910 Bradford Park Avenue 63 31
Distillery

McCleery, William (Billy) IL
b Belfast 25/1/1902
Caps: LoI 1/IrLge 12/Ireland Amat/Ireland 10
Cliftonville
Queen's Island
1924 1925 Blackburn Rovers 23 5
Queen's Island
Shelbourne
Linfield

McClelland, Hugh GK
b 1885
Glasgow Benburb
1914 Bury 1

McClelland, James (Jim) IR/RH/CF
b Dysart 11/5/1902
Rosslyn
Raith Rovers
1923 1924 Southend United 26 17
1924 1927 Middlesbrough 81 43
1927 1929 Bolton Wanderers 57 18
1929 1930 Preston North End 53 22
1930 1932 Blackpool 66 24
1933 1935 Bradford Park Avenue 100 10
1936 Manchester United 5 1

From To Apps Goal

McClennon, James William LB/RB
b Tynemouth 16/12/1900 d 1971
Walker Celtic
1923 1924 Grimsby Town 11
1925 Brentford 24
Walker Celtic
West Stanley

McCloud, Thomas Edward (Tom) OL
b Chevington 21/1/1898 d 1986
Chevington
Amble
1921 1922 Ashington 45 4

McCloy, James GK
b Howwood 1911
Petershill
Clyde
St Mirren
1938 Bradford City 37
1939 Swansea Town 0

McCloy, Philip (Phil) LB
b Uddingston 4/1896 d 1972
Caps: LoI 1/Scotland 2
Baillieston Juniors
Mossend Hibernian
Kilsyth Emmet
Parkhead
Ayr United
Clyde (loan)
1925 1929 Manchester City 147
Cork City
Chester
Stade Rennais Universite
Kidderminster Harriers

McCluggage, Andrew (Andy) RB/LB
b Larne 1/9/1900 d 1954
Caps: Ireland 13
Intervale
Cliftonville
1922 1924 Bradford Park Avenue 85 2
1925 1930 Burnley 204 22
Dundalk
1931 Preston North End 3
Morecambe
Larne

McClung, R OL
1896 Darwen 4 1

McClure, Alexander (Alex) CH
b Workington 3/4/1892 d 1973
Caps: FLge 1
Grangetown Juniors
1911 1923 Birmingham 192 4
1923 1924 Aston Villa 7
1924 1925 Stoke 28
1926 1927 Coventry City 49 7
1927 Walsall 11
1928 Luton Town 0
Market Harborough Town

McClure, David RB
b Slamannan
Caps: IrLge 2
Glenavon
1923 New Brigthon (trial) 0
Dunipace Juniors
St Johnstone
1927 Nelson 28 1
Dundee United
Portadown
Glentoran
Montrose

McClure, Joseph Henry (Joe) RH/CH
b Cockermouth 3/11/1907 d 1973
Workington
1926 Preston North End 0
Whitehaven
Leamington Town
Wallsend
1929 1932 Everton 29 1
1933 Brentford 1
1934 Exeter City 5
Nuneaton Town

McClure, Samuel (Sammy) CH/RH
b Workington 11/2/1878 d 1906
Black Diamonds
1898 Everton (trial) 0
1899 1905 Blackburn Rovers 144 12

McClure, Samuel Thompson IL
b Middlesbrough q4 1888
Grangetown
1910 Middlesbrough 11 3
1911 Aston Villa 0
Watford

McClure, W OL
1897 1898 Burton Swifts 11 2

From To | Apps Goal

McColgan, John LB
b Tollcross 2/1/1898
Caps: Lol 1
Vale of Clyde
Albion Rovers
1923 1929 Portsmouth 190
Waterford

McColgan, John (Jim) CF
b Ireland 20/6/1916
St Anthony's
1938 Plymouth Argyle 1
1939 Queen's Park Rangers 0
Tunbridge Wells Rangers
Ipswich Town

McColl, James (Jimmy) CF
b Glasgow 14/12/1892 d 1978
Anderston Thornbank
St Anthony's (Glasgow)
Celtic
Peebles Rovers (loan)
1920 Stoke 27 5
Partick Thistle
Hibernian
Leith Athletic

McColl, Robert Smyth (Bob) IL/CF
b Glasgow 13/4/1876 d 1959
Caps: SLge 1/Scotland 13
Benmore
Queen's Park
1901 1903 Newcastle United 64 18
Rangers
Queen's Park

McColl, William IR
b Drymen 1865
Caps: Scotland 1
Vale of Leven
Morton
Accrington
1889 Burnley 9 2
Ardwick
Renton
Vale of Leven

McCombe, James (Jimmy) OR
b Bothwell 4/6/1915
Bothwellhaugh A
Wishaw Thistle
Wishaw Juniors
Heart of Midlothian
Clyde
King's Park
1936 1937 Clapton Orient 45 8
Chelmsford City
Dartford

McCombie, Andrew (Andy) RB
b Inverness 30/6/1876 d 1952
Caps: Scotland 4
Inverness Thistle
1898 1903 Sunderland 157 6
1903 1909 Newcastle United 113

McCombie, W CF
1892 Northwich Victoria 3 1

McConachie, J Robert OL
1892 Sheffield Wednesday 1

McConnell, Alexander (Alex) RB/LB
b Glenbuck 1875
Glenbuck Athletic
1897 Everton 0
1897 1898 Woolwich Arsenal 37 1
Queen's Park Rangers
1901 1904 Grimsby Town 84

McConnell, James GK
Padiham
1889 Burnley 1
Brierfield

McConnell, James (Jimmy) CF
b Ayr 23/2/1899 d 1949
Auchinleck Talbot
Kilmarnock
Stevenston United
Nithsdale Wanderers
Celtic (loan)
Springfield Babes
Providence Clamdiggers
J & P Coats (Rhode Island)
Bethlehem Steel
1928 1931 Carlisle United 149 124
1932 Crewe Alexandra 36 22
1933 Rotherham United 21 4
Nithsdale Wanderers

From To | Apps Goal

McConnell, James English (English) CH/LH/RH
b Larne 1885 d 1928
Caps: IrLge 2/Ireland 12
Cliftonville
Glentoran
1905 1907 Sunderland 39
1908 1909 Sheffield Wednesday 44
1909 1910 Chelsea 21
South Shields
Linfield

McConnell, John LB/RB
b Glenbuck 1881
Glenbuck Athletic
Kilmarnock
1903 1905 Grimsby Town 49
Brentford
1907 Grimsby Town 6
Nithsdale Wanderers
St Cuthbert Wanderers
Hurlford

McConnell, John Morrison (Jock) LH
b Cambusnethan 9/12/1890
Motherwell Hearts
Glasgow Ashfield
Motherwell
Airdrieonians
1909 1911 Liverpool 50 1
Aberdeen

McConnell, Patrick (Pat) IL/IR
b Rasharkin 5/2/1900 d 1971
Caps: Ireland 2
Bellshill Athletic
Larkhall Thistle
Bathgate
1924 Bradford City 3
1925 1929 Doncaster Rovers 137 20
1930 1931 Southport 48 13
Shelbourne
Boston United
Grantham
Hibernian

McConnell, T OL
Mossend Swifts
1896 Manchester City 2
1897 Woolwich Arsenal 0

McConnell, William G (Bill) RB
b Ireland
1912 1914 Bradford Park Avenue 10

McConnell, William Henry (Billy 'Pat') LB
b Corbolis 2/9/??
Caps: Ireland 8
Slough YMCA
Slough Town
1922 Arsenal 0
Slough Town
1924 1927 Reading 142 1
Slough Town

McConville, Patrick (Paddy) LB/RB
b Gilford 25/3/1902
Portadown Celtic
Glenavon
1925 1931 Lincoln City 138
Glenavon

McCormack, John Andrew CH
b Scotland
Johnstone
1907 Newcastle United 2 1
1909 Everton 0
Johnstone
Dumbarton Harp

McCormick, Donald IL
1920 Gillingham 1
Sheppey United

McCormick, James RH
b Rotherham 28/4/1883 d 1935
Thornhill United
Attercliffe
1905 1906 Sheffield United 22 1
Plymouth Argyle
1910 Sheffield United 1
Plymouth Argyle
Ladysmith (Canada)

McCormick, James (Jimmy) OR/IR
b Rotherham 26/9/1912 d 1968
Rotherham YMCA
1930 1931 Rotherham United 19 2
Scarborough
1932 Chesterfield 15 2
1932 1938 Tottenham Hotspur 137 26
1946 Fulham 9 2
1947 1948 Lincoln City 64 6
1948 Crystal Palace 13 2
Sliema Wanderers

From To | Apps Goal

McCormick, John (Johnny) IL/OL
1893 1895 Rotherham Town 60 23

McCormick, Patrick IR/IL/CF
b Cleator Moor 7/1/1914 d 1991
Cleator Moor
1933 Preston North End 0
Dick, Kerr's XI
Lancaster Town
Morecambe
1936 1938 Oldham Athletic 38 13
Workington

McCormick, Robert (Bob) OR
b Paisley
Caps: Scotland 1
Abercorn
1889 Stoke 12 2
Abercorn

McCormick, Thomas CF
b Ireland
Linfield
Barrow Washington United
Cliftonville
1923 Barrow 1

McCorquodale, Douglas OR
1899 Middlesbrough 2

McCorry, Henry IR
b Felling 1888
South Shields
Ashington
Newburn
1913 Hull City 10 4
Chesterfield Town
Gateshead

McCosh, H IL
1898 1899 Glossop North End 10 3

McCosh, John McLoughlan IR
b Coylton 29/3/1904 d 1995
Auchinleck Talbot
Ayr United
Nithsdale Wanderers
Ayr United
Cowdenbeath
Clydebank (trial)
Third Lanark (trial)
East Stirlingshire (trial)
Morton (trial)
Queen of the South
1930 Exeter City 1
1931 New Brighton 24 2
Drumcondra

McCourt, James (Jimmy) CH
b Bellshill 8/9/1896
St Paul's Juniors
Bedlay Juniors
Mossend Hibernian
Third Lanark
1920 1923 Sheffield United 62 4
1924 Manchester City 4
Dykehead

McCourt, John Francis IL
b Rutherglen 9/7/1883
Ayr
Hibernian
Celtic
Brentford
1908 Fulham 2
Croydon Common

McCourty, William LH
b Morpeth 1884
North Seaton
1909 Birmingham 1
Ryton

McCowie, Andrew (Andy) IR/IL/OR
b Cambuslang 1876
Cambuslang Hibernian
1896 1898 Liverpool 33 11
1899 1900 Woolwich Arsenal 28 7
1900 Middlesbrough 16 5
1901 Chesterfield Town 17 7

McCracken, George OL
b Greenock
Port Glasgow Athletic
1922 South Shields 5
Jarrow

McCracken, Henry (Harry) CF
b Belfast
Caps: IrLge 5/Ireland Amat
Annsborough
Newry Town
1925 Cardiff City 0
1926 Charlton Athletic 1
Linfield
Portadown

From To | Apps Goal

McCracken, Peter John LH/LB
b Newton Stewart 1870
Caps: FAlliance 1
Third Lanark
Sunderland Albion
1892 1898 Nottingham Forest 113
1899 Middlesbrough 33
1900 1901 Chesterfield Town 52 1

McCracken, Robert (Bobby) RH
b Dromore 25/6/1890
Caps: IrLge 4/Ireland 4
Dromore United
Distillery
1920 1925 Crystal Palace 175 1
Portadown

McCracken, William Robert (Billy) RB
b Belfast 29/1/1883 d 1979
Caps: IrLge 5/Ireland 16
Distillery
1904 1922 Newcastle United 377 6

McCrae, David CF
b Kilbarchan 24/2/1901 d 1976
Caps: Scotland 1
Kilmacolm Juniors
Beith
1921 Manchester City (trial) 0
1921 Bury (trial) 0
Gainsborough Trinity
Denaby Main
Beith
St Mirren
Stade Rennais Universite
Morton (trial)
1934 New Brighton 11 1
Queen of the South
Stranraer
1934 Darlington 4 3
Beith
Glentoran

McCrae, James Clark Fulton (Jimmy) LH
b Bridge of Weir 2/9/1894 d 1974
Port Glasgow Juniors
Clyde
Rangers
Clyde
1919 1920 West Ham United 50
1920 1922 Bury 84 10
1923 Wigan Borough 32 5
1924 New Brighton 6
1925 Manchester United 9
Third Lanark (loan)
1926 Watford 2
Clyde

McCrae, Robert IR
Vale of Leven
1888 Burnley 2
Burnley Union Star

McCreadie, Andrew CH
b Girvan 19/11/1870
Caps: Scotland 2
Cowlairs
Rangers
1894 1895 Sunderland 42 8
Rangers
Bristol St George
Wishaw Thistle

McCreary, John RH
b Shotts 18/1/1909 d 1982
Falkirk
1936 Bury 0
1937 1938 Chester 56 2

McCree, James OR
b Cathcart 16/11/1902 d 1984
Queen's Park
London Caledonians
1924 Brentford 3
London Caledonians
1925 Fulham 2
1926 Watford 0
London Caledonians
1927 Middlesbrough 0
London Caledonians

McCrindle, J IR
1893 Rotherham Town 1

McCrindle, Robert CH
b Dreghorn 28/9/1869
Hurlford
1892 1893 Burslem Port Vale 48
Luton Town

From To Apps Goal

McCrorie, Thomas Shanks (Tom) IL
b Kirkintilloch 1/3/1902 d 1962
Renfrew St James
Kirkintilloch Rob Roy
Dundee
Hamilton Academical
1925 Charlton Athletic 5
1926 Aberdare Athletic 2
Dunfermline Athletic
Gurney (Canada)
Dunfermline Athletic
1928 Birmingham (trial) 0
Alloa Athletic
1928 Merthyr Town 2
Dumbarton
Olympique Marseille
New Bedford Whalers
1929 Barrow 3
Arbroath
Linfield
Shelbourne
Pawtucket Rangers
1932 Queen's Park Rangers 0
Beith (trial)
Coleraine
Ards

McCrory, Peter IR
1937 Darlington 1

McCubbin, Alexander C (Sandy) IR/IL
b Greenock 1888
Volunteer Amateurs
Morton
Bristol Rovers
Morton
1910 Huddersfield Town 11 5
1912 1913 Lincoln City 59 15
Newland Athletic
Lincoln Corinthians

McCudden, Joseph Francis (Frank) IR
b Edmonton 17/1/1899 d 1976
Park Avondale
Gnome Athletic
Royal Field Artillery
Edmonton
1921 Tottenham Hotspur 0
1922 Clapton Orient 0
1923 Tottenham Hotspur 0
1924 1925 Norwich City 38 14
1926 Clapton Orient 0
Grays Thurrock
Whitbreads

McCue, John William CH
b Longton q4 1899
Sandbach Ramblers
Stafford Rangers
1925 Oldham Athletic 1
Sandbach Ramblers
Oswestry Town
Denbigh

McCulloch, Alexander (Alex) IR/CF
b Edinburgh 4/1887 d 1962
Bonnyrigg Rose Athletic
Leith Athletic
1907 Middlesbrough 3 1
1907 Newcastle United 1
Brentford
1908 Bradford Park Avenue 7 1
Swindon Town
Bo'ness
Reading
Swindon Town
Coventry City
Raith Rovers
Alloa Athletic
St Bernard's
Broxburn United
Dunfermline Athletic
Heart of Midlothian
1919 Lincoln City 13 3
Aberaman
1920 Merthyr Town 3
Llanelly
Dundee Hibernian
Gala Fairydean

McCulloch, David (Dave) CF
b Hamilton 5/10/1911 d 1979
Caps: SLge 1/Scotland War 1/Scotland 7
Hamilton Amateurs
Hamilton Academical (trial)
Partick Thistle (trial)
Shotts United
Third Lanark
Heart of Midlothian
1935 1938 Brentford 117 85
1938 Derby County 31 16
1939 (Derby County) (3)
1946 Leicester City 4 2
Bath City
Waterford
Alloa Athletic

From To Apps Goal

McCulloch, J CH
1912 Blackpool 1

McCulloch, John Gordon (Gordon) IL/CF
b Hinckley 3/3/1888 d 1918
Ilkeston United
Ripley
Sutton Town
1911 Notts County 1
Sutton Town
1913 Lincoln City 11
Bentley Colliery

McCulloch, John Gray CF
b Rutherglen 15/7/1896
Vale of Clyde
Dumbarton
Rangers
Vale of Clyde
Dykehead
1921 Exeter City 1
Airdrieonians
New Bedford Whalers
J & P Coats (Rhode Island)

McCulloch, Michael Joseph (Mick) IL/RH
b Denny 26/4/1891 d 1973
Denny Hibernian
Falkirk
Heart of Midlothian
1922 1923 Nelson 49 8
1924 Chesterfield 3
1924 Bournemouth & Boscombe Ath 10 1
St Bernard's

McCulloch, Robert Gray (Bob) OL
b Glasgow 20/4/1900 d 1964
Auchinleck Talbot
Kilmarnock
Arbroath (loan)
1924 Bournemouth & Boscombe Ath 38 4
1925 Watford 14 2

McCulloch, Samuel Shaw (Sam) LH/CH
b Glasgow 21/5/1906
Petershill
1926 Blackburn Rovers 1
1930 Thames 20 1
1931 1935 Accrington Stanley 188 3
1936 Bury 0
Leyland Motors

McCulloch, Thomas LB/RB
b Strathblane 1868
Glasgow United
Partick Thistle
Rangers
1890 1892 West Bromwich Albion 46
Stirling

McCullough, Fred IL
b Liverpool
Liverpool White Star
1898 Barnsley 32 5
Liverpool White Star

McCullough, Keiller RH/IR/RB
b Larne 25/0/1905
Caps: IrLge 6/Ireland 5
Newington Rangers
Belfast Celtic
1935 1937 Manchester City 17 1
1937 1938 Northampton Town 35 1
1939 (Northampton Town) (3)

McCullough, Robert (Bob) IR
Radley (Gateshead)
1911 Sunderland 1
South Shields

McCullum, William David LB
b Paisley 1870
Celtic
1890 West Bromwich Albion 3
Dumbarton

McCurdy, William (Bill) LB/RB
b Bridgeton 4/9/1876
Vale of Clyde
1899 Luton Town 31
1900 1901 Nottingham Forest 11
New Brompton
Tottenham Hotspur
Luton Town

McCurley, John (Jock) IL/IR
b Kelty 17/3/1906 d 1969
Kelty Rangers
Third Lanark
1927 1929 Newcastle United 43 8
East Fife
Cowdenbeath

From To Apps Goal

McDade, Patrick CF
b Clydebank 22/11/1901 d 1974
Yoker Athletic
1926 Liverpool 0
1927 Exeter City 2
Morton
Yeovil & Petters United
1933 Clapton Orient 0

McDaid, John (Jock) IR
b Derry 1909
Derry City
Drumcondra
Heptonstall
1930 1931 Stoke City 4
Crusaders
Shelbourne

McDaniel, Edward RB
b Ireland
Belfast Celtic
1911 Leeds City 1

McDermid, Robert RB/LB
b Scotland 1870
Renton Thistle
Renton
Newcastle West End
Sunderland
Sunderland Albion
1890 Accrington 22
Burton Swifts
Stockton
1892 Lincoln City 2
Renton
Dundee Wanderers
1894 1896 Newcastle United 56 2
Hebburn Argyle
Warmley
South Shields

McDermott, Charles (Charlie) LB
b Goole 10/9/1912 d 1987
Goole Town
1932 1938 Bradford City 160 2
1939 (Bradford City) (1)

McDermott, John IL
Rossendale
1895 Sheffield United 3

McDermott, Joseph (Joe) IL/CF/OR
b Fencehouses
West Stanley
South Bank
Bishop Auckland
1932 Middlesbrough 0
1933 1938 Gateshead 104 28

McDermott, Thomas (Tommy) IR/IL
b Bridgeton 12/1/1878 d 1961
Rutherglen Rosebank
Cambuslang Hibernian
Dundee
Celtic
1903 1905 Everton 64 15
1905 1906 Chelsea 31 10
Dundee
1907 1908 Bradford City 8 1
1908 Gainsborough Trinity 1
Kilmarnock
1908 Bradford City 0
Dundee Hibernian
Anfield Royal
St Helens Recreation
Wirral Railways
Vale of Leven
Broxburn Shamrock
Clyde

McDevitt, William (Billy) IR/CH
b Belfast 5/1/1898 d 1966
Belfast United
1921 Swansea Town 5
Belfast United
1923 1924 Liverpool 4
1925 1929 Exeter City 125 9

McDiarmid, George CH/RH/LH
b Gartsherrie 1880 d 1946
Cambuslang
1900 Nottingham Forest 4
Northampton Town
Airdrieonians
1903 1905 Grimsby Town 64 1
1905 1906 Glossop 50 3
Clyde
1907 Grimsby Town 7

McDonagh, Charles RH
1931 Coventry City 0
1932 Southampton 0
1933 Bournemouth & Boscombe Ath 0
Kidderminster Harriers
1935 Cardiff City 2
Peterborough United

From To Apps Goal

McDonagh, Patrick (Pat) IL/IR
b Partick 5/11/1906
St Anthony's (Glasgow)
1927 Barnsley 9 2
1928 Nelson 5
Bangor City
Clydebank
Beith
Brechin City
Workington (trial)
Sligo Rovers

McDonald, Alexander (Alex) IR/IL
b Greenock 12/4/1878
Jarrow
1899 1900 Everton 23 6
Southampton
West Ham United
Portsmouth
Wellingborough
Luton Town
Croydon Common
Luton Town

McDonald, Alexander C (Alex) CF
b 1917
Haslingden Grange
1935 Accrington Stanley 2
Bacup Borough

McDonald, D RB/LB
1893 1894 Crewe Alexandra 2

McDonald, Daniel McIlroy (Roy) CH/RH
b East Wemyss 12/4/1894 d 1970
Wemyss Athletic
Kirkcaldy United
Dundee
1920 Tottenham Hotspur 0
1921 1922 Bradford Park Avenue 27

McDonald, David (Davie) IR
b Dundee 24/12/1872
Dundee Violet
Dundee Wanderers
Dundee
1895 Everton 0
1896 Leicester Fosse 16 5
Dundee
Millwall Athletic
Dundee Wanderers
Dundee

McDonald, Duncan RB
b Bo'ness
Duntocher Hibs
Glasgow Perthshire
Bo'ness
1909 1910 Woolwich Arsenal 26
Hartlepools United

McDonald, E RH
1910 Glossop 5

McDonald, Edward (Ted) LH/RH
b Newcastle-under-Lyme q4 1875 d 1938
Caps: FLge 1
Newcastle White Star
1894 1895 Burslem Port Vale 46 4
1896 Stoke 2
1898 1899 Burslem Port Vale 39 4
1899 1903 Notts County 139 3
Portsmouth

MacDonald, Elias OL
b Beswick 11/4/1898 d 1978
Ancoats Lads Club
1919 Derby County 0
Caerau
1921 Derby County 0
Burton All Saints
1923 Southampton 18
1924 Southend United 37 1
1925 Southport 42 5
1926 Doncaster Rovers 9
1926 1928 Barrow 97 13
Chorley
Ulverston Town
Morecambe
Chorley
Dalton Town
Rolls Royce Welfare

McDonald, George M (or John) IL
Glasgow Perthshire
Glasgow Ashfield
1895 Newcastle United 6 2
1899 Lincoln City 2

From To Apps Goal

McDonald, Hugh Lachlan GK
b Kilwinning 20/12/1881 d 1920
Ayr Westerlea
Maybole
Ayr Academicals
St Bernard's
Hearts o' Beath
Ayr
Hearts o' Beath
Ayr
Beith
1905 Woolwich Arsenal 2
Brighton & Hove Albion
1908 1909 Woolwich Arsenal 74
1910 1911 Oldham Athletic 41
1911 1912 Bradford Park Avenue 26
1912 Woolwich Arsenal 18
1913 Fulham 8
Bristol Rovers

McDonald, J CF
1896 Darwen 5 1

McDonald, James OL
Airdrieonians
1895 Bury 2

McDonald, James Alexander (Jimmy) LH/IL
b Peterhead 8/12/1883 d 1924
Inverness Citadel
Inverness Thistle
Aberdeen Favourites
St Bernard's
1906 1919 Bradford City 202 25
Raith Rovers
Wakefield City
Keighley Parkwood

McDonald, John IR
1900 Barnsley 1

McDonald, John RB
b Ayr 18/1/1883 d 1915
Arden Villa
Ayr
1903 Blackburn Rovers 1
1905 Leeds City 25
1906 Grimsby Town 16
Queen's Park Rangers
Mardy

McDonald, John OL/IR
b Kirkcaldy 6/1886 d 1943
Wemyss Harp
Vale of Wemyss
Raith Rovers
Rangers
1909 1911 Liverpool 76 4
1912 1913 Newcastle United 31 4
Raith Rovers

McDonald, John IR
b Glasgow 1894 d 1943
Linfield
Partick Thistle
Linfield
1919 1921 Blackburn Rovers 33 7
Dundee
Dundee United

McDonald, John (Jock) RB/LB
b Dykehead 4/1/1896
Caps: SLge 2
Shotts United
Barnsley 0
Motherwell
Airdrieonians
1920 1926 Everton 208
1927 1930 New Brighton 160 3
Connah's Quay & Shotton
Colwyn Bay United

McDonald, John Christopher (Jack) OL
b Maltby 27/8/1921 d 2007
1938 Wolverhampton Wanderers 2
1945 1947 Bournemouth & Boscombe Ath 80 36
1948 1951 Fulham 75 19
1952 Southampton 16 4
1953 1954 Southend United 28 6
Weymouth
Poole Town

From To Apps Goal

McDonald, Kenneth (Ken) CF
b Llanrwst 24/4/1898
Caps: WLge 1
Inverness Citadel
Inverness Clachnacuddin
Aberdeen
Caerau
1921 1922 Cardiff City 11 7
1922 1923 Manchester United 9 2
1923 1927 Bradford Park Avenue 145 135
1928 1929 Hull City 41 29
1929 Halifax Town 8 1
Inverness Caledonian
Coleraine
Walker Celtic
Spennymoor United
Walker Celtic
Blyth Spartans

McDonald, Murdoch (Murdo) IR/OR
b Redding 1/7/1901 d 1934
Grange Rovers (Grangemouth)
St Ninian's Thistle
Cowdenbeath
Bo'ness
Rangers
Bo'ness
1926 1929 Reading 65 13
1929 1930 Brighton & Hove Albion 10 1
Bo'ness
Bray Unknowns
Bo'ness

MacDonald, Robert James (Bob) LB/RB
b Inverness 25/2/1895 d 1971
Inverness Caledonian
1919 1924 Tottenham Hotspur 109
Heart of Midlothian (trial)
1927 1928 Clapton Orient 37

McDonald, Robert William (Roy) IL
b Penarth 11/7/1896 d 1970
Caps: Wales Amat
Lovells Athletic
Barry
1922 Newport County 9 1
Lovells Athletic

McDonald, Thomas (Tom) GK
b Longtown 28/11/1887 d 1947
High Blantyre Athletic
Bellshill Athletic
Blantyre Victoria
Motherwell
Portsmouth
Motherwell
Carlisle United
1911 1914 Bury 142
Tranmere Rovers
Rochdale

MacDonald, Thomas CF
b Portobello 1897
Musselburgh Comrades
Musselburgh Bruntonians
Portobello Thistle
Doncaster Rovers
Rossington Main
1921 Wigan Borough 1
Hibernian

McDonald, Thomas Henry (Tommy) IL
b Inverness 25/9/1895 d 1969
Inverness Thistle
Rangers
1920 1930 Newcastle United 341 100
1931 1932 York City 74 11
Goole Town
1934 York City 1
Usworth Colliery

McDonald, W LH
Darlington
1893 Walsall Town Swifts 2

McDonald, William LH
b Scotland 1883
Nithsdale Wanderers
Kilmarnock
Lanemark (loan)
Brighton & Hove Albion
1908 Leeds City 14
Nithsdale Wanderers
Lanemark

From To Apps Goal

McDonald, William (Billy) OR
b Quebec, County Durham q3 1892 d 1948
Craghead United
Shirebrook Moors Athletic
1911 1913 Hull City 69 5
Chesterfield Town
Durham City
1919 1922 Fulham 75 2
Shirebrook
1924 Durham City 6
Shirebrook
Alfreton Town
Hardwick Colliery
Grantham

Macdonald, William (Willie) IR/IL
b Coatbridge 9/7/1905 d 1979
Law Scotia
Dundee United
Broxburn United
Armadale
Airdrieonians
1931 1933 Manchester United 27 4
1934 1935 Tranmere Rovers 81 19
1936 1938 Coventry City 91 24
1939 Plymouth Argyle (2)

MacDonald, William James (Billy) IL
b Inverness 1877
Dundee
1898 1899 Derby County 23 4
1901 Stoke 9 3
Dundee
Montrose

McDonough, Francis John Bernard (Frank GK
b Haswell 24/12/1899 d 1976
Haswell
1922 Durham City 5
Horden Athletic
Wheatley Hill Colliery
Shotton Colliery Welfare
Annfield Plain
1930 Brentford 2
1931 Thames 26
1931 1933 Blackpool 82
1934 1937 Stockport County 132
Macclesfield
1939 Stockport County 0

McDonough, Francis Richard (Frank) LH
b Ponteland 27/2/1915 d 1976
Usworth Colliery
1934 Manchester City 0
Bromsgrove Rovers
1936 1937 Torquay United 23
1938 Watford 0
1945 Torquay United 0

MacDougall, Alexander Lindsay RH/LH
b Motherwell
Wishaw Juniors
1925 1927 Wolverhampton Wanderers 20 1
1928 Derby County 2

McDougall, Angus LH
b Glasgow 1891
Bathgate Linlithgow
1913 Lincoln City 9
Hartlepools United

McDougall, James (Jimmy) LH/IL/CH
b Port Glasgow 23/1/1904 d 1984
Caps: Scotland 2
Port Glasgow Athletic
Partick Thistle
1928 1937 Liverpool 339 12
South Liverpool

McDougall, John LH
b Hamilton 8/12/1900
Hamilton Intermediates
Larkhall Thistle
Motherwell
1925 Port Vale 0
1926 Accrington Stanley 1
Vale of Leven
New Bedford Whalers

McDougall, John (Jock) CH
b Port Glasgow 21/9/1901 d 1973
Caps: SLge 2/Scotland 1
Kilmacolm Amateurs
Port Glasgow Athletic
Airdrieonians
1929 1933 Sunderland 167 4
1934 1936 Leeds United 52

McDougall, John Lindsay (Jock) LB
b Buckhaven 24/2/1902 d 1976
Wellesley Juniors
Raith Rovers
Forfar Athletic (loan)
1932 1935 Aldershot 107 3

From To Apps Goal

McDougall, Laybourne RB/LB
b Tynemouth 12/5/1917 d 1994
1936 Derby County 0
1937 Carlisle United 3
1938 Preston North End 0
1939 Blackpool 0
1946 1948 Gateshead 60

McDougall, Robert (Bob) CF
b Glasgow 1894
St Cuthbert Wanderers
Dumfries
St Cuthbert Wanderers
1913 1914 Liverpool 7 1
Falkirk
Ayr United
Queen of the South
St Cuthbert Wanderers

McDowall, Leslie John (Les) CH/LH
b Gunga Pur, India 25/10/1912 d 1991
Glentyne Thistle
1934 1937 Sunderland 13
1937 1948 Manchester City 117 8
1939 (Manchester City) (3)
1949 Wrexham 3

McDowell, A RB
1893 Ardwick 4

McDowell, John LB
b Derry
Londonderry Distillery
1921 Accrington Stanley (trial) 1
Londonderry Distillery

McDuff, J OL
1894 Crewe Alexandra 1

McDuff, M IR
1892 Crewe Alexandra 3 2

Mace, Fred GK
b New Mills q4 1895 d 1962
Godley Athletic
Copley Celtic
1922 Stalybridge Celtic 1
1925 1926 Nelson 8
Macclesfield

Mace, Robert Stanley (Stan) CH
b Cleethorpes 2/12/1895 d 1974
Grimsby Rovers
1926 Sheffield United 4
1927 Brighton & Hove Albion 5

McEachran, David OL
b Clydebank 5/12/1903 d 1983
Brown's Welfare
Yoker Rob Roy
Clydebank
Vale of Leven
Clydebank
1925 Preston North End (trial) 1
Fall River Marksmen
Boston Wonder Workers
Boston Bears
New Bedford Whalers
Providence Gold Bugs
Montreal Carsteel
Beith
St Johnstone (trial)
Linfield

McEachran, Grant LB
b Barrow q2 1894 d 1966
Barrow
1919 1921 Grimsby Town 66
1923 Doncaster Rovers 16
1924 Halifax Town 1

MacEachrane, Roderick John (Roddy) LH
b Inverness 3/2/1877 d 1952
Inverness Thistle
Thames Ironworks
1902 1913 Woolwich Arsenal 313

McEleny, Charles Richard (Charlie) CH/RH
b Raymoghy 3/3/1873 d 1908
Greenock Volunteers
Abercorn
Celtic
1895 Burnley 15 1
Celtic
1898 New Brighton Tower 31
1899 Aston Villa 1
Swindon Town
Brentford
Morton

McEnaney, Francis Joseph (Joe) IL
b Gateshead 2/6/1911 d 1982
1932 Watford 0
1933 Northampton Town 0
Shildon
1934 Darlington 1

From To Apps Goal

McEwan, Marshall OL
b Rutherglen 1885 d 1966
Caps: IrLge 10
1903 1904 Blackpool 44 1
1904 1909 Bolton Wanderers 152 13
1909 1910 Chelsea 33 3
Linfield
Fleetwood

McEwan, Robert (Bob) LB
b Edinburgh 1881
Edinburgh Rosebery
St Bernard's
1903 1904 Bury 35
Rangers
Heart of Midlothian
1905 Chelsea 19
1906 1907 Glossop 55 1
Queen's Park Rangers
Dundee

McEwan, William (Billy) OR/IR
b Glasgow 29/8/1914 d 1991
Petershill
1938 1949 Queen's Park Rangers 96 17
1939 (Queen's Park Rangers) (1)
1949 1950 Leyton Orient 21 3
Gravesend & Northfleet

McEwen, James (Jimmy 'Punch') LB/RH
b Bootle 16/10/1872 d 1942
Lansdowne
1892 Bootle 14
Liverpool South End
1893 Everton 0
1897 Luton Town 30 1
1898 1899 Glossop North End 54 1
1900 1902 Bury 102
Luton Town
Norwich City
1911 Glossop 2

Macey, Frank Walter IL
b Brighton 6/11/1897 d 1972
Army
Kingstonian
1925 Plymouth Argyle 1
Kingstonian

McFadden, John RH
b Glengarnock 1891
Barrow
1913 1914 Lincoln City 19
Barrow

McFadden, Richard IL
b Cambuslang 1890 d 1916
Blyth Spartans
Wallsend Park Villa
1911 1914 Clapton Orient 137 66

McFadyen, Charles (Charlie) RB
b Inellan 1885 d 1947
1907 1913 Preston North End 164 1
1914 Everton 0

McFadyen, Ian CF
b Overtown 20/11/1909
Lanarkshire Steel
Motherwell
Clydebank
Dunfermline Athletic
1932 Bury 6 2

McFadyen, William (Willie) CF/IR
b Overtown 23/6/1904 d 1971
Caps: SLge 1/Scotland 2
Wishaw YMCA
Motherwell
Bo'ness (loan)
Clyde (loan)
1936 1937 Huddersfield Town 48 18
1939 Clapton Orient (3)

MacFarlane, Alexander (Sandy) IL/CF/OL
b Dundee 7/1878 d 1945
Caps: SLge 3/Scotland 5
Baillieston
Airdrieonians
1896 Woolwich Arsenal 5
Airdrieonians
1898 1901 Newcastle United 84 17
Dundee
1913 1914 Chelsea 4

McFarlane, Archibald E RB
b Scotland d 1902
1894 1895 Lincoln City 51
Glossop North End
1897 Lincoln City 10
Gravesend United
Sheppey United

From To Apps Goal

McFarlane, David IR
b 1890
Kirkintilloch Harp
1913 Lincoln City 7 2

MacFarlane, Dugald (Doug) IL/CF/OR
b Barrow 24/8/1880 d 1965
Barrow
1903 1907 Burnley 121 35
1908 1909 Tottenham Hotspur 21 2
Barrow

McFarlane, John IR
b Shettleston 1906
Cambuslang Rangers
Shawfield Juniors
Aberdeen
1928 1929 Liverpool 2
1930 1931 Halifax Town 65 15
1932 Northampton Town 3 1
Kidderminster Harriers
1935 1936 Darlington 18 1
Kidderminster Harriers
Worcester City
Bath City

MacFarlane, John LH/RH
b Bathgate 21/11/1899 d 1956
Caps: SLge 4
Denbeath Star
Wellesley Juniors
Cowdenbeath (trial)
Raith Rovers (trial)
Celtic
1929 1932 Middlesbrough 95
Shelbourne
Dunfermline Athletic

McFarlane, Peter LB
b Motherwell
Carfin
Motherwell
1894 Leicester Fosse 1

MacFarlane, Robert RB
St Mirren
1893 Blackburn Rovers 2
Nelson
1894 Blackburn Rovers 0
1894 Everton 0
1894 Liverpool 0

MacFarlane, Robert (Rab) GK
b Greenock 14/5/1876 d 1943
Caps: SLge 1/Scotland 1
Greenock Rosebery
Morton
Third Lanark
1897 Everton 9
East Stirlingshire
Bristol St George
New Brompton
1900 Grimsby Town 18
Celtic
1902 Middlesbrough 18
Aberdeen
Motherwell

McFarlane, Robert Robertson (Bobby) LH/RH
b Bo'ness 12/10/1913 d 1971
1936 Arsenal 0
1937 1947 Doncaster Rovers 131 4
1939 (Doncaster Rovers) (3)
Boston United

MacFarlane, Ronald Duff (Ron) OR
b Dundee 28/7/1912 d 1984
1937 Plymouth Argyle 0
CA Paris
1938 Barrow 1

MacFarlane, Thomas LB
b Scotland 1872
Caps: SLge 1
Hibernian
1898 1899 Burslem Port Vale 53
1900 Middlesbrough 2

McFarlane, William IR
1892 Burslem Port Vale 4

McFerran, Herbert John CF
b South Shields q4 1900
1921 1922 Darlington 4 3
1923 Durham City 0

McFetteridge, David OL/LH
b 1870
Cowlairs
1891 1892 Bolton Wanderers 25 5
Cowlairs
1894 Newton Heath 1
Stockport County

From To Apps Goal

McFettridge, William (Bill) RH/LH
b Govan 1862
Thornliebank
Padiham
1888 1892 Burnley 85 2

McGann, James Langley (Jimmy) GK
b Wilmslow q3 1908
Wilmslow
1929 1933 Stockport County 54
1934 Reading 14
Scarborough

McGarr, John George IL
b Dornock 17/10/1915 d 2003
1936 1937 Carlisle United 5 3

McGarry, Arthur Martin LH/RH
b Burslem q3 1898
1919 1920 Port Vale 33
1921 1922 Reading 62
1923 1924 Rochdale 42 1
1925 Hartlepools United (trial) 0

McGarry, Daniel (Danny) OL
b Howwood 9/2/1911
Port Glasgow Juniors
Dunfermline Athletic
Arthurlie
Morton
1938 Barnsley 41 12
1939 (Barnsley) (3) (1)
Morton
Stirling Albion

McGarry, Thomas (Tommy) CF/IR
b Heworth 28/9/1918 d 1983
Washington Colliery
1937 Newcastle United 0
1938 Hartlepools United 20 12
1938 Bradford Park Avenue 9 2
1939 (Bradford Park Avenue) (2) (1)
North Shields

McGeachan, Andrew IR
b Glasgow 1882 d 1943
Cambuslang Hibernian
Hibernian
1904 1905 Bradford City 34 9
Clyde

McGeachan, James (Jimmy) CH/LH
b Edinburgh 1871 d 1903
Hibernian
1894 1897 Bolton Wanderers 69 5
1897 Stoke 4
Hibernian
1899 Bolton Wanderers 0
Belfast Celtic

McGeachan, John IL
b Neilston 1892
1910 1911 Glossop 8

McGee, J IR
1895 Rotherham Town 7

McGee, J OL
Stalybridge Rovers
1898 Barnsley 3

McGee, John (Jock) CH/RB/LB
b Rothesay 13/7/1896
Bute Comrades
1920 Leeds United 0
Harrogate AFC
1922 1926 Hull City 70

McGeoch, Craig Archibald (Archie) CF
b Dunblane 1876
Dunblane
1897 1898 Woolwich Arsenal 35 13
Dundee
Dunblane
Portsmouth

McGeorge, Robert William (Bob) CH
b Islington q2 1876
Clapton Orient
Leytonstone
West Ham United
Finchley
1905 Clapton Orient 14
Finchley

From To Apps Goal

McGhee, George Dilworth IR
b Southwell q3 1883 d 1944
Newark
1904 Doncaster Rovers 11 3
1904 Nottingham Forest 0
1905 Gainsborough Trinity 2
Ipswich Town
Bitterne Guild
Southampton
Bitterne Guild
Vampires
Pirates
Southampton Cambridge

McGhee, (Dr) Samuel Wilson (Wilson) OL
Glasgow University
1921 Rochdale 2

McGhie, Alexander (Alex) OR/OL
b Liverpool
Kirkdale
Liscard Central
Ashton Town
1910 1919 Blackburn Rovers 23 3

McGhie, Joseph (Joe) CH
b Kilbirnie 22/3/1884 d 1976
Vale of Glengarnock Strollers
1906 1907 Sunderland 41
1908 Sheffield United 6
Brighton & Hove Albion
Stalybridge Celtic

McGibbon, Charles Edward (Charlie) CF
b Portsmouth 21/4/1880 d 1954
Royal Artillery
Eltham
1905 Woolwich Arsenal 0
Leyton
New Brompton
Crystal Palace
Southampton
1909 Woolwich Arsenal 4 3
Leyton
Reading
Southampton

McGibbon, Douglas (Doug) CF
b Netley 24/2/1919 d 2002
Air Service Training
1938 1946 Southampton 13 9
1946 1947 Fulham 42 18
1948 1950 Bournemouth & Boscombe Ath 103 65
Lovells Athletic

McGibbons, Terence (Terry) OR
b Irvine
Irvine Meadow
Galston (loan)
Kilmarnock
St Mirren
Partick Thistle
Ayr United
1938 Preston North End 22 2
Ayr United

McGiffen, James OL
b Stockton 30/1/1904 d 1929
Stockton
1927 1928 Darlington 23 4

McGill, John William LB
b Gateshead 10/11/1897 d 1972
1931 Carlisle United 16
Consett

McGill, Patrick IL
b Baillieston 1911
Baillieston
Clyde
Maryhill Hibernian
Heart of Midlothian
Raith Rovers (loan)
1936 1937 Exeter City 34 1
Distillery

McGill, Thomas IL/IR
b Wallsend 28/7/1901 d 1979
St Luke's
Scotswood
1921 Ashington 6
Wallsend
1922 Cardiff City 0
Scotswood
Shildon
Kettering Town
West Stanley
Ebbw Vale
1927 Charlton Athletic 5
Lovells Athletic

From To Apps Goal

McGillivray, Charles OR
b Kinlochleven 5/7/1912 d 1986
Dreghorn Juniors
Ayr United
Celtic
1933 Manchester United 8
Motherwell
Dundee
Dundee United
Stirling Albion
Arbroath

McGillivray, John (Jimmy) CH
b Broughton 1889
Berry's Association
1907 1908 Manchester United 3
Southport Central
Stoke
Dartford

McGinn, Alexander (Sandy) RH/IL
b New Cumnock 10/10/1891
Lanemark
1913 1919 Bradford City 5
1919 1924 Blackpool 134 2
1925 1926 Halifax Town 7
Great Harwood

McGinn, Hugh OR/CF
b Hewood 17/8/1896 d 1937
Glengarnock Vale
1923 Arsenal 0
1924 1925 Charlton Athletic 11
Dundee
Portadown
Glentoran

McGinn, James IL
Baillieston
Mossend Celtic
Celtic
Airdrieonians
1894 Bolton Wanderers 15 3
Airdrieonians

McGinnigle, Hugh CH
b Bargeddie 1/7/1906
Minerva Hibs
Falkirk
1930 1936 Luton Town 159 2
1937 Aldershot 2

McGlen, James (Jim) OR
b Sedgefield 17/1/1903 d 1986
Stakford United
1926 Hartlepools United 20 3
Bedlington United

McGloughlin, Francis J (Frank) RB
b Dublin 4/7/1898
Olympia
Shelbourne
Pontypridd
1921 1925 Bradford Park Avenue 77 1
1926 Bristol Rovers 0

McGorian, Isaac Moor (Ike) LH/RH
b Silksworth 19/10/1901
Thornley Albion
Silksworth Colliery
1925 1927 Sunderland 20 1
1928 Notts County 1
1929 Carlisle United 3
Shotton Colliery
Thurnscoe Victoria
Thurnscoe St Hilda's

McGough, Joseph (Joe) IR
b Tow Law 27/10/1909 d 1996
Middle Dock
1932 1937 Reading 142 50
1938 Chester 34 4
1939 (Chester) (3) (2)
1945 Southport 0
Runcorn

McGough, Richard CH
b Carlisle q3 1892 d 1917
Carlisle United
1914 Newcastle United 2

McGourty, John IR/IL
b Fauldhouse 10/7/1912 d 1999
Caps: LoI 1
Fauldhouse St John's
Partick Thistle
Edinburgh City (loan)
1932 1933 Everton 15 2
Hamilton Academical
Waterford
1938 Ipswich Town 1

From To Apps Goal

McGovern, John Thomas (Tom) IR/IL
b Old Kilpatrick 6/2/1901
Clydebank
1921 Millwall Athletic 0
Clydebank
1924 Bristol City 3 1
1925 Merthyr Town 28 8
Sheppey United
Queen of the South
1927 Torquay United 18 1
Sheppey United
Northfleet
Sittingbourne
Devon General Bus Co
Paignton Town

McGovern, Thomas (Tom) RH
b Glasgow
Leith Athletic
Halifax Town
Brentford
1920 Queen's Park Rangers 2

McGowan, Duncan OR
b Renton 1880
Renton
1901 Barnsley 3
Clyde

McGowan, Robert Nivison CF
b Sanquhar 2/6/1908 d 1984
Nithsdale Wanderers
Kello Rovers
Carlisle United
1928 Crewe Alexandra 0
Rangers
Kilmarnock (loan)
1932 Bournemouth & Boscombe Ath 6 1
Queen of the South
Ballymena
Dunfermline Athletic
Kilmarnock

McGrae, Joseph Russell (Joe) LH
b Kirkdale 24/10/1903 d 1975
Liverpool Royal Albion
1924 Everton 0
1925 Tranmere Rovers 8
1926 1928 Norwich City 114 3
1929 Bradford City 1
1930 Clapton Orient 4
1931 Halifax Town 32
Macclesfield
Littlewoods
Hyde United

McGraffin, George IR
1924 Halifax Town 3

McGrahan, John RH/CH/LH
b Leadgate 3/3/1898 d 1961
Leadgate Park
1922 Lincoln City 25 1
1922 1923 Wigan Borough 34 1
Boston Town
1925 1926 Lincoln City 26
Scarborough

McGrail, Daniel (Danny) IR
b Liverpool 25/10/1913 d 1982
St Sylvester's Boys Club
Llanrwst
Colwyn Bay United
Stalybridge Celtic
Winsford United
1934 Southport 3
Winsford United
1935 Southport 0
Stalybridge Celtic
Northwich Victoria

McGran, William (Willie) CH
b Lochwinnoch 21/4/1879 d 1922
Lochwinnoch North British
1902 Barnsley 7
Beith
Rangers
Airdrieonians
Hibernian
Glasgow Ashfield

McGrath, James (Jimmy) LH/OR/OL
b Washington 4/3/1907 d 1950
Ryhope Colliery
Washington Colliery
1928 1931 Cardiff City 33
1932 1933 Port Vale 66 11
1934 Notts County 11 3
1934 1937 Bradford Park Avenue 83 2

McGreevy, William James IR
b Fleetwood 11/11/1899 d 1981
Fleetwood Athletic
Fleetwood
1921 Nelson 3 1

From To Apps Goal

McGregor, Andrew Clark OR
b Wishaw 1867
Wishaw Thistle
1890 1892 Notts County 44 11
Notts Rovers

McGregor, George IR
b Saltcoats
Saltcoats Victoria
St Mirren
1929 Sunderland 1
Glasgow Benburb
1930 Norwich City (trial) 0
India of Inchinnan

McGregor, James RH
b Scotland
Queen's Park
Vale of Leven
1904 1906 Grimsby Town 93 3
1907 1909 Glossop 77 1

McGregor, John RB
b Darlington 2/8/1900 d 1993
Royal Navy
1930 1931 Gillingham 68 2
1932 Crystal Palace 4

McGregor, Robert CF
1913 Sheffield Wednesday 6 2
Portsmouth

McGregor, William (Bill) OL
b Levenbank 4/1904 d 1998
Levenbank Amateurs
Dumbarton Harp
Duntocher Hibs
1925 Coventry City 9 1
Burton Town
Stourbridge
Hinckley Town
Rugby Town
Leamington Town

McGrogan, Felix (Frank) OL
b Dumbarton 27/7/1914
Duntocher Hibs
Maryhill Hibernian
Renfrew Juniors
1935 Blackburn Rovers 4 1
Dunfermline Athletic
Cumbernauld United
Falkirk
Kilmarnock
Dumbarton
Third Lanark

McGrory, Robert Gerard (Bob) RB
b Erskine 17/10/1891 d 1954
Bishopton Boys Brigade
Houston St Fillan's
Cumbernauld United
Kilbarchan Athletic
Dumbarton
Partick Thistle (loan)
1920 Burnley 3
1920 1934 Stoke 479

McGuffie, A IL
1898 New Brighton Tower 2

McGuigan, Andrew (Andy) IL
b Newton Stewart 24/2/1878 d 1948
Newton Stewart
Hibernian
1900 1901 Liverpool 31 14
1903 Middlesbrough 1
Southport Central
Accrington Stanley
1906 Burslem Port Vale 0
1907 Bristol City 0
Barrow
Exeter City

McGuigan, Charles (Charlie) OR
b Thornley q1 1901 d 1949
Wheatley Hill Ramblers
Houghton Rovers
Wheatley Hill Alliance
1923 Newcastle United 0
1924 Brentford 2
Wheatley Hill Colliery
Weymouth
1926 Barrow 10
Sheppey United
Peterborough & Fletton United
Shildon Colliery Welfare
Horden Colliery Welfare (trial)
Thornley Colliery Welfare
Thornley St Godric's

McGuinness, H CF
1888 Bolton Wanderers 1 1

From To Apps Goal

McGuinness, William (Billy) IL
b Workington 30/11/1913 d 1978
1935 Blackpool 0
1936 Barnsley 1
Distillery

McGuire, Archibald Cook (Archie) IL
b Larkhall 27/12/1901
Pembroke Dock
Dundee
1927 Barrow 2

McGuire, James RH/LH
b Wallsend 10/12/1883
North Shields Athletic
1903 1904 Barnsley 34
North Shields Athletic
1906 1912 Sheffield United 61 1
North Shields

McGuire, James P (Jim) CH
b Edinburgh 1911 d 1974
Brooklyn Wanderers
Celtic
1932 1935 Northampton Town 70
St Mary's Celtic (Brooklyn)
Brooklyn Wanderers

McGuire, John CF/IL/LH
b Darlington q4 1900
Darlington Railway Athletic
Cockfield
1925 Charlton Athletic 6
1926 1927 Wigan Borough 33 14
1927 Nelson 20 2
1928 1929 Darlington 42 7

McGuire, Patrick (Paddy) RB/LB
b Manchester q2 1889 d 1916
Hurst
1912 1914 Manchester City 15

McGurk, Francis Reynolds OR
b Eddlewood 15/1/1909 d 1978
Caps: Scotland 1
Blantyre Celtic
Clyde
1933 1934 Birmingham 19 3
1935 Bristol City 3
Whittaker Ellis

McHale, John CH
b Maryhill
Maryhill Hibernian
Aberdeen
St Johnstone (loan)
Falkirk
Shelbourne
Keith
1932 1933 Doncaster Rovers 53
1934 Crewe Alexandra 7

Machant, JH GK
Eckington Red Rose
1909 Gainsborough Trinity 2

McHardie, D CH
Glossop North End
1897 Blackpool 27
Warmley

McHardy, G CH
b Scotland
Dundee Strathmore
Dundee
1892 Grimsby Town 3

Machent, Arthur RB/RH
b Chesterfield 22/6/1910 d 1996
Chesterfield Church Bible Class
1929 1931 Chesterfield 3
Buxton
Macclesfield

Machin, Peter IR
b 1883
Wallsend Park Villa
1905 1906 Lincoln City 54 21

Machin, Prestwood Udall RB
b Nottingham 1/7/1892 d 1948
Halifax Place Mission
1911 Nottingham Forest 1
1913 Notts County 1

Machin, WH RH/LH
1900 1903 Burslem Port Vale 8

From To Apps Goal

McHugh, John (Jock) GK
b Hamilton 13/8/1909 d 1966
Strathclyde
Burnbank Athletic
Dundee United
Montrose (loan)
1932 Portsmouth 3
1933 1938 Watford 38
1935 Southend United (loan) 0
1939 (Watford) (3)

McIlvanney, Michael RH/LH
b Glasgow 25/11/1902 d 1972
Kirkintilloch Rob Roy
Broxburn United
1925 1926 Coventry City 24 2
Thames

McIlvenny, James Robert (Jimmy) IL/IR/LH
b Tynemouth 11/5/1892 d 1970
Willington Athletic
South Shields
1910 1921 Bradford City 132 26
1922 Blackpool 16 4

McIlvenny, Patrick (Paddy) OR/CF
b Belfast 18/11/1900 d 1955
Caps: LoI 1/Ireland 1
Highfield
Distillery
1924 Cardiff City 5 2
1925 Sheffield Wednesday 1
Shelbourne
1928 Northampton Town 8 2
Boston Town
Hinckley United

McIlwane, John (Johnny) CH/CF
b Bonnybridge 12/6/1904 d 1980
Caps: SLge 1/WLge 1
Irvine Victoria
Falkirk
1927 1929 Portsmouth 56 5
1930 1931 Southampton 46 9
Llanelly
1933 1936 Southampton 81 9

McIlwraith, Francis (Frank) LB
b Kilkerran 1890
Ardeer Thistle
1911 1912 Bradford City 5
Stevenston United
Barrow

McInally, Thomas Bernard (Tommy) IL
b Partick 18/4/1900 d 1955
Caps: Scotland 2
St Mungo's Academy
Croy Celtic
St Anthony's (Glasgow)
Barrhead
Rangers (trial)
Celtic
Third Lanark
Celtic
1928 1929 Sunderland 35 3
1929 Bournemouth & Boscombe Ath 10 1
Morton
Derry City
Coleraine
Armadale
Nithsdale Wanderers

McInnes, Angus IR
St Bernard's
1897 1902 Burnley 38 4
Padiham
King's Park

McInnes, James Sloan (Jimmy) LH
b Ayr 17/2/1912 d 1965
Glasgow University
Ardeer Recreation
Third Lanark
1937 1938 Liverpool 45 1
1939 (Liverpool) (3) (1)
Distillery

McInnes, Thomas (Tom) IR/IL
b Glasgow 22/3/1870 d 1939
Caps: FLge 2
1889 1891 Notts County 54 14
Rangers
1892 Notts County 19 6
Third Lanark
1894 1895 Everton 42 18
1897 1899 Luton Town 93 21
Bedford Queens Engineers

From To Apps Goal

McInnes, Thomas (Tom) OL/OR
b Glasgow 29/8/1870 d 1937
Caps: SLge 1/Scotland 1
Dalmuir Thistle
Cowlairs
Newcastle East End
Newcastle West End
Clyde
1892 1898 Nottingham Forest 168 45
Bristol Rovers
1900 1902 Lincoln City 79 20
Port Glasgow Athletic

McInnes, William A (Willie) OL
b Beith
Kilbirnie Ladeside
Arthurlie
1929 Luton Town 22 1

McInroy, Albert GK
b Walton-le-Dale 23/4/1901 d 1985
Caps: England 1
Upper Walton
Coppull Central
1921 Preston North End 0
High Walton United
Great Harwood
Leyland
1923 1929 Sunderland 215
1929 1933 Newcastle United 143
1934 Sunderland 0
1935 1936 Leeds United 67
1937 1938 Gateshead 71

McIntosh, Alexander (Alex) IR
b Dunfermline 14/4/1916 d 1965
St Mirren
Hearts o' Beath
Folkestone
1937 1946 Wolverhampton Wanderers 44 7
1939 (Wolverhampton Wanderers) (3)
1946 1947 Birmingham City 23 4
1947 1948 Coventry City 20 3
Kidderminster Harriers
Bilston United

McIntosh, Angus Munro IR/CF/IL
b Birkenhead q3 1884
Inverness Thistle
1905 1908 Sunderland 40 9
1908 1909 Bury 36 13
Aberdeen
Buckie Thistle

McIntosh, George CH
b Govan 1899
Govan YMCA
Renfrew Juniors
Hibernian
Solway Star
Workington
1923 Exeter City 16
1924 Accrington Stanley 17 1
Boston Town

McIntosh, James Boyd LH/CH
b Glasgow 25/5/1886 d 1959
Wellwood Juveniles
Petershill
Reading (trial)
Glasgow Perthshire
Third Lanark
Aberdeen
Celtic
1909 Leeds City 0
1910 1913 Hull City 92 2
Scots Guards
Heart of Midlothian
Hibernian
Dumbarton (trial)

McIntosh, James McLauchlan (Jimmy) CF/OL
b Dumfries 5/4/1918 d 2000
Caps: IrLge 1
Droylsden
1935 1937 Blackpool 5
1937 1945 Preston North End 27 3
1946 1948 Blackpool 66 22
1948 1950 Everton 58 19
Distillery

McIntosh, John W (Jack) CF
Pallion Star
Tow Law Town
1896 Sunderland 1
Tow Law Town
1897 Sunderland 1
South Shields

McIntosh, Richard James OL
b Kingston 21/12/1916 d 1971
Caps: England Sch/England Amat
1934 1945 Barrow 42 9
1939 (Barrow) (2)

From To Apps Goal

McIntosh, Robert Anderson RH/CH
b Dundee 1/8/1892 d 1952
Thistle
Dundee Fairfield
Dundee
Motherwell (loan)
Motherwell
Dundee
1920 1923 Newcastle United 101 2
1924 Stockport County 8

MacIntosh, Stanley Wilson GK
b Brighton 26/11/1905 d 1976
London Caledonians
1930 Chelsea 1

McIntosh, Thomas OR
b Scotland
1892 1893 Sheffield Wednesday 9 1

McIntosh, William IL
b Scotland
Glasgow Meat Market
Clydebank
Strathclyde
St Mirren
Clyde
1924 Blackpool 1

McIntosh, William Walker OL
b Hutchestown 12/2/1884
Rutherglen Glencairn
Ardrossan Winton Rovers
1911 Fulham 6
Clydebank
St Mirren

McIntyre, Edward Patrick (Teddy) RH/LH/CF
b Newcastle q4 1881 d 1928
Caxton (Newcastle)
Allendale Park
1902 1904 Newcastle United 6 1
Fulham
Plymouth Argyle
Portsmouth
1910 Woolwich Arsenal 0
South Shields
West Stanley
Hartlepools United
West Stanley
South Shields Parkside
Ashington
Gateshead

McIntyre, James IL
1904 Doncaster Rovers 8

McIntyre, James Alfred (Jim) IL
b Darlaston 1881 d 1954
Witton
Darlaston
Wednesbury Old Athletic
Walsall
1902 Notts County 9 3
Northampton Town
Reading
Coventry City
Dudley & Bournbrook

McIntyre, John McGregor (Johnny) IL/IR/LH
b Glasgow 4/1/1895 d 1974
Denny Athletic
Partick Thistle
Vale of Leven (loan)
St Mirren (loan)
1919 Fulham 25 9
1919 1921 Sheffield Wednesday 67 36
1921 1927 Blackburn Rovers 175 38
1927 Blackpool 6 2
Chorley

McIntyre, John McMutrie (Johnny) RH
b Glasgow 19/10/1898 d 1974
Glasgow Perthshire
Stenhousemuir
1921 1931 Derby County 349 9
1931 1932 Chesterfield 58
Derby Co-op Welfare

McIntyre, Peter CH/OR
b Glenbuck 11/1875 d 1938
1895 Preston North End 0
Rangers
Abercorn
Wigan County
1898 1900 Preston North End 87 5
1901 Sheffield United 3
Hamilton Academical
Portsmouth
Hamilton Academical
Abercorn

From To Apps Goal

MacIntyre, Thomas Anderson (Tom) OR
b Dumfries 27/5/1894 d 1976
Carlisle United
1920 Exeter City 5
1921 Crewe Alexandra 23 5
1922 Wigan Borough 5 1
1923 Chesterfield 4

McIver, William (Willie) GK
b Whittle-le-Woods q1 1877 d 1934
Whittle-le-Woods
1898 Darwen 23
1901 1907 Blackburn Rovers 126
Brentford
Hartlepools United
1911 1912 Stockport County 68
Darwen
Nelson
Blackburn Trinity

McJennett, John James (Jack) RB
b Cardiff q1 1906 d 1954
1929 1931 Cardiff City 5
1932 Exeter City 0

Mack, S CH
Notts Rangers
Sheffield United
1892 Crewe Alexandra 1

McKane, Joseph LH
b Scotland
Clydebank
Newcastle East End
1893 1894 Newcastle United 41
Blyth

Mackay, Alexander (Alex) GK
b Darlington 3/8/1913 d 1984
Albert Hill Juniors
Darlington Railway Athletic
1929 Newcastle United (trial) 0
Crook Town
Stanley United
1930 Bolton Wanderers 0
1932 Bournemouth & Boscombe Ath 0
1933 Southport 1
Somerset Constabulary

McKay, Colin Campbell RH/CF/IL
b Portobello 24/8/1896 d 1978
Denbeath Star
Cowdenbeath
Raith Rovers
Heart of Midlothian
1919 Sheffield Wednesday 12 3
1920 1921 Huddersfield Town 18 2
1922 1923 Bradford City 26 4
Aberavon

McKay, D IL
1902 Bolton Wanderers 7

Mackay, Donald Morgan (Morgan) CF
b Edinburgh 23/6/1909
Clerwood Amateurs
Queen's Park
1930 Plymouth Argyle 0
1932 Northampton Town 0
Dundee
1935 Barnsley 1
Queen of the South
Leith Athletic (trial)

MacKay, G LH
1893 Middlesbrough Ironopolis 5

Mackay, Hugh Graham GK
1893 Rotherham Town 8
1893 Burslem Port Vale 16

McKay, J GK
1892 Bootle 1

McKay, James Alexander (Jim) CF/IL
b Custom House q2 1901 d 1997
Custom House
Dartford
1922 1923 Fulham 17 5
1924 1925 Clapton Orient 8 3
Aldershot Town

McKay, John (Jack) OL
b Hebburn 1885
Hebburn Argyle
1910 1911 Birmingham 19 2
Blyth Spartans

From To Apps Goal

McKay, John Reid (Jock) IL/IR
b Glasgow 1/11/1898 d 1970
Caps: Scotland 1
Townhead Benburb
St Anthony's (Glasgow)
Celtic
1921 1926 Blackburn Rovers 150 46
1926 1933 Middlesbrough 104 18
1935 Bolton Wanderers 0
Hibernian

McKay, Kenneth (Kenny) IR
b Wishaw 1877
1896 1897 Sheffield United 26 5
Tottenham Hotspur
Thames Ironworks
Wishaw United
Fulham
Royal Albert

Mackay, Norman RH/IR
b Edinburgh 26/5/1902
Edinburgh Royal
Leith Amateurs
Gala Fairydean
Hibernian
St Bernard's
Lochgelly United
Broxburn United
1923 Aston Villa 2
Lovells Athletic
Clydebank
Yoker Athletic
1927 1933 Plymouth Argyle 227 14
1934 Southend United 32
Clydebank

McKay, Norman IR
b Poole q3 1905
1927 Bournemouth & Boscombe Ath 1

McKay, P CF
1898 Bolton Wanderers 3

McKay, Robert (Bobby) IR
b Govan 2/9/1900 d 1977
Caps: SLge 1/Scotland 1
Parkhead White Rose
Vale of Clyde
Parkhead Juniors
Neilston Victoria
Morton
Rangers
1926 1928 Newcastle United 62 22
1928 1930 Sunderland 49 17
1930 1931 Charlton Athletic 49 8
1932 1934 Bristol Rovers 91 17
1935 Newport County 16 3

Mackay, Thomas (Tommy) IL
b Wishaw
Wishaw YMCA
St Mirren
1925 Brighton & Hove Albion 1
Aldershot

McKay, Thomas Galloway (Tommy) IL/IR
b Possilpark 16/7/1910 d 1988
Dreghorn
Glasgow Ashfield
Lyon Street Church
1930 1931 Nottingham Forest 4
Queen of the South
1936 1938 Southport 68 5
Wigan Athletic

McKay, W OL
1891 Accrington 3

McKay, William (Willie) IL
b Edinburgh
Heart of Midlothian
1888 Burnley 14 7
Newcastle West End
St Bernard's
Raith Rovers

McKay, William CF
b Scotland
Rangers
1895 Newcastle United 18 6

McKay, William (Billy) LH/IR
b West Benhar 24/8/1906
Shotts Battlefield
East Stirlingshire
Hamilton Academical
1929 1933 Bolton Wanderers 104 17
1933 1938 Manchester United 169 15
1939 (Manchester United) (2)
Stalybridge Celtic

From To Apps Goal

Mackay, William Alexander (Bill) OR
b Togston 19/3/1910 d 2001
Broomhill
Bedlington United
Ashington
1930 Gateshead 0
Pegswood United
1932 Sheffield Wednesday 0
1933 Tranmere Rovers 7 1
Linfield
1935 1936 Swansea Town 14 3
1937 Hull City 12
Ashington
Amble

McKay, William Boynes (Billy) RB
b Alves 24/8/1896
Elgin City
Darwen
1921 1923 Barrow 97
Mid-Rhondda United
Elgin City
(Canada)

McKechnie, ? OR
1898 Gainsborough Trinity 5 1

McKechnie, James OR
b Bonhill 15/4/1899
Duntocher Hibs
Helensburgh
1920 Luton Town 1
Mid-Rhondda United
1921 Manchester City (trial) 0
Partick Thistle
Raith Rovers
Helensburgh
1923 Reading 1
Helensburgh
Falkirk
East Stirlingshire
Helensburgh

McKechnie, John James (Jimmy) RB/LB
b Inverness
1919 Newcastle United 0
1920 Northampton Town 11
1921 Exeter City 18
1922 Stockport County 8
1923 1925 Clapton Orient 47
1926 Crewe Alexandra 15

McKee, Frederick W (Fred) GK
Caps: IrLge 5/Ireland Amat/Ireland 5
Belfast Celtic
Cliftonville
1907 Sunderland 0
Cliftonville
1911 Bradford City 1
Belfast Celtic
Linfield

McKee, Reginald (Reg) CF
b Erith 1900
Erith & Belvedere
1925 Gillingham 34 12
Erith & Belvedere
1926 Gillingham 4 2
Erith & Belvedere
1926 Charlton Athletic 2
Dartford
Erith & Belvedere

McKellar, Charles CF
1911 Preston North End 2
Galston
Girvan Athletic

McKellar, Matthew T CF
b Campsie 1887
Campsie
Kirkintilloch Harp
1909 Woolwich Arsenal 3 1

McKenna, Francis Charles (Frank) IL/OR/IR
b Walker 9/12/1902 d 1947
Swan Hunter
Spennymoor United
Wallsend
1922 1926 Grimsby Town 114 31
1927 Fulham 25 10
1928 Norwich City 41 18
1929 Newport County 24 4
Walker Celtic
1932 Wrexham 7 4
Walker Celtic

McKenna, Harold CH
b Yoker
Glasgow Ashfield
St Mirren
Rangers
Third Lanark
1924 Brighton & Hove Albion 7
Alloa Athletic

From To Apps Goal

McKenna, James Peter (Jim) GK
b Blackpool 18/4/1910 d 1986
1928 Port Vale 0
Great Harwood
1931 Leicester City 1
Bath City
Nuneaton Town
Market Harborough Town

McKenna, John OR
b Liverpool 1882
Old Xavierans
1906 Liverpool 1
Ashton Town
Chester

McKenna, John LH
b Belfast 1900 d 1933
St Malachy's College
Belfast United
Barrow St Patrick's
1921 Barrow 1
St Paul's Swifts
Ulverston St Mary's
Ards
Bohemians
Ards
1927 New Brighton 4
Mansfield Town
Shelbourne
Springfield Amateurs
Newry Town
Banbridge United

McKenna, John Guthrie RB/LB/OR
b Newcastle 28/10/1901 d 1974
Wallsend
1923 1924 Crystal Palace 3
Walker Celtic
1927 Bristol Rovers 10
Workington
Walker Celtic
Bristol St George

McKenna, Peter Joseph GK
b Toxteth Park 8/12/1901 d 1964
Bangor City
1924 1930 Chelsea 62
1931 Southend United 2

McKenna, Thomas Edward (Tom) GK
b Stewarton 27/9/1900 d 1938
Ardeer Thistle
Celtic
Dalry Thistle
1924 1925 Fulham 10
1926 South Shields 26
1927 Charlton Athletic 19
1928 Merthyr Town 37
1929 Southend United 10
Portadown

McKenna, Thomas Patrick (Tom) LB/LH/RH
b Tullamore 10/1891 d 1930
Lansdowne United
Shelbourne
Garston
Colne
1911 Burnley 0
Barrow
1913 1914 Grimsby Town 16
Belfast United
1921 Barrow 16
Morecambe
Kendal Town
Ulverston Town

McKennan, Hugh CF
b Airdrie 8/2/1905 d 1962
Airdrie Merchants
1927 Nottingham Forest 1
St Johnstone
Morton
Cowdenbeath

McKennie, William RH/OR/CF
b Renton 1868 d 1902
Royal Highlanders
1890 1891 Preston North End 11 2
Chorley
1892 1894 Darwen 70 21

McKenzie, Alexander IL/IR
b Leith 5/3/1896
Arniston Rangers
1920 1922 Arsenal 15 2
1923 Blackpool 6 1

From To Apps Goal

McKenzie, Archibald Denny IL/IR
b Greenock 1872
Clyde
Millwall Athletic
1895 Sunderland 2 1
Millwall Athletic
1897 1898 West Bromwich Albion 51 9
Portsmouth
Dumbarton

McKenzie, Crawford Leatham IR
b Newtongrange 7/10/1919 d 1999
Dalkeith Thistle
1939 Bradford Park Avenue (1)

McKenzie, Duncan RH
b Glasgow 10/8/1912 d 1987
Caps: Scotland 1
Milton Parish Church
Albion Rovers
1932 1937 Brentford 155 10
1938 Middlesbrough 28 1
1939 (Middlesbrough) (3)

McKenzie, Frank LB/RB
b Inverness 10/12/1896
Cameron Highlanders
Inverness Thistle
1919 1923 Rotherham County 84 4
1924 1925 Newport County 65
Scunthorpe & Lindsey United
Gainsborough Trinity
Newark Town

McKenzie, Frederick Taylor (Fred) CH
b Lochee 13/11/1903 d 1979
Lochee United
1924 1925 Newport County 66 1
1925 1933 Plymouth Argyle 203 13
1934 Newport County 22

MacKenzie, George C GK
b Dublin
Caps: Eire 9
Arthurlie
1934 Plymouth Argyle 1
1935 1938 Southend United 120
Hereford United

MacKenzie, (Dr) George Duncan OL
b Buckie 27/1/1908 d 1974
Caps: Scotland Amat
Buckie Thistle
Aberdeen University
Queen's Park
1933 Hull City 9 4
1934 Stockport County 7 3
Macclesfield

McKenzie, James R (Jim) OL
b Glasgow 11/1877
Gatmore
Possil Park
East Stirlingshire
Cowlairs
1896 Burton Swifts 26 5
Clyde
Southampton

McKenzie, John LH
1901 Doncaster Rovers 2

Mackenzie, John (Jock) LB
b Douglas 28/7/1885
Glenbuck Cherrypickers
Carlisle United
Norwich City
Heart of Midlothian
Millwall Athletic (trial) 0
1921 Walsall 4

Mackenzie, John Alick CF
b Aultbea 5/11/1915
Ross County
Nairn County
St Mirren
1938 Manchester United 0
1939 Swindon Town (1)

McKenzie, John D IL/OR/IR
b Sudbrook 1914
Chepstow
Gloucester City
1933 Bristol Rovers (trial) 0
1934 Leicester City (trial) 0
1935 1938 Cardiff City 35 6
1939 Notts County (1) (1)

McKenzie, John Wilson RB
b Montrose 9/1885 d 1943
Montrose
Dundee
1908 Aston Villa 5
Bristol Rovers

From To | Apps Goal

McKenzie, Kenneth RH
b Inverness 1888
Inverness Thistle
1910 Chelsea 1
Cardiff City

McKenzie, Kenneth Wilson CH/RH
b Montrose 1/5/1898 d 1960
Whitehill School
Queen's Park
1920 1921 Chelsea 21
1923 Cardiff City 0
Dalkeith

McKenzie, Murdoch IL
b Ayr 17/11/1899
Yoker Athletic
Ayr United
Stevenston United (loan)
1925 Darlington 37 17
1926 Portsmouth 4 1
Hamilton Academical
Glasgow Ashfield

MacKenzie, Roderick R (Roddie) RH
b Inverness 22/5/1901
Inverness Thistle
Inverness Clachnacuddin
Inverness Caledonian
1922 1933 Newcastle United 238 6
1935 1936 Gateshead 17 1
1937 Reading 0

Mackenzie, Ronald IL
b Scotland 1885
Inverness Clachnacuddin
Inverness Thistle
1907 Chelsea 0
1909 Lincoln City 28 6
Inverness Clachnacuddin

McKenzie, Thomas CF
b Petershill
Petershill
Third Lanark
1905 Sunderland 8 1
Plymouth Argyle
Portsmouth
1907 Glossop 6 1
Queen's Park Rangers
Brentford
Dunfermline Athletic

McKeown, Thomas Michael LB
b Dalmellington 3/1870 d 1903
Caps: Scotland 2
Lugar Boswell
Leith Harp
Hibernian
Celtic
1891 Blackburn Rovers 19
Cowlairs
Fair City Athletic
Motherwell
Morton
Royal Scots Fusiliers
Ayr Parkhouse
Hamilton Harp
Lugar Boswell
Hibernian
Carfin Shamrock
Camelon
Fair City Athletic
Lugar Boswell

Mackesy, John (Jack) LH/IL
b Deptford 1890
Deptford Invicta
1919 1922 West Ham United 10

Mackey, James Alfred (Jim) OR
b Ryton-on-Tyne 25/11/1897 d 1990
Newburn Colliery
1920 1921 Coventry City 12
Carlisle United
1923 Notts County 3 1
1923 Lincoln City 21 2
1924 Luton Town 10 1
1925 Crewe Alexandra 35 4
West Stanley
1927 1928 Torquay United 67 6
Dartford
Sheppey United
Bexleyheath & Welling
Dargas Sports
VCD Athletic

Mackey, Thomas Scott (Tom) LB/RB/CH
b Cassop 22/10/1908 d 1969
Cassop Celtic
Cassop Colliery
Ferryhill Athletic
1928 1929 Hartlepools United 30 1
1929 1931 Sheffield Wednesday 4
1932 1937 Luton Town 183 2

From To | Apps Goal

Mackie, Charles CF
b Peterhead 1882
Peterhead
Aberdeen
1904 Manchester United 5 3
West Ham United
Aberdeen
Lochgelly United

McKie, Daniel (Danny) IR/OL
b Walton-le-Dale q1 1885
Army
1904 Preston North End 3 2
1905 1906 Glossop 39 6
Bradford Park Avenue
Chorley
Queen's Park Rangers
Merthyr Town

McKie, James CF
b Arbroath 1873
Caps: Scotland 1
Dykehead
Heart of Midlothian
1896 Darwen 8 3
East Stirlingshire
1900 1902 Bolton Wanderers 81 19
Luton Town
New Brompton

Mackie, James (Jerry) IR
b Motherwell 1/1/1894 d 1959
Bo'ness
Motherwell
Blantyre Celtic
1920 1927 Portsmouth 247 78
1927 1930 Southampton 81 24
Cork FC

Mackie, James (Jimmy) OL
b Hebburn 1916
Hebburn Colliery
Washington Colliery
1936 Bolton Wanderers 0
1937 1938 Hartlepools United 6 2
Horden Colliery Welfare

Mackie, John RH/CH/IL
b Baillieston 11/3/1910 d 1960
Baillieston Park Vale
Bridgeton Waverley
1934 1935 Hull City 14 2
1935 1937 Bradford City 91 7
1938 Chesterfield 17 3

Mackie, John Alexander (Alex) RB
b Belfast 23/2/1904 d 1984
Caps: Ireland 3
Forth River
1922 1925 Arsenal 108
1928 1934 Portsmouth 257 2
1935 1936 Northampton Town 19

Mackie, Robert (Bob) RB/LB
b Dalry 7/9/1884 d 1943
Bannockburn
Cowie Wanderers
Stenhousemuir
Heart of Midlothian
1905 1907 Chelsea 44 1
1907 1908 Leicester Fosse 33
Darlington
Airdrieonians
Third Lanark
Albion Rovers

Mackie, Robert J OR
b Glasgow
Caps: IrLge 3
Coleraine
1930 Torquay United 6 2

McKiernan, Thomas IR
1902 Stockport County 5 1

McKinlay, A LB
1896 Darwen 4

McKinlay, Donald LB/LH/IR
b Newton Mearns 25/7/1891 d 1959
Caps: Scotland 2
Newton Swifts
Newton Villa
1909 1928 Liverpool 393 33
Prescot Cables

McKinlay, William Hodge (Billy) RH
b Dysart 23/8/1904 d 1976
Lochgelly United
Bathgate
1927 1936 Nottingham Forest 334 13

From To | Apps Goal

McKinley, Charles Albert OR
b Plaistow 13/9/1902 d 1983
Leyton
Southall
1927 Charlton Athletic 23 3
Leyton
1928 Brentford 15 1

McKinnell, James Templeton Broadfoot (Jimmy) LH/RH
b Dalbeattie 27/3/1893 d 1972
Dalbeattie Star
Ayr United
Nithsdale Wanderers
Queen of the South
1920 1925 Blackburn Rovers 111
1926 1928 Darlington 101 1
1929 Nelson 10

McKinney, Daniel OR/IR/CF
b Belfast 9/11/1898 d 1956
Caps: IrLge 1/Ireland 2
St Paul's Swifts
Belfast Celtic
1920 1922 Hull City 55 12
1923 Bradford City 31 1
1924 1925 Norwich City 48 4
Bangor

McKinney, Peter IR
b Consett 16/12/1897 d 1979
Consett
1920 Liverpool 3 1
New York Giants

McKinnon, Alex OR
b Edinburgh 1865
Hibernian
1888 Everton 6 5

McKinnon, Angus LH
b Paisley 6/12/1885 d 1968
Petershill
Heart of Midlothian (trial)
Carlisle United
1908 1921 Woolwich Arsenal 211 4
1922 Charlton Athletic 15
1923 Wigan Borough 0

McKnight, James (Jimmy) IR/IL
b 2/5/1892
Caps: IrLge 2/Ireland 2
Glentoran
1911 1912 Preston North End 12 2
Glentoran
1913 Nottingham Forest 9
Belfast Celtic

McKnight, John IR/CF
Hurlford
1892 1893 Darwen 24 10
1894 Burnley 22 6
St Bernard's
Lanemark

McKnight, Robert John IL
Hurlford
Dundee
Barrow
1914 Bury 22 5
Kilmarnock

McKnight, Thomas (Tom) IR
b Lichfield 4/1868 d 1930
Lichfield St Paul's
Burton Swifts
1890 Aston Villa 10 1
Leek Alexandra

Mackrell, James LB
b New Monkland 20/1/1909 d 1977
Longriggend Rob Roy
Falkirk
Motherwell
1933 1934 Portsmouth 3
1936 1938 Norwich City 38

Mackrill, Piercie Albert (Percy) LB
b Wynberg, South Africa 19/10/1894 d 1949
1913 Bradford Park Avenue 0
Rotherham County
1919 Coventry City 1
Pontypridd
1921 1922 Halifax Town 57
Pontypridd
1927 Torquay United 6

McLachlan, A GK
1892 Bootle 13
1893 Walsall Town Swifts 2

From To | Apps Goal

McLachlan, Albert James LH
b Kirkcudbright 2/1892 d 1956
Caps: SLge 1
St Cuthbert Wanderers
1913 Aston Villa 3
Aberdeen
Abercorn (loan)
Heart of Midlothian
Elgin City

McLachlan, Alexander (Alex) LH/RH
b Cardiff
1925 Cardiff City 0
1926 Darlington 2
1927 Merthyr Town 23 1

McLachlan, Edward Rolland OR/IR
b Glasgow 24/9/1903 d 1970
Glasgow Boys Brigade
Hibernian
Queen's Park
Clyde
Third Lanark
Vale of Leven
1926 Leicester City 0
1927 Nottingham Forest 8 2
Mansfield Town
1930 Northampton Town 11 1
1931 Mansfield Town 0

McLachlan, Frederick (Fred) RH/CH
b Kirkcudbright 21/8/1899 d 1982
St Cuthbert Wanderers
King's Own Scottish Borderers
Austin Motor Works
1914 Manchester United (trial)
Harold Johnson Motor Works
Partick Thistle
Aberdeen
Maidstone United
1923 1925 Coventry City 67
1925 1926 Grimsby Town 52
1927 Bury 2
1928 1931 Halifax Town 94 1

McLachlan, George Herbert OL/LH
b Glasgow 21/9/1902
Crosshill Amateurs
Parkhead Juniors
Rutherglen Glencairn
Queen's Park Strollers
Clyde
King's Park (loan)
Peebles Rovers (loan)
1925 1929 Cardiff City 140 22
1929 1932 Manchester United 110 4
1933 Chester 29 7
Le Havre

McLachlan, James (Jimmy) IR/OR
b Glasgow 1870
Vale of Leven
1890 1892 Derby County 55 15
1893 Notts County 2
1894 Derby County 8 2
Ilkeston Town

McLachlan, John Andrew IR/RH
b Dumfries 7/1888 d 1944
St Catherine's Boys Club
St Cuthbert Wanderers
Dundee
1912 1914 Aston Villa 17 3
Dundee
Partick Thistle

McLachlan, Peter OL/OR
b Didsbury q3 1879
1900 1903 Stockport County 46 11

McLachlan, Stephen (Steve) RH/CH
b Kirkcudbright 19/9/1918 d 1990
Dalbeattie Star
1938 1952 Derby County 58 1
Kilmarnock

McLafferty, Charles IL
1892 Bootle 22 9

McLardie, Alexander IL/IR
b Paisley 1868
Caps: SLge 1
St Mirren
1889 1891 Burnley 43 24
Abercorn

McLaren, Alexander (Sandy) GK
b Tibbermore 25/12/1910 d 1960
Caps: Scotland 5
Tulloch
Muirton
St Johnstone
1932 1938 Leicester City 239
1939 (Leicester City) (3)
Morton
St Johnstone

From To Apps Goal

McLaren, Hugh McDonald RH/LH/CH
b Kilbirnie 13/1/1901 d 1971
Dalry Thistle
Nithsdale Wanderers
Aberdeen
Kilmarnock (loan)
Workington
1933 1934 Bradford City 24 1
1935 1936 Tranmere Rovers 43 4
1936 1937 Rochdale 64 1
Astley Bridge

McLaren, James (Jimmy) GK
b Falkirk 12/7/1897 d 1975
Bonnybridge Heatherbell
Stenhousemuir
1922 1926 Bradford City 155
1926 1932 Leicester City 170
1933 1938 Watford 194

McLaren, Malcolm OL
b Glasgow
Strathclyde
1938 Blackpool 3
St Mirren
AS Cannes
AS Roma
Forfar Athletic

McLaren, William (Willie) RH/RB/CH
b Fauldhouse 1888
Duntocher Hibs
Cowdenbeath
1910 1913 Burnley 63
1913 1914 Huddersfield Town 31 2
Cowdenbeath

McLatchie, Colin Campbell OL
b New Cumnock 2/11/1876 d 1952
New Cumnock United
Lanemark
Dean Park (Kilmarnock)
Kilmarnock
1897 1898 Preston North End 9 2
1898 1902 Sunderland 122 33
1902 Grimsby Town 9 1
Lanemark
Nithsdale Wanderers
Lanemark

McLauchlan, Robert (Bob) LB
b Whitburn, County Durham 6/12/1910 d 1970
Whitburn St Mary's
Marsden Colliery Welfare
1931 1933 Gateshead 6
1934 Barnsley 3
Wigan Athletic

McLaughlan, George IL
b Bridgeton 18/1/1904
Greenhead Thistle Juniors
Celtic
Clydebank (loan)
Stenhousemuir (loan)
Clydebank
Mid-Rhondda United
Clyde
1925 Darlington 1
1926 Hull City 8 2
1927 1928 Accrington Stanley 76 21
1929 Nelson 29 2
Morecambe

McLaughlan, Hugh McCann LB
b Galston 20/7/1901 d 1983
Kilmarnock
Queen of the South
Bethlehem Steel
Detroit
Celtic
1929 Carlisle United 31
1930 1932 Barrow 80
1933 1934 Newport County 53

McLaughlan, Joseph James Simpson CF
b Edinburgh 5/2/1891 d 1971
Linlithgow
Bathgate
1911 1912 Woolwich Arsenal 16 3
Watford

McLaughlan, Robert (Bob) OL
b Kilwinning 1902
1923 Cardiff City 0
Kilwinning Rangers
1925 Clapton Orient 19 3

McLaughlin, James (Jimmy) IR
Vale of Clyde
1913 Bradford Park Avenue 1
Airdrieonians
Vale of Clyde
Dundee
Aberdeen
Clydebank

From To Apps Goal

McLaughlin, John W GK
b Newcastle
Wallsend Corinthians
1938 Gateshead 3
1939 (Gateshead) (3)

McLaughlin, Patrick (Pat) CF
b Jarrow q1 1883 d 1916
Blaydon United
Hebburn Argyle
Chorley
Hebburn Argyle
Blyth Spartans
South Shields Adelaide
1909 Fulham 2 1
Wallsend Park Villa
Southend United
Jarrow Caledonians
Scotswood

McLaughlin, William Joseph (Willie) IR/IL
b Cambuslang 22/6/1882 d 1946
Cambuslang Hibernian
Hamilton Academical
1904 1905 Everton 15 5
Plymouth Argyle
1907 Preston North End 1
Egremont Social (Wirral)
Hamilton Academical
Shelbourne

McLaverty, Bernard LH/CH/RH
b Cleator Moor 15/3/1898 d 1952
Cleator Moor
Leadgate Park
Durham City
1920 1927 Derby County 115 1
1927 1928 Norwich City 55 4
Heanor Town
Offilers Brewery

McLaverty, John George CH
b South Shields q4 1891 d 1957
Chester Moor
Sacriston United
Birtley Colliery
1913 Aston Villa 2
South Shields
1914 Aston Villa 0
West Stanley
Houghton Rovers
Shildon Athletic

McLean, Adam OL
b Glasgow 27/4/1897 d 1973
Caps: SLge 3
Whiteinch Oaklea Juveniles
Broomhill YMCA
Anderson Benburb
Anderson Thornbank
Celtic
1928 1930 Sunderland 67 14
Aberdeen
Partick Thistle

McLean, D OL
1893 Rotherham Town 2

McLean, David Prophet CF
b Forfar 13/12/1890 d 1967
Caps: Scotland 1
Forfar Half-Holiday
Forfar West End
Forfar Celtic
Forfar Athletic
Celtic
Forfar Athletic (loan)
Ayr (loan)
1909 1910 Preston North End 49 25
1910 1912 Sheffield Wednesday 84 57
Forfar Athletic
1913 1914 Sheffield Wednesday 48 31
Dykehead (loan)
Third Lanark
Rangers
Linfield (loan)
1919 Sheffield Wednesday 3
1919 1921 Bradford Park Avenue 85 49
Dundee
Forfar Athletic
Dykehead

McLean, Duncan LB/RB
b Dumbarton 12/9/1869
Caps: Scotland 2
Renton Union
Renton
1890 1891 Everton 25
1893 1894 Liverpool 52 5
St Bernard's

From To Apps Goal

McLean, George Thomson IR/IL
b Forfar 24/8/1897 d 1970
Yoker Athletic
Forfar Athletic
1921 1930 Bradford Park Avenue 250 136
1930 1933 Huddersfield Town 120 44
Forfar Athletic

McLean, James (Jimmy) RB
b Edinburgh 1880 d 1947
Edinburgh Thistle
Vale of Leven
1903 Liverpool 4

McLean, James C (Jimmy) RH/OR
b Stoke-on-Trent 1877 d 1914
Eastville Rovers
Worcester City
1899 1900 Walsall 59 5
1901 1902 West Bromwich Albion 57 10
1903 1910 Preston North End 185 4
(Australia)

McLean, James T (Jimmy) LB/LH/RB
b Inverness 1881
Inverness Clachnacuddin
1903 1904 Bradford City 29
1905 Clapton Orient 0
1906 1908 Bradford City 29
1908 1909 Burnley 41

McLean, John Calderwood (Jock) CH
b Busby 30/3/1908 d 1988
Kirkintilloch Rob Roy
1931 1932 Blackburn Rovers 8
1933 1937 Bristol Rovers 134 1
Street

McLean, John Cameron (Jock) CH/RH/LH
b Port Glasgow 22/5/1872
Greenock Volunteers
1894 1895 Liverpool 26
1897 Grimsby Town 30 2
1901 Bristol City 34 1
Bristol Rovers
Millwall Athletic
Queen's Park Rangers

McLean, John Stewart RH
b Clydebank 29/10/1898
Vale of Leven
1925 Bristol City 1
Taunton United

McLean, Joshua Buchanan CF
b Glasgow 29/11/1865 d 1936
1897 Loughborough 1

McLean, Lauchlan IL
b Inverness 1890
Inverness Clachnacuddin
Celtic
1910 Preston North End 1
St Mirren
Inverness Caledonian

McLean, Robert (Bob) IR
b Glasgow
Bo'ness
1908 1909 Clapton Orient 39 2
Leyton

McLean, Robert (Bob) RH
b Glasgow 9/6/??
St Bernard's
Airdrieonians
Alloa Athletic
1923 1929 Doncaster Rovers 136 4
Waterford Celtic
Hatfield Main Colliery

McLean, Robert CF
b 1917
Seaham Colliery Welfare
1937 Hartlepools United 1

McLean, Thomas (Tom) RB
b Alexandria 8/1866 d 1936
Vale of Leven
1888 1891 Notts County 12
Heanor Town
1889 1891 Notts County 54
1892 Derby County 2
1893 Notts County 0

McLean, Thomas (Tommy) IL/IR
b Lochgelly 26/12/1903 d 1983
Crosshill United
Bowhill Juniors
Arbroath
Lochgelly United
St Johnstone
1926 1934 Blackburn Rovers 247 44
1935 Exeter City 21 1
1936 Barrow 11 2

From To Apps Goal

McLellan, John (Jack) LB
Heart of Midlothian
1888 1892 Accrington 101
Bacup

McLenahan, Hugh CH/LH/RH
b West Gorton 23/3/1909 d 1988
Caps: England Sch
Ambrose
Longsight
Ashton Brothers
1926 Manchester United 0
Stalybridge Celtic
1926 Blackpool (trial) 0
1926 Stockport County (trial) 0
1927 1936 Manchester United 112 11
1936 1938 Notts County 54 1

McLeod, Donald RB
b Laurieston 28/5/1882 d 1917
Caps: SLge 2/Scotland 4
Stenhousemuir Thistle
Stenhousemuir
Ayr
Celtic
1908 1912 Middlesbrough 138
Inverness Caledonian (loan)

McLeod, Edward Hughes IL
b Glasgow 5/2/1914 d 1988
East Fife
1938 Manchester City 4 2
Hibernian
Shrewsbury Town

McLeod, James IL
b Glasgow 26/11/1905
Petershill
Partick Thistle
1929 Carlisle United 9 1
Raith Rovers
Havana

McLeod, John A RB
b Inverness 1888
Inverness Caledonian
1908 Hull City 0
1909 1910 Bury 2 1
Darlington
Hurst

McLeod, John Simpson CF
b Gorbals 20/4/1912
Neilston Victoria
Rangers
Heart of Midlothian
Queen of the South (loan)
Larne
1935 1936 Manchester City 12 9
1937 1938 Millwall 27 12
Hibernian

McLeod, Roderick (Roddie) IR
b Kilsyth 2/1872 d 1931
Westburn
Partick Thistle
1890 1896 West Bromwich Albion 149 50
1897 Leicester Fosse 28 13
Brighton United
Southampton
Brentford

McLeod, Thomas IL
b Airdrie 1904
Kirkintilloch Rob Roy
Aberdeen
1930 1931 Charlton Athletic 4

McLeod, William (Billy) CF/IL
b Hebburn 4/6/1887 d 1959
Hebburn Argyle
Peebles Rovers
1906 Lincoln City 13 8
1906 1919 Leeds City 289 172
1919 1920 Notts County 40 10
Doncaster Rovers

McLintock, Thomas (Tom) LB
b Maybole 1869
Clyde
Kilmarnock
1893 1901 Burnley 233 14
Kilmarnock

McLoughlin, William RH
Darwen
1908 1909 Burnley 6

McLuckie, James CF
b Glasgow 1/1/1878 d 1924
Jordanhill
1898 1901 Bury 94 31
1901 1903 Aston Villa 57 40
Plymouth Argyle
Dundee
Third Lanark
Hamilton Academical

From To Apps Goal

McLuckie, James Sime (Jimmy) LH/IR
b Stonehouse, Lanarkshire 2/4/1908 d 1986
Caps: Scotland 1
Tranent Juniors
Hamilton Academical
1933 1934 Manchester City 32 1
1934 1935 Aston Villa 15 1
1938 1945 Ipswich Town 41 1
1939 (Ipswich Town) (3)
Clacton Town

McLuggage, J OL
1889 Accrington 8 2

McMahon, Douglas Alexander (Doug) IR
b Winnipeg, Canada 1917 d 1997
Winnipeg Caledonian
1938 Wolverhampton Wanderers 1
Chicago Vikings
Montreal Carsteel

McMahon, Edward (Eddie) IL
b 1885
Kelty Rangers
Cowdenbeath
Bathgate
Portsmouth
Brentford
York City
1913 Clapton Orient 3
Boscombe

McMahon, Hugh CH
b Saltcoats 7/7/1906 d 1997
Saltcoats Victoria
Cowdenbeath
1930 Blackpool 26 1
1931 Stoke City 8 1
1932 1935 Wrexham 144 7
Workington
1936 Doncaster Rovers 5
Albion Rovers

McMahon, Hugh (Hughie) OL
b Grangetown 24/9/1909 d 1986
Upton's FC
South Bank St Peter's
Mexborough Town
1931 Sheffield Wednesday (trial) 0
1932 Reading 1
Mexborough Town (loan)
1933 Southend United 10 3
1934 1935 Reading 10 2
1936 1937 Queen's Park Rangers 41 3
1937 1938 Sunderland 8 1
1945 1947 Hartlepools United 28 7
1947 1948 Rotherham United 59 8
Stockton

McMahon, John (Johnny) RB/LB
b Scotland 1881 d 1933
Clyde
1900 1902 Preston North End 65
1902 1905 Manchester City 100 1
1906 1909 Bury 60

McMahon, Patrick (Pat) GK
b Glasgow 26/10/1908 d 1992
Pollokshaws Hibs
St Anthony's (Glasgow)
1932 1933 West Ham United 16
St Mirren
1934 1938 Wrexham 113
1939 Stoke City (3)

McMahon, Ross CF
Erin Rovers
1888 Burnley 2

McMain, Joseph (Joe) IR/CF
b Preston 1873
South Shore
1894 Preston North End 0
Stafford Rangers
Kettering
1896 1898 Wolverhampton Wanderers 46 19
1899 Notts County 26 13
Kettering
Wednesbury Old Athletic
Wellingborough Montrose

McManus, Peter Thomas LH/CH
b Winchburgh 4/1873 d 1936
Hibernian
Mossend Swifts
St Bernard's
Celtic
St Bernard's
1896 1897 West Bromwich Albion 28 1
Warmley
Thames Ironworks

From To Apps Goal

McMenemy, Francis (Frank) LH/RH/CH
b Rutherglen 5/12/1906
Burnbank Athletic
Hamilton Academical
St Cuthbert Wanderers (loan)
Nithsdale Wanderers (loan)
Airdrieonians
Tunbridge Wells Rangers
1933 1935 Northampton Town 57 3
1936 Crystal Palace 25 3
Guildford City

McMenemy, Harry IL/IR
b Glasgow 26/3/1910
Strathclyde Juniors
1931 1936 Newcastle United 138 34
Dundee
1939 Gateshead 0

McMillan, George RH
b Edinburgh
Leith Athletic
St Bernard's
Millwall Athletic
1893 Lincoln City 3

McMillan, George IR/IL
b Armadale 28/3/1904
Fauldhouse United
Armadale
Rangers
1930 1932 Bradford Park Avenue 54 10
Bath City
Lovells Athletic
Albion Rovers
East Stirlingshire

McMillan, James LB
Queen of the South Wanderers
1889 Notts County 22

McMillan, James (Jock) RB
b Seaton Delaval q1 1899
Caps: England Sch
Seaton Delaval
Newcastle United Swifts
1920 1921 Newport County 25

McMillan, James A IL
b 1870
Caps: Scotland 1
1892 1894 Everton 7 5
St Bernard's

McMillan, John Stuart (Johnny) IL/OL/CF
b Port Glasgow 16/2/1871 d 1941
Port Glasgow Athletic
St Bernard's
1890 1895 Derby County 116 45
1896 1900 Leicester Fosse 122 43
1900 1902 Small Heath 49 24
1903 1905 Bradford City 82 24
1906 1907 Glossop 27 1

McMillan, Stuart Thomas OR/IR
b Leicester 17/9/1896 d 1963
1914 Derby County 1
1919 Chelsea 0
1920 1921 Gillingham 30 2
1922 1923 Wolverhampton Wanderers 36 5
1924 1926 Bradford City 70 6
1927 Nottingham Forest 9
1928 1929 Clapton Orient 23 1

McMillan, William RB/CH
b Glespin 1878 d 1958
Lanark Athletic
1898 1903 Lincoln City 176 1
Newark Town
1905 Lincoln City 2
Newark Town
Castleford Town
Lincoln South End
RAMC
Waddington
Boston Town

McMillan, William RH/OL
b Dykehead 6/9/1876
Dykehead
Heart of Midlothian
Dykehead
Heart of Midlothian
Southampton
1898 1899 Burnley 3
St Mirren
Kilbarchan
Arthurlie
Morton
Arthurlie

McMillan, William H OR
Rothesay Royal Victoria
1930 Swansea Town 8

From To Apps Goal

McMillen, Walter S CH/RH
b Belfast 24/11/1913 d 1987
Caps: Ireland Amat/IrLge 1/NIRL 4/Ireland 7
Carrickfergus
Cliftonville
1932 Arsenal (trial) 0
1933 1934 Manchester United 27 2
1936 1938 Chesterfield 85 17
1939 Millwall (3)
Glentoran
Linfield
1946 1949 Millwall 91
Tonbridge

McMullan, David (Dave) LH/RH/IL
b Belfast 1901
Caps: IrLge 4/Ireland 2
Forth River
Distillery
1925 1927 Liverpool 31
New York Giants
Belfast Celtic
1929 Exeter City 19
Distillery

McMullan, James (Jimmy) LH/IL
b Denny 26/3/1895 d 1964
Caps: SLge 4/Scotland 16
Denny Hibernian
Third Lanark
Partick Thistle
Maidstone United
Partick Thistle
1925 1932 Manchester City 220 10

McMullan, Samuel (Sam) GK
b Belfast 2/7/1907 d 1952
Caps: IrLge 3
Deramore
Malone United
Clady
Forth River
Ards
Dundalk
Ards
1935 New Brighton 8
Brideville

McMurdo, Alexander Brown (Alex) OR/OL
b Cleland 9/4/1914
West Calder
1935 Bury 1
Queen of the South
1937 Rochdale 2

McMurray, Campbell CH/LB
b Glasgow 27/6/1893
Vale of Leven
Glasgow Ashfield
Strathclyde
1920 1921 Hull City 4
Workington
York City
Workington
1925 New Brighton 1

McMurray, Thomas (Tom) OR
b Belfast 24/7/1911 d 1964
Bexleyheath
1931 Millwall 0
1932 Tranmere Rovers 24 4
Guildford City
Glenavon
1937 Rochdale 23 1
Chelmsford City

McMurtrie, Andrew OR
b Dreghorn 30/10/1906
Dreghorn
Motherwell
1929 Bristol City 10 1
Cork FC
King's Park (trial)
1931 Rotherham United 0
Dreghorn

McNab, ? OR
1905 Burnley 1

McNab, Alexander (Sandy) LH/RH
b Glasgow 27/12/1911 d 1962
Caps: Scotland 2
Tuesday Waverley
Pollok Juniors
1932 1937 Sunderland 97 6
1937 1938 West Bromwich Albion 49 2
1939 (West Bromwich Albion) (3)
1946 Newport County 3
Dudley Town
Northwich Victoria

From To Apps Goal

McNab, Andrew CH
Dalziel Rovers
Motherwell
1905 Glossop 18
St Bernard's
Broxburn

McNab, David Stewart (Jock) CH
b Cleland 2/12/1897 d 1960
Newarthill Thistle
1923 Portsmouth 6
1925 1929 Fulham 158 21
1930 Coventry City 9
Llanelly
Walton-on-Thames

McNab, John Seymour (Jock) RH
b Cleland 17/4/1894 d 1949
Caps: Scotland 1
Bellshill Athletic
1919 1927 Liverpool 200 6
1928 1929 Queen's Park Rangers 54 2

McNab, William CF
b Glasgow 1870
1892 1893 Burnley 14 5
1893 Woolwich Arsenal 2 1
Royal Ordnance

McNair, Donald RH
b Glasgow
Partick Thistle
1893 Middlesbrough Ironopolis 26

McNally, John CH
b Thornaby 1875
Middlesbrough
Thornaby
1899 1900 Middlesbrough 3

McNally, Owen CF/IR
b Denny 20/6/1906 d 1973
Caps: IrLge 1
Denny Hibernian
Celtic
Arthurlie (loan)
Hamilton Academical (loan)
Bray Unknowns
1930 Norwich City (trial) 0
1931 Cardiff City 6
Bray Unknowns
Lausanne Sports
Sligo Rovers
Distillery
1935 1936 Leicester City 16 7
Racing Club Calais
Shamrock Rovers

McNaught, Hugh RB
b Greenock 1884
Glasgow University
Queen's Park
Dundee
Heart of Midlothian
1906 Sheffield United 1
Heart of Midlothian
1909 Nottingham Forest 0

McNaught, James Rankin CH/LH/IL
b Dumbarton 8/6/1870 d 1919
Dumbarton
Linfield
1893 1897 Newton Heath 141 12
Tottenham Hotspur
Maidstone United

McNaughton, George J RH
1893 Sunderland 0
1894 Bury 15

McNaughton, Gibson Norrie (Gibby) IL/LH
b Broughty Ferry 30/7/1911 d 1991
Dundee Violet
Clyde
Dundee
Dunfermline Athletic
East Fife
1936 1938 Nottingham Forest 66 12
1939 Notts County 0
Ilkeston Town

McNaughton, Harold (Harry) GK
b Edinburgh 6/4/1894
Tolbooth Juveniles
Edinburgh Renton
Heart of Midlothian
St Bernard's
1920 Liverpool 1
Broxburn United
Leith Athletic

McNaughton, John (Jock) LB
b Perth 19/1/1912 d 1986
Perth Roselea
1934 1935 Nottingham Forest 12
1936 1938 Brighton & Hove Albion 6

From	To		Apps	Goal
		McNaughton, William Frederick (Bill)	CF/IR	
		b Poplar 8/12/1905	d 1980	
		Barking Town		
1925		Millwall	0	
		Peterborough & Fletton United		
1928	1929	Northampton Town	11	2
1930	1931	Gateshead	63	46
1932	1934	Hull City	85	57
1934	1935	Stockport County	50	32
		Walker Celtic		
		City of Durham		
		McNeal, Robert (Bobby)	LH	
		b Hobson Village 15/1/1891	d 1956	
		Caps: FLge 5/England 2		
		Hobson Wanderers		
1910	1924	West Bromwich Albion	370	9
		McNee, John (Jack)	IL/OL	
		b Renton 1867		
		Renton Wanderers		
		Renton		
1889	1892	Bolton Wanderers	87	23
		Kingsland (Norfolk)		
1894		Newcastle United	21	4
		Gateshead NER		
		West Herts		
		Fulham		
		McNeil, John Law (Johnny)	CH/CF	
		b Inverkeithing 1906		
		Bo'ness		
		Musselburgh Bruntonians		
		Heart of Midlothian		
		Raith Rovers (loan)		
1928	1929	Portsmouth	12	5
1929	1931	Reading	39	5
		Airdrieonians (trial)		
		Shelbourne (trial)		
		Guildford City		
		Heart of Midlothian		
		Inverness Caledonian		
1934	1938	Plymouth Argyle	138	12
1939		Clapton Orient	(3)	
		McNeil, Robert William (Bobby)	OL	
		b Partick 10/3/1889		
		Caps: SLge 3		
		Wishaw Caledonians		
		Shettleston Juniors		
		Hamilton Academical		
1914		Chelsea	37	3
		Bathgate		
		Motherwell		
		Wishaw Thistle		
		Hamilton Academical		
1919	1926	Chelsea	242	24
		McNeill, D	RB/LB	
1894	1895	Burton Swifts	28	
		McNeill, Hamilton John (John)	CF	
		b Zabbar, Malta 13/5/1910	d 2002	
		Parkhead Juniors		
		Dunipace Juniors		
		Army		
1935		Leicester City	0	
		Ayr United		
1937	1938	Hull City	52	27
1938		Bury	15	6
1939		(Bury)	(3)	(1)
		McNeill, Robert	LB/RB	
		b Glasgow		
		Port Victoria		
		Port Glasgow Athletic		
		Vale of Leven		
		Clyde		
1894	1900	Sunderland	142	
		Morton		
		McNestry, George	OR/IR	
		b Chopwell 7/1/1908	d 1998	
		Chopwell Institute		
1926		Arsenal (trial)	0	
1926		Bradford Park Avenue	14	1
1927	1928	Doncaster Rovers	8	1
1928		Leeds United	3	
1929		Sunderland	4	
1930	1931	Luton Town	69	26
1932	1934	Bristol Rovers	112	42
1935	1936	Coventry City	46	21
		McNichol, Duncan	RB	
		b Alexandria 1876		
		Vale of Leven		
		St Bernard's		
1899	1902	Woolwich Arsenal	101	1
		Aberdeen		
		McNicol, D	RB	
1893		Darwen	1	

From	To		Apps	Goal
		Maconnachie, Alex	IR/OR	
		Glasgow Ashfield		
1897		Derby County	23	9
1898	1900	Notts County	76	26
		Third Lanark		
		Ripley Athletic		
		Newton Rovers		
		Ilkeston United		
		Alfreton Town		
		Tibshelf		
		Maconnachie, John Smith Jackson (Jock)	LB	
		b Aberdeen 8/5/1885	d 1956	
		Glasgow Perthshire		
		Hibernian		
1907	1919	Everton	245	6
		Shelbourne (loan)		
1920	1921	Swindon Town	55	3
		Djurgaarden		
1922		Swindon Town	1	
		Foleshill Great Heath		
1927		Barrow	2	
		Lowestoft Town		
		McOustra, William (Willie)	LH/IR	
		b Larbert 1881		
		Heather Rangers		
		Glasgow Ashfield		
		Celtic		
		Stenhousemuir (loan)		
1901	1906	Manchester City	65	6
1907		Blackpool	0	
		Stenhousemuir		
		Abercorn		
		Alloa Athletic		
		McOwen, William Arthur (Billy)	GK	
		b Blackburn q2 1871	d 1950	
		Cherry Tree		
		Blackburn Olympic		
1888	1889	Blackburn Rovers	14	
1891		Darwen	17	
1893		Liverpool	23	
		Blackpool		
		Nelson		
		McPhail, Daniel (Dan)	GK	
		b Campbeltown 9/2/1903	d 1987	
		Falkirk		
		Third Lanark (trial)		
1922	1928	Portsmouth	128	
1931	1938	Lincoln City	309	
		McPhail, Donald Douglas (Don)	OR/OL	
		b Dumbarton 17/2/1911	d 1992	
		Dumbarton Academy		
		Dumbarton		
		South Bank (loan)		
1930		Middlesbrough	4	1
1932		Bournemouth & Boscombe Ath	14	
1933		Barnsley	0	
1933		Carlisle United	5	
		Burton Town		
		Nuneaton Town		
1935	1936	Swindon Town	19	4
		Dunfermline Athletic		
		Dartford		
		Burton Town		
		McPheat, John	IR	
		b Longriggend 25/8/1911	d 1979	
		Rutherglen Glencairn		
1935		Hull City	9	
		Guildford City		
		McPhee, John	RB	
		b Scotland		
		Glasgow Perthshire		
1898		Woolwich Arsenal	7	
		McPhee, John (Johnny)	OR	
		b Stirling		
		Cowie Thistle Juveniles		
1929		Sunderland	4	
1930		Brentford	0	
		Albion Rovers		
		MacPhee, Magnus George (Tony)	CF	
		b Edinburgh 30/4/1914	d 1960	
		Wellington Rangers		
		Heart of Midlothian		
		Edina (loan)		
		Leith Athletic (loan)		
		Dunfermline Athletic		
		Bangor		
		Belfast Celtic		
		Workington		
1936		Bradford Park Avenue	30	18
1937		Coventry City	12	6
1938	1948	Reading	132	90
1939		(Reading)	(3)	(3)
		Banbury Spencer		

From	To		Apps	Goal
		McPherson, Archibald (Archie)	IL/LH	
		b Alva 10/2/1910	d 1969	
		Alva Albion Rovers		
		Rangers		
		Bathgate (loan)		
1929	1934	Liverpool	130	18
1934	1936	Sheffield United	57	1
		Falkirk		
		East Fife		
		Dundee United		
		McPherson, Francis Comber (Frank)	OL/CF	
		b Barrow 14/5/1901	d 1953	
		Barrow Shipbuilders		
		Partick Thistle		
		Barrow Shipbuilders		
		Chesterfield Municipal		
		Barrow Shipbuilders		
1921	1922	Barrow	53	3
1923	1927	Manchester United	159	45
		Manchester Central		
1928	1929	Watford	61	55
1929	1932	Reading	79	28
1933	1935	Watford	33	12
1936		Barrow	3	2
		McPherson, John	CH	
		b Motherwell 28/2/1867	d 1935	
		Caps: Scotland 1		
		Cambuslang		
		Heart of Midlothian		
		Nottingham Forest		
		Heart of Midlothian		
1892	1900	Nottingham Forest	226	25
		Motherwell		
		Cambuslang		
		McPherson, Lachlan (Lacky)	LH/RH/IR	
		b Dennistoun 11/7/1900		
		Cambuslang Juniors		
		Cambuslang Rangers		
1921	1923	Notts County	32	5
1924	1929	Swansea Town	199	29
1929	1931	Everton	30	1
1933	1934	New Brighton	53	3
		Hereford United		
		Milford United		
		McPherson, M	OR	
1890		Accrington	1	1
		McPherson, Peter Copeland	IL/OL	
		b Livingston Station 19/3/1912	d 1993	
		Shotts Battlefield		
		Dalkeith Thistle		
		Hibernian		
1933		Barnsley	1	
1934		Southport (trial)	4	1
1934		New Brighton	4	
		Le Havre		
		Portadown		
		Hibernian		
		Heart of Midlothian		
		Dudley Town		
		Waterford		
		St James's Gate (trial)		
		Cork City (trial)		
		Kodak Harrow		
		McPherson, William (Billy)	IL	
		b Beith 1880		
		Beith		
		St Mirren		
1906	1907	Liverpool	48	16
		Rangers		
		Heart of Midlothian		
		McPhillips, Laurence	IL	
		b Bathgate 6/5/1914	d 1994	
		Avonbridge Juveniles		
		Musselburgh Athletic		
		Heart of Midlothian		
		Albion Rovers		
		Belfast Celtic		
1939		Cardiff City	(3)	
		McPhillips, William Pearson (Bill)	GK	
		b Musselburgh 7/6/1910	d 1992	
		Musselburgh Bruntonians		
1933	1937	Newcastle United	33	
		Guildford City		
1939		Bradford City	(3)	
		McQuaker, Thomas	CH	
		b Glasgow 25/12/1867		
1896		Lincoln City (trial)	1	
		McQue, Joseph (Joe)	CH	
		b Glasgow 2/1870	d 1934	
		Pollokshields		
		Celtic		
1893	1897	Liverpool	103	10
		Third Lanark		

From	To		Apps	Goal
		McQueen, Hugh	OL/CF	
		b Harthill 1/10/1867	d 1944	
		Leith Athletic		
1893	1894	Liverpool	39	13
1895	1900	Derby County	150	18
		Queen's Park Rangers		
1902		Gainsborough Trinity	30	3
		Fulham		
		Kilmarnock (trial)		
		Hibernian		
		Norwich City		
		McQueen, Matthew (Matt)	GK/CF	
		b Harthill 18/5/1863	d 1944	
		Caps: Scotland 2		
		Leith Athletic		
		Heart of Midlothian		
		Leith Athletic		
1893	1898	Liverpool	77	1
		McQuillan, John (Jack)	LB	
		b Boldon Colliery q3 1885		
		Jarrow Town		
1905		Everton	0	
1906	1913	Hull City	239	2
1914		Leeds City	20	
		McRailt, William	CH	
		Barrow		
1913		Stockport County	1	
		Galston		
		McReddie, William (Wally)	IL/OL	
		b Lochee 1871		
		Lochee		
		Dundee Harp		
1889		Stoke	11	2
		Middlesbrough Ironopolis		
1893	1894	Stoke	33	10
1894	1895	Manchester City	31	12
1895		Bolton Wanderers	2	
		Celtic		
		Macrill, Frank	OR	
		b Lincoln q4 1875	d 1932	
		Grantham Rovers		
1896		Lincoln City	3	
		St Mary's (Lincoln)		
		McRobbie, Allan	RB/LB	
		b Elgin 13/11/1886	d 1967	
		Elgin City		
		Dundee		
1911	1912	Middlesbrough	7	
		Swindon Town		
		Aberdeen		
		McRoberts, Robert (Bobby)	CF/CH/IR	
		b Coatbridge 12/7/1874	d 1959	
		Coatbridge		
		Airdrieonians		
		Albion Rovers		
1896	1897	Gainsborough Trinity	52	15
1898	1904	Small Heath	173	70
1905	1908	Chelsea	104	10
		McRorie, Daniel M (Danny)	OR	
		b Glasgow 25/6/1906	d 1963	
		Caps: SLge 1/Scotland 1		
		Queen's Park Strollers		
		Queen of the South		
		Airdrieonians		
		Stenhousemuir		
		Morton		
1930	1932	Liverpool	33	6
1933		Millwall (trial)	0	
1933		Rochdale	5	
		Morton		
		Runcorn		
		Workington		
		McSevich, Peter	GK	
		b Stevenston 14/5/1902	d 1979	
		Newmains Juniors		
		Shieldmuir Celtic		
		Celtic		
		Aberdeen		
1928	1931	Bournemouth & Boscombe Ath	142	1
1932		Coventry City	34	
1933	1935	Walsall	102	
		Wellington Town		
		McShane, Henry (Harry)	OL/OR	
		b Holytown 8/4/1920		
		Bellshill Athletic		
1937		Blackburn Rovers	2	
1946		Huddersfield Town	15	1
1947	1950	Bolton Wanderers	93	6
1950	1953	Manchester United	56	8
1953	1954	Oldham Athletic	41	5
		Chorley		
		Wellington Town		
		Droylsden		

From To Apps Goal

McShea, Ernest (Ernie) CF
b Glasgow
Strathclyde
Port Glasgow Athletic
1907 Barnsley 20 8
Clyde
Rochdale
South Shields

McSkimming, Robert (Bob) IR
b Kilmarnock 1870
Hurlford
1888 Stoke 22 6
Burslem Port Vale
Stone Town

McSkimming, Robert Scott (Bob) CH/LB/LH
b Glenboig 1888
Douglas Park
Albion Rovers
1909 1914 Sheffield Wednesday 166
Wishaw Thistle
Motherwell
1919 Sheffield Wednesday 16
Albion Rovers
Ayr United
Helensburgh
Auchinstarry
Denny Hibernian
(New Zealand)

McTavish, John Kay (Jock) IR/OR
b Govan 7/6/1885 d 1926
Caps: SLge 2/Scotland 1
Petershill
Falkirk
1910 Oldham Athletic 10
1910 1911 Tottenham Hotspur 37 3
1911 1912 Newcastle United 34 6
Partick Thistle
Falkirk (loan)
East Fife
Dumbarton
East Stirlingshire
Dumbarton

McTavish, Robert (Bob) IL
b Govan 26/10/1888 d 1972
Ibrox Roselie
Glasgow Petershill
Falkirk
1910 Tottenham Hotspur 11 3
Brentford
Third Lanark
York City
Raith Rovers

McVean, Malcolm OR/IR
b Jamestown 7/3/1871 d 1907
Vale of Leven Wanderers
Clydebank
Vale of Leven
Rangers
Clydebank
Third Lanark
1893 1896 Liverpool 89 24
1896 Burnley 4
Dundee
Bedminster

McVee, William (Bill) LB
b Blackwood, Lanarkshire 26/11/1901 d 1977
Airdrieonians
Weymouth
1925 1926 Bradford Park Avenue 16
Weymouth
Poole

McVicker, John RB
b Belfast 29/4/1868
Caps: Ireland 2
Glentoran
Linfield
Glentoran
Birmingham St George's
1891 Accrington 19
1892 1893 Ardwick 26
Macclesfield

McWhinnie, Walter IR/IL
1893 1894 Walsall Town Swifts 29 11

McWhinnie, William G OR
b Scotland 1876 d 1936
Ayr
Bristol Eastville Rovers
Reading
Third Lanark
1900 Sheffield Wednesday 9
Hibernian
Third Lanark
Aberdeen
Staten Island

From To Apps Goal

McWhirr, James OR
b Partick 13/1/1905 d 1976
Glasgow Ashfield
1925 Gillingham 6
1926 Norwich City 1 1
1927 Merthyr Town 16 7
1927 Portsmouth 0
1928 Charlton Athletic 1

McWhirter, A LH
1889 Bolton Wanderers 4
Ardwick

McWhirter, Douglas RH
b Erith 13/8/1886 d 1966
Caps: England Amat
Bromley
1911 1913 Leicester Fosse 58 2
Southend United

McWhirter, Peter OR
b Glasgow 23/6/1871 d 1943
Toronto Scottish
Chicago Thistles
Morton
Clyde
1895 Leicester Fosse 17 1
Freemantle
Warmley
Brighton United
1899 Leicester Fosse 0

McWilliam, Peter LH
b Inveravon 22/9/1878 d 1951
Caps: Scotland 8
Heatherley
Inverness Thistle
Albion Rovers
Inverness Thistle
1902 1910 Newcastle United 199 11

McWilliams, P LB
1902 Bolton Wanderers 1

McWilliams, Robert (Bobby) OL
b Kirkintilloch 12/9/1907
Auchinsharry Juveniles
Denny Hibernian
Celtic
1929 1930 Watford 22 1
Leith Athletic
Celtic
Yeovil & Petters United
Newry Town (trial)
Celtic
Larne
Coleraine

Madden, G CF
1902 Burton United 4 1
Fulham

Madden, George IL
b Loftus
Saltburn Swifts
Loftus
Haverton Hill
1899 Middlesbrough 3
Gravesend United

Madden, MG CF
1901 Stockport County 23 4

Madden, Owen OL/IL
b Cork 5/12/1916 d 1991
Caps: LoI 2/Ireland 1/Eire 1
Cork Southern Rovers
Cork FC
1936 1937 Norwich City 22 1
1937 1938 Birmingham 12 1
Sligo Rovers
Cork United
Cork Athletic

Maddison, George (Geordie) GK
b Birtley 14/8/1902 d 1959
Birtley Colliery
1922 1923 Tottenham Hotspur 40
1924 1937 Hull City 430

Maddison, John Arden Brown (Arden) RH/LH
b Chester-le-Street 12/2/1900 d 1987
Usworth Colliery
1923 Stoke 1
1924 1926 Port Vale 53 1
1927 1928 Oldham Athletic 6
Burton Town
Prescot Cables
1933 Mansfield Town 0
Nimes
Gresley Rovers
Sutton Town
Gresley Rovers

From To Apps Goal

Maddock, John (Jack) RB/CH/LB
b Audley 24/11/1896 d 1972
Bignall
Audley Town
1919 1920 Stoke 23 4
Macclesfield
1923 1930 Port Vale 173 10
1931 1932 Crewe Alexandra 41 6
Nantwich
Audley United

Maddock, Joseph LH
b Northwich q1 1865 d 1906
Northwich Victoria
Ardwick
1892 Northwich Victoria 2

Maddocks, Emlyn CF
b Denbigh 6/7/1917 d 1995
Denbigh Red Dragons
1936 Tranmere Rovers 2

Magee, Thomas Patrick (Tommy) RH/OR/IR
b Widnes 6/5/1899 d 1974
Caps: England 5
Appleton Hornets
St Helens Recreation
Widnes Athletic
1919 1933 West Bromwich Albion 394 15
1934 Crystal Palace 0
Runcorn

Maggs, Percy GK
b Clutton 29/11/1906 d 1985
Bath City
1930 Aston Villa 12
1931 Blackpool 24
1932 1938 Torquay United 206

Maginnis, Hugh (Hughie) LH
b 5/9/1880
Caps: IrLge 3/Ireland 8
Linfield
1904 Glossop 20
Linfield
Distillery

Magner, Edward (Ted) CF
b Newcastle 1/1/1891 d 1948
Stainton Celtic
West Hartlepool Expansion
1909 Gainsborough Trinity 5 1
1910 Everton 6 2
St Mirren
South Liverpool
Shelbourne

Maguire, Hugh RB/LB
1892 1893 Preston North End 4

Maguire, James Edward (Teddy) OL/OR
b Meadowfield 23/7/1917 d 2000
Willington
1936 1938 Wolverhampton Wanderers 79 7
1939 (Wolverhampton Wanderers) (3)
1947 Swindon Town 28 4
1948 1949 Halifax Town 55 7
Spennymoor United

Maher, Cyril OR
b Liverpool q2 1918
South Liverpool
1936 Tranmere Rovers 1

Maher, David (Davie) OR/IR
Millwall Athletic
Brentford
1903 1905 Preston North End 24 2
Carlisle United

Maher, Edward John (Ted) GK
b Liverpool 31/7/1910 d 1979
1928 Everton 0
Rhyl Athletic
1929 New Brighton 4
St John's CEYMS

Mahon, John (Jack) RH
b Northwich 1886
Caps: SoLge 1
Clowne White Star
Worksop Town
1908 Gainsborough Trinity 16
New Brompton
Doncaster Rovers
Shirebrook

Mahon, John (Jack) OR/OL
b Gillingham 28/12/1911 d 1993
New Brompton Excelsior
1930 Doncaster Rovers 0
1931 1935 Leeds United 78 20
1935 1938 West Bromwich Albion 113 39
1938 Huddersfield Town 5
1939 (Huddersfield Town) (1)
1945 York City 0

From To Apps Goal

Mahon, Patrick RB
b Walker 27/2/1896 d 1975
Wallsend
1922 Ashington 24 3
Gosforth & Coxlodge British Legion

Maiden, Walter Henry RB
b Kidderminster 8/1896 d 1955
Kidderminster Harriers
1919 Aston Villa 1
Stourbridge

Maidment, Harry William OL
b Bournemouth 20/9/1901 d 1971
1924 1927 Bournemouth & Boscombe Ath 71 16
Thames

Maidment, James Henry C (Jimmy) GK
b Monkwearmouth 28/9/1901 d 1977
Robert Thompson's
1922 South Shields 0
1923 Southend United 13
1924 1929 Newport County 220 3
1930 Lincoln City 41
1931 1932 Notts County 44
1933 Accrington Stanley 37
Nottingham Co-op Diary

Maidment, Thomas (Tom) IR/RH
b Monkwearmouth 4/11/1905 d 1971
Southwick St Columba's
Robert Thompson's
1925 Sunderland 0
1925 1930 Lincoln City 126 43
1931 Portsmouth 3
Workington
1932 1933 Cardiff City 44 8
Blyth Spartans
South Shields

Mailey, James (Jim 'Ginger') OL
b Dundalk
Dundalk
1936 Fulham 0
Dundalk
1937 1938 Plymouth Argyle 15 1
1939 Swindon Town 0

Main, Alexander (Sandy) IR/IL/CH
b West Calder 1877
West Calder
Rangers
West Calder
Hibernian
1899 1902 Woolwich Arsenal 63 14
West Calder Swifts
Motherwell
Watford

Main, David (Davie) CF
b Falkirk 1888
Falkirk
1910 Sunderland 2
Aberdeen
Falkirk

Main, Frame Robert (Bobby) OR
b Airdrie 10/2/1909 d 1985
Caps: SLge 3/Scotland 1
Baillieston Juniors
Rangers
1939 New Brighton (3) (1)

Main, Walter Seymour IL
b Motherwell 1875
Airdrieonians
1899 1900 Small Heath 33 11
St Bernard's

Main, William OR
Ayr
1908 1909 Preston North End 12
Alloa Athletic
Wishaw Thistle
Barrow

Main, William Gay (Bill) LH
b St Monance 30/11/1915 d 1969
St Monance Juniors
Raith Rovers
1936 1938 Cardiff City 6
Colchester United

Mainman, Henry Layfield (Harry) CH/RH
b Liverpool 7/4/1877 d 1953
1896 Everton 0
1897 Liverpool 0
1898 1899 Burton Swifts 64 8
Reading
1901 1906 Notts County 130

From To Apps Goal

Mair, David (Davie) LH
b Dumbarton 1884
Renfrew Victoria
1905 1906 Glossop 74
Bradford Park Avenue
Dundee
Motherwell

Mair, Thomas (Tommy) OL
Galston
Ayr
Leyton
1908 1909 Chelsea 9 1

Maitland, Alfred Edward (Alf) LB/RB
b Leith 8/10/1896 d 1981
Caps: FLge 1
Leith
Benwell Adelaide
1919 1922 South Shields 151 4
1923 Middlesbrough 25
1924 1929 Newcastle United 156
Jarrow
Northfleet
Salisbury City
Shirley Town
Leamington Town

Maitland, Richard CH
b Wigan q2 1895 d 1972
Boscombe
1921 Portsmouth 2

Major, Arthur LH
b Nantwich q3 1912 d 1953
1932 Notts County 0
Sandbach Ramblers
Stalybridge Celtic
1935 1938 Crewe Alexandra 4

Major, William Henry (Bill) CH
b Poulton 14/1/1911 d 1969
Poulton
1932 1933 New Brighton 21 1
1934 1936 Tranmere Rovers 7

Makepeace, Joseph William Henry (Harry) LH/RH
b Middlesbrough 22/8/1881 d 1952
Caps: FLge 5/England 4
1902 1914 Everton 284 16

Makepeace, Ralph LH/CH
b Trimdon Grange 23/2/1909 d 1995
Blackhall Colliery Welfare
Trimdon Colliery Welfare
Penn XI (Canada)
1931 Sunderland (trial) 0
1932 1933 Hartlepools United 45 2
Blackhall Colliery Welfare
1934 Darlington 1
Altrincham
Blackhall Colliery Welfare

Makin, James (Jim) IR
b Radcliffe q1 1886
1909 1910 Stockport County 16 5
Heywood United
Accrington Stanley
1920 Exeter City 39 6
1921 1922 Accrington Stanley 40 16

Makinson, James (Jim) RH
b Aspull 25/1/1913 d 1979
Clitheroe
1935 1938 Leeds United 68

Malam, Albert IL/IR
b Liverpool 20/1/1913 d 1992
1930 Everton (trial) 0
Colwyn Bay United
1932 1934 Chesterfield 58 25
1934 Huddersfield Town 21 11
1936 1938 Doncaster Rovers 95 26
1939 (Doncaster Rovers) (3)
1946 Wrexham 6 1
Runcorn

Malcolm, George LH
b Thornaby 20/6/1889 d 1965
Thornaby St Mark's
Thornaby St Patrick's
Darlington St Augustine's
1909 Woolwich Arsenal (trial) 0
1909 Fulham 4 1
Plymouth Argyle
1912 1914 Middlesbrough 94 1
1921 1925 Darlington 166 7
1926 Durham City 33
Scarborough Penguins

Malcolm, William IL
b Alloa
Dunipace
1922 1923 Blackburn Rovers 2
Bo'ness

From To Apps Goal

Male, Charles George (George) RB
b Plaistow 8/5/1910 d 1998
Caps: FLge 2/England 19
Clapton
1930 1947 Arsenal 285
1939 (Arsenal) (3)

Male, Norman Alfred LB
b West Bromwich 27/5/1917 d 1992
Bush Rovers
1937 West Bromwich Albion 3 1
1938 1948 Walsall 70 2
1939 (Walsall) (3)

Maley, William (Willie) IR/LH
b Newry 4/1868 d 1958
Caps: SLge 2/Scotland 2
Cathcart Hazlebank
Third Lanark
Celtic
Ardwick (loan)
1895 Manchester City (loan) 1
1896 Everton (loan) 2

Mallalieu, Harry OL
b Rochdale 28/8/1896 d 1981
All Saints Oakenrod
1921 Rochdale 3

Mallett, Joseph (Joe) LH/IR
b Gateshead 8/1/1916 d 2004
Dunston CWS
1935 Charlton Athletic 0
1937 Queen's Park Rangers 29 4
1938 Charlton Athletic 2
1938 1946 Queen's Park Rangers 41 7
1939 (Queen's Park Rangers) (1)
1946 1952 Southampton 215 3
1953 1954 Leyton Orient 27 1

Mallinson, WH GK
Mexborough
1897 1899 Sheffield Wednesday 5
Royston

Malloch, Gavin Cooper LH
b Glasgow 18/7/1905 d 1974
Glasgow Benburb Juniors
1927 1931 Derby County 93
1931 1935 Sheffield Wednesday 84
1936 Millwall 15
1937 Barrow 40
Morton

Malloch, John Napier (Jock) IL/OL
b Lochee 2/11/1877 d 1935
East Craigie
Dundee
Brighton United
1900 1906 Sheffield Wednesday 143 11
1908 Barnsley 0
South Kirkby Colliery
Frickley Colliery

Malloy, William OR
b High Spen 2/4/1900 d 1967
Benwell Colliery
Spen Black & White
1924 Northampton Town 3
Spen Black & White
1926 Ashington 31 6
1927 Stockport County 9
Annfield Plain (trial)

Malone, Patrick GK
1902 Stockport County 1

Maloney, Robert John Herbert (Bob) CH
b Thringstone 8/6/1903 d 1981
Caps: LoI 1
Thrapston
Peterborough & Fletton United
Shepshed Albion
1925 Walsall 3
Peterborough & Fletton United
1926 1931 Northampton Town 183 4
Shelbourne
Racing Club Calais
Dundalk

Maloney, Timothy George (Tim) IL/OL
b South Bank 1909 d 1956
Grangetown
South Bank
1926 Middlesbrough 0
Grangetown
1927 Hull City 0
1928 Darlington 13 4
1931 Stoke City 8 1
South Bank

From To Apps Goal

Malpas, Edward (Ted) CH
b Wolverhampton 6/9/1904 d 1968
Chertington
Shrewsbury Town
Cannock Town
1924 Aston Villa 0
1927 Blackpool 1
1927 Oldham Athletic 3
Kidderminster Harriers

Malpass, A William (Billy) CH/RH/LH
b Wednesbury 5/3/1867 d 1939
Caps: FLge 1
Wednesbury Old Athletic
1891 1898 Wolverhampton Wanderers 133 6

Maltby, George Henry (Ginger) LB
b Long Eaton 16/4/1887 d 1950
Caps: FLge 3
Notts Rangers
1906 1913 Nottingham Forest 216 3
Doncaster Rovers

Manders, Frank IL/IR/OL
b Camberley 13/6/1914 d 1942
Camberley & York Town
Aldershot
1931 1935 Crystal Palace 97 31
1935 1938 Norwich City 130 40
1939 (Norwich City) (3)

Manderson, Robert (Bertie) RB
b Belfast 9/5/1893 d 1946
Caps: Ireland 5
Clifton
Dunedin (Belfast)
Macrory Memorial
Cliftonville Olympic
Derry Celtic
Belfast Celtic
Glenavon
Rangers
1927 Bradford Park Avenue 39

Mandley, John (Jack) OR
b Hanley 1/2/1909 d 1988
1928 1929 Port Vale 47 6
1929 1933 Aston Villa 106 25
Altrincham

Mandy, John Thomas (Tommy) OR/OL
b Bolton 8/12/1899 d 1971
Norwood Crescent
Crossens
Leyland
1922 1923 Southport 28
1925 1929 Wigan Borough 76 17
Burscough
Dick, Kerr's XI
Nelson
Dick, Kerr's XI
Liverpool Corporation Trams

Mandy, Leonard Aubrey (Aubrey) GK
b Transvaal, South Africa 1906 d 1957
State Mines Club
1929 Leicester City 3
State Mines Club

Mangham, James GK
b Cliviger 1/3/1907 d 1995
Worsthorne
Portsmouth Rovers
1927 1929 Nelson 2

Mangnall, David (Dave) CF/IR
b Wigan 21/9/1905 d 1962
Maltby New Church
Maltby Main Colliery Welfare
1922 Huddersfield Town (trial) 0
1922 Rotherham County (trial) 0
1923 Doncaster Rovers 0
Maltby Main Colliery Welfare
1929 Leeds United 9 6
1929 1933 Huddersfield Town 79 61
1933 1934 Birmingham 37 14
1934 1935 West Ham United 35 28
1936 1937 Millwall 58 32
1939 Queen's Park Rangers (3) (3)

Manley, Thomas Ronald (Tom) LH/OL
b Northwich 7/10/1912 d 1988
Brunner Mond
Norley United
Northwich Victoria
1931 1938 Manchester United 188 40
1939 1950 Brentford 116 7
1939 (Brentford) (3)

Mann, Christopher James CH
b West Smethwick 1/1877 d 1934
1897 West Bromwich Albion 0
1899 1900 Aston Villa 10
1901 1904 Burton United 114 8
Mickleover FRD

From To Apps Goal

Mann, Frank Drury IR/LH/CF
b Newark 3/1891 d 1959
Newark Castle Rovers
Newark Town
1909 Leeds City 0
1910 Lincoln City 0
1911 Aston Villa 1
1912 1922 Huddersfield Town 201 68
1922 1929 Manchester United 180 5
Mossley
Meltham Mills

Mann, George W RH
b 1873
St Bernard's
East Stirlingshire
1892 Blackburn Rovers 2 1
1894 1896 Manchester City 59 7
Bristol City

Mann, Herbert Harry (Bert) OR/OL
b Nuneaton 30/12/1907 d 1976
Griff Colliery
1928 Derby County 4
Grantham
1931 Manchester United 13 2
Ripley Town

Mann, J John GK
1895 Lincoln City 8

Mann, John Frederick (Jack) IR
b West Bromwich 1891
Bilston United
Great Bridge Juniors
1914 West Bromwich Albion 2
Newport County
Walsall

Mann, Richard John (Dick) GK
b Stourbridge 26/7/1898 d 1984
Burton All Saints
1921 South Shields 0
1922 Walsall 33
Brierley Hill Alliance

Mann, Samuel OR/OL
b Tipton q1 1910
Royal Woolwich Regiment
1929 Charlton Athletic 0
1930 1931 Thames 36 5
1932 Preston North End 0

Manners, John Albert (Jack) LH/CH
b Morpeth 3/1878 d 1946
Morpeth YMCA
Morpeth Harriers
1904 1911 West Bromwich Albion 193 7
Hartlepools United

Manning, Alfred IR
1919 Port Vale 1
Shildon Athletic
Middleton Athletic

Manning, John T (Jock) CH
b Burntisland
Kirkcaldy United
Raith Rovers
1907 Blackburn Rovers 4
Northampton Town

Manning, John Tom (Jack) OR
b Boston q2 1886 d 1946
Boston Swifts
Boston Town
1905 1906 Hull City 54 9
1908 1909 Bradford Park Avenue 47 9
Rochdale
1912 1914 Lincoln City 90 9
1919 Rotherham County 5
1920 Queen's Park Rangers 22 5
Boston Town

Mannion, Wilfred James (Wilf) IR/IL
b South Bank 16/5/1918 d 2000
Caps: England B/FLge 8/England War 4/ England 26
South Bank St Peter's
1936 1953 Middlesbrough 341 100
1939 (Middlesbrough) (3)
1954 Hull City 16 1
Poole Town
Cambridge United
King's Lynn
Haverhill Rovers
Earlestown

From To Apps Goal

Manns, Thomas (Tommy) LH/RH/RB
b Rotherham q1 1911
Eastwood United WMC
1931 Rotherham United 0
1932 Burnley 10
1933 Manchester United 2
1934 Clapton Orient 3 1
1935 Carlisle United 22
Yeovil & Petters United
Bridport

Manock, Edward (Ted) IR
b Salford 30/6/1904 d 1983
Chester
1929 1930 Nelson 18 2
Sandbach Ramblers
Pendleton Glassworks
CWS Glassworks (Worksop)

Mansfield, Eversley IR
b Barrow q3 1886 d 1954
Caps: England Amat
Preston Winckley
Preston North End 0
Manchester United 0
Preston North End 0
Barrow
Northern Nomads
1908 Preston North End 0
1908 Manchester City 1
Queen's Park
Northern Nomads
Rochdale

Manship, Ernest IL
b Leicester q2 1881 d 1956
Latimer
1902 Leicester Fosse 1
Humberstone Victoria
Clarence Hall

Mansley, Eric Holmes GK
b Chester 28/2/1917 d 1961
Llanerch Celts
1936 1938 Chester 9
1939 Liverpool 0

Manson, David Garrioch (Davie) IR
b Glasgow 20/8/1876
Ayr
Thistle
1894 Rotherham Town 19 5
1895 1896 Leicester Fosse 24 7
1896 Lincoln City 4
Bacup
Warmley
Gravesend United
Rushden
Coalville Town

Manson, Robert (Bob) IR
Brynn Central
1905 Stockport County 19 8
1905 1907 Blackburn Rovers 16 3

Mantle, Joseph (Joe) CF
b Hetton-le-Hole 9/5/1908 d 1977
Spennymoor Juniors
Hetton Juniors
1927 1930 Burnley 50 22
1930 1931 Plymouth Argyle 15 7
1932 1934 Chester 74 63
1935 1936 Carlisle United 55 38
1936 1937 Stockport County 22 12
Heart of Midlothian
1939 Hartlepools United (2) (1)

Manuel, Percival Edward (Percy) OL
b Wantage 21/2/1909
Marlborough
Oxford City
1933 Swindon Town 0
Stourbridge
1934 Wrexham 2
Montreal

Mapson, John (Johnny) GK
b Birkenhead 2/5/1917 d 1999
Caps: England War 1
Westrop Rovers
Highworth Town
1934 Swindon Town 0
Guildford City (loan)
1935 Reading 2
1935 1952 Sunderland 345
1939 (Sunderland) (3)

March, Harold James IL
b Gamston 30/1/1904 d 1977
Army
1929 Hull City 8
1930 1931 Lincoln City 10 5
Grantham

From To Apps Goal

March, Richard (Dickie) LH/RH
b Washington 9/10/1908 d 1987
Crawcrook Albion
1932 1938 Queen's Park Rangers 220 3
1939 (Queen's Park Rangers) (2)

March, Zillwood George (Zach) OL/OR
b Bosham 25/10/1892 d 1994
Bosham
1920 1921 Brighton & Hove Albion 56
1922 Portsmouth 4
Chichester City

Marcroft, Edward Hollows (Ted) OR/OL
b Rochdale 4/1910
Bacup Borough
Great Harwood
1931 Middlesbrough 1 1
1932 Queen's Park Rangers 29 8
1933 Cardiff City 28 2
1934 Accrington Stanley 24 4
Bacup Borough
1936 Rochdale 5
Macclesfield

Mardon, Harry James CF/IL
b Cardiff 8/6/1914 d 1981
Victoria Albion
Hereford United
1936 1937 Notts County 22 8
1937 1938 Bournemouth & Boscombe Ath 25 14
1938 Bristol City 13 3

Markham, Colin LH
b Clowne 2/3/1916 d 1967
1937 1946 Torquay United 25 1

Marklew, Herbert CF
b Dinnington 4/4/1910 d 1987
Dinnington Athletic
1932 Huddersfield Town (trial) 0
1933 1934 Lincoln City 7 3
Dinnington Main Colliery Welfare

Marks, William OR
b Worksop q2 1890
1910 1911 Gainsborough Trinity 3

Marks, William George (George) GK
b Amesbury 9/4/1915 d 1998
Caps: England War 8
Salisbury Corinthians
1936 Arsenal 0
Margate
1938 Arsenal 2
1939 (Arsenal) (3)
1946 1947 Blackburn Rovers 67
1948 Bristol City 9
1948 1952 Reading 118
Bulford United

Marlow, Geoffrey Arthur (Geoff) OL/IL
b Worksop 13/12/1914 d 1978
Dinnington Athletic
1937 1938 Lincoln City 16 5
Newark Town
1945 1948 Lincoln City 64 21
Grantham
Stalybridge Celtic
Skegness Town

Marlow, Leonard Frederick (Len) IL/CF
b Putney 30/4/1899 d 1975
Wimbledon
Old Kingstonians
1921 Huddersfield Town 1
1923 Reading 5 1
Ebbw Vale
Torquay United
Grays Thurrock
Thames Mills

Marlow, Owen GK
b Bolton q1 1909 d 1969
1926 Swansea Town 2
Mansfield Town

Marlow, T OL
1892 1893 Walsall Town Swifts 19 3

Marple, FA OL
1894 Burslem Port Vale 2 1

Marples, Emmerson Arthur RB
b Chesterfield q1 1879 d 1964
Dronfield Town
1901 1907 Chesterfield Town 146 10
1907 Sunderland 10
Chesterfield Town
Eckington Works

From To Apps Goal

Marquis, Frederick (Fred) IR/CF
b Kirkham 15/6/1899 d 1957
Rushden Town
Lancaster Town
1920 1924 Preston North End 35 9
1925 1926 Tranmere Rovers 70 32
Lancaster Town

Marr, Andrew (Andy) OR
b Newcastle 1892
Ashington
Coventry City
1913 Wolverhampton Wanderers 3
Gateshead

Marr, R IR
1893 Darwen 12 3

Marr, Reuben Charles RH
b Balby q2 1884 d 1961
Mexborough Town
1906 1919 Bristol City 178 11

Marr, Robert (Bobby) IL
b Bathgate 1870
Broxburn
1890 Burnley 9 4
St Bernard's

Marrable, Sidney Albert (Sid) CH
b Mile End 25/4/1895 d 1973
Leytonstone
1919 1920 Fulham 8
Wimbledon
1921 West Ham United 0
Leytonstone

Marriott, E IL/LH
1892 1897 Burton Swifts 3 1

Marriott, Ernest (Ernie) RB
b Sutton-in-Ashfield 25/1/1913 d 1989
Sutton Junction
1934 1947 Brighton & Hove Albion 163 1
1939 (Brighton & Hove Albion) (3)
Tonbridge
Eastbourne United

Marriott, Frank LB
b Sutton-in-Ashfield 26/10/1894 d 1947
Sutton Junction
1919 1922 Notts County 96 1
1923 Swansea Town 0
1924 Lincoln City 3
Grantham

Marriott, William OR
b Northampton 4/1880 d 1944
Wellingborough
1901 Aston Villa 8
Bristol Rovers
Northampton Town
New Brompton

Marrison, Thomas (Tom) IR/CF
b Darnall q2 1881 d 1926
1902 1904 Sheffield Wednesday 5 1
Rotherham Town
1906 1910 Nottingham Forest 163 38
1911 Oldham Athletic 17 4
1912 Bristol City 13 1

Marrow, Clifford Fallows IL
b Northwich q4 1870 d 1951
1894 Crewe Alexandra 1

Marsden, Ben RB
b Hanley q2 1898
1919 Port Vale 0
1920 1924 Queen's Park Rangers 126 6
1925 Reading 2

Marsden, Frederick (Fred) RB/LB
b Blackburn 6/9/1911 d 1989
Clitheroe
Manchester Central
1934 Accrington Stanley 5
1935 Wolverhampton Wanderers 1
1936 1948 Bournemouth & Boscombe Ath 194 1
1939 (Bournemouth & Boscombe Ath) (3) (1)
Weymouth

Marsden, Henry (Harry) RB
b Bentley 1902
Bentley Colliery
1923 Doncaster Rovers 0
Wombwell
1925 1928 Nottingham Forest 14
1929 1933 Brighton & Hove Albion 164
1934 Gillingham 31
1935 York City 0
Peterborough United

From To Apps Goal

Marsden, Joseph Thomas (Joe) RB
b Darwen q4 1868 d 1897
Caps: England 1
Padiham
Darwen
1891 Everton 1

Marsden, Joseph William RB
b Nottingham 6/1885
Stanton Hill Victoria
1909 Nottingham Forest 2

Marsden, Leonard IR
b Rotherham 4/2/1909 d 1992
1926 Rotherham United 1

Marsden, T LH/CF
1891 1894 Darwen 11 1

Marsden, WF IR
b 1872
1891 Darwen 19 7

Marsden, William (Billy) LH/CH
b Silksworth 10/11/1901 d 1983
Caps: FLge 1/England 3
Silksworth Colliery
1920 1923 Sunderland 3 2
1924 1929 Sheffield Wednesday 205 9

Marsh, Cecil William B IR/CF
b Darnall q4 1890 d 1956
Beighton Recreation
Heeley Friends
1919 1920 Blackpool 5
1921 Nelson 17 2
Fleetwood

Marsh, Frank Kitchener RH/OL
b Bolton 7/6/1916 d 1978
Stafford Rangers
1937 Crewe Alexandra 0
1938 Bolton Wanderers 3
1939 1947 Chester 69 2
1939 (Chester) (2)
Macclesfield Town

Marsh, Frederick James (Fred) GK
b Dudley q3 1914
Dudley Town
1936 Newport County 6

Marsh, G RB
1889 1891 Accrington 3

Marsh, Isaac William (Ike) CH/LH
b Burton-on-Trent 1/1877
Nottingham Jardines
Clifton Colliery
Hucknall Portland
1896 Burton Wanderers 0
Northfleet
West Herts
1898 Gainsborough Trinity 1
Hucknall Portland
1899 Notts County 3
Newark
1901 1902 Doncaster Rovers 33 3
Somercotes United
Worksop Town
Worksop North End
Dinnington Main Colliery Welfare
Birchwood Colliery
Denaby United
Chesterfield Town
Denaby United

Marsh, Joseph (Joe) OR
b Bolsover
1903 Chesterfield Town 2
Old Whittington Mutuals

Marsh, Joseph (Joe) IR
b Hemsworth
Hemsworth Colliery
Brierley
South Kirkby
1919 1921 Bradford City 24 4
Castleford Town

Marsh, Samuel (Sam) IR/RH/CF
b Westhoughton q1 1879
Daisy Hill
Hindley
Atherton Church House
1902 1911 Bolton Wanderers 185 72
1912 Bury 3

Marsh, William IR
b Brodsworth
Brodsworth Main Colliery
1931 Halifax Town 3

From To Apps Goal

Marsh, Wilson GK
b Hunslet q3 1894 d 1989
Normanton Springs
Eckington Works
1921 1923 Chelsea 10
Dundee
Kilmarnock

Marshall, Alfred Willis (Alf) RH/LH
b Darlington q1 1888 d 1923
Darlington St John's
Darlington St Augustine's
1909 1919 Fulham 100
1920 1922 Oldham Athletic 66 3

Marshall, Arthur George IL/RB
b Liverpool q3 1877
Kirkdale
1897 Everton (trial) 0
Chester
1899 Liverpool 0
Aberystwyth
Crewe Alexandra
1901 Leicester Fosse 15 3
1901 Stockport County 11 2
1902 Manchester United 6
Portsmouth
Hull City
Ashton Town
Earlestown
Chester

Marshall, Ernest (Ernie) LH/IR
b Dinnington 23/5/1918 d 1983
Dinnington Athletic
1934 Huddersfield Town (trial) 0
1936 1937 Sheffield United 13
1939 1946 Cardiff City 1
1939 (Cardiff City) (3)
Yeovil Town
Bath City

Marshall, FR CF
Wishaw Athletic
1899 Luton Town 3 1
Wishaw Athletic

Marshall, Frank IR/RH
b Shettleston 1904 d 1928
Shawfield Juniors
Shettleston
Rangers (trial)
Falkirk (trial)
1924 1926 Gillingham 101 16
1926 Brentford 21

Marshall, Frederick Arnold (Fred) OR
b Walsall 1/8/1870 d 1941
Birmingham St George's
Wednesbury Old Athletic
1890 Aston Villa 3
Birmingham St George's
Nechells
1892 Walsall Town Swifts 6 2
Bordesley Green Victoria

Marshall, George Harold LB
b Walker 3/3/1896
Shankhouse
Portsmouth (trial)
Newcastle City
Southend United
1920 1922 Wolverhampton Wanderers 102 1
1923 Walsall 11
1923 Reading 0
1924 Bournemouth & Boscombe Ath 20
Darlaston

Marshall, Henry James Hall (Harry) LH
b Portobello 24/11/1872 d 1936
Caps: SLge 4/Scotland 2
Portobello Thistle
St Bernard's
Heart of Midlothian
1892 1894 Blackburn Rovers 51 2
Heart of Midlothian
Celtic (loan)
1897 Blackburn Rovers (loan) 2
Celtic (loan)
Celtic
Alloa Athletic (loan)
Raith Rovers (loan)
Clyde
Broxburn Athletic

Marshall, James (Jimmy) LB
b Blowick 4/7/1899 d 1967
Blowick Juniors
Blowick Working Lads
1921 1925 Southport 25

From To Apps Goal

Marshall, (Dr) James (Jimmy) IR
b Avonbridge 3/1/1908 d 1977
Caps: SLge 1/Scotland 3
Shettleston Juniors
Rangers
1934 Arsenal 4
1934 1936 West Ham United 57 14
Ashford Town (Kent)

Marshall, James Hynd (Jimmy) CF/IL/OL
b Peterhead 9/6/1890 d 1958
Winchburgh
Vale of Grange
Bo'ness
Partick Thistle
1914 1920 Bradford City 33 12
Ayr United (loan)
1920 1922 Oldham Athletic 80 17
Bangor
1923 Southport 10 1
1924 Rotherham County 1
1924 Lincoln City 3 1
Queen of the South
Stranraer

Marshall, James Michael OL
b Bishop Auckland q3 1897
St Peter's Albion
1920 Hull City (trial) 1
Preston Colliery
1922 Ashington 0

Marshall, John IR/RH
b Stenhousemuir 1892
Bedlington United
1912 1913 Preston North End 26 4
1913 1914 Barnsley 14 1
Clyde

Marshall, John (Jack) CH
b Southport 31/7/1895 d 1968
St Paul's
Rochdale
Southport Central
Shelbourne
Southport
1919 1923 Preston North End 52
1924 Wigan Borough 34 2
1925 Southport 12 1
1925 Wigan Borough 7

Marshall, John (Jock) RB
b Saltcoats
Caps: WLge 1/Scotland 7/USA 1
Saltcoats Victoria
Shettleston
St Mirren
Stevenston United
St Mirren
Third Lanark
St Mirren
1919 1922 Middlesbrough 116
Llanelly
Belmont (New York)
Brooklyn Wanderers
Newark Skeeters
Brooklyn Wanderers
Bethlehem Steel

Marshall, John CF
b Aberdeen
Aberdeen Stonywood
1928 Liverpool 0
1929 Stockport County 2 1

Marshall, John G OR
b Hetton-le-Hole
1938 Wolverhampton Wanderers 1

Marshall, John Gilmore (Jack) LB
b Turton 29/5/1917 d 1998
Bacup Borough
1938 1946 Burnley 26
1939 (Burnley) (2)

Marshall, Joseph GK
b Ripley 24/4/1862 d 1913
Staveley
1888 Derby County 16
Derby Junction

Marshall, Kenneth C (Ken) GK
b Bournemouth
1923 Bournemouth & Boscombe Ath 2
Poole

Marshall, Lancelot Edwin (Lance) RB
b Birkdale 30/6/1914 d 1968
Huyton Quarry
Prescot Cables
1934 1935 Southport 21
Wigan Athletic
Prescot Cables
South Liverpool

From To Apps Goal

Marshall, Lester CF/LB
b Castleford 4/2/1902
Rowntree's
Selby Town
York City
1924 1926 Lincoln City 19 6
Scarborough
York City

Marshall, Owen Thomas LB/RB
b Nottingham 17/9/1892 d 1963
Ilkeston United
1913 1919 Chelsea 34
1921 1922 Gillingham 39
Maidstone United

Marshall, Robert (Rob) LB
b Dalry 13/3/1900
Dalry Thistle
1922 West Ham United (trial) 0
Kilmarnock
1923 Reading 1

Marshall, Robert Grant (Bobby) OR
b Edinburgh 1876
Leith Athletic
1897 1898 Liverpool 20 2
Portsmouth
Brighton & Hove Albion
St Bernard's

Marshall, Robert Samuel (Bobby) IR/CH/CF
b Hucknall 3/4/1903 d 1966
Hucknall Olympic
1920 1927 Sunderland 198 69
1927 1937 Manchester City 325 70
1938 Stockport County 0

Marshall, Thomas OR
St Mirren
1898 1902 Bolton Wanderers 4
1904 1905 Burnley 23 4

Marshall, Thomas Albert (Tommy) GK
b Blowick 2/9/1897 d 1964
Blowick Working Lads
Park Villa
Skelmersdale United
1921 1924 Southport 4
Skelmersdale United
1925 Accrington Stanley 3

Marshall, William CH
b Newcastle
Dunston Atlas Villa
1921 1922 Watford 2
Leadgate Park

Marshall, William (Bill) CH
b Falkirk 13/4/1914
Broxburn Athletic
1935 1937 Bradford Park Avenue 13

Marshall, William Edwin (Billy) OL
b Birmingham 1/10/1898 d 1966
Rotax Works
1921 1922 Chesterfield 67 10
1923 1931 Grimsby Town 340 59
1932 Reading 19 4
Boston Town

Marshall, William Henry (Bill) GK
b Liverpool 1880
1901 Liverpool 1

Marshall, William Henry OL
b Kilnhurst q1 1895
Silverwood Colliery
1914 Sheffield United 0
Silverwood Colliery
1919 Rotherham County 3

Marshall, William Henry (Harry) IL/IR/LH
b Hucknall 16/2/1905 d 1959
Hucknall Primitives
Bromley's Athletic
1923 1925 Nottingham Forest 19 3
1926 1927 Southport 54 27
1927 1929 Wolverhampton Wanderers 52 13
1929 1931 Port Vale 55 7
1931 Tottenham Hotspur 1
Kidderminster Harriers
Brierley Hill Alliance
1935 1937 Rochdale 95 22
Linfield

Marshalsey, William Henry Gray (Bill) RH
b Lochgelly 18/4/1910 d 1977
Denbeath Star
St Bernard's
Heart of Midlothian
St Bernard's (loan)
1933 Cardiff City 7 1
Brechin City
Peebles Rovers

From To Apps Goal

Marsland, Samuel IL
New Mills
1925 Stockport County 5

Marsland, William IR
1926 Stockport County 1

Marson, Fred OL/IL
b Darlaston 8/1/1900 d 1976
Darlaston
1923 1924 Wolverhampton Wanderers 8 4
1926 1927 Sheffield Wednesday 10
1928 Swansea Town 14 4
Darlaston
Wellington Town
Shrewsbury Town
Darlaston

Marston, John Pearson RH
b Gainsborough q1 1888 d 1921
1911 Gainsborough Trinity 1

Martin, Albert Ogden RH
b Lincoln 19/3/1896 d 1975
Rustons Staff
1919 Lincoln City 3
Rustons Staff
Retford Town

Martin, Alfred CF/RB
b Norton Canes
Hednesford Town
1925 Walsall 2
1926 Stockport County 4 2

Martin, Andrew Fitzsimmons (Andy) LH/OL/RH
b Wigtown 22/9/1896 d 1978
Kilwinning Rangers
Ardrossan Winton Rovers
1922 1923 Blackpool 16
1924 1927 Halifax Town 149 31
1928 Rochdale 32 1
1929 Torquay United 13

Martin, Blakey LH/RH
b Halifax q4 1891 d 1960
Caps: SoLge 1/WLge 2
Castleford Town
1914 Glossop 10 1
Castleford Town
1919 Derby County 6
1920 1921 Southend United 75 1
Llanelly

Martin, David Kirker (Davy 'Boy') CF
b Belfast 1/2/1914 d 1991
Caps: IrLge 4/NIRL 3/Ireland Amat/Ireland 10
Royal Ulster Rifles
Cliftonville
Belfast Celtic
1934 1935 Wolverhampton Wanderers 25 17
1936 1938 Nottingham Forest 81 41
1938 Notts County 26 16
1939 (Notts County) (2) (3)
Glentoran
Derry City
1945 Notts County 0

Martin, Edward (Ted) LB
b Greasley 15/5/1910 d 1990
Selston Amateurs
Heanor Town
1932 1945 Brighton & Hove Albion 155 4
1939 (Brighton & Hove Albion) (3)

Martin, Francis (Frank) LH/RB
b Gateshead 3/1/1887 d 1967
Gateshead Rodsley
1907 1910 Hull City 29 1
1911 1920 Grimsby Town 159 1
1921 Aberdare Athletic 10
Cleethorpes Town
Charlton's (Grimsby)

Martin, Frederick (Fred) CF/OR
b Clay Cross 1889 d 1932
Clay Cross Works
South Kirkby
1909 1911 Barnsley 10 2
1912 Sunderland 0
Raith Rovers

Martin, Frederick (Fred) RH/CH/LH
b Rotherhithe 28/12/1907 d 1978
Rotherhithe
1926 1930 Millwall 45 1
1932 Torquay United 11

Martin, George Ernest LH/IL
b Plumstead 8/5/1892 d 1979
Woolwich Polytechnic
1919 1923 Fulham 48

From	To		Apps	Goal
Martin, George Scott			IR/IL/OR	
b Bothwell 14/7/1899			d 1972	
		Cadzow St Anne's		
		Hamilton Academical		
		Bathgate (loan)		
		Bo'ness		
1922	1927	Hull City	204	55
1927	1931	Everton	85	31
1932		Middlesbrough	6	
1933	1936	Luton Town	98	27
Martin, Henry (Harry)			OL	
b Selston 5/12/1891			d 1974	
Caps: FLge 3/England 1				
		Sutton Junction		
1911	1921	Sunderland	213	23
1922	1924	Nottingham Forest	107	13
1925	1930	Rochdale	93	18
Martin, Henry J			IL	
b Chatham				
		Chatham Town		
1921	1922	Gillingham	7	2
Martin, Hugh Innes			CF	
b St Ninians, Stirlingshire 10/6/1903			d 1956	
		King's Park		
		Falkirk		
1929		Doncaster Rovers	2	
		King's Park		
Martin, Isaac George (Pompey)			CH/LH	
b Gateshead 25/5/1889			d 1962	
		Gateshead Rodsley		
		Windy Nook		
1908	1911	Sunderland	16	
		Portsmouth		
1920	1926	Norwich City	223	1
		Boulton & Paul		
		CEYMS (Norwich)		
Martin, James			OR	
1894	1895	Bolton Wanderers	7	1
Martin, James (Jimmy)			IL/CF/IR	
b Lancaster 1/1875				
1896	1897	Blackpool	52	17
1898	1900	Walsall	93	28
1901		Burton United	27	4
Martin, James (Jimmy)			LH	
b Bo'ness 21/8/1893			d 1940	
		Bo'ness		
		Heart of Midlothian		
		Rangers		
		Airdrieonians (loan)		
		Morton		
		Bo'ness		
		Dunfermline Athletic		
		Dumbarton		
1920	1926	Portsmouth	209	27
		Aldershot		
Martin, James Colin (Jimmy)			CF/IR/IL	
b Stoke-on-Trent 2/12/1898			d 1969	
		Stoke St Peter's		
		Basford		
1919	1920	Stoke	16	1
1921	1923	Aberdare Athletic	76	34
1923		Wolverhampton Wanderers	11	6
1924		Reading	18	2
1925		Aberdare Athletic	39	16
1926	1927	Bristol City	40	16
1928		Blackpool	4	2
1928		Southend United	3	1
1929		Halifax Town	18	4
		Congleton Town		
Martin, James Joseph			OL	
b Patricroft 28/11/1908			d 1980	
		Bacup Borough		
1935		Hull City	4	1
1936		Accrington Stanley	5	
		Macclesfield		
		Great Harwood		
1938		Bristol City (trial)	0	
Martin, John (Jack)			CF	
b South Shields 1882				
		Tyne Dock		
		Kingston Villa		
		South Shields		
1904	1905	Lincoln City	65	30
1906	1907	Blackburn Rovers	57	25
		Brighton & Hove Albion		
		Millwall Athletic		
		Hartlepools United		
		New Seaham Gymnasium		
		Seaham Albion		

From	To		Apps	Goal
Martin, John (Jack)			OL	
b Bishop Auckland 10/12/1904			d 1984	
		Hebburn Colliery		
1923		Darlington	6	
1924		Leeds United	2	
1926	1927	Accrington Stanley	44	8
		Connah's Quay & Shotton		
1929		Bury	1	1
1930		Reading	0	
		Guildford City		
1931	1933	Doncaster Rovers	26	5
Martin, John (Jack)			LH/RH	
b Sunderland 6/10/1912			d 1971	
		Horden Colliery Welfare		
1931		Portsmouth (trial)	0	
1932	1938	Middlesbrough	129	3
Martin, John Charles (Jack)			CH	
b Leeds 25/7/1903			d 1976	
		Barnoldswick Park Villa		
		Padiham Juniors		
1922		Burnley	0	
1924	1925	Accrington Stanley	28	1
1925	1926	Blackpool	4	
1927	1928	Southport	73	2
		Macclesfield		
1930		Southport	5	
1930		Nelson	27	1
1931		Wigan Borough	12	
1931		Oldham Athletic	11	1
Martin, John Rowland (Jackie)			IR	
b Hamstead 5/8/1914			d 1996	
Caps: England War 2				
		Combined London Colleges		
		Hednesford Town		
1936	1948	Aston Villa	81	22
1939		(Aston Villa)	(3)	(1)
Martin, Sydney H			IR	
b Durban, South Africa				
1927		Huddersfield Town	0	
1928		Grimsby Town	0	
1929		Gillingham	2	
Martin, T			GK	
1896	1897	Nottingham Forest	6	
Martin, Thomas B			RB	
b 1889				
		Mid Annandale		
1911		Bradford City	1	
Martin, Tudor James (Ted)			CF/OL	
b Caerau 20/4/1904			d 1979	
Caps: Wales 1				
		Caerau Corinthians		
		Bridgend Town		
1926		West Bromwich Albion	0	
1929		Newport County	29	34
1930	1931	Wolverhampton Wanderers	15	9
1932	1935	Swansea Town	117	46
1936		West Ham United	11	7
1936	1938	Southend United	57	28
1939		(Southend United)	(3)	
Martin, William John (Billy)			IR/IL	
b Glasgow 12/6/1913				
		Shawfield Juniors		
1936	1938	Bradford Park Avenue	60	8
1939		(Bradford Park Avenue)	(1)	
Martin, William Thomas James (Bill)			CF	
b Poplar 27/4/1883			d 1954	
		Millwall St John's		
		Millwall Athletic		
1905		Hull City	4	
1906	1907	Clapton Orient	61	28
1908		Stockport County	11	3
1908	1909	Oldham Athletic	7	
		Millwall Athletic		
Martin, William W			LB	
b London				
Caps: England Amat				
		Ilford		
1911		Huddersfield Town	5	
Martindale, Harling Richardson			IR	
b Beeston 10/9/1899				
		North Staffordshire Regiment		
1919		Nottingham Forest	1	
Martindale, Leonard (Len)			RH/LH	
b Bolton 30/6/1920			d 1971	
		Rossendale United (trial)		
1937	1950	Burnley	69	2
1951		Accrington Stanley	16	

From	To		Apps	Goal
Maskell, Leslie John (Les)			CF	
b Cowes 30/11/1918			d 1995	
		Cowes		
		Frost's Athletic		
1937	1938	Norwich City	7	2
		Lowestoft Town		
		Diss Town		
Maskill, George			RH	
b Great Ouseburn 4/10/1906			d 1969	
Caps: England Sch				
		Acomb WMC		
		York City		
		Scarborough		
1932		York City	3	
		York Post Office		
Maskill, Thomas (Tommy)			LH/RH	
b York 2/5/1903			d 1956	
Caps: England Sch				
		Poppleton Road Old Boys		
		Acomb WMC		
		York City		
1923	1925	Coventry City	59	1
		Caernarvon Athletic		
		Rhyl Athletic		
1928		Coventry City	10	
		Scarborough		
1930		Carlisle United	37	1
1931		Barnsley	17	3
1932		York City	29	3
		Selby Town		
Maskrey, Henry Mart (Harry)			GK	
b Unstone 8/10/1880			d 1927	
Caps: FLge 1/England 1				
		Ripley Athletic		
1902	1909	Derby County	197	
1909	1910	Bradford City	41	
		Ripley Town & Athletic		
		Stalybridge Celtic		
		Mansfield Mechanics		
		Mansfield Town		
		Celanese		
1920		Derby County	5	
		Burton All Saints		
Mason, Arthur			RB/LB	
b Cornsay Colliery 7/1895			d 1954	
		Cornsay Colliery		
		Craghead United		
		West Stanley		
1925	1926	Reading	6	
1927	1928	Norwich City	7	
1929	1931	Hartlepools United	18	
		Crook Town		
		Annfield Plain		
		Cornsay Welfare		
		Thorne Colliery		
		Blackhall Welfare		
		Hesleden Rising Star		
Mason, Charles (Charlie)			LB	
b Wolverhampton 13/4/1863			d 1941	
Caps: England 3				
1888	1891	Wolverhampton Wanderers	75	1
Mason, Charles			CF	
1894	1895	Burslem Port Vale	9	1
Mason, David W			CF	
		Cornsay Colliery		
1935		Newcastle United	0	
1936		Birmingham	0	
		Blyth Spartans		
1938		Darlington	6	5
Mason, Frederick C (Fred)			CF	
b Leeds				
1938		Halifax Town	2	1
Mason, Frederick Oliver (Fed)			RB/LB	
b Solihull 1/8/1901				
1921		Coventry City	0	
1922		Cardiff City	1	
1924	1926	Rochdale	49	
1927		Merthyr Town	7	
		Dundalk		
		Derry City		
Mason, George			OR	
b Church Gresley 16/9/1896			d 1987	
		Frickley Colliery		
1920	1922	Leeds United	65	5
1923		Swindon Town	1	
		Mexborough Town		
Mason, George William			CH	
b Birmingham 5/9/1913			d 1993	
Caps: England Sch/England War 2				
		Redhill Amateurs		
1930		Birmingham (trial)	0	
1931	1951	Coventry City	330	6
1939		(Coventry City)	(3)	(1)
		Nuneaton Borough		

From	To		Apps	Goal
Mason, James (Jim)			OL/IL	
1894	1895	Burslem Port Vale	36	8
Mason, Jeremiah (Jerry)			LB	
		Blakenhall St Luke's		
1889		Wolverhampton Wanderers	6	
		Willenhall Swifts		
Mason, John			CF/IL	
		Worcester City		
1907	1908	Wolverhampton Wanderers	8	1
		Bristol Rovers		
Mason, John Nicholson			OL	
b Percy Main 17/5/1901			d 1986	
1921	1922	South Shields	4	
Mason, Leslie			OR	
b Coleshill				
		Evesham Town		
		Nuneaton Town		
1929		Walsall	3	1
Mason, Robert (Bob)			GK	
b Burnbank 1884				
		Burnbank Athletic		
		Clyde		
		Hamilton Academical		
1909	1913	Bradford Park Avenue	118	
		Stalybridge Celtic		
		Burnbank Athletic		
		Hamilton Academical		
Mason, Robert (Bobby)			CH	
b Houghton-le-Spring 13/5/1901			d 1981	
		Whitburn		
1923	1924	Leeds United	15	
1927		Bristol Rovers	0	
1928		Hartlepools United	13	1
		West Stanley		
Mason, Samuel McAlonan (Sam)			CH	
b Fauldhouse 4/7/1906			d 1974	
		Partick Thistle		
1926		Gillingham	19	1
1927	1929	Exeter City	53	2
		Metropolitan Police		
Mason, SR			RH	
1910		Bristol City	3	
Mason, Thomas Edwin			OR	
b Hull 26/7/1893			d 1969	
1919	1920	Hull City	3	
		Rotherham Town		
Mason, Thomas Lot (Tom)			IR	
b Portsmouth 23/11/1886			d 1954	
1911		Tottenham Hotspur	7	1
		Southend United		
		Sittingbourne		
Mason, William			GK	
1892		Accrington	4	
Mason, William			OR	
1892		Nottingham Forest	5	
1892	1893	Burton Swifts	17	2
Mason, William			CH	
b Melbourne 1876				
		Melbourne Town		
1899		Leicester Fosse	0	
		Coalville Town		
1901		Chesterfield Town	2	
Mason, William Sidney (Bill)			GK	
b Earlsfield 31/10/1908			d 1995	
		Wimbledon		
1928	1929	Fulham	33	
1933	1938	Queen's Park Rangers	154	
		Wimbledon Police		
Massarella, Leonard			OR	
b Doncaster 14/2/1917			d 1999	
		Denaby United		
1937	1938	Sheffield Wednesday	31	10
Massey, Alfred Woolley (Alf)			RH	
b Normacot 16/10/1918				
		Caverswall Old Boys		
		Congleton Town		
1938		Stoke City	2	
1939		(Stoke City)	(3)	
		Stafford Rangers		
Massey, Frederick James (Fred)			IR	
b East Ham 2/11/1883			d 1953	
		Leyton		
1908		Tottenham Hotspur	1	
		West Ham United		
Massey, Frederick John (Fred)			OR	
b Helsby q1 1898			d 1965	
1921		Crewe Alexandra	4	
		Aldershot Old Boys		

From To | Apps | Goal

Massey, James (Jimmy) GK
b Wolverhampton 1869 d 1960
Denaby United
Doncaster Rovers
1894 1900 Sheffield Wednesday 159
Denaby United
South Kirkby Colliery

Massey, Kendrick Bernard (Bernard) IR/OR
b Ripley 5/11/1920 d 2006
Peterborough United
1938 1950 Halifax Town 83 7
Scarborough

Massie, Alexander (Alex) RH/IR
b Possilpark 13/3/1906 d 1977
Caps: SLge 6/Scotland 18
Blockairn Juniors
Shawfield Juniors
Petershill
Glasgow Perthshire
Glasgow Benburb
Glasgow Ashfield
Partick Thistle
Ayr United
1926 1927 Bury 17 4
Bethlehem Steel
Dolphin
Heart of Midlothian
1935 1938 Aston Villa 141 5
1939 (Aston Villa) (3)

Masterman, Wallace (Wally) IL
b Newcastle 29/1/1888 d 1965
Stockton
1910 1911 Gainsborough Trinity 41 4
1914 1919 Sheffield United 36 12
1920 Stoke 0

Masters, Arthur OR
b Coppull 17/8/1910 d 1998
Horwich RMI
1932 1936 Nottingham Forest 109 24
1937 1938 Port Vale 66 13

Mates, John (Jack) CH
b Chirk 28/2/1870 d 1938
Caps: Wales 3
Chirk
Northwich Victoria
Crewe Alexandra
1893 Northwich Victoria 7
Chirk
Chester
Gainsborough Trinity

Mather, Edward CF
b Westhoughton
Bolton League
1920 Southend United 3 1
Leyland

Mather, Stanley James E (Stan) OL
b Bolton 6/1/1905 d 1998
Horwich Central
Horwich RMI
1931 1932 Crewe Alexandra 14 3
1933 Southport 0

Mather, Stanley Joseph (Stan) GK
b Bolton
Bolton League
1920 Southend United 2

Mathieson, Allan IL/IR
b Belfast 22/7/1895 d 1953
Caps: Ireland 2
Parkside Rovers
Avondale
Glentoran
1920 1921 Luton Town 54 16
1922 Exeter City 26 4
Workington
1923 1926 New Brighton 128 37
Coleraine
Holywood Rangers
Glentoran

Mathieson, James Adamson (Jimmy) GK
b Methil 10/5/1905 d 1950
Dubbleside Hearts
Colinsburgh United
Partick Thistle
Raith Rovers
1926 1932 Middlesbrough 245
1934 1937 Brentford 126
Queen of the South

From To | Apps | Goal

Mathieson, John IL
b Belfast 7/10/1902 d 1958
Barn
Shelbourne
Glentoran
Sandown Park
Barn
1926 New Brighton 11 3
Dundalk
1929 New Brighton 0
Belfast Celtic
Coleraine
Glenavon
Carrickfergus
Larne
Glentoran
Ballymena United
Ballyclare Comrades

Mathieson, John Alexander CH
b Stevenston 9/12/1904 d 1984
Saltcoats Victoria
Kilmarnock
1929 Barrow 11 1
Distillery
Saltcoats Victoria

Mathieson, William OL
b Glasgow 1870
Clydesdale
Glasgow Thistle
1892 1893 Newton Heath 10 2
1895 Rotherham Town 3
Fairfield
Chorley
South Shore

Mathison, George LH/CH/RH
b Walker 24/11/1909 d 1989
Caps: England Sch
Walker Celtic
1928 1932 Newcastle United 20
1932 1933 Lincoln City 37
1934 1936 Gateshead 83 5
1937 Burnley 0
1937 Hartlepools United 0

Matier, Gerald (Gerry) GK
b Lisburn 1/12/1912 d 1984
Caps: LoI 7
Coleraine
1937 1938 Blackburn Rovers 20
Dundalk
Brideville
Glentoran
1945 Bradford City 0
1946 Plymouth Argyle 0
1946 Torquay United 17

Matson, Francis Robert (Frank) OR/IR
b Reading 21/11/1905 d 1985
Cardiff Corinthians
1925 Reading 0
1926 1929 Cardiff City 27 3
1930 Newport County 1 1
1931 Southampton 2

Matthew, Henry Moram LH
b Dundee 16/4/1870 d 1956
Darlington
1892 Bolton Wanderers 8
Dundee
Millwall Athletic
1897 Preston North End 18
Gravesend United
Distillery
Watford

Matthew, James CH
b Dundee
Lincoln City
1891 1892 Burnley 26 1
1892 Accrington 6
Millwall Athletic
Sheppey United

Matthews, Alfred William (Alf) OR
b Bristol 28/4/1901 d 1985
Parson Street Old Boys
1921 Bristol City 1
1922 1925 Exeter City 138 13
1925 1932 Plymouth Argyle 142 30
1933 Doncaster Rovers 8 1
1934 Crystal Palace 0

Matthews, Cecil Henry Wheeler (Cyril) OR
b Cowes 1/12/1901 d 1973
Cowes
Walney United
1921 1923 Barrow 84 16
1923 1927 Bury 67 14
1927 1929 Notts County 15
1929 Lincoln City 0
1930 Stockport County 34 10
1931 Chester 9 1
Hyde United

From To | Apps | Goal

Matthews, Charles Mosley IR
b Sheffield 11/8/1895 d 1977
Heeley Friends
Leeds City
1919 Barnsley 2
Scunthorpe & Lindsey United

Matthews, Ernest (Ernie) CF
b Chester-le-Street 9/11/1912
Kibblesworth Welfare
1935 1937 Bury 73 46
1937 Sheffield Wednesday 16 7
Colchester United
Ashington

Matthews, Frank OL/IL
b Wallsend 26/12/1902 d 1981
Washington Blue Star
Washington Colliery
Usworth Colliery
1922 Blackpool 0
1923 1924 Barnsley 34 5
1925 1926 Southampton 19 6
1927 Chesterfield 2 1
Usworth Colliery
1929 Carlisle United 0

Matthews, JR IR
1896 Burton Wanderers 9

Matthews, Robert William (Billy) CH
b Plas Bennion 16/4/1897 d 1987
Caps: Wales 3
1919 1921 Liverpool 9 4
1921 1923 Bristol City 42 1
1923 1924 Wrexham 62 1
Northwich Victoria
1925 Barrow 9 1
1925 1929 Bradford Park Avenue 112 5
1930 Stockport County 4
1930 1931 New Brighton 41 1
1931 Chester 5
Oswestry Town
Witton Albion
Sandbach Ramblers
Colwyn Bay United
Rossendale United

Matthews, (Sir) Stanley OR
b Hanley 1/2/1915 d 2000
Caps: England Sch/FLge 14/England War 29/England 54
Stoke St Peter's
1931 1946 Stoke City 259 51
1939 (Stoke City) (3)
1947 1961 Blackpool 381 17
1961 1964 Stoke City 59 3

Matthews, Vincent (Vince) CH
b Oxford 15/1/1896 d 1950
Caps: England 2
Oxford City
Boscombe
1922 1924 Bolton Wanderers 3
1925 1926 Tranmere Rovers 84 3
1927 1930 Sheffield United 125 2
Shamrock Rovers
Oswestry Town
Shrewsbury Town
Morris Motors

Matthews, William (Billy) IR
b Derby q4 1882 d 1916
1899 Nottingham Forest 0
Ripley Athletic
1903 1906 Aston Villa 26 12
1906 1911 Notts County 177 37
1912 Derby County 1
Newport County

Matthews, William Downes (Billy) CF
b Wrexham q4 1896 d 1964
1921 Wrexham 3 1

Matthews, William Howard (Howard) GK
b Roadend 29/11/1885 d 1963
Caps: FLge 1
Oldbury St John's
Langley St Michael's
1906 Burslem Port Vale 26
Burton United
1908 1925 Oldham Athletic 344
1926 1927 Port Vale 35
1928 1929 Halifax Town 40
Chester
Oswestry Town

Matthewson, George Thomas CH
b Gateshead 22/2/1910 d 1984
Pelaw CWS
Dunston CWS
1931 1938 Bury 213 11
1939 (Bury) (3)
Guildford City

From To | Apps | Goal

Matthewson, Thomas James (Tommy) OR
b Gateshead 9/5/1903 d 1966
Gateshead Town
Close Works
1921 Sheffield Wednesday 1
1923 1929 South Shields 220 44
North Shields
Pelaw Athletic
Dunston CWS

Matthias, Albert RH
b Wrexham q3 1902
Brymbo & Green United
1924 Wrexham 1

Matthias, James Thomas (Jimmy) CH
b Moss 13/2/1914 d 1980
Flint Town
1937 1938 Wrexham 27
1939 (Wrexham) (3)

Matthias, John Samuel RB/LB
b Broughton 6/1878 d 1938
Caps: Wales 5
Brymbo Institute
Shrewsbury Town
1897 1900 Wolverhampton Wanderers 44
Wrexham

Matthias, Thomas James (Tommy) RH/LH
b Brynteg 7/11/1890
Caps: Wales 12
Pentre Broughton
Mold Town
Saltney
Summerhill
Shrewsbury Town
Chester
1921 1926 Wrexham 150 8
Whitchurch
Oak Alyn Rovers

Mauchline, Robert Duff (Bob) OL
b Falkirk 15/12/1913 d 1999
East Stirlingshire
Grange Rovers
Falkirk (trial)
Bo'ness Cadora
Heart of Midlothian
1938 Blackpool 4
1938 Barrow 14 3
1939 1945 Accrington Stanley (3)

Maughan, John GK
b Byker 25/7/1904
Pandon Temperance
1925 1926 Darlington 28
1927 1928 Doncaster Rovers 69
1929 Bury 7
1931 Gateshead 0

Maughan, William Henry RH
b West Stanley q3 1894 d 1916
West Stanley
Easington Colliery Welfare
1913 1914 Fulham 22 1

Maund, John Henry (Jack) OR/OL
b Hednesford 5/1/1916 d 1994
Hednesford Town
1935 1937 Aston Villa 47 8
1939 Nottingham Forest (3) (1)
1946 1947 Walsall 32 7

Maven (Mavin), Frederick James (Fred) CH
b Newcastle q2 1884 d 1957
Tods Nook
Benwell Adelaide
Newcastle United Swifts
New Brompton
1909 1913 Fulham 140 27
1913 1914 Bradford Park Avenue 13 1
1920 Reading 24 3
Boscombe
Shildon Athletic

Maw, Arthur IR/IL
b Frodingham 29/12/1909 d 1964
Frodingham Athletic
Scunthorpe & Lindsey United
1928 1931 Notts County 35 11
1932 1938 Leicester City 179 58
Scunthorpe & Lindsey United

Mawson, Frank OL
b Ecclesfield q1 1875 d 1938
Mexborough Town
Kettering
Doncaster Rovers
1902 Barnsley 8
Ecclesfield Church

Mawson, Frederick (Fred) OL
b Ecclesfield q4 1877
1900 1902 Barnsley 52 8

From	To	Club	Apps	Goal
Mawson, Joseph Spence (Joe)			CF/IL/IR	
b Brandon Colliery 26/10/1905			d 1959	
		Crook Town		
		Washington Colliery		
1926		Durham City	0	
1927		Bishop Auckland		
1928	1933	Stoke City	86	46
1934		Nottingham Forest	2	
1935		Stockport County	3	
		Linfield		
1936		Crewe Alexandra	11	2
Maxwell, Alan			IR/CF	
b Glasgow 1870				
		Cambuslang		
1891	1893	Everton	43	13
1893	1895	Darwen	60	22
1895	1896	Stoke	31	4
		St Bernard's		
Maxwell, Alexander (Alex)			IR	
b 1888				
		Stenhousemuir		
1913		Bury	1	
Maxwell, James F (Jimmy)			LH/OL	
b Glasgow 1900				
		Neilston Victoria		
		Arbroath		
1925		Stoke City	10	
1926		Watford	4	1
Maxwell, James Morton			OR	
b New Cumnock 1882			d 1917	
Caps: SLge 1				
		Kilmarnock Shawbank		
		Petershill Juniors		
		Kilmarnock		
1906	1907	Sheffield Wednesday	27	6
1908		Woolwich Arsenal	2	
		Hurlford		
		Galston		
		Carlisle United		
		Lanemark		
		Kilmarnock		
		Nithsdale Wanderers		
Maxwell, James Morton (Bud)			CF	
b Kilmarnock 15/1/1913			d 1990	
Caps: Scotland Sch/SLge 1				
		Kilmarnock		
1934	1938	Preston North End	129	60
1939		Barnsley	(3)	(4)
		Kilmarnock		
		Shrewsbury Town		
Maxwell, R			CH	
1892	1893	Darwen	35	2
Maxwell, Thomas (Tommy)			IR	
b Dunfermline 1897				
		Cambuslang Rangers		
		Clyde		
		Dumbarton Harp		
		Dumbarton		
		Dunfermline Athletic		
1921		Arsenal	1	
		Bethlehem Steel		
		New Bedford Whalers		
		St Mary's Barn		
		Dulwich Hamlet		
		Mansfield Town		
Maxwell, William Sturrock (Willie)			IL/IR/OR	
b Arbroath 21/9/1876			d 1940	
Caps: Scotland 1				
		Hearts Strollers		
		Arbroath		
		Heart of Midlothian		
		Dundee		
1895	1900	Stoke	155	74
		Third Lanark		
1902		Sunderland	7	3
		Millwall Athletic		
1905	1908	Bristol City	120	58
		Leopold (Belgium)		
May, Edward Henry (Teddy)			OL/IR	
b Hull q4 1865			d 1941	
		Notts Rangers		
		Burslem Port Vale		
1888	1889	Notts County	29	4
		Nottingham Forest		
1892		Burton Swifts	19	5
		Mansfield Greenhalgh's		
		Mansfield Town		
		Mansfield		
1895		Burton Swifts	1	
May, George James (Kosher)			LH	
b Aston 5/1881			d 1947	
		Verity Athletic		
		Redditch Town		
1908	1909	Wolverhampton Wanderers	16	
		Nuneaton Town		
		Atherstone Town		

From	To	Club	Apps	Goal
May, Harry Clifford			IL/IR	
b Abingdon q2 1905				
		Woking		
1931	1933	Crystal Palace	31	10
		Dartford		
May, Hugh			CF	
b Dykehead 13/10/1882			d 1944	
		Montrose Works		
		Wishaw United		
		Rangers		
		Wishaw United		
		Rangers		
1902		Derby County	6	
		Fulham		
May, James			OR	
b Cambusnethan 1877				
		St Mirren		
1897		Preston North End	3	
May, John (Johnny)			LH/RH	
b Dykehead 15/4/1878			d 1933	
Caps: SLge 3/Scotland 5				
		Bo'ness		
		Paisley		
		Wishaw Thistle		
		Abercorn		
1898	1903	Derby County	179	17
		Rangers		
		Morton		
May, William Owen (Billy)			CF	
b Hull q4 1865			d 1936	
		Long Eaton Rangers		
1888		Notts County	4	
		Notts Rangers		
		Mansfield Greenhalgh		
		Mansfield Town		
		Mansfield		
1895		Burton Swifts	0	
Mayberry, Samuel (Sam)			GK	
b Bellshill 1918				
		Gainsborough Trinity		
1938		Luton Town	1	
Maybury, Alfred Edward			GK	
b Nantwich 1877				
		Nantwich		
1900		Burslem Port Vale	32	
1901		Chesterfield Town	9	
		Crewe Alexandra		
Maycock, Harry			OL	
b Rotherham 16/4/1890			d 1978	
		Parkgate Church		
		Scunthorpe & Lindsey United		
1923		Southend United	3	1
		Rotherham Town		
Maycock, Ranson (Rance)			CF/IR	
b Waterhouses q2 1905			d 1950	
		Tow Law Town		
1927	1929	South Shields	55	37
1930		Gateshead	16	4
		Guildford City		
1932		Accrington Stanley	18	3
		Guildford City		
Mayer, Wilfred (Wilf)			IR/IL	
b Etruria 18/2/1912			d 1979	
		Newcastle PSA		
		Downings Tileries		
1934		Stoke City	1	
1936	1937	Southampton	14	
		Wellington Town		
Mayers, HM			CH	
1898		Blackpool	1	
Mayes, Arnold Jack (Jack)			RH/LH	
b Wickford 8/12/1913			d 1994	
		Barking Town		
1933		Crystal Palace	0	
		Barking Town		
1935	1938	Chelsea	12	
1939		(Chelsea)	(1)	
Mayes, Kenneth William (Ken)			IL/OL	
b Wickford 8/10/1910			d 1975	
		Barking Town		
		Brentwood & Warley		
1931		Southend United	5	1
		Barking Town		
1934	1935	Fulham	2	
		Colchester Town		
		Chelmsford City		
Mayo, Alfred Charles			CF	
b Bridgend 19/6/1909			d 1970	
1930		Cardiff City	1	

From	To	Club	Apps	Goal
Mays, Albert William (Billy)			CF/IR	
b Ynyshir 18/7/1902			d 1959	
Caps: Wales 1				
		Ynyshir Swallows		
		Porth		
		Wattstown		
1923	1925	Bristol City	19	4
1926		Plymouth Argyle	0	
1927		Merthyr Town	35	14
1928	1929	Wrexham	54	41
1929		Notts County	8	4
1930		Burnley	2	
1930		Walsall	17	11
1931		Halifax Town	25	9
		Margate		
		Gresley Rovers		
		Shardlow St James		
Mayson, John Dunnett (Jackie)			OR/OL	
b Southport 24/10/1908			d 1991	
		Ainsdale		
1929		Southport	0	
		Burscough Rangers		
		Chorley		
1931		Bury (trial)	0	
1932		Bolton Wanderers	0	
1933	1935	Clapton Orient	79	22
1936		Hull City	23	8
1937		Tranmere Rovers	9	2
		Runcorn		
Mayson, Thomas (Tommy)			IL	
b Whitehaven 8/12/1886			d 1972	
		Walker Celtic		
1907	1911	Burnley	67	14
1911	1914	Grimsby Town	85	28
1919		Everton	1	1
		Pontypridd		
1921		Wolverhampton Wanderers	2	
1922		Aberdare Athletic	19	4
Meacock, William Richard (Bob)			CH/RH/IR	
b Hoole 26/7/1910			d 1980	
		Hoole & Newton		
1930		Blackpool	0	
1931		Torquay United	4	
1933	1934	Tranmere Rovers	57	3
1935	1937	Lincoln City	106	
1938		Birmingham	13	
1939		Bristol City	0	
Meade, Thomas George			IR	
b Plumstead 14/5/1877				
1894	1896	Woolwich Arsenal	11	5
		Tottenham Hotspur		
		Fulham		
Meadowcroft, Harold Chadwick			RH/OR	
b Cockermouth q1 1889				
		Whitworth		
		Rochdale		
1912		Glossop	10	
1913		Bury	5	
Meads, John (Jack)			RH	
b Grassmoor 5/8/1907			d 1980	
		Grassmoor Comrades		
		Grassmoor Ivanhoe		
1925	1926	Chesterfield	12	
		Scarborough		
1928		Middlesbrough	0	
		Poole		
		Frickley Colliery		
		Scarborough		
Meads, Thomas (Tommy)			LH/IL	
b Grassmoor 2/11/1900			d 1983	
		Grassmoor Ivanhoe		
		Clay Cross Town		
		Matlock Town		
1923	1926	Stockport County	117	21
1926	1928	Huddersfield Town	40	2
1928		Reading	31	4
1929	1934	Tottenham Hotspur	183	6
1935		Notts County	18	2
		Frickley Colliery		
		Dinnington Athletic		
		Frickley Colliery		
Mearns, Frederick Charles (Fred)			GK	
b Sunderland 31/3/1879			d 1931	
		Selbourne		
1901		Sunderland	2	
		Kettering		
		Tottenham Hotspur		
1904		Bradford City	21	
		Grays United		
		Southern United		
		Barrow		
1906	1907	Bury	10	
		Hartlepools United		
1909	1910	Barnsley	26	
1910	1912	Leicester Fosse	68	
		Newcastle City		
		West Stanley		
		Sunderland West End		

From	To	Club	Apps	Goal
Mears, Frank			CF/IL	
b Chorlton q2 1899			d 1964	
1920		Manchester United	0	
		Stalybridge Celtic		
1925	1926	Leeds United	2	
1928	1929	Barnsley	42	13
Meates, William Percival			GK	
b Bournemouth 1871				
		Eastbourne		
1895	1896	Small Heath	14	
		Warmley		
1898		Nottingham Forest (trial)	0	
Medcalf, James T			OL	
b Newark				
1913		Notts County	0	
1914		Hull City	2	
Medhurst, Henry Edward Pafford (Harry)			GK	
b Byfleet 5/2/1916			d 1984	
		Woking		
1938	1946	West Ham United	24	
1939		(West Ham United)	(3)	
1946	1951	Chelsea	143	
1952		Brighton & Hove Albion	12	
Medley, Lindon William			CF	
b Bradford 2/2/1909			d 1973	
		Yorkshire Amateurs		
1931		Bradford City	7	6
1932		Southport	5	4
		Blackpool Electricity & Trams		
		Ham's Hall		
Mee, Alfred			OR	
b Ruddington				
1898		Loughborough	13	2
Mee, Bertie			OL	
b Bulwell 25/12/1918			d 2001	
		Bulwell		
1937		Derby County	0	
1938		Mansfield Town	13	1
Mee, George Wilfred			OL	
b Bulwell 12/4/1900			d 1978	
		Highbury Vale Athletic		
1919		Notts County	0	
1920	1925	Blackpool	216	22
1925	1931	Derby County	148	15
1932		Burnley	18	3
1933		Mansfield Town	11	
		Morecambe		
		Great Harwood		
1935	1937	Accrington Stanley	106	8
1938		Rochdale	1	
1938		Accrington Stanley	17	2
Mee, Gordon			GK	
b Belper 13/5/1913			d 1975	
		Pottery Wesleyans (Belper)		
		Matlock Town		
1935	1938	Brighton & Hove Albion	41	
1939		(Brighton & Hove Albion)	(2)	
1945		Watford	0	
Mee, Peter			IL	
b Chorlton-cum-Hardy 30/3/1899			d 1923	
		Ashton National		
1921		Manchester City	0	
1923		Southport	13	6
Meechan, John Stewart			CF	
b Falkirk 4/5/1910				
		Grangemouth Sacred Heart		
		Maryhill Hibernian		
		St Mirren		
1933		Burnley	2	
		Falkirk		
		Kilmarnock		
		East Stirlingshire		
		St Johnstone		
		East Stirlingshire		
		Morton		
		Bo'ness		
		Forth Juniors		
		Polkemmet		
		East Stirlingshire		
Meehan, Peter			RB	
b Broxburn 28/2/1872			d 1915	
Caps: SLge 1				
		Broxburn Shamrock		
		Hibernian		
1893	1894	Sunderland	41	1
		Celtic		
1896	1897	Everton	24	
		Southampton		
1900		Manchester City	6	
		Barrow		
		Broxburn Athletic		
		Clyde		
		Broxburn Shamrock		

From To Apps Goal

Meehan, Thomas (Tommy) LH/RH
b Harpurhey q3 1896 d 1924
Caps: FLge 2/England 1
Newtown
Walkden Central
1919 1920 Manchester United 51 6
1920 1923 Chelsea 124 4

Meek, Hugh Leonard IL
b Belfast 1900
Caps: IrLge 1/Ireland 1
Belfast Rangers
Cliftonville
Glentoran
1925 Wolverhampton Wanderers 6 1
Shelbourne
Distillery
Ards
Burradon

Meek, Joseph (Joe) IR
b Hazlerigg 31/5/1910 d 1976
Burradon
Newcastle Co-op
Seaton Delaval
Bedlington United
1927 Liverpool (trial) 0
Stockton
1929 Middlesbrough 0
1930 1934 Gateshead 135 50
1934 1935 Bradford Park Avenue 31 11
1935 1938 Tottenham Hotspur 45 15
1938 Swansea Town 16 5
1939 (Swansea Town) (3) (1)

Meens, Harold CH
b Doncaster 15/10/1919 d 1987
Shepherd's Road Club
1938 1951 Hull City 146
1939 (Hull City) (2)
Hull Brunswick

Meeson, Arthur William GK
b Headington 10/4/1904 d 1971
Caps: England Amat
Oxford City
1927 Arsenal 0
1928 Fulham 1
1929 1930 Lincoln City 12
Osberton Radiators

Mehaffy, John Wesley GK
b Belfast 22/12/1896 d 1937
Caps: IrLge 2
Belfast Celtic
Glentoran
Ballyclare Comrades
Glentoran
1923 New Brighton 5
1924 1926 Rotherham County 79
Dundalk
Coleraine

Mehaffy, Joseph Alexander Cuthbert (Bert) GK
b Belfast 10/4/1895 d 1970
Caps: IrLge 2/Ireland 1
Queen's Park (Lurgan)
Belfast Celtic
Queen's Island
Belfast Celtic
Linfield
1919 Everton (trial) 0
Belfast Celtic
Glenavon
Queen's Island
1922 Tottenham Hotspur (trial) 0
Woodburn
1923 1928 New Brighton 218 1
Belfast Celtic

Meigh, Thomas (Tom) IR
b Stoke-on-Trent 6/6/1899 d 1972
Stoke United
Ravenscliffe Mission
Hanley Town
1923 Wrexham 3
1924 Port Vale 0
Blythe Bridge
Fenton Town

Meikle, Angus McLaren OR
b Dalserf 7/2/1900
Larkhall United
Royal Albert
Heart of Midlothian
Royal Albert
Heart of Midlothian
1922 1926 Portsmouth 152 22
1927 Grimsby Town 13 2
Bangor City
Coalburn Juniors

Meiklejohn, George CH
b Scotland 1873
1896 Everton 1

From To Apps Goal

Melaniphy, Eugene Michael Joseph Patrick (Ted) CF/IR/IL
b Westport 5/2/1912 d 1991
Redhill
Finchley Town
1931 1935 Plymouth Argyle 68 33
1936 1937 Cardiff City 20 8
Worcester City
1939 Northampton Town (3) (1)

Melia, James (Jimmy) RB
b Darlington 2/4/1874 d 1905
Stockton
1896 1897 Sheffield Wednesday 7
Tottenham Hotspur
1901 Preston North End 2

Mellan, David John Mead LH/OL
b Bill Quay 6/5/1899 d 1981
Wood Skinners
1920 Norwich City 1
Felling Colliery
1922 Aston Villa 0
1923 Chesterfield 1

Mellan, Joseph Mead (James) LB/RH
b Bill Quay 1903
1922 Barrow 0
Felling Colliery
1924 1927 Darlington 31
1928 Torquay United 10
Jarrow
1934 Gateshead 18

Mellen, Robert Henry OL
b 29/10/1911 d 1977
Vickerstown Athletic
1932 Barrow 1

Mellon, James (Jimmy) RH
b Kelvinside 22/12/1901
Caps: IrLge 1
Uddingston Juniors
Wishaw YMCA
Hibernian
1926 Brighton & Hove Albion 1
1927 Accrington Stanley 0
Distillery
Shelbourne
Rhyl Athletic

Mellor, Frank OL
b Willaston 1902
Willaston White Star
Nantwich
1920 1921 Bolton Wanderers 2
Chester
Oswestry Town

Mellor, Harold (Harry) CF
b Blackpool q3 1895
South Shore
1921 Nelson 1
South Shore
Eccles United
New Mills

Mellor, Harold Halden (Harry) IL/IR
b Stoke-on-Trent q4 1878
1895 Crewe Alexandra 2
Burslem Port Vale
Dresden United
1897 1899 Stoke 29 3
1900 Grimsby Town 33 4
Brighton & Hove Albion

Mellor, James (Jimmy) OL
b Stoke-on-Trent 1870
Dresden United
1894 Stoke 1
Stone BL

Mellor, John RB/LB
b Oldham
Greenacres Lads
Failsworth Trinity
Witton Albion
1930 1936 Manchester United 116
1936 1937 Cardiff City 28

Mellor, John William RH
b Buxton q3 1896
New Mills
1920 Port Vale 9
New Mills
1923 Port Vale 6
New Mills

Mellor, Sydney (Syd) IL
b Leek 1898
Leek Town
1920 1921 Stoke 11 1
Congleton Town

From To Apps Goal

Mellor, William Gladstone GK
b Stockport 3/4/1886 d 1969
Carlisle United
Norwich City
1913 1919 Newcastle United 23

Mellors, George Robert CH
b Lincoln q4 1885
Lincoln Liberal Club
1907 1908 Gainsborough Trinity 8 1
Worksop Town
Lincoln Liberal Club

Mellors, Mark GK
b Basford 30/4/1880 d 1961
Carrington
1900 Nottingham Forest (trial) 0
Bulwell United
1902 1903 Notts County 9
Brighton & Hove Albion
1907 Sheffield United 1
1908 1913 Bradford City 68

Mellors, Richard Dugdale (Dick) GK
b Mansfield 17/3/1905 d 1960
Mansfield Woodhouse
Welbeck Athletic
Chesterfield Municipal
Mansfield Town
1926 1930 Sheffield Wednesday 14
1931 1933 Reading 85
1934 1937 Bournemouth & Boscombe Ath 116
Queen of the South

Mellors, William (Billy) LB/RH
b Nottingham 11/1872 d 1950
Heywood Central
1892 Sheffield United 2
1893 Sheffield Wednesday 1
1895 Loughborough 3
Oldham County
Swindon Town
Wigan County
Darwen

Melville, David CH/LH/RH
b Tayport 1884
Buckhaven Juniors
East Fife
Partick Thistle
1907 1908 Bradford City 7
1909 1911 Stockport County 73 2
Southport Central

Melville, David CH
b Glasgow 1892
Arthurlie
1913 Hull City 5
East Fife
Clyde
Renton
Albion Rovers
Vale of Leven

Melville, James LB
b Dykehead
Vale of Clyde
Clyde
1921 Cardiff City 1
East Stirlingshire
Beith

Melville, James (Jim) CH/IL/LH
b Barrow 15/3/1909 d 1961
Vickerstown Athletic
1926 1927 Barrow 22 2
1929 1932 Blackburn Rovers 25
1933 Hull City 14 1
1934 1935 Northampton Town 20

Menham, Charles George Gordon GK
b Bromley 28/8/1896 d 1979
Northern Nomads
1925 Everton 3
Northern Nomads
1927 Bradford City 0
Northern Nomads

Menham, Robert William (Bob) GK
b North Shields 7/7/1871 d 1945
Luton Town
1896 Everton 18
Wigan County
Swindon Town

From To Apps Goal

Menlove, Bertie CF/IL
b St Albans 8/12/1892 d 1970
Barnet Alston
1919 Aston Villa 0
1920 1921 Crystal Palace 48 12
1921 1925 Sheffield United 74 42
Boston Town
Aldershot
Worksop Town (trial)
Bangor City
1929 Clapton Orient 0
Connah's Quay & Shotton
Coleraine
Ashford Town (Kent)

Menzies, Alexander William CF
b Blantyre 25/11/1882
Caps: Scotland 1
Blantyre Victoria
Heart of Midlothian
Motherwell
Arthurlie
Heart of Midlothian
1906 1907 Manchester United 23 4
Luton Town
Dundee
Hamilton Academical
Port Glasgow Athletic
Dumbarton

Menzies, William John (Bill) LB
b Bucksburn 10/7/1901 d 1970
Mugiemoss Juniors
1923 1931 Leeds United 248 1
Goole Town

Mercer, Alick (Alec) IR/CF/IL
b Tamworth 12/9/1891 d 1977
Kettlebrook
1913 1914 Bury 29 10
1919 1922 Coventry City 101 16
Kidderminster Harriers

Mercer, Arthur Stanley IR
b St Helens 28/12/1902 d 1994
Parr St Peter's
1921 1924 Wigan Borough 39 16
1925 Bury 11 3
1926 1927 Sheffield United 35 14
Rhyl Athletic
Connah's Quay & Shotton
1930 1931 Bristol City 31 8
1931 1933 Chester 63 18
1933 1934 Halifax Town 39 8
Dartford
Rhyl

Mercer, D LB
1888 Bolton Wanderers 1

Mercer, David William OR/IR
b St Helens 20/3/1893 d 1950
Caps: FLge 1/England 2
Prescot Athletic
Skelmersdale
1913 1920 Hull City 91 26
1920 1927 Sheffield United 223 22
Prescot Cables
Shirebrook
1929 Torquay United 28
Dartmouth United

Mercer, John Thompson (Johnnie 'Toby') OR
b Connswater 27/3/1877 d 1947
Caps: IrLge 6/Ireland 12
Belview
Ligoniel
81st North Lancashire Regiment
8th Belfast Boys Brigade
Linfield Swifts
1896 Preston North End (trial) 0
Distillery
Brighton United
1899 Leicester Fosse 9 1
Linfield
Distillery
1903 1904 Derby County 26 1
Distillery
Colne
Distillery

Mercer, Joseph (Joe) LH/RH
b Ellesmere Port 9/8/1914 d 1990
Caps: FLge 2/England War 27/England 5
Elton Green
Shell-Mex
Runcorn
Ellesmere Port Town
1931 Chester (trial) 0
1931 Blackburn Rovers (trial) 0
1931 Bolton Wanderers (trial) 0
1932 1946 Everton 170 1
1939 (Everton) (3)
1946 1953 Arsenal 247 2

From To Apps Goal

Mercer, Joseph Powell (Joe) CH
b Ellesmere Port 21/7/1890 d 1927
Burnell's Ironworks
Ellesmere Port
1910 1914 Nottingham Forest 149 6
Ellesmere Port
1921 Tranmere Rovers 16 1

Mercer, William OL
b Cowdenbeath 8/11/1874 d 1932
Cowdenbeath
Hibernian
1898 Glossop North End 2 1
Cowdenbeath

Mercer, William (Billy) LH/RH
b Preston 14/3/1896 d 1975
1919 1924 Preston North End 113
1925 Blackpool 1
Lancaster Town
Boston Town

Mercer, William Henry (Billy) GK
b Prescot 1892 d 1956
Grosvenor
Prescot
Prescot Athletic
1910 Huddersfield Town 0
Prescot Athletic
1914 1924 Hull City 193
1924 1927 Huddersfield Town 71
1928 Blackpool 19

Meredith, Jack OR
b Grimsby 12/9/1899 d 1970
Scunthorpe & Lindsey United
1923 1927 Blackpool 190 27
1928 1929 Chelsea 23 6
1930 Reading 5

Meredith, Samuel (Sam) RB
b Trefonen 5/9/1872 d 1921
Caps: Wales 8
Chirk
1901 1904 Stoke 45
Leyton

Meredith, William Henry (Billy) OR
b Chirk 28/7/1874 d 1958
Caps: Wales 48
Black Park
Chirk
1893 Northwich Victoria 11 5
Wrexham
1894 1904 Manchester City 338 145
1906 1920 Manchester United 303 35
1921 1923 Manchester City 28

Merrett, Graham Eric IR
b Grateley q2 1919
Aldershot United
Margate
1935 Arsenal 0
1936 Aldershot 1
Basingstoke Town

Merrick, Clifford LH/CH
b Salford 22/1/1910 d 1995
Walsden United
1931 1932 Burnley 12
1933 1934 Swindon Town 46

Merrick, Joseph GK
b Great Barr q3 1900
Queen's Park Rangers
1920 Birmingham 0
1921 Walsall 28
Nuneaton Town
1923 Manchester United 0

Merrie, Alexander Breckinridge (Alex) CF
b Saltcoats 20/5/1905
Saltcoats Victoria
Nithsdale Wanderers
St Mirren
St Bernard's (loan)
St Johnstone (loan)
Alloa Athletic (loan)
Stenhousemuir
1925 Portsmouth 7 2
Nithsdale Wanderers
Aberdeen
Ayr United
1933 Hull City 0
Clyde
1934 Crewe Alexandra 32 11
Brechin City
(France)
1935 Aldershot 4 2
Ross County
1935 Exeter City 4 2
Workington
Cork FC
Leith Athletic
Gloucester City
Evesham Town

From To Apps Goal

Merritt, Richard (Dickie) OL
b Shiney Row 22/7/1897 d 1978
Easington Colliery Welfare
1921 1922 South Shields 2
1923 1924 Durham City 72 13
1925 Lincoln City 22 3
Washington Colliery
York City
1929 Notts County 1
Easington Colliery Welfare

Merritt, Wilfred (Wilf) GK
b Leek 11/1864
Leek
1888 1889 Stoke 2
Leek

Merry, William (Bill) IR
b Fishguard 14/12/1910 d 1983
Fishguard Sports
1930 Cardiff City 8
Drumcondra
1934 Manchester United 0
1935 Halifax Town 11 1
St James's Gate

Messer, Alfred Thomas (Alf) CH
b Deptford 8/3/1900 d 1947
Sutton Town
Mansfield Town
1922 Nottingham Forest 0
1923 1929 Reading 271 18
1930 1931 Tottenham Hotspur 51 2
1934 1935 Bournemouth & Boscombe Ath 10

Messer, Brinley Charles (Bryn) LH
b Swansea 11/5/1895 d 1969
1920 Swansea Town 1
Bridgend Town

Messer, Robert OR
b Edinburgh 18/7/1887 d 1918
Broxburn Shamrock
King's Park
Bo'ness
1910 Leicester Fosse 2
Broxburn Shamrock
Broxburn United

Meston, Samuel (Sammy) IL/CH
b Arbroath 16/1/1872 d 1948
Arbroath Victoria
Arbroath
1893 1894 Stoke 11 2
Southampton
Salisbury City
Croydon Common
Salisbury City
Chandlers Ford
Eastleigh Athletic

Meston, Samuel William (Sammy) OR
b Southampton 30/5/1902 d 1953
Sholing Athletic
1921 1925 Southampton 10 2
1926 1927 Gillingham 61 8
1927 Everton 1
1929 1931 Tranmere Rovers 107 29
Newport (Isle of Wight)

Metcalf, Arthur IR/CF/IL
b Seaham Harbour 8/4/1889 d 1936
St George's (Seaham)
Herrington Swifts
Hebburn Argyle
North Shields Athletic
1909 1911 Newcastle United 12 2
1912 1914 Liverpool 52 23
1919 Stockport County 36 13
1920 1921 Swindon Town 31 6
1922 Accrington Stanley 31 18
1923 1924 Aberdare Athletic 72 10
1925 Norwich City 2

Metcalf, George William RH/CH
b Easington q2 1885 d 1963
Sunderland Black Watch
1906 Sunderland 1
North Shields Athletic
1910 1911 Huddersfield Town 6
Merthyr Town
Portsmouth

Metcalf, James (Jim) RH/LH/CH
b Sunderland 10/12/1899 d 1975
Sunderland Royal Rovers
Southwick (Co Durham)
1920 1926 South Shields 185 2
1927 Preston North End 16
1928 1929 Nelson 71 1

Metcalf, Thomas OR
1890 Preston North End 1 1

From To Apps Goal

Metcalf, Thomas Clarke (Tom) CH/RH
b Burton-on-Trent q4 1878 d 1938
1902 Burton United 0
Southampton
Salisbury City
1907 1908 Wolverhampton Wanderers 9

Metcalf, Walter Frederick LB
b Scarborough 15/12/1910 d 1981
Scarborough
1933 Sunderland 0
1934 1936 Brentford 7
1937 1945 Coventry City 76 1
1939 (Coventry City) (1)

Metcalfe, Edwin LB
b Sunderland q4 1895
Houghton Rovers
Jarrow
1922 1923 Durham City 12

Metcalfe, Robert Simon IL
b Sunderland q4 1884 d 1950
South Shields Parkside
1911 Blackpool 3

Methven, Harold CF
b Derby 9/10/1908 d 1987
Derby Municipal
Gresley Rovers
1930 Portsmouth 2
1931 Sheffield United (trial) 0
Scunthorpe & Lindsey United
Loughborough Corinthians
1933 Mansfield Town 10 9
Tunbridge Wells Rangers

Methven, James (Jimmy) RB
b Ceres 7/12/1868 d 1953
Leith Athletic
Heart of Midlothian
St Bernard's
1891 1906 Derby County 458

Methven, James IR
b Edinburgh 11/10/1890 d 1964
1913 Derby County 1
Cardiff City

Mettam, Edward (Ned) RH
b Lincoln 18/8/1868 d 1943
1892 1895 Lincoln City 85

Mettam, Ernest August IR/CF
b Shardlow q3 1886
Stapleford
Ilkeston United
1909 1910 Gainsborough Trinity 36 10
Ilkeston United
Holwell Works

Meunier, James Brown LB/RB
b Poynton 1885 d 1957
Heaton Chapel
1903 Stockport County 0
1904 Manchester City 0
Southport Central
1910 1911 Everton 5
1912 1913 Lincoln City 23
Coventry City
Hyde United
Macclesfield

Mew, John William (Jack) GK
b Sunderland 30/3/1889 d 1963
Caps: FLge 1/England 1
Marley Hill St Cuthbert's
Sunnyside
Blaydon United
Marley Hill United
1912 1925 Manchester United 186
1926 Barrow 29
Lyra

Meyer, Henry James IR
b Christchurch 4/3/1893
Bournemouth Tramways
1924 Bournemouth & Boscombe Ath 2
Bournemouth Tramways

Meynell, W Thomas CH
b Southwick, County Durham
Goole Town
1909 Clapton Orient 16 2
Rochdale
Goole Town

From To Apps Goal

Michael, William (Bill) IL
b Wishaw 1874 d 1938
Caps: SLge 1
Wishaw Thistle
Heart of Midlothian
1896 Liverpool 19 4
Wishaw Thistle
Heart of Midlothian
Bristol City
Falkirk
Wishaw United
Motherwell

Michaels, William OR
b Liverpool q1 1892 d 1952
1909 Everton 3
Egremont (Wirral)

Micklewright, William (Billy) OR
b Reading q4 1888
Wellington Town
1910 Wolverhampton Wanderers 5

Middleboe, Nils RH/CH/LH
b Copenhagen, Denmark 5/10/1887 d 1976
Caps: Denmark
KB Copenhagen
Casuals
1912 Newcastle United 0
1913 1921 Chelsea 41
Corinthians
Casuals

Middlehurst, James Henry RB
b Prescot q4 1892 d 1954
St Helens Recreation
1914 1919 Hull City 9

Middlemas, John Robert (Jack) RH
b Easington 17/1/1896 d 1984
Herrington Swifts
Blyth Spartans
1922 Hull City 10
York City
Blyth Spartans

Middlemiss, Herbert (Bert) OL
b Newcastle 19/12/1888 d 1941
Caps: FLge 1
Stalybridge Rovers
1907 Stockport County 0
1908 1919 Tottenham Hotspur 244 50
1920 Queen's Park Rangers 16 1

Middlemiss, James RH
b Benwell 10/1904 d 1961
Scotswood
1924 Crystal Palace 1

Middleton, Alexander (Alex) LH
b Port Gordon 2/6/1902
Buckie Wednesday
Buckie Thistle
Heart of Midlothian
1926 Charlton Athletic 5
Heart of Midlothian
Bo'ness
Clyde
Buckie Thistle

Middleton, Alfred IL
b Mansfield q1 1890
Mansfield Wesleyans
Mansfield Mechanics
1912 Stockport County 2
Mansfield Town
Sutton Junction
Grantham

Middleton, Charles William (Charlie) IL
b West Stanley 8/2/1914 d 1984
Walker Celtic
1934 Stoke City 0
West Stanley
1936 Hartlepools United 1
Walker Celtic

Middleton, Francis (Frank) OL
b Whitwick q2 1879 d 1943
Whitwick White Cross
1901 1905 Derby County 65 3
1906 1907 Leicester Fosse 49 10
Whitwick Imperial

Middleton, George Norman CF
b 1880 d 1937
1902 Stockport County 2 1

Middleton, Harry OR/CF
b Northwich 1902
Ashton Heys 4
Witton Albion 5
1923 1925 Oldham Athletic 22
Witton Albion
Northwich Victoria
Hurst
North Western Road Car Co

From To Apps Goal

Middleton, Henry (Harry) RH/CH
b Wednesbury q3 1870
Derby Junction
1892 1893 Ardwick 36 4
1895 1896 Loughborough 31 5

Middleton, Jack CH/LH/IR
b Sunderland 19/4/1898 d 1974
Herrington Swifts
Lambton Star
1922 1924 Leicester City 12 3
1925 1926 Queen's Park Rangers 54 9
1932 1936 Aldershot 103 3

Middleton, John IR
b Mickley 15/4/1910 d 1971
Mickley
1929 Swansea Town 1
Mickley
Waterford
Walker Celtic
1933 1934 Darlington 77 22
1935 1936 Blackpool 6 3
1937 Norwich City 3
South Shields

Middleton, Matthew Young (Matt) GK
b Boldon Colliery 24/10/1907 d 1979
Newcastle United Swifts
Boldon Colliery Welfare
1930 Charlton Athletic (trial) 0
1931 1932 Southport 63
1933 1938 Sunderland 57
1939 1945 Plymouth Argyle (3)
Horden Colliery Welfare
1946 1948 Bradford City 94
1948 1949 York City 55
Blyth Spartans
Murton Colliery Welfare

Middleton, Raymond (Ray) GK
b Boldon 6/9/1919 d 1977
Caps: England B
Ditchburn Sports
Washington Chemical Works
Boldon Colliery Welfare
Washington Church
North Shields
1938 1950 Chesterfield 250
1939 (Chesterfield) (2)
1951 1953 Derby County 116
Boston United

Middleton, Robert Connan (Bob) GK
b Brechin 15/1/1903 d 1996
Caps: Scotland 1
Brechin Victoria
Brechin City
Cowdenbeath
1930 1932 Sunderland 59
Burton Town
1933 1937 Chester 56
Congleton Town

Middleton, William (Billy) OR
b Hetton-le-Hole q1 1893
Boldon Colliery Welfare
Newcastle City
Brighton & Hove Albion
Ayr United
Aberdeen
1923 Southend United 30
Ayr United
Dumbarton

Middleton, William (Billy) RH
b Mickley
Mickley
1938 Darlington 2

Midgley, Jack Robinson LB
b Halifax 10/4/1910 d 1974
1931 Bradford City 0
1932 Halifax Town 1
Bedlington Town

Midgeley, Thomas IR
Burnley Rovers
1888 Burnley 1

Milarvie, Robert (Bob) OL
b Pollokshields 1864 d 1912
Pollokshields
Hibernian
1888 Stoke 15 5
Burslem Port Vale
1889 Derby County 14 4
Newton Heath
1892 1895 Ardwick/Manchester City 50 9

Milburn, ? RH
1899 Loughborough 1

From To Apps Goal

Milburn, George William RB
b Ashington 24/6/1910 d 1980
Ashington Colliery Welfare
1929 1936 Leeds United 152 1
1937 1947 Chesterfield 105 16
1939 (Chesterfield) (2)

Milburn, James (Jim) LB/RB/CF
b Ashington 21/6/1919 d 1985
Ashington
1939 1951 Leeds United 207 15
1939 (Leeds United) (1)
1952 1954 Bradford Park Avenue 90 10

Milburn, John (Jack) LB/RB
b Ashington 18/3/1908 d 1979
Seaton Hirst Corinthians
Spen Black & White
1928 1938 Leeds United 391 28
1938 Norwich City 15
1939 (Norwich City) (3)
1946 Bradford City 14 3

Miles, Alfred (Freddie) LB/RB
b Aston 1/1884 d 1926
Heath Villa
Aston St Mary's
1903 1913 Aston Villa 249

Miles, Alfred Edwin (Alfie) CF
b Treorchy 21/7/1906 d 1981
Bridgend Town
Mid-Rhondda United
1925 Luton Town (trial) 0
1926 Derby County (trial) 0
1927 1929 Cardiff City 16 8
1930 Crystal Palace 0
Yeovil & Petters United

Miles, Idris OR
b Neath 2/8/1908 d 1983
Radnor Road
1930 Cardiff City 3
Yeovil & Petters United
1932 Leicester City 7 1
1934 1936 Clapton Orient 73 6
1937 Exeter City 10
Yeovil & Petters United
Worcester City

Miles, Reginald (Reg) GK
b Enfield 8/7/1905 d 1978
Enfield
Army
1930 Aston Villa 16
1931 Millwall 0
Dulwich Hamlet

Miles, Robert (Bob) OL
b Rhosllanerchrugog 26/12/1898 d 1940
Ponciau
Rhos Athletic
Denbigh United
1924 Wrexham 4
Rhyl Athletic
Denbigh United

Miles, Uriah OR
b Newcastle-under-Lyme 4/1/1907 d 1970
Connah's Quay & Shotton
1926 Wrexham 12
1927 1928 Rochdale 10 2
Witton Albion
Bacup Borough

Miles, William Percy (Dossie) CH/IL
b Bournemouth 19/2/1898 d 1971
Bournemouth Tramways
1924 1928 Bournemouth & Boscombe Ath 94 10
1929 Watford 14 1
Bournemouth Tramways

Millar, Alexander (Alec) LB
b Markinch 1915 d 1973
Shawfield Juniors
Wellesley Juniors
Bowhill Rovers
East Fife
Margate
1937 1938 Bristol Rovers 52
1939 Bristol City (3)
Heart of Midlothian

Millar, Alexander (Alex) CH
b Mossend 21/10/1911 d 1978
Mossend Celtic
Parkhead Juniors
Shawfield Juniors
Celtic
1938 Preston North End 2
Motherwell
Dundee United
Morton
Inverness Caledonian (trial)
Stranraer

From To Apps Goal

Millar, Arthur Thomson LH/RH
b Montrose 26/1/1877 d 1929
Montrose
Millwall Athletic
1900 1901 Aston Villa 10
Millwall Athletic
Brighton & Hove Albion

Millar, David CF
1930 Doncaster Rovers 3

Millar, George RB
b South Shields
Birtley
Corinthians
Middlesbrough
Sunderland Albion
1893 Middlesbrough Ironopolis 1

Millar, George CF
Glasgow Perthshire
1894 Newton Heath 6 5
Chatham

Millar, Henry (Harry) CF
b Paisley 6/1874 d 1930
Abercorn
St Mirren
1893 Preston North End 2
1894 1897 Bury 109 38
Reading
1899 1900 Sheffield Wednesday 32 16
Queen's Park Rangers

Millar, Hugh RB/LB
b Glasgow 24/5/1898
Gillingham
St Roch's
1921 1923 Grimsby Town 26
Torquay United

Millar, J CH/RH/LB
1894 1895 Bolton Wanderers 9
1895 Manchester City 2
1896 Bolton Wanderers 0

Millar, James (Jimmy) CF/IL/IR
b Annbank 2/3/1870 d 1907
Caps: SLge 3/Scotland 3
Annbank
1890 1895 Sunderland 140 80
Rangers
1900 1903 Sunderland 98 27
1904 West Bromwich Albion 1
1905 Chelsea 0

Millar, James (Jimmy) LH/RH
b Elgin 1877 d 1932
Elgin City
Rangers
1900 1902 Middlesbrough 20
1903 1907 Bradford City 118 1
Aberdeen

Millar, John McVey (Jock) OL/OR
b Coatbridge 31/12/1907 d 1997
Bridgeton Waverley
Saltcoats Victoria
Kilmarnock
1928 Barnsley 17 5
1929 Hartlepools United 18 5
Bo'ness (trial)
Burton Town (trial)
Bo'ness
Workington
Lancaster Town
Glentoran
Lancaster Town
1937 New Brighton (trial) 1
1937 Rochdale 26 8
Glasgow Benburb
1938 Exeter City 9 3
Astley Bridge
Hyde United

Millar, Norman Henry RB
b Dunadry 30/11/1908 d 1998
Caps: IrLge 2
Linfield
Glentoran
1937 1938 Bournemouth & Boscombe Ath 22 1
Dundalk

Millar, Robert M (Bob) LH
b Dalry 26/12/??
Dalry Thistle
1920 1929 Luton Town 205 4
Belfast Celtic

Millar, William OL
Cowdenbeath
Hibernian
1898 Glossop North End 3 1

From To Apps Goal

Millar, William Mills (Willie) OL
b Carronshore 20/3/1901 d 1966
Dunipace Juniors
Bo'ness
Heart of Midlothian (trial)
Ayr United
Rhyl Athletic
1927 1928 Middlesbrough 16 6
1929 1930 York City 58 12
Glentoran
1931 Crewe Alexandra 0
Drumcondra
York Wednesday

Millar, William Thomas (Billy) CF/OR/IR
b Ballymena 25/10/1906
Caps: Ireland 2
Church Lads Brigade
South End Rangers
Linfield
1928 Liverpool 3 2
1929 1932 Barrow 103 67
1933 Newport County 7 1
1934 Carlisle United 33 9
Ballymena United
Short's
Sligo Rovers
Cork City
Drumcondra

Millard, Albert (Bert) CH/IL
b West Bromwich 1893
Coseley
Willenhall Swifts
Barry
Cardiff City
1919 1920 Birmingham 31 14
1920 1921 Coventry City 63 8
1922 1923 Crystal Palace 35 4
1924 1925 Charlton Athletic 38 5
Leamington Town

Millard, Albert Robert RH/LH/CH
b West Bromwich 1868
West Bromwich Victoria
1888 1891 West Bromwich Albion 5
Small Heath
Halesowen

Miller, Alforth Henry (Alf) RH/LH
b Gainsborough 27/9/1914 d 1987
Gainsborough Trinity
1934 Hull City 4
1935 Barrow 4
1935 1936 Tranmere Rovers 27 1
Shrewsbury Town
Linfield
Workington
Hereford United

Miller, Alfred George Abraham (Alf 'Dusty') RH/LH
b Portsmouth 5/3/1917 d 1999
1935 Portsmouth 0
Ryde
Margate
1936 Bristol Rovers 0
1937 1938 Southport 32 2
1946 1947 Plymouth Argyle 9
Colchester United

Miller, Andrew (Andy) IL
b Bo'ness 27/2/1899
Vale of Grange
Croy Celtic
Celtic
Dumbarton Harp (loan)
Dumbarton (loan)
1924 Nottingham Forest 5
Bo'ness
Camelon Juniors
Montrose

Miller, Charles OR
b Glasgow 1893
Glasgow Benburb
Cambuslang Rangers
1914 Fulham 6

Miller, Charles (Charlie) LB
b Bellshill 3/5/1904
Bellshill Athletic
St Roch's
1924 1925 Plymouth Argyle 4
1926 1935 Exeter City 274

Miller, David (Dave) LH
b Middlesbrough 21/1/1921 d 1989
1939 Middlesbrough (1)
1946 Wolverhampton Wanderers 2
1947 Derby County 1
1947 1952 Doncaster Rovers 140 3
1953 Aldershot 11
Boston United

From To Apps Goal

Miller, Edward Clementson OL
b Percy Main q1 1917
North Shields Athletic
1935 Fulham 0
1936 1938 Gateshead 97 23
1939 (Gateshead) (2)

Miller, Ernest OL
b Sheffield 1903
Rotherham Town
1924 Rotherham County 2
Mansfield Town

Miller, George LH
b New Monkland 1886
Larkhall United
1910 Lincoln City 22

Miller, Harold Sydney IL/LH
b St Albans 20/5/1902 d 1988
Caps: England 1
St Albans City
1922 Charlton Athletic 20 11
1923 1937 Chelsea 337 41
1939 Northampton Town (3)
Wellingborough Town

Miller, Henry Edwin James (Ted) OL
b Watford 14/12/1897 d 1985
Caps: England Amat
Watford Corinthians
St Albans City
1922 Watford 2
1923 Charlton Athletic 0
Barnet
Clapton
St Albans City
Chesham United
Hampstead Town

Miller, Henry James (Harry) IL/IR
b Preston
Fleetwood
Leyland
1922 Everton 2
1924 Preston North End 5
Lancaster Town

Miller, James LB
b Scotland
Newcastle East End
1893 Newcastle United 9
Hurlford

Miller, James (Jimmy) OR
b Tynemouth 10/5/1889
South Shields Albion
Wallsend Park Villa
1912 Newcastle United 0
1913 Grimsby Town 6 1
1919 Everton 8 1
1919 Coventry City 7
1919 Preston North End 15 1
Pontypridd
1921 Darlington 0
1922 Chesterfield 32 1
1923 Bournemouth & Boscombe Ath 38
1924 Swansea Town 25 1
1925 Luton Town 10 3

Miller, James (Jimmy) RH
b Glasgow 1891 d 1935
Maryhill
1912 1913 Sheffield Wednesday 30
Airdrieonians

Miller, James IL
b Greenock
Blantyre Victoria
Hamilton Academical
St Mirren
Morton
St Mirren
1921 1923 Grimsby Town 89 32
1923 Manchester United 4 1
York City
Boston Town
Shirebrook

Miller, James (Jim) LH/RH
b Glasgow 29/1/1904
Maryhill
Raith Rovers
1925 Preston North End (trial) 0
East Fife
Dumbarton
1930 1933 Swansea Town 135 2
1934 Millwall 33 3
Hibernian
Dunfermline Athletic
Albion Rovers
Cowdenbeath

From To Apps Goal

Miller, James William RH
b Felling 1902
Felling Colliery
1927 Liverpool 0
1928 Crewe Alexandra 13 1
1928 1933 Carlisle United 161 6

Miller, James William Guyett (Jem) GK
b Scotstoun 31/3/1911
Hamiltonhill Social
Glasgow Perthshire
Brechin City
1932 Liverpool 0
Kilmarnock
1937 Exeter City 1
Galston
Alloa Athletic
Allander United

Miller, John CF
b Dumbarton
Dumbarton
Liverpool
1893 Sheffield Wednesday 13 7
Airdrieonians

Miller, John CF/CH
b Dumbarton
Clyde
1895 1897 Derby County 62 20
1897 Bolton Wanderers 8

Miller, John OL
b Maryhill 1878
Birtley
1899 1900 Burnley 18 2

Miller, John IR
Hamilton Academical
1902 Manchester City 8 2
(South Africa)
Airdrieonians
Motherwell
Hamilton Academical

Miller, John (Jack) IR/OR
b Dalziel 12/3/1897
Larkhall Thistle
Blantyre Victoria
Hamilton Academical
1919 Liverpool 8
Heart of Midlothian
Aberdeen
Partick Thistle
Aberdeen
Clyde
Dundee
Dunfermline Athletic
Prescot Cables
1930 Barrow 13 2
1931 Carlisle United 0

Miller, John William OL
b Leyton 12/9/1912 d 1990
Tufnell Park
Dulwich Hamlet
1938 Fulham 4
Margate

Miller, Joseph (Joe) RH
b Belfast 27/4/1899
Caps: Ireland 3
Largs Thistle
Port Glasgow Thistle
Morton
Arthurlie (loan)
Johnstone
Nuneaton Town
1925 Aberdare Athletic 37 4
1926 1929 Middlesbrough 140
Dolphin
Hibernian
Ards
1931 1933 Bournemouth & Boscombe Ath 75
Ballymena
Ross County

Miller, Joseph OL
b Sheffield 1912
Rossington Main
1934 Rotherham United 15 2
1934 Wolverhampton Wanderers 0
1935 Chesterfield 38 13

Miller, Leslie Roy (Les) OL
b Romford 30/3/1911 d 1959
Caps: England Sch
Barking Town
1929 Northampton Town 0
Barking Town
Sochaux
1936 1938 Tottenham Hotspur 56 22
1939 Chesterfield (2)
Mansfield Town

From To Apps Goal

Miller, Percy C LB
1908 Blackpool 4

Miller, Peter CH
Dunfermline Athletic
1924 Doncaster Rovers 5 2
(Canada)

Miller, Peter Chippendale OR
b Blackpool q4 1883 d 1963
1903 Blackpool 3
Fleetwood

Miller, Peter Steedman IL/RH/OL
b Bo'ness 15/4/1908 d 1979
Bo'ness United
Grange Rovers
Falkirk
1930 Watford 14
1931 1934 New Brighton 140 22
Le Havre
1935 Rotherham United 11 2
1936 Port Vale 13 1
King's Park

Miller, Redvers Buller (Rev) OL
b Watford 24/10/1899 d 1995
Watford Corinthians
St Albans City
1922 Watford 1
1923 Charlton Athletic 0
1924 Millwall 0
Barnet
St Albans City
Chesham United
1926 Queen's Park Rangers 0

Miller, Stanley (Stan) OL
b Marple q2 1883
Eccles
Sale Holmfield
Springfield
Broughton
1909 1912 Oldham Athletic 39
Stalybridge Celtic

Miller, T John (Jack) OL
b Hednesford 1875
Caps: FLge 1
Hednesford Town
1895 1904 Wolverhampton Wanderers 251 47
1905 1906 Stoke 59 5
Willenhall

Miller, Thomas (Tommy) LB
b Falkirk 1884 d 1966
Caps: SLge 1
Edinburgh Myrtle
Falkirk
1905 1908 Chelsea 112
Falkirk
Dundee Hibernian
St Bernard's
Bathgate

Miller, Thomas (Tom) CF/IL
b Motherwell 29/6/1890 d 1958
Caps: Scotland 3
Larkhall Hearts
Glenview
Larkhall United
Third Lanark
Hamilton Academical
1911 1920 Liverpool 127 52
Hamilton Academical (loan)
Royal Albert (loan)
1920 Manchester United 25 7
Heart of Midlothian
Torquay United
Hamilton Academical
Raith Rovers

Miller, Thomas A (Tom) CF/IR
1896 1898 Bolton Wanderers 48 12

Miller, Thomas Hanning OL
b Hamilton
Heart of Midlothian
1932 Newcastle United 0
1933 Burnley 5 1
1934 Accrington Stanley 0

Miller, Walter CF/IR
b Newcastle 6/1882 d 1928
Wallsend Park Villa
Third Lanark
1907 Sheffield Wednesday 3
West Ham United
1909 1910 Blackpool 37 15
Third Lanark
1912 1913 Lincoln City 35 8
Merthyr Town
Dundee

From To Apps Goal

Miller, William RH
b Kilmarnock
Kilmarnock
Rangers (loan)
1895 1896 Newcastle United 42 2
Kilmarnock
Jarrow

Miller, William (Bill) IL
b Alnwick 1890
Ryhope Villa
1920 Brighton & Hove Albion 7
Hove
Redhill
Shoreham

Miller, William LH/IL
b Cowdenbeath 22/3/??
Dunfermline Athletic
Lochgelly United
1926 1928 Barrow 95 11
Bangor Athletic (trial)
1934 Carlisle United 0

Miller, William (Bill) CH
b Stockport 31/3/1908 d 1974
1927 Everton (trial) 0
Altrincham
1929 Bolton Wanderers 0
1931 Luton Town 3
Runcorn
1933 Stockport County 0
Stalybridge Celtic
1935 Southport 1
Stalybridge Celtic
Macclesfield
Lancaster City

Miller, William L CF
b Scotland 1880
St Bernard's
1903 Grimsby Town 4

Miller, William L (Willie) IL
b Perth
St Johnstone YM
1931 Torquay United 7 1

Miller, William Rennie (Willie) IR/IL
b Camelon 19/1/1910 d 1978
Caps: SLge 1
Alva Albion Rovers
Partick Thistle
1935 1936 Everton 16 2
1936 1938 Burnley 74 18
1938 Tranmere Rovers 11 1
Falkirk

Miller, William Thomas (Tout) CF
b Burton-on-Trent 15/8/1868 d 1950
Derby Junction
Burton Wanderers
1894 Leicester Fosse 10 2
Kettering
Northampton Town
Bedford Queens Engineers
Northampton Town

Millership, Harry RB/LB
b St Martin's, Shropshire 1890 d 1959
Caps: Wales 6
Chirk
Goole Town
1912 1914 Blackpool 30
1919 Leeds City 8
1919 1921 Rotherham County 81 7
1922 Barnsley 5
Castleford Town

Millership, Walter CH/IL/CF
b Warsop Vale 8/6/1910 d 1978
Warsop Main Colliery
Welbeck Athletic
Shirebrook
1927 1929 Bradford Park Avenue 30 13
1929 1938 Sheffield Wednesday 210 25
Denaby United

Milligan, A George IL
b Glasgow 1891
Glasgow Ashfield
1913 Burnley 2
Clyde
1920 Crystal Palace 2 1
Armadale

From To Apps Goal

Milligan, Dudley CF
b Johannesburg, South Africa 7/11/1916
Caps: South Africa 3/ Ireland 1
Johannesburg Rangers
Dundee (trial)
Clyde
1938 Chesterfield 28 12
1939 (Chesterfield) (2) (1)
Linfield
Distillery
Dundalk
Larne (trial)
1946 Chesterfield 19 6
1947 1948 Bournemouth & Boscombe Ath 45 25
1948 Walsall 5 1
Ballymena United

Milligan, George Henry LH
b Failsworth 31/8/1917 d 1983
Failsworth Hat Shop
Wilson's Brewery
Manchester North End
1935 1937 Oldham Athletic 82 2
1938 Everton 1

Milligan, Joseph (Joe) CH
b Birkenhead 29/9/1911 d 1980
Ellesmere Port Town
1934 1935 New Brighton 12
1936 Tranmere Rovers 0
1938 Barrow 0
Wigan Athletic
Bath City
Wigan Athletic

Millington, Benjamin (Ben) IL
b Lincoln 1/12/1889 d 1977
Lincoln South End
1908 Fulham 1

Millington, Charles (Charlie) OR/IR/IL
b Lincoln 25/4/1882 d 1945
Midland Athletic
Newark Avenue
Grantham
Ripley Athletic
1905 1907 Aston Villa 35 10
1907 1908 Fulham 57 18
1909 1911 Birmingham 83 13
Wellington Town
Brierley Hill Alliance
Stourbridge
Oakengates Town

Millington, E LH
1898 Walsall 1

Millington, George Edward RH
b Aston 1/11/1911 d 2000
1931 Arsenal 0
Shrewsbury Town
1932 Port Vale (trial) 0
1932 Northampton Town 0
Manchester North End
1934 1935 Halifax Town 11
Runcorn
1938 Bristol Rovers 3

Millington, John OL/OR
b Leigh 4/3/1912 d 1995
1933 Bolton Wanderers 0
1934 Clapton Orient 2
1935 1936 Notts County 15 2
1937 Birmingham 0
1937 1938 Swansea Town 44 7
Scunthorpe & Lindsey United

Millington, Melvyn CH
b Chesterfield 22/10/1911 d 1989
Frickley Colliery
1933 Rotherham United 2
1934 Torquay United 6
Scunthorpe & Lindsey United

Millington, Simeon (Sam) GK
b Walsall q4 1896 d 1941
Wellington Town
1926 1931 Chelsea 223

Millington, Thomas (Tom) LB
b Manchester 1887
Colne
Pendlebury
1908 1913 Bury 133
Queen's Park Rangers

From To Apps Goal

Millington, Thomas (Tommy) OR
b Wrexham 12/1/1906 d 1968
Oswestry Town
1923 Wrexham 2
Oswestry Town
1926 Everton 13
1927 1928 Gillingham 38 2
Oswestry Town
1930 Crewe Alexandra 38 6
Yeovil & Petters United
1932 Tottenham Hotspur 0
Oswestry Town
Brierley Hill Alliance
Treffach

Mills, Albert Henry (Mosky) OL
b Charlton 8/2/1889 d 1972
Crescent United
1921 Charlton Athletic 2
Catford Southend
Tunbridge Wells Rangers

Mills, Andrew (Andy) RB
b Hopesay 15/12/1876 d 1954
Knighton
1897 Blackburn Rovers 2
Swindon Town
Brighton United
1900 1902 Leicester Fosse 64 3
Shrewsbury Town (trial)

Mills, Arthur Sidney OR
b Karachi, India 29/9/1906 d 1979
Burton Town
Gainsborough Trinity
1932 Luton Town 37 14
1933 Gillingham 33 12
Burton Town
Gainsborough Trinity

Mills, Bertie Reginald (Paddy) CF/LH/IL
b Multan, India 23/2/1900 d 1994
Barton Town
1920 1925 Hull City 173 76
1925 1928 Notts County 76 35
1928 1929 Birmingham 13 3
1929 1932 Hull City 96 25
Scunthorpe & Lindsey United
Gainsborough Trinity
Barton Town

Mills, Charles (Charlie) IR
b Preston
Calder Vale
1928 Barrow 1

Mills, Frederick (Fred) RH/LH/IR
b Hanley 7/8/1911 d 1990
Middleport
1932 1933 Port Vale 73 4
1934 1938 Leeds United 67 2

Mills, George Robert CF/IR/IL
b Deptford 29/12/1908 d 1970
Caps: FLge 1/England 3
Emerald Athletic
Bromley
1929 1938 Chelsea 220 117

Mills, Hugh McMillan CF
b Dumbarton 9/3/1909 d 1949
Vale Oakville
Renton Thistle
Vale of Leven Academy
St Anthony's (Glasgow)
St Roch's
Bridgeton Waverley
1931 Portsmouth (trial)
1932 1934 West Ham United 21 15
Cannes (loan)
Celtic
1936 Luton Town 2
1936 1938 Carlisle United 54 28
1939 (Carlisle United) (2)
Stranraer (trial)

Mills, J RH
1902 Bury 1
Accrington Stanley

Mills, James (Jimmy) LH
b Dalton Brook 30/9/1915 d 1994
Bramley Park Rangers
Dinnington Athletic
1937 1945 Rotherham United 54 4
1939 (Rotherham United) (3)
1946 1947 Hull City 42 1
1947 Halifax Town 19
Gainsborough Trinity
Peterborough United

From To Apps Goal

Mills, James Thompson IR
b Rochdale 15/1/1898 d 1972
Rochdale All Saints
Rochdale
1921 Bolton Wanderers 0
1922 Norwich City 6 3
Torquay Athletic
Chester
Rochdale Tradesmen
Bury Co-op

Mills, John (Jock) IR
b Vale of Leven 5/4/??
Renfrew Juniors
1922 Blackpool 0
Fleetwood
1924 Rochdale 16 3
Lancaster Town
Morecambe
Standfast
Edmondsons

Mills, Joseph (Joe) RH/LH/IR
b Cresswell 10/4/1895 d 1938
Whitwell St Lawrence
1919 1923 Nottingham Forest 43
1924 Luton Town 31 2
Bentley Colliery

Mills, Joseph CF
b Wigan
Chorley
Clitheroe
1935 Halifax Town 3

Mills, Leslie Richard Robert IL/IR
b Newton Abbot 13/9/1910 d 1972
Dartmouth United
1932 1933 Torquay United 5 1

Mills, Percy Clifford RB/LB
b Barton-on-Humber 10/1/1909 d 1967
Barton Town
1926 Grimsby Town 0
1926 Hull City (trial) 0
1927 1938 Notts County 407 21
1939 (Notts County) (2)

Mills, Samuel OR
b Derby 1871
Alvaston
Derby Midland
1891 1892 Derby County 45 7
Leicester Fosse
Loughborough
1895 Woolwich Arsenal 24 3
Heanor Town

Mills, Thomas James (Tommy) IL/IR
b Ton Pentre 28/12/1911 d 1979
Caps: Wales Sch/Wales 4
Ton Pentre Boys Club
Trocadero Hotel
1929 1933 Clapton Orient 119 20
1934 1935 Leicester City 17 5
1936 1945 Bristol Rovers 99 17
1946 Chester 0
Kleen-e-Ze
1946 Notts County 0

Mills, Thomas Whitton (Tommy) GK
b Washington Station 16/9/1902
Washington Colliery
1929 Sheffield United 0
Washington Colliery
1931 1932 Bury 62

Mills, William (Billy) IR
b Hackney 1891
Barnet Alston
Vicar of Wakefield
1911 1914 Leicester Fosse 77 20

Mills, William (Willie) IL
b Alexandria 28/1/1915
Caps: Scotland 3
Bridgeton Waverley
Aberdeen
1937 1938 Huddersfield Town 27 7
1939 (Huddersfield Town) (3)
Dumbarton
Clyde
Lossiemouth
Huntly
Hamrun Spartans

Mills, William E CF
b 1903
Maple Star
1923 Hartlepools United 2
Fatfield Albion

From To Apps Goal

Millsom, Lawrence (Lawrie) GK
b Rotherham q2 1901 d 1959
1924 Rotherham County 5
Rotherham Amateurs
1927 1931 Torquay United 30

Millson, Ernest Dinsdale (Ernie) CH/RH
b Old Brumby 27/8/1901 d 1962
Ashby Mill Road
Scunthorpe & Lindsey United
1928 1930 Charlton Athletic 12
1931 Chester 11
Scunthorpe & Lindsey United

Mills-Roberts, (Dr) Robert Herbert GK
b Penmachno 5/8/1862 d 1935
Caps: Wales 8
Barnes
St Thomas' Hospital
Casuals
1888 Preston North End 2
Warwick County
Birmingham St George's
Llanberis

Millward, Alan Ernest GK
b Oldham 18/10/1910 d 1998
1931 Oldham Athletic 1
Northern Nomads
Middlesex Wanderers
1936 Oldham Athletic 0

Millward, Ernest Foster (Ernie) OL
b Hartshill, Staffordshire q4 1884 b 1962
Cobridge Church
Biddulph Mission
1905 Glossop 0
Wrexham
1906 Stoke 0
Hanley Swifts
Burslem Port Vale
Stoke
1910 Huddersfield Town 1
Crewe Alexandra

Milne, Alexander James (Alec) LB/RB
b Hebburn 29/9/1889 d 1970
West Stanley
Hebburn Argyle
1919 1925 Stoke 192
1926 1929 Doncaster Rovers 74

Milne, Alexander Simpson (Alec) IL
b Anderston 24/3/1915
Dunoon Athletic
Third Lanark
Lille
1937 Bournemouth & Boscombe Ath 3
Cowdenbeath
East Fife (loan)

Milne, James Low (Jimmy) LH
b Dundee 24/1/1911 d 1997
Lochee West Station
Dundee Arnot (trial)
Dundee Violet (trial)
Dundee United
1932 1938 Preston North End 230 9
1939 (Preston North End) (3)
Wigan Athletic
Morecambe

Milne, John IL/CH/IR
1888 1889 Bolton Wanderers 39 9
1892 1893 Ardwick 18 3

Milne, John Buchan (Johnny) RB
b Rosehearty 27/4/1911 d 1994
Rosehearty
Fraserburgh
1934 1936 Plymouth Argyle 3
1937 1938 Southend United 66 1
1946 Barrow 32
1947 Oldham Athletic 13

Milne, John Vance (Jackie) OL/OR
b Stirling 25/3/1911
Caps: Scotland War 1/Scotland 3
Glasgow Ashfield
1933 1934 Blackburn Rovers 45 13
1935 1937 Arsenal 49 19
1937 1938 Middlesbrough 59 7
1939 (Middlesbrough) (2)
Dumbarton

Milne, (Dr) Victor Edmond (Vic) CH
b Aberdeen 22/6/1897 d 1971
Aberdeen University
Aberdeen
1923 1928 Aston Villa 157 1

From To / Apps Goal

Milne, Walter LB
b Arbroath
Arbroath Woodside
1935 Blackburn Rovers 0
Brechin City
1937 Gateshead 26

Milne, Wilfred Ellis (Wilf) LB
b Hebburn 24/3/1899 d 1977
Caps: WLge 2
Walker Celtic
1920 1936 Swansea Town 587 7
Milford United

Milne, William (Bill) CF
b Montrose 1889
Montrose
1910 Glossop 4 1
1911 Blackpool 25 6
Aberdeen
Third Lanark
Dundee

Milne, William (Billy) RH
b Buckie 24/11/1895 d 1975
Buckie Thistle
Seaforth Highlanders
1920 Tottenham Hotspur (trial) 0
1921 1926 Arsenal 114 1

Milne, William J OR/IR
b Northumberland
Bedlington
Science & Art
Rutherford College
1894 Newcastle United 5 1
1895 Sunderland 0
1897 Newcastle United 1

Milner, Harold OL
b Beighton 10/7/1902 d 1971
Whitwell Colliery
1923 Chesterfield 4
Thurnscoe Victoria
Gainsborough Trinity
Loughborough Corinthians
1925 Chesterfield 0
Newark Town
Mansfield Town
Staveley Town
Frickley Colliery
Hurst
Ashton National
Winsford United
Mossley
Stalybridge Celtic

Milner, Leonard IL
b York q4 1917 d 1944
LNER Institute
1937 1938 York City 11 4

Milnes, Charles (Charlie) RH/CH
b Manchester q2 1885 d 1956
Doncaster St John's
1905 1906 Grimsby Town 35 1
1908 1910 Bradford Park Avenue 83 3
1912 Huddersfield Town 14
Rochdale
Halifax Town
Rochdale
Pontypridd
1921 Tranmere Rovers 16 2
1922 Rochdale 0

Milnes, Frederick Houghton (Fred) LB/RB
b Wortley 26/1/1878 d 1946
Caps: England Amat
Sheffield Wycliffe
Sheffield
1902 1904 Sheffield United 12
West Ham United
Tottenham Hotspur
1906 Manchester United 0
Reading
1906 Leicester Fosse 1
Northern Nomads
Ilford
Norwich City
Sheffield

Milnes, George RH/OR/LH
b Dronfield q1 1880 d 1930
Dronfield Town
1901 1907 Chesterfield Town 41 3
Rotherham County

From To / Apps Goal

Milsom, John (Jack) CF
b Bedminster 22/2/1907 d 1977
Hopewell Hill Mission
1926 Exeter City (trial) 0
1926 Bristol Rovers 0
Kettering Town
1928 1929 Rochdale 54 38
1929 1937 Bolton Wanderers 235 142
1937 1938 Manchester City 32 20
1939 (Manchester City) (1) (2)

Milsom, Percy IR/CF
b Basford q1 1884 d 1948
Sutton Town
1904 Gainsborough Trinity 27 7
Millwall Athletic
1908 Bradford Park Avenue 2

Milton, Albert LB
b High Green q4 1885 d 1917
South Kirkby
1907 Barnsley 15
1908 1913 Sunderland 125
Swindon Town

Milton, Alfred LB
b Masbrough 24/8/1895 d 1977
Rotherham County
Coventry City
Kimberworth Wesleyans
1920 Gillingham 1

Milton, Ernest LB
b Kimberworth 7/8/1897 d 1984
Parkgate Christ Church
1919 1926 Sheffield United 203 3

Milton, Stanley (Stan) GK
b Dewsbury 23/2/1913 d 1993
1933 1935 Halifax Town 8
1937 1938 York City 9

Milward, Alfred (Alf) OL
b Great Marlow 12/9/1870 d 1941
Caps: FLge 1/England 4
Old Borlasians
Marlow
1888 1896 Everton 201 84
1898 New Brighton Tower 32 19
Southampton
New Brompton
Southampton Cambridge

Milward, George (Paddy) CF
b 1879 d 1909
Poolsbrook United
New Whittington Exchange
1902 Chesterfield Town 24 13
Queen's Park Rangers

Mingay, Henry Joseph (Harry) GK
b Luton 19/10/1895 d 1969
RAMC
1919 1923 Blackpool 155
1924 Clapton Orient 0
1925 1926 Luton Town 29
1927 Watford 2
Bedford Town

Minion, Fred LH
b Bolton q4 1881
Bacup
1908 Burnley 2
Chorley
Bacup
Darwen

Minney, George CF
1920 Derby County 2

Minter, William James (Billy) IR/CF
b Woolwich 16/4/1888 d 1940
Norwich City
1905 Woolwich Arsenal 0
Reading
1908 1919 Tottenham Hotspur 245 95

Mitchell, Adam Edmond RH/LH/IR
b Prestonpans 14/12/1908 d 1989
Penicuik
Heart of Midlothian (trial)
Cowdenbeath (trial)
Bo'ness (trial)
1928 1935 Bradford City 143 12
1936 Wrexham 37 2
1937 1938 Doncaster Rovers 53 1
1939 (Doncaster Rovers) (1)
Coxhoe Albion
Peterborough United

Mitchell, Albert Edward IR
b Charlton 22/3/1892 d 1981
Charlton Invicta
1921 Charlton Athletic 1 1
Woolwich United

From To / Apps Goal

Mitchell, Andrew RB
b 1870
Airdrieonians
1892 1893 Newton Heath 54
1894 Burton Swifts 12

Mitchell, Andrew OL
b Scotland 1879
Albion Rovers
1898 Woolwich Arsenal 10 2

Mitchell, Andrew OR
1923 Lincoln City 1

Mitchell, Andrew (Andy) OR/OL
b Coxhoe 20/4/1907 d 1971
Ferryhill Athletic
Crook Town
1927 Sunderland 0
1928 Notts County 0
1929 1931 Darlington 99 32
1932 Manchester United 1
1933 Hull City 8
1933 Northampton Town 18 3
Rossendale United
Great Harwood
Rossendale United

Mitchell, Archibald P (Archie) CH
b Smethwick 15/12/1885 d 1949
Caps: SoLge 6
1906 Aston Villa 0
1920 Queen's Park Rangers 35 3
1921 Brentford 13 2

Mitchell, Charles CF
b Bradford
1906 Bradford City 2
Rochdale
Tonge

Mitchell, David OR
b Glasgow
Pembroke Dock
1926 Merthyr Town 18 2

Mitchell, Frank CF
1898 Burslem Port Vale 4 1

Mitchell, Frank William G GK
b Elgin 25/5/1890
Foundry Old Boys
Milngavie Allander
Maryhill
Motherwell
Celtic (loan)
1913 1919 Everton 23
1920 1921 Liverpool 18
1923 1924 Tranmere Rovers 55
Bangor City
Blue Circle Cement

Mitchell, Harold J OL
1906 1907 Stockport County 26 2

Mitchell, Harry OR
b Barrow Hill
1905 Derby County 1

Mitchell, Hodgson William OL
b Darlington 18/1/1900 d 1973
Royal Training Corps
1921 Darlington 2
Leadgate Park
Sheffield University

Mitchell, J LB
Newton Heath
1888 Bolton Wanderers 2
Newton Heath

Mitchell, J LH
b Belfast
Royal Field Artillery
1911 Leicester Fosse 1

Mitchell, James Frederick GK
b Manchester 18/11/1895 d 1975
Caps: England Amat/England 1
1914 Blackpool 5
Northern Nomads
Manchester University
1920 1921 Preston North End 21
1922 1925 Manchester City 99
1926 Leicester City 0

Mitchell, James William (Jimmy) OR/IR
b Barry 1/9/1918 d 2000
Caps: Wales Sch
1937 1938 Cardiff City 3
Barry Town

From To / Apps Goal

Mitchell, John IR
b 1885
Caps: IrLge 4
Glengowan Rangers
Airdrieonians
Glentoran
Distillery
Glentoran
1909 Oldham Athletic 4 1
Glentoran
Shelbourne

Mitchell, John Ernest (Johnny) RB
b Charlton 7/5/1888
1921 Charlton Athletic 16

Mitchell, Joseph Thomas (Joe) GK
b Darnall 1/1/1886 d 1964
Darnall Congregationals
Thorpe Hesley
1909 1912 Sheffield United 36
Luton Town
1919 South Shields 1
1919 1920 Coventry City 29
1921 Chesterfield 12
1922 Barnsley 0
Denaby United
Eckington Works

Mitchell, Michael Jeffray RH
b Glasgow 4/10/1903
Burnbank Athletic
1924 Notts County 5
New Bedford Whalers
J & P Coats (Rhode Island)
Brooklyn Wanderers

Mitchell, P IL
1894 Darwen 5 1

Mitchell, Robert (Bob) IR
b Paisley 1889
Cliftonville
1911 1912 Barnsley 4

Mitchell, Ronald LH/RH
b Birkenhead q3 1902
Dick, Kerr's XI
Skelmersdale United
1922 Liverpool 0
1924 1925 Hull City 27 1
1926 Nelson 32
1927 Bristol Rovers 0
Mossley
Great Harwood
Fleetwood Windsor Villa

Mitchell, Thomas (Tommy) OL/CF
b Trimdon Grange 27/6/1905 d 1970
Trimdon Grange
1922 1923 Hartlepools United 35 1
1924 1925 Stockport County 66 13
1925 1928 Blackburn Rovers 73 27
1929 Lincoln City 3
Horden Colliery Welfare

Mitchell, Thomas Morris (Tom) OL
b Spennymoor 30/9/1899 d 1984
Parkside United
Tudhoe United
Spennymoor United
Blyth Spartans
1920 1925 Newcastle United 60 5
1926 1930 Leeds United 142 19
1931 1932 York City 23 5

Mitchell, Thomas W (Tommy) OR
b Liversedge
Liversedge
1911 Blackpool 3
Watford

Mitchell, W OR
1888 Blackburn Rovers 1 2

Mitchell, William (Billy) RH
b Lurgan 22/11/1910 d 1978
Caps: IrLge 4/Ireland 15
Linfield Rangers
Cliftonville
Dundalk
Distillery
1933 1938 Chelsea 108 2
1939 (Chelsea) (2)
Bath City

Mitcheson, Frederick (Fred) RH/IR/IL
b Westerhope 20/3/1912 d 1994
1932 Wolverhampton Wanderers 0
1933 1935 Port Vale 49 8
1935 1938 Plymouth Argyle 93 25
1939 Ipswich Town (3) (1)
Yeovil Town

From	To		Apps	Goal
Mitcheson, Robert Erthington			OR	
b Blackhill q1 1901				
		Leadgate Park		
1922		Darlington	6	
		Leadgate Park		
Mite, Robert (Bob)			LH	
b Kimberworth 5/5/1889			d 1974	
		Rotherham County		
1911		Sheffield United	0	
		Rotherham Town		
		Goole Town		
		Rotherham County		
1919		Coventry City	7	
		Rotherham Town		
		Mansfield Town		
Mittell, James Lyons (Jackie)			GK	
b Merthyr Tydfil 28/2/1906			d 1976	
1922		Merthyr Town	0	
		Penrhiwceiber		
1927	1928	Rochdale	46	
1929		Wigan Borough	40	
		Connah's Quay & Shotton		
1930	1931	Wigan Borough	30	
1931	1932	Birmingham	6	
1933		Luton Town	8	
		Derry City		
1935	1936	Hartlepools United	65	
1937		Barrow	42	
		Tunbridge Wells Rangers		
Mitton, James (Jimmy)			CH/RH	
b Brierfield q1 1890			d 1949	
1909		Glossop	0	
1910	1920	Stockport County	88	6
1921	1922	Exeter City	72	2
1923		Nelson	0	
Mitton, John (Jack)			RH/LH/CH	
b Todmorden 7/11/1895			d 1983	
		Portsmouth Rovers		
		Padiham		
		Brierfield		
1914		Burnley	0	
1920		Exeter City	11	
1920	1923	Sunderland	79	8
1924	1926	Wolverhampton Wanderers	100	6
1927		Southampton	8	
Mizen, Henry James (Harry)			OR	
b Westbury 12/7/1910			d 1991	
		Salisbury City		
1932		Carlisle United	3	1
Mobbs, Frederick Wilfred (Fred)			GK	
b Gainsborough 29/7/1904			d 1973	
		Gainsborough Trinity		
1927		Blackpool	24	
		Aldershot		
		Newark Town		
		Grantham		
Mobley, Frank			CF	
b Handsworth 21/11/1868			d 1940	
		Hockley Belmont		
		Cape Hill		
		Singers		
1892	1895	Small Heath	96	62
1896		Bury	3	
		Gravesend United		
		Coventry City		
Mochan, Charles			LB	
b Glasgow 8/6/1879				
		Strathclyde		
1904		Grimsby Town	12	
		Brighton & Hove Albion		
		Renton		
Moffat, Andrew Naysmith (Andy)			CF	
b Rosewell 5/9/1900			d 1990	
		Glencraig Rangers		
		Kinglassie United		
		Glencraig Celtic		
		Lochgelly United		
		East Fife		
1920		Everton	1	
1922		Wrexham	8	
		East Fife		
		Lochgelly United		
		Dunfermline Athletic		
Moffat, Harold (Hugh)			OR	
b Camerton, Cumberland q1 1900			d 1968	
1923		Arsenal	0	
		Guildford United		
1925		Luton Town	33	4
1926		Everton	2	
1927		Oldham Athletic	0	
1928		Walsall	41	5
1929		Queen's Park Rangers	15	3
Moffat, Hugh			RH/LH/LB	
b Congleton 1/1885			d 1952	
Caps: FLge 2/England 1				
		Congleton Town		
		Congleton Swifts		
1903	1910	Burnley	201	13
1910	1914	Oldham Athletic	162	10
		Chesterfield Municipal		
		Congleton Town		
Moffat, Sidney Hugh (Sid)			OR	
b Congleton 16/9/1910			d 1981	
		Congleton Town		
1933	1934	Birmingham	18	3
1936		Millwall	2	
Moffatt, Joseph (Joe)			CF/LH/CH	
b Paisley 1875				
		Bo'ness		
		Abercorn		
		Bo'ness		
		Wishaw Thistle		
		Bo'ness		
		St Mirren		
		Chatham		
		Gravesend United		
1899		Walsall	27	13
		Tottenham Hotspur		
		Bo'ness		
		St Mirren		
1903	1905	Manchester City	20	4
		Kilmarnock		
		Nelson		
		Heart of Midlothian		
		Watford		
		Aberdeen		
Moffatt, Robert (Bobby)			RH	
b Dumfries 1873				
		St Mirren		
1895	1902	Manchester City	156	7
		Kilmarnock		
Moffatt, William John (Billy)			LH/RB/RH	
b Bellshill 30/6/1897			d 1952	
		Bellshill Athletic		
		Bo'ness		
1925	1928	Portsmouth	130	2
1930	1931	Brighton & Hove Albion	21	
Moger, Henry Herbert (Harry)			GK	
b Southampton 9/1879			d 1927	
		Forest Swifts		
		Freemantle		
		Southampton		
1903	1911	Manchester United	242	
Mogford, Reginald William James (Reg)			CF/IL	
b Newport 12/6/1919			d 1992	
1938	1947	Newport County	20	9
		Worcester City		
		Kidderminster Harriers		
		Bromsgrove Rovers		
Moir, David Leslie			CH	
b Heaton 2/5/1897			d 1969	
1921		Tottenham Hotspur	0	
		London University		
1923		Darlington	1	
Moir, Howard Lowndes			GK	
b Chorlton-cum-Hardy q3 1881			d 1923	
1902		Stockport County	1	
Moir, J			RH	
1903	1904	Burton United	6	
Moir, James (Jim)			CF/OR	
b Newcastle 23/3/1918			d 2000	
		Newcastle West End		
1937	1938	Accrington Stanley	20	9
1946	1947	Carlisle United	42	20
Moir, James Galbraith (Jimmy)			RH	
b Bonhill 11/11/1879				
		Bonhill Athletic		
		Vale of Leven		
		Celtic		
		Vale of Leven (loan)		
1900		Blackburn Rovers	32	
		Celtic		
1903	1905	Blackburn Rovers	45	
		Clyde		
Moir, James Glegg			RH	
b Inverbervie 7/1/1874			d 1953	
		Gowan Athletic		
1897		Sunderland	0	
1898	1899	Woolwich Arsenal	41	
		Gravesend United		
		Fulham		
Moir, Robert Marshall			CH	
b Maryhill 10/5/1904			d 1955	
		Vale of Clyde		
		Morton		
		St Johnstone		
1926		Luton Town	1	
Moiser, Gilbert			IR	
b Dewsbury q4 1895			d 1959	
1921		Rotherham County	1	
Mole, George (Barney)			OR/CF	
b Stockton q4 1878				
		Stockton St John's		
1899		Newcastle United	1	1
1900		Burnley	9	2
		South Bank		
Moles, James			LH	
b Tottenham q2 1884				
		Asplin Rovers		
		Tottenham Hotspur		
		Leyton		
1909	1910	Birmingham	33	
		Leyton		
		Edmonton		
Moles, Walter John			GK	
b Epping q4 1878			d 1954	
		Castle United		
		Waverley		
		Tottenham Hotspur		
1901		Bristol City	6	
		Tottenham Hotspur		
Molloy, John Thomas			RH/CH	
b Middlewich 30/4/1907			d 1978	
		Sandbach Ramblers		
1930		Arsenal (trial)	0	
		Witton Albion		
		Nantwich		
1932		Wrexham	1	
		Oswestry Town		
		Witton Albion		
		Winsford United		
		Mossley		
1936		Halifax Town	6	
		Macclesfield		
		Rhyl		
Molloy, Peter			LH/RH	
b Rossendale 20/4/1909			d 1993	
1930		Accrington Stanley	0	
1931		Fulham	4	
1933		Bristol Rovers	6	
1933	1934	Cardiff City	23	
1935		Queen's Park Rangers	3	
1936		Stockport County	10	
1937		Carlisle United	33	
1938		Bradford City	25	
1939		(Bradford City)	(3)	
1945		Accrington Stanley	0	
		Kettering Town		
		Stewart & Lloyds		
Molloy, William			CF	
		Dick, Kerr's XI		
1931		Notts County	2	1
		Dick, Kerr's XI		
Molloy, William Henry B			IL/IR	
b Barrow q3 1904				
		Dumbarton Harp		
		Celtic		
		Arthurlie (loan)		
		Ayr United (loan)		
		Arthurlie (loan)		
		Dumbarton		
		Yeovil & Petters United		
1932		Swansea Town	11	2
1933		Bristol City	7	2
		Falkirk		
		Dumbarton (trial)		
Molyneux, Frederick Leatherbarrow (Fred			CF	
b Bolton q2 1873				
		3rd Grenadiers		
1897	1898	Stoke	11	3
		Bristol City		
		Berwick Rangers (Worcester)		
		Dudley		
		Luton Town		
		Fulham		
		Kidderminster Harriers		
Molyneux, George			LB	
b Liverpool q3 1875			d 1942	
Caps: England 4				
		3rd Grenadiers		
		South Shore		
		Kirkdale		
1896		Everton	1	
		Wigan County		
1898	1899	Everton	42	
		Southampton		
		Portsmouth		
		Southend United		
		Colchester Town		
Molyneux, James (Jimmy)			GK	
b Port Sunlight q1 1887			d 1950	
		New Ferry Bible Class		
		Port Sunlight Works		
		Rock Ferry		
1906	1909	Stockport County	89	
1910	1921	Chelsea	210	
1924		Stockport County	8	
Molyneux, William			RH	
b St Helens				
		Alexandra Victoria		
		Heywood United		
		Norwich City		
1919		Liverpool	0	
1920	1923	Luton Town	80	1
		Kettering Town		
Monaghan, James (Jimmy)			OR	
b Newburn 1893			d 1916	
		Newburn		
1913		Sheffield Wednesday	2	
		Scunthorpe & Lindsey United		
Monaghan, Peter			LH	
b Stevenston 1917			d 1945	
		Ardeer Recreation		
1937	1938	Bournemouth & Boscombe Ath	63	1
1939		(Bournemouth & Boscombe Ath)	(3)	(1)
Monaghan, William (Billy)			CH	
1925		Halifax Town	4	
Monk, Frank Vivian			CH	
b Salisbury q3 1886			d 1962	
Caps: England Amat				
		St Mark's College		
1908		Chelsea	0	
		Salisbury City		
		Southampton		
1911		Glossop	2	
1911		Fulham	0	
		Southampton		
1911		Fulham	0	
		Salisbury City		
Monk, Wilfred (Wilf)			OL/OR	
b Burscough 22/4/1910			d 1988	
		Birkdale South End		
		High Park		
1931	1932	Southport	8	1
		Burscough Rangers		
1933		Blackburn Rovers	0	
		Lancaster Town		
		Fleetwood		
		Chorley		
		South Liverpool		
		Fleetwood Hesketh		
Monks (Monk), Albert			IR/CF/IL	
b Ashton-under-Lyne 6/5/1875			d 1936	
		Hurst Ramblers		
		Hadfield		
		Ashton North End		
1899		Glossop	13	1
		Stalybridge Rovers		
1901		Bury	16	7
1902		Everton	0	
1902	1903	Blackburn Rovers	24	4
		Nelson		
		Swindon Town		
		Stalybridge Rovers		
		Southport Central		
		Hyde		
		Hurst		
Monks, Albert			GK	
b Manchester				
1927		Rochdale	1	
Monks, Isaac			CH	
b Wilson 1863				
1888		Derby County	3	
Monks, James			GK	
b Chorley				
		Chorley		
1899		New Brighton Tower	7	
		Luton Town		

From	To	Club	Apps	Goal
Monteith, Hugh G			GK	
b New Cumnock 14/8/1874				
		Wellington Thistle		
		Parkhead Juniors		
		Celtic		
1895	1896	Loughborough	58	
		Bristol City		
		West Ham United		
1902	1905	Bury	77	
		Kilmarnock		
		Beith		
		Morton		
		Dundee Hibernian		
Monteith, James			OL	
b Ireland				
		Celtic		
1897		Woolwich Arsenal	6	1
		Distillery		
Montford, Edgar William John			RB	
b Newtown q2 1865			d 1940	
		Newtown		
1888	1889	Stoke	5	
		Leek		
Montford, James Henry Parker (Harry)			IL	
b Little Drayton q3 1863			d 1942	
		Newtown		
1888		Stoke	1	
		Leek		
Montgomery, A			OL	
1892		Bootle	20	9
Montgomery, Archibald (Archie)			GK	
b Chryston 27/1/1873			d 1922	
		Chryston Athletic		
		Rangers		
1894	1904	Bury	210	
1905		Manchester United	3	
1906		Bury	0	
Montgomery, Gerald John			CH	
b Birkenhead q4 1880			d 1938	
1900		Preston North End	4	
		Tottenham Hotspur		
1902		Preston North End	0	
Montgomery, Harold (Harry)			OR	
b Hadfield q1 1900				
		Glossop		
		Hyde United		
1922	1923	Crewe Alexandra	51	1
1924		Accrington Stanley	2	
Montgomery, James (Jim)			RH	
b Craghead				
		Bishop Auckland		
		Craghead United		
1912	1914	Glossop	67	1
1914	1920	Manchester United	27	1
1921		Crewe Alexandra	0	
Montgomery, John (Jack)			LB	
b Chryston 18/6/1876			d 1940	
		Tottenham Hotspur		
1898	1910	Notts County	316	2
Montgomery, John Joseph (Jack)			CF	
b Glasgow 26/6/1915			d 1973	
		Rothesay Royal Victoria		
		Glasgow Benburb (trial)		
		Renfrew Juniors (trial)		
		Coltness United		
1936		Manchester United	0	
1937	1938	New Brighton	57	34
1939		(New Brighton)	(1)	
Montgomery, William (Bill)			IL/IR	
b Gourock 1885			d 1953	
		Kilwinning Rangers		
		Rutherglen Glencairn		
1905	1906	Bradford City	17	3
1907	1908	Sunderland	11	2
1909	1911	Oldham Athletic	70	26
		Rangers		
		Dundee		
		Stevenston United		
		Ayr United		
Moody, Alfred George (Alf)			OL	
b Plumstead 11/4/1900			d 1971	
		Royal Ordnance Factory		
1921		Charlton Athletic	2	
1922		Arsenal	0	
		Erith & Belvedere		
Moody, Herbert			CF/IR	
b Luton q2 1880				
Caps: SoLge 6				
		Luton Stanley		
		Luton Town		
1905	1906	Leicester Fosse	54	11
		Luton Town		
		Millwall Athletic		

From	To	Club	Apps	Goal
Moody, James Henry (Harry)			GK	
b Rochdale 12/3/1896			d 1968	
		Mid-Rhondda		
1920	1921	Grimsby Town	33	
1922	1927	Rochdale	161	
Moody, John (Jack)			GK	
b Heeley 10/11/1903				
		Hathersage		
1924		Sheffield United (trial)	0	
		Norton Woodseats		
1926	1927	Arsenal	6	
1929		Bradford Park Avenue	6	
1930	1931	Doncaster Rovers	45	
1931	1932	Manchester United	50	
1933	1938	Chesterfield	186	
Moody, William Arthur			IL	
b Rochdale q2 1895				
		Mid-Rhondda		
1921		Cardiff City	0	
1922		Rochdale	1	
Moon, Albert			OL/IL	
b Preston 28/1/1904			d 1981	
		Chorley		
1928	1930	Accrington Stanley	3	
		Burscough Rangers		
		Rossendale United		
		Fleetwood		
Moon, George			RB	
b Blackhill				
		Consett		
		Shildon		
1930		Gateshead	1	
		Consett		
Moon, Thomas (Tommy)			OR	
b Preston 2/1/1900			d 1981	
		New Hall Lane Temperance		
		Dick, Kerr's XI		
		Horwich RMI		
1923		Preston North End	0	
		Dick, Kerr's XI		
1925		Southport	4	1
		Dick, Kerr's XI		
		Burscough Rangers (trial)		
		Chorley		
		Dick, Kerr's XI		
1928	1929	Bradford City	47	17
		Dick, Kerr's XI		
1930		Barrow	28	6
1931		Wigan Borough	10	1
		Frickley Colliery		
		Lytham		
		Drumcondra		
		Dick, Kerr's XI		
Mooney, Edward Peter (Peter)			LH/CH/RH	
b Walker 22/3/1897				
		Walker Celtic		
		Newcastle United Swifts		
1919	1926	Newcastle United	121	3
1927		Hull City	11	
		Scunthorpe & Lindsey United		
		Shildon		
		Northfleet (trial)		
		Walker Celtic		
Mooney, Felix			IL/CF	
		Bootle		
1892		Ardwick	9	4
1895		Bury	7	2
1896		Walsall	0	
Mooney, Hugh			LH	
b Belfast 23/5/1907			d 1975	
		Kilsyth Emmet		
		Belfast Celtic		
1930		Nottingham Forest	0	
		Stenhousemuir		
		Aberdeen		
1933		Gillingham	4	
		London Paper Mills		
Mooney, JM			CF	
1893		Middlesbrough Ironopolis	20	3
Mooney, John			IR	
b Dennistoun 13/6/1897				
		St Mirren Juniors		
		Glasgow Perthshire		
1921	1922	Bristol City	2	
		Cowdenbeath		
		Queen of the South		
1925		Barrow	14	2
1926		Clapton Orient	0	
Mooney, Joseph			RB	
1905		Burnley	1	

From	To	Club	Apps	Goal
Mooney, Paul			CH	
b Chapel, Lanarkshire 7/4/1901			d 1980	
		Vernon Athletic		
		Falkirk		
		Aberdeen		
		Clyde		
		East Stirlingshire		
1925	1935	Brighton & Hove Albion	283	10
Mooney, Thomas (Tom)			OL	
b Tollcross 31/10/1910			d 1981	
Caps: SLge 2				
		Kirkmuirhill		
		Stonehouse Victoria		
		Royal Albert		
		Larkhall Thistle		
		Celtic		
		Airdrieonians		
1936	1938	Newcastle United	75	17
1939		(Newcastle United)	(1)	
		Morton		
Moore, Albert Edward			IR	
b Nottingham q4 1863				
1888		Notts County	10	3
Moore, Albert Edward			IR	
b Longton 1898				
		Normacot		
1921		Stoke	1	
		Burslem Swifts		
Moore, Charles (Charlie)			RH/LH/CF	
b Worksop 23/9/1905			d 1972	
		Manton Colliery		
1926	1938	Bradford City	340	53
1939		(Bradford City)	(3)	
Moore, Charles William (Charlie)			RB/LB	
b Cheslyn Hay 3/6/1898				
		Hednesford Town		
1919	1929	Manchester United	309	
Moore, David			GK	
b Ashington q1 1905			d 1964	
		Ashington Welfare		
1927		Ashington	3	
		Wallaw United		
		Ashington Colliery Electricians		
		Ellington United		
		Ashington Colliery Electricians		
Moore, Ernest W			LB	
b Birmingham 1869				
		Sparkhill Alliance		
1894		Small Heath	1	
		Hockley Hill		
Moore, Everett W			IR	
b Aberdeen 1879				
		Rawdon		
1903		Bradford City	3	
Moore, F			RH	
1896		Walsall	2	
Moore, Frederick (Fred)			RH	
		Northwich Victoria		
1897	1898	Darwen	47	1
Moore, Frederick (Fred)			IL/OL	
b Worksop				
		Anston Athletic		
1926		Bradford City	6	3
		Worksop Town		
1929		Halifax Town	2	1
Moore, George Sinclair			IR	
b Nuneaton q3 1884				
		Nuneaton Town		
1907	1908	Birmingham	3	1
		Leamington Town		
Moore, George Wilfred			OL	
b Herrington 23/5/1908				
		Usworth Colliery		
		Tunbridge Wells Rangers		
1933		Charlton Athletic	1	1
		Yeovil & Petters United		
Moore, George William			IR	
b Newport, Shropshire q1 1887				
		Stafford Rangers		
1907		Notts County	1	
		Stafford Rangers		
		Siemens Institute		
Moore, Harold			RH	
		Halesowen Town		
1923		Portsmouth	1	1
		Kettering Town		

From	To	Club	Apps	Goal
Moore, Henry (Harry)			LH	
b Worksop 5/8/1896			d 1984	
		Worksop Congregationalists		
		Worksop Town		
1921		Notts County	16	
		Boston Town		
		Worksop Town		
		Mansfield Town		
		Worksop Town		
		Manton Colliery		
Moore, Isaac			LH/OR/IL	
b Dundee 8/4/1867			d 1954	
		Dundee Our Boys		
		Lincoln City		
1889		Aston Villa	5	3
		Newcastle West End		
1892		Lincoln City	22	3
1894		Burton Wanderers	10	3
		Swindon Town		
Moore, James (Jimmy)			IL/OL/CF	
b Felling 1/9/1891			d 1972	
		Boldon Colliery Welfare		
		Jarrow Croft		
1911	1914	Barnsley	101	23
1920		Southampton	42	12
1921		Leeds United	27	4
1922		Brighton & Hove Albion	6	2
1923		Halifax Town	40	6
1924		Queen's Park Rangers	26	5
1925		Crewe Alexandra	11	6
Moore, James (Jim)			IL/CF/IR	
b Handsworth 11/5/1889			d 1972	
Caps: England 1				
		Quebec Albion		
		Cradley Heath		
1911	1913	Glossop	67	35
1913	1925	Derby County	203	75
1925	1926	Chesterfield	41	21
		Mansfield Town		
		Worcester City		
Moore, James Alex Owen			LB	
b Middlesbrough 20/6/1877				
		Middlesbrough		
1898		Luton Town	19	
Moore, John (Jack)			OL/IL/IR	
b Wellington, Shropshire				
1904		Burton United	4	3
1904	1905	Derby County	5	
1907		Oldham Athletic	0	
		Watford		
Moore, John			RH	
b Inkerman, Renfrewshire				
		Kirkintilloch Rob Roy		
		(USA)		
		Saltcoats Victoria		
		Aberdeen		
1925		Crystal Palace	1	
		Hamilton Academical		
		Dundee United (loan)		
		Arthurlie		
Moore, John E			RH/IR/IL	
b Newcastle 1912				
		Annfield Plain		
		Hebburn Colliery		
1934		Hull City	5	
1935	1936	Gateshead	24	4
Moore, John H			RH	
1898		Loughborough	18	
Moore, Patrick (Paddy)			CH	
b Ballybough 4/8/1909			d 1951	
Caps: LoI 1/Ireland 1/Eire 9				
		Clonliffe Celtic		
		Bendigo (Dublin)		
		Richmond Rovers		
		Shamrock Rovers		
1929		Cardiff City	1	
1929		Merthyr Town	5	
1930		Tranmere Rovers	4	
		Shamrock Rovers		
		Brideville		
		Aberdeen		
		Shamrock Rovers		
		Shelbourne		
		Brideville		
		Shamrock Rovers		
Moore, Ralph			IL	
b Derby				
		Crewton United		
1919		Derby County	1	

From To Apps Goal

Moore, Stanley (Stan) GK
b Worksop 31/12/1909 d 1982
Anston Athletic
Worksop Town
1931 1934 Leeds United 78
1935 1938 Swansea Town 123
1939 (Swansea Town) (3)

Moore, Thomas CF
b Arbroath 1864
Arbroath
1888 Stoke 1
Arbroath

Moore, Thomas (Tom) IL
b Barrow q3 1905
Hawshead
1925 Barrow 4 2

Moore, Thomas D (Tommy) IL/OL
b Dudley Port 4/1910
Tipton All Souls
Stourbridge
1931 Aston Villa 1 1
Stourbridge
1934 Bournemouth & Boscombe Ath 6 2
Stourbridge
Dudley Town
1935 Birmingham 0
1936 Swansea Town 4
Stourbridge

Moore, Walter RB
b Darfield q1 1899
West Melton Excelsior
Darfield
1924 Nelson 5
Wath Athletic
Winterwell Athletic

Moore, William (Billy) RH/LH
b New Washington q2 1916 d 1982
Walker Celtic
1936 1937 Stoke City 4
1939 Mansfield Town (1)

Moore, William Albert (Billy) LH
b Llanbradach 14/10/1912 d 2002
Caps: Wales Amat
1934 Cardiff City 11
1935 Southampton 0
1936 Wolverhampton Wanderers 0

Moore, William C LB/RB/LH
Graham Street Primitives
1906 1908 Derby County 11
1909 Stockport County 2
Ilkeston United

Moore, William Gray Bruce (Billy) IL/IR
b Newcastle 6/10/1894 d 1968
Caps: England Amat/England 1
Seaton Delaval
1913 1921 Sunderland 46 11
1922 1928 West Ham United 181 42

Moore, William Henry OL
b York 17/10/1913 d 1978
1932 York City 2
1933 Bradford City 0
Goole Town

Moore, William John (Pal) OL
b Ballyclare 2/8/1895 d 1932
Caps: Ireland 1
Ollardale
Brantwood
Glentoran
Falkirk
1923 1924 Lincoln City 33 2
Ards
Glentoran

Moore, William Riddell (Billy) GK
b Sunderland 10/3/1903 d 1962
Limited Yard Apprentices
1922 Blackburn Rovers (trial) 0
Seaham Colliery
1924 Leeds United 6
1925 1935 Southend United 285
1936 Hartlepools United 16

Moores, J James GK
b West Kirby
West Kirby
Chester
Rock Ferry
1900 Stockport County 28
Chester

Moores, W LB
1892 1894 Crewe Alexandra 6

From To Apps Goal

Moorhead, George CH
b Christchurch, New Zealand 27/5/1895 d 1976
Caps: IrLge 9/Ireland 4
Glenavon
Royal Ulster Rifles
1920 Southampton 9
1922 Brighton & Hove Albion 1
Linfield
Glenavon
Linfield
Heart of Midlothian

Moorhouse, George OL
b Liverpool 4/4/1901 d 1943
Caps: USA 9
1920 Leeds United (trial) 0
1921 Tranmere Rovers 2
Montreal CPR
Brooklyn Wanderers
New York Giants
New York Soccer Club
New York Yankees
New York Americans

Moorwood, John Edwin (Jack) CH
b Sheffield q3 1896
Alfreton
1920 Stoke 9
1921 1923 Wrexham 65 2
Bangor City
Gleadless
Sheffield Forge
Woodhouse Working Mens Club

Moorwood, Thomas Leonard (Len) GK
b Wednesbury 21/9/1888 d 1976
Bilston United
1910 1919 West Bromwich Albion 30
1920 1922 Burnley 18
Weymouth
1924 Blackpool 0
Blackheath

Moralee, Matthew (Matt) IL/OL
b Mexborough 21/2/1912 d 1991
Ormsby United
Denaby United
Gainsborough Trinity
1931 1935 Grimsby Town 27 5
1936 Aston Villa 12 1
1937 1938 Leicester City 38 6
Shrewsbury Town
Denaby United
Manvers Main

Moralee, Matthew Whitfield (Matt) CH
b Newcastle 4/3/1878 d 1962
Blyth Spartans
Hebburn Argyle
1901 1903 Sheffield Wednesday 4 1
1904 Doncaster Rovers 32 2
Mexborough Town
Kilnhurst Town

Moralee, William Ernest (Bill)
b Crook 3/5/1906 d 1967
Crook Town
1927 Huddersfield Town 0
1928 1935 Bournemouth & Boscombe Ath 189 6
1936 1937 Queen's Park Rangers 22

Moran, James Joyce RB
b Sunderland 10/3/?? d 1973
Sheppey United
1929 1931 Millwall 18
Margate

Moran, John (Jack) RB/LB
b Haydock 9/2/1906 d 1959
Earlestown
1925 1930 Wigan Borough 201
1931 Tottenham Hotspur 12
1932 1935 Watford 100
1935 1936 Mansfield Town 30

Moran, John IL
b Ryton-on-Tyne
Scotswood
1928 Bury 3 1
1929 West Ham United 0
1930 Carlisle United 0
Consett
Crawcrook Albion

Moran, Joseph (Joe) OL
1902 Aston Villa 0
Doncaster Rovers
1904 Leicester Fosse 1

Moran, Joseph (Joe) LH
b Dublin 9/2/??
Caps: IrLge 1/Ireland 1
Shelbourne
1911 1912 Leeds City 25

From To Apps Goal

Moran, Martin (Marty) OR
b Bannockburn 19/12/1879
Glasgow Benburb
Celtic
Clyde
1899 Sheffield United 7
1900 1901 Middlesbrough 36 5
Millwall Athletic
Heart of Midlothian
1905 1907 Chelsea 63 7
Celtic
Hamilton Academical
Albion Rovers

Mordey, Henry Victor (Harold) LB
b Kuala Lumpur, Malaysia 4/5/1911 d 1986
Army
1936 1938 Charlton Athletic 10

Mordue, George Anthony RH/CH
b South Shields 3/11/1915 d 1999
Washington Colliery
1935 Wolverhampton Wanderers 0
1936 Bournemouth & Boscombe Ath 0
1936 1937 Aldershot 4
1938 Bradford City 7

Mordue, John (Jackie) OR/OL/IL
b Edmondsley 13/12/1886 d 1938
Caps: FLge 3/England 2
Sacriston
Spennymoor United
1906 Barnsley 24 12
1906 1907 Woolwich Arsenal 26 1
1908 1919 Sunderland 262 71
1920 1921 Middlesbrough 35 1
1922 1923 Durham City 6 1
Ryhope

Mordue, John (Jack) IR/OR
b Sacriston 11/9/1906 d 1991
Sacriston
Esh Winning
Langley Park
1927 1931 Hartlepools United 131 31
Annfield Plain

Mordue, Thomas (Tom 'Tucker') IL/CF/OR
b Horden 22/7/1905 d 1975
Herrington Swifts
1923 Hull City 6
Horden Athletic
1925 Newcastle United 5 2
1926 1927 Sheffield United 7
1928 1930 Hartlepools United 101 26
Horden Colliery Welfare
Shotton Colliery Welfare
Horden Coke Ovens

Mordue, William Michael (Billy) IL/RH/LH
b Horden 5/7/1903 d 1980
Horden St Mary's
Horden Athletic
1921 Middlesbrough 0
1922 Hartlepools United 8
Horden Athletic
1926 Blackpool 0
1927 1929 Hartlepools United 103 18
Crook Town
Horden Colliery Welfare
Easington Colliery Welfare

Moreland, Arthur Geoffrey (Geoffrey) IR/CF
b Wolverhampton 29/11/1914 d 1996
Stafford Rangers
1937 Swindon Town 0
1938 Birmingham 4
1938 Port Vale 7 3

Moreland, John IL/IR
Nelson
1897 1898 Blackburn Rovers 20 6

Moreton, John James (Jimmy) OR
b Birkenhead 22/9/1891 d 1942
Bebington St Andrew's
Cammell Laird
1921 1926 Tranmere Rovers 148 12

Morfitt, John William (Jack) CF/LH
b Sheffield 28/9/1908 d 1973
Heeley
Anston Athletic
1928 West Bromwich Albion 0
Mansfield Town
1930 Birmingham 1
1931 Blackpool 1
1931 Bradford Park Avenue 9 5
1932 1935 Southend United 66 16

From To Apps Goal

Morgan, Alfred Robert CH
b Caistor q4 1879
St Andrew's
Humber Trinity
Grimsby All Saints
1902 Grimsby Town 1
Grimsby All Saints
Grimsby Rangers

Morgan, Aneurin OR/OL/IL
b Merthyr Tydfil q1 1901
1922 1923 Merthyr Town 16
1926 Aberdare Athletic 8 1
1927 Merthyr Town 7 2

Morgan, Charles (Charlie) RH
b Bootle q3 1881
1903 Everton 0
Tottenham Hotspur
1905 1906 Leeds City 41 1
1909 Bradford Park Avenue 1
Halifax Town

Morgan, Clifford Ivor (Cliff) RH
b Bristol 26/9/1913 d 1975
Bristol Boys Brigade
1931 1948 Bristol City 245 11
1939 (Bristol City) (3)

Morgan, Douglas (Doug) LB
b Inverkeithing 1890 d 1917
Inverkeithing United
1913 1914 Hull City 52

Morgan, E RB
1891 Accrington 2

Morgan, Emlyn (Tom) RH
b Troedyrhiwfuwch 14/9/1914 d 1983
New Tredegar
1935 1938 Watford 108 6

Morgan, Francis Gerald (Gerry) CH
b Belfast 25/7/1899 d 1959
Caps: IrLge 1/Ireland 8
Cliftonville
Linfield
1922 1928 Nottingham Forest 200 6
1929 Luton Town 4
Grantham
Cork FC
Ballymena

Morgan, Frederick (Jerry) IR/IL
b Bristol 5/11/1897 d 1953
Horfield United
Bath City
1920 1924 Bristol Rovers 114 25
Brislington Wednesday
Showman's Guild
Bristol City Wednesday
Bristol South Wednesday

Morgan, Herbert Harry (Harry) IR
b Swansea q4 1913
1934 Newport County 4

Morgan, Hugh OR/IR/IL
b Shettleston 7/8/1874
Harthill Thistle
Airdrieonians
1896 1898 Sunderland 53 17
1898 1900 Bolton Wanderers 46 16
1900 Newton Heath 20 4
1901 Manchester City 12 1
Accrington Stanley
1904 Blackpool 24 4
North Wingfield St Lawrence
Hamilton Academical

Morgan, Hugh IL
b Longriggend 20/9/1869 d 1930
Caps: SLge 1/Scotland 2
Longriggend Wanderers
St Mirren
1897 1899 Liverpool 59 15
1900 1902 Blackburn Rovers 77 18
Dundee

Morgan, John (Jock) CH/LH
b Penicuik 18/8/1899 d 1983
Edinburgh Emmet
Third Lanark (trial)
Clyde (trial)
Ayr United
1924 Birmingham 1
Redditch
1925 1929 Doncaster Rovers 150 4
1930 Bristol City 1
1931 1932 Barrow 66
1933 Walsall 19
1934 Southport 10
Brideville
Worcester City
Atherstone Town

From To Apps Goal

Morgan, John W IR
1922 Aberdare Athletic 4 1

Morgan, Lewis (Lew) RB
b Cowdenbeath 30/4/1911 d 1988
Caps: SLge 1
Crossgates Primrose
Lochgelly Celtic
Bowhill Rovers
Dundee
1935 1945 Portsmouth 123
1939 (Portsmouth) (3)
1946 1947 Watford 50
Chelmsford City

Morgan, Llewellyn David (Llew) CH
b Aberdare 7/3/1905 d 1979
1928 Merthyr Town 0
Aberdare & Aberaman
1930 1931 Charlton Athletic 40
1932 Bradford City 1
1933 Aldershot 14
1934 1938 Walsall 192 1

Morgan, Matthew Black Biggar (Mattha) OR
b Glasgow 24/1/1900 d 1985
Renfrew Juniors
St Mirren
1930 Bournemouth & Boscombe Ath 6
Ayr United
Hibernian
Glentoran
Linfield (trial)
Coleraine
Shelbourne

Morgan, Morton Meredith (Monty) OR
b Mountain Ash 1/5/1910 d 1990
Penrhiwceiber
1932 Manchester United 0
1933 Swansea Town 3
1934 1936 Torquay United 121 22
1937 Plymouth Argyle 11 2
1938 Bristol City 2

Morgan, Reginald L OR
Clapton
Tooting Town
1926 Crystal Palace 1
Sutton United

Morgan, Ronald (Ron) CF/IR
b Twynrodyn 6/9/1915 d 1990
1932 Wolverhampton Wanderers 0
1935 Bournemouth & Boscombe Ath 2 1
Northfleet
1937 1938 Doncaster Rovers 6 1
1939 1946 Accrington Stanley 4
1939 (Accrington Stanley) (3) (1)
Worcester City

Morgan, Thomas (Tom) RH
b Bristol q4 1886
Fishponds
1912 Bristol City 2
Caerphilly

Morgan, William (Billy) RH/CH
b Leigh 1875
Horwich
1896 1902 Newton Heath/Manchester Utd 143 6
1902 Bolton Wanderers 3
Watford
1904 1905 Leicester Fosse 66 9
New Brompton
Kidderminster Harriers
Newton Heath Athletic

Morgan, William (Billy) LH
b Burnley 16/12/1896 d 1993
Burnley St Mary
Royal Navy
1921 1923 Burnley 28

Morgan, William (Bill) GK
b Ryton-on-Tyne 30/4/1914 d 1993
Chopwell Institute
Mickley Colliery Welfare
1931 Wolverhampton Wanderers 0
1932 1938 Coventry City 150
1939 (Coventry City) (3)

Morgan, William Albert L (Billy) IL/OL
b Old Hill 3/11/1891
Caps: FLge 1
Cradley Heath St Luke's
1912 1914 Birmingham 27 5
Motherwell
Third Lanark (loan)
1919 1920 Birmingham 33 6
1920 1921 Coventry City 53 14
1922 1924 Crystal Palace 76 14
Cradley Heath St Luke's
Shrewsbury Town

From To Apps Goal

Morgan-Owen, Morgan Maddox CH/RH/CF
b Cardiff 20/2/1877 d 1950
Caps: Wales 13
Oxford University
Corinthians
1900 Nottingham Forest 1
Corinthians
Casuals
1903 1905 Glossop 3

Morley, Ernest James (Ernie) RB/LB
b Sketty 11/9/1901 d 1975
Caps: WLge 2/Wales 4
Sketty
1921 1927 Swansea Town 123
1928 1930 Clapton Orient 71
Aberavon Harlequins

Morley, Fred CF
1905 1906 Gainsborough Trinity 33 8
Newark
Scunthorpe & Lindsey United

Morley, Frederick (Fred) IL/OR/CF
b Burslem 1/3/1890
Chesterton White Star
Reading
1909 1911 Blackpool 81 22
1920 Brentford 16
Philadelphia Field Club
J & P Coats (Rhode Island)
Fall River Marksmen
J & P Coats (Rhode Island)

Morley, Haydn Arthur LB/RB
b Derby 26/11/1860 d 1953
Derby Midland
Derby County
1888 Notts County 2
1888 Derby County 4
The Wednesday
Loughborough

Morley, Herbert (Bert) RB
b Kiveton Park 10/1882 d 1957
Caps: England 1
Kiveton Park
1904 1906 Grimsby Town 93 3
1906 1914 Notts County 258

Morley, John Bell OR/IR
b Carlisle 29/1/1884 d 1957
Workington
1907 Sunderland 5 1
1908 1911 Burnley 96 15
1911 1914 Preston North End 94 15
Dick, Kerr's XI

Morley, Joseph F IR
b Felling 5/11/1916
1938 Gateshead 1

Morley, Samuel Balshaw (Sam) IR
b Liverpool 18/11/1911 d 1986
Black Swan
Wallasey Services Club
1935 New Brighton 2
Prescot Cables

Morley, William Edward (Ted) OR/IL
b Chesterfield 1877 d 1954
Brampton Rising Star
New Whittington Exchange
1899 1900 Chesterfield Town 36 9

Morrall, George Alfred IL/IR
b Birmingham q2 1893 d 1964
Sparkhill Avon
Redditch Town
Nuneaton Town
Blackheath Town
1919 1920 Hull City 37 17
1920 1921 Grimsby Town 65 8
Redditch Town
Brierley Hill Alliance

Morrall, George Richard CH
b Smethwick 4/10/1905 d 1955
Gorse Street Prims
Chance's Glass Works
Littleton Harriers
Allen & Everitt's Sports
1926 West Bromwich Albion (trial) 0
1927 1935 Birmingham 243 5
1936 1938 Swindon Town 97 5

Morren, Thomas (Tom) CH
b Monkwearmouth q2 1871 d 1929
Caps: FLge 2/England 1
Middlesbrough Victoria
Middlesbrough Vulcan
Middlesbrough Ironopolis
Middlesbrough
1895 1902 Sheffield United 160 5

From To Apps Goal

Morris, Arthur IL
b Market Drayton 1882 d 1945
Shrewsbury Town
1906 1907 Birmingham 4 2
Shrewsbury Town
Wellington Town

Morris, Arthur Grenville (Grenville) IL
b Builth Wells 13/4/1877 d 1959
Caps: Wales 21
Builth Town
Aberystwyth
Swindon Town
1898 1912 Nottingham Forest 421 199

Morris, Austin RH
b Thurcroft 10/2/1913 d 1991
Thurcroft Main Colliery Welfare
1937 Mansfield Town 1
Gainsborough Trinity

Morris, Charles Richard (Charlie) LB
b Oswestry 29/8/1880 d 1952
Caps: Wales 27
Chirk
1900 1909 Derby County 276 1
1910 Huddersfield Town 16
Wrexham
Chirk

Morris, David Hyman (Harry) CF
b London 25/11/1900 d 1985
Vicar of Wakefield
1920 Fulham 6 2
1921 1922 Brentford 59 29
1922 1924 Millwall Athletic 74 30
1925 Swansea Town 9 5
1926 1932 Swindon Town 260 215
1933 Clapton Orient 13 8
Cheltenham Town

Morris, David Main Liston CH
b Leith 21/8/1899 d 1971
Caps: SLge 1/Scotland 6
Newtongrange Star
Arniston Rangers
Raith Rovers
1925 1929 Preston North End 146 7
Chester
Dundee United
Leith Athletic

Morris, David J IL
b Walsall 1888
Darlaston
1911 Birmingham 3
Tipton Town

Morris, Eric Leslie RB
b Cardiff
1931 1932 Cardiff City 16

Morris, Frederick (Fred) IL/IR/CF
b Tipton 27/8/1893 d 1962
Caps: FLge 1/England 2
Ball Street Primitives
Tipton Victoria
Redditch Town
1911 1923 West Bromwich Albion 263 112
1924 Coventry City 22 8
Oakengates Town

Morris, George Edward LB
b Birkenhead 22/6/1911 d 1984
1933 Tranmere Rovers 0
1934 Everton 0
1937 1938 New Brighton 14
South Liverpool

Morris, George R LH
b Manchester 1879
Manchester St Augustine's
1897 1899 Lincoln City 66 4
1899 Glossop 14
1900 Barnsley 23 1
Millwall Athletic

Morris, Harold (Harry) LH/RH/IL
b Bolsover 2/9/1902 d 1976
Bolsover Town
Bolsover Colliery
Worksop Town
Bolsover Colliery
1925 1927 Watford 51 4
Mansfield Town
1929 Barnsley 1
Shirebrook
Grantham
Shirebrook Supporters

Morris, Harold CH/RH/LH
b Fenton 25/8/1906
Whitchurch
1927 1933 Crewe Alexandra 118 7

From To Apps Goal

Morris, Harry LH
b Birmingham 11/4/1866 d 1931
Excelsior
1892 Small Heath 1

Morris, Henry (Harry) CH/LH
b Stoke-on-Trent
Prescot
1921 Manchester United 0
1923 Hartlepools United 7 2
1924 Wigan Borough 15
1925 1930 Crewe Alexandra 196 10

Morris, Hugh IR/OL
b Chirk q1 1872 d 1897
Caps: Wales 3
Chirk
1892 1893 Ardwick 28 12
1893 1895 Sheffield United 32 10
1895 Manchester City 16 9
1896 Grimsby Town 23 1
Millwall Athletic

Morris, Hugh OR/IL
b Giffnock 19/11/1900
Rutherglen Glencairn
Clyde
1922 1923 Manchester City 57
1924 Nottingham Forest 22 1
1924 Notts County 0
1925 1928 Southend United 117 14
1929 Newport County 22 5

Morris, J LH
1903 Burton United 1

Morris, James (Jimmy) GK
b London
1913 Bury 0
1914 Clapton Orient 4

Morris, James Henry CH/CF
b St Helens 16/11/1915
St Helens Town
1939 1948 Stockport County 61 3
1939 (Stockport County) (1)

Morris, John (Jack) GK
b Oswestry 1873 d 1914
Caps: Wales 1
Chirk
1893 Northwich Victoria 1
Chirk
Shrewsbury Town
Chirk

Morris, John CH/RH
b Leeds 18/10/1887
1905 1906 Leeds City 10

Morris, John CH
b Newarthill
Newarthill Thistle
1926 Hull City 1
1927 Bradford City 0

Morris, John James (Jack) IL/IR/OR
b Liscard q1 1876 d 1947
Liverpool South End
1898 Blackpool 6 4
1900 1902 Notts County 77 30
1903 Bristol City 29 11
New Brompton
Accrington Stanley
1906 Blackpool 18 4
Accrington Stanley
Darwen

Morris, R CF
1888 Everton 1

Morris, Richard (Dickie) IL
b Newtown 1879
Caps: Wales 11
Druids
Newtown
1901 1904 Liverpool 38 5
1905 Leeds City 25 5
1906 Grimsby Town 24 7
Plymouth Argyle
Reading
Huddersfield Town

Morris, Robert (Bob) OL/CF/IL
b Coppull
Crosland (Chorley)
1919 West Ham United 3
Fleetwood
1920 Barnsley 13 3
1922 Accrington Stanley 17 4
Lancaster Town

From To Apps Goal

Morris, Robert Arthur John (Roy) LH/RH
b Hatton, Middlesex 11/3/1913
1930 Brentford 0
Slough Town
Leyton
Southall
1933 1937 Norwich City 41
Colchester United

Morris, Samuel Herbert (Sam) RH
b Handsworth 2/1886
1906 Aston Villa 0
Queen's Park Rangers
1911 Birmingham 0
Bristol Rovers
1920 Brentford 27
Maidstone United

Morris, Samuel Walker (Sam) RH/LH
b Prescot 16/4/1907 d 1991
Prescot Cables
1928 1931 Sunderland 59
1932 Charlton Athletic 12
1933 Chester 5
Bath City
Weymouth

Morris, Seymour OL
b Ynyshir 15/2/1913 d 1991
Caps: Wales War 1/Wales 5
Lovells Athletic
Aberaman Athletic
1933 1934 Huddersfield Town 6 3
1934 1938 Birmingham 83 29

Morris, Thomas (Tom) CH/RH
b Grantham 9/2/1875 d 1942
Grantham Rovers
1897 1898 Gainsborough Trinity 61 4
1908 1911 Tottenham Hotspur 63 2

Morris, Thomas Henry (Tom) CH
b Caistor 1884 d 1915
Haycroft Rovers
Grimsby Rovers
1906 Grimsby Town 28
Brighton & Hove Albion
1908 1911 Leeds City 106 3
Scunthorpe & Lindsey United
Coventry City

Morris, Trevor IL
b Gorslas 6/9/1920 d 2003
1936 West Bromwich Albion 0
Caerphilly
1938 Ipswich Town 1
1939 Cardiff City 0

Morris, William (Billy) GK
Brunswick (Sheffield)
1908 Bury 1

Morris, William CH/RH
b Danesmoor 2/1888 d 1949
Clay Cross
1907 Derby County 0
Clay Cross
Alfreton Town
Chesterfield Town
1911 1914 Aston Villa 50
Shrewsbury Town
Cradley Heath
Clay Cross Zingari

Morris, William (Billy) IR
b Llanddulas 30/7/1918 d 2002
Caps: Wales War 1/Wales 5
Llandudno Town
1938 1952 Burnley 211 47

Morris, William Walker (Billy) RB/CH
b Handsworth 26/3/1913 d 1995
Caps: England 3
Handsworth Old Boys
1931 West Bromwich Albion (trial) 0
Halesowen Town
1933 1946 Wolverhampton Wanderers 175 2
1939 (Wolverhampton Wanderers) (3)
Dudley Town

Morrison, Evelyn S CF
b Wishaw
Hamilton Academy
Moorpark Amateurs
Motherwell (trial)
Stenhousemuir
Falkirk
1929 1930 Sunderland 15 7
Partick Thistle
Falkirk (trial)

From To Apps Goal

Morrison, Francis (Frank) LB/CH/LH
b Falkirk q1 1870 d 1940
Clyde
1896 Darwen 27 3
Millwall Athletic
1899 Luton Town 13
1899 1901 Barnsley 48

Morrison, John RH
b Jarrow q1 1886 d 1944
Jarrow
1908 Hull City 4
Swindon Town
1911 Sunderland 0
Jarrow

Morrison, John Alfred (Johnny) CF
b Belvedere 26/3/1911 d 1984
Bostall Heath
1929 Luton Town (trial) 0
Callenders Athletic
1931 Tottenham Hotspur 0
Northfleet
1932 1938 Tottenham Hotspur 133 87
1939 (Tottenham Hotspur) (1) (3)

Morrison, John Stanton Fleming LB
b Newcastle 17/4/1892 d 1961
Caps: England Amat
Corinthians
Old Carthusians
Jarrow
Cambridge University
Corinthians
1919 Sunderland 1
Corinthians

Morrison, Robert (Bobby) RH/LH
b Hyde 31/3/1896 d 1974
Hyde United
Stalybridge Celtic
Hyde United
1922 1924 Stockport County 30
1925 1930 New Brighton 168 4
Macclesfield

Morrison, Robert Graham (Bob) GK
b Glasgow 15/1/1905 d 1981
St Roch's
Airdrieonians
1934 Southport 19
Forfar Athletic (trial)
Falkirk (trial)
1935 Gateshead (trial) 0
Dundee United
Albion Rovers
Workington
Forfar Athletic
Glenavon

Morrison, Thomas (Tommy 'Ching') OR/IR
b Belfast 1874 d 1940
Caps: IrLge 2/Ireland 7
Stormont
Glentoran
1893 1894 Burnley 7 1
Glentoran
Celtic
1896 1902 Burnley 171 25
1902 1903 Manchester United 29 7
Colne
1906 Burnley 1
Glentoran

Morrison, Thomas (Tom) IL
b Liverpool
1925 Barrow (trial) 1

Morrison, Thomas Kelly (Tom) RH/RB
b Kilmarnock 21/7/1904
Caps: Scotland 1
Troon Athletic
St Mirren
1927 1934 Liverpool 240 4
1935 Sunderland 21
Gamlingay
Ayr United
Drumcondra

Morrison, William (Billy) CH
b West Benhar 25/6/1879 d 1937
East Lanarkshire
West Calder
St Bernard's
1907 1908 Fulham 31 1
1908 1909 Glossop 68 2
Clyde
Raith Rovers
St Bernard's (loan)
Morton
Falkirk

Morrison, William OR
b Bo'ness
Linlithgow Rose
1924 Chelsea 1

From To Apps Goal

Morrison, William Cockburn RB
b Musselburgh 3/7/1904 d 1977
Musselburgh Bruntonians
St Mirren
Pembroke Dock
Caernarvon Athletic
1928 Stockport County 2
Stockport Borough Police

Morse, Edward RB
b Hanley 1870
1894 1895 Burslem Port Vale 13

Mort, Enoch Francis CH
b Ogmore Vale 5/3/1912 d 1999
Caps: WLge 1
Gilfach Goch
1933 1937 Cardiff City 43
1938 Carlisle United 17

Mort, Thomas (Tommy) LB
b Kearsley 1/12/1897 d 1967
Caps: England 3
Kearsley St Stephen's
Newton Lads
Lancashire Fusiliers
Altrincham
1921 Rochdale 28
1921 1934 Aston Villa 337 2

Mortimer, Francis Ernest (Fred) CF
b Draycott q3 1890 d 1963
Grenadier Guards
Crystal Palace
1913 Leicester Fosse 22 8
Swansea Town
Bowmar's Athletic
Rugby Town
Coalville Swifts
Aylestone St James
Aylestone WMC

Mortimer, Peter OL
b Calton 17/8/1875 d 1951
Elm Park (Glasgow)
Cowlairs
Elm Park (Glasgow)
Glasgow Northern
Leith Athletic
1894 1895 Woolwich Arsenal 49 23
Chatham

Mortimer, Robert (Bob) CF/OR/IL
b Bolton 4/1908 d 1965
Park Street Wesleyans
1925 Bolton Wanderers 0
Connah's Quay & Shotton
Darwen
1926 1927 Barrow 24 10
1928 Bolton Wanderers 0
1931 1932 Northampton Town 62 22
1933 Brentford 0
1934 Bournemouth & Boscombe Ath 18 3
1935 Accrington Stanley 25 19
1935 Portsmouth 0
1936 1937 Accrington Stanley 45 37
1937 Blackburn Rovers 16 4
1938 York City 35 22
Bacup Borough
Horwich RMI

Morton, Alexander J (Alex) IR
b Darvel 1884
Darvel
1904 Bury 4
Clyde

Morton, Benjamin W (Ben) CF
b Sheffield 28/8/1910 d 1962
Stourbridge
1933 Wolverhampton Wanderers 0
Stourbridge
1935 Manchester United 1
1936 1937 Torquay United 49 33
1937 1938 Swindon Town 69 33
1939 (Swindon Town) (2)
Stourbridge

Morton, David IR
b Alva 1878
Berryhill (Stirling)
Millwall Athletic
1897 Sheffield United 2
Camelon
Wishaw
Falkirk
Camelon

From To Apps Goal

Morton, Harry GK
b Chadderton 7/1/1909 d 1974
Middleton Road Primitives
1929 Bury (trial) 0
1929 Bolton Wanderers (trial) 0
Royal Welch Fusiliers
1931 1936 Aston Villa 192
1936 1938 Everton 27
1939 Burnley 0
Ashton United

Morton, James CF
b Leith 22/8/1885 d 1926
Newtongrange Star
Hibernian
1907 Bradford City 0
1907 Stoke 0
1908 Tottenham Hotspur 2
Hibernian
St Bernard's
Bathgate
1913 Barnsley 18 3
1913 1914 Bristol City 12 7

Morton, John (Jackie) OL/IR/OR
b Sheffield 26/7/1914 d 1986
Caps: FLge 1/England 1
Sheffield Albion
Woodhouse Alliance
Gainsborough Trinity
1931 1938 West Ham United 258 54

Morton, Joseph (Joe) CH
b Newcastle
St Peter's Albion
Wallsend
1922 Ashington 9
Wallsend

Morton, JW GK
1893 Walsall Town Swifts 1

Morton, Robert (Bobby) OL
b Widdrington 3/3/1906 d 1990
Widdrington
Newbiggin
1922 1924 Ashington 3
Bedlington United
1927 Barnsley 1 1
1928 1929 Nottingham Forest 34 3
Newark Town
1931 Bradford Park Avenue 6
1932 1934 Port Vale 101 19
Throckley Welfare
Blyth Spartans
Jarrow
Blyth Spartans
North Shields

Morton, William (Bill) LH
b Bury 1877
Caps: IrLge 2
Chorley
1900 Bury 7
Chorley
Distillery
Nelson
Haslingden
Heywood United

Morton, William CF
Bedlington Primitive Methodists
Newbiggin West End
1927 Durham City 0
Craghead United
1928 Nelson 8 3
Craghead United
Bedlington United
Blyth Spartans
1930 Queen's Park Rangers 0
Craghead United
Ashington
Stakeford Albion

Morton, William Henry RH
b Ilkeston 16/12/1896
West Hallam
Ilkeston St John's
Ilkeston United
1920 1921 Derby County 24 1

Morton, William Howard OL/IL
b Newcastle 21/2/1903 d 1981
Walker Welbeck
Wallsend Town
1921 Newcastle United 0
1922 Lincoln City 21 4
1923 Wigan Borough 10 1
Jarrow
Scotswood
1927 Fulham 0
Consett
Washington Colliery
Blyth Spartans

From To Apps Goal

Morton, William Plant M (Billy) OL
b Hayfield 27/12/1902 d 1993
Tollcross
1925 Stockport County 3

Moseley, Horace Charles IR
b Lewisham 19/7/1912 d 1988
Bexleyheath
Dulwich Hamlet
1933 Millwall 0
1934 Bristol City 4
Dartford

Moseley, Robert Arthur IR
b St Pancras q1 1905 d 1967
1925 1926 Fulham 2
Dolcis

Moses, Jack (Jackie) IL
b Tow Law 1916
York Road Juniors
Trimdon Grange Colliery
1934 1936 Hartlepools United 21 3
Scunthorpe & Lindsey United
Blyth Spartans
Railway Athletic
Wingate Welfare

Mosley, Andrew RB
b Sneinton q1 1885 d 1917
Sneinton
1906 1909 Notts County 11

Mosley, Herbert Thomas OL
b Shuttlewood q1 1900 d 1962
Shuttlewood
Bolsover Colliery
1921 Chesterfield 3
1922 Luton Town 3
Sutton Town
Worksop Town

Moss, Albert E LH
b Walkden
1920 Bolton Wanderers 1

Moss, Arthur James RH/LH/CH
b Crewe 17/11/1887 d 1964
Crewe Central
Willaston White Star
Crewe Alexandra
Whitchurch
1909 1911 Aston Villa 5
1912 1914 Bristol City 85
Runcorn
1921 1924 Crewe Alexandra 134 1

Moss, Frank LH/RH
b Aston 17/4/1895 d 1965
Caps: FLge 2/England 5
Aston Manor
Walsall
1914 1928 Aston Villa 255 9
1928 Cardiff City 9
Bromsgrove Rovers
Worcester City

Moss, Frank GK
b Leyland 5/11/1909 d 1970
Caps: FLge 2/England 4
Farington Villa
Lostock Hall
Leyland Motors
Lostock Hall
1927 1928 Preston North End 24
1929 1931 Oldham Athletic 29
1931 1935 Arsenal 143 1

Moss, Frank CH/LH/RH
b Aston 16/9/1917 d 1997
Worcester Nondescripts
Worcester City
1935 Wolverhampton Wanderers 0
1936 1937 Sheffield Wednesday 22
1938 1954 Aston Villa 297 3

Moss, Ralph CF
Wellington Town
1901 Chesterfield Town 1

Mosscrop, Edwin (Eddie) OL/OR
b Southport 16/6/1892 d 1980
Caps: FLge 2/England 2
Blowick Wesleyans
Shepherds Bush
Middlesex
Southport YMCA
Southport Central
1912 1922 Burnley 176 19

Mould, William (Billy) RB/CH
b Great Chell 6/10/1919 d 1999
Summerbank
1937 1951 Stoke City 177
1939 (Stoke City) (2)
1952 1953 Crewe Alexandra 66 1

From To Apps Goal

Moule, Alfred Samuel (Alf) IR/IL
b Canning Town 31/7/1894 d 1973
West Ham Corinthians
Catford Southend
Leytonstone
1920 1926 Millwall Athletic 205 66
1927 Norwich City 32 11
1928 Watford 11 4
Margate

Moulson, Cornelius (Con) CH/LB
b Clogheen 3/9/1906 d 1989
Caps: Eire 5
Cleethorpes Town
1929 Grimsby Town 0
1931 Bristol City 11 1
1932 1936 Lincoln City 88
1936 1938 Notts County 97
1939 (Notts County) (2)

Mouncher, Frederick William (Fred) OL/LH
b Southampton 19/10/1883
Fitzhugh Rovers
Southampton Cambridge
Southampton
1907 1910 Fulham 43 10

Mount, Charles (Charlie) OL
b Cambuslang 1873
Cambuslang
1896 Blackpool 9 5
Cambuslang

Mount, Edward LH
b Cambuslang 18/1/1875
Cambuslang Hibernian
1897 Grimsby Town 4

Mountain, George (Bodge) RB/RH
b Grimsby q3 1874 d 1936
Grimsby White Star
Waltham Hornets
1895 Grimsby Town 1
Grimsby All Saints
Swindon Town (trial)
1897 1902 Grimsby Town 151 4
1903 Leicester Fosse 26
Grimsby Rangers

Mounteney, Arthur IL/IR/OL
b Belgrave 11/2/1883 d 1933
Belgrave Nonconformists
Leicester Imperial
1903 1904 Leicester Fosse 30 11
1905 1908 Birmingham 91 29
1909 1910 Preston North End 52 11
1911 1912 Grimsby Town 45 17
Portsmouth
Balmoral United
Hinckley United

Mountford, George OR
1892 Burslem Port Vale 3 2

Mountford, Harry Washington OL/IL/CF
b Hanley q2 1884
Hanley Swifts
1903 1906 Burslem Port Vale 96 28
1907 1910 Everton 25 5
1910 1913 Burnley 28 10
Third Lanark

Mountford, James OR
1892 Burslem Port Vale 1 1

Mountford, Reginald Charles (Reg) LB/RB
b Darlington 16/7/1908 d 1994
Caps: England War 1
1928 Darlington 12 3
1929 1938 Huddersfield Town 236 7
1939 (Huddersfield Town) (3)

Mountney, Charles Thomas CH
b Dinnington q2 1906
Gainsborough Trinity
1927 Rotherham United 2
Frickley Colliery
Denaby United
Stalybridge Celtic

Mowatt, Archibald (Archie) OR
b South Shields 1870
Wallsend Park Villa
Newcastle East End
Newcastle United
Hebburn Argyle
1898 Newcastle United 1
1899 Lincoln City 8 1
1900 Newcastle United 0

From To Apps Goal

Mowatt, Magnus James OR
b Fraserburgh 13/3/1917
St Francis
Morton Juniors
Clyde
Dumbarton
1937 Brentford 0
1938 Lincoln City 6 1
Morton
Clyde

Moyes, David (Davie) LB
b Donibristle 6/4/1899 d 1984
Cardwell
Kingseat Juniors
Hearts o' Beath
1919 Leicester City (trial) 0
Raith Rovers
1926 Leicester City 3
Cowdenbeath
East Fife
Cowdenbeath
Rosyth Recreation

Moyes, John IR
b Fife
Hearts o' Beath
Dundee
Scots Guards
1919 West Ham United 2 1
Clackmannan

Moyle, Walter RB/RH
b New Tredegar 10/1902
Barry
1925 Swansea Town 0
1926 Cardiff City 0
1927 Manchester United 0
1928 Crystal Palace 5 1
1929 Merthyr Town 14
1930 Swansea Town 0
Mexborough Athletic

Mudie, Leonard (Len) IL/CF
b Forfar 1872
1888 Burnley 1
1889 Stoke 3 1
Dundee Wanderers

Muir, J OL
1899 Glossop 3 2

Muir, James GK
b Longcroft
Clackmannan
1923 Plymouth Argyle 0
Lochgelly United
Dunfermline Athletic
Bo'ness
1927 Luton Town 10

Muir, John OL
Leith Athletic
1902 1903 Middlesbrough 13

Muir, John Baker LH
b Hamilton 18/11/1903 d 1959
Ayr United
Queen of the South
Broxburn United
1925 Stockport County 0
Dumbarton
Armadale
Falkirk
1930 Luton Town 4
1930 1931 Bristol Rovers 21 3
Bo'ness
Arbroath
East Stirlingshire

Muir, Malcolm McKenzie RB
b Campbeltown 20/1/1903
Kirkintilloch Rob Roy
Aberdeen
Peterhead
1930 Northampton Town 3
Peterhead

Muir, Robert GK
b St Ninians, Stirlingshire
Rutherglen Glencairn
Celtic (trial)
Hamilton Academical (trial)
1934 Portsmouth 1
Third Lanark
Rochdale 0

From To Apps Goal

Muir, Robert Bryce (Bobby) OR
b Kilmarnock 23/9/1876 d 1953
Kilmarnock Deanpark
Clyde
Kilmarnock
Bristol Rovers
Celtic
1904 Notts County 19
Norwich City
Toronto Eatonia

Muir, Samuel RB
1896 Loughborough 4

Muir, William (Willie) GK
b Ayr 22/9/1877 d 1941
Caps: SLge 2/Scotland 1
Glenbuck Athletic
Third Lanark
Kilmarnock
1897 1901 Everton 127
Dundee
1907 Bradford City 28
Heart of Midlothian
Dundee Hibernian
Dumbarton

Muir, William RH
Hamilton Academical
1902 Middlesbrough 4
1903 Bradford City 0

Mulcahy, Patrick Thomas IL/RH
b Tantobie q3 1904
White-le-Head Rangers
1924 Coventry City 0
1925 West Bromwich Albion 0
Annfield Plain
1927 1928 Crystal Palace 23 5
Eden Colliery

Muldoon, Thomas Patrick (Tommy) RH/LH
b Athlone 14/2/1901
Caps: Eire 1
Athlone Town
1924 1926 Aston Villa 33
1927 Tottenham Hotspur 0
1929 1930 Walsall 52

Mulford, Sidney Richard IR/IL
b Brentford 23/11/1896 d 1973
Kew Association
1922 1923 Brentford 21 3
Northfleet
Dartford
Ealing Celtic

Mulhall, John IR
b Dykehead 3/10/1902
Cleland
1923 Burnley 0
Dykehead
1924 Brighton & Hove Albion 2
Falkirk
Bethleham Steel
Dykehead

Mulholland, Thomas IR
b Wolverhampton 1880 d 1950
Stafford Rangers
Brierley Hill Colliery
1912 Wolverhampton Wanderers 6 1
Brewood
Coven Olympic

Mulholland, Thomas S (Tommy 'Steve') IR
b Carrickfergus 1888
Caps: Ireland 2
Belfast Celtic
Distillery
1909 1911 Leeds City 78 22
Distillery
Scunthorpe & Lindsey United
West Stanley
Halifax Town
Belfast Celtic
1921 Hartlepools United 5 1

Mullaney, Robert Vernon (Bob) IL
b Clydebank 24/5/1917
Clepington Juniors
1936 Leicester City 0
1937 Barrow 5 2
Distillery
Dundee United (trial)

Mullen, James (Jimmy) OL
b Newcastle 6/1/1923 d 1987
Caps: England Sch/England B/FLge 1/
England War 3/England 12
1938 1958 Wolverhampton Wanderers 445 98
1939 (Wolverhampton Wanderers) (3)

From To Apps Goal

Mullen, Matthew CF
b Scotland
St Mirren
1892 Grimsby Town 16 6
St Mirren
Dunblane

Mulligan, James Alphonsus (Jimmy) LB
b Bessbrook 27/4/1895 d 1966
Caps: Ireland 1
St Patrick's College
Bessbrook Strollers
St David's Swifts
Belfast Celtic
1921 1922 Manchester City 3
1923 1925 Southport 65
Manchester North End
Manchester Central

Mullineux, A RB
1893 Northwich Victoria 1

Mullineux, Ernest (Ernie) RB/LB
b Northwood, Staffordshire q1 1879 d 1960
Burslem Park
1900 1904 Burslem Port Vale 113 2
1904 1906 Bury 22
1906 1907 Stoke 29
Wellington Town

Mullineux, James EB RH
b Blackburn 1872
Lincoln City
1892 1894 Burnley 26
1894 Burton Wanderers 1

Mulloy, Thomas Francis OR
Barnoldswick Town
1923 Bradford City 2
Morecambe

Mulraney, Ambrose Aloysius (Jock) OR
b Wishaw 18/5/1916 d 2001
Wishaw White Rose
Carluke Rovers
Heart of Midlothian (trial)
Celtic
Hamilton Academical (trial)
Sligo Rovers (trial)
1935 Blackpool (trial) 0
1936 Clapton Orient (trial) 0
Dartford
1938 Ipswich Town 28 8
1939 (Ipswich Town) (3) (1)
1945 1946 Birmingham City 27 8
Shrewsbury Town
Kidderminster Harriers
1948 Aston Villa 12 2
Cradley Heath
Brierley Hill Alliance

Mulrenan, Bernard William (Barney) OR
b Bolsover 4/7/1912 d 1995
Caps: England Amat
Yorkshire Amateurs
Sheffield University
1934 Sheffield Wednesday 0
1935 Chesterfield 1
1936 Huddersfield Town 0
1937 Brighton & Hove Albion 0
Corinthians
Casuals
Yorkshire Amateurs

Mumford, Albert Corbett RH/GK/LB
b Wrockwardine Wood 7/6/1865 d 1926
Wrockwardine Wood
Berkley Star (Sheffield)
Bethel United (Sheffield)
Bethel Reds (Sheffield)
1892 1893 Sheffield Wednesday 24 1
1896 1899 Loughborough 87 1

Mumford, William Richard RB
b Stirchley 3/3/1894 d 1971
Bournville Athletic
1919 Birmingham 3
1920 Brighton & Hove Albion 0
Redditch Town
Bournville Athletic

Mummery, Albert Edward Pilkerton (Eddie LH/IL/OL
b Norwich 18/8/1897 d 1937
Coalville Swifts
1920 1925 Watford 119 23
1926 Clapton Orient 0
Yarmouth Town

From To Apps Goal

Muncie, William Paul (Bill) OR/OL/IL
b Carluke 28/8/1911 d 1992
Carluke Rovers
Shettleston Juniors
1934 1937 Leicester City 42 11
1938 Southend United 14 2
Hinckley United
1946 Crewe Alexandra 2
Sphinx (Coventry)

Munday, Herbert IL/LH
b Eckington 23/4/1876 d 1961
Caps: FLge 1
Eckington White Star
Eckington Works
1899 1908 Chesterfield Town 314 107
Eckington Red Rose

Munden, Stephen Harold (Steve) CF
b West Ham 30/5/1901 d 1981
1925 Queen's Park Rangers 1

Mundy, Frederick (Fred) IR/OL
b Stubley 7/10/1903 d 1981
1922 West Bromwich Albion 0
Dronfield Woodhouse
Norton Woodseats
1928 1929 Southport 15 5
Scarborough
1930 Chesterfield 0
Denaby United
Frickley Colliery
South Kirkby Colliery
Dronfield

Munn, Stuart RH/LH
b Greenock 22/12/1872 d 1959
Maryhill
Third Lanark
1894 Burnley 2
1895 1897 Grimsby Town 63
1897 1899 Manchester City 20
Watford
Hitchin Town

Munnings, Charles Edward (Eddie) OR
b Boston 6/7/1906 d 1995
Louth Town
Boston Town
1927 Grimsby Town 0
1930 Swindon Town 14 3
1931 Hull City 31 7
1932 Swindon Town 31 10
1933 Mansfield Town 29 7
Gresley Rovers
Boston United

Munro, Alexander Dewar (Alex) OR/IR
b Carriden 6/4/1912 d 1986
Caps: Scotland 3
Bo'ness United
Champfleurie
Newtongrange Star
Heart of Midlothian
1936 1948 Blackpool 142 17

Munro, Daniel (Dan) OR/OL
b Peterhead 2/3/1887
Forres Mechanics
Celtic
1910 1913 Bradford Park Avenue 85 3
Port Vale
Clydebank

Munro, David OL
b 1880
Petershill
Third Lanark
1907 Notts County 12 1
Glentoran

Munro, George E CF
b Elgin 19/7/1898 d 1980
Elgin City
1921 Barrow 27 6
Elgin City
(Canada)

Munro, Harry LH
b Scotland
Sheffield United
1896 1898 Gainsborough Trinity 89 2
South Shields

Munro, James (Jimmy) IL/OR/OL
b Dundee 23/1/1870 d 1899
Dundee Strathmore
1890 1892 Bolton Wanderers 50 20
1893 1894 Burton Swifts 54 15
Swindon Town

From To Apps Goal

Munro, James Auchterlonie (Jim) CF
b Glasgow 20/5/1905 d 1978
Ardrossan Winton Rovers
St Johnstone
Raith Rovers (loan)
1928 1929 Cardiff City 14 3
1929 Millwall 5 2
St Johnstone
Cork FC
Reds United

Munro, John Scott LB
b Burnside 13/8/1914
Burnside Rovers
Dundee North End
Dundee Violet
Dundee
1933 Birmingham (trial)
Heart of Midlothian
Hibernian (loan)
1936 1938 Nottingham Forest 93
1939 (Nottingham Forest) (3)

Murden, Egbert IL
b Nottingham 17/5/1906 d 1974
Wath Athletic
1929 1930 Rotherham United 43 25
Wombwell

Murfin, Clarence (Clarrie) OL/OR
b Barnsley 2/4/1909 d 1954
Barnsley West Ward
1930 1931 Barnsley 22 1
Scunthorpe & Lindsey United
1933 Rochdale 26 7
Gainsborough Trinity
1934 1935 Bradford Park Avenue 5 1
1937 Brighton & Hove Albion 1

Murphy, Bernard OL
Duntocher Hibs
1905 Burnley 6 2

Murphy, David Anthony LH
b South Bank 19/7/1917 d 1944
South Bank St Peter's
1937 1938 Middlesbrough 12
1939 (Middlesbrough) (1)
1939 Blackburn Rovers 0

Murphy, Edward (Eddie) OL/IL
b Tunstall 4/1881 d 1916
1902 1904 Glossop 86 18
1905 Bury 27 1
1906 Gainsborough Trinity 0
Swindon Town
Bristol Rovers

Murphy, George (Spud) IL/CF/RB
b Cwmfelinfach 22/7/1915 d 1983
Caps: Wales War 2
Pontllanfraith
Cwmfelinfach Colts
1934 1947 Bradford City 180 43
1939 (Bradford City) (3)
1947 Hull City 15 9
Scunthorpe & Lindsey United
Scarborough
Goole Town

Murphy, James (Jim) LH
b Hamilton 25/2/1902
Glasgow Perthshire
East Kilbride Thistle
Parkhead
Celtic
Ayr United (loan)
Clydebank (loan)
Ayr United
Mid-Rhondda United (loan)
1926 Charlton Athletic 17
1927 Merthyr Town (trial) 0
Morton

Murphy, James IL
b Edinburgh 1908
Leith Athletic
1938 Carlisle United 28 5

Murphy, James Joseph (Jimmy) OL
b Hulme 9/9/1907 d 1974
1929 Manchester City 0
Buxton
Droylsden
1931 Wigan Borough (trial) 2
Stalybridge Celtic
1935 Southport 10
Stalybridge Celtic
1936 Halifax Town 13 2
Northwich Victoria
Hyde United

From To Apps Goal

Murphy, James Patrick (Jimmy) RH
b Ton Pentre 8/8/1910 d 1989
Caps: Wales Sch/Wales 15
Treorchy Thursday
Treorchy Juniors
Mid-Rhondda United
1929 1938 West Bromwich Albion 204
1938 Swindon Town 4
Morris Commercial

Murphy, Jeremiah (Jerry) IL/IR
b Dowlais 16/3/1907 d 1992
1925 1926 Merthyr Town 18 4
1927 Cardiff City 1
1929 1930 Fulham 13 2
1931 Crystal Palace 8 2
Merthyr Town
Troedyrhiw
Dolphin
Barry

Murphy, John IL/IR/RH
b Nottingham q3 1872 d 1924
Hucknall St John's
1894 Leicester Fosse 0
Hucknall St John's
1896 1897 Notts County 37 24
Bristol City
South Shields
1901 1902 Doncaster Rovers 62 8

Murphy, John OR
1903 Stoke 0
1903 Bradford City 1

Murphy, John IR
b Ireland 1886
Caps: IrLge 2/Ireland 3
Shelbourne
1909 Bradford City 6
Shelbourne
Luton Town
Shamrock Rovers

Murphy, John IR
b Airdrie 4/1894 d 1921
Airdrie Shamrock
Glasgow Ashfield
Croy Celtic
Hamilton Academical
Airdrieonians
Hamilton Academical
1920 Bury 21 5
1921 Rotherham County 2

Murphy, John CF
b Blantyre 29/8/1912
Auchinleck Talbot
1934 Oldham Athletic 7 3
Workington
Ards

Murphy, John Edward CH
b Greenhead 3/11/1900 d 1973
Walker Celtic
1921 South Shields 0
Walker Celtic
1923 1925 Norwich City 35
1926 Southend United 3
Scunthorpe & Lindsey United
Newark Town
Loughborough Corinthians
Bath City
Frost's Athletic

Murphy, Joseph (Joe 'Judge') RH
b Stockton q1 1873
Hibernian
1897 1898 Stoke 49 2
1899 Woolwich Arsenal 27
Raith Rovers

Murphy, Joseph IL
b Ireland
1899 Middlesbrough 7 6

Murphy, Leslie A GK
b Dunnamanagh
Caps: IrLge 3
Belfast Celtic
1911 Leeds City 18
Glentoran
Linfield
1921 Wrexham 1
1923 Bristol Rovers 0
1924 Reading 0

From To Apps Goal

Murphy, Lionel (Spud) OL
b Hovingham 15/9/1895 d 1968
Melton Mowbray
Green Howards
1921 1927 Derby County 221 46
1927 1928 Bolton Wanderers 33 7
Mansfield Town
1931 1934 Norwich City 128 24
1934 Luton Town 0
British Celanese

Murphy, Michael IL
b South Bank q1 1875
South Bank
1899 Middlesbrough 1 1

Murphy, Neil OL
Caps: Ireland 3
1901 Sheffield United 0
Darlington St Augustine's
Queen's Park Rangers
Luton Town
1906 Aston Villa 0
1907 Gainsborough Trinity 19 3

Murphy, Robert P OR
b West Moor
Usworth Colliery
1928 South Shields 1

Murphy, Vincent J OL
b Limerick
Jarrow
1927 Grimsby Town 0
1928 Bournemouth & Boscombe Ath 6
1928 1930 Walsall 30 4
1931 Notts County 0
Wigan Athletic
1933 Gateshead 2
Ayr United
Crook Town

Murphy, William (Billy 'Spud') OL
b St Helens 23/5/1894 d 1975
Peasley Cross Juniors
Alexandra Victoria
1919 1925 Manchester City 209 30
1926 1928 Southampton 74 9
1929 Oldham Athletic 2 1
1930 Tranmere Rovers 3
Ellesmere Port Town
UBG

Murray, Allan Ferguson CH/RB/RH
b Heywood 16/3/1907 d 1995
Heywood St James'
1927 1929 Rochdale 12 1
Great Harwood
Darwen
1933 Fulham 1
1935 Bristol Rovers 13
1937 Crystal Palace 0
Bath City

Murray, David Bruce LB/RB
b Cathcart 4/12/1882 d 1915
Rangers
1903 Everton 2
1904 1905 Liverpool 15
1905 Hull City 0
1905 1908 Leeds City 83 7
Mexborough Town
Burslem Port Vale
Mexborough Town
Frickley Colliery

Murray, David William James CH/IL/IR
b Wynberg, South Africa 8/1902 d 1992
Clyde (Cape Town)
Wynberg
1925 1926 Everton 3 1
1926 1927 Bristol City 16
1928 1929 Bristol Rovers 39 12
1930 Swindon Town 1
1931 Rochdale 22 3
Bangor City

Murray, Frank IL
b Dundee 1894
Dunfermline Athletic
Dundee
1919 West Ham United 2
Dundee Hibernian

Murray, George William IL/OR
b Denny
Dunipace
1922 Reading 3
1923 1924 Exeter City 20 1
Stenhousemuir

Murray, J CF
Wellingborough
1898 Barnsley 4

From To Apps Goal

Murray, James Arthur (Jimmy) IR/OR
b Dalmellington 9/6/1880 d 1933
St Augustine's
Benwhat Heatherbell
Ayr
1900 1901 Aston Villa 2
1901 Small Heath 1 1
Watford
Kettering
Wellingborough
King's Heath Albion

Murray, James Marshall CF
b Kilmacrenan 14/3/1884
Caps: Ireland 3
Shettleston
Distillery
Motherwell
1909 1910 Sheffield Wednesday 13 4
Derry Celtic
Motherwell

Murray, JJ (Joey) GK/IR
Rangers
1891 1892 Everton 8
Swindon Town

Murray, John Black Ritchie CH
b Auchterderran 9/11/1915
Bowhill Juniors
Hamilton Academical
East Stirlingshire
1938 Plymouth Argyle 4
1939 Rotherham United 0

Murray, John James (Jimmy) LH/RH
b Saltcoats 10/8/1908
Saltcoats Victoria
Rangers
1932 1935 Newcastle United 92 10
Albion Rovers

Murray, John Winning LB/RB/LH
b Strathblane 24/4/1865 d 1922
Caps: Scotland 1
Cowdenbeath
Wanderers
Vale of Leven
1890 1891 Sunderland 41
1892 1895 Blackburn Rovers 109

Murray, Joseph OR
b Aberdeen
Dundee
1894 Grimsby Town 2

Murray, Joseph LH/IL/OL
b Hull 28/8/1908 d 1988
Dairycoates
1925 1930 Hull City 17 1
1931 Lincoln City 1

Murray, Joseph (Joe) GK
b Houghton-le-Spring 1916
1932 Birmingham 0
Shiney Row Swifts
1934 1935 Hartlepools United 7
Shotton Colliery Welfare

Murray, Joseph OL
b Uddingston 1914 d 1990
Overton Athletic
Hamilton Academical
1936 Brentford 1
Partick Thistle
Thorniewood United

Murray, Joseph Bell Gilk CH/RB
b Port Glasgow 10/5/1914 d 1991
Petershill
1934 1935 Millwall 6

Murray, Michael (Mick) OR
b North Leith 23/7/1901
Lochgelly United
East Fife
St Bernard's
Rhyl
Caernarvon Town
1930 Wigan Borough 27 2
1931 1932 Crewe Alexandra 54 5

From To Apps Goal

Murray, Patrick (Paddy) OR/IR
b Currie 13/3/1874 d 1925
Caps: SLge 1
Quarter Huttonbank
Royal Albert
Hibernian
1896 Darwen 5 1
East Stirlingshire
1898 1899 Preston North End 51 9
East Stirlingshire
Wishaw Thistle
Royal Albert
1900 1901 Nottingham Forest 27 2
Celtic
Portsmouth
East Stirlingshire
Royal Albert

Murray, R CF
1894 Nottingham Forest 2

Murray, R CH
1899 Nottingham Forest 1

Murray, Robert CF
b Grangemouth
Celtic
1937 Blackpool 2

Murray, Robert David (Bob) IR
b Newhaven, Midlothian 27/3/1915
Niddrie Strollers
Bo'ness Cadora
Newtongrange Star
Heart of Midlothian
Dunfermline Athletic (loan)
1937 Manchester United 4
Bath City
Colchester United

Murray, Robert William (Bobby) GK
b Alexandria
Crosshills
Darwen
1909 1910 Blackburn Rovers 10
Nelson
Darwen

Murray, T CF
Dundee Harp
1889 Burnley 7 1

Murray, Thomas IL/OL/IR
b Middlesbrough 7/4/1889 d 1976
1905 1906 Middlesbrough 12 2
Aberdeen
Rangers
Aberdeen
Heart of Midlothian
1913 Bradford City 6 1
1913 Hull City 2

Murray, Thomas CH
b Dundee
Dundee Hibernian
1920 Millwall Athletic 1

Murray, William IL/OL
b South Church q1 1898
Caps: England Amat
Eldon Lane
Bishop Auckland
1920 Derby County 31 3
1921 1922 Middlesbrough 15 1
Heart of Midlothian
Dunfermline Athletic

Murray, William (Bill) RB
b Aberdeen 10/3/1901 d 1961
Hall, Russell & Co
Aberdeen
Cowdenbeath
1927 1935 Sunderland 304
St Mirren

Murray, William IL
b Edmondsley
1937 Sheffield Wednesday 0
1938 Rotherham United 17 1

Murray, William Brunton (Willie) OL
b Forres 15/12/1881 d 1929
Forres Mechanics
Inverness
1901 1902 Sunderland 8 3
Northampton Town
Tottenham Hotspur
1906 Leeds City 8

From To Apps Goal

Murray, William Thomas (Bill) LH/RH
b Alexandria 9/11/1904 d 1940
Bonhill Celtic
Vale of Clyde
Clydebank
1925 Preston North End (trial) 0
1926 New Brighton 7
Clydebank
1927 1929 Liverpool 4 1
1929 1933 Barrow 137 9
1933 1934 Bristol Rovers 40
Folkestone
Racing Club de Roubaix

Murrell, Aubrey John (George) RH
b Grimsby q2 1870 d 1951
1892 1894 Grimsby Town 35 1
Grimsby All Saints
Newark
Wellingborough
Grimsby Tradesmen

Murrell, Harry Robert (Joe) LB
b Hounslow 19/11/1879 d 1952
Plumstead Albion
Middlesex Regiment
1899 Woolwich Arsenal 6
Clapton Orient

Musgrave, Archibald IR
b Carlisle q4 1883 d 1964
Workington
1909 1910 Hull City 7
1911 Grimsby Town (trial) 0
Southport Central
Carlisle United

Musgrave, Joseph (Joe) LH/IL
b Sedgefield 29/2/1908 d 1981
Willington
Spennymoor United
1930 1935 West Ham United 36 1
1936 1937 Swindon Town 23 3
1938 Hartlepools United 20 3
Spennymoor United

Musgrove, Charles CF
1905 Blackpool 3

Musgrove, James William IL/OL
b High Spen 18/2/1896 d 1969
Scotswood
1920 1921 Millwall Athletic 4

Musgrove, Robert (Bob) RH/RB/LH
b Silksworth 16/8/1893 d 1934
Caps: English Sch
Silksworth Colliery
1912 1914 Barnsley 12 2
Durham City
1920 Leeds United 36 2
1921 1923 Durham City 57 2

Mustard, John (Jack) OR/IR
b Boldon q1 1905 d 1958
Jarrow
Craghead United
Boldon Colliery Welfare
Crawcrook Albion
1926 1927 Queen's Park Rangers 37 4
1929 South Shields 31 4
1930 1931 Wrexham 70 17
1932 Preston North End 15 5
1932 1933 Burnley 15 4
1933 Southend United 20 3
1934 Crewe Alexandra 38 17
1935 Wrexham 16 1
1936 1937 New Brighton 78 11

Mutch, Adam IR/IL
b Aberdeen 7/3/1901 d 1930
Aberdeen
1924 Accrington Stanley 40 7
1925 Lincoln City 8 2
Forfar Athletic
Arbroath
1925 Walsall 4
Montrose
Forfar Athletic
Aberdeen Banks
Banks o' Dee
Marsh Lane Electrical

Mutch, Alexander (Alex) GK
b Inveraray 9/12/1884 d 1967
Inverurie Loco
Aberdeen
1910 1921 Huddersfield Town 229
1922 1924 Newcastle United 36

From To | Apps Goal

Mutch, George IR
b Ferryhill, Aberdeenshire 21/9/1912 d 2001
Caps: Scotland Sch/Scotland 1
Avondale
Hawthorn
Banks o' Dee
Arbroath
1934 1937 Manchester United 112 46
1937 1946 Preston North End 80 24
1939 (Preston North End) (3)
1946 Bury 21 8
1947 Southport 14 2
Banks o' Dee

Mutch, William James (Bill) OL
b Aberdeen 14/10/1914 d 1995
1934 Manchester United 0
1935 Accrington Stanley 19 2

Muttitt, Ernest (Ernie) IL/OL/LH
b Middlesbrough 24/7/1908 d 1996
South Bank
1929 1931 Middlesbrough 20 3
1932 1938 Brentford 92 25
Dartford
Dover

Myers, Ernest Colin (Colin) IL/IR
b Chapeltown 1894 d 1984
Northfleet
Crystal Palace
Hickleton Main Colliery
1919 Bradford City 1 1
1920 Southend United 22 2
1921 Aberdare Athletic 32 14
1922 1924 Northampton Town 72 29
1924 Queen's Park Rangers 17 3
1925 Exeter City 19 3
Grantham
1926 Hartlepools United 22 8
Gainsborough Trinity
Grantham
King's Lynn

Myers, James Henry (Jim) OL
b Barnsley 5/3/1920 d 1998
1937 Barnsley 0
1938 Wolverhampton Wanderers 3
1939 Cardiff City (3)

Myers, Joseph CF
b Sheffield
Meersbrook Congregationals
Heeley Friends
1925 Barnsley 3 2

Myerscough, Joseph (Joe) IR/IL
b Galgate 8/8/1893 d 1975
Lancaster Town
1920 1922 Manchester United 33 8
1923 1926 Bradford Park Avenue 120 47
Lancaster Town
Rossendale United
Morecambe
Fleetwood

Nairn, John OR/IL
b Johnstone 23/4/1903
Raith Rovers
Beith Rovers
1927 1928 Barrow 17 5
Ulverston Town
Morecambe

Nairn, William James (Billy) RH/CH
b Cowdenbeath 23/8/1898 d 1970
Caps: WLge 2
Cowdenbeath
Dundee
Ebbw Vale
1922 1930 Newport County 224 13

Naisby, Thomas Henry (Tom) GK
b Sunderland 12/3/1878 d 1927
Sunderland East End
1898 Sunderland 2
Sunderland West End
1902 Sunderland 0
Reading
1905 1906 Sunderland 35
1907 1909 Leeds City 63
South Shields
Luton Town
Darlington

From To | Apps Goal

Napier, Charles Edward (Charlie) IL/IR
b Bainsford 8/10/1910 d 1973
Caps: SLge 2/Scotland War 1/Scotland 5
Grangemouth Sacred Heart
Cowie Thistle Juveniles
Alva Albion Rovers
Maryhill Hibernian (loan)
Celtic
1935 1937 Derby County 80 24
1937 1938 Sheffield Wednesday 48 9
1939 (Sheffield Wednesday) (3) (2)
Falkirk
Stenhousemuir

Napier, Daniel RH
b Tynemouth q2 1884 d 1942
Wallsend Park Villa
1907 1908 Sheffield Wednesday 11 2
Northampton Town

Napier, Samuel (Sam) CF
Caps: IrLge 7
Glentoran
1905 Bolton Wanderers 4
1906 Glossop 27 14
Linfield
Glentoran

Napier, Walter GK
1895 Burnley 1

Narrowmore, William (Bill) CF
b Motherwell 4/4/1906
Queen's Park
Petershill
1927 Reading 0
1928 Walsall 3
Arbroath

Nash, Edward Montague (Teddy) GK
b Swindon 12/4/1902 d 1985
Gorse Hill Boys
North End Albion
1920 1929 Swindon Town 232
1930 1931 Brentford 56
1932 Crystal Palace 1

Nash, Frank Cooper (Paddy) GK
b South Bank 30/6/1918 d 1989
South Bank East End
1937 1947 Middlesbrough 19
1947 1950 Southend United 57
Annfield Plain

Nash, Harold Edward (Harry) LH/IL
b Fishponds 10/4/1892 d 1970
Caps: WLge 1
Brislington United
Mardy
Aberdare Town
Abertillery
Pontypridd
1914 1919 Aston Villa 12 5
1920 Coventry City 15 3
1920 1922 Cardiff City 30 6
1923 1924 Merthyr Town 62 4
Aberbargoed
Ystrad Mynach

Nash, Herbert (Bert) OR
b Sheffield 26/8/1893 d 1985
1919 Fulham 3
Gillingham
1920 Sheffield United 0
Northfleet
Rotherham Town
Prospect View

Nash, John Henry IL
b Burslem 12/1867 d 1939
1892 Burslem Port Vale 2

Nash, Joseph Henry LH/RH
b Uxbridge q2 1869
Uxbridge
1890 1892 Burnley 5
Nelson
1894 Manchester City 17 1

Nash, Leonard Thomas John CF/IR
b Sheerness 6/1/1911 d 1966
Sheppey United
1931 1932 Charlton Athletic 3 1
1933 Portsmouth 0

From To | Apps Goal

Naughton, William A (Billy 'Chippy') OR
b Gamkirk 16/7/1868
Carfin Shamrock
Hibernian (loan)
Uddingston (loan)
Celtic
Carfin Shamrock (loan)
Glasgow Hibernian
Wishaw Thistle
1891 1894 Stoke 85 22
Southampton
Carfin Rovers

Naylor, Bernard OL
b Sheffield q2 1897 d 1950
Darnall Old Boys
1920 Sheffield United 3
Doncaster Rovers

Naylor, Harry IR
Rotherwood Rovers
1898 Barnsley 1

Naylor, James (Jimmy) LH/RH
b High Crompton 2/3/1901 d 1983
Shawside
1922 1928 Oldham Athletic 238 5
1928 1929 Huddersfield Town 38 2
1930 1931 Newcastle United 30
1932 Manchester City 1
1932 Oldham Athletic (loan) 8
Macclesfield
Nelson
Wigan Athletic

Naylor, Thomas Holcroft (Tommy) RB/LB
b Prescot 24/2/1903 d 1962
Prescot
1924 1930 Tranmere Rovers 81 2
Prescot Cables

Neal, Arthur Marshall OR
b Rotherham 20/12/1903 d 1982
1924 Rotherham County 0
Gainsborough Trinity
Frickley Colliery
1927 Liverpool 0
1928 Darlington 2
Denaby United
Kettering Town

Neal, John Edward IL
b Llandudno 29/11/1898 d 1965
Caps: Wales 2
University College (Bangor)
Llandudno Town
Colwyn Bay
1928 1929 Wrexham 17 3
Colwyn Bay United

Neal, Reginald George IL
b Winchester q2 1913 d 1951
South Shore Wesleyans
1933 Blackpool 0
Altrincham
1935 Liverpool 0
1936 Bristol City 9
1937 Southport 0
1937 Gillingham 14 2

Neal, Richard Marshall (Dick) OR/OL/IR
b Fencehouses 14/1/1906 d 1986
Dinnington Main Colliery Welfare
1925 1930 Blackpool 85 17
1931 Derby County 10 1
1931 1936 Southampton 170 17
1937 Bristol City 6
1938 Accrington Stanley 21 7

Neal, Sidney (Sid) RH/OL/CH
b Mosborough q2 1899 d 1985
Dinnington Main Colliery Welfare
1922 Rotherham County 3
Mosborough
1924 1925 Luton Town 27
Frickley Colliery

Neal, Thomas Walker (Tom) LH
b New Washington 28/11/1910 d 1936
Usworth Colliery
1931 1935 Leeds United 20
1936 Hull City 0

Neale, Thomas (Tom) LH
b Ashby-de-la-Zouch 1/8/1908 d 1986
Ashby Town
1927 Birmingham 0
1928 Chesterfield 28 1
1929 Sheffield Wednesday 0
Worksop Town (loan)
Chester
Stourbridge
Dundalk
Macclesfield
Dudley Town

From To | Apps Goal

Neale, William CF
b West Bromwich q2 1872 d 1901
Grove Hill Saints
1892 1893 West Bromwich Albion 6 3
Brierley Hill Alliance

Neary, John CH
b Chorlton 14/12/1915 d 1996
1936 Chelsea 0
Manchester North End
1938 1945 Rochdale 1
Hurst

Neate, Thomas William J OL
b Chippenham q2 1903
Chippenham Town
1924 Bristol City 2
Chippenham Town

Neave, David OL
b Arbroath 1883
Forfar Athletic
Montrose
Arbroath
1904 Woolwich Arsenal 3
Leyton
1905 1911 Woolwich Arsenal 151 30
Merthyr Town
Dunfermline Athletic
Heart of Midlothian
Clyde
Arbroath

Neave, George D (Geordie) CH
1895 Lincoln City 29
Dundee

Neave, Robert A CH
b Lochee 23/5/1894 d 1951
Glasgow Perthshire
1912 Sheffield United 11
Chesterfield Town
Rochdale
Clyde
Abercorn (loan)
Kilmarnock
Johnstone
Helensburgh

Needham, Archibald (Archie) IR/IL
b Sheffield 8/1881 d 1950
1902 1903 Sheffield United 16 6
Crystal Palace
1909 Glossop 31 12
1910 Wolverhampton Wanderers 32 6
Brighton & Hove Albion

Needham, Ernest LH
b Whittington Moor 21/1/1873 d 1936
Caps: FLge 10/England 16
Waverley
Staveley
1892 1909 Sheffield United 464 51

Needham, Ernest Godfrey LH
b Staveley 5/3/1892 d 1975
Staveley Church
1912 Sheffield United 1
Staveley Town
Luton Town

Needham, George James LH/CH
b Shepshed 26/11/1884 d 1971
Shepshed Albion
1905 1914 Nottingham Forest 275 10

Needham, George Wright LH/RH/OL
b Staveley 28/4/1894 d 1967
Sherwood Foresters
Staveley
1919 Derby County 5
1920 1923 Gillingham 122 13
1923 1924 Northampton Town 35 1
Worksop Town

Needham, John (Jack) IL
b Newstead 4/3/1887
Langwith Rovers
Mansfield Invicta
Mansfield Wesleyans
1909 Birmingham 20 5
1909 1919 Wolverhampton Wanderers 187 57
1919 1920 Hull City 18 1
Scunthorpe & Lindsey United

Needham, Thomas IR/OR
1888 1889 Derby County 15 3

Neesam, Herbert (Bert) RH/IR/CF
b Brompton, North Yorkshire 2/6/1892 d 1959
Brompton
Grangetown Athletic
1913 1927 Bristol City 281 18
Bath City
George's Brewery

From To Apps Goal

Neil, Andrew (Andy) IR/LH/IL
b Kilmarnock 18/11/1892 d 1941
Ardeer Thistle
Kilmarnock
Galston (loan)
Clydebank (loan)
Third Lanark
Kilmarnock
Galston
Stevenston United
1920 1923 Brighton & Hove Albion 129 22
1923 1925 Arsenal 54 10
1925 1926 Brighton & Hove Albion 38 6
1927 1929 Queen's Park Rangers 106 1

Neil, Peter WH OR
b Methil 1898
Cambuslang Rangers
East Fife
1921 Birmingham 5
Heart of Midlothian
Alloa Athletic

Neil, Robert Scott Gibson (Bobby) CH
b Govan 24/9/1875 d 1913
Caps: Scotland 2
Glasgow Ashfield
Hibernian
1894 1896 Liverpool 22 2
Rangers
Airdrieonians

Neill, Quentin Durward RB
b Glasgow 1866 d 1901
Queen's Park
1892 1894 Lincoln City 59

Neilson, Adam OL
Lochgelly United
Falkirk
1927 South Shields 4

Neilson, Charles RH
1892 Bootle 7

Neilson, George Humble RH/LH/CH
b Thornley 28/8/1908 d 1999
Blackhall Wesleyans
Horden Athletic
Thornley Albion
Blackhall Colliery
1927 Durham City 3
1929 South Shields 37
1930 1938 Gateshead 273 15

Neilson, Peter M OL
b Glasgow 1890
Kilbirnie Ladeside
Airdrieonians
1913 Birmingham 3 1
Wallyford

Neilson, Richard (Dick) CH
b Blackhall 1/4/1916 d 2005
Easington Juniors
Blackhall Colliery Welfare
Dawdon Colliery
1935 1938 Manchester City 16 1
Droylsden

Neilson, Walter CH
b Glasgow
Strathclyde
1898 Bury 3

Neish, John OR
b Elgin 1910
Elgin City
Coleshill Hall
Buckie Thistle
Morton (trial)
Partick Thistle
1935 Hull City 1
Buckie Thistle
Coleshill Hall
Elgin Corinthains
Inverness Thistle

Nelis, Patrick (Pat) CF/IL
b Derry 5/10/1898 d 1970
Caps: IrLge 1/Ireland 1
Londonderry Distillery
1921 Accrington Stanley 11 14
1921 1924 Nottingham Forest 59 13
1925 Wigan Borough 16 1
Coleraine
Rossville Hall
Derry City

From To Apps Goal

Nelmes, Alfred LH
b Bristol q1 1871 d 1940
Saltburn
Middlesbrough
1898 1905 Grimsby Town 219 14
1906 Burton United 34 1
Brighton & Hove Albion
Ilkeston United
Gresley Rovers

Nelson, Albert Oswin IR
b Aberaman 7/3/1917 d 1997
Aberaman Athletic
1937 Wolverhampton Wanderers 0
1938 Wrexham 29 11
1939 (Wrexham) (2) (1)

Nelson, Alfred (Alf) IR
b Coventry
Foleshill Albion
1919 Coventry City 2
Foleshill Albion
Caerphilly
Leamington Town

Nelson, Arthur IR/CF
b Darnall 15/5/1909 d 1977
Sheffield Woodhouse
1927 1928 Hull City 21 8
Scarborough
1930 Notts County 0
1931 Stockport County 19 5
1932 Luton Town 21 6
Nuneaton Town
Wellington Town
Burton Town

Nelson, David (Dave) RH/IR/OR
b Douglas Water 3/2/1918 d 1988
Douglas Water Thistle
St Bernard's
1936 1946 Arsenal 27 4
1946 Fulham 23 3
1947 1949 Brentford 106 5
1949 1950 Queen's Park Rangers 31
1951 1952 Crystal Palace 12
Ashford Town (Kent)

Nelson, Edward (Ted) RH
b West Auckland 21/4/1907 d 1972
West Auckland
Crook Town
1926 Derby County 2
1928 Doncaster Rovers 1

Nelson, James (Jimmy) OL
1890 Derby County 4 2

Nelson, James (Jimmy) RB
b Greenock 7/1/1901 d 1965
Caps: Scotland 4
St Paul's (Belfast)
Glenavon
Crusaders
1921 1929 Cardiff City 240 2
1930 1934 Newcastle United 146
1935 1938 Southend United 73
Ekco Sports

Nelson, John H OR
b Manchester
1910 Manchester City 8

Nelson, John Henry (Jack) CH
b Chorley 15/3/1906 d 1986
Chorley All Saints
Chorley
1928 1932 Preston North End 71 2
1932 1934 Wolverhampton Wanderers 74 4
1935 1938 Luton Town 134

Nelson, William Francis RB
b Bamber Bridge 1/1/1919 d 1996
1938 Preston North End 0
1939 Mansfield Town (2)

Nesbitt, Robert Adam OL
b Sunderland 22/10/1884 d 1972
Blyth Spartans
1911 Blackpool 11 4

Nesbitt, William (Billy) OR
b Portsmouth, Lancashire 22/11/1891 d 1972
Portsmouth Rovers
Hebden Bridge
1911 1922 Burnley 172 19
1923 Bristol City 26
1924 Clapton Orient 0

From To Apps Goal

Ness, Harold Marshall (Harry) LB
b Scarborough q3 1885 d 1957
Sheffield
Rawmarsh Albion
Parkgate
1908 1910 Barnsley 70
1911 1919 Sunderland 93
Aberdeen

Nettleton, William (Willie) OR
1902 Doncaster Rovers 1 1

Neve, Edwin (Ned) OL
b Prescot 3/5/1885 d 1920
St Helens Recreation
1906 1911 Hull City 102 12
1912 1913 Derby County 47 1
1914 Nottingham Forest 35 3

Nevin, George William RB/LB
b Lintz 16/12/1907 d 1973
Lintz Colliery
Dipton United
1925 Newcastle United 0
White-le-Head Rangers
1929 Newcastle United 6
1932 Sheffield Wednesday 2
1933 Manchester United 4
1934 Sheffield Wednesday 0
1935 1936 Burnley 26
1937 1938 Lincoln City 8
1939 Rochdale 0

Nevin, John William CH
b Lintz 20/2/1886
Lintz Institute
Gateshead United
1908 Sunderland 0
Hobson Wanderers
1910 West Bromwich Albion 2
Bristol Rovers
Lintz Institute
Dolphin
Ayr United
West Stanley
Workington
1922 1923 Barrow 54 3
West Stanley
1924 Crewe Alexandra 23 1
Hobson Wanderers
Lintz Colliery
York City (trial)
Inverness Thistle
Fraserburgh

Nevin, William (Billy) CF
b Burnopfield 19/4/1916 d 1996
Ashington
1936 Sheffield Wednesday 0
1937 Hartlepools United 4 2

Nevins, Thomas (Tommy) RB/LB
b Washington q2 1886 d 1950
Washington Athletic
1907 1913 Hull City 130
Blyth Spartans
West Stanley

Newall, James Daniel (Danny) LH/RH/IR
b Newport 15/6/1921 d 1997
Melrose Stars
1938 1954 Newport County 232 4

Newall, John Thomas (Tommy) RH/CF
b West Bromwich q2 1890 d 1957
Great Bridge Celtic
1913 1921 West Bromwich Albion 21 3

Newall, William T OL
b Lye 1869 d 1954
Birmingham Carriage Works
Stourbridge
1894 West Bromwich Albion 14 2
Worcester Rovers
Singers
Smethwick Wesleyan Rovers

Newberry, Frank Orchard (Nobby) LH
b Cricklade 8/1/1908 d 1984
Rodbourne Athletic
Swindon Corinthians
1934 1935 Swindon Town 11 1
Bath City
Cheltenham Town

From To Apps Goal

Newbigging, Alexander (Alex) GK
b Larkhall 27/12/1879
Lanark Athletic
Abercorn
Lanark United
Queen's Park Rangers
1901 1904 Nottingham Forest 7
Reading
Rangers
Reading
Coventry City
Inverness Thistle

Newbigging, Henry (Harry) IL
b Douglas 25/5/1893
Douglas Water Thistle
Blantyre Victoria
Cambuslang Rangers
Raith Rovers
Cambuslang Rangers
Hamilton Academical
Raith Rovers
Abercorn
1919 Nottingham Forest 9 1
1920 Stockport County 15 1

Newcomb, Leamon Robinson (Lem) RH
b Stillington 28/11/1903 d 1964
Stillington Juniors
1920 Middlesbrough 0
Stockton Malleable
1926 Darlington 2
Sittingbourne
1928 1935 Millwall 187 2
1936 1938 Southport 79 1
1939 (Southport) (3)

Newcombe, Charles Niel IL
b Great Yarmouth 16/3/1891 d 1915
Sheepbridge Works
Creswell
Chesterfield Town
Rotherham Town
1913 Manchester United 0
1913 Glossop 2
Tibshelf Colliery

Newell, Percy RB
b Catshill 9/5/1893 d 1985
Stourbridge
1920 1922 Wolverhampton Wanderers 10
Stourbridge

Newlands, George GK
b Campbeltown 14/1/1906 d 1969
Shotts Battlefield
Armadale
1927 1931 Bristol City 90
Distillery

Newman, Alfred OR
b Birmingham
1924 Stockport County 4

Newman, Arthur Percy IL
b Smethwick 23/8/1895 d 1979
1919 1920 Stockport County 4
Kidderminster Harriers

Newman, Ernest Henry (Ernie) IR/IL
b Birmingham 27/12/1887 d 1945
Walsall
1909 Stockport County 19 5
1909 1913 Tottenham Hotspur 30 6

Newman, Frank OR
b Nuneaton 14/10/1898 d 1977
1919 Aston Villa 0
1920 Port Vale 20
1921 1922 Exeter City 42 1
1923 Halifax Town 4
1925 1926 Exeter City 16 1
Yeovil & Petters United

Newman, Robert T IL
b Newcastle
1922 Watford 1

Newnes, John (Jack) RH/CH
b Trefnant 4/6/1895 d 1969
Caps: Wales Sch/Wales 1
Whitchurch
Brymbo Institute
1922 Bolton Wanderers 7
1923 1925 Nelson 113 7
1926 1927 Southport 38 2
Mossley
Manchester North End
Winsford United
Glossop
Altrincham
Manchester North End

From To Apps Goal

Newton, Albert OL
b Barnsley 13/3/1894 d 1975
Barnsley St George's
1919 1925 Barnsley 222 21
1926 Bradford City 4

Newton, Cyril GK
b Hamsterley
Medomsley Juniors
Spen Black & White
1931 Birmingham 0
1932 1933 Gateshead 44
Consett
Hexham
Annfield Plain

Newton, Francis (Frank) RH
b Menston 28/10/1902
Menston
1921 Bradford City 1
1922 1923 Northampton Town 41 1
1924 Halifax Town 2

Newton, Frank CF
b Romiley 12/11/1902 d 1977
Ashton National
Pontypridd
1927 1930 Stockport County 94 86
1931 1933 Fulham 74 72
1933 1934 Reading 32 29
1934 Fulham 9 5

Newton, Frederick Arthur (Fred) GK
b Denaby 16/9/1884 d 1924
Grassmoor Red Rose
1905 1906 Chesterfield Town 2
Whitwell St Lawrence
Ling's Row Primitives

Newton, George William RB
b Middlesbrough q1 1900 d 1968
1921 Middlesbrough (trial) 0
1923 Durham City 2
Redcar United Automobile

Newton, Harry OR
1938 Rotherham United 4 1

Newton, James Israel (Jimmy 'Jack') GK
b Horsforth q1 1898
Anderston V
Glasgow Perthshire
Rutherglen Glencairn
Queen's Park
1924 Bradford City 5
1925 Halifax Town 40
1926 1927 Coventry City 70
1929 Brighton & Hove Albion 1
Otley
Burley Grove United
Otley

Newton, Leonard Francis (Frank) CF/IR
b Denaby 28/10/1883 d 1959
Caps: Wales 1
Grassmoor Red Rose
1902 1904 Chesterfield Town 98 23
Leyton
1906 Bradford City 17 5
1907 1909 Oldham Athletic 81 45
1909 1910 Bradford Park Avenue 33 13
1910 Burnley 6 2
Cardiff City
Cardiff Corinthians
Cardiff City
Cardiff Corinthians
Cardiff City
Cardiff Corinthians

Newton, Percy CH
b Whitchurch
Whitchurch
Sandbach Ramblers
1933 Manchester United 2
1934 1935 Tranmere Rovers 59

Newton, Sydney GK
b Tyldesley
1910 1911 Bolton Wanderers 15
1914 Preston North End 8

Newton, Thomas (Tom) GK
b Ryton-on-Tyne
Blaydon United
Croydon Common
Swindon Town
Scotswood
Newburn
1920 1922 Portsmouth 49
Scotswood
1924 Ashington 16
Crawcrook Albion

From To Apps Goal

Newton, Thomas (Tom) LB
b Ryton-on-Tyne
1927 Ashington 0
1928 Darlington 4

Newton, William (Billy) RH
b Cramlington 14/5/1893 d 1973
Blyth Spartans
Hartford Colliery
1919 Newcastle United 0
1920 1921 Cardiff City 6
1923 1925 Leicester City 87 1
1926 Grimsby Town 14
1927 1930 Stockport County 151 2
1931 Hull City 24
1932 Stockport County 0

Newton, William Alfred Andrew (Andy) LB/LH
b Romiley q1 1896
Droylsden
1919 Manchester City 2
1919 Port Vale 14
1920 Southend United 29 1
1921 Accrington Stanley 2
Hurst
Ashton National
Romiley
Marple
Congleton Town

Newton, William Griffiths LB
b Crewe q4 1900 d 1965
1923 Port Vale 1
Congleton Town
Oswestry Town

Neyland (Nalan), Martin CF
b Bolton 29/9/1877 d 1947
Chatham
New Brompton
1901 Bolton Wanderers 2
Swindon Town
Nelson

Niblo, Thomas Bruce (Tommy) CF/OL/OR
b Dunfermline 24/9/1877 d 1933
Caps: Scotland 1
Cadzow Oak
Hamilton Academical
Linthouse
1897 1901 Newcastle United 60 5
1899 Middlesbrough (loan) 3 2
1901 1903 Aston Villa 45 9
1904 1905 Nottingham Forest 46 9
Watford
1907 Newcastle United 0
Hebburn Argyle
Aberdeen
Raith Rovers
Cardiff City
Blyth Spartans

Nibloe, Joseph (Joe) RB/LB
b Corkerhill 23/11/1903 d 1976
Caps: SLge 2/Scotland 11
Shawfield Juniors
Rutherglen Glencairn
Kilmarnock
1932 1933 Aston Villa 48
1934 1937 Sheffield Wednesday 116

Nichol, James Baillie (Jimmy) RH/LH
b Tollcross 7/4/1903 d 1954
Vale of Clyde
Glasgow Perthshire
1925 1927 Gillingham 83 2
1927 1936 Portsmouth 353 10
1937 Gillingham 8
Bognor Regis Town

Nichol, James Brown IL
b Consett q4 1889
Dipton United
Spen Black & White
Allendale Park
1914 Fulham 3

Nichol, James Couttie CF
b Edinburgh 26/1/1908
Murrayfield Amateurs
Leith Athletic
1932 Portsmouth 3 1
1933 Aldershot 20 11
St Mirren
Burton Town
1935 Hull City 6 2
1936 York City 11 3
Scarborough
Bath City

Nichol, John OR
b Morpeth 1879
Morpeth Harriers
1903 Grimsby Town 16 3

From To Apps Goal

Nichol, William Bacon IL
b Lochgelly
Lochgelly Celtic
1928 Bournemouth & Boscombe Ath 2
1929 Gillingham 0
St Bernard's

Nichol, William Douglas (Willie) CF
b Easington 1/1887
Royal Warwickshire Regiment
Northumberland Fusiliers
1908 Nottingham Forest 0
1908 Notts County 0
Seaforth Highlanders
Fort George
Aberdeen
Celtic
Stenhousemuir (loan)
Ayr United (loan)
1912 Bristol City 3
Queen's Park Wednesday (Aberdeen)
Seaforth Highlanders

Nicholas, David Sidney (Dai) OL
b Aberdare 12/8/1897 d 1982
Caps: Wales Sch/WLge 1/Wales 3
Merthyr Town
Swansea Town
1920 1921 Merthyr Town 46 2
1921 1924 Stoke 54 3
Aberavon Athletic
1924 1929 Swansea Town 151 14

Nicholas, George Arthur CH
b Bedwellty 15/10/1911 d 1973
Treharris
1930 1933 Crystal Palace 39
Dartford
Burton Town

Nicholas, John Thomas (Jack) RH/RB
b Derby 26/11/1910 d 1977
Caps: Wales Sch
1927 Swansea Town 0
1928 1946 Derby County 347 14
1939 (Derby County) (3) (1)

Nicholas, William Joseph (Jack) RB/LB
b Staines q1 1885
Staines
1905 1910 Derby County 130
Swansea Town
Llanelly

Nicholl, James (Jimmy) OL/IL
b Port Glasgow 12/1/1887
Morningside Rangers
Cambuslang Rangers
Airdrieonians
1910 1913 Middlesbrough 52 13
1913 1914 Liverpool 52 12
Wishaw Thistle
Hamilton Academical

Nicholls, Alfred IR
b Birmingham 1875 d 1932
Wednesbury Old Athletic
1896 Wolverhampton Wanderers 3 2

Nicholls, Frederick OR
b Handsworth 1884
Handsworth Rovers
1905 West Bromwich Albion 7
Goldenhill Wanderers
Shrewsbury Town

Nicholls, George J OR
b Hackney 13/12/1890
1919 Chelsea 0
1920 Southend United 21
Ton Pentre
1922 Rochdale 17
Leyton

Nicholls, Herbert John (Jack) OL
b Walsall Wood 1891 d 1921
Hednesford Town
1913 West Bromwich Albion 4
Cannock Town

Nicholls, J LH
b West Bromwich 1867
St John's United
1889 West Bromwich Albion 4
Kidderminster Olympic

From To Apps Goal

Nicholls, James Henry GK
b Bilston 24/9/1908 d 1984
Sunbeam Motors
Bloxwich Strollers
Bilston Borough
1932 1933 Manchester City 16
1936 Brentford 7
1937 Port Vale 17

Nicholls, John Barry L (Jack) IR
b Cardiff 14/2/1898 d 1970
Caps: WLge 1/Wales Amat/Wales 4
Ton Pentre
Cardiff Corinthians
Pontypridd
Bridgend Town
1923 Newport County 11 4
1924 Cardiff City 2
1925 Swansea Town 0
Cardiff Corinthians

Nicholls, Joseph Edward (Joe) LB
b Bilston
1914 Wolverhampton Wanderers 0
Bilston United
1919 1924 Clapton Orient 117 2
Bilston United

Nicholls, Joseph Henry (Joe) GK
b Carlton, Nottinghamshire 8/3/1905 d 1973
Grenadier Guards
1924 Notts County (trial) 0
Darlaston
Northfleet
1926 1935 Tottenham Hotspur 124
1936 1938 Bristol Rovers 112
1939 (Bristol Rovers) (3)

Nicholls, Samuel (Sammy) IR/CF
b West Bromwich 1/1870 d 1912
Kidderminster Olympic
West Bromwich Victoria
1889 1891 West Bromwich Albion 33 11
London CBC
1893 West Bromwich Albion 8 3

Nichols, Harry RH
b Hednesford 1914
Hednesford Town
1934 Sheffield Wednesday 3
Wellington Town
Shrewsbury Town

Nichols, John Ernest CF
b Norwich 20/4/1878 d 1952
1898 Loughborough 9 2

Nicholson, Benjamin (Ben) LB
b Ashington 1884
Morpeth Harriers
1906 Newcastle United 1
Luton Town
West Stanley
Huddersfield Town (trial)

Nicholson, Benjamin Cummings (Ben) LH/CH
b Thornley 1898
Thornley Wesleyans
1921 1924 Hartlepools United 17
Thornley Dunelm
Thornley Albion
Thornley Dunelm

Nicholson, Fred LB
b Willington 23/8/1904 d 1992
Hunwick Villa
1925 Newcastle United 0
1927 Durham City 9
Annfield Plain
Walker Celtic
North Shields
Jarrow
Consett
West Stanley
Sunnybrow United

Nicholson, George RH/LH
b Pelaw 12/5/1905
Pelaw
1929 South Shields 0
Washington Colliery
1931 1935 Bolton Wanderers 67 1
1936 1938 Cardiff City 98
1939 Oldham Athletic 0

Nicholson, George H OR
b West Ham
1921 West Ham United 0
West Stanley
1923 Crystal Palace 2
Dundee United

Nicholson, Harry CF
1905 Gainsborough Trinity 18 3

From To Apps Goal

Nicholson, Horace RH/CH/LH
b Mexborough 19/7/1895
Mexborough Highthorne Mission
1913 Sheffield Wednesday 3
Mexborough Town
1920 1922 Bradford Park Avenue 25
Wath Athletic
Wombwell
Denaby United

Nicholson, James CH
b Morpeth 15/3/1901 d 1979
Caps: England Sch
Heart of Midlothian (trial)
1922 Ashington 3

Nicholson, John Andrew LH/RH
b Ayr 8/3/1888 d 1970
Glasgow Ashfield
1911 1920 Bristol City 196 4
Rangers
St Johnstone

Nicholson, Joseph Robinson (Joe) LH/RH
b Ryhope 4/6/1898 d 1974
Ryhope Colliery
1919 1923 Clapton Orient 145 4
1924 1925 Cardiff City 47 12
1926 Aston Villa 1
Bangor City
Spennymoor United

Nicholson, Mark D RB
b Oakengates 6/1871 d 1943
Oswestry Town
1891 1893 West Bromwich Albion 56
Luton Town
Cairo
Vienna

Nicholson, Sidney (Sid) CH/RB/LB
b Shildon q1 1912 d 1959
1929 Cardiff City 0
Merthyr Town
1931 1932 Bournemouth & Boscombe Ath 8
Scunthorpe & Lindsey United
1934 Chesterfield 0
1935 1937 Barnsley 7
Aberdeen

Nicholson, William Edward (Bill) RH/CH
b Scarborough 26/1/1919 d 2004
Caps: England B/FLge 1/England 1
Scarborough Working Mens Club
Scarborough Young Liberals
1935 Tottenham Hotspur (trial) 0
Northfleet
1938 1954 Tottenham Hotspur 314 6
1939 (Tottenham Hotspur) (3)

Nickalls, James Sproat (Jim) OR
b Amble 7/7/1903 d 1977
Bedlington United
Ashington
1930 Chelsea 0
1931 Swindon Town 13 1
Blyth Spartans

Nicol, Alfred OR
Stockton
1898 Burnley 2
1899 Gainsborough Trinity 7

Nicol, Andrew LH
b Lochgelly
Lochgelly United
Forfar Athletic
1925 1926 Aberdare Athletic 68 1
Kettering Town
Alloa Athletic

Nicol, Archibald (Archie) RH/LH
Lochgelly United
1897 1899 Bury 19
Dunfermline Athletic
Lochgelly United

Nicol, George (Geordie) CF
b Saltcoats 14/12/1903 d 1968
Ardrossan Winton Rovers
Kilwinning
Saltcoats Victoria
1927 1928 Manchester United 6 2
1929 1931 Brighton & Hove Albion 31 23
Glenavon
1932 1934 Gillingham 66 38
Racing Club de Roubaix

From To Apps Goal

Nicol, James McDonald (Jim) IL/IR
b Neilston
Montrose
1929 Middlesbrough 0
1930 Southend United 15 7
St Johnstone
Brechin City
1934 Rochdale 27 11
1935 1936 Crewe Alexandra 37 2

Nicol, John CH
Dundee
1930 Thames 2
1931 Clapton Orient 0

Nicol, Thomas H (Tom) OR/RB
b Whitburn, West Lothian 24/2/1870 d 1915
Mossend Swifts
1890 Burnley 3 3
Mossend Swifts
1891 1896 Burnley 137 41
1896 Blackburn Rovers 16 2
Southampton St Mary's
Southampton Wanderers

Nicoll, David CF
Western (Arbroath)
Victoria (Arbroath)
Wanderers (Arbroath)
Arbroath
1895 1898 Bolton Wanderers 59 11
Millwall Athletic
Bristol City
1901 Bolton Wanderers 2
Arbroath

Nidd, George Frederick (Fred) LB/RB
b Boston q1 1869 d 1956
Aintree Church
1889 Everton 0
Southport Central
1892 Everton 0
1893 Preston North End 3
Southport Central
1895 Bury 0
Stalybridge Rovers
Halliwell Rovers
1897 Lincoln City 9
1898 1899 Grimsby Town 50 1
Watford
Brentford
Fulham
Grays United
1905 Clapton Orient 0
Watford

Nieuwenhuys, Berry OR
b Boksburg, South Africa 5/11/1911 d 1984
Boksburg
Germiston Callies
1933 1946 Liverpool 236 74
1939 (Liverpool) (3)

Nightingale, Arthur OR
1898 Blackpool 3

Nightingale, James OR
1891 Darwen 18 2

Nightingale, James LB
b Edinburgh 1881
Bolton St Luke's
1901 Bolton Wanderers 0
Rochdale Town
Southport Central
Rossendale United
1905 Bradford City 10

Nightingale, John Gladstone (Jack) OR/IR
b Oldbury 6/1899 d 1967
Brandhall Rovers
Kidderminster Harriers
1919 Wolverhampton Wanderers 3
Shrewsbury Town
1921 1926 Brighton & Hove Albion 182 33
Shrewsbury Town

Nightingale, Samson IR
b Rotherham 5/11/1916 d 1982
Sheffield Woodhouse
1937 Lincoln City 2
Scunthorpe & Lindsey United
Doncaster Rovers

Nightingale, Thomas CH
1898 Darwen 3

Nimmo, James LH/LB
b Longridge, West Lothian
Broxburn United
1927 1929 Reading 24

From To Apps Goal

Nimmo, Michael (Mike) CH/RH
b Bothwell 27/10/1892
Glasgow Ashfield
Hamilton Academical
1921 1922 Barrow 54 2
Chatham

Nimrod, Joseph Dobson RH
b South Shields q2 1880 d 1914
Jarrow
1901 1902 Barnsley 13
Denaby United

Nisbet, Gavin RH
b Hamilton 11/10/1904 d 1967
Coalburn Juniors
Blantyre Victoria
1927 1934 Preston North End 139 6
1935 Burnley 2
1936 Accrington Stanley 31
Stalybridge Celtic

Nisbet, George CH/LH
Maxwelltown Volunteers
1906 1909 Lincoln City 62 1
Lanemark

Nisbet, James LB/RB
b Scotland 1865
1890 Accrington 5
1892 Northwich Victoria 13
1893 Rotherham Town 10

Nisbet, Kenneth Henry (Ken) IL/CF
b Rosyth 9/6/1907 d 1992
East Riding Amateurs
1930 Sunderland 0
1931 Rochdale 12 2
1931 Gateshead 1
West Stanley

Nisbet, Robert LB
b Carronshore 1910
Camelon Juniors
Motherwell
Dolphin
1932 Preston North End 2
East Stirlingshire (trial)
Falkirk
Dumbarton

Niven, James Bryden (Jimmy) RB/LB
b Moffat 8/9/1897 d 1984
1921 Tranmere Rovers 17
Flint Town
1923 1924 New Brighton 37
Flint Town
Chester
Bangor City
Llanelly

Nixon, Albert GK
1894 1895 Rotherham Town 25

Nixon, Ernest A CH
1905 Stockport County 4

Nixon, James GK
1893 Middlesbrough Ironopolis 2

Nixon, John OR
b Blackburn, West Lothian 1888
Hibernian
1907 Bristol City 7
Croydon Common
1909 1910 Stockport County 39 6
Halifax Town
Belfast Celtic
Halifax Town

Nixon, Joseph LB/CH/LH
b Prudhoe
Prudhoe Castle
1921 1926 Crystal Palace 29 1
Prudhoe Castle

Nixon, Thomas (Tom) LB/RB
b Wombwell 21/9/1867
Worsborough Common Gladstone
Old Association Club (Barnsley)
Sheffield Zulus (Lockwood Bros)
Ardsley
Barnsley St Peter's
1896 Darwen 9
1898 1899 Barnsley 40

Nixon, Thomas (Tom) CH/RB
b Newcastle 22/12/1905 d 1966
Crawcrook Albion
1928 1932 Queen's Park Rangers 56 1
1933 Crystal Palace 0
1933 1934 Swindon Town 53
1935 1936 Barrow 68
Felling Colliery

From To Apps Goal

Nixon, Wilfred (Wilf) GK
b Gateshead 22/10/1882 d 1985
Hexham
Carlisle United
Wallsend Park Villa
Haltwhistle Black Diamond
Newburn
1912 1920 Fulham 27

Noakes, George William OL
b Wednesbury 14/8/1899 d 1969
Stafford Rangers
Burton All Saints
1924 Walsall 12 1

Nobbs, Harold CH/RH
b Bishop Middleham 5/1/1903 d 1971
Stockton
1927 Durham City 0
South Bank
1929 1931 Hartlepools United 68 1
City of Durham

Nobbs, Walter LH/RH
b Ferryhill 14/5/1914 d 1995
Ferryhill Athletic
1935 1936 Hartlepools United 21 1
Horden Colliery Welfare

Noble, Alan Hugh OR/RH
b Southampton 19/6/1900 d 1973
1920 Southampton 0
Boscombe
1922 1924 Leeds United 60 4
1925 1926 Brentford 41
1927 Millwall 4

Noble, Arthur RB
b Norwich 15/11/1895 d 1990
Settlement House
St James
Royal Field Artillery
CEYMS (Norwich)
City Wanderers
1929 Norwich City 1
City Wanderers

Noble, James Frame IR
b Morpeth 21/3/1905 d 1988
1927 Ashington 1

Noble, Robert (Bob) IR/OR
b Buckhaven 29/9/1891 d 1976
Caps: Scotland Amat
Bromley
1910 Aston Villa 0
Queen's Park Rangers
Bromley
1912 Leicester Fosse 4
1920 Millwall Athletic 1
London Caledonians

Noble, William IR
b Edinburgh 1898
Cumnock Juniors
Ayr United
1920 Bristol City 6

Noble, William D (Bill) RB
b Wellingborough 1883 d 1947
Wellingborough
Northampton Town
Wellingborough
1905 1906 Barnsley 11 1
Northampton Town
Wellingborough
1909 Bradford Park Avenue 2
Rotherham Town
Fletton United
Market Harborough Town

Nock, Jack IL
b Stourbridge 1899
Caps: WLge 1
Cradley Heath
1921 1922 Cardiff City 3
1924 1925 Wrexham 65 22
Burton Town
Worcester City
Flint Town
Oswestry Town

Nock, John Edwin CF
b Rotherham 13/1/1909 d 1996
Dinnington Athletic
Silverwood Colliery
1931 1932 Rotherham United 25 15
Scarborough
Bacup Borough
1934 Accrington Stanley 1
Rossendale United

From	To		Apps	Goal
Nock, John F			OL	
b West Bromwich 1875				
		West Bromwich Swifts		
		Halesowen Town		
1897	1898	West Bromwich Albion	15	6
		Langley Richmond		
		Brierley Hill Alliance		
Nokes, George Stephen			LB	
b Sedgefield q4 1871			d 1946	
1893		Middlesbrough Ironopolis	1	
Nolan, Thomas Gerard (Tommy 'Wilf')			CF/IR	
b Preston 13/6/1909			d 1969	
		Preston Catholic College		
1929		Preston North End	0	
		Manchester Central		
1931	1934	Port Vale	107	54
1935	1936	Bradford Park Avenue	36	14
1936	1938	Port Vale	94	35
Noon, Michael			RB/LB/RH	
b Whitwick q4 1875			d 1939	
1897	1898	Burton Swifts	35	
1899	1905	Aston Villa	74	1
		Plymouth Argyle		
Nord, John Gaiger			OL	
b Sunderland 16/5/1895			d 1978	
		Shotton Colliery		
1920	1921	Oldham Athletic	3	
Norgrove, Frank			LB/RB/RH	
b Hyde q3 1878			d 1948	
1901	1903	Glossop	78	
1903	1911	Manchester City	94	1
Norman, Albert E Oliver (Oliver)			IR/OR	
b West Bromwich 1866			d 1943	
		Oldbury Town		
		Wednesbury Old Athletic		
1893	1895	West Bromwich Albion	18	4
		Hereford Town		
Norman, Alfred			OR	
b Leicester q1 1884				
		Oxford Victoria (Leicester)		
		St Andrew's (Leicester)		
		Leicester Imperial		
1906		Leicester Fosse	2	1
		Leicester Imperial		
Norman, James			OL	
b Hackney Wick 1893				
		Eton Mission		
		Walthamstow Grange		
1914		Arsenal	4	
Norrington, Cyril James			LB	
b Kensal Rise 3/6/1901			d 1972	
		Leytonstone		
		Barking Town		
1926		Leicester City	0	
1927	1928	West Ham United	27	
1929		Coventry City	0	
		Peterborough & Fletton United		
Norris, Frank			LB	
1891		Preston North End	3	
Norris, Frederick Harold (Fred)			RH/IR/LH	
b Aston 14/8/1903			d 1962	
		Adelaide		
		Halesowen		
1925	1926	Aston Villa	9	2
1928	1932	West Ham United	65	6
1933		Crystal Palace	11	4
		(France)		
Norris, Patrick			IR/IL	
b Broughton				
		Salford		
1919		Burnley	2	
1920		Stockport County	5	1
Norris, Robert (Bob)			LH	
b Preston q3 1875				
Caps: FLge 1				
		South Shore		
1896	1897	Blackpool	52	1
1898	1903	Nottingham Forest	129	7
1904		Doncaster Rovers	21	3
1905		Nottingham Forest	0	
North, Ernest Joseph (Joe)			CF/IL	
b Burton-on-Trent 23/9/1895			d 1955	
		Atlas & Norfolk		
1919		Sheffield United	0	
1919	1921	Arsenal	23	6
1922		Reading	4	
1923		Gillingham	39	11
1924	1925	Norwich City	56	19
1926		Watford	6	
		Northfleet		

From	To		Apps	Goal
North, James Thomas (Tommy)			CH	
b Codnor Park 7/8/1882			d 1943	
		Constitutional		
		Linby		
		Constitutional		
		Mansfield Mechanics		
1907		Sheffield United	4	
		Huddersfield Town		
Northam, Cyril George			OR	
b Hendon q4 1894				
		Dulwich Hamlet		
		Wrexham		
		Connah's Quay & Shotton		
		Dulwich Hamlet		
1921		Wrexham	16	4
		Connah's Quay & Shotton		
		Whitchurch		
Northey, George			IR	
		Green Waves		
1905		Aston Villa	0	
1906		Gainsborough Trinity	25	4
Norton, A			CF	
1903		Glossop	6	
Norton, Horace Arthur			IR/OL	
b Cleckheaton 15/9/1896			d 1976	
		Bowling Albion		
1919	1920	Bradford City	12	1
1921		Brentford	19	3
1922		Darlington	0	
Norton, John George (George)			IL	
b Stockton 18/11/1916				
		South Bank		
1938		Leicester City	0	
1939		Bradford Park Avenue	(1)	
		Blackhall Colliery Welfare		
Norton, Joseph (Joe)			OL/OR	
b Stoney Stanton 1/1/1891			d 1972	
		Avondale		
		Leicester British United		
		Leicester Imperial		
		Atherstone Town		
1911		Stockport County	8	1
		Atherstone Town		
		Nuneaton Town		
1913	1914	Manchester United	37	3
1919		Leicester City	11	
1920	1921	Bristol Rovers	38	2
1922		Swindon Town	26	2
		Kettering		
		Atherstone Town		
		Hinckley United		
		Ashby Town		
Norton, Percy			IL	
b Northampton q3 1883			d 1943	
		Wellingborough		
		Northampton Town		
		Wellingborough		
1906		Barnsley	1	
Norton, William (Billy)			RB	
b Bolton 1901				
1919		Bolton Wanderers	0	
1920		Bury	1	
1921		Bolton Wanderers	0	
Notley, Wilfred Samuel (Wilf)			CF	
b Bourne 25/5/1913			d 1972	
		Bourne Town		
		Stamford Town		
1933		Lincoln City (trial)		
1934		Tottenham Hotspur (trial)		
1935		Notts County	20	9
		Boston United		
Notton, Cecil Leonard Roger			IL	
b Northampton 12/3/1904			d 1971	
1922		Bury	0	
1923		Doncaster Rovers	1	
Nugent, John			GK	
1904		Notts County	3	
Nunn, Alfred Sydney (Alf)			OL	
b Holborn 15/11/1899			d 1946	
1920	1923	Clapton Orient	19	
		Folkestone		
1927		Luton Town	14	3
		Hugonians		
Nunnick, William			LH	
b Colne q3 1875			d 1948	
		Trawden Forest		
1898		Burnley	1	
		Nelson		

From	To		Apps	Goal
Nurse, Daniel George (Dan)			RH	
b Princes End 6/1873			d 1959	
Caps: FLge 1				
		Prince's End		
		Coseley		
1894	1900	Wolverhampton Wanderers	39	1
1901	1903	West Bromwich Albion	85	4
Nuttall, ?			CH	
1895		Darwen	1	
Nuttall, Henry (Harry)			RH	
b Oswaldtwistle				
1921		Accrington Stanley	2	
		Great Harwood		
		Darwen		
		Great Harwood		
Nuttall, Henry (Harry)			LH/RH/CH	
b Bolton 9/11/1897			d 1969	
Caps: England 3				
		St Mark's (Bolton)		
		Fleetwood		
		Atherton		
1921	1931	Bolton Wanderers	294	6
1932		Rochdale	35	
		Nelson		
Nuttall, James (Jimmy)			RB	
b Bolton 7/4/1900				
		Bolton Wanderers		
		Manchester United		
1921	1923	Rochdale	59	
Nuttall, Robert			CF	
b Tottington 1/5/1908			d 1983	
		Tottington		
1930		Nelson	4	
		Turton		
		Tottington St John's		
Nuttall, Thomas Albert B (Tommy)			IR/CF/IL	
b Bolton 2/1889				
		Heywood United		
1911	1912	Manchester United	16	4
1913	1914	Everton	19	7
		St Mirren		
		Northwich Victoria		
1920	1921	Southend United	57	10
		Leyland		
		Northwich Victoria		
		Eccles United		
		Chorley		
Nutter, Henry (Harry)			GK	
b Nelson q3 1900				
		Barnoldswick Town		
1923		Nelson	2	
Nutter, Walter			OL	
b Wath-on-Dearne q1 1904			d 1932	
		Darfield		
		Wombwell		
		Frickley Colliery		
1926	1927	Chesterfield	17	4
		Staveley Town (loan)		
		Scunthorpe & Lindsey United		
		Mexborough		
		Wombwell		
Oakden, Harry			OR	
b Derby q3 1877			d 1967	
		Alvaston & Boulton		
1898		Derby County	9	5
		Brighton United		
		Distillery		
		Swindon Town		
Oakes, Alfred William (Alf)			IL	
b Bewdley 22/7/1901			d 1967	
		RAF Uxbridge		
		Chesham United		
1923	1924	Millwall Athletic	6	2
1925		Reading	0	
		Rhyl Athletic (trial)		
		Wellington Town (trial)		
		Worcester City		
1926		Birmingham	1	
		Rhyl Athletic		
1929	1930	New Brighton	54	15
1931		Wigan Borough	11	4
		Frickley Colliery		
		Stalybridge Celtic		
		Buxton		
Oakes, Frederick (Fred)			OL	
b West Hartlepool 1880				
		New Clee Alexandra		
		Grimsby St John's		
1904		Grimsby Town	1	
		Grimsby St John's		
		Grimsby Rovers		

From	To		Apps	Goal
Oakes, James (Jimmy)			LB	
b Biddulph 12/7/1901			d 1974	
		Milton Albion		
1923	1932	Port Vale	288	3
1932	1938	Charlton Athletic	220	
1939		(Charlton Athletic)	(2)	
Oakes, John (Jack)			CH/CF	
b Winsford 13/9/1905			d 1992	
Caps: England War 1				
		Chilton Colliery Recreation Athletic		
		Cargo Fleet & Cochranes		
1929		Nottingham Forest	2	
		Newark Town		
1930		Clapton Orient (trial)	0	
		Crook Town		
1931		Southend United	2	
		Crook Town		
		Spennymoor United		
1934	1935	Aldershot	61	19
1935	1946	Charlton Athletic	130	3
1939		(Charlton Athletic)	(3)	
1947		Plymouth Argyle	36	
		Snowdown Colliery Welfare		
		Middlesbrough Police		
Oakes, Thomas Frederick			IR/OL/RH	
b King's Norton q2 1875			d 1926	
		Hereford Thistle		
1896	1899	Small Heath	35	8
		Gloucester City		
Oakes, William Henry (Bill)			LB/RB	
b Barking q4 1881			d 1927	
		Barking Lads Institute		
		Barking		
		Clapton		
		West Ham United		
1904	1906	Leicester Fosse	40	
Oakley, James Ernest			RB/LB	
b Tynemouth 10/11/1901			d 1972	
		Seaton Delaval		
		Blyth Spartans		
1922	1929	Sunderland	84	
1930		Reading	10	
1931	1932	Northampton Town	33	
		Kettering Town		
		Birtley		
Oakton, Albert Eric (Eric)			OR/OL	
b Kiveton Park 28/12/1906			d 1981	
		Kiveton Park		
1924		Grimsby Town	2	
1926		Rotherham United	7	3
		Worksop Town		
1928		Sheffield United	0	
		Scunthorpe & Lindsey United		
1931		Bristol Rovers	40	9
1932	1936	Chelsea	107	27
1937		Nottingham Forest	7	1
		Boston United		
O'Beirne, Patrick Joseph (Joe)			IL	
b Waterford 15/6/1900			d 1980	
		Norman Athletic		
1921	1922	Stalybridge Celtic	10	
1923		Burnley	5	
1924		Nelson	16	2
		Middlewich (loan)		
		Congleton Town		
		Manchester Central		
		Stalybridge Celtic		
Obrey, Alfred (Alf)			CH	
b Soke-on-Trent 3/6/1912			d 1986	
		Longton		
1936	1937	Port Vale	45	1
1938		Tranmere Rovers	17	
1939		(Tranmere Rovers)	(3)	
O'Brien, Joseph (Joe)			OL/IL	
1893		Ardwick	2	
1893	1894	Walsall Town Swifts	34	9
O'Brien, Joseph (Joe)			RB/LB	
b Shettleston 27/12/1875				
		Baillieston Thistle		
		Clitheroe		
		Sheffield		
		Reading		
1899	1900	Blackburn Rovers	3	
		Aberdeen		
		Swindon Town		
		Reading		
		Brighton & Hove Albion		
		Swindon Town		
		Stalybridge Rovers		
		Haslingden		

From To Apps Goal

O'Brien, Michael Terrence (Mick) CH/LH
b Kilcock 10/8/1893 d 1940
Caps: Ireland 10/Eire 4
Walker Celtic
Wallsend
Blyth Spartans
Newcastle East End
Celtic
Alloa Athletic (trial)
Brentford
Norwich City
1919 South Shields 3
1920 1921 Queen's Park Rangers 66 3
1921 1923 Leicester City 65 6
1924 1925 Hull City 74
Brooklyn Wanderers
1926 1927 Derby County 3
1928 Walsall 34
1929 1930 Norwich City 64 5
1931 1932 Watford 62 5

O'Brien, Patrick (Paddy) IL
b Glasgow 6/1873 d 1950
Elm Park (Glasgow)
Glasgow Northern
1894 1896 Woolwich Arsenal 63 27
1901 Bristol City 8 7
Swindon Town

O'Brien, Patrick G RB
b Edinburgh 1873
Broxburn Shamrock
Hibernian
Middlesbrough Ironopolis
1894 Sheffield United 0
1894 Newcastle United 9 2
Hebburn Argyle

O'Brien, Richard OL
b Dundee 1886
Leith Athletic
1911 1913 Stockport County 69 10

O'Brien, Ronald Victor (Vic) RB/RH/IL
b Coventry 1/5/1909 d 1997
Morris Motor Works
1930 1933 Coventry City 57 3
1934 1945 Watford 179 9
1939 (Watford) (3)
Bedworth Town

O'Brien, W George OL
1900 Everton 0
1901 Newton Heath 1

O'Brien, William IL/CH
b Glasgow
St Anthony's (Glasgow)
1936 1937 Bournemouth & Boscombe Ath 16 5
1938 Port Vale 4 1

O'Callaghan, Eugene (Taffy) IR/IL
b Ebbw Vale 6/10/1906 d 1956
Caps: Wales Sch/Wales 11
Victoria United
Ebbw Vale Corinthians
1925 Tottenham Hotspur 0
Barnet (loan)
Northfleet (loan)
1926 1934 Tottenham Hotspur 252 92
1934 1937 Leicester City 84 30
1937 1938 Fulham 39 6
1939 (Fulham) (2)

Occleshaw, Richard Henry GK
b Crewe 24/4/1900 d 1974
1923 Crewe Alexandra 1

O'Connell, Patrick Joseph (Pat) CH
b Dublin 8/3/1887 d 1959
Caps: Ireland 5
Frankfort (Dublin)
Strandville
Belfast Celtic
1908 1911 Sheffield Wednesday 18
1912 1913 Hull City 58 1
1914 Manchester United 34 2
Dumbarton
1921 Ashington 19 1

O'Connor, Francis Raymond (Frank) RH
b Jarrow 28/1/1913 d 1980
Jarrow
1936 Portsmouth 0
1937 Mansfield Town 18
1938 Darlington 19
Gillingham

O'Connor, James William (Jimmy) OR/IR
b Seaham Harbour 22/7/1917 d 1985
Murton Colliery Welfare
1935 1937 Barrow 14 1
Lancaster City

From To Apps Goal

O'Connor, John Patrick IR/OR
b Wolverhampton 27/6/1903 d 1986
1924 Wolverhampton Wanderers 11 2
1926 Gillingham 0
1927 Tranmere Rovers 2
1927 Darlington 1
1927 Crewe Alexandra 2 1
Flint Town
Darlaston

O'Connor, P CF
1896 Blackpool 4 1

Odell, George William LH/CH
b Hoddesdon 16/1/1901 d 1971
St Albans City
1927 1931 Northampton Town 147 11
Wigan Athletic
1934 Newport County 24

O'Dell, Joseph GK
b Nottingham 1890
Stapleford Rangers
1911 Gainsborough Trinity 1

Odell, Leslie Frank RB/LB
b Sandy q1 1903 d 1955
Biggleswade Town
1923 Luton Town 0
1924 1935 Chelsea 101 7

Odell, Walter Reginald LH
b Biggleswade 19/3/1912 d 1971
Sandy Albion
Biggleswade Town
Hitchin Town
1935 Tottenham Hotspur 0
Northfleet (loan)
1937 1938 Wrexham 61
1939 Darlington (3) (2)

Odenrode, Harold OR
b Ardwick 4/7/1903 d 1973
Ashton National
1926 1927 Stockport County 20 6
Witton Albion

Odhams, James Richard GK
b Hartlepool 3/11/1910 d 1984
Christ Church (Hartlepool)
1933 Hartlepools United 1
Murton Colliery Welfare

O'Doherty, Eugene FJ IL
b Ballaghaderreen 1896
1919 Blackpool 1
1920 Leeds United 0
Fleetwood
Wigan Borough
Ashton National
1922 Halifax Town 0
1922 Blackpool 1
1923 Walsall 18 2
Morecambe
Clitheroe

O'Donnell, Dennis IR/OR/CF
b Willington Quay q1 1880 d 1939
Willington Athletic
1901 1904 Lincoln City 118 31
1905 Sunderland 21 5
Queen's Park Rangers
1907 Notts County 18 4
1908 Bradford Park Avenue 10 1
North Shields Athletic

O'Donnell, Francis Joseph (Frank) CF/IL
b Buckhaven 31/8/1911 d 1952
Caps: Scotland 6
Denbeath Violet Juveniles
Wellesley Juniors
Celtic
1935 1937 Preston North End 92 36
1937 1938 Blackpool 30 17
1938 Aston Villa 29 14
1939 (Aston Villa) (3)
1946 Nottingham Forest 11 5
Buxton

O'Donnell, Hugh OL
b Buckhaven 15/2/1913 d 1965
Denbeath Violet Juveniles
Wellesley Juniors
Blantyre Victoria
Celtic
1935 1938 Preston North End 132 29
1938 1946 Blackpool 10 2
1939 (Blackpool) (3)
1946 1947 Rochdale 40 14
1947 1948 Halifax Town 13 1

From To Apps Goal

O'Donnell, John (Jack) LB/IL
b Gateshead 25/3/1897 d 1967
Felling Colliery
1923 1924 Darlington 30
1924 1929 Everton 188 10
1930 1931 Blackpool 55
1932 Hartlepools United 28 2
Wigan Athletic
Dolphin
Clitheroe
Wardley Welfare
West Stanley

O'Donnell, Magnus IL
b Willington Quay q4 1882
Wallsend Park Villa
1904 1905 Lincoln City 45 11
1906 Barnsley 19 4
Newark Town
Grantham Avenue
Castleford Town

O'Donnell, Rudolph Peter (Peter) GK
b Madras, India 8/1888 d 1961
Army
Shepherds Bush
Hanwell
Reading
1909 Fulham (loan) 3

O'Donnell, William James RB/OL/LB
b Felling q2 1908 d 1968
1927 Darlington 4
Connah's Quay & Shotton
1929 Everton 0
1930 Bury 0
1930 Stockport County 0
Felling Colliery
1931 Blackpool 0
Boston Town
1932 1934 Gateshead 61 1
Spennymoor United
West Stanley

O'Dowd, James Peter (Peter) CH/LH
b Halifax 26/2/1908 d 1964
Caps: FLge 1/England 3
Selby Town
1926 Bradford Park Avenue 0
1927 1929 Blackburn Rovers 50
1929 1931 Burnley 65 8
1931 1933 Chelsea 80
Valenciennes
1936 1937 Torquay United 7

O'Gara, James (Jimmy) IL
b Maryhill 1888
Airdrieonians
1907 Middlesbrough 0
Airdrieonians
1908 Clapton Orient 1
1909 Preston North End (trial) 0
Dundee Hibernian
Portsmouth

Ogden, Arthur IR/IL/CF
b Burnley
1906 1909 Burnley 45 12
Bacup

Ogden, Harold (Harry) RH
1922 Accrington Stanley 1

Ogden, Robert RH/RB
b Cheadle q1 1897
Cheadle
1922 1924 Bury 6 1
Flint

Ogden, William IL
1897 Gainsborough Trinity 5 3

Ogilvie, Adam GK/LH
b Scotland 1867
Forfar Athletic
1892 Grimsby Town 21
1893 1896 Blackburn Rovers 108
Shrewsbury Town

Ogilvie, Duncan Henderson OR
b Glasgow 8/10/1911 d 1970
Caps: Scotland 1
St Ninian's Thistle
Alva Albion Rovers
Motherwell
1935 1936 Huddersfield Town 28 4
Motherwell
Hamilton Academical
Dundee United

Ogilvie, Harold GK
b Carlisle 1909
1938 Carlisle United 2

Ogle, HE GK
1898 Gainsborough Trinity 6

From To Apps Goal

Ogle, Roger LB
b Bedlington 15/9/1904 d 1991
West Allotment Institute
Preston Colliery
Stakeford United
Barrington Colliery Welfare
Bebside Gordon
Shildon
1929 1930 Barnsley 11
1931 Norwich City 1
Netherford United
Stakeford Albion
Bedlington District Pit Welfare

Ogley, William (Bill) LB/LH
b Rotherham 1896
1920 Swansea Town 6 3
Porth
1922 1923 Newport County 39 2
1924 Queen's Park Rangers 36 2
Castleford Town
Denaby United
Denaby Welfare

O'Grady, Henry (Harry) IL/CF/IR
b Tunstall 16/3/1907 d 1990
Nantwich
Witton Albion
1929 Port Vale 1
1931 Southampton 7 2
1932 Leeds United 8 2
1933 Burnley 13 8
1934 Bury 15 4
1935 Millwall 4
1936 Carlisle United 28 9
1937 Accrington Stanley 23 2
Tunbridge Wells Rangers

O'Hagan, Charles (Charlie) IL
b Buncrana 28/7/1881 d 1931
Caps: Ireland 11
St Columb's College
Derry Celtic
Old Xavierans
1902 Everton 0
Tottenham Hotspur
1906 Middlesbrough 5 1
Aberdeen
Morton
Third Lanark

O'Hagan, William (Billy) GK
b Buncrana 8/8/1890 d 1972
Caps: Ireland 2
St Columb's College
Londonderry Guild
Derry Celtic
St Mirren
Third Lanark (loan)
Linfield (loan)
Airdrieonians
1921 1922 Norwich City 53
Fordsons
1924 Aberdare Athletic 3
Fordsons

O'Hara, Francis (Pat) IL
b Coatbridge
Albion Rovers
1905 Chelsea 1

O'Hare, John RB
b Armadale
Shawfield Juniors
1933 1938 Chelsea 102

O'Hare, William IL
b Hamilton 27/6/1904
Dalkeith Thistle
Dundee
St Mirren (loan)
1931 Portsmouth 1
Brechin City

O'Kane, Joseph (Joe) IR/IL
b Milngavie 12/1/1896
Maryhill Juniors
Celtic
Clydebank (loan)
Clydebank (loan)
Clydebank (loan)
Clyde (loan)
Airdrieonians (loan)
Stevenston United (loan)
1920 Stockport County (loan) 0
Stevenston United (loan)
1921 Stockport County (loan) 16 12
1922 Stalybridge Celtic (loan) 23 5
Dundee United (loan)
Dundee United (loan)
Arthurlie (loan)
Helensburgh

From To Apps Goal

Oldacre, Percy IR/CF
b Stoke-on-Trent 25/10/1892 d 1970
Stoke
Exeter City
Castleford Town
1921 1922 Sheffield United 6 5
1923 Halifax Town 8 1
1924 Crewe Alexandra 25 12
Mid-Rhondda United
Shrewsbury Town
1926 Port Vale 1
Hurst

Oldershaw, Harry James OL
b Basford q4 1898
Notts Magdala Amateurs
1921 Notts County 1
Boston Town
West Norwood

Oldershaw, Walter (Wally) LB
b Walsall 1867
Walsall Alma
1889 Wolverhampton Wanderers 1
Wednesbury Town

Oldfield, John Thomas (Tommy) CH
b Grimesthorpe 15/3/1908 d 1992
Cammell Laird
Grimethorpe Wesleyan Reform
Attercliffe
Bridlington
Norton Woodseats
1927 Halifax Town (trial) 0
1928 Southport 3
1929 Lincoln City (trial) 0
Stourbridge
Sheffield City Police

Oldham, George LB
b Tintwistle 20/4/1920 d 1993
Mottram Central
1938 Stoke City 2
1946 1947 Newport County 63
Hitchin Town

Oldham, Wilfred CF
b Accrington 1879
1898 1899 Everton 22 11
1900 Blackburn Rovers 9 1
Padiham
Oswaldtwistle Rovers

Oliver, Alfred OL
b Bangor 15/9/1882 d 1963
Caps: Wales 2
Beaumaris Town
Bangor City
1904 Blackburn Rovers 2
Bangor City
Llandegfen

Oliver, Ellison Douglas (Dougie) LB
b Ashington 9/9/1906 d 1992
Alnwick United
1929 1930 Rochdale 46
Guildford City

Oliver, Frank IL/CF
b Southampton
Brentford
1905 Everton 4 4
1906 1912 Clapton Orient 38 10
Southport Central
1912 Clapton Orient 1

Oliver, Frederick (Fred) IR
Shildon
1936 Aldershot 2
City of Durham
1937 Gateshead 0

Oliver, Harold CF
b Holloway
Great Eastern Rovers
1909 Woolwich Arsenal 1

Oliver, Harold Sidney M LB
b Birmingham 1863
Small Heath Alliance
1888 West Bromwich Albion 1
Small Heath

Oliver, Henry Spoors (Harry) CH/LB
b Sunderland 16/2/1921 d 1994
Caps: England Sch
Houghton Colliery Welfare
1937 Hartlepools United 9
1945 1947 Brentford 18
1948 1951 Watford 122 2
Canterbury City

From To Apps Goal

Oliver, John LB/CH
b Gateshead 1915
1933 Gateshead 0
Walker Celtic
1934 Stoke City 0
Spennymoor United
1935 1936 Burnley 3

Oliver, John Sidney (Sid) LB
b Southwick, County Durham 1867
Southwick (Co Durham)
1890 1891 Sunderland 22
1893 Middlesbrough Ironopolis 21
1894 1895 Small Heath 57
Durham

Oliver, Leonard Frederick (Len) RH
b Fulham 1/8/1905 d 1967
Caps: England 1
Alma Athletic
Tufnell Park
1924 1934 Fulham 406 3

Oliver, William OL
b Walthamstow 9/1892
1908 Tottenham Hotspur 0
Walthamstow Grange
1913 Tottenham Hotspur 2

Ollerenshaw, Ernest GK
b Hollingworth 11/4/1893 d 1965
1919 Manchester City 0
1920 Gillingham 1

Ollis, William (Billy) RH
b Birmingham 12/8/1871 d 1940
Newall Juniors
Southfield
Warwickshire County
1892 1895 Small Heath 99 2
Hereford Thistle

Olney, Benjamin Albert (Ben) GK
b Holborn 30/3/1899 d 1943
Caps: England 2
Fairleys Athletic
Aston Park Rangers
Stourbridge
1920 1927 Derby County 223
1927 1929 Aston Villa 84
Bilston United
1931 Walsall 3
Shrewsbury Town
Moor Green

Olney, James Ferd (Jim) LH/CH
b Aston 1/8/1914 d 1944
Redditch Town
1935 1936 Birmingham 3
1938 Swindon Town 10
1939 (Swindon Town) (3)

Olsen, Thomas Bernard (Tommy) IL/OL
b Tir Phil 13/1/1913 d 1969
Caps: Wales Sch/ WLge 1
New Tredegar
1931 1938 Swansea Town 194 50
1939 Bury 0

Olver, William Edward (Bill) IL
b Launceston 4/3/1918
Launceston
1938 Plymouth Argyle 2
St Austell

O'Mahony, Matthew Augustine (Matt) CH
b Mullinavat 19/1/1913 d 1992
Caps: Ireland 1/Eire 6
1933 Liverpool 0
1933 New Brighton 0
Hoylake
1934 Southport 12
1935 Wolverhampton Wanderers 0
1935 Newport County 8
1936 1938 Bristol Rovers 101 6
1939 1948 Ipswich Town 58 4
1939 (Ipswich Town) (3)
Yarmouth Town

O'Neil, John OR
b Coatbridge 26/4/1913 d 1992
Heart of Midlothian
East Stirlingshire
1935 Barrow 1

O'Neill, Harry CF
Earle
Runcorn
1931 Cardiff City 9 2
Young Boys Berne
Red Star 93 (Paris)
Hurst
1937 Stockport County 0
Wigan Athletic

From To Apps Goal

O'Neill, Henry (Harry) LB/RB
b Heddon 2/11/1894 d 1971
Wallsend
1919 1921 Sheffield Wednesday 49
1922 Bristol Rovers 17
1923 1927 Swindon Town 26 1

O'Neill, James RH
b Dumfries 26/8/1914
1936 Gateshead 0
1937 Gillingham 8
1938 Notts County 0
1939 Mansfield Town 0

Openshaw, James Eric (Eric) IR
b Droylsden 1/12/1910 d 1996
Taunton (Ashton)
Stalybridge Celtic
1927 Southport 1
Manchester Central
Droylsden
Pendleton Wednesday
Clayton Congregational Institute

Openshaw, William LB
b Manchester 1881 d 1945
Openshaw Clarence
Hooley Hill
1905 1906 Grimsby Town 5
Salford United
Rochdale
Macclesfield
Hurst
Eccles Borough

Oram, David Charles OL
b Ruabon 3/5/1914 d 1991
Druids
1934 1935 Blackpool 28 9
1936 Barnsley 10 1
Burton Town

O'Rawe, Francis (Frank) CH/IR
b Uphall 20/12/1900 d 1970
Bathgate
1923 Preston North End 4
1924 1925 Southend United 71 2
1926 Brighton & Hove Albion 1
Vernon Athletic
Whittaker Ellis Works (London)

Ord, Roger Gillis GK
b Cramlington q2 1871 d 1940
Hebburn Argyle
1893 Middlesbrough Ironopolis 26
Hebburn Argyle
1897 1899 Woolwich Arsenal 89
Luton Town
Wellingborough
Wellingborough Rodwell Stars

Ordish, Cyril Stanley LB/RB
b Chesterfield 23/5/1915 d 2007
Blackwell
1934 Chesterfield 1
1936 1937 Wolverhampton Wanderers 2
1937 1938 Reading 21

O'Reilly, John (Jack) OR
b Cobh 7/5/1914
Caps: LoI 5/Eire 20
Cork Bohemians
Cobh Wanderers
Cobh Ramblers
St Mary's (Cork)
Cork FC
1936 1938 Norwich City 33 11
Cork United
Cork Athletic

Orford, Charles Henry LH
b Hackney 12/1/1899 d 1977
1924 Gillingham 1

Ormandy, John (Jack) OL
b Knotty Ash 25/1/1912 d 1997
Prescot Cables
1932 1935 Bradford City 63 9
1936 1938 Bury 87 18
1939 Southend United (3) (1)
1946 Oldham Athletic 30 5
1947 Halifax Town 7

From To Apps Goal

Orme, Joseph Henry GK
b Staveley 8/11/1884 d 1935
Clay Cross Zingari
New Tupton Ivanhoe
Clay Cross Zingari
North Wingfield Red Rose
Chesterfield Town
Pinxton Colliery
Watford
Millwall Athletic
Ilkeston United
1919 1920 Nottingham Forest 11
Heanor Town
Shirebrook
Butterley Company Works

Ormiston, Andrew Paisley CH/LH
b Peebles 1/3/1884 d 1952
Peebles Rovers
Hebburn Argyle
1907 Lincoln City 24 2
1909 1913 Chelsea 95 1
1919 Lincoln City 20
Peebles Rovers

Ormston, Alexander (Alec) OL/IL/OR
b Stoke-on-Trent 10/2/1919 d 1975
Caps: NIRL 1/FLge 3
Summerbank
1937 1951 Stoke City 172 29
Linfield (loan)
Hereford United
Stafford Rangers

Ormston, Arthur CF
b Alnwick 3/6/1900 d 1947
Radcliffe United (Ashington)
1920 South Shields 0
1921 Chesterfield 22 6
1922 Durham City 16 2
1922 Coventry City 2
1923 Barrow 32 10
1923 1924 Wigan Borough 19 5
1925 1926 Oldham Athletic 40 22
1926 Bradford City 14 6
1927 1928 Bristol Rovers 27 15
1928 Oldham Athletic 3
Tunbridge Wells Rangers
Blyth Spartans
Stalybridge Celtic
Macclesfield

O'Rourke, Frank CF
b Bargeddie 5/12/1878 d 1954
Caps: Scotland 1
Kirkwood Juniors (Bargeddie)
Airdrieonians
Albion Rovers
Airdrieonians
1906 1914 Bradford City 192 88

O'Rourke, Harry RH
Bathgate
1908 Bradford Park Avenue 11

O'Rourke, James IR/LB
b Farnworth 28/12/1912 d 1986
1934 Bury 16 8
1935 1938 Northampton Town 14 1

O'Rourke, John CF
Willington Athletic
1900 Derby County 5

O'Rourke, Peter CH/RH
b Newmilns 22/9/1874 d 1956
Mossend Celtic
Hibernian (trial)
Celtic
New Brighton Tower
1897 1898 Burnley 18 1
1899 Lincoln City 32
Third Lanark
1901 1902 Chesterfield Town 39 1
1903 1905 Bradford City 43 1

O'Rourke, Peter IL
b Newmains 14/3/1903 d 1990
Dundee Hibernian
1924 Bradford Park Avenue 3 2
1925 Northampton Town 2
1926 Norwich City 0

Orpe, Thomas OR
b Hanley q3 1897
1922 Port Vale 8 2

Orr, Albert IR/OL/OR
b Eccles 5/9/1904 d 1974
Manchester Central
1928 1930 Rotherham United 89 24
1931 Chesterfield 0
1932 1933 Torquay United 68 7
1934 Gillingham 12
Stalybridge Celtic
Mossley

From To Apps Goal

Orr, James LB
b Dalry 24/7/1871 d 1942
Caps: Scotland 1
Kilmarnock Winton
Kilmarnock Roslyn
Kilmarnock Shawbank
Kilmarnock Athletic
Kilmarnock
1892 1894 Darwen 77 3
Celtic
Kilmarnock Athletic
Galston

Orr, John OL
1890 Accrington 2

Orr, John (Johnny) IR/CF
b Leith 1888
1907 1919 Blackburn Rovers 75 30

Orr, John GK
b Kilbirnie
Kilwinning Rangers
1923 Luton Town 9
Dunfermline Athletic

Orr, Robert John LB
b Hardgate 1888
Caps: SLge 2
Clydebank Juniors
Third Lanark
Morton
1926 1927 Crystal Palace 70 2
Dumbarton
Clydebank

Orr, Ronald IL/IR
b Bartonholm 6/8/1880 d 1924
Caps: Scotland 2
Kilwinning Eglinton
St Mirren
1901 1907 Newcastle United 160 61
1907 1911 Liverpool 108 35
Raith Rovers
South Shields

Orr, W CF
1889 Everton 1 1

Orr, William (Willie) LH
b Shotts 20/6/1873 d 1946
Caps: Scotland 3
Airdrie Fruitfield
Airdrieonians
1894 1896 Preston North End 62 3
Celtic

Orr, William (Willie) RB/LB
b Ayrshire 1875 d 1912
Ayr Parkhouse
1898 1900 Glossop North End 39
1901 1902 Manchester City 36
Fulham
1904 1905 Glossop 61
Watford
1907 Glossop 0

Orrell, Richard LB/RB
b Farington q4 1875 d 1919
1899 1905 Preston North End 140
Southport Central
Great Harwood
Higher Walton Albion
Great Harwood

Orrell, Roland CH
b Oldham 14/12/1896 d 1950
Hey Institute
1921 Southport 3
Hurst
Wesleyan Central Mission

Orrick, George OL
b Sunderland 10/7/1905 d 1989
1927 Torquay United 3
1927 Bristol City (trial) 0
Shiney Row Swifts
Easington Colliery Welfare

Orton, Richard William (Dick) CF
b London
1905 Clapton Orient 8 1

Osborn, Frederick (Freddie) CF/IL/IR
b Leicester 10/11/1889 d 1954
Avondale
Hinckley United
1910 1912 Leicester Fosse 67 29
1913 1919 Preston North End 68 40
Nuneaton Town

Osborne, Albert E LH
1910 1911 Bristol City 2

From To Apps Goal

Osborne, Archibald W (Archie) RH
b Lanarkshire 1869 b 1913
Vale of Leven Athletic
Vale of Leven
1890 1893 Notts County 46 1
Clyde

Osborne, Charles Henry LH
b Lincoln q1 1873
Adelaide (Lincoln)
1894 Lincoln City 6
Sheppey United

Osborne, E LH
1892 Crewe Alexandra 12

Osborne, Ernest OL
b Wolverhampton 12/5/1899 d 1958
Evesham Town
1923 1925 Crystal Palace 30 3
1926 Lincoln City 0

Osborne, Fergus IR
b Shotts 1875
Dykehead
1899 Middlesbrough 12 2

Osborne, Frank Raymond CF/IR/OR
b Wynberg, South Africa 14/10/1896 d 1988
Caps: England 4
Netley
Bromley
1921 1923 Fulham 67 18
1923 1930 Tottenham Hotspur 210 78
1931 1932 Southampton 17

Osborne, Harold OR
b Wynberg, South Africa 2/4/1904 d 1973
Chelmsford Town
1924 Norwich City 1

Osborne, John (Johnny) IL/LH
b Renfrew 14/10/1919 d 1981
Linwood Thistle
1939 1945 Leicester City (1)
1947 1948 Watford 34 12
Brush Sports
Rugby Town
Jones & Shipman

Osborne, John Edward (Jackie) LB
b Dundee 24/4/1902 d 1968
Lochee Central
Dundee United
Forfar Athletic
1928 Brighton & Hove Albion 3
Brechin City
Morton
1932 Norwich City (trial) 0
Forfar Athletic

Osborne, Reginald (Reg) LB
b Wynberg, South Africa 23/7/1898 d 1977
Caps: England Amat/England 1
RAMC
Bromley
Watling Street Boot Company
1922 1932 Leicester City 240 2
Folkestone

Osman, Harold James (Harry) OL
b Bentworth 29/1/1911 d 1998
Poole Town
1935 1936 Plymouth Argyle 5
1937 1938 Southampton 70 31
1938 1947 Millwall 35 3
1939 (Millwall) (2)
1947 Bristol City 18 1
Dartford

Osmond, Joseph Edward (Joe) RB/LB
b Seaham q2 1892 d 1955
Sunderland West End
1919 1922 Clapton Orient 50
1924 Hartlepools United 1

Ostick, Charles (Charlie) RB/LB
b Chorley q2 1875 d 1954
Chorley
1900 1905 Bolton Wanderers 84

Ostler, John (Jack) CH/IL
b Newarthill 1873 d 1958
Motherwell
1894 Bury 15 6
Motherwell
1896 1899 Newcastle United 67 3
1899 Middlesbrough (loan) 3

From To Apps Goal

Oswald, James (Jimmy) CF
b Greenock 3/1/1868 d 1948
Caps: SLge 3/Scotland 3
Clydebank
Govan Hill
Kilbirnie
Third Lanark
1889 1892 Notts County 95 55
St Bernard's
Rangers
Leith Athletic
Morton
Leith Athletic
Raith Rovers
Morton
Raith Rovers
Leith Athletic

Oswald, John IL/OR
b Greenock 1870
Third Lanark
1889 Notts County 22 6
1890 Burnley 15 1
Sunderland Albion

Oswald, Robert Ray Broome (Bert) OL
b Bo'ness 20/12/1904 d 1961
Linlithgow Rose
Heart of Midlothian
East Stirlingshire
Bo'ness
1928 1929 Reading 82 15
1930 1933 Sheffield United 106 23
1934 1938 Southend United 123 21

Oswald, William (Willie) CF/OR/IL
b Dundee 3/8/1900
Dundee Celtic
Dundee Hibernian (trial)
1922 Gillingham 13 3
St Johnstone
Dundee United
1926 1927 Brighton & Hove Albion 14 2
Providence Gold Bugs
Fall River FC
New York Yankees

Ottewell, Sidney (Sid) IL/IR/CF
b Horsley, Derbyshire 23/10/1919 d 2012
Holbrook Colliery Welfare
1936 1946 Chesterfield 42 12
1947 Birmingham City 5 2
1947 Luton Town 15 4
1948 1949 Nottingham Forest 32 3
1949 1951 Mansfield Town 67 21
1951 1952 Scunthorpe United 30 12
Whitstable Town
Spalding United
Heanor Town

Ouchterlonie, William Wood Mitchell CF/OR
b Dundee 29/12/1912 d 1984
Dundee Osborne
Raith Rovers (trial)
Dundee United
Raith Rovers
Portadown
Reds United (Dublin)
1936 Barrow 32 22
1937 Wrexham 3
Lochee Harp

Ovenstone, David Guthrie (Davie) OL
b St Monance 17/6/1913 d 1983
St Monance Swifts
Rosslyn Juniors
Raith Rovers
1934 Bristol Rovers 0
1935 Queen's Park Rangers 15 3
1936 Cardiff City 21 4
1937 Watford 1
1937 Southport 8 3
Barry
Ebbw Vale
Broughty Ex-Service Club
Forthill Athletic

Overend, Alexander (Alex) OR
b Paisley 14/1/1889 d 1961
Overend Victoria
Petershill
1912 Fulham 3

Owbridge, Charles Richard (Charlie) GK
b Hartlepool 7/3/1907 d 1989
Belle Vue Congregationalists
1931 1932 Hartlepools United 19
Trimdon Grange Colliery
St Oswald's (Hartlepool)

Owen, Alfred Arthur (Arthur) LB/LH
b Hoylake q2 1914
Hoylake
1936 1938 Tranmere Rovers 11
1939 (Tranmere Rovers) (3)
1939 Everton 0

From To Apps Goal

Owen, Alfred George OR
b Coalbrookdale 1880
Ironbridge
1903 1904 West Bromwich Albion 7 1
Walsall
Hereford Town
Rook End

Owen, Alfred Sydney (Syd) OL/IL
b Newcastle-under-Lyme q3 1885 d 1925
Caps: England Amat
North Staffs Nomads
Newcastle Town
Northern Nomads
1906 Stoke 1
1907 Stockport County 1
Burslem Port Vale
1907 Everton 0
1907 Stoke 5 4
Burslem Port Vale
1908 1910 Leicester Fosse 43 12
Northern Nomads
1911 Blackpool 2
Stoke

Owen, Clifford Lewis (Cliff) GK
b Barry 12/6/1908 d 2002
Barry
1934 Charlton Athletic 0
1935 1937 Halifax Town 102
1938 Chester 21
1939 Accrington Stanley (3)

Owen, David CH
1891 1893 Darwen 25

Owen, G OL
1888 Bolton Wanderers 7 3

Owen, Griffith Lawrence CF
b Liverpool 28/7/1897 d 1949
1923 Liverpool 0
1924 Hull City 2
Chester
1926 Rochdale 3
Flint Town
Liverpool Electric Cables

Owen, Hugh Glendwr Palmer GK
b Bath 19/5/1859 d 1912
Corpus Christi College
1888 Notts County 1
Nottingham Forest

Owen, James (Jimmy) CF
b Manchester 1864
Newton Heath
1889 Stoke 3 2
Newton Heath

Owen, James (Jimmy) IL
b Salford 1905
1924 1930 Crewe Alexandra 138 50
1931 Chester 0

Owen, John Russell (Jackie) IR/IL/CF
b Busby 1881 d 1924
Rutherglen Victoria
Leven Victoria
Hibernian
Aberdeen (loan)
1903 Barnsley 1
Morton
1905 1906 Barnsley 33 13
1906 1910 Bolton Wanderers 90 19
Chorley

Owen, Llewellyn Tudor GK
b Shrewsbury 16/12/1899 d 1988
1931 Crewe Alexandra 3

Owen, Trevor IR
b Llangollen 5/1873 d 1930
Caps: Wales 2
Wrexham
Druids
Crewe Alexandra
1899 Wolverhampton Wanderers 11 3

Owen, W OR
Holywell
1898 Newton Heath 1

Owen, William (Billy) CH/LH
b Brierley Hill 1869
Loughborough
1893 Wolverhampton Wanderers 18 3
Loughborough
1895 1897 Wolverhampton Wanderers 88 4
1898 Everton 13 3

From	To	Club	Apps	Goal
Owen, William			GK	
b Coventry 1906				
		Nuneaton Town		
1926		Birmingham	5	
1927		Fulham	0	
1930		Coventry City	5	
		Nuneaton Town		
		Stourbridge		
Owen, William (Billy)			OL	
b Northwich 17/9/1906			d 1981	
		Northwich Victoria		
		Macclesfield		
1934	1935	Manchester United	17	1
1935	1936	Reading	23	2
1936		Exeter City	24	6
1937	1938	Newport County	36	2
1939		(Newport County)	(3)	
Owen, William (Billy)			RH/CF	
b Llanfairfechan 30/6/1914			d 1976	
		Northwich Victoria		
1935		Manchester City	9	3
1935		Tranmere Rovers	6	4
1936	1946	Newport County	69	5
1939		(Newport County)	(3)	
1946		Exeter City	20	9
		Barry Town		
		Dartmouth United		
Owencroft, George Edward			OL	
b Prestwich 30/4/1911			d 1986	
		The Dragons (Colwyn Bay)		
		Llanfairfechan		
		Colwyn Bay United		
1931		Reading	0	
1932		Barnsley	5	2
1933		Southport	9	2
		Macclesfield		
Owens, Edward (Tussy)			RB/CF	
b Trimdon Grange 7/11/1913			d 1986	
		Trimdon St Mary's		
1928		Northampton Town (trial)	0	
1929		Stockport County	0	
1930	1933	Preston North End	19	7
1934	1938	Crystal Palace	165	
1939		(Crystal Palace)	(3)	
		Bath City		
Owens, Isaac (Ikey)			IL/CF	
b Darlington 1881				
		Darlington		
		Bishop Auckland		
		Crook Town		
1901		Woolwich Arsenal	9	2
		Darlington		
		Plymouth Argyle		
		Bristol Rovers		
		Crystal Palace		
1908		Grimsby Town	6	3
		Darlington		
Owens, John Reginald (Reg)			IR	
b Liverpool q1 1890			d 1967	
		Tranmere Rovers		
		Pontypridd		
1921		Rochdale	14	7
Owens, Maldwyn			OR	
b Pontypridd 24/11/1903			d 1982	
1932		Torquay United	1	
Owens, Patrick			LB	
1938		Stockport County	20	
1939		(Stockport County)	(2)	
Owens, Richard			IL	
b Hartlepool 1915				
		Dawdon Recreation		
		Trimdon Grange		
1935		Barrow (trial)	0	
1935		Hartlepools United	1	
1936		Southport	0	
Owens, Thomas Leslie (Les)			CF/IR	
b Monkwearmouth 17/10/1919			d 1974	
		Hylton Colliery Juniors		
		Ditchburn Social Club		
		Washington Chemical Works		
1937	1938	Charlton Athletic	12	5
1938	1947	Doncaster Rovers	21	11
1939		(Doncaster Rovers)	(1)	
1947	1948	Southport	53	11
1949		Hartlepools United	28	12
1949	1950	Norwich City	20	8
1951		Reading	8	4
1952		Brighton & Hove Albion	15	4
		Dartford		
		Hellesdon		

From	To	Club	Apps	Goal
Owers, Ebenezer Fuller			CF	
b Leytonstone 21/10/1888			d 1964	
		Bashford		
		Leytonstone		
		Leyton		
1907		Blackpool	9	3
1907		West Bromwich Albion	4	
1908		Chesterfield Town	15	3
		Darlington		
1910	1912	Bristol City	62	32
		Clyde		
		Celtic (loan)		
Oxberry, John (Jack)			IL/CF/IR	
b Sunderland 4/4/1901			d 1962	
		Boldon Colliery Welfare		
1919	1927	South Shields	170	63
1927	1931	Blackpool	74	20
1932	1934	Reading	87	24
1935		Aldershot	14	1
		Ashington		
Oxley, Albert			IL	
b Gateshead 21/10/1915			d 1994	
		Windy Nook		
1934	1946	Gateshead	120	25
Oxley, Bernard			OR/IR/CF	
b Whitwell 16/6/1907			d 1975	
		Whitwell Old Boys		
1925	1927	Chesterfield	37	10
1928	1933	Sheffield United	116	11
1933	1934	Sheffield Wednesday	14	4
1935		Plymouth Argyle	14	
1936	1937	Stockport County	68	10
		Worksop Town		
		Scunthorpe & Lindsey United		
Oxley, Cyril			OR/OL	
b Whitwell 2/5/1904			d 1984	
		Whitwell Old Boys		
		Wombwell		
		Whitwell Colliery		
1923	1925	Chesterfield	31	4
1925		Liverpool	31	6
1928		Southend United	15	6
		Kettering Town		
		Morecambe		
1931		Southend United	0	
Oxley, Richard Lambert (Dick)			OR/OL	
b Barrow 10/4/1893			d 1953	
		Wallsend		
1920		Newcastle United (trial)	0	
1921		Accrington Stanley	33	3
1922		Southport	8	
1923		Queen's Park Rangers	18	
1924		Northampton Town	1	
1926		Crystal Palace	0	
1927		Durham City	0	
		Blyth Spartans		
Oxley, William (Billy)			CF	
b Wallsend 4/12/1899			d 1951	
		Percy Main Amateurs		
		Wallsend		
1923		Middlesbrough	0	
		Willington Quay		
1923		Oldham Athletic (trial)	0	
1924		Rochdale	11	5
1925		Manchester City	0	
1925		Southport	11	1
1926		Merthyr Town (trial)	3	
1926		Northampton Town (trial)	3	1
1926		Durham City	14	15
1927		Wigan Borough	0	
1928		Darlington (trial)	1	1
		Consett		
1929		Carlisle United	1	
		Blyth Spartans		
		Scotswood		
Oxspring, Arnold			LH	
b Ecclesfield 11/10/1877			d 1951	
		Ecclesfield		
		Doncaster Rovers		
1901	1909	Barnsley	271	4
Pace, Arthur			OR	
b Newcastle q4 1885			d 1968	
		Hebburn Argyle		
1908	1909	Hull City	5	
		Rotherham Town		
		Croydon Common		
		Worksop Town		
Pacey, Harold John (Harry)			OR	
b Clophill 2/12/1912			d 1984	
		St Albans City		
1932		Luton Town	4	
		Bedford Town		
Pacey, Herbert Cornelius			LH	
b Nottingham q1 1890			d 1943	
		Beeston Ericssons		
1910	1911	Notts County	3	

From	To	Club	Apps	Goal
Packman, Frederick William (Fred)			OR	
b Birmingham 2/10/1901			d 1974	
		Barnet		
1924	1925	Fulham	5	
1926		Watford	5	
1927		Brighton & Hove Albion (trial)	0	
		Dartford		
		Hendon Garage		
		Cricklewood Garage		
Paddock, John William (William)			OR/OL	
b West Bromwich 1877			d 1928	
1894	1895	West Bromwich Albion	11	4
1896		Walsall	3	
		Brierley Hill Alliance		
1899		West Bromwich Albion	20	1
		Halesowen		
		Brierley Hill Alliance		
		Wellington Town		
1906		Burslem Port Vale	8	3
Padfield, William Albert (Billy)			LB	
b Bishopsworth q2 1885			d 1962	
1910		Bristol City	4	
		Swindon Town		
		Treharris		
		Bath City		
Padgett, Dan			LH	
b Deepcar q2 1871			d 1930	
		Ward Green		
1898		Barnsley	1	
Padgett, John Malcolm (Jack)			OR/IR	
b Ilkeston 30/11/1916			d 1985	
		Townend Juniors		
1937		Bradford City	2	1
1938		Bradford Park Avenue	1	1
		Peterborough United		
Padley, George			CF/IL	
b Grimsby q3 1882			d 1965	
		Albert Swifts		
		Grimsby St John's		
1904	1905	Grimsby Town	14	6
		Grimsby St John's		
		Worksop Town		
		Denaby United		
		Worksop Town		
		Cleethorpes Town		
		Goole Town		
		Cleethorpes Town		
		Grimsby Rovers		
1914		Grimsby Town	4	2
		Steam Trawler Co		
		Charlton's (Grimsby)		
Page, Albert Edward			CH	
b Walthamstow 18/3/1916			d 1995	
		Leyton		
		Colchester Town		
1936	1945	Tottenham Hotspur	55	
1939		(Tottenham Hotspur)	(1)	
		Colchester United		
		Chingford Town		
Page, George			CF	
b London				
		Cheshunt		
		Tottenham Hotspur		
1906		Leeds City	4	
		Redhill		
Page, George			LB	
b Darlington 30/11/1898			d 1931	
		Rise Carr		
		Doncaster Rovers		
1921		Barnsley	1	
1922		Accrington Stanley	31	1
1923		Ashington	36	2
1924	1925	Lincoln City	64	3
1926		Crewe Alexandra	17	1
		York City		
Page, John (Jack)			RB	
b Liverpool 24/3/1886			d 1951	
Caps: WLge 2				
		South Liverpool		
		Rochdale		
1913	1919	Everton	9	
1920	1925	Cardiff City	71	
1926	1928	Merthyr Town	100	1
Page, John Abraham (Jack)			OR	
b Sunderland q1 1893				
		Sunderland West End		
1919		Sunderland	3	
		Sunderland West End		
Page, John Elliot			IR/IL/LH	
b Grays 23/9/1901			d 1979	
1926	1929	Millwall	16	3
1930		Luton Town	4	1
		Chatham Town		

From	To	Club	Apps	Goal
Page, Louis Antonio			OL	
b Kirkdale 27/3/1899			d 1959	
Caps: FLge 1/England 7				
		Sudley Juniors		
		Everton		
		South Liverpool		
1919	1921	Stoke	21	1
1922	1924	Northampton Town	122	24
1925	1931	Burnley	248	111
1931	1932	Manchester United	12	
1932		Port Vale	18	2
		Yeovil & Petters United		
Page, Robert			LH/CH	
b Middlesbrough q1 1878			d 1949	
		Grove Hill		
1899	1904	Middlesbrough	22	2
Page, Samuel			GK	
b Blackheath, Worcestershire 10/6/1901			d 1973	
		Blackheath V		
		Halesowen Town		
1923	1924	Burnley	12	
		St Johnstone		
		Raith Rovers (loan)		
		St Mirren		
		Halesowen Town		
		Willenhall		
		Brierley Hill Alliance		
Page, Thomas (Tom)			IR/IL	
b Kirkdale 15/11/1888			d 1973	
		Canada (Bootle)		
		Selwyn		
		Pembroke (Liverpool)		
1910		Liverpool (trial)	0	
		Rochdale		
1913		Everton	7	2
		St Mirren		
1920	1928	Port Vale	285	59
1929		New Brighton	8	1
		Chorley		
Page, Walter			RH	
1904		Nottingham Forest	1	
Page, William (Willie)			IR	
b Liverpool 17/9/1896			d 1981	
		South Liverpool		
		Rochdale		
1921		Cardiff City	0	
1922		Northampton Town	13	1
		Bideford Town		
Paget, John William			LH	
b Gatley q2 1874			d 1941	
1897		Loughborough	2	
Paget, William Sidney Thomas (Tommy)			IL/OR/IR	
b Cardiff q3 1909			d 1960	
1932	1933	Cardiff City	6	
1934		Newport County	6	
1935		Clapton Orient	0	
		Barry		
Pagnam, Frederick (Fred)			CF/IR/OR	
b Poulton-le-Fylde 4/9/1891			d 1962	
		Lytham		
		Blackpool Wednesday		
1910		Huddersfield Town	0	
		Doncaster Rovers		
		Southport Central		
1912	1913	Blackpool	22	1
		Gainsborough Trinity		
1914	1919	Liverpool	37	28
1919	1920	Arsenal	50	26
1920	1921	Cardiff City	27	8
1921	1926	Watford	144	67
Pailor, Robert (Bob)			CF	
b Stockton 7/7/1887			d 1976	
		St Oswald's (Stockton)		
		West Hartlepool		
		Wingate Albion		
		West Hartlepool		
1908	1913	West Bromwich Albion	79	40
1914		Newcastle United	11	2
Pake, Ralph Robinson			CF	
b Tynemouth q2 1913			d 1942	
1935		Newcastle United	0	
1936		Burnley	5	1
Palethorpe, John Thomas (Jackie)			CF/IL	
b Leicester 23/11/1909			d 1984	
		Maidenhead United		
1929		Crystal Palace	0	
1930	1932	Reading	59	54
1932	1933	Stoke City	21	11
1933	1934	Preston North End	24	15
1934	1935	Sheffield Wednesday	28	13
1935		Aston Villa	6	2
1936	1937	Crystal Palace	39	11
		Chelmsford City		
		Shorts Sports		
		Colchester United		

From	To		Apps	Goal
Palin, Frank			CH	
b Whitwick q2 1876			d 1958	
		Hucknall St John's		
		Hucknall Torkard		
1898		Sheffield United	7	
		Newstead Byron		
		Scarborough		
Pallister, Gordon			LB	
b Howden-le-Wear 2/4/1917			d 1999	
Caps: FLge 1				
		Willington Juniors		
1937	1938	Bradford City	28	
1938	1951	Barnsley	220	3
1939		(Barnsley)	(1)	
Pallister, William			LB	
b Gateshead				
1898		Sunderland	1	
1902	1904	Lincoln City	59	
Palmer, James			OL/LH	
b London				
1919	1920	West Ham United	13	1
		Workington		
Palmer, John Frederick			GK	
1896		Everton	1	
		(London Junior Club)		
1898		Luton Town	1	
Palmer, Ronald W (Ron)			IL/RH	
b Tonbridge q4 1915				
Caps: England Sch				
		Northfleet		
1934	1936	Millwall	31	5
1939	1945	Aldershot	(3)	(1)
Palmer, Walter (Walt)			CF	
b Attercliffe 16/7/1907			d 1985	
		Tinsley Park Sports		
1931		Leeds United	0	
		Worksop Town		
1932		Burnley	0	
1932		Southport	1	
		Shelbourne		
		Woodhouse Albion		
		Tinsley Park Sports		
Palmer, William (Bill)			OL	
b Barnsley q4 1887			d 1955	
		Ardsley Nelson		
1907		Barnsley	0	
		Mexborough Town		
1909		Nottingham Forest	12	1
		Rotherham County		
		Bristol Rovers		
1913	1914	Everton	22	2
1920	1921	Bristol Rovers	43	10
1922		Gillingham	36	5
1923		Doncaster Rovers	2	
Palmer, William			OL	
1921		Durham City	1	
Paltridge, James William (Jim)			LH	
b Plymouth 24/7/1891			d 1980	
		Plymouth Argyle	0	
1921		Chesterfield	29	
		Alfreton Town		
Panes, William Charles Allen (Bill)			RB/LB	
b Bristol 9/10/1887			d 1961	
		Bath City		
1920	1921	Bristol Rovers	73	
		Sneyd Park		
Pangborn, Thomas (Tom)			OR/IL	
b Birmingham q1 1870			d 1926	
		Warwick County		
1892		Walsall Town Swifts	5	1
		Worcester Rovers		
1895		West Bromwich Albion	0	
		Ashton North End		
1896	1897	Bury	23	1
1898		Grimsby Town	3	
		Ashton North End		
		New Brompton		
		Tottenham Hotspur		
		Reading		
		Watford		
Pankhurst, Alfred Dillon			CF	
b Burslem q3 1878			d 1936	
		Smallthorne		
1900		Burslem Port Vale	5	
Panther, Frederick George (Fred)			CF	
b Manchester 4/4/1903			d 1971	
		Celtic (Lincoln)		
1922	1924	Lincoln City	15	3
		Newark Town		
		Peterborough & Fletton United		
1926	1927	Luton Town	8	3
1928		Brighton & Hove Albion	0	
		Folkestone		
		Raith Rovers		
Pantling, Harry Harold			RH	
b Leighton Buzzard 16/5/1891			d 1952	
Caps: England 1				
		Callow Land Juniors		
		Watford		
1914	1925	Sheffield United	224	1
1926		Rotherham United	12	
		Heanor Town		
Pape, Albert Arthur			CF	
b Elsecar 13/7/1897			d 1955	
		Wath Athletic		
		Yorkshire Light Infantry		
		Bolton-on-Dearne		
1919	1922	Rotherham County	113	41
1923		Notts County	6	2
1924		Clapton Orient	24	11
1924	1925	Manchester United	18	5
1925	1926	Fulham	42	12
		Rhyl Athletic		
		Hurst		
		Darwen		
		Manchester Central		
1929		Hartlepools United	37	21
1930		Halifax Town	26	15
		Burscough Rangers		
		Horwich RMI		
		Nelson		
Papworth, John Martin (Jack)			CF/CH	
b Deptford 8/11/1895			d 1942	
		St Nicholas (Deptford)		
1919	1924	Fulham	39	16
1924	1925	Watford	27	12
		Dartford		
Parden, Bernard			CF	
b Jump 13/4/1907			d 2005	
		Worksop Town		
1930	1931	Wrexham	12	9
		Rhyl Athletic		
		Denaby United		
Parfitt, George			LB	
b Stone q1 1891			d 1976	
		Newcastle St George's		
1914	1919	Wolverhampton Wanderers	4	
		Cocknage		
Park, John Bluey			OR	
b Douglas Water 7/10/1913			d 2002	
		Douglas Water Thistle		
		Partick Thistle (trial)		
		Hamilton Academical		
		Nithsdale Wanderers (loan)		
1936	1938	Newcastle United	60	11
Park, Oswald (Ossie)			CH	
b Darlington 7/2/1905			d 1957	
		Cockerton		
		Cockerton St Mary's		
		Darlington Railway Athletic		
1925	1930	Newcastle United	42	
		Connah's Quay (loan)		
1931	1933	Northampton Town	75	
1934	1936	Hartlepools United	98	1
		North Shields		
1937		Hartlepools United	6	
		Consett		
Park, W			GK	
1894		Bury	3	
		Horwich		
Park, William			CH/LB	
b Gateshead 13/2/1919			d 1999	
		Felling Red Star		
1938		Blackpool	3	
1946		York City	22	1
		Scarborough		
Parke, J			RH	
b Scotland 1871				
		Jordanhill		
1892		Notts County	1	
Parker, Arthur (Snowy)			RB	
b Cleethorpes q4 1878				
		Grimsby Rovers		
		Humber Rovers		
1897		Grimsby Town	1	
		Humber Rovers		
Parker, Charles William (Charlie)			CH/RH	
b Seaham Harbour 21/9/1891				
Caps: FLge 1				
		Seaham Albion		
		Seaham Harbour		
		Hartlepool BD		
1919	1920	Stoke	43	3
1920	1928	Sunderland	245	12
1929		Carlisle United	9	1
		Blyth Spartans		
		Chopwell Institute		
Parker, Eric			IL	
b Bradford 1/3/1912			d 1976	
		Barrow Grmmar School		
		Vickerstown Athletic		
1930	1933	Barrow	59	13
		Lancaster Town		
Parker, Ernest Simmonds Henry (Ernie)			OL	
b Anerley 18/12/1913			d 1983	
		Anerley Argyle		
		Croydon		
1933		Crystal Palace	2	
1934	1935	Mansfield Town	15	4
1936		Bournemouth & Boscombe Ath	7	
1937		Bristol Rovers	9	1
Parker, Frederick (Fred 'Spider')			OR/IR	
b Weymouth 18/6/1886			d 1963	
		Portland Grove		
		Weymouth		
		Salisbury City		
1907	1921	Clapton Orient	336	34
		Folkestone		
Parker, Frederick (Fred)			CH	
b New Seaham 1893				
		Seaham Young Albion		
		Seaham Harbour		
1914		Manchester City	0	
1919	1925	Nottingham Forest	157	6
1926		Southport	0	
Parker, Gilbert			OR	
b Eccles				
1931		Bristol City	3	
Parker, Harold			RB/LB	
1899	1900	Preston North End	3	
Parker, Harold Earl			OL	
b Penwortham 5/2/1905			d 1975	
		Penwortham St Leonard's		
		Coppull Central		
		Penwortham Amateurs		
1926	1928	Southport	24	3
		Northern Nomads		
		Fulwood Amateurs		
Parker, Henry (Harry)			OR/OL/IL	
b Herrington 1874				
1898	1899	Loughborough	54	4
		Castle Donington		
1901		Glossop	24	3
		Whitwick White Cross		
1903		Lincoln City	30	3
Parker, Henry Clifford (Cliff)			OL	
b Denaby 6/9/1913			d 1983	
		Denaby United		
1931	1933	Doncaster Rovers	52	11
1933	1950	Portsmouth	242	57
1939		(Portsmouth)	(3)	
		Denaby United		
Parker, James			OL	
		Brodsworth Main		
1923		Doncaster Rovers	3	1
		Brodsworth Main		
Parker, James			RH/OR	
b Carlisle 17/5/1914			d 2003	
1934	1935	Carlisle United	2	
Parker, John (Jim)			CH	
b Barrow q4 1884				
		Barrow St Matthew's		
1905	1908	Burnley	32	1
1908	1912	Bradford Park Avenue	80	4
		Barrow		
Parker, John			IR/CF	
b Edgmond q1 1899				
		Shrewsbury Town		
1919		Nottingham Forest	5	
		Tranmere Rovers		
		Shrewsbury Town		
1922	1923	Bristol Rovers	27	6
Parker, John			IR	
		Ashton National		
		Stalybridge Celtic		
1928		New Brighton	38	8
		Rhyl Athletic		
		Stafford Rangers		
		Witton Albion (trial)		
Parker, John Francis (Jack)			CF	
b Ellistown 16/1/1896			d 1973	
		Newhall UM		
		Midway Athletic		
		Royal Field Artillery		
		Newhall Swifts		
1919		Leicester City	5	1
1920		Norwich City	11	2
		Gresley Rovers		
		Burton All Saints		
		Gresley Rovers		
		Newhall United		
		Newhall Swifts		
Parker, John H			CF	
1902		Doncaster Rovers	2	1
Parker, Reginald			CF/IL	
b Willington Quay 8/7/??				
		Boldon Comrades		
1922	1925	Brentford	99	32
1925	1928	South Shields	102	41
1928	1929	Merthyr Town	44	15
		Tunbridge Wells Rangers		
Parker, Reginald William (Reg)			LB	
b Reading q1 1913				
		Tilehurst Wednesday		
1931	1934	Bournemouth & Boscombe Ath	49	
1935		West Ham United	2	
1936		Torquay United	16	
Parker, Richard (Dick)			CF	
b Stockton 14/9/1894			d 1969	
		Norton United		
		Thornaby Corinthians		
		South Bank		
		Stockton		
1919		Sunderland	6	2
1919	1920	Coventry City	26	11
1920		South Shields	9	5
		Wallsend		
1922	1923	Queen's Park Rangers	61	30
1924	1927	Millwall Athletic	88	62
1927		Watford	13	2
1928		Merthyr Town	0	
		Tunbridge Wells Rangers		
Parker, Robert Norris (Bobby)			CF	
b Possilpark 27/3/1891			d 1950	
		Glasgow Ashfield		
		Third Lanark		
		Glasgow Ashfield		
		Rangers		
1913	1920	Everton	84	68
		Rangers (loan)		
		Morton (loan)		
1921	1922	Nottingham Forest	46	11
		Fraserburgh		
Parker, Samuel			IL/IR	
b Riccarton 1872				
		Hurlford		
1893		Newton Heath	11	
1894		Burnley	5	
		Southport Central		
		Hurlford		
		Kilmarnock Athletic		
Parker, Thomas Albert (Albert)			CH	
b Eccles 22/11/1906			d 1964	
		Morton		
1930	1931	Manchester United	17	
1932	1933	Bristol City	54	1
1934		Carlisle United	18	
		Stalybridge Celtic		
Parker, Thomas Blood (Tom)			CH	
b Fenton q2 1893				
		Carr Vale (Sheffield)		
1914		Sheffield Wednesday	0	
		Bolsover Colliery		
1920	1921	Luton Town	36	
1922	1924	Portsmouth	43	1
1925		Wrexham	34	2
Parker, Thomas H			OR	
b Blackrod				
1926		Everton	6	
Parker, Thomas Robert (Tom)			RB	
b Woolston 19/11/1897			d 1987	
Caps: England 1				
		Sholing Rangers		
		Sholing Athletic		
		Woolston St Mark's		
1920	1925	Southampton	206	7
1925	1932	Arsenal	258	17

From	To	Club	Apps	Goal
Parker, William			IR/IL	
1900	1905	Stockport County	30	4
Parker, William			OL	
b St Helen Auckland q1 1889				
		Bishop Auckland		
1910	1911	Gainsborough Trinity	42	2
		Shildon Athletic		
Parker, William David (David)			LB/RB	
b Liverpool 27/5/1915			d 1980	
		Marine		
1937		Hull City	30	
1938		Wolverhampton Wanderers	3	
		South Liverpool		
		Formby		
Parker, William Edwin (Billy)			RH/LH	
b Sheffield 5/4/1880			d 1940	
		Malin Brothers		
1901	1908	Sheffield United	75	2
Parker, William Kirton			OL	
b Jarrow q3 1899				
		Jarrow		
1923		South Shields	8	1
1924		Swindon Town	0	
Parker, William S			OL	
1931		Gillingham	1	
Parker, Wilson			GK	
b Ryton-on-Tyne 11/4/1903				
		Crawcrook Albion		
		Scotswood		
1929	1932	Carlisle United	58	
1932	1938	Bradford City	125	
Parkes, David			CH	
b Lye 17/6/1892			d 1975	
		Newcastle Town		
		Brighton & Hove Albion		
1913	1914	Sheffield Wednesday	39	1
		Stourbridge		
1919		Sheffield Wednesday	8	
1920		Stoke	6	
		Llanelly		
1922	1927	Rochdale	209	11
		Macclesfield		
Parkes, Harold Arnold (Harry)			OR	
b Halesowen 9/1888			d 1947	
		Halesowen Amateurs		
		Coombs Wood		
		Halesowen		
1906	1907	West Bromwich Albion	19	4
		Coventry City		
1914		West Bromwich Albion	8	
		Newport County		
Parkes, Horace Bennett			RB	
b Tipton 14/10/1900			d 1989	
1922		Aston Villa	0	
1923		West Bromwich Albion	0	
1925		Barrow	1	
1926		Arsenal (trial)	0	
		Stafford Rangers		
Parkhouse, Richard McDonald			RB	
b Calne 30/8/1914			d 1992	
		Calne & Harris United		
1935	1946	Swindon Town	27	
1939		(Swindon Town)	(2)	
		Trowbridge Town		
		Cheltenham Town		
Parkin, Albert			CF	
b Wath-on-Dearne				
		Dearne Valley		
1926	1932	Rotherham United	83	45
		Stalybridge Celtic		
		Frickley Colliery		
		Denaby United		
Parkin, Frederick William (Fred)			GK	
b Basford q4 1911				
		Folkestone		
1936		Derby County	1	
1939		Notts County	0	
1945		Lincoln City	0	
		Scarborough		
Parkin, George			LH	
b Hunslet 20/8/1903			d 1971	
1921	1923	Halifax Town	36	
1923	1928	Burnley	125	2
		Chester		
1931		West Ham United	0	
1931		Torquay United	8	
1932		Halifax Town	19	
		Workington		

From	To	Club	Apps	Goal
Parkin, George Henry			CF	
b Pendleton 19/2/1900			d 1967	
		Redpath Brown's		
		Methley		
		West Salford		
1922	1923	Southport	10	3
1923		Tranmere Rovers	0	
		Chester		
		Northwich Victoria		
		Chester		
		Morecambe		
		BOCM		
Parkin, John Turnbull (Jack)			IR/CF	
b Byker 31/7/1900			d 1954	
		Walker Park		
		St Peter's Albion		
		Langley Moor		
		St Peter's Albion		
1924	1926	Durham City	68	20
1927	1928	Accrington Stanley	64	36
1929		Chesterfield	10	1
		Stalybridge Celtic		
Parkin, Raymond (Ray)			IR/RH	
b Crook 28/1/1911			d 1971	
1927		Newcastle United	0	
		Esh Winning		
1928	1935	Arsenal	25	11
1935	1936	Middlesbrough	6	
1937	1938	Southampton	56	10
1939		(Southampton)	(2)	
Parkin, Richard (Dick)			LB	
b Leeds 1886				
		Newton-le-Williams		
		Tranmere Rovers		
1908	1911	Bury	71	
		Tranmere Rovers		
Parkin, Thomas (Tommy)			OL/LH	
b Byker 5/2/1902			d 1984	
		North Shields		
		Wallsend		
		Preston Colliery		
1924		Coventry City	20	2
1925		Durham City	20	2
1926	1927	Exeter City	8	1
1928		Merthyr Town	23	1
		Yeovil & Petters United		
		Weymouth		
Parkinson, H			LH	
1888		Accrington	1	
Parkinson, Henry			LH	
1888		Everton	1	
Parkinson, Henry (Harry)			CF/IR	
b Little Hulton q2 1899			d 1994	
		Breightmet United		
		Altrincham		
1921	1922	Oldham Athletic	3	
		Macclesfield		
		Hazel Grove		
1923		Brentford	7	2
		Lytham		
		Lostock Hall		
		Lytham		
		Morecambe		
		Lytham		
		Ribble Motors		
Parkinson, James			GK/LB	
1888	1890	Bolton Wanderers	22	1
Parkinson, James			IR	
		Blackpool		
1895		Blackburn Rovers	1	
Parkinson, John (Jack)			CF/IL/IR	
b Bootle 13/9/1883			d 1942	
Caps: FLge 3/England 2				
		Hertford Albion		
		Valkyrie		
1903	1913	Liverpool	202	123
1914		Bury	4	3
Parkinson, John A (Jack)			CH/IL/CF	
b Blackpool 1877			d 1911	
		South Shore		
1896	1898	Blackpool	85	29
1899		Liverpool	1	
1900	1908	Blackpool	280	23
		Barrow		
Parkinson, Kenneth (Ken)			GK	
b Esh Winning 21/9/1911			d 1987	
		Esh Winning		
1934		Sheffield Wednesday	0	
		Shrewsbury Town		
1936	1938	Darlington	87	

From	To	Club	Apps	Goal
Parkinson, Robert (Bob)			CF/IL/OR	
b Preston 27/4/1873				
		Preston Ramblers		
		Preston Athletic		
		Fleetwood Rangers		
1894		Rotherham Town	14	4
		Luton Town		
1896		Blackpool	8	1
		Warmley		
1898		Nottingham Forest	2	
1899		Newton Heath	15	7
		Watford		
		Swindon Town		
Parkinson, Tom Oswald (Tot)			IR	
b West Hartlepool 30/4/1899				
		South Durham Iron & Steelworks		
1921	1924	Hartlepools United	60	19
		Shildon		
		Jarrow		
Parkinson, William			OR	
1900		Burnley	2	
Parle, James (Jimmy)			IL/OR/IR	
b Liverpool 7/7/1904			d 1986	
		Bootle Celtic		
1928		Birmingham	0	
1929		Chesterfield	12	1
1930		Walsall	23	1
1931	1932	New Brighton	65	9
1933		Crewe Alexandra (trial)	0	
		Worcester City		
		Yeovil & Petters United		
1935		Newport County	35	9
		Hereford United		
		Bath City		
		Rhyl Athletic		
		Hereford United		
		Wigan Athletic		
		Bangor City		
Parmley, James Smith (Jim)			CF	
b Felling 4/2/1908			d 1984	
		West Stanley		
		South Shields		
1934		Huddersfield Town	0	
1935		Swindon Town	14	9
1936		Darlington	12	4
Parnell, Gershom Frederick (Fred)			OR	
b Sutton-in-Ashfield q4 1883			d 1960	
		Skegby		
		Pinxton		
1903	1904	Derby County	9	
1905	1907	Leeds City	104	15
		Exeter City		
1909		Preston North End	15	1
		Exeter City		
		Sutton Junction		
		Mansfield Town		
Parr, Harry Cecil			RH	
b Newcastle 1914				
		Dawley Rovers		
		Wrockwardine Wood		
		Donnington Wood		
		Sankey's		
		Wellington Town		
1937		Birmingham	1	
		Dawley Rovers		
		Stafford Rangers		
Parr, Henry			RB	
b Blackpool 1869				
1896	1902	Blackpool	87	2
Parr, William Wilfred			OR	
b Fylde q2 1915			d 1942	
Caps: England Amat				
1935	1938	Blackpool	15	1
		Dulwich Hamlet		
Parris, John Edward (Eddie)			OL	
b Pwllmeyric 31/1/1911			d 1971	
Caps: Wales 1				
		Chepstow Town		
1928	1933	Bradford Park Avenue	133	38
1934	1936	Bournemouth & Boscombe Ath	103	23
1936	1937	Luton Town	7	2
1937	1938	Northampton Town	25	7
		Cheltenham Town		
Parrish, Herbert (Bert)			OR	
b Shelf				
		Farsley Celtic		
1929		Bradford Park Avenue	1	
Parry, Charles Frederick (Charlie)			LB/RH/LH	
b Llansillin q1 1870			d 1922	
		Chester St Oswald's		
1889	1895	Everton	86	5
1896		Manchester City	0	
		Newtown		
		Aberystwyth		
		Oswestry United		

From	To	Club	Apps	Goal
Parry, Edward (Ted)			LB/RB	
b Colwyn Bay 9/12/1892			d 1976	
Caps: Wales Amat/Wales 5				
		Colwyn Bay Celts		
		Colwyn Bay		
1920		Oldham Athletic	0	
1920	1924	Liverpool	13	
1926		Walsall	27	
		Colwyn Bay		
		Llandudno Town		
		Colwyn Bay		
Parry, Frank Thomas			OR	
b Aigburth 14/6/1898			d 1973	
1922	1925	Everton	12	
1926		Grimsby Town	1	
1927	1928	Accrington Stanley	81	10
1929		Nelson	24	2
		Felling Stanley		
Parry, George Henry			OL/IL	
b Ibstock q2 1906			d 1965	
		Hemsworth Colliery		
1927	1929	Preston North End	4	1
		Dick, Kerr's XI		
Parry, Henry (Harry)			LH/CH	
b Sutton, Lancashire 29/9/1905			d 1978	
		Peasley Cross		
		Sutton Rovers		
1929		Bolton Wanderers	5	
		Colwyn Bay		
		Peasley Cross		
1933		Southport	4	
		United Glass Blowers		
Parry, John			OL	
b Glanmule 1871				
		Newtown		
1894		West Bromwich Albion	1	
		Aberystwyth		
Parry, Maurice Pryce			RH	
b Trefonen 7/11/1877			d 1935	
Caps: Wales 16				
		Newtown		
		Oswestry United		
1897		Nottingham Forest (trial)	0	
		Long Eaton Rangers		
1898		Leicester Fosse	1	
1898		Loughborough	12	
		Brighton United		
1900	1908	Liverpool	207	3
		Partick Thistle		
		(South Africa)		
		Oswestry United		
Parry, Oswald (Ossie)			LB/RB	
b Dowlais 16/8/1908			d 1991	
		Wimbledon		
1931	1935	Crystal Palace	141	
1938	1948	Ipswich Town	104	
Parry, William (Bill)			LH	
b Denaby 20/10/1914				
		Mexborough		
		Denaby United		
		Frickley Colliery		
1938		Leeds United	6	
		Chelmsford City		
Parsonage, George			CH	
b Darwen 11/1880			d 1919	
		Oswaldtwistle		
1900		Blackburn Rovers	0	
		Accrington Stanley		
		Brentford		
1908		Fulham	22	3
1910		Oldham Athletic	0	
		Darwen		
Parsonage, Harold (Harry)			IR/CF	
b Aston 10/1889			d 1979	
		Walsall		
1911	1912	Wolverhampton Wanderers	20	6
		Dudley Town		
		Shrewsbury Town		
		Walsall		
		Worcester City		

From To Apps Goal

Parsons, David (Davie) IR/CF
b Redcar 1891 d 1953
Eston United
South Bank
Redcar
Eston United
1919 Lincoln City 12 4
Eston United
Ashington
1921 Hartlepools United 2
Redcar
Eston United
South Bank
Stockton
Scarborough
Loftus Albion
Eston United

Parsons, Edward (Teddy) RH/LH
b Stafford 1879
Stafford Rangers
1897 1900 Stoke 55 1
Featherstone Rangers
Distillery
Stafford Rangers
Brighton & Hove Albion

Parsons, Jacob CF
b Barrow 27/2/1903 d 1953
Whitehaven Athletic
1927 Southport 4 3
1927 1928 Barrow 30 15
1929 Accrington Stanley 15 12
1930 Exeter City 3
1931 Thames 4
1932 Mansfield Town 2
1932 Rotherham United (trial) 0

Parsons, James RB
b Newcastle
Heaton Stannington
1923 Durham City 1

Parsons, William J (Bill) CH
b Newport q4 1913
Windsor Juniors
1934 Newport County 4
1935 Swansea Town 0

Partington, Thomas (Tom) OL
b Bolton
Claremont Baptists
1922 Bury 2
Claremont Baptists
Heaton Stannington

Parton, James LH/RH
b Barrow 3/12/1902 d 1981
Barrow Submarine Engine Athletic
1922 1928 Barrow 45 2
1923 Bristol City (trial) 0
1923 Bolton Wanderers (trial) 0
Grantham (loan)
1929 Rochdale 7
Morecambe (trial)
Lancaster Town
1931 Barrow 0

Partridge, Albert Edward OR/LB/RB
b Birmingham 13/2/1901 d 1966
1921 Newcastle United 0
Redditch Town
1923 1928 Sheffield United 90 18
1929 1932 Bradford City 55 7
1933 Northampton Town 2

Partridge, Charles GK
b Wednesbury 1867
Wednesbury Old Athletic
1893 1895 Small Heath 29
Willenhall Town
Redditch Town
Headless Cross

Partridge, Edward Wooldridge (Ted) OL/IL
b Lye 13/2/1891 d 1970
Stambermill St Mark's
Ebbw Vale
1920 1928 Manchester United 148 16
1929 Halifax Town 15
Manchester Central
Altrincham
1930 Crewe Alexandra 13 2
Darwen

Partridge, William RB
b Birmingham
Cradley Heath
1923 Merthyr Town 5

Pashley, Thomas H GK
Whitby
1904 Bradford City 1

From To Apps Goal

Pass, James Ernest (Jimmy) IR/CF
b Juffulpore, India 6/11/1883 d 1956
1903 1906 Stockport County 59 18
Tottenham Hotspur
New Brompton

Patchett, George Henry GK
b East Rainton 29/7/1889 d 1972
Croxdale Villa
Shildon Athletic
1921 1922 Durham City 62
Shildon
Aveling & Porters

Pateman, George Edward CF/IL/CH
b Chatham 8/5/1910 d 1973
Aveling & Porters
Canterbury Waverley
1929 1930 Gillingham 17 5
1931 Portsmouth 2
1933 Oldham Athletic 7 4
1934 Bradford City 1
1935 Clapton Orient 9 1
1935 Reading 0
1936 Accrington Stanley 21 8
1936 Southport 13 4
1937 1938 Barrow 17 1
Shorts Sports

Paterson, Alexander Adam (Alex) IL
b Kirkfield Bank 18/5/1897
Lanark United
1920 Oldham Athletic 1

Paterson, Andrew (Andy) LH/RH
b Leeholm 19/1/1909 d 1989
Middle Dock
Hebburn Colliery
1931 1933 Gateshead 80
Wigan Athletic
1937 1938 Oldham Athletic 21 1
South Shields

Paterson, George CF
b Lochgelly 1904
Lochgelly United
Kelty Rangers
Lochgelly United
1925 Stoke City 7 4
Lochgelly United
East Fife
Rhyl Athletic

Paterson, George Longmore IL/IR
b Aberdeen 19/12/1916 d 1996
Hall, Russell & Co
1938 Liverpool 2
1946 1949 Swindon Town 53 6

Paterson, James (Jim) IL/IR/CF
b St Ninians 1908
Caps: Scotland 3
Causewayhead
Camelon Juniors
1926 Everton 0
St Johnstone
Cowdenbeath
1932 1934 Leicester City 48 17
1935 1937 Reading 72 23
1938 Clapton Orient 5

Paterson, (Dr) James Alexander (Jimmy) OL/OR
b Chelsea 9/5/1891
Caps: FLge 1
Bellahouston Academy
Queen's Park
Rangers
1920 1925 Arsenal 70 1

Paterson, John CF
Leith Athletic
1894 Burton Swifts 10 2

Paterson, John William (Jock) CF/IR/IL
b Dundee 14/12/1896
Caps: WLge 1/Scotland 1
Dundee Arnot
Dundee North End
Fort Hill
Dundee
1919 1921 Leicester City 81 34
1921 1924 Sunderland 73 37
1924 Preston North End 17
Mid-Rhondda United
1925 1927 Queen's Park Rangers 36 6
Wellesley Juniors
Mansfield Town
Airdrieonians
Montrose

From To Apps Goal

Paterson, John Wilson (Jock) IR/IL
b Kirkcaldy 13/4/1904
Edinburgh Emmet
Dundee in Spain
Bathgate
1927 1929 Bristol Rovers 46 5
St Saviour's (Canada)

Paterson, Marr IR
b Alva 1887
Leith Athletic
1910 1911 Sheffield Wednesday 21 2

Paterson, Peter IR/IL
b Glasgow 1880
Royal Albert
1901 Everton 5 1
1902 Grimsby Town 2

Paterson, Robert CH
b Glasgow
Clyde
1897 1899 Derby County 19 1
Coventry City

Paterson, Thomas OR
b Quarter 1874
Motherwell
1895 Burnley 7 3
Abercorn

Paterson, William (Willie) CF
b Hill o' Beath 5/3/1898 d 1970
Foulford White Rose
Cowdenbeath Wednesday
Cowdenbeath
Rangers (loan)
Cowdenbeath
1920 1923 Derby County 66 24
Armadale (loan)
Cowdenbeath
1925 Coventry City 40 25
Springfield Babes
Fall River Marksmen
New Bedford Whalers
Providence Gold Bugs
New Bedford Whalers
Brooklyn Wanderers
Fall River FC
Providence Gold Bugs
New York Nationals

Paterson, William (Willie) GK
b Dunfermline 1902 d 1967
Bungalow City (Rosyth)
Broomhall Juniors (Charlestown)
Dunfermline Athletic
Clydebank (loan)
Boston Wonder Workers
Dunfermline Athletic
Dundee United
1927 1928 Arsenal 15
Airdrieonians
Dundee United

Paterson, William CH
b Hamilton 4/3/1914
Quarter United
Denny Hibernian
Morton
Ballymena
Belfast Celtic
Distillery
East Fife (trial)`
Broadway United
Dundee
Arbroath
Raith Rovers
Stenhousemuir
1936 Lincoln City 2
1937 1938 Mansfield Town 61
1939 (Mansfield Town) (2)

Paterson, William Francis (Willie) RH
b Hamilton
Earnock Rovers
Petershill
Hamilton Academical
Motherwell
Bo'ness (loan)
1925 1927 Charlton Athletic 93
Bostall Heath

Paton, Alex RH
b Scotland
Vale of Leven
West Manchester
1890 1898 Bolton Wanderers 215 15

From To Apps Goal

Paton, Daniel John Ferguson CF
b Bonhill 1871
Caps: Scotland 1
Vale of Leven
1889 1890 Aston Villa 3 1
Vale of Leven
St Bernard's
1898 Aston Villa 0
Clyde

Paton, Harold D (Harry) IR
b Larkhall 23/5/1897
Larkhall Thistle
Queen's Park
Motherwell
Clydebank
1921 Newcastle United 13 2
St Mirren

Paton, Hugh M OR
b Glasgow 8/9/1918
Shettleston
1938 Bradford Park Avenue 13 1

Paton, James IL
1898 Glossop North End 1

Paton, James Arklay Jackson (Jim) LB
b Monikie 14/2/1903 d 1994
Kilmarnock
Dundee
1929 Watford 6
Training Battalion RE

Paton, James J IR
Vale of Leven
1892 Aston Villa 1
Dundee Harp

Paton, Thomas Gracie (Tommy) RH/IR/CH
b Saltcoats 22/12/1918 d 1991
Ardeer Thistle
1937 Wolverhampton Wanderers 0
1938 Swansea Town 6
1938 1947 Bournemouth & Boscombe Ath 46 8
1939 (Bournemouth & Boscombe Ath) (3) (1)
1947 1951 Watford 141 1
Folkestone Town

Paton, Thomas Henry (Tom) CF/IR
b Eat Kilbride 8/11/1881
Larkhall Thistle
Hamilton Academical
Royal Albert
Rangers
1904 1905 Derby County 35 4
1905 1906 Sheffield United 21 4
St Mirren
Airdrieonians
St Johnstone
Cowdenbeath
Stevenston United

Patrick, John GK
b Kilsyth 10/1/1870
Caps: SLge 2/Scotland 2
Grangemouth
Falkirk
St Mirren
1896 Everton 1
St Mirren

Patrick, Joseph Cookson (Joe) CF
b Carlisle 2/10/1910 d 1991
1932 Carlisle United 0
Lancaster Town
1934 1935 Bury 15 10
1936 Luton Town 0
1936 1938 Southport 118 76
1939 (Southport) (3) (1)
Queen of the South
Workington

Patrick, Ronald OR
1938 Bradford City 1

Pattemore, Herbert Alfred LB
b Bedwelly 16/11/1907 d 1972
Caps: Wales Sch
Blaenavon United
1928 Swansea Town 2
Llanelly
Epsom Town

Patten, John T (Jack) OR
b Tyneside
Trafalgar (Newcastle)
Newcastle West End
1893 Newcastle United 1
Hebburn Argyle

Patterson, Daniel Morrison (Jock) CF
b Leith 1896
Loanhead Mayflower
1922 Newport County 12 1
Bo'ness

From To Apps Goal

Patterson, John CF/IR
b Manchester
Rusholme
Talbot
1898 Manchester City 0
1900 1901 Stockport County 31 3

Patterson, Martin S LH
b Forest Hall 1909
1937 Carlisle United 2

Patterson, Michael Thomas IL/IR
b South Shields 24/3/1900 d 1995
The Dragon
Boldon Villa
Boldon Colliery Welfare
1925 1926 Bradford City 11 1
1927 1929 Doncaster Rovers 56 20
1930 Barnsley 5
1931 Southport 2
Shelbourne
Shamrock Rovers
Frickley Colliery
Pilkington Recreation

Patterson, T CH
1890 Burnley 2

Patterson, WH LH
b Scotland
1892 Sheffield United 1
Gainsborough Trinity

Patterson, William IL
Hibernian
1896 Manchester City 1
Stockport County

Pattinson, Daniel (Dan) IL
b Newcastle
Malcolm Juniors
Rutherford College
Willington Athletic
1901 Newcastle United 1 1

Pattinson, John Bouch OR/IR
b Worksop q4 1886 d 1918
1903 1904 Gainsborough Trinity 6 4
1905 1906 Sheffield United 4 1
1907 Grimsby Town 19 2
Doncaster Rovers
1908 1910 Gainsborough Trinity 86 14
1911 Manchester City 0
Doncaster Rovers
Rotherham County

Pattison, Ernest RH/CF
b Chesterfield 19/11/1905 d 1979
1928 West Bromwich Albion 0
1929 Rotherham United 24
Scunthorpe & Lindsey United
1931 Doncaster Rovers 18 7
Frickley Colliery
Scunthorpe & Lindsey United

Pattison, Frank OR/OL
b South Bank 7/3/1889 d 1950
South Bank Primitive Methodists
Saltburn
South Bank
Craghead United
1912 Sunderland 0
1913 Clapton Orient 7
1914 Lincoln City 11 2
Rustons Aircraftmen
Mid-Rhondda United
Boston Town

Pattison, George Charlton CH
b North Shields 20/2/1895 d 1972
Wallsend
1919 1921 Arsenal 9
1922 West Ham United 0

Pattison, John Mason RB
b Bedlington 3/5/1889 d 1978
Bedlington Colliery Welfare
1912 1914 Hull City 48
Scunthorpe & Lindsey United
Bridlington Town

Pattison, John Morris (Johnny) OL
b Glasgow 19/12/1918
Carntyne Thistle
St Anthony's (Glasgow)
Motherwell
1937 1949 Queen's Park Rangers 92 26
1949 1950 Leyton Orient 43 10
Dover

From To Apps Goal

Pattison, John William (Jack) OL
b Durham 10/4/1897 d 1970
Leadgate Park
Framwellgate Moor
Durham City
1920 Newcastle United 0
Durham City
1921 Derby County 15 2
1922 1923 Bristol Rovers 13 1
Leadgate Park
1924 South Shields 0
1925 Durham City 6 2
1925 South Shields 0
1927 Torquay United 26 5
Taunton United
Grays Thurrock United
Dunston United
Bath City
Grays Thurrock United
Frenchay United
Glastonbury
Warminster Town

Pattison, Joseph (Joe) GK
b Haslingden 3/6/1912 d 1988
1931 Burnley 0
1932 1934 Accrington Stanley 16
1935 Burnley 0
Haslingden St Mary's

Pattison, Samuel LH/OL
b Hazel Grove 1881
1900 1901 Glossop 17

Pattison, WJ RB/LB
1924 1926 South Shields 9

Patton, Alexander (Sandy) IR
b Belfast 23/12/1901 d 1980
Rockville
Mount Cuba
Ormiston
Glentoran
Ormiston
Falkirk
Ards
1928 1929 Barrow 57 10
Ards
Sunthorpe & Lindsey United (trial)
Morecambe

Paul, Arthur George GK
b Belfast 24/7/1864 d 1947
1889 Blackburn Rovers 1

Paul, John OR/OL/IR
b Glasgow 1874
Hibernian
1894 1897 Derby County 28 9
Bristol Rovers

Paul, John Campbell RH/IR/IL
b Glasgow 29/1/1904 d 1979
Torpedo A
Port Glasgow Athletic
1922 1929 Bristol City 206 49
Taunton Town

Pauls, Charles Alfred OL
b Stockton q1 1866 d 1929
1889 Preston North End 3

Pavey, Sydney Clement GK
b Taunton 27/7/1895 d 1979
Taunton United
1922 1925 Exeter City 27

Pawson, Thomas OL
b Hull 10/10/1909 d 1993
1934 York City 1 1

Payne, Charles Edgar OR
b Wednesfield 1888 d 1957
1907 1909 Wolverhampton Wanderers 12 1
Blakenhall
Worcester City

Payne, ER OR/GK
1892 1895 Crewe Alexandra 12 1

Payne, Ernest (Ernie) OR
b Worcester q1 1885
Worcester Rovers
Worcester City
1908 Manchester United 2 1
Worcester Rovers

From To Apps Goal

Payne, George Clark IL
b Hitchin 17/2/1887 d 1932
Hitchin Union Jack
Hitchin Town
Barnet Alston
Tottenham Hotspur
Crystal Palace
1911 Sunderland 2
Leyton
1912 Woolwich Arsenal 3

Payne, James Hance (Jimmy) RH/CH
b Barrow 14/12/1903 d 1983
Barrow YMCA
1923 1926 Barrow 73 1
Barrow Shipbuilders
Ulverston Town

Payne, John Frederick OL
b Southall 3/6/1906 d 1981
Botwell Mission
Lyons Athletic
Southall
1926 1928 West Ham United 4 1
1929 1930 Brentford 52 18
1931 1933 Manchester City 4 1
1934 Brighton & Hove Albion 8 1
1935 Millwall 7
Yeovil & Petters United

Payne, Joseph (Joe) CF
b Brinnington Common 17/1/1914 d 1975
Caps: England 1
Bolsover Colliery
Biggleswade Town
1934 1937 Luton Town 72 82
1937 1945 Chelsea 36 21
1939 (Chelsea) (1)
1946 West Ham United 10 6
1947 Millwall 0
Worcester City

Payne, Leslie Thomas (Les) LH
b Birmingham 20/3/1914
1936 Doncaster Rovers 0
1937 1938 Walsall 27

Peachey, Alfred (Alf) CH
b St Helens 16/10/1908 d 1993
Caps: LoI 3
St Helens Town
1927 Bolton Wanderers 0
Atherton
1929 1937 Bradford City 191 1
1938 Torquay United (trial) 0
Sligo Rovers

Peacock, Frederick (Fred) GK
b Altrincham q2 1891
Winsford United
1921 Accrington Stanley 4

Peacock, James (Jimmy) RH
b Stoke-on-Trent 1871
Dresden United
1896 Stoke 1
Saltgates

Peacock, John (Joe) LH/RH
b Wigan 15/3/1897 d 1979
Caps: England 3
Atherton
1919 1926 Everton 151 12
1927 1929 Middlesbrough 80 2
1930 Sheffield Wednesday 1
1931 1932 Clapton Orient 54
Sliepner (Sweden)

Peacock, Leo Vaughan LH
b Apperley Bridge q3 1903
Apperley Bridge
1924 1925 Bradford Park Avenue 9

Peacock, Thomas (Tom) IL
b Morton 14/9/1912
Nottingham University
1930 Chesterfield 0
Bath City
Melton Mowbray
1933 1938 Nottingham Forest 109 57

Peake, Ernest (Ernie) LH/CH
b Aberystwyth q4 1888 d 1931
Caps: Wales Amat/Wales 11
Aberystwyth
1908 1913 Liverpool 51 5
Third Lanark
Blyth Spartans
Aberaman Athletic
Caerphilly

From To Apps Goal

Peake, George GK
b Blackwell 8/5/1902
Blackwell
South Normanton Colliery
Blackwell Wesley Guild
Blackwell Colliery
1926 Sheffield United 0
South Normanton
1928 1929 Chesterfield 23
Ilkeston United
Sutton Town

Peake, James IL/CF
1893 1895 Crewe Alexandra 71 17
1898 Burslem Port Vale 22 11
Millwall Athletic
1900 Burslem Port Vale 28 7

Peake, William Edward (Billy) IR/RH/CH
b Bolton 1889
Northern Nomads
Eccles Borough
1909 1911 Sheffield United 27 6
1912 1921 Bury 168 35
Newcross
Macclesfield
Manchester North End

Pearce, Cyril CF
b Shirebrook 28/1/1908 d 1990
Shirebrook
Warsop Main Colliery
Staveley Town
Shirebrook
1929 Wolverhampton Wanderers 0
1930 Newport County 27 22
1931 Swansea Town 40 35
1932 1936 Charlton Athletic 68 52
1937 Swansea Town 15 8
Frickley Colliery
Shirebrook Miners Welfare

Pearce, Harold IL
b Oakengates
Oakengates Town
1928 Gillingham 9 2
1929 Charlton Athletic 0
Wellington Town
Hereford United

Pearce, Herbert John (Bert) CF
b Stratford q1 1889 d 1947
Wanstead
Ilford
Leytonstone
1911 1914 Fulham 90 46

Pearce, James G (Jim) CH
b Chirk
Caps: Wales Amat
Chirk
Army
1934 1938 Bristol City 148 2
1939 1945 Rochdale (3)
1946 Cardiff City 0

Pearce, James Henry (Jimmy) IL/LH
b Ulverston 31/7/1904 d 1980
Ulverston Town
1921 1922 Barrow 11 3

Pearce, Robert G OL
1919 Blackburn Rovers 1

Pearce, Thomas Herbert (Herbert) OR/OL
b Bethnal Green 1889 d 1961
1910 1911 Hull City 3
Portsmouth

Pearce, William RB/LB/CF
b Ilkeston 24/4/1899 d 1984
Ilkeston United
Long Eaton
Worksop Town
1920 1922 Norwich City 19 2
Ilkeston United
Grantham
Loughborough Corinthians

Pearman, James GK
b Lincoln q2 1877
Casuals (Lincoln)
St Mary's (Lincoln)
1899 Lincoln City 1

From	To		Apps	Goal
Pears, John (Jack)			OL	
b Ormskirk 23/2/1904				
		Westhead St James		
		Skelmersdale United		
		Burscough Rangers		
1927		Liverpool	0	
1928		Rotherham United	21	7
1929		Accrington Stanley	21	8
1930	1933	Oldham Athletic	92	34
1933	1934	Preston North End	18	4
1934		Sheffield United	13	3
1935	1936	Swansea Town	55	10
1937		Hull City	30	8
1938		Rochdale	0	
		Mossley		
Pears, William (Billy)			RH	
b Willington 15/11/1918			d 1992	
Caps: England Sch				
		Crook Town		
1938		Newcastle United	2	
Pearson, Albert Victor (Bert)			OL/LH/IL	
b Tynemouth 6/9/1892			d 1975	
Caps: WLge 1				
		Hebburn Argyle		
1912	1913	Sheffield United	6	
		Port Vale		
1919	1920	Liverpool	44	4
1921		Port Vale	19	1
		Llanelly		
1923	1925	Rochdale	52	12
1925	1928	Stockport County	69	6
		Ashton National		
Pearson, Alfred (Alf)			CH	
1906	1907	Blackpool	5	
Pearson, Andrew (Andy)			IR	
b New Brancepeth 1/8/1903			d 1980	
		Ushaw Moor		
		Shildon		
		West Stanley		
		Cockfield		
1928		Southport	1	1
		Union Cable Sports		
		Southend Services		
		Westcliff Motor Services		
Pearson, Charles James (Charlie)			GK	
b Sunderland				
1923		Liverpool	0	
1924		Derby County	0	
1925		South Shields	20	
1926		Newport County	0	
		Aldershot		
Pearson, Curtis			IL	
		Grantham		
1933		Birmingham	0	
1935		Walsall	9	
Pearson, Frank			CF/IL	
b Manchester 18/5/1884				
1901	1902	Preston North End	32	17
1903	1905	Manchester City	7	2
1905		Chelsea	29	18
1906		Hull City	13	6
		Luton Town		
		Rochdale		
		Eccles Borough		
Pearson, George			LH	
1893		Middlesbrough Ironopolis	5	
Pearson, George William M			OL	
b West Stanley 21/9/1907				
		West Stanley		
		Annfield Plain		
1924		Bury	0	
1925	1932	Chelsea	197	33
1933		Luton Town	14	1
1934		Walsall	12	
Pearson, Harold (Harry 'Tich')			OR/OL	
b Birkenhead q4 1910				
		Shaftesbury Boys Club		
1932	1933	Tranmere Rovers	30	
1934		Bournemouth & Boscombe Ath	0	
		Prescot Cables		
		Northwich Victoria		
1937		Coventry City	3	
1938		Queen's Park Rangers	11	1
1939		Barrow	0	
Pearson, Harold Frederick			GK	
b Tamworth 7/5/1908			d 1994	
Caps: England 1				
		Nuneaton Town		
		Tamworth Castle		
		Bromsgrove Rovers		
1927	1936	West Bromwich Albion	281	
1937	1938	Millwall	39	

From	To		Apps	Goal
Pearson, Harry			CF	
1905	1906	Preston North End	2	
		Colne		
		Oswaldtwistle Rovers		
		Earlestown		
		Great Harwood		
Pearson, Harry			OR/CF	
b Keswick 1884				
		Workington		
1907	1909	Bury	31	2
		Port Vale		
		Stafford Rangers		
Pearson, Harry			IR	
b 9/2/??				
		Bredbury		
		Stalybridge Celtic		
1921		Manchester City	1	
Pearson, Henry Harvey			OL	
1921		Barrow	16	1
		Pontypool		
Pearson, Herbert			CF/IR	
b Brierley Hill 7/1/1901			d 1972	
		Brierley Hill Alliance		
1923		Southampton	8	4
1924		Coventry City	5	1
		Nuneaton Town		
Pearson, Horace			GK	
b Tamworth 6/4/1907			d 1989	
		Tamworth Castle		
		Nuneaton Town		
1927		Luton Town	0	
		Nuneaton Town		
1929	1930	Blackpool	55	
1931	1932	Oldham Athletic	38	
1933	1935	Coventry City	108	
1937		Newport County	42	
		Barry		
1938		Bristol City	16	
		Scarborough		
Pearson, Hubert Pryer			GK	
b Kettlebrook 5/1886			d 1955	
Caps: FLge 2				
		Kettlebrook Oakfield		
		Tamworth Castle		
		Tamworth Athletic		
1907	1924	West Bromwich Albion	341	2
Pearson, Isaac			RB	
b North Shields 25/2/1908			d 1972	
		Hebburn Colliery		
		Hamilton Academical		
1929		Barrow	4	
		Wardley Colliery Welfare		
Pearson, James (Jim)			OR	
b Wardley 19/10/1906			d 1992	
		Washington Colliery		
1930	1931	Norwich City	19	3
1932		Aldershot	1	1
		Wardley Colliery Welfare		
		Cromer		
Pearson, James Stevens			LB	
b Heywood q1 1905			d 1962	
		Heywood		
1925	1927	Nelson	38	
		Hurst		
		Newark Town		
		Runcorn		
Pearson, John			LB	
b Arbroath 22/1/1892			d 1937	
		Arbroath Fairfield		
		Arbroath		
1914	1922	Tottenham Hotspur	47	
		Partick Thistle (loan)		
1923		Luton Town	1	
Pearson, John Cecil			RB	
b Dudley 14/3/1896			d 1979	
		Cradley Heath St Luke's		
		Halesowen Town		
1922		Burnley	1	
1923		Brentford	26	
1924	1925	Grimsby Town	5	
Pearson, John Hargreaves			IR/OR	
b Crewe 25/1/1868				
Caps: England 1				
1892	1894	Crewe Alexandra	14	3
Pearson, Joseph (Joe)			RH	
b Lancashire 1868				
1888	1889	Bolton Wanderers	1	
		Liverpool		
Pearson, Joseph Frank (Joe)			RH/CH	
b Brierley Hill 9/1877			d 1946	
		Saltley College		
1900	1906	Aston Villa	104	4

From	To		Apps	Goal
Pearson, Richard			RH/LH	
1893	1895	Darwen	10	2
Pearson, Richard (Dickie)			IL/CF	
b Broompark 25/6/1900				
		New Brancepeth Exiles		
		Broompark Comrades		
		Chopwell Institute		
		Crook Town		
		Langley Park		
1922		Durham City	2	2
		Chopwell Institute		
1922	1924	Rotherham County	97	24
		West Stanley		
		New Brancepeth Welfare		
1927		Durham City	22	4
		Craghead United		
		West Stanley		
		Craghead United		
1932		Bournemouth & Boscombe Ath	0	
		West Stanley		
		Pringle Place Villa		
Pearson, Stanley			OR	
b Sheffield q1 1896				
		Wycliffe		
1919		Sheffield Wednesday	2	
		Malin Bridge Old Boys		
1921		Huddersfield Town	1	
		Denaby United		
Pearson, Stanley Clare (Stan)			IL/IR	
b Salford 11/1/1919			d 1997	
Caps: FLge 1/England 8				
		Adelphi Lads Club		
1937	1953	Manchester United	312	127
1939		(Manchester United)	(3)	(1)
1953	1957	Bury	121	56
1957	1958	Chester	57	16
Pearson, Stephenson Chisholm (Chris)			LH	
b North Shields q1 1890				
		North Shields Athletic		
1919		South Shields	1	
Pearson, Thomas (Tom)			IL	
b West Bromwich 1866			d 1918	
		Oak Villa		
		West Bromwich Sandwell		
1888	1893	West Bromwich Albion	138	72
Pearson, Thomas (Tom)			IR	
b Aspull q2 1907				
		Aspull Amateurs		
1929	1931	Wigan Borough	5	2
Pearson, Thomas Usher (Tommy)			OL	
b Edinburgh 6/3/1913			d 1999	
Caps: FLge 1/SLge 1/England War 1/ Scotland 2				
		Murrayfield Amateurs		
		Heart of Midlothian (trial)		
1933	1947	Newcastle United	212	46
1939		(Newcastle United)	(2)	(2)
		Aberdeen		
Peart, Henry (Harry)			CH/RH	
b Newcastle 3/10/1889				
		Glasgow Strathclyde		
1910	1912	Bradford City	13	
1913	1914	Leeds City	7	
		Blyth Spartans		
Peart, John Charles			LB/RB	
b Tewkesbury 13/10/1884				
1910	1912	Woolwich Arsenal	57	
		Croydon Common		
1919	1920	Arsenal	6	
		Margate		
Peart, John George (Jack)			CF	
b South Shields 3/10/1888			d 1948	
Caps: SoLge 3/FLge 1				
		South Shields Adelaide		
		Treharris		
1907	1909	Sheffield United	27	8
		Stoke		
1911	1912	Newcastle United	17	6
1912	1919	Notts County	82	51
1919		Birmingham	3	
1919		Derby County	9	1
		Ebbw Vale		
1921		Port Vale	7	
1922		Norwich City	21	7
1922	1923	Rochdale	21	10
Peart, Ronald (Ron)			CH/RH/CF	
b Brandon, County Durham 8/3/1920			d 1999	
		Langley Moor		
1938		Hartlepools United	8	
1946		Derby County	1	
1948		York City	5	
		Spennymoor United		

From	To		Apps	Goal
Pease, William Harold (Billy)			OR	
b Leeds 30/9/1898			d 1955	
Caps: England 1				
1919		Leeds City	0	
1920	1925	Northampton Town	246	45
1926	1932	Middlesbrough	222	99
1933		Luton Town	33	8
Peddie, John Hope (Jock)			CF/IR/IL	
b Glasgow 21/3/1877			d 1928	
		Glasgow Benburb		
		Third Lanark		
1897	1901	Newcastle United	125	73
1902		Manchester United	30	11
		Plymouth Argyle		
1904	1906	Manchester United	82	41
		Heart of Midlothian		
		(USA)		
Peden, John			OL	
b Belfast 12/7/1863			d 1944	
Caps: IrLge 4/Ireland 24				
		Distillery		
		Linfield		
1893		Newton Heath	28	7
1894		Sheffield United	8	2
		Distillery		
		Linfield		
Pedlar, Philip			LB/RB	
b Merthyr Tydfil 30/4/1899			d 1955	
Caps: WLge 1				
		Merthyr Town		
		Rhymney		
1922		Chesterfield	15	
1923		Burnley	0	
1925	1927	Merthyr Town	86	6
		Ebbw Vale		
Pedley, John (Jack)			OL	
b West Bromwich 2/1881				
		Wednesbury Old Athletic		
1905	1909	Wolverhampton Wanderers	156	26
		Wrexham		
Pedwell, Ralph			OL	
b Durham q2 1908			d 1965	
		Durham West End		
1928		South Shields (trial)	0	
1929	1933	Hartlepools United	156	66
1934		Barnsley	10	2
		Frickley Colliery		
1936		Rotherham United	36	20
1937		Doncaster Rovers	1	2
		Spennymoor United		
Pee, Richard (Dick)			LH	
1900		Walsall	2	
Peed (Gonsalez), Francisco Enrique (Frank)			IR/CF	
b Venado Tuerto, Argentina 27/7/1905			d 1969	
Caps: WLge 1				
		Orb Villa		
		Lliswarry		
		South Wales Borderers		
		Brereton Social		
1928		Aston Villa	0	
1930		Bournemouth & Boscombe Ath	2	
1930		Norwich City	17	4
1932		Newport County	13	4
		Shelbourne		
1933	1934	Barrow	38	15
		Bath City		
		Nuneaton Town		
Peel, Harold Burston			IL/OL	
b Bradford 26/3/1900			d 1976	
		Calverley		
1920	1926	Bradford Park Avenue	207	37
1926	1929	Arsenal	47	5
1929	1935	Bradford City	186	26
Peers, Edward (Ted)			RB	
b Hednesford 1876				
		Hednesford Rovers		
1895		West Bromwich Albion	0	
1896	1898	Walsall	73	2
1899	1900	Nottingham Forest	56	
1901		Burton United	9	
		Swindon Town		
		Coventry City		
Peers, Edward John (Teddy)			GK	
b Connah's Quay 31/12/1886			d 1935	
Caps: Wales 12				
		Oswestry St Clare's		
		Chirk		
		Shrewsbury Town (trial)		
		Connah's Quay Juniors		
		Connah's Quay Victoria		
		Connah's Quay		
1911	1920	Wolverhampton Wanderers	186	
		Hednesford Town		
1921	1922	Port Vale	56	
		Hednesford Town		

From To Apps Goal

Peers, Harry IL
b Wednesfield 1875
Wednesfield
1898 Walsall 10 4

Peers, Samuel Abraham (Sam) IL/OL/CH
b Liverpool q3 1881 d 1942
Rudge-Whitworth
Lord Street
Foleshill Great Heath
Coventry City
1901 1903 Leicester Fosse 14 1
Swindon Town
Coventry City

Pegg, Ernest (Dick) CF
b Leicester q3 1878 d 1916
1896 Leicester Fosse 0
1897 1898 Loughborough 56 15
Kettering
Reading
1901 Preston North End 15 9
1902 1903 Manchester United 41 13
Fulham
1905 Barnsley 7 2

Pegg, Frank Edward OL
b Beeston 2/8/1902 d 1991
Sawley United
Loughborough Corinthians
1923 Derby County (trial) 0
1924 Blackpool (trial) 0
1924 Nelson (trial) 0
1925 Sunderland 1
1926 1930 Lincoln City 115 51
1931 Bradford City 3
1932 Norwich City 6 2
1933 New Brighton 41 8
Yarmouth Town

Peggie, James Nesbit CF
b Wemyss 1885
Saline
Lochgelly United
East Fife
Hibernian
Dunfermline Athletic (loan)
1910 Middlesbrough 6
East Fife

Pell, William RH
Kettering
Northampton Town
1902 1903 Glossop 62

Pember, Louis Charles IL
b Birmingham q3 1880 d 1959
1902 Aston Villa 0
Walsall
1904 Doncaster Rovers 17
Coventry City

Pemberton, Cecil CF
b Bury 19/2/1907 d 1970
Horwich RMI
1930 Burnley 0
Yeovil & Petters United
1932 Millwall 6 1

Pemberton, Frank Milton LH
b Hackney q3 1884 d 1965
1906 1907 Clapton Orient 4

Pemberton, Luther CH/LH/RH
b Oswaldtwistle q1 1866 d 1944
Bell's Temperance
1888 1890 Accrington 45
Bury

Pemble, Albert George GK
b Aston q2 1885 d 1946
1905 Stockport County 17

Pemble, Arthur James GK
b Aston q1 1890 d 1958
1908 Wolverhampton Wanderers 2
Willenhall Pickwick
Lowton Manor
Fordhouses

Pembleton, Arthur RH/LH/CH
b Palterton 25/1/1895 d 1976
Woodhouse Exchange
Mansfield Mechanics
Woodhouse Exchange
1919 1921 Notts County 71
1922 1926 Millwall Athletic 127
1927 Norwich City 18

From To Apps Goal

Pender, Robert LH/IL
b Coatbridge 5/11/1891
Kirkintilloch Harp
Dumbarton
St Mirren (trial) -
Johnstone
Dumbarton Harp
Raith Rovers
Johnstone
Dumbarton Harp (loan)
Renton
1919 1923 Middlesbrough 104 10
St Johnstone

Pendergast, Thomas CF/IL
b Oswaldtwistle q1 1870 d 1946
1889 1891 Accrington 36 12
Accrington Stanley

Pendergast, William James (Bill) CF/IL
b Pen-y-groes 13/4/1915 d 2001
Rhyl Athletic
1934 Crewe Alexandra 0
1935 Wrexham 0
1935 Manchester United 0
1935 Wolverhampton Wanderers 0
1936 1937 Bristol Rovers 7 3
Colchester United
1938 Chester 34 26
1939 (Chester) (3) (1)
1946 1947 New Brighton 69 26
Rhyl

Pendleton, John James (Jack) RH/CH
b Liverpool 13/1/1894 d 1939
South Liverpool
1919 Aston Villa 6
1922 1923 Wigan Borough 39 1
1924 Walsall 39

Penman, James (Jim) LB
b Kelty 26/5/1896 d 1976
Glasgow Ashfield
1920 Liverpool 1
Lochgelly United

Penman, James IR
Bowhill
1923 Doncaster Rovers 1
Lochgelly United

Penman, Thomas (Tom) CH
b 1887 d 1915
Darlington St Augustine's
Crook Town
1908 Bristol City 1
Shildon Athletic
Wingate Albion
Hartlepools United
Wingate Albion

Penman, William CH
b Falkirk 1886 d 1907
Glasgow Ashfield
1906 Bradford City 15 1

Penn, Francis John (Frank) OL
b Edmonton 5/4/1896 d 1966
Alston Rangers
Vicar of Wakefield
1919 1933 Fulham 427 45

Penn, Thomas (Tom) RB/LB
b Heath Common 11/10/1897 d 1978
Altofts
1925 Bristol City 6
1927 Darlington 14
Gainsborough Trinity
1929 1930 Swindon Town 27
Yeovil & Petters United
Bath City

Pennington, Alfred RB
b Burslem 1875
Bristol Eastville Rovers
1898 Grimsby Town 1
Folkestone
Shrewsbury Town

Pennington, Henry (Harry) GK
b Farnworth 1/9/1875
First Scots Guards
Brentford
Chorley
1900 1904 Notts County 126
Atherton Church House

Pennington, James IL
b Prescot q2 1915
Rainhill
1933 Tranmere Rovers 2 1

From To Apps Goal

Pennington, Jesse LB/RB
b West Bromwich 23/8/1883 d 1970
Caps: FLge 9/England 25
Langley Villa
Langley St Michael's
Dudley Town
1901 Aston Villa 0
Dudley Town
1903 1921 West Bromwich Albion 455

Pennington, John GK
b Bolton
1927 Halifax Town 28
1928 Stockport County 6

Pennington, Rowland GK
b St Helens 1870
St Helens
Whiston
1890 1892 Blackburn Rovers 8
1892 Northwich Victoria 4

Pennington, Thomas (Tom) GK
b 1887
Newtown
Whitchurch
Reading
Saltney
1909 Oldham Athletic 1

Penny, Hubert G (Bert) CH
b Reading 1894 d 1961
British Workers' Institute
1922 Reading 1

Pentland, Frederick Beaconsfield (Fred) OR/CF
b Wolverhampton 18/9/1883 d 1962
Caps: England 5
Avondale Juniors
Willenhall Swifts
1901 Small Heath 0
1903 Blackpool 8 5
1903 1905 Blackburn Rovers 51 9
Brentford
Queen's Park Rangers
1908 1911 Middlesbrough 92 11
Halifax Town
Stoke
Halifax Town

Peplow, William (Billy) OR
b Derby q2 1885 d 1957
Redditch Town
1907 Birmingham 17
Bristol Rovers

Pepper, Francis (Frank) CH
b Sheffield q3 1875 d 1914
Greasborough
1897 Sheffield United 0
1898 Newton Heath 7
1899 1901 Barnsley 58
1901 Doncaster Rovers 1
Rotherham Town
South Kirkby

Pepper, Frederick W RH/LH
Netherfield Rangers
1909 1911 Notts County 5
Hamilton Lancashire (Canada)
Bethlehem Steel
Harrison FC (USA)
Fall River Marksmen
New York Giants

Pepper, William George (Bill) GK
b Faversham q2 1895 d 1918
Sheppey United
1912 Leicester Fosse 1
Gillingham

Peppitt, Sydney (Syd) CF/IR/IL
b Stoke-on-Trent 8/9/1919 d 1992
Caps: England Sch
1936 1949 Stoke City 94 29
1950 Port Vale 11 3
Worcester City

Percival, John Robert (Jack) RH/LH
b Pittington 16/5/1913 d 1976
Low Pittington
Durham City
1933 1946 Manchester City 161 8
1947 1948 Bournemouth & Boscombe Ath 52 1
Murton
Shotton Colliery Welfare

Percival, Peter OR
b Reddish 23/2/1911 d 1960
Hurst
Buxton
Ashton National
1933 Manchester City 2
1934 Sheffield Wednesday 0
1936 Chester 2
Hurst

From To Apps Goal

Percy, Andrew Alfred (Alf) OL
b Ilford 1912
Ilford
1938 Clapton Orient 4
1939 Plymouth Argyle 0

Perfect, Frank Thomas RB
b Gorleston 9/3/1915 d 1977
Gorleston
1933 Norwich City 1
1936 Mansfield Town 13
1936 Wolverhampton Wanderers 0
1938 Tranmere Rovers 13
1938 Southampton 15
1939 (Southampton) (2)

Perkins, Edward E OL
b Astwood Bank 26/11/1874 d 1941
Astwood Bank
Worcester City
1905 1906 West Bromwich Albion 33 1
Worcester City
Redditch

Perkins, George Henry GK
b Rothwell, Northamptonshire q2 1882
Rothwell Britannia
Rothwell
Market Harborough Town
1904 Leicester Fosse 1
Hinckley United
Market Harborough Excelsior
Market Harborough Town
Rothwell Town

Perkins, George T OL
b Bolton
Folds Road Methodists
1920 Bury 4

Perkins, W LH
Newark
1902 1903 Burslem Port Vale 58 3
Newark

Perkins, William Henry (Bill) GK
b Wellingborough 26/1/1876
Wellingborough Trinity
Kettering
1898 Luton Town 26
1898 1902 Liverpool 107
Northampton Town

Perks, Henry (Harry) OL
b Cardiff 15/2/1912 d 1983
1933 Cardiff City 9 1
1934 Newport County 8 1
Barry

Perrett, George Richard RH
b Kenilworth 2/5/1915 d 1952
Woking
1935 Fulham 0
1938 1949 Ipswich Town 131 4

Perrett, Robert Frederick OL
b Bournemouth 23/11/1919 d 1994
1937 Bournemouth & Boscombe Ath 0
1938 Huddersfield Town 1
1939 Southampton (3)

Perrett, William James (Billy) CH
b Carlisle 10/6/1886 d 1969
Wood Cross Links
Fazeley Rovers
Bilston United
1909 1911 Wolverhampton Wanderers 4
Dudley Town
Halesowen

Perrins, George RH/LH
b Birmingham 24/2/1873 d 1947
Birmingham St George's
1892 1895 Newton Heath 92
1897 Luton Town 6
Chatham
1901 Stockport County 29

Perry, Arthur Arnold LB/RB
b West Bromwich 7/1897 d 1977
West Bromwich Baptists
1923 1926 West Bromwich Albion 74
Wellington Town
1927 Crystal Palace 0
1928 Merthyr Town 0

Perry, Charles (Charlie) CH
b West Bromwich 1/1866 d 1927
Caps: FLge 1/England 3
West Bromwich Strollers
1888 1895 West Bromwich Albion 171 12

From To Apps Goal

Perry, Colin OR
b Kiveton Park q4 1916 d 1942
Kiveton Park
1933 Sheffield United 0
Gainsborough Trinity
1938 Aston Villa 0
1939 Nottingham Forest (3) (2)

Perry, Edwin (Eddie) CF
b Rhymney 19/1/1909 d 1996
Caps: Wales War 1/Wales 3
Tredomen Engineering Works
Rhymney
1926 Swansea Town (trial) 0
1927 Merthyr Town 0
1928 Bournemouth & Boscombe Ath 0
1930 Thames 25 16
1931 1936 Fulham 64 36
1936 1938 Doncaster Rovers 98 45
1939 (Doncaster Rovers) (3) (2)
1945 Fulham 0

Perry, Eric RB/LB
b West Bromwich 13/7/1907 d 1988
Brierley Hill Alliance
1931 West Bromwich Albion 0
1932 1933 Coventry City 40 4
Dudley Town

Perry, Ernest William (Ernie) CH
b Wednesbury 3/11/1891 d 1979
1919 1920 Port Vale 44 2
1921 1923 Crewe Alexandra 62

Perry, Hubert IL
b Manchester 15/4/1911 d 1998
Bridgwater Town
1929 Bristol City 1
Bath City

Perry, Ivor Leslie CH
b Ystrad 8/1904 d 1965
Ystrad Rovers
1924 Tottenham Hotspur (trial) 0
Pontypridd
Torquay United
1927 1928 Bristol Rovers 35 1
1929 Middlesbrough (trial) 0
Walton-on-Thames

Perry, Josiah (Joe) RB
b Brierley Hill q1 1893 d 1947
Brockmoor St John's
Pensnett Victoria
Brierley Hill Associates
Newport County
Stourbridge
1914 Notts County 18
Ebbw Vale

Perry, Robert (Bob) RH/RB
b Airdrie 1893
King's Park
1912 1922 Bury 137 18
J & P Coats (Rhode Island)
Fall River Marksmen
New Bedford Whalers
Hartford Americans
J & P Coats (Rhode Island)
Pawtucket Rangers

Perry, Sidney J (Sid) LB
b Walsall
1937 Grimsby Town 0
1938 Torquay United 4
Peterborough United

Perry, Thomas (Tom) RH/IR
b West Bromwich 8/1871 d 1927
Caps: FLge 3/England 1
Christ Church (West Bromwich)
West Bromwich Baptists
Stourbridge
1890 1900 West Bromwich Albion 248 14
1901 1902 Aston Villa 27 1

Perry, Walter OR/LH/IR
b West Bromwich 10/1868 d 1928
West Bromwich Excelsior
1888 West Bromwich Albion 9 4
1889 Wolverhampton Wanderers 8 3
Warwickshire County
1892 1893 Burton Swifts 40 7
1894 West Bromwich Albion 1
1895 Burton Swifts 0

Pescod, George RH
b Sunderland 31/10/1909 d 1978
1932 Liverpool 0
1933 Halifax Town 8 1
1934 Hartlepools United 0
Horden Colliery Welfare
Easington Colliery Welfare

From To Apps Goal

Peters, Frank OR
b Crewe 26/2/1910 d 1990
Wellington St George's
1928 Coventry City 0
Wellington St George's
1930 1931 Charlton Athletic 29 7
1931 Fulham 1 1
1933 1935 Swindon Town 100 45
1936 1938 Bristol City 113 22

Peters, Harold IL
b Salford 15/3/1903 d 1968
West Salford
1922 1923 Southport 10 2
Altrincham
Chester
Macclesfield
1931 Stockport County 0
Mossley
Witton Albion
Mossley
Great Harwood

Peters, James (Jack) OL
Heywood Central
1894 1895 Newton Heath 45 13
New Brompton
Sheppey United

Peters, Keith LB
b Port Sunlight 19/7/1915 d 1989
1938 Liverpool 1

Peters, Samuel (Sam) RH
b West Bromwich 1886
Carters Green Juniors
Churchfields
1905 West Bromwich Albion 6 1
Crewe Alexandra
Brierley Hill Alliance

Peters, William T RH
b Motherwell 1906
1932 Bournemouth & Boscombe Ath 0
1933 Rochdale 1
Burton Town

Petrie, Charles (Charlie) IL
b Chorlton q3 1895 d 1972
Openshaw
1920 Manchester City 0
1921 Stalybridge Celtic 22 14
1921 1924 Sheffield Wednesday 57 22
1925 1926 Swindon Town 32 12
1927 1928 Southampton 24 7
1929 York City 0
Stalybridge Celtic

Petrie, Robert (Bob) LH/RH
b Dundee 25/10/1874 d 1947
Arbroath
Dundee East End
Dundee
1894 1896 Sheffield Wednesday 52 3
Southampton
Dundee Wanderers
1900 New Brighton Tower 28
Dundee Wanderers
Arbroath
Dundee Wanderers
Brechin City
Dundee Wanderers
Arbroath

Pett, Ernest Frank (Ernie) OR
b Edmonton q3 1892 d 1953
Barnet
1920 Luton Town 1

Pettit, Harold Henry C LH
b Sydenham 23/5/1906 d 1988
Kingstonian
1924 1925 Crystal Palace 2

Pettitt, James H RH
1902 Doncaster Rovers 1

Pheasant, Edward (Ted) CH
b Wednesbury q2 1875 d 1910
Wednesbury Excelsior
Wednesbury Old Athletic
1896 1903 Wolverhampton Wanderers 159 19
1904 1909 West Bromwich Albion 140 20
Darlaston

Philbin, John (Jack) IR/IL
b Jarrow 6/9/1913 d 1983
Washington Colliery
1934 Derby County 1
1936 1937 Torquay United 69 10
1938 Brighton & Hove Albion 6 1

From To Apps Goal

Philip, George C CF
b Newport-on-Tay 1891
Heart of Midlothian
Dundee
1914 Sunderland 37 22
St Mirren
Dundee
1919 Sunderland 0
Dundee

Philipson, John OL
b Newburn 18/11/1905 d 1984
Willington
1925 Durham City 0
1926 Bury 0
1927 Doncaster Rovers 28 4
1928 Norwich City 1
Throckley Welfare
Clara Vale United

Phillips, Alan Hedley IL
b Oxford 13/2/1899 d 1975
Oxford University
Oxford City
Corinthians
Sheringham
1923 Norwich City 4 3
Holt
Corinthians

Phillips, Cuthbert (Charlie) OR/CF/IR
b Victoria, Monmouthshire 23/6/1910 d 1969
Caps: Wales Sch/Wales 13
Ebbw Vale
1928 Plymouth Argyle (trial) 0
1929 1935 Wolverhampton Wanderers 191 59
1935 1937 Aston Villa 22 5
1937 1938 Birmingham 24 9
Chelmsford City

Phillips, David CH
b Glasgow 25/12/1917
Haddon United
1938 Bradford Park Avenue 1

Phillips, David Samuel (Dai) IL/IR
b Bala 27/3/1916 d 1945
Bala Town
Blaenau Ffestiniog
1935 Blackburn Rovers 0
1936 1938 Wrexham 14 1
Bangor City

Phillips, Ernest H CH
b Birmingham 12/2/1897
Redditch Town
1922 Tranmere Rovers 19 1
Wallasey Town

Phillips, George Raymond IR/IL
b Tottenham 11/10/1912 d 1993
Northfleet
1932 Clapton Orient 3 1
1933 1934 Millwall 18 5

Phillips, Henry George (Harry) CF
b Staffordshire 1882
Sandford Hill
1899 Lincoln City 2 1
Stockton
1903 1904 Grimsby Town 21 9
New Brompton

Phillips, John (Jack) CF/IR
b Barry 1903
Barry Brooklands
1923 West Bromwich Albion 0
1923 Rochdale (trial) 0
1924 Southend United 8 1
1925 1926 Merthyr Town 57 31
1927 1928 Brentford 29 22
1928 1929 Bristol Rovers 65 37
1930 Coventry City 25 17
Merthyr Town
Barry
Troedyrhiw

Phillips, John R GK
b Weston Rhyn
Chirk
1925 Manchester City 1
Oswestry Town

Phillips, Leonard A IR
1925 Walsall 1 1

Phillips, Reginald (Reg) OL
b Hove q1 1899 d 1924
Brighton & Hove Amateurs
1921 Brighton & Hove Albion 3

Phillips, Reginald RB
b Trecynon
1923 1924 Merthyr Town 29

From To Apps Goal

Phillips, Thomas LH/RH
b Leeds 1882
Alloa Vale of Forth
Alloa Athletic
1904 1905 Glossop 41 1

Phillips, Wilfred John (Wilf) IL/IR
b Brierley Hill 9/8/1895 d 1973
Bilston United
1919 Stoke 13 3
Ebbw Vale
Darlaston
Bilston United
1923 1925 Bristol Rovers 90 35
1925 1929 Millwall 109 58
1930 Thames 35 7
1931 West Ham United 21 3
1932 Clapton Orient 24 4
Stourbridge

Phillips, William Michael OR
b 23/5/??
1927 Rotherham United 19 6
Scunthorpe & Lindsey United

Phillipson, Thomas Featherstone (Tom) IL
b Stanhope q1 1885 d 1965
Bishop Auckland
1904 Middlesbrough 2 1
Fulham (trial)
1904 Middlesbrough 1 1
Spennymoor United
West Stanley
South Shields
Shildon
West Stanley

Phillipson, Thomas William (Tom) CF/IR/OR
b Ryton-on-Tyne 31/10/1898 d 1965
Caps: England Sch
Scotswood
1919 1920 Newcastle United 14 4
1921 1923 Swindon Town 87 24
1923 1927 Wolverhampton Wanderers 144 104
1927 1929 Sheffield United 56 26
Bilston United
1931 Walsall 7 3

Philp, John Bain RH
b Kelty 5/9/1911
Kelty Boys
Inverkeithing
1933 Leicester City 1
Rhyl Athletic
Alloa Athletic
Raith Rovers
Glenavon

Philpott, William RH
1898 1900 Walsall 7

Phipps, Cecil Harry IL/IR
b Leicester 25/10/1896 d 1968
1919 West Ham United 1
Coalville Swifts
1921 Halifax Town 5
Coalville Swifts
Loughborough Corinthians
Whitwick Imperial
Burton All Saints
Shepshed Albion
Holy Trinity Pilots
Municipal Offices

Phipps, W OL
1893 Lincoln City 2

Phizacklea, James Robert LB/RB
b Barrow 29/9/1898 d 1971
Barrow Hindpool Athletic
Barrow Submarine Engine Athletic
1921 1923 Barrow 71 3
1924 Nelson 19
1924 1925 Preston North End 22
1926 1927 South Shields 68
Thames
1930 Stockport County 0
Guildford City
Roneo Sports (Romford)

From To | Apps | Goal

Phoenix, Albert Frederick (Ginger) RH/IR
b Patricroft 5/7/1897 d 1979
Hadfield
Glossop
1923 Birmingham 3
1924 Aston Villa 3 2
1925 Barnsley 2
1926 1928 Exeter City 52 9
1929 Wigan Borough 25
Bath City
1930 Torquay United 18
1931 Mansfield Town 3
Racing Club de Paris
Sandbach Ramblers
Shelbourne
Colwyn Bay United
Brierley Hill Alliance
Ballymena United
Nelson
Mossley

Phypers, Ernest (Ernie) LH/RH
b Walthamstow 13/9/1910 d 1960
Walthamstow Avenue
1932 Aston Villa 0
1933 Tottenham Hotspur 0
Northfleet
1934 1936 Tottenham Hotspur 30
1939 Doncaster Rovers (2)

Pick, William Edward (Billy) OL
b Danesmoor 5/6/1903 d 1981
Caps: WLge 1
Danesmoor Miners Welfare
Danesmoor Rovers
1924 Bury 0
1925 Lincoln City 2
1926 Portsmouth 0
1927 1928 Newport County 20 4
1928 1930 Coventry City 74 25
1930 1931 Watford 26 5
1932 Barrow 39 7
1933 Stockport County 1
Bath City
Sutton Town
Danesmoor Miners Welfare

Pickard, Frank CF/OR
b Darlington 1912
Ferryhill Athletic
City of Durham
Chilton Colliery Recreation Athletic
1935 Hartlepools United 3 1
Blyth Spartans
1936 Gateshead 4 2
Blyth Spartans

Pickard, Herbert RH/LH
Upper Armley Christ Church
1906 1909 Leeds City 8

Pickard, John William OR
b Syston q3 1873 d 1933
Syston Swifts
1895 Leicester Fosse 1

Pickard, Thomas James GK
b Amble 4/6/1911 d 1967
Caps: England Sch
Amble
1929 Sunderland 0
1930 Gateshead 17
1931 Bradford City 6
1932 1936 Barrow 174

Pickard, William Cuthbert CF/IR
b Whitchurch, Shropshire q2 1873 d 1939
1892 1894 Crewe Alexandra 27 14

Picken, Albert Henry OL
b Wellington 4/8/1904 d 1989
Audley
1922 1924 Wolverhampton Wanderers 12
1925 1927 Bolton Wanderers 18 2
1927 Derby County 0
1928 Gillingham 8 1
Wellington Town
1930 Crewe Alexandra 0

Picken, John Barclay IL/IR
b Hurlford 1880 d 1952
Hurlford Thistle
Kilmarnock Shawbank
1899 1902 Bolton Wanderers 101 22
Plymouth Argyle
1905 1910 Manchester United 113 39
1911 1912 Burnley 18 10
1913 1914 Bristol City 51 13

From To | Apps | Goal

Picken, Thomas (Tom) GK
b Hednesford 5/1883
Hednesford Town
Shrewsbury Town
1905 West Bromwich Albion 2
Hednesford Town
Rood End
Oldbury Town
Dudley Phoenix

Picken, Walter CH
b Rotherham 1/2/1900 d 1981
Tinsley United
1920 1925 Rotherham County 86 1

Picken, William (Billy) LB
b Glasgow 29/3/1916
Bridgeton Waverley
1936 1938 Bradford Park Avenue 34

Pickering, Archibald (Archie) IR
b Murton Colliery 26/12/1913 d 1961
Murton Colliery Welfare
1933 1934 Southport 26
Rossendale United
Workington
Murton Colliery Welfare
1937 Hartlepools United 1
Murton Colliery Welfare
Dawdon Colliery

Pickering, Francis Guy CF
b Burton-on-Trent q1 1891 d 1966
Sutton Town
1912 Grimsby Town 2
Sutton Town

Pickering, Francis O OR
1924 Preston North End 1

Pickering, John IL
b Newcastle 1884
Willington Athletic
1904 Bury 5
Luton Town
New Brompton
1908 Bury 0

Pickering, John (Jack) IL/IR
b Chapeltown 18/12/1908 d 1977
Caps: FLge 1/England 1
Mortomley St Saviour's
1926 1947 Sheffield United 344 102
1939 (Sheffield United) (1)

Pickering, John William (Jack) OL
b Clowne
Frickley Colliery
1913 Sheffield Wednesday 4
Sutton Town
Rotherham County
Clowne Colliery
Clowne Town

Pickering, Thomas (Tom) CF
b Egremont, Cumberland q4 1906
Egremont
1926 Nelson 1
Egremont
Parton Athletic

Pickering, Thomas George IR
b Wednesbury 1879
Wednesbury Town
Brierley Hill Alliance
1900 West Bromwich Albion 10 2
Kettering
Brierley Hill Alliance

Pickering, W Alfred (Alf) OL
1893 Rotherham Town 7 1

Pickering, William CF
b Glasgow 1894 d 1917
1913 1914 Burnley 13 6
Morton

Pickering, William Harold (Bill) RB/LB
b Birmingham 1/11/1901 d 1971
Latch & Batchelors
1924 Sunderland 0
1925 Merthyr Town 9
1926 1927 Gillingham 45
1927 1928 Huddersfield Town 1
1929 Reading 20
Colwyn Bay
1931 1936 Bristol Rovers 215 1
1937 Accrington Stanley 29
Oswestry Town
Cradley Heath

From To | Apps | Goal

Pickering, William Henry (Bill) LB
b Sheffield 10/12/1919 d 1983
Caps: England Amat
1938 1945 Sheffield Wednesday 3
1948 1949 Oldham Athletic 78
Gainsborough Trinity

Pickering, William Hunter (Billy) CH/LH/RH
b Murton Colliery 13/11/1906 d 1952
Bishop Auckland
Murton Colliery Welfare
1930 1931 Southport 16
1932 Clapton Orient 12
1933 Southport 5

Pickersgill, Thomas (Tommy) LH
b St Helens 19/2/1908 d 1991
Runcorn
1931 1932 Oldham Athletic 39
Rhyl
1933 1934 Torquay United 33
1935 Accrington Stanley 0
Fleetwood
Rhyl

Pickett, Thomas Alfred (Tommy) GK
b Merthyr Tydfil 5/2/1909 d 2001
Kentish Town
1929 1931 Queen's Park Rangers 46
1932 Bristol City 6
Yeovil & Petters United
1934 Clapton Orient 0

Pickford, E OR
1893 Ardwick 8 3

Pickford, Percy RH
b Macclesfield q3 1879 d 1957
Macclesfield
1900 1902 Stockport County 59 1
1903 Blackpool 1

Pickles, Albert E OR
b Leeds 1905
Castleford Town
1926 Bradford City 2

Pickrell, John (Jack) IL
b Bilston q1 1866 d 1931
Dudley Road Swifts
1889 Wolverhampton Wanderers 1
Dudley Town
Netherton St Luke's

Pickup, John Henry (Jack) OR
b Bolton q1 1893 d 1968
1919 Bolton Wanderers 1

Pickup, Thomas (Tom) OR
b Blackburn q2 1908 d 1959
1929 Blackburn Rovers 0
1930 Accrington Stanley 5
Great Harwood
Mossley

Picton, Henry Vivian LH/RH
b Trehafod 28/6/1915 d 1974
1936 1937 Bournemouth & Boscombe Ath 7
1938 Crewe Alexandra 25 1
1939 (Crewe Alexandra) (2)

Pidgeon, Henry Thomas (Harry) CF/OR
b Tottenham q2 1899
Gnome Athletic
Queen's Park Rangers
1921 1922 Southend United 17 4
Yeovil & Petters United

Pierce, John Warbrick (Jackie) IL/IR
b Preston q2 1873 d 1908
1894 1900 Preston North End 74 16
Bristol Rovers

Pierce, William (Bill) RB/LB
b Ashington 29/10/1907 d 1976
Bedlington Colliery Welfare
1923 1930 Queen's Park Rangers 179 2
1931 Carlisle United 19

Piercy, Frank LB/LH
b Haverton Hill q3 1879 d 1931
South Bank
1899 1902 Middlesbrough 4
West Ham United

Piercy, Robert Henry (Bob) CH
b Haverton Hill q2 1874 d 1929
Port Clarence
1899 Middlesbrough 8 1

From To | Apps | Goal

Pigg, Albert CF
b Medomsley 6/0/1903 d 1944
Allendale Park
1924 Newcastle United (trial) 0
1925 Crewe Alexandra 0
Carlisle United
Raith Rovers
1929 Barnsley 5 1
Consett
Annfield Plain

Pigg, William (Bill) LH/RH
b High Spen 27/1/1898 d 1976
Chopwell Institute
Hamsterley Juniors
Spen Black & White
1921 1923 Ashington 95 1
1924 1925 Queen's Park Rangers 21
1928 1929 Carlisle United 68 7
1930 Accrington Stanley 10

Piggin, Albert CF
b Norwich 29/12/1894 d 1967
CEYMS (Norwich)
1920 Norwich City 2

Pike, Horace OL/OR/IL
b Keyworth q1 1870
Keyworth
1892 1895 Nottingham Forest 91 22
1897 1899 Loughborough 66 7

Pike, Richard Sidney George Arthur CF
b Finchley 15/3/1917 d 1988
Banbury Spencer
1938 West Bromwich Albion 1
Banbury Spencer

Pike, Theophilus (Theo 'Tot') IL/OL
b Sunderland 25/3/1907 d 1967
Sunderland Co-op Wednesday
1925 Southend United (trial) 0
1926 Fulham 3
1927 Bournemouth & Boscombe Ath 16 3
1927 1928 Birmingham 15 4
1930 1932 Southend United 69 19
1933 1934 Norwich City 20 7
Bury Town

Pilgrim, James Ernest (Jim) RB/LB
b Holmes q3 1874 d 1939
Parkgate
Thornhill United
Rotherham Swifts
1898 Sheffield United 15
1899 1900 Chesterfield Town 54
Thornhill United
Rotherham Town

Pilkington, Elliot CH/IR/RH
b Radcliffe 2/4/1890 d 1945
Radcliffe St Thomas's
Rossendale United
Salford United
1911 1925 Oldham Athletic 269 14
Llandudno Town
Macclesfield

Pilkington, Frederick Alfred (Alf) RB/LH
b Camberwell 22/4/1901 d 1986
Dulwich Hamlet
1924 1926 Fulham 4 1
Sheppey United

Pilkington, Oliver IL
b Darwen q1 1874 d 1946
1898 Darwen 18 4

Pilkington, Samuel Turnell (Sam) OR
b Accrington 14/12/1889 d 1970
Accrington Stanley
1906 Burnley 0
Colne
Haslingden
1910 Oldham Athletic 5
Haslingden
Accrington Stanley

Pilkington, Saville Henry OL
b Hathern q2 1893 d 1957
Hathern
Loughborough Corinthians
1913 Leicester Fosse 1

Pilkington, William OR
b 1906
Leyland
Chorley
1926 Blackpool 0
1927 Preston North End 1
Chorley
Lancaster Town

From To Apps Goal

Pillinger, William (Billy) RH
b Keynsham q2 1895 d 1964
Warmley
Aberdare Town
Aberaman Athletic
1921 Plymouth Argyle 0
1922 Merthyr Town 36 1
Weymouth

Pilsbury, Charles CF
b Bilston 1881 d 1964
Queen Street Methodists
Dudley Central
1903 Wolverhampton Wanderers 1 1
Bilston Swifts
Tipton Victoria

Pimlott, Arthur OL
b Hanley q1 1872 d 1895
1892 Burslem Port Vale 1

Pinch, Charles Edwin (Charlie) LH
b Cardiff 3/1/1890 d 1978
Southport Central
1913 Preston North End 3
Scunthorpe & Lindsey United
Swansea Town

Pinches, Alick LB
b Twitchen, Shropshire q2 1865 d 1926
1892 1896 Walsall Town Swifts 72

Pincott, Frederick (Fred) CH
b Bristol 19/3/1913 d 2000
Bristol Royal Victoria
1932 Wolverhampton Wanderers 2
1934 1938 Bournemouth & Boscombe Ath 196
1939 (Bournemouth & Boscombe Ath) (3)
Dartford
Gravesend United
1947 Newport County 14
Bideford Town

Pinder, John James (Jack) RB/LB
b Acomb 1/12/1912 d 2004
Caps: England Sch
1932 1947 York City 199 4

Pinder, William P CH
Sheffield University
1906 Chesterfield Town 3

Pinkerton, Henry IL/LH
b Dunipace 7/5/1916 d 1986
Caps: Scotland War 1
Kilsyth A
Banknock
Dunipace Juniors
1934 Hull City 2 1
1935 Port Vale 3
1936 1937 Burnley 3
Falkirk
Bo'ness United

Pinkerton, James Ross OL
b Rothesay 21/9/1911
Rothesay Royal Victoria
Bute Athletic
Partick Thistle
Montrose
1935 Blackburn Rovers 1
St Bernard's
Dundee United

Pinkney, Ernest (Ernie) OR
b Glasgow 23/11/1887 d 1975
Christ Church
West Hartlepool
1909 1910 Everton 8 1
Barrow
Gillingham
Liverpool
Tranmere Rovers
1921 Halifax Town 30 2
1922 Accrington Stanley 12 3

Pinnell, Archibald GK/OR
1892 Everton 3
1893 Preston North End 1
Chorley
1898 Burnley 5
New Brompton
Plymouth Argyle

Pinxton, Albert Edward IR
b Hanley 24/5/1912 d 1992
1931 Stoke City 0
Stoke St Peter's
Nantwich
1935 Blackburn Rovers 3
1936 Cardiff City 20 3
1937 Torquay United 4

From To Apps Goal

Pipe, James Joyce (Jimmy) LB
b Blackheath 1/3/1909 d 1987
Grays Thurrock
1926 1933 Millwall 196

Pirie, Thomas Stuart (Tom) CH
b Gorbals 9/12/1896 d 1966
Battlefield Juniors
Bathgate
Queen's Park
1923 Manchester United (trial) 0
Aberdeen
1926 Cardiff City 5
1928 Bristol Rovers 12
1928 Brighton & Hove Albion 0
Ross County

Pitcairn, John Watt (Johnny) RH
b Kelvinside 29/1/1904 d 1987
Maryhill Juniors
Raith Rovers
Connah's Quay & Shotton
1930 1931 Charlton Athletic 55
1932 1936 Chester 135
Wigan Athletic

Pither, George OL
b Kew 24/6/1899 d 1966
Richmond Wednesday
Isleworth Town
1921 Brentford 7
1922 1923 Millwall Athletic 18
1924 Bristol Rovers 2
Torquay United
1926 Merthyr Town 16 5
1926 1927 Liverpool 12 1
1928 Crewe Alexandra 38 11
1929 1930 New Brighton 79 10
Tunbridge Wells Rangers
Chatham Town (trial)
Margate

Pitman, Reuben John GK
b Derby 1865 d 1933
1888 1889 Derby County 5

Pitt, Albert Edward OL/IL
b Shardlow 1880
Stone Town
1903 1904 Stoke 7 1
Birmingham University
Canterbury Provinces (NZ)
Stoke
(Canada)
Trentham
Stoke
Norton Bridge

Pitt, Clifford (Cliff) GK
b Moston 26/6/1911 d 1991
Newton Heath Parish Church WM
Acme
Bacup Borough
Acme
1933 Southport 16
Ferguson Pailin
1934 Manchester City 0
Manchester North End
Macclesfield
Bangor City

Pitt, Howard Vincent OL/OR
b Wrexham q1 1907 d 1963
Caps: Wales Amat
1924 1925 Wrexham 7
Northern Nomads

Pitt, John E (Jack) CF
b Walsall
1924 Wolverhampton Wanderers 0
1925 Walsall 4 2

Pittaway, James CF
b West Bromwich 1867
West Bromwich Wednesday
1889 West Bromwich Albion 1 1
Stourbridge
Oldbury Town

Pitts, Harold Frederick (Harry) LB/RB
b Leyton 29/4/1915 d 1998
1931 Fulham 0
Woking
Islington Corinthians
1935 1938 Fulham 9
1939 (Fulham) (1)
Chelmsford City

Place, Walter (Junior) OL/IL/LH
b Burnley q4 1872 d 1928
Blue Star (Burnley)
Union Stars
1893 1899 Burnley 152 30
1900 1901 Woolwich Arsenal 42 6
Trawden Forest
Padiham

From To Apps Goal

Place, Walter (Senior) RH/IL/CH
b Burnley 22/3/1870 d 1948
Burnley
Colne
Bacup
Burnley Union Star
1890 1899 Burnley 136 7
Burnley Belvedere

Plackett, Everard Vernon Sydney (Syd) LH
b Loughborough 21/9/1896 d 1959
Sawley United Church
Sawley Discharged Soldiers Fed
1921 1926 Derby County 140 3
1926 1929 Notts County 84

Plackett, Henry (Harry) IL
b Breaston q2 1871 d 1948
Long Eaton Midland
1888 Derby County 16 2
Nottingham Forest

Plackett, John William LH/RH
b Derby q4 1865 d 1931
Long Eaton Rangers
1896 1897 Loughborough 8

Plackett, Laurence (Lol) IL
b Breaston q1 1869 d 1939
Long Eaton Alexandra
1888 Derby County 22 7
Nottingham Forest

Plane, Edward (Eddie) GK
b 27/9/1907 d 1969
1927 Rochdale 2
Halford Congregationalists

Plant, James Arthur (Jim) LH
b Creswell q3 1898 d 1952
Creswell Colliery
Whitwell Discharged Soldiers
1919 1923 Sheffield United 55 1
Macclesfield
Worksop Town
Ripley Town
Whitwell Old Boys
Whitwell Colliery

Plant, John (Jack) OL
b Bollington 3/1871
Caps: England 1
Heaton Norris
1894 1897 Bury 111 30
Reading
1899 1906 Bury 208 27
Heywood United

Platt, Frederick Douglas (Douglas) OR
b Wolverhampton 1869 d 1940
Lanesford Boys
1898 1899 Wolverhampton Wanderers 6
Oxley
Castle Hill Rovers
St Augustine's

Platt, Harry RH/CH
b Rochdale
Park Bridge St James
1930 1931 Rochdale 16
Hartford Works

Platt, Henry George LB
1898 Burslem Port Vale 2

Platt, John (Jack) IR/CF
b Preston 1880
1901 Preston North End 0
Kettering
Portsmouth
Northampton Town
1908 1910 Preston North End 30 7
St Helens Recreation
Chorley

Platt, John GK
1930 Accrington Stanley 1

Platt, JW CF
1896 Manchester City 1

Platt, Peter GK
b Rishton 23/1/1883 d 1922
Great Harwood
Oswaldtwistle Rovers
1900 Blackburn Rovers 1
1902 1903 Liverpool 44
Luton Town
Nuneaton Town

Platt, Richard (Dick) RB
b Huyton
Huyton Quarry
1932 1936 Tranmere Rovers 173
1937 1938 Northampton Town 3

From To Apps Goal

Platts, Albert John OL/IL
b Worksop q1 1885
Ashton Juniors
Worksop Town
1910 1913 Lincoln City 29 4
Scunthorpe & Lindsey United
Rotherham Town

Platts, Henry CF
Silverwood Colliery
1911 Gainsborough Trinity 1
Silverwood Colliery
1913 Sheffield Wednesday 0

Platts, Robert (Bob) OR
b Anston q1 1900
Anston United
1920 1924 Notts County 50 3
1925 Southend United 0
Heanor Town
British Celanese
Nottingham Co-operative Dairy

Pleasant, George GK
b Plumstead 23/8/1896 d 1976
Ramsgate
1921 Charlton Athletic 2
Northfleet

Plenderleith, Joseph Forsyth CH
b Carluke 1902
1929 Carlisle United 5
Glentoran

Plenderleith, Robert (Bob) CH
b Hamilton 20/6/1909 d 1974
Blantyre Victoria
Peebles Rovers
East Fife
1928 Sunderland 0
1929 Bristol Rovers 22
Sunderland Borough Police

Plum, Seth Lewis LH/RH
b Tottenham 15/7/1899 d 1969
Caps: England 1
Tottenham Park
Avondale
Barnet
1922 1923 Charlton Athletic 47
1924 1925 Chelsea 26 1
1927 Southend United 10

Plummer, Arthur Edward RB
b Bristol q1 1907
Bedminster Down Sports
1927 Bristol City 0
Welton Rovers
Bath City
1930 1931 Coventry City 25
Boston Town
1933 Walsall 3
Dundalk
Valenciennes
Albert (France)
1936 Bristol Rovers 0
Gloucester City

Plummer, Harold George RB/LB
b Bristol 23/3/1904 d 1973
Army (Catterick)
1929 Burnley 0
1930 1932 Darlington 30

Plunkett, Adam Gordon TB LB
b Blantyre 16/3/1903 d 1992
Blantyre Celtic
1924 Bury 0
1925 Queen's Park Rangers 15
Guildford United
1927 Walsall 25
1928 Coventry City 23
1929 Crystal Palace 0
1929 Southend United 0
Oswestry Town
Hinckley Athletic
Loughborough Corinthians
1930 1931 Rochdale 18
Stalybridge Celtic
Hinckley Athletic

Plunkett, Sidney Ernest (Sid) OR
b Norwich 2/10/1920 d 1986
Esdelle Shoe Works
Norwich YMCA
1938 Norwich City 3
1939 Wolverhampton Wanderers 0
1945 1946 Norwich City 28 7
Chelmsford City
Yarmouth Town
Gorleston
Yarmouth Town

From To Apps Goal

Pocock, James Henry (Jimmy) RH
b Bristol q3 1896 d 1956
Imperial Rovers
1920 1921 Swindon Town 11

Pocock, William Thomas (Billy) IL/OL
b Bristol 24/2/1894 d 1959
Bedminster St Francis
Reading
1919 1925 Bristol City 238 46
St Johnstone
Bath City
Bedminster Down Sports

Pointer, Ernest GK
b Sparkbrook 1872
Redditch Town
1896 Small Heath 28
Berwick Rangers (Worcester)
1900 Small Heath 0
Kidderminster Harriers

Pointon, Joe OR/CF
b Leek 1/2/1905 d 1939
Leek Wesleyans
Leek National
Congleton Town
1923 1925 Port Vale 10
1926 1927 Luton Town 65 12
1928 Brighton & Hove Albion 16 5
1929 Torquay United 27 18
1930 Bristol Rovers 9 1
1931 Walsall 17 4

Pointon, Thomas Cecil (Tom) OL
b Middlesbrough q2 1890 d 1966
Redditch Town
1913 Birmingham 4 1
Redditch Town
Walsall
Nuneaton Town
1920 Coventry City 2
Redditch Town

Poland, Frederick (Fred) CF
b Dundee
Our Boys (Dundee)
Burnley
Newton Heath
1888 Burnley 9 5

Poland, George GK
b Penarth 21/9/1913 d 1988
Caps: Wales War 4/Wales 2
Cogan
Penarth Mission
1934 Swindon Town 0
1935 1936 Cardiff City 24
1938 Wrexham 39
1939 Liverpool 0
1946 Cardiff City 2
Lovells Athletic
Penarth Albion

Pole, Eric OR
b Sheffield 8/8/1912 d 1993
1933 Rotherham United 2 1

Pollard, Henry IL/IR/CH
b Liverpool
1935 Sheffield Wednesday 0
1936 1937 Exeter City 4
1939 Rochdale (2)

Pollard, Robert (Bob) RB/LB/RH
b Platt Bridge 25/8/1899
Plank Lane
1920 1928 Exeter City 246
1929 1931 Queen's Park Rangers 66
1932 Cardiff City 31
St Etienne

Pollard, Walter IR/IL
b Burnley 26/9/1906 d 1945
1925 1927 Burnley 20 4
1929 1932 West Ham United 37 3
Sochaux
1933 Fulham 0
1934 1935 Southampton 23 3
1936 Brighton & Hove Albion 0
Tunbridge Wells Rangers

Pollock, Archibald (Archie) RH
b Galston 25/11/1904 d 1988
Peasley Cross Athletic
1930 1931 New Brighton 26

Pollock, Hugh RH
b Newmilns 1865 d 1910
Kilmarnock Athletic
Liverpool Stanley
1888 Everton 1

From To Apps Goal

Pollock, Robert (Bob) LH/RH/LB
b Wishaw 1/6/1880
Wishaw Thistle
Third Lanark
Wishaw Thistle
Bristol City
Kettering
1901 Notts County 0
1902 1908 Leicester Fosse 211 14
Leyton
Leicester Imperial

Pollock, Thomas Alfred OR
b Newcastle 19/6/1905 d 1990
Armstrong Whitworth
1925 Hartlepools United 0
Armstrong Whitworth
1926 Preston North End (trial) 0
Jarrow
Annfield Plain
White-le-Head Rangers
1930 Carlisle United 1
White-le-Head Rangers

Pollock, William OL
b Wishaw 1911
Royal Albert
Cambuslang Rangers
1932 Chelsea 0
Dunfermline Athletic
Dundee
1935 Stockport County 7
Hamilton Academical

Pond, Harold LH
b Kilnhurst 19/4/1917 d 1990
1937 Barnsley 0
1938 1945 Carlisle United 11
1939 (Carlisle United) (2)

Ponsonby, Joseph (Joe) RH
b Dumbarton 1876
Caps: IrLge 6/Ireland 9
Distillery
1897 Stoke 5
Distillery

Ponting, Walter Thomas (Wally) CF
b Grimsby 23/4/1913 d 1960
Humber United
1930 1935 Grimsby Town 13 3
1936 1938 Chesterfield 81 35
1938 Lincoln City 23 15
1939 (Lincoln City) (3) (3)

Pool, Alexander CH/RH
b Annan 1901
Solway Star
1921 1924 Blackburn Rovers 17
1925 Bristol City 12
1926 1928 Exeter City 74 3
Stalybridge Celtic

Poole, Arthur RH
1920 Port Vale 9

Poole, Cyril John LB/OL
b Mansfield 13/3/1921 d 1996
Annesley Colliery Welfare
1936 Mansfield Town 1
1937 Wolverhampton Wanderers 0
Gillingham
1949 1950 Mansfield Town 16 1
Clipstone Colliery Welfare
Corby Town

Poole, Harold CF
b Bulwell 30/7/1894
Newstead Rangers
1911 Nottingham Forest 1
Coventry City
Sutton Town

Poole, John Smith (Jack) LH/CH
b Codnor q4 1892 d 1967
Sutton United (Notts)
Sutton Junction
1914 Nottingham Forest 0
1919 1923 Sunderland 144 1
1924 1927 Bradford City 97

Poole, R Frederick CF/IR
1893 Preston North End 2
1895 Rotherham Town 3

Poole, Thomas GK
Crewe Carriage Works
1899 1900 Burslem Port Vale 17

Poole, William IR
b Keyworth 16/9/1900
Boots Athletic
Basford United
1919 Notts County 1
1920 Coventry City 0
Boston Town

From To Apps Goal

Poole, William Arthur (Billy) CF/CH/IR
b West Bromwich q1 1900
Kidderminster Harriers
1921 Merthyr Town 11 1
1921 1922 Stoke 12
1923 1924 Watford 42 8
1925 Coventry City 17 6
Kidderminster Harriers
Yeovil & Petters United
1928 Merthyr Town 2
Wellington Town
Stourbridge
1931 Walsall 2
Dudley Town

Pooley, Ernest OR
Chorley
1897 Bury 2
Chorley

Pope, Alfred Leslie LB
b Lofthouse 8/1/1913 d 1987
Harrogate AFC
1931 Leeds United 0
1934 Rotherham United (trial) 0
1935 1936 Halifax Town 53
Heart of Midlothian
Darwen

Pope, Francis James L (Frankie) IR/CF
b Brierley Hill q4 1884 d 1953
Pensnett Albion
Cradley Heath
1900 Wolverhampton Wanderers 0
Stourbridge
1905 Wolverhampton Wanderers 8 3
1906 Notts County 2
Walsall
Stourbridge
Netherton

Pope, Harvey Frank (Frank) CF/IR
b Wolverhampton 1879
Compton Rovers
1900 1901 Wolverhampton Wanderers 5 1
Darlaston

Pope, Stanley GN (Stan) IL
b Tiverton q2 1913
Tiverton Town
1936 1937 Exeter City 26 10
1938 Torquay United 13

Poppitt, James IR/IL/CF
b Lilleshall q2 1875 d 1930
Wellington Town
1900 1901 Wolverhampton Wanderers 21 3
Swindon Town
Reading
Swindon Town
1905 1906 Notts County 15 2
1907 Lincoln City 23 3

Popplewell, Stanley CH/RH
b Bolton 2/9/1892 d 1956
Barrow
Exeter City
1920 Blackpool 1
1921 1923 Accrington Stanley 71 4
Darwen
Clitheroe
Colne Town
1927 Accrington Stanley 0

Porritt, Walter OR/IL/RH
b Heckmondwike 19/7/1914 d 1993
1935 Huddersfield Town 0
1936 1946 York City 40 5

Porteous, David (Dave) CH/LH
b Kilmarnock 1874 d 1920
1894 1895 Rotherham Town 51 5
1896 Darwen 3
1898 Barnsley 31
Monckton Athletic

Porteous, George CH/LH
b Stranraer 1890
Govan St Anthony's
1912 1913 Blackburn Rovers 6
Clyde

Porteous, Thomas Stoddart (Tom) RB
b Newcastle q4 1865 d 1919
Caps: England 1
Heart of Midlothian
Kilmarnock
1890 1893 Sunderland 79
1894 1895 Rotherham Town 49
1895 Manchester City 5
South Shore

From To Apps Goal

Porter, Ernest Wesley (Ernie) OR
b Annfield Plain q1 1901
Ouston Rovers
Birtley
1924 Sheffield United 0
Boston Town
1926 Reading 15 3
1927 1930 Norwich City 130 30
Tunbridge Wells Rangers

Porter, John CH
b Stockton 1886
Skinningrove
1909 Grimsby Town 1

Porter, Robert OR
1888 Blackburn Rovers 1

Porter, Thomas Christopher (Chris) IR/IL
b Stockport 25/10/1885 d 1915
Caps: England Amat
Northern Nomads
1905 1908 Stockport County 66 23
1909 1911 Glossop 44 11
Northern Nomads

Porter, W James (Jimmy) RH
b Hamilton 31/7/1901 d 1967
Wishaw YMCA
1921 1935 Bury 396 7

Porter, Walter S LB
b Mellor
Mellor St John's
1895 1896 Blackburn Rovers 6
Mellor Thursday Rangers
St Silas

Porter, William (Billy) CF
b Allithwaite q2 1904
Allithwaite
1926 Barrow 1

Porter, William (Billy) LB
b Fleetwood 7/1905 d 1946
Windsor Villa (Fleetwood)
Fleetwood
1927 1934 Oldham Athletic 274 1
1934 1937 Manchester United 61
Hyde United

Porter, William Alfred (Willie) OL
b London q2 1884
London Caledonians
Fulham
London Caledonians
1905 1906 Chelsea 2
Brighton & Hove Albion
Luton Town
London Caledonians
Ilford

Porter, William Carr CH
b Sunderland 24/1/1908 d 1987
Hylton Colliery
Nottingham University
1931 1934 Nottingham Forest 14

Porterfield, Alfred GK
b 1869
King's Park
1894 Burnley 2

Portman, Horace CH/LB
b High Green 8/12/1906 d 1996
High Green Swifts
1928 1929 Rotherham United 20
Mexborough Athletic

Poskett, Thomas William (Tom) GK
b Esh Winning 26/12/1909 d 1972
Chopwell Institute
Crook Town
1928 1930 Grimsby Town 2
1933 Lincoln City 10
1934 Notts County 10
1935 1936 Tranmere Rovers 22
1937 1946 Crewe Alexandra 99
1939 (Crewe Alexandra) (2)
Northwich Victoria

Posnett, Arthur Thorpe OR
b Lincoln 21/5/1887 d 1950
Lincoln Liberal Club
1906 Lincoln City 3 1
1907 Gainsborough Trinity 0
Lincoln Liberal Club
Grantham Avenue
South End
Newland Athletic
Horncastle Town

From To Apps Goal

Postin, Eli IR/OR
b Darby End 3/6/1908 d 1991
Rowley Village
Warley Institute
Whiteheath Juniors
Whiteheath
Ham Bakers
Crosswells Road Star
Blackheath Town
Halesowen Town
1928 West Bromwich Albion 0
Cradley Heath
1930 West Bromwich Albion 0
1933 Cardiff City 33 13
1934 1935 Bristol Rovers 4 1
1935 Wrexham 10 2
Brierley Hill Alliance
Dudley Town
Hednesford Town
Darlaston
Hednesford Town
Marsh & Baxter
Samuel Taylor
BSA Redditch
Marsh & Baxter
BTH Blackheath
Marsh & Baxter

Postles, George Henry LB/RB
b Northwich q3 1869 d 1936
1892 1893 Northwich Victoria 45
1894 Crewe Alexandra 3

Postlethwaite, Thomas William (Tom) LH/IR
b Haverthwaite 4/9/1909 d 1984
Haverthwaite
Ulverston Town
1927 Barrow 9
Bouth Athletic
Ulverston Town
1930 Bolton Wanderers 0
1931 1933 Barrow 74 10
1934 Bradford Park Avenue 19 1
Northwich Victoria
1937 1938 Northampton Town 61 1
1939 Watford (2)

Potter, Albert Edward LH/LB
b Exeter 23/9/1897 d 1942
Woodbury
Pinhoe
1923 1926 Exeter City 89 3
1927 1928 Wigan Borough 67 4
Colwyn Bay United
Devon General Bus Company

Potter, Arthur IR
b Nottingham 1874
1897 Notts County 2
Bristol City

Potter, Cecil Bertram RH
b West Hoathly 14/11/1888 d 1975
Melton Asylum
Ipswich Town
Norwich City
1919 Hull City 10
1921 Hartlepools United 0

Potter, John J OR
b Birmingham
Redditch Town
1925 Walsall 16 1

Potter, John M CF/CH
Herrington Welfare
1931 1932 Doncaster Rovers 17 8
Denaby United

Potter, Leonard F (Len) IL
b Bedford
Bedford Town
1934 1935 Northampton Town 20 6
Wellingborough Town

Potter Smith, Thomas IL/IR/RH
b Newcastle 7/6/1901 d 1978
Caps: WLge 2
St Peter's Albion
1922 Merthyr Town 18 6
1923 Hull City 8 2
1924 Hartlepools United 30 7
1925 Merthyr Town 14 4
1925 1928 Cardiff City 42 7
1929 1936 Brighton & Hove Albion 282 40
1937 Crystal Palace 0
Gloucester City

From To Apps Goal

Potts, Arthur IL/IR
b Cannock 26/5/1888 d 1981
Willenhall Pickwick
Hednesford Town
Willenhall Swifts
1913 1919 Manchester United 27 5
1920 1921 Wolverhampton Wanderers 35 9
1922 Walsall 1
Bloxwich Strollers
Dudley Town
Red White & Blue (Wolverhampton)

Potts, Harry Archibald IR/IL
Sheffield
1897 1898 Sheffield Wednesday 2 1
Sheffield

Potts, James Forster (Jimmy) GK
b Morpeth 22/1/1904 d 1986
Blyth Spartans
1925 1932 Leeds United 247
1934 1935 Port Vale 82

Potts, Joseph (Joe) LB/RB
b Newcastle 25/2/1889
Ashington
1912 1913 Hull City 5
1920 Portsmouth 5
1921 1922 Leeds United 10
1923 1924 Chesterfield 53
1925 1926 Bradford Park Avenue 38

Potts, Robert Frederick (Fred) RB
b Congleton 11/3/1893 d 1953
1910 Manchester United 0
Bacup Borough
1912 1921 Bradford City 136
Congleton Town

Potts, Victor Ernest (Vic) RB
b Birmingham 20/8/1915 d 1996
Metro Welfare
Northfleet
1934 Tottenham Hotspur 0
1937 1938 Doncaster Rovers 27
1945 1947 Aston Villa 62

Poulter, Henry (Harry) CF
b Sunderland 24/4/1910 d 1985
Royal Navy
Shiney Row Swifts
1931 Sunderland 0
1932 1935 Exeter City 50 33
1936 Hartlepools United 0

Poulton, Alonzo (Jerry) IL/IR/CF
b Wolverhampton 28/3/1890 d 1966
Monmore Green
Priestfield Albion
1912 West Bromwich Albion 0
Worcester City (loan)
1914 West Bromwich Albion 9 1
Merthyr Town
1919 1921 Middlesbrough 18 5
1921 1922 Bristol City 28 9
1922 Reading 25 3
Llanelly

Powell, Albert Elyston Edgar OR
b Bargoed 22/6/1908 d 1940
Bargoed United
1928 Swindon Town 3
1929 Coventry City 0
Merthyr Town

Powell, Alfred Charles Henry (Alf) OL
b Pontnewydd 1912
Pontnewydd
1934 Bolton Wanderers 0
1935 Plymouth Argyle 2
1936 Leeds United 0

Powell, Alfred Frank IL
1904 Nottingham Forest 1
Cardiff City
Hyde

Powell, Aubrey IR/OR/IL
b Cwmtwrch 19/4/1918 d 2009
Caps: Wales War 4/Wales 8
Cwm Wanderers
1934 Swansea Town 0
1936 1947 Leeds United 112 25
1939 (Leeds United) (2)
1948 1949 Everton 35 5
1950 Birmingham City 15 1
Wellington Town

From To Apps Goal

Powell, Edgar Frederick IL
b Cardiff 6/1/1899 d 1955
Caps: Wales Sch
Barry
Pembroke Dock
Denaby United
1923 Huddersfield Town 0
1924 Stoke 2
1925 1926 Accrington Stanley 65 17
1927 Merthyr Town 23 4
1928 Barrow 1
Taunton Town
Street
Frome Town

Powell, Herbert (Bert) IL/CF
b Colwick q1 1886
Treharris
1903 Nottingham Forest 0
Gresley Rovers
Grantham Avenue
1906 Chesterfield Town 6 1
1906 Barnsley 6 2
Sutton Town
Carlisle United
New Brompton
Coventry City
1910 Birmingham 4 1
Rotherham Town
Portsmouth
Boscombe
Worksop Town
Grantham
Retford Town
Sutton Town

Powell, Ivor Verdun RH/LH
b Gilfach 5/7/1916
Caps: Wales War 4/Wales 8
Bargoed
1935 Queen's Park Rangers (trial) 0
Barnet
1938 1948 Queen's Park Rangers 110 2
1948 1950 Aston Villa 79 5
1951 Port Vale 6
Barry Town
1952 1954 Bradford City 83 9

Powell, John GK
b Burslem 3/6/1892 d 1961
Port Vale
Walsall
1914 Nottingham Forest 24

Powell, Joseph Joshua (Joe) RB
b Bristol 1870 d 1896
Walsall
80th Staffordshire Regiment
1893 1896 Woolwich Arsenal 86 1

Powell, Samuel (Sam) IL/CF/IR
b Holmes 25/5/1899 d 1961
Thornhill United
1920 1924 Leeds United 28 7
1924 1927 Sheffield Wednesday 25 9
Stafford Rangers

Powell, Seth LB
b Cerney 1862 d 1945
Caps: Wales 7
Oswestry White Star
Oswestry Town
1889 1891 West Bromwich Albion 30
1892 Burton Swifts 0
Chester
Oswestry United

Powell, WE LB
1892 Burslem Port Vale 3

Powell, William H (Billy) LB
Merthyr Town
1932 Lincoln City 4
Dundalk
Newry Town
Sligo Rovers
Limerick

Powell, William Methuen Phillips (Billy) LH
b Sutton-in-Ashfield 21/1/1901 d 1981
Retford Town
Sutton Town
1924 Sheffield Wednesday 20
1927 1929 Grimsby Town 78 1
1930 Southend United 1
Sutton Town

From To Apps Goal

Power, Geoffrey Frank (Geoff) IR
b Grangetown 7/4/1899 d 1963
Grangetown St Mary's
1920 Sunderland 10
1921 Blackpool 16 6
Darwen
Fleetwood
Denaby United
Eston United
Scarborough
Grangetown St Mary's

Power, George GK
b Bolton 10/4/1904 d 1985
1927 Manchester City 0
1928 Rochdale 3
Darwen

Pownell, James LH
b Hoyland q4 1888 d 1966
1911 Blackpool 1

Poxton, James Harold (Jimmy) OL
b Staveley 2/2/1904 d 1971
Staveley Town
1926 1927 West Bromwich Albion 9 1
1927 1928 Gillingham 43 8
1929 1933 Millwall 147 30
1934 Watford 23 9
1935 Walsall 25 5
1936 Bristol City 0
1937 Reading 0

Poynton, Cecil LB/LH
b Brownhills 10/8/1901 d 1983
Ton Pentre
1923 1932 Tottenham Hotspur 150 3
Margate
Northmet

Poynton, William OR
b Hill Top 1883
Wednesbury Old Athletic
Britannia Victoria
1901 West Bromwich Albion 2 2

Poynton, William LH
b West Bromwich
Kynoch Works
1931 Aston Villa 0
1932 1933 Chesterfield 14
Buxton

Poyntz, William Ivor (Billy) IR/CH
b Tylorstown 18/3/1894 d 1966
Gorseinon United
Llanelly
1921 1922 Leeds United 29 7
1923 Doncaster Rovers 29 10
1924 Northampton Town 29 4
1925 1926 Bradford Park Avenue 33 5
1926 Crewe Alexandra 10 1
1927 Hartlepools United 31

Poyser, George Henry LB
b Stanton Hill 6/2/1910 d 1995
Teversall Colliery
Mansfield Town (trial)
Stanton Hill
1928 Wolverhampton Wanderers 0
Stourbridge
Mansfield Town
1931 1933 Port Vale 72
1934 1945 Brentford 149
1946 Plymouth Argyle 3
Dover

Pratt, Charles Bertie CH
b Aston 7/6/1886 d 1973
Barrow
1909 Everton 2
Exeter City

Pratt, David LH/CH/CF
b Lochore 5/3/1896
Lochore Welfare
Lochgelly United
Hearts o' Beath
Celtic
Bo'ness (loan)
1921 1922 Bradford City 50 5
1922 1926 Liverpool 77 1
1927 1928 Bury 51
Yeovil & Petters United

Pratt, John OL
1898 Walsall 1 1

Pratt, John T GK
b Workington q2 1916
1935 Preston North End 0
1935 1936 Blackburn Rovers 6
Distillery
Workington
1939 Carlisle United 0

From	To		Apps	Goal
Pratt, Richard			IL	
b Middlesbrough q2 1876				
1897		Sheffield United	0	
		South Bank		
1899		Middlesbrough	16	1
Pratt, Thomas Peet (Tom)			IR/CF/IL	
b Fleetwood 28/8/1873			d 1935	
		Fleetwood Rangers		
1895		Grimsby Town	29	15
1896	1898	Preston North End	71	24
		Tottenham Hotspur		
1900	1902	Preston North End	54	16
		Fleetwood		
1902		Preston North End	19	3
1903		Woolwich Arsenal	8	2
		Fulham		
1904		Blackpool	8	2
		Fleetwood		
1906		Blackpool	0	
Pratt, William			LB	
b Highgate, Warwickshire 1872				
		Hoskins & Sewell		
1895	1901	Small Heath	129	
Pray, John (Jack)			RH	
b Falkirk 1873			d 1948	
		Rangers		
1895	1901	Bury	185	8
		St Bernard's		
Preece, John Causer (Jack)			LB/RB	
b Wolverhampton 30/4/1914			d 2003	
		Sunbeam Motors		
1933		Wolverhampton Wanderers	2	
1935	1937	Bristol Rovers	79	
1938		Bradford City	3	
1939	1946	Southport	36	
1939		(Southport)	(3)	
1947		Swindon Town	7	
		Chippenham United		
Preece, William			RB	
b Ashton-under-Lyne				
1921	1922	Stalybridge Celtic	8	
Preedy, Charles James Fane (Charlie)			GK	
b Neemuch, India 11/1/1900			d 1978	
		British Motor Cab		
		Bostall Heath		
		Redhill		
1923	1927	Charlton Athletic	131	
1928		Wigan Borough	41	
1929	1932	Arsenal	37	
1933		Bristol Rovers	39	
1934		Luton Town	5	
		Margate		
Prentice, David			IL/IR	
b Alloa 29/7/1908			d 1984	
		Alva Albion Rovers		
		Celtic		
		Stranraer (loan)		
		Ayr United (loan)		
		Nithsdale Wanderers (loan)		
1930		Plymouth Argyle	0	
1931		Walsall	23	4
1932		Bournemouth & Boscombe Ath	0	
		Raith Rovers		
1933		Mansfield Town	21	1
		Bath City		
		Trowbridge Town		
Prentice, Horace			OR	
b Weldon 23/10/1900			d 1978	
		Brickstock St Peters		
1923		Luton Town	1	
Prentice, John Harkness			OL	
b Glasgow 19/10/1898				
1919		Manchester United	1	
1920		Swansea Town	3	
1921		Tranmere Rovers	23	3
		Manchester North End		
		Hurst		
		Chester		
		Great Harwood		
		Manchester North End		
		Hurst		
Prentice, William			OR	
1904		Glossop	9	3
Prescott, James R			OL/OR	
b Waterloo, Lancashire				
1932		Everton	0	
1933		Southport	0	
		Marine		
1935		Liverpool	0	
1936	1938	Cardiff City	31	7
1939		Hull City	0	
1945		Plymouth Argyle	0	

From	To		Apps	Goal
Prescott, Thomas George (Tom)			RB	
b Attercliffe 8/1/1875			d 1957	
Caps: FLge 1				
		Liverpool East End		
		Hamilton Athletic		
		Crosse		
		Liverpool South End		
1896	1904	Notts County	212	1
Prescott, Thomas Harry			RB	
1902	1907	Gainsborough Trinity	32	
Presgrave, Gordon Edwin			OR	
b Kippax 5/1/1915			d 1976	
		Worksop Town		
1933	1935	Halifax Town	21	5
1936		Carlisle United	5	1
1936		Mansfield Town	5	1
		Worksop Town		
Preskett, Frank Matthew			IR	
b Woking 1/11/1916			d 2002	
		Woking		
1935	1937	Plymouth Argyle	3	1
1937	1938	Torquay United	32	8
1939		(Torquay United)	(3)	(1)
Prest, Thomas Walsh (Tommy)			IL/IR/OL	
b Darwen 4/2/1908			d 1987	
		Darwen		
1929	1934	Burnley	80	16
1935	1936	Brighton & Hove Albion	27	5
1937		Aldershot	16	1
		Tuckholes		
1938		Rochdale	21	6
Preston, Alfred			OL/CF	
1906	1907	Gainsborough Trinity	3	
Preston, Ernest			LB	
b Middlesbrough q4 1901			d 1966	
Caps: England Amat				
		South Bank		
1922		Durham City	8	
		South Bank		
Preston, Gerald			RH	
b Northwich 1873				
1893		Northwich Victoria	9	
Preston, Henry (Harry)			IL/CF	
b Shropshire 1880				
		Ironbridge		
1901	1904	Wolverhampton Wanderers	26	1
		Kidderminster Harriers		
		Hatherley		
Preston, Josiah			RB	
b Derby 1885				
		Derby Midland		
		Burton United		
1909		Birmingham	7	
		Halesowen		
Preston, Robert (Bob)			RH/CH	
b Loanhead 1895			d 1945	
		Loanhead Mayflower		
		Heart of Midlothian		
		Torquay United		
1923	1927	Plymouth Argyle	143	3
1928		Torquay United	15	
		Llanelly		
		Bray Unknowns		
		Shelbourne		
		Sligo Rovers		
Preston, Stephen			CF/IL	
b Gorton q4 1879				
1901	1902	Newton Heath/Manchester Utd	33	13
1902		Stockport County	11	2
1903		Manchester United	0	
Preston, William			RH	
1906		Middlesbrough	1	
Prew, James Herbert (Jimmy)			OR	
b Coventry 2/1914			d 1940	
		Hinckley United		
1936		West Bromwich Albion	7	1
1937		Walsall	4	
		Hinckley United		
Price, Albert James William (Billy)			CF	
b Hadley 10/4/1917			d 1995	
		Wrockwardine Wood Juniors		
1937	1947	Huddersfield Town	51	23
1939		(Huddersfield Town)	(3)	(1)
1947	1948	Reading	15	2
1948		Hull City	8	5
1949	1951	Bradford City	54	28
		Winsford United		

From	To		Apps	Goal
Price, Alfred H (Alf)			LH	
1904		Bristol City	3	
		Worcester City		
		Bournville		
		Worcester City		
		Walsall		
		Redditch		
Price, Arthur			LH/IR/IL	
b Sheffield q3 1892			d 1954	
		Sharrow Old Boys		
		Worksop Town		
1912	1919	Leeds City	78	26
1919	1921	Sheffield Wednesday	78	3
1922		Southend United	1	
		Scunthorpe & Lindsey United		
		Bakewell		
Price, Arthur Bertrand R			IR	
b Birmingham 1883			d 1941	
		Sheldon Heath		
		Moor Green		
1906		Wolverhampton Wanderers	1	
		Acocks Green		
Price, Cyril			IL/CF/IR	
b South Elmsall 10/3/1908			d 1998	
		South Kirkby Colliery		
1928	1930	Doncaster Rovers	24	5
1931		Wrexham	2	1
		Scunthorpe & Lindsey United		
		Frickley Colliery		
Price, David William (Billy)			CF	
b New Tredegar q1 1898				
		Barry		
		Pontypridd		
		Ebbw Vale		
1926		Newport County	23	8
		Barry		
Price, Edward (Ted)			GK	
b Walsall q3 1883				
		Walsall		
1909	1910	Stockport County	34	
		Croydon Common		
		Brentford		
1920		Queen's Park Rangers	7	
Price, Eric			IL/CF	
b Hemsworth 3/9/1905			d 1976	
		Wilmslow		
		Sandbach Ramblers		
1925		Manchester City	0	
1926		Norwich City	16	6
1927		Northampton Town	4	2
1928		Torquay United	3	1
Price, Ernest Clifford (Cliff)			IL	
b Ibstock 13/6/1895			d 1955	
		Ibstock Albion		
		Coalville Swifts		
1919	1921	Leicester City	28	8
		Coalville Swifts (loan)		
1922	1923	Halifax Town	44	15
1923	1925	Southampton	59	16
1926	1927	Nottingham Forest	20	5
		Loughborough Corinthians		
		Nuneaton Town		
		Gresley Rovers		
		Snibston United		
Price, Frederick (Freddie)			RH/OR	
b Brierley Hill 1888			d 1960	
		Aston		
		Wellington Street Citadels		
		Dudley Town		
1912	1919	Wolverhampton Wanderers	116	
		Sunbeam Motors		
1920		Port Vale	19	1
1921		Newport County	27	1
Price, Frederick Thomas (Fred)			OL	
b Ibstock 24/10/1901			d 1985	
		Coalville Swifts		
		Whitwick Imperial		
1922	1923	Leicester City	4	
1924		Southampton	9	
1925	1926	Wolverhampton Wanderers	39	8
1927		Chesterfield	25	6
		Burton Town		
		Nuneaton Town		
		Midland Red Sports (Coalville)		
Price, George Jabez			IR/IL/RH	
b Wolstanton q1 1878			d 1938	
1895	1906	Burslem Port Vale	223	39
Price, George Leonard			GK	
b Cudworth q2 1902			d 1942	
		Fryston Colliery		
1924		Halifax Town	11	

From	To		Apps	Goal
Price, Gilbert Walter			CF	
b Wolverhampton 1888			d 1955	
		Chillington Rangers		
1909		West Bromwich Albion	1	
		Cradley Heath St Luke's		
		Rawmarsh Town		
Price, Ioan Haydn (Haydn)			LH	
b Mardy q2 1883			d 1964	
Caps: Wales 5				
		Mardy Corinthians		
		Riverside		
		Aberdare Town		
1906		Burton United	1	
1907		Aston Villa	0	
		Wrexham		
1909		Leeds City	8	
		Shrewsbury Town		
		Walsall		
Price, James (Jimmy)			CH	
b Annbank 24/4/1896			d 1970	
		Cumnock Juniors		
		Celtic		
		Dumbarton (loan)		
		Airdrieonians		
1921	1922	Nelson	24	
1922	1928	Ashington	235	10
		North Shields		
		Ashington		
		Wallaw United		
Price, Jeremiah (Jerry)			IL	
1930		Doncaster Rovers	9	2
		Boston Town		
Price, John (Jack)			IL/OR	
b Shotton 29/8/1918				
		Easington Juniors		
		Blackhall Colliery Welfare		
		Horden Colliery Welfare		
1936		Portsmouth	0	
1937		Wolverhampton Wanderers	0	
1938	1948	Hartlepools United	89	12
1939		(Hartlepools United)	(1)	
1948		York City	2	2
		Horden Colliery Welfare		
		Stockton		
		Murton Colliery Welfare		
Price, John A			OR/CF	
b Blackburn				
1920	1921	Wolverhampton Wanderers	13	1
Price, John Charles			RH	
b New Washington				
1923		Bristol City	3	
		Workington		
Price, John Leonard (Jack)			IR/CF	
b Birmingham 1877				
		Shenstone Boys Club		
1898		Small Heath	1	
		Watford		
1901	1902	Doncaster Rovers	59	17
1903		Stockport County	11	1
Price, John William (Jack)			LB/RB	
b Ibstock 9/6/1900			d 1984	
		Coalville Swifts		
1920		Leicester City	0	
1923		Bristol Rovers	5	
1924		Swindon Town	2	
1925		Brentford	12	
1927	1928	Torquay United	31	
Price, Llewellyn Percy (Lew)			OL	
b Caersws 12/8/1896			d 1969	
Caps: Wales Amat				
		Barmouth		
		Hampstead Town		
		Mansfield Town		
1920	1921	Aston Villa	10	
1922	1927	Notts County	66	6
1928		Queen's Park Rangers	3	
		Grantham		
		Basford United		
Price, Norman Malcolm			LB	
b Dumfries 2/3/1904			d 1977	
		Dumfries		
		Glasgow Ashfield		
		Ayr United		
1930		Bristol Rovers	0	
		Nithsdale Wanderers (loan)		
1931	1933	Accrington Stanley	88	8
		Coleraine		
		Stalybridge Celtic		
1936	1937	Oldham Athletic	73	
		Gainsborough Trinity		
Price, Thomas			CF	
b Barlestone q4 1879				
		Whitwick White Cross		
1902		Lincoln City	11	3

From To Apps Goal

Price, Walter RB/LB
b Aberdare 13/8/1896
1921 1922 Aberdare Athletic 36
Pontypridd
1924 Aberdare Athletic 7
1924 1929 Plymouth Argyle 63
1930 Bristol Rovers 13

Price, William John (Johnny) IL
b Mhow, India 4/12/1903 d 1987
Caps: England Amat
Coldstream Guards
10th Hussars
Woking
1927 Brentford 1 1
Woking
1928 1936 Fulham 189 49
1937 Port Vale 13 2

Priest, Alfred Ernest (Fred) OL/IL/LB
b Guisborough q3 1875 d 1922
Caps: England 1
South Bank
1896 1905 Sheffield United 209 72
South Bank
1906 Middlesbrough 13
Hartlepools United

Priestley, John (Jock) RH/CH
b Johnstone 19/8/1900 d 1980
Johnstone
1920 1927 Chelsea 191 18
1928 1931 Grimsby Town 139 7
St Johnstone
Cowdenbeath
Keith

Priestley, Robert Irwin IR
b Sheffield q2 1873 d 1941
1894 Sheffield Wednesday 2 1

Priestley, Thomas John McKee (Tom) IR
b Belfast 11/3/1911 d 1985
Caps: LoI 3/Ireland Amat/Ireland 2
Cookstown
Coleraine
Linfield
1933 Chelsea 23 1
Shelbourne

Priestman, Joseph James (James) OL
b Melton Mowbray q2 1870 d 1940
Melton Rovers
Melton Town
1894 Leicester Fosse 8 2
Melton Town

Prince, Albert J IL
Stafford Rangers
1914 Manchester United 1

Prince, Arthur OL
b Bucknall 8/12/1902 d 1980
Bucknall
1922 1923 Port Vale 43 1
1924 1927 Sheffield Wednesday 53 7
1928 Hull City 5
Chester
1929 Walsall 1
1930 Bristol Rovers 0
Dorden Institute

Prince, D OL
1893 Newton Heath 2

Prince, E IL
1892 Crewe Alexandra 1

Prince, John (Jack) GK
b Crewe 6/6/1906 d 1971
Nantwich
1927 Oldham Athletic 1
1928 1929 Port Vale 43
1930 Rochdale 15
1931 Wrexham 3
Shrewsbury Town
1932 Derby County 0
Northwich Victoria
Nantwich
1937 Crewe Alexandra 0

Prince, Thomas OL/IL
Selbourne
1897 1900 Sunderland 4

Pringle, Allen LH/RH
b Craghead 26/3/1914 d 1990
West Pelton
1935 1937 Portsmouth 26 2
1939 1945 Chesterfield (2)
Shrewsbury Town

From To Apps Goal

Pringle, Charles Ross (Charlie) LH/RH
b Nitshill 18/10/1894
Caps: SLge 1/Scotland 1
Inkerman Rangers
Maryhill
St Mirren
1922 1927 Manchester City 197 1
Manchester Central
Inkerman Rangers
1929 1930 Bradford Park Avenue 44 1
1931 1932 Lincoln City 58 1
1932 Stockport County 0
FC Zurich
Hurst
Waterford

Pringle, Henry (Harry) IR/IL/OR
b Perkinsville 8/4/1900 d 1965
Craghead United
1920 Arsenal 0
Chester-le-Street
1922 1933 Lincoln City 292 60
Grantham

Pringle, Robert J RB
b Stockton 21/9/1897
1921 Middlesbrough 0
1922 1923 Bradford City 31
1924 1933 Crewe Alexandra 290 7

Prior, George CF
b Edinburgh
St Bernard's
1901 Sunderland 5
Third Lanark

Prior, George (Geordie) RB/LB
b Ashington 2/3/1898 d 1977
Blyth Spartans
1920 1923 Sheffield Wednesday 37
1924 1929 Watford 172
Ashington

Prior, Jack OR
b Choppington 2/7/1904 d 1982
Choppington Colliery
Blyth Spartans
1922 1926 Sunderland 67 10
1926 1931 Grimsby Town 160 34
Ashington
1932 Mansfield Town 32 7
Stalybridge Celtic
Pressed Steel (Oxford)

Prior, Philip OR
b Bethnal Green q2 1889 d 1966
1909 1911 Clapton Orient 19 3
1912 1913 Bury 33
Darlington

Prior, Stanley John (Stan) CF
b Swindon 20/12/1910 d 1972
Swindon Corinthians
1933 1936 Charlton Athletic 50 32
1937 Queen's Park Rangers 6 3
Cheltenham Town

Prior, William Dinsdale RB
b Choppington 8/8/1985 d 1986
Blyth Spartans
Bedlington United
Stakeford United
Choppington
1924 Ashington 1

Pritchard, Andrew Smart RH
b Airdrie 23/6/1912
Glasgow Ashfield
Partick Thistle
Ards
1937 Halifax Town 15 2
1938 Clapton Orient 1

Pritchard, Arthur Brynley OR
b Newport 22/10/1917 d 2005
Oakdale
1935 1936 Newport County 4
Yeovil & Petters United
Colchester United

Pritchard, Harvey John (Jack) OR/LH/OL
b Meriden 30/1/1913 d 2000
Exhall Colliery
1936 Coventry City 5 2
1937 Crystal Palace 30 6
1937 1945 Manchester City 22 5
1946 1951 Southend United 71 8
Folkestone Town

From To Apps Goal

Pritchard, Thomas Francis (Tommy) CH
b Wellington 18/6/1904 d 1980
GWR (Wolverhampton)
1924 Wolverhampton Wandrs (trial) 0
Sunbeam Motors
1925 Stockport County 2
1926 1927 Newport County 23 1
1927 1928 Wolverhampton Wanderers 56 3
1929 1931 Charlton Athletic 43
1931 Thames 27 1
Olympique Marseille
1933 Preston North End 1
Lancaster Town
1935 Mansfield Town 1
Lancaster Town

Pritchard, Tilson RB
b Walsall Wood 1872
Burntwood Swifts
1894 Small Heath 1
Lichfield Town

Pritty, George Joseph RH/LH
b Birmingham 4/3/1915 d 1996
HB Metro
1932 Newport County 0
1936 1937 Aston Villa 3
1938 1947 Nottingham Forest 49 1
1939 (Nottingham Forest) (3)
Cheltenham Town

Probert, William Henry (Billy) RB/LB
b Worksop 15/1/1893 d 1948
Kilton Rovers
Portsmouth
Southend United
1920 1924 Portsmouth 176
1925 1926 Fulham 16
Emsworth

Procter, Benjamin OR
Blackburn 19/2/1890 d 1977
Lower Darwen
1910 1911 Blackburn Rovers 2
1913 1914 Stockport County 37 6

Proctor, Edward (Ted) CF
b Barlaston 1870 d 1944
Leek
1893 Sheffield United 0
Royal Dublin Fusiliers
1895 Stoke 3 2
Burslem Port Vale

Proctor, James Alston OR
b Burnley q4 1874 d 1911
1897 Darwen 10 2

Proctor, James Frederick IR
b Canning Town 7/3/1890 d 1976
Custom House
1911 Huddersfield Town 4
1912 Leicester Fosse 7 1
1913 Stockport County 0

Proctor, Jeremiah CH
b Burnley q1 1876 d 1955
1897 Darwen 3 1

Proctor, John (Jack) CH
b Stoke-on-Trent 1871 d 1893
Fenton
Dresden United
1891 1893 Stoke 52 1

Proctor, John Roxby (Jack) RB
b New Delaval 10/8/1910 d 1978
New Delaval Villa
1930 Huddersfield Town 0
1932 1933 Bournemouth & Boscombe Ath 53
1934 1937 Hartlepools United 149 20
Blyth Spartans

Proctor, John William (Jack) CF
b South Bank 15/4/1904 d 1970
South Bank
1926 Middlesbrough 0
South Bank
1928 Barrow 5 2

Proctor, Michael Henry (Harry) LH/IR
b Ushaw Moor 10/7/1912 d 1984
Esh Winning Juniors
Washington Colliery
1931 Portsmouth 0
1932 1933 Hartlepools United 61 14
1934 1946 Norwich City 108 3

From To Apps Goal

Proctor, Norman LH/IL/IR
b Alnwick 11/5/1896 d 1947
Spen Black & White
Scotswood
Blyth Spartans
1922 Rotherham County 22 1
1923 West Ham United 7 1
1924 Leicester City 5
1925 1926 Tranmere Rovers 56 13
1927 1930 Halifax Town 126 3
Workington
Newbiggin West End

Proctor, Wilfred (Wyn) OL
b Fenton 23/11/1893 d 1980
South Shore
1920 Blackpool 0
1921 Nelson 14 1
Fleetwood
Lancaster Town

Proffitt, Wilfred IL
b Walsall 9/1/1906 d 1981
Pelsall
1925 Walsall 21 2

Prosser, Benjamin (Ben) CF
b Stoke-on-Trent q1 1878 d 1936
Leeds
1902 Stoke 1
1903 Bradford City 15 1

Prosser, WH RH
1908 Gainsborough Trinity 1

Protheroe, Sydney (Syd) OL
b Dowlais 16/12/1910 d 1982
1928 Merthyr Town 0
Machynlleth
Merthyr Town
1931 Charlton Athletic 0
1933 Wolverhampton Wanderers 0
1934 1935 Torquay United 38 3
1936 1937 Rochdale 63 14
1938 Notts County 2

Proud, Joseph (Joe) OR/OL
b Dipton 13/11/1905 d 1977
Dipton
Boldon Colliery Welfare
Spennymoor United
1930 1931 Fulham 12 3
Llanelly
1932 1938 Aldershot 126 17
1939 (Aldershot) (1)

Proud, Pattison LH
b Bishop Auckland q3 1883 d 1937
Bishop Auckland
1906 Sheffield Wednesday 1

Proudfoot, David CH
b Dunfermline 1/4/1872 d 1941
Whiteinch Juniors
Partick Thistle
1896 1897 Leicester Fosse 25
Bedminster
Partick Thistle

Proudfoot, J LB
1931 Thames 1

Proudfoot, James (Jimmy) IL/IR/RH
b Usworth Colliery 31/1/1906 d 1963
Fatfield Juniors
Usworth Juniors
Washington Colliery
Usworth Colliery
1927 1931 Barnsley 143 28
1932 Notts County 10
1933 Southend United 10 1
Yeovil & Petters United
1934 1935 Southport 67 2
Ashington
Murton Colliery Welfare
Blue Bus Company

Proudfoot, John CF/IR
b Airdrie 27/2/1874 d 1934
Partick Thistle
1896 1897 Blackburn Rovers 36 14
1898 1901 Everton 84 30
Watford
Partick Thistle
Hamilton Academical

From	To	Club	Apps	Goal
Proudfoot, Peter			IR/CH/RH	
b Wishaw 25/11/1880			d 1941	
		Wishaw Victoria		
		Airdrieonians		
		Wishaw Thistle		
		Wishaw United		
1899		Sheffield Wednesday	0	
1900	1902	Lincoln City	79	20
		St Mirren		
		Albion Rovers		
		Millwall Athletic		
1905		Clapton Orient	26	
1905	1907	Chelsea	12	
1907		Manchester United	0	
1908		Stockport County	34	1
		Morton		
		Wishaw Thistle		
1910	1912	Stockport County	11	
Proudlock, George Thomas			IL	
b Morpeth 19/9/1919			d 2006	
		Amble Juniors		
1938	1947	West Ham United	18	5
		Workington		
Prouse, William Horatio Redvers (Bill)			IR	
b Birmingham 1/2/1900			d 1984	
		Redditch Town		
		Dogpool		
1922	1923	Rochdale	51	18
1924	1926	Fulham	76	31
		Wellington Town		
		Cradley Heath		
		Wellington St George's		
Prout, George William			GK	
b Dalton-in-Furness 3/11/1902			d 1960	
		Dalton Casuals		
1923	1925	Preston North End	46	
1926		Grimsby Town	4	
1928	1929	Carlisle United	66	
		Bath City		
		Cheltenham Town		
Prout, Stanley Sylvester (Stan)			OL	
b Fulham 22/1/1911			d 1996	
		Leytonstone		
1930		Fulham	0	
		Park Royal		
1932		Chelsea	16	3
1934	1935	Bristol Rovers	39	5
1936		Chester	2	1
		Dartford		
Prout, Sylvester Charles (Dick)			CF/RH/IR	
b Fulham q2 1888			d 1949	
		Silverdale (Fulham)		
		Fulham Old Town		
		Fulham Amateurs		
		Tunbridge Wells Rangers		
1909		Fulham	7	
1910	1912	Stockport County	59	19
		Plymouth Argyle		
Provan, John			CF	
		West Calder		
1895		Burnley	4	
		St Bernard's		
Pryce, John (Jack)			IR/IL/CF	
b Renton 25/1/1874			d 1905	
		Renton		
		Hibernian		
1898		Glossop North End	20	6
1898	1900	Sheffield Wednesday	54	5
		Queen's Park Rangers		
		Brighton & Hove Albion		
Pryce-Williams, Price			LH	
1909		Glossop	5	
Pryde, David (Dave)			LH/RH	
b Newtongrange 10/11/1913			d 1987	
		Newtongrange Star		
		St Bernard's		
		Peebles Rovers		
1935		Arsenal	0	
		Margate		
1938		Arsenal	4	
1946	1949	Torquay United	64	
		Bonnyrigg Rose Athletic		
Pryde, Robert Ireland (Bob)			CH/LH	
b Methil 25/4/1913			d 1998	
Caps: FLge 2				
		Windygates Thistle		
		Thornton Rangers		
		East Fife (trial)		
		St Johnstone		
		Brechin City (loan)		
1933	1948	Blackburn Rovers	320	11
1939		(Blackburn Rovers)	(3)	
		Wigan Athletic		

From	To	Club	Apps	Goal
Pudan, Albert Ernest (Dick)			LB/RB	
b East Ham q3 1881			d 1957	
		Clapton		
		West Ham United		
		Bristol Rovers		
1907	1908	Newcastle United	24	
1909		Leicester Fosse	29	7
1910		Huddersfield Town	0	
1912	1913	Leicester Fosse	17	
Puddefoot, Sydney Charles (Syd)			IR/CF	
b Limehouse 17/10/1894			d 1972	
Caps: SoLge 1/FLge 2/England 2				
		Condor Athletic		
		Limehouse Town		
		West Ham United		
		Falkirk		
1919	1921	West Ham United	103	64
		Falkirk		
1924	1931	Blackburn Rovers	250	79
1931	1932	West Ham United	22	3
		Fenerbahce		
Pugh, David Henry (Harry)			OR	
b Wrexham q1 1875			d 1945	
Caps: Wales 7				
		Wrexham Grosvenor		
		Wrexham		
1897		Stoke	18	1
1897	1901	Lincoln City	91	11
1905		Lincoln City	0	
Pugh, Edwin Charles (Charles)			OL	
b Middlesbrough q2 1876			d 1943	
		St Augustine's		
1899		Middlesbrough	31	7
Pugh, James William (Jimmy)			LB	
b Hereford q3 1891				
		Brighton & Hove Albion		
		Hereford		
		Bridgend Town		
		Abertillery		
1921	1922	Manchester United	2	
1923	1924	Wrexham	40	
		Rhos Athletic		
		Bangor City		
		Buckley United		
		Holywell Town		
		Denbigh United		
Pugh, Reginald (Reg)			OR	
b Aberaman 7/1917				
		Aberaman Athletic		
1934	1938	Cardiff City	166	25
1939		(Cardiff City)	(3)	(1)
Pugh, Robert Archibald Lewis (Bob)			LH/IL	
b Symonds Yat 16/9/1909			d 1986	
		Chepstow		
		Hereford United		
1926	1928	Newport County	64	13
1929	1930	Bury	28	10
1930	1938	Nottingham Forest	248	19
Pugh, Sidney John			LH	
b Dartford 10/10/1919			d 1944	
		Nunhead		
		Margate		
1938		Arsenal	1	
Pugsley, John			LH/RH/CH	
b Grangetown 1/4/1900			d 1976	
Caps: Wales 1				
		Grangeway YMCA		
1922		Cardiff City	0	
1925	1926	Grimsby Town	80	6
1927		Bristol City	16	
1928	1933	Charlton Athletic	215	8
		Lovells Athletic		
Pullan, Robert Lander (Bob)			RH/IR	
b Darlington 19/2/1898			d 1983	
		Dawdon		
1921	1923	Bristol City	18	1
1924	1926	Exeter City	103	2
		Yeovil & Petters United		
Pullen, Harry			LB	
b Wellingborough q4 1888			d 1937	
		Kettering		
		Queen's Park Rangers		
1920		Newport County	22	
1921		Hartlepools United	0	
		Kettering		
Pullen, William John (John)			CH	
b Victoria, Monmouthshire 1/11/1901			d 1969	
Caps: Wales 1				
		Ebbw Vale		
1924	1934	Plymouth Argyle	194	16
Pulman, John			RH	
1909		Bolton Wanderers	1	

From	To	Club	Apps	Goal
Pumford, George Leslie			IL/CF	
b Ruabon 23/4/1902			d 1972	
		Manchester North End		
1924		Derby County	2	
1926		Walsall	6	2
Pumfrey, Bernard			LB/RB	
b Stirchley 5/1873			d 1930	
Caps: FLge 1				
		Birmingham St Mark's		
1892	1893	Small Heath	11	1
1896	1900	Gainsborough Trinity	121	1
Pumfrey, Paul			IL	
b Birmingham q4 1875			d 1911	
1899		Gainsborough Trinity	1	
Purcell, Albert			OL	
b Burslem 3/7/1913			d 2001	
1933	1934	Port Vale	4	
Purcell, George William			OR/IR	
b Barnsley 18/2/1901			d 1968	
		Victory WMC		
1922	1923	Stockport County	20	4
1924	1925	Swindon Town	18	2
1926	1931	Exeter City	227	51
1932	1933	Gillingham	47	18
		Gainsborough Trinity		
Purcell, Llewellyn			IL	
b Boothstown 30/4/1909			d 1980	
		Pendlebury		
		Winsford United		
1931		Oldham Athletic	1	
1932		Stockport County	0	
		Winsford United		
		Witton Albion		
		Rossendale United		
		Mossley Common United		
Purcell, Mark			LB	
b Barnsley 26/7/1902			d 1978	
		Attercliffe		
		Mexborough		
1926	1927	Barrow	28	
		Dick, Kerr's XI		
		Scunthorpe & Lindsey United (trial)		
1928		Exeter City	0	
		Dick, Kerr's XI		
		Lancaster Town		
		Peterborough United (trial)		
Purcell, Oswald Jack (Ossie)			IR	
b Crewe 7/6/1895			d 1985	
		Nantwich		
1922	1924	Crewe Alexandra	8	5
Purdon, James Small (Jimmy)			RB/OR	
b Springburn 14/3/1906			d 1985	
		Baillieston Juniors		
		Tweedhill		
		Rangers		
		Clyde (loan)		
		Ayr United (loan)		
		Celtic (loan)		
1931	1933	Bradford Park Avenue	44	
1934	1935	Crystal Palace	14	2
1936		Southport	28	
		Montrose		
Purdy, Albert			RH/CH	
b Edmonton 15/3/1899			d 1991	
1920		Tottenham Hotspur	0	
1921	1924	Charlton Athletic	99	
1925	1927	Southend United	43	
1928		Brentford	1	
		Dartford		
Purdy, Arthur			GK	
b Evenwood 23/7/1904			d 1970	
		Evenwood Juniors		
		Cockfield St Mary's		
		Coundon United		
1923		Tottenham Hotspur	0	
1925		Luton Town	24	
1926		Southend United	2	
1927		Durham City	27	
1927	1928	Blackpool	31	
		Colwyn Bay United		
1930		Norwich City	11	
		Fleetwood		
		Evenwood Comrades		
		Throckley Welfare		
Pursell, Peter			LB/CH/LH	
b Campbeltown 1/7/1894			d 1968	
Caps: Scotland 1				
		Campbeltown Academicals		
		Queen's Park		
		Rangers		
1919	1923	Port Vale	162	
1924	1925	Wigan Borough	35	
		Congleton Town		
		Dordrecht		

From	To	Club	Apps	Goal
Pursell, Robert Russell (Bob)			LB/RB	
b Campbeltown 18/3/1889			d 1974	
Caps: Scotland Amat				
		Aberdeen University		
		Queen's Park		
1911	1919	Liverpool	99	
1920	1921	Port Vale	66	
Purslow, Thomas			IL	
b Perry Barr 6/1870			d 1937	
		Nechells Old Boys		
1894		Aston Villa	1	1
		Walsall		
		Darlaston		
		Willenhall Pickwick		
Purves, William Michael			RB	
b Belfast 1870				
Caps: IrLge 3				
		Glentoran		
1893	1895	Small Heath	41	
		Glentoran		
Pybus, George			IR	
b Brandon, County Durham 22/7/1911			d 2001	
		Chester-le-Street		
1932		Bradford City	0	
		Altrincham		
1934		Chelsea	0	
1935		Gillingham	6	1
		Folkestone		
Pycock, Arthur			RB/RH	
b Kirton-in-Lindsey 11/3/1876			d 1970	
1899	1902	Gainsborough Trinity	117	3
		Worksop Town		
Pye, Reginald			RB	
b Woodhouse q3 1898			d 1969	
		Beighton		
1919		Sheffield United	0	
		Beighton		
1924		Rotherham County	1	
		Loughborough Corinthians		
		Staveley Town		
		Dinnington Main Athletic		
Pyke, George Woolston			CF	
b Gateshead 28/8/1893			d 1977	
		Rutherford College		
1919	1921	Newcastle United	13	3
		Blyth Spartans		
Pyle, Arthur			IR	
b Doncaster q4 1881			d 1922	
		Doncaster St James		
1902		Doncaster Rovers	5	2
		Rotherham Town		
Pyle, Thomas (Tom)			OL/IL	
b Lincoln 1875			d 1958	
		Princess (Lincoln)		
1894	1899	Lincoln City	27	3
		Adelaide (Lincoln)		
Pym, James Coleman			IL	
b Bedminster q3 1876			d 1962	
1897		Loughborough	2	
Pym, Richard Henry (Dick)			GK	
b Topsham 2/2/1893			d 1988	
Caps: FLge 2/England 3				
		Topsham		
1920		Exeter City	39	
1921	1930	Bolton Wanderers	301	
		Yeovil & Petters United		
		Topsham		
Pynegar, Albert			IR/IL/CF	
b Basford 24/9/1895			d 1978	
		Awsworth Amateurs		
		Eastwood Rangers		
		Sutton Town		
1920	1923	Leicester City	44	20
1923	1924	Coventry City	54	27
1925	1928	Oldham Athletic	131	51
1928	1930	Port Vale	56	34
1930	1931	Chesterfield	64	39
1932		Rotherham United	17	4
		Sutton Town		
Pynegar, Algernon			CF/IR	
b Marlpool 22/10/1883			d 1948	
		Marlpool		
		Whitwick White Cross		
1904		Derby County	1	
1905		Grimsby Town	2	
		Rotherham Town		
		Rotherham County		
		Tottenham Hotspur		
		Denaby United		
		Heanor United		

From To Apps Goal

Quantick, John Henry RB
b Cwm 7/7/1910 d 1972
Ebbw Vale
1930 West Bromwich Albion 0
Dudley Town
1933 1936 Hull City 88 1
Worcester City

Quantrill, Alfred Edward (Alf) OL/OR
b Rawalpindi, India 22/1/1897 d 1968
Caps: England 4
Boston Swifts
1914 1920 Derby County 72 5
1921 1923 Preston North End 64 7
Chorley
1924 1929 Bradford Park Avenue 191 57
1930 1931 Nottingham Forest 15 2

Quayle, Charles James (Charlie) CF
b Kirkdale 11/4/1907 d 1984
Seventh Kings
1932 New Brighton 11 2
1933 Accrington Stanley 0
Shrewsbury Town
Drumcondra
1936 1937 Crystal Palace 10 3
1938 Bradford City 0

Quayle, James Alfred LB
b Camden Town q3 1890
Fossdene Old Boys
1907 Woolwich Arsenal 0
Northfleet
1910 Woolwich Arsenal 1

Quigley, Dennis OR
b St Andrews 7/12/1913 d 1984
St Andrews United
Dundee
Brechin City
1936 1938 Grimsby Town 23 2
1939 Hull City (2)
Forfar Athletic

Quigley, James Alexander OR/LH/OL
b Gateshead 13/9/1911 d 1989
Mickley
Crawcrook Albion
1934 1936 Gateshead 22 3

Quigley, Patrick Hugh (Paddy) OL
b Derry 1899 d 1976
Londonderry Distillery
Glentoran
1921 Accrington Stanley 13 1
Rossendale United
1923 Accrington Stanley 26 4
1924 Preston North End (trial) 0
Rossendale United
Chorley
Darwen

Quin, William John Joseph (John) OR/CF
b Barrhead 1886 d 1957
Manchester Xavieran College
Higher Broughton
Cheetham Hill
1907 Manchester City 0
1908 1909 Manchester United 2
Nelson
Chorley
Eccles Borough
1912 1914 Grimsby Town 61 5
Arthurlie
Clyde
Ayr United

Quinn, C OR
b Tyneside
1893 Newcastle United 23 5
1894 Manchester City 0
1895 Newcastle United 1

Quinn, Charles Joseph (Joe) LB/RB
b Kilmarnock 11/3/1902
Guildford United
1922 1923 Portsmouth 21
(USA)
Peterborough & Fletton United

Quinn, Cyril OR/OL
b Ilkeston 29/1/1910 d 1968
Ilkeston
Grantham
1929 1931 Blackpool 37 6
Fleetwood (loan)
1932 Swindon Town 30 3
Fleetwood
Grantham

From To Apps Goal

Quinn, Peter (MM) OL
b Sunderland 3/12/1892 d 1976
Bankhead Albion
Spennymoor United
1910 1919 Blackpool 155 16
1919 1922 Preston North End 87 10
Fleetwood
1922 Bury 6 1
1923 New Brighton 30 2

Quinn, Peter IL
b North Shields
North Shields Athletic
1919 Bradford City 4 1
1919 Coventry City 15 3

Quinton, Walter (Wally) LB/RB
b Anston 13/12/1917 d 1996
Dinnington
1938 Rotherham United 32
1947 1948 Birmingham City 8
1948 1950 Brentford 42
1952 Southend United (trial) 0
1952 Shrewsbury Town 3

Raby, Walter Leslie IL
b Lincoln 23/9/1902 d 1973
Robeys
Lincoln City
Grantham
1921 Grimsby Town 2 1
1922 Clapton Orient 0
Scunthorpe & Lindsey United
Gainsborough Trinity
Poole
1926 Doncaster Rovers 0

Raby, William (Joe) IL/IR/OL
b Heighington 3/7/1873 d 1954
St Catherine's (Lincoln)
1892 1893 Lincoln City 23 7
1896 Gainsborough Trinity 5 1
1896 Lincoln City 3
1897 Gainsborough Trinity 11 4
Tottenham Hotspur
Wellingborough
1900 1901 Gainsborough Trinity 60 20
1902 1903 Stockport County 52 12
1904 Doncaster Rovers 2

Race, Henry (Harry) IR/IL
b Evenwood 7/1/1906 d 1942
Raby United
1927 1929 Liverpool 43 18
1930 1932 Manchester City 10 3
1933 1936 Nottingham Forest 115 26
Shrewsbury Town
1938 Hartlepools United 3

Race, William (Billy) OR
b Horden 5/2/1896 d 1974
Spennymoor United
1925 1927 Darlington 40 8
Spennymoor United
1929 1930 Hartlepools United 19 2
Horden Colliery Welfare

Radford, Arthur OL/IL
b Eastwood q3 1877
1897 1898 Nottingham Forest 4
1899 1900 Gainsborough Trinity 64 21

Radford, Arthur Henry Hart RB/LB
b East Ham 12/2/1902 d 1962
Bromley
1923 1924 Millwall Athletic 2

Radford, Bernard CF/IL
b West Melton 23/1/1908 d 1986
Dearne Valley Old Boys
Wath Athletic
Wombwell
Darfield
1927 1928 Nelson 55 41
1929 1930 Sheffield United 20 7
1931 Northampton Town 8
Royal Naval Depot (Chatham)
Banstead Mental Hospital

Radford, Charles (Charlie) RB
b Walsall 19/3/1900 d 1924
Caps: England Sch
Walsall
1920 1923 Manchester United 91 1

Radford, Robert Baden GK
b Lichfield 19/10/1900 d 1970
Brereton Social
1923 Port Vale 3

Radford, Thomas IR
b Bristol q3 1886 d 1946
Salisbury City
1908 Bristol City 1
Treharris

From To Apps Goal

Radford, Walter Robert IL
b Wolverhampton 7/1886 d 1940
1905 Wolverhampton Wanderers 2
Southampton
1907 1909 Wolverhampton Wanderers 83 41
Southport Central

Rae, George OL
b Paisley
Kilwinning Rangers
1923 Wigan Borough 19 1

Rae, Henry S (Harry) CH
b Glasgow 1896
Glasgow Benburb
Clyde
Morton
Clyde
1925 1926 Brentford 67 7
Hamilton Academical

Rae, James Clarkson (Jimmy) LB
b Bothkennar 22/11/1907 d 1958
Gairdoch United
King's Park
Partick Thistle
1932 1938 Plymouth Argyle 246
1939 (Plymouth Argyle) (3)

Rae, John CF
b Blackmill, Argyllshire 1912
Camelon
Clyde
East Stirlingshire (loan)
Dumbarton
East Stirlingshire
Partick Thistle
1937 Bristol City 2
Bristol Aeroplane Company

Rae, Peter LH/CF/OL
Mansfield Greenhalgh
1892 Burton Swifts 1
1892 1893 Northwich Victoria 9 2
1893 Rotherham Town 19 5
Mansfield
1896 1897 Burton Swifts 48 5

Rae, Thomas (Tommy) LH/RH/CH
b Kilwinning 1883
Morton
1906 1910 Bury 72 1
St Mirren

Rae, William CF
Castle Donington
1901 Glossop 13 2

Raeside, Henry (Harry) CF
b Renfrew 1864
Abercorn
1890 Preston North End 2
Abercorn

Raeside, James Smith GK
b Parkhead 1879 d 1946
Caps: Scotland 1
Parkhead
Third Lanark
1906 1911 Bury 156 3

Rafferty, Daniel RH/OR
Blantyre Victoria
1907 1909 Everton 7
Royal Albert
Airdrieonians

Raine, James Edmundson OR
b Newcastle 3/1886 d 1928
Caps: FLge 1/England Amat 1
Rydal Mount (Colwyn Bay)
Scotswood
1904 Sheffield United 1
1905 Newcastle United 4 1
1906 1907 Sunderland 25 6
Bohemians (Newcastle)
Reading
1908 1910 Glossop 52 4

Raine, Thomas Anthony (Tommy) IR
b Leadgate 29/5/1903 d 1987
Consett Celtic
Leadgate Park
1924 South Shields (trial)
Consett Celtic
1924 Chelsea 0
Annfield Plain
Dipton United
1927 Durham City 12 3
Crookhall Colliery Welfare
Wath Athletic
Easington Colliery Welfare
Crookhall Rovers
Crookhall Colliery Welfare

From To Apps Goal

Rainford, William (Billy) IL/CF
b Prescot 26/2/1892 d 1968
1920 Manchester United 0
1921 1922 Tranmere Rovers 22 6
Wallasey United

Rainnie, Alexander (Alex) RH/LH
b Banff 22/6/1891 d 1965
South Shields
1919 Newcastle United 1
1921 Darlington 8
1923 Ashington 1

Raisbeck, Alexander Galloway (Alex) CH
b Wallacestone 26/12/1878 d 1949
Caps: SLge 3/Scotland 8
Blantyre Boys Brigade
Larkhall Thistle
Royal Albert
Hibernian
1897 Stoke 4
1898 1908 Liverpool 312 19
Partick Thistle
Hamilton Academical

Raisbeck, Andrew LH
b Slamannan 1881
Hibernian
1901 Liverpool 0
1905 1906 Hull City 47 5
(Canada)

Raisbeck, Leslie CF
b Shotley Bridge 23/5/1907 d 1990
Benfieldside St Cuthbert's
Willington
Tow Law Town
1928 Stockport County 1 1
1930 Nelson 29 11
1931 Stockport County 1
Stalybridge Celtic
Buxton
Northwich Victoria

Raisbeck, Luke CH/LH
b Polmont 1879
Airdrieonians
1898 Sheffield United 0
Third Lanark
1899 Middlesbrough 19 1
West Ham United
Port Glasgow Athletic
1905 Blackpool 18
Lancaster
Ashton Town
Barrow

Raisbeck, William M (Bill) LH
b Wallacestone 22/12/1875 d 1946
Larkhall Thistle
Hibernian
Clyde
1896 Sunderland 0
Royal Albert
Clyde
1898 1900 Sunderland 69 8
1901 Derby County 3
New Brompton
Reading
Falkirk
(Canada)

Raitt, David RB
b Buckhaven 7/12/1884 d 1969
Buckhaven Victoria
Buckhaven Thistle
Dundee
1922 1927 Everton 122
1928 Blackburn Rovers 4
Forfar Athletic

Raitt, George P LH
b Glasgow
Cambuslang
1911 Huddersfield Town 6

Raleigh, Simeon CF/IL
b Brinsworth 24/3/1909 d 1934
Silverwood Colliery
1929 Huddersfield Town 0
1930 1931 Hull City 31 21
1932 1934 Gillingham 83 34

Ralley, William CH/LH
b Luton q4 1878 d 1939
Luton Stanley
1898 1899 Luton Town 21
Bedford Queens Engineers

From	To	Club	Apps	Goal
Ralphs, Albert			OR	
b Nantwich 2/1892			d 1964	
		Nantwich		
		Burnell's Ironworks		
		Whitchurch		
1911		Aston Villa	1	
		Chester		
		Mold		
Ralphs, Bertram Victor H (Bert)			OR/OL	
b Handsworth q4 1896			d 1942	
		Dennison's		
		Reading		
		Nuneaton Town		
1920	1921	Blackburn Rovers	40	6
1922	1925	Stoke	91	6
1926		Chesterfield	32	7
1927	1928	Crewe Alexandra	57	4
		Stafford Rangers		
		Colwyn Bay		
		Northwich Victoria		
Ramage, Andrew			CF	
b Edinburgh 27/2/1904				
		Orwell United		
		Musselburgh Bruntonians		
		Dunfermline Athletic (trial)		
		St Bernard's		
		Dundee		
1927		South Shields	3	1
		St Bernard's		
		Penicuik Athletic		
Ramage, John (Jock)			CH/RH	
b Lasswade 4/10/1899				
		Bonnyrigg Rose Athletic		
		Heart of Midlothian		
1926	1927	Coventry City	11	2
1927		Luton Town	9	
		Heart of Midlothian		
		Ross County		
		Chirnside United		
Ramage, Peter Martin Fairgrieve			IL	
b Bonnyrigg 26/3/1908			d 1982	
		Bonnyrigg Rose Athletic		
		Tranent Juniors		
		Newtongrange Star		
1927		Coventry City	26	5
1928	1936	Derby County	233	55
1937	1938	Chesterfield	71	4
		Chelmsford City		
		Heanor Town		
		Atherstone Town		
		Ilkeston Town		
Rampton, George			CF/IL	
b Brighton 28/10/1888			d 1971	
		Nuneaton PSA		
		Atherstone Town		
		Nuneaton Town		
		Stafford Rangers		
		Walsall		
1911	1914	Grimsby Town	73	30
Ramsay, Alexander Parrott (Alex)			OL	
b Gateshead q1 1899			d 1957	
		Spen Black & White		
		Swalwell		
1919	1920	Newcastle United	34	2
1921		Queen's Park Rangers	6	
		Aberaman Athletic		
Ramsay, Andrew			GK	
b Scotland				
		Newcastle East End		
		Newcastle United		
		Stockton		
1893		Newcastle United	1	
		Dundee		
Ramsay, Andrew			LB	
b East Benhar 1877			d 1908	
		East Benhar		
1899	1903	Middlesbrough	124	1
		Leyton		
Ramsay, David Robert (Bob)			RH/RB/CH	
b Stoke-on-Trent 1864				
		Burslem Port Vale		
1888	1889	Stoke	43	4
		Newton Heath		
		West Manchester		
1892	1893	Northwich Victoria	29	4
1893		Burslem Port Vale	16	
Ramsay, James Howie (Jimmy)			IL	
b Clydebank 7/8/1898			d 1969	
		Moor Park		
		Arthurlie		
		Renfrew Victoria		
		Kilmarnock		
1923	1926	Arsenal	69	11
		Kilmarnock		
		Galston		

From	To	Club	Apps	Goal
Ramsay, Raymond			OR/OL	
1921		Walsall	2	
1922		Gillingham	3	
Ramsay, Stanley Hunter (Stan)			LB/IL/CH	
b Ryton-on-Tyne 10/8/1904			d 1989	
		Ryton		
		Stargate Rovers		
1925	1927	Sunderland	24	14
1927	1931	Blackpool	104	2
1932	1934	Norwich City	79	1
		Shrewsbury Town		
		Dereham Town		
Ramsbottom, Thomas			LB	
b Idle 13/1/1901			d 1972	
		Idle		
1920		Bradford City	0	
		Pontypridd		
1921		Sheffield Wednesday	12	
Ramsden, Bernard (Barney)			LB/RB	
b Sheffield 8/11/1917			d 1976	
		Hampton Sports		
		Sheffield Victoria		
1937	1947	Liverpool	57	
1939		(Liverpool)	(3)	
1947	1948	Sunderland	12	
1949		Hartlepools United	13	
		(USA)		
Ramsden, Charles William			OR	
b South Normanton q1 1903			d 1949	
		South Normanton Colliery		
1925	1926	Rotherham United	50	15
1927	1930	Manchester United	14	3
1927		Stockport County (loan)	21	9
		Manchester North End		
Ramsden, Ernest			LB	
b Sheffield 1882				
		Denaby United		
		Brentford		
1909		Grimsby Town	5	
		Mexborough Town		
Ramsell, Ernest Arthur			RH	
b Stanton, Staffordshire 1883			d 1954	
		Stanton		
1905		Derby County	5	
Ramsell, Leonard Thomas			IL	
b Gillingham 20/8/1897			d 1975	
		RGA		
		Gillingham		
		Chatham Town		
1924		Gillingham	10	2
		Chatham Town		
1926		Brentford	0	
Ramsey, Alexander R			RB	
b Collington 1867			d 1935	
		Kidderminster Harriers		
1888		West Bromwich Albion	1	
		Kidderminster Harriers		
Ramsey, J David			LH	
		Wishaw		
1908		Manchester City	1	
Ramsey, John			LB	
b Bordesley Green 9/1870			d 1942	
		Church (Birmingham)		
1892		Aston Villa	4	
		Ward End		
Ranby, Samuel (Sam)			IR	
b Hull 29/10/1897			d 1958	
		Gilberdyke		
1920		Hull City	1	
		Reckitt's (Hull)		
		Selby Town		
		York City		
		Selby Town		
Rance, Charles Stanley (Charlie)			CH	
b Bow 28/2/1889			d 1966	
		Clapton		
1910	1920	Tottenham Hotspur	103	
1920	1921	Derby County	23	
1922		Queen's Park Rangers	13	
		Guildford United		
Rand, John Edward (Jack)			IR	
b Cockfield 19/6/1902			d 1970	
		Cockfield		
1925		Everton	0	
1926		Watford	6	
		Flint Town		
		Connah's Quay & Shotton		
1929		Darlington	10	7
		Scarborough		
		Tunbridge Wells Rangers		
		West Stanley		

From	To	Club	Apps	Goal
Randall, CH			GK	
1906		Nottingham Forest	1	
Randall, Charles Edward			IL	
b Bearpark q1 1884			d 1916	
		Hobson Wanderers		
1908	1910	Newcastle United	18	6
		Huddersfield Town (loan)		
		Castleford Town (loan)		
1911	1913	Woolwich Arsenal	43	12
		North Shields Athletic		
Randall, James (Jimmy)			OL/IL/OR	
b Guide Post 12/12/1904			d 1995	
		Ashington Colliery Welfare		
		Sleekburn Albion		
		Bedlington United		
1925	1928	Ashington	124	32
1928	1929	Bradford City	57	15
1930	1934	Derby County	52	4
1935		Bristol City	19	
		Ashington		
		Crookhill Colliery		
Randall, Oswald James Henry (Ossie)			GK	
b Thatcham 13/8/1895			d 1978	
1920		Brighton & Hove Albion	1	
1923	1925	Swindon Town	71	
1926		Exeter City	14	
Randle, Arthur John			RH	
b West Bromwich 3/12/1880			d 1913	
		Lyng Rovers		
		Oldbury Town		
		Darlaston		
1901	1907	West Bromwich Albion	132	1
1908	1912	Leicester Fosse	123	2
Randle, Herbert Clarence (Harry)			RH/CH/RB	
b Stonebroom 31/7/1906			d 1976	
		Stonebroom United		
		Mansfield Town		
		Shirebrook		
1930		Birmingham	0	
1932	1933	Southend United	40	
1934	1936	Gillingham	110	2
1937	1938	Accrington Stanley	74	1
1939		Barrow	0	
Randle, John (Jackie)			LB	
b Bedworth 23/8/1902			d 1990	
		Bedworth Juniors		
		Exhall Colliery		
1923	1927	Coventry City	149	
1927	1932	Birmingham	111	
1933		Bournemouth & Boscombe Ath	28	
		Guildford City		
		Newdigate		
Randle, Walter William			OR	
b Aston 8/1870			d 1931	
		Aston Unity		
1893		Aston Villa	1	
		Leek		
		Aston Victoria		
Randles, Joshua			OL/LB/CH	
b Burslem 6/1865			d 1925	
1892	1895	Burslem Port Vale	11	4
Randles, Robert			IL	
b Birkenhead q1 1888				
1906		Liverpool	0	
		Tranmere Rovers		
1908		Chesterfield Town	4	1
		Tranmere Rovers		
Rankin, Arthur			OL	
b Glasgow 30/4/1904			d 1962	
		Rutherglen Glencairn		
		Clyde		
		Dykehead		
1926	1928	Bristol City	70	12
1929		Charlton Athletic	0	
		Yeovil & Petters United		
Rankin, Bruce			OR	
b Glasgow 1880				
		White Star Wanderers		
		Kirkdale		
		Tranmere Rovers (trial)		
1901	1905	Everton	37	7
1905	1906	West Bromwich Albion	29	5
1906		Manchester City	2	
		Luton Town		
		Egremont Social (Wirral)		
		Wrexham		

From	To	Club	Apps	Goal
Rankin, John Patterson (Johnnie)			IL/IR/LH	
b Coatbridge 10/5/1901				
		Bellshill Athletic		
		Hamilton Academical		
1924		Doncaster Rovers	6	
		Dundee		
1925	1929	Charlton Athletic	187	34
1930	1933	Chelsea	62	9
1934	1935	Notts County	25	2
		Burton Town		
Rankin, William (Willie)			CH	
b Dumbarton 20/3/1901			d 1968	
		Parkhead Juniors		
		Vale of Clyde		
		Dundee		
1926	1931	Blackburn Rovers	144	4
1931	1932	Charlton Athletic	26	
		Burton Town		
Ransford, Herbert			IL	
b Blackwell, Derbyshire 25/9/1901			d 1983	
		South Normanton		
1923		Nottingham Forest	4	1
		Alfreton Town		
Ransford, James			CF	
b Blackwell, Derbyshire q2 1884			d 1929	
		Blackwell		
		Ripley Athletic		
		Blackwell		
		Alfreton Town		
1906		Derby County	15	3
		Alfreton Town		
		Sutton Junction		
Ransom, Frank			LH	
b Ireland				
1903		Woolwich Arsenal	1	
		Southern United		
		Crystal Palace		
Ranson, John George (Jack)			CF/IR	
b Norwich 1/4/1909			d 1992	
1928		Norwich City	0	
1930		Swansea Town	2	
1931		Chester	8	1
		Colwyn Bay United		
1932		Gateshead	32	21
1933		Millwall	14	3
		Burton Town		
1934		Carlisle United	15	9
1935		Lincoln City	5	1
		Blyth Spartans		
		Spennymoor United		
		Durham City		
		Horden Colliery Welfare		
		Durham City		
Ranson, Ronald (Ronnie)			LB	
b Pelton 12/9/1913			d 1983	
		Birtley		
1937		Portsmouth	0	
1938		Bournemouth & Boscombe Ath	1	
1939		Clapton Orient	0	
		Weymouth		
Ratcliffe, Beaumont (Bill)			CH/RB	
b Bolton-on-Dearne 24/4/1909			d 2003	
		Mexborough		
		Thurnscoe Victoria		
		Bolton Albion		
1930		Bradford Park Avenue	0	
1931		Charlton Athletic (trial)	0	
1931	1934	New Brighton	131	4
		Le Havre		
1935	1938	Oldham Athletic	156	1
1939		(Oldham Athletic)	(3)	
1946	1947	Reading	32	
1948		Watford	24	
		Runcorn		
		Earlestown		
Ratcliffe, Emor (Jack)			RB/LB/LH	
b Hyde q2 1880			d 1948	
		Loughborough Corinthians		
1902	1905	Derby County	16	
1905	1906	Middlesbrough	9	
Ratcliffe, George			OR	
b Lathom q3 1877				
1898		Newton Heath	1	
Ratcliffe, George Albert			IL/OL	
b Hanley q1 1877			d 1944	
		Stone Town		
1895		Crewe Alexandra	0	
		South Shore		
1897		Sheffield United	0	
1898	1899	Grimsby Town	57	19
		West Ham United		
1902		Doncaster Rovers	27	7
Ratcliffe, JR			LH/IR	
1896	1898	Darwen	23	3

From To Apps Goal

Ratcliffe, Milton Archie (Archie) CF
b Blackburn 30/1/1893 d 1981
Nelson
1920 Blackpool 13 2
1921 Sheffield Wednesday 12 4
1922 Tranmere Rovers 1

Ratcliffe, NR OR
1894 Darwen 1

Rathbone, Fred GK
b Meir 1886
Newcastle Rangers
1906 1907 Stoke 3
Whitchurch
Stoke
Winsford

Rathbone, H LH
1902 Stockport County 6

Rathbone, Matthew OR
1930 Stockport County 2

Rattray, Charles Robert (Charlie) OR
b Fleetwood 10/5/1911 d 1995
Fleetwood Windsor Villa
1929 1933 Blackpool 54 9
1934 Watford 19
1936 Mansfield Town 36 5
1937 Port Vale 22 1
1938 Accrington Stanley 19 1
Mossley
Fleetwood

Rattray, Hardie Wilson IR
b Glasgow 11/7/1901
Glasgow Benburb
Kilmarnock
1924 Bournemouth & Boscombe Ath 11 1
Arthurlie

Raven, James RH
b Nottingham 29/3/1908 d 1965
1931 Notts County 0
Folkestone
1934 Brentford 1
1936 Bristol Rovers 7
1937 1938 Wrexham 55 1
Nottingham Corinthians
East End (Nottingham)
Nottingham Co-operative Dairy

Raw, Henry (Harry) RH/IL/IR
b Tow Law 6/7/1903 d 1965
Tow Law Town
1925 1930 Huddersfield Town 63 11
1930 1932 West Bromwich Albion 25 7
1936 1937 Lincoln City 66 7

Rawcliffe, Roland RH
b Accrington 17/8/1900 d 1987
1923 Accrington Stanley 1
1924 Burnley (trial) 0

Rawlings, Archibald (Archie) OR
b Leicester 2/10/1891 d 1952
Caps: England 1
Shirebrook
Wombwell
Darfield United
1911 Barnsley 0
Shirebrook
Northampton Town
Rochdale
Dundee
1920 1923 Preston North End 147 17
1923 1925 Liverpool 63 8
1926 Walsall 23
1926 1927 Bradford Park Avenue 21 5
1928 Southport 9 3
Dick, Kerr's XI
Fleetwood
Burton Town

Rawlings, James Sydney Dean (Syd) OR
b Wombwell 5/5/1913 d 1956
Dick, Kerr's XI
1933 Preston North End 12
1933 1934 Huddersfield Town 11 2
1934 1935 West Bromwich Albion 10 1
1936 1937 Northampton Town 48 18
1937 1938 Millwall 53 27
1945 Everton 0
1946 1947 Plymouth Argyle 56 20

Rawlings, William Ernest (Bill) CF
b Andover 3/1/1896 d 1972
Caps: England 2
Andover
1920 1927 Southampton 294 156
1927 1929 Manchester United 35 19
1929 Port Vale 5 2
New Milton
Newport (Isle of Wight)

From To Apps Goal

Rawlins, Nathan (Nat) OL
b Blowick 26/7/1896 d 1979
All Saints
Blowick Working Lads
1921 Southport 1 1
Burscough Rangers

Rawlinson, Norris RB
b Rochdale q2 1906 d 1968
1933 Halifax Town 4
Macclesfield

Rawlinson, Percy OR
b Barrow 29/9/1907 d 1987
Marsh Albion Junior Unionists
Barrow Templar Crusaders
Vickerstown
1926 1927 Barrow 11 1
Ulverston Town
Kirkby United
Crow Nest Sports

Rawlinson, Thomas IL
b Barrow 28/8/1903 d 1992
1925 Barrow 12 3

Rawson, Albert Noble CF/IR
b Rotherham q4 1896 d 1949
Darnall Old Boys
1919 1922 Sheffield United 18 7
1922 1923 Birmingham 19 9
1924 Barnsley 15 6
Worksop Town

Rawsthorne, Joseph (Joe) CF
b Liverpool 30/4/1908 d 1978
Runcorn
1930 Tranmere Rovers 0
Rhyl Athletic
1931 New Brighton 9 2
Northwich Victoria
Winsford United

Ray, Cecil Holmes CF
b West Grinstead 25/10/1911 d 1995
Lewes United
1935 1946 Aldershot 89 39
1939 (Aldershot) (3)
Cuckfield

Ray, George Browne RH
b Whitehaven 5/9/1902 d 1985
Frizington
1927 Bradford City 2
Derry City

Ray, Richard (Dick) LB/RB
b Newcastle-under-Lyme 4/2/1876 d 1952
Audley
Macclesfield
1894 Burslem Port Vale 29 1
1895 Crewe Alexandra 0
1896 1900 Manchester City 83 3
Macclesfield
1902 Manchester City 0
Coventry City
1903 Stockport County 34
1904 Chesterfield Town 31
1905 1906 Leeds City 38
Huddersfield Town

Raybould, Samuel (Sam) CF/IL/OR
b Chesterfield 11/6/1875 d 1953
Caps: FLge 3
Poolsbrook United
Staveley Colliery
North Staveley
Chesterfield Town (trial)
Ilkeston Town
1894 Derby County 5 2
Ilkeston Town
Poolsbrook United
Ilkeston Town
Bolsover Colliery
1899 New Brighton Tower 13 10
1899 1906 Liverpool 211 119
1907 Sunderland 27 12
1908 Woolwich Arsenal 26 6
Chesterfield Town
Sutton Town
Barlborough United

Raybould, Thomas (Tom) RH/CH
b Wilden 7/1884 d 1944
Kidderminster Harriers
1905 1906 Wolverhampton Wanderers 15 1
1907 Grimsby Town 0
Worksop Town
Stourbridge

Rayment, Joseph Watson (Joe) OR
b Hartlpool 17/1/1906 d 1969
West Hartlepool Perseverance
1927 Hartlepools United 19 2
West Hartlepool Perseverance
Gas & Water

From To Apps Goal

Raymond, Harry W IL/IR
b Plymouth
Caps: SoLge 1/England Amat
Woodland Villa
1920 1923 Plymouth Argyle 67 10
Torquay United

Rayner, Frank Walter RH/IR
b Goldthorpe 1913
1930 Charlton Athletic 0
1931 Barnsley 0
1932 Rotherham United 0
Frickley Colliery
1933 Mansfield Town 15 8
Mexborough
1934 1938 Burnley 79 7
1939 Notts County (2)

Raynes, Charles Bernal RB/CF
b Walsall q1 1899
1925 1926 Walsall 5 1

Raynor, E GK
1898 1899 Gainsborough Trinity 23

Raynor, George OR
b Hoyland 13/1/1907 d 1985
Elsecar Bible Class
Mexborough Athletic
Wombwell Town
1930 Sheffield United 0
1932 Mansfield Town 9 1
1933 1934 Rotherham United 59 17
1934 1937 Bury 54 4
1938 Aldershot 33 4
1939 (Aldershot) (2)

Raynor, Harold A (Harry) RH/CF/IL
b Hipperholme
1923 Huddersfield Town 0
Selby Town
1925 Halifax Town 1
1926 1928 Coventry City 12
Colwyn Bay
Lancaster Town

Raysen, Leonard OL
b 1908
1926 Lincoln City 1
Grantham

Rea, John Charles OL
b Lledrod 1868 d 1944
Caps: Wales 9
Ardwyn
Upton Excelsiors
London Caledonians
London Welsh
Aberystwyth Town
1894 West Bromwich Albion 1
Aberystwyth Town
1896 West Bromwich Albion 0
Aberystwyth Town

Rea, Robert OR
Caps: Ireland 1
Glentoran
1901 Burton United 2

Read, Arthur Henry LH/CH/RH
b Saxilby q3 1894
Saxilby
Bargoed United
1921 Aberdare Athletic 32
1922 1923 Gillingham 61 3
1924 Lincoln City 8

Read, Edward (Teddy) CH/LH
b Rhosllanerchrugog 16/6/1903 d 1997
Rhos Athletic
Penycae
1927 1929 Wrexham 39
Macclesfield
1931 1932 Halifax Town 52 1
Bellfield St Anne's

Read, Thomas Albert (Tommy) GK
b West Bromwich 2/4/1900 d 1956
West Cannock Colliery
Darlaston
1926 Stockport County 11
1927 1933 Grimsby Town 247
1935 Crystal Palace 16
Shirley Town

Read, Thomas Herbert RB/LB
b Manchester
Stretford
1895 1901 Manchester City 115 2
1902 1903 Manchester United 35

Read, Trevett William GK
b Chatham 9/2/1893 d 1976
Royal Navy
1923 Gillingham 1

From To Apps Goal

Read, William Henry (Harry) OR
b Blackpool q4 1885 d 1951
Lytham
1907 1908 Blackpool 30 3
Colne
1909 1910 Sunderland 4 2
1911 Chelsea 3
Dundee
Swansea Town
Chesterfield Municipal

Reader, George CF
b Nuneaton 22/11/1896 d 1978
St Luke's College
Exeter City
1920 Southampton 3
Harland & Wolff
Cowes

Reader, Josiah (Joe) GK
b West Bromwich 2/1866 d 1954
Caps: FLge 3/England 1
1889 1900 West Bromwich Albion 315

Reader, Richard (Dickie) OR
b Derby 3/6/1894
Belper Town
Ripley Athletic
1912 Leicester Fosse 0
Ripley Athletic
1913 Derby County 4
1914 1921 Bristol City 51 4
1922 Luton Town 7
(USA)

Readett, Harold (Harry) RB
b Darwen 15/10/1910 d 1990
Blackburn Corinthians
1930 Blackburn Rovers 0
Manchester Central
Horwich RMI
Hurst
1934 Burnley 3
1936 Wrexham 1
Stalybridge Celtic
Hurst
Rossendale United
Droylsden
Hurst
Audenshaw United

Readman, John (Jack) GK
b Skelton q4 1913
1933 Wolverhampton Wandrs (trial) 0
1933 Lincoln City (trial) 0
1934 Walsall 1
1935 Hartlepools United 0

Readman, Joseph Andrew (Joe) IR/IL/RH
b West Hartlepool 20/11/1901 d 1973
Wheatley Hill Alliance
1923 Bolton Wanderers 0
1924 1926 Bournemouth & Boscombe Ath 48 20
1927 Brighton & Hove Albion 6
1928 1930 Millwall 56 20
1931 1932 Mansfield Town 73 12
Ramsgate
Ramsgate Press Wanderers

Reaney, Thomas RB
Bridgetown Amateurs
1904 Burslem Port Vale 3

Reason, Herbert (Bert 'Jumbo') LB
b Wanstead
Woodford
1905 1909 Clapton Orient 91 4

Reay, Albert Frederick (Archie) LB
b West Derby 15/9/1901 d 1962
Gnome Athletic
1921 Brentford 0
1922 Gillingham 15
1923 Norwich City 2
Guildford United
Sheppey United

Reay, Edwin Peel (Ted) LB/RB
b Tynemouth 5/8/1914 d 1992
Washington Colliery
Washington Chemical Works
Ferryhill Athletic
North Shields
1936 Sheffield United 0
1937 1949 Queen's Park Rangers 34
1939 (Queen's Park Rangers) (3)

From To Apps Goal

Reay, George Turnbull OR
b East Howden 2/1903 d 1962
Percy Main Amateurs
1922 South Shields 4
Blyth Spartans
1923 Reading 1
Kettering Town
Raith Rovers
1928 1929 Bristol Rovers 67 9
1930 Coventry City 11 3
Burton Town
Rushden Town
Kettering Town
Gresley Rovers

Reay, Harold OL
b Sunderland q2 1896 d 1959
Margate
1922 Sunderland 0
1923 Preston North End 1
1924 Grimsby Town 1

Reay, Harry OR
b Tyneside
Gateshead
Shankhouse Black Watch
Newcastle East End
Newcastle United
1893 1894 Everton 1 1

Reay, John C OR
Blyth Spartans
1935 Chesterfield 0
Chester-le-Street
1936 Gateshead 15 2
1937 Hull City 0

Record, Charles Reuben IL
b Gillingham 26/7/1902 d 1985
1925 Gillingham 3 1

Redding, James GK
b London
Amersham
1905 Clapton Orient 7
Amersham

Reddish, JH IR
1900 Bury 1
Rochdale

Reddish, John (Jack) LB/RB
b Nottingham 22/12/1904 d 1989
Boots Athletic
1929 1931 Tottenham Hotspur 6
1933 1934 Lincoln City 53
1935 Notts County 0
Dundee

Reddock, Charles (Charlie) LH
b Rutherglen 1902
Shettleston
1925 Gillingham 29
1926 1928 Brentford 9
1930 1931 Thames 34

Reddyhough, Herbert CF
b Bolton 23/7/1900 d 1964
Adlington
1929 Wigan Borough 3 1
Burscough Rangers

Redfern, Albert IL
b Wombwell
1920 Rotherham County 2

Redfern, J LH
1899 Middlesbrough 3

Redfern, Leslie (Les) IL/IR
b Burton-on-Trent 6/12/1911
1931 1932 Wolverhampton Wanderers 6 1
1933 Southend United 3
1934 Crewe Alexandra 16 4
Folkestone

Redfern, Levi RH/LH
b Burton-on-Trent 18/2/1905 d 1976
Conisbrough Discharged Soldiers
Denaby United
York City
1927 1930 Huddersfield Town 52 1
1932 Bradford City 6
1934 Rochdale 25 3
1935 Sheffield United 2

Redfern, Robert (Bob) OR
b Crook 3/3/1918 d 2002
Tow Law Town
1936 Wolverhampton Wanderers 0
Cradley Heath
1936 1946 Bournemouth & Boscombe Ath 89 4
1939 (Bournemouth & Boscombe Ath) (3) (3)
1947 Brighton & Hove Albion 5 1
Weymouth
Bournemouth FC

From To Apps Goal

Redfern, TW OL
1906 Glossop 3

Redfern, William Joseph (Billy) IR
b Connah's Quay 15/10/1910 d 1988
Caps: IrLge 1/Wales War 1
Holywell Arcadians
Bangor City
Marine
Newry Town
1937 1938 Luton Town 41 19
1939 Derby County (2) (1)

Redpath, Ernest (Ernie) LB
b Newcastle
Stockton
1921 Durham City 1

Redwood, Douglas James (Doug) OL
b Ebbw Vale 24/10/1918 d 1979
Caps: Wales Sch
Ebbw Vale
1935 1936 Cardiff City 13
1937 1938 Walsall 27 6
1939 Rochdale 0

Redwood, George Edward LB
b Shoreditch q2 1885 d 1956
Tottenham St Louis
Enfield Town
Royal Fusiliers
1910 Fulham 7
West Ham United

Redwood, Hubert RB
b St Helens q3 1913 d 1943
Shirdley Albion
1935 1938 Manchester United 86 3
1939 (Manchester United) (3)

Reece, George CF
Soho Villa
1894 Woolwich Arsenal 1

Reece, Harry Joseph LB
b Darlaston 26/7/1911 d 1981
FH Lloyd's
Darlaston Town
1931 1932 Blackpool 4
1933 1934 Luton Town 29
1935 Barrow 18
Worcester City
Darlaston Town

Reece, Thomas Samuel (Tom) LH
b Wolverhampton 17/5/1919 d 1990
1937 Wolverhampton Wanderers 0
1938 1947 Crystal Palace 76 5
1939 (Crystal Palace) (2)
Kidderminster Harriers

Reed, Albert (Arthur) CH
b Ealing 1899
Caps: England Amat/ England 1
Tufnell Park
1921 Queen's Park Rangers 21
1922 Reading 3

Reed, Alfred George (Alf) LH/RH
b Exeter 21/3/1911 d 1961
Llanelly
Lovells Athletic
1933 Charlton Athletic 1
1934 1938 Watford 126 5
1939 (Watford) (1)

Reed, Arthur IR/IL/CF
b Sheffield 1883
Leadmill St Mary's
Doncaster Rovers
1911 1914 Birmingham 28 12

Reed, Charles LB
b Sunderland 1885
Sunderland West End
1905 Barnsley 11
Sunderland West End
1907 Barnsley 16

Reed, Charles LB
b Durham
Darlington
1909 Clapton Orient 2

From To Apps Goal

Reed, Charles William (Charlie 'Chick') IL/CF/LH
b Holbeach 21/3/1912 d 1964
Little London Vics
Spalding Institute
Spalding United
1931 Sheffield United 2 1
1932 1934 Lincoln City 55 24
1934 1935 Southport 35 9
1935 1936 Chesterfield 37 10
Spalding United
1937 Mansfield Town 22 9
1938 Notts County 36 2
Pinchbeck
Crowland

Reed, Ebor CH/LH
b Spennymoor 30/11/1899 d 1971
Caps: IrLge 1
1924 Newcastle United 0
1925 Cardiff City 6
1926 Nottingham Forest 5
1927 1928 Rotherham United 60
Derry City
Dundalk
Portadown

Reed, Frederick William Marshall (Fred) CH
b Scotswood 3/1894 d 1967
Newburn
Wesley Hall
Benwell
Lintz Institute
1914 1926 West Bromwich Albion 138 4

Reed, George LH
b Altofts 7/2/1904 d 1958
Altofts
1925 1929 Leeds United 141 2
1931 1933 Plymouth Argyle 46 1
1934 Crystal Palace 2
1935 Clapton Orient 1
King's Lynn
Haverfordwest Athletic

Reed, Gordon CF
b Spennymoor 5/1913
Spennymoor United
1930 Huddersfield Town 0
1931 Everton 0
1931 1933 Bristol City 12 4
1933 Newport County 16 11
1934 Queen's Park Rangers 9 4
1935 Darlington 18 7
1936 Gateshead 23 2

Reed, Johnson (Jack) RH/LH
b Brusselton 31/3/1910 d 1983
Spennymoor United
Walsall Miners Welfare
Dudley White Star
Beaverbrook Swifts
1930 Wolverhampton Wanderers 1
Dudley Town
1931 1936 Walsall 124 6

Reed, Percy CH/RH
b Stokesley 5/12/1890 d 1970
Royal Navy
1919 1920 Sheffield Wednesday 14
1921 Chesterfield 5
Doncaster Rovers
Denaby United
York City
Heanor Town
City Surveyors (Sheffield)
Staveley Town

Reeday, Maurice LB/RB
b Darwen 28/8/1909 d 1979
Darwen
1935 Blackpool 0
1936 Accrington Stanley 22
1937 1938 Leicester City 74 2
1939 (Leicester City) (3)
Darwen

Rees, Abraham IL
Bentley Colliery
1924 Doncaster Rovers 1
Bentley Colliery
1925 Merthyr Town 0

Rees, David OR
1928 Merthyr Town 1

Rees, Edwin James LH/CF
b Llanelli 1899
Ton Pentre
1922 1924 Charlton Athletic 63 14
1925 Bradford City 2

From To Apps Goal

Rees, Evan Glasnant (Gus) RB/LH/RH
b Loughor 26/10/1904 d 1991
Loughor Juniors
1927 Swansea Town 0
Loughor Stars
1930 1932 Swansea Town 9
1933 1934 Torquay United 46 2
Altrincham

Rees, John GK
b Ebbw Vale 10/1909
Ebbw Vale
1930 Bristol City 1
1931 Southampton 0

Reeve, Frank D IL/OR
b Nuneaton
Rugby Town
1927 Coventry City 2
1927 Walsall 1
Rugby Town

Reeve, Frederick William (Fred) LH
b Clapton 1/5/1918 d 1994
Ashford Town (Kent)
1936 Crystal Palace 1
1937 Tottenham Hotspur 0
1938 Rochdale 27 3
1939 1947 Grimsby Town 46
1939 (Grimsby Town) (2)
1948 1949 Reading 34 1
Ashford Town (Kent)
Hastings United

Reeves, Frederick (Fred) OR
b Mexborough
Bentley Colliery
Mexborough
1920 Sheffield Wednesday 1
Mexborough

Reeves, George IR/OR/CF
b Hucknall 7/1884 d 1954
Sutton-in-Ashfield
Ripley Athletic
Sutton Town
1906 1907 Barnsley 30 27
1907 1908 Aston Villa 35 11
1909 1912 Bradford Park Avenue 58 17
1912 Blackpool 3

Regan, Edward Gerald Patrick (Ted) RH
b Chester 27/12/1900 d 1973
Saltney
Crichton's Athletic
1921 1927 Wrexham 188 14
Manchester Central
1929 Fulham 1
Derry City (trial)
Belfast Celtic
Connah's Quay & Shotton
Colwyn Bay United
Milford United
Rustproof Athletic (Chester)
Buckley Town

Regan, EJ LH
1893 Ardwick 21
1894 Burslem Port Vale 5

Regan, Robert Hunter (Bobby) OL
b Falkirk 21/8/1915
Grangetown Thistle
Queen of the South
Linlithgow Rose
Partick Thistle
1936 Manchester City 4
Dundee
Rhyl Athletic

Regan, Sydney Eugene RB
b Woolwich q2 1899
1922 Millwall Athletic 7

Regan, William (Bill) RH/LH
Sheffield Wednesday 0
Fairfield
1896 1897 Sheffield Wednesday 9
Millwall Athletic
Brentford

Reid, Alexander Laing (Alec) OR
b West Calder 9/2/1896 d 1969
Glasgow Ashfield
Airdrieonians
Third Lanark
Aberdeen
1927 1932 Preston North End 193 50
1932 Blackpool 13 1
Chorley
Darwen
Aberdeen North End
Tunbridge Wells Rangers
Babcock & Wilcox

From To Apps Goal

Reid, Andrew (Andy) RB/LB
b Aberdeen
Bo'ness
1926 1927 Burnley 3
1928 1929 Bradford Park Avenue 12
1930 Reading 0
Burton Town

Reid, David CH/LH/IR
b Glasgow
Caps: IrLge 4
Distillery
1920 1926 Everton 97 11
Distillery
Ballymena

Reid, David (Dave) RH
b Glasgow
1920 Aston Villa 0
Worcester City
1921 1922 Southend United 40
1923 Barrow 29
Mid-Rhondda United
Worcester City
Wellington Town
Shrewsbury Town

Reid, Ernest James (Ernie) RB/LH/IR
b Pentrebach 25/3/1914
Troedyrhiw
Plymouth United
1932 Swansea Town 1
1938 Chelsea 1
1939 Swansea Town 0
1945 1946 Norwich City 5
Bedford Town

Reid, George Albert CF
b Handsworth, Yorkshire 2/1872 d 1934
Attercliffe
1896 Sheffield Wednesday 0
1897 West Bromwich Albion 11 3
Warmley
Thames Ironworks
1899 Middlesbrough 15 5
Millwall Athletic

Reid, George Hull CF/IL
b Belfast 1/1896
Caps: Ireland 1
Distillery
1920 Blackpool 3 2
1921 1922 Walsall 47 31
1922 Cardiff City 7 4
1923 Fulham 2
1924 Stockport County 11 3
1924 Rotherham County 12 4
Mid-Rhondda United

Reid, George T (Geordie) IL/CF
b Paisley 1882
Caps: SoLge 2
St Mirren
1905 Middlesbrough 24 5
Johnstone
1908 Bradford Park Avenue 5
Brentford
Clyde
Johnstone
Clydebank

Reid, James (Jimmy) CF/IR/IL
b Bellshill 18/11/1879
Petershill
Hibernian
1899 Burslem Port Vale 17 2
West Ham United
Fulham
1901 Gainsborough Trinity 31 8
Worksop Town
1903 1904 Notts County 16 2
Watford
Tottenham Hotspur
Reading
New Brompton
Worksop Town
Gainsborough WMC & Institute

Reid, James (Jimmy) RH/IR
b Kilmarnock 1887
Caps: IrLge 4
Belfast Celtic
Glentoran
1908 1909 Oldham Athletic 5 2
Glentoran

Reid, James CF
b Blantyre d 1933
Blantyre Victoria
Motherwell
Blantyre Celtic
1920 Portsmouth 7 2
Armadale

From To Apps Goal

Reid, James Forsyth (Jimmy) OR/OL
b Shettleston 6/8/1907 d 1967
Caps: Scotland Sch
Shettleston Juniors
Townsend Waverley
Airdrieonians
1927 Luton Town 0
1929 1930 Barrow 52 6
Hamilton Academical (trial)
Dolphin
Alloa Athletic
1933 Southport 33 4
1934 1938 Rotherham United 168 13
1939 (Rotherham United) (1)

Reid, James Greig (Jimmy) IR
b Peebles 1/5/1890 d 1938
Caps: SLge 3/Scotland 3
Peebles Rovers
Partick Thistle (trial)
1908 Chelsea (trial) 0
1909 1910 Lincoln City 36 3
Airdrieonians
Clydebank

Reid, John Douglas Jamieson (Duggie) IR/CF/CH
b Mauchline 3/10/1917 d 2002
Heaton Chapel
1936 1938 Stockport County 84 23
1939 (Stockport County) (2)
1946 1955 Portsmouth 308 129
Tonbridge

Reid, John Walkinshaw (Jack) CH
b Riccarton 18/6/1898
Dunraven Star
Bloomfield United
Castleview
Distillery
1923 1927 New Brighton 167 9
Ballymena United
Bangor
1930 New Brighton 7
Distillery

Reid, Joseph Edmund (Joe) LB/LH
b Hebburn 30/6/1896 d 1936
Hebburn Argyle
South Shields
1919 Manchester City 3 1
1920 1925 Stockport County 145 1
Carlisle United
Boston Town
1928 1929 Newport County 61 1
1930 Fulham 7
Annfield Plain

Reid, Maxwell Walkinshaw (Max) RH
b Riccarton 1/6/1893
Victoria FC
Distillery
1923 1926 New Brighton 109 2
Portadown
Carrickfergus
(Canada)

Reid, Robert (Bob) RB
b Newtongrange 1887
Cowdenbeath
1910 1913 Burnley 84
1914 Huddersfield Town 26
1920 Southend United 28

Reid, Robert (Bobby) OL
b Hamilton 19/2/1911 d 1987
Caps: SLge 2/Scotland 2
Ferniegair Violet
Hamilton Academical
Stranraer (loan)
1935 1938 Brentford 103 33
1938 1946 Sheffield United 14 4
1939 (Sheffield United) (3)
1946 Bury 17 1
Third Lanark

Reid, Robert T IR
Larkhall
1912 Nottingham Forest 9 1

Reid, Sidney Edward (Sid) LB/RB
b Belfast 20/6/1908
Caps: IrLge 1/Ireland 3
Cliftonville Strollers
Distillery
1931 1935 Derby County 16
1936 Reading 2

Reid, Sydney CF/IL/IR
b Troedyrhiw
Troedyrhiw Star
1921 1927 Luton Town 134 70
Luton Amateurs

From To Apps Goal

Reid, Thomas (Tom) CF
b Calderbank 1901
Bedlay Juniors
New Stevenston United
Clyde (trial)
Albion Rovers (trial)
Dundee (trial)
Ayr United
1922 1925 Port Vale 25 3
1926 Clapton Orient 7 2
Northwich Victoria
1928 1929 New Brighton 7 1

Reid, Thomas Joseph (Tommy) CF
b Motherwell 15/8/1905 d 1972
Blantyre Victoria
Clydebank
1925 1928 Liverpool 51 31
1928 1932 Manchester United 96 63
1932 1934 Oldham Athletic 67 34
1935 Barrow 31 17
Prescot Cables
Rhyl Athletic

Reid, Thomas Stewart (Tom) CH
b Newcastle 1915
North Shields
1937 Hartlepools United 7
North Shields

Reid, Walter LB
b Scotland 1869
St Bernard's
1892 Grimsby Town 10

Reid, William (Billy) LH/OL/IL
b Rotherham
1894 1895 Rotherham Town 32 4
1895 Newcastle United 2
1896 Darwen 2
Rotherham Town
Attercliffe
1899 Barnsley 6

Reid, William IL
b Mauchline 1876 d 1923
Stevenston Thistle
Kilmarnock Athletic
Kilmarnock
1898 Newcastle United (loan) 4 1
Partick Thistle
Galston
Thornhill
Kilmarnock
Galston

Reilly, Edward W IR
1908 Chelsea 1
1909 Fulham 0
Shepherds Bush

Reilly, Francis (Frank) CH
b Perth 26/5/1894 d 1956
Caps: WLge 1
Perth Roselea
Falkirk
1919 1922 Blackburn Rovers 127 8
Llanelly
1923 Swansea Town 0
Llanelly
Weymouth
Lancaster City

Reilly, James H LB/OL
1904 1905 Blackpool 3

Reilly, John (Paddy) OR
b 1897
Ryhope Colliery
Sheffield Tramways
1920 Sheffield Wednesday 2
Castleford Town
Sheffield Tramways

Reilly, Leonard Harold (Len) CH
b Rotherhithe 31/1/1917 d 1998
Diss Town
1937 1946 Norwich City 30
1939 (Norwich City) (3)
Chelmsford City
Gorleston

Reilly, Matthew Michael (Matt 'Gunner') GK
b Donnybrook 22/3/1874 d 1954
Caps: Ireland 2
Glasgow Benburb
Royal Artillery (Portsmouth)
Southampton St Mary's (loan)
Freemantle (loan)
Portsmouth
Dundee
1905 Notts County 16
Tottenham Hotspur
Shelbourne

From To Apps Goal

Reilly, Peter IR
East Fife
1924 Hartlepools United 1
East Fife

Reilly, William J (Billy) LH
b Lanark 24/12/1902
Lanark United
Shieldmuir Celtic
St Roch's
Kilmarnock
1928 1929 South Shields 75 4
1930 Gateshead 26 1
1930 Chelsea 0
1931 Chester 35 1
1932 Southend United 2
1933 Hartlepools United 7
Ashington
Jarrow
Walker Celtic

Reinhardt, (Dr) Cecil Goodwin GK
b Lewisham 3/3/1888
Leeds University
1911 Leeds City 12

Relph, William (Billy) IR/OL/OR
b Morpeth 26/1/1900 d 1978
Seaton Delaval
Blyth Spartans
1921 1923 Ashington 32 14
1924 Brentford 7 1
Blyth Spartans
Morpeth Church Institute
Pegswood United
Morpeth Town

Rendell, Thomas LH
b Tyneside
Shankhouse Black Watch
1894 Newcastle United 23
Shankhouse Black Watch

Render, James CH
b Newcastle 12/7/1914 d 2003
1938 Gateshead 2

Renneville, William Thomas James CF
b Mullingar 16/4/1884 d 1948
Caps: Ireland 4
Leyton
1910 Aston Villa 2 1
Walsall
Worcester City

Rennie, Alex GK
Halliwell
1892 Everton 4
1893 Liverpool 0
Liverpool Police Athletic

Rennie, Andrew (Andy) CF/IL/CH
b Baillieston 1901 d 1938
Paisley Waverley
Kilwinning Rangers
1925 1934 Luton Town 307 146
1935 Newport County 3

Rennie, John (Jack) RB
b Largs 1916 d 2007
Hibernian
1938 Clapton Orient 6
Selby Town

Rennie, Joseph (Joe) LH
Maryhill Hibernian
1933 Luton Town 4

Rennox, Clatworthy (Charlie) IL/CF/IR
b Shotts 25/2/1897 d 1967
Dykehead
Wishaw YMCA
1921 1924 Clapton Orient 101 24
1924 1926 Manchester United 60 24
1927 Grimsby Town 0
Bangor City
1928 Accrington Stanley 0

Renshaw, Brien CH
1907 Sheffield United 0
Catcliffe
Rotherham Town
1910 Gainsborough Trinity 1

Renshaw, William IL/OL
b Doncaster
Balby Athletic
1932 1933 Doncaster Rovers 4 1
Frickley Colliery

From To Apps Goal

Renwick, John Loudon CF
b Larkhall 4/6/1906
Royal Albert
Dumbarton (trial)
Falkirk (trial)
East Stirlingshire
1931 Gillingham (trial) 5 3
Albion Rovers
Heart of Midlothian (loan)
Distillery (loan)
Excelsior Roubaix
Queen of the South
1937 Barrow 25 4

Resoli, Daniel John OR
b Maerdy 28/7/1908 d 1977
1928 Brighton & Hove Albion 0
1929 Merthyr Town 7 1
1930 Brighton & Hove Albion 0

Retford, James (Jimmy 'Jack') CF
Aberdeen Mugiemoss
1921 Barnsley 3 2
Scunthorpe & Lindsey United

Revill, James William (Jimmy) OL
b Sutton-in-Ashfield q3 1891 d 1917
Sutton Junction
Tibshelf
1910 1914 Sheffield United 60 3

Reynolds, Arnold (Arthur) GK
b Dartford 30/6/1889 d 1970
Caps: FLge 1
Dartford Albion
Dartford
1909 1924 Fulham 399
Heart of Midlothian (trial)
Hibernian (loan)
1925 Clapton Orient 0
Dartford

Reynolds, Charles (Jasper) OR
b Wolverhampton 1873
Church Taveners
1894 Wolverhampton Wanderers 14 5
Berwick Rangers (Worcester)
Banbury

Reynolds, Jeremiah (Jerry) RB
b Maryhill 15/4/1867 d 1944
Drumpellier
Cowlairs
Hibernian
Cowlairs
Carfin Shamrock
Celtic (loan)
Glasgow Hibernian (loan)
Celtic
1895 1899 Burnley 107
Mossend Swifts

Reynolds, John (Jack 'Baldy') RH
b Blackburn 21/2/1869 d 1917
Caps: FLge 4/Ireland 5/England 8
Park Road (Blackburn)
Witton (Blackburn)
Blackburn Rovers
Park Road (Blackburn)
East Lancashire Regiment
Distillery
Ulster
1891 West Bromwich Albion 17 2
Droitwich Town
1892 West Bromwich Albion 20 1
1893 1896 Aston Villa 96 17
Celtic
Southampton
Bristol St George
(New Zealand)
1903 Stockport County 1
Willesden Town

Reynolds, John W (Jack) OR
b Manchester 23/9/1881 d 1962
1902 Manchester City 0
1903 Burton United 32 3
1904 Grimsby Town 29 3
1905 1906 Sheffield Wednesday 2
Watford
New Brompton
Rochdale

Reynolds, Joseph William (Joe) RH
b Leicester 25/12/1906 d 1993
Mountsorrel
1927 Luton Town 2
1930 Watford 6

From To Apps Goal

Reynolds, Walter OR
b Syston q3 1894
All Souls
Belvoir Street Sunday School
1912 Leicester Fosse 1
Leicester Imperial
Eccles United
Whitwick Imperial
Barwell United

Reynolds, Walter (Wally) OR
b Ecclesall 24/11/1906 d 1995
Hathersage
1929 Sheffield Wednesday 0
1930 Leeds United 0
1931 Clapton Orient 2
1932 Burnley 19 3
1933 1934 Newport County 59 4
1935 1937 Accrington Stanley 125 28
1938 York City 3
1938 1945 Rochdale 22 4
1939 (Rochdale) (2) (1)

Reynolds, William CF/IL
b County Tyrone 22/7/1879
1902 Manchester City 0
1903 Burton United 7 1
Clapton Orient
1905 Grimsby Town 6
Swindon Town
Croydon Common

Reynolds, William Thomas LB
b Tewkesbury 1870
St Luke's
1893 Small Heath 12
Berwick Rangers (Worcester)

Rhodes, Arthur IR/OR
b Devon 1920
1936 Stockport County 0
1937 Bournemouth & Boscombe Ath 8 3
1938 Torquay United 7
1938 Cardiff City 5

Rhodes, Cyril RH
b Sheffield q1 1903
Caps: England Sch
Birtley
1924 Rotherham County 1
Mansfield Town
Staveley Town

Rhodes, Ernest (Ernie) LB
Gravesend United
1920 1922 Crystal Palace 89 1
Sheppey United

Rhodes, Ephraim (Dusty) RB/LB
b South Bank q3 1882 d 1960
Grangetown
1902 1907 Sunderland 115 5
Brentford

Rhodes, Fred Foster IR/CF
b Gomersal 21/3/1904 d 1988
Liversedge
1922 1925 Bradford City 52 14
Poole

Rhodes, Harold CH
1930 Accrington Stanley 1
Lancaster Town
Nelson
Morecambe
Great Harwood
Morecambe

Rhodes, Irwin LB
b Rotherham q3 1916 d 1965
West Melton
1935 Sheffield United 0
1935 Accrington Stanley 0
1936 Rotherham United 2 1
Great Harwood
1937 Preston North End 0
1937 Accrington Stanley 5
Boston United

Rhodes, Leonard OL
b Darlaston 15/4/1897 d 1984
Willenhall
1922 Wolverhampton Wanderers 19 1
Shrewsbury Town

Rhodes, Richard Alma (Dickie) RH/IR
b Wolverhampton 18/2/1908 d 1993
Redditch Town
1928 1935 Wolverhampton Wanderers 149 7
1935 1937 Sheffield Wednesday 57
1938 Swansea Town 25 1
1939 Rochdale (3)

From To Apps Goal

Rhodes, William Henry IR
b Clay Cross q3 1881 d 1934
Clay Cross Zingari
1903 Chesterfield Town 1
Worksop Town
Thornhill United
Newark Town
Clay Cross Zingari

Rhodes, William T RB
1893 Burslem Port Vale 1

Rhodes, William Trevor (Trevor) IR/CF/RH
b Leeds 10/11/1909 d 1993
Castleford Town
Yorkshire Amateurs
1928 1932 Bradford Park Avenue 57 39
1933 1937 Port Vale 139 28

Rice, Arthur IR/IL
b Liverpool 25/7/1914 d 1988
1933 New Brighton 1
1934 Manchester United 0
Albion Rovers
1936 1937 Stockport County 15
1938 Crewe Alexandra 29 12
1939 (Crewe Alexandra) (2)

Rice, Harold Ernest (Harry) IR
b Torpoint q1 1908 d 1964
Shrewsbury Town
1929 Torquay United 3
Evesham Town

Rice, James (Jimmy) CF
Holytown United
1934 Manchester United (trial) 0
1934 Wrexham 5 5
Albion Rovers
Falkirk
Alloa Athletic

Rich, Leonard Thomas (Len) OR/OL
b Camelford 3/11/1912 d 1994
Torpoint
1935 Plymouth Argyle 3 1
1935 1936 Luton Town 19 5
1938 Exeter City 31 4
1939 1945 Stockport County (2)

Richards, Albert Charles OL/OR
b Chatham 18/7/1903 d 1973
Chatham Town
1923 1924 Charlton Athletic 20 3
1924 Luton Town 2
Chatham Town
1925 Gillingham 25 4
Chatham Town
1928 Brentford 2
Dartford

Richards, Aneurin Glyndwr (Nai) LB/RB
b Maerdy 24/8/1902 d 1976
Caps: Wales 1
Mardy Albion
Mardy
Tylorstown
Pontypridd
Bridgend Town
1927 Hull City (trial) 0
1927 1933 Barnsley 123
1934 Southport 1
Bexhill

Richards, Anthony D OR
Stourbridge
1895 Sheffield Wednesday 7 1

Richards, Arthur John RB
b Knighton 1888
New Invention
1910 West Bromwich Albion 1
Kilnhurst

Richards, C Samuel (Sam) OL
b Birmingham
Ruskin Social
1925 Coventry City 9

Richards, Charles Henry IR/CF
b Burton-on-Trent 9/8/1875
Caps: England 1
Gresley Rovers
Newstead Byron
1895 Notts County 0
1895 1898 Nottingham Forest 74 20
1898 1900 Grimsby Town 80 42
1901 Leicester Fosse 25 5
1902 Manchester United 8 1
1902 Doncaster Rovers 7

From To Apps Goal

Richards, David (Dave) LB/RB/RH
b Wolverhampton 1/10/1896 d 1971
Larkhall Thistle
1922 Port Vale 1
Dundee United
1925 1930 Luton Town 147
1931 1932 Watford 35

Richards, David LH/RH/LB
b Pentrebach
Pentrebach
1927 1928 Merthyr Town 13
1928 Aston Villa (trial) 0
1928 Middlesbrough 0
Merthyr Town
1931 Bolton Wanderers 0
1934 1935 Wrexham 50
1936 Newport County 1
Burton Town

Richards, David Thomas (Dai) LH
b Abercanaid 31/10/1906 d 1969
Caps: Wales 21
Riverfield
Bedlinog
1926 Merthyr Town 0
1927 1935 Wolverhampton Wanderers 218 5
1935 1936 Brentford 55
1936 1938 Birmingham 62 2
1939 Walsall (3)

Richards, Frederick (Fred) IR
b Burton-on-Trent q1 1879
Burton Wanderers
1898 Derby County 2
1898 Sheffield Wednesday 2 1
Burton Wanderers
Woodville Excelsior
Trent Rovers

Richards, George Henry LH/IL
b Bulwell 10/5/1880 d 1950
Caps: England 1
Castle Donington Juniors
Whitwick White Cross
1901 1913 Derby County 284 33

Richards, Iorwerth IL
b Rhosllanerchrugog
Rhos Church
Johnstown
1929 Wrexham 2
Oswestry Town
Llanerch Celts
Blaenau Ffestiniog

Richards, John CF
b Martley 1873
City Ramblers (London)
1895 West Bromwich Albion 14
1896 Loughborough 0
Shepshed Albion

Richards, John William (Jack) RH
b Rhosllanerchrugog 16/5/1909 d 1965
Denbigh United
1929 Wrexham 4
1930 1931 Blackburn Rovers 2
1932 Chester 0
Colwyn Bay United
1934 Accrington Stanley (trial) 0
Darwen

Richards, Leonard George (Len) LB
b Barry 13/4/1911 d 1985
Caps: Wales Sch/LoI 1
Canton Institute
1931 Tottenham Hotspur 0
1932 Cardiff City 1
Dundalk
Balfast Celtic
Dundalk
Dundee
Barry
Dundee
1938 Newport County 30
1939 Newport County (3)

Richards, Leonard Joseph GK
b Bilston 10/1892 d 1954
Hurst Hill Wesleyans
Stourbridge
1911 1913 Aston Villa 7
Bilston United

Richards, Percy CF
b Manchester 15/5/1905
New Mills
1925 1927 Burnley 9 8
1927 1929 Plymouth Argyle 29 15
Tunbridge Wells Rangers
Folkestone

Richards, Percy — OL
b Merthyr Tydfil q3 1906 — d 1967
Caps: Wales Sch

From	To	Club	Apps	Goal
		Merthyr Vale		
1926		Cardiff City	3	
1927		Chesterfield	0	
1928		Tranmere Rovers	5	1
1929		Newport County (trial)	4	1
		Merthyr Town		
1930	1931	Leicester City	10	2
1932	1933	Coventry City	46	7
		Bath City		
		Brierley Hill Alliance		
		Kidderminster Harriers		
		Hereford United		

Richards, Richard William (Dick) — IL/OR/OL
b Glyncorrwg 14/2/1890 — d 1934
Caps: Wales 9

From	To	Club	Apps	Goal
		Bronygarth		
		Chirk		
		Oswestry United		
1913	1921	Wolverhampton Wanderers	88	22
1922	1923	West Ham United	43	5
1924		Fulham	21	2
		Mold Town		
		Colwyn Bay		

Richards, Samuel (Sam) — IL
b Bulwell q2 1889 — d 1962

From	To	Club	Apps	Goal
		Bulwell Forest Villa		
1910	1921	Notts County	179	69

Richards, Stanley — LB/RH
b Beeston 15/4/1916

From	To	Club	Apps	Goal
		Beeston St John's		
1937	1938	Nottingham Forest	2	

Richards, William — IL/CF
b West Bromwich 6/10/1874 — d 1926

From	To	Club	Apps	Goal
		Wordsley		
		Singers		
		West Bromwich Standard		
1894	1900	West Bromwich Albion	123	35
1901		Newton Heath	9	1
		Stourbridge		
		Halesowen Town		

Richards, William (Billy) — OR
b Heaton Park 1878 — d 1947

From	To	Club	Apps	Goal
		Middleton		
1898	1907	Bury	233	24
		Heywood United		

Richards, William Edward (Billy) — OR
b Abercanaid 8/1905 — d 1956
Caps: Wales 1

From	To	Club	Apps	Goal
		Troedyrhiw Carlton		
		Mid-Rhondda United		
1925		Merthyr Town	1	
1927	1928	Wolverhampton Wanderers	30	2
1928	1930	Coventry City	77	12
1931	1933	Fulham	76	14
1935	1936	Brighton & Hove Albion	44	8
1937		Bristol Rovers	4	
		Folkestone		

Richardson, Arthur — CF
b Wigan 15/1/1913 — d 1993

From	To	Club	Apps	Goal
		Calderstones		
1936	1937	Burnley	11	2
1938		Chesterfield	4	1
1939		Rochdale	0	

Richardson, Ernest William — OR
b Bishop Burton 8/3/1916 — d 1977

From	To	Club	Apps	Goal
		Leven (East Yorkshire)		
1935	1936	Birmingham	3	
1938		Swansea Town	19	2
1939		Aldershot	0	

Richardson, Frank — CF/IL
b Barking 29/1/1897 — d 1987

From	To	Club	Apps	Goal
		Barking Town		
1921	1922	Plymouth Argyle	63	37
1922	1923	Stoke	14	3
1923		West Ham United	10	2
1924	1925	Swindon Town	53	33
1925	1929	Reading	91	44
1930		Swindon Town	38	11
1931		Mansfield Town	0	
		Guildford City		

Richardson, George — RH

From	To	Club	Apps	Goal
1897		Nottingham Forest	1	

Richardson, George — IR

From	To	Club	Apps	Goal
1903		Gainsborough Trinity	14	3
		Worksop Town		

Richardson, George — IR/IL
b Worksop 12/12/1912 — d 1968

From	To	Club	Apps	Goal
		Manton Colliery		
1933		Huddersfield Town	1	
1935	1938	Sheffield United	32	9
1938	1947	Hull City	36	15
1939		(Hull City)	(2)	
		Ransome & Marles (loan)		
		Bangor City		

Richardson, George Coulthard — CF
b Tynemouth q3 1879

From	To	Club	Apps	Goal
		Willington Athletic		
1902		Barnsley	5	1

Richardson, George Edward (Ted) — OL
b Easington 4/7/1902

From	To	Club	Apps	Goal
		Easington Colliery		
1919	1921	South Shields	35	4
1922		Newcastle United	2	
1923	1924	Huddersfield Town	6	
1924		Sheffield Wednesday	9	
1925		South Shields	0	
		York City		
1926	1927	Bradford City	50	10
		Easington Colliery		
1928		Ashington	23	5
		Whitburn		

Richardson, George Edward Holland — OR
b Seaham Harbour 4/12/1891 — d 1969

From	To	Club	Apps	Goal
		Seaham Rising Star		
		Seaham Young Albion		
		Seaham Harbour		
		Seaham Colliery		
1914	1923	Huddersfield Town	110	7
1923	1925	Hull City	40	2
1926		Bradford City (trial)	0	
1927		Hartlepools United	3	
		Lancaster Town		

Richardson, George William — LH/CF
b East Rainton 1901

From	To	Club	Apps	Goal
		Horden Athletic		
1920		Sunderland (trial)	0	
1921	1922	Burnley	9	5
1923		Derby County	0	
1924	1927	Hartlepools United	106	13
1928	1929	Newport County	31	14
		Aldershot		
		Blackhall Colliery Welfare		

Richardson, George William Richard — LH
b Gainsborough q1 1899 — d 1963

From	To	Club	Apps	Goal
		Gainsborough Wednesday		
1921		Lincoln City	12	
1921	1922	Sheffield United	13	
1924		Bournemouth & Boscombe Ath	9	
		Boston Town		

Richardson, Harry — GK

From	To	Club	Apps	Goal
1898		Gainsborough Trinity	1	

Richardson, Jack — CF

From	To	Club	Apps	Goal
		Kettering Town		
1934		Bournemouth & Boscombe Ath	1	

Richardson, James (Jimmy) — CF
b Bridgeton 1885 — d 1951
Caps: SLge 2

From	To	Club	Apps	Goal
		Gleniffer		
		Blantyre Victoria		
		Kirkintilloch Rob Roy		
		Third Lanark		
1910	1911	Huddersfield Town	42	24
1912	1913	Sunderland	35	20
		Ayr United		
		Partick Thistle (loan)		
1921		Millwall Athletic	19	4

Richardson, James Robert (Jimmy) — IR/IL
b Ashington 8/2/1911 — d 1964
Caps: England Sch/FLge 1/England 2

From	To	Club	Apps	Goal
		Blyth Spartans		
1929	1934	Newcastle United	136	42
1934	1937	Huddersfield Town	120	32
1937		Newcastle United	14	4
1937	1945	Millwall	52	16
1939		(Millwall)	(3)	(3)
1947		Leyton Orient	15	

Richardson, John — RB
b Church q2 1895 — d 1957

From	To	Club	Apps	Goal
		Great Harwood		
		Accrington Stanley (trial)		
		Moscow Mill United Methodists		
1921	1924	Accrington Stanley	95	
		Great Harwood		

Richardson, John (Jock) — LB/RB
b Motherwell 11/11/1906 — d 1986

From	To	Club	Apps	Goal
		Motherwell		
		Northfleet		
1926	1928	Tottenham Hotspur	39	
1929	1933	Reading	125	
1934		Bournemouth & Boscombe Ath	7	
		Folkestone		

Richardson, John — IR
b Johannesburg, South Africa 1909 — d 1977

From	To	Club	Apps	Goal
		Wallacestone Wesleyans		
		Wallacestone Welfare		
1930		Bristol Rovers	8	
		Falkirk		
		Alloa Athletic		
		Leith Athletic		
		East Stirlingshire		

Richardson, John Mettam (Mick) — CH/LH
b Lincoln q4 1872 — d 1920

From	To	Club	Apps	Goal
		St Catherine's		
1892	1895	Lincoln City	64	6
1896		Gainsborough Trinity	8	
		Constitutional Club (Lincoln)		

Richardson, John Pattison — OR
b Bedlington 9/7/1909 — d 1979

From	To	Club	Apps	Goal
		Ashington Colliery Welfare		
		Newbiggin		
1935		Oldham Athletic	3	
		Newbiggin West End		
		Ashington		

Richardson, Jonathan T — LB
b Durham 1905
Caps: IrLge 1

From	To	Club	Apps	Goal
		Spen Black & White		
1929		Wolverhampton Wanderers	3	
1930		Southend United	0	
		Waterford Celtic		
		Linfield		

Richardson, Joseph (Joe) — RB
b Bedlington 24/8/1908 — d 1977
Caps: England War 1

From	To	Club	Apps	Goal
		New Delaval Villa		
		Blyth Spartans		
1929	1938	Newcastle United	208	1

Richardson, JW — OR/IL

From	To	Club	Apps	Goal
		South Bank		
		Middlesbrough		
1895		Sheffield United	1	1
		South Bank		
1898		Grimsby Town	1	

Richardson, Lancelot Holliday (Lance) — GK
b Tow Law q3 1899 — d 1958

From	To	Club	Apps	Goal
		Shildon Athletic		
1923	1925	South Shields	56	
1925	1928	Manchester United	38	
1929	1931	Reading	80	
1932		Bournemouth & Boscombe Ath	0	
		Rowland's Gill		

Richardson, Norman — LB/RB
b Hamsterley 15/4/1915 — d 1991

From	To	Club	Apps	Goal
		Medomsley Juniors		
1933		Bolton Wanderers	0	
1935	1950	New Brighton	213	
1939		(New Brighton)	(2)	
		Chorley		

Richardson, Ord — IR
b Newcastle q2 1875 — d 1958

From	To	Club	Apps	Goal
		Wallsend Park Villa		
1902		Newcastle United	1	

Richardson, Samuel (Sammy) — RH/LH
b Great Bridge 11/8/1894 — d 1960
Caps: FLge 1

From	To	Club	Apps	Goal
		Greets Green Primitives		
		Great Bridge Juniors		
		Great Bridge Celtic		
1914	1926	West Bromwich Albion	191	1
1927	1930	Newport County	127	1
		Aldershot		
		Kidderminster Harriers		

Richardson, Thomas (Tom) — LB
b Worksop q3 1891

From	To	Club	Apps	Goal
		Worksop Town		
		Retford Town		
1912	1913	Sheffield United	2	
		Worksop Town		
		Worksop West End		

Richardson, William — IR
b Denton 20/10/1878 — d 1950

From	To	Club	Apps	Goal
		Rycroft Albion		
		Denton Victoria		
		Ashton Victoria		
		Hurst Ramblers		
		Fairfield		
1897		Grimsby Town	1	
		Swindon Town		

Richardson, William (Billy) — GK
b Scotswood 1897 — d 1959

From	To	Club	Apps	Goal
		Scotswood		
1920	1921	Blackpool	32	
1922	1928	Bury	216	
1929	1930	Stockport County	41	

Richardson, William (Billy) — RB/LB
b Hebburn q2 1898

From	To	Club	Apps	Goal
		Jarrow		
		Wallsend		
1921	1925	Stockport County	159	
		Poole		
1927		Ashington	2	
1927		Durham City	14	1
1928		Ashington	10	
		Craghead United		
		Crook Hall Colliery Welfare		

Richardson, William (Bill) — CH/RH
b Great Bridge 14/2/1908 — d 1985

From	To	Club	Apps	Goal
		Greets Green Primitives		
		Great Bridge Celtic		
1928	1936	West Bromwich Albion	319	1
1937		Swindon Town	9	
		Dudley Town		
		Vono Sports		

Richardson, William (Billy 'Ginger') — CF
b Framwellgate Moor 29/5/1909 — d 1959
Caps: England 1

From	To	Club	Apps	Goal
		Horden Wednesday		
		United Bus Company (Hartlepool)		
1928		Hartlepools United	29	19
1929	1938	West Bromwich Albion	320	202
		Shrewsbury Town		

Richardson, William Frederick — OR
b St Albans q4 1888

From	To	Club	Apps	Goal
		Barnet Alston		
1914		Leeds City	2	

Riches, Leonard Arthur — RH/OR/IR
b Broughton, Northamptonshire 5/5/1906 — d 1980

From	To	Club	Apps	Goal
		Kettering Town		
1929	1937	Northampton Town	136	8
		Kettering Town		

Richmond, Gilbert — RB/LB
b Bolton 2/4/1909 — d 1958

From	To	Club	Apps	Goal
1929		Burnley	0	
1929	1930	Nelson	21	
		Clitheroe		
1932	1938	Burnley	176	1

Richmond, Hugh — CH/CF/IR
b Kilmarnock 9/3/1893 — d 1940

From	To	Club	Apps	Goal
		Kilbirnie Ladeside		
		Kilmarnock		
		Galston		
		Arthurlie		
1919	1921	Leicester City	24	2
		Nuneaton Town (loan)		
1922	1924	Coventry City	65	16
1925		Queen's Park Rangers	10	
		Blyth Spartans		
		Spennymoor United		

Richmond, James Hart (Jimmy) — RH
b Auchinleck 12/12/1903 — d 1967

From	To	Club	Apps	Goal
		Kello Rovers		
		Partick Thistle		
		Morton		
1930		Luton Town	2	
		Cork FC		
		Linfield		
		Larne		

Richmond, Joseph (Joe) — CF/LB
b Leasingthorne 26/2/1897 — d 1953

From	To	Club	Apps	Goal
		Sittingbourne		
		Shildon Athletic		
1922	1924	Leeds United	56	19
1925		Barnsley	13	5
1926	1929	Norwich City	124	9

Richmond, Philip — IR

From	To	Club	Apps	Goal
1913		Bury	1	

From To Apps Goal

Richmond, William Crichton (Bill) RH/LH
b Kirkcaldy 24/6/1910 d 1973
Raith Rovers
Dundee United
Montrose
1929 1931 Carlisle United 39
Ayr United (trial)
1932 1934 Bournemouth & Boscombe Ath 27
1935 1937 Walsall 89
1938 Clapton Orient 1
Guildford City
St Bernard's
Valentine Thistle

Rickards, Charles Thomas (Tom 'Tex') IR/OR
b Giltbrook 19/2/1915 d 1980
Giltbrook Villa
Johnson & Barnes
1932 1937 Notts County 112 22
1938 Cardiff City 20 5
Scunthorpe & Lindsey United
Peterborough United

Rickards, Richard IL
1925 Crewe Alexandra 1

Rickett, William J (Billy) IR
b Plaistow
Colchester United
1930 Luton Town 1
1931 Gateshead 0

Riddell, Frank IR
b Burton-on-Trent q3 1887
1908 Derby County 3
Bristol Rovers

Riddell, Frederick William (Fred) IR
b Newhall q3 1887 d 1959
Newhall Swifts
1907 Derby County 3 1
Watford
Norwich City
Newhall Swifts
Wrexham
Newhall Swifts

Riddell, James Hamilton (Jim) CH/LH
b Hutchesontown 6/2/1891 d 1952
Fern Thistle
Bellevue Hearts
Glasgow Ashfield
Rangers
Dumbarton
Renton
Rangers
Clyde
Rangers
Partick Thistle (loan)
Kilmarnock
Dumbarton (loan)
St Mirren
1920 1922 Millwall Athletic 105 5
1923 1925 Fulham 37
1925 1927 Wigan Borough 88 3
Caernarvon Town

Riddell, Norman Grey LB
b Morpeth q1 1887 d 1918
Blyth Spartans
Morpeth Harriers
Choppington St Paul's
Rochdale
1911 Clapton Orient 11
Rossendale United

Ridding, William (Bill) CF/IR
b Heswall 4/4/1911 d 1981
Heswall PSA
1928 1929 Tranmere Rovers 17 13
1929 1931 Manchester City 9 4
1931 1933 Manchester United 42 14
1934 Northampton Town 0
1935 Tranmere Rovers 1
1935 Oldham Athletic 1

Riddoch, David (Dave) OL/IL
b Edinburgh 1864 d 1926
Edina
Heart of Midlothian
St Bernard's
Berwick Rangers
1892 1894 Grimsby Town 59 18

Ridge, Dennis Hazelwood CH
b Wortley 18/3/1904 d 1966
Ecclesfield United
1926 Halifax Town 0
1927 Nelson 8
Scarborough
Scarborough Electric

Ridgway, John Henry RB
b Cannock q1 1905 d 1968
1927 Cardiff City 0
1928 Tranmere Rovers 2

From To Apps Goal

Ridgway, Joseph Arthur GK
b Chorlton-cum-Hardy q2 1873 d 1930
West Manchester
1895 1897 Newton Heath 14
Rochdale Town

Ridgway, William H CF/IL
1902 1904 Glossop 7 1

Ridings, Frank IR
b Radcliffe 30/4/1910 d 1969
Heywood St James'
1929 Bury 0
Stalybridge Celtic
Great Harwood
Glossop
1931 Blackburn Rovers 0
Burscough Rangers
1932 Oldham Athletic 2
Nelson

Ridley, Frederick (Fred) OL
b St Pancras q1 1889
Barnet Alston
1913 Leicester Fosse 1

Ridley, Henry (Harry) OL
b Sunderland 25/11/1904 d 1989
Spennymoor United
1926 Fulham (trial) 0
Aldershot
1928 Nelson 31 7
West Stanley
Workington
Spennymoor United
Blyth Spartans
Murton Colliery Welfare
Spennymoor United

Ridley, James OL
b Newcastle 1889
Byker East End
Willington Athletic
1907 1910 Newcastle United 17 2
1910 Nottingham Forest 4 1
Wallsend
Newcastle City
Ashington
Hartlepools United
Wallsend

Ridley, James (Jimmy) OR
b Tanfield Lea 19/1/1903
Tow Law Town
Annfield Plain
1932 Hartlepools United 8 1
Annfield Plain

Ridley, John George RB
b Bardon Mill 19/1/1898 d 1977
Mickley
1920 1926 South Shields 182 4
1927 1932 Manchester City 174
1933 Reading 28
1934 Queen's Park Rangers 17
North Shields

Ridley, Ralph Henry GK
b Haltwhistle 14/4/1904 d 1936
Chopwell Institute
1924 1927 Ashington 74
1929 1931 York City 46
Consett
Workington (trial)
Throckley Welfare
Usworth Colliery Welfare

Ridley, Robert (Bobby) OL
South Shields
Seaham Harbour
Sunderland Royal Rovers
1914 Clapton Orient 17 1
Seaham Colliery

Ridsdale, George RH
b Blackburn q4 1876
1901 Burnley 3

Ridsdale, J RH
1888 Burnley 1
Brierfield

Ridyard, Alfred (Alf) CH/CF
b Cudworth 5/3/1908 d 1981
Shafton
1930 1931 Barnsley 21 3
1932 1936 West Bromwich Albion 31
1937 1947 Queen's Park Rangers 28
1939 (Queen's Park Rangers) (3)
Tunbridge Wells Rangers (loan)

From To Apps Goal

Rigby, Arthur OL/IL
b Chorlton 7/6/1900 d 1960
Caps: FLge 1/England 5
1919 Stockport County (trial) 0
Crewe Alexandra
1920 1924 Bradford City 120 21
1924 1929 Blackburn Rovers 156 41
1929 1931 Everton 42 11
1932 Middlesbrough 10 3
1933 1934 Clapton Orient 70 18
1935 1936 Crewe Alexandra 69 13

Rigby, James Richard (Jimmy) RH
b Bolton q4 1885 d 1954
Atherton
1906 Bolton Wanderers 0
Accrington Stanley
1920 1922 Exeter City 60

Rigby, Norman GK
Atherton Town
1930 Wrexham 2
1931 Wigan Borough 0

Rigby, Walter GK
b Warsop
Shrewsbury Town
1937 1938 Stockport County 11

Rigby, William CF
b Liverpool q1 1896 d 1941
Burscough Rangers
Southport Central
1921 Wigan Borough 15 6
Burscough Rangers

Rigby, William (Will) OR
b Atherton q3 1904
Atlas Mills
1926 Bolton Wanderers 0
Atherton
Clitheroe
1930 Wigan Borough 8 1
1931 Stockport County 3
1932 1933 Rochdale 46 5
Peterborough United
Glentoran
Derry City

Rigg, Clement (Clem) LB
b Lydgate, Todmorden 7/2/1899 d 1966
Todmorden
Portsmouth Rovers
1919 Burnley (trial) 0
1921 1928 Nelson 254 4
Stalybridge Celtic (trial)
1929 Newcastle United (trial) 0

Rigg, Tweedale LH/RB
b Rochdale 1/11/1896 d 1973
Rochdale
1919 Blackburn Rovers 12
1924 Rochdale 2

Rigsby, Herbert (Bert) IL
b Aintree 22/7/1894 d 1972
Hartley's
Inglewood
1919 Everton 14 5
1920 Swansea Town 10
1921 1922 Southport 49 10
Burscough Rangers
Marine
Hartley's

Riley, Alfred (Alf) LH/CH
b Stafford 7/12/1889 d 1958
Wellington Town
Stafford Rangers
1913 1922 Wolverhampton Wanderers 112 1

Riley, Arthur Jack GK
b Boksburg, South Africa 26/12/1903
Boksburg
1925 1938 Liverpool 322

Riley, Harold (Harry) IL/IR
b Hollinwood 22/11/1909 d 1982
Altrincham
Hurst
1928 Birmingham 1
Ashton National
1930 Accrington Stanley 32 18
1931 1932 Lincoln City 57 25
1933 Notts County 16 3
1934 1935 Cardiff City 61 13
1936 1937 Northampton Town 22 4
1938 Exeter City 26 9
1939 (Exeter City) (2) (2)
Newark Town
Ruston-Bucyrus

Riley, James E RB/LH
1905 1906 Burnley 3

From To Apps Goal

Riley, James Harold LH
b West Bromwich 1869
Wednesbury Old Athletic
1890 West Bromwich Albion 3 1
Walsall Town Swifts

Riley, John Leonard OR
b Riddings 1888
Sutton Town
1913 Lincoln City 6

Riley, Joseph (Joe) CF
b Sheffield q2 1910
Conisbrough Welfare
Denaby United
Goldthorpe United
1931 1932 Bristol Rovers 9 4
1933 1934 Bristol City 59 21
1935 1937 Bournemouth & Boscombe Ath 93 57
1937 Notts County 7 1
Gloucester City
Cheltenham Town

Riley, Richard OL
b Padiham q2 1891
Colne
1912 Burnley 3 2
Third Lanark

Riley, Solomon OR
Macclesfield
1894 1895 Crewe Alexandra 43 2

Riley, Thomas (Tom) LB/RB
b Blackburn 3/1882 d 1939
Chorley
1902 1904 Blackburn Rovers 22
Brentford
1905 1907 Aston Villa 16
Brentford
Southampton

Riley, Valentine (Val) LH
b Hebburn 1/1/1904 d 1966
Washington Colliery
1923 Middlesbrough 0
Hebburn Argyle
Wood Skinners
1924 Leeds United 0
Annfield Plain
1928 1930 Newport County 82 4
West Stanley
1932 Southampton 0
Jarrow

Riley, William OR
b Carlisle 19/10/1898
Mid Annandale
1928 Carlisle United 1

Rimmer, Albert RH/OR/IR
b Scarisbrick 27/2/1908 d 1980
Crossens Juniors
1927 1932 Southport 27 2
Lancaster Town
1934 Clapton Orient 0
Ashford Town (Kent)
Fleetwood
1936 Accrington Stanley 2
Fleetwood
Hartwood Hosiery
High Park

Rimmer, Arthur LB
b Wigan 8/6/1904 d 1973
Old Ashtonians
1926 Wigan Borough 0
Ashton St Thomas
1929 Wigan Borough 1

Rimmer, Ellis James OL
b Birkenhead 2/1/1907 d 1965
Caps: England 4
Parkside
Northern Nomads
Whitchurch
1924 1927 Tranmere Rovers 62 20
1927 1937 Sheffield Wednesday 382 122
1938 Ipswich Town 3

Rimmer, Hugh RB
1906 1907 Blackpool 21

Rimmer, John Woolfall (Jackie) OL
b Southport 15/3/1910 d 1989
Caps: England Amat
Mornington Road Juniors
Birkdale South End
1928 1929 Southport 20 6
1930 1936 Bolton Wanderers 82 16
1936 Burnley 0
1937 Reading 8 1
Macclesfield

From To Apps Goal

Ringland, Robert (Bob) CF
1927 Torquay United 14 9
Broadway United

Ringrose, Albert Arthur (Bert) RB/LB
b Edmonton 8/11/1916 d 1968
Tottenham Juniors
1934 Tottenham Hotspur 0
Northfleet
1936 Tottenham Hotspur 10
1939 Notts County (1)

Rippon, Thomas (Pip) IR/CF
b Beighton 4/2/1891 d 1979
1911 1919 Grimsby Town 121 37
1921 Lincoln City 33 10
Worksop Town
York City
Wath Athletic
Grantham

Rippon, Willis CF
b Beighton 15/5/1886 d 1956
Hackenthorpe
Rawmarsh Albion
Sandhill Rovers
Kilnhurst Town
1907 1909 Bristol City 36 13
1910 Woolwich Arsenal 9 2
Brentford
Hamilton Academical
1913 Grimsby Town 23 12
Rotherham County
Rotherham Town

Risdon, Stanley William (Stan) RH/IR/CH
b Exeter 13/8/1913 d 1979
Tipton St John's
St Mary's Majors
1933 1935 Exeter City 35 1
1936 1946 Brighton & Hove Albion 23
Hastings United

Rist, Frank Henry CH/RH
b Leyton 30/3/1914 d 2001
Grays Athletic
1932 Clapton Orient 0
1934 1946 Charlton Athletic 47 1
Colchester United
Tonbridge

Ritchie, Alexander Watson (Alex) OR/IR
b Airdrie 2/4/1904 d 1954
Glasgow Ashfield
Faulhouse United
Airdrieonians
Armadale
St Bernard's
Peebles Rovers (loan)
Raith Rovers
Dunfermline Athletic (loan)
1928 1930 Blackpool 31 5
1930 1932 Reading 72 35
1933 Watford 17 3
1934 Bournemouth & Boscombe Ath 33 12
Third Lanark
Hibernian
Albion Rovers

Ritchie, Archibald (Archie) RB
b Kirkcaldy 12/4/1872 d 1932
Caps: Scotland 1
East Stirlingshire
1892 1898 Nottingham Forest 156
Bristol Rovers
Swindon Town

Ritchie, Archibald (Archie) LB
b Stenhousemuir 11/5/1894 d 1973
Denny Hibernian
Stenhousemuir
Dumbarton
Rangers
1920 1926 Derby County 87 1
Guildford City

Ritchie, Duncan OR/OL
b Renton 1886
Strathleven
Renton
Hibernian
Dumbarton
Raith Rovers
1912 Sheffield United 13 1
1913 Derby County 2
Renton

Ritchie, George Thompson LH
b Maryhill 16/1/1904 d 1978
Maryhill
1922 Blackburn Rovers 2
Royal Albert
Falkirk
1928 1936 Leicester City 247 12
Colchester United

From To Apps Goal

Ritchie, George Wright IL/IR
b West Derby q3 1889 d 1960
Rossendale United
Chester
1912 Preston North End 0
Norwich City
1920 Brighton & Hove Albion 3
1921 Reading 16 4
Northfleet

Ritchie, Henry McGill (Harry) OR
b Scone 27/10/1898 d 1941
Caps: SLge 5/Scotland 2
Perth Violet
Hibernian
1928 1929 Everton 28 5
Dundee
St Johnstone
Brechin City
Arbroath

Ritchie, Robert (Bob) RH
Stockton
Barnsley St Peter's
Stockton
1898 Barnsley 3
Middlesbrough

Ritchie, Robert OL
Victoria United (Aberdeen)
1899 Lincoln City 1

Ritchie, Samuel J CH
Caps: IrLge 4
Glentoran
1913 Nottingham Forest 7
Belfast Celtic

Ritchie, William (Billy) OR
b Renton 1895
Renton
Dumbarton
1919 1921 Bury 62 15
1922 Grimsby Town 25 4

Ritchie, William (Billy) OR/IR
b Carlisle 3/1/1897 d 1987
1919 Derby County 4 1
Porth
Sittingbourne
1923 Millwall Athletic 3
1924 Ashington 19 3
1925 Barrow 27 1
Montreal Scottish
New Bedford Whalers
J & P Coats (Rhode Island)
Boston Wonder Workers
New Bedford Whalers
Boston Bears

Rivers, James Embleton (Jimmy) GK
b Kirk Merrington 23/4/1908 d 1990
Kirk Merrington RA
1928 1932 Hartlepools United 129
Page Bank
Spennymoor United

Rivers, Walter (Wally) IL/IR/LH
b Throckley 8/1/1909 d 1956
Throckley Welfare
1928 Gillingham 5 1
1929 1932 Crystal Palace 81 2
1933 Queen's Park Rangers 3
1934 1935 Gateshead 59 12
1935 Aldershot 12 1
1936 Carlisle United 2 1
1936 1937 Accrington Stanley 56 4
Scarborough

Rix, John (Jack) LH/RH
b Lintz 12/7/1908 d 1979
Lintz Colliery
1927 1937 West Bromwich Albion 64
1939 Lincoln City (3)

Roach, James GK
b West Bromwich 12/1/1864 d 1955
Hereford Thistle
Saltley Gas Company
1895 Small Heath 15
Eastville Rovers

Roach, John IR
b Dalston
Clapton Wanderers
1905 1907 Clapton Orient 1

From To Apps Goal

Robb, David LH/RH
b Leith 18/2/1903 d 1992
Leith Athletic
Musselburgh Bruntonians
Dundee
Arbroath (loan)
1926 Charlton Athletic (trial) 0
1926 1929 Wigan Borough 107 3
1930 Chesterfield 23 1
1932 New Brighton 34

Robb, Thomas (Tommy) RH
b Bellshill 25/1/1899
Kirkintilloch Harp
1919 Bradford City 0
Bathgate
1921 Bradford City 11 1
Bathgate
Hamilton Academical
New York Giants

Robb, William (Willie) GK
b Walker q3 1902
Eastern Burnside
Walker Amateurs
Wallsend
1923 Cardiff City 0
Wallsend
1924 Barrow 33
1925 Bradford Park Avenue 0
Walker Celtic
West Stanley
Crawcrook Albion

Robb, William (Willie) GK
b Rutherglen 20/3/1895 d 1976
Caps: SLge 2/Scotland 2
Rutherglen Welfare
Eastern Burnside
Kirkintilloch Rob Roy
1913 1914 Birmingham 40
Vale of Leven
Royal Albert
Third Lanark
Armadale
Rangers
Hibernian
1932 1936 Aldershot 177
Guildford City
Regent Star

Robbie, David Middleton OR
b Motherwell 6/10/1899 d 1978
Bathgate
1921 1934 Bury 420 102
1935 Plymouth Argyle 3
1935 Manchester United 1
Margate

Robbins, Albert IL
b Penrhiwceiber
Abertysswg
1928 Coventry City 2
Hereford United
Barry

Robbins, Patrick (Paddy) IL/OL
b Birr 18/11/1913 d 1986
Thornaby St Patrick's
Stockton
1933 Middlesbrough 0
1934 Blackburn Rovers 0
1935 1937 Oldham Athletic 80 15
1938 Hartlepools United 24 5
1939 Accrington Stanley (3) (2)
1945 York City 0

Robbins, Walter William OL/IL
b Cardiff 24/11/1910 d 1979
Caps: Wales 11
Ely Brewery
Ely United
1928 1931 Cardiff City 86 38
1931 1938 West Bromwich Albion 84 28
1939 Newport County 0

Roberts, ? CH
1888 Everton 1

Roberts, Albert (Arthur) LB
b Goldthorpe 27/1/1907 d 1957
Goldthorpe United
Ardsley Athletic
1930 1937 Southampton 156
1938 Swansea Town 16
1946 York City 1

Roberts, Albert Victor (Vic) RH
b Shrewsbury 14/2/1902 d 1967
1924 Crewe Alexandra 3
Shrewsbury Town

Roberts, Alfred (Alf) OL
1894 Walsall Town Swifts 5

From To Apps Goal

Roberts, Arthur IL
b Newcastle-under-Lyme 1876
Newcastle Casuals
1899 Stoke 2
Tunstall Rangers

Roberts, Charles (Charlie) CH
b Rise Carr 6/4/1883 d 1939
Caps: FLge 9/England 3
Rise Carr Rangers
Darlington St Augustine's
Bishop Auckland
1903 Grimsby Town 31 4
1903 1912 Manchester United 271 22
1913 1914 Oldham Athletic 72 2

Roberts, Charles Leslie (Les) IL/IR
b Halesowen 28/2/1901 d 1980
Cradley Heath St Luke's
1921 Aston Villa 0
Redditch
1921 Bristol Rovers 0
1922 Chesterfield 6 4
1923 Sheffield Wednesday 0
1923 Bristol Rovers 0
1924 Merthyr Town 12 2
1924 1925 Bournemouth & Boscombe Ath 51 11
1925 1926 Bolton Wanderers 6 2
1927 1929 Swindon Town 106 32
1930 Brentford 5
1930 Manchester City 8 2
1931 Exeter City 11 4
1932 1933 Crystal Palace 47 18
1933 Chester 5 2
1934 Rotherham United 9 5
Scunthorpe & Lindsey United
1936 1937 New Brighton 40 11
South Liverpool

Roberts, Cyril RB
1925 Coventry City 1

Roberts, David A CF
b Tipton
Caps: LoI 3
Shrewsbury Town
1922 Walsall 3
Bohemians

Roberts, Dennis CH
b Monk Bretton 5/2/1918 d 2001
1937 Notts County 0
1938 1953 Bristol City 303 2
1939 (Bristol City) (3)

Roberts, E Thomas IR
1901 1902 Nottingham Forest 6

Roberts, Edgar F OR
b Shrewsbury 1900
1921 1922 Bolton Wanderers 5
Rhos
1926 Crewe Alexandra 8
Shrewsbury Town

Roberts, Edward (Ted) CF/IL/IR
b Chesterfield 2/11/1916 d 1970
Lea Mission
Glapwell Colliery
1935 Derby County 4
1936 1951 Coventry City 211 85
King's Lynn
Banbury Spencer
Bedworth Town

Roberts, Edward Daniel (ED) LH
b Rhosllanerchrugog 20/2/1891 d 1970
Chirk
Druids
Rhos Athletic
1920 Bristol City 0
1921 1922 Wrexham 43
Rhos Athletic
Druids

Roberts, Evan Evans GK
b Bolton q3 1870
1891 Bolton Wanderers 0
Kettering
1894 Lincoln City 23
1894 Rotherham Town 0

Roberts, Francis (Frank) RH
b Motherwell 1902
Cadzow St Anne's
Queen's Park
Rangers
Cowdenbeath
Rangers
St Johnstone
Rangers
Alloa Athletic
Rangers
1924 Bristol Rovers 2
Ayr United

From To Apps Goal

Roberts, Frank CF/IR
b Sandbach 3/4/1893 d 1961
Caps: FLge 1/England 4
Sandbach Villa
Sandbach Ramblers
Crewe Alexandra
1914 1922 Bolton Wanderers 157 79
1922 1928 Manchester City 216 116
Manchester Central
Horwich RMI

Roberts, Frank CF
b Llangollen
Chester
1925 Wrexham 7 3
Shell-Mex (Chester)

Roberts, Frederick (Fred) IL/LH
b Greets Green 9/10/1908 d 1979
Thomas Pigot's Works
1933 1934 Birmingham 29 9
1934 1938 Luton Town 180 38
1939 (Luton Town) (3)
Kettering Town

Roberts, Frederick (Fred) OR
b Rhyl 7/5/1916 d 1985
Rhyl
1938 1946 Bury 12 5
1939 (Bury) (3) (1)
1946 Leyton Orient 18 2
Rhyl

Roberts, Gerald Stanley (Gerry) LB
b Bromborough q2 1908 d 1944
Bromborough Pool
1932 Tranmere Rovers 2

Roberts, Harry CF
Doncaster St James
1902 1904 Doncaster Rovers 5 2
Doncaster St James

Roberts, Henry (Harry) IR/IL/CF
b Barrow 1/9/1907 d 1984
Caps: England 1
Barrow Wireworks
1925 Barrow 17 3
1926 1927 Chesterfield 17 3
1928 1929 Lincoln City 33 23
1930 Port Vale 24 9
1930 1934 Millwall 115 25
1935 Sheffield Wednesday (trial) 0
Peterborough United
Spalding United

Roberts, Henry LH/RH
b Ardsley q3 1912
Frickley Colliery
1935 1936 Rotherham United 9
1938 Rochdale 0

Roberts, Henry Bromley (Harry) RB
b Crofton 12/5/1906 d 1963
Castleford Town
1925 1930 Leeds United 84 2
1930 1936 Plymouth Argyle 248 21
1937 1938 Bristol Rovers 77
Frickley Colliery

Roberts, Herbert (Herbie) CH
b Oswestry 19/2/1905 d 1944
Caps: England 1
Oswestry Town
1926 1937 Arsenal 297 4

Roberts, Hopkin John (Jackie) RB/IR
b Swansea 30/6/1918 d 2001
Caps: Wales Sch/Wales 1
Cwmbwrla Juniors
1937 1950 Bolton Wanderers 162 19
1950 Swansea Town 16 1
Llanelly

Roberts, Hugh Pierce OR
b Rhyl 14/10/1882
Port Sunlight
St Helens Recreation
Southport Central
1909 1912 Leeds City 108 14
Scunthorpe & Lindsey United
Luton Town

Roberts, J OL
1906 Middlesbrough 1

Roberts, Jack OL
b Wednesbury 1873
Swan Athletic (West Bromwich)
Tipton Excelsior
1894 Wolverhampton Wanderers 1
Ewells (Wednesbury)

Roberts, James OL
1893 Northwich Victoria 1

From To Apps Goal

Roberts, James (Jimmy) LB/RB
b Chirk 1878
Caps: Wales 2
Chirk
Crewe Alexandra
1904 1908 Bradford City 24
Huddersfield Town

Roberts, James (Jas) OL
b Mold 7/1/1891
Caps: Wales Amat/Wales 2
Mold Villa
Mold Town
Wrexham
Crewe Alexandra
1914 Everton 1
1921 Tranmere Rovers 32 1
1921 Crewe Alexandra 0
1922 Wrexham 6
Mold Town

Roberts, James W RH
1893 Northwich Victoria 1

Roberts, John IL
b Walsall 1885
Darlaston
1906 Wolverhampton Wanderers 24 14
Bristol Rovers
Stourbridge
Walsall Phoenix

Roberts, John Edgar (Jack 'Nipper') CF
b Anfield 15/3/1910 d 1985
Caps: England Amat
Marine
Orrell
Northern Nomads
Blundellsands
1931 1932 Southport 18 8
1933 Liverpool 1
Wigan Athletic
1935 1938 Port Vale 93 56
1939 (Port Vale) (2)

Roberts, John William (Billy) IL
b Liverpool 1880
White Star Wanderers
Tottenham Hotsur
1901 Stockport County 0
Grays United
Brighton & Hove Albion
Queen's Park Rangers
1906 Preston North End 2
1907 Leicester Fosse (trial) 0

Roberts, Joseph (Joe) OL
b Birkenhead 2/9/1900 d 1984
Oswestry Town
1926 Watford 20 5
1927 Queen's Park Rangers 4
York City
1929 Halifax Town 22 1
1929 1930 Southport 44
1931 Clapton Orient 2
1932 Luton Town 17 2
1932 Millwall 0
1933 Barrow 41 14
Peterborough United
1935 Cardiff City 22 5
Dartford
Worcester City

Roberts, Josiah Edmund RB
b West Smethwick 1871
Birmingham St George's
1892 Small Heath 1
Walsall Wood

Roberts, Lawrence CF
b Kirkintilloch
Dykehead
Rangers
St Mirren (loan)
Renton
1919 Burnley 1
Hamilton Academical
Dumbarton Harp
Dykehead
Airdrieonians
Vale of Leven
Old Kilpatrick
Helensburgh
Dumbarton Harp
Helensburgh

Roberts, Leonard (Len) LH
b Rotherham
1931 1933 Halifax Town 23 1

From To Apps Goal

Roberts, Norman OL
b Penmachno q2 1915
Penmachno
1933 Chester 1 1
Bangor City
1935 Wolverhampton Wanderers 0
1936 Barnsley 7
1936 1937 Carlisle United 30 6
Shrewsbury Town

Roberts, Percy CF
b Wrexham
Oak Alyn Rovers
1924 Wrexham 0
Oswestry Town
1926 Nelson 1
Macclesfield
Birmingham City Police

Roberts, Richard Edward (Dick) LB
b Rhyl q1 1891
Rhyl United
1910 Leeds City 0
1919 Coventry City 18
Rhyl United
Nuneaton Town
Atherstone Town
Barwell United

Roberts, Richard James OL/OR
b Bromsgrove 1878 d 1931
Redditch Excelsior
1899 1900 West Bromwich Albion 43 8
1901 1903 Newcastle United 51 17
1903 1904 Middlesbrough 23 5
Crystal Palace

Roberts, Robert (Bob) LH/CH
b Penycae 7/1864 d 1932
Caps: Wales 9
Druids
1888 1891 Bolton Wanderers 71 3
1891 Preston North End 5
1892 Lincoln City 16 3

Roberts, Robert OL
b Rhosllanerchrugog 1865 d 1945
Caps: Wales 2
Rhosllanerchrugog
Witton Britannia
Wrexham (trial)
1890 West Bromwich Albion 1
Wrexham
1892 1893 Crewe Alexandra 38 17

Roberts, Robert HA RB
b Earlestown
Altrincham
1913 Manchester United 2

Roberts, Robert John (Bob) GK
b West Bromwich 4/1859 d 1933
Caps: England 3
George Salter's Works
West Bromwich Strollers
1888 1889 West Bromwich Albion 40
Sunderland Albion
1891 West Bromwich Albion 9
1892 Aston Villa 4
Sunderland Albion

Roberts, Samuel (Sam) OL
b Connah's Quay
Holywell
Connah's Quay & Shotton
Flint Town
Rhyl Athletic
1932 Halifax Town 9
Rhyl Athletic
Newry Town
Rangers
Kilmarnock
Dundee
Glasgow Benburb

Roberts, Samuel Grenville (Grenville) IR
b Blackwell 16/8/1919 d 1940
Huthwaite CWS
1937 1938 Nottingham Forest 6

Roberts, Sydney (Syd) IL/IR/OL
b Bootle 3/1911
Bootle Junior Ordnance Corps
1931 1936 Liverpool 57 10
Shrewsbury Town
1937 1938 Chester 29 6
Northfleet

Roberts, T IL
1899 New Brighton Tower 4 1

Roberts, Thomas (Tom) LH/OL
b Bristol 4/8/1903 d 1970
Trowbridge Town
1925 1929 Bristol Rovers 120 6
Lovells Athletic

From To Apps Goal

Roberts, Thomas Frederick (Frederick) LB/CH/LH
b Smethwick 1868
1890 West Bromwich Albion 1
Birmingham St George's
1893 1894 West Bromwich Albion 3

Roberts, Vivian GK
1919 West Ham United 1

Roberts, W IR
1894 Walsall Town Swifts 16 6

Roberts, Walter OR
1905 Stockport County 3

Roberts, Walter (Wally) CH/RH/LH
b Wrexham 23/11/1917 d 2006
1938 1947 Wrexham 60 1
1948 1949 Bournemouth & Boscombe Ath 15
Ellesmere Port Town
Winsford United
Blaenau Ffestiniog

Roberts, William RB
b Nottingham d 1937
Sherwood Foresters
1890 Derby County 5

Roberts, William IR/OL
1902 1903 Glossop 5 1

Roberts, William A (Bogie) OL
1898 1899 Newton Heath 9 2

Roberts, William David (Billy) CF/IR
b Rainhill 9/1/1901 d 1960
Saltney
Northwich Victoria
1923 Huddersfield Town 0
1925 Tranmere Rovers 6 1
Winsford United
Buckley United
1926 Bolton Wanderers 5 4
Flint Town
1927 New Brighton 16 10
Prescot Cables
Hurst
Connah's Quay & Shotton

Roberts, William Henry (Bill) RH
b Connah's Quay 3/3/1914 d 2002
Newry Town
1937 West Ham United 1
1939 Crystal Palace 0

Roberts, William J (Bill) LB
b Birmingham
Flint Town
1928 1932 Cardiff City 130 1

Roberts, William S OL
1905 Sheffield United 0
1906 1907 Middlesbrough 12
Hartlepools United

Roberts, William Samuel (Bill) RB
b Bargoed 12/7/1908 d 1976
Army
1932 Tottenham Hotspur 0
1933 1936 Bristol City 135 7
1938 1945 Newport County 41

Roberts, William Thomas (Tommy) CF
b Handsworth 29/11/1898 d 1965
Caps: FLge 2/England 2
Soho Villa
1914 Leicester Fosse 0
1919 1924 Preston North End 199 118
1924 1925 Burnley 49 28
1926 1927 Preston North End 55 39
1928 Tottenham Hotspur 4 2
Dick, Kerr's XI
Chorley

Robertson, Albert Christopher (Chris) CH/RB
b Mablethorpe 25/3/1914 d 1995
1935 1937 Grimsby Town 5
1938 Chester 13
Hereford United

Robertson, Alexander CF/OL
b Dundee 1878
Dundee Violet
Dundee
1900 1902 Middlesbrough 48 24
1903 1904 Manchester United 28 10
Bradford Park Avenue

Robertson, Alexander LH
b Perth 1878
Fair City Athletic
Hibernian
Fair City Athletic
Hibernian
1903 1905 Manchester United 33 1
Fair City Athletic

From To Apps Goal

Robertson, Alexander (Alec) IL
b Kilbirnie 1911
Beith Athletic
Aberdeen
Kilmarnock
1935 1937 Hartlepools United 79 16
Horden Colliery Welfare

Robertson, Alexander Harper (Alex) CH
b Liverpool q4 1895 d 1966
Caps: England Amat
Harrowby
Northern Nomads
Tranmere Rovers
Liverpool
1921 Oldham Athletic 0
Harrowby
1923 1924 New Brighton 3
Northern Nomads
1928 New Brighton 0
Northern Nomads

Robertson, Alexander S (Sandy) RH/LH
b Edinburgh 12/1860 d 1927
1888 1889 Preston North End 28 3

Robertson, Alfred Joseph (Alf) GK
b Sunderland 3/7/1908 d 1984
Bank Head
1927 Newcastle United (trial) 0
1929 Notts County 0
Grantham
1930 1932 Bradford Park Avenue 45
1933 1934 Clapton Orient 50
1935 Bristol Rovers 8
1936 1938 Accrington Stanley 81
Dunkenhalgh

Robertson, D CF
1893 Ardwick 7 3

Robertson, Edward (Ted) IL
b Trimdon Colliery q2 1897
Wingate Albion
Trimdon Grange Colliery
1923 Durham City 1 1
Trimdon Grange Colliery
Ferryhill Athletic
Willington
Trimdon Grange Colliery

Robertson, George LH/IL
b Glasgow 1883
Rutherglen Glencairn
Clyde
Rangers
Clyde
1902 Blackburn Rovers 10 1
Clyde
1910 1913 Birmingham 84 17
Bloxwich Strollers
Brierley Hill Alliance

Robertson, George RB/LB/LH
b Failsworth
Ashton National
1927 1932 Manchester City 14
Cambuslang Rangers
1933 1934 Southend United 43
1935 Chesterfield 2

Robertson, George Clarke OL
b Menstrie 7/3/1885 d 1962
Caps: Scotland 4
Yoker Athletic
Port Glasgow Athletic
Motherwell
1909 1919 Sheffield Wednesday 163 30
East Fife

Robertson, Hope Ramsey LH/RB/OR
b Whiteinch 17/1/1868 d 1947
Minerva
Partick Thistle
Woolwich Arsenal
1890 1892 Everton 29 1
1892 Bootle 10 1
1894 Walsall Town Swifts 12

Robertson, Hugh CF
b Cambusnethan 24/9/1872
1893 Everton 0
Millwall Athletic
1895 1896 Burnley 40 15
1897 1898 Lincoln City 64 34
Millwall Athletic
1899 Woolwich Arsenal 0
Dundee
1900 Leicester Fosse (trial) 5 1

Robertson, Hugh RB/RH
b Perth
St Johnstone YMCA
1936 1937 Wrexham 6
St Johnstone

From To Apps Goal

Robertson, J IR
1888 Accrington 3

Robertson, James (Jimmie) CF
b Dundee 1868
Dundee Our Boys
1892 1894 Stoke 60 19
Ashton North End
1895 Manchester City 3 2

Robertson, James (Jimmy) OR
Abercorn
Third Lanark
1901 1902 Middlesbrough 32 3
New Brompton
Aberdeen

Robertson, James (Jimmy) IR
b Glasgow 1880
Glasgow United
Crewe Alexandra
1903 Small Heath 6 2
1905 1906 Chelsea 29 21
1907 1908 Glossop 70 28
Leyton
Partick Thistle
Ayr United
Barrow
1912 Leeds City 27 7
Gateshead

Robertson, James (Jimmy) IR
b Scotland
Vale of Leven
Distillery
1905 1907 Blackburn Rovers 78 22
Brighton & Hove Albion
Vale of Leven
Falkirk
Dunfermline Athletic (loan)
Armadale
Falkirk
Vale of Leven
Dumbarton Harp
Dumbarton

Robertson, James OR
b Glasgow
1923 Barrow 16
Runcorn
Clitheroe

Robertson, James E CF
b Dundee 1910
Caps: Scotland 1
Logie United
Logie Thistle
Dundee
1933 Birmingham 6 1
Kilmarnock
Elgin City

Robertson, James Henry (Jimmy) IR
b Berwick-on-Tweed 22/3/1913 d 1973
1930 Notts County (trial) 0
Welbeck Colliery
1932 1937 Bradford Park Avenue 130 58
1937 1938 Bradford City 36 17
Tunbridge Wells Rangers

Robertson, James S GK
b 1873
Chatham
New Brompton
1901 Bristol City 12
Accrington Stanley

Robertson, James Walter (Jim 'Jock') RB
b Chatham 21/2/1898 d 1970
Caps: SoLge 1
Chatham Central
1920 1932 Gillingham 358 1
Canterbury Waverley

Robertson, John Nicol RH/LH
b Coylton 1884 d 1937
Caps: SoLge 2
Drongan
Rangers
1903 1905 Bolton Wanderers 15
Southampton
Rangers

Robertson, John Tait (Jack) LH/IL/OL
b Dumbarton 25/2/1877 d 1935
Caps: SLge 6/Scotland 16
Poinfield
Sinclair Swifts
Morton
1897 Everton 26 1
Southampton
Rangers
1905 1906 Chelsea 36 4
1906 1908 Glossop 45 10

From To Apps Goal

Robertson, John Thomas (Jack) RB/RH/CH
b Newton Mearns 6/1877
Newton Thistle
St Bernard's
1894 1895 Stoke 24 1
Hibernian
Millwall Athletic
1897 1899 Stoke 88 2
1900 1901 Liverpool 42 1
Southampton
Brighton & Hove Albion

Robertson, Peter RH
Polton Vale
1895 Burnley 1

Robertson, Peter CH
b Dundee 1881
Providence
Dundee
1904 Nottingham Forest 7
Dundee

Robertson, Peter IR/IL
b Port Glasgow 1891
Port Glasgow Athletic
Morton
1921 1922 Hartlepools United 36 18
1923 Doncaster Rovers 16 4
Somaphore (South Australia)

Robertson, Peter GK
b Dundee 2/1908 d 1964
Lochee United
Dundee
1929 1932 Charlton Athletic 117
1933 Crystal Palace 4
Dundee United
Brechin City
Arbroath
1939 Rochdale (3)

Robertson, Samuel RB
b Cowdenbeath 1882
Dundee
1905 Notts County 2

Robertson, Samuel P (Sam) RH/IL
b Hebburn 1887
Hebburn Argyle
1904 1905 Barnsley 22 1

Robertson, Thomas RH
b Torrance 12/1864
Queen's Park
1892 Nottingham Forest 1
Queen's Park

Robertson, Thomas (Tom) CH
1895 1896 Everton 4

Robertson, Thomas (Tommy) OL
b Renton 1877
Caps: Scotland 1
East Benhar Heatherbell
Motherwell
Fauldhouse
Heart of Midlothian
1897 1901 Liverpool 126 34
Heart of Midlothian
Dundee
1903 Manchester United 3
Bathgate

Robertson, Thomas (Tommy) LB/RB
b Trimdon Colliery 1906
Trimdon Grange
Ferryhill Athletic
Trimdon Colliery
1927 1928 Hartlepools United 35
1928 1930 Bury 13
Morecambe
Darwen

Robertson, Thomas Henry (Tom) CF
b Gateshead 6/8/1889 d 1950
Wallsend Park Villa
1910 Lincoln City 8 1
Wallsend Park Villa
Cardiff City
1921 1925 Ashington 149 61

Robertson, William LH/IR
b Pontypool 1873
Abercarn
1895 1898 Small Heath 91 14
Bristol Rovers
1902 Small Heath 0
Bristol Rovers

From To Apps Goal

Robertson, William (Bill) LH
b Falkirk
Glasgow Perthshire
1920 Portsmouth 0
Lancaster Town
1922 1923 Barrow 41 1
Lancaster Town
Ulverston Town
Lancaster Town

Robertson, William CF
Shaftesbury Boys Club
1936 Tranmere Rovers 1

Robertson, William P (Billy) GK
b Glasgow
Oatlands
Morton
1919 Bury 6
Beith
Vale of Clyde

Robertson, William S (Billy) RH
b Falkirk 20/4/1907
Camelon Juniors
King's Park
Third Lanark
Ayr United
1929 1933 Stoke City 117 3
1933 1935 Manchester United 47 1
1935 1936 Reading 24
East Stirlingshire

Robertson, William Smith (Willie) OL
b Stirling 7/6/1887 d 1960
Denny Hibernian
Celtic
1910 Preston North End 2
St Mirren
York City

Robey, James Henry RB
b Radcliffe 1/3/1913 d 1992
Heywood St James
Stalybridge Celtic
1936 Aston Villa 3
Aberdeen
Wigan Athletic

Robins, Arthur OR
b Northampton 1888 d 1924
Raunds St Peter's
1908 1909 Sheffield United 7
Castleford Town

Robins, Robert Walter Vivian (Walter) OR
b Stafford 3/6/1906 d 1968
1929 1930 Nottingham Forest 2

Robinson, Albert OL
b Doncaster q2 1882
Doncaster St James
1902 Doncaster Rovers 3
Doncaster St James

Robinson, Albert GK
b Sheffield
Hillsborough Ex-Servicemens' FC
Shirebrook
1923 Rotherham County 0
1924 Sheffield United 3
Worksop Town
Bilsthorpe Colliery
Ilkeston
Alfreton Welfare
Heanor Town
Ranleigh Athletic
Ilkeston
South Normanton Welfare

Robinson, Albert RB
b South Normanton 1913
South Normanton
1931 1932 Mansfield Town 12
1933 Derby County 0
Sutton Town

Robinson, Alfred IL/OL
b West Hartlepool 1883
Stranton Parish Church
West Hartlepool
1904 Sunderland 0
1905 1906 Stockport County 20 3
Carlisle United
1909 Sheffield United 0
Spennymoor United

Robinson, Alfred GK
b Manchester 1888
Chapel-en-le-Frith
1908 1910 Gainsborough Trinity 54
1911 1920 Blackburn Rovers 144
Darwen

From To Apps Goal

Robinson, Alfred OR
b Grimsby 1887 d 1945
St James (Grimsby)
Grimsby St John's
Grimsby Rovers
1909 Grimsby Town 2
Grimsby Rovers
Cleethorpes Town
Immingham

Robinson, Alfred (Alf) LH
b Belfast
South Liverpool
1921 Accrington Stanley 3

Robinson, Alfred IL
b Boldon 1916
Washington Colliery
1934 Bolton Wanderers 0
1935 York City 3
Scarborough

Robinson, Alfred John IR/IL
b Birkenhead 30/1/1898 d 1980
1919 Everton 1
1921 1922 Tranmere Rovers 7 1
Wallasey United

Robinson, Alick LH/RB
b Leigh 17/4/1906 d 1977
Caps: FLge 2
Hindley Green
1926 1933 Bury 169 4
1933 1938 Burnley 204 8
1939 (Burnley) (2)

Robinson, Arnold OL
Alfreton Town
Tibshelf Colliery
1909 Derby County 1
Tibshelf Colliery

Robinson, Arthur IR
b Middlestone Moor
Cockfield
1931 Hartlepools United 1
Crook Town
Heart of Midlothian
Crook Town

Robinson, Arthur Charles (Nat) GK
b Coventry 28/2/1878 d 1929
Caps: FLge 2
Allesley
Coventry Stars
Singers
1899 1907 Small Heath/Birmingham 283
1908 1909 Chelsea 3
Coventry City

Robinson, Benjamin (Benny) RH
b Broughton
Swinburn
1919 1921 Coventry City 27
Nuneaton Town

Robinson, Bernard Cecil RH/RB
b Cambridge 5/12/1911 d 2004
King's Lynn
1931 1948 Norwich City 360 13
1939 (Norwich City) (3)

Robinson, Bethel RB/LB
b Wheelton 1862
Preston North End
1888 Bolton Wanderers 16
1888 West Bromwich Albion 0
1888 Bolton Wanderers 2
1888 West Bromwich Albion 0
1889 1890 Bolton Wanderers 20
Newton Heath (loan)
1890 West Bromwich Albion 0
Hyde
1892 Darwen 0
Bootle

Robinson, Charles (Charlie) RH
b Rotherham 20/8/1905 d 1972
Parkgate Church Lads
Silverwood Colliery
1929 Rotherham United 12
1930 Wolverhampton Wanderers 0
1931 Coventry City 0
1932 1935 Stockport County 115 11
1936 Plymouth Argyle 0
1937 1938 Hull City 68 4
1939 (Hull City) (1)

Robinson, Charles Alexander (Charlie) RH/CH/OR
b Pegswood q2 1906
Pegswood United
Amble
Stakeford United
1926 1927 Ashington 29 5
Bedlington United
1928 Blackpool 5
1931 1932 Exeter City 8
1933 1934 Gillingham 34
1935 Accrington Stanley 24
1936 1937 Rochdale 18
Blyth Spartans

Robinson, Cyril IR
1935 Northampton Town 1

Robinson, David (Dave) LB/RB
b Longtown 4/7/1900 d 1986
Lockerbie
1921 Aston Villa (trial) 0
Eskdale
Carlisle United
Solway Star
Workington
1926 1927 Leeds United 5
1928 1938 Southend United 317 1
1939 (Southend United) (3)

Robinson, Edward (Ted) LB
b Hindley 27/9/1904 d 1972
Hindley St Benedict's
Castle Hill
Hindley Rovers
Hindley St Benedict's
Hindley Green Athletic
Chorley
1927 Southampton 1
1930 1932 Southport 108 6
Wigan Athletic

Robinson, Ernest George SR (Ernie) RB/RH
b Shiney Row 21/1/1908 d 1990
Shiney Row Swifts
Houghton Colliery
Shildon
York City
1929 Notts County 0
1930 Nelson 27
1930 Northampton Town (trial) 0
Tunbridge Wells Rangers
1932 Barnsley 23
1933 Sheffield United 17
1934 Carlisle United 38
1935 1938 Lincoln City 64

Robinson, Foster Wilson G OL
b South Shields 6/2/1901 d 1975
Simonside
1921 Coventry City 0
Nuneaton Town (loan)
1922 Coventry City 5
1923 Bournemouth & Boscombe Ath 31 1
1925 Luton Town 1 1

Robinson, Fred IL/IR
b Belper 1881
Belper Town
1905 1906 Grimsby Town 32 8
Rotherham County

Robinson, George Henry RH/CH
b Basford 1877 d 1945
Nottingham Jardines Athletic
Newark
1898 1902 Nottingham Forest 85 1
1903 1914 Bradford City 343 16

Robinson, George Henry IR/OR
b Marlpool 11/1/1908 d 1963
Ilkeston Rangers
Ilkeston United
1927 1930 Sunderland 31 8
1931 1932 Charlton Athletic 40 5
Burton Town
1934 1946 Charlton Athletic 198 37
1939 (Charlton Athletic) (2)

Robinson, Gladney IR/OR
b Settle 14/10/1915 d 1991
Settle
1936 1937 Halifax Town 23 2
Lancaster City

Robinson, Harold OR
b Middlesbrough q1 1901
Haverton Hill
Darlington
South Bank
1922 Durham City 9

Robinson, Harry OR
Newton Rangers
1900 Chesterfield Town 2

Robinson, Henry RH/OR
Wednesbury Old Athletic
1892 1893 Walsall Town Swifts 27 1

Robinson, Henry OL/OR
b Chilton 1909
Kirk Merrington
Shildon
Chilton Colliery Recreation Athletic
1929 Sunderland 0
1930 Nelson 20 3
1930 Hartlepools United 6 1
Spennymoor United
1932 Darlington 1
Crook Town
Horden Colliery Welfare

Robinson, Herbert (Bert) IL/CF
b Grimsby
Grimsby All Saints
1895 1898 Grimsby Town 8 5
Cyclists FC
Grimsby Rangers

Robinson, Herve Josse (Hervey) IL
b Grimsby q4 1874 d 1954
Grimsby All Saints
1893 Grimsby Town 2 4
Grimsby All Saints

Robinson, Ian H RH
1921 Ashington 1

Robinson, Isaac (Ike) LB
b Bishop Auckland 16/7/1915 d 1979
Brotherton Colliery Welfare
1934 Leeds United 0
Scarborough
1936 Grimsby Town 3
Boston United

Robinson, J William GK
1895 Crewe Alexandra 10

Robinson, James Walter RH/LH
b Ryton-on-Tyne q3 1901
Stargate Rovers
1923 Burnley 4
1925 Nelson 0
1926 Bradford City 0
Workington
1929 Doncaster Rovers 17
Scarborough
1930 Newcastle United 1
Crawcrook Albion

Robinson, James Wilson OL
b Belfast 8/1/1898
1919 1921 Manchester United 21 3
1923 Tranmere Rovers 4

Robinson, JM CF
1894 Burton Swifts 1

Robinson, John OR
b Leeds 1/4/1913 d 1989
1936 Huddersfield Town 0
1937 1938 Sheffield United 3
1939 Hull City 0

Robinson, John Allan (Jackie) IR
b Shiremoor 10/8/1917 d 1972
Caps: FLge 1/England 4
West Wylam Colliery
Shiremoor
1934 1946 Sheffield Wednesday 108 34
1939 (Sheffield Wednesday) (2)
1946 1948 Sunderland 82 32
1949 Lincoln City 8 5

Robinson, John James (Jack) GK
b Oswaldtwistle 23/4/1918 d 1993
Sacred Heart
1935 1936 Accrington Stanley 16
1938 1946 Manchester City 2
1946 Bury 12
1947 Southend United 6

Robinson, John William (Jack) GK
b Derby 22/4/1870 d 1931
Caps: England 11
Derby St Neots
Derby Midland
Lincoln City
1891 1896 Derby County 163
New Brighton Tower
Southampton
Plymouth Argyle
Millwall Athletic
Exeter City
Green Waves
Exeter City
Stoke
Rochester (New York)

Robinson, John William LH/IL
b Grangetown
1919 Middlesbrough 1
1921 1922 Portsmouth 26 2
Guildford United
1923 Queen's Park Rangers 5 1

Robinson, Joseph (Joe) GK
b Morpeth 4/3/1919 d 1991
Morpeth Town
Ashington
1938 Hartlepools United 11
1939 (Hartlepools United) (2)
1947 1948 Blackpool 25
1948 1952 Hull City 70
Hexham Hearts
Wisbech Town

Robinson, Leslie St John (Les) IR/IL
b Romford 2/5/1898 d 1965
Sterling Athletic
1920 1923 West Ham United 19 2
1925 1926 Northampton Town 73 32
1927 Norwich City 31 10
Thames
1929 Torquay United 23 16

Robinson, LG OL
1895 Notts County 0
1896 Manchester City 3 2

Robinson, Matthew (Matt) IL/LH/OL
b Felling 21/4/1907 d 1987
Pelaw
1928 1930 Cardiff City 18 2
1931 Manchester United 10
1931 Chester 6 1
1932 1937 Barrow 226 52

Robinson, Patrick (Pat) OR
b Belfast 1892
Caps: IrLge 2/Ireland 2
Distillery
1920 Blackburn Rovers 18 2
Caerphilly
Linfield
Brooklyn Wanderers

Robinson, Ralph (Robby) RB/LB
b Annfield Plain 1906
Tow Law Town
1925 Durham City (trial) 0
1925 Huddersfield Town (trial) 0
1926 Arsenal 0
1933 1934 Newport County 71
1935 Gateshead 19

Robinson, Raymond Wilson (Ray) OR
b Blaydon q3 1895 d 1964
Scotswood
1919 Newcastle United 27 4
1920 Sunderland 10 2
1921 Grimsby Town 9
1922 Sunderland 0
Eden Colliery
Lancaster Town
Liverpool Police
Shirebrook
Silverwood Colliery

Robinson, Reginald (Reg) CH/LH
b Scunthorpe
Scunthorpe & Lindsey United
1933 1934 Huddersfield Town 2
1935 Exeter City 30 1
1937 Watford 2

Robinson, Robert (Bob) GK
b Leamside 27/3/1910 d 1989
Lamton & Hetton
South Hetton Colliery Welfare
Hebburn Colliery Welfare
1929 1930 Sunderland 34
Guildford City
1932 Norwich City 34
1935 1936 Barrow 32
Scarborough
Gainsborough Trinity

Robinson, Robert Breckell IL
b Preston q2 1871
1893 Ardwick 4 2
1894 Preston North End 0
1895 Wolverhampton Wanderers 0

Robinson, Robert John C CH
b Bordon 9/11/1906 d 1990
Caps: England Amat
RAF
1929 Gillingham 2

From To Apps Goal

Robinson, Robert Smith (Robbie) IR/RH
b Sunderland 1/10/1879 d 1950
South Hylton
Sunderland Royal Rovers
1902 1903 Sunderland 24 7
1903 1911 Liverpool 254 64
Tranmere Rovers

Robinson, Roland T CF
1923 Walsall 4 1
Worcester City

Robinson, Samuel Blighton LB
b Grimsby q1 1878
Humber Rovers
Grimsby Rovers
1899 Grimsby Town 1
Grimsby Rovers
Grimsby Rangers
Grimsby St John's

Robinson, Samuel Henry (Sam) CH
b Hucknall 15/12/1910
1928 Luton Town 0
1929 1930 Bournemouth & Boscombe Ath 11 1
1930 Derby County 0
1931 1933 Mansfield Town 61 1
1933 Clapton Orient 2
Guildford City

Robinson, Thomas Charles (Tom) LH/RH
b Burton-on-Trent 2/10/1903 d 1981
1927 1929 Derby County 9
1930 1931 Bury 2
1932 Torquay United 24

Robinson, Thomas Edward (Tommy) IL
b Coalville 11/2/1909 d 1982
Coalville YMCA
Gresley Rovers
1929 1932 Birmingham 11 1
1933 Blackpool 2
1933 Chesterfield 22 7
1934 Lincoln City 33 14
1935 Northampton Town 4 2
1936 Gillingham 35 12
1937 Walsall 15 1
Tunbridge Wells Rangers
Nuneaton Borough

Robinson, Thomas James Douglas IL
b Liverpool 14/9/1893 d 1951
1919 Everton 0
1920 Gillingham 2 1

Robinson, W OR
1905 1906 Burton United 12

Robinson, W CF
1906 Grimsby Town (trial) 1

Robinson, Walter Lawrence RH/LB/RB
b Raunds q2 1878
Finedon
Irthlingborough Town
1898 1904 Leicester Fosse 177 3
1905 1906 Burton United 70 3
Winnipeg Celtic

Robinson, William OR
Walsall
Lincoln City
Walsall
1909 Derby County 3
Walsall

Robinson, William (Billy) LH/RH
b Birkenhead 1900
1919 Everton 7
Saltney Athletic
Chester
1923 Wrexham 1
Mold Town

Robinson, William (Billy) CH
b Darlington 24/8/1903
Croft
1921 1926 Darlington 143
1927 Southend United 4
1927 Torquay United 0
1928 Carlisle United 4 1

Robinson, William (Bill) IL
b Hyde 9/6/1905 d 1936
New Moss Colliery
Droylsden
1927 1929 Southport 58 12
Hyde United
Ashton National

Robinson, William (Bill) LB
b Birkenhead
1929 New Brighton 1
West Kirby

From To Apps Goal

Robinson, William (Bill) CF/OR
b Whitburn, County Durham 4/4/1919 d 1992
Hylton Colliery Juniors
1937 1938 Sunderland 24 14
1939 (Sunderland) (3)
1946 1948 Charlton Athletic 52 16
1948 1951 West Ham United 101 60

Robinson, William Atkin (Billy) CF/IL
b Pegswood Colliery 30/12/1898 d 1975
Pegswood Colliery
1924 1927 Hartlepools United 62 38
1928 Bradford Park Avenue 5 1
1929 Lincoln City 17 7
Gainsborough Trinity
Ashington
Crook Town

Robinson, William Samuel CH
b Prescot q3 1880 d 1926
1902 Bolton Wanderers 0
1903 Manchester City 1
1905 1908 Hull City 119 6
1908 1910 Bolton Wanderers 31
Accrington Stanley

Robotham, Horace Osborne (Harry) RH
b Heath Town q3 1879 d 1916
Wolverhampton Post Office
Redshaw Albion
Ossett
Hunslet
1901 1902 Wolverhampton Wanderers 7 1
Fulham
Brentford
1906 Glossop 23 4
New Brompton

Robson, Albert Proud (Bert) CF/IR
b Crook 14/11/1916 d 1990
Godalming
1936 1947 Crystal Palace 85 22
1939 (Crystal Palace) (3) (1)
Tunbridge Wells

Robson, Arnold RH
b Felling 30/4/1897
Felling Colliery
1929 South Shields 0
1930 1931 Carlisle United 8
1932 Wrexham 0
Wigan Athletic

Robson, Cuthbert (Cud) OR/OL
b High Wheatley 19/10/1900 d 1972
Thornley Albion
Crook Town
Cockfield
1924 Leeds United 17 4
1926 Southend United 5 1
1927 Hartlepools United 20 5
Connah's Quay & Shotton
1930 1931 Bristol City 25 2
1931 Chester 13 4

Robson, David LB
Ayr
1892 1893 Ardwick 39
1893 1894 Wolverhampton Wanderers 5
1894 1895 Manchester City 47 1
Millwall Athletic

Robson, Edward Riddell (Ted) GK
b Hexham 21/8/1890 d 1977
Caps: WLge 1
Gateshead
Watford
1920 1921 Portsmouth 75
1922 1923 Sunderland 38
1924 1925 Swansea Town 29
1926 1927 Wrexham 69
1928 Grimsby Town 0
1928 Rochdale 12

Robson, Ernest (Ernie) CH/CF
b Gateshead
1934 1935 Gateshead 7 4
1935 1937 Aldershot 72 4
1938 Rochdale 0

Robson, Frederick (Fred) RB/LB
b Sunderland 3/5/1892 d 1960
Ryhope Villa
Southend United
1920 1921 Swansea Town 76
Easington Colliery Welfare
1923 1924 Durham City 77 5
1925 Hartlepools United 12
1926 Durham City 0

Robson, George IR/IL
b New Delaval 1901
New Delaval Villa
1926 1929 Walsall 80 27
1929 Coventry City 4
Ashington

From To Apps Goal

Robson, George Arnold LB/RB
b Cambois 22/4/1897 d 1984
Cambois United
Blyth Spartans
Raith Rovers
St Mirren
1919 1925 South Shields 77
1926 Southampton 0
1927 1928 Ashington 21
Blyth Spartans

Robson, George Chippendale IR
b Newcastle 17/6/1905 d 1982
St Peter's Albion
1925 Newcastle United 0
1927 1930 West Ham United 17 2
1930 1935 Brentford 124 32
Heart of Midlothian

Robson, James OL
b Durham 1900
Low Fell
1922 Blackburn Rovers 0
1923 Lincoln City 10

Robson, James CF
1935 Gateshead 4 2

Robson, James William CH
b Cambois 16/8/1900
Seaton Delaval
1921 Derby County 3
1924 Durham City 0

Robson, John OL
1935 Gateshead 2 1

Robson, John Cecil (Jack) OL
b Birtley 24/3/1906 d 1966
Berwick Main
Durham County Amateurs
1922 Burnley (trial) 0
Birtley
1924 Hull City 1
1925 1927 Reading 108 22
1928 1931 Derby County 38 10
1932 Southend United 23 5
1932 Chester 0
1933 Rochdale 28 10
1934 1935 Oldham Athletic 37 8
Hull Brewery

Robson, John Hardy (Jock) GK
b Innerleithen 15/4/1899 d 1995
Vale of Leithen
1922 1925 Arsenal 97
1926 1927 Bournemouth & Boscombe Ath 42
Montrose

Robson, John William CF
b Cambois
Bedlington United
1924 Ashington 3 1
Silksworth Colliery
1926 1928 Ashington 21 9
Silksworth Colliery
Blyth Spartans
Pegswood United
Ashington (trial)
Blyth Spartans
Bedlington United
Pegswood United
Newbiggin West End

Robson, Joseph RH
b Scotland 1878 d 1929
Birkenhead Loco Swifts
Haydock
LNW Locos
Tranmere Rovers
1898 New Brighton Tower 1
South Liverpool
Tranmere Rovers

Robson, Joseph (Joe) CF
b Gateshead 21/3/1903 d 1969
Craghead United
Saltwell Villa
1924 1930 Grimsby Town 161 123
1930 1931 Huddersfield Town 30 20
1932 Bradford Park Avenue 15 4
Gainsborough Trinity
Nuneaton Town
Burton Town

From To Apps Goal

Robson, Joseph William (Joe) CH/LH/LB
b Ryhope 26/10/1899 d 1961
Caps: England Sch
Marsden Rescue
1920 1922 South Shields 21
1923 Southend United 5
1923 1924 Durham City 58 1
1925 Rochdale 4
1925 1927 Lincoln City 60 1
Durham City
Pegswood United
Horden Colliery Welfare
Blyth Spartans
Ashington (trial)
Bedlington United
Pegswood United
Seaton Burn Welfare
Burradon Welfare

Robson, Matthew Henry (Matt) RH/LH
b Eighton Banks q2 1889 d 1929
Washington United
Wallsend Park Villa
1909 1914 Lincoln City 121 3
Scunthorpe & Lindsey United
Boston Town

Robson, Norman CF/IR
b Ryton-on-Tyne 1908
West Stanley
1926 1929 Preston North End 41 30
1930 1932 Derby County 35 6
1932 1933 Bradford City 20 9
Wigan Athletic

Robson, Percy T IL
b Scotswood
Wallsend
1929 Wolverhampton Wanderers 0
1930 Hartlepools United 3 1
West Stanley

Robson, Robert (Bob) RB
b Gateshead 1897
Usworth Colliery
1925 Stoke City 1
1926 Southport 0

Robson, Thomas OR
1895 Darwen 6 3

Robson, Thomas (Tommy) RB
b Scotswood 1892
1914 1922 Stockport County 93

Robson, Thomas (Tommy) OL
b Gosforth
Gosforth
Bedlington United
1922 Ashington 1
1925 1927 Durham City 34 5
1928 Carlisle United 0

Robson, Thomas (Tom) LH/RH
b Morpeth 1909
Blyth Spartans
1929 Everton 27
1930 1931 Sheffield Wednesday 3
Yeovil & Petters United
1934 1937 Northampton Town 38
Kettering Town

Robson, William CF
1895 Crewe Alexandra 2 1

Robson, William LB/RB
b Usworth 1891
Hebburn Argyle
1910 1911 Hull City 8

Robson, William RB
1913 1914 Blackpool 46

Robson, William (Bill) IR
b Shildon 1900
Shildon Athletic
Cockfield
1921 1922 Leeds United 10
Mansfield Town
Frickley Colliery
Gainsborough Trinity
1926 Ashington 0

Robson, William (Bill) LB
b Southwick, County Durham 1906 d 1960
Hylton Colliery
1927 1931 Derby County 13
1933 West Ham United 3
1934 1937 Reading 134 1

From	To	Club	Apps	Goal
Robson, William Paisley (Billy)			CF	
b Newcastle 20/12/1907			d 1985	
		Walker Celtic		
1930		Huddersfield Town	0	
		Washington Colliery		
1933	1937	Stoke City	13	5
1937		Burnley	10	2
Roche, George			LH	
b Birkenhead 1889				
		Northern Nomads		
1909		Preston North End	3	
		Liverpool University		
		Stoke		
		Lancaster Town		
Roche, William			OR	
b 1879				
1901		Everton	1	
Rochford, William (Bill)			LB/RB	
b Esh Winning 27/5/1913			d 1984	
Caps: FLge 1				
		Cuckfield		
		Esh Winning Juniors		
1932	1938	Portsmouth	137	1
1939		(Portsmouth)	(3)	
1946	1949	Southampton	128	
1950		Colchester United	2	
Rock, Robert Munro (Bobby)			CF	
b Camlachie 11/2/1905			d 1984	
		Kilsyth Rangers		
		Kilsyth Emmet		
		Glasgow Ashfield		
		Kilmarnock		
		Airdrieonians		
		Alloa Athletic		
		Fall River Marksmen		
		J & P Coats (Rhode Island)		
		Philadelphia Field Club		
		Airdrieonians		
1929		Barrow	26	11
		Stenhousemuir (trial)		
		Armadale		
Roddes, AE			IR	
1903		Gainsborough Trinity	1	
Rodger, Charles Colin (Colin 'Fally')			OL/CF/IL	
b Ayr 3/3/1909			d 1982	
Caps: SLge 1				
		Craigview Athletic		
		Ayr United		
1935	1937	Manchester City	19	7
1937	1938	Northampton Town	35	4
1939		Ipswich Town	0	
Rodger, George B			CH	
b Cambuslang 18/12/1899			d 1982	
		Kilsyth Rangers		
1924	1930	Chelsea	119	2
		Inverness Clachnacuddin		
		Nimes		
		Inverness Clachnacuddin		
Rodger, James			OL	
b Scotland				
		St Mirren		
		Renton		
1907		Woolwich Arsenal	1	
Rodger, John James (Jimmy)			CH	
b Sunderland 17/11/1913			d 1993	
1936		Sunderland	0	
1937		Hartlepools United	12	
Rodger, Robert (Bob)			CH	
b Dumbarton 1917				
		Hibernian		
		Distillery		
		Rhyl Athletic		
1938		Ipswich Town	9	
1939		Hull City	0	
Rodger, Thomas (Tom)			OR/IL/OL	
b Dundee 9/6/1882				
		Dundee		
1903		Manchester United	0	
1904		Preston North End	5	1
1906		Grimsby Town	34	13
		Reading		
		Brighton & Hove Albion		
1908		Leeds City	25	4
Rodgers, Albert			CH	
1893		Rotherham Town	9	2
Rodgers, Arthur			LB	
b Mexborough 8/2/1907			d 1986	
		Frickley Colliery		
		Denaby United		
1928	1932	Hull City	67	
		Merthyr Town		
1933	1938	Doncaster Rovers	175	1

From	To	Club	Apps	Goal
Rodgers, Norman			IR/CF	
b Stockport 1891			d 1947	
		Park Albion (Heaton Norris)		
		Hooley Hill		
1911	1919	Stockport County	156	72
1919	1922	Blackburn Rovers	43	21
Rodgers, Walter Ronald			OR	
b Ecclesall 14/12/1911			d 1985	
		Norton Woodseats		
1932		Rotherham United	9	1
		Norton Woodseats		
Rodgerson, Edward (Ted)			IL	
b Sunderland q2 1891			d 1962	
		Boldon Colliery		
1913		Huddersfield Town	0	
		Castleford Town		
		Southend United		
1919		Bury	13	3
1920	1921	Brighton & Hove Albion	53	11
1922		Clapton Orient	0	
Rodgerson, Ralph			LB/RB	
b Sunderland 30/12/1892			d 1939	
		Pallion Institute		
1912		Burnley	0	
1914	1920	Huddersfield Town	26	
		Dundee (loan)		
1920	1921	Leeds United	27	
		Sunderland West End		
		Dundee		
		Spennymoor United		
		Carlisle United		
Rodgerson, Ralph			LB	
b Sunderland 25/12/1913			d 1972	
		Shotton Colliery		
1935	1938	Sunderland	5	
Rodway, Thomas William (Tommy)			LB	
b Dudley q2 1879			d 1959	
Caps: FLge 1				
		Wellingborough		
1903	1914	Preston North End	335	9
		Chorley		
		Fleetwood		
		Dick, Kerr's XI		
Roe, Archibald (Archie)			CF	
b Hull 9/12/1893			d 1947	
1914		Sheffield Wednesday	0	
1919		South Shields	2	1
1919		Birmingham	3	
1920		Gillingham	16	2
		Castleford Town		
1922		Arsenal	4	1
1923	1924	Lincoln City	27	12
1924		Rotherham County	7	3
Roe, Arthur			LH/CH/RH	
b South Normanton q1 1892			d 1960	
		South Normanton		
1920	1924	Luton Town	93	1
1924		Arsenal	1	
1925	1926	Bournemouth & Boscombe Ath	50	2
		Mansfield Town		
Roe, John Thomas			GK	
b Clowne 20/1/1907			d 1995	
		Brodsworth Main		
1929		Doncaster Rovers	2	
		Brodsworth Main		
Roe, Thomas William (Tommy)			IR/CF	
b Evenwood 8/12/1900			d 1972	
		Evenwood Town		
		Cockfield		
		Esperley Rovers		
		Willington Athletic		
1922		Durham City	17	8
		Shildon		
		Cockfield		
		Northfleet		
1925	1926	Tottenham Hotspur	7	4
1927		Nottingham Forest	9	4
1928		Luton Town	17	7
1929		Walsall	41	8
1930		Coventry City	4	
		Heanor Town		
		Nottingham City Transport		
Roebuck, Frederick (Fred)			LB	
b Silverhill 6/11/1902			d 2001	
1925		Huddersfield Town	0	
		Mansfield Town		
1927		Barrow	24	
		Peterborough & Fletton United		
		Dinnington Athletic		
		City Surveyors (Sheffield)		
Roebuck, Larrett			LB	
b Jump 3/1889			d 1914	
		Silverwood Colliery		
1913		Huddersfield Town	17	

From	To	Club	Apps	Goal
Rogers, Albert J			IL	
b Manchester				
		Southall		
1928	1929	Queen's Park Rangers	12	4
Rogers, Charles William (Bill)			LH	
b Bradford 9/10/1901			d 1977	
1924		Liverpool	0	
1925		Bradford Park Avenue	4	
Rogers, David (Dave)			RH/LH/CF	
b Stockport 3/2/1892			d 1975	
1920	1925	Swindon Town	138	12
1926	1927	Gillingham	58	
Rogers, Ehud (Tim)			OR	
b Chirk 15/10/1909			d 1996	
Caps: Wales Amat/Wales War 2				
		Weston Rhyn		
		Llanerch Celts		
		Chirk		
		Oswestry Town		
1934		Wrexham	11	2
1934	1935	Arsenal	16	5
1936	1938	Newcastle United	56	10
1939		Swansea Town	(3)	
1945	1946	Wrexham	1	
		Oswestry Town		
Rogers, Frederick (Fred)			CH/RH	
b Frodsham 17/4/1910			d 1967	
		Helsby Athletic		
1934	1938	Liverpool	70	
Rogers, John (Jack)			IR/CF	
b Helston 20/6/1895			d 1977	
		Crystal Palace		
1921	1922	Aberdare Athletic	59	10
1923	1924	Sunderland	7	2
1925		Norwich City	12	4
		Newquay		
		Helston British Legion		
Rogers, Joseph Henry (Joe)			LH/OL	
b Normanton q1 1915				
		Oswestry Town		
1935	1937	Manchester City	11	1
1938		Chester	8	1
		Shrewsbury Town		
Rogers, Joseph James (Joe)			OR	
b Coventry 5/11/1874			d 1955	
		Stoke United		
		Macclesfield		
		Southampton St Mary's		
1896	1897	Grimsby Town	53	23
1898	1900	Newcastle United	54	10
1900	1901	Preston North End	39	11
		(Germany)		
		Tivoli (Grimsby)		
Rogers, Lionel J			RB	
		Thorne Colliery		
1932		Doncaster Rovers	2	
Rogers, Thomas (Tom)			LB	
b Scotland				
		Perth Juniors		
		Newcastle East End		
1893	1894	Newcastle United	22	
Rogers, Thomas (Tom)			LB/RB	
b Prescot 1885				
		Rossendale United		
1906	1910	Liverpool	38	
Rogers, Thomas			OL	
b Willenhall				
1921		Walsall	1	
Rogers, Thomas W			OR	
b South Wales				
1933		Cardiff City	2	1
Rogers, Walter			LH	
b Stoke-on-Trent 1883				
1906		Burslem Port Vale	0	
1907		Stoke	1	
		Reading		
Rogers, William			CF	
		Abercorn		
1896		Lincoln City	1	
Rogers, William (Billie)			RH/IR/OR	
b Summerhill q4 1905			d 1936	
Caps: Wales 2				
		Summerhill		
		Oak Alyn Rovers		
		Flint Town		
1926	1931	Wrexham	170	23
1932		Newport County	22	3
1933		Bristol Rovers	0	
1933		Clapton Orient	3	
		Bangor City		

From	To	Club	Apps	Goal
Rogers, William (Billy)			RH/OR/IR	
b Ulverston 3/7/1919			d 1974	
		Swarth Moor		
1937		Preston North End	0	
1938	1947	Blackburn Rovers	73	24
1939		(Blackburn Rovers)	(3)	(2)
1947	1952	Barrow	196	14
Rollinson, Frank			IL	
b Ecclesall 21/6/1884			d 1927	
		Heeley Friends		
1906	1910	Sheffield Wednesday	41	15
1911		Leicester Fosse	17	2
		Portsmouth		
		Luton Town		
Rollinson, Thomas			GK	
b Bolton q2 1885			d 1945	
1907		Bolton Wanderers	1	
		Hyde		
		Accrington Stanley		
Rollo, David (Dave)			RB	
b Belfast 26/8/1890			d 1963	
Caps: IrLge 5/Ireland 16				
		Linfield		
1919	1926	Blackburn Rovers	207	5
1927		Port Vale	2	
Ronald, Peter Mann			IR/CF	
b Wallsend 15/11/1889			d 1953	
		Watford		
		Hebburn Argyle		
1920		Watford	29	10
1921	1922	Nottingham Forest	4	
		West Stanley		
Ronaldson, Duncan McKay			IR	
b Blythswood 21/4/1879			d 1947	
		Vale of Clyde		
		Rutherglen Glencairn		
		Queen's Park Rangers		
1901	1902	Grimsby Town	64	19
1903		Bury	15	4
		Queen's Park Rangers		
		Norwich City		
		Brighton & Hove Albion		
		Southend United		
		Norwich City		
		Dunfermline Athletic		
Ronan, Peter			LH/RH	
b Dysart 16/3/1909			d 1973	
		Rosslyn Juniors		
1931	1932	Cardiff City	30	1
		East Fife		
Rooke, Edward			CH/LH	
b Hockley 1/11/1899			d 1974	
		Brierley Hill Alliance		
1924	1927	West Bromwich Albion	41	1
		Nuneaton Town		
Rooke, John			IR	
b Keynsham q4 1878			d 1938	
1903		Blackpool	21	5
Rooke, Ronald Leslie (Ronnie)			CF	
b Guildford 7/12/1911			d 1985	
Caps: England War 1				
		Guildford City		
1931		Stoke City (trial)	0	
		Woking		
1933	1936	Crystal Palace	18	6
1936	1946	Fulham	105	70
1939		(Fulham)	(3)	(2)
1946	1948	Arsenal	88	68
1949	1950	Crystal Palace	45	26
		Bedford Town		
Rooke, William			RH	
b Keynsham q1 1877			d 1950	
1903		Stockport County	16	
		Bristol East		
		Oldham Athletic		
		Staple Hill		
		Merthyr Vale		
Rookes, Philip William (Phil)			RB/LB	
b Dulverton 23/4/1919			d 2003	
		Worksop Town		
1937		Bradford City	11	
1938	1950	Portsmouth	114	
1951	1952	Colchester United	68	
		Chichester City		
Rooks, William (Billy)			LH/LB/CH	
b Sunderland 14/12/1890			d 1972	
		Willington		
		Sunderland Rovers		
1913	1921	Blackpool	101	4
1922	1926	Accrington Stanley	132	4
		Hurst		
		Great Harwood		

From To | Apps Goal

Rooney, Joseph CH
b Wolverhampton 1920 d 1943
1938 Wolverhampton Wanderers 2

Rooney, Thomas CH
b Felling q3 1893 d 1936
Gateshead
1914 Barnsley 25
Durham City

Rooney, Walter Francis LH/RH
b Liverpool 31/3/1902 d 1963
1924 1929 Everton 14
1929 Wrexham 12
Runcorn
Northwich Victoria

Roose, (Dr) Leigh Richmond (Dick) GK
b Holt 27/11/1877 d 1916
Caps: Wales Amat/Wales 24
UCW Aberystwyth
Aberystwyth Town
Druids
London Welsh
1901 1903 Stoke 81
1904 Everton 18
1905 1907 Stoke 66
1907 1910 Sunderland 92
Celtic (loan)
Port Vale (loan)
1910 Huddersfield Town 5
1911 Aston Villa 10
1911 Fulham 0
1911 Woolwich Arsenal 13
Aberystwyth Town
Llandudno Town

Rooth, William Benjamin OR
b North Wingfield 10/11/1897 d 1962
North Wingfield St Lawrence
Hardwick Colliery
1921 Chesterfield 1
Shirebrook

Roper, Francis Leonard CF
b Wolverhampton 16/12/1892 d 1969
1919 Wolverhampton Wanderers 1

Roper, Harry IR/LH
b Romiley 13/4/1910 d 1983
New Mills
1932 1934 Leeds United 18 3
1935 1936 Cardiff City 31 2
1937 Stockport County 0

Roper, William H GK
b Birkenhead q2 1914 d 1960
Caps: England Sch
1931 Liverpool 0
1932 1934 Tranmere Rovers 3
South Liverpool

Rorrison, James Armstrong (Jim) OR/IL
b Kirkconnel 21/6/1908 d 1981
Kello Rovers
St Mirren
1930 Carlisle United 2
1931 Doncaster Rovers 1
Cork FC
Workington
Distillery
Dolphin
Bray Unknowns

Rosbotham, Arthur IL/IR
b Lower Ince 18/2/1892 d 1941
Atherton
Eccles Borough
Nelson
1919 Preston North End 0
Chorley
1920 Arsenal 0
1920 1921 Stockport County 21 2
1922 Southport 17 2
Chorley
1924 Barrow 17 7
Chorley
Rossendale United
Colwyn Bay
Winsford United

Roscamp, John (Jack) RH/CF/LH
b Blaydon 8/8/1901 d 1939
Wallsend Celtic
Wallsend
1923 1931 Blackburn Rovers 223 37
1931 1933 Bradford City 27
Shrewsbury Town

From To | Apps Goal

Roscoe, Jack Houghton CF
b Oldham 28/1/1906 d 1969
Werneth Athletic
Witton Albion
Mossley
1931 Oldham Athletic 19 8
1932 Chester 1 1
Macclesfield
Hyde United
Mossley
Hope Congregational

Roscoe, John (Jack) OR/IR
b Prescot 22/10/1909 d 1996
Prescot Cables
1928 Everton 0
1929 New Brighton 16 5
Prescot Cables
1931 Rotherham United 5 3
Prescot Cables
Lancaster Town
Prescot Cables
South Liverpool

Rose, Charles Herebert IL/CF
b Derby q2 1872 d 1949
Derby Midland
1891 1892 Derby County 5
1899 Loughborough 23 2
Ilkeston United

Rose, Frederick CH
1907 Blackpool 3

Rose, Harold Bernard (Harry) CH/RH
b Reading 5/1900 d 1941
Reading Liberal Club
Imperial
1920 Reading 5
1922 1923 Bristol Rovers 14
Mid-Rhondda United

Rose, Ivor Stewart OL
b Cardiff 25/8/1902 d 1974
1925 Aberdare Athletic 5 1
Hereford United
Manchester Central

Rose, James OR
b Leeds
1936 Bradford City 0
1937 Halifax Town 6

Rose, James (Jim) GK
b Clayton-le-Moors 4/3/1918 d 1989
Clayton Villa
1938 1946 Accrington Stanley 20

Rose, Leslie Arthur OL
b Bedminster 25/9/1890 d 1983
Clifton St Vincent's
1913 Bristol City 4
St Pancras

Rose, Leslie Eric Ronald (Les) LH/IL
b Weston-super-Mare 30/11/1914 d 1987
Trowbridge Town
1934 Everton (trial) 0
1934 Bristol Rovers 0
Bath City
1935 New Brighton (trial) 2
1938 Hartlepools United 12
Trowbridge Town

Rose, R OR
1894 1895 Burton Wanderers 26 6

Rose, Stephen Benjamin LH
b Islington 10/1/1891 d 1961
1919 Arsenal 0
1922 Clapton Orient 3

Rose, Thomas CF
b Breaston q3 1872
1893 1895 Nottingham Forest 30 9

Rose, Thomas Harry (Harry) OR
b Lowestoft q4 1870 d 1946
1892 1894 Grimsby Town 31 7
Grimsby All Saints
1895 Grimsby Town 3
Grimsby All Saints

Rose, Walter RH
b Borrowash 13/1/1870 d 1953
Draycott
Breaston
Derby Midland
1891 1892 Derby County 5
1895 Loughborough 30 1
Ilkeston Town
1899 Loughborough 31 1
Whitwick White Cross
Draycott

From To | Apps Goal

Rose, William Crispin (Billy) GK
b St Pancras 3/4/1861 d 1937
Caps: England 5
Small Heath Alliance
London Swifts
Swindon Town
Preston North End
Stoke
1888 1893 Wolverhampton Wanderers 115
Loughborough
1895 Wolverhampton Wanderers 19

Rose, William Wilkinson (Billy) IL/LH
b Sunderland 31/1/1904 d 1982
Methley Perseverance
1925 Bury 1
1926 Fulham (trial) 0
1926 Barrow 14 3
Sunderland West End
Spennymoor United
Aldershot
Annfield Plain
Horden Colliery Welfare
Millfield

Roseboom, Edward (Teddy) IR/IL
b Govan 24/11/1896 d 1980
Strathclyde
1919 Fulham (trial) 0
Ton Pentre
Pontypridd
1920 Cardiff City 0
1921 1922 Blackpool 20 2
1923 Nelson 12 1
1923 Clapton Orient 3
1924 Rochdale 30 4
1925 1928 Chesterfield 124 38
Mansfield Town
Newark Town
Mexborough

Rosenthal, Abram Wallace (Abe) IL/CF
b Liverpool 12/10/1921 d 1986
1938 Liverpool 0
1938 1946 Tranmere Rovers 27 8
1939 (Tranmere Rovers) (3) (1)
1946 1948 Bradford City 44 11
1948 Oldham Athletic (trial) 0
1949 1951 Tranmere Rovers 69 24
1952 1953 Bradford City 63 32
1954 Tranmere Rovers 21 3
1955 Bradford City 1

Rosevear, Charles CF
b Stafford q1 1879 d 1961
Leicester Imperial
1901 Leicester Fosse 3
Leicester Imperial
Leicester Olympic

Rosie, J CH
1893 Crewe Alexandra 4

Rosier, Herbert Leonard (Bert) LB/RB
b Hanwell 21/3/1893 d 1939
Hanwell North End
Uxbridge Town
Southall
1920 1922 Brentford 92
1922 1926 Clapton Orient 136 1
1927 Southend United 41
1928 1929 Fulham 52
Folkestone

Ross, Albert Cyril RB/LB
b York 7/10/1916 d 1998
Caps: England Sch
1933 Arsenal 0
Gainsborough Trinity
1935 1936 Middlesbrough 11
1936 1937 Bradford Park Avenue 20
1938 Chester 1

Ross, Alexander (Alec) CF
b Aberdeen
Aberdeen Richmond
Dundee
Arbroath (loan)
1926 Rochdale 1 1

Ross, Andrew OL
b Hurlford 17/2/1878
Hurlford Thistle
Kilmarnock (trial)
Celtic
Galston
Barrow
1904 Burnley 24 2

From To | Apps Goal

Ross, David IL/IR
b Over Darwen 8/1/1884 d 1947
Heywood United
1903 Bury 4 1
Luton Town
Norwich City
1906 1911 Manchester City 61 19
Dundee
Rochdale

Ross, George Adams OR/IR
b Bonnyrigg 21/2/1908 d 1980
Dalkeith Thistle
Arbroath (trial)
Dundee United
1929 1930 Portsmouth 5 2
Bray Unknowns
Dundee United
Leith Athletic

Ross, George William LH
b Melbairn 29/11/1869 d 1928
Bury Unitarians
1894 1905 Bury 366 10
Rochdale

Ross, Henry (Harry) RB
b Brechin 4/4/1881 d 1953
Lochee Harp
Brechin Harp
1899 1903 Burnley 106 2
1907 1908 Fulham 29 3
St Mirren
Southport Central
Darwen
Brechin City

Ross, James CH
1892 Northwich Victoria 1

Ross, James David (Jimmy) IR/CF
b Edinburgh 28/3/1866 d 1902
St Bernard's
1888 1893 Preston North End 130 85
1894 1896 Liverpool 73 37
1896 1898 Burnley 51 29
1898 1901 Manchester City 67 21

Ross, James Donaldson (Jimmy) RB
b Bonnyrigg 7/3/1895
Raith Rovers
1922 1923 Tottenham Hotspur 7

Ross, John OR
1937 Gateshead 3
Gillingham

Ross, Nicholas John (Nick) LB/CF
b Edinburgh 2/1/1863 d 1894
Caps: FLge 1
Heart of Midlothian
Preston North End
1888 Everton 19 4
Linfield
1889 1893 Preston North End 95 25

Ross, Robert (Bob) CH
b Stenhousemuir 27/12/1898
Camelon Juniors
Falkirk
Stenhousemuir
1923 Plymouth Argyle 2
1924 Coventry City 20
Workington
1928 Carlisle United 22 2
1929 Wrexham 29 1
Scunthorpe & Lindsey United
Boston Town
Hyde United

Ross, Thomas (Tommy) CF
b Croft
1922 Darlington 2

Ross, William OL/CF/IL
b Kiveton Park q1 1874
Chesterfield Town
1895 1896 Sheffield United 19 3
1897 Gainsborough Trinity (loan) 0
1897 Lincoln City 22 3
Gravesend United
Reading
1900 1903 Notts County 110 28
1904 Grimsby Town 32 7
1905 1907 Glossop 51 21

Rossiter, Ambrose (Bud) RB/CF
b Ashford, Kent 24/11/1907 d 1993
Margate
Folkestone
1933 1934 Crystal Palace 23
1935 Gillingham 19
1936 Clapton Orient 7 2

From To | Apps Goal

Rosson, Sydney (Syd) RH
b Sandbach 17/4/1908 d 1980
Sandbach Ramblers
1933 Crewe Alexandra 11

Rostance, James Colin (Jack) GK
b Penkridge q2 1891 d 1955
1919 Wolverhampton Wanderers 9
Hednesford Town

Rotherforth, Edmund GK
b Fryston q4 1906 d 1968
Pontefract
1929 Halifax Town 1

Rotherham, Albert Edward RH/RB/LB
b Wednesbury 11/1903 d 1966
Lloyds AFC
Wednesbury Town
Darlaston
1925 1928 Bristol Rovers 46
1929 Coventry City 0
Bath City
1931 Gillingham 4

Rothery, Harry OL
b Royston, West Yorkshire q2 1881 d 1965
Wath Athletic
Mexborough West End
Mexborough Town
1905 Sheffield United 4
1905 1906 Nottingham Forest 5
Rawmarsh Albion

Rothwell, Alfred (Alf) OR
Accrington Stanley
1914 Leeds City 1
Accrington Stanley

Rothwell, Charles OR/IR
b Newton Heath q4 1874
1893 1896 Newton Heath 2 1

Rothwell, Edward (Teddy) OR/OL/IR
b Atherton 3/9/1917 d 2000
1937 1948 Bolton Wanderers 48 2
1939 (Bolton Wanderers) (3) (1)
1949 1950 Southport 40 5

Rothwell, Herbert RB
Newton Heath Athletic
1897 Newton Heath 0
1898 1901 Glossop North End 69 3
1902 Manchester United 22
1903 Manchester City 0
Newton Heath Athletic
Failsworth
1907 Lincoln City 0
Chorlton

Rothwell, John (Jack) CF/OR
b Kearsley 29/3/1920 d 1991
Whitworths
Walkden Primitive Methodists
St Thomas Sunday School
1938 1946 Southport 18 9
1947 Birmingham City 0
1949 Southport 0
1949 Crewe Alexandra 3 1
Wellington Town

Rothwell, Peter Joseph IL/IR
b Birkenhead q2 1898
Chester
1923 1924 Tranmere Rovers 8
Northwich Victoria

Rotton, William Harry (Billy) CF/IL
b Wednesbury 29/3/1906 d 1991
1927 Wolverhampton Wanderers 4 1
Shrewsbury Town
1929 West Bromwich Albion 0
Brierley Hill Alliance
1931 Walsall 7 3

Roughley, Edward (Ed) GK
b Prescot q4 1880 d 1948
Skelmersdale United
St Helens Recreation
1906 1911 Hull City 157
Chesterfield Town
Rugby Town

Roughton, William George (George) LB
b Manchester 11/5/1909 d 1989
Caps: FLge 1
Droylsden
1928 1935 Huddersfield Town 164
1936 1938 Manchester United 86
1945 Exeter City 0

From To | Apps Goal

Roulson, Joseph (Joe) RH/LH
b Sheffield 7/10/1891 d 1952
Cammell Laird
1912 1921 Birmingham 116 4
1922 1923 Swansea Town 49 2
1924 Clapton Orient 16

Roulstone, Arthur LH/OR/OL
b Castle Donington q1 1878 d 1945
Castle Donington
1895 1899 Loughborough 123 11
Kettering
1901 1902 Leicester Fosse 68 1
Whitwick White Cross
Ilkeston United
Long Eaton Rangers
Castle Donington Town
Long Eaton St Helens

Roulstone, Francis (Frank) LB
b Radcliffe-on-Trent q4 1862 d 1939
Sawley Rangers
1888 Derby County 1

Roulstone, Walter LH
b Castle Donington 1866 d 1953
Sawley Rangers
1888 1894 Derby County 118 4
Heanor Town
Castle Donington Town
Heanor Town
Castle Donington Town

Rounce, George Alfred IL
b Orsett q4 1905 d 1936
Grays Athletic
Tilbury
Uxbridge Town
1927 1932 Queen's Park Rangers 171 59
1932 1933 Fulham 12 1
1935 Bristol Rovers 0

Round, Elijah GK
b Stoke-on-Trent q1 1882 d 1943
Mexborough West End
1904 1907 Barnsley 45
1907 1908 Oldham Athletic 10
1909 Manchester United 2
Worksop Town
Mexborough Town
Castleford Town

Round, Freeman GK
b West Bromwich q4 1900 d 1966
Rogerstone
1923 Newport County 1
Ebbw Vale

Round, H OR
1913 Glossop 2

Round, Howard CF
b Newcastle-under-Lyme q4 1878 d 1957
Tunstall Casuals
1900 Burslem Port Vale 1

Round, John Henry (Jack) CH
b Brierley Hill 20/5/1901 d 1936
Brierley Hill Alliance
Cradley Heath
1925 1929 Bolton Wanderers 56 1
1930 1934 Port Vale 128 5
1935 1936 Carlisle United 37

Round, Kenneth Arthur LH
b Dudley 13/10/1917 d 1988
Dudley Town
1938 Lincoln City 3

Rounsfull, Reginald Edward IL
b St Austell 25/3/1906 d 1974
Plymouth United
1929 Millwall 2 1

Rourke, James CH
1911 Stockport County 12

Rouse, Frederick William (Fred) IR/CF
b Cranford 28/11/1881 d 1953
Caps: FLge 2
Southall
Wycombe Wanderers
Brentford
Shepherds Bush
1902 1903 Grimsby Town 37 15
1903 1906 Stoke 69 26
1906 1907 Everton 9 2
1907 1908 Chelsea 38 11
1909 West Bromwich Albion 5 2
Croydon Common
Brentford

From To | Apps Goal

Rouse, Valentine Alfred (Val) LH
b Hoddesdon 14/2/1898 d 1961
Llanelly
Pontypridd
1921 Wolverhampton Wanderers 5
1922 1924 Stoke 92 2
1925 Swansea Town 4
1926 1928 Port Vale 95
1929 1930 Crewe Alexandra 83 1
Connah's Quay & Shotton

Routledge, William H (Bill) CH/RH
b Haltwhistle 28/10/1907 d 1972
Stakeford United
1927 South Shields 0
1928 Crystal Palace 0
Bangor City
Colwyn Bay
1930 Chelsea 0
1931 1933 Bristol Rovers 64 5
1934 1935 York City 78 1
1936 Carlisle United 16

Rowan, Alexander (Sandy) CF
b Hamilton 1868
Albion Rovers
Nottingham Forest
Albion Rovers
1892 1893 Sheffield Wednesday 29 12
1893 Burton Swifts 16 9
1894 1895 Manchester City 45 23

Rowan, Frederick Septimus (Fred) OR/IR
b Sunderland q4 1883 d 1951
Sunderland Royal Rovers
1908 1909 Nottingham Forest 2
Wingate Albion
Sunderland Rovers

Rowbotham, Henry (Harry) IR
b Willington Quay 22/4/1911 d 1979
Cheddleton Mental Hospital
1930 1931 Port Vale 7 2
Hyde United
1932 Southampton 0
1933 Accrington Stanley 4
Jarrow
North Shields
1934 1935 Barrow 59 14
1936 Rochdale 19 1
Tunbridge Wells Rangers
Walker Celtic

Rowbotham, Samuel (Sam) LH/IL
b Rotherham
1931 1932 Rotherham United 3 1
Scarborough
1934 1935 Darlington 17 1
Peterborough United

Rowden, Horace Leonard CH/RH
b Gillingham 4/3/1900 d 1938
Chatham Central
1921 1923 Gillingham 9

Rowe, Alfred James (Alf) LH/OL
b Poplar q1 1896 d 1965
Barking Town
1921 1924 Plymouth Argyle 41
1925 Queen's Park Rangers 4 1

Rowe, Arthur Sydney CH
b Tottenham 1/9/1906 d 1993
Caps: England 1
1923 Tottenham Hotspur 0
Cheshunt
Northfleet
1931 1937 Tottenham Hotspur 182

Rowe, Douglas Heath (Doug) OL
b Nottingham 9/7/1909 d 1978
Sneinton
1931 1932 Luton Town 23 8
1933 Lincoln City 11 5
1934 Southampton 2 1
Union Sportif Tourcoing

Rowe, George William OL/LB
b Saltburn 22/5/1899 d 1966
Loftus Albion
1921 1922 Hartlepools United 28 1
1925 Derby County 1
1927 Norwich City 3
1928 Chesterfield 0
Coleraine
Loughborough Corinthians
Chester
Trent Motors

Rowe, Jocelyn A RB
b Kingston 1886
Caps: IrLge 1
Bohemians
1913 Manchester United 1
Bohemians
Kingstonian

From To | Apps Goal

Rowe, Jonathan (Jonty) LB/RB
b Packmoor q4 1907 d 1953
Manchester Central
1932 1934 Reading 77
1935 1936 Queen's Park Rangers 52
1937 1938 Port Vale 72
1939 (Port Vale) (2)

Rowe, Leslie OR
b Hednesford 1915
Hednesford Town
1934 Chesterfield 8 3

Rowe, Robert Kerr CF
b Herrington q1 1911
Herrington Colliery
1932 Rochdale 1
Jarrow

Rowe, Ronald George (Ronnie) RH
b Fulham 11/10/1902
Wimbledon
1924 Brentford 8
Wimbledon
Hampstead Town
Hayes
Hampstead Town
Uxbridge

Rowe, Thomas (Tommy) CH
b Poole 13/8/1913 d 2006
Parkstone Institute
Poole Town
1934 1938 Portsmouth 81
1939 (Portsmouth) (3)
Ayr United

Rowe, Vivian Frederick IL
Lambeth 18/2/1901
Wimbledon
1924 Brentford 4 1
Wimbledon

Rowell, Joseph Peter (Joe) OR
b Norwich 19/10/1901 d 1985
CEYMS (Norwich)
1922 Norwich City 1
1923 Millwall Athletic 0
Gorleston
CEYMS (Norwich)
Sexton, Son & Everards

Rowell, Thomas (Tom) RB
b Birtley 1875
Hedley Harriers
Dipton Wanderers
Birtley
1897 Leicester Fosse 5
Annfield Plain Celtic

Rowlands, Alfred Stanley (Stan) CF
b Coedway 12/11/1889 d 1974
Caps: Wales 1
Snailbeach White Stars
Abbey Juniors
Welshpool
Wellington Town
Birkenhead North End
Wrexham
South Liverpool
1910 Nottingham Forest 1
South Liverpool
1911 Liverpool 0
Wrexham
Tranmere Rovers
Reading
1921 Crewe Alexandra 23 8
1922 Wrexham 9
Oswestry Town
South Molton

Rowlands, Herbert L CF
b Brecon
Brecon
1921 Aberdare Athletic 3 2

Rowlandson, Thomas Sowerby (Tom) GK
b Darlington q2 1880 d 1916
Caps: England Amat
Cambridge University
Corinthians
1902 Preston North End 0
1903 1904 Sunderland 12
Corinthians
1905 Newcastle United 1
Corinthians
Old Carthusians
Corinthians
Darlington

Rowles, Alfred John (Alf) CF
b Bristol 6/5/1916
St Francis (Bristol)
Weston-super-Mare
1937 1938 Bristol City 24 20

From To Apps Goal

Rowles, Reginald RB
1930 Cardiff City 0
1931 Tranmere Rovers 2

Rowley, Arthur LB/RH/LH
b Leek 1870
Leek
Distillery
North Staffordshire Regiment
1896 1898 Stoke 57
Bristol Rovers
1902 1903 Burslem Port Vale 57 4

Rowley, Enoch OL
Biddulph
1904 Burslem Port Vale 1
Biddulph Mission
Leek United

Rowley, Henry Bowater (Harry) IL/IR
b Bilston 23/1/1904 d 1985
Bilston United
1926 Southend United (trial) 0
Walsall Wood
Burton Town
Shrewsbury Town
1928 1931 Manchester United 95 24
1931 1932 Manchester City 18 4
1932 1934 Oldham Athletic 70 13
1934 1936 Manchester United 78 31
Burton Town
Gillingham

Rowley, J IR
1894 Burton Swifts 1

Rowley, John Frederick (Jack) OL/CF/IL
b Wolverhampton 7/10/1918 d 1998
Caps: FLge 3/England B/England War 1/England 6
Dudley Old Boys
1935 Wolverhampton Wanderers 0
Cradley Heath (loan)
1936 1937 Bournemouth & Boscombe Ath 23 12
1937 1954 Manchester United 380 182
1954 1956 Plymouth Argyle 56 14

Rowley, Joseph (Joe) LH/RH
b Wellington 13/10/1899 d 1982
Oakengates Town
1922 1925 Coventry City 148 2
1926 1927 Bristol Rovers 61 1
Oswestry Town

Rowley, Richard William Morris (Dick) IR/IL/CF
b Enniskillen 13/1/1904 d 1984
Caps: Ireland 6
Tidworth United
Andover
1925 Swindon Town 2 2
London Casuals
1926 1929 Southampton 104 52
1929 1931 Tottenham Hotspur 24 10
1931 1933 Preston North End 51 14

Rowley, Walter James CH/RH/LH
b Little Hulton 14/4/1891 d 1976
Farnworth Wednesday
Walkden Wednesday
Little Hulton Wednesday
1910 Oldham Athletic 0
1912 1924 Bolton Wanderers 175 7

Rowley, William Leslie (Bill) RB/LB
b Chester 10/11/1912 d 1986
Ellesmere Port
1934 1935 Chester 2

Rowley, William Spencer (Billy) GK
b Hanley 3/1865 d 1939
Caps: FLge 1/England 2
Hanley Orion
Stoke
Burslem Port Vale
1888 1896 Stoke 118
1898 Leicester Fosse 1

Rowson, Arthur Edward OL
b Shrewsbury q3 1892 d 1941
Shrewsbury Town
Bargoed (trial)
1921 Barrow 4 1
Ebbw Vale
Shrewsbury Town

Rowston, Charles Ernest OR
b Grimsby q2 1887 d 1946
Cleethorpes Town
1909 Grimsby Town 15 1
Cleethorpes Town
Grimsby Rovers
Gainsborough Trinity
Cleethorpes Town
Grimsby Rovers
Cleethorpes Town

From To Apps Goal

Roxburgh, Alexander White (Alex) GK
b Manchester 19/9/1910 d 1985
Caps: England War 1
Nuneaton Town
1928 Manchester City 0
1932 1938 Blackpool 62
1946 1947 Barrow 69
Hyde United

Roxburgh, Andrew (Andy) IL
b Leith 4/4/1900 d 1981
Rugby Town
1920 1921 Leicester City 19 2
Rugby Town
Leicester Nomads
Rugby Town

Roxburgh, John (Jack) OR/IR/IL
b Granton 10/11/1901 d 1977
Caps: Scotland Amat
Rugby Town
1920 1922 Leicester City 48 2
1922 Aston Villa 12 3
1923 Stoke 14 1
1925 1926 Sheffield United 5 2
Sheffield
Leicester Nomads

Roxburgh, Robert RB/LB
b Morpeth 5/2/1896 d 1974
Morpeth Comrades
1920 1923 Newcastle United 24
1924 1929 Blackburn Rovers 114

Roy, James CF
1893 Preston North End 1

Roy, James CH
b Carlisle 23/3/1902
1926 Hull City 0
St Ninian's Thistle
1928 Carlisle United 10 1
Rhyl Athletic

Roy, John Robin (Jack) OL/OR
b Woolston 23/3/1914 d 1980
Sholing Athletic
1934 1935 Norwich City 6
1936 Mansfield Town 25 2
1936 1937 Sheffield Wednesday 15 1
1937 1938 Notts County 15
1938 Tranmere Rovers 20 2
Yeovil & Petters United
1946 Ipswich Town 15 2
Gravesend & Northfleet
Yeovil Town

Royals, Ezra John GK
b Fenton q1 1882
Chesterton White Star
1911 1913 Manchester United 7
Northwich Victoria

Royan, William Osgood Hamlett CF
b Friockheim 9/12/1914
Greenhead Thistle
Glasgow Perthshire
Heart of Midlothian
Chirnside United (loan)
1936 Queen's Park Rangers 0
Queen of the South
1938 Rochdale 5 1
Glasgow Perthshire

Royle, Stanley OR
b Stockport q2 1897
Heaton Chapel
1921 Manchester City 1

Royston, Robert (Bob 'Roy') RB
b Gallowgate 1/12/1915 d 1996
Seaham Colliery
1935 Sunderland 0
1937 1938 Southport 70 2
1938 1946 Plymouth Argyle 39
1939 (Plymouth Argyle) (2)
Hambledon

Roystone, Albert IL
b Rawmarsh 2/2/1892 d 1960
Redfearns
1911 1913 Barnsley 1
Doncaster Rovers

Rudd, Archibald Charles RB
b Nottingham q4 1887 d 1957
Nottingham Olympic
1907 Grimsby Town 1

Ruddlesdin, Arthur IR/CF/IL
b Hoyland 7/2/1899 d 1972
Tankersley United
1920 1922 Barnsley 4 1
1923 1925 Swindon Town 30 12
Poole Town

From To Apps Goal

Ruddlesdin, Frank LH
b Hoyland q1 1895 d 1962
Tankersley United
1913 Barnsley 1

Ruddlesdin, Herod LH/RH
b Birdwell q3 1876 d 1910
Caps: England 3
Birdwell
1898 1907 Sheffield Wednesday 259 7
Northampton Town

Ruddlesdin, William RH
b Birdwell q1 1884 d 1937
Birdwell
1906 Barnsley 14
Birdwell

Ruddock, William Edwin (Bill) CF
b Ryhope Colliery 16/7/1898 d 1986
1920 Sheffield Wednesday 0
1921 Southend United 8 4

Ruddy, Thomas (Tom) CF/IL
b Stockton 1/3/1902 d 1979
Stockton Shamrocks
1924 1927 Darlington 66 37
1928 1931 Derby County 22 9
1931 Chesterfield 18 6
1932 1933 Southampton 24 3
Spennymoor United
Linfield

Rudkin, George William IL
b Horncastle 1/3/1912
Grantham
1937 Mansfield Town 1
1938 Carlisle United 16 1
Boston United
1945 Chesterfield 0

Rudkin, Thomas William (Tommy) OL/OR
b Peterborough 16/6/1919 d 1969
Creswell
1937 Wolverhampton Wanderers 0
1938 Lincoln City 2 1
Peterborough United
1946 Arsenal 5 2
1947 1948 Southampton 9
1949 1950 Bristol City 34 4
Weston-super-Mare
Hastings United
Peterborough United

Ruecroft, Jacob (Jake) LB/LH/CH
b Lanchester 1/5/1915 d 2005
Goole Town
1938 1946 Halifax Town 60 2
1939 (Halifax Town) (3)
Scarborough
1947 1948 Bradford City 43
Goole Town

Ruffell, James William (Jimmy) OL
b Barnsley 11/8/1900 d 1989
Caps: FLge 3/England 6
Chadwell Heath United
Manor Park Albion
East Ham
Walls End United
1921 1936 West Ham United 505 159
1938 Aldershot 2 1

Ruffell, William George (Bill) IL
b Poplar 29/4/1905 d 1988
1925 West Ham United 0
1927 Nelson 12 3
1928 Crewe Alexandra (trial) 0
1928 Stockport County (trial) 0
Epsom Town

Rumbold, George Arthur LB/RB
b Alton 10/7/1911 d 1995
Faringdon
1935 Crystal Palace 5
1937 1945 Clapton Orient 52
1939 (Clapton Orient) (3)
1946 1949 Ipswich Town 121 11
King's Lynn
Whitton United

Rumney, John CF
b Dipton 1/5/1898 d 1969
Annfield Plain
Leadgate Park
Preston Colliery
1922 1923 Hull City 13 4
1924 Chesterfield 11 4
1925 Merthyr Town 38 24
1926 Bristol Rovers 8 2
Consett

From To Apps Goal

Rumney, William (Bill) CH
b West Hartlepool 13/8/1893 d 1936
St George's (Hartlepool)
Hartlepools United
St Oswald's (Hartlepool)
Horden Athletic
Hartlepools United
Dick, Kerr's XI
1922 Barrow 6
Dick, Kerr's XI
Ashton National
Dick, Kerr's XI

Rushby, William RH/LH
b Cleethorpes 18/11/1888 d 1981
Cleethorpes Town
1912 1913 Grimsby Town 5
Castleford Town
Grimsby Rovers
Cleethorpes Town
Haycroft Rovers

Rushforth, Stanley CF
b Rotherham 15/7/1912 d 1988
1935 Rotherham United 4
Cheltenham Town

Rushton, Frank RB
Hamilton Central
1913 Blackpool 1
Barry Dock
Chorley
Darwen
Clitheroe

Rushton, George CF/OR
b Chatterley 10/1881 d 1964
Leek Broughs
1901 1902 Burslem Port Vale 20 5
Barrow
1902 Burslem Port Vale 2 2
Brighton & Hove Albion
1905 1906 Hull City 29 14
Swindon Town
Brentford
Swindon Town
Goole Town

Rushton, Richard LH/RH/CH
b Willenhall 18/9/1902 d 1981
Bloxwich Strollers
Willenhall Swifts
1924 1925 Lincoln City 44 1
1925 Sheffield Wednesday 0
1926 Barnsley 6
Wombwell Town
Connah's Quay & Shotton
1929 Bury 5
1930 Swindon Town 7
Wellington Town

Rushton, Walter IR
Blackburn Rovers
1888 1889 Bolton Wanderers 2
Ardwick

Russell, Andrew (Andy) RH
b Airdrie 3/9/1904
Harthill Athletic
Airdrieonians
Ayr United (loan)
1927 Leicester City 1
Falkirk
Morton
Queen of the South
Coleraine

Russell, Cecil John (Jack) OL/IL
b Northfield 19/6/1904 d 1995
Northfield
Bournville
Bromsgrove Rovers
1923 1926 Birmingham 27 1
1927 Bristol Rovers 22 6
Worcester City
1930 1933 Bournemouth & Boscombe Ath 138 43
1934 Luton Town 8 1
1934 1935 Norwich City 56 23
Worcester City
Shirley Town
Solihull Town

Russell, Colin H CF
b Potterspury
1931 Northampton Town 7 8
Wolverton

From To Apps Goal

Russell, David (Dave) CH/CF
b Airdrie 6/4/1868
Caps: SLge 1/Scotland 6
East Benhar Heatherbell
Shotts Minors
Stewarton
Broxburn
Heart of Midlothian
1892 Preston North End 18 14
Heart of Midlothian
Celtic
1898 Preston North End 26 3
Celtic
Broxburn

Russell, David Kennedy (Dave) CH
b Beith 1862 d 1918
Stewaton Cunningham
1888 1889 Preston North End 39 4
Nottingham Forest
1892 Ardwick 17 3
1895 Notts County 9

Russell, David Page (Dave) GK
b Crossgates 13/11/1895 d 1972
Hearts o' Beath
Kilsyth Rangers
1923 1924 Doncaster Rovers 27
1924 Leeds United 9
1926 Watford 7
1927 Lincoln City 0

Russell, David Wallace (Dave) RH
b Methil 7/4/1914 d 2000
Dundee Violet
Dundee
East Fife
1938 Sheffield Wednesday 42
1939 (Sheffield Wednesday) (1)

Russell, George LH
b Ayrshire 8/1869 d 1930
Ayr
1893 1894 Aston Villa 32 1
Glasgow United

Russell, George Henry LB/RB
b Atherstone 1/8/1902 d 1963
Atherstone Town
1925 Portsmouth 0
1926 Watford 12 1
1927 1930 Northampton Town 53
1930 1931 Bristol Rovers 55 1
Atherstone Town
1932 1933 Cardiff City 56 1
1933 Sheffield United (trial) 0
1934 Newport County 16
Stafford Rangers
Bangor City
Cradley Heath
Stafford Rangers

Russell, George Thomas OR
b Chatham 7/7/1893
1920 Gillingham 3

Russell, Harold George (Harry) CF
b Burton-on-Trent 25/6/1898
Burton All Saints
1923 Barnsley 2
Burton All Saints
1924 Southend United 3 1
1925 Burnley 0

Russell, Henry James (Harry) CH/RH
b Chalk q1 1890 d 1946
Army
1912 1924 Fulham 137 7
Sheppey United
Bevan's Works (Northfleet)

Russell, James LH
b Scotland
Cambuslang
1893 Grimsby Town 25 4
St Bernard's

Russell, James RH
1925 Aberdare Athletic 16 1

Russell, James Walker (Jim) IR/IL
b Edinburgh 14/9/1916 d 1994
Caps: Scotland Sch
Craigmer Juveniles
Murrayfield Amateurs
Queen's Park (trial)
Heart of Midlothian (trial)
1935 1937 Sunderland 5
1938 1946 Norwich City 12 2
1946 1947 Crystal Palace 43 6
1948 New Brighton 24 1
Fleetwood

Russell, JH CF
1892 Walsall Town Swifts 2

From To Apps Goal

Russell, John (Jock) OL
b Carstairs 29/12/1872 d 1905
Wishaw Thistle
Leith Athletic
St Mirren
1896 Woolwich Arsenal 23 4
Bristol City
1901 Blackburn Rovers 1
Brighton & Hove Albion (loan)
Port Glasgow Athletic
Motherwell
1904 Doncaster Rovers 3

Russell, John IR
1898 Derby County 2

Russell, John CH
1902 Everton 3
West Ham United
Clyde

Russell, Leslie LB
b Atherton q3 1909 d 1967
Atherton
1930 Wigan Borough 19
Ashton National
Chorley

Russell, Moses Richard LB/RB
b New Tredegar 20/5/1888 d 1946
Caps: Wales 23
Ton Pentre
Merthyr Town
Southport Central
Merthyr Town
1920 1929 Plymouth Argyle 314 5
1930 Thames 13
Llanelly

Russell, Robert CH
b Paisley
Bo'ness
Glasgow Perthshire
Heart of Midlothian
1911 Stockport County 27

Russell, Samuel R (Sam) RB
b Downpatrick 2/1/1900
Caps: LoI 2/Ireland 3
Distillery
Old Park Corinthians
1920 1924 Newcastle United 28
Shelbourne
1926 1929 Bradford City 134 1
Derry City

Russell, Sidney Ernest James (Sid) LB/RB
b Feltham 16/11/1911 d 1994
Tunbridge Wells Rangers
1932 1935 Queen's Park Rangers 42
1935 1938 Northampton Town 109

Russell, Thomas (Tom) LB
b Cowdenbeath 23/11/1909
Cowdenbeath Wednesday
Cowdenbeath
Rangers
1934 Newcastle United 7
Horden Colliery Welfare

Russell, William RB/LH
1890 1891 Bolton Wanderers 6

Russell, William LB
1894 Darwen 1

Russell, William (Willie) RH
b Hamilton 1903
Larkhall Juniors
Blantyre Celtic
1927 1934 Chelsea 150 6
Heart of Midlothian
Rhyl Athletic

Russell, William Edward OR
b Croydon q4 1892
West Norwood
1913 Leicester Fosse 5
West Norwood

Russell, William Fraser (Willie) IR/RH
b Falkirk 6/12/1901 d 1944
Caps: SLge 2/Scotland 2
Petershill
Glasgow Benburb
Airdrieonians
1925 1930 Preston North End 133 35
Shelbourne

Rutherford, George OL
b Hebburn
Usworth Colliery
1929 Newport County 2

From To Apps Goal

Rutherford, James (Jim) LB
b Bedlington 1894 d 1924
Ashington
1920 Brighton & Hove Albion 26
(USA)

Rutherford, James B CF/IL
d 1902
St Mirren
1898 Derby County 1 1
1898 Darwen 5 1

Rutherford, John (Jock) OR
b Percy Main 12/10/1884 d 1963
Caps: FLge 1/England 11
Percy Main
Willington Athletic
1901 1912 Newcastle United 290 78
1913 1922 Woolwich Arsenal 177 21
1922 Stoke 0
1923 1925 Arsenal 45 4
1926 Clapton Orient 9
Tunbridge Wells Rangers

Rutherford, John (Jack) CH
b Bedlington 1892 d 1930
Ashington
Bedlington
1914 Tottenham Hotspur 0
Blyth Spartans
Luton Town
1920 Brighton & Hove Albion 29 2
1921 Cardiff City 0
(USA)
1922 Bristol Rovers 29 1
Mold Town
York City
1924 1926 Gillingham 84 2

Rutherford, John (Jack) GK
b Nenthead 6/11/1908
Crawcrook Albion
1928 1930 Gillingham 44
1931 1932 Watford 31
1933 West Ham United 33
1935 Swindon Town 30
Dartford
1937 Hartlepools United 4
1938 Barrow 34
1939 (Barrow) (3)

Rutherford, John Burnet CF
b Edinburgh 9/11/1899 d 1975
Winchburgh Violet
Hibernian
Falkirk
Workington
Aberaman Athletic
Bridgend Town
1924 Swindon Town 5

Rutherford, John James OR
b South Shields 4/3/1907
Ilford
1925 Arsenal 1
1927 West Ham United 0
Tunbridge Wells Rangers

Rutherford, Joseph Henry Hamilton (Joe) GK
b Fatfield 20/9/1914 d 1994
Fatfield Juniors
Blyth Spartans (trial)
Chester Moor Temperance
Ferryhill Athletic
Chester-le-Street
Birtley Colliery
1936 1938 Southport 88
1938 1951 Aston Villa 148
1939 (Aston Villa) (2)

Rutherford, Robert Edward CH
b Gateshead q2 1878
1905 Newcastle United 1

Rutherford, Septimus Eric (Sep) OL
b Percy Main 29/11/1907 d 1975
Caps: England Sch
Blyth Spartans
1927 1935 Portsmouth 121 33
1936 Blackburn Rovers 13 1

Rutter, Arthur CF
b South Shields q1 1888
South Shields Parkside
1909 Bradford City 3
South Shields
1910 Barnsley 16 5
Exeter City
Plymouth Argyle

Rutter, Edward Lewis (Lewis) LH
b West Kirby 2/7/1898 d 1984
West Kirby
1924 Tranmere Rovers 14
Pontypridd

From To Apps Goal

Rutter, Hubert RB
b Walsall 1869
Bradley Swifts
1890 Wolverhampton Wanderers 2
Ashwood Villa
Tutbury Town
Dresden Celtic

Ryalls, Joseph (Joe) OR
b Sheffield q1 1881 d 1952
Montrose Works (Sheffield)
1902 1903 Sheffield Wednesday 2
1905 Barnsley 17
Fulham
Rotherham Town
Brentford
1909 Nottingham Forest 9
Brentford
Chesterfield Town

Ryan, John OR
1893 Northwich Victoria 4

Ryan, Thomas (Tommy) LH/RH
b Holytown 31/1/1914 d 2001
Celtic
1936 1938 Plymouth Argyle 7
1939 Swindon Town (2)
1945 Torquay United 0

Ryan, William GK
1892 Burnley 1
Padiham

Ryder, Frank OR/OL/IR
b Summerseat 7/3/1909 d 1978
Prescot Cables
Sunny Brow Olympic
1931 1932 Bury 6 3
1933 Torquay United 21 9
1934 Rochdale 6
Ards
Altrincham
1935 1936 Port Vale 23 4
Altrincham

Ryder, George Frederick IL
b Newcastle q4 1882
Caps: IrLge 3
Queen's Park Rangers
1906 1907 Bolton Wanderers 4
Leyton
Distillery
Leyton
Blyth Spartans
Croydon Common
Linfield
Blyth Spartans

Ryder, Isaac J IL
b Newcastle 1872
1893 Newcastle United 1

Ryder, Isaac Terence (Terry) CF
b Norwich 4/9/1904 d 1977
Hoigham YMCA
City Wanderers
1924 1925 Norwich City 3
Gorleston
CEYMS (Norwich)
Boulton & Paul

Ryder, Joseph (Joe) GK
b Tyneside
Newcastle Albion
Newcastle West End
Newcastle East End
1893 1894 Newcastle United 2
Hebburn Argyle
South Shields

Ryley, Herbert Sidney A OL
b Bolton q1 1893 d 1952
Barrow
1920 Hull City (trial) 1

Ryott, William R IR/CF
b Newcastle q1 1911 d 1932
Newcastle United Swifts
1930 1931 Carlisle United 4 1
1932 Liverpool 0

Sabin, Alfred James RH
b Oldbury 7/4/1905 d 1982
Accles & Pollock
1929 Birmingham 2
Oldbury United
Dudley Town
Leamington Town
Kidderminster Harriers
Leamington Town

Saddington, H OL
1893 Ardwick 6

From To Apps Goal
Sadler, Arthur OL
b Eckington 1915
Ilford
Romford
1937 Chesterfield 4
Chesterfield Ramblers

Sadler, Joseph LH
b Newport 18/4/1914 d 1987
1932 Coventry City 0
Windsor Juniors
1935 Newport County 2

Sadler, JZ OR
1892 Walsall Town Swifts 1

Saer, Charles (Charlie) GK
b St Clears q3 1871 d 1958
Fleetwood Rangers
1896 Blackburn Rovers 0
1897 Leicester Fosse 28
Stockport County
Fleetwood Rangers

Sagar, Charles IL/CF
b Daisy Hill 28/3/1878 d 1919
Caps: FLge 4/England 2
Edgeworth Rovers
Turton Rovers
1898 1904 Bury 186 71
1905 1906 Manchester United 30 20
Atherton
Haslingden

Sagar, Edward (Ted) GK
b Campsall 7/2/1910 d 1986
Caps: NIRL 1/FLge 5/England 4
Thorne Colliery
1928 Hull City (trial) 0
1929 1938 Everton 299
1939 (Everton) (3)
Portadown
1946 1952 Everton 164

Sagar, James (Jim) OR
b Padiham 1901
Padiham
1923 Accrington Stanley 10
Barnoldswick Town

Sage, William (Billy) RH/CH
b Edmonton 11/11/1893 d 1968
Tottenham Thursday
Corinthians
1919 1925 Tottenham Hotspur 12
1927 Clapton Orient 12
Dartford

St Pier, Stanley Walter (Wally) CH/RH
b Becontree Heath 8/10/1904 d 1989
Ilford
1929 1932 West Ham United 24

Sale, Thomas (Tommy) CF/IL
b Stoke-on-Trent 30/4/1910 d 1990
Stoke St Peter's
1930 1935 Stoke City 161 75
1935 1937 Blackburn Rovers 65 25
1937 1945 Stoke City 42 23
1939 (Stoke City) (3) (3)
Northwich Victoria
Hednesford Town

Sales, Arthur Alfred RH/CH
b Lewes 4/3/1900 d 1977
Redhill
1924 1927 Chelsea 7
1930 1931 Queen's Park Rangers 35
Ales (France)
1933 Bournemouth & Boscombe Ath 0

Salisbury, J CF
1897 Darwen 2

Salisbury, John Henry OR
1894 Crewe Alexandra 9 1

Salisbury, William (Bill) CF
b Glasgow 23/2/1899 d 1965
St Anthony's (Glasgow)
Partick Thistle
1928 Liverpool 16 2
Bangor
Distillery
Shelbourne
Bangor
Partick Thistle

Salkeld, George OL
b Blackburn 1877
1897 Darwen 2

From To Apps Goal
Salley, George CH
b Newcastle q1 1886 d 1938
Wallsend Park Villa
1911 Oldham Athletic 3
Southport Central
Hurst

Salmon, Harry CH/LH/CF
b Fenton 14/3/1910 d 1944
Stoke St Peter's
Longton Hall
Macclesfield
1932 Stoke City 3 1
1934 1935 Millwall 27 1
Wellington Town
1937 Southport 24
Shrewsbury Town

Salmon, Leonard Alexander (Len) RH/LH
b West Kirby 24/6/1912 d 1995
West Kirby
Hoylake
1934 1935 New Brighton 30 2
South Liverpool
1945 Burnley 0
1946 1947 Tranmere Rovers 30 1
Runcorn

Salmond, Robert C (Bob) CH
b Kilmarnock 22/9/1911 d 1997
Dundee North End
1930 1938 Portsmouth 135
1938 Chelsea 24
1939 (Chelsea) (3)
Banbury Spencer

Salt, Ernest (Ernie) GK
b Walsall 10/2/1897 d 1940
Walsall
Talbot Stead Tube Works
1921 Everton 4
1923 1924 Accrington Stanley 72
1925 Wigan Borough 26

Salt, George Oscar OL
b Barton-on-Irwell q2 1883 d 1959
Northern Nomads
1910 Manchester City 1
Northern Nomads

Salt, Harold OL
Ravensdale
1925 Port Vale 5

Salt, Harry LH/CH/RH
b Sheffield 20/11/1899 d 1971
Ecclesfield United
1921 Brighton & Hove Albion 6 2
Mexborough
Peterborough & Fletton United
1926 Queen's Park Rangers 5
Grays Thurrock
1927 1928 Crystal Palace 42 1
1929 1931 Brentford 78
1932 Walsall 10
Yeovil & Petters United
Tunbridge Wells Rangers

Salt, Herbert Arthur GK
b Stoke-on-Trent q3 1882 d 1967
Newcastle St Peter's
1902 Stoke 1
Stafford Rangers

Salt, HR RH
1894 Walsall Town Swifts 11

Salt, Jonathan GK
1894 Burton Wanderers 1

Salter, John MacGregor IL
b Bitterne 3/8/1898 d 1982
Bitterne Sports
1923 Southampton 1
Southampton Civil Service
Thorneycrofts

Salvidge, George Brown OR
b Bridlington q4 1919 d 1941
Southcoates Lane Old Boys
Beverley White Star
1938 Hull City 4 1
Burton Town

Sambidge, Ernest Baden (Ernie) LB
b Newcastle 7/8/1900 d 1979
Spennymoor United
1922 1924 Bristol Rovers 23
Bath City
Street
Trowbridge Town

From To Apps Goal
Sambrook, John Henry (Jack) CF/IL
b Wednesfield 10/3/1899 d 1973
Willenhall Town
1919 1920 Wolverhampton Wanderers 21 7
1922 Liverpool 2
1923 Stockport County 17 4
1924 1925 Southport 65 31
Willenhall Town
C & L Hills

Sambrooke, Christopher Lockley (Chris) CF
b Oldbury 5/1/1893 d 1959
Kidderminster Harriers
Oldbury Town
1919 Coventry City 6
Nuneaton Town
1921 West Bromwich Albion 0
Wellington Town
1922 Stalybridge Celtic 19 9
Redditch Town

Samms, Anthony CH
b Hunslet q2 1894 d 1954
Ulverston St Mary's
1921 Barrow 1
Ulverston St Mary's

Sampy, Thomas (Tommy) RH/IR
b Backworth 14/3/1899 d 1978
Seaton Delaval
Chopwell Institute
1920 1933 Sheffield United 340 27
1934 Barnsley 1

Sampy, William Albert (Bill) RB/LB
b Backworth 21/1/1901 d 1973
Chopwell Institute
1924 1926 Sheffield United 34
1926 1929 Swansea Town 41
Waterford
Nelson

Sams, Alfred (Alfie) IL
b Craghead 10/11/1911 d 1990
Whitby United
Shildon
Trimdon Grange Colliery
Shildon
Grantham
1937 Mansfield Town 11 2
1938 Reading 10
1939 Accrington Stanley (1)
Grantham

Samson, Ambrose Arthur (Arthur) GK
b Measham 14/10/1897 d 1980
Measham Town
1922 Birmingham 2
Burton Town

Samuel, Daniel John (Dan) IR/OR/IL
b Swansea 23/8/1910 d 1980
Caps: WLge 1
Llanelly
1932 Southend United 7 3
1933 1934 Reading 4 1
Glenavon (loan)
1935 Queen's Park Rangers 9 3
Tunbridge Wells Rangers
1937 1938 Barrow 78 11
1939 (Barrow) (3) (1)

Sanaghan, Joseph (Joe) LB
b Motherwell 12/12/1914
Caps: NIRL 2
Blantyre Celtic
1935 Bradford Park Avenue 4
1937 1938 Bournemouth & Boscombe Ath 49
1939 (Bournemouth & Boscombe Ath) (2)
Distillery
1946 1948 Bournemouth & Boscombe Ath 120
1949 1950 Stockport County 52

Sandbach, Charles (Charlie) LH
b Bury 8/12/1909 d 1990
1930 Nelson 2
1931 Northampton Town 0
Northwich Victoria

Sanders, Arthur William RH/CF
b Edmonton 8/5/1901 d 1983
London University
Peterborough & Fletton United
Northfleet
1926 1927 Tottenham Hotspur 13 7
Northfleet
1929 1932 Clapton Orient 53 5

Sanders, Moses CH/LB/LH
b Preston 26/9/1873 d 1941
Crewe Alexandra
1890 Accrington 17 1
1891 1898 Preston North End 210 20
1899 Woolwich Arsenal 4 1
Dartford

From To Apps Goal
Sanders, Robert Morgan (Bob) IL/OL/IR
b Leeswood 20/8/1913 d 1979
Caps: England Amat
Brickfields Athletic
1935 1938 Chester 44 23

Sanderson, Benjamin Salisbury RH
b Preston 30/4/1879 d 1946
1899 1902 Preston North End 6

Sanderson, Charles A RH
b Wombwell
Wombwell
1923 1925 Barnsley 24
Mexborough Athletic

Sanderson, Edgar John LH/RH
b Elkington 16/3/1874
1895 Stoke 0
Jarrow
1897 1898 Notts County 34

Sanderson, Frederick Cecil (Fred) IR/RH/LH
b Seaton Delaval 13/9/1902 d 1977
Caps: WLge 2
Bates United
Blyth Spartans
1923 1925 Newport County 14
1926 Stockport County 2
1927 New Brighton 11 1
Blyth Spartans
North Shields

Sanderson, George A IR/CF
1891 1892 Blackburn Rovers 4

Sanderson, John IR
1937 Newcastle United 0
1938 Port Vale 1
1939 (Port Vale) (2)

Sanderson, John Robert McDevitt LB
b Carlisle 5/2/1918 d 1993
1938 Carlisle United 15
1939 Wolverhampton Wanderers 0
1946 Luton Town 6
Berwick Rangers

Sanderson, Richard RH
b Pembroke
Pembroke Dock
1922 1923 Aberdare Athletic 16

Sanderson, Robert OL
Sunderland Royal Rovers
1907 Barnsley 5

Sanderson, Thomas IL
b Chorley 8/1880
1905 Blackpool 2 1

Sanderson, William OL
b Walbottle
Scotswood
Barrow
1906 1909 Preston North End 45 6

Sandford, Edward Albert (Teddy) IL/CH
b Handsworth 22/10/1910 d 1995
Caps: England 1
Tantany Athletic
Overend Wesley
Birmingham Carriage Works
Smethwick Highfield
1930 1938 West Bromwich Albion 286 67
1938 Sheffield United 5 1
Morris Commercial

Sandham, Joseph Benton CF
b Newcastle-under-Lyme q3 1871 d 1948
1892 Stoke 0
1893 1894 Crewe Alexandra 28 9
1895 Burslem Port Vale 4 2
Dresden United

Sandham, William IR/CF
b Fleetwood q3 1898 d 1963
Fleetwood
1920 Blackpool 0
1920 Blackburn Rovers 4 1
1922 Rochdale 22 7
Fleetwood

Sandiford, Robert (Bob) IR/IL
b Rochdale q3 1900 d 1967
Rochdale St Peter's
1921 Rochdale 12 2
Bacup Borough
1923 1924 Rochdale 4 2
York City

Sandland, Edwin Thomas (Teddy) IL
b Stoke-on-Trent q3 1873
Newcastle Swifts
1894 1895 Stoke 13 3
Congleton Hornets

From To Apps Goal

Sands, Alexander (Alex) OR
b Dunoon 1870
Dunoon
1893 Burslem Port Vale 1 1

Sands, Joseph Irving B OL
b Nottingham q2 1882 d 1960
Lawrence Athletic
1903 Notts County 2
1904 Nottingham Forest 0

Sands, Percy Robert CH
b Norwood q4 1881 d 1965
Caps: FLge 1
Cheltenham Town
1903 1914 Woolwich Arsenal 327 10
Southend United

Sang, Robert IL
St Anthony's
1922 Stalybridge Celtic 4 1

Sankey, John (Jack) RH/LH
b Winsford 19/3/1912 d 1985
Moulton Wanderers
Winsford United
1933 1938 West Bromwich Albion 144 5
1939 (West Bromwich Albion) (3)
1945 1947 Northampton Town 42
Hereford United

Sankey, Thomas (Tom) CF
b Stanton Hill 24/10/1891 d 1974
Huthwaite Colliery
1920 Grimsby Town 4

Sapsford, George Douglas IL
b Higher Broughton 10/3/1896 d 1970
South Salford Lads Club
Clarendon
1919 1921 Manchester United 52 16
1921 1925 Preston North End 36 9
1925 1926 Southport 69 24

Sargeant, Charles (Charlie) OL
b Cornsay 2/2/1909 d 1988
Cornsay Park Albion
White-le-Head Rangers
Ushaw Moor
Washington Colliery
Bishop Auckland
Tow Law Town
Bishop Auckland
1930 Norwich City 13 1
1931 Bristol City 27 10
1932 1933 Hull City 60 16
1933 1937 Chester 153 51
1937 1938 Stockport County 49 19
1939 Plymouth Argyle (3) (2)
Blackhall Colliery Welfare
Cornsay Park Albion
Murton Colliery Welfare
Blackhall Colliery Welfare

Sargeaunt, Henry (Harry) IL
b Richmond, Yorkshire q1 1892 d 1960
Felling Colliery
Seaton Delaval
1920 1921 Hull City 19 8
1922 Brighton & Hove Albion 0
Blyth Spartans
Seaton Delaval
Penkridge
1926 Durham City 28 7
Preston Colliery

Sargent, Frank A OR
b London
1919 Fulham 0
1920 Southend United 2

Sargent, Frederick Albert (Fred) OR
b Islington 7/3/1912 d 1948
Barnsbury
Tufnell Park
1933 Tottenham Hotspur 0
Northfleet
1934 1938 Tottenham Hotspur 93 24
1939 (Tottenham Hotspur) (3) (1)
Chelmsford City

Sarvis, William Isaac IR/CF
b Merthyr Tydfil q3 1898 d 1968
1921 Merthyr Town 5 1
1922 Manchester United 1
1925 Bradford City 1
1926 Walsall 9 2

From To Apps Goal

Satterthwaite, Charles Oliver (Charlie) IL/OL
b Cockermouth 4/1877 d 1948
Black Diamonds
1895 Bury 4 2
1897 Burton Swifts 8
1899 1901 Liverpool 46 12
New Brompton
West Ham United
1904 1909 Woolwich Arsenal 129 45

Satterthwaite, Joseph Norman (Joe) IL
b Cockermouth q3 1885 d 1916
Workington
1907 Woolwich Arsenal 5 1
1908 Grimsby Town 20 2
New Brompton
Mexborough (trial)
Shirebrook
Mansfield Mechanics

Saul, Charles Ernest CH
b Kimberworth q2 1878 d 1948
Kimberworth
Thornhill United
1900 Sheffield United 1
Thornhill United

Saul, Mark (Monty) OR
b Manchester 24/6/1899 d 1980
1922 Stalybridge Celtic 1

Saul, Percy RH/RB/LB
b Rotherham q4 1881 d 1965
Thornhill United
1901 1903 Gainsborough Trinity 68 8
Plymouth Argyle
1906 1908 Liverpool 75 1
Coventry City
Rotherham Town
Rotherham County

Saunders, Edgar CF
b Birmingham
Birmingham Tramways
1922 Brighton & Hove Albion 2
Pontypridd
Peterborough & Fletton United

Saunders, Frank Victor CF
b Dudley q2 1888 d 1946
Wednesbury Old Athletic
1911 Nottingham Forest 28 7
1912 Huddersfield Town 0

Saunders, James E GK
b Birmingham
1899 Glossop 1
1900 Middlesbrough 0
1901 1902 Newton Heath/Manchester Utd 12
Nelson
1906 1907 Lincoln City 65
1909 Chelsea 2
Watford
Lincoln Liberal Club

Saunders, Percy Kitchener IL/LH
b Newhaven q3 1916 d 1942
Newhaven
1936 1938 Sunderland 26 6
1939 Brentford (2) (1)

Saunders, Samuel LH
Alfreton Town
1904 1905 Derby County 8
Sutton Town

Saunders, Sidney OL
b West Bromwich 1872
Unity Gas
1895 West Bromwich Albion 2
Birmingham Centinels

Saunders, Wilfred William (Wilf) GK
b Banbury q2 1916
Banbury Spencer
1938 West Bromwich Albion 2
Banbury Spencer

Saunders, William GK
1899 Burslem Port Vale 1

Savage, George LH
1893 Northwich Victoria 6

Savage, George LH/CH
b Aston q1 1896 d 1968
Willenhall Swifts
1921 West Bromwich Albion 2
1922 1924 Wrexham 111 1
Shrewsbury Town
Alfreton Town
Cradley Heath

From To Apps Goal

Savage, Harry OL
b Frodsham q1 1897 d 1968
Crewe Alexandra
1920 Sheffield United 10
1921 Watford 7 1
Connah's Quay & Shotton
Mold Town
Frodsham

Savage, Jack (MM) LB
b Belfast
Caps: IrLge 2
Botanic
Dundela
Distillery
Larne
1926 New Brighton 11
Larne

Savage, James OL
b Withnell 12/5/1876
Nelson
1900 1901 Burnley 36 11
Trawden Forest

Savage, Reginald (Reg) GK
b Eccles 5/7/1912 d 1997
Taylor Brothers
Stalybridge Celtic
1934 1938 Leeds United 79
Queen of the South
1945 1946 Nottingham Forest 20
1947 Accrington Stanley 0

Savage, Robert Edward (Ted) RH
b Louth 2/1912 d 1964
Stewton
1928 1930 Lincoln City 96 3
1931 1937 Liverpool 100 2
1937 Manchester United 4
1938 Wrexham 26
1939 (Wrexham) (1)

Savage (Finnigan), Thomas Finnigan (Tommy) CF
b West Stanley 13/7/1913 d 1937
Craghead United
1933 Middlesbrough 0
Hurst
1934 Barnsley 4 1
1935 1936 Southport 32 14
Stalybridge Celtic
Peterborough United

Savage, William Henry Marcus CF
b Chatham 3/1896 d 1975
1923 Gillingham 4

Saville, William RH
b Sheffield 18/5/1908 d 1988
1926 1927 Rotherham United 7
Shirebrook

Sawers, Alexander LB
b Glasgow 1861
Kilmarnock
Third Lanark
Clyde
1892 Burnley 2

Sawers, William (Bill) IL/IR
b Bridgeton 13/6/1871 d 1927
Caps: Scotland 1
Clyde
1892 Blackburn Rovers 24 11
1893 Stoke 17 5
Dundee
1895 Stoke 1
Dundee
Kilmarnock
Abercorn
Clyde

Sawley, Alfred IR/CF
b Worsthorne q2 1880
1900 1902 Burnley 13 1
Trawden

Sawyer, Thomas E OR/IR
1894 Derby County 2
Macclesfield
Stockport County
1899 1900 Newton Heath 6
Chorley
1901 Chesterfield Town 9
Coventry City

Saxby, Alfred (Alf) RB
b Bolsover 11/3/1897 d 1966
New Bolsover Wesleyans
Bolsover Colliery
1921 1927 Chesterfield 186

From To Apps Goal

Saxton, Arthur William OL/OR
b Breaston 28/8/1874
Glossop North End
Stalybridge Rovers
1897 1898 Sunderland 19 2
Bedminster
Luton Town
Northampton Town
1901 Nottingham Forest (trial) 1
Long Eaton St Helen's
Perks Athletic

Saxton, Edgar RB
b Carlton, West Yorkshire q1 1897 d 1966
Carlton Victoria
1919 1920 Barnsley 3
1923 1927 Bournemouth & Boscombe Ath 77

Saxton, Fred OR
b Mansfield 6/3/1916 d 2000
Sutton-in-Ashfield
1934 Nottingham Forest 1

Saxton, John (Jack) RH
b Kimberley 18/11/1902 d 1964
Bentley Colliery
1925 1926 Nottingham Forest 11
1927 Southport 35
Scunthorpe & Lindsey United
Bentley Colliery

Sayer, James (Jimmy) OR
b Mexborough q3 1862 d 1922
Caps: England 1
Mexborough
Heeley
Sheffield Wednesday
1888 1889 Stoke 14 1
Mexborough

Sayer, Stanley Charles (Stan) CF/IR/IL
b Chatham 2/2/1895 d 1982
Ramsgate Town
1920 1921 Millwall Athletic 30 2
Northfleet
1922 1924 Tranmere Rovers 79 30
1925 New Brighton 12 5
1925 Wigan Borough 16 7
1925 1926 Lincoln City 32 6
1927 1928 Southend United 32 1
Dartford
Ramsgate
Folkestone
Bexleyheath & Welling
Dagenham Town

Sayles, George RB/LB
b Wales, Nottinghamshire 26/3/1899 d 1971
1920 Cardiff City 0
1921 1923 Reading 21
York City
1925 Reading 0

Sayles, Thomas (Tommy) RB/LB
b Wales, Nottinghamshire q2 1892 d 1940
Sheffield
1920 Cardiff City 0
1921 1922 Barnsley 20
1923 1926 Southend United 94 2
Worksop Town
Shirebrook

Scaife, George RB
b Bradford 23/12/1914 d 1990
1938 Leeds United 9

Scanlan, T LB
1892 1893 Northwich Victoria 39 6

Scanlon, Edward IR/LH
b Hebburn 14/5/1890 d 1939
Wallsend
North Shields Athletic
Jarrow
1909 1910 Lincoln City 29 3
South Shields
Jarrow
Swindon Town
Hamilton Academical

Scarr, John Geoffrey S RH/LB
b Blackpool q4 1874 d 1961
1896 1898 Blackpool 9

Scarratt, James OR/OL
b Wellington, Shropshire q4 1868 d 1933
Wellington St George's
1892 1894 Burslem Port Vale 59 9

Scarratt, W CF
1899 Glossop 7

From To Apps Goal

Scattergood, Ernald Oak (Ernie) GK
b Riddings 29/5/1887 d 1932
Caps: England 1
Ripley Athletic
1907 1914 Derby County 182 3
1914 1924 Bradford Park Avenue 268 5
Alfreton Town

Scattergood, Kenneth (Ken) GK
b Bradford 6/4/1912 d 1988
1931 Sheffield Wednesday 0
1932 Wolverhampton Wanderers 0
1933 Bristol City 39
1934 Stoke City 4
1936 1937 Derby County 22

Schofield, Alfred John (Alf) OR
b Blackburn q4 1876 d 1953
1895 1899 Everton 13 2
1900 1906 Newton Heath/Manchester Utd 157 29

Schofield, Frederick (Fred) LH
b Greenfield 15/9/1912 d 1975
Brunswick Wesleyans
Crompton Albion
New Mills
1933 1935 Oldham Athletic 82 3

Schofield, George William OR/OL
b Southport 6/8/1896
1914 Liverpool 0
1919 Bury 1
1920 Manchester United 1
1922 Crewe Alexandra 18 1
Altofts WR Colliery

Schofield, Harold LB/RB
b Manchester 25/5/1903 d 1975
1925 1928 Bradford Park Avenue 17
1929 1931 Chesterfield 88 3
1932 1934 Doncaster Rovers 66
1935 Queen's Park Rangers 0
Tunbridge Wells Rangers

Schofield, Harry LB
Manchester St Augustine's
1897 1899 Lincoln City 17

Schofield, John (Jack) RH
b Waterfoot 1913
Bacup Borough
1931 1932 Burnley 9
1935 Accrington Stanley 10
Rossendale United

Schofield, Joseph (Joe) OR/OL
b Wigan
Brynn Central
Ashton Town
1903 Manchester United 2
1905 Stockport County 33 3
Luton Town

Schofield, Joseph Alfred (Joe) OL/CF/IL
b Hanley 1/1/1871 d 1929
Caps: FLge 2/England 3
1891 1898 Stoke 199 81

Schofield, Percy IL
b Bolton
Eccles Borough
1921 Manchester United 1
Eccles Borough
Hurst
Stalybridge Celtic

Schofield, Robert IL
b Rochdale 7/11/1904 d 1978
1926 1927 Rochdale 17 6
Newton Heath
1929 Halifax Town 6
1930 Rochdale 0
Bacup Borough
1932 Accrington Stanley 1

Scholes, Joseph OL
1919 Bury 2

Scholes, Robert (Bob) CF/OL
b Oldham 1903 d 1987
Hurst
1923 Oldham Athletic 0
Glossop
1924 Oldham Athletic 5
1926 Walsall 4
Hurst
Mid-Rhondda United
Hurst
Stalybridge Celtic
Mossley
1935 Accrington Stanley (trial) 0
Ashton National
Crompton Albion

From To Apps Goal

Scholfield, Jack CF
b Todmorden 8/9/1902 d 1979
Portsmouth Rovers
Bury (trial) 0
1922 Aberdare Athletic 4
Atherton
Lancaster Town
1925 Barrow 5 4
1925 1926 Oldham Athletic 4 1
Lancaster Town
Middlewich
Chester
Llandudno
Oakhill United (Todmorden)
Bourillion (Todmorden)

Scorer, Robert (Bob) LH/CH
b Felling 5/10/1898 d 1971
Felling Colliery
1921 1922 Hull City 5
1923 1924 Bristol Rovers 37
1925 Wigan Borough 21
1925 1926 Crewe Alexandra 7
Shrewsbury Town

Scorgie, John OL
b Aberdeen 9/1/1892
Aberdeen Parkvale
Aberdeen
1919 Birmingham 0
Nuneaton Town
1921 Hartlepools United 4 2
Redditch Town
1922 Tranmere Rovers 0
Aberdeen
Worcester City (trial)
Aberdeen Parkvale

Scotchbrook, Frederick (Fred) LH/RH/IL
b Willenhall q2 1874 d 1948
1896 1899 Bolton Wanderers 5

Scotson, James (Jimmy) IL
1900 1901 Manchester City 8 3
1903 Stockport County 6

Scott, Adam LB
b Coatbridge 1871
Albion Rovers
1892 1899 Nottingham Forest 179 4

Scott, Alexander (Alex) IL/CF
b South Shields 11/7/1915 d 1958
Harton Colliery Welfare
1934 1936 Stockport County 11 6
1936 1937 Carlisle United 27 2
1938 Southport 30 7
1939 Barrow (1)
1945 Southport 0

Scott, Allan IR/CF
b Tranmere 8/1910 d 1967
Liverpool Pemblians
1929 1930 Liverpool 3 2
1932 Swindon Town 18 3
1933 Gillingham 25 11
London Paper Mills

Scott, Archibald Teasdale (Archie) CH/RH/LH
b Airdrie 22/7/1905 d 1990
Bellshill Athletic
Gartsherrie Athletic
Airdrieonians
1927 1933 Derby County 27
1934 1937 Brentford 6

Scott, David IR
b Backworth
Palmersville Villa Welfare
1927 Sunderland 0
Backworth
1927 Durham City 4

Scott, David Stanley LH
b Abercanaid q4 1900
1920 1922 Merthyr Town 53

Scott, Edwin John (Eddie) OL
b Portsmouth 21/5/1917 d 2007
1935 1937 Gillingham 50 3

Scott, Elisha GK
b Belfast 24/8/1893 d 1959
Caps: IrLge 2/Ireland 31
Belfast Boys Brigade
Linfield
Broadway United
1912 1933 Liverpool 430
Belfast Celtic

Scott, Frank IR/IL
b Boultham 1876 d 1937
Adelaide (Lincoln)
1897 1900 Lincoln City 45 8
New Brompton
Brighton & Hove Albion

From To Apps Goal

Scott, Frederick Hind (Freddie) OR/IR
b Fatfield 6/10/1916 d 1995
Caps: England Sch
Fatfield Juniors
1935 Bolton Wanderers 0
1936 Bradford Park Avenue 0
1936 1946 York City 74 16
1939 (York City) (3)
1946 1956 Nottingham Forest 301 40

Scott, George CF/IL/RH
b Monkwearmouth q2 1886 d 1916
Braeside
Sunderland West End
1908 1914 Clapton Orient 205 33

Scott, George OL
b Blackhill 14/8/??
Crawcrook Albion
1923 Durham City 0
1924 Tottenham Hotspur (trial) 0
White-le-Head Rangers
1926 1928 South Shields 67 10
1929 Newcastle United 7 2
1930 1931 Gillingham 39 7
North Shields
Wigan Athletic

Scott, Harold (Harry) OR
b Horbury
Horbury Spring End
1937 1938 Halifax Town 11 2

Scott, Henry (Harry) IL/IR
b Newburn 4/8/1897
Bankhead Albion
Newburn Grange
Bankhead
1924 Sunderland 2
1925 1926 Wolverhampton Wanderers 35 6
1926 1927 Hull City 29 8
1928 1931 Bradford Park Avenue 69 20
1932 Swansea Town 40 7
1933 Watford 1
Nuneaton Town
Vauxhall Motors

Scott, James GK
b 1881
St Mirren
1905 Bradford City 2

Scott, James CF
1925 Nottingham Forest 1

Scott, James LB
b Greenock
1925 Accrington Stanley 0
1926 Charlton Athletic 1
1928 1929 Merthyr Town 65

Scott, James Edgar (Jim) LH/CH
b Stevenston 1892
Ardeer Thistle
1911 1912 Liverpool 10
Dumbarton
Third Lanark
New York Giants

Scott, John (Jock) OL/IL
b Scotland
Albion Rovers
1890 1895 Sunderland 96 25
South Shields

Scott, John OR
b Crieff 1898
Muirkirk Athletic
Norwich City
East Stirlingshire
Ayr United
1921 1922 Reading 54 8

Scott, John CH/LH
b Hamsterley 1909
Chopwell Institute
1927 Oldham Athletic 0
1928 1929 South Shields 15
1930 1933 Gateshead 82
1934 1938 Crewe Alexandra 170 3

Scott, John (Jack) OR
b Sunderland 5/2/1908 d 1992
Seaham Harbour
1926 Sunderland 0
1927 Crystal Palace 0
Kettering Town
1929 1930 Nottingham Forest 47 3
1931 Northampton Town 22
1932 1935 Exeter City 133 20
1936 1937 Hartlepools United 70 20
Blyth Spartans

From To Apps Goal

Scott, John A (Jack) LB/RB
Albion Rovers
1897 Sunderland 0
1898 1908 Blackpool 311 16
Rossendale United

Scott, John C (Jack) IL/CF
Cameron Highlanders
Leith Athletic
1892 Sheffield United 5 2
1896 1899 Gainsborough Trinity 90 18

Scott, John Frederick IL
b Sheffield 14/1/1909 d 1997
Gainsborough Trinity
1927 Portsmouth 0
Worksop Town
1930 Bristol Rovers 6 1
Kiveton Park Colliery
Dinnington Athletic

Scott, John George OL
b Wallsend q1 1890
Wallsend Slipway
1910 1912 Newcastle United 8 1
1913 1914 Grimsby Town 47 1
Cleethorpes Town
Charlton's (Grimsby)

Scott, John MA (Jack) LH
b Shieldmuir 1890
Wishaw Rovers
Cambuslang Rangers
Hamilton Academical
1909 1920 Bradford Park Avenue 245 3
Clydebank (loan)
1921 Manchester United 23
St Mirren
New York Giants

Scott, John McRae (Jock) RH/LH/IL
b Sanquhar 3/11/1906 d 1981
Euchan Thistle
Kello Rovers
Nithsdale Wanderers
1928 Luton Town 0
Loughborough Corinthians
1929 Norwich City 10 4
1930 Bristol Rovers 0
1931 1932 Walsall 45 2
1933 York City 34 1
1934 Southport 22 2
Workington

Scott, John Redvers (Jack) CH
b Grimethorpe 4/12/1905 d 1976
Pilkington Recreation (Doncaster)
1929 1930 Doncaster Rovers 29 1
1931 1936 Norwich City 33
1937 Southampton 1

Scott, Joseph (Joe) IR
b Newcastle 15/3/1901 d 1972
Pandon Tempest Colliery
1923 Sunderland 2
1925 1927 Darlington 43 12
1928 Ashington 0
1928 South Shields 2

Scott, Joseph (Joe) OL
b Lye 6/7/1900 d 1962
Cradley Heath
1923 1927 Rotherham County 167 54
1927 Barnsley 10 3
1928 1930 Tottenham Hotspur 18 4
Cradley Heath

Scott, Lawrence (Laurie) RB
b Sheffield 23/4/1917 d 1999
Caps: FLge 5/England B/England War 16/England 17
Bolton Woods
1935 1936 Bradford City 39
1945 1951 Arsenal 115
1951 1952 Crystal Palace 28

Scott, Leslie GK
b Sunderland q2 1895
Fulwell
St Andrew's (Sunderland)
1913 1921 Sunderland 91
1922 Stoke 20
1923 Preston North End 2
Sunderland Corporation

Scott, Matthew GK
Elswick Rangers
Newcastle East End
1893 Sunderland 1
1895 Newcastle United 0
South Shields

From To Apps Goal

Scott, Matthew McLintock LB
b Airdrie 11/7/1872
Caps: Scotland 1
Airdrieonians
1900 Newcastle United 5
Albion Rovers
Airdrieonians

Scott, Reuben Handley (Ben) LH
b Roslin 1/5/1918 d 1989
Fatfield Juniors
1936 Manchester United 0
1937 1938 Southport 49
1939 (Southport) (3)
Roddy Athletic

Scott, Richard James GK
b Liverpool 19/12/1897
1921 1925 Crewe Alexandra 156

Scott, Robert Alexander GK
b Liverpool 26/10/1913 d 1962
Caps: England Sch
1931 Liverpool 0
1933 1935 Burnley 57
1935 1938 Wolverhampton Wanderers 119
1939 (Wolverhampton Wanderers) (3)
1947 1948 Crewe Alexandra 44

Scott, Samuel LB
b Port Glasgow 1873
Port Glasgow Athletic
1896 1897 Bolton Wanderers 19
Rangers
Port Glasgow Athletic
Barrow
Port Glasgow Athletic

Scott, Samuel (Sammy) OL
b Wheatley Hill
Wheatley Hill Juniors
Bishop Auckland
1935 Sunderland 0
1936 Torquay United 4

Scott, Sidney (Sid) CH
b Macclesfield 11/2/1892 d 1947
Castle Primitives
Northwich Victoria
1919 1920 Manchester City 15
Tranmere Rovers
1921 Norwich City 21
New Brighton
Stafford Rangers
Altrincham

Scott, Thomas CF
b County Durham
Tyzacks
Seaham Colliery Welfare
Horden Colliery Welfare
Ferryhill Athletic
Ashburne
1922 Blackpool 0
1923 Durham City 1 1
Ferryhill Athletic

Scott, Thomas (Tom) IR/IL
b Newcastle 6/4/1904 d 1979
Swifts (Newcastle)
Pandon Temperance
1923 Sunderland 0
1924 Darlington 7 3
1924 1927 Liverpool 17 4
1928 1929 Bristol City 35 6
1930 1931 Preston North End 41 23
1932 1934 Norwich City 53 26
1934 1936 Exeter City 56 16
Bangor City

Scott, Thomas (Tom) OR
b Newcastle 1917
Seaham Colliery Welfare
Horden Colliery Welfare
Easington Colliery Welfare
1936 Hartlepools United 6
Chilton Colliery Recreation Athletic

Scott, Walter GK
b Worksop q1 1886 d 1955
Caps: IrLge 5
Worksop West End
Worksop Central
Worksop Town
1907 1909 Grimsby Town 80
1909 1910 Everton 18
1911 1912 Sunderland 34
Shelbourne
Worksop Town
1919 Grimsby Town 19
Gainsborough Trinity

Scott, Walter James CH/RH
b Willington Quay 7/1/1890 d 1973
Bedlington United
Heart of Midlothian
Raith Rovers
St Bernard's
Dunfermline Athletic
Broxburn United
Falkirk
Hartlepools United
Blyth Spartans
1921 South Shields 3
Close Works
1921 Ashington 1
Seaton Delaval
New Delaval Villa
Bebside Gordon

Scott, William (Billy) GK
b Belfast 1884
Caps: IrLge 3/Ireland 25
Cliftonville
Linfield
1904 1911 Everton 251
1912 1913 Leeds City 26

Scott, William (Willie) IR/CF
b Bucksburn 10/10/1916 d 1994
Woodside
Aberdeen
1938 Newcastle United 6 2
1939 (Newcastle United) (3) (1)
Consett

Scott, William H CF
b Scotland
Larkhall Thistle
Airdrieonians
1922 1923 Newcastle United 4

Scott, William Harrison (Harry) IR/IL
b Grimethorpe 16/9/1905 d 1990
Pilkington Recreation (Doncaster)
1929 1931 Bournemouth & Boscombe Ath 81 36
1932 Swindon Town 18 5
Pilkington Recreation (Doncaster)

Scott, William John (Bill) LB/RB
b Glasgow 1906
Caps: IrLge 3
Bellshill Academy
Woodburn
Belfast Celtic
Lancaster Town
Manchester Central
Macclesfield
1933 1934 Darlington 73
1935 Stockport County 11
1936 Cardiff City 17
Wigan Athletic

Scott, William Reed (Billy) IR/IL/RH
b Willington Quay 6/12/1907 d 1969
Caps: England 1
Howdon British Legion
1930 1931 Middlesbrough 26 5
1932 1946 Brentford 273 84
1939 (Brentford) (2)
1947 Aldershot 21
Dover

Scowcroft, J CH
1888 1889 Bolton Wanderers 9 1

Screen, John (Jack) LB/RB
b Oldbury 3/1/1915 d 2004
Smethwick Highfield
1934 West Bromwich Albion 1
1939 Wrexham (3)
Banbury Spencer

Scrimshaw, Charles Thomas (Charlie) LB
b Heanor 3/4/1909 d 1973
Hebden Bridge
1929 1938 Stoke City 124
1938 Middlesbrough 9

Scrimshaw, Stanley (Stan) CH/RH/IR
b Hartlepool 7/8/1915 d 1988
Easington Colliery Welfare
1935 1936 Hartlepools United 18 1
1937 1946 Bradford City 20
1939 (Bradford City) (1)
Frickley Colliery
1947 1949 Halifax Town 52

Scriven, Aubrey OL
b Cleobury Mortimer 7/7/1904 d 1988
Highley
Denaby United
1924 1926 Birmingham 51 9
1927 1931 Bradford City 105 37
1932 1933 Bristol City 54 12
Worcester City
Brierley Hill Alliance

Scriven, Herbert Richard (Bert) GK
b Winsor 2/2/1908 d 2001
Totton
1930 1936 Southampton 225
Salisbury City

Scrivens, Thomas (Tom) IR
b Walsall 1876
Walsall Star
1897 Small Heath 0
Wellingborough
1899 Small Heath 13 5
Northampton Town
Willenhall

Scull, John Alfred (Jack) LB
b Saltaire 15/9/1897 d 1977
Idle
1921 Halifax Town 8

Scullion, James Peter (Jimmy) IR/CF/OL
b Holytown 4/8/1900 d 1981
Carluke Rovers
1922 Bury 0
King's Park
Albion Rovers
Workington
1926 Fulham 1
Lytham
1927 Stockport County 18 5
1928 1929 Crewe Alexandra 73 41
1930 Wigan Borough 27 11
1931 Stockport County 15 5
Mossley
Stalybridge Celtic
Hurst
Buxton
Darwen
Bacup Borough
Droylsden
Mossley

Scully, Thomas LB
b Billinge q4 1894 d 1964
Our Lady's
1921 Wigan Borough 6

Scurr, Thompson Wilson (Tommy) OL
b Tudhoe 9/1/1897 d 1947
Tudhoe United
Willington
1919 Bolton Wanderers (trial) 0
Spennymoor United
Ferryhill Athletic
Willington
Crook Town
Scarborough
Bishop Auckland
Chilton Colliery Recreation Athletic
1925 1927 Stockport County 61 10
Peterborough & Fletton United
1929 Wigan Borough 19 6
Macclesfield
Crook Town

Seabrook, Arthur IR/OR
b Luton 2/10/1895 d 1981
Luton Clarence
1921 1923 Northampton Town 36 9
1924 1927 Halifax Town 104 35
1928 Crewe Alexandra 35 7
1929 Stockport County 3 1

Seabrook, Edward CH
b Wigan 8/1909 d 1995
Wigan Parish Church
1929 Bolton Wanderers 0
1930 Wigan Borough 4
1931 Chesterfield 2
1932 Swindon Town 3
Chorley
Dick, Kerr's XI
Leyland Motors
South Liverpool (trial)

Seagrave, J OL
1896 1897 Gainsborough Trinity 2

Seagrave, John William (Jack) RB/CH/RH
b South Elmsall 16/4/1912 d 1965
South Elmsall
Frickley Colliery
1929 Grimsby Town 0
1930 1935 Southport 168 3
1935 1938 Chesterfield 84
1939 Stockport County (2)

Seal, Christopher (Chris) LB
b Nottingham q1 1885 d 1949
Hyson Green
1905 Derby County 1
Mansfield Woodhouse
Basford United

Search, John CF
b Liverpool 5/2/1915 d 1988
Liobians
Lucern (Liverpool)
1933 Liverpool 0
1935 New Brighton 6 3
Runcorn
1936 Arsenal (trial) 0

Searle, Frank Burnett RB/LB/LH
b Hednesford 30/1/1906 d 1977
1924 Stoke 0
Willenhall Town
1927 Bristol City 1
1928 1932 Charlton Athletic 66 2
1932 Chester 4
1933 Watford 4
1934 1937 Clapton Orient 122 1

Seaton, Robert Henry LH
b Burslem 9/10/1879 d 1969
1900 Burslem Port Vale 12

Seddon, James (Jimmy) CH/RH
b Bolton 20/5/1895 d 1971
Caps: England 6
Hamilton Central
1913 1931 Bolton Wanderers 337 4
Mossley

Seddon, Roger Cowburn OL
b Bradley Fold 19/11/1903 d 1955
Black Lane Temperance
1924 Manchester United (trial) 0
Leyland
Congleton Town
Chorley
1925 Oldham Athletic 1
1926 Southport 6 1
Winsford United
Rossendale United

Seddon, Sidney (Sid) OR
b Kettering 21/11/1898 d 1982
Rushden
1926 Northampton Town 1
Rushden

Seddon, William Charles (Bill) RH/CH
b Clapton 28/7/1901 d 1993
Villa Athletic
1923 Gillingham 0
1924 Aston Villa (trial) 0
1925 1931 Arsenal 69
1931 1932 Grimsby Town 20 1
1933 Luton Town 0

Sedgwick, Patrick CH
b Ince-in-Makerfield 16/8/1898 d 1969
Ince Labour Club
1921 Wigan Borough 4
Horwich RMI
Atherton
Fleetwood
Atherton
Horwich RMI

Seeburg, Max Paul RH/OR
b Leipzig, Germany 19/9/1884 d 1972
Park (Tottenham)
Cheshunt
1906 Chelsea 0
1908 Tottenham Hotspur 1
Leyton
1910 Burnley 17
1911 Grimsby Town 20
Reading

Seed, Angus Cameron RB
b Lanchester 6/2/1893 d 1953
Whitburn
South Shields
Seaham Harbour
1913 Everton (trial) 0
1913 Leicester Fosse 3
Reading
St Bernard's
Mid-Rhondda
Ebbw Vale
Broxburn United
Workington

Seed, James Marshall (Jimmy) IR/IL
b Blackhill 25/3/1895 d 1966
Caps: England 5
Whitburn Villa
Whitburn
1914 Sunderland 0
Mid-Rhondda
1919 1926 Tottenham Hotspur 229 65
1927 1930 Sheffield Wednesday 134 32
1931 Clapton Orient 0

From To Apps Goal

Self, Edward Richard (Eddie) OL
b South Shields 30/7/1912 d 1982
Chester-le-Street
1933 1935 Bury 32 2
1936 1938 Hartlepools United 114 16
1939 Hull City 0

Sellars, Harry LH/RH
b Beamish 9/4/1902 d 1978
1921 Darlington 0
Leadgate Park
1923 1935 Stoke 370 18
Congleton Town
1937 Port Vale 0

Sellars, William IR
b Burton-on-Trent 1880
1899 1900 Burton Swifts 22 2

Sellars, William (Billy) OR
b Park, Yorkshire 7/10/1907 d 1987
Park Labour
1927 1931 Rotherham United 165 36
1932 Southport 39 11
1933 Burnley 19 2
1934 Bradford Park Avenue 2 1
1935 Lincoln City 33 2
Norton Woodseats

Sellars, William GK
b Glasgow
St Anthony's (Glasgow)
1937 1938 Bournemouth & Boscombe Ath 23
1939 (Bournemouth & Boscombe Ath) (3)
Wolverhampton Wanderers

Sellman, Alfred CH
b Exeter 1881
Bridgetown Amateurs
1904 Small Heath 1
Leyton
Newton Abbot

Selvey, Scotch LH
b Derby 1/11/1863 d 1947
Derby St Luke's
Derby Midland
1888 Derby County 1

Selvey, Walter IR
b Derby q1 1866 d 1944
Derby Midland
1888 Derby County 1
Derby Junction

Semple, James LB
b Belfast
1925 Charlton Athletic 2
Ards
Philadelphia

Semple, John RB
b Kirkintilloch 28/5/1889
Kirkintilloch Rob Roy
Ayr United
Dumbarton (loan)
Renton (loan)
1920 Luton Town 7

Semple, William (Billy) OL
b West Maryston 18/4/1886 d 1965
Baillieston Thistle
Rutherglen Glencairn
Celtic
Millwall Athletic
Carlisle United
Haslingden
1921 1922 Southport 38 3

Senior, Harold OL
b Cleckheaton 1908
Norristhorpe
1927 1928 Bradford City 6 1
Derry City
Peterborough & Fletton United
Frickley Colliery

Senior, James OL
b Grantham q1 1873
Grantham Rovers
1894 Sheffield United 1
Grantham Rovers

Senior, Wilfred OL
b Rotherham 29/12/1911 d 1983
1935 Rotherham United 1

Sergeant, Archibald John IR
b 29/12/1903 d 1991
Royal Engineers
1928 Millwall 1

From To Apps Goal

Settle, Alfred (Alf) LH
b Barugh Green 17/9/1912 d 1988
Barugh Green
1935 1938 Sheffield United 70 2
1939 (Sheffield United) (3)
1945 Lincoln City 0

Settle, James (Jimmy) IL/IR
b Millom q4 1875
Caps: FLge 4/England 6
1894 Bolton Wanderers 13 4
Halliwell
1896 1898 Bury 63 28
1898 1907 Everton 237 84
1908 Stockport County 26 2

Settle, John Arthur Frederick LB
b Chester q2 1895 d 1955
Chester
1921 1922 Wrexham 24
Bangor City
Chester
Holyhead Town
Caernarvon Athletic
Rhyl

Severn, Walter GK
b Ilkeston 29/1/1876 d 1965
1894 Nottingham Forest 2

Sewell, Albert LH
b Crewe
Nantwich
1927 1928 Crewe Alexandra 51
Nantwich

Sewell, Charles A LB
1904 Burton United 2

Sewell, George William LH
b Newcastle 3/6/1898
1921 Barnsley 0
1922 Tranmere Rovers 33
1923 Merthyr Town 14

Sewell, Joseph OR
1931 1932 Darlington 11

Sewell, William Ronald (Ronnie) GK
b Wingate 19/7/1890 d 1945
Caps: England 1
Wingate Albion
1911 Gainsborough Trinity 37
1912 1919 Burnley 23
1919 1926 Blackburn Rovers 227
Gainsborough Trinity

Seymour, Arthur GK
b Stockton q3 1878 d 1931
Hebburn Argyle
1901 1902 Barnsley 60
1903 Bradford City 34

Seymour, Charles (Charlie) IR
b Hebburn q1 1907
Hebburn Colliery
1929 1930 Newport County 37 12

Seymour, George Stanley (Stan) OL
b Kelloe 25/5/1892 d 1978
Caps: FLge 2
1909 Newcastle United 0
Shildon Athletic
Coxhoe
1911 Bradford City 1
Morton
1920 1928 Newcastle United 242 73

Seymour, Thomas (Tom) RH
b Ahoghill 7/6/1866 d 1951
Arthurlie
Middlesbrough Ironopolis
1894 Leicester Fosse 19 1
Arthurlie

Seymour, Thomas Gilbert (Tommy) RB/LB/LH
b Yarm 2/5/1906 d 1983
Langley Park
Crook Town
Faversham United
1924 Bury 0
1927 Swansea Town 0
Connah's Quay & Shotton
1929 1935 Oldham Athletic 127
Shrewsbury Town

Shackleton, John OR
b 1882
Darlington
Tottenham Hotspur
1906 Bury 4
Heckmondwike
Huddersfield Town
Heckmondwike

From To Apps Goal

Shadbolt, Joseph Arthur (Joe) IR
b Warrington 1/8/1874 d 1967
Birkdale South End
Southport Central
1907 1908 Oldham Athletic 27 9
Hyde

Shadwell, William John (John) RH/LH
b Bury
Turton
1934 Manchester City 2
1936 1938 Exeter City 85 2

Shaffery, John (Jack) OR
b Hanley q1 1877 d 1934
Northwood
1897 Stoke 4
Hanley Swifts

Shafto, John CF
b Humshaugh 8/11/1918 d 1978
Hexham
1937 1938 Liverpool 17 6

Shand, Hector Mackenzie RH
b Inverness 1/5/1879
Citadel
Inverness Thistle
Southampton
Inverness Thistle
1906 Middlesbrough 2
Millwall Athletic

Shankland, John IR
b Kirkconnel 13/2/1893
Kilmarnock Juveniles
Ardeer Thistle
Kilmarnock
Hurlford (loan)
Nithsdale Wanderers
1920 Luton Town 3
Galston

Shankly, James Blyth (Jimmy) CF
b Glenbuck 19/6/1901 d 1978
Glenbuck Cherrypickers
Bedlington United
1922 Portsmouth 0
Guildford United
1924 Halifax Town 7 2
Nuneaton Town
1925 Coventry City 8 2
Carlisle United
1926 1927 Sheffield United 7 4
1928 1932 Southend United 147 97
1933 1934 Barrow 78 47
1935 Carlisle United 6 3

Shankly, John Dunlop IR/OR
b Glenbuck 4/11/1903 d 1960
Glenbuck Cherrypickers
Nithsdale Wanderers
1922 1923 Portsmouth 3 1
1924 1925 Luton Town 46 20
Alloa Athletic
1930 Blackpool 5
Morton
King's Park
Alloa Athletic
Dalbeattie Star

Shankly, Robert (Bob) IR/IL
b Douglas 11/2/1909
Douglas Dale
Douglas Water Thistle
1931 Hull City 0
Carluke Rovers
Brechin City
Rutherglen Glencairn
1934 Newcastle United 6
1935 Aldershot 28 6
1936 Barrow 30 5
1937 1938 Clapton Orient 13

Shankly, William (Bill) RH
b Glenbuck 2/9/1913 d 1981
Caps: Scottish War 7/Scotland 5
Glenbuck Cherrypickers
Cronberry
1932 Carlisle United 16
1933 1948 Preston North End 297 13
1939 (Preston North End) (3)

Shanks, Albert V OR
b Leamington Spa
George Ellison (Birmingham)
Leamington Town
1926 Coventry City 1
Leamington Town
Banbury Spencer

From To Apps Goal

Shanks, Robert LB
b Cowpen Bewley q2 1905
Stockton
York City
1927 Huddersfield Town 0
Connah's Quay & Shotton
1929 1930 Exeter City 41 1
1931 Stockport County 13 1

Shanks, Robert (Bob) CH
b Sunniside 14/12/1911 d 1989
1934 Leeds United 0
1935 1936 Swindon Town 25 1
1937 1938 Crystal Palace 18
1939 (Crystal Palace) (3)
1946 Swindon Town 1
Chippenham Town
Gloucester City
Tonbridge
Ilfracombe Town

Shanks, Thomas (Tommy) IL/IR
b Wexford 30/3/1882
Caps: Ireland 3
Derby West End
Derby Fosse
1898 1900 Derby County 27 9
Brentford
1902 1903 Woolwich Arsenal 44 28
Brentford
1906 1908 Leicester Fosse 57 16
Leyton
1911 Clapton Orient 0
York City

Shanley, Frank GK
1913 Preston North End 1

Sharkey, Bernard Joseph IR
b Middlesbrough 25/3/1894 d 1958
Grangetown St Mary's
1920 Preston North End 1
1921 Barrow 36 14
1922 Tranmere Rovers 22 4

Sharkey, Hugh RH
b Livingston Station
Bo'ness
Hibernian
Waterford
Sligo Rovers
1936 Barnsley 1

Sharman, Frederick (Fred) CH/CF
b Loughborough 19/11/1912 d 1976
Loughborough Red Triangle
Brush Sports
Loughborough Corinthians
1933 1938 Leicester City 190 18
1939 (Leicester City) (3) (1)
Brush Sports

Sharman, J GK
Beeston Humber
1897 1899 Notts County 2
1900 Grimsby Town 0

Sharman, Richard GK
b Lincoln q3 1874
Nondescripts
1896 Gainsborough Trinity 0
1897 1898 Lincoln City 6
Adelaide (Lincoln)

Sharp, Alexander (Alex) CH
b Prestonpans 12/11/1910 d 1982
Tranent Juniors
Heart of Midlothian
Ayr United
1929 Southampton (trial) 1
East Fife
1930 Tranmere Rovers 3
East Fife
Leith Athletic
Duns

Sharp, Alexander (Alex) IL
b Dundee 12/10/1910
Dundee Violet
East Fife
1934 1935 Blackburn Rovers 9 1
1935 Hull City 18 4
Raith Rovers
Falkirk
Raith Rovers

From To | Apps Goal

Sharp, Arthur Allen IL/IR
b Nottingham 9/7/1905 d 1991
Nottingham St Mark's
Loughborough Corinthians
Mansfield Town
1927 Blackpool 0
1928 Reading 0
1928 West Ham United 0
Newark Town
1930 1931 Carlisle United 69 15
1932 Bristol City 28 9
1933 Aldershot 34 3
1934 Oldham Athletic 1
Shrewsbury Town
1936 Darlington 8
Shrewsbury Town
Scarborough
Peterborough United

Sharp, Bertram (Bert) RH/RB/LB
b Hereford 1/1876 d 1944
Hereford Comrades
Hereford Town
Hereford Thistle
1897 1898 Aston Villa 22
1899 Everton 3
Southampton
1901 Everton 6
Kirkdale
Southport Central

Sharp, Brittain Cooper IL/IR
b Lincoln q4 1883 d 1966
St Catherine's (Lincoln)
1904 1905 Lincoln City 11
Newark Town
1907 Lincoln City 3 1
Worksop Town
Lincoln City

Sharp, Buchanan (Kenny) IL/IR
b Alexandria 2/11/1894 d 1956
Vale of Leven
Clydebank Juniors
1919 1922 Chelsea 65 20
1922 1924 Tottenham Hotspur 3
1924 1925 Leicester City 12 2
1926 1928 Nelson 80 35
1928 Southport 4 1

Sharp, CB IR
1913 Blackpool 3

Sharp, Frank IL/IR
b Tintwistle 1900
Barton BSC
Mossley
1922 Birmingham 5
1922 1923 Chesterfield 22 7
Stourbridge
Stalybridge Celtic
Mossley

Sharp, Henry (Harry) OR
b Ardwick 29/11/1899 d 1931
Mossley
1920 Manchester City 0
Levenshulme Zion
1922 Southport 1
Levenshulme Zion

Sharp, James RH
b Jamestown 1869
1891 1895 Preston North End 93 3
1896 Darwen 24 2
Reading

Sharp, James (Jimmy) LB
b Jordanstone 11/10/1880 d 1949
Caps: SLge 2/Scotland 5
East Craigie
Dundee
Fulham
1905 1907 Woolwich Arsenal 103 4
Rangers
1908 1912 Fulham 97
1912 1914 Chelsea 61
1919 Fulham 1 1

Sharp, James CH
b Motherwell
Craigneuk Juniors
Hamilton Academical
1928 1929 Rotherham United 6 1

Sharp, John (Jack) OR
b Hereford 15/2/1878 d 1938
Caps: FLge 3/England 2
Hereford Thistle
1897 1898 Aston Villa 23 15
1899 1909 Everton 300 70

From To | Apps Goal

Sharp, Samuel (Sammy) RH
b Ardwick q2 1896 d 1936
1919 1927 Manchester City 176
1929 1930 Crewe Alexandra 60
1931 Wigan Borough 4
Bacup Borough
Whitchurch

Sharp, WA OR
b Leicester
Leicester Imperial
1902 Leicester Fosse 1
Leicester Old Boys

Sharp, Wilfred (Wilf) RH/RB
b Bathgate 8/4/1907 d 1981
Pumpherston Rangers
Bathgate
Kirkintilloch Rob Roy
Clydebank
Airdrieonians
Tunbridge Wells Rangers
Airdrieonians
1934 1935 Sheffield Wednesday 48 2
1936 Bradford Park Avenue 17 1
Burton Town

Sharpe, Claude Young RB
b Springburn 3/11/1909
Kirkintilloch Rob Roy
Aberdeen
1936 1937 Doncaster Rovers 2
Clyde

Sharpe, David Albert CH
b Glasgow
Glasgow Ashfield
1898 Luton Town 21

Sharpe, George W IL/OR
b York 2/9/1912 d 1984
1929 1930 York City 23 2
Selby Town

Sharpe, Harry IR
1913 Bury 0
1914 Glossop 30 6

Sharpe, Ivan Gordon OL
b St Albans 15/6/1889 d 1968
Caps: England Amat
St Albans Abbey
Watford
1908 1910 Glossop 86 16
Brighton & Hove Albion
1911 1912 Derby County 54 12
1913 1914 Leeds City 61 16
Glossop
1920 Leeds United 1
Yorkshire Amateurs

Sharpe, John William (Jack) OL
b Ruddington 9/12/1866 d 1936
1889 Notts County 3
West Herts

Sharpe, Robert C OL
1932 Darlington 4

Sharpe, William Henry OL
Loughborough
1894 Woolwich Arsenal 13 4
Glossop North End

Sharples, Harry RB
Macclesfield
1932 Rochdale 2
Ashton National

Sharples, James (Jimmy) IL/OL
b Blackburn 1872 d 1920
Rossendale
1894 1896 Manchester City 39 20
Wigan County
Swindon Town
Millwall Athletic

Sharpley, Herbert Joshua LH/CH
b Stockport q3 1877
1900 1903 Stockport County 37 3

Sharpley, William Albert LB
b Bow q2 1891 d 1916
Essex Regiment
1911 Leicester Fosse (trial) 1

Shaw, Albert E (Basher) OR
Chilton Colliery Recreation Athletic
1923 Grimsby Town (trial) 5
Chilton Colliery Recreation Athletic

From To | Apps Goal

Shaw, Arthur Frederick IL/IR/OR
b Basford 1/8/1869 d 1946
Notts Rangers
1888 1889 Notts County 4
1892 1897 Nottingham Forest 79 14
1897 Loughborough 11 3

Shaw, B OL
b Willenhall 1862
Wolverhampton Wanderers
1888 West Bromwich Albion 1 1
Oldbury Town

Shaw, Cecil Ernest LB
b Mansfield 22/6/1911 d 1977
Caps: FLge 1
Blidworth Juniors
Rainworth Church
Rufford Colliery
1929 1936 Wolverhampton Wanderers 177 8
1936 1946 West Bromwich Albion 110 10
1939 (West Bromwich Albion) (3)
Hereford United

Shaw, Charles J (Shiner) CH/RH
b Walsall 1/1866 d 1942
Walsall Town
1892 1893 Walsall Town Swifts 22 1

Shaw, Cyril IR
1927 Crewe Alexandra 1
Chester

Shaw, Fred RH/CH
b Milnthorpe 15/6/1908 d 1991
1930 1931 Barrow 5
Lancaster Town
Morecambe
Milnthorpe Corinthians

Shaw, Frederick Elliott OL
b Newcastle 1891
Wallsend
1911 1912 Hull City 9 1
Portsmouth
Boscombe

Shaw, George RH/OL
b Lincoln q3 1865 d 1928
Lincoln Ramblers
1892 1895 Lincoln City 13

Shaw, George OR
b Hyde 1887
Hyde
Denton
Hyde
1908 Oldham Athletic 10 1
Hyde
Denton

Shaw, George OR
1909 1910 Blackpool 6

Shaw, George Edward RB/LB
b Swinton 13/10/1899 d 1973
Caps: FLge 1/England 1
Bolton-on-Dearne
Rossington Colliery
Doncaster Rovers
1920 Gillingham 3
1923 Doncaster Rovers 26
1923 1926 Huddersfield Town 29
1926 1937 West Bromwich Albion 393 11
Stalybridge Celtic
Worcester City
Floriana

Shaw, George Rickerby OL/OR
b Withnell Mill 7/4/1904 d 1987
Withnell St Joseph's
Horwich RMI
Brinscall
1925 Accrington Stanley 7 1
1926 Preston North End 3
1927 Wigan Borough (trial) 2
1927 Southport 1
Darwen

Shaw, Gilbert Alexander OL/IL
b Pwllheli 4/4/1906 d 1980
1922 Aston Villa 0
Wellington Town
Brierley Hill Alliance
1926 1927 Blackburn Rovers 5 2
1928 Grimsby Town 0
1929 Bristol Rovers 20 6
1930 Walsall 10 1

Shaw, GT RB
1894 Walsall Town Swifts 1

From To | Apps Goal

Shaw, Harold Victor (Harry) LB
b Hednesford 22/5/1905 d 1984
Hednesford Town
1923 1929 Wolverhampton Wanderers 235
1929 1935 Sunderland 195 4

Shaw, Herbert OL
b Davenham q4 1878
Haverton Hill
1898 1899 Woolwich Arsenal 26 9

Shaw, Herbert (Bert) OR
b Sheffield 1919
Broadway Amateurs
Dronfield Town
Boston United
1937 1938 Grimsby Town 15 3
Chelmsford City

Shaw, James IR/IL
b Goldenhill 8/8/1904
Goldenhill Wanderers
1925 Bolton Wanderers 0
Frickley Colliery
1926 1927 Arsenal 11 4
1930 Brentford 1
1931 Gillingham 9

Shaw, John OR/IR
1903 1904 Bolton Wanderers 8
Arbroath

Shaw, John IL
Darlington
1905 Sunderland 1

Shaw, John (Jack) CH
b Oswaldtwistle
St Mary's RC (Oswaldtwistle)
1922 Accrington Stanley 3

Shaw, John LH/RH/CH
b Oldham 2/10/1916 d 1973
South Shore Wesleyans
Lytham
1934 1935 Oldham Athletic 2
Mossley
1937 1938 Grimsby Town 7
1938 Birmingham 11
1945 Watford 0
Mossley

Shaw, Jonathan Frederick CF
b North East
Wallsend Park Villa
1908 Clapton Orient 19 2

Shaw, Joseph Ebenezer (Joe) RB/LB
b Bury 7/5/1883 d 1963
Bury Athenaeum
Accrington Stanley
1907 1921 Woolwich Arsenal 309

Shaw, Joseph F (Joe) CF
b Durham 1882
St Mark's (Sunderland)
Sunderland West End
Armstrong College
Durham University
Bishop Auckland
Darlington
1905 1906 Sunderland 31 14
1907 1908 Hull City 46 20
1909 Grimsby Town 6

Shaw, Michael Victor (Mike) CF/RH/LH
b Stockport 3/2/1901 d 1976
Cheshire Regiment
1925 Barnsley 5 1
1926 1928 Crewe Alexandra 104 29
Chester

Shaw, R RH/RB
1893 1895 Darwen 70 6

Shaw, Raymond (Ray) LH/RH/CF
b Walsall 18/5/1913 d 1980
1934 Walsall 0
Streetly Works
Darlaston
1937 1946 Birmingham 12
1939 (Birmingham) (3)

Shaw, Richard (Dick) IL
b Kilnhurst
Sheffield United
Mexborough
1920 1921 Rotherham County 29 2
Wath Athletic
Denaby United
Wombwell
Wath Athletic
Mexborough

From To Apps Goal

Shaw, Richardson GK
b Halifax q3 1876 d 1953
Peterborough GN Loco
1894 1895 Lincoln City 7
Peterborough GN Loco

Shaw, Robert A RH
b South Hylton 1900
Robert Thompson's
1923 Hartlepools United 12

Shaw, Robert Eric CF
b Litherland 29/4/1911 d 1984
1929 Liverpool 0
Runcorn
Liverpool Cables
1932 New Brighton 6 3

Shaw, Samuel Henry IL
1897 Burton Swifts 7

Shaw, Thomas (Tom) CH
b London
1920 Southend United 1
Darwen

Shaw, Thomas Frederick (Fred) IL/IR
b Hucknall 27/3/1909 d 1994
Annesley Colliery
Darlaston
1933 Birmingham 6
1934 1936 Notts County 56 21
1937 Mansfield Town 22 1
1938 Bournemouth & Boscombe Ath 10 1
Ollerton Colliery

Shaw, Thomas William RB
b Davenham q1 1876
Stockton
1899 Middlesbrough 12

Shaw, Wainwright GK
b Sheffield q1 1870 d 1946
Basford Wanderers
Mansfield
Bulwell
Grantham Rovers
1897 Lincoln City 8

Shaw, Walter OR
1900 Nottingham Forest 0
1901 Gainsborough Trinity 5

Shaw, Walter James CF/IL
b Small Heath 1870
Singers
Unity Gas
Birmingham St George's
1893 1894 Woolwich Arsenal 19 11

Shaw, Wilfred (Wilf) RB
b Rossington 21/4/1912 d 1945
Rossington Main
1930 1938 Doncaster Rovers 181
1939 (Doncaster Rovers) (3)

Shaw, William IL/CF
b Kilnhurst 3/10/1897
Frickley Colliery
1921 1922 Bradford City 15 4
1923 Chesterfield 2
Scunthorpe & Lindsey United
1925 Southend United 34 19
Gainsborough Trinity
1928 Cardiff City 2
Gainsborough Trinity
Mansfield Town

Shaw, William H IL/LH
b Durham 1902
Scarborough
Barcelona
1925 1930 Northampton Town 74 15
1931 Crystal Palace 0
Kettering Town

Shawcroft, Edward CF
b Chesterfield q1 1893 d 1968
Welbeck
1921 Watford 1

Shea, Daniel Harold (Danny) IR
b Wapping 6/11/1887 d 1960
Caps: SoLge 3/FLge 2/England 2
Builders Arms
Pearl United
Manor Park Albion
West Ham United
1912 1919 Blackburn Rovers 97 61
Celtic (loan)
1920 West Ham United 16 1
1920 1922 Fulham 100 23
1923 1924 Coventry City 60 11
1924 1925 Clapton Orient 33 8
Sheppey United

Shearer, James (Jimmy) OR
b Inverkeithing
Dundee Hibernian
1920 Clapton Orient 4

Shearer, Samuel (Sammy) OL
Nithsdale Wanderers
1912 Bradford Park Avenue 1

Sheargold, Arthur L CH
b Tipton 4/1888
Great Bridge Celtic
1911 Wolverhampton Wanderers 4
Dudley Town
Netherton
Gornal Town

Shearman, Benjamin W (Ben) OL
b Lincoln 6/1884 d 1958
Caps: FLge 2
Attercliffe
High Hazels
1907 Nottingham Forest 0
Rotherham Town
1909 1910 Bristol City 60 4
1911 1914 West Bromwich Albion 126 18
1919 Nottingham Forest 31 1
Gainsborough Trinity
Norton Woodseats

Shearman, Frederick P (Fred) OR
b Bristol 1873 d 1953
Wainfleet
1895 1896 Lincoln City 17 3
Skegness Town

Shearman, William James IR/OR
b Keswick 22/5/1879
Caps: FLge 2
1903 1908 Nottingham Forest 110 39

Shears, Albert Edward (Bert) CH/RH/CF
b Newcastle 12/5/1900 d 1954
Close Works
Spen Black & White
1921 Preston North End 2
1923 Doncaster Rovers 3
Aberaman
1925 1928 Liverpool 16
1930 Tranmere Rovers 27
1931 Wigan Borough 4
1931 Barnsley 0
1932 Aldershot 0
Morecambe
Leyland Motors

Sheehan, William Joseph (Joe) LB
b Rochdale
Rochdale St John's
1921 Rochdale 1
Rochdale Civil Service

Sheffield, Alec RH
b Nottingham 4/4/1908 d 1992
Caps: England Sch
Shirebrook
Mansfield Town
1928 1929 Exeter City 24
1930 Bristol City 0
Folkestone
Margate
1933 Rochdale 0
Paris CIP
Tunbridge Wells Rangers

Sheffield, George CF
b Barrow-on-Soar q1 1896 d 1964
Loughborough Corinthians
1920 Plymouth Argyle 19 4
Kettering

Sheffield, John Davenport (Jack) OR
b Coalville q3 1879 d 1915
Coalville Albion
Whitwick White Cross
Coalville Town
Coalville Wednesday
1902 1903 Burton United 12
Coalville Town
1904 Leicester Fosse 2
Loughborough Corinthians
Ibstock Albion
Coalville Excelsior
Ibstock Albion
Coalville Wednesday
Coalville Town
Coalville Swifts

Sheldon, Albert Edward OL
b Barrow 13/6/1902 d 1983
Barrow Wireworks
1925 Barrow 3

Sheldon, Alfred (Alf) OL
b Smethwick q4 1886
Good Shepherd
Portway Villa
Rowley United
Coombs Wood
Worcester City
Dudley
1919 Coventry City 12 1
Wellington Town
1922 Wrexham 36 5
Wellington Town
Shrewsbury Town
Redditch

Sheldon, Frank IR/CF
b Liverpool 26/4/1891 d 1981
Southport Central
1922 Everton 0
1923 Clapton Orient 0
Llanelly
Tranmere Rovers (trial)
1924 Merthyr Town (trial) 1
1926 Wigan Borough 2 1
1926 Northampton Town (trial) 0
Chester (trial)
Mold Town
Liverpool Meat Traders

Sheldon, Frederick RH/OR/LH
b West Bromwich 10/12/1891 d 1973
Barry
Swansea Town
1921 1926 Aberdare Athletic 178 11
Barry

Sheldon, Frederick L (Fred) GK
b Stoke-on-Trent 1871
Stoke St Peter's
1896 1897 Stoke 8
Eccleshall C

Sheldon, John (Jackie) OR
b Clay Cross 11/2/1888 d 1941
Nuneaton Progress
Coton Villa
Bedworth ECS
Nuneaton Town
1910 1912 Manchester United 26 1
1913 1920 Liverpool 129 17

Sheldon, Lancelot Bowmer (Lance) OR
b Selston q1 1896 d 1963
Selston Town
Notts County
1919 Coventry City 6
Heanor Town
Mansfield Town

Sheldon, Wilfred (Wilf) OR
b Bulwell 11/7/1908 d 1992
Hawley's Dye Works
Bulwell Wesleyan Mission
Mansfield Town
Grantham
1929 Luton Town 2
Shirebrook
Sutton Town
Nottingham Water Department

Shell, Francis Henry (Frank) CF
b Hackney 2/1/1912 d 1988
Barking Town
Ford Sports
1937 1938 Aston Villa 23 8
1946 Birmingham City 0
Hereford United
1947 Mansfield Town 22 1
Stafford Rangers
Hinckley Athletic

Shelley, Albert OR/OL/CF
b Birmingham
Birmingham 0
Oakengates Town
1934 Southampton 0
1935 Bournemouth & Boscombe Ath 0
Gloucester City
1936 Sheffield Wednesday 3 2
1937 1938 Torquay United 36 10
Gloucester City

Shelley, Arthur CH
Chesterton
1905 Burslem Port Vale 1

Shelley, Frederick Albert (Albert) RH/CH
b Romsey 11/8/1899 d 1971
Romsey Comrades
Eastleigh Athletic
1920 1931 Southampton 392 8

Shelley, Geoffrey Leonard CH
b Fulham 12/3/1885 d 1975
Fulham
Tunbridge Wells Rangers
1907 1908 Clapton Orient 9
Tunbridge Wells Rangers
1910 Clapton Orient 0

Shelmerdine, Thomas (Tom) LH
b Hyde q4 1892 d 1964
1921 Crewe Alexandra 4

Shelton, Alfred (Alf) LH
b Nottingham 11/9/1865 d 1923
Caps: England 6
Notts Rangers
1888 1895 Notts County 195 5
1896 Loughborough 15 1
Ilkeston Town

Shelton, Charles CH/RB/LH
b Nottingham 22/1/1864 d 1951
Caps: England 1
Notts Rangers
1888 1891 Notts County 20 1

Shelton, George OL/LH/IL
b Sheffield 25/9/1899 d 1934
Attercliffe
Star Inn Club
1919 1921 Sheffield Wednesday 17
1922 1925 Exeter City 75 8
1926 New Brighton 24 3
Okehampton

Shelton, George Henry IR
b Wolverhampton q3 1894 d 1960
1919 Port Vale 2

Shelton, John (Jack) IR
b Wolverhampton q2 1886
Willenhall Pickwick
Crompton Rovers
1907 1909 Wolverhampton Wanderers 83 16
Burslem Port Vale
Stourbridge
Dudley Town

Shelton, John (Jack) CF
b Monmouth
Ynysddu
1921 Newport County 3 1
1922 Merthyr Town (trial) 0

Shelton, John Benjamin Thomas (Jack) RB/IR/LH
b Wollaston 9/11/1912 d 1992
Chase Terrace United
1932 Wolverhampton Wanderers 0
Hednesford Town
1934 1946 Walsall 103 5
Worcester City

Shelton, Thomas (Tom) CF/OR
b Nottingham 1907
1931 1933 Hull City 5 1

Shelton, Wallis LH
1920 Stockport County 3 1

Shelton, William OL
Arnold St Mary's
1910 Lincoln City 2
Netherfield Rangers

Shenton, George RB
b Hanley 15/6/1899 d 1978
Downings Tileries
Naybro Stone
Blythe Bridge
1928 1935 Port Vale 187
Shelton Iron & Steel

Shepherd, Albert CF
b Great Lever 10/12/1885 d 1929
Caps: FLge 2/England 2
St Mark's (Bolton)
Bolton Temperance
1901 Bolton Wanderers 0
1902 Blackburn Rovers 0
1902 Bolton Wanderers 0
St Luke's (Bolton)
1904 1908 Bolton Wanderers 115 85
1908 1913 Newcastle United 104 76
1914 Bradford City 22 10

Shepherd, Edward A LB
b Wembley
Harrow Weald
1924 Brentford 2

From To Apps Goal

Shepherd, Ernest (Ernie) OL
b Wombwell 14/8/1919 d 2001
Bradford Rovers
1939 1948 Fulham 72 13
1939 (Fulham) (1)
1948 West Bromwich Albion 4
1948 1949 Hull City 15 3
1950 1955 Queen's Park Rangers 219 51
Hastings United

Shepherd, George IL/OL
Rocester
1919 1920 Derby County 2

Shepherd, James RH
b Scotland 1867 d 1925
1893 Sheffield Wednesday 2
Chesterfield Town
Barnsley St Peter's

Shepherd, John IL
1911 Leicester Fosse 1

Shepherd, John William Veitch (Billy) GK
b Harton 1894 d 1936
Harton Colliery
Jarrow
Newcastle Swifts
Jarrow
1921 1922 Ashington 41
1923 Luton Town 3
Workington
West Stanley

Shepherd, Thomas LH
Castleton Baptists
1933 Rochdale 4
Ashton National

Shepherdson, Harold CH
b Middlesbrough 28/10/1918 d 1995
South Bank East End
1936 1946 Middlesbrough 17
1947 Southend United 0

Sheppard, ? CH
1898 Glossop North End 1

Sheppard, Horace Hedley (Hedley) LB/RB
b West Ham 26/11/1909 d 2006
Ilford
Barking Town
1932 West Ham United 0
1934 1948 Aldershot 249 1
Fleet Town

Sheppard, William (Bill) IL/OL
b Ferryhill 1907 d 1950
Ferryhill Athletic
Chilton Colliery Recreation Athletic
Crook Town
1926 Liverpool 0
1927 1929 Watford 89 37
1930 Queen's Park Rangers 13 4
1931 1932 Coventry City 22 8
1932 1933 Walsall 58 20
1934 Chester 1
1934 Walsall 13 7
Tunbridge Wells Rangers
Odhams

Shepperson, George IR/OR
Nottingham Forest
1892 Northwich Victoria 0
1893 1895 Notts County 5

Sherborne, John Lewis (Jack) IL
b Bolton 1/5/1916
Chorley
1937 Chelsea 5

Sheridan, James (Jimmy 'Paddy') IL
b Belfast 15/5/1882
Caps: Ireland 6
Cambuslang Hibernian
1902 1903 Everton 20 4
1904 Stoke 12 1
New Brompton
Shelbourne
Hamilton Academical

Sherlaw, David Drummond OR/CF
b Penicuik 17/9/1901
Dalkeith Thistle
Bathgate
St Bernard's (loan)
1925 Bristol City 20 6
1926 1928 Charlton Athletic 78 32
1928 1930 Brentford 34 10
St Johnstone
Montrose (loan)

From To Apps Goal

Sherlock, Harold GK
b Hoylake 2/2/1909 d 1956
Ellesmere Port Cement Works
West Kirby
1934 Southport 5
Hoylake
1936 Tranmere Rovers 1
Hoylake

Sherlock, John S RH
b Hanley
Hanley YMCA
1929 1932 Port Vale 48 3
Colwyn Bay United

Sherman, Edward IL
b Liverpool q4 1882
Hudson's (Liverpool)
Chester
1903 Barnsley 3 1
Rotherham Town
Rotherham County
Rotherham Town

Sherman, Frederick Henry (Harry) OR
b Edmonton 16/10/1906 d 1985
Cheshunt
Hampstead Town
1930 1931 Bournemouth & Boscombe Ath 25 4

Sherrington, Jack LH
b Blackburn
Blackburn Vale
1896 Blackburn Rovers 1
1897 Darwen 9
Nelson
Park Road
Great Harwood

Sherry, Alexander Patterson (Alex) LB
b Banknock 8/2/1908 d 1966
Denny Hibernian
1929 1931 Preston North End 14
Olympique Marseille
Leyland Motors

Sherwin, Harry RH/CH
b Walsall 11/10/1893 d 1953
Caps: England Sch
Darlaston
1913 1920 Sunderland 28
1921 1924 Leeds United 98 2
1924 1925 Barnsley 14

Sherwin, Mordecai GK
b Kimberley 26/2/1851 d 1910
1888 Notts County 1

Sherwood, Clifford H OR
b Merthyr Tydfil 21/3/1916
Aberaman Athletic
1937 Wolverhampton Wanderers 0
1938 Hull City 4

Sherwood, George William IL
b Selby 14/3/1917 d 2003
1937 Huddersfield Town 0
1938 Stockport County 39 10
Selby Town
Goole Town

Sherwood, Henry William (Jack) RH
b Reading 3/9/1913 d 1985
Maidenhead United
Islington Corinthians
1938 Reading 9 1
1947 1948 Aldershot 47 5
1949 Crystal Palace 2

Shevlin, Peter GK
b Wishaw 18/11/1905 d 1948
St Mary's (Hamilton)
Uddingston St John's
Pollok Juniors
St Roch's
Celtic
1927 1928 South Shields 66
1929 1930 Nelson 53
Shelbourne
Hamilton Academical
Celtic (loan)
Albion Rovers
Hexham Town
Jarrow
Chopwell Colliery

Shiel, John CF/IL
b Seahouses 13/5/1917
Seahouses
1937 Newcastle United 1
North Shields
1938 Huddersfield Town 1
Seahouses

From To Apps Goal

Shield, John George LH
b South Shields 10/4/1915 d 1981
Durham University
Evenwood Town
Sacriston United
1933 Hartlepools United 0
Bishop Auckland
1935 Liverpool 1
Bishop Auckland
Wolverhampton Wanderers 0
West Bromwich Albion 0

Shields, Ralph CF/IR
b Newbiggin
Choppington
1913 Newcastle United 0
1914 1920 Huddersfield Town 45 21
1920 Exeter City 19 4
1921 Brentford 8 1
Sittingbourne
Blyth Spartans

Shiels, James Patrick (Paddy) OL
b Longford, Ireland 5/2/1909
Ballymoney United
Dunmurry
Ballymena United
Dolphin
Belfast Celtic
1936 1937 New Brighton 57 8
Coleraine
Solihull Town
Ballymoney United

Shiner, Albert James CF
b St Helen's, Isle of Wight 1899 d 1961
Seaview (Isle of Wight)
1920 Derby County 1

Shinner, James Herbert (Bert) CF
b Dudley q4 1877
Dudley
1902 Middlesbrough 0
Aberdeen
1904 Bradford City 4 4
1904 Doncaster Rovers 12 3
Brentford
1905 Bradford City 0
Barrow
1907 Bristol City 0
Southend United
Watford
1909 Bristol City 0
Spennymoor United

Shinton, Bertram IR
b Wednesbury 11/1885
Bilston United
1909 Wolverhampton Wanderers 1 1

Shinton, Frederick (Fred) CF/IR
b Wednesbury 3/1883 d 1923
Hawthorn Villa
Moxley White Star
Wednesbury Old Athletic
Hednesford Town
1904 1907 West Bromwich Albion 64 46
1907 1909 Leicester Fosse 78 51
1910 Bolton Wanderers 7 1
1910 Leicester Fosse 14 5
Wednesbury Old Athletic

Shipley, Arthur OR
1896 Gainsborough Trinity 1

Shipley, Arthur G CF
b Kettering
Desborough Town
1926 Northampton Town 1
Wellingborough Town

Shipley, Thomas LB/RB
b Durham
Hetton Juniors
1930 Portsmouth 0
1931 1932 Gillingham 16 1

Shipman, Thomas Eric Rollason (Tom) LB
b Langwith 4/8/1910 d 1972
Norwood Rangers
Shirebrook
1931 Birmingham 0
1933 1936 Blackpool 36
1937 Reading 2
1938 1945 Oldham Athletic 40
1939 (Oldham Athletic) (3)
Mossley

Shipton, Ronald RB
1939 Northampton Town (1)

From To Apps Goal

Shirlaw, Walter Paterson (Wattie) GK
b Wishaw 24/6/1901 d 1981
Larkhall Thistle
1925 Bradford City 2
1926 Rochdale 0
1927 1931 Bradford City 97
1932 1934 Halifax Town 121
Workington

Shirley, Jack H IL
b Crewe 1902
Whitchurch
1927 1929 Stoke City 30 11
Hednesford Town
Macclesfield

Shirtcliffe, Edward OR
1901 Derby County 4
Ripley Town

Shonakan, Joseph Francis (Joe) OR
b Bolton 29/11/1913 d 1973
Bolton Boys Federation
1931 Bolton Wanderers 0
1932 Rochdale 27 2
1933 Wrexham 4
Horwich RMI
1934 Southport (trial) 1
Chorley
CW Norris (Bolton)

Shone, Daniel (Danny) IL/CF
b Wirral 27/4/1892 d 1974
Earle
Liverpool
Grayson's
1921 1925 Liverpool 76 23
1928 West Ham United 12 5
1928 Coventry City 8 1

Shooter, Francis Arthur CF
b Ilkeston 21/1/1906 d 1980
Ilkeston Town
Ransome & Marles
Newark Town
1930 Notts County 2
1931 Mansfield Town 0
Matlock Town

Shore, Albert Victor (Victor) IR/IL
b Wednesbury q1 1897
Deans Works (Birmingham)
1919 1920 Sunderland 5 1
1921 Stoke 3
Brierley Hill Alliance
Cottage Spring (Wednesbury)
Whitburn

Shore, Ernest William (Ernie) RB
b Wednesbury 12/10/1891
Wednesbury United
Willenhall Swifts
1914 West Bromwich Albion 5
Stourbridge

Shorrock, James OL
1902 Preston North End 1

Shorrock, Richard LB/RB
b Blackburn q2 1901
Brinscall
Darwen
1921 1922 Accrington Stanley 3
Darwen

Short, George Frederick RB/LB
b Birmingham 1866
Unity Gas
1892 1893 Small Heath 18 1
Oldbury Town

Short, James William (Jimmy) IR
b Bedlington 9/12/1911 d 1995
Jarrow
1931 Sheffield Wednesday 2
1933 1934 Brighton & Hove Albion 37 11
1935 Barrow 9 4
South Shields
Walker Celtic
Middle Dock

Short, John James (James) IL/IR/CF
b Hucknall 4/1896
Arnold St Mary's
1919 Birmingham 16 10
1920 1921 Watford 21 7
Ilkeston United
1923 Norwich City 11 3
Newark Town
Lewisons

Short, John Samuel (Sammy) II
b Norbrigg 10/5/1903 d 1955
Seamore
1926 1928 West Bromwich Albion 39 17

From	To	Club	Apps	Goal
Short, Wilfred			IL	
		Bacup		
1907		Burnley	3	
		Nelson		
Short, William (Billy)			LH/IR	
b Gosforth 1893				
		Pandon Temperance		
1919		Leeds City	5	
1921		Hartlepools United	18	
Short, William John			IR	
1936		Gateshead	2	
Shortt, Matthew			IL	
b Dumfries 5/2/1889			d 1974	
		Nithbank		
		Balmoral		
		Skares Burnock		
		Dumfries		
		Dalbeattie Star (loan)		
		Millwall Athletic (trial)		
1910		Woolwich Arsenal	4	
		Kilmarnock		
		Clydebank		
		Kilmarnock		
		Llanelly		
		Fall River Marksmen		
		Brooklyn Wanderers		
		Philadelphia Field Club		
		Boston Wonder Workers		
		Brooklyn Wanderers		
Shotton, Robert (Bob)			LB/RB	
b Witton Gilbert 17/10/1910			d 1999	
		Bearpark		
1927		Durham City	0	
1928		Bolton Wanderers	0	
		West Stanley		
1930		Leeds United	0	
1931		Hartlepools United	33	
1932	1938	Barnsley	221	8
1939		(Barnsley)	(1)	
Shreeve, Frederick Daniel (Fred)			RB	
b Newhall 17/12/1882			d 1962	
		Stanton		
		Newhall Swifts		
		Gresley Rovers		
1905		Burton United	34	
		Millwall Athletic		
		West Ham United		
		Doncaster Rovers		
		Bentley Colliery		
		Methley Perseverance		
Shreeve, John Thomas Thornton (Jack)			RB/LB	
b Boldon 18/8/1917			d 1966	
		Boldon Villa		
1936	1950	Charlton Athletic	145	
1939		(Charlton Athletic)	(1)	
Shrewsbury, Thomas Peace			RH/CH	
b Basford q2 1872			d 1949	
1894		Nottingham Forest	4	
1895		Darwen	3	
1896	1897	Woolwich Arsenal	3	
Shufflebotham, John (Jack)			CH	
b Macclesfield 11/4/1885			d 1951	
		Hanley Town		
		Loughborough Corinthians		
1903		Aston Villa	0	
1904		Notts County	1	
		Old Mill		
1905		Birmingham	1	
1907	1908	Oldham Athletic	7	1
		Portsmouth		
		Southport Central		
Shufflebotham, Thomas			CH	
b Macclesfield q4 1880			d 1959	
1901		Stoke	0	
		Brentford		
1903		Chesterfield Town	33	
		Queen's Park Rangers		
		Rotherham Town		
		Workington		
1907		Oldham Athletic	0	
1907		Lincoln City	0	
		Nuneaton Town		
		Ilkeston United		
Shufflebottom, Frank			LB/RB	
b Chesterfield 9/10/1917				
		Norton Woodseats		
1934		Sheffield United	0	
		Margate		
1938		Ipswich Town	2	
1946		Nottingham Forest	2	
1946	1947	Bradford City	56	

From	To	Club	Apps	Goal
Shutt, George			CH	
b Stoke-on-Trent q4 1861			d 1936	
Caps: England 1				
		Stoke Priory		
1888		Stoke	21	1
		Burslem Port Vale		
		Hanley Town		
Shutt, Hartley (Jack)			RB/LB	
b Burnley 9/11/1874			d 1950	
		Brierfield		
		Nelson		
1895		Bolton Wanderers	0	
		Swindon Town		
		Notts Rangers		
		Millwall Athletic		
1901	1903	Aston Villa	40	
		Hucknall		
		Beasley RCA		
Shuttleworth, Thomas			GK	
1893	1894	Bolton Wanderers	2	
Shuttleworth, W			LH/RH	
1890	1892	Accrington	39	
Sibbald, John Patrick (Jack)			CF/IL/IR	
b Wallsend 12/9/1890			d 1956	
		Walker St Christopher		
		Wallsend Elm Villa		
		Brentford		
1914	1919	Blackpool	59	13
		Wallsend		
		West Stanley		
1921		Blackpool	15	2
1922	1923	Southport	69	16
1924		Walsall	39	12
		Wallsend		
Sibley, Albert (Joe)			OR	
b West Thurrock 6/10/1919			d 2008	
		Barking Town		
1939	1946	Southend United	21	3
1939		(Southend United)	(3)	
1946	1949	Newcastle United	31	6
1950	1955	Southend United	192	36
		Folkestone Town		
Sibley, Eric Seymour			RB/LB/CH	
b Christchurch 17/11/1915			d 1996	
1934		Tottenham Hotspur	0	
1937		Bournemouth & Boscombe Ath	7	
1937	1946	Blackpool	83	
1939		(Blackpool)	(3)	
1947	1948	Grimsby Town	23	
1949		Chester	7	
		Lytham		
Siddle, Reginald Nevison (Reg)			IR/RH	
b Darlington 15/6/1906			d 1995	
		Albert Hill		
1929	1932	Darlington	31	8
		Spennymoor United		
Siddons, E			LB	
1888		Bolton Wanderers	1	
Siddons, William Henry			LB/RB	
b West Bromwich q3 1864			d 1893	
		Aston Villa		
		Excelsior		
		Birmingham St George's		
1891		Darwen	16	1
1892		Walsall Town Swifts	4	
		Redditch		
Sidebottom, James			OL	
1898		Glossop North End	1	
Sidebottom, Walter			OL	
b Hunslet q1 1921			d 1943	
1938		Bolton Wanderers	1	
Sidey, Norman William			CH/RH	
b Nunhead 31/5/1907			d 1969	
		Nunhead		
1932	1937	Arsenal	40	
Sidlow, Cyril			GK	
b Colwyn Bay 26/11/1915			d 2005	
Caps: Wales Amat/Wales War 11/Wales 7				
		Colwyn Bay United		
		Abergele		
		Colwyn Bay United		
		Flint Town		
		Llandudno Town		
1937	1938	Wolverhampton Wanderers	4	
1946	1950	Liverpool	149	
		New Brighton		
1953		Wolverhampton Wanderers	0	
		Sittingbourne		
Sidlow, Eric			GK	
		Wharton Prebyterians		
1913	1914	Bolton Wanderers	19	

From	To	Club	Apps	Goal
Sidney, Hilton			OL	
b Sunderland 14/4/1895			d 1957	
		Horden Athletic		
1920		Luton Town	2	
		Mansfield Town		
Silcock, John (Jack)			LB	
b New Springs 15/1/1898			d 1966	
Caps: FLge 3/England 3				
		Atherton		
1919	1933	Manchester United	423	2
1934		Oldham Athletic (trial)	0	
		Droylsden United		
Silcock, Joseph Ernest (Ernie)			GK	
b Brampton q1 1881				
		Brampton		
1901	1903	Chesterfield Town	18	
		Grassmoor Red Rose		
1905	1906	Chesterfield Town	5	
		Brampton Social		
Silk, George Henry			RB/LB	
b Orrell Park 18/10/1916			d 1969	
		Miranda		
1935	1936	Southport	14	
1937	1950	Plymouth Argyle	86	1
		Newquay		
Sillett, Charles Thomas (Charlie)			RB/LB/CF	
b Plumstead 29/10/1906			d 1945	
		Barking Town		
		Tidworth		
1931	1937	Southampton	175	9
		Guildford City		
Sillito, Henry (Harry)			OL	
b Chester-le-Street 10/7/1901			d 1993	
		Chester-le-Street		
		Washington Colliery		
1921		Chelsea	0	
1922	1923	Lincoln City	48	2
1924		Merthyr Town	19	
		Grantham		
Silto, William Alfred (Billy)			CH	
b Washington q4 1883			d 1959	
		Washington		
		Hebburn Argyle		
1904	1908	Barnsley	92	3
		Swindon Town		
Silverthorne, James			CF	
b Bedminster 3/8/1894			d 1962	
		Harwich & Parkeston		
		Gorleston		
1921		Norwich City	15	6
		Gorleston		
1923		Norwich City	5	1
		Weymouth		
		Parkeston Railway		
		Harwich & Parkeston		
Silverwood, Eric			IR	
b Rochdale 25/7/1906			d 1973	
		Rochdale St Clement's		
1928		Rochdale	2	
Silvester, Bertie Edward			RH	
b Bishops Stortford 14/9/1890			d 1974	
1911		Clapton Orient	1	
Silvester, Walter			IL	
b Sheffield q1 1871				
1893		Rotherham Town	6	1
Simm, William			OR	
b Tyneside				
		Newcastle Rangers		
		Trafalgar (Newcastle)		
1893		Newcastle United	1	
		Hebburn Argyle		
Simmers, W			CH	
1888		Bolton Wanderers	2	
Simmon, Henry (Harry)			OR/LH	
b Bearpark q2 1879			d 1951	
		Bearpark		
		Leadgate Park		
1905	1907	Hull City	17	
Simmonite, Horace			RH/LB	
b Rotherham 1868			d 1914	
1893	1895	Rotherham Town	3	
Simmonite, Wilfred			RH	
b Rotherham 18/11/1895			d 1972	
1919	1920	Rotherham County	8	
		Worksop Town		

From	To	Club	Apps	Goal
Simmons, Charles (Charlie 'Chippy')			IR/CF	
b West Bromwich 9/1878			d 1937	
		Trinity Victoria		
		Oldbury Town		
		Worcester Rovers		
1898	1903	West Bromwich Albion	142	57
		West Ham United		
1905	1906	West Bromwich Albion	36	18
1907		Chesterfield Town	32	7
		Wellington Town		
		Royal Rovers (Canada)		
Simmons, Harvey V			OR	
b Cleethorpes				
1930		Stockport County	2	
Simmons, Henry Richard (Harry)			IR/CF	
b Sunderland 11/12/1908			d 1968	
		Pallion		
		Bankhead Albion		
1928		West Ham United (trial)	0	
1928		Sunderland (trial)	0	
		Bankhead Albion		
1930		Hartlepools United	31	17
1931		Preston North End	8	3
		Chorley		
		Oxford City		
1933		Aldershot	17	3
Simmons, James William (Jim)			IR/OR/IL	
b Blackwell 27/6/1889			d 1972	
		Blackwell Colliery		
1908	1919	Sheffield United	204	43
1920	1921	West Ham United	27	1
Simmons, John			IR	
b Wigan 7/10/1904			d 1977	
		Aspull Amateurs		
1929		Wigan Borough	2	
Simmons, William			OR	
b Sheffield 1879			d 1911	
		Parkgate United		
1899		Sheffield Wednesday	1	
1899		Barnsley	15	6
1900		Sheffield Wednesday	0	
1902		Doncaster Rovers	0	
Simmons, William A			CF	
b Walkden				
1921		Stalybridge Celtic	4	
Simms, Charles (Charlie)			CH	
b Birmingham 12/2/1859			d 1935	
		Calthorpe		
		Mitchell St George's		
1892		Small Heath	1	
Simms, Ernest (Ernie)			CF	
b Scotland 1896				
		Vale of Clyde		
		Clyde		
		Vale of Leven		
		Abercorn		
		Vale of Clyde		
1920		Reading	1	
Simms, Ernest (Ernie)			CF	
b Murton 23/7/1891			d 1971	
Caps: SoLge 1/England 1				
		South Shields Adelaide		
		Murton Colliery Welfare		
1912		Barnsley	0	
1920	1921	Luton Town	65	46
1921	1923	South Shields	48	17
1923	1925	Stockport County	66	20
		Scunthorpe & Lindsey United		
		York City		
		Vauxhall Motors		
Simms, Hedley Arthur			CF	
b Jacksdale 4/6/1913			d 1993	
Caps: England Amat				
		Northern Nomads		
1934		Chester	1	1
		Northern Nomads		
		Wellington Town		
Simms, John			OL	
b Burslem 1903				
		Whitfield Colliery		
		Leek Alexandra		
1926	1930	Port Vale	81	25
1931		Swansea Town	4	2
		Winsford United		
		Macclesfield		
		Northwich Victoria		
Simms, Robert			LH	
b Horsforth 13/5/1896				
		Castleford Town		
1923		Halifax Town	2	

From To Apps Goal

Simms, Samuel (Sammy) RH/CF
b Atherton q1 1888 d 1952
Tyldesley Colliery
Ton Pentre
Atherton
1912 Everton 2 1
Swindon Town
1914 Leicester Fosse 16 5
1920 Swindon Town 11 3
1921 Gillingham 7 1

Simms, Willard CF
b Mansfield q4 1891 d 1935
South Normanton Colliery
1913 Nottingham Forest 3

Simon, Frank Wilfred CH
b Nantwich q3 1899 d 1956
1919 Manchester City 0
Crewe Alexandra
Altrincham
1920 1921 Port Vale 10 1
Winsford United
Nantwich

Simons, Henry Thomas (Tommy) IL/IR/CF
b Hackney 26/11/1887 d 1956
Peel Institute
1905 1906 Clapton Orient 7 1
Tufnell Park
Leyton
Doncaster Rovers
1910 1911 Sheffield United 9 2
Halifax Town
Merthyr Town
Brentford
1914 Fulham 9 4
Queen's Park Rangers
1920 Norwich City 3
Margate

Simons, Reuben Rhys CH
b Swansea 16/10/1908 d 1991
Beaufort (Gorseinon)
1933 1938 Swansea Town 107
1939 Northampton Town (3)
Llanelly

Simpson, Albert IR/IL
b Salford
1921 Manchester City 1
1923 Bournemouth & Boscombe Ath 12 3
Peterborough & Fletton United

Simpson, Charles Fred (Freddy) IL/OL
b Lincon q3 1882 d 1961
Midland Athletic
1902 1907 Lincoln City 124 37
Newark Town
Worksop Town

Simpson, Daniel IL/CF/CH
b Burslem
Tunstall Town
1895 1902 Burslem Port Vale 83 23

Simpson, Edwin LH
b Bristol 20/12/??
Ton Pentre
1921 Barrow 25

Simpson, Edwin LH
b Chilton 21/1/1909 d 1973
Chilton Colliery Recreation Athletic
1926 Blackburn Rovers (trial) 0
1926 1927 Nelson 17
1928 Crewe Alexandra 0
Craghead United
South Moor Colliery

Simpson, Frank CH
b Manchester
Belsize Athletic
1921 Crewe Alexandra 10 1

Simpson, Francis Larratt (Frank) OR
b Syston q1 1880 d 1953
Syston Victoria
1902 Leicester Fosse (trial) 0
Leicester Imperial
1903 Leicester Fosse 2
Humberstone Victoria
Leicester Imperial
Syston Victoria
Thursday Excelsior
Melton Mowbray
Leicester Nomads
Wand's United
Hinckley United

Simpson, Frederick Hall (Fred) RH/CH
b Fulwell, County Durham 18/7/1908 d 1990
Marsden Colliery Welfare
1930 1932 Coventry City 14

Simpson, George OL/LH
b Jarrow 1883
Jarrow
1902 1908 Sheffield Wednesday 141 31
1908 1910 West Bromwich Albion 19 5
North Shields

Simpson, George Robert RB/LB
b Newbold q2 1876 d 1955
Sheepbridge
1897 1899 Sheffield United 10
1901 1902 Doncaster Rovers 64 2
1903 Chesterfield Town 21
Rotherham Town

Simpson, H RB
1893 Rotherham Town 2

Simpson, Harry OR
b Scotland 1864
East Stirlingshire
1889 Stoke 10 3
Forfar Athletic

Simpson, Harry RH/CH
b Stoke-on-Trent 1875
1895 Crewe Alexandra 26 2
1896 Stoke 8
New Brighton Tower

Simpson, Henry Coutts (Harry) IR
b Peterhead 10/10/1888 d 1951
Peterhead
St Bernard's
1909 Leicester Fosse 7 1
Raith Rovers
Ayr United
East Stirlingshire

Simpson, Herbert LB
b Sleaford q4 1863 d 1929
Lincoln Rovers
1893 Lincoln City 3

Simpson, Herbert OL
b Nantwich 24/2/1900 d 1966
Nantwich
1921 1923 Bolton Wanderers 9 1
1924 1925 Wigan Borough 69 7
Nantwich
Congleton Town
Stalybridge Celtic
Winsford United

Simpson, Hugh IR
Shettleston
Bo'ness
1904 Glossop 10 2
Raith Rovers
Leith Athletic
Abercorn
Cowdenbeath

Simpson, John (Jock) OR
b Pendleton 25/12/1886 d 1959
Caps: SLge 1/FLge 5/England 8
Grange Rovers
Laurieston Juniors
Rangers (trial)
Falkirk
1910 1914 Blackburn Rovers 151 16
Falkirk

Simpson, John (Johnny) CF
b Glasgow 2/2/1908 d 1999
Maryhill Juniors
Partick Thistle
1932 Plymouth Argyle 5 2
Ayr United
Stranraer
Sligo Rovers
Stranraer

Simpson, John W IL
Lincoln Rovers
1919 Lincoln City 4
Scunthorpe & Lindsey United
Grantham

Simpson, Joseph W (Joe) LB/RB
1894 1895 Lincoln City 21
Newark Town
Kettering
1896 1897 Lincoln City 41
St Mary's (Lincoln)
1899 1900 Lincoln City 8

Simpson, Peter CF
b Leith 13/11/1904 d 1974
Leith Amateurs
St Bernard's
Kettering Town
1929 1934 Crystal Palace 180 154
1935 1936 West Ham United 32 12
1937 Reading 19 4

Simpson, Peter IR/IL
Fraserburgh
1933 1934 Plymouth Argyle 6 1
Ayr United
1937 1938 Aldershot 37 5

Simpson, Robert (Bobby) OR/OL
b Bishop Auckland 15/9/1915 d 1994
West Auckland
1936 1946 Darlington 96 14
1939 (Darlington) (3)
1947 Hartlepools United 13 1
Stockton

Simpson, Robert Albert (Bobby) IR/IL
b Chorlton-cum-Hardy q3 1888
Westburn (Aberdeen)
Aberdeen
1910 1912 Bradford Park Avenue 53 8
Brighton & Hove Albion

Simpson, Robert Henry (Bobby) RB/LB
b Redcar q2 1889
Redcar Juniors
Old Corinthians
Teesside Amateurs
South Bank
1910 Blackburn Rovers (trial) 0
Grangetown Athletic
1911 Bradford City (trial) 0
1912 1914 Everton 21
1921 Wrexham 24
Chester

Simpson, Samuel (Sam) LB
b Bothwell 28/2/1914 d 1992
Shettleston Rovers
1936 Hull City 0
1937 Accrington Stanley 26
1938 1945 Barrow 42
1939 (Barrow) (3)

Simpson, Thomas (Tom) OL/OR
b Keyworth 13/8/1879 d 1961
Keyworth
1899 1901 Notts County 7
1902 Leicester Fosse 27 5
1903 Everton 1
Nelson

Simpson, Thomas (Tommy) CF/CH/OR
b 1880
Cross Heath
1900 Stoke 0
1901 1904 Burslem Port Vale 51 16
1904 1905 Bury 20 8
Stafford Rangers
Hanley Swifts

Simpson, Thomas M (Tommy) OR
b Dundee 1904
Dundee Osborne
Dundee United
1927 Brighton & Hove Albion 30 6
Montrose

Simpson, Vivien Sumner, MC IL/IR/CF
b Sheffield q1 1883 d 1918
Sheffield
1901 1906 Sheffield Wednesday 30 8
Sheffield
Norwich City
Northern Nomads

Simpson, Walter LB
1897 Lincoln City 2

Simpson, William (Billy) LB/CH
b Sunderland 1878 d 1962
Selbourne
1898 Sunderland 3 1
1902 1907 Lincoln City 140

Simpson, William (Billy) OL
b Jarrow 26/1/1907 d 1970
Howdon British Legion
Jarrow
1928 Sheffield Wednesday 0
Jarrow
1929 Barrow 8 2
Washington Colliery Welfare
1929 1936 Nottingham Forest 229 36
Jarrow
North Shields

Simpson, William Stewart LH
b Annan 1897
Solway Star
1921 Blackburn Rovers 4
Aberaman Athletic
Aberavon
Morton

Simpson, William Swan (Billy) LH/IL
b Cowdenbeath 1/5/1907 d 1986
Donibristle Colliery
Cowdenbeath YMCA
Fulford White Rose
Dunbar
Musselburgh Bruntonians
Clyde
1931 1934 Aston Villa 29 1
Cowdenbeath
1936 Northampton Town 42
1937 1938 Walsall 67 4
Bromsgrove Rovers

Sims, Stephen CH/CF
b Bedminster 11/12/1895 d 1973
Bath City
1914 Leicester Fosse 11 2
1920 1921 Bristol Rovers 66 8
1922 1923 Burnley 11
Weymouth
1925 Bristol City 0
1926 Bristol Rovers 13 1
1927 Newport County 4

Sims, Sydney OL
b West Yorkshire 1916
Hatfield Main Colliery
Thorne Colliery
1934 Hull City 3
Scarborough
Boston United
Peterborough United
Ollerton Colliery

Sims, Thomas LB
b Hawthorn, County Durham 22/11/1900 d 1985
Shildon Athletic
1922 Durham City 1

Sinclair, Archibald RH
1898 Darwen 1

Sinclair, Finlay LB
b Glasgow 18/6/1871
Clutha Swifts
Elderslie
Linthouse
Rangers
1896 Woolwich Arsenal 26
Bristol City

Sinclair, Harry RB/LB
b High Park 9/5/1900 d 1983
Park Royal
Albion
Norwood Crescent
1921 1923 Southport 31
Bangor City
Winsford United
Burscough Rangers

Sinclair, Robert Dunlop OR
b Winchburgh 29/6/1915 d 1993
Musselburgh Athletic
Heat of Midlothian
Musselburgh Athletic
Falkirk
1939 1945 Chesterfield (2)
1946 1947 Darlington 68 11

Sinclair, Thomas (Tommy) RH/LH
b Southport 27/8/1897 d 1967
Southport Central
Norwood Crescent
1919 Port Vale 0
1921 1929 Southport 320 21
Macclesfield
Nelson
Burscough Rangers

Sinclair, Thomas Mackie RB
b Alva 13/3/1907
Alva Albion Rovers
Celtic
1928 1929 South Shields 84
1930 1932 Gateshead 91 1
Alloa Athletic (trial)

Sinclair, Thomas McKenzie IR
Shettleston
1938 Bolton Wanderers 10 5

Sinclair, Thomas S GK
b Glasgow
Rutherglen Glencairn
Morton
Rangers
Celtic (loan)
1906 1911 Newcastle United 8
Dumbarton Harp
Dunfermline Athletic
Stevenston United
Kilmarnock
Stevenston United

From	To	Club	Apps	Goal
Singleton, Albert			CF	
1919		Preston North End	0	
1920		Bury	0	
1921		Stalybridge Celtic	1	
Singleton, Edward Alfred (Ted)			CF	
b Hackney 27/11/1919			d 2002	
1938		Southend United	2	
Singleton, Harry Bertram			OL	
b Prescot q4 1877			d 1948	
1900		Stockport County	1	
1900		Bury	0	
1901		Everton	3	
1902		Grimsby Town	18	2
		New Brompton		
		Queen's Park Rangers		
1905	1906	Leeds City	45	7
		Huddersfield Town		
Singleton, Herbert			GK	
b Manchester 6/1900			d 1958	
		Manchester Central		
1923		Aston Villa	2	
Singleton, James (Jim)			IR	
b Egremont, Cumberland 11/3/1917			d 1999	
1934		West Bromwich Albion	0	
1936		Accrington Stanley	5	
1936		Carlisle United	1	
1937		Bournemouth & Boscombe Ath	0	
Singleton, Stephen Smith			LB	
b Earby q4 1866			d 1915	
1888		Accrington	4	
1894		Sheffield United	0	
Singleton, Thomas			IR	
1895		Darwen	1	
Sinkinson, Frederick (Fred)			OR	
b Middleton 1916				
		Buxton		
		Manchester North End		
1937		Oldham Athletic	2	
Sinning, Arthur Edward			OL	
b Tottenham 30/4/1901			d 1985	
1922		Tottenham Hotspur	0	
1923		Gillingham	12	2
1925		Clapton Orient	0	
Sinton, Leslie Warnford			OR	
b Newcastle 30/12/1915				
1938		Gateshead	3	
Sisson, Thomas (Tom)			LB/RB/LH	
b Basford 19/10/1894			d 1976	
		Players Athletic		
		Ripley's Athletic		
1914		Notts County	3	
		Hucknall Byron		
1920	1922	Gillingham	73	
1923		Barrow (trial)	2	
1923	1925	Lincoln City	75	1
		Peterborough & Fletton United		
		Sutton Town		
Sissons, Albert Edward			OR	
b Kiveton Park 5/7/1903			d 1975	
		Kiveton Park Colliery		
1922		Arsenal (trial)	0	
1923	1925	Doncaster Rovers	80	2
1925	1927	Leeds United	30	1
1928		Southport	30	3
1929		Northampton Town	19	4
		Worksop Town		
Sissons, Henry Peter			CF	
b Worksop q2 1874			d 1961	
1892		Burton Swifts	3	2
		Worksop Town		
1894		Notts County	0	
		Mansfield Town		
Sissons, William Stanley (Bill)			GK	
b Kiveton Park 1/2/1901			d 1988	
		Kiveton Park		
1924	1925	Lincoln City	74	
Siviter, Elijah (Eli)			RH	
b Clowne 11/12/1910			d 1993	
		Langwith Colliery		
		Shirebrook		
1932	1933	Mansfield Town	2	
		Ollerton Colliery		
		Ripley Town		
		Ilkeston Town		
		Sutton Town		
		Creswell Colliery		
Skaife, Samuel (Sam)			RH/LH	
b Otley 10/2/1909			d 1981	
		Yeadon Celtic		
1932		Bradford Park Avenue	2	
1934	1936	Rochdale	60	

From	To	Club	Apps	Goal
Skea, David Findlay			IL	
b Arbroath 5/10/1870			d 1939	
		Arbroath		
1892		Aston Villa	1	1
		Dundee Thistle		
1893		Darwen	1	
		Bury		
1894	1895	Leicester Fosse	45	29
		Swindon Town		
		Chatham		
		New Brompton		
		Cowes		
Skene, (Dr) Leslie Henderson			GK	
b Larbert 22/8/1882				
Caps: SLge 1/IrLge 1/Scotland 1				
		George Watson's College		
		Edinburgh University		
		Queen's Park		
		Hibernian		
		Stenhousemuir		
		Queen's Park		
		Stenhousemuir		
1907	1909	Fulham	88	
		Glentoran		
Skermer, Herbert Edward			GK	
b Selston 19/2/1896			d 1954	
		Hartshay Colliery		
1920	1921	Norwich City	67	
		Ramsgate		
		Coalville Swifts		
		Loughborough Corinthians		
Skidmore, Joseph (Joe)			IL	
1930		Darlington	2	
Skillen, James (Jim)			IL	
b Ballochmyle 27/5/1893				
		Auchinleck Talbot		
		Kilmarnock		
1924		Accrington Stanley	25	8
1925		Barrow	28	14
		Morton		
		Royal Albert		
Skiller, Leon Ferdinand (Len)			GK	
b Madron 30/9/1885			d 1964	
		Leytonstone		
		Leyton		
1908		Aston Villa	1	
1920	1921	Swindon Town	70	
		Truro City		
Skinner, Albert James			LB	
b Burslem q1 1868				
1892		Burslem Port Vale	1	
Skinner, George Watson Smith			LH/IR	
b Camlachie 14/10/1897			d 1946	
		Saltcoats Victoria		
		Strathclyde Juniors		
		Eastern Athletic		
		Skatby Clyde		
		Armadale		
1920		Blackburn Rovers	0	
1921	1922	Southport	16	
Skinner, Henry (Harry)			LH	
b Windsor 1878				
		Windsor		
		Uxbridge		
		Queen's Park Rangers		
1901		Grimsby Town	1	
		Queen's Park Rangers		
Skinner, James Frederick (Jimmy)			LH/RH	
b Beckenham 11/10/1898			d 1984	
		Beckenham		
1919	1925	Tottenham Hotspur	89	3
Skitt, Harry			CH/RH	
b Portobello, Staffordshire 26/6/1901			d 1976	
		Darlaston		
		Northfleet		
1924	1930	Tottenham Hotspur	212	
1931	1935	Chester	101	
		Congleton Town		
Skull, Frank William			RH/LH	
b Swindon 26/10/1902			d 1977	
1922		Middlesbrough	0	
1923		Merthyr Town	3	
		Scunthorpe & Lindsey United		
1930	1931	Rotherham United	39	1
		Newark Town		
		Scunthorpe & Lindsey United		

From	To	Club	Apps	Goal
Slack, Samuel (Sam)			RB	
b Skegby q4 1907				
		Sutton Town		
		Frickley Colliery		
		Shirebrook		
1928		Charlton Athletic	3	
		Mansfield Town		
		Sutton Town		
		Edwinstowe Welfare		
Slack, William (Bill)			LH/OL	
b Skegby 20/1/1906			d 1989	
		Sutton Junction		
		Shirebrook		
		Sutton Junction		
1927		Blackpool	0	
1927		Nelson	10	3
1928		Portsmouth	0	
1929		Merthyr Town	42	5
1930		Norwich City	29	2
1932	1935	Mansfield Town	120	1
		Sutton Town		
		Ripley Town		
Slade, Donald			CF/IR	
b Southampton 26/11/1888			d 1980	
		Shirley Warren		
		Southampton Ramblers		
1908		Blackpool (trial)	0	
		Southampton		
1912	1913	Lincoln City	23	9
1913		Woolwich Arsenal	12	4
1914		Fulham	17	4
		Dumbarton		
		Dundee		
		Ayr United		
		Dundee United		
Slade, Howard Charles (Charlie)			RH/LH/IR	
b Bath 29/1/1891			d 1971	
		Bath City		
		Stourbridge		
1913		Aston Villa	3	
1913	1922	Huddersfield Town	111	6
1922	1924	Middlesbrough	68	2
1925	1926	Darlington	23	
		Folkestone		
Slade, Ralph (Reg)			RB/LB	
b Amersham q2 1896			d 1983	
		Amersham		
1920	1929	Watford	119	
Slater, Frank			OR	
b Blackburn q2 1907				
1925		Bolton Wanderers	0	
1926	1927	Accrington Stanley	17	1
		Stalybridge Celtic		
1930		Manchester City	0	
		Manchester Central		
		Hurst		
		Stalybridge Celtic		
Slater, George			IL	
b Walsall 1864				
		Hanley United		
1888		Stoke	2	1
Slater, Harold			OL	
b Bradford 1900				
		Saltaire		
		Harrogate AFC		
1921	1922	Hull City	3	
		Castleford Town		
		Scunthorpe & Lindsey United		
Slater, Herbert			IL	
b Langley Mill 11/11/1881			d 1958	
		Creswell Colliery		
1901		Chesterfield Town	1	
		Shirebrook		
		Creswell United		
		Langwith Colliery		
Slater, Herbert			CF	
b Aston q2 1888				
		Atherstone Town		
		Stourbridge		
1909		Aston Villa	0	
1910		Nottingham Forest	2	
Slater, John (MP) (Jack)			LB	
b Adlington 6/4/1889			d 1935	
		Adlington		
1906	1912	Bolton Wanderers	92	
		South Liverpool		
Slater, John Albert (Jackie)			IL	
b Sheffield q1 1899			d 1961	
1920	1921	Swansea Town	10	3
1922	1924	Southend United	92	15
		Grays Thurrock		

From	To	Club	Apps	Goal
Slater, Percival (Percy)			LB/RB	
b Adlington q1 1879				
1898		Blackburn Rovers	0	
		Chorley		
1900	1903	Manchester City	20	
1904	1905	Bury	28	
		Oldham Athletic		
		Chorley		
Slater, Thomas			OL	
1891		Darwen	7	
Slater, Thomas Arthur W (Arthur)			GK	
b Chester-le-Street 25/2/1908			d 1976	
		Horden Colliery		
		Easington Colliery		
		Murton Colliery Welfare		
1926	1929	Clapton Orient	20	
1930	1931	Port Vale	20	
1932	1933	Watford	29	
		Vauxhall Motors		
Slavin, Hugh			LB/RB	
b Kirkdale q2 1882			d 1947	
		Birkenhead		
1904	1909	Sheffield Wednesday	48	
Sleight, Harold			GK	
b Sleaford 2/7/1907				
1936		Carlisle United	9	
1937	1938	Rotherham United	51	
Slemin, Jack C			OL	
b Ireland				
Caps: Ireland Amat/Ireland 1				
		Bohemians		
1909		Bradford City	3	
		Distillery		
Slicer, John (Jackie)			OL	
b Bramley 24/11/1902			d 1979	
		Bullcroft Main Colliery		
1923		Doncaster Rovers	0	
1924		Chesterfield	0	
		Mexborough Town		
1926		Huddersfield Town	7	2
1927	1929	Norwich City	125	12
1930	1931	Luton Town	45	13
		Ashton National		
1933		York City	6	
1934		Bury	0	
Slicer, Walter			LB	
1932		Luton Town	0	
1933		Rochdale	4	
		Oswestry Town		
1935		Crewe Alexandra	0	
Sliman, Allan Melrose			CH	
b Busby 27/2/1906			d 1945	
		Arthurlie		
1928	1931	Bristol City	136	1
1931	1937	Chesterfield	241	9
		Chelmsford City		
Slinger, James William (Bill)			CF	
b Leeds 13/8/1906			d 1978	
		Army		
1931	1934	Carlisle United	80	54
1935		Accrington Stanley	2	
Sloan, Andrew S			CF	
b Ireland				
Caps: Ireland Amat/Ireland 1				
		Cliftonville		
		London Caledonians		
1924		Charlton Athletic	1	
1925		Millwall	0	
		Catford Wanderers		
Sloan, Donald			GK	
b Rankinston 31/7/1883			d 1917	
Caps: IrLge 1				
		Distillery		
1906	1907	Everton	6	
1908		Liverpool	6	
		Distillery		
Sloan, Francis John (Frank)			IR	
b Chapelhall 26/12/1904			d 1974	
		Shieldmuir Celtic		
1923	1935	Plymouth Argyle	207	49
1935	1936	Luton Town	4	

From To Apps Goal

Sloan, Josiah Walter (Paddy) RH/IR/IL
b Lurgan 30/4/1920 d 1993
Caps: Ireland War 1/Ireland 1/Eire 2
Glenavon
1937 Manchester United 0
1939 Tranmere Rovers (3) (2)
1946 1947 Arsenal 33 1
1947 Sheffield United 12 2
AC Milan
Torino
Udinese
Brescia
1951 Norwich City 6
Peterborough United
Rabat (Malta)
Hastings United
Lockheed Leamington
Bath City

Sloan, Thomas OR
b Craghead 11/9/1905 d 1987
Craghead United
1928 Southampton 1

Sloan, Thomas Milne (Tom) CH
b Portadown 23/9/1898
Caps: IrLge 1/Ireland 11
Crusaders
Linfield
1924 1928 Cardiff City 79 1
Linfield

Sloane, James (Jimmy) CF
b Glasgow 1864
Rangers
1888 Stoke 11 2
Rangers

Sloane, John Joseph (Joe) GK
b Preston
1920 Preston North End 0
Morecambe
1921 1922 Accrington Stanley 33
Morecambe

Sloley, Richard (Dick) IR
b Barnstaple 20/8/1891 d 1946
Caps: England Amat
Corinthians
Cambridge University
Brentford
Corinthians
1919 Aston Villa 2
Corinthians
Ealing

Sly, Harold LH/IR/LB
b Appley Bridge 26/2/1904
Rover Motor Company
1922 Birmingham 0
Tamworth Castle
1927 1928 Gillingham 15 1
1929 1932 Brighton & Hove Albion 22
FC Sete

Smailes, Andrew (Andy) LH/IL/CH
b Radcliffe, Northumberland 21/5/1895 d 1978
Blyth Spartans
1919 1922 Newcastle United 73 30
1922 1923 Sheffield Wednesday 37 13
1923 1928 Bristol City 162 14
1929 1931 Rotherham United 26 1

Smailes, James (Jimmy) OL
b South Moor 9/6/1907 d 1986
Tow Law Town
1927 1930 Huddersfield Town 32 8
1930 1931 Tottenham Hotspur 16 3
1932 1934 Blackpool 92 23
1935 Grimsby Town 10
1936 1937 Stockport County 63 17
1938 Bradford City 34 13
1939 (Bradford City) (2)
Waterhouses Sports Club

Smailes, Matthew (Matt) RH/CH
b Milkwell Burn 25/3/1899 d 1946
Annfield Plain
1925 1926 Blackburn Rovers 4
1928 West Ham United 7
1930 Coventry City 11
Ashington

Smale, Douglas Martin OL
b Victoria, London 27/3/1916 d 2006
Kingstonian
1936 1938 Chelsea 9

Small, Horace Hardman OR
b Connah's Quay 10/11/1914 d 1990
Caps: Wales Sch
Flint Amateurs
Connah's Quay & Shotton
1937 1938 New Brighton 60 2

From To Apps Goal

Small, John (Jack) RH
b South Bank 29/10/1889 d 1946
South Bank North End
Craghead United
1912 Sunderland 1
Southampton
Thorneycrofts
Mid-Rhondda
Harland & Wolff

Small, Samuel John (Sam) CF/LH/RB
b Birmingham 15/5/1912 d 1993
Bromsgrove Rovers
1934 1936 Birmingham 6
1936 1947 West Ham United 108 39
1947 1949 Brighton & Hove Albion 38

Small, Thomas OR
b Scarborough 2/9/1907 d 1993
Scarborough
1930 Aston Villa 0
1931 Mansfield Town 2
Scarborough

Smalley, Arthur LH/OL/IR
b Scunthorpe
Scunthorpe & Lindsey United
1929 1932 Blackpool 23 1
Scunthorpe & Lindsey United

Smalley, Leslie Wilfred OR
b Blackburn 10/9/1911 d 1983
Audley Range
Clitheroe
1931 1932 Oldham Athletic 20 5
1933 Southport (trial) 0
1933 Accrington Stanley (trial) 0
Hereford United
Clitheroe
Morecambe
Moffatt's Works

Smalley, Robert Edwin GK
b Darwen q2 1867 d 1947
Preston North End
1888 1890 Everton 36

Smalley, Thomas (Tom) RB/RH/LH
b Kinsley 13/1/1912 d 1984
Caps: England 1
South Kirkby Colliery
1931 1937 Wolverhampton Wanderers 179 11
1938 Norwich City 42 1
1939 (Norwich City) (3)
1945 1950 Northampton Town 200 2
Lower Gornal

Smalley, William (Bill) IR
b Lancaster 1864
1888 Preston North End 0
1888 Stoke (loan) 1

Smallman, Francis Joseph Bruce (Frank) OR
b Gainsborough q1 1869 d 1941
St John's (Lincoln)
1892 Lincoln City 22 17
Burton Wanderers
1894 1895 Lincoln City 36 6

Smallwood, Frederick (Fred) OL
b Brynteg 16/9/1910
Caps: Wales Amat
Llanerch Celts
1933 Wrexham 1 1
1934 Chester 1
Macclesfield
1936 1937 Southampton 48 10
1938 Reading 40 10
1939 (Reading) (3) (2)

Smallwood, William RH
1893 Crewe Alexandra 2

Smart, Bertie LB
b Hednesford q1 1891
Hednesford St Mary's
Hednesford Town
1912 Wolverhampton Wanderers 3
Cannock Town
Bloxwich Strollers

Smart, Ernest (Ernie) OL
b Kinsley
Frickley Colliery
1923 1924 Barnsley 3
1924 Doncaster Rovers 0

Smart, Frederick L IL
b Birmingham
1921 Wolverhampton Wanderers 3 1

Smart, George W RB
b Bristol 1890
Treharris
1919 Stoke 4
Stafford Rangers

From To Apps Goal

Smart, Herbert Horace IL
b Smethwick 4/1892 d 1951
Bilston United
1913 Aston Villa 1
1919 Wolverhampton Wanderers 4 1
Willenhall
Dudley Town

Smart, Leonard OL
1937 Wolverhampton Wanderers 0
1938 Port Vale 13 5
1945 Bournemouth & Boscombe Ath 0

Smart, Thomas (Tommy) RB
b Blackheath, Worcestershire 20/9/1896 d 1968
Caps: FLge 1/England 5
Blackheath Town
Halesowen
1919 1932 Aston Villa 405 8
Brierley Hill Alliance

Smeaton, Alexander Richardson (Alec) LH/IL/RH
b South Shields 27/9/1900 d 1956
Middle Dock
Hebburn Colliery
1923 Bristol Rovers 4 1
1925 1927 Halifax Town 77 6
1928 Torquay United 27 4
1929 Luton Town 6
1930 Gillingham 3

Smeaton, John Raymond (Jock) IL
b Perth 29/7/1914 d 1984
Scone Thistle
St Johnstone
1936 1937 Blackburn Rovers 38 9
1938 Sunderland 28 4
1939 (Sunderland) (3)
Jeanfield Swifts
Albion Rovers
East Fife
St Johnstone

Smedley, James Henry (Jimmy) LH/RH
b Stapleford 12/7/1904 d 1979
Sandiacre Swifts
1923 Notts County 0
Worksop Town
Johnson & Barnes Athletic
Chester (trial)
1926 Bolton Wanderers (trial) 0
1927 1934 New Brighton 279 12
Johnson & Barnes Athletic

Smellie, Richard David (David) CF
b Scotland
Albion Rovers
1895 Nottingham Forest 16 3
1896 Newcastle United 26 15
Bristol Eastville Rovers

Smellie, Robert LB
1893 Walsall Town Swifts 14

Smellie, Robert J LB
b Dalziel 15/10/1865
Caps: Scotland 6
Clydesdale Colts
Hamilton Academical
Queen's Park
1892 Sunderland 23
Queen's Park
Motherwell
St Bernard's

Smelt, Alfred (Alf) LB
b Rotherham 1888
Mansfield Mechanics
Chesterfield Town
Mexborough Town
1920 Leeds United 1

Smelt, John William (Jack) OR
b Rotherham q4 1895 d 1968
Mansfield Mechanics
Chesterfield Municipal
1919 Rotherham County 0
1920 Portsmouth 1
1920 1921 Sheffield Wednesday 16 2
Bangor City
1922 Barrow 0
Thatched House
Bradgate WMC

From To Apps Goal

Smelt, Leonard (Len) RB
b Rotherham 10/12/1883 d 1933
Kimberworth Wesleyans
Rotherham Main Institute
Rotherham County
1908 Gainsborough Trinity 7 1
Sutton Junction
Rotherham Town
Masbrough Thursday
Rotherham County
Chesterfield Town
1919 1924 Burnley 229
1926 Barrow 37
Frickley Colliery
Scunthorpe & Lindsey United (trial)
Hurst

Smelt, Thomas (Tom) IR/CF
b Rotherham 25/11/1900 d 1980
Mexborough Town
Chesterfield Municipal
Rotherham Town
1920 Burnley 0
Wombwell
1922 1923 Accrington Stanley 40 16
1924 Exeter City 5 1
1925 Chesterfield 3 1
Morecambe
1927 Manchester City 2 1
1929 Oldham Athletic 2
1930 Crewe Alexandra 37 11
Scunthorpe & Lindsey United
1932 Rotherham United 2

Smethams, John Charles (Charlie) OL/OR
b Congleton 1886
Congleton Town
1907 1909 Burnley 60 4
1910 Blackburn Rovers 3
Southport Central

Smethurst, Henry (Harry) CH
b Burnley q2 1893
1921 Accrington Stanley 8

Smiles, James (Jimmy) RB
b North Shields 1900
Preston Colliery
1928 1930 Carlisle United 43
North Shields

Smiles, Thomas W (Tom) IL
19th Regiment (York)
1929 York City 8

Smirk, Alfred Henry (Alf) IR/OR
b Penshaw 14/3/1917 d 1996
Caps: England Sch
1936 Sheffield Wednesday 0
Sunderland District Omnibus Co
1938 1947 Southend United 100 26
1939 (Southend United) (3)
1947 Gateshead 11 4
Chingford Town
Tonbridge
Brush Sports

Smith, A Joseph RH
1927 Merthyr Town 11 4

Smith, A Richard (Dickie) LH
b Newcastle-under-Lyme 1890
Newcastle Town
Crewe Alexandra
1919 1922 Stoke 107 2

Smith, Abraham (Abe) RH/LH
b Mansfield 17/12/1910 d 1974
Mansfield Town
1931 1938 Portsmouth 75
1939 (Portsmouth) (3)

Smith, Albert RH
1891 Blackburn Rovers 7

Smith, Albert LH
1899 Loughborough 1

Smith, Albert OL
b Burnley 28/4/1887 d 1929
Caps: FLge 1
Foulridge
Healey Wood
1905 1908 Burnley 105 21
1908 1909 Bradford Park Avenue 55 10
Rochdale
1919 1921 Grimsby Town 89 15
1923 1924 Rochdale 13

Smith, Albert RB
b Sheffield
Silverwood Colliery
1920 Grimsby Town 1
Charlton's (Grimsby)

From To Apps Goal

Smith, Albert CF
1923 Millwall Athletic 1

Smith, Albert GK
Brodsworth Colliery
1924 Doncaster Rovers 3
Wombwell
1928 Leicester City 0
1929 Watford 5
Denaby United

Smith, Albert A CF
b Bolsover 1911
1930 Sheffield Wednesday 0
1931 Gillingham 2 1

Smith, Albert Charles OR/CF/IR
b Drumoyne 1905
Barclay Curle Athletic
Third Lanark (trial)
Petershill
1926 Manchester United 5 1
1927 1930 Preston North End 39 10
Morton (trial)
Dolphin
1932 Carlisle United 33 1
Glenavon
Belfast Celtic
Derry City
Ayr United

Smith, Albert W RH
b Nottingham 23/7/1869 d 1921
Caps: England 3
Notts Rangers
Long Eaton Rangers
Derby County
Nottingham Forest
1889 Notts County 4
1892 1893 Nottingham Forest 26 1

Smith, Albert William Thomas (Bertie) CH/CF/RH
b Camberwell 22/4/1900 d 1957
Nunhead
1922 1925 Huddersfield Town 12 1
1926 Bradford City 17 5
Rhyl Athletic
Bangor City
1928 Bournemouth & Boscombe Ath 28
Streatham Town

Smith, Alexander (Alec) IR/LH
b Old Kilpatrick 7/11/1873 d 1908
St Mirren
1895 1896 Lincoln City 45 9
Third Lanark
Swindon Town

Smith, Alexander CF
b Buckie 17/1/1915
Buckie Thistle
1937 Liverpool 1
1939 Crewe Alexandra 0

Smith, Alexander Mason (Alec) RH/CH
b Scotland 1911
Vickerstown Athletic
1930 1932 Barrow 4
Lancaster Town

Smith, Alexander McDO RH
b Forfar 1915
Hall, Russell & Co
Forfar Athletic
Forfar East End
1937 Wrexham 6
Forfar Athletic

Smith, Alfred (Alf) IL
b Longton 1880
1902 Burton United 0
1903 1905 Stoke 3
Wrexham
Crewe Alexandra
Stoke

Smith, Alfred (Alf) IL
b Bury 1890
Bury Tradesmen
1909 1910 Bury 5 3
Stalybridge Celtic
Hamilton Academical
Stalybridge Celtic

Smith, Alfred Roy (Alf) RH
b Elswick 19/2/1904 d 1985
Scotswood
South Benwell
Felling Colliery
1924 Liverpool 0
1926 Southport 5
Scotswood
Consett
Throckley Welfare

Smith, Alfred William CF/IR
b Langley Green q4 1890 d 1958
Langley Green Juniors
Crosswells Brewery
1912 1914 Birmingham 54 33
1919 1922 West Bromwich Albion 79 20
1922 1923 Stoke 5
1923 Wigan Borough 3 1

Smith, Andrew CF/IL
b Slamannan 12/1877
East Stirlingshire
Vale of Garron
1898 Stoke 0
1899 Newton Heath 0
1900 1902 West Bromwich Albion 23 8
Bristol Rovers
Millwall Athletic
Swindon Town
Leyton
Bristol Rovers
East Stirlingshire
Wednesbury Old Athletic
Brierley Hill Alliance

Smith, Archibald OR
b West Bromwich 1880
Worcester City
1903 West Bromwich Albion 8 1
Brierley Hill Alliance
Worcester City
Wellington Town

Smith, Archibald (Archie) IR
b Birmingham
Birmingham
1919 Coventry City 1
Worcester City
Stourbridge

Smith, Arthur IR/CF
b West Bromwich 1878 d 1948
West Bromwich Baptists
1898 1899 West Bromwich Albion 6 1

Smith, Arthur Harold GK
b Marchwiel
1927 Wrexham 3

Smith, Arthur Hoyle OR
b Bury 8/5/1915
Bury Co-op
1934 Bury 4
1938 Leicester City 8
1939 (Leicester City) (2) (2)

Smith, Arthur John (Jack) LB/LH
b Aberaman 27/10/1911 d 1975
Caps: Wales War 1
Aberdare & Aberaman
1928 West Bromwich Albion (trial) 0
1929 Merthyr Town 2
1930 1933 Wolverhampton Wanderers 30
1934 Bristol Rovers 4
1935 1937 Swindon Town 114
1937 1938 Chelsea 45
1939 (Chelsea) (3)

Smith, Arthur L OL
Wenlock
1919 South Shields 4
Wallsend

Smith, Arthur Richard OR/OL
b Stourbridge q1 1888
Brierley Hill Alliance
Queen's Park Rangers
1912 1913 Birmingham 51 3
Brierley Hill Alliance

Smith, Benjamin George (Bennie) LB
b Norwich 21/9/1892 d 1972
CEYMS (Norwich)
1920 1923 Norwich City 73

Smith, Bernard LB
b Sileby 1908
Loughborough Corinthians
1931 Derby County (trial) 0
1932 1934 Birmingham 12
1935 1938 Coventry City 54
1939 (Coventry City) (2)

Smith, Bertram (Bert) RH
b Higham, Kent 7/3/1892 d 1969
Caps: FLge 1/England 2
Vanbrugh Park
Crawford United
Metrogas
1913 1914 Huddersfield Town 16 5
1919 1928 Tottenham Hotspur 291 9
Northfleet
Sheppey United
Young Boys Berne

Smith, Cecil Sidney Frank LH
b Hounslow 16/6/1907 d 1990
Brentford Market
1933 1936 Brentford 3
1936 1938 Doncaster Rovers 68 2

Smith, Charles F LH/CH
b Newcastle
Spen Black & White
1921 1922 Bolton Wanderers 7
1923 1928 Bournemouth & Boscombe Ath 173 6

Smith, Charles Godfrey CH
b Ecclesall 12/1/1903 d 1986
1924 Barnsley 0
1925 Doncaster Rovers 1
Scunthorpe & Lindsey United
1928 Notts County 0
Grantham

Smith, Charles Henry (Charlie) IL/OR
b Small Heath
Nuneaton Town
Northampton Town
1919 1920 Coventry City 8 2
Stourbridge
Worcester City

Smith, Charles James (Charlie) OR
b Cardiff 26/8/1915 d 1984
Exeter Toc H
1936 Exeter City 5
Yeovil & Petters United
Aberdeen
1946 Torquay United 23

Smith, Clement (Clem) IR
b Wath-on-Dearne 28/7/1910 d 1970
South Kirkby Colliery
1935 1936 Halifax Town 55 12
1937 Chester 26 3
1937 1938 Stoke City 25 7
1939 (Stoke City) (3) (2)

Smith, Clifford F (Cliff) CF
b Bradford
1919 Bradford Park Avenue 3 1

Smith, Cyril IL
b Knighton 1893
Army
Aberdare Town
Croydon Common
Crystal Palace
1921 Charlton Athletic 7

Smith, David OR
b Ayrshire
Stewarton
1919 West Ham United 1

Smith, David GK
1922 Port Vale 1

Smith, David (Dave) IR
b South Shields 12/10/1915 d 1997
Middle Dock
Reyrolles
1935 Newcastle United 1
South Shields
1945 1950 Northampton Town 128 31

Smith, David Lamont McQueen (Dave) GK
b Coatbridge 6/7/1903
Pollok
Albion Rovers
Mid Annandale
Albion Rovers
Queen of the South
Hamilton Academical
1929 1930 Gillingham 26
1931 Brentford 7

Smith, David Wilson RH
b Lochgelly 7/7/1875 d 1947
Lochgelly United
Cowdenbeath
Lochgelly United
Third Lanark
Chatham
Millwall Athletic
1900 Notts County 5
1900 1904 Middlesbrough 108 12

Smith, Duncan IL
Albion Rovers
1890 Accrington 2
Albion Rovers

Smith, DW (Paddy) GK/CH
Duntocher Harp
Partick Thistle
1895 1896 Bolton Wanderers 3

Smith, E David CF/IL
1893 1895 Preston North End 33 14

Smith, Edward (Ted) IL/IR
b Old Hill 1880 d 1954
Old Hill Wanderers
1899 West Bromwich Albion 0
Brierley Hill Alliance
1901 1903 West Bromwich Albion 10 5
Brierley Hill Alliance

Smith, Edward (Ted) LB
b Sunderland 22/2/1902 d 1972
Robert Thompson's
1923 1924 Hartlepools United 56
1925 1926 Newport County 53 2
1926 Portsmouth 12
1928 Reading 26
1929 1930 Luton Town 32
1931 Preston North End 0
1931 Bristol Rovers 8
Vauxhall Motors

Smith, Edward George GK
1899 Middlesbrough 10

Smith, Edward William John (Ted) RB
b Grays 3/9/1914 d 1989
Grays Albion
Grays Athletic
Barking Town
Tilbury
1935 1947 Millwall 143 1
1939 (Millwall) (2)

Smith, Edwin LH/LB
b Wednesbury q4 1880
Walsall Unity
Wednesbury Old Athletic
Bilston United
1903 1904 Wolverhampton Wanderers 13
Dudley Town

Smith, Edwin Arthur CF/IL
b Birmingham q2 1884 d 1965
Brierley Hill Alliance
1910 1911 Hull City 9
1920 1921 Crystal Palace 25 11

Smith, Elijah M (Father) LH
b Stoke-on-Trent 1860
Tunstall
1888 1889 Stoke 25
Stafford Road

Smith, Ernest (Ernie) OR
b Bradford 1900
Bradford Park Avenue
1921 Halifax Town 4 1
Wakefield City

Smith, Ernest (Ernie) IL/CF/IR
b Shirebrook 13/1/1912 d 1996
Sutton Junction
1931 1932 Burnley 7 1
1934 Nottingham Forest 2 1
1935 1938 Rotherham United 107 44
1938 Plymouth Argyle 12 5

Smith, Ernest Edwin (Bert) CH
b Donegal 4/1/1890
Caps: Ireland 4
1920 1923 Cardiff City 105 2
1923 1924 Middlesbrough 21
1925 1926 Watford 50 1
Emsworth

Smith, Frank RH/LH
b Darnall 22/11/1889 d 1982
Sheffield
1914 1919 Barnsley 26
1920 Swansea Town 1
1921 Grimsby Town 4
Charlton's (Grimsby)
Haycroft Rovers
Louth Town

Smith, Frank William RH/IR
b Kettering 13/10/1897 d 1988
Kettering
1920 1930 Watford 319 30

Smith, Frederick (Fred) CF
b Howden
1908 Liverpool 0
North Shields Athletic
Heart of Midlothian
1911 1912 Stockport County 48 19

Smith, Frederick (Fred) LB
b Waterfoot 26/11/1898 d 1971
Rossendale United
1921 1931 Bury 116 4
Ashton National

Smith, Frederick (Fred) IR
b Crook
1922 Middlesbrough 0
1923 Crewe Alexandra 18 1

From To Apps Goal

Smith, Frederick (Fred) CF/IL
b Blackburn 1901
1922 Blackburn Rovers 0
Barnoldswick Town (trial)
1924 1925 Nelson 2
Fleetwood
Darwen
William Dickinson & Son (Blackburn)

Smith, Frederick (Fred) OR
b Oldham
Chadderton
Hurst
1931 Stockport County 17 1
Ashton National
Hurst
1935 Darlington 27 8
1936 Exeter City 24 4
1937 Gillingham 15 2

Smith, Frederick Arthur (Fred) CF
b Liverpool 16/4/1914 d 1982
Cadby Hall
1936 1937 Bury 6
1938 Bradford Park Avenue 29 21
1939 (Bradford Park Avenue) (2)

Smith, Frederick Augustus F LB/CH/RB
b Buxton q2 1887 d 1958
Buxton
1906 1908 Stockport County 27
1909 Derby County 5
Macclesfield
Southampton

Smith, Frederick C OL
b Stafford
1925 1926 Port Vale 4

Smith, Frederick Cecil (Cecil) CF
b Marchwiel 30/10/1904 d 1977
Marchwiel
Oswestry Town
Welshpool
1926 1927 Wrexham 46 26
1928 1929 Wigan Borough 38 22
1929 Notts County 0
Macclesfield
Stalybridge Celtic
1932 1935 Burnley 106 49
1936 Cardiff City 16 8
Stalybridge Celtic
Rhyl
Bangor City

Smith, Frederick L OR
b Gainsborough
1923 1925 Doncaster Rovers 8 2

Smith, George RH
Hednesford Town
1898 Walsall 10

Smith, George IR/OR
b Preston 7/1879 d 1908
St Christopher's
Leyland
1899 1900 Preston North End 28 1
1901 Aston Villa 5
New Brompton
1903 1905 Blackburn Rovers 58 4
Plymouth Argyle
Southampton

Smith, George OR/CF
2nd Scots Guards
1905 1906 Gainsborough Trinity 17 6
1906 Bristol City 11 2
Crystal Palace

Smith, George GK
b London
1913 Tottenham Hotspur 0
1914 Clapton Orient (loan) 2

Smith, George RH/LH/IL
b Liverpool 1902
Caps: England Sch
Runcorn
1922 Liverpool 0
1923 Gillingham 11 1
1924 1925 Tranmere Rovers 35
1926 Coventry City 5
Runcorn

Smith, George RB
b Glasgow 20/5/1901
Strathclyde
1924 1927 Notts County 83
1928 West Ham United 0

Smith, George GK
b Sherburn 1905
Sherburn Hill United
1927 Arsenal 0
1928 Hartlepools United 4

From To Apps Goal

Smith, George LB
b Connah's Quay 1910
Connah's Quay & Shotton
1928 Bristol City 0
1930 1931 Thames 73
1932 Bradford City 1
1933 Newport County 4
1934 Wolverhampton Wanderers 0
1934 Bournemouth & Boscombe Ath 16
Bath City
Colchester United
Clacton Town

Smith, George LH/CH
b Sunderland 20/11/1908
Easington Colliery
1930 Watford 1
1932 Clapton Orient 2
1933 Darlington 13 1
Yeovil & Petters United
Bath City

Smith, George RH
1936 Gateshead 2

Smith, George Casper CH
b Bromley-by-Bow 23/4/1915 d 1983
Caps: England War 1
Bexleyheath & Welling
1938 Charlton Athletic 1
1945 1946 Brentford 41 1
1947 1948 Queen's Park Rangers 75 1
1949 Ipswich Town 8
Chelmsford City

Smith, George Clarence Bassett RH/LH
b Portsmouth 24/3/1919 d 2001
Guernsey Rovers
1938 1948 Southampton 95 1
1939 (Southampton) (1)
1950 Crystal Palace 7

Smith, George E OR
b South Shields
1919 South Shields 0
1920 Brentford 9

Smith, George Henry RB
b Sheffield 2/9/1872
Westminster Amateurs (Nottingham)
Mapperley
Sneinton Institute
Bulwell
Hinckley Athletic
1894 Leicester Fosse 24
1895 Preston North End (trial) 0
Ilkeston Town

Smith, George Henry GK
1898 Luton Town 1

Smith, George Henry LB
b Netherton 6/6/1901
1922 Chelsea 0
1923 Gillingham 0
1924 1926 Walsall 92 2
1927 Torquay United 6
Exmouth Town
Newton Abbot Spurs

Smith, George Rowley OR
1906 Stockport County 1 1

Smith, George W RB/LB
b Parkhead
Parkhead
1921 1931 Chelsea 351
East Fife

Smith, Gilbert RB
b Oldbury 1869
Causeway Green Villa
1893 Small Heath 14
Berwick Rangers (Worcester)

Smith, H Charles GK
b Litchborough 1894
1920 1925 Northampton Town 173
Higham Town

Smith, Harold (Harry) IR
1925 Crewe Alexandra 3

Smith, Harold (Harry) IL
b North Shields 10/3/??
Cullercoats
1926 Newcastle United 0
1927 West Ham United 1
Blyth Spartans
West Stanley

From To Apps Goal

Smith, Harold Roberts CH/LH/RH
b Watford 12/3/1907 d 1979
Wealdstone
1930 1934 Notts County 117
1935 1936 Cardiff City 50 3
Peterborough United

Smith, Harry CF
Worcester Rovers
Kidderminster Olympic
Kidderminster
Kidderminster Harriers
Berwick Rangers (Worcester)
1897 Leicester Fosse 15 4
Bedminster

Smith, Harry LB
b Cannock 1885
Walsall
1907 Stoke 1
Walsall

Smith, Harry LB
Rotherham Town
1911 Gainsborough Trinity 3

Smith, Harry IR
b Fishponds 21/5/1890 d 1937
Bath City
Bristol Rovers
Bath City
1913 Bolton Wanderers 8 1

Smith, Harry GK
b South Shields 20/6/1916 d 2006
Wenlock Juniors
Kingston Rovers
Middle Dock
Boldon Villa
1937 Charlton Athletic 0
1938 Southport 3
1938 Middlesbrough 0
Stockton
Horden Colliery Welfare
Throckley Welfare
Chopwell
Seaton Burn

Smith, Harry McPherson IL/IR
b Dundee 14/10/1911
Logie Juniors
Dundee United
Dunfermline Athletic
Dundee
Raith Rovers
1934 1938 Clapton Orient 148 34
1939 (Clapton Orient) (1)

Smith, HE RB
1893 Blackburn Rovers 0
1894 Manchester City 18
Stalybridge Rovers

Smith, Henry OR
Whitchurch
Chirk
Neston
1907 Lincoln City 2
Chirk

Smith, Henry (Harry) OR/CF
b Walthamstow 14/10/1901
1919 1924 Clapton Orient 167 9
Royal London United Sports

Smith, Henry Stanley (Harry) CH/RB/LH
b Throckley 11/10/1908 d 1993
Throckley Welfare
1929 1936 Nottingham Forest 157 1
1937 1938 Darlington 65
1945 1946 Bristol Rovers 3

Smith, Herbert LB
b Witney 22/11/1879 d 1951
Caps: England Amat/England 4
Witney
Richmond
Reading
1902 Stoke 3
Oxford City
Reading
1906 Derby County 1
Reading
Oxford City

Smith, Herbert OL
b Bradford
Liversedge
1925 Bradford City 5

Smith, Herbert William RH/LH
b Stafford
Littleworth
1925 1928 Port Vale 60
Stafford Rangers

From To Apps Goal

Smith, Horace OL
b Netherton 26/8/1903 d 1954
Hingley's
1923 West Bromwich Albion 2
1927 Blackpool 0
1928 Walsall 16 4
Worcester City

Smith, Horace RH/LH
b Stourbridge 5/7/1908
Stourbridge
1930 Coventry City 5
Merthyr Town
1935 Stoke City 0
1936 Nottingham Forest 1
Shrewsbury Town
Revo Athletic

Smith, Howard CH
b Walsall
Pleck Old Boys
1925 Walsall 8

Smith, Ian OL
b Langley Park
Langley Park
1920 Hull City 1

Smith, Isaac LH
b Wednesbury
Wednesbury
Darlaston
Oldbury Town
1919 Leicester City 2

Smith, J CH
1888 1889 Derby County 12

Smith, Jack IR
b Wolverhampton 1875 d 1929
Springfield Royal Star
1897 Wolverhampton Wanderers 1
Dudley Town

Smith, Jack GK
b Bolton
Breightmet United
1930 Bury 11

Smith, Jack CF/IR
b Batley 17/2/1915 d 1975
Whitehall Printeries
Dewsbury Moor Welfare
1932 1934 Huddersfield Town 45 24
1934 1937 Newcastle United 104 69
1937 1945 Manchester United 36 14
1939 (Manchester United) (1)
1946 Blackburn Rovers 30 12
1946 1947 Port Vale 29 10
Macclesfield Town

Smith, James GK
b Sheffield 11/4/1863 d 1937
All Saints Wanderers
Nether Club
The Wednesday
1893 Rotherham Town 1

Smith, James OL
b 1876
Kilmarnock
1894 Burslem Port Vale 20 4

Smith, James IL
1895 Preston North End 5

Smith, James (Jim) OR
b Preston 27/3/1887
1903 1904 Bury 6
Stalybridge Rovers
Accrington Stanley
Chorley
Nelson
Chorley
1908 1914 Fulham 183 19
1920 Arsenal 10 1
Chorley

Smith, James (Jimmy) CF
b Stafford 1889 d 1918
Hanley PSA
Hanley Swifts
Brighton & Hove Albion
1912 1914 Bradford Park Avenue 90 52

Smith, James CF
b Falkirk
Clydebank
1921 Plymouth Argyle 1
Clydebank

Smith, James IL
b Dundee 21/10/1902
Pembroke Dock
1926 1927 Wrexham 64 21

From To Apps Goal

Smith, James A (Jim) LB
b Thurnscoe 6/5/1908 d 1956
Brodsworth Main Colliery
1929 1930 Doncaster Rovers 20
1931 1935 Lincoln City 116 3
1936 Bradford City 1
Peterborough United

Smith, James A CH/LB
b Worcester
Army
1936 1937 Cardiff City 13
1938 Wrexham 22
Bangor City

Smith (Schmidt), James Christopher Reginald (Reg) OL
b Battersea 20/1/1912 d 2004
Caps: England War 3/England 2
Pirton
Hitchin Town
1931 Crystal Palace (trial) 0
1932 Tottenham Hotspur 0
Northfleet
St Albans City
1935 1945 Millwall 117 21
1939 (Millwall) (3)
Dundee
Corby Town
Dundee

Smith, James D CF
b Glasgow 26/7/??
Rutherglen Hawthorn
Rutherglen Glencairn
Third Lanark
Abercorn
Glentoran
Third Lanark
Clydebank (loan)
Clyde
Dunfermline Athletic (loan)
1921 Plymouth Argyle 0
1922 Port Vale 7 2
1922 Fulham 5 1
Dartford
Dundee United
Dumbarton Harp
Clydebank

Smith, James McQueen Anderson (Jimmy GK
b Leith 28/11/1901 d 1964
Rosyth Juniors
Rosyth Recreation
East Fife
1925 1926 Tottenham Hotspur 30
St Johnstone
1930 Norwich City 31
Ayr United

Smith, James Terence (Jimmy) CF/IL
b Old Kilpatrick 12/3/1902 d 1975
Dumbarton Harp Juniors
Clydebank
Rangers
Ayr United
1929 1931 Liverpool 61 38
Tunbridge Wells Rangers
1933 1934 Bristol Rovers 25 13
1935 Newport County 26 10
1936 Notts County 4 1
Dumbarton

Smith, John (Jock) CF/OR/IR
b Ayrshire 1866 d 1911
Kilmarnock
Newcastle East End
Kilmarnock
1890 1891 Sunderland 24 2
Liverpool
1893 Sheffield Wednesday 18 1
1894 Newcastle United 25 10
1895 Loughborough 14 1

Smith, John IR
1892 Nottingham Forest 1

Smith, John IL/CF
b Wednesfield 1882
Cannock
Stafford Road
1902 1905 Wolverhampton Wanderers 104 38
1905 1906 Birmingham 6 1
Bristol Rovers
Norwich City
Luton Town
Millwall Athletic
Coventry City

From To Apps Goal

Smith, John (Jackie) IR/CF
b Wardley 15/9/1886 d 1916
Caps: FLge 1
Hebburn Argyle
West Stanley
1905 1910 Hull City 156 98
1910 Sheffield United 12 6
1910 Nottingham Forest 3 1
Nelson
York City
Hebburn Argyle
Heckmonwike

Smith, John (Jack) RB
b Fulwood 1885
Moor Park
1907 Blackburn Rovers 0
Portsmouth
1920 Reading 32

Smith, John RH
Leadgate Park
1921 Ashington 1

Smith, John (Jock) RB/LB
b Dalbeattie 7/12/1898
Caps: SLge 1/Scotland 1
Beith
Neilston Victoria
Ayr United
1926 1929 Middlesbrough 113
1930 1931 Cardiff City 61
Distillery

Smith, John OL
Haswell
1927 Darlington 1
Durham City

Smith, John (Jackie) IR
b Littletown
Sherburn Hill
West Stanley
1932 1934 Barnsley 104 26
1935 1945 Plymouth Argyle 79 9
1939 (Plymouth Argyle) (2)

Smith, John IL
1931 Derby County 0
1932 Port Vale 6
1933 Carlisle United 0

Smith, John RB
b Hurlford
Dalbeattie Star
Queen of the South
1933 Middlesbrough 1
Nithsdale Wanderers (loan)
Queen of the South
Dumbarton

Smith, John RH
1935 Exeter City 0
Maidstone United
1937 Gillingham 14

Smith, John Alfred LH
b West Melton 27/8/1905
Manningham Mills
1926 1932 Bradford Park Avenue 57 4

Smith, John Clayton (Jack) GK
b Stocksbridge 15/9/1910 d 1986
Bolderstone
Worksop Town
1930 1949 Sheffield United 347
1939 (Sheffield United) (3)

Smith, John F IR
b Stoke-on-Trent 1921
1938 Port Vale 13
1939 Chelsea (3) (2)

Smith, John H OR
b Barnsley
Wombwell
1922 Huddersfield Town 0
1923 1925 Reading 102 19

Smith, John Joseph IR
b Clydebank 1910
Clydebank
Heart of Midlothian
Hibernian
1936 Wrexham 12 1
Bray Unknowns
Babcock & Wilcox

Smith, John R CF
1931 Stockport County 1 1

From To Apps Goal

Smith, John Reid CF/IR
b Pollokshaws 2/4/1895 d 1946
Battlefield Swifts
Albion Rovers
Kilmarnock
Cowdenbeath
Rangers
1922 1927 Bolton Wanderers 147 72
1927 1932 Bury 157 107
1933 Rochdale 25 8
Ashton National
Whistons Temperance

Smith, John Richard (Jack) CF
b Bristol
Victoria Albion
1921 1923 Bristol City 27 12
1923 Plymouth Argyle 6 4
1924 1926 Aberdare Athletic 66 44
1926 1927 Fulham 34 9
Guildford City
1928 Rochdale 0
Caernarvon Athletic
1929 Wrexham 6 2
Burton Town

Smith, John S (Jack) IR/CF
b Eccleshill 1901
Harrogate AFC
1923 1925 Bradford City 38 6
1926 Blackburn Rovers 0
Harrogate AFC

Smith, John Thomas CF/OR
b Chester Moor 8/4/1915
West Stanley
Annfield Plain
Blyth Spartans
1933 Blackpool 0
Blyth Spartans
West Stanley
1934 Sheffield Wednesday 1
1937 1938 Gateshead 51 33

Smith, John Trevor (Trevor) IR/IL
b West Stanley 8/9/1910 d 1997
South Moor
Annfield Plain
1930 Portsmouth (trial) 0
1933 1934 Charlton Athletic 24 6
1934 1937 Fulham 93 19
1937 1945 Crystal Palace 57 14
1939 (Crystal Palace) (3) (1)
Yeovil Town
Colchester United
1947 Watford 10
Bedford Town

Smith, John W (Jack) RH/CH
1892 1894 Burslem Port Vale 26

Smith, John William GK
b Beeston
Long Eaton St Helen's
1903 1906 Derby County 9
Newark Town
1909 1910 Nottingham Forest 29
Ilkeston United

Smith, John William (Jack) IR
b Whitburn, County Durham 28/10/1898 d 1977
Caps: FLge 2/England 3
North Shields Athletic
1919 1927 South Shields 264 84
1927 1934 Portsmouth 261 61
1934 1935 Bournemouth & Boscombe Ath 41 2
1936 Clapton Orient 5

Smith, Jonathan William (Jack) CF
b Burton-on-Trent q2 1891
Wirksworth
Burton United
1910 1911 Manchester City 18 6
Mansfield Mechanics
Chesterfield Town
Rotherham County
Hartlepools United
Third Lanark
1920 1921 Queen's Park Rangers 75 28
1922 1923 Swansea Town 66 33
1924 Brighton & Hove Albion 14 4
Burton Town
Burton Wednesday

Smith, Joseph (Joe) IL/CF
b Dudley Port 25/6/1889 d 1971
Caps: England 5
Newcastle St Luke's
1908 1926 Bolton Wanderers 449 254
1926 1928 Stockport County 70 61
Darwen
Manchester Central
Hyde United

From To Apps Goal

Smith, Joseph (Joe) RB/LB
b Sutton-on-Trent 1887
Worksop North End
Kiveton Park
1909 1912 Sheffield United 48
South Shields
1914 Derby County 6

Smith, Joseph (Joe) RB
b Darby End 17/4/1890 d 1956
Caps: England 2
Netherton St Andrew's
Darby End Victoria
Cradley Heath St Luke's
1910 1925 West Bromwich Albion 434
1926 1928 Birmingham 48
Worcester City

Smith, Joseph Edward (Joe 'Stanley') OR/OL/CF
b West Stanley 1886
Caps: IrLge 3
West Stanley
1905 1911 Hull City 213 46
1911 1912 Everton 10
Distillery
1913 1914 Bury 53 1
West Stanley

Smith, Joseph Enoch (Joe) LH
b Kilnhurst 1889 d 1916
Hickleton Main Colliery
1912 1913 Birmingham 8
Chesterfield Town

Smith, Joseph Kirby (Joe) LB
b Whitburn, County Durham 11/6/1908 d 1993
Whitburn
1929 Leicester City 0
1930 Watford 1
Market Harborough Town
Bentley Engineering

Smith, Joseph Stanley (Joe) OL
Keswick
1904 Burnley 15 1

Smith, Joseph William (Jack) RH
b Blackheath, Worcestershire 23/11/1904 d 1948
Halesowen Town
1926 Aston Villa 0
Halesowen Town
1928 1931 Barnsley 118 1
1932 Notts County 23 1
Scunthorpe & Lindsey United (trial)

Smith, Lawrence OL
b Manchester 1881 d 1912
Army
1902 Manchester United 8 1
New Brompton
Earlestown

Smith, Leonard (Len) LH
b Worcester q4 1895
Redditch Town
1922 1925 Leeds United 32
1926 1928 Bristol Rovers 45 1
1929 Merthyr Town 25
1930 Wolverhampton Wanderers 0
Evesham Town
Witley Wanderers

Smith, Leslie CF/IL
b Brighton
Redhill
1930 1931 Millwall 31 20

Smith, Leslie George Frederick OL/OR
b Ealing 13/5/1918 d 1995
Caps: England War 13/England 1
1933 Brentford 0
Petersham
Wimbledon
Hayes
1936 1938 Brentford 62 6
1939 (Brentford) (3)
1945 1951 Aston Villa 181 31
1952 Brentford 14 1
Kidderminster Harriers

Smith, Lewis Frederick CH
b Blisworth 23/3/1902 d 1990
1923 Northampton Town 0
Hampstead Town
1925 1928 Crystal Palace 45 1

Smith, Matthew CH
b Grimsby
1936 Watford 0
1937 1938 Clapton Orient 5
Tunbridge Wells Rangers

From To Apps Goal

Smith, Norman RB
b Newburn 20/9/1897 d 1978
Wedworth Colliery
1921 Tottenham Hotspur 0
1922 1935 Charlton Athletic 417 16
1937 1938 Queen's Park Rangers 68 2
1939 Chelsea 0

Smith, Norman RH/LH
b Newburn 15/12/1897 d 1978
Mickley
Ryton United
1924 1927 Huddersfield Town 24
1927 Sheffield Wednesday 19
1930 1931 Queen's Park Rangers 26
Kseuzlingern (Switzerland)

Smith, Norman IR
1938 Walsall 1

Smith, Norman CF/OR
b Boldon 23/11/1919 d 2010
Standard Apprentices
1938 1947 Coventry City 13
1947 Millwall 10
Bedworth Town

Smith, Norman H CF
b Rotherham
1925 Rotherham United 1 1

Smith, Paul IR
Clay Cross Zingari
1904 Chesterfield Town 5

Smith, Percy James CH/CF/IR
b Burbage Spring q2 1880 d 1959
Hinckley Town
1902 1909 Preston North End 240 94
1910 1919 Blackburn Rovers 172 5
Fleetwood
1921 Barrow 5

Smith, Philip (Phil) CF
b Newcastle-under-Lyme q1 1885
Knutton
1905 Burslem Port Vale 25 8
Crewe Alexandra
1909 Chelsea 1
1910 Burnley 7
Crewe Alexandra
Stalybridge Celtic

Smith, Ralph Albert IL
b Hartlepool q4 1898 d 1950
Caps: England Amat
South Bank East End
South Bank
Darlington Forge Albion
Stockton
1925 Middlesbrough 0
Stockton
1928 Barrow 2
Stockton
Whitby United

Smith, Redvers (Reg) RB/LB
b Rotherham 3/12/1901
Scunthorpe & Lindsey United
1923 1929 Brighton & Hove Albion 143 1
Shoreham

Smith, Reginald George Charles (Reg) CF/IL/OR
b Westbury q1 1916
Westbury United
Trowbridge Town
1935 1936 Bristol City 7 1
Colchester United
1937 Wolverhampton Wanderers 2
1938 Tranmere Rovers 1
Yeovil & Petters United

Smith, Richard IL/OL/IR
b Halliwell
Halliwell Rovers
Heywood Central
1894 1897 Newton Heath 77 32
Halliwell Rovers
Wigan County
1899 1900 Newton Heath 17 2
1900 Bolton Wanderers 0
Wigan United

Smith, Richard (Dick) CF
b Workington 29/10/1877
Workington
1904 1909 Burnley 174 71
Workington

Smith, Richard CF
Barrow
1908 Preston North End 6 1
Haslingden
Mansfield Town

From To Apps Goal

Smith, Richard (Ritchie) OL
b Nigg, Aberdeen 1911
Caps: Scotland Sch
Aberdeen Mugiemoss
Aberdeen East End
Aberdeen
1938 Cardiff City 11 2
Clyde
Arbroath

Smith, Robert LH
b Newcastle-under-Lyme 1870
Newcastle Swifts
1891 Stoke 1
1892 Burslem Port Vale 0

Smith, Robert IL/OL
1891 1893 Darwen 36 7

Smith, Robert (Bob) LH
b Walkden
Walkden
1923 Manchester City 6
Pontypridd
1925 1926 Plymouth Argyle 31 1
1928 1931 Torquay United 139 3

Smith, Robert (Bobby) IR/IL
b Kirkcaldy 1/3/??
Raith Rovers
Aldershot
1929 1936 Doncaster Rovers 264 36

Smith, Robert (Bob) RB
b Atherton 15/12/??
Atherton
1932 1935 Bolton Wanderers 89
Colwyn Bay United
1936 Huddersfield Town 0

Smith, Royston Leonard (Roy) GK
b Shirebrook 22/9/1916 d 1971
Selby Town
1936 1947 Sheffield Wednesday 84
1939 (Sheffield Wednesday) (3)
1948 1952 Notts County 110

Smith, Samuel RH
1896 Burton Swifts 3

Smith, Samuel RB
1901 Stockport County 30
Stalybridge United
Hurst

Smith, Samuel James (Sam) CF/IR
b Pelsall 7/9/1909 d 1994
Darlaston
Cannock Town
Walsall LMS
1931 1933 Birmingham 31 13
1934 Chelsea 0
1935 Norwich City 1
1935 Walsall 14 4
Stourbridge

Smith, Samuel James William (Sam) IL/IR
b Stafford 14/11/1904 d 1988
Darby End Victoria
Cradley Heath
1925 1926 Cardiff City 4
1927 Port Vale 4
1928 Hull City 14 2
1929 Millwall 1
Kidderminster Harriers

Smith, Septimus Charles (Sep) RH/CH/IL
b Whitburn, County Durham 15/3/1912 d 2006
Caps: England Sch/FLge 1/England 1
Whitburn
1929 1948 Leicester City 350 35
1939 (Leicester City) (3)

Smith, Sidney LH
b Gateshead 1900
St Peter's Albion
1923 1924 Bristol Rovers 39

Smith, Stephen (Steve) OL
b Abbots Bromley 14/1/1874 d 1935
Caps: FLge 2/England 1
Cannock Town
Rugeley Coal
Hednesford Town
1893 1900 Aston Villa 162 35
Portsmouth
New Brompton

Smith, Stephen RB/LH
b Bykor 1898
1921 1922 Chelsea 22 1
1923 1924 Merthyr Town 49

From To Apps Goal

Smith, Stephen Charles (Steve) OL
b Hednesford 27/3/1896 d 1980
1919 1921 West Ham United 27
1922 1924 Charlton Athletic 90 8
1925 1926 Southend United 79 10
1927 Clapton Orient 6 1
1928 Queen's Park Rangers 24 1
Mansfield Town (loan)

Smith, Stephen R GK
Guildford United
1925 Queen's Park Rangers 2
Guildford United
Mansfield Town

Smith, Sydney E IL
1908 Glossop 2
Partick Thistle

Smith, Sydney Joseph (Syd) IR/IL/CF
b Aston 11/7/1895
Aston Manor
Aston Park Rangers
Stourbridge
Cradley Heath St Luke's
1922 Derby County 1
1923 Norwich City 3
1924 Gillingham 4

Smith, Sydney Warwick (Syd) CF
b Liverpool 1875
1903 Liverpool 2 1
Southport Central

Smith, Thomas (Tom) OR
b Maryport 26/11/1876 d 1937
1895 1897 Preston North End 53 8
Tottenham Hotspur
1903 Preston North End 8 3
Carlisle United
Workington
Maryport Tradesmen

Smith, Thomas (Tom) IR
b Ecclesfield 7/1869
Ecclesfield Church Juniors
Ecclesfield
Sheffield United
Sheffield Strollers
1898 1899 Barnsley 11

Smith, Thomas (Tom) OR
b Ashton-in-Makerfield 1876
Ashton Athletic
Ashton Town
1897 Preston North End 4
Southampton
Queen's Park Rangers
1900 Preston North End 2

Smith, Thomas OR
1910 Lincoln City 1

Smith, Thomas LH
b 6/10/??
Trimdon Grange
1931 Sunderland 0
1932 Crystal Palace 9

Smith, Thomas F LH
b Luncarty 1911
Caps: SLge 1
Luncarty
Dundee
1939 Hull City (2)

Smith, Thomas Gable (Tom) IR/OR
b Whitburn, County Durham 18/10/1900 d 1934
Marsden Villa
Whitburn
1919 South Shields 8 1
1919 1923 Leicester City 72 12
1923 1926 Manchester United 83 12
1927 1929 Northampton Town 112 22
1930 Norwich City 1
Whitburn

Smith, Thomas George (George) IR
b Handsworth 1881
1900 Bolton Wanderers 1

Smith, Thomas McCall (Tom) CH
b Fenwick 4/10/1908 d 1998
Caps: SLge 1/Scotland War 1/Scotland 2
Cumnock Juveniles
Sinclair Celtic
Cumnock Townhead Thistle
Kilmarnock
Galston (loan)
1936 1938 Preston North End 44

From To Apps Goal

Smith, Thomas Stanley (Tom) LB/CH/LH
b Higham
Higham
Nelson
1933 Rochdale 25
1934 1938 Luton Town 157 1
1939 Burnley 0

Smith, Valentine OR
b Sandiacre 14/2/1903
Newark Town
1925 1926 Derby County 4
Newark Town

Smith, Wallace (Wally) IL/IR/CF
b Coventry 12/1880 d 1917
Rothwell Town
Kettering
Northampton Town
1905 1908 Bradford City 112 54
1908 Leicester Fosse 5
1908 1911 Hull City 91 32
Worksop Town

Smith, Walter OR
b Grimsby
Grimsby All Saints
1892 Grimsby Town 2 1
Grimsby All Saints

Smith, Walter CF
South Liverpool
1899 Notts County 2

Smith, Walter (Wally) IL
b Lincoln q2 1880 d 1917
Blue Star (Lincoln)
Grantham Avenue
1899 1902 Lincoln City 90 21
1903 Small Heath 0
Newark
Brighton & Hove Albion
Norwich City
Southend United
Lincoln Liberal Club
Sutton Junction
Mansfield Mechanics
Mansfield Town

Smith, Walter (Wally) IL/IR
b Bootle 1885
1907 Liverpool (trial) 0
Southend United
Chester
1911 1913 Bury 74 26
1913 1914 Birmingham 26 4
Altrincham

Smith, Walter IL
b Airdrie 1912
Fruitfields
Kirkintilloch Rob Roy
St Mirren
Kirkintilloch Rob Roy
East Stirlingshire
Stranraer
Portadown
1937 1938 New Brighton 17 3
1939 (New Brighton) (2)

Smith, Walter Ernest GK
b Leicester 25/3/1884 d 1972
Caps: FLge 1
Crafton Swifts
Leicester Imperial
1903 1905 Leicester Fosse 79
1906 1919 Manchester City 232
1920 1921 Port Vale 41
1922 Plymouth Argyle 0
1922 Grimsby Town 10

Smith, Wilfred RB/LB
b Sheffield 28/3/1910
1931 West Bromwich Albion 0
1932 Blackpool 1
1933 1934 Burnley 29
1935 Crystal Palace 2

Smith, Wilfred RB
1933 Rotherham United 26

Smith, Wilfred LH/RB/RH
b Stoke-on-Trent 18/4/1917 d 1995
Sneyd Colliery
1936 1948 Port Vale 87
1939 (Port Vale) (2)

Smith, Wilfred Victor (Wilf) LB/RB/CH
b Pucklechurch 7/4/1918 d 1968
Clevedon Town
1937 1946 Bristol Rovers 26
1946 1947 Newport County 9
Abergavenny Thistle

From To Apps Goal

Smith, William (Tich) RH/IR/OR
b Sawley 10/11/1868 d 1907
Caps: FAlliance 1
Long Eaton Rangers
Derby County
1889 Notts County 15 7
Long Eaton Rangers
1892 1893 Nottingham Forest 36 6
Long Eaton Rangers
1896 Notts County 8 4
1897 Loughborough 27 1
1898 Lincoln City 33
1899 Burton Swifts 0

Smith, William (Billy) IL
b Bilston 1872
Willenhall
1896 1898 Wolverhampton Wanderers 58 19
Portsmouth
Gosport United

Smith, William (Buxton) CH/RH
b Buxton 1875
Buxton
1897 1901 Manchester City 144 5

Smith, William (Stockport) IR/LH
b Manchester 1874
Stockport County
1897 1899 Manchester City 54 22
1900 Stockport County 25 2
1901 Newton Heath 16 1

Smith, William IL
b Scotland 1873
Hibernian
1897 1898 Newcastle United 15 4
Swindon Town

Smith, William CF
b Worcester
1920 Merthyr Town 1

Smith, William LB
1926 Barrow 1

Smith, William (Willie) RH
b Cellardyke
Anstruther Amateurs
St Monance Swifts
St Andrews Athletic
1933 Wolverhampton Wanderers 0
1934 1938 Bournemouth & Boscombe Ath 154 8
1939 (Bournemouth & Boscombe Ath) (3)
Dundee United

Smith, William (Bill) LH/RH/CH
b Boldon 12/3/1907
Boldon Colliery
1934 1935 Stockport County 3
1936 1938 Carlisle United 70
1939 Darlington (3)

Smith, William CH
b Rochdale 1912
1935 Halifax Town 0
1936 Rochdale 4 1
Lancaster City
Mossley

Smith, William (Billie) RH
b Kirkcaldy 1914
Newburgh West End
1936 Doncaster Rovers 0
1937 Hartlepools United 28 1
1938 Barrow (trial) 0
Queen of the South

Smith, William IR
b Bo'ness 18/9/1915 d 1973
Kirkintilloch Rob Roy
1938 Tranmere Rovers 1

Smith, William A LB
b Blackburn
Kearsley
1892 Blackburn Rovers 1

Smith, William Alfred (Billy) IR/OR
b Bedworth 1882
Old Hill Wanderers
Worcester City
1902 1904 West Bromwich Albion 21 2
Brierley Hill Alliance
Tipton Excelsior
Coventry City
1908 Birmingham 17 5
Coventry City
Nuneaton Town
Coventry City
Tipton Excelsior

From To Apps Goal

Smith, William Alfred LB/RB
b Corsham 29/9/1900 d 1990
Bath City
1923 1926 Notts County 41 4
1927 1928 West Ham United 2

Smith, William Courtney RB/CH/RH
b Aberaman 1912
Denaby United
1932 Wolverhampton Wanderers 5
1933 1935 Southend United 16

Smith, William E (Billy) IL/CF
b Sheffield 19/11/1900
1920 1921 Huddersfield Town 3
1923 Southend United (trial) 0
1923 1924 Hartlepools United 44 21
1925 Rochdale 10 2
1926 Halifax Town 33 10
1927 Barrow 36 7
Manchester Central
Caernarvon Town

Smith, William Ernest (Billy) IR
b Lostock Hall 1886
Darwen
Nelson
1908 Bradford City 3
Huddersfield Town
Stoke
1914 Preston North End 0

Smith, William Harris (Bill) LB
b Kelvin 23/3/1906 d 1979
Old Kilpatrick
Burnbank Athletic
1930 1933 Norwich City 98 1
1933 1934 Exeter City 13
Stenhousemuir

Smith, William Henry (Billy) OL/OR
b Tantobie 23/5/1895 d 1951
Caps: FLge 3/England 3
West Stanley Seniors
Hobson Welfare
Tantobie
1913 1933 Huddersfield Town 521 114
1934 Rochdale 3 1

Smith, William Henry (Billy) LB/RB
b Whitburn, County Durham 9/6/1906 d 1983
Whitburn
1924 Tottenham Hotspur 0
Northfleet (loan)
Whitburn
1926 1927 South Shields 22
1928 1936 Portsmouth 311 2
1938 Stockport County 34
1939 (Stockport County) (2)

Smith, William S GK
b Haggate
Haggate
1888 1894 Burnley 7

Smith, William Shiel LH
b South Shields 22/10/1903
Jarrow
1929 1932 Sheffield Wednesday 29 1
1933 Brentford 1
1933 1935 Crystal Palace 37 1
1936 1938 Burnley 53
1939 Accrington Stanley (1)

Smith, William Thomas (Bill) LH
b Langley Park 9/4/1894
Langley Park
1920 Hull City 0
Leadgate Park
1921 Durham City 34 3
York City
1924 Stockport County 0

Smithies, George Herbert CF
b Ribchester 22/11/1906 d 1980
Caps: England Amat
Northern Nomads
1929 1930 Preston North End 20 10
1931 Birmingham 1
Darley Dale

Smithson, Albert CF/IR
b Blackhall q2 1911 d 1963
Horden Colliery Welfare
1931 Southampton 0
1932 1934 Aldershot 35 14
Scarborough
Scunthorpe & Lindsey United

Smithurst, Charles Freeman Vincent RH/CH
b Bolsover 30/12/1913 d 1985
Bolsover Colliery
1934 1935 Halifax Town 16 2
1936 Gillingham 3

From To Apps Goal

Smithurst, Edgar Ishmael OR
b Eastwood 5/11/1895 d 1978
Warmsworth
Doncaster West End
Doncaster Main Colliery
1919 Oldham Athletic 2
1919 1920 West Ham United 3
1921 Chesterfield 14 1
Doncaster Rovers
Brodsworth Main Colliery

Smy, James (Jimmy) IL
b Edmonton 24/11/1907
Hampstead Town
1928 1930 Tottenham Hotspur 17 6
Sittingbourne

Smyth, David CF
1936 Newcastle United 0
1937 Darlington 19 6

Snaith, John William IR
b Newcastle 9/6/1908 d 2000
Scotswood
1930 Bury 3
Wigan Athletic

Snaith, William Arnold (Bill) CF
b Stockton 14/9/1911 d 1986
Shildon
1933 Millwall 3

Snape, John (Jack) RH
b Birmingham 2/7/1917 d 2000
Shirley Town
Solihull Town
1937 1949 Coventry City 106 2
Bedworth Town

Snarey, Charles RB
b Oakham q4 1881 d 1950
1903 Lincoln City 3

Snary, John Edward (Jack) RB
b Washington 17/3/1907 d 1974
Washington Colliery
1930 Accrington Stanley 4

Sneddon, John CF
1890 Accrington 1
Newton Heath

Sneddon, Robert IR
b Kilwinning 1908
Kilwinning Eglinton
Kilmarnock
1933 Carlisle United 17 3
Beith
Galston

Sneddon, Thomas (Tom) LB
b Livingston 22/8/1912 d 1983
Whithorn Juniors
Queen of the South
1937 1946 Rochdale 67
1939 (Rochdale) (3)

Sneddon, William Cleland (Billy) LH
b Wishaw 1/4/1914 d 1995
Rutherglen Glencairn
Falkirk
1937 1938 Brentford 66 2
1939 1946 Swansea Town 2
1939 (Swansea Town) (3)
1946 Newport County 18
Milford United

Snee, John Edward RH
b Sheffield 22/6/1904 d 1985
1925 1928 Rotherham United 69 1

Sneyd, William GK
b Oldham
1921 Rochdale 4

Snook, Herbert Durrant LB
b Nottingham 23/12/1867 d 1947
Trent College
1888 Notts County 1

Snow, George Edward Gardiner IL/LH
b Newcastle 9/2/1910 d 1977
Walker Park
1931 Leeds United 0
1932 Rochdale 41 12
1933 1938 Wrexham 207 45
1939 (Wrexham) (3)

Snowdon, Thomas Henry OR
b Jarrow q1 1887 d 1950
1909 Newcastle United 0
South Shields
1911 Burnley 14

From To Apps Goal

Soar, George CF
Castleford Town
1907 Gainsborough Trinity 3
Castleford Town

Soar, Thomas Albert (Albert) OR
b Heanor 20/5/1881 d 1940
Heanor St Mary's
Langley Mill Rovers
Heanor Town
1897 Nottingham Forest 0
Alfreton Town
Newark Town
1902 Derby County 2
Fulham
Watford

Solly, Alfred William (Alf) GK
b Battersea 6/8/1906 d 1954
Caps: England Amat
Dulwich Hamlet
1931 Arsenal 0
1932 Newport County 38
1933 Portsmouth 0
1934 Aldershot (trial) 2

Solly, Charles Basil (Bert) IR
b Battersea 28/3/1912 d 1978
Wimbledon
1932 Newport County 1
Sutton United

Somerfield, Alfred George (Alf) CF/IL/OR
b South Kirkby 22/3/1918 d 1985
Minthorpe WMC
Frickley Colliery
1938 Mansfield Town 14 6
1939 Wolverhampton Wanderers 0
Chelmsford City
1946 Wrexham 2 1
1947 Crystal Palace 10 3
Worcester City
Kidderminster Harriers

Somers, Peter IR
b Avondale 3/6/1878 d 1914
Caps: SLge 3/Scotland 4
Mossend Celtic
Cadzow Oak
Hamilton Athletic
Celtic
Clyde (loan)
1899 Blackburn Rovers (loan) 14 2
1900 1901 Blackburn Rovers 62 11
Celtic
Hamilton Academical

Somerville, John RB
b Ayr 1868 d 1917
Ayr Parkhouse
1890 1900 Bolton Wanderers 265 2

Sommerville, George Liddell GK
b Dalziel 21/12/1900 d 1984
Holytown Violet
Strathclyde Juniors
Hamilton Academical
1926 1931 Burnley 118
1932 1933 Bristol City 34
Burton Town
Yeovil & Petters United

Soo, Hong Ying (Frank) RH/LH/IL
b Buxton 12/3/1914 d 1991
Caps: England War 9
West Derby Boys Club
Prescot Cables
1933 1938 Stoke City 173 5
1939 (Stoke City) (3) (1)
1945 Leicester City 0
1946 1947 Luton Town 71 4
Chelmsford City

Sorenson, Ian Maclagan CF
b Bromley 13/11/1900 d 1973
Northampton Nomads
1923 Northampton Town 1

Sorley, John (Jock) CF/OL
b Muirkirk 1870
Newmilns
Newcastle East End
1893 Newcastle United 1 1
Middlesbrough
1893 1894 Blackburn Rovers 26 9
1895 Burton Swifts 26 1
Hebburn Argyle

From To Apps Goal

Soulsby, John Norman (James) OR/CF
b South Shields 6/12/1897 d 1980
Gateshead Rodsley
West Stanley
1914 Newcastle United 1
1919 South Shields 1
Darlington
Wallsend
Blyth Spartans
1922 Ashington 32 6
Blyth Spartans
Whitburn
Spennymoor United
Carlisle United

Soulsby, Thomas (Tom) OR
b Mickley 24/10/1876
Mickley
1899 Liverpool 0
Tottenham Hotspur
Mickley
1905 Lincoln City 3 1

Soutar, Henry William (Harry) GK
b Invergowrie 18/9/1902
Dundee Violet
Dundee (loan)
Rhyl Athletic
1929 Accrington Stanley 7
1930 Notts County 7
1931 Rotherham United 23
Rhyl Athletic
Shelbourne
Dartford
Brechin City

Southall, George OL
b Cradley Heath 1880
Halesowen Royal
Redditch Excelsior
Stourbridge
1905 1906 Birmingham 14
Halesowen
Dudley Town
Lye Town

Southcombe, Roy OR
b South Molton 18/4/1915 d 1974
Bideford Town
1938 Exeter City 2

Southway, Leonard Frederick CH/RB
b Bristol 22/7/1893 d 1982
1919 1921 Bristol City 27
1922 Exeter City 15
1923 Aberdare Athletic 32
1924 Merthyr Town 22 1
1925 Bristol City 0

Southworth, James RB/OR
b Blackburn 1864
Silver Star
Blackburn Olympic
Chester
Blackburn Olympic
1888 1889 Blackburn Rovers 21

Southworth, John (Jack) CF
b Blackburn 12/12/1866 d 1956
Caps: FLge 1/England 3
Brookhouse Perseverance
Blackburn Olympic
Higher Walton
Inkerman Rangers
Chester
Blackburn Olympic
1888 1892 Blackburn Rovers 108 97
1893 1894 Everton 31 36

Soye, James (Jimmy) IL/CF
b Govan 14/4/1885 d 1975
Caps: SLge 1
Rutherglen Glencairn
Celtic
Hibernian (trial)
Distillery
Southampton
1906 1907 Newcastle United 7 2
Aberdeen
Distillery
Glenavon

Spargo, Stephen (Steve) CH/RH
b Burnley 29/12/1903 d 1972
Mount Olivet
1925 1926 Burnley 3
1929 Nelson 21
1930 1931 Doncaster Rovers 48
1932 York City 35
1933 Rochdale 4
Burton Town

From To Apps Goal

Sparke, Cecil Frederick OL
b Lambeth q3 1909 d 1968
1927 Fulham 2
Peterborough & Fletton United
1930 Bristol City 0
1931 Tottenham Hotspur 0
Northfleet
Folkestone
1933 Crystal Palace 0

Sparkes, Harold CF
b Glossop q1 1896 d 1917
1914 Glossop 3

Sparrow, Harry CF
b Faversham 13/6/1889 d 1973
Faversham Thursday
Portsmouth
Sittingbourne
Croydon Common
1911 1913 Leicester Fosse 48 29
1913 1914 Tottenham Hotspur 18 7
Margate

Spaven, John Richard (Jack) IR
b Scarborough 22/11/1891 d 1971
Scarborough St James
Scarborough North End
Scarborough
Goole Town
Scunthorpe & Lindsey United
1919 1925 Nottingham Forest 157 46
Grantham

Speak, George LB
b Blackburn 7/11/1890 d 1953
Clitheroe Central
Darwen
1910 Liverpool (trial) 0
1910 West Bromwich Albion 0
1911 1912 Grimsby Town 4
Gainsborough Trinity
West Ham United
1919 1922 Preston North End 65
1923 1924 Leeds United 28

Speakman, James OR
b Huyton Quarry q4 1888 d 1962
1909 1912 Liverpool 8 1

Speakman, Samuel (Sam) RB/LB/LH
b Huyton Quarry 9/8/1884 d 1934
Colne
1913 1919 Liverpool 25
South Liverpool

Spear, Arthur Thomas RH/LH/CH
b Bedminster q1 1883 d 1946
1904 1910 Bristol City 136 1

Spedding, John James (James) RH
b Keighley 1/10/1912 d 1982
Rosehill Villa
1933 1935 Gateshead 88 14
1936 Huddersfield Town 4
1937 1938 Chesterfield 19 1
1939 Darlington (3) (1)
Worksop Town

Spedding, Stanley GK
b Lanchester 15/3/1909 d 1975
Throckley
1936 Gateshead 2

Speed, Frederick (Fred) LH
b Newcastle 1909
Newark Town
1930 1933 Hull City 49 15
1934 1935 York City 79 15
1936 1938 Mansfield Town 100 6
1939 Exeter City (2)

Speed, John G OL
Royal Naval Depot
1929 Gillingham 6 1

Speedie, Finlay Ballantyne IL/CH/IR
b Dumbarton 18/8/1880 d 1953
Caps: SLge 1/Scotland 3
Artizan Thistle
Clydebank Juniors
Dumbarton
Duntocher Hibs
Strathclyde
Rangers
1906 1907 Newcastle United 52 13
1908 Oldham Athletic 15 6
1908 Bradford Park Avenue 5 1
Dumbarton

Speight, Thomas OR
1900 Blackpool 5

From To Apps Goal

Speight, Walter (Wally) IL
b Elsecar q1 1881
1903 Grimsby Town 6 1
Rotherham Town
Worksop Town

Speirs, James Hamilton (Jimmy) IL/IR
b Glasgow 22/3/1886 d 1917
Caps: Scotland 1
Glasgow Annandale
Maryhill
Rangers
Clyde
1909 1912 Bradford City 86 29
1912 1914 Leeds City 73 31

Speller, Francis (Frank) LB
b Marlow q3 1867
Great Marlow
1892 1893 Small Heath 11

Spelman, Isaac (Taffy) RH
b Newcastle 9/3/1914 d 2003
Usworth Colliery
1933 Leeds United 0
1935 1936 Southend United 43 3
1937 1938 Tottenham Hotspur 28 2
1946 Hartlepools United 25

Spence, Arthur IR
1894 Bolton Wanderers 4 2

Spence, David McLachlan OL/OR
b Paisley 9/3/1896 d 1961
St Mirren
1920 Reading 20 1
1921 1922 Walsall 44 4
1922 Oldham Athletic 4
Pontypridd
1923 Aberdare Athletic 0
1924 Coventry City 0
Taunton United
Reading Serpills (Green Waves)

Spence, George IR/IL
b Rothesay 27/9/1877
St Mirren
1897 Derby County 0
1898 Gainsborough Trinity 26 10
Reading
1901 Preston North End 19 7
Reading
Southampton
1905 Hull City 19 2
Clyde
Albion Rovers
Cowdenbeath

Spence, George Robert OR
b Burnley 6/4/1904
Colne Town
1927 Nelson 13 2
Rossendale United
Great Harwood
B Thornber's Sports (Burnley)
A Cuerdale's Mill (Burnley)
Accrington Road Unity

Spence, James RB
b Belfast
1930 Tranmere Rovers 2

Spence, James Frederick V CH
b Uphall 19/1/1904 d 1968
Pumpherston Rangers
1925 Watford 0
1926 1929 Clapton Orient 30 3
1930 1931 Thames 49
1932 Aldershot 17
Tunbridge Wells Rangers

Spence, John LH
Kilmarnock
1890 Sunderland 5 2
Newcastle East End

Spence, Joseph Waters (Joe) OR/CF
b Throckley 13/12/1898 d 1966
Caps: FLge 1/England 2
Throckley Celtic
Scotswood
1919 1932 Manchester United 481 158
1933 1934 Bradford City 75 27
1935 1937 Chesterfield 57 10

Spence, Marshall Bonwell (Bonwell) LB/RH/CH
b Ferryhill 21/2/1899 d 1982
Ferryhill Athletic
1924 1932 Huddersfield Town 69

From To Apps Goal

Spence, Richard (Dickie) OR/OL
b Platts Common 18/7/1908 d 1983
Caps: England 2
Thorpe Colliery
Platts Common WMC
1932 1934 Barnsley 64 25
1934 1947 Chelsea 221 62
1939 (Chelsea) (3) (1)

Spence, William CF
b Throckley 31/10/1907
Throckley
1927 Bradford City 2 1
West Stanley

Spence, William E IR/IL
Blyth Spartans
1909 1910 Preston North End 2 1
South Shields
North Shields Athletic
Blyth Spartans
Newbiggin Athletic

Spencer, Albert R IR/IL
1922 1923 Port Vale 4

Spencer, Alexander Reginald Bruce (Reg) LH
b North Queensferry 1/12/1908 d 1981
Caps: England Sch
Army
1931 1938 Tranmere Rovers 235 3

Spencer, Alfred (Alf) IR
Army (India)
1913 Clapton Orient 1

Spencer, Charles William (Charlie) CH
b Washington 4/12/1899 d 1953
Caps: FLge 2/England 2
Glebe Rovers
Washington Chemicals
1921 1927 Newcastle United 161 1
1928 1929 Manchester United 46
Tunbridge Wells Rangers
Wigan Athletic

Spencer, Clarence Grenville OL/IL
b Bestwood 5/8/1909 d 1979
Butler's Hill United
1928 Birmingham 0
1930 1931 Port Vale 15 1
1932 Norwich City 0
1933 Barrow 1
1934 Carlisle United 12 1
Bestwood Colliery

Spencer, Edward W (Teddy) IL
b London
1931 Aston Villa 0
1932 1933 Tranmere Rovers 15 2
Leamington Town
Tamworth
Shirley Town

Spencer, Frederick (Fred) OR/IR
b Nottingham 1873
1895 1899 Nottingham Forest 43 19
1900 1901 Notts County 15 2
St Andrew's (Nottingham)

Spencer, Geoffrey (Geoff) OR
b Shavington 9/11/1913
Willaston White Star
Whitchurch
Nantwich
1938 West Bromwich Albion 13 2
1939 Brighton & Hove Albion (3)

Spencer, Henry George IR/IL
b Farnham 17/7/1897
Bursledon
1921 Everton 9 2
1922 1924 Wigan Borough 35 7
1924 Walsall 2

Spencer, Howard RB
b Edgbaston 23/8/1875 d 1940
Caps: FLge 9/England 6
Stamford
Birchfield All Saints
Birchfield Trinity
1894 1907 Aston Villa 258 2

Spencer, James Lawrence OR
b Mosborough 1/1902 d 1961
Caps: FLge 1
Beighton Victoria
1922 1925 West Bromwich Albion 59 3
1927 Aston Villa 0
Tamworth

From To | Apps Goal

Spencer, Jonathan Thomas OR
b Stockton 1898
Grangetown St Mary's
Eston United
Crook Town
1920 1921 Stoke 17
South Bank
1922 Hartlepools United 1
South Bank

Spencer, Joseph LB
b Newcastle
South Shields Parkside
1911 Blackpool 2
Southend United

Spencer, Samuel (Sam) RH/CH/IL
b Stoke-on-Trent 18/1/1902 d 1987
Trent Vale
Oakhill
1921 Stoke 0
1923 1924 New Brighton 8
Mid-Rhondda United
Aberdeen
1928 Bristol Rovers 2
1929 Port Vale 0
Newry Town
1931 New Brighton 8
Winsford United

Spencer, Stanley IR
1903 Blackpool 1 1

Spencer, Thomas William (Tom) OL
b Deptford 22/3/1914 d 1995
Hastings & St Leonards
Tunbridge Wells Rangers
1936 Fulham 0
1936 Lincoln City 4 1
Ashford Town (Kent)
Watford

Spencer, William (Billy) LB/RB
b Nelson 15/5/1904
Hebden Bridge
1925 1935 Stoke City 338
1935 1938 Crewe Alexandra 3

Spendiff, Martin Nelson GK
b North Shields 24/6/1880 d 1943
North Shields Athletic
1902 1904 Grimsby Town 66
1905 1907 Hull City 104
1907 1911 Bradford City 54
Millwall Athletic
1913 1919 Grimsby Town 57

Sperry, Edward LB
b Warsop Vale 15/7/1913 d 1980
Shirebrook
1933 Notts County 0
Sutton Town
Ollerton Colliery
1937 Rochdale 3

Spiby, Samuel (Sam) IL
b Ashton-under-Lyne q3 1877 d 1953
1900 Glossop 1

Spicer, Thomas Ashby (Tommy) GK
b Brighton q2 1876 d 1958
Silver Star (Brighton)
Sheppey United
Brighton United
1899 1900 Woolwich Arsenal 4
Brentford
Leyton
Brentford

Spicer, Walter IR/IL
b Sheffield 7/5/1909 d 1981
Norton Woodseats
1930 Sheffield United 3
1931 1933 Rotherham United 66 16
Sheffield

Spickett-Jones, Edwin Ambrey (Ted) LB
b Newport 3/7/1892 d 1978
Oak Villa
Newport County
Lysaght's Excelsior
1920 Newport County 8
Caerphilly

Spiers, Cyril Henry GK
b Witton 4/4/1902 d 1967
Caps: FLge 1
Brookvale United
Handsworth Central
Halesowen
1920 1926 Aston Villa 104
1927 1931 Tottenham Hotspur 158
1933 1934 Wolverhampton Wanderers 8

From To | Apps Goal

Spiers, Daniel CH
b Saltcoats 1866
Morton
1889 1891 Burnley 27 1

Spiksley, Frederick (Fred) OL
b Gainsborough 25/1/1870 d 1948
Caps: FLge 2/England 7
Gainsborough Jubilee Swifts
Gainsborough Trinity
1892 1902 Sheffield Wednesday 293 100
1904 Glossop 4
Leeds City
Southern United
Watford

Spilman, George LH/RB
b Scunthorpe q2 1889 d 1922
North Lindsey United
York College
1909 1911 Gainsborough Trinity 30

Spilsbury, Albert William Joseph GK
b Ledbury q4 1894 d 1959
1919 Newcastle United 0
1920 Bury 3

Spilsbury, Benjamin Ward IR
b Findern 1/8/1864 d 1938
Caps: England 3
Derby County
Cambridge University
Corinthians
1888 Derby County 1 1

Spilsbury, John Thomas LB/RB
b Stoke-on-Trent q3 1874 d 1947
Dresden United
1898 1899 Burslem Port Vale 16

Spink, Henry (Harry) OL
b Blackburn 21/9/1912 d 1979
Blackburn GSOB
Darwen
Lancaster Town
1933 1934 Oldham Athletic 20 1
Rossendale United
Lancaster Town
1936 Accrington Stanley 0
Bacup Borough

Spink, James (Jimmy) RH
b Dipton q3 1890 d 1943
Dipton United
Craghead United
1913 1914 Newcastle United 20
Hartlepools United

Spink, Thomas William (Tommy) OR
b Dipton 13/11/1887 d 1966
Dipton United
Craghead United
West Stanley
1910 1911 Fulham 9 1
Rochdale
1914 1921 Grimsby Town 116 3
Hibernian (loan)
Worksop Town

Spinks, Fred RB
1895 Darwen 4
Southport Central

Spiring, Gordon OL
b Bristol 25/8/1918 d 1997
1938 Bristol City 4 1
Glastonbury

Spittle, Arthur IR
b Wednesbury q2 1868
1893 Ardwick 1 1

Spittle, Thomas RB
b Whitechapel q3 1888
1912 Glossop 15
Newport County

Spittle, William Arthur (Billy) IR/IL
b Southfields 19/3/1894
Southfields Juniors
1912 1913 Woolwich Arsenal 7
1919 1920 Leicester City 26 3
Nuneaton Town
Tamworth Castle

Spivey, Richard (Dick) OL
b Hull 18/8/1916 d 1973
Southcoates Lane Old Boys
1934 1936 Hull City 21 5
1937 Torquay United 28 1
1938 Bristol Rovers 10 4
1939 Southport (3) (1)

From To | Apps Goal

Splevens, Ernest IL
b Witton Park q1 1885 d 1951
Cambridge House
Saltburn
Darlington
1908 1909 Gainsborough Trinity 39 15
Ilkeston United
Bristol Rovers

Splitt, Thomas LB
b Lochgelly 1886 d 1954
Dunfermline Athletic
Lochgelly United
Cowdenbeath
1909 1912 Burnley 47
Halifax Town
Nelson

Spooner, James CF
b Wednesbury q2 1875
Hednesford Town
1895 West Bromwich Albion 2
New Brompton

Spooner, Peter Goodwill OL
b Hepscott 30/8/1909 d 1987
Newbiggin United
1928 Ashington 0
1929 Newcastle United (trial) 0
1930 Bradford Park Avenue 5 1
1931 1932 York City 57 13
1933 1934 Sheffield United 17 2
1935 1938 York City 132 29
1939 Gateshead (3) (2)

Spoors, James (Jimmy) RB/LB/CH
b Jarrow q3 1887 d 1960
Jarrow
1908 1919 Sheffield Wednesday 253 5
1920 1921 Barnsley 23 10

Spottiswood, Joseph Dominic (Joe) OL
b Carlisle q2 1893 d 1960
Catholic Young Men's Society
Carlisle United
1913 Manchester City 6
1914 Bury 6 1
1919 Chelsea 1
1920 1924 Swansea Town 159 9
1925 Queen's Park Rangers 22 2

Spottiswood, Robert (Bob) RH
b Carlisle 20/1/1884 d 1966
Caps: SoLge 1
Carlisle United
Croydon Common
Crystal Palace
1919 Clapton Orient 1
Caerphilly
Aberdare Athletic
1920 Queen's Park Rangers 0
Inter Milan

Spouncer, William Alfred (Alf) OL
b Gainsborough 1/7/1877 d 1962
Caps: England 1
Gainsborough Trinity
1895 Sheffield United 0
1896 Gainsborough Trinity 27 15
1897 1909 Nottingham Forest 300 47

Spratt, Walter LB
b Huddersfield 15/8/1892 d 1973
Meadow Hall
Rotherham Town
Brentford
1914 1919 Manchester United 13
1920 Brentford 4
Sittingbourne
Elsecar Main

Spratt, William CF
1907 Chesterfield Town 11 5

Spreadbury, Bertie Arthur Sydney CF
b Plumstead q2 1892 d 1956
Ordnance
1920 Brentford 12 2
Woolwich

Spriggs, Charles OL
b Smethwick 1889
Smethwick Centaur
Bilston United
1912 Birmingham 5
Redditch Town
1914 Birmingham 9
Moor Green

From To | Apps Goal

Spriggs, Frank CF
b Leicester q4 1882 d 1947
Leicester Old Boys
Leicester Imperial
1901 1902 Leicester Fosse 1 2
Oxford Victoria (Leicester)
Leicester Imperial
Hitchin Town
New Brompton
1909 Leicester Fosse 1
Merthyr Town
Rochdale
Heywood United
Ilkeston United
Mansfield Town
Leicester Imperial

Springell, George William OL
b Tilehurst q4 1900 d 1938
Norcot Rovers
Windsor & Eton
1922 1926 Reading 75 2
1927 Walsall 33 1
Thames

Springett, Frederick (Fred) RB
b Brotton 22/7/1915 d 2002
Whitby United
1937 Middlesbrough 0
1938 York City 17
1939 Gateshead 0

Springthorpe, Harold Thomas (Harry) IR/IL
b Tinwell 28/4/1886 d 1915
Caps: England Amat
Stamford Town
Wolverton
Northampton Town
1908 1909 Grimsby Town 22 6
Grimsby Rangers
1911 1912 Grimsby Town 3

Springthorpe, James Alfred OR
b Ockbrook 28/10/1888 d 1979
Draycott
1907 Derby County 2
Draycott

Sproat, Herbert OL
b Windermere 16/12/1904 d 1983
1925 Barrow 3

Sproson, George RH
b Crewe 20/11/1909 d 1983
1929 Crewe Alexandra 4

Sproson, Thomas GK
b Stoke-on-Trent 9/12/1903 d 1976
Audley
1925 1927 West Bromwich Albion 9
1928 Port Vale 0
Burton United

Sproston, Arthur RB
b Northampton 1889 d 1934
1920 Northampton Town 5
Desborough Town

Sproston, Bert RB
b Elworth 22/6/1915 d 2000
Caps: FLge 4/England War 2/England 11
Sandbach Ramblers
1932 Huddersfield Town (trial) 0
1933 1937 Leeds United 130 1
1938 Tottenham Hotspur 9
1938 1949 Manchester City 125 5
1939 (Manchester City) (3)
Ashton United

Sproston, JB LH/CH/RH
1892 1895 Crewe Alexandra 34 2

Sproston, William Thomas CH
b Wybunbury q1 1873 d 1925
1892 1894 Crewe Alexandra 24

Spruce, Samuel (Sam) LH
b Rochdale
Stalybridge Celtic
Hooley Hill Independents
Hurst
Rochdale
1919 Bury 1
Mid-Rhondda
Eccles
Hyde United
Ashton Brothers

Spry, William Hedley (Billy) OR
b West Cramlington 1/7/1904 d 1975
Seaton Delaval
Bedlington United
1927 Blackpool 0
1928 Hartlepools United 15 2
Blyth Spartans

From To Apps Goal

Spuhler, John Oswald (Johnny) OR/CF
b Sunderland 18/9/1917 d 2007
Caps: England Sch
1936 1938 Sunderland 35 5
1945 1953 Middlesbrough 216 69
1954 1955 Darlington 67 19
Spennymoor United

Squires, Charles RH
b Mardy
Mardy
1921 Exeter City 2
Torquay United

Stabb, George Herbert CF/RH/IL
b Paignton 26/9/1912 d 1994
Paignton Town
Dartmouth United
1931 1934 Torquay United 93 44
1934 Notts County 24 5
1935 1936 Port Vale 32 9
1936 1946 Bradford Park Avenue 94 4
1939 (Bradford Park Avenue) (3)

Stables, John (Jack) GK
b Wath-on-Dearne q4 1879 d 1962
Mexborough Olympic
1902 Doncaster Rovers 1
Denaby United

Stacey, Alexander (Alec) RH
b London 3/6/1904 d 1993
Grove House Lads Club
New Mills
Northwich Victoria
1927 1933 Leeds United 51
1933 1936 Sheffield United 64 3
Kidderminster Harriers
Workington

Stacey, George William LB/RB
b Thorpe Hesley q2 1887 d 1956
Thorpe Hesley
1903 Sheffield Wednesday 0
Thornhill United
1905 1906 Barnsley 64 6
1907 1914 Manchester United 241 9

Stafford, Harold (Harry) OR
b Clayton q3 1899
1921 1922 Stalybridge Celtic 53 2
1923 Manchester United 0
1924 Crewe Alexandra 22 1
1925 Accrington Stanley (trial) 1

Stafford, Harry RB
b Nantwich q4 1869
Southport Central
1892 1895 Crewe Alexandra 88 3
1895 1902 Newton Heath/Manchester Utd 183
Crewe Alexandra

Stafford, Henry Elijah (Harry) RB
b Heywood 6/2/1907 d 1989
Heywood St James'
1928 1933 Oldham Athletic 17

Stafford, Joseph (Joe) LB
b New Mills 14/8/1879 d 1957
Pine Villa
Newton Heath Athletic
1907 Oldham Athletic 1

Stage, William (Billy) IR
b Whitby 22/3/1893 d 1957
Willington
1913 Middlesbrough 3
Hibernian
St Bernard's
1921 1927 Bury 202 33
1928 1929 Burnley 25 2
1930 Southampton 4 1
Darwen
Rossendale United
Fleetwood

Stainton, Ronald George (George) LB
b Bournville 10/6/1909 d 1965
Caps: England Sch
Bournville
1927 Birmingham 1
King's Heath
Worcester City
Shirley Town

Staley, Clive Howard Victor (Victor) CF
b Newhall 14/5/1899 d 1985
Newhall Swifts
1921 Sunderland 1
1922 Stoke 0
Newhall Swifts
Burton All Saints

From To Apps Goal

Staley, Henry Ernest (Harry) RH
b Small Heath 1/1/1904 d 1972
1926 Birmingham 0
1927 Walsall 25
Worcester City
Kidderminster Harriers

Staley, Jonathan LB/RH/LH
b Newhall q4 1868 d 1917
Derby Midland
1891 1900 Derby County 128
Ripley Athletic

Stallard, Trevor (Ivor) CH
b Cwmparc 6/3/1905 d 1999
Cwmparc
1924 West Bromwich Albion (trial) 0
1925 Aberdare Athletic 0
Weymouth
1925 Bristol Rovers 2
Weymouth

Stamps, John David (Jackie) CF/IR/IL
b Thrybergh 2/12/1918 d 1991
Silverwood Colliery
1937 Mansfield Town 1
1938 New Brighton 11 5
1938 1953 Derby County 233 100
1939 (Derby County) (3)
1953 Shrewsbury Town 22 4
Burton Albion

Stanbury, George Horace Joshua GK
b Plymouth 24/10/1905 d 1957
1924 Exeter City 0
Torpoint
1927 1931 Plymouth Argyle 33
1933 Gillingham 1
1936 Crystal Palace 1

Stanford, Harry GK
b Birmingham
Earle Bourne
1923 Walsall 0
1924 Southend United 0
1925 Brentford 2
1926 Bristol Rovers 0
Brierley Hill Alliance
1927 Coventry City 11

Stanford, James IL
1911 Manchester United 0
Rochdale
1913 Glossop 4

Stanger, John OR
b Carlisle 18/7/1912 d 1997
Workington
1934 1935 Stockport County 14 2
1936 Darlington 21 5

Staniforth, Archer Christopher (Chris) CF/IR/IL
b Carrington 26/9/1895 d 1954
Creswell Athletic
Creswell Colliery
Mansfield Town
1922 1923 Oldham Athletic 35 7
Mansfield Town
1924 1925 Notts County 39 8
Mansfield Town
1927 Notts County 27 14
Mansfield Town
Shirebrook
Grantham
1931 Mansfield Town 8 2
Sutton Town
Worksop Town
Creswell Colliery

Staniforth, Frederick Walter (Fred) OR
b Kilnhurst q4 1884 d 1955
Kilnhurst Town
Rawmarsh
Kilnhurst Town
Rotherham Main Institute
Mexborough Town
1906 1910 Bristol City 134 14
1911 1912 Grimsby Town 67 8
1913 Liverpool 3

Staniforth, Harry OR
Louth Town
1932 Rotherham United 6 2
1932 Hull City 0

Stanley, Frederick RH
b Burton-on-Trent 12/1884
1905 1906 Burton United 52
1907 Nottingham Forest 1
Burton United
Crewe Alexandra

From To Apps Goal

Stanley, Jesse LH/RB
b Stoke-on-Trent 1870
Northwich Victoria
1891 Stoke 3
1892 1893 Northwich Victoria 35

Stanley, John (Jack) LB
b Longton q2 1883
1905 Wolverhampton Wanderers 20
1905 1909 Bolton Wanderers 67
Crewe Alexandra

Stanley, Thomas (Tom) LB/RB
b Liverpool q2 1899 d 1958
1919 Liverpool 0
1919 West Ham United 1
1921 Crewe Alexandra 1

Stannard, Paul CF
b Warwick 17/1/1895 d 1982
Tamworth Castle
1921 1923 Sunderland 13 2
1923 South Shields 2 1
Carlisle United
Workington
West Stanley
Jarrow

Stansbridge, Leonard Edward Charles (Len) GK
b Southampton 19/2/1919 d 1986
1937 1951 Southampton 48
Basingstoke Town

Stansfield, Charles J (Charlie) IR
b London 13/12/1885
Nunhead
1909 Bury 6 2
1909 Preston North End 0

Stansfield, Harold (Harry) OR
b Manchester 21/7/1878 d 1963
1895 Manchester City 0
Fallowfield
Berry's
1899 Preston North End 4 1
1900 1903 Stockport County 88 11
Tottenham Hotspur
Luton Town

Stansfield, Harold Forbes RB
b Bolton 9/12/1906 d 1971
1929 Bolton Wanderers 0
1930 1932 Swindon Town 48 1
1933 Southport 0
Rossendale United

Stansfield, Harold Henry (Harry) GK
b Todmorden 2/1891 d 1961
1907 Bolton Wanderers 0
Bolton Collingwood
1911 Barnsley (trial) 0
Bath City
1920 Bristol Rovers 3

Stansfield, James William (Jimmy) LB
b Liverpool q4 1900
1919 Liverpool 0
1920 Manchester City 0
1920 Bury 2
Tranmere Rovers

Stansfield, John (Jack) OL
b Bradford 14/7/1896 d 1980
1914 Bradford Park Avenue 0
Castleford Town
1919 Bradford City 2
Castleford Town
1921 Hull City 12 1
Castleford Town

Stanton, Arthur LB/RB
b Bloxwich q4 1892 d 1915
Bloxwich Strollers
1913 1914 Birmingham 6
Oldbury

Stanton, Clifford (Cliff) CF/OR
b Stockport 12/8/1908 d 1970
Greek Street Baptists (Stockport)
Altrincham
1927 1928 Oldham Athletic 13 4
Macclesfield
1930 Oldham Athletic 5 1

Stanton, William Waymark (Bill) LH/RH
b Poplar 9/5/1890 d 1977
1919 Rotherham County 27 1
1920 1922 Millwall Athletic 60 3
Llanelly

Stanton, WW CF
1910 Gainsborough Trinity 9

From To Apps Goal

Stanway, Reginald Ewart RH
b Langley Mill 25/4/1892 d 1972
1911 Nottingham Forest 1

Staples, Arthur GK
b Newstead 4/2/1899 d 1965
Newstead
1927 Notts County 0
Newark Town
Mansfield Town
1930 Bournemouth & Boscombe Ath 0
1931 Mansfield Town 13
Ilkeston Town

Staples, John William OL
b Shardlow q3 1879
Castle Donington
Whitwick White Cross
1902 Leicester Fosse 5
Whitwick White Cross
Ilkeston United
Heanor Rangers
Castle Donington Town
Shardlow St James

Stapleton, Albert OR
b Salford 3/12/1916 d 1988
Urmston
Langley Road Social Club
1936 Manchester United 0
1937 1938 Southport 49 9
1939 (Southport) (2)

Stapleton, Laurence OL
b Nottingham 19/5/1893 d 1969
Basford United
1919 1920 Nottingham Forest 11
Heanor Town
Shirebrook

Stapleton, William RB
b Sheffield 1891 d 1929
Silverwood Colliery
Mexborough Town
1919 Sheffield Wednesday 19
1920 1921 Swansea Town 7

Stapley, Henry (Harry) CF/IR
b Southborough 24/4/1883 d 1937
Caps: England Amat
Bromley
Reading
Woodford Town
West Ham United
1908 1913 Glossop 188 93

Stapley, William John CH
b Southborough q1 1887 d 1964
Caps: England Amat
Dulwich Hamlet
West Ham United
1908 1914 Glossop 120 1

Starbuck, Jonathan (Jonty) GK
b Measham q1 1884 d 1939
Measham United
1905 1906 Burton United 74
1907 1911 Leicester Fosse 77
Ilkeston United
Burton All Saints

Stark, James CH
b Ruchzie 1880 d 1949
Caps: SLge 2/Scotland 2
Mansewood
Pollokshaws Eastwood
Glasgow Perthshire
Rangers
1907 Chelsea 30 2
Rangers
Morton

Stark, James IR/CF
b Glasgow
Petershill
St Roch's
1926 1927 Barnsley 8 2
1928 Bradford City 0

Starkey, Arthur Edwin OR
b Coalville 10/2/1887 d 1971
Hugglescote St John's
Gresley Rovers
Coalville Amateurs
Coalville Town
Hugglescote United
Coalville Swifts
Shepshed Albion
1910 Leicester Fosse 8
Whitwick Imperial
Coalville Town
Ibstock Albion
Coalville Swifts
Shepshed Albion
Coalville Swifts

From To Apps Goal

Starling, Ronald William (Ronnie) IR/IL
b Pelaw 11/10/1909 d 1991
Caps: England 2
Usworth Colliery
Washington Colliery
1927 1929 Hull City 78 13
1930 1931 Newcastle United 51 8
1932 1936 Sheffield Wednesday 176 31
1936 1946 Aston Villa 88 11
1939 (Aston Villa) (2)
Beighton Miners Welfare

Starsmore, John George (Jack) IR/CF
b Kettering 20/12/1901 d 1983
Brigstock St Peter's
Kettering
Desborough Town
Kettering Town
1928 1929 Coventry City 51 17
Kettering Town
1931 1932 Swindon Town 66 15
1933 Barrow 9 1
Dartford
Kettering Town

Statham, Alwyne LH
b Sleaford 28/1/1920 d 2003
Caps: England Sch
1937 Wolverhampton Wanderers 0
1938 Mansfield Town 3

Staton, Frank CF
b Stoke-on-Trent 1864
Goldenhill Wanderers
1888 Stoke 4 2
Stafford Rangers

Steadman, Joseph OR
Newchapel q2 1878
1900 Burslem Port Vale 3 1

Steel, Alexander (Alex) RH
b Newmilns 25/7/1886
Newmilns
Ayr
1905 1907 Manchester City 30 1
Galston
1909 Tottenham Hotspur 1
Kilmarnock
Southend United
Gillingham

Steel, Daniel (Danny) CH/RH
b Newmilns 2/5/1884 d 1931
Newmilns
Airdrieonians
Rangers
1908 1911 Tottenham Hotspur 128 3
Third Lanark
1914 Clapton Orient 23

Steel, John RH
b Denny 24/10/1902
Banknock
Hamilton Academical
1925 1930 Burnley 145 5
Hamilton Academical

Steel, John Hay LB/RB
b Glasgow 1895 d 1953
Queen's Park
Third Lanark
1921 1923 Nelson 50
Arthurlie
1924 Arsenal (trial) 0
1924 Brentford 16

Steel, Robert Loudoun (Bobby) IL/CH
b Newmilns 25/6/1888 d 1972
Newmilns
Kilwinning
Morton
Port Glasgow Athletic
1908 1914 Tottenham Hotspur 227 41
Gillingham

Steel, William Gilbert (Willie) LB/RB
b Blantyre 6/2/1908
Bellhaven Oak
Bridgeton Waverley
St Johnstone
1931 1934 Liverpool 120
1934 1938 Birmingham 91
1938 Derby County 11

Steele, Alexander (Alex) LH/IR/IL
b Belfast 19/3/1899 d 1980
Caps: Ireland Amat/Ireland 4
Barnville
Dunmurry
Glenavon
1921 1925 Charlton Athletic 132 26
1926 Swansea Town 2
1927 1929 Fulham 49
Distillery

From To Apps Goal

Steele, David Morton RH/LH
b Carluke 26/7/1894 d 1964
Caps: Scotland 3
Armadale
St Mirren
Douglas Water Thistle
1920 1921 Bristol Rovers 67 2
1922 1928 Huddersfield Town 186 1
1929 Preston North End 29 2
1930 Bury 0
Ashton National

Steele, Ernest (Ernie) OR/IR
b Leigh 28/10/1911 d 1997
Middleton
Hurst
Mossley
1931 Rochdale 19 3
1932 Oldham Athletic 14 1
1933 1934 Torquay United 38 7
1934 1935 Notts County 54 9
Bath City
1936 1937 Millwall 37 9
1938 Crystal Palace 30 8
1939 (Crystal Palace) (3) (1)
1939 Rochdale 0
Barry Town
Hurst
Northwich Victoria
Ossett Town

Steele, F RB/CF
1892 1893 Ardwick 17 1

Steele, Frederick Charles (Freddie) CF/IR
b Hanley 6/5/1916 d 1976
Caps: FLge 2/England 6
Downings Tileries
1934 1948 Stoke City 224 140
1949 1951 Mansfield Town 53 39
1951 1952 Port Vale 25 12

Steele, Gilbert CF/IL/CH
b Prestwick 12/2/1892
Glenburn Rovers
Ayr United
Glenburn Rovers
1921 Stockport County 15 4
1922 1924 Crewe Alexandra 23 2

Steele, Herbert G OL
Leyton
1925 Charlton Athletic 3

Steele, John (Johnny) IR
b Glasgow 24/11/1916 d 2008
Barony Parish Church
Lesmahagow Juniors
East Fife
Raith Rovers (loan)
Ayr United
Raith Rovers (loan)
1938 1948 Barnsley 49 21
1939 (Barnsley) (3) (2)

Steele, Murray Arthur GK
b Mansfield 7/1891 d 1922
Mansfield Wednesday
Mansfield Amateurs
Mansfield Mechanics
1912 Notts County 3
Mansfield Town

Steele, Parkin Helliwell LH
b Wortley q1 1902
1925 Gillingham 0
Shirebrook
1926 Rotherham United 16
Worksop Town

Steele, William OL
b Glasgow 20/5/1875 d 1962
Royal Albert
St Mirren
Royal Albert
1902 Chesterfield Town 32 9

Steen, Alan William OL/OR
b Crewe 26/6/1922
1938 Wolverhampton Wanderers 1 1
1946 Luton Town 10
Northwich Victoria
1949 Aldershot 9
1950 1951 Rochdale 45 8
1951 Carlisle United 19 2

Steer, William Henry Owen IR
b Kingston 10/10/1888 d 1969
Caps: SoLge 1/England Amat
Old Kingstonians
Kingston Town
Queen's Park Rangers
1912 Chelsea 4 1
Newry County

From To Apps Goal

Stein, James (Jimmy) OL/OR
b Coatbridge 7/11/1907 d 1979
Blackburn Rovers (West Lothian)
Dunfermline Athletic
1928 1934 Everton 199 57
1936 1937 Burnley 42 8
1938 New Brighton 39 5
1939 (New Brighton) (3)

Stenhouse, Henry (Harry) OR
b Blyth 1882
Blyth Spartans
1902 Newcastle United 6
Ashington
Blyth Spartans

Stenson, Frederick Alan LB
b Kegworth q1 1877 d 1956
1899 Loughborough 3

Stenson, James RB
1893 Ardwick 2

Stenson, John William GK
b Langley Mill q1 1887
Langley Mill
1906 Chesterfield Town 7

Stentiford, George Robert RH/CH
b Brentford 7/5/1900 d 1976
Kingstonian
1922 Huddersfield Town 0
1923 1924 Stoke 11
1924 1925 Stockport County 43
Guildford United

Stephen, James Findlay (Jimmy) RB
b Fettercairn 23/8/1922
Caps: Scotland War 5/Scotland 2
Johnshaven Dauntless
1939 1948 Bradford Park Avenue 94 1
1939 (Bradford Park Avenue) (2)
1949 1954 Portsmouth 100
Yeovil Town
Bridgwater Town

Stephens, Herbert James (Bert) OL/OR
b Chatham 13/5/1909 d 1987
Ealing Association
1931 1932 Brentford 6 1
1935 1947 Brighton & Hove Albion 180 86
1939 (Brighton & Hove Albion) (3) (1)

Stephenson, Clement (Clem) IL/IR
b Seaton Delaval 6/2/1890 d 1961
Caps: FLge 3/England 1
New Delaval Villa
West Stanley
Blyth Spartans
Durham City
1910 1920 Aston Villa 192 85
Stourbridge (loan)
1920 1928 Huddersfield Town 248 42

Stephenson, George RH
1888 Everton 1

Stephenson, George Henry OL
b Stillington 9/1908
Carlton Iron Works
Stillington St John's
1927 Durham City 0
Stillington St John's
1929 Huddersfield Town (trial) 0
1931 Aston Villa 2 1
1934 1938 Luton Town 192 59
1939 (Luton Town) (3)
1939 Leeds United 0

Stephenson, George Ternent IL/IR
b New Delaval 3/9/1900 d 1971
Caps: England 3
New Delaval Villa
1919 Leeds City 0
1919 Aston Villa 0
Stourbridge (loan)
1921 1927 Aston Villa 93 22
1927 1930 Derby County 111 53
1930 1932 Sheffield Wednesday 39 17
1933 Preston North End 25 16
1934 1936 Charlton Athletic 50 12

Stephenson, Herbert Leon IR
b Hendon q3 1904
1930 Queen's Park Rangers 2

Stephenson, James (Jimmy) OR
b New Delaval 2/1895 d 1958
New Delaval Villa
1914 1920 Aston Villa 31 2
1921 Sunderland 21 2
1922 1926 Watford 195 18
1927 Queen's Park Rangers 18
Boston Town
New Delaval Villa
Ashington
New Delaval Villa

From To Apps Goal

Stephenson, John RB/LB
b Croxdale q1 1896
Croxdale
Horden Athletic
1921 South Shields (trial) 0
1921 1922 Luton Town 10
Kettering
1924 1927 Durham City 130
1927 Rochdale 22
1928 Ashington 42 1

Stephenson, John (Jackie) IR/IL
b Crawcrook 1/6/1899 d 1969
Crawcrook Amateurs
Prudhoe Castle
Craghead United
1924 1927 Durham City 121 19
1928 Norwich City 19 2
1929 Hartlepools United 11
Grantham (trial)
Crawcrook Albion
Cork FC
Wallsend
West Stanley

Stephenson, John Wallace RB
b Leigh-on-Sea 8/2/1874 d 1908
1897 Liverpool 0
1898 1899 New Brighton Tower 45 1
Swindon Town
Tottenham Hotspur

Stephenson, Joseph Eric (Eric) IL
b Bexleyheath 9/1914 d 1944
Caps: England 2
Outwood Stormcocks
Harrogate AFC
1934 1938 Leeds United 108 21
1939 (Leeds United) (3)

Stephenson, R IL
Talbot
1895 1896 Newton Heath 1 1
Northern Nomads

Stephenson, William RB
b Whitburn, County Durham 1888
Jarrow
Whitburn
1907 1909 Hull City 55
1910 Tottenham Hotspur 0
Wingate Albion
1919 Hull City 9
Hartlepools United

Stephenson, William RH
b Ryton-on-Tyne 1899
Mickley Colliery Welfare
1920 Coventry City 1
Nuneaton Town
Scotswood

Steven, Andrew IR
b Bathgate 1875
Bathgate
1897 Woolwich Arsenal 5 1
Dartford

Steven, David OL
b Dundee 16/3/1878 d 1903
Dundee Violet
Dundee
1896 Bury 3
Southampton
Dundee
Montrose

Stevens, Charles IL
1905 Bristol City 1

Stevens, George IL/OL
b Dundee 24/2/1891
Dundee Violet
Dundee
St Johnstone (loan)
Third Lanark
Dundee
1921 1925 Darlington 130 38
1926 Crewe Alexandra 6

Stevens, George OL
b London
1931 Chelsea 0
1932 Bournemouth & Boscombe Ath 1

Stevens, George James IL
b Hackney
1914 Clapton Orient 1

From To Apps Goal

Stevens, George Leopold (Leo) CF
b Wallasey 18/3/1910 d 1987
Wallasey Trams
1930 1931 New Brighton 54 33
1932 Everton 2
1933 1935 Southend United 72 45
1936 1937 Stockport County 28 9
1938 Crewe Alexandra 24 23
1939 (Crewe Alexandra) (2)

Stevens, Harold (Harry) LH
b Morton, Derbyshire 27/3/1917 d 1998
Stretton Institute
1937 Sheffield United 7
Clay Cross Park House

Stevens, John (Jack) CH
b Broomhill, Northumberland 1/2/1909 d 1994
1928 Ashington 2
Bangor City (trial)
Middlewich
1929 Manchester City 0
Ashton National
Yeovil & Petters United
1932 1933 Stockport County 66
1934 1938 Brighton & Hove Albion 137
1939 (Brighton & Hove Albion) (2)

Stevens, John Norman (Jack) CF
b Wallasey 11/11/1908 d 1990
Wallasey
1932 New Brighton 3 3
Runcorn
Ellesmere Port Town

Stevens, Robert C IR
b Maryhill 1886
Rangers
1909 Woolwich Arsenal 7 1

Stevens, Ronald Frederick (Ron) OL
b Luton 26/11/1914 d 1999
Hitchin Town
1936 1938 Luton Town 7 1
1938 Queen's Park Rangers 0

Stevens, Samuel (Sammy) CF
b Netherton 18/11/1890 d 1948
Cradley Heath St Luke's
1911 1919 Hull City 150 84
1920 Notts County 22 9
1920 1922 Coventry City 59 25
Dudley Bean
Lichfield City
Dudley Bean

Stevens, Thomas OL
b 1888
Aylesbury United
Chesterfield Town
Clyde
1912 Everton 5
Chesterfield Town
Doncaster Rovers

Stevenson, Albert CF
b Partick 27/2/1901
Chryston Athletic
1924 Wigan Borough 7 2
Mid-Rhondda United (trial)
1924 Sheffield United 0

Stevenson, Alexander (Alex) RB
b Airdrie 24/10/1903
Airdrieonians
Detroit R
Airdrieonians
Armadale
1927 1933 Brentford 125
1934 Southend United 11
Ards
Ross County

Stevenson, Alexander Ernest (Alex) IL
b Dublin 10/8/1912 d 1985
Caps: Ireland War 1/Ireland 17/Eire 7
St Barnabas
Dolphin
Rangers
1933 1948 Everton 255 82
1939 (Everton) (3)
Bootle

Stevenson, Alfred Edward CF
b Broughton, Northants q2 1902 d 1960
Keyworth
Carlton Athletic
Worksop Town
1926 Notts County 3
Chatham Town
Rothwell Town
Melton Mowbray Army Remt Depot
Ashfordby Old Boys
Melton Mowbray

From To Apps Goal

Stevenson, Arthur Brown OL
b Padiham 24/8/1896 d 1976
Accrington Stanley
Darwen
1922 1923 Wigan Borough 41 1
1923 Middlesbrough 8
Mid-Rhondda United
1924 1927 Sheffield United 3
1930 Bristol City 5 1
1931 Wigan Borough 4 1
Chorley
Stalybridge Celtic

Stevenson, Charles IR
1907 Everton 0
1908 Blackpool 1
Huddersfield Town

Stevenson, General RB
b Hapton q1 1875 d 1961
Hapton
Padiham
1898 1899 Liverpool 21
1900 1901 Barnsley 54
Wellingborough
Millwall Athletic
Accrington Stanley

Stevenson, George Henry IL
b Nottingham 1905
Lenton
Stamford Town
1925 1926 Lincoln City 11 6
Shirebrook

Stevenson, Harry GK
b Pendlebury 19/6/1916 d 1980
Wharton Presbyterians
Little Hulton Albion
Bacup Borough
1938 Southport 11
1939 (Southport) (3)

Stevenson, Hugh CH/RH/LH
b Paisley 1888
Maryhill
1906 1910 Blackburn Rovers 58 3
Great Harwood
St Mirren

Stevenson, James (Jimmy) IL/IR
b Paisley 1/2/1877 d 1916
Glasgow Ashfield
Clyde
1894 1898 Derby County 73 31
1898 1899 Newcastle United 33 12
Bristol City
1901 Grimsby Town 8 1
1901 Leicester Fosse 7 1
Clyde
St Mirren

Stevenson, James (Jim) CH/CF/IR
b Bonhill 8/1875 d 1925
Dumbarton Fereday
Dumbarton
1895 1897 Preston North End 51 21
Bristol St George
1899 1900 Preston North End 31 5
1900 1903 West Bromwich Albion 120 9
Dumbarton

Stevenson, James (Jim) IR
b Govan 2/2/1881 d 1946
Abington
Leith Athletic
Morton
1902 Nottingham Forest 6 1
New Brompton
Morton
Belfast Celtic
Port Glasgow Athletic
Morton
Arthurlie
Morton
Kilmarnock (loan)
Clyde (loan)
Arthurlie

Stevenson, James Tervit (Jimmy) IR/IL
b Newmains 10/11/1903 d 1973
Newmains
Overtown Rangers
Third Lanark
1926 1928 South Shields 62 25
1929 1930 Bradford City 10 1
Aldershot
1932 1934 Stockport County 96 38
1935 Walsall 3
1935 Stockport County 1
Macclesfield

Stevenson, John RB/RH
b Scotland 1862
Arthurlie
1888 1892 Accrington 81

From To Apps Goal

Stevenson, John CH
1894 Bolton Wanderers 2

Stevenson, John Alexander IR/OR/IL
b Wigan 27/2/1898 d 1979
Kilbirnie Ladeside
1919 Sunderland (trial)
Ayr United
Aberdeen
1921 Middlesbrough (trial)
Beith
1922 1924 Bury 9 1
1924 1926 Nelson 73 26
St Johnstone
Falkirk
1932 Chester 11 2
1932 Bristol Rovers 7 1
Motherwell (trial)
1933 1934 Carlisle United 65 11

Stevenson, Robert RH
b Barrhead 10/5/1869
Third Lanark
1894 Woolwich Arsenal 7
Old Castle Swifts
Thames Ironworks
Arthurlie

Stevenson, Robert RB
b Craigneuk 1898
Motherwell YMCA
1921 1922 Grimsby Town 8

Stevenson, Thomas LH
b Glasgow 1873
Clyde
1897 Sheffield Wednesday 2
Clyde

Stevenson, Walter Herbert CF
b Asfordby 19/11/1908 d 1988
Hyde United
1924 Manchester United 0
Buxton
1927 Chesterfield 3 1
Staveley Town
Shirebrook

Stevenson, William RB
b Accrington 1886
Accrington Stanley
1907 1913 Everton 111

Steventon, Edwin Herbert (Ted) GK
b Nantwich q3 1891 d 1961
Nantwich
1914 Aston Villa 0
Nantwich
1920 Stoke 3
Nantwich
1922 Wolverhampton Wanderers 0
Tettenhall

Steward, Alfred (Alf) GK
b Manchester 18/9/1896
Stalybridge Celtic
Heaton Park
1920 1931 Manchester United 309
Manchester North End
Altrincham

Stewart, Alexander (Alec) LH/RH/IL
b Greenock 11/11/1868
Morton
1889 1892 Burnley 57 7
1892 Everton 12 1
1893 1896 Nottingham Forest 97 1
1896 1897 Notts County 35 3
Bedminster
Northampton Town
1901 Burnley 9 1
1902 Leicester Fosse 1 1

Stewart, Andrew IL
1913 Fulham 3

Stewart, Duncan Smart RB
b Dundee 8/9/1900
1922 Sunderland 1
1924 Southend United 1

Stewart, F Harry OL
Dundee
1899 Derby County 2 1
1900 Blackburn Rovers 0

Stewart, George OR
b Wishaw 1883
Caps: SLge 2/Scotland 4
Strathclyde
Hibernian
1906 1910 Manchester City 93 11
Partick Thistle

Stewart, HA LH
1895 Rotherham Town 2

From To Apps Goal

Stewart, Henry (Harry) LB
b 1888
Tillicoultry
Leith Athletic
1911 Bury 1
East Stirlingshire
St Bernard's
Kirkcaldy United

Stewart, James (Jimmy) IL/IR
b Gateshead 7/6/1883 d 1957
Caps: FLge 4/England 3
Todds Nook
Gateshead NER
1902 1907 Sheffield Wednesday 123 51
1908 1912 Newcastle United 121 49
Rangers
North Shields Athletic

Stewart, James Mundell (Jimmy) IR/IL
b Dumbarton 1882
Glasgow Ashfield
Motherwell
1909 1913 Liverpool 64 27
Hamilton Academical
Dumbarton
Hamilton Academical

Stewart, John RH
b County Derry
Ashton National
1930 Rotherham United 6

Stewart, Robert (Bob) LB
b Loanhead 13/3/1894 d 1969
Broxburn United
1919 1920 Oldham Athletic 34
1921 Exeter City 25
1922 Wigan Borough 3

Stewart, Robert Whyte IL
b Paisley 19/12/1899 d 1950
Stevenston United
St Mirren
1922 Norwich City 15

Stewart, S CF
1892 Bootle 4

Stewart, Thomas (Tom) RB
b Lanarkshire
Motherwell
1896 1897 Newcastle United 27
1898 Grimsby Town 1

Stewart, Thomas RB
Wycliffe (Sheffield)
1905 Sheffield United 2

Stewart, Thomas Earley (Tommy) RH
b Renfrew 28/6/1888
Cambuslang Rangers
Rutherglen Glencairn
1912 1913 Fulham 12
Dumbarton Harp
Celtic (loan)
St Mirren (loan)

Stewart, Thomas Worley (Tommy) LB/RB
b Sunderland q2 1881 d 1955
Sunderland Royal Rovers
1904 Sunderland 3
Portsmouth
Sunderland Royal Rovers
1906 1907 Clapton Orient 50
Brighton & Hove Albion
Brentford
Wingate Albion

Stewart, William Graham (Willie) OR
b Glasgow 29/2/1876
Caps: Scotland 2
Third Lanark
Queen's Park
1901 1902 Newcastle United 37 4

Stewart, William S (Billy) LH
b Arbroath 1867
Strathmore
Arbroath
Black Watch Regiment
Distillery
1890 1892 Preston North End 69 4
1893 1897 Everton 122 6
Bristol City

From To Apps Goal

Stewart, William S CH/LH
b Coupar Angus 11/2/1870 d 1945
Dundee Our Boys
Warwickshire County
1892 1894 Newton Heath 74 5
1897 Luton Town 30 10
Millwall Athletic
1899 Luton Town 15
Thames Ironworks
Millwall Athletic
Dundee

Stewart, William Todd OL
b Glasgow 29/4/1910
Shettleston Juniors
Cowdenbeath
1932 1933 Manchester United 46 7
Motherwell
Albion Rovers
Alloa Athletic

Still, Robert Arthur (Bob) LH
b Brinscall 15/12/1912 d 1983
Brinscall
Tocholes
1932 Burnley 0
Chorley
1934 1938 Stockport County 155 2
1939 1946 Crewe Alexandra 1
1939 (Crewe Alexandra) (1)

Stimpson, George Henry RB/LB/LH
b Giltbrook 25/1/1910 d 1983
Kimberley Amateurs
1930 1933 Notts County 90
Rhyl Athletic
1936 Exeter City 29
1937 1938 Mansfield Town 82
1939 (Mansfield Town) (3)
Giltbrook Villa
Brinsley

Stimpson, Reginald Redvers (Reg) CF
b Lincoln 25/8/1900 d 1977
Robeys
1921 Lincoln City 1
Worksop Town

Stirling, Edward RB
b Arbroath
Dundee Hibernian
1924 Rochdale 13

Stirling, James OR
Third Lanark
1894 Leicester Fosse 4 1
Partick Thistle

Stirling, James IR
Polton Vale
1895 Burnley 2

Stirling, John (Jock) OR
b Clydebank d 1924
Clydebank Juniors
Rangers (trial)
Clyde
1911 1913 Middlesbrough 103 8
1914 Bradford Park Avenue 31 2
1919 Stoke 20 1
1919 Coventry City 5
Alloa Athletic

Stirling, Robert Laidlaw OR
b Kelvin 26/2/1883
Heart of Midlothian
Plymouth Argyle
1908 Blackpool 2
Morton
Millwall Athletic

Stirling, William RB
1921 Chesterfield 7

Stirzaker, Henry (Harry) CH/LB
b Fleetwood q3 1869 d 1938
Fleetwood Rangers
1896 1902 Blackpool 153 13

Stoakes, James Henry (Jimmy) OL
b Newark 17/12/1895 d 1979
Newark Athletic
1919 Notts County 2
1921 1925 Norwich City 140 5
Newark Town
Ransome & Marles

Stock, Alexander William Alfred (Alec) CF/OR
b Peasedown St John 30/3/1917 d 2001
Wilmington Village
Redhill
1935 Tottenham Hotspur 0
1936 Charlton Athletic 0
1937 1945 Queen's Park Rangers 16 3
1939 (Queen's Park Rangers) (2)
Yeovil Town

Stock, Harold (Harry) IR
b Stockport 31/7/1918 d 1977
Cheadle
1938 1947 Stockport County 19 5
1948 1950 Oldham Athletic 35 10

Stockdale, Thomas William (Tom) LH
b South Elmsall 3/4/1903 d 1977
1927 Manchester United 0
1928 1929 Halifax Town 12 1
Scarborough

Stockill, Reginald Robert (Reg) IR/CF/IL
b York 24/11/1913 d 1995
Caps: England Sch
1929 1930 York City 2 1
Scarborough
1931 1932 Arsenal 7 4
1934 1938 Derby County 66 29
1939 Luton Town (3) (2)

Stockley, George Thomas LB
b Hockley Heath 26/11/1891 d 1971
Worcester City
Brierley Hill Alliance
1921 Bristol Rovers 5
Aberaman Athletic

Stocks, Cyril William IR
b Pinxton 3/5/1905 d 1989
South Normanton Amateurs
South Normanton Colliery
1924 1933 Nottingham Forest 241 76
Grantham

Stockton, Colin Moffat OR
b Ellesmere Port q1 1881 d 1931
Ellesmere Port Town
Melrose (Cheshire)
Ellesmere Port Town
Wrexham
Chester
1908 Chelsea 0
1909 Leeds City 3

Stockton, George IR
b Chesterton q3 1905
Chesterton
Army
1929 Port Vale 6 4

Stoddart, George Graham IR
b Kirkcaldy 9/3/1897 d 1961
Inverkeithing United
Leslie Hearts
Raith Rovers
1920 Hull City 7
Dundee Hibernian

Stoddart, William Michael E (Bill) CH/RH/CF
b Leadgate 29/10/1907 d 1972
West Stanley
1926 Manchester City 0
1927 Coventry City 6 1
1928 1929 Southampton 12
1931 1932 Bristol Rovers 40
1933 Accrington Stanley 31 1
Annfield Plain

Stoker, Lewis (Lew) RH
b Wheatley Hill 31/3/1910 d 1979
Caps: FLge 1/England 3
Brandon Juniors
Esh Winning Juniors
Bearpark
West Stanley
1930 1937 Birmingham 230 2
1938 Nottingham Forest 11

Stoker, Robert (Bob) OR
b Bearpark 17/4/1908
Bearpark
1930 Bolton Wanderers 0
West Stanley
1932 Huddersfield Town 0
1933 Southend United 2
West Stanley

Stokes, Alfred (Fred) RH
b West Bromwich q4 1904 d 1960
Allen & Everitt's Sports
1926 1928 Notts County 13
1929 1930 Coventry City 45
1931 1932 Watford 38

Stokes, Archer LB
b West Ella 5/1/1920
Hull Nomads
1938 Hull City 1
Boston United
Scarborough

Stokes, Arthur Wilberforce RB/RH
b West Bromwich 4/1867 d 1939
White Hill
Wednesbury Old Athletic
Walsall
1892 Aston Villa 13
1892 1893 Burton Swifts 6 1
1894 Walsall Town Swifts 2

Stokes, David OR
b Ketley 1880
Caps: FLge 4
Kingswinford Albion
Wordsley Olympic
Halesowen
Brierley Hill Alliance
1900 Aston Villa 0
Brierley Hill Alliance
1901 1919 Bolton Wanderers 387 43
Brierley Hill Alliance
1920 Wolverhampton Wanderers 7

Stokes, Ernest Stanley (Ernie) LB
b West Ella 16/1/1916 d 2000
1936 Sheffield Wednesday 0
1937 Torquay United 30
1937 1938 Southend United 11

Stokes, Frank LB/RB
b Burslem 7/6/1881 d 1945
Burslem Park
1898 1900 Burslem Port Vale 67
Reading
1903 1909 Small Heath/Birmingham 199 1
Worcester City

Stokes, Patrick (Paddy) OR/IL
b Stockton q1 1883 d 1959
Shildon Athletic
Denaby United
1907 Grimsby Town 6 1
Shildon Athletic
1908 Grimsby Town 8 1
1908 Oldham Athletic 2 1
Shildon Athletic
1910 Oldham Athletic 0
Shildon Athletic
Hartlepools United (trial)

Stokes, Thomas (Tom) IL
1906 Stockport County 1

Stokoe, James (Jimmy) OR/IR
b Jarrow 12/7/1888 d 1970
Jarrow Croft
Hartlepools United
Jarrow
1920 1921 Swindon Town 18 7
1922 Derby County 8 1
1923 1927 Durham City 151 17
Spen Black & White
Mickley

Stolz, Wilhelm Lewin (William) OR
b Pontefract q2 1879 d 1947
Bedminster St Francis
Bedminster
Bedminster St Francis
1904 Bristol City 1
Bedminster St Francis
Bath City

Stone, Arthur GK
1904 Burton United 1

Stone, George OL/OR
b 27/7/1894 d 1940
Hemel Hempstead
1925 1926 Chelsea 25 2
1927 Watford 0

Stone, Herbert Henry CH
b St Albans q2 1873 d 1946
1893 1894 Newton Heath 6
Ashton North End

Stone, Joseph (Joe) OR
b Willenhall
Willenhall Swifts
1914 Wolverhampton Wanderers 0
Dudley Town
1919 Coventry City 2

Stone, Norman Willoughby B CF
b Brentford q3 1904 d 1957
Bank of England
Corinthians
1928 Brentford 4 2

Stoneham, John GK
b Witham 15/6/1892 d 1950
Carlisle United
1923 1925 Sunderland 13
1927 Nelson 6

Stonehouse, George CH
b Percy Main q4 1887 d 1961
Wallsend Park Villa
1911 Clapton Orient 3

Stones, H GK
b Manchester
West Manchester
1892 1893 Ardwick 12

Stonley, Stephen J CF
b Sunderland 1891
Seaham
Northampton Town
Newcastle City
1912 1913 Woolwich Arsenal 38 14
Brentford

Stoodley, Henry Claude (Claude) IR/IL
b Plumstead q4 1889 d 1963
Walthamstow Grange
1912 Glossop 12 2
1913 Leicester Fosse 25 3
Merthyr Town
1920 Norwich City 0

Storer, Charles (Charlie) CH/CF
b Ibstock 29/3/1891
Ibstock Albion
Gresley Rovers
1912 1923 Bradford City 208 13
1924 1925 Hartlepools United 31

Storer, Harry GK
b Butterley 24/7/1870 d 1908
Caps: FLge 1
Ripley Town
Derby Midland
1890 Derby County 0
Gainsborough Trinity
Loughborough
1894 1895 Woolwich Arsenal 40
1895 1899 Liverpool 102

Storer, Harry LH/IL/CF
b West Derby 2/2/1898 d 1967
Caps: England 2
Ripley Town
Eastwood Town
Notts County
1919 1920 Grimsby Town 64 18
1920 1928 Derby County 257 60
1928 1930 Burnley 52 5

Storer, John Arthur (Jackie) OR
b Swinton-on-Dearne 3/1/1908 d 1972
Mexborough Athletic
Scarborough
1928 1930 Barnsley 22 6
1931 Bristol Rovers 1
1931 Mansfield Town 13 1
Distillery

Storer, William IL/CF
b Butterley 25/1/1867 d 1912
Derby Midland
1891 1892 Derby County 25 10
Loughborough
Glossop North End

Storey, Cuthbert William IR
b Burnley q4 1878 d 1955
Burnley Belvedere
1902 Burnley 4 1

Storey, Ernest GK
b Birtley q1 1888
1908 Hull City 3
Spennymoor United
1911 Bradford City 3
Blyth Spartans
Distillery
Swansea Town
Distillery

Storey, George Christopher CF
b Dudley 20/10/1877
Formby
1898 Everton 0
Aberystwyth
Oswestry Town
St Helens Recreation
1902 Bury 3 1
Luton Town
Fulham
Stockport County

Storey, John LB
b Marley Hill 14/2/1901
Whickham Park Villa
Scotswood
Chopwell Institute
1922 Preston North End 1
1923 Hartlepools United 13
1924 Grimsby Town 0

From	To		Apps	Goal
		Storey, Thomas (Tom)	IR/OR	
		b Crook 23/11/1892		
		Crook Town		
1913	1919	Middlesbrough	33	1
1920	1921	Crystal Palace	51	4
1922	1924	Coventry City	59	3
		Storey, Thomas (Tom)	OR	
		b Foulridge 23/11/1914		
		Darwen		
		Nelson		
1935	1937	Burnley	35	7
1938		Accrington Stanley	26	3
		Storey, William Crosby (Bill)	IR/IL	
		b South Shields 2/5/1912	d 1993	
		Washington Colliery		
1934		Bolton Wanderers	0	
1935	1936	Swindon Town	17	2
1937		Exeter City	5	2
1937		Gateshead	3	
		Stormont, Robert (Bob)	CF	
		b Dundee 12/4/1872		
		Johnstone Wanderers		
1893		Preston North End	9	
		Dundee		
		Tottenham Hotspur		
		Brentford		
		Maidstone United		
		Storrier, David	RB/LB/CH	
		b Arbroath 25/10/1872	d 1910	
		Caps: SLge 2/Scotland 3		
		Arbroath Dauntless		
		Arbroath		
1893	1897	Everton	55	
		Celtic		
		Dundee		
		Millwall Athletic		
		Storrs, John Alfred	LB	
		b Owston Ferry q2 1872	d 1939	
		Lincolnshire Regiment		
1893		Woolwich Arsenal	12	
		Stothard, Edward	RH/CH	
		b Benwell 16/11/1893	d 1955	
		Scotswood		
1919	1923	South Shields	32	
		West Stanley		
		Stothert, James	LB/RB/LH	
		b Blackburn q2 1870		
		Braeside		
		Bohemians (Blackburn)		
1888		Blackburn Rovers	1	1
		Bohemians (Blackburn)		
1891		Blackburn Rovers	0	
		Darwen Dimmocks		
		Knuzden Rovers		
		Brierfield		
1893		Lincoln City	18	
1894	1895	Notts County	23	
		Bacup		
		Barnsley		
		Crewe Alexandra		
		Stott, George Rae Burns	OR	
		b North Shields 31/1/1906	d 1963	
		Percy Main Colliery		
		Chilton Colliery Recreation Athletic		
		Monckton Athletic		
1926		Barnsley	2	
		Bedlington United		
1928	1930	Rochdale	109	30
1931		Bradford City	5	
1932		Hull City	4	
		Macclesfield		
		Frickley Colliery		
		Stott, Henry (Harry)	OL	
		b North Shields 20/7/1899	d 1978	
1921		Aston Villa	0	
1922		Brentford	24	
		Preston Colliery		
1927		Barnsley	0	
		Stott, James (Jimmy)	LH/CH/IL	
		b Darlington q4 1870	d 1908	
		South Bank		
		Middlesbrough		
1893		Liverpool	15	14
1894		Grimsby Town	29	4
1895	1898	Newcastle United	113	9
1899		Middlesbrough	1	
		Stott, Thomas (Tom)	IR	
		b Guisborough q3 1886	d 1929	
		Thornaby St Patrick		
		Brighton & Hove Albion		
		Southend United		
		Ebbw Vale		
		Halifax Town		
1921		Tranmere Rovers	1	

From	To		Apps	Goal
		Stott, William Healie	RB	
		b Northwich q1 1885	d 1941	
1908	1913	Bolton Wanderers	63	
		South Shields		
		Strain, David	LB	
		b Kilmarnock 1909		
		Galston		
		Irvine Meadow		
		St Mirren		
1933		York City	13	
		Galston		
		Ayr United		
		Strain, Joseph (Jock)	CH/LH	
		b Baillieston 25/7/1894	d 1973	
		Baillieston Juniors		
		Shettleston Juniors		
		Bo'ness		
1921	1926	Watford	178	6
		Hamilton Academical		
		Baillieston Juniors		
		Strang, Richard (Dick)	CH	
		b Rutherglen 19/3/1900	d 1971	
1923		Birmingham	0	
1924	1925	Crystal Palace	24	
		Worcester City		
		Poole		
1929	1931	Halifax Town	99	2
1932		Northampton Town	7	
1933	1937	Darlington	171	2
		Strang, Thomas William	IL	
		b West Calder 1882		
		Plains		
		Celtic		
1902		Bolton Wanderers	3	
		Aberdeen		
		Bristol Rovers		
		New Brompton		
		Strange, Alfred Henry (Alf)	RH/IL/IR	
		b Marehay 2/4/1900	d 1978	
		Caps: FLge 3/England 20		
		Marehay Colliery		
		Ripley		
1922	1923	Portsmouth	24	16
1924	1926	Port Vale	95	25
1926	1934	Sheffield Wednesday	253	22
1935		Bradford Park Avenue	10	
		Ripley Town		
		Raleigh Cycles (Nottingham)		
		Corsham United		
		Strange, Edmund Wallis	LH	
		b Bordesley Green 3/1871	d 1925	
		Small Heath Ravenhurst		
		Hoskins & Sewell		
1892		Small Heath	0	
		Langley Mill		
		Unity Gas		
1897		Aston Villa	2	
		Langley St Michael's		
		Strathie, William James (James)	CH/LB/RB	
		b Beancross 12/2/1913	d 1976	
		Camelon Juniors		
		Falkirk		
		King's Park		
		St Bernard's		
1937	1938	Luton Town	2	
1939	1946	Northampton Town	6	
1939		(Northampton Town)	(3)	
		Kettering Town		
		Corby Town		
		Rothwell Town		
		Straughton, James	CF	
		b Workington 20/9/1889	d 1958	
		Army		
1912	1913	Leicester Fosse	15	2
		Pontypridd		
		Leicester Imperial		
		Grantham		
		Flimby Rangers		
		Street, Ernest	IR	
		b Altrincham q3 1878		
		Sale Holmfield		
1902		Manchester United	1	
		Sale Holmfield		
		Streets, George Henry	GK	
		b Nottingham 5/4/1893	d 1958	
		Nottingham St Margaret's		
		Raleigh Athletic		
		Mansfield Mechanics		
1913		Sheffield Wednesday	2	
1919	1927	Notts County	133	
		Boston Town		
		Newark Town		

From	To		Apps	Goal
		Streets, John William	IR	
		b Nottingham 11/1893	d 1949	
		Long Eaton Rangers		
1913		Wolverhampton Wanderers	2	
1914		Notts County	0	
		Mansfield Invicta		
		Mansfield Town		
		Streets, Stanley Ernest Edward	IR	
		b Grantham 25/6/1901	d 1961	
		Grantham		
1924	1925	Blackpool	16	2
1925	1927	Clapton Orient	12	1
1928		Exeter City	9	2
		Tunbridge Wells Rangers		
		Cork FC		
		West Stanley		
		Strettle, Samuel	RB/LB	
		b Warrington q4 1885	d 1926	
1906	1908	Everton	4	
		Chesterfield Town		
		Exeter City		
		Northwich Victoria		
		Stretton, William	CF	
		b Stapenhill q1 1876		
1899	1900	Burton Swifts	17	4
		Strevett, John William Vincent (Jack)	IL	
		b Shanklin 28/11/1903	d 1990	
		Portsmouth	0	
1926		Barrow (loan)	7	1
		Emsworth Sports		
		Stringer, James (Jimmy)	GK	
		b Netherton 5/1878	d 1933	
		Netherton Rovers		
1901	1903	Wolverhampton Wanderers	15	
1904	1909	West Bromwich Albion	160	
		Dudley Town		
		Stringfellow, Frank	IR/IL	
		b Sutton-in-Ashfield q1 1889	d 1948	
		Ilkeston United		
1908	1910	Sheffield Wednesday	20	5
1920	1921	Portsmouth	60	26
		Heart of Midlothian		
		Weymouth		
		Pontypridd		
1925	1928	Bournemouth & Boscombe Ath	117	30
		Scunthorpe & Lindsey United		
		Stringfellow, Henry (Harry)	CH/RH	
		b Lathom 1/10/1874	d 1956	
		Southport Central		
1898		Everton	0	
		Portsmouth		
		Swindon Town		
1905		Leeds City	13	1
		Wigan Town		
1906	1907	Preston North End	39	2
		Wigan Town		
		Stringfellow, John	LH	
1891		Blackburn Rovers	4	
		Strong, George James (Jimmy)	GK	
		b Morpeth 7/6/1916	d 1989	
		Choppington Welfare		
		Pegswood United		
1933		Hartlepools United	1	
1934		Chesterfield	18	
1934	1937	Portsmouth	59	
		Gillingham		
1939	1945	(Walsall)	(3)	
1946	1952	Burnley	264	
		Strong, Thomas Philips (Tommy)	LB/LH	
		b Newcastle q4 1890	d 1917	
1913	1914	Lincoln City	8	
		Stroud, William Harman	RB	
		b Southampton 4/4/1902	d 1959	
1920		Everton	0	
1921		Blackpool	2	
		Chester		
1924		Merthyr Town (trial)	1	
		Struthers, Robert John (Bob)	LB	
		b Liverpool q1 1879	d 1959	
		Temple (Liverpool)		
		Kirkdale		
		Rock Ferry		
1897		Everton	0	
		Gravesend United		
		Portsmouth		
1901	1906	Bolton Wanderers	130	
		Bradford Park Avenue		
		Stuart, Alex	RH/LH	
1896	1898	Blackpool	45	1

From	To		Apps	Goal
		Stuart, George Ernest	LH	
		b East Wemyss 4/7/1895	d 1989	
		Dundee		
1920		Leeds United	1	
		Stuart, James (Jim)	CF	
		b Coatbridge		
		Albion Rovers		
1894		Blackburn Rovers	13	4
		Rossendale		
1896		Blackburn Rovers	2	1
1897		Woolwich Arsenal	2	1
		Northfleet		
		New Brompton		
		Stuart, Robert William (Bobby)	LB/RB	
		b Middlesbrough 9/10/1913	d 1987	
		Caps: England Sch		
		South Bank		
1931	1947	Middlesbrough	247	2
1939		(Middlesbrough)	(3)	
1947		Plymouth Argyle	20	
		Whitby United		
		Stuart, Thomas Andrew M (Tom)	LB/RB	
		b Liverpool 25/10/1893	d 1957	
		Bootle Albion		
1921	1927	Tranmere Rovers	192	13
		Stuart, William	IL	
		Birkenhead		
1907	1909	Bolton Wanderers	7	1
1910		Liverpool	0	
		Stubbins, Albert	CF/IR	
		b Wallsend 13/7/1919	d 2002	
		Caps: FLge 4/England War 1		
		Whitley & Monkseaton		
1936		Sunderland	0	
1937	1946	Newcastle United	27	5
1939		(Newcastle United)	(1)	
1946	1952	Liverpool	161	75
		Ashington		
		Stubbs, Francis Lloyd (Frank)	GK	
		b Woodhouse Eaves 13/4/1878	d 1944	
		Coalville		
1899		Loughborough	33	
1900	1902	Sheffield Wednesday	18	
		Loughborough Wednesday		
		Stubbs, Philip Eric Gordon (Eric)	OL/OR	
		b Chester 10/9/1912		
		Winsford United		
		Nantwich		
1933		Bolton Wanderers	0	
1934		Wrexham	28	10
1935	1936	Nottingham Forest	22	6
1936	1938	Leicester City	74	14
1939		(Leicester City)	(3)	(1)
1945		Chester	0	
		Sturgess, Albert	LH/RB/RH	
		b Etruria 21/10/1882	d 1957	
		Caps: England 2		
		Tunstall Crosswells		
1902	1907	Stoke	124	3
1908	1922	Sheffield United	353	5
1923	1924	Norwich City	47	
		Sturgess, Arthur Henry	IL	
		b Conisbrough 26/7/1912	d 2000	
		Frickley Colliery		
1933		Rotherham United	2	1
		Sturton, Thomas William (William)	LH	
		b Basford 25/9/1908	d 1966	
1927		Nottingham Forest	1	
		Stuttard, John Ellis (Ellis)	RB/LB/LH	
		b Padiham 24/4/1920	d 1983	
1937		Burnley	0	
1938	1946	Plymouth Argyle	29	1
1947	1950	Torquay United	82	
		Bideford		
		Sete (France)		
		Suart, Robert (Bob)	RH/LH	
		b Stockport q4 1882	d 1918	
		Edgeley		
1903	1907	Stockport County	109	9
1907	1910	Fulham	97	1
		Port Vale		
		Suddick, George	LB	
		b Fatfield 6/10/1907	d 1987	
1931		Barnsley	1	
		Suddick, James	OR/CF/IR	
		b Middlesbrough 8/1873	d 1932	
		Middlesbrough		
1897		Aston Villa	2	1
1898		Nottingham Forest	14	4
		Thornaby		
1903		Middlesbrough	1	1

From To Apps Goal

Sugarman, Barnett (Barney) IR
b Abercynon 10/11/1903 d 1947
Abercynon United
Aberdare & Aberaman
Abertysswg
1929 Merthyr Town 13 6

Sugden, ? CH
1895 Rotherham Town 1

Sugden, Arthur RB
b Gorton q4 1891 d 1941
Droylsden
1919 Manchester City 6
1921 1922 Tranmere Rovers 4
1923 Southport 0

Sugden, Herbert OR
1897 1898 Darwen 19 1

Sugden, Sidney Herbert CF/OR
b Battersea 30/10/1880
Ilford
West Ham United
1902 1904 Nottingham Forest 47 16
Queen's Park Rangers
Brentford
Southend United

Sugden, Thomas GK
1901 Burnley 7

Sugg, Frank Howe CF/CH
b Ilkeston 11/1/1862 d 1933
Bolton Wanderers
The Wednesday
Derby County
Burnley
1888 1889 Everton 10
1890 Burnley 0

Suggett, Ernest James (Ernie) OR
b Pelaw 3/12/1905 d 1971
Willington
Usworth Colliery
Crawcrook Albion
Ayr United
1930 Gateshead (trial) 0
1931 Barrow 35 21
1932 1935 Bradford Park Avenue 108 42

Sullivan, Cornelius (Con) RH/LH
b Tynemouth 6/6/1903 d 1988
Newburn Grange
1922 Preston North End 0
1923 Swansea Town 0
1924 Southend United 1
Newburn
1926 1928 Hull City 65 3
1929 Bradford Park Avenue 2
1930 Carlisle United 10
Wallsend

Sullivan, James Henry (Jim) CF
b Burnley 14/11/1904
1922 Burnley 0
1922 Barrow 0
Crewe College
1924 1925 Crewe Alexandra 35 22
1925 1927 Notts County 22 10
Grantham
Loughborough Corinthians
Gainsborough Trinity

Sullivan, Leslie Gordon (Les) OL
b Croydon 6/8/1912 d 1996
Fleetwood
1932 Blackburn Rovers 0
Lytham
1934 Rochdale 32 9
1935 Brentford 0
1936 1937 Bristol Rovers 39 10
1938 Chesterfield 7
1939 Stockport County (1)
Macclesfield

Sullivan, Maurice Jeremiah IL/IR
b Newport 30/8/1915 d 1979
Pontymister United
1936 1937 Newport County 38 8
1938 Derby County 0
1939 Mansfield Town (3)

Sullivan, William (Billy) OL
1935 1937 Stockport County 27 8
1938 Hull City 0

From To Apps Goal

Summerbee, George Morley LH/RH/RB
b Winchester 22/10/1914 d 1955
Winchester City
Basingstoke Town
1932 Stockport County (trial) 0
1933 1934 Aldershot 19
1937 1945 Preston North End 3
1946 Chester 9
1947 1949 Barrow 122
Cheltenham Town

Summerbee, Gordon Charles Scott CH/LH/LB
b Winchester 8/2/1913 d 1983
Basingstoke Town
1934 1945 Aldershot 112
1939 (Aldershot) (3)
Weymouth
Dorchester Town

Summerfield, William Henry (Harry) GK
b Haverton Hill 5/7/1890 d 1962
Haverton Hill
1921 1924 Hartlepools United 59
Snook End Athletic
Furness Athletic

Summers, George Moffett OL
b Durham 30/10/1906 d 1979
Willington
1929 Huddersfield Town 0
1930 Accrington Stanley 26 2
1931 Barrow 20
Lancaster Town
Ashington
City of Durham
West Stanley

Summers, John Lawrence (Jack) OR
b Chorlton 8/2/1915 d 1991
Manchester North End
1931 Burnley (trial) 0
Fleetwood
1932 Preston North End (trial) 0
Tunbridge Wells Rangers
1934 Leicester City 11 2
1935 Derby County 2
1936 1937 Southampton 31 7
Southampton Police

Summers, Percy GK
b Chesterfield 1889
Wales FC
Chesterfield Town
1914 Grimsby Town 34
Luton Town
Margate

Summers, William (Willie) CH
b Burnbank 14/7/1893 d 1972
Caps: Scotland 1
Burnbank Athletic
Bellshill Athletic
Airdrieonians
St Bernard's (loan)
St Mirren
1927 1931 Bradford City 120 1
1932 Newport County 36

Sumner, Thomas William LH
b Northwich q1 1872 d 1946
1893 Northwich Victoria 3

Sunter, John CF
1914 Glossop 1

Surrey, Thomas Hindmore CF
b Gateshead 31/10/1907 d 1976
Scotswood
1929 Hull City 1

Surtees, Albert Edward CF/IR/IL
b Willington Quay 2/1900 d 1963
1922 Durham City 0
1923 1924 Aston Villa 11 1
1925 West Ham United 0
1926 Southend United 5
1927 Clapton Orient 1
Wellington Town

Surtees, Ernest (Ernie) IL
b Rotherham 1/1/1885 d 1971
Rotherham County
Rotherham Town
Parkgate
1907 Barnsley 10 3
Rotherham County

From To Apps Goal

Surtees, John (Jack) IR/IL
b Percy Main 1/7/1911 d 1992
Percy Main
1931 Middlesbrough 1
1932 Portsmouth 1
1933 Bournemouth & Boscombe Ath 21 4
1933 Northampton Town 0
1934 1936 Sheffield Wednesday 40 5
1936 1938 Nottingham Forest 96 24
1939 (Nottingham Forest) 93 23

Surtees, Joseph (Joe) OR
b Littleburn q4 1896 d 1957
Spennymoor United
1921 1922 Durham City 14 1
York City

Sutcliffe, Arnold OR
Breda Visada
1937 Rochdale 2

Sutcliffe, Charles Spencer GK
b Bradford 7/10/1890 d 1964
Heckmondwike
Halifax Town
York City
1919 Leeds City 0
1920 1924 Rotherham County 102
1924 1926 Sheffield United 45

Sutcliffe, John William GK
b Shibden 14/4/1868 d 1947
Caps: FLge 5/England 5
1889 1901 Bolton Wanderers 332
Millwall Athletic
1903 Manchester United 21
Plymouth Argyle
Southend United

Sutcliffe, Percy CH
b Ramsbottom 28/7/1889 d 1971
Ramsbottom
Haslingden
Norwich City
1921 1922 Darlington 53
1923 Hartlepools United 19

Sutcliffe, R LH
1898 Glossop North End 8

Suter, Ernest Robert (Bob) GK
b Epperstone 10/7/1880 d 1945
Southwell Church Lads Brigade
Southwell St Mary's
Nottingham Park (loan)
1898 1901 Notts County 38
Alnoea
Newark Town
1906 Notts County 4
Goole Town
1921 1928 Halifax Town 4

Suter, Fergus (Fergie) GK
b Blythswood 21/11/1857 d 1916
Partick Thistle
Rangers
Turton
Darwen
1888 Blackburn Rovers 1

Suter, Francis Robert (Bob) GK
b Basford 11/4/1911 d 1987
1931 Bradford Park Avenue 0
1932 Halifax Town 3

Sutherland, Arthur Gordon LH
b North Shields 10/12/1914 d 1995
Throckley Welfare
North Shields
1938 Chesterfield 3
1939 (Chesterfield) (2)

Sutherland, Charles Christison IL/IR
b Brechin 4/2/1898
Petershill
Third Lanark
Abercorn (loan)
Clydebank
St Mirren
1920 1921 Millwall Athletic 57 8
1922 1925 Bristol City 103 23
1926 Merthyr Town 34 6
St Mirren

Sutherland, Donald James LH
b Lerwick 1867
St Bernard's
Grimsby Town
1892 Burton Swifts 7

Sutherland, George RB
b New Scone 1876
1894 Sheffield Wednesday 3

From To Apps Goal

Sutherland, Harry Ross CF/IR
b Salford 30/7/1915
Sedgley Park
Mossley
1938 Leeds United 3 1
1946 1947 Exeter City 14 3
1948 Bournemouth & Boscombe Ath 0

Sutherland, James OL
b Inverness 1881
Inverness Caledonian
1899 1900 Burnley 11 1

Sutherland, Joseph William Russell (Russell) LH
b Clyne 16/11/1896
Dundee Hibernian
Dundee
1921 Barrow 9
(Canada)

Sutherland, Malcolm Nicolson IL
b Greenock 9/1868
1892 1893 Darwen 51 19
1894 Burnley 1

Sutherley, Charles Edwin OL
b Chudleigh 30/3/1920 d 2002
Chudleigh
1938 Exeter City 9 1
1939 (Exeter City) (3)
Penzance

Suttie, David Shand LH
b Lochgelly 18/12/1906 d 1985
1927 Blackburn Rovers 0
1928 1930 Nelson 104 2
Manchester Central
Ashton National
1933 Carlisle United 1
Stalybridge Celtic

Suttie, Thomas (Tommy) LB
b Lochgelly 1883 d 1954
Lochgelly Rangers
Lochgelly United
Cowdenbeath
Leith Athletic
1906 1914 Blackburn Rovers 102
Accrington Stanley
Darwen
Great Harwood

Sutton, William GK
1894 Everton 1

Swaby, Henry Northing (Harry) CH/LH
b Grimsby 22/1/1906 d 1982
Grimsby YMCA
Cleethorpes Town
1926 1931 Grimsby Town 44 2
1932 Barnsley 18
Scarborough
Grantham
Gainsborough Trinity

Swain, John Sanderson (Jack) OL
b Grimsby 13/4/1914 d 2000
1936 1938 Grimsby Town 22 6
Scunthorpe & Lindsey United

Swain, Joseph LH
1903 Burnley 1

Swainston, Henry (Harry) CF
b Richmond 16/1/1877 d 1967
Darlington
1899 Burnley 2

Swales, Norman LH/RH
b New Marske 10/1903 d 1961
Scarborough
1925 Middlesbrough 2
Scarborough
1928 1929 Aston Villa 6
Scarborough
Whitley Bay

Swales, Stuart Allison OL
b Bradford 7/12/1912 d 1975
1937 Bradford City 13

Swallow, Andrew E IR/RH/LH
b Bellshill 23/11/1906 d 1969
Shettleston Celtic
Shettleston Juniors
St Johnstone
1930 1934 Millwall 40 3
Morton

Swallow, John E GK
1895 Wolverhampton Wanderers 2
Darlaston
1897 Walsall 0
Dudley Phoenix
Hill Top Vics

From To Apps Goal

Swan, Christopher Samuel (Chris) IR/RH/OR
b Byker 4/12/1900 d 1979
Caps: England Sch/Lol 1
Tyneside Juniors
1919 1921 Newcastle United 4
1923 1924 Stockport County 32 4
1925 1928 Hull City 73 8
1929 Crystal Palace 6
Waterford
Scarborough

Swan, Edward (Eddie) IL
b Glasgow 28/7/1897
St Roch's
Aberdeen
New York Giants
1924 Barnsley 2
Dumbarton
Nairn County
Forres Mechanics

Swan, John (Jack) IL
b Easington 10/7/1892 d 1990
Seaham Colliery
1919 1921 Huddersfield Town 67 30
1921 1924 Leeds United 108 47
1925 1926 Watford 54 27
1926 1927 Queen's Park Rangers 28 5
Thames
Lovells Athletic

Swann, Andrew CF/IR
b Dalbeattie 1878
Dalbeattie
1898 Lincoln City 13 10
New Brompton
1900 Barnsley 29 18
1901 Woolwich Arsenal 7 2
1901 Gainsborough Trinity 0
1901 Stockport County 14 4
Mexborough United
St Mirren
Tottenham Hotspur
Partick Thistle
1906 1908 Blackpool 26 1
Workington

Swann, Herbert CF
b Lytham 28/3/1882 d 1954
Lytham Institute
1903 1905 Bury 40 11
Plymouth Argyle
Crystal Palace
Queen's Park Rangers

Swann, John William GK
b Broughton 1882
Northern Nomads
1909 Manchester City 1
Northern Nomads
Rochdale

Swarbrick, James (Jimmy) OL
b Lytham St Annes 1881
Blackpool Red Star
Marton Combination
Blackpool Etrurians
1901 1902 Blackburn Rovers 15
Accrington Stanley (loan)
Brentford
1905 1906 Grimsby Town 67 12
1907 1908 Oldham Athletic 4 2
Southport Central
Stoke
Port Vale
Swansea Town
Swansea Albion

Swarbrick, Robert Lewis (Lewis) OL
b Blackpool q4 1881 d 1917
1903 Blackpool 1

Swarbrick, William OL
Blackpool Athletic
Rossendale United
Fleetwood
1912 1913 Preston North End 4 2

Sweeney, Eric E IL/IR
b Rock Ferry 3/10/1905
Flint Town
1925 1929 Manchester United 27 6
1930 Charlton Athletic 9 4
1931 Crewe Alexandra 27 13
1932 Carlisle United 27 3

Sweet, Frank George CH
b Barton Regis q4 1885 d 1956
St Michael's
1910 1911 Bristol City 4 1

Sweetman, Sydney Charles (Syd) RB
b Hendon 2/3/1903 d 1980
Hampstead Town
1924 1928 Queen's Park Rangers 100
1929 1933 Millwall 123 1

From To Apps Goal

Swift, Arnold GK
b West Hartlepool 21/4/1910 d 1966
St James' (Hartlepool)
South Durham Steel & Ironworks
1930 Hartlepools United 3
Trimdon Grange Colliery
1932 1933 Southport 24
1934 1936 Crewe Alexandra 123
South Shields

Swift, Arthur CF
b West Hartlepool 27/11/1889 d 1954
Seaton Carew Ironworks
West Hartlepool Expansion
Hartlepools United
West Hartlepool Perseverance
West Hartlepool Expansion
Seaton Carew Ironworks
West Hartlepool Expansion
1913 West Bromwich Albion 13 4
Worcester City
1914 West Bromwich Albion 15 7
1920 Crystal Palace 1

Swift, Edward S RH
Black Diamonds
1899 Blackburn Rovers 2

Swift, Frank Victor GK
b Blackpool 26/12/1913 d 1958
Caps: FLge 3/England War 14/England 19
Blackpool Corporation Gasworks
Fleetwood
1933 1949 Manchester City 338
1939 (Manchester City) (3)

Swift, Fred GK
b Royton 13/2/1908 d 1971
Lytham
1928 1929 Blackpool 3
Dick, Kerr's XI
Chorley
1933 1934 Oldham Athletic 54
1935 1937 Bolton Wanderers 62
Shrewsbury Town
1939 Swansea Town 0

Swift, George IR
b Coseley 1874 d 1938
Coseley Town
1901 Wolverhampton Wanderers 1 1

Swift, George Harold LB
b St George's, Shropshire 3/2/1870 d 1956
Caps: FLge 1
St George's Swifts
Wellington Town
Wellington St George's
Stoke (trial)
Crewe Alexandra
1891 1893 Wolverhampton Wanderers 59 1
1895 Loughborough 26 1
1896 1901 Leicester Fosse 186 5
1902 Notts County 16
1905 Leeds City 1

Swift, Henry (Harry) CH/RH
b Accrington q4 1885
Accrington Stanley
1909 1912 Burnley 64 2
Third Lanark
Pontypridd

Swift, James IL
b St Helens 6/1/1903 d 1993
Runcorn
1924 Wigan Borough 1
Pilkington's Recreation
1928 Doncaster Rovers 0
Pilkington's Recreation

Swift, Webster RH/CF
b Wombwell q1 1902 d 1967
Wombwell
1927 Halifax Town 14
1928 Barnsley 0
1929 Crewe Alexandra 0
Wombwell
1931 Stockport County 3 1

Swinburne, Thomas Anderson (Tom) GK
b Houghton-le-Spring 9/8/1915 d 1969
Caps: England War 1
East Rainton
1932 Hull City 0
Herrington Colliery
1934 1946 Newcastle United 77
1939 (Newcastle United) (3)
Consett
Horden Colliery Welfare

From To Apps Goal

Swindale, Lancelot (Lance) OR
b Newcastle q4 1903 d 1960
Preston Colliery
Blyth Spartans
1921 Coventry City 4
Shildon Athletic
Blyth Spartans
Pembroke Dock

Swindells, Herbert (Bert) CF/IR
b Stockport 13/8/1909 d 2001
Stockport Sunday School
Alderley Edge United
1927 1936 Crewe Alexandra 247 127
1937 Chesterfield 0
Chelmsford City
1937 Barrow 23 7
1938 Bradford City 15 5
Hyde United
Hurst

Swindells, James OR/OL
1902 1906 Glossop 7 1

Swinden, James Frederick IR
b Fulham 30/1/1905 d 1971
Salisbury City
Pirelli General
1926 1927 Southampton 3
Newport (Isle of Wight)

Swinden, Sidney Allan RB/LB
b King's Norton 17/8/1913 d 1987
Smethwick Highfield
1936 West Bromwich Albion 4
1937 1938 Swindon Town 36
1939 Accrington Stanley (3) (1)
Oldbury Town

Swindin, George Hedley GK
b Campsall 4/12/1914 d 2005
Rotherham YMCA
New Stubbin Colliery
1932 Rotherham United 0
1934 1935 Bradford City 26
1936 1953 Arsenal 271
Peterborough United

Swinfen, Reginald (Reg) RB/CF/IR
b Battersea 4/5/1915 d 1996
Civil Service
1936 1946 Queen's Park Rangers 26 5
1939 (Queen's Park Rangers) (2) (1)
Yeovil Town
Tonbridge
Crawley Town

Sword, Ronald RH
b Dundee 6/5/1916 d 2010
Dunfermline Athletic
1938 Carlisle United 6 1
Buxton

Sykes, Albert LH
b Shirebrook 29/9/1900 d 1994
Maltby Victoria
Maltby Main Colliery Welfare
1924 Birmingham 1
1926 1927 Brighton & Hove Albion 16
1928 1930 Lincoln City 42 1
Peterborough & Fletton United
1932 Luton Town 0
Grantham

Sykes, Arthur Broughton OR
b Grimsby 16/6/1897 d 1978
Grimsby Rovers
1920 Grimsby Town 1
Grimsby Rovers
Louth Town

Sykes, Arthur Victor GK
b Swindon 1902
Maidstone United
1924 1925 Gillingham 7
Folkestone

Sykes, Ernest Alfred RB/LB
b Temple Normanton 27/11/1915 d 1997
Sutton Town
1936 1938 Birmingham 8
1939 Cardiff City (3)

Sykes, Herbert OL
b Barnsley
Houghton Main Colliery
1921 1922 Chesterfield 4 1

Sykes, John George (Jack) LH
b Wombwell q3 1915 d 1948
Wombwell
1933 1936 Birmingham 33
1937 1938 Millwall 7

From To Apps Goal

Sykes, Joseph (Joe) CH/RH/LH
b Sheffield 8/1/1898 d 1974
Caps: WLge 2
1919 1923 Sheffield Wednesday 29 1
1924 1934 Swansea Town 314 7

Sykes, Richard CH/IL
b South Elmsall 28/11/1910 d 1988
South Kirkby Colliery
1932 1934 Rotherham United 54 2

Sykes, William RH
b Sheffield
Atlas & Norfolk
1919 Sheffield United 1

Sylph, James LB
b Chirton q1 1882 d 1947
Jarrow
1903 Barnsley 1

Sylvester, Henry (Harry) IR
b Loughborough q4 1880
1899 Loughborough 1

Sylvester, Thomas (Tom) RB
1908 Derby County 2
Loughborough Corinthians
Mansfield Town
Holwell Works

Syme, Robert Graham CF
b South Queensferry 13/12/1907 d 1972
Hearts o' Beath
Blairhall
Dunfermline Athletic
1931 1933 Manchester City 11 2
1934 Burnley 9
Dunfermline Athletic
Dundee United

Symes, Herbert Charles (Ernie) LB
b Fulham 22/8/1892 d 1977
Acton
1920 1922 Fulham 6
1923 Aberdare Athletic 31
1924 1925 Queen's Park Rangers 26
Grays Thurrock

Symon, James Scotland (Scot) LH/RH
b Errol 9/5/1911 d 1985
Caps: Scotland 1
Errol Amateurs
Perth North End
Dundee Violet
Dundee
1935 1937 Portsmouth 66 6
Rangers

Symons, John J RB
b London
1937 Aldershot 1

Synott, William James RB
b Widnes q4 1882 d 1916
1904 1905 Glossop 27

Syred, Thomas George OR/CF
b Gillingham 2/11/1912 d 1979
1933 1934 Gillingham 9 1
1935 Burnley 0

Tabram, Philip (Phil) CH
b Swansea 11/11/1917 d 1989
Cwm Mission
1938 Swansea Town 11 1
1939 (Swansea Town) (3)
Merthyr Tydfil
Hafod Brotherhood

Tabram, William David (Billy) CH/RH/LH
b Swansea 19/1/1909 d 1992
Caps: Wales Sch
Cwm Mission
Cwm Athletic
1928 Preston North End (trial) 0
1929 1932 Swansea Town 20
1933 Port Vale 35 1
1934 1936 Hull City 106 5
South Shields
Haverfordwest Athletic

Tadman, George Henry OR/CF
b Rainham, Kent 5/1/1914 d 1994
Rainham
1932 Gillingham 0
1933 1934 Bristol Rovers 5 2
1935 Gillingham 40 18
1936 1938 Charlton Athletic 87 47
1939 (Charlton Athletic) (3) (2)
Cheltenham Town

Taft, Henry Edward (Harry) GK
b Melbourne, Derbyshire q1 1875 d 1937
1902 Burton United 1

From To | Apps Goal

Tagg, Ernest (Ernie) RH/IL/IR
b Crewe 15/9/1917 d 2006
1937 Crewe Alexandra 19 7
1938 Wolverhampton Wanderers 1
1945 1948 Bournemouth & Boscombe Ath 80 8
1948 Carlisle United 5 1

Taggart, John (Jack 'Mit') LH
b Belfast 3/2/1872 d 1927
Caps: Ireland 1
Distillery
Middlesbrough
1892 1895 West Bromwich Albion 68 4
1896 1900 Walsall 113 1

Tainton, Walter RH
b Smethwick 8/1882 d 1937
Smethwick Centaur
1906 Aston Villa 1
Birmingham Welfare
Hockley Hill Methodists

Tait, Alexander Gilchrist (Sandy) LB/RB
b Glenbuck 1873 d 1949
Glenbuck Athletic
Ayr
Royal Albert (loan)
Rangers
Motherwell
1894 1898 Preston North End 76
Tottenham Hotspur
Leyton
Croydon Common

Tait, David RH
Renton
1896 Manchester City 4 2
1898 Darwen 4

Tait, James (Jimmy) IL
b Edinburgh
Petershill
Bo'ness
Heart of Midlothian
Broxburn United (loan)
1923 Bournemouth & Boscombe Ath 12 4

Tait, John Fordyce (James) IL
b Newcastle q4 1896 d 1934
Lintz Institute
Ashington
Scotswood
1921 Newcastle United 0
Lintz Institute
1922 Ashington 8 1

Tait, Thomas (Tommy) CF/IR
b Hetton-le-Hole 20/11/1908 d 1976
Caps: England Sch
1923 Sunderland 0
Hetton
1927 Middlesbrough 0
1927 Southport 15 10
1927 1930 Manchester City 61 43
1930 Bolton Wanderers 9 4
1931 1933 Luton Town 84 50
1934 Bournemouth & Boscombe Ath 12 5
1934 1938 Reading 144 79
1939 1945 Torquay United (3)

Tait, Thomas Somerville (Tommy) RH
b Carluke 13/9/1879
Caps: Scotland 1
Cambuslang Rangers
Airdrieonians
Bristol Rovers
1906 1911 Sunderland 182 2
Dundee
Wishaw Thistle
Jarrow
Armadale

Tait, William IR
b Glasgow 1863
Glasgow Parkside
Glasgow Pilgrims
Third Lanark
Newton Heath
1888 Burnley 5 5
Newton Heath
West Manchester
Ardwick

Talbot, Alexander Douglas (Alec) CH
b Cannock 13/7/1902 d 1975
Caps: FLge 1
Hednesford Primitives
Hednesford Town
1923 1934 Aston Villa 240 7
1935 Bradford Park Avenue 6 1
Brierley Hill Alliance
Stourbridge

Talbot, Arthur GK
Hednesford Town
1896 Woolwich Arsenal 5

From To | Apps Goal

Talbot, Frank Leslie (Les) IL/IR
b Hednesford 3/8/1910 d 1983
Hednesford Town
1930 1935 Blackburn Rovers 90 20
1936 1938 Cardiff City 94 21
1939 1946 Walsall 18 5
1939 (Walsall) (3)

Talbot, Fred IR
b 1886
Newton-le-Willows
1906 1907 Bury 3
Ashton Town

Talbot, George Robson GK
b Willington Quay 15/7/1910 d 1990
Willington Athletic
Wallsend
1933 Liverpool 0
1934 Oldham Athletic 2
1935 Gateshead 13
1935 1936 Southport 32

Talbot, James Hunter (Jimmy) OL
b Craghead 3/11/1905 d 1983
Ravensworth Albion
Craghead United
1928 1929 South Shields 35 5
1930 Gateshead 16 3
1931 Barrow 18 5
Wallsend Town
Blyth Spartans
West Stanley

Talbot, Robert Curry LB/RB
b North Hylton 20/9/1908 d 1971
Hetton United
1930 West Ham United 0
1931 Burnley 0
West Stanley
1932 Newport County 10
Wigan Athletic
1935 Oldham Athletic 13

Talbot-Lewis, Albert Edward GK
b Bedminster 20/1/1877 d 1956
Bedminster
Bristol City
1898 Everton 0
Bristol City
Walsall
1902 1903 Sheffield United 15
1904 Sunderland 4
Luton Town
1906 Leicester Fosse 38
1907 Bristol City 21

Talks, Thomas (Tommy) CF
b Lincoln 15/5/1897 d 1987
1919 Lincoln City 0
Grimsby Rovers
1920 1921 Grimsby Town 15 4
Boston Town

Tann, Bertram James (Bert) RH/IR/CH
b Plaistow 4/5/1914 d 1972
1931 Clapton Orient 0
Romford
1933 1938 Charlton Athletic 19 2

Tannahill, Robert OR
b Kilmarnock 1870 d 1950
Kilmarnock
1892 Blackburn Rovers 0
1892 1896 Bolton Wanderers 67 8
Tottenham Hotspur
Millwall Athletic
1899 Chesterfield (loan) 4 2
Fulham
Grays United
Oldham Athletic

Tapken, Norman GK
b Wallsend 21/2/1913 d 1996
Caps: Lol 2
Wallsend Thermal Welfare
1934 1937 Newcastle United 106
1938 Manchester United 14
1946 1947 Darlington 31
Shelbourne

Tapp, Lewis John Henry (Lew) LB
b Taunton 20/11/1910 d 1964
Newton Abbot Corinthians
1931 1936 Torquay United 158
Newton Abbot

Tarbuck, Frederick LB
b St Helens
1921 Stockport County 1

From To | Apps Goal

Targett, Alfred Nicholas (Alf) LH
b Southampton 14/1/1916 d 1983
1931 Arsenal 0
Bournemouth Gasworks
1932 Southampton 0
1936 Fulham 1

Tarplin, Walter IL/CF
b Small Heath 30/3/1879 d 1937
Small Heath Albion
Coventry City
1903 1907 Notts County 97 25
Reading
Stafford Rangers
Shrewsbury Town

Tarrant, Frederick (Fred) CF
b Hoylake 28/7/1913 d 1970
Hoylake
1934 New Brighton 1

Tarrant, Harold Henry C OR
b New Milton 28/12/1915 d 2002
New Milton
1936 Bournemouth & Boscombe Ath 1
Poole Town

Tart, William (Billy) OL
b Whittington q3 1876 d 1951
New Whittington Exchange
1899 Chesterfield Town 2
New Whittington Exchange

Tasker, Ernest RB
b Basford q1 1898 d 1934
Hucknall George Street WMC
1919 Notts County 1
Hucknall Byron
Shirebrook

Tasker, Hiram CF
b Bradford 6/11/1898 d 1968
1923 Bradford Park Avenue 4

Tasker, Ronald Henry IL
b Bedminster q3 1891
1913 Bristol City 1

Tate, Isaac Holliday (Hal) GK
b Gateshead 21/7/1906 d 1986
Marley Hill
1924 Newcastle United 4
1927 1928 West Ham United 14
1929 1934 Doncaster Rovers 127

Tate, John Anthony GK
b Chester-le-Street 6/12/1892
West Stanley
1912 1913 Tottenham Hotspur 4
West Stanley

Tate, Joseph Thomas (Joe) LH
b Old Hill 4/8/1904 d 1973
Caps: FLge 1/England 3
Grainger's Lane Primitives
Round Oaks Works
Cradley Heath
1927 1933 Aston Villa 180 2
Brierley Hill Alliance

Tate, William George OR
b Sunderland 1/8/1915 d 2005
Hetton United
1937 Carlisle United 14 3
Horden Colliery Welfare

Tatem, Frank E GK
b West Bromwich 1888
Willenhall Pickwick
1907 Wolverhampton Wanderers 2
Brierley Hill Alliance
Hednesford Town
Stourbridge
Netherton

Tatham, William (Willie) GK
b Burnley
1895 1896 Burnley 45
1897 Bolton Wanderers 2
1898 1900 Burnley 6
Nelson

Tattersall, Harold (Harry) RH
Haslingden
1912 1913 Stockport County 34
Rossendale United
Mossley

Tattersall, James LH/CH
1888 1892 Accrington 100 2
Southport Central

From To | Apps Goal

Tattersall, John GK
b Church
St Mary's RC (Oswaldtwistle)
1921 Accrington Stanley 3
Barnoldswick Town

Tattersall, John Garner (Garner) IL
b Hull 13/9/1910 d 1984
Warley Circuit
1936 Halifax Town 4

Tattersall, Walter Scott (Wally) OR/OL
b Warsop 4/9/1888 d 1968
Mansfield Wesleyans
Warsop United
Moores Athletic (Shirebrook)
1907 Chesterfield Town 3
Mansfield Mechanics
Watford
1911 1914 Tottenham Hotspur 44 3
Shirebrook
Welbeck Colliery
Sutton Junction

Tattersall, William RB
Heywood
1894 1895 Burnley 5
Nelson

Tatton, John Henry (Jack) OR
b Dunston-on-Tyne 23/11/1894 d 1973
Dunston Atlas Villa
1911 Newcastle United 0
Gillingham
1919 Preston North End 18 1
1919 1921 Oldham Athletic 67 2

Taylor, ? OR
1894 Crewe Alexandra 1

Taylor, Albert CF
Stockport County
1893 Walsall Town Swifts 1

Taylor, Albert OL/CF
b Ashington 10/7/1908 d 1957
1928 Ashington 1
Armstrong Whitworth
Blyth Spartans
Bedlington United
1929 South Shields 18 7
1930 Gateshead 27 3
1931 Chelsea 0
1933 1935 Bristol Rovers 54 17
1936 Lincoln City 4
1937 Gillingham 9 3
Bexleyheath & Welling

Taylor, Alec OR
b Maltby 21/12/1906 d 1993
Maltby Main Colliery Welfare
1927 Rotherham United 2

Taylor, Alexander (Alex) CH/LB
b Menstrie 25/12/1916 d 1982
King's Park
1938 1946 Carlisle United 24
1939 (Reading) (2)

Taylor, Allan GK
b North Shields 1/12/1905 d 1981
North Shields
1925 Newcastle United 1
1926 1928 South Shields 34
1931 1935 Tottenham Hotspur 60
1937 Hartlepools United 25

Taylor, Archibald (Archie) LB/RB
b Dundee 28/11/1879 d 1966
Dundee East Craigie
1904 Bolton Wanderers 3
Bristol Rovers
Brentford
West Ham United
Dundee
Falkirk
1910 Huddersfield Town 29
1911 1912 Barnsley 57
York City

Taylor, Archibald (Archie) RH/IL/IR
b Glasgow 4/10/1918 d 1976
Cambuslang
1938 Burnley 3 1
1939 1947 Reading 15 2
1939 (Carlisle United) (2)
1948 1950 Leyton Orient 46 1
Bath City

Taylor, Arthur B CH
b 1879 d 1947
Midland Athletic
1899 Lincoln City 0
Midland Athletic
Grantham Avenue
1905 Lincoln City 6

From To Apps Goal

Taylor, Charles IR
b Sheffield 1907
Dinnington
1927 Manchester United 0
1928 Halifax Town 6 1

Taylor, Charles Stanley (Stan) IR/CF
b Sheffield q3 1897 d 1963
Norfolk Amateurs
1919 Sheffield Wednesday 7
Norton Woodseats
1923 Sheffield United 1 1
Denaby United
Mexborough Athletic
Worksop Town
Mexborough Athletic
Worksop Town

Taylor, Christopher CH/IR
b Small Heath q3 1904
Evesham Town
Redditch
1924 1929 Manchester United 28 6
Hyde United

Taylor, David LB/CH
b Bannockburn 5/8/1884 d 1949
Bannockburn Juniors
Falkirk (trial)
Glasgow Ashfield
Rangers
Motherwell (loan)
1910 1911 Bradford City 45 1
1911 1923 Burnley 221 5
Ayr United (loan)
Rangers (loan)
Falkirk (loan)
Celtic (loan)

Taylor, David IR/OR
b Cwmbran q4 1909
2nd Monmouthshire Regiment
1927 1928 Newport County 7

Taylor, Eden IR
b Sheffield 1916
1936 Wolverhampton Wanderers 0
1937 Bournemouth & Boscombe Ath 4 2
Ipswich Town
1938 Portsmouth 4 1
1939 Watford 0

Taylor, Edward Hallows (Ted) GK
b Liverpool 7/3/1887 d 1956
Caps: FLge 2/England 8
Marlborough Old Boys (Liverpool)
Liverpool Balmoral
1912 1921 Oldham Athletic 87
1922 1926 Huddersfield Town 119
1926 1927 Everton 40
Ashton National
1928 Wrexham 25

Taylor, Ernest (Ernie) RB
b Mansfield 1901
Mansfield Town
1923 Southend United 5
Frickley Colliery

Taylor, Francis Edward (Frank) IR/IL/CF
b Wolverhampton 16/7/1901 d 1973
Sunbeam Motors
1921 Port Vale 0
Sunbeam Motors
1923 1925 Newport County 34 12
1926 1927 Bournemouth & Boscombe Ath 61 21
1928 Gillingham 29 8
Shrewsbury Town

Taylor, Frank OL/CF
b 1887 d 1928
Lincoln Liberal Club
1905 1907 Lincoln City 36 10
Worksop Town
Merthyr Town

Taylor, Frank LB/RB
b Hemsworth 30/4/1916 d 1970
Caps: England War 1
1936 1938 Wolverhampton Wanderers 48
1939 (Wolverhampton Wanderers) (3)

Taylor, Fred LH
b Grimsby q2 1877
Grimsby All Saints
1897 Grimsby Town 1
Grimsby All Saints

Taylor, Fred OR
b Heywood 1914
Heywood St James'
1935 Rochdale 6 3

From To Apps Goal

Taylor, Frederick (Fred) RH/IR
b Rotherham 1884
Caps: FLge 1
Rotherham Town
1905 Gainsborough Trinity 21 10
Kimberworth
1907 1909 Gainsborough Trinity 84 1
1909 1914 Chelsea 155 4
Brentford
Maidstone United
1921 Rochdale 19
Fletton United

Taylor, Frederick (Fred) OR
b Burnley 24/2/1920 d 1983
Briercliffe St James
1937 1946 Burnley 49 7
1948 1949 New Brighton 55 10

Taylor, George LH
b Burtonwood
Skelmersdale United
1920 Exeter City 6
Skelmersdale United

Taylor, George IR/IL
b Cramlington
Bedlington United
1921 1922 Ashington 7 1
Craghead United
Cramlington Rovers

Taylor, George CF/IR
b Failsworth 23/1/1901
Ferranti
Hurst
1924 1928 Oldham Athletic 71 22
Macclesfield
Sandbach Ramblers
Hurst
1933 Newport County 11 6
Hurst

Taylor, George LH
b Ashton-under-Lyne 23/4/1909
Caps: England Sch
1930 1938 Bolton Wanderers 220 3
1939 (Bolton Wanderers) (3)

Taylor, George Arthur GK
b Grimsby q1 1916
Boston United
1938 Notts County 6

Taylor, George E GK
Worksop Town
1931 Halifax Town 7

Taylor, George Hector OR
b Brentford 2/6/1900 d 1982
Brentford Thursday
1920 Brentford 23
1921 1922 Millwall Athletic 23
1923 Clapton Orient 0

Taylor, George Thomas OR/OL
b Walsall 23/4/1907
Caps: England Sch
Walsall Wood
Bloxwich Strollers
Stourbridge
1925 1933 Notts County 265 46
1933 1937 Bolton Wanderers 150 27
1937 1938 Coventry City 65 11

Taylor, Harold (Harry) CF
b Dudley 9/1893 d 1974
Dudley Bean
1920 West Bromwich Albion 9 2
1921 Barrow 9 4
Shrewsbury Town
Bilston
Brierley Hill Alliance
Bristol Steel Works

Taylor, Harold (Harry) OL
b Ripley
Ripley Town
1926 1927 Nelson 17 4
Mossley
Horwich RMI

Taylor, Harold (Harry) OR/LH/OL
b Hanley 1912
Stoke St Peter's
1929 1931 Stoke City 24 11
1932 1936 Liverpool 69 6

Taylor, Harold (Lal) RH/IR
b Boston 20/12/1910 d 1970
Vulcan
High Park
1931 Southport 1
1933 1938 Clapton Orient 174 13
1939 (Clapton Orient) (2)

From To Apps Goal

Taylor, Harold William RH
b Frizinghall 18/11/1902 d 1963
Little Hoton Moravian Church
Marshfield Athletic
1921 1931 Bradford Park Avenue 335 15
1932 Southport 24 1
1933 Oldham Athletic (trial) 0
1933 1934 Stockport County 9

Taylor, Harry OR
b Chesterfield 1874 d 1955
Brampton Works
Sheepbridge Works
1900 Chesterfield Town 3 1
Sheepbridge Works
1902 Chesterfield Town 0

Taylor, Henry George (Harry) IR/CF/IL
b Fegg Hayes 1889
Chell Heath
Fegg Hayes
Stoke
1911 Huddersfield Town 15 5
Port Vale
1912 1920 Manchester City 91 27
1921 Port Vale 0

Taylor, Herbert GK
b Burbage q4 1880 d 1928
Hinckley Town
1903 1913 Preston North End 108

Taylor, Hiram Alfred (Dick) LB
b Earl Shilton 24/10/1891 d 1962
Earl Shilton Town
Earl Shilton Victor
Earl Shilton Town
1914 Leicester Fosse 14
Nuneaton Town
Hinckley United

Taylor, James LH
Wallsend Park Villa
1907 1909 Sheffield Wednesday 20
1910 Leicester Fosse 0
Doncaster Rovers

Taylor, James IR
1922 Stalybridge Celtic 10

Taylor, James CF
Lincoln Butchers
1922 Coventry City (trial) 0
1923 Lincoln City 1

Taylor, James RH
b Ashton-under-Lyne
Droylsden
1928 Exeter City 2
1928 Southport 0
Hurst

Taylor, James Henry (Harry) IR
b Derby q2 1888
1907 Derby County 0
Langley Mill
Sutton Town
1909 1910 Barnsley 16 7
Ilkeston United
Portsmouth

Taylor, Job LH/CF/RH
b Wigan 29/11/1908 d 1981
Tyldesley
1929 1930 New Brighton 43 21
1930 1935 Stockport County 80 10
1935 1936 Chesterfield 22 1
1937 Crewe Alexandra 10 1
Chorley

Taylor, John (Jock) IR
b Elgin 1886 d 1916
Parkhead
1907 1908 Hull City 9 3
Tunbridge Wells Rangers
New Brompton
Leith Athletic

Taylor, John (Jack) CF
b Newcastle 1900
Christ Church
Jarrow
St Peter's Albion
1923 Bristol Rovers 5 1
Leadgate Park

Taylor, John (Jack) LB/RB
b Barnsley 15/2/1914 d 1978
Worsborough Bridge Athletic
1935 1937 Wolverhampton Wanderers 79
1938 1946 Norwich City 50
1939 (Norwich City) (3)
1947 1949 Hull City 72
Weymouth

From To Apps Goal

Taylor, John Arthur (Arthur) CF/IR
b Chesterfield q3 1880 d 1963
Newbold White Star
1901 1907 Chesterfield Town 126 21
Rotherham County
Worksop Town
Chesterfield Town
Shirebrook

Taylor, John Davidson (Jack) CH/OR/IR
b Dumbarton 27/1/1872 d 1949
Caps: SLge 6/Scotland 4
Dumbarton Albion
Dumbarton
St Mirren
1896 1909 Everton 400 66
South Liverpool

Taylor, John Swinley (Jack) LB/LH/CH
b Cowdenbeath 17/8/1909 d 1964
Raith Rovers
1927 1933 Bristol City 148
1934 Halifax Town 32
1935 1936 Clapton Orient 30
1937 Bristol City 0

Taylor, John W IR
1930 Northampton Town 1
Bedford Town

Taylor, Joseph (Joe) CH/LH
b Burnley q1 1874 d 1938
Bacup Borough
1894 1906 Burnley 323 12

Taylor, Joseph (Joe) IR/CF
b Nottingham 13/4/1905
Lenton United
1925 1926 Nottingham Forest 2
Ilkeston United
1928 Blackpool 4 1
1929 1930 Oldham Athletic 12 7
Hurst
Yeovil & Petters United
Nuneaton Town
Nottingham LMS

Taylor, Joseph Thomas (Joe) LH/IL/OL
b West Bromwich 23/7/1909 d 1977
Wednesbury
Leamington Town
Shrewsbury Town
1934 Luton Town 1
1935 1936 Carlisle United 58 11
1936 1937 Stockport County 19 4
1938 Oldham Athletic 13 6

Taylor, JS IL
1891 Preston North End 1 1

Taylor, Martin Seymour CF
b Annfield Plain 5/1899 d 1962
Annfield Plain
1921 Aston Villa 1
1922 Durham City 0

Taylor, Oliver GK
b Wednesfield 1880
Bilston United
1901 1902 West Bromwich Albion 5
Coventry City

Taylor, Philip Henry (Phil) RH/IR
b Bristol 18/9/1917
Caps: England Sch/FLge 4/England B/England 3
Bristol St George
1935 Bristol Rovers 21 2
1935 1953 Liverpool 312 32
1939 (Liverpool) (2) (2)

Taylor, Richard Eric (Dick) CH
b Wolverhampton 9/4/1918 d 1995
1934 Wolverhampton Wanderers 0
1938 1947 Grimsby Town 36
1950 1953 Scunthorpe United 131 2
RTM

Taylor, Robert (Bob) OL/LH/CH
b Daubhill 1876 d 1919
Willow Dale
Black Lane
1900 Everton 0
1901 1906 Bolton Wanderers 104 18
Atherton
Bacup
Oswaldtwistle Rovers

From	To		Apps	Goal
Taylor, Robert (Bob)			IR	
b Stirling 24/9/1904			d 1962	
		Sauchie United		
		Alva Albion Rovers		
		St Bernard's		
		Stenhousemuir		
		Third Lanark		
1927		Middlesbrough	0	
1928		Southport	31	11
		Connah's Quay & Shotton		
		Stafford Rangers		
		Stenhousemuir		
		Bo'ness		
Taylor, Robert Craig			OL	
b 4/1/1897				
		Seaton Delaval		
1921		Derby County	2	
Taylor, Samuel (Sam)			IL/IR	
b Birmingham 20/11/1902			d 1975	
		Cradley Heath		
1926		Birmingham	0	
		Stourbridge		
1928	1929	Chesterfield	59	26
1930	1931	Wrexham	81	26
1932		Walsall	20	4
		Hereford United		
		Gaskell & Chambers		
Taylor, Samuel James (Sam)			IL/IR/CF	
b Sheffield 17/9/1893			d 1973	
		Atlas & Norfolk Works		
		Silverwood Colliery		
1919	1920	Huddersfield Town	61	39
1920	1924	Sheffield Wednesday	120	36
		Mansfield Town		
1926	1927	Southampton	69	17
1928		Halifax Town	13	3
		Grantham		
1929	1930	Chesterfield	24	8
		Llanelly		
		Loughborough Corinthians		
Taylor, Sidney G			OL	
1934		Cardiff City	1	
Taylor, Stanley			RH	
1935		Rochdale	2	
Taylor, Thomas			IR	
1900		Blackpool	1	
Taylor, Thomas (Tom)			IR/IL	
b St Helens 1901				
		Rhos		
1926		Manchester City	0	
1927	1928	Southampton	8	4
		Rhyl		
		Caernarvon Athletic		
Taylor, Thomas (Tommy)			OR	
b Walsall 1916				
		Streetly Works		
1938		Notts County	25	1
1939		Walsall	0	
Taylor, Thomas C			OR	
b Gillingham				
1925		Gillingham	1	
1926		New Brighton	0	
Taylor, Walter			OR	
b 1901				
		New Mills		
1921		Manchester United	1	
		Chester		
Taylor, Walter Joseph (Wally)			LH/CF	
b Norwich 6/6/1887			d 1961	
		St James (Norwich)		
		Norwich City		
		Doncaster Rovers		
1921	1922	Norwich City	2	
		Phoenix Works		
Taylor, William			OR	
b Edinburgh 1870			d 1949	
Caps: Scotland 1				
		Dalry Primrose		
		Heart of Midlothian		
1892		Blackburn Rovers	10	1
		Heart of Midlothian		
		Leith Athletic		
Taylor, William (Bill 'Artful')			CH/OL	
1892		West Bromwich Albion	0	
		Walsall Unity		
1894	1896	Walsall Town Swifts	27	6

From	To		Apps	Goal
Taylor, William			LB	
b Edinburgh 1885				
		Dudley		
1905		Gainsborough Trinity	4	
		West Ham United		
		Croydon Common		
		Airdrieonians		
		Dunfermline Athletic		
		Newport County		
		Glentoran		
		Hartlepools United		
Taylor, William (Bill)			LH/CH	
b Southwell 1886			d 1966	
		Southwell		
		Mansfield Mechanics		
1913		Notts County	0	
		Mansfield Mechanics		
		Shirebrook		
1919	1920	Burnley	17	2
1920	1924	Oldham Athletic	109	1
		Newark Town		
Taylor, William (Billy)			IL	
b Crook 1899				
		Durham City		
		Crook Town		
		Norwich City (trial)		
1919	1921	Sheffield Wednesday	16	4
		Doncaster Rovers		
		Mansfield Town		
		Mexborough Town		
		Mansfield Town		
1925		Doncaster Rovers	19	5
		Denaby United		
		Mexborough Town		
		Worksop Town		
Taylor, William (Billy)			OL/OR	
b Langley Green 5/6/1898			d 1965	
Caps: WLge 1				
		Langley Green Zion		
1920		West Bromwich Albion (trial)	0	
		Redditch Town		
		Stourbridge		
1922	1924	Cardiff City	6	
1924	1925	Aberdare Athletic	47	10
1926	1930	Hull City	152	17
1931		Norwich City	13	2
		Llanelly		
1933		Aldershot	4	
		Chance & Hunt		
Taylor, William (Billy)			IR	
		Coxhoe United		
		Crook Town		
		Durham City		
		Coxhoe United		
1923		Durham City	1	
		Wingate Albion Comrades		
		Ferryhill Athletic		
Taylor, William			LB	
b Consett				
		Consett		
1929	1930	Darlington	3	
Taylor, William Thomas (Will)			IL	
b Millwall 29/10/1893				
		Christ Church Athletic		
		Tower Hamlets		
		Metrogas		
1912	1920	Fulham	49	9
		St Mary's Recreation (Putney)		
Tebb, Thomas Edward (Tommy)			IL/IR	
b Westerhope q1 1911			d 1957	
		Throckley Welfare		
		Scotswood		
1929		Aston Villa (trial)	0	
1929		Hull City (trial)	0	
		Washington Colliery		
1930		Nelson	14	2
1931		Wigan Borough	6	
		Chopwell		
		Lancaster Town		
1933		Tottenham Hotspur	0	
		Northfleet (loan)		
		Blyth Spartans		
Tebbs, John			OL	
b Loughborough 1881				
1898	1899	Loughborough	33	5
1900	1901	Small Heath	4	1
		Leicester United		
Tebbutt, Thomas			GK	
1895		Nottingham Forest	1	
Telford, Robert (Bob)			IR/CF	
b Invergarry				
		Leith Athletic		
1926		Hartlepools United	3	
1926		Doncaster Rovers	1	1

From	To		Apps	Goal
Telling, Hubert			RH/LH/CH	
b Swindon 28/3/1913			d 1989	
		Swindon Victoria		
1934		Reading	1	
1936		Crystal Palace	3	
1937		Hartlepools United	2	
Tellum, James			RH/LH/IL	
b West Sleekburn q4 1883			d 1967	
		Ashington		
		Bedlington United		
1906		Sheffield Wednesday	0	
1907		Gainsborough Trinity	33	6
		Millwall Athletic		
1909	1911	Gainsborough Trinity	103	3
Tempest, William (Billy)			OL	
b Stoke-on-Trent 8/1/1893			d 1945	
1911		Huddersfield Town	0	
		Trentham		
1919	1923	Stoke	164	22
1924	1925	Port Vale	45	3
Temple, Ernest Daniel (Ernie)			GK	
b West Kirby 5/3/1910			d 1975	
		Heswall		
		Hoylake		
		West Kirby		
1932		Tranmere Rovers	1	
1935		New Brighton	18	
1936		Tranmere Rovers	1	
		Northwich Victoria		
		Macclesfield		
Temple, George Arthur (Arthur)			IL/IR/CF	
b Newcastle 1887			d 1959	
		Newcastle East End		
		Wallsend Park Villa		
1907	1913	Hull City	173	77
		Blyth Spartans		
Temple, James Leslie (Jimmy)			OR	
b Scarborough 16/9/1904			d 1943	
		Tyneside Juniors (Wallsend)		
		Preston Colliery		
		Wallsend		
1926	1930	Fulham	156	58
1931	1932	Sunderland	31	12
1933		Gateshead	18	4
		Crook Town		
		Ashington		
		Murton Colliery Welfare		
Temple, William (Bill)			IL/IR	
b Winlaton 12/12/1914			d 2006	
		Newbiggin Juniors		
		Newbiggin West End		
1934	1936	Aldershot	14	2
1937		Carlisle United	11	4
1938		Grimsby Town	2	
1946		Gateshead	10	1
Templeman, Joseph (Joe)			OR/IL	
b Liverpool 27/10/1906			d 1994	
1927		Everton	0	
1929	1930	New Brighton	9	1
Templeton, Robert Bryson (Bobby)			OL/OR	
b Coylton 22/6/1879			d 1919	
Caps: SLge 3/Scotland 11				
		Irvine Heatherbell		
		Westmount		
		Neilston Victoria		
		Rosslyn (Irvine)		
		Kilmarnock Rugby XI		
		Kilmarnock (trial)		
		Hibernian		
1898	1902	Aston Villa	64	7
1902	1904	Newcastle United	51	4
1904	1905	Woolwich Arsenal	33	1
		Celtic		
		Kilmarnock		
1913	1914	Fulham	32	
		Kilmarnock		
Tennant, James (Jimmy)			OL	
b Parkhead 1878				
Caps: SLge 1				
		Linton Villa		
		Parkhead		
		St Bernard's		
1899	1900	Woolwich Arsenal	51	8
1901		Middlesbrough	17	7
		Watford		
		Royal Albert		
		Stenhousemuir		
		St Bernard's		
Tennant, James (Jim)			OR	
b Glasgow				
1932		Cardiff City	2	
		St Johnstone		

From	To		Apps	Goal
Tennant, John Willie (Jack)			RB/LB	
b Newcastle 3/8/1907			d 1978	
		Washington Colliery		
1926		Newcastle United	0	
		Washington Colliery		
1930		Stoke City	1	
1932		Torquay United	42	
1933	1934	Liverpool	39	
1935	1938	Bolton Wanderers	99	1
1938		Stoke City	26	
1939		(Stoke City)	(3)	
Tennant, William (Billy)			GK	
b Wolverhampton 12/7/1865			d 1927	
		Willenhall Pickwick		
		Hartshill Unity		
1895	1896	Wolverhampton Wanderers	39	
1898	1900	Walsall	100	
1901		Grimsby Town	13	
		RTM		
Tennant, William			CF	
b Kirkfieldbank 13/9/1904				
		Motherwell		
1930		Norwich City	10	1
Tepper, George Samuel Beverley			OL/OR	
b Doncaster 27/2/1913			d 1985	
		Roman Terrace		
		Thurnscoe Victoria		
		Mexborough		
1930		Chesterfield	3	
1931		Blackpool	0	
1932		Bristol Rovers	0	
		Goldthorpe United		
1933		Plymouth Argyle	1	
		Bath City		
		Thurnscoe Victoria		
Terris, James Lonie			CH	
b Cowdenbeath 21/12/1894				
		Victoria Hawthorn		
		Inverkeithing		
		Cowdenbeath		
		Heart of Midlothian (loan)		
1921		Millwall Athletic	3	
		Falkirk		
1923		Liverpool	0	
		New York Field Club		
		Indiana Flooring		
		New York Giants		
Terry, James Cyril (Cyril)			RB/LB	
b Bloxwich 9/7/1909			d 1956	
		Bloxwich Strollers		
		Stafford Rangers		
1928		Manchester City	0	
1931		Bristol City	5	
		Yeovil & Petters United		
1933		Bristol Rovers	4	
		Kidderminster Harriers		
Tetlow, Albert			IR	
b Ashton-under-Lyne 15/12/1900			d 1993	
		New Moss Colliery		
1921	1922	Stalybridge Celtic	29	14
1923		Nottingham Forest	0	
1924		Walsall	18	7
Tewkesbury, Kenneth Cyril (Ken)			GK	
b Hove 10/4/1909			d 1970	
Caps: England Amat				
		Birmingham University		
		Casuals		
1929	1931	Birmingham	5	
1931		Aston Villa	0	
1932		Notts County	7	
1932		Aston Villa	1	
1935		Bradford Park Avenue	14	
1936	1938	Walsall	75	
Thacker, Francis William (Frank)			LH/IR	
b Sheepbridge q3 1876			d 1949	
		Sheepbridge Red Rose		
		Sheepbridge Works		
1898		Sheffield United	2	
1899	1905	Chesterfield Town	228	25
1906	1907	Clapton Orient	34	1
		Rotherham Town		
		Chesterfield Town		
		Sheepbridge		
		Chesterfield Town		
Thacker, Jack			GK	
b 1919				
		Sunbeam Motors		
1938		Lincoln City	1	
		Sunbeam Motors		

From To Apps Goal

Thackeray, David LH
b Hamilton 16/11/1902 d 1954
Caps: SLge 1
Banknock
Law Winnings
Alloa Athletic
Motherwell
1928 1935 Portsmouth 280 9

Thackeray, Fred LB/RB/CH
b Sheffield 1878
Montrose Works
1900 1902 Sheffield Wednesday 9
1904 Gainsborough Trinity 11
Rotherham County
Eccles Borough

Thackeray, James (Jim) OL
b Hebburn q1 1882
Hebburn Argyle
1904 1909 Middlesbrough 157 16
1910 Bradford Park Avenue 33 3
West Stanley

Thain, Albert Edward IR/IL
b Southall 20/4/1900 d 1979
Southall
Metropolitan Railway
1922 1929 Chelsea 144 44
1931 Bournemouth & Boscombe Ath 20 6

Thain, John William OR
b Pelaw q1 1903
Pelaw
1921 Newcastle United 1
1922 Brentford 5 1
Peterborough & Fletton United
1924 Grimsby Town 26 4
Peterborough & Fletton United

Thayne, William (Billy) CH/RH
b West Hartlepool 13/12/1909 d 1986
Hesleden Wesleyans
Docklands AFC
West Hartlepool Perseverance
Shotton Colliery Welfare
1929 Crystal Palace 0
1930 1933 Hartlepools United 101 8
1934 1935 Luton Town 30
1935 1938 Northampton Town 133
1939 Walsall (3)

Theaker, Clarence Alfred (Cam) GK
b Spalding 8/12/1912 d 1992
Spalding Town
1935 1938 Grimsby Town 5
1938 1946 Newcastle United 13
1947 Hartlepools United 14

Theobald, William Stephen (Stephen) CH
b Plumstead q2 1877 d 1936
St Andrew's (Woolwich)
Woolwich Polytechnic
1902 1908 Woolwich Arsenal 24

Thickett, Henry (Harry) RB
b Hexthorpe 28/3/1873 d 1920
Caps: FLge 2/England 2
Hexthorpe Wanderers
Sheffield United
Doncaster Rovers
1893 Rotherham Town 10
1893 1903 Sheffield United 259 1
1904 Bristol City 14

Thirkell, Percy LB
b Tyne Dock 13/2/1900 d 1997
Darlington
Jarrow
1922 Bolton Wanderers 14
1925 1929 Tranmere Rovers 175
Congleton Town
Whitchurch

Thirlaway, William (Billy) OR/OL
b New Washington 10/10/1896 d 1983
Usworth Colliery
1921 1923 West Ham United 36 2
1924 Southend United 8
1924 Luton Town 13
1925 South Shields 29 4
1926 Birmingham 22 1
1926 1929 Cardiff City 108 22
Tunbridge Wells Rangers
Usworth Colliery

Thirlwell, Thomas William (Tom) RH
b Ashington 4/4/1904 d 1969
West Sleekburn
1928 Ashington 6
Cambois Welfare

From To Apps Goal

Thom, Alexander (Alec) OL
b Stevenston 10/10/1894 d 1973
Leven Academy
Leven Amateurs
Yoker Athletic
Dumbarton
Kilmarnock (loan)
Ayr United (loan)
Motherwell (loan)
Morton
Airdrieonians
1922 1925 Hull City 131 18
1926 1929 Swindon Town 100 24

Thom, John (Jock) IR/CF
b Hurlford 18/5/1899 d 1966
Hurlford Thistle
1921 Birmingham (trial) 0
1922 Nottingham Forest 0
Workington
1924 Leeds United 7 3
1927 Bristol Rovers 6 4
Workington
1932 Aldershot 16 6
Guildford City

Thomas, Albert RH
b Birmingham
1920 1921 Wolverhampton Wanderers 11

Thomas, Albert Brandon LH
b Birmingham 25/4/1899 d 1990
1923 Merthyr Town 21
1924 Walsall 25

Thomas, Alfred Charles (Alf) OR
b Hetton-le-Hole 17/8/1895
Llanelly
Houghton Main Colliery
1921 1922 Bradford City 14 1
1922 Merthyr Town 15
1923 1924 Hull City 36 4
1925 South Shields 0
1926 Ashington 0
Hetton United

Thomas, Alwyn IR/IL
b Tonypandy
Pontypridd
1927 1928 Torquay United 15 2
1929 Exeter City 1

Thomas, Cecil Edward Sidney OL/CF
b Pill 9/8/1909 d 1972
Pill Athletic
1929 Bristol Rovers 4 1
1930 Thames 14 2
Bath City
Pill Athletic

Thomas, David Watkin John (Dave) CF
b Stepney 6/7/1917 d 1991
Romford
1938 1947 Plymouth Argyle 74 29
1947 1950 Watford 105 41
1950 1952 Gillingham 80 42
Sittingbourne

Thomas, Ernest (Ernie) CH
b Rhos 1915
Caps: Wales Amat
Llanerch Celts
Northfleet
1936 Tottenham Hotspur 0
1937 1938 Hartlepools United 62
1939 (Hartlepools United) (1)

Thomas, G CH
1893 Northwich Victoria 2

Thomas, George OR
b Wrexham
Caps: WLge 2
Chirk
1925 1930 Swansea Town 64 10

Thomas, Gwyn IR
1929 Merthyr Town 3

Thomas, Harry LH
1892 Northwich Victoria 1

Thomas, Henry (Harry) OL
b Swansea 28/2/1901
Caps: WLge 1/Wales 1
Swansea Town
Porth
1921 1929 Manchester United 128 12
Waterford
Merthyr Town
Abercarn
Aberavon Harlequins

From To Apps Goal

Thomas, James RH
b Wigan q1 1900
Wigan United
Nondescripts
1921 Wigan Borough 1

Thomas, John William (Jack) IR
b Sacriston 1891
Spennymoor United
Brighton & Hove Albion
1911 Newcastle United 1
Spennymoor United

Thomas, Joseph (Joe) LH
1912 1914 Bolton Wanderers 30

Thomas, Leonard (Len) OR
b Dartford q3 1901
Dartford
Bromley
1922 Fulham 1
Bromley
Dartford
Northfleet
Sheppey United
Chatham
London Paper Mills

Thomas, Levi John LB
b Blaen Clydach 4/10/1902 d 1986
1927 Crewe Alexandra 1
Oswestry Town
Bangor City
Hurst

Thomas, Louis Llewellyn IL
b Fulham q2 1884 d 1949
Bromley
Fulham Amateurs
Fulham
1906 Clapton Orient 6 1
Tunbridge Wells Rangers

Thomas, Reginald George RB
b Weymouth 2/1/1912 d 1983
Weymouth
1931 Southampton 8
Folkestone
Bath City
Guildford City
Sittingbourne
Margate

Thomas, Robert Sherwood (Bob) OR
b Durham q4 1911
Trimdon Grange
1934 Blackpool 6 2
1934 1935 Barnsley 39 2
1936 Millwall 7 1
1938 Tranmere Rovers 9 1

Thomas, Ronald F (Bob) OR
b Swansea 1913
1935 Charlton Athletic 0
1936 Aldershot 35 4
1937 Charlton Athletic 0

Thomas, William IR/IL
b Liverpool 1885
Newcastle Swifts
1904 1905 Burslem Port Vale 11 1
1906 Everton 0
1907 Leeds City 9 2
1908 Barnsley 3
Huddersfield Town

Thomas, William C RB
1921 Aberdare Athletic 1

Thomas, William D IL
b Croydon
1920 Northampton Town 21 2
1921 Millwall Athletic 0

Thomas, William Edward (Billy) RH/CH/RB
b Chorlton 16/3/1906 d 1956
Sutton Rovers
St Helens Town
Runcorn
1927 Liverpool 0
1928 1932 Oldham Athletic 22
1933 Tranmere Rovers 6
1934 Rochdale 6 1
Ashton National
Runcorn

Thomas, William Rees (Billy) OL/IL
b Port Talbot 20/8/1903
Caps: WLge 1/Wales 2
Port Talbot Steelworks
Bridgend
Lovells Athletic
1927 1936 Newport County 285 53
Barry
Aberdare Town

From To Apps Goal

Thomas, William W GK
b 1870
1892 Everton 1

Thomas, Wynford Glyn (Wyn) LH
b Swansea 12/4/1915 d 1987
1935 Swansea Town 0
1936 1937 Halifax Town 50
Runcorn

Thompson, Albert CF
b Llanbradach 1912
Barry
1934 1936 Bradford Park Avenue 11 2
1936 York City 24 24
1937 Swansea Town 4
Wellington Town

Thompson, Albert John OL
b Louth q3 1885 d 1956
Grimsby Rovers
1904 Grimsby Town 2
Grimsby Rovers
Grimsby St John's
Grimsby Rovers

Thompson, Alfred CF
b Padiham 1891 d 1922
Grimsby Rovers
1912 Grimsby Town 0
Grimsby Rovers
1919 Grimsby Town 3 1
Cleethorpes Town
Charlton's (Grimsby)

Thompson, Alfred Alexander IR/IL
b Liverpool 28/4/1891 d 1969
1910 Liverpool 0
1913 Glossop 5 2
1914 Arsenal 0
1920 Brentford 15 2
Guildford United
Tunbridge Wells Rangers

Thompson, Alfred Stanley (Stan) OR
b Durham
Durham City
1929 1934 Brighton & Hove Albion 57 14
1935 Hartlepools United 34 11
1936 Exeter City 3
1937 Hartlepools United 0

Thompson, Andrew (Andy) OR
b Sunderland
Sunderland West End
1904 Sunderland 2
Queen's Park Rangers

Thompson, Andrew (Andy) OR/IR/IL
b Newcastle 21/1/1899 d 1970
Whickham Park Villa
1920 1930 Tottenham Hotspur 153 19
1931 Chester 7 2
1931 Norwich City 12 2
1932 Clapton Orient 18 5
Ashford Town (Kent)
Northfleet

Thompson, Arthur OR
b Durham q1 1900
Esh Brockwell
Durham City
Shildon Athletic
1921 Liverpool (trial) 0
1922 Durham City 2

Thompson, Benjamin Swinhoe (Benny) OL
b Southwick, County Durham 7/1882
Southwick (Co Durham)
1903 Sunderland 0
Southwick (Co Durham)
Fulham
1908 Clapton Orient 6
Hartlepools United

Thompson, Charles RB
b Wrekenton
1920 Newcastle United 0
1921 Queen's Park Rangers 1

Thompson, Charles (Charlie) OL
b Kimberworth 11/7/1903 d 1971
Garrotree Nibs
Rotherham Town
1920 Rotherham County (trial) 0
1921 Chesterfield 2
1922 Birmingham 0
New Brimington
1923 Swindon Town 2
1925 West Ham United 0
1926 Southend United 1 1
Sheppey United

From To Apps Goal

Thompson, Charles (Charlie) LH/RH
b Forest Hall 4/1909
Wallsend
1929 1930 Liverpool 5
1931 Blackpool 0
1932 Barrow 19
Walker Celtic

Thompson, Charles Henry LH
Wolseley Motors
1924 Preston North End 1

Thompson, Cyril IL
Crittall Athletic
1935 Bournemouth & Boscombe Ath 5 1

Thompson, Edward William LB
b Prudhoe q3 1894 d 1918
Spen Black & White
1914 Fulham 1

Thompson, Ernest (Ernie) OR
b Rotherham 1892
South Shields
Rotherham County
1920 Portsmouth 36 1
1921 Sheffield Wednesday 23
1922 1923 Bradford Park Avenue 50 2
1924 Grimsby Town 7
Castleford Town
Scunthorpe & Lindsey United

Thompson, Francis William (Frank) OL
b Ballynahinch 2/10/1885 d 1950
Caps: IrLge 3/Ireland Amat/Ireland 12
Cliftonville
Black Diamonds
Linfield
1910 1912 Bradford City 51 11
Clyde

Thompson, Frank RB/LB/CH
b Egerton 16/5/1897 d 1983
Atherton
1921 1926 Manchester City 33
1927 Swindon Town 7
1928 Halifax Town 19
Horwich RMI

Thompson, Frank CF
b Birtley
St Peter's Albion
1923 Newcastle United 2 1

Thompson, Fred CH
1896 Blackpool 6
Stalybridge Rovers

Thompson, Fred GK
Fleetwood
1914 Blackpool 3

Thompson, Frederick (Fred) RH
b Sheffield 1870 d 1898
Hastings (Sheffield)
The Wednesday
1892 Nottingham Forest 1

Thompson, Frederick T (Fred) GK
b South Hetton 28/7/1875 d 1958
Sunderland West End
1895 Sunderland 2
1896 1901 Bury 65
1902 Bolton Wanderers 20
Luton Town
Portsmouth
Fulham
Norwich City
Doncaster Rovers
Denaby United
Brodsworth Colliery

Thompson, George RB/RH
b Ashington q1 1895
Bedlington United
1919 Burnley 5
1921 1922 Rotherham County 35
1923 1925 Ashington 59 2
Pegswood United
1928 Ashington 1

Thompson, George Alexander OR
b South Shields 23/3/1884
South Shields Bertram
South Shields Adelaide
North Shields Athletic
1906 1908 Sheffield United 40 4
1908 1910 Derby County 46 5
1911 Newcastle United 0

Thompson, George Alfred OR
b Wolverhampton 1878 d 1943
Halesowen
1903 1904 Newcastle United 1
Crystal Palace
Carlisle United

From To Apps Goal

Thompson, George Harry IR
Ticknall
1920 Derby County 4

Thompson, George Herbert GK
b Treeton q4 1900 d 1968
Treeton Reading Rooms
York City
1927 1929 Southampton 14
Dinnington Main Colliery Welfare

Thompson, George Wilfred RH/CH
b Sunderland 15/4/1896 d 1976
Caps: England Sch
Castletown
Southwick (Co Durham)
Norwich City
Croydon Common
Durham City
Norwich City
Aberdare Athletic
Dundee
Torquay United
1923 Reading 23 2
1924 Coventry City 2
Nuneaton Town
1925 Walsall 1
Caernarvon Athletic
Scarborough
Rhyl Athletic
Larne

Thompson, Harold (Harry) IL/IR/CF
b Mansfield 29/4/1915
Mansfield Invicta
1932 Mansfield Town 0
1935 1938 Wolverhampton Wanderers 69 16
1938 Sunderland 11 1
1945 York City 0
1946 1948 Northampton Town 38 2
Headington United

Thompson, Harold John LH
1898 Sheffield United 2

Thompson, Henry LB
b South Hetton 1886
North Shields Athletic
1909 Newcastle United 2
Crystal Palace

Thompson, James LH
1897 Derby County 1

Thompson, James (Jimmy) IR/OL/OR
b Chadderton 24/1/1899 d 1961
Bradbury's Works (Oldham)
1919 Oldham Athletic 2
1920 Manchester City 2
1921 Stalybridge Celtic 31 11
Ashton National
1922 Port Vale 8 3
1923 Blackpool 6 1
1924 Accrington Stanley 42 8
1925 Swindon Town 7 1
1926 Crewe Alexandra 32 4
Hurst
Wilson's Brewery

Thompson, James Edward (Jimmy) IR
b Thornaby 1908
Stockton
Marsden
Weymouth
Whitby United
1929 1931 Hartlepools United 67 22
Falkirk

Thompson, James Gilbert (Jack) RB
b Crewe 7/1900
Nantwich
Ashington
1919 1920 Aston Villa 26
1921 1923 Brighton & Hove Albion 94
Chesterton

From To Apps Goal

Thompson, James William (Jimmy) CF/IL
b West Ham 19/4/1898 d 1984
Custom House
1921 Charlton Athletic 2
Wimbledon
1921 Millwall Athletic 7 3
1923 Coventry City 2
1924 Clapton Orient 1
1925 1926 Luton Town 72 41
1927 1928 Chelsea 37 33
1929 Norwich City 29 17
1929 Sunderland 0
1930 Fulham 4 2
1931 Hull City 1
Tunbridge Wells Rangers
1932 Tranmere Rovers 0
Sittingbourne
Peterborough United
Linfield
1936 Aldershot 0
Lucerne

Thompson, John (Jack) OR
b Redcar 22/7/1892 d 1970
South Bank
Scunthorpe & Lindsey United
1914 1920 Sheffield United 21 2
1920 1921 Bristol City 29 1
Bath City
JS Fry

Thompson, John GK
b Barrow
Southport
1921 Barrow 1
Morecambe
Morecambe Park Villa

Thompson, John CH/RH
b Willesden
Yeovil & Petters United
1924 1925 Queen's Park Rangers 22

Thompson, John (Jack) IR/IL/CF
b Cramlington 21/3/1915 d 1996
Hartford Celtic
Blyth Spartans
1933 1945 Sheffield Wednesday 36 9
1946 1947 Doncaster Rovers 59 17
1948 1952 Chesterfield 82 8

Thompson, John E CF
b Stockport
New Mills
1920 Stockport County 6 2

Thompson, John Ernest (Ernie) CF/OR
b Newbiggin 23/2/1903
Consett
1925 Ashington 0
Stakeford United
1927 Bradford Park Avenue (trial) 0
1928 Carlisle United 2 1
1929 Bristol City 0
Bath City
1931 1936 Blackburn Rovers 171 82
1936 1937 Manchester United 3 1
1937 1938 Gateshead 24 7
1939 York City (3) (1)

Thompson, John William OR
b Alnwick 1888
Alnwick Town
North Shields Athletic
1907 1909 Sunderland 34 15
1910 1911 Preston North End 58 9

Thompson, Leonard (Len) IL
b Sheffield 18/2/1901
Caps: England Sch
Shiregreen Primitive Methodists
Norfolk Amateurs
Hallam
1919 Barnsley 0
Hallam
1921 1922 Birmingham 3
1922 1927 Swansea Town 188 89
1927 1931 Arsenal 26 6
1933 Crystal Palace 2
Islington Corinthians

Thompson, Norman IL
b Forest Hall 5/9/1900 d 1989
1919 Newcastle United 0
Seaton Delaval
Backworth
1922 1924 South Shields 43 7
1925 Middlesbrough 8 3
1926 Barnsley 4
Chilton Colliery Recreation Athletic
York City
West Stanley
1927 1929 Nottingham Forest 12 3
West Stanley
1931 Carlisle United 0
West Stanley

From To Apps Goal

Thompson, Norman CF
b West Moor 5/10/1915 d 1991
Whitley & Monkseaton
1936 Sheffield United 4 1
1937 Hartlepools United 1
Ashington
Blyth Spartans
Jarrow
West Stanley

Thompson, Oliver (Ollie) LH/RH
b Wheatley Hill 11/5/1900 d 1975
Spen Black & White
Spennymoor United
1921 Merthyr Town 0
1922 1927 Chesterfield 219 3
1928 Queen's Park Rangers 18
1929 1931 York City 121 2
1932 Halifax Town 41 1
1933 Chesterfield 0

Thompson, Peter GK
b Rothesay 23/4/1877
Bute Rangers
St Mirren
Partick Thistle
1901 Chesterfield Town 4

Thompson, Ralph Motson OL
b Grimsby q1 1892 d 1916
George Street Wesleyans
Grimsby Rovers
Grimsby St John's
Grimsby Rovers
Haycroft Rovers
1913 1914 Grimsby Town 12

Thompson, Robert LB
b 1870
1892 Everton 1

Thompson, Robert LB
b Crook
1896 Loughborough 30
1897 Gainsborough Trinity 0

Thompson, Robert GK
b Whalley 11/2/1878
Whalley
1898 1899 Blackburn Rovers 9

Thompson, Robert (Bob) CF/OR/IL
b Coundon Grange 1890
Caps: WLge 1
Wingate Albion
1910 1912 Preston North End 17 2
1912 1914 Glossop 47 14
Durham City
1920 Leeds United 23 11
1921 Ashington 17 2
1922 Luton Town 17 7
Pontypridd
1924 Accrington Stanley 33 17
1925 Bury 1
1925 Tranmere Rovers (trial) 0
1926 Hartlepools United 4 3
Goole Town (trial)
York City

Thompson, Robert (Bob) RB/LB
b Newcastle 27/2/1890 d 1958
Blaydon
Swalwell
Scotswood
1911 1912 Leicester Fosse 27
1913 1920 Everton 83
1921 Millwall Athletic 9
1922 Tranmere Rovers 35 5

Thompson, Robert IR
b County Durham 1896
Annfield Plain
1919 Barnsley 2

Thompson, Robert CF
b Liverpool
1925 Bolton Wanderers 0
1926 Tranmere Rovers 1

Thompson, Robert Alfred (Bob) RB/RH
b Derby q3 1876
1894 1898 Leicester Fosse 4
Leicester Banks
South Wigston Albion

Thompson, Sydney CH
b Wallsend 1892
Wallsend Villa
1910 Bradford City 1
Luton Town
Pontypridd

Thompson, Thomas OL
b Smethwick 1879 d 1939
Nettlefolds
1902 Small Heath 1
Oldbury Town

From To Apps Goal

Thompson, Thomas IR
Southwick (Co Durham)
1903 Lincoln City 6
Southwick (Co Durham)

Thompson, Thomas GK
Norwich City
1906 Clapton Orient 1

Thompson, Thomas Henry Fryer (Harry) IL
b Darlington 22/9/1894 d 1980
Spennymoor United
1922 West Ham United 0
1923 New Brighton 6 2

Thompson, Thomas Norman (Tom) CH/RH/LH
b Seaham Harbour 9/3/1893 d 1976
Seaham Bible Class
Seaham Albion
1919 Sunderland 0
1920 1923 Gillingham 73 2
Guildford United

Thompson, Thomas Russell (Tommy) OR
b South Shields 1903 d 1968
Seaton Delaval
1921 1922 Hartlepools United 10
Jarrow

Thompson, Walter J LB
b Sheffield 1911
1932 Aston Villa 0
1933 Northampton Town 2
Scarborough

Thompson, William IR
Dumbarton
1893 Aston Villa 0
1893 Newton Heath 3

Thompson, William RB
South Shields
1902 1905 Gainsborough Trinity 122 2
Fulham
1907 1908 Gainsborough Trinity 33 1

Thompson, William (Billy) OR/IL
b Morpeth 8/1886 d 1933
Caps: SoLge 1
Grangetown Athletic
1905 Middlesbrough 6 2
Morpeth Harriers
1907 1910 West Bromwich Albion 54 6
1911 Sunderland 0
Plymouth Argyle
Queen's Park Rangers
1919 South Shields 0
Queen's Park Rangers
1920 Newport County 18
1921 Hartlepools United 1
Jarrow

Thompson, William K (Willie) CF/OR
b North Seaton 1862
Bedlington Burdon
Shankhouse Black Watch
Newcastle East End
1893 1896 Newcastle United 80 33
Jarrow
Ashington

Thompson, William Potter (Bill) RB/LB
b Derby 17/9/1899
Caps: England Sch
Rolls Royce
1922 1934 Nottingham Forest 364 4
Burton Town

Thompson, William S RB
b Croydon 1910
Wellingborough Town
1934 1935 Northampton Town 7

Thoms, Henry James (Harry) CH/RH
b Greatham 19/11/1896 d 1970
Greatham
1921 Hartlepools United 33 1
1922 1927 Derby County 179 4
1928 Crystal Palace 6 1
Glentoran

Thomson, Alexander (Alex) CF/IR
1900 1902 Middlesbrough 7 3
West Ham United
1905 Chesterfield Town 7 2
West Stanley

Thomson, Arthur IL/IR/CF
b West Stanley q3 1903
West Stanley
Morecambe
1928 1930 Manchester United 3 1
1931 Southend United 14 6
1932 Coventry City 1
1933 Tranmere Rovers 0
Morecambe

From To Apps Goal

Thomson, Charles Bellany (Charlie) CH
b Prestonpans 12/6/1878 d 1936
Caps: SLge 5/Scotland 21
Prestonpans
Heart of Midlothian
1908 1914 Sunderland 236 3

Thomson, Charles Marshall (Charlie) GK
b Perth 25/10/1905
St Johnstone YMCA
Arbroath (trial)
Raith Rovers
Alloa Athletic
Falkirk
1934 1938 Brighton & Hove Albion 169
1939 1945 Exeter City (3)
Dundee United

Thomson, Charles Morgan (Charlie) RH
b Glasgow 11/12/1910 d 1984
Caps: Scotland 1
Pollok
1931 1938 Sunderland 237 7

Thomson, Daniel (Dan) OL
b Dundee 10/8/1891
Aberdeen
St Johnstone
1925 Bristol City 6
1926 Bournemouth & Boscombe Ath 20 2
1927 Torquay United 11 2
1928 Walsall 2

Thomson, Douglas IR
b Dundee 10/8/1891
Dundee Violet
Minnedosa (Canada)
Winnipeg Scottish
Dundee Hibernian
Millwall Athletic
Aberdeen
1923 Grimsby Town 25 3
Dartford

Thomson, Ernest CH/LH
b 1884
Darwen
1907 1908 Manchester United 4
Nelson
Cardiff City
Nelson

Thomson, Gavin CF
b Scotland
Third Lanark
The Wednesday
Stockton
1895 Lincoln City 5 3

Thomson, James OL
b Dumbarton
Clydebank
Renton
1913 Manchester United 6 1
Dumbarton Harp
Clyde
Dumbarton Harp
St Mirren

Thomson, James Hunter (Jimmy) RB
b Deepdale, Shetland 9/5/1884 d 1959
Edinburgh Myrtle
Leith Athletic
Heart of Midlothian
Abercorn
Leith Athletic
Portsmouth
Coventry City
1913 1914 Bury 58
Nelson

Thomson, James Pender OL
b Larkhall 10/11/1908 d 1984
Larkhall Academy
Larkhall Thistle
Strathclyde Juniors
Kilmarnock
Third Lanark
1929 Carlisle United 16 3
Dunfermline Athletic
Newry Town
Larne
Blairhall Colliery

Thomson, John LH/RH
1912 1913 Bradford Park Avenue 8

Thomson, John GK
b Dundee 1897
Shettleston
Dundee
1921 1922 Gillingham 39
1923 Barrow 18
1923 Nelson 2
Glasgow Benburb

From To Apps Goal

Thomson, John IR
b Loanhead 14/4/1916 d 1976
Loanhead Steelworks
1936 1938 Leeds United 41 11
1939 Grimsby Town 0
Worcester City
Hereford United
1948 York City 0

Thomson, John Ross (Jock) LH
b Thornton 6/7/1906 d 1979
Caps: SLge 1/Scotland 1
Thornton Rangers
Dundee
1929 1938 Everton 272 5
Carnoustie Panmure

Thomson, John Yungmann (Jack) GK
b Greenock 27/7/1896 d 1980
Caledonian Juniors
Glasgow Benburb
1921 Bristol Rovers 6
Alloa Athletic
Partick Thistle
Aberaman Athletic
1924 Aberdare Athletic 20
1925 Brentford 40
1926 Plymouth Argyle 7
1927 Chesterfield 22
1927 Coventry City 3
Aberdare & Aberaman
New York Nationals
Nuneaton Town

Thomson, Matthew CH/RH
b Maryhill 5/1886 d 1956
Maryhill
1908 1913 Woolwich Arsenal 89 1
Swindon Town

Thomson, Norman Shaw IR/IL
b Glasgow 20/2/1901 d 1984
St Anthony's (Glasgow)
Dumbarton
Hibernian
1925 1926 Luton Town 43 10
1926 Clapton Orient 10 2
1927 Brighton & Hove Albion 11 5
1928 Walsall 38 13
1929 Norwich City 15
1930 Brentford 1
1932 Swindon Town 3
Folkestone

Thomson, Robert LB
b Glasgow
1911 Huddersfield Town 5

Thomson, Robert Austin (Bertie) OR
b Johnstone 12/7/1907 d 1937
Caps: SLge 2/Scotland 1
Bloomfield Juveniles
Possil Hawthorn
Glasgow Perthshire
Celtic
1933 Blackpool 24 1
Motherwell
Brideville

Thomson, Robert John (Bobby) CF/IL/IR
b Croydon 29/12/1890 d 1971
Dartford
Croydon Common
1911 1920 Chelsea 83 23
1921 1924 Charlton Athletic 70 15
Dartford

Thomson, Robert W (Bob) LB
b Falkirk 24/10/1905
Caps: SLge 1/Scotland 1
Lauriston Villa
Falkirk Amateurs
Falkirk
1927 Sunderland 19
1928 1933 Newcastle United 73
1934 Hull City 4
Olympique Marseille
Racing Club de Paris
Ipswich Town

Thomson, Samuel (Sammy) CF/IL/OL
b Lugar 14/2/1862 d 1943
Caps: Scotland 2
Lugar Boswell
Rangers
1888 1889 Preston North End 34 10
1890 Wolverhampton Wanderers 21 9
1891 Everton 3 1
1891 Accrington 19 5

Thomson, Thomas IL
1890 Accrington 10 2

From To Apps Goal

Thomson, William (Billy) OR
b Dundee
Caps: Scotland 1
Clydemore
Dundee Our Boys
Dundee
1896 1898 Bolton Wanderers 45 5

Thomson, William (Billy) LH/RH
b Parkhead 3/1/1895
Blantyre Victoria
Parkhead
Clyde
1914 1923 Leicester City 197 3
Arthurlie (loan)
1924 Bristol Rovers 21
Inverness Citadel

Thomson, William James G (Dave) LB
b New Brompton q3 1873 d 1940
Strathmore
1892 1893 Stoke 9
Southampton
Cowes

Thorley, Ernest (Cliff) OL
b West Melton 12/11/1913
Dearne Valley
Sandymount United
Wath National Old Boys
Denaby United
Frickley Colliery
1932 1934 Sunderland 4
1934 1935 Hull City 34 5
Kidderminster Harriers
Cheltenham Town
1937 1938 Bristol City 14 3

Thornber, Richard RH
b Darwen 1867
1891 Darwen 18 3
1892 Preston North End 3

Thornborough, Elijah Holden (Ernie) LH/RH
b Bolton 17/1/1902 d 1976
Halliwell United
1925 1929 Bolton Wanderers 69
1930 1931 Preston North End 20
Horwich RMI
Chorley

Thorne, Charles OR
b Birmingham 1902
Stourbridge
1923 1924 Merthyr Town 45 2

Thorne, Frank Lewis Charles RB
b Swindon 23/2/1910 d 1996
Swindon Corinthians
1932 Swindon Town 1
Swindon Corinthians

Thornett, Charles William Frederick GK
b Chelsea q3 1901 d 1985
Barnet
1928 Charlton Athletic 4

Thornewell, George OR
b Romiley 8/7/1898 d 1986
Caps: England 4
Rolls Royce
1919 1927 Derby County 275 23
1927 1928 Blackburn Rovers 41 4
1929 1931 Chesterfield 84 10
Newark Town

Thornhill, F GK
1892 Nottingham Forest 3

Thornley, Ernest Harry IL
b Compstall q1 1902 d 1965
1921 Accrington Stanley 0
1922 Stalybridge Celtic 5 1

Thornley, Hartley LH
b Hayfield q2 1884 d 1959
1901 Glossop 1

Thornley, Irvine CF/IR
b Glossop q4 1883 d 1955
Caps: FLge 2/England 1
Glossop Villa
Glossop St James
1901 1903 Glossop 79 42
1903 1911 Manchester City 195 92
South Shields Adelaide
Clydebank
Hamilton Academical
Houghton

Thornley, John Fearn CH/RH
b Coalville q3 1875 d 1956
1897 1898 Nottingham Forest 6
1899 1901 Gainsborough Trinity 88

From To | Apps Goal

Thornley, Jonathan (John) CF/OR
1902 1906 Glossop 5

Thornley, Thomas (Tom) LB/RB
b Bolton
Bolton Juniors
1927 1931 Crewe Alexandra 48
Stalybridge Celtic
Macclesfield

Thornton, Edwin John IL
b Barrow q4 1899 d 1966
Vickerstown
1921 Barrow 2
Morecambe
Barrow YMCA
Ulverston Town

Thornton, Percy LH/RH
b Wigton 28/7/1901 d 1975
West Stanley
Tow Law Town
1928 Grimsby Town (trial) 0
1929 1932 Hartlepools United 97 10
Workington
Spennymoor United

Thornton, Richard G (Dick) GK
b Bearpark
Esh Winning
Bearpark
1925 Leeds United 1
1928 1930 Accrington Stanley 61
1931 York City 11
Bridlington Town
Leyland Motors
Selby Town

Thornton, William (Billy) RH
b Sheffield q4 1883 d 1966
Mexborough Victoria
1904 Doncaster Rovers 0
1905 Hull City 1
Denaby United

Thornton, William IR
b Aston q4 1899
Bathurst Works
1919 Leicester City 11 2
Wellington Town

Thorogood, Jack OL
b Dinnington 4/4/1911 d 1970
Frickley Colliery
1930 1933 Birmingham 23 2
1934 1938 Millwall 74 24
1939 Doncaster Rovers 0

Thorpe, Albert RH
Loughborough Corinthians
1920 Plymouth Argyle 3
1921 Burnley 0

Thorpe, Albert Edward (Ted) RB
b Pilsley 14/7/1910 d 1971
Langwith Colliery
Shirebrook
1928 Wolverhampton Wanderers 1
Mansfield Town
1931 Notts County 1
1932 1935 Norwich City 61
1935 Crystal Palace 4
Bath City
Scunthorpe & Lindsey United
Hereford United

Thorpe, Edwin (Ted) RB/LB
b Kiveton Park 1898
Sheffield Wednesday
1919 Lincoln City 12
Doncaster Rovers
York City
1923 Reading 3

Thorpe, Frank CH
b Hayfield 13/11/1879 d 1928
Stalybridge Rovers
1900 Newton Heath 0
1901 1905 Bury 130 6
Plymouth Argyle
Southampton
1909 Bury 0

Thorpe, George GK
b Farnworth 1910
1930 Leeds United 0
1931 Huddersfield Town 8
1933 Chester 0

Thorpe, Harry Cheetham RB/LB
b Barrow Hill q1 1880 d 1908
Poolsbrook United
1900 1902 Chesterfield Town 64
1903 Woolwich Arsenal 10
Fulham
1907 Leicester Fosse 26

From To | Apps Goal

Thorpe, James LH/OL
b 1885
1906 Bolton Wanderers 2
1907 Leeds City 9
Crystal Palace
Darwen

Thorpe, James Horatio (Jimmy) GK
b Jarrow 16/9/1913 d 1936
Jarrow Imperial
Jarrow
1930 1935 Sunderland 123

Thorpe, John (Jack) OL
b Heanor q3 1875
Heanor Town
Kettering
1895 Sheffield United 1
Heanor Town
Huddersfield

Thorpe, John Henry RH
b Skegby q2 1892
Stanton Hill Victoria
Mansfield Mechanics
1911 Leicester Fosse 2
Mansfield Mechanics
Sutton Town
Shirebrook

Thorpe, Levi (Levy) RH/LH
b Seaham Harbour 18/11/1889 d 1935
Seaham Albion
Seaham Harbour
1910 1913 Blackpool 92 1
1913 Bradford City (trial) 0
1913 1919 Burnley 72 3
1919 1921 Blackburn Rovers 85 1
1922 1923 Lincoln City 69 9
1924 1925 Rochdale 31

Thorpe, Percy RB
b Nottingham 18/7/1899 d 1972
Sutton Town
1924 1927 Blackpool 113 5
Connah's Quay & Shotton
1928 1929 Reading 72
1930 1932 Sheffield United 103
1933 West Ham United 3
1934 Accrington Stanley 2
1934 Port Vale 1

Thorpe, Thomas (Tommy) GK
b Kilnhurst 19/5/1881 d 1953
Caps: SoLge 3
Rawmarsh Athletic
1904 Doncaster Rovers 31
1905 1908 Barnsley 105 1
1920 Northampton Town 22
1921 Barnsley 13

Thorpe, W Thomas (Tommy) GK
1900 Walsall 2

Thorpe, William OL
1900 Burton Swifts 1

Thraves, James (Jimmy) GK
b Normanton q1 1869 d 1936
Notts St John's
1890 1891 Notts County 4
1894 1896 Leicester Fosse 80
Long Eaton Rangers

Threlfall, Edward RH
b Kirkham q1 1880
Kirkham
1900 1910 Blackpool 317 11

Threlfall, Frederick (Fred) OL/OR
b Preston q3 1879 d 1957
Hyde
1899 1904 Manchester City 67 8
1907 1908 Fulham 33 4
1909 1910 Leicester Fosse 50 6
Cliftonville

Threlfall, Thomas LB
b Preston q2 1900 d 1956
1919 Preston North End 2

Threlfall, Wilfred (Wilf) OL
b Morecambe 19/10/1906 d 1988
Morecambe
1926 Sunderland 0
1927 Birmingham 5
1927 Bournemouth & Boscombe Ath 3
Morecambe
Lancaster Town
Morecambe
Rossendale United
Morecambe Victoria

From To | Apps Goal

Thurley, Arthur CH
b Bishops Stortford 17/5/1908 d 1972
Bishops Stortford
1931 Watford 4
Racing Club de Calais
Red Star Olympique
Olympique Lyonnais
Villourbanne
Watford Labour Club

Thurman, Arthur John RH
b Nottingham 8/5/1874 d 1900
Gedling Grove
1898 Notts County 2

Thursby, Robert Stanley (Stan) OR
b Lincoln 5/3/1909 d 1998
Burton Road
1929 1931 Lincoln City 21 6
City School Old Boys

Tice, W GK
Army
1893 Lincoln City 10

Tickle, Bert RH/LH
1901 1903 Preston North End 6
Southport Central

Tickle, Charles Henry (Charlie) OR
b Selly Oak q4 1883 d 1960
Caps: FLge 1
Selly Oak St Mary's
Bournbrook
1902 1907 Small Heath/Birmingham 88 14
Coventry City
Bristol Rovers
Bournbrook

Tidman, Oliver Eustace OL
b Margate 16/3/1911 d 2000
Tufnell Park
1932 Aston Villa 1
1935 Stockport County 24 4
1936 Bristol Rovers 16 1
1937 Clapton Orient 1
Chelmsford City

Tierney, Cornelius (Con) OL
b Kilbirnie 22/4/1909
Caps: IrLge 1
Rosewell Rosedale
Bo'ness
Celtic
St Johnstone (loan)
Forfar Athletic (loan)
Belfast Celtic (loan)
Guildford City
1934 Exeter City 18 1
Glenavon

Tierney, Herbert RH/CH
b Rochdale q3 1888
Heaton Park
1907 Bolton Wanderers 1
Exeter City
Haslingden
Darlington
1912 Lincoln City 2
Castleford Town
Goole Town
Rochdale
Aberaman Athletic

Tierney, Patrick (Pat) GK
b Renfrew
Vale of Clyde
1936 1937 Exeter City 29
1938 Crystal Palace 0

Tierney, Thomas Timothy (Tommy) IL/CF/OR
b Cheshire 1875
Witton Albion
1893 Northwich Victoria 4 1
Chorley
1895 1896 Blackburn Rovers 20 3
New Brighton Tower
1897 Blackburn Rovers (loan) 1
Chorley
1899 New Brighton Tower 30 5
Luton Town
1902 Gainsborough Trinity 3
Barrow
Glentoran
Watford
Chorley

From To | Apps Goal

Tilbrook, Charles (Charlie) IR
b Sheffield 11/7/1901 d 1975
1924 Sheffield United 0
1925 Blackpool 1
1926 Barrow 32 4
1927 Wigan Borough 1
Mexborough Athletic
Gainsborough Trinity
Dinnington Main Athletic
Tinsley Athletic

Tildesley, James (Jim) RB
b Halesowen 7/10/1881 d 1963
Halesowen St John
1903 1905 Newcastle United 21
1906 Middlesbrough 23
Luton Town
1909 Leeds City 6

Tilford, Arthur LB
b Ilkeston 14/5/1903 d 1993
Trowell St Helens
1924 1925 Nottingham Forest 8
1926 1928 Blackpool 54
1929 1931 Coventry City 57
1931 1932 Fulham 36
1932 Southampton 10
1933 Fulham 5
1934 Walsall 25

Till, Joseph Henry (Joe) LB
b Stoke-on-Trent q3 1892 d 1955
Wellington Town
Dumbarton
St Mirren
1923 1927 Luton Town 138 1
1928 Crewe Alexandra (trial) 0

Tilley, Arthur William OR
b Wellingborough 6/3/1892 d 1984
Fletton United
1912 Clapton Orient 1
1913 Lincoln City (trial) 0

Tilling, Horace W RB/LB
b New Cross
Army
1922 1927 Millwall Athletic 51 1
1928 Northampton Town 0

Tillotson, Arthur LB
b Hunslet 7/2/1894 d 1984
Castleford Town
1920 Leeds United 2
Castleford Town

Tillotson, Stephen GK
b Brierfield q2 1884 d 1961
Colne
1907 1908 Blackpool 19
1909 1910 Burnley 9

Tilson, Samuel Frederick (Fred) IL/CF/IR
b Barnsley 19/4/1904 d 1972
Caps: FLge 3/England 4
Regent Street Congregationals
1926 1927 Barnsley 61 23
1927 1937 Manchester City 245 110
1937 1938 Northampton Town 41 10
1939 York City (3)

Timbrell, Herbert John (Harry) OL/IL
b Swindon 30/8/1912 d 1982
Municipal Offices
1931 1933 Swindon Town 7 3
Oxford City

Timmins, Beniah (Ben) LB
b Great Barr 8/1898 d 1965
Caps: England Sch
Beeches Road Methodists
Dartmouth Victoria (West Brom)
1921 1923 Walsall 104
1923 1925 Wolverhampton Wanderers 11
Kidderminster Harriers
Bridgnorth

Timmins, George LH
b West Bromwich q1 1864 d 1926
George Salter's Works
1888 1890 West Bromwich Albion 36
Old Hill Wanderers

Timmins, George RH
1903 Burton United 3

Timmins, Samuel (Sammy) LH/RH/CH
b West Bromwich q1 1881
Dudley Town
1899 1900 Walsall 30
1900 1905 Nottingham Forest 125 5
1906 1910 West Bromwich Albion 111 3
Sutton Junction
Mansfield Town
Sutton Town

From To Apps Goal

Timmis, Samuel CH
b Audley q1 1872 d 1952
Audley
1896 Lincoln City 18 2

Timms, George Henry OR
b West Bromwich 24/10/1906 d 1968
1925 Walsall 1

Tindall, Thomas Jackson (Jack) LB
b Barnsley 12/5/1891 d 1971
St Barnabas (Barnsley)
1913 1922 Barnsley 140
1924 Accrington Stanley 12
Shirebrook

Tinkler, Alfred CH/RH
b Openshaw q3 1886 d 1950
Ilkeston United
1909 Derby County 2
Heanor United
Ilkeston United
1911 1914 Birmingham 96 3
Burton United

Tinklin, Herbert Frank (Bert) OL
b Nottingham 16/6/1910 d 1980
Grantham
Nuneaton Town
Folkestone
1934 1935 Aldershot 33 8
1936 Watford 8

Tinning, George E RB
b Kirkintilloch 21/10/1906 d 1968
Clydebank Juniors
1925 1928 Coventry City 26

Tinnion, James (Jim) RH
b Burnopfield 19/12/1904 d 1977
Lintz Colliery
1928 Darlington 1
1929 Huddersfield Town 0
North Shields
1931 1934 Barrow 120 8
Blyth Spartans
Horden Colliery Welfare
West Stanley
Horden Colliery Welfare
Chopwell Institute
Hexham
Annfield Plain

Tinsley, Walter Edward IL
b Ironville 10/8/1891 d 1966
Alfreton Town
Sutton Town
1911 1913 Sunderland 10 3
1913 1920 Middlesbrough 86 46
1921 1923 Nottingham Forest 61 13
1924 1926 Reading 55 13

Tinto, Richard IR
b Easington q4 1875
Rangers
1898 Glossop North End 6 4

Tippett, Thomas (Tommy) CF/OR/IL
b Gateshead 10/7/1904 d 1997
Twizell United
Craghead United
1925 Stoke City (trial) 0
1927 1928 Doncaster Rovers 31 4
1929 1930 Rochdale 70 47
1931 1932 Port Vale 39 11
1932 Stoke City 0
1933 1935 West Ham United 27 10

Tipping, Alfred (Alf) IL
b Barrow q4 1899 d 1955
1921 Barrow 1

Tipping, Charles (Charlie) CH
b Barrow q1 1912 d 1960
Vickerstown Athletic
1930 Barrow 0
Vickerstown Athletic
1936 Barrow 1

Tirrell, Alfred (Alf) LB
b Desborough 7/2/1894 d 1944
Peterborough City
1919 West Ham United 1
1920 1923 Luton Town 122 5

Tither, John (Jack) LH
b South Shields 19/9/1907 d 1974
South Shields Corinthians
1929 1932 Hartlepools United 15 1
Spennymoor United
1933 Darlington 0
North Shields
Jarrow
West Stanley

From To Apps Goal

Titley, Albert OL
b Middleport 18/11/1911 d 1986
Leek Alexandra
1933 West Bromwich Albion 0
1934 Port Vale 4

Titmuss, Frederick (Fred) LB
b Pirton q2 1895 d 1966
Caps: England 2
Pirton United
Hitchin Town
1920 1925 Southampton 188
1925 1931 Plymouth Argyle 166
St Austell

Titterington, William (Bill) IL/IR/RH
b Darwen 17/12/1911
Caps: England Yth
Blackburn St Philip's
1928 Blackburn Rovers 0
Great Harwood
Fleetwood
Hurst
1934 1938 Stockport County 113 11
1939 (Stockport County) (1)

Tizard, Charles Walter GK
b Blandford Forum 10/10/1914 d 1988
Caps: Lol 2
Winchester City
1934 Crystal Palace 4
1935 Mansfield Town 0
1936 Northampton Town 0
Dundalk
Glentoran

Tod, George LH/RB
b Glasgow 1880 d 1930
Linthouse
1900 1906 Preston North End 131 4
1907 Grimsby Town 0

Todd, Alan GK
b Leslie 1912
Leith Athletic
Cowdenbeath
1932 1936 Port Vale 78
1937 1938 Nottingham Forest 17
1939 Darlington (3)

Todd, John George (Jack) LH
b New Brancepeth 7/9/1904 d 1987
Broompark Comrades
1923 Durham City 1
Consett
Esh Winning

Toll, John Patrick (Jack) IR
b Bradford 7/12/1914 d 1972
Bridlington Town
1936 1937 Burnley 20 9

Tolland, Daniel (Danny) IL/IR
b Coatbridge 31/12/1902 d 1945
Well Park
Shettleston
Ayr United
Galston (loan)
1933 1937 Northampton Town 138 26
1937 1938 Bristol Rovers 34 3
(USA)

Toman, Michael OL
b Cleator Moor 15/12/1913 d 1944
1937 Preston North End 0
1938 Bristol City 2

Toman, Wilfred (Wilf) CF
b Bishop Auckland q4 1874 d 1917
Caps: FLge 1
Victoria United (Aberdeen)
Aberdeen Strollers
Dundee
Victoria United (Aberdeen)
1896 1898 Burnley 63 30
1898 1899 Everton 27 9
Southampton
1901 Everton 2 1
1903 Stockport County 5 1
Oldham Athletic (trial)
1906 Newcastle United 0

Tomkin, Albert Henry OL
b Barrow 23/12/1915 d 1989
Formby
1937 Tottenham Hotspur 0
Northfleet
1938 Tottenham Hotspur 2
1939 (Tottenham Hotspur) (2)

From To Apps Goal

Tomkins, Eric Feltham LH/RH
b Rushden 18/12/1892 d 1980
Rushden Fosse
1920 1922 Northampton Town 75
Rushden Town
1925 1926 Northampton Town 7
Rushden Town

Tomkinson, Alfred IL
b Burslem 1/5/1887 d 1973
1910 Glossop 8 4
Exeter City
Doncaster Rovers
Leek United

Tomkinson, GE IR
1902 Stockport County 3 1

Tomkys, Thomas CF
1888 Wolverhampton Wanderers 1

Tomlin, John (Jack) CH
b Kildare 1882 d 1941
Seaham White Star
1905 Sunderland 13 1
1906 Middlesbrough 4
Murton Red Star

Tomlinson, Frederick Charles T (Fred) RH
b South Shields q2 1885
South Shields Primtve Methodists
Workington United
West Stanley
1907 1908 Barnsley 16 1
Stoke
Washington Sentinel

Tomlinson, George Harold GK
b Heywood q1 1909 d 1945
1930 Leeds United 0
1931 Manchester City 0
1932 Bury 1

Tomlinson, Isaac OR
b Clay Cross 16/4/1880 d 1970
North Wingfield Red Rose
1900 1902 Chesterfield Town 58 9
1903 Woolwich Arsenal 0
1904 Chesterfield Town 33 8
Southampton
Portsmouth
Heart of Midlothian
Clay Cross Works

Tomlinson, James (Jimmy) CH
b Darwen q1 1875
1900 Blackburn Rovers 1
Nelson
Darwen
Brentford
Norwich City
1909 Bolton Wanderers 0
Reading

Tomlinson, James (Jim) RH/CH
b Leyland q3 1904
Leyland
1925 1928 Accrington Stanley 20 1
Morecambe

Tomlinson, James OL
b Horwich 17/5/1911 d 1997
White Horse Temperance
1934 Bristol City 1
Leyland Motors

Tomlinson, Reginald William (Reg) CF
b Sleaford 2/7/1914 d 1971
Horncastle Town
1935 1937 Grimsby Town 20 2
1938 Southampton 36 12
1939 (Southampton) (2)
Southampton Police

Tomlinson, Robert (Bob) OL
b Castleford
Castleford Town
Harrogate AFC
1930 York City 3 1
Castleford Town

Tomlinson, Thomas (Tommy) OL
b Chesterfield q1 1887
Newbold United
Birdholme Rovers
1906 1907 Chesterfield Town 19 5
Worksop Town
1908 Chesterfield Town 0
1909 Bradford Park Avenue 4 4
Mexborough
1912 Notts County 7
Newport County

From To Apps Goal

Tomlinson, Thomas (Tom) CH
b Sheffield
Shiregreen WMC
1932 Darlington 1

Tompkin, Maurice IL/OR
b Countesthorpe 17/2/1919 d 1956
Countesthorpe United
1937 Leicester City 1
1945 Bury 0
1946 Huddersfield Town 10 1
Kettering Town

Tompkin, Percy Lord OL
b Salford 28/1/1894 d 1948
Countesthorpe United
Leicester Imperial
Sutton Junction
Hinckley United
Nuneaton Town
1919 Huddersfield Town 1
1920 1923 Leicester City 87 4
Nuneaton Town

Tompkins, James John (Jimmy) LH
b Edmonton q2 1914 d 1944
Woking
1933 1938 Fulham 154 5
1939 (Fulham) (3)

Tompkins, Thomas (Tom) RH
b 1884
1904 Doncaster Rovers 15 1
Denaby United
1907 Leeds City 11
Mexborough Town

Tompkinson, GH OR
1892 Northwich Victoria 2

Tompkinson, Harry OR
Longsight St John's
1894 Manchester City 6 1

Tompkinson, William Vincent (Billy) OR
b Stone 18/6/1895 d 1968
Caps: WLge 1
1914 Wolverhampton Wanderers 0
1919 Stoke 1
1921 1922 Aberdare Athletic 41 4
1923 1927 Rochdale 162 45
1928 1929 Stockport County 76 26
Connah's Quay & Shotton

Toms, William Edward (Bill) IL/CF/OL
b The Curragh 19/5/1896
Altrincham
Eccles Borough
1919 1920 Manchester United 13 3
1920 Plymouth Argyle 24 3
1921 Oldham Athletic 20 5
1922 Coventry City 30 19
1923 Stockport County 5 1
1923 1924 Wrexham 42 10
1924 Crewe Alexandra 25 8
Great Harwood
Winsford United
Eccles United
CWS Margarine Works (Manchester)

Toner, Francis (Frank) OL
b Troon
Troon Athletic
Hamilton Academical
1924 Stockport County 0
1925 Portsmouth 3
Providence Clamdiggers
J & P Coats (Rhode Island)
Brooklyn Wanderers
New Bedford Whalers

Toner, Joseph Samuel (Joe) OL
b Castlewellan 30/3/1894 d 1954
Caps: Ireland 8
Castlewellan
Whitehaven Athletic
Whitehaven Recreation
Annsboro
St Peter's Swifts
Belfast Celtic
Belfast United
1919 1925 Arsenal 89 6
St Johnstone
Coleraine
Castlewellan Star
Annsboro
Castlewellan Star

Tong, Robert OL/OR
b Birkenhead q2 1911 d 1982
Shaftesbury Boys Club
1932 1933 Tranmere Rovers 7 1
Witton Albion

From To Apps Goal

Tonge, Benjamin (Ben) IR
b Barton-on-Irwell q4 1887
Atherton
1908 Blackpool 4
Darwen

Tonge, James OR
1896 1899 Manchester City 4

Tonks, Joseph (Jack) OR
b Wednesfield 7/1872 d 1951
Walsall Unity
Walsall
1894 1899 Wolverhampton Wanderers 106 20
Walsall

Tonner, Arthur Edward McSorley RB
b Govanhill 10/3/1909 d 1983
St Anthony's (Glasgow)
1935 West Ham United 1
St Mirren
1937 1938 Swindon Town 41
1939 Swansea Town 0

Tonner, James Edward (Jimmy) OL/OR
b Bridgeton 31/3/1896 d 1985
Bungalow City (Rosyth)
Inverkeithing United
Dunfermline Juniors
Dunfermline Athletic
East Fife
Linlithgow Rose
1919 Clapton Orient 12
Lochgelly United
Bo'ness
1924 1925 Burnley 37 2
Hamilton Academical
(USA)
1932 Portsmouth 0

Tonner, John (Jack) IL/CF/IR
b Holytown 20/2/1898 d 1978
Dunfermline Athletic
1919 1925 Clapton Orient 143 35
1926 Fulham 28 13
1927 Crystal Palace 24 8
Thames

Tonner, Samuel (Sam) RB
b Dunfermline 10/8/1894 d 1976
Inverkeithing
Dunfermline Athletic
1919 1924 Clapton Orient 186 13
1925 Bristol City 6 1
1926 Crystal Palace 2
Armadale

Toone, George GK
b Nottingham 10/6/1868 d 1943
Caps: England 2
Forest Olympic
St Saviour's (Nottingham)
Lincoln City
Nottingham Jardines
Notts Rangers
1889 1898 Notts County 262
Bedminster
Bristol City
1901 Notts County 3

Toone, George RH/CH
b Nottingham 6/9/1893 d 1950
Northvale
Sneinton Institute
Sherwood
Sneinton Institute
1913 Notts County 1
Mansfield Mechanics
1920 1923 Watford 165
1924 Sheffield Wednesday 19
Ilkeston United
Scarborough Penguins

Toone, Percy GK
b Colchester 27/7/1883 d 1955
Army
1907 Woolwich Arsenal 0
Leyton
Southend United
1911 1912 Preston North End 14
Barrow
Southend United
1914 Bolton Wanderers 3
Plymouth Argyle
1920 Newport County 1

Tooth, George OL
b Stoke-on-Trent 1874
Congleton Hornets
1898 1899 Stoke 5 1
Stafford Rangers

From To Apps Goal

Tooth, John Godfrey OL
b Norwich q4 1882
1904 Aston Villa 0
1905 Burton United 11
Coventry City
1908 1911 Gainsborough Trinity 65 1

Tootill, Alfred (Alf) GK
b Stubbins 12/11/1908 d 1975
Ramsbottom United
1925 Accrington Stanley (trial) 0
Ramsbottom United
1927 1928 Accrington Stanley 31
1928 1932 Wolverhampton Wanderers 138
1932 1937 Fulham 203
1938 Crystal Palace 1
1939 (Crystal Palace) (1)

Tootill, George Albert (Alf) CH
b Walkden 20/10/1913 d 1984
Chorley
1936 1937 Plymouth Argyle 9
1938 Sheffield United 12
1947 Hartlepools United 18

Tootle, James (Jimmy) LB/RB
b Skelmersdale 22/4/1899 d 1947
Old Skelmersdale Rangers
Skelmersdale United
1922 1924 Southport 60 2
1924 1925 Derby County 7
Chester
Skelmersdale United

Topham, John H (Jack) OL
Staveley
1898 1899 Sheffield Wednesday 12 1

Topham, Robert (Dick) OR/CF
b Ellesmere 3/11/1867 d 1951
Caps: England 2
Oswestry
Casuals
Chiswick Park
1890 1892 Wolverhampton Wanderers 21 13
Casuals
Corinthians
1895 Wolverhampton Wanderers 2 1
Corinthians

Topping, Henry (Harry) LB
b Manchester 27/10/1908 d 1977
United Glassblowers
1932 1934 Manchester United 12 1
1935 Barnsley 14 2
Macclesfield
Manchester North End
Wigan Athletic

Topping, Henry (Harry) LB/RB
b Kearsley 21/9/1913 d 2001
Horwich RMI
1933 Swindon Town 0
1934 Hull City (trial) 0
1934 Charlton Athletic (trial) 0
1934 Barrow (trial) 0
1934 Tranmere Rovers (trial) 0
Bath City (trial)
1935 Manchester City 0
1937 Exeter City 1
1938 New Brighton 5
1938 Stockport County 0
1945 Bristol Rovers 0

Topping, Henry Westby (Harry) RB
b Prescot 28/9/1915 d 2004
Rossendale United
1938 1945 Stockport County 3
1946 1947 New Brighton 67
Prescot Cables

Topping, Robert William OL
b Blackpool 4/6/1886 d 1984
1905 Blackpool 7
Fleetwood

Torbet, John McDowall OL
b Benwhat 25/9/1903 d 1957
New Cumnock United
Partick Thistle
1933 Preston North End 11 4
Burton Town
1935 Stockport County 6 1
Ayr United
Alloa Athletic
Leith Athletic

Tordoff, Harry CH/RH
b Barnsley 25/11/1905 d 1976
1928 1929 Nelson 9
1929 Sheffield United 0
1931 Rotherham United 2
Boston Town (trial)
1933 Barnsley 0
Worksop Town
Horwich RMI

From To Apps Goal

Torr, Frank OL
b Coundon 26/7/1906 d 1981
1931 Bradford Park Avenue 0
1932 Gillingham 1
1933 Aldershot 5
Ashford Town (Kent)

Torrance, Alexander LH
b Glasgow 29/9/1901 d 1941
Renfrew Juniors
1921 1927 Bristol City 167 10
Bath City

Torrance, George IL
b Glasgow 1/3/1914
Glasgow Benburb
1933 Bradford Park Avenue 1

Torrance, James (Jimmy) CH/LH/IL
b Coatbridge 28/7/1889 d 1949
Kirkintilloch Rob Roy
Glasgow Ashfield
1910 1925 Fulham 338 35
1925 1926 Walsall 38
Standard Telephone & Cables

Torrance, Robert (Bob) CH/RB
b Kirkintilloch 1888 d 1918
Kirkintilloch Rob Roy
1908 1914 Bradford City 161

Toseland, Ernest (Ernie) OR
b Northampton 17/3/1905 d 1987
Caps: FLge 1
Higham Ferrers Town
1928 Coventry City 22 11
1928 1938 Manchester City 368 61
1938 Sheffield Wednesday 12 2
1939 (Sheffield Wednesday) (3)
Mossley

Toser, Ernest William (Ernie) CH
b Old Ford 30/11/1912 d 2002
Caps: England Sch
Eton Manor
1930 Luton Town 0
Dulwich Hamlet
1931 Southampton 0
1933 Crystal Palace 0
Dulwich Hamlet
1937 Millwall 2
1946 Notts County 2
Bognor Regis Town

Tosswill, John Speare IR
b Eastbourne 6/8/1890 d 1915
Eastbourne
Hastings & St Leonards
Aberdare Town
Tunbridge Wells Rangers
Maidstone United
Queen's Park Rangers
1912 Liverpool 11 1
Southend United
Coventry City

Tout, William Edwin Brown (Billy) LB
b Hereford 1884 d 1960
Caps: SoLge 1
Redfield Rangers
Bristol Rovers
Bristol East
1920 Swindon Town 4
Bath City

Toward, Alfred Vickers (Alf) CF/CH
b Castleside q3 1882 d 1962
Leadgate Park
1908 1909 Hull City 10 6
1909 1913 Oldham Athletic 72 30
1913 1914 Preston North End 30 8
Darlington
Leadgate Park

Toward, Ralph William OR
b Lanchester q2 1889 d 1963
Leadgate Park
Craghead United
1912 1914 Glossop 66 4
Durham City
Hartlepools United
1920 Swindon Town 0
Durham City
Jarrow

Towe, Joseph (Dick) GK
b Wednesbury q2 1873 d 1951
1896 Walsall 3

Towers, Jack S LH
b Darlington 1901
1929 Cockfield
1930 Everton 0
1931 Southport 0
1932 Carlisle United 2
1932 Hartlepools United 0

From To Apps Goal

Towers, John IR/IL/LH
b Willington 21/12/1913 d 1979
1934 1938 Darlington 94 22
Willington
1945 1946 Darlington 13

Towie, Thomas IL/OL
Dumbarton Union
1891 Preston North End 22 9
Renton
Celtic (loan)
1893 Derby County 8 1
Rossendale
Renton

Towler, Bernard Edward OL/IL
b Ipswich 13/3/1912 d 1992
Lincoln Corinthians
1932 1937 Lincoln City 68 32
1938 Notts County 22 9
Ruston-Bucyrus
Boston United

Towler, Edwin GK
b Burnley q4 1883
1902 1903 Burnley 23

Townend, Harry Vincent (Vinney) OR
b Selby q3 1889 d 1958
Selby Town
Selby Robins
1909 1911 Hull City 12 1
Goole Town

Townley, James Chadwick (Jimmy) OL/IL
b Blackburn 2/5/1902 d 1983
Hamburg Victoria
St Gallen
1924 Chelsea (trial) 0
1927 Tottenham Hotspur 3 2
1928 Brighton & Hove Albion 9
1929 1930 Clapton Orient 19 2
(Switzerland)

Townley, William (Billy) OL
b Blackburn 4/2/1866 d 1950
Caps: England 2
Blackburn Swifts
Blackburn Olympic
1888 1891 Blackburn Rovers 77 27
Stockton
1893 Blackburn Rovers 20 10
1894 1895 Darwen 42 15
1896 Manchester City 3

Townrow, Frank Albert LH/IL/IR
b West Ham 27/11/1902 d 1958
Caps: England Sch
Barking Town
1920 Chelsea 0
Northfleet
1922 1923 Arsenal 8 2
Dundee
1930 Bristol City 22 5
1931 1932 Bristol Rovers 50 6
Taunton Town

Townrow, John Ernest (Jack) CH
b Stratford 28/3/1901 d 1969
Caps: England Sch/England 2
Fairbairn House
1919 1926 Clapton Orient 253 5
1926 1931 Chelsea 130 3
1932 Bristol Rovers 10

Townsend, Alfred Harold (Alf) OL
b Nuneaton 25/8/1902 d 1980
1925 Cardiff City 0
1926 1927 Nottingham Forest 15 4
1928 Stockport County 7
Connah's Quay & Shotton

Townsend, Charles Noel Rogers LH/RH
b Reading q1 1911
Oxford City
1932 1934 Reading 11

Townsend, Eric Esme CF
b Hove 14/2/1914 d 1976
1931 1933 Brighton & Hove Albion 15 9
1934 Bournemouth & Boscombe Ath 0
Shoreham
Hove

Townsend, Ernest IL
b Bristol
1930 Thames 10 2

Townsend, John IR
b Ebbw Vale
Ebbw Vale
1928 Southend United 6 1
Grays Thurrock

From To Apps Goal

Townsend, John Sidney (Jack) OL
b Nuneaton q2 1906
Griff Colliery
Nuneaton Town
1927 1928 Coventry City 31 4
Hinckley United
Nuneaton Town
Newdigate Colliery

Townsend, Leonard Francis (Len) IR/CF
b Brentford 31/8/1917 d 1997
Caps: NIRL 1
Isleworth Town
Hayes
1938 Brentford 4 4
Belfast Celtic
1945 1946 Brentford 29 8
1947 1948 Bristol City 74 45
1949 Millwall 5 1
Guildford City
Hayes
Slough Town
Maidenhead United

Townsend, Thomas IL
b Babbacombe
Torquay Town
1921 Exeter City 7
Torquay United

Townsend, W IL/IR
1894 1895 Darwen 13 6

Townsley, Thomas (Tom) RB/CH
b Polmont 28/4/1898 d 1976
Caps: SLge 4/Scotland 1
Lauriston Villa
Cowie Wanderers
California Celtic
Falkirk
1925 1930 Leeds United 159 2
Falkirk
Bo'ness
Peterhead

Towse, Thomas (Tom) CF
b Lazenby q2 1894 d 1961
South Bank
1921 1922 Hartlepools United 13 5
Trimdon Grange

Toyne, George Edward LB
b Caistor q3 1880 d 1961
1899 1900 Gainsborough Trinity 18
1900 Nottingham Forest 0

Tracey, Charles Patrick (Charlie) OL
b Glasgow 17/8/1909
Douglas Water Thistle
Kirkmuirhill Juniors
1930 Watford 3 1
Morton
King's Park
Morecambe
Newry Town
Bacup Borough
Morton

Tracey, Daniel (Dan) IL
1893 Walsall Town Swifts 3 1

Tracey, William Michael OL
b Shrewsbury 4/11/1876 d 1945
Shrewsbury Town
1900 1902 Bolton Wanderers 56 11
Shrewsbury Town
Chirk

Trainer, Harry IL/CF
b Wrexham 1872 d 1924
Caps: Wales 3
Wrexham Victoria
Wrexham Grosvenor
Westminster Rovers
Wrexham
1894 West Bromwich Albion (trial) 0
1895 1896 Leicester Fosse 31 13
Sheppey United
Wrexham
Oxcroft Colliery
Poolsbrook United

Trainer, James (Jimmy) GK
b Wrexham 7/1/1863 d 1915
Caps: FLge 1/Wales 20
Wrexham Victoria
Wrexham Grosvenor
Wrexham
Great Lever
Bolton Wanderers
1888 1897 Preston North End 253

From To Apps Goal

Trainer, John (Jack) CF
b Norham-on-Tweed
Berwick Rangers
Duns
Ashington
1936 1937 Leeds United 3
1938 Southend United 25 6

Trainer, T Stephen OR
b Coatbridge
1906 Burnley 3

Trainor, Peter CH
b Cockermouth 2/3/1915 d 1979
Workington
1937 Preston North End 0
1938 1947 Brighton & Hove Albion 71 4
1939 (Brighton & Hove Albion) (1)
Workington

Tranter, George Henry RH
b Quarry Bank 4/1887 d 1940
Netherton Recreation
Brierley Hill Alliance
Stourbridge
1907 1913 Aston Villa 162 1

Tranter, Richard Arthur IL
b Bolton q3 1893 d 1957
Padiham
1913 1914 Burnley 5

Travers, Bernard (Barney) CF
b Sunderland q4 1894 d 1949
Sunderland Co-op Wednesday
Oak Villa
New Lambton Star
Sunderland West End
1919 1920 Sunderland 58 25
1920 1921 Fulham 46 28

Travers, George Edward (George) IR/CF
b Birmingham 1886 d 1943
Bilston United
Rowley United
1906 Wolverhampton Wanderers 0
1907 1908 Birmingham 2
1908 Aston Villa 4 4
Queen's Park Rangers
1910 Leicester Fosse 12 5
1910 1913 Barnsley 84 23
1913 1914 Manchester United 21 4
Swindon Town
1920 Millwall Athletic 2
1920 Norwich City 29 14
1921 Gillingham 10 1
Nuneaton Town
Cradley Heath St Luke's
Bilston United

Travers, Patrick (Paddy) IL/IR
b Renfrew 28/5/1883 d 1962
Renfrew Victoria
Thornliebank
1901 Barnsley 13 4
Thornliebank
1903 Barnsley 8
Thornliebank
New Brompton
Renton
Clyde
Aberdeen
Celtic
Aberdeen
Dumbarton
Clydebank
Vale of Leven
Dumbarton Harp
Dumbarton

Travis, Aaron CF
b Manchester 28/3/1890 d 1966
Hurst
1912 Manchester United 0
Hurst
1921 Darlington 11 6
Hurst Albion
Ashton PSI

Travis, Henry (Harry) CF
b Manchester 13/12/1911 d 1982
1931 Manchester City 0
1932 Oldham Athletic 0
1933 Accrington Stanley 4 1
1934 Leeds United 0
1935 1936 Bradford City 44 20
1936 1938 Derby County 12 4
1938 Tranmere Rovers 13 3
Kidderminster Harriers

Trayler, Frederick Cyril (Fred) IL
b Stratford 30/6/1903 d 1981
1923 Clapton Orient 0
1924 Charlton Athletic 6

From To Apps Goal

Traynor, John William LB
b Grangetown 16/1/1910 d 1994
1932 Leicester City 0
1933 Crystal Palace 0
1934 Gateshead 2

Traynor, Thomas Smith LH
b South Shields 23/12/1894 d 1985
1914 Preston North End 0
1919 South Shields 4
Ebbw Vale

Treadwell, Joseph William OL
b West Ham 8/9/1896 d 1967
1923 Gillingham 2

Treanor, James Leslie (Jim) LH/RH
b Heap 11/10/1913 d 1966
Winsford United
1933 1934 Bury 11
1935 1936 Accrington Stanley 40
1936 1938 Hull City 44 1
Chorley

Treasure, Charles James (Cyril) RB
b Farrington Gurney 1/9/1896 d 1985
Paulton Rovers
1919 1921 Bristol City 63
1922 Halifax Town 8
Taunton United

Trechmann, Otto Leopold CF
b Hartlepool q2 1884 d 1950
West Hartlepool
1905 Middlesbrough 1
West Hartlepool

Tremain, Sidney (Syd) GK
b North Skelton 10/1/1911 d 1973
Guisborough Brigantes
Pease & Partners
1932 Hartlepools United 16
1933 Preston North End 0

Tremelling, Elijah Solomon (Sol) CH/CF
b Newhall q2 1887 d 1960
Newhall Swifts
1905 1907 Derby County 2
Burton United
Ilkeston United
Gresley Rovers
Shirebrook Forest
1913 1914 Bradford City 2
Mansfield Town
Gresley Rovers

Tremelling, Richard Daniel (Dan) GK
b Newhall 12/12/1897 d 1970
Caps: FLge 1/England 1
Langwith Junction Wagon Works
Mansfield Town
Shirebrook
1919 1930 Birmingham 382
1933 1934 Bury 57

Tremelling, William Reuben (Billy) CH/CF/LH
b Newhall 9/5/1904 d 1961
Shirebrook
Kirkby Colliery
Mansfield Town
Welbeck Colliery
Retford Town
Worksop Town
1924 1930 Blackpool 114 43
1930 1937 Preston North End 209 11

Trentham, Douglas Harold OL
b Chirbury 2/11/1917 d 2003
Mickle Trafford
1937 1938 Everton 16 7
Ellesmere Port Town

Trentham, Herbert Francis (Bert) LB
b Chirbury 22/4/1908 d 1979
Caps: FLge 1
Knighton Town
Knighton Victoria
Knighton United
Hereford United
1928 Aston Villa (trial) 0
1929 1936 West Bromwich Albion 246
Hereford United
Darlaston

Tresadern, John (Jack) LH/RH
b Leytonstone 26/9/1890 d 1959
Caps: England 2
Wanstead
Barking
1919 1924 West Ham United 144 5
1924 Burnley 22
1925 1926 Northampton Town 34 1

From To Apps Goal

Trevis, Arthur Stanley Sackville Redvers Trevor Boscawen Griffith (Bos) RH
b Blackheath, Worcestershire 20/10/1912 d 1997
Leamington Town
Old Hill Amateurs
1933 West Bromwich Albion 1
1936 1938 Chester 29 2
Worcester City

Trevisone, Luigi Roberto (Robert) GK
b Bournemouth q4 1907 d 1969
Bournemouth Gasworks
1933 Bournemouth & Boscombe Ath 1
Poole Town

Trewick, Henry CH
b Lanchester 14/5/1898 d 1966
Scotswood
Tanfield Lea Institute
1921 Ashington 2

Tricker, Reginald William (Reg) CF/IR/IL
b Karachi, India 5/10/1905 d 1990
Beccles Town
Alexandra Park (London)
1924 Luton Town 4
Beccles Town
1925 1926 Charlton Athletic 41 17
1926 1928 Arsenal 12 5
1928 1932 Clapton Orient 131 60
Margate
Ramsgate

Trigg, Charles IL
b Cardiff 13/9/1902 d 1973
Barry
Ebbw Vale
1927 Merthyr Town 2

Trigg, Cyril CF/RB
b Measham 8/4/1917 d 1993
Binley Welfare
1933 Coventry City (trial) 0
Bedworth Town
1935 1953 Birmingham 268 67
1939 (Birmingham) (3)
Stourbridge

Trim, Reginald Frederick (Reg) RB/LB
b Portsmouth 1/10/1913 d 1997
Caps: England Sch
Bournemouth Postal
Winton & Moordown
1930 1932 Bournemouth & Boscombe Ath 22
1934 Arsenal 1
1937 1938 Nottingham Forest 70
1939 (Nottingham Forest) (3)
1945 Derby County 0
1946 Swindon Town 15

Triner, Donald Arthur (Don) OR/IR
b Longton 21/8/1919 d 2002
Downings Tileries
1938 1947 Port Vale 25 7
Witton Albion
Buxton
Biggleswade Town
Leek Town

Trippier, Austin Wilkinson OR/OL
b Ramsbottom 30/8/1909 d 1993
Rochdale St Clement's
1929 1930 Rochdale 12 1
1930 Bury (trial) 0
1931 Oldham Athletic 6 1
1932 Southport 2
Chorley
Macclesfield
Bacup Borough

Trodd, William RH
Leyton
1934 Queen's Park Rangers 6

Trotman, Reginald Wilfred (Reg) IL/IR
b Bristol 10/7/1906 d 1970
Kingswood AFC
1927 Bristol Rovers 3 1
1928 Rochdale 23 10
1929 Sheffield Wednesday 0
Worksop Town
Mansfield Town
Dartford
Bath City
Bristol St George
Trowbridge Town

From To Apps Goal

Trotter, Alexander Elliot (Sandy) OL
b Jarrow q3 1893
Jarrow Croft
Newburn
Ashington
Raith Rovers
Dumbarton
Renton
Ashington
1920 1923 Leicester City 96 10
1924 1926 South Shields 120 15
1927 Port Vale 16 3
Manchester Central
Bedlington United
West Stanley

Trotter, Alexander John (Alex) IL
b Renfrew 9/7/1910
Glasgow Ashfield
1930 Wolverhampton Wanderers 0
1931 Arsenal 0
1932 Preston North End 0
1933 Carlisle United 2
Shelbourne
Portadown
Shelbourne
Morecambe (trial)
Albion Rovers

Trotter, George OR
b Newcastle
Blyth Spartans
1911 1912 Stockport County 15 1

Trotter, James William (Jimmy) CF
b Easington 25/11/1899 d 1984
Parsons Turbine Works
1919 1921 Bury 48 20
1921 1928 Sheffield Wednesday 154 109
1930 1931 Torquay United 56 36
1931 1932 Watford 4 1

Trotter, Walter OL
b Oldham 4/07 1905 d 1975
Chamber Colliery
1926 1927 Oldham Athletic 5 1
Manchester North End
Manchester Central
Altrincham
Buxton

Troughear, Thomas (Tom) RB/CH/RH
b Carlisle 15/12/1906 d 1975
Cumberland County
1928 1934 Carlisle United 58

Troughear, William (Billy) RB
b Workington q2 1885 d 1955
Workington Marsh Mission
Workington
1909 1912 Sunderland 100
1914 Leicester Fosse 15
Flimby Rangers
Workington

Troup, Alexander (Alec) OL
b Forfar 4/5/1895 d 1951
Caps: SLge 2/Scotland 5
Forfar North End
Forfar Athletic
Dundee
Ayr United (loan)
1922 1929 Everton 249 32
Dundee
Forfar Athletic

Truelove, James Rowland (Jim) IL
b Manchester 25/8/1908 d 1973
1928 1930 Crewe Alexandra 8 1
Mossley

Trueman, Albert Harry Cowell LH
b Leicester q2 1882 d 1961
Caps: SoLge 4
Wigston Excelsior
Grasmere Swifts
1899 Leicester Fosse 0
Grasmere Swifts
Coalville Town
Hinckley Town
Coalville Town
St Andrew's (Leicester)
1905 1907 Leicester Fosse 43 2
Southampton
1910 1912 Sheffield United 55
Darlington
Leicester Imperial
Clydebank

Trueman, James Ronald (Ronald) OR
b Whaley Bridge 1882
Macclesfield
1908 1909 Derby County 16
Sutton Town
Macclesfield
Sutton Town

From To Apps Goal

Tubb, Albert Ernest LH/RH
b Eston 24/7/1893 d 1978
South Bank
Normanby Magnesite
South Bank
1922 1924 Ashington 36
1925 Barrow 34
Boston Town
Shirebrook
1928 Chesterfield 3
Mexborough Athletic

Tucker, Charles Garman GK
b Preston 14/4/1914 d 1996
Hoylake
Lytham
1936 Tranmere Rovers 1

Tucker, Cyril RB
1939 Southend United (1)

Tucker, William Henry CF
1906 Middlesbrough 4 1

Tucker, William J OR
1934 York City 2 1

Tuckett, Ernest William (Ernie) IR/CH
b Lingdale 1/1/1914 d 1945
Guisborough Brigantes
Scarborough
1932 Arsenal 0
Margate
1935 Arsenal 2
1936 1937 Bradford City 13 4
1938 Fulham 1

Tuckley, William Lee CF
b Aston 25/3/1904 d 1975
Wellington St George's
Leamington Town
1924 Wolverhampton Wanderers 0
1925 Leicester City 0
Hinckley United
1927 Chesterfield 4 1
Hinckley United
Leamington Town
Nuneaton Town
Loughborough Corinthians
Atherstone Town
Hinckley United
Nichols & Wileman (Earl Shilton)

Tudor, William Henry (Billy) CH/LH
b Shotton 14/2/1918 d 1965
Caps: Wales Sch
Llanerch Celts
Lavender
1938 West Bromwich Albion 31
1946 1948 Wrexham 56 2
Bangor City
Pwllheli & District
Flint Town United
Llandudno Junction
Mancot

Tufnell, Ernest (Ernie) IL
b Burton-on-Trent q3 1884 d 1949
Long Eaton
Worcester City
1907 Glossop 7 1
Kidderminster Harriers
Stourbridge

Tufnell, Henry (Harry) IL/IR
b Burton-on-Trent 2/3/1886 d 1959
Long Eaton
Worcester City
1907 1908 Bury 13 3
1909 1919 Barnsley 200 60
Wakefield City
Doncaster Rovers

Tufnell, Sidney James LH/IL
b Sheffield 11/10/1904
Worksop Town
1927 1932 Blackpool 90 4

Tuft, William LB/RB
b Wolverhampton 1874
Coseley United
1897 1899 Wolverhampton Wanderers 8
1900 Walsall 33
1901 1905 Bristol City 137

Tull, Walter Daniel John CF
b Folkestone 28/4/1888 d 1918
Clapton
1909 1910 Tottenham Hotspur 10 2
Northampton Town

Tulloch, Albert (Bert) RB/LB
b North Shields 23/2/1889 d 1953
Scotswood
1914 1923 Blackpool 185

From To Apps Goal

Tully, Frederick Charles Arnold (Fred) OR/IR/OL
b St Pancras 4/7/1907 d 1969
Rosehill Villa
Preston Colliery
1927 1928 Aston Villa 7
1933 1936 Southampton 97 9
1937 1938 Clapton Orient 57 18

Tully, James Andrew (Jim) LH/RH/IL
b Newcastle q4 1885
West Stanley
1909 1910 Clapton Orient 5 1
West Stanley
Rochdale
Pontypridd
1921 1922 Rochdale 40

Tumelty, James RH
b Shotts 5/11/1898 d 1979
Royal Naval Depot (Chatham)
1922 Portsmouth 5
Workington

Tummon, Oliver (Ollie) OR/OL
b Sheffield 3/3/1884 d 1955
South Street New Connexion
1901 Gainsborough Trinity 0
1905 1909 Sheffield Wednesday 40 9
1910 1911 Gainsborough Trinity 76 20
1912 1914 Oldham Athletic 108 19
1919 Sheffield United 23 2
1920 Barnsley 1
Sir Albert Hawkes FC
Nether Edge

Tunbridge, Alec Walter LB/RB
b Burnham-on-Crouch 29/11/1909 d 1990
Burnham-on-Crouch
1930 1931 Southend United 3

Tunney, Edward Luton (Eddie) RB
b Liverpool 23/9/1915 d 2011
1936 Everton 0
1937 1951 Wrexham 222
1939 (Wrexham) (3)
Winsford United

Tunnicliffe, John IL
b Hanley 1864
Longton Atlas
1891 Stoke 3
Audlem

Tunnicliffe, William (Billy) OL
b Hanley 1866
Hanley Town
1888 Stoke 8 4
Middlewich

Tunnicliffe, William Francis (Billy) OL
b Stoke-on-Trent 5/1/1920 d 1997
1936 1937 Port Vale 3
1938 1946 Bournemouth & Boscombe Ath 50 7
1939 (Bournemouth & Boscombe Ath) (3) (1)
1947 1952 Wrexham 236 74
1952 1954 Bradford City 89 20
Stafford Rangers
Congleton Town

Tunstall, Fred OL
b Darfield 28/5/1897 d 1971
Caps: FLge 4/England 7
Darfield St George's
Scunthorpe & Lindsey United
1920 1931 Sheffield United 437 129
1932 1935 Halifax Town 105 40
Boston United

Tunstall, William IR/IL
Hanley Swifts
1901 1903 Burslem Port Vale 13 1

Tunstall, William Henry (Bill) CF
b St Helens 19/1/1905 d 1983
Prescot Cables
1932 Aston Villa 0
1933 Bournemouth & Boscombe Ath 8 2

Turley, Harry IR
b Snedshill 4/1/1891 d 1971
Wellington St George's
1911 Wolverhampton Wanderers 0
1913 1914 Blackpool 11 1

Turley, Robert (Pat) LH/IL
b Newry 1908
Caps: IrLge 2
Newry Town
1928 1930 Stoke City 5
St Patrick's Athletic

Turnbull, Alexander (Sandy) IL/IR
b Hurlford 1884 d 1917
Hurlford
1902 1905 Manchester City 110 53
1906 1914 Manchester United 220 90

From To Apps Goal

Turnbull, Alexander Stewart OR
b Partick 1917
Yoker Athletic
Albion Rovers
East Stirlingshire
1937 Manchester City 0
Droylsden (loan)
1938 Exeter City 14 1

Turnbull, George LB
b South Shields 21/8/1899 d 1928
South Shields Rosedale
1919 South Shields 0
Ebbw Vale
1921 1922 Durham City 52
1923 Sunderland 0
Spennymoor United
1925 1926 Durham City 22
1926 1927 Bradford Park Avenue 27

Turnbull, George GK
b Douglas
Stakeford United
Blyth Spartans
1927 Sheffield United 1
Blyth Spartans

Turnbull, George E CF/IL
1930 Rochdale 10 2
1930 Newcastle United (trial) 0
1931 Darlington 5 1

Turnbull, Henry Wilkinson IR/OR
b Earsdon 31/12/1902 d 1970
Newbiggin West End
1926 1927 Ashington 9 3
Blyth Spartans (trial)
Newbiggin West End
Bedlington United
Blyth Spartans
Newbiggin West End

Turnbull, James Malcolm (Jimmy) CF
b Ashington 19/6/1910 d 1986
Caps: IrLge 1
Brooklyn A
Hakoah
1932 Barnsley 1
Tunbridge Wells Rangers
Ashington
Tunbridge Wells Rangers
Ashington
1934 Gateshead 13 6
Stakeford Albion
Cork FC
Belfast Celtic
Cork FC
Evergreen United
Cork United

Turnbull, James McLachlan (Jimmy) CF
b Bannockburn 23/5/1884
Falkirk
East Stirlingshire
Dundee
Falkirk
Rangers
1904 1905 Preston North End 13
Leyton
1907 1909 Manchester United 67 36
1910 1911 Bradford Park Avenue 49 19
1912 1913 Chelsea 20 8
1914 Manchester United (trial) 0
Hurst

Turnbull, John CF
b Carronshore 1908
Dunblane Rovers
Bonnyrigg Rose
Leith Athletic
Stenhousemuir (loan)
Stenhousemuir
1932 York City 1

Turnbull, Peter CF/IR/IL
b Sanquhar 30/12/1873 d 1942
Rangers
Glasgow Thistle
1892 1894 Burnley 46 23
1894 Bolton Wanderers 4 5
1895 Blackburn Rovers 25 7
Rangers
1897 Blackburn Rovers (loan) 1
Millwall Athletic
Queen's Park Rangers
Brentford
Barrow
Tranmere Rovers

From To — Apps Goal

Turnbull, Robert Armstrong (Bob) LB/RB/CH
b Allendale 1909
Esh Winning Juniors
West Stanley
1927 1929 South Shields 49
1930 1932 Gateshead 120 1
1933 1935 Millwall 88 1
1935 Halifax Town 0
1936 1937 Crewe Alexandra 40

Turnbull, Robert Hamilton (Bobby) CF
b Dumbarton 22/6/1894 d 1944
Royal Engineers
1921 1924 Arsenal 59 26
1924 Charlton Athletic 6 2
1924 1927 Chelsea 80 51
1927 1929 Clapton Orient 39 18
1929 Southend United 2
Chatham
1932 Crystal Palace 2

Turnbull, Robert Joseph (Bobby) OR/IL
b South Bank 17/12/1895 d 1952
Caps: England 1
South Bank East End
1919 1924 Bradford Park Avenue 207 47
1925 1931 Leeds United 204 45
Rhyl Athletic
Smith's Clock (Teesside)

Turnbull, Thomas RB
Falkirk
East Stirlingshire
Celtic
Partick Thistle
1900 Sheffield United 2
Stenhousemuir
Partick Thistle

Turnbull, Thomas OL
b Morpeth 11/1906
Gainsborough Trinity
1930 Bristol Rovers 1
Ashington
1934 Gateshead 5

Turnbull, William (Billy) OR/CF/RB
b Blyth 21/12/1900
Caps: WLge 1
Blyth United
New Delaval Villa
Blyth Spartans (trial)
West Stanley
1922 Cardiff City 1
1924 Newport County 5 3
1925 Ashington 34 18
1925 Manchester City 0
1927 Chesterfield 29 11
1928 Brighton & Hove Albion 5
Ashington
Blyth Spartans
Wallsend Town
1932 1933 Gateshead 10
1934 Oldham Athletic 0

Turnell, Reginald L (Reg) OR
1913 Glossop 3

Turner, Albert (Bert) OL/IL
b Sheffield 3/9/1907
Grimethorpe Wesleyan
Mansfield & Howell SC
Ecclesfield United
1925 Halifax Town (trial) 0
Denaby United
1928 1930 Hull City 19 2
1931 1932 Walsall 56 21
1933 1936 Doncaster Rovers 119 51
1937 1938 Cardiff City 42 20
1938 Bristol Rovers 21 4
Bath City

Turner, Albert James RH
b Blackpool 7/4/1901 d 1985
South Shore
1921 Nelson 1
Lytham

Turner, Alfred Docwra (Alf) OR
b Islington 25/6/1879 d 1926
West Herts
Crouch End Vampires
Watford
Upton Park
1902 1903 Nottingham Forest 9

Turner, Arthur (Archie) OR
b Farnborough, Hampshire 6/1877 d 1925
Caps: England 2
Aldershot North End
South Farnborough
Camberley St Michael's
Brentford (trial)
Reading (trial)
Southampton St Mary's
1902 Derby County 21 1
1902 1903 Newcastle United 13 1
Tottenham Hotspur
Southampton
1904 Bristol City (loan) 1
South Farnborough Athletic

Turner, Arthur LB
b Plymouth
Royal Artillery
Bolsover Town
1931 Plymouth Argyle 0
1932 1933 Bristol City 16
1934 York City 12
Cheltenham Town

Turner, Arthur Owen CH
b Chesterton 1/4/1909 d 1994
Downings Tileries
Wolstanton PSA
1929 West Bromwich Albion 0
1930 1938 Stoke City 290 17
1938 1946 Birmingham 39
1939 (Birmingham) (3)
1947 1948 Southport 28

Turner, Cecil LH
b Medomsley q3 1906
Chilton Colliery Recreation Athletic
1927 Middlesbrough 0
1928 Stockport County 1

Turner, Charles LB
Bangor City
1936 Cardiff City 2
Workington

Turner, Charles J (Charlie) CH
b Athlone 1911
Caps: Eire 10
Manchester Central
Stalybridge Celtic
1933 1934 Leeds United 13
1935 1937 Southend United 99
1937 1938 West Ham United 11
1939 Hartlepools United (3)

Turner, Charles John (Charlie) GK
b Newport 1/7/1919 d 1999
Dewstonians
Ebbw Junction
1938 1947 Newport County 37
1948 Swansea Town 2
Yeovil Town

Turner, Cyril T RB
b Berkshire
1919 1921 West Ham United 7 1

Turner, David William RH
b Wallsend 12/5/1905 d 1978
Burnhope Institute
Spennymoor United
Burnhope Institute
1930 Norwich City 3
Horden Colliery Welfare
Crook Town
Hexham

Turner, Douglas (Doug) OL
b Sheffield
1937 Sheffield United 0
1938 Aldershot 1

Turner, Edward (Old Hookey) RB
b Skerton q1 1874
Skerton
Kendal
1898 Everton 2
Royal Artillery (Portsmouth)
Portsmouth
Northampton Town
Portsmouth
Fulham
Luton Town
Carlisle Co-operative

Turner, Eli Fearn LH/RB
b Stoke-on-Trent q1 1893
1921 1926 Crewe Alexandra 206 6
Oswestry Town

Turner, Ernest CF/IR
b Brithdir 1898 d 1951
Bargoed
Caerphilly
1922 1924 Merthyr Town 96 31
1925 Southampton 16 3

Turner, Everard Edley LH
b Ecclesfield q1 1879 d 1947
Sheffield
Rotherham Town
1903 1904 Gainsborough Trinity 35 1
Rotherham Town

Turner, F LB
1893 Rotherham Town 10 1

Turner, Fred OR
1893 1894 Rotherham Town 13 2

Turner, George GK
1929 Rotherham United 4

Turner, George Jones GK
b Swallownest 2/10/1909 d 1982
Frickley Colliery
Scarborough
1933 Rotherham United 22
Gainsborough Trinity

Turner, George William OL
b Mansfield 5/5/1910 d 1996
Mansfield Athletic
Sneinton
1930 Notts County 3 1
1931 Luton Town 16 4
1932 Everton 2
1934 Bradford City 16 2
1935 Luton Town 4 1
1935 1936 Northampton Town 22 3
Newark Town

Turner, Gilbert GK
b Bolton q1 1877
Victoria Wesleyans (Bolton)
Bolton St Luke's
Accrington Stanley
1907 1910 Aston Villa 15
Pontypridd
1913 Everton 0
1921 Bury 2

Turner, Harold (Harry) LB
b Birmingham 1880
Royal Artillery (Portsmouth)
Portsmouth
1900 New Brighton Tower 14
Portsmouth
1903 Leicester Fosse 0

Turner, Harold CF/IL
b Whitwell 1913 d 1961
Whitwell Colliery
1934 Chesterfield 7 3
1935 Bristol City 6

Turner, Harold Lovett RH
b Desborough 16/3/1907 d 1987
Harborough Town
1930 Bournemouth & Boscombe Ath 9

Turner, Henry CH
b Wallsend
Wallsend Elm Villa
1914 Hull City 6 3
Hartlepools United
Workington
Shildon Athletic

Turner, Herbert Gwyn (Bert) RB/CH/LB
b Rhymney 19/6/1909 d 1981
Caps: Wales War 8/Wales 8
Brithdir
1933 1946 Charlton Athletic 176 2
1939 (Charlton Athletic) (3)
Dartford

Turner, Herbert Lewis (Bert) IR/IL/CF
b King's Norton 17/2/1899 d 1953
Darlaston
1919 Birmingham 0
1920 1924 Merthyr Town 138 35
1924 1925 Coventry City 30 7
Brierley Hill Alliance
1927 Torquay United 38 11
1928 Bristol Rovers 9 2
Brierley Hill Alliance
Standard Athletic

Turner, Hugh GK
b Wigan 6/8/1904 d 1996
Caps: FLge 1/England 2
Felling Colliery
1924 Darlington 0
High Fell
1926 1936 Huddersfield Town 364
1937 1938 Fulham 68
1939 (Fulham) (3)
Hurst

Turner, Isaiah (Ike) GK
b Netherton 7/1876 d 1936
Dudley St James
1898 West Bromwich Albion 1
Stourbridge
Dudley Town
Kidderminster Harriers
1906 Stoke 7
Worcester City
Old Hill Wanderers

Turner, James LB/RB
b Swallownest 20/2/1898 d 1973
1923 1934 Rotherham County 337 2

Turner, James Albert (Jimmy) LH/RH/IR
b Black Bull 1866 d 1904
Caps: FLge 3/England 3
Black Lane Rovers
1888 1893 Bolton Wanderers 96 8
1894 1895 Stoke 52 1
1896 1897 Derby County 51 1
1898 Stoke 7

Turner, John CH
Gravesend United
1898 Newton Heath 3

Turner, John Allan GK
b Swallownest
Silverwood Colliery
1926 1927 Stockport County 38
1928 Wolverhampton Wanderers 7
1929 Watford 13
1929 Rotherham United 1

Turner, John Kipling OR
b Worksop 1914
Worksop Town
Northern Rubber Works (Retford)
1935 1937 Leeds United 14
1937 1938 Mansfield Town 58 9
1939 Bristol City (3) (1)

Turner, John Thomas RB/LB
b Wednesbury 30/10/1915 d 1985
Caps: England Sch
1932 Wolverhampton Wanderers 0
1933 West Bromwich Albion 0
1934 1935 Bournemouth & Boscombe Ath 40 1
1936 1937 Chester 4
1937 1938 Bristol City 23
1939 Clapton Orient 0

Turner, Joseph (Joe) CF
1892 Walsall Town Swifts 14 7

Turner, Joseph (Joe) LH
b Leyland 1894
Leyland
1920 1921 Portsmouth 28 3
1922 Preston North End 0

Turner, Joseph H (Joe) OL
b Burslem 3/1872 d 1950
Newcastle Swifts
Dresden United
Southampton
1898 1899 Stoke 57 15
1899 1900 Everton 32 8
Southampton
New Brompton
Northampton Town
Eastleigh Athletic
South Farnborough Athletic

Turner, Joseph Herbert (Joe) OL
b Sheffield 12/5/1892 d 1964
Rotherham Town
1920 1921 Barnsley 12
Worksop Town

Turner, Leslie Appleby (Les) LH/RH
b Dinnington 25/11/1909 d 1965
Warmsworth
Denaby United
Conisbrough Welfare
1929 Doncaster Rovers (trial) 0
1930 Huddersfield Town 0
1932 1934 Crewe Alexandra 112 2
1935 1936 Doncaster Rovers 13
1938 New Brighton 38 1
1939 (New Brighton) (3)

From To Apps Goal

Turner, Maurice OL/LH/RB
1905 1908 Gainsborough Trinity 38 2

Turner, Neil McDougall OR
b Glasgow 7/10/1892
Petershill
1913 Leeds City 4 2
Raith Rovers
St Mirren
Vale of Leven
Kilmarnock
1919 Sunderland 1
1921 Aberdare Athletic 22 2
Dundee
Bethlehem Steel
New Bedford Whalers
Springfield Babes

Turner, Oliver Charles (Charlie) OL
b Warminster q1 1898 d 1968
Warminster
1921 1922 Swindon Town 17 1
Bridgend Town

Turner, Percy George IL/IR
b Mountsorrel q3 1879
1897 1898 Loughborough 7
Swindon Town
1900 Barnsley 5 1
1900 Chesterfield Town 14 4
Wellingborough
Brentford
1904 Grimsby Town 14

Turner, Peter J IL
b Glasgow 18/12/1876 d 1970
Parkhead
St Bernard's
1900 Woolwich Arsenal 33 5
1901 Middlesbrough 23 6
Royal Albert
Luton Town
Watford
Leyton
Doncaster Rovers

Turner, Richard RB
b Whitburn, County Durham Colliery 1918
Marsden Colliery
Hetton United
1937 Hartlepools United 1

Turner, Richard William (Billy) IL
b Leicester q3 1883
Leicester Imperial
1905 1909 Leicester Fosse 14 2
Portsmouth
Leyton

Turner, Robert (Bob) RH
b Manchester 1877
Red Rock
Gravesend United
1898 Newton Heath 2
Brighton United
Thames Ironworks
Fulham
Glentoran
Cray Wanderers
Watford
Rossendale United

Turner, Robert Frewen (Bob) OL
b Leicester 15/7/1885 d 1959
Grasmere Swifts
St Andrew's (Leicester)
St Mark's
Leicester Imperial
1906 1908 Leicester Fosse 56 7
1908 1910 Everton 34 1
1911 Preston North End 8
Darlington
Coventry City
Durham City

Turner, Robert Frewen (Bobby) LH/OL/RH
b Leicester 14/2/1910 d 1978
Blyth Spartans
Darlington Alliance Juniors
Darlington Railway Athletic
Albert Hill United
Cockfield
1930 Newcastle United 0
1931 Hull City 1
1932 Southport 20 8
1933 Swindon Town 4
1933 Carlisle United 28 4
1934 York City 9
Blyth Spartans

From To Apps Goal

Turner, Samuel Isaiah (Isaiah) IL
b Langley, Worcestershire 1882
Oldbury Town
Darlaston
1904 West Bromwich Albion 1
Brierley Hill Alliance
Bristol Rovers
Coventry City
Dudley Town

Turner, Thomas (Tom) LH
b Whittle-le-Woods q3 1903 d 1941
Whittle-le-Woods
Chorley
1928 Nottingham Forest 1
Chorley
Lytham
Fleetwood
Lytham

Turner, Thomas Stuart (Tom 'Tucker') OL/IL
b Glasgow
Commercial Athletic
St Roch's
Raith Rovers
1929 1935 Blackburn Rovers 113 24
Arbroath
Albion Rovers

Turner, William (Bill) LH
b South Moor 22/12/1894 d 1970
Dipton United
Scotswood
Leadgate Park
1920 1923 Southampton 149 1
1924 1926 Bury 76
1927 Queen's Park Rangers 38

Turner, William (Bill) IR/RH/OR
b Tipton 16/11/1901 d 1989
Bromsgrove Rovers
1925 1935 Crystal Palace 282 36
Worcester City
Bromsgrove Rovers

Turner, Wilmot Arthur CF
b Brierley Hill q2 1865 d 1931
Chester
1891 1892 Stoke 32 8
1892 Ardwick 1

Turton, Jeffrey RB
b Wortley 21/4/1912 d 1981
Chapeltown
1934 West Bromwich Albion 0
1935 Gillingham 11
1935 1937 Crystal Palace 12
Folkestone

Turton, Samuel Frederick LH
b Burton-on-Trent q4 1867
1894 Burton Swifts 1

Tustin, William Arthur GK
b Birmingham q2 1882
Bournbrook
Soho Villa
Kidderminster
Stafford Rangers
1906 1907 Glossop 48
Brighton & Hove Albion

Tuthill, George Robert LH/IL
b Southwold 30/7/1878 d 1974
Army
1897 1898 Loughborough 26 1
Wellingborough
Fulham
Grays United
Northfleet

Tutin, Arthur RH
b Coundon q2 1907 d 1961
Shildon
Newton Aycliffe
Ferryhill Athletic
Bishop Auckland
Consett
Chilton Colliery Recreation Athletic
Spennymoor United
1930 Sheffield Wednesday (trial) 0
1930 Bradford Park Avenue (trial) 0
Crook Town
1932 1933 Aldershot 12
1933 1938 Stoke City 183 3
1939 (Stoke City) (1)

Tutt, Walter Reginald OL
b Dover 15/2/1906 d 1978
Canterbury Waverley
1930 1931 Queen's Park Rangers 7 3

Tuxford, William RB/LH/RH
1892 1895 Crewe Alexandra 23 1

From To Apps Goal

Tweddle, Frederick (Freddie) OR
b Middlesbrough q1 1887 d 1976
Darlington St Augustine's
Saltburn
Hartlepools United
1910 Sheffield United 10
Hartlepools United
Shildon Athletic

Tweed, George Edward LB/RB
b Newmarket 4/12/1910 d 1971
Newmarket Town
Bury Town
Newmarket Town
1935 Coventry City 0
1936 1937 Bristol Rovers 25
1937 Gillingham 31
Bath City
Gloucester City

Tweedy, George Jacob GK
b Bedlington 8/1/1913 d 1987
Caps: England 1
Willington
1932 1952 Grimsby Town 347
1939 (Grimsby Town) (3)

Twell, Ben CF/IR
b Temple Normanton 30/8/1903 d 1986
Staveley Town
Matlock Town
Hardwick Colliery
Grassmoor Ivanhoe
1927 Grimsby Town 3 1
1929 1930 Southport 21 25
1931 New Brighton 11 1
1932 Port Vale (trial) 0
Fleetwood
Sutton Town
Temple Normanton Old Boys
Clay Cross Rangers
Temple Normanton Red Rose

Twemlow, Charles (Charlie) OR
b Macclesfield 1900
Macclesfield
Congleton Town
1921 Stoke 1 1
Macclesfield

Twemlow, William (Billy) LB/RB
b Hanley q3 1892 d 1933
Sandbach Ramblers
1919 1920 Stoke 36 2
1921 1922 Port Vale 21
Macclesfield

Twigg, John Alfred (Alf) CF/IL
b Ashby-de-la-Zouch q3 1882
1902 Burton United 23 2
Hinckley Town
1904 Gainsborough Trinity 32 16
Millwall Athletic

Twine, Frank William RB/LB
b Holborn 1903
Caps: England Amat
Army
1926 1927 Middlesbrough 52
Aldershot
1931 Rochdale 10
Caernarvon United

Twiss, James CF
b Haydock q2 1897 d 1961
Atherton
Skelmersdale United
1919 Burnley 4 1
1921 Wigan Borough 7 3
Chester

Twiss, Richard (Dickie) LH/CF/IL
b Ashton-in-Makerfield 11/11/1909 d 1970
1932 Wolverhampton Wanderers 0
1933 Port Vale 1
1934 1935 Bournemouth & Boscombe Ath 4

Twist, Richard GK
b Chorley
1931 Burnley 10
1932 Preston North End 3

Twomey, James Francis (Jim) GK
b Newry 13/4/1914 d 1984
Caps: Irl.ge 2/Ireland 2
Newry Town
1937 1948 Leeds United 106
1939 (Leeds United) (1)
1949 Halifax Town 0

Tye, Albert Edward LH/LB
b Birmingham 1883
1903 Burton United 5
1904 1905 Chesterfield Town 26
Tutbury Town

From To Apps Goal

Tye, Edward LB
b Stanford
Stanford
1914 Chelsea 1

Tyldesley, James Darbyshire GK
b Ashton-in-Makerfield 10/8/1889 d 1923
1911 1913 Bolton Wanderers 10

Tyler, Herbert Ernest CH/LH
b Ecclesall 4/9/1889
Firth's Works (Tinsley)
Castleford Town
1914 Sheffield Wednesday 0
1919 1920 Manchester City 44
1921 1922 Stalybridge Celtic 73 1
1923 1924 Chesterfield 32

Tyler, Sidney (Syd) LB/RB
b Wolverhampton 7/12/1904 d 1971
Stourbridge
1923 Manchester United 1
1924 1926 Wolverhampton Wanderers 18
1927 1928 Gillingham 76
1929 Norwich City (trial) 0
1929 1930 Millwall 29
Colwyn Bay United

Tyler, William (Billy) RB/RH
b Bradford, Lancashire 28/5/1900 d 1974
The Beech
New Cross (Manchester)
1923 Manchester United 0
1925 Southport 30 3
1926 Bradford City 11
1927 Bournemouth & B Ath (trial) 1
1927 Grimsby Town 1
Hurst
1929 Accrington Stanley 7
Ashton National

Tyrer, Henry (Harry) IL/CH/IR
b Halsall 26/7/1868 d 1935
Turton
1888 Bolton Wanderers 14 2
Blackpool
1895 1897 Darwen 83 21
1898 Newcastle United 0
Turton

Tysoe, Frank OR/OL
b Northampton 14/11/1902 d 1996
1920 Northampton Town 1
Birmingham Tramways
1926 Cardiff City 2
1927 Charlton Athletic 0
1929 Crewe Alexandra 12
Derry City

Tyson, William George (Billy) IL
b Skerton 2/2/1916 d 1987
Skerton Athletic
1933 Southport 0
Morecambe
Glentoran
Lancaster Town
1936 1937 Accrington Stanley 26 12
1937 Blackburn Rovers 6 2
Boston United
1938 Accrington Stanley 5 1
1939 Southport 0
Lancaster Moor Hospital

Udall, Harry IR
b Tutbury q3 1872 d 1943
1894 Burton Wanderers 1

Udall, William Edward Gisbourne (Ted) RB
b Atherstone 28/5/1910 d 1982
Atherstone Town
1932 Leicester City 0
1934 1936 Derby County 81

Ullathorne, Thomas (Tom) RH
1898 Gainsborough Trinity 1

Underwood, Albert IL
b Darlington q1 1879
Rutherglen Glencairn
1902 Barnsley 13 3
Airdrieonians

Underwood, Alexander Austin ('Tosher') OL
b Street q1 1878 d 1960
Fulham
Grays United
Fulham (loan)
Brentford
1908 Glossop 18
1909 Clapton Orient 37 1

From To Apps Goal

Underwood, Alfred (Alf) LB
b Hanley q2 1869 d 1928
Caps: England 2
Hanley Tabernacle
Etruria
1888 1894 Stoke 94

Underwood, Benjamin Riley (Ben) RH/LH
b Newton, Derbyshire 30/9/1901 d 1958
New Hucknall Colliery
Sutton Town
1925 Derby County 0
1926 1928 Doncaster Rovers 101 1
1928 1930 Leeds United 6
1931 1932 Coventry City 20

Unwin, Matthew James CF/LB
b Clay Cross q4 1879 d 1930
Clay Cross
North Wingfield
Clay Cross Zingari
1902 1904 Chesterfield Town 13 3
Clay Cross Zingari
Clay Cross Works
Stanton Hill
Clay Cross Town

Upex, Dick IL
b Peterborough 26/6/1892 d 1979
GER Locomotive Works (Peterborough)
Peterborough City
Croydon Common
Southend United
1921 Charlton Athletic 3

Upton, C RH
1892 Burton Swifts 2

Upton, Mark RB
b Guisborough q1 1867 d 1941
1893 Middlesbrough Ironopolis 16
Saltburn Swifts

Upton, Solomon OR
b Higham Ferrers 7/2/1891 d 1972
Kettering
1912 Tottenham Hotspur 2
Portsmouth
Plymouth Argyle

Upton, William John (Billy) IR/IL
b Coatbridge 11/6/??
NB Athletic
Albion Rovers
1928 1933 Blackpool 74 26
1933 Chester 2
Albion Rovers
Waterford
Peterborough United

Uren, Harold John OL
b Barton Regis 23/8/1885 d 1955
Millbank Juniors
Northern Nomads
Wrexham
Hoylake
1907 Liverpool 2
Wrexham
1908 1911 Liverpool 41 2
1911 1912 Everton 24 3
Wrexham
Lochgelly United

Urmson, Fred OL/IL
b Little Hulton 26/11/1907 d 1985
Atherton
1927 1935 Tranmere Rovers 310 94
1936 Exeter City 10
Stalybridge Celtic
South Liverpool
Mossley

Urquhart, Arthur OR
b Glasgow 1886
Glasgow Ashfield
Linthouse
Morton
1907 Middlesbrough 4
Johnstone
Dumbarton

Urquhart, Duncan LB
b Gorgie 18/8/1908 d 1960
Caps: LoI 1/Scotland 1
Clinton Vale
Newtongrange Star
Hibernian
Aberdeen
1937 Barnsley (trial) 0
1937 Barrow 19
Cork City
1938 Clapton Orient 0
Waterford

From To Apps Goal

Urwin, Joseph Sydney (Sydney) OR/CF
b High Spen 25/2/1912
Tanfield Lea Institute
1930 Bradford City 1
1931 Chesterfield 0
Throckley Welfare
1933 Lincoln City 8 1
1934 Stockport County 6 2

Urwin, Thomas (Tommy) OL/OR/IR
b Haswell 5/2/1896 d 1968
Caps: FLge 1/England 4
Fulwell
Lambton Star
Shildon Athletic
1914 1923 Middlesbrough 192 14
1924 1929 Newcastle United 188 23
1929 1934 Sunderland 50 5

Urwin, Thomas A LH
b Scotswood
Newburn
1913 Sheffield United 2
Luton Town

Usherwood, Arthur OL
b Congleton 1884
Congleton Excelsior
1904 Stoke 6 1
Ashton Town

Utley, George LH
b Elsecar 16/5/1887 d 1966
Caps: FLge 1/England 1
Elsecar
Wentworth
1906 Sheffield Wednesday (trial) 0
Elsecar
1908 1913 Barnsley 170 8
1913 1921 Sheffield United 107 4
1922 Manchester City 1

Utterson, James (Jimmy) GK
b Gateshead 26/11/1914 d 1935
Caps: IrLge 2
Glenavon
1934 1935 Wolverhampton Wanderers 12

Vail, Thomas (Tommy) CF
b Auchterderran 1873
Lochgelly United
Dundee
1895 Bolton Wanderers 3 1
Lochgelly United
Chatham
1898 Walsall 30 16
Bristol Rovers
1899 Gainsborough Trinity 22 13
Doncaster Rovers
Lochgelly United
Dunfermline Athletic

Valentine, Albert Finch CF
b Higher Ince 3/6/1907 d 1990
Ince St Mary's
1927 Liverpool (trial) 0
Abram Colliery
Ashton St Thomas
Horwich RMI
Ince St Mary's
1928 Liverpool (trial) 0
1928 Southport 21 17
1929 1930 Cardiff City 16 3
1931 Wigan Borough 12 1
1931 Chester 2 1
Prescot Cables
1932 Crewe Alexandra 5 2
Macclesfield
1934 1936 Halifax Town 114 88
1937 Stockport County 0
1937 Accrington Stanley 7 1
1938 Oldham Athletic 2 1
1939 (Oldham Athletic) (2) (2)
Ince St Mary's

Valentine, Frederick (Fred) OR/IR
Earlestown
Ashton Town
1907 1909 Burnley 18 3
Accrington Stanley

Valentine, Frederick Edward (Fred) OR
b Birkenhead q2 1909
Whitchurch
Oswestry Town
Runcorn
Hyde United
1936 Oldham Athletic 5

Valentine, Robert GK
1904 1905 Manchester United 10

From To Apps Goal

Vallance, Hugh Baird CF
b Wolverhampton 14/6/1905 d 1973
Kidderminster Harriers
1927 Aston Villa 0
1928 Queen's Park Rangers 1
1929 1930 Brighton & Hove Albion 44 32
Worcester City
Evesham Town
Tunbridge Wells Rangers
1931 Gillingham 13 7
Kidderminster Harriers
Olympique Alesien
Basle
Brierley Hill Alliance
1934 Gillingham 5 3
Racing Club de Paris
Cork FC
Evesham Town

Vallance, James (Jimmy) OR
b Glasgow 1885 d 1956
Postal Athletic
Glasgow Civil Service
Queen's Park Rangers
1907 Bradford City 3
St Johnstone
Beith

Vallance, Robert (Bob) LH
b Stanley Common 19/9/1901 d 1980
Heanor Town
Ilkeston Town
Grantham
1929 Notts County 8
Grantham
Gainsborough Trinity
Stanley Common Miners Welfare
Smalley United
Stanley Excelsior

Vallance, William (Bill) IL
b Bridgeton 2/10/1916 d 1982
Congleton Town
1938 Oldham Athletic 1

Vallis, Frank GK
b Ashley Down 5/5/1896 d 1957
Horfield United
1919 1925 Bristol City 219
1926 Merthyr Town 2

Vallis, Gilbert Arthur OR
b Ashley Down q1 1898 d 1962
Horfield United
1919 Bristol City 6
Bridgend Town
Barry
1922 Halifax Town 12 1

Vallis, Henry John (Jack) GK
b Ashley Down q1 1892 d 1968
Horfield United
Dundee
Barry
1921 Bristol City 10
Yeovil & Petters United

Van Den Berg, Herman Hubert Christophe OL
b Cape Town, South Africa 21/3/1918 d 2006
Peninsula (Cape Town)
1937 1938 Liverpool 19 3
1939 (Liverpool) (3) (1)

Van Den Eynden, Isaac (Ike) CH
b Belgium
Caps: Belgium
(Belgium)
1913 Clapton Orient 12
(Belgium)

Vance, James IL
b Stevenston 1876
Annbank
1895 1896 Newton Heath 11 1
Fairfield
Annbank

Vango, Alfred James (Alf) CH/LH
b Bethnal Green 23/12/1900 d 1977
Gnome Athletic
1924 Gillingham 5
Barking Town
Walthamstow Avenue
1930 1931 Queen's Park Rangers 12
1932 Clapton Orient 23
London Paper Mills

Vann, Arthur Harrison Allard OL
b Bugbrooke q2 1884 d 1915
Northampton Town
1906 Burton United 2 1
1907 Derby County 0

From To Apps Goal

Vann, Bernard William, VC, MC and bar OL/CF
b Rushden 9/7/1887 d 1918
Hugglescote United
Irthlingborough
Northampton Town
1906 Burton United 12
1906 Derby County 3
1907 Leicester Fosse 0
Mansfield Wesleyans

Vanner, Henry John (Harry) OR
b Haggerston 27/12/1898 d 1975
RN Depot (Chatham)
1924 Charlton Athletic 2
1927 1928 Watford 2
Grays Athletic
Hampstead Town
Erith & Belvedere

Vanner, Richard Thomas (Dick) OR
b Farnham 14/11/1903 d 1978
Aldershot Traction Company
1928 Tottenham Hotspur 0
1929 1930 Clapton Orient 35 4
Aldershot

Varco, Percy Seymour CF/IR
b Fowey 17/4/1904 d 1982
Fowey Town
Torquay United
1923 1924 Aston Villa 10 2
1926 Queen's Park Rangers 16 4
1927 1929 Norwich City 57 37
1929 1931 Exeter City 81 41
1932 Brighton & Hove Albion 1
St Austell
St Blazey

Varney, Frank LB
1924 Nottingham Forest 0
1925 Doncaster Rovers 1
Oswestry Town

Varney, Herbert OR
b Belper 2/2/1885 d 1952
Whitwick White Cross
Belper Town
1901 1902 Derby County 2
Belper Town
1905 West Bromwich Albion 5
Belper Town

Varty, James William LH
b Scotswood 1890 d 1958
Shildon Athletic
Scotswood Rovers
1912 West Bromwich Albion 3
Hartlepools United
Heart of Midlothian
Scotswood

Varty, William C OL
b Throckley 25/6/1906 d 1965
1933 Blackpool 2
1934 Gillingham 10 2
1935 Gateshead 5 1
1935 Carlisle United 16 4

Vasey, Robert Henry (Bob) LH/RH
b Annfield Plain 16/12/1907 d 1979
Annfield Plain
Consett
1932 1934 Nottingham Forest 23
1936 1937 Notts County 27 1
1938 Brighton & Hove Albion 15 1

Vaughan, Alfred CH
1898 Everton 1

Vaughan, Harry IR
b Wath-on-Dearne 6/9/1897
Wath Athletic
1919 Barnsley 5 1

Vaughan, Thomas (Tommy) IR/CF
b Cardiff
Treorchy
1932 1933 Chester 2
1934 Cardiff City 12 3
Folkestone

Vaughan, Thomas W (Tommy) OL
Stourbridge
1929 West Bromwich Albion 0
Shrewsbury Town
1931 Walsall 2

Vaughan, William OL
Whitchurch
1909 Nottingham Forest 4

From To Apps Goal

Vaughan, William (Billy) IL
b Willenhall 18/12/1898 d 1976
Willenhall
1920 Bristol Rovers 6 1
Stafford Rangers
1922 Merthyr Town 0
Shrewsbury Town
1924 Wrexham 11 2
Bilston United
Burton Town
1927 Exeter City 33 9
1928 Merthyr Town 9
1928 Luton Town 3 2
Brierley Hill Alliance
Gresley Rovers
1930 Exeter City 0
Bloxwich Strollers
Cheltenham Town
Walsall Wood
Winsford United
Knotty Ash Athletic

Vaughton, Willis RB
b Sheffield 20/1/1911 d 2007
Chapel-en-le-Frith
Atlas & Norfolk
1933 Huddersfield Town 2 1
1934 Sheffield United 3
Boston United
1936 1938 New Brighton 110

Vause, Peter Granville OL
b Chorley 17/6/1914 d 1986
Leyland Motors
1935 1936 Blackburn Rovers 7 1
1938 Blackpool 0
Darwen
1938 Rochdale 20 13
1939 (Rochdale) (3)

Vaux, Edward (Ted) RB/LB
b Goole 2/9/1916 d 2002
Thorne Colliery
Goole Town
1934 Doncaster Rovers 0
1936 1937 Mansfield Town 29
1938 Chelsea 0
Peterborough United

Vavasor, Vernon Ernest IL
b Exeter 26/8/1902 d 1980
1924 Crewe Alexandra 1

Veitch, Colin Campbell McKechnie CH/RH/IL
b Newcastle 22/5/1881 d 1938
Caps: FLge 4/England 6
Rutherford College
1899 1914 Newcastle United 276 43

Venables, Albert CF
b Aston 28/12/1899 d 1976
Cardiff Camerons
1922 Newport County 1
Minehead

Venters, John Cook IR
b Cowdenbeath 22/8/1910
Lochore Thistle
Dunniker Juniors
1927 Preston North End 0
1929 Nottingham Forest 1
1930 Thames 1
Morton
Young Boys Berne

Verdin, George Eliis CF
b Liverpool 11/7/1908 d 1975
Morecambe
1936 Crewe Alexandra 2 1

Vernon, Douglas Sydney CF
b Devonport 19/5/1905 d 1979
RAF
1928 Southampton 5
Wycombe Wanderers
Leyton

Vernon, Harry James OL
1899 Burton Swifts 1

Vernon, Joseph Leslie (Les) CF/IL/IR
b Sheffield 27/12/1905 d 1979
Netherton United
Worksop Town
1927 1934 Bury 127 50
1934 1936 Preston North End 14 2
1937 Swansea Town 7
Lancaster Town

Verrill, Edward (Teddy) LH
b Staithes 9/10/1884 d 1962
South Bank
1907 1914 Middlesbrough 181 4

From To Apps Goal

Verrill, George RH
b Staithes 17/4/1889 d 1949
1909 Middlesbrough 0
1910 1911 Gainsborough Trinity 45
Hibernian

Veysey, Arthur John OR
b Chorlton q1 1881
1904 Wolverhampton Wanderers 2 2

Vials, Percival Arthur (Percy) CF
b Market Harborough 31/1/1908 d 1983
Little Rowden Albion
1925 Leicester City (trial) 0
Kettering Town
Market Harborough Town
1928 1931 Bristol City 73 36
1932 Middlesbrough 0
Hinckley United
Atherstone Town
Tamworth

Vickers, Harry LH
1896 Preston North End 1

Vickers, John (Jack) LB/RB/RH
b Auckland Park 7/8/1908 d 1980
Eldon Juniors
Bishop Auckland
1928 Hull City 2
1929 Darlington 14
1930 1931 Doncaster Rovers 39 2
1932 Charlton Athletic 10
1933 1935 Port Vale 73
1936 Newport County 19
South Shields
1938 Hartlepools United 0
Stockton

Vickers, Simeon GK
b Preston 24/8/1892 d 1970
1913 Preston North End 1

Vickers, Thomas Hedley (Hedley) LH/RH
b Lincoln q3 1877 d 1955
London Hospitals
1895 1897 Lincoln City 12
Lindum

Vickerstaffe, Ernest RB/CF
b Hanley 1884
Cheltenham Town
Eastville Athletic
1901 Bristol City (trial) 1
Leicester Old Boys
1903 Leicester Fosse 1
Leicester Old Boys
Leicester Nomads
Hinckley United

Vidler, Horace Jack (Jack) CF/OL/IL
b Portsmouth 13/6/1905 d 1953
Army
1928 1938 Plymouth Argyle 243 96
1939 Bristol City (3)

Viggars, Ralph William LH/RH
b Audley 15/7/1901 d 1971
AVIC Chiseldon
1928 1929 Swindon Town 15 1
Bath City

Vigrass, John CH
b Leek 4/1/1898 d 1986
Leek Alexandra
1921 1923 Queen's Park Rangers 66 1
Macclesfield

Vigrow, Scott IL
b Muirhead 1878
Dundee
1896 West Bromwich Albion 1
Airdrieonians
Ayr

Villiers, Henry George RH
b Faversham 29/6/1892 d 1972
Bedford Town
Rugby Town
1920 Leicester City 5
Hinckley United
Mansfield Town
Nuneaton Town
Rugby Town
Hinckley United

From To Apps Goal

Vinall, Edward John (Jack) CF
b Witton 16/12/1910 d 1997
Allen & Everitt's Sports
Ellisons
1929 Birmingham 0
Folkestone
1931 1932 Sunderland 16 3
1933 1937 Norwich City 168 72
1937 1945 Luton Town 44 18
1946 Walsall 2
Worcester City

Vincent, Alexander (Alec) RH
b Spennymoor 19/5/1896 d 1963
Seaham Harbour
1921 1923 Durham City 65 1

Vincent, Ernest (Ernie) RH/CH
b Washington 28/10/1907 d 1978
Dawdon Colliery
Ryhope Colliery
Seaham Colliery
Washington Colliery
1930 1931 Southport 58
1931 1933 Manchester United 64 1
1935 1936 Queen's Park Rangers 28
1937 Doncaster Rovers 1
Stamford Town
Grantham

Vincent, Norman Edwin (Ned) RB/LH/LB
b Prudhoe 3/3/1909 d 1980
Prudhoe United
Spennymoor United
1928 1933 Stockport County 132 20
1934 1946 Grimsby Town 144 2
1939 (Grimsby Town) (3)
Stalybridge Celtic

Vincett, John Herbert LB
b Hastings 24/3/1883 d 1953
Hastings Rovers
Old Hastonians
St Leonards
Hastings
St Leonards United
1907 Grimsby Town 32
1908 Leicester Fosse 1
1908 Barnsley 0
Hastings & St Leonards
1910 Tottenham Hotspur 0

Vine, Reuben OL
b Leadgate q4 1903 d 1969
Stanley United
Eden Colliery
1929 1930 Darlington 48 12
1931 Gateshead 0

Viner, Francis Ronald Jesse (Ron) CH
b Reading q4 1904 d 1955
1923 Reading 0
Kettering Town
1925 Leicester City 0
Guildford City
1930 1932 Accrington Stanley 96 2
1932 Chester 1
1933 Barrow 15
Nelson

Viner, Horace GK
b Tipton q2 1877 d 1935
Birkenhead
1903 Stoke 1
Rhyl

Viney, Edward Evan CF
b New Tredegar 10/5/1904 d 1996
Bangor City
1931 Gateshead 1

Vinson, Harry LH/RH
b Inverness 1889
Inverness Thistle
1909 1911 Bury 3

Virr, Albert Edward LH
b Liverpool q4 1902 d 1959
Lyndholm
1924 1929 Everton 117 2

Vizard, Edward Thomas (Ted) OL
b Cogan 7/6/1889 d 1973
Caps: Wales 22
Cogan Old Boys
Penarth RFC
Barry
1910 1930 Bolton Wanderers 467 64

Voisey, William (Bill) RH/LH/RB
b Millwall 19/11/1891 d 1964
Glengall Rovers
St John's
1920 1922 Millwall Athletic 78 3
1923 Bournemouth & Boscombe Ath 26 2
Leytonstone

From To Apps Goal

Vose, George CH
b St Helens 4/10/1911 d 1981
Peasley Cross Athletic
1933 1938 Manchester United 195 1
1939 (Manchester United) (2)
Runcorn

Vowles, Charles James (Charlie) IL/CF/IR
b Bedminster q3 1895 d 1965
1920 1922 Exeter City 64 20
Boston Town
Bath City (trial)
1924 Barrow 38 13
Scunthorpe & Lindsey United
Newark Town
Ilkeston United

Voysey, Clement Ross (Clem) CH/IR/OL
b New Cross 27/12/1897 d 1989
Royal Naval Air Service
1919 1925 Arsenal 35 6

Waddell, George Barr RH/LH
b Lesmahagow 29/11/1888 d 1966
Dalziel Rovers
Burnbank Athletic
Larkhall United
Rangers
Kilmarnock (loan)
1914 1920 Bradford City 23
Royal Albert (loan)
Stevenston United (loan)
Ayr United (loan)
Ayr United (loan)
Abercorn (loan)
1920 1921 Preston North End 51 2
1922 Oldham Athletic 1
1922 Birmingham 2
Hamilton Academical
1923 New Brighton (trial) 3
1923 Wolverhampton Wanderers 0
Aberaman Athletic
Chorley
Fraserburgh
(Germany)
Dick, Kerr's XI
Ribble Motors

Waddell, Thomas MR CF
Caps: Ireland 1
Cliftonville
1906 1907 Glossop 7 1

Waddington, Abraham (Abe) GK
b Clayton, West Yorkshire 4/2/1893 d 1959
Bradford Central
1920 Bradford City 0
1921 Halifax Town 7
Yorkshire Amateurs
1922 Bradford City 0

Waddington, John OL
Caps: IrLge 1
Glentoran
1904 Blackpool 23 6
Chorley
1907 Blackpool 9

Waddington, John Mercer IR
b Clayton-le-Moors 26/8/1914 d 2000
Stanhill
1938 Accrington Stanley 5 1
Clitheroe

Wade, Edward (Ted) IR/CF
b Blackpool 29/9/1901 d 1966
Central Amateurs
1919 Liverpool 0
South Shore
1922 Burnley 0
Lytham
1924 1927 New Brighton 74 24
1928 Exeter City 9 5
Aldershot (trial)
Margate

Wade, John James OR/OL
1891 1894 Darwen 47 12
1894 Blackburn Rovers 1 2
1896 Darwen 2 1

Wade, Reginald Thomas (Reg) RB/LB
b Stoke Newington q1 1907
Barking Town
1925 Millwall 0
Ilford
1929 1931 West Ham United 37
1932 1936 Aldershot 186 1

Wade, Thomas LB
b Leeds
Methley Perseverance
1929 Huddersfield Town 1
1930 Darlington 0

From To Apps Goal

Wade, William Alexander (Bill) RB
b Jarrow 22/3/1901 d 1958
Bertram FC
Smith's High Docks
Jarrow
1923 1928 Preston North End 139
1929 West Ham United 11
1931 Wigan Borough 8
Frickley Colliery (loan)
Nelson

Wadley, HE IL
1904 Bristol City 1

Wadsley, Harold IL
Netherfield Rangers
1909 Lincoln City 2 1
Sutton Junction
Peterborough GN Loco
Grantham Avenue

Wadsworth, Charles Edward CF
b Rotherham 6/1917 d 1979
1938 Rotherham United 7 2

Wadsworth, Eric Appleyard IR
b Goole q2 1894 d 1934
1919 Hull City 1
Hornsea Town

Wadsworth, Harold OL/OR
b Bootle 1/10/1898 d 1975
Bootle St Matthew's
Tranmere Rovers
1919 1923 Liverpool 54 3
1924 1926 Leicester City 98 7
1927 Nottingham Forest 30 9
1928 1930 Millwall 70 9
Cray Wanderers

Wadsworth, Samuel John (Sam) LB
b Darwen 13/9/1896 d 1961
Caps: FLge 6/England 9
Darwen
1914 Blackburn Rovers 0
Nelson
1920 1929 Huddersfield Town 281 4
1929 1930 Burnley 7
Lytham

Wadsworth, Walter CH
b Bootle 7/10/1890 d 1951
Caps: FLge 1
Lingdale
Ormskirk
1914 1925 Liverpool 217 7
1926 1927 Bristol City 67 1
Flint Town
1928 1929 New Brighton 55 3
Oswestry Town

Wadsworth, Walter OR/OL
b Kilnhurst 9/6/1904 d 1990
Denaby United
1927 Southend United 0
Scunthorpe & Lindsey United
1929 1931 Doncaster Rovers 67 11
1932 Barnsley 17 4

Waggott, David CF
b Chester-le-Street q2 1878 d 1954
Scotswood
1905 Gainsborough Trinity 4 1
1906 Sheffield Wednesday 0
West Stanley
West Ham United

Wagstaff, James Thompson RB/LB
b Middlewich 17/8/1901 d 1976
Witton Albion
1925 1931 Bolton Wanderers 50 1
Horwich RMI

Wagstaff, John George GK
b Nottingham 27/9/1899 d 1932
Arnold St Mary's
1919 Nottingham Forest 1
Arnold St Mary's

Wagstaffe, Edward Herbert (Teddy) CH
b Bethnal Green 2/3/1885 d 1965
Walthamstow Grange
South Weald
Norwich City
West Ham United
Doncaster Rovers
1911 Sheffield United 2
Halifax Town
Scunthorpe & Lindsey United

Wagstaffe, Ralph Thompson OL
b Northwich 19/7/1897 d 1986
1922 1923 Crewe Alexandra 10 2

From To Apps Goal

Wagstaffe, Thomas Daniel (Tom) IR/CF
b Dinapore, India
Fleetwood
1922 Sunderland 2
1923 Oldham Athletic 0
Fleetwood
Morecambe
1926 Crewe Alexandra 3 1
Mossley

Wainscoat, William Russell (Russell) IL/CF
b Maltby 28/7/1898 d 1967
Caps: England 1
Maltby Main Colliery Welfare
1919 1923 Barnsley 144 54
1923 1924 Middlesbrough 34 5
1924 1931 Leeds United 215 87
1931 1933 Hull City 79 42

Wainwright, Arthur Henry OR/IL
b Tinsley 11/1894 d 1968
Tinsley Working Mens Club
1919 Leeds City 0
1919 Grimsby Town 8 2
Gresley Rovers
1922 1923 Bristol Rovers 16
1924 Barrow 34 3
Hednesford Town
Walsall LMS
Bloxwich Strollers
Scarborough
Tinsley Working Mens Club

Wainwright, Barnet OL
b Walsall q3 1901 d 1954
1923 Walsall 1

Wainwright, H James (Jimmy) LB
b Newton Heath 1872
Earlestown Albion
Haydock
1900 Stockport County 29

Wainwright, Harry IR/OR
b Sheffield q3 1899
Highfields
1919 Port Vale 4
Doncaster Rovers
Brodsworth Main Colliery
Frickley Colliery
1924 1925 Sheffield United 2
Boston Town
Scunthorpe & Lindsey United
Newark Town
Scunthorpe & Lindsey United

Wainwright, Thomas (Tom) IL
b Stoke-on-Trent 1864
Stoke St Jude's
1888 Stoke 1
Stoke Priory

Wainwright, Thomas LH/CH
b Nantwich q2 1879
Nantwich
Crewe Carriage Works
1900 1901 Burslem Port Vale 21
Crewe Alexandra
Wellington Town
1904 1905 Notts County 8
Wellington Town
Nantwich

Wainwright, Thomas Goddard GK
b Ecclesfield q3 1897
Brunswick Wesleyans
Thorpe Hesley
1922 Sheffield United 0
Rotherham Town
1924 Notts County 0
Boston Town
1926 Cardiff City 0
1927 Exeter City 13
Tunbridge Wells Rangers
Shirebrook
Loughborough Corinthians
Thorpe Hesley
Park Labour
Alliance Sports (Sheffield)

Wainwright, William Thomas (Bill) LH/CH
b Worksop 28/10/1917
Worksop Town
1936 Mansfield Town 3
1938 1945 Aldershot 10

Wainwright, Wilson LH
b Morley 24/7/1892 d 1952
Morley
1914 Leeds City 2

Wait, Harold (Harry) GK
b Darlaston 3/1892 d 1975
Darlaston
1923 1935 Walsall 264

From To Apps Goal

Waite, George Henry IR/CF/OR
b Bradford 1/3/1894 d 1972
Royal Artillery
1919 Bradford Park Avenue 6
Heart of Midlothian (loan)
Raith Rovers
Clydebank
Pontypridd
1921 1922 Leicester City 28 12
1922 1925 Clapton Orient 62 9
1926 Hartlepools United 26 7
York City

Waite, Norman IR
b Windy Nook 15/2/1898 d 1970
Preston Colliery
1921 1922 Crystal Palace 16 3
1923 Hartlepools United (trial) 0

Waite, Robert Aitcheson CH
b Watch Hill 29/5/1904 d 1991
1924 1925 Swindon Town 4
Bath City

Waites, Sydney Hastings (Syd) OR
b Gateshead 20/9/1901
Technical School Old Boys
Lincoln YMCA
1922 1923 Lincoln City 3
Newark Town
1925 1927 Halifax Town 96 14
1928 Stockport County 2
Boston Town
1930 New Brighton 37 6
Workington
Tunbridge Wells Rangers

Wake, Bertram (Bert) CF
b Wincanton q1 1885 d 1955
1906 Blackpool 4
1907 Wolverhampton Wanderers 0
Salisbury City
1907 Wolverhampton Wanderers 4 1

Wake, Henry Williamson (Harry) RH/IR
b Seaton Delaval 27/1/1901 d 1978
Caps: England Sch/WLge 1
Bigges Main Colliery
Birtley
1919 1921 Newcastle United 3
1923 1930 Cardiff City 149 9
1931 Mansfield Town 20
1932 Gateshead 0

Wakefield, George Edward RH
b Bradford
1920 Bradford City 0
1921 Gillingham 10

Wakefield, John IL
b Golborne 8/1/1909 d 1992
Brynn Central
Ashton Central
1928 Wigan Borough 1

Wakefield, Joseph Henry (Joe) RH
b Barrow 12/2/1901 d 1981
Barrow YMCA
1925 Barrow 9
Barrow YMCA
Barrow Shipbuilders
Ulverston Town
Morecambe
Barrow Paper Mills

Wakeman, Alan GK
b Walsall 20/11/1920 d 2002
Caps: England Sch
Bloxwich Strollers
1938 1949 Aston Villa 12
1950 1951 Doncaster Rovers 5
Bloxwich Strollers
1952 1953 Shrewsbury Town 6
1959 Shrewsbury Town 0

Walden, Frederick Ingram (Fanny) OR
b Wellingborough 1/3/1888 d 1949
Caps: SoLge 3/FLge 1/England 2
White Cross
All Saints
Rodwell
Wellingborough
Northampton Town
1912 1923 Tottenham Hotspur 214 21
1926 Northampton Town 20 1

Walden, George Joseph CF
b Poplar q2 1888 d 1944
1909 Hull City 2 1
Rotherham Town
Denaby United
Luton Town
Scunthorpe & Lindsey United

From To Apps Goal

Walden, Harold Adrian CF
b Umballa, India 10/10/1887 d 1955
Caps: IrLge 1
Linfield
Army
Northern Nomads
Linfield
Halifax Town
1911 1919 Bradford City 54 22
1920 Arsenal 2 1
1921 Bradford Park Avenue 0

Walders, David CH
b Barrow q3 1879 d 1929
Barrow
1903 1905 Burnley 93 3
1907 1911 Oldham Athletic 112 8
Southport Central

Walders, Jonathan (Jack) OR
b Barrow q4 1881 d 1924
Barrow
1904 1905 Burnley 48 2
Oldham Athletic
Luton Town
Chorley

Waldron, Ernest (Ernie) IL/IR
b Birmingham 3/6/1913 d 1994
Bromsgrove Rovers
1934 1946 Crystal Palace 80 30
1939 (Crystal Palace) (3) (5)
Aberdeen

Waldron, Harry CF
b Sheffield
Attercliffe
1899 Barnsley 14 1

Wales, Abraham IR
b Kilwinning 4/10/1907 d 1980
Bartonholm United
Kilwinning Rangers
Kilmarnock
Galston (loan)
Montrose
1931 Luton Town 3
Kilwinning Eglinton
1932 Leicester City trial) 0
Queen of the South
Scottish Aviation

Walkden, Edgar Vivian CH
Stockport 4/11/1914 d 2001
1936 Everton 0
1938 Tranmere Rovers 21
1939 (Tranmere Rovers) (3)

Walker, A RH
1898 Darwen 5

Walker, Albert OL/IL
b Ripley 8/1888
South Wingfield
Ripley Athletic
1906 Nottingham Forest 0
Queen's Park Rangers
1908 1911 Notts County 53 9
Croydon Common

Walker, Albert LB/OL
b Little Lever 4/2/1910 d 1993
Little Lever United
1928 Southport 0
1928 Bolton Wanderers 0
1929 1931 Barrow 72 11
1932 1937 West Ham United 162
1938 Doncaster Rovers 37
1939 (Doncaster Rovers) (3)
Colchester United

Walker, Albert H CH
b Manchester
Eccles United
1922 1923 Crewe Alexandra 25

Walker, Alfred Samuel (Alf) OL
b Upper Holloway q4 1884 d 1961
Wolverton
Northampton Town
Brentford
1909 1910 Wolverhampton Wanderers 32 2
Port Vale
Dunfermline Athletic

Walker, Andrew H (Andy) CH
b Paisley 27/9/1900 d 1963
Renfrew Juniors
Bo'ness
St Mirren (trial)
1928 Reading 0
Bo'ness
1930 Watford 2
Dunfermline Athletic

From	To		Apps	Goal
Walker, Andrew McQueen (Andy)			RH/LH	
b Dalkeith 6/1892			d 1961	
		Lumphinnans Swifts		
		Dundee		
1913	1919	Chelsea	18	2
		Raith Rovers (loan)		
1920	1921	Newport County	74	14
1922		Accrington Stanley	13	
		(USA)		
Walker, Carl Reginald Wilfred			RH	
b Dudley 8/6/1910			d 1983	
1932		Walsall	2	
Walker, Charles Edward (Charlie)			LB	
b Nottingham				
		Margate		
1935		Arsenal	0	
1936	1938	West Ham United	110	
1939		(West Ham United)	(3)	
		Margate		
		Ashford Town (Kent)		
Walker, Cyril John			IR	
b Newport Pagnell 24/2/1914			d 2002	
		Hitchin Town		
		Leavesden Mental Hospital		
1935		Watford	0	
1937		Gillingham	10	3
1937		Sheffield Wednesday	4	
		Chelmsford City		
		Shorts Sports		
1946		Norwich City	3	2
		Dartford		
		Chatham		
		Snowdown Colliery Welfare		
		Dartford		
		Margate		
Walker, David (Davie)			IL	
b Walsall q1 1884			d 1935	
		Walsall White Star		
		Birchfield Villa		
1904		Wolverhampton Wanderers	2	
		Bristol Rovers		
1907		West Bromwich Albion	36	15
1908	1910	Leicester Fosse	73	26
		Bristol Rovers		
		Willenhall Swifts		
		Walsall		
Walker, David J (Dave)			LH/CF/IL	
b Walsall 1908				
		Walsall Town		
		Walsall LMS		
1927	1928	Walsall	20	7
1929	1938	Brighton & Hove Albion	310	28
Walker, Duncan Campbell			CF	
b Alloa 12/9/1902				
		Kilsyth Rangers		
		Dumbarton		
		Bo'ness (loan)		
		St Mirren		
1923	1926	Nottingham Forest	82	29
		Bo'ness (loan)		
Walker, Edward Richard Walter (Dick)			CH	
b Hackney 22/7/1913			d 1988	
		Park Royal		
1934	1952	West Ham United	292	2
1939		(West Ham United)	(3)	
Walker, Ernest Edwin D (Ernie)			OL/LB	
b Hinckley 24/11/1889			d 1958	
		South Wigston Albion		
		17th Regimental District		
		Holwell Works		
		Hinckley United		
1919	1923	Leicester City	64	3
		Hinckley United		
Walker, Frank			RH/LH	
b Newport q3 1906				
		St John's (Newport)		
1926	1927	Newport County	6	1
Walker, Frederick (Fred)			CH	
		Barrow		
1905	1906	Leeds City	26	
		Huddersfield Town		
Walker, Frederick (Fred)			RH/LH	
b Wednesbury 3/7/1913			d 1978	
		Metro Shaft		
		Wednesbury		
1936		Walsall	3	
1937	1938	Sheffield Wednesday	10	1
1939		(Sheffield Wednesday)	(2)	
		Chelmsford City		
Walker, George			CH	
b Musselburgh 24/5/1904				
Caps: SLge 2/Scotland 4				
		Rosslyn Juniors		
		St Mirren		
1933	1935	Notts County	100	1
1936	1938	Crystal Palace	102	1
1939		Watford	0	
Walker, George Henry (Harry)			GK	
b Aysgarth 20/5/1916			d 1976	
		Leyburn		
1935	1937	Darlington	50	
1937	1946	Portsmouth	49	
1939		(Portsmouth)	(3)	
1946	1954	Nottingham Forest	293	
Walker, George Samuel			CH	
b Oldham q4 1905				
		Chadderton Amateurs		
		Hyde United		
1925		Oldham Athletic	2	
		Buxton		
		Manchester North End		
		Buxton		
Walker, Harold			OR	
		Throckley Welfare		
		Usworth Colliery		
1934	1935	Lincoln City	18	2
1936	1937	Gateshead	40	12
Walker, Harry			LH	
b Leeds				
1923		Halifax Town	5	
Walker, Hugh			IR	
b Edinburgh 27/11/??				
		St Bernard's		
1927		Barrow	17	1
		Distillery		
		Worcester City		
		Bo'ness		
Walker, J			LH	
		Coseley		
1903		Wolverhampton Wanderers	2	
Walker, James			OL	
b Glasgow 1902				
		Bathgate Northern		
		Livingstone Juniors		
		Arniston Rangers		
		Dundee		
		Dundee United		
		Broxburn United		
1925		Coventry City	16	1
		Bathgate		
		Bo'ness		
		Armadale		
Walker, James Henry (Harry)			RH/LH/IR	
b Wirksworth q1 1890			d 1934	
		Wirksworth Boys Brigade		
		Clay Cross		
1911	1919	Derby County	84	4
1920		Notts County	5	
1920		Fulham	8	
1923		Aberdare Athletic	5	
1923		Bournemouth & Boscombe Ath	1	
1924		Chesterfield	0	
1925		Derby County	0	
Walker, James R (Jimmy)			IL/LH/RH	
b Rutherglen 20/1/1895				
		Rutherglen Glencairn		
		Kilsyth Emmet		
		Rutherglen Waverley		
1922	1925	Plymouth Argyle	21	1
1926		Exeter City	12	2
1927		Wigan Borough	8	1
		Darwen		
		Bath City		
Walker, James Richard (Jimmy)			RH/CH	
b Port Glasgow				
		Port Glasgow Athletic		
1920	1925	Luton Town	133	4
Walker, John			RB	
1890	1891	Burnley	40	
		Clyde		
1893		Sunderland	6	
1895		Stoke	0	
Walker, John (Jack)			RB/CH	
b Bonhill 4/11/1868				
		Vale of Leven		
1892		Grimsby Town	13	
		Gainsborough Trinity		
1893		Everton	3	1
1894		Manchester City	19	1
1895	1898	Leicester Fosse	113	
Walker, John			IR	
b Coatbridge 31/5/1874			d 1940	
Caps: SLge 2/Scotland 5				
		Armadale		
		Heart of Midlothian		
1897	1901	Liverpool	109	28
		Rangers		
		Morton		
Walker, John			OL	
b 1878			d 1900	
		Leith Primrose		
		Leith Athletic		
		Heart of Midlothian		
1899		Lincoln City	6	
Walker, John			OL	
b Glasgow 1891				
Caps: Ireland 1				
		Belfast Celtic		
1909	1911	Bury	18	
		Glentoran		
Walker, John (Jock)			OL	
b Clydebank 1903				
		Kirkintilloch Rob Roy		
		Rangers		
		Hibernian		
1927	1928	Swindon Town	20	4
		Ebbw Vale		
		Bath City		
Walker, John A			LB	
b Beith 8/10/1882			d 1968	
Caps: SoLge 4/Scotland 9				
		Eastern Burnside		
		Cambuslang Rangers		
		Burnbank Athletic		
		Raith Rovers		
		Beith		
		Rangers		
		Cowdenbeath		
		Swindon Town		
1913	1920	Middlesbrough	106	
1921	1922	Reading	59	
Walker, John Allsop			RH/IL/IR	
b Plumtree 30/11/1871			d 1951	
		Shrewsbury School		
		Derby Junction		
1889	1890	Derby County	11	
		Magdalen College (Oxford)		
1891	1892	Notts County	4	
		Corinthians		
Walker, John D (Jack)			RH	
b Great Wyrley 1900				
		Cannock Town		
1924	1925	Stoke	35	1
1926		Walsall	12	
Walker, John Robert			RB	
b Wheatley Hill 1901				
		Wheatley Hill		
1922	1923	Hartlepools United	24	
		Spennymoor United		
Walker, John William (William)			IR	
b High Spen 1899				
		Langley Park		
1923		Hull City	5	1
		Leadgate Park		
Walker, Joseph (Joe)			RB	
b Farnworth 26/2/1912			d 1983	
		Kearsley Celtic		
		Bridgewater Celtic		
		Astley Bridge		
1934	1935	Southport	24	
Walker, Luther			LB/RB	
b West Bromwich q2 1864			d 1903	
		West Bromwich Royal		
1888	1889	West Bromwich Albion	18	
		West Bromwich Standard		
Walker, Richard Stringer			OL	
b Tonge, Lancashire q4 1889				
		Tonge		
1910	1911	Bury	23	1
		Eccles United		
Walker, Robert			CH	
1897		Notts County	0	
1898		Newton Heath (trial)	2	
Walker, Robert (Bob)			RB	
b Bradford 6/4/1903			d 1952	
		Wibsey		
1920		Bradford City	1	
1921		Barrow	0	
1921		Bradford City	0	
1923		Bradford Park Avenue	4	
1924		New Brighton	16	
Walker, Robert (Bob)			RH	
b Beith				
		Arthurlie		
1929		Luton Town	5	
Walker, Robert George			LB	
b Southampton				
		Cowes		
1926	1928	Bournemouth & Boscombe Ath	21	
Walker, Robert Henry (Bob)			IL	
b Northallerton q1 1884				
		Heart of Midlothian		
1905		Middlesbrough	9	2
		Tottenham Hotspur		
		New Brompton		
		Northampton Town		
		Millwall Athletic		
		Luton Town		
		Bristol Rovers		
Walker, Stanley (Stan)			CF	
1930		Nelson	2	
		Clitheroe		
		Brierfield Mills		
		Brierfield Legion		
		Brierfield Old Boys		
Walker, Stephen (Steve)			LH/CH/RH	
b Sheffield 16/10/1914			d 1987	
1935		Leeds United	0	
		Gainsborough Trinity		
1937		Sheffield United	0	
1938	1949	Exeter City	141	3
1939		(Exeter City)	(3)	
		Minehead		
Walker, Thomas			OL	
1892		Northwich Victoria	1	
Walker, Thomas			LB	
1900	1901	Gainsborough Trinity	46	
Walker, Thomas			IL	
b Seaton Delaval				
		Thornley		
1903		Sunderland	0	
		West Stanley		
1907		Fulham	0	
		Watford		
1908		Blackpool	8	3
Walker, Thomas (Tommy)			RB	
b Cross Colls 4/3/1902			d 1973	
		Vale of Grange		
1924	1925	Bradford City	54	4
1925	1934	Sheffield Wednesday	258	3
Walker, Thomas J			OR/OL	
1892		Burslem Port Vale	15	3
1892	1894	Burton Swifts	16	4
Walker, Thomas T (Tom)			IL/OL	
1894	1896	Nottingham Forest	4	
1897		Loughborough	16	4
Walker, W George			CH/LB/RB	
b Wednesfield 1877				
		Willenhall Pickwick		
1900	1904	Wolverhampton Wanderers	121	2
		Crystal Palace		
		New Brompton		
		Crystal Palace		
Walker, Walter W			IL	
1911		Nottingham Forest	1	
Walker, Walter William (Billy)			IL/OL	
b Horseley Heath 1879				
		Toll End Wesley		
1899	1901	West Bromwich Albion	34	6
		Brierley Hill Alliance		
		Dudley		
Walker, WH			OL	
1894	1895	Rotherham Town	3	
Walker, Wilfred Stanley (Stan)			GK	
b Waddington 15/12/1907			d 1983	
		Waddington		
1925		Lincoln City	0	
		Gainsborough Trinity		
		Grantham		
1929		Wolverhampton Wanderers	1	
1931		New Brighton	40	
1932		Doncaster Rovers	20	
		Grantham		
		Peterborough United		
		Grantham		

From To Apps Goal

Walker, William d 1907
b Broxburn
Cardross Swifts
Broxburn Athletic
Leith Athletic
1897 Liverpool 12 2
Leith Athletic

Walker, William CF
b Walsall 1888
Walsall
Darlaston
Halesowen
1910 West Bromwich Albion 1 1
Willenhall Swifts

Walker, William OL
1919 Stockport County 6 3

Walker, William Baird (Billy) IR/IL/CF
b New Cumnock 5/5/1893
New Cumnock
Lugar Boswell
1911 1912 Bradford City 5
Lanemark
1913 1919 Birmingham 28 10
1919 Coventry City 20 7
1920 1922 Merthyr Town 82 24
1922 1923 Bristol City 37 7
1923 Sheffield Wednesday 18 5
Weymouth
Leamington Town
Redditch Town
Leamington Town
Halesowen Town

Walker, William Burn (Willie) OL
b Darlington q2 1891 d 1968
Darlington Albion
Darlington (trial)
Darlington St Augustine's
1909 1920 Fulham 168 24
1921 Lincoln City 33 5
1923 Lincoln City (trial) 3

Walker, William Henry (Billy) IL/CF
b Wednesbury 29/10/1897 d 1964
Caps: FLge 6/England 18
Hednesford Town
Darlaston
Wednesbury Old Park
1919 1933 Aston Villa 478 214

Walker, Willis GK
b Gosforth 24/11/1892 d 1991
1911 Sheffield United 0
Doncaster Rovers
1914 1919 Leeds City 22
1919 1924 South Shields 192
1925 Bradford Park Avenue 34
1926 Stockport County 19

Walkerdine, Garnet Coxon OL/IL
b Nottingham q4 1882 d 1965
1903 Notts County 1
1904 Gainsborough Trinity 3
Sutton Town
Mansfield Mechanics

Walkerdine, Henry (Harry) IL/OR
b Nottingham 1870 d 1949
1889 Notts County 2
Gainsborough Trinity
1891 1892 Notts County 36 16
Mansfield
Mansfield Foresters

Wall, Alexander (Alec) IR/IL
b Liverpool 31/10/1899 d 1978
Caps: England Sch
Bootle Secondary School Old Boys
1919 1924 Everton 16 3
1925 1926 Swindon Town 56 20

Wall, Anthony John (Tony) OL
b Chester 15/11/1907 d 1984
1928 New Brighton 1

Wall, George OL
b Boldon Colliery 20/2/1885 d 1962
Caps: FLge 5/England 7
Boldon Royal Rovers
Whitburn
Jarrow
1903 1905 Barnsley 75 24
1905 1914 Manchester United 287 89
Cowdenbeath (loan)
1919 1920 Oldham Athletic 74 12
Hamilton Academical
1922 Rochdale 30 1
Ashton National
Manchester Ship Canal

From To Apps Goal

Wall, Leonard John (Len) LH/IL/CH
b Ditherington q2 1889 d 1951
Ditherington Athletic
Shrewsbury All Saints
Welshpool
Shrewsbury Town
1909 1910 Glossop 10 1
1910 1913 Manchester City 41 2
Dundee
Crystal Palace
Wellington Town
Shrewsbury Town
1921 Walsall 3
Bargoed
Bloxwich Strollers
West Cannock Colliery

Wall, Thomas Henry (Tom) GK
b Nottingham 29/5/1909 d 1989
Ripley Town
Clifton Colliery
1932 Notts County 3
1933 Tottenham Hotspur 0
1934 Nottingham Forest 1
Ripley Town

Wallace, Alexander (Sandy) IR/OL
Abercorn
1892 Sheffield United 16 3
1893 Middlesbrough Ironopolis 12 2

Wallace, Alexander (Alec) IL/OL
b Darwen 1872 d 1950
Blackpool
1894 Manchester City 6 1
Baltimore
1897 Small Heath 2 1
Hereford Thistle

Wallace, Alexander James John GK
b Sheffield 1874 d 1899
Attercliffe
1896 Grimsby Town 20

Wallace, Bertram OL
b Stoke-on-Trent 1880
Stoke St Jude's
1901 Stoke 1
Stoke Town

Wallace, Bruce OR
b Kilmarnock 27/10/1904
Muirkirk Ex-Servicemen
Bathgate
Hamilton Academical
1924 Plymouth Argyle 1
Torquay United
Taunton Town
Falkirk

Wallace, Charles William (Charlie) OR
b Southwick, County Durham 20/1/1885 d 1970
Caps: FLge 5/England 3
Rectory Park
Southwick (Co Durham)
Crystal Palace
1907 1920 Aston Villa 314 54
1921 1922 Oldham Athletic 47 3

Wallace, Francis Jardine IL
b Dumfries 10/5/1909 d 1994
1927 1930 Darlington 43 7
1931 Queen's Park Rangers 0
Tunbridge Wells Rangers

Wallace, Hugh GK
Dumbarton
1911 Bradford Park Avenue 4

Wallace, James IR
b Milton of Campsie
Milton Battle
Pollok
Clyde
1928 1929 Burnley 39 8
Chester
Bo'ness
Hibernian
Rutherglen Glencairn
Clyde

Wallace, John (Jack) GK
b Blantyre 20/6/1910 d 1992
Blantyre Victoria
Stonehouse Violet
Celtic
East Stirlingshire (loan)
Coleraine
Derry City
1938 Hartlepools United 31
1939 (Hartlepools United) (1)
Belfast Celtic

Wallace, John Fawcett IR
b Spennymoor 9/1/1895 d 1973
1919 1921 Rotherham County 32 6

From To Apps Goal

Wallace, John Martin (Jock) GK
b Wallyford 13/4/1911 d 1978
Wallyford Bluebell
Raith Rovers
1933 1947 Blackpool 235
1939 (Blackpool) (3)
1947 Derby County 16
Leith Athletic

Wallace, Joseph OL
b Ayrshire
Glenbuck Cherrypickers
Newmilns
Newcastle West End
Newcastle East End
1893 1894 Newcastle United 42 19
Rendel (Newcastle)

Wallace, Lawrence Mervyn OL
b Sandown q2 1917 d 2007
University College (Southampton)
1938 Southampton 1

Wallace, Robert IR
b Paisley 1905
Cambuslang Rangers
Cowdenbeath
1928 Sunderland 5
Third Lanark
Bo'ness
Raleigh Athletic (Nottingham)
Blantyre Victoria
Hamilton Academical
Bo'ness (loan)

Wallace, Robert (Bob) LB/RB
b Tanfield 25/9/1909 d 1938
1933 Bolton Wanderers 0
1934 Swindon Town 12
1936 Plymouth Argyle 9
1937 1938 Exeter City 38

Wallace, Robert Stewart (Bob) LH
b Greenock 20/1/1893 d 1970
Caps: IrLge 5
Linfield
1923 1930 Nottingham Forest 248 2
Burton Town

Wallace, Thomas Hall CH
b Jarrow 1/7/1906 d 1939
South Shields
1931 Sunderland 0
1933 1935 Burnley 61 1

Wallace, W LH
1898 Blackpool 1

Wallace, William OL
1901 Glossop 18 1

Wallace, William OL
b Blaydon
Newburn
1912 1913 Manchester City 43 9
1914 Bolton Wanderers 2 1

Wallach, Alexander T (Thedy) OR
b Castle Douglas 1881
Castle Douglas Juniors
Castle Douglas Wanderers
Dumfries Hibernians
1900 Chesterfield Town 1 2

Wallbanks, Frederick (Fred) LB/OL
b Platt Bridge 14/5/1908 d 1948
Crook Town
Consett
Annfield Plain
1929 Bury 0
1930 Chesterfield 6 3
Scarborough
1932 1934 Bradford City 15
1934 West Ham United 0
1935 Nottingham Forest 8
1936 Northampton Town 0

Wallbanks, James (Jimmy) CH/RB/LH
b Platt Bridge 12/9/1909 d 1979
Annfield Plain
1930 Barnsley 9
1931 Norwich City 3
1932 Northampton Town 2
Chopwell Institute
Wigan Athletic
1934 1938 Millwall 89
1938 1946 Reading 48 1
Ramsgate Athletic

From To Apps Goal

Wallbanks, John CF
b Hindley 7/7/1905 d 1987
Annfield Plain
Crook Town
1929 1932 Barnsley 118 65
1933 Portsmouth 0
1933 1934 Chester 38 36
1934 Bradford Park Avenue 11 2
Glenavon
Wigan Athletic

Waller, Charles GK
b Plymouth
Army
1920 Exeter City 3
Army

Waller, George LH/OL
b Pitsmoor 3/12/1863 d 1937
Pyebank (Sheffield)
Park Grange (Sheffield)
The Wednesday
Middlesbrough
1892 1895 Sheffield United 6 2

Waller, Henry W (Harry) OL/OR
b Annfield Plain 2/5/1902
Annfield Plain
1927 Bury 0
1928 1931 Torquay United 114 23
1932 1934 Wrexham 93 33
Wellington Town

Waller, Horace CF
West Hartlepool Perseverance
1930 1931 Hartlepools United 10 7
Blackhall Colliery Welfare
Seaton Holy Trinity
St Oswald's

Waller, Wilfred Hugh GK
b South Africa 27/7/1877
Vampires
Corinthians
Richmond Association
Tottenham Hotspur
1899 1900 Bolton Wanderers 6
Queen's Park
Southampton
Watford
Aylesbury United

Waller, William IL
b Bolton q4 1894 d 1985
Horwich RMI
1921 Nelson 25 7
1922 Burnley 1
Chorley
1923 Queen's Park Rangers 2

Walley, Hugh OL
1905 1906 Burslem Port Vale 10 1

Wallington, Edward Ernest (Ernie) OR
b Rickmansworth 8/7/1895 d 1959
Rickmansworth Town
1920 1922 Watford 51 5
1923 Arsenal 1
Watford Old Boys

Wallington, Sidney Percival (Sid) RH
b Small Heath 15/10/1908 d 1989
Wolseley Sports
1931 Birmingham 2
Shirley Town
1933 1935 Bristol Rovers 92 1
Guildford City
1936 Bristol Rovers 2
Worcester City
Cradley Heath

Wallis, George Henry IL/CF
b Sawley 11/3/1910 d 1988
Sandiacre Excelsior
1933 Birmingham 0
1934 1936 Bristol City 42 14
Bath City
Colchester United

Wallis, Robert GK
b Hanley
1924 Port Vale 1

Walls, Frank Brown (Frankie) CF
b Stranraer 8/11/1901 d 1966
Caps: IrLge 1
Stranraer
Newton Stewart
Larne
1923 Hull City (trial) 0
Stranraer
1926 Ashington 8
1926 Newcastle United 0
Larne
Stranraer

From	To		Apps	Goal
		Walls, George	CF	
		b Edinburgh 20/1/1874		
		Heart of Midlothian		
1896		Sheffield United	16	4
		Walls, Nicholas (Nick)	RH	
		b Perkinsville 22/1/1901	d 1957	
		Caps: England Sch		
		Birtley		
		Annfield Plain		
		Chester-le-Street		
1925	1926	Norwich City	30	2
		Annfield Plain		
		Jarrow		
		Crook Town		
		Jarrow		
		Spennymoor United		
		Horden Colliery Welfare		
		Walls, Robert McKenzie (Rab)	OR	
		b Leith 13/7/1908	d 1992	
		Leith Emmet		
		Rosslyn Juniors		
		Wemyss Athletic		
		Heart of Midlothian		
		St Bernard's		
		Hibernian		
1936		Aldershot	20	9
		Waterford		
		Cowdenbeath		
		Wallwork, Robert Thomas	OR	
		b Haslingden q4 1885	d 1947	
1902	1903	Stockport County	7	1
		Walmsley, Albert	RH	
		b Blackburn 21/10/1885		
		St Peter's (Blackburn)		
		Darwen		
1907	1919	Blackburn Rovers	272	6
1920	1922	Stockport County	80	3
		Walmsley, Clifford (Cliff)	GK	
		b Burnley 25/11/1910	d 1983	
1930		Burnley	0	
1931		Manchester City	2	
1932		Reading	3	
1933	1934	Rochdale	59	
		Stalybridge Celtic		
		Walmsley, John William	RH/RB/CH	
		b Accrington 22/4/1903	d 1970	
		Accrington St Peter's		
		Bacup Borough		
1921		Nelson	1	
		Barnoldswick Town		
1924	1925	Accrington Stanley	17	
		Barnoldswick Town		
		Great Harwood		
		Horwich RMI		
		St Ignatius (Preston)		
		Howard & Bullough		
		Higher Walton		
		Walmsley, Richard	RB	
		b Blackburn 1894		
		Blackburn Trinity		
1919	1922	Blackburn Rovers	38	
		Lancaster Town		
		Walsh, Charles (Charlie)	RH/LH	
		b Glossop 1/11/1894	d 1964	
		Glossop		
1921		Stalybridge Celtic	1	
1923		Birmingham	0	
1924		Halifax Town	19	
1925		Preston North End	4	
1926		Barnsley	6	
		Walsh, Charles Henry (Charlie)	IR	
		b London 27/10/1910		
		Hampstead Town		
1932		Arsenal	0	
1932		Brentford	10	3
		Walsh, James Arthur (Jimmy)	IR/RH/CF	
		b Stockport 15/5/1901	d 1971	
		Stockport Lads Club		
1920	1921	Stockport County	38	5
1923	1927	Liverpool	69	24
1928	1930	Hull City	82	9
		Colwyn Bay United		
1931		Crewe Alexandra	0	
		Colwyn Bay United		
		Rhyl Town		
		Walsh, John J (Jack)	RB	
		b Blackburn 11/2/1901	d 1965	
		Darwen		
1925	1926	Aberdare Athletic	51	3
1926	1931	Bristol City	164	1
1931	1935	Millwall	140	

From	To		Apps	Goal
		Walsh, Thomas (Tommy 'Tot')	CF	
		b Bolton		
1920	1923	Bolton Wanderers	22	4
1923	1927	Bristol City	142	88
1928		Crystal Palace	8	1
		Hurst		
		Chorley		
		Mossley		
		Walsh, Wilfred (Wilf)	IR/OR	
		b Pontlottyn 29/7/1917	d 1977	
1936		Arsenal	0	
		Margate		
1938		Arsenal	3	
1939	1946	Derby County	1	
1939		(Derby County)	(3)	
1946	1947	Walsall	33	4
		Hednesford Town		
		Redditch Town		
		Hednesford Town		
		Walsh, William (Billy)	CH/LH	
		b Littletown		
1914		Grimsby Town	0	
		Scotswood		
		Horden Athletic		
1920	1921	Luton Town	17	2
		Horden Athletic		
1923	1924	Hartlepools United	28	
		Walsh, William	IR	
		b Stourbridge		
		Bridgend Town		
1923		Charlton Athletic	9	2
		Walsh, William (Bill)	CF/IR/IL	
		b Blackpool q4 1909	d 1965	
		South Shore Wednesday		
		Fleetwood		
1931		Bolton Wanderers	0	
		Fleetwood		
1933	1935	Oldham Athletic	78	49
		Heart of Midlothian		
1937	1938	Millwall	42	19
		Walter, Joseph Dorville (Joe)	OR	
		b Eastville 16/8/1895	d 1995	
		Caps: SoLge 1		
		Horfield United		
1920	1921	Bristol Rovers	75	11
1922	1924	Huddersfield Town	55	5
		Taunton United		
1925	1927	Blackburn Rovers	27	2
1928		Bristol Rovers	7	1
		Bath City		
		Walters, Albert Victor	CF	
		b Wolverhampton 5/1902		
		Heanor Town		
1927		Portsmouth	0	
		Aldershot		
1928		Luton Town	1	
1929	1930	Walsall	50	30
		Shrewsbury Town		
		Walters, Charles	IR	
1898		Gainsborough Trinity	18	4
1899		Burslem Port Vale	10	2
		Walters, Charles (Charlie)	CH	
		b Sandford-on-Thames 1/4/1897	d 1971	
		Oxford City		
1919	1925	Tottenham Hotspur	106	
1926	1927	Fulham	17	
		Mansfield Town		
		Walters, Charles Edwin	CH	
		b Bradeley 1890		
1910		Blackpool	6	
		Walters, Frederick Clement (Fred)	RB/IL/CF	
		b Walsall 15/5/1903	d 1992	
		Shrewsbury Town		
1924	1931	Walsall	133	20
		Walters, Joseph (Joe)	IR/IL/OL	
		b Stourbridge 4/1886	d 1923	
		Wordsley Athletic		
		Stourbridge		
1905	1911	Aston Villa	113	41
1912	1919	Oldham Athletic	110	35
		Accrington Stanley		
1920		Southend United	28	5
1921		Millwall Athletic	22	5
1922		Rochdale	24	6
		Manchester North End		
1923		Crewe Alexandra	1	

From	To		Apps	Goal
		Walters, Thomas Charles (Tom)	CF/IR/IL	
		b Trealaw 15/6/1909	d 1968	
		Caps: Wales Sch		
		Merthyr Town		
1931		Bolton Wanderers	5	1
1932		Crystal Palace	14	4
1933		Exeter City	6	4
1933	1934	Torquay United	25	12
1935	1937	Watford	57	24
1938		Clapton Orient	23	9
		Dartford		
		Walters, Trevor Bowen	CH	
		b Aberdare 13/1/1916	d 1989	
		Dundee		
1934		Hull City	0	
1935		Wolverhampton Wanderers	0	
		Aberaman Athletic		
1937	1948	Chester	151	1
1939		(Chester)	(3)	
		Caernarvon Town		
		Walters, Victor	OL	
		Walthamstow Grange		
		Gravesend United		
1913		Leicester Fosse	11	2
		Abertillery		
		Walton, Frank Hillard	LB/OL	
		b Southend-on-Sea 9/4/1918	d 1986	
1937	1950	Southend United	144	
		Dartford		
		Walton, George	IR/IL	
		b Burnley q1 1911		
		Burnley Works XI		
1929	1932	Accrington Stanley	79	21
1932	1936	Bolton Wanderers	26	1
1936	1938	Cardiff City	84	16
1939	1945	Walsall	(3)	
		Walton, Gordon	RB	
		Sevenoaks		
1905		Derby County	1	
		Walton, James Jackson (Jimmy)	LH/IL	
		b Sacriston 3/11/1898	d 1989	
		Cleator Moor		
		West Stanley		
1920	1922	Leeds United	69	4
1923		Bristol Rovers	40	1
1924	1925	Brentford	59	
1926		Hartlepools United	2	
		Walton, John	RH/LH	
		b Chester-le-Street		
		West Stanley		
1921		Derby County	7	
1922	1923	Walsall	69	1
		Walton, Joseph	GK	
1891		Darwen	4	
		Walton, Joseph (Joe)	OR/IR	
		b Lunes 8/1/1881		
1901	1902	Preston North End	25	4
1908		Tottenham Hotspur	24	2
1909	1910	Sheffield United	60	6
		Stalybridge Celtic		
		Walton, Joseph (Joe)	RB/LB	
		b North Shields q3 1882		
		Wallsend Park Villa		
1903		Sheffield Wednesday	0	
		New Brompton		
1906	1909	Chelsea	53	
		Barry		
		Swansea Town		
		Bridgend Town		
		Walton, Joseph William (Joe)	GK	
		b Bishop Auckland 25/4/1907	d 1940	
		Close House Friends		
1925		Hartlepools United	0	
		Eldon Lane United		
		Bishop Auckland		
1931		Huddersfield Town	0	
1932	1934	Swansea Town	64	
1935		Preston North End	0	
		Kidderminster Harriers		
		Walton, Nathaniel (Nat)	IL/GK/IR	
		b Preston q3 1867	d 1930	
		Caps: England 1		
		Witton (Blackburn)		
1888	1892	Blackburn Rovers	110	37
		Nelson		

From	To		Apps	Goal
		Walton, Robert (Bob)	CF	
		b Kirkdale 4/9/1909	d 1985	
		Miranda		
1929		Everton (trial)	0	
1929		Manchester City (trial)	0	
1933		Southport	1	
1933		Blackpool	0	
		Miranda		
		Burscough		
		Port Sunlight		
		Miranda		
		Walton, Robert W (Bob)	RB	
1906		Newcastle United	0	
1908		Bradford Park Avenue	8	
		Walton, William Ewart	RB/RH	
		b Ribchester q3 1871		
		Clitheroe		
		Fleetwood Rangers		
1894	1895	Blackburn Rovers	5	1
		Blackburn Park Road		
		Walton, William Howard T (Billy)	IR/RH/LH	
		b Hockley Brook 6/8/1871	d 1963	
		Hockley Belmont		
1892	1901	Small Heath	169	49
		Dudley		
		Walvin, George	OR	
		b Blackwell, Derbyshire q2 1877	d 1969	
		Clay Cross Zingari		
1903		Chesterfield Town	7	
		North Wingfield St Lawrence		
		Wanless, Robert (Bob)	OR	
		b Middlesbrough 19/7/1876	d 1963	
1899		Middlesbrough	10	
		Waplington, Samuel	RH	
		b Basford 13/4/1896		
1919		Nottingham Forest	1	
		Warburton, Arthur	IR/RH/IL	
		b Whitefield 10/9/1909	d 1972	
		Sedgley Park		
1929	1933	Manchester United	35	10
1933		Burnley	25	4
		Nelson		
1934	1937	Fulham	45	6
1938		Queen's Park Rangers	17	
1945		Southport	0	
		Warburton, Benjamin Frederick (Ben)	CH	
		b Worksop q3 1864	d 1943	
1888		Notts County	2	
		Warburton, Fred	IL/CF	
		b Astley Bridge 1880	d 1948	
1903		Bolton Wanderers	1	
		Brynn Central		
1905	1906	Bury	11	5
		Swindon Town		
		Plymouth Argyle		
		Accrington Stanley		
		Warburton, George Albert	OL	
		b Holland 12/12/1915	d 1996	
		Morecambe		
1937		Aston Villa	0	
		Morecambe		
1938		Preston North End	0	
1938		Chester	10	2
1939		(Chester)	(1)	(1)
		Morecambe		
		Netherfield		
		Lancaster City		
		Ingleborough		
		Trimpell		
		Warburton, John	LB	
		b Tyneside		
1895		Newcastle United	3	
		Hebburn Argyle		
		Warburton, John	LB	
		b Bolton		
1924	1925	Doncaster Rovers	13	
		Warburton, John Salmon	OL	
		b Crewe q1 1903		
		Rhyl		
		Bangor City		
		Mold Town		
1924		Wrexham	1	
		Mold Town		
		Macclesfield		
		Congleton Town		
1928		Crewe Alexandra	2	
		Warburton, Richard	OR	
		Manchester City		
1922		Wrexham	6	1
		Rhos Athletic		
		Mold Town		

From	To	Club	Apps	Goal
Warburton, T			OR	
1896		Burnley	1	
		South Shore		
Warburton, Thomas Charnley			OL	
b Bury 11/9/1910			d 1985	
		Bury GSOB		
1930		Rochdale	2	
Warburton, William (Billy)			RH	
b Bradford, Lancashire 20/1/1903			d 1976	
		Bradford Parish		
1927		Southport	2	
		Manchester North End		
Ward, Albert			GK	
b Mexborough				
		St Albans City		
1928		Fulham	0	
		Mexborough Athletic		
1930		Rotherham United	7	
		Wombwell		
Ward, Alfred			OR	
b Eastwood q2 1883			d 1926	
		Clowne White Star		
1903		Notts County	7	
		Brighton & Hove Albion		
		Aberdeen		
		Bradford Park Avenue		
		Southampton		
Ward, Allen			CH/LH	
b Parkgate 1872				
		Barnsley St Peter's		
1893		Sheffield Wednesday	0	
1894		Burton Wanderers	28	
1895		Woolwich Arsenal	7	
Ward, Arthur Jackson			IL	
b Gainsborough q2 1874				
		Gainsborough Trinity		
1895		Loughborough	11	
Ward, David (Dai)			CF	
b Barry 19/7/1901			d 1959	
Caps: WLge 2				
		Pentrebach Harlequins		
1924		Merthyr Town	21	6
		Aberaman Athletic		
		Barry		
1927	1928	Coventry City	11	2
1928		Newport County	6	1
		Barry		
Ward, Edward (Ted)			IR/IL	
b Cowpen 16/6/1896				
		Blyth Shamrocks		
		Blyth Spartans		
		Bedlington United		
		Blyth Spartans		
1920		Newcastle United	21	5
1922		Crystal Palace	4	
1923		Nelson	2	
1924		Darlington	5	
1925	1926	Ashington	25	10
		Workington		
		West Stanley		
1929		Carlisle United	0	
		Blyth Spartans		
Ward, Felix			OL/OR	
b Seaham Harbour 1882			d 1941	
		Seaham White Star		
1907		Fulham	4	
1908		Clapton Orient	33	1
		Southend United		
Ward, Frank			RB/RH/LH	
b Leigh 21/1/1903				
		Walshaw United		
1923	1926	Bury	44	
1927	1932	Preston North End	208	3
1933	1934	Southampton	27	
		Folkestone		
		Worcester City		
Ward, Fred (Yaffer)			LB	
b Lincoln q1 1895			d 1953	
		Stamp End		
		South Bar		
		West End (Lincoln)		
1914	1922	Lincoln City	99	8
1922	1924	Wigan Borough	70	
1925		Lincoln City	7	2
1926	1927	Rochdale	67	
1930		Lincoln City	2	
Ward, George			RB/CF	
		Barrow Rising Star		
1897	1899	Loughborough	32	
Ward, George			LB/RH	
		Gresley Rovers		
1900	1901	Glossop	3	
Ward, George			IR	
b 1887				
		Kirkby Rovers		
1907	1909	Gainsborough Trinity	47	10
Ward, George			LH	
		Macclesfield		
1930	1931	Rochdale	34	
		Bury Co-op		
Ward, Henry			GK	
b Wallasey				
		Old Xavierans		
1929		New Brighton	1	
		Winsford United (trial)		
Ward, James (Tim)			IR	
		Nondescripts		
1896		Lincoln City	4	
Ward, John			RH	
		Wallsend Park Villa		
1903		Barnsley	8	
Ward, John			GK/CF	
b Birtley				
1920		Fulham		
1921	1923	Darlington	18	
1925		Gillingham	2	
		Fatfield Albion		
1927		Bradford City	5	
Ward, Joseph			LH	
b County Tyrone				
		St Johnstone		
1920	1921	Chelsea	14	
1922		Swansea Town	1	
Ward, Ralph Arthur			RB	
b Oadby 5/2/1911			d 1983	
Caps: England Sch				
		Kettering Town		
		Hinckley United		
1928		Leicester City	0	
		Hinckley United		
1930	1935	Bradford Park Avenue	129	
1935	1945	Tottenham Hotspur	115	10
1939		(Tottenham Hotspur)	(3)	
1946	1948	Crewe Alexandra	91	7
		Oadby Town		
Ward, Robert (Bob)			GK	
b Glasgow 1881				
		Abercorn		
		Port Glasgow Athletic		
1906	1907	Sunderland	48	
1908		Bradford Park Avenue	7	
		Marsden Rescue		
Ward, Robert (Bob)			RH/CH	
b Manchester				
1928		Manchester United	0	
1929	1930	Southend United	39	2
		Altrincham		
1931	1932	Crewe Alexandra	68	
		Rhyl Athletic		
		Altrincham		
		Buxton		
Ward, Samuel			LB/RB	
b Wolverhampton 1880				
		Springfield		
1906	1909	Wolverhampton Wanderers	45	1
		Wednesbury Old Athletic		
		Dudley Town		
		Brierley Hill Alliance		
		Worcester City		
Ward, Samuel			CH	
b Dennistoun 1/6/1906				
		Shawfield Juniors		
		Morton		
1927		Brentford	7	
Ward, Thomas Edward George (Tommy)			CF/IL/LH	
b Chatham 28/4/1913			d 1997	
		Chatham		
1933		Crystal Palace	7	
1934		Grimsby Town	0	
1936	1937	Port Vale	38	18
1937		Stoke City	5	4
1938		Port Vale	12	4
1939		Mansfield Town	(3)	(3)
Ward, Thomas Henry (Tom)			OR	
b Padiham q2 1901				
1922	1923	Accrington Stanley	20	
1923		Burnley (trial)	0	
1924		Wigan Borough (trial)	0	
Ward, Victor Timothy (Tim)			RH/LH	
b Cheltenham 16/9/1917			d 1993	
Caps: England 2				
		Cheltenham Town		
1936		Leicester City (trial)	0	
1937	1950	Derby County	238	4
1939		(Derby County)	(2)	
1950	1952	Barnsley	33	
Ward, WA			GK	
		Loughborough		
1894	1895	Newcastle United	18	
Ward, Walter			OL	
b Gainsborough q2 1871			d 1902	
		Gainsborough Trinity		
1895	1896	Loughborough	48	10
Ward, Wilkin (Wilkie)			OR	
b Rochdale q4 1884			d 1958	
		Whitworth		
1907		Oldham Athletic	15	1
1908		Bradford Park Avenue	18	2
		Rossendale United		
Ward, William			LB	
1909		Sheffield United	0	
		Castleford Town		
1914		Glossop	19	
Ward, William (Billy)			IL	
b Carlisle 1894				
		Carlisle YMCA		
1928	1929	Carlisle United	36	9
Wardell, Albert (Nippy)			OR	
b Bilston 12/1/1908			d 1987	
Caps: Wales Sch/Wales Amat				
		Newport Amateurs		
1926	1928	Newport County	41	9
1929		Chelsea (loan)	0	
1929		Wolverhampton Wandrs (loan)	0	
1930		Darlington	5	2
1930		Newport County	2	
		Hereford United		
		Shrewsbury Town		
		Taylor Brothers		
Wardle, Edwin Silvester			OL	
b Nottingham 11/1/1870				
1888		Notts County	2	
Wardle, George			RH/OR/OL	
b Kibblesworth 24/9/1919			d 1991	
		Durham Boys Club		
1937		Middlesbrough	1	
1939	1946	Exeter City	38	6
1939		(Exeter City)	(3)	
1946	1948	Cardiff City	40	11
1948	1950	Queen's Park Rangers	53	4
1951	1953	Darlington	95	6
		Crook Town		
Wardle, Henry (Harry)			IL	
b Sunderland				
1903	1904	Sunderland	4	2
		South Shields		
		North Shields		
Wardle, William (Billy)			OL	
b Houghton-le-Spring 20/1/1918			d 1989	
		Fatfield Juniors		
		Houghton Colliery Welfare		
1936	1937	Southport	14	
1937		Manchester City	6	
1939	1947	Grimsby Town	73	11
1939		(Grimsby Town)	(2)	
1948	1950	Blackpool	60	1
1951	1952	Birmingham City	60	5
1953	1954	Barnsley	28	1
		Skegness Town		
Wardrope, Alexander C (Sandy)			CH	
b Stewarton 1886				
		Broxburn		
		Kilbirnie Ladeside		
		Airdrieonians		
1910		Middlesbrough	10	
		Portsmouth		
		Nithsdale Wanderers		
Wardrope, William			CH	
1893	1894	Darwen	10	1
Wardrope, William (Willie)			OL/OR	
b Maryhill 14/2/1876				
Caps: SLge 1				
		Dalziel Rovers		
		Motherwell		
		Linthouse		
1895	1899	Newcastle United	127	44
1899	1901	Middlesbrough	62	21
		Third Lanark		
		Fulham		
		Swindon Town		
		Hamilton Academical		
		Third Lanark		
		Raith Rovers		
Wardropper, Frederick (Fred)			RH	
b Newcastle q1 1895			d 1922	
		Darwen		
1921	1922	Barrow	13	
Ware, Edward Alfred George (Teddy)			LH	
b Chatham 17/9/1906			d 1976	
		Chatham		
1928	1932	Brentford	96	
1933	1935	Clapton Orient	106	3
1936		Swindon Town	5	
1937	1938	Crewe Alexandra	61	
Ware, Harry			IR/CF	
b Birmingham 22/10/1911			d 1970	
		Hanley St Luke's		
		Cobridge Celtic		
		Stoke St Peter's		
1930	1934	Stoke City	53	15
1935	1936	Newcastle United	44	9
1937		Sheffield Wednesday	12	1
1937	1945	Norwich City	43	13
		Northwich Victoria		
Ware, Thomas (Tommy)			GK	
b Bristol q2 1885			d 1915	
		Army		
1911	1913	Bristol City	51	
Ware, Thomas (Tom)			LB	
b Cardiff				
1930		Cardiff City	12	
Wareham, John			OL	
b Alsagers Bank q2 1901				
1924		Port Vale	2	
1925	1927	Crewe Alexandra	33	4
		Winsford United		
Wareing, William (Billy)			LH/CH	
b Southport 1/1887			d 1955	
		St Helens Recreation		
		Chorley		
1910	1912	Preston North End	79	2
1912	1919	Everton	64	4
1920	1924	Swindon Town	156	8
Warhurst, Frank			CH	
b Sheffield 5/4/1917			d 2002	
1936		Sheffield United	0	
		Bath City		
1938		Bristol Rovers	4	
1945		Plymouth Argyle	0	
1945		Newport County	0	
Warhurst, Philip Ewart			RB	
b Chapel-en-le-Frith q1 1889			d 1935	
1909		Gainsborough Trinity	14	
1910		Stockport County	0	
1910		Glossop	0	
		Tranmere Rovers		
Warhurst, Samuel Lee (Sam)			GK	
b Nelson 29/12/1907			d 1981	
		Nelson British Legion		
1927	1930	Nelson	76	
		Stalybridge Celtic		
1933	1936	Bradford City	66	
1937	1938	Southampton	78	
1939		(Southampton)	(3)	
Waring, Bernard			OL	
b Sheffield				
		Kiveton Park		
1927		Wolverhampton Wandrs (trial)	0	
1928		Southend United	1	
		Worksop Town		
Waring, Clement			CF	
1899		Blackburn Rovers	1	
Waring, John (Jack)			OR	
b Wombwell 13/7/1909			d 1991	
		Wombwell		
1933		Grimsby Town	2	
1934		Crewe Alexandra	3	1
1934		Sheffield Wednesday	0	
1935	1938	Crewe Alexandra	168	56
1939		(Crewe Alexandra)	(2)	

From To | Apps Goal

Waring, Thomas (Tom 'Pongo') CF/IR
b High Tranmere 12/10/1906 d 1980
Caps: England 5
Tranmere Celtic
1927 Tranmere Rovers 24 23
1927 1935 Aston Villa 215 159
1935 Barnsley 18 7
1936 Wolverhampton Wanderers 10 3
1936 1938 Tranmere Rovers 74 42
1938 Accrington Stanley 22 10
Bath City
South Liverpool
Ellesmere Port Town
Grayson's FC
Birkenhead Dockers
Harrowby FC

Waring, William IL
1889 Blackburn Rovers 1
Darwen

Waring, William Stanley OR
b Dewsbury 23/8/1908 d 1972
1928 Cardiff City 0
1929 Rotherham United 6 1

Warmby, Harry CH
Derby County
1888 Everton 1

Warner, Alfred Cragg (Alf) IR/IL
b Hyson Green 4/1879
Notts Rangers
Nottingham Olympic
Weal
1899 1901 Notts County 49 14
Tottenham Hotspur
Luton Town
1907 Notts County 7 1

Warner, James (Jimmy) GK
b Lozells 4/1865 d 1929
Milton
1888 1891 Aston Villa 75
1892 Newton Heath 22
1893 Walsall Town Swifts 12

Warner, James A (Percy) IL
b Birdwell
Birdwell
1905 Barnsley 3 2

Warner, John (Jack) LB/RB
b Preston 1883 d 1948
St Michael's (Preston)
1902 1903 Preston North End 11
Southampton
Portsmouth

Warner, John (Jack) IR/RH
b Woolwich 1898 d 1950
Custom House
1919 Burnley 0
1920 1925 Manchester City 76 15
1926 1929 Watford 110 22
1930 1931 Thames 57 2

Warner, John (Jack) RH
b Tonyrefail 21/9/1911 d 1980
Caps: Wales War 1/Wales 2
Treorchy Juniors
Trealaw Rangers
Treorchy Athletic
Aberaman Athletic
1933 1937 Swansea Town 135 9
1938 1949 Manchester United 102 1
1939 (Manchester United) (3)
1951 Oldham Athletic 34 2
1952 Rochdale 21

Warner, Leslie Horace (Les) OR
b Birmingham 19/12/1918 d 1982
Shirley Juniors
Jack Moulds Athletic
1937 1953 Coventry City 199 19

Warner, Thomas (Tom) LH
b Sheffield 28/2/1895 d 1972
1919 Sheffield United 2

Warnes, Frederick W (Fred) CF/RB
b Tynemouth q1 1915
1936 1937 Bradford City 3 1
Peterborough United

Warnes, William Henry (Billy) OR
b Rotherhithe 14/11/1907 d 1997
Caps: England Amat
Cambridge University Mission
Nunhead
West Norwood
Woking
1932 Arsenal 0
1933 1936 Norwich City 112 45
1937 Aldershot 23 2

From To | Apps Goal

Warren, ? RB
1892 Burton Swifts 1

Warren, Arnold OR
b Codnor 2/4/1875 d 1951
Heanor Town
Ripley Athletic
1899 Glossop 0
Ripley Athletic
1901 Derby County 8 2
Brentford
Ripley Athletic

Warren, Benjamin (Ben) RH/IL
b Newhall q3 1879 d 1917
Caps: FLge 5/England 22
Newhall Town
Newhall Swifts
1899 1907 Derby County 242 19
1908 1911 Chelsea 92 4

Warren, Clement Edwin (Clem) IR
b Nuneaton 28/7/1899
Herberts Athletic
1921 1922 Coventry City 18 3
Yeovil & Petters United
1924 Walsall 0
Worcester City

Warren, Emrys John LB
b Troedyrhiw 9/4/1909 d 1988
Troedyrhiw Welfare
1932 Bristol City (trial)
1933 1934 Tranmere Rovers 7
Aberaman
Dundee
Hereford Town

Warren, Ernest Thorne (Ernie) LH/RH/IL
b Sunderland 14/9/1910
Usworth Colliery
1928 Lincoln City (trial) 0
1929 Southampton 1
Burton Town
1933 Northampton Town 2 1
1934 Hartlepools United 15
South Shields

Warren, F CF
1904 Burton United 6

Warren, Frederick Arthur CH
b Newhall 12/1878
Derby Hills Ivanhoe
1902 1903 Nottingham Forest 25 2
Alfreton Town

Warren, Frederick Windsor (Freddie) OL
b Cardiff 23/12/1907 d 1986
Caps: Wales 6
Whitchurch
1927 1929 Cardiff City 37 8
1929 1935 Middlesbrough 160 49
Heart of Midlothian

Warren, George CF/IR
b Burton-on-Trent q2 1880 d 1917
Rangemoor Albion
1898 Burton Swifts 2
Sheppey United
Hinckley Town
1903 Leicester Fosse 21 7
Gresley Rovers
Hinckley United
Nuneaton Town
Coventry City
Willenhall Swifts
1911 Stockport County 3
Dudley
Nuneaton Town
Hinckley United

Warren, Harry CH/LH
b Newhall q2 1902 d 1968
Gresley Rovers
1924 1926 Blackpool 5
1927 Exeter City 1
1928 Merthyr Town 26 4
1929 Sheffield United 2
1930 Notts County 0
Folkestone

Warren, James H RB
1906 Burton United 16

Warren, Peter LB
b Dublin 1887
Caps: Ireland 2
Belfast Celtic
1909 1911 Sheffield Wednesday 6
Shelbourne
Millwall Athletic
Shelbourne

From To | Apps Goal

Warren, Raymond Richard (Ray) CH/RH
b Bristol 23/6/1918 d 1988
Parson Street Old Boys
1935 1955 Bristol Rovers 450 28
1939 (Bristol Rovers) (3) (1)

Warren, Robert Adolphus CF
b Newhall q3 1886 d 1963
1909 Grimsby Town 1
Shrewsbury Town
Newhall Swifts

Warrilow, Frank OL
b Walsall 4/4/1909 d 1971
Rushall Olympic
Cannock Town
1930 West Bromwich Albion 0
1931 Millwall 0
Cannock Town
Dudley Town
Wellington Town
1935 Barnsley 13 4
Dudley Town
Cradley Heath

Warrington, Joseph (Joe) OR/IL
b Macclesfield q1 1882 d 1924
Derby Wanderers
1901 1903 Derby County 29 7
Brentford
Portsmouth
New Brompton
Macclesfield
1907 Chesterfield Town 20
Macclesfield
Leek United
Hurst

Warters, George LH
1896 Darwen 2

Wass, Edwin (Ted) CH/RB/LB
b Chesterfield q3 1910 d 1955
Sheepbridge
Old Whittington Evening School
1929 Chesterfield 3
1931 1938 York City 222

Wass, Horace RH/RB
b Old Whittington 26/8/1903 d 1969
Clay Cross Zingari
Whittington Moor Victoria
1923 1936 Chesterfield 413 6
1937 Southport 20 1
Chelmsford City

Wassall, John Victor IR/OR
b Shrewsbury 11/2/1917 d 1994
Wellington Town
1935 1938 Manchester United 45 6
1939 (Manchester United) (1)
1946 1947 Stockport County 19 2

Wassell, Gilbert (Gillie) RB/LB
b Tipton 9/4/1910 d 1966
Cradley Heath
1932 1935 Blackpool 97
1936 Millwall 4
1937 1938 Tranmere Rovers 60 2

Wassell, Harold LB/RB
b Stourbridge 21/9/1879 d 1951
Brierley Hill Alliance
1901 1903 Small Heath 56
Bristol Rovers
Queen's Park Rangers

Wassell, Leonard Richard (Len) LB
b Parkgate 14/11/1906 d 1994
Goldthorpe United
Thurnscoe Victoria
Mexborough
1931 Sheffield Wednesday 0
1933 1934 Barrow 49 1
Thurnscoe Victoria
Mexborough Athletic
Scarborough

Waterall, Albert RH/IL/LH
b Radford q2 1890 d 1963
Radford Institute
Sneinton
1910 1912 Notts County 26 1
1913 1925 Stockport County 290 35
1926 Queen's Park Rangers 2
1926 Clapton Orient 2 1
Grantham

From To | Apps Goal

Waterall, Isaac (Ike) OR/OL
b Radford 3/10/1888 d 1970
Caps: WLge 1
Radford Woodhouse
Heanor United
1906 Notts County 6
Doncaster Rovers
Rotherham County
Rotherham Town
1909 1919 Notts County 178 12
1920 Millwall Athletic 26 3
Ebbw Vale

Waterall, Thomas William (Tommy) OL
b Radford 24/10/1884 d 1951
Radford Institute
Heanor United
1905 1907 Notts County 28 5
1908 Bradford Park Avenue 4
Mansfield Mechanics
1913 Leicester Fosse 31 6
1920 Watford 36 4
1921 Gillingham 18 1
Sheppey United
Sittingbourne
Sheppey United
Canning Town Glass Works

Waterfield, George Smith LB
b Swinton 2/6/1901 d 1988
Caps: England 1
Swinton
Mexborough Town
1923 1934 Burnley 371 5
1935 Crystal Palace 2
Nelson

Waterhouse, Frank RH/CH
b Langley Green 7/1889
Langley St Michael's Guild
Langley St Michael's
Wednesbury Old Athletic
1909 1919 West Bromwich Albion 171 6
1919 1920 Derby County 26

Waters, Arthur LB
b Birmingham q1 1879 d 1952
1900 Small Heath 0
Walsall
Swindon Town
1905 1910 Stockport County 158 8
Cardiff City

Waterson, Frederick (Fred) RH/CF
b Burton-on-Trent 1880 d 1918
1896 1900 Burton Swifts 103 2
1901 1902 Burton United 62 1
1907 1908 Fulham 2
Doncaster Rovers

Waterson, James LH
b Scotland
Arbroath
1894 Grimsby Town 20
Hull Albany
Hull Town

Waterston, Archibald Rutherford (Archie) CF
b Musselburgh 13/10/1902 d 1982
Musselburgh Bruntonians
1923 Leicester City 0
Cowdenbeath
1927 1928 Newport County 43 36
1928 Southampton 6 1
1929 Tranmere Rovers 30 18
1930 1931 Southport 58 44
1932 1933 Doncaster Rovers 43 27
1934 Aldershot 20 4
Edinburgh City

Watford, Albert RB/RH
b Chesterfield 12/2/1917 d 1982
Mosborough
1938 Chester 1
1939 Bradford Park Avenue 0
1945 Chesterfield 0
1946 Lincoln City 14
Scunthorpe & Lindsey United
Boston United

Wathey, Frank OR
b Barnsley q1 1888
Denaby United
Conisbrough Swifts
Mexborough
1912 Notts County 7

Watkin, Arthur Dennis (Dennis) OR
b Stapleford 28/6/1912 d 1983
Stapleford
1932 1935 Aston Villa 21 5
1936 1938 Reading 86 22

From To Apps Goal

Watkin, Arthur Edward IL/CF
b Burslem 30/7/1895 d 1972
Hanley Swifts
1919 1922 Stoke 115 33
Congleton Town
1924 1925 Stoke 16 3
Congleton Town

Watkin, Frank IL/CF
b Stoke-on-Trent 30/3/1904 d 1979
Congleton Town
1926 Stoke City 5 3
Stoke St Peter's
1929 Port Vale 13 9

Watkin, Frank Harcourt OL
b Gainsborough q3 1891 d 1957
Newark Castle Rovers
1909 Leeds City (trial) 0
1910 Leicester Fosse 4 1
1912 Notts County 0
Scunthorpe & Lindsey United

Watkins, Alfred Ernest (Fred) OL
b Llanwnog 6/1878 d 1957
Caps: Wales 5
Caersws
Oswestry
1897 1898 Leicester Fosse 31 12
1899 Aston Villa 1
1900 Grimsby Town 11 5
Millwall Athletic
Southend United

Watkins, Alfred Whittingham (Alf) IR
b Skipton q1 1880
Nelson
Accrington Stanley
Nelson
1904 Leicester Fosse 4
1904 Blackburn Rovers 0
Nelson

Watkins, Ernest Thomas (Ernie) CF/IL
b Finchley 3/4/1898 d 1976
Barnet
Finchley
1922 Birmingham 8 1
1923 1925 Southend United 32 15
1925 1929 Brentford 120 55
1929 Millwall 6 1
1930 Fulham 17 10
1931 Gillingham 4
1931 Charlton Athletic 15 6

Watkins, Wallace Gwynfryn OL
b Trehafod 17/7/1917 d 1989
Trehafod Ex-Schoolboys
1934 Swansea Town 0
1934 Bolton Wanderers 0
1936 New Brighton 1
1937 Oldham Athletic (trial) 0
Macclesfield
Margate

Watkins, Walter Martin (Mart) CF/IR
b Caersws q2 1880 d 1942
Caps: Wales 10
Caersws
Oswestry Town
1900 1903 Stoke 108 44
1903 1904 Aston Villa 6 1
1904 Sunderland 15 9
Crystal Palace
Northampton Town
1907 Stoke 17 4
Crewe Alexandra
Stafford Rangers
Tunstall
Stoke

Watkins, William IR
Trawden Forest
1898 1901 Burnley 44 7
Trawden Forest

Watkinson, Albert OR
b Westhoughton q3 1900
Atherton
1921 1922 Blackpool 9 1

Watkinson, John W OL
b Bradford 29/1/1901
Queensbury United
1921 Accrington Stanley 8 1

Watmough, Frank RB/LB
b Bury 1891
St Stephen's Mission
1919 1920 Bury 7
1921 Southport 0

From To Apps Goal

Watmough, Richard (Dickie) OR
b Idle 1912 d 1962
Calverley
Thackley
Greengates United
Idle
1931 1934 Bradford City 94 25
1934 1937 Blackpool 100 32
1937 Preston North End 20 4

Watson, Albert RH/IR
b Felling 19/8/1903
Felling Colliery
1923 1935 Blackpool 353 22
1936 Halifax Town 29 2
1937 1938 Gateshead 67 24

Watson, Albert LH
b Darlington
1923 Darlington 8

Watson, Albert OR
b 1904
Yorkshire Amateurs
1924 Lincoln City 1

Watson, Albert LH/RH
b Bolton-on-Dearne 1/6/1918 d 2009
1937 1947 Huddersfield Town 17
1948 1949 Oldham Athletic 42

Watson, Alexander (Sandy) RB/LB
b Stirling 2/8/1889
St Ninian's Thistle
Clyde
1911 1919 Bradford Park Avenue 151
Pontypridd
1921 Halifax Town 8

Watson, Andrew G RB
b Kirkcaldy 1894
Kirkcaldy
1919 1921 Bolton Wanderers 35
1922 Bradford City 7

Watson, Arnold RH
b Ferryhill 26/12/1903 d 1978
Chilton Colliery Recreation Athletic
1925 Middlesbrough 8
1926 Darlington 0

Watson, Arthur OL
b Ecclesfield q1 1870 d 1931
Rotherham Swifts
1892 1895 Sheffield United 59 14

Watson, Arthur RB/LB
b South Hiendley 12/7/1913 d 1995
Monckton Colliery Welfare
1934 1935 Lincoln City 37
1936 1938 Chesterfield 10
1939 1946 Hull City 35 2
1939 (Hull City) (2)

Watson, Arthur Edwin Cooke OR/OL
b Hucknall Torkard q2 1870 d 1937
University College
Mansfield Greenhalgh
Mansfield Town
1893 1894 Notts County 22 13
Mansfield Town
1896 1897 West Bromwich Albion 28 2
1898 Lincoln City 0
Mansfield

Watson, B OL/OR
1894 1895 Darwen 20 8

Watson, David OR
Annbank
1893 Burnley 2
Annbank

Watson, David IL
b Cowie 2/10/1896 d 1978
Falkirk
Bo'ness
Sunderland
1920 1929 Portsmouth 276 61
Bo'ness

Watson, Edward RB/RH
b Sunderland 1899
Caps: England Sch
Sunderland West End
1920 Sunderland 1
Dundee Hibernian
1922 Queen's Park Rangers 8
1923 Rochdale 1

From To Apps Goal

Watson, Edward George (Ted) RB/LB
b Felling 28/4/1895
Felling Colliery
Portsmouth
Pontypridd
1921 1928 Wolverhampton Wanderers 193 4
1928 1931 Coventry City 85
Oakengates Town

Watson, Edwin CF/IL
b Pittenweem 28/5/1914
Crossgates Primrose
Partick Thistle
1937 Huddersfield Town 3
1939 Bradford Park Avenue (1) (1)

Watson, Ernest RH
b West Bromwich 12/1901
Tanfield Lea Rovers
1921 West Bromwich Albion 1
Hereford United
Kidderminster Harriers

Watson, Frank IL/IR/OR
b Nottingham 15/11/1902
Ilkeston Town
1921 Aston Villa 0
1922 Blackpool 2
1923 Leeds United 0
1925 Brentford 7
1926 Southend United 0
Ilkeston Town
Grantham
1928 Crewe Alexandra 1
Grantham
1931 Mansfield Town 0

Watson, George Edward OL
b Shotton Colliery 1914
Durham City
1934 Queen's Park Rangers 8 1
London Paper Mills

Watson, George Sutton OR/IR
b Milton Regis 10/4/1907 d 1974
Caps: England Amat
Casuals
1929 Charlton Athletic 14 2
Maidstone United
1930 Crystal Palace 2
1931 Clapton Orient 2
Nuneaton Town
Tunbridge Wells Rangers

Watson, George Whyte OR
b Newcastle q1 1912
Army
Motherwell
Partick Thistle
1933 Halifax Town 2
Coleraine
Dunfermline Athletic
Cowdenbeath

Watson, George William Robert GK
b Forest Gate 4/12/1905 d 1991
Ilford
Abbey Langthorne Works
1932 1934 West Ham United 33

Watson, Harold (Harry) RH/CH/LH
b Wath-on-Dearne 13/3/1908 d 1982
Wath Athletic
1926 1929 Stoke City 4
1931 1932 Brighton & Hove Albion 6
Kidderminster Harriers

Watson, Harry IR
1932 Stockport County 1

Watson, Herbert Leonard (Bert) RH/LH
b Springwell 20/11/1908 d 1939
Pelton Fell
1929 1931 Middlesbrough 13 1
1932 1935 Brentford 108 1
1936 Bristol Rovers 19

Watson, James (Dougal) IR/RH/RB
b Inverness 1883
Inverness Thistle
1903 1904 Sunderland 5
Portsmouth
1905 Chelsea 13

Watson, James Boyd (Jimmy) IR/CF/OL
b Govan 14/4/1910 d 1978
St Anthony's (Glasgow)
Tunbridge Wells Rangers
1933 Bristol Rovers 14 2
1934 Northampton Town 7 3
1935 1937 Gillingham 110 38
1938 Notts County 17 4
1939 Bristol Rovers (2) (1)
1945 Brighton & Hove Albion 0

From To Apps Goal

Watson, James Marshall (Jim) GK
b Maryhill 1886
Cambuslang Rangers
Earnock Rovers
Hamilton Academical
Ayr United (loan)
Dundee
1920 Luton Town 4
1921 Exeter City 10
Armadale

Watson, James Miller (Jimmy) LB
b Motherwell 4/10/1877 d 1915
Caps: Scotland 6
Burnbank Athletic
Clyde
1898 Sheffield United (trial) 0
1899 1906 Sunderland 211
1906 1909 Middlesbrough 103
Shildon Athletic

Watson, James William (William) RH/LH
b Darwen q3 1896
Darwen Olympic
1920 1922 Blackburn Rovers 12
1923 1924 Accrington Stanley 72 3
Clitheroe
Darwen

Watson, John LB
b Dundee 1877
Dundee Wanderers
New Brompton
Dundee
1899 1901 Everton 44
Tottenham Hotspur

Watson, John (Jock) RB
b Newarthill
Clyde
1902 Newcastle United 3
New Brompton
Brentford
1908 1909 Leeds City 45
Clyde

Watson, John Fox (Jack) CH
b Hamilton 31/12/1917 d 1976
Douglas Water Thistle
1938 1945 Bury 6
1946 1947 Fulham 71 2
Real Madrid
1949 1950 Crystal Palace 61 1
Canterbury City

Watson, John G IR
Seghill
Carlisle United
1928 Barrow 1 1
Ulverston Town

Watson, John George (Jack) CH/IR
b Edinburgh 3/12/1911 d 1944
Milton Rovers
1933 1935 Tranmere Rovers 4 1
South Liverpool

Watson, John Gordon OR/IL
b Wolsingham q4 1912
Blyth Spartans
1932 1933 Everton 2
1934 1935 Coventry City 17 1
1936 Crystal Palace 12 3
Ashington

Watson, John Innes RH/CH
b Aberdeen 24/6/1906
Aberdeen Richmond
1927 1930 Hull City 47

Watson, John S (Jack) RB
b Bulwell 1892 d 1957
Bulwell
1912 Manchester City 0
1913 Oldham Athletic 0
Bloxwich Strollers
1919 Birmingham 2
Measham Town

Watson, Joseph (Joe) RB
b Swalwell
White-le-Head Rangers
Lintz Colliery
1928 Darlington 11

Watson, Joseph (Joe) LB
St Chad's
Theatre Gospel Hall
Derby Wednesday
1932 1933 Notts County 10

From To Apps Goal

Watson, Lionel P IL/CF/IR
b Southport 1881
Laurel Rovers (Southport)
High Park
Southport Central
1901 Manchester City 1
1902 1904 Blackburn Rovers 55 18
West Ham United
1908 Blackpool 1

Watson, Norman CH/LH/RH
b Chester-le-Street 21/12/1899
Hylton Colliery
Southwick (Co Durham)
Chester-le-Street
1922 1931 Leicester City 173 1
1932 Notts County 5
Workington
Wigan Athletic
Horwich RMI
Wigan Athletic

Watson, Percy C Thomas LB
b Barnsley 3/1869 d 1944
1893 Rotherham Town 8
1893 Small Heath 2
Denaby

Watson, Philip Ross (Phil) CH/RB
b Dykehead 23/2/1907
Caps: SLge 1/Scotland 1
Lakeland A
Wishaw YMCA
Hamilton Academical
1931 1937 Blackpool 171 11
1937 Barnsley 4
Queen of the South

Watson, Reginald Herbert (Bert) OL
b Thelwall 26/8/1900 d 1971
Witton Albion
1921 1928 Oldham Athletic 233 64
1929 1930 Southampton 19 5
1931 Rochdale 17 8

Watson, Robert IR
1888 Everton 18 5
Gorton Villa

Watson, Robert (Bob) IR/OR
b Middlesbrough q4 1880
South Bank
1901 1902 Middlesbrough 16 5
1903 1904 Woolwich Arsenal 9 1
1905 1907 Leeds City 83 21
Exeter City
Stalybridge Celtic
Rochdale

Watson, Ronald (Ron) LH
1933 Darlington 7

Watson, Thomas GK
b Birmingham 1870
Yardley Victoria
1894 Small Heath 2
Birmingham City Police

Watson, Thomas Andrew (Tom) LB/RB
b South Shields q2 1904
Consett
1928 1930 Rochdale 91
Guildford City

Watson, Thomas Gordon (Gordon) LH
b Wolsingham 1/3/1914 d 2001
Blyth Spartans
1936 1948 Everton 61 1
1939 (Everton) (3)

Watson, Thomas Houston (Tommy) LB
b Belfast 4/10/1900
Caps: Ireland 1
Crusaders
1925 1928 Cardiff City 85
Linfield

Watson, Thomas Linton (Tom) CF
b Shiney Row 10/1912
Shiney Row Swifts
1930 Grimsby Town 0
1931 Accrington Stanley 19 9
1932 Rochdale 7 6

Watson, Victor Martin (Vic) CF/IL
b Girton 10/11/1897 d 1988
Caps: England 5
Girton
Cambridge Town
Peterborough & Fletton United
Wellingborough Town
1920 1934 West Ham United 462 299
1935 Southampton 36 14

From To Apps Goal

Watson, Walter OL
b Sheffield 11/1890 d 1956
Worksop Town
1911 Aston Villa 3
Rotherham Town
Kilmarnock
Chesterfield Town
Worksop Town

Watson, William OR/IL
South Bank
1903 1906 Lincoln City 120 28
Newark Town
Lincoln City
Castleford Town

Watson, William (Billy) LH
b Birkdale 11/9/1890 d 1955
Caps: FLge 5/England 3
Blowick Wesleyans
Southport Central
1908 1924 Burnley 346 18
1925 Accrington Stanley 6
1926 Blackburn Rovers 0

Watson, William (Billy) LH
b Bolton-on-Dearne 31/12/1893 d 1962
Bolton United
1912 1926 Huddersfield Town 292

Watson, William (Willie) LB
b Larkhall 29/7/1894 d 1950
Larkhall United
Airdrieonians
1921 1930 Bradford City 330 1
1931 Walsall 35

Watson, William CH
b Scotland 1902
Vale of Clyde
Ayr United
Vale of Leven
1925 Coventry City 32 1
Bathgate
Clydebank
Bethlehem Steel
New Bedford Whalers
Providence Gold Bugs
Fall River FC
New Bedford Whalers
Stix Baer & Fuller (St Louis)

Watson, William (Bill) RB/CH
b South Hiendley 29/5/1916 d 1986
Monckton Colliery Welfare
1934 1935 Lincoln City 9
1946 1947 Chesterfield 36
1948 1953 Rochdale 200

Watson, William (Willie) RH/IL
b Bolton-on-Dearne 7/3/1920 d 2004
Caps: England B/England War 1/England 4
1938 Huddersfield Town 11
1946 1953 Sunderland 211 15
1954 1955 Halifax Town 33 1

Watson, William J RB
b Carlisle
Carlisle United
1920 1928 Northampton Town 326 4

Watson, William Thomas (Bill) OL/IL
b Cambois 16/3/1899 d 1969
Bolckow's United
Seaton Delaval
Blyth Spartans
1923 1927 Ashington 200 36
1928 1931 Carlisle United 141 38
1932 Rochdale 39 12
1933 Accrington Stanley 25 3

Watt, James (Jimmy) LH/CH
b Bellshill 24/12/1904 d 1980
Caps: Lol 1
Bellshill Juniors
Mossend Swifts
1927 Charlton Athletic 0
1929 1930 Barrow 71 2
Dolphin
1933 Southport 41 2
Shelbourne
Dolphin
Bangor City
Wigan Athletic (trial)

Wattam, Frank LH
b Grimsby 12/11/1908 d 1984
Grimsby YMCA
Grimsby Albion
Cleethorpes Town
Louth Town
1932 1938 Grimsby Town 27

From To Apps Goal

Watters, John IR/OR
b Glasgow 24/9/1913 d 1989
Glasgow Perthshire
Ayr United
1936 New Brighton 19 2
Cowdenbeath
1947 Stockport County 5 1

Watts, Charles (Charlie) GK
b Middlesbrough 1875 d 1924
Middlesbrough Ironopolis
1893 Blackburn Rovers 9
1894 1895 Burton Wanderers 51
Blackburn Brooks (loan)
1896 1905 Newcastle United 89

Watts, Ernest OR
1924 Merthyr Town 4 1

Watts, Ernest Arthur (Ernie) RH/GK
b Woolhampton 1872
Reading
1898 Notts County 17
Reading
West Ham United
New Brompton
Grays Athletic
Reading
1906 Clapton Orient 2
Reading

Watts, Farewell IR
b Sheffield 10/3/1904 d 1970
Gainsborough Trinity
1927 Portsmouth 0
1928 Newport County 5 1
1929 1933 Tranmere Rovers 115 53

Watts, Henry P (Harry) IL/CF
b Liverpool
Failsworth
1907 1909 Oldham Athletic 13 4
Haslingden
Hurst

Watts, Joseph GK
1900 Burton Swifts 2
1900 Leicester Fosse 0

Watts, T Frederick LB
b London
1920 1922 Queen's Park Rangers 4
Yeovil & Petters United

Watts, TH CF
Notts Magdala Amateurs
1906 Notts County 3

Waugh, David IR
b 1866
Padiham
Burnley
1888 Everton 7 2

Waugh, James (Jimmy) CH
b Chopwell 12/8/1898 d 1968
Chopwell Institute
1921 1926 Sheffield United 126 2
1926 1932 Darlington 236 10

Waugh, John CH
b Slamannan 1887
Bo'ness
1913 Sunderland 1
Newarthill Thistle
Dundee Hibernian
1920 1921 Gillingham 60 4
1922 Darlington 0
Guildford United

Waugh, Lyle Sidney CH
b Newcastle q4 1899 d 1957
Bedlington United
1923 Queen's Park Rangers 5
Cramlington WE
West Cramlington Welfare

Waugh, Robert (Bob) LB/RB
b Newcastle
Newcastle Bentonians
1909 1911 Newcastle United 11 1
1912 1914 Derby County 28
Palmer's (Jarrow)

Waugh, William T RB
b Bedlington
Bedlington United
1921 West Ham United 6

Wayman, Brian Oswald IL/CF
b Basford q2 1902 d 1962
1919 Nottingham Forest 0
Ebbw Vale
1923 Aberdare Athletic 3 1
1924 Hartlepools United 5

From To Apps Goal

Weale, Robert Henry (Bobby) OR
b Troedyrhiw 12/1905 d 1952
Caps: Wales Sch
Troedyrhiw
1924 Luton Town (trial) 0
1925 West Ham United 3
1927 1928 Swindon Town 20 7
1928 1929 Southampton 45 10
Guildford City
Boston Town
Guildford City
Merthyr Town (trial)
1932 Newport County 26 7
1932 1934 Wrexham 23 4
Glentoran
Cheltenham Town
Bath City

Weale, Thomas James (Tommy) OL
b Troedyrhiw 31/12/1910 d 1971
Folkestone
1929 Swindon Town 2 1
1930 Cardiff City 5
1931 1933 Crewe Alexandra 100 27
1933 1934 Burnley 15 2

Weare, Arthur John (Jack) GK
b Newport 21/9/1912 d 1994
Lovells Athletic
1933 1936 Wolverhampton Wanderers 42
1936 1937 West Ham United 57
St Mirren
1946 1949 Bristol Rovers 141
Barry Town

Weaver, Alexander Edward (Alex) CF
b Weymouth 22/6/1902 d 1976
RAF
Weymouth
Wycombe Wanderers
1924 Sheffield Wednesday 6 1
Weymouth

Weaver, Francis Robert (Frank) CF
b Chester q4 1905 d 1964
Connah's Quay & Shotton
Colwyn Bay
Connah's Quay & Shotton
Flint Town
1925 Wrexham 1
Mold Town
Whitchurch
1927 Wrexham 0
Mold Town
Connah's Quay & Shotton
Oswestry Town

Weaver, Reginald William (Reg) CF/OR/IR
b Clutton 14/9/1905 d 1970
Caps: WLge 1
Llanhilleth United
1926 1927 Newport County 23 13
1927 1928 Wolverhampton Wanderers 50 29
1928 1931 Chelsea 20 8
1932 Bradford City 8 3
1932 1933 Chesterfield 11 2
1934 Newport County 29 8
Bath City
Gloucester City

Weaver, Robert Samuel (Bob) OR/CF
b Ponkey 1912
Holyhead
Manchester Central
Altrincham
1930 1931 Burnley 6
1932 Luton Town 3 1
1933 Bristol City 3

Weaver, Samuel (Sam) LH
b Pilsley 8/2/1909 d 1985
Caps: FLge 2/England 3
Pilsley Red Rose
Sutton Junction (trial)
Sutton Town
1928 1929 Hull City 48 5
1929 1935 Newcastle United 204 41
1936 1938 Chelsea 116 4
1939 (Chelsea) (3)
1946 Stockport County 2

Weaver, Walter OL
b Birkenhead 9/11/1898 d 1965
South Liverpool
1919 1924 Burnley 106 15
1924 1926 Everton 18 3
1926 1927 Wolverhampton Wanderers 43 11

From To Apps Goal

Weaver, William (Billy) OR
b Shropshire 5/11/1885
Nantwich
Crewe Alexandra
Whitchurch
1906 Bolton Wanderers 4 1
Wellington Town
Nantwich
Hurst

Webb, Alfred (Alf) GK
b Dawley q1 1878 d 1932
Mansfield
1899 1903 Lincoln City 131
Mansfield Mechanics

Webb, Alfred Henry (Alf) IL
b Stafford q4 1901
Hednesford Town
Stafford Rangers
1922 Barrow 24 9

Webb, Charles OR
b Higham Ferrers 4/3/1879 d 1939
Chesham Generals
Higham Ferrers
Rushden
Kettering
1901 Leicester Fosse 32 3
Wellingborough
Kettering
Southampton
1904 Blackpool 0
Dundee
1907 1908 Manchester City 22 3
Airdrieonians

Webb, Geoffrey John H OL
b Rotherham q4 1903 d 1963
1927 Rotherham United 2

Webb, George Henry CH/LH
b Wolverhampton q2 1896 d 1968
1919 Aston Villa 0
Nuneaton Town
1921 Derby County 2
1922 Bristol Rovers 2
Wellington Town

Webb, George William CF
b Poplar q3 1888 d 1915
Caps: SoLge 1/England Amat/England 2
Ilford Alliance
Wanstead
West Ham United
1912 Manchester City 2

Webb, Harold James (Harry) CH/LH/RB
b Fulham 15/5/1910
Park Royal
Walthamstow Avenue
1930 1932 Fulham 7 1
1932 1934 Exeter City 69 5
1935 Coventry City 3
1936 1937 Newport County 54 3
1938 Bristol Rovers 1

Webb, Isaac (Ike) GK
b Worcester 10/10/1874 d 1950
St Clement's Rangers
Berwick Rangers (Worcester)
Worcester Olympic
Evesham Town
Wellington Town
1897 1900 Small Heath 6
1901 1904 West Bromwich Albion 96
1904 1905 Sunderland 22
Queen's Park Rangers

Webb, John Armstrong (Jack) RB/LB
b Southwick, County Durham 19/5/1908 d 1984
Southwick Juniors
1929 1936 Derby County 25
1937 1945 Newport County 33
1939 (Newport County) (3)
Ilkeston Town

Webb, Sidney IL
b Coventry 2/1884 d 1956
St Saviour's
Stourbridge
1908 Aston Villa 0
Burton United
Wednesbury Old Athletic
1911 Birmingham 3
Worcester City

Webb, Sydney John (Stan) GK
b Portslade 6/1/1906 d 1994
Portslade Gasworks
Hove
Tunbridge Wells Rangers
1925 1933 Brighton & Hove Albion 205
Tunbridge Wells Rangers
Southwick (Sussex)

From To Apps Goal

Webb, William George (Willie) IL/OL
b Shettleston 12/7/1906
Cambuslang Rangers
1925 Leicester City 1
St Johnstone
1930 1932 Bournemouth & Boscombe Ath 57 6
Ramsgate Press Wanderers
Guildford City
Third Lanark
Bo'ness
Hinckley United

Webber, Eric Victor CH
b Steyning 22/12/1919 d 1996
Gosport Athletic
1938 1950 Southampton 182
1951 1951 Torquay United 149 2

Webber, George William RH
b Bristol 24/6/1911 d 1989
1934 Bristol City 1

Webster, Arnold (Arnie) CF
b Birchover 3/3/1913 d 1982
Birchover
1936 Sheffield Wednesday 1
Frickley Colliery
Mill Close Mine
Darley Dale United

Webster, Ernest (Ernie) RH
b Leigh 15/9/1903 d 1989
1928 Bolton Wanderers 0
1929 Reading 0
1930 Brighton & Hove Albion 0
1931 Bournemouth & Boscombe Ath 6
Ramsgate Press Wanderers

Webster, Francis Reginald (Frank) CH
b Shepshed q2 1887 d 1960
Shepshed Albion
1908 Leicester Fosse 7
1909 Everton 0
Long Eaton St Helen's

Webster, Frederick Joseph (Fred) RB/LB
b Sheffield 3/4/1887
Crown & Victoria (Sheffield)
1907 1910 Gainsborough Trinity 91
1911 1914 Tottenham Hotspur 82
Brentford
Gainsborough Trinity

Webster, Herbert GK
b Walsall 5/10/1910 d 1970
Cannock Town
Burntwood Villa
1928 West Bromwich Albion 1
1929 1930 Swindon Town 7
Walsall United
Hednesford Town
Lichfield Rangers

Webster, John OR
b Sheffield
Attercliffe
1893 1894 Sheffield Wednesday 23 5
1895 Rotherham Town 23 3
1896 1897 Gainsborough Trinity 47 7

Webster, Joseph (Joe) GK
b Ilkeston 1886 d 1927
Caps: SoLge 2
Ilkeston United
Watford
1919 West Ham United 2

Webster, Maurice CH/RH
b Blackpool 13/11/1899 d 1978
Caps: FLge 1/England 3
South Shore Wednesday
Fleetwood
Lytham
1920 Blackburn Rovers (trial) 0
1921 Stalybridge Celtic 11 1
1921 1933 Middlesbrough 262 3
1935 Carlisle United 14

Webster, Montague Victor IR
b Catford 19/5/1898 d 1969
1919 Blackburn Rovers 2
1920 Watford 0
1923 Barrow 1

Webster, Richard (Dick) LB/LH/RB
b Accrington 6/8/1919 d 1979
Woodnook Amateurs
1937 1938 Accrington Stanley 41
1939 Sheffield United 0
1945 1950 Accrington Stanley 186 3

Webster, Thomas IR
b Loughborough 1878
1897 Loughborough 1

From To Apps Goal

Webster, Walter CH/IL
b Rochdale 3/6/1906 d 1942
1927 1928 Rochdale 22 1
1929 Sheffield Wednesday 0
Oswestry Town
1931 Rochdale 14
Guildford City

Webster, Walter George (Wally) RB/LB
b West Bromwich 22/5/1895 d 1980
Kingsbury Colliery
West Bromwich United
1921 1924 Walsall 132 3
1925 Lincoln City 12
1925 1929 Sheffield United 35
Worksop Town
Scunthorpe & Lindsey United
1931 1932 Torquay United 28
1933 Rochdale 38
Stalybridge Celtic
1934 Barrow 4
Workington

Webster, William T (Billy) OL
b Sunderland 1909
Usworth Colliery
1930 1931 Stockport County 73 17
1932 Bradford City 16 4
1933 Port Vale 0
1934 Accrington Stanley 0
1935 Gateshead 24 4
Stalybridge Celtic
Horden Colliery Welfare

Weddle, John Robson (Jack) CF
b Fatfield 5/11/1905 d 1979
Fatfield Albion
1924 Middlesbrough (trial) 0
1927 1937 Portsmouth 368 171
1938 Blackburn Rovers 42 16
1939 (Blackburn Rovers) (3)

Wedge, Alfred (Alf) LB
b Chadsmoor q3 1877 d 1956
1897 1898 Walsall 6 1

Wedge, Francis Edgar IR
b Sedgley q3 1876 d 1955
Talbot
1897 Newton Heath 2 1
Chorlton-cum-Hardy

Wedlock, William John (Billy) CH
b Bedminster 28/10/1880 d 1965
Caps: FLge 3/England 26
Melrose (Bristol)
Arlington Rovers
Bristol City
Gloucester County
Aberdare Town
1905 1920 Bristol City 362 17

Weedall, John Thomas OL
b Bolton 24/10/1907 d 1979
1929 Nelson 7 3
Chorley
Breightmet United
Holden's Temperance (Bolton)
Breightmet United

Weeks, Edward Charles (Jessie) GK
b Wilton q2 1908 d 1949
Salisbury City
1932 Portsmouth 1
1935 Clapton Orient 0

Weeks, George B LB
b London
Millwall United
Southall
1931 Brentford 2
1932 Watford 1
Ford Motors
Dagenham

Weightman, Agur Francis (Frank) IL
b Coddington, Nottinghamshire 21/10/1864 d 1945
1899 Loughborough 1

Weightman, Arthur William LH/RH
b Newark 1/5/1910 d 1979
Newark Town
1930 Torquay United 4
1931 1932 Mansfield Town 45 1
Newark Town
Tunbridge Wells Rangers

Weightman, David CF/IL
b Coatbridge 1890
Baillieston
1909 Burnley 3
Royal Albert
1911 Burnley 1

From To Apps Goal

Weightman, Eric LH
b York 4/5/1910 d 2002
Scarborough
1933 1935 Middlesbrough 3
1936 1938 Chesterfield 79 1
1939 Notts County (2)

Weightman, Frederick Hugh (Fred) IL
b Newark q1 1863 d 1897
Notts Rangers
Nottingham Forest
Notts Wanderers
1888 Notts County 1 1
Nottingham Forest

Weir, Alexander (Alex) LH
Reading
1907 1908 Glossop 69

Weir, Alexander (Alex) LH
1909 Stockport County 1

Weir, Alexander IL
1912 Bolton Wanderers 2 2
Merthyr Town

Weir, David (Davie) CH/IL/LB
b Aldershot 1863 d 1933
Caps: England 2
Maybole
Glasgow Thistle
Halliwell
1888 1889 Bolton Wanderers 43 21
1892 Ardwick 14 8
1892 1894 Bolton Wanderers 43 10
Maybole

Weir, James (Jimmy) RH/LH
b Edinburgh 1864
Hibernian
Third Lanark
1888 1889 Everton 19
Sunderland Albion

Weir, James (Jimmy) LB
b Burnfoothill 23/8/1887
Burnfoothill Thistle
Dunaskin Lads
Ayr
Celtic
1910 1914 Middlesbrough 113

Weir, James IR
b Glasgow 12/6/1901 d 1984
Kilsyth Rangers
Kilmarnock
Hamilton Academical (loan)
Queen of the South
1930 Norwich City 9
Armadale
Bo'ness
Dunfermline Athletic
Dundee United
Dunfermline Athletic

Weir, John (Jock) CF
b Scotland
Caps: SoLge 1
Bellshill Athletic
1912 Fulham 1
Swansea Town
Reading
Pembroke Dock
Clydebank
Cowdenbeath

Weir, William Findlay (Findlay) RH/LH/CH
b Glasgow 18/4/1889 d 1918
Campvale
Waverley
Maryhill
1909 1911 Sheffield Wednesday 71 1
1912 1914 Tottenham Hotspur 96 2

Welch, Herbert (Bert) GK
b Pendleton 1912
Whitworth Valley
1931 1934 Rochdale 57
Bangor City
Bacup Borough
Mossley

From To Apps Goal

Weldon, Anthony (Tony) IL
b Croy 12/11/1900 d 1953
Caps: IrLge 1
Croy Celtic
Kilsyth Rangers
Airdrieonians
1926 1929 Everton 70 13
1930 Hull City 31 6
1931 West Ham United 20 3
Lovells Athletic
Dolphin
1933 Rochdale 27 7
Dundalk
Bangor
Distillery
Bangor
Distillery
Larne

Weldrick, Robert Pickering GK
b Beverley q1 1873 d 1956
1897 Gainsborough Trinity 1

Welfare, Henry (Harry) OL
b Liverpool 8/1888 d 1961
St Helens Recreation
Southport Central
Northern Nomads
Wrexham
1912 Liverpool 4 1
Corinthians (Rio de Janeiro)
Fluminense

Welford, James William (Jimmy) LB
b Barnard Castle 27/3/1869 d 1945
Barnard Castle
Stockton
Bishop Auckland
Birmingham St George's
1893 1896 Aston Villa 79 1
Celtic
Belfast Celtic (loan)
Distillery
Hamilton Academical

Weller, Louis Charles LB/RH/LH
b Stoke-on-Trent 7/5/1887 d 1952
1908 Chesterfield Town 0
Leek United
1909 1911 Everton 7 1
Chesterfield Town
1913 1921 Everton 58 1

Wellock, Maurice CF/RB/IL
b Bradford 15/6/1902 d 1967
Caps: England Sch
1919 Bradford City 0
1921 1922 Halifax Town 33 3
1923 1926 Blackpool 27 7
1926 Oldham Athletic 5 6
1927 Torquay United 27 3
Peterborough & Fletton United
1929 1931 Darlington 104 71
1932 1933 Halifax Town 82 21

Wells, Albert F RH/CH
b Watford
Ramsgate
1921 1922 Crystal Palace 5

Wells, Thomas Charles (Tommy) OL
b Nunhead 21/9/1905 d 1971
1925 Arsenal 0
1926 1934 Northampton Town 277 73
1935 Swindon Town 34 7
1936 Clapton Orient 4 1

Welsby, Arthur LH/OL/OR
b Ashton-in-Makerfield 17/11/1902 d 1980
Ashton St Mary's
1923 1930 Wigan Borough 220 31
1931 Sunderland 3 1
1932 1933 Exeter City 39 8
1934 Stockport County 4 2
1935 Southport 21 1
1936 Cardiff City 3
Mossley

Welsh, Andrew (Andy) LB
b Annfield Plain 28/6/1917 d 1990
1935 Charlton Athletic 0
1936 Manchester City 0
1937 1938 Darlington 46
1945 Northampton Town 0

Welsh, Christopher LB/RB
b Hebburn q1 1877 d 1922
Hebburn Athletic
Bristol Rovers
Hebburn Argyle
1901 1903 Barnsley 57
Denaby United

From To Apps Goal

Welsh, Donald (Don) LH/CH/IL
b Manchester 25/2/1911 d 1990
Caps: FLge 1/England War 9/England 3
Royal Navy (Devonport)
1932 1934 Torquay United 79 4
1934 1947 Charlton Athletic 199 43
1939 (Charlton Athletic) (1)

Welsh, Fletcher CF
b Galashiels 16/8/1893 d 1963
Tranent Juniors
Leith Athletic
Raith Rovers
Heart of Midlothian (loan)
1919 1920 Sheffield Wednesday 12 4
Third Lanark
East Stirlingshire

Welsh, Frederick (Fred) GK
Bacup
1902 Burnley 1

Welsh, Roderick Ernest (Rod) RB/LB
b Newcastle q4 1908
Dipton United
Annfield Plain
Durham City
1932 Portsmouth 1
1935 1937 Port Vale 64

Welsh, William RH
1919 Grimsby Town 5

Welsh, William (Billy) IR/CF/IL
b Douglas Water 2/5/1904 d 1978
Lanark Technical College
Douglas Water Thistle
Heart of Midlothian
Dundee United
1927 1928 Charlton Athletic 28 7
1928 1929 Wigan Borough 55 16
1929 Southport 11 3
1930 Newport County 6 1
Connah's Quay & Shotton (loan)
1930 Wrexham 9 1
1931 1933 Gateshead 58 22
1933 Hartlepools United 3
Jarrow

Wensley, Henry (Harry) CF/OL
b Eldon q3 1893 d 1959
Shildon Athletic
Stanley United
Darlington
Bishop Auckland
1921 Durham City 25 7
Shildon Athletic
1925 1926 Hartlepools United 76 37
Shildon

Wesley, Frederick (Fred) CF
b Derby 21/4/1898 d 1992
Midland Railway (Derby)
1919 Sheffield United 0
Long Eaton
1921 Chesterfield 2
Long Eaton

Wesley, George Thomas CF
b Barrow-on-Soar q4 1882
Army
Leicester Imperial
1906 Leicester Fosse (trial) 1
Ryde

Wesley, John Crawshay (Jack) IL/CF
b Cheltenham 19/1/1908 d 1946
St Austell
1932 1934 Gateshead 52 31
1934 1938 Bradford Park Avenue 141 25
1939 (Bradford Park Avenue) (1)

West, Abraham Kendall (Abe) GK
b Cockermouth q3 1887 d 1952
1912 Notts County 1
Sutton Town
Mansfield Mechanics

West, Alfred (Alf) RB/LB
b Nottingham 15/12/1881 d 1944
Nottingham Jardines Athletic
Radford Congregationals
Ilkeston Town
1902 1903 Barnsley 42
1903 1908 Liverpool 124 5
Reading
1910 Liverpool 4
1911 1914 Notts County 130 4
Mansfield Town
Shirebrook

From To Apps Goal

West, Alfred (Alf) LB
b Enderby 24/5/1879
Enderby
1903 Leicester Fosse 3
Enderby Town
Earl Shilton United
Enderby Town
Enderby Granite
Enderby Town

West, Enoch James (Knocker) CF/IL/IR
b Hucknall Torkard 31/3/1886 d 1965
Caps: FLge 2
Linby
1903 Sheffield United 0
Hucknall Constitutionals
1905 1909 Nottingham Forest 169 93
1910 1914 Manchester United 166 72

West, G IL
Great Northern Loco
1896 Lincoln City 1

West, George IL/IR
b Wardley q4 1889
Wallsend
1920 1921 Cardiff City 25 5
1921 Stockport County 3

West, Henry LH
b Cottingham q2 1883
Army
1906 Hull City 1

West, James (Jack) OL
b Enderby q3 1885
Enderby Granite
1908 1909 Leicester Fosse 10 2
Leyton
Enderby Town

West, John (Jack) IL
b Oldham
Northern Nomads
1908 Oldham Athletic 1
1910 Aston Villa 0
Exeter City

West, John William CH
1892 1897 Burton Swifts 102 11

West, Joseph (Joe) CF
b Walker q1 1910 d 1965
Walker Park
1932 Newcastle United 0
1933 Cardiff City 6 2
1934 Darlington 2 1

West, Norman IL
b Walker q4 1917
Walker Celtic
1937 1945 Hartlepools United 19 7
1939 (Hartlepools United) (3)
Washington Colliery

West, Thomas Norton (Tom) CF
b Salford 8/12/1916 d 1987
1937 1938 Stockport County 3 1
1945 Oldham Athletic 0
1946 Rochdale 4 2
Nelson
McMahon's

Westbrook, Henry Alfred GK
b Chertsey 24/5/1896 d 1977
1921 Lincoln City 2

Westby, Jack Leslie RB
b Aintree 20/5/1917 d 2006
Orrell
Burscough
1937 Blackburn Rovers 2
1945 Liverpool 0
1947 Southport 13
Runcorn
Ellesmere Port Town
Bootle

Westcott, Dennis CF
b Wallasey 2/7/1917 d 1960
Caps: FLge 1/England War 4
Wallasey Grocers
Leasowe Road Brickworks
1934 Everton (trial) 0
1934 West Ham United (trial) 0
1935 New Brighton 18 10
1936 1947 Wolverhampton Wanderers 128 105
1939 (Wolverhampton Wanderers) (3) (1)
1948 1949 Blackburn Rovers 63 37
1949 1951 Manchester City 72 37
1952 Chesterfield 40 21
Stafford Rangers

From To Apps Goal

Westcott, Ronald (Ronnie) CF
b Wallasey 19/9/1910
Banbury Spencer
1935 Arsenal 2 1

Western, Frederick Charles CF
b Ton Pentre 19/10/1906 d 1985
Lovells Athletic
1928 Charlton Athletic 0
1929 Merthyr Town 2
Yeovil & Petters United

Westgarth, Michael Hills (Mike) OL
b Hetton-le-Hole 29/7/1908 d 1972
Trimdon Grange
Ashburn Colliery Welfare
Shildon
Stockton
1930 1931 Darlington 11 1
Shildon

Westlake, Francis Arthur (Frank) RB
b Bolton-on-Dearne 11/8/1915 d 1999
Thurnscoe Victoria
1937 1949 Sheffield Wednesday 110
1950 Halifax Town 2
Denaby United

Westland, Douglas George (Doug) GK
b Aberdeen 5/2/1915
Banks o' Dee
Aberdeen
1936 1938 Stoke City 5
Belfast Celtic
Barlaston St Giles
Raith Rovers

Westland, James (Jim) IL
b Aberdeen 21/7/1916 d 1972
Inchgarth
Banks o' Dee
Aberdeen
1935 1938 Stoke City 60 16
1946 Mansfield Town 10

Westley, Charles T RB
1939 Rotherham United (3)

Westmoreland, William (Bill) IR
b New Herrington 6/1909
Fatfield Juniors
Herrington Colliery Welfare
Royal Artillery
1934 Hartlepools United 7
Herrington Colliery Welfare
Easington Colliery Welfare

Weston, Albert Mark (Tober) LB/RB
b Calne 26/2/1888 d 1966
Calne
1920 1928 Swindon Town 270 9

Weston, Cyril Arthur CF/RH
b Kettering 19/7/1899 d 1977
Kettering Atlas
1920 1921 Northampton Town 4
Kettering

Weston, Harold (Harry) CF/IR
b Birmingham
Chatham
1920 1921 Reading 26 6
Northfleet

Weston, John Matthew OR/OL
b Dudley 19/10/1900 d 1984
Halesowen
1927 Burnley 2 1
1928 1931 Northampton Town 45 15
Shelbourne

Weston, Thomas (Tommy) LB
b Halesowen 8/1890 d 1952
Quarry Bank
Old Hill Comrades
Coombs Wood
Stourbridge
1911 1921 Aston Villa 154
1922 Stoke 4

Weston, William IL
b Southwick, County Durham q4 1882 d 1948
1905 Sunderland 0
Crystal Palace
1906 Burslem Port Vale 0
1907 1908 Blackpool 46 9
Nelson
Spennymoor United

From To Apps Goal

Westwood, Eric LB/OL
b Manchester 25/9/1917 d 2001
Caps: FLge 2/England B
Fairfield
Stretford Rovers
1936 Manchester United 0
1938 1952 Manchester City 248 3
1939 (Manchester City) (3)
Altrincham

Westwood, John William LH/RH
b 1886
Rotherham Town
1904 1905 Gainsborough Trinity 40 2
Denaby United
Bristol Rovers

Westwood, William Raymond (Ray) IL/OL
b Kingswinford 14/4/1912 d 1982
Caps: FLge 5/England 6
Stourbridge
Brierley Hill Alliance
1928 Aston Villa (trial) 0
1930 1947 Bolton Wanderers 301 127
1939 (Bolton Wanderers) (3) (1)
1947 1948 Chester 38 13
Darwen

Wetherell, Joseph GK
b Oswaldtwistle q4 1872
1896 Newton Heath 2

Wethersby, Thomas (Tom) RB
b Worcester 1/4/1901 d 1979
Caps: WLge 1
1922 Plymouth Argyle 0
Royal Navy
1924 1927 Newport County 40 3
1928 1930 Crystal Palace 65

Whaites, John Alexander (Alex) OL
b Liverpool 22/6/1885 d 1946
1901 New Brighton Tower
Linfield
1904 1906 Bradford City 12
1907 1908 Oldham Athletic 42 7

Whalley, Arthur CH/LH/RH
b Rainford 17/2/1886 d 1952
Caps: FLge 1
Brynn Central
Wigan Town
1908 Blackpool 6 2
1909 1919 Manchester United 97 6
1920 Southend United 30 5
1921 1923 Charlton Athletic 88 8
1924 Millwall Athletic 8
1926 Barrow 1

Whalley, Frederick Harold (Fred) GK
b Salford 9/10/1898 d 1976
1919 Preston North End 8
1920 Grimsby Town 23
1921 1923 Leeds United 87
1923 1924 Fulham 8

Whalley, Herbert (Bert) LH/RH/CH
b Ashton-under-Lyne 6/8/1913 d 1958
Stalybridge Celtic
1935 1946 Manchester United 32
1939 (Manchester United) (1)

Whalley, John William (Johnny) OL
b Bradford 17/2/1897 d 1972
1919 Sheffield Wednesday 5
1921 1925 Halifax Town 141 17
Harrogate AFC

Whalley, Robert IR/OL
b Flimby q4 1905
Workington
1928 Nottingham Forest 0
Peterborough & Fletton United
1930 Lincoln City 9 4
Peterborough & Fletton United
1932 Luton Town 4 1

Wharton, Arthur GK
b Jamestown, Ghana 28/10/1865 d 1930
Cannock
Cannock White Cross
Darlington
Preston North End
Darlington
1893 Rotherham Town 19
1894 Sheffield United 1
1895 Rotherham Town 15
Stalybridge Rovers
Ashton North End
Stalybridge Rovers
1901 Stockport County 6

Wharton, Clarence Norman (Norman) GK
b Askam-in-Furness q4 1904 d 1961
Askam
1922 1924 Barrow 44
1925 1926 Preston North End 13
1927 Barrow 27
1928 1929 Sheffield United 70
1931 1934 Norwich City 101
1935 Doncaster Rovers 5
1936 1938 York City 117
1939 Leeds United (2)

Wharton, Guy LH/RH
b Darfield 5/12/1916 d 1990
Broomhill
1935 Chester 12 5
1936 1937 Wolverhampton Wanderers 29 2
1937 1947 Portsmouth 93 4
1939 (Portsmouth) (3)
Wellington Town
1948 1949 Darlington 39 2
Darlaston

Wharton, John Edwin (Jackie) OL/OR
b Bolton 18/6/1920 d 1997
1935 Bolton Wanderers 0
1938 Plymouth Argyle 11 2
1939 1946 Preston North End 25 7
1939 (Preston North End) (3)
1946 1947 Manchester City 23 2
1948 1952 Blackburn Rovers 129 14
1952 1954 Newport County 74 10
Wigan Athletic

Wharton, Sidney Emmanuel (Sid) OL
b Birmingham 19/12/1875 d 1951
Caps: FLge 1
Smethwick Wesleyan Rovers
1897 1902 Small Heath 151 19

Whatley, Jesse Winter GK
b Trowbridge 20/1/1895 d 1982
Trowbridge Town
1920 1929 Bristol Rovers 371
Stapleton Institute

Whatley, William John (Billy) LB
b Ebbw Vale 12/10/1912 d 1974
Caps: Wales Sch/Wales War 1/Wales 2
Hayward Sports
Ebbw Vale
Northfleet
1932 1938 Tottenham Hotspur 226 2

Whatmore, Ernest (Ernie) IL/LH/CF
b Kidderminster 25/4/1900 d 1991
Stourbridge
1922 Wolverhampton Wandrs (trial) 2
Shrewsbury Town
1923 1927 Bristol Rovers 134 38
1928 1931 Queen's Park Rangers 78 3
Shepherds Bush

Wheat, John Herbert RH
b Worksop 4/11/1913 d 1974
1937 Barnsley 0
1938 Carlisle United 11
1939 Bradford City 0

Wheatcroft, Edwin CF/OR
b Laughton q3 1872 d 1950
1893 1895 Rotherham Town 21 6

Wheatcroft, Frederick George (Freddie) IL/CF
b Alfreton q3 1882 d 1917
Caps: England Amat
Alfreton Town
1903 1904 Derby County 4 3
Swindon Town
1905 Derby County 1 1
Swindon Town
Fulham
1905 1907 Derby County 20 4
Reading
Swindon Town

Wheatley, Ernest LB
b Staveley 14/7/1899 d 1995
1920 1921 Rotherham County 27 1
Mansfield Town
Wath Athletic

Wheatley, Harold Joseph (Joe) RH/IR
b Eastham 9/5/1920
Ellesmere Port Town
1938 Port Vale 2
1950 Shrewsbury Town 7
Ellesmere Port Town

Wheatley, James Henry (Jimmy) IR
b Clowne q4 1883
Clowne Rovers
Whitwell St Lawrence
1906 1907 Chesterfield Town 6 2
Mansfield Mechanics
Mansfield Town

Wheeler, Alexander (Alex) GK
b Barrow 2/6/1898 d 1979
Dalton Casuals
1924 Barrow 3

Wheeler, Alfred James (Alf) IL/OL
b Bilston 4/4/1910 d 1978
1931 Walsall 11 3
Mossley
1932 Brentford 1
1933 Northampton Town 5 1
1934 Southampton 11 6
1935 Barnsley 0
1935 Norwich City 0
1936 Gillingham 8 3

Wheeler, Frank Charles OL
b Rotherham 24/7/1909 d 1986
Broom Sports
1929 1933 Rotherham United 69 11

Wheeler, George Harold LB
b Newport 19/2/1910 d 1995
Caps: Wales Sch/WLge 2/Wales Amat
1928 1932 Newport County 60 1
Lovells Athletic

Wheeler, James Arthur (Jim) RB
b Newport 7/6/1916 d 1994
Caps: Wales Sch
Lovells Athletic
1937 1938 Newport County 7

Wheeler, William (Billy) OL
b Chesham 1886
Chesham Town
Watford
1910 Derby County 1
Watford
Peterborough City

Wheeler, William John (Jack) GK
b North Littleton 13/7/1919 d 2009
Cheltenham Town
1938 1947 Birmingham 12
1948 1955 Huddersfield Town 166
Kettering Town
Evesham Town

Wheelhouse, Ben RB/LB
b Rothwell 23/9/1902 d 1985
Rothwell Athletic
1923 Halifax Town 24
1923 1924 Burnley 13
Denaby United
1926 1931 Halifax Town 165 4
1932 1933 Rochdale 66 2

Wheelhouse, Sidney (Sid) RB
b Darlington q3 1888 d 1916
Bishop Auckland
Shildon Athletic
1907 1914 Grimsby Town 234 3

Whelan, George Patrick OL
b Wallasey 11/12/1911 d 1976
Poulton Villa
1931 New Brighton 6

Whelan, Hugh CH
b Airdrie 15/8/??
1922 Bradford City 0
1923 Exeter City 2

Whelan, Michael (Micky) OR
b Port Clarence 1876
South Bank
Whitby Town
Millwall Athletic
1898 Sheffield United 13 1
Bedminster
Bristol City

Whelan, William (Billy) RB/LH/LB
b Airdrie 20/2/1906 d 1982
Gartsherrie Athletic
Coatbridge
1927 1930 Sunderland 19
1932 Southend United 8
1933 1934 Darlington 10

Wheldon, George Frederick (Fred) IL
b Langley Green 1/11/1869 d 1924
Caps: FLge 4/England 4
Rood End White Star
Langley Green Victoria
1889 West Bromwich Albion (trial) 0
1892 1895 Small Heath 109 65
1896 1899 Aston Villa 123 68
1900 West Bromwich Albion 26 3
Queen's Park Rangers
Portsmouth
Worcester City
Coventry City
Worcester City

Wheldon, Samuel RB
b Smethwick 1865 d 1930
Langley Green Victoria
1891 West Bromwich Albion 1
1892 Walsall Town Swifts 0
Erdington Wood

Whelpton, James Isaac (Ike) GK
b Sheffield 1887 d 1944
1909 Lincoln City 0
1910 Birmingham 0
Castleford Town
1911 Huddersfield Town 2
Guildford United
Mexborough Town
West Ham United (trial)
1913 Grimsby Town 1
Guildford United
1923 Bournemouth & Boscombe Ath 1

Whewell, William Charles (Bill) CF/IL
b Liverpool 23/4/1903 d 1969
Army
Poole
1928 New Brighton 30 13
Connah's Quay & Shotton
1930 New Brighton 16 5
Goodison Victoria

Whewell, William Thomas (Bill) CH
b Blackburn 18/7/1905 d 1940
Caps: England Amat
Cambridge University
Corinthians
1929 Charlton Athletic 4
Casuals
Cambridge Town

Whibley, John OL
b Sittingbourne 7/7/1891 d 1972
Sittingbourne
1920 1922 Crystal Palace 90 15
Sittingbourne

Whing, John Thomas Anderson CF
b Percy Main 23/4/1895 d 1972
Gordon Villa
Teamby United
Whitburn Park Villa
1921 Norwich City 7
West Stanley
Chester-le-Street
Marley Hill United
Watergate Colliery
Bensham St Hilda's

Whipp, Percy Leonard IR
b Glasgow 28/6/1893 d 1962
West London Old Boys
Ton Pentre
1921 Clapton Orient 20 8
1922 Sunderland 1
1922 1926 Leeds United 145 44
1927 1928 Clapton Orient 68 17
1929 Brentford 7 2
1930 Swindon Town 9 5
Bath City
Worcester City

Whitbourn, John Giles GK
b Farnham q1 1885 d 1936
South Bank
1904 Sunderland 3
Tottenham Hotspur
Leyton

Whitchurch, Ernest (Ernie) LH
b Sheffield 7/8/1891 d 1957
Sharrow Reform
1912 1919 Grimsby Town 30
Rotherham Town
Wombwell

Whitchurch, Herbert IL/CF
b Ilkeston 26/3/1886 d 1973
1905 1909 Nottingham Forest 24 8
Ilkeston United
Sutton Town
Grantham

Whitcombe, George Charles RH/CH
b Cardiff 21/1/1902 d 1986
1924 Cardiff City 0
1925 Stockport County 15
1926 1930 Port Vale 51
1930 Notts County 7
Ashton National
Colwyn Bay United

White, Alfred (Alfie) IR/IL/CF
b Spennymoor q2 1909
Spennymoor United
1927 1931 Derby County 4
1931 1935 Bournemouth & Boscombe Ath 124 33
1936 Wrexham 21 5
Spennymoor United

From To Apps Goal

White, Alfred (Alf) IR
Great Western Colliery
Aberaman
Bangor City
Northwich Victoria
1937 New Brighton (trial) 1
Witton Albion

White, Arthur LH
Heanor
1897 Loughborough 29 1

White, Cecil John RH/CH
b Hendon q2 1903
New Albion
Ashton Moss Colliery
Macclesfield
Denton Brotherhood
New Mills
1925 Leeds United 0
1928 West Ham United 0
1929 Torquay United 5
1930 Wigan Borough 32
Ashton National
Congleton Town
Hurst

White, Charles William (Charlie) IL
b Chesham 13/1/1889 d 1925
Caps: SoLge 1
Chesham Generals
Chesham Town
1920 1924 Watford 134 24

White, Charlie Harry OL
Gateshead NER
1903 Bury 2 1

White, Claude RB
b Mansfield 12/1/1904 d 1981
Hillstown Welfare
Shirebrook
Wombwell
1931 Mansfield Town 1

White, Cornelius IL/CF
b Leicester 10/3/1901 d 1975
Whitwick Imperial
1924 Birmingham (trial) 0
1924 1925 Oldham Athletic 5
Llandudno
Bangor City
1928 Bradford City 4 4
Loughborough Corinthians
Hereford United
Nuneaton Town

White, Earl Thomas IL
b Barnsley 2/12/1898 d 1977
Bolton United
Dearne Athletic
1919 Barnsley 1
Wakefield City
1923 Doncaster Rovers 25 4

White, Edward IL
b Wolverhampton
Wellington Town
1922 Wolverhampton Wanderers 11 3
Wellington Town

White, Edward Thomas (Tom) CH
b Uxbridge q4 1866
Uxbridge
1889 Burnley 21

White, Francis (Frank) OR
b Warwick 30/6/1910 d 1981
Warwick Town
1930 West Bromwich Albion 0
1931 1934 Coventry City 119 26
1935 Newport County 17 3
Dudley Town
Racing Club de Paris
Grantham
Peterborough United

White, Frank Robert Henry OR/OL
b Kingsbury, Warwickshire 14/4/1911 d 1987
Tamworth Juniors
Stoneware Limited (Tamworth)
1932 1938 Birmingham 147 46
1938 Preston North End 19 10
1939 (Preston North End) (3)
Redditch Town

White, Fred IL/OL
b Nottingham
1923 1924 Stockport County 9 1

White, George CF
1930 Hull City 0
1931 Rochdale 1

From To Apps Goal

White, Harold (Harry) IL
b West Bromwich 2/1902 d 1927
1923 West Bromwich Albion 0
1924 Newport County 1 1

White, Harold A RB
b Wednesbury 16/6/1916 d 1981
Darlaston
1938 West Bromwich Albion 36
1939 (West Bromwich Albion) (3)
Worcester City

White, Henry CF
Hibernian
Hamilton Academical
1897 Sheffield United 6

White, Henry Albert (Bert) IR/CF
b Watford 8/8/1895 d 1972
Wharncliffe Athletic (London)
Brentford
1919 1922 Arsenal 101 40
1922 1924 Blackpool 69 18
1925 Fulham 7 1
1925 1926 Walsall 39 29
1926 1927 Nelson 22 15
1927 Walsall 5
Stafford Rangers
Thames
Columbia (Earlsfield)

White, J Harold (Harry) CF/LH
b Leyton
Leigh Ramblers
1921 1922 Southend United 4

White, John LB/RB
b Galston 1870
Kilmarnock
St Mirren
Clyde
1896 1897 Newcastle United 48 1
Dundee
1899 Leicester Fosse 0

White, John IR
b Coatbridge 27/8/1897 d 1986
Caps: SLge 4/Scotland 2
Bedlay Juniors
Clyde
Albion Rovers
Maidstone United
Heart of Midlothian
1926 1929 Leeds United 102 36
Heart of Midlothian
Margate
Leith Athletic

White, John F IL
Selby Town
1924 Doncaster Rovers 5
Frickley Colliery

White, John W RB
1901 1902 Nottingham Forest 24
New Brompton

White, John William (Jack) LB/RB
b Droylsden q4 1877
Ollenshaw United
Grays Anchor
Swanscombe
Grays United
Queen's Park Rangers
1908 1910 Leeds City 60
Merthyr Town
Hurst

White, Jonathan RH
b Paisley 1872
St Mirren
1894 Bury 13

White, Joseph IR
b Wolverhampton
Wellington Town
1922 Wolverhampton Wanderers 1

White, Robert Nelson (Bob) CF/OR
b Walbottle 5/12/1901 d 1977
Prudhoe Castle
1923 Huddersfield Town 0
1924 Stoke 3
1925 1926 Tranmere Rovers 45 16
Yeovil & Petters United
1929 Wolverhampton Wanderers 3 2
1930 1931 Watford 21 17
1931 Portsmouth 0
1932 Carlisle United 22 7
North Shields

From To Apps Goal

White, Samuel (Sam) OR
b Newburn
1926 Leeds United 0
1927 Torquay United 0
1928 Hull City 0
1929 Darlington 9 2

White, Sidney Ernest (Sid) LH
b Tottenham 15/2/1899 d 1968
Edmonton Ramblers
1923 1925 Tottenham Hotspur 20

White, Thomas G (Tommy) CH
Skelmersdale United
1938 Chester 1

White, Thomas Henry (Tommy) OR
b Tring 12/11/1881
Chesham Generals
Grays United
Brighton & Hove Albion
1906 Stockport County 32 1
Carlisle United
Exeter City
Watford

White, Tom Angus (Tommy) CH/CF/IR
b Pendleton 29/7/1908 d 1967
Caps: England 1
Holy Trinity Old Boys
1925 1926 Southport 17 5
1927 1936 Everton 193 66
1937 Northampton Town (trial) 0
1938 New Brighton 0

White, V Thomas Wilson RB/LB
b West Bromwich 9/1896 d 1960
Notts County
1919 1920 Birmingham 15
Worksop Town
1922 1924 Newport County 40
Kidderminster Harriers

White, Vincent Harold RH/LH
b Walsall 22/10/1897 d 1972
Erdington
Wednesbury Old Athletic
1921 Birmingham 2
Ellesmere Port
Redditch Town
1923 Watford 7 1

White, Walter IL
b Halesowen 1864
Coombs Wood
1888 Wolverhampton Wanderers 4 2
Cradley Heath St Luke's

White, Walter (Wattie) IL/LH/IR
b Hurlford 15/5/1882 d 1950
Caps: Scotland 2
Hurlford Britannia
Portland Thistle (Kilmarnock)
Hurlford Thistle
1902 1908 Bolton Wanderers 196 88
1908 1910 Everton 43 10
1910 1922 Fulham 191 16

White, William (Billy) OL/IR
b Edinburgh 1872
Edinburgh Thistle
Broxburn Athletic
Heart of Midlothian
1897 1898 Woolwich Arsenal 39 16
New Brompton
West Calder
Queen's Park Rangers
1901 Liverpool 6 1
Sandyford

White, William IR
b Broxburn
Dundee
1903 Middlesbrough 6
Motherwell
Aberdeen

White, William Collins (Willy) GK
b Kerry Cowdie 5/3/1895 d 1974
Caps: SLge 4
Bedlay Juniors
Hamilton Academical
Heart of Midlothian
1928 1931 Southampton 101
1932 Aldershot 0
Weymouth
Wellington Town

From To Apps Goal

White, William Walter (Willie) IR/IL
b Kirkcaldy 26/7/1907
Musselburgh Bruntonians
1927 Reading 0
1928 Bristol Rovers 8
1929 Southport 0
1930 Charlton Athletic 0
1930 1931 Gillingham 64 18
1932 1933 Aldershot 71 10
1934 Carlisle United 8 2
1934 Manchester City 0
1934 Newport County 19 3
1935 1936 Bristol City 50 15
1936 1937 Lincoln City 46 11
1938 Hull City 2

Whitehead, Harry RB/RH
b Barlestone 19/9/1874 d 1944
Barlestone
1896 Loughborough 2
Hinckley Town
1902 Leicester Fosse 3
Hinckley Town

Whitehead, James W IR
b Church 1870 d 1929
Caps: England 2
Peel Bank Rovers
1890 1892 Accrington 73 23
1893 1896 Blackburn Rovers 85 22
1897 1898 Manchester City 24 7
Accrington Stanley

Whitehead, John GK
b Liverpool 1871
1892 Bootle 7
1893 Everton 2
1894 1895 Liverpool 2

Whitehead, Norman Jarrett OR
b Tamworth 27/7/1914 d 1987
Birmingham University
1934 West Bromwich Albion 1
1935 Birmingham 0

Whitehead, William OL/OR
1890 1892 Blackburn Rovers 3 1

Whitehead, William Thomas CF
b Saffron Walden 11/9/1897 d 1986
Caps: WLge 1
March Great Eastern United
Boston Town
1923 1924 Swansea Town 4 1
1925 Queen's Park Rangers 24 5
1926 Preston North End 3 1
1927 Manchester City 0
Boston Town
Yeovil & Petters United
Taunton Town
Westland United

Whitehouse, AF LH
1892 Walsall Town Swifts 6

Whitehouse, Benjamin (Ben) IR/IL
b Coseley
Wolverhampton Wanderers 0
Bilston United
1906 1907 Chelsea 10 1
1908 1910 Stockport County 75 21

Whitehouse, Charles Henry (Charlie) RH
b Newport 12/11/1910 d 1957
Windsor Juniors
1933 1935 Newport County 42 1
Lovells Athletic

Whitehouse, Frank (Tinker) IR/OR
b Newcastle-under-Lyme 1876
Bucknall
1899 Burslem Port Vale 19 1
1900 1904 Stoke 88 23
1905 Glossop 20 4
Stafford Rangers
Dresden Queen's Park

Whitehouse, Fred OR
1933 1934 Walsall 5

Whitehouse, James (Jimmy) GK
b Birmingham 4/1873 d 1934
Albion Swifts
Birmingham St George's
1892 1895 Grimsby Town 110
1896 1897 Aston Villa 40
Bedminster
1899 Grimsby Town 27
1900 1902 Newton Heath/Manchester Utd 59
1902 Manchester City 0
Third Lanark
Hull City
Southend United

From To Apps Goal

Whitehouse, John Charles (Jack) IR/IL/LB
b Smethwick 4/3/1897 d 1948
Blackheath Town
Redditch Town
Smethwick Hall
1919 1922 Birmingham 110 31
1923 1928 Derby County 186 82
1928 1929 Sheffield Wednesday 10 1
1930 1932 Bournemouth & Boscombe Ath 105 17
Folkestone
Worcester City

Whitehouse, John Frank CF
b Dudley 5/10/1906 d 1993
Sunbeam Motors
Wellington St George's
Stafford Rangers
1928 Swansea Town 2
Stourbridge
Manchester Central
Burton Town
Stafford Rangers

Whitehouse, John Thomas (Jack) RH
b West Bromwich 1878
Wednesbury Town
1901 1905 Wolverhampton Wanderers 147
Halesowen Town
1906 Stoke 2
Stourbridge
Bloxwich Strollers
Darlaston
Dudley

Whitehouse, William IR
1933 Walsall 3 1

Whitehurst, Albert John (Bert) CF/IL/CH
b Fenton 22/6/1898 d 1976
New Haden Colliery
1920 1922 Stoke 18 4
1923 1927 Rochdale 169 117
1928 Liverpool 8 2
1928 1930 Bradford City 38 30
1931 1933 Tranmere Rovers 80 29

Whitelaw, Andrew RB
b Jamestown 19/5/1865 d 1938
Caps: Scotland 2
Vale of Leven
Heanor Town
1891 1892 Notts County 41
Heanor Town
1894 Leicester Fosse 16
Heanor Town
Ilkeston Town

Whitelaw, David Logan (Dave) GK
b Anderston 9/8/1909 d 1989
Hill of Beath Star
Cadder United
1930 Bristol City 12
1931 1934 Southend United 92
1935 1937 Gillingham 114
1945 Wrexham 0

Whitelaw, John IL/IR
b Falkirk
Shettleston
Douglas Water Thistle
St Mirren
1925 Stockport County 8 2
Rhyl Athletic
Ebbw Vale
1927 Stockport County 12 3
London (Canada)
Rhyl Athletic
Chorley
1930 Barrow (trial) 0
1931 Rochdale 1

Whitelaw, John IR
b Cowdenbeath 1914
Lochgelly Celtic
Dunniker
Inverkeithing
Cowdenbeath
Racing Club de Paris
1936 York City 10 4
Raith Rovers
St Bernard's

From To Apps Goal

Whitelaw, Robert (Bobby) RH/LH
b Stonehouse, Lanarkshire 2/11/1902 d 1965
Larkhall Thistle
1926 1929 Doncaster Rovers 31 1
Celtic
Albion Rovers (loan)
1932 Bournemouth & Boscombe Ath 10 2
Glentoran
Queen of the South
Celtic
Coleraine
Linfield
Cowdenbeath
Hamilton Academical (loan)
Albion Rovers
Glentoran
1936 Southampton 20 1
Kidderminster Harriers

Whitelaw, William OR
Duns Athletic
1933 York City 2

Whiteley, Charles OR
b Burnley 1885
1905 1906 Burnley 3
Clitheroe Central
Great Harwood

Whitelum, Clifford (Cliff) CF
b Farnworth 2/12/1919 d 2000
Doncaster Co-operative Society
Bentley Colliery
1938 1947 Sunderland 43 18
1947 1948 Sheffield United 41 14
King's Lynn
Stowmarket

Whiteside, Arnold RH/LH
b Garstang 6/11/1911 d 1994
Woodplumpton Juniors
1932 1948 Blackburn Rovers 218 3
1939 (Blackburn Rovers) (3)
Wigan Athletic

Whiteside, Edward (Eddie) IR
b Fylde q1 1884
1908 Blackpool 6
Rossendale United
Norwich City
New Brompton

Whiteside, Ernest (Ernie) LH
b Lytham q2 1889 d 1953
Lytham St John's
Lytham Institute
Kirkham
1908 1913 Bolton Wanderers 84
York City
Shelbourne
Halifax Town
1921 Rochdale 3

Whiteside, James (Jimmy) OR
b Fleetwood q1 1890
Fleetwood Amateurs
1908 1910 Bolton Wanderers 7 1
Nelson
Fleetwood

Whiteside, Kerr Douglas RH
b Irvine 1885
Irvine Victoria
1907 Manchester United 1
Hurst

Whitfield, Frank CH
b South Anston 15/12/1897 d 1984
Anston White Star
1920 Huddersfield Town 0
1922 1924 Wigan Borough 68 6
1924 Lincoln City 23 1
Anston Athletic
1925 Southend United 2
1926 Doncaster Rovers 6 1
1926 Wigan Borough 0
Middlewich
1927 Chesterfield 0
Middlewich

Whitfield, Job RB
b Wolsingham q3 1870 d 1909
Howden-le-Wear
1896 Woolwich Arsenal 2

Whitfield, Norman IL
b Prudhoe 3/4/1896
Prudhoe Celtic Juniors
Jarrow Croft
1913 1919 Leicester Fosse 24 6
Hednesford Town
1922 1926 Chesterfield 120 60
Worcester City
Nuneaton Town
Hinckley United

From To Apps Goal

Whitfield, Wilfred (Wilf 'Baggy') LH/RH
b Chesterfield 17/11/1916 d 1971
Worksop Town
1938 1946 Bristol Rovers 26 1
1939 (Bristol Rovers) (3)
1949 1950 Torquay United 47 1
Bath City

Whitfield, William (Billy) LH/IL
b Bewick Main 22/3/1905 d 1971
Birtley Colliery
1931 1938 Bury 208 13

Whitham, Machin OR
b Ecclesfield 1874
1894 Rotherham Town 1

Whitham, Michael (Mick) RB/CH
b Ecclesfield 6/11/1867 d 1924
Caps: England 1
Atlas Rovers
Thorpe Hesley
Rawmarsh
Ecclesfield
Lockwood Brothers
The Wednesday
Rotherham Swifts
1892 1897 Sheffield United 86 1

Whitham, Victor (Vic) IR/IL
b Burnley 12/2/1894 d 1962
Kimberworth Congregationals
Rotherham County
Kimberworth Old Boys
1919 Barnsley 3
1920 Norwich City 9 3
Scunthorpe & Lindsey United
1923 Southend United 20 10
Boston Town
Scunthorpe & Lindsey United

Whiting, Robert (Bob) GK
b West Ham 6/1/1883 d 1917
South West Ham
West Ham United
Tunbridge Wells Rangers
1905 1907 Chelsea 52
Brighton & Hove Albion

Whitley, John (Jack) GK
b Seacombe 20/4/1880 d 1955
Seacombe YMCA
Liscard YMCA
1898 Darwen 14
1900 1901 Aston Villa 11
1902 1903 Everton 11
1904 1905 Stoke 36
1905 1906 Leeds City 7
1906 Lincoln City 0
1907 1913 Chelsea 127

Whitlow, Frederick William James (Fred) CF
b Bristol 3/9/1904 d 1978
Barry YMCA
Barry
1926 Cardiff City 0
1927 Charlton Athletic 3 1
Dundee
1928 1930 Charlton Athletic 92 59
1931 1933 Exeter City 83 61
1934 Cardiff City 7 1
Barry

Whitney, John Henry LH
b Newton Heath q2 1874 d 1932
1895 1900 Newton Heath 3

Whitson, Thomas Thompson (Tony) LB
b Cape Town, South Africa 1885 d 1945
Caps: FLge 1
Walker Athletic
Walker Parish
1905 1913 Newcastle United 124
Carlisle United

Whittaker, Arnold (Arnie) OR
b Blackburn q3 1879
Caps: FLge 1
Queen's Park (Blackburn)
Accrington
1899 1907 Blackburn Rovers 250 57
Accrington Stanley
1909 Bury 0

Whittaker, Bernard IL
b Blackburn q4 1865
1888 Blackburn Rovers 4 1

Whittaker, Edgar GK
Burnley Belvedere
1902 Burnley 1

Whittaker, Edward W CH
1909 1910 Gainsborough Trinity 7
Tibshelf Colliery

From To Apps Goal

Whittaker, Frederick (Fred) IR
b Burnley
1905 1908 Burnley 60 21
1908 Bradford City 9 1
Northampton Town
Exeter City
Millwall Athletic

Whittaker, George F OR
Maltby
1904 Doncaster Rovers 2
Doncaster Thursday

Whittaker, GF CH
Accrington Stanley
1901 Chesterfield Town 1

Whittaker, Harvey OR
b Congleton 1875
Congleton Hornets
1899 Stoke 4 1
Newcastle Town

Whittaker, James Henry OL
b Bolton
1904 Barnsley 0
1905 Manchester City 6 1
1907 Clapton Orient 17 1

Whittaker, John GK
1898 Darwen 13

Whittaker, John CF
1922 Stalybridge Celtic 6

Whittaker, Mark CF
b Bradford
Clarence Mills (Bradford)
1923 Rotherham County 1

Whittaker, Percy GK
b Rotherham 19/11/1905 d 1973
Wath Athletic
Grantham
Wath Athletic
Shirebrook
1930 1932 Wolverhampton Wanderers 6
1933 1938 Reading 185
Redditch United

Whittaker, Samson Clement LH/RH/IR
b Shelfield 8/1888
Shelfield Methodists
Rushall Red Cross
Bloxwich Strollers
1908 1914 Aston Villa 62 6
Walsall

Whittaker, Thomas (Tom) LB
b Boothstown 12/5/1899
Skelmersdale United
Darwen
1925 1930 Accrington Stanley 221
Stalybridge Celtic
Rossendale United

Whittaker, Thomas James (Tom) LH/LB
b Aldershot 21/7/1898 d 1956
Newcastle Swifts
1919 1924 Arsenal 64 2

Whittaker, Walter GK
b Manchester 20/9/1878 d 1917
Molyneaux
Buxton
1895 Newton Heath 3
Fairfield
1897 Grimsby Town 28
Reading
1899 1901 Blackburn Rovers 52
1901 1902 Grimsby Town 47
1903 Derby County 12
Brentford
Reading
1907 1909 Clapton Orient 90
Exeter City
Swansea Town
Llanelly

Whittam, Arthur CF
1903 Burnley 4 1

Whittam, Ernest Alfred (Ernie) IR/IL
b Wealdstone 7/1/1911 d 1951
1929 1932 Huddersfield Town 19 4
1933 1934 Chester 54 20
1935 Mansfield Town 20 4
1935 Wolverhampton Wanderers 1
1936 1938 Bournemouth & Boscombe Ath 106 27
1939 Reading (1)
Mossley

From To Apps Goal

Whitter, Ernest (Ernie) OR
b Didsbury 26/10/1900 d 1930
Didsbury
1921 Nelson (trial) 0
1922 Bradford City 1
1923 1927 New Brighton 172 33
Ashton National

Whittick, Edward A (Ted) CH
Stockton
Walsall Town Swifts
Northwich Victoria
1892 Walsall Town Swifts 1

Whittingham, Alfred (Alf) CF/OR/IR
b Altofts 19/6/1914 d 1993
Altofts WR Colliery
1936 1946 Bradford City 87 24
1939 (Bradford City) (2) (1)
1946 1948 Huddersfield Town 67 17
1948 1949 Halifax Town 39 9

Whittingham, Robert (Bob) IR/CF/IL
b Goldenhill q1 1889 d 1926
Caps: FLge 1
Goldenhill Wanderers
1904 Stoke 0
Goldenhill Wanderers
Crewe Alexandra
1906 Burslem Port Vale 0
1907 1908 Blackpool 54 28
1908 1909 Bradford City 45 31
1909 1913 Chelsea 113 70
South Shields
1919 Chelsea 6 1
1919 Stoke 18 8
1920 Port Vale 0
Stoke United
Macclesfield
Scunthorpe & Lindsey United
1923 Wrexham 0
Goldenhill Wanderers

Whittingham, Samuel LH/LB/CH
b Sandyford 1881
Goldenhill Wanderers
1902 Stoke 0
1903 1905 Burslem Port Vale 69 3
Crewe Alexandra
1908 1909 Blackpool 48
1910 Huddersfield Town 0
Mirfield United

Whittle, Daniel CH
Halliwell
1892 1893 Ardwick 30 3
1894 Bolton Wanderers 0

Whittle, Daniel IL/CF/OL
1897 1899 Preston North End 5
Chorley
1899 Preston North End 5

Whittle, Harry CF
1903 Blackpool 2

Whittle, John Robert RB
1938 Port Vale 4
Peterborough United

Whittle, John T OL
b Leigh
Hindsford
1931 Manchester United 1
Rossendale United
Fleetwood
Hindsford

Whittle, Richard RB
1888 Preston North End 1 1

Whitton, Percival Albert (Percy) RB/CF/RH
b Creech St Michael 14/1/1892 d 1974
Taunton Town
Bristol Rovers
Aberaman Athletic
1922 1924 Newport County 78 6
1925 Brentford 25 5

Whitton, William A (Willie) CF
b Aldershot
Inverness Caledonian
1921 Tottenham Hotspur 0
1922 1924 Chelsea 38 19

Whitty, Ernest OR
b Warrington 7/7/1907 d 1985
Skelmersdale
1931 Burnley 2
Skelmersdale
Darwen
Chorley

From To Apps Goal

Whitworth, Ernest (Ernie) LH/CH
b Dinnington 14/3/1907 d 1974
Treeton
1927 Chesterfield 17
Wath Athletic
Dinnington Main Colliery Welfare
1930 1931 Rotherham United 64
1932 1934 Barnsley 78 4
1935 1936 Aldershot 27

Whitworth, George H CF/IR
b Northampton 14/7/1896 d 1979
Grafton Excelsior
Rushden Windmill
1920 1921 Northampton Town 67 42
1921 1924 Crystal Palace 111 48
1924 Sheffield Wednesday 0
1925 1927 Hull City 67 31
1928 South Shields 0
Peterborough & Fletton United
Blyth Spartans

Whitworth, John W (Jack) LB
b Brimington 31/1/??
West Hallam
Ripley Athletic
1921 1922 Chesterfield 56
Shirebrook
1924 1925 Chesterfield 3
Newark Town

Whysall, John IR
b Loscoe 1886
Clay Cross Tradesmen
Clay Cross Zingari
Clay Cross Works
Clay Cross Zingari
1908 Chesterfield Town 1
Clay Cross Town

Whyte, Campbell OR
b Auchterderran 27/6/1907 d 1984
Inverkeithing
Denbeath Star
Lochgelly Celtic
Third Lanark
Cowdenbeath
Third Lanark
1929 Gillingham 24 3
1930 Northampton Town 5 1
1931 Rochdale 0

Whyte, Charles (Charlie) OR
b Bridgemill 20/9/1911
Arbroath Ardenlea Juniors
Dundee United
Arbroath
1934 Rochdale (trial) 9 1
1934 Oldham Athletic (trial) 2
Nelson
Montrose
Raith Rovers
Yeovil & Petters United

Whyte, Crawford LB
b Wallsend 4/12/1907 d 1984
Walker Park
Crawcrook Albion
1930 1934 Blackburn Rovers 87
1935 Bradford Park Avenue 9
1936 Tranmere Rovers 11
Ashington
1937 Hartlepools United 5
1938 Clapton Orient 6
Floriana

Whyte, George LH/OL
b Cowdenbeath 24/3/1909 d 1992
Kelty Rangers
Dunfermline Athletic
Rhyl Athletic
1929 1930 Accrington Stanley 73 15
1931 1938 Lincoln City 299 35
Gainsborough Trinity

Whyte, John LH/RH
b Leven 1906
Denbeath Star
East Fife Juniors
St Johnstone
1926 1928 Blackburn Rovers 26 2
1929 Everton 0
Dundee

Whyte, Peter OR
1902 Notts County 3
Renton
Albion Rovers

Wicks, John R (Jim) GK
b Reading
Wycombe Wanderers
1922 Nottingham Forest 0
1923 Reading 6
1924 Queen's Park Rangers 5

From To Apps Goal

Widdowfield, Edward (Ted) CF/OR
b Hetton-le-Hole 25/3/1915 d 1983
Birtley Colliery
Hetton Juniors
Crystal Palace (trial)
Hartlepools United
1935 Huddersfield Town 5
1936 1945 Halifax Town 83 36
1939 (Halifax Town) (3) (2)
Ransome & Marles
Peterborough United

Widdowson, Albert OR
b Bingham q2 1864
Nottingham Forest
1891 Notts County 3

Widdowson, Alfred (Alf) CF/IR/IL
b Keyworth 16/9/1900 d 1970
Boots Athletic
1919 1927 Notts County 141 39
1927 1930 Coventry City 69 16
Newark Town
Heanor Town

Widdowson, Fred LH
b Dronfield q3 1873
Sheepbridge Works
Chesterfield Town
1894 1895 Rotherham Town 32
Barnsley St Peter's
Chesterfield Town
Dronfield Town

Widdowson, Thomas Haslam (Tom) GK
b Hucknall q1 1862 d 1944
Nottingham Forest
1888 Notts County 12
Nottingham Forest
Kimberley

Wield, Thomas William (Tommy) LH/RH
b Lincoln q1 1886 d 1963
St Catherine's
1904 1905 Lincoln City 13
Grantham Avenue
1909 1914 Lincoln City 118 5
Scunthorpe & Lindsey United
Gainsborough Trinity
Grantham
Horncastle Town
Lincoln Claytons

Wienand, George Victor (Tolley) OR
b East London, South Africa 27/4/1910
Transvaal
1937 1938 Huddersfield Town 28 3
1938 Hull City 15 3
(South Africa)

Wigg, Percival Frederick (Percy) OR
b Lowestoft 5/10/1899 d 1985
Pakefield Harriers
Vickers Works
Lowestoft Town
1926 Norwich City 9 3
Lowestoft Town

Wiggins, Edward RH
b Haslingden q3 1877 d 1955
1898 Darwen 3

Wiggins, Joseph Albert (Joe) CF/RB/LB
b Alperton 1/4/1909 d 1982
Hanwell Town
Grays Thurrock
1927 Brentford 4 2
1930 1932 Leicester City 9
1934 Gillingham (loan) 12
1935 Rochdale 27 14
1936 Oldham Athletic 3
Stalybridge Celtic
Hurst
Rhyl

Wigglesworth, Arthur RB
b Hull 26/10/1891 d 1974
Goole Town
1919 Hull City 7
1923 1925 Doncaster Rovers 67
Goole Town

Wigglesworth, Johnson OR
b Burnley q1 1876
1898 Darwen 2

Wigham, John (Johnny) IL/IR
b Hebburn q3 1909 d 1959
Hebburn Colliery
1931 1938 Hartlepools United 264 95

From To Apps Goal

Wightman, Harold (Harry) CH/RB
b Sutton-in-Ashfield 19/6/1894 d 1945
Sutton Town
Eastwood Rangers
Chesterfield Town
1919 1927 Derby County 180 9
1929 Chesterfield 38 2
1930 Notts County 0

Wightman, John Renton (Jock) LH/RH
b Duns 2/11/1912 d 1964
Duns Athletic
Scarborough
1933 York City 5
1934 Bradford Park Avenue 17
1934 1936 Huddersfield Town 64
1936 1946 Blackburn Rovers 66 2
1947 Carlisle United 36

Wigmore, Cuthbert (Clive) LH
b Kiveton Park q1 1892 d 1969
Dinnington Main Colliery
1911 Barnsley 2
Rotherham Town
Dinnington Main Colliery
1913 1914 Barnsley 58 5
1919 Aston Villa 0
1920 Gillingham 9

Wigmore, Joe Francis RB
b Kiveton Park q1 1891 d 1949
Glossop 0
Dinnington Main Colliery
1911 Blackpool 0
Dinnington Main Colliery
1912 Huddersfield Town 1

Wigmore, Walter CH/CF/RB
b Chipping Sodbury 25/2/1873 d 1931
Caps: FLge 1
Kiveton Park
Worksop Town
1892 Sheffield United 0
Worksop Town
1895 Sheffield United 1
1896 1898 Gainsborough Trinity 78 42
1898 1911 Small Heath/Birmingham 329 23
Brierley Hill Alliance

Wilbourn, Henry (Harry) OL
b Eckington 10/2/1905 d 1991
Anston Athletic
1926 Sheffield United 0
1927 Watford 2
1928 Halifax Town 7
Mexborough Athletic
Gainsborough Trinity
Grantham

Wilce, William George Ivor (George) CF
b Plymouth 8/4/1898 d 1975
1922 Barrow 5 1

Wilcock, George Harrie GK
b Edinburgh 24/1/1890 d 1962
1909 Bradford Park Avenue 0
1911 Barnsley 4
Goole Town
Brighton & Hove Albion
Southampton
1920 Preston North End 7
Caerphilly
Southampton Docks & Marine

Wilcockson, Ernest Stanley (Stan) LH
b Poplar 11/5/1905 d 1965
Crittall Athletic
1930 1931 Crystal Palace 5 1
Dartford
1933 York City 39 5
1934 Leeds United 4
1935 1938 Swindon Town 134 5
Tunbridge Wells Rangers

Wilcox, Frederick Jeremiah (Freddie) IL/CH
b Bristol 7/7/1880 d 1954
Glendale
Bristol Rovers
1902 1905 Small Heath/Birmingham 78 32
1905 1909 Middlesbrough 106 22
Plymouth Argyle

Wilcox, George Edwin RB/LB
b Treeton 23/8/1917 d 1991
Denaby United
1937 1946 Derby County 12
1939 (Derby County) (2)
1948 Rotherham United 1

From To Apps Goal

Wilcox, Harry Melbourne IR/CF
b Dalston 17/1/1878 d 1937
Caps: SoLge 1
Bromsgrove Rovers
1898 1899 Small Heath 15 3
Watford
1901 1904 Preston North End 99 42
Plymouth Argyle
1906 1907 Leicester Fosse 44 16
1907 West Bromwich Albion 17 5
Plymouth Argyle

Wilcox, Herbert LB
1906 Bury 0
1907 1908 Burnley 3
Chorley
Rossendale United

Wilcox, John Mitchell OR
b Stourbridge 1/1886 d 1940
Stourbridge Standard
Cradley Heath
Dudley Town
1907 1908 Aston Villa 6
1908 1910 Birmingham 47 1
Southampton
Wellington Town
Walsall

Wilcox, Jonah Charles (Joe) CF/IR/IL
b Coleford 19/1/1894 d 1956
Coleford Athletic
Frome Town
Abertillery
1919 1921 Bristol City 59 20
1922 1923 Bradford Park Avenue 21 5
1924 New Brighton 41 35
1925 Bristol Rovers 32 19
1926 Queen's Park Rangers 9 2
1927 1928 Gillingham 56 26
Kidderminster Harriers
Taunton United
Frome Town

Wilcox, Thomas Walter James (Tom) GK
b at sea 1879 d 1952
Millwall Athletic
Cray Wanderers
1904 Woolwich Arsenal 0
Norwich City
1906 Blackpool 37
1908 Manchester United 2
Carlisle United
1910 Huddersfield Town 2
Goole Town
Abergavenny

Wilcox, William A IR
1923 Crewe Alexandra 1

Wild, George Henry IR
b Sowerby Bridge 31/8/1887 d 1970
Sowerby Bridge Institute
Halifax Town
1913 Bradford City 2 1
1921 Halifax Town 13 2

Wild, Robert Durham (Bob) RH
b Windhill, Shipley q4 1895 d 1939
1919 1920 Bradford City 4
1921 Nelson 36
1922 1923 Halifax Town 51
Barnoldswick Town

Wilde, Arthur Leslie (Leslie) GK
b Liverpool q1 1890
Pontypridd
Aberaman
1923 Tranmere Rovers 1
Pontypridd

Wilde, Arthur Thomas (Archie) IL
d Derby q2 1879 d 1952
Wigston Excelsior
Market Harborough
1902 Leicester Fosse 1
Wigston Excelsior

Wilde, James Frederick (Jimmy) LB/LH
b Tinsley q2 1889 d 1953
Rotherham Town
1914 Burnley 1
1920 Reading 24
1921 1923 Accrington Stanley 34

Wilde, William Charles (Jimmy) CH/RH
b Lyndhurst 24/9/1904 d 1976
Royal Tank Corps
1928 1936 Crystal Palace 270 5

Wildes, H OR
1899 1900 Burton Swifts 51 10

From To Apps Goal

Wildin, William LH
1899 1900 Burton Swifts 34
Newhall
1904 Burton United 34

Wilding, Harry Thomas Oulton CH/RH
b Wolverhampton 27/6/1894 d 1958
Grenadier Guards
1919 1927 Chelsea 241 22
1928 Tottenham Hotspur 12 1
1930 Bristol Rovers 0

Wildman, Frank Reginald GK
b South Kirkby 11/6/1908 d 1994
South Kirkby
1932 1934 Wolverhampton Wanderers 54
1934 1935 Reading 14
1936 1945 Swindon Town 94
1939 (Swindon Town) (3)
Frickley Colliery

Wildman, Walter Ross (Wally) OR
b Wombwell 22/9/1919 d 1972
1938 Torquay United 2 1

Wildman, William RB/LB
b Liverpool 1883
1904 1905 Everton 2
West Ham United

Wildsmith, John Bennison IR/OR
b Darlington 17/6/1911 d 2003
Darlington GSOB
1931 1933 Darlington 6

Wildsmith, Thomas (Tom) RH
b Sheffield 8/1/1913 d 1976
Hadfield Sports
1932 Wolverhampton Wanderers 1
1934 1935 Bristol Rovers 24 2
1936 Doncaster Rovers 4
Frickley Colliery

Wileman, George IR
b Newhall 1879
1899 Loughborough 9

Wileman, Harold Arthur (Arthur), MM IR
b Newhall q1 1886 d 1918
1906 Burton United 8 2
1909 Chelsea 14 5
Millwall Athletic
Luton Town
Southend United

Wileman, Henage (Harry) RH
b Newhall q4 1888 d 1926
Burton United
1909 Chelsea 0
1920 1921 Southend United 58 2

Wileman, Sydney IL/LH/CF
b Coalville 26/4/1910 d 1985
Hugglescote Wesleyans
Gresley Rovers
1933 1936 Derby County 9 1
1938 Port Vale 4
Hinckley United

Wiles, George Harold LB/LH
b East Ham 25/3/1905 d 1986
Sittingbourne
1929 1931 Queen's Park Rangers 18
1932 1937 Walsall 167 2
Halesowen Town

Wiles, Henry John (Harry) CF/IR/OR
b East Ham 31/12/1902 d 1974
Sittingbourne
1929 1932 Queen's Park Rangers 42 25
1933 1934 Walsall 11 5

Wilkes, Albert LH/RH/CH
b Birmingham 10/1874 d 1936
Caps: England 5
Oldbury Town
1896 1897 Walsall 45 6
1898 1906 Aston Villa 141 7
1907 1908 Fulham 16 1
1908 Chesterfield Town 3

Wilkes, Dennis Henry GK
b Redditch 3/3/1896 d 1970
Stafford Rangers
1924 Crewe Alexandra 1

Wilkes, Frederick (Fred) LB
b Bidford-on-Avon 26/8/1883 d 1942
Reading
1908 1911 Tottenham Hotspur 57

Wilkes, George Harry IL
1905 Wolverhampton Wanderers 1

From To Apps Goal

Wilkes, Harry Theodore GK
b Sedgley 24/6/1907 d 1984
Sedgley Congregationals
Wellington Town
1927 1932 Derby County 208
1933 1934 Sheffield United 13
Rhyl Athletic
Heanor Town

Wilkes, Thomas Henry (Tom) GK
b Alcester 19/6/1873 d 1921
Redditch Town
1894 1898 Aston Villa 66
1897 Stoke (loan) 5
1899 1902 Stoke 74

Wilkie, Charles Henry (Charlie) OL
b Cardiff 19/7/1909 d 2002
Merthyr Town
1932 Swansea Town 5
Burton Town
Hednesford Town
Worcester City
Evesham Town
Hednesford Town
Stafford Rangers
Worcester City

Wilkie, John IL/OL
b Govan
Partick Thistle
1895 1897 Blackburn Rovers 75 17
Rangers
1900 Middlesbrough 28 8
Rangers
Partick Thistle
Hibernian
Ayr Parkhouse

Wilkie, T GK
b Glasgow
United Abstainers
1889 Blackburn Rovers 5

Wilkie, Thomas (Tom) LB
b Edinburgh 1876 d 1932
Heart of Midlothian
1895 1898 Liverpool 58 1
Portsmouth

Wilkie, Thomas GK
Caps: SLge 1
Clyde
St Bernard's
Partick Thistle
1900 Preston North End (loan) 3
Rangers (loan)

Wilkins, Arthur Ashley IR
b Packington q4 1887 d 1953
1906 Burton United 11 4

Wilkins, Ernest George (George) IL/IR
b Hackney 27/10/1919 d 1999
Hayes
1938 1946 Brentford 29 7
1946 1947 Bradford Park Avenue 27 6
1947 1948 Nottingham Forest 24 6
1949 Leeds United 3

Wilkins, Leslie (Les) IL/RH/IR
b Swansea 21/7/1907 d 1979
Swansea Red Triangle
1928 Swansea Town 0
1929 Merthyr Town 7 4
1929 Sunderland 2
1930 West Ham United 0
1930 1931 Brentford 19 1
1932 Swindon Town 20 8
1933 Stockport County 3 1
Yeovil & Petters United

Wilkinson, Alfred CF
1904 Doncaster Rovers 2

Wilkinson, Algernon (Algy) GK
b Greasbrough 21/1/1894 d 1967
Rotherham Town
1919 1921 Bradford City 12
1922 Liverpool 0
1924 Blackpool 5
Mold Town
1925 Wrexham 35
Flint Town
Mold Town
Little Sutton Victoria

Wilkinson, Arthur OR/OL
1888 1890 Accrington 23 13
Bury
Accrington Stanley

From To Apps Goal

Wilkinson, Bernard CH
b Thorpe Hesley 12/9/1879 d 1949
Caps: England 1
Thorpe Hesley Parish Church
Shiregreen
Atlas & Norfolk
Thorpe Hesley
1899 1912 Sheffield United 373 14
Rotherham Town

Wilkinson, Charles Edward (Charlie) LB
b Medomsley 7/5/1907 d 1975
Wallsend
Consett
1931 1933 Leeds United 3
1933 1937 Sheffield United 120
1938 Southampton 3
1939 Bournemouth & Boscombe Ath (1)

Wilkinson, Cyril GK
b Rotherham q1 1918
1937 1938 Rotherham United 33
1939 (Rotherham United) (3)

Wilkinson, Frank CH/LH/RH
b Radcliffe-on-Trent 8/1/1867
Wilkinson's (Beeston)
1889 1893 Notts County 9

Wilkinson, Fred (Sonny) LH/IL
b Bury q2 1889
St Augustine's
Lancaster City
Norwich City
Darlington
1912 Blackpool 15 1
Newport County
Stalybridge Celtic
1920 Watford 37
1921 Stoke 3
Bury St Edmunds

Wilkinson, Frederick (Freddy) IL
b Bishop Auckland q4 1878
Bishop Auckland
1903 Grimsby Town 16 2
Norwich City
Shildon Athletic
1908 Barnsley 15
Shildon Athletic
Darlington

Wilkinson, George Alfred LH/IR/RH
b Lower Ince 5/3/1895 d 1964
Atherton
1921 Oldham Athletic 0
1922 1925 Southport 46 9
High Park

Wilkinson, Gilbert George CF
b Clandown 20/4/1910 d 1978
Clandown
1926 1927 Watford 9 2
Sheppey United
Taunton Town
Taunton GWR

Wilkinson, H LH
1909 Bolton Wanderers 1

Wilkinson, Harry OL/OR
b Bury 1883
Newton Heath Alliance
1903 Manchester United 8
Hull City
West Ham United
1905 Manchester United 0
Haslingden
St Helens Recreation
1907 Bury 2
Oswaldtwistle Rovers
Rochdale

Wilkinson, Harry CH/LH
b Derker 2/5/1903 d 1997
Albert Mount
Wellington Albion
Werneth Amateurs
1923 1925 Oldham Athletic 17
1926 Bolton Wanderers 0
Mossley
1928 Southport 4
Ashton National

Wilkinson, Jack CH
b Ilkeston
Hickleton Main Colliery
1905 1907 Barnsley 24 2

Wilkinson, John CH
b Darlington 1888
Darlington St Agnes
1906 1910 Manchester City 31 2

From	To	Club	Apps	Goal
		Wilkinson, John (Jack)	OL	
		b Wath-on-Dearne 13/6/1902	d 1979	
		Dearne Valley Old Boys		
		Wath Athletic		
1925	1929	Sheffield Wednesday	72	16
1930		Newcastle United	30	7
1932	1934	Lincoln City	93	19
1935		Sunderland	0	
1936		Hull City	17	2
		Scunthorpe & Lindsey United		
		Burton Town		
		Wilkinson, John T (Jack)	OL	
		b Durham		
		Consett Celtic		
1921	1923	Watford	61	7
1925		Hartlepools United	0	
		Wilkinson, John William	LB/RB	
		b Hucknall Torkard 10/1882		
		Hucknall White Star		
1904	1905	Notts County	7	
		Tottenham Hotspur		
		Wilkinson, Jonathan Montague (Monty)	OR/CF	
		b Esh Winning 18/7/1908	d 1979	
		Esh Winning		
		Kelloe Colliery		
1924		Sunderland (trial)	0	
		Esh Winning		
1925		Durham City	0	
		Crook Town		
1927	1928	Newcastle United	27	11
1929	1930	Everton	11	2
1931	1932	Blackpool	60	15
1932	1938	Charlton Athletic	224	48
1939		(Charlton Athletic)	(1)	
		Wilkinson, Jonathan T	CH/RH	
1888	1890	Accrington	6	
		Wilkinson, Joseph Hargreaves (Joe)	CH/GK	
		b Darfield 27/10/1905	d 1978	
		Wombwell		
		Mexborough Athletic		
1926		Sheffield United	0	
1928	1929	Doncaster Rovers	12	1
		Wilkinson, Norman	GK	
		b Tantobie 9/6/1910	d 1975	
		Tanfield Lea		
1932		Huddersfield Town	0	
1935	1951	Stoke City	186	
		Oswestry Town		
		Wilkinson, Reginald George (Reg)	RH	
		b Norwich 26/3/1899	d 1946	
		CEYMS (Norwich)		
1920	1922	Norwich City	102	7
1923		Sunderland	2	
1924	1933	Brighton & Hove Albion	361	14
		Frost's Athletic		
		Norwich Electricty Works		
		Wilkinson, Thomas	CF	
		b Glasgow		
		Maryhill Youth Club		
1924		Gillingham	5	
		Wilkinson, Thomas (Tom)	IL	
		b Newfield, Co Durham 8/2/1902		
		Beamish Athletic		
		Tanfield Lea Institute		
		Pelton Fell Institute		
1924	1925	Hull City	4	2
		Chester-le-Street		
		Blyth Spartans		
1927		Everton	0	
1928		Nelson	17	5
		Twizell United		
		Annfield Plain		
		Craghead United		
		Shildon		
		Beamish Athletic		
		Lumley United		
		Consett		
		Beamish Rovers		
		Wilkinson, Thomas W	OL	
		b Marsden		
1926	1927	South Shields	5	
		Wilkinson, William Henry	GK	
1894	1895	Rotherham Town	9	
		South Shore		
1897		Lincoln City	20	
		Chatham		
		Gravesend United		
		Wilkinson, William Herbert (Billy)	RH/IL/CH	
		b Thorpe Hesley 12/3/1881	d 1961	
		Thorpe Hesley		
1901	1908	Sheffield United	58	7
1909		Bolton Wanderers	0	
		Wilks, Alwyne	OR	
		b Staveley 4/9/1906	d 1980	
		Brodsworth Main Colliery		
1926		Doncaster Rovers	14	3
1926	1928	Sunderland	52	2
1929		Reading	0	
1929		Barrow	6	
		Loughborough Corinthians		
		Owston Park Rangers (Doncaster)		
		Wilks, Fred	GK	
		b Haverton Hill		
1930		Sheffield Wednesday	0	
		Furness Shipyard Athletic		
1932		Hartlepools United	15	
		Billingham Synthonia		
		Wilks, Samuel (Sam)	IL	
		b Sheffield q4 1903		
1924		Rotherham County	17	1
		Wilks, William	RH	
		b Staveley 8/10/1917	d 1986	
		Staveley Gas Works		
1936	1937	Reading	3	
		Willacy, David Lewis	OR	
		b Barrow 13/6/1916	d 1941	
		Greenbrae Juveniles		
		Queen of the South		
1938		Preston North End	1	
		Willacy, Wilson	OL	
		b Annan 1/8/1911		
		Annan Athletic		
1931		Carlisle United	4	
		Willett, Charles (Charlie)	CF	
1895		Burton Swifts	7	1
		Willey, William	CF	
1893		Ardwick	1	
		Williams, Albert	CH	
1903		Stockport County	6	1
		Williams, Albert Leslie (Bert)	OR/OL	
		b Newtown 1/5/1905	d 1974	
		Caps: Wales 1		
		Chester		
1929	1930	Wrexham	24	3
1931		Gillingham	39	5
1932		York City	7	
1933	1934	Gillingham	11	1
		Burton Town		
		Williams, Archibald McLeish (Archie)	CF/IL	
		b Wavertree 16/2/1898	d 1961	
		Liverpool		
		Northern Nomads		
		Northwich Victoria		
		Runcorn		
1922	1923	Wigan Borough	24	10
1923	1924	Southport	9	4
		Williams, Austin	OR/OL	
		b Aberdare 13/3/1914	d 1984	
		Porth		
1936	1938	Swansea Town	12	
1939		Chester	0	
		Williams, Benjamin David (Ben)	RB	
		b Penrhiwceiber 29/10/1900	d 1968	
		Caps: WLge 1/Wales 10		
		Penrhiwceiber		
1925	1929	Swansea Town	101	
1929	1935	Everton	131	
1936		Newport County	18	
		Williams, Bert Frederick	GK	
		b Bradley, Staffordshire 31/1/1920		
		Caps: England B/FLge 5/England War 4/ England 24		
		Thompson's (Wolverhampton)		
1937	1938	Walsall	25	
1945	1956	Wolverhampton Wanderers	381	
		Williams, Bertram (Bertie)	IR/OR/OL	
		b Merthyr Tydfil 4/3/1907	d 1968	
		Caps: Wales 1		
		Cyfartha Stars		
1926		Merthyr Town	0	
1927	1931	Bristol City	103	26
1931	1936	Sheffield United	113	16
		Williams, Charles	GK	
		b Clowne q3 1912		
		Clowne Welfare		
		Shirebrook		
1933		Mansfield Town	22	
		Rhyl Athletic		
		Williams, Charles Albert (Charlie)	GK	
		b Welling 19/11/1873	d 1952	
		Caps: FLge 1		
		Phoenix		
		Clarence		
		Erith		
1893		Woolwich Arsenal	19	
1894	1901	Manchester City	221	1
		Tottenham Hotspur		
		Norwich City		
		Brentford		
		Williams, Daniel J	CF	
		b Cardiff		
1935	1936	Cardiff City	20	10
		Williams, David H (Dai)	CF/IR	
		b Liverpool		
		St Helens Recreation		
1912		Glossop	6	2
1912	1913	Notts County	31	5
		Belfast Celtic		
		Cliftonville		
		Luton Town		
1920		Brighton & Hove Albion	20	2
		Maidstone United		
		Williams, David Rees (Rees)	OR/OL	
		b Abercanaid 1900	d 1963	
		Caps: Wales 8		
		Pentrebach		
1920	1921	Merthyr Town	65	6
1922	1927	Sheffield Wednesday	163	8
1927	1928	Manchester United	31	2
		Thames		
		Aldershot		
		Merthyr Town		
		Glenavon		
		Williams, Edward	IL	
		East Vale		
1904		Burslem Port Vale	5	
		Williams, Edwin H (Ted)	CH/IL	
		b Hawarden 1868		
		Caps: Wales 2		
		Saltney		
		Saltney Victoria		
		Over Wanderers		
		Chester		
1892	1895	Crewe Alexandra	40	6
		Williams, Emlyn	CF/IL	
		b Aberaman 1903		
1926		Aberdare Athletic	12	9
1928		Clapton Orient	3	1
1929		Hull City	1	
		Merthyr Town		
1931		Bournemouth & Boscombe Ath	6	2
		Ramsgate Press Wanderers		
		Williams, Emlyn	RB/CH	
		b Maesteg 15/1/1912	d 1989	
1934		Wrexham	0	
		Burton Town		
1936	1938	Barnsley	88	
1939	1947	Preston North End	62	
1939		(Preston North End)	(3)	
1947	1948	Barnsley	17	
1948		Accrington Stanley	15	
		Williams, Eric RT	CH	
		Connah's Quay & Shotton		
1925		Wrexham	1	
		Connah's Quay & Shotton		
		Winsford United		
		Williams, Ernest Harold (Ernie)	RB	
		b Wales		
		Rhyl		
1907		Clapton Orient	5	
		Williams, Ernest William	OL	
		b Ryde q3 1882		
		Caps: England Amat		
		Ryde		
		Portsmouth		
1909		Chelsea	6	
		Portsmouth		
		Southampton		
		Williams, Frank H	RH	
		b Kearsley 1908		
		Stalybridge Celtic		
1930		Manchester United	3	
		Altrincham		
		Williams, Frank Harold	OR/OL	
		b Cefn-y-Bedd 10/3/1906	d 1982	
		Caps: Wales Amat		
		Oak Alyn Rovers		
1924	1925	Wrexham	3	
1926		Preston North End	8	
1928		Port Vale	1	
		Oswestry Town		
		Northern Nomads		
		Rhyl		
		Ashton National Gas		
		Cross Street		
		Altrincham		
		Shrewsbury Town		
		Buxton		
		Williams, Frederick (Fred)	IL/OL	
		b Manchester		
		South Shore		
1896	1901	Manchester City	125	38
1902		Manchester United	8	
		Williams, Frederick (Fred)	CH	
		South Shore		
1898		Blackpool	27	1
		Williams, Frederick Arthur	RB	
		b Hucknall 15/4/1918	d 1994	
		Hucknall Colts		
1938		Southampton	22	
1939		(Southampton)	(1)	
1945		Stockport County	0	
		Altrincham		
		Williams, George	RH	
		b Wolverhampton 1882	d 1939	
		Blakenhall		
1905		Wolverhampton Wanderers	22	
		Tettenhall Rovers		
		Williams, George	LB	
		b Ynysddu 19/5/1914	d 1993	
		Caps: Wales War 2		
1934		Charlton Athletic	0	
1936	1938	Aldershot	68	
1938	1946	Millwall	25	
1939		(Millwall)	(3)	
		South Shields		
		Williams, George E	IR	
1924		Walsall	7	1
		Williams, George Henry	IL/IR	
		b Ventnor 10/1/1897	d 1957	
1920		Southampton	2	1
1921		Exeter City	11	1
		Netley Sports		
		Williams, George Owen	CH/LH	
		b Birmingham 9/1879		
		Caps: Wales 1		
		Monway		
		Oldbury		
		Wednesbury Old Athletic		
1900	1901	West Bromwich Albion	16	
		Brierley Hill Alliance		
		Kidderminster Harriers		
		Wrexham		
		Stafford Rangers		
		Willenhall Swifts		
		Walsall		
		Williams, Harry	RB	
		b Aston 1875		
		Aston Unity		
		Aston Manor		
1896		Small Heath	1	
		Nechells		
		Williams, Harry	LB/LH	
		St Albans City		
		Hitchin Town		
1898	1899	Luton Town	54	2
		Reading		
		Williams, Henry (Harry)	OL	
		b Farnworth 1883		
		Walkden St Mary's		
		Turton		
1900		Bury	0	
1901	1902	Bolton Wanderers	16	6
1903		Burnley	32	8
1904	1907	Manchester United	33	7
1908		Leeds City	0	
		Williams, Henry (Harry)	IL	
		b Hucknall Torkard 1899		
		Hucknall Olympic		
1920		Sunderland	1	
1921		Chesterfield	28	10
1922		Manchester United	5	2
1923	1924	Brentford	52	7

From To Apps Goal

Williams, Horace Frederick CF
b Liverpool q3 1898 d 1960
Liverpool Regiment
Hibernian
St Johnstone
Hibernian
St Johnstone
Dundee Hibernian
1922 Gillingham 26 10
St Bernard's
1923 Wrexham (trial) 0
Mold Town
1926 1927 New Brighton 46 38
1927 Blackpool 5 3
Peterborough & Fletton United
Macclesfield (trial)
Caernarvon Athletic (trial)
Lovells Athletic (trial)
Hereford United
Amiens
Hereford United
Tunbridge Wells Rangers
Connah's Quay & Shotton
Abergele
Lucerne
Denbigh Mental Hospital
Northwich Victoria
Burton Town

Williams, Idris RH
b Treharris
1928 Swansea Town 0
1929 1931 Rochdale 83 5

Williams, Idris LB
b Merthyr Tydfil
Merthyr Town
1933 Blackpool 0
Burton Town
1935 Halifax Town 14
Tredomen
1937 Rochdale 4
Rossendale United

Williams, Iorwerth RB/LH
b Wales 1914
Merthyr Town
1932 1934 Lincoln City 3
Crittall Athletic

Williams, Jack Walter CF/IR
b Washington 12/1885
Hebburn Argyle
1904 1905 Bury 15 7
1909 Clapton Orient 12 3
Leyton

Williams, James (Jimmy) RB/OR
b Brownhills 1882
Lichfield
Brownhills Albion
1903 Aston Villa 0
1904 1907 West Bromwich Albion 31 1
Brownhills Albion

Williams, Jesse Thomas OL/OR
b Cefn-y-Bedd 24/6/1903 d 1972
Caps: Wales 1
Caergwrle
Oak Alyn Rovers
1923 Wrexham 33 3
1924 1926 Middlesbrough 37 8
1927 1928 Clapton Orient 32 3
Rhyl Athletic
Ashton National
Shrewsbury Town
Wellington Town
Colwyn Bay United

Williams, John CF
b Pendleton
Bacup Borough
Rossendale United
1924 Burnley 4 2

Williams, John Boar OL
1893 Rotherham Town 2 1

Williams, John Henry LH/RH
b Staincross 17/5/1890 d 1973
Staincross
1919 1920 Barnsley 39
Doncaster Rovers

Williams, John James (Jackie) OR
b Aberdare 29/3/1911 d 1979
Caps: Wales 1
Aberaman
Llanelly
1932 1935 Huddersfield Town 50 15
1935 Aston Villa 17 5
1938 Ipswich Town 9
1938 Wrexham 25 4
1939 (Wrexham) (2)
Colwyn Bay
Runcorn

From To Apps Goal

Williams, John Lewis James (Jack) LH/RH/CF
b Rhayader 15/1/1890 d 1969
Builth Wells
1911 Nottingham Forest 4 1
1912 Tottenham Hotspur 0
1920 1922 Swansea Town 85 4
Mold Town

Williams, John S OL
b Broughton
Brymbo Green
1921 Wrexham 2
Brymbo Green

Williams, John Thomas (Johnny) CH/LB
b West Hartlepool
South Durham S & I
1927 1928 Hartlepools United 41 1
1929 Grimsby Town 0
Scarborough

Williams, John William IL
b Buckley 5/1884 d 1916
Caps: Wales 2
1906 Bury 0
Accrington Stanley
1908 Birmingham 12 3
Accrington Stanley
Crystal Palace
Millwall Athletic

Williams, Joseph IR
Macclesfield
1906 Manchester United 3 1

Williams, Joseph E IR
b Rugby
Rugby Town
1921 Northampton Town 2

Williams, Joseph E OR
b Saltney Ferry
1923 Wrexham 3

Williams, Joseph Joshua (Joey) OR/OL
b Rotherham 4/6/1902 d 1978
Rotherham Town
1921 1923 Rotherham County 95 7
1924 1925 Huddersfield Town 58 6
1925 1928 Stoke City 82 17
1929 1931 Arsenal 22 5
1931 1934 Middlesbrough 78 11
1935 1936 Carlisle United 20 2

Williams, Leonard Horace (Len) RB/LB
b Dalton, West Yorkshire 17/5/1898 d 1932
Caps: WLge 1
Silverwood Colliery
Wath Athletic
1923 1925 Sheffield Wednesday 9
1926 Stockport County 39
1927 1929 Wolverhampton Wanderers 49
1929 1930 Swansea Town 42
Wellington Town
Oswestry Town

Williams, Leonard Stanley (Len) OR/OL
b Cefn-y-Bedd 2/5/1910 d 1990
Spennymoor United
1929 1932 Bournemouth & Boscombe Ath 90 18
Macclesfield
1933 Portsmouth 1
1934 1935 Aldershot 64 19
1936 1937 Charlton Athletic 3
1938 Aldershot 14 1
Worcester City

Williams, Leslie OR
1929 Wrexham 1
1930 Wolverhampton Wanderers 0
1931 Gillingham 0

Williams, Leslie Thomas RH
b Chatham q1 1916
Chatham Town
1937 Gillingham 1
Chatham Town

Williams, Louis CH
b Longton 1889
North Staffs Nomads
1907 Stoke 33 1
1908 Bradford City 10
Bristol Rovers
Port Vale

Williams, Owen IL
b Smethwick 11/1874
Oldbury Town
1893 1895 West Bromwich Albion 14 7
Oldbury Town
Smethwick Centaur

From To Apps Goal

Williams, Owen OL
b Ryhope 23/9/1896 d 1960
Caps: England Sch/England 2
Ryhope Colliery
1913 Sunderland (trial) 0
1914 Manchester United (trial) 0
Easington Colliery
1919 1923 Clapton Orient 162 33
1923 1929 Middlesbrough 184 39
1930 Southend United 16 4
Shildon

Williams, Owen LH
b Holyhead 2/10/1896
South Liverpool
1919 Everton 2
1921 1922 Wigan Borough 57
Holyhead
1924 Wigan Borough 1

Williams, Ralph Shipley CF/IL
b Aberaman 2/10/1905 d 1985
Aberaman Athletic
1923 Aberdare Athletic 2
1924 Brentford 7 1
Aberaman Athletic
Poole
1927 Chesterfield 31 15
Manchester Central
Colwyn Bay
1929 1930 Cardiff City 30 17
1931 Crewe Alexandra 13 16
1932 Southport 12 3
1932 Rochdale 8 1
Merthyr Town
Lovells Athletic
Aberdare Town
Bangor City
Rhyl
Aberdare Town

Williams, Reginald George (Reg 'Skilly') GK
b Watford 4/1/1890 d 1959
Caps: SoLge 1
Leavesden Mental Hospital
1920 1925 Watford 240
1926 1928 Brighton & Hove Albion 101
Watford National
Watford Wanderers

Williams, Richard GK
Bromborough Pool
1891 1894 Everton 58
1897 Luton Town 30
1898 1899 Glossop North End 52

Williams, Richard (Dick) GK
b Newcastle-under-Lyme 15/12/1905 d 1983
Jarrow
1926 1929 Stoke City 61
1930 Reading 4
1931 Chester 0

Williams, Robert Daniel (Bob) OR
b Brymbo q3 1902
Rhos Church
Brymbo
1923 Wrexham 3
Brymbo
Llandudno
Oswestry Town

Williams, Roderick (Rod) CF
b Newport 2/12/1909 d 1987
Sutton United
Epsom Town
Uxbridge Town
1932 Crystal Palace 0
1933 1935 Norwich City 19 9
1936 Exeter City 41 29
1937 Reading 14 12
1937 West Ham United 9 5
1938 Clapton Orient 35 16
1939 (Clapton Orient) (3) (2)

Williams, Ronald (Ron) CF/IR/OR
b Llansamlet 23/1/1907 d 1987
Caps: WLge 3/Wales 2
National Oil Refinery (Skewen)
Bethel Juniors
Swansea Amateurs
Llanelly
1929 1933 Swansea Town 137 46
1933 1934 Newcastle United 35 14
1935 Chester 24 15
1936 1937 Swansea Town 39 5
Lovells Athletic
Llanelly
Milford United
Haverfordwest Athletic

From To Apps Goal

Williams, Thomas Hutchinson (Tommy) IR/CF/IL
b Easington 23/5/1899 d 1960
Ryhope Colliery
1920 Huddersfield Town (trial) 0
1921 1922 Clapton Orient 26 6
1923 Charlton Athletic 5 2
1923 Gillingham 16 6
1924 Ashington 10 4
Mid-Rhondda United
1925 1927 Bristol Rovers 75 28
1928 Bristol City 8 4
1928 1929 Merthyr Town 46 19
1930 1931 Norwich City 27 13
Easington Colliery Welfare
Frost's Athletic

Williams, Thomas P CH
b Cardiff 1915
Caps: Wales Sch/Wales Amat
1937 1938 Cardiff City 6
Salisbury City

Williams, Trevor OL
Grimsby Rangers
1903 Grimsby Town 4 1
Grimsby Rovers
Hull City
Grimsby Rangers
Grimsby Victoria
Grimsby Rangers

Williams, Victor (Vic) RH
b Birmingham 27/10/1901
Redditch Town
1926 Sheffield United 3
Redditch Town

Williams, Walter IL
Bostall Rovers
1893 Woolwich Arsenal 1

Williams, Walter OR/LH/OL
1904 1907 Wolverhampton Wanderers 58 4

Williams, Walter John (Jack) CH
b Wolverhampton 18/7/1906 d 1982
Wednesfield Roves
1927 Wolverhampton Wanderers 3
1928 Gillingham 9
1928 1929 Brighton & Hove Albion 42 1

Williams, William (Bill) OR/IR
Caps: FLge 2
1894 1897 Everton 23 4
1898 1899 Blackburn Rovers 31 1
Bristol Rovers
1901 Newton Heath 4

Williams, William (Billy) LB/RB
b West Smethwick 6/1875 d 1929
Caps: FLge 5/England 6
West Smethwick
Old Hill Wanderers
1894 1900 West Bromwich Albion 180 8

Williams, William (Billy) LH
b Llantwit Vardre 1896
Caps: Wales 1
Pontypridd
1920 Cardiff City 0
1921 1926 Northampton Town 187 3
1927 Newport County 6

Williams, William Alfred (Billy) RH
b Edmonton q1 1910
1933 Sheffield Wednesday 0
1934 Southend United 1

Williams, William David IL
b Manchester 16/11/?? d 1926
Darwen
1922 1924 Everton 39 14
1924 1925 Blackpool 22 10

Williams, William Dennis (Billy) IL/CF/IR
b Leytonstone 27/9/1905 d 1993
Caps: England Sch
Fairbairn House
1921 1926 West Ham United 35 8
1927 Chelsea 2

Williams, William Hugh LB
b Wrexham 9/1886 d 1957
Chirk
Wrexham
Chester
1913 Aston Villa 1
Chirk
Mold Town
St Asaph
Chester Lymphets

From To Apps Goal

Williams, William Llewellyn (Bill) RH/IL
b Swansea 1914
1933 Southampton 0
St Budeaux
Cork FC
1936 Watford 1
1937 Gillingham 1

Williamson, Albert RH
b Sawley q2 1866 d 1951
Sawley Rangers
1888 1890 Derby County 41
1891 Notts County 2
Nottingham Forest

Williamson, Alfred William (Alf) CF
b Wallasey q1 1909 d 1941
1929 New Brighton 1 1
Costain's
1930 Southport 0

Williamson, Charles W OR
Preston Winckley
1907 Preston North End 1

Williamson, David Leslie (Len) GK
b Llanelli 3/9/1914 d 1989
1933 Swansea Town 0
1934 1935 Newport County 7
Guildford City

Williamson, Ernest Clark (Tim) GK
b Murton Colliery 24/5/1890 d 1964
Caps: England 2
Murton Red Star
Wingate Albion
Croydon Common
1919 1922 Arsenal 105
1923 1924 Norwich City 43

Williamson, John IR/RH
b Manchester
Ancoats Lads Club
St Mirren
1919 Manchester United 2
1921 Bury 12
1922 Crewe Alexandra 15 2
British Dyestuffs

Williamson, John (Johnny) LH/RH
b Fauldhouse 16/10/1895 d 1979
Armadale
1921 1925 Preston North End 63 2
1926 Grimsby Town 1
Lancaster Town
Darwen
Morecambe

Williamson, John Robert RB
b Gateshead q1 1887
Annfield Plain Celtic
1911 Aston Villa 0
Stourbridge
Gainsborough Trinity
1914 Sunderland 5

Williamson, Reginald Garnet (Reg 'Tim') GK
b North Ormesby 6/6/1884 d 1943
Caps: FLge 5/England 7
Redcar Crusaders
1901 1922 Middlesbrough 564 2

Williamson, Thomas (Tommy) RH/CH
b Salford 16/3/1913 d 1992
Pendleton Wednesday
1932 Leeds United 0
Nantwich
Northwich Victoria
1935 1946 Oldham Athletic 157 4
1939 (Oldham Athletic) (3)
Fleetwood

Williamson, Thomas Robertson (Tom) CH
b Dalmuir 8/2/1901 d 1988
Kilbowie Ross Dhu
Kirkintilloch Rob Roy
1922 1923 Blackburn Rovers 19 1
Third Lanark
1926 1930 Stoke City 152 14
1931 1933 Norwich City 82 4
Frost's Athletic

From To Apps Goal

Williamson, William Gallacher (Tim) IL/CF/IR
b Pollokshaws 7/4/1900 d 1976
Caps: WLge 1
Glencraig Celtic
Lochgelly United
Broxburn United
Heart of Midlothian
1924 1925 Portsmouth 12 3
Clyde
Hamilton Academical
Dunfermline Athletic
1927 Crystal Palace 6 1
Dunfermline Athletic
Ebbw Vale
Montrose
Clyde
Shirebrook
Dundee United
1931 Accrington Stanley 27 14
1931 1932 Southport 10 5
1932 Rochdale 7 2
Montrose
Distillery
Alloa Athletic
Leith Athletic
Montrose

Williamson, William Mountford (Billy) OR
b Stone q4 1887
North Staffs Nomads
1906 1907 Stoke 8
Crewe Alexandra
1910 Leicester Fosse 2
Stoke
Wellington Town

Willighan, Thomas (Tommy) RB
b Belfast 23/2/1903 d 1936
Caps: Ireland 2
Willowfield
1929 1933 Burnley 59

Willingham, Charles Kenneth (Ken) RH/LH
b Sheffield 1/12/1912 d 1975
Caps: FLge 7/England War 6/England 12
Ecclesfield
Worksop Town
1932 1938 Huddersfield Town 247 4
1939 (Huddersfield Town) (3)
1945 1946 Sunderland 14
1946 1947 Leeds United 35

Willingham, D Alfred (Alf) CF
b East London
1910 Clapton Orient 1
Millwall Athletic (trial)

Willis, David Lalty RH/LH
b Byker 7/1881 d 1949
Gateshead NER
1902 Sunderland 1
Reading
1904 1906 Sunderland 47 2
1907 1912 Newcastle United 95 3
Reading
Palmer's (Jarrow)

Willis, Herbert LH
b Clapton q3 1886
Clapton Warwick
1908 1913 Clapton Orient 136 1
Maidstone United

Willis, Jonathan LH/CF
b Easington q3 1885 d 1914
1910 1911 Gainsborough Trinity 5

Willis, Robert (Bobby) IR
b Cramlington 1871
Shankhouse Black Watch
1893 1894 Newcastle United 34 19
Shankhouse Black Watch

Willis, Robert Smith (Bobby) RH
b Cramlington 31/1/1901 d 1974
Shankhouse
Blyth Spartans
Dundee
1923 1925 Rochdale 64 1
1926 Halifax Town 2
1927 Rochdale 0

Willocks, David King (Davie) IR/IL
b Arbroath 6/1/1871
Arbroath
1892 1893 Bolton Wanderers 32 8
1894 1895 Burton Swifts 58 25
Dundee
Brighton United
Arbroath

Willows, William Henry (Billy) OL
b New Tupton q3 1884 d 1961
New Tupton Ivanhoe
1906 Chesterfield Town 20 2

From To Apps Goal

Wills, Thomas LB
b Kilmarnock d 1912
Ayr
1903 1904 Newcastle United 18
Crystal Palace
Ayr
Carlisle United
Johannesburg

Willshaw, George James OL
b Hackney 18/10/1912 d 1993
Southall
Walthamstow Avenue
1935 1937 Southend United 28 6
1938 Bristol City 34 9
1939 1946 Clapton Orient 12 2
1939 (Clapton Orient) (3)

Wilmington, Thomas OR
b Oswaldtwistle 1875 d 1947
Accrington Stanley
Accrington
1895 Burnley 0
1896 Blackburn Rovers 9
Nelson
Southport Central
Accrington Stanley

Wilmot, James RB
b Newcastle q3 1883 d 1965
Dunston
Shildon Athletic
1910 Lincoln City 2
Abertillery
Carlisle United

Wilmot, Kilburn (Ken) LB
b Chilvers Coton 3/4/1911 d 1996
Hinckley United
1932 Coventry City 12
Nuneaton Town
1935 Walsall 3
Dudley Town

Wilshaw, John Henry IR
b Stafford q4 1896
Bedlington United
1927 Barnsley 2
Wath Athletic
Stakeford Albion

Wilson, Albert CF
b Lochee
Dundee Violet
1929 1930 Preston North End 10 1
Cowdenbeath

Wilson, Albert OR/OL
b Rotherham 28/1/1915 d 1998
Rotherham YMCA
Rawmarsh Welfare
Stafford Rangers
1936 Derby County 1
1938 Mansfield Town 20 2
1938 1945 Crystal Palace 20 6
1939 (Crystal Palace) (3)
1946 Rotherham United 38 19
1947 Grimsby Town 17 1
Boston United
Scunthorpe & Lindsey United

Wilson, Albert Edward IL
b Galgate 4/12/1896 d 1977
Lancaster Town (trial)
Lancaster United
Lancaster Town
1923 Barrow 17 1
Lancaster Town
Morecambe

Wilson, Albert Sidney OL
b Hetton-le-Hole 26/11/1903 d 1973
Dawdon Colliery
1924 Durham City 2
Seaham Harbour

Wilson, Alexander Adams (Alex) GK
b Wishaw 29/10/1908 d 1971
Overtown Rangers
Morton
1933 1938 Arsenal 82
St Mirren
1947 Brighton & Hove Albion 1

Wilson, Alfred Royle RB
b Wortley q1 1890
Malin Bridge
1912 Sheffield Wednesday 0
Rotherham Town
1919 Birmingham 2
Rotherham Town

From To Apps Goal

Wilson, Andrew IR
b Strathclyde
Strathclyde
1896 Sunderland 2
Partick Thistle
Motherwell
Partick Thistle
Motherwell

Wilson, Andrew OR
b Dunipace
Dunipace Thistle
1922 Plymouth Argyle 3
Alloa Athletic

Wilson, Andrew McCrindle (Andy) CF/IL
b Irvine 10/12/1880 d 1945
Caps: Scotland 6
Irvine Meadow
Clyde
1900 1919 Sheffield Wednesday 501 199

Wilson, Andrew Nisbet (Andy) IL/CF/IR
b Newmains 14/2/1895 d 1973
Caps: Scotland 12
Cambuslang Rangers
1914 Middlesbrough 8 5
Hamilton Academical
Heart of Midlothian
Dunfermline Athletic
1921 1923 Middlesbrough 77 51
1923 1931 Chelsea 238 59
1931 Queen's Park Rangers 20 3
Nimes
Clacton Town

Wilson, Angus OR
1898 Derby County 1
1898 Darwen 0

Wilson, Archibald (Archie) OR
b Cambuslang 1890 d 1916
Newmilns
1909 Tottenham Hotspur 0
Southend United
1914 Middlesbrough 21 4

Wilson, Arthur CH/IL/RH
b Newcastle 6/10/1908 d 2000
Scotswood
1929 1931 Southampton 62 12
1932 1933 West Ham United 29 14
1933 1937 Chester 136 6
1937 Wolverhampton Wanderers 0
1938 Torquay United 7
1939 (Torquay United) (3)

Wilson, Charles (Charlie) RH/LH/CH
b Stockport 2/1877
1897 1904 Liverpool 84 3

Wilson, Charles (Charlie) CF
b Atherstone 30/3/1895 d 1971
Coventry City
1919 1922 Tottenham Hotspur 55 27
1922 1925 Huddersfield Town 99 57
1925 1930 Stoke City 156 112
Stafford Rangers
1933 Wrexham 0
Shrewsbury Town

Wilson, Charles (Charlie) IL/LH/IR
b Heeley 20/7/1905 d 1985
Sheffield Hallam
Chesterfield Municipal (trial)
1920 Sheffield United (trial) 0
1921 1927 West Bromwich Albion 125 41
1927 1931 Sheffield Wednesday 57 5
1931 1932 Grimsby Town 27 2
1933 Aston Villa 0
1934 Coventry City 10 4
Kidderminster Harriers
Worcester City
Kidderminster Harriers
Kidderminster Police

Wilson, Charles Henry (Charlie) RB/RH
b Cleethorpes 10/2/1904 d 1994
Cleethorpes Town
1923 1932 Grimsby Town 273 2
1933 Bournemouth & Boscombe Ath 11
Grantham
Peterborough United

Wilson, Charles William LH
b Whitburn, County Durham q3 1900
Whitburn
1920 Sunderland (trial) 0
Carlisle United
1926 Newport County 2
Lovells Athletic

From To Apps Goal

Wilson, Clare LH/IL/CH
b Boroughbridge q2 1886
Wallsend Park Villa
Gateshead
1908 Bradford City 2
1908 1911 Glossop 109 6
1911 1912 Oldham Athletic 21
Gateshead

Wilson, Cyril Kershaw IL
b Kirkby-in-Ashfield q1 1904
1921 West Bromwich Albion 0
1922 Derby County 1
Worcester City

Wilson, Daniel OR
b Liverpool 1875
East Bontas
1899 Liverpool 2

Wilson, David IL
b Lochgelly 1883
Lochgelly Rangers
Buckhaven United
Lochgelly Rangers
1901 Gainsborough Trinity 15
Cowdenbeath
East Fife
Heart of Midlothian
1906 Everton 5
Distillery
Portsmouth

Wilson, David LH/RH/RB
b Irvine 14/1/1884
Caps: Scotland 1
Irvine Meadow
St Mirren
Hamilton Academical
1904 1905 Bradford City 12 1
1907 1920 Oldham Athletic 368 16
1921 1923 Nelson 95 3

Wilson, David 'Soldier' CF
b Hebburn 23/7/1883 d 1906
Black Watch
Raith Rovers
Dundee
Heart of Midlothian
1905 Hull City 10 3
1905 1906 Leeds City 21 13

Wilson, Ernest (Ernie 'Tug') OL
b Beighton 11/7/1899 d 1955
Silverwood Colliery
Beighton Recreation
Denaby United
1922 1935 Brighton & Hove Albion 509 68
Vernon Athletic

Wilson, Francis (Frank) OR
b Motherwell 1904
Motherwell Juniors
Mid Annandale
Motherwell
Hamilton Academical
1933 Preston North End 6 1
Falkirk
Glentoran
Alloa Athletic
1937 Rochdale 7 1

Wilson, Frank RH
b 1875 d 1898
Bishop Auckland
1896 Aston Villa 0
Tottenham Hotspur
1897 Blackpool 25 1

Wilson, Frank CF/IL
Chorley
1913 1914 Bury 16 6

Wilson, Frank IR
b Kettering
Rothwell Town
1926 Northampton Town 1
Higham Town

Wilson, Frederick Charles (Fred) CH
b Nottingham 10/11/1918 d 1993
Mansfield Baptists
1935 Mansfield Town 0
1936 Wolverhampton Wanderers 0
1938 1950 Bournemouth & Boscombe Ath 98
Weymouth

Wilson, Frederick William (Fred) IR
b Windermere
Bowness Rovers
1931 1932 Bolton Wanderers 4 1
1933 Bournemouth & Boscombe Ath 3 1
1934 Barnsley 0
Lancaster Town

From To Apps Goal

Wilson, George CH/CF
b Blackpool 14/1/1892 d 1961
Caps: FLge 4/England 12
Willows Rovers
Stanley Villa
Fleetwood
Willows Rovers
Morecambe
1911 1919 Blackpool 88 14
1919 1924 Sheffield Wednesday 185 5
1925 1929 Nelson 160 18

Wilson, George LB
Chorley
1914 Bolton Wanderers 26

Wilson, George Alfred OR
b Seaham Colliery 27/2/1910 d 1988
Seaham Colliery Welfare
1931 Southport 2
Murton Colliery Welfare

Wilson, George McIntyre IR/IL/OR
b Portobello 23/5/1905 d 1984
Portobello Thistle
Clydebank
Alloa Athletic
1927 Huddersfield Town 1 1
1928 Leeds United 3
1930 Chesterfield 3 1

Wilson, George Rupert GK
b Dublin
Dublin Amateurs
Bohemians
Bray Unknowns
1923 Clapton Orient 0
1924 1925 Bournemouth & Boscombe Ath 81
Witton Albion
Connah's Quay & Shotton
1927 New Brighton 0
1927 Notts County 0
Mold Town
Llanelly
Waterford
Bray Unknowns
Belfast Celtic
Larne

Wilson, George T GK
b Hull 1912
Deghorn
Galston
Ayr United
1935 York City 39

Wilson, George Wilfred RB
b Arlecdon 21/12/1906 d 1971
Workington
1934 Stockport County 2
1935 1936 Accrington Stanley 73

Wilson, George Williamson OL/IL
b Lochgelly 1884 d 1960
Caps: SLge 1/IrLge 1/Scotland 6
Thomson Rovers
Lochgelly Rangers
Buckhaven United
Cowdenbeath
Heart of Midlothian
1906 Everton 28 3
Distillery (loan)
1907 1914 Newcastle United 176 25
Raith Rovers
East Fife
Albion Rovers
St Andrew's (Vancouver)

Wilson, Gordon Gill LB
b West Auckland 19/6/1904 d 1947
Evenwood Juniors
1921 Middlesbrough (trial) 0
Evenwood Town
West Auckland
Scotswood
1925 1930 Hull City 28 1
1931 Luton Town 7
1932 1933 Norwich City 2
1934 Barrow 19
Linfield

Wilson, Henry (Harry) RH/LH/IL
b Marsden 3/5/1897
Marsden Rescue
1919 1927 South Shields 221 20
1928 1930 Blackpool 32 1
Aldershot

From To Apps Goal

Wilson, Henry (Harry) OL
b Belfast 1896
Caps: IrLge 3
Distillery
Belfast Celtic
Dunmurry
Glenavon
1920 Hull City 30 2
1921 Charlton Athletic 24 1
Aberaman Athletic
Linfield
Larne

Wilson, Henry LH
b Exeter
1921 Exeter City 4

Wilson, Hugh (Hughie) RH/LH/IL
b Mauchline 18/3/1869 d 1940
Caps: FLge 1/SLge 1/Scotland 4
Mauchline
2nd Ayrshire Rifle Volunteers
Newmilns
1890 1898 Sunderland 227 42
Bedminster
Bristol City
Third Lanark
Kilmarnock

Wilson, J OL
1892 Wolverhampton Wanderers 2

Wilson, Jack (Jock) RB/CH
b Ayrshire 1870
Caps: SLge 1
St Bernard's
New Brompton
1896 1897 Lincoln City 35
1897 Manchester City 1
1898 Small Heath 0
Swindon Town

Wilson, James (Jim) OR
b Scotland
Ayr Parkhouse
1892 1893 Bolton Wanderers 36 7
Millwall Athletic

Wilson, James OR/OL/IL
1894 1898 Darwen 32 8

Wilson, James IR/IL
b Glasgow 1880
St Mirren
1903 1910 Preston North End 162 32
1911 Oldham Athletic 0

Wilson, James OR
b Barrow q2 1891
Barrow North End
Dalton Casuals
Morecambe
1924 Barrow 2

Wilson, James (Jimmy) IR
b Seaham Harbour 1916
Seaham Colliery
1937 1938 Lincoln City 36 8
1939 Derby County (1)
Linfield

Wilson, James E (Jimmy) GK
b Garforth 1/1/1909
Rothwell Amateurs
1928 Leeds United 3
1929 Halifax Town 8
Shrewsbury Town
Shirebrook
1931 1932 Mansfield Town 41
Sutton Town
1933 Bradford Park Avenue 1
1934 1937 Bristol City 67
1938 Bristol Rovers 0

Wilson, James H GK
b Newcastle
Newcastle Bentonians
1912 1913 Newcastle United 3
North Shields Athletic

Wilson, James Joseph (Joe) OL
b Handsworth 1/1861 d 1952
Hamstead Swifts
Aston Unity
Stoke
Walsall Town
Aston Villa
Walsall Town
1888 1889 West Bromwich Albion 40 8
Kidderminster Harriers
Birmingham St George's

From To Apps Goal

Wilson, John RB
b Chilton 29/10/1904
Chilton Colliery Recreation Athletic
1924 1926 Middlesbrough 18
1927 Southend United 3

Wilson, John LB
b Trimdon 1909
Blackhall Colliery Welfare
Horden Colliery Welfare
1930 Hartlepools United 1

Wilson, John OL
b Rotherham
1935 Stockport County 0
Cradley Heath
1937 Wrexham 7

Wilson, John Ball (Jack) LB/OR
b New Washington 1/5/1916 d 1984
Blackhall Colliery Welfare
1935 Barnsley 3
Peterborough United
Margate
1938 Hartlepools United 25
1939 (Hartlepools United) (1)

Wilson, John Grant IR
b Edinburgh 1908
Dalkeith Thistle
1931 Swindon Town 0
1931 Plymouth Argyle 2
Cowdenbeath
St Bernard's
Banbury Spencer

Wilson, John Marshall RB/LB
b Dublin
Richmond United
Shelbourne
1933 Southport 0
1933 1937 Crewe Alexandra 112

Wilson, John Richard Montague IR
b Lanchester 30/10/1914 d 1988
Consett Parish Church
Medomsley Juniors
1934 West Bromwich Albion 0
1935 Port Vale 3

Wilson, John Robert (Jock) RH/LH
b Cambois
Bedlington United
1921 1922 Portsmouth 61
1923 1926 Reading 119 1
1927 1929 Northampton Town 24 1

Wilson, John Thomas (Jack) LH/IL/CF
b Leadgate 8/3/1897
Leadgate St Ives
Leadgate United
1919 Newcastle United 7 2
Leadgate Park
1921 Durham City 9 5
1922 1925 Stockport County 131 12
1926 1931 Manchester United 130 3
1932 Bristol City 18

Wilson, Joseph (Joe) CH
b Wigan 1884
Caps: SoLge 1
Wigan County
Darwen
1905 1907 Blackburn Rovers 42 4
Brighton & Hove Albion
Millwall Athletic
Rochdale
Fleetwood

Wilson, Joseph (Joe) OL
b Southwick, County Durham q2 1901
Southwick (Co Durham)
Leadgate Park
1920 Manchester United 0
1921 1922 Durham City 49 7
1923 Sheffield Wednesday 3
1924 1925 Norwich City 41 4
Southwick (Co Durham)

Wilson, Joseph (Joe) LB/RB
b Spennymoor
1928 1929 Gillingham 31
1930 Walsall 9

Wilson, Joseph (Joe) IL/IR
b Murton Colliery 1/9/1907 d 1985
Seaham Harbour
Murton Colliery Welfare
South Hetton Colliery Welfare
1930 Southport 12 8
1931 Barrow 26 12
1932 Watford 0
1933 Southport (trial) 1
Murton Colliery Welfare
Vauxhall Motor Works

From To | Apps Goal

Wilson, Joseph Alexander (Joe) IR
b High Spen 23/3/1911 d 1984
Spen Black & White
Winlaton Celtic
Tanfield Lea Institute
1934 1935 Newcastle United 28 5
1936 1946 Brighton & Hove Albion 156 15
1939 (Brighton & Hove Albion) (2) (1)

Wilson, Joseph William (Joe) CH/RB
b West Butsfield 29/9/1910 d 1996
Crook Town
Annfield Plain
Stanley United
1929 Newcastle United 1
1930 1934 Southend United 164 4
1935 1938 Brentford 60 2
1939 Reading (3)
1945 1946 Barnsley 20
Blyth Spartans

Wilson, Norman Henry RH
b Bishop Auckland q3 1901 d 1945
New Delaval Villa
Blyth Spartans
Dundee
1925 Bury 13
1926 Accrington Stanley 32
Aldershot

Wilson, Oliver GK
Leyton
1912 Woolwich Arsenal 1

Wilson, Peter IL
b Scotland
1911 Bristol City 10

Wilson, Robert GK
b Blantyre 1916
Bellshill Athletic
1937 Blackburn Rovers 3
Falkirk
Nelson

Wilson, Robert D LH
1922 Watford 1

Wilson, Robert S (Bob) CF
b Cambuslang
Cambuslang Rangers
Third Lanark
1924 Bradford Park Avenue 27 22
Shawsheen Indians
Fall River Marksmen
J & P Coats (Rhode Island)

Wilson, Samuel George OL
b Dublin
Caps: IrLge 1
Tritonville
Wilton YMCA
Shelbourne
1924 Liverpool (trial) 0
1925 New Brighton 12
1926 Clapton Orient 0
Bray Unknowns
St James's Gate

Wilson, Thomas IL
b 1875
Army
1895 Lincoln City 2
Oldham County

Wilson, Thomas (Tommy) CH
b Seaham 16/4/1896 d 1948
Caps: FLge 3/England 1
Seaham Albion
1913 Sunderland 0
Seaham Colliery
1919 1931 Huddersfield Town 448 4
1931 Blackpool 18

Wilson, Thomas LB
b Belfast
Caps: Ireland Amat
Portadown
1925 Stockport County 4

Wilson, Thomas RH
b Cambois
Cambois Athletic
Shankhouse
1927 Bradford Park Avenue (trial) 0
1927 Sheffield Wednesday (trial) 0
New Delaval Villa
1928 Ashington 22
Wallaw United
Blyth Spartans
Cambois Welfare
Morpeth Town

From To | Apps Goal

Wilson, Thomas (Tom) IL
b Coppull 31/1/1910 d 1986
Adlington
Darwen
Blackburn Rovers 0
Chorley
Darwen
1930 Wigan Borough (trial) 5 2
Morecambe
Coppull Moor
Heskin Parish
Cheshall Hall Colliery

Wilson, Thomas Carter (Tom) OL
b Preston 20/10/1877 d 1940
Fishwick Ramblers
Ashton-in-Makerfield
West Manchester
Ashton Town
Ashton North End
Oldham County
Swindon Town
1898 Blackburn Rovers 1
Swindon Town
Millwall Athletic
1900 1901 Aston Villa 5
London Caledonians
Queen's Park Rangers
Kensal Rise United
1904 1905 Bolton Wanderers 20 5
1906 Leeds City 20 2
1907 Manchester United 1
Queen's Park Rangers

Wilson, Thomas Harold (Tom) IL/IR
b Lewisham 23/11/1917 d 1959
Sheppey United
1936 1937 Gillingham 66 4
Gravesend & Northfleet

Wilson, Thomas Henry (Tom) CH/RH/CF
b Lambeth 9/12/1902 d 1992
Walthamstow Avenue
1924 1925 Charlton Athletic 15 4
1926 1929 Wigan Borough 108 4
1930 Cardiff City 1
1931 Charlton Athletic 18
1932 1934 Southend United 12

Wilson, Thomas T CH/LH
b Newcastle
Morpeth Harriers
1907 1909 Middlesbrough 10
Heart of Midlothian

Wilson, Walter LB
b 1865
1888 Everton 1

Wilson, Walter RH
Mansfield Town
1894 Burslem Port Vale 5
Nelson

Wilson, Walter (Wattie) LB
b Armadale 4/11/1879 d 1926
Dykehead
Queen's Park
Celtic
Clyde
Dykehead
Albion Rovers
Bathgate
Peebles Rovers
1907 1914 Lincoln City 171 6
Fosdyke Watermen

Wilson, Walter LH
1908 Stockport County 6
Denton

Wilson, William (Billy) RH
b 1876
Maybole
1897 Bury 1

Wilson, William (Billy) RB
b Tyneside
South Shields Athletic
1902 Newcastle United 4
1903 1904 Bradford City 58 1
Oldham Athletic
Failsworth

Wilson, William (Bill) CH/RH/OL
b Seaham 1902
Seaham Harbour
Portsmouth
1920 Port Vale 2
1921 Walsall 19
Stafford Rangers
Worcester City
1925 Bristol Rovers 24
Willenhall
1927 Brighton & Hove Albion 0

From To | Apps Goal

Wilson, William (Billy) OR
b Burnley q1 1899
1921 Nelson 1
Morecambe

Wilson, William (Billy) LB/LH/RB
b Middlesbrough 26/7/??
Hurst
1921 1926 Manchester City 48
1927 1929 Stockport County 108 1
Ashton National

Wilson, William (Willie) GK
b Port Seaton 7/9/1900
Musselburgh Bruntonians
Peebles Rovers
1925 1928 Newcastle United 127
1929 1933 Millwall 148
Duns
Dunfermline Athletic
Peebles Rovers
Penicuik Athletic

Wilson, William IR
b Sheffield
1930 Watford 1

Wilson, William RH
b Sheffield 1915
Lopham Street WMC
1934 Bradford City 1
Newark Town

Wilson, William (Billy) IL
b New Seaham
1935 Millwall 1
1937 1938 Aldershot 18 1
Tunbridge Wells Rangers

Wilson, William Arthur (Billy) RH
b Newcastle 17/3/1896 d 1996
1919 Newcastle United 0
1922 Merthyr Town 2
West Stanley
Carlisle United

Wilson, William Raymond LH/RH/CH
b Rotherham q4 1910
Scarborough
Scunthorpe & Lindsey United
Frickley Colliery
1933 Rotherham United 11
1934 1935 Bristol Rovers 6
1936 Gillingham 5

Wilson, William Thomas GK
b Belper q2 1878
Heanor
Alfreton
1901 1902 Leicester Fosse 5
Whitwick White Cross
Heanor United

Wiltshire, Herbert LH
b Birmingham q3 1871
1893 Lincoln City 27

Wimbs, Patrick J RH
b 1896 d 1966
1923 Merthyr Town 2

Winchester, John RB
b Kirkham q3 1886 d 1960
1906 1909 Preston North End 37
Eccles Borough

Windle, Charles OR
b Barnsley 8/1/1917 d 1975
1938 Bury 0
1939 Exeter City (2)
1946 Bristol Rovers 7 1
Hurst

Windle, Edward Roebuck (Paddy) LH
b Rotherham 6/9/1899 d 1980
Dalton Juniors
Kilnhurst Colliery
Frickley Colliery
1923 Rotherham County 2
Denaby United
Shirebrook
Denaby United
Wath Athletic

Windmill, Joseph William LH
b Brierley Hill q3 1881 d 1927
Saltley College
Halesowen
1903 1908 Aston Villa 42 1

From To | Apps Goal

Windridge, James Edwin (Jimmy) IL
b Sparkbrook 21/10/1882 d 1939
Caps: England 8
Small Heath Alma
1902 1904 Small Heath 26 7
1905 1911 Chelsea 143 54
1911 1913 Middlesbrough 68 11
1913 1914 Birmingham 29 11

Windsor, Foster (Frank) GK
b Bristol 9/3/1908 d 1985
Wesley Rovers
1932 1933 Bristol Rovers 20
Bath City

Winfield, William OL
b Gresley 1/11/1896 d 1982
Hallam
Frickley Colliery
1927 Chesterfield 1

Wingham, Harold Charles (Harry) LB/RB
b Selsey 25/6/1895 d 1969
Thorneycrofts
1923 Bournemouth & Boscombe Ath 18
1924 Clapton Orient 5
1925 1926 Norwich City 43 1
Salisbury City

Wingrove, Joseph LB
b Southall q2 1894 d 1922
Uxbridge
1920 Queen's Park Rangers 24

Winn, Edward W CH
b Ormskirk
South Liverpool
1921 Tranmere Rovers 1

Winn, Norman Joseph OL
b Lancaster 24/8/1900 d 1972
Lancaster Town
Morecambe
1921 1925 Bradford City 86 10
Chorley
Lancaster Town
Morecambe

Winnell, Walter IR
b Sheffield 4/2/1908 d 1986
Park Labour
1928 Luton Town 0
1929 Bristol Rovers 4 1
1930 Chesterfield 0
Grantham
Wombwell

Winship, Edward (Teddy) LB/RB
b Prudhoe 1901 d 1929
Prudhoe Castle
1920 Crystal Palace 0
Prudhoe Castle
1922 1924 Coventry City 79
Kidderminster Harriers
1926 1928 Brentford 86

Winship, Thomas (Wee) OL
b Byker 14/7/1890 d 1976
Sleekburn Villa
Wallsend Park Villa
1910 1912 Woolwich Arsenal 28 3
1912 Fulham 2
1913 1914 Woolwich Arsenal 27 4
1921 1925 Darlington 146 17
1926 Crewe Alexandra 21 1
Wallsend
Trimdon Grange Colliery
Cockfield
Spen Black & White
Marley Hill UCG

Winskill, William (Bill) IR
b Salford q1 1906 d 1954
Manchester North End
1924 Manchester City 0
Ashton National
Congleton Town
1928 Accrington Stanley 5

Winsper, Thomas (Tom) RH
b West Bromwich q2 1895 d 1968
Halesowen Town
Hednesford Town
1921 Bristol Rovers 22
Willenhall
Shrewsbury Town

Winstanley, George IR
1896 Blackpool 2

Winstanley, Ira William (Bill) RB
b Prestwich 26/10/1911 d 1985
Altrincham
1935 1938 Stoke City 48
Trafford Park

From To Apps Goal

Winster, Richard Carl (Carl) OR
b Shap 11/4/1900 d 1978
Penrith
1928 1929 Carlisle United 5 1

Winter, Clifford IL
b Gateshead q2 1884
1904 Newcastle United 0
1905 Gainsborough Trinity 6 1
South Shields Adelaide
Byker East End

Winter, Daniel Thomas (Danny) RB
b Tonypandy 14/6/1918 d 2004
Caps: Wales War 2
Maes-y-Hof
1936 1938 Bolton Wanderers 34
1939 (Bolton Wanderers) (3)
1945 1950 Chelsea 131
Worcester City

Winter, George OL
b Carlisle 1908
1935 Carlisle United 1

Winter, Percy OR
Chesham United
1924 1925 Charlton Athletic 6
Chesham United
St Albans City

Winter, Wallace OR
b Todmorden 25/5/1918 d 1999
1938 Halifax Town 2

Winter, William (Billy) GK
b Liverpool 15/2/1904
Bootle Celtic
1925 1927 Wigan Borough 83
Brenka

Winterbottom, (Sir) Walter CH
b Oldham 31/3/1913 d 2002
Mossley
1936 1937 Manchester United 25
Mossley

Winterburn, Alfred (Alf) IL/OL
b Bury 29/5/1902 d 1988
1919 Bolton Wanderers 1
Hurst
1921 1922 Crewe Alexandra 34 9

Winterhalder, Arthur OL/OR
b Oxford q4 1884 d 1937
West Ham United
1907 Everton 4
1908 1910 Preston North End 54 6
Accrington Stanley
1911 Preston North End 2

Winterhalder, Herbert Tirrell OR
b Kettering q2 1879 d 1946
Kettering
1902 Sheffield United 11 2
Plymouth Argyle
Wellingborough
West Ham United
Kettering

Winthrop, Senhouse Wilfred (Wilfred) IR
b Brampton, Cumberland 12/8/1909 d 1977
1934 Carlisle United 2

Wipfler, Charles John (Charlie) OL/IL
b Trowbridge 15/7/1915 d 1983
McCall's
Trowbridge Town
1934 Bristol Rovers 18 5
Heart of Midlothian
1937 1938 Watford 22 7
Frickley Colliery
Canterbury City
1946 Watford 13 1
Gravesend & Northfleet

Wisden, Alan Leslie CF
b Hastings 31/1/1896 d 1978
Rock-a-Nore (Hastings)
1920 Brighton & Hove Albion 1
Hastings & St Leonards

Wise, Albert William (Micky) GK
b Olney q4 1884 d 1965
Irthlingborough
Wellingborough
1905 Chelsea 0
1906 1908 Bradford City 22
Brentford

Wise, Harold Arter IR
b Bow q2 1895 d 1957
Custom House
1914 Leicester Fosse 11 1
Charlton Athletic

From To Apps Goal

Wise, Kenneth Kitchener (Ken) OL/CF
b Swindon 26/11/1914 d 1981
Swindon Corinthians
1935 West Ham United 0
1936 1938 Swindon Town 13 1

Wishart, James Walker McNab (McNab) CH
b Darvel 1886 d 1967
Darvel
Kilmarnock
Carlisle United
1909 Sheffield United 2
Carlisle United
Haslingden
Halifax Town

Witcomb, Douglas Frank (Doug) RH/LH
b Cwm 18/4/1918 d 1997
Caps: Wales War 7/Wales 3
Cwm Villa
1935 Tottenham Hotspur 0
Northfleet
Enfield
1938 1946 West Bromwich Albion 55 3
1946 1952 Sheffield Wednesday 224 12
1953 Newport County 25
Llandudno Town
Redditch United
IHB Alloys & Alkamatic Works

Witham, Richard (Dick) LB
b Bowburn 4/5/1915 d 1999
Durham City
1933 Huddersfield Town 4
1933 1937 Blackpool 149
1946 Oldham Athletic 5

Witheridge, Thomas Henry (Tommy) IR
b Amersham 25/5/1911 d 1985
1930 Tottenham Hotspur 0
1931 Clapton Orient 1

Withers, Edward Peter (Peter 'Tosh') IR
b Ower 8/9/1915 d 1994
Clarke's College
1936 Southampton 6
1937 Bristol Rovers 17 4
Bramtoco Sports

Withington, Sidney Harry (Harry) RB
1892 Walsall Town Swifts 20

Witton, Joseph (Joe) CF
b Newport 14/12/1908
1928 1930 Newport County 15 5
GPO

Woffinden, Richard Shaw LH/RH
b Rotherham 20/2/1917 d 1987
Winterwell Athletic
1938 Barnsley 2
1938 Hartlepools United 15 1
1939 Barnsley 0
Peterborough United

Wolf, George GK
b Newcastle 23/4/1903 d 1978
Walker Celtic
1929 1930 Blackpool 28
1931 1932 Preston North End 45
1933 1934 Carlisle United 63
Blyth Spartans

Wolfe, George CH
b Plumstead q4 1878 d 1958
Northfleet
Folkestone
1900 1902 Woolwich Arsenal 5
Swindon Town
1905 1910 Nottingham Forest 128 1

Wolfe, Thomas Henry (Tom) IL/LH/CH
b Barry Dock 7/3/1900 d 1954
Caps: Wales Amat
Atlantic Mills
Barry
1921 Swansea Town 0
1922 Sheffield Wednesday 0
1923 Coventry City 10 1
1924 Southend United 11
1924 1926 Fulham 27 2
1927 1928 Charlton Athletic 10
1929 Bristol Rovers 2
Westerham

Wollaston, Arthur Wilbert RH
b Shrewsbury 3/1865 d 1933
Stafford Road
1888 Aston Villa 4
Chirk

Wollaston, William OR
b Willenhall 6/12/1866 d 1933
Willenhall Pickwick
1910 1911 West Bromwich Albion 25 2
Darlaston

From To Apps Goal

Wolstencroft, Albert IR
Northwich Victoria
1921 Rochdale 1

Wolstenholme, Arthur IR/IL/CF
b Bolton 14/5/1889 d 1958
Tonge
1907 1909 Oldham Athletic 30 10
1909 1911 Blackpool 77 14
New Brompton
Norwich City
1914 Lincoln City 30 7
1919 Oldham Athletic 22 2
1920 Newport County 29 8
1921 Darlington 29 17
1922 1924 Nelson 68 17

Wolstenholme, John GK
b Bury 1880 d 1950
Bury Unitarians
1905 1908 Bury 18

Wolstenholme, Samuel (Sam) RH
b Little Lever 16/3/1878 d 1933
Caps: FLge 2/England 3
Farnworth Alliance
Horwich
1897 1903 Everton 160 8
1904 1907 Blackburn Rovers 97 1
Croydon Common
Norwich City
Chester

Wolstenholme, Thomas (Tom) LH
b Little Lever q1 1882
1902 1904 Blackpool 93
1905 1906 Bolton Wanderers 9
1907 Burnley 38
1908 1909 Bradford Park Avenue 39 1
Nelson

Womack, Francis (Frank) LB/RB
b Wortley 16/9/1888 d 1968
Caps: FLge 2
Lopham Street
Rawmarsh Albion
1908 1927 Birmingham 491
Worcester City
1929 Torquay United 20

Wombwell, Richard (Dicky) OL/IL/OR
b Nottingham q3 1877 d 1943
Red Hill
Bulwell
Ilkeston Town
1899 1901 Derby County 85 17
1902 1904 Bristol City 92 19
1904 1906 Manchester United 47 3
Heart of Midlothian
Brighton & Hove Albion
1907 1908 Blackburn Rovers 15 1
Ilkeston United

Wonnacott, Clarence Benjamin (Ben) IL
b Clowne 31/12/1909 d 1989
Caps: LoI 1
Clipstone Colliery Welfare
Mansfield Town
1930 1931 Northampton Town 13 4
Shelbourne
1932 Mansfield Town 15 2
Racing Club Calais
Kidderminster Harriers

Wood, Alan Esplin OL/IL
b Walsall
Talbot Stead Tube Works
1920 1921 Crystal Palace 35 9
1922 1924 Coventry City 82 17
Willenhall

Wood, Albert IL/IR
b Seaham Harbour 25/4/1903 d 1965
Seaham Harbour
1927 1930 Sunderland 30 11
1931 1934 Fulham 22 9
1935 Crewe Alexandra 42 14
1936 Tranmere Rovers 37 11
1937 1938 New Brighton 46 11
1939 Hartlepools United 0

Wood, Alexander (Alex) IR/IL
b Glasgow 1906
Greenock Overton
Airdrieonians
Albion Rovers (loan)
1928 Brentford 1
1929 Charlton Athletic 1
1930 Fulham 0
Larne

From To Apps Goal

Wood, Alexander Lochlan (Sandy) LB
b Lochgelly 12/6/1907 d 1987
Caps: Scotland Sch/USA
Gary Soccer Club
Chicago Bricklayers
Holley Carburetors (Detroit)
Brooklyn Wanderers
1932 1935 Leicester City 52
1936 Nottingham Forest 21
Colchester United
Chelmsford City

Wood, Alexander M LB
St Bernard's
1900 1901 Sheffield United 6
St Bernard's

Wood, Alfred CF
b Workington
1904 Blackpool 0
1905 Burnley 5 1
Workington

Wood, Alfred (Alf) OR
1926 Crewe Alexandra 2

Wood, Alfred Josiah Edward (Alf) CH/LH/IL
b Smallthorne 6/1876 d 1919
Smallthorne Albion
1892 1894 Burslem Port Vale 63 20
1895 1900 Stoke 118 10
1900 1904 Aston Villa 103 7
1905 1906 Derby County 60 2
Bradford Park Avenue

Wood, Alfred Robert (Alf) GK
b Aldridge 14/5/1915 d 2001
Sutton Town
Nuneaton Town
1937 1951 Coventry City 221
1951 1954 Northampton Town 139
1955 1958 Coventry City 13

Wood, Arthur CF
b 1884
Wingate
Crook Town
Charlton Rovers
1907 1909 Gainsborough Trinity 40 15
Doncaster Rovers

Wood, Arthur GK
b Walsall 14/1/1894 d 1941
Portsmouth
1920 Southampton 2
1921 1930 Clapton Orient 373
Ryde Sports
Newport (Isle of Wight)

Wood, Arthur Basil IR/IL/CF
b Southampton 8/5/1890 d 1977
St Mary's Athletic
Eastleigh Athletic
1911 1914 Fulham 21 1
1920 1921 Gillingham 49 11
Hamilton Academical
Northfleet
1922 Newport County 12 3
1923 1924 Queen's Park Rangers 20
Regent Palace Hotel Staff

Wood, Basil OL
b Stocksbridge 9/11/1900 d 1977
Crook Town
1920 1921 Leeds United 56 2
1922 Sheffield Wednesday 0

Wood, Cecil John Burditt IL/RH
b Northampton 21/11/1875 d 1960
Leicester YMCA
Market Harborough
1896 1899 Leicester Fosse 3 1
Market Harborough
Leicester Banks
Leicester Amateurs

Wood, Edmund Eli (Ed) CH
b Shirley 10/12/1903 d 1986
Rhyl Athletic
1922 1924 Northampton Town 49 3
1926 Birmingham 1
Rhyl Athletic
1928 1929 Newcastle United 9
Rhyl Athletic
Runcorn

Wood, Edward John (Jackie) IL/OL/IR
b Canning Town 23/10/1919 d 1993
Caps: England Amat
Leytonstone
1937 1948 West Ham United 58 13
1939 (West Ham United) (3) (2)
1949 Leyton Orient 9 1
Margate

From To Apps Goal

Wood, Frederick W Raymond (Freddy) GK
b Bromley
Tufnell Park
Clapton
Crystal Palace
1920 1921 Millwall Athletic 4
1922 1924 Charlton Athletic 92
Grays Thurrock
Bostall Heath

Wood, Harold F OL
b West Bromwich 1870 d 1929
West Bromwich Sandwell
Oldbury Town
1892 West Bromwich Albion 1 1
Walsall Victoria
Oldbury Town

Wood, Harry IL/LB/IR
b Walsall 2/8/1868 d 1951
Caps: FLge 4/England 3
Walsall Swifts
1888 1890 Wolverhampton Wanderers 60 35
Walsall Town Swifts
1891 1897 Wolverhampton Wanderers 181 74
Southampton

Wood, Harry 'Bud' IL/IR
b Barrow 31/12/1911 d 1994
Vickers Athletic
1932 1936 Barrow 10 2
Netherfield
1947 1948 Barrow 11 1

Wood, James (Jimmy) OR
b Royton
Crompton Albion
Hyde United
1926 Bournemouth & Boscombe Ath 7 1
Hyde United
1929 1934 West Ham United 63 13
1935 Crystal Palace 10 4

Wood, James Lindsay CF
b Byker 15/1/1901 d 1982
Close Works
Methley
1922 Hull City 2 2
Bedlington United
Jarrow
Workington

Wood, James William RB
b Sunderland 8/3/1893
Hylton Colliery
1912 Sunderland 0
South Shields
1914 1922 Huddersfield Town 127
1922 1925 Blackpool 55
Fall River Marksmen
Springfield Babes
Providence Clamdiggers

Wood, John IR/IL
b Seacombe 1885
Port Sunlight
Southern United
1905 1906 Derby County 37 7
1907 1908 Manchester City 28 6
Plymouth Argyle
1910 Huddersfield Town 10
Aberdeen
Hibernian

Wood, John OR
b Leven 17/2/?? d 1971
Montraive Juniors
Black Watch
Hibernian
Dunfermline Athletic
Lochgelly United
Dumbarton
1922 Manchester United 15 1
Lochgelly United
St Mirren
East Stirlingshire
Hamilton Academical
Cowdenbeath
East Fife
Alloa Athletic (trial)

Wood, John LH
1925 Coventry City 1

Wood, John T OR
b 1902
Daventry
1921 Northampton Town 1

From To Apps Goal

Wood, Leonard (Len) CF
b Wednesbury q1 1903
Stourbridge
1924 Fulham 4 2
1926 Accrington Stanley 0
Dartford
Chatham
Hounslow Ramblers

Wood, Leonard LH/RH
1934 Huddersfield Town 0
1935 1937 Mansfield Town 46 3

Wood, Matthew Currie (Matt) LB/RB
b Hobson Village 1892 d 1923
Hobson Wanderers
1911 1914 West Bromwich Albion 17
Kidderminster Harriers

Wood, Norman Arthur IL
b Tooting 1889 d 1916
Crystal Palace
Plymouth Argyle
Croydon Common
1912 Chelsea 0
1913 1914 Stockport County 58 12

Wood, Robert R RB
1905 1906 Burton United 19

Wood, Samuel F IL
b West Bromwich 1915
1935 Walsall 4 1
1936 Accrington Stanley 0

Wood, Stanley (Stan) OL
b Winsford 1/7/1905 d 1967
Caps: FLge 1
Whitegate Victoria
Winsford United
1928 1937 West Bromwich Albion 256 58
1938 1945 Halifax Town 35 6
1939 (Halifax Town) (3) (1)

Wood, Thomas (Tommy) IL/LH/IR
b Wednesbury 4/1908
Wednesbury United
Shrewsbury Town
1930 1936 Aston Villa 62 2
1936 1938 Newport County 104 25
1939 (Newport County) (3)

Wood, William (Willie) IR/CF
b Middleton 1878 d 1947
Caps: FLge 1
Middleton
1898 1904 Bury 189 63
Fulham
Norwich City
Leyton
New Brompton

Wood, William IR
b Parkgate 1/1/1900
Retford
Wombwell
1921 1922 Oldham Athletic 24 3
1923 Northampton Town 32 6
1924 Swansea Town 0
Wellingborough Town
Rugby Town

Wood, William OR
b Stoke-on-Trent
1924 Stoke 0
1925 Aberdare Athletic 2

Wood, William LH/OL/RH
b Blackburn
1931 1932 Blackburn Rovers 7
1932 Burnley 7
1933 Mansfield Town 5
Chorley
Darwen

Wood, William C GK
1926 Newcastle United 0
1927 Rochdale 1

Wood, William Horace RB
b Mereclough 5/4/1910
1930 1933 Burnley 32
Yeovil & Petters United

Woodall, Harry CF
b Newport 1900
1920 Newport County 1

Woodards, Charles Ernest CF
b East Ham 6/10/1902 d 1965
Guildford City
1928 1929 Millwall 8 4

From To Apps Goal

Woodards, Daniel James (Dan) CH/LH
b Upton Park 18/11/1886 d 1964
St Ethelburga's
West Ham United
Hastings & St Leonards
1919 1920 West Ham United 16

Woodburn, James (Jimmy) LH/IL/RH
b Rutherglen 29/1/1917 d 1978
Kilsyth Emmet
Coltness United
1938 1947 Newcastle United 44 4
1939 (Newcastle United) (3)
1948 1951 Gateshead 131 10

Woodburn, John CH
b Darvel
Hurlford
1919 West Ham United 4
Peterborough & Fletton United

Woodcock, Wilfrid (Wilf) IR/CF/IL
b Ashton-under-Lyne 15/2/1892 d 1966
Waterloo
Abbey Hey
Hindley Central (trial)
Stalybridge Celtic
1913 1919 Manchester United 58 20
1920 1921 Manchester City 15 2
1921 1923 Stockport County 75 23
1924 Wigan Borough 14 2
Sandbach Ramblers
CWS Balloon Street

Woodfield, John OR
1897 Lincoln City 1
Kettering

Woodford, George Arthur LB/RB
b Lymington 22/4/1915 d 1966
Lymington
1935 1936 Norwich City 10
1937 1938 Southampton 7
Lymington

Woodgate, John Terence (Terry) OR/OL
b East Ham 11/12/1919 d 1985
Beckton
1938 1952 West Ham United 259 48
Peterborough United

Woodger, George (Lady) IL
b Croydon 3/9/1883 d 1961
Caps: England 1
Thornton Heath Wednesday
Croydon Glenrose
Croydon Wanderers
Crystal Palace
1910 1913 Oldham Athletic 115 22
1914 Tottenham Hotspur 0

Woodhall, George (Spry) OR/CF
b West Bromwich 5/9/1863 d 1924
Caps: England 2
West Bromwich All Saints
Churchfield Foresters
1888 1891 West Bromwich Albion 44 10
1892 1893 Wolverhampton Wanderers 18 1
Berwick Rangers (Worcester)
Oldbury Town

Woodhall, William Henry (Billy) CF
b Lower Gornal 12/1900 d 1963
Bilston United
1923 1924 Bristol Rovers 38 13
Dudley Bean

Woodhead, Clifford (Cliff) LB/RB
b Darfield 17/8/1908 d 1985
Dearne Valley Old Boys
Ardsley Athletic
1928 Southport (trial) 0
Denaby United
1930 1938 Hull City 305
1939 (Hull City) (2)
Goole Town

Woodhouse, Christopher Henry (Charlie) OL
b Sheringham 5/2/1902 d 1978
Sheringham
1921 Norwich City 13 3
Sheringham

Woodhouse, Harry OL
b Chesterfield 24/4/1904 d 1981
Staveley
1925 Arsenal 0
Workington
Markham Sports
Staveley Town
1928 Chesterfield 2
Buxton

From To Apps Goal

Woodhouse, John (Jack) RH/LH
b Smethwick
Caps: SoLge 1
Cheddleton Asylum
1920 1923 Brighton & Hove Albion 117

Woodhouse, Robert Henry (Bob) LH
b Middlesbrough 8/1/1897 d 1974
Spennymoor United
1922 1923 Durham City 57 1
Spennymoor United
1925 1926 Durham City 54 2

Woodhouse, Roland Thomas IL/IR
b Leyland 15/1/1897 d 1969
1919 1925 Preston North End 206 52
1926 Everton 2
1927 1929 Wrexham 113 21
1930 Halifax Town 13 2
Chorley

Woodhouse, Samuel Herbert GK
b Walton-le-Dale q4 1881
Walton-le-Dale
1900 Preston North End 2
Walton-le-Dale

Woodhouse, Stanley (Stan) LH/RH/IL
b Warrington 10/2/1899 d 1977
Monks Hall
1921 1923 Bury 23 5
1924 1935 Southampton 351 5
Basingstoke Town

Woodland, Arthur LH/RH
b Mount Pleasant, Liverpool 3/8/1889 d 1941
St Polycarp's
Kirkdale
Zingari
St Helens Town
Norwich City
1919 1921 Notts County 48 1
1922 Southend United 31 1
Pontypridd
Leamington Town

Woodland, Thomas (Tommy) OL/OR
b Alfreton
Riddings St James'
1902 Doncaster Rovers 4
1903 Chesterfield Town 10 2
Worksop Town
Rotherham County
1906 1907 Nottingham Forest 5 2
Rotherham County
Alfreton Town
Burton United

Woodley, Victor Robert (Vic) GK
b Cippenham 26/2/1910 d 1978
Caps: FLge 4/England War 2/England 19
Cippenham
Windsor & Eton
1931 1938 Chelsea 252
1939 (Chelsea) (3)
Bath City
1945 1946 Derby County 30
Bath City

Woodley, William Percy LB
b Bromley-by-Bow q1 1897
Millwall Athletic
Grenadier Guards
1920 1921 Millwall Athletic 50

Woodman, John Albert Edward (Jack) CF
b Bristol 9/7/1914 d 1984
Melrose (Bristol)
1935 1936 Bristol Rovers 39 21
1937 Preston North End 0
1938 Swindon Town 0
1939 Wrexham (3) (1)

Woodruff, Arthur RB/CH
b Barnsley 12/4/1913 d 1983
Caps: FLge 2
1934 Bradford City 0
1936 1951 Burnley 271
1939 (Burnley) (2)
1952 Workington 11
Worcester City
Northwich Victoria

Woodruff, Charles Lewis (Charlie) OR
b Grantham 19/1/1884 d 1943
Grantham Avenue
1908 1909 Tottenham Hotspur 10 1
Doncaster Rovers
Grantham

Woods, Albert LH
b Faversham 24/7/1907 d 1982
1930 Gillingham 2
1931 Brentford 0

From	To		Apps	Goal
Woods, Cyril			IR/CF	
b Tinsley 6/3/1915			d 1999	
1935		Bolton Wanderers	0	
1937		Swindon Town	4	
1938		Hartlepools United	25	6
1939		Hull City	0	
Woods, F			CH	
1889		Bolton Wanderers	5	
Woods, Harold (Harry)			IL/IR/CF	
b St Helens 12/3/1890				
		St Helens Recreation		
		Ashton Town		
		St Helens Town		
		Norwich City		
1919	1921	South Shields	92	23
1921	1922	Newcastle United	14	2
1923	1925	Arsenal	70	21
1926	1929	Luton Town	97	22
		North Shields		
Woods, Henry (Harry)			CF	
b Wallasey q1 1911				
		Rainford North End		
1933		New Brighton	1	
Woods, J			LB	
1888		Accrington	2	
Woods, James			IL	
1888		Burnley	1	
Woods, James (Jimmy)			GK	
b Bolton				
1914		Bolton Wanderers	0	
1919		Bury	3	
Woods, John (Jack)			CF	
b St Helens q4 1896				
		Stalybridge Celtic		
1921		Halifax Town	21	12
		York City		
Woods, Jonathan			CF/OL	
b Workington 1889				
		Workington		
1910	1911	Burnley	2	
Woods, Leonard George			OL	
		St Helens Town		
1907		Everton	4	
Woods, Samuel			IL	
b Glasgow 1871				
		Morton		
1896		Stoke	1	
		Morton		
Woods, Samuel			IR/CF	
		Earlestown		
1908	1909	Bolton Wanderers	5	2
		Accrington Stanley		
Woods, Thomas			LH	
b Atherton				
		Daisy Hill United		
1936		Plymouth Argyle	0	
1937		Bristol City	7	
Woodvine, Albert			OR	
b Kirk Sandall 16/6/1917			d 1972	
		Pilkington Recreation		
1937		Leicester City	1	
Woodward, Arthur			LH/CH/LB	
b Watford 18/11/1906			d 1984	
		Watford St Mary's		
1926	1938	Watford	388	16
1939		(Watford)	(3)	
		Scammells		
Woodward, Benjamin			OR/OL	
b Rotherham 18/2/1914			d 2001	
		St Ann's Rovers		
1934	1935	Rotherham United	2	
Woodward, Fred			RH	
b Ashton-under-Lyne q4 1899			d 1963	
		Hindley Wesleyans		
		Wellington Temperance		
1920		Burnley	0	
1921		Wigan Borough	3	
Woodward, Harry			LB/RB	
		Hednesford Town		
1908	1909	Burnley	3	
Woodward, Harry			OR	
b Troedyrhiw				
1921		Merthyr Town	2	
Woodward, J			RB	
1892		Walsall Town Swifts	9	

From	To		Apps	Goal
Woodward, John			RH/CH/RB	
b Halesowen				
1923	1926	Merthyr Town	126	6
Woodward, Joseph Henry (Joe)			GK	
b Catford 2/1904			d 1974	
		Catford Southend		
1926		Watford	2	
1927		Southend United	2	
1927		Clapton Orient	1	
1927	1928	Queen's Park Rangers	10	
1929		Merthyr Town	19	
		Bexleyheath & Welling		
		Canterbury Waverley		
Woodward, Laurence (Dai)			RH/LH	
b Troedyrhiw 5/7/1918			d 1997	
		Folkestone		
1938		Wolverhampton Wanderers	0	
1938		Walsall (loan)	29	
1946	1953	Bournemouth & Boscombe Ath	272	7
Woodward, Maurice			CH/LB/RH	
b Enderby 12/10/1891			d 1950	
		Enderby Granite		
		Enderby Town		
1913		Leicester Fosse	2	
		Southend United		
1919	1921	Wolverhampton Wanderers	33	1
1922		Bristol Rovers	0	
Woodward, Thomas (Tom)			OR/OL	
b Westhoughton 8/12/1917			d 1994	
		White Horse Temperance		
1935	1949	Bolton Wanderers	152	18
1949	1950	Middlesbrough	19	6
		Wigan Athletic		
Woodward, Thomas George			RH	
b Troedyrhiw 13/11/1900			d 1981	
Caps: WLge 1				
		Troedyrhiw Stars		
		Merthyr Thursdays		
1921		Merthyr Town	0	
1922		Chesterfield	4	
		Bridgend		
		Llanelly		
1924	1925	Preston North End	24	1
1926	1928	Swansea Town	59	
1929		Merthyr Town	35	2
		Llanelly		
		Taunton Town		
		Troedyrhiw		
Woodward, Vivian			IR/IL/LH	
b Troedyrhiw 20/5/1914				
Caps: Wales War 1				
		Troedyrhiw		
		Folkestone		
1935	1946	Fulham	92	25
1939		(Fulham)	(3)	(1)
1946	1947	Millwall	42	13
1948	1949	Brentford	20	4
1949	1950	Aldershot	53	5
		Bedford Town		
Woodward, Vivian John			CF/IL/IR	
b Kennington 3/6/1879			d 1954	
Caps: FLge 3/England Amat/England 23				
		Ascham College		
		Clacton		
		Harwich & Parkeston		
		Chelmsford Town		
1908		Tottenham Hotspur	27	18
		Chelmsford Town		
1909	1914	Chelsea	106	30
Woodward, William (Billy)			IL	
b West Auckland 2/7/1907			d 1975	
		Evenwood Colliery		
1927		Hartlepools United (trial)	0	
		Chilton Colliery Recreation Athletic		
1929		Newcastle United	0	
		West Stanley		
		Crook Town		
		Spennymoor United		
1931		Exeter City	7	2
		Bath City		
1932		Manchester United	0	
1933	1935	Tranmere Rovers	102	38
1936	1937	Chesterfield	29	13
1937		Stockport County	7	
Wooldridge, William Thomas (Billy)			CF/CH/IL	
b Netherton 10/8/1878			d 1945	
Caps: FLge 1				
		Netherton St Mary's		
		Dudley Royal		
		Cradley Heath St Luke's		
		Wednesbury Old Athletic		
1900	1910	Wolverhampton Wanderers	328	81
		Croydon Common		

From	To		Apps	Goal
Woolf, Levi James			IR	
b Johannesburg, South Africa 28/1/1916			d 2003	
		JRAS (Johannesburg)		
1937		Southampton (trial)	1	
		Guildford City		
Woolfall, Thomas			RB/LB	
b Darwen				
1898		Darwen	30	
1899		Burnley	33	
1900	1901	Bolton Wanderers	21	
Woolfe, J			IR	
1893	1895	Crewe Alexandra	17	2
Woolfe, S			OR	
1892	1895	Crewe Alexandra	12	
Woolhouse, Henry (Harry)			CF/IL	
b Ecclesfield q4 1867			d 1911	
		Sheffield		
1892	1894	Sheffield Wednesday	16	10
Woolhouse, Reuben (Ben)			OR	
b Sheffield 25/11/1904			d 1986	
		Ecclesfield United		
1927		Birmingham	0	
1928		Southend United	2	1
		Loughborough Corinthians		
1930	1931	Bradford City	26	5
1932		Coventry City	7	1
1933	1937	Walsall	181	43
1938		Swindon Town	4	
Woolley, ?			CF	
1892		Crewe Alexandra	3	
Woolley, Albert			OL	
b Hockley 6/1870			d 1896	
		Park Mills		
1892	1894	Aston Villa	20	13
1894		Derby County	6	3
Woolley, George Arthur (Arthur)			GK	
b Staveley				
		Ilkeston Town		
1901		Chesterfield Town	4	
Woolley, Gordon Horace Alfred (Horace)			OR	
b Rutherglen 5/6/1912				
		Larbert Amateurs		
		East Kilbride Thistle		
		Vale Ocoba		
		Partick Thistle		
1937		Blackburn Rovers	1	
		Dundee United		
		Morton		
		East Kilbride Amateurs		
Woolley, Jim Horobin			RB/LB	
b Kegworth 24/10/1889			d 1980	
		Kegworth		
1912	1914	Notts County	3	
Woolley, Robert George (Bob)			RB/LB	
b Chatham 22/1/1899			d 1970	
		Lowestoft Town		
1922	1923	Norwich City	3	
		Lowestoft Town		
Woolliscroft, Arthur			IL/IR	
b Salford 17/2/1904			d 1977	
		Salford		
		Manchester Ship Canal		
1927		Manchester City	0	
		Caernarvon Athletic		
1929		Leicester City	1	
1929	1932	Watford	63	14
1933		Newport County	15	
		Northwich Victoria		
Woolridge, John			OL	
		Hanley Swifts		
1900		Leicester Fosse	3	
		Stafford Rangers		
		Hanley Swifts		
Woolven, Lewis Edgar			OL	
b Chatham 8/12/1907			d 1978	
		Whitstable Town		
1929	1931	Gillingham	6	
		Maidstone United		
Woosnam, Martin Herbert			LH	
b Clun q3 1903			d 1962	
Caps: Wales Amat				
1927		Manchester City	0	
		Ealing Association		
1928		Brentford	1	
1931		Thames	21	
		Club Francais		

From	To		Apps	Goal
Woosnam, Maxwell (Max)			CH	
b Liverpool 6/9/1892			d 1965	
Caps: England Amat/England 1				
		Trinity College		
		Corinthians		
1913		Chelsea	3	
		Corinthians		
1919		Manchester City	16	
		Corinthians		
1920		Manchester City	34	
		Corinthians		
1921	1924	Manchester City	36	4
		Northwich Victoria		
Wootten, James Thomas			CF	
b Walsall q1 1877				
1903		Aston Villa	0	
		Leyton		
1905		Clapton Orient	10	2
		Leyton		
Wootton, Harold (Harry)			LB/RB	
b Hanley q1 1897			d 1964	
		Stafford Rangers		
1919		Stoke	1	
		Stafford Rangers		
1923	1927	Crewe Alexandra	131	
Wootton, James			OL	
b Bloxwich q3 1895			d 1960	
		Leek Alexandra		
1919	1920	Port Vale	43	2
		Nuneaton Town		
1921		Nelson	14	1
		Hereford United		
		Rugby Town		
		Oakengates Town		
		Walsall Early Closers		
Wootton, William (Billy)			RB/LB	
b Longton 27/8/1904			d 2000	
1923		Stoke	0	
		Congleton Town		
1925	1931	Port Vale	56	
1932		Southend United	2	
		Northwich Victoria		
Worboys, Allen Albert Alfred (Alf)			CH/RH/LH	
b Barnet 7/11/1899			d 1980	
1919	1922	Clapton Orient	43	1
		Crawford United		
Wordley, Edward Henry			IL	
b Burslem 30/5/1897			d 1961	
		Leek Alexandra		
1922		Stalybridge Celtic	21	3
		Congleton Town		
Worgan, Albert			IR/CF	
b Helwith Bridge q2 1872			d 1920	
		Aigburth Vale		
1893	1894	Liverpool	2	2
		Chester		
Worlock, Charles Samuel Robert			OR	
b Bristol 24/2/1895			d 1973	
		St Philip's Adult School		
1922	1924	Bristol City	73	9
1925		Bradford Park Avenue	0	
Worrall, Arthur			CF	
		Sandbach Ramblers		
1932		Rochdale	1	
Worrall, Arthur John			CF/OR/IR	
b Wolverhampton 8/9/1869				
Caps: IrLge 2				
		Goldthorne Villa		
1889	1890	Wolverhampton Wanderers	29	10
1892		Burton Swifts	17	13
		Leicester Fosse		
1893		Woolwich Arsenal	4	1
		Nelson		
		Stockport County		
		Crewe Alexandra		
1898		Barnsley	7	
		Distillery		
		Kettering		
Worrall, Fred			OR	
b Warrington 8/9/1910			d 1979	
Caps: FLge 2/England 2				
		Witton Albion		
		Nantwich		
1928		Bolton Wanderers	0	
1928	1931	Oldham Athletic	105	21
1931	1945	Portsmouth	313	68
1939		(Portsmouth)	(3)	(1)
1946		Crewe Alexandra	7	1
1946		Stockport County	0	

From	To		Apps	Goal
		Worrall, John Edwin (Ted)	RB	
		b Buxton 2/10/1891	d 1980	
		The Comrades (Buxton)		
1910	1914	Sheffield Wednesday	105	
1919	1922	Fulham	88	
1923	1924	Aberdare Athletic	50	1
1924		Watford	4	
1925	1926	New Brighton	84	2
1927	1928	Southport	71	4
		Shirebrook		
		Gresley Rovers		
		Ripley Town		
		Worrall, William Edward (Bill)	GK	
		b Shildon 1886		
		South Bank		
1905		Middlesbrough	1	
		Shildon Athletic		
1910		Sunderland	12	
		Sunderland West End Wednesday		
		Wingate Albion		
		Worrell, Joseph Eric	LH	
		b Stourbridge 7/1886	d 1970	
		Stourbridge Swifts		
		Stourbridge		
1919		Aston Villa	4	
		Cradley Heath St Luke's		
		Netherton		
		Dudley Town		
		Old Hill Wanderers		
		Brierley Hill Alliance		
		Worsley, Arthur	RB	
1905	1906	Stockport County	7	
		Worsley, Herbert (Bert)	OR/IR	
		b Stockport 20/9/1911	d 1971	
		Altrincham		
		Manchester North End		
1930		Bolton Wanderers	0	
		Manchester North End		
1934		Leeds United	3	
1935	1938	Fulham	106	15
1939		(Fulham)	(1)	
		Worswick, Randall (Ray)	CF/IL	
		b Wavertree 28/12/1911	d 1983	
		Woodville Juniors		
		Wavertree United		
1934	1935	Southport	38	21
		Macclesfield		
		Northwich Victoria		
		South Liverpool		
1938		Chester	8	4
1939		(Chester)	(1)	
		Prescot Cables		
		Worth, Albert	OL	
		b Manchester 1888		
1907	1908	Stockport County	21	1
		Rochdale		
1911		Grimsby Town	20	2
		Luton Town		
		Heywood United		
		Worthington, John	OL	
1901		Bolton Wanderers	3	1
		Hyde		
		Hurst		
		Worthington, William (Bill)	IL	
1928		Accrington Stanley	2	
		Stalybridge Celtic		
		Worthy, Albert	RB	
		b Pilsley 1/11/1905	d 1978	
		Holmewood		
		Danesmoor		
1926		Chesterfield	7	
1927	1932	Lincoln City	198	5
1933		Southend United	28	
1934	1936	Rochdale	99	1
		Gainsborough Trinity		
		Shrewsbury Town		
		Worthy, Reginald Francis (Reg)	CH	
		b Newport q3 1903	d 1958	
		Cwmbran Town		
1929		Newport County	3	
		Worton, Alfred James (Alf)	LB	
		b Wolverhampton 4/4/1914		
		Priestfield Albion		
		Ettingshall Westley		
		Bilston United		
1933		Walsall	0	
1934	1937	Norwich City	23	
		Colchester United		
		Worton, Thomas (Tommy)	IL/IR	
		b Wolverhampton 2/1878		
1898	1900	Wolverhampton Wanderers	57	12
1901	1903	West Bromwich Albion	72	23
		Wrack, Charles (Charlie)	CH	
		b Boston 28/12/1899	d 1979	
		Boston West End		
		Boston Town		
		Cleethorpes Town		
1925	1930	Grimsby Town	125	2
1931		Hull City	3	
		Boston Town		
		Louth Town		
		Wragg, William (Willie)	LH/LB/RB	
		b Lenton q3 1875	d 1950	
		Notts Olympic		
		Sutton-in-Ashfield		
		Newstead Byron		
		Hucknall Portland		
1896	1898	Nottingham Forest	49	1
1898	1900	Leicester Fosse	49	4
1900		Small Heath	1	
		Watford		
		Hinckley Town		
1903		Chesterfield Town	20	
		Accrington Stanley		
		Doncaster Rovers		
		Brighton & Hove Albion		
		Wragge, Frank	CH	
		b Wolverhampton 9/2/1898	d 1973	
1919		Wolverhampton Wanderers	0	
		Oakengates Town		
1921		Wolverhampton Wanderers	0	
		Oakengates Town		
1923	1925	Bristol Rovers	62	1
		Stafford Rangers		
1927		Torquay United	27	
1928		Walsall	2	
		Madeley Miners Welfare		
		Wray, Arthur	CF	
1921		Crewe Alexandra	1	
		Wray, James Herbert (Jimmy)	CF	
		b Didsbury 17/11/1893	d 1963	
		Norman Athletic		
		Bolton Wanderers		
		Manchester City (trial)		
1920		Reading	2	1
1921		Southport	19	2
		Chorley		
1923		Exeter City	0	
		Ottery St Mary		
		Chard Town		
		Wren, Cecil	RH	
		b Hemsworth q1 1891	d 1966	
		South Kirkby		
1909		Barnsley	2	
		Wren, John Edward (Jack)	CH/RH/LH	
		b Bristol 30/1/1894	d 1948	
		Greenbank		
		Bristol Rovers		
1919	1921	Bristol City	104	1
1922	1925	Notts County	63	
1926		Southport	6	
		Wren, Thomas James (Tom)	RB/LB	
		b Rossington 4/3/1907	d 1973	
		Rossington Main		
1927		Huddersfield Town	0	
1928	1929	Bradford City	2	
1930		Portsmouth	0	
1931		Norwich City	2	
1932		Bristol City	0	
		Tunbridge Wells Rangers		
		Wrigglesworth, William Herbert (Billy)	OL/OR	
		b South Elmsall 12/11/1912	d 1980	
		Frickley Colliery		
1932	1934	Chesterfield	34	6
1934	1936	Wolverhampton Wanderers	50	21
1936	1946	Manchester United	27	7
1939		(Manchester United)	(3)	(1)
1946	1947	Bolton Wanderers	13	1
1947		Southampton	12	4
1948		Reading	5	
		Burton Albion		
		Scarborough		
		Wright, Albert	IR	
		b Blackburn 1903		
1923		Halifax Town	1	
		Chorley		
		Stalybridge Celtic		
1929		Blackburn Rovers	0	
		Stalybridge Celtic		
		Chorley		
		Wright, Alexander (Alex)	GK	
		b Kilmarnock 5/1904	d 1934	
		Queen of the South		
		Irvine Meadow		
1932	1934	Charlton Athletic	63	
		Wright, Arthur (Ticker)	RH	
		b Watford		
1920		Watford	1	
		Wright, Arthur William Tempest	LH	
		b Burradon 23/9/1919	d 1985	
		Caps: England Sch/FLge 2		
		Hylton Colliery		
1937	1954	Sunderland	270	13
		Wright, David (Dave)	IL/CF	
		b Kirkcaldy 5/10/1905	d 1955	
		Dunniker Juniors		
		Raith Rovers		
		East Fife		
		Cowdenbeath		
1927	1929	Sunderland	52	7
1929	1933	Liverpool	93	35
1934		Hull City	32	11
1935		Bradford Park Avenue	20	1
		Wright, Edgar	OL	
		b Oakenholt q3 1910		
		Oakenholt		
1930		Wrexham	2	
		Connah's Quay & Shotton		
		Wright, Edmund	GK	
		b London 3/1902		
		High Wycombe		
1920		Aston Villa	2	
1922		Brentford	6	
		Wright, Edward Gordon Dundas (Gordon)	OL	
		b Earlsfield Green 3/10/1884	d 1947	
		Caps: England Amat/England 1		
		Cambridge University		
		Corinthians		
		Portsmouth		
1905		Hull City	1	1
		Corinthians		
1906	1909	Hull City	92	11
		Leyton		
1910	1912	Hull City	59	2
		Worthing		
		Reigate Priory		
		Wright, Ellis	LH	
		b Shiregreen q3 1873	d 1940	
		Ecclesfield		
1901	1904	Doncaster Rovers	80	
		Wright, Ernest	CH/LH	
		b 1912		
1932		Huddersfield Town	0	
1933		Bradford City	0	
1934	1935	Mansfield Town	47	
		Boston United		
		Wright, Ernest (Ernie)	IR/IL	
		b Middleton 1912		
		Sedgley Park		
1934		Queen's Park Rangers	1	
1935	1936	Crewe Alexandra	4	
1937		Chesterfield	1	
1938		Oldham Athletic	37	5
1939		(Oldham Athletic)	(1)	
		Wright, Ernest J	OR	
1903		Nottingham Forest	4	
		Wright, Ernest Victor (Vic)	IR/IL	
		b Bloxwich 24/1/1909	d 1964	
		Bloxwich Strollers		
1928		Bristol City	0	
1929	1930	Rotherham United	40	20
1931		Sheffield Wednesday	2	
1932	1933	Rotherham United	48	18
1933	1936	Liverpool	81	31
1937		Plymouth Argyle	18	7
		Chelmsford City		
		Wright, Frank	LH	
		b Wednesbury 1872		
		Smethwick Centaur		
		Smethwick Carriage Works		
1895		West Bromwich Albion	2	
		Stourbridge		
		Coventry City		
		Wright, Frank	OR	
		b Birmingham 1898		
		Hamstead Colliery		
1920		Southampton	1	
		Wright, Frederick (Fred)	RB/LB	
		b Ruddington q4 1908		
		Ruddington		
1928		Notts County	1	
		Grantham		
1930		Hull City	2	
		Loughborough Corinthians		
		Leicester City Police		
		Wright, George	OL/CF	
1897	1898	Loughborough	8	
		Wright, George William	GK	
		b Plymouth 10/10/1919	d 2008	
		Kitto Institute		
1938	1946	Plymouth Argyle	12	
1950	1954	Colchester United	151	
		Sudbury Town		
		Wright, Grayson	IR	
		b Sheffield q2 1889	d 1925	
		Darnall Congregationals		
		Worksop Town		
1909		Sheffield United	2	
		Rotherham Town		
		Worksop Town		
		Rotherham County		
		Wright, Harold (Harry)	OL	
		b Staveley 5/4/1900		
		Welbeck Colliery		
1920	1921	Gillingham	33	
		Welbeck Colliery		
1922	1926	Bradford City	68	4
		Staveley Town		
		Wright, Harry Fereday	IR/IL/OR	
		b West Bromwich 12/10/1888	d 1950	
		West Bromwich St Mark's		
		Wednesbury Athletic		
1907	1908	West Bromwich Albion	5	1
		Stourbridge		
1910	1914	West Bromwich Albion	83	16
1919		Wolverhampton Wanderers	18	4
1920		Newport County	17	4
1921		Chesterfield	1	
		Wright, Henry (Harry)	GK	
		b High Park 7/2/1909	d 1979	
		Fleetwood Hesketh		
1934		Southport	7	
		Fleetwood Hesketh		
		Leyland Motors		
		Crossens		
		Wright, Henry Edward (Harry)	GK	
		b Tottenham 3/6/1909	d 1994	
		Harwich & Parkeston		
1932	1935	Charlton Athletic	39	
1936	1937	Aldershot	28	
1937	1938	Derby County	25	
1938		Aldershot (loan)	0	
		Chelmsford City		
		Colchester United		
		Guildford City		
		Wright, Horace Duncan	OR	
		b Ilkeston q2 1892		
		Ilkeston United		
		Wath Athletic		
		Bulwell White Star		
1910	1911	Derby County	15	2
		Portsmouth		
		Darlington		
		Mansfield Mechanics		
1919		Coventry City	10	
1920		Exeter City	0	
		Aberaman Athletic		
		Abertillery		
1923		Chesterfield	0	
		Coalville Town		
		Wright, Horace Raymond (Ray)	IL	
		b Pontefract 6/9/1918	d 1987	
		Woodbourne Athletic		
1937	1938	Wolverhampton Wanderers	8	1
1946	1947	Exeter City	56	11
		Yeovil Town		
		Wright, James (Jim)	RB/LB	
		b Okehampton 11/9/1910	d 1978	
		Okehampton		
1930	1931	Torquay United	28	1
1932	1934	Grimsby Town	27	
1934	1935	Sheffield Wednesday	3	
		Guildford City		
1937		Swansea Town	4	
1938		Hartlepools United	34	
1939		(Hartlepools United)	(3)	
		Wright, John	GK	
1895		Preston North End	2	
		Fleetwood Rangers		
		Wright, John (Jocky)	IL	
		b Hamilton 4/2/1873	d 1946	
		Hamilton Academical		
		Motherwell		
		Hamilton Academical		
		Clyde		
1895	1898	Bolton Wanderers	85	14
1898	1901	Sheffield Wednesday	103	42
		Hamilton Academical		
1902	1903	Bolton Wanderers	34	5
		Plymouth Argyle		
		Watford		
		Southend United		

From To Apps Goal

Wright, John (Jack) RH
Caps: IrLge 7/Ireland Amat/Ireland 6
Cliftonville
1910 Huddersfield Town 2
Cliftonville

Wright, John LH
b Blackhall
Easington Juniors
1932 Hartlepools United 0
Easington Colliery Welfare
1934 Derby County 0
1937 1938 Darlington 37 4
Denaby United

Wright, John Douglas (Doug) RH/LH
b Rochford 29/4/1917 d 1992
Caps: England 1
Chelmsford City
1936 1937 Southend United 31 2
1938 1946 Newcastle United 72 1
1939 (Newcastle United) (2)
1948 1954 Lincoln City 233 2
Blyth Spartans

Wright, John E (Jack) CF
b North Wingfield
Alfreton Town
Staveley Town
Matlock Town
1931 Notts County 1 1
Ilkeston United
Sutton Town
Grantham

Wright, John Ernest GK
b Swallownest
Woodhouse Brunswick
1932 Sheffield United 0
1933 Rotherham United 11

Wright, John H LH/IR
b Southport
1921 1923 Crewe Alexandra 11

Wright, John M OL
Doncaster YC
1933 1934 Doncaster Rovers 2
Scunthorpe & Lindsey United

Wright, John William (Bill) GK
b Banks q4 1883
1902 Blackpool 7
St Cuthbert's (Churchtown)
Lytham
Blackpool 0
1907 Oldham Athletic 3
Southport Central
Accrington Stanley
1914 Manchester United 0

Wright, Joseph (Joe) GK
b Gateshead q1 1907 d 1936
Birtley
1929 Leicester City 15
1930 1931 Torquay United 69
1932 1933 Brighton & Hove Albion 14

Wright, Levi George CH
b Oxford 15/1/1862 d 1953
Derby Midland
1888 Derby County 4 1
1889 Notts County 0

Wright, Norman OL
b Ushaw Moor 27/12/1908 d 1974
Esh Winning
1927 1929 Grimsby Town 17 3
1930 Crewe Alexandra 30 4
1931 1932 Accrington Stanley 78 21
1933 1934 Manchester City 3 1
1935 Watford 21 3
South Shields

Wright, Percy Lionel OL
b Darley Dale 6/6/1890 d 1971
Darley Harriers
Heanor Town
1910 1913 Sheffield Wednesday 20 6
West Ham United
Chesterfield Municipal

Wright, Peter RB
b Hebburn 1882
Hebburn Argyle
1904 Barnsley 2

From To Apps Goal

Wright, Reginald (Reg) LB/RH/RB
b Dronfield 17/1/1901 d 1973
Mosborough Trinity
1921 Sheffield Wednesday 0
Worksop Town
Mansfield Town (trial)
1925 1927 Blackpool 43 1
1928 1930 Bournemouth & Boscombe Ath 31
1931 Chesterfield 11
Frickley Colliery
Worksop Town
Buxton
Mosborough Trinity

Wright, Robert RH/CF
1905 Everton 1
1907 Burnley 2

Wright, Robert IL
AVTC Chiseldon
1934 Swindon Town 11

Wright, Robert Cooper Allen (Bob) LH/CH
b Glasgow 20/2/1913 d 1998
1931 Hartlepools United 0
Crook Town
1935 Manchester United (trial) 0
1935 Millwall (trial) 0
Horden Colliery Welfare
1938 1946 Charlton Athletic 28
1939 (Charlton Athletic) (3)

Wright, Ronald Leslie IL
b Kettering 1903
Northampton Amateurs
1923 Northampton Town 1
Kettering Town

Wright, Stephen (Steve) LH/CH
b Leicester 24/12/1882 d 1959
Bohemians
1920 1921 Bolton Wanderers 10
1922 Norwich City 36 1
1923 Brighton & Hove Albion 4

Wright, William (Billy) RH
b South Hiendley 1913
Frickley Colliery
1934 Bolton Wanderers 0
1935 1938 New Brighton 124
1939 (New Brighton) (3)

Wright, William Bullock (Billy) LH/IL/IR
b Sheffield 25/12/1899
1921 Southend United 0
1922 1932 Bolton Wanderers 154 21
1933 1937 Reading 173 3
Wachat Rouen

Wright, William J (Tim) RH/LH/OR
b Patrington 1891 d 1951
Patrington
Withernsea
1908 1920 Hull City 153 5

Wright, William Pountney (Bill) CF
b Seaforth q4 1892 d 1945
Egremont
1914 Everton 2
South Liverpool
St Mirren
Tranmere Rovers
1920 Exeter City 17 9
1920 Huddersfield Town 9 4
Mid-Rhondda United
Yeovil & Petters United

Wright, William Pretty (Bill) CH
b Southwark 8/5/1903 d 1983
1931 Clapton Orient 1

Wright, William Samuel (Bill) LB
b Hanley q3 1914
Milton True Blues
1934 Stoke City 0
Burton Town
1936 Port Vale 0
1936 Birmingham (trial) 0
Glentoran
1938 Barrow 1

Wrightson, Frank Lawrence (Paddy) IR/CF
b Shildon 9/1/1906 d 1979
Ferryhill Athletic
1928 1929 Darlington 36 16
1929 1931 Manchester City 22 4
1931 1932 Fulham 18 5
1932 1934 Exeter City 71 25
1935 1938 Chester 89 73

Wrightson, John Mawson IL
b Sunderland q1 1901
Robert Thompson's
1923 Hartlepools United 1
West Stanley
Willington Athletic

From To Apps Goal

Wrigley, Bernard GK
b Clitheroe q1 1894
Clitheroe Royal Blues
Clitheroe Amateurs
Great Harwood
1921 Blackburn Rovers 1
1923 1924 Lincoln City 9
Grantham
Great Harwood

Wroe, Harold OR
b Birdwell q2 1906 d 1960
Birdwell
1925 Barnsley 1
Wombwell Town
Denaby United
Mansfield Town
Sutton Town (loan)
Denaby United (loan)
Welbeck Colliery
Shirebrook
Mexborough Athletic
Welbeck Athletic
Ardsley

Wykes, David OR/IR/OL
b Walsall 15/9/1867 d 1895
Caps: FLge 1
Bloxwich Strollers
Wednesbury Town
Walsall Swifts
1888 1895 Wolverhampton Wanderers 151 57

Wylie, Thomas (Tom) LB
b Darvel 3/1896 d 1956
Queen of the South
1920 1925 Blackburn Rovers 174
Darwen
1926 1929 Swindon Town 82

Wylie, Thomas (Tom) CF
b Linwood 10/11/1907
Glasgow Benburb
Motherwell
1936 Sunderland 7 3
Queen of the South
Peebles Rovers

Wyllie, David CF
b Hurlford 1880
Renfrew Victoria
St Mirren
1908 Fulham 7
Dunfermline Athletic
St Mirren

Wyllie, James CH/RH
1895 1897 Burton Swifts 57 2

Wyllie, James RB
b Hurlford
Caps: SLge 1
North Sea Viking
Clyde
Aberdeen
1912 Bradford City 24
Aberdeen
Fraserburgh

Wyllie, John LH
b Maybole 1914
Glenafton Athletic
Partick Thistle
Ayr United
Partick Thistle
1936 Bury 0
1937 Lincoln City 0
1938 Notts County 1
Stranraer (loan)

Wyllie, Thomas (Tom) OR/IR
b Maybole 5/4/1870 d 1943
Caps: Scotland 1
Maybole
Rangers
1890 1891 Everton 20 5
Liverpool
1894 1896 Bury 73 15
Bristol City

Wyness, George Dow CH
b Monkwearmouth 12/8/1907 d 1993
Tyzack
Jarrow
Houghton Colliery Welfare
1927 Leicester City (trial) 0
Falkirk
1929 1932 Southport 88
1933 Chester 8
1934 1935 Rochdale 70
1936 Notts County 10
1937 Gateshead 0
Jarrow

From To Apps Goal

Wyness, William Dow (Bill) IL
b Monkwearmouth 29/12/1909 d 1998
Hetton United
1929 Southport (trial) 0
Crook Town
1932 Aldershot 0
Blyth Spartans
Spennymoor United
1934 Wrexham 1
Spennymoor United
Shrewsbury Town
Spennymoor United
South Shields
Sunderland Fire Brigade

Wynn, George Arthur IR
b Treflach 14/10/1886 d 1966
Caps: Wales 1
Pant Glas
Chirk
Oswestry United
Wrexham
1909 1919 Manchester City 119 54
1919 1920 Coventry City 24 3
Llandudno Town
1921 Halifax Town 1
Mansfield Town
Mossley

Wynn, James (Jimmy) IR/CF
b Wallsend 4/9/1910 d 1986
Swan Hunter
Blyth Spartans
Wallsend
1933 Sheffield Wednesday 0
1935 Southport 31 6
1936 Rotherham United 5 1
1936 1938 Rochdale 86 64
1939 (Rochdale) (3) (1)
Scunthorpe & Lindsey United

Wynn, Richard OL
Chester
1913 1914 Middlesbrough 7 1

Wynne, Fred GK
b Todmorden
1902 Burnley 10

Wynne, George OL
b Wrexham 3/5/1910 d 1991
Flint Town
Oak Alyn Rovers
1929 Wrexham 8 1
Colwyn Bay
Denbigh Town

Wynne, Samuel (Sam) RB
b Neston 26/4/1897 d 1927
Neston Colliery
Connah's Quay & Shotton
1921 1926 Oldham Athletic 145 9
1926 Bury 18 1

Wyper, Henry Thomas Hartley (Tommy) OR
b Calton 8/10/1900 d 1974
Glengarnock Vale
1921 Southport 7
Motherwell
1922 Southport 2
1923 Burnley (trial) 0
Wallasey United
Burscough Rangers
1925 1926 Accrington Stanley 61 14
1926 1927 Hull City 40 2
1928 Arsenal (trial) 0
1928 1930 Charlton Athletic 82 12
1931 Queen's Park Rangers 11
1931 1932 Chester 24 7
1932 Bristol Rovers 11 2
1933 Accrington Stanley 29 7
1934 Crewe Alexandra 0
Rossendale United

Yardley, Herbert IR/CF
b Brownhills q1 1873 d 1932
1896 1900 Burton Swifts 57 10
1901 1902 Burton United 5 1

Yardley, James (Jimmy) CF/IR
b Wishaw 16/4/1903 d 1959
Lorne Thistle
Overton Rangers
Bellhaven Oak
1924 1926 Clapton Orient 29 3
1926 1931 Luton Town 173 78
1931 1933 Charlton Athletic 51 26
1933 1935 Millwall 76 24
Third Lanark
Ayr United
Morton

From To Apps Goal
Yarnall, Herbert George IL/CF
b Goole q4 1892 d 1943
Kidsgrove Wellington
1914 Blackpool 9 1
Airdrieonians
Clydebank
Dumbarton
1920 Reading 5 1
Oswestry Town

Yarwood, Harold Randle IR
b Stourbridge 21/8/1906 d 1988
Worcester City
Stourbridge Town
Shrewsbury Town
1927 Birmingham 0
1928 Chesterfield 13 3
Brierley Hill Alliance

Yarwood, James William (Jack) CH
b Stockport 1891
Merthyr Town
1921 Rochdale 11

Yarwood, John CH
b Bacup
Accrington
1895 Blackburn Rovers 1

Yarwood, Jonathan (Jonty) LB
b Huyton Quarry 9/1/1899 d 1939
Blackmore Wanderers
1920 Bury 0
Atherton
1922 Everton 0
1922 1923 Oldham Athletic 11
Liverpool Warehousing

Yates, George Herbert CF
b Westhoughton 21/1/1906 d 1975
Horwich RMI
1925 1927 Wigan Borough 35 10
Horwich RMI
Darwen
Rossendale United

Yates, Harry R LH/CH/RH
b Walsall 8/1861 d 1932
Walsall Swifts
1888 1889 Aston Villa 14
Birmingham St George's
1898 Walsall 4

Yates, Herbert LB
b Barnoldswick
1924 1926 Rotherham County 60 12

Yates, James (Jimmy) OR
b Tunstall 2/11/1869 d 1922
1891 Burnley 0
1892 1893 Ardwick 20 9
1893 1896 Sheffield United 80 8
Southampton
Gravesend United
Southampton
St Leonards United
Copenhagen
Southampton
Gravesend United
Hastings & St Leonards
Salisbury City

Yates, John (Jack) OL/IL
b Blackburn 1861 d 1917
Caps: England 1
Blackburn Olympic
Accrington
1888 1893 Burnley 29 7

Yates, John (Jack) RH
b Little Lever 19/6/1904 d 1980
Little Lever
1927 Watford 2
Bangor City

Yates, John LH
b Manchester 26/9/1903
Manchester Central
Boston Town
1925 Coventry City 0
1926 Chesterfield 0
1927 1928 Aston Villa 14
1929 Queen's Park Rangers 10
Stourbridge

Yates, Levi CF
b Burton-on-Trent q3 1891 d 1934
Gresley Villa
Gresley Rovers
1913 Nottingham Forest 10 1

Yates, Richard E RB/OL
1897 1898 Darwen 11 1

From To Apps Goal
Yates, Thomas (Tom) LH
b Blackburn 1915
Lancashire Amateurs
1936 Accrington Stanley 3
1939 Accrington Stanley 0

Yates, Wilfred James (Wilf) RB/LB
b Southport 5/11/1897 d 1981
Southport
1921 1924 Preston North End 63
1925 Crewe Alexandra 36
1926 1928 Tranmere Rovers 92
Mansfield Town
1930 Preston North End 0

Yates, William RH
1891 1895 Darwen 11 1

Yates, William IR
b Birmingham 1883
Witton Shell Shop
Erdington
1903 Aston Villa 0
Brighton & Hove Albion
1906 Manchester United 3
Heart of Midlothian
Portsmouth
Coventry City

Yates, William (Bill) GK
b Little Lever 20/3/1903 d 1978
Little Lever St Matthew's
1925 1926 Bolton Wanderers 6
1926 1928 Watford 47
Northfleet

Yeardley, James CF
b Doncaster 8/4/1911 d 1991
Balby Athletic
1931 Doncaster Rovers 2
Thorne Town

Yeates, Richard CF
1924 Bradford City 3

Yenson, William (Billy) CF
b Kingston Bagpuize 1880
West Ham United
1903 1904 Bolton Wanderers 28 8
Queen's Park Rangers
West Ham United
Croydon Common

Yeomans, Harry Arthur GK
b Farnborough 11/4/1901 d 1965
Camberley & York Town
1924 1925 Southampton 12
Southampton Police

Yews, Thomas Peace (Tommy) OR
b Wingate 28/2/1902 d 1966
NER Athletic
1921 1922 Hartlepools United 39 3
1923 1932 West Ham United 332 46
1933 Clapton Orient 3

York, Andrew (Andy) LB
b Blyth 14/6/1894 d 1977
Sleekburn Albion
Bedlington United
Blyth Spartans
1921 Sunderland 1
1923 1924 Coventry City 16
1925 1926 Northampton Town 24
1927 1929 Lincoln City 106 6
Newark Town
Scarborough

York, Charles H (Charlie) CF/IR
b Edinburgh 1882
Swindon Town
Reading
1902 1903 Derby County 24 6
1903 Sunderland 2
Heart of Midlothian
Southampton
Sheppey United
South Farnborough

York, Richard Ernest (Dicky) OR
b Handsworth 25/4/1899 d 1969
Caps: England Sch/FLge 2/England 2
Handsworth Royal
Birchfield Rangers
1919 1930 Aston Villa 356 79
1931 Port Vale 26 5
Brierley Hill Alliance

York, Roland CF
b Kettering q1 1897 d 1944
Higham Town
1923 Northampton Town 3
Higham Town

York, Walter George IL
b Loughborough q2 1877 d 1927
1897 Loughborough 1

From To Apps Goal
Yorke, Charles IR
1927 Darlington 1

Yorke, Robert Johnstone (Bob) LH
b Haddington 8/3/1911
Rosyth Recreation
Thornton Rangers
Ayr United
Dunfermline Athletic
1932 1933 Aldershot 14
Dundee United
1935 Hull City 9
Dundee United
Montrose

Yorston, Benjamin Collard (Benny) IR/CF/IL
b Nigg 14/10/1905 d 1977
Caps: Scotland 1
Kittybrewster
Aberdeen Mugiemoss
Alloa Athletic (trial)
Aberdeen Richmond
Hibernian (trial)
Montrose
Aberdeen
1931 1933 Sunderland 49 25
1933 1938 Middlesbrough 152 54
1939 (Middlesbrough) (2)

Youds, George LB
b Wolstanton q1 1872 d 1937
Kettering
1892 1895 Burslem Port Vale 53

Young, Alexander Simpson (Sandy) CF/IL
b Slamannan 23/6/1880 d 1959
Caps: Scotland 2
St Mirren
Falkirk
1901 1910 Everton 275 109
1911 Tottenham Hotspur 5 3
1911 Manchester City 13 2
South Liverpool

Young, Alfred (Alf) CH/LH/RH
b Wingate 27/11/1900 d 1975
Trimdon Grange
Wingate Albion
1923 1927 Hartlepools United 123 1
1928 Gillingham 18
Workington
1929 1933 Lincoln City 148 5

Young, Alfred (Alf) CH
b Sunderland 4/11/1905 d 1977
Caps: FLge 2/England 9
Sunderland West End
1926 Durham City 0
1929 1938 Huddersfield Town 283 6
1939 (Huddersfield Town) (3)
1945 York City 0

Young, Andrew CF/LH/RH
b Darlington 17/9/1896 d 1964
Blyth Spartans
1919 1921 Aston Villa 26 11
1921 1926 Arsenal 68 9
1927 Bournemouth & Boscombe Ath 2
Kidderminster Harriers

Young, Archibald (Archie) RH/LH
b Paisley 1/1/1915
Clydebank Juniors
1937 Portsmouth 2
1938 Notts County 11

Young, Archibald Wishart (Archie) LH/IL
b Twechar 10/12/1906 d 1980
Kilsyth Rangers
Dunipace
1929 Preston North End (trial) 0
Dunfermline Athletic
1932 1934 Leicester City 14
1935 Bristol Rovers 24
1936 Exeter City 19
1937 Gillingham 21
1938 Rochdale 1

Young, Arthur OR
b Scotland
Hurlford Thistle
1906 Manchester United 2

Young, Christopher (Chris) CF
b Cleethorpes 26/5/1886 d 1956
Grimsby Rovers
Cleethorpes Town
1905 1907 Grimsby Town 5 2
Cleethorpes Town
Grimsby Rovers
1911 Gainsborough Trinity 27 14
1912 Tottenham Hotspur 4
Port Vale
Cleethorpes Town
Charlton's (Grimsby)

From To Apps Goal
Young, David CF
1921 Stockport County 2

Young, Edward OR
b 1915
West Wylam Colliery Welfare
1937 Lincoln City 5 1

Young, Ernest Albert (Ernie) IL/CF
b Sunderland q3 1892 d 1962
Thompson's Munition Works
Horsley Hill
1919 South Shields 10 4
1921 1922 Durham City 50 18
Spennymoor United

Young, Ernest Wilson (Ernie) CF
b Middlesbrough q2 1893
1920 Middlesbrough 1
1922 Darlington 13 4
Leadgate Park

Young, George RB
b Kirkintilloch 1880
Dumbarton
Beith
Rangers
Beith
Portsmouth
1905 West Bromwich Albion 16
West Bromwich Strollers
Kidderminster Harriers
Worcester City

Young, Harold LH/RB/LB
b Hull
1935 1937 York City 10
Goole Town

Young, Herbert (Bert) OL
b Liverpool 4/9/1899 d 1976
1922 Everton 0
1923 1924 Aberdare Athletic 68 5
1924 1925 Brentford 33 2
Bangor City
1927 1928 Newport County 64 6
1929 Queen's Park Rangers 14 1
1930 1931 Bristol Rovers 75 11
1932 Swindon Town 14 2

Young, J LH
1919 Lincoln City 1

Young, James RH
Cambuslang Hibernian
Port Glasgow Athletic
1905 Manchester City 1
Port Glasgow Athletic
St Johnstone

Young, Jerry Lythgoe OR/OL
b Farnworth 11/3/1915
Morecambe
Horwich RMI
1936 1938 Accrington Stanley 4
Horwich RMI

Young, John (Jack) CF
b Burnbank 1889
Burnbank Athletic
1910 1911 Bradford City 10 8
1911 Sunderland 13 2
Port Vale
Hamilton Academical

Young, John (Jack) LB/OL
b Whitburn, County Durham 1895 d 1952
Whitburn Villa
South Shields
Southend United
1919 1925 West Ham United 124 3
1926 1928 Queen's Park Rangers 89 12
1929 Accrington Stanley 4

Young, John RB
b Lanarkshire
Petershill
Morton
Clydebank
1921 Barrow 13
Lancaster Town

Young, John William CH
b Kilmarnock 26/12/1903
Auchinleck Talbot
Cowdenbeath
Rhyl Athletic
Cowdenbeath
1928 Southampton 0
1928 Crewe Alexandra 6

From	To	Club	Apps	Goal
Young, Joseph (Joe)			OR	
b Whitehaven q1 1896				
		Whitburn		
		Kells		
		Carlisle United		
1921		Preston North End	0	
1921		Barrow	2	
		Lancaster Town		
		Leyland		
		Kendal Town		
		Lancaster Town		
		Morecambe		
Young, Joseph W (Joe)			IR/CF	
b Flimby 1906				
1926		Leeds United	0	
1927	1928	Hartlepools United	19	4
		Spennymoor United		
1929		Luton Town	3	
1929		Northampton Town	2	2
Young, Leonard Archibald (Len)			CH/LH/RH	
b West Ham 23/2/1912				
		Colchester Town		
		Ilford		
1933	1937	West Ham United	12	
1937	1947	Reading	84	
1939		(Reading)	(2)	
1947	1948	Brighton & Hove Albion	8	
Young, Matthew Sprott (Matty)			OR	
b Cambois q1 1901				
		Preston Colliery		
1923		Hartlepools United	29	3
1924		Reading	6	
		Workington		
1926		Preston North End	6	1
		Aldershot		
Young, Norman James			RB	
b Solihull 1/6/1906			d 1977	
		Cobden Works		
		Redditch Town		
1935		Aston Villa	9	
1936		Barnsley	22	
		Brierley Hill Alliance		
Young, Richard H			LH	
b Southend-on-Sea				
		Grays Thurrock		
1923		Southend United	1	
Young, Richard Harter (Dick)			LB/CH/RB	
b Gateshead 17/4/1918			d 1989	
		Wardley Colliery Welfare		
		Hebburn St Cuthbert's		
1936	1948	Sheffield United	71	
1939		(Sheffield United)	(3)	
1948	1953	Lincoln City	100	2
Young, Robert K			RB/RH	
b Guard Bridge 1886				
		Dundee Violet		
1907	1919	Bristol City	167	
Young, Robert T			OL	
b Catrine 1894				
		Queen's Park		
		Albion Rovers (loan)		
		Airdrieonians		
		Albion Rovers		
		Ayr United		
1921		South Shields	1	
		Sleekburn Albion		
Young, Robert Thomson			CH/RH	
b Stonehouse, Lanarkshire 7/9/1886			d 1955	
		Swinhill Hearts		
		Larkhall Thistle		
		St Mirren		
		West Ham United		
1908	1909	Middlesbrough	34	5
1910	1911	Everton	38	7
1911	1913	Wolverhampton Wanderers	67	10
Young, Robert Thornton (Bob)			LB	
b Brandon, County Durham 5/9/1893			d 1960	
		New Brancepeth Juniors		
		New Brancepeth Villa		
		Esh Winning Rangers		
1914	1924	Sunderland	50	
1926		Norwich City	0	
Young, William			GK	
b Whitburn, County Durham				
		Whitburn		
1920	1924	Brentford	169	
Young, William			IR	
1922		Stalybridge Celtic	2	
Young, William			IR/IL	
b Ferrybridge 1898				
		Tyneside District		
1924	1925	Queen's Park Rangers	8	2
		Kettering Town		
		Jarrow		
1930		Barnsley	0	
1931		Gillingham	0	
1932		Carlisle United	2	
1933		Barnsley	0	
Young, William			RH	
b Paisley 1916				
		Mossvale YMCA		
		Clydebank Juniors		
1936		Blackburn Rovers	6	
		St Mirren		
		Dumbarton		
Young, William Craig			RH	
b Chadsmoor 1884			d 1917	
		Chadsmoor Celtic		
		Hednesford Victoria		
		Hednesford Town		
1907	1909	West Bromwich Albion	19	2
		Hednesford Town		
		Wednesbury		
		Worcester City		
		Kidderminster Harriers		
Younger, James (Jimmy)			OL	
b Pelton				
		Winsford United		
1933		Bury	2	1
1934		Gateshead	19	1
Youtman, Bert Alfred			OL	
b Eastleigh 1/6/1893				
		Thorneycrofts		
1920		Portsmouth	1	
		Harland & Wolff		
Yuill, Duncan			GK	
b Shettleston 19/3/1901			d 1977	
		Clydebank Juniors		
		St Mirren		
		Dumbarton		
		Rangers		
		Aberdeen		
1930	1938	Millwall	187	
1939		(Millwall)	(3)	
		Dumbarton		
Yuill, John Crawford			OL	
b Coltness 1915				
		Coltness United		
		Falkirk (trial)		
1935		Huddersfield Town	1	
		Arbroath		
		Distillery		
Yuill, John George (Jack)			OR	
b Hendon q4 1885			d 1916	
		Northern Nomads		
		Sale Holmfield		
1906		Manchester City	0	
1907		Oldham Athletic	0	
1907		Stockport County	1	
		Wrexham		
1908		Manchester City	3	1
		Chester		
		Wrexham		
		Chester		
		Port Vale		
		Chester		
		Northern Nomads		
Yule, Thomas (Tommy)			OL	
b Douglas Water 4/2/1888				
		Douglas Water Thistle		
		Portobello		
1909	1910	Lincoln City	63	8
1911	1912	Wolverhampton Wanderers	33	7
		Port Vale		
		Ayr United		

WIGAN BOROUGH OPPONENTS 1931-1932

These appearances were expunged from the official records.

From	To	App	Goal
Anderson, Robert (Bobby)			
1931	Lincoln City	1	
Armes, Samuel (Sammy)			
1931	Carlisle United	1	
Bamford, Thomas (Tommy)			
1931	Wrexham	1	1
Barley, Henry Frank (Harry)			
1931	Hull City	1	
Bilcliff, Bernard			
1931	Halifax Town	1	
Boland, George (Dicky)			
1931	Gateshead	1	
Bowron, Stephen (Steve)			
1931	Hartlepools United	1	
Bradford, John William (Bill)			
1931	Walsall	1	
Brown, Arthur Ivor			
1931	Crewe Alexandra	1	
Brown, Herbert Archibald			
1931	Darlington	1	
Brown, John Thomas (Jack)			
1931	Wrexham	1	
Buckley, Walter			
1931	Lincoln City	2	
Burkinshaw, Ralph			
1931	Wrexham	1	
Burrows, Wilfred (Wilf)			
1931	Wrexham	1	
Bushell, William			
1931	Walsall	1	
Cartwright, Herbert Philip (Phil)			
1931	Lincoln City	2	1
Charlton, Thomas			
1931	Gateshead	1	
Clayton, John			
1931	Wrexham	1	
Crawford, Edmund C (Ted)			
1931	Halifax Town	1	1
Cresswell, Frank			
1931	Chester	1	1
Crowther, George E			
1931	Gateshead	1	
Davidson, James (Jack)			
1931	Carlisle United	1	
Davies, Edward			
1931	Halifax Town	1	
Davies, James			
1931	Gateshead	1	
Dawson, William John			
1931	Crewe Alexandra	1	
Deacon, Henry (Harry)			
1931	Crewe Alexandra	1	1
Dickson, Hubert (Hugh)			
1931	Darlington	1	
Dixon, Robert Hall (Bobby)			
1931	Hartlepools United	1	
Donoghue, John			
1931	Wrexham	1	
Duncan, Andrew (Andy)			
1931	Hull City	1	
Duncan, Douglas (Dally)			
1931	Hull City	1	
Duthie, John Flett			
1931	Crewe Alexandra	1	
Ferguson, Christopher (Chris)			
1931	Wrexham	1	
Gardner, William (Bill)			
1931	Crewe Alexandra	1	
Gibson, Frederick William (Fred)			
1931	Hull City	1	
Goldsmith, George			
1931	Hull City	1	
Gomm, Archibald Frank (Archie)			
1931	Carlisle United	1	
Gowdy, William Alexander (Bill)			
1931	Hull City	1	
Graham, Robert Henry (Bob)			
1931	Halifax Town	1	
Hall, Berthold Alan Couldwell (Alan)			
1931	Lincoln City	2	2
Halliday, John Hastings (Jack)			
1931	Lincoln City	1	
Halliday, Thomas (Tom)			
1931	Darlington	1	
Hamilton, James (Jimmy)			
1931	Hartlepools United	1	
Harker, Stanley J			
1931	Halifax Town	1	
Hedley, Foster			
1931	Chester	1	1
Helliwell, Sidney (Sid)			
1931	Walsall	1	1
Henderson, Joseph Robert			
1931	Carlisle United	1	
Henry, Charles E (Charlie)			
1931	Walsall	1	
Herod, Edwin Redvers Baden (Baden)			
1931	Chester	1	
Hewitt, John Joseph (Joss)			
1931	Hartlepools United	1	
Hopkinson, Frederick (Fred)			
1931	Darlington	1	
Hunter, Albert Edward			
1931	Walsall	1	
Hurst, George			
1931	Darlington	1	
Jennings, Thomas Hamilton Oliver (Tommy)			
1931	Chester	1	1
John, William Ronald (Roy)			
1931	Walsall	1	
Johnson, William (Bill)			
1931	Chester	1	
Jones, Alfred (Alf)			
1931	Wrexham	1	
Jones, Walter			
1931	Chester	1	
Keeley, Ernest (Ernie)			
1931	Chester	1	
Keenor, Frederick Charles (Fred)			
1931	Crewe Alexandra	1	
Keetley, Frank			
1931	Lincoln City	1	
Knox, Thomas (Tommy)			
1931	Darlington	1	

WIGAN BOROUGH OPPONENTS 1931-1932

Continued

From	To		App	Goal
Lewis, Thomas Hewitt (Tommy)				
1931		Wrexham	1	2
Lincoln, Andrew (Andy)				
1931		Lincoln City	1	
McConnell, James (Jimmy)				
1931		Carlisle United	1	1
McConville, Patrick (Paddy)				
1931		Lincoln City	2	
McGrae, Joseph Russell (Joe)				
1931		Halifax Town	1	
McLachlan, Frederick (Fred)				
1931		Halifax Town	1	
McNaughton, William Frederick (Bill)				
1931		Gateshead	1	
McPhail, Daniel (Dan)				
1931		Lincoln City	2	
Marsh, William				
1931		Halifax Town	1	
Matthews, Cyril Henry Wheeler				
1931		Chester	1	
Mays, Albert William (Billy)				
1931		Halifax Town	1	
Meek, Joseph (Joe)				
1931		Gateshead	1	
Miller, James William				
1931		Carlisle United	1	1
Mills, Bertie Reginald (Paddy)				
1931		Hull City	1	
Mitchell, Andrew (Andy)				
1931		Darlington	1	1
Mordue, John (Jack)				
1931		Hartlepools United	1	
Murray, Michael				
1931		Crewe Alexandra	1	1
Neilson, George Humble				
1931		Gateshead	1	
Newton, William (Billy)				
1931		Hull City	1	
Parker, Wilson				
1931		Carlisle United	1	
Pierce, William (Bill)				
1931		Carlisle United	1	
Pointon, Joseph (Joe)				
1931		Walsall	1	1
Prentice, David				
1931		Walsall	1	
Pringle, Charles Ross (Charlie)				
1931		Lincoln City	2	
Pringle, Robert J				
1931		Crewe Alexandra	1	
Raleigh, Simeon				
1931		Hull City	1	1
Ranson, John George (Jack)				
1931		Chester	1	1
Read, Edward				
1931		Halifax Town	1	
Reilly, William J (Billy)				
1931		Chester	1	
Richmond, William Crichton (Bill)				
1931		Carlisle United	1	
Riley, Harold (Harry)				
1931		Lincoln City	1	2
Rivers, James Embleton (Jimmy)				
1931		Hartlepools United	1	
Robson, Arnold				
1931		Carlisle United	1	
Rodgers, Arthur				
1931		Hull City	1	

From	To		App	Goal
Rogers, William (Billie)				
1931		Wrexham	1	
Scott, John				
1931		Gateshead	1	
Scott, John McRae (Jock)				
1931		Walsall	1	
Shotton, Robert (Bob)				
1931		Hartlepools United	1	
Siddle, Reginald N (Reg)				
1931		Darlington	1	1
Sinclair, Thomas Mackie				
1931		Gateshead	1	
Skitt, Harry				
1931		Chester	1	
Taylor, Samuel (Sam)				
1931		Wrexham	1	2
Thayne, William (Billy)				
1931		Hartlepools United	1	
Thornton, Percy				
1931		Hartlepools United	1	1
Turnbull, Robert Armstrong (Bob)				
1931		Gateshead	1	
Turner, Albert (Bert)				
1931		Walsall	1	1
Waller, Horace				
1931		Hartlepools United	1	
Ward, Robert (Bob)				
1931		Crewe Alexandra	1	1
Watson, William (Willie)				
1931		Walsall	1	
Waugh, James (Jimmy)				
1931		Darlington	1	
Weale, Thomas James (Tommy)				
1931		Crewe Alexandra	1	
Wellock, Maurice				
1931		Darlington	1	3
Welsh, William (Billy)				
1931		Gateshead	1	1
Westgarth, Michael H (Mike)				
1931		Darlington	1	
Wheelhouse, Benjamin (Ben)				
1931		Halifax Town	1	
Whyte, George				
1931		Lincoln City	2	1
Wigham, John (Johnny)				
1931		Hartlepools United	1	
Willacy, Wilson				
1931		Carlisle United	1	
Williams, Ralph Shipley				
1931		Crewe Alexandra	1	1
Worthy, Albert				
1931		Lincoln City	1	
Wrack, Charles (Charlie)				
1931		Hull City	1	
Young, Alfred (Alf)				
1931		Lincoln City	2	

TEST MATCHES

Matches played 1893 to 1896 to settle promotion and relegation.

			App	Goal
Abbott, Walter				
1895		Small Heath	1	1
Aitken, Andrew				
1897		Newcastle United	4	1
Allan, George Horsburgh				
1895		Liverpool	4	3
Allan, John				
1894	1896	Notts County	5	
Allsopp, Elijah				
1894		Notts County	1	
Anderson, George E				
1897		Blackburn Rovers	4	1
Banks, John				
1895		West Bromwich Albion	2	
Barbour, William				
1894		Bury	1	
Barrett, Francis				
1896		Newton Heath	4	
Battles, Bernard				
1895		Liverpool	3	
Bayley, John Thomas				
1892		Small Heath	2	
Becton, Francis				
1895		Liverpool	4	
Beveridge, David				
1897		Burnley	4	
Blackburn, Frederick				
1897		Blackburn Rovers	2	1
Bloomer, Stephen				
1894		Derby County	1	1
Booth, Thomas Edward				
1897		Blackburn Rovers	3	
Boucher, Thomas				
1896		Notts County	4	1
Bowes, William				
1896	1897	Burnley	8	1
Bowie, W				
1892		Accrington	1	
Boyd, Henry				
1896		Newton Heath	3	2
Boyle, Peter				
1896		Sunderland	2	
Bradshaw, Thomas Henry				
1893	1895	Liverpool	6	3
Bramley, Charles				
1892	1894	Notts County	3	
Brandon, Thomas				
1897		Blackburn Rovers	3	
Brealey, H				
1896		Notts County	1	1
Briercliffe, Thomas				
1897		Blackburn Rovers	1	1
Briggs, HF				
1893		Darwen	1	
Brodie, David				
1894		Stoke	1	
Brown, David C				
1896		Burnley	4	1
Bruce, Daniel				
1892	1893	Notts County	2	1
Bryant, William				
1896		Newton Heath	4	
Bull, Walter				
1896		Notts County	3	
Burke, James				
1892		Notts County	1	
Cain, Robert				
1892		Sheffield United	1	
Calderhead, David				
1892	1896	Notts County	7	
Campbell, John				
1897		Blackburn Rovers	2	
Campbell, John Middleton				
1896		Sunderland	4	
1897		Newcastle United	3	1
Campbell, William Cecil				
1892		Darwen	1	
Carter, James				
1897		Blackburn Rovers	4	
Cartwright, Walter G				
1896		Newton Heath	2	
Cassidy, J				
1892		Newton Heath	2	1
Cassidy, Joseph				
1894	1896	Newton Heath	5	
Chadburn, John				
1894		Notts County	1	
Chapman, Thomas				
1895		Ardwick	2	
Charsley, Charles Christopher				
1892	1893	Small Heath	3	
Clare, Thomas				
1894		Stoke	1	
Clarkin, John				
1893	1894	Newton Heath	2	
Clawley, George				
1894		Stoke	1	
Clegg, Joseph R				
1894		Bury	1	
Cleghorn, Thomas				
1895		Liverpool	4	
Cleland, James W				
1894		Liverpool	1	

			App	Goal
Clements, John E				
1892		Newton Heath	2	
Cookson, Harry				
1892		Accrington	1	
Coupar, James				
1892		Newton Heath	2	1
Cowan, John				
1893		Preston North End	1	
Cowan, WG				
1896		Sunderland	2	
Cox, John Davies				
1894		Derby County	1	
Crone, Robert				
1896		Notts County	4	
Cunningham, John				
1893		Preston North End	1	1
Curran, John				
1894		Liverpool	1	
Daft, Harry Butler				
1893		Notts County	1	
Davidson, Thomas				
1894		Bury	1	
Davidson, William R				
1893		Newton Heath	1	
Davies, J				
1892		Newton Heath	2	
Davies, Joseph				
1895		Ardwick	2	1
Davies, Samuel				
1894		Bury	1	
Devey, Edwin James				
1893		Small Heath	1	
Dickson, William Alexander				
1894		Stoke	1	
Ditchfield, J Charles				
1892		Accrington	1	
1895		Ardwick	1	
Doig, John Edward				
1896		Sunderland	4	
Donaldson, Robert				
1892	1896	Newton Heath	8	
Donnelly, Samuel				
1893		Notts County	1	
Doughty, Roger				
1896		Newton Heath	3	
Douglas, William				
1894		Newton Heath	1	
Dow, John M				
1894		Newton Heath	1	
Draycott, William Levi				
1896		Newton Heath	4	
Drummond, George				
1893		Preston North End	1	1
Drummond, John				
1892		Sheffield United	1	1
1894		Liverpool	1	
Dunlop, Thomas				
1895		Small Heath	1	
Dunlop, William TP				
1894		Liverpool	1	
Dunn, Hugh				
1893		Preston North End	1	
Eccles, John				
1894	1897	Stoke	5	
Erentz, Fred Charles				
1892	1896	Newton Heath	7	
Fall, John Walter				
1893		Newton Heath	1	
Farman, Alfred H				
1892	1893	Newton Heath	3	4
Farnall, Thomas				
1895		Small Heath	3	
Farrell, Jack				
1894		Stoke	1	1
Ferguson, Matthew				
1896		Sunderland	4	
Ferguson, William				
1896		Burnley	2	1
Finnerhan, Patrick				
1895		Ardwick	4	
Fish, R				
1892		Darwen	1	
Fitzsimmons, Thomas				
1892		Newton Heath	2	
Fletcher, Frederick				
1894		Notts County	1	1
Flewitt, Albert William				
1895		West Bromwich Albion	4	2
Francis, Percy Ollivant				
1894		Derby County	1	
Fraser, Adam				
1895		Small Heath	4	
Gallacher, Hugh M				
1892		Sheffield United	1	
Geary, Fred				
1895		Liverpool	1	
Ghee, T				
1893		Darwen	1	
Ghee, Thomas				
1897		Newcastle United	4	1
Gibson, William				
1896		Notts County	4	

TEST MATCHES - CONTINUED

Player / Season	Club	App	Goal
Gillespie, James			
1896	Sunderland	4	2
Gillespie, Matthew			
1896	Newton Heath	4	
Gillies, Alexander			
1895	Ardwick	2	
Glover, John William			
1897	Blackburn Rovers	1	
Goldie, Archibald			
1895	Liverpool	4	
Goodall, Archibald Lee			
1894	Derby County	1	
Goodall, John			
1894	Derby County	1	
Gordon, Patrick			
1893	Liverpool	1	1
Gow, Donald Robertson			
1896	Sunderland	4	
Greer, William H			
1893	Preston North End	1	
Grewer, James			
1894	Stoke	1	
Haddow, David			
1896	Burnley	4	
Hallam, John			
1892 1895	Small Heath	6	2
Hammond, Walter Henry			
1892	Sheffield United	1	
Hands, Thomas			
1892 1895	Small Heath	5	
Hannah, Andrew Boyd			
1893	Liverpool	1	
Hannah, James			
1896	Sunderland	4	
Hargreaves, Joshua			
1897	Blackburn Rovers	2	
Harper, James			
1895	Ardwick	3	
Harper, Theophilus			
1893	Notts County	1	
Harvey, John			
1896	Sunderland	2	
1897	Newcastle United	4	2
Henderson, Adam			
1893	Preston North End	1	1
Henderson, David			
1893	Liverpool	1	
Henderson, James			
1894	Bury	1	
Hendry, Jack			
1892 1894	Notts County	2	
Hendry, William Harold			
1892	Sheffield United	1	
Higgins, John Thomas			
1895	West Bromwich Albion	4	1
Hill, Robert			
1892	Sheffield United	1	
1895	Ardwick	1	
Hillman, John			
1897	Burnley	4	
Hodge, William			
1892	Accrington	1	
Holmes, Robert			
1893	Preston North End	1	
Hood, William			
1892 1893	Newton Heath	2	
Horton, John H			
1895	West Bromwich Albion	4	
Houlker, Albert Edward			
1897	Blackburn Rovers	3	
Howell, Raby			
1892	Sheffield United	1	
Howlett, Charles H			
1892	Sheffield United	1	
Hulse, Benjamin Daniel			
1897	Blackburn Rovers	3	
Hurst, Daniel James			
1897	Blackburn Rovers	2	2
Hutchinson, Thomas			
1895	West Bromwich Albion	2	
Hyslop, Thomas			
1894	Stoke	1	
Jackson, James			
1897	Newcastle United	4	1
Jackson, J Thomas			
1897	Blackburn Rovers	2	
Jenkyns, Caesar Augustus Llewellyn			
1892 1893	Small Heath	3	
1896	Newton Heath	4	1
Johnson, Frederick J			
1897	Stoke	4	
Johnson, George			
1895	West Bromwich Albion	1	1
Jones, John Thomas			
1895	Small Heath	4	3
Kennedy, John			
1897	Stoke	4	1
Kenyon, A			
1892	Darwen	1	
Killean, Edward			
1897	Blackburn Rovers	3	
Kirkham, John B			
1892	Accrington	1	
Langham, William			
1896	Notts County	4	1
Lea, H			
1892	Accrington	1	
Lea, T			
1892	Accrington	1	
Leach, John R			
1892 1893	Darwen	2	
Leake, Alexander			
1895	Small Heath	4	
Leiper, Joseph			
1894	Derby County	1	
Lester, Frank			
1895	Small Heath	4	
Lindsay, William			
1897	Newcastle United	2	
Livingstone, Archibald Lang			
1897	Burnley	4	
Lockie, James C			
1897	Newcastle United	2	
Logan, James			
1893	Notts County	1	
McAllister, Alexander			
1896	Sunderland	2	
McAvoy, M			
1892	Darwen	1	
McBride, James			
1893	Liverpool	1	
1895	Ardwick	4	1
McCartney, John			
1893 1895	Liverpool	5	1
McCartney, W John			
1894	Newton Heath	1	
McInnes, Thomas			
1892	Notts County	1	
McKennie, William			
1892 1893	Darwen	2	
McKnight, John			
1893	Darwen	1	1
McLean, Duncan			
1893	Liverpool	1	
McLean, John C			
1894	Liverpool	1	
McLeod, Roderick			
1895	West Bromwich Albion	4	
McLintock, Thomas			
1896 1897	Burnley	8	
McMillan, John Stuart			
1894	Derby County	1	1
McNaught, James Rankin			
1893 1896	Newton Heath	5	
McNaughton, George J			
1894	Bury	1	
McNeill, Robert			
1896	Sunderland	4	
McQue, Joseph			
1893 1895	Liverpool	5	
McQueen, Hugh			
1893	Liverpool	1	
McQueen, Matthew			
1893 1894	Liverpool	2	
McVean, Malcolm			
1893 1895	Liverpool	5	
1896	Burnley	4	
Mann, George W			
1895	Ardwick	4	
Marshall, Harry			
1897	Blackburn Rovers	4	
Mason, W			
1892	Accrington	1	
Maxwell, Alan			
1893	Darwen	1	
Maxwell, R			
1892	Darwen	1	1
Maxwell, William Sturrock			
1897	Stoke	3	1
Meates, William Percival			
1895	Small Heath	3	
Mellor, Harry			
1897	Stoke	3	
Meredith, William Henry			
1895	Ardwick	4	1
Methven, James			
1894	Derby County	1	
Millar, Harry			
1894	Bury	1	1
Millar, J			
1895	Ardwick	2	
Mills, Andrew			
1897	Blackburn Rovers	1	
Mitchell, Andrew			
1892 1893	Newton Heath	3	
Mobley, Frank			
1892 1895	Small Heath	4	1
Molyneux, Fred			
1897	Stoke	2	
Montgomery, Archibald			
1894	Bury	1	
Moreland, John			
1897	Blackburn Rovers	1	
Morgan, Hugh			
1896	Sunderland	4	1
Morris, Harry			
1892	Small Heath	1	
Morris, Hugh			
1895	Ardwick	4	
Morrison, Thomas			
1896 1897	Burnley	5	
Murphy, John			
1896	Notts County	4	
Murphy, Joseph			
1897	Stoke	4	
Naughton, William A			
1894	Stoke	1	
Needham, Ernest			
1892	Sheffield United	1	
Neil, Robert Scott Gibson			
1894	Liverpool	1	
Oliver, John Sidney			
1895	Small Heath	3	
Ollis, William			
1892 1893	Small Heath	3	
Orr, James			
1892 1893	Darwen	2	
Ostler, Jack			
1897	Newcastle United	4	
Oswald, James			
1892	Notts County	1	
Owen, David			
1892	Darwen	1	1
Paul, John			
1894	Derby County	1	
Pearson, Richard			
1893	Darwen	1	
Peddie, John H			
1897	Newcastle United	1	
Peden, John			
1893	Newton Heath	1	
Perrins, George			
1892 1894	Newton Heath	4	
Perry, Thomas			
1895	West Bromwich Albion	3	1
Peters, Jack			
1894	Newton Heath	1	
Pinnell, Archibald			
1893	Preston North End	1	
Place, Walter (Junior)			
1896 1897	Burnley	6	
Place, Walter (Senior)			
1896	Burnley	4	
Plant, John			
1894	Bury	1	
Prescott, Thomas G			
1896	Notts County	4	
Proudfoot, John			
1897	Blackburn Rovers	1	
Pumfrey, Bernard			
1892	Small Heath	2	
Purves, William Michael			
1893	Small Heath	1	
Raisbeck, Alexander Galloway			
1897	Stoke	4	1
Reader, Josiah			
1895	West Bromwich Albion	4	
Reynolds, Jeremiah			
1896 1897	Burnley	8	
Richards, John			
1895	West Bromwich Albion	4	1
Richards, William			
1895	West Bromwich Albion	4	1
Roach, James			
1895	Small Heath	1	
Robertson, Hugh			
1896	Burnley	3	
Robertson, John Thomas			
1897	Stoke	2	
Robertson, William			
1895	Small Heath	4	
Robinson, John William			
1894	Derby County	1	
Robson, David			
1895	Ardwick	4	
Ross, George William			
1894	Bury	1	
Ross, James D			
1893	Preston North End	1	1
1894 1895	Liverpool	5	
1896 1897	Burnley	7	1
Rowan, Alexander			
1895	Ardwick	3	2
Rowley, Arthur			
1897	Stoke	2	
Sanders, Moses			
1893	Preston North End	1	
Schofield, Joseph Alfred			
1894 1897	Stoke	5	3
Sharp, James			
1893	Preston North End	1	
Shaw, R			
1893	Darwen	1	
Shelton, Alfred			
1892 1894	Notts County	3	
Short, George Frederick			
1892 1893	Small Heath	3	
Sissons, Henry P			
1894	Notts County	1	
Smith, Richard			
1894	Newton Heath	1	
Smith, William			
1897	Newcastle United	4	2
Staley, Jonathan			
1894	Derby County	1	
Stevenson, John			
1892	Accrington	1	
Stewart, Alexander			
1896	Notts County	4	
Stewart, William S			
1892 1894	Newton Heath	2	
Stone, Herbert Henry			
1894	Newton Heath	1	
Storer, Harry			
1895	Liverpool	4	
Stothert, James			
1894	Notts County	1	
Stott, James			
1897	Newcastle United	4	
Sutherland, Malcolm			
1892 1893	Darwen	2	
Taggart, John			
1895	West Bromwich Albion	4	
Tattersall, James			
1892	Accrington	1	
Taylor, Joseph			
1896 1897	Burnley	8	
Toman, Wilfred			
1896 1897	Burnley	5	4
Toone, George			
1892 1896	Notts County	7	
Turner, James Albert			
1894	Stoke	1	
Wade, John James			
1892 1893	Darwen	2	
Walkerdine, Harry			
1892	Notts County	1	
Walton, William Howard T			
1892 1895	Small Heath	4	2
Wardrope, William			
1897	Newcastle United	4	1
Watson, Arthur			
1892	Sheffield United	1	
Watson, Arthur EC			
1893	Notts County	1	
Watts, Charles			
1897	Newcastle United	4	
Wheldon, George Frederick			
1892 1895	Small Heath	7	5
Whitehead, James W			
1892	Accrington	1	
Whitehead, John			
1894	Liverpool	1	
Whitelaw, Andrew			
1892	Notts County	1	
Whitham, Michael			
1892	Sheffield United	1	
Wilkes, Thomas Henry			
1897	Stoke	4	
Wilkie, John			
1897	Blackburn Rovers	2	
Wilkie, Thomas			
1895	Liverpool	1	
Wilkinson, Frank			
1893	Notts County	1	
Williams, Charles Albert			
1895	Ardwick	4	
Williams, William			
1895	West Bromwich Albion	4	2
Wilson, Hugh			
1896	Sunderland	4	
Wood, Alfred Josiah Edward			
1897	Stoke	4	
Wylie, Thomas G			
1894	Bury	1	

The National Football Archive

at www.enfa.co.uk

Further information on every player in this book can be found in the web site of the English National Football Archive. The archive contains a database of 400,000 match line-ups, 41,000 players and 600,000 goals. Details of every Football League and Premier League game since 1888 are included, together with the FA Cup, League Cup and a host of other tournaments. Every team member and every scorer can be clicked-through to open new pages that show their complete career at every club they played for.

Match details can be found from a calendar showing every date on which a game has been played, or by looking at the season-by-season record of every League club. If you are researching a player's career, you can see his appearance totals for each season, then click-through to club and match details. You can also see all meetings between any two clubs, in League and cups. Again, you can click-through on the match result to see the line-ups and goal scorers of the two teams.

The match results and dates, the complete player list, and the club v club meetings are available to all users free of charge. We ask you to register an email address first, after which we will send you a user name and password. Match line-ups and full player details require you to take out a weekly or yearly subscription.

In subsequent phases of development, it is planned to add digital content, such as match videos, newspaper reports and player photographs. The database will act as the search tool for such content, with icons alongside the match detail to indicate when additional material can be seen.

The ENFA web site is provided by Soccerdata Limited, a trading company of Tony Brown and partners.